YEARBOOK OF THE
UNITED NATIONS
1989

Volume 43

Yearbook of the United Nations, 1989

Volume 43   Sales No. E.97.I.11

Prepared by the Yearbook Section of the Department of Public Information, United Nations, New York. Although the *Yearbook* is based on official sources, it is not an official record.

Chief Editor: Elizabeth Flynn-Connors

Senior Editors: Christine B. Koerner, Kathryn Gordon

Editors/Writers: Melody C. Pfeiffer, Elizabeth Baldwin-Penn, Peter Jackson, Kikko Maeyama, Dmitri Marchenkov, Louis Germain

Contributing Editors/Writers: Keith Beavan, Igor Khvorostiany, Nancy Seufert-Barr

Copy Editors: Alison M. Koppelman, Janet E. Root, Bruce F. Murphy

Copy Co-ordinator: Leonard M. Simon

Editorial Assistants: Nidia H. Morisset, Lawri M. Moore, Dan Rustin

Research Assistant: Anahit Turabian

Chief Typesetter: Sunita Chabra

Jacket Design: James Eschinger

YEARBOOK
OF THE
UNITED
NATIONS
1989

Volume 43

Department of Public Information
United Nations, New York

Martinus Nijhoff Publishers
THE HAGUE / BOSTON / LONDON

Published for and on behalf of the United Nations by Martinus Nijhoff Publishers
P.O. Box 85889, 2508 CN The Hague, Netherlands

Kluwer Law International incorporates the
publishing programmes of Martinus Nijhoff Publishers

Sold and distributed in North and South America
by Kluwer Law International,
675 Massachusetts Avenue, Cambridge, MA 02139, U.S.A.

In all other countries, sold and distributed
by Kluwer Law International,
P.O. Box 85889, 2508 CN The Hague, Netherlands

Yearbook of the United Nations, 1989
Vol. 43
ISBN: 90-411-0451-8
ISSN: 0082-8521

UNITED NATIONS PUBLICATION
SALES NO. E.97.I.11

Printed in the United States of America

Foreword

THE CLOSE OF THE DECADE OF THE 1980s brought with it new hopes and challenges, and, as cold-war tensions eased, the United Nations began to assume a significantly larger international role. The stage was set for the fulfilment of two long-pursued United Nations objectives—the independence of Namibia and the creation of a united, non-racial and democratic society in South Africa. The cease-fire between Iran and Iraq negotiated by the United Nations remained in place, and both sides continued their talks on the full restoration of peace following a long and sanguinary conflict. Efforts towards peace in Cambodia and Central America also seemed capable of finally bearing fruit.

At the same time, many issues remained unresolved and new problems arose which required the attention of the international community, particularly in the area of development. The revitalization of economic growth in developing countries, especially in Africa, continued to be a priority in 1989. Action to protect the environment was high on the agenda, with particular emphasis on climate change, toxic waste and drift-net fishing. The Organization also led the global fight against the spread of HIV/AIDS and continued to promote the world-wide campaign to combat drug abuse and illicit drug trafficking.

Major natural disasters occurred throughout the year, including Hurricane Hugo, which devastated many islands in the Caribbean; heavy floods in Democratic Yemen and Djibouti; earthquakes in Algeria, China and Tajikistan; and relentless drought and desertification in the Sudano-Sahel region and elsewhere. The United Nations provided much-needed relief to address these and other critical emergency situations and to mitigate the suffering of millions of refugees and displaced persons world-wide. Operation Lifeline Sudan was launched, setting a historic precedent for complex relief operations.

I was honoured to serve as Secretary-General of the United Nations and to participate in the work chronicled in this volume of the *Yearbook of the United Nations*. As the United Nations continues its unremitting efforts to contribute to the betterment of humanity and to realize the noble objectives of the Charter, I offer my best wishes to the current Secretary-General, Kofi A. Annan, for success in this most important endeavour.

JAVIER PÉREZ DE CUÉLLAR
Former Secretary-General of the United Nations
New York, July 1997

Contents

Part One: *Political and security questions*

Part Two: *Regional questions*

Part Three: *Economic and social questions*

Part Six: *Administrative and budgetary questions*

Part Seven: *Intergovernmental organizations related to the United Nations*

Appendices

Indexes

About the 1989 edition of the *Yearbook*

The 1989 *YEARBOOK OF THE UNITED NATIONS* is the second of three backlog editions (1988, 1989, 1990) to be published. As the publication of *Yearbook* volumes had been falling behind over a period of time, it was decided to focus on the production of current volumes, with the backlog editions to be done concurrently through the provision of funds by the publisher. The 1988 edition was published in 1994. The 1990 edition is under preparation. The scope, content and breadth of coverage of these volumes have been restructured and redefined to enhance the presentation of the main activities and events of each year. The Department of Public Information of the United Nations is committed to clear the backlog and maintain the publication of the current volumes of the *Yearbook* on a timely annual schedule. As in previous volumes, this volume has been designed to serve as the most comprehensive reference tool for use by the research community and those interested in the activities of the United Nations and its related organizations.

Structure and scope of articles

The *Yearbook* is subject-oriented, divided into seven major parts: political and security questions, regional questions, economic and social questions, trusteeship and decolonization, legal questions, administrative and budgetary questions, and intergovernmental organizations related to the United Nations.

Information includes summaries of major reports, Secretariat activities and, in selected cases, the views of States in written communications. REFERENCES are listed at the end of chapters or sub-chapters, linked to the text by numerical indicators.

Activities of United Nations bodies. All resolutions, decisions and other major activities of the principal organs and, where applicable, those of subsidiary bodies are either reproduced or summarized in the respective articles. The texts of all resolutions and decisions of a substantive nature adopted in 1989 by the General Assembly, the Security Council and the Economic and Social Council are reproduced or summarized under the relevant topic. These texts are followed by the procedural details giving date of adoption, meeting number and vote totals (in favour-against-abstaining); information on their approval by a sessional or subsidiary body prior to final adoption, with document symbols of drafts, approved amendments and committee reports; and in most cases a list of sponsors. Also given are the document symbols of any financial implications and relevant meeting numbers. Details of any recorded or roll-call vote on the resolution/decision as a whole also follow the text. The texts of resolutions and decisions of a purely procedural nature are not reproduced, but are summarized and their numbers highlighted in bold type.

Major reports. Most 1989 reports of the Secretary-General, along with selected reports from other United Nations sources, such as seminars and working groups, are summarized briefly.

Secretariat activities. The operational activities of the United Nations for development and humanitarian assistance are described under the relevant topics. Information is also provided on major activities financed outside the United Nations regular budget, wherever available.

Views of States. Written communications sent to the United Nations by Member States and circulated as documents of the principal organs have been summarized in selected cases, under the relevant topic. Substantive actions by the Security Council have been analysed and brief reviews of the Council's deliberations given, particularly in cases where an issue was taken up but no resolution was adopted.

Related organizations. The *Yearbook* also briefly describes the 1989 activities of the specialized agencies and other related organizations of the United Nations.

Terminology

Formal titles of bodies, organizational units, conventions, declarations and officials are given in full on first mention in an article or sequence of articles. They are also used in resolution/decision texts, and in the SUBJECT INDEX under the key word of the title. Short titles may be used in subsequent references.

How to find information in the *Yearbook*

The user may locate information in the 1989 edition in a number of ways: by the table of contents, which highlights the broad subjects and subheadings; by the SUBJECT INDEX, which may be used to locate individual topics and specific references to the bodies dealing with each topic; and by the INDEX OF RESOLUTIONS AND DECISIONS, which provides a numerical list of all resolutions and substantive decisions adopted in 1989 by the principal organs, with page numbers for their text. The *Yearbook* also contains five appendices. APPENDIX I comprises a list of Member States with dates of their admission to the United Nations; APPENDIX II reproduces the Charter of the United Nations, including the Statute of the International Court of Justice; APPENDIX III gives the structure of the principal organs of the United Nations; APPENDIX IV provides the agenda for each session of the principal organs in 1989; and APPENDIX V gives the location and addresses of the United Nations Information Centres and Services world wide.

ABBREVIATIONS COMMONLY USED IN THE *YEARBOOK*

ACABQ	Advisory Committee on Administrative and Budgetary Questions
ACC	Administrative Committee on Co-ordination
ANC	African National Congress of South Africa
ASEAN	Association of South-East Asian Nations
CDP	Committee for Development Planning
CEDAW	Committee on the Elimination of Discrimination against Women
CERD	Committee on the Elimination of Racial Discrimination
CFA	Committee on Food Aid Policies and Programmes (WFP)
CMEA	Council for Mutual Economic Assistance
CPC	Committee for Programme and Co-ordination
CSDHA	Centre for Social Development and Humanitarian Affairs
DIEC	Development and International Economic Co-operation
DIESA	Department of International Economic and Social Affairs
DPI	Department of Public Information
DTCD	Department of Technical Co-operation for Development
EC	European Community
ECA	Economic Commission for Africa
ECDC	economic co-operation among developing countries
ECE	Economic Commission for Europe
ECLAC	Economic Commission for Latin America and the Caribbean
ECOWAS	Economic Community of West African States
EEC	European Economic Community
ESC	Economic and Social Council
ESCAP	Economic and Social Commission for Asia and the Pacific
ESCWA	Economic and Social Commission for Western Asia
FAO	Food and Agriculture Organization of the United Nations
GA	General Assembly
GATT	General Agreement on Tariffs and Trade
GDP	gross domestic product
GEMS	Global Environment Monitoring System
GNP	gross national product
IAEA	International Atomic Energy Agency
ICAO	International Civil Aviation Organization
ICJ	International Court of Justice
ICRC	International Committee of the Red Cross
ICSC	International Civil Service Commission
IDA	International Development Association
IDDA	Industrial Development Decade for Africa
IFAD	International Fund for Agricultural Development
IFC	International Finance Corporation
ILC	International Law Commission
ILO	International Labour Organisation
IMF	International Monetary Fund
IMO	International Maritime Organization
INCB	International Narcotics Control Board
INSTRAW	International Research and Training Institute for the Advancement of Women
IPF	indicative planning figure (UNDP)
ITC	International Trade Centre (UNCTAD/GATT)
ITU	International Telecommunication Union
JAG	Joint Advisory Group on the International Trade Centre
JIU	Joint Inspection Unit
JUNIC	Joint United Nations Information Committee
LDC	least developed country
NATO	North Atlantic Treaty Organization
NGO	non-governmental organization
NPT	Treaty on the Non-Proliferation of Nuclear Weapons
NSGT	Non-Self-Governing Territory
OAS	Organization of American States
OAU	Organization of African Unity
ODA	official development assistance
OECD	Organisation for Economic Co-operation and Development
OPEC	Organization of Petroleum Exporting Countries
PAC	Pan Africanist Congress of Azania
PLO	Palestine Liberation Organization
SC	Security Council
SDR	special drawing right
S-G	Secretary-General
SNPA	Substantial New Programme of Action for the 1980s for the Least Developed Countries
SPC	Special Political Committee
SWAPO	South West Africa People's Organization (Namibia)
TC	Trusteeship Council
TCDC	technical co-operation among developing countries
TDB	Trade and Development Board (UNCTAD)
TNC	transnational corporation
UN	United Nations
UNCDF	United Nations Capital Development Fund
UNCHS	United Nations Centre for Human Settlements (Habitat)
UNCITRAL	United Nations Commission on International Trade Law
UNCTAD	United Nations Conference on Trade and Development
UNDOF	United Nations Disengagement Observer Force (Golan Heights)
UNDP	United Nations Development Programme
UNDRO	Office of the United Nations Disaster Relief Co-ordinator
UNEP	United Nations Environment Programme
UNESCO	United Nations Educational, Scientific and Cultural Organization
UNFDAC	United Nations Fund for Drug Abuse Control
UNFICYP	United Nations Peace-keeping Force in Cyprus
UNFPA	United Nations Population Fund
UNFSTD	United Nations Fund for Science and Technolgy for Development
UNHCR	Office of the United Nations High Commissioner for Refugees
UNIC	United Nations Information Centre
UNICEF	United Nations Children's Fund
UNIDIR	United Nations Institute for Disarmament Research
UNIDO	United Nations Industrial Development Organization
UNIFIL	United Nations Interim Force in Lebanon
UNIIMOG	United Nations Iran-Iraq Military Observer Group
UNITAR	United Nations Institute for Training and Research
UNPAAERD	United Nations Programme of Action for African Economic Recovery and Development 1986-1990
UNRFNRE	United Nations Revolving Fund for Natural Resources Exploration
UNRISD	United Nations Research Institute for Social Development
UNRWA	United Nations Relief and Works Agency for Palestine Refugees in the Near East
UNSO	United Nations Sudano-Sahelian Office
UNTAG	United Nations Transition Assistance Group (Namibia)
UNTSO	United Nations Truce Supervision Organization (Israel and neighbouring States)
UNU	United Nations University
UNV	United Nations Volunteers
UPU	Universal Postal Union
WFC	World Food Council
WFP	World Food Programme
WHO	World Health Organization
WIPO	World Intellectual Property Organization
WMO	World Meteorological Organization
YUN	*Yearbook of the United Nations*

EXPLANATORY NOTE ON DOCUMENTS

References at the end of each article in Parts One to Six of this volume give the symbols of the main documents issued in 1989 on the topic, arranged in the order in which they are referred to in the text. The following is a guide to the principal document symbols:

A/- refers to documents of the General Assembly, numbered in separate series by session. Thus, A/44/- refers to documents issued for consideration at the forty-fourth session, beginning with A/44/1. Documents of special and emergency special sessions are identified as A/S- and A/ES-, followed by the session number.

A/C.- refers to documents of six of the Assembly's Main Committees, e.g. A/C.1/- is a document of the First Committee, A/C.6/-, a document of the Sixth Committee. The symbol for documents of the seventh Main Committee, the Special Political Committee, is A/SPC/-. A/BUR/- refers to documents of the General Committee. A/AC.- documents are those of the Assembly's *ad hoc* bodies and A/CN.-, of its commissions; e.g. A/AC.105/- identifies documents of the Assembly's Committee on the Peaceful Uses of Outer Space, A/CN.4/-, of its International Law Commission. Assembly resolutions and decisions since the thirty-first (1976) session have been identified by two arabic numerals: the first indicates the session of adoption; the second, the sequential number in the series. Resolutions are numbered consecutively from 1 at each session. Decisions of regular sessions are numbered consecutively, from 301 for those concerned with elections and appointments, and from 401 for all other decisions. Decisions of special and emergency special sessions are numbered consecutively, from 11 for those concerned with elections and appointments, and from 21 for all other decisions.

E/- refers to documents of the Economic and Social Council, numbered in separate series by year. Thus, E/1989/- refers to documents issued for consideration by the Council at its 1989 sessions, beginning with E/1989/1. E/AC.-, E/C.- and E/CN.-, followed by identifying numbers, refer to documents of the Council's subsidiary *ad hoc* bodies, committees and commissions. For example, E/C.1/-, E/C.2/- and E/C.3/- refer to documents of the Council's sessional committees, namely, the First (Economic), Second (Social) and Third (Programme and Co-ordination) Committees, respectively; E/CN.5/- refers to documents of the Council's Commission for Social Development, E/CN.7/-, to documents of its Committee on Natural Resources. E/ICEF/- documents are those of the United Nations Children's Fund. Symbols for the Council's resolutions and decisions, since 1978, consist of two arabic numerals: the first indicates the year of adoption and the second, the sequential number in the series. There are two series: one for resolutions, beginning with 1 (resolution 1989/1); and one for decisions, beginning, since 1983, with 101 (decision 1989/101).

S/- refers to documents of the Security Council. Its resolutions are identified by consecutive numbers followed by the year of adoption in parentheses, beginning with resolution 1(1946).

ST/-, followed by symbols representing the issuing department or office, refers to documents of the United Nations Secretariat.

T/- refers to documents of the Trusteeship Council.

Documents of certain bodies bear special symbols, including the following:

ACC/-	Administrative Committee on Co-ordination
CD/-	Conference on Disarmament
CERD/-	Committee on the Elimination of Racial Discrimination
DC/-	Disarmament Commission
DP/-	United Nations Development Programme
HS/-	Commission on Human Settlements
ITC/-	International Trade Centre
LOS/PCN/-	Preparatory Commission for the International Sea-Bed Authority and for the International Tribunal for the Law of the Sea
TD/-	United Nations Conference on Trade and Development
UNEP/-	United Nations Environment Programme
UNITAR/-	United Nations Institute for Training and Research

Many documents of the regional commissions bear special symbols. These are sometimes preceded by the following:

E/ECA/-	Economic Commission for Africa
E/ECE/-	Economic Commission for Europe
E/ESCAP/-	Economic and Social Commission for Asia and the Pacific
E/ESCWA/-	Economic and Social Commission for Western Asia
LC/G.-	Economic Commission for Latin America and the Caribbean

"CONF." in a symbol refers to documents of a conference; "INF." to those of general information; "L." to documents of limited distribution, such as draft resolutions. Summary records are designated by "SR.", verbatim records by "PV.", each followed by the meeting number.

United Nations sales publications each carry a sales number with the following components separated by periods: a capital letter indicating the language(s) of the publication; two arabic numerals indicating the year; a Roman numeral indicating the subject category; a capital letter indicating a subdivision of the category, if any; and an arabic numeral indicating the number of the publication within the category. Examples: E.89.V.4; E/F/R.89.II.E.8; E.89.IX.3.

Report of the Secretary-General

Report of the Secretary-General on the work of the Organization

*Following is the Secretary-General's report on the work of the Organization, submitted to the General Assembly and dated 12 September 1989. The Assembly took note of it on 17 October (**decision 44/404**).*

I

Fifty years ago this very month, Europe was plunged into a conflict that eventually engulfed other continents and became known as the Second World War. As the event had been preceded by a similar one only a quarter-century earlier, it was a stark revelation of the destructive nature of the international system that prevailed at the time. The havoc it wrought moved all the then sovereign States to join and make a radical new departure in international relations. At the conclusion of the war, they founded the United Nations to give peace a more secure foundation.

How secure the new foundation is or is likely to prove in different contingencies has remained an open question through much of the intervening period.

There is no doubt that peace has gained a meaning and dimension that it lacked before—above all, the dimension of multilateral endeavour. No realistic view of human experience from 1945 to the present can ignore the transformation of the world scene reflected by the presence and working of the United Nations. It is under the auspices of the Organization that an international agenda encompassing all matters of common concern to nations has taken shape and a massive change in international life has been effected and, by and large, peacefully absorbed.

But there remained a gaping void—not an institutional one—at the core of the whole enterprise. Ambiguity corroded the answer to the central question of the strength and durability of world peace. Collective security became a hostage of the cold war. Because of this, no major issue of war or peace could be examined on its merits. Disputes festered; wars were waged by proxy; tensions became chronic. The imagery and rhetoric suggestive of an Armageddon entered the language of political discourse. The effect on the United Nations of the policies generated by this state of relations has been amply noted in previous reports. To put it mildly, it left the United Nations in a waiting position—waiting until common sense and the dynamics of the world situation would induce a return to the way of handling international affairs outlined in its Charter.

It has not been fully two years since we have begun to witness signs of such a return. The two major Power blocs have started an assiduous search for bases of stable peace between them. A growing determination on the part of the permanent members of the Security Council to work together has facilitated purposeful diplomatic effort towards the resolution of some of the long-standing disputes. In regional contexts also, approaches are being made and important initiatives taken to reconcile conflicting positions, or achieve a compromise between them. And there is a heightened awareness of a new generation of problems common to all nations.

The year under review has been largely a year for the consolidation and extension of those trends and efforts. I mentioned the negativities of the earlier phase to emphasize the scope and degree of the transition we are now witnessing. By its nature, this transition could be neither abrupt nor smooth. Problems that should have been solved years ago did not just remain unsolved because of differences between the major Powers: they became more complicated as subsidiary problems were added to them. But now, after years of frustration, they are being seriously addressed. That this means the end of the era of sterile confrontations that began immediately after the Second World War can be a helpful assumption. But though easy to launch, it is the kind of assumption that can float only on a tide of confirmations.

II

During the year, the United Nations has been intensely involved in activities to bring peace to troubled regions of the world. In an increasing number of cases, its role has been, and is being, looked upon as pivotal to the settlement of problems that not too long ago appeared intractable. Indeed, the assistance of the world Organization is being sought as never before in its history. There has been a palpable change stemming from the recognition that, if there are to be lasting solutions to international problems, these must be based on universally accepted principles as laid down in the Charter. I cannot fail to record my deep gratification at this renewal of confidence in multilateralism and its agents. Today, at diverse points of the globe, representatives of the United Nations and its Secretary-General are engaged in the arduous tasks of peace and my own visits to different areas of conflict have vividly impressed on me the great degree of trust and responsibility placed in the Organization. That the expectations should be fulfilled and not defeated is a matter of the utmost importance to peace.

To bring independence to Namibia has been a fundamental objective of the United Nations and, for me personally, an unremitting concern. The year has been one of major advance towards that goal. The establishment of the United Nations Transition Assistance Group (UNTAG) on Namibian soil and the efforts under way to hold free and fair elections under the supervision and control of the United Nations constitute one of the most challenging and significant operations ever undertaken by the world Organization. Its success depends on scrupulous observance of all the provisions of the United Nations plan, the cease-fire arrangements and related undertakings. At the time of writing, there are still serious problems to be overcome. However, the multilateral efforts of the Security Council, the concerned parties and the Secretariat have brought us to a stage where, despite the many difficulties, past and present, the implementation of the plan for the independence of the Territory must be considered irreversible.

It bears repeating in this context that UNTAG, the military component of which does not have powers of enforcement, requires the full cooperation of the parties, all of whom must continuously respect their obligations and strictly adhere to the agreements and understandings to which they have committed themselves.

The overwhelming majority of the Namibian refugees who had registered for repatriation have now returned under the auspices of the Office of the United Nations High Commissioner for Refugees. The voter registration process and the election campaign are now well advanced and special care is being taken to ensure that the elections are completely free and fair and that they take place under the effective supervision and control of the United Nations. A draft electoral law is currently the subject of active discussion in order to remove a number of unsatisfactory features; it will be promulgated only when the United Nations is satisfied with the text. The same is the case with the law relating to the powers of the Constituent Assembly. Other major issues that continue to require the most careful attention include the continuing presence in the South West Africa Police Force of former members of a counter-insurgency unit, who are now being confined to base; the complete dismantling of the command structures of the South West African Territorial Force; the release of any remaining political detainees; the assurance of impartial coverage of the elections by the media; and arrangements in the Territory for the period between the elections and independence. Each of those matters is being actively pursued by my Special Representative and is receiving my close personal attention.

The unique international collaboration that has been forged over the last few years, involving the efforts of many parties, must be maintained until the process of bringing independence to Namibia through free and fair elections under the supervision and control of the United Nations is duly accomplished.

In the effort to close a decade of turmoil in the Central American region, the Presidents of Costa Rica, El Salvador, Guatemala, Honduras and Nicaragua have laid down concrete plans for the implementation of the goals of peace and democratization that they set themselves two years ago in the Agreement known as Esquipulas II (A/42/521-S/19085, annex). The monitoring of the electoral process in Nicaragua by the United Nations is under way with a view to ensuring its purity and transparency and thus contributing to national reconciliation. A reconnaissance mission is now in the region to prepare the basis for consideration by the Security Council of a proposal for the verification, by military observers deployed throughout the region by the United Nations, of compliance with the commitments that aid incompatible with Esquipulas II to irregular forces and insurrectionist movements shall cease and that the territory of one State shall not be used to attack another. The United Nations will also be undertaking broad responsibilities in all phases of the voluntary demobilization, repatriation or resettlement of the Nicaraguan resistance and their families. That major project may well require a military component and, in due course, the full use of UNHCR as well as other programmes and agencies of the United Nations system.

While the war rages on in El Salvador, accompanied by widespread suffering, it is to be hoped that new political developments will lead towards dialogue and reconciliation in that country as well. The unequivocal appeal from all five Governments issued at the recent summit at Tela, Honduras (see A/44/451-S/20778), must not go unheeded. The deployment of United Nations military observers throughout the region could provide a new opportunity to render assistance in those efforts.

The Security Council, in resolution 637(1989), has now given strong backing to the peace process, which entered into a new phase with the signing of the Esquipulas II Agreement. It has encouraged me to continue to lend my good offices, which I intend to do, and for which I will continue to consult with the Security Council and seek its approval as needed. States from outside the Central American region have an important role to play in assisting the States of the region in their endeavours. A sustained effort is required to ensure that irregular forces and insurrectionist movements in the region co-operate in the implementation of Esquipulas II.

The international community at large, and in particular the major donors to humanitarian and development efforts, have given considerable assistance in the early phases of the Special Plan of Economic Co-operation for Central America, prepared in accordance with General Assembly resolutions 42/1 of 7 October 1987 and 42/204 of 11 December 1987, pursuant to the request of the five Presidents contained in Esquipulas II. The time has now come to buttress the emerging peace by providing the massive support that the region needs to overcome its age-old problems. Similarly, we may well have reached the stage where the plans laid down at the International Conference on Central American Refugees, held at Guatemala City in May 1989, can be put into effect, but these will also require substantial additional support. It is through those efforts in the development and humanitarian fields that the vast number of refugees and displaced persons in this beleaguered region will feel that they have a true stake in peace.

Following a number of encouraging developments that had taken place earlier this year, a conference on Cambodia was convened in Paris last month at the initiative of the Government of France. While the Conference succeeded in working out various elements of a comprehensive settlement, certain substantive political issues stood in the way of the total package needed to bring back to the Khmer people the stable peace that they desperately need after two decades of intense suffering, war and destruction.

I believe that attention should be focused now on preventing a recurrence of fighting, with its readily foreseeable consequences and the uncertainty it implies for all concerned. The follow-up mechanism established by the Paris Conference, under the leadership of the French and the Indonesian Co-Chairmen, offers some hope, however, for the continuation of the diplomatic process and for the reconvening of the Conference. For my part, I intend to continue the efforts I have made in the exercise of my good offices.

In recent months, there have been further constructive developments towards ending the 14-year-old dispute in Western Sahara. Although in August 1988 the parties signified their acceptance, with some remarks and comments, of the peace plan presented to them by the Chairman of the Organization of African Unity (OAU) and myself, practical discussions as to its implementation were required. Following a recent tour of the region, I proposed that a technical commission be established at United Nations Headquarters to work out the details of the implementation of the settlement plan. That proposal was accepted and the first

meeting of the commission took place in July. During these meetings, which include representatives of the two parties to the conflict, the Chairman of OAU and the Secretary-General of the United Nations, clarification of the arrangements and modalities for the implementation of the peace plan is being provided by the United Nations. The meetings also allow the two parties to express their concerns on each step of the process. A number of sensitive issues remain, which will require the active involvement on a continuing basis of the Chairman of OAU and myself.

Despite the conclusion at Geneva, on 14 April 1988, of the Agreements on the Settlement of the Situation relating to Afghanistan and the unanimous adoption of General Assembly resolution 43/20 on 3 November 1988, the suffering of the people of Afghanistan has not yet been brought to an end. The total withdrawal of foreign troops, which took place in February, was a major step towards a peaceful settlement; further progress requires, however, the full implementation of all parts of the Agreements as well as of the Assembly resolution. There has been an escalation in fighting, with massive infusion of war *matériel*. In the current circumstances, the programme of the United Nations to render humanitarian assistance has, despite every effort, been severely impeded.

The problem relating to Afghanistan cannot be solved except by political means. For this, a consensus is needed at both the international and the national levels. While such a consensus has not yet emerged, efforts are under way to narrow the gulf between the positions taken by the countries neighbouring Afghanistan and other concerned countries. In addition, however, there is a fundamental need for a structure through which the wishes of the various segments of the people of Afghanistan can be validly expressed. In pursuance of the mandate entrusted to me by the General Assembly, I shall persevere in my efforts during the months ahead.

On 20 August 1988, fighting stopped between the Islamic Republic of Iran and Iraq, and United Nations military observers took up the challenge of monitoring compliance with the cease-fire, which, one year later, remains in place.

While the heavy toll in human lives has thus come to an end, this has been only the beginning of the implementation of Security Council resolution 598(1987). The other steps called for in that resolution towards the restoration of security and stability in the region have yet to be taken. For over a year, my Personal Representative and I have held several inconclusive rounds of direct talks with the Foreign Ministers of the Islamic Republic of Iran and Iraq, as agreed on 8 August 1988, and presented suggestions to facilitate the fulfilment of the resolution in a manner that would generate mutual confidence. Eight years of sanguinary war have resulted in deep mistrust. The question we, therefore, continue to face is how to secure the implementation of a unanimously adopted and mandatory resolution in such circumstances. Lasting peace in the region depends on a way being found to achieve that objective.

Since my last annual report, the search for a solution to the Cyprus question has been particularly active. For the first time in the 25-year history of the problem, the leaders of the Greek Cypriot and Turkish Cypriot communities have personally committed themselves to a sustained effort to achieve an overall settlement. To that end, and in line with my initiative in August 1988, my Special Representative in Cyprus has hosted regular meetings between the two leaders since September 1988. They also met with me at United Nations Headquarters in November 1988 and April and June 1989 in order to review the results achieved and agree on how to proceed. Those discussions have been useful in revealing possible options for resolving the issues that comprise the Cyprus problem. While I do not wish to minimize the difficulties and distrust that remain to be overcome, I believe that we have now reached the critical juncture where an overall settlement that will safeguard the legitimate interests and meet the concerns of both communities seems possible. I shall, in keeping with the mandate of good offices entrusted to me by the Security Council, continue to make every conceivable effort to help the two sides seize the opportunity that could now be within their grasp.

Progress towards resolving the outstanding issues relating to the situation in Korea depends on sustained dialogue between North and South Korea. The conciliatory atmosphere around the world and the urge to settle problems that are the legacies of former conflicts will, I hope, facilitate an amicable solution of differences between the two sides. I remain available to render whatever assistance the two Governments may desire towards this end.

The eradication of the unjust and anachronistic system of *apartheid* in South Africa has been a prime responsibility and a universally acknowledged goal of the United Nations. The positive turn of events in Namibia and a political climate conducive to the resolution of regional problems should encourage the prospects of fundamental change in South Africa. It is clear that a mere dilution or softening of *apartheid* will not answer the expectations of the majority of the people of South Africa or of the world as a whole. The United Nations has indicated the steps that the Government of South Africa must take to create an appropriate atmosphere for a national dialogue with the genuine representatives of the majority in order to set in motion a democratic process aimed at shaping the political future of the country. These measures include the release of all political prisoners, the lifting of restrictions on political organizations and individuals, the restoration of freedom of speech and movement and the ending of all other manifestations of the state of emergency.

The General Assembly will devote a special session to this issue in December. I would appeal to the Government of South Africa to frame a positive and credible response to the unequivocal call for the dismantlement of *apartheid*. The opportunity has arrived for it to chart a courageous new course that will allay all fears about its intent and put an end, once and for all, to the oppression and violence that the system of institutionalized racial discrimination and minority rule inevitably entails.

The situation in the Middle East remains a source of profound and intense concern, not only because of the political principles and issues at stake, but also because of the widespread human suffering caused by the failure to resolve those issues. Hopes for early progress in the peace process, which were encouraged by the diplomatic momentum following the decisions taken by the Palestinian National Council at Algiers in November 1988, and at Geneva a month later, have sadly given way to mistrust and doubt among the parties concerned. Bilateral efforts to promote a dialogue between Israelis and Palestinians have thus far been unsuccessful. My constant attempts to pave the way to an effective negotiating process, which have included repeated contacts at the highest level with the parties directly concerned and with the permanent members of the Security Council, have also until now proved frustratingly inconclusive. Moreover, I am troubled by recent declarations that, in effect, question the applicability of Security Council resolution 242(1967). Since its unanimous adoption, the resolution has been regarded as the corner-stone of any comprehensive settlement to be reached. Unless there is agreement on that point, it is unlikely that real progress will be achieved.

Meanwhile, the situation in the Israeli-occupied territories grows steadily worse, with hundreds of people killed and thousands wounded or detained since the beginning of the *intifadah* nearly two years ago. The Security Council has repeatedly called on Israel to abide by its obligations under the Geneva Convention relative to the Protection of Civilian Persons in Time of War and I have voiced my deep concern that, despite the appeals of the international community, widespread violation of human rights persists. However, it is the political aspects of the problem that have to be addressed if an end is to be put to the confrontations that occur almost daily throughout the occupied territories. I would, therefore, remind all concerned of the urgent need for an effective negotiating process based on Security Council resolutions 242 (1967) and 338(1973) and taking fully into account the legitimate rights of the Palestinian people, including that of self-determination. The longer such a process is delayed, the greater will be the difficulties in initiating it and the more explosive the situation can become.

The world is appalled by the steady disintegration of the institutions of government and society in Lebanon and by the resort to unprecedented violence by all the parties involved in the Lebanese conflict. On 15 August 1989, after an alarming escalation in the military confrontation in and around Beirut, and with the danger of even further involvement of outside parties, I requested the President of the Security Council to convene an urgent meeting of the Council in view of the serious threat to international peace and security. The Council met the same day and expressed its deep concern at the further deterioration of the situation and appealed to all the parties to observe a total and immediate cease-fire. The Council also expressed its full support for the efforts of the Tripartite Committee of the Arab Heads of State and appealed to all to support those efforts likewise. In accordance with the Council's statement, I am pursuing all appropriate contacts in liaison with the Tripartite Committee to ensure the fulfilment of the Council's intent.

I strongly believe that the international community bears a responsibility to ensure that the unity, sovereignty, territorial integrity and independence of Lebanon are restored. A Member State of the United Nations deserves no less.

III

With the extraordinary improvement of the international climate during the past three years, there has been a new demand—and a new enthusiasm—for peace-keeping operations. Four new operations have been set up, and at least three are at present being actively considered. The seeds planted in earlier, less clement years are growing and proliferating. The wide recognition of the value of those operations is reflected in the award to the peace-keeping forces of the Nobel Peace Prize last year. New ideas and new directions for peace-keeping are being discussed, both within and outside the United Nations.

All this is encouraging and promising. It is imperative, however, that we keep the peace-keeping situation under constant scrutiny so that the best use is made of the Organization's capacity and so that we develop this important and valuable activity in a positive and constructive way. There are three main areas that need to be kept under constant review: function, capacity and performance, and support.

As far as function is concerned, we seem to be moving into a number of situations where, although there is a connection with international peace and security, the peace-keeping action is mainly concerned with the situation within the boundaries of a State, instead of taking place on the borders between States or between conflicting parties. Peace-keeping operations are being called on for a wider range of tasks, including the supervision of elections and the monitoring of the implementation of complex agreements.

I believe that it is important to maintain a rigorous analysis of what the United Nations can, and cannot, do, and how it should do it. Here the basic principles on which peace-keeping operations have always been based are a good guide for our actions: a workable mandate; the consistent support of the Security Council; the co-operation of the parties in conflict; the readiness of Member States to make available personnel and resources; a geographically balanced and representative force; an effective and integrated United Nations command; and adequate financial and logistical support.

The method of operation also needs to be kept under constant review. Until now, the use of force by peace-keeping operations has, with one exception, been permitted solely for self-defence in the last resort. We would be wise to stick to that principle. These are not, after all, enforcement operations. But I believe that the new and positive consensus, which for the first time animates the political role of the United Nations, also entitles us to consider how the strength and credibility of peace-keeping forces on the ground can be enhanced. Strength does not necessarily mean using force. Very often it means being strong enough not to use force. Before we embark on too many new and demanding ventures, I should like to see a serious discussion among Member States of the ways in which our soldiers in distant conflict areas can be given the means and the support to command respect and compliance with the decisions of the United Nations to a far greater degree than hitherto. The question of enhancing the credibility and authority of peace-keeping operations needs to be examined here at the United Nations by the Member States, and especially by the members of the Security Council.

Traditionally the personnel of peace-keeping operations have been overwhelmingly military. In Namibia we see a variant of that practice. With the multiplicity of functions now being discussed for peace-keeping, we would do well to consider new combinations of military, police and civilian personnel.

As regards capacity and performance, we have traditionally operated on a shoe-string in peace-keeping. With several new operations impending in different parts of the world, I am very conscious of our need to underpin our peace-keeping capacity here at Headquarters. I believe that Member States can also help—and some have done so already—by reviewing possibilities for earmarking stand-by troops for peace-keeping. I think we should also look at the training situation and see what can be done to enhance the degree of training for peace-keeping in national armies as a measure of readiness for United Nations peace-keeping duties. Rosters of available senior officers and staff officers might also be helpful in the future.

Support is inevitably the key to capacity and performance. The financing of peace-keeping has a long and not very creditable history. Many of the financial problems of the past had to do with political differences which are, I hope, no longer with us. None the less we still face a large and debilitating problem in relation to financing peace-keeping.

The truth is that the expense of peace-keeping is minimal by comparison with the costs—human, financial, military—of the alternative. Peace-keeping costs are infinitesimal by comparison with national military expenditures. And peace-keeping could be an important part of plans to reduce these national expenditures.

The current financial arrangements are not only dangerously limiting during the period in which a complex operation is being mounted; they also put an inequitable financial burden on troop-contributing countries. In addition, they tend to diminish the perception of collective responsibility, which is psychologically essential to peace-keeping operations.

I hope that Member States will address the financial problems of peace-keeping urgently and with imagination. A promising one among many possibilities would seem to be the establishment of a special reserve fund for peace-keeping, supported by all Member States. Such a fund would vastly facilitate the timely launching of operations mandated by the Security Council. Contributions to it, whatever its size, would, incidentally, represent a minuscule percentage of current national military expenditures.

Nowhere has the inadequacy of present arrangements been more evident than in the logistical support of United Nations peace-keeping operations. Here again the new political climate should allow a much freer exchange and more co-operation. In particular, I hope that countries with large and far-ranging military establishments will work together to see what can be done to establish a more reliable and responsive logistical framework for United Nations peace-keeping operations.

These are relatively short-term goals. For the longer term, we need to speculate on where peace-keeping fits into the underlying effort to build the international rule of law and a reliable system for the maintenance of international peace and security. When nations work together for those aims, as they now appear to be doing, the effect of representation and of symbolic presences is vastly increased. Peace-keeping is, and always has been, a dramatic way of representing the international will to peace and conciliation in the conflict areas of the world. If it is backed by an international consensus and sustained by a genuinely international effort, it can become a reliable and extremely important part of our broader effort to build a world at peace.

IV

Efforts to prevent possible conflicts, reduce the risk of war and achieve definitive settlements of disputes, whether long-standing or new, are part and parcel of a credible strategy for peace.

The United Nations needs to demonstrate its capacity to function as guardian of the world's security. Neither any alterations in the structure of the Organization nor in the distribution of competence among its respective organs are needed for that purpose. What is needed is an improvement of existing mechanisms and capabilities in the light of the demands of the unfolding international situation.

The prevention of armed conflicts is a mandate envisaged in the provisions of the Charter relating both to the Security Council and to the responsibilities of the Secretary-General. Article 34 speaks of any situation which might lead to international friction or give rise to a dispute and Article 99 of any matter which in the Secretary-General's opinion may threaten the maintenance of international peace and security. However, as has been repeatedly observed, it has been the general practice over the years to address a particular situation only after it has clearly taken a turn towards the use of force. Experience has shown that it is far more difficult to stop hostilities after their outbreak than to restrain Governments from heading towards the point of no return.

In order to activate the potential of the Organization for averting wars, the necessity of earlier discussion of situations threatening to explode needs to be clearly recognized. Timely, accurate and unbiased information is a prerequisite for that purpose. At present, the pool of material available to the Secretary-General consists of information provided by government representatives supplemented by the collection and analyses of published reports and comments. This is manifestly insufficient in cases where more than anticipatory diplomacy is required. Even for such measures as the establishment of observation posts or the dispatch of fact-finding teams, not to speak of the appointment of military observer missions in situations where fighting appears imminent, the Secretary-General needs to have at his disposal information that is dependable *prima facie*, even though it might be subject to further inquiry or verification. Only then can he be in a position to assess whether and when an issue needs to be brought to the attention of the Security Council under Article 99 of the Charter. The invocation of this Article is discretionary and the discretion has to be exercised with a most careful consideration of its possible outcome. There are situations where quiet diplomacy can be more effective in moderating a conflict. In any case, the lack or paucity of objective information can have most deleterious results. But in a setting in which incipient conflicts are under a global watch there will be less likelihood of confusion and, therefore, of indecision on the part of the Security Council in the matter of halting their escalation. Arrangements, for instance, could be made to receive information from space-based and other technical surveillance systems, which would enable the Secretariat to monitor potential conflict situations from a clearly impartial standpoint, but the question is whether the potential of modern technology can be placed in the service of peace.

More importantly, the Security Council could meet periodically to consider the state of international peace and security in different regions. For such meetings sufficiently to guide and influence the necessary supportive diplomacy, it might be helpful to hold them at the level of foreign ministers and, when appropriate, in closed session. That simple expedient could help ensure that the United Nations would not be caught unready by developments threatening the peace. Where international friction appears likely, the Security Council could act on its own or request the Secretary-General to exercise his good offices directly or through a special representative. When appropriate, the Council could also enlist the co-operation of the concerned regional organization in averting a crisis.

It cannot be stressed too often that there is usually a point in an impending crisis at which the potential adversaries are readier to make concessions that subsequently they are apt to regard as surrender. Such points offer opportunities for multilateral diplomacy to be at its best in allaying the fears and suspicions that so often lead to belligerency. If difficulties arise at the first turn, it can use other means of contact and communication between the Governments involved. All this implies a conscious policy decision on the part of Member States to strengthen and use the mediatory capacity of the Organization.

It also implies a resolve to use the leverage that lies with the United Nations, particularly with the Security Council, in the form of the collective influence that it can bring to bear on a situation. The invocation of the provisions of Chapter VII of the Charter is an extreme: in the intermediate stages of a party's obduracy against a settlement or against initiating a credible negotiating process to evolve a settlement, the United Nations can mobilize governmental and public opinion and also give salutary warnings of the consequences of a negative stand. Such warnings need not be public; in certain cases, they may be more effective if conveyed in private. However, they will fail to be persuasive if they are not backed, or are not seen to be backed, by the united will of the membership of the United Nations to avert a conflict. While a certain degree of partisanship among Member States on the merits of a dispute is unavoidable, and can even be suggestive of balanced solutions by exposing different viewpoints, there cannot be any division on the primary obligation flowing from the Charter, namely, the prevention of war.

To ''settle international disputes by peaceful means in such a manner that international peace and security, and justice, are not endangered'' is one of the principles set forth in the Charter. The conjunction of peace and justice is less liable to be overlooked by the conduct of multilateral diplomacy than by its alternatives. I am all too conscious how thorny is often the path leading to a just and lasting settlement and how hard is the resistance encountered. But I firmly believe that the United Nations can fulfil its mandate only if it is not daunted by the difficulties involved. By itself, the passage of time rarely brings about solutions to problems. The expectation of disputes ending through sheer attrition is certainly not supported by the experience of the Organization with regard to situations that involve issues of a fundamental nature such as the territorial integrity or political independence of a State or the self-determination of a people.

The United Nations can take credit for recommending the terms of equitable and comprehensive settlement of many disputes of this character that have been brought before it. However, nothing short of concerted or, at the very least, convergent action on the part of Member States, especially the permanent members of the Security Council, designed to bring about the acceptance and implementation of those terms, can suffice to resolve a conflict. Lacking such effort, the mounting of peace-keeping operations or mediation can produce an illusion of calm, beneath which disputes fester and resentments grow, threatening new outbreaks of hostilities. The pain of conflicts needs more than palliatives.

Political and moral suasion, combined with a judicious use of leverage, has been the main basis of multilateral efforts aimed at the settlement of disputes. However, there are categories of disputes that lend themselves to settlement by other means. Article 36 of the Charter requires that "legal disputes should as a general rule be referred by the parties to the International Court of Justice in accordance with the provisions of the Statute of the Court". I warmly welcome recent pronouncements made in that context.

As legal disputes arise in various parts of the world over a wide range of issues, there may be cases where the parties concerned are prepared to seek settlement through the International Court of Justice, but cannot proceed owing to a lack of legal expertise or funds. There may also be cases where the parties are unable to implement a decision of the Court for similar reasons. Considering this, I have established a special voluntary trust fund, which, under certain conditions, will be used to assist developing countries that lack the necessary means for recourse to the Court or for implementing its decisions.

Moreover, there have been, and in all likelihood there will be, many disputes that have a clearly legal component; assuming respect for judicial opinion, a reference to the Court on that aspect of the issue could at least help make the whole dispute more amenable to solution. There are also cases that are arbitrable. International arbitration has been resorted to with benefit to peace in many cases during the existence of the United Nations but its use needs greater encouragement in all situations to which it is applicable.

V

Progress towards arms limitation and disarmament demands persistence and considerable hard work. Beyond this, as we have seen, it requires the stimulus and guidance that only inspired political leadership can provide. In one area of major importance in this field, all these have been in evidence in the past year. As we survey the entire scene, however, global stability and peace are still in danger. The steps towards arms reduction taken by the two militarily most powerful States and the proposals under consideration between the two major alliances present a marked contrast to the lack of comparable progress elsewhere.

No complacency is reflected in noting the credit side of the balance. It is apparent that, even when all their proposed reductions are achieved, the members of the two military alliances will still have far more weapons than all others together. Nor can the stresses and strains that exist in so many other parts of the world be ignored. But the fact remains that in areas where confrontation has been the norm for so many years, major changes in attitudes and perceptions are taking place and long-standing differences are being reconciled.

In this regard I warmly welcome the proposals that have been put forward concerning conventional arms reductions in Europe. Furthermore, over half the intermediate-range and shorter-range missiles affected by the Treaty between the United States of America and the Union of Soviet Socialist Republics on the Elimination of Their Intermediate-Range and Shorter-Range Missiles (INF Treaty) have already been removed and physically destroyed. To complement those actions with major reductions in conventional weapons and forces would signify a change of fundamental importance.

With the resumption of the bilateral negotiations between the Soviet Union and the United States on the reduction of strategic offensive weapons, the pursuit of a 50 per cent cut in these arms should occupy the centre stage of nuclear disarmament efforts. It is imperative that the momentum established by the agreement and subsequent successful implementation of the INF Treaty should not falter. The world awaits a successful outcome on this issue. A slowing down and reversal of the vertical arms race would be all the more important in view of the forthcoming Review Conference of the Parties to the Treaty on the Non-Proliferation of Nuclear Weapons due to open at Geneva in August 1990.

At the Paris Conference on chemical weapons held in January 1989, 149 States unanimously called for early agreement on a convention on the prohibition of the development, production, stockpiling, acquisition, transfer and use of chemical weapons—and on their destruction. This has intensified the effort being made in the Conference on Disarmament at Geneva to achieve a complete ban on those weapons. The problems still impeding the attainment of this objective, including the question of verification in particular, are complex and difficult but not insurmountable. Considering the horrifying prospect of the spread of these weapons, the present opportunity to agree on a complete ban must be seized. I strongly urge all concerned to demonstrate a concerted will to achieve that goal at an early date.

For several years I have called for action on two particular issues: nuclear tests and conventional weapons. Although no specific agreement has yet evolved on either, some constructive negotiations are now taking place bilaterally and regionally. These are encouraging signs. I remain convinced that significant additional restrictions on nuclear testing beyond the Treaty Banning Nuclear Weapon Tests in the Atmosphere, in Outer Space and under Water of 1963, leading progressively to a complete halt, together with major reductions in nuclear weapons, offer the best way to release the world from the fearful possibility of nuclear war. I hope that the Conference on Disarmament will soon be associated with the bilateral efforts on the nuclear-test-ban issue. These measures, supported by conventional arms reductions such as those now being negotiated at Vienna, would do much to solidify the growing sense of confidence and trust.

The issue of conventional disarmament is beset with many regional and local implications. Even so, if dangers to peace around the globe are to be overcome, one of the essential requirements is that means be found to regulate the transfer of arms. The need for action both within and outside this Organization towards this end becomes ever more pressing. Many developing countries are draining their economies to purchase highly sophisticated weapons. On their side, arms-producing countries are vigorously pursuing weapon sales and transfers to bolster their trade balances. Efforts at the United Nations, with the help of governmental experts, to introduce greater transparency into arms transfers would be a necessary first step in arresting this alarming trend.

Apart from arms transfers, the increasing sophistication of new weapons and their proliferation, due to wider knowledge of the technologies involved, aggravate the already existing difficulties. The spread of knowledge, not only of nuclear weapons, but of chemical weapons and missile technology, introduces another potentially destabilizing factor. It is important to ensure that a qualitative arms race will not follow quantitative disarmament. This presents the challenge of harnessing scientific and technological progress for humanity's benefit rather than for armed confrontations.

A quarter of the resolutions adopted each year by the General Assembly address issues of disarmament. This, of course, indicates the depth and continuity of the Assembly's concern with these issues; it also reflects the consideration that the United Nations should continue to be at the forefront of multilateral efforts in this field. However, the number of resolutions and a reiteration of old positions does not meet the demands of new circumstances. To give an example of the questions that need to be faced now, the United Nations will be convening a conference on conversion of military to civilian industries next year in Moscow. The magnitude and complexity of the issues involved in the multilateral disarmament process demand that we explore all avenues to strengthen the role of the United Nations in this field and make more effective use of its deliberative machinery.

By in-depth study and careful analysis, by providing objective data and stimulating informed discussion, the Secretariat will play its part. It is also ready to undertake a role in multilateral verification of disarmament agreements, a subject on which a group of governmental experts has already been at work. However, the responsibility for action and leadership rests with Member States, particularly in addressing issues of specific relevance to their own regions.

With the new turn in the global situation, the broad objectives of arms limitation and disarmament, which were regarded as utopian, have begun to appear practical and achievable. But it is tangible progress towards these objectives that will lend permanence to the change.

VI

One of the most deplorable phenomena of current international life is the incidence of international terrorism. Calculated as it is to cause panic and disorder and to inspire and manipulate fear for the achievement of political ends, it violates human rights, and also lends a note of dangerous ambiguity to the dividing line between war and peace. It thus impinges directly on relations among States and shows how, thanks to the uncontrolled or indiscriminate supply of sophisticated weapons, organized violence is being increasingly privatized.

The firm and consistent position of the United Nations with regard to the prevention of international terrorism leaves no room for doubt or equivocation. Both the General Assembly, in its resolution 40/61 of 9 December 1985, and the Security Council, in resolution 579(1985), have taken pronounced stands on the question. The resolution of the Council unanimously condemned all acts of hostage-taking and it was recalled on 31 July when the news was received that a senior official serving with the United Nations Interim Force in Lebanon (UNIFIL) had, in all probability, been killed following his abduction months earlier. By its resolution 638(1989), the Security Council reiterated its condemnation of all acts of hostage-taking and abduction and demanded the immediate safe release of all hostages and abducted persons wherever and by whomever they were being held. For my part, I have repeatedly condemned this inhuman practice and, as requested by the Council, I will continue my efforts to seek the release of all hostages and abducted persons. In this connection, I will maintain my contacts with all those who might be in a position to use their influence towards achievement of this objective and the prevention of further acts of hostage-taking and abduction.

The question of defining terrorism and investigating its underlying causes does not diminish the urgency of taking preventive measures. There may be varying perceptions of the threat but no country is guaranteed safety from the danger. It is in the interest of all to deny to the perpetrators of terrorist acts the facilities and instruments they use.

Six specific conventions related to international terrorism have been elaborated since 1969; they have at least curbed terrorist activity in some spheres. The International Civil Aviation Organization (ICAO) has urged its member States to expedite research on means of detecting explosives and on security equipment. The work of ICAO is complemented by Security Council resolution 635(1989), which calls upon all States to share the results of such research and co-operation with a view to devising an international régime for the marking of plastic or sheet explosives for the purpose of detection. Such a régime would contribute significantly to safeguarding civil aviation and other potential targets. The problem is one that the United Nations will need to keep under continuous review until the time when the spill-over of political violence into the international domain will finally have been checked.

VII

To promote and encourage respect for human rights is not only a matter of legitimate international concern; it is also one of the main purposes and principles of the United Nations, as proclaimed by its Charter. Like every other purpose, it demands consistent pursuit, undeflected by considerations of short-term expediency. Like every other principle, it suffers discredit if it is selectively invoked.

Under the International Bill of Human Rights, consisting of the Universal Declaration and the two International Covenants based thereon, the international community has accepted the protection of human rights as a permanent obligation. A number of legal instruments have been adopted under the auspices of the United Nations that define fundamental rights in various contexts. Last December, the Body of Principles for the Protection of All Persons under Any Form of Detention or Imprisonment was added to this corpus (General Assembly resolution 43/173, annex). This year the General Assembly will consider two significant draft instruments: an optional protocol for the abolition of the death penalty and a draft convention on the rights of the child. Intense thought and effort have been devoted over recent years to the question of how to assure the rights of children, whom all societies and cultures look upon as humanity's most cherished and also its most vulnerable resource. This shared concern is reflected in the draft convention.

The elaboration of this considerable body of international law has been one of the main accomplishments of the United Nations in laying the foundation of a universal culture of human rights, transcending the differences among nations on account of ancestral traditions, systems of thought or belief, world-views and levels of social and economic development. The concern has been not only normative or theoretical, however: it has taken practical shape in efforts to secure adherence to the commonly accepted obligations in particular cases brought to the attention of the United Nations. This is done through examination of alleged violations, through public discussion in, and pronouncements by, the Commission on Human Rights and the various Sub-Commissions and, in certain cases, through confidential representations by the Secretary-General. Moreover, under a variety of legal instruments, mechanisms have been established for monitoring the observance of human rights. Currently, priority is being given to strengthening national infrastructures for the observance of human rights by providing advisory services and technical assistance. As greater awareness on the part of individuals is the key to assuring the protection of human rights, the United Nations, within the means available to it, is launching a world public information campaign on human rights.

Despite this effort towards the fulfilment of one of the main conditions of an international order of justice, sombre realities are facing us still. Nothing that has been done can lighten the burden on the human conscience imposed by the frequent, sometimes massive, violations of human rights in different parts of the world. The institutionalized system of racial discrimination in South Africa continues to be a most glaring example; in other areas also, the gross mistreatment of ethnic groups, the systematic practice of torture, the killings of unarmed demonstrators, the disappearances of individuals, summary arrests and executions furnish a most deplorable record. The year under review has brought little relief.

Such acts not only cause moral outrage; they also lead to political consequences injurious to the long-term interests of peace. If anything is writ large on current experience it is the truth that the stability of national and international society can only rest upon a foundation of assured human rights. Issues of human rights provide the deeper tones and shadings to political and social relations within and among nations. Governments, of course, have the right—indeed even the obligation—to maintain civil order and to use proportionate force in their territories against terrorism or other forms of violence. However, it is becoming increasingly plain that no Government can expect immunity from international exposure and criticism if it flouts human rights in trying to overcome political dissidence or ethnic unrest. The damage done to the self-confidence of its people and to its international prestige may be ignored in the short term but it will not be negligible over the long run.

I must pay tribute here to the efforts of non-governmental organizations and concerned individuals throughout the world who are championing the cause of human rights. Sincere efforts untainted by ulterior political considerations are bound to yield beneficial results.

The United Nations has done much to illuminate the interrelationship of peace, justice, freedom and human rights. But it is Governments that must realize this interrelationship in their laws and legal procedures. Far-sightedness on their part is required to help make a reality of what is meant to be a common condition of civilized life.

VIII

It is apparent from the current status of the questions relating to regional conflicts and to arms limitation that much ground is yet to be covered if the world is to move to conditions of lasting peace. Over and above these specific questions, the flux observable at many points of the political landscape is likely to present challenges different from those encountered before. Not only diplomacy but the attitudes of Governments will need to respond to these challenges in such a manner as to reduce disharmony and avert disruptions to peace.

The fact that there is now a fluidity in international relations, in marked contrast to the rigidity of the recent past, argues for greater care in handling the situations that may arise from time to time. In the first place, no change for the better in the political climate of the globe can be regarded as irreversible; to ignore the provisional element in it would be to lapse into complacency. Secondly, a movement away from entrenched positions holds no guarantee by itself that knotty issues will not arise which will need to be unravelled with a deft and high-minded approach. Thirdly, we seem to have reached one of those turning points in the evolution of international life at which personal contacts and greater ease of communication between the leaders of nations can play a larger role than they do in phases which follow a set pattern.

Apart from this aspect of world affairs, which affects diplomacy, especially of the most influential States, there is a ferment in large sections of the global society—and no policy on either the national or the international plane can be viable if it is based on a faulty diagnosis of the various causes of unrest. Whatever shape the turmoil takes, whether it be the assertion of ethnic identities or the demand for a better deal in political or economic terms, or even if it leads to upheavals within States, two requirements seem to be paramount: the stability of international relations must be preserved to the maximum possible extent and the universal standards of respect for human rights must be maintained.

At this critical stage, the mandatory principle of non-intervention by States in one another's internal affairs acquires added importance. Prudence and restraint will need to be fully employed to prevent internal upheavals in any State from becoming the cause of international conflicts. No State can, of course, insulate itself completely from the currents of information and opinion flowing in the world, but ultimately each national society must find its own equilibrium in accordance with its own genius. Considering the web of memories, perceptions, aspirations and cultural values that constitute national life, any forceful pressures from outside to give it a particular form can hold little constructive promise in the long run. More often than not, they provoke a reaction different from the one desired. I am conscious that no precise formula in terms of law or international ethics can be laid down in this context because definition in such matters can prove treacherous. However, the principles of the Charter do provide the necessary guidance.

If political wisdom and caution on all sides were needed at times of crises in the past, and did indeed serve to avert wider conflict, the kinds of situations that can arise in the future will make even greater calls on statesmanship. As myriad forces that shape the future become less and less manageable by Governments acting alone, States will need more and more to co-operate with one another and adopt practices and policies that will support the emergence and the consolidation of the rule of law. Certainly, the rampant violence that at present scars large parts of the world and the menace of terrorism from which no nation is immune cannot be overcome by recourse to methods contrary to international law.

The historic moment we have reached abounds with opportunities. If seized with an open mind, and with no intent to take advantage of any country's difficulties, they can lead us to a fruitful phase of international relations unrecognizable in traditional terms. By the same token, if they are misused, even the older civilities will not hold if the more vulnerable among societies around the world slide into chaos.

IX

The prospects of war or peace, regional or global, will no doubt always be the overarching concern of the international community. However, the state of the world economy and the possibilities it opens for sustainable development and social progress in disadvantaged sections of the globe also have major political implications. So, in an increasing degree, do certain social issues.

I would like to see the United Nations play a key role, as envisaged in the Charter, in promoting social progress and better standards of life for people throughout the world. This role becomes all the more important in the situation we are facing at present. There is an opportunity to extend to the economic and social spheres the same spirit of co-operation as has recently emerged in the political field. Indeed, the progress we have achieved in the global political climate can prove precarious if the economic climate remains adverse for the majority of the world's population.

During the past year there has been an apparent improvement in world economic conditions as world output and international trade in particular showed significant growth. However, the expansion of the world economy has not been even: some areas have enjoyed continuing prosperity while others are persistently plagued by depression and economic disorder. It would be inaccurate and facile to assume that the present lopsided growth patterns are due in all cases to inherent differences in underlying potential or to unsound policies. Nor should we expect these persistent imbalances automatically to correct themselves.

I remain deeply concerned about certain aspects of the current economic situation, particularly the widening economic and technological gap between the developing and the developed countries. The situation of the developing countries is being worsened by the continuing net transfer of resources to the developed countries. In much of the developing world, particularly in Africa and Latin America, most economies continue to stagnate if not regress, while in the industrialized world the central issue is the need to maintain inflation-free growth.

Debt remains a major constraint to the resumption of growth in many developing countries. It is clear that a common understanding on a solution to the problem of the external indebtedness of developing countries must now be reached quickly in the context of their growth and development. A review and strengthening of the current debt strategy is an urgent necessity. While the new thinking on debt in official circles is a welcome development, what is needed is a broad-based approach that includes substantial debt reduction. Every effort must be made to ensure that the measures taken are adequate and timely. Failure to find a just and equitable solution to the debt crisis in the near future can lead to a collapse of social and political structures in many developing countries.

It is encouraging that the major industrialized countries have committed themselves to achieving substantial progress in the Uruguay Round of multilateral trade negotiations in order to complete it by the end of 1990. These trade negotiations must lead to significant benefits and address the problems of the developing countries. Real progress has also to be made in alleviating the difficulties faced by developing countries that are dependent on commodity exports.

During the past year I have visited a large number of developing countries and I have been deeply impressed by the strenuous efforts they are making, often against formidable odds, for the welfare of their peoples. However, the external economic environment aggravates the difficulties they face in the process of adjustment. I believe that it is now essential to resume a broad-based North-South dialogue on international economic co-operation that takes fully into account the views of all countries. The special session of the General Assembly scheduled for early next year can provide an excellent opportunity for it. I trust that the session as well as the preparatory process for the international development strategy for the fourth United Nations development decade will lend fresh impetus to thinking and action on international co-operation for development.

Discussions are continuing for the restructuring of the intergovernmental machinery in the economic and social sectors, including the revitalization of the Economic and Social Council. Although the Council has made progress in enhancing its effectiveness, what is required above all at this juncture is an increased commitment by Member States to utilize and support the Organization in its economic and social activities. Only thus can the full potential of the United Nations in this sphere be realized.

X

At the present stage of the evolution of global society, the impact of technology has radically altered the means and methods of production and communications and, in the field of health, made rapid strides towards enhancing life expectancy and reducing disease. This has constituted genuine human advance in diverse respects. However, it is ironical that, at the same stage, certain processes are bringing civilization to a crisis. I refer in particular to the deterioration of the natural environment, the explosive growth in the world's population and the emergence of a variety of social trends that are steadily gnawing at the fabric of society.

The United Nations perceived the coming of the environmental crisis years before the phenomenon became a matter of public debate and policy in individual countries. The United Nations Conference on the Human Environment, held at Stockholm in 1972, sought to address the question comprehensively. Now, with the possibilities of disastrous change in climate no longer dismissible, daily signs of an ailing and exhausted Earth are evoking universal concern.

Two trends in the matter of treating the planet's affliction are currently discernible. One of them is reassuring; the other can be cause for apprehension.

The positive trend stems from the increased recognition in all countries, from the most industrialized to the least developed, of the gravity of the problem and the urgent need to deal with it in a practical way. This has been highlighted by pronouncements made and initiatives announced at the highest level of the world's leadership. It represents a most welcome step forward and may well signify the birth of a new kind of loyalty, an Earth-patriotism, a looking at the planet and its atmosphere as an object for protection and not for aggression and pillage.

The cause for apprehension, however, is that Governments may adopt unilateral approaches that will lead to overlapping, duplication and waste of resources. The problem of the environment is *sui generis* in many respects; agreement about its gravity notwithstanding, different countries may have different perceptions of its implications and, therefore, different priorities. This underscores the need to evolve an integrated response and establish the forms of international co-operation that the situation so clearly demands.

The environmental crisis is manifested in many forms, ranging from the depletion of the ozone layer, the greenhouse effect, global warming, desertification, land degradation and impoverishment of the Earth's biological diversity to the vexatious issue of the transborder disposal of hazardous wastes.

Since the emergence of the crisis, the United Nations has taken a number of steps to promote an understanding of the magnitude of the problem and to find means for arresting the degradation of the natural resources of our planet. The 1987 Montreal Protocol on Substances that Deplete the Ozone Layer, which came into force this year, prescribed the action to address the problem of ozone depletion. The Basel Convention on the Control of Transboundary Movements of Hazardous Wastes and Their Disposal was adopted in March 1989. A joint United Nations Environment Programme/World Meteorological Organization panel is studying the pace and nature of climate change and its likely environmental and economic impact and will report to the Second World Climate Conference in 1990. The United Nations has launched a major study, which will address several key environmental issues, including its link with development. Moreover, United Nations agencies are now pressing vigorously to integrate environment and natural resources protection into development programmes.

Nevertheless, much still remains to be done. It is imperative that Member States frame co-ordinated plans of international action that will ease and gradually resolve the crisis. The responsibility, of course, is shared by all countries; but the industrialized countries have a special obligation to check and mitigate the damage caused to the global environment and to assist the developing countries in achieving environmentally sound and sustainable development. There is also the need to address the question of the environment as a totality and to establish clear and equitable norms for the environmental behaviour of States through international law.

The proposed international conference on environment and development to be held in 1992, 20 years after the Stockholm Conference, will provide an occasion for developing a universal response in order to protect our planet for future generations. An opportunity lies here to redefine the relationship between man and nature and thus give a new turn to civilization.

XI

The current rate of increase in the world's population has most disturbing implications for sustainable development and social progress, especially in countries where larger increments still occur. Accompanying the explosive population growth is the rapid pace of urbanization in developing countries, making heavy demands on their ability to provide employment, housing, infrastructure and related services. One consequence is that the number of people living in absolute poverty, without adequate food or shelter, has increased at an alarming rate.

International efforts, including the Global Strategy for Shelter to the Year 2000 adopted by the General Assembly in its resolution 43/181 of 20 December 1988, will be crucial in meeting the challenge posed by the present population growth rates and the destitution in which people are condemned to live. At a time of vast expansion in the world's total wealth, the hunger and homelessness of millions remain a rebuke to civilization.

XII

Throughout the world the pace of social change has so accelerated that the pressures on individuals and on basic social institutions severely constrain the effective operation of the agencies of civil order. Frequent incidents of lawlessness cause widespread fear and, for the individual, a haunting sense of insecurity. This new generation of problems affects the growth and preservation of civil institutions and the process of development generally. Moreover, since they easily cross the boundaries of States they affect the stability of international relations as well.

The internationalization of certain major social issues can, therefore, no longer be discounted. There is a growing realization that the social crisis affects all countries, even if in varying degrees, and that there is none among them which can regard itself as immune from danger. Essential as it is, therefore, jointly to devise and implement strategies to reduce and gradually to eliminate these new sources of disorder and potential conflict, it is also necessary to acknowledge that their roots lie deep in conditions of imbalance between the different components of society.

In recent years, the United Nations has been the catalyst for the adoption of a corpus of internationally agreed plans of action and guidelines that in fact provide the elements of a global social strategy. This encompasses the guiding principles for developmental social welfare policies and programmes, the strategies adopted at Nairobi for the advancement of women, global documents in the field of youth, disabled persons and aging, the results of the International Conference on Drug Abuse and Illicit Trafficking, as well as the recommendations of the United Nations Congresses on the Prevention of Crime and the Treatment of Offenders. Thus a set of principles and norms, together with operational guidelines, is at our disposal.

Drug abuse, the incidence of the acquired immunodeficiency syndrome (AIDS) and international crime have reached such proportions that a new sense of urgency is needed to deal with them. Each is of a nature that not even the most resourceful States can solve by themselves; each, therefore, underscores the need for nations to act in concert.

Illicit use and traffic of drugs is now recognized as a social plague afflicting both developed and developing countries. Although efforts to combat this scourge have intensified in recent years, estimates suggest that the monetary value of drug trafficking has recently surpassed that of international trade in oil and is second only to the arms trade. It is a chastening observation that humanity is so deeply mired in the commerce of degradation and death.

The misery caused by drug addiction is immeasurable. Moreover, in a number of countries, the vast profits derived from this illicit production and traffic have the direct effect of making sections of local economies dependent on the trade and thus creating militant constituencies for its continuance. In some cases, administrative and judicial structures are being undermined to the extent of endangering political stability. Financial systems and banking institutions are frequently used to disguise vast sums acquired through drug trade and, in a number of developing countries, underground economies are expanded by its profits. There are also reported cases of collaboration between terrorists and those involved in drug trafficking in subverting civic peace. Indeed, the Government of a Member State has been confronted with an appalling situation: a cartel of drug dealers has openly embarked on armed conflict with it and, through assassinations and other terrorist acts, has tried to intimidate the body politic as a whole.

It is now generally recognized that both the supply of and the demand for drugs should be reduced and action should be taken to break the link between consumers and producers. A major step in this direction was taken in December 1988 with the adoption of the United Nations Convention against Illicit Traffic in Narcotic Drugs and Psychotropic Substances. The onus, of course, falls on Governments concerned to exercise the wide powers that the Convention vests in them and ensure that it is fully implemented. However, international understanding and co-ordination, together with increased resources, are indispensable in bringing this problem under control.

The United Nations Fund for Drug Abuse Control is working with other United Nations bodies and multilateral organizations to restrict cultivation of drug-producing crops and to stop trade in drugs through appropriate programmes, technical assistance and social measures taken largely at the community level. If decisive action is to be taken in solving the drug problem, it is essential that international support be available whenever and wherever requested. I would, therefore, appeal to all Member States to accede to the Convention and contribute generously to the United Nations Fund for Drug Abuse Control.

A related and tragic social problem is the rapid spread of AIDS, with a clear upward trend in all regions. The World Health Organization (WHO) is leading the global effort on AIDS in collaboration with intergovernmental and other bodies. In over 150 countries, WHO is monitoring and evaluating national AIDS programmes, co-ordinating with relevant United Nations entities in addressing the practical issues involved.

The socio-economic and humanitarian aspects of the AIDS pandemic must also be addressed. In response to General Assembly resolution 43/15 of 27 October 1988, I have sought to ensure a co-ordinated system-wide approach through the establishment of the United Nations inter-agency advisory group on AIDS and focal points have been created in all relevant United Nations entities.

The rising crime rate, particularly in its transnational and organized forms, has also become a threat to global society as a whole. The menace cannot be overcome without full co-operation on a multilateral basis. There is need for Governments to co-ordinate the relevant policies and judicial procedures and co-operate in law enforcement. Preparations are under way for a United Nations Congress on the Prevention of Crime and the Treatment of Offenders next year. It is not beyond the combined capacities of Governments to ensure that no corner of the globe will serve as sanctuary for the perpetrators of international crime nor any laxity in vigilance afford them the impunity of which they have been taking advantage so far.

Though there is world-wide concern about the use of narcotics and the incidence of crime, particularly in their international aspects, additional factors cause major social upheavals in many developing countries. The mass migrations due to hunger and natural and man-made disasters tell their own tale of human distress. The quest for global tranquillity will lack balance if the problem of the displacement of an untold number of human beings is not addressed with the sense of urgency it deserves.

XIII

The large number of refugees and displaced persons around the world continues to be a sombre commentary on the present state of affairs. While several important advances have been made in addressing and resolving the problems of refugees, asylum-seekers and related humanitarian categories, other developments are posing difficult new challenges. In seeking to meet those challenges, the Office of the United Nations High Commissioner for Refugees (UNHCR) takes the lead in working closely with other United Nations entities such as the United Nations Development Programme (UNDP), the World Food Programme (WFP) and the Office of the United Nations Disaster Relief Co-ordinator (UNDRO) in order to assure a co-ordinated and timely response.

The world's largest single refugee group is the Afghans, who have yet to be repatriated on a large scale. Such repatriation over the past year has occurred largely in Africa, where large numbers of refugees from several countries have returned home. UNHCR is currently overseeing the organized return of several thousand Namibian refugees. Assistance has also been planned for the repatriation of refugees in South-East Asia and Central America.

More States have acceded to the major international and regional instruments on refugees. However, this further validation of the international humanitarian law of refugees was offset by an increase in unilateral measures by States that has not only worsened the plight of asylum-seekers and refugees, but even poses a threat to the humanitarian institution of asylum.

I have been particularly concerned with the complex emergency situations that have developed in Africa as a result of severe civil conflicts often compounded by other factors. These situations generally exceed the response capacity of any single agency or organization of the United Nations system and require co-ordinated action by several of these entities. Complex emergency situations lead to large-scale internal displacement in addition to the exodus of people to countries that are themselves, in many cases, among the least developed.

In response to requests from affected Governments, I have organized inter-agency missions on several occasions to help assess the scope of humanitarian and rehabilitation needs for their particular situations. The final reports of such missions provide the basis for launching appeals to the international donor community for urgent assistance. During the past year I have, *inter alia*, appealed to Member States to support emergency humanitarian and rehabilitation programmes for Burundi, Ethiopia, Mauritania, Mozambique, Senegal, Somalia and the Sudan.

Natural disasters are too frequently a cause of human loss, economic and social hardship. In recognition of the importance of international efforts in early warning and disaster relief, the General Assembly has designated the 1990s as an International Decade for Natural Disaster Reduction. It is hoped that this will enhance the ability of the international community to answer situations of human distress due to causes beyond human control.

XIV

The administrative and financial situation of the Organization differs significantly from previous years. This is because of the impact of administrative reform, the addition of major new peacekeeping responsibilities and the continuing financial crisis.

The programme of administrative reforms initiated in 1986, based on the recommendations of the Group of High-level Intergovernmental Experts to Review the Efficiency of the Administrative and Financial Functioning of the United Nations, has been largely implemented. However, administrative reform is essentially a continuing process. The reforms have unquestionably produced a leaner and, in many ways, a more efficient Secretariat. Staff reductions undertaken since 1986 are now nearing the recommended target of 15 per cent. Unfortunately, in several areas, the capacity of the Secretariat to fulfil its tasks is already under considerable strain. In view of additional responsibilities placed on the Secretariat, it may well be necessary to limit the cuts to the level already attained. Several offices have been restructured in order to provide a more effective response to new demands while also adjusting to continuing constraints on available resources. Management information systems and the introduction of new technologies have yielded benefits in substantive, conference and administrative services.

Despite these changes, other factors have detracted from their potential net benefit. Although the Group of High-level Intergovernmental Experts envisaged less demand for conference and documentation services owing to the reductions and reforms, such a decrease has not occurred. Few bodies have decided to schedule biennial rather than annual meetings, or to reduce the duration of their sessions. As a result, the calendar of meetings is not significantly different this year from 1986, before the reform process began.

The mounting of 4 new peace-keeping operations in 1988-1989, as against 13 operations over the previous 40 years, and the planning of others have stretched to the limit the human and financial resources of the Organization. The demands on the Secretariat for additional services required a re-examination of programme priorities following on reform. In this context, I wish to mention that the staff as a whole have responded to this challenge with unfailing devotion to the mandate of the Organization. Many staff members have volunteered for service in overseas missions, fully aware of the personal sacrifice or physical hardship involved. Their enthusiasm and dedication to the realization of the goals of the United Nations provide a living testament to the vibrancy of international co-operation and multilateralism. On a recent visit to Namibia, I was deeply moved to see personnel drawn from as many as 109 States serving together under the flag of the United Nations with the single purpose of bringing that country to independence in the manner laid down by the Security Council.

The United Nations is now at the forefront of international efforts in a variety of areas. Demand for additional operations is likely in the coming months; these will entail more expense. At a time when the Organization continues to be short of funds, it is imperative that Governments ensure the regular and timely payment of their dues. However, the present financial position is not reassuring. As at 31 August, outstanding contributions to the regular budget exceeded $688 million, out of which $347 million were owed for the current year and $341 million for earlier years. For peace-keeping operations, the arrears totalled $661 million. All outstanding contributions thus amounted to $1,349 million. Only with a secure financial foundation can the Secretariat respond to requests for assistance with the speed and the resources requisite to a particular situation. It is high time that the United Nations is able to leave its financial worries behind.

In this context, it must also be recognized that the employment of the staff so as to secure the highest standards of efficiency, competence and integrity is an obligation under the Charter. The erosion of the conditions of service has made it increasingly difficult to comply with this requirement and to attract and retain staff with the necessary qualifications. The International Civil Service Commission has undertaken a comprehensive review of this situation and its findings will be presented to the Assembly.

The security of international civil servants also remains a cause of anxiety. There is an urgent need to ensure that the Organization is able to discharge its responsibilities without having the safety and sometimes the lives of its personnel endangered while serving in the field. I would urge Governments of all Member States to extend to them not only the protection that they need but also the treatment to which they are entitled by virtue of their being servants of all. The terms of service and the security of the staff are, I believe, matters of great importance for the Organization as a whole.

XV

The present report began with a retrospective glance at the different phases of international relations prior to the one ushered in only recently. I believe that the way public attitudes with regard to peace have varied and evolved through all these phases deserves to be borne in mind at this time when we may be witnessing a new turn in international affairs.

At the time the Charter of the United Nations was adopted, there was a sense of a new beginning around the world. For the first time in history, the prospect of the banishment of war from international relations ceased to look utopian. This evoked a kind of enthusiasm that had never been experienced before.

But the optimism was soon dispelled by the discord between the principal architects of the world Organization and the consequent impasse on all major questions of international peace and security. The world did escape another global war but the balance of terror between the major nuclear-weapon Powers provided no reliable insurance against the danger and little comfort to those outside the great-Power equation. There was no shortage of the rhetoric of peace but doubts grew as to whether war was a totally unacceptable option. A fearful, fatalistic sense attended an unending arms race.

This sense of a loss of purpose lasted for decades. Now that it has begun to lighten, there is a return to the earlier hope that had greeted the birth of the world Organization, but a hope tempered by a firmer sense of realities. When people think better of the United Nations and when it succeeds in its efforts, they are more hopeful about peace; the reverse also holds. This is borne out by all indications of opinion around the world. If anything is clear in the present situation, it is that war and the preparations for war have dwindling constituencies, while peace has a growing one.

For the size and strength of the constituency of peace, a great deal of credit is due to non-governmental organizations around the world. Their tireless work in many vital areas has complemented and supported the efforts of the United Nations.

But the noticeable improvement in public perceptions of the Organization intensifies an obligation—the obligation to avert another crisis of confidence. I am certain that, given the necessary support from Member States, the Secretariat of the Organization will respond fully to whatever calls are made upon it. However, its capabilities will be best employed if the Organization as a whole is used more purposefully by its Member States than it was in the recent past. The decision-making process on political matters has vastly improved with the emergence of a collegial spirit among the permanent members of the Security Council and with the daily co-operation between the Council as a whole and the Secretary-General. While this no doubt satisfies a basic condition for successful action, the changing times demand more. Agreement among the major Powers must carry with it the support of a majority of Member States if it is to make the desired impact on the world situation.

We will soon be entering a new decade. This, of course, means little by itself but not many decades can have opened at truly historic points. The present is such a point. There is a ubiquitous desire to turn over a new leaf, to try innovative approaches for the solution of old problems. In diverse regions, there is weariness with wars and there is recognition of their futility. Nor do the postures of hostile competition have the appeal to public opinion that they unfortunately exerted not too long ago. Instead, it is the combat against the causes of conflict, the struggle against economic inequities, and social evils and the degradation of the environment that must evoke all the courage and determination of battle. Obstacles to stable peace and balanced progress are many and the world's political, intellectual and moral imagination will need to be fully employed in overcoming them. The United Nations stands ready as the instrument for the effort.

Javier PÉREZ DE CUÉLLAR
Secretary-General

PART ONE

Political and security questions

Chapter I

International peace and security

The United Nations continued in 1989 to safeguard international peace and security. The General Assembly, noting that conflicts and hostilities were giving way to negotiations and co-operation, stressed the need to enhance the effectiveness of the Security Council in maintaining international peace and security as well as its preventive role, authority and enforcement capacity (resolution 44/126). The Assembly also reaffirmed its support for the validity and relevance of the Charter of the United Nations and encouraged Member States to implement and strengthen the principles of international peace, security and international co-operation (44/21).

During the year, new peace-keeping operations were established in Namibia and Central America and others were being actively considered. The Assembly adopted the recommendations of the Special Committee on Peace-keeping Operations for strengthening peace-keeping operations and making them more effective (44/49).

The Assembly expressed concern at the persistent tension in parts of the Mediterranean region and urged States to co-operate in reducing tension and promoting peace and security (44/125). It also called on States to promote the objectives established in its 1986 declaration of the zone of peace and co-operation of the South Atlantic and to refrain from actions that might create or aggravate tension and potential conflict in the region (44/20).

The Assembly expressed concern over attempts by mercenaries to infringe upon the sovereignty and territorial integrity of small States and urged the Secretary-General to monitor the security of those States and to bring such attempts to the attention of the Security Council (44/51).

In other action, the Assembly recognized the important contribution of the 1986 International Year of Peace and supported the efforts of the international community in strengthening the United Nations as an instrument of peace (44/11).

Strengthening of international security

Implementation of the 1970 Declaration

In December 1989, the General Assembly reaffirmed the validity of the 1970 Declaration on the Strengthening of International Security[1] and urged States, particularly the nuclear-weapon States and other militarily significant States, to promote and use effectively the system of collective security as envisaged in the Charter.

In February,[2] responding to a 1987 Assembly invitation,[3] Chile submitted its views on the implementation of the Declaration. In November,[4] the Secretary-General transmitted the views received from seven Member States in response to a 1988 Assembly request.[5]

GENERAL ASSEMBLY ACTION

On 15 December 1989, on the recommendation of the First Committee, the General Assembly adopted **resolution 44/126** by recorded vote.

Review of the implementation of the Declaration on the Strengthening of International Security

The General Assembly,

Conscious that the present stage of mankind's development is distinctive for its technological, economic and political changes, making overall progress possible, but at the same time also for its many obstacles, old and new, to the building of a more peaceful, secure, just, equitable, democratic and humane world,

Considering that events of significant bearing on international security are taking place, including a wide-ranging dialogue between the Union of Soviet Socialist Republics and the United States of America, with their positive effect on world developments and establishment of new trends in international relations,

Noting with satisfaction that conflicts and hostilities are giving way to negotiations, understanding and co-operation in a number of instances,

Mindful that the use of nuclear weapons could lead to the extinction of human life on earth,

Stressing the need for the strengthening of international security through disarmament and restraints on the qualitative and quantitive escalation of the arms race,

Expressing its expectation that the Treaty between the United States of America and the Union of Soviet Socialist Republics on the Elimination of Their Intermediate-Range and Shorter-Range Missiles, of 8 December 1987, would be a precursor to the adoption of further concrete disarmament measures leading to the complete elimination of nuclear weapons,

Emphasizing that the existing sombre contrast between enormous military expenditures and dire poverty underlines the importance of giving concrete shape to the concept of the link between disarmament and development,

Stressing also that disarmament, the relaxation of international tension, respect for the purposes and principles of the Charter of the United Nations, especially the principles of the sovereign equality of States and the peaceful settlement of disputes and the injunction to refrain from the use or threat of use of force in international relations; respect for the right to self-determination and national independence, economic and social development, the complete eradication of colonialism, *apartheid* and all other forms of racism and racial discrimination, aggression and occupation; respect for human rights, and the strengthening of international peace and security are closely related to each other,

Expressing its support for all efforts towards a successful resolution of hotbeds of crisis in the world, irrespective of their historical or contemporary causes, ensuring that the solutions are not imposed by outside Powers to the detriment of the interest of the parties directly concerned,

Expressing its conviction that the gradual military disengagement of the great Powers and their military alliances from various parts of the world should be promoted,

Considering that a détente devoid of economic content is unlikely to endure, and that if economic imperatives, particularly the requirements of developing countries, are not accommodated, the resulting strains may very well undermine the current trends towards global peace and harmony,

Considering also that the economic situation in the vast majority of the developing countries has deteriorated dramatically, especially in the least developed ones, and that the fruits of development should benefit the largest segments of population,

Stressing that the present asymmetry in economic and technological development can only be redressed through a balanced development of the entire international community and through efforts aimed at the broadest possible democratization of international relations,

Stressing also the need for structural adjustments in all spheres, in accordance with the development objectives and priorities of the countries concerned, in order to respond to the challenges of advanced technology, especially the technology of tomorrow,

Noting with satisfaction that the important process of decolonization from which a large number of sovereign States have emerged is entering a decisive stage,

Concerned over the growing environmental problems, which pose a threat to the very survival of mankind and testify to the interdependence of interests of all nations,

Stressing further that the promotion of freedom and human rights is one of the basic objectives of the world community,

Deeply concerned that racism and discrimination based on colour, creed, ethnic origin, culture or way of life are still practised,

Strongly emphasizing that *apartheid* is a particular and repugnant form of institutionalized racism which civilized nations have rightly condemned as a crime against humanity,

Reaffirming that the United Nations is an irreplaceable instrument for regulating international relations and resolving international problems and that its main organs, particularly the Security Council, are responsible for the maintenance and effective promotion of international peace and security,

1. *Reaffirms* the validity of the Declaration on the Strengthening of International Security, and calls upon all States to contribute effectively to its implementation;

2. *Urges once again* all States to abide strictly, in their international relations, by their commitment to the Charter of the United Nations;

3. *Emphasizes* that, until an enduring and stable peace based on a comprehensive, viable and readily implementable structure of international security is established, peace, the achievement of disarmament and the settlement of disputes by peaceful means continue to be the first and foremost task of the international community;

4. *Calls upon* all States to refrain from the use or threat of use of force, intervention, interference, aggression, foreign occupation and colonial domination or measures of political and economic coercion which violate the sovereignty, territorial integrity, independence and security of other States, as well as the permanent sovereignty of peoples over their natural resources;

5. *Also calls upon* all States to seek, through more effective utilization of the means provided for in the Charter, the peaceful settlement of disputes and the elimination of the focal points of crisis and tension, which constitute a threat to international peace and security;

6. *Urges* all States, in particular the nuclear-weapon States and other militarily significant States, to take immediate steps aimed at promoting and using effectively the system of collective security as envisaged in the Charter, as well as halting effectively the arms race with the aim of achieving general and complete disarmament under effective international control, and implementing the recommendations and decisions contained in the Final Document of the Tenth Special Session of the General Assembly;

7. *Stresses* that there is a need further to enhance the effectiveness of the Security Council in discharging its principal responsibility of maintaining international peace and security and to enhance the preventive role, authority and enforcement capacity of the Council in accordance with the Charter;

8. *Emphasizes* the role that the United Nations has in the maintenance of international peace and security and in economic and social development and progress for the benefit of mankind;

9. *Considers* that the management of the world economy needs to be more broad-based so as to reflect the interests of all countries and groups of countries and to evolve policies which can be supported by all, as well as that the current economic and social problems and the needs of the future are such that no single nation or group of nations can solve them in isolation;

10. *Emphasizes also* that there can be no lasting peace and security in the world without the solution of the international economic problems, particularly those of the developing countries, and the ensuring of the sustained growth and development of the world economy;

11. *Reaffirms* that the total eradication of colonialism and the economic emancipation of all peoples as an indispensable pre-condition for maintaining and strengthening their political independence remain priority tasks;

12. *Considers* that the protection of the environment has emerged as a major global concern, dramatically emphasizing the growing interdependence of the world, which calls for urgent co-operative measures and a global compact ensuring a sustainable and environmentally sound development;

13. *Considers also* that respect for and promotion of human rights and fundamental freedoms in their civil,

political, economic, social and cultural aspects, on the one hand, and the strengthening of international peace and security, on the other, mutually reinforce each other;

14. *Reaffirms also* the legitimacy of the struggle of peoples under colonial domination, foreign occupation or racist régimes and their inalienable right to self-determination and independence;

15. *Reaffirms further* that the democratization of international relations is an imperative necessity enabling, under the conditions of interdependence, the full development and independence of all States, as well as the attainment of genuine security, peace and co-operation in the world, and stresses its firm belief that the United Nations offers the best framework for the promotion of these goals;

16. *Emphasizes* the role that the United Nations has to play in promoting respect for international law as a basis of peace and security;

17. *Invites* Member States to submit their views on the question of the implementation of the Declaration on the Strengthening of International Security, and requests the Secretary-General to submit a report to the General Assembly at its forty-fifth session on the basis of the replies received;

18. *Decides* to include in the provisional agenda of its forty-fifth session the item entitled ''Review of the implementation of the Declaration on the Strengthening of International Security''.

General Assembly resolution 44/126

15 December 1989   Meeting 81   128-1-24 (recorded vote)

Approved by First Committee (A/44/821) by recorded vote (98-1-23), 30 November (meeting 52); 14-nation draft (A/C.1/44/L.71/Rev.1); agenda item 72.
Sponsors: Algeria, Bangladesh, Cuba, Egypt, India, Indonesia, Madagascar, Malaysia, Mali, Pakistan, Romania, Sri Lanka, Uganda, Yugoslavia.
Meeting numbers. GA 44th session: 1st Committee 46-52; plenary 81.

Recorded vote in Assembly as follows:

In favour: Afghanistan, Albania, Algeria, Angola, Antigua and Barbuda, Argentina, Bahamas, Bahrain, Bangladesh, Barbados, Benin, Bhutan, Bolivia, Botswana, Brazil, Brunei Darussalam, Bulgaria, Burkina Faso, Burundi, Byelorussian SSR, Cameroon, Cape Verde, Central African Republic, Chad, Chile, China, Colombia, Congo, Costa Rica, Côte d'Ivoire, Cuba, Cyprus, Czechoslovakia, Democratic Kampuchea, Democratic Yemen, Djibouti, Dominica, Dominican Republic, Ecuador, Egypt, Ethiopia, Fiji, Gabon, Gambia, German Democratic Republic, Ghana, Guatemala, Guinea, Guinea-Bissau, Guyana, Haiti, Honduras, Hungary, India, Indonesia, Iran, Iraq, Jamaica, Jordan, Kenya, Kuwait, Lao People's Democratic Republic, Lebanon, Lesotho, Liberia, Libyan Arab Jamahiriya, Madagascar, Malawi, Malaysia, Maldives, Mali, Mauritania, Mauritius, Mexico, Mongolia, Morocco, Mozambique, Myanmar, Nepal, Nicaragua, Niger, Nigeria, Oman, Pakistan, Panama, Papua New Guinea, Paraguay, Peru, Philippines, Poland, Qatar, Romania, Rwanda, Saint Kitts and Nevis, Saint Lucia, Saint Vincent and the Grenadines, Samoa, Sao Tome and Principe, Saudi Arabia, Senegal, Seychelles, Sierra Leone, Singapore, Solomon Islands, Somalia, Sri Lanka, Sudan, Suriname, Swaziland, Syrian Arab Republic, Thailand, Togo, Trinidad and Tobago, Tunisia, Uganda, Ukrainian SSR, USSR, United Arab Emirates, United Republic of Tanzania, Uruguay, Vanuatu, Venezuela, Viet Nam, Yemen, Yugoslavia, Zaire, Zambia, Zimbabwe.
Against: United States.
Abstaining: Australia, Austria, Belgium, Canada, Denmark, Finland, France, Germany, Federal Republic of, Greece, Iceland, Ireland, Israel, Italy, Japan, Luxembourg, Malta, Netherlands, New Zealand, Norway, Portugal, Spain, Sweden, Turkey, United Kingdom.

Enhancing international peace and security

The Special Committee on the Charter of the United Nations and on the Strengthening of the Role of the Organization, at its March/April 1989 meetings,[6] considered working papers submitted by Belgium, the Federal Republic of Germany, Italy, Japan, New Zealand and Spain[7] and by Czechoslovakia and the German Democratic Republic,[8] on fact-finding activities by the United Nations in the context of the maintenance of international peace and security.

The Special Committee was of the opinion that States should consider the proposals submitted by Romania[9] on the resort to a commission of good offices, mediation or conciliation within the United Nations as useful guidance when resorting to such measures to settle disputes, and recommended that the General Assembly bring those proposals to the attention of States.

The Assembly, in **resolution 44/37**, asked the Special Committee to give priority to the question of the maintenance of international peace and security in all its aspects in order to strengthen United Nations fact-finding activities and to examine the Secretary-General's report on the elaboration of a draft handbook on the peaceful settlement of disputes between States.[10] In **resolution 44/32**, the Assembly invited the International Law Commission to continue work on elaborating a draft Code of Crimes against the Peace and Security of Mankind.

On 29 September, the Ministers for Foreign Affairs of the five permanent members of the Security Council met with the Secretary-General to exchange views and review developments on a wide range of international issues. In a statement following their meeting,[11] the Ministers agreed that at the current time of positive change in the international political climate, from confrontation to relaxation and interaction among States, the United Nations had an important role to play. They placed particular emphasis on efforts to resolve current regional conflicts, noted with satisfaction the trend towards dialogue and peaceful settlement of disputes which had developed in recent years and welcomed the active involvement of the United Nations in that process. They commended United Nations peace-keeping operations in preventing and resolving regional disputes and underlined the importance of their effective functioning. The Ministers expressed satisfaction at the improved working relations within the Security Council and with the Secretary-General and expressed their determination to continue to work together and in co-operation with him for the prevention and resolution of international conflicts.

On 3 November,[12] the USSR and the United States jointly requested inclusion in the Assembly's agenda of an item on enhancing international peace, security and international co-operation in all its aspects in accordance with the Charter. They explained that recent developments offered renewed prospects for international co-operation towards common goals and new importance to the further strengthening of the role and effectiveness of the United Nations in maintaining international peace and security through respect for its Charter and better international co-operation in resolving international problems of a political, social, cultural or humanitarian character.

Appended to the request was a draft resolution which the two States said reflected a commitment to a renewed relationship in the United Nations based on enhanced consultation and co-operation to implement and strengthen the principles and system of peace, security and international co-operation laid down in the Charter. In that connection, it was particularly relevant to intensify co-operative efforts towards ensuring international peace and security in accordance with the Charter, and to consult and co-operate within the framework of the United Nations, particularly through the Security Council, the General Assembly and the appropriate subsidiary bodies.

On 9 November, the Assembly, on the recommendation of the General Committee,[13] decided in **decision 44/402 A** to include the additional item.

GENERAL ASSEMBLY ACTION

On 15 November 1989, the General Assembly adopted **resolution 44/21** without vote.

Enhancing international peace, security and international co-operation in all its aspects in accordance with the Charter of the United Nations
The General Assembly,
Desiring to strengthen further the role and effectiveness of the United Nations in maintaining international peace and security for all States on the basis of full and universal respect for the Charter of the United Nations and through better international co-operation in resolving international problems of a political, economic, social, cultural or humanitarian character,
Mindful of the potential of the United Nations to be even more effective in achieving international co-operation,
1. *Calls upon* all States to intensify their practical efforts towards ensuring international peace and security in all its aspects through co-operative means in accordance with the Charter of the United Nations;
2. *Reaffirms* its support for the validity and relevance of the Charter and urges all States to abide by it and, in particular, to respect the principles of sovereign equality, political independence and territorial integrity of States and non-intervention in internal affairs, refrain from the threat or use of force inconsistent with the Charter, settle disputes peacefully, adhere to the principles of equal rights and self-determination of peoples, respect for human rights and fundamental freedoms, and co-operation among States, and comply in good faith with their obligations assumed in accordance with the Charter;
3. *Encourages* Member States to consult and co-operate within the framework of the United Nations, the Security Council, the General Assembly and their appropriate subsidiary bodies in order to find multifaceted approaches to implement and strengthen the principles and the system

of international peace, security and international co-operation laid down in the Charter.

General Assembly resolution 44/21

15 November 1989   Meeting 56   Adopted without vote

43-nation draft (A/44/L.38 & Add.1); agenda item 158.
Sponsors: Argentina, Australia, Austria, Belgium, Bulgaria, Byelorussian SSR, Canada, Colombia, Czechoslovakia, Denmark, Ecuador, Ethiopia, Finland, France, German Democratic Republic, Germany, Federal Republic of, Greece, Hungary, Iceland, Ireland, Italy, Luxembourg, Malaysia, Malta, Mauritius, Mongolia, Nepal, Netherlands, New Zealand, Norway, Poland, Portugal, Romania, Senegal, Spain, Suriname, Sweden, Turkey, Ukrainian SSR, USSR, United Kingdom, United States, Yugoslavia.

On 14 November,[14] Argentina, in requesting that it be added to the sponsors of the draft resolution, said that in the new international climate of trust and co-operation, the Assembly was able to take up again ideas and concepts that constituted the foundations of the United Nations, which now had before it reasonable prospects of building a world in which democracy, freedom and human rights would prevail.

The First Committee considered the item on a comprehensive approach to strengthening international peace and security in accordance with the Charter of the United Nations from 22 to 30 November. It had before it several communications, including a Soviet *aide-mémoire* on strengthening the preventive functions of the United Nations and related international organizations in an interdependent world.[15]

The Committee reported[16] to the Assembly that it had considered the item jointly with those on strengthening security and co-operation in the Mediterranean region (see below) and review of the implementation of the 1970 Declaration on the Strengthening of International Security (see above), but had not taken any action.

On 15 December, by **decision 44/433**, the Assembly took note of the First Committee's report.

On 4 December, by **resolution 44/31**, the Assembly had called on Member States to make full use, in accordance with the Charter, of the framework provided by the United Nations for the peaceful settlement of disputes and international problems.

REFERENCES
[1]YUN 1970, p. 105, GA res. 2734(XXV), 16 Dec. 1970. [2]A/44/121. [3]YUN 1987, p. 114, GA res. 42/92, 7 Dec. 1987. [4]A/44/722 & Add.1. [5]YUN 1988, p. 20, GA res. 43/88, 7 Dec. 1988. [6]A/44/33. [7]A/AC.182/L.60. [8]A/AC.182/L.62. [9]A/AC.182/L.52/Rev.2. [10]A/AC.182/L.61. [11]S/20880. [12]A/44/245. [13]A/44/250/Add.4. [14]A/44/727. [15]A/44/602. [16]A/44/822.

Review of peace-keeping operations

In 1989, two new peace-keeping operations were established: the United Nations Transition Assistance Group in Namibia (see PART FOUR, Chapter III) and the United Nations Observer Group in Central America (see PART TWO, Chapter II). There were also other potential new missions under active consideration.

The Special Committee on Peace-keeping Operations held four meetings between 10 April and 1 June.[1] It had before it a March report with later addenda[2] of the Secretary-General, containing replies from 22 Governments to a 1988 General Assembly request[3] for their views on United Nations peace-keeping operations. The Committee recommended that the Assembly request the Secretary-General to provide Member States with information on personnel, material and technical requirements for peace-keeping operations; invite them to identify the resources they would, in principle, contribute to those operations and establish a registry of potential contributions based on their replies; and undertake a study of those tasks and services that could be performed by civilian personnel. The Committee also recommended that States exchange experiences and establish national training programmes for military and civilian personnel for the operations and that the Secretary-General prepare the necessary training manuals. It recommended full support of host countries to the operations; the conclusion of status-of-forces agreements; that Member States pay assessed contributions in full and on time; and that voluntary contributions be encouraged.

On 22 May,[4] Sweden transmitted the 14 April final statement of the Palme Commission on Disarmament and Security Issues containing, among other things, suggestions for improving United Nations peace-keeping capabilities.

In October, the Secretary-General, in a report[5] on the administrative and budgetary aspects of financing United Nations peace-keeping operations, addressed the issues of the economies of scale, civilian personnel provided by Governments, start-up problems and the feasibility and cost-effectiveness of maintaining a reserve stock of equipment and supply items. He noted the need to maintain a high degree of readiness in the Organizations's ability to emplace new peace-keeping operations and proposed measures to cover the financial and physical arrangements for their implementation.

In a December report to the Assembly's Fifth (Administrative and Budgetary) Committee,[6] the Secretary-General proposed the establishment within the Secretariat of a Senior Planning and Monitoring Group, which would also review and make recommendations regarding the Secretariat's organizational structure in relation to peace-keeping matters. He also made proposals for financing (see PART FIVE, Chapter I) and backstopping peace-keeping operations, and for providing additional support for the Office for Special Political Affairs.

GENERAL ASSEMBLY ACTION

On 8 December 1989, on the recommendation of the Special Political Committee, the General Assembly adopted **resolution 44/49** without vote.

Comprehensive review of the whole question of peace-keeping operations in all their aspects

The General Assembly,

Recalling its resolutions 1874(S-IV) of 27 June 1963, 2006(XIX) of 18 February 1965, 2053 A (XX) of 15 December 1965, 2249(S-V) of 23 May 1967, 2308(XXII) of 13 December 1967, 2451(XXIII) of 19 December 1968, 2670(XXV) of 8 December 1970, 2835(XXVI) of 17 December 1971, 2965(XXVII) of 13 December 1972, 3091(XXVIII) of 7 December 1973, 3239(XXIX) of 29 November 1974, 3457(XXX) of 10 December 1975, 31/105 of 15 December 1976, 32/106 of 15 December 1977, 33/114 of 18 December 1978, 34/53 of 23 November 1979, 35/121 of 11 December 1980, 36/37 of 18 November 1981, 37/93 of 10 December 1982, 38/81 of 15 December 1983, 39/97 of 14 December 1984, 40/163 of 16 December 1985, 41/67 of 3 December 1986, 42/161 of 8 December 1987 and 43/59 A of 6 December 1988,

Welcoming the progress made by the Special Committee on Peace-keeping Operations during its session in 1989 and, in particular, the agreement reached on a number of conclusions and recommendations,

Convinced that the United Nations peace-keeping operations are an integral component of enhancing the effectiveness of the United Nations in the maintenance of international peace and security,

Taking into account that increasing activities in the field of United Nations peace-keeping require increasing human, financial and material resources for the Organization,

Aware of the extremely difficult financial situation of the United Nations peace-keeping forces and of the heavy burden on the troop contributors, especially those from developing countries,

Emphasizing that the current political atmosphere is propitious for achieving further progress in the work of the Special Committee,

Bearing in mind the fact that constructive exchanges of views on various practical aspects of peace-keeping operations can contribute favourably to the smooth and effective functioning of these operations,

Taking note of the report of the Secretary-General on the work of the Organization,

Having examined the report of the Special Committee,

1. *Takes note* of the report of the Special Committee on Peace-keeping Operations;

2. *Requests* the Secretary-General to provide Member States with the relevant information with respect to the requirements for United Nations peace-keeping operations of personnel, material and technical resources and services and, at the same time, to invite Member States, by means of a questionnaire, to identify those personnel, material and technical resources and services which they would be ready, in principle, to contribute to United Nations peace-keeping operations;

3. *Also requests* the Secretary-General, on the basis of the responses by States to the questionnaire, to establish a registry, indicative in nature, of potential contributions by Member States of personnel, material and

technical resources and services, and to invite Member States to bring their responses up to date as necessary;

4. *Further requests* the Secretary-General to undertake a study to identify those tasks and services which could be performed by civilian personnel in peace-keeping operations and to inform the Special Committee of the conclusions of the study as soon as possible, taking into account the study requested by the General Assembly in resolution 43/230 of 21 December 1988;

5. *Encourages* Member States to exchange the experiences acquired through their participation in peace-keeping operations and encourages Member States and interested organizations to hold, in consultation with the Secretariat, as appropriate, regional and international seminars on peace-keeping operations;

6. *Also encourages* Member States to establish national training programmes for military and civilian personnel for peace-keeping operations and, in this connection, requests the Secretary-General to prepare training manuals, which Member States might wish to use as guidelines for their national or regional training programmes;

7. *Emphasizes* the need to ensure a secure and sound financial basis for United Nations peace-keeping operations;

8. *Urges* all Member States to pay their assessed contributions in full and on time and also encourages those States which can do so to make voluntary contributions that are acceptable to the Secretary-General;

9. *Urges* host countries of any United Nations peace-keeping operation and all directly interested parties to extend all possible support in order to facilitate the deployment and functioning of such operations;

10. *Considers* that status-of-forces agreements should be concluded between host countries of any United Nations peace-keeping operation and the United Nations and, to this end, urges host countries of any United Nations peace-keeping operation to conclude status-of-forces agreements with the United Nations as soon as possible after the establishment of the operation;

11. *Requests* the Secretary-General to prepare a model status-of-forces agreement between the United Nations and host countries, while maintaining the flexibility needed to encompass different possible operations, and to make the model agreement available to Member States;

12. *Welcomes* the initiative of the Secretary-General in preparing standard operating procedures, and expresses the hope that this work will be completed as soon as possible and made available to Member States;

13. *Requests* the Secretary-General to publish an updated version of *The Blue Helmets* and to include therein a summary of the practice of United Nations peace-keeping operations, in time for the forty-fifth session of the General Assembly and, thereafter, to bring it up to date as necessary;

14. *Considers* it useful to have further discussions, in the appropriate forums, including the Special Committee, on the possible fields for peace-keeping and on the further development of peace-keeping operations;

15. *Urges* the Special Committee, in accordance with its mandate, to continue its efforts for a comprehensive review of the whole question of peace-keeping operations in all their aspects with a view to strengthening the role of the United Nations in this field, taking into account the difficult financial situation of peace-keeping operations and the need for maximum cost efficiency;

16. *Decides* that the Special Committee shall accept the participation of observers of Member States, including in the meetings of its working groups;

17. *Invites* Member States to submit any further observations and suggestions to the Secretary-General by 1 March 1990 on peace-keeping operations in all their aspects, with particular emphasis on practical proposals to make these operations more effective;

18. *Requests* the Secretary-General to prepare, within existing resources, a compilation of the above-mentioned observations and suggestions and to submit it to the Special Committee during its session in 1990;

19. *Requests* the Special Committee to submit a report on its work to the General Assembly at its forty-fifth session;

20. *Decides* to include in the provisional agenda of its forty-fifth session the item entitled "Comprehensive review of the whole question of peace-keeping operations in all their aspects".

General Assembly resolution 44/49

8 December 1989   Meeting 78   Adopted without vote

Approved by Special Political Committee (A/44/734) without vote, 2 November (meeting 12); 6-nation draft (A/SPC/44/L.6 & Corr.1), orally revised; agenda item 78.

Sponsors: Argentina, Canada, Egypt, German Democratic Republic, Japan, Nigeria.

Financial implications. 5th Committee, A/44/808; S-G, A/C.5/44/23, A/SPC/44/L.7.

Meeting numbers. GA 44th session: 5th Committee 48; SPC 9-12; plenary 78.

REFERENCES

[1]A/44/301. [2]A/AC.121/36 & Add.1-4. [3]YUN 1988, p. 30, GA res. 43/59 A, 6 Dec. 1988. [4]A/44/293-S/20653. [5]A/44/605 & Add.1,2. [6]A/C.5/44/45.

Regional aspects of international peace and security

Security and co-operation in the Mediterranean

In accordance with a 1988 General Assembly resolution,[1] the Secretary-General submitted in November 1989 a report[2] on the strengthening of security and co-operation in the Mediterranean region, in which he presented a summary of the debate on the question during the 1988 Assembly session. Also included were the views of 10 Member States submitted in response to his request.

In related developments, the heads of State or Government of the Movement of Non-Aligned Countries, at their Ninth Conference (Belgrade, Yugoslavia, 4-7 September),[3] reaffirmed their support for the transformation of the Mediterranean into a region of peace, security and co-operation, free from conflict and confrontation. They also expressed the hope that the 1990 meeting of the Conference on Security and Co-operation in Europe on the Mediterranean would contribute to the strengthening of confidence and security in the region. On 19 September,[4] the

Libyan Arab Jamahiriya drew attention to media reports on the launching by Israel (referred to by the Jamahiriya as the Zionist entity) on 14 September of a medium-range missile capable of carrying nuclear warheads, which fell into the Mediterranean north of the Libyan city of Benghazi. The incident, it said, represented a further escalation of tension in the region, endangered air and sea navigation and economic activity, and nullified efforts to strengthen peace and co-operation and to make the region a zone of peace. On 20 October,[5] the Libyan Arab Jamahiriya referred to military manoeuvres conducted by the North Atlantic Treaty Organization in the western part of the Mediterranean, which it said turned the region into an area of tension and international conflict and which were incompatible with the call to make the Mediterranean a zone of security and co-operation.

On 29 September,[6] Algeria, the Libyan Arab Jamahiriya, Mauritania, Morocco and Tunisia transmitted to the Secretary-General the texts of the Treaty and Declaration creating the Arab Maghreb Union. Signed on 17 February by those five States, the Treaty aimed, *inter alia*, at achieving progress and prosperity of their societies and the preservation of peace. It entered into force on 1 July.

GENERAL ASSEMBLY ACTION

On 15 December 1989, on the recommendation of the First Committee, the General Assembly adopted **resolution 44/125** without vote.

Strengthening of security and co-operation in the Mediterranean region

The General Assembly,

Recalling its resolutions 36/102 of 9 December 1981, 37/118 of 16 December 1982, 38/189 of 20 December 1983, 39/153 of 17 December 1984, 40/157 of 16 December 1985, 41/89 of 4 December 1986, 42/90 of 7 December 1987 and 43/84 of 7 December 1988,

Recognizing the importance of promoting peace, security and co-operation in the Mediterranean region and of strengthening further the economic, commercial and cultural links in the region,

Reaffirming the primary role of the Mediterranean countries in the promotion of security and co-operation in the Mediterranean region,

Expressing concern at the persistent tension in parts of the Mediterranean region and the consequent threat to peace,

Welcoming the favourable developments in the international situation, and expressing hope that these developments will have a positive impact on the Mediterranean region,

Concerned at the continuing military operations and reports of recent activities in the Mediterranean and the danger that they create for peace, security and general equilibrium in the region,

Reaffirming the responsibility of all States to conform in their actions to the purposes and principles of the Charter of the United Nations, as well as to the provisions of the Declaration on Principles of International Law concerning Friendly Relations and Co-operation among States in accordance with the Charter of the United Nations,

Reaffirming also the need to intensify and promote peace and security and to strengthen co-operation in the region, as provided for in the Mediterranean chapter of the Final Act of the Conference on Security and Co-operation in Europe, signed at Helsinki on 1 August 1975,

Recalling the declarations of successive meetings of non-aligned countries concerning the Mediterranean, as well as official declarations on, and contributions to, peace and security in the Mediterranean region made by individual countries,

Welcoming the efforts realized by the Mediterranean members of the Movement of Non-Aligned Countries to strengthen regional co-operation in various fields among themselves and between them and the European countries,

Recognizing the desire of Mediterranean countries that the needs of their region be taken into account in ongoing and future negotiations relating to international security and disarmament,

Recognizing also the desire of the non-aligned Mediterranean countries to intensify the process of dialogue and consultations with European-Mediterranean and other European countries aimed at strengthening efforts towards the promotion of peace, security and co-operation in the region, thus contributing to the stabilization of the situation in the Mediterranean,

Noting the results of the Stockholm Conference on Confidence- and Security-building Measures and Disarmament in Europe and the Concluding Document of the Vienna Follow-up Meeting of the Conference on Security and Co-operation in Europe, where all the participating States reaffirmed their resolve fully to implement unilaterally, bilaterally and multilaterally all the provisions of the Final Act and of the other documents of the Conference on Security and Co-operation in Europe,

Taking note of the debate on this item during its various sessions and, in particular, of the report of the Secretary-General on this item,

1. *Reaffirms:*

(a) That the security of the Mediterranean is closely linked with European security and with international peace and security;

(b) That further efforts are necessary for the reduction of tension and of armaments and for the creation of conditions of security and fruitful co-operation in all fields for all countries and peoples of the Mediterranean, on the basis of the principles of sovereignty, independence, territorial integrity, security, non-intervention and non-interference, non-violation of international borders, non-use of force or threat of use of force, the inadmissibility of the acquisition of territory by force, peaceful settlement of disputes and respect for permanent sovereignty over natural resources;

(c) That just and viable solutions are needed for existing problems and crises in the region on the basis of the provisions of the Charter and of relevant resolutions of the United Nations, the withdrawal of foreign forces of occupation and the right of peoples under colonial or foreign domination to self-determination and independence;

2. *Takes note* of the final documents of the Ninth Conference of Heads of State or Government of Non-Aligned Countries, held at Belgrade from 4 to 7 September 1989, and in particular paragraph 25 of the final document on international security and disarmament, which, *inter alia*, supported the transformation of the Mediterranean region into a region of peace, security and co-operation, free from conflict and confrontation;

3. *Expresses satisfaction* that important negotiations on confidence- and security-building measures are currently taking place at Vienna aimed at building upon and expanding the militarily significant and politically binding achievements of the Stockholm Conference on Confidence- and Security-building Measures and Disarmament in Europe, which, in relation to the Mediterranean, *inter alia*, confirmed the intention of the participants in the Conference on Security and Co-operation in Europe to develop good-neighbourly relations with all States of the region, with due regard to reciprocity, and in the spirit of the principles contained in the Declaration on Principles Guiding Relations between Participating States, so as to promote confidence and security and make peace prevail in the region, in accordance with the provisions contained in the Mediterranean chapter of the Final Act of the Conference on Security and Co-operation in Europe;

4. *Welcomes* the agreement reached by the States participating in the Vienna Follow-up Meeting of the Conference on Security and Co-operation in Europe to convene a meeting on the Mediterranean at Palma de Mallorca in 1990, in order to consider ways and means of further enhancing various aspects of co-operation, including the protection and improvement of Mediterranean ecosystems, with the aim of widening the scope of their co-operation with the non-participating Mediterranean States and contributing to the strengthening of confidence and security in the region;

5. *Urges* all States to co-operate with the Mediterranean States in the further efforts required to reduce tension and promote peace, security and co-operation in the region in accordance with the purposes and principles of the Charter of the United Nations and with the provisions of the Declaration on Principles of International Law concerning Friendly Relations and Co-operation among States in accordance with the Charter of the United Nations;

6. *Encourages once again* efforts to intensify existing forms and to promote new forms of co-operation in various fields, particularly those aimed at reducing tension and strengthening confidence and security in the region;

7. *Reaffirms* the importance of intensifying and constantly promoting contacts in all fields where common interests exist in order to eliminate gradually, through co-operation, the causes preventing the faster social and economic development of the Mediterranean States, particularly the developing States of the region;

8. *Welcomes* any further communication to the Secretary-General from all States of proposals, declarations and recommendations on strengthening peace, security and co-operation in the Mediterranean region;

9. *Also welcomes* the creation of the Arab Maghreb Union at Marrakesh, Morocco, on 17 February 1989, and greets this event as a factor of peace, stability, security and development in the region;

10. *Invites* the States members of the relevant regional organizations to lend support and to submit to the Secretary-General concrete ideas and suggestions on their potential contribution to the strengthening of peace and co-operation in the Mediterranean region;

11. *Renews its invitation* to the Secretary-General to give due attention to the question of peace, security and co-operation in the Mediterranean region and, if requested to do so, to render advice and assistance to Mediterranean countries in their concerted efforts in promoting peace, security and co-operation in the region;

12. *Requests* the Secretary-General to submit to the General Assembly at its forty-fifth session, on the basis of all replies received and notifications submitted in the implementation of the present resolution and taking into account the debate on this question during its forty-fourth session, a detailed report on the strengthening of security and co-operation in the Mediterranean region;

13. *Decides* to include in the provisional agenda of its forty-fifth session the item entitled "Strengthening of security and co-operation in the Mediterranean region".

General Assembly resolution 44/125

15 December 1989   Meeting 81   Adopted without vote

Approved by First Committee (A/44/820) without vote, 30 November (meeting 52); 7-nation draft (A/C.1/44/L.70), orally revised; agenda item 71.
Sponsors: Algeria, Cyprus, Libyan Arab Jamahiriya, Malta, Morocco, Tunisia, Yugoslavia.
Meeting numbers. GA 44th session: 1st Committee 46-52; plenary 81.

South Atlantic zone of peace

In 1986,[7] the General Assembly had declared the Atlantic Ocean, in the region between Africa and South America, a zone of peace and co-operation.

In 1988,[8] the Assembly called on States to co-operate in promoting the objectives of the declaration and to refrain from any action inconsistent with those objectives. It requested relevant organizations, organs and bodies of the United Nations to assist States of the zone in implementing the declaration. The Secretary-General in October 1989 transmitted replies from nine Governments on its implementation.[9]

The Presidents of Argentina, Brazil, Colombia, Mexico, Peru, Uruguay and Venezuela, at the Third Meeting of the Permanent Mechanism for Consultation and Concerted Political Action (Ica, Peru, 11 and 12 October) issued a declaration[10] in which they expressed satisfaction at the imminent resumption of negotiations between Argentina and the United Kingdom, which would promote the objectives of the declaration.

GENERAL ASSEMBLY ACTION

On 14 November 1989, the General Assembly adopted **resolution 44/20** by recorded vote.

Zone of peace and co-operation of the South Atlantic

The General Assembly,

Recalling its resolution 41/11 of 27 October 1986, in which it solemnly declared the Atlantic Ocean, in the region situated between Africa and South America, the "Zone of peace and co-operation of the South Atlantic",

Recalling also its resolution 42/16 of 10 November 1987, in which it urged States of the region to continue their actions aiming at fulfilling the goals of the declaration, especially through the adoption and implementation of specific programmes for this purpose, and its resolution 43/23 of 14 November 1988, in which it commended initiatives by States of the zone to promote peace and regional co-operation in the South Atlantic,

Reaffirming that the questions of peace and security and those of development are interrelated and inseparable, and considering that co-operation among all States, in particular those of the region, for peace and development is essential to promote the objectives of the zone of peace and co-operation of the South Atlantic,

Aware of the importance that the States of the zone attach to the preservation of the region's environment and recognizing the threat that pollution from any source poses to the marine and coastal environment, its ecological balance and its resources,

Noting with appreciation the efforts of States of the zone towards fulfilling the goals of the declaration,

1. *Takes note* of the report submitted by the Secretary-General in accordance with resolution 43/23;

2. *Calls upon* all States to co-operate in the promotion of the objectives of peace and co-operation established in the declaration of the zone of peace and co-operation of the South Atlantic and to refrain from any action inconsistent with those objectives, particularly actions which may create or aggravate situations of tension and potential conflict in the region;

3. *Welcomes* the beginning in April 1989 of the implementation of the United Nations plan for the independence of Namibia and looks forward to receiving Namibia very soon as a member of the community of the States of the zone;

4. *Emphasizes* the imperative need to preserve the environment of the region and urges all States to take the necessary measures in order to ensure its protection from environmental damage;

5. *Urges* all States to abstain from transferring to and disposing in the region hazardous, toxic and nuclear wastes;

6. *Welcomes* the assistance that the Office for Ocean Affairs and the Law of the Sea of the Secretariat and the United Nations Development Programme are extending towards the convening by the States of the zone of two seminars, to be held in the Congo in 1990 and in Uruguay in 1991, devoted to the review of the development and implementation of the legal régime established by the United Nations Convention on the Law of the Sea;

7. *Requests* the Secretary-General to keep the implementation of resolution 41/11 under review and to submit a report to the General Assembly at its forty-fifth session, taking into account, *inter alia*, the views expressed by Member States;

8. *Decides* to include in the provisional agenda of its forty-fifth session the item entitled "Zone of peace and co-operation of the South Atlantic".

General Assembly resolution 44/20

14 November 1989   Meeting 55   146-1-2 (recorded vote)

22-nation draft (A/44/L.24); agenda item 33.

Sponsors: Angola, Argentina, Benin, Brazil, Cameroon, Cape Verde, Congo, Côte d'Ivoire, Equatorial Guinea, Gabon, Gambia, Ghana, Guinea, Guinea-Bissau, Liberia, Nigeria, Sao Tome and Principe, Senegal, Sierra Leone, Togo, Uruguay, Zaire.

Recorded vote in Assembly as follows:

In favour: Afghanistan, Albania, Algeria, Angola, Argentina, Australia, Austria, Bahamas, Bahrain, Bangladesh, Barbados, Belgium, Benin, Bhutan, Bolivia, Botswana, Brazil, Brunei Darussalam, Bulgaria, Burkina Faso, Burundi, Byelorussian SSR, Cameroon, Cape Verde, Central African Republic, Chad, Chile, China, Colombia, Comoros, Congo, Costa Rica, Côte d'Ivoire, Cuba, Cyprus, Czechoslovakia, Democratic Kampuchea, Democratic Yemen, Denmark, Djibouti, Dominican Republic, Ecuador, Egypt, El Salvador, Equatorial Guinea, Ethiopia, Fiji, Finland, France, Gabon, Gambia, German Democratic Republic, Germany, Federal Republic of, Ghana, Greece, Guatemala, Guinea, Guinea-Bissau, Guyana, Haiti, Honduras, Hungary, Iceland, India, Indonesia, Iran, Iraq, Ireland, Israel, Italy, Jamaica, Jordan, Kenya, Kuwait, Lao People's Democratic Republic, Lebanon, Lesotho, Liberia, Libyan Arab Jamahiriya, Luxembourg, Madagascar, Malawi, Malaysia, Maldives, Mali, Malta, Mauritania, Mauritius, Mexico, Mongolia, Morocco, Mozambique, Myanmar, Nepal, Netherlands, New Zealand, Nicaragua, Niger, Nigeria, Norway, Oman, Pakistan, Panama, Peru, Philippines, Poland, Portugal, Qatar, Romania, Rwanda, Saint Lucia, Saint Vincent and the Grenadines, Samoa, Sao Tome and Principe, Saudi Arabia, Senegal, Seychelles, Sierra Leone, Singapore, Solomon Islands, Somalia, Spain, Sri Lanka, Sudan, Suriname, Swaziland, Sweden, Syrian Arab Republic, Thailand, Togo, Trinidad and Tobago, Tunisia, Turkey, Uganda, Ukrainian SSR, USSR, United Arab Emirates, United Kingdom, United Republic of Tanzania, Uruguay, Venezuela, Viet Nam, Yemen, Yugoslavia, Zaire, Zambia.

Against: United States.

Abstaining: Canada, Japan.

REFERENCES

[1]YUN 1988, p. 27, GA res. 43/84, 7 Dec. 1988. [2]A/44/676. [3]A/44/551-S/20870. [4]A/44/542-S/20854. [5]A/44/667. [6]A/44/594. [7]YUN 1986, p. 369, GA res. 41/11, 27 Oct. 1986. [8]YUN 1988, p. 26, GA res. 43/23, 14 Nov. 1988. [9]A/44/536. [10]A/44/694.

Protection and security of small States

On 9 August 1989, Maldives requested inclusion in the agenda of the General Assembly's forty-fourth session of an item on the protection and security of small States.[1] In the accompanying memorandum, Maldives referred to the attempted invasion of its territory by mercenaries in November 1988, with the aim of overthrowing the legitimate Government. It said that small island States were particularly vulnerable to such aggression and their best defence should be found in the Charter and the machinery established thereby. Small States faced a cruel choice of either putting their trust in international machinery, especially the Security Council, or diverting scarce resources to military purposes and engaging in possibly encumbering defence agreements with larger Powers. Maldives proposed a number of measures for strengthening the norms conducive to good order, including giving highest priority to finalizing and adopting the draft convention against the recruitment, use, financing and training of mercenaries.

GENERAL ASSEMBLY ACTION

On 8 December, the General Assembly, on the recommendation of the Special Political Committee, adopted **resolution 44/51** without vote.

Protection and security of small States

The General Assembly,

Reaffirming its commitment to international peace and security,

Recalling the Declaration on Principles of International Law concerning Friendly Relations and Co-operation among States in accordance with the Charter of the United Nations,

Conscious that small States may be particularly vulnerable to external threats and acts of interference in their internal affairs and may have special needs consonant with the right to sovereignty and territorial integrity that they share with all nations,

Concerned at the danger that mercenaries can represent for small States,

Recalling with deep concern the various incidents in which groups of mercenaries have attempted to infringe upon the sovereignty and territorial integrity of small States, including the attempted invasion of Maldives in November 1988,

1. *Recognizes* that small States may be particularly vulnerable to external threats and acts of interference in their internal affairs;

2. *Stresses* in this regard the significance of the obligation of all States to respect the principle of territorial integrity and the other principles of the Charter of the United Nations;

3. *Appeals* to the relevant regional and international organizations to provide assistance when requested by small States for the strengthening of their security in accordance with the purposes and principles of the Charter;

4. *Urges* the Secretary-General to pay special attention to monitoring the security situation of small States and to consider making use of the provisions of Article 99 of the Charter;

5. *Invites* the Secretary-General to explore ways and means, within the United Nations and in accordance with the Charter, of preserving the security of small States;

6. *Requests* the Secretary-General to hold consultations with the members of the Security Council and interested Governments and to submit a report to it at its forty-sixth session on the implementation of the present resolution;

7. *Decides* to include in the provisional agenda of its forty-sixth session the item entitled "Protection and security of small States".

General Assembly resolution 44/51

8 December 1989   Meeting 78   Adopted without vote

Approved by Special Political Committee (A/44/707) without vote, 24 October (meeting 5); 55-nation draft (A/SPC/44/L.4); agenda item 150.
Sponsors: Afghanistan, Antigua and Barbuda, Australia, Bahamas, Bangladesh, Barbados, Belize, Brunei Darussalam, Colombia, Comoros, Cuba, Cyprus, Democratic Yemen, Djibouti, Dominica, Fiji, Grenada, Guyana, India, Indonesia, Jamaica, Lesotho, Libyan Arab Jamahiriya, Madagascar, Malaysia, Maldives, Mali, Malta, Mauritania, Mauritius, Morocco, Nepal, New Zealand, Nicaragua, Niger, Oman, Pakistan, Panama, Papua New Guinea, Philippines, Qatar, Saint Lucia, Saint Vincent and the Grenadines, Samoa, Seychelles, Sierra Leone, Singapore, Solomon Islands, Sri Lanka, Swaziland, Trinidad and Tobago, Tunisia, United Arab Emirates, Viet Nam, Yugoslavia.
Meeting numbers. GA 44th session: SPC 4, 5; plenary 78.

On 4 December, the Assembly, by **resolution 44/34**, adopted the International Convention against the Recruitment, Use, Financing and Training of Mercenaries.

REFERENCE

[1]A/44/192.

Follow-up to
International Year of Peace (1986)

In response to a 1987 General Assembly request,[1] the Secretary-General in October 1989[2] reported on the achievements of the International Year of Peace (IYP), proclaimed by the Assembly in 1985[3] and observed in 1986.[4] The IYP programme, designed to stimulate action in the promotion of peace, international security and co-operation, strengthen the United Nations as an instrument of peace and focus attention on the basic requirements for peace, encouraged participation at the international, national and grass-roots levels. IYP activities were coordinated by the Peace Studies Unit of the Department of Political and Security Council Affairs and financed from the Voluntary Trust Fund for the Promotion of Peace. As at 31 August 1989, the Fund totalled $22,000 in convertible currencies and $790,000 in non-convertible currencies.

In 1989, the theme for International Day of Peace, "Peace for the Future of the Earth", was highlighted in a television programme produced by the United Nations in collaboration with the International Peace Child Foundation. Among other peace activities were: an international conference (Mt. Abu, India, February 1989) at which the Mt. Abu Declaration of Principles for Co-operation was adopted;[5] the second meeting of Peace Messenger cities (Warsaw, Poland, September) for the promotion of peace and fostering greater global awareness, which adopted the Warsaw Peace Appeal marking the fiftieth anniversary of the outbreak of the Second World War;[6] a Conference on Visions of a Peaceful World, organized by the Polish Peace Committee in April, and two international conferences on the role of women in the promotion of peace and the preservation of the environment, hosted by the Soviet Women's Peace Committee; an International Congress on Peace in the Minds of Men, sponsored by the United Nations Educational, Scientific and Cultural Organization (Yamoussoukro, Côte d'Ivoire, June/July); and the first International Peace Olympiad organized by Greece in March. In addition, a variety of information materials were prepared and disseminated by the Peace Studies Unit, non-governmental organizations and academic institutions.

Other developments in the promotion of peace included the growing interest in the study and practice of conflict resolution and mediation, through a variety of conferences, courses and seminars; the increased emphasis on peace education in primary and secondary schools; new initiatives in the field of science and technology for peace, including the 1988 General Assembly proclamation[7] of the "International Week of Science and Peace" to be observed each November; the Conference in Search of the True Meaning of Peace (San José, Costa Rica, June),[8] which adopted the Declaration of Human Responsibilities for Peace and Sustainable Development; and increased academic research on aspects of peace-keeping, peacemaking and peace-building. The Secretary-General noted that the United Nations was an important centre and catalyst for the promotion of peace efforts and suggested that Member States and interested organizations should keep it informed of relevant peace initiatives.

GENERAL ASSEMBLY ACTION

On 24 October 1989, the General Assembly adopted **resolution 44/11** without vote.

Achievements of the International Year of Peace

The General Assembly,

Recalling its resolution 40/3 of 24 October 1985, in the annex to which it solemnly proclaimed 1986 to be the International Year of Peace,

Recalling also its resolution 40/10 of 11 November 1985, in which it took note of the programme of the International Year of Peace,

Recalling further its resolution 42/13 of 28 October 1987, in which it requested the Secretary-General to submit a report on the achievements of the International Year of Peace to the General Assembly at its forty-fourth session,

Noting that the numerous efforts and activities undertaken by Member States and by non-governmental organizations have inspired a concrete and substantive dialogue among nations, peoples and persons in pursuit of the goal of true peace,

Recognizing that the objectives of the Year helped to strengthen the United Nations as an instrument of peace, stimulating action for the promotion of international peace and security, co-operation and the peaceful settlement of disputes,

Welcoming the positive change in the international political climate from confrontation to co-operation, understanding among States and the pursuit of dialogue,

1. *Takes note with appreciation* of the report on the achievements of the International Year of Peace submitted by the Secretary-General in accordance with resolution 42/13;

2. *Expresses its satisfaction* at the activities which have taken place since the Proclamation of the International Year of Peace, as documented in the report of the Secretary-General;

3. *Recognizes* the important contribution of the International Year of Peace and supports the efforts made by the international community in carrying out activities designed to strengthen the United Nations as an instrument of peace and to focus attention on the basic elements of peace, such as social and economic development, disarmament, human rights and fundamental freedoms, preparation for life in peace, the ecological balance, protection of the environment and improvement of the quality of life;

4. *Commends* the initiative taken by the Secretary-General to place greater and greater emphasis each year on the observance, on the third Tuesday of September, of the International Day of Peace, established by the General Assembly in its resolution 36/67 of 30 November 1981, as a reminder that the Assembly meets every year at that time to work for peace;

5. *Emphasizes* the importance of education for peace, especially at the primary and secondary levels, and expresses satisfaction at its inclusion in many education and teacher-training programmes that have been launched and have received favourable evaluations;

6. *Urges* all those interested in the promotion and attainment of the goals of the International Year of Peace to support the programmes of the Peace Studies Unit of the Department of Political and Security Council Affairs of the Secretariat by making voluntary contributions to the Trust Fund for the Promotion of Peace;

7. *Urges* Member States, intergovernmental and non-governmental organizations and the world community to persevere in these efforts, developing initiatives conducive to the objectives of the Year, and to join the United Nations in its noble purpose of ensuring that humanity reaches the threshold of the twenty-first century in the full enjoyment of a stable and lasting peace;

8. *Requests* the Secretary-General to invite Member States and interested organizations to inform the Secretariat of their activities and initiatives in pursuit of those ends and to submit to the General Assembly at its forty-sixth session, under an item entitled "Programmes and activities to promote peace in the world", a report on the development of relevant programmes and activities.

General Assembly resolution 44/11

24 October 1989   Meeting 37   Adopted without vote

46-nation draft (A/44/L.15 & Add.1); agenda item 21.

Sponsors: Antigua and Barbuda, Argentina, Bahamas, Bangladesh, Barbados, Bolivia, Cameroon, Colombia, Costa Rica, Côte d'Ivoire, Chile, Cyprus, Dominican Republic, Ecuador, El Salvador, Fiji, German Democratic Republic, Grenada, Guatemala, Guyana, Honduras, Jamaica, Mauritius, Mexico, Morocco, Nepal, Nicaragua, Pakistan, Papua New Guinea, Paraguay, Peru, Philippines, Poland, Romania, Saint Lucia, Samoa, Senegal, Sierra Leone, Singapore, Sri Lanka, Suriname, Thailand, Togo, Ukrainian SSR, Uruguay, Yugoslavia.

Meeting numbers. GA 44th session: plenary 37, 43, 55.

REFERENCES

[1]YUN 1987, p. 123, GA res. 42/13, 28 Oct. 1987. [2]A/44/615. [3]YUN 1985, p. 123, GA res. 40/3, annex, 24 Oct. 1985. [4]YUN 1986, p. 115. [5]A/44/549. [6]A/45/94. [7]YUN 1988, p. 32, GA res. 43/61, 6 Dec. 1988. [8]A/44/626.

Chapter II

Disarmament

During the year, the international community noted some positive developments towards meaningful arms limitation and disarmament, including actual reductions as a result of the 1987 Treaty between the United States of America and the Union of Soviet Socialist Republics on the Elimination of Their Intermediate-Range and Shorter-Range Missiles. By the end of 1989, following the entry into force of the Treaty the previous year, on 1 June 1988, some 2,000 of the 2,700 intermediate-range and shorter-range Soviet and United States missiles affected by the Treaty had been eliminated and the verification arrangements were reported to be working well.

The issue of nuclear testing remained prominent on the agendas of United Nations disarmament bodies, and many States continued to press for a comprehensive nuclear-test ban. In April, 41 States parties to the 1963 Treaty Banning Nuclear Weapon Tests in the Atmosphere, in Outer Space and under Water (the partial test-ban Treaty) requested the depositary States to convene a conference in 1990 to consider a proposal to amend the treaty to convert it into a comprehensive nuclear-test-ban treaty. During the year, preparatory work was begun for the Fourth Review Conference of the Treaty on the Non-Proliferation of Nuclear Weapons, scheduled to be held in 1990.

At its 1989 session, the General Assembly, on the recommendation of the First Committee, adopted 57 resolutions and two decisions on disarmament issues.

The Disarmament Commission (New York, 8-31 May), a deliberative body composed of all United Nations Member States, took on one new agenda item in 1989—consideration of the declaration of the 1990s as the Third Disarmament Decade.

The Conference on Disarmament (Geneva, 7 February–27 April and 13 June–31 August) was asked by the General Assembly to commence negotiations on an international convention prohibiting the use of nuclear weapons. Efforts to elaborate a global, comprehensive ban on chemical weapons intensified. A large number of proposals and documents dealing with many aspects of a draft convention on chemical weapons were put forward, but divergent views persisted on a number of issues.

Comprehensive approaches to disarmament

UN disarmament bodies and their activities in 1989

The United Nations continued its disarmament efforts in 1989 mainly through the General Assembly and its First Committee, the Disarmament Commission (a subsidiary organ of the Assembly) and the Conference on Disarmament (a multilateral negotiating forum at Geneva).

Disarmament Commission

The Disarmament Commission, composed of all United Nations Member States, at its 1989 session (New York, 8-31 May) held eight plenary meetings.[1] It also met on 1 and 7 December to elect its officers and consider its provisional agenda for 1990.

The Commission's 1989 agenda included items on aspects of the arms race, particularly a general approach to negotiations on nuclear and conventional disarmament; reduction of military budgets; South Africa's nuclear capability; the role of the United Nations in disarmament; naval armaments and disarmament; and conventional disarmament. A new item on the agenda concerned the declaration of the 1990s as the Third Disarmament Decade.

The Commission established a contact group to deal with negotiations on nuclear and conventional disarmament; a consultation group on the reduction of military budgets; and working groups to deal with, respectively, South Africa's nuclear capability, the role of the United Nations in the field of disarmament, conventional disarmament, and declaration of the 1990s as the Third Disarmament Decade. The Chairman of the Commission held substantive and open-ended consultations on naval armaments and disarmament. His report on the topic was incorporated into the Commission's 1989 report.[1] Since it was not possible to conclude consideration of any agenda item during the session, many delegations urged examination of the situation. The Chairman held consultations in an informal working group to consider proposals to improve the Commission's functioning. Proposals made on the subject included streamlining the agenda in order to concentrate on the most promising items; limiting the number of subsidiary bodies; making the duration of the session flexible; encouraging high-level and active participation; establishing procedures to allow the Commission to conclude items within a certain period; rotating the chairmanship of working bodies; and holding extensive consultations year round. The deliberations resulted in a text outlining ways and means to enhance the Commission's functioning (see the annex to resolution 44/119 C below).

GENERAL ASSEMBLY ACTION

On 15 December 1989, on the recommendation of the First Committee, the General Assembly adopted **resolution 44/119 C** without vote.

Report of the Disarmament Commission
The General Assembly,

Having considered the annual report of the Disarmament Commission,

Emphasizing again the importance of an effective follow-up to the relevant recommendations and decisions contained in the Final Document of the Tenth Special Session of the General Assembly, the first special session devoted to disarmament,

Taking into account the relevant sections of the Concluding Document of the Twelfth Special Session of the General Assembly, the second special session devoted to disarmament,

Also taking into account widespread views expressed during the fifteenth special session of the General Assembly, the third special session devoted to disarmament,

Considering the role that the Disarmament Commission has been called upon to play and the contribution that it should make in examining and submitting recommendations on various problems in the field of disarmament and in the promotion of the implementation of the relevant decisions of the tenth special session,

Recalling its resolutions 33/71 H of 14 December 1978, 34/83 H of 11 December 1979, 35/152 F of 12 December 1980, 36/92 B of 9 December 1981, 37/78 H of 9 December 1982, 38/183 E of 20 December 1983, 39/148 R of 17 December 1984, 40/152 F of 16 December 1985, 41/86 E of 4 December 1986, 42/42 G of 30 November 1987 and 43/78 A of 7 December 1988,

1. *Takes note* of the annual report of the Disarmament Commission;

2. *Notes* that the Disarmament Commission has yet to conclude its consideration of some items on its agenda, but notes also with appreciation the progress achieved on some of these;

3. *Recalls* the role of the Disarmament Commission as the specialized, deliberative body within the United Nations multilateral disarmament machinery that allows for in-depth deliberations on specific disarmament issues, leading to the submission of concrete recommendations on those issues;

4. *Stresses* the importance for the Disarmament Commission to work on the basis of a relevant agenda of disarmament topics, thereby enabling the Commission to concentrate its efforts and thus optimize its progress on specific subjects in accordance with resolution 37/78 H;

5. *Notes also* that consultations have been held on the question of ways and means to enhance the functioning of the Disarmament Commission in the field of disarmament;

6. *Takes note with satisfaction* of the results of those consultations on ways and means to enhance the functioning of the Disarmament Commission, as annexed to the present resolution;

7. *Requests* the Disarmament Commission to continue its work in accordance with its mandate, as set forth in paragraph 118 of the Final Document of the Tenth Special Session of the General Assembly, and with paragraph 3 of resolution 37/78 H, and to that end to make every effort to achieve specific recommendations, at its 1990 substantive session, on the outstanding items on its agenda, taking into account the relevant resolutions of the General Assembly as well as the results of its 1989 substantive session;

8. *Also requests* the Disarmament Commission to meet for a period not exceeding four weeks during 1990 and to submit a substantive report, containing specific recommendations on the items included in its agenda, to the General Assembly at its forty-fifth session;

9. *Requests* the Secretary-General to transmit to the Disarmament Commission the annual report of the Conference on Disarmament, together with all the official records of the forty-fourth session of the General Assembly relating to disarmament matters, and to render all assistance that the Commission may require for implementing the present resolution;

10. *Also requests* the Secretary-General to ensure full provision to the Commission and its subsidiary bodies of interpretation and translation facilities in the official languages and to assign, as a matter of priority, all the necessary resources and services to that end;

11. *Decides* to include in the provisional agenda of its forty-fifth session the item entitled ''Report of the Disarmament Commission''.

ANNEX
Ways and means to enhance the functioning of the Disarmament Commission

1. *Mandate*
The Disarmament Commission reaffirms its mandate contained in paragraph 118 (*a*) of the Final Document of the Tenth Special Session of the General Assembly, the first special session devoted to disarmament (hereinafter referred to as the ''Final Document'').

2. *Decision-making method*
The decision-making method described in paragraph 118 (*b*) of the Final Document should be maintained.

3. *Agenda items*
1. The Disarmament Commission could have a general agenda and a working agenda for each substantive session. The working agenda should be agreed at the Commission's organizational session.

2. For each session, the working agenda should be limited to a maximum of four substantive items for in-depth consideration.

3. From 1991, no subject should, in principle, be maintained on the working agenda for more than three consecutive years. At each session, the Commission should review, for possible reconsideration, any subject that had been suspended.

4. If no agreement can be reached on a specific agenda item, the report of the Commission should contain a joint statement or a Chairman's summary of the proceedings to reflect views or positions of different delegations, particularly in the case of those agenda items to be suspended for a period of time.

5. At its 1990 session, the Commission should make every effort to conclude all its agenda items, except the new substantive items.

4. *Subsidiary bodies*

1. At each annual session, the Disarmament Commission should not establish more than four subsidiary bodies for its substantive agenda items. The allocation of the agenda items to the four subsidiary bodies and the appointment of chairmen for these subsidiary bodies should be decided at the organizational session of the Commission, taking into account the principle of equitable geographical distribution.

2. The chairmanship of subsidiary bodies should, in principle, be rotated each year; however, at its organizational session, the Commission may decide to extend the term of office of any chairman in the interest of effective work and the speedy conclusion of an item.

5. *Duration of the substantive session*

1. The Disarmament Commission should meet for a period not exceeding four weeks for in-depth deliberations on substantive items.

2. The duration of each substantive session, in accordance with the established practice, should be flexible and could be shortened. In order to utilize efficiently the conference-servicing resources available, the Commission should decide the duration of each substantive session at its organizational session.

6. *Organization of work of the session*

1. Each session may have a general debate on agenda items in the plenary meetings, not exceeding three days' duration.

2. Except in the case of new items, there should be no general exchange of views in the subsidiary bodies. The general exchange of views on new items should not exceed two meetings.

3. Subsidiary bodies could begin their work in parallel with the general exchange of views in the plenary meetings.

4. No more than two official meetings should be held simultaneously. This restriction, however, would not apply to informal consultations.

5. The meetings of the Commission and its subsidiary bodies should be provided with full meeting services.

6. All the officers of the Commission should be elected at its organizational session.

7. *Consultations*

The Chairman of the Disarmament Commission should conduct consultations on matters relating to the work of the Commission, in particular on its working agenda, year round, especially during the meetings of the First Committee of the General Assembly.

General Assembly resolution 44/119 C

15 December 1989   Meeting 81   Adopted without vote

Approved by First Committee (A/44/788) without vote, 16 November (meeting 39); 17-nation draft (A/C.1/44/L.8/Rev.1), orally revised; agenda item 66 *(a)*.

Sponsors: Austria, Bahrain, Belgium, Byelorussian SSR, Cameroon, China, Costa Rica, Denmark, German Democratic Republic, Haiti, Indonesia, Nigeria, Romania, Sri Lanka, Sweden, Togo, Zaire.
Meeting numbers. GA 44th session: 1st Committee 3-25, 30, 39; plenary 81.

Conference on Disarmament

The Conference on Disarmament, the 40-member multilateral negotiating body, met twice in 1989 at Geneva (7 February–27 April and 13 June–31 August).[2] During 48 formal plenary meetings and 11 informal meetings, it considered a nuclear-test ban, cessation of the nuclear-arms race and nuclear disarmament, prevention of nuclear war, chemical weapons, prevention of an arms race in outer space, security assurances to non-nuclear-weapon States, radiological weapons and a comprehensive programme of disarmament. (Details of those questions are discussed elsewhere in this chapter.)

The Conference re-established *ad hoc* committees on chemical weapons, prevention of an arms race in outer space, assurances to non-nuclear-weapon States, and radiological weapons. There was no need to re-establish the *Ad Hoc* Committee on the Comprehensive Programme of Disarmament as its mandate extended up to the General Assembly's forty-fourth (1989) session.

The Conference reaffirmed its 1988 decision[3] that its membership might be increased by not more than four States and that candidates for membership should be nominated, two by the Group of 21 neutral and non-aligned States (Algeria, Argentina, Brazil, Cuba, Egypt, Ethiopia, India, Indonesia, Iran, Kenya, Mexico, Morocco, Myanmar, Nigeria, Pakistan, Peru, Sri Lanka, Sweden, Venezuela, Yugoslavia, Zaire), one by the Socialist Group and one by the Western Group, so as to maintain a balance in the membership of the Conference, but no action was taken.

GENERAL ASSEMBLY ACTION

On 15 December 1989, on the recommendation of the First Committee, the General Assembly adopted **resolution 44/119 D** by recorded vote.

Report of the Conference on Disarmament

The General Assembly,

Recalling its resolutions 34/83 B of 11 December 1979, 35/152 J of 12 December 1980, 36/92 F of 9 December 1981, 37/78 G of 9 December 1982, 38/183 I of 20 December 1983, 39/148 N of 17 December 1984, 40/152 M of 16 December 1985, 41/86 M of 4 December 1986, 42/42 L of 30 November 1987 and 43/78 M of 7 December 1988,

Having considered the report of the Conference on Disarmament,

Convinced that the Conference on Disarmament, as the single multilateral negotiating body on disarmament, should play the central role in substantive negotiations on priority questions of disarmament,

Expressing its regret that the Conference on Disarmament was not able in 1989 either to establish *ad hoc* committees or to commence negotiations on the nuclear issues on its agenda,

Expressing its expectation that the Conference on Disarmament, in view of the positive current processes in some important fields of disarmament, would be in a position to reach concrete agreements on disarmament issues to which the United Nations has assigned the greatest priority and urgency and which have been under consideration for a number of years,

Considering that it is more than ever imperative in the present circumstances to give an additional impetus to negotiations on disarmament at all levels and to achieve genuine progress in the immediate future,

1. *Reaffirms* the role of the Conference on Disarmament as the single multilateral disarmament negotiating forum of the international community;

2. *Notes with satisfaction* that further progress has been made in the negotiations on the elaboration of a draft convention on the complete and effective prohibition of the development, production and stockpiling of all chemical weapons and on their destruction, and urges the Conference on Disarmament to intensify further its work with a view to completing negotiations on such a draft convention as soon as possible;

3. *Calls upon* the Conference on Disarmament to intensify its work, to further its mandate more earnestly through substantive negotiations, within the framework of *ad hoc* committees as the most appropriate mechanism, and to adopt concrete measures on the specific priority issues of disarmament on its agenda, in accordance with the Programme of Action set forth in section III of the Final Document of the Tenth Special Session of the General Assembly;

4. *Urges* the Conference on Disarmament to provide negotiating mandates to *ad hoc* committees on all agenda items, in keeping with the fundamental role of the Conference as identified in the Final Document of the Tenth Special Session;

5. *Requests* the Conference on Disarmament to submit a report on its work to the General Assembly at its forty-fifth session;

6. *Decides* to include in the provisional agenda of its forty-fifth session the item entitled ''Report of the Conference on Disarmament''.

General Assembly resolution 44/119 D

15 December 1989   Meeting 81   138-8-9 (recorded vote)

Approved by First Committee (A/44/788) by recorded vote (119-7-10), 15 November (meeting 37); 27-nation draft (A/C.1/44/L.30); agenda item 66 *(b)*.
Sponsors: Algeria, Bangladesh, Brazil, Cuba, Ecuador, Egypt, Ethiopia, India, Indonesia, Iran, Kenya, Madagascar, Malaysia, Mexico, Morocco, Myanmar, Nigeria, Pakistan, Peru, Romania, Sri Lanka, Sweden, Tunisia, Venezuela, Viet Nam, Yugoslavia, Zaire.
Meeting numbers. GA 44th session: 1st Committee 3-25, 30, 37; plenary 81.

Recorded vote in Assembly as follows:

In favour: Afghanistan, Albania, Algeria, Angola, Antigua and Barbuda, Argentina, Australia, Austria, Bahamas, Bahrain, Bangladesh, Barbados, Benin, Bhutan, Bolivia, Botswana, Brazil, Brunei Darussalam, Bulgaria, Burkina Faso, Burundi, Byelorussian SSR, Cameroon, Cape Verde, Central African Republic, Chad, Chile, China, Colombia, Congo, Costa Rica, Côte d'Ivoire, Cuba, Cyprus, Czechoslovakia, Democratic Kampuchea, Democratic Yemen, Djibouti, Dominica, Dominican Republic, Ecuador, Egypt, El Salvador, Ethiopia, Fiji, Finland, Gabon, Gambia, German Democratic Republic, Ghana, Greece, Grenada, Guatemala, Guinea, Guinea-Bissau, Guyana, Haiti, Honduras, Hungary, India, Indonesia, Iran, Iraq, Ireland, Jamaica, Jordan, Kenya, Kuwait, Lao People's Democratic Republic, Lebanon, Lesotho, Liberia, Libyan Arab Jamahiriya, Madagascar, Malawi, Malaysia, Maldives, Mali, Malta, Mauritania, Mauritius, Mexico, Mongolia, Morocco, Mozambique, Myanmar, Nepal, New Zealand, Nicaragua, Niger, Nigeria, Oman, Pakistan, Panama, Papua New Guinea, Paraguay, Peru, Philippines, Poland, Qatar, Romania, Rwanda, Saint Kitts

and Nevis, Saint Lucia, Saint Vincent and the Grenadines, Samoa, Sao Tome and Principe, Saudi Arabia, Senegal, Seychelles, Sierra Leone, Singapore, Solomon Islands, Somalia, Sri Lanka, Sudan, Suriname, Swaziland, Sweden, Syrian Arab Republic, Thailand, Togo, Trinidad and Tobago, Tunisia, Uganda, Ukrainian SSR, USSR, United Arab Emirates, United Republic of Tanzania, Uruguay, Vanuatu, Venezuela, Viet Nam, Yemen, Yugoslavia, Zaire, Zambia, Zimbabwe.
Against: Belgium, France, Germany, Federal Republic of, Italy, Luxembourg, Netherlands, United Kingdom, United States.
Abstaining: Canada, Denmark, Iceland, Israel, Japan, Norway, Portugal, Spain, Turkey.

UN role in disarmament

In accordance with a General Assembly request of 1988,[4] the Disarmament Commission continued its consideration of the role of the United Nations in disarmament.[1] Working Group II, established to develop recommendations and proposals on the topic, held three meetings between 10 and 26 May. The proposals, contained in 37 papers before the Group, were also considered in informal consultations. At the third meeting, the Group's Chairman submitted a new working paper containing proposals resulting from the consultations but, owing to lack of time, the Group was unable to address the new text. It agreed to annex the Chairman's working paper to the Commission's 1989 report in the belief that it might assist future deliberations.

GENERAL ASSEMBLY ACTION

On 15 December 1989, on the recommendation of the First Committee, the General Assembly adopted **resolution 44/116 Q** without vote.

Review of the role of the United Nations in the field of disarmament

The General Assembly,

Recalling its resolutions 39/151 G of 17 December 1984, 40/94 O of 12 December 1985, 41/59 O of 3 December 1986, 42/38 O of 30 November 1987 and 43/75 R of 7 December 1988,

Bearing in mind that the primary purpose of the United Nations is to maintain international peace and security,

Reaffirming its conviction that genuine and lasting peace can be created only through the effective implementation of the security system provided for in the Charter of the United Nations and the speedy and substantial reduction of arms and armed forces, by international agreement and mutual example, leading ultimately to general and complete disarmament under effective international control,

Reaffirming that the United Nations, in accordance with its Charter, has a central role and primary responsibility in the sphere of disarmament,

Recognizing the need for the United Nations, in discharging its central role and primary responsibility in the sphere of disarmament, to play a more active role in the field of disarmament in accordance with its primary purpose under the Charter to maintain international peace and security,

Taking into account the part of the report of the Disarmament Commission relating to this question, and noting the progress made in the consideration of the question at the fifteenth special session of the General

Assembly, the third special session devoted to disarmament,

Bearing in mind the common desire expressed at the third special session devoted to disarmament to strengthen the role of the United Nations in the field of disarmament and the increased reaffirmation of faith in the United Nations as an indispensable instrument for international peace and security,

1. *Requests* the Disarmament Commission to continue its consideration of the role of the United Nations in the field of disarmament as a matter of priority at its next substantive session, in 1990, with a view to the elaboration of concrete recommendations and proposals, as appropriate, taking into account, *inter alia*, the views and suggestions of Member States as well as the aforementioned documents on the subject;

2. *Also requests* the Disarmament Commission to submit its report on the subject, including findings, recommendations and proposals, as appropriate, to the General Assembly at its forty-fifth session;

3. *Decides* to include in the provisional agenda of its forty-fifth session the item entitled "Review of the role of the United Nations in the field of disarmament: report of the Disarmament Commission".

General Assembly resolution 44/116 Q

15 December 1989   Meeting 81   Adopted without vote

Approved by First Committee (A/44/785) without vote, 9 November (meeting 32); 2-nation draft (A/C.1/44/L.51); agenda item 63 *(l)*.
Sponsors: Cameroon, Romania.
Meeting numbers. GA 44th session: 1st Committee 3-25, 32; plenary 81.

UN resolutions on disarmament

In response to a 1988 General Assembly request,[5] the Secretary-General submitted in September 1989 a report with a later addendum, containing the views of four Member States on the implementation of General Assembly resolutions in the field of disarmament.[6]

GENERAL ASSEMBLY ACTION

On 15 December, the General Assembly, on the recommendation of the First Committee, adopted **resolution 44/116 G** by recorded vote.

Implementation of General Assembly resolutions in the field of disarmament

The General Assembly,

Taking note of the report of the Secretary-General,

Recalling paragraph 115 of the Final Document of the Tenth Special Session of the General Assembly, in which it is stated, *inter alia*, that the Assembly has been and should remain the main deliberative organ of the United Nations in the field of disarmament and should make every effort to facilitate the implementation of disarmament measures,

Considering that the implementation of the recommendations of the General Assembly in the field of disarmament can play a significant role in the attainment of the purposes of the Charter of the United Nations,

1. *Deems it important* that all Member States show their resolve to arrive at mutually acceptable, comprehensively verifiable and effective disarmament measures, including through the implementation of General Assembly resolutions in the field of disarmament;

2. *Invites* all Member States to contribute to the elaboration of draft resolutions in the field of disarmament that will permit, in so far as possible, their adoption without a vote, in order to facilitate their appropriate implementation;

3. *Also invites* Member States to consider the proposals and ideas contained in the report of the Secretary-General;

4. *Invites* all Member States that have not yet done so to make available to the Secretary-General their views and suggestions on ways and means to enhance the implementation of General Assembly resolutions in the field of disarmament;

5. *Requests* the Secretary-General to submit to the General Assembly at its forty-sixth session a progress report on the implementation of the present resolution;

6. *Decides* to continue its consideration of the issue of the implementation of General Assembly resolutions in the field of disarmament at its forty-sixth session.

General Assembly resolution 44/116 G

15 December 1989   Meeting 81   129-1-25 (recorded vote)

Approved by First Committee (A/44/785) by recorded vote (105-1-27), 14 November (meeting 36); 3-nation draft (A/C.1/44/L.22/Rev.1); agenda item 63 *(g)*.
Sponsors: Cameroon, Czechoslovakia, Ukrainian SSR.
Meeting numbers. GA 44th session: 1st Committee 3-25, 27, 36; plenary 81.

Recorded vote in Assembly as follows:

In favour: Afghanistan, Albania, Algeria, Angola, Antigua and Barbuda, Argentina, Bahamas, Bahrain, Bangladesh, Barbados, Benin, Bhutan, Bolivia, Botswana, Brazil, Brunei Darussalam, Bulgaria, Burkina Faso, Burundi, Byelorussian SSR, Cameroon, Cape Verde, Central African Republic, Chad, China, Colombia, Congo, Costa Rica, Côte d'Ivoire, Cuba, Cyprus, Czechoslovakia, Democratic Kampuchea, Democratic Yemen, Djibouti, Dominica, Dominican Republic, Ecuador, Egypt, El Salvador, Ethiopia, Fiji, Gabon, Gambia, German Democratic Republic, Ghana, Grenada, Guatemala, Guinea, Guinea-Bissau, Guyana, Haiti, Honduras, Hungary, India, Indonesia, Iran, Iraq, Jamaica, Jordan, Kenya, Kuwait, Lao People's Democratic Republic, Lebanon, Lesotho, Liberia, Libyan Arab Jamahiriya, Madagascar, Malawi, Malaysia, Maldives, Mali, Mauritania, Mauritius, Mongolia, Morocco, Mozambique, Myanmar, Nepal, New Zealand, Nicaragua, Niger, Nigeria, Oman, Pakistan, Panama, Papua New Guinea, Paraguay, Peru, Philippines, Poland, Qatar, Romania, Rwanda, Saint Kitts and Nevis, Saint Lucia, Saint Vincent and the Grenadines, Samoa, Sao Tome and Principe, Saudi Arabia, Senegal, Seychelles, Sierra Leone, Singapore, Solomon Islands, Somalia, Sri Lanka, Sudan, Suriname, Swaziland, Syrian Arab Republic, Thailand, Togo, Trinidad and Tobago, Tunisia, Uganda, Ukrainian SSR, USSR, United Arab Emirates, United Republic of Tanzania, Uruguay, Vanuatu, Venezuela, Viet Nam, Yemen, Yugoslavia, Zaire, Zambia, Zimbabwe.
Against: United States.
Abstaining: Australia, Austria, Belgium, Canada, Chile, Denmark, Finland, France, Germany, Federal Republic of, Greece, Iceland, Ireland, Israel, Italy, Japan, Luxembourg, Malta, Mexico, Netherlands, Norway, Portugal, Spain, Sweden, Turkey, United Kingdom.

International co-operation for disarmament

By **decision 44/432** of 15 December, the General Assembly reaffirmed the importance of strengthening international co-operation in the field of disarmament and called on all States to contribute to increasing the effectiveness of the United Nations in fulfilling its role and responsibility in that area.

Disarmament agreements

Parties and signatories

In October 1989, the Secretary-General submitted to the General Assembly his annual report on the status of multilateral disarmament agreements,[7] based on information received from the depositaries of those instruments. It listed the parties to and signatories of those agreements as at 31 July 1989.

As at 31 December 1989, the following numbers of States had become parties to the multilateral agreements covered in the Secretary-General's report (listed in chronological order, with the years in which they were initially signed or opened for signature).[8]

(Geneva) Protocol for the Prohibition of the Use in War of Asphyxiating, Poisonous or Other Gases, and of Bacteriological Methods of Warfare (1925): 122 parties

The Antarctic Treaty (1959): 39 parties

Treaty Banning Nuclear Weapon Tests in the Atmosphere, in Outer Space and under Water (1963): 118 parties

Treaty on Principles Governing the Activities of States in the Exploration and Use of Outer Space, including the Moon and Other Celestial Bodies (1967): 91 parties

Treaty for the Prohibition of Nuclear Weapons in Latin America (Treaty of Tlatelolco) (1967): 31 parties

Treaty on the Non-Proliferation of Nuclear Weapons (1968): 141 parties

Treaty on the Prohibition of the Emplacement of Nuclear Weapons and Other Weapons of Mass Destruction on the Sea-Bed and the Ocean Floor and in the Subsoil Thereof (1971): 82 parties

Convention on the Prohibition of the Development, Production and Stockpiling of Bacteriological (Biological) and Toxin Weapons and on Their Destruction (1972): 111 parties

Convention on the Prohibition of Military or Any Other Hostile Use of Environmental Modification Techniques (1977): 55 parties

Agreement Governing the Activities of States on the Moon and Other Celestial Bodies (1979): 7 parties

Convention on Prohibitions or Restrictions on the Use of Certain Conventional Weapons Which May Be Deemed to Be Excessively Injurious or to Have Indiscriminate Effects (1981): 32 parties

South Pacific Nuclear Free Zone Treaty (Treaty of Rarotonga) (1985): 13 parties

Compliance

On 15 December 1989, on the recommendation of the First Committee, the General Assembly adopted **resolution 44/122** without vote.

Compliance with arms limitation and disarmament agreements

The General Assembly,

Reaffirming its resolution 43/81 A of 7 December 1988,

Aware of the profound concern of all Member States for maintaining respect for rights and obligations arising from treaties and other sources of international law,

Convinced that observance of the Charter of the United Nations, relevant treaties and other sources of international law is essential for the strengthening of international security,

Mindful, in particular, of the fundamental importance of full implementation and strict observance of agreements on arms limitation and disarmament so that individual nations and the international community can derive enhanced security from them,

Stressing that any violation of such agreements not only adversely affects the security of States parties but can also create security risks for other States relying on the constraints and commitments stipulated in those agreements,

Stressing also that any weakening of confidence in such agreements diminishes their contribution to global or regional stability and to further disarmament and arms limitation efforts and undermines the credibility and effectiveness of the international legal system,

Recognizing in this context, *inter alia*, the contribution that full compliance with existing agreements can make to progress in the negotiation of arms limitation and disarmament agreements,

Believing that compliance with arms limitation and disarmament agreements by States parties is, therefore, a matter of interest and concern to all members of the international community, and noting the role that the United Nations might play in this regard,

Convinced that resolution of non-compliance questions that have arisen with regard to agreements on arms limitation and disarmament would contribute to better relations among States and the strengthening of world peace and security,

Welcoming the universal recognition of the importance of the question of compliance in the context of arms limitation and disarmament agreements,

1. *Urges* all States parties to arms limitation and disarmament agreements to implement and comply with the entirety of the provisions of such agreements;

2. *Calls upon* all Member States to consider fully the adverse implications of non-compliance with those obligations for international security and stability, as well as for the prospects for further progress in the field of disarmament;

3. *Also calls upon* all Member States to support efforts aimed at the resolution of non-compliance questions, with a view to encouraging strict observance by all parties of the provisions of arms limitation and disarmament agreements and maintaining or restoring the integrity of such agreements;

4. *Requests* the Secretary-General to provide Member States with assistance that may be necessary in this regard;

5. *Welcomes* efforts by States parties to develop additional co-operative measures, as appropriate, aimed at increasing confidence in compliance with arms limitation and disarmament agreements and reducing any possibility of misinterpretation and misunderstanding;

6. *Notes* in this connection the contribution that verification experiments can make in confirming and perfecting verification procedures in arms limitation and disarmament agreements under negotiation, thereby providing an opportunity, from the time that such agreements enter into force, for enhanced confidence in the effectiveness of verification procedures as a basis for determining compliance;

7. *Decides* to include in the provisional agenda of its forty-sixth session the item entitled "Compliance with arms limitation and disarmament agreements".

General Assembly resolution 44/122

15 December 1989   Meeting 81   Adopted without vote

Approved by First Committee (A/44/791) without vote, 17 November (meeting 41); draft by Chairman (A/C.1/44/L.67); agenda item 69.
Meeting numbers. GA 44th session: 1st Committee 3-25, 29, 40, 41; plenary 81.

Second Disarmament Decade (1980s)

In its review and appraisal of the Declaration of the 1980s as the Second Disarmament Decade, declared by the General Assembly in 1980,[9] the Assembly, in 1985, had requested the Secretary-General to report annually on the Declaration's implementation.[10]

In an August 1989 report with later addendum, the Secretary-General provided the views and suggestions of five Governments on implementing the Declaration.[11]

Declaration of the 1990s
as the Third Disarmament Decade

The General Assembly in 1988 declared the 1990s as the Third Disarmament Decade,[12] requesting the Secretary-General to seek views on elements for a declaration and to report to the Disarmament Commission in 1989.

In a May report, with later addenda, the Secretary-General transmitted the views of 11 Member States (one on behalf of the 12 member States of the European Community (EC)) and one specialized agency on the future Declaration.[13]

In May,[1] Working Group IV of the Disarmament Commission stated that it had not completed its work on the Declaration and invited the Assembly to consider further action on the matter.

GENERAL ASSEMBLY ACTION

On 15 December 1989, the General Assembly, on the recommendation of the First Committee, adopted **resolution 44/119 H** without vote.

Declaration of the 1990s as the
Third Disarmament Decade

The General Assembly,

Recalling its resolution 35/46 of 3 December 1980, in which it declared the 1980s as the Second Disarmament Decade,

Recalling also its resolution 34/75 of 11 December 1979, in which it directed the Disarmament Commission to prepare elements of a draft resolution entitled "Declaration of the 1980s as the Second Disarmament Decade" for submission to the General Assembly at its thirty-fifth session for consideration and adoption,

Bearing in mind that the Second Disarmament Decade declared by its resolution 35/46 is coming to an end,

Recalling further its resolution 43/78 L of 7 December 1988, in which it decided to declare the decade of the 1990s as the Third Disarmament Decade,

Reaffirming the responsibility of the United Nations in the attainment of disarmament,

Noting the progress in the disarmament talks between the Union of Soviet Socialist Republics and the United States of America and its positive impact on the attainment of global peace and security,

Desirous of maintaining the current momentum in the disarmament process,

Convinced that a third disarmament decade will accelerate the disarmament process,

1. *Takes note* of the work of the Disarmament Commission at its 1989 session on the declaration of the 1990s as the Third Disarmament Decade;

2. *Directs* the Disarmament Commission, at its 1990 substantive session, to finalize the preparation of elements of a draft resolution to be entitled "Declaration of the 1990s as the Third Disarmament Decade" and to submit them to the General Assembly at its forty-fifth session for consideration and adoption;

3. *Requests* the Secretary-General to render all necessary assistance to the Disarmament Commission in implementing the present resolution;

4. *Decides* to include in the provisional agenda of its forty-fifth session the item entitled "Declaration of the 1990s as the Third Disarmament Decade".

General Assembly resolution 44/119 H

15 December 1989   Meeting 81   Adopted without vote

Approved by First Committee (A/44/788) without vote, 9 November (meeting 32); 2-nation draft (A/C.1/44/L.62); agenda item 66 *(m)*.
Sponsors: Nigeria, Romania.
Meeting numbers. GA 44th session: 1st Committee 3-25, 32; plenary 81.

Comprehensive programme of disarmament

In 1989, limited progress was made in the Conference on Disarmament towards a comprehensive programme of disarmament, first envisaged in the Final Document of the General Assembly's first special session on disarmament in 1978[14] and considered annually since 1980.

The Conference continued its consideration of a draft programme from 10 to 14 April and from 7 to 11 August 1989. Its *Ad Hoc* Committee on the Comprehensive Programme of Disarmament held 23 formal meetings between 7 February and 24 August. In addition, it organized contact groups and informal consultations to deal with various sections of the draft in order to concentrate on the unresolved issues, with a view to reaching consensus on them. In its report to the Conference,[2] the *Ad Hoc* Committee stated that some progress had been made towards harmonizing positions and narrowing areas of disagreement, but that it had not been possible to reconcile differences on a number of issues.

GENERAL ASSEMBLY ACTION

On 15 December 1989, the General Assembly, on the recommendation of the First Committee, adopted **resolution 44/119 A** by recorded vote.

Comprehensive programme of disarmament

The General Assembly,

Recalling its resolution 2602 E (XXIV) of 16 December 1969, in which it declared the decade of the 1970s as a Disarmament Decade and requested, *inter alia*, the then Conference of the Committee on Disarmament to work out "a comprehensive programme, dealing with all aspects of the problem of the cessation of the arms race and general and complete disarmament under effective international control, which would provide the Conference with a guideline to chart the course of its further work and its negotiations",

Recalling also its resolution 35/46 of 3 December 1980, by which it adopted the Declaration of the 1980s as the Second Disarmament Decade, which, *inter alia*, called for the elaboration of the comprehensive programme of disarmament with the utmost urgency,

Recalling further its resolution 43/78 K of 7 December 1988, in which it noted the agreement of the *Ad Hoc* Committee on the Comprehensive Programme of Disarmament of the Conference on Disarmament to "resume its work at the outset of the 1989 session of the Conference with the firm intention of completing the elaboration of the programme for its submission to the General Assembly, at the latest at its forty-fourth session",

Having examined the report of the *Ad Hoc* Committee on the Comprehensive Programme of Disarmament concerning its work during the 1989 session of the Conference on Disarmament, which is an integral part of the report of the Conference,

Recognizing the efforts of the *Ad Hoc* Committee on the Comprehensive Programme of Disarmament and the substantial progress achieved thus far,

Conscious of the need to continue the work on the comprehensive programme of disarmament, building on the texts already agreed to, with a view to resolving the outstanding issues and thus concluding negotiations on it,

Recalling its resolution 43/78 L of 7 December 1988, in which it declared the decade of the 1990s as the Third Disarmament Decade,

Considering that the conclusion of the elaboration of the comprehensive programme of disarmament would constitute an important contribution to the success of the Third Disarmament Decade and to the role of the United Nations in the field of disarmament,

1. *Calls upon* the Conference on Disarmament to consider, at the beginning of its 1991 session, the resumption of the work of the *Ad Hoc* Committee on the Comprehensive Programme of Disarmament with the aim of resolving the outstanding issues in order to conclude the elaboration of the programme;

2. *Decides* to include in the provisional agenda of its forty-sixth session the item entitled "Comprehensive programme of disarmament".

General Assembly resolution 44/119 A

15 December 1989   Meeting 81   154-0-1 (recorded vote)

Approved by First Committee (A/44/788) by recorded vote (129-0-1), 16 November (meeting 38); draft by Mexico (A/C.1/44/L.2/Rev.1); agenda item 66 (*I*).

Meeting numbers. GA 44th session: 1st Committee 3-25, 27, 38; plenary 81.

Recorded vote in Assembly as follows:

In favour: Afghanistan, Albania, Algeria, Angola, Antigua and Barbuda, Argentina, Australia, Austria, Bahamas, Bahrain, Bangladesh, Barbados, Belgium, Benin, Bhutan, Bolivia, Botswana, Brazil, Brunei Darussalam, Bulgaria, Burkina Faso, Burundi, Byelorussian SSR, Cameroon, Canada, Cape Verde, Central African Republic, Chad, Chile, China, Colombia, Congo, Costa Rica, Côte d'Ivoire, Cuba, Cyprus, Czechoslovakia, Democratic Kampuchea, Democratic Yemen, Denmark, Djibouti, Dominica, Dominican Republic, Ecuador, Egypt, El Salvador, Ethiopia, Fiji, Finland, France, Gabon, Gambia, German Democratic Republic, Germany, Federal Republic of, Ghana, Greece, Grenada, Guatemala, Guinea, Guinea-Bissau, Guyana, Haiti, Honduras, Hungary, Iceland, India, Indonesia, Iran, Iraq, Ireland, Is-

rael, Italy, Jamaica, Japan, Jordan, Kenya, Kuwait, Lao People's Democratic Republic, Lebanon, Lesotho, Liberia, Libyan Arab Jamahiriya, Luxembourg, Madagascar, Malawi, Malaysia, Maldives, Mali, Malta, Mauritania, Mauritius, Mexico, Mongolia, Morocco, Mozambique, Myanmar, Nepal, Netherlands, New Zealand, Nicaragua, Niger, Nigeria, Norway, Oman, Pakistan, Panama, Papua New Guinea, Paraguay, Peru, Philippines, Poland, Portugal, Qatar, Romania, Rwanda, Saint Kitts and Nevis, Saint Lucia, Saint Vincent and the Grenadines, Samoa, Sao Tome and Principe, Saudi Arabia, Senegal, Seychelles, Sierra Leone, Singapore, Solomon Islands, Somalia, Spain, Sri Lanka, Sudan, Suriname, Swaziland, Sweden, Syrian Arab Republic, Thailand, Togo, Trinidad and Tobago, Tunisia, Turkey, Uganda, Ukrainian SSR, United Arab Emirates, United Kingdom, United Republic of Tanzania, Uruguay, Vanuatu, Venezuela, Viet Nam, Yemen, Yugoslavia, Zaire, Zambia, Zimbabwe.

Against: None.

Abstaining: United States.

In the Committee, paragraph 1 was approved by a recorded vote of 112 to none, with 17 abstentions. A separate vote was also requested in the Assembly; the paragraph was adopted by a recorded vote of 137 to none, with 17 abstentions.

Confidence-building measures

In 1989, agreements of a confidence-building nature were signed between the United States and the USSR.

An agreement between the two parties, signed in Moscow on 12 June, dealt with the prevention of dangerous military activities.[15] It provided for direct communications between the military units of the two sides when they were in the field, in order to prevent any possible misunderstandings, and also covered a number of activities or situations that could give rise to incidents during peacetime. At meetings held in September at Jackson Hole (Wyoming, United States), the United States and the USSR signed an agreement on advance notification of strategic exercises and another on verification and stability measures.[16]

(For further information and General Assembly action concerning confidence-building measures in Europe, see below, under "Prohibition or restriction of other weapons".)

Naval armaments and disarmament

In 1989, the Disarmament Commission continued to consider naval armaments and disarmament in a consultation group, which held seven meetings between 10 and 26 May. The group subscribed to the general approach of retaining and consolidating elements and principles that had been accepted earlier and incorporated into the Chairman's paper in 1988.[17]

Four working papers were submitted on the item: one by Bulgaria, the German Democratic Republic and the USSR, on confidence-building measures at sea and limitation and reduction of naval armaments;[18] two by Sweden, concerning proposals on a multilateral agreement for the prevention of incidents at sea[19] and on a protocol on sea mines;[20] and one by Finland, Indonesia and Sweden, on the general topic of naval armaments and disarmament.[21]

The Chairman of the Commission prepared a paper containing recommendations that had been agreed on previously, as well as a number of new proposals.[22] However, it was not possible to reach agreement on all elements of the paper and the Group recommended that the topic should be considered again in 1990. The Group's report was incorporated into the Commission's report to the General Assembly.[1]

GENERAL ASSEMBLY ACTION

On 15 December 1989, the General Assembly, on the recommendation of the First Committee, adopted **resolution 44/116 M** by recorded vote.

Naval armaments and disarmament

The General Assembly,

Recalling its resolution 38/188 G of 20 December 1983, in which it requested the Secretary-General, with the assistance of qualified governmental experts, to carry out a comprehensive study on the naval arms race,

Recalling also its resolution 40/94 F of 12 December 1985, in which it requested the Disarmament Commission to consider the issues contained in the study entitled *The Naval Arms Race*, both its substantive content and its conclusions, taking into account all other relevant present and future proposals, with a view to facilitating the identification of possible measures in the field of naval arms reductions and disarmament, pursued within the framework of progress towards general and complete disarmament, as well as confidence-building measures in this field,

Recalling further its resolution 43/75 L of 7 December 1988, in which it requested the Disarmament Commission to continue, at its 1989 session, the substantive consideration of the question and to report on its deliberations and recommendations to the General Assembly at its forty-fourth session,

Having examined the report of the Chairman of the Disarmament Commission on the substantive consideration of the question of the naval arms race and disarmament during the 1989 session of the Commission, which met with the approval of all delegations participating in the substantive consultations and which, in their view, could form the basis of further deliberations on the subject,

1. *Takes notes with satisfaction* of the report of the Chairman of the Disarmament Commission on the substantive consideration of the question of the naval arms race and disarmament;

2. *Requests* the Disarmament Commission to inscribe on the agenda for its 1990 session the item entitled "Naval armaments and disarmament";

3. *Also requests* the Disarmament Commission to continue, at its forthcoming session in 1990, the substantive consideration of the question and to report on its deliberations and recommendations to the General Assembly at its forty-fifth session;

4. *Decides* to include in the provisional agenda of its forty-fifth session the item entitled "Naval armaments and disarmament".

General Assembly resolution 44/116 M

15 December 1989   Meeting 81   154-1 (recorded vote)

Approved by First Committee (A/44/785) by recorded vote (132-1), 15 November (meeting 37); 15-nation draft (A/C.1/44/L.35); agenda item 63 *(j)*.

Sponsors: Australia, Austria, Bulgaria, China, Finland, German Democratic Republic, Iceland, Indonesia, Malaysia, Mexico, New Zealand, Nigeria, Sri Lanka, Sweden, Yugoslavia.

Meeting numbers. GA 44th session: 1st Committee 3-25, 28, 37; plenary 81.

Recorded vote in Assembly as follows:

In favour: Afghanistan, Albania, Algeria, Angola, Antigua and Barbuda, Argentina, Australia, Austria, Bahamas, Bahrain, Bangladesh, Barbados, Belgium, Benin, Bhutan, Bolivia, Botswana, Brazil, Brunei Darussalam, Bulgaria, Burkina Faso, Burundi, Byelorussian SSR, Cameroon, Canada, Cape Verde, Central African Republic, Chad, Chile, China, Colombia, Congo, Costa Rica, Côte d'Ivoire, Cuba, Cyprus, Czechoslovakia, Democratic Kampuchea, Democratic Yemen, Denmark, Djibouti, Dominica, Dominican Republic, Ecuador, Egypt, El Salvador, Ethiopia, Fiji, Finland, France, Gabon, Gambia, German Democratic Republic, Germany, Federal Republic of, Ghana, Greece, Grenada, Guatemala, Guinea, Guinea-Bissau, Guyana, Haiti, Honduras, Hungary, Iceland, India, Indonesia, Iran, Iraq, Ireland, Israel, Italy, Jamaica, Japan, Jordan, Kenya, Kuwait, Lao People's Democratic Republic, Lebanon, Lesotho, Liberia, Libyan Arab Jamahiriya, Luxembourg, Madagascar, Malawi, Malaysia, Maldives, Mali, Malta, Mauritania, Mauritius, Mexico, Mongolia, Morocco, Mozambique, Myanmar, Nepal, Netherlands, New Zealand, Nicaragua, Niger, Nigeria, Norway, Oman, Pakistan, Panama, Papua New Guinea, Paraguay, Peru, Philippines, Poland, Portugal, Qatar, Romania, Rwanda, Saint Kitts and Nevis, Saint Lucia, Saint Vincent and the Grenadines, Samoa, Sao Tome and Principe, Saudi Arabia, Senegal, Seychelles, Sierra Leone, Singapore, Solomon Islands, Somalia, Spain, Sri Lanka, Sudan, Suriname, Swaziland, Sweden, Syrian Arab Republic, Thailand, Togo, Trinidad and Tobago, Tunisia, Turkey, Uganda, Ukrainian SSR, USSR, United Arab Emirates, United Kingdom, United Republic of Tanzania, Uruguay, Vanuatu, Venezuela, Viet Nam, Yemen, Yugoslavia, Zaire, Zambia, Zimbabwe.

Against: United States.

Defensive security concepts and policies

In 1989, an area of growing interest to European States in particular was defensive security concepts and policies.

GENERAL ASSEMBLY ACTION

On 15 December 1989, the General Assembly, on the recommendation of the First Committee, adopted **resolution 44/116 P** by recorded vote.

Defensive security concepts and policies

The General Assembly,

Recalling the principle that States shall refrain in their international relations from the threat or use of force against the territorial integrity or political independence of any State, or in any other manner inconsistent with the purposes of the United Nations,

Reaffirming the obligation to maintain international peace and security in conformity with the purposes and principles of the United Nations,

Bearing in mind the reports of the Secretary-General transmitting the study on the relationship between disarmament and international security and the study undertaken by the Group of Governmental Experts to Carry Out a Comprehensive Study of Concepts of Security submitted to the General Assembly in 1981 and 1985, respectively,

Recognizing that since then a number of important developments have taken place in the areas of disarmament and security concepts and that new opportunities have emerged for arms limitation and disarmament, for ending regional conflicts and for developing among States constructive and co-operative relations,

Noting the ongoing international dialogue on matters of security, including the renewed search for common security as well as for common denominators for the security requirements in different regions,

Convinced that in the nuclear age national policies of restraint and co-operative efforts are essential to eliminate eventually the risk of war and global destruction,

Stressing that a nuclear war cannot be won and must never be fought,

Believing that security concepts and policies should be aimed at removing the danger of war and securing peace at progressively lower levels of armaments and armed forces, and welcoming activities by States to implement this goal by negotiated disarmament measures,

Bearing in mind the specific political and security requirements in different regions,

1. *Considers* the development of an international dialogue on defensive security concepts and policies to be of great importance for promoting the process of achieving disarmament and strengthening international security;

2. *Invites* Member States to initiate or intensify the dialogue on defensive security concepts and policies at the bilateral, regional or multilateral level and to keep the General Assembly informed about the progress achieved;

3. *Decides* to include in the provisional agenda of its forty-fifth session an item entitled ''Defensive security concepts and policies''.

General Assembly resolution 44/116 P

15 December 1989   Meeting 81   131-0-19 (recorded vote)

Approved by First Committee (A/44/785) by recorded vote (107-0-18), 17 November (meeting 40); 5-nation draft (A/C.1/44/L.45/Rev.2); agenda item 63.
Sponsors: Byelorussian SSR, Czechoslovakia, German Democratic Republic, Poland, USSR.
Meeting numbers. GA 44th session: 1st Committee 3-25, 31, 40; plenary 81.

Recorded vote in Assembly as follows:

In favour: Afghanistan, Algeria, Angola, Antigua and Barbuda, Argentina, Australia, Austria, Bahamas, Bahrain, Bangladesh, Barbados, Benin, Bhutan, Bolivia, Botswana, Brazil, Brunei Darussalam, Bulgaria, Burkina Faso, Burundi, Byelorussian SSR, Cameroon, Cape Verde, Central African Republic, Chad, Congo, Costa Rica, Côte d'Ivoire, Cuba, Cyprus, Czechoslovakia, Democratic Yemen, Djibouti, Dominica, Dominican Republic, Ecuador, Egypt, El Salvador, Ethiopia, Fiji, Finland, Gabon, Gambia, German Democratic Republic, Ghana, Grenada, Guatemala, Guinea, Guinea-Bissau, Guyana, Haiti, Honduras, Hungary, India, Indonesia, Iran, Iraq, Ireland, Jamaica, Jordan, Kenya, Kuwait, Lao People's Democratic Republic, Lebanon, Lesotho, Liberia, Libyan Arab Jamahiriya, Madagascar, Malawi, Malaysia, Maldives, Mali, Malta, Mauritania, Mauritius, Mexico, Mongolia, Morocco, Mozambique, Myanmar, Nepal, New Zealand, Nicaragua, Niger, Nigeria, Oman, Pakistan, Panama, Papua New Guinea, Paraguay, Peru, Philippines, Poland, Qatar, Romania, Rwanda, Saint Kitts and Nevis, Saint Lucia, Saint Vincent and the Grenadines, Samoa, Sao Tome and Principe, Saudi Arabia, Senegal, Seychelles, Sierra Leone, Solomon Islands, Somalia, Sri Lanka, Sudan, Suriname, Swaziland, Sweden, Syrian Arab Republic, Thailand, Togo, Trinidad and Tobago, Tunisia, Uganda, Ukrainian SSR, USSR, United Arab Emirates, United Republic of Tanzania, Uruguay, Vanuatu, Venezuela, Viet Nam, Yemen, Yugoslavia, Zaire, Zambia, Zimbabwe.
Against: None.
Abstaining: Belgium, Canada, Chile, Denmark, France, Germany, Federal Republic of, Greece, Iceland, Israel, Italy, Japan, Luxembourg, Netherlands, Norway, Portugal, Spain, Turkey, United Kingdom, United States.

REFERENCES

[1]A/44/42. [2]A/44/27. [3]YUN 1988, p. 38. [4]*Ibid.*, p. 39, GA res. 43/75 R, 7 Dec. 1988. [5]*Ibid.*, p. 40, GA res. 43/75 H, 7 Dec. 1988. [6]A/44/495 & Add.1. [7]A/44/619. [8]*The United Nations Disarmament Yearbook*, vol. 14: *1989*, Sales No. E.90.IX.4. [9]YUN 1980, p. 102, GA res. 35/46, annex, 3 Dec. 1980. [10]YUN 1985, p. 22, GA res. 40/152 L, 16 Dec. 1985.

[11]A/44/435 & Add.1. [12]YUN 1988, p. 46, GA res. 43/78 L, 7 Dec. 1988. [13]A/CN.10/115 & Add.1-4 & Add.4/Corr.1. & Add.5. [14]YUN 1978, p. 39, GA res. S-10/2, 30 June 1978. [15]CD/943. [16]A/44/578-S/20868. [17]YUN 1988, p. 48. [18]A/CN.10/119. [19]A/CN.10/121. [20]A/CN.10/129. [21]A/CN.10/130. [22]A/CN.10/134.

Nuclear disarmament

Nuclear arms limitation and disarmament

Disarmament Commission consideration. In 1989, the Disarmament Commission considered various aspects of the arms race, particularly the nuclear-arms race, nuclear disarmament, the prevention of nuclear war and conventional disarmament by establishing a contact group within the framework of the Committee of the Whole.[1] The group held 12 meetings between 10 and 26 May, basing its work on the compilation of proposals for recommendations contained in the report of the Commission to the General Assembly at its fifteenth (1988) special session.[2] It also had before it a working paper on negotiations on nuclear disarmament submitted by Bulgaria, Czechoslovakia, the German Democratic Republic and the USSR.[3] While the group made some progress towards narrowing areas of disagreement on a basic recommendation on nuclear disarmament and another one on conventional disarmament, it was unable to reach a consensus on a complete set of recommendations. Consequently, it recommended that the Commission should continue its efforts with a view to reaching agreement on a complete set of recommendations.

Consideration by the Conference on Disarmament. The Conference on Disarmament considered the cessation of the nuclear-arms race and nuclear disarmament from 20 February to 3 March and from 19 to 30 June 1989.[4] As in previous years, no consensus was reached on a mandate proposed by the Group of 21 to establish an *ad hoc* committee to consider proposals on the subject.[5]

(For General Assembly action on cessation of the nuclear-arms race and nuclear disarmament and prevention of nuclear war, see **resolution 44/119 E** below.)

GENERAL ASSEMBLY ACTION

On 15 December 1989, the General Assembly, on the recommendation of the First Committee, adopted **resolution 44/116 D** without vote.

Nuclear disarmament

The General Assembly,

Recalling its resolutions 41/59 F of 3 December 1986, 42/38 H of 30 November 1987 and 43/75 E of 7 December 1988,

Reaffirming the determination to save succeeding generations from the scourge of war as expressed in the Preamble to the Charter of the United Nations,

Convinced that the most acute and urgent task of the present day is to remove the threat of a world war—a nuclear war,

Recalling and reaffirming the statements and provisions on nuclear disarmament set forth in the Final Document of the Tenth Special Session of the General Assembly, and, in particular, provisions that "effective measures of nuclear disarmament and the prevention of nuclear war have the highest priority", contained in paragraph 20, and that "in the task of achieving the goals of nuclear disarmament, all the nuclear-weapon States, in particular those among them which possess the most important nuclear arsenals, bear a special responsibility", contained in paragraph 48,

Also recalling that paragraph 55 of the same document states that "Real progress in the field of nuclear disarmament could create an atmosphere conducive to progress in conventional disarmament on a world-wide basis",

Bearing in mind that the ultimate goal of nuclear disarmament is the complete elimination of nuclear weapons,

Noting that the leaders of the Union of Soviet Socialist Republics and the United States of America agreed in their joint statement issued at Geneva on 21 November 1985 that "a nuclear war cannot be won and must never be fought" and the common desire they expressed in the same statement calling for early progress in areas where there is common ground, including the principle of a 50 per cent reduction in the nuclear arms of the Soviet Union and the United States appropriately applied,

Noting also that the Union of Soviet Socialist Republics and the United States of America have conducted intensive negotiations on various issues of disarmament,

Noting further that the Conference on Disarmament has not played its due role in the field of nuclear disarmament,

Believing that the qualitative aspect of the arms race needs to be addressed along with its quantitative aspect,

Bearing in mind that the Governments and peoples of various countries expect that the Union of Soviet Socialist Republics and the United States of America will reach agreement on halting the nuclear-arms race and further reducing nuclear weapons,

1. *Welcomes* the continued implementation of the Treaty between the United States of America and the Union of Soviet Socialist Republics on the Elimination of Their Intermediate-Range and Shorter-Range Missiles;

2. *Urges* the Union of Soviet Socialist Republics and the United States of America, which possess the most important nuclear arsenals, further to discharge their special responsibility for nuclear disarmament, to take the lead in halting the nuclear-arms race and to accelerate negotiations with a view to reaching early agreement on the drastic reduction of their nuclear arsenals;

3. *Reiterates its belief* that bilateral and multilateral efforts for nuclear disarmament should complement and facilitate each other;

4. *Decides* to include in the provisional agenda of its forty-fifth session the item entitled "Nuclear disarmament".

General Assembly resolution 44/116 D

15 December 1989   Meeting 81   Adopted without vote

Approved by First Committee (A/44/785) without vote, 10 November (meeting 33); draft by China (A/C.1/44/L.14); agenda item 63 *(e)*.
Meeting numbers. GA 44th session: 1st Committee 3-25, 31, 33; plenary 81.

USSR–United States nuclear-arms negotiations

Following the signing in 1987[6] and the entry into force in 1988[7] of the Treaty between the United States of America and the Union of Soviet Socialist Republics on the Elimination of Their Intermediate-Range and Shorter-Range Missiles, the two parties sought to negotiate a 50 per cent reduction in their strategic arms. In a joint statement of 23 September 1989, they indicated that they had removed a number of obstacles to the conclusion of an agreement on the subject.[8] In December, Presidents George Bush of the United States and Mikhail S. Gorbachev of the USSR agreed to accelerate the strategic arms reduction negotiations in order to resolve all substantive issues and to conclude a treaty before the end of 1990.

GENERAL ASSEMBLY ACTION

On 15 December 1989, the General Assembly, on the recommendation of the First Committee, adopted **resolution 44/116 B** by recorded vote.

Bilateral nuclear-arms negotiations

The General Assembly,

Recalling that at their meeting at Geneva in November 1985 the leaders of the Union of Soviet Socialist Republics and the United States of America committed themselves to the objective of working out effective agreements aimed at preventing an arms race in space and terminating it on Earth,

Noting the progress reflected in the joint statement issued by the Union of Soviet Socialist Republics and the United States of America following their meetings in Washington and Wyoming from 21 to 23 September 1989,

Noting also that, since their meetings in Moscow from 29 May to 1 June 1988, bilateral nuclear-arms negotiations have been intensified,

Noting further the importance of the verification procedures contained in the Treaty between the United States of America and the Union of Soviet Socialist Republics on the Elimination of Their Intermediate-Range and Shorter-Range Missiles as an example of the high standards of verification that are now achievable in arms control agreements, both bilateral and multilateral,

Believing that, through negotiations pursued in a spirit of flexibility and with full account taken of the security interests of all States, it is possible to achieve far-reaching and effectively verifiable agreements,

Firmly convinced that early agreement in these negotiations, in accordance with the principle of undiminished security at the lowest possible level of armaments, would be of crucial importance for the strengthening of international peace and security,

Convinced that the international community should encourage the Government of the Union of Soviet Socialist

Republics and the Government of the United States of America in their endeavours, taking into account both the importance and the complexity of their negotiations,

1. *Welcomes* the fact that the provisions of the Treaty between the United States of America and the Union of Soviet Socialist Republics on the Elimination of Their Intermediate-Range and Shorter-Range Missiles are being implemented by the United States of America and the Union of Soviet Socialist Republics;

2. *Calls upon* the Government of the Union of Soviet Socialist Republics and the Government of the United States of America to spare no effort in seeking, in accordance with the security interests of all States and the universal desire for progress towards disarmament, the attainment of all the agreed objectives in the negotiations, that is, the resolution of a complex of questions concerning space and strategic nuclear arms with all these questions considered and resolved in their interrelationship;

3. *Invites* the two Governments concerned to keep other States Members of the United Nations duly informed of progress in their negotiations, in accordance with paragraph 114 of the Final Document of the Tenth Special Session of the General Assembly;

4. *Expresses its firmest possible encouragement and support* for the bilateral negotiations and their successful conclusion.

General Assembly resolution 44/116 B

15 December 1989   Meeting 81   91-0-61 (recorded vote)

Approved by First Committee (A/44/785) by recorded vote (71-0-64), 13 November (meeting 35); 17-nation draft (A/C.1/44/L.12); agenda item 63.
Sponsors: Australia, Belgium, Canada, Denmark, France, Germany, Federal Republic of, Greece, Iceland, Italy, Japan, Luxembourg, Netherlands, Norway, Portugal, Spain, Turkey, United Kingdom.
Meeting numbers. GA 44th session: 1st Committee 3-25, 29, 35; plenary 81.

Recorded vote in Assembly as follows:

In favour: Antigua and Barbuda, Australia, Austria, Bahamas, Bahrain, Barbados, Belgium, Bhutan, Brunei Darussalam, Bulgaria, Burkina Faso, Byelorussian SSR, Canada, Cape Verde, Central African Republic, Chad, Chile, China, Colombia, Costa Rica, Côte d'Ivoire, Czechoslovakia, Democratic Kampuchea, Denmark, Djibouti, Dominica, Fiji, Finland, France, Gambia, German Democratic Republic, Germany, Federal Republic of, Greece, Grenada, Guatemala, Guinea, Guinea-Bissau, Honduras, Hungary, Iceland, Ireland, Israel, Italy, Jamaica, Japan, Lao People's Democratic Republic, Lebanon, Lesotho, Liberia, Luxembourg, Malawi, Malta, Mauritius, Mongolia, Morocco, Myanmar, Netherlands, New Zealand, Norway, Papua New Guinea, Paraguay, Philippines, Poland, Portugal, Romania, Rwanda, Saint Kitts and Nevis, Saint Lucia, Saint Vincent and the Grenadines, Samoa, Sao Tome and Principe, Saudi Arabia, Senegal, Seychelles, Sierra Leone, Singapore, Solomon Islands, Somalia, Spain, Sudan, Sweden, Thailand, Togo, Turkey, Ukrainian SSR, USSR, United Kingdom, United States, Uruguay, Viet Nam, Zaire.

Against: None.

Abstaining: Afghanistan, Algeria, Angola, Argentina, Bangladesh, Benin, Bolivia, Botswana, Brazil, Burundi, Cameroon, Congo, Cuba, Cyprus, Democratic Yemen, Dominican Republic, Ecuador, Egypt, Ethiopia, Gabon, Ghana, Guyana, India, Indonesia, Iran, Iraq, Jordan, Kenya, Kuwait, Libyan Arab Jamahiriya, Madagascar, Malaysia, Maldives, Mali, Mauritania, Mexico, Mozambique, Nepal, Nicaragua, Niger, Nigeria, Oman, Pakistan, Panama, Peru, Qatar, Sri Lanka, Suriname, Swaziland, Syrian Arab Republic, Trinidad and Tobago, Tunisia, Uganda, United Arab Emirates, United Republic of Tanzania, Vanuatu, Venezuela, Yemen, Yugoslavia, Zambia, Zimbabwe.

On the same day, also on the recommendation of the First Committee, the Assembly adopted **resolution 44/116 K** by recorded vote.

Bilateral nuclear-arms negotiations

The General Assembly,

Recalling its resolution 43/75 A of 7 December 1988,

Recalling also the Declaration and the final document on international security and disarmament adopted by the Ninth Conference of Heads of State or Government of Non-Aligned Countries, held at Belgrade from 4 to 7 September 1989,[a]

Stressing that general *rapprochement* between the Union of Soviet Socialist Republics and the United States of America contributes to the relaxation of international tensions and the creation of basic prerequisites for establishing lasting peace,

Encouraged by the positive developments in the field of disarmament brought about by the implementation of the Treaty between the United States of America and the Union of Soviet Socialist Republics on the Elimination of Their Intermediate-Range and Shorter-Range Missiles and by recent agreements between the two sides,

Concerned, however, that the world is still threatened by the massive nuclear arsenals, which are being further refined and added to, and that the only hope for nuclear disarmament lies in discarding the balance of fear and in the nuclear-weapon Powers' embracing the objective of the total elimination of nuclear weapons,

Stressing also the importance of the strengthening of international security through disarmament and the halting of the qualitative and quantitative escalation of the arms race,

Aware of the fact that both the nuclear and the conventional disarmament processes cannot be carried out without a contribution by all States and especially by the major military Powers and their alliances, which have the greatest responsibility in that regard,

Mindful that, while it is the responsibility and obligation of all States to speed up the emerging process and to channel it in a direction that would benefit all, lasting peace and security can only be achieved by pooling the efforts of the international community and with all countries participating and contributing on the basis of equality,

Stressing further that general and complete disarmament under effective international control is by its very nature unattainable unless all countries join in its implementation,

Emphasizing that, since nuclear war threatens the very right to live, the prevention of nuclear war remains the principal task of our times,

Affirming that bilateral and multilateral negotiations on disarmament should facilitate and complement each other and that progress at the bilateral level should not be used to postpone or impede action at the multilateral level,

1. *Welcomes* the positive developments in the bilateral negotiations between the Union of Soviet Socialist Republics and the United States of America on disarmament issues, as well as the commencement of the implementation of the Treaty between the United States of America and the Union of Soviet Socialist Republics on the Elimination of Their Intermediate-Range and Shorter-Range Missiles;

2. *Calls upon* the Union of Soviet Socialist Republics and the United States of America to exert every effort to achieve the goal they set themselves of a treaty on a 50 per cent reduction in strategic offensive arms as part

---

[a]A/44/551-S/20870.

of the process leading to the complete elimination of nuclear weapons;

3. *Also calls upon* the two Governments to intensify their efforts to achieve agreements in other areas, in particular the issue of a comprehensive nuclear-test ban as a matter of urgency;

4. *Further calls upon* the two Governments to reach agreement to ensure that outer space is kept free of all weapons;

5. *Invites* the Governments of the Union of Soviet Socialist Republics and the United States of America to keep the General Assembly and the Conference on Disarmament duly informed of progress made in their negotiations.

General Assembly resolution 44/116 K

15 December 1989   Meeting 81   134-0-18 (recorded vote)

Approved by First Committee (A/44/785) by recorded vote (119-0-19), 13 November (meeting 35); draft by Romania and Yugoslavia for Non-Aligned Group (A/C.1/44/L.31/Rev.1); agenda item 63.
Meeting numbers. GA 44th session: 1st Committee 3-25, 35; plenary 81.

Recorded vote in Assembly as follows:

In favour: Afghanistan, Algeria, Angola, Antigua and Barbuda, Argentina, Australia, Austria, Bahamas, Bahrain, Bangladesh, Barbados, Benin, Bhutan, Bolivia, Botswana, Brazil, Brunei Darussalam, Bulgaria, Burkina Faso, Burundi, Byelorussian SSR, Cameroon, Cape Verde, Central African Republic, Chad, Chile, China, Colombia, Congo, Costa Rica, Côte d'Ivoire, Cuba, Cyprus, Czechoslovakia, Democratic Kampuchea, Democratic Yemen, Djibouti, Dominica, Dominican Republic, Ecuador, Egypt, El Salvador, Ethiopia, Fiji, Finland, Gabon, Gambia, German Democratic Republic, Ghana, Grenada, Guatemala, Guinea, Guinea-Bissau, Guyana, Honduras, Hungary, India, Indonesia, Iran, Iraq, Ireland, Jamaica, Jordan, Kenya, Kuwait, Lao People's Democratic Republic, Lebanon, Lesotho, Liberia, Libyan Arab Jamahiriya, Madagascar, Malawi, Malaysia, Maldives, Mali, Malta, Mauritania, Mauritius, Mexico, Mongolia, Morocco, Mozambique, Myanmar, Nepal, New Zealand, Nicaragua, Niger, Nigeria, Oman, Pakistan, Panama, Papua New Guinea, Paraguay, Peru, Philippines, Poland, Qatar, Romania, Rwanda, Saint Kitts and Nevis, Saint Lucia, Saint Vincent and the Grenadines, Samoa, Sao Tome and Principe, Saudi Arabia, Senegal, Seychelles, Sierra Leone, Singapore, Solomon Islands, Somalia, Sri Lanka, Sudan, Suriname, Swaziland, Sweden, Syrian Arab Republic, Thailand, Togo, Trinidad and Tobago, Tunisia, Uganda, Ukrainian SSR, USSR, United Republic of Tanzania, Uruguay, Vanuatu, Venezuela, Viet Nam, Yemen, Yugoslavia, Zaire, Zambia, Zimbabwe.

Against: None.

Abstaining: Belgium, Canada, Denmark, France, Germany, Federal Republic of, Greece, Iceland, Israel, Italy, Japan, Luxembourg, Netherlands, Norway, Portugal, Spain, Turkey, United Kingdom, United States.

Nuclear-weapons freeze

Since 1982, the General Assembly annually called for a freeze on nuclear weapons, but no action was taken by the nuclear-weapon States. In 1989, the Assembly again considered the issue of a nuclear-arms freeze.

GENERAL ASSEMBLY ACTION

On 15 December 1989, the General Assembly, on the recommendation of the First Committee, adopted **resolution 44/117 D** by recorded vote.

Nuclear-arms freeze

The General Assembly,

Recalling that, in the Final Document of the Tenth Special Session of the General Assembly, the first special session devoted to disarmament, adopted in 1978 and unanimously and categorically reaffirmed in 1982 during the twelfth special session of the General Assembly, the second special session devoted to disarmament, the Assembly expressed deep concern over the threat to the very survival of mankind posed by the existence of nuclear weapons and the continuing arms race,

Convinced that, in this nuclear age, lasting world peace can be based only on the attainment of the goal of general and complete disarmament under effective international control,

Welcoming the new trends that have led to an improvement in the international security environment,

Convinced also of the urgency further to pursue negotiations for the substantial reduction and qualitative limitation of existing nuclear arms,

Considering that a nuclear-arms freeze, while not an end in itself, would constitute an effective step to prevent the continued increase and qualitative improvement of existing nuclear weaponry during the period when the negotiations take place, and that at the same time it would provide a favourable environment for the conduct of negotiations to reduce and eventually eliminate nuclear weapons,

Convinced further that the undertakings derived from the freeze can be effectively verified,

Welcoming the announcement that the Union of Soviet Socialist Republics will cease production of highly enriched uranium for nuclear weapons purposes by the end of 1989 and had begun the process of shutting down its reactors producing weapons-grade plutonium,

Noting with deep concern that all nuclear-weapon States have not so far taken any collective action in response to the call made in the relevant resolutions on the question of a nuclear-arms freeze,

1. *Urges once more* both the Union of Soviet Socialist Republics and the United States of America, as the two major nuclear-weapon States, to reach agreement on an immediate nuclear-arms freeze, which would, *inter alia*, provide for a simultaneous total stoppage of any further production of nuclear weapons and a complete cut-off in the production of fissionable material for weapons purposes;

2. *Calls upon* all nuclear-weapon States to agree, through a joint declaration, to a comprehensive nuclear-arms freeze, whose structure and scope would be the following:

(a) It would embrace:

(i) A comprehensive test ban on nuclear weapons and on their delivery vehicles;

(ii) The complete cessation of the manufacture of nuclear weapons and of their delivery vehicles;

(iii) A ban on all further deployment of nuclear weapons and of their delivery vehicles;

(iv) The complete cessation of the production of fissionable material for weapons purposes;

(b) It would be subject to appropriate and effective measures and procedures of verification;

3. *Requests* the nuclear-weapon States to submit a joint report, or separate reports, to the General Assembly, prior to the opening of its forty-fifth session, on the implementation of the present resolution;

4. *Decides* to include in the provisional agenda of its forty-fifth session the item entitled "Nuclear-arms freeze".

General Assembly resolution 44/117 D

15 December 1989   Meeting 81   136-13-5 (recorded vote)

Approved by First Committee (A/44/786) by recorded vote (115-13-4), 15 November (meeting 37); 7-nation draft (A/C.1/44/L.40/Rev.1); agenda item 64 (c).
Sponsors: India, Indonesia, Mexico, Pakistan, Peru, Romania, Sweden.
Meeting numbers. GA 44th session: 1st Committee 3-25, 31, 37; plenary 81.

Recorded vote in Assembly as follows:

In favour: Afghanistan, Albania, Algeria, Angola, Antigua and Barbuda, Argentina, Australia, Austria, Bahamas, Bahrain, Bangladesh, Barbados,

Benin, Bhutan, Bolivia, Botswana, Brazil, Brunei Darussalam, Bulgaria, Burkina Faso, Burundi, Byelorussian SSR, Cameroon, Cape Verde, Central African Republic, Chad, Chile, Colombia, Congo, Côte d'Ivoire, Cuba, Cyprus, Czechoslovakia, Democratic Yemen, Denmark, Djibouti, Dominica, Dominican Republic, Ecuador, Egypt, Ethiopia, Fiji, Finland, Gabon, Gambia, German Democratic Republic, Ghana, Greece, Grenada, Guatemala, Guinea, Guinea-Bissau, Guyana, Haiti, Honduras, Hungary, India, Indonesia, Iran, Iraq, Ireland, Jamaica, Jordan, Kenya, Kuwait, Lao People's Democratic Republic, Lebanon, Lesotho, Liberia, Libyan Arab Jamahiriya, Madagascar, Malawi, Malaysia, Maldives, Mali, Malta, Mauritania, Mauritius, Mexico, Mongolia, Morocco, Mozambique, Myanmar, Nepal, New Zealand, Nicaragua, Niger, Nigeria, Norway, Oman, Pakistan, Panama, Papua New Guinea, Paraguay, Peru, Philippines, Poland, Qatar, Romania, Rwanda, Saint Kitts and Nevis, Saint Lucia, Saint Vincent and the Grenadines, Samoa, Sao Tome and Principe, Saudi Arabia, Senegal, Seychelles, Sierra Leone, Singapore, Solomon Islands, Somalia, Sri Lanka, Sudan, Suriname, Swaziland, Sweden, Syrian Arab Republic, Thailand, Togo, Trinidad and Tobago, Tunisia, Uganda, Ukrainian SSR, USSR, United Arab Emirates, United Republic of Tanzania, Uruguay, Vanuatu, Venezuela, Viet Nam, Yemen, Yugoslavia, Zaire, Zambia, Zimbabwe.

Against: Belgium, Canada, France, Germany, Federal Republic of, Israel, Italy, Japan, Luxembourg, Netherlands, Portugal, Turkey, United Kingdom, United States.

Abstaining: China, Costa Rica, El Salvador, Iceland, Spain.

Prohibition of nuclear weapons

On 15 December 1989, the General Assembly, on the recommendation of the First Committee, adopted **resolution 44/116 H** by recorded vote.

Prohibition of the production of fissionable material for weapons purposes

The General Assembly,

Recalling its resolutions 33/91 H of 16 December 1978, 34/87 D of 11 December 1979, 35/156 H of 12 December 1980, 36/97 G of 9 December 1981, 37/99 E of 13 December 1982, 38/188 E of 20 December 1983, 39/151 H of 17 December 1984, 40/94 G of 12 December 1985, 41/59 L of 3 December 1986, 42/38 L of 30 November 1987 and 43/75 K of 7 December 1988, in which it requested the Conference on Disarmament, at an appropriate stage of the implementation of the Programme of Action set forth in section III of the Final Document of the Tenth Special Session of the General Assembly, the first special session devoted to disarmament, and of its work on the item entitled "Nuclear weapons in all aspects", to consider urgently the question of adequately verified cessation and prohibition of the production of fissionable material for nuclear weapons and other nuclear explosive devices and to keep the Assembly informed of the progress of that consideration,

Noting that the agenda of the Conference on Disarmament for 1989 included the item entitled "Nuclear weapons in all aspects" and that the programme of work of the Conference for both parts of its 1989 session contained the item entitled "Cessation of the nuclear-arms race and nuclear disarmament",

Recalling the proposals and statements made in the Conference on Disarmament on those items,

Considering that the cessation of production of fissionable material for weapons purposes and the progressive conversion and transfer of stocks to peaceful uses would be a significant step towards halting and reversing the nuclear-arms race,

Considering also that the prohibition of the production of fissionable material for nuclear weapons and other explosive devices would be an important measure in facilitating the prevention of the proliferation of nuclear weapons and explosive devices,

Requests the Conference on Disarmament, at an appropriate stage of its work on the item entitled "Nuclear weapons in all aspects", to pursue its consideration of the question of adequately verified cessation and prohibition of the production of fissionable material for nuclear weapons and other nuclear explosive devices and to keep the General Assembly informed of the progress of that consideration.

General Assembly resolution 44/116 H

15 December 1989   Meeting 81   147-1-6 (recorded vote)

Approved by First Committee (A/44/785) by recorded vote (126-1-6), 10 November (meeting 34); 23-nation draft (A/C.1/44/L.24); agenda item 63 *(i)*.

Sponsors: Australia, Austria, Bahamas, Bangladesh, Botswana, Byelorussian SSR, Cameroon, Canada, Denmark, Finland, German Democratic Republic, Greece, Indonesia, Ireland, Japan, Netherlands, New Zealand, Norway, Philippines, Romania, Samoa, Sweden, Uruguay.

Meeting numbers. GA 44th session: 1st Committee 3-25, 29, 34; plenary 81.

Recorded vote in Assembly as follows:

In favour: Afghanistan, Albania, Algeria, Angola, Antigua and Barbuda, Australia, Austria, Bahamas, Bahrain, Bangladesh, Barbados, Belgium, Benin, Bhutan, Bolivia, Botswana, Brunei Darussalam, Bulgaria, Burkina Faso, Burundi, Byelorussian SSR, Cameroon, Canada, Cape Verde, Central African Republic, Chad, Chile, Colombia, Congo, Costa Rica, Côte d'Ivoire, Cuba, Cyprus, Czechoslovakia, Democratic Yemen, Denmark, Djibouti, Dominica, Dominican Republic, Ecuador, Egypt, El Salvador, Ethiopia, Fiji, Finland, Gabon, Gambia, German Democratic Republic, Germany, Federal Republic of, Ghana, Greece, Grenada, Guatemala, Guinea, Guinea-Bissau, Guyana, Haiti, Honduras, Hungary, Iceland, Indonesia, Iran, Iraq, Ireland, Israel, Italy, Jamaica, Japan, Jordan, Kenya, Kuwait, Lao People's Democratic Republic, Lebanon, Lesotho, Liberia, Libyan Arab Jamahiriya, Luxembourg, Madagascar, Malawi, Malaysia, Maldives, Mali, Malta, Mauritania, Mauritius, Mexico, Mongolia, Morocco, Mozambique, Myanmar, Nepal, Netherlands, New Zealand, Nicaragua, Niger, Nigeria, Norway, Oman, Pakistan, Panama, Papua New Guinea, Paraguay, Peru, Philippines, Poland, Portugal, Qatar, Romania, Rwanda, Saint Kitts and Nevis, Saint Lucia, Saint Vincent and the Grenadines, Samoa, Sao Tome and Principe, Saudi Arabia, Senegal, Seychelles, Sierra Leone, Singapore, Solomon Islands, Somalia, Spain, Sri Lanka, Sudan, Suriname, Swaziland, Sweden, Syrian Arab Republic, Thailand, Togo, Trinidad and Tobago, Tunisia, Turkey, Uganda, Ukrainian SSR, USSR, United Arab Emirates, United Republic of Tanzania, Uruguay, Vanuatu, Venezuela, Viet Nam, Yemen, Yugoslavia, Zaire, Zambia, Zimbabwe.

Against: France.

Abstaining: Argentina, Brazil, China, India, United Kingdom, United States.

Prevention of nuclear war

Consideration by the Conference on Disarmament. The Conference on Disarmament considered the topic of the prevention of nuclear war from 6 to 10 March and from 10 to 14 July 1989.[4] As in previous years, no consensus was reached on a mandate proposed by the Group of 21 for an *ad hoc* committee to consider all relevant proposals, including appropriate and practical measures for preventing nuclear war.[9]

Other action. In 1989, the USSR and the United States signed a new accord on the avoidance of accidental war—the Agreement on the Prevention of Dangerous Military Activities.[10] It was aimed at reducing the risk of the outbreak of war, including nuclear war, in particular as a result of misinterpretation, miscalculation or accident.

GENERAL ASSEMBLY ACTION

On 15 December 1989, the General Assembly, on the recommendation of the First Committee, adopted **resolution 44/119 B** by recorded vote.

Non-use of nuclear weapons and prevention of nuclear war

The General Assembly,

Recalling that, in accordance with paragraph 20 of the Final Document of the Tenth Special Session of the General Assembly, the first special session devoted to disarmament, effective measures of nuclear disarmament and the prevention of nuclear war have the highest priority and that this commitment was reaffirmed by the Assembly at its twelfth special session, the second special session devoted to disarmament,

Recalling also that, in paragraph 58 of the Final Document, it is stated that all States, in particular nuclear-weapon States, should consider as soon as possible various proposals designed to secure the avoidance of the use of nuclear weapons, the prevention of nuclear war and related objectives, where possible through international agreement, and thereby ensure that the survival of mankind is not endangered,

Recalling further that at its fifteenth special session, the third special session devoted to disarmament, it was generally recognized that the prevention of nuclear war was of utmost concern and that specific efforts, bilateral, regional or multilateral, should be vigorously pursued and measures should be strengthened to reduce and ultimately eliminate the risk of nuclear war,

Reaffirming that the nuclear-weapon States have the primary responsibility for nuclear disarmament and for undertaking measures aimed at preventing the outbreak of nuclear war, and that in the task of achieving the goals of nuclear disarmament all the nuclear-weapon States, in particular those among them which possess the most important nuclear arsenals, bear a special responsibility,

Stressing that a nuclear war cannot be won and must never be fought,

Welcoming the entry into force and implementation of the Treaty between the United States of America and the Union of Soviet Socialist Republics on the Elimination of Their Intermediate-Range and Shorter-Range Missiles as a first valuable step towards the reduction of nuclear weapons, as well as measures taken by the two States to reduce the risk of nuclear war, including the establishment and operation of nuclear risk reduction centres,

Expressing the hope that further measures will be undertaken to reduce and ultimately eliminate the risk of nuclear war,

Taking note of ideas directed to that end, including the suggestion to consider the establishment of a multilateral nuclear alert centre to reduce the risk of fatal misinterpretation of unintentional nuclear launchings,

Noting that, in its final document on international security and disarmament,[a] the Ninth Conference of Heads of State or Government of Non-Aligned Countries, held at Belgrade from 4 to 7 September 1989, stressed the need for the conclusion of an international agreement prohibiting all use of nuclear weapons,

Welcoming recent progress in the field of disarmament, including the beginning at Vienna of new negotiations on conventional armed forces and on confidence- and security-building measures in Europe,

Emphasizing that, for the sake of international peace and security, military concepts and doctrines must be of a strictly defensive character,

1. *Considers* that the solemn declarations by two nuclear-weapon States made or reiterated at the twelfth special session of the General Assembly, concerning their respective obligations not to be the first to use nuclear weapons, offer an important avenue to decrease the danger of nuclear war;

2. *Expresses the hope* that those nuclear-weapon States that have not yet done so will consider making similar declarations with respect to not being the first to use nuclear weapons;

3. *Requests* the Conference on Disarmament to commence negotiations on the item in its agenda concerning prevention of nuclear war and to consider, *inter alia*, the elaboration of an international instrument of a legally binding character laying down the obligation not to be the first to use nuclear weapons;

4. *Decides* to include in the provisional agenda of its forty-fifth session the item entitled ''Non-use of nuclear weapons and prevention of nuclear war''.

---

[a]A/44/551-S/20870.

General Assembly resolution 44/119 B

15 December 1989   Meeting 81   129-17-7 (recorded vote)

Approved by First Committee (A/44/788) by recorded vote (106-16-8), 10 November (meeting 33); 6-nation draft (A/C.1/44/L.3), orally revised; agenda item 66 *(g)*.

Sponsors: Bulgaria, Cuba, German Democratic Republic, Hungary, Mongolia, Romania.

Meeting numbers. GA 44th session: 1st Committee 3-25, 27, 33; plenary 81.

Recorded vote in Assembly as follows:

In favour: Afghanistan, Algeria, Angola, Antigua and Barbuda, Argentina, Austria, Bahamas, Bahrain, Bangladesh, Barbados, Benin, Bhutan, Bolivia, Botswana, Brazil, Brunei Darussalam, Bulgaria, Burkina Faso, Burundi, Byelorussian SSR, Cameroon, Cape Verde, Central African Republic, Chad, China, Congo, Côte d'Ivoire, Cuba, Cyprus, Czechoslovakia, Democratic Kampuchea, Democratic Yemen, Djibouti, Dominica, Dominican Republic, Ecuador, Egypt, El Salvador, Ethiopia, Fiji, Finland, Gabon, Gambia, German Democratic Republic, Ghana, Grenada, Guatemala, Guinea, Guinea-Bissau, Guyana, Haiti, Honduras, Hungary, India, Indonesia, Iran, Iraq, Jamaica, Jordan, Kenya, Kuwait, Lao People's Democratic Republic, Lebanon, Lesotho, Liberia, Libyan Arab Jamahiriya, Madagascar, Malawi, Malaysia, Maldives, Mali, Malta, Mauritania, Mauritius, Mexico, Mongolia, Morocco, Mozambique, Myanmar, Nepal, Nicaragua, Niger, Nigeria, Oman, Pakistan, Panama, Papua New Guinea, Paraguay, Peru, Philippines, Poland, Qatar, Romania, Rwanda, Saint Kitts and Nevis, Saint Lucia, Saint Vincent and the Grenadines, Sao Tome and Principe, Saudi Arabia, Senegal, Seychelles, Sierra Leone, Singapore, Solomon Islands, Somalia, Sri Lanka, Sudan, Suriname, Swaziland, Sweden, Syrian Arab Republic, Thailand, Togo, Trinidad and Tobago, Tunisia, Uganda, Ukrainian SSR, USSR, United Arab Emirates, United Republic of Tanzania, Uruguay, Vanuatu, Venezuela, Viet Nam, Yemen, Yugoslavia, Zaire, Zambia, Zimbabwe.

Against: Australia, Belgium, Canada, Denmark, France, Germany, Federal Republic of, Italy, Japan, Luxembourg, Netherlands, Norway, Portugal, Spain, Turkey, United Kingdom, United States.

Abstaining: Chile, Colombia, Costa Rica, Greece, Iceland, Ireland, Israel.

The Assembly adopted **resolution 44/119 E** on 15 December, also on the recommendation of the First Committee and by recorded vote.

Cessation of the nuclear-arms race and nuclear disarmament and prevention of nuclear war

The General Assembly,

Believing that all nations have a vital interest in negotiations on nuclear disarmament because the existence of nuclear weapons jeopardizes the vital security interests of both nuclear and non-nuclear-weapon States alike,

Recalling its resolutions 43/78 E and F of 7 December 1988,

Recalling also that the international community, through the Final Document of the Tenth Special Session of the General Assembly, has agreed that the nuclear-arms race, far from contributing to the strengthening of the security of all States, increases the danger of the outbreak of a nuclear war,

Welcoming the reaffirmation by the Ninth Conference of Heads of State or Government of Non-Aligned Countries, held at Belgrade from 4 to 7 September 1989, in its final document on international security and disarmament,[a] that nuclear disarmament is a process in which all nations should participate, and its view that the ongoing process of disarmament could be accelerated and its coverage widened through the common endeavour of the entire international community,

Taking into account that all nuclear-weapon States, in particular those with the most important nuclear arsenals, bear a special responsibility for the fulfilment of the task of achieving the goals of nuclear disarmament,

Convinced that the prevention of nuclear war and the reduction of the risk of nuclear war are matters of the highest priority and of vital interest to all people of the world,

Encouraged by the continued recognition by the Union of Soviet Socialist Republics and the United States of America that a nuclear war cannot be won and must never be fought,

Aware of the fact that the prevention of nuclear war and the reduction of the risk of nuclear war are inextricably linked with the cessation of the nuclear-arms race and nuclear disarmament, and that consequently they should be viewed in their interrelationship as essential elements of a process of general and complete disarmament,

Convinced that all avenues should be explored to ensure that progress is made in these two vital fields, and also convinced of the imperative need to take constructive multilateral action to complement and reinforce the bilateral process under way,

1. *Reaffirms* that multilateral and bilateral negotiations on nuclear questions should complement and facilitate each other;

2. *Believes* that efforts should be intensified in order to initiate multilateral negotiations in accordance with the provisions of paragraph 50 of the Final Document of the Tenth Special Session of the General Assembly;

3. *Reiterates* that, in view of the importance of the matter, it is equally necessary to devise suitable steps to expedite effective action for the prevention of nuclear war;

4. *Requests* the Conference on Disarmament to establish *ad hoc* committees at the beginning of its 1990 session on both the cessation of the nuclear-arms race and nuclear disarmament and the prevention of nuclear war with adequate mandates in order to allow a structured and practical analysis of how the Conference on Disarmament can best contribute to progress on these two urgent matters;

5. *Also requests* the Conference on Disarmament to report to the General Assembly at its forty-fifth session on its consideration of those subjects;

6. *Decides* to include in the provisional agenda of its forty-fifth session the items entitled ''Cessation of the nuclear-arms race and nuclear disarmament'' and ''Prevention of nuclear war''.

---

[a]A/44/551-S/20870.

General Assembly resolution 44/119 E

15 December 1989   Meeting 81   138-11-6 (recorded vote)

Approved by First Committee (A/44/788) by recorded vote (114-12-5), 10 November (meeting 33); 17-nation draft (A/C.1/44/L.34); agenda item 66 *(i)* and *(j)*.

Sponsors: Argentina, Brazil, Byelorussian SSR, Colombia, Costa Rica, Ecuador, German Democratic Republic, Guatemala, Malaysia, Mexico, Mongolia, Nigeria, Romania, Sweden, Uruguay, Venezuela, Viet Nam.

Meeting numbers. GA 44th session: 1st Committee 3-25, 33; plenary 81.

Recorded vote in Assembly as follows:

In favour: Afghanistan, Albania, Algeria, Angola, Antigua and Barbuda, Argentina, Australia, Austria, Bahamas, Bahrain, Bangladesh, Barbados, Benin, Bhutan, Bolivia, Botswana, Brazil, Brunei Darussalam, Bulgaria, Burkina Faso, Burundi, Byelorussian SSR, Cameroon, Cape Verde, Central African Republic, Chad, Chile, China, Colombia, Congo, Costa Rica, Côte d'Ivoire, Cuba, Cyprus, Czechoslovakia, Democratic Kampuchea, Democratic Yemen, Djibouti, Dominica, Dominican Republic, Ecuador, Egypt, El Salvador, Ethiopia, Fiji, Finland, Gabon, Gambia, German Democratic Republic, Ghana, Greece, Grenada, Guatemala, Guinea, Guinea-Bissau, Guyana, Haiti, Honduras, Hungary, India, Indonesia, Iran, Iraq, Ireland, Jamaica, Jordan, Kenya, Kuwait, Lao People's Democratic Republic, Lebanon, Lesotho, Liberia, Libyan Arab Jamahiriya, Madagascar, Malawi, Malaysia, Maldives, Mali, Malta, Mauritania, Mauritius, Mexico, Mongolia, Morocco, Mozambique, Myanmar, Nepal, New Zealand, Nicaragua, Niger, Nigeria, Oman, Pakistan, Panama, Papua New Guinea, Paraguay, Peru, Philippines, Poland, Qatar, Romania, Rwanda, Saint Kitts and Nevis, Saint Lucia, Saint Vincent and the Grenadines, Samoa, Sao Tome and Principe, Saudi Arabia, Senegal, Seychelles, Sierra Leone, Singapore, Solomon Islands, Somalia, Sri Lanka, Sudan, Suriname, Swaziland, Sweden, Syrian Arab Republic, Thailand, Togo, Trinidad and Tobago, Tunisia, Uganda, Ukrainian SSR, USSR, United Arab Emirates, United Republic of Tanzania, Uruguay, Vanuatu, Venezuela, Viet Nam, Yemen, Yugoslavia, Zaire, Zambia, Zimbabwe.

Against: Belgium, Canada, France, Germany, Federal Republic of, Italy, Luxembourg, Netherlands, Portugal, Turkey, United Kingdom, United States.

Abstaining: Denmark, Iceland, Israel, Japan, Norway, Spain.

On the same date, the Assembly, on the recommendation of the First Committee, adopted **resolution 44/117 C** by recorded vote.

Convention on the Prohibition of the Use of Nuclear Weapons

The General Assembly,

Convinced that the existence and use of nuclear weapons pose the greatest threat to the survival of mankind,

Conscious that the ongoing nuclear-arms race increases the danger of the use of nuclear weapons,

Convinced also that nuclear disarmament is the only ultimate guarantee against the use of nuclear weapons,

Convinced further that a multilateral agreement prohibiting the use or threat of use of nuclear weapons should strengthen international security and help to create the climate for negotiations leading to the complete elimination of nuclear weapons,

Recalling that, in paragraph 58 of the Final Document of the Tenth Special Session of the General Assembly, it is stated that all States should actively participate in efforts to bring about conditions in international relations among States in which a code of peaceful conduct of nations in international affairs could be agreed upon and that would preclude the use or threat of use of nuclear weapons,

Reaffirming that the use of nuclear weapons would be a violation of the Charter of the United Nations and a crime against humanity, as declared in its resolutions 1653(XVI) of 24 November 1961, 33/71 B of 14 December 1978, 34/83 G of 11 December 1979, 35/152 D of 12 December 1980 and 36/92 I of 9 December 1981,

Noting with regret that the Conference on Disarmament, during its 1989 session, was not able to undertake negotiations with a view to achieving agreement on an international convention prohibiting the use or threat of use of nuclear weapons under any circumstances, taking as a basis the text annexed to General Assembly resolution 43/76 E of 7 December 1988,

1. *Reiterates its request* to the Conference on Disarmament to commence negotiations, as a matter of priority, in order to reach agreement on an international convention prohibiting the use or threat of use of nuclear weapons under any circumstances, taking as a basis the draft Convention on the Prohibition of the Use of Nuclear Weapons annexed to the present resolution;

2. *Also requests* the Conference on Disarmament to report to the General Assembly at its forty-fifth session on the results of those negotiations.

ANNEX
Draft Convention on the Prohibition of the Use of Nuclear Weapons

The States Parties to this Convention,

Alarmed by the threat to the very survival of mankind posed by the existence of nuclear weapons,

Convinced that any use of nuclear weapons constitutes a violation of the Charter of the United Nations and a crime against humanity,

Convinced that this Convention would be a step towards the complete elimination of nuclear weapons leading to general and complete disarmament under strict and effective international control,

Determined to continue negotiations for the achievement of this goal,

Have agreed as follows:

Article 1
The States Parties to this Convention solemnly undertake not to use or threaten to use nuclear weapons under any circumstances.

Article 2
This Convention shall be of unlimited duration.

Article 3
1. This Convention shall be open to all States for signature. Any State that does not sign the Convention before its entry into force in accordance with paragraph 3 of this article may accede to it at any time.

2. This Convention shall be subject to ratification by signatory States. Instruments of ratification or accession shall be deposited with the Secretary-General of the United Nations.

3. This Convention shall enter into force on the deposit of instruments of ratification by twenty-five Governments, including the Governments of the five nuclear-weapon States, in accordance with paragraph 2 of this article.

4. For States whose instruments of ratification or accession are deposited after the entry into force of the Convention, it shall enter into force on the date of the deposit of their instruments of ratification or accession.

5. The depositary shall promptly inform all signatory and acceding States of the date of each signature, the date of deposit of each instrument of ratification or accession and the date of the entry into force of this Convention, as well as of the receipt of other notices.

6. This Convention shall be registered by the depositary in accordance with Article 102 of the Charter of the United Nations.

Article 4
This Convention, of which the Arabic, Chinese, English, French, Russian and Spanish texts are equally authentic, shall be deposited with the Secretary-General of the United Nations, who shall send duly certified copies thereof to the Government of the signatory and acceding States.

IN WITNESS WHEREOF, the undersigned, being duly authorized thereto by their respective Governments, have signed this Convention, opened for signature at _____ on the _____ day of _____ one thousand nine hundred and _____.

General Assembly resolution 44/117 C

15 December 1989   Meeting 81   134-17-4 (recorded vote)

Approved by First Committee (A/44/786) by recorded vote (113-17-4), 10 November (meeting 33); 12-nation draft (A/C.1/44/L.39); agenda item 64 *(f)*.

Sponsors: Algeria, Bangladesh, Bhutan, Ecuador, Egypt, India, Indonesia, Madagascar, Malaysia, Romania, Viet Nam, Yugoslavia.

Meeting numbers. GA 44th session: 1st Committee 3-25, 31, 33; plenary 81.

Recorded vote in Assembly as follows:

In favour: Afghanistan, Albania, Algeria, Angola, Antigua and Barbuda, Argentina, Austria, Bahamas, Bahrain, Bangladesh, Barbados, Benin, Bhutan, Bolivia, Botswana, Brazil, Brunei Darussalam, Bulgaria, Burkina Faso, Burundi, Byelorussian SSR, Cameroon, Cape Verde, Central African Republic, Chad, Chile, China, Colombia, Congo, Costa Rica, Côte d'Ivoire, Cuba, Cyprus, Czechoslovakia, Democratic Kampuchea, Democratic Yemen, Djibouti, Dominica, Dominican Republic, Ecuador, Egypt, El Salvador, Ethiopia, Fiji, Finland, Gabon, Gambia, German Democratic Republic, Ghana, Grenada, Guatemala, Guinea, Guinea-Bissau, Guyana, Haiti, Honduras, Hungary, India, Indonesia, Iran, Iraq, Jamaica, Jordan, Kenya, Kuwait, Lao People's Democratic Republic, Lebanon, Lesotho, Liberia, Libyan Arab Jamahiriya, Madagascar, Malawi, Malaysia, Maldives, Mali, Malta, Mauritania, Mauritius, Mexico, Mongolia, Morocco, Mozambique, Myanmar, Nepal, Nicaragua, Niger, Nigeria, Oman, Pakistan, Panama, Papua New Guinea, Paraguay, Peru, Philippines, Poland, Qatar, Romania, Rwanda, Saint Kitts and Nevis, Saint Lucia, Saint Vincent and the Grenadines, Samoa, Sao Tome and Principe, Saudi Arabia, Senegal, Seychelles, Sierra Leone, Singapore, Solomon Islands, Somalia, Sri Lanka, Sudan, Suriname, Swaziland, Sweden, Syrian Arab Republic, Thailand, Togo, Trinidad and Tobago, Tunisia, Uganda, Ukrainian SSR, USSR, United Arab Emirates, United Republic of Tanzania, Uruguay, Vanuatu, Venezuela, Viet Nam, Yemen, Yugoslavia, Zaire, Zambia, Zimbabwe.

Against: Australia, Belgium, Canada, Denmark, France, Germany, Federal Republic of, Iceland, Italy, Luxembourg, Netherlands, New Zealand, Norway, Portugal, Spain, Turkey, United Kingdom, United States.

Abstaining: Greece, Ireland, Israel, Japan.

Climatic effects of nuclear war

As requested by the General Assembly in 1988,[11] the Secretary-General submitted in September 1989 a report, with later addenda,[12] containing the views of 10 Member States on a 1988 expert study on the climatic effects of nuclear war, including nuclear winter.[13]

Cessation of nuclear-weapon tests

In 1989, it was reported that the USSR and United States negotiators had agreed, in bilateral talks, on the text for the required protocol to the 1976 Treaty on Underground Nuclear Explosions for Peaceful Purposes (peaceful nuclear explosions Treaty), and were moving along well with the protocol to the 1974 Treaty on the Limitation of Underground Nuclear Weapon Tests (threshold test-ban Treaty). Because of the complementary nature of the two Treaties, it was generally understood that the two protocols would be governmentally considered as a package. According to a joint statement issued by the two parties in September, they had reached, *ad referendum*, agreement on the proposed protocol to the peaceful nuclear explosions Treaty and had arrived at certain understandings with regard to the protocol for the threshold test-ban Treaty.[8] The 1989 negotiations concluded in mid-December with the text of the protocol to the threshold test-ban Treaty yet to be finalized and considerable documentation involved in the two protocols still requiring official approval.

Notes by the Secretary-General. By a January note with later addenda,[14] prepared pursuant to a 1987 General Assembly request,[15] the Secretary-General provided data on nuclear explosions received from three Member States (Australia, New Zealand, USSR) during the period January 1987 to October 1989. In October,[16] he submitted the annual register for 1989, compiled on the basis of the information provided. It concerned various periods from January 1987 to September 1989 and consolidated information received from the same three States.

Conference on Disarmament consideration. The Conference on Disarmament considered the question of a nuclear-test ban from 20 February to 3 March and from 19 to 30 June 1989.[4] For the sixth successive year, it was unable to reach consensus on a mandate for a subsidiary body to deal with the question of a nuclear-test ban.

New documents were submitted by the German Democratic Republic[17] and Norway[18] on verification.

The *Ad Hoc* Group of Scientific Experts to Consider International Co-operative Measures to Detect and Identify Seismic Events held two sessions at Geneva in 1989 (twenty-seventh session, 6-17 March;[19] twenty-eighth session, 24 July–4 August[20]). During those sessions the *Ad Hoc* Group adopted its fifth report to the Conference,[21] describing initial concepts for a modern international seismic-data exchange system based on the expeditious exchange of wave-form (Level II) and parameter (Level I) data and the processing of such data at international data centres. The Group also continued its discussion of plans for conducting its second technical test (GSETT-2) and decided that phase 2 of GSETT-2 would start in January 1990.

GENERAL ASSEMBLY ACTION

On 15 December 1989, the General Assembly, on the recommendation of the First Committee, adopted **resolution 44/105** by recorded vote.

Cessation of all nuclear-test explosions

The General Assembly,

Bearing in mind that the complete cessation of nuclear-weapon tests, which has been examined for more than thirty years and on which the General Assembly has adopted more than fifty resolutions, is a basic objective of the United Nations in the sphere of disarmament, to the attainment of which it has repeatedly assigned the highest priority,

Stressing that on eight different occasions it has condemned such tests in the strongest terms and that, since 1974, it has stated its conviction that the continuance of nuclear-weapon testing will intensify the arms race, thus increasing the danger of nuclear war,

Recalling that the Secretary-General, addressing a plenary meeting of the General Assembly on 12 December 1984, after appealing for a renewed effort towards a comprehensive test-ban treaty, emphasized that no single multilateral agreement could have a greater effect on limiting the further refinement of nuclear weapons and that a comprehensive test-ban treaty is the litmus test of the real willingness to pursue nuclear disarmament,

Taking into account that the three nuclear-weapon States that act as depositaries of the 1963 Treaty Banning Nuclear Weapon Tests in the Atmosphere, in Outer Space and under Water undertook in article I of that Treaty to conclude a treaty resulting in the permanent banning of all nuclear-test explosions, including all those explosions underground, and that such an undertaking was reiterated in 1968 in the preamble to the Treaty on the Non-Proliferation of Nuclear Weapons, article VI of which further embodies their solemn and legally binding commitment to take effective measures relating to cessation of the nuclear-arms race at an early date and to nuclear disarmament,

Noting that the Third Review Conference of the Parties to the Treaty on the Non-Proliferation of Nuclear Weapons, in its Final Declaration, adopted on 21 September 1985, called upon the nuclear-weapon States parties to the Treaty to resume trilateral negotiations in 1985 and upon all the nuclear-weapon States to participate in the urgent negotiation and conclusion of a comprehensive nuclear-test-ban treaty, as a matter of the highest priority, in the Conference on Disarmament,

Recalling the final document on international security and disarmament adopted by the Ninth Conference of Heads of State or Government of Non-Aligned Countries, held at Belgrade from 4 to 7 September 1989,[a] which underlined that the immediate suspension of and comprehensive ban on nuclear tests remained one of the highest priorities of nuclear disarmament,

Recalling also that the leaders of the States associated with the Six-Nation Initiative on peace and disarmament affirmed in the Stockholm Declaration, adopted on 21 January 1988, that "Any agreement that leaves room for continued testing would not be acceptable",

Taking note with satisfaction of the continuing progress made in the Conference on Disarmament by the *Ad Hoc* Group of Scientific Experts to Consider International Co-operative Measures to Detect and Identify Seismic Events on the seismic verification of a comprehensive test ban,

Expressing its concern that, after six years of efforts, the Conference on Disarmament has not yet succeeded in establishing an *ad hoc* committee on item 1 of its agenda, entitled "Nuclear-test ban",

---

[a]A/44/551-S/20870.

1. *Reiterates once again its grave concern* that nuclear-weapon testing continues unabated, against the wishes of the overwhelming majority of Member States;

2. *Reaffirms its conviction* that a treaty to achieve the prohibition of all nuclear-test explosions by all States for all time is a matter of the highest priority;

3. *Reaffirms also its conviction* that such a treaty would constitute a contribution of the utmost importance to the cessation of the nuclear-arms race;

4. *Urges once more* all nuclear-weapon States, in particular the three depositary Powers of the Treaty Banning Nuclear Weapons Tests in the Atmosphere, in Outer Space and under Water and of the Treaty on the Non-Proliferation of Nuclear Weapons, to seek to achieve the early discontinuance of all test explosions of nuclear weapons for all time and to expedite negotiations to this end;

5. *Appeals* to all States members of the Conference on Disarmament to promote the establishment by the Conference at the beginning of its 1990 session of an *ad hoc* committee with the objective of carrying out the multilateral negotiation of a treaty on the complete cessation of nuclear-test explosions;

6. *Recommends* to the Conference on Disarmament that such an *ad hoc* committee should comprise two working groups dealing, respectively, with the following interrelated questions: contents and scope of the treaty, and compliance and verification;

7. *Decides* to include in the provisional agenda of its forty-fifth session the item entitled "Cessation of all nuclear-test explosions".

General Assembly resolution 44/105

15 December 1989   Meeting 81   136-3-13 (recorded vote)

Approved by First Committee (A/44/772) by recorded vote (117-3-13), 16 November (meeting 38); 12-nation draft (A/C.1/44/L.11); agenda item 50.
Sponsors: Costa Rica, Ecuador, Indonesia, Ireland, Mexico, Myanmar, Peru, Romania, Sri Lanka, Sweden, Venezuela, Yugoslavia.
Meeting numbers. GA 44th session: 1st Committee 3-25, 31, 38; plenary 81.

Recorded vote in Assembly as follows:

In favour: Afghanistan, Albania, Algeria, Antigua and Barbuda, Argentina, Australia, Austria, Bahamas, Bahrain, Bangladesh, Barbados, Benin, Bhutan, Bolivia, Botswana, Brazil, Brunei Darussalam, Bulgaria, Burkina Faso, Burundi, Byelorussian SSR, Cameroon, Cape Verde, Central African Republic, Chad, Chile, Colombia, Congo, Costa Rica, Côte d'Ivoire, Cuba, Cyprus, Czechoslovakia, Democratic Yemen, Denmark, Djibouti, Dominica, Dominican Republic, Ecuador, Egypt, Ethiopia, Fiji, Finland, Gabon, Gambia, German Democratic Republic, Ghana, Greece, Grenada, Guatemala, Guinea, Guinea-Bissau, Guyana, Haiti, Honduras, Hungary, India, Indonesia, Iran, Iraq, Ireland, Jamaica, Jordan, Kenya, Kuwait, Lao People's Democratic Republic, Lebanon, Lesotho, Liberia, Libyan Arab Jamahiriya, Madagascar, Malawi, Malaysia, Maldives, Mali, Malta, Mauritania, Mauritius, Mexico, Mongolia, Morocco, Mozambique, Myanmar, Nepal, New Zealand, Nicaragua, Niger, Nigeria, Norway, Oman, Pakistan, Panama, Papua New Guinea, Paraguay, Peru, Philippines, Poland, Qatar, Romania, Rwanda, Saint Kitts and Nevis, Saint Lucia, Saint Vincent and the Grenadines, Samoa, Sao Tome and Principe, Saudi Arabia, Senegal, Seychelles, Sierra Leone, Singapore, Solomon Islands, Somalia, Sri Lanka, Sudan, Suriname, Swaziland, Sweden, Syrian Arab Republic, Thailand, Togo, Trinidad and Tobago, Tunisia, Uganda, Ukrainian SSR, USSR, United Arab Emirates, United Republic of Tanzania, Uruguay, Vanuatu, Venezuela, Viet Nam, Yemen, Yugoslavia, Zaire, Zambia, Zimbabwe.

Against: France, United Kingdom, United States.

Abstaining: Belgium, Canada, China, Germany, Federal Republic of, Iceland, Israel, Italy, Japan, Luxembourg, Netherlands, Portugal, Spain, Turkey.

Also on 15 December and on the recommendation of the First Committee, the Assembly adopted **resolution 44/107** by recorded vote.

Urgent need for a comprehensive nuclear-test-ban treaty

The General Assembly,

Convinced that a nuclear war cannot be won and must never be fought,

Convinced also of the consequent urgent need for an end to the nuclear-arms race and the immediate and verifiable reduction and ultimate elimination of nuclear weapons,

Convinced further that an end to nuclear testing by all States in all environments for all time is an essential step in order to prevent the qualitative improvement and development of nuclear weapons and their further proliferation and to contribute, along with other concurrent efforts to reduce nuclear arms, to the eventual elimination of nuclear weapons,

Recognizing the recent progress made in the negotiations between the Union of Soviet Socialist Republics and the United States of America, as reflected in their joint statement of 23 September 1989, towards improved verification arrangements and the ratification of the Treaty between the United States of America and the Union of Soviet Socialist Republics on the Limitation of Underground Nuclear Weapon Tests, signed on 3 July 1974, and the Treaty between the United States of America and the Union of Soviet Socialist Republics on Underground Nuclear Explosions for Peaceful Purposes, signed on 28 May 1976, and urging both countries to complete that process,

Welcoming the ongoing implementation of the Treaty between the United States of America and the Union of Soviet Socialist Republics on the Elimination of Their Intermediate-Range and Shorter-Range Missiles and the agreement in principle on and further progress made towards an agreement for 50 per cent reductions in their strategic nuclear forces,

Recalling the final document on international security and disarmament adopted by the Ninth Conference of Heads of State or Government of Non-Aligned Countries, held at Belgrade from 4 to 7 September 1989,[a]

Recalling also the proposals by the leaders of the Six-Nation Initiative to promote an end to nuclear testing,

Convinced that the most effective way to achieve the discontinuance of all nuclear tests by all States in all environments for all time is through the conclusion, at an early date, of a verifiable, comprehensive nuclear-test-ban treaty that will attract the adherence of all States,

Reaffirming the particular responsibilities of the Conference on Disarmament in the negotiation of a comprehensive nuclear-test-ban treaty,

Taking note of the work being undertaken within the Conference on Disarmament by the *Ad Hoc* Group of Scientific Experts to Consider International Cooperative Measures to Detect and Identify Seismic Events in preparation for the next phase of the technical test, to take place in 1990, concerning the global exchange and analysis of seismic data,

1. *Reaffirms its conviction* that a treaty to achieve the prohibition of all nuclear-test explosions by all States in all environments for all time is a matter of fundamental importance;

2. *Urges,* therefore, that the following actions be taken in order that a comprehensive nuclear-test-ban treaty may be concluded at an early date:

---

[a]A/44/551-S/20870.

(a) The Conference on Disarmament should intensify its consideration of item 1 of its agenda, entitled "Nuclear-test ban", and initiate substantive work on all aspects of a nuclear-test-ban treaty at the beginning of its 1990 session;

(b) States members of the Conference on Disarmament, in particular the nuclear-weapon States, and all other States should co-operate in order to facilitate and promote such work;

(c) The nuclear-weapon States, especially those which possess the most important nuclear arsenals, should agree promptly to appropriate verifiable and militarily significant interim measures, with a view to realizing a comprehensive nuclear-test-ban treaty;

(d) Those nuclear-weapon States which have not yet done so should adhere to the Treaty Banning Nuclear Weapon Tests in the Atmosphere, in Outer Space and under Water;

3. *Also urges* the Conference on Disarmament:

(a) To take immediate steps for the establishment, with the widest possible participation, of an international seismic monitoring network with a view to the further development of its potential to monitor and verify compliance with a comprehensive nuclear-test-ban treaty;

(b) To take into account, in this context, the progress achieved by the *Ad Hoc* Group of Scientific Experts to Consider International Co-operative Measures to Detect and Identify Seismic Events, including work on the routine exchange and use of wave-form data, and other relevant initiatives or experiments by individual States and groups of States;

(c) To encourage the widest possible participation by States in the technical test that will take place in 1990 concerning the global exchange and analysis of seismic data;

(d) To initiate detailed investigation of other measures to monitor and verify compliance with such a treaty, including an international network to monitor atmospheric radioactivity;

4. *Calls upon* the Conference on Disarmament to report to the General Assembly at its forty-fifth session on progress made;

5. *Decides* to include in the provisional agenda of its forty-fifth session the item entitled "Urgent need for a comprehensive nuclear-test-ban treaty".

General Assembly resolution 44/107

15 December 1989   Meeting 81   145-2-6 (recorded vote)

Approved by First Committee (A/44/774) by recorded vote (124-2-7), 16 November (meeting 38); 30-nation draft (A/C.1/44/L.50/Rev.1); agenda item 52.
Sponsors: Australia, Austria, Bahamas, Barbados, Brunei Darussalam, Cameroon, Canada, Colombia, Costa Rica, Denmark, Ecuador, Fiji, Finland, Greece, Iceland, Ireland, Japan, Malaysia, New Zealand, Nigeria, Norway, Papua New Guinea, Philippines, Samoa, Singapore, Solomon Islands, Sweden, Thailand, Vanuatu, Zaire.
Meeting numbers. GA 44th session: 1st Committee 3-25, 29, 38; plenary 81.

Recorded vote in Assembly as follows:

In favour: Afghanistan, Albania, Algeria, Angola, Antigua and Barbuda, Australia, Austria, Bahamas, Bahrain, Bangladesh, Barbados, Belgium, Benin, Bhutan, Bolivia, Botswana, Brunei Darussalam, Bulgaria, Burkina Faso, Burundi, Byelorussian SSR, Cameroon, Canada, Cape Verde, Central African Republic, Chad, Chile, Colombia, Congo, Côte d'Ivoire, Cuba, Cyprus, Czechoslovakia, Democratic Kampuchea, Democratic Yemen, Denmark, Djibouti, Dominica, Dominican Republic, Ecuador, Egypt, Ethiopia, Fiji, Finland, Gabon, Gambia, German Democratic Republic, Germany, Federal Republic of, Ghana, Greece, Grenada, Guatemala, Guinea, Guinea-Bissau, Guyana, Haiti, Honduras, Hungary, Iceland, Indonesia, Iran, Iraq, Ireland, Italy, Jamaica, Japan, Jordan, Kenya, Kuwait, Lao People's Democratic Republic, Lebanon, Lesotho, Liberia, Libyan Arab Jamahiriya, Luxembourg, Madagascar, Malawi, Malaysia, Maldives, Mali, Malta, Mauritania, Mauritius, Mexico, Mongo-

lia, Morocco, Mozambique, Myanmar, Nepal, Netherlands, New Zealand, Nicaragua, Niger, Nigeria, Norway, Oman, Pakistan, Panama, Papua New Guinea, Paraguay, Peru, Philippines, Poland, Portugal, Qatar, Romania, Rwanda, Saint Kitts and Nevis, Saint Lucia, Saint Vincent and the Grenadines, Samoa, Sao Tome and Principe, Saudi Arabia, Senegal, Seychelles, Sierra Leone, Singapore, Solomon Islands, Somalia, Spain, Sri Lanka, Sudan, Suriname, Swaziland, Sweden, Syrian Arab Republic, Thailand, Togo, Trinidad and Tobago, Tunisia, Turkey, Uganda, Ukrainian SSR, USSR, United Arab Emirates, United Republic of Tanzania, Uruguay, Vanuatu, Venezuela, Viet Nam, Yemen, Yugoslavia, Zaire, Zambia, Zimbabwe.
Against: France, United States.
Abstaining: Argentina, Brazil, China, India, Israel, United Kingdom.

Amendment conference of States parties to the partial test-ban Treaty

By early April 1989,[22] more than one third of the parties to the 1963 Treaty Banning Nuclear Weapon Tests in the Atmosphere, in Outer Space and under Water (also known as the partial test-ban Treaty)[23] had formally requested the convening of a conference to consider amendments to the Treaty, in accordance with the provisions of article II of the Treaty.[24] The amendments would convert the Treaty into a comprehensive test-ban treaty, one that included underground nuclear tests in addition to those already prohibited.

GENERAL ASSEMBLY ACTION

On 15 December 1989, the General Assembly, on the recommendation of the First Committee, adopted **resolution 44/106** by recorded vote.

Amendment of the Treaty Banning Nuclear Weapon Tests in the Atmosphere, in Outer Space and under Water

The General Assembly,

Reiterating its conviction that a comprehensive nuclear-test-ban treaty is the highest-priority step towards nuclear disarmament,

Recalling its resolution 1910(XVIII) of 27 November 1963, in which it noted with approval the Treaty Banning Nuclear Weapon Tests in the Atmosphere, in Outer Space and under Water, signed on 5 August 1963, and requested the Conference of the Eighteen-Nation Committee on Disarmament[a] to continue with a sense of urgency its negotiations to achieve the objectives set forth in the preamble to the Treaty,

Convinced that, pending the conclusion of a comprehensive nuclear-test-ban treaty, the nuclear-weapon States should suspend all nuclear-test explosions through an agreed moratorium or unilateral moratoria,

Noting that article II of the Treaty provides a procedure for convening a conference of the parties to the Treaty to consider amendments to the Treaty,

Noting also that, in its resolution 42/26 B of 30 November 1987, it recommended that the non-nuclear-weapon States parties to the Treaty formally submit an amendment proposal to the Depositary Governments with a view to convening a conference at the earliest possible date to consider amendments to the Treaty that would convert it into a comprehensive nuclear-test-ban treaty and that, by its resolution 43/63 B of 7 December 1988, it welcomed the submission of such an amendment proposal,

---

[a]The Committee on Disarmament was redesignated the Conference on Disarmament as from 7 February 1984.

Noting further that the Ninth Conference of Heads of State or Government of Non-Aligned Countries, held at Belgrade from 4 to 7 September 1989, supported the initiative to convene, as soon as possible in 1990, an amendment conference to convert the Treaty into a comprehensive nuclear-test-ban treaty,[b]

Considering that more than one third of the parties have requested the convening of a conference to consider such an amendment and that Depositary Governments have announced their intention to comply with their obligations under the Treaty,

Convinced that such a conference will serve to strengthen the Treaty,

1. *Recommends* that a preparatory committee, open to all parties to the Treaty Banning Nuclear Weapon Tests in the Atmosphere, in Outer Space and under Water, should be established to make arrangements for the amendment conference and that the preparatory committee should meet at United Nations Headquarters from 29 May to 1 June 1990, followed by a one-week session of the conference from 4 to 8 June 1990 and a second substantive session from 7 to 18 January 1991;

2. *Recommends also* that the costs of the amendment conference and its preparatory committee should be shared among the States parties to the Treaty, on the basis of the present scale of assessments of the United Nations;

3. *Requests* the Secretary-General to render the necessary assistance and provide such services, including summary records, as may be required for the amendment conference and its preparation;

4. *Invites* the amendment conference to transmit to the General Assembly the documents it deems appropriate to keep the Assembly duly informed of its ongoing work;

5. *Decides* to include in the provisional agenda of its forty-fifth session the item entitled "Amendment of the Treaty Banning Nuclear Weapon Tests in the Atmosphere, in Outer Space and under Water".

---

[b]A/44/551-S/20870.

General Assembly resolution 44/106

15 December 1989   Meeting 81   127-2-22 (recorded vote)

Approved by First Committee (A/44/773) by recorded vote (108-2-21), 17 November (meeting 41); 57-nation draft (A/C.1/44/L.25/Rev.1); agenda item 51.

Sponsors: Afghanistan, Bahamas, Bangladesh, Benin, Bolivia, Cape Verde, Colombia, Costa Rica, Cyprus, Democratic Yemen, Dominican Republic, Ecuador, Egypt, El Salvador, Fiji, Gabon, Gambia, Ghana, Guatemala, Honduras, India, Indonesia, Iran, Iraq, Jordan, Lebanon, Liberia, Libyan Arab Jamahiriya, Madagascar, Malaysia, Mauritius, Mexico, Mongolia, Nepal, Nicaragua, Nigeria, Pakistan, Panama, Papua New Guinea, Peru, Philippines, Romania, Singapore, Sri Lanka, Sudan, Suriname, Swaziland, Thailand, Togo, Uganda, United Republic of Tanzania, Uruguay, Venezuela, Yugoslavia, Zaire, Zambia, Zimbabwe.

Meeting numbers. GA 44th session: 1st Committee 3-26, 40, 41; plenary 81.

Recorded vote in the Assembly as follows:

In favour: Afghanistan, Albania, Algeria, Antigua and Barbuda, Argentina, Bahamas, Bahrain, Bangladesh, Barbados, Benin, Bhutan, Bolivia, Botswana, Brazil, Brunei Darussalam, Bulgaria, Burkina Faso, Burundi, Byelorussian SSR, Cameroon, Cape Verde, Central African Republic, Chad, Chile, Colombia, Congo, Costa Rica, Côte d'Ivoire, Cuba, Cyprus, Czechoslovakia, Democratic Kampuchea, Democratic Yemen, Djibouti, Dominica, Dominican Republic, Ecuador, Egypt, Ethiopia, Fiji, Gabon, Gambia, German Democratic Republic, Ghana, Grenada, Guatemala, Guinea, Guinea-Bissau, Guyana, Haiti, Honduras, Hungary, India, Indonesia, Iran, Iraq, Jamaica, Jordan, Kenya, Kuwait, Lao People's Democratic Republic, Lebanon, Lesotho, Liberia, Libyan Arab Jamahiriya, Madagascar, Malawi, Malaysia, Maldives, Mali, Mauritania, Mauritius, Mexico, Mongolia,

Morocco, Mozambique, Myanmar, Nepal, Nicaragua, Niger, Nigeria, Oman, Pakistan, Panama, Papua New Guinea, Paraguay, Peru, Philippines, Poland, Qatar, Romania, Rwanda, Saint Kitts and Nevis, Saint Lucia, Saint Vincent and the Grenadines, Samoa, Sao Tome and Principe, Saudi Arabia, Senegal, Seychelles, Sierra Leone, Singapore, Solomon Islands, Somalia, Sri Lanka, Sudan, Suriname, Swaziland, Syrian Arab Republic, Thailand, Togo, Trinidad and Tobago, Tunisia, Uganda, Ukrainian SSR, USSR, United Arab Emirates, United Republic of Tanzania, Uruguay, Vanuatu, Venezuela, Viet Nam, Yemen, Yugoslavia, Zaire, Zambia, Zimbabwe.

Against: United Kingdom, United States.

Abstaining: Australia, Austria, Belgium, Canada, Denmark, Finland, Germany, Federal Republic of, Greece, Iceland, Ireland, Israel, Italy, Japan, Luxembourg, Malta, Netherlands, New Zealand, Norway, Portugal, Spain, Sweden, Turkey.

France indicated that it did not participate in the vote because it was not a party to the 1963 Treaty. It wished that action to be reflected in the record.

In the Committee, before adopting the text as a whole, separate recorded votes were taken: the phrase "at United Nations Headquarters" in paragraph 1 was retained by 105 to 1, with 22 abstentions, and that paragraph as a whole was approved by 106 to 10, with 13 abstentions. Paragraph 2 was approved by 105 to 9, with 14 abstentions, as was the third preambular paragraph, by 116 to 6, with 10 abstentions.

Strengthening the security of non-nuclear-weapon States

The Conference on Disarmament considered, from 3 to 7 April and from 31 July to 4 August 1989, effective international arrangements to assure non-nuclear-weapon States against the use or threat of use of nuclear weapons (also known as negative security assurances).[4] On 7 February,[25] it had re-established an *ad hoc* committee to negotiate an agreement on such arrangements.

In its conclusions and recommendations,[26] the *Ad Hoc* Committee stated that agreement on a common formula of assurance could not be reached due to specific difficulties relating to differing perceptions of security interests. It was generally agreed that the *Ad Hoc* Committee should be re-established in 1990.

GENERAL ASSEMBLY ACTION

On 15 December 1989, the General Assembly, on the recommendation of the First Committee, adopted **resolution 44/110** by recorded vote.

Conclusion of effective international arrangements on the strengthening of the security of non-nuclear-weapon States against the use or threat of use of nuclear weapons

The General Assembly,

Deeply concerned at the arms race, in particular the nuclear-arms race, and the possibility of the use or threat of use of nuclear weapons,

Convinced that nuclear disarmament and the complete elimination of nuclear weapons are essential to remove the danger of nuclear war,

Considering that, until complete nuclear disarmament is achieved on a universal basis, it is imperative for the international community to develop effective arrangements to ensure the security of non-nuclear-weapon States against the use or threat of use of nuclear weapons,

Noting the general desire to conclude effective international measures to that end at an early date,

Taking note of the unilateral declarations on the security of non-nuclear-weapon States against the use or threat of use of nuclear weapons, made by all nuclear-weapon States,

Desirous of promoting the implementation of paragraph 59 of the Final Document of the Tenth Special Session of the General Assembly, the first special session devoted to disarmament,

Recognizing that effective measures of such security assurances to non-nuclear-weapon States would constitute an important contribution to the non-proliferation of nuclear weapons,

Aware of the in-depth negotiations on this subject in the Conference on Disarmament during the past ten years,

Recalling the relevant parts of the special report of the Committee on Disarmament[a] submitted to the General Assembly at its twelfth special session, the second special session devoted to disarmament, and of the special report of the Conference on Disarmament submitted to the Assembly at its fifteenth special session, the third special session devoted to disarmament, as well as of the annual report of the Conference on its 1989 session,

Welcoming the unanimous support in the Conference on Disarmament for continuing the search for a common approach to the substance of negative security assurances, which could be included in a legally binding instrument,

Recognizing the need for a fresh look at the issue, in particular by the nuclear-weapon States, in order to overcome the difficulties encountered at the negotiations in previous years,

Taking note of the proposals on this subject submitted to the Conference on Disarmament,

1. *Reaffirms* the urgent need, pending the achievement of complete nuclear disarmament, to reach an early agreement on effective international arrangements to assure non-nuclear-weapon States against the use or threat of use of nuclear weapons;

2. *Recommends* that the Conference on Disarmament pursue intensive negotiations in its *Ad Hoc* Committee on Effective International Arrangements to Assure Non-Nuclear-Weapon States against the Use or Threat of Use of Nuclear Weapons at the beginning of its 1990 session, with a view to reaching such an agreement, taking into account the widespread support in the Conference for conclusion of an international convention and giving consideration to any other proposals designed to secure the same objective;

3. *Appeals* to all States, in particular the nuclear-weapon States, to demonstrate willingness and to exercise the flexibility necessary to reach agreement on a common approach to, including the possibility of a common formula in, an international instrument or instruments of a legally binding character to assure the non-nuclear-weapon States against the use or threat of use of nuclear weapons;

4. *Decides* to include in the provisional agenda of its forty-fifth session the item entitled ''Conclusion of effective international arrangements on the strengthening of the security of non-nuclear-weapon States against the use or threat of use of nuclear weapons''.

---

[a]The Committee on Disarmament was redesignated the Conference on Disarmament as from 7 February 1984.

General Assembly resolution 44/110

15 December 1989   Meeting 81   131-0-21 (recorded vote)

Approved by First Committee (A/44/778) by recorded vote (113-1-20), 13 November (meeting 35); 2-nation draft (A/C.1/44/L.23/Rev.1); agenda item 56.

Sponsors: Bulgaria, Nigeria.

Meeting numbers. GA 44th session: 1st Committee 3-25, 30, 35; plenary 81.

Recorded vote in Assembly as follows:

In favour: Afghanistan, Albania, Algeria, Angola, Antigua and Barbuda, Australia, Austria, Bahamas, Bahrain, Bangladesh, Barbados, Benin, Bhutan, Bolivia, Botswana, Bulgaria, Burkina Faso, Burundi, Byelorussian SSR, Cameroon, Canada, Cape Verde, Central African Republic, Chad, China, Colombia, Congo, Costa Rica, Côte d'Ivoire, Cuba, Cyprus, Czechoslovakia, Democratic Kampuchea, Democratic Yemen, Djibouti, Dominica, Dominican Republic, Ecuador, Egypt, Ethiopia, Fiji, Finland, Gabon, Gambia, German Democratic Republic, Ghana, Grenada, Guatemala, Guinea, Guinea-Bissau, Guyana, Haiti, Honduras, Hungary, India, Indonesia, Iran, Iraq, Ireland, Jamaica, Jordan, Kenya, Kuwait, Lao People's Democratic Republic, Lebanon, Lesotho, Liberia, Libyan Arab Jamahiriya, Madagascar, Malawi, Malaysia, Maldives, Mali, Malta, Mauritania, Mauritius, Mexico, Mongolia, Morocco, Mozambique, Myanmar, Nepal, New Zealand, Nicaragua, Niger, Nigeria, Oman, Pakistan, Panama, Papua New Guinea, Paraguay, Peru, Philippines, Poland, Qatar, Romania, Rwanda, Saint Kitts and Nevis, Saint Lucia, Saint Vincent and the Grenadines, Samoa, Saudi Arabia, Senegal, Seychelles, Sierra Leone, Singapore, Solomon Islands, Somalia, Sri Lanka, Sudan, Suriname, Swaziland, Sweden, Syrian Arab Republic, Thailand, Togo, Trinidad and Tobago, Tunisia, Uganda, Ukrainian SSR, USSR, United Arab Emirates, United Republic of Tanzania, Vanuatu, Venezuela, Viet Nam, Yemen, Yugoslavia, Zaire, Zambia, Zimbabwe.

Against: None.

Abstaining: Argentina, Belgium, Brazil, Chile, Denmark, France, Germany, Federal Republic of, Greece, Iceland, Israel, Italy, Japan, Luxembourg, Netherlands, Norway, Portugal, Spain, Turkey, United Kingdom, United States, Uruguay.

On the same day, the Assembly, also on the First Committee's recommendation, adopted **resolution 44/111** by recorded vote.

Conclusion of effective international arrangements to assure non-nuclear-weapon States against the use or threat of use of nuclear weapons

The General Assembly,

Bearing in mind the need to allay the legitimate concern of the States of the world with regard to ensuring lasting security for their peoples,

Convinced that nuclear weapons pose the greatest threat to mankind and to the survival of civilization,

Deeply concerned at the continuing escalation of the arms race, in particular the nuclear-arms race, and the possibility of the use or threat of use of nuclear weapons,

Also convinced that nuclear disarmament and the complete elimination of nuclear weapons are essential to remove the danger of nuclear war,

Taking into account the principle of the non-use of force or threat of force enshrined in the Charter of the United Nations,

Deeply concerned also about the possibility of the use or threat of use of nuclear weapons,

Recognizing that the independence, territorial integrity and sovereignty of non-nuclear-weapon States need to be safeguarded against the use or threat of use of force, including the use or threat of use of nuclear weapons,

Considering that, until nuclear disarmament is achieved on a universal basis, it is imperative for the international community to develop effective measures to ensure the security of non-nuclear-weapon States against the use or threat of use of nuclear weapons from any quarter,

Recognizing also that effective measures to assure the non-nuclear-weapon States against the use or threat of use of nuclear weapons can constitute a positive contribution to the prevention of the spread of nuclear weapons,

Recalling its resolutions 3261 G (XXIX) of 9 December 1974 and 31/189 C of 21 December 1976,

Bearing in mind paragraph 59 of the Final Document of the Tenth Special Session of the General Assembly, in which it urged the nuclear-weapon States to pursue efforts to conclude, as appropriate, effective arrangements to assure non-nuclear-weapon States against the use or threat of use of nuclear weapons,

Desirous of promoting the implementation of the relevant provisions of the Final Document of the Tenth Special Session,

Recalling also its resolutions 33/72 B of 14 December 1978, 34/85 of 11 December 1979, 35/155 of 12 December 1980, 36/95 of 9 December 1981, 37/81 of 9 December 1982, 38/68 of 15 December 1983, 39/58 of 12 December 1984, 40/86 of 12 December 1985, 41/52 of 3 December 1986, 42/32 of 30 November 1987 and 43/69 of 7 December 1988,

Recalling further paragraph 12 of the Declaration of the 1980s as the Second Disarmament Decade, contained in the annex to its resolution 35/46 of 3 December 1980, which states, *inter alia*, that all efforts should be exerted by the Committee on Disarmament[a] urgently to negotiate with a view to reaching agreement on effective international arrangements to assure non-nuclear-weapon States against the use or threat of use of nuclear weapons,

Noting the in-depth negotiations undertaken in the Conference on Disarmament and its *Ad Hoc* Committee on Effective International Arrangements to Assure Non-Nuclear-Weapon States against the Use or Threat of Use of Nuclear Weapons, with a view to reaching agreement on this item,

Taking note of the proposals submitted under that item in the Conference on Disarmament, including the drafts of an international convention,

Taking note also of the final document on international security and disarmament adopted by the Ninth Conference of Heads of State or Government of Non-Aligned Countries, held at Belgrade from 4 to 7 September 1989,[b] as well as the relevant recommendations of the Organization of the Islamic Conference reiterated in the Final Communiqué of the Eighteenth Islamic Conference of Foreign Ministers, held at Riyadh from 13 to 16 March 1989, calling upon the Conference on Disarmament to work urgently towards an agreement on an international convention to assure non-nuclear-weapon States against the use or threat of use of nuclear weapons,[c]

Noting also the support expressed in the Conference on Disarmament and in the General Assembly for the elaboration of an international convention to assure non-nuclear-weapon States against the use or threat of use

of nuclear weapons, as well as the difficulties pointed out in evolving a common approach acceptable to all,

1. *Reaffirms* the urgent need to reach agreement on effective international arrangements to assure non-nuclear-weapon States against the use or threat of use of nuclear weapons;

2. *Notes with satisfaction* that in the Conference on Disarmament there is no objection, in principle, to the idea of an international convention to assure non-nuclear-weapon States against the use or threat of use of nuclear weapons, although the difficulties as regards evolving a common approach acceptable to all have also been pointed out;

3. *Appeals* to all States, especially the nuclear-weapon States, to demonstrate the political will necessary to reach agreement on a common approach and, in particular, on a common formula that could be included in an international instrument of a legally binding character;

4. *Recommends* that further intensive efforts should be devoted to the search for such a common approach or common formula and that the various alternative approaches, including, in particular, those considered in the Conference on Disarmament, should be further explored in order to overcome the difficulties;

5. *Recommends also* that the Conference on Disarmament should actively continue negotiations with a view to reaching early agreement and concluding effective international arrangements to assure non-nuclear-weapon States against the use or threat of use of nuclear weapons, taking into account the widespread support for the conclusion of an international convention and giving consideration to any other proposals designed to secure the same objective;

6. *Decides* to include in the provisional agenda of its forty-fifth session the item entitled "Conclusion of effective international arrangements to assure non-nuclear-weapon States against the use or threat of use of nuclear weapons".

---

[a]The Committee on Disarmament was redesignated the Conference on Disarmament as from 7 February 1984.
[b]A/44/551-S/20870.
[c]A/44/235-S/20600.

General Assembly resolution 44/111

15 December 1989   Meeting 81   151-0-3 (recorded vote)

Approved by First Committee (A/44/779) by recorded vote (133-0-3), 13 November (meeting 35); 6-nation draft (A/C.1/44/L.49); agenda item 57.
Sponsors: Bangladesh, Iran, Madagascar, Nepal, Pakistan, Sri Lanka.
Meeting numbers. GA 44th session: 1st Committee 3-25, 35; plenary 81.

Recorded vote in Assembly as follows:

In favour: Afghanistan, Albania, Algeria, Angola, Antigua and Barbuda, Argentina, Australia, Austria, Bahamas, Bahrain, Bangladesh, Barbados, Belgium, Benin, Bhutan, Bolivia, Botswana, Brunei Darussalam, Bulgaria, Burkina Faso, Burundi, Byelorussian SSR, Cameroon, Canada, Cape Verde, Central African Republic, Chad, Chile, China, Colombia, Congo, Costa Rica, Côte d'Ivoire, Cuba, Cyprus, Czechoslovakia, Democratic Kampuchea, Democratic Yemen, Denmark, Djibouti, Dominica, Dominican Republic, Ecuador, Egypt, Ethiopia, Fiji, Finland, France, Gabon, Gambia, German Democratic Republic, Germany, Federal Republic of, Ghana, Greece, Grenada, Guatemala, Guinea, Guinea-Bissau, Guyana, Haiti, Honduras, Hungary, Iceland, Indonesia, Iran, Iraq, Ireland, Israel, Italy, Jamaica, Japan, Jordan, Kenya, Kuwait, Lao People's Democratic Republic, Lebanon, Lesotho, Liberia, Libyan Arab Jamahiriya, Luxembourg, Madagascar, Malawi, Malaysia, Maldives, Mali, Malta, Mauritania, Mauritius, Mexico, Mongolia, Morocco, Mozambique, Myanmar, Nepal, Netherlands, New Zealand, Nicaragua, Niger, Nigeria, Norway, Oman, Pakistan, Panama, Papua New Guinea, Paraguay, Peru, Philippines, Poland, Portugal, Qatar, Romania,

Rwanda, Saint Kitts and Nevis, Saint Lucia, Saint Vincent and the Grenadines, Samoa, Sao Tome and Principe, Saudi Arabia, Senegal, Seychelles, Sierra Leone, Singapore, Solomon Islands, Somalia, Spain, Sri Lanka, Sudan, Suriname, Swaziland, Sweden, Syrian Arab Republic, Thailand, Togo, Trinidad and Tobago, Tunisia, Turkey, Uganda, Ukrainian SSR, USSR, United Arab Emirates, United Kingdom, United Republic of Tanzania, Uruguay, Vanuatu, Venezuela, Viet Nam, Yemen, Yugoslavia, Zaire, Zambia, Zimbabwe.

Against: None.

Abstaining: Brazil, India, United States.

Nuclear non-proliferation

Nuclear-weapon-free zones and zones of peace

In 1989, the international community again discussed the establishment of nuclear-weapon-free zones and zones of peace in various regions of the world. Debate in the General Assembly focused primarily on the desirability and feasibility of setting up nuclear-weapon-free zones in Africa, the Middle East and South Asia, with the two existing nuclear-free zones, Latin America and the South Pacific, generally acknowledged as valuable measures of regional arms control. As to the establishment of the Indian Ocean as a zone of peace, despite a 1988 Assembly decision to convene the Conference on the Indian Ocean in 1990,[27] the Assembly in 1989 called for its postponement until 1991 (**resolution 44/120**).

Africa

Since 1964, when the Declaration on the Denuclearization of Africa was adopted by the Organization of African Unity (OAU),[28] the General Assembly had annually called for its implementation. In 1989, the Assembly again adopted two resolutions—one on the implementation of the Declaration and the other on the nuclear capability of South Africa.

Disarmament Commission consideration. The Disarmament Commission continued consideration in 1989 of South Africa's nuclear capability,[1] in response to a 1988 General Assembly request.[29] The Commission established Working Group I, which, at 13 meetings between 10 and 26 May, based its work on the working paper contained in the report of the Commission to the General Assembly at the third special session devoted to disarmament.[2] Nigeria submitted a new working paper in 1989.[30]

Although the Group had reached agreement on a number of points, it was not possible to reach consensus on the remaining text, and it recommended that the Commission continue consideration of the topic in 1990.

Report of the Secretary-General. In an October report on the nuclear capability of South Africa,[31] the Secretary-General stated that he had continued to follow nuclear developments in that country. He had been in contact with the International Atomic Energy Agency (IAEA) and OAU. Annexed to the report was a resolution on

South Africa's nuclear capabilities adopted on 29 September 1989 by the IAEA General Conference.

GENERAL ASSEMBLY ACTION

On 15 December 1989, the General Assembly, on the recommendation of the First Committee, adopted **resolution 44/113 A** by recorded vote.

Implementation of the Declaration

The General Assembly,

Bearing in mind the Declaration on the Denuclearization of Africa adopted by the Assembly of Heads of State and Government of the Organization of African Unity at its first ordinary session, held at Cairo from 17 to 21 July 1964,

Recalling its resolution 1652(XVI) of 24 November 1961, its earliest on the subject, as well as its resolutions 2033(XX) of 3 December 1965, 31/69 of 10 December 1976, 32/81 of 12 December 1977, 33/63 of 14 December 1978, 34/76 A of 11 December 1979, 35/146 B of 12 December 1980, 36/86 B of 9 December 1981, 37/74 A of 9 December 1982, 38/181 A of 20 December 1983, 39/61 A of 12 December 1984, 40/89 A of 12 December 1985, 41/55 A of 3 December 1986, 42/34 A of 30 November 1987 and 43/71 A of 7 December 1988, in which it called upon all States to consider and respect the continent of Africa and its surrounding areas as a nuclear-weapon-free zone,

Recalling that in its resolution 33/63 it vigorously condemned any overt or covert attempt by South Africa to introduce nuclear weapons into the continent of Africa and demanded that South Africa refrain forthwith from conducting any nuclear explosion in the continent or elsewhere,

Bearing in mind the provisions of resolution CM/Res.1101(XLVI)/Rev.1 on the denuclearization of Africa adopted by the Council of Ministers of the Organization of African Unity at its forty-sixth ordinary session, held at Addis Ababa from 20 to 25 July 1987,

Having taken note of the report of the United Nations Institute for Disarmament Research entitled "South Africa's nuclear capability", undertaken in co-operation with the Department for Disarmament Affairs of the Secretariat and in consultation with the Organization of African Unity, as well as of the report of the Disarmament Commission,

Noting the actions taken by those Governments which have taken measures to restrict co-operation with South Africa in nuclear and other fields,

Expressing regret that, despite the threat that South Africa's nuclear capability constitutes to international peace and security and, in particular, to the realization of the objective of the Declaration on the Denuclearization of Africa, the Disarmament Commission, although it considered the question during its substantive session in 1989, failed once again to reach a consensus on this important item on its agenda,

1. *Strongly renews its call* upon all States to consider and respect the continent of Africa and its surrounding areas as a nuclear-weapon-free zone;

2. *Reaffirms* that the implementation of the Declaration on the Denuclearization of Africa adopted by the Assembly of Heads of State and Government of the Organization of African Unity would be an important

measure to prevent the proliferation of nuclear weapons and to promote international peace and security;

3. *Expresses once again its grave alarm* at South Africa's possession and continued development of nuclear-weapon capability;

4. *Condemns* South Africa's continued pursuit of a nuclear capability and all forms of nuclear collaboration by any State, corporation, institution or individual with the racist régime that enable it to frustrate the objective of the Declaration on the Denuclearization of Africa, which seeks to keep Africa free from nuclear weapons;

5. *Calls upon* all States, corporations, institutions and individuals to desist from further collaboration with the racist régime that may enable it to frustrate the objective of the Declaration on the Denuclearization of Africa;

6. *Demands once again* that the racist régime of South Africa refrain from manufacturing, testing, deploying, transporting, storing, using or threatening to use nuclear weapons;

7. *Appeals* to all States that have the means to do so to monitor South Africa's research on and development and production of nuclear weapons and to publicize any information in that regard;

8. *Demands once again* that South Africa submit forthwith all its nuclear installations and facilities to inspection by the International Atomic Energy Agency;

9. *Requests* the Secretary-General to provide all necessary assistance that the Organization of African Unity may seek regarding the modalities and elements for the preparation and implementation of the relevant convention or treaty on the denuclearization of Africa;

10. *Decides* to include in the provisional agenda of its forty-fifth session the item entitled "Implementation of the Declaration on the Denuclearization of Africa".

General Assembly resolution 44/113 A

15 December 1989   Meeting 81   147-0-4 (recorded vote)

Approved by First Committee (A/44/781) by recorded vote (129-0-4), 16 November (meeting 39); draft by Kenya, for African Group (A/C.1/44/L.53/Rev.3, part A); agenda item 59.
Financial implications. 5th Committee, A/44/810; S-G, A/C.1/44/L.65, A/C.5/44/37.
Meeting numbers. GA 44th session: 1st Committee 3-25, 39; 5th Committee 48; plenary 81.

Recorded vote in Assembly as follows:

In favour: Afghanistan, Albania, Algeria, Angola, Antigua and Barbuda, Argentina, Australia, Austria, Bahamas, Bahrain, Bangladesh, Barbados, Belgium, Benin, Bhutan, Bolivia, Botswana, Brazil, Brunei Darussalam, Bulgaria, Burkina Faso, Burundi, Byelorussian SSR, Cameroon, Canada, Cape Verde, Central African Republic, Chad, Chile, China, Colombia, Congo, Costa Rica, Côte d'Ivoire, Cuba, Cyprus, Czechoslovakia, Democratic Kampuchea, Democratic Yemen, Denmark, Djibouti, Dominica, Dominican Republic, Ecuador, Egypt, Ethiopia, Fiji, Finland, Gabon, Gambia, German Democratic Republic, Germany, Federal Republic of, Ghana, Greece, Grenada, Guatemala, Guinea, Guinea-Bissau, Guyana, Haiti, Honduras, Hungary, Iceland, India, Indonesia, Iran, Iraq, Ireland, Italy, Jamaica, Japan, Jordan, Kenya, Kuwait, Lao People's Democratic Republic, Lebanon, Lesotho, Liberia, Libyan Arab Jamahiriya, Luxembourg, Madagascar, Malaysia, Maldives, Mali, Malta, Mauritania, Mauritius, Mexico, Morocco, Mozambique, Myanmar, Nepal, Netherlands, New Zealand, Nicaragua, Niger, Nigeria, Norway, Oman, Pakistan, Panama, Papua New Guinea, Paraguay, Peru, Philippines, Poland, Portugal, Qatar, Romania, Saint Kitts and Nevis, Saint Lucia, Saint Vincent and the Grenadines, Samoa, Sao Tome and Principe, Saudi Arabia, Senegal, Seychelles, Sierra Leone, Singapore, Solomon Islands, Somalia, Spain, Sri Lanka, Sudan, Suriname, Swaziland, Sweden, Syrian Arab Republic, Thailand, Togo, Trinidad and Tobago, Tunisia, Turkey, Uganda, Ukrainian SSR, USSR, United Arab Emirates, United Republic of Tanzania, Uruguay, Vanuatu, Venezuela, Viet Nam, Yemen, Yugoslavia, Zaire, Zambia, Zimbabwe.
Against: None.
Abstaining: France, Israel, United Kingdom, United States.

On the same date, on the First Committee's recommendation, the General Assembly adopted **resolution 44/113 B**, also by recorded vote.

Nuclear capability of South Africa

The General Assembly,

Having considered the report of the Secretary-General on South Africa's nuclear capability,

Recalling its resolutions 34/76 B of 11 December 1979, 35/146 A of 12 December 1980, 36/86 A of 9 December 1981, 37/74 B of 9 December 1982, 38/181 B of 20 December 1983, 39/61 B of 12 December 1984, 40/89 B of 12 December 1985, 41/55 B of 3 December 1986, 42/34 B of 30 November 1987 and 43/71 B of 7 December 1988,

Bearing in mind the Declaration on the Denuclearization of Africa adopted by the Assembly of Heads of State and Government of the Organization of African Unity at its first ordinary session, held at Cairo from 17 to 21 July 1964,

Recalling that, in paragraph 12 of the Final Document of the Tenth Special Session of the General Assembly, it noted that the massive accumulation of armaments and the acquisition of armaments technology by racist régimes, as well as their possible acquisition of nuclear weapons, present a challenging and increasingly dangerous obstacle to a world community faced with the urgent need to disarm,

Recalling also that, in its resolution 33/63 of 14 December 1978, it vigorously condemned any overt or covert attempt by South Africa to introduce nuclear weapons into the continent of Africa and demanded that South Africa refrain forthwith from conducting any nuclear explosion in the continent or elsewhere,

Bearing in mind the provisions of resolution CM/Res.1101(XLVI)/Rev.1 on the denuclearization of Africa adopted by the Council of Ministers of the Organization of African Unity at its forty-sixth ordinary session, held at Addis Ababa from 20 to 25 July 1987,

Noting with regret the non-implementation by *apartheid* South Africa of resolution GC(XXX)/RES/468 adopted on 3 October 1986 by the General Conference of the International Atomic Energy Agency during its thirtieth regular session,

Having taken note of the report of the United Nations Institute for Disarmament Research entitled "South Africa's nuclear capability", undertaken in co-operation with the Department for Disarmament Affairs of the Secretariat and in consultation with the Organization of African Unity,

Expressing regret that, despite the threat that South Africa's nuclear capability constitutes to international peace and security and, in particular, to the realization of the objective of the Declaration on the Denuclearization of Africa, the Disarmament Commission, although it considered the question during its substantive session in 1989, failed once again to reach a consensus on this important item on its agenda,

Alarmed that South Africa's nuclear facilities, particularly those that remain unsafeguarded, enable it to develop and acquire the capability of producing fissionable material for nuclear weapons,

Also alarmed that, by its own public admission at Vienna on 13 August 1988, the *apartheid* South African régime has now acquired nuclear-weapon capability,

Deeply concerned about recent reports of *apartheid* South Africa's active military collaboration with Israel in the production of nuclear-tipped medium-range missiles with completed testing facilities and the consequences for the peace and security of African States,

Gravely concerned that South Africa, in flagrant violation of international law and the relevant provisions of the Charter of the United Nations, has continued its acts of aggression and subversion against the peoples of the independent States of southern Africa,

Deeply indignant at the persistent policy of hostility by the racist régime of South Africa as demonstrated by its constant encroachment into the territory of neighbouring States, which constitutes an act of aggression against the sovereignty and territorial integrity of those countries,

Expressing its grave disappointment that, despite appeals by the international community, certain Western States and Israel have continued to collaborate with the racist régime of South Africa in the military and nuclear fields and that some of these States have, by a ready recourse to the use of veto, consistently frustrated every effort in the Security Council to deal decisively with the question of South Africa,

Recalling its decision taken at the tenth special session that the Security Council should take appropriate effective steps to prevent the frustration of the implementation of the decision of the Organization of African Unity for the denuclearization of Africa,

Stressing the need to preserve peace and security in Africa by ensuring that the continent is a nuclear-weapon-free zone,

1. *Takes note* of the report of the Secretary-General on South Africa's nuclear capability;

2. *Condemns* the massive buildup of South Africa's military machine, in particular its frenzied acquisition of nuclear-weapon capability for repressive and aggressive purposes and as an instrument of blackmail;

3. *Also condemns* all forms of nuclear collaboration by any State, corporation, institution or individual with the racist régime of South Africa, in particular the decision by some Member States to grant licences to several corporations in their territories to provide equipment and technical and maintenance services for nuclear installations in South Africa;

4. *Takes note with great concern* of recent reports that collaboration between Israel and South Africa has resulted in the development by South Africa of a nuclear-tipped missile;

5. *Calls upon* the Secretary-General, with the assistance of a group of qualified experts, to investigate those reports, bearing in mind their implications for the implementation of the policy of denuclearization of Africa and for the security of African States and, in particular, the front-line and other neighbouring States;

6. *Requests* the Secretary-General to submit a preliminary report on his investigation to the Disarmament Commission at its substantive session in 1990 and a final report to the General Assembly at its forty-fifth session;

7. *Reaffirms* that the acquisition of nuclear-weapon capability by the racist régime constitutes a very grave danger to international peace and security and, in particular, jeopardizes the security of African States and increases the danger of the proliferation of nuclear weapons;

8. *Expresses its full support* for the African States faced with the danger of South Africa's nuclear capability;

9. *Commends* the actions of those Governments that have taken measures to restrict co-operation with South Africa in nuclear and other fields;

10. *Demands* that South Africa and all other foreign interests put an immediate end to the exploration for and exploitation of uranium resources in Namibia;

11. *Calls upon* all States, corporations, institutions and individuals to terminate forthwith all forms of military and nuclear collaboration with the racist régime;

12. *Requests* the Disarmament Commission to consider once again as a matter of priority during its substantive session in 1990 South Africa's nuclear capability, taking into account, *inter alia*, the findings of the report of the United Nations Institute for Disarmament Research on South Africa's nuclear capability;

13. *Requests* the Secretary-General to provide all necessary assistance that the Organization of African Unity may seek regarding the modalities and elements for the preparation and implementation of the relevant convention or treaty on the denuclearization of Africa;

14. *Commends* the adoption by the Security Council of resolutions 558(1984) of 13 December 1984 and 591(1986) of 28 November 1986 on the question of South Africa, with a view to blocking the existing loopholes in the arms embargo so as to render it more effective and to prohibiting, in particular, all forms of co-operation and collaboration with the racist régime of South Africa in the nuclear field;

15. *Demands once again* that South Africa submit forthwith all its nuclear installations and facilities to inspection by the International Atomic Energy Agency;

16. *Requests* the Secretary-General to follow very closely South Africa's evolution in the nuclear field and to report thereon to the General Assembly at its forty-fifth session;

17. *Also requests* the Secretary-General to report to the General Assembly at its forty-fifth session on the military assistance that *apartheid* South Africa is receiving from Israel and any other sources in advanced missile technology as well as the supporting technical facilities.

General Assembly resolution 44/113 B

15 December 1989   Meeting 81   137-4-10 (recorded vote)

Approved by First Committee (A/44/781) by recorded vote (118-4-10), 16 November (meeting 39); draft by Kenya, for African Group (A/C.1/44/L.53/Rev.3, part B); agenda item 59.

Meeting numbers. GA 44th session: 1st Committee 3-25, 39; plenary 81.

Recorded vote in Assembly as follows:

In favour: Afghanistan, Albania, Algeria, Angola, Antigua and Barbuda, Argentina, Austria, Bahamas, Bahrain, Bangladesh, Barbados, Benin, Bhutan, Bolivia, Botswana, Brazil, Brunei Darussalam, Bulgaria, Burkina Faso, Burundi, Byelorussian SSR, Cameroon, Cape Verde, Central African Republic, Chad, Chile, China, Colombia, Congo, Costa Rica, Côte d'Ivoire, Cuba, Cyprus, Czechoslovakia, Democratic Kampuchea, Democratic Yemen, Denmark, Djibouti, Dominica, Dominican Republic, Ecuador, Egypt, Ethiopia, Fiji, Finland, Gabon, Gambia, German Democratic Republic, Ghana, Greece, Grenada, Guatemala, Guinea, Guinea-Bissau, Guyana, Haiti, Honduras, Hungary, Iceland, India, Indonesia, Iran, Iraq, Ireland, Jamaica, Jordan, Kenya, Kuwait, Lao People's Democratic Republic, Lebanon, Lesotho, Liberia, Libyan Arab Jamahiriya, Madagascar, Malaysia, Maldives, Mali, Malta, Mauritania, Mauritius, Mexico, Morocco, Mozambique, Myanmar, Nepal, New Zealand, Nicaragua, Niger, Nigeria, Norway, Oman, Pakistan, Panama, Papua New Guinea, Paraguay, Peru, Philippines, Poland, Qatar, Romania, Rwanda, Saint Kitts and Nevis, Saint Lucia, Saint Vincent and the Grenadines, Samoa, Sao Tome and Principe, Saudi Arabia, Senegal, Seychelles, Sierra Leone, Singapore, Solomon Islands, Somalia, Sri Lanka, Sudan, Suriname, Swaziland, Sweden, Syrian Arab Republic, Thailand, Togo, Trinidad and Tobago, Tunisia, Turkey, Uganda, Ukrainian SSR, USSR,

United Republic of Tanzania, Uruguay, Vanuatu, Venezuela, Viet Nam, Yemen, Yugoslavia, Zaire, Zambia, Zimbabwe.
Against: France, Israel, United Kingdom, United States.
Abstaining: Australia, Belgium, Canada, Germany, Federal Republic of, Italy, Japan, Luxembourg, Netherlands, Portugal, Spain.

Latin America

The General Assembly again considered in 1989 the item on the signature and ratification of Additional Protocol I of the 1967 Treaty for the Prohibition of Nuclear Weapons in Latin America (Treaty of Tlatelolco), concerning the application of the Treaty to territories in the region for which outside States had *de jure* or *de facto* responsibility. Three of the four States to which the Protocol was open were already parties to it (Netherlands, United Kingdom, United States). France, the fourth State, had signed the Protocol, but had not ratified it.

GENERAL ASSEMBLY ACTION

On 15 December 1989, the General Assembly, on the recommendation of the First Committee, adopted **resolution 44/104** by recorded vote.

Implementation of General Assembly resolution 43/62 concerning the signature and ratification of Additional Protocol I of the Treaty for the Prohibition of Nuclear Weapons in Latin America (Treaty of Tlatelolco)

The General Assembly,

Recalling its resolutions 2286(XXII) of 5 December 1967, 3262(XXIX) of 9 December 1974, 3473(XXX) of 11 December 1975, 32/76 of 12 December 1977, S-10/2 of 30 June 1978, 33/58 of 14 December 1978, 34/71 of 11 December 1979, 35/143 of 12 December 1980, 36/83 of 9 December 1981, 37/71 of 9 December 1982, 38/61 of 15 December 1983, 39/51 of 12 December 1984, 40/79 of 12 December 1985, 41/45 of 3 December 1986, 42/25 of 30 November 1987 and 43/62 of 7 December 1988 concerning the signature and ratification of Additional Protocol I of the Treaty for the Prohibition of Nuclear Weapons in Latin America (Treaty of Tlatelolco),

Taking into account that within the zone of application of that Treaty, to which twenty-three sovereign States are already parties, there are some territories which, in spite of not being sovereign political entities, are nevertheless in a position to receive the benefits deriving from the Treaty through its Additional Protocol I, to which the four States that *de jure* or *de facto* are internationally responsible for those territories may become parties,

Considering that it is not fair that the peoples of some of those territories are deprived of such benefits without being given the opportunity to express their opinion in this connection,

Recalling that three of the States to which Additional Protocol I is open—the United Kingdom of Great Britain and Northern Ireland, the Kingdom of the Netherlands and the United States of America—became parties to the Protocol in 1969, 1971 and 1981, respectively,

1. *Deplores* that the signature of Additional Protocol I by France, which took place on 2 March 1979, has not yet been followed by the corresponding ratification, notwithstanding the time already elapsed and the press-

ing invitations which the General Assembly has addressed to it;

2. *Once more urges* France not to delay any further such ratification, which has been requested so many times and which appears all the more advisable, since France is the only one of the four States to which the Protocol is open that is not yet party to it;

3. *Decides* to include in the provisional agenda of its forty-fifth session an item entitled "Implementation of General Assembly resolution 44/104 concerning the signature and ratification of Additional Protocol I of the Treaty for the Prohibition of Nuclear Weapons in Latin America (Treaty of Tlatelolco)".

General Assembly resolution 44/104

15 December 1989   Meeting 81   147-0-3 (recorded vote)

Approved by First Committee (A/44/771) by recorded vote (132-0-3), 10 November (meeting 33); 18-nation draft (A/C.1/44/L.5); agenda item 49.
Sponsors: Bahamas, Barbados, Bolivia, Costa Rica, Dominican Republic, Ecuador, El Salvador, Guatemala, Haiti, Honduras, Mexico, Nicaragua, Panama, Paraguay, Suriname, Trinidad and Tobago, Uruguay, Venezuela.
Meeting numbers. GA 44th session: 1st Committee 3-26, 33; plenary 81.

Recorded vote in Assembly as follows:

In favour: Afghanistan, Albania, Algeria, Antigua and Barbuda, Australia, Austria, Bahamas, Bahrain, Bangladesh, Barbados, Belgium, Benin, Bhutan, Bolivia, Botswana, Brazil, Brunei Darussalam, Bulgaria, Burkina Faso, Burundi, Byelorussian SSR, Cameroon, Canada, Cape Verde, Central African Republic, Chad, Chile, China, Colombia, Congo, Côte d'Ivoire, Cyprus, Czechoslovakia, Democratic Kampuchea, Democratic Yemen, Denmark, Djibouti, Dominica, Dominican Republic, Ecuador, Egypt, Ethiopia, Fiji, Finland, Gabon, Gambia, German Democratic Republic, Germany, Federal Republic of, Ghana, Greece, Guatemala, Guinea, Guinea-Bissau, Guyana, Haiti, Honduras, Hungary, Iceland, India, Indonesia, Iran, Iraq, Ireland, Israel, Italy, Jamaica, Japan, Jordan, Kenya, Kuwait, Lao People's Democratic Republic, Lebanon, Lesotho, Liberia, Libyan Arab Jamahiriya, Luxembourg, Madagascar, Malawi, Malaysia, Maldives, Mali, Malta, Mauritania, Mauritius, Mexico, Mongolia, Morocco, Mozambique, Myanmar, Nepal, Netherlands, New Zealand, Nicaragua, Niger, Nigeria, Norway, Oman, Pakistan, Panama, Papua New Guinea, Paraguay, Peru, Philippines, Poland, Portugal, Qatar, Romania, Rwanda, Saint Kitts and Nevis, Saint Lucia, Saint Vincent and the Grenadines, Samoa, Sao Tome and Principe, Saudi Arabia, Senegal, Seychelles, Sierra Leone, Singapore, Solomon Islands, Somalia, Spain, Sri Lanka, Sudan, Suriname, Sweden, Syrian Arab Republic, Thailand, Togo, Trinidad and Tobago, Tunisia, Turkey, Uganda, Ukrainian SSR, USSR, United Arab Emirates, United Kingdom, United Republic of Tanzania, United States, Uruguay, Vanuatu, Venezuela, Viet Nam, Yemen, Yugoslavia, Zaire, Zambia, Zimbabwe.
Against: None.
Abstaining: Argentina, Cuba, France.

Middle East

In an August 1989 report, with later addenda,[32] submitted in response to a 1988 General Assembly request,[33] the Secretary-General transmitted the views of five Member States on the establishment of a nuclear-weapon-free zone in the Middle East.

GENERAL ASSEMBLY ACTION

On 15 December, on the recommendation of the First Committee, the General Assembly adopted **resolution 44/108** without vote.

Establishment of a nuclear-weapon-free zone in the region of the Middle East

The General Assembly,

Recalling its resolutions 3263(XXIX) of 9 December 1974, 3474(XXX) of 11 December 1975, 31/71 of 10 December 1976, 32/82 of 12 December 1977, 33/64 of 14 December 1978, 34/77 of 11 December 1979, 35/147 of 12 December 1980, 36/87 of 9 December 1981, 37/75 of 9 December 1982, 38/64 of 15 December 1983, 39/54 of 12 December 1984, 40/82 of 12 December 1985, 41/48 of 3 December 1986, 42/28 of 30 November 1987 and 43/65 of 7 December 1988 on the establishment of a nuclear-weapon-free zone in the region of the Middle East,

Recalling also the recommendations for the establishment of such a zone in the Middle East consistent with paragraphs 60 to 63, and in particular paragraph 63 *(d)*, of the Final Document of the Tenth Special Session of the General Assembly,

Emphasizing the basic provisions of the above-mentioned resolutions, which call upon all parties directly concerned to consider taking the practical and urgent steps required for the implementation of the proposal to establish a nuclear-weapon-free zone in the region of the Middle East and, pending and during the establishment of such a zone, to declare solemnly that they will refrain, on a reciprocal basis, from producing, acquiring or in any other way possessing nuclear weapons and nuclear explosive devices and from permitting the stationing of nuclear weapons on their territory by any third party, to agree to place all their nuclear facilities under International Atomic Energy Agency safeguards and to declare their support for the establishment of the zone and deposit such declarations with the Security Council for consideration, as appropriate,

Reaffirming the inalienable right of all States to acquire and develop nuclear energy for peaceful purposes,

Emphasizing also the need for appropriate measures on the question of the prohibition of military attacks on nuclear facilities,

Bearing in mind the consensus reached by the General Assembly at its thirty-fifth session that the establishment of a nuclear-weapon-free zone in the region of the Middle East would greatly enhance international peace and security,

Desirous of building on that consensus so that substantial progress can be made towards establishing a nuclear-weapon-free zone in the region of the Middle East,

Emphasizing further the essential role of the United Nations in the establishment of a nuclear-weapon-free zone in the region of the Middle East,

Having examined the report of the Secretary-General,

1. *Urges* all parties directly concerned to consider seriously taking the practical and urgent steps required for the implementation of the proposal to establish a nuclear-weapon-free zone in the region of the Middle East in accordance with the relevant resolutions of the General Assembly and, as a means of promoting this objective, invites the countries concerned to adhere to the Treaty on the Non-Proliferation of Nuclear Weapons;

2. *Calls upon* all countries of the region that have not done so, pending the establishment of the zone, to agree to place all their nuclear activities under International Atomic Energy Agency safeguards;

3. *Takes note* of the request made by the General Conference of the International Atomic Energy Agency to its Director General in resolution GC(XXXIII)/RES/506 "to consult with the States concerned in the Middle East area with a view to applying Agency safeguards to all nuclear installations in the area, keeping in mind the relevant recommendations contained in paragraph 75 of the report attached to document GC(XXXIII)/887

and the situation in the area of the Middle East, and to report on the matter to the Board of Governors and to the General Conference at its thirty-fourth regular session'';

4. *Invites* all countries of the region, pending the establishment of a nuclear-weapon-free zone in the region of the Middle East, to declare their support for establishing such a zone, consistent with paragraph 63 *(d)* of the Final Document of the Tenth Special Session of the General Assembly, and to deposit those declarations with the Security Council;

5. *Also invites* those countries, pending the establishment of the zone, not to develop, produce, test or otherwise acquire nuclear weapons or permit the stationing on their territories, or territories under their control, of nuclear weapons or nuclear explosive devices;

6. *Invites* the nuclear-weapon States and all other States to render their assistance in the establishment of the zone and at the same time to refrain from any action that runs counter to both the letter and the spirit of the present resolution;

7. *Extends its thanks* to the Secretary-General for his report containing the views of parties concerned regarding the establishment of a nuclear-weapon-free zone in the region of the Middle East;

8. *Takes note* of the report of the Secretary-General;

9. *Requests* parties of the region to submit to the Secretary-General their views and suggestions with respect to the measures called for in paragraph 8 of resolution 43/65;

10. *Requests* the Secretary-General to submit to the General Assembly at its forty-fifth session a progress report on the implementation of the present resolution;

11. *Decides* to include in the provisional agenda of its forty-fifth session the item entitled "Establishment of a nuclear-weapon-free zone in the region of the Middle East".

General Assembly resolution 44/108

15 December 1989   Meeting 81   Adopted without vote

Approved by First Committee (A/44/775) without vote, 10 November (meeting 33); draft by Egypt (A/C.1/44/L.9); agenda item 53.
Meeting numbers. GA 44th session: 1st Committee 3-26, 33; plenary 81.

Israeli nuclear armaments

In an October 1989 report,[34] submitted in response to a 1988 Assembly request,[35] the Secretary-General indicated that he had continued to follow closely Israeli nuclear activities. Apart from the text of a resolution adopted by the IAEA General Conference on 29 September, which was annexed to his report, no other information had been transmitted to him.

GENERAL ASSEMBLY ACTION

On 15 December 1989, on the recommendation of the First Committee, the General Assembly adopted **resolution 44/121** by recorded vote.

Israeli nuclear armament

The General Assembly,

Bearing in mind its previous resolutions on Israeli nuclear armament, the latest of which is resolution 43/80 of 7 December 1988,

Recalling its resolution 43/65 of 7 December 1988, in which, *inter alia*, it called for placing all nuclear facilities in the region under International Atomic Energy Agency safeguards, pending the establishment of a nuclear-weapon-free zone in the Middle East,

Recalling also Security Council resolution 487(1981) of 19 June 1981, in which, *inter alia*, the Council called upon Israel urgently to place all its nuclear facilities under International Atomic Energy Agency safeguards,

Noting that only Israel has been specifically called upon by the Security Council to place its nuclear facilities under International Atomic Energy Agency safeguards,

Noting with grave concern Israel's persistent refusal to commit itself not to manufacture or acquire nuclear weapons, despite repeated calls by the General Assembly, the Security Council and the International Atomic Energy Agency,

Taking into consideration resolution GC(XXXIII)/RES/506 of 29 September 1989 adopted by the General Conference of the International Atomic Energy Agency, in which the General Conference deprecated Israel's refusal to place all its nuclear installations under the Agency's safeguards and called upon Israel to comply with Security Council resolution 487(1981),

Also taking into consideration the final document on international security and disarmament adopted by the Ninth Conference of Heads of State or Government of Non-Aligned Countries, held at Belgrade from 4 to 7 September 1989,[a] in paragraph 12 of which Israel was condemned for continuing to develop its nuclear military programmes and weapons of mass destruction and for its refusal to implement the resolutions of the United Nations and the International Atomic Energy Agency in this regard,

Deeply alarmed by the information with regard to the continuing production, development and acquisition of nuclear weapons by Israel and its testing of their delivery systems in the Mediterranean, thus threatening the peace and security of the region,

Aware of the grave consequences that endanger international peace and security as a result of Israel's development and acquisition of nuclear weapons and Israel's collaboration with South Africa to develop nuclear weapons and their delivery systems,

Deeply concerned that the declared Israeli policy of attacking and destroying nuclear facilities devoted to peaceful purposes is a part of its nuclear armament policy,

1. *Reiterates its condemnation* of Israel's refusal to renounce any possession of nuclear weapons;

2. *Reiterates also its condemnation* of the co-operation between Israel and South Africa;

3. *Expresses its deep concern* at Israel's continuing production, development and acquisition of nuclear weapons and testing of their delivery systems;

4. *Requests once more* the Security Council to take urgent and effective measures to ensure that Israel complies with Council resolution 487(1981);

5. *Demands once more* that Israel place all its nuclear facilities under International Atomic Energy Agency safeguards;

6. *Calls upon* all States and organizations that have not yet done so to discontinue co-operating with and giving assistance to Israel in the nuclear field;

7. *Reiterates its request* to the International Atomic Energy Agency to suspend any co-operation with Israel that could contribute to its nuclear capabilities;

8. *Requests also* the International Atomic Energy Agency to inform the Secretary-General of any steps Israel may take to place its nuclear facilities under Agency safeguards;

9. *Requests* the Secretary-General to follow closely Israeli nuclear activities and to report thereon to the General Assembly at its forty-fifth session;

10. *Decides* to include in the provisional agenda of its forty-fifth session the item entitled ''Israeli nuclear armament''.

---

[a]A/44/551-S/20870.

General Assembly resolution 44/121

15 December 1989   Meeting 81   104-2-43 (recorded vote)

Approved by First Committee (A/44/790) by recorded vote (91-2-34), 17 November (meeting 41); 21-nation draft (A/C.1/44/L.21); agenda item 68.

Sponsors: Algeria, Bahrain, Democratic Yemen, Djibouti, Egypt, Iraq, Jordan, Kuwait, Lebanon, Libyan Arab Jamahiriya, Mauritania, Morocco, Oman, Qatar, Saudi Arabia, Somalia, Sudan, Syrian Arab Republic, Tunisia, United Arab Emirates, Yemen.

Meeting numbers. GA 44th session: 1st Committee 3-25, 30, 41; plenary 81.

Recorded vote in Assembly as follows:

In favour: Afghanistan, Albania, Algeria, Angola, Argentina, Bahrain, Bangladesh, Barbados, Benin, Bhutan, Bolivia, Botswana, Brazil, Brunei Darussalam, Bulgaria, Burkina Faso, Burundi, Byelorussian SSR, Cameroon, Cape Verde, Chad, China, Colombia, Congo, Cuba, Cyprus, Czechoslovakia, Democratic Kampuchea, Democratic Yemen, Djibouti, Ecuador, Egypt, Ethiopia, Gabon, Gambia, German Democratic Republic, Ghana, Guatemala, Guinea, Guinea-Bissau, Guyana, Haiti, Hungary, India, Indonesia, Iran, Iraq, Jordan, Kenya, Kuwait, Lao People's Democratic Republic, Lebanon, Lesotho, Liberia, Libyan Arab Jamahiriya, Madagascar, Malaysia, Maldives, Mali, Mauritania, Mexico, Mongolia, Morocco, Mozambique, Nicaragua, Niger, Nigeria, Oman, Pakistan, Paraguay, Peru, Philippines, Poland, Qatar, Romania, Rwanda, Sao Tome and Principe, Saudi Arabia, Senegal, Seychelles, Sierra Leone, Somalia, Sri Lanka, Sudan, Suriname, Swaziland, Syrian Arab Republic, Thailand, Togo, Trinidad and Tobago, Tunisia, Turkey, Uganda, Ukrainian SSR, USSR, United Arab Emirates, United Republic of Tanzania, Vanuatu, Venezuela, Viet Nam, Yemen, Yugoslavia, Zambia, Zimbabwe.

Against: Israel, United States.

Abstaining: Antigua and Barbuda, Australia, Austria, Bahamas, Belgium, Canada, Central African Republic, Chile, Costa Rica, Denmark, Dominica, Dominican Republic, El Salvador, Fiji, Finland, France, Germany, Federal Republic of, Greece, Grenada, Honduras, Iceland, Ireland, Italy, Jamaica, Japan, Luxembourg, Malawi, Malta, Netherlands, New Zealand, Norway, Papua New Guinea, Portugal, Saint Kitts and Nevis, Saint Lucia, Saint Vincent and the Grenadines, Samoa, Singapore, Solomon Islands, Spain, Sweden, United Kingdom, Uruguay.

The Assembly adopted, by separate recorded votes, paragraph 2 by 102 to 20, with 22 abstentions; paragraph 6 by 91 to 23, with 28 abstentions; paragraph 7 by 78 to 23, with 37 abstentions; and the sixth and tenth preambular paragraphs by 101 to 20, with 21 abstentions, and 84 to 22, with 33 abstentions, respectively.

The First Committee also approved those paragraphs by recorded votes. Paragraphs 2, 6 and 7 were retained by 88 votes to 20, with 17 abstentions, 78 to 22, with 22 abstentions, and 68 votes to 22, with 31 abstentions, respectively. The sixth and tenth preambular paragraphs were approved by 86 to 20, with 18 abstentions, and 73 to 22, with 24 abstentions, respectively.

South Asia

As requested by the General Assembly in 1988,[36] the Secretary-General transmitted in

July 1989 the views of two Governments (China and Maldives) on the establishment of a nuclear-weapon-free zone in South Asia.[37]

GENERAL ASSEMBLY ACTION

On 15 December, the General Assembly, on the recommendation of the First Committee, adopted **resolution 44/109** by recorded vote.

Establishment of a nuclear-weapon-free zone in South Asia

The General Assembly,

Recalling its resolutions 3265 B (XXIX) of 9 December 1974, 3476 B (XXX) of 11 December 1975, 31/73 of 10 December 1976, 32/83 of 12 December 1977, 33/65 of 14 December 1978, 34/78 of 11 December 1979, 35/148 of 12 December 1980, 36/88 of 9 December 1981, 37/76 of 9 December 1982, 38/65 of 15 December 1983, 39/55 of 12 December 1984, 40/83 of 12 December 1985, 41/49 of 3 December 1986, 42/29 of 30 November 1987 and 43/66 of 7 December 1988 concerning the establishment of a nuclear-weapon-free zone in South Asia,

Reiterating its conviction that the establishment of nuclear-weapon-free zones in various regions of the world is one of the measures that can contribute effectively to the objectives of non-proliferation of nuclear weapons and general and complete disarmament,

Believing that the establishment of a nuclear-weapon-free zone in South Asia, as in other regions, will assist in the strengthening of the security of the States of the region against the use or threat of use of nuclear weapons,

Noting with appreciation the declarations issued at the highest level by the Governments of South Asian States that are developing their peaceful nuclear programmes, reaffirming their undertaking not to acquire or manufacture nuclear weapons and to devote their nuclear programmes exclusively to the economic and social advancement of their peoples,

Welcoming the recent proposal for the conclusion of a bilateral or regional nuclear-test-ban agreement in South Asia,

Taking note of the proposal to convene, under the auspices of the United Nations, a conference on nuclear non-proliferation in South Asia, as soon as possible, with the participation of the regional and other concerned States,

Bearing in mind the provisions of paragraphs 60 to 63 of the Final Document of the Tenth Special Session of the General Assembly regarding the establishment of nuclear-weapon-free zones, including in the region of South Asia,

Taking note of the report of the Secretary-General,

1. *Reaffirms* its endorsement, in principle, of the concept of a nuclear-weapon-free zone in South Asia;

2. *Urges once again* the States of South Asia to continue to make all possible efforts to establish a nuclear-weapon-free zone in South Asia and to refrain, in the mean time, from any action contrary to that objective;

3. *Calls upon* those nuclear-weapon States that have not done so to respond positively to this proposal and to extend the necessary co-operation in the efforts to establish a nuclear-weapon-free zone in South Asia;

4. *Requests* the Secretary-General to communicate with the States of the region and other concerned States

in order to ascertain their views on the issue and to promote consultations among them with a view to exploring the best possibilities of furthering the efforts for the establishment of a nuclear-weapon-free zone in South Asia;

5. *Also requests* the Secretary-General to report on the subject to the General Assembly at its forty-fifth session;

6. *Decides* to include in the provisional agenda of its forty-fifth session the item entitled "Establishment of a nuclear-weapon-free zone in South Asia".

General Assembly resolution 44/109

15 December 1989   Meeting 81   116-3-32 (recorded vote)

Approved by First Committee (A/44/776) by recorded vote (102-3-30), 10 November (meeting 33); 2-nation draft (A/C.1/44/L.48); agenda item 54.
Sponsors: Bangladesh, Pakistan.
Meeting numbers. GA 44th session: 1st Committee 3-25, 33; plenary 81.

Recorded vote in Assembly as follows:

In favour: Albania, Antigua and Barbuda, Australia, Bahamas, Bahrain, Bangladesh, Barbados, Belgium, Benin, Bolivia, Botswana, Brunei Darussalam, Burkina Faso, Burundi, Cameroon, Canada, Cape Verde, Central African Republic, Chad, Chile, China, Colombia, Congo, Costa Rica, Côte d'Ivoire, Democratic Kampuchea, Djibouti, Dominica, Dominican Republic, Ecuador, Egypt, Fiji, Finland, Gabon, Gambia, Germany, Federal Republic of, Ghana, Greece, Grenada, Guatemala, Guinea, Guinea-Bissau, Guyana, Haiti, Honduras, Iran, Iraq, Ireland, Israel, Italy, Jamaica, Japan, Jordan, Kenya, Kuwait, Lebanon, Lesotho, Liberia, Libyan Arab Jamahiriya, Malawi, Malaysia, Maldives, Mali, Malta, Mauritania, Mexico, Morocco, Mozambique, Nepal, New Zealand, Nicaragua,[a] Niger, Nigeria, Oman, Pakistan, Panama, Papua New Guinea, Paraguay, Peru, Philippines, Portugal, Qatar, Romania, Rwanda, Saint Kitts and Nevis, Saint Lucia, Saint Vincent and the Grenadines, Samoa, Saudi Arabia, Senegal, Sierra Leone, Singapore, Solomon Islands, Somalia, Spain, Sri Lanka, Sudan, Suriname, Swaziland, Thailand, Togo, Trinidad and Tobago, Tunisia, Turkey, Uganda, United Arab Emirates, United Kingdom, United Republic of Tanzania, United States, Uruguay, Vanuatu, Venezuela, Yemen, Zaire, Zambia, Zimbabwe.

Against: Bhutan, India, Mauritius.

Abstaining: Afghanistan, Algeria, Angola, Argentina, Austria, Brazil, Bulgaria, Byelorussian SSR, Cuba, Cyprus, Czechoslovakia, Democratic Yemen, Denmark, Ethiopia, France, German Democratic Republic, Iceland, Indonesia, Lao People's Democratic Republic, Luxembourg,[b] Madagascar, Mongolia, Myanmar, Netherlands,[b] Norway, Poland, Seychelles, Sweden, Ukrainian SSR, USSR, Viet Nam, Yugoslavia.

[a]Later advised the Secretariat it had intended to abstain.
[b]Later advised the Secretariat it had intended to vote in favour.

South Pacific

In 1989, the General Assembly commended the South Pacific Nuclear Free Zone Treaty (the Treaty of Rarotonga), which opened for signature in 1985[38] and entered into force in 1986,[39] for the consideration of all Member States.

GENERAL ASSEMBLY ACTION

On 15 December 1989, the General Assembly, on the recommendation of the First Committee, adopted **resolution 44/119 F** by recorded vote.

South Pacific Nuclear Free Zone Treaty

The General Assembly,

Recalling its resolution 3477(XXX) of 11 December 1975, in which it endorsed the idea of the establishment of a nuclear-weapon-free zone in the South Pacific and invited the countries concerned to carry forward consultations about ways and means of realizing that objective,

Recalling also article VII of the Treaty on the Non-Proliferation of Nuclear Weapons, which acknowledges the right of any group of States to conclude regional treaties in order to assure the total absence of nuclear weapons in their respective territories,

Bearing in mind paragraph 60 of the Final Document of the Tenth Special Session of the General Assembly, the first special session devoted to disarmament, which states that the establishment of nuclear-weapon-free zones on the basis of arrangements freely arrived at among the States of the region concerned constitutes an important disarmament measure,

Noting the adoption on 6 August 1985 by the heads of Government of the independent or self-governing members of the South Pacific Forum, meeting at Rarotonga, of the South Pacific Nuclear Free Zone Treaty (also known as the Treaty of Rarotonga), and their adoption on 8 August 1986 of three Protocols to the Treaty,

Noting also that the Treaty entered into force upon the deposit of the eighth instrument of ratification, on 11 December 1986,

Recognizing that the Treaty reflects the particular circumstances of the South Pacific region,

1. *Notes with satisfaction* that eleven members of the South Pacific Forum have now ratified the South Pacific Nuclear Free Zone Treaty and that China and the Union of Soviet Socialist Republics have adhered to Protocols 2 and 3 of the Treaty;

2. *Notes also* that the United Kingdom of Great Britain and Northern Ireland and the United States of America have stated that none of their practices and activities within the Treaty area are inconsistent with the Treaty or its Protocols;

3. *Commends* the Treaty and its Protocols for the consideration of all Member States.

General Assembly resolution 44/119 F

15 December 1989   Meeting 81   151-0-4 (recorded vote)

Approved by First Committee (A/44/788) by recorded vote (132-0-5), 10 November (meeting 33); 5-nation draft (A/C.1/44/L.42); agenda item 66.
Sponsors: Australia, Fiji, New Zealand, Samoa, Solomon Islands.
Meeting numbers. GA 44th session: 1st Committee 3-25, 27, 33; plenary 81.

Recorded vote in Assembly as follows:

In favour: Afghanistan, Albania, Algeria, Angola, Antigua and Barbuda, Argentina, Australia, Austria, Bahamas, Bahrain, Bangladesh, Barbados, Belgium, Benin, Bhutan, Bolivia, Botswana, Brazil, Brunei Darussalam, Bulgaria, Burkina Faso, Burundi, Byelorussian SSR, Cameroon, Canada, Cape Verde, Central African Republic, Chad, Chile, China, Colombia, Congo, Costa Rica, Côte d'Ivoire, Cuba, Cyprus, Czechoslovakia, Democratic Kampuchea, Democratic Yemen, Denmark, Djibouti, Dominica, Dominican Republic, Ecuador, Egypt, El Salvador, Ethiopia, Fiji, Finland, Gabon, Gambia, German Democratic Republic, Germany, Federal Republic of, Ghana, Greece, Grenada, Guatemala, Guinea, Guinea-Bissau, Guyana, Haiti, Honduras, Hungary, Iceland, India, Indonesia, Iran, Iraq, Ireland, Israel, Italy, Jamaica, Japan, Jordan, Kenya, Kuwait, Lao People's Democratic Republic, Lebanon, Lesotho, Liberia, Libyan Arab Jamahiriya, Luxembourg, Madagascar, Malawi, Malaysia, Maldives, Mali, Malta, Mauritania, Mauritius, Mexico, Mongolia, Morocco, Mozambique, Myanmar, Nepal, Netherlands, New Zealand, Nicaragua, Niger, Nigeria, Norway, Oman, Pakistan, Panama, Papua New Guinea, Paraguay, Peru, Philippines, Poland, Portugal, Qatar, Romania, Rwanda, Saint Kitts and Nevis, Saint Lucia, Saint Vincent and the Grenadines, Samoa, Sao Tome and Principe, Saudi Arabia, Senegal, Seychelles, Sierra Leone, Singapore, Solomon Islands, Somalia, Spain, Sri Lanka, Sudan, Suriname, Swaziland, Sweden, Syrian Arab Republic, Thailand, Togo, Trinidad and Tobago, Tunisia, Turkey, Uganda, Ukrainian SSR, USSR, United Arab Emirates, United Republic of Tanzania, Uruguay, Venezuela, Viet Nam, Yemen, Yugoslavia, Zaire, Zambia, Zimbabwe.
Against: None.
Abstaining: France, United Kingdom, United States, Vanuatu.

1971 Declaration of the Indian Ocean as a Zone of Peace

The *Ad Hoc* Committee on the Indian Ocean held two sessions in 1989 (New York, 10-14 April, 5-19 July)[40] as it continued to study practical

measures for achieving the objectives of the 1971 Declaration of the Indian Ocean as a Zone of Peace.[41]

In April, the Committee's open-ended Working Group discussed 20 substantive issues and principles submitted by the Chairman of the Group relating to the establishment of the zone of peace. In July, it considered 19 revised substantive issues and principles, also submitted by the Chairman, reflecting further views and observations of the Group's members. Formal and informal Committee exchanges of views took place on the provisional agenda for the United Nations Conference on the Indian Ocean, its rules of procedure and structure. The Government of Sri Lanka said it was prepared to hold the Conference from 2 to 13 July 1990, but the General Assembly subsequently deferred it to 1991, requesting the *Ad Hoc* Committee to meet again in 1990 (see below).

As requested by the Assembly in 1988,[42] the Committee held a special meeting in July 1989 to commemorate the tenth anniversary of the Meeting of the Littoral and Hinterland States of the Indian Ocean.[43]

GENERAL ASSEMBLY ACTION

On 15 December 1989, on the First Committee's recommendation, the General Assembly adopted **resolution 44/120** by recorded vote.

Implementation of the Declaration of the Indian Ocean as a Zone of Peace

The General Assembly,

Recalling the Declaration of the Indian Ocean as a Zone of Peace, contained in its resolution 2832(XXVI) of 16 December 1971, and recalling also its resolutions 2992(XXVII) of 15 December 1972, 3080(XXVIII) of 6 December 1973, 3259 A (XXIX) of 9 December 1974, 3468(XXX) of 11 December 1975, 31/88 of 14 December 1976, 32/86 of 12 December 1977, S-10/2 of 30 June 1978, 33/68 of 14 December 1978, 34/80 A and B of 11 December 1979, 35/150 of 12 December 1980, 36/90 of 9 December 1981, 37/96 of 13 December 1982, 38/185 of 20 December 1983, 39/149 of 17 December 1984, 40/153 of 16 December 1985, 41/87 of 4 December 1986, 42/43 of 30 November 1987, 43/79 of 7 December 1988 and other relevant resolutions,

Reaffirming that the establishment of zones of peace in various regions of the world under appropriate conditions, to be clearly defined and determined freely by the States concerned in the zone, taking into account the characteristics of the zone and the principles of the Charter of the United Nations, and in conformity with international law, can contribute to strengthening the security of States within such zones and to international peace and security as a whole,

Recalling also the report of the Meeting of the Littoral and Hinterland States of the Indian Ocean,

Noting that the *Ad Hoc* Committee on the Indian Ocean, during its preparatory session in July 1989, commemorated the tenth anniversary of the Meeting of the Littoral and Hinterland States of the Indian Ocean, which took place on 13 July 1979,

Recalling further paragraph 22 of the final document on international security and disarmament adopted by the Ninth Conference of Heads of State or Government of Non-Aligned Countries, held at Belgrade from 4 to 7 September 1989,[a]

Reaffirming its conviction that concrete action for the achievement of the objectives of the Declaration of the Indian Ocean as a Zone of Peace would be a substantial contribution to the strengthening of international peace and security, as well as to the independence, sovereignty, territorial integrity and peaceful development of the States of the region,

Convinced that agreement on such action should be facilitated by encouraging developments in international relations that could have beneficial effects on the region,

Also convinced that the continued military presence of the great Powers in the Indian Ocean area, conceived in the context of their confrontation, gives urgency to the need to take practical steps for the early achievement of the objectives of the Declaration,

Considering that the creation of a zone of peace requires co-operation and agreement among the States of the region to ensure conditions of peace and security within the area, as envisaged in the Declaration,

Noting with appreciation the offer made by the Government of Sri Lanka to host the Conference on the Indian Ocean at Colombo, from 2 to 13 July 1990,

Regretting that it is not possible to hold the Conference in 1990, as scheduled, in spite of the generous offer of the Government of Sri Lanka,

1. *Takes note* of the report of the *Ad Hoc* Committee on the Indian Ocean;

2. *Reaffirms* full support for the achievement of the objectives of the Declaration of the Indian Ocean as a Zone of Peace;

3. *Reiterates and emphasizes* its decision to convene the Conference on the Indian Ocean at Colombo, as a necessary step for the implementation of the Declaration of the Indian Ocean as a Zone of Peace, adopted in 1971;

4. *Renews* the mandate of the *Ad Hoc* Committee as defined in the relevant resolutions, and requests the Committee to intensify its work with regard to the implementation of its mandate;

5. *Notes with satisfaction* that, in the implementation of the mandate of the *Ad Hoc* Committee, including the preparatory work for the convening of the Conference, as called for in the relevant resolutions recommended by the Committee and adopted by the General Assembly by consensus, considerable progress has been made by the Working Group of the *Ad Hoc* Committee in its meetings during the sessions of the Committee in 1989 and that the Chairman of the Working Group submitted his report to the *Ad Hoc* Committee;

6. *Urges* the *Ad Hoc* Committee to intensify its discussions on substantive issues and principles, including those identified by the Chairman of the Working Group in his report dated 12 July 1989, with the aim of elaborating elements that might be taken into consideration during the subsequent preparation of a draft final document of the Conference;

7. *Requests* the *Ad Hoc* Committee to hold two preparatory sessions during the first half of 1990, the first with a duration of one week and the second with a duration of two weeks, for completion of the remaining preparatory work relating to the Conference on the Indian Ocean to enable the convening of the Conference at Colombo in 1991 in consultation with the host country;

8. *Requests* the Chairman of the *Ad Hoc* Committee to continue his consultations on the participation in the work of the Committee by States Members of the United Nations which are not members of the Committee, with the aim of resolving this matter at the earliest possible date;

9. *Also requests* the Chairman of the *Ad Hoc* Committee to consult the Secretary-General at the appropriate time on the establishment of a secretariat for the Conference;

10. *Requests* the *Ad Hoc* Committee to submit to the General Assembly at its forty-fifth session a full report on the implementation of the present resolution;

11. *Requests* the Secretary-General to continue to render all necessary assistance to the *Ad Hoc* Committee, including the provision of summary records, in recognition of its preparatory function.

---

[a]A/44/551-S/20870.

General Assembly resolution 44/120

15 December 1989   Meeting 81   137-4-14 (recorded vote)

Approved by First Committee (A/44/789) by recorded vote (112-4-14), 30 November (meeting 53); draft by Bulgaria, German Democratic Republic and Yugoslavia, for Non-Aligned Group (A/C.1/44/L.33/Rev.1); agenda item 67.

Financial implications. 5th Committee, A/44/869; S-G, A/C.1/44/L.66, A/C.5/44/44.

Meeting numbers. GA 44th session: 1st Committee 3-25, 29, 31, 53; 5th Committee 54; plenary 81.

Recorded vote in Assembly as follows:

In favour: Afghanistan, Albania, Algeria, Angola, Antigua and Barbuda, Argentina, Australia, Austria, Bahamas, Bahrain, Bangladesh, Barbados, Benin, Bhutan, Bolivia, Botswana, Brazil, Brunei Darussalam, Bulgaria, Burkina Faso, Burundi, Byelorussian SSR, Cameroon, Cape Verde, Central African Republic, Chad, Chile, China, Colombia, Congo, Costa Rica, Côte d'Ivoire, Cuba, Cyprus, Czechoslovakia, Democratic Kampuchea, Democratic Yemen, Djibouti, Dominica, Dominican Republic, Ecuador, Egypt, El Salvador, Ethiopia, Fiji, Finland, Gabon, Gambia, German Democratic Republic, Ghana, Grenada, Guatemala, Guinea, Guinea-Bissau, Guyana, Haiti, Honduras, Hungary, India, Indonesia, Iran, Iraq, Ireland, Jamaica, Jordan, Kenya, Kuwait, Lao People's Democratic Republic, Lebanon, Lesotho, Liberia, Libyan Arab Jamahiriya, Madagascar, Malawi, Malaysia, Maldives, Mali, Malta, Mauritania, Mauritius, Mexico, Mongolia, Morocco, Mozambique, Myanmar, Nepal, New Zealand, Nicaragua, Niger, Nigeria, Oman, Pakistan, Panama, Papua New Guinea, Paraguay, Peru, Philippines, Poland, Qatar, Romania, Rwanda, Saint Kitts and Nevis, Saint Lucia, Saint Vincent and the Grenadines, Samoa, Sao Tome and Principe, Saudi Arabia, Senegal, Seychelles, Sierra Leone, Singapore, Solomon Islands, Somalia, Sri Lanka, Sudan, Suriname, Swaziland, Sweden, Syrian Arab Republic, Thailand, Togo, Trinidad and Tobago, Tunisia, Uganda, Ukrainian SSR, USSR, United Arab Emirates, United Republic of Tanzania, Uruguay, Vanuatu, Venezuela, Viet Nam, Yemen, Yugoslavia, Zaire, Zambia, Zimbabwe.

Against: France, Japan, United Kingdom, United States.

Abstaining: Belgium, Canada, Denmark, Germany, Federal Republic of, Greece, Iceland, Israel, Italy, Luxembourg, Netherlands, Norway, Portugal, Spain, Turkey.

Preparation for the 1990 Review Conference on NPT

Following the entry into force on 5 March 1970 of the 1968 Treaty on the Non-Proliferation of Nuclear Weapons (NPT),[44] quinquennial review conferences were held in 1975,[45] 1980[46] and 1985.[47] The Final Declaration of the Third

(1985) Review Conference recommended that a fourth conference be convened in 1990.

An open-ended Preparatory Committee of parties to NPT, meeting in New York from 1 to 5 May 1989, decided on a number of organizational matters and agreed that the 1990 Conference would take place at Geneva from 20 August to 14 September. At its second session (Geneva, 11-15 September), the Committee focused on the financing of the Conference, its agenda and background documentation. The third and final session of the Committee was scheduled for April/May 1990.

REFERENCES

[1]A/44/42. [2]YUN 1988, p. 34. [3]A/CN.10/117. [4]A/44/27. [5]CD/819/Rev.1. [6]YUN 1987, p. 47. [7]YUN 1988, p. 56. [8]A/44/578-S/20868. [9]CD/515/Rev.5. [10]CD/942 & CD/943. [11]YUN 1988, p. 55, GA res. 43/78 D, 7 Dec. 1988. [12]A/44/514 & Add.1,2. [13]YUN 1988, p. 55. [14]A/44/87 & Add.1-7. [15]YUN 1987, p. 54, GA res. 42/38 C, 30 Nov. 1987. [16]A/44/648. [17]CD/902. [18]CD/935. [19]CD/904. [20]CD/944. [21]CD/903 & Corr.1. [22]A/44/211. [23]YUN 1963, p. 137. [24]*Status of Multilateral Arms Regulation and Disarmament Agreements*, 3rd edition: *1987*, Sales No. E.88.IX.5. [25]CD/885. [26]CD/938. [27]YUN 1988, p. 73, GA res. 43/79, 7 Dec. 1988. [28]YUN 1964, p. 69. [29]YUN 1988, p. 68, GA res. 43/71 B, 7 Dec. 1988. [30]A/CN.10/131. [31]A/44/655. [32]A/44/430 & Add.1,2. [33]YUN 1988, p. 70, GA res. 43/65, 7 Dec. 1988. [34]A/44/658. [35]YUN 1988, p. 71, GA res. 43/80, 7 Dec. 1988. [36]*Ibid.*, p. 72, GA res. 43/66, 7 Dec. 1988. [37]A/44/363 & Corr.1. [38]YUN 1985, p. 58. [39]YUN 1986, p. 54. [40]A/44/29. [41]YUN 1971, p. 34, GA res. 2832(XXVI), 16 Dec. 1971. [42]YUN 1988, p. 73, GA res. 43/79, 7 Dec. 1988. [43]YUN 1979, p. 49. [44]YUN 1968, p. 17, GA res. 2373(XXII) annex, 12 June 1968. [45]YUN 1975, p. 27. [46]YUN 1980, p. 51. [47]YUN 1985, p. 56.

Prohibition or restriction of other weapons

Chemical and biological weapons

The Conference of States Parties to the 1925 Geneva Protocol and Other Interested States (Paris, 7-11 January 1989), known as the Paris Conference, in its Final Declaration, reaffirmed the authority of the 1925 Protocol for the Prohibition of the Use in War of Asphyxiating, Poisonous or Other Gases, and of Bacteriological Methods of Warfare and called on the Conference on Disarmament to redouble its efforts to conclude a convention prohibiting chemical weapons.[1] The Conference was proposed by the United States in 1988 to uphold the authority and, in its words, to reverse the serious erosion of the Geneva Protocol.[2]

Consideration by the Conference on Disarmament. In response to a recommendation of the Paris Conference, the Conference on Disarmament intensified its negotiations on a chemical weapons convention from 20 to 31 March and from 17 to 28 July 1989.[3]

The *Ad Hoc* Committee on Chemical Weapons, re-established by the Conference on 16 February,[4] held 26 meetings between 17 February and 18 August. In addition, the Committee Chairman held a number of informal consultations with delegations. The Committee had before it a report on its inter-sessional work, which contained the rolling text of the draft convention, reflecting the stage that the negotiations had reached by the beginning of the 1989 session of the Conference.[5] It established five working groups to deal with aspects of the convention, as follows: verification; legal and political questions; institutional; technical; and transition. The Committee Chairman undertook intensive consultations on challenge inspections; sanctions; the size, composition and decision-making process of the executive council; and universal adherence to the convention. Progress was achieved in elaborating several draft provisions of the rolling text, including those concerning institutional and technical aspects. The Committee recommended that it hold a resumed session from 16 January to 1 February 1990 and, in preparation for that session, have informal open-ended consultations from 28 November to 14 December 1989. It also recommended that it be re-established at the outset of the 1990 session of the Conference on Disarmament and that a decision on the mandate be taken at the beginning of that session.

New documents were submitted by Australia[6] and Czechoslovakia[7] on their chemical production/consumption and on their facilities relevant to the convention; by Canada, on a workshop concerning IAEA safeguards as a model for verification of a chemical weapons convention;[8] by the Federal Republic of Germany, on the validity of *ad hoc* on-site verification;[9] by Finland, on standard operating procedures for verification;[10] by France, transmitting the Final Act and Final Declaration of the Paris Conference,[11] and two proposals, one concerning the establishment of a high-level advisory body for the various organs of the convention, to be called the scientific advisory council,[12] and another on protecting the confidentiality of any information in the military, commercial and industrial fields that might be handled in the course of verification arrangements;[13] by Italy, on an international forum on the problems of verification of a chemical weapons convention;[14] by Norway, on headspace gas chromatography, a new approach to verification of alleged chemical weapons use;[15] and by the United Kingdom, on verification of the convention.[16] In addition, a large number of States submitted reports on national trial inspections.

Report of the Secretary-General. As requested by the General Assembly in 1988,[17] the Secretary-General, in October 1989, transmitted a report of the group of qualified experts to develop further technical guidelines and procedures available to the Secretary-General for the timely and efficient investigation of reports of the possible use of chemical and bacteriological (biological) or toxin weapons.[18] The six-member group, appointed by the Secretary-General in 1988,[19] met twice in 1989 (Geneva, 6-17 February and 31 July–11 August) and completed its work on the technical guidelines for investigating possible violations of the Geneva Protocol. The report dealt with principles and other general aspects of investigations, including assessment and decision by the Secretary-General following submission of a report of alleged use; involvement of Member States, consultants, experts and laboratories; activities of the Secretary-General; and technical procedures and other practical aspects of investigations.

In separate addenda,[20] the Secretary-General provided information received from two Member States (Israel and Iran), containing the names of persons those States considered to be qualified experts to investigate reports of the possible use of chemical and biological or toxin weapons, as requested by the Assembly in 1987.[21]

Other action. Sixty-seven delegates from 23 nations in the South-East Asian and South Pacific region attended a seminar convened by the Government of Australia (Canberra, 2-4 August 1989) to increase support in the region for the early conclusion of a chemical weapons convention.[22]

Wishing to build on the Final Declaration of the Paris Conference, Australia convened the Government-Industry Conference against Chemical Weapons, which brought together Governments as well as representatives of the world's chemical industry (Canberra, 18-22 September).[23] At the conclusion of the Conference, the Chairman stated that it had affirmed the commitment of Governments and the world's chemical industry to work together to bring to fruition at the earliest possible date a comprehensive, global chemical weapons convention. Representatives of the chemical industry adopted a statement, by which they declared their support for efforts to conclude the convention.

The United States and the USSR issued a joint statement reaffirming their commitment to pursue aggressively the prohibition of chemical weapons and the destruction of all stockpiles of such weapons.[24] The statement was issued at the conclusion of talks held on 22 and 23 September at Jackson Hole, Wyoming (United States).

GENERAL ASSEMBLY ACTION

On 15 December 1989, the General Assembly, on the recommendation of the First Committee, adopted **resolution 44/115 A** without vote.

Chemical and bacteriological (biological) weapons

The General Assembly,

Recalling its previous resolutions relating to the complete and effective prohibition of the development, production and stockpiling of all chemical weapons and to their destruction,

Reaffirming the urgent necessity, particularly following recent United Nations reports, of strict observance by all States of the principles and objectives of the Protocol for the Prohibition of the Use in War of Asphyxiating, Poisonous or Other Gases, and of Bacteriological Methods of Warfare, signed at Geneva on 17 June 1925,

Welcoming the broad participation in and the positive results of the Conference of States Parties to the 1925 Geneva Protocol and Other Interested States on the prohibition of chemical weapons, held in Paris from 7 to 11 January 1989, and noting with satisfaction the resulting additional accession of States to the 1925 Protocol,

Endorsing the Final Declaration of the Paris Conference as an important contribution to the aim of the total elimination of chemical weapons,

Recognizing that the effectiveness of a convention for the prohibition of the development, production, stockpiling and use of chemical weapons and for their destruction will benefit from the support and co-operation of the chemical industry,

Commending, in that regard, the initiative of the Government of Australia to strengthen and expand the co-operation of the chemical industry with Governments by convening at Canberra from 18 to 22 September 1989 a Government-Industry Conference against Chemical Weapons,

Reaffirming the urgent necessity of the adherence by all States to the Convention on the Prohibition of the Development, Production and Stockpiling of Bacteriological (Biological) and Toxin Weapons and on Their Destruction, signed in London, Moscow and Washington on 10 April 1972,

Taking note of the Final Document of the Second Review Conference of the Parties to the Convention on the Prohibition of the Development, Production and Stockpiling of Bacteriological (Biological) and Toxin Weapons and on Their Destruction, adopted by consensus on 26 September 1986, and, in particular, of article IX of the Final Declaration of the Conference,

Having considered the report of the Conference on Disarmament, which incorporates, *inter alia,* the report of its *Ad Hoc* Committee on Chemical Weapons, and noting that, following the precedents set over the past five years, consultations are continuing during the intersessional period, thus increasing the time devoted to negotiation,

Convinced of the necessity that all efforts be exerted for the continuation and successful conclusion of negotiations on the prohibition of the development, production, stockpiling and use of all chemical weapons and on their destruction,

Emphasizing the importance of the widest possible participation of States in the negotiations on the draft convention in order to ensure universal adherence on its conclusion,

Conscious of the need to share data relevant to the negotiations on a future convention banning all chemical weapons on a global basis and of the fact that the provision of such data would be an important confidence-building measure,

Noting the bilateral and other discussions, including the ongoing exchange of views between the Union of Soviet Socialist Republics and the United States of America in the framework of the multilateral negotiations, on issues related to the prohibition of chemical weapons,

Noting with appreciation the efforts made at all levels by States to facilitate the earliest conclusion of a convention for the prohibition of the development, production, stockpiling and use of chemical weapons and on their destruction and, in particular, the concrete steps designed to promote confidence and to contribute directly to that goal,

1. *Notes with satisfaction* the work of the Conference on Disarmament during its 1989 session regarding the prohibition of chemical weapons, and, in particular, appreciates the progress in the work of its *Ad Hoc* Committee on Chemical Weapons on that question and the tangible results recorded in its report;

2. *Notes*, while regretting that a convention on the prohibition of the development, production, stockpiling and use of chemical weapons and on their destruction has not yet been concluded, that there exists an ever-growing will to resolve the pending problems at the earliest possible date;

3. *Again urges* the Conference on Disarmament, as a matter of high priority, to intensify, during its 1990 session, which will be of pivotal importance, the negotiations on such a convention and to reinforce its efforts further by, *inter alia*, increasing the time that it devotes to such negotiations, taking into account all existing proposals and future initiatives, with a view to the final elaboration of a convention at the earliest possible date, and to re-establish its *Ad Hoc* Committee on Chemical Weapons for that purpose with the mandate to be agreed upon by the Conference at the beginning of its 1990 session;

4. *Requests* the Conference on Disarmament to use the political momentum generated by the Conference of States Parties to the 1925 Geneva Protocol and Other Interested States, held in Paris from 7 to 11 January 1989, and the recognition by that conference that a global ban on chemical weapons is of universal concern and interest, to achieve the conclusion at the earliest possible date of such a convention;

5. *Also requests* the Conference on Disarmament to report to the General Assembly at its forty-fifth session on the results of its negotiations;

6. *Calls upon* all States to abide by the commitments undertaken in the Final Declaration of the Paris Conference;

7. *Welcomes* the renewed declarations of commitment by Governments represented at the Government-Industry Conference against Chemical Weapons to conclude and implement a convention at the earliest possible date, and welcomes also the first collective statement by representatives of the chemical industry of their commitment to co-operate with Governments to that end;

8. *Recognizes* that constructive proposals were discussed at the Government-Industry Conference against Chemical Weapons that could contribute momentum to the Geneva negotiations and assist in the conclusion and early implementation of such a convention;

9. *Recognizes also* the importance of declarations made by States on whether or not they possess chemical weapons and of further international exchanges of data

in connection with the negotiations on such a convention;

10. *Encourages* Member States to take further initiatives to promote confidence and openness in the negotiations and to provide further information to facilitate prompt resolution of outstanding issues, thus contributing to an early agreement on, and universal adherence to, such a convention.

General Assembly resolution 44/115 A

15 December 1989   Meeting 81   Adopted without vote

Approved by First Committee (A/44/784) without vote, 17 November (meeting 41); 37-nation draft (A/C.1/44/L.38/Rev.1); agenda item 62.
Sponsors: Argentina, Australia, Austria, Belgium, Bulgaria, Byelorussian SSR, Canada, Costa Rica, Denmark, Finland, France, German Democratic Republic, Germany, Federal Republic of, Greece, Hungary, Iceland, Ireland, Italy, Japan, Malaysia, Mongolia, Myanmar, Netherlands, Norway, Philippines, Poland, Portugal, Samoa, Spain, Sweden, Turkey, Ukrainian SSR, USSR, United Kingdom, United States, Uruguay, Viet Nam.
Meeting numbers. GA 44th session: 1st Committee 3-25, 31, 41; plenary 81.

Also on 15 December, the Assembly, on the recommendation of the First Committee, adopted **resolution 44/115 B** without vote.

Chemical and bacteriological (biological) weapons: measures to uphold the authority of the 1925 Geneva Protocol and to support the conclusion of a chemical weapons convention

The General Assembly,

Recalling its previous resolutions, and those adopted by the Security Council, on the use of chemical weapons,

Recalling also the provisions of the Protocol for the Prohibition of the Use in War of Asphyxiating, Poisonous or Other Gases, and of Bacteriological Methods of Warfare, signed at Geneva on 17 June 1925, and of other rules and principles of international humanitarian law applicable in armed conflict,

Welcoming in that regard the reaffirmation in the Final Declaration of the Conference of States Parties to the 1925 Geneva Protocol and Other Interested States, held in Paris from 7 to 11 January 1989, of the importance and the continuing validity of the 1925 Protocol,

Recalling further the necessity of the adherence by all States to the Convention on the Prohibition of the Development, Production and Stockpiling of Bacteriological (Biological) and Toxin Weapons and on Their Destruction, signed in London, Moscow and Washington on 10 April 1972,

Expressing deep dismay at the use and the risk of use of chemical weapons as long as such weapons remain and are spread,

Acknowledging that prompt and impartial investigation of reports of possible use of chemical and bacteriological weapons will further enhance the authority of the 1925 Geneva Protocol,

Taking note of the report of the Secretary-General on the proposals of the group of qualified experts established in pursuance of General Assembly resolution 42/37 C of 30 November 1987, concerning technical guidelines and procedures available to the Secretary-General for the timely and efficient investigation of reports of the possible use of chemical and bacteriological (biological) or toxin weapons,

Noting that, upon conclusion of a chemical weapons convention, these guidelines and procedures should be adapted in the light of the obligations under the convention,

1. *Renews its call* to all States to observe strictly the principles and objectives of the Protocol for the Prohibition of the Use in War of Asphyxiating, Poisonous or Other Gases, and of Bacteriological Methods of Warfare, and condemns vigorously all actions that violate that obligation;

2. *Calls upon* all States that have not yet done so to accede to the 1925 Geneva Protocol;

3. *Urges* the Conference on Disarmament to pursue as a matter of continuing urgency its negotiations on a convention on the prohibition of the development, production, stockpiling and use of all chemical weapons and on their destruction;

4. *Requests* the Secretary-General to carry out promptly investigations in response to reports that may be brought to his attention by any Member State concerning the possible use of chemical and bacteriological (biological) or toxin weapons that may constitute a violation of the 1925 Geneva Protocol or other relevant rules of customary international law in order to ascertain the facts of the matter, and to report promptly the results of any such investigation to all Member States;

5. *Welcomes*, in that regard, the proposals of the group of qualified experts concerning technical guidelines and procedures to guide the Secretary-General in the conduct of timely and efficient investigation of the reports of use of chemical and bacteriological (biological) or toxin weapons;

6. *Calls upon* all States to consider the implementation of those guidelines and procedures for investigation, *inter alia*, by putting at the disposal of the Secretary-General qualified experts and/or consultants as well as laboratories for analysis;

7. *Notes with satisfaction* that the Security Council decided to consider immediately, taking into account the investigations of the Secretary-General, appropriate and effective measures in accordance with the Charter of the United Nations;

8. *Urges* all States to exercise restraint and to act responsibly in accordance with the need for the early conclusion and entry into force of a convention on the prohibition of the development, production, stockpiling and use of all chemical weapons and on their destruction;

9. *Decides* to include in the provisional agenda of its forty-fifth session the item entitled "Chemical and bacteriological (biological) weapons".

General Assembly resolution 44/115 B

15 December 1989   Meeting 81   Adopted without vote

Approved by First Committee (A/44/784) without vote, 17 November (meeting 41); 32-nation draft (A/C.1/44.L.47/Rev.1), orally revised; agenda item 62.

Sponsors: Antigua and Barbuda, Australia, Austria, Belgium, Bulgaria, Cameroon, Canada, Colombia, Costa Rica, Denmark, Ecuador, Finland, France, German Democratic Republic, Germany, Federal Republic of, Greece, Iceland, Italy, Japan, Netherlands, New Zealand, Norway, Poland, Portugal, Samoa, Spain, Sweden, Thailand, Turkey, USSR, United Kingdom, United States.

Meeting numbers. GA 44th session: 1st Committee 3-25, 37, 41; plenary 81.

Review conferences of the parties to the Convention on biological weapons

Review conferences of the parties to the Convention on the Prohibition of the Development, Production and Stockpiling of Bacteriological (Biological) and Toxin Weapons and on Their Destruction[25] were held in 1980[26] and 1986,[27] and a third conference was scheduled to be held not later than 1991. The Convention opened for signature on 10 April 1972 and entered into force on 26 March 1975.

GENERAL ASSEMBLY ACTION

On 15 December 1989, the General Assembly, on the recommendation of the First Committee, adopted **resolution 44/115 C** without vote.

Implementation of the recommendations of the Second Review Conference of the Parties to the Convention on the Prohibition of the Development, Production and Stockpiling of Bacteriological (Biological) and Toxin Weapons and on Their Destruction

The General Assembly,

Recalling its resolution 2826(XXVI) of 16 December 1971, in which it commended the Convention on the Prohibition of the Development, Production and Stockpiling of Bacteriological (Biological) and Toxin Weapons and on Their Destruction,

Recalling also that the Second Review Conference of the Parties to the Convention was held at Geneva from 8 to 26 September 1986 in order to review the operation of the Convention with a view to assuring that the purposes of the preamble to and the provisions of the Convention, including the provisions concerning negotiations on chemical weapons, were being realized,

Taking note of the confidence-building measures agreed upon by the Second Review Conference for further strengthening the authority of the Convention and for enhancing confidence among States,

Acknowledging that the Final Declaration of the Second Review Conference expressed the need to give further consideration to, *inter alia*, the implementation of the Convention in all its aspects,

Confirming the common interest in strengthening the authority and the effectiveness of the Convention to promote confidence and co-operation among Member States as well as the necessity to comply with the obligations set forth in the Convention,

1. *Notes with appreciation* that, in accordance with the Final Declaration of the Second Review Conference of the Parties to the Convention on the Prohibition of the Development, Production and Stockpiling of Bacteriological (Biological) and Toxin Weapons and on Their Destruction, an *Ad Hoc* Meeting of Scientific and Technical Experts from States parties to the Convention was held at Geneva from 31 March to 15 April 1987, which adopted by consensus a report finalizing the modalities for the exchange of information and data agreed to in the Final Declaration, thus enabling States parties to follow a standardized procedure;

2. *Calls upon* all States parties to the Convention to provide such information and data to the Secretary-General on an annual basis and not later than 15 April;

3. *Requests* the Secretary-General to render the necessary assistance and to provide such services as may be required for the implementation of the relevant parts of the Final Declaration;

4. *Notes* that the Second Review Conference decided, in its Final Declaration, that a Third Review Confer-

ence should be held at Geneva at the request of a majority of States parties not later than 1991;

5. *Recalls* in that regard the decision that the Third Review Conference should consider, *inter alia*, the issues set out in article XII of the Final Declaration of the Second Review Conference;

6. *Also requests* the Secretary-General to circulate to the States parties to the Convention not later than four months prior to the convening of the Third Review Conference a report on the implementation of the confidence-building measures agreed upon by the *Ad Hoc* Meeting of Scientific and Technical Experts from States parties;

7. *Welcomes* the fact that there are more than one hundred States parties to the Convention, including all the permanent members of the Security Council, and that since the holding of the Second Review Conference four more States have forwarded their instruments of ratification of the Convention, two more States have declared their accession to the Convention and one State has withdrawn its reservations to it;

8. *Calls upon* all States that have not ratified or acceded to the Convention to do so without delay, thus contributing to the achievement of universal adherence to the Convention and to the strengthening of international confidence.

General Assembly resolution 44/115 C

15 December 1989   Meeting 81   Adopted without vote

Approved by First Committee (A/44/784) without vote, 9 November (meeting 32); 40-nation draft (A/C.1/44/L.52); agenda item 62.

Sponsors: Argentina, Australia, Austria, Bangladesh, Belgium, Bolivia, Bulgaria, Byelorussian SSR, Canada, Chile, China, Czechoslovakia, Denmark, Finland, France, German Democratic Republic, Germany, Federal Republic of, Greece, Hungary, Iran, Ireland, Italy, Japan, Liberia, Luxembourg, Mongolia, Netherlands, New Zealand, Norway, Pakistan, Peru, Poland, Romania, Spain, Sweden, Ukrainian SSR, USSR, United Kingdom, United States, Zaire.

Meeting numbers. GA 44th session: 1st Committee 3-25, 32; plenary 81.

New weapons of mass destruction, including radiological weapons

For the first time since 1975, the General Assembly in 1989 did not adopt a resolution on the question of prohibiting the development and manufacture of weapons of mass destruction and new systems of such weapons. In addition, the subject attracted little attention in the disarmament bodies, although differences of view concerning the imminence of the emergence of such weapons persisted.

Consideration by the Conference on Disarmament. The Conference on Disarmament considered the item "New types of weapons of mass destruction and new systems of such weapons; radiological weapons" from 3 to 7 April and from 31 July to 4 August.[3]

The *Ad Hoc* Committee on Radiological Weapons, re-established on 7 February, held six meetings between 20 February and 7 August; informal consultations also took place. It re-established contact group A to consider the prohibition of radiological weapons in the "traditional" sense and contact group B, the prohibi-

tion of attacks against nuclear facilities. The reports of the two groups were annexed to the Committee's report.[28] Hungary submitted a paper on suggested scopes for prohibiting radiological weapons,[29] and Peru, a draft convention on the prohibition of attacks against nuclear installations.[30]

The Committee concluded that its work had contributed to clarifying and making more concise the different approaches which continued to exist with regard to both subjects under consideration and recommended that the Conference re-establish it in 1990.

Report of the Secretary-General. In response to a 1988 General Assembly request,[31] the Secretary-General, in October 1989,[32] drew the attention of Member States to sections of the report of the Conference on Disarmament dealing with new types of weapons of mass destruction and new systems of such weapons; radiological weapons.[3]

GENERAL ASSEMBLY ACTION

On 15 December 1989, the General Assembly, on the recommendation of the First Committee, adopted **resolution 44/116 A** by recorded vote.

Prohibition of the development, production, stockpiling and use of radiological weapons

The General Assembly,

Recalling its resolutions 37/99 C of 13 December 1982, 38/188 D of 20 December 1983, 39/151 J of 17 December 1984, 40/94 D of 12 December 1985, 41/59 A and I of 3 December 1986, 42/38 F of 30 November 1987 and 43/75 J of 7 December 1988 on, *inter alia*, the conclusion of an agreement prohibiting military attacks against nuclear facilities,

Taking note of the report of the Secretary-General on this subject submitted pursuant to resolution 43/75 J,

Gravely concerned that armed attacks against nuclear facilities, though carried out with conventional weapons, could be tantamount to the use of radiological weapons,

Recalling also that Additional Protocol I of 1977 to the Geneva Conventions of 12 August 1949 prohibits attacks on nuclear electricity-generating stations,

Deeply concerned that the destruction of nuclear facilities by conventional weapons causes the release into the environment of huge amounts of dangerous radioactive material, which results in serious radioactive contamination,

Firmly convinced that the Israeli attack against the safeguarded nuclear facilities in Iraq constitutes an unprecedented danger to international peace and security,

Recalling further resolutions GC(XXVII)/RES/407 and GC(XXVII)/RES/409, adopted in 1983 by the General Conference of the International Atomic Energy Agency, in which the Conference urged all member States to support actions in international forums to reach an international agreement that prohibits armed attacks against nuclear installations devoted to peaceful purposes,

1. *Reaffirms* that armed attacks of any kind against nuclear facilities are tantamount to the use of radiolog-

ical weapons, owing to the dangerous radioactive forces that such attacks cause to be released;

2. *Requests once again* the Conference on Disarmament to intensify further its efforts to reach, as early as possible, an agreement prohibiting armed attacks against nuclear facilities;

3. *Requests again* the International Atomic Energy Agency to provide the Conference on Disarmament with the technical studies that could facilitate the conclusion of such an agreement;

4. *Requests* the Secretary-General to report to the General Assembly at its forty-fifth session on the progress made in the implementation of the present resolution.

General Assembly resolution 44/116 A

15 December 1989   Meeting 81   124-2-26 (recorded vote)

Approved by First Committee (A/44/785) by recorded vote (104-2-28), 13 November (meeting 35); 5-nation draft (A/C.1/44/L.1); agenda item 63 *(c)*.
Sponsors: Iraq, Jordan, Libyan Arab Jamahiriya, Oman, Yemen.
Meeting numbers. GA 44th session: 1st Committee 3-25, 31, 35; plenary 81.

Recorded vote in Assembly as follows:

In favour: Afghanistan, Albania, Algeria, Angola, Antigua and Barbuda, Argentina, Bahamas, Bahrain, Bangladesh, Barbados, Benin, Bhutan, Bolivia, Botswana, Brazil, Brunei Darussalam, Bulgaria, Burkina Faso, Burundi, Byelorussian SSR, Cameroon, Cape Verde, Central African Republic, Chad, China, Colombia, Congo, Costa Rica, Côte d'Ivoire, Cuba, Cyprus, Czechoslovakia, Democratic Kampuchea, Democratic Yemen, Djibouti, Dominica, Dominican Republic, Ecuador, Egypt, El Salvador, Fiji, Gabon, Gambia, German Democratic Republic, Ghana, Grenada, Guatemala, Guinea, Guinea-Bissau, Guyana, Haiti, Honduras, Hungary, India, Indonesia, Iran, Iraq, Jamaica, Jordan, Kenya, Kuwait, Lao People's Democratic Republic, Lebanon, Lesotho, Liberia, Libyan Arab Jamahiriya, Madagascar, Malawi, Malaysia, Maldives, Mali, Mauritania, Mauritius, Mexico, Mongolia, Morocco, Mozambique, Myanmar, Nepal, Nicaragua, Niger, Nigeria, Oman, Pakistan, Panama, Papua New Guinea, Paraguay, Peru, Philippines, Poland, Qatar, Romania, Rwanda, Saint Kitts and Nevis, Saint Lucia, Saint Vincent and the Grenadines, Sao Tome and Principe, Saudi Arabia, Senegal, Seychelles, Sierra Leone, Solomon Islands, Somalia, Sri Lanka, Sudan, Suriname, Swaziland, Syrian Arab Republic, Togo, Trinidad and Tobago, Tunisia, Turkey, Uganda, Ukrainian SSR, USSR, United Arab Emirates, United Republic of Tanzania, Vanuatu, Viet Nam, Yemen, Yugoslavia, Zaire, Zambia, Zimbabwe.

Against: Israel, United States.

Abstaining: Australia, Austria, Belgium, Canada, Chile, Denmark, Finland, France, Germany, Federal Republic of, Greece, Iceland, Ireland, Italy, Japan, Luxembourg, Malta, Netherlands, New Zealand, Norway, Portugal, Samoa, Spain, Sweden, United Kingdom, Uruguay, Venezuela.

On the same date and on the recommendation of the First Committee, the Assembly adopted **resolution 44/116 T** without vote.

Prohibition of the development, production, stockpiling and use of radiological weapons

The General Assembly,

Recalling its resolution 43/75 C of 7 December 1988,

1. *Takes note* of the part of the report of the Conference on Disarmament on its 1989 session that deals with the question of radiological weapons, in particular the report of the *Ad Hoc* Committee on Radiological Weapons;

2. *Recognizes* that in 1989 the *Ad Hoc* Committee made a further contribution to the clarification and better understanding of different approaches that continue to exist with regard to both of the important matters under consideration;

3. *Takes note also* of the recommendation of the Conference on Disarmament that the *Ad Hoc* Committee on Radiological Weapons should be re-established at the beginning of its 1990 session;

4. *Requests* the Conference on Disarmament to continue its substantive negotiation on the subject with a view to the prompt conclusion of its work, taking into account all proposals presented to the Conference to this end and drawing upon the annexes to its report as a basis of its future work, the result of which should be submitted to the General Assembly at its forty-fifth session;

5. *Requests* the Secretary-General to transmit to the Conference on Disarmament all relevant documents relating to the discussion of all aspects of the issue by the General Assembly at its forty-fourth session;

6. *Decides* to include in the provisional agenda of its forty-fifth session the item entitled "Prohibition of the development, production, stockpiling and use of radiological weapons".

General Assembly resolution 44/116 T

15 December 1989   Meeting 81   Adopted without vote

Approved by First Committee (A/44/785) without vote, 13 November (meeting 35); 7-nation draft (A/C.1/44/L.57); agenda item 63 *(c)*.
Sponsors: Austria, Byelorussian SSR, Hungary, Netherlands, Peru, Sweden, USSR.
Meeting numbers. GA 44th session: 1st Committee 3-25, 31, 35; plenary 81.

By **decision 44/431** of 15 December, the Assembly took note of the First Committee's report on the prohibition of the development and manufacture of new types of weapons of mass destruction and new systems of such weapons.[33] No proposal was submitted for consideration by the Committee.

Dumping of radioactive wastes

In accordance with a 1988 General Assembly request,[34] the Secretary-General, in October 1989, provided information received from the United Nations Environment Programme, the International Maritime Organization, IAEA and OAU on the dumping of radioactive wastes in Africa, including all steps taken or envisaged to monitor, control and put an end to such activities.[35]

GENERAL ASSEMBLY ACTION

On 15 December 1989, the General Assembly, on the recommendation of the First Committee, adopted **resolution 44/116 R** by recorded vote.

Prohibition of the dumping of radioactive wastes

The General Assembly,

Bearing in mind resolution CM/Res.1153(XLVIII) concerning the dumping of nuclear and industrial wastes in Africa, adopted on 25 May 1988 by the Council of Ministers of the Organization of African Unity at its forty-eighth ordinary session, held at Addis Ababa from 19 to 23 May 1988,

Bearing in mind also resolution CM/Res.1225(L) adopted by the Council of Ministers of the Organization of African Unity at its fiftieth ordinary session, held at Addis Ababa from 17 to 22 July 1989,[a]

Welcoming resolution GC(XXXIII)/RES/509 on the dumping of nuclear wastes, adopted on 29 September 1989 by the General Conference of the International Atomic Energy Agency at its thirty-third regular session,

---

[a]A/44/603.

Considering its resolution 2602 C (XXIV) of 16 December 1969, in which it requested the Conference of the Committee on Disarmament,[b] *inter alia*, to consider effective methods of control against the use of radiological methods of warfare,

Aware of the potential hazards underlying any use of nuclear wastes which would constitute radiological warfare and its implications for regional and international security and in particular for the security of developing countries,

Desirous of promoting the implementation of paragraph 76 of the Final Document of the Tenth Special Session of the General Assembly, the first special session devoted to disarmament,

Aware also of the consideration of the question of dumping of radioactive wastes in the Conference on Disarmament during its 1989 session,

Recalling its resolution 43/75 Q of 7 December 1988, in which it requested the Conference on Disarmament to include in its report to the General Assembly at its forty-fourth session the developments in the ongoing negotiations on this subject,

Recalling also its resolution 43/75 T of 7 December 1988, in which it requested the Secretary-General, *inter alia*, "to prepare a report, in consultation with relevant international organizations, on the dumping of radioactive wastes in all its aspects in Africa, including all steps taken or envisaged to monitor, control and put a halt to such activities",

Having considered the report of the Secretary-General on the dumping of radioactive wastes,

1. *Takes note* of the report of the Secretary-General;

2. *Takes note also* of the part of the report of the Conference on Disarmament relating to the dumping of radioactive wastes;

3. *Expresses grave concern* regarding any use of nuclear waste that would constitute radiological warfare and have grave implications for the national security of all States;

4. *Calls upon* all States to take appropriate measures with a view to preventing any dumping of nuclear wastes that would infringe upon the sovereignty of States;

5. *Requests* the Conference on Disarmament to continue to take into account, in the ongoing negotiations for a convention on the prohibition of radiological weapons, the deliberate employment of nuclear wastes to cause destruction, damage or injury by means of radiation produced by the decay of such material;

6. *Requests* the Secretary-General to transmit to the Conference on Disarmament all documents relating to the consideration of this item by the General Assembly at its forty-fourth session;

7. *Also requests* the Conference on Disarmament to include in its report to the General Assembly at its forty-fifth session the developments in the ongoing negotiations on this subject;

8. *Decides* to include in the provisional agenda of its forty-fifth session an item entitled "Prohibition of the dumping of radioactive wastes".

---

[b]The Committee on Disarmament was redesignated the Conference on Disarmament as from 7 February 1984.

General Assembly resolution 44/116 R

15 December 1989   Meeting 81   150-0-4 (recorded vote)

Approved by First Committee (A/44/785) without vote, 17 November (meeting 41); draft by Kenya, for African Group, and Romania (A/C.1/44/L.55/Rev.1); agenda item 63 *(n)*.

Meeting numbers. GA 44th session: 1st Committee 3-25, 41; plenary 81.

Recorded vote in Assembly as follows:

In favour: Afghanistan, Albania, Algeria, Angola, Antigua and Barbuda, Argentina, Australia, Austria, Bahamas, Bahrain, Bangladesh, Barbados, Benin, Bhutan, Bolivia, Botswana, Brazil, Brunei Darussalam, Bulgaria, Burkina Faso, Burundi, Byelorussian SSR, Cameroon, Canada, Cape Verde, Central African Republic, Chad, Chile, China, Colombia, Congo, Costa Rica, Côte d'Ivoire, Cuba, Cyprus, Czechoslovakia, Democratic Kampuchea, Democratic Yemen, Denmark, Djibouti, Dominica, Dominican Republic, Ecuador, Egypt, El Salvador, Ethiopia, Fiji, Finland, Gabon, Gambia, German Democratic Republic, Ghana, Greece, Grenada, Guatemala, Guinea, Guinea-Bissau, Guyana, Haiti, Honduras, Hungary, Iceland, India, Indonesia, Iran, Iraq, Ireland, Israel, Jamaica, Japan, Jordan, Kenya, Kuwait, Lao People's Democratic Republic, Lebanon, Lesotho, Liberia, Libyan Arab Jamahiriya, Luxembourg, Madagascar, Malawi, Malaysia, Maldives, Mali, Malta, Mauritania, Mauritius, Mexico, Mongolia, Morocco, Mozambique, Myanmar, Nepal, Netherlands, New Zealand, Nicaragua, Niger, Nigeria, Norway, Oman, Pakistan, Panama, Papua New Guinea, Paraguay, Peru, Philippines, Poland, Portugal, Qatar, Romania, Rwanda, Saint Kitts and Nevis, Saint Lucia, Saint Vincent and the Grenadines, Samoa, Sao Tome and Principe, Saudi Arabia, Senegal, Seychelles, Sierra Leone, Singapore, Solomon Islands, Somalia, Spain, Sri Lanka, Sudan, Suriname, Swaziland, Sweden, Syrian Arab Republic, Togo, Trinidad and Tobago, Tunisia, Turkey, Uganda, Ukrainian SSR, USSR, United Arab Emirates, United Kingdom, United Republic of Tanzania, United States, Uruguay, Vanuatu, Venezuela, Viet Nam, Yemen, Yugoslavia, Zaire, Zambia, Zimbabwe.

Against: None.

Abstaining: Belgium, France, Germany, Federal Republic of, Italy.

Advanced technology

In response to a 1988 General Assembly request,[36] the Secretary-General, in a September 1989 report with later addenda,[37] described action he had taken to follow scientific and technological developments and to evaluate their impact on international security. A consultative meeting was held (New York, 31 May 1989) to assist him in identifying the broad areas of scientific and technological developments which might have potential military applications. He planned to invite qualified consultants to prepare individual assessments covering information technology, biotechnology, materials technology, space technology and nuclear technology. Those assessments would be discussed by a wider group of experts and the outcome included in a report to the Assembly in 1990.

The Secretary-General presented the views and proposals of seven Member States on the establishment of panels at the national level to monitor and evaluate such scientific and technological developments, as well as evaluations of the panels.

GENERAL ASSEMBLY ACTION

On 15 December 1989, on the recommendation of the First Committee, the General Assembly adopted **resolution 44/118 A** by recorded vote.

Scientific and technological developments and their impact on international security

The General Assembly,

Recalling its resolution 43/77 A of 7 December 1988,

Noting with concern the potential in technological advances for application to military purposes, which could lead to the emergence of an entirely new class of weapon systems,

Recognizing that such a development will have a negative impact on the security environment and cause a major setback to disarmament efforts,

Stressing, in this context, the importance of preventing this negative impact by effectively addressing this problem and ensuring that scientific and technological developments are harnessed for the common benefit of mankind,

Recognizing also the interests of the international community in the subject and the need to follow closely such developments,

Recognizing further that scientific and technological developments can have both civilian and military applications and that progress in science and technology for civilian applications needs to be maintained and encouraged,

Emphasizing that the proposal contained in resolution 43/77 A is without prejudice to research and development efforts being undertaken for peaceful purposes,

Having examined the report of the Secretary-General on this question,

1. *Takes note* of the preliminary work undertaken by the Secretary-General to follow future scientific and technological developments, especially those which have potential military applications, and to evaluate their impact on international security;

2. *Requests* the Secretary-General to conclude this work so that a report can be submitted to the General Assembly at its forty-fifth session;

3. *Notes* that the process of establishing national expert panels by Member States has already begun;

4. *Encourages* Member States to participate by communicating their views to the Secretary-General, and invites them to establish panels at the national level to monitor and evaluate developments;

5. *Decides* to include in the provisional agenda of its forty-fifth session the item entitled ''Scientific and technological developments and their impact on international security''.

General Assembly resolution 44/118 A

15 December 1989   Meeting 81   137-3-14 (recorded vote)

Approved by First Committee (A/44/787) by recorded vote (113-3-15), 17 November (meeting 40); 10-nation draft (A/C.1/44/L.41/Rev.2); agenda item 65.
Sponsors: Byelorussian SSR, Czechoslovakia, German Democratic Republic, Hungary, India, Indonesia, Poland, Romania, Sri Lanka, Venezuela.
Meeting numbers. GA 44th session: 1st Committee 3-25, 31, 40; plenary 81.

Recorded vote in Assembly as follows:

In favour: Afghanistan, Albania, Algeria, Angola, Antigua and Barbuda, Argentina, Australia, Austria, Bahamas, Bahrain, Bangladesh, Barbados, Benin, Bhutan, Bolivia, Botswana, Brazil, Bulgaria, Burkina Faso, Burundi, Byelorussian SSR, Cameroon, Cape Verde, Central African Republic, Chad, Chile, China, Colombia, Congo, Costa Rica, Côte d'Ivoire, Cuba, Cyprus, Czechoslovakia, Democratic Kampuchea, Democratic Yemen, Djibouti, Dominica, Dominican Republic, Ecuador, Egypt, El Salvador, Ethiopia, Fiji, Finland, Gabon, Gambia, German Democratic Republic, Ghana, Grenada, Guatemala, Guinea, Guinea-Bissau, Guyana, Haiti, Honduras, Hungary, India, Indonesia, Iran, Iraq, Ireland, Italy,* Jamaica, Jordan, Kenya, Kuwait, Lao People's Democratic Republic, Lebanon, Lesotho, Liberia, Libyan Arab Jamahiriya, Madagascar, Malawi, Malaysia, Maldives, Mali, Malta, Mauritania, Mauritius, Mexico, Mongolia, Morocco, Mozambique, Myanmar, Nepal, New Zealand, Nicaragua, Niger, Nigeria, Oman, Pakistan, Panama, Papua New Guinea, Paraguay, Peru, Philippines, Poland, Qatar, Romania, Rwanda, Saint Kitts and Nevis, Saint Lucia, Saint Vincent and the Grenadines, Samoa, Sao Tome and Principe, Saudi Arabia, Senegal, Seychelles, Sierra Leone, Singapore, Solomon Islands, Somalia, Sri Lanka, Sudan, Suriname, Swaziland, Sweden, Syrian Arab Republic, Thailand, Togo, Trinidad and Tobago, Tunisia, Uganda, Ukrainian SSR, USSR, United Arab Emirates, United Republic of Tanzania, Uruguay, Vanuatu, Venezuela, Viet Nam, Yemen, Yugoslavia, Zaire, Zambia, Zimbabwe.

Against: France, United Kingdom, United States.

Abstaining: Belgium, Canada, Denmark, Germany, Federal Republic of, Greece, Iceland, Israel, Japan, Luxembourg, Netherlands, Norway, Portugal, Spain, Turkey.

*Later advised the Secretariat it had intended to abstain.

On the same date and on a recommendation of the First Committee, the General Assembly adopted **resolution 44/118 B**, also by recorded vote.

Science and technology for disarmament
The General Assembly,

Considering that science and technology can profoundly contribute to solving the problems of mankind, especially to promoting its social and economic development,

Noting the interest of the international community in the peaceful uses of scientific and technological achievements,

Recognizing the vast possibilities that scientific and technological progress offers for supporting disarmament negotiations and implementing their results, *inter alia,* in the fields of verification of compliance with agreements on arms limitation and disarmament as well as conversion of military industry to civilian production,

Welcoming respective activities undertaken so far in this area by States and national and international scientific and technological institutions,

Taking into account that scientifically and technologically more advanced States bear a special responsibility for disseminating information on and promoting the application of science and technology in the field of disarmament,

Considering the need for an intensification and extension of such activities, as well as international co-operation, with a view to using scientific and technological achievements for disarmament-related purposes, *inter alia,* in the fields of verification of compliance with agreements on arms limitation and disarmament, application of technologies for improved means of verification and conversion of military industry to civilian production,

1. *Takes note* of national and international activities to use scientific and technological achievements for disarmament-related purposes;

2. *Calls upon* Member States and intergovernmental and non-governmental organizations to intensify and extend such activities, to develop international co-operation in this area and to keep the United Nations informed about progress in this field;

3. *Decides* to include in the provisional agenda of its forty-fifth session an item entitled ''Science and technology for disarmament''.

General Assembly resolution 44/118 B

15 December 1989   Meeting 81   154-0-1 (recorded vote)

Approved by First Committee (A/44/787) by recorded vote (133-0-1), 16 November (meeting 39); 4-nation draft (A/C.1/44/L.46/Rev.1); agenda item 65.
Sponsors: Byelorussian SSR, Czechoslovakia, German Democratic Republic, Mexico.
Meeting numbers. GA 44th session: 1st Committee 3-25, 31, 39; plenary 81.

Recorded vote in Assembly as follows:

In favour: Afghanistan, Albania, Algeria, Angola, Antigua and Barbuda, Argentina, Australia, Austria, Bahamas, Bahrain, Bangladesh, Barbados, Belgium, Benin, Bhutan, Bolivia, Botswana, Brazil, Brunei Darussalam, Bulgaria, Burkina Faso, Burundi, Byelorussian SSR, Cameroon, Canada, Cape Verde, Central African Republic, Chad, Chile, China, Colombia, Congo, Costa Rica, Côte d'Ivoire, Cuba, Cyprus, Czechoslovakia, Democratic Kampuchea, Democratic Yemen, Denmark, Djibouti, Dominica, Dominican Republic, Ecuador, Egypt, El Salvador, Ethiopia, Fiji, Finland, France, Gabon, Gambia, German Democratic Republic, Germany, Federal Republic of, Ghana, Greece, Grenada, Guatemala, Guinea, Guinea-Bissau, Guyana, Haiti, Honduras, Hungary, Iceland, India, Indonesia, Iran, Iraq, Ireland, Israel, Italy, Jamaica, Japan, Jordan, Kenya, Kuwait, Lao People's Democratic Republic, Lebanon, Lesotho, Liberia, Libyan Arab Jamahiriya, Luxembourg,

Madagascar, Malawi, Malaysia, Maldives, Mali, Malta, Mauritania, Mauritius, Mexico, Mongolia, Morocco, Mozambique, Myanmar, Nepal, Netherlands, New Zealand, Nicaragua, Niger, Nigeria, Norway, Oman, Pakistan, Panama, Papua New Guinea, Paraguay, Peru, Philippines, Poland, Portugal, Qatar, Romania, Rwanda, Saint Kitts and Nevis, Saint Lucia, Saint Vincent and the Grenadines, Samoa, Sao Tome and Principe, Saudi Arabia, Senegal, Seychelles, Sierra Leone, Singapore, Solomon Islands, Somalia, Spain, Sri Lanka, Sudan, Suriname, Swaziland, Sweden, Syrian Arab Republic, Thailand, Togo, Trinidad and Tobago, Tunisia, Turkey, Uganda, Ukrainian SSR, USSR, United Arab Emirates, United Kingdom, United Republic of Tanzania, Uruguay, Vanuatu, Venezuela, Viet Nam, Yemen, Yugoslavia, Zaire, Zambia, Zimbabwe.
Against: None.
Abstaining: United States.

Conventional weapons

Conventional disarmament

Disarmament Commission consideration. Working Group III, established by the Disarmament Commission on 8 May 1989 to deal with the question of conventional disarmament, held 13 meetings between 10 and 26 May.[38] Within that general topic, the Commission was called on, pursuant to a 1988 General Assembly resolution,[39] to take into account arms transfers in all their aspects and possible measures to monitor and regulate them. Working papers on arms transfers were submitted by China[40] and Cosa Rica,[41] while a paper on a variety of measures was submitted by Nigeria.[42] The Working Group was unable to reach agreement on a complete text and therefore submitted a procedural consensus report to the Commission,[38] proposing that the Commission recommend to the Assembly that it continue its work in 1990.

Report of the Secretary-General. In an August report with later addenda, the Secretary-General presented the views of 11 Member States (one on behalf of EC members) concerning arms transfers and measures to regulate and control them.[43]

GENERAL ASSEMBLY ACTION

On 15 December 1989, the General Assembly, on the recommendation of the First Committee, adopted **resolution 44/116 F** without vote.

Conventional disarmament
The General Assembly,
Recalling its resolution 43/75 D of 7 December 1988,
Taking into account the decisions and recommendations appearing in the Final Document of the Tenth Special Session of the General Assembly, particularly in paragraph 114,
Also taking into account that conventional disarmament is a necessary part of the disarmament process,
Having examined the report of the Disarmament Commission,
1. *Takes note with satisfaction* of the extensive discussion of the question of conventional disarmament during the 1989 session of the Disarmament Commission;
2. *Recommends* that the report should provide a basis for further deliberations on the subject by the Disarmament Commission;

3. *Requests* the Disarmament Commission to continue at its 1990 session the substantive consideration of issues related to conventional disarmament and to report to the General Assembly at its forty-fifth session with a view to facilitating possible measures in the field of conventional arms reduction and disarmament;
4. *Also requests* the Disarmament Commission for this purpose to include in the agenda for its 1990 session the item entitled "Substantive consideration of issues related to conventional disarmament";
5. *Decides* to include in the provisional agenda of its forty-fifth session the item entitled "Conventional disarmament".

General Assembly resolution 44/116 F

15 December 1989   Meeting 81   Adopted without vote

Approved by First Committee (A/44/785) without vote, 16 November (meeting 38); draft by Denmark (A/C.1/44/L.20/Rev.1); agenda item 63 (d).
Meeting numbers. GA 44th session: 1st Committee 3-25, 38; plenary 81.

Also on 15 December and on the First Committee's recommendation, the General Assembly adopted **resolution 44/116 C** without vote.

Conventional disarmament
The General Assembly,
Reaffirming the determination to save succeeding generations from the scourge of war as expressed in the Preamble to the Charter of the United Nations,
Recalling the Final Document of the Tenth Special Session of the General Assembly, and particularly its paragraph 81, which provides that, together with negotiations on nuclear disarmament measures, the limitation and gradual reduction of armed forces and conventional weapons should be resolutely pursued within the framework of progress towards general and complete disarmament, and which stresses that States with the largest military arsenals have a special responsibility in pursuing the process of conventional armaments reductions,
Also recalling that in the same document it is stated, *inter alia,* that priorities in disarmament negotiations shall be: nuclear weapons; other weapons of mass destruction, including chemical weapons; conventional weapons, including any which may be deemed to be excessively injurious or to have indiscriminate effects; and reduction of armed forces, and that it stresses that nothing should preclude States from conducting negotiations on all priority items concurrently,
Further recalling that in the same document it is stated that effective measures of nuclear disarmament and the prevention of nuclear war have the highest priority, and that real progress in the field of nuclear disarmament could create an atmosphere conducive to progress in conventional disarmament on a world-wide basis,
Aware of the dangers to world peace and security originating from, and the loss in human life and property caused by, wars and conflicts fought with conventional weapons, as well as of their possible escalation into a nuclear war in regions with a high concentration of conventional and nuclear weapons,
Also aware that with the advance in science and technology, conventional weapons tend to become increasingly lethal and destructive and that conventional armaments consume large amounts of resources,
Believing that resources released through disarmament, including conventional disarmament, can be used for

the social and economic development of people of all countries, particularly the developing countries,

Noting that the ongoing conventional disarmament negotiations in Europe have gained increasing importance,

Bearing in mind its resolution 36/97 A of 9 December 1981 and the *Study on Conventional Disarmament* conducted in accordance with that resolution, as well as its resolutions 41/59 C and 41/59 G of 3 December 1986, 42/38 E and 42/38 G of 30 November 1987 and 43/75 D and 43/75 F of 7 December 1988, and the consideration by the Disarmament Commission at its 1989 session of the question of conventional disarmament,

Bearing in mind also the efforts made to promote conventional disarmament and the related proposals and suggestions, as well as the initiatives taken by various countries in this regard,

1. *Reaffirms* the importance of the efforts aimed at resolutely pursuing the limitation and gradual reduction of armed forces and conventional weapons within the framework of progress towards general and complete disarmament;

2. *Believes* that the military forces of all countries should not be used other than for the purpose of self-defence;

3. *Welcomes* the new negotiation on conventional armed forces in Europe;

4. *Urges* the countries with the largest military arsenals, which bear a special responsibility in pursuing the process of conventional armaments reductions, and the States members of the two major military alliances to continue their intensive negotiations on conventional armaments, through appropriate forums, with a view to reaching early agreement on the establishment of a stable and secure balance of conventional armaments and forces at lower levels under effective international control in their respective regions, particularly in Europe, which has the largest concentration of arms and forces in the world;

5. *Encourages* all States, while taking into account the need to protect security and maintain necessary defensive capabilities, to intensify their efforts and take, either on their own or in a regional context, appropriate steps to promote progress in conventional disarmament and enhance peace and security;

6. *Requests* the Disarmament Commission to consider further, at its 1990 substantive session, issues related to conventional disarmament;

7. *Decides* to include in the provisional agenda of its forty-fifth session the item entitled ''Conventional disarmament''.

General Assembly resolution 44/116 C

15 December 1989   Meeting 81   Adopted without vote

Approved by First Committee (A/44/785) without vote, 13 November (meeting 35); draft by China (A/C.1/44/L.13/Rev.1); agenda 63 *(d)*.
Meeting numbers. GA 44th session: 1st Committee 3-25, 31, 35; plenary 81.

On the same date and on a recommendation of the First Committee, the Assembly adopted **resolution 44/116 N** by recorded vote.

International arms transfers

The General Assembly,

Taking note of its resolution 43/75 I of 7 December 1988,

Noting the views of Member States submitted to the Secretary-General in the past year on this issue,

Looking forward to the United Nations study on international arms transfers and the report of the study group to be submitted to the General Assembly at its forty-sixth session,

Also noting the substantive deliberations initiated within the Disarmament Commission on matters related to the issue of international arms transfers,

1. *Invites* all Member States that have not yet done so to make available to the Secretary-General their views and proposals on the matters contained in paragraphs 1 and 2 of resolution 43/75 I;

2. *Requests* the Disarmament Commission to continue its deliberation on the matters contained in the above-mentioned resolution during its 1990 session under the item of conventional disarmament;

3. *Requests* the Secretary-General to continue to make available within the framework of resolution 43/75 I all relevant information on this matter;

4. *Decides* to include in the provisional agenda of its forty-fifth session the item entitled ''International arms transfers''.

General Assembly resolution 44/116 N

15 December 1989   Meeting 81   143-0-12 (recorded vote)

Approved by First Committee (A/44/785) by recorded vote (95-0-31), 16 November (meeting 38); 28-nation draft (A/C.1/44/L.37); amended in Assembly by Colombia (A/44/L.59); agenda item 63 *(h)*.
Sponsors: Australia, Austria, Bahamas, Bolivia, Bulgaria, Cameroon, Canada, Colombia, Costa Rica, Dominican Republic, Ecuador, El Salvador, Fiji, Germany, Federal Republic of, Greece, Guatemala, Honduras, Italy, Netherlands, Nigeria, Norway, Paraguay, Peru, Philippines, Samoa, Singapore, Sweden, United Kingdom.
Meeting numbers. GA 44th session: 1st Committee 3-25, 29, 38; plenary 81.

Recorded vote in Assembly as follows:

In favour: Albania, Algeria, Antigua and Barbuda, Argentina, Australia, Austria, Bahamas, Bahrain, Bangladesh, Barbados, Belgium, Benin, Bhutan, Bolivia, Brazil, Brunei Darussalam, Bulgaria, Burkina Faso, Burundi, Byelorussian SSR, Cameroon, Canada, Cape Verde, Central African Republic, Chad, Chile, China, Colombia, Congo, Costa Rica, Côte d'Ivoire, Cuba, Cyprus, Czechoslovakia, Democratic Kampuchea, Democratic Yemen, Denmark, Djibouti, Dominica, Dominican Republic, Ecuador, Egypt, El Salvador, Fiji, Finland, France, Gabon, Gambia, German Democratic Republic, Germany, Federal Republic of, Ghana, Greece, Grenada, Guatemala, Guinea, Guinea-Bissau, Guyana, Haiti, Honduras, Hungary, Iceland, Indonesia, Ireland, Israel, Italy, Jamaica, Japan, Jordan, Kenya, Kuwait, Lao People's Democratic Republic, Lebanon, Lesotho, Liberia, Libyan Arab Jamahiriya, Luxembourg, Madagascar, Malawi, Malaysia, Maldives, Mali, Malta, Mauritania, Mauritius, Mexico, Mongolia, Morocco, Mozambique, Myanmar, Nepal, Netherlands, New Zealand, Nicaragua, Niger, Nigeria, Norway, Oman, Panama, Papua New Guinea, Paraguay, Peru, Philippines, Poland, Portugal, Qatar, Romania, Rwanda, Saint Kitts and Nevis, Saint Lucia, Saint Vincent and the Grenadines, Samoa, Sao Tome and Principe, Saudi Arabia, Senegal, Seychelles, Sierra Leone, Singapore, Solomon Islands, Somalia, Spain, Sri Lanka, Sudan, Suriname, Swaziland, Sweden, Syrian Arab Republic, Thailand, Togo, Trinidad and Tobago, Tunisia, Turkey, Ukrainian SSR, USSR, United Arab Emirates, United Kingdom, United States, Uruguay, Vanuatu, Venezuela, Viet Nam, Yemen, Yugoslavia, Zaire.
Against: None.
Abstaining: Afghanistan, Angola, Botswana, Ethiopia, India, Iran, Iraq, Pakistan, Uganda, United Republic of Tanzania, Zambia, Zimbabwe.

In the Assembly, prior to voting on the text as a whole, the sponsors called for a vote on a series of amendments, which were adopted by a recorded vote of 141 to none, with 6 abstentions.

Regional approach to conventional disarmament

In accordance with a 1987 General Assembly request,[44] the Secretary-General, in October 1989, described activities for regional disarmament taken by the United Nations Department for Disarmament Affairs (DDA) and the United Nations Institute for Disarmament Research (UNIDIR).[45] DDA organized seminars on verification, African disarmament and security, the Indian Ocean as a zone of peace, and multilateral confidence-building measures and the prevention of war. UNIDIR published two reports on conventional disarmament in Europe and one on confidence-building measures in Africa, and helped organize a conference on problems and perspectives of conventional disarmament in Europe (Vienna, 23-25 January 1989).

GENERAL ASSEMBLY ACTION

On 15 December 1989, the General Assembly, on the recommendation of the First Committee, adopted **resolution 44/117 B** without vote.

Regional disarmament

The General Assembly,

Recalling its resolutions 37/100 F of 13 December 1982, 38/73 J of 15 December 1983, 39/63 F of 12 December 1984, 40/94 A of 12 December 1985, 41/59 M of 3 December 1986 and 42/39 E of 30 November 1987, relating to regional disarmament,

Reaffirming that all States, in particular nuclear-weapon States and other militarily significant States, have the responsibility of halting and reversing the arms race,

Considering that regional disarmament measures enable all States to contribute to the general process of arms reduction and disarmament,

Confirming the importance and potential effectiveness of regional disarmament measures taken at the initiative of the region and with the participation of all the States concerned, in that they can contribute to the realization of general and complete disarmament under strict and effective international control and therefore to security and stability,

Stressing that any regional disarmament enterprise must take into account the specific conditions characteristic of each region,

Also stressing that it is for the countries themselves of a region to take appropriate initiatives in common and to prepare agreements that will allow the achievement of regional disarmament,

Further stressing that disarmament efforts in a region cannot be isolated either from the disarmament efforts in other regions or from global disarmament efforts both in the nuclear and conventional field,

Taking into account Chapter VIII of the Charter of the United Nations and the decisions and recommendations appearing in the Final Document of the Tenth Special Session of the General Assembly, particularly in paragraph 114,

Aware of those studies which have already been carried out and of the views of States which are of interest for regional disarmament,

1. *Expresses its thanks* to the Secretary-General for his report submitted pursuant to resolution 42/39 E;

2. *Notes with concern* that conflicts continue to threaten regional and global peace and security but that prospects are emerging for the peaceful settlement of certain regional conflicts;

3. *Notes with satisfaction* the importance of the regional measures that have already been adopted and the regional efforts undertaken in the field of nuclear and conventional disarmament;

4. *Welcomes* the progress made since its forty-second session with respect to:

(*a*) The process initiated by the agreement on "Procedures for the establishment of a firm and lasting peace in Central America" signed by the Central American Presidents at Guatemala City on 7 August 1987 at the Esquipulas II summit meeting in order to arrive at a lasting peace in that region and that has resulted in the agreements concluded at Tela, Honduras, on 7 August 1989;[a]

(*b*) The resumption, at Vienna, of negotiations in the area of confidence- and security-building measures, as well as the new negotiation on conventional armed forces in Europe, both within the framework of the process of the Conference on Security and Co-operation in Europe, which have been characterized by rapid progress since they began in March 1989;

5. *Encourages* all States to consider and develop, as far as possible, regional solutions in the matter of arms reduction and disarmament;

6. *Invites* all States and regional institutions associated with regional disarmament efforts to report thereon to the Secretary-General;

7. *Requests* the United Nations to lend its assistance to States and regional institutions that may request it, with the view to the institution of measures within the framework of an effort for regional disarmament;

8. *Requests* the Secretary-General to keep the General Assembly regularly informed of the implementation of resolutions on regional disarmament and of the activities which the Secretariat, in particular the Department for Disarmament Affairs, and the United Nations Institute for Disarmament Research are conducting in the field of regional disarmament;

9. *Decides* to include in the provisional agenda of its forty-sixth session the item entitled "Regional disarmament: report of the Secretary-General".

---

[a]A/44/451-S/20778.

General Assembly resolution 44/117 B

15 December 1989   Meeting 81   Adopted without vote

Approved by First Committee (A/44/786) without vote, 13 November (meeting 35); 26-nation draft (A/C.1/44/L.27); agenda item 64 *(a)*.
Sponsors: Austria, Bangladesh, Belgium, Bulgaria, Canada, Czechoslovakia, Denmark, France, German Democratic Republic, Germany, Federal Republic of, Greece, Ireland, Italy, Luxembourg, Malawi, Malta, Netherlands, New Zealand, Norway, Poland, Portugal, Romania, Spain, USSR, United Kingdom, Zaire.
Meeting numbers. GA 44th session: 1st Committee 3-25, 35; plenary 81.

Also on 15 December, the General Assembly, on the recommendation of the First Committee, adopted **resolution 44/116 S** by recorded vote.

Conventional disarmament on a regional scale

The General Assembly,

Recalling its resolutions 40/94 A of 12 December 1985, 41/59 M of 3 December 1986, 42/38 N of 30 November 1987 and 43/75 S of 7 December 1988,

Taking note of the final documents of the Ninth Conference of Heads of State or Government of Non-Aligned Countries, held at Belgrade from 4 to 7 September 1989,[a]

Reiterating the primary responsibility of nuclear-weapon States and militarily significant States for halting and reversing the arms race, particularly the nuclear-arms race,

Convinced that effective measures of nuclear disarmament and the prevention of nuclear war have the highest priority,

Drawing attention to the fact that, together with negotiations on nuclear disarmament measures, negotiations should be carried out on the balanced reduction of armed forces and on conventional disarmament, based on the principle of equal and undiminished security of the parties with a view to promoting or enhancing stability at a lower level of military forces, taking into account the need of all States to protect their security,

Aware that, as a consequence of the continuing military application of scientific and technological developments, conventional weapons have become more lethal and destructive,

Taking into account the fact that conventional weapons consume large amounts of resources, especially in militarily significant States, which could be utilized for the social and economic development of the people of all countries, particularly the developing countries,

Affirming that regional and subregional disarmament processes that take into account the characteristics of each region, as well as the views of all parties concerned, and are implemented in accordance with the principles and norms embodied in the Charter of the United Nations enhance and complement global disarmament efforts,

Noting with satisfaction the positive trend towards the peaceful settlement of various regional and subregional conflicts and the important role played in that regard by the United Nations,

1. *Welcomes* the initiatives towards arms limitation and disarmament undertaken jointly or unilaterally by some countries at the regional and subregional levels, as well as the systematic implementation of confidence-building measures, limitations of the acquisition of conventional weapons and the reduction of military spending, with a view to achieving equal and undiminished security at a lower level of armaments, as well as to allocating the resources thus released to the social and economic development of the people of all countries, particularly the developing countries;

2. *Again expresses its firm support* for the United Nations system, and for the Secretary-General in particular, in the efforts to find solutions to conflict situations, thereby reaffirming a fundamental role of the United Nations in promoting peace and disarmament, and for the strict observance of the principles and norms embodied in the Charter of the United Nations;

3. *Urges* all States, in particular the nuclear-weapon States and militarily significant States, to intensify their efforts in the negotiation and implementation, in appropriate forums, of regional and subregional disarmament and arms limitation measures, taking into account their particular responsibility in this matter and the principle of equal and undiminished security for all parties, aimed at enhancing international peace and security;

4. *Requests* the United Nations, in conformity with its mandate to promote international peace and security, to provide assistance to States that might request it with a view to establishing disarmament measures at the regional and subregional levels;

5. *Appeals* to all States to facilitate the progress of regional disarmament, refraining from any action, including the use or threat of use of force against the sovereignty and territorial integrity of States and intervention or interference in internal affairs of States, that might hinder the achievement of this objective;

6. *Invites* all Member States to convey to the Secretary-General their views on ways and means aimed at strengthening regional and subregional disarmament and arms limitation efforts, taking into account recent developments that have taken place in this sphere;

7. *Requests* the Secretary-General to submit a report to the General Assembly at its forty-fifth session on the implementation of the present resolution, taking into consideration the views expressed by Member States in accordance with paragraph 6 above;

8. *Decides* to include in the provisional agenda of its forty-fifth session the item entitled "Conventional disarmament on a regional scale".

---

[a]A/44/551-S/20870.

General Assembly resolution 44/116 S

15 December 1989   Meeting 81   119-1-31 (recorded vote)

Approved by First Committee (A/44/785) by recorded vote (98-1-31), 17 November (meeting 41); 15-nation draft (A/C.1/44/L.56/Rev.2); agenda item 63 *(m)*.

Sponsors: Bangladesh, Bolivia, Colombia, Costa Rica, Dominican Republic, Ecuador, Guatemala, Iran, Pakistan, Panama, Paraguay, Peru, Philippines, Romania, Uruguay.

Meeting numbers. GA 44th session: 1st Committee 3-25, 31, 41; plenary 81.

Recorded vote in Assembly as follows:

In favour: Algeria, Antigua and Barbuda, Argentina, Australia, Austria, Bahamas, Bangladesh, Barbados, Benin, Bhutan, Bolivia, Brazil, Brunei Darussalam, Bulgaria, Burkina Faso, Burundi, Byelorussian SSR, Cameroon, Cape Verde, Central African Republic, Chad, Chile, China, Colombia, Congo, Costa Rica, Côte d'Ivoire, Cyprus, Czechoslovakia, Democratic Kampuchea, Denmark, Djibouti, Dominica, Dominican Republic, Ecuador, Egypt, El Salvador, Fiji, Finland, Gabon, Gambia, German Democratic Republic, Ghana, Greece, Grenada, Guatemala, Guinea, Guinea-Bissau, Guyana, Haiti, Honduras, Hungary, Iceland, Indonesia, Iran, Ireland, Jamaica, Lao People's Democratic Republic, Lebanon, Lesotho, Liberia, Madagascar, Malawi, Malaysia, Maldives, Mali, Malta, Mauritania, Mauritius, Mexico, Mongolia, Morocco, Myanmar, Nepal, New Zealand, Nicaragua, Niger, Nigeria, Norway, Pakistan, Panama, Papua New Guinea, Paraguay, Peru, Philippines, Poland, Romania, Rwanda, Saint Kitts and Nevis, Saint Lucia, Saint Vincent and the Grenadines, Samoa, Sao Tome and Principe, Saudi Arabia, Senegal, Seychelles, Sierra Leone, Singapore, Solomon Islands, Somalia, Spain, Sri Lanka, Sudan, Suriname, Swaziland, Sweden, Thailand, Togo, Trinidad and Tobago, Tunisia, Turkey, Ukrainian SSR, USSR, Uruguay, Vanuatu, Venezuela, Yugoslavia, Zaire, Zambia.*

Against: United States.

Abstaining: Afghanistan, Angola, Bahrain, Belgium, Botswana, Canada, Cuba, Ethiopia, France, Germany, Federal Republic of, India, Iraq, Israel, Italy, Japan, Jordan, Kenya, Libyan Arab Jamahiriya, Luxembourg, Mozambique, Netherlands, Portugal, Qatar, Syrian Arab Republic, Uganda, United Arab Emirates, United Kingdom, United Republic of Tanzania, Viet Nam, Yemen, Zimbabwe.

*Later advised the Secretariat it had intended to abstain.

Europe

In January 1989, the "Group of 23" (representatives of the 16 members of the North Atlantic Treaty Organization—Belgium, Canada, Denmark, France, Federal Republic of Germany, Greece, Iceland, Italy, Luxembourg, Netherlands,

Norway, Portugal, Spain, Turkey, United Kingdom, United States—and seven members of the Warsaw Treaty Organization—Bulgaria, Czechoslovakia, German Democratic Republic, Hungary, Poland, Romania, USSR), which had met throughout 1988, completed their work on the mandate for the new Negotiation on Conventional Armed Forces in Europe (CFE).[46] The first four rounds of the CFE talks took place from 9 to 23 March, 5 May to 14 July, 7 September to 10 October and 10 November to 21 December.

In the area of conventional disarmament, the pace of change in the European region outside the CFE context was manifested by many and substantial unilateral cuts in armed forces and armaments, announced throughout the year by individual Eastern European States.

GENERAL ASSEMBLY ACTION

On 15 December 1989, the General Assembly, on the recommendation of the First Committee, adopted **resolution 44/116 I** without vote.

Confidence- and security-building measures and conventional disarmament in Europe

The General Assembly,

Determined to achieve progress in disarmament,

Recalling its resolution 43/75 P of 7 December 1988,

1. *Notes with satisfaction* the successful conclusion of the deliberations of the Vienna Follow-up Meeting of the Conference on Security and Co-operation in Europe;

2. *Welcomes* the opening of two negotiations in the framework of the process of the Conference on Security and Co-operation in Europe, one on the elaboration of new confidence- and security-building measures and the other on conventional armed forces in Europe;

3. *Also welcomes* the progress achieved so far in those negotiations, and expresses the hope that they will be successfully concluded at an early date.

General Assembly resolution 44/116 I

15 December 1989   Meeting 81   Adopted without vote

Approved by First Committee (A/44/785) without vote, 17 November (meeting 41);

14-nation draft (A/C.1/44/L.26/Rev.2); agenda item 63.

Sponsors: Austria, Belgium, Cyprus, Finland, France, German Democratic Republic, Germany, Federal Republic of, Greece, Hungary, Italy, Luxembourg, Poland, Sweden, Yugoslavia.

Meeting numbers. GA 44th session: 1st Committee 3-25, 41; plenary 81.

On the same date and on the First Committee's recommendation, the General Assembly adopted **resolution 44/116 U**, also without vote.

Contribution of confidence- and security-building measures to international peace and security

The General Assembly,

Mindful of the importance of confidence-building in the bilateral, regional and global context for the peaceful settlement of existing international problems and for the improvement and promotion of international relations based on justice, co-operation and solidarity,

Recognizing that commitment to confidence-building measures could significantly contribute to preparing for further progress in disarmament,

Recalling previous resolutions on the subject of confidence-building, in particular resolution 43/78 H of 7 December 1988,

1. *Welcomes* the implementation of confidence-building measures as contained in the Final Act of Helsinki and on that basis the positive experience gathered since 1987 with the implementation, by the thirty-five States participating in the Conference on Security and Co-operation in Europe, of the measures agreed at the Stockholm Conference on Confidence- and Security-building Measures and Disarmament in Europe;

2. *Expects* the ongoing Vienna negotiations on confidence- and security-building measures to build upon and expand the results already achieved at the Stockholm Conference with the aim of elaborating and adopting a new set of mutually complementary confidence- and security-building measures designed to reduce the risk of military confrontation in Europe;

3. *Reaffirms* its invitation to all States to consider the possible introduction of confidence-building measures in their particular regions and, where possible, on the basis of initiatives of the States of the region concerned, to negotiate on them in keeping with conditions and requirements prevailing in the respective region;

4. *Also welcomes* the consideration, *inter alia,* of confidence-building measures in United Nations regional disarmament workshops and in the United Nations regional centres for peace and disarmament in Africa, Asia and Latin America and the Caribbean.

General Assembly resolution 44/116 U

15 December 1989   Meeting 81   Adopted without vote

Approved by First Committee (A/44/785) without vote, 14 November (meeting 36); 32-nation draft (A/C.1/44/L.58/Rev.2); agenda item 63.

Sponsors: Australia, Austria, Belgium, Byelorussian SSR, Cameroon, Canada, Colombia, Denmark, Ecuador, Finland, France, Gabon, German Democratic Republic, Germany, Federal Republic of, Greece, Hungary, Ireland, Italy, Luxembourg, Nepal, Netherlands, Norway, Pakistan, Peru, Poland, Portugal, Spain, Sweden, Togo, Turkey, USSR, United Kingdom.

Meeting numbers. GA 44th session: 1st Committee 3-25, 30, 36; plenary 81.

Convention on excessively injurious conventional weapons and its Protocols

As at 31 December 1989,[47] the number of States parties to the Convention on Prohibitions or Restrictions on the Use of Certain Conventional Weapons Which May Be Deemed to Be Excessively Injurious or to Have Indiscriminate Effects and its three Protocols (dealing with non-detectable fragments; mines, booby traps and other devices; and incendiary weapons)[48] increased to 32. During the year, Benin acceded to the Convention and Liechtenstein ratified it. The Convention and Protocols had entered into force in 1983.[49]

The Secretary-General submitted, in response to a 1988 General Assembly request,[50] a report containing information on action taken with respect to the Convention and Protocols between 1 September 1988 and 31 August 1989.[51]

On 15 December, by **decision 44/430**, the Assembly took note of the Secretary-General's report and decided to include in the provisional agenda of its forty-fifth (1990) session the item entitled "Convention on Prohibitions or Restrictions on the Use of Certain Conventional Weapons Which May Be Deemed to Be Excessively Injurious or to Have Indiscriminate Effects".

Prevention of an arms race in outer space

The Conference on Disarmament considered the item on preventing an arms race in outer space from 6 to 10 March and from 3 to 7 July 1989.[3]

The *Ad Hoc* Committee on the topic, re-established by the Conference on 9 March, held 17 meetings between 14 March and 24 August to examine and identify relevant issues.

New documents submitted dealing with the legal aspects of the item included: a survey of relevant international law, by Bulgaria, the German Democratic Republic and Hungary;[52] a document on legal problems raised by the militarization of outer space, by Chile;[53] and a proposed amendment to the 1967 Treaty on Principles Governing the Activities of States in the Exploration and Use of Outer Space, including the Moon and Other Celestial Bodies, by Peru.[54] Documents relating to verification were transmitted to the Conference by the German Democratic Republic[55] and by France.[56]

In its report to the Conference,[57] the *Ad Hoc* Committee concluded that there had been continued general recognition of the importance and urgency of preventing an arms race in outer space. It noted the significant role that the existing legal régime played in preventing an arms race in that environment and the need to consolidate and reinforce that régime. The Committee acknowledged the importance of strict compliance with existing agreements, both bilateral and multilateral. It recommended that it be re-established with an adequate mandate at the beginning of the 1990 session.

GENERAL ASSEMBLY ACTION

On 15 December 1989, the General Assembly, on the recommendation of the First Committee, adopted **resolution 44/112** by recorded vote.

Prevention of an arms race in outer space
The General Assembly,

Inspired by the great prospects opening up before mankind as a result of man's entry into outer space,

Recognizing the common interest of all mankind in the exploration and use of outer space for peaceful purposes,

Reaffirming that the exploration and use of outer space, including the Moon and other celestial bodies, shall be carried out for the benefit and in the interest of all countries, irrespective of their degree of economic or scientific development, and shall be the province of all mankind,

Reaffirming also the will of all States that the exploration and use of outer space, including the Moon and other celestial bodies, shall be for peaceful purposes,

Recalling the obligation of all States, in accordance with the Charter of the United Nations, to refrain from the threat or use of force, including in their space activities,

Recalling also that the States parties to the Treaty on Principles Governing the Activities of States in the Exploration and Use of Outer Space, including the Moon and Other Celestial Bodies have undertaken, in article III, to carry on activities in the exploration and use of outer space, including the Moon and other celestial bodies, in accordance with international law and the Charter of the United Nations, in the interests of maintaining international peace and security and promoting international co-operation and understanding,

Reaffirming, in particular, article IV of the above-mentioned Treaty, which stipulates that States parties to the Treaty undertake not to place in orbit around the Earth any objects carrying nuclear weapons or any other kinds of weapons of mass destruction, install such weapons on celestial bodies or station such weapons in outer space in any other manner,

Reaffirming also paragraph 80 of the Final Document of the Tenth Special Session of the General Assembly, in which it is stated that in order to prevent an arms race in outer space further measures should be taken and appropriate international negotiations held in accordance with the spirit of the Treaty,

Noting its resolutions 36/97 C and 36/99 of 9 December 1981, as well as resolutions 37/83 of 9 December 1982, 37/99 D of 13 December 1982, 38/70 of 15 December 1983, 39/59 of 12 December 1984, 40/87 of 12 December 1985, 41/53 of 3 December 1986, 42/33 of 30 November 1987 and 43/70 of 7 December 1988 and the relevant paragraphs of the final document on international security and disarmament adopted by the Ninth Conference of Heads of State or Government of Non-Aligned Countries, held at Belgrade from 4 to 7 September 1989,[a]

Recognizing the importance and urgency of preventing an arms race in outer space and the readiness of all States to contribute to that common objective,

Gravely concerned at the danger posed to all mankind by an arms race in outer space and, in particular, by developments that could further undermine international peace and security and retard the pursuit of general and complete disarmament,

Encouraged by the widespread interest expressed by Member States in the course of negotiations on and following the adoption of the above-mentioned Treaty in ensuring that the exploration and use of outer space should be for peaceful purposes, and taking note of proposals submitted to the General Assembly at its tenth special session and at its regular sessions and to the Conference on Disarmament,

Noting the grave concern expressed by the Second United Nations Conference on the Exploration and Peaceful Uses of Outer Space at the extension of an arms race into outer space and the recommendations made to the competent organs of the United Nations, in particular the General Assembly, and also to the Committee on Disarmament,[b]

Noting also that in 1989 the *Ad Hoc* Committee on the Prevention of an Arms Race in Outer Space, taking into

---

[a]A/44/551-S/20870.

[b]The Committee on Disarmament was redesignated the Conference on Disarmament as from 7 February 1984.

account its previous efforts since its establishment, undertook the examination and identification of various issues, existing agreements and existing proposals, as well as future initiatives relevant to the prevention of an arms race in outer space, and that this contributed to a better understanding of a number of problems and to a clearer perception of the various positions,

Convinced that additional measures should be examined in the search for effective and verifiable bilateral and multilateral agreements in order to prevent an arms race in outer space,

Emphasizing the paramount importance of strict compliance with existing arms limitation and disarmament agreements relevant to outer space, and with the existing legal régime concerning the use of outer space,

Emphasizing also the necessity of maintaining the effectiveness of relevant existing treaties, and in this context reaffirming the vital importance of a strict compliance with the Treaty on the Limitation of Anti-Ballistic Missile Systems,

Recognizing that bilateral negotiations between the Union of Soviet Socialist Republics and the United States of America could facilitate the multilateral negotiations for the prevention of an arms race in outer space in accordance with paragraph 27 of the Final Document of the Tenth Special Session of the General Assembly,

Noting the importance in this context of bilateral negotiations between the Union of Soviet Socialist Republics and the United States of America that have continued since 1985, including at their summit meetings in Washington and Moscow on a complex of questions concerning space and nuclear arms,

Hopeful that concrete results would emerge from these negotiations as soon as possible,

Emphasizing the mutually complementary nature of bilateral and multilateral efforts in the field of preventing an arms race in outer space,

Taking note of that part of the report of the Conference on Disarmament relating to this question,

Welcoming the re-establishment of an *Ad Hoc* Committee on the Prevention of an Arms Race in Outer Space during the 1989 session of the Conference on Disarmament, in the exercise of the negotiating responsibilities of this sole multilateral negotiating body on disarmament, to continue to examine and to identify, through substantive and general consideration, issues relevant to the prevention of an arms race in outer space,

1. *Reaffirms* that general and complete disarmament under effective international control warrants that outer space shall be used exclusively for peaceful purposes and that it shall not become an arena for an arms race;

2. *Recognizes*, as stated in the report of the *Ad Hoc* Committee on the Prevention of an Arms Race in Outer Space, that the legal régime applicable to outer space by itself does not guarantee the prevention of an arms race in outer space, that this legal régime plays a significant role in the prevention of an arms race in that environment, the need to consolidate and reinforce that régime and enhance its effectiveness, and the importance of strict compliance with existing agreements, both bilateral and multilateral;

3. *Emphasizes* that further measures with appropriate and effective provisions for verification to prevent an arms race in outer space should be adopted by the international community;

4. *Calls upon* all States, in particular those with major space capabilities, to contribute actively to the objective of the peaceful use of outer space and to take immediate measures to prevent an arms race in outer space in the interest of maintaining international peace and security and promoting international co-operation and understanding;

5. *Reiterates* that the Conference on Disarmament, as the single multilateral disarmament negotiating forum, has the primary role in the negotiation of a multilateral agreement or agreements, as appropriate, on the prevention of an arms race in outer space in all its aspects;

6. *Requests* the Conference on Disarmament to consider as a matter of priority the question of preventing an arms race in outer space;

7. *Also requests* the Conference on Disarmament to intensify its consideration of the question of the prevention of an arms race in outer space in all its aspects, taking into account relevant proposals and initiatives, including those presented in the *Ad Hoc* Committee at the 1989 session of the Conference and at the forty-fourth session of the General Assembly;

8. *Further requests* the Conference on Disarmament to re-establish an *ad hoc* committee with an adequate mandate at the beginning of its 1990 session, with a view to undertaking negotiations for the conclusion of an agreement or agreements, as appropriate, to prevent an arms race in outer space in all its aspects;

9. *Urges* the Union of Soviet Socialist Republics and the United States of America to pursue intensively their bilateral negotiations in a constructive spirit aimed at reaching early agreement for preventing an arms race in outer space, and to advise the Conference on Disarmament periodically of the progress of their bilateral sessions so as to facilitate its work;

10. *Calls upon* all States, especially those with major space capabilities, to refrain, in their activities relating to outer space, from actions contrary to the observance of the relevant existing treaties or to the objective of preventing an arms race in outer space;

11. *Takes note* of the report of the Secretary-General on the question of the prevention of an arms race in outer space, submitted in accordance with resolution 42/33 of 30 November 1987;

12. *Requests* the Conference on Disarmament to report on its consideration of this subject to the General Assembly at its forty-fifth session;

13. *Requests* the Secretary-General to transmit to the Conference on Disarmament all documents relating to the consideration of this subject by the General Assembly at its forty-fourth session;

14. *Decides* to include in the provisional agenda of its forty-fifth session the item entitled ''Prevention of an arms race in outer space''.

General Assembly resolution 44/112

15 December 1989   Meeting 81   153-1 (recorded vote)

Approved by First Committee (A/44/780) by recorded vote (132-1), 17 November (meeting 40); 22-nation draft (A/C.1/44/L.10); agenda item 58.
Sponsors: Argentina, Bangladesh, Brazil, Cameroon, Egypt, Ethiopia, German Democratic Republic, India, Indonesia, Iran, Ireland, Jordan, Malaysia, Mexico, Myanmar, Peru, Romania, Sri Lanka, Sweden, Venezuela, Viet Nam, Yugoslavia.
Meeting numbers. GA 44th session: 1st Committee 3-25, 40; plenary 81.

Recorded vote in Assembly as follows:

In favour: Afghanistan, Albania, Algeria, Angola, Antigua and Barbuda, Argentina, Australia, Austria, Bahamas, Bahrain, Bangladesh, Barbados, Belgium, Benin, Bhutan, Bolivia, Botswana, Brazil, Brunei Darussalam, Bulgaria, Burkina Faso, Burundi, Byelorussian SSR, Cameroon, Canada, Cape Verde, Central African Republic, Chad, Chile, China, Colombia, Congo, Costa Rica, Côte d'Ivoire, Cuba, Cyprus, Czechoslovakia, Democratic Kampuchea, Democratic Yemen, Denmark, Djibouti, Dominica, Dominican Republic, Ecuador, Egypt, Ethiopia, Fiji, Finland, France, Gabon, Gambia, German Democratic Republic, Germany, Federal Republic of, Ghana, Greece, Grenada, Guatemala, Guinea, Guinea-Bissau, Guyana, Haiti, Honduras, Hungary, Iceland, India, Indonesia, Iran, Iraq, Ireland, Israel, Italy, Jamaica, Japan, Jordan, Kenya, Kuwait, Lao People's Democratic Republic, Lebanon, Lesotho, Liberia, Libyan Arab Jamahiriya, Luxembourg, Madagascar, Malawi, Malaysia, Maldives, Mali, Malta, Mauritania, Mauritius, Mexico, Mongolia, Morocco, Mozambique, Myanmar, Nepal, Netherlands, New Zealand, Nicaragua, Niger, Nigeria, Norway, Oman, Pakistan, Panama, Papua New Guinea, Paraguay, Peru, Philippines, Poland, Portugal, Qatar, Romania, Rwanda, Saint Kitts and Nevis, Saint Lucia, Saint Vincent and the Grenadines, Samoa, Sao Tome and Principe, Saudi Arabia, Senegal, Seychelles, Sierra Leone, Singapore, Solomon Islands, Somalia, Spain, Sri Lanka, Sudan, Suriname, Swaziland, Sweden, Syrian Arab Republic, Thailand, Togo, Trinidad and Tobago, Tunisia, Turkey, Uganda, Ukrainian SSR, USSR, United Arab Emirates, United Kingdom, United Republic of Tanzania, Uruguay, Vanuatu, Venezuela, Viet Nam, Yemen, Yugoslavia, Zaire, Zambia, Zimbabwe.

Against: United States.

Before acting on the text as a whole, the Assembly adopted paragraph 1 by a recorded vote of 136 to 1, with 13 abstentions, and paragraphs 3 and 8 each by 139 to 1, with 13 abstentions. The eleventh and eighteenth preambular paragraphs were adopted by recorded votes of 139 to 1, with 13 abstentions, and 137 to 1, with 13 abstentions, respectively.

In the Committee, paragraphs 1 and 3 were each approved by recorded votes of 119 to 1, with 13 abstentions, and paragraph 8, by 118 to 1, with 13 abstentions. The eleventh and eighteenth preambular paragraphs were retained by recorded votes of 119 to 1, with 13 abstentions, and 117 to 1, with 13 abstentions, respectively.

On 30 October, three draft resolutions on the prevention of an arms race in outer space were submitted in the First Committee.[58] At the request of the sponsors, no action was taken on them.

Review Conference on the 1971 Sea-Bed Treaty

The Third Review Conference of the Parties to the Treaty on the Prohibition of the Emplacement of Nuclear Weapons and Other Weapons of Mass Destruction on the Sea-Bed and the Ocean Floor and in the Subsoil Thereof met at Geneva from 19 to 28 September,[59] with the participation of 53 of the 82 States parties, two signatories and 13 observer States. It adopted a Final Document, which contained the Final Declaration consisting of a preamble and the Conference's article-by-article review of the Treaty. The other two parts of the Final Document dealt with the organization and work of the Conference, and summary records of the plenary meetings.

The Treaty, which was concluded in 1970 and commended to Member States by the General Assembly,[60] was opened for signature on 11 February 1971 and entered into force on 18 May 1972. The first and second Review Conferences were held in 1977[61] and 1983.[62]

GENERAL ASSEMBLY ACTION

On 15 December 1989, the General Assembly, on the recommendation of the First Committee, adopted **resolution 44/116 O** without vote.

Review Conference of the Parties to the Treaty on the Prohibition of the Emplacement of Nuclear Weapons and Other Weapons of Mass Destruction on the Sea-Bed and the Ocean Floor and in the Subsoil Thereof

The General Assembly,

Recalling its resolution 2660(XXV) of 7 December 1970, in which it commended the Treaty on the Prohibition of the Emplacement of Nuclear Weapons and Other Weapons of Mass Destruction on the Sea-Bed and the Ocean Floor and in the Subsoil Thereof,

Convinced that the Treaty constitutes a step towards the exclusion of the sea-bed, the ocean floor and the subsoil thereof from the arms race and towards a treaty or treaties on general and complete disarmament under strict and effective international control,

Recalling also that the States parties to the Treaty met at Geneva from 19 to 28 September 1989 to review the operation of the Treaty with a view to assuring that the purposes of the preamble and the provisions of the Treaty were being realized,

Noting with satisfaction that the Third Review Conference of the Parties to the Treaty on the Prohibition of the Emplacement of Nuclear Weapons and Other Weapons of Mass Destruction on the Sea-Bed and the Ocean Floor and in the Subsoil Thereof concluded that the obligations assumed under article I of the Treaty had been faithfully observed by the States parties,

Noting that in its Final Declaration the Third Review Conference affirmed its belief that universal adherence to the Treaty, particularly by those States possessing nuclear weapons or any other weapons of mass destruction, would enhance international peace and security,

Noting also that the States parties to the Treaty reaffirmed their strong support for and continued dedication to the principles and objectives of the Treaty, as well as their commitment to implement effectively its provisions,

Noting further that all States parties to the Treaty confirmed that they had not emplaced any nuclear weapons or other weapons of mass destruction on the sea-bed outside the zone of application of the Treaty as defined by its article II and had no intention to do so,

Recognizing that in the Final Declaration the States parties to the Treaty reaffirmed the commitment undertaken in article V to continue negotiations in good faith concerning further measures in the field of disarmament for the prevention of an arms race on the sea-bed and the ocean floor and in the subsoil thereof,

1. *Welcomes with satisfaction* the positive assessment by the Third Review Conference of the Parties to the Treaty on the Prohibition of the Emplacement of Nuclear Weapons and Other Weapons of Mass Destruction on the Sea-Bed and the Ocean Floor and in the Subsoil Thereof of the effectiveness of the Treaty since its entry into force, as reflected in its Final Declaration;

2. *Reiterates its expressed hope* for the widest possible adherence to the Treaty, and invites all States that have not yet done so, particularly those possessing nuclear weapons or any other types of weapons of mass destruction, to ratify or accede to the Treaty as a significant contribution to international peace and security;

3. *Affirms* its strong interest in avoiding an arms race in nuclear weapons or any other types of weapons of mass destruction on the sea-bed and the ocean floor and in the subsoil thereof;

4. *Calls again upon* all States to refrain from any action which might lead to the extension of the arms race to the sea-bed and the ocean floor and the subsoil thereof;

5. *Requests* the Conference on Disarmament, in consultation with the States parties to the Treaty, taking into account existing proposals and any relevant technological developments, to proceed promptly with consideration of further measures in the field of disarmament for the prevention of an arms race on the sea-bed and the ocean floor and in the subsoil thereof;

6. *Requests* the Secretary-General to transmit to the Conference on Disarmament all documents of the forty-fourth session of the General Assembly relevant to further measures in the field of disarmament for the prevention of an arms race on the sea-bed and the ocean floor and in the subsoil thereof;

7. *Also requests* the Conference on Disarmament to report on its consideration of further measures in the field of disarmament for the prevention of an arms race on the sea-bed and the ocean floor and in the subsoil thereof to the General Assembly at its forty-seventh session;

8. *Also requests* the Secretary-General to report by 1992, and every three years thereafter until the fourth Review Conference is convened, on technological developments relevant to the Treaty and to the verification of compliance with the Treaty, including dual-purpose technologies for peaceful and specified military ends; in carrying out this task he should draw from official sources and from contributions by States parties to the Treaty and may use the assistance of appropriate expertise;

9. *Urges* all States parties to the Treaty to assist the Secretary-General accordingly by providing information and drawing his attention to suitable sources;

10. *Decides* to include in the provisional agenda of its forty-seventh session an item entitled ''Further measures in the field of disarmament for the prevention of an arms race on the sea-bed and the ocean floor and in the subsoil thereof''.

General Assembly resolution 44/116 O

15 December 1989   Meeting 81   Adopted without vote

Approved by First Committee (A/44/785) without vote, 9 November (meeting 32); 38-nation draft (A/C.1/44/L.43); agenda item 63.
Sponsors: Australia, Austria, Botswana, Brazil, Bulgaria, Byelorussian SSR, Canada, Costa Rica, Cuba, Czechoslovakia, Denmark, Finland, German Democratic Republic, Germany, Federal Republic of, Greece, Hungary, Iceland, India, Iran, Ireland, Italy, Japan, Malaysia, Mongolia, Netherlands, New Zealand, Norway, Panama, Poland, Portugal, Romania, Sweden, Ukrainian SSR, USSR, United Kingdom, United States, Viet Nam, Yugoslavia.
Meeting numbers. GA 44th session: 1st Committee 3-25, 31, 32; plenary 81.

REFERENCES

[1]A/44/88. [2]YUN 1988, p. 75. [3]A/44/27. [4]CD/889. [5]CD/881. [6]CD/907. [7]CD/949. [8]CD/947. [9]CD/950. [10]CD/932. [11]CD/880. [12]CD/916. [13]CD/901. [14]CD/877. [15]CD/936 & CD/940. [16]CD/909 & CD/921. [17]YUN 1988, p. 76, GA res. 43/74 A, 7 Dec. 1988. [18]A/44/561. [19]YUN 1988, p. 76. [20]A/44/561/Add.1,2. [21]YUN 1987, p. 70, GA res. 42/37 C, 30 Nov. 1987. [22]A/C.1/44/5. [23]A/C.1/44/4. [24]A/C.1/44/2. [25]YUN 1971, p. 19, GA res. 2826(XXVI), annex, 16 Dec. 1971. [26]YUN 1980, p. 70. [27]YUN 1986, p. 64. [28]CD/946. [29]CD/928. [30]CD/929. [31]YUN 1988, p. 80, GA res. 43/75 J, 7 Dec. 1988. [32]A/44/621. [33]A/44/782. [34]YUN 1988, p. 82, GA res. 43/75 T, 7 Dec. 1988. [35]A/44/652. [36]YUN 1988, p. 43, GA res. 43/77 A, 7 Dec. 1988. [37]A/44/487 & Add.1,2. [38]A/44/42. [39]YUN 1988, p. 42, GA res. 43/75 I, 7 Dec. 1988. [40]A/CN.10/118. [41]A/CN.10/125. [42]A/CN.10/124. [43]A/44/444 & Add.1-3. [44]YUN 1987, p. 32, GA res. 42/39 E, 30 Nov. 1987. [45]A/44/513. [46]YUN 1988, p. 86. [47]*Multilateral Treaties Deposited with the Secretary-General: Status as at 31 December 1989* (ST/LEG/SER.E/8), Sales No. E.90.V.6. [48]YUN 1980, p. 76. [49]YUN 1983, p. 66. [50]YUN 1988, p. 86, GA res. 43/67, 7 Dec. 1988. [51]A/44/569. [52]CD/933. [53]CD/915. [54]CD/939. [55]CD/927. [56]CD/937 & CD/945. [57]CD/954. [58]A/C.1/44/L.16, A/C.1/44/L.19 & A/C.1/44/L.28. [59]SBT/CONF.III/15. [60]YUN 1970, p. 18, GA res. 2660(XXV), annex, 7 Dec. 1970. [61]YUN 1977, p. 44. [62]YUN 1983, p. 47.

Reduction of military expenditures

The subject of conversion of military resources to civilian purposes gained wider attention during 1989 and was for the first time the focus of a General Assembly resolution (44/116 J).

Eastern European States emphasized the need for negotiations on the reduction of military budgets. Some of them pointed to the steps they had taken to cut military spending and unilaterally to reduce armed forces and armaments. Bulgaria decided to reduce its military budget by 12 per cent;[1] Czechoslovakia planned to reduce its defence expenses for 1989-1990 by 15 per cent;[2] and the German Democratic Republic announced that its national outlay for defence would be cut back by 10 per cent.[3] Poland stated that it had been systematically lowering its national defence expenditure since 1987.[4]

Disarmament Commission consideration. Pursuant to a 1988 General Assembly request,[5] the Disarmament Commission continued to consider the reduction of military budgets and to conclude its work on the last outstanding paragraph of the ''Principles which should govern further actions of States in the field of freezing and reduction of military budgets''.[6] The Commission had before it the text of the principles as elaborated in 1986 and further considered in 1987 and 1988.

A consultation group held six meetings and a series of informal consultations between 10 and 22 May and continued its consideration of paragraph 7 on the basis of the text discussed in 1988,[7] with a view to reaching agreement on that paragraph. As no agreement on the text of paragraph 7 or on the text of the principles as a whole could be reached in the consultation group, the matter was referred to the Commission itself for consideration, which transmitted to the General Assembly the same text of the principles as it had in 1988.[7]

Reports of the Secretary-General. In an August report, with a later addendum,[8] the Secretary-General submitted his annual report on military expenditures in standardized form reported by 22 States. Annexed to the report was the standard reporting instrument consisting of a matrix designed to show how much each force group (such as land, naval and air forces) spent in each resource category (such as personnel, procurement and operations).

In a July report, with later addenda,[9] the Secretary-General submitted information received from nine States (including one on behalf of the 12 States members of EC) on further consolidating the emerging trend towards greater openness in military matters, specifically with regard to the provisions of objective information on such matters.

GENERAL ASSEMBLY ACTION

On 15 December 1989, on the recommendation of the First Committee, the General Assembly adopted **resolution 44/114 A** by recorded vote.

Reduction of military budgets

The General Assembly,

Desirous of reversing the arms race and military expenditures, which constitute a heavy burden for the economies of all nations and have harmful effects on world peace and security,

Convinced that the reduction of military expenditures as a result of the progress in disarmament negotiations will have favourable consequences on the world economic and financial situation,

Reaffirming that the resources released through the reduction of military expenditures could be reallocated to the economic and social development of all States, particularly for the benefit of the developing countries,

Firmly convinced that the reduction of military expenditures will have a positive impact on the process of strengthening confidence and improving international security and co-operation among States,

Desirous of bringing its contribution to the achievement of these goals,

1. *Welcomes* the work of the Disarmament Commission on the identification and elaboration of a set of principles that should govern further actions of States in the field of the freezing and reduction of military budgets;

2. *Takes note* of these principles, as annexed to the present resolution, and decides to bring them to the attention of Member States and of the Conference on Disarmament as useful guidelines for further action in the field of the freezing and reduction of military budgets;

3. *Requests* the Secretary-General to submit to the General Assembly at its forty-sixth session a progress report on the implementation of the present resolution;

4. *Decides* to include in the provisional agenda of its forty-sixth session the item entitled ''Reduction of military budgets''.

ANNEX

Principles that should govern further actions of States in the field of the freezing and reduction of military budgets

1. Concerted efforts should be made by all States, in particular by those States with the largest military arsenals and by the appropriate negotiating forums, with the objective of concluding international agreements to freeze and reduce military budgets, including adequate verification measures acceptable to all parties. Such agreements should contribute to genuine reductions of armed forces and armaments of States parties, with the aim of strengthening international peace and security at lower levels of armed forces and armaments. Definite agreements on the freezing and reduction of military expenditures are assuming special importance and should be reached within the shortest period of time in order to contribute to the curbing of the arms race, alleviate international tensions and increase the possibilities of reallocation of resources now being used for military purposes to economic and social development, particularly for the benefit of the developing countries.

2. All efforts in the field of the freezing and reduction of military expenditures should take into account the principles and purposes of the Charter of the United Nations and the relevant paragraphs of the Final Document of the Tenth Special Session of the General Assembly.

3. Pending the conclusion of agreements to freeze and reduce military expenditures, all States, in particular the most heavily armed States, should exercise self-restraint in their military expenditures.

4. The reduction of military expenditures on a mutually agreed basis should be implemented gradually and in a balanced manner, either on a percentage or on an absolute basis, so as to ensure that no individual State or group of States may obtain advantages over others at any stage, and without prejudice to the right of all States to undiminished security and sovereignty and to undertake the necessary measures of self-defence.

5. While the freezing and reduction of military budgets is the responsibility of all States, to be implemented in stages in accordance with the principle of greatest responsibility, the process should begin with those nuclear-weapon States with the largest military arsenals and the biggest military expenditures, to be followed immediately by other nuclear-weapon States and militarily significant States. This should not prevent other States from initiating negotiations and reaching agreements on the balanced reduction of their respective military budgets at any time during this process.

6. Human and material resources released through the reduction of military expenditures should be devoted to economic and social development, particularly for the benefit of the developing countries.

7. Meaningful negotiations on the freezing and reduction of military budgets would require that all parties to such negotiations have accepted and implemented transparency and comparability. The elaboration of agreed methods of measuring and comparing military expenditures between specified periods of time and between countries with different budgeting systems would be required. To this end States should utilize the reporting system adopted by the General Assembly in 1980.

8. Armaments and military activities that would be the subject of physical reductions within the limits provided for in any agreement to reduce military ex-

penditures will be identified by every State party to such agreements.

9. The agreements to freeze and reduce military expenditures should contain adequate and efficient measures of verification, satisfactory to all parties, in order to ensure that their provisions are strictly applied and fulfilled by all States parties. The specific methods of verification or other compliance procedure should be agreed upon in the process of negotiation depending upon the purposes, scope and nature of the agreement.

10. Unilateral measures undertaken by States concerning the freezing and reduction of military expenditures, especially when they are followed by similar measures adopted by other States on the basis of mutual example, could contribute to favourable conditions for the negotiation and conclusion of international agreements to freeze and reduce military expenditures.

11. Confidence-building measures could help to create a political climate conducive to the freezing and reduction of military expenditures. Conversely, the freezing and reduction of military expenditures could contribute to the increase of confidence among States.

12. The United Nations should play a central role in orienting, stimulating and initiating negotiations on freezing and reducing military expenditures, and all Member States should co-operate with the Organization and among themselves, with a view to solving the problems implied by this process.

13. The freezing and reduction of military expenditures may be achieved, as appropriate, on a global, regional or subregional level, with the agreement of all States concerned.

14. The agreements on the freezing and reduction of military budgets should be viewed in a broader perspective, including respect for and implementation of the security system of the United Nations, and be interrelated with other measures of disarmament, within the context of progress towards general and complete disarmament under effective international control. The reduction of military budgets should therefore be complementary to agreements on the limitation of armaments and disarmament and should not be considered as a substitute for such agreements.

15. The adoption of the above principles should be regarded as a means of facilitating meaningful negotiations on concrete agreements on the freezing and reduction of military budgets.

General Assembly resolution 44/114 A

15 December 1989   Meeting 81   116-10-19 (recorded vote)

Approved by First Committee (A/44/783) by recorded vote (94-10-18), 16 November (meeting 38); 18-nation draft (A/C.1/44/L.36); agenda item 61.
Sponsors: Angola, Benin, Byelorussian SSR, Cameroon, Central African Republic, Chile, Colombia, Costa Rica, Gambia, German Democratic Republic, Indonesia, Lesotho, Nigeria, Peru, Philippines, Romania, Suriname, USSR.
Meeting numbers. GA 44th session: 1st Committee 3-25, 27, 38; plenary 81.

Recorded vote in Assembly as follows:

In favour: Afghanistan, Angola, Antigua and Barbuda, Argentina, Australia, Austria, Bahamas, Bahrain, Bangladesh, Barbados, Benin, Bhutan, Bolivia, Botswana, Brunei Darussalam, Bulgaria, Burkina Faso, Burundi, Byelorussian SSR, Cameroon, Cape Verde, Central African Republic, Chad, Chile, China, Colombia, Congo, Costa Rica, Côte d'Ivoire, Cuba, Cyprus, Czechoslovakia, Democratic Kampuchea, Democratic Yemen, Dominica, Dominican Republic, Ecuador, Ethiopia, Fiji, Finland, Gabon, Gambia, German Democratic Republic, Ghana, Greece, Grenada, Guatemala, Guinea, Guinea-Bissau, Guyana, Haiti, Honduras, Hungary, Indonesia, Iran, Ireland, Jamaica, Lao People's Democratic Republic, Lesotho, Liberia, Libyan Arab Jamahiriya,* Madagascar, Malawi, Malaysia, Maldives, Mali, Malta, Mauritania, Mauritius, Mexico, Mongolia, Mozambique, Myanmar, Nepal,

New Zealand, Nicaragua, Niger, Nigeria, Pakistan, Panama, Papua New Guinea, Paraguay, Peru, Philippines, Poland, Romania, Rwanda, Saint Kitts and Nevis, Saint Lucia, Saint Vincent and the Grenadines, Samoa, Sao Tome and Principe, Senegal, Seychelles, Sierra Leone, Solomon Islands, Sri Lanka, Sudan, Suriname, Swaziland, Sweden, Thailand, Togo, Trinidad and Tobago, Uganda, Ukrainian SSR, USSR, United Republic of Tanzania, Uruguay, Vanuatu, Venezuela, Viet Nam, Yugoslavia, Zaire, Zambia, Zimbabwe.

Against: Belgium, Canada, France, Germany, Federal Republic of, Italy, Luxembourg, Netherlands, Portugal, United Kingdom, United States.

Abstaining: Algeria, Brazil, Denmark, Egypt, Iceland, India, Iraq, Israel, Japan, Jordan, Norway, Saudi Arabia, Somalia, Spain, Syrian Arab Republic, Tunisia, Turkey, United Arab Emirates, Yemen.

*Later advised the Secretariat it had intended to abstain.

On the same date and on the First Committee's recommendation, the Assembly adopted **resolution 44/114 B**, also by recorded vote.

Military budgets

The General Assembly,

Welcoming the encouraging progress achieved in arms limitations and disarmament,

Noting that further progress in disarmament negotiations could also lead to reductions in military expenditures,

Stressing that increased information on military matters is an important prerequisite for achieving agreements on the reduction of armed forces,

Recalling that an international system for the standardized reporting of military expenditures has been introduced in pursuance of General Assembly resolution 35/142 B of 12 December 1980, and that national reports on military expenditures have been received from a number of Member States belonging to different geographic regions and having different budgeting and accounting systems,

Convinced that more transparency and comparability could be reached through broader participation in the standardized system of the United Nations for reporting military expenditures,

1. *Considers* that transparency requires also agreed methods of measuring and comparing military expenditures between specified periods of time and between countries with different budgeting systems;

2. *Accordingly calls upon* all States to make use of the reporting system adopted by the General Assembly;

3. *Decides* to include in the provisional agenda of its forty-sixth session an item entitled ''Transparency and reduction of military budgets''.

General Assembly resolution 44/114 B

15 December 1989   Meeting 81   127-0-15 (recorded vote)

Approved by First Committee (A/44/783) by recorded vote (105-0-16), 16 November (meeting 38); 13-nation draft (A/C.1/44/L.44/Rev.1); agenda item 61.
Sponsors: Byelorussian SSR, Cameroon, Denmark, Gabon, Germany, Federal Republic of, Italy, Luxembourg, Netherlands, Nigeria, Norway, Portugal, Turkey, USSR.
Meeting numbers. GA 44th session: 1st Committee 3-25, 31, 38; plenary 81.

Recorded vote in Assembly as follows:

In favour: Afghanistan, Antigua and Barbuda, Argentina, Australia, Austria, Bahamas, Bangladesh, Barbados, Belgium, Benin, Bhutan, Bolivia, Botswana, Brazil, Brunei Darussalam, Bulgaria, Burkina Faso, Burundi, Byelorussian SSR, Cameroon, Canada, Cape Verde, Central African Republic, Chad, Chile, Colombia, Congo, Costa Rica, Côte d'Ivoire, Cyprus, Czechoslovakia, Denmark, Dominica, Dominican Republic, Ecuador, Fiji, Finland, France, Gabon, Gambia, German Democratic Republic, Germany, Federal Republic of, Ghana, Greece, Grenada, Guatemala, Guinea, Guinea-Bissau, Guyana, Haiti, Honduras, Hungary, Iceland, Indonesia, Iran, Ireland, Israel, Italy, Jamaica, Japan, Kenya, Lao People's Democratic Republic, Lesotho, Liberia, Libyan Arab Jamahiriya,* Luxembourg, Madagascar, Malawi, Malaysia, Maldives, Mali, Malta, Mauritius, Mexico, Mongolia, Mozam-

bique, Myanmar, Nepal, Netherlands, New Zealand, Nicaragua, Niger, Ni-
geria, Norway, Pakistan, Panama, Papua New Guinea, Paraguay, Peru,
Philippines, Poland, Portugal, Romania, Rwanda, Saint Kitts and Nevis,
Saint Lucia, Saint Vincent and the Grenadines, Samoa, Sao Tome and Prin-
cipe, Senegal, Seychelles, Sierra Leone, Singapore, Solomon Islands, Spain,
Sri Lanka, Sudan,* Suriname, Swaziland, Sweden, Thailand, Togo, Trinidad
and Tobago, Turkey, Uganda, Ukrainian SSR, USSR, United Kingdom,
United Republic of Tanzania, United States, Uruguay, Vanuatu, Venezuela,
Viet Nam, Yugoslavia, Zaire, Zimbabwe.

Against: None.

Abstaining: Algeria, Angola, Bahrain, Cuba, Egypt, India, Iraq, Jordan,
Saudi Arabia, Somalia, Syrian Arab Republic, Tunisia, United Arab Emirates,
Yemen, Zambia.

*Later advised the Secretariat it had intended to abstain.

On 15 December, the Assembly, again on the
recommendation of the First Committee, also
adopted **resolution 44/116 E** by recorded vote.

Objective information on military matters
The General Assembly,

Recalling paragraph 105 of the Final Document of the
Tenth Special Session of the General Assembly, the first
special session devoted to disarmament, in which the
Assembly encouraged Member States to ensure a better flow of information with regard to the various aspects
of disarmament to avoid dissemination of false and ten-
dentious information concerning armaments and to concentrate on the danger of escalation of the arms race
and on the need for general and complete disarmament
under effective international control,

Taking into account the attention paid to the questions
of openness and of ensuring an exchange of objective
information in the military field at its fifteenth special
session, the third special session devoted to disarmament,

Noting with satisfaction that recent agreements in the field
of arms limitation and disarmament have provided for
qualitatively new standards of openness,

Noting also with satisfaction an increased number of steps
and proposals by different States aimed at achieving
openness and transparency in military activities,

Believing that the adoption of confidence-building
measures to promote openness and transparency would
reduce the risk of misperceptions of military capabilities and intentions which could induce military rival-
ries between States, leading to their undertaking armaments programmes and the acceleration of the arms
race, in particular the nuclear-arms race, to heightened
international tensions and, ultimately, to conflict,

Believing also that balanced and objective information
on all military matters, in particular of nuclear-weapon
States and other militarily significant States, would contribute to the building of confidence among States and
to the conclusion of concrete disarmament agreements,
and thereby help to halt and reverse the arms race,

Recognizing that greater openness and transparency
would contribute to enhancing security,

Convinced that greater openness on military activities,
inter alia, through the transmittal of relevant information on these activities, including on the levels of military budgets, would contribute to increased confidence
among States,

Taking into account the work undertaken in the Disarmament Commission on the reduction of military budgets,

Noting with satisfaction that an increased number of
States have provided annual reports on military expenditures in conformity with the international system for
the standardized reporting of military expenditures
under the auspices of the United Nations,

Recalling its resolution 43/75 G of 7 December 1988,
in which it invited all Member States to communicate
to the Secretary-General their views on ways and means
of further consolidating the emerging trend towards
greater openness in military matters, specifically with
regard to the provision of objective information on military matters, for consideration by the Disarmament
Commission at its 1990 session,

1. *Takes note* of the report of the Secretary-General
on this subject to the third special session of the General
Assembly devoted to disarmament;

2. *Reaffirms its firm conviction* that a better flow of objective information on military capabilities would help
to relieve international tension and contribute to the
building of confidence among States on a global,
regional or subregional level and to the conclusion of
concrete disarmament agreements;

3. *Recommends* that those States and global, regional
and subregional organizations which have already expressed support for the principle of practical and concrete confidence-building measures of a military nature
on a global, regional or subregional level should intensify their efforts with a view to adopting such measures;

4. *Recommends* that all States, in particular nuclear-
weapon States and other militarily significant States,
should implement the international system for the standardized reporting of military expenditure, with the aim
of achieving a realistic comparison of military budgets,
facilitating the availability of objective information on,
as well as objective assessment of, military capabilities
and contributing to the process of disarmament;

5. *Invites* all Member States to communicate to the
Secretary-General before 30 April 1990 measures they
have adopted towards these ends, for submission to the
General Assembly at its forty-fifth session;

6. *Requests* the Disarmament Commission to include
in the agenda for its 1990 session an item entitled "Objective information on military matters";

7. *Decides* to include in the provisional agenda of its
forty-fifth session the item entitled "Objective information on military matters".

General Assembly resolution 44/116 E

15 December 1989   Meeting 81   132-0-13 (recorded vote)

Approved by First Committee (A/44/785) by recorded vote (110-0-15), 14
November (meeting 36); 31-nation draft (A/C.1/44/L.15/Rev.1); agenda item
63 (f).

Sponsors: Australia, Austria, Belgium, Botswana, Bulgaria, Canada, Czechoslovakia, Denmark, France, German Democratic Republic, Germany, Federal Republic of, Greece, Hungary, Iceland, Italy, Japan, Luxembourg,
Netherlands, New Zealand, Norway, Philippines, Poland, Portugal, Samoa,
Spain, Sweden, Thailand, Turkey, USSR, United Kingdom, United States.

Meeting numbers. GA 44th Session: 1st Committee 3-25, 29, 36; plenary 81.

Recorded vote in Assembly as follows:

In favour: Afghanistan, Antigua and Barbuda, Argentina, Australia, Austria, Bahamas, Bangladesh, Barbados, Belgium, Benin, Bhutan, Bolivia, Botswana, Brazil, Brunei Darussalam, Bulgaria, Burkina Faso, Burundi, Byelorussian SSR, Cameroon, Canada, Cape Verde, Central African Republic,
Chad, Chile, Colombia, Congo, Costa Rica, Côte d'Ivoire, Cyprus, Czechoslovakia, Democratic Kampuchea, Denmark, Djibouti, Dominica, Dominican Republic, Ecuador, El Salvador, Fiji, Finland, France, Gabon, Gambia,
German Democratic Republic, Germany, Federal Republic of, Ghana,
Greece, Grenada, Guatemala, Guinea, Guinea-Bissau, Guyana, Haiti, Hon-
duras, Hungary, Iceland, Indonesia, Iran, Ireland, Israel, Italy, Jamaica,
Japan, Kenya, Lao People's Democratic Republic, Lesotho, Liberia, Lux-
embourg, Madagascar, Malawi, Malaysia, Maldives, Mali, Malta, Mauritius,
Mexico, Mongolia, Mozambique, Myanmar, Nepal, Netherlands, New
Zealand, Nicaragua, Niger, Nigeria, Norway, Oman,* Pakistan, Panama,
Papua New Guinea, Paraguay, Peru, Philippines, Poland, Romania, Roma-
nia, Rwanda, Saint Kitts and Nevis, Saint Lucia, Saint Vincent and the
Grenadines, Samoa, Sao Tome and Principe, Saudi Arabia, Senegal,

Seychelles, Sierra Leone, Singapore, Solomon Islands, Spain, Sri Lanka, Sudan, Suriname, Swaziland, Sweden, Thailand, Togo, Trinidad and Tobago, Turkey, Uganda, Ukrainian SSR, USSR, United Kingdom, United Republic of Tanzania, United States, Uruguay, Vanuatu, Venezuela, Viet Nam, Yemen, Yugoslavia, Zaire, Zimbabwe.

Against: None.

Abstaining: Algeria, Bahrain, Cuba, Egypt, India, Iraq, Jordan, Libyan Arab Jamahiriya, Qatar, Somalia, Tunisia, United Arab Emirates, Zambia.

*Later advised the Secretariat it had not intended to vote in favour.

Disarmament and development

In accordance with a 1988 General Assembly request,[10] the Secretary-General described in September 1989[11] activities undertaken by the Secretariat to implement the action programme contained in the Final Document adopted at the 1987 International Conference on the Relationship between Disarmament and Development.[12] A high-level intra-secretariat task force was established in 1987 to identify activities to be carried out during the period 1988 to 1990, which included monitoring trends in military spending; facilitating exchanges of experience in conversion from military to civilian production; and promoting collective knowledge of non-military threats to international security.

GENERAL ASSEMBLY ACTION

On 15 December 1989, on the recommendation of the First Committee, the General Assembly adopted **resolution 44/116 L** without vote.

Relationship between disarmament and development

The General Assembly,

Recalling the provisions of the Final Document of the Tenth Special Session of the General Assembly related to the relationship between disarmament and development,

Recalling also the adoption on 11 September 1987 of the Final Document of the International Conference on the Relationship between Disarmament and Development,

1.   *Welcomes* the report of the Secretary-General and actions undertaken in accordance with the Final Document of the International Conference on the Relationship between Disarmament and Development;

2.   *Requests* the Secretary-General to continue to take action, through the appropriate organs and within available resources, for the implementation of the action programme adopted at the International Conference;

3.   *Also requests* the Secretary-General to submit a report to the General Assembly at its forty-fifth session;

4.   *Decides* to include in the provisional agenda of its forty-fifth session the item entitled ''Relationship between disarmament and development''.

General Assembly resolution 44/116 L

15 December 1989   Meeting 81   Adopted without vote

Approved by First Committee (A/44/785) without vote, 9 November (meeting 32); draft by German Democratic Republic, Romania and Yugoslavia, for Non-Aligned Group (A/C.1/44/L.32); agenda item 63 *(b)*.

Meeting numbers. GA 44th session: 1st Committee 3-25, 31, 32; plenary 81.

Also on 15 December, on the recommendation of the First Committee, the Assembly adopted **resolution 44/116 J** by recorded vote.

Conversion of military resources

The General Assembly,

Conscious that many States wish to convert their military resources to civilian purposes,

Noting that such conversion ought to be carried out gradually following a careful study of the basic aspects and practical details of the reorientation of military production and personnel,

Noting also the importance of the appropriate knowledge and reporting of military expenditure,

Noting further that the efficient conversion of military production may require relevant administrative and legislative measures, as well as appropriate organizational, financial and other mechanisms,

Aware that economic, social, financial and other aspects ought to be taken into account in elaborating a national conversion programme,

Recalling its resolution 43/73 of 7 December 1988 on the reduction of military budgets,

Recalling also that there exist studies on certain aspects of conversion which could be used by the international community,

Desirous of promoting an exchange of experience, within the United Nations framework, on modalities for the conversion of military resources to civilian purposes,

1.   *Invites* Member States to submit to the Secretary-General by 30 April 1991 their views concerning various aspects of the conversion of military resources to civilian purposes;

2.   *Decides* to include in the provisional agenda of its forty-sixth session an item entitled ''Conversion of military resources to civilian purposes''.

General Assembly resolution 44/116 J

15 December 1989   Meeting 81   153-0-1 (recorded vote)

Approved by First Committee (A/44/785) by recorded vote (134-0-1), 15 November (meeting 37); 2-nation draft (A/C.1/44/L.29), orally revised; agenda item 63.

Sponsors: Bulgaria, German Democratic Republic.

Meeting numbers. GA 44th session: 1st Committee 3-25, 30, 37; plenary 81.

Recorded vote in Assembly as follows:

In favour: Afghanistan, Albania, Algeria, Angola, Antigua and Barbuda, Argentina, Australia, Austria, Bahamas, Bahrain, Bangladesh, Barbados, Belgium, Benin, Bhutan, Bolivia, Botswana, Brazil, Brunei Darussalam, Bulgaria, Burkina Faso, Burundi, Byelorussian SSR, Cameroon, Canada, Cape Verde, Central African Republic, Chad, Chile, China, Colombia, Congo, Costa Rica, Côte d'Ivoire, Cuba, Cyprus, Czechoslovakia, Democratic Kampuchea, Democratic Yemen, Denmark, Djibouti, Dominica, Dominican Republic, Ecuador, Egypt, El Salvador, Ethiopia, Fiji, Finland, France, Gabon, Gambia, German Democratic Republic, Germany, Federal Republic of, Ghana, Greece, Grenada, Guatemala, Guinea, Guinea-Bissau, Guyana, Haiti, Honduras, Hungary, Iceland, India, Indonesia, Iran, Iraq, Ireland, Israel, Italy, Jamaica, Japan, Jordan, Kenya, Kuwait, Lao People's Democratic Republic, Lebanon, Lesotho, Liberia, Libyan Arab Jamahiriya, Luxembourg, Madagascar, Malawi, Malaysia, Maldives, Mali, Malta, Mauritania, Mauritius, Mexico, Mongolia, Morocco, Mozambique, Myanmar, Nepal, Netherlands, New Zealand, Nicaragua, Niger, Nigeria, Norway, Oman, Pakistan, Panama, Papua New Guinea, Paraguay, Peru, Philippines, Poland, Portugal, Qatar, Romania, Rwanda, Saint Kitts and Nevis, Saint Lucia, Saint Vincent and the Grenadines, Samoa, Sao Tome and Principe, Saudi Arabia, Senegal, Seychelles, Sierra Leone, Singapore, Solomon Islands, Somalia, Spain, Sri Lanka, Sudan, Suriname, Swaziland, Sweden, Syrian Arab Republic, Thailand, Togo, Trinidad and Tobago, Tunisia, Turkey, Uganda, Ukrainian SSR, USSR, United Arab Emirates, United Kingdom, United Republic of Tanzania, Uruguay, Vanuatu, Venezuela, Viet Nam, Yemen, Yugoslavia, Zambia, Zimbabwe.

Against: None.

Abstaining: United States.

REFERENCES

[1]A/44/113. [2]A/44/163. [3]A/44/96. [4]A/44/165. [5]YUN 1988, p. 90, GA res. 43/73, 7 Dec. 1988. [6]A/44/42. [7]YUN 1988, p. 89. [8]A/44/422 & Add.1. [9]A/44/396 & Add.1,2. [10]YUN

1988, p. 49, GA res. 43/75 B, 7 Dec. 1988. [11]A/44/449. [12]YUN 1987, p. 82.

Information and studies

World Disarmament Campaign

As in previous years, the World Disarmament Campaign—launched by the General Assembly in 1982 at the start of its second special session devoted to disarmament[1]—continued to inform, educate and generate public understanding and support for the disarmament objectives of the United Nations.

The Seventh United Nations Pledging Conference for the Campaign was convened in New York during Disarmament Week and the Assembly decided to hold an eighth conference in 1990 (resolution 44/117 A).

Financial difficulties persisted, making it necessary again to adjust some projects. Nevertheless, the Campaign carried out a large number of activities.

Report of the Secretary-General. In October 1989,[2] in his annual report on implementing the Campaign's objectives, the Secretary-General informed the Assembly of activities carried out by the United Nations system, including information materials, special events and publicity programmes. DDA organized a seminar on African disarmament and security (Cairo, Egypt, 20-23 March) and a regional conference (Dagomys, USSR, 12-16 June). The Department of Public Information continued to inform the public of United Nations activities in the disarmament area by providing radio and television coverage, arranging briefings for non-governmental organizations (NGOs) and organizing other events at Headquarters and United Nations information centres around the world.

Financing

The Seventh United Nations Pledging Conference for the World Disarmament Campaign was held in New York on 25 October, with 80 delegates participating.[3]

Either during the Conference or at other times during the year, the following pledges were earmarked for the Campaign: Australia ($A 30,000), Austria ($10,000), Bulgaria (50,000 leva), Byelorussian SSR (200,000 roubles for 1990-1993), China ($10,000), Ecuador ($1,000), Finland (50,000 markkaa), Greece ($5,000), Indonesia ($5,000), Kuwait ($5,000), Norway ($6,000), Saudi Arabia ($5,000), Sweden (150,000 kronor), Ukrainian SSR (300,000 roubles for 1990-1993), USSR (500,000 roubles for 1990-1993), Zaire ($1,000); for

UNIDIR, Australia ($A 20,000), Bulgaria (65,000 leva), Canada ($Can 10,000), Finland (75,000 markkaa), Nigeria ($10,000), Norway ($49,975), Spain ($10,000 for 1990 and $15,000 for 1991), Sweden ($40,000), USSR (250,000 roubles and $20,000); for the regional centre in Latin America and the Caribbean, Ecuador ($757), Norway ($10,000), Peru ($5,000), Spain ($5,000 for 1989 and $5,000 for 1990), Uruguay ($1,000); for the seminar on confidence-building measures in the maritime domain (Helsingör, Denmark), Finland (100,000 markkaa), Sweden ($30,000); for the regional centre in Asia, Federal Republic of Germany ($15,000), Nepal ($7,000), Norway ($10,000), Philippines (22,000 pesos); for the regional centre in Africa, Norway ($10,000); for the disarmament training programme for Asia and the Pacific, Norway ($15,000); and New Zealand, an unallocated pledge ($NZ 15,000).

GENERAL ASSEMBLY ACTION

On 15 December 1989, the General Assembly, on the recommendation of the First Committee, adopted **resolution 44/117 A** by recorded vote.

World Disarmament Campaign

The General Assembly,

Recalling that in paragraph 15 of the Final Document of the Tenth Special Session of the General Assembly, the first special session devoted to disarmament, it declared that it was essential that not only Governments but also the peoples of the world recognize and understand the dangers in the present situation and stressed the importance of mobilizing world public opinion on behalf of disarmament,

Recalling also its resolution 43/76 C of 7 December 1988,

Having examined the report of the Secretary-General of 20 October 1989 on the implementation of the programme of activities of the World Disarmament Campaign by the United Nations system,

Having also examined the part of the report of the Secretary-General of 26 October 1989 dealing with the activities of the Advisory Board on Disarmament Matters relating to the implementation of the World Disarmament Campaign, as well as the Final Act of the Seventh United Nations Pledging Conference for the Campaign, held on 25 October 1989,

Noting with appreciation the contributions that Member States have already made to the Campaign,

1. *Reiterates its commendation* of the manner in which, as described in the above-mentioned reports, the World Disarmament Campaign has been geared by the Secretary-General in order to guarantee "the widest possible dissemination of information and unimpeded access for all sectors of the public to a broad range of information and opinions on questions of arms limitation and disarmament and the dangers relating to all aspects of the arms race and war, in particular nuclear war'';

2. *Recalls* that, as was also agreed by consensus in the Concluding Document of the Twelfth Special Session of the General Assembly, the second special session devoted to disarmament, it is likewise an essential

requisite for the universality of the Campaign that it receive the co-operation and participation of all States;

3. *Endorses once more* the statement made by the Secretary-General on the occasion of the Third United Nations Pledging Conference for the World Disarmament Campaign to the effect that such co-operation implies that adequate funds be made available and that consequently the criterion of universality also applies to pledges, since a campaign without world-wide participation and funding will have difficulty in reflecting this principle in its implementation;

4. *Urges* States that have not yet done so, especially those with the largest military expenditures, to make an initial financial contribution to the Campaign;

5. *Decides* that at its forty-fifth session there should be an eighth United Nations Pledging Conference for the World Disarmament Campaign, and expresses the hope that on that occasion all those Member States that have not yet announced any voluntary contributions will do so, bearing in mind the objectives of the Third Disarmament Decade and the need to ensure its success;

6. *Reiterates its recommendation* that the voluntary contributions made by Member States to the World Disarmament Campaign Voluntary Trust Fund should not be earmarked for specific activities inasmuch as it is most desirable that the Secretary-General enjoy full freedom to take the decisions he deems fit within the framework of the Campaign previously approved by the General Assembly and in exercise of the powers vested in him in connection with the Campaign;

7. *Notes with appreciation* that the Secretary-General has given permanent character to his instructions to the United Nations information centres and regional commissions to give wide publicity to the Campaign and, whenever necessary, to adapt, as far as possible, United Nations information materials to local languages;

8. *Requests* the Secretary-General to submit to the General Assembly at its forty-fifth session a report covering both the implementation of the programme of activities of the Campaign by the United Nations system during 1990 and the programme of activities contemplated by the system for 1991;

9. *Also requests* the Secretary-General to assess the achievements and shortcomings of the World Disarmament Campaign so far and to submit a brief report in this regard to the General Assembly at its forty-fifth session;

10. *Decides* to include in the provisional agenda of its forty-fifth session the item entitled "World Disarmament Campaign".

General Assembly resolution 44/117 A

15 December 1989   Meeting 81   144-0-10 (recorded vote)

Approved by First Committee (A/44/786) by recorded vote (117-0-9), 9 November (meeting 32); 15-nation draft (A/C.1/44/L.4); agenda item 64 *(d)*.
Sponsors: Bangladesh, Bulgaria, Byelorussian SSR, Egypt, German Democratic Republic, Indonesia, Mexico, Mongolia, Peru, Philippines, Romania, Sri Lanka, Sweden, Venezuela, Yugoslavia.
Meeting numbers. GA 44th session: 1st Committee 3-25, 29, 32; plenary 81.

Recorded vote in Assembly as follows:

In favour: Afghanistan, Albania, Algeria, Angola, Antigua and Barbuda, Argentina, Australia, Austria, Bahamas, Bahrain, Bangladesh, Barbados, Benin, Bhutan, Bolivia, Botswana, Brazil, Brunei Darussalam, Bulgaria, Burkina Faso, Burundi, Byelorussian SSR, Cameroon, Cape Verde, Central African Republic, Chad, Chile, China, Colombia, Congo, Costa Rica, Côte d'Ivoire, Cuba, Cyprus, Czechoslovakia, Democratic Kampuchea, Democratic Yemen, Denmark, Djibouti, Dominica, Dominican Republic, Ecuador, Egypt, El Salvador, Ethiopia, Fiji, Finland, Gabon, Gambia, German Democratic Republic, Ghana, Greece, Grenada, Guatemala, Guinea, Guinea-Bissau, Guyana, Haiti, Honduras, Hungary, Iceland, India, Indonesia, Iran, Iraq, Ireland, Israel,

Jamaica, Japan, Jordan, Kenya, Kuwait, Lao People's Democratic Republic, Lebanon, Lesotho, Liberia, Libyan Arab Jamahiriya, Madagascar, Malawi, Malaysia, Maldives, Mali, Malta, Mauritania, Mauritius, Mexico, Mongolia, Morocco, Mozambique, Myanmar, Nepal, New Zealand, Nicaragua, Niger, Nigeria, Norway, Oman, Pakistan, Panama, Papua New Guinea, Paraguay, Peru, Philippines, Poland, Qatar, Romania, Rwanda, Saint Lucia, Saint Vincent and the Grenadines, Samoa, Sao Tome and Principe, Saudi Arabia, Senegal, Seychelles, Sierra Leone, Singapore, Solomon Islands, Somalia, Spain, Sri Lanka, Sudan, Suriname, Swaziland, Sweden, Syrian Arab Republic, Thailand, Togo, Trinidad and Tobago, Tunisia, Turkey, Uganda, Ukrainian SSR, USSR, United Arab Emirates, United Republic of Tanzania, Uruguay, Vanuatu, Venezuela, Viet Nam, Yemen, Yugoslavia, Zaire, Zambia, Zimbabwe.
Against: None.
Abstaining: Belgium, Canada, France, Germany, Federal Republic of, Italy, Luxembourg, Netherlands, Portugal, United Kingdom, United States.

Regional centres for peace and disarmament

In October 1989, the Secretary-General reported to the General Assembly on the activities of the United Nations Regional Centre for Peace and Disarmament in Africa,[4] which had been inaugurated in 1986 at Lomé, Togo.[5] The Centre held a high-level experts' workshop (14-18 August), which focused on the main sources of threats to peace, regional and subregional security in Africa; ways and means of preventing and resolving conflicts in Africa by peaceful means; and the relationship between national, regional and global security, disarmament and development. It continued to disseminate information relating to peace, security and development.

As decided by the Assembly in 1986,[6] the United Nations Regional Centre for Peace, Disarmament and Development in Latin America and the Caribbean was established on 1 January 1987 and inaugurated at Lima, Peru, on 9 October of that year.[7] In October 1989,[8] the Secretary-General noted that the Centre had expanded its contacts with organizations and individuals in the region and had taken steps towards establishing a reference and documentation service on issues of peace, security, disarmament and development. During the year, the Centre provided assistance to NGOs.

Also in October,[9] the Secretary-General reported that the United Nations Regional Centre for Peace and Disarmament in Asia, established in 1987,[10] was inaugurated at Kathmandu, Nepal, on 30 January 1989. The initial activities of the Centre focused on the dissemination of information on United Nations activities in the area of arms limitation and disarmament.

GENERAL ASSEMBLY ACTION

On 15 December 1989, the General Assembly, on the recommendation of the First Committee, adopted **resolution 44/117 F** by recorded vote.

United Nations Regional Centre for Peace and Disarmament in Africa, United Nations Regional Centre for Peace and Disarmament in Asia and United Nations Regional Centre for Peace, Disarmament and Development in Latin America and the Caribbean

The General Assembly,

Recalling its resolutions 40/151 G of 16 December 1985, 41/60 D of 3 December 1986, 42/39 J of 30 November

1987 and 43/76 D of 7 December 1988 on the United Nations Regional Centre for Peace and Disarmament in Africa, 41/60 J of 3 December 1986, 42/39 K of 30 November 1987 and 43/76 H of 7 December 1988 on the United Nations Regional Centre for Peace, Disarmament and Development in Latin America and the Caribbean, and 42/39 D of 30 November 1987 and 43/76 G of 7 December 1988 on the United Nations Regional Centre for Peace and Disarmament in Asia,

Reaffirming its resolutions 37/100 F of 13 December 1982, 38/73 J of 15 December 1983, 39/63 F of 12 December 1984, 40/94 A of 12 December 1985, 41/59 M of 3 December 1986 and 42/39 E of 30 November 1987 on regional disarmament,

Taking note of the final documents of the Ninth Conference of Heads of State or Government of Non-Aligned Countries, held at Belgrade from 4 to 7 September 1989,[a] and noting in particular the importance placed by the heads of State or Government on the activities of the United Nations regional centres in Africa, Asia and Latin America and the Caribbean,

Convinced that the initiatives and activities mutually agreed upon by Member States of the respective regions aimed at fostering mutual confidence and security, as well as the implementation and co-ordination of regional activities under the World Disarmament Campaign, would encourage and facilitate the development of effective measures of confidence-building, arms limitation and disarmament in these regions,

Expressing its gratitude to the Member States and international governmental and non-governmental organizations that have contributed to the trust funds of the three regional centres,

Bearing in mind the need to provide the centres with financial stability so as to facilitate the planning of their activities,

Taking note with appreciation of the reports of the Secretary-General on the regional centres in Africa, Asia and Latin America and the Caribbean, and of the efforts of the Secretary-General in providing the necessary administrative measures to permit the establishment of the three centres,

Convinced that the appointment of a Director to head each of the three regional centres is essential to ensure the continued effective functioning of the centres,

Noting that the responsibilities of the United Nations Regional Centre for Peace and Disarmament in Asia include the Asia-Pacific region,

1. *Appeals once again* to Member States, as well as to international governmental and non-governmental organizations, to make voluntary contributions in order to strengthen the effective operational activities of the centres;

2. *Commends* the Secretary-General for all the efforts he has made in favour of the centres, and requests him to continue to provide all the necessary support to their activities;

3. *Requests* the Secretary-General to establish, as soon as practicable, the post of Director at each of the regional centres so as to ensure the effective functioning of the centres;

4. *Decides* to rename the United Nations Regional Centre for Peace and Disarmament in Asia as the United Nations Regional Centre for Peace and Disarmament in Asia and the Pacific;

5. *Also requests* the Secretary-General to report to the General Assembly at its forty-fifth session on the implementation of the present resolution.

---

[a]A/44/551-S/20870.

General Assembly resolution 44/117 F

15 December 1989   Meeting 81   153-1-1 (recorded vote)

Approved by First Committee (A/44/786) by recorded vote (130-1-1), 16 November (meeting 38); draft by Bangladesh, China, Democratic Yemen, Iran, Japan, Kenya for African Group, Malaysia, Mongolia, Myanmar, Nepal, New Zealand, Pakistan, Peru for Latin American and Caribbean Group, Philippines, Singapore and Sri Lanka (A/C.1/44/L.63/Rev.1); agenda item 64 *(e)*, *(h)* and *(i)*.

Financial implications. 5th Committee, A/44/810; S-G, A/C.1/44/L.64/Rev.1, A/C.5/44/36.

Meeting numbers. GA 44th session: 1st Committee 3-25, 38; 5th Committee 48; plenary 81.

Recorded vote in Assembly as follows:

In favour: Afghanistan, Albania, Algeria, Angola, Antigua and Barbuda, Argentina, Australia, Austria, Bahamas, Bahrain, Bangladesh, Barbados, Belgium, Benin, Bhutan, Bolivia, Botswana, Brazil, Brunei Darussalam, Bulgaria, Burkina Faso, Burundi, Byelorussian SSR, Cameroon, Canada, Cape Verde, Central African Republic, Chad, Chile, China, Colombia, Congo, Costa Rica, Côte d'Ivoire, Cuba, Cyprus, Czechoslovakia, Democratic Kampuchea, Democratic Yemen, Denmark, Djibouti, Dominica, Dominican Republic, Ecuador, Egypt, El Salvador, Ethiopia, Fiji, Finland, France, Gabon, Gambia, German Democratic Republic, Germany, Federal Republic of, Ghana, Greece, Grenada, Guatemala, Guinea, Guinea-Bissau, Guyana, Haiti, Honduras, Hungary, Iceland, India, Indonesia, Iran, Iraq, Ireland, Israel, Italy, Jamaica, Japan, Jordan, Kenya, Kuwait, Lao People's Democratic Republic, Lebanon, Lesotho, Liberia, Libyan Arab Jamahiriya, Luxembourg, Madagascar, Malawi, Malaysia, Maldives, Mali, Malta, Mauritania, Mauritius, Mexico, Mongolia, Morocco, Mozambique, Myanmar, Nepal, Netherlands, New Zealand, Nicaragua, Niger, Nigeria, Norway, Oman, Pakistan, Panama, Papua New Guinea, Paraguay, Peru, Philippines, Poland, Portugal, Qatar, Romania, Rwanda, Saint Kitts and Nevis, Saint Lucia, Saint Vincent and the Grenadines, Samoa, Sao Tome and Principe, Saudi Arabia, Senegal, Seychelles, Sierra Leone, Singapore, Solomon Islands, Somalia, Spain, Sri Lanka, Sudan, Suriname, Swaziland, Sweden, Syrian Arab Republic, Thailand, Togo, Trinidad and Tobago, Tunisia, Turkey, Uganda, Ukrainian SSR, USSR, United Arab Emirates, United Republic of Tanzania, Uruguay, Vanuatu, Venezuela, Viet Nam, Yemen, Yugoslavia, Zaire, Zambia, Zimbabwe.

Against: United States.

Abstaining: United Kingdom.

Disarmament Week

Disarmament Week, an annual event starting on United Nations Day, 24 October, and aimed at fostering the objectives of disarmament, was observed on 25 October 1989 at United Nations Headquarters at a special meeting of the General Assembly's First Committee, where statements were made by the President of the General Assembly, the Secretary-General and the Chairman of the First Committee.

In an August report with later addenda,[11] the Secretary-General submitted information received from 11 Member States, as well as from the United Nations system and international NGOs on their activities to promote the Week's objectives.

GENERAL ASSEMBLY ACTION

On 15 December 1989, on the recommendation of the First Committee, the General Assembly adopted **resolution 44/119 G** without vote.

Disarmament Week

The General Assembly,

Noting that there have been important developments of late in the areas of arms limitation and disarmament efforts which provide a sense of encouragement and hope for a more secure world,

Noting at the same time that, despite the positive developments, the arms race still poses a grave threat to world peace and security,

Stressing the vital importance of eliminating the threat of nuclear and conventional war, ending the nuclear and conventional arms race and bringing about disarmament,

Emphasizing anew the need for and the importance of world public opinion in support of halting and reversing the global arms race in all its aspects,

Taking into account the aspirations of the world public to prevent an arms race in space and to terminate it on Earth,

Noting with satisfaction the broad and active support by Governments and international and national organizations of the decision taken by the General Assembly at its tenth special session, the first special session devoted to disarmament, regarding the proclamation of the week starting 24 October, the day of the foundation of the United Nations, as a week devoted to fostering the objectives of disarmament,

Recalling the recommendations concerning the World Disarmament Campaign contained in annex V to the Concluding Document of the Twelfth Special Session of the General Assembly, the second special session devoted to disarmament, in particular the recommendation that Disarmament Week should continue to be widely observed,

Noting the support for the further observance of Disarmament Week expressed by Member States at the fifteenth special session of the General Assembly, the third special session devoted to disarmament,

Recognizing the significance of the annual observance of Disarmament Week, including by the United Nations,

1. *Takes note with satisfaction* of the report of the Secretary-General on the follow-up measures undertaken by States, governmental and non-governmental organizations in holding Disarmament Week;

2. *Commends* all States, international and national governmental and non-governmental organizations for their active support for and participation in Disarmament Week;

3. *Invites* all States that so desire, in carrying out appropriate measures at the local level on the occasion of Disarmament Week, to take into account the elements of the model programme for Disarmament Week prepared by the Secretary-General;

4. *Invites* Governments to continue, in accordance with General Assembly resolution 33/71 D of 14 December 1978, to inform the Secretary-General of activities undertaken to promote the objectives of Disarmament Week;

5. *Invites* international and national non-governmental organizations to continue to take an active part in Disarmament Week and to inform the Secretary-General of the activities undertaken;

6. *Invites* the Secretary-General to continue to use the United Nations information organs as widely as possible to promote better understanding among the world public of disarmament problems and the objectives of Disarmament Week;

7. *Requests* the Secretary-General, in accordance with paragraph 4 of resolution 33/71 D, to submit to the General Assembly at its forty-seventh session a report on the implementation of the present resolution.

General Assembly resolution 44/119 G

15 December 1989   Meeting 81   Adopted without vote

Approved by First Committee (A/44/788) without vote, 9 November (meeting 32); 15-nation draft (A/C.1/44/L.61); agenda item 66 (k).

Sponsors: Angola, Bulgaria, Byelorussian SSR, Cuba, Czechoslovakia, German Democratic Republic, Japan, Lao People's Democratic Republic, Mongolia, New Zealand, Papua New Guinea, Philippines, Samoa, Ukrainian SSR, Viet Nam.

Meeting numbers. GA 44th session: 1st Committee 3-25, 31, 32; plenary 81.

Disarmament studies and research

Advisory Board on Disarmament Matters

Following the Advisory Board's 1988 deliberations concerning its own role,[12] and taking into account other suggestions for improvements, the Secretary-General decided in early 1989 to make a number of changes in the functioning of the Board. With effect from 1 January 1989, the title of the Board was changed from Advisory Board on Disarmament Studies to Advisory Board on Disarmament Matters. That change was in line with the Board's views and suggestions made by many delegations in order to reflect more accurately the functions set out in the Board's mandate, which remained unchanged.

In its new form (twentieth session, New York, 6-11 July),[13] the Board discussed the implementation of the World Disarmament Campaign and its own activities in its capacity as Board of Trustees of UNIDIR. In addition, it held a discussion on the topic "The changing world—implications for arms limitation and disarmament".

The Board approved UNIDIR's programme of work for 1990 and recommended a subvention of $220,000 from the United Nations regular budget for 1990.

The General Assembly approved the subvention by **resolution 44/202 A**.

UN Institute for Disarmament Research

In August 1989, the Secretary-General transmitted to the General Assembly the report of UNIDIR covering the period from October 1988 to June 1989.[14] In addition to its ongoing research projects, UNIDIR, in co-operation with the Institut française des rélations internationales, organized a conference on problems and perspectives of conventional disarmament in Europe (Geneva, 23-25 January).

By **resolution 44/201 B, section IV**, the General Assembly requested the Secretary-General, without prejudice to the UNIDIR statute, to intensify his efforts to attract voluntary contributions to the Institute in order to obviate the need for a subvention from the regular budget. It also requested him to review the question of programme support costs and to report annually on the situation of the Institute.

UN disarmament studies programme

In 1989, no new studies were mandated by the General Assembly, nor were any study reports completed for the Secretary-General to transmit to the Assembly. Several studies requested in 1988, however, were under preparation, concerning the role of the United Nations in the field of verification; an update of the 1980 *Comprehensive Study on Nuclear Weapons*;[15] international arms transfers; the establishment of a nuclear-weapon-free zone in the Middle East; and scientific and technological developments and their impact on international security.

Education and information for disarmament

On 15 December 1989, the General Assembly, on the recommendation of the First Committee, adopted **resolution 44/123** by recorded vote.

Education for disarmament

The General Assembly,

Firmly convinced that the United Nations was established for the purpose of laying the foundations of a new world order whose general lines are set out in Article 2 of the Charter of the United Nations,

Fully aware that a peace based exclusively upon the political and economic arrangements of Governments would not be a peace that could secure the unanimous, lasting and sincere support of the world, and that the peace must be founded, if it is not to fail, upon the intellectual and moral solidarity of mankind,

Fully persuaded that, since wars begin in the minds of men, it is in the minds of men that the defences of peace must be constructed,

Taking into account the Final Document of the Tenth Special Session of the General Assembly, in particular paragraph 106 thereof, in which the Assembly urged Governments and governmental and non-governmental international organizations to take steps to develop programmes of education for disarmament and peace studies at all levels,

Considering that paragraphs 99, 100 and 101 of the Final Document provide for the mechanisms of a programme to mobilize world public opinion on behalf of disarmament, including the dissemination of supplementary information and publicity as part of its educational work,

Also considering that the World Disarmament Campaign plays an important supplementary role in the educational efforts on behalf of disarmament carried out by Member States within their own educational and cultural development systems, but that it cannot achieve irreversible results until training programmes are carried out at all levels of formal education for the purpose of changing basic attitudes with respect to aggression, violence, armaments and war,

1.   *Invites* Member States and international governmental and non-governmental organizations to inform the Secretary-General about all the efforts that they have made to respond to the call made in paragraph 106 of the Final Document of the Tenth Special Session of the General Assembly;

2.   *Requests* the Secretary-General to prepare a report, within available resources, on the current state of education for disarmament, taking into account the reports of Member States and international governmental and non-governmental organizations and based on information available from other kinds of sources;

3.   *Also requests* the Secretary-General to submit the reports requested in paragraphs 1 and 2 above to the General Assembly at its forty-sixth session;

4.   *Decides* to include in the provisional agenda of its forty-fifth session the item entitled "Education and information for disarmament".

General Assembly resolution 44/123

15 December 1989   Meeting 81   149-0-5 (recorded vote)

Approved by First Committee (A/44/792) by recorded vote (130-0-4), 10 November (meeting 34); 2-nation draft (A/C.1/44/L.17/Rev.1); agenda item 151.

Sponsors: Costa Rica, Côte d'Ivoire.

Meeting numbers. GA 44th session: 1st Committee 3-25, 31, 34; plenary 81.

Recorded vote in Assembly as follows:

In favour: Afghanistan, Albania, Algeria, Angola, Antigua and Barbuda, Argentina, Australia, Austria, Bahamas, Bahrain, Bangladesh, Barbados, Belgium, Benin, Bhutan, Bolivia, Botswana, Brazil, Brunei Darussalam, Bulgaria, Burkina Faso, Burundi, Byelorussian SSR, Cameroon, Canada, Cape Verde, Central African Republic, Chad, Chile, China, Colombia, Congo, Costa Rica, Côte d'Ivoire, Cuba, Cyprus, Czechoslovakia, Democratic Kampuchea, Democratic Yemen, Denmark, Djibouti, Dominica, Dominican Republic, Ecuador, Egypt, El Salvador, Ethiopia, Fiji, Finland, Gabon, Gambia, German Democratic Republic, Ghana, Greece, Guatemala, Guinea, Guinea-Bissau, Guyana, Haiti, Honduras, Hungary, Iceland, India, Indonesia, Iran, Iraq, Ireland, Israel, Jamaica, Japan, Jordan, Kenya, Kuwait, Lao People's Democratic Republic, Lebanon, Lesotho, Liberia, Libyan Arab Jamahiriya, Luxembourg, Madagascar, Malawi, Malaysia, Maldives, Mali, Malta, Mauritania, Mauritius, Mexico, Mongolia, Morocco, Mozambique, Myanmar, Nepal, Netherlands, New Zealand, Nicaragua, Niger, Nigeria, Norway, Oman, Pakistan, Panama, Papua New Guinea, Paraguay, Peru, Philippines, Poland, Portugal, Qatar, Romania, Rwanda, Saint Kitts and Nevis, Saint Lucia, Saint Vincent and the Grenadines, Samoa, Sao Tome and Principe, Saudi Arabia, Senegal, Seychelles, Sierra Leone, Singapore, Solomon Islands, Somalia, Spain, Sri Lanka, Sudan, Suriname, Swaziland, Sweden, Syrian Arab Republic, Thailand, Togo, Trinidad and Tobago, Tunisia, Turkey, Uganda, Ukrainian SSR, USSR, United Arab Emirates, United Republic of Tanzania, Uruguay, Vanuatu, Venezuela, Viet Nam, Yemen, Yugoslavia, Zaire, Zambia, Zimbabwe.

Against: None.

Abstaining: France, Germany, Federal Republic of, Italy,* United Kingdom, United States.

*Later advised the Secretariat it had intended to vote in favour.

Fellowship, training and advisory services programme

In October 1989,[16] the Secretary-General submitted his annual report on the United Nations disarmament fellowship, training and advisory services programme, stating that 24 fellows had been selected to participate in 1989. The programme—comprising lectures, seminars and panel discussions, research projects on peace and disarmament, simulation exercises and study visits—began on 3 July at Geneva and ended in New York on 23 November. During the first part of the programme, the fellows followed meetings of the Conference on Disarmament and, during the latter part, the work of the First Committee. In the course of their work, they also made study visits to IAEA headquarters at Vienna and, at the invitation of the States concerned, to offices and institutions in the German Democratic Republic, the Federal Republic of Germany, Japan, Sweden, the USSR and the United States.

GENERAL ASSEMBLY ACTION

On 15 December 1989, on the recommendation of the First Committee, the General Assembly adopted **resolution 44/117 E** without vote.

United Nations disarmament fellowship, training and advisory services programme

The General Assembly,

Recalling its decision, contained in paragraph 108 of the Final Document of the Tenth Special Session of the General Assembly, the first special session devoted to disarmament, to establish a programme of fellowships on disarmament, as well as its decisions contained in annex IV to the Concluding Document of the Twelfth Special Session of the General Assembly, the second special session devoted to disarmament, in which it decided, *inter alia*, to continue the programme and to increase the number of fellowships from 20 to 25 as from 1983,

Noting with satisfaction that the programme has already trained an appreciable number of public officials selected from geographical regions represented in the United Nations system, most of whom are now in positions of responsibility in the field of disarmament affairs in their respective countries or Governments,

Recalling also its resolutions 37/100 G of 13 December 1982, 38/73 C of 15 December 1983, 39/63 B of 12 December 1984, 40/151 H of 16 December 1985, 41/60 H of 3 December 1986, 42/39 I of 30 November 1987 and 43/76 F of 7 December 1988,

Noting also with satisfaction that the programme, as designed, has enabled an increased number of public officials, particularly from the developing countries, to acquire more expertise in the sphere of disarmament,

Believing that the forms of assistance available to Member States, particularly to developing countries, under the programme will enhance the capabilities of their officials to follow ongoing deliberations and negotiations on disarmament, both bilateral and multilateral,

1. *Reaffirms* its decisions contained in annex IV to the Concluding Document of the Twelfth Special Session of the General Assembly and in the report of the Secretary-General approved by resolution 33/71 E of 14 December 1978;

2. *Expresses its appreciation* to the Governments of the German Democratic Republic, the Federal Republic of Germany, Japan, Sweden, the Union of Soviet Socialist Republics and the United States of America for inviting the 1989 fellows to study selected activities in the field of disarmament, thereby contributing to the fulfilment of the overall objectives of the programme;

3. *Expresses its gratitude* to the Government of Nigeria for serving as host to the United Nations Regional Disarmament Workshop for Africa, which examined African security perceptions and requirements, including related regional issues, and to the Government of Norway for making financial contributions for the Workshop;

4. *Commends* the Secretary-General for the diligence with which the programme has continued to be carried out;

5. *Requests* the Secretary-General to continue the implementation of the programme within existing resources;

6. *Also requests* the Secretary-General to report to the General Assembly at its forty-fifth session on the implementation of the programme.

General Assembly resolution 44/117 E

15 December 1989   Meeting 81   Adopted without vote

Approved by First Committee (A/44/786) without vote, 9 November (meeting 32); 22-nation draft (A/C.1/44/L.59/Rev.1); agenda item 64 *(g)*.

Sponsors: Algeria, Argentina, Bolivia, Colombia, Cuba, Ethiopia, German Democratic Republic, Germany, Federal Republic of, Greece, Hungary, Indonesia, Liberia, Morocco, Myanmar, New Zealand, Nigeria, Pakistan, Philippines, Sweden, USSR, Venezuela, Zaire.

Meeting numbers. GA 44th session: 1st Committee 3-25, 32; plenary 81.

REFERENCES

[1]YUN 1982, p. 31. [2]A/44/647. [3]A/CONF.149/2. [4]A/44/582. [5]YUN 1986, p. 85. [6]*Ibid.*, p. 86, GA res. 41/60 J, 3 Dec. 1986. [7]YUN 1987, p. 88. [8]A/44/584. [9]A/44/583. [10]YUN 1987, p. 89, GA res. 42/39 D, 30 Nov. 1987. [11]A/44/446 & Add.1,2. [12]YUN 1988, p. 97. [13]A/44/654. [14]A/44/421. [15]YUN 1980, p. 109. [16]A/44/663.

Chapter III

Peaceful uses of outer space

During 1989, the Committee on the Peaceful Uses of Outer Space (Committee on outer space) and its Scientific and Technical and Legal Sub-Committees continued consideration of international co-operation in the peaceful uses of outer space.

In December, the General Assembly endorsed the Committee's recommendations regarding international co-operation in outer space and the initiative of international organizations and bodies to designate 1992 as International Space Year (resolution 44/46).

Science, technology and law

General aspects

The Committee on outer space,[1] in accordance with a 1988 General Assembly resolution,[2] continued its consideration, as a matter of priority, of ways and means of maintaining outer space for peaceful purposes. The Committee, at its thirty-second session (New York, 5-15 June), felt that it had, through its work in the scientific, technical and legal fields, an important role to play in assuring that outer space was maintained for peaceful purposes. It had responsibilities for strengthening the international basis for peaceful co-operation which could cover, among other things, further developments of international space law, including preparation of international agreements governing various practical peaceful applications of the achievements of space science and technology.

Implementation of the recommendations of the 1982 Conference on outer space

The Secretary-General, in August,[3] reported on the progress made in implementing the recommendations of the Second (1982) United Nations Conference on the Exploration and Peaceful Uses of Outer Space (UNISPACE-82).[4] The report covered the Working Group of the Whole to Evaluate the Implementation of the Recommendations of UNISPACE-82, inter-agency and regional co-operation, various studies, the United Nations Programme on Space Applications, technical advisory services, the International Space Information Service and voluntary contributions.

The Working Group was re-established in 1989[5] by the Scientific and Technical Sub-Committee with a view to improving the execution of international co-operation activities, particularly those included in the United Nations Programme on Space Applications (see below), and to increase such co-operation and make it more efficient.

The Working Group met in New York between 22 February and 1 March. Since many of the UNISPACE-82 recommendations had still not been fully implemented, the Working Group proposed that the emphasis of the Programme on Space Applications should remain on long-term, project-oriented, on-the-job training in specific application areas of space technology; and that activities recommended in the report of the Expert on Space Applications for 1989[6] should be carried out (see below). Other recommendations included the following: promotion of better access to higher education in space-related subjects, with the United Nations providing on request experts in preparing national plans of action; participation of international and regional financial and development institutions; regional co-operation through resource sharing, with United Nations assistance in establishing a regional programme if requested; constant review by the Programme on Space Applications of recommendations of regional meetings of experts; greater specialist interaction for promoting wider application of the results of scientific research; encouragement to non-governmental organizations (NGOs) in integrating regional and interregional efforts by means of conferences, publications and other activities; updated Outer Space Affairs Division reports on the resources of States; and provision to developing countries, by countries with relevant capabilities, of assistance in developing low-cost community receivers for communication satellites and low-cost, preferably renewable, power sources to operate them in unelectrified locations; also, continual provision of data by satellite-operating States in a form compatible with current systems, and increase by the Outer Space Affairs Division of the number of fellowships in space technology application for scientists and technicians from developing countries. The Working Group recommended that it be reconvened in 1990.

In addition, the Working Group renewed its 1988 recommendation that the Committee on outer space request all Member States and international organizations with space-related activities to inform the Secretary-General of activities that could be the subject of greater international co-operation.

Five Member States (Bulgaria, German Democratic Republic, Hungary, Syrian Arab Republic, USSR) responded to the Secretary-General's request for such information.[7]

The Group's report and recommendation were adopted by the Scientific and Technical Sub-Committee and annexed to its report and endorsed by the Committee on outer space.[1]

One of the recommendations of UNISPACE-82 was that an international space information service be established within the Outer Space Affairs Division of the United Nations. In 1989, the Division issued a revised edition of the directory on education, training, research and fellowship opportunities in space science and technology and its applications[8] and an addendum to the directory on information systems on space science and technology.[9]

UN Programme on Space Applications

In 1989, the United Nations Programme on Space Applications focused on providing long-range fellowships for in-depth training and technical advisory services to Member States and regional institutions; organizing regional and international workshops, training courses, seminars and expert meetings; provision and development of indigenous capability; and promoting greater co-operation in space science and technology. Programme activities were described in a December report of the United Nations Expert on Space Applications to the Scientific and Technical Sub-Committee.[6] The Programme received offers to renew the following fellowships: Austria, two one-year fellowships in microwave technology; Brazil, 10 nine-month fellowships for training and research in remote-sensing technology; the German Democratic Republic, three fellowships in basic space sciences, satellite geodesy and remote sensing; the USSR, 15 fellowships in geodesy, cartography and aerial photography and six new fellowships in different fields of space science and technology; and the European Space Agency (ESA), four fellowships for studies in communications engineering, telecommunications, remote-sensing information systems and satellite meteorology.

In 1989, the Programme conducted four training courses, two meetings of experts and one workshop: the United Nations/United Nations Development Programme (UNDP)/Food and Agriculture Organization of the United Nations (FAO)/ESA Meeting of Experts on Remote Sensing and Satellite Meteorology Applications to Marine Resources and Coastal Management, for the benefit of Member States of the Atlantic coast of Africa region (Maspalomas, Canary Islands, Spain, 8-12 May);[10] the United Nations Meeting of Experts on the Development of Remote-Sensing Skills and Knowledge (Dundee, United Kingdom, 26-30 June);[11] the fifth United Nations/FAO/World Meteorological Organization (WMO)/ESA Training Course on the Use of Remote Sensor Systems (visible, infrared and microwave) in Agrometeorological and Hydrological Applications, organized for members of the Economic and Social Commission for Asia and the Pacific (Canberra, Australia, 15 May–2 June),[12] with a follow-up course on digital image processing (MicroBRIAN) (Brisbane, Australia, 5-16 June); a United Nations International Training Course on the Use of Remote-Sensing Data in Agriculture Management (Moscow, 25 September–6 October);[13] the second International Training Course on Remote-Sensing Applications to Geological Sciences (Potsdam, German Democratic Republic, 5-22 October);[14] the fourteenth United Nations/FAO International Training Course on Applications of Remote Sensing to Land Resources (Rome, Italy, 6-24 November);[15] and a United Nations/Indian Ocean Marine Affairs Co-operation Conference (IOMAC) Workshop on Oceanographic/Marine Space Information Systems (Karachi, Pakistan, 2-6 July).[16]

Publication began in 1989 of a series of papers selected from those presented under the auspices of the Programme, in the language of presentation. The first publication was entitled *Seminars of the United Nations Programme on Space Applications: Selected Papers on Remote Sensing Technology.*[17]

Programme activities were supported in 1989 with voluntary contributions from Australia, Austria, Brazil, Canada, France, the German Democratic Republic, Italy, Nigeria, Pakistan, Spain, the USSR, the United Kingdom and the United States.

The United Nations Expert on Space Applications, in a 1988 report[18] considered by the Scientific and Technical Sub-Committee in 1989, appealed to Member States and international organizations either to provide support for the Programme as a whole or to identify specific activities of the Programme they would like to support and inform the Secretariat accordingly.

The Scientific and Technical Sub-Committee[5] expressed concern over the meagre financial resources available to the Expert on Space Applications for carrying out the Programme and appealed to Member States to support the Programme through voluntary contributions, noting that the Programme was a priority activity.

The Committee on outer space[1] expressed appreciation to the Expert for the effective manner in which he had implemented the Programme within the limited funds at his disposal. The General Assembly, by its **resolution 44/46** of 8 December, endorsed the Programme for 1990, as proposed to the Committee by the Expert, and urged States to make voluntary contributions to the Programme.

Co-ordination in the UN system

The Scientific and Technical Sub-Committee[5] continued to stress the necessity of ensuring continuous and effective consultations and co-ordination in the field of outer space activities among organizations within the United Nations system and the avoidance of duplication of activities. It noted with satisfaction that an Inter-Agency Meeting on Outer Space Activities was being planned to consider, in particular, participation of the specialized agencies and other organizations within the United Nations system in the implementation of the recommendations of UNISPACE-82. It reaffirmed its view that the United Nations should continue to seek the support of UNDP and that of other international funding organizations in carrying out UNISPACE-82 recommendations, while at the same time noting that UNDP was supporting the 1989 Programme and expressing hope for future support.

The *Ad Hoc* Inter-Agency Meeting on Outer Space Activities (Geneva, 27-29 September),[19] convened by the Administrative Committee on Co-ordination (ACC), recommended that the 1990 inter-agency meeting consider a number of items, including co-ordination of plans and programmes in the application of space technology and activities of UNISPACE-82, an in-depth review of co-operation in remote-sensing activities and planning for International Space Year 1992. In addition, the meeting approved the programmes subsequently included in an October report[20] of the Secretary-General on the co-ordination of outer space activities in 1990, 1991 and future years. Activities in 1989 included education, training and information dissemination regarding remote sensing, communications, meteorology and aspects of space science and technology.

The Committee on outer space[1] reiterated the Scientific and Technical Sub-Committee's call for consultations among United Nations organizations and the avoidance of duplication of work, and endorsed the Sub-Committee's view that the United Nations should continue to seek the support of UNDP and other international funding institutions and that the Secretariat should operate within UNDP funding procedures.

Science and technology aspects

At its twenty-sixth session (New York, 21 February–3 March 1989),[5] the Scientific and Technical Sub-Committee paid particular attention to the question of remote sensing as applied to environmental problems, particularly of the developing countries, while continuing its work on nuclear power sources and safety in spacecraft, technical aspects of the geostationary orbit, life sciences including space medicine, the geosphere-biosphere (global change) programme, planetary exploration and astronomy.

Space technology and environmental problems

The theme of the Sub-Committee's 1989 session, "Space technology as an instrument for combating environmental problems, particularly those of developing countries", addressed problems such as desertification, deforestation, floods, erosion and pest infestation.

In accordance with a 1988 General Assembly resolution[2] and at the invitation of the Committee on Space Research (COSPAR), the Sub-Committee, with the participation of the Scientific Committee on Problems of the Environment (SCOPE), organized a symposium (New York, 21 and 22 February) on remote sensing applied to environmental problems, particularly of developing nations. Presentations were made on such matters as ecological control of the environment; tropical deforestation; the geosphere-biosphere (global change) programme; and the Egyptian, European, Indian and United States experiences.

Remote sensing of the Earth by satellites

The Scientific and Technical Sub-Committee[5] reiterated its view that remote sensing from outer space should be carried out, taking into account the urgent need to assist the developing countries, and emphasized the importance of the availability of remote-sensing data and analysed data at reasonable cost and in a timely manner, as well as the need for free access to data from operational meteorological satellites. It noted the continuing programmes of China, France, India, Japan, the USSR and the United States for remote-sensing satellites as well as the planned remote-sensing satellite systems of Brazil, Canada and ESA. Poland said it would establish a United Nations inter-regional remote-sensing training centre for the benefit of developing countries. An expert from the United States made a presentation on remote sensing for disaster mitigation.

The Committee on outer space[1] recognized the importance of continuing international efforts to ensure the continuity, compatibility and complementarity of remote-sensing systems. It urged all countries and agencies to continue the free distribution of meteorological information. The Committee considered a paper on education and training opportunities in the United States in satellite remote sensing and related space sciences and applications.[21] It endorsed a recommendation by the Sub-Committee that the item be retained on its agenda as a priority item in 1990.

Nuclear power sources and safety in spacecraft

The Scientific and Technical Sub-Committee reconvened the Working Group on the Use of Nuclear Power Sources in Outer Space, which met in New York from 27 February to 2 March.[5]

The Working Group was informed that the Cosmos 1900 satellite, following the loss of radio contact with the ground, had automatically shut down its reactor, separated it, and boosted it into a higher orbit, thereby allowing time for radioactive decay to a safe level prior to re-entry into the atmosphere. The lifetime of the parking orbit of the nuclear power device was about 200 years, and of the thermal element assembly more than 300 years.

The Working Group noted Member States' concern over the growing quantity of space debris and collision possibilities with space objects with nuclear power sources. It recommended that nuclear reactors used in Earth orbit should be stored, after their mission, in a parking orbit until radioactivity had decayed to an acceptable minimum level before re-entering the Earth's atmosphere; that, in view of possible failures in the systems of nuclear power sources or satellites during operations in orbit, there be a reliable operational system to ensure disposal of the reactor; and that, in the case of radioisotope generators, due to the presence of radioactive materials from the beginning of the flight, the containment for the radionuclide materials should be such that the probability of release of radioisotopes would be minimized. The Group considered it important to ensure protection of the environment in the event of the re-entry of a nuclear power source into the atmosphere. In particular, measures should be taken to prevent contamination of the surface of the Earth, and, if radioactive material reached the ground, to protect human health and the environment.

The Group agreed that safety standards for nuclear power sources in space should be formulated in terms of the objectives to be met by designers rather than in terms of technical solutions or choices, since a variety of technical solutions was acceptable. Safety standards needed to distinguish provisions required during normal operation (including all planned situations anticipated to occur perhaps only once during the lifetime of the mission) from provisions under accident conditions.

The Committee on outer space[1] endorsed the Sub-Committee's recommendation that the agenda item be retained as a priority and that the Working Group continue its work at its 1990 session.

Technical aspects of the geostationary orbit

The Scientific and Technical Sub-Committee[5] continued consideration of the utilization and technical aspects of the geostationary orbit, in which satellites maintain an altitude of about 36,000 kilometres above the equator.

The Committee on outer space[1] endorsed the recommendation of the Sub-Committee that it continue consideration of the item at its next session.

International Space Year (1992)

In accordance with a General Assembly request of 1988,[2] the Committee on outer space and its Scientific and Technical Sub-Committee considered the advisability of declaring 1992 as international space year. The Sub-Committee reviewed working papers submitted by the USSR[22] on its budget and by the United States,[23] outlining possible activities during an international space year. The Committee on outer space took note of the plans of COSPAR and the International Astronautical Federation (IAF) to celebrate 1992 as international space year with a joint world space congress and a major programme on "Mission to Planet Earth", and recommended that the international space year promote international cooperation for the benefit and in the interest of all States, with an emphasis on the needs of developing countries. The Committee considered that activities during the year should be organized through the United Nations Programme on Space Applications and international organizations such as COSPAR, IAF, the International Civil Service Union and the Space Agency Forum for the International Space Year, and that such activities should be undertaken through voluntary contributions by Member States and without any impact on the United Nations regular budget or existing programmes.

The Committee recommended that the General Assembly endorse the initiative to designate 1992 as international space year, which the Assembly did in December in adopting the omnibus resolution on outer space matters (see below).

Spin-off benefits of space technology

In accordance with a 1988 General Assembly resolution,[2] the Committee on outer space took up a new item on the current status of spin-off benefits of space technology. It took note of a working paper submitted by the USSR,[24] outlining the Soviet activities regarding spin-off benefits; a working paper of the United States,[25] suggesting ways to enhance the information exchange on such benefits and the convening of a future seminar on spin-offs in the context of the United Nations Programme on Space Applications; "Spinoff

1988",[26] regarding activities of the United States National Aeronautics and Space Administration; and a contribution by FAO on the spin-off benefits in agriculture, forestry, fisheries and in the field of environmental protection. The Committee agreed that spin-offs were yielding substantial benefits in many fields, particularly energy, environmental protection, agriculture, forestry, marine fisheries, geophysical prospecting and medicine, including eye disease detection, heart attack protection, implantable medication systems and magnetic resonance imaging systems for diagnosing diseases. In the field of safety, spin-off applications resulted in the development of fire-resistant fabrics, fire-extinguishing materials and breathing systems for firefighters; industrial spin-offs included precision machine tools, testing and quality-control instruments, optical instruments and techniques, electronics and computer programmes. The Committee noted that the economic importance of these benefits was growing rapidly and in some cases was greater than the cost of the space programmes themselves. It also noted the importance of international co-operation in developing spin-off benefits and ensuring that all countries, in particular developing countries, had access to them.[1]

Other questions

The Scientific and Technical Sub-Committee[5] heard special presentations by France and the United States on life sciences in space and on terrestrial benefits derived from space research, respectively. The Sub-Committee noted that studies of human physiology under conditions of manned space flight had led to advances in medical knowledge in such areas as blood circulation, heart function and metabolism and that effects of microgravity on the human cardiovascular and nervous sytems, as well as on animals and individual cells, had been investigated by astronauts from France, the USSR and the United States. It also took note of efforts to study the feasibility of developing biospheric monitoring and disease prediction systems which would apply remote-sensing technology to malaria and other vector-borne diseases.

The Sub-Committee said progress being made through international co-operation in the planning of the international geosphere-biosphere (global change) programme for the 1990s was of fundamental importance for examining the future habitability of the planet and managing the common natural resources of the Earth and that COSPAR should arrange a special presentation on the programme. In relation to planetary exploration, the Sub-Committee heard special presentations by Czechoslovakia on planetary science, by the United States on the Galileo mission to Jupi-

ter, arriving in 1995, and by the Federal Republic of Germany and the United States on astronomy. Other special presentations included the International Space University (United States); life sciences in outer space (France); and the FY-1 meteorological satellite (China).

The Scientific and Technical Sub-Committee, after noting developments in the space transportation system programmes in China, India, Japan, the USSR, the United Kingdom and the United States and binational and international space transportation system programmes, stressed the importance of international co-operation in providing access to the benefits of such programmes for all countries. Experts from Bulgaria and the USSR made special presentations.

The Committee on outer space[1] endorsed the recommendation of the Sub-Committee to continue consideration of the item on space transportation in 1990.

Regarding the problem of collisions with and other aspects of space debris, the Committee on outer space considered it essential that more attention be paid to this problem by Member States and called for the continuation of national research on the question. It took note of a working paper[27] submitted by Australia, Belgium, Canada, the Federal Republic of Germany, the Netherlands, Nigeria and Sweden, which contained a proposal to put the issue of space debris on the agenda of the Scientific and Technical Sub-Committee at its 1990 session.

The Committee endorsed the decision of the Scientific and Technical Sub-Committee to continue consideration at its next session of items on the life sciences, including space medicine, progress in the geosphere-biosphere (global change) programme, matters relating to planetary exploration, and matters relating to astronomy, noting with satisfaction that special presentations by various experts were made under those items. It further endorsed the Sub-Committee's recommendation that COSPAR and IAF be invited to present reports and that COSPAR arrange a special presentation on progress in the global change programme.

The Committee endorsed the Sub-Committee's recommendation that the new theme at the 1990 Sub-Committee session should be "The use of space technology in terrestrial search and rescue and in disaster relief activities". It further endorsed the recommendation that COSPAR and IAF be invited to arrange a symposium on that theme.

Legal aspects

The Legal Sub-Committee of the Committee on outer space held its twenty-eighth session in New York from 20 March to 7 April.[28] It continued to consider the elaboration of draft principles relevant to the use of nuclear power sources in outer space; matters relating to the definition and delimitation of outer space; ways to ensure the rational and equitable use of the geostationary orbit; and the legal aspects of the application of the principle that outer space activities should be carried out for the benefit and in the interests of all States, taking into particular account the needs of developing countries, a new item agreed to in 1988.[29]

Nuclear power sources in outer space

The Legal Sub-Committee's Working Group on the elaboration of draft principles relevant to the use of nuclear power sources in outer space considered at its 1989 session a revised working paper[30] and two new working papers[31] presented by Canada. The revised paper proposed 11 principles, of which 3 had been agreed to by the Sub-Committee. The three agreed concerned applicability of international law; notification of re-entry; and assistance to States. The eight still under consideration concerned notification of the presence on board a space object of a nuclear power source; guidelines and criteria for safe use; safety assessment; consultations; responsibility of States; compensation; settlement of disputes; and relation with international treaties. The Sub-Committee also received papers by France[32] and the United Kingdom,[33] and another by Canada, France, the Federal Republic of Germany, Sweden and the United Kingdom.[34] The latter paper concerned guidelines and criteria for safe use, incorporating ideas on the same subject put forward in the papers by France and the United Kingdom.

By the end of the session, the Working Group recorded consensus[28] on principles concerning consultations and the settlement of disputes.

The Committee on outer space[1] recommended that the Legal Sub-Committee continue consideration of the item in 1990.

Geostationary orbit and definition of outer space

Matters relating to the definition and delimitation of outer space and to the character and utilization of the geostationary orbit were considered in the Legal Sub-Committee's Working Group, re-established by the Sub-Committee on 20 March 1989. The Working Group continued discussion of issues raised in previous years.[35] In the discussions, the Working Group considered working papers submitted to the Sub-Committee's previous sessions and exchanged views on a "working non-paper" on the geostationary orbit introduced by a number of members of the Group of 77.

The Working Group Chairman stated that the exchange of ideas with regard to the "non-paper" was substantive, useful and constructive, and

would constitute a positive platform for future debate.

Benefits from the exploration of outer space

Pursuant to a 1988 General Assembly resolution,[2] the Legal Sub-Committee considered the legal aspects related to the application of the principle that the exploration and utilization of outer space should be carried out for the benefit and in the interests of all States, taking into particular account the needs of developing countries. The Assembly had urged the Sub-Committee to pursue the question of the establishment of a working group on this item.

The Sub-Committee reviewed the replies[36] to the Secretary-General's note verbale of 26 September 1988, inviting Member States to submit their views on the priority of subjects under the item and provide information on their national legal frameworks relating to the application of the principle contained in article 1 of the 1967 Treaty on Principles Governing the Activities of States in the Exploration and Use of Outer Space, including the Moon and Other Celestial Bodies.[37]

The Sub-Committee adopted a proposal by Austria on the method of work on this item.

The Committee on outer space recommended that the Sub-Committee continue consideration of the item at its 1990 session.[1]

GENERAL ASSEMBLY ACTION

On 8 December 1989, on the recommendation of the Special Political Committee, the General Assembly adopted without vote **resolution 44/46.**

International co-operation in the peaceful uses of outer space

The General Assembly,

Recalling its resolution 43/56 of 6 December 1988,

Deeply convinced of the common interest of mankind in promoting the exploration and use of outer space for peaceful purposes and in continuing efforts to extend to all States the benefits derived therefrom, and of the importance of international co-operation in this field, for which the United Nations should continue to provide a focal point,

Reaffirming the importance of international co-operation in developing the rule of law, including the relevant norms of space law and their important role in international co-operation for the exploration and use of outer space for peaceful purposes,

Gravely concerned at the extension of an arms race into outer space,

Recognizing that all States, in particular those with major space capabilities, should contribute actively to the goal of preventing an arms race in outer space as an essential condition for the promotion of international co-operation in the exploration and use of outer space for peaceful purposes,

Aware of the need to increase the benefits of space technology and its applications and to contribute to an orderly growth of space activities favourable to the socio-economic advancement of mankind, in particular that of the peoples of developing countries,

Considering that space debris is an issue of concern to all nations,

Noting the progress achieved in the further development of peaceful space exploration and application as well as in various national and co-operative space projects, which contribute to international co-operation in this field,

Taking note of the report of the Secretary-General on the implementation of the recommendations of the Second United Nations Conference on the Exploration and Peaceful Uses of Outer Space,

Having considered the report of the Committee on the Peaceful Uses of Outer Space on the work of its thirty-second session,

1. *Endorses* the report of the Committee on the Peaceful Uses of Outer Space;

2. *Invites* States that have not yet become parties to the international treaties governing the uses of outer space to give consideration to ratifying or acceding to those treaties;

3. *Notes* that, at its twenty-eighth session, the Legal Sub-Committee of the Committee on the Peaceful Uses of Outer Space, in its working groups, continued its work as mandated by the General Assembly in resolution 43/56;

4. *Endorses* the recommendations of the Committee that the Legal Sub-Committee, at its twenty-ninth session, taking into account the concerns of all countries, particularly those of developing countries, should:

(*a*) Continue, through its working group, the elaboration of draft principles relevant to the use of nuclear-power sources in outer space;

(*b*) Continue, through its working group, its consideration of matters relating to the definition and delimitation of outer space and to the character and utilization of the geostationary orbit, including consideration of ways and means to ensure the rational and equitable use of the geostationary orbit without prejudice to the role of the International Telecommunication Union;

(*c*) Continue its consideration of the legal aspects related to the application of the principle that the exploration and utilization of outer space should be carried out for the benefit and in the interests of all States, taking into particular account the needs of developing countries;

5. *Endorses* the recommendations of the Legal Sub-Committee on the method of work concerning the agenda item referred to in paragraph 4 (*c*) above, and notes that the working group will be established in 1990 and convened in 1991 in accordance with paragraph 53 (*c*) of the report of the Legal Sub-Committee;

6. *Calls upon* Member States to respond promptly to the requests issued by the Secretary-General in connection with paragraphs 53 (*a*) and (*b*) of the report of the Legal Sub-Committee;

7. *Notes* that, at its twenty-sixth session, the Scientific and Technical Sub-Committee of the Committee on the Peaceful Uses of Outer Space continued its work as mandated by the General Assembly in resolution 43/56;

8. *Endorses* the recommendations of the Committee that the Scientific and Technical Sub-Committee, at its twenty-seventh session, taking into account the concerns of all countries, particularly those of developing countries, should:

(*a*) Consider the following items on a priority basis:

(i) United Nations Programme on Space Applications and the co-ordination of space activities within the United Nations system;

(ii) Implementation of the recommendations of the Second United Nations Conference on the Exploration and Peaceful Uses of Outer Space;

(iii) Matters relating to remote sensing of the Earth by satellites, including, *inter alia*, applications for developing countries;

(iv) Use of nuclear-power sources in outer space;

(*b*) Consider the following items:

(i) Questions relating to space transportation systems and their implications for future activities in space;

(ii) Examination of the physical nature and technical attributes of the geostationary orbit; examination of its utilization and applications, including, *inter alia*, in the field of space communications, as well as other questions relating to space communications developments, taking particular account of the needs and interests of developing countries;

(iii) Matters relating to life sciences, including space medicine;

(iv) Progress in the geosphere-biosphere (global change) programme; the Committee on Space Research and the International Astronautical Federation should be invited to present reports and arrange a special presentation on this subject;

(v) Matters relating to planetary exploration;

(vi) Matters relating to astronomy;

(vii) The theme fixed for special attention at the 1990 session of the Scientific and Technical Sub-Committee: ''The use of space technology in terrestrial search and rescue and in disaster relief activities''; the Committee on Space Research and the International Astronautical Federation should be invited to arrange a symposium, with as wide a participation as possible, to be held during the first week of the Sub-Committee's session, after the adjournment of its meetings, to complement discussions within the Sub-Committee;

9. *Considers*, in the context of paragraph 8 (*a*) (ii) above, that it is particularly urgent to implement the following recommendations:

(*a*) All countries should have the opportunity to use the techniques resulting from medical studies in space;

(*b*) Data banks at the national and regional levels should be strengthened and expanded and an international space information service should be established to function as a centre of co-ordination;

(*c*) The United Nations should support the creation of adequate training centres at the regional level, linked, whenever possible, to institutions implementing space programmes; necessary funding for the development of such centres should be made available through financial institutions;

(*d*) The United Nations should organize a fellowship programme through which selected graduates or post-graduates from developing countries should get in-depth, long-term exposure to space technology or applications; it is also desirable to encourage the availability of opportunities for such exposures on other bilateral and multilateral bases outside the United Nations system;

10. *Endorses* the recommendation of the Committee that the Scientific and Technical Sub-Committee should reconvene, at its twenty-seventh session, the Working Group of the Whole to Evaluate the Implementation of the Recommendations of the Second United Nations Conference on the Exploration and Peaceful Uses of Outer Space, with a view to improving the execution of activities relating to international co-operation, particularly those included within the United Nations Programme on Space Applications, and to proposing concrete steps to increase such co-operation, as well as to make it more efficient;

11. *Also endorses* the recommendations of the Working Group of the Whole, as endorsed by the Committee and as contained in paragraphs 4, 5 and 6 of the report of the Working Group of the Whole;

12. *Decides* that, during the twenty-seventh session of the Scientific and Technical Sub-Committee, the Working Group on the Use of Nuclear Power Sources in Outer Space shall be reconvened to conduct additional work on the basis of its previous reports and of subsequent reports of the Sub-Committee;

13. *Endorses* the United Nations Programme on Space Applications for 1990, as proposed to the Committee by the Expert on Space Applications, and urges all States to make voluntary contributions to the Programme in order to enhance its effectiveness;

14. *Emphasizes* the urgency and importance of implementing fully the recommendations of the Second United Nations Conference on the Exploration and Peaceful Uses of Outer Space as early as possible;

15. *Reaffirms* its approval of the recommendation of the Conference regarding the establishment and strengthening of regional mechanisms of co-operation and their promotion and creation through the United Nations system;

16. *Expresses its appreciation* to all Governments that have made or expressed their intention to make contributions towards carrying out the recommendations of the Conference;

17. *Invites* all Governments to take effective action for the implementation of the recommendations of the Conference;

18. *Requests* all organs, organizations and bodies of the United Nations system and other intergovernmental organizations working in the field of outer space or on space-related matters to co-operate in the implementation of the recommendations of the Conference;

19. *Requests* the Secretary-General to report to the General Assembly at its forty-fifth session on the implementation of the recommendations of the Conference;

20. *Endorses* the initiative of international scientific organizations and bodies to designate 1992 as International Space Year;

21. *Endorses* the recommendation of the Committee that international co-operation should be promoted through the International Space Year, which should be carried out for the benefit and in the interests of all States, taking into particular account the needs of developing countries, and that, in that context, the train-

ing and educational capabilities of the United Nations Programme on Space Applications should be utilized to bring about a meaningful role for the United Nations, through voluntary contributions by Member States and without any impact on the regular budget of the United Nations or the existing programme of work of the Programme;

22. *Recommends* that more attention should be paid to all aspects related to the protection and the preservation of the outer space environment, especially those potentially affecting the Earth's environment;

23. *Considers* that it is essential that Member States pay more attention to the problem of collisions with space debris and other aspects of space debris, and calls for the continuation of national research on that question;

24. *Urges* all States, in particular those with major space capabilities, to contribute actively to the goal of preventing an arms race in outer space as an essential condition for the promotion of international co-operation in the exploration and uses of outer space for peaceful purposes;

25. *Takes note* of the views expressed and documents circulated during the thirty-second session of the Committee and during the forty-fourth session of the General Assembly concerning ways and means of maintaining outer space for peaceful purposes;

26. *Requests* the Committee to continue to consider, as a matter of priority, ways and means of maintaining outer space for peaceful purposes and to report thereon to the General Assembly at its forty-fifth session;

27. *Also requests* the Committee to continue to consider at its thirty-third session its agenda item entitled "Spin-off benefits of space technology: review of current status";

28. *Affirms* that the interference that satellite systems to be newly established may cause to systems already registered with the International Telecommunication Union shall not exceed the limits specified in the relevant provision of the Radio Regulations of the Union applicable to space services;

29. *Requests* the specialized agencies and other international organizations to continue and, where appropriate, enhance their co-operation with the Committee and to provide it with progress reports on their work relating to the peaceful uses of outer space;

30. *Requests* the Committee to continue its work, in accordance with the present resolution, to consider, as appropriate, new projects in outer space activities and to submit a report to the General Assembly at its forty-fifth session, including its views on which subjects should be studied in the future.

General Assembly resolution 44/46

8 December 1989   Meeting 78   Adopted without vote

Approved by Special Political Committee (A/44/814) without vote, 17 November (meeting 21); draft by Austria for Working Group on International Co-operation in the Peaceful Uses of Outer Space (A/SPC/44/L.18); agenda item 75.

Meeting numbers. GA 44th session: SPC 19-21; plenary 78.

In **resolution 44/112**, the Assembly again called on all States, in particular those with major space capabilities, to contribute actively to the objective of the peaceful use of outer space and to take immediate measures to prevent an arms race in outer space. It urged the USSR and the United States to pursue intensively their bilateral negotiations aimed at reaching early agreement on the matter and requested the Conference on Disarmament to consider as a priority matter prevention of an arms race in outer space.

REFERENCES

[1]A/44/20. [2]YUN 1988, p. 104, GA res. 43/56, 6 Dec. 1988. [3]A/44/469. [4]YUN 1982, p. 162. [5]A/AC.105/429. [6]A/AC.105/446. [7]A/AC.105/458. [8]A/AC.105/432/Add.1. [9]A/AC.105/397/Rev.1/Add.1. [10]A/AC.105/436. [11]A/AC.105/438. [12]A/AC.105/437. [13]A/AC.105/440. [14]A/AC.105/441. [15]A/AC.105/442. [16]A/AC.105/439. [17]A/AC.105/443. [18]YUN 1988, p. 101. [19]ACC/1989/PG/8. [20]A/AC.105/444. [21]A/AC.105/L.183 & Corr.1. [22]A/AC.105/C.1/L.161. [23]A/AC.105/C.1/L.160. [24]A/AC.105/L.180. [25]A/AC.105/L.182. [26]COPUOS/1989/CRP.2. [27]A/AC.105/L.179. [28]A/AC.105/430. [29]YUN 1988, p. 104. [30]A/AC.105/C.2/L.154/Rev.4. [31]A/AC.105/C.2/L.169, A/AC.105/C.2/L.172. [32]A/AC.105/C.2/L.170. [33]A/AC.105/C.2/L.168. [34]A/AC.105/C.2/L.173. [35]YUN 1987, p. 101. [36]A/AC.105/C.2/15 & Add.1-7. [37]YUN 1966, p. 41, GA res. 2222(XXI), annex, 19 Dec. 1966.

Spacecraft launchings

During 1989, eight countries (Australia, Czechoslovakia, France, Japan, Sweden, USSR, United Kingdom, United States)[1] provided information to the United Nations on the launching of objects into orbit or beyond, in accordance with a 1961 General Assembly resolution[2] and article IV of the Convention on Registration of Objects Launched into Outer Space,[3] which had entered into force in 1976.

REFERENCES

[1]ST/SG/SER.E/196-201, 203-213. [2]YUN 1961, p. 35, GA res. 1721 B (XVI), 20 Dec. 1961. [3]YUN 1974, p. 63, GA res. 3235(XXIX), annex, 12 Nov. 1974.

Chapter IV

Other political questions

In 1989, questions related to information, effects of atomic radiation and Antarctica were again on the General Assembly's agenda. United Nations public information policies and activities were assessed and recommendations made (resolution 44/50) and the United Nations Educational, Scientific and Cultural Organization agreed by consensus upon a new strategy for the development of communication and the free flow of information. As to atomic radiation, the Assembly requested the United Nations Scientific Committee on the Effects of Atomic Radiation to continue its work on the levels, effects and risks of ionizing radiation from all sources (44/45). On the issue of Antarctica, the Assembly underlined its significance for international peace and security, environment, global climate conditions, economy and scientific research (44/124 B). It appealed again for the exclusion of South Africa from the meetings of the Antarctic Treaty Consultative Parties until the system and practices of *apartheid* were eliminated (44/124 A).

In the ongoing efforts towards finding a solution to the Cyprus question, the Secretary-General, in exercise of his good offices, met with the two leaders of the island communities and presented ideas to assist them in reaching agreement, proposing resumed talks between them for February 1990.

During 1989, the Security Council held a total of 69 meetings and adopted 20 resolutions. The Assembly resumed and concluded its forty-third session and held the major part of its forty-fourth session with 161 items on the agenda. It also held its sixteenth special session, covering *apartheid* and its destructive consequences in southern Africa.

The Assembly requested strengthened co-operation between the United Nations and the League of Arab States (44/7), and the Organization of the Islamic Conference (44/8). It also invited the Council of Europe to participate in its work in the capacity of observer (44/6).

As there were no new admissions to the United Nations during 1989, its membership remained 159.

Information

The public information activities of the United Nations in 1989 continued to focus on two broad objectives: enhancing the information and commu-

nication capabilities of the developing countries and promoting an informed understanding of the work and purpose of the United Nations system among the peoples of the world. Those activities were carried out by the Department of Public Information (DPI) of the Secretariat and the United Nations Educational, Scientific and Cultural Organization (UNESCO).

Information policies and activities were also reviewed at the eleventh session of the General Assembly's Committee on Information (New York, 13-28 April), following an organizational session on 6 March.[1] Recommendations were not annexed to the Committee's report since it was agreed to continue consultations during the Assembly session. The report was considered by the Special Political Committee in November and acted on by the Assembly in December in resolution 44/50. The Assembly, by **decisions 44/418** and **44/313** of 8 December, increased the Committee on Information's membership from 73 to 74 and appointed Nepal as additional member.

Mass communication

At its 1989 session, the Committee on Information elaborated on the establishment of a new, more just and more effective world information and communication order, and examined United Nations public information policies and activities in the light of the evolution of international relations and the progress achieved by the United Nations system in the field of information and communication.

Proposed new world
information and communication order

The Committee on Information continued to examine the question of the establishment of a new world information and communication order. Delegations generally emphasized the need for consensus, and many of them felt that separating the Committee's mandate to the Department of Public Information from the broader questions would break the deadlock in the Committee and steer it towards a more progressive path.

UNESCO continued its collaborative research into the impact of new communication technologies, supported the preparation of a communication research catalogue in Western Europe, and took part in setting up an information network for Latin America. In March, UNESCO awarded its third IPDC-UNESCO Prize for Rural Communication to two projects: People's Cultural Action of Colombia and National Association of Small Farmers of Cuba.

At its twenty-fifth session (Paris, 17 October–16 November),[2] the General Conference of UNESCO agreed by consensus upon a new strategy for the development of communications and the free flow of information as part of UNESCO's 1990-1995 medium-term plan. Entitled "Communication in the service of humanity", it included: encouragement of the free flow of information at both international and national levels and promotion of wider and better balanced dissemination of information; enhancement of communication capacities of developing countries to increase their participation in the development process, including strengthening the International Programme for the Development of Communication (IPDC), providing training in media and communications fields, and enhancing technological capabilities; and advancement of mutual knowledge and understanding in the world through mass communication. The new strategy unequivocally supported freedom of the press and called on the United Nations to strive for the development of free, independent and pluralistic media in the public and private sectors.

International Programme for the Development of Communication

Pursuant to a 1988 General Assembly resolution,[3] the Director-General of UNESCO, in September 1989, submitted to the Assembly a report[4] examining the application of IPDC—a project aimed at helping developing countries to build communication infrastructure—and the social, economic and cultural effects of the accelerated development of communication technologies.

At its tenth session (Paris, 7-13 March), the IPDC Intergovernmental Council concentrated its future actions on a limited number of projects with multiplier effects and decided that a country could obtain financing for only one project at each session, regardless of its stage of implementation, thus reducing the number of approved and financed projects from 55 with an average of $35,000 per project in 1988 to 18 with an average of $88,700 per project. Two of the projects were interregional, 5 regional and 11 national.

African States received allocations of $613,000; Asian and Pacific States $422,000; interregional projects $100,000; and regional projects $461,500. Among the interregional projects were allocations to the development of the network of the Pool of News Agencies of Non-Aligned Countries, and the regional projects included training for audience research specialists in eight Central African countries,

development of the rural press in South-East Asia, and increasing regional television co-production in the Caribbean. Among projects in African States were establishment of community radio stations in Ethiopia; communications training for social change in the Gambia; resource extension and development of professional training for the Mauritanian Broadcasting Service; rehabilitation of Zanzibar television; manpower planning and development for Uganda's Ministry of Information and Broadcasting; and rescuing and safeguarding Sudan's audio-visual heritage. Projects in Asia and the Pacific included development of Bangladesh's film training facilities; mass media training in the Lao People's Democratic Republic; television programme production in Maldives; Nepal's folk music recording project; and a rural radio project in Samoa.

UN public information

DPI activities

During 1989, DPI, through its radio, visual and publications services and information centres, continued to implement United Nations information activities.

In accordance with a request from the General Assembly regarding implementation of its main 1988 resolution on information,[5] the Secretary-General submitted a report in October 1989.[6]

Pursuant to the resolution,[5] the Committee on Information also had before it the following reports pertaining to the work of DPI: assessment of the effectiveness of the *UN Chronicle*: 1988 survey;[7] application of modern technologies within DPI;[8] public information activities of the United Nations pertaining to the situation in the Middle East and the question of Palestine;[9] public information activities pertaining to the policies and practices of *apartheid*;[10] a progress report on the staff of DPI in posts subject to geographical distribution[11] prepared by the Secretariat; and two reports submitted by the Secretary-General: a review of public information activities in the Secretariat external to DPI;[12] and the implementation of recommendation 37[13] of the Group of High-Level Intergovernmental Experts to Review the Efficiency of the Administrative and Financial Functioning of the United Nations concerning a thorough review of DPI's functions, working methods and policies, with a view to consolidating functions and improving the quality of its activities.[14]

The ninth annual training programme for broadcasters and journalists from developing countries (New York, 12 September–20 October) was held to provide training and briefings on major issues before the United Nations for 17 young journalists. This included an international seminar on sex role stereotyping in the media's portrayal of women and its implications, organized in co-operation with Columbia University, New York. The United Nations Fellowship Programme for Educators—formerly called the Triangular Fellowship Programme—was held to promote education about the United Nations system in teacher education programmes (Dakar, Senegal, 4-13 December). The Department also co-sponsored an all-day symposium and workshop on human rights (19 October) and continued its full coverage of the meetings of all United Nations bodies concerned with this issue.

In July, DPI held a number of regional and national encounters of journalists and experts on the question of Palestine, and issued a booklet entitled *The United Nations and the Question of Palestine*. It prepared a comprehensive press kit in connection with the Economic Commission for Africa's report on an African Alternative Framework to Structural Adjustment Programmes for Socio-Economic Recovery and Transformation,[15] and a kit on the Secretary-General's report reviewing the implementation of the United Nations Programme of Action for African Economic Recovery and Development 1986-1990.[16] The Department also prepared two press kits on the United Nations Transition Assistance Group for Namibia (UNTAG).

Through its internal and external publications, DPI continued to disseminate relevant information on disarmament. It co-published a number of studies on this issue and produced a brochure entitled *Disarmament: A Global Concern*.

The Department continued to strengthen its ties with the News Agencies Pool of Non-Aligned Countries by sending daily news dispatches to its members and by participating in the Pool's Fifth General Conference (Luanda, Angola, 1-5 June).

UN information centres

The United Nations information centres (UNICs) continued to assist press and information media in their respective countries and intensified direct and systematic communication exchange with local media, educational institutions and non-governmental organizations (NGOs). United Nations information was regularly disseminated through UNICs for immediate distribution to local radio stations and newspapers. In order to improve co-ordination of field office and Headquarters activities on both programme and administrative issues, DPI continued to organize regional meetings with UNIC directors. It held such a regional meeting for directors in the Americas (Mexico City, February) and conducted a number of staff training programmes and workshops, including a training seminar for information assistants from 13 centres in different regions (New York, June); a workshop for administrative assistants from

centres in Europe (Geneva, August); and a training programme for reference assistants from 12 centres in English-speaking African countries (Nairobi, December).

Co-ordination within the UN system

The Joint United Nations Information Committee (JUNIC)—the inter-agency co-ordinating body for information activities in the United Nations system—did not hold its annual session in 1989. The inter-sessional period was used to prepare a revision of the Committee's terms of reference, in order to make it a more effective and action-oriented body.

Consultations between the Under-Secretary-General for Public Information and information directors of several United Nations specialized agencies and programmes resulted in an issues paper entitled "Enhancing the public image of the United Nations system",[17] which was considered by the Administrative Committee on Co-ordination (ACC) in October.[18] ACC adopted recommendations on improving inter-agency co-ordination in the field of information and a revision of JUNIC's terms of reference aimed at projecting a more coherent image of the United Nations system as a whole and making optimal use of the system's scarce resources.

DPI signed an initial agreement with the United Nations Development Programme (UNDP) on rationalizing United Nations field representation, intended to strengthen their co-operation in the field, make their relationship more mutually beneficial and reduce potential areas of duplication.

In November, the Special Political Committee[19] considered two reports submitted by the Joint Inspection Unit (JIU) in response to a 1986 General Assembly resolution:[20] "Review of UN public information networks—Reorganization of the Department of Public Information"[21] and "Review of UN public information networks—United Nations information centres",[22] and the related comments of the Secretary-General.[23] The Committee also had before it two non-papers with the Committee on Information's recommendations.[19]

On 8 December, on the recommendation of the Special Political Committee, the General Assembly adopted **resolution 44/50** by recorded vote.

Questions relating to information

The General Assembly,

Recalling its previous resolutions on questions relating to information,

Reaffirming the mandate given to the Committee on Information by the General Assembly in its resolution 34/182 of 18 December 1979,

Taking note of the report of the Secretary-General on questions relating to information,

Also taking note of the report of the Joint Inspection Unit and the conclusions and recommendations therein concerning the reorganization of the Department of Public Information of the Secretariat, as well as the comments of the Secretary-General thereon,

Encouraging the Secretary-General to continue necessary action in order to increase the efficiency and effectiveness of the Department of Public Information, with particular emphasis on securing a co-ordinated approach to priority issues before the Organization,

Further taking note of the comprehensive report of the Committee on Information, which served as an important basis and stimulated further deliberations,

I

Information in the service of mankind

Urges the full implementation of the following recommendations:

(1) All countries, the United Nations system as a whole and all others concerned, reaffirming their commitment to the principles of the Charter of the United Nations and adhering to the principles of freedom of the press and freedom of information, as well as to those of the independence, pluralism and diversity of the media, should co-operate and interact in responding to the call for the establishment of a new world information and communication order, seen as an evolving and continuous process, aimed at eliminating the existing imbalances between developed and developing countries in the field of information and communication, at reducing existing disparities in information flows at the international as well as the national level and at improving the media infrastructure and communication technology in the developing countries in order to increase their participation in the communication process, based on the free flow and wider and better balanced dissemination of information as well as on the meaningful and equal participation of all countries in the field of information and communication, ensuring the diversity of sources of and free access to information and intended to advance the mutual knowledge and understanding of peoples through all means of mass communication as an important contribution towards strengthening international peace and understanding. The central role of the United Nations Educational, Scientific and Cultural Organization in this regard, in line with that organization's strategies, should be reaffirmed;

(2) Fully aware of the important role that the media worldwide can freely play, the mass media should be encouraged to give wider and more objective coverage to the efforts of the international community towards global development and, in particular, the efforts of the developing countries to achieve economic, social and cultural progress;

(3) All countries are urged to assure to journalists the free and effective performance of their professional tasks; all physical attacks against them should be resolutely condemned;

(4) Aware of the existing imbalances in the international distribution of news, particularly that affecting the developing countries, it is recommended that urgent attention should be given to the elimination of existing inequalities and the reduction of existing disparities in information flows at the international as well as the national level, to the encouragement of the free flow and the promotion of wider and better balanced dissemination of information, without any obstacle to freedom of expression, and to the advancement of mutual knowledge and understanding of peoples through the diversification of sources of information, respecting the interests, aspirations and socio-cultural values of all peoples;

(5) The United Nations system as a whole, particularly the United Nations Educational, Scientific and Cultural Organization, and the developed countries should be urged to co-operate in a concerted manner with the developing countries and their media, public and private or other, with a view to strengthening the information and communication infrastructure in the developing countries and promoting their access to advanced communication technology, in accordance with their needs and the priorities attached to such areas by the developing countries, so as to enable them and their media to develop their own information and communication policies freely and independently and in the light of their social and cultural values, adhering to the principles of freedom of information and freedom of the press. In this regard, support should be provided for the continuation and strengthening of practical training programmes for broadcasters and journalists from developing countries;

(6) Regional efforts and co-operation among developing countries, as well as co-operation between developed and developing countries, to strengthen communication capacities and to develop further the media infrastructure in the developing countries, especially in the areas of training and dissemination of information, should be enhanced so as to encourage the free flow of information and promote its wider and better balanced dissemination;

(7) In addition to bilateral co-operation, the United Nations system, particularly the United Nations Educational, Scientific and Cultural Organization, should aim at providing all possible support and assistance to the developing countries and their media, public and private or other, with due regard to their interests and needs in the field of information and to action already adopted within the United Nations system, including in particular:

(a) The development of the human and technical resources that are indispensable for the improvement of information and communication systems in developing countries and support for the continuation and strengthening of practical training programmes, such as those already operating under both public and private auspices throughout the developing world;

(b) The creation of conditions that will enable developing countries and their media, public and private or other, by using their national and regional resources, to have the communication technology suited to their national needs, as well as the necessary programme material, especially for radio and television broadcasting;

(c) Assistance in establishing and promoting telecommunication links at the subregional, regional and interregional levels, especially among developing countries;

(8) Full support should be provided for the International Programme for the Development of Communication of the United Nations Educational, Scientific

and Cultural Organization, which should support both public and private media;

II
United Nations public information policies and activities

1. *Calls upon* the Secretary-General, in respect of United Nations public information policies and activities, to implement the following recommendations:

(1) The United Nations system as a whole should co-operate in a concerted manner, through its information services, in promoting a more comprehensive and realistic image of the activities and potential of the United Nations system in all its endeavours, in accordance with the purposes and principles of the Charter of the United Nations, with particular emphasis on the creation of a climate of confidence, the strengthening of multilateralism and the promotion of the development activities in the United Nations system;

(2) Reaffirming the primary role of the General Assembly in elaborating, co-ordinating and harmonizing United Nations policies and activities in the field of information, the Secretary-General is requested to ensure that the activities of the Department of Public Information of the Secretariat, as the focal point of the public information tasks of the United Nations, are strengthened and improved, keeping in view the purposes and principles of the Charter, the priority areas defined by the Assembly and the recommendations of the Committee on Information, so as to ensure an objective and more coherent coverage of, as well as better knowledge about, the United Nations and its work. The Secretary-General should ensure that the Department of Public Information:

(a) Co-operate more regularly with the United Nations Educational, Scientific and Cultural Organization, especially at the working level, with a view to maximizing the contribution of the Department to the efforts of that organization in:

(i) Encouraging the free flow of information, at the international as well as the national level;

(ii) Promoting the wider and better balanced dissemination of information, without any obstacle to freedom of expression;

(iii) Developing all the appropriate means of strengthening communication capacities in the developing countries in order to increase their participation in the communication process;

(iv) Advancing the mutual knowledge and understanding of peoples through all means of mass communication and, to that end, recommending such international agreements as may be necessary to promote the free flow of ideas by word and image;

(b) Enhance its co-operation with news agencies of and in the developing countries, in particular the News Agencies Pool of Non-Aligned Countries, the Eco-Pool of the News Agencies of Non-Aligned Countries and the Broadcasting Organization of Non-Aligned Countries, as well as with other news agencies and intergovernmental and regional organizations;

(c) Continue to disseminate, in co-ordination with the information services of other relevant agencies, information about United Nations activities pertaining, in particular, to:

(i) International peace and security;

(ii) Disarmament;

(iii) Peace-keeping operations;

(iv) Decolonization and the situation in the Non-Self-Governing Territories;

(v) The elimination of foreign occupation;

(vi) Human rights;

(vii) The elimination of all forms of racial discrimination;

(viii) The advancement of the status of women and their role in society;

(ix) Problems of economic and social development, as well as international economic co-operation aimed at resolving external debt problems;

(x) The environment;

(xi) The campaign against terrorism in all its forms, bearing in mind General Assembly resolution 40/61 of 9 December 1985;

(xii) The international campaign against drug abuse and illicit trafficking, including adequate coverage of the special session of the General Assembly, to be held from 20 to 23 February 1990, to consider the question of international co-operation against illicit production, supply, demand, trafficking and distribution of narcotic drugs, with a view to expanding the scope and increasing the effectiveness of such co-operation;

(d) Do its utmost to disseminate widely and to publicize the United Nations Programme of Action for African Economic Recovery and Development 1986-1990 and the tremendous efforts of the African countries towards recovery and development, as well as the positive response by the international community to alleviate the serious economic situation prevailing in Africa;

(e) Strengthen its activities and the dissemination of information on United Nations activities against the policies and practices of *apartheid*, giving due attention to the unilateral measures and official censorship imposed on the local and international media with regard to all aspects of that issue; provide adequate coverage of the sixteenth special session of the General Assembly on *apartheid* and its destructive consequences in southern Africa, to be held from 12 to 14 December 1989, and report thereon to the Committee on Information at its twelfth session, in 1990;

(f) Continue to disseminate information about activities of the United Nations directed at a comprehensive, just and lasting solution of international conflicts by exclusively peaceful means;

(g) Continue to cover all United Nations activities pertaining to the situation in the Middle East, and the question of Palestine in particular, and current developments in the region, in accordance with relevant United Nations resolutions, and report thereon to the Committee on Information at its twelfth session, in 1990;

(h) Continue to disseminate information about Namibia, in particular the current independence process as provided for in Security Council resolution 435(1978) of 29 September 1978; the Department should make adequate plans for the establishment of an information centre in Namibia, in consultation with the government of the new nation immediately after independence;

(i) Ensure the provision of coverage of the special session of the General Assembly devoted to international economic co-operation, in particular to the revitalization of economic growth and development of the developing countries, to be held from 23 to 27 April 1990;

(3) The Department of Public Information should continue its efforts in promoting an informed understanding of the work and purposes of the United Nations system among the peoples of the world and in strengthening the image of the United Nations system as a whole. The Secretary-General should ensure that the Department:

(a) Continue to maintain consistent editorial independence and accuracy in reporting in all the material it produces, taking necessary measures to ensure that its output contains adequate, objective and impartial information about issues before the Organization, reflecting divergent opinions where they occur;

(b) In the context of the review of its role, performance and methods of work, continue to apply appropriate modern technologies for the collection, production, storage, dissemination and distribution of information materials, including the use of satellite facilities;

(c) Consider expanding the programme of telephone news bulletins that are paid for by its users;

(d) Continue its co-operation with those countries that have expressed readiness to assist the United Nations in resuming short-wave broadcasts through their respective national networks free of charge, and encourage expansion of that type of co-operation with those developed and developing countries having recognized capabilities in this field;

(e) Take adequate measures to resume taped radio programmes, which it has temporarily curtailed, if so requested by broadcasting stations;

(f) Continue its briefing, assistance and orientation programme for broadcasters and journalists from developing countries focused on issues related to the United Nations;

(g) Identify new forms of co-operation, at the regional and subregional level, for the training of media professionals and for the improvement of the information and communication infrastructure of developing countries;

(h) Co-operate with educational institutions of Member States and with educators and education policy-makers, informing them about United Nations activities;

(i) Ensure adequate daily coverage of United Nations open meetings in the two working languages of the Secretariat, reflecting the views of all delegations with accuracy and objectivity. The Department should also continue to co-operate closely with and provide assistance to members of the United Nations Correspondents Association, taking into account their needs and requirements, especially in the area of press releases, press conferences and briefings, which provide them with basic information for reporting;

(j) Use the official languages of the United Nations adequately in its written and audio-visual materials and make balanced use of the two working languages of the Secretariat;

(k) Ensure timely distribution of its materials to subscribers and to United Nations information centres;

(4) The Department of Public Information should produce and distribute its publications in a timely manner. In particular, the Secretary-General is requested to make further efforts regarding the timely appearance of the *United Nations Yearbook*. The improvement in format and printing of the *United Nations Chronicle* is welcome. The Department is encouraged to continue to consider the interests of specific target audiences as it formulates its editorial policies;

(5) The Secretary-General is urged to continue his efforts to secure a sound and stable financial basis for the publications *Development Forum* and *Africa Recovery*;

(6) It is recognized that United Nations information centres constitute an important means of disseminating information about the United Nations among the peoples of the world. In this regard, the centres should intensify direct and systematic communication exchange with local media, information and educational institutions and non-governmental organizations. The Department should arrange for periodic evaluation of the activities of the centres in this regard. Every effort should be made to establish close co-ordination with other field offices of the United Nations system, particularly those of the United Nations Development Programme, in order to avoid duplication of work, taking into account the functional autonomy that the United Nations information centres should have. A report should be submitted to the Committee on Information after the first year of the provisional understanding between the Department and the United Nations Development Programme, reached in accordance with recommendation 37 (3) of the Group of High-level Intergovernmental Experts to Review the Efficiency of the Administrative and Financial Functioning of the United Nations. The Department should provide open and unhindered access by all people to all United Nations information centres and to all materials distributed through the centres. It is also urged to accelerate the process of linking the remaining United Nations information centres that have not been linked with electronic mail;

(7) Stressing the need for co-ordinating the information activities of the United Nations system and recognizing the important role that the Joint United Nations Information Committee plays in that regard, the Department of Public Information is encouraged to continue its active participation in the work of the Committee;

(8) It is recognized that free distribution of materials is necessary in the public information activities of the United Nations. However, as demands increase and whenever it is desirable and possible, the Department of Public Information should actively encourage the sale of its materials;

(9) The Secretary-General is requested to ensure that the reorganization and restructuring of the Department of Public Information strengthen and improve the output of the mandated programmes and activities of the Department, taking into account, in conformity with the relevant provisions of the Charter and of General Assembly resolution 41/213 of 19 December 1986, the need for equitable geographical distribution of posts and especially keeping in mind the levels at which developing countries are underrepresented;

(10) In view of the importance of radio programmes in developing countries, the Secretary-General is requested to enhance the efficiency of and to ensure full programme delivery by all regional radio units, namely, the African, Asian, Caribbean, European, Latin American and Middle Eastern Units and the Anti-*Apartheid* Programmes Section, including production of radio programmes called for by the General Assembly in resolution 38/82 B of 15 December 1983;

(11) All reports of the Secretary-General, as well as reports by representatives of the Department of Public Information, to the Committee on Information and the General Assembly, in particular those on new programmes or on the expansion of existing programmes, should contain:

(a) Detailed information on the output of the Department on each topic included in its work programme, which forms the basis of its programme budget;

(b) The costs of the activities undertaken on each topic;

(c) Adequate information on target audiences, end-use of the Department's products and analysis of feedback data received by the Department;

(d) A statement detailing the priority level that the Secretary-General has attached to current or future activities of the Department in documents dealing with such activities;

(e) Evaluation by the Department of the effectiveness of its different programmes and activities, with particular reference to the need constantly to review internal programme elements and activities;

2. *Requests* the Secretary-General to implement the recommendations relating to the activities of the Department of Public Information in accordance with the budgetary procedures as approved by the General Assembly in its resolutions 41/213, 42/211 of 21 December 1987 and 43/213 of 21 December 1988, and taking into account the priorities set by the Assembly;

3. *Supports* the Secretary-General in his continuing efforts to restructure and revitalize the Department of Public Information, based on the relevant provisions of General Assembly resolution 41/213;

4. *Also requests* the Secretary-General to report to the Committee on Information at its twelfth session, in 1990, on the activities of the Department of Public Information and on the implementation of the recommendations in the present resolution;

5. *Further requests* the Secretary-General to report to the General Assembly at its forty-fifth session on the implementation of the present resolution;

6. *Requests* the Committee on Information to report to the General Assembly at its forty-fifth session;

7. *Decides* to include in the provisional agenda of its forty-fifth session the item entitled "Questions relating to information".

General Assembly resolution 44/50

8 December 1989   Meeting 78   127-2-21 (recorded vote)

Approved by Special Political Committee (A/44/817) by recorded vote (107-2-20), 22 November (meeting 25); draft by Malaysia for Group of 77 (A/SPC/44/L.26); agenda item 79.

Meeting numbers. GA 44th session: SPC 15-19, 25; plenary 78.

Recorded vote in Assembly as follows:

In favour: Afghanistan, Algeria, Angola, Antigua and Barbuda, Argentina, Austria, Bahamas, Bahrain, Bangladesh, Barbados, Benin, Bhutan, Bolivia, Botswana, Brazil, Brunei Darussalam, Bulgaria, Burkina Faso, Burundi, Byelorussian SSR, Cameroon, Cape Verde, Central African Republic, Chad, Chile, China, Colombia, Comoros, Costa Rica, Côte d'Ivoire, Cuba, Cyprus, Czechoslovakia, Democratic Kampuchea, Democratic Yemen, Djibouti, Dominica, Dominican Republic, Ecuador, Egypt, Equatorial Guinea, Ethiopia, Fiji, Gabon, German Democratic Republic, Ghana, Grenada, Guatemala, Guinea, Guinea-Bissau, Guyana, Honduras, Hungary, India, Indonesia, Iran, Iraq, Jamaica, Jordan, Kenya, Kuwait, Lao People's Democratic Republic, Lebanon, Lesotho, Liberia, Libyan Arab Jamahiriya, Madagascar, Malawi, Malaysia, Maldives, Mali, Mauritania, Mauritius, Mexico, Mongolia, Morocco, Mozambique, Myanmar, Nepal, Nicaragua, Niger, Nigeria, Oman, Pakistan, Panama, Papua New Guinea, Paraguay, Peru, Philippines, Poland, Qatar, Romania, Rwanda, Saint Lucia, Saint Vincent and the Grenadines, Sao Tome and Principe, Saudi Arabia, Senegal,

Seychelles, Sierra Leone, Singapore, Solomon Islands, Somalia, Sri Lanka, Sudan, Suriname, Swaziland, Sweden, Syrian Arab Republic, Thailand, Togo, Trinidad and Tobago, Tunisia, Uganda, Ukrainian SSR, USSR, United Arab Emirates, United Republic of Tanzania, Uruguay, Vanuatu, Venezuela, Viet Nam, Yemen, Yugoslavia, Zaire, Zambia, Zimbabwe.

Against: Israel, United States.

Abstaining: Australia, Belgium, Canada, Denmark, Finland, France, Germany, Federal Republic of, Greece, Iceland, Ireland, Italy, Japan, Luxembourg, Malta, Netherlands, New Zealand, Norway, Portugal, Spain, Turkey, United Kingdom.

Also on 8 December, on the recommendation of the Third (Social, Humanitarian and Cultural) Committee, the Assembly adopted without vote **resolution 44/61** on the development of public information activities in the field of human rights.

The Assembly adopted other resolutions relating to information issues. By **resolution 44/201 A**, section VI, it took note of the JIU reports and the Secretary-General's related comments. In **resolution 44/201 B**, section XII, it requested the Secretary-General to ensure that the new DPI structure provided for full implementation of all mandated programmes and activities, to strengthen UNIC activities and to ensure that those activities fully reflected the General Assembly mandates.

REFERENCES

[1]A/44/21. [2]UNESCO 25 C/4. [3]YUN 1988, p. 109, GA res. 43/60 B, 6 Dec. 1988. [4]A/44/509. [5]YUN 1988, p. 112, GA res. 43/60 A, 6 Dec. 1988. [6]A/44/653. [7]A/AC.198/1989/3. [8]A/AC.198/1989/4. [9]A/AC.198/1989/5. [10]A/AC.198/1989/7. [11]A/AC.198/1989/6. [12]A/AC.198/1989/8. [13]YUN 1986, p. 1022. [14]A/AC.198/1989/9. [15]E/1989/35. [16]A/43/500 & Corr.1 & Add.1,2. [17]ACC/1989/CRP.10. [18]ACC/1989/DEC/24-32. [19]A/44/817. [20]YUN 1986, p. 1024, GA res. 41/213, 19 Dec. 1986. [21]A/44/433. [22]A/44/329. [23]A/44/433/Add.1, A/44/329/Add.1.

Radiation effects

The United Nations Scientific Committee on the Effects of Atomic Radiation at its thirty-eighth session (Vienna, 8-12 May) continued to review important problems on radiation doses and effects, as requested by the General Assembly in 1988.[1] In its report, presented to the Assembly in 1989,[2] the Committee made proposals for future work, including studies in: doses from natural sources of radiation; doses from man-made sources of radiation in the environment; medical radiation exposures; occupational radiation exposures and trends; effects of radiation exposures on plants and animals in the environment; epidemiological study of radiation effects in human populations; effects on the developing human brain from pre-natal radiation exposures; dose and dose-rate effects on radiation response; mechanisms by which radiation causes cancer; stimulation effects of low doses of radiation; hereditary effects of radiation in human populations; and perception of radiation risks. Concepts and methodologies for comparative assessment of effects, interactions and risks of toxic chemicals and radiation were also kept under consideration.

The Committee noted with satisfaction that its 1988 report to the General Assembly,[3] containing the Committee's basic radiation evaluations, had been issued as a United Nations sales publication. The Committee reiterated its earlier request that more adequate support be given to its secretariat.

GENERAL ASSEMBLY ACTION

On 8 December, on the recommendation of the Special Political Committee, the General Assembly adopted **resolution 44/45** without vote.

Effects of atomic radiation

The General Assembly,

Recalling its resolution 913(X) of 3 December 1955, by which it established the United Nations Scientific Committee on the Effects of Atomic Radiation, and its subsequent resolutions on the subject, including resolution 43/55 of 6 December 1988, in which, *inter alia*, it requested the Scientific Committee to continue its work,

Taking note with appreciation of the report of the United Nations Scientific Committee on the Effects of Atomic Radiation,

Reaffirming the desirability of the Scientific Committee continuing its work,

Concerned about the potentially harmful effects on present and future generations resulting from the levels of radiation to which man is exposed,

Conscious of the continued need to examine and compile information about atomic and ionizing radiation and to analyse its effects on man and his environment,

Bearing in mind the decision of the Scientific Committee to submit, as soon as the relevant studies are completed, shorter reports with supporting scientific documents on the specialized topics mentioned by the Committee,

1. *Commends* the United Nations Scientific Committee on the Effects of Atomic Radiation for the valuable contribution it has been making in the course of the past thirty-four years, since its inception, to wider knowledge and understanding of the levels, effects and risks of atomic radiation and for fulfilling its original mandate with scientific authority and independence of judgement;

2. *Notes with satisfaction* the continued and growing scientific co-operation between the Scientific Committee and the United Nations Environment Programme;

3. *Requests* the Scientific Committee to continue its work, including its important co-ordinating activities, to increase knowledge of the levels, effects and risks of ionizing radiation from all sources;

4. *Endorses* the intentions and plans of the Scientific Committee for its future activities of scientific review and assessment on behalf of the General Assembly;

5. *Also requests* the Scientific Committee to continue at its next session the review of the important problems in the field of radiation and to report thereon to the General Assembly at its forty-fifth session;

6. *Requests* the United Nations Environment Programme to continue providing support for the effective conduct of the work of the Scientific Committee and for the dissemination of its findings to the General Assembly, the scientific community and the public;

7. *Expresses its appreciation* for the assistance rendered to the Scientific Committee by Member States, the specialized agencies, the International Atomic Energy Agency and non-governmental organizations, and invites them to increase their co-operation in this field;

8. *Invites* Member States, the organizations of the United Nations system and non-governmental organizations concerned to provide further relevant data about doses, effects and risks from various sources of radiation, which would greatly help in the preparation of future reports of the Scientific Committee to the General Assembly.

General Assembly resolution 44/45

8 December 1989   Meeting 78   Adopted without vote

Approved by Special Political Committee (A/44/718) without vote, 19 October (meeting 4); 27-nation draft (A/SPC/44/L.3); agenda item 74.
Sponsors: Argentina, Australia, Austria, Bangladesh, Canada, China, Costa Rica, Czechoslovakia, Denmark, Egypt, France, Germany, Federal Republic of, India, Indonesia, Japan, Netherlands, New Zealand, Nigeria, Poland, Saint Lucia, Samoa, Swaziland, Sweden, USSR, United Kingdom, United States, Uruguay.
Meeting numbers. GA 44th session: SPC 3, 4; plenary 78.

REFERENCES

[1]YUN 1988, p. 116, GA res. 43/55, 6 Dec. 1988. [2]A/44/587. [3]YUN 1988, p. 116.

Antarctica

Minerals régime

Pursuant to a 1988 General Assembly resolution,[1] the Secretary-General submitted in October 1989 a report reviewing the question of a minerals régime on Antarctica.[2] In 1988, the Assembly had expressed its deep regret over the adoption by the Antarctic Treaty Consultative Parties on 2 June 1988 of a Convention on the Regulation of Antarctic Mineral Resource Activities, notwithstanding 1986[3] and 1987[4] Assembly resolutions calling for a moratorium on any such matter until all members of the international community could fully participate in negotiations. On 19 April, in response to the Secretary-General's note verbale on the issue, Australia, on behalf of the States parties to the Antarctic Treaty, emphasized the Parties' continuing belief that consideration of Antarctica by the General Assembly should proceed only on the basis of consensus. The Secretary-General noted further that the General Assembly had reiterated its call to the Antarctic Treaty Consultative Parties to invite the Secretary-General or his representative to all their meetings and reported that he had not been invited. He noted that, on 6 July, France conveyed a press release[5] of the Preparatory Meeting of the XVth Antarctic Treaty Consultative Meeting (Paris, 9-

13 May), which prepared a draft agenda for the next Consultative Meeting (Paris, 9-19 October), with items such as human impact on the Antarctic environment, including waste disposal; effects of tourism; protected areas; marine pollution and maritime safety; and the role of Antarctica in global change, including the ozone layer.

Communications. On 13 February, Malaysia transmitted a statement[6] by Antigua and Barbuda, Bangladesh, Ghana, Kenya, Malaysia, Nepal, Nigeria, Oman, Pakistan, Rwanda, Sri Lanka, the Sudan, Uganda and Zambia. Following a damaging oil spill from the supply ship *Bahía Paraíso*, which sank on 1 February off the Antarctic western coast, the countries urged the Antarctic Treaty Consultative Parties to reconsider the ratification of the Convention on the Regulation of Antarctic Mineral Resource Activities.

The Ministerial Meeting of the Co-ordinating Bureau of the Movement of Non-Aligned Countries (Harare, 17-19 May)[7] reaffirmed the conviction that Antarctica should be accessible to all nations and that any exploitation of the Antarctic resources should ensure the maintenance of international peace and security on the continent.

The Ninth Conference of Heads of State or Government of the Movement of Non-Aligned Countries (Belgrade, 4-7 September)[8] recognized the interest of mankind as a whole in ensuring the protection and conservation of the Antarctic environment, as well as its dependent and associated ecosystems, and considered the adoption by the Antarctic Treaty Consultative Parties of a Convention on the Regulation of Antarctic Mineral Resources to be detrimental to efforts at a consensus on the issue of Antarctica in the General Assembly.

The Commonwealth Heads of Government, in a communiqué adopted at their meeting (Kuala Lumpur, 18-24 October),[9] recognized Antarctica's critical impact on the environment and shared the conviction that every effort should be made to protect and conserve that unique territory.

GENERAL ASSEMBLY ACTION

On 15 December, the General Assembly, on the recommendation of the First Committee, adopted **resolution 44/124 B** by roll-call vote.

Question of Antarctica

The General Assembly,

Having considered the item entitled "Question of Antarctica",

Recalling its resolutions 38/77 of 15 December 1983, 39/152 of 17 December 1984, 40/156 A and B of 16 December 1985, 41/88 A and B of 4 December 1986, 42/46 A and B of 30 November 1987 and 43/83 A and B of 7 December 1988,

Recalling also the relevant paragraphs of the Political Declaration adopted by the Eighth Conference of Heads of State or Government of Non-Aligned Countries, held at Harare from 1 to 6 September 1986, and the resolution on Antarctica adopted by the Council of Ministers of the Organization of African Unity at its forty-second ordinary session, held at Addis Ababa from 10 to 17 July 1985, as well as the relevant paragraphs of the decision of the Council of Ministers of the League of Arab States meeting at Tunis on 17 and 18 September 1986 and resolution 25/5-P(IS) adopted by the Fifth Islamic Summit Conference of the Organization of the Islamic Conference, held at Kuwait from 26 to 29 January 1987, the final document on Antarctica adopted by the Ninth Conference of Heads of State or Government of Non-Aligned Countries, held at Belgrade from 4 to 7 September 1989 and the communiqué issued by Commonwealth Heads of Government at Kuala Lumpur on 24 October 1989,

Taking into account the debates on this item held since its thirty-eighth session,

Welcoming the increasing awareness of and interest in Antarctica shown by the international community,

Convinced of the advantages to the whole of mankind of a better knowledge of Antarctica,

Affirming its conviction that, in the interest of all mankind, Antarctica should continue forever to be used exclusively for peaceful purposes and that it should not become the scene or object of international discord,

Reaffirming the principle that the international community is entitled to information covering all aspects of Antarctica and that the United Nations should be made the repository for all such information in accordance with General Assembly resolutions 41/88 A, 42/46 B and 43/83 A,

Conscious of the particular significance of Antarctica to the international community in terms, *inter alia,* of international peace and security, environment, its effects on global climatic conditions, economy and scientific research,

Conscious also of the interrelationship between Antarctica and the physical, chemical and biological processes that regulate the total Earth system,

Reaffirming that the management and use of Antarctica should be conducted in accordance with the purposes and principles of the Charter of the United Nations and in the interest of maintaining international peace and security and of promoting international co-operation for the benefit of mankind as a whole,

Affirming the necessity of ensuring, in the interest of all mankind, comprehensive environmental protection and conservation of the Antarctic environment and its dependent and associated ecosystems through negotiations with the full participation of all members of the international community,

Conscious of the environmental degradation that prospecting and mining in and around Antarctica would pose to the Antarctic and global environment and ecosystems,

Convinced of the need to prevent or minimize any impact of human activity resulting from the large number of scientific stations and expeditions in Antarctica on the environment and its dependent and associated ecosystems,

Taking into account all aspects pertaining to all areas covered by the Antarctic Treaty system,

Taking note with appreciation of the reports of the Secretary-General on the question of Antarctica,

1. *Expresses its regret* that, despite the numerous resolutions in which it has called upon the Antarctic Treaty Consultative Parties to invite the Secretary-General or his representative to their meetings, including their consultative meetings, the Secretary-General was not invited to the Preparatory Meeting of the XVth Antarctic Treaty Consultative Meeting or to the XVth Consultative Meeting, held in Paris from 9 to 13 May and from 9 to 20 October 1989, respectively;

2. *Reiterates its call* upon the Antarctic Treaty Consultative Parties to invite the Secretary-General or his representative to all meetings of the Treaty parties, including their consultative meetings;

3. *Requests* the Secretary-General to submit a report on his evaluations thereon to the General Assembly at its forty-fifth session;

4. *Expresses the conviction* that, in view of the significant impact that Antarctica exerts on the global environment and ecosystems, any régime to be established for the protection and conservation of the Antarctic environment and its dependent and associated ecosystems, in order to be for the benefit of mankind as a whole and in order to gain the universal acceptability necessary to ensure full compliance and enforcement, must be negotiated with the full participation of all members of the international community;

5. *Urges* all members of the international community to support all efforts to ban prospecting and mining in and around Antarctica and to ensure that all activities are carried out exclusively for the purpose of peaceful scientific investigation and that all such activities ensure the maintenance of international peace and security in Antarctica and the protection of its environment and are for the benefit of all mankind;

6. *Expresses its conviction* that the establishment, through negotiations with the full participation of all members of the international community, of Antarctica as a nature reserve or a world park would ensure the protection and conservation of its environment and its dependent and associated ecosystems for the benefit of all mankind;

7. *Also expresses its conviction*, in view of the large number of scientific stations and expeditions, that international scientific research should be enhanced through the establishment of international stations devoted to scientific investigations of global significance, regulated by stringent environmental safeguards, so as to avoid or minimize any adverse impact of human activities on the Antarctic environment and its dependent and associated ecosystems;

8. *Urges* all States Members of the United Nations to co-operate with the Secretary-General and to continue consultations on all aspects relating to Antarctica;

9. *Decides* to include in the provisional agenda of its forty-fifth session the item entitled ''Question of Antarctica''.

General Assembly resolution 44/124 B

15 December 1989   Meeting 81   101-0-8 (roll-call vote)

Approved by First Committee (A/44/819) by roll-call vote (85-0-7), 22 November (meeting 46); 26-nation draft (A/C.1/44/L.69); agenda item 70.
Sponsors: Antigua and Barbuda, Bangladesh, Brunei Darussalam, Cameroon, Congo, Ghana, Indonesia, Iran, Kenya, Kuwait, Lesotho, Malaysia, Mali, Mexico, Nepal, Nigeria, Oman, Pakistan, Rwanda, Sri Lanka, Sudan, Uganda, United Republic of Tanzania, Zaire, Zambia, Zimbabwe.
Meeting numbers. GA 44th session: 1st Committee 42-46; plenary 81.

Roll-call vote in Assembly as follows:

In favour: Albania, Algeria, Angola, Antigua and Barbuda, Bahamas, Bahrain, Bangladesh, Barbados, Benin, Bhutan, Bolivia, Botswana, Brunei Darussalam, Burkina Faso, Burundi, Cameroon, Cape Verde, Central African Republic, Chad, Congo, Costa Rica, Côte d'Ivoire, Cyprus, Democratic Kampuchea, Djibouti, Dominica, Dominican Republic, Egypt, El Salvador, Ethiopia, Gabon, Gambia, Ghana, Grenada, Guatemala, Guinea, Guinea-Bissau, Guyana, Haiti, Honduras, Indonesia, Iran, Iraq, Jamaica, Jordan, Kenya, Kuwait, Lebanon, Lesotho, Liberia, Libyan Arab Jamahiriya, Madagascar, Malawi, Malaysia, Maldives, Mali, Mauritania, Mauritius, Mexico, Morocco, Mozambique, Myanmar, Nepal, Niger, Nigeria, Oman, Pakistan, Panama, Philippines, Qatar, Romania, Rwanda, Saint Kitts and Nevis, Saint Lucia, Saint Vincent and the Grenadines, Sao Tome and Principe, Saudi Arabia, Senegal, Seychelles, Sierra Leone, Singapore, Solomon Islands, Somalia, Sri Lanka, Sudan, Suriname, Syrian Arab Republic, Thailand, Togo, Trinidad and Tobago, Tunisia, Uganda, United Arab Emirates, United Republic of Tanzania, Vanuatu, Venezuela, Yemen, Yugoslavia, Zaire, Zambia, Zimbabwe.
Against: None.
Abstaining: China, Fiji, Ireland, Luxembourg, Malta, Portugal, Swaziland, Turkey.

During the roll-call vote in plenary the following 44 States announced they were not participating: Afghanistan, Argentina, Australia, Austria, Belgium, Brazil, Bulgaria, Byelorussian SSR, Canada, Chile, Colombia, Cuba, Czechoslovakia, Denmark, Ecuador, Finland, France, German Democratic Republic, Germany, Federal Republic of, Greece, Hungary, Iceland, India, Israel, Italy, Japan, Lao People's Democratic Republic, Mongolia, Netherlands, New Zealand, Nicaragua, Norway, Papua New Guinea, Paraguay, Peru, Poland, Spain, Sweden, Ukrainian SSR, USSR, United Kingdom, United States, Uruguay, Viet Nam.

Participation of South Africa

In September,[10] the Secretary-General submitted a report in response to a 1988 General Assembly resolution,[11] by which the Assembly had viewed with concern the continuing participation of South Africa in meetings of the Antarctic Treaty Consultative Parties and had appealed once again to those Parties to exclude the racist *apartheid* régime of South Africa from participation in their meetings and invited them to inform the Secretary-General on the relevant actions. In an April 1989 reply[10] to a note verbale of the Secretary-General, Australia, on behalf of the States Parties, recalled an earlier vote on the subject reproduced in a 1987 report of the Secretary-General.[12] That note, Australia stated, continued to reflect the Parties' position.

In its final document, the Ninth Conference of Heads of State or Government of Non-Aligned Countries (Belgrade, 4-7 September)[8] reiterated its regret over the continuing membership of the racist *apartheid* régime of South Africa as a Consultative Party of the Antarctic Treaty, urging the Consultative Parties to exclude that régime from participation in their meetings.

GENERAL ASSEMBLY ACTION

On 15 December, the General Assembly, on the recommendation of the First Committee, adopted **resolution 44/124 A** by roll-call vote.

Question of Antarctica

The General Assembly,

Recalling its resolution 43/83 B of 7 December 1988,

Having considered the item entitled ''Question of Antarctica'',

Noting with regret that the racist *apartheid* régime of South Africa, which has been suspended from participation in the General Assembly of the United Nations, has continued to participate in the meetings of the Antarctic Treaty Consultative Parties,

Recalling the resolution adopted by the Council of Ministers of the Organization of African Unity at its fiftieth ordinary session, held at Addis Ababa from 17 to 22 July 1989,

Recalling also the final document on Antarctica adopted by the Ninth Conference of Heads of State or Government of Non-Aligned Countries, held at Belgrade from 4 to 7 September 1989,

Recalling further that the Antarctic Treaty is, by its terms, intended to further the purposes and principles embodied in the Charter of the United Nations,

Noting that the policy of *apartheid* practised by the racist minority régime of South Africa, which has been universally condemned, constitutes a threat to regional and international peace and security,

1. *Views with concern* the continuing participation of the *apartheid* régime of South Africa in the meetings of the Antarctic Treaty Consultative Parties;

2. *Appeals once again* to the Antarctic Treaty Consultative Parties to take urgent measures to exclude the racist *apartheid* régime of South Africa from participation in the meetings of the Consultative Parties at the earliest possible date;

3. *Invites* the States parties to the Antarctic Treaty to inform the Secretary-General of the actions taken regarding the provisions of the present resolution;

4. *Requests* the Secretary-General to submit a report in this regard to the General Assembly at its forty-fifth session;

5. *Decides* to include in the provisional agenda of its forty-fifth session the item entitled ''Question of Antarctica''.

General Assembly resolution 44/124 A

15 December 1989   Meeting 81   114-0-7 (roll-call vote)

Approved by First Committee (A/44/819) by roll-call vote (94-0-6), 22 November (meeting 46); draft by Lesotho for Group of African States (A/C.1/44/L.68); agenda item 70.

Meeting numbers. GA 44th session: 1st Committee 42-46; plenary 81.

Roll-call vote in Assembly as follows:

In favour: Afghanistan, Albania, Algeria, Angola, Antigua and Barbuda, Argentina, Bahamas, Bahrain, Bangladesh, Barbados, Benin, Bhutan, Bolivia, Brazil, Brunei Darussalam, Burkina Faso, Burundi, Cameroon, Cape Verde, Central African Republic, Chad, China, Colombia, Congo, Costa Rica, Côte d'Ivoire, Cuba, Cyprus, Democratic Kampuchea, Democratic Yemen, Djibouti, Dominica, Dominican Republic, Ecuador, Egypt, El Salvador, Ethiopia, Fiji, Gabon, Gambia, Ghana, Grenada, Guatemala, Guinea, Guinea-Bissau, Guyana, Haiti, Honduras, India, Indonesia, Iran, Iraq, Jamaica, Jordan, Kenya, Kuwait, Lao People's Democratic Republic, Lebanon, Lesotho, Liberia, Libyan Arab Jamahiriya, Madagascar, Malawi, Malaysia, Maldives, Mali, Mauritania, Mexico, Mongolia, Morocco, Mozambique, Myanmar, Nepal, Nicaragua, Niger, Nigeria, Oman, Pakistan, Panama, Peru, Philippines, Qatar, Romania, Rwanda, Saint Kitts and Nevis, Saint Lucia, Saint Vincent and the Grenadines, Sao Tome and Principe, Saudi Arabia, Senegal, Seychelles, Sierra Leone, Singapore, Solomon Islands, Somalia, Sri Lanka, Sudan, Suriname, Syrian Arab Republic, Thailand, Togo, Trinidad and Tobago, Tunisia, Uganda, United Arab Emirates, United Republic of Tanzania, Vanuatu, Venezuela, Viet Nam, Yemen, Yugoslavia, Zaire, Zambia, Zimbabwe.

Against: None.

Abstaining: Botswana, Ireland, Luxembourg, Malta, Mauritius, Portugal, Swaziland.

During the roll-call vote in plenary, the following 31 States announced they were not participating: Australia, Austria, Belgium, Bulgaria, Byelorussian SSR, Canada, Chile, Czechoslovakia, Denmark, Finland, France, German Democratic Republic, Germany, Federal Republic of, Greece, Hungary, Iceland, Israel, Italy, Japan, Netherlands, New Zealand, Norway, Papua New Guinea, Paraguay, Poland, Spain, Sweden, Turkey, Ukrainian SSR, USSR, United Kingdom, United States, Uruguay.

REFERENCES

[1]YUN 1988, p. 118, GA res. 43/83 A, 7 Dec. 1988. [2]A/44/586. [3]YUN 1986, p. 373, GA res. 41/88 B, 4 Dec. 1986. [4]YUN 1987, p. 358, GA res. 42/46 B, 30 Nov. 1987. [5]A/44/383. [6]A/44/125. [7]A/44/409 & Corr.1,2. [8]A/44/551. [9]A/44/689. [10]A/44/518. [11]YUN 1988, p. 119, GA res. 43/83 B, 7 Dec. 1988. [12]YUN 1987, p. 357.

Cyprus question

Throughout 1989, the Secretary-General continued his mission of good offices concerning Cyprus, entrusted to him by the Security Council. Following their agreement in August 1988 to meet without any pre-conditions and to attempt to achieve a negotiated settlement of all aspects of the Cyprus problem by 1 June 1989, the leaders of the two sides in Cyprus held direct talks on an ongoing basis with the Secretary-General's Special Representative in Nicosia. In the second round of talks (January-March 1989), the two leaders agreed to develop, on a non-committal basis, a wide range of options for each of the issues making up the Cyprus problem.[1] On 9 June, the President of the Security Council issued a statement[2] on behalf of the members, urging the parties to redouble their efforts. At the end of June, the Secretary-General met with the two leaders and, on 25 July, the Secretary-General's ideas to assist in achieving an agreement were presented, confidentially, as food for thought. Resumed talks between the two leaders did not, however, prove possible and the Secretary-General's efforts for the remainder of 1989 were concentrated in trying to achieve their resumption, including separate meetings with the two leaders from October to December. The Special Representative then undertook contacts aimed at achieving resumption.[3]

The Security Council twice extended the mandate of the United Nations Peace-keeping Force in Cyprus (UNFICYP)—on 9 June and 14 December—which continued its peace-keeping and humanitarian tasks.

Although the question of Cyprus was included in the agenda of the forty-fourth (1989) General Assembly session (**decision 43/464**, 18 September 1989), it was not discussed.

Cyprus and Turkey addressed communications to the Secretary-General on various aspects of the situation throughout the year. Those from Turkey forwarded letters from the Turkish Cypriot community signed by Rauf R. Denktas as "President of the Turkish Republic of Northern Cyprus", or by Ozer Koray as "representative" of that "Republic".

Report of the Secretary-General (May/June). In his report to the Security Council on the United Nations operation in Cyprus from 1 December 1988 to 31 May 1989,[1] the Secretary-General summarized UNFICYP activities and his good offices mission and reported on the situation regarding maintenance of the *status quo*.

Cyprus again protested about desecration of churches in the north, the changing of place names in the northern part and expropriation of immovable properties. UNFICYP raised the matters with the Turkish Cypriot authorities.

The Committee on Missing Persons in Cyprus continued to discuss reports submitted by the two sides. Additional investigations regarding some of the 169 cases under consideration were carried out in the field, as well as investigations regarding 168 new cases submitted by both sides.

The Secretary-General recommended extension of UNFICYP's mandate for a further six months. He reported that Cyprus, Greece and the United Kingdom had agreed, while Turkey, supporting the position of the Turkish Cypriot side, had indicated that the draft resolution (see below) was unacceptable as a basis for extending the stationing of UNFICYP, but that its stance would be explained before the Council.[4]

SECURITY COUNCIL ACTION (June)

The Security Council met on 9 June to consider the Secretary-General's report and recommendation to extend UNFICYP's mandate. Cyprus, Greece and Turkey were invited, at their request, to participate in the discussion without the right to vote. The Council also extended an invitation to Ozer Koray under rule 39 of its provisional rules of procedure.[a]

On the same day, the Council unanimously adopted **resolution 634(1989)**.

The Security Council,

Taking note of the report of the Secretary-General on the United Nations operation in Cyprus of 31 May and 8 June 1989,

Taking note also of the recommendation by the Secretary-General that the Security Council extend the stationing of the United Nations Peace-keeping Force in Cyprus for a further period of six months,

Noting that the Government of Cyprus has agreed that in view of the prevailing conditions in the island it is necessary to keep the Force in Cyprus beyond 15 June 1989,

Reaffirming the provisions of resolution 186(1964) of 4 March 1964 and other relevant resolutions,

1. *Extends once more* the stationing in Cyprus of the United Nations Peace-keeping Force established under resolution 186(1964) for a further period ending on 15 December 1989;

2. *Requests* the Secretary-General to continue his mission of good offices, to keep the Security Council informed of the progress made and to submit a report on the implementation of the present resolution by 30 November 1989;

3. *Calls upon* all the parties concerned to continue to co-operate with the Force on the basis of the present mandate.

Security Council resolution 634(1989)

9 June 1989   Meeting 2868   Adopted unanimously

Draft prepared in consultations among Council members (S/20679).

Mr. Koray repeated previous rejections of similar resolutions by the Turkish Cypriot side since it could not accept any resolution which purported to endorse the Greek Cypriot side as the so-called "Government of the Republic of Cyprus". Turkey supported this position and said it could not consent to renewal of UNFICYP's mandate on that basis.

Report of the Secretary-General (November/December). Reporting to the Security Council on the United Nations operation in Cyprus from 1 June to 4 December 1989,[3] the Secretary-General updated information on UNFICYP activities, his good offices mission and the question of the maintenance of the *status quo*.

The Secretary-General met the leaders of the two sides on 28 and 29 June and the leaders agreed to resume talks in Nicosia on 26 July. On 25 July, the Special Representative forwarded to both leaders, as "food for thought", the Secretary-General's written summary of the ideas discussed, with the aim of facilitating the preparation of an outline of a comprehensive agreement by September 1989. On 29 July, the Turkish Cypriot side, which had previously expressed its reservations about the process, informed the Special Representative that its participation in the talks as scheduled was impossible because of tensions over the 19 July incident (see below). On various separate occasions, the Secretary-General further met with President Vassiliou (4 October and 29 November) and with Mr. Denktas (11 October and 4 December) and stressed the importance of a commitment to resume the talks on a meaningful basis. Pres-

[a]Rule 39 of the Council's provisional rules of procedure states: "The Security Council may invite members of the Secretariat or other persons, whom it considers competent for the purpose, to supply it with information or to give other assistance in examining matters within its competence."

ident Vassiliou expressed his readiness to resume direct talks, while Mr. Denktas made a number of suggestions for resuming the process, including a joint declaration of intent that would define the new pattern of relationship between the two communities.

Following the meetings, the Secretary-General instructed his Special Representative to pursue his contacts at Nicosia in order to prepare for the early continuation of the high-level talks, which the Secretary-General had proposed for two weeks' duration in February 1990 at a venue to be decided.

The Committee on Missing Persons in Cyprus underlined in a press statement issued on 25 October that it had to "rely entirely on the files and documents transmitted to it by both sides but, finally, and above all, on the testimony of the witnesses interviewed, on their co-operation, and on their willingness and knowledge to give complete and precise information".

As in his previous report, the Secretary-General, referring to his recommendation that the Council extend UNFICYP's mandate for a further six months, indicated that Cyprus, Greece and the United Kingdom had agreed, while Turkey, supporting the position of the Turkish Cypriot side, indicated that the draft resolution (see below) was unacceptable as a basis for UNFICYP's extension and that its position would be explained before the Council.[5]

SECURITY COUNCIL ACTION (December)

On 14 December, the Security Council considered the Secretary-General's report and recommendation to extend the UNFICYP mandate. Cyprus, Greece and Turkey were invited, at their request, to participate without the right to vote. Ozer Koray was also invited to participate under rule 39 of the provisional rules of procedure.[a]

On the same day, the Security Council unanimously adopted **resolution 646(1989)**.

The Security Council,

Taking note of the report of the Secretary-General on the United Nations operation in Cyprus of 7 and 13 December 1989,

Taking note also of the recommendation by the Secretary-General that the Security Council extend the stationing of the United Nations Peace-keeping Force in Cyprus for a further period of six months,

Noting that the Government of Cyprus has agreed that in view of the prevailing conditions in the island it is necessary to keep the Force in Cyprus beyond 15 December 1989,

Reaffirming the provisions of resolution 186(1964) of 4 March 1964 and other relevant resolutions,

1. *Extends once more* the stationing in Cyprus of the United Nations Peace-keeping Force established under resolution 186(1964) for a further period ending on 15 June 1990;

2. *Requests* the Secretary-General to continue his mission of good offices, to keep the Security Council informed of the progress made and to submit a report on the implementation of the present resolution by 31 May 1990;

3. *Calls upon* all the parties concerned to continue to co-operate with the Force on the basis of the present mandate.

Security Council resolution 646(1989)

14 December 1989   Meeting 2898   Adopted unanimously

Draft prepared in consultations among Council members (S/21020).

Peace-keeping and humanitarian assistance

The United Nations Peace-keeping Force in Cyprus, established in 1964 in accordance with a Security Council resolution,[6] continued throughout 1989 to supervise the cease-fire lines of the Cyprus National Guard and of the Turkish and Turkish Cypriot forces. On 10 April 1989, Major-General Günther G. Greindl of Austria, who had commanded UNFICYP since March 1981, relinquished his command and returned to his national service. On the same date, command was assumed by Major-General Clive Milner of Canada.

In 1989, UNFICYP continued full liaison and co-operation at all levels with the two sides and pursued efforts to improve its freedom of movement in the northern part of the island. Through a system of 146 observation posts, 54 of which were permanently manned, UNFICYP kept under constant surveillance the area between the cease-fire lines, known as the United Nations buffer zone, extending approximately 180 kilometres from the north-west to the south-east coasts and covering about 3 per cent of the island.

Following the December 1988 shooting and killing of a Turkish Cypriot soldier, UNFICYP succeeded in getting both sides to unman their forward military positions and cease patrolling in three sensitive areas in Nicosia, with a view to keeping their troops further apart and thereby reducing the risk of incidents.

In March 1989, considerable tension occurred over the well-publicized plans of a Greek Cypriot women's group to organize a large demonstration with the announced intention of crossing the Turkish forces' cease-fire line. The demonstration, however, passed without serious incident. Altogether 54 demonstrators were arrested by the Turkish Cypriot police and were released to UNFICYP the same day.

A serious situation arose on 19 July, when some 1,000 Greek Cypriot demonstrators, mostly women, forced their way into the United Nations buffer zone. Turkish Cypriot police forced their way into the area and arrested 111 people. On 21 July and succeeding days, Greek Cypriot demonstrators protesting the detention blocked all United

Nations traffic through the main entrance to the protected area in Nicosia until 30 July, when the Turkish Cypriot authorities released the last two detainees. The President of the Security Council conveyed to the representatives of all the parties the Council's deep concern at the tense situation created by the 19 July incidents. During the period there were three other occasions, two in July and one in October, when 150 to 250 Greek Cypriots entered the United Nations buffer zone. United Nations officials conveyed to the authorities of the Government of Cyprus their expectation that the police would take effective measures to prevent demonstrators from entering the United Nations buffer zone. President Vassiliou made a public statement to that effect.

Overflights of the buffer zone continued, with 12 by civilian aircraft from the north and 19 from the south in the period of the Secretary-General's two reports. In addition, National Guard aircraft overflew the buffer zone three times and Turkish forces' aircraft six times. Civilian aircraft of other nationalities accounted for nine further overflights. UNFICYP investigated and protested as appropriate.

UNFICYP continued to assist in organizing the electricity and water supply and mail delivery across the buffer zone, and facilitated meetings of trade unionists, journalists and other groups from the two communities, in addition to joint meetings arranged by the United Nations Development Programme (UNDP) and the Office of the United Nations High Commissioner for Refugees (UNHCR). As part of its efforts to promote a return to normal conditions, UNFICYP facilitated economic and other civilian activities in the areas between and adjacent to the cease-fire lines, in particular farming.. The UNFICYP civilian police (UN-CIVPOL) maintained close co-operation with the Cyprus police and the Turkish Cypriot police on matters having inter-communal aspects. UNFICYP distributed 604 tons of foodstuffs and other supplies, as well as social welfare and pension benefits among the Greek Cypriots in the north, delivered 331 tons of foodstuffs and other supplies to the Maronites on the two sides of the cease-fire lines, and continued periodic visits to Turkish Cypriots living in the south. UNFICYP continued to provide emergency medical services to members of both communities and to co-operate with UNHCR and UNDP, which, in their turn, increased and broadened their activities in Cyprus.

In 1989, the total strength of UNFICYP remained 2,126, including 2,091 military personnel and 35 civilian police. The countries which contributed their military personnel were Austria (410), Canada (575), Denmark (342), Finland (7), Ireland (8), Sweden (7) and the United Kingdom (742). Civilian police were staffed by Australia (20)

and Sweden (15). One member of UNFICYP died as a result of a traffic accident, which was the 147th fatality in the Force since its inception.

UNFICYP financing

The cost to the United Nations of maintaining UNFICYP in 1989 amounted to some $26.9 million, $13.1 million for the first extension and an estimated $13.8 million for the second (June-December 1989 and December 1989–May 1990). In his reports, the Secretary-General emphasized that the United Nations financing of the Force depended entirely on voluntary contributions from Governments; however, despite his letters of 15 March[7] and 20 October[8] to Member States and the United Nations specialized agencies, containing appeals for contributions to UNFICYP, only $8.1 million was contributed by Member States in 1989. As these contributions were insufficient to meet the cost of the Force, the reimbursement claims from the troop-contributing countries had been met only up to June 1980, and the accumulated deficit in the UNFICYP Special Account from the inception of the Force to the end of 1989 was estimated at $174.6 million. In their letters of 22 May[9] and 1 June[10] addressed to the Secretary-General, the Governments of the troop-contributing countries expressed their grave concern at the growing deficit in the UNFICYP Special Account and their disappointment at the further decline in the level of voluntary contributions. The letters also conveyed the Governments' belief that the Security Council would agree to the proposal, formulated in a 1986 report[11] of the Secretary-General, to finance the United Nations share of UNFICYP's cost from assessed contributions rather than from voluntary contributions.

REFERENCES

[1]S/20663. [2]S/20682. [3]S/21010. [4]S/20663/Add.1. [5]S/21010/Add.1. [6]YUN 1964, p. 165, SC res. 186(1964), 4 Mar. 1964. [7]S/20560. [8]S/20933. [9]S/20650. [10]S/20666. [11]YUN 1986, p. 246.

Institutional machinery

Security Council

The Security Council held 69 meetings in 1989 and adopted 20 resolutions. Twenty-six meetings were devoted to the situation in the Middle East and related questions; 11 concerned Namibia; seven related to Afghanistan; six each concerned complaints by the Libyan Arab Jamahiriya and the situation in Panama; four were devoted to the situation in Central America; two each concerned the Iran-Iraq conflict, UNFICYP, terrorist activities and an election to the International Court of Justice; and one (private) related to the Council's annual report to the General Assembly.

Agenda

During 1989, its forty-fourth year, the Security Council considered 22 agenda items. It continued the practice of adopting at each meeting the agenda for that meeting. (For list of agenda items, see APPENDIX IV). Seven items were included in the agenda for the first time. They concerned: marking of plastic or sheet explosives for the purpose of detection; Central America—efforts towards peace; the question of hostage-taking and abduction; the situation in Panama; and communications from Member States to the President of the Security Council (Libyan Arab Jamahiriya v. United States regarding the downing of two Libyan military aircraft; Panama v. United States wherein Panama contested actions of the United States military in Panama while the United States alleged election fraud in Panama; El Salvador v. Sandinista Government of Nicaragua).

On 15 September,[1] the Secretary-General notified the General Assembly, in accordance with Article 12, paragraph 2, of the Charter of the United Nations, of 14 matters relative to the maintenance of international peace and security discussed by the Security Council since his previous annual notification. He listed 130 other matters not discussed during the period but of which the Council remained seized, and notified the Assembly of the matter contained in the letter of 3 September 1964 from Malaysia, with which the Council had ceased to deal, pursuant to the request from Indonesia and Malaysia of 15 September 1989.[2] By **decision 44/409** of 13 November, the Assembly took note of these matters.

Membership

In 1989, the question of equitable representation on the Security Council and increase in its membership was not considered. Draft resolutions proposing an increase in membership from 15 to 21 had been discussed in 1979[3] and in 1980,[4] but no action had been taken.

On 22 December, by **decision 44/460**, the Assembly decided to include the item in the provisional agenda of its forty-fifth (1990) session.

Pursuant to rule 15 of the provisional rules of procedure of the Security Council, the Secretary-General, in December,[5] reported to the Council the credentials of Côte d'Ivoire, Cuba, Democratic Yemen, Romania and Zaire, which had been elected by the General Assembly on 18 October as non-permanent members for a two-year term beginning 1 January 1990. In his opinion, those credentials were in order.

Report for 1988/89

At a private meeting on 17 November, the Security Council unanimously adopted its report covering the period 16 June 1988 to 15 June 1989.[6] The General Assembly took note of the report of the Security Council by **decision 44/424** of 11 December.

General Assembly

The General Assembly met in three sessions during 1989—to resume and conclude its forty-third (1988) session and the major part of its forty-fourth session, as well as its sixteenth special session.

The first part of the forty-third session had been held from 20 September to 22 December 1988,[7] and resumed in 1989 on 14, 16 and 21 February, on 1 and 7 March, from 18 to 20 April, on 11 July and on 18 September, when it was declared closed. The sixteenth special session on *apartheid* and its destructive consequences in southern Africa was held from 12 to 14 December. The forty-fourth regular session opened on 19 September 1989 and continued until its suspension on 29 December.

Agenda

The General Assembly resumed its forty-third session in February 1989 to consider seven items retained on that session's agenda by a 1988 decision.[8] On 14 and 21 February, the Assembly, by **decision 43/402 B**, on the proposals of the Secretary-General,[9] added to the agenda items on the financing of the United Nations Angola Verification Mission and of the Transition Assistance Group and allocated them to the Fifth Committee. On 11 July, acting on the proposal contained in the Secretary-General's note,[10] the Assembly, by **decision 43/402 C**, reopened agenda item 36, on policies of *apartheid* of the Government of South Africa.

On 18 September, by **decisions 43/464** and **43/465**, respectively, the Assembly included the questions of Cyprus and of the consequences of the prolongation of the armed conflict between Iran and Iraq in the draft agenda of its forty-fourth session.

Pursuant to **decisions 43/462** of 11 July and **44/408** of 13 November, adopted at the Assembly's forty-third and forty-fourth sessions, respectively, the sixteenth special session was held in New York from 12 to 14 December to consider the question of *apartheid* and its destructive consequences in southern Africa. The session had seven items on its agenda (see APPENDIX IV). On 14 December, the Assembly adopted **resolution S-16/1**, the Declaration on *Apartheid* and its Destructive Consequences in Southern Africa.

The forty-fourth session initially had 154 items on its agenda, which was adopted by the Assembly on 22 September; seven others were later added. (For list and allocation of agenda items, see APPENDIX IV.) The agenda was adopted by **decision 44/402 A**. Under the same decision, the Assembly allocated the items to the appropriate Main Committees and plenary. Inclusion of the items and their allocation to the Assembly's Main Committees or plenary meetings had been recommended by the General Committee[11] on the basis of the preliminary[12] and annotated preliminary[13] list of items, a 154-item provisional agenda[14] and a five-item supplementary list.[15]

On 7 December, by **decision 44/417**, the Assembly deferred consideration of the Declaration of the Assembly of Heads of State and Government of the Organization of African Unity on the aerial and naval military attack against the Socialist People's Libyan Arab Jamahiriya by the then current United States administration in April 1986 and included this item in the provisional agenda of its forty-fifth session.

On 22 December, by **decision 44/458**, the Assembly included in the provisional agenda of its forty-fifth session the item entitled ''Implementation of the resolutions of the United Nations''.

Organization of the 1989 session

On 22 September and 8 December, by **decision 44/401**, the General Assembly, on the recommendation of the General Committee,[11] adopted a number of provisions concerning the organization of the forty-fourth (1989) session.

The Committee's recommendations concerned rationalization of the Assembly's work; the schedule of meetings; meeting records; the general debate; explanations of vote, right of reply and length of statements; concluding statements; questions related to the programme budget; documentation; resolutions; special conferences; meetings of subsidiary organs; and the closing date of the 1989 session.

Subsidiary organs

By **decisions 44/403 A** of 19 September and **44/403 B** of 22 September, **44/403 C** of 4 December and **44/403 D** of 8 December, the General Assembly, on the recommendation of the General Committee,[11] decided that the following subsidiary organs should be authorized to hold meetings during the session: High-level Committee on the Review of Technical Co-operation among Developing Countries; Advisory Committee on the United Nations Educational and Training Programme for Southern Africa; Committee of Trustees of the United Nations Trust Fund for South Africa; Committee on Relations with the Host Country; Committee on the Exercise of the

Inalienable Rights of the Palestinian People; Intergovernmental Group to Monitor the Supply and Shipping of Oil and Petroleum Products to South Africa; Special Committee against *Apartheid*; United Nations Council for Namibia; Working Group on the Financing of the United Nations Relief and Works Agency for Palestinian Refugees in the Near East; Special Committee on the Situation with regard to the Implementation of the Declaration on the Granting of Independence to Colonial Countries and Peoples; and Executive Board of the United Nations Children's Fund.

Representatives' credentials

At its first meeting on 11 October, the Credentials Committee examined the Secretary-General's memorandum of the previous day, reporting on the status of credentials of representatives to the forty-fourth regular session and to the sixteenth special session, indicating that credentials had been submitted by 125 Member States for the forty-fourth regular session and by 34 Member States for the sixteenth special session. The Legal Counsel informed the Committee on additional credentials received from 11 Member States for the forty-fourth session and four Member States for the sixteenth session.

On 6 December, at its second meeting, the Committee examined the Secretary-General's memorandum from the previous day, concerning the credentials of representatives of Member States other than those which had been already accepted. The memorandum indicated that additional credentials had been submitted by 17 Member States for the forty-fourth session and by 25 Member States for the sixteenth special session. It also indicated that communications on the appointment of representatives had been received from six Member States for the forty-fourth session and 65 Member States for the sixteenth special session. Another 31 Member States had previously empowered their Permanent Representatives to represent them in all organs of the United Nations without limitation as to session.

At each meeting, acting without vote on an oral proposal by its Chairman, the Committee accepted the credentials received. The Committee also recommended two draft resolutions to the Assembly. On 17 October and 11 December, the Assembly, by **resolutions 44/5 A and 44/5 B**, respectively, approved the first[16] and second[17] reports of the Credentials Committee.

REFERENCES

[1]A/44/528. [2]A/44/528/Add.1. [3]YUN 1979, p. 435. [4]YUN 1980, p. 461. [5]S/21062. [6]A/44/2. [7]YUN 1988, p. 125. [8]YUN 1988, p. 125, GA dec. 43/459, 22 Dec. 1988. [9]A/43/249, A/43/997. [10]A/43/1010. [11]A/44/250 & Corr.1,2 & Add.1-7. [12]A/44/50. [13]A/44/100. [14]A/44/150. [15]A/44/200. [16]A/44/639. [17]A/44/639/Add.1.

PUBLICATIONS

Index to Proceedings of the General Assembly, Forty-fourth session—1989/1990, Part I—Subject Index; Conclusion of the Forty-third session—1988/1989 (ST/LIB/SER.B/A.45 (Part I)), Sales No. E.90.I.25 (Part I); Part II—Index to Speeches (ST/LIB/SER.B/A.45 (Part II)), Sales No. E.90.I.10 (Part II). *Index to Proceedings of the Security Council, Forty-fourth year—1989,* (ST/LIB/SER.B/S.26), Sales No. E.90.I.7.

Co-operation with other intergovernmental organizations

League of Arab States

In accordance with a 1988 General Assembly resolution,[1] the Secretary-General reported in September 1989 on co-operation between the United Nations and the League of Arab States.[2]

The report described consultations and exchanges of information which had taken place between the two organizations since 1988 and summarized follow-up action on proposals for co-operation in accordance with their 1983[3] and 1988[4] agreements.

On 6 October, the United Nations and the League of Arab States signed an Agreement of Co-operation, as called for by the Assembly in 1988.[1]

GENERAL ASSEMBLY ACTION

On 17 October, the General Assembly adopted **resolution 44/7** by recorded vote.

Co-operation between the United Nations and the League of Arab States

The General Assembly,

Recalling its previous resolutions on the promotion of co-operation between the United Nations and the League of Arab States, in particular resolution 43/3 of 17 October 1988,

Having considered the report of the Secretary-General on co-operation between the United Nations and the League of Arab States,

Recalling also the Articles of the Charter of the United Nations which encourage activities through regional arrangements for the promotion of the purposes and principles of the United Nations,

Noting with appreciation the desire of the League of Arab States to consolidate and develop the existing ties with the United Nations in all areas relating to the maintenance of international peace and security, and to co-operate in every possible way with the United Nations in the implementation of United Nations resolutions relating to Lebanon and to the question of Palestine and the situation in the Middle East,

Aware of the vital importance for the countries members of the League of Arab States of achieving a just, comprehensive and durable solution to the Middle East conflict and the question of Palestine, the core of the conflict,

Realizing that the strengthening of international peace and security is directly related, *inter alia,* to disarmament, decolonization, self-determination and the eradication of all forms of racism and racial discrimination,

Taking note with satisfaction of the progress so far achieved with regard to the recommendations adopted at the second joint meeting of the representatives of the United Nations and other organizations of the United Nations system and the representatives of the League of Arab States and its specialized organizations, held at Geneva from 29 June to 1 July 1988,

Convinced that the maintenance and further strengthening of co-operation between the United Nations and other organizations of the United Nations system and the League of Arab States contribute to the work of the United Nations system and to the promotion of the purposes and principles of the United Nations,

Recognizing the need for closer co-operation between the United Nations system and the League of Arab States and its specialized organizations in realizing the goals and objectives set forth in the Strategy for Joint Arab Economic Development adopted by the Eleventh Arab Summit Conference, held at Amman from 25 to 27 November 1980,

Noting with satisfaction the signing on 6 October 1989 of the Agreement of Co-operation between the United Nations and the League of Arab States, as called for in paragraph 10 of General Assembly resolution 43/3,

Also noting with satisfaction the progress so far achieved between the Arab Interior Ministers Council and the Office of the United Nations Disaster Relief Co-ordinator with regard to the holding in 1990, with the participation of the League of Arab States, of the joint seminar on disaster preparedness and prevention in the Arab countries,

Having heard the statement of the Permanent Observer of the League of Arab States of 17 October 1989 on co-operation between the United Nations and the League of Arab States, and having noted the emphasis placed therein on follow-up actions and procedures on the recommendations in the political, social and cultural fields adopted at the meetings between the representatives of the General Secretariat of the League of Arab States and its specialized organizations and the secretariats of the United Nations and other organizations of the United Nations system, held at Tunis from 28 June to 1 July 1983 and at Geneva from 29 June to 1 July 1988, as well as on the recommendations relating to political matters contained in the relevant resolutions of the General Assembly,

1. *Takes note with satisfaction* of the report of the Secretary-General;

2. *Expresses its appreciation* to the Secretary-General for the follow-up action taken by him to implement the proposals adopted at the meetings between representatives of the secretariats of the United Nations and other organizations of the United Nations system and the General Secretariat of the League of Arab States and its specialized organizations held at Tunis and Geneva and the sectoral meeting on social development in the Arab region, held at Amman from 19 to 21 August 1985;

3. *Commends* the League of Arab States for its efforts and endeavours and those of its Tripartite High Committee in resolving the crisis in Lebanon;

4. *Requests* the Secretary-General to continue to strengthen co-operation with the General Secretariat of

the League of Arab States for the purpose of implementing United Nations resolutions relating to Lebanon and to the question of Palestine and the situation in the Middle East in order to achieve a just, comprehensive and durable solution to the Middle East conflict and the question of Palestine, the core of the conflict;

5. *Requests* the Secretariat of the United Nations and the General Secretariat of the League of Arab States, within their respective fields of competence, further to intensify their co-operation towards the realization of the purposes and principles of the Charter of the United Nations, the strengthening of international peace and security, disarmament, decolonization, self-determination and the eradication of all forms of racism and racial discrimination;

6. *Also requests* the Secretary-General to continue his efforts to strengthen co-operation and co-ordination between the United Nations and other organizations of the United Nations system and the League of Arab States and its specialized organizations in order to enhance their capacity to serve the mutual interests of the two organizations in the political, economic, social and cultural fields;

7. *Further requests* the Secretary-General to continue to co-ordinate the follow-up action to facilitate the implementation of the proposals of a multilateral nature adopted at the Tunis meeting in 1983, and to take appropriate action regarding the multilateral proposals adopted at the Amman meeting in 1985, and at the Geneva meeting in 1988, including the following measures:

(*a*) Promotion of contacts and consultations between the counterpart programmes, organizations and agencies concerned;

(*b*) Setting-up of joint sectoral inter-agency working groups;

8. *Calls upon* the specialized agencies and other organizations and programmes of the United Nations system:

(*a*) To continue to co-operate with the Secretary-General and the programmes, organizations and agencies concerned within the United Nations system and the League of Arab States and its specialized organizations in the follow-up of multilateral proposals aimed at strengthening and expanding co-operation in all fields between the United Nations system and the League of Arab States and its specialized organizations;

(*b*) To maintain and increase contacts and consultations with the counterpart programmes, organizations and agencies concerned regarding projects of a bilateral nature, in order to facilitate their implementation;

(*c*) To associate whenever possible with organizations and institutions of the League of Arab States in the execution and implementation of development projects in the Arab region;

(*d*) To inform the Secretary-General, not later than 15 May 1990, of the progress of their co-operation with the League of Arab States and its specialized organizations, in particular the follow-up action taken on the multilateral and bilateral proposals adopted at the Tunis, Amman and Geneva meetings;

9. *Decides* that, in order to intensify co-operation and for the purpose of review and appraisal of progress as well as to prepare comprehensive periodic reports, a general meeting between the United Nations system and the League of Arab States should take place once every three years and inter-agency sectoral meetings should be organized annually on areas of priority and wide importance in the development of the Arab States, the time and place to be determined by consultations between the United Nations and the League of Arab States;

10. *Invites* the Secretary-General of the United Nations and the Secretary-General of the League of Arab States to ensure the continuation of the consultations between the Department for Disarmament Affairs of the United Nations Secretariat and the League of Arab States with a view to considering the possibility of holding a seminar on disarmament matters in the Arab region in 1990 or 1991;

11. *Recommends* that the United Nations and the other organizations of the United Nations system should utilize Arab expertise to the extent possible in projects undertaken in the Arab region;

12. *Requests* the Secretary-General of the United Nations, in close co-operation with the Secretary-General of the League of Arab States, to hold periodic consultations, as and when appropriate, between representatives of the Secretariat of the United Nations and of the General Secretariat of the League of Arab States on follow-up policies, projects, actions and procedures;

13. *Also requests* the Secretary-General to arrange for a joint meeting to be held in 1990 between representatives of the organizations of the United Nations system and of the League of Arab States and its specialized organizations in order to review the progress achieved in the implementation of the multilateral proposals, especially those adopted at the Geneva meeting, and to develop a two-year programme of co-operation between the United Nations and the League of Arab States;

14. *Further requests* the Secretary-General to submit to the General Assembly at its forty-fifth session a progress report on the implementation of the present resolution;

15. *Decides* to include in the provisional agenda of its forty-fifth session the item entitled "Co-operation between the United Nations and the League of Arab States".

General Assembly resolution 44/7

17 October 1989   Meeting 33   143-2-0 (recorded vote)

21-nation draft (A/44/L.7/Rev.1); agenda item 23.
Sponsors: Algeria, Bahrain, Democratic Yemen, Djibouti, Egypt, Iraq, Jordan, Kuwait, Lebanon, Libyan Arab Jamahiriya, Mauritania, Morocco, Oman, Qatar, Saudi Arabia, Somalia, Sudan, Syrian Arab Republic, Tunisia, United Arab Emirates, Yemen.

Recorded vote in Assembly as follows:

In favour: Afghanistan, Albania, Algeria, Angola, Argentina, Australia, Austria, Bahamas, Bahrain, Bangladesh, Barbados, Belgium, Belize, Benin, Bhutan, Bolivia, Botswana, Brazil, Brunei Darussalam, Bulgaria, Burkina Faso, Burundi, Byelorussian SSR, Cameroon, Canada, Central African Republic, Chad, Chile, China, Colombia, Congo, Côte d'Ivoire, Cuba, Cyprus, Czechoslovakia, Democratic Kampuchea, Democratic Yemen, Denmark, Djibouti, Dominican Republic, Ecuador, Egypt, Equatorial Guinea, Ethiopia, Fiji, Finland, France, Gabon, Gambia, German Democratic Republic, Germany, Federal Republic of, Ghana, Greece, Grenada, Guatemala, Guinea, Guinea-Bissau, Guyana, Haiti, Hungary, Iceland, India, Indonesia, Iran, Iraq, Ireland, Italy, Jamaica, Japan, Jordan, Kenya, Kuwait, Lao People's Democratic Republic, Lebanon, Lesotho, Liberia, Libyan Arab Jamahiriya, Luxembourg, Madagascar, Malawi, Malaysia, Maldives, Mali, Malta, Mauritania, Mauritius, Mexico, Morocco, Mozambique, Myanmar, Nepal, Netherlands, New Zealand, Nicaragua, Niger, Nigeria, Norway, Oman, Pakistan, Panama, Papua New Guinea, Paraguay, Peru, Philippines, Poland, Portugal, Qatar, Romania, Rwanda, Samoa, Sao Tome and Principe, Saudi Arabia, Senegal, Seychelles, Sierra Leone, Singapore, Solomon Islands, Somalia, Spain, Sri Lanka, Sudan, Suriname, Sweden, Syrian Arab Republic, Togo, Trinidad and Tobago, Tunisia, Turkey, Uganda,

Ukrainian SSR, USSR, United Arab Emirates, United Kingdom, United Republic of Tanzania, Uruguay, Vanuatu, Venezuela, Viet Nam, Yemen, Yugoslavia, Zaire, Zambia, Zimbabwe.
Against: Israel, United States.
Abstaining: None.

Organization of the Islamic Conference

In response to a 1988 General Assembly resolution,[5] the Secretary-General submitted in August 1989 a report on co-operation between the United Nations and the Organization of the Islamic Conference (OIC).[6]

The report described consultations which had taken place between representatives of the two organizations and their representation at meetings since the Secretary-General's 1988 report and summarized the follow-up action on the recommendations of the third United Nations/OIC meeting.[7]

In October, the Secretary-General submitted an addendum to his report,[8] transmitting conclusions and recommendations of the co-ordination meeting of the focal points of the lead agencies of the United Nations and OIC (Geneva, 13-15 September).

On 18 April,[9] Saudi Arabia transmitted the final communiqué of the Eighteenth Islamic Conference of Foreign Ministers (Riyadh, 13-16 March). On 31 October, Saudi Arabia transmitted the communiqué of the Co-ordination Meeting of the Ministers for Foreign Affairs of the Organization of the Islamic Conference (New York, 4 October).[10]

GENERAL ASSEMBLY ACTION

On 18 October, the General Assembly adopted without vote **resolution 44/8**.

Co-operation between the United Nations and the Organization of the Islamic Conference

The General Assembly,

Having considered the report of the Secretary-General on co-operation between the United Nations and the Organization of the Islamic Conference,

Taking into account the desire of both organizations to co-operate more closely in their common search for solutions to global problems, such as questions relating to international peace and security, disarmament, self-determination, decolonization, fundamental human rights and the establishment of a new international economic order,

Recalling the Articles of the Charter of the United Nations which encourage activities through regional co-operation for the promotion of the purposes and principles of the United Nations,

Noting the strengthening of co-operation between the specialized agencies and other organizations of the United Nations system and the Organization of the Islamic Conference and its specialized institutions,

Noting with satisfaction the co-ordination meeting of the focal points of the lead agencies of the United Nations and the Organization of the Islamic Conference, held

at Geneva from 13 to 15 September 1989, as called for in General Assembly resolution 43/2 of 17 October 1988,

Noting also the encouraging progress made in the seven priority areas of co-operation as well as in the identification of other areas of co-operation,

Convinced that the strengthening of co-operation between the United Nations and other organizations of the United Nations system and the Organization of the Islamic Conference contributes to the promotion of the purposes and principles of the United Nations,

Noting with appreciation the desire of both organizations to strengthen further the existing co-operation by developing specific proposals in the designated priority areas of co-operation,

Recognizing the need for closer co-operation between the specialized agencies and other organizations of the United Nations system and the Organization of the Islamic Conference and its specialized institutions in the implementation of the proposals adopted at the co-ordination meeting of the focal points of the lead agencies of the two organizations,

Recalling its resolutions 37/4 of 22 October 1982, 38/4 of 28 October 1983, 39/7 of 8 November 1984, 40/4 of 25 October 1985, 41/3 of 16 October 1986, 42/4 of 15 October 1987 and 43/2 of 17 October 1988,

1. *Takes note with satisfaction* of the report of the Secretary-General;

2. *Approves* the conclusions and recommendations of the co-ordination meeting of the focal points of the lead agencies of the United Nations and the Organization of the Islamic Conference;

3. *Notes with satisfaction* the active participation of the Organization of the Islamic Conference in the work of the United Nations towards the realization of the purposes and principles of the Charter of the United Nations;

4. *Requests* the United Nations and the Organization of the Islamic Conference to continue co-operation in their common search for solutions to global problems, such as questions relating to international peace and security, disarmament, self-determination, decolonization, fundamental human rights and the establishment of a new international economic order;

5. *Encourages* the specialized agencies and other organizations of the United Nations system to continue to expand their co-operation with the Organization of the Islamic Conference, particularly by negotiating co-operation agreements, and invites them to multiply the contacts and meetings of focal points for co-operation in priority areas of interest to the United Nations and the Organization of the Islamic Conference;

6. *Recommends* that a meeting of the focal points of the lead agencies of the United Nations and the Organization of the Islamic Conference and its specialized institutions should be organized in 1990 to review the progress in the implementation of the plan of action adopted at the co-ordination meeting held between the two organizations in 1989, and that that meeting should be followed by a general meeting in 1991 between representatives of the secretariats of the organizations of the United Nations system and the Organization of the Islamic Conference;

7. *Urges* the organizations of the United Nations system, especially the lead agencies, to provide increased technical and other forms of assistance to the Organi-

zation of the Islamic Conference and its specialized institutions in order to enhance co-operation;

8. *Requests* the Secretary-General to strengthen co-operation and co-ordination between the United Nations and other organizations of the United Nations system and the Organization of the Islamic Conference to serve the mutual interests of the two organizations in the political, economic, social and cultural fields;

9. *Requests* the United Nations and the Organization of the Islamic Conference to arrange for the holding of consultations, as and when appropriate, between representatives of the Secretariat of the United Nations and the General Secretariat of the Organization of the Islamic Conference on the implementation of projects and follow-up action;

10. *Also requests* the Secretary-General of the United Nations, in consultation with the Secretary-General of the Organization of the Islamic Conference, to encourage the convening of sectoral meetings between the two organizations on the priority areas of co-operation;

11. *Expresses its appreciation* for the efforts of the Secretary-General in the promotion of co-operation between the United Nations and the Organization of the Islamic Conference, and expresses the hope that he will continue to strengthen the mechanisms of co-operation between the two organizations;

12. *Further requests* the Secretary-General to report to the General Assembly at its forty-fifth session on the state of co-operation between the United Nations and the Organization of the Islamic Conference;

13. *Decides* to include in the provisional agenda of its forty-fifth session the item entitled ''Co-operation between the United Nations and the Organization of the Islamic Conference''.

General Assembly resolution 44/8

18 October 1989   Meeting 34   Adopted without vote

Draft by Saudi Arabia (A/44/L.5); agenda item 22.

Observer status for the Council of Europe

By a letter dated 6 July 1989,[11] Luxembourg, the Netherlands, Norway and Portugal requested inclusion of an item in the General Assembly's agenda on granting observer status to the Council of Europe. On 22 September, the Assembly decided to include the item and to consider it directly in plenary.

GENERAL ASSEMBLY ACTION

On 17 October, the General Assembly adopted without vote **resolution 44/6**.

Observer status for the Council of Europe in the General Assembly

The General Assembly,

Wishing to promote co-operation between the United Nations and the Council of Europe,

Requests the Secretary-General to invite the Council of Europe to participate in the sessions and the work of the General Assembly in the capacity of observer.

General Assembly resolution 44/6

17 October 1989   Meeting 33   Adopted without vote

20-nation draft (A/44/L.4); agenda item 148.

Sponsors: Austria, Belgium, Cyprus, Denmark, Finland, France, Germany, Federal Republic of, Greece, Iceland, Ireland, Italy, Luxembourg, Malta, Netherlands, Norway, Portugal, Spain, Sweden, Turkey, United Kingdom.

REFERENCES

[1]YUN 1988, p. 127, GA res. 43/3, 17 Oct. 1988. [2]A/44/478 & Corr.1. [3]YUN 1983, p. 394. [4]YUN 1988, p. 126. [5]YUN 1988, p. 129, GA res. 43/2, 17 Oct. 1988. [6]A/44/424. [7]YUN 1988, p. 128. [8]A/44/424/Add.1. [9]A/44/235-S/20600. [10]A/44/700-S/20934. [11]A/44/141.

Other institutional questions

Composition of UN organs

In 1989, as in every year since 1979, consideration of the question of the composition of the relevant organs of the United Nations was deferred, based on the recommendation of the Special Political Committee, which reported that none of its members had requested to speak on the substance of the item.[1] Acting on the Committee's recommendation, the General Assembly, on 8 December, adopted **decision 44/420** by which it included the item in the provisional agenda of its forty-fifth (1990) session.

Implementation of UN resolutions

On 22 December, by **decision 44/458**, the General Assembly deferred consideration of the item on implementation of the resolutions of the United Nations and decided to include it in the provisional agenda of its forty-fifth session.

REFERENCE

[1]A/44/686.

PART TWO

Regional questions

Chapter I

Africa

In 1989, a major goal for Africa remained the elimination of *apartheid* and a peaceful transformation of South Africa into a united, non-racial and democratic society. The anti-*apartheid* struggle intensified inside and outside South Africa, and the leadership of the ruling National Party changed following the resignation in August of President P. W. Botha. In September, elections were held for the racially segregated Parliament, again excluding the African majority. However, the new President, F. W. de Klerk, described the election results as a mandate for orderly reform. The African National Congress (ANC) proposed a process of constitutional change through peaceful negotiations, and, on 21 August, the Organization of African Unity (OAU) adopted the Harare Declaration on the conditions necessary for a negotiated solution to the political conflict. Towards the end of the year, President de Klerk undertook a number of liberalization measures and held discussions on the country's political future with the still-imprisoned ANC leader, Nelson Mandela. In December, the Pan Africanist Movement was formed, and the first Conference for a Democratic Future was held, with more than 4,600 delegates attending.

The United Nations during 1989 continued its support for the anti-*apartheid* struggle. The General Assembly adopted 12 resolutions to strengthen international pressure against South Africa, including intensifying economic and financial sanctions and tightening the oil embargo. The Assembly also called on South Africa to commute the death sentence of Mangena Jeffrey Boesman, as well as those for all political prisoners (resolution 44/1).

In December, the Assembly held its sixteenth special session, at which the question of *apartheid* was discussed. It adopted the Declaration on *Apartheid* and its Destructive Consequences in Southern Africa, which for the first time laid down internationally agreed steps towards a negotiating climate and principles for a united, non-racial and democratic South Africa. It also prescribed a programme of work to achieve that end (resolution S-16/1).

Major advances were made by the United Nations in 1989 towards the independence of Namibia, once the territory of South West Africa administered by South Africa. Agreements signed in 1988 between Angola, Cuba and South Africa resulted in the withdrawal of Cuban troops from Angola and the withdrawal of South Africa from Namibia. The deployment in April in Namibia of the UN Transition Assistance Group led to democratic elections in November—setting the stage for independence in early 1990 (see PART FOUR, Chapter III). During the year, United Nations Angola Verification Mission also became operational.

In other developments, the Security Council considered the downing of two aircraft of the Libyan Arab Jamahiriya by the United States, but adopted no decision due to the negative vote of a permanent member. The Assembly again reaffirmed the sovereignty of the Comoros over the island of Mayotte. Noting the increasing co-operation between OAU and the United Nations, it requested the United Nations to support the efforts of OAU to establish an African economic community and endorsed the convening of a meeting between the secretariats of the two organizations to consider expanding and strengthening co-operation in the economic and social sectors.

South Africa and *apartheid*

The situation in South Africa remained at an impasse for the greater part of 1989. Despite signing agreements with Angola and Cuba in December 1988[1] to bring about the independence of Namibia, Pretoria undertook no fundamental initiatives to dismantle the *apartheid* system. In June, it announced its five-year plan for political reform, which failed to fulfil the demands of the black majority for full political rights and maintained the fundamental aspects of white minority rule. The plan also envisaged that municipal representatives elected in 1988 would become political representatives to the National Council, which would devise a new constitution.

Pretoria also undertook further repressive measures to eliminate opposition to its rule. It announced the renewal of the state of emergency for the fourth consecutive year, and in March adopted the Disclosure of Foreign Funding Act designed to control the activities of anti-*apartheid* organizations. Police violence increased, as did attacks by vigilante groups and death squads, creating growing numbers of internal refugees and displaced persons. The court system became an increasingly important instrument of repression and a draconian press censorship hid from world scrutiny human rights violations, including detentions and forced removal of populations.

Meanwhile, differences within the National Party as to the future direction of South Africa led to the resignation on 14 August of P. W. Botha as leader and the subsequent election of Frederick Willem de Klerk as leader and later President.

On 6 September, elections were held for the three houses of the racially segregated Parliament (Whites, Coloured and Indians), again excluding the African majority, and were widely boycotted by the Indian and Coloured populations. The National Party lost ground to the Conservative Party and the newly formed Democratic Party. However, President de Klerk described the election results as a mandate for the National Party's policy of orderly reform, and spoke of launching a negotiating forum and developing a new constitution without domination of one group over another.

Against this background, internal resistance experienced a resurgence as *apartheid* opponents undertook a co-ordinated Campaign of Defiance. The Campaign, launched by the Mass Democratic Movement, focused on the defiance of *apartheid* laws and included several acts of civil disobedience and economic pressure through the successful boycott of white-owned businesses. In May, some 10,000 blacks and whites defied emergency regulations to attend funeral services for the assassinated white democrat, David Webster. Political activity at the community level was also renewed. The trade union movement took a leading role in the political activity, intensifying its campaign against the labour laws and other forms of repression. Religious organizations became even more prominent in the anti-*apartheid* opposition, calling on Pretoria to create the conditions for a peaceful resolution of the conflict. The continuing crisis in *apartheid* education initiated renewed student activity, involving the boycott of classes and protests in schools and universities.

There was also a growing involvement of whites in organized opposition to *apartheid*. The Campaign of Defiance reached a high point in September in a week of protest against the elections for the racially segregated tri-cameral Parliament. It continued in the following months in the homelands and in urban areas. The formation of the Pan Africanist Movement in December further mobilized the forces opposed to the *apartheid* régime. An extended hunger strike by political detainees drew the attention of the international community to detentions without trial and forced the régime to release hundreds of detainees, including several leaders of anti-*apartheid* organizations. It also transferred ANC leader Nelson Mandela to a private prison and released Zephania Mothopeng, leader of the Pan Africanist Congress of Azania (PAC).

Meanwhile, ANC began a process of consultations with the anti-*apartheid* opposition within and outside the country on the basis of its 1987 Constitutional Guidelines for South Africa as a non-racial, united and democratic society. It proposed a process for constitutional change through peaceful negotiations that would include a cease-fire, the formation of an interim government to oversee the transition to a non-racial political system and negotiations for a new constitution. In July, the then President, P. W. Botha, met with Nelson Mandela. In a statement issued following the meeting, Mr. Mandela reiterated his position that dialogue with the Mass Democratic Movement, and, in particular, with ANC, was the only path to peace in the country. He stressed his desire to contribute to the creation of a climate that would promote peace in South Africa.

On 21 August,[2] the OAU *Ad Hoc* Committee on Southern Africa on the question of South Africa, meeting at Harare, Zimbabwe, adopted a declaration based on the ANC position for constitutional change. The Declaration outlined the conditions necessary for a negotiated solution to the political conflict in South Africa, notably the unconditional release of all political prisoners and detainees; the lifting of all bans and restrictions on organizations and individuals; the removal of troops from townships; an end to the state of emergency; repeal of all repressive legislation; and cessation of all political trials and executions.

Also in August, the Mass Democratic Movement, the Black Consciousness Movement, trade unions and religious bodies announced the convening of a Conference for a Democratic Future. Held on 9 and 10 December, the Conference, attended by more than 4,600 delegates representing 2,100 organizations, discussed a programme to intensify and to bring greater unity to the anti-*apartheid* struggle. The Conference adopted the OAU Harare Declaration and called for a non-racial constituent assembly, representing all the peoples of South Africa, to draw up a new constitution.

Towards the end of the year, President de Klerk undertook a number of liberalization measures, such as allowing mass demonstrations, releasing several long-term political prisoners, reducing the length of national service from two years to one year, and dismantling the military-controlled National Management System and replacing it by the National Co-ordinating Mechanism under civilian control. He also announced measures that were being considered for improving the climate for constitutional change.

In December, together with several of his cabinet members, he held consultations on the country's political future with the still-imprisoned Mr. Mandela.

GENERAL ASSEMBLY ACTION

On 22 November 1989, the General Assembly adopted **resolution 44/27 A** by recorded vote.

International solidarity with the liberation struggle in South Africa

The General Assembly,

Having considered the report of the Special Committee against *Apartheid,*

Gravely concerned at the continuing repression of the majority population in South Africa and the continuation of the state of emergency,

Expressing particular concern at the continuing practice of arbitrary detentions and trials, including those of women and children, executions of political prisoners, the ongoing use of vigilante groups and the stifling of the press,

Noting with serious concern the régime's acts of aggression and destabilization against neighbouring independent African States,

1. *Reaffirms* the legitimacy of the struggle of the South African people for the total eradication of *apartheid* and for the establishment of a united, non-racial and democratic society in which all the people of South Africa, irrespective of race, colour or creed, enjoy the same fundamental freedoms and human rights;

2. *Reaffirms also* its full support to the national liberation movements, the African National Congress of South Africa and the Pan Africanist Congress of Azania, which pursue their noble objective to eliminate *apartheid* through political, armed and other forms of struggle and have reiterated their preference for reaching their legitimate objectives through peaceful means;

3. *Condemns* the régime's continuing practice of sentencing to death and executing its opponents and demands that it annul the capital punishment imposed on opponents of *apartheid*, including the "Upington Fourteen", and confer prisoner-of-war status on captured freedom fighters in accordance with the Geneva Conventions of 12 August 1949 and Additional Protocol I of 1977 thereto;

4. *Demands* that all political prisoners and detainees, particularly children, be released unconditionally and without subsequent restrictions and that the abhorrent practice of applying repressive measures to children and minors cease immediately;

5. *Calls upon* Governments, intergovernmental and non-governmental organizations and individuals to extend all possible assistance to the struggling people of South Africa, their national liberation movements and South African refugees, particularly women and children;

6. *Also calls upon* all Governments, intergovernmental and non-governmental organizations to step up material, financial and other forms of support to the front-line and other neighbouring independent States that are subject to acts of destabilization by South Africa;

7. *Appeals* to all Governments, intergovernmental and non-governmental organizations to contribute generously to the Action for Resisting Invasion, Colonialism and *Apartheid* Fund set up by the Eighth Conference of Heads of State or Government of Non-Aligned Countries, held at Harare from 1 to 6 September 1986;

8. *Decides* to continue the authorization of adequate financial provision in the regular budget of the United Nations to enable the South African liberation movements recognized by the Organization of African Unity—namely, the African National Congress of South Africa and the Pan Africanist Congress of Azania—to maintain offices in New York in order to participate effectively in the deliberations of the Special Committee against *Apartheid* and other appropriate bodies.

General Assembly resolution 44/27 A

22 November 1989   Meeting 63   129-4-21 (recorded vote)

69-nation draft (A/44/L.26 & Add.1); agenda item 28.

Sponsors: Afghanistan, Albania, Algeria, Angola, Antigua and Barbuda, Barbados, Benin, Botswana, Bulgaria, Burundi, Byelorussian SSR, Cameroon, Comoros, Congo, Cuba, Czechoslovakia, Djibouti, Ethiopia, Gambia, German Democratic Republic, Ghana, Guinea, Haiti, India, Indonesia, Iran, Iraq, Jamaica, Jordan, Kenya, Kuwait, Lesotho, Liberia, Libyan Arab Jamahiriya, Madagascar, Malaysia, Mali, Mauritania, Mauritius, Mongolia, Morocco, Mozambique, Myanmar, Nepal, Nicaragua, Niger, Nigeria, Pakistan, Panama, Philippines, Qatar, Rwanda, Senegal, Sierra Leone, Somalia, Sudan, Syrian Arab Republic, Togo, Trinidad and Tobago, Tunisia, Uganda, Ukrainian SSR, USSR, United Republic of Tanzania, Vanuatu, Viet Nam, Yugoslavia, Zambia, Zimbabwe.

Financial implications. 5th Committee, A/44/758; S-G, A/C.5/44/29.

Meeting numbers. GA 44th session: 5th Committee 46; plenary 11, 46, 47, 49-53, 63.

Recorded vote in Assembly as follows:

In favour: Afghanistan, Albania, Algeria, Angola, Antigua and Barbuda, Argentina, Bahamas, Bahrain, Barbados, Belize, Benin, Bhutan, Bolivia, Botswana, Brazil, Brunei Darussalam, Bulgaria, Burkina Faso, Burundi, Byelorussian SSR, Cameroon, Cape Verde, Central African Republic, Chad, China, Colombia, Comoros, Congo, Costa Rica, Côte d'Ivoire, Cuba, Cyprus, Czechoslovakia, Democratic Kampuchea, Democratic Yemen, Djibouti, Dominica, Dominican Republic, Ecuador, Egypt, Equatorial Guinea, Ethiopia, Fiji, Gabon, Gambia, German Democratic Republic, Ghana, Grenada, Guatemala, Guinea, Guinea-Bissau, Guyana, Haiti, Honduras, India, Indonesia, Iran, Iraq, Jamaica, Jordan, Kenya, Kuwait, Lao People's Democratic Republic, Lebanon, Lesotho, Liberia, Libyan Arab Jamahiriya, Madagascar, Malawi, Malaysia, Maldives, Mali, Mauritania, Mauritius, Mexico, Mongolia, Morocco, Mozambique, Myanmar, Nepal, Nicaragua, Niger, Nigeria, Oman, Pakistan, Panama, Papua New Guinea, Peru, Philippines, Poland, Qatar, Romania, Rwanda, Saint Kitts and Nevis, Saint Lucia, Saint Vincent and the Grenadines, Samoa, Sao Tome and Principe, Saudi Arabia, Senegal, Seychelles, Sierra Leone, Singapore, Solomon Islands, Somalia, Sri Lanka, Sudan, Suriname, Swaziland, Syrian Arab Republic, Thailand, Togo, Trinidad and Tobago, Tunisia, Turkey, Uganda, Ukrainian SSR, USSR, United Arab Emirates, United Republic of Tanzania, Uruguay, Vanuatu, Venezuela, Viet Nam, Yemen, Yugoslavia, Zaire, Zambia, Zimbabwe.

Against: Israel, Portugal, United Kingdom, United States.

Abstaining: Australia, Austria, Belgium, Canada, Denmark, Finland, France, Germany, Federal Republic of, Greece, Hungary, Iceland, Ireland, Italy, Japan, Luxembourg, Malta, Netherlands, New Zealand, Norway, Spain, Sweden.

On the same date, the Assembly adopted **resolution 44/27 B** without vote.

International support for the eradication of *apartheid* in South Africa through genuine negotiations

The General Assembly,

Condemning once again the policy and practice of *apartheid,*

Convinced that the continuation of the policy and practice of *apartheid* will lead to further violence and is detrimental to the vital interests of all the people of South Africa,

Convinced that the system of *apartheid* cannot be reformed but must be eliminated,

Taking note of the Declaration of the *Ad Hoc* Committee of the Organization of African Unity on Southern Africa on the question of South Africa, adopted at Harare on 21 August 1989,

1. *Reaffirms* its support for the establishment of a united, non-racial and democratic society in which all the people of South Africa, irrespective of race, colour

or creed, will enjoy the same fundamental freedoms and human rights;

2. *Fully supports* the efforts of the South African people to arrive at a peaceful settlement of the conflict in their country through genuine negotiations;

3. *Strongly demands:*

(a) The lifting of the state of emergency;

(b) The immediate and unconditional release of Nelson Mandela and all other political prisoners and detainees;

(c) The lifting of the ban on all individuals and political organizations opposing *apartheid* and the repeal of restrictions on the press;

(d) The withdrawal of the troops from black townships;

(e) The cessation of all political trials and political executions;

4. *Considers* that the implementation of the above demands would help create the necessary climate for genuine negotiations and calls upon all parties to take full advantage of opportunities arising therefrom, and further considers that this could also promote an agreement to end *apartheid* and bring about the cessation of violence;

5. *Calls upon* all Member States to use concerted and effective measures to ensure the prompt implementation of the present resolution;

6. *Requests* the Secretary-General to continue to promote efforts leading to the eradication of *apartheid* through genuine negotiations.

General Assembly resolution 44/27 B

22 November 1989   Meeting 63   Adopted without vote

85-nation draft (A/44/L.27 & Add.1); agenda item 28.

Sponsors: Afghanistan, Albania, Angola, Antigua and Barbuda, Australia, Austria, Barbados, Benin, Botswana, Bulgaria, Burundi, Byelorussian SSR, Cameroon, Canada, Comoros, Congo, Côte d'Ivoire, Cuba, Czechoslovakia, Djibouti, Egypt, Ethiopia, France, Gabon, Gambia, German Democratic Republic, Ghana, Greece, Guinea, Haiti, Hungary, India, Indonesia, Iraq, Ireland, Jamaica, Jordan, Kenya, Kuwait, Lesotho, Liberia, Libyan Arab Jamahiriya, Madagascar, Malaysia, Mali, Mauritania, Mauritius, Mongolia, Morocco, Mozambique, Myanmar, Nepal, New Zealand, Nicaragua, Niger, Nigeria, Pakistan, Panama, Peru, Philippines, Qatar, Rwanda, Saint Lucia, Samoa, Senegal, Sierra Leone, Somalia, Spain, Sudan, Suriname, Sweden, Syrian Arab Republic, Togo, Trinidad and Tobago, Tunisia, Turkey, Uganda, Ukrainian SSR, USSR, United Republic of Tanzania, Vanuatu, Viet Nam, Yugoslavia, Zambia, Zimbabwe.

Financial implications. 5th Committee, A/44/758; S-G, A/C.5/44/29.

Meeting numbers. GA 44th session: 5th Committee 46; plenary 11, 46, 47, 49-53, 63.

General Assembly special session on *apartheid*

In 1988,[3] the General Assembly had decided to convene, prior to its forty-fourth (1989) session, a special session on *apartheid* and its destructive consequences at a date to be determined by the Secretary-General in consultation with the Special Committee against *Apartheid*. The Secretary-General, in June 1989,[4] transmitted the recommendation of the Chairman of the Special Committee that the special session be held in December, to be preceded by the debate on the agenda item entitled "Policies of *apartheid* of the Government of South Africa". The Secretary-General proposed that the Assembly reopen the debate on

that agenda item to enable it to consider the Special Committee's recommendations.

On 11 July, at its resumed forty-third session, the Assembly, by **decision 43/402 C**, approved the Secretary-General's proposal. By **decision 43/462** of the same date, it decided that its sixteenth special session would be held from 12 to 14 December 1989, on the understanding that the debate on "Policies of *apartheid* of the Government of South Africa" would be held three to four weeks earlier.

On 19 October,[5] the Acting Chairman of the Special Committee against *Apartheid* submitted organizational proposals for the special session, including the establishment of an *Ad Hoc* Committee of the Whole to hear non-governmental organizations (NGOs) and individuals and to finalize a draft declaration; and that the OAU Chairman and South African national liberation movements recognized by it be allowed to participate.

On 13 November, by **decision 44/408**, the Assembly approved those proposals. It also requested the bureau of the Special Committee, in co-operation with the front-line States, to consult with interested delegations concerning the preparation of a draft declaration to be submitted to the *Ad Hoc* Committee for finalization.

On 12 December, the Assembly, at the special session, adopted its agenda (**decision S-16/23**), established the *Ad Hoc* Committee of the Whole (**decision S-16/22**) and noted that the credentials of representatives to the session had already been approved by its resolutions 44/5 A and B (**decision S/16-21**).

The *Ad Hoc* Committee held five meetings between 12 and 14 December.[6] It considered the draft declaration submitted by the bureau of the Special Committee against *Apartheid* and heard statements by Member States, the representatives of ANC, PAC and NGOs and individuals. The *Ad Hoc* Committee recommended to the Assembly a draft resolution, to which was annexed the Declaration on *Apartheid* and its Destructive Consequences in Southern Africa, as well as a draft decision. The Assembly, on 14 December, adopted the Declaration and decided to reopen the forty-fourth session's item entitled "Policies of *apartheid* of the Government of South Africa" to consider a report of the Secretary-General on progress made in implementing the Declaration, which was to be submitted by 1 July 1990 (**decision S-16/24**).

Prior to the special session, the South African Minister for Foreign Affairs, in a 7 December letter[7] to the Secretary-General, declared that adoption of the draft Declaration, support for which was being canvassed at that time, would be a blatant intervention in the domestic affairs of a Member State. He referred to the policies of the South African Government in the political, social and economic fields, the pursuit of which would be made more difficult by adoption of the Declaration, which would also have a negative effect on and complicate negotiations between the relevant parties in South Africa. He saw the Declaration as an attempt to incorporate as much as possible of the Harare Declaration,[2] which incorporated the position of only one (ANC) of the parties likely to participate in future negotiations. The special session, he said, offered the United Nations the opportunity to acknowledge and promote the emerging new realism that was developing in South Africa.

GENERAL ASSEMBLY ACTION

On 14 December 1989, the General Assembly adopted **resolution S-16/1** without vote.

Declaration on *Apartheid* and its Destructive Consequences in Southern Africa

The General Assembly

Adopts the Declaration on *Apartheid* and its Destructive Consequences in Southern Africa, annexed to the present resolution.

ANNEX
Declaration on *Apartheid* and its Destructive Consequences in Southern Africa

We, the States Members of the United Nations,

Assembled at the sixteenth special session of the General Assembly, a special session on *apartheid* and its destructive consequences in southern Africa, guided by the fundamental and universal principles enshrined in the Charter of the United Nations and the Universal Declaration of Human Rights, in the context of our efforts to establish peace throughout the world by ending all conflicts through negotiations, and desirous of making serious efforts to bring an end to the unacceptable situation prevailing in southern Africa, which is a result of the policies and practices of *apartheid*, through negotiations based on the principle of justice and peace for all:

Reaffirming our conviction, which history confirms, that where colonial and racial domination or *apartheid* exist, there can be neither peace nor justice,

Reiterating, accordingly, that while the *apartheid* system in South Africa persists, the peoples of Africa as a whole cannot achieve the fundamental objectives of justice, human dignity and peace which are both crucial in themselves and fundamental to the stability and development of the continent,

Recognizing that, with regard to southern Africa, the entire world is vitally interested that the processes in which that region is involved, leading to the genuine national independence of Namibia and peace in Angola and Mozambique, should succeed in the shortest possible time, and equally recognizing that the world is deeply concerned that destabilization by South Africa of the countries of the region, whether through direct aggression, sponsorship of surrogates, economic subversion or other means, is unacceptable in all its forms and must not occur,

Also recognizing the reality that permanent peace and stability in southern Africa can only be achieved when the system of *apartheid* in South Africa has been eradicated and South Africa has been transformed into a united, democratic and non-racial country, and therefore reiterating that all the necessary measures should be adopted now to bring a speedy end to the *apartheid* system in the interest of all the people of southern Africa, the continent and the world at large,

Believing that, as a result of the legitimate struggle of the South African people for the elimination of *apartheid*, and of international pressure against that system, as well as global efforts to resolve regional conflicts, possibilities exist for further movement towards the resolution of the problems facing the people of South Africa,

Reaffirming the right of all peoples, including the people of South Africa, to determine their own destiny and to work out for themselves the institutions and the system of government under which they will, by general consent, live and work together to build a harmonious society, and remaining committed to doing everything possible and necessary to assist the people of South Africa, in such ways as they may, through their genuine representatives, determine to achieve this objective,

Making these commitments because we believe that all people are equal and have equal rights to human dignity and respect, regardless of colour, race, sex or creed, that all men and women have the right and duty to participate in their own government, as equal members of society, and that no individual or group of individuals has any right to govern others without their democratic consent, and reiterating that the *apartheid* system violates all these fundamental and universal principles,

Affirming that *apartheid*, characterized as a crime against the conscience and dignity of mankind, is responsible for the death of countless numbers of people in South Africa, has sought to dehumanize entire peoples and has imposed a brutal war on the region of southern Africa, which has resulted in untold loss of life, destruction of property and massive displacement of innocent men, women and children and which is a scourge and affront to humanity that must be fought and eradicated in its totality,

Therefore we support and continue to support all those in South Africa who pursue this noble objective. We believe this to be our duty, carried out in the interest of all humanity,

While extending this support to those who strive for a non-racial and democratic society in South Africa, a point on which no compromise is possible, we have repeatedly expressed our objective of a solution arrived at by peaceful means; we note that the people of South Africa, and their liberation movements who felt compelled to take up arms, have also upheld their preference for this position for many decades and continue to do so,

Welcoming the Declaration of the *Ad Hoc* Committee of the Organization of African Unity on Southern Africa on the question of South Africa, adopted at Harare on 21 August 1989, and subsequently endorsed by the Heads of State or Government of Non-Aligned Countries at their Ninth Conference, held at Belgrade from 4 to 7 September 1989, as a reaffirmation of readiness to resolve the problems of South Africa through negotiations. The Declaration is consistent with the positions contained in the Lusaka Manifesto of two decades ago, in particular regarding the preference of the African people for peaceful change, and takes into account the changes that have taken place in southern Africa since then. The Declaration constitutes a new challenge to the Pretoria régime to join in the noble efforts to end the *apartheid* system, an objective to which the United Nations has always been committed,

Noting with appreciation that the Commonwealth Heads of Government, at their meeting held at Kuala Lumpur from 18 to 24 October 1989, noted with satisfaction the strong preference for the path of negotiated and peaceful settlement inherent in the Declaration adopted at Harare on 21 August 1989, and considered what further steps they might take to advance the prospects for negotiations,

Also noting with appreciation that the Third Francophone Conference of Heads of State and Government, held at Dakar from 24 to 26 May 1989, likewise called for negotiations between Pretoria and representatives of the majority of the people with a view to the establishment of a democratic and egalitarian system in South Africa,

Consequently, we shall continue to do everything in our power to increase support for the legitimate struggle of the South African people, including maintaining international pressure against the system of *apartheid* until that system is ended and South Africa is transformed into a united, democratic and non-racial country, with justice and security for all its citizens,

In keeping with this solemn resolve, and responding directly to the wishes of the majority of the people of South Africa, we publicly pledge ourselves to the positions contained hereunder, convinced that their implementation will lead to a speedy end of the *apartheid* system and herald the dawn of a new era of peace for all the peoples of Africa, in a continent finally free from racism, white minority rule and colonial domination,

Declare as follows:

1.   A conjuncture of circumstances exists, which, if there is a demonstrable readiness on the part of the South African régime to engage in negotiations genuinely and seriously, given the repeated expression of the majority of the people of South Africa of their long-standing preference to arrive at a political settlement, could create the possibility to end *apartheid* through negotiations.

2.   We would therefore encourage the people of South Africa, as part of their legitimate struggle, to join together to negotiate an end to the *apartheid* system and agree on all the measures that are necessary to transform their country into a non-racial democracy. We support the position held by the majority of the people of South Africa that these objectives, and not the amendment or reform of the *apartheid* system, should be the goals of the negotiations.

3.   We are at one with the people of South Africa that the outcome of such a process should be a new constitutional order determined by them and based on the Charter of the United Nations and the Universal Declaration of Human Rights. We therefore hold the following fundamental principles to be of importance:

(a)   South Africa shall become a united, non-racial and democratic State;

(b)   All its people shall enjoy common and equal citizenship and nationality, regardless of race, colour, sex or creed;

(c)   All its people shall have the right to participate in the government and administration of the country on the basis of universal, equal suffrage, under a non-racial voters' roll, and by secret ballot, in a united and non-fragmented South Africa;

(d)   All shall have the right to form and join any political party of their choice, provided that this is not in furtherance of racism;

(e)   All shall enjoy universally recognized human rights, freedoms and civil liberties, protected under an entrenched bill of rights;

(f)   South Africa shall have a legal system that will guarantee equality of all before the law;

(g)   South Africa shall have an independent and non-racial judiciary;

(h)   There shall be created an economic order that will promote and advance the well-being of all South Africans;

(i)   A democratic South Africa shall respect the rights, sovereignty and territorial integrity of all countries and pursue a policy of peace, friendship and mutually beneficial co-operation with all peoples.

4.   We believe that acceptance of these fundamental principles could constitute the basis for an internationally acceptable solution that will enable South Africa to take its rightful place as an equal partner among the world community of nations.

A.   Climate for negotiations

5.   We believe that it is essential that the necessary climate be created for negotiations. There is an urgent need to respond positively to this universally acclaimed demand and thus create this climate.

6.   Accordingly, the present South African régime should, at the least:

(a)   Release all political prisoners and detainees unconditionally and refrain from imposing any restrictions on them;

(b)   Lift all bans and restrictions on all proscribed and restricted organizations and persons;

(c)   Remove all troops from the townships;

(d)   End the state of emergency and repeal all legislation, such as the Internal Security Act, designed to circumscribe political activity;

(e)   Cease all political trials and political executions.

7.   These measures would help create the necessary climate in which free political discussion can take place—an essential condition to ensure that the people themselves participate in the process of remaking their country.

B.   Guidelines to the process of negotiations

8.   We are of the view that the parties concerned should, in the context of the necessary climate, negotiate the future of their country and its people in good faith and in an atmosphere which, by mutual agreement between the liberation movements and the South African régime, would be free of violence. The process could commence along the following guidelines:

(a)   Agreement on the mechanism for the drawing up of a new constitution, based on, among others, the principles enunciated above, and the basis for its adoption;

(b)   Agreement on the role to be played by the international community in ensuring a successful transition to a democratic order;

(c)   Agreed transitional arrangements and modalities for the process of the drawing up and adoption of a new constitution, and for the transition to a democratic order, including the holding of elections.

C. Programme of action

9. In pursuance of the objectives stated in this Declaration, we hereby decide:

(a) To remain seized of the issue of a political resolution of the South African question;

(b) To step up all-round support for the opponents of *apartheid* and to campaign internationally in pursuance of this objective;

(c) To use concerted and effective measures, including the full observance by all countries of the mandatory arms embargo, aimed at applying pressure to ensure a speedy end to *apartheid;*

(d) To ensure that the international community does not relax existing measures aimed at encouraging the South African régime to eradicate *apartheid* until there is clear evidence of profound and irreversible changes, bearing in mind the objectives of this Declaration;

(e) To render all possible assistance to the front-line and neighbouring States to enable them: to rebuild their economies, which have been adversely affected by South Africa's acts of aggression and destabilization; to withstand any further such acts; and to continue to support the peoples of Namibia and South Africa;

(f) To extend such assistance to the Governments of Angola and Mozambique as they may request in order to secure peace for their peoples, and to encourage and support peace initiatives undertaken by the Governments of Angola and Mozambique aimed at bringing about peace and normalization of life in their countries;

(g) The new South Africa shall, upon adoption of the new constitution, participate fully in relevant organs and specialized agencies of the United Nations.

10. We request the Secretary-General to transmit copies of the present Declaration to the South African Government and the representatives of the oppressed people of South Africa and also request the Secretary-General to prepare a report and submit it to the General Assembly by 1 July 1990 on the progress made in the implementation of the present Declaration.

General Assembly resolution S-16/1

14 December 1989   Meeting 6   Adopted without vote

Draft by *Ad Hoc* Committee (A/S-16/4); agenda item 7.
Meeting numbers. GA 16th special session: *Ad Hoc* Committee 1-5; plenary 1-6.

General aspects

Activities of the Special Committee against *Apartheid.* The Special Committee against *Apartheid*, in its annual report covering the period August 1988 to August 1989,[8] reviewed the political developments and economic and social conditions in South Africa, the external relations of South Africa and international action against *apartheid*. Developments later in the year were described in the Committee's 1990 report.[9]

During the period under review, the Special Committee monitored the situation in South Africa and promoted international campaigns to isolate the *apartheid* régime, focusing on activities aimed at influencing and mobilizing world opinion. It organized and sponsored seminars and hearings, promoted contacts among opponents of *apartheid* and assisted the anti-*apartheid* resistance

both inside and outside South Africa. The Special Committee also encouraged and generated support to anti-*apartheid* forces and to the victims of *apartheid*, and issued statements and messages against their repression in South Africa. The Committee denounced the régime's decisions to hold elections and to renew the state of emergency, and expressed solidarity with the detainees on hunger strikes in prisons throughout South Africa. It continued to persuade Governments to end their economic, military and other relations with South Africa and expressed appreciation to those States that had taken action in that regard.

In its conclusions, the Special Committee noted that, after a year of continued resistance, it had become clear that the new leadership of Pretoria was facing a formidable domestic and international challenge, while the international community was expecting initiatives for real change in South Africa. However, that new leadership still had not fully understood the imperative for fundamental change towards the eradication of *apartheid* and the establishment of a democratic and non-racial society. It continued to suppress with savagery any peaceful opposition to its policies. Under the circumstances, the international community had no other option for a peaceful end to *apartheid* than to step up pressure by adopting comprehensive and mandatory sanctions directed at the vulnerable areas of the South African economy. The liberation struggle and international pressure, facilitated by recent positive developments on the world political scene, had opened new possibilities for a peaceful end to *apartheid*. Intensified and coordinated pressure by the international community could induce Pretoria to take steps conducive to a climate for negotiations.

The Special Committee recommended that the General Assembly demand that Pretoria annul capital punishment imposed on the opponents of *apartheid*, support a political settlement through negotiations and call on South Africa to create the climate necessary for negotiations by lifting the state of emergency, unconditionally releasing Nelson Mandela and other political prisoners and detainees, lifting the ban on individuals and anti-*apartheid* organizations, withdrawing troops from the black townships and ceasing all political trials and executions.

The Committee recommended that the Assembly urge the Security Council to apply comprehensive and mandatory sanctions and to implement strictly the mandatory arms embargo; and urge States to stop collaborating with South Africa in the military intelligence and technology fields. It also recommended that States, pending the adoption of comprehensive and mandatory sanctions, impose embargoes on the supply of oil, petroleum products and technology, investments, loans and credits, computer and communications equipment and other high-technology products having military application; prohibit the import of coal, gold and other minerals, and agricultural products from South Africa; deny landing and port rights to South African air and sea carriers and sever direct transportation links; and induce transnational corporations (TNCs), banks and financial institutions to withdraw effectively from South Africa by ceasing equity investments and cutting off non-equity links. The Committee further proposed that the Assembly urge governmental and private financial institutions not to reschedule South Africa's foreign debt and to end financial support and favourable treatment; and urge Governments and NGOs to ensure the effectiveness of the cultural and sports boycott and extend all possible assistance to the national liberation movements, refugees, particularly women and children, and the front-line States.

Among other recommendations were that the Assembly: authorize the Special Committee to continue to monitor the imposition and implementation of sanctions and their impact on South Africa and to mobilize international action against *apartheid;* request the Secretary-General to co-ordinate United Nations activities and facilitate efforts leading to a peaceful eradication of *apartheid;* and appeal to Governments, intergovernmental and non-governmental organizations, the information media and individuals to co-operate with the Centre against *Apartheid* and the Department of Public Information in monitoring international action against *apartheid* and in disseminating information on the situation in South Africa.

International action to eliminate *apartheid*

In accordance with a 1988 General Assembly resolution,[10] the Secretary-General in October 1989[11] submitted replies from 33 Governments to his request for information regarding the Assembly's renewed appeal to consider, pending mandatory sanctions by the Security Council, national legislative or other measures to increase pressure on the South African régime. Such measures included cessation of further investment in and financial loans to South Africa; an end to all promotion of and support for trade with South Africa; prohibition of the sale of krugerrand and all other coins minted in South Africa; cessation of all military, police or intelligence co-operation, in particular the sale of computer equipment; an end to nuclear collaboration; cessation of export and sale of oil to South Africa; and other measures within the economic and commercial fields.

In submitting the report, the Secretary-General suggested that the information he had presented in his four reports since 1986 was sufficient for an ample review of the implementation of Assembly resolutions concerning concerted international action for the elimination of *apartheid*.

The Special Committee against *Apartheid* concluded that, although proposals were made to impose further sanctions and to strengthen current measures, Governments and intergovernmental organizations had adopted few significant measures in that regard. The urgent task confronting the international community was how to make sanctions effective by targeting the key areas of the highly vulnerable South African economy. Intensified and co-ordinated pressure by the international community could induce Pretoria to take the steps conducive to a climate for negotiations.

In May, the Economic and Social Council, in **resolution 1989/83**, decided to give priority attention to the specific activities of the Programme of Action for the Second Decade to Combat Racism and Racial Discrimination that were directed towards the elimination of *apartheid*, in view of the explosive situation in southern Africa. By **decision 1989/136**, the Council approved the decision of the Commission on Human Rights to renew the mandate of its *Ad Hoc* Working Group of Experts on Southern Africa. In **resolution 1989/82**, it requested the *Ad Hoc* Working Group to continue to study the situation of trade unions in South Africa, in consultation with the International Labour Organisation (ILO), the Special Committee against *Apartheid* and international and African trade union confederations. The Council, by **decision 1989/137**, approved a Commission request that its Group of Three, established under the 1973 International Convention on the Suppression and Punishment of the Crime of *Apartheid*,[12] should meet to consider reports of States parties to the Convention.

In June, at the seventy-sixth session of the International Labour Conference, the ILO Committee on Action against *Apartheid* called on Governments, employers' and workers' organizations and the International Labour Office to promote the implementation of ILO's updated Declaration and Programme of Action concerning Action against *Apartheid* in South Africa as well as other action intended to end *apartheid*. It recommended the adoption of sanctions, including financial sanctions, the imposition of a coal embargo and the adoption of legislation to prevent the transport of oil. The Committee supported the establishment of a Group of Three Independent Experts to monitor and evaluate the implementation of sanctions and other measures.

In August, the Commonwealth Committee of Foreign Ministers on Southern Africa agreed to secure a more co-ordinated approach to global sanctions.

On 11 September,[13] the Chairman of the Special Committee against *Apartheid* transmitted to the Secretary-General the text of the conclusions and recommendations adopted by the International Non-Governmental Organizations Seminar on Education against *Apartheid* (Geneva, 4-6 September). The Seminar recommended the integration of teaching against *apartheid* into school curricula at all levels, and the expansion and regular production of news about South Africa. It also recommended that education against *apartheid* should support the international solidarity campaigns aimed at putting pressure on the *apartheid* régime.

GENERAL ASSEMBLY ACTION

On 22 November, the General Assembly adopted **resolution 44/27 K** by recorded vote.

Concerted international action for the elimination of *apartheid*

The General Assembly,

Alarmed by the critical situation in South Africa caused by the policy of *apartheid* and in particular by the extension of the nation-wide state of emergency,

Convinced that the root-cause of the crisis in southern Africa is the policy of *apartheid*,

Noting with grave concern that in order to perpetuate *apartheid* in South Africa the authorities there have committed acts of aggression and breaches of the peace,

Recognizing that the policy of bantustanization deprives the majority of the people of their citizenship and makes them foreigners in their own country,

Noting that the so-called reforms in South Africa have had the effect of further entrenching the *apartheid* system and further dividing the people of South Africa,

Convinced that only the total eradication of *apartheid* and the establishment of majority rule on the basis of the free and fair exercise of universal adult suffrage can lead to a peaceful and lasting solution in South Africa,

Also convinced that broad-based negotiations involving the genuine representatives of South Africa's majority population should be initiated immediately by the South African authorities with a view to establishing a free, democratic, united and non-racial South Africa,

Recognizing the responsibility of the United Nations and the international community to take all necessary action for the eradication of *apartheid*, and, in particular, the need for effective pressure on the South African authorities as a peaceful means of achieving the abolition of *apartheid*,

Encouraged, in this context, by the growing international consensus, as demonstrated by the adoption of Security Council resolution 569(1985) of 26 July 1985, and the increase in and expansion of national, regional and intergovernmental measures to this end,

Considering sanctions to be the most effective peaceful means available to the international community to increase pressure on the South African authorities,

Convinced of the vital importance of the strict observance of Security Council resolution 418(1977) of 4 November 1977, by which the Council instituted a mandatory arms embargo against South Africa, and Council resolution 558(1984) of 13 December 1984 concerning the import of arms, ammunition and military

vehicles produced in South Africa, and of the need to make these embargoes fully effective in conformity with Council resolution 591(1986) of 28 November 1986,

Commending the national policies not to sell and export oil to South Africa,

Considering that measures to ensure effective and scrupulous implementation of such embargoes through international co-operation are essential and urgent,

Noting, in this respect, the efforts undertaken by the Intergovernmental Group to Monitor the Supply and Shipping of Oil and Petroleum Products to South Africa,

Noting with deep concern that, through a combination of military and economic pressures, in violation of international law, the authorities of South Africa have resorted to economic reprisals and aggression against and destabilization of neighbouring States,

Alarmed by the deteriorating situation of millions of refugees, returnees and displaced persons in southern Africa caused by these policies and actions,

Considering that contacts between *apartheid* South Africa and the front-line and other neighbouring States, necessitated by geography, colonial legacy and other reasons, should not be used by other States as a pretext for legitimizing the *apartheid* system or justifying attempts to break the international isolation of that system,

Convinced that the existence of *apartheid* will continue to lead to ever-increasing resistance by the oppressed people, by all possible means, and increased tension and conflict that will have far-reaching consequences for southern Africa and the world,

Also convinced that policies of collaboration with the *apartheid* régime, instead of respect for the legitimate aspirations of the genuine representatives of the great majority of the people, will encourage its repression and aggression against neighbouring States and its defiance of the United Nations,

Expressing its full support for the legitimate aspiration of African States and peoples and of the Organization of African Unity for the total liberation of the continent of Africa from colonialism and racism,

1. *Strongly condemns* the policy of *apartheid* that deprives the majority of the South African population of their dignity, fundamental freedoms and human rights;

2. *Also strongly condemns* the South African authorities for the killings, arbitrary mass arrests and the detention of members of mass organizations as well as other individuals who are opposing the *apartheid* system and the state of emergency, and for the detention of and even the use of violence against children;

3. *Condemns* the overt and the covert aggressive actions which South Africa has carried out for the destabilization of neighbouring States, as well as those aimed against refugees from South Africa;

4. *Demands* that the authorities of South Africa:

(a) Release immediately, unconditionally and effectively Nelson Mandela and all other political prisoners, detainees and restrictees;

(b) Immediately lift the state of emergency;

(c) Abrogate discriminatory laws and lift bans on all organizations and individuals, as well as end restrictions on and censorship of news media;

(d) Cease all political trials and political executions;

(e) Grant freedom of association and full trade union rights to all workers of South Africa;

(f) Initiate a political dialogue with genuine leaders of the majority population with a view to eradicating *apartheid* without delay and establishing a representative government;

(g) Eradicate the bantustan structures;

(h) Immediately end the destabilization of front-line and neighbouring States;

5. *Urges* the Security Council to consider without delay the adoption of effective mandatory sanctions against South Africa;

6. *Also urges* the Security Council to take steps for the strict implementation of the mandatory arms embargo instituted by it in resolution 418(1977) and of the arms embargo requested in its resolution 558(1984) and, within the context of the relevant resolutions, to secure an end to military and nuclear co-operation with South Africa and the import of military equipment or supplies from South Africa;

7. *Appeals* to all States that have not yet done so, pending mandatory sanctions by the Security Council, to consider national legislative or other appropriate measures to exert pressure on the *apartheid* régime of South Africa, such as:

(a) Cessation of further investment in and financial loans to South Africa;

(b) An end to all promotion of and support for trade with South Africa;

(c) Prohibition of the sale of krugerrand and all other coins minted in South Africa;

(d) Cessation of all forms of military, police or intelligence co-operation with the authorities of South Africa, in particular the sale of computer equipment;

(e) An end to nuclear collaboration with South Africa;

(f) Cessation of export and sale of oil and petroleum products to South Africa;

(g) Other measures within the economic and commercial fields;

8. *Recognizes* the pressing need, existing and potential, of South Africa's neighbouring States for economic assistance, as a complement and not as an alternative to sanctions against South Africa, and appeals to all States, organizations and institutions:

(a) To increase assistance to the front-line States and the Southern African Development Co-ordination Conference in order to increase their economic strength and independence from South Africa;

(b) To increase humanitarian, legal, educational and other such assistance and support to the victims of *apartheid*, to the liberation movements recognized by the Organization of African Unity and to all those struggling against *apartheid* and for a non-racial, democratic society in South Africa;

9. *Appeals* to all Governments and organizations to take appropriate action for the cessation of all academic, cultural, scientific and sports relations that would support the *apartheid* régime of South Africa, as well as relations with individuals, institutions and other bodies endorsing or based on *apartheid;*

10. *Commends* the States that have already adopted voluntary measures against the *apartheid* régime of South Africa in accordance with General Assembly resolution 43/50 K of 5 December 1988 and invites those which have not yet done so to follow their example;

11. *Reaffirms* the legitimacy of the struggle of the oppressed people of South Africa for the total eradication of *apartheid* and for the establishment of a non-racial, democratic society in which all the people, irrespective

of race, colour or creed, enjoy fundamental freedoms and human rights;

12. *Pays tribute to and expresses solidarity with* organizations and individuals struggling against *apartheid* and for a non-racial, democratic society in accordance with the principles of the Universal Declaration of Human Rights;

13. *Requests* the Secretary-General to report to the General Assembly at its forty-fifth session on the implementation of the present resolution.

General Assembly resolution 44/27 K

22 November 1989   Meeting 63   151-2-3 (recorded vote)

24-nation draft (A/44/L.36 & Add.1); agenda item 28.

Sponsors: Angola, Antigua and Barbuda, Australia, Austria, Denmark, Egypt, Finland, Ghana, Greece, Haiti, Iceland, India, Ireland, Jamaica, Madagascar, New Zealand, Nigeria, Norway, Pakistan, Peru, Sweden, United Republic of Tanzania, Zambia, Zimbabwe.

Financial implications. 5th Committee, A/44/758; S-G, A/C.5/44/29.

Meeting numbers. GA 44th session: 5th Committee 46; plenary 11, 46, 47, 49-53, 63.

Recorded vote in Assembly as follows:

In favour: Afghanistan, Albania, Algeria, Angola, Antigua and Barbuda, Argentina, Australia, Austria, Bahamas, Bahrain, Barbados, Belgium, Belize, Benin, Bhutan, Bolivia, Botswana, Brazil, Brunei Darussalam, Bulgaria, Burkina Faso, Burundi, Byelorussian SSR, Cameroon, Canada, Cape Verde, Central African Republic, Chad, Chile, China, Colombia, Comoros, Congo, Costa Rica, Côte d'Ivoire, Cuba, Cyprus, Czechoslovakia, Democratic Kampuchea, Democratic Yemen, Denmark, Djibouti, Dominica, Dominican Republic, Ecuador, Egypt, El Salvador, Equatorial Guinea, Ethiopia, Fiji, Finland, France, Gabon, Gambia, German Democratic Republic, Ghana, Greece, Grenada, Guatemala, Guinea, Guinea-Bissau, Guyana, Haiti, Honduras, Hungary, Iceland, India, Indonesia, Iran, Iraq, Ireland, Israel, Italy, Jamaica, Japan, Jordan, Kenya, Kuwait, Lao People's Democratic Republic, Lebanon, Liberia, Libyan Arab Jamahiriya, Luxembourg, Madagascar, Malawi, Malaysia, Maldives, Mali, Malta, Mauritania, Mauritius, Mexico, Mongolia, Morocco, Mozambique, Myanmar, Nepal, Netherlands, New Zealand, Nicaragua, Niger, Nigeria, Norway, Oman, Pakistan, Panama, Papua New Guinea, Peru, Philippines, Poland, Qatar, Romania, Rwanda, Saint Kitts and Nevis, Saint Lucia, Saint Vincent and the Grenadines, Samoa, Sao Tome and Principe, Saudi Arabia, Senegal, Seychelles, Sierra Leone, Singapore, Solomon Islands, Somalia, Spain, Sri Lanka, Sudan, Suriname, Swaziland, Sweden, Syrian Arab Republic, Thailand, Togo, Trinidad and Tobago, Tunisia, Turkey, Uganda, Ukrainian SSR, USSR, United Arab Emirates, United Republic of Tanzania, Uruguay, Vanuatu, Venezuela, Viet Nam, Yemen, Yugoslavia, Zaire, Zambia, Zimbabwe.

Against: United Kingdom, United States.

Abstaining: Germany, Federal Republic of, Lesotho, Portugal.

In **resolution 44/84**, the General Assembly appealed to mass media, trade unions, NGOs and individuals to co-ordinate efforts to mobilize international public opinion against the policy of the *apartheid* régime of South Africa, and to work for the enforcement of economic and other sanctions against it and for encouraging a policy of systematic and genuine divestment from corporations doing business in South Africa.

Relations with South Africa

Economic relations

In an overview of the economic situation in South Africa, the Special Committee against *Apartheid*, in its annual report,[8] said that the effects of sanctions, the shortage of investment capital, the lack of foreign financing, the burden of external debt payments and the withdrawal of TNCs continued to put strains on the South African economy. The reduction of its trade surplus in 1988 and its substantial debt-servicing obligations led to the introduction of deflationary measures in its March 1989 budget.

The rate of economic growth declined to 2.1 per cent compared to 3.2 per cent in 1988 and total output contracted by 1.5 per cent in the first quarter of 1989, signalling the beginning of a recessionary phase. Inflation reached 14.7 per cent compared with 12.9 per cent in 1988, while the exchange rate of the South African rand declined by 3.8 per cent in 1989. In the area of trade, imports declined steadily in the second half of 1989, though export performance improved. Overall, the volume of merchandise exports, excluding gold, was 17 per cent higher than in 1988. This led to an improvement in the balance of payments, which reflected an increase in the current account surplus to R 4.1 billion, against R 2.9 billion in 1988. At the end of 1988, South Africa's total foreign debt stood at just under $21.2 billion.

The authorities announced the creation of a R 3 billion Special Trust Fund to address "economic backlogs", particularly concerning housing and education for black South Africans. However, the income inequalities between whites and blacks continued to widen.

Sanctions and boycott

The Special Committee said that the economic sanctions against South Africa had contributed to positive developments in the region, as Pretoria appeared to have felt even their current limited impact. However, they had not so far succeeded in pressing the régime to the point of abandoning its *apartheid* policies. Loopholes, avoidance measures and increased third-party trading practices had lessened their impact, and the oil and arms embargoes were openly violated.

The Special Committee reported that data compiled by the Independent Expert Study on the Evaluation of the Application and Impact of Sanctions showed that total trade between South Africa and nine major Western States (Australia, Canada, Denmark, Finland, France, New Zealand, Norway, Sweden, United States), which had decreased between 1983 and 1985 and in 1987, had increased in value in 1988. Quoting the *Monthly Statistics of Foreign Trade* of the Organisation for Economic Co-operation and Development, it said that the main exporters to South Africa in 1989 were the Federal Republic of Germany ($3.3 billion), Japan ($1.7 billion), the United Kingdom ($1.7 billion) and the United States ($1.7 billion), followed by Belgium-Luxembourg ($732 million) and Italy ($673 million). The Committee observed that as the Nordic countries, the United States and the Commonwealth countries reduced their trade with South Africa, some Far Eastern and Western European States were taking their place. The increase

in trade between South Africa and some of its trading partners in recent years underscored the need for new mechanisms to tighten and strengthen trade sanctions. South Africa continued to purchase oil and petroleum products at premium prices and had managed to expand parts of its armaments production and secure markets for them. There was also evidence that the financial community was taking action to lessen the debt-related financial pressures on South Africa.

The Special Committee said that the uneven effectiveness of current government sanctions was due to the lack of co-ordination, enforcement and political will.

To achieve maximum effectiveness, the Committee concluded, sanctions had to be mandatory and comprehensive. Further sanctions should target the main areas of dependence and vulnerability in the South African economy, and they should be adopted in unison, strictly monitored and enforced. A powerful weapon against the régime would be the imposition of a mandatory oil embargo and, short of that, a widening and tightening of the voluntary embargo in effect. The mandatory arms embargo also had to be monitored and enforced more strictly. In addition, all sanctions should apply to South African-controlled firms to prevent them from assisting Pretoria in evading sanctions. The Special Committee proposed that measures be adopted to prevent States from benefiting from the vacuum created by other States that had imposed sanctions.

In June, the International Labour Conference noted that ILO was to constitute a group of three independent experts to monitor and evaluate progress made in relation to the implementation of sanctions.

In accordance with a 1988 General Assembly resolution,[14] the Secretary-General in October 1989[15] transmitted a report of the Centre against *Apartheid* on restrictive measures affecting externally dependent areas of the South African economy. The report focused on the main areas of external dependence, including external trade, finance and foreign capital flows and services, and examined the scope, implementation and impact of the restrictive measures.

The report stated that restrictive measures against South Africa, affecting both the country's foreign trade and the inflow of foreign capital, had had a discernible impact to the extent that, with the curtailment of foreign investment capital and long-term loans, foreign trade had become particularly important as a provider of foreign exchange for South Africa.

It concluded that while official sanctions had been limited in scope and had not always targeted the main areas of South African dependence on the rest of the world, their cumulative effect had imposed important constraints on the economy.

South Africa had been able to circumvent, albeit at a cost, sanctions on its essential imports, such as oil, petroleum products, capital goods, production material, spare parts and technology and, to a lesser degree, official financial measures. In addition, market pressures played a major role in constraining the South African economy. States had implemented some of the General Assembly recommendations, although in an uneven and unco-ordinated way.

GENERAL ASSEMBLY ACTION

On 22 November 1989, the General Assembly adopted **resolution 44/27 C** by recorded vote.

Comprehensive and mandatory sanctions against the racist régime of South Africa

The General Assembly,

Recalling its earlier resolutions and those of the Security Council calling for concerted international action to force the racist régime of South Africa to eradicate *apartheid,*

Having considered the report of the Special Committee against *Apartheid,* in particular paragraphs 255 to 275, and the report of the Commission against *Apartheid* in Sports,

Gravely concerned that, in spite of recent developments in South Africa, the system of *apartheid* remains intact and the régime maintains its repressive domestic practices, its policies of destabilization against neighbouring independent States and its intransigence towards the will of the international community for the prompt elimination of *apartheid,*

Noting with grave concern that sanctions and other measures recommended by the General Assembly, as well as measures introduced unilaterally by a number of States, lack comprehensiveness, co-ordination and adequate monitoring mechanisms,

Gravely concerned that some Member States and transnational corporations have continued economic relations with South Africa, while others continue to exploit opportunities created by sanctions imposed by other States, thus substantially increasing their trade with that country, as indicated in paragraphs 109, 110, 112 and 265 of the report of the Special Committee against *Apartheid,*

Convinced that the imposition of comprehensive and mandatory sanctions by the Security Council under Chapter VII of the Charter of the United Nations remains the most appropriate and effective means to bring about a peaceful end to *apartheid,*

1. *Reaffirms* that *apartheid* is a crime against humanity and a threat to international peace and security, and that it is a primary responsibility of the United Nations to assist in efforts to eliminate *apartheid* peacefully without further delay;

2. *Calls upon* those States that have increased their trade with South Africa and, particularly, the Federal Republic of Germany, which recently emerged as the leading trading partner of South Africa, to sever trade relations with South Africa;

3. *Calls upon* those Governments that are still opposed to the application of comprehensive and mandatory sanctions to reassess their policies and cease their op-

position to the application of such sanctions by the Security Council;

4. *Urges* the Security Council to consider immediate action under Chapter VII of the Charter of the United Nations with a view to applying comprehensive and mandatory sanctions against the racist régime of South Africa as long as it continues to disregard the demands of the majority of the people of South Africa and of the international community to eradicate *apartheid.*

General Assembly resolution 44/27 C

22 November 1989   Meeting 63   118-11-22 (recorded vote)

46-nation draft (A/44/L.28 & Add.1); agenda item 28.
Sponsors: Afghanistan, Algeria, Angola, Antigua and Barbuda, Benin, Burundi, Byelorussian SSR, Cameroon, Congo, Cuba, Djibouti, Ethiopia, Gambia, German Democratic Republic, Ghana, Guinea, Haiti, India, Indonesia, Iran, Iraq, Kenya, Kuwait, Liberia, Libyan Arab Jamahiriya, Madagascar, Malaysia, Mauritania, Mongolia, Nicaragua, Niger, Nigeria, Pakistan, Panama, Qatar, Saint Lucia, Senegal, Sudan, Syrian Arab Republic, Tunisia, Uganda, Ukrainian SSR, United Republic of Tanzania, Vanuatu, Zambia, Zimbabwe.
Meeting numbers. GA 44th session: plenary 11, 46, 47, 49-53, 63.

Recorded vote in Assembly as follows:

In favour: Afghanistan, Albania, Algeria, Angola, Argentina, Bahamas, Bahrain, Barbados, Benin, Bhutan, Bolivia, Brazil, Brunei Darussalam, Bulgaria, Burkina Faso, Burundi, Byelorussian SSR, Cameroon, Cape Verde, Central African Republic, Chad, China, Colombia, Comoros, Congo, Costa Rica, Côte d'Ivoire, Cuba, Cyprus, Czechoslovakia, Democratic Kampuchea, Democratic Yemen, Djibouti, Dominica, Dominican Republic, Ecuador, Egypt, Equatorial Guinea, Ethiopia, Fiji, Gambia, German Democratic Republic, Ghana, Grenada, Guatemala, Guinea, Guinea-Bissau, Guyana, Haiti, India, Indonesia, Iran, Iraq, Jamaica, Jordan, Kenya, Kuwait, Lao People's Democratic Republic, Lebanon, Liberia, Libyan Arab Jamahiriya, Madagascar, Malaysia, Maldives, Mali, Mauritania, Mauritius, Mexico, Mongolia, Morocco, Mozambique, Myanmar, Nepal, Nicaragua, Nigeria, Oman, Pakistan, Panama, Peru, Philippines, Poland, Qatar, Romania, Rwanda, Saint Kitts and Nevis, Saint Vincent and the Grenadines, Samoa, Sao Tome and Principe, Saudi Arabia, Senegal, Seychelles, Sierra Leone, Singapore, Solomon Islands, Somalia, Sri Lanka, Sudan, Suriname, Syrian Arab Republic, Thailand, Togo, Trinidad and Tobago, Tunisia, Turkey, Uganda, Ukrainian SSR, USSR, United Arab Emirates, United Republic of Tanzania, Uruguay, Vanuatu, Venezuela, Viet Nam, Yemen, Yugoslavia, Zaire, Zambia, Zimbabwe.

Against: Belgium, France, Germany, Federal Republic of, Israel, Italy, Japan, Luxembourg, Netherlands, Portugal, United Kingdom, United States.

Abstaining: Antigua and Barbuda, Australia, Austria, Belize, Botswana, Canada, Denmark, Finland, Greece, Hungary, Iceland, Ireland, Lesotho, Malawi, Malta, New Zealand, Norway, Papua New Guinea,* Saint Lucia, Spain, Swaziland, Sweden.

*Later advised the Secretariat it had intended to vote in favour.

Before adopting the resolution, the Assembly, by a recorded vote of 53 to 40, with 41 abstentions, retained the words ''and, particularly, the Federal Republic of Germany, which recently emerged as the leading trading partner of South Africa,'' in paragraph 2.

Oil embargo

In response to a 1988 General Assembly request,[16] the Intergovernmental Group to Monitor the Supply and Shipping of Oil and Petroleum Products to South Africa, established in 1986,[17] and the Special Committee against *Apartheid* held hearings on the oil embargo against South Africa. The Panel established for that purpose met in New York on 12 and 13 April 1989. In its report,[18] the Panel stated that the oil embargo was being violated because of a lack of effective co-operation and enforcement measures. In addition, steps taken by

States to deal with reported violations were inadequate. The Panel examined existing legislative and enforcement measures, co-operation with the Intergovernmental Group in monitoring violations, and between Governments and other organizations, the role of TNCs and oil traders, the transfer of relevant oil industry technology and issues of financing and insurance. The Panel said that an effective oil embargo would further increase the economic and political pressure on South Africa, but would have to comprise, in addition to the supply, shipping and handling of oil to South Africa, financing and investment in the petroleum industry. It recommended measures for tightening the embargo against South Africa.

The Intergovernmental Group, in an October report,[(19)] said that certain trends during 1989 suggested that South Africa would face increasing difficulties in evading the oil embargo. These included the return to normal maritime navigation in the Persian Gulf region, thus facilitating the monitoring of oil tankers; improvement in the producer/demand/supply situation; and the reduction of the amount of oil passing through spot markets on which South Africa depended for most of its supply. In addition, the number of independent oil traders which South Africa had used extensively was declining, while increasing quantities of Middle East oil to Europe were being transported through pipelines terminating in Mediterranean ports, thereby reducing the tanker traffic passing the southern tip of Africa.

The Intergovernmental Group concluded that an effective oil embargo against South Africa was feasible, but its implementation would depend on enforcement and co-ordination internationally of measures by oil-producing, shipping and handling States. The Group recommended that the Assembly request the Security Council to invoke Chapter VII of the Charter and impose a mandatory embargo; request States, pending that decision, to expedite legislative or comparable measures to impose an oil embargo, including measures to prevent the transfer of financial resources, technical assistance and energy technology; co-operate with the Intergovernmental Group in detecting, investigating and preventing violations and in taking action against violators; disseminate information on violations and their prevention; make the conveying of petroleum products to South Africa a punishable offence and publicize cases of successful prosecution; and co-operate with local governmental and non-governmental organizations in exposing violators.

GENERAL ASSEMBLY ACTION

On 22 November 1989, the General Assembly adopted **resolution 44/27 H** by recorded vote.

Oil embargo against South Africa

The General Assembly,

Having considered the report of the Intergovernmental Group to Monitor the Supply and Shipping of Oil and Petroleum Products to South Africa,

Recalling its resolutions on an oil embargo against South Africa, in particular resolution 43/50 J of 5 December 1988,

Noting that, while oil-exporting States have committed themselves to an oil embargo against South Africa, very few major shipping States have done so,

Concerned that the racist régime of South Africa has been able to circumvent the oil embargoes and comparable measures adopted by States,

Commending action taken by labour unions, student groups and anti-*apartheid* organizations against companies involved in the violation of the oil embargo against South Africa, and for the enforcement of the embargo,

Convinced that an effective oil embargo against South Africa would complement the arms embargo against the *apartheid* régime and serve to curtail both its acts of aggression against the front-line States and its repression of the people of South Africa,

1. *Takes note* of the report of the Intergovernmental Group to Monitor the Supply and Shipping of Oil and Petroleum Products to South Africa;

2. *Notes* the intention of the Intergovernmental Group to submit an interim report to the General Assembly at its forty-fourth session, in keeping with paragraph 44 of the Group's report;

3. *Takes note also* of the report of the Panel on the Hearings on the Oil Embargo against South Africa held in New York on 12 and 13 April 1989;

4. *Urges* the Security Council to take action without further delay to impose a mandatory embargo on the supply and shipping of oil and petroleum products to South Africa as well as on the supply of equipment and technology to, financing of and investment in its oil industry and coal liquefaction projects;

5. *Requests* all States concerned, pending a decision by the Security Council, to adopt effective measures and/or legislation to broaden the scope of the oil embargo in order to ensure the complete cessation of the supply and shipping of oil and petroleum products to South Africa, whether directly or indirectly, and in particular:

(*a*) To apply strictly the "end users" clause and other conditions concerning restriction on destination to ensure compliance with the embargo;

(*b*) To compel the companies originally selling or purchasing oil or petroleum products, as appropriate to each nation, to desist from selling, reselling or otherwise transferring oil and petroleum products to South Africa, whether directly or indirectly;

(*c*) To establish strict control over the supply of oil and petroleum products to South Africa by intermediaries, oil companies and traders by placing responsibility for the fulfilment of the contract on the first buyer or seller of oil and petroleum products who would, therefore, be liable for the actions of these parties;

(*d*) To prevent access by South Africa to other sources of energy, including the supply of raw materials, technical know-how, financial assistance and transport;

(*e*) To prohibit all assistance to *apartheid* South Africa, including the provision of finance, technology, equipment or personnel for the prospecting, development or production of hydrocarbon resources, the construction or operation of oil-from-coal or oil-from-gas plants or the development and operation of plants producing fuel substitutes and additives such as ethanol and methanol;

(f) To prevent South African corporations from maintaining or expanding their holdings in oil companies or properties outside South Africa;

(g) To terminate the transport of oil and petroleum products to South Africa by ships flying their flags, or by ships that are ultimately owned, managed or chartered by their nationals or by companies within their jurisdiction;

(h) To develop a system for registration of ships, registered or owned by their nationals, that have unloaded oil or petroleum products in South Africa in contravention of embargoes imposed, and to discourage such ships from calling at South African ports;

(i) To impose penal action against companies and individuals that have been involved in violating the oil embargo, and to publicize cases of successful prosecutions in conformity with their national laws;

(j) To gather, exchange and disseminate information regarding violations of the oil embargo, including ways and means to prevent such violations, and to take concerted measures against violators;

6. *Authorizes* the Intergovernmental Group to take action to promote public awareness of the oil embargo against South Africa, including, when necessary, sending missions and participating in relevant conferences and meetings;

7. *Requests* the Intergovernmental Group to submit to the General Assembly at its forty-fifth session a report on the implementation of the present resolution, including proposals for strengthening the mechanism to monitor the supply and shipment of oil and petroleum products to South Africa;

8. *Requests* all States to extend their co-operation to the Intergovernmental Group in the implementation of the present resolution, including submission of proposals for strengthening the mechanism to monitor the supply and shipment of oil and petroleum products to South Africa;

9. *Requests* the Secretary-General to provide the Intergovernmental Group with all necessary assistance for the implementation of the present resolution.

General Assembly resolution 44/27 H

22 November 1989   Meeting 63   139-2-14 (recorded vote)

15-nation draft (A/44/L.33 & Add.1); agenda item 28.

Sponsors: Algeria, Cuba, German Democratic Republic, Haiti, Indonesia, Iran, Kuwait, New Zealand, Nicaragua, Nigeria, Norway, Ukrainian SSR, United Republic of Tanzania, Vanuatu, Venezuela.

Financial implications. 5th Committee, A/44/758; S-G, A/C.5/44/29.

Meeting numbers. GA 44th session: 5th Committee 46; plenary 11, 46, 47, 49-53, 63.

Recorded vote in Assembly as follows:

In favour: Afghanistan, Albania, Algeria, Angola, Antigua and Barbuda, Argentina, Australia, Austria, Bahamas, Bahrain, Barbados, Belize, Benin, Bhutan, Bolivia, Brazil, Brunei Darussalam, Bulgaria, Burkina Faso, Burundi, Byelorussian SSR, Cameroon, Cape Verde, Central African Republic, Chad, Chile, China, Colombia, Comoros, Congo, Costa Rica, Côte d'Ivoire, Cuba, Cyprus, Czechoslovakia, Democratic Kampuchea, Democratic Yemen, Denmark, Djibouti, Dominica, Dominican Republic, Ecuador, Egypt, Equatorial Guinea, Ethiopia, Fiji, Finland, Gabon, Gambia, German Democratic Republic, Ghana, Grenada, Guatemala, Guinea, Guinea-Bissau, Guyana, Haiti, Honduras, Hungary, Iceland, India, Indonesia, Iran, Iraq, Ireland, Italy, Jamaica, Jordan, Kenya, Kuwait, Lao People's Democratic Republic, Lebanon, Liberia, Libyan Arab Jamahiriya, Madagascar, Malaysia, Maldives, Mali, Malta, Mauritania, Mauritius, Mexico, Mongolia, Morocco, Mozambique, Myanmar, Nepal, New Zealand, Nicaragua, Niger,

Nigeria, Norway, Oman, Pakistan, Panama, Papua New Guinea, Peru, Philippines, Poland, Qatar, Romania, Rwanda, Saint Kitts and Nevis, Saint Lucia, Saint Vincent and the Grenadines, Samoa, Sao Tome and Principe, Saudi Arabia, Senegal, Seychelles, Sierra Leone, Singapore, Solomon Islands, Somalia, Spain, Sri Lanka, Sudan, Suriname, Sweden, Syrian Arab Republic, Thailand, Togo, Trinidad and Tobago, Tunisia, Turkey, Uganda, Ukrainian SSR, USSR, United Arab Emirates, United Republic of Tanzania, Uruguay, Vanuatu, Venezuela, Viet Nam, Yemen, Yugoslavia, Zaire, Zambia, Zimbabwe.

Against: United Kingdom, United States.

Abstaining: Belgium, Botswana, Canada, France, Germany, Federal Republic of, Greece, Israel, Japan, Lesotho, Luxembourg, Malawi, Netherlands, Portugal, Swaziland.

In **resolution 44/84**, the Assembly also called on those oil-producing and oil-exporting countries that had not done so to take effective measures against the oil companies concerned so as to terminate the supply of crude oil and petroleum products to the racist régime of South Africa.

Foreign investments and credits

The international banking community was taking action to ease the debt-related financial pressure on South Africa, said the Special Committee against *Apartheid.* By the end of 1988, some Swiss banks had agreed to "roll over" some of South Africa's short-term debt. In early 1989, South Africa's foreign creditor banks had taken up an option in financing arrangements allowing them to escape from negotiations on South African debts and to cease being a lender to it by 1997. Some banks had also exchanged some $3.5 billion in loans for special exit securities. Thus, in May, the South African Finance Minister announced that over a two-month period $1.1 billion of short-term debt had been converted into long-term debt, enabling the country to make debt repayments of $1.3 billion in 1989.

On 18 October, South Africa concluded a Third Interim Agreement with major creditor banks, covering $8.1 billion, making it possible for the régime to reschedule repayment of its foreign debt obligations over a longer period and providing financial relief in the face of a looming debt crisis. On 26 October, the Acting Chairman of the Special Committee condemned the Third Interim Agreement, which the Committee considered as giving favourable treatment to, and undermining the international economic pressure on, South Africa.

The Special Committee said that with the application of sanctions to new loans to South Africa, trade credits were virtually the only source of new foreign financing available. South Africa acknowledged that there had been an increase in trade credits, which had eased its balance-of-payments constraints. The Committee noted that while some States had banned some types of trade credits to South Africa, the ban was not complete. The United States General Accounting Office calculated that from June 1986 to June 1989, new guaranteed trade-related credits amounted to $1,066 million.

In October,[20] heads of Government of the Commonwealth (Kuala Lumpur, Malaysia) decided to develop new forms of financial pressure on South Africa by calling on banks and financial institutions to impose tougher conditions on day-to-day trade financing, specifically by reducing the maximum credit terms to 90 days. They called on relevant Governments to make it harder for South Africa to get trade credits by taking it "off cover" with official government agencies for official trade credit and insurance purposes. They endorsed the establishment of an independent agency to review and report regularly on South Africa's international financial links and to publicize information on financial policies and flows to South Africa.

GENERAL ASSEMBLY ACTION

On 22 November 1989, the General Assembly adopted **resolution 44/27 E** by recorded vote.

International financial pressure on the *apartheid* economy of South Africa

The General Assembly,

Noting that the maintenance of the *apartheid* economy and the expansion of military and police expenditures substantially depend on the supply of further credits and loans by the international financial community,

Deeply regretting that the participating banks in the Third Interim Agreement with the *apartheid* régime, in spite of demands by the international community, have recently announced the rescheduling of South Africa's external debt, which was due for repayment in 1990,

Considering that the rescheduling of South Africa's external debt at this particular time represents an attempt to undermine the efforts of the international community to promote a peaceful resolution of the conflict in that country,

Taking note of the Kuala Lumpur Statement on Southern Africa adopted by the Commonwealth Heads of Government Meeting on 21 October 1989,

1. *Deplores* the Third Interim Agreement, particularly its terms and timing, which, by providing for the rescheduling over a period of three and a half years of a significant part of South Africa's debt, lessens the financial pressure on the *apartheid* régime;

2. *Strongly urges* Governments and private financial institutions to deny new bank loans to South Africa, whether to the public or private sectors;

3. *Calls upon* those States which continue to maintain trade and financial links with South Africa to restrict the provision of trade credits and cease loan insurance, in particular:

(*a*) By calling upon all the relevant banks and financial institutions to impose stricter conditions on day-to-day trade financing, specifically through reducing the maximum credit terms to 90 days;

(*b*) By taking South Africa "off cover" with official government agencies for official trade credit and insurance purposes, thus making its acquisition of trade credits more difficult;

4. *Calls upon* all Governments, intergovernmental and non-governmental organizations to use all appropriate

means to induce banks and other financial institutions to give effect to the measures outlined above;

5. *Requests* the Secretary-General to report to the General Assembly at its forty-fifth session on the implementation of the present resolution.

General Assembly resolution 44/27 E

22 November 1989   Meeting 63   140-4-11 (recorded vote)

64-nation draft (A/44/L.30 & Add.1); agenda item 28.
Sponsors: Afghanistan, Albania, Algeria, Angola, Antigua and Barbuda, Australia, Benin, Burundi, Byelorussian SSR, Cameroon, Comoros, Congo, Cuba, Djibouti, Ethiopia, Gambia, German Democratic Republic, Ghana, Guinea, Haiti, Hungary, India, Indonesia, Iraq, Jamaica, Jordan, Kenya, Kuwait, Liberia, Libyan Arab Jamahiriya, Madagascar, Malaysia, Mali, Mauritania, Mauritius, Mozambique, Myanmar, Nepal, New Zealand, Nicaragua, Niger, Nigeria, Pakistan, Panama, Philippines, Qatar, Saint Lucia, Samoa, Senegal, Sierra Leone, Somalia, Sudan, Suriname, Syrian Arab Republic, Trinidad and Tobago, Tunisia, Uganda, Ukrainian SSR, United Republic of Tanzania, Vanuatu, Viet Nam, Yugoslavia, Zambia, Zimbabwe.
Financial implications. 5th Committee, A/44/758; S-G, A/C.5/44/29.
Meeting numbers. GA 44th session: 5th Committee 46; plenary 11, 46, 47, 49-53, 63.

Recorded vote in Assembly as follows:

In favour: Afghanistan, Albania, Algeria, Angola, Antigua and Barbuda, Argentina, Australia, Austria, Bahamas, Bahrain, Barbados, Belize, Benin, Bhutan, Bolivia, Brazil, Brunei Darussalam, Bulgaria, Burkina Faso, Burundi, Byelorussian SSR, Cameroon, Canada, Cape Verde, Central African Republic, Chad, Chile, China, Colombia, Comoros, Congo, Costa Rica, Côte d'Ivoire, Cuba, Cyprus, Czechoslovakia, Democratic Kampuchea, Democratic Yemen, Denmark, Djibouti, Dominica, Dominican Republic, Ecuador, Egypt, Equatorial Guinea, Ethiopia, Fiji, Finland, Gabon, Gambia, German Democratic Republic, Ghana, Greece, Grenada, Guatemala, Guinea, Guinea-Bissau, Guyana, Haiti, Honduras, Hungary, Iceland, India, Indonesia, Iran, Iraq, Ireland, Jamaica, Jordan, Kenya, Kuwait, Lao People's Democratic Republic, Lebanon, Liberia, Libyan Arab Jamahiriya, Madagascar, Malaysia, Maldives, Mali, Malta, Mauritania, Mauritius, Mexico, Mongolia, Morocco, Mozambique, Myanmar, Nepal, New Zealand, Nicaragua, Niger, Nigeria, Norway, Oman, Pakistan, Panama, Papua New Guinea, Peru, Philippines, Poland, Qatar, Romania, Rwanda, Saint Kitts and Nevis, Saint Lucia, Saint Vincent and the Grenadines, Samoa, Sao Tome and Principe, Saudi Arabia, Senegal, Seychelles, Sierra Leone, Singapore, Solomon Islands, Somalia, Spain, Sri Lanka, Sudan, Suriname, Sweden, Syrian Arab Republic, Thailand, Togo, Trinidad and Tobago, Tunisia, Turkey, Uganda, Ukrainian SSR, USSR, United Arab Emirates, United Republic of Tanzania, Uruguay, Vanuatu, Venezuela, Viet Nam, Yemen, Yugoslavia, Zaire, Zambia, Zimbabwe.

Against: Germany, Federal Republic of, Netherlands, United Kingdom, United States.

Abstaining: Belgium, Botswana, France, Israel, Italy, Japan, Lesotho, Luxembourg, Malawi, Portugal, Swaziland.

Transnational corporations

Among the documents considered at the April 1989 session of the Commission on Transnational Corporations[21] were reports submitted by the Secretary-General on the follow-up to the recommendations of the Panel of Eminent Persons established to conduct the public hearings on the activities of TNCs in South Africa and Namibia;[22] on the activities of TNCs in South Africa and Namibia and collaboration of such corporations with the racist minority régime in that area;[23] and on the responsibilities of home countries with respect to TNCs operating in South Africa and Namibia in violation of relevant resolutions and decisions of the United Nations.[24]

In May, the Economic and Social Council, by **resolution 1989/27**, urged all TNCs to stop operations in South Africa and all forms of trade and economic links with the racist minority régime, and called on multilateral financial and development institutions to cease any kind of support to or collaboration with South Africa.

(For further details on TNCs, see PART THREE, Chapter V.)

Hearings on TNC activities in South Africa and Namibia

The Secretary-General transmitted to the General Assembly in October the report and recommendations of the Panel of Eminent Persons established to conduct the second public hearings on the activities of TNCs in South Africa and Namibia (Geneva, 4-6 September).[25] The first public hearings were held in 1985.[26] The aim of the hearings was to examine the process of change in South Africa and investigate action which the international community could take to accelerate the abolition of *apartheid* and contribute to a post-*apartheid* society. The Panel heard views from Governments, the South African business community, trade union leaders, church organizations and the academic community.

The report examined the current situation in South Africa, the impact of sanctions and the future of South Africa, and made specific recommendations relating to financial, investment and trade sanctions as well as proposals for their monitoring. The Panel called upon the international community to reflect the will of the United Nations in adopting universal, comprehensive and mandatory sanctions, and upon the General Assembly to appoint an independent group to prepare a detailed report on sanctions abuses. Among its specific recommendations was that Governments forbid South Africa from raising money either through gold swaps or the sale of gold in the forward market. The Panel endorsed the demands of anti-*apartheid* groups, including the freeing of political prisoners, ending the state of emergency, unbanning political organizations, repeal of the Group Areas Act and other legislation, and the beginning of meaningful negotiations, as a precondition for debt rescheduling. It also considered the rescheduling of the Second Interim Agreement in 1990 and the repayment on guaranteed credits in 1990-1991 as opportunities to put additional pressure on South Africa.

The Panel recommended the enactment of disinvestment laws according to the Nordic model; the repeal of double taxation agreements granting tax credits; the adoption of legislation to cover non-equity ties; and ensuring the fair and just treatment of the black work-force affected by disinvestment. The Panel endorsed the recommendations of the Commonwealth Committee of Foreign Ministers on Southern Africa (Canberra, Australia, 7-9 August)[27] on trade sanctions and demanded that the mandatory arms embargo be strengthened, particularly with regard to "dual-

use" items and technology transfer, and that international arms exporters cease the trade of military equipment and "dual-use" items.

It recommended that licensing and franchise agreements and the export of technology should be subject to wider trade sanctions; a complete ban on imports of South African gold; and the establishment by gold-consuming countries of a system for certifying the origin of gold. The Panel urged closer official monitoring of oil flows to ensure that shippers and middlemen were not circumventing sanctions. It called for the mandatory prohibition of the purchase of South African coal and the banning of the export of machine tools and capital equipment to South Africa.

The Panel noted that the absence of a comprehensive monitoring system had reduced the efficacy of sanctions. It recommended that the United Nations organize and co-ordinate monitoring activities and create for that purpose a comprehensive information system on the South African economy and on the impact and efficacy of sanctions. The monitoring system should also standardize reporting procedures on investment and trade links, maintain a register of investment and disinvestment and ensure maximum publicity of the findings. The Panel urged the International Chamber of Commerce to put pressure on its members to increase their participation in sanctions programmes.

In relation to the post-*apartheid* era, the Panel recommended that the General Assembly request that a comprehensive study be prepared, detailing the scope, responsibilities and likely costs of a comprehensive training and education programme for black South Africans, to be considered by a conference convened by the United Nations.

GENERAL ASSEMBLY ACTION

On 22 November 1989, the General Assembly adopted **resolution 44/27 D** by recorded vote.

Imposition, co-ordination and strict monitoring of measures against racist South Africa

The General Assembly,

Recalling its resolutions on sanctions against South Africa, in particular resolution 43/50 D of 5 December 1988,

Taking note of the report of the Special Committee against *Apartheid* and of the report of the Secretary-General on restrictive measures affecting externally dependent areas of the South African economy,

Taking note with appreciation of the recommendations made in the report of the Panel of Eminent Persons that held public hearings, at Geneva from 4 to 6 September 1989, on the activities of transnational corporations in South Africa and Namibia,

Convinced that sanctions and other restrictive measures have had a significant impact on recent developments in South Africa and remain a most effective and necessary instrument of pressure in contributing to a political solution to the crisis in that country,

Considering that measures taken by States individually or collectively, while commendable, vary in coverage and degree of enforcement and monitoring and are not always addressed to those areas of the South African economy which are vulnerable to international pressure,

Concerned at the increasing number of States that exploit the trade gaps created by the uneven and uncoordinated imposition of restrictive measures,

Noting with concern that a number of transnational corporations, including banks, continue to provide support to the *apartheid* economy by maintaining financial and technological and other ties with South Africa,

Commending those States which have already adopted strict measures against the *apartheid* régime in accordance with United Nations resolutions, as well as non-governmental organizations and individuals, for their contribution to the isolation of the *apartheid* régime,

1. *Urges* all States that have not yet done so, pending the imposition of comprehensive and mandatory sanctions, to adopt legislative and/or comparable measures to impose effective sanctions against South Africa and, in particular:

(a) To impose embargoes on the supply of all products, in particular computer and communications equipment, technologies, skills and services, including military intelligence, that can be used for the military and nuclear industry of South Africa;

(b) To impose embargoes on the supply of oil and petroleum products and oil technology;

(c) To prohibit the import of coal, gold, other minerals and agricultural products from South Africa;

(d) To induce transnational corporations, banks and financial institutions to withdraw effectively from South Africa by ceasing equity investment and cutting off non-equity links, particularly those involving transfer of high technology and know-how;

(e) To induce banks to cease the provision of new credits and loans;

(f) To consider ending promptly double taxation agreements with South Africa and any form of tax relief in respect of income from investments in that country;

(g) To restrict landing and port rights to South African air and sea carriers and to sever direct air, sea and other transport links with South Africa;

(h) To ensure, through appropriate measures, that their citizens refrain from serving in South Africa's armed forces and other sensitive sectors;

(i) To take appropriate measures to ensure the effectiveness of the sports and cultural boycott of *apartheid* South Africa;

2. *Also urges* all States to monitor strictly the implementation of the above measures and adopt, when necessary, legislation providing for penalties on individuals and enterprises violating those measures;

3. *Calls upon* Governments, intergovernmental organizations, the specialized agencies of the United Nations, non-governmental organizations and the public at large to take full account of the recommendations of the Panel of Eminent Persons that held public hearings on the activities of transnational corporations in South Africa and Namibia;

4. *Requests* the Secretary-General to report to the General Assembly at its forty-fifth session on measures to monitor sanctions undertaken by the United Nations system, governments and non-governmental agencies, taking fully into account reports of existing intergovernmental monitoring mechanisms.

General Assembly resolution 44/27 D

22 November 1989   Meeting 63   135-3-15 (recorded vote)

62-nation draft (A/44/L.29 & Add.1); agenda item 28.

Sponsors: Afghanistan, Albania, Algeria, Angola, Antigua and Barbuda, Barbados, Benin, Burundi, Byelorussian SSR, Cameroon, Comoros, Congo, Cuba, Djibouti, Ethiopia, Gambia, German Democratic Republic, Ghana, Guinea, Haiti, Hungary, India, Indonesia, Iraq, Jamaica, Jordan, Kenya, Kuwait, Liberia, Libyan Arab Jamahiriya, Madagascar, Malaysia, Mali, Mauritania, Mozambique, Myanmar, Nepal, Nicaragua, Niger, Nigeria, Pakistan, Panama, Philippines, Qatar, Saint Lucia, Senegal, Sierra Leone, Somalia, Sudan, Suriname, Syrian Arab Republic, Trinidad and Tobago, Tunisia, Uganda, Ukrainian SSR, USSR, United Republic of Tanzania, Vanuatu, Viet Nam, Yugoslavia, Zambia, Zimbabwe.

Financial implications. 5th Committee, A/44/758; S-G, A/C.5/44/29.

Meeting numbers. GA 44th session: 5th Committee 46; plenary 11, 46, 47, 49-53, 63.

Recorded vote in Assembly as follows:

In favour: Afghanistan, Albania, Algeria, Angola, Antigua and Barbuda, Argentina, Australia, Bahamas, Bahrain, Barbados, Belize, Benin, Bhutan, Bolivia, Brazil, Brunei Darussalam, Bulgaria, Burkina Faso, Burundi, Byelorussian SSR, Cameroon, Canada, Cape Verde, Central African Republic, Chad, China, Colombia, Comoros, Congo, Costa Rica, Côte d'Ivoire, Cuba, Cyprus, Czechoslovakia, Democratic Kampuchea, Democratic Yemen, Denmark, Djibouti, Dominica, Dominican Republic, Ecuador, Egypt, Equatorial Guinea, Ethiopia, Fiji, Finland, Gabon, Gambia, German Democratic Republic, Ghana, Grenada, Guatemala, Guinea, Guinea-Bissau, Guyana, Haiti, Honduras, Hungary, Iceland, India, Indonesia, Iran, Iraq, Jamaica, Jordan, Kenya, Kuwait, Lao People's Democratic Republic, Lebanon, Liberia, Libyan Arab Jamahiriya, Madagascar, Malaysia, Maldives, Mali, Malta, Mauritania, Mexico, Mongolia, Morocco, Mozambique, Myanmar, Nepal, New Zealand, Nicaragua, Niger, Nigeria, Norway, Oman, Pakistan, Panama, Papua New Guinea, Peru, Philippines, Poland, Qatar, Romania, Rwanda, Saint Kitts and Nevis, Saint Lucia, Saint Vincent and the Grenadines, Samoa, Sao Tome and Principe, Saudi Arabia, Senegal, Seychelles, Sierra Leone, Singapore, Solomon Islands, Somalia, Sri Lanka, Sudan, Suriname, Swaziland, Sweden, Syrian Arab Republic, Thailand, Togo, Trinidad and Tobago, Tunisia, Turkey, Uganda, Ukrainian SSR, USSR, United Arab Emirates, United Republic of Tanzania, Uruguay, Vanuatu, Venezuela, Viet Nam, Yemen, Yugoslavia, Zaire, Zambia, Zimbabwe.

Against: Portugal, United Kingdom, United States.

Abstaining: Austria, Belgium, Botswana, France, Germany, Federal Republic of, Greece, Ireland, Israel, Italy, Japan, Lesotho, Luxembourg, Malawi, Netherlands, Spain.

Military and nuclear collaboration

The Special Committee against *Apartheid* continued to monitor the implementation of the arms embargo against South Africa. It collaborated with the World Campaign against Military and Nuclear Collaboration with South Africa in organizing consultations on the implementation by the Federal Republic of Germany of the arms embargo against South Africa (Bonn, 27 April). The meeting discussed cases of alleged violations of the arms embargo, particularly the transfer of submarine blueprints to South Africa, and proposed legal and other actions which the Federal Republic could take to make the arms embargo more effective. In response to a communication from the Chairman of the Special Committee, the Federal Republic of Germany said that the investigations into the delivery of submarine blueprints were probes not into a possible infringement of the arms embargo but into a suspected infringement of official secrets regulations. However, in August it was revealed that South Africa was in fact constructing submarines, contrary to official denials, and that a third country was involved in the project. The Special Committee welcomed the withdrawal of the licence granted by the Federal Republic in 1985 for the export to South Africa of high-technology dual-use multi-sensor platforms and related electronic and other equipment.

In other developments, the Special Committee expressed concern over the visit to Chile by the South African Minister of Defence to discuss closer military collaboration between the two countries. That visit, which took place in February and March, revealed the extent of their co-operation, in particular their joint weapons and ammunition production projects. South Africa had assisted Chile in producing the G.5 155-millimetre artillery gun and was involved in the construction of a shipyard at Punta Arenas. Chile explained that the extent of its collaboration was limited to the acquisition of technology from South Africa for manufacturing the gun and that the shipyard was engaged solely in non-military activities. In April, five men were arrested in Paris while handing over to an official accredited to the South African Embassy parts of an anti-aircraft Blowpipe missile stolen from the British army in Northern Ireland. In May, South Africa participated in the International Defence Equipment and Avionics Exhibition held at Ankara, Turkey. In response to a letter from the Chairman of the Special Committee, Turkey stated that South Africa's participation was an "unfortunate incident" owing to an oversight by the private company that had organized the exhibition.

In a December report on activities between 1980 and 1989,[28] the Security Council Committee on the question of South Africa reviewed the implementation of the arms embargo against South Africa, including ways it had been circumvented.

The Special Committee noted several convictions in a number of States for the illegal sale of arms to South Africa, indicating the need for stricter enforcement of the embargo.

In the area of nuclear collaboration, an investigation conducted by the Federal Republic of Germany revealed that one of its domestic companies had delivered nuclear technology to South Africa and another was involved with a Swiss company in supplying nuclear materials as well. The activities of the companies involved were being investigated by the respective Governments and the United States. It was also reported that South Africa had successfully tested a modified version of the Israeli missile Jericho II, which was capable of launching nuclear warheads over a distance of 1,000 kilometres.

The Special Committee concluded that although the arms embargo had had a considerable effect on the South African defence establishment, arms and related *matériel* continued to reach South

Africa. The Committee appealed to States to tighten and to increase their vigilance regarding licensing procedures for the export and re-export of military equipment; to implement fully the provisions of the embargo in their national legislation; and to investigate reported violations. It recommended that Governments close any loopholes.

GENERAL ASSEMBLY ACTION

On 22 November 1989, the General Assembly adopted **resolution 44/27 I** by recorded vote.

Military collaboration with South Africa

The General Assembly,

Recalling its resolutions and those of the Security Council on the arms embargo, as well as other resolutions on collaboration with South Africa,

Taking note of the report of the Special Committee against *Apartheid,*

Reiterating that the full implementation of an arms embargo against South Africa is an essential element of international action against *apartheid,*

Taking note of the statement adopted on 18 December 1987 by the Security Council Committee established by Council resolution 421(1977), of 9 December 1977, concerning the question of South Africa, which "noted with alarm and great concern that large quantities of arms and military equipment, including highly sophisticated *matériel,* were still reaching South Africa directly or via clandestine routes",

Expressing serious concern at the increasing number of violations of the mandatory arms embargo against South Africa,

Regretting that some countries surreptitiously continue to deal in arms with South Africa and allow South Africa to participate in international arms exhibitions,

1. *Strongly deplores* the actions of those States and organizations which directly or indirectly continue to violate the arms embargo and collaborate with South Africa in the military, nuclear, intelligence and technology fields and, in particular, Israel, for providing nuclear technology and two corporations based in the Federal Republic of Germany, for supplying blueprints for the manufacture of submarines and other related military *matériel;* and calls upon Israel to terminate forthwith such hostile acts and upon the Government of the Federal Republic of Germany to honour its obligations under Security Council resolution 421(1977) by prosecuting the said corporations;

2. *Deplores* the actions of Chile, which has become an important outlet for the sale of South Africa's military hardware, and strongly urges it to refrain forthwith from such acts;

3. *Urges* the Security Council to consider immediate steps to ensure the scrupulous and full implementation of the arms embargo imposed by the Council in resolutions 418(1977) of 4 November 1977 and 558(1984) of 13 December 1984 and its effective monitoring;

4. *Requests* the Special Committee against *Apartheid* to keep the matter under constant review and to report thereon to the General Assembly and the Security Council as appropriate.

General Assembly resolution 44/27 I

22 November 1989   Meeting 63   106-17-26 (recorded vote)

26-nation draft (A/44/L.34/Rev.1 & Add.1); agenda item 28.

Sponsors: Afghanistan, Algeria, Angola, Botswana, Congo, Cuba, Ethiopia, Ghana, Guinea, Indonesia, Iraq, Kuwait, Libyan Arab Jamahiriya, Mauritania, Mozambique, Nigeria, Qatar, Senegal, Sudan, Syrian Arab Republic, Tunisia, Uganda, United Republic of Tanzania, Vanuatu, Zambia, Zimbabwe.

Financial implications. 5th Committee, A/44/758; S-G, A/C.5/44/29.

Meeting numbers. GA 44th session: 5th Committee 46; plenary 11, 46, 47, 49-53, 63.

Recorded vote in Assembly as follows:

In favour: Afghanistan, Albania, Algeria, Angola, Argentina, Bahrain, Barbados, Bhutan, Bolivia, Botswana, Brazil, Brunei Darussalam, Bulgaria, Burkina Faso, Burundi, Byelorussian SSR, Cape Verde, Chad, China, Colombia, Comoros, Congo, Cuba, Cyprus, Czechoslovakia, Democratic Kampuchea, Democratic Yemen, Djibouti, Dominica, Dominican Republic, Ecuador, Egypt, Equatorial Guinea, Ethiopia, Gambia, German Democratic Republic, Ghana, Guatemala, Guinea, Guinea-Bissau, Guyana, Haiti, India, Indonesia, Iran, Iraq, Jamaica, Jordan, Kuwait, Lao People's Democratic Republic, Lebanon, Lesotho, Liberia, Libyan Arab Jamahiriya, Malaysia, Maldives, Mali, Mauritania, Mexico, Mongolia, Morocco, Mozambique, Myanmar, Nepal, Nicaragua, Nigeria, Oman, Pakistan, Panama, Peru, Philippines, Poland, Qatar, Romania, Rwanda, Sao Tome and Principe, Saudi Arabia, Senegal, Seychelles, Sierra Leone, Singapore, Solomon Islands, Somalia, Sri Lanka, Sudan, Suriname, Swaziland, Syrian Arab Republic, Thailand, Trinidad and Tobago, Tunisia, Turkey, Uganda, Ukrainian SSR, USSR, United Arab Emirates, United Republic of Tanzania, Uruguay, Vanuatu, Venezuela, Viet Nam, Yemen, Yugoslavia, Zaire, Zambia, Zimbabwe.

Against: Belgium, Chile, Denmark, France, Germany, Federal Republic of, Greece, Honduras, Ireland, Israel, Italy, Japan, Luxembourg, Netherlands, Portugal, Spain, United Kingdom, United States.

Abstaining: Antigua and Barbuda, Australia, Austria, Belize, Cameroon, Canada, Central African Republic, Costa Rica, Côte d'Ivoire, El Salvador, Fiji, Finland, Grenada, Iceland, Kenya, Malawi, Malta, New Zealand, Norway, Papua New Guinea,* Saint Kitts and Nevis, Saint Lucia, Saint Vincent and the Grenadines, Samoa, Sweden, Togo.

*Later advised the Secretariat it had intended to vote in favour.

The two phrases in paragraph 1 referring to the Federal Republic of Germany were retained by a recorded vote of 53 to 45, with 38 abstentions.

In **resolution 44/113 A**, the Assembly condemned South Africa's continued pursuit of a nuclear capability and all forms of nuclear collaboration; called on States, corporations, institutions and individuals to desist from further collaboration with the racist régime; and appealed to those States with the capability to do so to monitor South Africa's research on and development and production of nuclear weapons and to publicize any information in that regard.

The Assembly, in **resolution 44/84**, strongly condemned the collaboration of certain Western Powers, Israel and other countries with South Africa in the nuclear field and called on them and other Governments concerned to refrain from supplying the régime with installations, equipment or material that might enable it to produce uranium, plutonium and other materials, reactors or military equipment.

Israel–South Africa relations

The Special Committee against *Apartheid*, in the second part of its report,[8] prepared in response to a 1988 General Assembly resolution,[29] examined recent developments concerning relations between Israel and South Africa. The Special Committee said that media and intelligence reports had revealed collaboration between the two countries in the joint production of armaments. Israel had provided South Africa with military technology for its growing armaments industry and was helping it to expand the military capability of its defence force. Attention was drawn to their reported collaboration in the development and preparation for testing of an intermediate-range ballistic missile capable of carrying nuclear devices. Israel was also assisting South Africa in developing the CAVA twin-engine multi-role combat aircraft, and in converting the old Mirage III into the Cheetah aircraft. Israel was also refurbishing 16 old F-5 aircraft from Chile for delivery to South Africa.

In its report covering the second half of 1989,[9] the Special Committee noted intelligence reports that Israel had received from South Africa permission to use its long-range test site and enriched uranium for its nuclear warheads in exchange for Israeli missile technology. According to the United States Central Intelligence Agency, the first missile flight of the South African–Israeli project took place on 5 July. In response to such reports, the Israeli Prime Minister, on 15 November, said Israel had contractual arrangements with South Africa that it intended to adhere to. On 22 November, the Acting Chairman of the Special Committee issued a statement expressing the Committee's concern over the military and nuclear collaboration between the two countries.

Other reported collaboration included the importation by Israel of coal from South Africa and the use of Israel as a conduit for South African coal going to Western Europe. The Special Committee suggested that Western European Governments and anti-*apartheid* organizations should maintain vigilance to prevent such circumvention of restrictions on the import of South African coal. It was also reported that the Israeli Kibbutz Ayelet Hashahar was planning to sell a complete automotive tyre factory to South Africa. In February, a delegation from the independent homeland of Bophuthatswana visited Israel to encourage Israeli investment there.

The Special Committee said Israel should abrogate its existing secret agreements and arrangements with South Africa for the supply of weapons and military technology. It recommended that the General Assembly call on Israel to cease its collaboration with South Africa, particularly in the military field, and authorize the Committee to continue to monitor the relations between the two countries.

The Ninth Conference of Heads of State or Government of Non-Aligned Countries (Belgrade, Yugoslavia, 4-7 September)[30] condemned the increasing co-operation between what it called the racist régimes of South Africa and Israel and called on States to refrain from co-operation with those régimes in the nuclear field.

On 22 November 1989, the General Assembly adopted **resolution 44/27 F** by recorded vote.

Relations between South Africa and Israel

The General Assembly,

Recalling all its previous resolutions concerning the relations between South Africa and Israel and, in particular, its resolution 43/50 E of 5 December 1988,

Having considered the report of the Special Committee against *Apartheid* on recent developments concerning relations between South Africa and Israel,

Noting with concern that the military relations between South Africa and Israel, especially in the area of military technology and, in particular, the collaboration in the recent production and testing of nuclear missiles, continue unabated,

Taking note of the relevant provision of the final document on southern Africa adopted by the Ninth Conference of Heads of State or Government of Non-Aligned Countries, held at Belgrade from 4 to 7 September 1989,

1. *Condemns* the collaboration of Israel with the racist minority régime of South Africa in the military and nuclear fields;

2. *Reiterates its demand* that Israel desist from and terminate forthwith all forms of collaboration with South Africa, particularly in the military and nuclear fields;

3. *Requests* the Special Committee against *Apartheid* to continue to monitor the relations between South Africa and Israel and keep them under constant review and report to the General Assembly and the Security Council as appropriate.

General Assembly resolution 44/27 F

22 November 1989   Meeting 63   114-22-18 (recorded vote)

54-nation draft (A/44/L.31 & Corr.1 & Add.1); agenda item 28.

Sponsors: Afghanistan, Albania, Algeria, Angola, Benin, Botswana, Burundi, Byelorussian SSR, Comoros, Cuba, Djibouti, Ethiopia, Gambia, German Democratic Republic, Ghana, Guinea, Haiti, Hungary, India, Indonesia, Iran, Iraq, Jordan, Kenya, Kuwait, Liberia, Libyan Arab Jamahiriya, Madagascar, Malaysia, Mali, Mauritania, Mongolia, Morocco, Mozambique, Nicaragua, Niger, Nigeria, Pakistan, Qatar, Rwanda, Senegal, Sierra Leone, Somalia, Sudan, Syrian Arab Republic, Tunisia, Uganda, Ukrainian SSR, USSR, United Republic of Tanzania, Vanuatu, Viet Nam, Zambia, Zimbabwe.

Financial implications. 5th Committee, A/44/758; S-G, A/C.5/44/29.

Meeting numbers. GA 44th session: 5th Committee 46; plenary 11, 46, 47, 49-53, 63.

Recorded vote in Assembly as follows:

In favour: Afghanistan, Albania, Algeria, Angola, Argentina, Bahrain, Barbados, Benin, Bhutan, Bolivia, Angola, Brazil, Brunei Darussalam, Bulgaria, Burkina Faso, Burundi, Byelorussian SSR, Cape Verde, Central African Republic, Chad, China, Colombia, Comoros, Congo, Côte d'Ivoire, Cuba, Cyprus, Czechoslovakia, Democratic Kampuchea, Democratic Yemen, Djibouti, Ecuador, Egypt, Equatorial Guinea, Ethiopia, Gabon, Gambia, German Democratic Republic, Ghana, Guatemala, Guinea, Guinea-Bissau, Guyana, Haiti, Hungary, India, Indonesia, Iran, Iraq, Jamaica, Jordan, Kenya, Kuwait, Lao People's Democratic Republic, Lebanon, Lesotho, Liberia, Libyan Arab Jamahiriya, Madagascar, Malaysia, Maldives, Mali, Mauritania, Mauritius, Mexico, Mongolia, Morocco, Mozambique, Myanmar, Nepal, Nicaragua, Niger, Nigeria, Oman, Pakistan, Panama, Papua New Guinea, Peru, Philippines, Poland, Qatar, Romania, Rwanda, Sao Tome and Principe, Saudi Arabia, Senegal, Seychelles, Sierra Leone, Singapore, Solomon Islands, Somalia, Sri Lanka, Sudan, Suriname, Swaziland, Syrian Arab Republic, Thailand, Togo, Trinidad and Tobago, Tunisia, Turkey, Uganda, Ukrainian SSR, USSR, United Arab Emirates, United Republic of Tanzania, Vanuatu, Venezuela, Viet Nam, Yemen, Yugoslavia, Zaire, Zambia, Zimbabwe.

Against: Australia, Austria, Belgium, Canada, Denmark, Finland, France, Germany, Federal Republic of, Greece, Iceland, Ireland, Israel, Italy, Luxembourg, Netherlands, New Zealand, Norway, Portugal, Spain, Sweden, United Kingdom, United States.

Abstaining: Antigua and Barbuda, Bahamas, Belize, Cameroon, Chile, Costa Rica, Dominica, Dominican Republic, Fiji, Grenada, Japan, Malawi, Malta, Saint Kitts and Nevis, Saint Lucia, Saint Vincent and the Grenadines, Samoa, Uruguay.

In **resolution 44/113 B**, the Assembly requested the Secretary-General to investigate reports that collaboration between Israel and South Africa had resulted in the development by South Africa of a nuclear-tipped missile.

Sports and cultural boycott

The Special Committee against *Apartheid*, on 13 June 1989, released the Register of Sports Contacts with South Africa, containing information on such contacts during 1988. Of the 3,404 sportspersons mentioned, 650 participated in sports activities in South Africa, although most were not renowned. The highest numbers came from the United States and the United Kingdom. Between April 1988 and April 1989, 91 sportspersons pledged not to participate in sporting activities in South Africa.

The Special Committee observed that tennis and golf associations still allowed South African individuals and teams to compete in their events. While tennis associations had considered ending contacts with South Africa, no similar action had been forthcoming from the golf associations. The International Cricket Conference agreed to ban any player who participated in cricket events in South Africa after 31 March 1989. However, in a widely criticized move, a group of individual cricketers from the United Kingdom agreed to play in South Africa in 1990 and 1991. Reports about the participation of individual players from Australia, France and the United Kingdom in the centenary rugby games in South Africa in August 1989 became a matter of concern, especially to the organizers of the Commonwealth Games in Auckland, New Zealand, in 1990.

In May, ANC called on the international community to support current efforts in South Africa to create broad non-racial governing bodies in every major sports discipline in the country.

In August,[27] the Commonwealth Committee of Foreign Ministers on Southern Africa reaffirmed their support for the sports boycott of South Africa. It called for rigorous enforcement of the penalties agreed in 1989 by the International Cricket Conference and called on other sporting bodies to develop and apply similar rules and penalty structures.

The Commission against *Apartheid* in Sports, in a report on its 1989 session (New York, 18-20 October),[31] reported that the 1985 International Convention against *Apartheid* in Sports,[32] which entered into force on 4 April 1988, had been ratified or acceded to by 43 States and signed by 35.

The Commission consulted with international and national sporting organizations. It urged those international sports federations in which South Africa still maintained membership to expel South Africa and to persuade their affiliated teams and individuals not to engage in sporting activities in South Africa and not to compete abroad with South African sportspersons.

The Commission recognized the progress achieved in the international boycott of *apartheid* sports, but felt that further action was needed at the national and international levels, particularly with regard to golf, rugby and other sports. It recommended that the International Boxing Federation and the World Boxing Organization be included in the Register of Sports Contacts with South Africa and that they terminate any contacts with South Africa.

The Commission recommended that the Assembly urge those States that had not done so to sign and ratify the 1985 Convention; call on States to co-operate with the Commission and the Committee against *Apartheid* in matters relating to the boycott of *apartheid* sports; urge States, organizations and individuals to achieve the total isolation of *apartheid* in sports and terminate any sports contacts with South Africa; and request the Secretary-General to support the Commission, particularly in respect to publicity against *apartheid* sports.

With respect to the cultural boycott, the Special Committee continued to publish the Register of Entertainers, Actors and Others Who Have Performed in *Apartheid* South Africa. Between September 1988 and August 1989, the names of 23 artists were deleted from the list. The Special Committee and anti-*apartheid* groups continued to monitor activities connected with the production of films, in violation of the United Nations cultural boycott, and to persuade individuals and companies involved to cease their collaboration with South Africa. They were particularly concerned with the upsurge of foreign films made in South Africa involving producers from the United States. In May, the ANC made public its redefinition of the cultural boycott, stating that cultural and academic contacts should be permitted only in furtherance of the national democratic struggle or its objectives. The international community gave financial, technical and other forms of assistance to developing cultural alternatives inside South Africa and increased cultural exchanges. The Special Committee established a scholarship fund for young South African artists, as well as a board of international representatives to advise the Committee on the cultural boycott and a cultural resistance desk.

GENERAL ASSEMBLY ACTION

On 22 November 1989, the General Assembly adopted **resolution 44/27 L** by recorded vote.

Support for the work of the Commission against *Apartheid* in Sports

The General Assembly,

Recalling its resolutions on the boycott of *apartheid* in sports and in particular resolution 32/105 M of 14 December 1977 by which it adopted the International Declaration against *Apartheid* in Sports and resolution 40/64 G of 10 December 1985, the annex to which contains the International Convention against *Apartheid* in Sports,

Having considered the report of the Commission against *Apartheid* in Sports and the relevant sections of the report of the Special Committee against *Apartheid*,

1. *Takes note* of the report of the Commission against *Apartheid* in Sports;

2. *Calls upon* those States that have signed the International Convention against *Apartheid* in Sports to ratify it and also calls upon other States to accede to it as soon as possible;

3. *Commends* those Governments, organizations and individual sportsmen and sportswomen that have taken action in accordance with the Register of Sports Contacts with South Africa with a view to achieving a total isolation of *apartheid* in sports;

4. *Requests* the Special Committee against *Apartheid* to continue issuing the Register of Sports Contacts with South Africa;

5. *Calls upon* those international sports organizations and federations that have not yet expelled South Africa or suspended its membership to do so without further delay;

6. *Requests* the Secretary-General to provide the Commission against *Apartheid* in Sports with all needed assistance.

General Assembly resolution 44/27 L

22 November 1989   Meeting 63   127-1-23 (recorded vote)

22-nation draft (A/44/L.40 & Add.1); agenda item 28.
Sponsors: Algeria, Bangladesh, Barbados, Congo, Ethiopia, German Democratic Republic, Ghana, Haiti, Indonesia, Malaysia, Mongolia, Nigeria, Peru, Philippines, Qatar, Senegal, Somalia, Syrian Arab Republic, Ukrainian SSR, United Republic of Tanzania, Vanuatu, Zimbabwe.
Financial implications. 5th Committee, A/44/758; S-G, A/C.5/44/29.
Meeting numbers. GA 44th session: 5th Committee 46; plenary 11, 46, 47, 49-53, 63.

Recorded vote in Assembly as follows:

In favour: Afghanistan, Albania, Algeria, Angola, Antigua and Barbuda, Argentina, Bahamas, Bahrain, Barbados, Belize, Benin, Bhutan, Bolivia, Botswana, Brazil, Brunei Darussalam, Bulgaria, Burkina Faso, Burundi, Byelorussian SSR, Cameroon, Cape Verde, Central African Republic, Chad, Chile, China, Colombia, Comoros, Congo, Costa Rica, Cuba, Cyprus, Czechoslovakia, Democratic Kampuchea, Democratic Yemen, Djibouti, Dominica, Dominican Republic, Ecuador, Egypt, El Salvador, Equatorial Guinea, Ethiopia, Fiji, Gabon, Gambia, German Democratic Republic, Ghana, Grenada, Guatemala, Guinea, Guinea-Bissau, Guyana, Haiti, Honduras, India, Indonesia, Iran, Iraq, Jamaica, Jordan, Kenya, Kuwait, Lao People's Democratic Republic, Lebanon, Lesotho, Liberia, Libyan Arab Jamahiriya, Madagascar, Malawi, Malaysia, Maldives, Mali, Mexico, Mongolia, Morocco, Mozambique, Myanmar, Nepal, Nicaragua, Niger, Nigeria, Oman, Pakistan, Panama, Papua New Guinea, Peru, Philippines, Poland, Qatar, Romania, Rwanda, Saint Kitts and Nevis, Saint Lucia, Saint Vincent and the Grenadines, Sao Tome and Principe, Saudi Arabia, Senegal, Seychelles, Sierra Leone, Singapore, Solomon Islands, Somalia, Sri Lanka, Sudan, Suriname, Swaziland, Syrian Arab Republic, Thailand, Togo, Trinidad and Tobago, Tunisia, Turkey, Uganda, Ukrainian SSR, USSR, United Arab Emirates, United Republic of Tanzania, Uruguay, Vanuatu, Venezuela, Viet Nam, Yemen, Yugoslavia, Zaire, Zambia, Zimbabwe.

The Assembly, in **resolution 44/27 K**, appealed to Governments and organizations to cease all academic, cultural, scientific and sports relations that would support the *apartheid* régime of South Africa, as well as relations with individuals, institutions and other bodies endorsing or based on *apartheid*.

Situation in South Africa

Political prisoners and detainees

The Special Committee against *Apartheid* estimated that, by January 1989, the number of persons being held in South African prisons for political activities was 804, which did not include the large number of children and youth under 21 years of age serving prison terms. There had been a decrease in the number of detainees, although the period of detention had increased, making detainees, in effect, long-term prisoners. On 25 January, the plight of detainees was underscored by the indefinite hunger strike of 20 detainees at Diepkloof Prison. Their demand for the immediate and unconditional release of all detainees sparked off a wave of hunger-strike protests, as well as solidarity actions in South Africa and around the world. The resulting crisis led to the release of hundreds of detainees by the South African authorities.

Another disturbing aspect of Pretoria's repression was the number of prisoners on death row, which as at June 1989 stood at 88. In May, 14 persons were sentenced to death under the principle of "common purpose" for the murder of a policeman at Upington in 1985. They constituted the largest number of people to be sentenced to death at a single trial for a politically related incident. Their appeal was rejected in July. The increasing number of executions for political offences generated a renewed discussion on the question of the death penalty. By June 1989, 37 persons had been executed at Pretoria Central Prison. Several anti-*apartheid* organizations both inside and outside South Africa called for a judicial commission to inquire into the death penalty and for a moratorium on all executions pending the report of the commission.

The Special Committee appealed to the international community and, in particular, the media to take appropriate action for the immediate release of journalists arrested for participating in and covering demonstrations on the eve of the September elections, and to step up efforts to save the life of ANC activist Mangena Jeffrey Boesman and all other political prisoners on death row. It demanded the release of all political prisoners and detainees.

On 11 October, the Committee observed the Day of Solidarity with South African Political Prisoners. In October, eight long-term political prisoners, including Walter Sisulu, were released. Three more were released in December.

The Economic and Social Council, by **resolution 1989/82**, had demanded the immediate and unconditional release of all trade unionists imprisoned for exercising their legitimate trade union rights.

Death sentence of South African patriot

On 27 September,[33] the Chairman of the African Group requested the General Assembly to consider urgently a draft resolution entitled "Death sentence of South African patriot". In introducing the draft before the Assembly, he said that the execution of ANC activist Mangena Jeffrey Boesman could only exacerbate the situation in South Africa, thereby leading to increased violence. The Chairman, calling on South African leaders to take decisions that went beyond speeches and to abolish *apartheid*, said that saving the life of one man could preserve the lives of thousands of others.

GENERAL ASSEMBLY ACTION

On 28 September 1989, the General Assembly adopted **resolution 44/1** by recorded vote.

Death sentence passed on a South African patriot

The General Assembly,

Having considered the question of the death sentence passed in October 1988 at Grahamstown, South Africa, on Mangena Jeffrey Boesman, a member of the African National Congress of South Africa,

Gravely concerned about the decision of the South African authorities on 22 September 1989 to refuse executive clemency in respect of the appeal against the death sentence,

Conscious that the carrying out of this death sentence would aggravate the situation in South Africa and thereby deal a severe blow to the prospects for negotiations to end *apartheid*,

1. *Calls upon* the South African authorities as a matter of urgency to commute the death sentence imposed on Mangena Jeffrey Boesman;

2. *Urges* all States and organizations to use their influence and to take urgent measures, in conformity with the Charter of the United Nations, the resolutions of the Security Council and relevant international instruments to save the life of Mangena Jeffrey Boesman;

3. *Also calls upon* the South African authorities to commute the death sentences passed on all political prisoners as a means of creating an environment conducive to the peaceful resolution of the situation in South Africa.

General Assembly resolution 44/1

28 September 1989   Meeting 11   149-0-2 (recorded vote)

47-nation draft (A/44/L.1 & Add.1); agenda item 28.

Sponsors: Algeria, Angola, Barbados, Benin, Botswana, Burkina Faso, Burundi, Cameroon, Colombia, Comoros, Congo, Costa Rica, Côte d'Ivoire, Cuba,

Djibouti, Egypt, Ethiopia, Gabon, Guinea, Guinea-Bissau, Guyana, Honduras, India, Lesotho, Liberia, Libyan Arab Jamahiriya, Madagascar, Mali, Mauritania, Mauritius, Morocco, Niger, Nigeria, Papua New Guinea, Philippines, Sao Tome and Principe, Senegal, Somalia, Sudan, Suriname, Togo, Tunisia, Uganda, United Republic of Tanzania, Vanuatu, Zambia, Zimbabwe.

Recorded vote in Assembly as follows:

In favour: Afghanistan, Albania, Algeria, Angola, Antigua and Barbuda, Argentina, Australia, Austria, Bahamas, Bahrain, Bangladesh, Barbados, Belgium, Belize, Benin, Bhutan, Bolivia, Botswana, Brazil, Brunei Darussalam, Bulgaria, Burkina Faso, Burundi, Byelorussian SSR, Cameroon, Canada, Cape Verde, Central African Republic, Chile, China, Colombia, Comoros, Congo, Costa Rica, Côte d'Ivoire, Cuba, Cyprus, Czechoslovakia, Democratic Kampuchea, Democratic Yemen, Denmark, Djibouti, Dominica, Ecuador, Egypt, El Salvador, Ethiopia, Fiji, Finland, France, Gabon, Gambia, German Democratic Republic, Germany, Federal Republic of, Greece, Guatemala, Guinea, Guinea-Bissau, Guyana, Haiti, Honduras, Hungary, Iceland, India, Indonesia, Iran, Iraq, Ireland, Israel, Italy, Jamaica, Japan, Jordan, Kenya, Kuwait, Lao People's Democratic Republic, Lebanon, Lesotho, Liberia, Libyan Arab Jamahiriya, Luxembourg, Madagascar, Malawi, Malaysia, Maldives, Mali, Malta, Mauritania, Mauritius, Mexico, Mongolia, Morocco, Mozambique, Myanmar, Nepal, Netherlands, New Zealand, Nicaragua, Niger, Nigeria, Norway, Oman, Pakistan, Panama, Papua New Guinea, Paraguay, Peru, Philippines, Poland, Portugal, Qatar, Romania, Rwanda, Saint Lucia, Saint Vincent and the Grenadines, Samoa, Sao Tome and Principe, Saudi Arabia, Senegal, Seychelles, Sierra Leone, Singapore, Solomon Islands, Somalia, Spain, Sri Lanka, Sudan, Suriname, Sweden, Syrian Arab Republic, Thailand, Togo, Trinidad and Tobago, Tunisia, Turkey, Uganda, Ukrainian SSR, USSR, United Arab Emirates, United Republic of Tanzania, Uruguay, Vanuatu, Venezuela, Viet Nam, Yemen, Yugoslavia, Zaire, Zambia, Zimbabwe.

Against: None.

Abstaining: United Kingdom, United States.

Women and children under *apartheid*

Responding to a 1988 Economic and Social Council request,[34] the Secretary-General transmitted in January to the 1989 session of the Commission on the Status of Women (see PART THREE, Chapter XIII) a report on developments from 1 October 1987 to 30 November 1988 concerning the situation of women under *apartheid* in South Africa and Namibia and measures of assistance to women in those countries.[35] The report stated that the situation of women and children living under *apartheid* had not changed appreciably except in the political field, where the hardening of the position of the *apartheid* régime had resulted in massive arrests of children. According to the Special Committee against *Apartheid*, by July 1988 some 40 per cent of the more than 30,000 persons detained since the imposition of the state of emergency in June 1986 were children 18 years or younger, who were subjected to prolonged incarceration, torture and even death. Information from the Centre against *Apartheid* indicated that black women in South Africa, particularly their leaders, were subject to police repression and harassment. In the social and economic fields, most women and children continued to live in urban slums or impoverished rural areas, and women suffered from discrimination in employment, education and health. The report also summarized action taken by United Nations organizations and the international community to provide assistance to women and children under *apartheid*.

A seminar on the special needs of South African and Namibian refugee women and children, organized by the Special Committee in co-operation with the Association of Women's Clubs of Zimbabwe (Harare, 16-18 January), urged the international community to publicize the special situation of women and children in those countries and to provide them with political, economic, legal, humanitarian and other assistance. A mission by a delegation of the Support Group of Eminent Women, in co-ordination with the Office of the United Nations High Commissioner for Refugees,[36] visited Namibia, Zambia and Zimbabwe in November to assess the needs of South African and Namibian refugee women and children. It made recommendations for action by the United Nations, intergovernmental organizations, NGOs and host and donor Governments.

The United Nations Children's Fund issued an updated edition of its 1987 report *Children on the front line—The impact of* apartheid, *destabilization and warfare on children in southern and South Africa.*

ECONOMIC AND SOCIAL COUNCIL ACTION

On 24 May 1989, the Economic and Social Council, on the recommendation of its Second (Social) Committee, adopted **resolution 1989/33** by recorded vote.

Women and children under *apartheid*

The Economic and Social Council,

Recalling its resolution 1988/23 of 26 May 1988,

Noting the concern of women throughout the world about the continuing degradation and abuse to which African women and children are subjected daily by the white minority régime of South Africa,

Recalling that this concern was expressed in the Nairobi Forward-looking Strategies for the Advancement of Women, which also contain proposals for various forms of assistance to be rendered to women and children inside South Africa and to those who have become refugees,

Recognizing that the inhuman exploitation and dispossession of the African people by the white minority régime is directly responsible for the appalling conditions in which African women and children live,

Also recognizing that the equality of women cannot be achieved without the success of the struggle for national liberation and self-determination of the people of South Africa against the racist régime of Pretoria,

Having considered the report of the Secretary-General on new developments concerning the situation of women under *apartheid* in South Africa and Namibia and measures of assistance to women in South Africa and Namibia,

1. *Commends* the tenacity and bravery of those women both inside and outside South Africa who have resisted oppression, who have been detained, tortured or killed, and of those whose husbands, children and relatives have been detained, tortured or killed and who, despite this, have remained steadfast in their opposition to the racist régime;

2. *Acknowledges* the efforts of those Governments, intergovernmental and non-governmental organizations and individuals that have campaigned for and applied sanctions against the racist régime;

3. *Condemns unequivocally* the South African régime for the imposition of the state of emergency, the forcible separation of black families, the detention and imprisonment of women and children and the restrictions on non-violent anti-*apartheid* democratic organizations and individuals;

4. *Urges* the South African régime to accord prisoner-of-war status to captured freedom fighters, in accordance with the Geneva Conventions of 12 August 1949 and the Protocol Additional to the Geneva Conventions of 12 August 1949 relating to the protection of victims of international armed conflicts (Protocol I), adopted in 1977, to accord all political prisoners sentenced to death, among whom are women, a fair trial based on international legal standards, and to stop the execution of political prisoners;

5. *Demands* the immediate and unconditional release of all political prisoners and detainees, among whom are an increasing number of women and children;

6. *Again calls upon* Governments, in view of the deterioration of the situation in South Africa, to impose, as a matter of urgency, comprehensive sanctions in accordance with the resolutions of the Security Council and the Nairobi Forward-looking Strategies for the Advancement of Women;

7. *Appeals* to all countries to support educational, health and social welfare programmes for women and children under *apartheid;*

8. *Also appeals* to the international community for increased assistance for women and children refugees in southern Africa;

9. *Urges* the international community to look into the newly developing situation of refugees and displaced persons, with a view to providing material assistance for them;

10. *Urges* Member States and United Nations bodies, in consultation with liberation movements, to give effect forthwith to the Nairobi Forward-looking Strategies that deal with women and children under *apartheid*, giving particular attention to education, health, vocational training and employment opportunities and to the strengthening of the women's sections of the liberation movements;

11. *Requests* the Commission on the Status of Women to work closely with women in the liberation movements in order to disseminate information and to ensure a proper assessment of the needs and aspirations of the women and children living under *apartheid;*

12. *Requests* the Secretary-General to submit to the Commission on the Status of Women at its thirty-fourth session a comprehensive report on the implementation and monitoring of the Nairobi Forward-looking Strategies in regard to women and children under *apartheid*.

Economic and Social Council resolution 1989/33

24 May 1989   Meeting 15   44-2-8 (recorded vote)

Approved by Second Committee (E/1989/90) by recorded vote (37-2-9), 16 May (meeting 16); draft by Commission on women (E/1989/27); agenda item 10.

Recorded vote in Council as follows:

In favour: Bahamas, Belize, Bolivia, Brazil, Bulgaria, Cameroon, China, Colombia, Cuba, Czechoslovakia, Denmark, Ghana, Greece, Guinea, India, Indonesia, Iran, Iraq, Jordan, Kenya, Lesotho, Liberia, Libyan Arab Jamahiriya, New Zealand, Nicaragua, Niger, Norway, Oman, Poland, Rwanda, Saudi Arabia, Somalia, Sri Lanka, Sudan, Thailand, Trinidad and Tobago, Tunisia, Ukrainian SSR, USSR, Uruguay, Venezuela, Yugoslavia, Zaire, Zambia.

Against: United Kingdom, United States.

Abstaining: Canada, France, Germany, Federal Republic of, Ireland, Italy, Japan, Netherlands, Portugal.

GENERAL ASSEMBLY ACTION

The General Assembly, by **resolution 44/143**, condemned the *apartheid* racist régime for the increasing detention, torture and inhuman treatment of children in South Africa and requested United Nations bodies and NGOs to intensify the world-wide campaign to monitor those practices.

Aid programmes and inter-agency co-operation

United Nations aid to victims of *apartheid* was provided through national liberation movements recognized by OAU and directly to individuals for education and training. Legal assistance, relief and education grants were given by the United Nations Trust Fund for South Africa to persons persecuted under repressive and discriminatory South African legislation. The United Nations Educational and Training Programme for Southern Africa offered additional educational assistance.

Assistance to national liberation movements

In June 1989,[37] the Governing Council of the United Nations Development Programme (UNDP) noted that, within the priorities set in the first programme of assistance to national liberation movements, new areas of assistance had been identified and programmes were being formulated. It requested the Administrator to review the South West Africa People's Organization (SWAPO) component of the ongoing programme of assistance to maximize funding that could be transferred to the technical assistance programme in an independent Namibia; to plan and implement an orderly winding down and transfer of projects to Namibia; and to ensure, during the transitional period leading to Namibia's independence, that the use of indicative planning figure (IPF) resources for national liberation movements be governed by the principle of impartiality in accordance with the United Nations plan for implementing Security Council resolution 435(1978).[38]

The Administrator reported[39] that in 1989 the main emphasis of UNDP assistance to national liberation movements continued to be on providing educational and health services. Projects to provide repair and maintenance services were submitted for approval and a project on the involvement of women in development was being formulated. In the light of the forthcoming independence of Namibia, assistance to SWAPO was scaled down, while the transfer of development assistance for SWAPO to technical assistance for Namibia had commenced.

During 1989, 16 projects were operational under IPF funding for national liberation movements. ANC and PAC had three ongoing projects each, SWAPO benefited from seven projects and three projects covered all three national liberation movements. However, SWAPO was no longer eligible to participate in the last three projects after 1 April 1989. Total UNDP commitments under the national liberation movement IPF amounted to $13.4 million. The sectoral distribution of the projects remained the same except for changes in the number of projects and IPF allocations among sectors. Following the winding down of the SWAPO projects, seven projects remained in the education sector, valued at $7 million; two projects in the planning and co-ordination sector, valued at $500,000; two in the health sector with a combined allocation of $3.1 million; and one in the agricultural sector with a budget of $900,000. There were five pipeline projects with ANC and two with PAC, with resources amounting to $2.8 million.

GENERAL ASSEMBLY ACTION

The General Assembly, by **resolution 44/27 A**, reaffirmed its full support for ANC and PAC. It decided to continue the authorization of adequate financial provision in the regular budget of the United Nations to enable them to maintain offices in New York in order to participate effectively in the deliberations of the Special Committee against *Apartheid* and other bodies. In **resolution 44/27 K**, it appealed to States to increase humanitarian, legal, educational and other assistance and support to the liberation movements recognized by OAU.

UN Trust Fund for South Africa

In October 1989,[40] the Secretary-General reported that the United Nations Trust Fund for South Africa had made seven grants totalling $3,650,000 during the preceding 12 months and had extended five grants totalling $1,504,000. It had received contributions totalling $3,473,775. Since its inception in 1965,[41] the Fund's total income was $36,769,314 with grants awarded for legal assistance, relief and education of refugee victims of South Africa and Namibia amounting to $35,521,560, leaving a balance of $1,931,751 as at 31 August 1989. As of that date, pledges of $633,080 were outstanding.

The Committee of Trustees of the Fund continued to encourage direct contributions to voluntary organizations providing assistance to victims of *apartheid*. It appealed for greater legal, humanitarian and relief assistance to those victims. It also decided to keep under review the situation resulting from the March 1989 Disclosure of Foreign Funding Act, adopted by the South African Parliament.

GENERAL ASSEMBLY ACTION

On 22 November 1989, the General Assembly adopted **resolution 44/27 J** without vote.

United Nations Trust Fund for South Africa

The General Assembly,

Recalling its earlier resolutions on the United Nations Trust Fund for South Africa, in particular resolution 43/50 I of 5 December 1988,

Having considered the report of the Secretary-General on the United Nations Trust Fund for South Africa, to which is annexed the report of the Committee of Trustees of the Trust Fund,

Gravely concerned at the continued nation-wide state of emergency and security regulations which criminalize political dissent and protest,

Alarmed by the continued detentions without trials, forced removals, bannings, restriction orders, political trials, death sentences imposed on opponents of *apartheid* and harassment of trade unions, church and other organizations and individuals involved in peaceful protest and dissent,

Reaffirming that increased humanitarian and legal assistance by the international community to those persecuted under repressive and discriminatory legislation in South Africa is more than ever necessary to alleviate their plight and sustain their efforts,

Strongly convinced that increased contributions to the Trust Fund and to the voluntary agencies concerned are necessary to enable them to meet the extensive needs for humanitarian and legal assistance,

1. *Endorses* the report of the Secretary-General on the United Nations Trust Fund for South Africa;

2. *Expresses its appreciation* to the Governments, organizations and individuals that have contributed to the Trust Fund and to the voluntary agencies engaged in rendering humanitarian and legal assistance to the victims of *apartheid* and racial discrimination;

3. *Appeals* for generous and increased contributions to the Trust Fund;

4. *Also appeals* for direct contributions to the voluntary agencies engaged in rendering assistance to the victims of *apartheid* and racial discrimination in South Africa;

5. *Commends* the Secretary-General and the Committee of Trustees of the Trust Fund for their persistent efforts to promote humanitarian and legal assistance to persons persecuted under repressive and discriminatory legislation in South Africa and Namibia, as well as assistance to their families and to refugees from South Africa.

General Assembly resolution 44/27 J

22 November 1989   Meeting 63   Adopted without vote

31-nation draft (A/44/L.35 & Add.1); agenda item 28.
Sponsors: Antigua and Barbuda, Argentina, Australia, Austria, Brazil, Canada, China, Denmark, Egypt, Finland, France, Germany, Federal Republic of, Greece, Haiti, Iceland, India, Indonesia, Ireland, Italy, Japan, Morocco, Netherlands, Nigeria, Norway, Pakistan, Sweden, Tunisia, Turkey, Vanuatu, Venezuela, Yugoslavia.
Meeting numbers. GA 44th session: plenary 11, 46, 47, 49-53, 63.

Assistance for public information

In 1988,[42] the General Assembly had requested the Secretary-General to expand United Nations anti-*apartheid* broadcasts to South Africa, as well as the production of audio-visual material, and to provide technical and financial assistance to radio stations of those States broadcasting or willing to broadcast to South Africa. In response to that request, the Secretary-General in November 1989 presented a report on the assessment needs for technical assistance to those radio stations.[43] He suggested a phased approach for the implementation of the request, beginning with a programming and technical study to determine the extent of assistance needed. The report outlined the results of that study, which was completed by the International Telecommunication Union (ITU). It recommended financial outlays totalling $9,700,000 in capital costs and $750,000 in annual operating costs for the transmission of broadcasts from Angola, the United Republic of Tanzania, Zambia and Zimbabwe. The Secretary-General proposed consulting with ITU, the United Nations Educational, Scientific and Cultural Organization and other agencies in respect of those needs. He also proposed to submit a single report in 1990 on the two remaining studies to determine the existing and potential interest in broadcasting United Nations anti-*apartheid* radio programmes, and the extent of the audience for those programmes in South Africa.

Work programme of the Special Committee

In its 1989 report,[8] the Special Committee against *Apartheid* recommended that the General Assembly authorize it to continue as a focal point in monitoring the situation in South Africa, especially the impact of sanctions, and to continue mobilizing international action against *apartheid*.

Its main focus was directed at activities having the potential for influencing decision-making and for mobilizing world public opinion. It organized and sponsored seminars and hearings, promoted contacts among opponents of *apartheid* and assisted the anti-*apartheid* resistance inside and outside South Africa.

GENERAL ASSEMBLY ACTION

On 22 November 1989, the General Assembly adopted **resolution 44/27 G** by recorded vote.

Programme of work of the Special Committee against *Apartheid*

The General Assembly,

Having considered the report of the Special Committee against *Apartheid*,

1. *Commends* the Special Committee against *Apartheid* for its work in the discharge of its responsibilities in promoting international action against *apartheid;*

2. *Takes note* of the report of the Special Committee and endorses the recommendations contained in paragraph 275 of the report relating to its programme of work;

3. *Authorizes* the Special Committee, in accordance with its mandate and acting as a focal point for the international campaign against *apartheid* and with the support services of the Centre against *Apartheid* of the Secretariat, to continue:

(a) To monitor closely the situation in South Africa and the actions of the international community regarding the imposition and implementation of sanctions and other restrictive measures and their impact on *apartheid* South Africa;

(b) To mobilize international action against *apartheid*, *inter alia*, through collection, analysis and dissemination of information, through liaison with non-governmental organizations and relevant individuals and groups able to influence public opinion and decision-making, and through hearings, conferences, consultations, missions, publicity and other relevant activities;

4. *Appeals* to all Governments, intergovernmental and non-governmental organizations to increase their co-operation with the Special Committee in the discharge of its mandate;

5. *Requests* all United Nations bodies, organs and agencies to co-operate with the Special Committee and the Centre against *Apartheid* in their activities in order to ensure consistency and improve co-ordination and the greatest use of available resources in the implementation of the relevant resolutions of the General Assembly and the Security Council;

6. *Requests* Governments and organizations to provide financial and other assistance for the special projects of the Special Committee and to make generous contributions to the Trust Fund for Publicity against *Apartheid;*

7. *Appeals* to all Governments, intergovernmental organizations, information media, non-governmental organizations and individuals to co-operate with the Centre against *Apartheid* and the Department of Public Information of the Secretariat in their activities relating to *apartheid* and, in particular, in disseminating information on the situation in South Africa in order to mitigate the effects of the restraints on the press in South Africa and to counteract South African propaganda effectively;

8. *Decides* to make a special allocation of 430,000 United States dollars to the Special Committee for 1990 from the regular budget of the United Nations to cover the cost of special projects to be decided upon by the Committee.

General Assembly resolution 44/27 G

22 November 1989   Meeting 63   145-0-10 (recorded vote)

66-nation draft (A/44/L.32 & Add.1); agenda item 28.
Sponsors: Afghanistan, Albania, Algeria, Angola, Antigua and Barbuda, Benin, Botswana, Burundi, Cameroon, Comoros, Congo, Cuba, Czechoslovakia, Djibouti, Ethiopia, Gambia, German Democratic Republic, Ghana, Guinea, Haiti, Hungary, India, Indonesia, Iran, Iraq, Jordan, Kenya, Kuwait, Liberia, Libyan Arab Jamahiriya, Madagascar, Malaysia, Mali, Mauritania, Mauritius, Mongolia, Mozambique, Myanmar, Nepal, Nicaragua, Niger, Nigeria, Pakistan, Panama, Peru, Philippines, Qatar, Rwanda, Saint Lucia, Senegal, Sierra Leone, Somalia, Sudan, Syrian Arab Republic, Togo, Trinidad and Tobago, Tunisia, Uganda, Ukrainian SSR, USSR, United Republic of Tanzania, Vanuatu, Viet Nam, Yugoslavia, Zambia, Zimbabwe.
Financial implications. 5th Committee, A/44/758; S-G, A/C.5/44/29.
Meeting numbers. GA 44th session: 5th Committee 46; plenary 11, 46, 47, 49-53, 63.

Recorded vote in Assembly as follows:

In favour: Afghanistan, Albania, Algeria, Angola, Antigua and Barbuda, Argentina, Australia, Austria, Bahamas, Bahrain, Barbados, Belize, Benin, Bhutan, Bolivia, Botswana, Brazil, Brunei Darussalam, Bulgaria, Burkina Faso, Burundi, Byelorussian SSR, Cameroon, Canada, Cape Verde, Central African Republic, Chad, Chile, China, Colombia, Comoros, Congo, Costa Rica, Côte d'Ivoire, Cuba, Cyprus, Czechoslovakia, Democratic Kampuchea, Democratic Yemen, Denmark, Djibouti, Dominica, Dominican Republic, Ecuador, Egypt, Equatorial Guinea, Ethiopia, Fiji, Finland, Gabon, Gambia, German Democratic Republic, Ghana, Greece, Grenada, Guatemala, Guinea, Guinea-Bissau, Guyana, Haiti, Honduras, Hungary, Iceland, India, Indonesia, Iran, Iraq, Ireland, Jamaica, Japan, Jordan, Kenya, Kuwait, Lao People's Democratic Republic, Lebanon, Lesotho, Liberia, Libyan Arab Jamahiriya, Madagascar, Malawi, Malaysia, Maldives, Mali, Malta, Mauritania, Mauritius, Mexico, Mongolia, Morocco, Mozambique, Myanmar, Nepal, New Zealand, Nicaragua, Niger, Nigeria, Norway, Oman, Pakistan, Panama, Papua New Guinea, Peru, Philippines, Poland, Qatar, Romania, Rwanda, Saint Kitts and Nevis, Saint Lucia, Saint Vincent and the Grenadines, Samoa, Sao Tome and Principe, Saudi Arabia, Senegal, Seychelles, Sierra Leone, Singapore, Solomon Islands, Somalia, Spain, Sri Lanka, Sudan, Suriname, Swaziland, Sweden, Syrian Arab Republic, Thailand, Togo, Trinidad and Tobago, Tunisia, Turkey, Uganda, Ukrainian SSR, USSR, United Arab Emirates, United Republic of Tanzania, Uruguay, Vanuatu, Venezuela, Viet Nam, Yemen, Yugoslavia, Zaire, Zambia, Zimbabwe.

Against: None.

Abstaining: Belgium, France, Germany, Federal Republic of, Israel, Italy, Luxembourg, Netherlands, Portugal, United Kingdom, United States.

On 7 November, by **decision 44/407 A**, the Assembly took note of the Special Political Committee's report[44] on hearings of organizations and individuals in connection with South Africa's *apartheid* policies. Altogether, the Committee heard statements by 18 persons.

REFERENCES

[1]YUN 1988, p. 159. [2]A/44/697. [3]YUN 1988, p. 157, GA res. 43/50 G, 5 Dec. 1988. [4]A/43/1010. [5]A/44/681. [6]A/S-16/4. [7]A/S-16/6. [8]A/44/22. [9]A/45/22. [10]YUN 1988, p. 139, GA res. 43/50 D, 5 Dec. 1988. [11]A/44/533. [12]YUN 1973, p. 103, GA res. 3068(XXVII), annex, 30 Nov. 1973. [13]A/44/522-S/20844. [14]YUN 1988, p. 139, GA res. 43/50 D, 5 Dec. 1988. [15]A/44/555 & Corr.1. [16]YUN 1988, p. 141, GA res. 43/50 J, 5 Dec. 1988. [17]YUN 1986, p. 137, GA res. 41/35 F, 10 Nov. 1986. [18]A/44/279-S/20634. [19]A/44/44-S/20926. [20]A/44/672-S/20914. [21]E/1989/28/Rev.1. [22]E/1989/17. [23]E/C.10/1989/8 & Corr.1. [24]E/C.10/1989/9. [25]A/44/576-S/20867. [26]YUN 1985, p. 149. [27]A/44/501-S/20831. [28]S/21015. [29]YUN 1988, p. 146, GA res. 43/50 E, 5 Dec. 1988. [30]A/44/551-S/20870. [31]A/44/47. [32]YUN 1985, p. 166, GA res. 40/64 G, annex, 10 Dec. 1985. [33]A/44/577. [34]YUN 1988, p. 153, ESC res. 1988/23, 26 May 1988. [35]E/CN.6/1989/3. [36]A/AC.115/L.665. [37]E/1989/32 (dec. 89/30). [38]YUN 1978, p. 915, SC res. 435(1978), 29 Sep. 1978. [39]DP/1990/29. [40]A/44/556. [41]YUN 1965, p. 115, GA res. 2054 B (XX), 15 Dec. 1965. [42]YUN 1988, p. 155, GA res. 43/50 H, 5 Dec. 1988. [43]A/44/698. [44]A/44/709.

Other States

Angola

Prospects for peace in Angola increased as the 1988 agreements[1] involving Angola, Cuba and South Africa and between Cuba and South Africa went into effect with the start of the withdrawal of Cuban forces from Angola and the start of oper-ations of the United Nations Angola Verification Mission (UNAVEM).

On 16 January, the Security Council, by **resolution 628(1989)**, expressed full support for those agreements and called on all parties to co-operate in their implementation.

The Joint Commission established under the tripartite agreement held an extraordinary meeting from 16 to 18 October at Johannesburg and Pretoria, South Africa.[2] The Commission welcomed the decision of Angola and South Africa to improve the mechanism to register and investigate alleged security breaches of the settlement plan for south-western Africa.

In other developments, on 22 June, Angola and the União Nacional para a Independência Total de Angola (UNITA), following the intervention of 18 African heads of State, signed the Gbadolite Agreement, which led to a fragile cease-fire between the two parties.

UNAVEM

In May,[3] the Secretary-General reported on developments relating to UNAVEM, established in 1988[4] to verify the redeployment northwards and the total withdrawal of Cuban troops from the territory of Angola. He said that the Mission, headquartered at Luanda, consisted of 70 military observers drawn from 10 countries and was assisted by 22 international and 15 local staff. By 1 April, it had deployed a number of military teams at the ports and airports to be used by Cuban troops over the 27-month period of their withdrawal. The first withdrawal began on 10 January.

In August,[5] the Secretary-General reported that by 31 July the total departures had reached 15,927, which was consistent with the timetable established. UNAVEM had also verified the withdrawal of Cuban military equipment. The Secretary-General confirmed that, in accordance with the agreement between the two countries, all Cuban troops had been withdrawn north of the adjusted 15th parallel by 1 August.

In a letter dated 16 August,[6] Cuba complained that on 14 August a Cuban lorry was ambushed by UNITA forces and six of its soldiers killed. In denouncing this act, Cuba warned that it might have an adverse effect on compliance with the timetable for the withdrawal of its troops from Angola.

The Secretary-General further reported, in November,[7] that by 31 October total departures recorded since the start of the withdrawal of Cuban troops in January stood at 25,510. It had also been verified that all Cuban troops had, in accordance with the agreement, completed their deployment to locations north of the adjusted 13th parallel by that day. The Secretary-General said that the success of the Mission illustrated what could be achieved by a United Nations peace-keeping operation when it received the full co-operation of the parties concerned.

Financing of UNAVEM

On 31 January,[8] the Secretary-General requested the inclusion of an item on the financing of UNAVEM in the agenda of the resumed forty-third session of the General Assembly. In an addendum to that request,[9] he indicated that, to meet the immediate requirements of the Mission, he sought and had received the concurrence of the Advisory Committee on Administrative and Budgetary Questions (ACABQ), under the terms of the 1987 Assembly resolution on unforeseen and extraordinary expenses,[10] to enter into commitments with respect to UNAVEM in an amount not exceeding $4.2 million. Cost estimates for UNAVEM for the period 3 January 1989 to 2 August 1991, inclusive of that amount, were $19.4 million gross ($18.8 million net). However, he was seeking an appropriation of $9.2 million gross ($9 million net) for the initial 12-month period from 3 January 1989 to 2 January 1990.

ACABQ[11] recommended approval of $9,193,000 gross ($8,962,000 net) for that period, including the $4.2 million previously committed.

GENERAL ASSEMBLY ACTION (February)

On 16 February 1989, on the recommendation of the Fifth (Administrative and Budgetary) Committee, the General Assembly adopted **resolution 43/231** without vote.

Financing of the United Nations Angola Verification Mission

The General Assembly,

Having considered the report of the Secretary-General on the financing of the United Nations Angola Verification Mission and the related report of the Advisory Committee on Administrative and Budgetary Questions,

Bearing in mind Security Council resolution 626(1988) of 20 December 1988, by which the Council established the United Nations Angola Verification Mission for a period of thirty-one months,

Recognizing that the costs of the United Nations Angola Verification Mission are expenses of the Organization to be borne by Member States in accordance with Article 17, paragraph 2, of the Charter of the United Nations,

Mindful of the fact that it is essential to provide the United Nations Angola Verification Mission with the necessary financial resources to enable it to fulfil its responsibilities under the relevant resolution of the Security Council,

Urging all Member States to make every possible effort to ensure payment of their assessed contributions to the United Nations Angola Verification Mission in full and on time,

Taking into account the nature and the mandate of the United Nations Angola Verification Mission,

Recognizing that in order to meet the expenditures caused by the United Nations Angola Verification Mis-

sion, a different procedure from the one applied to meet expenditures of the regular budget of the United Nations is required,

Taking into account the fact that the economically more developed countries are in a position to make relatively larger contributions and that the economically less developed countries have a relatively limited capacity to contribute towards such an operation,

Bearing in mind the special responsibilities of the States permanent members of the Security Council, as indicated in General Assembly resolution 1874(S-IV) of 27 June 1963, in the financing of the United Nations Angola Verification Mission,

1. *Decides* to appropriate an amount of 9,193,000 United States dollars, inclusive of the amount of 4.2 million dollars authorized with the concurrence of the Advisory Committee on Administrative and Budgetary Questions, under the terms of General Assembly resolution 42/227 of 21 December 1987, for the operation of the United Nations Angola Verification Mission for an initial period of twelve months, from 3 January 1989 to 2 January 1990, of the mandate period of thirty-one months authorized by the Security Council, and requests the Secretary-General to establish a special account for the Mission;

2. *Decides,* as an *ad hoc* arrangement, to apportion:

(a) An amount of 5,303,438 dollars for the above-mentioned initial period among the States permanent members of the Security Council in the proportions determined by the scale of assessments for the years 1989, 1990 and 1991;

(b) An amount of 3,646,863 dollars for the above-mentioned initial period among the economically developed Member States that are not permanent members of the Security Council in the proportions determined by the scale of assessment for the years 1989, 1990 and 1991;

(c) An amount of 238,283 dollars for the above-mentioned initial period among the economically less developed Member States in the proportions determined by the scale of assessments for the years 1989, 1990 and 1991;

(d) An amount of 4,416 dollars for the above-mentioned initial period to the following of the economically less developed Member States in the proportions determined by the scale of assessments for the years 1989, 1990 and 1991: Afghanistan, Angola, Antigua and Barbuda, Bangladesh, Belize, Benin, Bhutan, Botswana, Burkina Faso, Burundi, Cape Verde, Chad, Comoros, Democratic Yemen, Djibouti, Dominica, Ethiopia, Grenada, Guinea, Guinea-Bissau, Haiti, Lao People's Democratic Republic, Lesotho, Malawi, Maldives, Mali, Mozambique, Nepal, Niger, Papua New Guinea, Rwanda, Saint Kitts and Nevis, Saint Lucia, Saint Vincent and the Grenadines, Samoa, Sao Tome and Principe, Senegal, Seychelles, Solomon Islands, Somalia, Sudan, Suriname, Uganda, United Republic of Tanzania, Vanuatu, Yemen and Zimbabwe;

3. *Decides* that, for the purpose of the present resolution, the term "economically less developed Member States" in paragraph 2 *(c)* above shall mean all Member States except Australia, Austria, Belgium, the Byelorussian Soviet Socialist Republic, Canada, Czechoslovakia, Denmark, Finland, the German Democratic Republic, Germany, Federal Republic of, Iceland, Ireland, Italy, Japan, Luxembourg, the Netherlands, New

Zealand, Norway, Poland, South Africa, Sweden, the Ukrainian Soviet Socialist Republic and the Member States referred to in paragraphs 2 *(a)* and *(d)* above;

4. *Decides* that, in accordance with the provisions of its resolution 973(X) of 15 December 1955, there shall be set off against the apportionment among Member States, as provided for in paragraph 2 above, their respective share in the Tax Equalization Fund of the estimated staff assessment income of 231,000 dollars approved for the above-mentioned initial period;

5. *Invites* voluntary contributions to the United Nations Angola Verification Mission both in cash and in the form of services and supplies acceptable to the Secretary-General, to be administered, as appropriate, in accordance with the procedure established by the General Assembly in section II of its resolution 43/230 of 21 December 1988;

6. *Requests* the Secretary-General to take all necessary action to ensure that the United Nations Angola Verification Mission is administered with the maximum of efficiency and economy bearing in mind the relevant observations contained in the report of the Advisory Committee on Administrative and Budgetary Questions,

7. *Decides* to include in the provisional agenda of its forty-fourth session the item entitled "Financing of the United Nations Angola Verification Mission".

General Assembly resolution 43/231

16 February 1989   Meeting 87   Adopted without vote

Approved by Fifth Committee (A/43/996) without vote, 16 February (meeting 53); draft by Chairman (A/C.5/43/L.23); agenda item 153.
Meeting numbers. GA 43rd session: 5th Committee 52, 53; plenary 87.

In December, the Secretary-General reported[12] that, of the assessment totalling $9,033,059 apportioned among Member States for the period 3 January 1989 to 2 January 1990, contributions totalling $7,421,587 had been received as at 30 November 1989, with $1,611,472 still outstanding. Savings for the period from 3 January 1989 to 2 January 1990 were projected in the amount of $861,100 gross ($806,100 net). In the light of outstanding assessed contributions, the Secretary-General recommended no action in respect of such savings. For the period 3 January 1990 to 2 August 1991, estimates were revised downward to $9.5 million gross ($9.2 million net), of which $5,826,400 gross ($5,616,450 net) related to the period 3 January 1990 to 2 January 1991, and $3,704,600 gross ($3,564,600 net) to the period 3 January to 2 August 1991.

ACABQ recommended approval of $5,826,400 gross ($5,616,400 net) for the period 3 January 1990 to 2 January 1991.[13]

GENERAL ASSEMBLY ACTION (December)

On 21 December, on the recommendation of the Fifth Committee, the General Assembly adopted **resolution 44/190** without vote.

Financing of the United Nations Angola Verification Mission

The General Assembly,

Having considered the report of the Secretary-General on the financing of the United Nations Angola Verifi-

cation Mission and the related report of the Advisory Committee on Administrative and Budgetary Questions,

Bearing in mind Security Council resolution 626(1988) of 20 December 1988, by which the Council established the United Nations Angola Verification Mission for a period of thirty-one months,

Recognizing that the costs of the Verification Mission are expenses of the Organization to be borne by Member States in accordance with Article 17, paragraph 2, of the Charter of the United Nations,

Mindful of the fact that it is essential to provide the Verification Mission with the necessary financial resources to enable it to fulfil its responsibilities under the relevant resolution of the Security Council,

Recognizing that, in order to meet the expenditures caused by the Verification Mission, a different procedure is required from the one applied to meet expenditures of the regular budget of the United Nations,

Taking into account the fact that the economically more developed countries are in a position to make relatively larger contributions and that the economically less developed countries have a relatively limited capacity to contribute towards such an operation,

Bearing in mind the special responsibilities of the States permanent members of the Security Council in the financing of such operations, as indicated in General Assembly resolution 1874(S-IV) of 27 June 1963,

Mindful of the views expressed in the Fifth Committee on the requests of some Member States to change their placement in the existing groups "b", "c" and "d" of Member States, on the basis of the criteria set out in General Assembly resolution 3101(XXVIII) of 11 December 1973,

1. *Concurs* with the observations, recommendations and conclusions contained in the report of the Advisory Committee on Administrative and Budgetary Questions;

2. *Urges* all Member States to make every possible effort to ensure payment of their assessed contributions to the United Nations Angola Verification Mission in full and on time;

3. *Decides*, taking into account the outstanding assessed contributions due to the Special Account of the United Nations Angola Verification Mission, to defer any action on the estimated unencumbered balance of the appropriations as may be called for until its forty-fifth session;

4. *Decides also* to appropriate an amount of 5,826,400 United States dollars for the operations of the Verification Mission from 3 January 1990 to 2 January 1991, inclusive;

5. *Decides further*, as an *ad hoc* arrangement, to apportion the amount of 5,826,400 dollars for the above-mentioned period among Member States in accordance with the composition of groups set out in paragraphs 3 and 4 of General Assembly resolution 43/232 of 1 March 1989, to be adjusted by the decision to be taken by the Assembly at its forty-fourth session on the composition of groups "a", "b", "c" and "d" of Member States and taking into account the scale of assessments for the years 1989, 1990 and 1991;

6. *Decides* that, in accordance with the provisions of its resolution 973(X) of 15 December 1955, there shall be set off against the apportionment among the Member States, as provided for in paragraph 5 of the present resolution, their respective share in the Tax Equalization Fund of the estimated staff assessment income

of 210,000 dollars approved for the above-mentioned period;

7. *Invites* voluntary contributions to the Verification Mission both in cash and in the form of services and supplies acceptable to the Secretary-General, to be administered, as appropriate, in accordance with the procedure to be established by the General Assembly at its forty-fourth session;

8. *Requests* the Secretary-General to take all necessary action to ensure that the Verification Mission is administered with the maximum of efficiency and economy, bearing in mind the relevant observations contained in the report of the Advisory Committee;

9. *Decides* to include in the provisional agenda of its forty-fifth session the item entitled "Financing of the United Nations Angola Verification Mission" and to request the Secretary-General to submit to the General Assembly at its forty-fifth session a report on the implementation of the present resolution.

General Assembly resolution 44/190

21 December 1989   Meeting 84   Adopted without vote

Approved by Fifth Committee (A/44/890) without vote, 18 December (meeting 58); draft by Chairman (A/C.5/44/L.16); agenda item 135.

Comoros

Comorian island of Mayotte

The question of the Comorian island of Mayotte—one of a group of four islands in the Indian Ocean Comoro Archipelago—was the subject of further consideration by the General Assembly in 1989. The Islamic Federal Republic of the Comoros acceded to independence on 6 July 1975, following a referendum in 1974. France, the former colonial Power, had since continued to administer the island of Mayotte.

Report of the Secretary-General. In an October report to the General Assembly,[14] the Secretary-General said that he had addressed a note verbale to the Comoros and France, drawing their attention to a 1988 Assembly resolution on the question of the island of Mayotte[15] and inviting them to provide him with any pertinent information for inclusion in his report. A similar communication had been sent to OAU.

France, in its response, reiterated that Mayotte had, since December 1976, been a territorial collectivity of France, which did not close the door to any further developments. France had demonstrated its readiness to seek actively a solution to the problem in keeping with national and international law and its own Constitution, taking into account the will of the populations concerned. Accordingly, it was maintaining a continuing dialogue at the highest level with the Comoros.

In its note verbale to the Secretary-General, the Comoros said that it had always preferred dialogue and concerted action in conformity with the principles of the United Nations Charter and the recommendations of international organizations for negotiations. It had increased its contacts at

the highest governmental level with the French authorities.

In May 1989, President Ahmed Abdallah Abderemane discussed the question with the French President during a private visit to France. At the summit meeting of French-speaking countries at Dakar, Senegal, he expressed the hope that the recent détente in international relations might have a favourable impact on the matter. The Comoros said that during 1989 the issue of Mayotte had been discussed at several international forums, all of which expressed support for the Comoros in recovering its territorial integrity. It appealed to the Secretary-General to continue his role as a mediator with a view to bringing the two parties closer together in the search for a fair and equitable settlement.

OAU quoted a resolution adopted by its Council of Ministers (Addis Ababa, Ethiopia, 17-22 July), reaffirming the sovereignty of the Comoros over Mayotte and inviting OAU member States to sensitize French and international public opinion to the question and to convince the French Government to end its illegal occupation of the island. OAU mandated its *Ad Hoc* Committee of Seven on the question of Mayotte to resume dialogue with the French authorities in order to restore Mayotte to the Federal Islamic Republic of the Comoros.

GENERAL ASSEMBLY ACTION

On 18 October 1989, the General Assembly adopted **resolution 44/9** by recorded vote.

Question of the Comorian island of Mayotte
The General Assembly,

Recalling its resolutions 1514(XV) of 14 December 1960, containing the Declaration on the Granting of Independence to Colonial Countries and Peoples, and 2621(XXV) of 12 October 1970, containing the programme of action for the full implementation of the Declaration,

Recalling also its previous resolutions, in particular resolutions 3161(XXVIII) of 14 December 1973, 3291(XXIX) of 13 December 1974, 31/4 of 21 October 1976, 32/7 of 1 November 1977, 34/69 of 6 December 1979, 35/43 of 28 November 1980, 36/105 of 10 December 1981, 37/65 of 3 December 1982, 38/13 of 21 November 1983, 39/48 of 11 December 1984, 40/62 of 9 December 1985, 41/30 of 3 November 1986, 42/17 of 11 November 1987 and 43/14 of 26 October 1988, in which, *inter alia*, it affirmed the unity and territorial integrity of the Comoros,

Recalling, in particular, its resolution 3385(XXX) of 12 November 1975 on the admission of the Comoros to membership in the United Nations, in which it reaffirmed the necessity of respecting the unity and territorial integrity of the Comoro Archipelago, composed of the islands of Anjouan, Grande-Comore, Mayotte and Mohéli,

Recalling further that, in accordance with the agreements between the Comoros and France, signed on 15 June

1973, concerning the accession of the Comoros to independence, the results of the referendum of 22 December 1974 were to be considered on a global basis and not island by island,

Convinced that a just and lasting solution to the question of Mayotte is to be found in respect for the sovereignty, unity and territorial integrity of the Comoro Archipelago,

Convinced also that a speedy solution of the problem is essential for the preservation of the peace and security which prevail in the region,

Bearing in mind the wish expressed by the President of the French Republic to seek actively a just solution to that problem,

Taking note of the repeated wish of the Government of the Comoros to initiate as soon as possible a frank and serious dialogue with the French Government with a view to accelerating the return of the Comorian island of Mayotte to the Islamic Federal Republic of the Comoros,

Taking note of the report of the Secretary-General,

Bearing in mind also the decisions of the Organization of African Unity, the Movement of Non-Aligned Countries and the Organization of the Islamic Conference on this question,

1. *Reaffirms* the sovereignty of the Islamic Federal Republic of the Comoros over the island of Mayotte;

2. *Invites* the Government of France to honour the commitments entered into prior to the referendum on the self-determination of the Comoro Archipelago of 22 December 1974 concerning respect for the unity and territorial integrity of the Comoros;

3. *Calls* for the translation into practice of the wish expressed by the President of the French Republic to seek actively a just solution to the question of Mayotte;

4. *Urges* the Government of France to accelerate the process of negotiations with the Government of the Comoros with a view to ensuring the effective and prompt return of the island of Mayotte to the Comoros;

5. *Requests* the Secretary-General of the United Nations to maintain continuous contact with the Secretary-General of the Organization of African Unity with regard to this problem and to make available his good offices in the search for a peaceful negotiated solution to the problem;

6. *Also requests* the Secretary-General to report on this matter to the General Assembly at its forty-fifth session;

7. *Decides* to include in the provisional agenda of its forty-fifth session the item entitled "Question of the Comorian island of Mayotte".

General Assembly resolution 44/9

18 October 1989   Meeting 34   128-1-24 (recorded vote)

35-nation draft (A/44/L.10); agenda item 29.

Sponsors: Algeria, Bahrain, Benin, Botswana, Burkina Faso, Burundi, Comoros, Cuba, Democratic Yemen, Equatorial Guinea, Gabon, Gambia, Guinea, Guinea-Bissau, Kenya, Lesotho, Liberia, Libyan Arab Jamahiriya, Madagascar, Mali, Mauritius, Morocco, Oman, Qatar, Sao Tome and Principe, Senegal, Somalia, Sudan, Swaziland, Uganda, United Arab Emirates, United Republic of Tanzania, Yemen, Zambia, Zimbabwe.

Recorded vote in Assembly as follows:

In favour: Afghanistan, Albania, Algeria, Angola, Antigua and Barbuda, Argentina, Australia, Bahamas, Bahrain, Bangladesh, Barbados, Benin, Bhutan, Bolivia, Botswana, Brazil, Brunei Darussalam, Bulgaria, Burkina Faso, Burundi, Byelorussian SSR, Cameroon, Cape Verde, Central African Republic, Chad, Chile, China, Colombia, Comoros, Congo, Costa Rica, Côte d'Ivoire, Cuba, Czechoslovakia, Democratic Kampuchea, Democratic Yemen, Djibouti, Ecuador, Egypt, El Salvador, Equatorial Guinea, Ethiopia, Fiji, Finland, Gabon, Gambia, German Democratic Republic, Ghana, Grenada, Guatemala, Guinea, Guinea-Bissau, Guyana, Haiti, Honduras, Hungary, India, Indonesia, Iran, Iraq, Jamaica, Jordan, Kenya, Kuwait, Lao People's Democratic Republic, Lesotho, Liberia, Libyan Arab Jamahiriya, Madagascar, Malawi, Malaysia, Maldives, Mali, Mauritania, Mauritius, Mexico, Mongolia, Morocco, Mozambique, Myanmar, Nepal, New Zealand, Nicaragua, Niger, Nigeria, Oman, Pakistan, Panama, Papua New Guinea, Paraguay, Peru, Philippines, Poland, Qatar, Romania, Saint Lucia, Sao Tome and Principe, Saudi Arabia, Senegal, Sierra Leone, Singapore, Solomon Islands, Somalia, Sri Lanka, Sudan, Suriname, Swaziland, Sweden, Syrian Arab Republic, Thailand, Togo, Trinidad and Tobago, Tunisia, Turkey, Uganda, Ukrainian SSR, USSR, United Arab Emirates, United Republic of Tanzania, Uruguay, Vanuatu, Venezuela, Viet Nam, Yemen, Yugoslavia, Zaire, Zambia, Zimbabwe.

Against: France.

Abstaining: Austria, Belgium, Canada, Cyprus, Denmark, Dominica, Dominican Republic, Germany, Federal Republic of, Greece, Iceland, Ireland, Israel, Italy, Japan, Luxembourg, Malta, Netherlands, Norway, Portugal, Saint Kitts and Nevis, Saint Vincent and the Grenadines, Spain, United Kingdom, United States.

Situation in the Comoros

On 14 December,[16] the Islamic Group requested the inclusion in the agenda of the General Assembly of an item entitled "Grave situation in the Comoros". In an explanatory memorandum, it stated that an armed group of mercenaries had assassinated President Ahmed Abdallah Abderemane of the Comoros and had disarmed the national armed forces with the intention of seizing control of the country. This constituted a flagrant violation of the United Nations Charter and international law. The international community was being called upon to use its influence to end this brutal interference in the internal affairs of a sovereign State and to enable its legitimate constitutional institutions to function. Appended to the request was a draft resolution for adoption by the Assembly.

During consideration of the request by the General Committee on 15 December, the representative of the Comoros expressed gratitude to those Governments that had helped to oust the mercenaries. He reported that, as of that morning, all mercenary elements had left the Comoros and national sovereignty had been re-established. France indicated its willingness to provide military assistance to the Comoros for an unspecified period.

On the same day, the General Assembly was informed that the General Committee had made no recommendation on the request by the Islamic Group.

Libyan Arab Jamahiriya

On 3 January,[17] the Co-ordinating Bureau of Non-Aligned Countries issued a communiqué in which it recalled that threats of aggression and media campaigns had preceded the 15 April 1986[18] aerial and naval attacks by the United States against the Libyan Arab Jamahiriya and warned that the current campaign might serve as a pretext for launching fresh acts of aggression against that country. It noted the offer of the Jamahiriya to allow international inspection of the pharmaceutical factories alleged to be producing chemical weapons.

On 4 January,[19] the Libyan Arab Jamahiriya requested an immediate meeting of the Security Council in order to halt the aggression by the United States, which, it said, had that morning downed two Libyan reconnaissance aircraft over international waters.

The United States[20] on the same day, in a letter to the President of the Security Council, said that it had acted in accordance with Article 51 of the Charter in exercising its inherent right of self-defence by taking defensive action in response to hostile action by Libyan military forces against United States aircraft lawfully operating above international waters of the Mediterranean. It had shot down the two Libyan aircraft in self-defence. The Arab Group,[21] also on the same day, requested the Council to meet on the issue.

On 5 January,[22] the Co-ordinating Bureau of Non-Aligned Countries, recalling its communiqué of 3 January, condemned the attack and called on the United States to withdraw its forces from the area.

SECURITY COUNCIL CONSIDERATION

The Security Council held six meetings at the request of the Libyan Arab Jamahiriya and the Arab Group between 5 and 11 January.

Meeting numbers. SC 2835-2837, 2839-2841.

At their request, the President of the Security Council, under rule 37[a] of the provisional rules of procedure, invited the following States to participate in the discussion without the right to vote: Afghanistan, Bahrain, Bangladesh, Bulgaria, Burkina Faso, Byelorussian SSR, Cuba, Czechoslovakia, Democratic Yemen, German Democratic Republic, India, Iran, Lao People's Democratic Republic, Libyan Arab Jamahiriya, Madagascar, Mali, Malta, Mongolia, Morocco, Nicaragua, Pakistan, Poland, Romania, Sudan, Syrian Arab Republic, Tunisia, Uganda, United Arab Emirates, Yemen, Zimbabwe.

At the request of Algeria, invitations were extended under rule 39[b] to the Acting Permanent Observer[23] and the Permanent Observer[24] of the League of Arab States, the Permanent Observer of the Organization of the Islamic Conference,[25] a representative of the Pan Africanist Congress of Azania[26] and a representative of the African National Congress of South Africa.[27]

At his request,[28] the Council decided, by 11 votes to 1 (United States), with 3 abstentions (Canada, France, United Kingdom), that an invitation should be extended to the Alternate Permanent Observer of Palestine to the United Nations. The invitation would confer upon him the same rights of participation as those conferred on

a Member State when it was invited to participate under rule 37.

During the debate, the Libyan Arab Jamahiriya said that, prior to the incident, the United States had dispatched a 13-vessel task force from Norfolk, Virginia, to support its Sixth Fleet, which was deployed off the Libyan coast. By shooting down without any justification two unarmed Libyan reconnaissance aircraft on routine patrol near the Libyan coast, the United States action was premeditated and a prelude to large-scale aggression. It called on the Council to condemn the American military aggression, to take all measures to stop it and to call on the United States to withdraw its naval fleet.

The United States said that the aircraft carrier *Kennedy* was on an easterly transit through the Mediterranean Sea, 170 miles north of the border between the Libyan Arab Jamahiriya and Egypt. Its naval aircraft were operating on a training mission over international waters, some 70 miles off the Libyan coast, north of Tobruk, when they were aggressively and hostilely challenged by the Libyan Air Force. The American pilots exercised restraint under the circumstances and repeatedly made attempts to avoid the Libyan aircraft which were closing in on them. When the section leader determined that his aircraft was in jeopardy, the United States aircraft fired on the Libyan planes.

The United States also stated that the incident was unrelated to concerns about Libya's chemical-warfare plant and should not be associated with the routine rotation of the United States Sixth Fleet in and out of the Mediterranean.

On 11 January, the Council received a draft resolution,[29] sponsored by Algeria, Colombia, Ethiopia, Malaysia, Nepal, Senegal and Yugoslavia, which would have had the Council deplore the downing of the two Libyan reconnaissance planes by the United States, and call on the United States to suspend military manoeuvres off the Libyan coast and on the parties to refrain from the use of force, to exercise restraint and to resolve their differences by peaceful means. It would also have called on the United States and the Libyan Arab Jamahiriya to co-operate with the Secretary-General in bringing about a peaceful settlement of their differences.

[a]Rule 37 of the Council's provisional rules of procedure states: "Any Member of the United Nations which is not a member of the Security Council may be invited, as the result of a decision of the Security Council, to participate, without vote, in the discussion of any question brought before the Security Council when the Security Council considers that the interests of that Member are specially affected, or when a Member brings a matter to the attention of the Security Council in accordance with Article 35 (1) of the Charter."

[b]Rule 39 of the Council's provisional rules of procedure states: "The Security Council may invite members of the Secretariat or other persons, whom it considers competent for the purpose, to supply it with information or to give other assistance in examining matters within its competence."

The vote on the draft was 9 votes to 4 (Canada, France, United Kingdom, United States), with 2 abstentions (Brazil, Finland); the draft was not adopted owing to the negative vote of a permanent member.

GENERAL ASSEMBLY ACTION

On 7 December 1989, the General Assembly, by **decision 44/417**, decided to defer consideration of an item on the 1986 Declaration of the Assembly of Heads of State and Government of OAU on the aerial and naval military attack against the Libyan Arab Jamahiriya by the United States in April of that year[30] and to include it in the provisional agenda of its forty-fifth (1990) session.

Malagasy islands of Glorieuses, Juan de Nova, Europa and Bassas da India

The item on the question of the Malagasy islands of Glorieuses, Juan de Nova, Europa and Bassas da India was included in the provisional agenda of the General Assembly's 1989 regular session, in accordance with a 1988 Assembly decision.[31] On 22 September, by **decision 44/402 A**, the Assembly, on the recommendation of the General Committee, included the item in its agenda and allocated it to the Special Political Committee.

On 19 October, the Chairman informed the Committee that he had held consultations with the delegations concerned, particularly France and Madagascar. In view of the ongoing periodic contacts between the two countries, it was requested that the Committee postpone consideration of the item to the 1990 regular Assembly session.

On 8 December, by **decision 44/419**, the Assembly, on the recommendation of the Committee,[32] included the item in the provisional agenda of its 1990 session.

Relations between Mauritania and Senegal

Senegal, on 19 July,[33] informed the President of the Security Council of the situation existing between it and Mauritania, arising from the murder in April of two Senegalese nationals in Senegalese territory by the Mauritanian National Guard and the taking hostage of 13 Senegalese nationals. At Senegal's request, the President of Mali, as current Chairman of OAU, had been acting as mediator, but no progress had been made in resolving the conflict. In May, Mauritania expelled 26,000 of its nationals belonging to ethnic groups also to be found in Senegal. The deportation intensified in July, creating tension between the two countries. Senegal, considering the situation a threat to peace and security in the West African subregion, was informing the Council so that it could take appropriate action.

Mauritania, in a letter of 24 July to the President of the Security Council,[34] refuted Senegal's account of the incident. It said that the incident had occurred on Mauritanian territory between stock-raisers and farmers and was used as a pretext by Senegal to implement a plan against Mauritania and Mauritanians living in Senegal. Mauritania rejected the delaying tactics of Senegal in refusing to welcome its nationals repatriated from Mauritania on the pretext that they were Mauritanians. It also said that the repatriation of Senegalese living in Mauritania had ceased. Mauritania was therefore drawing the attention of the Security Council to the aggressive designs of Senegal.

REFERENCES

[1]YUN 1988, p. 159. [2]S/20910. [3]S/20625. [4]YUN 1988, p. 160, SC res. 626(1988), 20 Dec. 1988. [5]S/20783. [6]S/20799. [7]S/20955. [8]A/43/249. [9]A/43/249/Add.1. [10]YUN 1987, p. 1110, GA res. 42/227, 21 Dec. 1987. [11]A/43/249/Add.2. [12]A/44/877. [13]A/44/881. [14]A/44/633. [15]YUN 1988, p. 162, GA res. 43/14, 26 Oct. 1988. [16]A/44/249. [17]A/44/66-S/20369. [18]YUN 1986, p. 247. [19]S/20364. [20]S/20366. [21]S/20367. [22]A/44/69-S/20377. [23]S/20371. [24]S/20390. [25]S/20382. [26]S/20384. [27]S/20387. [28]S/20392. [29]S/20378. [30]YUN 1986, p. 257. [31]YUN 1988, p. 163, GA dec. 43/419, 6 Dec. 1988. [32]A/44/685. [33]S/20739. [34]S/20747.

UN Educational and Training Programme for Southern Africa

Scholarships awarded under the United Nations Educational and Training Programme for Southern Africa reached 1,208 in 1988/89 compared with 1,358 in 1987/88, according to the Secretary-General's September 1989 report.[1] The Programme was administered by the Secretary-General in consultation with the Advisory Committee on the Programme and was financed from a Trust Fund made up of voluntary contributions from States, organizations and individuals. For the 1988/89 period, there were 442 scholarship holders from Namibia and 766 from South Africa. With the independence of Namibia imminent, educational assistance to Namibian students would be provided for a transitional period.

For the period 1 September 1988 to 31 August 1989, a total of $4,238,446 in contributions had been received from 28 countries. In addition, pledges for 1989 amounted to $460,928. The 1989 contributions and pledges totalling $4,699,374 represented an increase over the previous year's total of $4,675,510.

The Secretary-General appealed to States, institutions, organizations and individuals for generous financial and other support to the Programme.

The Advisory Committee decided that the Programme should be evaluated in 1989, in view of the independence of Namibia and the need to outline the Programme's future focus, as well as to assess the needs for educational and training assistance to students from South Africa.

GENERAL ASSEMBLY ACTION

On 11 December 1989, on the recommendation of the Fourth Committee, the General Assembly adopted **resolution 44/86** without vote.

United Nations Educational and Training Programme for Southern Africa

The General Assembly,

Recalling its earlier resolutions on the United Nations Educational and Training Programme for Southern Africa, in particular resolution 43/31 of 22 November 1988,

Having considered the report of the Secretary-General containing an account of the work of the Advisory Committee on the United Nations Educational and Training Programme for Southern Africa and the administration of the Programme for the period from 1 September 1988 to 31 August 1989,

Taking note of the ongoing evaluation of the Programme,

Recognizing the valuable assistance rendered by the Programme to the peoples of South Africa and Namibia,

Noting with satisfaction that educational and technical assistance for southern Africa has become a growing concern of the international community,

Fully recognizing the need to provide continuing educational opportunities and counselling to a greater number of student refugees from South Africa and Namibia in a wide variety of professional, cultural and linguistic disciplines, as well as opportunities for vocational and technical training and for advanced studies at graduate and post-graduate levels in the priority fields of study,

Strongly convinced that the continuation and steady expansion of the Programme is essential in order to meet the ever-increasing demand for educational and training assistance to students from South Africa and Namibia,

1. *Endorses* the report of the Secretary-General on the United Nations Educational and Training Programme for Southern Africa;

2. *Commends* the Secretary-General and the Advisory Committee on the United Nations Educational and Training Programme for Southern Africa for their continuing efforts further to promote generous contributions to the Programme and to enhance co-operation with governmental, intergovernmental and non-governmental agencies involved in educational and technical assistance to southern Africa;

3. *Expresses its appreciation* to all those that have supported the Programme by providing contributions, scholarships or places in their educational institutions;

4. *Appeals* to all States, institutions, organizations and individuals to offer greater financial and other support to the Programme in order to secure its continuation and steady expansion.

General Assembly resolution 44/86

11 December 1989   Meeting 80   Adopted without vote

Approved by Fourth Committee (A/44/741) without vote, 20 October (meeting 12); 60-nation draft (A/C.4/44/L.3); agenda item 119.

Sponsors: Algeria, Argentina, Australia, Austria, Bangladesh, Belgium, Bolivia, Brazil, Burundi, Byelorussian SSR, Cameroon, Canada, Chile, Denmark, Djibouti, Finland, France, Germany, Federal Republic of, Greece, Guyana, Iceland, India, Indonesia, Ireland, Italy, Japan, Liberia, Madagascar, Malaysia, Mali, Mexico, Morocco, Myanmar, Netherland, New Zealand, Nicaragua, Nigeria, Norway, Pakistan, Papua New Guinea, Philippines, Portugal, Romania, Senegal, Spain, Sudan, Suriname, Sweden, Thailand, Tunisia, Turkey, Ukrainian SSR, United Kingdom, United Republic of Tanzania, United States, Vanuatu, Venezuela, Zaire, Zambia, Zimbabwe.

Meeting numbers. GA 44th session: 4th Committee 5, 9-16; plenary 80.

REFERENCE

(1)A/44/557.

Co-operation between OAU and the UN system

Co-operation between the United Nations and the Organization of African Unity intensified during 1989. In an August report,[1] prepared in response to a 1988 General Assembly request,[2] the Secretary-General outlined the nature and extent of that co-operation, as well as United Nations responses to the measures called for by the Assembly.

Co-operation between the two organizations covered four major areas: consultations and exchange of information; co-operation with regard to the situation in southern Africa; co-operation in the field of economic and social development; and co-operation in the field of information and publicity. The report also spoke of the discussions between the Secretaries-General of the United Nations and OAU in March on the establishment of an OAU observer mission in Namibia, modalities for the repatriation of Namibian refugees and matters relating to the election process in that country. At the Summit Conference of OAU (Addis Ababa, 24-26 July), the United Nations Secretary-General addressed the questions of Namibia, Western Sahara, the United Nations Programme of Action for African Economic Recovery and Development 1986-1990,[3] environment, human rights, the draft convention on the rights of the child, and the problems of African refugees and displaced persons. Consultations also took place between the two organizations on proposals for reactivating the machinery for co-operation between the secretariats of the United Nations system and of OAU and its affiliated organizations. It was decided that further consultations should take place later in 1989, in preparation for a joint meeting in 1990.

Also submitted to the General Assembly were the texts of resolutions adopted by the Council of Ministers of OAU at its fiftieth ordinary session

(Addis Abada, 17-22 July).[4] The President of Egypt, Mohamed Hosni Mubarak, in an address to the Assembly, outlined the political and economic problems facing Africa, including the debt problem, and the impact of the region's environmental problems.

In May, the Economic and Social Council, by **resolution 1989/59**, acknowledged the efforts made by the Economic Commission for Africa, in co-operation with OAU and the Crime Prevention and Criminal Justice Branch of the Centre for Social Development and Humanitarian Affairs of the Secretariat, during the initial phase of the operation of the African Institute for the Prevention of Crime and the Treatment of Offenders.

GENERAL ASSEMBLY ACTION

On 1 November, the General Assembly adopted without vote **resolution 44/17**.

Co-operation between the United Nations and the Organization of African Unity

The General Assembly,

Having considered the report of the Secretary-General on co-operation between the United Nations and the Organization of African Unity,

Recalling its previous resolutions on the enhancement of co-operation between the United Nations and the Organization of African Unity and the practical measures taken for their implementation,

Recalling also its resolutions S-13/2 of 1 June 1986, the annex to which contains the United Nations Programme of Action for African Economic Recovery and Development 1986-1990, 43/12 of 25 October 1988 and 43/27 of 18 November 1988 on the mid-term review and appraisal of the implementation of the Programme,

Taking note of the relevant resolutions, decisions and declarations adopted by the Council of Ministers of the Organization of African Unity at its fiftieth ordinary session, held at Addis Ababa from 17 to 22 July 1989, and by the Assembly of Heads of State and Government of that organization at its twenty-fifth ordinary session, held at Addis Ababa from 24 to 26 July 1989,

Considering the important statement made by the current Chairman of the Assembly of Heads of State and Government of the Organization of African Unity before the General Assembly on 29 September 1989,

Mindful of the need for continued and closer co-operation between the United Nations and the specialized agencies and the Organization of African Unity,

Concerned at the situation in southern Africa arising from the continued domination and oppression of the people of South Africa by the minority racist régime and conscious of the need to provide increased assistance to the people of South Africa and to their national liberation movements in their legitimate struggle to eradicate the policies of *apartheid,*

Reiterating that Security Council resolution 435(1978) of 29 September 1978 must be implemented in its original and definitive form to ensure those conditions in Namibia which will allow the Namibian people to participate freely and without intimidation and harassment in the electoral process under the supervision and control of the United Nations, leading to the early independence of the Territory,

Deeply concerned that the critical economic situation persists in Africa despite the policies of reform being implemented by African countries,

Also concerned that some constraints continue to pose critical obstacles to African economic recovery and development, including those in the external arena, resulting in weak export earnings, severe debt-servicing burdens and limited availability of finance,

Mindful of the efforts under way by the Organization of African Unity and its member States in the area of economic integration and, in particular, towards the establishment of an African economic community,

Conscious of its responsibilities to provide economic, material and humanitarian assistance to independent States in southern Africa to help them cope with the situation resulting from the acts of aggression and destabilization committed by the *apartheid* régime of South Africa,

Deeply concerned also at the gravity of the situation of the refugees and displaced persons in Africa and the urgent need for increased international assistance to help African countries of asylum,

Recognizing the important role that the United Nations information system could play in disseminating information to bring about a greater awareness of the grave situation prevailing in southern Africa as well as the social and economic problems and the needs of African States and their regional and subregional institutions,

Expressing its gratitude for the continued financial and other support extended to Africa by the international community and especially by certain countries,

1. *Takes note* of the report of the Secretary-General on co-operation between the United Nations and the Organization of African Unity and of his efforts to strengthen co-operation;

2. *Notes with appreciation* the increasing and continued participation of the Organization of African Unity in the work of the United Nations and the specialized agencies and its constructive contribution to that work;

3. *Notes* those efforts of the Secretary-General which are under way in order to implement General Assembly resolution 43/12 of 1 November 1988, particularly with regard to the establishment of a group of experts to undertake an in-depth assessment of the question of commodities of interest to Africa and the scope for export diversification;

4. *Commends* the continued efforts of the Organization of African Unity to promote multilateral co-operation among African States and to find solutions to African problems of vital importance to the international community;

5. *Reaffirms* that the implementation of the United Nations Programme of Action for African Economic Recovery and Development 1986-1990 is the responsibility of the international community as a whole and commends the efforts undertaken by African countries in spite of the effects of the adverse international economic environment;

6. *Calls upon* the Secretary-General of the United Nations to continue to ensure closer co-operation and co-ordination with the Secretary-General of the Organization of African Unity in the implementation and monitoring of the Programme of Action;

7. *Also calls upon* the Secretary-General of the United Nations, notwithstanding the competence of the multi-

lateral financial institutions, to co-operate with the Secretary-General of the Organization of African Unity to contribute to the implementation of measures aimed at a lasting solution to Africa's debt and debt-servicing burden, taking into account Africa's common position on its external debt, adopted by the Assembly of Heads of State and Government of the Organization of African Unity at its third extraordinary session, held at Addis Ababa on 30 November and 1 December 1987;

8. *Urges* all Member States and regional and international organizations, in particular those of the United Nations system, to continue to extend maximum support to Africa's Priority Programme for Economic Recovery 1986-1990;

9. *Requests* all Member States, United Nations bodies, the specialized agencies and all other relevant organs of the United Nations, as well as non-governmental organizations, to activate and increase their programme of assistance to African subregional organizations for drought and desertification control such as the Permanent Inter-State Committee on Drought Control in the Sahel and the Intergovernmental Authority for Drought and Development;

10. *Reiterates its appreciation* to the Secretary-General for his efforts, on behalf of the international community, to organize and mobilize special programmes of economic assistance for those African States facing grave economic difficulties, the front-line States and other independent States of southern Africa to help them to withstand the effects of the acts of aggression and destabilization committed by the *apartheid* régime of South Africa;

11. *Requests* the Secretary-General of the United Nations and relevant agencies of the United Nations system to extend their support and co-operation to the Secretary-General of the Organization of African Unity in the efforts to establish an African economic community, in accordance with resolutions AHG/Res.161 (XXIII) and AHG/Res.179(XXV) adopted by the Assembly of Heads of State and Government of the Organization of African Unity in July 1987 and July 1989, respectively;

12. *Also requests* the Secretary-General to continue to keep the Organization of African Unity informed periodically of the response of the international community to the special programmes of economic assistance and to continue to co-ordinate efforts with all similar programmes initiated by that organization;

13. *Expresses its appreciation* to the United Nations Development Programme, the Office of the United Nations Disaster Relief Co-ordinator, the World Food Programme, the World Food Council, the Food and Agriculture Organization of the United Nations, the World Health Organization, the United Nations Children's Fund, the Office of the United Nations High Commissioner for Refugees and the United Nations Institute for Training and Research for the assistance so far rendered to the African States in dealing with the emergency situation as well as with the critical economic problems that exist on the African continent;

14. *Endorses* the agreement reached between the organizations of the United Nations system and the Organization of African Unity for the convening of a meeting between the secretariats of those organizations, to be held at the headquarters of the Organization of African Unity from 2 to 5 April 1990 in order to discuss ways and means of expanding and strengthening areas of co-operation in the social and economic sectors;

15. *Requests* the United Nations and the Organization of African Unity to continue to hold regular consultations, as and when appropriate, between representatives of the Secretariat of the United Nations and the General Secretariat of the Organization of African Unity on the implementation of the present resolution;

16. *Reiterates* the determination of the United Nations, in co-operation with the Organization of African Unity, to intensify its efforts to eliminate colonialism, racial discrimination and *apartheid* in southern Africa;

17. *Urges* the international community to extend full support to the Secretary-General in his effort to ensure that Security Council resolution 435(1978) is implemented in its original and definitive form;

18. *Requests* the Secretary-General to take the necessary measures to strengthen co-operation at the political, economic, cultural and administrative levels between the United Nations and the Organization of African Unity in accordance with the relevant resolutions of the General Assembly, particularly with regard to the provision of assistance to the victims of colonialism and *apartheid* in southern Africa;

19. *Also urges* the international community to contribute generously to the Assistance Fund for the Struggle against Colonialism and *Apartheid*, established by the Organization of African Unity, and to the Action for Resisting Invasion, Colonialism and *Apartheid* Fund, established by the Movement of Non-Aligned Countries;

20. *Calls upon* the competent organs of the United Nations and the specialized agencies to continue to ensure the just and equitable representation of Africa at senior and policy levels at their respective headquarters and in their regional and field operations;

21. *Urges* all Member States and regional and international organizations, in particular those of the United Nations system, as well as non-governmental organizations to provide material and economic assistance to African countries of asylum to enable them to withstand the heavy burden imposed on their limited resources and weak infrastructure by the presence in their countries of large numbers of refugees;

22. *Calls upon* the United Nations organs—in particular the Security Council, the Economic and Social Council, the Special Committee on the Situation with regard to the Implementation of the Declaration on the Granting of Independence to Colonial Countries and Peoples and the Special Committee against *Apartheid*— to continue to associate closely the Organization of African Unity with all their activities concerning Africa;

23. *Expresses appreciation* to the Secretary-General of the United Nations and the Secretary-General of the Organization of African Unity for reactivating the machinery for co-operation of the two organizations and encourages them to further strengthen that machinery;

24. *Requests* the Secretary-General of the United Nations to continue to invite the representative of the Secretary-General of the Organization of African Unity to participate in the meetings of the United Nations Steering Committee and its Inter-Agency Task Force and working groups on the implementation of the United Nations Programme of Action for African Economic Recovery and Development 1986-1990;

25. *Also requests* the Secretary-General to ensure that adequate facilities continue to be made available to facili-

tate continued liaison and consultations on matters of common interest as well as the provision of technical assistance to the General Secretariat of the Organization of African Unity, as required;

26. *Further requests* the Secretary-General to report to the General Assembly at its forty-fifth session on the implementation of the present resolution and on the development of co-operation between the Organization of African Unity and the organizations within the United Nations system.

General Assembly resolution 44/17

1 November 1989   Meeting 44   Adopted without vote

2-nation draft (A/44/L.6/Rev.1); agenda item 27.
Sponsors: Kenya, Lesotho.

REFERENCES

[1]A/44/425. [2]YUN 1988, p. 165, GA res. 43/12, 25 Oct. 1988. [3]YUN 1986, p. 446, GA res. S-13/2, annex, 1 June 1986. [4]A/44/603.

Chapter II

Americas

The United Nations played a pivotal role in 1989 in assisting Central American countries to achieve peace in the region. In February, August and December, the five Central American Presidents (Costa Rica, El Salvador, Guatemala, Honduras, Nicaragua) and Panama agreed on further measures to implement the security undertakings of their 1987 Esquipulas II summit. In July, the Security Council called on the Presidents to continue their efforts to achieve a firm and lasting peace in Central America and expressed support for the Secretary-General's mission of good offices (resolution 637(1989)). At the request of the Presidents, the United Nations, in co-operation with the Organization of American States, set up the International Support and Verification Commission to promote compliance with the agreements reached by the Central American Presidents. The Security Council, on the Secretary-General's recommendation, established the United Nations Observer Group in Central America, for an initial six months, to verify the cessation of aid to irregular forces and insurrectionist movements and the non-use of the territory of one State for attacks on another (resolution 644(1989)). The General Assembly approved funds for its financing (resolution 44/44).

In preparation for national elections in Nicaragua, scheduled for February 1990, the Secretary-General established the United Nations Observer Mission for the Verification of the Electoral Process in Nicaragua. In December, the Assembly deplored the continuation of the trade embargo against Nicaragua (resolution 44/217). The Secretary-General also remained engaged in negotiations between the Government and the opposition party in El Salvador, which reached an agreement on 15 September 1989. In October, the Assembly requested him to continue to support the Central American Governments in their efforts to achieve peace (resolution 44/10).

In December, the Council and the Assembly also met to consider the situation resulting from the United States military intervention in Panama. The Assembly deplored the intervention, demanded the withdrawal of United States forces from Panama and called for respect of the 1977 Torrijos-Carter Treaties (resolution 44/240).

Central America

In 1989, Central American countries took initiatives to accelerate the peace process in the region, in accordance with the agreements reached at the 1987 Esquipulas II summit[1] and the commitments made in their 1988 Declaration.[2] Most notable was the adoption on 14 February 1989[3] of the Joint Declaration of the Central American Presidents at Costa del Sol, El Salvador, by which they agreed, following Nicaragua's undertaking to initiate a process of democratization and national reconciliation and hold elections by 25 February 1990, to draw up within 90 days a joint plan for the voluntary demobilization, repatriation or relocation of members of the Nicaraguan resistance. International observers were to be invited to verify that the electoral process was genuine.

The Presidents, meeting in Honduras from 5 to 7 August 1989,[4] adopted the Tela Declaration, endorsing that plan, as well as assistance in the voluntary demobilization of all those involved in armed action in the countries of the region. They endorsed a 7 August agreement between Honduras and Nicaragua by which the former would request the Security Council to dispatch to Honduras an international peace-keeping force and Nicaragua, upon the receipt of an official report on the implementation of the joint plan for demobilization, would withdraw the application it had filed against Honduras before the International Court of Justice (ICJ) in 1986,[5] charging it with border and transborder armed actions. On 14 August 1989,[6] the Central American countries officially requested the United Nations and the Organization of American States (OAS) to set up an International Support and Verification Commission (CIAV) to implement the demobilization and repatriation plan provided for in the Tela Declaration.

The Central American Presidents, meeting again in December,[7] reaffirmed in the Declaration of San Isidro de Coronado (Costa Rica) their condemnation of the armed action and terrorism by irregular forces in Central America and reiterated their conviction that the people of the region must reject the use of force and terror to achieve political ends. They expressed their support for the Government of El Salvador, appealed to Frente

Farabundo Martí para la Liberación Nacional (FMLN) to cease hostilities and requested the Secretary-General to ensure resumption of the dialogue between the Government and FMLN. The Presidents called on Nicaragua to contact the United Nations Observer Group in Central America (ONUCA) and CIAV so that the demobilization of the Nicaraguan resistance in Honduras could begin. They appealed to Nicaragua and El Salvador to end their estrangement through negotiation and to continue their diplomatic and consular relations.

The necessity to establish a firm and lasting peace in Central America was emphasized by the Secretary-General at the International Conference on Central American Refugees (Guatemala City, 29-31 May) (see PART THREE, Chapter XV). On 15 December, the General Assembly, in **resolution 44/139**, expressed satisfaction with the adoption by the Conference of the Declaration and Concerted Plan of Action in favour of Central American Refugees, Returnees and Displaced Persons.

Women and peace in Central America and women, human rights and development in Central America were related items considered by the Economic and Social Council. The Council, in **resolution 1989/35**, welcomed progress in the peace process and exhorted the Governments of Central America to ensure full participation of women at all levels in the search for peace, pluralism, democracy and overall development. In **resolution 1989/39**, the Council urged the international community to support greater participation of women in the processes of change and in the bodies involved in negotiations and dialogue.

Report of the Secretary-General (June). Responding to a 1988 General Assembly request,[8] the Secretary-General submitted in June 1989 a report[9] on the situation in Central America. In his continuing efforts to assist the peace process, he had met in New York on 8 February with the Foreign Ministers of the five Central American countries. At their request, he had appointed a technical group of the Secretariat to draft proposals for establishing machinery to verify security commitments. Those proposals, which were considered at a technical meeting held in New York on 14 and 15 March with Central American Governments, provided for the creation of ONUCA, to be deployed in the territorities of the five Central American countries. On 31 March,[10] the Ministers requested the Secretary-General to set in motion the verification mechanism. However, on 14 April,[11] the Secretary-General informed the Ministers that, due to the reservation of Honduras subordinating establishment of the mechanism to the effective fulfilment of the February commitment of Central American Presidents to seek negotiated solutions, he was

unable to respond to their request; efforts to overcome that obstacle had so far been unsuccessful.

Also in April,[12] he had informed the President of the General Assembly of Nicaragua's request for him to set up a group of observers to verify implementation of the democratization and national reconciliation measures in that country, as well as the genuineness of the electoral process (see below).

SECURITY COUNCIL ACTION

On 27 July, the Security Council met in accordance with the understanding reached at prior consultations. The Council, having considered the Secretary-General's report, unanimously adopted **resolution 637(1989)**.

The Security Council,

Recalling its resolutions 530(1983) of 19 May 1983 and 562(1985) of 10 May 1985 and General Assembly resolutions 38/10 of 11 November 1983, 39/4 of 26 October 1984, 41/37 of 18 November 1986, 42/1 of 7 October 1987 and 43/24 of 15 November 1988, as well as the initiative that the Secretary-General of the United Nations undertook on 18 November 1986 together with the Secretary General of the Organization of American States,

Convinced that the peoples of Central America wish to achieve a peaceful settlement of their conflicts without outside interference, including support for irregular forces, with respect for the principles of self-determination and non-intervention while ensuring full respect for human rights,

Taking note of the report of the Secretary-General of 26 June 1989 submitted in pursuance of Security Council resolutions 530(1983) and 562(1985),

Recognizing the important contribution of the Contadora Group and its Support Group in favour of peace in Central America,

Welcoming the agreement on "Procedures for the establishment of a firm and lasting peace in Central America" signed at Guatemala City on 7 August 1987 by the Presidents of the Republics of Costa Rica, El Salvador, Guatemala, Honduras and Nicaragua as the manifestation of the will of the peoples of Central America to achieve peace, democratization, reconciliation, development and justice, in accordance with their decision to meet the historical challenge of forging a peaceful destiny for the region,

Welcoming also the subsequent Joint Declarations issued by the Central American Presidents on 16 January 1988 at Alajuela, Costa Rica and on 14 February 1989 at Costa del Sol, El Salvador,

Aware of the importance which the Central American Presidents attach to the role of international verification as an essential component for the implementation of the above-mentioned instruments, including, in particular, their commitments relating to regional security, especially non-use of territory to support destabilization of neighbouring countries, and democratization, especially free and fair elections, as well as to the voluntary demobilization, repatriation or relocation of irregular forces, as agreed in the Costa del Sol accord of 14 February 1989,

Aware also that the commitments enshrined in the Guatemala agreement form a harmonious and indivisible whole,

Noting with appreciation the efforts undertaken to date by the Secretary-General in support of the Central American peace process, including his assistance in the establishment of appropriate mechanisms to verify compliance with the provisions of the Guatemala agreement and of the Joint Declaration adopted by the Central American Presidents at their meeting held in El Salvador on 14 February 1989, and particularly the Secretary-General's agreement with Nicaragua to deploy a United Nations observer mission to verify the electoral process,

1. *Commends* the desire for peace expressed by the Central American Presidents in signing on 7 August 1987 at Guatemala City the agreement on "Procedures for the establishment of a firm and lasting peace in Central America" and in the Joint Declarations subsequently signed in pursuance of it;

2. *Expresses its firmest support* for the Guatemala agreement and the Joint Declarations;

3. *Calls upon* the Presidents to continue their efforts to achieve a firm and lasting peace in Central America through the faithful implementation of the commitments entered into in the Guatemala agreement and in the expressions of good will contained in the Joint Declaration of 14 February 1989;

4. *Appeals* to all States, in particular to those which have links with the region and interests in it, to back the political will of the Central American countries to comply with the provisions of the Guatemala agreement and of the Joint Declaration, particularly that regional and extra-regional Governments which either openly or covertly supply aid to irregular forces or insurrectional movements in the area immediately halt such aid, with the exception of the humanitarian aid that contributes to the goals of the Costa del Sol accord;

5. *Lends* its full support to the Secretary-General to continue his mission of good offices, in consultation with the Security Council, in support of the Central American Governments in their effort to achieve the goals set forth in the Guatemala agreement;

6. *Requests* the Secretary-General to report to the Security Council regularly on the implementation of the present resolution.

Security Council resolution 637(1989)

27 July 1989   Meeting 2871   Adopted unanimously

Draft prepared in consultations among Council members (S/20752)

Report of the Secretary-General (October). In an October addendum to his June report,[13] the Secretary-General noted that the Central American Presidents, in the Tela Declaration adopted at their August summit,[4] had invited him and the Secretary General of the Organization of American States (OAS) to establish ONUCA and CIAV. The invitation to set up CIAV was reiterated in a letter of 14 August.[6] By a letter of 10 August,[14] Honduras confirmed that it had withdrawn its reservation regarding the establishment of ONUCA. In response, he sent a reconnaissance mission to the region in September, headed by

Brigadier Péricles Ferreira Gomes of the United Nations Angola Verification Mission. He undertook to submit a report to the Security Council based on the mission's recommendations.

The Secretary-General had agreed with the Secretary General of OAS to establish CIAV with effect from 6 September and they had defined its terms of reference. The Security Council approved the steps taken and welcomed the Secretary-General's intention to establish a military unit to ensure the collection and custody of weapons and other military equipment. The United Nations High Commissioner for Refugees (UNHCR) had been requested to assist in the voluntary relocation and protection of members of the Nicaraguan resistance and their families. Further assistance to the returnees would be provided under the United Nations Special Plan of Economic Co-operation for Central America (see PART THREE, Chapter III).

Since the establishment of CIAV, frequent consultations had been held with Central American Governments, the United States and the Nicaraguan resistance on the establishment of the bases for the execution of the joint plan of demobilization.

According to the Secretary-General, the new climate of détente had been strengthened by the agreement reached on 15 September in Mexico City between El Salvador and FMLN to initiate dialogue for a political settlement of the armed conflict in El Salvador. He had accepted the invitation of both parties to attend their next meeting, scheduled for 16 and 17 October at San José, Costa Rica, and on 1 September had appointed Alvaro de Soto as his personal representative for the peace process in Central America.

The Secretary-General concluded that the situation in Central America had considerably improved since his last report, to the point where political solutions to the main conflicts in the region could be envisaged. The electoral process in Nicaragua and the execution of the joint plan provided an opportunity for national reconciliation. The establishment of ONUCA similarly would contribute to creating confidence in the region and should help promote an environment more favourable to dialogue, particularly the one initiated between the Government of El Salvador and FMLN.

GENERAL ASSEMBLY ACTION

On 23 October, the General Assembly adopted without vote **resolution 44/10**.

**The situation in Central America:
threats to international peace and
security and peace initiatives**

The General Assembly,

Recalling Security Council resolutions 530(1983) of 19 May 1983, 562(1985) of 10 May 1985 and 637(1989) of

27 July 1989 and its resolutions 38/10 of 11 November 1983, 39/4 of 26 October 1984, 41/37 of 18 November 1986, 42/1 of 7 October 1987 and 43/24 of 15 November 1988, as well as the initiative of the Secretaries-General of the United Nations and of the Organization of American States of 18 November 1986,

Taking note of the reports of the Secretary-General of 26 June and 17 October 1989, submitted in pursuance of General Assembly resolution 43/24,

Convinced that the peoples of Central America wish to achieve peace, reconciliation, development and justice, without outside interference, in accordance with their own decision and their own historical experience, and without sacrificing the principles of self-determination and non-intervention,

Aware that the agreement on "Procedures for the establishment of a firm and lasting peace in Central America" signed at Guatemala City on 7 August 1987 by the Presidents of the Republics of Costa Rica, El Salvador, Guatemala, Honduras and Nicaragua, at the Esquipulas II summit meeting, is the outcome of the decision by Central Americans to take up fully the historical challenge of forging a peaceful destiny for Central America,

Aware also of the political will which inspires them to settle their differences by means of dialogue, negotiation and respect for the legitimate interests of all States, establishing commitments to be fulfilled in good faith, through the verifiable performance of actions aimed at achieving peace, democracy, security, co-operation and respect for human rights,

Welcoming the joint declarations adopted by the Central American Presidents at Alajuela, Costa Rica, on 16 January 1988, and at Costa del Sol, El Salvador, on 14 February 1989,

Taking note with special satisfaction of the agreements reached by the Central American Presidents at Tela, Honduras, on 7 August 1989, comprising the Tela Declaration, the Joint Plan for the voluntary demobilization, repatriation or relocation in Nicaragua or third countries of the members of the Nicaraguan resistance and their families, as well as assistance for the demobilization of all those involved in armed actions in the countries of the region when such persons voluntarily request it, and the agreement signed by Honduras and Nicaragua with the moral support of the leaders of Costa Rica, El Salvador and Guatemala,

Noting the action taken by the Secretaries-General of the United Nations and of the Organization of American States in support of the agreements of the Central American Presidents, in particular those relating to the establishment and functioning of the International Support and Verification Commission entrusted with the implementation of the Joint Plan for the voluntary demobilization, repatriation or relocation of the members of the Nicaraguan resistance and their families, and of other irregular forces when they request it,

Recognizing the importance of the action taken by the Secretary-General for the establishment of the United Nations Observer Group in Central America at the request of the Governments of the region, with a view to the adoption of the necessary measures for setting in motion the on-site verification machinery in fulfilment of the security commitments emanating from the agreement signed at the Esquipulas II summit meeting and subsequent declarations,

Noting the importance attached by the Central American Presidents to the function of international verification of the electoral processes in the region, in accordance with the provisions of the agreement signed at the Esquipulas II summit meeting, and the declaration adopted at Costa del Sol,

Welcoming the invitation extended through a sovereign decision by the Government of Nicaragua to the Secretary-General to establish, within the context of the Central American peace process, a group of observers to verify each and every stage of the electoral process in Nicaragua, a process that is to culminate in national elections scheduled for 25 February 1990, as well as the positive response of the Secretary-General,

Noting with interest the agreement signed on 15 September 1989 at Mexico City by the Government of El Salvador and the Frente Farabundo Martí para la Liberación Nacional to continue the process of dialogue in an effort to reach an understanding through political agreements that would put an end to the armed conflict by political means in the shortest possible time, as well as to encourage the democratization of the country and to reunify Salvadorian society, and the decision of the Secretary-General to accept the invitation extended to him by the above-mentioned parties for the United Nations to participate as a witness in the meeting held at San José from 16 to 18 October 1989,

Recognizing the unfailing determination and the decisive contribution of the Contadora Group and its Support Group in favour of peace in Central America,

Bearing in mind the particular importance which the implementation of its resolution 42/231 of 12 May 1988 concerning the Special Plan of Economic Co-operation for Central America and other relevant resolutions has for the improvement of the living standards of the Central American people,

1. *Commends* the desire for peace expressed by the Central American Presidents in signing on 7 August 1987 at Guatemala City the agreement on "Procedures for the establishment of a firm and lasting peace in Central America" and in issuing their subsequent declarations and agreements;

2. *Expresses* its strongest support for these agreements;

3. *Exhorts* the Governments to continue their efforts to achieve a firm and lasting peace in Central America and expresses its fervent hopes for the effective implementation of the agreements signed at Tela, Honduras, on 7 August 1989;

4. *Appeals* to the countries which are outside the region but which have links with it and interests in it to facilitate the implementation of the agreements concluded by the Central American Presidents and to abstain from any action which may impede such implementation;

5. *Fully supports* the Secretary-General of the United Nations in the performance of the functions which the Central American Presidents, at the Tela summit meeting, entrusted to him as a member of the International Support and Verification Commission, together with the Secretary General of the Organization of American States;

6. *Requests* the Secretary-General to continue to afford the fullest possible support to the Central American Governments in their efforts to achieve peace, especially by taking the measures necessary for the

establishment and effective functioning of the verification machinery in respect of security, through the United Nations Observer Group in Central America;

7. *Supports* the agreement of the Secretary-General with the Government of Nicaragua concerning the establishment of the United Nations Observer Mission to verify the electoral process in Nicaragua, contained in the letter dated 6 July 1989 from the Secretary-General to the President of the General Assembly;

8. *Requests* the Secretary-General to report to it periodically during the present session on the progress of the United Nations Observer Mission to verify the electoral process in Nicaragua, which he established as an extraordinary measure related to the maintenance of international peace and security, as well as on the electoral process in Nicaragua, and to submit a final report to it on the results thereof;

9. *Urges* the international community and international organizations to increase their technical, economic and financial co-operation with the Central American countries for the implementation of the goals and objectives of the Special Plan of Economic Co-operation for Central America, as stipulated in General Assembly resolution 42/231, and as a way of assisting the efforts being made by the countries of the region to achieve peace and development;

10. *Requests* the Secretary-General to submit a preliminary report to the General Assembly during the first two weeks of December 1989 on progress made in implementing the present resolution and to submit a report thereon to the Assembly at its forty-fifth session;

11. *Decides* to include in the provisional agenda of its forty-fifth session the item entitled "The situation in Central America: threats to international peace and security and peace initiatives".

General Assembly resolution 44/10

23 October 1989   Meeting 35   Adopted without vote

17-nation draft (A/44/L.14/Rev.1 & Add.1); agenda item 34.

Sponsors: Argentina, Bolivia, Brazil, Chile, Colombia, Costa Rica, Ecuador, El Salvador, Guatemala, Honduras, Mexico, Nicaragua, Panama, Paraguay, Peru, Uruguay, Venezuela.

Report of the Secretary-General (December).
In a December report on the situation in Central America,[15] the Secretary-General detailed the continuing consultations by CIAV with the parties to the conflict and its proposals for: the creation of a climate of trust to encourage repatriation; the establishment of direct contact between the Nicaraguan Government and the resistance; a census of the members of the resistance and their families; and a survey mission to assess personnel and equipment requirements for the collection and custody of arms and other military equipment. However, in view of the persisting differences between the Government and the resistance relating to the implementation of the joint plan, CIAV had proposed that the two parties hold direct talks. At the same time, there was a breach of the cease-fire in Nicaragua and the Government announced its decision, with effect from 1 November, not to extend the unilateral declaration of the cease-fire which it had renewed on a monthly basis since

March 1988. After various initiatives, meetings between the two sides were held in November under the auspices of CIAV.

On 5 December, the Secretary General and the Secretary General of OAS were obliged to report to the five Central American Presidents that they had been unable to set in motion the joint plan contained in the Tela Declaration. Nevertheless, the Secretary-General noted, preliminary steps had been taken to lay the foundation for implementation of the plan, in conjunction with measures taken by UNHCR, the United Nations Development Programme and specialized agencies.

Based on his proposals, the Security Council on 7 November approved the establishment of ONUCA (see below).

The Secretary-General also reported on the United Nations Observer Mission for the Verification of the Electoral Process in Nicaragua (ONUVEN) and its work (see below). He also followed with concern the deteriorating situation in El Salvador (see below) and considered it urgent that substantive conversations be resumed between the Government and FMLN. He stated that he was prepared to make every effort to contribute to a just and lasting peace in that country.

Responding to the requests made to him by the Central American Presidents at San Isidro de Coronado, in December,[7] to ensure acceleration of the deployment and functioning of ONUCA and an expansion of its mandate to include verification of any cessation of hostilities and demobilization of irregular forces, as well as reinitiation of the dialogue between the Government of El Salvador and FMLN, the Secretary-General reported that he was taking steps to carry out those tasks.

UN Observer Group in Central America

On 7 November 1989, the Security Council, by **resolution 644(1989)**, established under its authority a United Nations Observer Group in Central America (ONUCA) as part of impartial machinery to verify implementation of the security provisions of Esquipulas II and the commitments made by the Central American Governments in subsequent joint declarations (see above). The Group's mandate was for an initial period of six months.

Reports of the Secretary-General. In his reports of June,[9] October[13] and December[15] on the Central American situation, the Secretary-General described the steps he had taken to respond to the requests of the five Central American Presidents to establish ONUCA to verify compliance with the security undertakings in respect of the 1987 Esquipulas II Agreements. An October report to the Council[16] reflected the operational concept of ONUCA, taking into account the findings and recommendations of a reconnaissance mission which had visited the region in September.

As requested by the Central American Governments, ONUCA's mandate would be to conduct on-site verification of the cessation of aid to irregular forces and insurrectionist movements and the non-use of the territory of one State for attacks on other States. Its monitoring and investigative functions would be performed by mobile teams of military observers. The Group would be under the command of a Chief Military Observer appointed by the Secretary-General. Headquartered at Tegucigalpa, Honduras, it would have liaison offices in each of the capitals of the five Central American countries and 33 verification centres, as well as a naval unit and an air wing. At full deployment, ONUCA would require a staff of about 260 military observers, 115 air crew and support personnel, 50 crew and support personnel for the naval unit, 14 medical staff, 104 international staff and 82 locally recruited civilians. The Secretary-General recommended that ONUCA be established for an initial six months, at an estimated cost of $41 million to be borne by Member States.

SECURITY COUNCIL ACTION

On 7 November, the Security Council met in accordance with the understanding reached in prior consultations. On the same date, the Council unanimously adopted **resolution 644(1989)**.

The Security Council,

Recalling its resolution 637(1989) of 27 July 1989,

1. *Approves* the report of the Secretary-General of 11 October 1989;

2. *Decides* to set up immediately, under its authority, a United Nations Observer Group in Central America and requests the Secretary-General to take the necessary steps to this effect, in accordance with his above-mentioned report, bearing in mind the need to continue to monitor expenditures carefully during this period of increasing demands on peace-keeping resources;

3. *Also decides* that the United Nations Observer Group in Central America shall be established for a period of six months, unless the Security Council decides otherwise;

4. *Requests* the Secretary-General to keep the Security Council fully informed of further developments.

Security Council resolution 644(1989)

7 November 1989   Meeting 2890   Adopted unanimously

Draft prepared in consultations among Council members (S/20951).

Following the vote, the President, after consultations with Council members, made a statement on their behalf:

"The members of the Security Council reaffirm their full support for the Secretary-General's efforts to assist the Central American Governments in their efforts to achieve the goals set forth in the Guatemala Agreement of 7 August 1987 and in the Joint Declarations subsequently signed in pursuance of it. In any consideration of the renewal of the mandate of ONUCA, they will wish to assure themselves that the presence of the observer group is continuing to contribute actively to the achievement of a firm and lasting peace in Central America."

Composition

On 16 November,[17] the Secretary-General, following consultations with the parties, proposed to the Security Council that the following countries should contribute personnel to ONUCA: *(a)* military observers: Canada, Colombia, Ireland, Spain and Venezuela; *(b)* logistics units: Canada, Venezuela and civilian elements from the Federal Republic of Germany. On the same date,[18] he informed the Council of his intention to appoint Major-General Agustín Quesada Gómez of Spain as ONUCA's Chief Military Observer.

The Council agreed to the Secretary-General's proposals on 21 November.[19]

Financing

On 20 November, at the request of the Secretary-General,[20] the General Assembly, by **decision 44/402**, included an additional item on financing of ONUCA in the agenda of its 1989 session. In a report accompanying his request,[21] the Secretary-General set out ONUCA's financial requirements, including cost estimates totalling $40.8 million gross ($40.2 million net) for the initial six-month period. That figure incorporated commitments of $3,450,000 to meet expenses of an immediate nature.

The Advisory Committee on Administrative and Budgetary Questions (ACABQ)[22] recommended approval of an appropriation of $40.8 million gross ($40.2 million net) for ONUCA from 7 November 1989 to 6 May 1990, including the commitments of $3,450,000 to meet initial expenses, and authorization for commitments not to exceed $4,524,100 gross per month for the period beginning 7 May 1990, should the Security Council renew ONUCA's mandate. At the same time, the Advisory Committee emphasized that the Secretary-General should endeavour to maximize savings through efficient use of resources; as uncertainties diminished, he should adjust expenditure estimates in line with the actual situation.

GENERAL ASSEMBLY ACTION

On 7 December, on the recommendation of the Fifth (Administrative and Budgetary) Committee, the General Assembly adopted without vote **resolution 44/44.**

Financing of the United Nations Observer Group in Central America

The General Assembly,

Having considered the report of the Secretary-General on the financing of the United Nations Observer Group in Central America and the related report of the Advisory Committee on Administrative and Budgetary Questions,

Bearing in mind Security Council resolution 644(1989) of 7 November 1989, by which the Council established the United Nations Observer Group in Central America for a period of six months,

Recognizing that the costs of the Group are expenses of the Organization to be borne by Member States in accordance with Article 17, paragraph 2, of the Charter of the United Nations,

Mindful of the fact that it is essential to provide the Group with the necessary financial resources to enable it to fulfil its responsibilities under the relevant resolution of the Security Council,

Urging all Member States to make every effort to ensure payment of their assessed contributions to the Group in full and on time,

Recognizing that in order to meet the expenditures caused by the Group, a different procedure from the one applied to meet expenditures of the regular budget of the United Nations is required,

Taking into account the fact that the economically more developed countries are in a position to make relatively larger contributions and that the economically less developed countries have a relatively limited capacity to contribute towards such an operation,

Bearing in mind the special responsibilities of the States permanent members of the Security Council, as indicated in General Assembly resolution 1874(S-IV) of 27 June 1963, in the financing of the Group,

Mindful of the views expressed in the Fifth Committee on the requests of some Member States to change their placement in the existing groups ''b'', ''c'' and ''d'' of Member States, on the basis of the criteria set out in General Assembly resolution 3101(XXVIII) of 11 December 1973,

1. *Concurs* with the observations, recommendations and conclusions contained in the report of the Advisory Committee on Administrative and Budgetary Questions;

2. *Decides* to appropriate an amount of 40.8 million United States dollars, inclusive of the amount of 3,450,000 dollars authorized with the concurrence of the Advisory Committee, under the terms of General Assembly resolution 42/227 of 21 December 1987, for the operation of the United Nations Observer Group in Central America from 7 November 1989 to 6 May 1990, inclusive, and requests the Secretary-General to establish a special account for the Group;

3. *Decides also*, as an *ad hoc* arrangement, to apportion the amount of 40.8 million dollars for the above-mentioned period among the States Members of the United Nations, in accordance with the composition of groups set out in paragraphs 3 and 4 of General Assembly resolution 43/232 of 1 March 1989, to be adjusted by the decision to be taken by the Assembly, at its forty-fourth session, on the composition of groups ''a'', ''b'', ''c'' and ''d'' of Member States and taking into account the scale of assessments for the years 1989, 1990 and 1991;

4. *Decides further* that, in accordance with the provisions of its resolution 973(X) of 15 December 1955, there shall be set off against the apportionment among the Member States, as provided for in paragraph 3 of the present resolution, their respective share in the Tax Equalization Fund of the estimated staff assessment income of 600,000 dollars approved for the above-mentioned period;

5. *Authorizes* the Secretary-General to enter into commitments for the Group at a rate not to exceed 4,524,100 dollars gross (4,389,500 dollars net) per month, with the prior concurrence of the Advisory Committee, for the twelve-month period beginning 7 May 1990, should the Security Council decide to renew the mandate of the Group beyond the period of six months authorized under its resolution 644(1989), the said amount to be apportioned among Member States in accordance with the scheme set out in paragraphs 3 and 4 of the present resolution;

6. *Invites* voluntary contributions to the Group both in cash and in the form of services and supplies acceptable to the Secretary-General, to be administered, as appropriate, in accordance with the procedure to be established by the General Assembly at its forty-fourth session;

7. *Requests* the Secretary-General to take all necessary action to ensure that the Group is administered with the maximum of efficiency and economy, bearing in mind the relevant observations contained in the report of the Advisory Committee;

8. *Decides* to include in the provisional agenda of its forty-fifth session the item entitled ''Financing of the United Nations Observer Group in Central America'' and in this connection requests the Secretary-General to submit appropriate documentation.

General Assembly resolution 44/44

7 December 1989   Meeting 77   Adopted without vote

Approved by Fifth Committee (A/44/847) without vote, 5 December (meeting 53); 12-nation draft (A/C.5/44/L.9/Rev.1); agenda item 159.

Sponsors: Canada, Colombia, Costa Rica, El Salvador, Germany, Federal Republic of, Guatemala, Honduras, Ireland, Japan, Nicaragua, Spain, Venezuela.

Meeting numbers. GA 44th session: 5th Committee 50-53; plenary 61, 77.

Nicaragua

In February 1989, Nicaragua announced its decision to hold national elections no later than 25 February 1990 and, referring to the Joint Declaration of the five Central American Presidents,[3] requested the Secretary-General to establish a group of observers to verify that the electoral process was genuine.

On 6 June,[23] the Secretary-General reported to the President of the General Assembly that he had sent several missions to Nicaragua in connection with that request, primarily to make contact with Government and electoral authorities as well as opposition parties, and to observe the debate in the National Assembly on the reforms of the electoral laws and those regulating the mass media and to study the new legislation. He had also suggested to the Secretary General of OAS that the two organizations jointly carry out Nicaragua's request with respect to creating a verification machinery. The Secretary General of OAS replied on 22 June that OAS had already begun the observation, but that he attached special importance to an exchange of views and dialogue on the possible form and modalities of collaboration.

On 6 July,[24] the Secretary-General informed the Assembly President of his decision to establish a United Nations Observer Mission to verify the electoral process in Nicaragua, referring to a 1988 Assembly resolution on the situation in Central America[8] as authority for his action. The Secretary-General explained that his decision should not be construed as any kind of value judgement as to the laws in force governing the electoral process. He also proposed that the Mission have unrestricted freedom of movement within all electoral districts, unrestricted access to all polling stations and unimpeded contacts with all political parties.

The Security Council, in **resolution 637(1989)**, noted with appreciation the Secretary-General's agreement with Nicaragua to deploy a United Nations election observer mission to the country.

On 4 August, the President of Nicaragua and the political parties, in the presence of observers from the United Nations, OAS and the Centre for Democracy and in accordance with the February Agreement of Central American Presidents, signed an agreement setting out legal and political conditions for a free and just electoral process.[25]

UN Observer Mission for electoral verification

The United Nations Observer Mission for the Verification of the Electoral Process in Nicaragua (ONUVEN) was established on 25 August. The Secretary-General appointed Elliott Richardson as his Personal Representative to oversee the Mission's activities, Iqbal Riza as Chief of Mission and Horatio Boneo as Deputy Chief.

Under ONUVEN's terms of reference, as agreed between the United Nations and the Government, it was to verify that political parties were equitably represented in the Supreme Electoral Council and its subsidiary bodies, that they enjoyed complete freedom of organization and mobilization and equal access to State television and radio, and that electoral rolls were properly drawn up; inform the Supreme Electoral Council of complaints and irregularities; and report to the Secretary-General.

ONUVEN's first report,[26] which covered the period from 5 July, i.e., the date of the exchange of letters between Nicaragua and the Secretary-General regarding the establishment of the Mission, to 30 September, outlined the steps taken by Nicaragua in preparation for national elections,

including amendments to the Constitution introduced by a new Electoral Act and the establishment of the Supreme Electoral Council. The report described the organization of Nicaraguan political parties and coalitions; the initiation of political and electoral activity; and co-operation between the United Nations and OAS. In its conclusion, the report stated that all levels of the electoral authority were put in place and the organization of parties and coalitions almost completed.

The Mission's second report,[27] covering events in October and November, analysed the functioning of the electoral authority; the preparation of the electoral rolls; the organization of political parties; the progress of the electoral campaign; and the use of the mass media.

Summarizing ONUVEN's main observations, the report noted that voter registration had been satisfactorily concluded. However, there was concern that the electoral process would be threatened by the increase in political tension resulting partly from a resumption of military activity and interruption of the cease-fire. In addition, the political debate was surprisingly aggressive and attacks on opponents had reached unacceptable levels. Another source of concern was the persistence in discrediting the electoral authority, predictions of electoral fraud and reiteration of the argument that fraud would be the only possible explanation for any defeat in the election. Also alarming was the violence of the language used in the media and the manipulation of information on both sides.

In his December report on the situation in Central America (see above),[15] the Secretary-General said that, despite interruption of the cease-fire, the electoral process in Nicaragua was proceeding in a generally positive way.

Financing

In December,[28] the Secretary-General reported to the Fifth Committee that commitments for ONUVEN were entered into for 1989 with the concurrence of ACABQ, under the 1987 General Assembly resolution on unforeseen and extraordinary expenses for the 1988-1989 biennium.[29] Requirements of ONUVEN up to 31 December 1989 amounted to $3,166,700, i.e., $296,500 lower than the initial amount of $3,463,200 authorized by the Advisory Committee in September. For the completion of the Mission during the period 1 January to 30 April 1990, the Secretary-General estimated requirements of $2,398,300. ACABQ, in December,[30] recommended approval of that additional appropriation.

Other developments

On 20 March 1989,[31] Honduras, in response to a 15 March communiqué of the Co-ordinating Bureau of the Movement of Non-Aligned Countries,[32] denied having received any request by the United States to keep Nicaraguan insurgent forces in its territory. However, on 29 March[33] and again on 6 April,[34] Nicaragua, by letters to the Secretary-General, said that the bipartisan agreement announced by the United States Administration and Congress on 24 March to continue funding counter-revolutionary forces based in Honduras until February 1990 was an outrage against international law and a disregard for the spirit of the agreements concluded by the five Central American Governments.

On 16 April,[35] Nicaragua called on the United States to halt immediately all aid for irregular forces and insurrectionist movements, except humanitarian aid, and declared its willingness to discuss with the United States mutual security interests and to work towards establishing relations of mutual trust and respect. The United States responded on 21 April[36] that Nicaragua's charges were unfounded and that its aid fell clearly within the definition of humanitarian assistance in the Esquipulas II Agreement and was supported by all signatories except Nicaragua.

In May,[37] Nicaragua alleged that the United States was continuing to foment war in Central America and referred to incidents between 1 January and 15 May, in which hundreds of civilians were killed or wounded by counter-revolutionary forces and casualties were sustained by both its forces and the mercenary forces. In June,[38] Nicaragua protested to the United States continued acts of terrorism perpetrated by mercenary forces, citing an 8 June attack on a hydroelectric plant. Also in June, it protested to Honduras[39] against the continued presence of mercenaries on Honduran territory, in disregard of the Esquipulas Agreements and to the United States[40] for intervening in its internal affairs through the reported backing by representatives of the United States Congress of covert assistance to opposition parties in Nicaragua.

Further attacks on Nicaraguan civilians during the period from 21 to 24 June were brought by Nicaragua to the attention of the United States,[41] and of the Secretary-General for the period from 3 to 11 July.[42] By another letter to the United States,[43] Nicaragua complained that on 21 October counter-revolutionary forces had ambushed two trucks of the Sandinist People's Army, killing 17 persons and wounding 8 others.

By a communiqué of 1 November,[44] Nicaragua requested a meeting at United Nations Headquarters on 6 and 7 November between Honduras and Nicaragua, CIAV and representatives of the counter-revolutionary forces to agree on the logistical and other technical arrangements for the relocation, repatriation and integration into the political process of persons linked to counter-revolutionary activity. On 2 November,[45] Nicaragua announced its decision not to extend the unilateral cease-fire, in view of increased military activity by the counter-revolutionary forces, which, it charged, threatened the electoral process.

On 12 December 1989, in connection with the Application filed in 1986 by Nicaragua against Honduras before the International Court of Justice (ICJ), relating to alleged border and transborder armed activities,[5] both countries agreed to set up a bilateral commission to seek an out-of-court settlement to the dispute within six months, to communicate this agreement immediately to ICJ and to request the Court to postpone until 11 June 1990 the setting of the deadline for submission of the Honduran counter-memorial. The two countries also agreed, in the event that no settlement was reached within the specified time, to request ICJ to allow Honduras six months for submitting the counter-memorial (see PART FIVE, Chapter I).

Compliance with 1986 ICJ Judgment

Responding to a 1988 General Assembly resolution,[46] the Secretary-General, in November 1989,[47] reported that there had been no new developments regarding compliance with ICJ's 1986 Judgment concerning military and paramilitary activities in and against Nicaragua (Nicaragua v. United States).[48] In its annual report,[49] the Court pointed out that, failing agreement between the parties and at Nicaragua's request, it was in the process of deciding, in accordance with the 1986 Judgment on the merits of the case, the form and amount of the reparation owed by the United States to Nicaragua for "all injury caused to Nicaragua by certain breaches of obligations under international law committed by the United States". The Secretary-General noted that the United States had not participated in the proceedings to date, remaining of the view that ICJ was without jurisdiction to entertain the dispute. The Assembly, in **resolution 44/43**, reiterated once again its urgent call for full and immediate compliance with the Judgment, in conformity with the Charter.

Trade embargo

In response to a 1988 General Assembly resolution,[50] the Secretary-General, in November 1989,[51] submitted a report containing replies from Côte d'Ivoire, Ecuador, the German Democratic Republic, Nicaragua, Nigeria and the USSR in response to a note verbale of the Economic Commission for Latin America and the Caribbean requesting information from States on action undertaken in the context of the 1988 resolution deploring the trade embargo against Nicaragua. The replies conveyed the opposition of those countries to the embargo and their appeal for compliance with the relevant Assembly resolutions.

GENERAL ASSEMBLY ACTION

On 22 December 1989, on the recommendation of the Second (Economic and Financial) Committee, the General Assembly adopted **resolution 44/217** by recorded vote.

Trade embargo against Nicaragua

The General Assembly,

Recalling its resolutions 40/188 of 17 December 1985, 41/164 of 5 December 1986, 42/176 of 11 December 1987 and 43/185 of 20 December 1988, as well as its resolutions 42/204 of 11 December 1987, 42/231 of 12 May 1988 and 43/210 of 20 December 1988,

Taking note of the report of the Secretary-General on the trade embargo against Nicaragua,

1. *Deplores* the continuation of the trade embargo contrary to its resolutions 40/188, 41/164, 42/176 and 43/185 and to the Judgment of the International Court of Justice of 27 June 1986, and once again requests that those measures be immediately revoked;

2. *Requests* the Secretary-General to report to the General Assembly at its forty-fifth session on the implementation of the present resolution.

General Assembly resolution 44/217

22 December 1989   Meeting 85   82-2-47 (recorded vote)

Approved by Second Committee (A/44/746/Add.2) by recorded vote (78-2-32), 4 December (meeting 48); 8-nation draft (A/C.2/44/L.51); agenda item 82 *(b)*.

Sponsors: Algeria, Democratic Yemen, Libyan Arab Jamahiriya, Mexico, Nicaragua, Panama, Peru, Zimbabwe.

Meeting numbers. GA 44th session: 2nd Committee 44, 48; plenary 85.

Recorded vote in Assembly as follows:

In favour: Afghanistan, Albania, Algeria, Angola, Argentina, Australia, Austria, Bahamas, Barbados, Bolivia, Botswana, Brazil, Bulgaria, Burkina Faso, Byelorussian SSR, Cameroon, Cape Verde, China, Colombia, Congo, Cuba, Cyprus, Czechoslovakia, Democratic Yemen, Denmark, Ethiopia, Finland, German Democratic Republic, Ghana, Guinea, Guyana, Hungary, Iceland, India, Indonesia, Iran, Iraq, Ireland, Kenya, Kuwait, Lao People's Democratic Republic, Lesotho, Liberia, Libyan Arab Jamahiriya, Madagascar, Malawi, Malaysia, Mali, Mexico, Mongolia, Morocco, Mozambique, Myanmar, Nepal, New Zealand, Nicaragua, Nigeria, Norway, Pakistan, Papua New Guinea, Peru, Philippines, Romania, Sao Tome and Principe, Solomon Islands, Sudan, Suriname, Sweden, Syrian Arab Republic, Uganda, Ukrainian SSR, USSR, United Arab Emirates, United Republic of Tanzania, Uruguay, Vanuatu, Venezuela, Viet Nam, Yugoslavia, Zaire, Zambia, Zimbabwe.

Against: Israel, United States.

Abstaining: Antigua and Barbuda, Bahrain, Belgium, Brunei Darussalam, Burundi, Canada, Central African Republic, Chad, Chile, Costa Rica, Côte d'Ivoire, Djibouti, Dominica, Dominican Republic, Egypt, Fiji, France, Gambia, Germany, Federal Republic of, Greece, Italy, Jamaica, Japan, Jordan, Lebanon, Luxembourg, Malta, Netherlands, Niger, Oman, Portugal, Rwanda, Saint Lucia, Saint Vincent and the Grenadines, Samoa, Senegal, Sierra Leone, Singapore, Somalia, Spain, Sri Lanka, Togo, Trinidad and Tobago, Tunisia, Turkey, United Kingdom, Yemen.

Speaking after the vote in the Committee, the United States said it could not accept that the trade measures it had taken against Nicaragua were inappropriate or illegal; neither international law nor the United Nations Charter prohibited a State from protecting its security through the organization of its bilateral trade relations. The resolution furthermore did not take into account Nicaragua's destabilizing activities in the region nor its repressive domestic policies. In Nicaragua's view, however, the United States had not offered any new arguments to justify the trade embargo which, it believed, would not promote but only hinder democratic change.

El Salvador

In 1989, El Salvador continued to accuse the Frente Farabundo Martí para La Liberación Nacional–Frente Democrático Revolucionario (FMLN-FDR)—the Salvadorian opposition movement—of terrorist activities that it said were part of a guerrilla war designed to achieve a violent take-over of power. By a note of 9 June,[52] El Salvador informed the Secretary-General of the assassination that morning of the recently appointed Minister for the Presidency, Dr. José Antonio Rodríguez-Porth which, it charged, was perpetrated by FMLN as part of its irrational use of violence and terror. By a letter of 27 June,[53] El Salvador condemned the assassination of the Director-General of the National Firefighting Corps by FMLN Urban Commandos. Less than a month after the new Government had taken power, it said, FMLN was undermining the process of democratization by increasing violence and terror. By a 23 October communiqué,[54] El Salvador announced measures it had adopted to deal with the repatriation from Honduras of over 13,000 Salvadorian refugees. A Tripartite Commission, comprising El Salvador, Honduras and UNHCR, had established an operational plan for their repatriation, and the National Committee for returnees had prepared a national action plan, which was adopted by the Council of Ministers on 26 September.

The Co-ordinating Bureau of the Movement of Non-Aligned Countries, by a communiqué issued on 20 November[55] condemning indiscriminate acts of violence against the civilian population, appealed for an immediate cease-fire and called on the Government of El Salvador and FMLN to resume negotiations. Similar requests were made on 24 November[56] by Argentina, Brazil, Colombia, Mexico, Peru, Uruguay and Venezuela, members of the Permanent Mechanism for Consultation and Concerted Political Action.

On 27 November,[57] El Salvador requested the convening of the Security Council to consider actions by Nicaragua which it considered breaches of the agreements concluded by the Central American Presidents. Unless those breaches were brought to an end, El Salvador believed that not only would peace in Central America be threatened, but a conflict with incalculable consequences might be unleashed in the region. On 28 November,[58] Nicaragua requested that the scope of the Council meeting be expanded to include consider-

ation of the repercussions of the serious deterioration of the situation in El Salvador on the peace
process in Central America. On 29 November,
Nicaragua submitted a draft resolution[59] for
consideration by the Council calling for an immediate cease-fire.

SECURITY COUNCIL ACTION

The Security Council met on 30 November and
invited El Salvador and Nicaragua, at their request, to participate in the discussion without the
right to vote, in accordance with rule 37 of the
Council's provisional rules of procedure.[a]

On 8 December, following consultations among
the Security Council members, the Council President made a statement on their behalf:[60]

"The members of the Security Council, after hearing statements by the representatives of El Salvador
and Nicaragua at the 2896th meeting of the Security
Council, on 30 November 1989, express their grave
concern over the present situation in Central America,
in particular over the numerous acts of violence resulting in loss of lives and sufferings of the civilian population.

"The members of the Council reiterate their firm
support for the Esquipulas process of peaceful settlement in Central America and appeal to all States to
contribute to the urgent implementation of the agreements reached by the five Central American Presidents. In this regard the members of the Council welcome the announcement by the five Central American
Presidents to meet on 10 and 11 December at San José,
Costa Rica, in order to discuss, within the framework
of the Esquipulas peace process, solutions to the problems confronting them.

"The members of the Council consider that it is
primarily the responsibility of the five Central American Presidents to find solutions to the regional problems, in accordance with the Esquipulas Agreements.
Therefore, they reiterate their appeal to all States, including those with links to the region and interests
in it, to refrain from all actions that could impede the
achievement of a real and lasting settlement in Central America through negotiations.

"The members of the Security Council urge all parties concerned to co-operate in the search for peace
and a political solution.

"They also express their firm support for the ef-
forts being made by the Secretary-General of the
United Nations and the Secretary-General of the Or-
ganization of American States in the peace process.
In particular, they reiterate their full support for the
Secretary-General of the United Nations in the exer-
cise of the missions entrusted to him by the General
Assembly and the Security Council, as well as for the
early deployment of the United Nations Observer
Group in Central America."

Meeting numbers. SC 2896, 2897.

GENERAL ASSEMBLY ACTION

On 15 December, the General Assembly, by
resolution 44/165 appealed to the Government of

El Salvador and FMLN to end the armed conflict
and to resume the suspended dialogue in order to
end all hostilities within an agreed time-frame. It
supported the readiness of the Secretary-General
to help bring about an immediate agreement on
the cessation of the armed conflict and expressed
concern about the persistence of and increase
in the alleged activities of the so-called "death
squads" operating in El Salvador.

REFERENCES
[1]YUN 1987, p. 188. [2]YUN 1988, p. 169. [3]A/44/140-S/20491.
[4]A/44/451. [5]YUN 1986, p. 983. [6]A/44/464-S/20791.
[7]A/44/872-S/21019. [8]YUN 1988, p. 169, GA res. 43/24, 15
Nov. 1988. [9]A/44/344-S/20699. [10]A/44/287-S/20642.
[11]A/44/288-S/20643. [12]A/44/210. [13]A/44/344/Add.1-
S/20699/Add.1. [14]A/44/459-S/20786. [15]A/44/886-S/21029.
[16]S/20895. [17]S/20979. [18]S/20981. [19]S/20980, S/20982.
[20]A/44/246. [21]A/44/246/Add.1. [22]A/44/246/Add.2.
[23]A/44/304. [24]A/44/375. [25]A/44/445-S/20774. [26]A/44/642
& Corr.1. [27]A/44/834. [28]A/C.5/44/51. [29]YUN 1987, p. 1110,
GA res. 42/227, 21 Dec. 1987. [30]A/44/7/Add.8. [31]A/44/181-
S/20536. [32]A/44/177-S/20534. [33]A/44/205-S/20559.
[34]A/44/212-S/20570. [35]S/20599. [36]A/44/253-S/20605.
[37]A/44/286-S/20641. [38]S/20686. [39]A/44/335-S/20696.
[40]A/44/391-S/20731. [41]A/44/359-S/20705. [42]A/44/399-
S/20737. [43]S/20929. [44]A/44/701-S/20935. [45]A/44/704-
S/20939. [46]YUN 1988, p. 793, GA res. 43/11, 25 Oct. 1988.
[47]A/44/760. [48]YUN 1986, p. 981. [49]A/44/4. [50]YUN 1988,
p. 173, GA res. 43/185, 20 Dec. 1988. [51]A/44/581.
[52]A/44/320. [53]A/44/381. [54]A/44/688. [55]A/44/794-S/20985.
[56]S/20994. [57]S/20991. [58]S/20999. [59]S/21000. [60]S/21011.

Other questions
relating to the Americas

Panama–United States

In 1989, relations between Panama and the
United States worsened, with the former accusing the latter of interfering in its internal affairs
and violating the 1977 Panama Canal Treaties. In
elections held on 7 May, Guillermo Endara was
elected President. However, the country continued to be ruled by General Manuel Antonio
Noriega, who on 15 December declared a state of
war with the United States. In response, the
United States on 20 December sent military forces
into Panama.

Communication. By a statement issued on 24
April,[1] the President of Panama accused the
United States of further meddling in Panama's in-
ternal affairs by providing $10 million to opposi-

[a]Rule 37 of the Council's provisional rules of procedure states: "Any
Member of the United Nations which is not a member of the Security
Council may be invited, as the result of a decision of the Security Council, to participate, without vote, in the discussion of any question brought
before the Security Council when the Security Council considers that
the interests of that Member are specially affected, or when a Member
brings a matter to the attention of the Council in accordance with Article 35 (1) of the Charter."

tion groups for use in the election scheduled for 7 May, as well as through further military aggression, electronic warfare and bribery. Panama said it would take steps in international forums to denounce the violations by the United States of the Charters of the United Nations and of OAS.

SECURITY COUNCIL CONSIDERATION (April)

At the request of Panama,[2] the Security Council met on 28 April to consider what Panama called the grave situation resulting from flagrant intervention in its internal affairs by the United States, the policy of destabilization and coercion pursued by that country and the permanent threat of the use of force against Panama.

The President, with the consent of the Council, invited Panama, at its request, to participate in the discussion without the right to vote, in accordance with the relevant provisions of the Charter and rule 37ᵃ of the Council's provisional rules of procedure.

Addressing the Council, Panama accused the United States of interfering in its affairs, citing reports that the United States had approved a covert plan of operation which included the possible assassination of the Commander-in-Chief of the Panamanian Defence Forces and assistance to an opposition candidate. Panama said it also had to contend with the movement of United States armed units outside their defence sites, violations of its airspace, infiltration by United States intelligence units, overflights of Panamanian military defence installations, acts endangering civilian aviation in Panama, and allowing explosive devices to fall near Panamanian towns or abandoning them outside firing ranges. In addition, the United States had brought to Panama an offensive military team that had never before been part of the forces used to defend the Panama Canal. Panama further accused the United States of attempting to discredit the Panamanian electoral process by making accusations of alleged fraud and prejudicing international public opinion in advance with regard to the results. It charged that the United States planned to destabilize the country as a pretext for military intervention.

The United States replied that it had grave doubts over the fairness and freedom of the coming elections. Panama's crisis was not the result of United States interference, but of the policies of General Manuel Antonio Noriega who had arrogated to himself complete power over civic life and sponsored and countenanced widespread corruption, including drug trafficking and gunrunning. The Inter-American Commission on Human Rights of OAS had expressed serious concern about the extensive irregularities in the election process and evidence continued to mount that the military régime was subverting the election

through fraud, coercion and intimidation. The United States supported the Panamanian people in restoring genuine civilian democracy and was committed to the Panama Canal Treaties.

The Council President, before adjourning the meeting, said that the timing of the next meeting to continue consideration of the agenda item would be fixed in consultation with Council members.

Meeting number. SC 2861.

Further developments (May-July). On 11 May,[3] the European Community issued a declaration condemning the annulment of the Panamanian elections and the violence which took place during that process, particularly the aggression towards opposition leaders. On the same day,[4] the President of the United States, in announcing his country's support for initiatives by Governments in the hemisphere and in OAS to address the crisis, said he was recalling the United States Ambassador to Panama, reducing the embassy staff and relocating United States government employees and their dependants. He also said that the United States would continue economic sanctions, assert and enforce its rights under the Panama Canal Treaties, and augment its military forces in Panama.

On 18 May,[5] the Secretary General of OAS transmitted to the United Nations Secretary-General the decision of the Twenty-first Meeting of Consultation of Ministers of Foreign Affairs of OAS to entrust to the Foreign Ministers of Ecuador, Guatemala and Trinidad and Tobago the mission of urgently promoting compromise formulas leading to a national agreement which would ensure the early transfer of power in accordance with democratic mechanisms and on the basis of full respect for the sovereign wishes of the Panamanian people. By a communiqué of 22 May,[6] the Cabinet of Panama said the OAS action was outside the competence of the OAS Charter and incompatible with the United Nations Charter, ran counter to inter-American agreements and affronted Panama's national dignity. Panama welcomed any initiative that could establish the truth about the current crisis, but would never accept any act that interfered in matters of a sovereign nature.

In July,[7] Panama denounced what it called acts of provocation and military intimidation by United States forces, accused the United States[8] of making an incursion into Panamanian territory on 8 July and drew attention to press statements by the Chief of the United States Army Southern Command in Panama to the effect that the United States should impose a military solution.

On 7 August,[9] Panama requested a reconvening of the Security Council, in view of what it called a dangerous escalation of intimidation, provocation and aggression by the United States against it. The Council met on 11 August to resume its consideration of the situation in Panama. In accordance with its decision taken in April, the President invited Panama to participate in the debate without the right to vote.

Speaking before the Council, Panama said the increased activities of the United States armed forces, in violation of Panama's territorial integrity, had forced it to draw the Council's attention to the need to take specific measures to avert armed conflict. The situation had been worsened by United States measures violating the Panama Canal Treaties and other agreements. In 1977, Panama and the United States had signed treaties guaranteeing Panama full jurisdiction over the whole of its territory and providing the world with a neutral, safe Panama Canal open to ships of all flags. Panama called for military observers to be sent to the area immediately, and for a good offices mission by the Secretary-General, to avert an imminent breach of peace in the region.

The United States replied that it had augmented its military forces in Panama in direct response to the hostile actions of the Noriega régime. It accused Panama of violating the Panama Canal Treaties and wanting to divert attention from the OAS efforts to promote the surrender of power and a transition to legitimate, representative and democratic Government.

The Council took no action at this stage, and the President stated that the Council would reconvene at a later date to continue consideration of the item.

Meeting number. SC 2874

Further developments (August-December).
By a Proclamation issued on 31 August,[10] the General Council of State of Panama announced the establishment of a provisional Government and the assignment of Francisco Rodríguez-Poveda as Provisional President and Carlos Ozores Typaldos as Provisional Vice-President.

By a letter to the Secretary-General of 3 November[11] and a communiqué of 21 November,[12] Panama denounced the military actions by the United States between 30 October and 21 November. On 11 December,[13] the Provisional President informed the Secretary-General of statements made by senior United States officials that, although obliged to do so by the 1977 Panama Canal Treaties, their Government would not appoint the Panamanian national proposed by Panama to fill the post of Administrator of the Canal.

On 20 December,[14] the United States reported to the Security Council that, in accordance with Article 51 of the United Nations Charter, its forces had exercised their inherent right of self-defence by taking action in Panama in response to armed attacks by forces under the direction of Manuel Noriega following his 15 December declaration that a state of war existed with the United States.

On 20 December, the Security Council, at the request of Nicaragua,[15] resumed consideration of the situation in Panama. Following consultation among Council members, the President invited Nicaragua, at its request, to participate in the discussion without the right to vote, in accordance with rule 37[a] of the Council's provisional rules of procedure.

Nicaragua opened the debate charging that the United States, under the pretext of protecting American citizens, had committed an act of aggression by invading Panama and was trying to conceal a new and dramatic manifestation of its interventionist policy of force in Latin America. It had violated the United Nations Charter and international law, posing a threat not only to Latin America, but to international peace and security. The Security Council must condemn this outrage and demand immediate withdrawal of the invading troops.

The United States responded that its action in Panama was, in the light of armed attacks by General Noriega's forces, designed to protect American lives and fulfil its obligation to defend the integrity of the Panama Canal Treaties. An intolerable situation had built up in Panama over the preceding two years, with General Noriega having obstructed the elections of 7 May, while being involved in drug trafficking, endangering United States military personnel and jeopardizing the functioning of the Panama Canal. The United States acted in Panama with the approval of that country's democratically elected leaders; it intended to withdraw its forces as quickly as possible and was eager to work with the Panamanian people to rebuild their economy.

At the resumed meeting on 21 December, the President, with the consent of the Council, invited Cuba, El Salvador, the Libyan Arab Jamahiriya and Peru, at their request, to participate in the discussion without the right to vote, in accordance with rule 37[a] of the Council's provisional rules of procedure. The Council decided by a vote of 14 in favour (Algeria, Brazil, Canada, China, Colombia, Ethiopia, Finland, France, Malaysia, Nepal, Senegal, USSR, United Kingdom, Yugoslavia) to none, with 1 abstention (United States), that Panama should participate in the discussion without the right to vote, in accordance with rule 37.[a]

However, it requested the Secretary-General to report on the credentials of persons requesting participation in the debate as representatives of Panama.

When the Council resumed consideration of the item on 23 December, it considered the Secretary-General's report on the credentials of the representatives of Panama,[16] which indicated that the two requests to represent Panama at the Council meeting had emanated from contending authorities. The Secretary-General said that he was not in a position to formulate an opinion as to the adequacy of the credentials submitted. The Council noted the report and was informed by each of the requestors that they did not maintain their requests.

Following the debate, the Council put to the vote a draft resolution submitted by Algeria, Colombia, Ethiopia, Malaysia, Nepal, Senegal and Yugoslavia.[17] The resolution would have strongly deplored the United States intervention and demanded immediate withdrawal of United States forces. The text received 10 votes in favour (Algeria, Brazil, China, Colombia, Ethiopia, Malaysia, Nepal, Senegal, USSR, Yugoslavia), 4 against (Canada, France, United Kingdom, United States), with one abstention (Finland), and was not adopted due to the negative vote of three permanent Council members.

Meeting numbers. SC 2899-2902.

GENERAL ASSEMBLY ACTION

By a letter dated 20 December,[18] Cuba and Nicaragua requested the General Assembly to include a priority item entitled "Grave situation in Panama" in the agenda of its 1989 session, to be considered in plenary. In an explanatory memorandum, they said that on 20 December, the United States had invaded Panama, thereby committing a flagrant violation of the Charter and international law. Also appended was a draft resolution for consideration by the Assembly.

On 29 December, the Assembly adopted **resolution 44/240** by recorded vote.

Effects of the military intervention by the United States of America in Panama on the situation in Central America

The General Assembly,

Taking note of the statements made in the General Assembly and the Security Council regarding the invasion of Panama,

Reaffirming the sovereign and inalienable right of Panama to determine freely its social, economic and political system and to develop its international relations without any form of foreign intervention, interference, subversion, coercion or threat,

Recalling that, in accordance with Article 2, paragraph 4, of the Charter of the United Nations, all Member States shall refrain in their international relations from the threat or use of force against the territorial integrity or political independence of any State, or in any other manner inconsistent with the purposes of the United Nations,

Reaffirming the need to restore conditions which will guarantee the full exercise of the human rights and fundamental freedoms of the Panamanian people,

Expressing its profound concern at the serious consequences the armed intervention by the United States of America in Panama might have for peace and security in the Central American region,

1. *Strongly deplores* the intervention in Panama by the armed forces of the United States of America, which constitutes a flagrant violation of international law and of the independence, sovereignty and territorial integrity of States;

2. *Demands* the immediate cessation of the intervention and the withdrawal from Panama of the armed invasion forces of the United States;

3. *Demands also* full respect for and strict observance of the letter and spirit of the Torrijos-Carter Treaties;

4. *Calls upon* all States to uphold and respect the sovereignty, independence and territorial integrity of Panama;

5. *Requests* the Secretary-General to monitor the developments in Panama and to report to the General Assembly within twenty-four hours after the adoption of the present resolution.

General Assembly resolution 44/240

29 December 1989   Meeting 88   75-20-40 (recorded vote)

10-nation draft (A/44/L.63 & Add.1); agenda item 34.
Sponsors: Cuba, Ethiopia, Iran, Libyan Arab Jamahiriya, Mongolia, Nicaragua, United Republic of Tanzania, Viet Nam, Zambia, Zimbabwe.
Meeting numbers. GA 44th session: plenary 35, 86-88.

Recorded vote in Assembly as follows:

In favour: Afghanistan, Albania, Algeria, Angola, Argentina, Austria, Barbados, Belize, Bhutan, Bolivia, Botswana, Brazil, Bulgaria, Burkina Faso, Burundi, Byelorussian SSR, Chile, China, Colombia, Congo, Cuba, Cyprus, Czechoslovakia, Democratic Yemen, Ecuador, Equatorial Guinea, Ethiopia, Finland, German Democratic Republic, Ghana, Guatemala, Guinea, Guyana, Haiti, Hungary, India, Indonesia, Iran, Iraq, Jamaica, Jordan, Kuwait, Lao People's Democratic Republic, Libyan Arab Jamahiriya, Malaysia, Mali, Mauritius, Mexico, Mongolia, Myanmar, Nepal, Nicaragua, Pakistan, Paraguay, Peru, Romania, Solomon Islands, Spain, Sri Lanka, Sudan, Suriname, Sweden, Syrian Arab Republic, Trinidad and Tobago, Uganda, Ukrainian SSR, USSR, United Republic of Tanzania, Uruguay, Vanuatu, Venezuela, Viet Nam, Yugoslavia, Zambia, Zimbabwe.
Against: Australia, Belgium, Canada, Denmark, Dominica, El Salvador, France, Germany, Federal Republic of, Israel, Italy, Japan, Luxembourg, Netherlands, New Zealand, Norway, Panama, Portugal, Turkey, United Kingdom, United States.
Abstaining: Antigua and Barbuda, Bahrain, Brunei Darussalam, Cape Verde,* Central African Republic, Chad, Costa Rica, Egypt, Fiji, Greece, Grenada, Honduras, Iceland, Ireland, Kenya, Lebanon, Liberia, Madagascar, Malawi, Malta, Morocco, Niger, Oman, Papua New Guinea, Philippines, Poland, Qatar, Rwanda, Saint Lucia, Saint Vincent and the Grenadines, Samoa, Saudi Arabia, Singapore, Somalia, Thailand, Togo, Tunisia, United Arab Emirates, Yemen, Zaire.

*Subsequently informed the Secretariat that it had intended not to participate in the voting.

Speaking before the vote, the United States said it had acted for legitimate reasons of self-defence and defence of the integrity of the Panama Canal, in full conformity with the United Nations Charter, the Charter of OAS and the Panama Canal Treaties. Its goals had been to safeguard the lives of Americans, to defend democracy in Panama, to combat illicit drug trafficking and to protect the integrity of the Panama Canal Treaties after the many attempts at negotiations had been rejected by General Noriega, whose response to successive diplomatic efforts was increased violence. It urged the Assembly to vote against that draft resolution, which it called flawed and unbalanced, in order to send a signal of support for the democratically elected Endara Government and to send a message of rejection to those who would keep alive any vestige of Noriega's cruel reign.

After the vote, Panama stated that the United States intervention had been provoked by General Noriega's criminal irresponsibilities, had been aimed at his dictatorship and had made possible the restoration of democracy to Panama.

Related developments. On 21 December,[19] Cuba informed the Secretary-General of measures taken by the United States, following its invasion of Panama, against the Cuban Embassy in Panama City. Cuba said it held the United States responsible for anything that might happen to its officials or facilities in its embassy. Nicaragua, on the same date,[20] also reported to the Secretary-General that United States troops had surrounded its embassy in Panama. It condemned the presence of United States troops and demanded their withdrawal.

By a 26 December communication to the President of the Security Council,[21] Cuba said that since the guarantees and assurances given by the United States regarding the safety of its diplomatic representatives had not been matched by the attitude of the military forces surrounding the residence of the Cuban Ambassador, and in view of the gravity of the situation, it was requesting an urgent meeting of the Council to consider the matter and find an immediate solution. On 27 December,[22] Nicaragua transmitted to the Secretary-General the text of a letter addressed the previous day to the United States Secretary of State protesting arbitrary acts committed against Nicaraguan citizens and its diplomatic mission and State property in Panama.

On 29 December,[23] following what it called an unlawful and unjustifiable outrage against the residence of its Ambassador in Panama, Nicaragua notified the United States of measures taken in response, such as limiting the number of diplomatic and consular officers at the United States Embassy in Nicaragua to 15, the number of United States Marine Corps personnel there to 9, and administrative, technical and service personnel to 100. It also ordered the expulsion of 20 United States Embassy officials.

Report of the Secretary-General. On 30 December,[24] the Secretary-General, responding to the Assembly's request in its resolution of the previous day to report within 24 hours on developments in Panama, said that while he continued to follow the situation as closely as possible, he did not have at his disposal sources of information other than those publicly available and was therefore not in a position to monitor the developments in such a way as to provide a substantive report.

REFERENCES

[1]A/44/254-S/20607. [2]S/20606. [3]S/20627. [4]S/20628. [5]S/20646. [6]S/20652. [7]S/20719. [8]S/20729. [9]S/20773. [10]S/20828. [11]S/20944. [12]S/20989. [13]A/45/62. [14]S/21035. [15]S/21034. [16]S/21047. [17]S/21048. [18]A/44/906. [19]S/21043. [20]A/44/907-S/21046. [21]S/21053. [22]A/44/910-S/21059. [23]A/44/912-S/21064. [24]A/44/911.

Chapter III

Asia and the Pacific

The situation in Asia and the Pacific, aggravated by certain long-standing conflicts, remained tense in 1989. The United Nations Command continued to report violations of the 1953 Armistice Agreement between the Democratic People's Republic of Korea and the Republic of Korea. Following the withdrawal of Soviet troops from Afghanistan, completed in February, fighting in the country escalated and caused more people to seek refugee status in Pakistan and Iran. Viet Nam's announcement of its complete troop withdrawal from Kampuchea in September was refuted by the opposition parties to the conflict because of the lack of a proper international control mechanism.

In those circumstances, United Nations efforts aimed at restoring peace in the region were concentrated on the implementation of resolutions and agreements concluded in preceding years. The dialogue on national reconciliation in Kampuchea resulted in a basic agreement over the conditions essential for a peaceful settlement of the conflict. The United Nations and non-governmental organizations providing humanitarian aid to the Kampuchean people introduced a number of new relief programmes and began preparatory work for repatriation of the Indo-Chinese refugees.

Throughout the year, the Secretary-General and his Personal Representative, with the assistance of the United Nations Good Offices Mission in Afghanistan and Pakistan, were unremitting in their efforts to achieve a comprehensive solution of the Afghanistan problem, based on the 1988 Geneva Accords concluded under United Nations auspices. The United Nations Iran-Iraq Military Observer Group, established in 1988 to monitor the cease-fire between Iran and Iraq and the withdrawal of their troops to internationally recognized boundaries, continued its mission in 1989, and the Security Council twice extended its mandate. In December, the General Assembly approved the Group's financing up to 31 March 1991.

East Asia

Korean question

The annual report of the United Nations Command (UNC) concerning the maintenance in 1988

of the 1953 Armistice Agreement[1] was submitted to the Security Council on 8 May 1989[2] by the United States on behalf of the Unified Command established pursuant to a 1950 Council resolution.[3] The report provided background information on UNC and its mission, as well as on the Armistice mechanism and procedures.

The report stated that the Korean People's Army and the Chinese People's Volunteers continued to frustrate the investigative function of the Military Armistice Commission (MAC) by refusing to participate in its joint investigations and to misuse MAC as a propaganda forum for presenting political statements unrelated to the Agreement. Set up to supervise the Agreement's implementation and settle any violations of it through negotiations, MAC held four meetings in 1988 to consider, among other matters, five serious violations. One of them was the bombing of a Korean Air Lines passenger plane on 29 November 1987, allegedly by two terrorists from the Democratic People's Republic of Korea (DPRK), which resulted in the death of all 115 people aboard.[4] In February 1988,[5] the Senior Member representing UNC at MAC charged the DPRK with a flagrant violation of the Armistice Agreement and presented evidence to support this charge. He demanded a public apology, severe punishment of those responsible for the incident and compensation to the victims' families.

Other charges of violations included the continued acquisition and deployment by the DPRK of modern and sophisticated weapons from outside Korea; firing across the military demarcation line into UNC's portion of the demilitarized zone (DMZ); introduction of unauthorized weapons; and construction of illegal fortifications in the DMZ.

In 1988, the DPRK reiterated its call for discontinuance of the annual military training exercise "Team Spirit", conducted jointly by the United States and the Republic of Korea. In that regard, UNC pointed out that such exercises were not addressed by the Armistice Agreement and thus could not constitute a violation of it, as the DPRK maintained. On the other hand, UNC noted, the secret exercises routinely held by the DPRK were a cause for genuine concern. In order to demonstrate its good faith, UNC provided on 28 January 1988 a prior notification to the DPRK of "Team Spirit 88" to be conducted in March, with an invitation to observe.

The issue of Korean War remains found in the territory of either side and their return through MAC, as stipulated by the Armistice Agreement, was raised again in 1988. On 2 February, the DPRK officially informed UNC that it had the remains of two UNC soldiers from the United States Army in its possession, but decided later not to return them, citing reasons unrelated to the Agreement.

During 1988, UNC presented a number of proposals to assist in reducing military tensions. The proposals addressed confidence-building measures, such as the restoration of joint observer teams to investigate serious violations, prior notification and observation of training exercises, removal of propaganda signs in the DMZ and establishment of a viable verification system for Armistice compliance in the DMZ and in the joint security area (Panmunjom). The DPRK, however, did not respond positively to most of UNC's initiatives.

REFERENCES

(1)YUN 1953, p. 136, GA res. 725(VIII), annex, 7 Dec. 1953. (2)S/20622. (3)YUN 1950, p. 230, SC res. 84(1950), 7 July 1950. (4)YUN 1988, p. 179. (5)S/19488.

South-East Asia

On 7 December 1989, the General Assembly, by **decision 44/416**, deferred consideration of the item entitled ''Question of peace, stability and co-operation in South-East Asia'' and included it in the provisional agenda of its forty-fifth (1990) session.

Kampuchea situation

In 1989, the dialogue and negotiations on Kampuchea gathered unprecedented momentum. At the second Jakarta informal meeting (19-21 February),(1) the four parties to the Kampuchea conflict (National United Front for an Independent, Neutral, Peaceful and Cooperative Cambodia; Khmer People's National Liberation Front; Party of Democratic Kampuchea; People's Revolutionary Party of Kampuchea) reached a basic agreement on the conditions required for a peaceful settlement, which included the withdrawal of Vietnamese forces from Kampuchea under the supervision of an international control mechanism; prevention of the recurrence of genocidal policies and practices; cessation of foreign interference and external arms supplies to the opposing Kampuchean forces; and the holding of free and democratic general elections. Yet the meeting revealed disagreements on internal aspects of the settlement, particularly the establishment of a pro-

visional quadripartite authority of national reconciliation under the leadership of Prince Samdech Norodom Sihanouk.

On 5 April, Viet Nam announced the decision to withdraw all of its troops from Kampuchea by the end of September,(2) and later informed the Secretary-General that the withdrawal had been completed between 21 and 26 September.(3) The Cambodian National Resistance and the Coalition Government of Democratic Kampuchea, however, repeatedly denounced Viet Nam's statement as non-credible, given the absence of an international verification mechanism.(4)

The conclusions of the Jakarta meeting were echoed in the 1989 report(5) by the *Ad Hoc* Committee of the International Conference on Kampuchea, established in 1981.(6) Pursuant to a 1988 General Assembly resolution,(7) the Committee continued to seek the implementation of the 1981 Declaration on Kampuchea(6) and, for that purpose, set up a mission which held extensive consultations in July with Association of South-East Asian Nations officials, the competing Kampuchean factions and other parties concerned on the prospects for a comprehensive political solution. It was emphasized that a negotiated settlement leading to the establishment of a sovereign, independent, neutral and non-aligned Kampuchea was in the long-term interests of all parties to the conflict.

Paris Conference on Cambodia

In 1989, following the agreement reached at the second Jakarta informal meeting(1) and at Prince Sihanouk's request,(8) France initiated the International Conference on Cambodia, which held its first session from 30 July to 30 August in Paris.(9) The Conference participants included Australia; Brunei Darussalam; Cambodia, represented by the four parties to the conflict; Canada; China; France; India; Indonesia; Japan; the Lao People's Democratic Republic; Malaysia; the Philippines; Singapore; Thailand; the USSR; the United Kingdom; the United States; Viet Nam; Zimbabwe; and the Secretary-General of the United Nations.

In his address to the Conference,(10) the Secretary-General pointed out, *inter alia*, that the establishment of a credible international control mechanism, essential for a comprehensive political settlement, was contingent on the adoption of an effective decision-making process and the provision of the necessary human, logistical and financial resources. He suggested that a precise evaluation of such resources could only be made by a fact-finding mission. From 6 to 19 August, following a decision of the Conference, a preliminary mission visited the area to gather on-the-spot technical information. The Conference further elaborated a variety of elements for the framework of the settlement process, established four working committees and suspended the session, to be reconvened in due time.

Report of the Secretary-General. In October, pursuant to a 1988 General Assembly resolution,[7] the Secretary-General reported[11] on the situation in Kampuchea. He stated that, in 1989, he and his Special Representative, Rafeeuddin Ahmed, had maintained regular contacts with the parties and countries concerned, including consultations with the leaders of the Kampuchean factions, which focused on issues related to national reconciliation.

Humanitarian assistance in Kampuchea continued to be provided through the United Nations and voluntary agencies represented in Phnom Penh. The United Nations Children's Fund was engaged in relief efforts for mothers and children; the Food and Agriculture Organization of the United Nations supplied agricultural inputs; the World Food Programme provided food assistance; and the International Committee of the Red Cross (ICRC) and five national Red Cross societies were involved in medical relief work. The Office of the United Nations High Commissioner for Refugees (UNHCR), designated by the Secretary-General in July as the lead agency for repatriation in Kampuchea, and the United Nations Border Relief Operation (UNBRO) were responsible for relief assistance in the encampments and evacuation sites along the Thai-Kampuchean border, which had some 309,000 people as at the end of September. According to the estimate, however, some 40,000 more Kampucheans who needed assistance were still living in areas inaccessible to the international community. In preparation for repatriation, UNHCR and UNBRO, with the assistance of the United Nations Educational, Scientific and Cultural Organization and the International Labour Organisation, introduced a variety of vocational and educational training programmes for the potential returnees, notwithstanding the shortfall of some $5 million that, despite an increase in contributions, the relief project faced in 1989.

With the deployment of a new Displaced Persons Protection Unit by Thailand and the retention of five senior police officers from developed countries to assist in training Khmer civilian police, the security and protection of the border population improved. The food situation was expected to show some improvement, though the effects of the 1987 drought were still felt in certain provinces. It was hoped that the food-supply deficit might be reduced to less than 50,000 tons of rice.

Since the beginning of the year, the Secretary-General noted, the process of dialogue and negotiations had gathered unprecedented momentum, culminating in the Paris Conference; it was of utmost importance that that momentum not be lost.

Since the suspension of the Conference, there were two main developments: the reported withdrawal by Viet Nam of its troops from Kampuchea in September and the increased hostilities during the past few weeks. The Secretary-General believed that there could be no military solution and every effort should be made to spare the Kampucheans further bloodshed and suffering. He remained convinced that the only constructive course of action was the early resumption of the negotiating process; he hoped that the consultations conducted to that end would reach fruition in the near future.

The most important outstanding issue was national reconciliation, which had to begin with the definition of viable administrative arrangements for the transitional period leading to the holding of free, fair and internationally supervised elections. At the same time, the Secretary-General said, attention should focus on the modalities of the cease-fire, especially with respect to the disposition of the armed forces of the parties; on the adoption of measures to ensure the non-return to the universally condemned policies and practices of the 1975-1978 period; and on the mandate and *modus operandi* of an effective international control mechanism for all the elements of a comprehensive political settlement.

The Secretary-General believed that the establishment of a firm basis of negotiations required a genuine spirit of compromise and readiness for mutual concessions; only in that way could the ground be prepared for the conclusion of a comprehensive agreement necessary to establish a durable peace. He appealed to all parties to work towards such an agreement with renewed vigour and a sense of urgency. He himself intended to continue his effort in the exercise of his good offices and do whatever he could to further the negotiating process and steer it towards a successful outcome. In the final analysis, however, such success depended on whether the parties most directly concerned mustered the will to face the challenge of peace and recognized that peace could only be more rewarding than the prolongation of a sterile and fratricidal war.

International Conference on Indo-Chinese Refugees. Issues related to the Kampuchea conflict were the subject of the International Conference on Indo-Chinese Refugees (Geneva, 13 and 14 June),[12] convened by the Secretary-General. In December, the General Assembly, by **resolution 44/138**, acted on the results of the Conference. (For details, see PART THREE, Chapter XV.)

GENERAL ASSEMBLY ACTION

On 16 November, the General Assembly, having reviewed the Secretary-General's report, adopted **resolution 44/22** by recorded vote.

The situation in Kampuchea

The General Assembly,

Recalling its resolutions 34/22 of 14 November 1979, 35/6 of 22 October 1980, 36/5 of 21 October 1981, 37/6 of 28 October 1982, 38/3 of 27 October 1983, 39/5 of 30 October 1984, 40/7 of 5 November 1985, 41/6 of 21 October 1986, 42/3 of 14 October 1987 and 43/19 of 3 November 1988,

Recalling also the Declaration on Kampuchea and resolution 1(I) adopted by the International Conference on Kampuchea,

Taking note of the report of the Secretary-General on the implementation of General Assembly resolution 43/19,

Deploring foreign armed intervention and occupation in Kampuchea, the cause of continuing hostilities in that country, seriously threatening international peace and security,

Noting the continued and effective struggle of the Kampuchean people under the leadership of Samdech Norodom Sihanouk to achieve the independence, sovereignty, territorial integrity and neutral and non-aligned status of Kampuchea,

Taking note of Economic and Social Council decision 1989/156 of 24 May 1989 on the right of peoples to self-determination and its application to peoples under colonial or alien domination or foreign occupation,

Greatly disturbed that the continued fighting and instability in Kampuchea have forced an additional large number of Kampucheans to flee to the Thai-Kampuchean border in search of food and safety,

Recognizing that the assistance extended by the international community has continued to reduce the food shortages and health problems of the Kampuchean people,

Emphasizing that it is the inalienable right of the Kampuchean people who have sought refuge in neighbouring countries to return safely to their homeland,

Emphasizing also that no effective solution to the humanitarian problems can be achieved without a comprehensive political settlement of the Kampuchean conflict,

Seriously concerned about reported demographic changes imposed in Kampuchea as a result of foreign occupation,

Convinced that, to bring about lasting peace in South-East Asia and to reduce the threat to international peace and security, there is an urgent need for the international community to find a comprehensive political settlement of the Kampuchean problem, with effective guarantees, that must include the total withdrawal of all foreign forces from Kampuchea under supervision and control of the United Nations and will provide for the creation of an interim administering authority, the promotion of national reconciliation among all Kampucheans under the leadership of Samdech Norodom Sihanouk and the non-return to the universally condemned policies and practices of a recent past and ensure respect for the sovereignty, independence, territorial integrity and neutral and non-aligned status of Kampuchea, as well as the right of the Kampuchean people to self-determination free from outside interference,

Recognizing that the informal meetings held at Jakarta from 25 to 28 July 1988 and from 19 to 21 February 1989 have made a significant contribution towards achieving a comprehensive political settlement of the Kampuchean problem,

Recognizing also that the Paris Conference on Cambodia, which met from 30 July to 30 August 1989, made progress in elaborating a wide variety of elements necessary for reaching a comprehensive settlement, although it was not yet possible to achieve a comprehensive political settlement, and that the Conference should be reconvened in due time after consultations by the Co-Presidents with the participants,

Noting the announced withdrawal of foreign forces from Kampuchea, but emphasizing that it has not been verified under supervision and control of the United Nations and is not within the framework of a comprehensive political settlement,

Reiterating its conviction that, after the comprehensive political settlement of the Kampuchean question through peaceful means, the countries of the South-East Asian region can pursue efforts to establish a zone of peace, freedom and neutrality in South-East Asia so as to lessen international tensions and to achieve lasting peace in the region,

Reaffirming the need for all States to adhere strictly to the principles of the Charter of the United Nations, which call for respect for the national independence, sovereignty and territorial integrity of all States, non-intervention and non-interference in the internal affairs of States, non-recourse to the threat or use of force and peaceful settlement of disputes,

1. *Reaffirms* its resolutions 34/22, 35/6, 36/5, 37/6, 38/3, 39/5, 40/7, 41/6, 42/3 and 43/19 and calls for their full implementation;

2. *Reiterates its conviction* that the withdrawal of all foreign forces from Kampuchea under supervision and control of the United Nations, the creation of an interim administering authority, the promotion of national reconciliation among all Kampucheans under the leadership of Samdech Norodom Sihanouk, the non-return to the universally condemned policies and practices of a recent past, the restoration and preservation of the independence, sovereignty, territorial integrity and neutral and non-aligned status of Kampuchea, the reaffirmation of the right of the Kampuchean people to determine their own destiny and the commitment by all States to non-interference and non-intervention in the internal affairs of Kampuchea, with effective guarantees, are the principal components of any just, lasting and comprehensive political settlement of the Kampuchean problem;

3. *Emphasizes* that the Kampuchean people should be allowed to exercise their inalienable right to self-determination through internationally supervised free, fair and democratic elections;

4. *Affirms* that any withdrawal of foreign forces from Kampuchea without United Nations supervision, control and verification is not within the framework of a comprehensive political settlement;

5. *Calls upon* all parties concerned to intensify urgently all efforts towards ensuring that the Kampuchean problem be resolved through a comprehensive political settlement in order to prevent further hostilities and subsequent loss of life and the continued suffering of the Kampuchean people, and to ensure the independence, sovereignty, territorial integrity, neutral and non-aligned status of Kampuchea and the non-return to the universally condemned policies and practices of a recent past;

6. *Takes note with appreciation* of the report of the *Ad Hoc* Committee of the International Conference on

Kampuchea on its activities during 1988-1989 and requests that the Committee continue its work;

7. *Authorizes* the *Ad Hoc* Committee to convene when necessary and to carry out the tasks entrusted to it in its mandate;

8. *Reaffirms* its commitment to reconvene the Conference at an appropriate time, in accordance with Conference resolution 1(I), and its readiness to support any other conference of an international nature under the auspices of the Secretary-General;

9. *Requests* the Secretary-General to continue to consult with and assist the Conference and the *Ad Hoc* Committee and to provide them on a regular basis with the necessary facilities to carry out their functions;

10. *Expresses its appreciation once again* to the Secretary-General for taking appropriate steps in following the situation closely and requests him to continue to do so and to exercise his good offices in order to contribute to a comprehensive political settlement;

11. *Invites* the Co-Presidents of the Paris Conference on Cambodia to intensify their consultations with a view to reconvening the Conference and its committees at an appropriate time;

12. *Expresses its deep appreciation once again* to donor countries, the United Nations and its agencies and other humanitarian organizations, national and international, that have rendered relief assistance to the Kampuchean people, and appeals to them to continue to provide emergency assistance to those Kampucheans who are still in need, especially along the Thai-Kampuchean border and in the various encampments in Thailand;

13. *Reiterates its deep appreciation* to the Secretary-General for his efforts in co-ordinating humanitarian relief assistance and in monitoring its distribution, and requests him to intensify such efforts as necessary;

14. *Urges* the States of South-East Asia, once a comprehensive political settlement to the Kampuchean conflict is achieved, to exert renewed efforts to establish a zone of peace, freedom and neutrality in South-East Asia;

15. *Reiterates the hope* that, following a comprehensive political settlement, an intergovernmental committee will be established to consider a programme of assistance to Kampuchea for the reconstruction of its economy and for the economic and social development of all States in the region;

16. *Requests* the Secretary-General to report to the General Assembly at its forty-fifth session on the implementation of the present resolution;

17. *Decides* to include in the provisional agenda of its forty-fifth session the item entitled "The situation in Kampuchea".

General Assembly resolution 44/22

16 November 1989   Meeting 58   124-17-12 (recorded vote)

79-nation draft (A/44/L.23 & Add.1); agenda item 31.

Sponsors: Antigua and Barbuda, Australia, Bahamas, Bangladesh, Barbados, Belize, Brunei Darussalam, Burundi, Cameroon, Canada, Cape Verde, Central African Republic, Chad, Chile, Colombia, Comoros, Costa Rica, Denmark, Djibouti, Dominica, Dominican Republic, Ecuador, El Salvador, Equatorial Guinea, Fiji, France, Gabon, Gambia, Germany, Federal Republic of, Greece, Grenada, Guatemala, Guinea-Bissau, Haiti, Honduras, Iceland, Indonesia, Italy, Japan, Lesotho, Liberia, Luxembourg, Malawi, Malaysia, Maldives, Mauritania, Mauritius, Morocco, Nepal, Netherlands, New Zealand, Niger, Nigeria, Norway, Oman, Pakistan, Papua New Guinea, Paraguay, Philippines, Saint Kitts and Nevis, Saint Lucia, Saint Vincent and the Grenadines, Samoa, Saudi Arabia, Senegal, Sierra Leone, Singapore, Solomon Islands, Somalia, Spain, Sudan, Swaziland, Thailand, Togo, Turkey, United Kingdom, Uruguay, Zaire, Zambia.

Financial implications. 5th Committee, A/44/732; S-G, A/C.5/44/25.
Meeting numbers. GA 44th session: 5th Committee 40; plenary 56-58.

Recorded vote in Assembly as follows:

In favour: Antigua and Barbuda, Argentina, Australia, Austria, Bahamas, Bahrain, Bangladesh, Barbados, Belgium, Belize, Benin, Bhutan, Bolivia, Botswana, Brazil, Brunei Darussalam, Burkina Faso, Burundi, Cameroon, Canada, Cape Verde, Central African Republic, Chad, Chile, China, Colombia, Comoros, Costa Rica, Côte d'Ivoire, Cyprus, Democratic Kampuchea, Denmark, Djibouti, Dominica, Dominican Republic, Ecuador, Egypt, El Salvador, Equatorial Guinea, Fiji, France, Gabon, Gambia, Germany, Federal Republic of, Ghana, Greece, Grenada, Guatemala, Guinea, Guinea-Bissau, Guyana, Haiti, Honduras, Iceland, Indonesia, Ireland, Israel, Italy, Jamaica, Japan, Jordan, Kenya, Kuwait, Lesotho, Liberia, Libyan Arab Jamahiriya, Luxembourg, Malawi, Malaysia, Maldives, Mali, Malta, Mauritania, Mauritius, Mexico, Morocco, Myanmar, Nepal, Netherlands, New Zealand, Niger, Nigeria, Norway, Oman, Pakistan, Panama, Papua New Guinea, Paraguay, Peru, Philippines, Portugal, Qatar, Rwanda, Saint Kitts and Nevis, Saint Lucia, Saint Vincent and the Grenadines, Samoa, Sao Tome and Principe, Saudi Arabia, Senegal, Sierra Leone, Singapore, Solomon Islands, Somalia, Spain, Sri Lanka, Sudan, Suriname, Swaziland, Thailand, Togo, Trinidad and Tobago, Tunisia, Turkey, United Arab Emirates, United Kingdom, United States, Uruguay, Vanuatu, Venezuela, Yugoslavia, Zaire, Zambia, Zimbabwe.

Against: Afghanistan, Albania, Bulgaria, Byelorussian SSR, Cuba, Czechoslovakia, Democratic Yemen, Ethiopia, German Democratic Republic, Lao People's Democratic Republic, Mongolia, Nicaragua, Poland, Syrian Arab Republic, Ukrainian SSR, USSR, Viet Nam.

Abstaining: Algeria, Congo, Finland, India, Iraq, Lebanon, Madagascar, Mozambique, Sweden, Uganda, United Republic of Tanzania, Yemen.

REFERENCES

[1]A/44/138-S/20477 & Corr.1. [2]A/44/214-S/20572. [3]A/44/596-S/20879. [4]A/44/213-S/20571, A/44/219-S/20583, A/44/530-S/20849. [5]A/CONF.109/15. [6]YUN 1981, p. 239. [7]YUN 1988, p. 182, GA res. 43/19, 3 Nov. 1988. [8]A/44/213-S/20571, annex II. [9]A/44/720-S/20959. [10]S/20768. [11]A/44/670. [12]A/44/523.

Western and south-western Asia

Afghanistan situation

On 15 February 1989,[1] the USSR announced the complete withdrawal of its troops from Afghanistan, in compliance with the 1988 Agreements on the Settlement of the Situation Relating to Afghanistan,[2] concluded under United Nations auspices. Referred to as the Geneva Agreements, they comprised four instruments: a bilateral agreement between Afghanistan and Pakistan on the principles of mutual relations, in particular on non-interference and non-intervention; a declaration on international guarantees; a bilateral agreement between Afghanistan and Pakistan on the voluntary return of refugees; and an agreement on the interrelationships for the settlement of the situation relating to Afghanistan. They were also signed by the USSR and the United States as State guarantors.

The withdrawal, executed in two phases, was monitored by the United Nations Good Offices Mission in Afghanistan and Pakistan (UNGOMAP), established under the Geneva Agreements. In a 15 February 1989 report,[3] submitted in pursuance of a 1988 Security Council resolution,[4] UNGOMAP expressed satisfaction at the scrupulous manner in which the withdrawal time-frame was observed and reviewed the steps being taken to implement other provisions of the Agreements.

During the initial period of its operation, UN-GOMAP encountered a number of difficulties in connection with the arrangements for monitoring the implementation of the non-interference and non-intervention obligations set out in the first instrument of the Geneva Agreements. Some difficulties, particularly those of a logistical character, were resolved, but a large number of complaints of alleged violations continued to be exchanged. UNGOMAP made every effort to investigate all alleged violations and work out with both sides measures to ensure compliance. Two permanent outposts were established in November 1988 on the Pakistan side, at Peshawar and Quetta, to enhance UNGOMAP's capacity to carry out investigations in a more timely manner. UNGOMAP further endeavoured to obtain the parties' agreement, as envisaged in the Agreements, regarding their meetings to consider alleged violations and reports of their investigation. UNGOMAP pointed out to both parties that most of the allegations had not been accompanied by sufficient information to permit a practical and effective investigation. Difficulties had also been encountered owing to the extremely rough terrain, time lapsed from the alleged incidents and security conditions in the area of investigation.

In connection with the agreement regarding the voluntary return of refugees, UNGOMAP reached an understanding with the United Nations High Commissioner for Refugees (UNHCR), shortly before the entry into force of the Agreements, concerning the functions that devolved on each of them in connection with the Agreements' relevant provisions. UNGOMAP stood ready to monitor and inform UNHCR of the conditions of safety which were essential for the return and resettlement of the refugees, a very limited number of whom had returned to Afghanistan.

In a 20 October report,[5] the Secretary-General stated that he had initiated a series of intensive consultations with various segments of the Afghan people, the two parties and the two guarantors of the Geneva Agreements, as well as with other Governments concerned, to encourage and facilitate the early realization of a comprehensive political settlement. On 1 February, 14 April and 3 August, the Secretary-General publicly expressed his grave concern over the escalation in fighting and emphasized the necessity to find a political, not military, solution. His Personal Representative in Afghanistan and Pakistan, Benon Sevan, who replaced Diego Cordovez in that capacity in May, maintained regular contacts with government authorities in the two countries, all Afghan leaders based at Peshawar,

Pakistan, and Tehran, Iran, and military commanders of the Afghan opposition groups. That effort required continuous shuttling between Islamabad, Pakistan, and Kabul, Afghanistan.

UNGOMAP, with headquarters units in those two cities, assisted the Secretary-General in his activities, as mandated by the Geneva Agreements. In October, in addition to a small civilian auxiliary staff, UNGOMAP retained 40 military officers from Austria, Canada, Denmark, Fiji, Finland, Ghana, Ireland, Nepal, Poland and Sweden, temporarily detached from other peace-keeping operations. In May, Colonel Heikki Happonen of Finland assumed duties as the Deputy to the Secretary-General's Personal Representative.

By the end of September 1989, UNGOMAP had received over 5,000 complaints from Afghanistan and 1,000 from Pakistan dealing with hostile political activities and propaganda, border crossings and cross-border firings, rocket attacks, acts of sabotage and airspace violations. The Mission submitted 76 reports to the parties; however, in the circumstances, it was practically impossible to investigate all the cases.

In addition to the existing outposts at Peshawar and Quetta, UNGOMAP established three more "permanent presences" in 1989 on the Pakistani side of the border to increase its monitoring capability. At the same time, after the withdrawal of foreign troops, the Mission closed three permanent outposts in Afghanistan.

With regard to the implementation of the agreement on the voluntary return of refugees, differences between Afghanistan and Pakistan had prevented the establishment of the mixed commissions envisaged to co-ordinate and supervise repatriation. The continued fighting caused many Afghans to move from their homes and even to cross the border into Pakistan, seeking refugee status. None the less, UNGOMAP, in co-operation with UNHCR, took a number of measures to help create conditions conducive to repatriation, including the establishment of a comprehensive communication network throughout the operational area and the setting up of the United Nations Logistic Operations to serve international relief and rehabilitation efforts as well as repatriation needs.

Under the guidance of the Secretary-General's Co-ordinator for United Nations Humanitarian and Economic Assistance Programmes relating to Afghanistan, Sadruddin Aga Khan, a plan of action was developed jointly by United Nations agencies and programmes, notably the United Nations Children's Fund, the United Nations Development Programme, the World Food Programme, UNHCR, the Food and Agriculture Organization of the United Nations, the United Nations Educational, Scientific and Cultural Organization and the World Health Organization.

Under that plan, several projects were launched either directly by the United Nations or through non-governmental organizations in the field of agriculture, food aid, public health, mother and child health care, emergency aid to vulnerable groups, vocational training, rural reconstruction, economic recovery and rehabilitation. Another important programme initiated in 1989 provided training for Afghan volunteers to clear the land and access roads of mines and unexploded ordnance.

A number of other planned activities, however, such as road repair, shelter, anti-narcotic programmes and human resources development, suffered from lack of financial support. The Secretary-General noted that 70 per cent of the pledges, amounting to almost $1 billion, were in kind, therefore restricting operational flexibility.

For a comprehensive political solution to be achieved, the Secretary-General believed it necessary to secure an international as well as national consensus. While such a consensus had not yet emerged, efforts were under way to narrow the gulf between the positions taken by the neighbouring and other concerned countries. In addition, the Secretary-General felt that there was a fundamental need for a structure through which the wishes of the various segments of the Afghan people could be expressed. He remained confident that, despite their differences and diversity, they would achieve a comprehensive political settlement and he counted on the international community to encourage them in that direction.

GENERAL ASSEMBLY ACTION

On 1 November, the General Assembly adopted **resolution 44/15** without vote.

The situation in Afghanistan and its implications for international peace and security
The General Assembly,

Having considered the item entitled "The situation in Afghanistan and its implications for international peace and security",

Recalling its resolution 43/20 of 3 November 1988,

Reaffirming the purposes and principles of the Charter of the United Nations and the obligation of all States to refrain in their international relations from the threat or use of force against the sovereignty, territorial integrity and political independence of any State,

Reaffirming also the inalienable right of all peoples to determine their own form of government and to choose their own economic, political and social system free from outside intervention, subversion, coercion or constraint of any kind whatsoever,

Gravely concerned at the situation in Afghanistan, which resulted from the violation of principles of the Charter and of the recognized norms of inter-State conduct,

Noting the conclusion at Geneva, on 14 April 1988, of the Agreements on the Settlement of the Situation Relating to Afghanistan and the completion of the withdrawal of foreign troops in accordance with those Agreements,

Aware of the continuing concern of the international community at the sufferings of the Afghan people and the magnitude of the social and economic problems posed to Pakistan and Iran by the presence on their soil of millions of Afghan refugees,

Deeply conscious of the urgent need for a comprehensive political solution of the situation in respect of Afghanistan,

Conscious that a successful final political settlement of the Afghanistan problem would have a favourable impact on the international situation and provide an impetus for the resolution of other acute regional conflicts,

Expressing its appreciation to the Secretary-General for his efforts to bring about peace and security,

Taking note of the report of the Secretary-General and the status of the process of political settlement,

1. *Emphasizes* the importance of the Agreements on the Settlement of the Situation Relating to Afghanistan, hereinafter referred to as the "Geneva Agreements", concluded at Geneva on 14 April 1988 under United Nations auspices, which constitute an important step towards a comprehensive political solution of the Afghanistan problem;

2. *Welcomes* the completion on 15 February 1989 of the withdrawal of Soviet troops from Afghanistan in accordance with the Geneva Agreements;

3. *Expresses its deep appreciation* to the Secretary-General for his constant efforts to achieve a political solution of the Afghanistan problem;

4. *Calls* for the scrupulous respect for and faithful implementation of the Geneva Agreements by all parties concerned, who should fully abide by their letter and spirit;

5. *Reiterates* that the preservation of the sovereignty, territorial integrity, political independence and non-aligned and Islamic character of Afghanistan is essential for a peaceful solution of the Afghanistan problem;

6. *Reaffirms* the right of the Afghan people to determine their own form of government and to choose their economic, political and social system free from outside intervention, subversion, coercion or constraint of any kind whatsoever;

7. *Calls upon* all parties concerned to work urgently for the achievement of a comprehensive political solution, the cessation of hostilities and the creation of the necessary conditions of peace and normalcy that would enable the Afghan refugees to return voluntarily to their homeland in safety and honour;

8. *Emphasizes* the need for an early start of the intra-Afghan dialogue for the establishment of a broad-based government to ensure the broadest support and immediate participation of all segments of the Afghan people;

9. *Calls upon* all parties concerned to exert every effort to promote a political settlement acceptable to the Afghan people in order to bring to an end the protracted conflict that has prevailed in Afghanistan for the past several years;

10. *Requests* the Secretary-General to encourage and facilitate the early realization of a comprehensive political settlement in Afghanistan in accordance with the provisions of the Geneva Agreements and of the present resolution;

11. *Expresses its appreciation* for the work of the United Nations Good Offices Mission in Afghanistan and Pakistan in the implementation of the Geneva Agreements and emphasizes that it should continue to discharge its

functions in strict compliance with the Agreements, and requests Afghanistan and Pakistan to provide full assistance to it;

12. *Renews its appeal* to all States and national and international organizations to continue to extend humanitarian relief assistance with a view to alleviating the hardship of the Afghan refugees, in co-ordination with the United Nations High Commissioner for Refugees;

13. *Calls upon* all States to provide adequate financial and material resources to the Co-ordinator for Humanitarian and Economic Assistance Programmes Relating to Afghanistan for the purposes of achieving the speedy repatriation and rehabilitation of the Afghan refugees, as well as for the economic and social reconstruction of the country;

14. *Requests* the Secretary-General to keep Member States and the Security Council informed of progress towards the implementation of the present resolution and to submit to the General Assembly at its forty-fifth session a report on the situation in Afghanistan and on progress achieved in the implementation of the Geneva Agreements and the political settlement relating to Afghanistan;

15. *Decides* to include in the provisional agenda of its forty-fifth session the item entitled ''The situation in Afghanistan and its implications for international peace and security''.

General Assembly resolution 44/15

1 November 1989   Meeting 43   Adopted without vote

Draft by President (A/44/L.17); agenda item 32.
Financial implications. 5th Committee, A/44/679; S-G, A/C.5/44/15.
Meeting numbers. GA 44th session: 5th Committee 20, 22; plenary 43.

Introducing the draft, the President said it was the result of a consensus of the parties; as part of the understanding between those directly concerned, it was agreed that there should be no debate in order to permit the broadest possible support for the text.

Iran-Iraq situation

United Nations efforts towards a peaceful settlement of the hostilities between Iran and Iraq continued to focus during 1989 on the full implementation of Security Council resolution 598(1987).[6] The basic framework for such a settlement, provided by the Council's resolution, particularly included the discontinuance of military activities, observance of a cease-fire and withdrawal of the parties' troops to the internationally recognized boundaries as described in the 1975 Treaty concerning the State Frontier and Neighbourly Relations between Iran and Iraq, and its protocols and annexes. In 1989, the Security Council twice extended the mandate of the United Nations Iran-Iraq Military Observer Group (UNIIMOG), set up in 1988[7] to verify, confirm and supervise the implementation of resolution 598(1987). On 18 September 1989, at its resumed forty-third session, the General Assembly, by **decision 43/465**, included the item entitled ''Con-

sequences of the prolongation of the armed conflict between Iran and Iraq'' in the agenda of its forty-fourth (1989) session.

UN Iran-Iraq Military Observer Group

Report of the Secretary-General (February). As requested by the Security Council in 1988,[7] the Secretary-General on 2 February 1989 submitted a report[8] covering UNIIMOG's activities during its first mandate period, from 9 August 1988 to 2 February 1989. The report provided information on the Group's deployment and structure and described the steps taken to monitor compliance with the cease-fire, which came into effect on 20 August 1988,[9] and to investigate alleged violations of it. As of 20 January 1989, UNIIMOG had received 1,960 complaints of such violations; however, only 25 per cent of them had been confirmed by UNIIMOG as violations.

One of the most serious incidents was the flooding by Iran of no man's land in the Khusk region starting on 13 September 1988 in order to create a water obstacle between the forward positions of the two armies. UNIIMOG requested Iran to stop the flooding, but it was resumed, increasing tension along the cease-fire line and leading to an exchange of artillery, small arms and rocket fire on 11 December 1988 which resulted in the death of two Iranians. The Group's prompt reaction prevented an escalation of artillery fire, but the situation in the area remained tense. Three burning oil wells on the Iranian side of no man's land constituted another source of tension, as the Iraqi authorities refused to co-operate on the measures necessary to extinguish the fire.

The Chief Military Observer (CMO) pursued a number of confidence-building initiatives between the two parties, including the exchange of a small number of prisoners on 4 October 1988, the negotiation of agreement for locust spraying along the cease-fire line, and the exchange of war dead found in no man's land or behind the forward defended localities. By 20 January, Iran and Iraq had exchanged the remains of 1,237 such victims. They also reached an agreement to establish a mixed military working group under the CMO's chairmanship, as proposed by the Secretary-General, and signed memoranda of understanding with ICRC on 14 November 1988 concerning the release and repatriation of sick and wounded prisoners of war. On 5 November, the United Nations and Iraq concluded a preliminary agreement on the status of UNIIMOG. A similar agreement with Iran was still being discussed.

At joint meetings of the foreign ministers of the two countries, held at the Secretary-General's initiative, the Secretary-General provided the parties with specific ideas regarding implementation of resolution 598(1987); yet the parties continued to hold divergent views on the constituent elements of the cease-fire and the subjects falling within the resolution's framework. In January 1989, Ambassador Jan Eliasson, appointed on 1 September 1988 as the Secretary-General's Personal Representative on Issues Pertaining to the Implementation of Security Council Resolution 598(1987), visited Tehran and Baghdad for consultations with senior government officials. The report indicated that the exchanges which had taken place during the visit could add momentum to the peace process.

Summing up the conditions essential for further progress towards a peaceful settlement of the Iran-Iraq conflict, the Secretary-General recommended to the Security Council a renewal of UNIIMOG's mandate until 30 September 1989, which he considered essential for further progress, adding that both parties had assured him of their support for UNIIMOG.

SECURITY COUNCIL ACTION (February)

On 8 February, the Security Council considered the Secretary-General's report and unanimously adopted **resolution 631(1989)**.

The Security Council,

Recalling its resolutions 598(1987) of 20 July 1987 and 619(1988) of 9 August 1988,

Having considered the report of the Secretary-General on the United Nations Iran-Iraq Military Observer Group of 2 February 1989, and taking note of the observations expressed therein,

Decides:

(a) To call upon the parties concerned to implement immediately Security Council resolution 598(1987);

(b) To renew the mandate of the United Nations Iran-Iraq Military Observer Group for a period of seven months and twenty-two days, that is, until 30 September 1989;

(c) To request the Secretary-General to submit, at the end of this period, a report on the developments in the situation and the measures taken to implement resolution 598(1987).

Security Council resolution 631(1989)

8 February 1989   Meeting 2844   Adopted unanimously

Draft prepared in consultations among Council members (S/20449).

Report of the Secretary-General (September). In a report[10] covering the period from 3 February to 22 September 1989, submitted pursuant to the Security Council's February resolution, the Secretary-General noted that, although UNIIMOG continued successfully to carry out its mandate in monitoring the cease-fire lines, the withdrawal of forces had not yet taken place and resolution 598(1987)[6] remained partly unimplemented. By 31 August 1989, UNIIMOG had confirmed 1,435 cease-fire violations, of which 80 per cent were minor, and recorded six local-

ized firing incidents. The flooding of no man's land by Iran continued and extended southwards, and UNIIMOG's efforts to persuade Iraq to allow the burning oil wells to be extinguished were unsuccessful.

The CMO continued to pursue measures aimed at easing tension between the parties. A total of 955 Iranian and 973 Iraqi war dead were repatriated during the period under review, and on several occasions the Group monitored reconstruction activities close to the cease-fire line, to assure the other party that the work had no military purpose. On 28 March, the United Nations and Iran concluded a preliminary agreement on the status of UNIIMOG.

Joint ministerial meetings between Iran and Iraq continued. Meetings were held in New York (10 February) and Geneva (20-23 April), followed by extensive consultations with senior government officials in May and June. At separate meetings with the Secretary-General in Belgrade, Yugoslavia, on 4 and 5 September, both parties agreed that another round of talks would not be fruitful at that stage but favoured the Secretary-General's suggestion that his Personal Representative would visit the area later in 1989, in an effort to further the implementation of resolution 598(1987). The report indicated that Iran and Iraq had repeatedly expressed their commitment to achieving a peaceful settlement, but diverged on the priority of troop withdrawal and other provisions of that resolution.

Emphasizing UNIIMOG's indispensable role in ensuring the maintenance of the cease-fire, the Secretary-General recommended its extension for a period of six months, until 31 March 1990.

SECURITY COUNCIL ACTION (September)

Having reviewed the Secretary-General's report, the Security Council on 29 September 1989 unanimously adopted **resolution 642(1989)**.

The Security Council,

Recalling its resolution 598(1987) of 20 July 1987, 619(1988) of 9 August 1988 and 631(1989) of 8 February 1989,

Having considered the report of the Secretary-General on the United Nations Iran-Iraq Military Observer Group of 22 September 1989, and taking note of the observations expressed therein,

Decides:

(a) To call once again upon the parties concerned to implement immediately Security Council resolution 598(1987);

(b) To extend the mandate of the United Nations Iran-Iraq Military Observer Group for a further period of six months, that is, until 31 March 1990;

(c) To request the Secretary-General to submit, at the end of this period, a report on the developments in the situation and the measures taken to implement resolution 598(1987).

Security Council resolution 642(1989)
29 September 1989   Meeting 2885   Adopted unanimously
Draft prepared in consultations among Council members (S/20873).

Composition

As of September 1989,[10] UNIIMOG, including headquarters staff at Baghdad and Tehran, had a total strength of 408, as compared to 409 in February. That number included 351 military observers (as compared to 350 in February) from 26 countries (Argentina, Australia, Austria, Bangladesh, Canada, Denmark, Finland, Ghana, Hungary, India, Indonesia, Ireland, Italy, Kenya, Malaysia, New Zealand, Nigeria, Norway, Peru, Poland, Senegal, Sweden, Turkey, Uruguay, Yugoslavia, Zambia); 17 in the air unit from New Zealand; 36 military police from Ireland; and 4 military medical personnel from Austria. The international staff in the mission area was reduced from 117 in February to 105 in September, while local civilian staff increased from 41 to 93, which was still substantially less than the number of authorized posts.

On 9 September, Brigadier-General T. Källstrom of Sweden assumed duties as Assistant Chief Military Observer (ACMO) on the Iranian side, replacing Brigadier-General J. Kelly of Ireland. Major-General Slavko Jovic of Yugoslavia remained in command of the Group as CMO, and Brigadier V. M. Patil of India continued to be ACMO on the Iraqi side.

Financing

In December 1988,[11] the General Assembly appropriated for UNIIMOG $18.3 million gross, in addition to the $35.7 million gross it had appropriated in August 1988[12] for the initial six-month period from 9 August 1988 to 8 February 1989. It also authorized the Secretary-General to enter into commitments for UNIIMOG at a rate not to exceed $7,986,000 gross ($7,889,000 net) per month, with the prior concurrence of the Advisory Committee on Administrative and Budgetary Questions (ACABQ), for the 12 months beyond 9 February 1989.

After the Security Council, in February, renewed UNIIMOG's mandate for a period of seven months and 22 days, i.e., until 30 September 1989, the Advisory Committee concurred with the request that the Secretary-General enter into commitments for that period in the amount of $61,678,175 gross ($60,929,016 net), to be assessed on Member States.

Following the extension of UNIIMOG's mandate for a further six months, from 1 October 1989 to 31 March 1990, the Controller again requested ACABQ's concurrence for the Secretary-General to enter into commitments in an amount not to exceed $34,153,825 gross ($33,738,984 net) for that mandate period.

In a December report,[13] the Secretary-General expressed the view that the authorization given for the period from 1 October 1989 to 8 February 1990 would be sufficient to meet the cost of UNIIMOG for the full six months up to 31 March 1990; accordingly, he proposed that the authorization be extended until that date.

As at 31 October 1989, the Secretary-General noted, assessments totalling $114,812,611 net had been apportioned among Member States in respect of UNIIMOG for the period from its inception to 30 September 1989. Contributions received for that period amounted to $105,591,613, representing a shortfall of $9,220,998. Assessments totalling $33,866,585 net had been apportioned among Member States for the period from 1 October 1989 to 8 February 1990, against which contributions in the amount of $2,155 had been received as at 31 October 1989. Voluntary contributions since UNIIMOG's inception included supplies, services and $11 million cash.

As at 31 October 1989, an unencumbered balance of $18.3 million existed for UNIIMOG for the period since its inception until 30 September 1989, resulting mainly from a less than full implementation of the original plan of deployment. The Secretary-General proposed that a maximum amount of $10 million be credited to Member States against future assessments, taking into account the need to provide a reserve of approximately $10 million for six weeks' expenditure pending the receipt of contributions for new mandate periods.

The Advisory Committee agreed[14] with the Secretary-General's proposal that, in the interest of administrative efficiency, the first two mandate periods, comprising 13 months and 23 days, be considered as one accounting or financial period. However, in its understanding, this would be an exception and Member States would continue to be assessed according to mandate periods.

The Committee also agreed to the amount requested for the mandate period from 1 October 1989 to 8 February 1990, noting that the Secretary-General had indicated that the financing authority already granted by the Assembly would be sufficient to finance UNIIMOG until 31 March 1990. With regard to estimates for the 12-month period beginning 1 April 1990, ACABQ recommended that the Secretary-General be authorized to enter into commitments at a rate not to exceed $6,401,333 gross. Member States would be credited $10 million against the assessments for that period.

On 21 December, the General Assembly, on the recommendation of the Fifth Committee, adopted **resolution 44/189** without vote.

Financing of the United Nations Iran-Iraq Military Observer Group

The General Assembly,

Having considered the report of the Secretary-General on the financing of the United Nations Iran-Iraq Military Observer Group and the related report of the Advisory Committee on Administrative and Budgetary Questions,

Bearing in mind Security Council resolution 619(1988) of 9 August 1988, by which the Council established the United Nations Iran-Iraq Military Observer Group, and the subsequent resolutions by which the Council extended the mandate of the Military Observer Group, the latest of which was resolution 642(1989) of 29 September 1989,

Recalling its resolutions 42/233 of 17 August 1988 and 43/230 of 21 December 1988 on the financing of the Military Observer Group,

Recognizing that the costs of the Military Observer Group are expenses of the Organization to be borne by Member States in accordance with Article 17, paragraph 2, of the Charter of the United Nations,

Mindful of the fact that it is essential to provide the Military Observer Group with the necessary financial resources to enable it to fulfil its responsibilities under the relevant resolutions of the Security Council,

Urging all Member States to make every possible effort to ensure payment of their assessed contributions to the Military Observer Group in full and on time,

Reaffirming its previous decisions regarding the fact that, in order to meet the expenditures caused by such operations, a different procedure is required from the one applied to meet expenditures of the regular budget of the United Nations,

Taking into account the fact that the economically more developed countries are in a position to make relatively larger contributions and that the economically less developed countries have a relatively limited capacity to contribute towards peace-keeping operations involving heavy expenditures,

Bearing in mind the special responsibilities of the States permanent members of the Security Council in the financing of such operations, as indicated in General Assembly resolution 1874(S-IV) of 27 June 1963 and other resolutions of the Assembly,

Noting with appreciation that voluntary contributions in cash and in kind have been made to the Military Observer Group by certain Governments,

Mindful of the views expressed in the Fifth Committee on the requests of some Member States to change their placement in the existing groups "b", "c" and "d" of Member States, on the basis of the criteria set out in General Assembly resolution 3101(XXVIII) of 11 December 1973,

1. *Concurs* with the observations and recommendations contained in the report of the Advisory Committee on Administrative and Budgetary Questions;

2. *Decides* that the authorization provided by its resolution 43/230 for the period from 9 February 1989 to 8 February 1990, inclusive, shall be extended to include the period up to and including 31 March 1990;

3. *Decides also* to appropriate to the Special Account referred to in paragraph 1 of General Assembly resolution 42/233 an amount of 61,678,175 United States dollars gross (60,929,016 dollars net) authorized by the Assembly and apportioned in accordance with section I, paragraph 4, of its resolution 43/230 for the period from 9 February to 30 September 1989, inclusive;

4. *Decides further* to appropriate to the Special Account the amount of 34,153,825 dollars gross (33,738,984 dollars net) authorized by the Assembly and apportioned in accordance with section I, paragraph 4, of its resolution 43/230 for the period from 1 October 1989 to 31 March 1990, inclusive;

5. *Authorizes* the Secretary-General to enter into commitments for the operation of the United Nations Iran-Iraq Military Observer Group at a rate not to exceed 6,401,333 dollars gross (6,237,333 dollars net) per month for the six-month period from 1 April to 30 September 1990, inclusive, subject to obtaining the prior concurrence of the Advisory Committee for the actual level of commitments to be entered into, should the Security Council decide to continue the Military Observer Group beyond the period of six months authorized under its resolution 642(1989);

6. *Also authorizes* the Secretary-General to enter into commitments for the operation of the Military Observer Group at a rate not to exceed 7,068,000 dollars gross (6,904,000 dollars net) per month for the six-month period from 1 October 1990 to 31 March 1991, subject to obtaining the prior concurrence of the Advisory Committee for the actual level of commitments to be entered into, should the Security Council decide to continue the Military Observer Group beyond 30 September 1990;

7. *Decides*, as an *ad hoc* arrangement, to apportion the amounts referred to in paragraphs 5 and 6 of the present resolution among Member States in accordance with the composition of groups set out in paragraphs 3 and 4 of General Assembly resolution 43/232 of 1 March 1989, to be adjusted by the decision to be taken by the Assembly at its forty-fourth session on the composition of groups "a", "b", "c" and "d" of Member States and taking into account the scale of assessments for the years 1989, 1990 and 1991;

8. *Also decides*, on an exceptional basis, that the appropriations provided for the first two mandate periods of the Military Observer Group, that is, from 9 August 1988 to 30 September 1989, inclusive, be administered as one financial period;

9. *Further decides* that the special financial period of the Military Observer Group shall be for twelve months, beginning on 1 October of one year and ending on 30 September of the next, effective from 1 October 1989, subject to the renewal of the mandate of the Military Observer Group by the Security Council;

10. *Decides* that 10 million dollars of the unencumbered balance in respect of the period from the inception of the Military Observer Group on 9 August 1988 to 30 September 1989 shall be credited to Member States against their assessments in respect of such mandate periods as may be approved by the Security Council for the twelve months subsequent to 31 March 1990;

11. *Also decides* that the remaining 10,117,762 dollars of the unencumbered balance shall be retained in the

Special Account subject to the review to be undertaken by the Advisory Committee as to the level of commitments to be authorized for the Military Observer Group for the mandate period from 1 April to 30 September 1990, taking into account the status of the receipt of assessed contributions for the period from 1 October 1989 to 31 March 1990, inclusive;

12.   *Invites* voluntary contributions to the Military Observer Group, acceptable to the Secretary-General, in cash, in convertible or readily usable currencies and in the form of supplies and services;

13.   *Requests* the Secretary-General to take all necessary measures to ensure that the Military Observer Group is administered with a maximum of efficiency and economy.

General Assembly resolution 44/189

21 December 1989   Meeting 84   Adopted without vote

Approved by Fifth Committee (A/44/889) without vote, 18 December (meeting 58); draft by Chairman (A/C.5/44/L.14); agenda item 134.
Meeting numbers. GA 44th session: 5th Committee 45, 47, 49, 58; plenary 84.

REFERENCES

[1]A/44/131-S/20472. [2]YUN 1988, p. 184. [3]S/20465. [4]YUN 1988, p. 187, SC res. 622(1988), 31 Oct. 1988. [5]A/44/661-S/20911. [6]YUN 1987, p. 223, SC res. 598(1987), 20 July 1987. [7]YUN 1988, p. 194, SC res. 619(1988), 9 Aug. 1988. [8]S/20442. [9]YUN 1988, p. 193. [10]S/20862. [11]YUN 1988, p. 197, GA res. 43/230, 21 Dec. 1988. [12]*Ibid.*, p. 196, GA res. 42/233, 17 Aug. 1988. [13]A/44/835. [14]A/44/874 & Corr.1.

Chapter IV

Middle East

Throughout 1989, the United Nations continued its efforts for a peaceful settlement of the Middle East conflict. The Palestinian uprising in the West Bank and Gaza Strip—known in Arabic as *intifadah*—intensified, as did Israeli countermeasures. Military confrontation escalated in Lebanon, where the assassination of the newly elected President in November demonstrated the fragility of the reconciliation process.

The question of Palestine was reaffirmed from various sides as the core of the Arab-Israeli conflict and it was stressed that no comprehensive, just and lasting peace in the region would be achieved without the full exercise by the Palestinian people of its inalienable national rights and the immediate, unconditional and total withdrawal of Israel from the occupied Palestinian territory and the other occupied Arab territories. The General Assembly reaffirmed that such a peace could not be achieved without the participation on an equal footing of all the parties to the conflict, including the Palestine Liberation Organization, and called for the convening of an international peace conference on the Middle East under UN auspices.

The Security Council met on several occasions to discuss the situation in the Middle East and in the territories occupied by Israel. In July and August, it adopted resolutions by which it expressed its regret over the continuing deportation by Israel of Palestinian civilians and called on Israel to ensure the safe and immediate return of those deported and to desist from deporting others. The Council also issued a number of statements on the situation in Lebanon, expressing grave concern at the deterioration of the situation there and urging all the parties immediately to end the confrontation and support all efforts to find a peaceful solution to the Lebanese crisis.

During the year, the Council twice extended, for periods of six months each, the mandates of the United Nations Interim Force in Lebanon (UNIFIL) and the United Nations Disengagement Observer Force (UNDOF). The United Nations Truce Supervision Organization continued to assist UNDOF and UNIFIL in their tasks.

The Committee on the Exercise of the Inalienable Rights of the Palestinian People (Committee on Palestinian rights), which kept under review the Palestine question, reported continuing serious aggravation of the situation in the occupied territory. The Special Committee to Investigate Israeli Prac-

tices Affecting the Human Rights of the Population of the Occupied Territories (Committee on Israeli practices) reported that the situation in the occupied territories was marked by a dangerous level of violence and repression, which had constantly escalated since the start of the Palestinian uprising in 1987. Both Committees stressed the need for urgent measures to ensure the safety of the Palestinians and protect their rights.

Economic and social developments in the occupied Palestinian and other Arab territories were monitored by the Economic and Social Council, which adopted during the year resolutions on Israeli economic practices, assistance to the Palestinian people and the situation of Palestinian women.

Assistance to Palestinians was provided by various UN organizations. Notable among them was the United Nations Relief and Work Agency for Palestinian Refugees in the Near East (UNRWA) which continued to deliver education, health and relief services to more than 2.3 million Palestinian refugees in Jordan, Lebanon, the Syrian Arab Republic, the West Bank and the Gaza Strip. As the Palestinian uprising and its consequences produced sudden and unprecedented demands for additional assistance, UNRWA introduced its emergency programme, which included increased medical and relief services.

Middle East situation

The escalation of the Israeli-Palestinian conflict, as well as the military confrontation in Lebanon, underlined the urgency for an effective negotiated settlement. While the necessity to convene an international conference on the Middle East as a major political instrument in attaining a comprehensive, just and lasting solution of the conflict was widely supported by the international community, negotiations remained at a standstill and no consensus was found on the modalities of setting in motion such a conference (see below, under "Palestine question").

However, the search for a peaceful negotiated solution of the conflict continued throughout the year. The United States, Israel and Egypt launched their own initiatives. To promote a dialogue between the parties, the United States established contact with them and in November presented a five-point proposal as a basis for such dialogue. Israel accepted the proposal,[1] while stressing that any discussion had to start with its own peace initiative of 14 May 1989.[2] Egypt put forward the idea of holding a dialogue in Cairo between an Israeli government delegation and a mandated Palestinian delegation, during which each party would be free to present its position on the settlement process and to discuss the question of elections and any other related matter.[3]

There were also proposals to consider placing the territories occupied by Israel under international supervision to ensure the protection and security of the inhabitants, pending a definitive solution and the establishment of total peace in the region, as suggested by, among others, the Committee on Palestinian rights.[4]

Reports of the Secretary-General. In accordance with a 1988 request of the General Assembly,[5] the Secretary-General submitted in November 1989 a comprehensive report[6] on the developments in the Middle East in all their aspects. The report addressed such issues as UN peace-keeping activities, the situation in the occupied territories, the Palestine refugee problem, the question of Palestine and the situation in the Middle East.

The Secretary-General stated that expectations for progress in the Middle East peace process were heightened by a number of dramatic political developments, notably the decision by the United States to begin a dialogue with the Palestine Liberation Organization (PLO) and other important proposals aimed primarily at launching a dialogue between Israelis and Palestinians. However, he expressed concern over the fact that valuable time was passing and the willingness to negotiate might be eroded by bitterness resulting from events on the ground. The *intifadah*, in contrast to the nuances of the diplomatic process, gave a direct and unequivocal message of rejection of the Israeli occupation and commitment to the exercise of legitimate Palestinian rights, including self-determination.

The Secretary-General reported that he had endeavoured to launch a process of consultations, initially with the permanent members of the Security Council, and remained in continuous contact with the parties to the conflict to discuss ways of advancing the peace process, including the prospects for an international peace conference on the Middle East.

He reiterated that he was troubled by some declarations that questioned the applicability of Security Council resolution 242(1967),[7] since he believed that any deviation from it imperilled the prospects for a comprehensive settlement and that

the Council could make an important contribution to the process by renewing its commitment to that resolution as well as Council resolution 338(1973).[8]

By an October report with later addendum,[9] the Secretary-General submitted to the Assembly replies from four Member States to his request for information on steps taken to implement three 1988 Assembly resolutions on the Middle East situation. By those resolutions—dealing with general aspects of the Middle East situation,[5] Israeli policy in the Syrian Arab Golan occupied by Israel since 1967[10] and the transfer by some States of their diplomatic missions to Jerusalem[11]—the Assembly had called on States to adopt a number of measures concerning their relations with Israel and on the States concerned to abide by the relevant Assembly resolutions.

GENERAL ASSEMBLY ACTION

On 4 December 1989, the General Assembly adopted **resolution 44/40 A** by recorded vote.

The General Assembly,

Having discussed the item entitled ''The situation in the Middle East'',

Reaffirming its resolutions 36/226 A and B of 17 December 1981, ES-9/1 of 5 February 1982, 37/123 F of 20 December 1982, 38/58 A to E of 13 December 1983, 38/180 A to D of 19 December 1983, 39/146 A to C of 14 December 1984, 40/168 A to C of 16 December 1985, 41/162 A to C of 4 December 1986, 42/209 A to D of 11 December 1987 and 43/54 A to C of 6 December 1988,

Recalling Security Council resolutions 425(1978) of 19 March 1978, 497(1981) of 17 December 1981, 508(1982) of 5 June 1982, 509(1982) of 6 June 1982, 511(1982) of 18 June 1982, 512(1982) of 19 June 1982, 513(1982) of 4 July 1982, 515(1982) of 29 July 1982, 516(1982) of 1 August 1982, 517(1982) of 4 August 1982, 518(1982) of 12 August 1982, 519(1982) of 17 August 1982, 520(1982) of 17 September 1982, 521(1982) of 19 September 1982 and 555(1984) of 12 October 1984 and other relevant resolutions,

Taking note of the reports of the Secretary-General of 27 October 1989, 16 November 1989 and 22 November 1989,

Reaffirming the need for continued collective support for the decisions adopted by the Twelfth Arab Summit Conference, held at Fez, Morocco, on 25 November 1981 and from 6 to 9 September 1982, which were confirmed by subsequent Arab summit conferences, including the Extraordinary Arab Summit Conference held at Casablanca, Morocco, from 23 to 26 May 1989, reiterating its previous resolutions on the question of Palestine and its support for the Palestine Liberation Organization as the sole legitimate representative of the Palestinian people, and considering that the convening of the International Peace Conference on the Middle East, under the auspices of the United Nations, in accordance with General Assembly resolution 38/58 C and other resolutions related to the question of Palestine, would contribute to the promotion of peace in the region,

Welcoming all efforts contributing towards the realization of the inalienable rights of the Palestinian people through the achievement of a comprehensive, just and lasting peace in the Middle East, in accordance with the United Nations resolutions relating to the question of Palestine and to the situation in the Middle East,

Welcoming the world-wide support extended to the just cause of the Palestinian people and the other Arab countries in their struggle against Israeli aggression and occupation in order to achieve a comprehensive, just and lasting peace in the Middle East and the full exercise by the Palestinian people of its inalienable national rights, as affirmed by previous resolutions of the General Assembly on the question of Palestine and on the situation in the Middle East,

Gravely concerned that the Palestinian territory occupied since 1967, including Jerusalem, and the other occupied Arab territories still remain under Israeli occupation, that the relevant resolutions of the United Nations have not been implemented and that the Palestinian people is still denied the restoration of its land and the exercise of its inalienable national rights in conformity with international law, as reaffirmed by resolutions of the United Nations,

Reaffirming the applicability of the Geneva Convention relative to the Protection of Civilian Persons in Time of War, of 12 August 1949, to the Palestinian territory occupied since 1967, including Jerusalem, and the other occupied Arab territories,

Reaffirming also all relevant United Nations resolutions which stipulate that the acquisition of territory by force is inadmissible under the Charter of the United Nations and the principles of international law and that Israel must withdraw unconditionally from the Palestinian territory occupied since 1967, including Jerusalem, and the other occupied Arab territories,

Reaffirming further the imperative necessity of establishing a comprehensive, just and lasting peace in the region, based on full respect for the Charter and the principles of international law,

Gravely concerned also at the continuing Israeli policies involving the escalation and expansion of the conflict in the region, which further violate the principles of international law and endanger international peace and security,

Stressing once again the great importance of the time factor in the endeavours to achieve an early comprehensive, just and lasting peace in the Middle East,

1. *Reaffirms its conviction* that the question of Palestine is the core of the conflict in the Middle East and that no comprehensive, just and lasting peace in the region will be achieved without the full exercise by the Palestinian people of its inalienable national rights and the immediate, unconditional and total withdrawal of Israel from the Palestinian territory occupied since 1967, including Jerusalem, and the other occupied Arab territories;

2. *Reaffirms* that a just and comprehensive settlement of the situation in the Middle East cannot be achieved without the participation on an equal footing of all the parties to the conflict, including the Palestine Liberation Organization, the representative of the Palestinian people;

3. *Declares once more* that peace in the Middle East is indivisible and must be based on a comprehensive, just and lasting solution of the Middle East problem, under the auspices of the United Nations and on the basis of its relevant resolutions, which ensures the complete and unconditional withdrawal of Israel from the Palestinian territory occupied since 1967, including Jerusalem, and the other occupied Arab territories, and which enables the Palestinian people, under the leadership of the Palestine Liberation Organization, to exercise its inalienable rights, including the right to return and the right to self-determination, national independence and the establishment of its independent sovereign State in Palestine, in accordance with the resolutions of the United Nations relating to the question of Palestine, in particular General Assembly resolutions ES-7/2 of 29 July 1980, 36/120 A to F of 10 December 1981, 37/86 A to D of 10 December 1982, 37/86 E of 20 December 1982, 38/58 A to E of 13 December 1983, 39/49 A to D of 11 December 1984, 40/96 A to D of 12 December 1985, 41/43 A to D of 2 December 1986, 42/66 A to D of 2 December 1987, 43/54 A to C of 6 December 1988, and 43/175 A to C, 43/176 and 43/177 of 15 December 1988;

4. *Considers* the Arab peace plan adopted unanimously at the Twelfth Arab Summit Conference, held at Fez, Morocco, on 25 November 1981 and from 6 to 9 September 1982, which was confirmed by subsequent Arab summit conferences, including the Extraordinary Arab Summit Conference held at Casablanca, Morocco, from 23 to 26 May 1989, as well as relevant efforts and action to implement the Fez plan, as an important contribution towards the realization of the inalienable rights of the Palestinian people through the achievement of a comprehensive, just and lasting peace in the Middle East;

5. *Condemns* Israel's continued occupation of the Palestinian territory occupied since 1967, including Jerusalem, and the other occupied Arab territories, in violation of the Charter of the United Nations, the principles of international law and the relevant resolutions of the United Nations, and demands the immediate, unconditional and total withdrawal of Israel from all the territories occupied since 1967;

6. *Rejects* all agreements and arrangements which violate the inalienable rights of the Palestinian people and contradict the principles of a just and comprehensive solution to the Middle East problem to ensure the establishment of a just peace in the area;

7. *Deplores* Israel's failure to comply with Security Council resolutions 476(1980) of 30 June 1980 and 478(1980) of 20 August 1980 and General Assembly resolutions 35/207 of 16 December 1980 and 36/226 A and B of 17 December 1981; determines that Israel's decision to annex Jerusalem and to declare it as its "capital" as well as the measures to alter its physical character, demographic composition, institutional structure and status are null and void and demands that they be rescinded immediately; and calls upon all Member States, the specialized agencies and all other international organizations to abide by the present resolution and all other relevant resolutions and decisions;

8. *Condemns* Israel's aggression, policies and practices against the Palestinian people in the occupied Palestinian territory and outside this territory, including expropriation, establishment of settlements, annexation and other terrorist, aggressive and repressive measures, which are in violation of the Charter and the principles of international law and the relevant international conventions;

9. *Strongly condemns* the imposition by Israel of its laws, jurisdiction and administration on the occupied Syrian Arab Golan, its annexationist policies and practices, the establishment of settlements, the confiscation of lands, the diversion of water resources and the imposition of Israeli citizenship on Syrian nationals, and declares that all these measures are null and void and constitute a violation of the rules and principles of international law relative to belligerent occupation, in particular the Geneva Convention relative to the Protection of Civilian Persons in Time of War, of 12 August 1949;

10. *Considers* that the agreements on strategic co-operation between the United States of America and Israel, signed on 30 November 1981, and the continued supply of modern arms and *matériel* to Israel, augmented by substantial economic aid, including the Agreement on the Establishment of a Free Trade Area between the two Governments, have encouraged Israel to pursue its aggressive and expansionist policies and practices in the Palestinian territory occupied since 1967, including Jerusalem, and the other occupied Arab territories, and have had adverse effects on efforts for the establishment of a comprehensive, just and lasting peace in the Middle East and pose a threat to the security of the region;

11. *Calls once more upon* all States to put an end to the flow to Israel of any military, economic, financial and technological aid, as well as of human resources, aimed at encouraging it to pursue its aggressive policies against the Arab countries and the Palestinian people;

12. *Strongly condemns* the continuing and increasing collaboration between Israel and the racist régime of South Africa, especially in the economic, military and nuclear fields, which constitutes a hostile act against the African and Arab States and enables Israel to enhance its nuclear capabilities, thus subjecting the States of the region to nuclear blackmail;

13. *Reaffirms its call* for convening the International Peace Conference on the Middle East, under the auspices of the United Nations, with the participation of the five permanent members of the Security Council and all parties to the conflict, including the Palestine Liberation Organization, the sole legitimate representative of the Palestinian people, on an equal footing, and that the Conference should be effective with full authority, in order to achieve a comprehensive and just solution based on the withdrawal of Israel from the occupied Palestinian territory, including Jerusalem, and the other occupied Arab territories, and the attainment of the inalienable rights of the Palestinian people in accordance with United Nations resolutions relevant to the question of Palestine and the situation in the Middle East;

14. *Endorses the call* for setting up a preparatory committee, within the framework of the Security Council, with the participation of the permanent members of the Council, to take the necessary action to convene the Conference;

15. *Requests* the Secretary-General to report to the Security Council periodically on the development of the situation and to submit to the General Assembly at its forty-fifth session a comprehensive report covering the developments in the Middle East in all their aspects.

General Assembly resolution 44/40 A

4 December 1989   Meeting 73   109-18-31 (recorded vote)

12-nation draft (A/44/L.47 & Add.1); agenda item 37.
Sponsors: Afghanistan, Albania, Bahrain, Cuba, Djibouti, Indonesia, Kuwait, Malaysia, Mauritania, Morocco, Oman, Pakistan.
Meeting numbers. GA 44th session: plenary 64-66, 73.

Recorded vote in Assembly as follows:

In favour: Afghanistan, Albania, Algeria, Angola, Argentina, Bahrain, Bangladesh, Belize, Benin, Bhutan, Bolivia, Botswana, Brazil, Brunei Darussalam, Bulgaria, Burkina Faso, Burundi, Byelorussian SSR, Cameroon, Cape Verde, Chad, China, Colombia, Comoros, Congo, Côte d'Ivoire, Cuba, Cyprus, Czechoslovakia, Democratic Kampuchea, Democratic Yemen, Djibouti, Ecuador, Egypt, Ethiopia, Gabon, Gambia, German Democratic Republic, Ghana, Greece, Guatemala, Guinea, Guinea-Bissau, Guyana, Haiti, Hungary, India, Indonesia, Iran, Iraq, Jordan, Kuwait, Lao People's Democratic Republic, Lebanon, Lesotho, Libyan Arab Jamahiriya, Madagascar, Malaysia, Maldives, Mali, Mauritania, Mauritius, Mexico, Mongolia, Morocco, Mozambique, Myanmar, Nepal, Nicaragua, Niger, Nigeria, Oman, Pakistan, Peru, Philippines, Poland, Qatar, Romania, Rwanda, Sao Tome and Principe, Saudi Arabia, Senegal, Seychelles, Sierra Leone, Singapore, Somalia, Sri Lanka, Sudan, Suriname, Swaziland, Syrian Arab Republic, Thailand, Togo, Trinidad and Tobago, Tunisia, Turkey, Uganda, Ukrainian SSR, USSR, United Arab Emirates, United Republic of Tanzania, Vanuatu, Venezuela, Viet Nam, Yemen, Yugoslavia, Zaire, Zambia, Zimbabwe.
Against: Australia, Belgium, Canada, Denmark, Dominica, France, Germany, Federal Republic of, Iceland, Ireland, Israel, Italy, Luxembourg, Netherlands, New Zealand, Norway, Portugal, United Kingdom, United States.
Abstaining: Antigua and Barbuda, Austria, Bahamas, Barbados, Central African Republic, Chile, Costa Rica, Dominican Republic, El Salvador, Equatorial Guinea, Fiji, Finland, Grenada, Honduras, Jamaica, Japan, Kenya, Liberia, Malawi, Malta, Panama, Papua New Guinea, Paraguay, Saint Kitts and Nevis, Saint Lucia, Saint Vincent and the Grenadines, Samoa, Solomon Islands, Spain, Sweden, Uruguay.

UN Truce Supervision Organization

In his November report on the Middle East,[6] the Secretary-General provided information on the activities of three UN peace-keeping operations in the region: two peace-keeping forces—UNDOF and UNIFIL—and one observer mission, the United Nations Truce Supervision Organization (UNTSO). Apart from assisting UNDOF and UNIFIL, UNTSO maintained two observer groups of its own in Beirut, Lebanon, and in Egypt. The Observer Group in Beirut, set up by the Security Council in 1982 following the occupation of West Beirut by Israeli troops,[12] stood at a reduced strength of 14 observers, some of whom were withdrawn temporarily during hostilities in 1989. The Observer Group in Egypt, established when the second United Nations Emergency Force was withdrawn in 1979,[13] had a total strength of 50 observers. In addition to liaison offices in Cairo and Ismailia, it maintained six observation posts in the Sinai.

On 15 November, the Secretary-General informed the President of the Security Council[14] that total UNTSO strength was at its authorized level of 298 officers, contributed by 10 countries. China and Switzerland had each recently offered five observers. The Council agreed with the proposed change in the composition of UNTSO.[15]

REFERENCES

[1]A/44/721-S/20960. [2]A/44/282-S/20637. [3]A/44/796-S/20987. [4]A/44/35. [5]YUN 1988, p. 202, GA res. 43/54 A, 6 Dec. 1988. [6]A/44/737-S/20971. [7]YUN 1967, p. 257, SC res. 242(1967), 22 Nov. 1967. [8]YUN 1973, p. 213, SC

res. 338(1973), 22 Oct. 1973. [9]A/44/690 & Add.1. [10]YUN 1988, p. 246, GA res. 43/54 B, 6 Dec. 1988. [11]*Ibid.*, p. 212, GA res. 43/54 C, 6 Dec. 1988. [12]YUN 1982, p. 475, SC res. 516(1982), 1 Aug. 1982. [13]YUN 1979, p. 318. [14]S/20977. [15]S/20978.

Palestine question

The question of Palestine remained at the core of an intensifying Arab-Israeli conflict which brought with it an escalating uprising against Israeli occupation in the West Bank, Gaza Strip and East Jerusalem. In April, at the request of the Chairman of the Arab Group at the United Nations, the Assembly resumed its consideration of the question and adopted a resolution condemning the latest action of members of the Israeli armed forces in the Palestinian town of Nahalin and requesting the Security Council to consider measures to provide international protection to the Palestinian civilians (see below, under ''Territories occupied by Israel''). Under the same agenda item, the Assembly in October adopted a resolution on the *intifadah*. In December, following its consideration of the 1989 report of the Committee on Palestinian rights,[1] the Assembly adopted three resolutions addressing the Palestine question.

The International Day of Solidarity with the Palestinian People was observed on 29 November at United Nations Headquarters in New York and at the United Nations Offices at Geneva and Vienna.

GENERAL ASSEMBLY ACTION

On 20 April, the General Assembly adopted **resolution 43/233** by recorded vote.

Question of Palestine

The General Assembly,

Having considered the item entitled ''Question of Palestine'',

Guided by the principles of the Charter of the United Nations and the provisions of the Universal Declaration of Human Rights,

Gravely concerned at and alarmed by the deteriorating situation in the Palestinian territory occupied by Israel since 1967, including Jerusalem,

Expressing its profound shock at the latest action of members of the Israeli armed forces on 13 April 1989, which resulted in the killing and wounding of Palestinian civilians in the town of Nahalin,

Having considered the statement of the Secretary-General on 13 April 1989 relative to that raid,

Aware that Israel, the occupying Power, has imposed limitations on Palestinian Muslims that restrict their participation in the life of their community and in the observance of their religious rites and obligations,

Taking into account the need to consider means for the impartial protection of the Palestinian civilian population under Israeli occupation,

Considering that the current policies and practices of Israel, the occupying Power, in the occupied Palestinian territory are bound to have grave consequences for the endeavours to achieve a comprehensive, just and lasting peace in the Middle East,

Reaffirming once again that the Geneva Convention relative to the Protection of Civilian Persons in Time of War, of 12 August 1949, is applicable to the Palestinian and other Arab territories occupied by Israel, including Jerusalem,

1. *Condemns* those policies and practices of Israel, the occupying Power, which violate the human rights of the Palestinian people in the occupied territory, including the right of freedom of worship, and, in particular, the opening of fire by Israeli armed forces, which has resulted in the killing and wounding of defenceless Palestinian civilians, and specifically the latest action of members of the Israeli armed forces against the defenceless civilians in the Palestinian town of Nahalin;

2. *Demands* that Israel, the occupying Power, abide scrupulously by the Geneva Convention relative to the Protection of Civilian Persons in Time of War, of 12 August 1949, and that it desist immediately from those policies and practices which are in violation of the provisions of the Convention;

3. *Requests* the Security Council to consider with urgency the situation in the occupied Palestinian territory with a view to considering measures needed to provide international protection to the Palestinian civilians in the Palestinian territory occupied by Israel since 1967, including Jerusalem;

4. *Stresses* the urgent need to expedite the convening of the International Peace Conference on the Middle East, under the auspices of the United Nations and in conformity with the provisions of General Assembly resolution 43/176 of 15 December 1988;

5. *Requests* the Secretary-General to submit periodic reports on developments in the occupied Palestinian territory.

General Assembly resolution 43/233

20 April 1989   Meeting 94   129-2-1 (recorded vote)

38-nation draft (A/43/L.55 & Add.1); agenda item 37.
Sponsors: Afghanistan, Algeria, Bahrain, Bangladesh, Democratic Yemen, Djibouti, Egypt, German Democratic Republic, India, Indonesia, Iraq, Jordan, Kuwait, Lebanon, Libyan Arab Jamahiriya, Madagascar, Malaysia, Mali, Malta, Mauritania, Mongolia, Morocco, Oman, Qatar, Saudi Arabia, Senegal, Somalia, Sudan, Tunisia, Uganda, Ukrainian SSR, United Arab Emirates, Vanuatu, Viet Nam, Yemen, Yugoslavia, Zambia.
Meeting numbers. GA 43rd session: plenary 92-94.

Recorded vote in Assembly as follows:

In favour: Afghanistan, Albania, Algeria, Angola, Argentina, Australia, Austria, Bahamas, Bahrain, Bangladesh, Barbados, Belgium, Bhutan, Bolivia, Botswana, Brazil, Brunei Darussalam, Bulgaria, Burkina Faso, Burma, Burundi, Byelorussian SSR, Canada, Cape Verde, Chad, China, Colombia, Comoros, Côte d'Ivoire, Cuba, Cyprus, Czechoslovakia, Democratic Yemen, Denmark, Djibouti, Egypt, Ethiopia, Fiji, Finland, France, Gabon, Gambia, German Democratic Republic, Germany, Federal Republic of, Ghana, Greece, Guatemala, Guinea-Bissau, Guyana, Haiti, Hungary, Iceland, India, Indonesia, Iran, Iraq, Ireland, Italy, Jamaica, Japan, Jordan, Kenya, Kuwait, Lao People's Democratic Republic, Lebanon, Lesotho, Libyan Arab Jamahiriya, Luxembourg, Madagascar, Malaysia, Maldives, Mali, Malta, Mauritania, Mauritius, Mexico, Mongolia, Morocco, Mozambique, Nepal, Netherlands, New Zealand, Nicaragua, Niger, Nigeria, Norway, Oman, Pakistan, Panama, Papua New Guinea, Paraguay, Peru, Philippines, Poland, Portugal, Qatar, Rwanda, Saint Vincent and the Grenadines, Samoa, Sao Tome and Principe, Saudi Arabia, Senegal, Sierra Leone, Singapore, Somalia, Spain, Sri Lanka, Sudan, Suriname, Sweden, Syrian Arab Republic, Thailand, Trinidad and Tobago, Tunisia, Turkey, Uganda, Ukrainian USSR, United Arab Emirates, United Kingdom, United Repub-

lic of Tanzania, Uruguay, Venezuela, Viet Nam, Yemen, Yugoslavia, Zaire, Zambia, Zimbabwe.
Against: Israel, United States.
Abstaining: Liberia.

Activities of the Committee on Palestinian rights. As mandated by the General Assembly in 1988,[2] the Committee on Palestinian rights, established in 1975,[3] continued to review the situation relating to the Palestine question in the light of new developments and to promote the exercise by the Palestinian people of its rights.

In November, the Committee submitted to the Assembly its annual report[1] with recommendations. The Committee acknowledged that the year under review had brought about events of momentous significance in the history of the struggle of the Palestinians to regain and exercise their rights. Their continuing uprising, the proclamation of the State of Palestine and the Palestinian peace initiative announced in December 1988 by Yasser Arafat had in the Committee's view created new conditions and opportunities for concerted international action aimed at achieving a comprehensive, just and lasting settlement. The growing deterioration of the situation in the occupied Palestinian territory was, according to the Committee, a matter of utmost concern that imposed a moral duty on the international community to bring about such a settlement expeditiously. The Committee considered it incumbent on the Security Council to take concrete and effective action to secure those goals. It believed that its 1976 recommendations,[4] endorsed by the Assembly,[5] provided a constructive programme for implementing Palestinian rights; it therefore called for urgent positive action on those recommendations by the Security Council and reaffirmed that the recognition, attainment and exercise of the rights of the Palestinians were indispensable conditions in the solution of the Palestine question. The Committee reasserted that the Israeli evacuation of the occupied territories was a *conditio sine qua non* for the exercise of those rights.

The Committee reaffirmed the international consensus that PLO was the sole and legitimate representative of the Palestinians, whose participation on an equal footing was indispensable in any efforts and deliberations aimed at achieving a comprehensive, just and lasting Middle East peace. It considered that the State of Palestine should be accorded its rightful place within the international community and the United Nations. It noted the widespread international support for the Palestinian peace initiative and deeply regretted that Israel so far had failed to respond positively to it and continued to refuse to acknowledge Palestinian national rights; it accordingly urged Israel to reverse its position and join the international consensus.

The Committee considered it imperative for the Security Council to take positive action towards the convening of an international peace conference on the Middle East (see below), on the basis of a 1988 General Assembly resolution on the Palestine question,[6] which had the international community's overwhelming support. The Committee reaffirmed the principles for achieving a comprehensive peace contained in that resolution, namely: Israeli withdrawal from the Palestinian territory occupied since 1967, including Jerusalem, and from the other occupied Arab territories; guaranteeing arrangements for the security of all States in the region, including those mentioned in the 1947 resolution on the future Government of Palestine,[7] within secure and internationally recognized boundaries; resolving the problem of the Palestine refugees in conformity with a 1948 Assembly resolution[8] and subsequent relevant resolutions; dismantling the Israeli settlements in the occupied territories; and guaranteeing freedom of access to Holy Places, religious buildings and sites.

The Committee urged the Secretary-General to do everything in his power to ensure that active consultations were undertaken within the Security Council towards the convening of an international conference; the Committee itself intended to continue to intensify its efforts towards that objective and make it once again the focal point of its work programme in the coming year. Noting that the Secretary-General had reported that his attempts to pave the way to an effective negotiating process had so far proved inconclusive, the Committee recommended that the Assembly call once again on the Council, particularly its permanent members, to consider measures needed to convene such a conference, including the establishment of a preparatory committee, and to consider guarantees for security measures in accordance with the 1988 resolution.[6]

The Committee protested in the strongest terms the intensification of Israeli repression against Palestinians in the occupied territory, including children, particularly the liberal use of live ammunition, random beatings, raids and mass arrests, the increased use of administrative detention, deportations and collective punishment. It condemned the unchecked violence of Israeli settlers and the measures taken by the occupying Power to deprive the Palestinians of their right to education, as well as administrative, economic and other measures to control all aspects of Palestinian life and prevent the development of autonomous socio-economic structures. The Committee welcomed the action by Governments, non-governmental organizations (NGOs) and other bodies to denounce those measures and welcomed the partial opening of schools as a result of that international pressure. It called on all concerned to redouble their efforts to expose, protest and put an end to those Israeli policies and practices which violated the 1949 Geneva Convention relative to the Protection of Civilian Persons in Time of War (fourth Geneva Convention). Given the grave situation created by such policies and practices, the Committee called once again on the Security Council to consider urgently measures to provide international protection to the Palestinians in the occupied territory, including Jerusalem. It also called for international action to alleviate the sufferings of the Palestinians living under occupation, especially women and children.

The Committee reasserted that the United Nations had a historical duty and responsibility to render all assistance necessary to promote the autonomous economic development of the occupied territory in preparation for the attainment of independence; it accordingly reiterated its call on the UN system, as well as on Governments, intergovernmental organizations and NGOs, to sustain and increase their economic and social assistance, in close co-operation with PLO.

The Committee noted with satisfaction the increased awareness and mobilization of international public opinion in support of the attainment of Palestinian rights and UN recommendations for a comprehensive, just and lasting solution to the Palestine question. It believed that its regional seminars and meetings and symposia of NGOs, as well as the journalists' encounters and other informational activities it sponsored, had played a valuable role in that process; it would continue to strive for maximum effectiveness in carrying out that programme and to intensify its efforts in implementation of its mandate.

In order to promote international awareness of the Palestine question and create conditions favourable for implementation of its recommendations, the Committee and, under its guidance, the Division for Palestinian Rights continued to expand co-operation with NGOs. To that end, it held a regional symposium and seminar in Africa (Cairo, Egypt, 18-22 December 1988); a North American regional seminar (New York, 19-20 June); a North American regional NGO symposium (New York, 21-23 June 1989); a regional symposium in Europe (Vienna, 28-29 August); an international NGO meeting (Vienna, 30 August-1 September); and an Asian regional NGO symposium (Kuala Lumpur, Malaysia, 18-21 December). The conclusions, recommendations and declarations of the symposia and seminars were annexed to the Committee's report. The Committee was represented at a number of international conferences and meetings, including an international NGO symposium on the role of foreign assistance in meeting the economic and social development requirements of the Palestinian people (Vienna, 27 August).

GENERAL ASSEMBLY ACTION

Following consideration of the report of the Committee on Palestinian rights, the General Assembly adopted on 6 December resolutions on the question of Palestine. **Resolution 44/41 A** was adopted by recorded vote.

The General Assembly,

Recalling its resolutions 181(II) of 29 November 1947, 194(III) of 11 December 1948, 3236(XXIX) of 22 November 1974, 3375(XXX) and 3376(XXX) of 10 November 1975, 31/20 of 24 November 1976, 32/40 of 2 December 1977, 33/28 of 7 December 1978, 34/65 A and B of 29 November 1979 and 34/65 C and D of 12 December 1979, ES-7/2 of 29 July 1980, 35/169 of 15 December 1980, 36/120 of 10 December 1981, ES-7/4 of 28 April 1982, ES-7/5 of 26 June 1982, ES-7/9 of 24 September 1982, 37/86 A of 10 December 1982, 38/58 A of 13 December 1983, 39/49 A of 11 December 1984, 40/96 A of 12 December 1985, 41/43 A of 2 December 1986, 42/66 A of 2 December 1987 and 43/175 A of 15 December 1988,

Having considered the report of the Committee on the Exercise of the Inalienable Rights of the Palestinian People,

1. *Expresses its appreciation* to the Committee on the Exercise of the Inalienable Rights of the Palestinian People for its efforts in performing the tasks assigned to it by the General Assembly;

2. *Endorses* the recommendations of the Committee contained in paragraphs 110 to 118 of its report and draws the attention of the Security Council to the fact that action on the Committee's recommendations, as repeatedly endorsed by the General Assembly at its thirty-first session and subsequently, is still awaited;

3. *Requests* the Committee to continue to keep under review the situation relating to the question of Palestine as well as the implementation of the Programme of Action for the Achievement of Palestinian Rights and to report and make suggestions to the General Assembly or the Security Council, as appropriate;

4. *Authorizes* the Committee to continue to exert all efforts to promote the implementation of its recommendations, including representation at conferences and meetings and the sending of delegations, to make such adjustments in its approved programme of seminars and symposia and meetings for non-governmental organizations as it may consider necessary, and to report thereon to the General Assembly at its forty-fifth session and thereafter;

5. *Also requests* the Committee to continue to extend its co-operation to non-governmental organizations in their contribution towards heightening international awareness of the facts relating to the question of Palestine and creating a more favourable atmosphere for the full implementation of the Committee's recommendations, and to take the necessary steps to expand its contacts with those organizations;

6. *Requests* the United Nations Conciliation Commission for Palestine, established under General Assembly resolution 194(III), as well as other United Nations bodies associated with the question of Palestine, to continue to co-operate fully with the Committee and to make available to it, at its request, the relevant in-

formation and documentation which they have at their disposal;

7. *Decides* to circulate the report of the Committee to all the competent bodies of the United Nations and urges them to take the necessary action, as appropriate, in accordance with the Committee's programme of implementation;

8. *Requests* the Secretary-General to continue to provide the Committee with all the necessary facilities for the performance of its tasks.

General Assembly resolution 44/41 A

6 December 1989   Meeting 76   132-3-21 (recorded vote)

14-nation draft (A/44/L.43 & Add.1); agenda item 39.
Sponsors: Afghanistan, Bangladesh, Cuba, German Democratic Republic, Guyana, India, Indonesia, Madagascar, Malaysia, Mali, Pakistan, Senegal, Ukrainian SSR, Yugoslavia.
Financial implications. 5th Committee, A/44/846; S-G, A/C.5/44/43.
Meeting numbers. GA 44th session: 5th Committee 53; plenary 23, 67-71, 73, 76.

Recorded vote in Assembly as follows:

In favour: Afghanistan, Albania, Algeria, Angola, Antigua and Barbuda, Argentina, Bahamas, Bahrain, Bangladesh, Barbados, Benin, Bhutan, Bolivia, Botswana, Brazil, Brunei Darussalam, Bulgaria, Burkina Faso, Burundi, Byelorussian SSR, Cameroon, Cape Verde, Central African Republic, Chad, Chile, China, Colombia, Comoros, Congo, Costa Rica, Côte d'Ivoire, Cuba, Cyprus, Czechoslovakia, Democratic Kampuchea, Democratic Yemen, Djibouti, Ecuador, Egypt, El Salvador, Ethiopia, Fiji, Gabon, Gambia, German Democratic Republic, Ghana, Greece, Grenada, Guatemala, Guinea, Guinea-Bissau, Guyana, Haiti, Hungary, India, Indonesia, Iran, Iraq, Jamaica, Jordan, Kenya, Kuwait, Lao People's Democratic Republic, Lebanon, Lesotho, Liberia, Libyan Arab Jamahiriya, Madagascar, Malawi, Malaysia, Maldives, Mali, Malta, Mauritania, Mauritius, Mexico, Mongolia, Morocco, Mozambique, Myanmar, Nepal, Nicaragua, Niger, Nigeria, Oman, Pakistan, Panama, Papua New Guinea, Paraguay, Peru, Philippines, Poland, Qatar, Romania, Rwanda, Saint Kitts and Nevis, Saint Lucia, Saint Vincent and the Grenadines, Samoa, Sao Tome and Principe, Saudi Arabia, Senegal, Seychelles, Sierra Leone, Singapore, Solomon Islands, Somalia, Spain, Sri Lanka, Sudan, Suriname, Swaziland, Syrian Arab Republic, Thailand, Togo, Trinidad and Tobago, Tunisia, Turkey, Uganda, Ukrainian SSR, USSR, United Arab Emirates, United Republic of Tanzania, Uruguay, Vanuatu, Venezuela, Viet Nam, Yemen, Yugoslavia, Zaire, Zambia, Zimbabwe.
Against: Dominica, Israel, United States.
Abstaining: Australia, Austria, Belgium, Belize, Canada, Denmark, Equatorial Guinea, Finland, France, Germany, Federal Republic of, Iceland, Ireland, Italy, Japan, Luxembourg, Netherlands, New Zealand, Norway, Portugal, Sweden, United Kingdom.

On the same date, the Assembly also adopted **resolution 44/41 B** by recorded vote.

The General Assembly,

Having considered the report of the Committee on the Exercise of the Inalienable Rights of the Palestinian People,

Taking note, in particular, of the relevant information contained in paragraphs 64 to 93 of that report,

Recalling its resolutions 32/40 B of 2 December 1977, 33/28 C of 7 December 1978, 34/65 D of 12 December 1979, 35/169 D of 15 December 1980, 36/120 B of 10 December 1981, 37/86 B of 10 December 1982, 38/58 B of 13 December 1983, 39/49 B of 11 December 1984, 40/96 B of 12 December 1985, 41/43 B of 2 December 1986, 42/66 B of 2 December 1987 and 43/175 B of 15 December 1988,

1. *Takes note with appreciation* of the action taken by the Secretary-General in compliance with General Assembly resolution 43/175 B;

2. *Requests* the Secretary-General to provide the Division for Palestinian Rights of the Secretariat with the necessary resources and to ensure that it continues to discharge the tasks detailed in paragraph 1 of General

Assembly resolution 32/40 B, paragraph 2 *(b)* of resolution 34/65 D, paragraph 3 of resolution 36/120 B, paragraph 3 of resolution 38/58 B, paragraph 3 of resolution 40/96 B and paragraph 2 of resolution 42/66 B, in consultation with the Committee on the Exercise of the Inalienable Rights of the Palestinian People and under its guidance;

3. *Also requests* the Secretary-General to ensure the continued co-operation of the Department of Public Information and other units of the Secretariat in enabling the Division for Palestinian Rights to perform its tasks and in covering adequately the various aspects of the question of Palestine;

4. *Invites* all Governments and organizations to lend their co-operation to the Committee on the Exercise of the Inalienable Rights of the Palestinian People and the Division for Palestinian Rights in the performance of their tasks;

5. *Takes note with appreciation* of the action taken by Member States to observe annually on 29 November the International Day of Solidarity with the Palestinian People.

General Assembly resolution 44/41 B

6 December 1989   Meeting 76   133-3-20 (recorded vote)

14-nation draft (A/44/L.44 & Add.1); agenda item 39.
Sponsors: Afghanistan, Bangladesh, Cuba, German Democratic Republic, Guyana, India, Indonesia, Madagascar, Malaysia, Mali, Pakistan, Senegal, Ukrainian SSR, Yugoslavia.
Financial implications. 5th Committee, A/44/846; S-G, A/C.5/44/43.
Meeting numbers. GA 44th session: 5th Committee 53; plenary 23, 67-71, 73, 76.

Recorded vote in Assembly as follows:

In favour: Afghanistan, Albania, Algeria, Angola, Antigua and Barbuda, Argentina, Bahamas, Bahrain, Bangladesh, Barbados, Benin, Bhutan, Bolivia, Botswana, Brazil, Brunei Darussalam, Bulgaria, Burkina Faso, Burundi, Byelorussian SSR, Cameroon, Cape Verde, Central African Republic, Chad, Chile, China, Colombia, Comoros, Congo, Costa Rica, Côte d'Ivoire, Cuba, Cyprus, Czechoslovakia, Democratic Kampuchea, Democratic Yemen, Djibouti, Ecuador, Egypt, El Salvador, Equatorial Guinea, Ethiopia, Fiji, Gabon, Gambia, German Democratic Republic, Ghana, Greece, Grenada, Guatemala, Guinea, Guinea-Bissau, Guyana, Haiti, Hungary, India, Indonesia, Iran, Iraq, Jamaica, Jordan, Kenya, Kuwait, Lao People's Democratic Republic, Lebanon, Lesotho, Liberia, Libyan Arab Jamahiriya, Madagascar, Malawi, Malaysia, Maldives, Mali, Malta, Mauritania, Mauritius, Mexico, Mongolia, Morocco, Mozambique, Myanmar, Nepal, Nicaragua, Niger, Nigeria, Oman, Pakistan, Panama, Papua New Guinea, Paraguay, Peru, Philippines, Poland, Qatar, Romania, Rwanda, Saint Kitts and Nevis, Saint Lucia, Saint Vincent and the Grenadines, Samoa, Sao Tome and Principe, Saudi Arabia, Senegal, Seychelles, Sierra Leone, Singapore, Solomon Islands, Somalia, Spain, Sri Lanka, Sudan, Suriname, Swaziland, Syrian Arab Republic, Thailand, Togo, Trinidad and Tobago, Tunisia, Turkey, Uganda, Ukrainian SSR, USSR, United Arab Emirates, United Republic of Tanzania, Uruguay, Vanuatu, Venezuela, Viet Nam, Yemen, Yugoslavia, Zaire, Zambia, Zimbabwe.
Against: Dominica, Israel, United States.
Abstaining: Australia, Austria, Belgium, Belize, Canada, Denmark, Finland, France, Germany, Federal Republic of, Iceland, Ireland, Italy, Japan, Luxembourg, Netherlands, New Zealand, Norway, Portugal, Sweden, United Kingdom.

Proposed peace conference under UN auspices

In accordance with a 1988 General Assembly request,[6] the Secretary General in 1989 continued his efforts with the parties concerned and, in consultation with the Security Council, to facilitate the convening of an international peace conference on the Middle East. In November, he submitted a progress report[9] setting out the results of the Security Council President's consultations with Council members and statements of concerned parties, as well as his own observations.

The Council President stated that the Council members had noted with appreciation some positive steps and initiatives undertaken in the past year, but remained preoccupied with the continuing lack of progress in achieving peace and the increasingly serious situation in the occupied territories. They reaffirmed their support for an active peace process and invited the Secretary-General to pursue his efforts and consultations with respect to the convening of an international peace conference. Most Council members stressed that the conference should be organized on the basis of a 1988 Assembly resolution on the question of Palestine,[6] in which the Assembly called for convening the conference under UN auspices, with the participation of all parties, including PLO, on an equal footing. Several Council members said the Council should begin urgent consideration of the Middle East situation with a view to reaching early agreement, in particular on the establishment of a preparatory committee for the conference, while others indicated that the parties directly concerned must reach agreement on the exact form of the conference, which should not prejudge the outcome of negotiations. However, one member could not support the convening of a conference on the basis of the 1988 resolution, since in its view the formula it contained failed to address the centrality of direct negotiations among the parties and purported to determine in advance the outcome of issues which had to be resolved in the course of negotiations. That member considered that the time was not right to convene an international conference.

In statements of concerned parties, submitted in response to a note verbale of the Secretary-General of 21 September, Egypt and Jordan supported the conference's convening and presented suggestions for its terms of reference and other aspects pertaining to it. Israel objected to convening a conference and advocated direct negotiations, stating that PLO could not be considered a partner to peace negotiations. Lebanon agreed in principle to convening a conference, but did not support any linkage of the solution of its own problem with that of the Middle East issue. The Syrian Arab Republic emphasized the need to continue efforts for convening the conference based on UN resolutions, complete Israeli withdrawal from all occupied Arab territories and guarantee of the national rights of the Palestinians. PLO stressed that all peace endeavours had to be carried out under UN auspices and on the basis of the principles of the Charter and the 1988 Assembly resolution.

The Secretary-General concluded that sufficient agreement did not exist, within the Council or among parties to the conflict, to permit the convening of a peace conference. He was deeply concerned that the opportunities which had emerged in the previous 12 months might slip away, but said he would spare no efforts to carry out the responsibilities entrusted to him in that regard.

In its annual report,[1] the Committee on Palestinian rights reiterated its firm conviction that the proposed conference provided the only comprehensive, practical and overwhelmingly accepted framework for peace in the Middle East. It believed that continuation of the *intifadah* and the intensification of repressive measures by Israel had created a critical situation making it imperative to advance towards a settlement of the Palestine question. The Committee stressed the urgent need for the Council and the parties directly concerned to take positive action towards convening the conference.

GENERAL ASSEMBLY ACTION

On 6 December, the General Assembly adopted **resolution 44/42** by recorded vote.

Question of Palestine

The General Assembly,

Having considered the report of the Secretary-General of 16 November 1989,

Having heard the statement made on 29 November 1989 by the chairman of the observer delegation of Palestine,

Stressing that achieving a comprehensive settlement of the Middle East conflict, the core of which is the question of Palestine, will constitute a significant contribution to international peace and security,

Aware of the overwhelming support for the convening of the International Peace Conference on the Middle East,

Noting with appreciation the endeavours of the Secretary-General to achieve the convening of the Conference,

Preoccupied by the increasingly serious situation in the occupied Palestinian territory as a result of persistent policies and practices of Israel, the occupying Power, and by the continuing lack of progress in achieving peace in the Middle East,

Aware of the ongoing uprising *(intifadah)* of the Palestinian people since 9 December 1987, aimed at ending Israeli occupation of Palestinian territory occupied since 1967,

1. *Reaffirms* the urgent need to achieve a just and comprehensive settlement of the Arab-Israeli conflict, the core of which is the question of Palestine;

2. *Calls once again* for the convening of the International Peace Conference on the Middle East, under the auspices of the United Nations, with the participation of all parties to the conflict, including the Palestine Liberation Organization, on an equal footing, and the five permanent members of the Security Council, based on Security Council resolutions 242(1967) of 22 November 1967 and 338(1973) of 22 October 1973 and the legitimate national rights of the Palestinian people, primarily the right to self-determination;

3. *Reaffirms* the following principles for the achievement of comprehensive peace:

(a) The withdrawal of Israel from the Palestinian territory occupied since 1967, including Jerusalem, and from the other occupied Arab territories;

(b) Guaranteeing arrangements for security of all States in the region, including those named in resolution 181(II) of 29 November 1947, within secure and internationally recognized boundaries;

(c) Resolving the problem of the Palestine refugees in conformity with General Assembly resolution 194(III) of 11 December 1948, and subsequent relevant resolutions;

(d) Dismantling the Israeli settlements in the territories occupied since 1967;

(e) Guaranteeing freedom of access to Holy Places, religious buildings and sites;

4. *Notes* the expressed desire and endeavours to place the Palestinian territory occupied since 1967, including Jerusalem, under the supervision of the United Nations for a limited period, as part of the peace process;

5. *Once again invites* the Security Council to consider measures needed to convene the International Peace Conference on the Middle East, including the establishment of a preparatory committee, and to consider guarantees for security measures agreed upon by the Conference for all States in the region;

6. *Requests* the Secretary-General to continue his efforts with the parties concerned, and in consultation with the Security Council, to facilitate the convening of the Conference, and to submit progress reports on developments in this matter.

General Assembly resolution 44/42

6 December 1989   Meeting 76   151-3-1 (recorded vote)

36-nation draft (A/44/L.51/Rev.1 & Add.1); agenda item 39.

Sponsors: Afghanistan, Bahrain, Bangladesh, Cuba, Cyprus, Democratic Yemen, Djibouti, Egypt, German Democratic Republic, Hungary, India, Indonesia, Iraq, Kuwait, Lebanon, Madagascar, Malaysia, Mali, Malta, Mauritania, Mongolia, Morocco, Oman, Pakistan, Qatar, Saudi Arabia, Senegal, Somalia, Sudan, Ukrainian SSR, United Arab Emirates, Vanuatu, Viet Nam, Yemen, Yugoslavia, Zambia.

Meeting numbers. GA 44th session: plenary 23, 67-71, 73, 76.

Recorded vote in Assembly as follows:

In favour: Afghanistan, Albania, Algeria, Angola, Antigua and Barbuda, Argentina, Australia, Austria, Bahamas, Bahrain, Bangladesh, Barbados, Belgium, Benin, Bhutan, Bolivia, Botswana, Brazil, Brunei Darussalam, Bulgaria, Burkina Faso, Burundi, Byelorussian SSR, Cameroon, Canada, Cape Verde, Central African Republic, Chad, Chile, China, Colombia, Comoros, Congo, Costa Rica, Côte d'Ivoire, Cuba, Cyprus, Czechoslovakia, Democratic Kampuchea, Democratic Yemen, Denmark, Djibouti, Ecuador, Egypt, El Salvador, Equatorial Guinea, Ethiopia, Fiji, Finland, France, Gabon, Gambia, German Democratic Republic, Germany, Federal Republic of, Ghana, Greece, Grenada, Guatemala, Guinea, Guinea-Bissau, Guyana, Haiti, Hungary, Iceland, India, Indonesia, Iraq, Ireland, Italy, Jamaica, Japan, Jordan, Kenya, Kuwait, Lao People's Democratic Republic, Lebanon, Lesotho, Liberia, Libyan Arab Jamahiriya, Luxembourg, Madagascar, Malawi, Malaysia, Maldives, Mali, Malta, Mauritania, Mauritius, Mexico, Mongolia, Morocco, Mozambique, Myanmar, Nepal, Netherlands, New Zealand, Nicaragua, Niger, Nigeria, Norway, Oman, Pakistan, Panama, Papua New Guinea, Paraguay, Peru, Philippines, Poland, Portugal, Qatar, Romania, Rwanda, Saint Kitts and Nevis, Saint Lucia, Saint Vincent and the Grenadines, Samoa, Sao Tome and Principe, Saudi Arabia, Senegal, Seychelles, Sierra Leone, Singapore, Solomon Islands, Somalia, Spain, Sri Lanka, Sudan, Suriname, Swaziland, Sweden, Syrian Arab Republic, Thailand, Togo, Trinidad and Tobago, Tunisia, Turkey, Uganda, Ukrainian SSR, USSR, United Arab Emirates, United Kingdom, United Republic of Tanzania, Uruguay, Vanuatu, Venezuela, Viet Nam, Yemen, Yugoslavia, Zaire, Zambia, Zimbabwe.

Against: Dominica, Israel, United States.

Abstaining: Belize.

Iran announced that it was not participating in the vote.

Speaking before the Assembly, the Observer for Palestine said that PLO accepted a preliminary

Palestinian-Israeli dialogue, provided that each party nominated the members of its own delegation without interference from any other side; that the agenda of the dialogue should be open; that the dialogue should be held under the auspices of the five permanent Security Council members; and that the dialogue should be a preparatory step towards convening the envisaged international conference.

Earlier, the Assembly, in **resolution 43/233**, stressed the urgent need to expedite the convening of an international conference under UN auspices and in conformity with its 1988 resolution on the question.[6]

Public information activities

In compliance with a 1988 General Assembly resolution,[10] the Department of Public Information (DPI) of the UN Secretariat continued in 1989, in full co-operation with the Committee on Palestinian rights, its special information programme on the Palestine question. DPI disseminated press releases, publications and audio-visual materials, and organized fact-finding missions and regional and national encounters for journalists. It provided press coverage of all UN meetings relevant to the question, as well as seminars and symposia held by the Committee, focusing increasingly on news items and information concerning the situation in the occupied territories and efforts to convene an international peace conference on the Middle East under UN auspices.

The *UN Chronicle* reported extensively on the consideration given to the Palestine question by the Assembly and the Security Council. During 1989, DPI issued in Arabic, English, French, German and Spanish two new booklets, on the work of the Committee on Palestinian rights and of the Committee on Israeli practices. DPI also produced a widely circulated poster on the proposed international peace conference.

The Department produced radio features on various aspects of the Palestine question. Extensive radio coverage was given to the North American regional seminar on the question, the Latin American regional journalists' encounter and the International Day of Solidarity with the Palestinian People.

Meetings of the Assembly and Security Council on the question received full television coverage, as did meetings and seminars of the Committee on Palestinian rights. Three editions of the weekly video programme entitled "UN in Action" were devoted to various aspects of the question. A total of 138 video news packages relating to the question were disseminated world wide.

In order to acquaint the media with the facts and developments pertaining to the question, DPI organized a news mission of 13 high-level journalists to the Middle East. From 7 to 23 May, they visited Tunis (Tunisia), Damascus (Syrian Arab Republic), Amman (Jordan) and Cairo (Egypt). No reply was received to DPI's formal request for the mission to visit Israel and the West Bank. The Department also organized two regional encounters for journalists in Singapore (30 January–1 February) and Kingston, Jamaica (26-28 July). Three series of national expert encounters in the form of press conferences were held in London and Berlin (16-19 January); New Delhi (India), Bangkok (Thailand), Sydney and Canberra (Australia), Wellington (New Zealand) and Tokyo (Japan) (24 January–13 February); and Bogotá (Colombia), Quito (Ecuador) and Santiago (Chile) (19-24 July).

UN information centres throughout the world distributed publications on the topic, and organized exhibitions, meetings and other activities to observe the International Day of Solidarity with the Palestinian People on 29 November.

GENERAL ASSEMBLY ACTION

On 6 December, the General Assembly adopted **resolution 44/41 C** by recorded vote.

The General Assembly,

Having considered the report of the Committee on the Exercise of the Inalienable Rights of the Palestinian People,

Taking note, in particular, of the information contained in paragraphs 94 to 109 of that report,

Recalling its resolutions 43/175 C, 43/176 and 43/177 of 15 December 1988,

Convinced that the world-wide dissemination of accurate and comprehensive information and the role of non-governmental organizations and institutions remain of vital importance in heightening awareness of and support for the inalienable rights of the Palestinian people to self-determination and to the establishment of an independent sovereign Palestinian State,

1. *Takes note with appreciation* of the action taken by the Department of Public Information of the Secretariat in compliance with General Assembly resolution 43/175 C;

2. *Requests* the Department of Public Information, in full co-operation and co-ordination with the Committee on the Exercise of the Inalienable Rights of the Palestinian People, to continue its special information programme on the question of Palestine for the biennium 1990-1991, with particular emphasis on public opinion in Europe and North America and, in particular:

(a) To disseminate information on all the activities of the United Nations system relating to the question of Palestine, including reports of the work carried out by the relevant United Nations organs;

(b) To continue to issue and update publications on the various aspects of the question of Palestine, including Israeli violations of the human rights of the Arab inhabitants of the occupied territories as reported by the relevant United Nations organs;

(c) To expand its audio-visual material on the question of Palestine, including the production of special series of radio programmes and television broadcasts;

(d) To organize fact-finding news missions to the area for journalists;

(e) To organize regional and national encounters for journalists.

General Assembly resolution 44/41 C

6 December 1989   Meeting 76   136-3-17 (recorded vote)

14-nation draft (A/44/L.45 & Add.1); agenda item 39.

Sponsors: Afghanistan, Bangladesh, Cuba, German Democratic Republic, Guyana, India, Indonesia, Madagascar, Malaysia, Mali, Pakistan, Senegal, Ukrainian SSR, Yugoslavia.

Financial implications. 5th Committee, A/44/846; S-G, A/C.5/44/43.

Meeting numbers. GA 44th session: 5th Committee 53; plenary 23, 67-71, 73, 76.

Recorded vote in Assembly as follows:

In favour: Afghanistan, Albania, Algeria, Angola, Antigua and Barbuda, Argentina, Austria, Bahamas, Bahrain, Bangladesh, Barbados, Benin, Bhutan, Bolivia, Botswana, Brazil, Brunei Darussalam, Bulgaria, Burkina Faso, Burundi, Byelorussian SSR, Cameroon, Cape Verde, Central African Republic, Chad, Chile, China, Colombia, Comoros, Congo, Costa Rica, Côte d'Ivoire, Cuba, Cyprus, Czechoslovakia, Democratic Kampuchea, Democratic Yemen, Djibouti, Ecuador, Egypt, El Salvador, Equatorial Guinea, Ethiopia, Fiji, Finland, Gabon, Gambia, German Democratic Republic, Ghana, Greece, Grenada, Guatemala, Guinea, Guinea-Bissau, Guyana, Haiti, Hungary, India, Indonesia, Iran, Iraq, Jamaica, Jordan, Kenya, Kuwait, Lao People's Democratic Republic, Lebanon, Lesotho, Liberia, Libyan Arab Jamahiriya, Madagascar, Malawi, Malaysia, Maldives, Mali, Malta, Mauritania, Mauritius, Mexico, Mongolia, Morocco, Mozambique, Myanmar, Nepal, Nicaragua, Niger, Nigeria, Oman, Pakistan, Panama, Papua New Guinea, Paraguay, Peru, Philippines, Poland, Qatar, Romania, Rwanda, Saint Kitts and Nevis, Saint Lucia, Saint Vincent and the Grenadines, Samoa, Sao Tome and Principe, Saudi Arabia, Senegal, Seychelles, Sierra Leone, Singapore, Solomon Islands, Somalia, Spain, Sri Lanka, Sudan, Suriname, Swaziland, Sweden, Syrian Arab Republic, Thailand, Togo, Trinidad and Tobago, Tunisia, Turkey, Uganda, Ukrainian SSR, USSR, United Arab Emirates, United Republic of Tanzania, Uruguay, Vanuatu, Venezuela, Viet Nam, Yemen, Yugoslavia, Zaire, Zambia, Zimbabwe.

Against: Dominica, Israel, United States.

Abstaining: Australia, Belgium, Belize, Canada, Denmark, France, Germany, Federal Republic of, Iceland, Ireland, Italy, Japan, Luxembourg, Netherlands, New Zealand, Norway, Portugal, United Kingdom.

Jerusalem

In October 1989, the Secretary-General reported[11] to the General Assembly on steps he had taken in response to a 1988 resolution[12] regarding the transfer by some States of their diplomatic missions to Jerusalem in violation of a 1980 Security Council resolution.[13] In May 1989, he had sent notes verbales to Member States, but received no replies specific to that question at the time of his report.

GENERAL ASSEMBLY ACTION

On 4 December, the General Assembly adopted **resolution 44/40 C** by recorded vote.

The General Assembly,

Recalling its resolutions 36/120 E of 10 December 1981, 37/123 C of 16 December 1982, 38/180 C of 19 December 1983, 39/146 C of 14 December 1984, 40/168 C of 16 December 1985, 41/162 C of 4 December 1986, 42/209 D of 11 December 1987 and 43/54 C of 6 December 1988, in which it determined that all legislative and administrative measures and actions taken by Israel, the occupying Power, which had altered or purported to alter the character and status of the Holy City of Jerusalem, in particular the so-called "Basic Law" on Jerusalem and the proclamation of Jerusalem as the capital of Israel, were null and void and must be rescinded forthwith,

Recalling Security Council resolution 478(1980) of 20 August 1980, in which the Council, *inter alia*, decided not to recognize the "Basic Law" and called upon those States that had established diplomatic missions at Jerusalem to withdraw such missions from the Holy City,

Having considered the report of the Secretary-General of 22 November 1989,

1. *Determines* that Israel's decision to impose its laws, jurisdiction and administration on the Holy City of Jerusalem is illegal and therefore null and void and has no validity whatsoever;

2. *Deplores* the transfer by some States of their diplomatic missions to Jerusalem in violation of Security Council resolution 478(1980), and their refusal to comply with the provisions of that resolution;

3. *Calls once more upon* those States to abide by the provisions of the relevant United Nations resolutions, in conformity with the Charter of the United Nations;

4. *Requests* the Secretary-General to report to the General Assembly at its forty-fifth session on the implementation of the present resolution.

General Assembly resolution 44/40 C

4 December 1989   Meeting 73   147-2-8 (recorded vote)

16-nation draft (A/44/L.49 & Add.1); agenda item 37.
Sponsors: Afghanistan, Algeria, Bahrain, Cuba, Djibouti, Egypt, Indonesia, Kuwait, Malaysia, Mali, Mauritania, Morocco, Oman, Pakistan, Syrian Arab Republic, Yugoslavia.
Meeting numbers. GA 44th session: plenary 64-66, 73.

Recorded vote in Assembly as follows:

In favour: Afghanistan, Albania, Algeria, Angola, Antigua and Barbuda, Argentina, Australia, Austria, Bahamas, Bahrain, Bangladesh, Barbados, Belgium, Benin, Bhutan, Bolivia, Botswana, Brazil, Brunei Darussalam, Bulgaria, Burkina Faso, Burundi, Byelorussian SSR, Cameroon, Canada, Cape Verde, Central African Republic, Chad, Chile, China, Colombia, Comoros, Congo, Côte d'Ivoire, Cuba, Cyprus, Czechoslovakia, Democratic Kampuchea, Democratic Yemen, Denmark, Djibouti, Dominican Republic, Ecuador, Egypt, Ethiopia, Fiji, Finland, France, Gabon, Gambia, German Democratic Republic, Germany, Federal Republic of, Ghana, Greece, Grenada, Guatemala, Guinea, Guinea-Bissau, Guyana, Haiti, Hungary, Iceland, India, Indonesia, Iran, Iraq, Ireland, Italy, Jamaica, Japan, Jordan, Kuwait, Lao People's Democratic Republic, Lebanon, Lesotho, Libyan Arab Jamahiriya, Luxembourg, Madagascar, Malaysia, Maldives, Mali, Malta, Mauritania, Mauritius, Mexico, Mongolia, Morocco, Mozambique, Myanmar, Nepal, Netherlands, New Zealand, Nicaragua, Niger, Nigeria, Norway, Oman, Pakistan, Panama, Papua New Guinea, Paraguay, Peru, Philippines, Poland, Portugal, Qatar, Romania, Rwanda, Saint Kitts and Nevis, Saint Lucia, Saint Vincent and the Grenadines, Samoa, Sao Tome and Principe, Saudi Arabia, Senegal, Seychelles, Sierra Leone, Singapore, Solomon Islands, Somalia, Spain, Sri Lanka, Sudan, Suriname, Swaziland, Sweden, Syrian Arab Republic, Thailand, Togo, Trinidad and Tobago, Tunisia, Turkey, Uganda, Ukrainian SSR, USSR, United Arab Emirates, United Kingdom, United Republic of Tanzania, Uruguay, Vanuatu, Venezuela, Viet Nam, Yemen, Yugoslavia, Zaire, Zambia, Zimbabwe.

Against: Costa Rica, Israel.

Abstaining: Belize, Dominica, El Salvador, Equatorial Guinea, Honduras, Kenya, Malawi, United States.

Assistance to Palestinians

Under their respective mandates, various organizations of the UN system continued in 1989 to provide economic and social assistance to the Palestinian people. An overview of their activities was contained in an October report[14] submitted by the Secretary-General in response to a 1988 General Assembly resolution.[15] The Assembly, by that resolution, had requested the Secretary-General to entrust the United Nations Centre for Human Settlements (UNCHS) with supervising the development of the programme of economic and social assistance to the Palestinians, in close cooperation with PLO. In June, UNCHS submitted an interim report[16] outlining steps taken in that regard. It had met with PLO representatives and selected experts to determine the scope of the programme and identified 30 projects. By October, it had received 26 project proposals, which were summarized in an appendix to the Secretary-General's report.

The United Nations Development Programme (UNDP), whose economic and social assistance was primarily for non-refugee Palestinian population in the occupied territory, was implementing in 1989 some 15 projects with a total budget of over $15 million. Its assistance programme included manpower development, industrial development, improvement of water supply systems, sewage disposal and effluent recycling, strengthening of educational and health institutions, assistance to municipalities and establishment of a business development course. UNDP submitted to the Israeli authorities for approval projects to develop women's institutions and the poultry industry. Among contributors to the programme were Canada, Italy, Japan, Tunisia, the United States and the Arab Gulf Fund for United Nations Development Organizations.

In response to additional needs for assistance as a consequence of the *intifadah*, the United Nations Relief and Works Agency for Palestine Refugees in the Near East (UNRWA) introduced a programme of extraordinary measures and an expanded programme of assistance to improve living conditions in the occupied territory, including additional medical supplies and equipment. UNRWA also continued to provide education, health and relief services to Palestine refugees in the West Bank and Gaza Strip, as well as in Jordan, Lebanon and the Syrian Arab Republic (see below, under "Palestine refugees").

The United Nations Conference on Trade and Development (UNCTAD) focused its Palestine-related activities on three main areas: monitoring and analysing policies and measures of the Israeli occupation authorities that affected the economy of the occupied Palestinian territory; investigating the impact of such policies on key economic sectors and examining feasible solutions; and developing a data base for the dissemination of information on the economy of the occupied territory. Within the framework of the latter, UNCTAD issued selected statistical tables on the economy of the occupied Palestinian territory (West Bank and Gaza Strip), and data-base extracts of economic issues and related Israeli practices in the occupied Palestinian territory (West Bank and Gaza Strip, 1987-1988), as well as an in-depth study analysing Palestinian external trade under Israeli occupation and examining the potential for its development.

Assistance to Palestinian children and mothers was provided by the United Nations Children's Fund (UNICEF), concentrating on six areas: immunization, oral rehydration therapy, training of traditional birth attendants, establishment and operation of four child development centres, training of village health workers and kindergarten teacher training. In co-operation with the Palestinian Red Crescent Society, UNICEF was implementing water and sanitation projects in villages of the Hebron district. Through UNRWA, UNICEF also provided primary health care services for Palestinian refugees in the occupied territory.

Focusing its attention on assistance in the industrial and the livestock resource sectors, the Economic and Social Commission for Western Asia (ESCWA) in 1989 was preparing a survey of the industrial sector in the West Bank and Gaza Strip and produced two pre-feasibility studies: one for a dairy farm project and the other for an animal breeding station project, both in the West Bank.

The technical co-operation programme of the International Labour Organisation was organized around three main subjects: vocational training in general, entrepreneur training and trade union training. Projects dealing with activities for women in the field of co-operatives and activities to help the disabled were also set in motion.

Two projects aimed at enhancing training for the Palestinians and funded by the Near East Co-operative Programme were implemented by the Food and Agriculture Organization of the United Nations (FAO). Under the first, FAO organized three post-graduate training fellowships in agricultural economics and animal production. Under the second, it provided short-term consultancies and audio-visual equipment to assist the Al-Quds Open University in developing its curriculum and programmes relating to land and community development.

The United Nations Industrial Development Organization (UNIDO) completed a study on the establishment of a Palestinian industrial development bank, a feasibility study on a canning plant for citrus fruit and, in co-operation with Bir Zeit University, a study to identify industrial priority projects. In October, UNIDO organized in Vienna a seminar on prospects for the Palestinian industrial sector.

The United Nations Environment Programme (UNEP) in February, in co-operation with the World Health Organization (WHO), launched a training course on water supply, sanitation and health for environmental health officers working with the Palestinians. The UNEP Executive Director initiated consultations on the preparation of a report on the environmental situation in the oc-

cupied territories, requested by the UNEP Governing Council in May.[17]

The forty-second World Health Assembly, also in May, adopted two resolutions, regarding the request of Palestine for admission as a member of WHO and on the health conditions of the Arab population in the occupied Arab territories, including Palestine. A WHO mission visited the occupied territories in July to identify priority health needs with a view to providing intensified assistance to the Palestinians. In consultation with several parties concerned, WHO started preparing a two-year plan of action, with special emphasis on primary health care.

The United Nations Population Fund (UNFPA) supported activities of other UN organizations within the UNDP-financed educational programme. It funded fellowships for post-graduate studies in demography and related topics, and helped finance mother and child health research and training activities at WHO collaborating centres for primary health care research. It allocated funds to examine information on maternal and reproductive health and health care coverage for Palestine refugees, and to draft a plan for an expanded UNRWA mother and child health and feeding programme. It also funded several technical advisory missions by the ESCWA Regional Adviser in Demography and in Population Statistics to the Palestinian Central Bureau of Statistics.

ECONOMIC AND SOCIAL COUNCIL ACTION

On 26 July, the Economic and Social Council, on the recommendation of its Third (Programme and Co-ordination) Committee, adopted **resolution 1989/96** by vote.

Assistance to the Palestinian people

The Economic and Social Council,

Recalling General Assembly resolution 43/178 of 20 December 1988,

Recalling also Economic and Social Council resolution 1988/54 of 26 July 1988,

Taking into account the *intifadah* of the Palestinian people in the occupied Palestinian territory against the Israeli occupation, including its economic and social policies and practices,

Affirming that the Palestinian people cannot develop their national economy as long as the Israeli occupation persists,

Gravely concerned at the serious repercussions, especially for Palestinian children, of Israeli practices, in particular the prolonged blanket closure in the West Bank of Palestinian institutions of learning, including kindergartens, schools operated by the United Nations Relief and Works Agency for Palestine Refugees in the Near East and other schools,

Rejecting Israeli restrictions on external economic and social assistance to the Palestinian people in the occupied Palestinian territory,

Aware of the increasing need to provide economic and social assistance to the Palestinian people,

Noting with regret that a full report on the implementation of General Assembly resolution 43/178 has not been prepared,

1. *Expresses its appreciation* to the States, United Nations bodies and intergovernmental and non-governmental organizations that have provided assistance to the Palestinian people;

2. *Requests* the international community, the United Nations system and intergovernmental and non-governmental organizations to sustain and increase their assistance to the Palestinian people, in close co-operation with the Palestine Liberation Organization;

3. *Requests* the United Nations Children's Fund and other appropriate United Nations bodies to address the special needs of Palestinian children suffering from Israeli practices and their repercussions;

4. *Calls* for the immediate reopening of all Palestinian institutions of learning;

5. *Also calls* for the immediate lifting of Israeli restrictions and obstacles hindering the implementation of assistance projects by the United Nations Development Programme, other United Nations bodies and others providing economic and social assistance to the Palestinian people in the occupied Palestinian territory;

6. *Further calls* for the implementation of development projects in the occupied Palestinian territory, including the facilitation by all concerned of the establishment of the cement plant referred to in General Assembly resolution 39/223 of 18 December 1984;

7. *Requests* the Secretary-General to report in full on the implementation of General Assembly resolution 43/178 and the present resolution to the Assembly at its forty-fourth session.

Economic and Social Council resolution 1989/96

26 July 1989   Meeting 35   48-1

Approved by Third Committee (E/1989/130) by vote (41-1-1), 18 July (meeting 13); 18-nation draft (E/1989/C.3/L.3/Rev.1), orally revised; agenda item 10.

Sponsors: Algeria, Bangladesh, Byelorussian SSR, Cuba, Egypt, German Democratic Republic, Indonesia, Jordan, Kuwait, Libyan Arab Jamahiriya, Malaysia, Morocco, Niger, Saudi Arabia, Sudan, Syrian Arab Republic, Tunisia, Zambia.

Speaking in explanation of vote, the United States said it firmly supported assistance to the Palestinians, but did not believe that UN organizations should channel funds destined for them through PLO.

GENERAL ASSEMBLY ACTION

On 22 December, the General Assembly, on the recommendation of the Second (Economic and Financial) Committee, adopted **resolution 44/235** by recorded vote.

Assistance to the Palestinian people

The General Assembly,

Recalling its resolution 43/178 of 20 December 1988,

Taking note of Economic and Social Council resolution 1989/96 of 26 July 1989,

Taking into account the *intifadah* of the Palestinian people in the occupied Palestinian territory against the Israeli occupation, including Israeli economic and social policies and practices,

Rejecting Israeli restrictions on external economic and social assistance to the Palestinian people in the occupied Palestinian territory,

Aware of the increasing need to provide economic and social assistance to the Palestinian people,

Affirming that the Palestinian people cannot develop their national economy as long as the Israeli occupation persists,

1. *Takes note* of the report annexed to the note by the Secretary-General on assistance to the Palestinian people;

2. *Expresses its appreciation* to the States, United Nations bodies and intergovernmental and non-governmental organizations that have provided assistance to the Palestinian people;

3. *Requests* the international community, the organizations of the United Nations system and intergovernmental and non-governmental organizations to sustain and increase their assistance to the Palestinian people, in close co-operation with the Palestine Liberation Organization;

4. *Calls* for the treatment on a transit basis of Palestinian exports and imports passing through neighbouring ports and points of exit and entry;

5. *Also calls* for the granting of trade concessions and concrete preferential measures for Palestinian exports on the basis of Palestinian certificates of origin;

6. *Further calls* for the immediate lifting of Israeli restrictions and obstacles hindering the implementation of assistance projects by the United Nations Development Programme, other United Nations bodies and others providing economic and social assistance to the Palestinian people in the occupied Palestinian territory;

7. *Reiterates its call* for the implementation of development projects in the occupied Palestinian territory, including the projects mentioned in its resolution 39/223 of 18 December 1984;

8. *Requests* the Secretary-General to report to the General Assembly at its forty-fifth session, through the Economic and Social Council, on the progress made in the implementation of the present resolution.

General Assembly resolution 44/235

22 December 1989   Meeting 85   146-2-1 (recorded vote)

Approved by Second Committee (A/44/832/Add.1) by recorded vote (132-2-2), 21 November (meeting 41); 7-nation draft (A/C.2/44/L.25), orally revised; agenda item 12.

Sponsors: Algeria, Bahrain, Cuba, Egypt, Mali, Mauritania, Pakistan.

Meeting numbers. GA 44th session: 2nd Committee 15-17, 19, 20, 29, 41; plenary 85.

Recorded vote in Assembly as follows:

In favour: Afghanistan, Albania, Algeria, Angola, Antigua and Barbuda, Argentina, Australia, Austria, Bahamas, Bahrain, Bangladesh, Barbados, Belgium, Belize, Benin, Bhutan, Bolivia, Botswana, Brazil, Brunei Darussalam, Bulgaria, Burkina Faso, Burundi, Byelorussian SSR, Cameroon, Cape Verde, Central African Republic, Chad, Chile, China, Colombia, Congo, Costa Rica, Côte d'Ivoire, Cuba, Cyprus, Czechoslovakia, Democratic Kampuchea, Democratic Yemen, Denmark, Djibouti, Dominica, Dominican Republic, Ecuador, Egypt, El Salvador, Ethiopia, Fiji, Finland, France, Gabon, Gambia, German Democratic Republic, Germany, Federal Republic of, Ghana, Greece, Guatemala, Guinea, Guinea-Bissau, Guyana, Haiti, Honduras, Hungary, Iceland, India, Indonesia, Iran, Iraq, Ireland, Italy, Jamaica, Japan, Jordan, Kuwait, Lao People's Democratic Republic, Lebanon, Lesotho, Liberia, Libyan Arab Jamahiriya, Luxembourg, Madagascar, Malawi, Malaysia, Maldives, Mali, Malta, Mauritania, Mauritius, Mexico, Mongolia, Morocco, Mozambique, Myanmar, Nepal, Netherlands, New Zealand, Nicaragua, Niger, Nigeria, Norway, Oman, Pakistan, Papua New Guinea, Peru, Philippines, Poland, Portugal, Qatar, Romania, Rwanda, Saint Lucia, Saint Vincent and the Grenadines, Samoa, Sao Tome and Principe, Saudi Arabia, Senegal, Sierra Leone, Singapore, Solomon Islands, Somalia, Spain, Sri Lanka, Sudan, Suriname, Sweden, Syrian Arab Republic, Thailand, Togo,

Trinidad and Tobago, Tunisia, Turkey, Uganda, Ukrainian SSR, USSR, United Arab Emirates, United Kingdom, United Republic of Tanzania, Uruguay, Vanuatu, Venezuela, Viet Nam, Yemen, Yugoslavia, Zaire, Zambia, Zimbabwe.
Against: Israel, United States.
Abstaining: Canada.

REFERENCES

[1]A/44/35. [2]YUN 1988, p. 209, GA res. 43/175 A, 15 Dec. 1988. [3]YUN 1975, p. 248, GA res. 3376(XXX), 10 Nov. 1975. [4]YUN 1976, p. 235. [5]*Ibid.*, p. 246, GA res. 31/20, 24 Nov. 1976. [6]YUN 1988, p. 206, GA res. 43/176, 15 Dec. 1988. [7]YUN 1947-48, p. 247, GA res. 181 A (II), 29 Nov. 1947. [8]YUN 1948-49, p. 174, GA res. 194(III), 11 Dec. 1948. [9]A/44/731-S/20968. [10]YUN 1988, p. 211, GA res. 43/175 C, 15 Dec. 1988. [11]A/44/690 & Add.1. [12]YUN 1988, p. 212, GA res. 43/54 C, 6 Dec. 1988. [13]YUN 1980, p. 426, SC res. 478(1980), 20 Aug. 1980. [14]A/44/637. [15]YUN 1988, p. 216, GA res. 43/178, 20 Dec. 1988. [16]E/1989/113. [17]A/44/25 (dec. 15/8).

Incidents and disputes involving Arab countries and Israel

Israel and Iraq

By **decision 43/463** of 18 September 1989, the General Assembly decided to include in the draft agenda of its forty-fourth session the item on armed Israeli aggression against Iraqi nuclear installations. The item had been inscribed yearly on the Assembly's agenda since 1981,[1] following the bombing by Israel of a nuclear research centre near Baghdad. No action had been taken on the item by the time the Assembly was suspended in December 1989.

Lebanon

Military confrontation and violence in and around Beirut intensified during 1989, producing some devastating casualties. Security Council members, in a 7 November statement,[2] supported action by the Tripartite High Committee of the League of Arab States for the implementation of a settlement plan for the Lebanese crisis. Council members also welcomed the election of René Moawad as the President of the Lebanese Republic and ratification of the Taif Agreement by the Lebanese Parliament.

In a statement on 22 November,[3] they condemned the assassination of President Moawad, and called for the continued establishment of renovated institutions as part of the process of national reconciliation. In a 27 December statement[4], Council members welcomed the election of Elias Hrawi as the new President of Lebanon and supported his efforts in implementation of the Taif Agreement to deploy Lebanese government forces in order to restore central government authority over all Lebanese territory.

Following the announcement by a group in Lebanon that it had executed Lieutenant-Colonel William Richard Higgins, a United States national who had been serving with UNIFIL when abducted in February 1988,[5] the Secretary-General sent to Lebanon the Under-Secretary-General for Special Political Affairs. Unfortunately, he could not obtain definite proof of Colonel Higgins' fate. On 31 July 1989, in a Council statement,[6] members noted reports that Colonel Higgins may have been murdered and, if those reports were true, expressed outrage that such a cruel and criminal act should have been committed against an officer who served the United Nations on a peace-keeping mission. They condemned all acts of hostage-taking and abduction and demanded the safe release of all hostages and abducted persons wherever and by whomever they were being held.

The fate of Alec Collett, a British journalist kidnapped near the Beirut airport in March 1985[7] while on assignment for UNRWA, remained unresolved, no word having been received from his kidnappers since 1986.

Israel and Lebanon

During 1989, the situation between Israel and Lebanon remained tense. Israel Defence Forces (IDF) continued to control parts of southern Lebanon, which Israel declared its "security zone". The boundaries of the Israeli-controlled area were not clearly defined, but determined *de facto* by the forward positions of IDF and the so-called South Lebanon Army (SLA). IDF and SLA remained targets for attacks by Lebanese groups opposed to the occupation; in retaliation, they often used heavy artillery, tanks and helicopters.

UNIFIL reported a further strengthening of Israeli control over parts of southern Lebanon. The control was exercised through the military activities of IDF and SLA and through "civilian administration offices" that had been opened in a number of towns and villages. There had been also an increase in the number of IDF and SLA positions in the area.

Throughout the year, Lebanon addressed numerous communications to the Secretary-General accusing Israel of ongoing attacks against its territory, causing death and injury to civilians and destruction of property. Lebanon also complained about forcible expulsion of Lebanese from the "security zone", forcible conscription of men into SLA, confiscation of farmland and other acts.

The Security Council met on several occasions to consider developments in Lebanon and specific charges against Israeli actions there. On 31 March, the President of the Council, following consultations, made a statement[8] on behalf of the Council members, expressing their grave concern at the recent deterioration of the situation in Lebanon, which had left many victims among the civilian population and caused considerable material damage.

On 24 April, the Council President made another statement[9] in which the members of the Council once again expressed grave concern over the suffering caused to the civilian population by the worsening situation in Lebanon.

On 31 July, the Council President, in a statement,[6] said that Council members reaffirmed their profound concern over the safety and security of UNIFIL personnel, who were exposed to constant threats and danger.

On 15 August, the Secretary-General addressed a letter[10] to the Council President stating that the crisis which, in his opinion, had escalated to a level unprecedented in 14 years of conflict, posed a serious threat to international peace and security. He therefore requested the President to convene an urgent Council meeting. The Council did so immediately and adopted a statement,[11] by which Council members expressed deep concern over the further deterioration of the situation and profoundly deplored the intensification of shelling and bitter fighting in recent days.

On 20 September, the Council, following consultations among its members and consideration of Lebanon's accusation of new aggressive acts by the Israeli army, resumed its consideration of the situation in Lebanon. On behalf of the Council, the President made another statement[12] strongly urging respect for the appeal by the Tripartite High Committee for an immediate and comprehensive cease-fire.

UNIFIL

Established by the Security Council in 1978[13] following Israel's invasion of Lebanon in March of that year,[14] the United Nations Interim Force in Lebanon was entrusted with restoring international peace and security, confirming the withdrawal of Israeli forces from Lebanese territory and re-establishing the Lebanese Government's effective authority in the area. After a second Israeli invasion in June 1982,[15] the Council authorized the Force also to provide protection and humanitarian assistance to the local population.[16]

During 1989, at the request of Lebanon and on the recommendation of the Secretary-General, the Council twice extended the UNIFIL mandate, in January and July, each time for six months.

Composition

As of July 1989,[17] UNIFIL had a strength of 5,854 military personnel provided by nine countries: Fiji, Finland, France, Ghana, Ireland, Italy, Nepal, Norway and Sweden. By January 1990,[18] its total strength had slightly increased, to 5,876. The Commander of UNIFIL continued to be Lieutenant-General Lars-Eric Wahlgren of Sweden, who had assumed his responsibilities on 1 July 1988.[19] During 1989, UNIFIL was assisted

by 65 military observers of UNTSO, 64 of whom maintained five observation posts along the Lebanese side of the Israel-Lebanon armistice demarcation line and also operated four mobile teams in parts of the area of operation, including those under Israeli control. One military observer was attached to UNIFIL headquarters. The strength of the Lebanese army unit serving with UNIFIL during the year decreased from 200 to 128 personnel.

Developments in the UNIFIL area

Report of the Secretary-General (January). In a January 1989 report,[20] the Secretary-General informed the Security Council of developments in the UNIFIL area of operation between 26 July 1988 and 24 January 1989, as well as organizational and financial aspects of the Force.

During the reporting period, three members of the Force, an Irish, a Norwegian and a Swedish soldier, lost their lives in accidents. Seventeen soldiers suffered injuries, 5 as a result of hostile fire, 5 from mine explosions and the others in accidents. Since UNIFIL's establishment, 156 members of the Force had died, 60 from firing and mine or bomb explosions, 68 in accidents and 28 from other causes. Some 230 had been wounded by firing and mine or bomb explosions. On 24 January, one more Irish soldier was wounded when SLA fired towards the Irish position.

The situation in the UNIFIL area of operation remained essentially unchanged. UNIFIL still was not able to extend its area up to the Israel-Lebanon armistice demarcation line, as envisaged in Security Council resolution 425(1978),[13] while IDF and SLA continued to control the "security zone", maintaining 54 positions within the UNIFIL area.

Armed resistance groups continued operations against IDF and SLA using small arms, rocket-propelled grenades, rockets and mortars, as well as mines and roadside bombs. UNIFIL recorded a total of 114 such operations, including 10 of them in January 1989, which indicated a marked intensification of activities in some of the northern parts of the UNIFIL area, especially in the Finnish battalion sector.

IDF and SLA forces, whether in retaliation or unprovoked, often used heavy artillery, tank and mortar shelling and Israeli helicopter gunships. Fire from those forces was close to UNIFIL positions and vehicles, sometimes hitting them. Some 108 unprovoked firings were protested by UNIFIL to the Israeli authorities. Resistance groups also opened fire close to UNIFIL positions; however, warning shots by UNIFIL in most cases stopped that fire. There were some other incidents between UNIFIL and armed elements, mainly due to their passage through UNIFIL checkpoints being denied. A serious incident happened on 15 December 1988, near the village of Jumayjimah, where about

20 armed elements fired at and stopped an Irish armoured personnel carrier. The incident was quickly resolved through negotiations. In an apparently related incident on the following day, five armed elements fired at and overran an Irish battalion checkpoint near Tibnin and kidnapped three soldiers; however, with the assistance of the Amal Movement they were released the next day.

Protection and security of the civilian population continued to be an important part of UNIFIL activities. The Force detonated mines and roadside bombs, as well as unexploded remnants of war, in its area of operation. UNIFIL consistently protested to IDF about forced expulsion of Lebanese civilians from their homes by SLA and forced recruitment of local men to that army.

UNIFIL continued to provide humanitarian assistance, mainly in the medical and health areas and to welfare institutions, using funds provided by the troop-contributing Governments. A large number of civilians were treated at UNIFIL medical centres, including the UNIFIL hospital at Naqoura, where nearly 6,500 Lebanese patients were treated, 561 of them as in-patients.

In his observations, the Secretary-General noted that UNIFIL's ability to carry out the tasks which the Security Council had assigned to it in 1978 was still blocked. Israel continued to refuse to withdraw its forces from Lebanon, and its "security zone" had become a focus of attack, both by those aiming to attack Israel itself and by those with the aim of liberating Lebanese territory from foreign occupation. Attempts by armed elements to infiltrate Israel, which increased substantially during 1988, and retaliatory air and commando raids by Israel, often far to the north of the UNIFIL area of operation, meant that international peace and security were a long way from being restored. The failure to elect a new President of Lebanon and the subsequent existence of two rival Governments in Beirut had prevented UNIFIL from making any progress in helping ensure the return of the Lebanese Government's effective authority in southern Lebanon.

On 19 January 1989,[21] the Secretary-General received a request from Lebanon for an extension of UNIFIL's mandate for a further six-month period. Meanwhile, he reported that Israel continued to take the position that its presence in Lebanon was a temporary arrangement necessary for ensuring the security of northern Israel as long as the Lebanese Government was not able to exercise effective authority and prevent its territory from being used to launch attacks against Israel. The Israeli authorities did not consider that UNIFIL, as a peace-keeping force, could assume that responsibility.

Given the negative developments he had reported and UNIFIL's continuing inability to carry out its original mandate, the Secretary-General observed that it was understandable that doubts had been expressed as to whether the Force should maintain its current strength. He presented four points that, he said, the Security Council should take into account when considering Lebanon's request for a mandate extension: the Council's conviction that a solution to the problems of southern Lebanon lay in the full implementation of resolution 425(1978);[13] the important role the Force played in controlling the level of violence in southern Lebanon; UNIFIL's humanitarian support to the population in the area of its operation; and UNIFIL's role as a symbol of the international community's commitment to the sovereignty, independence and territorial integrity of Lebanon.

The Secretary-General recommended that the Council renew UNIFIL's mandate for a further six months.

SECURITY COUNCIL ACTION (January)

The Security Council met on 30 January to consider the Secretary-General's report and, without debate, unanimously adopted **resolution 630(1989)**.

The Security Council,

Recalling its resolutions 425(1978) and 426(1978) of 19 March 1978, 501(1982) of 25 February 1982, 508(1982) of 5 June 1982, 509(1982) of 6 June 1982 and 520(1982) of 17 September 1982, as well as all its resolutions on the situation in Lebanon,

Having studied the report of the Secretary-General on the United Nations Interim Force in Lebanon of 24 and 27 January 1989, and taking note of the observations expressed therein,

Taking note of the letter dated 19 January 1989 from the Permanent Representative of Lebanon to the United Nations addressed to the Secretary-General,

Responding to the request of the Government of Lebanon,

1. *Decides* to extend the present mandate of the United Nations Interim Force in Lebanon for a further interim period of six months, that is, until 31 July 1989;

2. *Reiterates* its strong support for the territorial integrity, sovereignty and independence of Lebanon within its internationally recognized boundaries;

3. *Re-emphasizes* the terms of reference and general guidelines of the Force as stated in the report of the Secretary-General of 19 March 1978, approved by resolution 426(1978), and calls upon all parties concerned to co-operate fully with the Force for the full implementation of its mandate;

4. *Reiterates* that the Force should fully implement its mandate as defined in resolutions 425(1978), 426(1978) and all other relevant resolutions;

5. *Requests* the Secretary-General to continue consultations with the Government of Lebanon and other parties directly concerned with the implementation of the present resolution and to report to the Security Council thereon.

Security Council resolution 630(1989)
30 January 1989   Meeting 2843   Adopted unanimously
Draft prepared in consultations among Council members (S/20429).

Report of the Secretary-General (July). In a report[17] on UNIFIL activities and developments in the area of its operation, covering the period from 25 January to 21 July 1989, the Secretary-General informed the Security Council that the situation remained essentially unchanged, with IDF and SLA continuing to control the "security zone" in southern Lebanon. There had been a notable increase in the number of their positions, from 54 to 64.

UNIFIL recorded 98 operations by resistance groups against IDF and SLA targets with the use of small arms, rocket-propelled grenades, rockets and mortars. Whether in retaliation to those operations or unprovoked, IDF and SLA often used heavy artillery, tanks, mortars and helicopters. During the reporting period, UNIFIL registered 112 unprovoked firings close to its positions. In view of the seriousness of some of those incidents, in May the matter was taken up with the Israeli authorities at a senior level, which resulted in a marked decrease of such firings.

The Secretary-General reported several serious incidents, resulting in the death of three Irish soldiers and injury to a Fijian, an Irish and two Norwegian soldiers. During the period under review, eight UNIFIL members—five Irish, two Norwegians and one Swede—lost their lives from firing, mine or bomb explosions, accidents and natural causes. Fifteen others suffered injuries.

UNIFIL continued to provide protection, security and assistance to the civilian population. Its troops removed in the area of operation mines, roadside bombs and remnants of war. The Secretary-General reported that Ireland had agreed to provide expert teams as part of the Irish contingent to search for, and dispose of, explosive ordnance in the Irish battalion sector. Those teams would also train personnel from the other UNIFIL battalions.

In conclusion, the Secretary-General regretted that, after another difficult mandate period, UNIFIL remained far from being able to implement its mandate of confirming Israeli withdrawal from Lebanese territory, restoring international peace and security, and assisting the Lebanese Government to return its effective authority in the area. UNIFIL had again been unable to make progress towards deployment to the international border, while Israel had strengthened its hold on the so-called "security zone" where positions occupied by its own forces and those of SLA had increased by 18.5 per cent during the reporting period.

However, the Secretary-General considered as positive achievements the significant role UNIFIL played in controlling the level of violence in its area and in providing humanitarian assistance. He once again recommended extending the Force's mandate for a further six months, until 31 January 1990, in response to Lebanon's request of 13 July.[22]

SECURITY COUNCIL ACTION (July)

On 31 July 1989, again without debate, the Security Council, having considered the Secretary-General's report, unanimously adopted **resolution 639(1989)**.

The Security Council,

Recalling its resolutions 425(1978) and 426(1978) of 19 March 1978, 501(1982) of 25 February 1982, 508(1982) of 5 June 1982, 509(1982) of 6 June 1982 and 520(1982) of 17 September 1982, as well as all its resolutions on the situation in Lebanon,

Having studied the report of the Secretary-General on the United Nations Interim Force in Lebanon of 21 July 1989, and taking note of the observations expressed therein,

Taking note of the letter dated 13 July 1989 from the representative of Lebanon to the United Nations addressed to the Secretary-General,

Responding to the request of the Government of Lebanon,

1. *Decides* to extend the present mandate of the United Nations Interim Force in Lebanon for a further interim period of six months, that is, until 31 January 1990;

2. *Reiterates* its strong support for the territorial integrity, sovereignty and independence of Lebanon within its internationally recognized boundaries;

3. *Re-emphasizes* the terms of reference and general guidelines of the Force as stated in the report of the Secretary-General of 19 March 1978, approved by resolution 426(1978), and calls upon all parties concerned to co-operate fully with the Force for the full implementation of its mandate;

4. *Reiterates* that the Force should fully implement its mandate as defined in resolutions 425(1978), 426(1978) and all other relevant resolutions;

5. *Requests* the Secretary-General to continue consultations with the Government of Lebanon and other parties directly concerned with the implementation of the present resolution and to report to the Security Council thereon.

Security Council resolution 639(1989)
31 July 1989   Meeting 2873   Adopted unanimously
Draft prepared in consultations among Council members (S/20755).

Financing

The Secretary-General reported in December 1989[23] that, as at 30 September, contributions totalling $1,324.4 million had been received for the operation of UNIFIL out of $1,691.7 million apportioned among Member States for the periods from the inception of the Force on 19 March 1978 to 31 January 1990. Of the unpaid balance of $367.3 million, only $138.7 million could be considered collectible, leaving a shortfall of $228.6 million, including $19.6 million transferred to a special account in accordance with a 1981 General Assembly resolution.[24] As a consequence, UNIFIL was unable to meet its obligations on a current basis, particularly to the troop-contributing countries, which had never been paid on a current and full basis in accordance with established rates. The UNIFIL Suspense Account, set up in 1979[25] to facilitate reimbursement to them for equipment and supplies, had so far not achieved its purpose. The troop-contributing countries had expressed to the Secretary-General their serious concern over that situation.

As at 30 September 1989, voluntary contributions totalling $2.9 million had been received from Governments, of which $1.6 million was contributed by Switzerland. A $3 million contribution made by Japan in 1988 was utilized to defray expenses arising from the acquisition of logistic equipment and supplies that had not been previously budgeted for.

For the mandate periods from 1 February 1989 to 31 January 1990, $142,842,000 gross ($140,574,000 net) had been authorized for UNIFIL by the General Assembly.[26] The costs of UNIFIL for the 12-month period beginning 1 February 1990 were estimated at $12,001,000 gross ($11,806,000 net) per month, based on an average Force strength of 5,850 troops, for a total of $144,012,000 gross ($141,672,000 net). On a net basis, that was $1,098,000 (0.8 per cent) more than the estimate for the previous 12 months.

The Advisory Committee on Administrative and Budgetary Questions (ACABQ) recommended[27] that the Assembly approve the Secretary-General's estimate for UNIFIL for the one-year period beginning 1 February 1990.

GENERAL ASSEMBLY ACTION

On 21 December, on the recommendation of the Fifth (Administrative and Budgetary) Committee, the General Assembly adopted **resolution 44/188** without vote.

Financing of the United Nations Interim Force in Lebanon

The General Assembly,

Having considered the report of the Secretary-General on the financing of the United Nations Interim Force in Lebanon and the related report of the Advisory Committee on Administrative and Budgetary Questions,

Bearing in mind Security Council resolution 425(1978) of 19 March 1978, by which the Council established the United Nations Interim Force in Lebanon, and the subsequent resolutions by which the Council extended the mandate of the Force, the latest of which was resolution 639(1989) of 31 July 1989,

Recalling its resolution S-8/2 of 21 April 1978 on the financing of the United Nations Interim Force in Lebanon and its subsequent resolutions thereon, the latest of which was resolution 43/229 of 21 December 1988,

Reaffirming its previous decisions regarding the fact that, in order to meet the expenditures caused by such operations, a different procedure from the one applied to meet expenditures of the regular budget of the United Nations is required,

Taking into account the fact that the economically more developed countries are in a position to make relatively larger contributions and that the economically less developed countries have a relatively limited capacity to contribute towards peace-keeping operations involving heavy expenditures,

Bearing in mind the special responsibilities of the States permanent members of the Security Council in the financing of such operations, as indicated in General Assembly resolution 1874(S-IV) of 27 June 1963 and other resolutions of the Assembly,

Having regard to the financial position of the Special Account for the United Nations Interim Force in Lebanon, as set forth in the report of the Secretary-General, and referring to paragraph 23 of the report of the Advisory Committee on Administrative and Budgetary Questions,

Recalling its resolution 34/9 E of 17 December 1979 and the subsequent resolutions in which it decided that the provisions of regulations 5.2 (b), 5.2 (d), 4.3 and 4.4 of the Financial Regulations of the United Nations should be suspended, the latest of which was resolution 43/229,

Mindful of the fact that it is essential to provide the United Nations Interim Force in Lebanon with the necessary financial resources to enable it to fulfil its responsibilities under the relevant resolutions of the Security Council,

Noting with appreciation that voluntary contributions have been made to the United Nations Interim Force in Lebanon by certain Governments,

Concerned that the Secretary-General is continuing to face increasing difficulties in meeting the obligations of the United Nations Interim Force in Lebanon on a current basis, including reimbursement to current and former troop-contributing States, resulting from the withholding of contributions by certain Member States,

Concerned also that the surplus balances in the Special Account for the United Nations Interim Force in Lebanon have, in effect, been drawn upon to the full extent to supplement the income received from contributions for meeting expenses of the Force,

Concerned further that the application of the provisions of regulations 5.2 (b), 5.2 (d), 4.3 and 4.4 of the Financial Regulations of the United Nations would aggravate the already difficult financial situation of the United Nations Interim Force in Lebanon,

Mindful of the views expressed in the Fifth Committee on the requests of some Member States to change their placement in the existing groups "b", "c" and "d" of Member States, on the basis of the criteria set out in General Assembly resolution 3101(XXVIII) of 11 December 1973,

1. *Decides* to appropriate to the Special Account referred to in section I, paragraph 1, of General Assembly resolution S-8/2 an amount of 142,842,000 United States dollars gross (140,574,000 dollars net) authorized by the Assembly and apportioned in paragraph 5 of its resolution 43/229 for the operation of the United Nations Interim Force in Lebanon from 1 February 1989 to 31 January 1990, inclusive;

2. *Authorizes* the Secretary-General to enter into commitments for the operation of the United Nations Interim Force in Lebanon at a rate not to exceed 12,001,000 dollars gross (11,806,000 dollars net) per month for the twelve-month period beginning 1 February 1990, should the Security Council decide to continue the Force beyond the period of six months authorized under its resolution 639(1989);

3. *Decides*, as an *ad hoc* arrangement, to apportion the amounts referred to in paragraph 2 of the present resolution among Member States, in accordance with the composition of groups set out in paragraphs 3 and 4 of General Assembly resolution 43/232 of 1 March 1989, to be adjusted by the decision to be taken by the Assembly at its forty-fourth session on the composition of groups "a", "b", "c" and "d" of Member States and taking into account the scale of assessments for the years 1989, 1990 and 1991;

4. *Decides also* that the provisions of regulations 5.2 *(b)*, 5.2 *(d)*, 4.3 and 4.4 of the Financial Regulations of the United Nations shall be suspended in respect of the amount of 3,078,849 dollars, which otherwise would have to be surrendered pursuant to those provisions, this amount to be entered in the account referred to in the operative part of General Assembly resolution 34/9 E and held in suspense until a further decision is taken by the Assembly;

5. *Requests* the Secretary-General to take all necessary measures to ensure that the United Nations Interim Force in Lebanon shall be administered with a maximum of efficiency and economy;

6. *Renews its invitation* to Member States and other interested parties to make voluntary contributions to the United Nations Interim Force in Lebanon both in cash and in the form of services and supplies acceptable to the Secretary-General and also to make voluntary contributions in cash to the Suspense Account established in accordance with General Assembly resolution 34/9 D of 17 December 1979.

General Assembly resolution 44/188

21 December 1989   Meeting 84   Adopted without vote

Approved by Fifth Committee (A/44/888) without vote, 18 December (meeting 58); 18-nation draft (A/C.5/44/L.12); agenda item 133 *(b)*.
Sponsors: Austria, Canada, Denmark, Fiji, Finland, France, Germany, Federal Republic of, Ghana, Iceland, Ireland, Italy, Lebanon, Nepal, Netherlands, New Zealand, Norway, Samoa, Sweden.

Israel and the Syrian Arab Republic

UNDOF

The United Nations Disengagement Observer Force, established by the Security Council in 1974[28] and headquartered in Damascus, continued to supervise the observance of the cease-fire in the Golan Heights, as called for by the Agreement on Disengagement between Israeli and Syrian Forces.[29] Its mandate was renewed in May and November 1989, each time for six months.

The issue of the human rights of the population in the occupied territories was continuously monitored by the Committee on Israeli practices and the Commission on Human Rights (see below and PART THREE, Chapter X).

Composition

As of November 1989, UNDOF had a strength of 1,327 military troops (reduced from 1,344 in May) from four countries—Austria, 531; Canada, 227; Finland, 410; and Poland, 159—including four Polish officers deployed to the United Nations Good Offices Mission in Afghanistan and Pakistan. Seven military observers were assigned to UNDOF from UNTSO. In addition, UNTSO observers assigned to the Israel-Syria Mixed Armistice Commission assisted UNDOF as needed.

Activities

Reports of the Secretary-General. Before the expiration of the mandate of UNDOF on 31 May and 30 November 1989, the Secretary-General reported to the Security Council on UNDOF activities during the periods from 18 November 1988 to 22 May 1989[30] and from 23 May to 21 November 1989.[31]

In accordance with its mandate[28] and in cooperation with the parties, UNDOF continued to supervise the cease-fire between Israel and the Syrian Arab Republic and monitor the area of separation to ensure that there were no military forces within it. It also conducted fortnightly inspections of armament and forces in the area of limitation. UNDOF carried out its duties from static positions and observation posts, which were manned 24 hours a day, and by foot and mobile patrols operating at irregular intervals on predetermined routes by day and night. In addition, temporary outposts were established and patrols were conducted from time to time to perform specific tasks.

The safety of Syrian shepherds grazing their flocks close to and west of the separation area continued to be of concern to UNDOF, and intensified patrolling of new mine-cleared paths helped to prevent incidents. Since mines continued to pose a threat to the Force and the population in the area of separation, UNDOF conducted mine-clearing operations there. During the two reporting periods, the Force cleared 71,930 and 43,790 square metres, respectively. UNDOF also assisted the International Committee of the Red Cross in its humanitarian activities.

The Secretary-General concluded that despite the current quiet in the Israel-Syria sector, the situation in the Middle East as a whole continued to be potentially dangerous and was likely to remain so, unless and until a comprehensive settlement covering all aspects of the Middle East problem could be reached. Therefore, he considered the presence of UNDOF in the area to be essential and recommended in his two reports, with the agreement of the Syrian Arab Republic and Israel, that the Security Council extend the mandate of the Force for a further six months, until 30 November 1989 and 31 May 1990, respectively.

On 30 May 1989, without debate, the Security Council unanimously adopted **resolution 633(1989)**.

The Security Council,
Having considered the report of the Secretary-General on the United Nations Disengagement Observer Force,
Decides:
(a) To call upon the parties concerned to implement immediately Security Council resolution 338(1973) of 22 October 1973;
(b) To renew the mandate of the United Nations Disengagement Observer Force for another period of six months, that is, until 30 November 1989;
(c) To request the Secretary-General to submit, at the end of this period, a report on the developments in the situation and the measures taken to implement Security Council resolution 338(1973).

Security Council resolution 633(1989)
30 May 1989   Meeting 2862   Adopted unanimously
Draft prepared in consultations among Council members (S/20656).

On 29 November, again without debate, the Council unanimously adopted **resolution 645(1989)**.

The Security Council,
Having considered the report of the Secretary-General on the United Nations Disengagement Observer Force,
*Decides:*t
(a) To call upon the parties concerned to implement immediately Security Council resolution 338(1973) of 22 October 1973;
(b) To renew the mandate of the United Nations Disengagement Observer Force for another period of six months, that is, until 31 May 1990;
(c) To request the Secretary-General to submit, at the end of this period, a report on the developments in the situation and the measures taken to implement resolution 338(1973).

Security Council resolution 645(1989)
29 November 1989   Meeting 2895   Adopted unanimously
Draft prepared in consultations among Council members (S/20996).

Following the adoption of each resolution, the President of the Council made the following statement:[32]

"As is known, the report of the Secretary-General on the United Nations Disengagement Observer Force states, in paragraph 24: 'Despite the present quiet in the Israel-Syria sector, the situation in the Middle East as a whole continues to be potentially dangerous and is likely to remain so, unless and until a comprehensive settlement covering all aspects of the Middle East problem can be reached.' That statement of the Secretary-General reflects the view of the Security Council."

Financing

In October 1989,[33] the Secretary-General reported that, as at 30 September 1989, assessments totalling $879.2 million had been apportioned among Member States for UNDOF since its inception on 31 May 1974[28] to 30 November 1989 and for the second United Nations Emergency Force, established in 1973[34] and liquidated in 1980.[35] Contributions received from 1973 to 1989 amounted to $801 million. Of the unpaid assessed balance of $78.2 million, only $10 million could be considered collectible, leaving a shortfall of $68.2 million, including $36 million transferred to a special account in accordance with a 1981 General Assembly resolution.[24] Therefore, troop-contributing countries had not been reimbursed on time.

In 1988,[36] the Assembly had appropriated $18,114,000 for UNDOF for the period from 1 December 1988 to 31 May 1989 and authorized the Secretary-General to enter into commitments for UNDOF at a rate not to exceed $3,019,000 gross ($2,963,000 net) per month for the period from 1 June to 30 November 1989, should the Security Council decide to continue UNDOF beyond 31 May 1989. The Secretary-General estimated the costs of the Force to be $3,368,000 gross ($3,283,000 net) per month from 1 December 1989.

In December,[27] ACABQ recommended approval of the Secretary-General's cost estimate for the period from 1 December 1989 to 30 November 1990 not exceeding $40,416,000 gross ($39,396,000 net).

On 21 December, the General Assembly, on the recommendation of the Fifth Committee, adopted **resolution 44/187** without vote.

Financing of the United Nations Disengagement Observer Force

The General Assembly,
Having considered the report of the Secretary-General on the financing of the United Nations Disengagement Observer Force, as well as the related report of the Advisory Committee on Administrative and Budgetary Questions,
Bearing in mind Security Council resolution 350(1974) of 31 May 1974, by which the Council established the United Nations Disengagement Observer Force, and the subsequent resolutions by which the Council extended the mandate of the Force, the latest of which was resolution 645(1989) of 29 November 1989,
Recalling its resolution 3211 B (XXIX) of 29 November 1974 on the financing of the United Nations Emergency Force and the United Nations Disengagement Observer Force and its subsequent resolutions thereon, the latest of which was resolution 43/228 of 21 December 1988,
Reaffirming its previous decisions regarding the fact that, in order to meet the expenditures caused by such operations, a different procedure from the one applied to meet expenditures of the regular budget of the United Nations is required,

Taking into account the fact that the economically more developed countries are in a position to make relatively larger contributions and that the economically less developed countries have a relatively limited capacity to contribute towards peace-keeping operations involving heavy expenditures,

Bearing in mind the special responsibilities of the States permanent members of the Security Council in the financing of such operations, as indicated in General Assembly resolution 1874(S-IV) of 27 June 1963 and other resolutions of the Assembly,

Having regard to the financial position of the Special Account for the United Nations Emergency Force and the United Nations Disengagement Observer Force, as set forth in the report of the Secretary-General, and referring to paragraph 5 of the report of the Advisory Committee on Administrative and Budgetary Questions,

Recalling its resolution 33/13 E of 14 December 1978 and subsequent resolutions in which it decided that the provisions of regulations 5.2 *(b)*, 5.2 *(d)*, 4.3 and 4.4 of the Financial Regulations of the United Nations should be suspended, the latest of which was resolution 43/228,

Mindful of the fact that it is essential to provide the United Nations Disengagement Observer Force with the necessary financial resources to enable it to fulfil its responsibilities under the relevant resolutions of the Security Council,

Concerned that the Secretary-General continues to face difficulties in meeting the obligations of the Forces on a current basis, particularly those due to the Governments of troop-contributing States,

Recognizing that, in consequence of the withholding of contributions by certain Member States, the surplus balances in the Special Account for the United Nations Emergency Force and the United Nations Disengagement Observer Force have, in effect, been drawn upon to the full extent to supplement the income received from contributions for meeting expenses of the Forces,

Concerned that the application of the provisions of regulations 5.2 *(b)*, 5.2 *(d)*, 4.3 and 4.4 of the Financial Regulations of the United Nations would aggravate the already difficult financial situation of the Forces,

Mindful of the views expressed in the Fifth Committee on the requests of some Member States to change their placement in the existing groups "b", "c" and "d" of Member States, on the basis of the criteria set out in General Assembly resolution 3101(XXVIII) of 11 December 1973,

1.   *Decides* to appropriate to the Special Account referred to in section II, paragraph 1, of General Assembly resolution 3211 B (XXIX) the amount of 18,114,000 United States dollars gross (17,778,000 dollars net) authorized and apportioned in paragraph 6 of Assembly resolution 43/228 for the operation of the United Nations Disengagement Observer Force for the period from 1 June to 30 November 1989, inclusive;

2.   *Decides also* to appropriate to the Special Account an amount of 20,208,000 dollars for the operation of the United Nations Disengagement Observer Force for the period from 1 December 1989 to 31 May 1990, inclusive;

3.   *Decides further*, as an *ad hoc* arrangement, to apportion the amount of 20,208,000 dollars for the above-mentioned period among Member States, in accordance with the composition of groups set out in paragraphs 3 and 4 of General Assembly resolution 43/232 of 1 March 1989, to be adjusted by the decision to be taken by the Assembly at its forty-fourth session on the composition

of groups "a", "b", "c" and "d" of Member States and taking into account the scale of assessments for the years 1989, 1990 and 1991;

4.   *Decides* that there shall be set off against the apportionment among Member States, as provided for in paragraph 3 of the present resolution, their respective share in the estimated income of 6,500 dollars other than staff assessment income approved for the period from 1 December 1989 to 31 May 1990, inclusive;

5.   *Decides also* that, in accordance with the provisions of its resolution 973(X) of 15 December 1955, there shall be set off against the apportionment among Member States, as provided for in paragraph 3 of the present resolution, their respective share in the Tax Equalization Fund of the estimated staff assessment income of 503,500 dollars approved for the period from 1 December 1989 to 31 May 1990, inclusive;

6.   *Authorizes* the Secretary-General to enter into commitments for the United Nations Disengagement Observer Force at a rate not to exceed 3,368,000 dollars gross (3,283,000 dollars net) per month for the period from 1 June to 30 November 1990, inclusive, should the Security Council decide to continue the Force beyond the period of six months authorized under its resolution 645(1989), the said amount to be apportioned among Member States in accordance with the scheme set out in the present resolution;

7.   *Decides* that the provisions of regulations 5.2 *(b)*, 5.2 *(d)*, 4.3 and 4.4 of the Financial Regulations of the United Nations shall be suspended in respect of the amount of 2,024,706 dollars, which otherwise would have to be surrendered pursuant to those provisions, this amount to be entered into the account referred to in the operative part of General Assembly resolution 33/13 E and held in suspense until a further decision is taken by the Assembly;

8.   *Stresses* the need for voluntary contributions to the United Nations Disengagement Observer Force, both in cash and in the form of services and supplies acceptable to the Secretary-General;

9.   *Requests* the Secretary-General to take all necessary action to ensure that the United Nations Disengagement Observer Force is administered with a maximum of efficiency and economy.

General Assembly resolution 44/187

21 December 1989   Meeting 84   Adopted without vote

Approved by Fifth Committee (A/44/887) without vote, 18 December (meeting 58); 13-nation draft (A/C.5/44/L.11); agenda item 133 *(a)*.

Sponsors: Australia, Austria, Canada, Denmark, Finland, Germany, Federal Republic of, Ghana, Ireland, Nepal, New Zealand, Norway, Poland, Sweden.

REFERENCES

[1]YUN 1981, p. 275. [2]S/20953. [3]S/20988. [4]S/21056. [5]YUN 1988, p. 225. [6]S/20758. [7]YUN 1985, p. 353. [8]S/20554. [9]S/20602. [10]S/20789. [11]S/20790. [12]S/20855. [13]YUN 1978, p. 312, SC res. 425(1978), 19 Mar. 1978. [14]*Ibid.*, p. 296. [15]YUN 1982, p. 428. [16]*Ibid.*, p. 450, SC res. 511(1982), 18 June 1982. [17]S/20742. [18]S/21102. [19]YUN 1988, p. 221. [20]S/20416 & Add.1 & Add.1/Corr.1 & Add.2. [21]S/20410. [22]S/20733. [23]A/44/818. [24]YUN 1981, p. 1299, GA res. 36/116 A, 10 Dec. 1981. [25]YUN 1979, p. 352, GA res. 34/9 D, 17 Dec. 1979. [26]YUN 1988, p. 224, GA res. 43/229, 21 Dec. 1988. [27]A/44/867. [28]YUN 1974, p. 205, SC res. 350(1974), 31 May 1974. [29]*Ibid.*, p. 198. [30]S/20651. [31]S/20976 & Corr.1. [32]S/20659, S/20998. [33]A/44/630. [34]YUN 1973, p. 213, SC res. 340(1973), 25 Oct. 1973. [35]YUN 1980, p. 361. [36]YUN 1988, p. 227, GA res. 43/228, 21 Dec. 1988.

Territories occupied by Israel

The territories occupied by Israel as a result of armed conflicts in the Middle East comprised the West Bank of the Jordan River, including East Jerusalem, the Gaza Strip and the Golan Heights in the Syrian Arab Republic. The United Nations continued in 1989 to monitor the situation and take appropriate action on various aspects of it.

In April, the General Assembly, at the request of the Chairman of the Group of Arab States, resumed its consideration of the item on the question of Palestine, and subsequently condemned Israeli policies and practices which violated the human rights of the Palestinians in the occupied territory. In October, the Assembly, in adopting a resolution on the uprising (*intifadah*) of the Palestinians, condemned human rights violations in the occupied Palestinian territory, in particular such acts as the opening of fire by the Israeli army and settlers that resulted in the killing and wounding of defenceless Palestinian civilians, beating, deportation, imposition of restrictive economic measures, demolition of houses and so forth.

After considering reports of the Special Committee to Investigate Israeli Practices Affecting the Human Rights of the Population of the Occupied Territories (Committee on Israeli practices), the Assembly adopted in December seven resolutions condemning various types of human rights violations in the territories.

In 1989, the Security Council discussed the situation in the occupied Arab territories at meetings held in February, June, July, August and November. In July, the Council adopted a resolution by which it deeply regretted the continuing deportation by Israel of Palestinian civilians and called on Israel to ensure the safe and immediate return of those deported. In August, the Council again deplored the continuing deportation of Palestinian civilians from the occupied territories.

The Committee on the Inalienable Rights of the Palestinian People (Committee on Palestinian rights) monitored the situation in the occupied territory on an ongoing basis, drawing the attention of the General Assembly and the Security Council to Israeli policies and practices there. In its annual report, the Committee protested the intensification of what it called Israeli repression of Palestinians.

The Committee on Israeli practices continued to collect from various sources, including oral testimony and written communications, information on developments in the occupied territories, reviewing that information and assessing the overall human rights situation. On that basis, the Committee concluded in October that the situation in the territories had been marked by a dangerous level of violence and repression, which had constantly escalated since the beginning of the *intifadah* in December 1987.

The Economic and Social Council in May strongly condemned the continuation of Israel's "iron-fist" policy against Palestinian women and their families in the occupied territories. In July, it adopted a resolution on Israeli economic practices in the occupied Palestinian and other Arab territories.

The United Nations Conference on Trade and Development reported on economic issues and related Israeli practices in the West Bank and the Gaza Strip.

In February, the Commission on Human Rights adopted three resolutions related to the occupied territories. In one, it declared that the continued Israeli occupation of the Syrian Arab Golan and Israel's decision of 14 December 1981 to impose its laws, jurisdiction and administration there constituted an act of aggression and that the decision was null and void and without international legal validity or effect. In the two other resolutions, the Commission condemned Israeli policies and practices in the occupied territories.

Report of the Committee on Palestinian rights. In its annual report,[1] the Committee expressed alarm at the further aggravation of the situation in the occupied territory as a result of intensified Israeli efforts to suppress the Palestinian uprising, including the increasing resort to armed force and settler vigilantism. Use of force resulted in an extensive and unprecedented range of human rights violations. Thousands of Palestinians were the victims of beatings while in the hands of the Israeli army or security personnel, it was reported.

As of 15 September 1989, Palestinians shot to death by the Israeli forces or armed settlers numbered 537. Another 212 had died from beatings, suffocation from tear gas and other actions, the Committee stated. It was, it said, particularly alarmed that a high proportion of victims were children—at least 20 per cent of fatalities were children under the age of 16. That percentage had increased to 46 per cent during August.

The Committee also reported campaigns of mass arrests. As of September 1989, more than 40,000 Palestinians had been in prison at one time or another, only 18,000 of whom had actually been sentenced. Israeli authorities, after removing previously existing judicial safeguards for detainees, increasingly relied on the use of administrative detention without charges or trial. In August, the standard period of administrative detention was doubled from six months to a year. As of September, about 13,600 Palestinians, including children, were reported to be in detention.

Violations of the Palestinians' right to education intensifed, with the complete closure of universities, long-term and repeated closure of schools, the use of schools as military outposts and the destruction of school property. It was estimated that some 400,000 primary and secondary schoolchildren were in school for only about five months between the autumn of 1987 and June 1989.

The Committee also was concerned over the health situation in the occupied territory, which it said continued to deteriorate. Sanitary infrastructure, quantity and quality of medical services, and medical equipment and supplies were increasingly insufficient.

Concluding its assessment of the situation, the Committee reiterated its urgent appeal to the Security Council and the international community as a whole to take measures to ensure the safety and protection of the Palestinians, pending the withdrawal of Israeli forces and the achievement of a settlement. The Committee called on all concerned to sustain and increase their assistance to the Palestinians, in close co-operation with PLO.

Report of the Committee on Israeli practices. In October 1989, the Committee on Israeli practices, established by the General Assembly in 1968,[2] submitted its twenty-first report,[3] covering the period from 26 August 1988 to 25 August 1989; in July, a periodic report[4] covering the period from 26 August 1988 to 31 March 1989 had been provided. While the latter contained mostly factual information about developments affecting the human rights of the civilian population in the occupied territories, the main report also transmitted information on Committee activities and conclusions.

The Committee held a series of meetings in Geneva (3-6 January, 22-23 May, 21-25 August), Damascus (24-27 May), Amman (28 May–1 June) and Cairo (2-7 June) to examine information on developments in the occupied territories, as well as to consider communications addressed to it in connection with its mandate by Governments, organizations and individuals. The Committee worked in close co-operation with the Governments of Egypt, Jordan and the Syrian Arab Republic and with various Palestinian representatives. Israel, as in previous years, did not participate in its work.

The Committee concluded that Israel was continuing its policy of annexation towards the occupied territories, by establishing settlements, expropriating property, transferring Israeli citizens to the occupied territories and encouraging or compelling Palestinians to leave their homeland. There also had been a considerable increase in the number of deportations from the occupied territories, as well as detentions, the Committee stated.

As a consequence of the arrests of tens of thousands of Palestinians since the uprising began, the situation of detainees had further deteriorated, with their being subjected to various forms of ill-treatment, both physical and psychological, a lack of adequate sanitary and medical facilities, nutrition and clothing, and overcrowding of cells.

Freedom of association and freedom of the press were affected by closure of newspapers and detention of journalists. Freedom of education was seriously hampered by prolonged closure of educational institutions. Freedom of movement was affected by arbitrary orders and curfews.

The Committee, in view of the gravity of the situation in the territories, stressed that urgent measures had to be taken in order to ensure an effective protection of the basic rights and freedoms of the civilians. The Committee called again for the full application by Israel of the relevant provisions of the fourth Geneva Convention, the full co-operation of the Israeli authorities with the International Committee of the Red Cross (ICRC) to ensure access of ICRC representatives to detainees, and the full support by Member States of UNRWA activities in order to enable that Agency to improve general assistance to refugees.

Report of the Secretary-General. In pursuance of a 1988 General Assembly resolution,[5] the Secretary-General in May requested that Israel inform him of any steps taken or envisaged to implement relevant provisions of that resolution. In October, the Secretary-General reported[6] that, in a note verbale, Israel had categorically rejected all allegations contained in that resolution and in the 1988 report[7] of the Committee on Israeli practices.

GENERAL ASSEMBLY ACTION

On 8 December, following consideration of the report of the Committee on Israeli practices and acting on the recommendation of the Special Political Committee, the General Assembly adopted **resolution 44/48 A** by recorded vote.

The General Assembly,

Guided by the purposes and principles of the Charter of the United Nations and by the principles and provisions of the Universal Declaration of Human Rights,

Aware of the uprising *(intifadah)* of the Palestinian people since 9 December 1987 against Israeli occupation, which has received significant attention and sympathy from world public opinion,

Deeply concerned at the alarming situation in the Palestinian territory occupied since 1967, including Jerusalem, as well as in the other occupied Arab territories, as a result of the continued occupation by Israel, the occupying Power, and of its persistent policies against the Palestinian people,

Bearing in mind the provisions of the Geneva Convention relative to the Protection of Civilian Persons in Time of War, of 12 August 1949, as well as of other relevant conventions and regulations,

Taking into account the need to consider measures for the impartial protection of the Palestinian people under the Israeli occupation,

Recalling all its resolutions on the subject, in particular resolutions 32/91 B and C of 13 December 1977, 33/113 C of 18 December 1978, 34/90 A of 12 December 1979, 35/122 C of 11 December 1980, 36/147 C of 16 December 1981, ES-9/1 of 5 February 1982, 37/88 C of 10 December 1982, 38/79 D of 15 December 1983, 39/95 D of 14 December 1984, 40/161 D of 16 December 1985, 41/63 D of 3 December 1986, 42/160 D of 8 December 1987, 43/21 of 3 November 1988, 43/58 A of 6 December 1988 and 44/2 of 6 October 1989,

Recalling also the relevant Security Council resolutions, in particular resolutions 605(1987) of 22 December 1987, 607(1988) of 5 January 1988, 608(1988) of 14 January 1988, 636(1989) of 6 July 1989 and 641(1989) of 30 August 1989,

Recalling further the relevant resolutions adopted by the Commission on Human Rights, in particular resolutions 1983/1 of 15 February 1983, 1984/1 of 20 February 1984, 1985/1 A and B and 1985/2 of 19 February 1985, 1986/1 A and B and 1986/2 of 20 February 1986, 1987/1, 1987/2 A and B and 1987/4 of 19 February 1987, 1988/1 A and B and 1988/2 of 15 February 1988 and 1988/3 of 22 February 1988, 1989/1 and 1989/2 of 17 February 1989 and 1989/19 of 6 March 1989, and by other United Nations organs concerned and the specialized agencies,

Having considered the reports of the Special Committee to Investigate Israeli Practices Affecting the Human Rights of the Population of the Occupied Territories, which contain, *inter alia*, self-incriminating public statements made by officials of Israel, the occupying Power,

Having also considered the reports of the Secretary-General of 21 January 1988 and 20 October 1989,

1. *Commends* the Special Committee to Investigate Israeli Practices Affecting the Human Rights of the Population of the Occupied Territories for its efforts in performing the tasks assigned to it by the General Assembly and for its impartiality;

2. *Deplores* the continued refusal by Israel to allow the Special Committee access to the occupied Palestinian territory, including Jerusalem, and other Arab territories occupied by Israel since 1967;

3. *Demands* that Israel allow the Special Committee access to those occupied territories;

4. *Reaffirms* the fact that occupation itself constitutes a grave violation of the human rights of the Palestinian people in the occupied Palestinian territory, including Jerusalem, and other Arab territories occupied by Israel since 1967;

5. *Condemns* the continued and persistent violation by Israel of the Geneva Convention relative to the Protection of Civilian Persons in Time of War, of 12 August 1949, and other applicable international instruments, and condemns in particular those violations which the Convention designates as "grave breaches" thereof;

6. *Declares once more* that Israel's grave breaches of that Convention are war crimes and an affront to humanity;

7. *Reaffirms*, in accordance with the Convention, that the Israeli military occupation of the Palestinian territory, including Jerusalem, and other Arab territories is of a temporary nature, thus giving no right whatsoever to the occupying Power over the territorial integrity of the occupied territories;

8. *Strongly condemns* the following Israeli policies and practices:

(*a*) Annexation of parts of the occupied Palestinian territory, including Jerusalem;

(*b*) Imposition of Israeli laws, jurisdiction and administration on the Syrian Arab Golan, which has resulted in the effective annexation of that territory;

(*c*) Illegal imposition and levy of taxes and dues;

(*d*) Establishment of new Israeli settlements and expansion of the existing settlements on private and public Palestinian and other Arab lands, and transfer of an alien population thereto;

(*e*) Eviction, deportation, expulsion, displacement and transfer of Palestinians and other Arabs of those occupied territories and denial of their right to return;

(*f*) Confiscation and expropriation of private and public Palestinian and other Arab property in those occupied territories and all other transactions for the acquisition of land by the Israeli authorities, institutions or nationals;

(*g*) Excavation and transformation of the landscape and the historical, cultural and religious sites, especially at Jerusalem;

(*h*) Pillaging of archaeological and cultural property;

(*i*) Destruction and demolition of Palestinian and other Arab houses;

(*j*) Collective punishment, mass arrests, administrative detention and ill-treatment of Palestinians and other Arabs;

(*k*) Torture of Palestinians and other Arabs;

(*l*) Interference with religious freedoms and practices, as well as family rights and customs;

(*m*) Interference with the system of education and with the social and economic and health development of the Palestinians and other Arabs in those occupied territories;

(*n*) Interference with the freedom of movement of individuals within the occupied Palestinian territory, including Jerusalem, and other Arab territories occupied by Israel since 1967;

(*o*) Illegal exploitation of the natural wealth, resources and labour of those occupied territories;

9. *Strongly condemns*, in particular, the following Israeli policies and practices:

(*a*) Implementation of an "iron-fist" policy against the Palestinian people in the occupied Palestinian territory;

(*b*) Escalation of Israeli brutality since the beginning of the uprising (*intifadah*) on 9 December 1987;

(*c*) Ill-treatment and torture of children and minors under detention and/or imprisonment;

(*d*) Closure of headquarters and offices of trade unions and social organizations and harassment, including expulsion of their leaders, as well as attacks on hospitals and their personnel;

(*e*) Interference with the freedom of the press, including censorship, detention or expulsion of journalists, closure and suspension of newspapers and magazines, as well as denial of access to international media;

(*f*) Killing and wounding of defenceless demonstrators;

(*g*) Breaking of bones and limbs of thousands of civilians;

(*h*) House and/or town arrests;

(i) Use of toxic gas, which has resulted, *inter alia*, in the killing of many Palestinians;

10. *Condemns* the Israeli repression against and closing of the educational institutions in the occupied Syrian Arab Golan, particularly the prohibition of Syrian textbooks and the Syrian educational system, the deprivation of Syrian students from pursuing their higher education in Syrian universities, the denial of the right to return to Syrian students receiving their higher education in the Syrian Arab Republic, the forcing of Hebrew on Syrian students, the imposition of courses that promote hatred, prejudice and religious intolerance, and the dismissal of teachers, all in clear violation of the Geneva Convention;

11. *Strongly condemns* the arming of Israeli settlers in those occupied territories to perpetrate and commit acts of violence against Palestinians and other Arabs, causing deaths and injuries;

12. *Requests* the Security Council to ensure Israel's respect for and compliance with all the provisions of the Geneva Convention relative to the Protection of Civilian Persons in Time of War, of 12 August 1949, in the occupied Palestinian territory, including Jerusalem, and other Arab territories occupied by Israel since 1967, and to initiate measures to halt Israeli policies and practices in those territories;

13. *Urges* the Security Council to consider the current situation in the Palestinian territory occupied by Israel since 1967, taking into account the recommendations contained in the reports of the Secretary-General, and with a view to securing international protection for the defenceless Palestinian people until the withdrawal of Israel, the occupying Power, from the occupied Palestinian territory;

14. *Reaffirms* that all measures taken by Israel to change the physical character, demographic composition, institutional structure or legal status of those occupied territories, or any part thereof, including Jerusalem, are null and void, and that Israel's policy of settling parts of its population and new immigrants in those occupied territories constitutes a flagrant violation of the Geneva Convention and of the relevant resolutions of the United Nations;

15. *Demands* that Israel desist forthwith from the policies and practices referred to in paragraphs 8, 9, 10 and 11 above;

16. *Calls upon* Israel, the occupying Power, to allow the reopening of the Roman Catholic Medical Facility Hospice in Jerusalem in order to continue to provide needed health and medical services to the Palestinians in the city;

17. *Also calls upon* Israel, the occupying Power, to take immediate steps for the return of all displaced Arab and Palestinian inhabitants to their homes or former places of residence in the territories occupied by Israel since 1967, in implementation of Security Council resolution 237(1967) of 14 June 1967;

18. *Urges* international organizations, including the specialized agencies, in particular the International Labour Organisation, the United Nations Educational, Scientific and Cultural Organization and the World Health Organization, to continue to examine the educational and health conditions in the occupied Palestinian territory, including Jerusalem, and other Arab territories occupied by Israel since 1967;

19. *Reiterates its call* upon all States, in particular those States parties to the Geneva Convention, in accordance with article 1 of that Convention, and upon international organizations, including the specialized agencies, not to recognize any changes carried out by Israel, the occupying Power, in those occupied territories and to avoid actions, including those in the field of aid, which might be used by Israel in its pursuit of the policies of annexation and colonization or any of the other policies and practices referred to in the present resolution;

20. *Requests* the Special Committee, pending early termination of Israeli occupation, to continue to investigate Israeli policies and practices in the occupied Palestinian territory, including Jerusalem, and other Arab territories occupied by Israel since 1967, to consult, as appropriate, with the International Committee of the Red Cross in order to ensure the safeguarding of the welfare and human rights of the peoples of those occupied territories and to report to the Secretary-General as soon as possible and whenever the need arises thereafter;

21. *Also requests* the Special Committee to submit regularly to the Secretary-General periodic reports on the present situation in the occupied Palestinian territory;

22. *Further requests* the Special Committee to continue to investigate the treatment of prisoners in the occupied Palestinian territory, including Jerusalem, and other Arab territories occupied by Israel since 1967;

23. *Condemns* Israel's refusal to permit persons from the occupied Palestinian territory to appear as witnesses before the Special Committee and to participate in conferences and meetings held outside the occupied Palestinian territory;

24. *Requests* the Secretary-General:

(a) To provide all necessary facilities to the Special Committee, including those required for its visits to those occupied territories, so that it may investigate the Israeli policies and practices referred to in the present resolution;

(b) To continue to make available additional staff as may be necessary to assist the Special Committee in the performance of its tasks;

(c) To circulate regularly and periodically the reports mentioned in paragraph 21 above to the States Members of the United Nations;

(d) To ensure the widest circulation of the reports of the Special Committee and of information regarding its activities and findings, by all means available, through the Department of Public Information of the Secretariat and, where necessary, to reprint those reports of the Special Committee which are no longer available;

(e) To report to the General Assembly at its forty-fifth session on the tasks entrusted to him in the present resolution;

25. *Decides* to change the name of the Special Committee to: "the Special Committee to Investigate Israeli Practices Affecting the Human Rights of the Palestinian People and Other Arabs of the Occupied Territories";

26. *Also decides* to include in the provisional agenda of its forty-fifth session an item entitled "Report of the Special Committee to Investigate Israeli Practices Affecting the Human Rights of the Palestinian People and Other Arabs of the Occupied Territories".

General Assembly resolution 44/48 A

8 December 1989   Meeting 78   107-2-41 (recorded vote)

Approved by Special Political Committee (A/44/816) by recorded vote (93-2-31), 22 November (meeting 25); 13-nation draft (A/SPC/44/L.19 & Corr.1); agenda item 77.

Sponsors: Afghanistan, Bangladesh, Brunei Darussalam, Burkina Faso, Comoros, Cuba, India, Indonesia, Madagascar, Malaysia, Nicaragua, Pakistan, Zambia.

Meeting numbers. GA 44th session: SPC 22-25; plenary 78.

Recorded vote in Assembly as follows:

In favour: Afghanistan, Albania, Algeria, Angola, Argentina, Bahrain, Bangladesh, Benin, Bhutan, Bolivia, Botswana, Brazil, Brunei Darussalam, Bulgaria, Burkina Faso, Burundi, Byelorussian SSR, Cape Verde, Chad, China, Colombia, Comoros, Costa Rica, Cuba, Cyprus, Czechoslovakia, Democratic Kampuchea, Democratic Yemen, Djibouti, Dominican Republic, Ecuador, Egypt, Ethiopia, Gabon, German Democratic Republic, Ghana, Guatemala, Guinea, Guinea-Bissau, Guyana, Honduras, Hungary, India, Indonesia, Iran, Iraq, Jordan, Kuwait, Lao People's Democratic Republic, Lebanon, Lesotho, Liberia, Libyan Arab Jamahiriya, Madagascar, Malaysia, Maldives, Mali, Mauritania, Mauritius, Mexico, Mongolia, Morocco, Mozambique, Myanmar, Nepal, Nicaragua, Nigeria, Oman, Pakistan, Panama, Papua New Guinea, Paraguay, Peru, Philippines, Poland, Qatar, Romania, Rwanda, Sao Tome and Principe, Saudi Arabia, Senegal, Seychelles, Sierra Leone, Singapore, Solomon Islands, Somalia, Sri Lanka, Sudan, Suriname, Swaziland, Syrian Arab Republic, Thailand, Trinidad and Tobago, Tunisia, Turkey, Uganda, Ukrainian SSR, USSR, United Arab Emirates, United Republic of Tanzania, Vanuatu, Venezuela, Viet Nam, Yemen, Yugoslavia, Zambia, Zimbabwe.

Against: Israel, United States.

Abstaining: Antigua and Barbuda, Australia, Austria, Bahamas, Barbados, Belgium, Cameroon, Canada, Central African Republic, Côte d'Ivoire, Denmark, Dominica, Equatorial Guinea, Fiji, Finland, France, Germany, Federal Republic of, Greece, Grenada, Iceland, Ireland, Italy, Jamaica, Japan, Kenya, Luxembourg, Malawi, Malta, Netherlands, New Zealand, Norway, Portugal, Saint Lucia, Saint Vincent and the Grenadines, Samoa, Spain, Sweden, Togo, United Kingdom, Uruguay, Zaire.

Paragraph 6 of the resolution was adopted by the Committee and the Assembly by recorded votes of 75 to 20, with 28 abstentions, and 81 to 21, with 43 abstentions, respectively.

The Palestinian uprising (*intifadah*)

During 1989, the Palestinian uprising (*intifadah*) in the occupied territory continued unabated. As the Secretary-General reported,[8] the message of the *intifadah* was direct and unequivocal, namely, that the Israeli occupation would continue to be rejected, and that the Palestinian people would remain committed to the exercise of their legitimate political rights, including self-determination.

The Committee on Palestinian rights reported[1] in November that it was alarmed by a further aggravation of the situation in the occupied Palestinian territory as a result of the intensification of efforts by Israel to suppress the *intifadah*. The Committee expressed the view that the continuation of the *intifadah* and the intensification of repressive measures by Israel had created a critical situation that made it imperative to advance towards a comprehensive, just and lasting settlement of the question of Palestine.

GENERAL ASSEMBLY ACTION

On 6 October, the General Assembly adopted **resolution 44/2** by recorded vote.

The uprising (*intifadah*) of the Palestinian people

The General Assembly,

Aware of the uprising (*intifadah*) of the Palestinian people since 9 December 1987 against Israeli occupation, which has received significant attention and sympathy from world public opinion,

Deeply concerned at the alarming situation in the Palestinian territory occupied since 1967, as a result of the continued occupation by Israel, the occupying Power, and of its persistent policies and practices against the Palestinian people,

Reaffirming that the Geneva Convention relative to the Protection of Civilian Persons in Time of War, of 12 August 1949, is applicable to the Palestinian territory occupied by Israel since 1967, including Jerusalem, and to the other occupied Arab territories,

Expressing its profound shock at the continued measures by Israel, the occupying Power, including the killing and wounding of Palestinian civilians and the recent action of ransacking the houses of defenceless civilians in the Palestinian town of Beit Sahour,

Stressing the need to promote international protection to the Palestinian civilians in the occupied Palestinian territory,

Recognizing the need for increased support to, aid for and solidarity with the Palestinian people under Israeli occupation,

Having considered the recommendations contained in the report of the Secretary-General,

Recalling its relevant resolutions as well as the relevant Security Council resolutions,

1. *Condemns* those policies and practices of Israel, the occupying Power, which violate the human rights of the Palestinian people in the occupied Palestinian territory, including Jerusalem, and, in particular, such acts as the opening of fire by the Israeli army and settlers that result in the killing and wounding of defenceless Palestinian civilians, the beating and breaking of bones, the deportation of Palestinian civilians, the imposition of restrictive economic measures, the demolition of houses, the ransacking of real or personal property belonging individually or collectively to private persons, collective punishment and detentions, and so forth;

2. *Demands* that Israel, the occupying Power, abide scrupulously by the Geneva Convention relative to the Protection of Civilian Persons in Time of War, of 12 August 1949, and desist immediately from those policies and practices which are in violation of the provisions of the Convention;

3. *Calls upon* all the High Contracting Parties to the Convention to ensure respect by Israel, the occupying Power, for the Convention in all circumstances, in conformity with their obligation under article 1 thereof;

4. *Strongly deplores* the continuing disregard by Israel, the occupying Power, of the relevant decisions of the Security Council;

5. *Reaffirms* that the occupation by Israel of the Palestinian territory since 1967, including Jerusalem, and of the other Arab territories in no way changes the legal status of those territories;

6. *Requests* the Security Council to examine with urgency the situation in the occupied Palestinian territory with a view to considering measures needed to provide

international protection to the Palestinian civilians in the Palestinian territory occupied by Israel since 1967, including Jerusalem;

7. *Invites* Member States, the organizations of the United Nations system, governmental, intergovernmental and non-governmental organizations, and the mass communications media to continue and enhance their support for the Palestinian people;

8. *Requests* the Secretary-General to examine the present situation in the Palestinian territory occupied since 1967, including Jerusalem, by all means available to him and to submit periodic reports thereon, the first such report as soon as possible.

General Assembly resolution 44/2

6 October 1989   Meeting 23   140-2-6 (recorded vote)

32-nation draft (A/44/L.2/Rev.1); agenda item 39.

Sponsors: Algeria, Bahrain, Bangladesh, Colombia, Cuba, Democratic Yemen, Djibouti, Egypt, Indonesia, Iraq, Jordan, Kuwait, Lebanon, Libyan Arab Jamahiriya, Madagascar, Malaysia, Mali, Mauritania, Morocco, Oman, Pakistan, Qatar, Saudi Arabia, Senegal, Somalia, Sudan, Syrian Arab Republic, Tunisia, Ukrainian SSR, United Arab Emirates, Yemen, Yugoslavia.

Recorded vote in Assembly as follows:

In favour: Afghanistan, Albania, Algeria, Angola, Argentina, Australia, Austria, Bahamas, Bahrain, Bangladesh, Barbados, Belgium, Belize, Benin, Bhutan, Bolivia, Botswana, Brazil, Brunei Darussalam, Bulgaria, Burkina Faso, Burundi, Byelorussian SSR, Cameroon, Canada, Chad, Chile, China, Colombia, Comoros, Congo, Costa Rica, Côte d'Ivoire, Cuba, Cyprus, Czechoslovakia, Democratic Kampuchea, Democratic Yemen, Denmark, Djibouti, Ecuador, Egypt, Ethiopia, Fiji, Finland, France, Gabon, Gambia, German Democratic Republic, Germany, Federal Republic of, Ghana, Greece, Guatemala, Guinea, Guinea-Bissau, Guyana, Haiti, Hungary, Iceland, India, Indonesia, Iran, Iraq, Ireland, Italy, Jamaica, Japan, Jordan, Kenya, Kuwait, Lao People's Democratic Republic, Lebanon, Lesotho, Liberia, Libyan Arab Jamahiriya, Luxembourg, Madagascar, Malaysia, Maldives, Mali, Malta, Mauritania, Mauritius, Mexico, Mongolia, Morocco, Mozambique, Myanmar, Nepal, Netherlands, New Zealand, Nicaragua, Niger, Nigeria, Norway, Oman, Pakistan, Panama, Papua New Guinea, Paraguay, Peru, Philippines, Poland, Portugal, Qatar, Romania, Rwanda, Samoa, Sao Tome and Principe, Saudi Arabia, Senegal, Seychelles, Sierra Leone, Singapore, Somalia, Spain, Sri Lanka, Sudan, Suriname, Swaziland, Sweden, Syrian Arab Republic, Thailand, Togo, Trinidad and Tobago, Tunisia, Turkey, Uganda, Ukrainian SSR, USSR, United Arab Emirates, United Kingdom, United Republic of Tanzania, Vanuatu, Venezuela, Viet Nam, Yemen, Yugoslavia, Zambia, Zimbabwe.

Against: Israel, United States.

Abstaining: Antigua and Barbuda, El Salvador, Grenada, Saint Vincent and the Grenadines, Uruguay, Zaire.*

*Later advised the Secretariat it had intended to vote in favour.

SECURITY COUNCIL CONSIDERATION (February, June and November)

The Security Council convened throughout 1989 to consider the situation in the occupied territories. At the request[9] of the Chairman of the Group of Arab States, the Security Council met on 10, 13, 14 and 17 February.

Meeting numbers. SC 2845-2847, 2849, 2850.

The Palestine Observer's request[10] to participate in the meetings was approved by 11 votes to 1 (United States), with 3 abstentions (Canada, France, United Kingdom). The United States, which requested the vote, took the position that, under the Council's provisional rules of procedure, rule 39[a] was the only legal basis on which the Council might grant a hearing to non-governmental entities. It also pointed out that observers did not have the right to speak in the Coun-

cil on their own request; a request must be made on the observer's behalf by a Member State. The United States concluded that it believed in listening to all points of view, but not if that required violating the rules.

On 17 February, after debate, the Council voted on a draft resolution[11] submitted by Algeria, Colombia, Ethiopia, Malaysia, Nepal, Senegal and Yugoslavia. By the text, the Council would have strongly deplored the continuing disregard by Israel of the relevant decisions of the Council and would have called on it to abide by the relevant Council resolutions, as well as to comply with its obligations under the fourth Geneva Convention and to desist forthwith from its policies and practices that were in violation of the provisions of the Convention.

The vote was 14 to 1, as follows:

In favour: Algeria, Brazil, Canada, China, Colombia, Ethiopia, Finland, France, Malaysia, Nepal, Senegal, USSR, United Kingdom, Yugoslavia.

Against: United States.

The draft was not adopted owing to the negative vote of a permanent Council member.

At the request[12] of the Chairman of the Arab Group, the Council held further meetings on the situation in the occupied territories on 6, 7, 8 and 9 June.

Meeting numbers. SC 2863-2867.

Approval of the request by the Palestine Observer[13] to participate was by the same vote as in February, after the United States had restated its negative position on such participation (see above).

On 9 June, the Council voted on a draft resolution[14] put forward by the same seven States that had proposed the February text. By the text, the Council would have strongly deplored Israeli policies and practices which violated Palestinian human rights, as well as vigilante attacks against Palestinian towns and villages and desecration of the Holy Koran; called on Israel to comply with its obligation under the fourth Geneva Convention; demanded that Israel desist forthwith from deporting Palestinian civilians from the occupied territory and ensure the safe and immediate return of those already deported; and expressed great concern over the prolonged closure of schools in parts of the occupied territory and called for their reopening.

The vote was 14 to 1, following the same voting pattern as in February. The draft was rejected

[a]Rule 39 of the Council's provisional rules of procedure states: "The Security Council may invite members of the Secretariat or other persons, whom it considers competent for the purpose, to supply it with information or to give other assistance in examining matters within its competence."

owing to the negative vote of a permanent member.

In a statement before the vote, the United States stressed that while the draft contained much with which it could agree, the text was unbalanced in making sweeping condemnations of Israeli policies and practices without reference to any of the serious acts of violence by the other side.

Speaking after the vote, the Permanent Observer of Palestine expressed regret that the Council had not succeeded in bringing to fruition the work that had been undertaken for months and years, but he believed that the debate would contribute to the cause of peace.

At the request[15] of the Chairman of the Arab Group, the Council met again on 6 and 7 November to discuss the situation in the occupied territories.

Meeting numbers. SC 2887-2889.

The request for participation by the Palestine Observer[16] was approved by the same vote as earlier, with the United States reiterating its negative position.

On 7 November, the Council voted on a revised draft resolution[17] proposed by the seven States which had sponsored the two earlier drafts (see above). By the text, the Council would have expressed alarm at the deteriorating situation in the Palestinian territory occupied by Israel since 1967, including Jerusalem; strongly deplored Israeli policies and practices violating the human rights of the Palestinian people, in particular the siege of towns, the ransacking of the homes of inhabitants, as had happened at Beit Sahur, and the confiscation of their property and valuables; reaffirmed once again the applicability of the fourth Geneva Convention and called once again on Israel to abide by it; demanded that Israel return confiscated property to its owners; and requested the Secretary-General to conduct on-site monitoring of the current situation and to submit periodic reports.

The vote was 14 to 1 (United States); the draft was rejected owing to the negative vote of a permanent member.

After the vote, the United States said that it was engaged in intensive efforts to help launch an Israeli-Palestinian dialogue; repeated recourse to the Security Council with one-sided draft resolutions did not contribute to that process or to a real reduction of confrontation in the occupied territories. The United States also did not agree with the request that the Secretary-General conduct on-site monitoring since that connoted a permanent, ongoing presence on the ground. However, it did support the Secretary-General's efforts and those of his representatives to visit the occupied territo-

ries in order to report periodically on the situation there.

Israel stated that the drastic increase in violence was PLO's direct response to the challenge posed by Israel's peace initiative. The violence was intended to intimidate the local population and ensure the complete domination of PLO terror. Israel rejected the charge that it violated international law by collecting taxes in Beit Sahur and said that the taxes levied in the territories were used solely to finance the provision of services to the Palestinian residents.

In a statement after the vote, the Palestine Observer said it was distressing that a concern expressed so overwhelmingly by the Council had been undermined by a permanent member. It was his understanding that the United States was tying the hands of the Secretary-General, preventing him from pursuing his endeavours. By opposing on-site monitoring, it was trying to cover up what Israel was doing. The position taken by the Palestinians, as expressed by the National Council, was a peace initiative supported by the entire international community in a 1988 General Assembly resolution.

Fourth Geneva Convention

In 1989, the General Assembly and the Commission on Human Rights (see PART THREE, Chapter X) again reaffirmed that the Geneva Convention relative to the Protection of Civilian Persons in Time of War, of 12 August 1949, applied to the Palestinian and other Arab territories occupied by Israel. Continuing disregard of that main international instrument in humanitarian law that applied to the occupied territories was reported throughout the year by the Committee on Israeli practices.

Report of Committee on Israeli practices. In the opinion of the Committee,[3] the provisions of the fourth Geneva Convention continued to be disregarded and violated. In violation of its obligation as a State party to the Convention, Israel, the Committee said, pursued a policy of annexation, which had led to establishing settlements, expropriating property, transferring Israeli citizens to the occupied territories and encouraging or compelling Palestinians to leave their homeland. Deportations from the occupied territories also violated article 49 of the Convention. In violation of article 76, detainees had continued to be held in prisons and detention centres.

The Committee once again stressed that urgent measures had to be taken in order to ensure an effective protection of the basic rights and freedoms of the civilians in the occupied territories and it again called for full application by Israel of the relevant Convention provisions.

Report of Secretary-General. In pursuance of a 1988 General Assembly resolution,[18] the Secretary-General reported[19] in September 1989 that he had sent a note verbale to the Minister for Foreign Affairs of Israel and that, in its reply of 18 August, Israel had stated that, while reserving its position on the *de jure* applicability of the fourth Geneva Convention, due to the question of the political status of the areas, Israel's official position was to conform with the provisions of the Convention and implement them on a *de facto* basis in its administration in those areas. That was not an engagement in semantics, it said, but rather a fundamental principle which was the basis of the policy of the Government of Israel.

GENERAL ASSEMBLY ACTION

On 8 December 1989, the General Assembly, having considered the report of the Committee on Israeli practices and on the recommendation of the Special Political Committee, adopted **resolution 44/48 B** by recorded vote.

The General Assembly,

Recalling Security Council resolution 465(1980) of 1 March 1980, in which, *inter alia,* the Council affirmed that the Geneva Convention relative to the Protection of Civilian Persons in Time of War, of 12 August 1949, is applicable to the Arab territories occupied by Israel since 1967, including Jerusalem,

Recalling also its resolutions 3092 A (XXVIII) of 7 December 1973, 3240 B (XXIX) of 29 November 1974, 3525 B (XXX) of 15 December 1975, 31/106 B of 16 December 1976, 32/91 A of 13 December 1977, 33/113 A of 18 December 1978, 34/90 B of 12 December 1979, 35/122 A of 11 December 1980, 36/147 A of 16 December 1981, 37/88 A of 10 December 1982, 38/79 B of 15 December 1983, 39/95 B of 14 December 1984, 40/161 B of 16 December 1985, 41/63 B of 3 December 1986, 42/160 B of 8 December 1987 and 43/58 B of 6 December 1988,

Taking note of the reports of the Secretary-General of 21 January 1988 and 28 September 1989,

Considering that the promotion of respect for the obligations arising from the Charter of the United Nations and other instruments and rules of international law is among the basic purposes and principles of the United Nations,

Bearing in mind the provisions of the Geneva Convention,

Noting that Israel and the concerned Arab States whose territories have been occupied by Israel since June 1967 are parties to the Convention,

Taking into account that States parties to the Convention undertake, in accordance with article 1 thereof, not only to respect but also to ensure respect for the Convention in all circumstances,

1. *Reaffirms* that the Geneva Convention relative to the Protection of Civilian Persons in Time of War, of 12 August 1949, is applicable to the Palestinian and other Arab territories occupied by Israel since 1967, including Jerusalem;

2. *Condemns once again* the failure of Israel, the occupying Power, to acknowledge the applicability of the Convention to the territories it has occupied since 1967, including Jerusalem;

3. *Strongly demands* that Israel acknowledge and comply with the provisions of the Convention in the Palestinian and other Arab territories it has occupied since 1967, including Jerusalem;

4. *Urgently calls upon* all States parties to the Convention to exert all efforts in order to ensure respect for and compliance with its provisions in the Palestinian and other Arab territories occupied by Israel since 1967, including Jerusalem;

5. *Requests* the Secretary-General to report to the General Assembly at its forty-fifth session on the implementation of the present resolution.

General Assembly resolution 44/48 B

8 December 1989   Meeting 78   149-1-2 (recorded vote)

Approved by Special Political Committee (A/44/816) by recorded vote (124-1-3), 22 November (meeting 25); 13-nation draft (A/SPC/44/L.20); agenda item 77.

Sponsors: Afghanistan, Bangladesh, Brunei Darussalam, Burkina Faso, Comoros, Cuba, India, Indonesia, Madagascar, Malaysia, Nicaragua, Pakistan, Zambia.

Meeting numbers. GA 44th session: SPC 22-25; plenary 78.

Recorded vote in Assembly as follows:

In favour: Afghanistan, Albania, Algeria, Angola, Antigua and Barbuda, Argentina, Australia, Austria, Bahamas, Bahrain, Bangladesh, Barbados, Belgium, Benin, Bhutan, Bolivia, Botswana, Brazil, Brunei Darussalam, Bulgaria, Burkina Faso, Burundi, Byelorussian SSR, Cameroon, Canada, Cape Verde, Central African Republic, Chad, Chile, China, Colombia, Comoros, Costa Rica, Côte d'Ivoire, Cuba, Cyprus, Czechoslovakia, Democratic Kampuchea, Democratic Yemen, Denmark, Djibouti, Dominican Republic, Ecuador, Egypt, Equatorial Guinea, Ethiopia, Fiji, Finland, France, Gabon, German Democratic Republic, Germany, Federal Republic of, Ghana, Greece, Grenada, Guatemala, Guinea, Guinea-Bissau, Guyana, Haiti, Honduras, Hungary, Iceland, India, Indonesia, Iran, Iraq, Ireland, Italy, Jamaica, Japan, Jordan, Kenya, Kuwait, Lao People's Democratic Republic, Lebanon, Lesotho, Liberia, Libyan Arab Jamahiriya, Luxembourg, Madagascar, Malawi, Malaysia, Maldives, Mali, Malta, Mauritania, Mauritius, Mexico, Mongolia, Morocco, Mozambique, Myanmar, Nepal, Netherlands, New Zealand, Nicaragua, Nigeria, Norway, Oman, Pakistan, Panama, Papua New Guinea, Paraguay, Peru, Philippines, Poland, Portugal, Qatar, Romania, Rwanda, Saint Lucia, Saint Vincent and the Grenadines, Samoa, Sao Tome and Principe, Saudi Arabia, Senegal, Seychelles, Sierra Leone, Singapore, Solomon Islands, Somalia, Spain, Sri Lanka, Sudan, Suriname, Swaziland, Sweden, Syrian Arab Republic, Thailand, Togo, Trinidad and Tobago, Tunisia, Turkey, Uganda, Ukrainian SSR, USSR, United Arab Emirates, United Kingdom, United Republic of Tanzania, Uruguay, Vanuatu, Venezuela, Viet Nam, Yemen, Yugoslavia, Zaire, Zambia, Zimbabwe.

Against: Israel.

Abstaining: Dominica, United States.

Paragraph 1 of the resolution was adopted by the Committee by a recorded vote of 124 to 1, with 2 abstentions, and by the Assembly by 146 to 1, with 1 abstention.

Deportation of Palestinians

The Committee on Israeli practices reported[3] a considerable increase in the number of deportations from the occupied territories, carried out in spite of a wave of protests by the international community, including unanimous resolutions by the Security Council, against such illegal practice. According to the Committee, many witnesses stressed the fact that the intended deportees had not been given the opportunity to see the allegations leading to their expulsion.

The Committee on Palestinian rights also reported[1] in November that deportations had increased; 60 Palestinians had been deported during the year.

Detailed reports of deportations were conveyed to the Secretary-General in letters from the Permanent Representative of Lebanon, the Permanent Observer of Palestine and the Chairman of the Committee on Palestinian rights and in reports of the Committee on Israeli practices. On 3 January, the Lebanese Government reaffirmed its complete rejection of illegal deportations across the international boundaries, since they were an encroachment on Lebanon's sovereignty and a flagrant breach of the inviolability of its borders and of its territorial integrity. During 1988, it reported, expulsions and deportations to Lebanon involved 48 Palestinians.[20]

Report of the Secretary-General. In a September report,[21] issued in response to a 1988 Assembly resolution,[22] the Secretary-General stated that on 18 August he had received a reply from the Foreign Minister of Israel to his note verbale of 30 May. Israel stated that its position on that resolution had been set out fully previously. The continuing threat which terrorist activity posed to Israel's security accounted for its measures to ensure the maintenance of public order as contemplated by international law. Expulsion orders against individuals had been issued in the most extreme cases and were subject first to the review of an advisory committee and afterwards to Israel's High Court of Justice, Israel said.

SECURITY COUNCIL ACTION (July and August)

At the request of the Arab Group,[23] the Security Council convened on 6 July to consider deportations of Palestinians from the occupied territories.

The Palestine Observer's request[24] to participate was approved by 11 votes to 1 (United States), with 3 abstentions (Canada, France, United Kingdom). The United States reiterated its views concerning the request (see above, under "The Palestinian uprising *(intifadah)*").

Speaking before the Council, Israel said that while facing continuous and escalating violence, owing to deliberate PLO incitement intended to undermine Israel's peace initiative, it had acted with utmost restraint within the confines of local and international law. It had chosen not to use the death penalty expressly contemplated by the fourth Geneva Convention, but had preferred to exercise less severe measures in conformity with article 63 of the Hague regulations, which permitted the expulsion of individuals who posed an immediate and grave threat to security and public order.

The United States expressed opposition to the practice of deportations as a violation of article 49

of the fourth Geneva Convention and agreed with the call on Israel to desist from further deportations (see resolution below). However, the United States did not believe that raising the issue in the Council at the current time, in the form in which it was being presented, would help reduce tension or restore calm.

The Council adopted **resolution 636 (1989)**.

The Security Council,

Reaffirming its resolutions 607(1988) of 5 January 1988 and 608(1988) of 14 January 1988,

Having been apprised that Israel, the occupying Power, has once again, in defiance of those resolutions, deported eight Palestinian civilians on 29 June 1989,

Expressing grave concern over the situation in the occupied Palestinian territories,

Recalling the Geneva Convention relative to the Protection of Civilian Persons in Time of War, of 12 August 1949, and in particular articles 47 and 49 thereof,

1. *Deeply regrets* the continuing deportation by Israel, the occupying Power, of Palestinian civilians;

2. *Calls upon* Israel to ensure the safe and immediate return to the occupied Palestinian territories of those deported and to desist forthwith from deporting any other Palestinian civilians;

3. *Reaffirms* that the Geneva Convention relative to the Protection of Civilian Persons in time of War, of 12 August 1949, is applicable to the Palestinian territories, occupied by Israel since 1967, including Jerusalem, and to the other occupied Arab territories;

4. *Decides* to keep the situation under review.

Security Council resolution 636(1989)

6 July 1989   Meeting 2870   14-0-1

7-nation draft (S/20710).
Sponsors: Algeria, Colombia, Ethiopia, Malaysia, Nepal, Senegal, Yugoslavia.
Vote in Council as follows:
In favour: Algeria, Brazil, Canada, China, Colombia, Ethiopia, Finland, France, Malaysia, Nepal, Senegal, USSR, United Kingdom, Yugoslavia.
Against: None.
Abstaining: United States.

At the request[25] of the Chairman of the Arab Group, the Security Council again took up the question of deportations on 30 August.

The Palestine Observer's request[26] to participate was approved by the same vote as in July and the United States again made a statement concerning the request (see above).

Israel stated that the drastic increase in violence in recent months was intended to intimidate the local population and ensure PLO domination. It regarded expulsions as the most severe measure, which was taken only after careful consideration and upon the conclusion that all other means had failed in curbing the violence and preventing grave risks to public safety.

The United States reiterated its position, opposing the deportations in principle, but did not believe that resort to the Council would help address the underlying problems of finding peace or facilitate negotiations between the parties.

The Council adopted **resolution 641(1989)**.

The Security Council,

Reaffirming its resolutions 607(1988) of 5 January 1988, 608 (1988) of 14 January 1988 and 636(1989) of 6 July 1989,

Having been apprised that Israel, the occupying Power, has once again, in defiance of those resolutions, deported five Palestinian civilians on 27 August 1989,

Expressing grave concern over the situation in the occupied Palestinian territories,

Recalling the Geneva Convention relative to the Protection of Civilian Persons in Time of War, of 12 August 1949, and in particular articles 47 and 49 thereof,

1. *Deplores* the continuing deportation by Israel, the occupying Power, of Palestinian civilians;

2. *Calls upon* Israel to ensure the safe and immediate return to the occupied Palestinian territories of those deported and to desist forthwith from deporting any other Palestinian civilians;

3. *Reaffirms* that the Geneva Convention relative to the Protection of Civilian Persons in Time of War, of 12 August 1949, is applicable to the Palestinian territories, occupied by Israel since 1967, including Jerusalem, and to the other occupied Arab territories;

4. *Decides* to keep the situation under review.

Security Council resolution 641(1989)

30 August 1989   Meeting 2883   14-0-1

7-nation draft (S/20820).
Sponsors: Algeria, Colombia, Ethiopia, Malaysia, Nepal, Senegal, Yugoslavia.
Vote in Council as follows:
   In favour: Algeria, Brazil, Canada, China, Colombia, Ethiopia, Finland, France, Malaysia, Nepal, Senegal, USSR, United Kingdom, Yugoslavia.
   Against: None.
   Abstaining: United States.

GENERAL ASSEMBLY ACTION

On 8 December, the General Assembly, on the recommendation of the Special Political Committee, adopted **resolution 44/48 E** by recorded vote.

The General Assembly,

Recalling Security Council resolutions 605(1987) of 22 December 1987, 607(1988) of 5 January 1988, 608(1988) of 14 January 1988, 636(1989) of 6 July 1989 and 641(1989) of 30 August 1989,

Taking note of the reports of the Secretary-General of 21 January 1988 and 28 September 1989,

Alarmed by the continuing deportation of Palestinians from the occupied Palestinian territory by the Israeli authorities,

Recalling the Geneva Convention relative to the Protection of Civilian Persons in Time of War, of 12 August 1949, in particular article 1 and the first paragraph of article 49, which read as follows:

"*Article 1*

"The High Contracting Parties undertake to respect and to ensure respect for the present Convention in all circumstances."

"*Article 49*

"Individual or mass forcible transfers, as well as deportations of protected persons from occupied territory to the territory of the occupying Power or to that of any other country, occupied or not, are prohibited, regardless of their motive . . .",

Reaffirming the applicability of the Geneva Convention to the Palestinian and other Arab territories occupied by Israel since 1967, including Jerusalem,

1. *Strongly deplores* the continuing disregard by Israel, the occupying Power, of the relevant decisions of the Security Council and resolutions of the General Assembly;

2. *Demands* that the Government of Israel, the occupying Power, rescind the illegal measures taken by the Israeli authorities in deporting Palestinians and that it facilitate their immediate return;

3. *Calls upon* Israel, the occupying Power, to cease forthwith the deportation of Palestinians and to abide scrupulously by the provisions of the Geneva Convention relative to the Protection of Civilian Persons in Time of War, of 12 August 1949;

4. *Requests* the Secretary-General to report to the General Assembly as soon as possible but not later than the beginning of its forty-fifth session on the implementation of the present resolution.

General Assembly resolution 44/48 E

8 December 1989   Meeting 78   150-1-2 (recorded vote)

Approved by Special Political Committee (A/44/816) by recorded vote (125-1-1), 22 November (meeting 25); 13-nation draft (A/SPC/44/L.23); agenda item 77.
Sponsors: Afghanistan, Bangladesh, Brunei Darussalam, Burkina Faso, Comoros, Cuba, India, Indonesia, Madagascar, Malaysia, Nicaragua, Pakistan, Zambia.
Meeting numbers. GA 44th session: SPC 22-25; plenary 78.

Recorded vote in Assembly as follows:

   In favour: Afghanistan, Albania, Algeria, Angola, Antigua and Barbuda, Argentina, Australia, Austria, Bahamas, Bahrain, Bangladesh, Barbados, Belgium, Benin, Bhutan, Bolivia, Botswana, Brazil, Brunei Darussalam, Bulgaria, Burkina Faso, Burundi, Byelorussian SSR, Cameroon, Canada, Cape Verde, Central African Republic, Chad, Chile, China, Colombia, Comoros, Costa Rica, Côte d'Ivoire, Cuba, Cyprus, Czechoslovakia, Democratic Kampuchea, Democratic Yemen, Denmark, Djibouti, Dominican Republic, Ecuador, Egypt, Equatorial Guinea, Ethiopia, Fiji, Finland, France, Gabon, German Democratic Republic, Germany, Federal Republic of, Ghana, Greece, Grenada, Guatemala, Guinea, Guinea-Bissau, Guyana, Haiti, Honduras, Hungary, Iceland, India, Indonesia, Iran, Iraq, Ireland, Italy, Jamaica, Japan, Jordan, Kenya, Kuwait, Lao People's Democratic Republic, Lebanon, Lesotho, Liberia, Libyan Arab Jamahiriya, Luxembourg, Madagascar, Malawi, Malaysia, Maldives, Mali, Malta, Mauritania, Mauritius, Mexico, Mongolia, Morocco, Mozambique, Myanmar, Nepal, Netherlands, New Zealand, Nicaragua, Niger, Nigeria, Norway, Oman, Pakistan, Panama, Papua New Guinea, Paraguay, Peru, Philippines, Poland, Portugal, Qatar, Romania, Rwanda, Saint Lucia, Saint Vincent and the Grenadines, Samoa, Sao Tome and Principe, Saudi Arabia, Senegal, Seychelles, Sierra Leone, Singapore, Solomon Islands, Somalia, Spain, Sri Lanka, Sudan, Suriname, Swaziland, Sweden, Syrian Arab Republic, Thailand, Togo, Trinidad and Tobago, Tunisia, Turkey, Uganda, Ukrainian SSR, USSR, United Arab Emirates, United Kingdom, United Republic of Tanzania, Uruguay, Vanuatu, Venezuela, Viet Nam, Yemen, Yugoslavia, Zaire, Zambia, Zimbabwe.
   Against: Israel.
   Abstaining: Dominica, United States.

Palestinian detainees

The Committee on Israeli practices reported[3] in October that the administration of justice in the occupied territories had deteriorated considerably. The "quick justice" had continued to characterize court procedures, provoking many protests from lawyers and human rights activists. The situation of detainees, as a consequence of the arrests of many Palestinians since the outbreak of the uprising, had also further deteriorated. The great increase in the number of detainees led the Israeli authorities to convert governmental buildings and even schools into temporary detention centres and use army detention centres for civilians. Detainees were denied humane prison conditions and endured serious physical and psychological hardship.

The Committee heard several witnesses who presented extensive accounts of conditions in detention. Most testimonies denounced the various forms of ill-treatment, such as torture and violence, intimidation, solitary confinement, overcrowding of cells, lack of sanitary facilities, inadequate nutrition, and the denial of the right to receive visits and of access to lawyers. Very harsh conditions were endured by prisoners in the Ansar 3 (Ketziot) detention camp in the Negev desert inside Israel, where detainees were reported to have been shot. Conditions of detention often gave rise to hunger strikes, which sometimes led to the death of hunger strikers seeking to ameliorate their treatment.

Report of the Secretary-General. In compliance with a 1988 General Assembly resolution,[27] the Secretary-General reported[28] in September 1989 that, in reply to his note verbale to the Minister for Foreign Affairs of Israel, he received on 18 August a response in which Israel rejected the resolution in question. It also stated that, in view of the resolution's unconcealed bias, it must be noted that detention and imprisonment in Judea, Samaria and Gaza were legal measures taken against terrorism and violence. It was Israel's duty under international law to maintain public order and security in those areas, a duty carried out with the utmost regard for the protection of human rights in keeping with the provisions of the Geneva Conventions. Israel stated that due process of law was guaranteed also by allowing detainees and prisoners to petition Israel's High Court of Justice. Representatives of ICRC were authorized regularly to visit prisons and detention centres where they could interview in complete privacy any prisoner or detainee.

GENERAL ASSEMBLY ACTION

On 8 December, on the recommendation of the Special Political Committee, the General Assembly adopted **resolution 44/48 D** by recorded vote.

The General Assembly,

Recalling Security Council resolution 605(1987) of 22 December 1987,

Recalling also its resolutions 38/79 A of 15 December 1983, 39/95 A of 14 December 1984, 40/161 A of 16 December 1985, 41/63 A of 3 December 1986, 42/160 A of 8 December 1987, 43/21 of 3 November 1988, 43/58 D of 6 December 1988 and 44/2 of 6 October 1989,

Taking note of the reports of the Special Committee to Investigate Israeli Practices Affecting the Human Rights of the Population of the Occupied Territories,

Taking note also of the reports of the Secretary-General of 21 January 1988, 28 September 1989 and 20 October 1989,

1. *Deplores* the arbitrary detention or imprisonment by Israel of thousands of Palestinians as a result of their resistance against occupation in order to attain self-determination;

2. *Calls upon* Israel, the occupying Power, to release all Palestinians and other Arabs arbitrarily detained or imprisoned;

3. *Requests* the Secretary-General to report to the General Assembly as soon as possible but not later than the beginning of its forty-fifth session on the implementation of the present resolution.

General Assembly resolution 44/48 D

8 December 1989   Meeting 78   145-2-2 (recorded vote)

Approved by Special Political Committee (A/44/816) by recorded vote (124-2-1), 22 November (meeting 25); 13-nation draft (A/SPC/44/L.22); agenda item 77.

Sponsors: Afghanistan, Bangladesh, Brunei Darussalam, Burkina Faso, Comoros, Cuba, India, Indonesia, Madagascar, Malaysia, Nicaragua, Pakistan, Zambia.

Meeting numbers. GA 44th session: SPC 22-25; plenary 78.

Recorded vote in Assembly as follows:

In favour: Afghanistan, Albania, Algeria, Angola, Antigua and Barbuda, Argentina, Australia, Austria, Bahamas, Bahrain, Bangladesh, Barbados, Belgium, Benin, Bhutan, Bolivia, Botswana, Brazil, Brunei Darussalam, Bulgaria, Burkina Faso, Burundi, Byelorussian SSR, Cameroon, Canada, Cape Verde, Central African Republic, Chad, China, Colombia, Comoros, Costa Rica, Côte d'Ivoire, Cuba, Cyprus, Czechoslovakia, Democratic Kampuchea, Democratic Yemen, Denmark, Djibouti, Dominican Republic, Ecuador, Egypt, Equatorial Guinea, Ethiopia, Fiji, Finland, France, Gabon, German Democratic Republic, Germany, Federal Republic of, Ghana, Greece, Grenada, Guatemala, Guinea, Guinea-Bissau, Guyana, Honduras, Hungary, Iceland, India, Indonesia, Iran, Iraq, Ireland, Italy, Jamaica, Japan, Jordan, Kuwait, Lao People's Democratic Republic, Lebanon, Lesotho, Liberia, Libyan Arab Jamahiriya, Luxembourg, Madagascar, Malawi, Malaysia, Maldives, Mali, Malta, Mauritania, Mauritius, Mexico, Mongolia, Morocco, Mozambique, Myanmar, Nepal, Netherlands, New Zealand, Nicaragua, Nigeria, Norway, Oman, Pakistan, Panama, Papua New Guinea, Paraguay, Peru, Philippines, Poland, Portugal, Qatar, Romania, Rwanda, Saint Lucia, Saint Vincent and the Grenadines, Samoa, Sao Tome and Principe, Saudi Arabia, Senegal, Seychelles, Sierra Leone, Singapore, Solomon Islands, Somalia, Spain, Sri Lanka, Sudan, Suriname, Swaziland, Sweden, Syrian Arab Republic, Togo, Trinidad and Tobago, Tunisia, Turkey, Uganda, Ukrainian SSR, USSR, United Arab Emirates, United Kingdom, United Republic of Tanzania, Uruguay, Vanuatu, Venezuela, Viet Nam, Yemen, Yugoslavia, Zaire, Zambia, Zimbabwe.

Against: Israel, United States.

Abstaining: Dominica, Kenya.

Israeli settlements

The Committee on Israeli practices reported in July[4] and October[3] that Israel had continued in 1989 to annex Palestinian territory and establish settlements. In March, Jewish residents of the West Bank established a new settlement 8 kilometres north-west of Ramallah. In April, an inauguration ceremony was held for the new settlement of Tzufim, east of Kalkilya. Two new settlements were established in May—Tzoref, in the Etzion bloc, and Ofarim, south of Beit-Arye, in the Binyamin district. The Israeli Central Bureau of Statistics reported on 7 August that some 6,000 people had settled in the territories over the past year.

According to the Committee, acts of violence and aggression by Israeli settlers against the Palestinian population had increased during the year, in both scope and gravity. *Ha'aretz* and the *Jerusalem Post* reported on 31 May that a group of 30 settlers had raided on 29 May the village of Kifl

Harith, where they reportedly carried out a methodical and prolonged rampage, involving arson and vandalism, and shot a 13-year-old girl. The same newspapers reported on 18 April that settlers created vigilante intervention forces.

The Committee also reported cases of settlers' retaliatory actions against the Arab population. On 9 February, following the death of a settler, a group of Jewish settlers raided the village of Haris. On 22 May, hundreds of settlers from Maaleh Adumim carried out a retaliation action in nearby Eizariya after a settler family's car was stoned and its four passengers injured. The settlers set fire to a truck and overturned two others, smashed windows of cars and homes and fired in the air.

The Committee on Palestinian rights in November[1] condemned the unchecked violence of settlers. It also stressed that there had been a dramatic increase in the number of house demolitions in 1989. At least 236 Palestinian homes were destroyed for "security" reasons between December 1987 and August 1989, while another 675 buildings were destroyed on the pretext that they had been built illegally.

Report of the Secretary-General. In September, the Secretary-General reported[29] that, in accordance with a 1988 General Assembly resolution,[30] he had sent a note verbale to Israel requesting information on steps it had taken or envisaged taking in implementation of the relevant provisions of that resolution. On 18 August, Israel stated that its position had been set out previously.

GENERAL ASSEMBLY ACTION

On 8 December, on the recommendation of the Special Political Committee, the General Assembly adopted **resolution 44/48 C** by recorded vote.

The General Assembly,

Recalling Security Council resolution 465(1980) of 1 March 1980,

Recalling also its resolutions 32/5 of 28 October 1977, 33/113 B of 18 December 1978, 34/90 C of 12 December 1979, 35/122 B of 11 December 1980, 36/147 B of 16 December 1981, 37/88 B of 10 December 1982, 38/79 C of 15 December 1983, 39/95 C of 14 December 1984, 40/161 C of 16 December 1985, 41/63 C of 3 December 1986, 42/160 C of 8 December 1987 and 43/58 C of 6 December 1988,

Expressing grave anxiety and concern at the present serious situation in the Palestinian and other occupied Arab territories, including Jerusalem, as a result of the continued Israeli occupation and the measures and actions taken by Israel, the occupying Power, designed to change the legal status, geographical nature and demographic composition of those territories,

Taking note of the reports of the Secretary-General of 21 January 1988 and 28 September 1989,

Confirming that the Geneva Convention relative to the Protection of Civilian Persons in Time of War, of 12 August 1949, is applicable to all Palestinian and other Arab territories occupied by Israel since June 1967, including Jerusalem,

1. *Determines* that all such measures and actions taken by Israel in the Palestinian and other Arab territories occupied since 1967, including Jerusalem, are in violation of the relevant provisions of the Geneva Convention relative to the Protection of Civilian Persons in Time of War, of 12 August 1949, and constitute a serious obstacle to the efforts to achieve a comprehensive, just and lasting peace in the Middle East and therefore have no legal validity;

2. *Strongly deplores* the persistence of Israel in carrying out such measures, in particular the establishment of settlements in the Palestinian and other occupied Arab territories, including Jerusalem;

3. *Demands* that Israel comply strictly with its international obligations in accordance with the principles of international law and the provisions of the Geneva Convention;

4. *Demands once more* that Israel, the occupying Power, desist forthwith from taking any action that would result in changing the legal status, geographical nature or demographic composition of the Palestinian and other Arab territories occupied since 1967, including Jerusalem;

5. *Urgently calls upon* all States parties to the Geneva Convention to respect and to exert all efforts in order to ensure respect for and compliance with its provisions in all Palestinian and other Arab territories occupied by Israel since 1967, including Jerusalem;

6. *Requests* the Secretary-General to report to the General Assembly at its forty-fifth session on the implementation of the present resolution.

General Assembly resolution 44/48 C

8 December 1989   Meeting 78   146-1-3 (recorded vote)

Approved by Special Political Committee (A/44/816) by recorded vote (123-1-3), 22 November (meeting 25); 13-nation draft (A/SPC/44/L.21); agenda item 77.

Sponsors: Afghanistan, Bangladesh, Brunei Darussalam, Burkina Faso, Comoros, Cuba, India, Indonesia, Madagascar, Malaysia, Nicaragua, Pakistan, Zambia.

Meeting numbers. GA 44th session: SPC 22-25; plenary 78.

Recorded vote in Assembly as follows:

In favour: Afghanistan, Albania, Algeria, Angola, Antigua and Barbuda, Argentina, Australia, Austria, Bahamas, Bahrain, Bangladesh, Barbados, Belgium, Benin, Bhutan, Bolivia, Botswana, Brazil, Brunei Darussalam, Bulgaria, Burkina Faso, Burundi, Byelorussian SSR, Cameroon, Canada, Cape Verde, Central African Republic, Chad, Chile, China, Colombia, Comoros, Costa Rica, Côte d'Ivoire, Cuba, Cyprus, Czechoslovakia, Democratic Kampuchea, Democratic Yemen, Denmark, Djibouti, Dominican Republic, Ecuador, Egypt, Equatorial Guinea, Ethiopia, Fiji, Finland, France, Gabon, German Democratic Republic, Germany, Federal Republic of, Ghana, Greece, Grenada, Guatemala, Guinea, Guinea-Bissau, Guyana, Honduras, Hungary, Iceland, India, Indonesia, Iran, Iraq, Ireland, Italy, Jamaica, Japan, Jordan, Kuwait, Lao People's Democratic Republic, Lebanon, Lesotho, Liberia, Libyan Arab Jamahiriya, Luxembourg, Madagascar, Malawi, Malaysia, Maldives, Mali, Malta, Mauritania, Mauritius, Mexico, Mongolia, Morocco, Mozambique, Myanmar, Nepal, Netherlands, New Zealand, Nicaragua, Nigeria, Norway, Oman, Pakistan, Panama, Papua New Guinea, Paraguay, Peru, Philippines, Poland, Portugal, Qatar, Romania, Rwanda, Saint Vincent and the Grenadines, Samoa, Sao Tome and Principe, Saudi Arabia, Senegal, Seychelles, Sierra Leone, Singapore, Solomon Islands, Somalia, Spain, Sri Lanka, Sudan, Suriname, Swaziland, Sweden, Syrian Arab Republic, Thailand, Togo, Trinidad and Tobago, Tunisia, Turkey, Uganda, Ukrainian SSR, USSR, United Arab Emirates, United Kingdom, United Republic of Tanzania, Uruguay, Vanuatu, Venezuela, Viet Nam, Yemen, Yugoslavia, Zaire, Zambia, Zimbabwe.

Against: Israel.

Abstaining: Dominica, Kenya, United States.

Golan Heights

Report of the Committee on Israeli practices.
The October 1989 report[3] of the Committee on Israeli practices contained information on the situation in the occupied Syrian Golan, submitted by the Ministry of Foreign Affairs of the Syrian Arab Republic. Israel was accused of imposing its laws, administration, religion and collective economic punishment by closing the market for apple production, a main source of local income.

On the basis of some newspaper reports, the Committee cited several cases of arrests of Arabs for participating in demonstrations, distributing anti-Israel leaflets and burning an Israeli flag. In May, Israeli police were said to have used rubber bullets and tear-gas to disperse hundreds of demonstrators in Mas'ada. Over 40 villagers were detained.

Report of the Secretary-General. In response to a 1988 resolution of the General Assembly[31] calling on Member States not to recognize Israel's imposition of its laws, jurisdiction and administration on the occupied Syrian Arab Golan, the Secretary-General reported[32] in October that five States had expressed support for the provisions of that resolution. Israel's position remained as first expressed in 1981,[33] namely, that it could not be expected to maintain indefinitely a military administration merely to accommodate the Syrian Arab Republic's interest in persistent conflict and that its legislation did not diminish the local population's rights.

GENERAL ASSEMBLY ACTION

On 4 December, the General Assembly adopted **resolution 44/40 B** by recorded vote.

The General Assembly,
Having discussed the item entitled ''The situation in the Middle East'',
Taking note of the report of the Secretary-General of 22 November 1989,
Recalling Security Council resolution 497(1981) of 17 December 1981,
Reaffirming its resolutions 36/226 B of 17 December 1981, ES-9/1 of 5 February 1982, 37/123 A of 16 December 1982, 38/180 A of 19 December 1983, 39/146 B of 14 December 1984, 40/168 B of 16 December 1985, 41/162 B of 4 December 1986, 42/209 C of 11 December 1987 and 43/54 B of 6 December 1988,
Recalling its resolution 3314(XXIX) of 14 December 1974, in which it defined an act of aggression, *inter alia*, as ''the invasion or attack by the armed forces of a State of the territory of another State, or any military occupation, however temporary, resulting from such invasion or attack, or any annexation by the use of force of the territory of another State or part thereof'' and provided that ''no consideration of whatever nature, whether political, economic, military or otherwise, may serve as a justification for aggression'',
Reaffirming the fundamental principle of the inadmissibility of the acquisition of territory by force,

Reaffirming once more the applicability of the Geneva Convention relative to the Protection of Civilian Persons in Time of War, of 12 August 1949, to the Palestinian territory occupied since 1967, including Jerusalem, and the other occupied Arab territories,
Noting that Israel's record, policies and actions establish conclusively that it is not a peace-loving Member State and that it has not carried out its obligations under the Charter of the United Nations,
Noting also that Israel has refused, in violation of Article 25 of the Charter, to accept and carry out the numerous relevant decisions of the Security Council, in particular resolution 497(1981), thus failing to carry out its obligations under the Charter,

1. *Strongly condemns* Israel for its failure to comply with Security Council resolution 497(1981) and General Assembly resolutions 36/226 B, ES-9/1, 37/123 A, 38/180 A, 39/146 B, 40/168 B, 41/162 B, 42/209 C and 43/54 B;

2. *Declares once more* that Israel's continued occupation of the Syrian Arab Golan and its decision of 14 December 1981 to impose its laws, jurisdiction and administration on the occupied Syrian Arab Golan constitute an act of aggression under the provisions of Article 39 of the Charter of the United Nations and General Assembly resolution 3314(XXIX);

3. *Declares once more* that Israel's decision to impose its laws, jurisdiction and administration on the occupied Syrian Arab Golan is illegal and therefore null and void and has no validity whatsoever;

4. *Declares* all Israeli policies and practices of, or aimed at, annexation of the Palestinian territory occupied since 1967, including Jerusalem, and of the other occupied Arab territories to be illegal and in violation of international law and of the relevant United Nations resolutions;

5. *Determines once more* that all actions taken by Israel to give effect to its decision relating to the occupied Syrian Arab Golan are illegal and invalid and shall not be recognized;

6. *Reaffirms its determination* that all relevant provisions of the Regulations annexed to the Hague Convention IV of 1907, and the Geneva Convention relative to the Protection of Civilian Persons in Time of War, of 12 August 1949, continue to apply to the Syrian territory occupied by Israel since 1967, and calls upon the parties thereto to respect and ensure respect for their obligations under these instruments in all circumstances;

7. *Determines once more* that the continued occupation of the Syrian Arab Golan since 1967 and its annexation by Israel on 14 December 1981, following Israel's decision to impose its laws, jurisdiction and administration on that territory, constitute a continuing threat to international peace and security;

8. *Strongly deplores* the negative vote by a permanent member of the Security Council which prevented the Council from adopting against Israel, under Chapter VII of the Charter, the ''appropriate measures'' referred to in resolution 497(1981) unanimously adopted by the Council;

9. *Further deplores* any political, economic, financial, military and technological support to Israel that encourages it to commit acts of aggression and to consolidate and perpetuate its occupation and annexation of the Palestinian territory occupied since 1967, including Jerusalem, and the other occupied Arab territories;

Regional questions

10. *Firmly emphasizes once more* its demand that Israel, the occupying Power, rescind forthwith its illegal decision of 14 December 1981 to impose its laws, jurisdiction and administration on the Syrian Arab Golan, which resulted in the effective annexation of that territory;

11. *Reaffirms once more* the overriding necessity of the total and unconditional withdrawal by Israel from the Palestinian territory occupied since 1967, including Jerusalem, and the other occupied Arab territories, which is an essential prerequisite for the establishment of a comprehensive and just peace in the Middle East;

12. *Determines once more* that Israel's record, policies and actions confirm that it is not a peace-loving Member State, that it has persistently violated the principles contained in the Charter and that it has carried out neither its obligations under the Charter nor its commitment under General Assembly resolution 273(III) of 11 May 1949;

13. *Calls once more upon* all Member States to apply the following measures:

(a) To refrain from supplying Israel with any weapons and related equipment and to suspend any military assistance that Israel receives from them;

(b) To refrain from acquiring any weapons or military equipment from Israel;

(c) To suspend economic, financial and technological assistance to and co-operation with Israel;

(d) To sever diplomatic, trade and cultural relations with Israel;

14. *Reiterates its call* to all Member States to cease forthwith, individually and collectively, all dealings with Israel in order totally to isolate it in all fields;

15. *Urges* non-member States to act in accordance with the provisions of the present resolution;

16. *Calls upon* the specialized agencies and other international organizations to conform their relations with Israel to the terms of the present resolution;

17. *Requests* the Secretary-General to report to the General Assembly at its forty-fifth session on the implementation of the present resolution.

General Assembly resolution 44/40 B

4 December 1989   Meeting 73   84-22-49 (recorded vote)

14-nation draft (A/44/L.48 & Add.1); agenda item 37.

Sponsors: Afghanistan, Albania, Algeria, Bahrain, Cuba, Djibouti, Indonesia, Kuwait, Malaysia, Mauritania, Morocco, Oman, Pakistan, Syrian Arab Republic.

Meeting numbers. GA 44th session: plenary 64-66, 73.

Recorded vote in Assembly as follows:

In favour: Afghanistan, Albania, Algeria, Angola, Bahrain, Bangladesh, Benin, Bhutan, Botswana, Brunei Darussalam, Bulgaria, Burkina Faso, Byelorussian SSR, Cameroon, Cape Verde, Chad, China, Comoros, Congo, Cuba, Cyprus, Czechoslovakia, Democratic Kampuchea, Democratic Yemen, Djibouti, Gabon, Gambia, German Democratic Republic, Ghana, Greece, Guatemala, Guinea, Guinea-Bissau, Guyana, India, Indonesia, Iran, Iraq, Jordan, Kuwait, Lao People's Democratic Republic, Lebanon, Lesotho, Libyan Arab Jamahiriya, Madagascar, Malaysia, Maldives, Mali, Mauritania, Mauritius, Mexico, Mongolia, Morocco, Nicaragua, Niger, Nigeria, Oman, Pakistan, Poland, Qatar, Rwanda, Sao Tome and Principe, Saudi Arabia, Senegal, Seychelles, Sierra Leone, Somalia, Sri Lanka, Sudan, Swaziland, Syrian Arab Republic, Tunisia, Turkey, Uganda, Ukrainian SSR, USSR, United Arab Emirates, United Republic of Tanzania, Vanuatu, Viet Nam, Yemen, Yugoslavia, Zambia, Zimbabwe.

Against: Australia, Belgium, Canada, Denmark, Dominica, Finland, France, Germany, Federal Republic of, Iceland, Ireland, Israel, Italy, Japan, Kenya, Luxembourg, Netherlands, New Zealand, Norway, Portugal, Sweden, United Kingdom, United States.

Abstaining: Antigua and Barbuda, Argentina, Austria, Bahamas, Barbados, Belize, Bolivia, Brazil, Burundi, Central African Republic, Colombia, Costa Rica, Côte d'Ivoire, Dominican Republic, Ecuador, Egypt, El Sal-

vador, Equatorial Guinea, Ethiopia, Fiji, Grenada, Haiti, Honduras, Hungary, Jamaica, Liberia, Malawi, Malta, Myanmar, Nepal, Panama, Papua New Guinea, Paraguay, Peru, Philippines, Saint Kitts and Nevis, Saint Lucia, Saint Vincent and the Grenadines, Samoa, Singapore, Solomon Islands, Spain, Suriname, Thailand, Togo, Trinidad and Tobago, Uruguay, Venezuela, Zaire.

On 8 December, on the recommendation of the Special Political Committee, the Assembly adopted **resolution** 44/48 F by recorded vote.

The General Assembly,

Deeply concerned that the Arab territories occupied since 1967 have been under continued Israeli military occupation,

Recalling Security Council resolution 497(1981) of 17 December 1981,

Recalling also its resolutions 36/226 B of 17 December 1981, ES-9/1 of 5 February 1982, 37/88 E of 10 December 1982, 38/79 F of 15 December 1983, 39/95 F of 14 December 1984, 40/161 F of 16 December 1985, 41/63 F of 3 December 1986, 42/160 F of 8 December 1987, 43/21 of 3 November 1988, 43/58 F of 6 December 1988 and 44/2 of 6 October 1989,

Having considered the report of the Secretary-General of 20 October 1989,

Recalling its previous resolutions, in particular resolutions 3414(XXX) of 5 December 1975, 31/61 of 9 December 1976, 32/20 of 25 November 1977, 33/28 and 33/29 of 7 December 1978, 34/70 of 6 December 1979 and 35/122 E of 11 December 1980, in which, *inter alia,* it called upon Israel to put an end to its occupation of the Arab territories and to withdraw from all those territories,

Reaffirming once more the illegality of Israel's decision of 14 December 1981 to impose its laws, jurisdiction and administration on the Syrian Arab Golan, which has resulted in the effective annexation of that territory,

Reaffirming that the acquisition of territory by force is inadmissible under the Charter of the United Nations and that all territories thus occupied by Israel must be returned,

Recalling the Geneva Convention relative to the Protection of Civilian Persons in Time of War, of 12 August 1949,

1. *Strongly condemns* Israel, the occupying Power, for its refusal to comply with the relevant resolutions of the General Assembly and the Security Council, particularly Council resolution 497(1981), in which the Council, *inter alia,* decided that the Israeli decision to impose its laws, jurisdiction and administration on the occupied Syrian Arab Golan was null and void and without international legal effect and demanded that Israel, the occupying Power, should rescind forthwith its decision;

2. *Condemns* the persistence of Israel in changing the physical character, demographic composition, institutional structure and legal status of the occupied Syrian Arab Golan;

3. *Determines* that all legislative and administrative measures and actions taken or to be taken by Israel, the occupying Power, that purport to alter the character and legal status of the Syrian Arab Golan are null and void and constitute a flagrant violation of international law and of the Geneva Convention relative to the Protection of Civilian Persons in Time of War, of 12 August 1949, and have no legal effect;

4. *Strongly condemns* Israel for its attempts to impose forcibly Israeli citizenship and Israeli identity cards on

the Syrian citizens in the occupied Syrian Arab Golan, and calls upon it to desist from its repressive measures against the population of the Syrian Arab Golan;

5. *Calls once again upon* Member States not to recognize any of the legislative or administrative measures and actions referred to above;

6. *Requests* the Secretary-General to report to the General Assembly at its forty-fifth session on the implementation of the present resolution.

General Assembly resolution 44/48 F

8 December 1989   Meeting 78   148-1-4 (recorded vote)

Approved by Special Political Committee (A/44/816) by recorded vote (122-1-4), 22 November (meeting 25); 13-nation draft (A/SPC/44/L.24); agenda item 77.
Sponsors: Afghanistan, Bangladesh, Brunei Darussalam, Burkina Faso, Comoros, Cuba, India, Indonesia, Madagascar, Malaysia, Nicaragua, Pakistan, Zambia.
Meeting numbers. GA 44th session: SPC 22-25; plenary 78.

Recorded vote in Assembly as follows:

In favour: Afghanistan, Albania, Algeria, Angola, Antigua and Barbuda, Argentina, Australia, Austria, Bahamas, Bahrain, Bangladesh, Barbados, Belgium, Benin, Bhutan, Bolivia, Botswana, Brazil, Brunei Darussalam, Bulgaria, Burkina Faso, Burundi, Byelorussian SSR, Cameroon, Canada, Cape Verde, Central African Republic, Chad, Chile, China, Colombia, Comoros, Côte d'Ivoire, Cuba, Cyprus, Czechoslovakia, Democratic Kampuchea, Democratic Yemen, Denmark, Djibouti, Dominican Republic, Ecuador, Egypt, Equatorial Guinea, Ethiopia, Fiji, Finland, France, Gabon, German Democratic Republic, Germany, Federal Republic of, Ghana, Greece, Grenada, Guatemala, Guinea, Guinea-Bissau, Guyana, Haiti, Honduras, Hungary, Iceland, India, Indonesia, Iran, Iraq, Ireland, Italy, Jamaica, Japan, Jordan, Kuwait, Lao People's Democratic Republic, Lebanon, Lesotho, Liberia, Libyan Arab Jamahiriya, Luxembourg, Madagascar, Malawi, Malaysia, Maldives, Mali, Malta, Mauritania, Mauritius, Mexico, Mongolia, Morocco, Mozambique, Myanmar, Nepal, Netherlands, New Zealand, Nicaragua, Niger, Nigeria, Norway, Oman, Pakistan, Panama, Papua New Guinea, Paraguay, Peru, Philippines, Poland, Portugal, Qatar, Romania, Rwanda, Saint Lucia, Saint Vincent and the Grenadines, Samoa, Sao Tome and Principe, Saudi Arabia, Senegal, Seychelles, Sierra Leone, Singapore, Solomon Islands, Somalia, Spain, Sri Lanka, Sudan, Suriname, Swaziland, Sweden, Syrian Arab Republic, Thailand, Togo, Trinidad and Tobago, Tunisia, Turkey, Uganda, Ukrainian SSR, USSR, United Arab Emirates, United Kingdom, United Republic of Tanzania, Uruguay, Vanuatu, Venezuela, Viet Nam, Yemen, Yugoslavia, Zaire, Zambia, Zimbabwe.
Against: Israel.
Abstaining: Costa Rica, Dominica, Kenya, United States.

Measures regarding educational institutions

Report of the Committee on Palestinian rights. In its November report,[1] the Committee on Palestinian rights expressed concern over the intensification during the second year of the uprising of violations of the Palestinians' right to education. According to the Committee, measures taken by Israel included the complete closure of universities and long-term and repeated closure of schools, prohibition of home study and compensation classes in alternative locations, the use of schools as military outposts, destruction of school property, and military raids on schools and alternative classes.

Arrests, deportations and administrative detention were used against faculty, administrators and students. The Committee noted with great concern the assessment by educators that the imposition of those measures penalized current and future generations of Palestinians and would create serious dysfunctions in the educational system which would be extremely difficult to compensate

at a later stage. The Committee also welcomed the partial opening of schools as a result of international pressure.

Report of the Committee on Israeli practices. The Committee on Israeli practices also reported on freedom of education for Palestinians in the occupied territories. In its October report,[3] it concluded that freedom of education had been seriously hampered by the prolonged closure of educational institutions, including all universities, schools and even kindergartens. The efforts by the Palestinians to provide children with some kind of "popular teaching" in order to compensate for the lack of public education were also jeopardized by the Israeli authorities.

According to a number of testimonies obtained by the Committee, teachers and students experienced various forms of harassment, including detention, raiding of schools, deportation or expulsion.

The Committee reported that on 12 July the Israeli Defence Minister and the army Chief of Staff had ordered the beginning of preparations to re-open schools in the West Bank, which had been closed since the beginning of the uprising. On 22 July, some 183,000 elementary school pupils and 10,700 pre-matriculation class students returned to school, while universities and several colleges remained closed. In August, after a six-month closure, some 69,000 junior high school pupils returned to classes at 324 schools in the West Bank.

Report of the Secretary-General. In September, the Secretary-General informed the General Assembly[34] that no reply had been received from Israel to his 30 May request for information on steps it had taken or envisaged taking in implementation of a 1988 Assembly demand[35] that it rescind all actions and measures against all educational institutions, ensure the freedom of those institutions and refrain from hindering the effective operation of universities, schools and other educational institutions.

However, in a letter of 17 July[36] to the Secretary-General, Israel stated that since 1967 it had contributed to the development of the educational system of the occupied territories. The number of pupils, teachers and classrooms had more than doubled. Many new institutes of learning were established with the assistance of the Israeli authorities, including five universities. However, since December 1987, the schools had frequently been exploited as centres for organizing and launching violent activity. Israel said it had had no choice, therefore, but to close the schools in Judea and Samaria, while in the Gaza District, where the schools had not succumbed to the violence, they remained open. Israel also informed about its decision to gradually reopen schools in Judea and Samaria.

On 8 December 1989, on the recommendation of the Special Political Committee, the General Assembly adopted **resolution** 44/48 G by recorded vote.

The General Assembly,

Bearing in mind the Geneva Convention relative to the Protection of Civilian Persons in Time of War, of 12 August 1949,

Deeply concerned at the continued and intensified harassment by Israel, the occupying Power, against educational institutions in the occupied Palestinian territory,

Recalling Security Council resolution 605(1987) of 22 December 1987,

Recalling also its resolutions 38/79 G of 15 December 1983, 39/95 G of 14 December 1984, 40/161 G of 16 December 1985, 41/63 G of 3 December 1986, 42/160 G of 8 December 1987, 43/21 of 3 November 1988, 43/58 G of 6 December 1988 and 44/2 of 6 October 1989,

Taking note of the reports of the Secretary-General of 21 January 1988 and 28 September 1989,

Taking note also of the relevant decisions adopted by the Executive Board of the United Nations Educational, Scientific and Cultural Organization concerning the educational and cultural situation in the occupied Palestinian territory,

1. *Reaffirms* the applicability of the Geneva Convention relative to the Protection of Civilian Persons in Time of War, of 12 August 1949, to the occupied Palestinian territory, including Jerusalem, and other Arab territories occupied by Israel since 1967;

2. *Condemns* Israeli policies and practices against Palestinian students and faculties in schools, universities and other educational institutions in the occupied Palestinian territory, especially the opening of fire on defenceless students, causing many casualties;

3. *Also condemns* the systematic Israeli campaign of repression against and closing of universities, schools and other educational and vocational institutions in the occupied Palestinian territory, in large numbers and for prolonged periods, restricting and impeding the academic activities of Palestinian universities by subjecting the selection of courses, textbooks and educational programmes, the admission of students and the appointment of faculty members to the control and supervision of the military occupation authorities, in flagrant contravention of the Geneva Convention;

4. *Demands* that Israel, the occupying Power, comply with the provisions of that Convention, rescind all actions and measures against all educational institutions, ensure the freedom of those institutions and refrain forthwith from hindering the effective operation of the universities, schools and other educational institutions;

5. *Requests* the Secretary-General to report to the General Assembly as soon as possible but not later than the beginning of its forty-fifth session on the implementation of the present resolution.

General Assembly resolution 44/48 G

8 December 1989   Meeting 78   150-2-1 (recorded vote)

Approved by Special Political Committee (A/44/816) by recorded vote (125-2-1), 22 November (meeting 25); 13-nation draft (A/SPC/44/L.25); agenda item 77.

Sponsors: Afghanistan, Bangladesh, Brunei Darussalam, Burkina Faso, Comoros, Cuba, India, Indonesia, Madagascar, Malaysia, Nicaragua, Pakistan, Zambia.

Meeting numbers. GA 44th session: SPC 22-25; plenary 78.

Recorded vote in Assembly as follows:

In favour: Afghanistan, Albania, Algeria, Angola, Antigua and Barbuda, Argentina, Australia, Austria, Bahamas, Bahrain, Bangladesh, Barbados, Belgium, Benin, Bhutan, Bolivia, Botswana, Brazil, Brunei Darussalam, Bulgaria, Burkina Faso, Burundi, Byelorussian SSR, Cameroon, Canada, Cape Verde, Central African Republic, Chad, Chile, China, Colombia, Comoros, Costa Rica, Côte d'Ivoire, Cuba, Cyprus, Czechoslovakia, Democratic Kampuchea, Democratic Yemen, Denmark, Djibouti, Dominican Republic, Ecuador, Egypt, Equatorial Guinea, Ethiopia, Fiji, Finland, France, Gabon, German Democratic Republic, Germany, Federal Republic of, Ghana, Greece, Grenada, Guatemala, Guinea, Guinea-Bissau, Guyana, Haiti, Honduras, Hungary, Iceland, India, Indonesia, Iran, Iraq, Ireland, Italy, Jamaica, Japan, Jordan, Kenya, Kuwait, Lao People's Democratic Republic, Lebanon, Lesotho, Liberia, Libyan Arab Jamahiriya, Luxembourg, Madagascar, Malawi, Malaysia, Maldives, Mali, Malta, Mauritania, Mauritius, Mexico, Mongolia, Morocco, Mozambique, Myanmar, Nepal, Netherlands, New Zealand, Nicaragua, Niger, Nigeria, Norway, Oman, Pakistan, Panama, Papua New Guinea, Paraguay, Peru, Philippines, Poland, Portugal, Qatar, Romania, Rwanda, Saint Lucia, Saint Vincent and the Grenadines, Samoa, Sao Tome and Principe, Saudi Arabia, Senegal, Seychelles, Sierra Leone, Singapore, Solomon Islands, Somalia, Spain, Sri Lanka, Sudan, Suriname, Swaziland, Sweden, Syrian Arab Republic, Thailand, Togo, Trinidad and Tobago, Tunisia, Turkey, Uganda, Ukrainian SSR, USSR, United Arab Emirates, United Kingdom, United Republic of Tanzania, Uruguay, Vanuatu, Venezuela, Viet Nam, Yemen, Yugoslavia, Zaire, Zambia, Zimbabwe.

Against: Israel, United States.

Abstaining: Dominica.

Economic and social conditions of Palestinians

According to a report of the UNCTAD secretariat,[37] the first two decades of Israeli occupation of the Palestinian territory had been characterized by drastic changes in the structure and performance of the Palestinian economy. There had been a decline in the share of agriculture, industrial stagnation, chronic trade and payments deficits, growing unemployment and massive labour migration, and financial disarray and insecurity. Since the beginning of the uprising in 1987, the Palestinians had activated a new and independent economic policy aimed at boosting self-reliance in agricultural and industrial production, investment and marketing, restructuring the domestic productive base and disengaging from dependence on the Israeli economy.

In response, the Israeli authorities introduced some measures in order to contain Palestinian initiatives. They included demolition of houses, expropriation of land and increase in Israeli settlements, uprooting of orchards, destruction of crops, bans on fishing off the Gaza coast, restriction on the movement of Palestinian workers, and increased administrative control over Palestinian domestic trade and exports. All those measures had increased the already severe pressure on the Palestinian economy. As a result, Palestinian economic performance in 1989 maintained its downward trend.

Per capita gross national product in the occupied territory was estimated at no more than $1,300, or 25 per cent below the level in 1987. At the same time, the cost-of-living index rose by over 20 per cent. There appeared alarming signs of growing poverty in remote areas.

The international response to the growing crisis in the Palestinian economy considerably supported the population in the occupied territory. Contributions from some Arab States and regional organizations for emergency relief, provision of transit facilities and direct access to regional markets helped to ease the crisis. The United Nations and a number of its specialized agencies had intensified their assistance to the Palestinian people.

In accordance with a 1987 General Assembly resolution,[38] the Secretary-General entrusted the United Nations Centre for Human Settlements (Habitat) with the preparation of an in-depth study on future infrastructure needs of the Palestinians in the occupied territory. In October 1989, Habitat submitted its first study[39] focusing on transport infrastructure. It was stated that the transportation sector in the West Bank and the Gaza Strip, like other economic sectors, was unable to develop to a level that would have enabled it to provide effective transport services for those regions. At the same time, Israel had developed a transportation network aimed at enhancing Jewish settlement activities by providing relatively higher quality roads to link settlements with each other and with the metropolitan Israeli road network. That situation hindered the evolution of a national Palestinian transportation system, the report stated.

Report of the Committee on Palestinian rights. In its November report,[1] the Committee on Palestinian rights condemned administrative, economic and other measures taken by Israel to control all aspects of Palestinian life and to prevent the development of autonomous socio-economic structures. The Committee stressed that Israeli policies had resulted in a lack of basic sanitary infrastructure and health services and led to a substantial deterioration in the standard of living of the Palestinians in general.

GENERAL ASSEMBLY ACTION

On 19 December, the General Assembly, on the recommendation of the Second Committee, adopted **resolution 44/174** by recorded vote.

Living conditions of the Palestinian people in the occupied Palestinian territory

The General Assembly,

Recalling the Vancouver Declaration on Human Settlements, 1976, and the relevant recommendations for national action adopted by Habitat: United Nations Conference on Human Settlements,

Recalling also its resolution 42/190 of 11 December 1987,

Taking into account the *intifadah* of the Palestinian people against the Israeli occupation, including its economic and social policies and practices,

Gravely alarmed by the continuation of the Israeli settlement policies in the Palestinian territory occupied by Israel since 1967, including Jerusalem, which have been declared null and void and a major obstacle to peace,

Taking into account the need of the secretariat of the United Nations Conference on Trade and Development for extra funds to prepare the comprehensive study on the economy of the occupied Palestinian territory requested by the Trade and Development Board in its resolution 239(XXIII) of 9 October 1981,

1. *Takes note* of the study annexed to the note by the Secretary-General concerning the infrastructure needs of the Palestinian people;

2. *Calls* for the immediate cessation of the Israeli practices against the Palestinian people, particularly in the economic and social fields;

3. *Expresses its alarm* at the deterioration, as a result of the Israeli occupation, in the living conditions of the Palestinian people in the Palestinian territory, including Jerusalem, occupied since 1967;

4. *Affirms* that the Israeli occupation is contradictory to the basic requirements for the social and economic development of the Palestinian people in the occupied Palestinian territory;

5. *Rejects* the Israeli plans and actions intended to change the demographic composition of the occupied Palestinian territory, in particular the increase and expansion of the Israeli settlements;

6. *Requests* the Secretary-General to make available to the secretariat of the United Nations Conference on Trade and Development from the United Nations regular budget the extra funds needed to prepare the comprehensive study on the economy of the occupied Palestinian territory;

7. *Also requests* the Secretary-General to report to the General Assembly at its forty-sixth session, through the Economic and Social Council, on the progress made in the implementation of the present resolution.

General Assembly resolution 44/174

19 December 1989   Meeting 83   146-2-8 (recorded vote)

Approved by Second Committee (A/44/746/Add.9) by recorded vote (127-2-7), 21 November (meeting 41); 8-nation draft (A/C.2/44/L.24/Rev.2), orally revised; agenda item 82 *(h)*.
Sponsors: Algeria, Bahrain, Cuba, Egypt, Malaysia, Mali, Mauritania, Pakistan.
Financial implications. 5th Committee, A/44/831; S-G, A/C.2/44/L.35/Rev.1, A/C.5/44/39.
Meeting numbers. GA 44th session: 2nd Committee 10-13, 29, 30, 35, 41; 5th Committee 50; plenary 83.

Recorded vote in Assembly as follows:

In favour: Afghanistan, Albania, Algeria, Angola, Antigua and Barbuda, Argentina, Australia, Austria, Bahamas, Bahrain, Bangladesh, Barbados, Belgium, Benin, Bhutan, Bolivia, Botswana, Brazil, Brunei Darussalam, Bulgaria, Burkina Faso, Burundi, Byelorussian SSR, Cameroon, Cape Verde, Central African Republic, Chad, Chile, China, Colombia, Comoros, Congo, Costa Rica, Côte d'Ivoire, Cuba, Cyprus, Czechoslovakia, Democratic Kampuchea, Democratic Yemen, Denmark, Djibouti, Dominican Republic, Ecuador, Egypt, Ethiopia, Fiji, Finland, France, Gabon, Gambia, German Democratic Republic, Ghana, Greece, Guatemala, Guinea, Guinea-Bissau, Guyana, Haiti, Honduras, Hungary, Iceland, India, Indonesia, Iran, Iraq, Ireland, Italy, Jamaica, Japan, Jordan, Kenya, Kuwait, Lao People's Democratic Republic, Lebanon, Lesotho, Liberia, Libyan Arab Jamahiriya, Luxembourg, Madagascar, Malawi, Malaysia, Maldives, Mali, Malta, Mauritania, Mauritius, Mexico, Mongolia, Morocco, Mozambique, Myanmar, Nepal, New Zealand, Nicaragua, Niger, Nigeria, Norway, Oman, Pakistan, Panama, Papua New Guinea, Paraguay, Peru, Philippines, Poland, Portugal, Qatar, Romania, Rwanda, Saint Lucia, Saint Vincent and the Grenadines, Samoa, Sao Tome and Principe, Saudi Arabia, Senegal, Seychelles, Sierra Leone, Singapore, Solomon Islands, Somalia, Spain, Sri Lanka, Sudan, Suriname, Swaziland, Sweden, Syrian Arab Republic, Thailand, Togo, Trinidad and Tobago, Tunisia, Turkey, Uganda, Ukrainian SSR, USSR, United Arab Emirates, United Republic of Tanzania, Uruguay, Vanuatu, Venezuela, Viet Nam, Yemen, Yugoslavia, Zaire, Zambia, Zimbabwe.
Against: Israel, United States.
Abstaining: Canada, Dominica, El Salvador, Equatorial Guinea, Germany, Federal Republic of, Grenada, Netherlands, United Kingdom.

Finance and trade

In response to a 1988 Economic and Social Council resolution,[40] the Secretary-General submitted a survey by the Economic and Social Commission for Western Asia on the Israeli financial and trade practices in the occupied Syrian Arab Golan,[41] which was subject to the same discriminatory financial policy and practices as the occupied Palestinian territory. After the occupation, the only local bank was forced to close and Syrian currency was replaced by that of Israel. Existing Israeli banks, which did not offer a full range of services, mostly facilitated trade between the inhabitants of the occupied Syrian Arab Golan, Israel and the occupied Palestinian territory. Their credit policies hampered the emergence of a strong local production base. The informal monetary sector in Syrian villages was much less developed than in the occupied Palestinian territory. There was no access to external funding sources and, in contrast to the occupied Palestinian territory, no foreign agencies or NGOs were operating there.

The survey stressed that internal trade had flourished as a result of a marked rise in per capita income and a conversion to a market-oriented economy. External trade, especially export of agricultural products (mostly apples) to Israel, was under strict Israeli control. Since the occupation, there had been no trade relations between the Syrian Arab Republic and the occupied Syrian Arab Golan.

Report of the Secretary-General. In accordance with a 1988 Economic and Social Council resolution,[40] requesting the Secretary-General to speed up preparation of a report on the trade practices of the Israeli authorities in the occupied Palestinian territories, the Secretary-General submitted in May 1989[42] the main findings and recommendations of an UNCTAD in-depth study on the external trade of the territories, carried out in 1988.[43] The study examined the role of trade and services in promoting Palestinian economic development; the performance of the external trade sector; major factors affecting the external trade of the territories, including policies, practices and structural limitations; the potentials for expansion and diversification of external trade in the territories; and requisite policies and measures for the long-term development of the Palestinian external trade sector.

ECONOMIC AND SOCIAL COUNCIL ACTION

On 26 July 1989, the Economic and Social Council adopted **resolution 1989/86** by roll-call vote.

Israeli economic practices in the occupied Palestinian and other Arab territories

The Economic and Social Council,

Recalling General Assembly decision 40/432 of 17 December 1985, in which the Assembly requested the Secretary-General to prepare a report on the financial and trade practices of the Israeli occupation authorities in the occupied Palestinian and other Arab territories,

Recalling also Economic and Social Council resolution 1988/65 of 28 July 1988 and General Assembly decision 43/430 of 20 December 1988,

Having considered the reports of the Secretary-General on Israeli trade practices in the occupied Palestinian territories and on Israeli financial and trade practices in the occupied Syrian Arab Golan,

Taking into account the fact that land and water are basic national resources in the occupied Palestinian and other Arab territories,

1. *Takes note with concern* of the reports of the Secretary-General on Israeli trade practices in the occupied Palestinian territories and on Israeli financial and trade practices in the occupied Syrian Arab Golan, prepared in pursuance of General Assembly decisions 40/432 and 43/430 and Economic and Social Council resolution 1988/65;

2. *Requests* the Secretary-General to prepare a comprehensive report on Israeli land and water policies and practices in the occupied Palestinian and other Arab territories and to submit the report to the General Assembly at its forty-fifth session, through the Economic and Social Council.

Economic and Social Council resolution 1989/86

26 July 1989   Meeting 35   48-1 (roll-call vote)

25-nation draft (E/1989/L.38/Rev.1); agenda item 5.

Sponsors: Algeria, Bahrain, Bangladesh, Bulgaria, Cuba, Czechoslovakia, Democratic Yemen, Egypt, German Democratic Republic, Iran, Jordan, Kuwait, Libyan Arab Jamahiriya, Madagascar, Morocco, Nicaragua, Oman, Saudi Arabia, Somalia, Sudan, Syrian Arab Republic, Tunisia, Ukrainian SSR, United Arab Emirates, Yemen.

Meeting numbers. ESC 32, 33, 35.

Roll-call vote in Council as follows:

In favour: Bolivia, Brazil, Bulgaria, Cameroon, Canada, China, Colombia, Cuba, Czechoslovakia, Denmark, France, Germany, Federal Republic of, Ghana, Greece, Guinea, India, Indonesia, Iran, Iraq, Ireland, Italy, Japan, Jordan, Kenya, Libyan Arab Jamahiriya, Netherlands, New Zealand, Nicaragua, Niger, Norway, Poland, Portugal, Rwanda, Saudi Arabia, Somalia, Sri Lanka, Sudan, Thailand, Trinidad and Tobago, Tunisia, Ukrainian SSR, USSR, United Kingdom, Uruguay, Venezuela, Yugoslavia, Zaire, Zambia.

Against: United States.

Palestinian women

In response to a 1988 Economic and Social Council resolution,[44] the Secretary-General submitted in February 1989 to the Commission on the Status of Women a report on the situation of Palestinian women.[45] Following consideration of the report, the Council on 24 May adopted **resolution 1989/34** condemning the continuation of the ''iron-fist'' policy practised by Israel against Palestinian women and their families in the occupied territories and requesting the Commission to monitor implementation of the Nairobi Forward-looking Strategies for the Advancement of Women[46] concerning assistance to Palestinian women and children inside and outside the occupied territories. The Council reaffirmed that Palestinian women, as an integral part of a nation whose people were prevented from exercising their basic human and political rights, could not fully participate in the attainment of the objectives of equality, development and peace without the realization of their inalienable rights to return to their homes, to self-determination and to establish an independent State. The Secretary-General was requested to send a mission composed of experts on the status of women to investigate the condition of Palestinian women and children, in the light of the drastic deteriorating situation in the territories.

REFERENCES

[1]A/44/35. [2]YUN 1968, p. 555, GA res. 2443(XXIII), 19 Dec. 1968. [3]A/44/599. [4]A/44/352. [5]YUN 1988, p. 232, GA res. 43/58 A, 6 Dec. 1988. [6]A/44/640. [7]YUN 1988, p. 231. [8]A/44/737-S/20971. [9]S/20454. [10]S/20456. [11]S/20463. [12]S/20662. [13]S/20669. [14]S/20677. [15]S/20942. [16]S/20949. [17]S/20945/Rev.1. [18]YUN 1988, p. 240, GA res. 43/58 B, 6 Dec. 1988. [19]A/44/565. [20]A/44/62-S/20361. [21]A/44/565. [22]YUN 1988, p. 243, GA res. 43/58 E, 6 Dec. 1988. [23]S/20709. [24]S/20711. [25]S/20817. [26]S/20823. [27]YUN 1988, p. 244, GA res. 43/58 D, 6 Dec. 1988. [28]A/44/564. [29]A/44/563. [30]YUN 1988, p. 245, GA res. 43/58 C, 6 Dec. 1988. [31]*Ibid.*, p. 247, GA res. 43/58 F, 6 Dec. 1988. [32]A/44/643. [33]YUN 1981, p. 312. [34]A/44/566. [35]YUN 1988, p. 248, GA res. 43/58 G, 6 Dec. 1988. [36]A/44/397-S/20734. [37]TD/B/1266 & Corr.1. [38]YUN 1987, p. 321, GA res. 42/190, 11 Dec. 1987. [39]A/44/534. [40]YUN 1988, p. 250, ESC res. 1988/65, 28 July 1988. [41]A/44/338-E/1989/118. [42]A/44/277-E/1989/82. [43]YUN 1988, p. 250. [44]YUN 1988, p. 634, ESC res. 1988/25, 26 May 1988. [45]E/CN.6/1989/4 & Corr.1. [46]YUN 1985, p. 937.

Palestine refugees

The year 1989 marked the fortieth anniversary of the establishment of the United Nations Relief and Works Agency for Palestine Refugees in the Near East (UNRWA),[1] an anniversary which the UNRWA Commissioner-General said provided a stark reminder to the international community of the failure to resolve one of the most unsettling political and humanitarian issues.[2]

More than 2.3 million refugees were registered with UNRWA as at 30 June 1989 in five areas of the Middle East: in and outside camps in the Israeli-occupied West Bank (398,391) and Gaza Strip (469,385); Jordan (899,811); Lebanon (294,272); and the Syrian Arab Republic (272,778). Overall, about a third of the total were in 61 camps. An estimated further 52,000 persons, not registered refugees, also lived in camps, about 37,000 being people displaced as a result of the 1967 hostilities.

In 1989, the General Assembly addressed the work of UNRWA and the situation of Palestine refugees in 11 resolutions, dealing with: assistance to Palestine refugees (44/47 A) and displaced persons (44/47 C); the Working Group on the Financing of UNRWA (44/47 B); scholarships for higher education and vocational training (44/47 D); a proposed University of Jerusalem "Al-Quds" for Palestine refugees (44/47 J); Palestine refugees in Palestinian territory occupied by Israel since 1967 (44/47 E); resumption of the ration distribution to Palestine refugees (44/47 F); refugee protection (44/47 I); revenues from refugee properties (44/47 H); return of population and refugees displaced since 1967 (44/47 G); and protection of Palestinian students and educational institutions and safeguarding UNRWA facilities in the occupied territories (44/47 K).

Work of UNRWA

As at 30 June 1989,[2] Palestine refugees numbering 2,334,637 were registered with UNRWA in its five areas of operation. The Agency was providing educational, health and relief services, as well as undertaking emergency measures in response to the *intifadah* and continuing upheavals in Lebanon, where major clashes had erupted again beginning in February 1989. The UNRWA Commissioner-General reported on the Agency's work—from 1 July 1988 to 30 June 1989,[2] and from 1 July 1989 to 30 June 1990.[3] He stated that with the continuing Palestinian uprising in the occupied territories, while contacts and co-operation at the higher official levels remained normal, there was heightened tension on the ground. Agency premises were violated and used as observation posts and interrogation or detention centres. There was deliberate large-scale destruction of Agency property and increased interference with the freedom of movement of staff. Local staff were arrested and detained without charge and many complained of maltreatment by the authorities, while physical harassment, and even detention, of international staff during the performance of official duties increased. In Lebanon, it was remarkable that services to Palestine refugees had continued in spite of the chaotic situation and dangers involved.

UNRWA's educational programme included nine grades of general education, vocational and technical training, in-service teacher training and some higher education for Palestine refugees. The curricula followed those prescribed in the respective host countries. During the 1988/89 academic year, 351,100 refugee children were enrolled through six years of elementary education and three years of secondary education in 628 elementary and preparatory schools. However, 90 of 98 schools in the West Bank, with a pupil population of more than 39,000, had been closed by Israeli military order, disrupting and shortening the school year, until permitted to reopen in July. Pupils witnessed scenes of violence, a pervasive presence of security forces, intrusion of soldiers into school compounds and classrooms, involving at times the firing of ammunition, rubber bullets and tear-gas, and detention of students and teachers.

During the 1988/89 academic year, UNRWA provided places for 4,100 vocational trainees and

850 teacher trainees in eight training centres, but those places were reduced to 3,160 and 300, respectively, owing to the closure of the three centres in the West Bank by order of Israeli authorities. Total expenditure for education in 1989 was $108.8 million.

The UNRWA health programme was community-based, with 100 centres providing sanitation services, curative and preventive medical services and maternal and child health services. Events in the occupied territories created a high demand for emergency and casualty care, reflected in health programme expenditures of $45.7 million, as against $38.4 million in 1988.

Under the relief services programme, the major goal was assistance to destitute refugee families. The special hardship case programme, providing food, blankets, clothing and shelter, in 1989 serviced 146,800 beneficiaries from more than 33,000 families. Special hardship cases comprised families with no males between the ages of 18 and 55 in the household, or with one medically incapable of earning a living. The cost in 1989 of the relief services programme was $23.1 million.

Lebanon. UNRWA work was affected by widespread and serious hostilities in east and west Beirut, beginning in February 1989, and by parallel random violence, kidnapping and strikes throughout the country. There was consequent displacement of several thousand Palestinians and the killing of at least 40 registered refugees during 1989. Nevertheless, refugee camps were not generally physically affected. However, in April, shelling of west Beirut caused heavy damage to offices and vehicles at the Agency's central warehouse compound, and essential field staff and operations were moved from Beirut to Saida. Given the prevailing circumstances, UNRWA continued to extend emergency assistance, as well as most of its regular programmes, including education, to the entire Palestinian community, not merely to registered refugees, and to participate actively with other United Nations agencies in providing assistance to the Lebanese population in general.

West Bank and Gaza Strip. The *intifadah* and the Israeli response thereto continued to affect virtually all UNRWA operations. Between 1 July 1988 and 30 June 1989, 107 Palestinian refugees were killed in Gaza and 196 in the West Bank. It was reported that since the beginning of the *intifadah* more than 30,000 Palestinians had sought medical attention for injuries, and that the Agency's health services were stretched to the limit. Individuals were arrested or detained without charge or trial in substantial numbers, it was reported, and there had been indiscriminate beatings and curfews severely affecting the mobility of people and their capacity to work. While schools had reopened in July 1989, selective closure orders, as well as strikes, continued severely to disrupt school life. Palestinians in the occupied territories continued to be a major concern of the Agency. Schools were again closed in November 1989 on the West Bank.

Jordan and the Syrian Arab Republic. The deterioration of the Jordanian and Syrian economies caused difficulties for refugees, with the price of basic commodities rising. At the same time, economic retrenchment in the Persian Gulf States meant fewer opportunities for employment. Palestinians returned in increasing numbers to their families, with resulting loss of income. Growing demands on UNRWA health and welfare services were related to those economic hardships. In early December, demonstrations to support the *intifadah* took place in some refugee camps in Jordan.

GENERAL ASSEMBLY ACTION

On 8 December, on the recommendation of the Special Political Committee, the General Assembly adopted **resolution 44/47 A** by recorded vote.

Assistance to Palestine refugees
The General Assembly,

Recalling its resolution 43/57 A of 6 December 1988 and all its previous resolutions on the question, including resolution 194(III) of 11 December 1948,

Taking note of the report of the Commissioner-General of the United Nations Relief and Works Agency for Palestine Refugees in the Near East, covering the period from 1 July 1988 to 30 June 1989,

1. *Notes with deep regret* that repatriation or compensation of the refugees as provided for in paragraph 11 of General Assembly resolution 194(III) has not been effected, that no substantial progress has been made in the programme endorsed by the Assembly in paragraph 2 of its resolution 513(VI) of 26 January 1952 for the reintegration of refugees either by repatriation or resettlement and that, therefore, the situation of the refugees continues to be a matter of serious concern;

2. *Expresses its thanks* to the Commissioner-General and to all the staff of the United Nations Relief and Works Agency for Palestine Refugees in the Near East, recognizing that the Agency is doing all it can within the limits of available resources, and also expresses its thanks to the specialized agencies and private organizations for their valuable work in assisting the refugees;

3. *Reiterates its request* that the headquarters of the Agency should be relocated to its former site within its area of operations as soon as practicable;

4. *Notes with regret* that the United Nations Conciliation Commission for Palestine has been unable to find a means of achieving progress in the implementation of paragraph 11 of General Assembly resolution 194(III), and requests the Commission to exert continued efforts towards the implementation of that paragraph and to report to the Assembly as appropriate, but no later than 1 September 1990;

5. *Directs attention* to the continuing seriousness of the financial position of the Agency, as outlined in the report of the Commissioner-General;

6. *Notes with profound concern* that, despite the commendable and successful efforts of the Commissioner-

General to collect additional contributions, this increased level of income to the Agency is still insufficient to cover essential budget requirements in the present year and that, at currently foreseen levels of giving, deficits will recur each year;

7. *Calls upon* all Governments, as a matter of urgency, to make the most generous efforts possible to meet the anticipated needs of the Agency, particularly in the light of the budgetary deficit projected in the report of the Commissioner-General, and therefore urges non-contributing Governments to contribute regularly and contributing Governments to consider increasing their regular contributions;

8. *Decides* to extend the mandate of the Agency until 30 June 1993, without prejudice to the provisions of paragraph 11 of General Assembly resolution 194(III).

General Assembly resolution 44/47 A

8 December 1989   Meeting 78   134-0-1 (recorded vote)

Approved by Special Political Committee (A/44/815) by recorded vote (130-0-2), 22 November (meeting 25); draft by United States (A/SPC/44/L.5 & Corr.1); agenda item 76.

Meeting numbers. GA 44th session: SPC 5-8, 25; plenary 78.

Recorded vote in Assembly as follows:

In favour: Afghanistan, Algeria, Angola, Antigua and Barbuda, Argentina, Australia, Austria, Bahamas, Bahrain, Bangladesh, Barbados, Belgium, Benin, Bhutan, Bolivia, Botswana, Brazil, Brunei Darussalam, Burkina Faso, Burundi, Byelorussian SSR, Cameroon, Canada, Cape Verde, Central African Republic, Chad, Chile, China, Colombia, Costa Rica, Côte d'Ivoire, Cuba, Cyprus, Czechoslovakia, Democratic Kampuchea, Democratic Yemen, Denmark, Dominica,* Dominican Republic, Ecuador, Egypt, Equatorial Guinea, Ethiopia, Fiji, Finland, German Democratic Republic, Germany, Federal Republic of, Greece, Grenada, Guinea, Guinea-Bissau, Guyana, Haiti, Honduras, Hungary, Iceland, India, Indonesia, Iran, Iraq, Ireland, Italy, Jamaica, Japan, Jordan, Kenya, Kuwait, Lao People's Democratic Republic, Lebanon, Lesotho, Liberia, Libyan Arab Jamahiriya, Luxembourg, Madagascar, Malawi, Malaysia, Maldives, Mali, Malta, Mauritania, Mauritius, Mexico, Mongolia, Morocco, Mozambique, Myanmar, Nepal, Netherlands, New Zealand, Norway, Oman, Pakistan, Panama, Paraguay, Peru, Philippines, Poland, Portugal, Qatar, Romania, Rwanda, Saint Lucia, Samoa, Sao Tome and Principe, Saudi Arabia, Senegal, Seychelles, Sierra Leone, Singapore, Solomon Islands, Somalia, Spain, Sri Lanka, Suriname, Sweden, Syrian Arab Republic, Thailand, Togo, Trinidad and Tobago, Tunisia, Turkey, Ukrainian SSR, USSR, United Arab Emirates, United Kingdom, United States, Uruguay, Vanuatu, Venezuela, Viet Nam, Yemen, Yugoslavia, Zaire, Zambia.

Against: None.

Abstaining: Israel.

*Later advised the Secretariat it had intended to abstain.

UNRWA financing

Agency income for its General Fund and on-going activities amounted to $210.9 million in 1989.[3] To maintain regular programmes at planned levels, UNRWA spent $201.8 million. That fully expended its net income, after reallocating $7.7 million to partially fund emergency-related programmes in Lebanon and the occupied territory, and $1.4 million to project funds, mainly for urgent school construction in Jordan. Thus, the UNRWA working capital reserve—$28.9 million—was not increased in 1989.

According to financial report and statements for the year ended 31 December 1989,[4] the UNRWA 1989 expenditures amounted to $265 million, of which $222.2 million was for the General Fund. Project funds were $20.4 million for ongoing activities and $5.9 million for capital and special projects, leaving $228.1 million for the regular budget.

Extraordinary emergency expenditures included the Lebanon Emergency Fund of $10.9 million. The Extraordinary Measures in the Occupied Territories Fund had a budget of $23.5 million, used to alleviate the hardship of the Palestine refugees owing to civil unrest. Another fund—the Expanded Programme of Assistance—was used to improve the infrastructure in terms of better housing and new or expanded sewage systems, and to provide UNRWA with better facilities to run its education, health and relief programmes in the territories. Some $2.5 million was expended on that programme in 1989.

On 19 December, the General Assembly, by **resolution 44/183**, accepted the financial report and audited financial statements of UNRWA for the year ended 31 December 1988,[5] together with the report of the Board of Auditors, and requested the Commissioner-General to report in 1990 on steps taken to implement the Board's recommendations.

Working Group on UNRWA financing

In a report[6] on its meetings of 11 September and 10 October 1989, the Working Group on the Financing of UNRWA stated that, at the beginning of 1989, it had been apparent that the fall in the value of one of the major local currencies would significantly reduce the dollar cost of budgeted expenditure. The Commissioner-General therefore had taken the decision to reduce the 1989 budget by $6 million, from $233 million to $227 million. The salaries of the area staff, however, had to be increased in several fields of operation to compensate the staff for the loss of purchasing power, thereby reducing the dollar value of exchange-rate savings.

Although it appeared that UNRWA would be able to meet its expenses for the remainder of 1989, there was cause for serious concern for 1990—an increase of 5 per cent in budgeted expenditure for the regular programme was anticipated. That figure had been used for planning purposes and in discussions with donors as the minimum increase in contributions needed to meet Agency requirements for its regular programme in 1990. In addition, funding would be required to maintain emergency-related programmes in Lebanon, the West Bank and the Gaza Strip. At the end of 1989, the balances remaining in those funds could be quite small and, at the most, would last only a month or so. If the programmes were to be maintained at 1989 levels, contributions of between $25 million and $30 million would be required over and above the increased contributions that would be needed to finance the regular programme.

The Working Group was pleased to note that UNRWA had received sufficient funding to deliver the essential parts of its regular and emergency-related programmes in 1988 and expected to do so again in 1989. It expressed its appreciation to donors, especially to those which had increased their contributions, for making those results possible. It noted, however, that in both years the construction budget had been underfunded and that much-needed construction work would therefore have to be postponed again.

The Working Group shared the Commissioner-General's concern about the financial outlook for 1990. In that connection, it noted that the favourable financial outcome in 1988, as well as the satisfactory projection for 1989, was attributable not so much to increased contributions as to reductions in costs owing to favourable movements in exchange rates against the dollar. As the Working Group had pointed out earlier, exchange-rate fluctuations could easily reverse their current trends and unfavourably affect the Agency's finances. It was therefore necessary to continue to stimulate higher contributions not only from traditional donors, but perhaps more importantly from new ones. The Working Group commended the Agency for its efforts in those directions and the Commissioner-General for his efforts, including a rigorous schedule of personal fund-raising visits, to attract an increased level of contributions. It noted that the Commissioner-General continued to envisage an annual growth of 5 per cent in expenditures in order to maintain the regular programme at its current level.

The Working Group was particularly concerned about future funding for the emergency-related programmes, which were in operation in three of its five fields.

GENERAL ASSEMBLY ACTION

On 8 December 1989, on the recommendation of the Special Political Committee, the General Assembly adopted **resolution 44/47 B** without vote.

Working Group on the Financing of the United Nations Relief and Works Agency for Palestine Refugees in the Near East

The General Assembly,

Recalling its resolutions 2656(XXV) of 7 December 1970, 2728(XXV) of 15 December 1970, 2791(XXVI) of 6 December 1971, 2964(XXVII) of 13 December 1972, 3090(XXVIII) of 7 December 1973, 3330(XXIX) of 17 December 1974, 3419 D (XXX) of 8 December 1975, 31/15 C of 23 November 1976, 32/90 D of 13 December 1977, 33/112 D of 18 December 1978, 34/52 D of 23 November 1979, 35/13 D of 3 November 1980, 36/146 E of 16 December 1981, 37/120 A of 16 December 1982, 38/83 B of 15 December 1983, 39/99 B of 14 December 1984, 40/165 B of 16 December 1985, 41/69 B of 3 December 1986, 42/69 B of 2 December 1987 and 43/57 B of 6 December 1988,

Recalling also its decision 36/462 of 16 March 1982, whereby it took note of the special report of the Working Group on the Financing of the United Nations Re-

lief and Works Agency for Palestine Refugees in the Near East and adopted the recommendations contained therein,

Having considered the report of the Working Group,

Taking into account the report of the Commissioner-General of the United Nations Relief and Works Agency for Palestine Refugees in the Near East, covering the period from 1 July 1988 to 30 June 1989,

Deeply concerned at the critical financial situation of the Agency, which has affected and affects the continuation of the provision of the necessary Agency services to the Palestine refugees, including the emergency-related programmes,

Emphasizing the continuing need for extraordinary efforts in order to maintain, at least at their present minimum level, the activities of the Agency, as well as to enable the Agency to carry out essential construction,

1. *Commends* the Working Group on the Financing of the United Nations Relief and Works Agency for Palestine Refugees in the Near East for its efforts to assist in ensuring the Agency's financial security;

2. *Takes note with approval* of the report of the Working Group;

3. *Requests* the Working Group to continue its efforts, in co-operation with the Secretary-General and the Commissioner-General, for the financing of the Agency for a further period of one year;

4. *Requests* the Secretary-General to provide the necessary services and assistance to the Working Group for the conduct of its work.

General Assembly resolution 44/47 B

8 December 1989   Meeting 78   Adopted without vote

Approved by Special Political Committee (A/44/815) without vote, 22 November (meeting 25); 16-nation draft (A/SPC/44/L.9); agenda item 76.

Sponsors: Austria, Bangladesh, Canada, Denmark, Germany, Federal Republic of, India, Indonesia, Liberia, Malaysia, Netherlands, New Zealand, Pakistan, Philippines, Spain, Sweden, Yugoslavia.

Meeting numbers. GA 44th session: SPC 5-8, 25; plenary 78.

Protection of Palestinian students and UNRWA staff and premises

During the 1988/89 reporting period, there was a substantial increase in the number of staff arrested and detained without charge or trial in the occupied territory as compared with previous years. Israeli occupation authorities also deported a staff member from the Gaza Strip. In Lebanon, however, the total number of staff kidnapped or detained decreased.

Since UNRWA remained unable to obtain adequate, timely information on the reasons for the arrests and detentions, it was unable to ascertain whether the staff members' official functions had been involved or whether their rights and duties flowing from the Charter, the 1946 Convention on the Privileges and Immunities of the United Nations[7] and UNRWA Staff Regulations and Rules had been duly respected.

The treatment of staff in detention continued to be cause for concern, with many staff members complaining of beatings and other forms of brutality. The Commissioner-General said that in addition Agency staff, including international staff, had been subjected to physical abuse and, at times, undisciplined behaviour by Israeli soldiers in the West Bank and Gaza Strip. Difficulties continued regarding movement of staff into and out of the West Bank and Gaza Strip, with entry permits sometimes refused. Only a small proportion of staff were issued curfew permits. As a result Agency operations were impeded.

According to the Commissioner-General, between September 1988 and June 1989 two students were killed inside Agency schools, 376 were injured by live rounds and rubber bullets and 76 were detained, while outside the schools 11 were killed, 3,655 injured and 657 detained.

GENERAL ASSEMBLY ACTION

On 8 December, on the recommendation of the Special Political Committee, the General Assembly adopted **resolution 44/47 K** by recorded vote.

Protection of Palestinian students and educational institutions and safeguarding of the security of the facilities of the United Nations Relief and Works Agency for Palestine Refugees in the Near East in the occupied Palestinian territory

The General Assembly,

Recalling Security Council resolution 605(1987) of 22 December 1987,

Recalling its resolutions 43/21 of 3 November 1988, 43/57 I of 6 December 1988 and 44/2 of 6 October 1989,

Taking note of the report of the Secretary-General of 21 January 1988, submitted in accordance with Security Council resolution 605(1987),

Having considered the statement of the Secretary-General of 19 October 1989 on the incidents in which Israeli soldiers broke into the premises of installations of the United Nations Relief and Works Agency for Palestine Refugees in the Near East in the occupied Palestinian territory,

Having also considered the report of the Commissioner-General of the United Nations Relief and Works Agency for Palestine Refugees in the Near East, covering the period from 1 July 1988 to 30 June 1989,

Taking note, in particular, of paragraph 104 of that report, in which it is stated that, in the occupied Gaza Strip "between September 1988 and June 1989, two students were killed inside Agency schools, 376 were injured by live rounds and rubber bullets and 76 were detained. Outside the schools, 11 were killed, 3,655 injured and 657 detained",

Gravely concerned and alarmed by the deteriorating situation in the Palestinian territory occupied by Israel since 1967, including Jerusalem,

1. *Condemns* the repeated Israeli raids on the premises and installations of the United Nations Relief and Works Agency for Palestine Refugees in the Near East, and calls upon Israel, the occupying Power, to refrain from such raids;

2. *Also condemns,* in particular, Israeli policies and practices against Palestinian students and faculties in educational institutions in the occupied Palestinian territory, especially the opening of fire on defenceless students, causing many casualties;

3. *Deplores* the policy and practices of Israel, the occupying Power, which have led to the prolonged closure of educational institutions, a large number of which are operated by the Agency, and the repeated disruption of medical services;

4. *Calls upon* Israel, the occupying Power, to open immediately all closed educational institutions and to refrain from closing them thereafter;

5. *Requests* the Secretary-General to report to the General Assembly at its forty-fifth session on the implementation of the present resolution.

General Assembly resolution 44/47 K

8 December 1989   Meeting 78   146-2-1 (recorded vote)

Approved by Special Political Committee (A/44/815) by recorded vote (127-2-1),
22 November (meeting 25); 13-nation draft (A/SPC/44/L.17); agenda item 76.
Sponsors: Afghanistan, Bangladesh, Brunei Darussalam, Burkina Faso, Comoros, Cuba, Indonesia, Madagascar, Malaysia, Nicaragua, Pakistan, Yugoslavia, Zambia.
Meeting numbers. GA 44th session: SPC 5-8, 25; plenary 78.

Recorded vote in Assembly as follows:

In favour: Afghanistan, Albania, Algeria, Angola, Antigua and Barbuda, Argentina, Australia, Austria, Bahamas, Bahrain, Bangladesh, Barbados, Belgium, Benin, Bhutan, Bolivia, Botswana, Brazil, Brunei Darussalam, Bulgaria, Burkina Faso, Burundi, Byelorussian SSR, Cameroon, Canada, Cape Verde, Central African Republic, Chad, Chile, China, Colombia, Costa Rica, Côte d'Ivoire, Cuba, Cyprus, Czechoslovakia, Democratic Kampuchea, Democratic Yemen, Denmark, Djibouti, Dominican Republic, Ecuador, Egypt, Equatorial Guinea, Ethiopia, Fiji, Finland, France, German Democratic Republic, Germany, Federal Republic of, Ghana, Greece, Grenada, Guatemala, Guinea, Guinea-Bissau, Guyana, Haiti, Honduras, Hungary, India, Indonesia, Iran, Iraq, Ireland, Italy, Jamaica, Japan, Jordan, Kenya, Kuwait, Lao People's Democratic Republic, Lebanon, Lesotho, Liberia, Libyan Arab Jamahiriya, Luxembourg, Madagascar, Malawi, Malaysia, Maldives, Mali, Malta, Mauritania, Mauritius, Mexico, Mongolia, Morocco, Mozambique, Myanmar, Nepal, Netherlands, New Zealand, Nicaragua, Nigeria, Norway, Oman, Pakistan, Panama, Papua New Guinea, Paraguay, Peru, Philippines, Poland, Portugal, Qatar, Romania, Rwanda, Saint Lucia, Saint Vincent and the Grenadines, Samoa, Sao Tome and Principe, Saudi Arabia, Senegal, Seychelles, Sierra Leone, Singapore, Solomon Islands, Somalia, Spain, Sri Lanka, Sudan, Suriname, Swaziland, Sweden, Syrian Arab Republic, Thailand, Togo, Trinidad and Tobago, Tunisia, Turkey, Uganda, Ukrainian SSR, USSR, United Arab Emirates, United Kingdom, United Republic of Tanzania, Uruguay, Vanuatu, Venezuela, Viet Nam, Yemen, Yugoslavia, Zaire, Zambia, Zimbabwe.
Against: Israel, United States.
Abstaining: Dominica.

Compensation claims

In 1989, UNRWA reported that no progress had been made with regard to claims against the Governments of: Israel (for loss of and damage to UNRWA property during the 1967 hostilities, Israel's invasion of Lebanon in 1982 and its military action before then); Jordan (arising from the 1967 hostilities and the disturbances in 1970 and 1971); and the Syrian Arab Republic (relating mainly to the levy of certain taxes from which UNRWA believed it was exempt under existing agreements). Those claims had been reported in 1986.[8]

In **resolution 44/47 I**, the General Assembly called anew on Israel to compensate UNRWA for damage to its property and facilities resulting from Israel's invasion of Lebanon, without prejudice to Israel's responsibility for all damages resulting from that invasion.

Israel had informed UNRWA in July 1988[9] that, because of temporary budgetary constraints, it was withholding payment of clearance, warehousing and transport charges payable to the Agency under the 1967 provisional agreement concerning assistance to Palestine refugees. Israel had not reverted to payments in 1989, which stood at more than $3 million.[3]

Other aspects

Humanitarian assistance to displaced and other persons

During 1989, in addition to providing relief in the form of basic food commodities, blankets, clothing, shelter repair and cash grants, UNRWA continued to provide a small measure of humanitarian assistance to persons who had been displaced as a result of the June 1967 and subsequent hostilities, but who were not registered with UNRWA as refugees.

The Agency remained concerned about the future of the Palestine refugees who had been stranded at Canada Camp on the Egyptian side of the international border, at Rafah, when Israel withdrew from the Sinai in April 1982. Under an agreement between Israel and Egypt, they were to return to the Gaza Strip where they would be reunited with their families. In August 1989, a group of 20 families were accommodated at Rafah, Gaza, and UNRWA was assisting them with rations for a six-month initial period. The agreement between the Israeli and Egyptian authorities for the other families, who numbered over 800, was that they should return to the Tel el-Sultan housing project in a phased transfer. The compensation provided by the Egyptian Government to each family for the housing they would leave behind was, however, a fraction of the cost of a simple house of sufficient size to accommodate the household, and few families were able to accumulate savings with which to supplement the compensation. By the end of 1989, only a small number of heads of family had begun to build their new homes, which had to be completed before families were permitted to return. Consequently, plans were postponed under which UNDP was to have constructed a centre in Tel el-Sultan to provide shops and workshops for the returnees to rent. Meanwhile, UNRWA continued to provide food rations to some 4,000 refugees in Canada Camp who were mostly unemployed and living in poverty.

GENERAL ASSEMBLY ACTION

On 8 December, the General Assembly, on the recommendation of the Special Political Committee, adopted **resolution 44/47 C** without vote.

Assistance to persons displaced as a result of the June 1967 and subsequent hostilities

The General Assembly,

Recalling its resolution 43/57 C of 6 December 1988 and all its previous resolutions on the question,

Taking note of the report of the Commissioner-General of the United Nations Relief and Works Agency for Palestine Refugees in the Near East, covering the period from 1 July 1988 to 30 June 1989,

Concerned about the continued human suffering resulting from the hostilities in the Middle East,

1. *Reaffirms* its resolution 43/57 C and all its previous resolutions on the question;

2. *Endorses*, bearing in mind the objectives of those resolutions, the efforts of the Commissioner-General of the United Nations Relief and Works Agency for Palestine Refugees in the Near East to continue to provide humanitarian assistance as far as practicable, on an emergency basis and as a temporary measure, to other persons in the area who are at present displaced and in serious need of continued assistance as a result of the June 1967 and subsequent hostilities;

3. *Strongly appeals* to all Governments and to organizations and individuals to contribute generously for the above purposes to the United Nations Relief and Works Agency for Palestine Refugees in the Near East and to the other intergovernmental and non-governmental organizations concerned.

General Assembly resolution 44/47 C

8 December 1989   Meeting 78   Adopted without vote

Approved by Special Political Committee (A/44/815) without vote, 22 November (meeting 25); 20-nation draft (A/SPC/44/L.8); agenda item 76.
Sponsors: Austria, Belgium, Canada, Denmark, Finland, Germany, Federal Republic of, Greece, India, Indonesia, Ireland, Italy, Japan, Malaysia, Mali, Netherlands, Norway, Pakistan, Philippines, Sri Lanka, Sweden.
Meeting numbers. GA 44th session: SPC 5-8, 25; plenary 78.

Repatriation of refugees

In September 1989, the Secretary-General reported[10] on compliance with the General Assembly's 1988 call[11] on Israel to take immediate steps for the return of all displaced persons to their homes or former places of residence in the territories occupied by Israel since 1967, and to desist from measures obstructing their return. By a note verbale of 28 June, Israel stated that its position had been detailed fully in successive replies to the Secretary-General in previous years, most recently in 1988.[12] It continued to make every effort to review individual cases of resettlement, based on their merits, and, as a result, some 75,600 persons had returned to the administered territories.

UNRWA had not been involved in arrangements for the return of either refugees or displaced persons who were not registered. Agency information was based on requests made by returning registered refugees who wanted a transfer of their benefit entitlements and correction of their records; thus it would not necessarily be aware of the return of any registered refugees who had not requested services. As far as was known to UNRWA, between 1 July 1988 and 30 June 1989, 172 registered refugees had returned to the West Bank and 21 to the Gaza Strip. The number of displaced registered refugees who were known to UNRWA to have returned to the occupied territories since June 1967 was about 11,500. Those records, however, might be incomplete, it was reported.

On 8 December, on the recommendation of the Special Political Committee, the General Assembly adopted **resolution 44/47 G** by recorded vote.

Return of population and refugees displaced since 1967

The General Assembly,

Recalling Security Council resolution 237(1967) of 14 June 1967,

Recalling also its resolutions 2252(ES-V) of 4 July 1967, 2452 A (XXIII) of 19 December 1968, 2535 B (XXIV) of 10 December 1969, 2672 D (XXV) of 8 December 1970, 2792 E (XXVI) of 6 December 1971, 2963 C and D (XXVII) of 13 December 1972, 3089 C (XXVIII) of 7 December 1973, 3331 D (XXIX) of 17 December 1974, 3419 C (XXX) of 8 December 1975, 31/15 D of 23 November 1976, 32/90 E of 13 December 1977, 33/112 F of 18 December 1978, 34/52 E of 23 November 1979, ES-7/2 of 29 July 1980, 35/13 E of 3 November 1980, 36/146 B of 16 December 1981, 37/120 G of 16 December 1982, 38/83 G of 15 December 1983, 39/99 G of 14 December 1984, 40/165 G of 16 December 1985, 41/69 G of 3 December 1986, 42/69 G of 2 December 1987 and 43/57 G of 6 December 1988,

Having considered the report of the Commissioner-General of the United Nations Relief and Works Agency for Palestine Refugees in the Near East, covering the period from 1 July 1988 to 30 June 1989, and the report of the Secretary-General,

1. *Reaffirms* the inalienable right of all displaced inhabitants to return to their homes or former places of residence in the territories occupied by Israel since 1967, and declares once more that any attempt to restrict, or to attach conditions to, the free exercise of the right to return by any displaced person is inconsistent with that inalienable right and is inadmissible;

2. *Considers* any and all agreements embodying any restriction on, or condition for, the return of the displaced inhabitants as null and void;

3. *Strongly deplores* the continued refusal of the Israeli authorities to take steps for the return of the displaced inhabitants;

4. *Calls once more upon* Israel:

(*a*) To take immediate steps for the return of all displaced inhabitants;

(*b*) To desist from all measures that obstruct the return of the displaced inhabitants, including measures affecting the physical and demographic structure of the occupied territories;

5. *Requests* the Secretary-General, after consulting with the Commissioner-General of the United Nations Relief and Works Agency for Palestine Refugees in the Near East, to report to the General Assembly, before the opening of its forty-fifth session, on Israel's compliance with paragraph 4 above.

General Assembly resolution 44/47 G

8 December 1989   Meeting 78   126-2-19 (recorded vote)

Approved by Special Political Committee (A/44/815) by recorded vote (108-2-22), 22 November (meeting 25); 15-nation draft (A/SPC/44/L.13); agenda item 76.

Sponsors: Afghanistan, Bangladesh, Brunei Darussalam, Burkina Faso, Comoros, Cuba, India, Indonesia, Madagascar, Malaysia, Mali, Nicaragua, Pakistan, Yugoslavia, Zambia.

Meeting numbers. GA 44th session: SPC 5-8, 25; plenary 78.

Recorded vote in Assembly as follows:

In favour: Afghanistan, Albania, Algeria, Angola, Antigua and Barbuda, Argentina, Bahamas, Bahrain, Bangladesh, Barbados, Benin, Bhutan, Bolivia, Botswana, Brazil, Brunei Darussalam, Bulgaria, Burkina Faso, Burundi, Byelorussian SSR, Cameroon, Cape Verde, Central African Republic, Chad, Chile, China, Colombia, Costa Rica, Côte d'Ivoire, Cuba, Cyprus, Czechoslovakia, Democratic Kampuchea, Democratic Yemen, Djibouti, Dominican Republic, Ecuador, Egypt, Equatorial Guinea, Ethiopia, Fiji, German Democratic Republic, Ghana, Greece, Grenada, Guatemala, Guinea, Guinea-Bissau, Guyana, Haiti, Honduras, Hungary, India, Indonesia, Iran, Iraq, Jamaica, Japan, Jordan, Kenya, Kuwait, Lao People's Democratic Republic, Lebanon, Lesotho, Liberia, Libyan Arab Jamahiriya, Madagascar, Malawi, Malaysia, Maldives, Mali, Malta, Mauritania, Mauritius, Mexico, Mongolia, Morocco, Mozambique, Myanmar, Nepal, Nigeria, Oman, Pakistan, Panama, Papua New Guinea, Paraguay, Peru, Philippines, Poland, Qatar, Romania, Rwanda, Saint Lucia, Saint Vincent and the Grenadines, Samoa, Sao Tome and Principe, Saudi Arabia, Senegal, Seychelles, Sierra Leone, Singapore, Solomon Islands, Somalia, Spain, Sri Lanka, Suriname, Syrian Arab Republic, Thailand, Togo, Trinidad and Tobago, Tunisia, Turkey, Uganda, Ukrainian SSR, USSR, United Arab Emirates, United Republic of Tanzania, Uruguay, Vanuatu, Venezuela, Viet Nam, Yemen, Yugoslavia, Zaire, Zambia, Zimbabwe.

Against: Israel, United States.

Abstaining: Australia, Austria, Belgium, Canada, Denmark, Dominica, Finland, France, Germany, Federal Republic of, Iceland, Ireland, Italy, Luxembourg, Netherlands, New Zealand, Norway, Portugal, Sweden, United Kingdom.

Food aid

The Secretary-General reported[13] in September 1989, pursuant to a 1988 General Assembly resolution,[14] that UNRWA had continued to distribute rations to the most needy sector of the refugee population, known as special hardship cases; those cases numbered 137,963 in December 1988. In Lebanon, a one-time emergency distribution of food was made in 1988 to some 220,000 refugees and, in the West Bank, approximately 680,000 food packages were distributed. Food commodities were also distributed on three occasions to refugee families through some 90,000 schoolchildren in the Gaza Strip. Food would continue to be distributed, as long as the emergency need remained and supplies were available. However, owing to continuing financial constraints and lack of donations, it had not been possible to resume the general ration distribution to all refugees.

On 8 December, on the recommendation of the Special Political Committee, the General Assembly adopted **resolution 44/47 F** by recorded vote.

Resumption of the ration distribution to Palestine refugees

The General Assembly,

Recalling its resolutions 36/146 F of 16 December 1981, 37/120 F of 16 December 1982, 38/83 F of 15 December 1983, 39/99 F of 14 December 1984, 40/165 F of 16 December 1985, 41/69 F of 3 December 1986, 42/69 F of 2 December 1987, 43/57 F of 6 December 1988 and all its previous resolutions on the question, including resolution 302(IV) of 8 December 1949,

Having considered the report of the Commissioner-General of the United Nations Relief and Works Agency for Palestine Refugees in the Near East, covering the period from 1 July 1988 to 30 June 1989, and the report of the Secretary-General,

Deeply concerned at the interruption by the Agency, owing to financial difficulties, of the general ration distribution to Palestine refugees in all fields,

1. *Regrets* that its resolutions 37/120 F, 38/83 F, 39/99 F, 40/165 F, 41/69 F, 42/69 F and 43/57 F have not been implemented;

2. *Calls once again upon* all Governments, as a matter of urgency, to make the most generous efforts possible and to offer the necessary resources to meet the needs of the United Nations Relief and Works Agency for Palestine Refugees in the Near East, particularly in the light of the interruption by the Agency of the general ration distribution to Palestine refugees in all fields, and therefore urges non-contributing Governments to contribute regularly and contributing Governments to consider increasing their regular contributions;

3. *Requests* the Commissioner-General of the United Nations Relief and Works Agency for Palestine Refugees in the Near East to resume on a continuing basis the interrupted general ration distribution to Palestine refugees in all fields;

4. *Requests* the Secretary-General, in consultation with the Commissioner-General, to report to the General Assembly at its forty-fifth session on the implementation of the present resolution.

General Assembly resolution 44/47 F

8 December 1989   Meeting 78   121-20-3 (recorded vote)

Approved by Special Political Committee (A/44/815) by recorded vote (108-20-4), 22 November (meeting 25); 14-nation draft (A/SPC/44/L.12); agenda item 76.

Sponsors: Afghanistan, Bangladesh, Brunei Darussalam, Burkina Faso, Comoros, Cuba, Indonesia, Madagascar, Malaysia, Mali, Nicaragua, Pakistan, Yugoslavia, Zambia.

Meeting numbers. GA 44th session: SPC 5-8, 25; plenary 78.

Recorded vote in Assembly as follows:

In favour: Afghanistan, Albania, Algeria, Angola, Antigua and Barbuda, Argentina, Bahamas, Bahrain, Bangladesh, Barbados, Benin, Bhutan, Bolivia, Botswana, Brazil, Brunei Darussalam, Bulgaria, Burkina Faso, Burundi, Byelorussian SSR, Cameroon, Cape Verde, Central African Republic, Chad, Chile, China, Colombia, Costa Rica, Côte d'Ivoire, Cuba, Cyprus, Czechoslovakia, Democratic Kampuchea, Democratic Yemen, Djibouti, Dominica,* Dominican Republic, Ecuador, Egypt, Equatorial Guinea, Ethiopia, Fiji, German Democratic Republic, Ghana, Grenada, Guinea, Guinea-Bissau, Guyana, Haiti, Honduras, Hungary, India, Indonesia, Iran, Iraq, Jamaica, Jordan, Kenya, Kuwait, Lao People's Democratic Republic, Lebanon, Lesotho, Liberia, Libyan Arab Jamahiriya, Madagascar, Malawi, Malaysia, Maldives, Mali, Malta, Mauritania, Mauritius, Mexico, Mongolia, Morocco, Mozambique, Myanmar, Nepal, Nigeria, Oman, Pakistan, Panama, Papua New Guinea, Paraguay, Peru, Philippines, Poland, Qatar, Romania, Rwanda, Saint Lucia, Saint Vincent and the Grenadines, Samoa, Sao Tome and Principe, Saudi Arabia, Senegal, Seychelles, Sierra Leone, Singapore, Solomon Islands, Somalia, Sri Lanka, Suriname, Syrian Arab Republic, Thailand, Togo, Trinidad and Tobago, Tunisia, Turkey, Ukrainian SSR, USSR, United Arab Emirates, Uruguay, Vanuatu, Venezuela, Viet Nam, Yemen, Yugoslavia, Zaire, Zambia, Zimbabwe.

Against: Australia, Belgium, Canada, Denmark, Finland, France, Germany, Federal Republic of, Iceland, Ireland, Israel, Italy, Japan, Luxembourg, Netherlands, New Zealand, Norway, Portugal, Sweden, United Kingdom, United States.

Abstaining: Austria, Greece, Spain.

*Later advised the Secretariat it had intended to abstain.

Education and training services

Schools and teacher training

The UNWRA education programme continued to provide nine grades of general education, vocational and technical training, pre-service and in-service teacher training and scholarships for higher education for Palestine refugees. The programme operated with technical assistance from the United

Nations Educational, Scientific and Cultural Organization (UNESCO).

In 1989, expenditures for the education programme amounted to $108.8 million: $32.8 million in Jordan; $30.7 million in the Gaza Strip; $17.5 million in the Syrian Arab Republic; $16.6 million in the West Bank; $8.8 million in Lebanon; and $2.4 million at UNRWA headquarters in Vienna.

As at 15 October, 357,706 pupils, some 6,570 more than the previous year, were enrolled in UNRWA schools, as follows: 133,808 in Jordan; 95,597, Gaza Strip; 55,546, Syrian Arab Republic; 39,456, West Bank; and 33,299, Lebanon. In addition, 115,300 refugee pupils attended government and private schools.

During the 1988/89 academic year, UNRWA provided places for 4,108 vocational trainees and 850 teacher trainees at eight centres.

Proposed University of Jerusalem "Al-Quds"

In August, the Secretary-General submitted a report,[15] as requested by the General Assembly in 1988,[16] on the establishment of a university for Palestine refugees in Jerusalem. The proposed "Al-Quds" University, first considered by the Assembly in 1980,[17] had since been the subject of annual reports by the Secretary-General with regard to measures taken towards its establishment, including a functional feasibility study. The Secretary-General was assisted by the Rector of the United Nations University, who provided a highly qualified expert.

On 15 May 1989, the Secretary-General requested Israel to facilitate the expert's visit. On 6 July, Israel replied that its position remained unchanged; it had consistently voted against the resolution calling for the establishment of the University, whose sponsors, it said, sought to exploit higher education in order to politicize issues totally extraneous to genuine academic pursuits. Therefore, Israel was unable to assist in taking the matter further.

The Secretary-General reported that, in view of Israel's position, the feasibility study could not be completed as planned.

GENERAL ASSEMBLY ACTION

On 8 December, on the recommendation of the Special Political Committee, the General Assembly adopted **resolution 44/47 J** by recorded vote.

**University of Jerusalem "Al-Quds"
for Palestine refugees**

The General Assembly,

Recalling its resolutions 36/146 G of 16 December 1981, 37/120 C of 16 December 1982, 38/83 K of 15 December 1983, 39/99 K of 14 December 1984, 40/165 D and K of 16 December 1985, 41/69 K of 3 December 1986,

42/69 K of 2 December 1987 and 43/57 J of 6 December 1988,

Having considered the report of the Secretary-General,

Having also considered the report of the Commissioner-General of the United Nations Relief and Works Agency for Palestine Refugees in the Near East, covering the period from 1 July 1988 to 30 June 1989,

1. *Emphasizes* the need for strengthening the educational system in the Palestinian territory occupied by Israel since 5 June 1967, including Jerusalem, and specifically the need for the establishment of the proposed university;

2. *Requests* the Secretary-General to continue to take all necessary measures for establishing the University of Jerusalem ''Al-Quds'', in accordance with Assembly resolution 35/13 B of 3 November 1980, giving due consideration to the recommendations consistent with the provisions of that resolution;

3. *Calls once more upon* Israel, the occupying Power, to co-operate in the implementation of the present resolution and to remove the hindrances that it has put in the way of establishing the University of Jerusalem ''Al-Quds'';

4. *Requests* the Secretary-General to report to the General Assembly at its forty-fifth session on the progress made in the implementation of the present resolution.

General Assembly resolution 44/47 J

8 December 1989   Meeting 78   147-2-1 (recorded vote)

Approved by Special Political Committee (A/44/815) by recorded vote (130-2), 22 November (meeting 25); 16-nation draft (A/SPC/44/L.16); agenda item 76.

Sponsors: Afghanistan, Bangladesh, Brunei Darussalam, Burkina Faso, Comoros, Cuba, India, Indonesia, Jordan, Madagascar, Malaysia, Mali, Nicaragua, Pakistan, Yugoslavia, Zambia.

Meeting numbers. GA 44th session: SPC 5-8, 25; plenary 78.

Recorded vote in Assembly as follows:

In favour: Afghanistan, Albania, Algeria, Angola, Antigua and Barbuda, Argentina, Australia, Austria, Bahamas, Bahrain, Bangladesh, Barbados, Belgium, Benin, Bhutan, Bolivia, Botswana, Brazil, Brunei Darussalam, Bulgaria, Burkina Faso, Burundi, Byelorussian SSR, Cameroon, Canada, Cape Verde, Central African Republic, Chad, Chile, China, Colombia, Costa Rica, Côte d'Ivoire, Cuba, Cyprus, Czechoslovakia, Democratic Kampuchea, Democratic Yemen, Denmark, Djibouti, Dominican Republic, Ecuador, Egypt, Equatorial Guinea, Ethiopia, Fiji, Finland, France, German Democratic Republic, Germany, Federal Republic of, Ghana, Greece, Grenada, Guatemala, Guinea, Guinea-Bissau, Guyana, Haiti, Honduras, Hungary, Iceland, India, Indonesia, Iran, Iraq, Ireland, Italy, Jamaica, Japan, Jordan, Kenya, Kuwait, Lao People's Democratic Republic, Lebanon, Lesotho, Liberia, Libyan Arab Jamahiriya, Luxembourg, Madagascar, Malawi, Malaysia, Maldives, Mali, Malta, Mauritania, Mauritius, Mexico, Mongolia, Morocco, Mozambique, Myanmar, Nepal, Netherlands, New Zealand, Nicaragua, Nigeria, Norway, Oman, Pakistan, Panama, Papua New Guinea, Paraguay, Peru, Philippines, Poland, Portugal, Qatar, Romania, Rwanda, Saint Lucia, Saint Vincent and the Grenadines, Samoa, Sao Tome and Principe, Saudi Arabia, Senegal, Seychelles, Sierra Leone, Singapore, Solomon Islands, Somalia, Spain, Sri Lanka, Sudan, Suriname, Swaziland, Sweden, Syrian Arab Republic, Thailand, Togo, Trinidad and Tobago, Tunisia, Turkey, Uganda, Ukrainian SSR, USSR, United Arab Emirates, United Kingdom, United Republic of Tanzania, Uruguay, Vanuatu, Venezuela, Viet Nam, Yemen,' Yugoslavia, Zaire, Zambia, Zimbabwe.

Against: Israel, United States.

Abstaining: Dominica.

Scholarships

The Secretary-General reported in September[18] on responses to the General Assembly's 1988 appeal[19] for augmentation of special allocations for scholarships and grants to Palestine refugees, for which UNRWA acted as recipient and trustee.

The 1989 activities of responding States and institutions included 25 scholarships awarded by the Federal Republic of Germany to Palestine refugee graduates of UNRWA vocational training centres, and provision by Japan of 15 fellowships to UNRWA vocational training instructors. UNESCO, IMO, FAO, UPU and WHO provided fellowships and scholarships within their areas of competence.

GENERAL ASSEMBLY ACTION

On 8 December, on the recommendation of the Special Political Committee, the General Assembly adopted **resolution 44/47 D** by recorded vote.

Offers by Member States of grants and scholarships for higher education, including vocational training, for Palestine refugees

The General Assembly,

Recalling its resolution 212(III) of 19 November 1948 on assistance to Palestine refugees,

Recalling also its resolutions 35/13 B of 3 November 1980, 36/146 H of 16 December 1981, 37/120 D of 16 December 1982, 38/83 D of 15 December 1983, 39/99 D of 14 December 1984, 40/165 D of 16 December 1985, 41/69 D of 3 December 1986, 42/69 D of 2 December 1987 and 43/57 D of 6 December 1988,

Cognizant of the fact that the Palestine refugees have, for the last four decades, lost their homes, lands and means of livelihood,

Having considered the report of the Secretary-General,

Having also considered the report of the Commissioner-General of the United Nations Relief and Works Agency for Palestine Refugees in the Near East, covering the period from 1 July 1988 to 30 June 1989,

1. *Urges* all States to respond to the appeal contained in General Assembly resolution 32/90 F of 13 December 1977 and reiterated in subsequent relevant resolutions in a manner commensurate with the needs of Palestine refugees for higher education, including vocational training;

2. *Strongly appeals* to all States, specialized agencies and non-governmental organizations to augment the special allocations for grants and scholarships to Palestine refugees in addition to their contributions to the regular budget of the United Nations Relief and Works Agency for Palestine Refugees in the Near East;

3. *Expresses its appreciation* to all Governments, specialized agencies and non-governmental organizations that responded favourably to General Assembly resolutions 41/69 D, 42/69 D and 43/57 D;

4. *Invites* the relevant specialized agencies and other organizations of the United Nations system to continue, within their respective spheres of competence, to extend assistance for higher education to Palestine refugee students;

5. *Appeals* to all States, specialized agencies and the United Nations University to contribute generously to the Palestinian universities in the Palestinian territory occupied by Israel since 1967, including, in due course, the proposed University of Jerusalem ''Al-Quds'' for Palestine refugees;

6. *Also appeals* to all States, specialized agencies and other international bodies to contribute towards the establishment of vocational training centres for Palestine refugees;

7. *Requests* the Agency to act as the recipient and trustee for the special allocations for grants and scholarships and to award them to qualified Palestine refugee candidates;

8. *Requests* the Secretary-General to report to the General Assembly at its forty-fifth session on the implementation of the present resolution.

General Assembly resolution 44/47 D

8 December 1989   Meeting 78   141-0-1 (recorded vote)

Approved by Special Political Committee (A/44/815) by recorded vote (131-0-1), 22 November (meeting 25); 15-nation draft (A/SPC/44/L.10); agenda item 76.
Sponsors: Afghanistan, Bangladesh, Brunei Darussalam, Burkina Faso, Comoros, Cuba, Indonesia, Jordan, Madagascar, Malaysia, Mali, Nicaragua, Pakistan, Yugoslavia, Zambia.
Meeting numbers. GA 44th session: SPC 5-8, 25; plenary 78.

Recorded vote in Assembly as follows:

In favour: Afghanistan, Albania, Algeria, Angola, Antigua and Barbuda, Argentina, Australia, Austria, Bahamas, Bahrain, Bangladesh, Barbados, Belgium, Benin, Bhutan, Bolivia, Botswana, Brazil, Brunei Darussalam, Bulgaria, Burkina Faso, Burundi, Byelorussian SSR, Cameroon, Canada, Cape Verde, Central African Republic, Chad, Chile, China, Colombia, Costa Rica, Côte d'Ivoire, Cuba, Cyprus, Czechoslovakia, Democratic Kampuchea, Democratic Yemen, Denmark, Dominica,* Dominican Republic, Ecuador, Egypt, Equatorial Guinea, Ethiopia, Fiji, Finland, France, German Democratic Republic, Germany, Federal Republic of, Ghana, Greece, Grenada, Guinea, Guinea-Bissau, Guyana, Haiti, Honduras, Hungary, Iceland, India, Indonesia, Iran, Iraq, Ireland, Italy, Jamaica, Japan, Jordan, Kenya, Kuwait, Lao People's Democratic Republic, Lebanon, Lesotho, Liberia, Libyan Arab Jamahiriya, Luxembourg, Madagascar, Malawi, Malaysia, Maldives, Mali, Malta, Mauritania, Mauritius, Mexico, Mongolia, Morocco, Mozambique, Myanmar, Nepal, Netherlands, New Zealand, Nigeria, Norway, Oman, Pakistan, Panama, Papua New Guinea, Paraguay, Peru, Philippines, Poland, Portugal, Qatar, Romania, Rwanda, Saint Lucia, Samoa, Sao Tome and Principe, Saudi Arabia, Senegal, Seychelles, Sierra Leone, Singapore, Solomon Islands, Somalia, Spain, Sri Lanka, Suriname, Sweden, Syrian Arab Republic, Thailand, Togo, Trinidad and Tobago, Tunisia, Turkey, Ukrainian SSR, USSR, United Arab Emirates, United Kingdom, United States, Uruguay, Vanuatu, Venezuela, Viet Nam, Yemen, Yugoslavia, Zaire, Zambia, Zimbabwe.

Against: None.

Abstaining: Israel.

*Later advised the Secretariat it had intended to abstain.

Property rights

Report of Secretary-General. In August, the Secretary-General reported[20] on responses to his request for information on steps taken to implement the 1988 General Assembly resolution[21] concerning revenues derived from Palestine refugee properties.

In its 28 June reply, Israel reiterated its position, as set out previously in statements to the Special Political Committee and in a 1988 report of the Secretary-General,[22] that there was no legal basis for taking the steps proposed, as property rights within the borders of a sovereign State were subjected exclusively to the domestic laws of that State. The right of States to regulate and dispose of property within their territory and the income derived from that property was a generally accepted principle, Israel stated. Significantly, the resolution's sponsors had made no suggestion regarding confiscated property in Arab countries of some 800,000 Jewish refugees as a result of the 1948 war, estimated to be worth billions of dollars. Israel stressed that there could be no difference in law, justice or equity between the claims of Arab and of Jewish property owners.

No reply had been received from any other Member State regarding implementation of the resolution, the Secretary-General reported.

Report of Conciliation Commission. The United Nations Conciliation Commission for Palestine, in its report[23] covering the period from 1 September 1988 to 31 August 1989, stated that events that had occurred in the area since the preceding reporting period had further complicated an already very complex situation. As far as the Commission was concerned, the circumstances that had limited its possibilities of action remained essentially unchanged. Nevertheless, it continued to hope that the situation would improve towards the achievement of a comprehensive, just and lasting peace in the Middle East, thus enabling it to carry forward its work in accordance with its mandate as defined by the Assembly in 1948.[24]

GENERAL ASSEMBLY ACTION

On 8 December, on the recommendation of the Special Political Committee, the General Assembly adopted **resolution 44/47 H** by recorded vote.

Revenues derived from Palestine refugee properties
The General Assembly,

Recalling its resolutions 35/13 A to F of 3 November 1980, 36/146 C of 16 December 1981, 37/120 H of 16 December 1982, 38/83 H of 15 December 1983, 39/99 H of 14 December 1984, 40/165 H of 16 December 1985, 41/69 H of 3 December 1986, 42/69 H of 2 December 1987, 43/57 H of 6 December 1988 and all its previous resolutions on the question, including resolution 194(III) of 11 December 1948,

Taking note of the report of the Secretary-General,

Taking note also of the report of the United Nations Conciliation Commission for Palestine, covering the period from 1 September 1988 to 31 August 1989,

Recalling that the Universal Declaration of Human Rights and the principles of international law uphold the principle that no one shall be arbitrarily deprived of his or her private property,

Considering that the Palestine Arab refugees are entitled to their property and to the income derived therefrom, in conformity with the principles of justice and equity,

Recalling in particular its resolution 394(V) of 14 December 1950, in which it directed the United Nations Conciliation Commission for Palestine, in consultation with the parties concerned, to prescribe measures for the protection of the rights, property and interests of the Palestine Arab refugees,

Taking note of the completion of the programme of identification and evaluation of Arab property, as announced by the United Nations Conciliation Commission for Palestine in its twenty-second progress report, and of the fact that the Land Office had a schedule of Arab owners and file of documents defining the location, area and other particulars of Arab property,

1. *Requests* the Secretary-General to take all appropriate steps, in consultation with the United Nations Conciliation Commission for Palestine, for the protection

and administration of Arab property, assets and property rights in Israel and to establish a fund for the receipt of income derived therefrom, on behalf of the rightful owners;

2. *Calls once more upon* Israel to render all facilities and assistance to the Secretary-General in the implementation of the present resolution;

3. *Calls upon* the Governments of all the other Member States concerned to provide the Secretary-General with any pertinent information in their possession concerning Arab property, assets and property rights in Israel which would assist the Secretary-General in the implementation of the present resolution;

4. *Deplores* Israel's refusal to co-operate with the Secretary-General in the implementation of the resolutions on the question;

5. *Requests* the Secretary-General to report to the General Assembly at its forty-fifth session on the implementation of the present resolution.

General Assembly resolution 44/47 H

8 December 1989   Meeting 78   125-2-21 (recorded vote)

Approved by Special Political Committee (A/44/815) by recorded vote (107-2-23), 22 November (meeting 25); 15-nation draft (A/SPC/44/L.14); agenda item 76.
Sponsors: Afghanistan, Bangladesh, Brunei Darussalam, Burkina Faso, Comoros, Cuba, India, Indonesia, Madagascar, Malaysia, Mali, Nicaragua, Pakistan, Yugoslavia, Zambia.
Meeting numbers. GA 44th session: SPC 5-8, 25; plenary 78.

Recorded vote in Assembly as follows:

In favour: Afghanistan, Albania, Algeria, Angola, Antigua and Barbuda, Argentina, Bahamas, Bahrain, Bangladesh, Barbados, Benin, Bhutan, Bolivia, Botswana, Brazil, Brunei Darussalam, Bulgaria, Burkina Faso, Burundi, Byelorussian SSR, Cameroon, Cape Verde, Central African Republic, Chad, Chile, China, Colombia, Costa Rica, Côte d'Ivoire, Cuba, Cyprus, Czechoslovakia, Democratic Kampuchea, Democratic Yemen, Djibouti, Dominican Republic, Ecuador, Egypt, Equatorial Guinea, Ethiopia, Fiji, German Democratic Republic, Ghana, Greece, Grenada, Guatemala, Guinea, Guinea-Bissau, Guyana, Haiti, Honduras, Hungary, India, Indonesia, Iran, Iraq, Jamaica, Jordan, Kenya, Kuwait, Lao People's Democratic Republic, Lebanon, Lesotho, Libyan Arab Jamahiriya, Madagascar, Malawi, Malaysia, Maldives, Mali, Malta, Mauritania, Mauritius, Mexico, Mongolia, Morocco, Mozambique, Myanmar, Nepal, Nicaragua, Nigeria, Oman, Pakistan, Panama, Papua New Guinea, Paraguay, Peru, Philippines, Poland, Qatar, Romania, Rwanda, Saint Lucia, Saint Vincent and the Grenadines, Samoa, Sao Tome and Principe, Saudi Arabia, Senegal, Seychelles, Sierra Leone, Singapore, Solomon Islands, Somalia, Spain, Sri Lanka, Suriname, Syrian Arab Republic, Thailand, Togo, Trinidad and Tobago, Tunisia, Turkey, Uganda, Ukrainian SSR, USSR, United Arab Emirates, United Republic of Tanzania, Uruguay, Vanuatu, Venezuela, Viet Nam, Yemen, Yugoslavia, Zaire, Zambia, Zimbabwe.

Against: Israel, United States.

Abstaining: Australia, Austria, Belgium, Canada, Denmark, Dominica, Finland, France, Germany, Federal Republic of, Iceland, Ireland, Italy, Japan, Liberia, Luxembourg, Netherlands, New Zealand, Norway, Portugal, Sweden, United Kingdom.

Refugee protection

The Secretary-General reported[25] in September on implementation of a 1988 Assembly resolution[26] holding Israel responsible for the security of the Palestine refugees in the occupied territories and calling on it to compensate UNRWA for the damage to its property and facilities resulting from Israel's 1982 invasion of Lebanon.

The report reproduced Israel's reply of 28 June 1989 to the Secretary-General's request for information on any steps taken or envisaged to comply with the resolution. Israel stated it had fully set forth its position on the subject in statements to the Special Political Committee and in a 1988

report of the Secretary-General.[27] The adoption of the resolution, Israel maintained, was hypocritical, anachronistic and out of place. Despite its withdrawal from Lebanon in 1985, Israel was still being blamed for the ''suffering'' of Palestinians in Lebanon and, not surprisingly, for Arab persecution of Palestinian refugees. In recent years, thousands of Palestinians had been killed and wounded in Lebanese refugee camps in vicious fighting totally unconnected with Israel; likewise, Palestinian refugee camps in Jordan and the Syrian Arab Republic were the scene of considerable human misery. The selective and distorted presentation of the Palestinian refugees' situation in Arab countries, Israel said, clearly illustrated the resolution's double standards and its disregard for the refugees' general welfare. Israel emphasized that, in keeping with international law, it alone was competent to ensure full protection to all the inhabitants of Judea, Samara and the Gaza District.

The Secretary-General cited the UNRWA Commissioner-General's report for the period 1 July 1988 to 30 June 1989,[2] stating that efforts had continued to ensure that everything feasible was being done to contribute to the refugees' safety and security. There had been no progress on UNRWA's claim against the Government of Israel regarding damage to its property and facilities resulting from the 1982 invasion of Lebanon.

GENERAL ASSEMBLY ACTION

On 8 December, on the recommendation of the Special Political Committee, the General Assembly adopted **resolution 44/47 I** by recorded vote.

Protection of Palestine refugees

The General Assembly,

Recalling Security Council resolutions 508(1982) of 5 June 1982, 509(1982) of 6 June 1982, 520(1982) of 17 September 1982 and 523(1982) of 18 October 1982,

Also recalling, in particular, recent Security Council resolutions 605(1987) of 22 December 1987, 607(1988) of 5 January 1988, 608(1988) of 14 January 1988, 636(1989) of 6 July 1989 and 641(1989) of 30 August 1989,

Further recalling its resolutions ES-7/5 of 26 June 1982, ES-7/6 and ES-7/8 of 19 August 1982, ES-7/9 of 24 September 1982, 37/120 J of 16 December 1982, 38/83 I of 15 December 1983, 39/99 I of 14 December 1984, 40/165 I of 16 December 1985, 41/69 I of 3 December 1986, 42/69 I of 2 December 1987, 43/21 of 3 November 1988 and 43/57 I of 6 December 1988,

Taking note of the report of the Secretary-General of 21 January 1988, submitted in accordance with Security Council resolution 605(1987),

Having considered the report of the Secretary-General,

Having also considered the report of the Commissioner-General of the United Nations Relief and Works Agency for Palestine Refugees in the Near East, covering the period from 1 July 1988 to 30 June 1989,

Gravely concerned and alarmed by the deteriorating situation in the Palestinian territory occupied by Israel since 1967, including Jerusalem,

Taking into account the need to consider measures for the impartial protection of the Palestinian civilian population under Israeli occupation,

Referring to the humanitarian principles of the Geneva Convention relative to the Protection of Civilian Persons in Time of War, of 12 August 1949, and to the obligations arising from the regulations annexed to the Hague Convention IV of 1907,

Deeply concerned at the marked deterioration in the security situation experienced by the Palestine refugees as stated by the Commissioner-General in his report,

Deeply distressed at the suffering of the Palestinian and Lebanese population which has resulted from continuing Israeli acts of aggression against Lebanon and other hostile acts,

Deeply distressed also at the continuing tragic, difficult and uncertain situation of the civilian population in and around the Palestinian refugee camps in Lebanon,

Reaffirming its support for the sovereignty, unity and territorial integrity of Lebanon, within its internationally recognized boundaries,

1. *Holds* Israel responsible for the security of the Palestine refugees in the occupied Palestinian territory, including Jerusalem, and other Arab territories occupied by Israel since 1967, and calls upon it to fulfil its obligations as the occupying Power in this regard, in accordance with the pertinent provisions of the Geneva Convention relative to the Protection of Civilian Persons in Time of War, of 12 August 1949;

2. *Calls upon* all the High Contracting Parties to the Convention to take appropriate measures to ensure respect by Israel, the occupying Power, for the Convention in all circumstances in conformity with their obligation under article 1 thereof;

3. *Urges* the Security Council to consider the current situation in the occupied Palestinian territory, taking into account the recommendations contained in the report of the Secretary-General;

4. *Urges* the Secretary-General, in consultation with the Commissioner-General of the United Nations Relief and Works Agency for Palestine Refugees in the Near East, to continue his efforts in support of the upholding of the safety and security and the legal and human rights of the Palestine refugees in all the territories under Israeli occupation in 1967 and thereafter;

5. *Calls once again upon* Israel, the occupying Power, to release forthwith all arbitrarily detained Palestine refugees, including the employees of the United Nations Relief and Works Agency for Palestine Refugees in the Near East;

6. *Welcomes* the provision by the Commissioner-General, in consultation with the Government of Lebanon, to provide housing to the Palestine refugees whose houses were demolished or razed;

7. *Calls once again upon* Israel to compensate the Agency for the damage to its property and facilities resulting from the Israeli invasion of Lebanon, without prejudice to Israel's responsibility for all damages resulting from that invasion;

8. *Requests* the Secretary-General, in consultation with the Commissioner-General, to report to the General Assembly, before the opening of its forty-fifth session, on the implementation of the present resolution.

General Assembly resolution 44/47 I

8 December 1989   Meeting 78   146-2-1 (recorded vote)

Approved by Special Political Committee (A/44/815) by recorded vote (130-2), 22 November (meeting 25); 14-nation draft (A/SPC/44/L.15 & Corr.1), orally revised; agenda item 76.
Sponsors: Afghanistan, Bangladesh, Brunei Darussalam, Burkina Faso, Comoros, Cuba, Indonesia, Madagascar, Malaysia, Mali, Nicaragua, Pakistan, Yugoslavia, Zambia.
Meeting numbers. GA 44th session: SPC 5-8, 25; plenary 78.

Recorded vote in Assembly as follows:

In favour: Afghanistan, Albania, Algeria, Angola, Antigua and Barbuda, Argentina, Australia, Austria, Bahamas, Bahrain, Bangladesh, Barbados, Belgium, Benin, Bhutan, Bolivia, Botswana, Brazil, Brunei Darussalam, Bulgaria, Burkina Faso, Burundi, Byelorussian SSR, Cameroon, Canada, Cape Verde, Central African Republic, Chad, Chile, China, Colombia, Costa Rica, Côte d'Ivoire, Cuba, Cyprus, Czechoslovakia, Democratic Kampuchea, Democratic Yemen, Denmark, Djibouti, Dominican Republic, Ecuador, Egypt, Equatorial Guinea, Ethiopia, Fiji, Finland, France, German Democratic Republic, Germany, Federal Republic of, Ghana, Greece, Grenada, Guatemala, Guinea, Guinea-Bissau, Guyana, Haiti, Honduras, Hungary, Iceland, India, Indonesia, Iran, Iraq, Ireland, Italy, Jamaica, Japan, Jordan, Kenya, Kuwait, Lao People's Democratic Republic, Lebanon, Lesotho, Liberia, Libyan Arab Jamahiriya, Luxembourg, Madagascar, Malawi, Malaysia, Maldives, Mali, Malta, Mauritania, Mauritius, Mexico, Mongolia, Morocco, Mozambique, Myanmar, Nepal, Netherlands, New Zealand, Nicaragua, Nigeria, Norway, Oman, Pakistan, Panama, Papua New Guinea, Paraguay, Peru, Philippines, Poland, Portugal, Qatar, Romania, Rwanda, Saint Lucia, Saint Vincent and the Grenadines, Samoa, Sao Tome and Principe, Saudi Arabia, Senegal, Seychelles, Sierra Leone, Singapore, Solomon Islands, Somalia, Spain, Sri Lanka, Sudan, Suriname, Sweden, Syrian Arab Republic, Thailand, Togo, Trinidad and Tobago, Tunisia, Turkey, Uganda, Ukrainian SSR, USSR, United Arab Emirates, United Kingdom, United Republic of Tanzania, Uruguay, Vanuatu, Venezuela, Viet Nam, Yemen, Yugoslavia, Zaire, Zambia, Zimbabwe.
Against: Israel, United States.
Abstaining: Dominica.

Removal and resettlement of refugees

The Secretary-General reported[28] in October that, in response to his request for information on steps taken to implement a 1988 General Assembly resolution[29] calling on Israel to refrain from resettling Palestine refugees in the occupied territories and from destroying their shelters, Israel replied on 28 June 1989 that its position had been set out in annual statements to the Special Political Committee and in a 1988 report of the Secretary-General.[30] It called the resolution unbalanced and distorted, intentionally ignoring improved living conditions in the Gaza District since 1967. There had been, Israel said, a considerable increase of pupils attending school, a significant drop in illiteracy, extensive development of medical care, and improvement of environmental services, including water supply, sewerage and refuse disposal. Community development projects initiated by Israel had enabled 15,000 families—about 120,000 persons—to leave the refugee camps voluntarily and relocate to nearby residential areas. Israel was determined to pursue the humanitarian task of improving refugee living conditions and welcomed all international assistance to that end.

The Secretary-General, basing his comments on reports from the Commissioner-General, said that in the Gaza Strip, as well as the West Bank, refugee shelters had been demolished and sealed on punitive grounds by the Israeli authorities. With regard to families affected by demolitions as far back as 1971, including those categorized as living in hardship conditions, repeated assurances had been made that they would be housed. The Israeli authorities had assured UNRWA that a solution had been developed and would be implemented as soon as possible.

UNRWA objected also to the Israeli practice of requiring refugee families to demolish their shelters as a pre-condition for moving to new housing, because of practical complications in the case of extended families who shared the same shelter where only one family wished to move, and because of overcrowded conditions and an urgent need for accommodation for refugee families.

The Secretary-General regretted not being able to comply with the Assembly's request[29] to resume issuing identification cards to all Palestine refugees and their descendants in the occupied Palestinian territory, irrespective of whether or not they were recipients of Agency rations and services. For almost 40 years, all registered refugee families had had Agency registration cards, but they were not identification cards as such. The Commissioner-General did not have the means to issue such cards. He would review the situation regarding possible appropriate documentation for individual family members.

According to available information, Israeli authorities had to date allocated approximately 3,914 plots of land in the Gaza Strip for housing projects. A total of 2,605 plots had been built on by 3,714 refugee families, comprising 22,946 persons. Buildings on 236 plots were under construction, 936 plots were vacant and 137 had been built on by non-refugee families. In addition, 3,034 families, consisting of 18,823 persons, had moved into 2,666 completed housing units, consisting of 5,893 rooms.

GENERAL ASSEMBLY ACTION

On 8 December, on the recommendation of the Special Political Committee, the General Assembly adopted **resolution 44/47 E** by recorded vote.

Palestine refugees in the Palestinian territory occupied by Israel since 1967

The General Assembly,

Recalling Security Council resolution 237(1967) of 14 June 1967,

Recalling also its resolutions 2792 C (XXVI) of 6 December 1971, 2963 C (XXVII) of 13 December 1972, 3089 C (XXVIII) of 7 December 1973, 3331 D (XXIX) of 17 December 1974, 3419 C (XXX) of 8 December 1975, 31/15 E of 23 November 1976, 32/90 C of 13 December 1977, 33/112 E of 18 December 1978, 34/52 F of 23 November 1979, 35/13 F of 3 November 1980, 36/146 A of 16 December 1981, 37/120 E and I of 16 December 1982, 38/83 E and J of 15 December 1983, 39/99 E and J of 14 December 1984, 40/165 E and J of 16 December 1985, 41/69 E and J of 3 December 1986,

42/69 E and J of 2 December 1987 and 43/57 E of 6 December 1988,

Having considered the report of the Commissioner-General of the United Nations Relief and Works Agency for Palestine Refugees in the Near East, covering the period from 1 July 1988 to 30 June 1989 and the report of the Secretary-General,

Recalling the provisions of paragraph 11 of its resolution 194(III) of 11 December 1948, and considering that measures to resettle Palestine refugees in the Palestinian territory occupied by Israel since 1967 away from their homes and property from which they were displaced constitute a violation of their inalienable right of return,

Alarmed by the reports received from the Commissioner-General that the Israeli occupying authorities, in contravention of Israel's obligation under international law, persist in their policy of demolishing shelters occupied by refugee families,

1. *Strongly reiterates its demand* that Israel desist from the removal and resettlement of Palestine refugees in the Palestinian territory occupied by Israel since 1967 and from the destruction of their shelters;

2. *Requests* the Commissioner-General of the United Nations Relief and Works Agency for Palestine Refugees in the Near East to address the acute situation of the Palestine refugees in the Palestinian territory occupied by Israel since 1967 and accordingly to extend all the services of the Agency to those refugees;

3. *Requests* the Secretary-General, in co-operation with the Commissioner-General, to resume issuing identification cards to all Palestine refugees and their descendants in the occupied Palestinian territory, irrespective of whether or not they are recipients of rations and services of the Agency;

4. *Requests* the Secretary-General, after consulting with the Commissioner-General, to report to the General Assembly, before the opening of its forty-fifth session, on the implementation of the present resolution and in particular on Israel's compliance with paragraph 1 above.

General Assembly resolution 44/47 E

8 December 1989   Meeting 78   140-2-1 (recorded vote)

Approved by Special Political Committee (A/44/815) by recorded vote (130-2), 22 November (meeting 25); 15-nation draft (A/SPC/44/L.11); agenda item 76.

Sponsors: Afghanistan, Bangladesh, Brunei Darussalam, Burkina Faso, Comoros, Cuba, India, Indonesia, Madagascar, Malaysia, Mali, Nicaragua, Pakistan, Yugoslavia, Zambia.

Meeting numbers. GA 44th session: SPC 5-8, 25; plenary 78.

Recorded vote in Assembly as follows:

In favour: Afghanistan, Albania, Algeria, Angola, Antigua and Barbuda, Argentina, Australia, Austria, Bahamas, Bahrain, Bangladesh, Barbados, Belgium, Benin, Bhutan, Bolivia, Botswana, Brazil, Brunei Darussalam, Bulgaria, Burkina Faso, Burundi, Byelorussian SSR, Cameroon, Canada, Cape Verde, Central African Republic, Chad, Chile, China, Colombia, Costa Rica, Côte d'Ivoire, Cuba, Cyprus, Czechoslovakia, Democratic Kampuchea, Democratic Yemen, Denmark, Dominican Republic, Ecuador, Egypt, Equatorial Guinea, Ethiopia, Fiji, Finland, France, German Democratic Republic, Germany, Federal Republic of, Ghana, Greece, Grenada, Guinea, Guinea-Bissau, Guyana, Haiti, Honduras, Hungary, Iceland, India, Indonesia, Iran, Iraq, Ireland, Italy, Jamaica, Japan, Jordan, Kenya, Kuwait, Lao People's Democratic Republic, Lebanon, Lesotho, Liberia, Libyan Arab Jamahiriya, Luxembourg, Madagascar, Malawi, Malaysia, Maldives, Mali, Malta, Mauritania, Mauritius, Mexico, Mongolia, Morocco, Mozambique, Myanmar, Nepal, Netherlands, New Zealand, Nigeria, Norway, Oman, Pakistan, Panama, Papua New Guinea, Paraguay, Peru, Philippines, Poland, Portugal, Qatar, Romania, Rwanda, Saint Lucia, Saint Vincent and the Grenadines, Samoa, Sao Tome and Principe, Saudi Arabia, Senegal, Seychelles, Sierra Leone, Singapore, Solomon Islands, Somalia, Spain, Sri

Lanka, Suriname, Sweden, Syrian Arab Republic, Thailand, Togo, Trinidad and Tobago, Tunisia, Turkey, Ukrainian SSR, USSR, United Arab Emirates, United Kingdom, Uruguay, Vanuatu, Venezuela, Viet Nam, Yemen, Yugoslavia, Zaire, Zambia, Zimbabwe.

Against: Israel, United States.

Abstaining: Dominica.

REFERENCES

[1]YUN 1948-49, p 211, GA res. 302(IV), 8 Dec. 1949. [2]A/44/13 & Corr.1 & Add.1. [3]A/45/13 & Add.1. [4]A/45/5/Add.3. [5]YUN 1988, p. 255. [6]A/44/641. [7]YUN 1946-47, p. 100, GA res. 22 A (I), annex, 13 Feb. 1946. [8]YUN 1986, p. 342. [9]YUN 1988, p. 257. [10]A/44/507. [11]YUN 1988, p. 258, GA res. 43/57 G, 6 Dec. 1988. [12]*Ibid.*, p. 258. [13]A/44/506. [14]YUN 1988, p. 259, GA res. 43/57 F, 6 Dec. 1988. [15]A/44/474. [16]YUN 1988, p. 260, GA res. 43/57 J, 6 Dec. 1988. [17]YUN 1980, p. 443, GA res. 35/13 B, 3 Nov. 1980. [18]A/44/505. [19]YUN 1988, p. 261, GA res. 43/57 D, 6 Dec. 1988. [20]A/44/431. [21]YUN 1988, p. 262, GA res. 43/57 H, 6 Dec. 1988. [22]*Ibid.*, p. 261. [23]A/44/497. [24]YUN 1948-49, p. 174, GA res. 194(III), 11 Dec. 1948. [25]A/44/508. [26]YUN 1988, p. 263, GA res. 43/57 I, 6 Dec. 1988. [27]*Ibid.*, p. 263. [28]A/44/608. [29]YUN 1988, p. 265, GA res. 43/57 E, 6 Dec. 1988. [30]*Ibid.*, p. 265.

Chapter V

Regional economic and social activities

The five United Nations regional commissions continued to promote economic and social development in their respective regions during 1989. Four commissions held their regular sessions in March and April—the Economic and Social Commission for Asia and the Pacific (ESCAP), the Economic Commission for Europe (ECE), the Economic Commission for Africa (ECA) and the Economic and Social Commission for Western Asia (ESCWA). The Economic Commission for Latin America and the Caribbean (ECLAC) did not meet in a regular session, but its Committees of the Whole and of High-Level Government Experts held biennial meetings in March.

In December, the General Assembly proclaimed 1991-2000 as the Second Industrial Development Decade for Africa, and invited international financial and development bodies to consider the African Alternative Framework to Structural Adjustment Programmes for Socio-Economic Recovery and Transformation, which had been adopted by ECA as a basis for dialogue and consultation. The Economic and Social Council adopted resolutions on the African Institute for Economic Development and Planning, interregional co-operation for facilitation of international trade, and the Europe-Africa permanent link through the Strait of Gibraltar. The General Assembly adopted texts on co-operation between the United Nations and the Latin American Economic System and between the United Nations and the Southern African Development Co-ordination Conference. ESCAP worked on a strategy for regional social development towards the year 2000 and beyond. ECE addressed ongoing economic reforms in centrally planned economy nations, and adopted a Charter on Ground-Water Management. ESCWA and ECLAC sought ways to contribute to the Fourth United Nations Development Decade, and continued work to improve regional economic performance.

Regional co-operation

The Executive Secretaries of the five regional commissions, under the chairmanship of the Director-General for Development and International Economic Co-operation, met twice in 1989 (New York, 18 January; Santiago, Chile, 27 and 28 April). In April, they reviewed activities in mutual priority areas, including debt, human resource development, the role of the commissions in reconstruction and development of war-ravaged countries, and economic reforms in centrally planned economies. Also discussed were preparations for a General Assembly special session on international economic co-operation, especially revitalization of economic growth and development in developing countries, and the new International Development Strategy for the fourth United Nations Development Decade (see PART THREE, Chapter I). The importance of the commissions' participation in those preparatory processes was stressed.

The Executive Secretaries reviewed progress in improving links between the commissions and the Economic and Social Council, and reaffirmed the role and potential of the regional commissions in UN operational activities.

In June, the Secretary-General reported on regional co-operation,[1] describing commission progress achieved in promoting interregional economic and technical co-operation among developing countries, and reviewing their co-operation in international trade facilitation (see below) as well as progress in promoting interregional economic and technical co-operation among developing countries.

On 28 July, the Economic and Social Council noted the Secretary-General's report (**decision 1989/191**) and documents on international economic and social policy (**decision 1989/182**), including the summaries of: the survey of economic and social conditions in Africa, 1987-1988;[2] the economic and social survey of Asia and the Pacific, 1988;[3] the economic survey of Europe in 1988-1989;[4] the economic survey of Latin America and the Caribbean, 1988;[5] the survey of economic and social developments in the Economic and Social Council for Western Asia (ESCWA) region during the Third United Nations Development Decade.[6]

On 22 December, the General Assembly, by **resolution 44/226**, requested regional commissions to contribute to preventing illegal traffic in toxic and dangerous products and wastes by continuous monitoring and regional assessments of such traffic and its environmental and health implications, through interaction among themselves and in co-operation with UNEP and other relevant UN bodies (see also PART THREE, Chapter VIII).

Trade facilitation

On 10 February, the Economic and Social Council, acting on joint recommendations made by the commission Executive Secretaries pursuant to a 1982 decision,[7] decided to consider in 1989 interregional co-operation in international trade facilitation (**decision 1989/101**).

In April, the Executive Secretaries formulated proposals for co-operation between the commissions to establish a trade facilitation network and trade facilitation activities in the regions and promote the UN Rules for Electronic Data Interchange for Administration, Commerce and Transport (UN/EDIFACT), being developed by ECE (see below).

ECONOMIC AND SOCIAL COUNCIL ACTION

On 28 July, the Economic and Social Council, on the recommendation of its First (Economic) Committee, adopted **resolution 1989/118** without vote.

Interregional co-operation for facilitation of international trade

The Economic and Social Council,

Recalling its decision 1982/174 of 30 July 1982, in which it requested the executive secretaries of the regional commissions to submit recommendations concerning a subject for interregional co-operation of common interest to all regions, and noting ongoing activities undertaken by the regional commissions within this framework,

Taking note of the report of the Secretary-General on regional co-operation, in particular section IV thereof,

Conscious of the global importance of trade facilitation and of the work carried out by the regional commissions to reduce, simplify and harmonize formalities, procedures and documentation for the development of international trade, and of the technical co-operation activities carried out by the United Nations Conference on Trade and Development to promote and implement such measures pursuant to the decision adopted by the Economic and Social Council on 31 July 1969,

Noting that the Rules for Electronic Data Interchange for Administration, Commerce and Transport (EDIFACT) being developed and maintained within the Economic Commission for Europe allow for the progressive replacement of trade documents by electronic messages,

Recalling, in the light of Economic Commission for Europe decision L(44) of 21 April 1989, that consideration should be given to augmenting the existing facilities in the Commission for the development and the maintenance of EDIFACT, given the central importance of these facilities for the use of EDIFACT by all countries concerned,

Recognizing that the introduction of trade facilitation measures leading to simpler, faster and more economical documentary procedures might require the modification of trade-related practices,

Noting that the introduction of electronic data interchange is contingent upon the availability of appropriate data-processing equipment and telecommunications facilities, as well as relevant business management techniques, which have still to be established in many countries, particularly developing countries,

1. *Invites* the regional commissions to formulate, jointly with the United Nations Conference on Trade and Development, within existing resources, a draft proposal for interregional co-operation based on projects detailing technical and resource requirements, duly taking into account the national laws and regulations and the needs and concerns of the various regions, especially those of the developing countries, in the area of trade facilitation, and in particular the phased application of EDIFACT, wherever appropriate, and to submit the draft proposal for approval to the Council at its second regular session of 1990;

2. *Requests* the regional commissions to consult with funding organizations, notably the United Nations Development Programme, concerning the financial resources available for possible execution of the draft proposal after approval by the Council at its second regular session of 1990;

3. *Recommends* to the Executive Secretary of the Economic Commission for Europe that, in examining closely the resources required for maintenance and development activity now under way, consideration be given to the issue of what resources, from within existing resources of the Commission, might be made available to support this activity.

Economic and Social Council resolution 1989/118

28 July 1989   Meeting 37   Adopted without vote

Approved by First Committee (E/1989/142) without vote, 20 July (meeting 24); 16-nation draft (E/1989/C.1/L.7), based on recommendation in report of Secretary-General (E/1989/96) and orally revised; agenda item 6.

REFERENCES

[1]E/1989/96. [2]E/1989/68. [3]E/1989/55. [4]E/1989/61. [5]E/1989/59. [6]E/1989/67. [7]YUN 1982, p. 797, ESC dec. 1982/174, 30 July 1982.

Africa

The Economic Commission for Africa (ECA) held its twenty-fourth session (fifteenth meeting of the Conference of Ministers) at Addis Ababa, Ethiopia, from 6 to 10 April.[1]

Major agenda items dealt with the search for an African Alternative to Structural Adjustment Programmes; review and appraisal of progress made in the implementation of the UN Programme of Action for African Economic Recovery and Development 1986-1990 (UNPAAERD)[2] and Africa's Priority Programme for Economic Recovery, 1986-1990 (APPER), as well as the report and recommendations of the tenth meeting of the Technical Preparatory Committee of the Whole[3] (Addis Ababa, 27 March–3 April), which dealt with a whole range of specific issues, from food, agriculture, environment, industrial development, transport and communications to social development, population and operational activities.

The Conference of Ministers of the Commission adopted resolutions covering the UN Trust Fund for African Development, prevention of crime, the current African economic situation, meteorology and development, information systems for development, the fight against locusts, industrial development, creation of an African Economic Association, establishment of the African Monetary Fund, integration of women in development, popular participation in Africa's recovery, resource mobilization for operational activities, and programme questions.

Six resolutions were proposed for adoption by the Economic and Social Council. They dealt with: proclamation of a second Industrial Development Decade for Africa; strengthening of Multinational Programming and Operations Centres (MULPOCs); measures for strengthening ECA's special programme for least developed, land-locked and island countries; the African Institute for Economic Development and Planning; a proposed programme of work and priorities for the biennium 1990-1991; and the African Alternative Framework for Structural Adjustment Programmes for Socio-economic Recovery and Transformation. (See below, under specific headings.)

ECA subsidiary bodies meeting in 1989 included the Joint Intergovernmental Regional Committee on Human Settlements and Environment (Addis Ababa, 13-17 February); the Conference of African Ministers of Finance on the African Framework for Structural Adjustment Programmes (Blantyre, Malawi, 6-8 March), which adopted the Blantyre Statement on the Alternative Framework for Structural Adjustment Programmes; the Intergovernmental Committee of Experts of African Least Developed Countries (Addis Ababa, 22-25 March); the Conference of Ministers of African Least Developed Countries (Addis Ababa, 4-5 April), which adopted a declaration to the second United Nations Conference on Least Developed Countries for acceleration of the development process; the Conference of African Ministers of Industry (Harare, Zimbabwe, 29-31 May); the Conference of African Ministers of Social Affairs (Arusha, United Republic of Tanzania, 27-28 October); the Intergovernmental Committee of Experts for Science and Technology Development (Addis Ababa, 6-9 November); the Conference of African Ministers of Transport, Communications and Planning (Tangier, Morocco, 15-16 November); the Conference of African Ministers of Trade (Addis Ababa, 17-18 November) and the Conference of African Ministers of Tourism (Addis Ababa, 20-25 November). These and other developments were reflected in the biennial report of the Executive Secretary for 1988-89.[4]

Economic and social trends

The ECA summary of the survey of economic and social conditions in Africa 1988-1989[5] indicated that after crises in the 1980s, including prolonged and widespread droughts, economic performance had improved modestly in 1988 and 1989. Nevertheless, the economic situation remained extremely fragile and highly susceptible to exogenous factors and domestic structural limitations. Structural rigidities, notably fragmentation, narrowness and backwardness of the production base and infrastructure, as well as continued external resource constraints, dampened recovery. Inadequate findings for policy reforms and escalating debt service obligations negatively affected the region's development efforts. Coffee and cocoa prices fell to a 14-year low, with devastating effects on the economies of a number of countries, notably Cameroon, the Central African Republic, Côte d'Ivoire, Kenya, Rwanda and Uganda.

The gross domestic product (GDP) at factor cost grew by 2.9 per cent, up from 2.4 per cent in 1988 and 0.4 per cent in 1987. A major factor in the modest recovery was two years of good weather for agriculture, reinforced by the favourable impact of domestic policy reforms. The agricultural output rise of 3.1 per cent, up from 2.8 per cent in 1988, together with improving food supply, helped boost the allied sectors, notably agro-based industries, trade and transport. Further growth impetus came from the mining sector and higher export earnings.

Growth in manufacturing output rose from 2.6 per cent in 1987 and 4.5 per cent in 1988 to 4.9 per cent in 1989, despite intensified protectionism in many developed countries and increasingly discriminatory technological policies seriously eroding African manufacturing export competitiveness.

Cereal output was estimated at 77.9 million tons in 1989—15.4 per cent higher than in 1987, but 2.6 per cent lower than the 1988 bumper crop, partly due to locust infestation of the eastern Sahelian zone. An increasing number of countries held food grain surpluses for export in 1989, totalling 1.2 million tons. However, the food grain import requirements of Africa's food-deficit countries were estimated to have risen by about 3.8 per cent, to reach 18.4 million tons. Except for cocoa and tobacco, production of major industrial crops increased in 1989. Producer prices, however, fell.

The bleak social situation persisted, with families facing growing financial and food insecurity and inaccessibility to basic goods, including decent housing and minimal medical care. The number of refugees swelled to 6 million, mostly women and children, following frequent natural and man-made disasters, civil conflicts and war; the disabled were estimated at 10 per cent of the population. The African population growth rate increased much more rapidly than elsewhere, with a high percentage of persons—45 per cent—under 15 years old, compared to 22 per cent in developed regions.

The subregions encompassing East and southern Africa and West Africa showed rates of growth around 3 per cent—generally better than 1988. Performance in Central and North Africa continued to be weak, with GDP growing at 1.6 per cent and 2.8 per cent respectively, well below the rates of population growth. Growth in African least developed countries (LDCs) was generally higher than in other economic groupings, although they remained structurally and economically the weakest. The number of countries experiencing negative growth rates sharply declined from 15 in 1987 to four in 1989. However, only Botswana and Mauritius were able to record consistently high rates of growth over this period.

The slow growth in investment spending during the 1980s resulted in a precipitous erosion of capital stock and the rundown of physical and infrastructure facilities. The 1989 current account deficit stagnated at a high $13.8 billion. External debt rose by about 2.9 per cent to $256.9 billion.

Intensified efforts at policy reforms gave increased priority to the agricultural sector. Several countries, including Egypt, the Libyan Arab Jamahiriya, Nigeria, Senegal and Uganda, achieved the 20 to 25 per cent ratio in total investment allocation recommended by APPER to upgrade production techniques and agricultural infrastructure. A number of initiatives to strengthen the agricultural sector and improve food security were launched at the subregional level.

In a 7 April resolution,[6] the Conference of Ministers requested the Executive Secretary to continue preparing the annual survey of African economic and social conditions and to present annually the economic report on Africa as a summary preview of the survey to ECA. Member States were urged to respond promptly to requests for information on their economic conditions. In another resolution,[7] the Ministers expressed deep concern that the World Bank/UNDP report on Africa's adjustment and growth in the 1980s was, in many respects, at variance with the mid-term review of UNPAAERD and with the reality of the African economic situation. They called on the Executive Secretary to publish, for an objective evaluation of the continent's economic situation, the technical and statistical variances contained in the report.

Activities in 1989

Development policy and regional economic co-operation

In his biennial report for 1988-1989,[4] the Executive Secretary reviewed activities aimed at in-

itiating actions at the national, subregional, regional and international levels to implement a process of sustained socio-economic growth and development in African countries.[8] Legislative organs of all the MULPOCs met during 1989. They were based at Tangier; Niamey, Niger; Gisenyi, Rwanda; Lusaka, Zambia; and Yaoundé, Cameroon.

In response to a 1988 General Assembly resolution,[9] ECA prepared the commission's contribution to the preparation of the International Development Strategy for the fourth United Nations Development Decade. Noting the disappointing development experience during the third United Nations Decade, the contribution particularly emphasized the necessity of an equitable and just international economic order regarding commodity issues, resource flows and transfer of technology.

Alternative framework to structural adjustment programmes

The ECA secretariat promoted the search for an alternative to existing policy frameworks, particularly those associated with conventional structural adjustment programmes, to make them more coherent and consistent with Africa's real development priorities and objectives as stipulated in regionally agreed development strategies.

In May, Ethiopia transmitted to the Economic and Social Council the African Alternative Framework to Structural Adjustment Programmes for Socio-Economic Recovery and Transformation (AAF-SAP),[10] adopted by the Conference of Ministers in April, and endorsed a Joint Statement by African Ministers of Economic Planning and Development and Ministers of Finance, declaring that AAF-SAP should constitute a basis for constructive dialogue between African countries and their development partners in implementing and financing country programmes. The alternative framework gave a structural analysis of the political economy of Africa, asserting that policy reform aimed merely at improvements in financial balances and price structures were unlikely to succeed. It reiterated the development objectives of APPER and UNPAAERD, within the contemporary imperatives of recovery with transformation, concluding that stabilization and structural adjustment programmes in Africa were inadequate to address the region's real causes of economic, financial and social problems. The proposed alternative framework was based on three sets of macroentities: operative forces, available resources and needs.

ECONOMIC AND SOCIAL COUNCIL ACTION

On 28 July 1989, the Economic and Social Council, on the recommendation of its First Committee, adopted **resolution 1989/116** without vote.

African Alternative Framework to Structural Adjustment Programmes for Socio-Economic Recovery and Transformation

The Economic and Social Council,

Recalling General Assembly resolution 43/27 of 18 November 1988, in particular paragraph 55(c) of the annex, in which the Assembly recommended that African countries increase their efforts in the search for a viable conceptual and practical framework for economic structural adjustment programmes in keeping with long-term development objectives and strategies at the national, subregional and regional levels,

Convinced of the urgent need for African economies to bring about structural transformation and sustained growth and development,

1. *Takes note with interest* of the African Alternative Framework to Structural Adjustment Programmes for Socio-Economic Recovery and Transformation, adopted by the Conference of Ministers of the Economic Commission for Africa in resolution 676(XXIV) of 7 April 1989, and the joint statement on Africa's long-term development adopted by the meeting of agencies concerned with Africa's economic and social progress held at Washington, D.C., on 10 May 1989;

2. *Requests* the General Assembly to consider taking action on the Framework, as appropriate;

3. *Calls upon* the international community, especially developed countries and multilateral institutions, to consider requests to provide support to the country programmes prepared by African countries.

Economic and Social Council resolution 1989/116

28 July 1989   Meeting 37   Adopted without vote

Approved by First Committee (E/1989/142) without vote, 21 July (meeting 25); draft by Ethiopia for ECA Conference of Ministers (E/1989/C.1/L.5), orally revised; agenda item 6.

GENERAL ASSEMBLY ACTION

By **decision 44/411** of 17 November, the General Assembly, acting on the question of AAF-SAP, decided that activities supporting UNPAAERD[2] should be continued pending its final review and appraisal by the Assembly at the forty-sixth (1991) session, in accordance with its 1988 resolution.[11]

On the same date, the General Assembly adopted **resolution 44/24** by recorded vote.

African Alternative Framework to Structural Adjustment Programmes for Socio-Economic Recovery and Transformation

The General Assembly,

Recalling its resolution S-13/2 of 1 June 1986, the annex to which contains the United Nations Programme of Action for African Economic Recovery and Development 1986-1990,

Recalling also its resolution 43/27 of 18 November 1988 and, in particular, paragraph 55 (c) of the annex to that resolution, in which African countries were urged to increase their efforts in the search for a viable conceptual and practical framework for economic structural adjustment programmes in keeping with the long-term development objectives and strategies at the national, subregional and regional levels,

Taking note of the final document on the critical economic situation in Africa adopted by the Ninth Con-

ference of Heads of State or Government of Non-Aligned Countries, held at Belgrade from 4 to 7 September 1989, as well as paragraph 12 of section II of the Caracas Declaration of the Ministers for Foreign Affairs of the member countries of the Group of Seventy-seven, adopted at the special ministerial meeting of the Group, held at Caracas from 21 to 23 June 1989,

Recalling resolution CM/RES.1222(L) adopted by the Council of Ministers of the Organization of African Unity at its fiftieth ordinary session, held at Addis Ababa from 17 to 22 July 1989,

Recalling also Economic and Social Council resolution 1989/116 of 28 July 1989,

1. *Takes note with interest* of the African Alternative Framework to Structural Adjustment Programmes for Socio-Economic Recovery and Transformation;

2. *Invites* the international community, including the multilateral financial and development institutions, to consider the African Alternative Framework as a basis for constructive dialogue and fruitful consultation.

General Assembly resolution 44/24

17 November 1989   Meeting 60   137-1-0 (recorded vote)

Draft by Lesotho (A/44/L.20/Rev.1); agenda item 155.

Recorded vote in Assembly as follows:

In favour: Afghanistan, Albania, Algeria, Angola, Antigua and Barbuda, Australia, Austria, Bahamas, Bahrain, Bangladesh, Barbados, Belgium, Benin, Bhutan, Bolivia, Botswana, Brazil, Brunei Darussalam, Bulgaria, Burkina Faso, Burundi, Byelorussian SSR, Cameroon, Canada, Cape Verde, Central African Republic, Chad, Chile, China, Colombia, Comoros, Congo, Côte d'Ivoire, Cuba, Cyprus, Czechoslovakia, Democratic Yemen, Denmark, Djibouti, Ecuador, Egypt, El Salvador, Ethiopia, Fiji, Finland, France, Gabon, Gambia, German Democratic Republic, Germany, Federal Republic of, Ghana, Greece, Guatemala, Guinea, Guinea-Bissau, Guyana, Haiti, Honduras, Hungary, India, Iran, Iraq, Ireland, Israel, Italy, Jamaica, Japan, Jordan, Kenya, Lesotho, Liberia, Libyan Arab Jamahiriya, Luxembourg, Madagascar, Malawi, Malaysia, Maldives, Mali, Malta, Mauritania, Mauritius, Mexico, Mongolia, Morocco, Mozambique, Myanmar, Nepal, Netherlands, New Zealand, Nicaragua, Niger, Norway, Oman, Pakistan, Panama, Papua New Guinea, Peru, Philippines, Poland, Portugal, Qatar, Romania, Rwanda, Saint Vincent and the Grenadines, Sao Tome and Principe, Saudi Arabia, Senegal, Seychelles, Sierra Leone, Singapore, Solomon Islands, Somalia, Spain, Sudan, Suriname, Swaziland, Sweden, Syrian Arab Republic, Thailand, Togo, Trinidad and Tobago, Tunisia, Turkey, Uganda, Ukrainian SSR, USSR, United Arab Emirates, United Kingdom, United Republic of Tanzania, Uruguay, Venezuela, Viet Nam, Yemen, Yugoslavia, Zaire, Zambia, Zimbabwe.

Against:: United States.

Abstaining: None.

African Institute for Economic Development and Planning

The African Institute for Economic Development and Planning (IDEP) faced a critical financial crisis in 1989 with the decline in contributions from member States and UNDP's decision to withdraw its assistance for the Institute's training activities and the funding of its core staff by the end of the year. The IDEP Governing Council, at its thirty-first session (Addis Ababa, 20-22 March), adopted a special memorandum, noting that the non-payment of contributions and the withdrawal of UNDP's assistance would provoke an imminent collapse of the Institute. The Governing Council appointed a sub-committee to review IDEP's structure and management and make recommendations for restructuring. In a 7 April resolution,[12] the ECA Conference of Ministers urged the UNDP Administrator to reconsider the decision, and appealed to the General Assembly to approve the incorporation of four core posts at the Institute in the UN regular budget.

On 28 July, the Economic and Social Council, on the recommendation of its First Committee, adopted **resolution 1989/117** without vote.

African Institute for Economic Development and Planning

The Economic and Social Council,

Recalling its resolution 1985/62 of 26 July 1985,

Noting with satisfaction the achievements of the African Institute for Economic Development and Planning, the services it has rendered to African Governments and the increasing and continued interest of Member States in its activities,

Considering the critical financial crisis facing the Institute, the decline in the contributions of member States and the decision of the United Nations Development Programme to withdraw its assistance for training at the Institute and funding of its core staff at the end of 1989,

Noting with satisfaction that the Governing Council of the Institute has appointed a sub-committee to review the structure and management of the Institute and make recommendations on its restructuring,

Expressing appreciation for the support that the United Nations Development Programme has so far given the Institute,

1. *Urges* the Governing Council of the African Institute for Economic Development and Planning to expedite the work of restructuring and rationalizing the activities and means of the Institute in order to establish, as early as possible, a renewed and financially viable Institute for the benefit of African development;

2. *Invites* the Administrator of the United Nations Development Programme to reconsider, in the light of the progress made in the restructuring process, the decision to cease the funding of the Institute after December 1989 and to provide support, as appropriate;

3. *Earnestly urges* African Governments to pay their contributions in a regular and timely manner and make plans to pay gradually their accumulated arrears.

Economic and Social Council resolution 1989/117
28 July 1989   Meeting 37   Adopted without vote

Approved by First Committee (E/1989/142) without vote, 21 July (meeting 25); draft by Ethiopia for ECA Conference of Ministers (E/1989/C.1/L.6), based on recommendation in report of Secretary-General (E/1989/96) and orally revised; agenda item 6.
Financial implications. S-G, E/1989/C.1/L.11.

Least developed countries

The ECA secretariat continued to implement the Substantial New Programme of Action (SNPA) for the 1980s for LDCs (see PART THREE, Chapter I) and participated in country round tables on Burundi, Lesotho and Sao Tome and Principe.

The ninth meeting of the Conference of Ministers of African LDCs (Addis Ababa, 4 and 5 April) prepared for the second UN conference on LDCs,[13] to be held in 1990, drawing up a declaration reviewing the implementation of SNPA

and containing proposals on policies and measures for the 1990s.

Food and agriculture

During 1989, ECA, in collaboration with the Food and Agriculture Organization of the United Nations (FAO), continued to carry out substantive agricultural activities. To build national capabilities in agricultural development policy, planning and programming, field missions were undertaken in the eastern, southern, West African and Central African subregions. Reports submitted to member countries suggested measures for harmonizing national food plans and policies. The reports highlighted problems of institutional inadequacies, limitations on grass-roots participation in planning and policy-making, unrealistic planning and policy objectives due to lack of data, and scarcity of funds. ECA assisted member countries in developing systems for collection, synthesis, analysis, processing and storage of agricultural data, and, in particular, improved the agricultural data base.

ECA activities to strengthen co-operation and trade in food and agricultural products aimed to improve institutions and increase food crop and livestock production. ECA reports were prepared on the importance of sub-regional co-operation in the area of cereals and tubers; non-conventional food sources; strategic food commodities; women's land rights; and multinational co-operation in fishery development.

Activities in agricultural marketing services concentrated in the areas of credit institutions, price policies, and training and manpower.

ECA continued to assist member countries to formulate policies aimed at efficient organization and distribution of agricultural inputs to small farmers, and to harmonize pricing policies on staple food crops to stimulate interregional trade.

Population

Population policies and development planning, demographic analysis in the context of economic and social development planning, and regional training and research continued to be concerns of the ECA population programme in 1989. Provision of advisory services to member States was also emphasized.

ECA studied the implications of demographic patterns for implementing APPER and UNPAAERD. Reports were completed for the sixth Joint Conference of Planners, Statisticians and Demographers on: age-sex data evaluation of recent African censuses; national experiences in implementing population policies in ECA member States in relation to the Kilimanjaro Programme of Action; fertility influences of the relative roles of maternal and child health care and family planning programmes, proximate determinants and socio-economic correlates; methodological and technological innovations in demographic data collection, processing and analysis; and the biennial report on activities of the population information network for Africa (POPIN-Africa).

Other studies concerned the impact of maternal and child health and family planning programmes on fertility, infant and childhood mortality and maternal health; the effect of nuptiality variables on fertility in selected African countries; a comparison of infant and childhood mortality and its relationship to fertility, cultural factors and socio-economic development in selected African countries; patterns, causes and consequences of urbanization in Africa; and status and prospects of population policies in ECA member countries.

Assistance continued for the Regional Institute for Population Studies (RIPS) in Ghana, the Institut de formation et de recherche démographiques (IFORD) in Cameroon and the Sahel Institute in Mali.

On 26 July, the Economic and Social Council adopted **resolution 1989/94** requesting the UN system to give priority to population needs and problems in Africa in accordance with UN-PAAERD. The Secretary-General was asked to ensure continued fund availability for technical co-operation in the population field, particularly with the UN-supported Cairo Demographic Centre, RIPS, IFORD and other UN demographic centres and programmes serving African countries.

Natural resources and energy

ECA continued technical and administrative assistance to member States, as well as to the Central African Mineral Resources Development Centre (CAMRDC) and the Eastern and Southern African Mineral Resources Development Centre (ESAMRDC), located respectively at Brazzaville, Congo, and Dodoma, United Republic of Tanzania. An evaluation was made of CAMRDC, and advice was provided to ESAMRDC on the development of infrastructual facilities, comprising a mineral dressing laboratory, a rock and soil mechanics laboratory, an industrial minerals laboratory and a library and documentation unit. To increase knowledge of continental mineral potentials, studies were made of copper and bauxite/alumina/aluminium and on iron ore production and its future in West Africa. A study on the exploitation of the mineral, trona, in Chad continued.

In promoting river and lake basin development and as part of the continuing co-operation between ECA and UNDP, a ministerial meeting was held at Addis Ababa on 10 January. The second meeting of the Committee on River and Lake Basins took place at Harare on 27 and 28 April. ECA also ad-

vised Lesotho on its highlands water project. A fact-finding mission visited eight Nile riparian countries in May and June to help develop the river basin's resources with UNDP assisting.

Energy activities were aimed at assisting ECA members develop indigenous resources and integrate energy policies into their overall socio-economic development and economic growth policies. Missions were sent to Burundi, Rwanda, Sudan, Uganda, Zaire, Zambia and Zimbabwe. A study was made of inter-connecting the electrical grids of neighbouring States of the Economic Community of the Great Lakes Countries.

A meeting of plenipotentiaries took place (Addis Ababa, 22-25 May) on the establishment of the African Nuclear Energy Commission.

Science and technology

ECA continued to strive to increase the awareness of member States regarding the applications of science and technology in socio-economic development, seeking to strengthen policies and institutions, develop and mobilize endogenous manpower and achieve greater collaboration in regional and interregional projects. It also organized the sixth meeting of the Intergovernmental Committee of Experts for Science and Technology Development (Addis Ababa, 6-9 November).

Support was given to the planning and servicing of the second meeting (25-26 January) of the North African subregional Working Group of the Intergovernmental Committee of Experts for Science and Technology Development; participation in a round table (Nairobi, Kenya, 1-3 February) on invention licensing and commercialization options for research; and a symposium (Arusha, 27 February–3 March) on technological development and transfer for rural development, held in collaboration with the African Regional Centre for Technology (ARCT).

The ECA, in collaboration with the Organization of African Unity (OAU), helped organize the sixth meeting (Addis Ababa, 6-9 November) of the Intergovernmental Committee of Experts for Science and Technology Development, which reviewed, among other things, the implementation of the Vienna Programme of Action on Science and Technology for Development[14] and made recommendations for the coming decade. An ECA-supported training workshop was held (Oshodi, Nigeria, 24-28 July) on developing capabilities in handling scientific and technological information.

Environment

Development of environmental capabilities, including the conservation of resources and pollution control, was the focus of ECA effort in this area. Combating drought and controlling desertification were considered priority areas to help alleviate Africa's social and economic crises. Several subregional intergovernmental organizations addressed those issues, including the Permanent Inter-State Committee for Combating Drought in the Sahel (CILSS), the Inter-governmental Authority on Drought and Development in the Horn of Africa, the Southern African Development Co-ordination Conference (SADCC), and the Ministerial Conference on Desertification and the Arid Lands Committee of the African Ministerial Conference on the Environment.

At the fifth meeting of the Joint Intergovernmental Regional Committee on Human Settlements and Environment (Addis Ababa, 13-17 February),[4] two reports were presented: on the development of suitable measures for combating desertification, and on modalities for incorporating the Cairo Programme of the African Ministerial Conference on the Environment into ongoing programmes of ECA member States. Another report—on the management of environmental degradation, particularly drought and desertification aspects, in the implementation of APPER—was presented in April to the ECA Conference of Ministers.

The UNEP Environmental Perspective to the Year 2000 and Beyond[15] and the report of the World Commission on Environment and Development[16] generated ECA action on environmental management for sustainable development, including preparations for a ministerial-level regional conference on environmental and sustainable development in Africa, scheduled for Kampala in June.

On 27 July, the Economic and Social Council adopted **resolution 1989/103**, by which it urgently appealed to the international community, particularly donor countries, to support efforts towards a joint policy to combat desertification by the Permanent Inter-State Committee on Drought Control in the Sahel and the Intergovernmental Authority on Drought and Development and the Ministerial Conference. The United Nations Sudano-Sahelian Office was urged to assist Sudano-Sahelian countries to prepare for the UN Conference on Environment and Development. The Secretary-General was requested to place greater emphasis in the World Economic Survey on the situation of countries stricken by desertification and drought.

Transport, communications and tourism

ECA continued to support advisory services, studies, technical publications and professional meetings on transport, communications and tourism. The Conference of African Ministers of Transport, Communications and Planning[17] met in Tangier from 15 to 16 November. Recommendations were made to help open up land-locked countries.

Guidelines for evaluating international practices in road transport were prepared. Attention was given to promoting an African industry to manufacture transport equipment and spare parts in order to reduce imports. Advisory services in general and multimodal transport were rendered to Burundi, Rwanda and Zaire to determine capacity to "containerize" exports or imports through the ports of Dar es Salaam, United Republic of Tanzania, and Mombasa, Kenya.

In shipping, the ECA assessed Africa's capabilities for a shipbuilding and repair industry and identified existing bottle-necks hampering the smooth flow of African maritime trade. Work continued towards convening a ministerial conference on maritime transport for eastern and southern Africa. Regarding inland water transport, the major activities included identification of transport facilitation problems, ways to ease Africa's international traffic flow, and a study of activities to ensure the safety of navigation on Lakes Kivu and Tanganyika.

ECA spearheaded preparations for an African policy to deal with changes in the air transport environment, stemming from deregulation in the United States, liberalization in Europe, noise restrictions, and introduction of a computerized reservation system. The first Inter-agency Co-ordinating Committee meeting of the second United Nations Transport and Communications Decade for Africa was held in Addis Ababa on 16 and 17 March. The ECA also organized a meeting of the five ministers responsible for co-ordinating the implementation at the subregional level of the Yamoussoukro Declaration, adopted in 1988 by the Special Conference of African Ministers of Civil Aviation,[18] and conducted studies on the western, eastern and southern African subregions.

In the area of communications, ECA conducted studies, organized seminars, provided technical assistance to member States, and issued technical publications. A report on the telecommunications development process and policy in Africa was presented to meetings of the Councils of Ministers of the MULPOCs.

The Conference of African Ministers of Tourism[4] (Addis Ababa, 20-25 November) set up mechanisms for co-operation between African intergovernmental organizations, as well as with institutions outside Africa. ECA organized in Paris on 25 August the first meeting on preparations for African Tourism Year in 1991. The General Assembly of the World Tourism Organization (WTO) (Paris, 28 August–2 September) adopted the WTO Commission for Africa programme.

Missions were undertaken to the Preferential Trade Area of Eastern and Southern African States, SADCC, the Organization for the Development of the Senegal River, the African Development Bank, West Africa and southern Africa. An inter-agency committee for tourism development in Africa was established in November 1989.

Transport and Communications Decade

The twelfth meeting of the Inter-Agency Co-ordinating Committee (Addis Ababa, 14-17 March) formally began preparations for the Second Transport and Communications Decade in Africa (1991-2000).[19] Following a further meeting in June, a draft policy document was prepared containing proposed global and sectoral objectives and strategies.

By **decision 44/455** on 22 December, the General Assembly noted the Secretary-General's progress report[20] on the Second Decade.

An evaluation of the first Transport and Communications Decade (1978-1988) showed that ten years was hardly sufficient to complete so gigantic a task as was envisaged during the Decade, the Secretary-General reported.

Europe-Africa Link

In April, the Secretary-General reported[21] on the Europe/Africa permanent link through the Strait of Gibraltar, as requested by the Economic and Social Council in 1987.[22] He reviewed recent studies on reconnaissance of the physical structure (geodesy, cartography, bathymetry, seismic reflection, refraction, physical oceanography, meteorology, geology and geotechnics), as well as engineering, economic and financial and legal aspects. The economic studies dealt with the analysis of the flow of transport through the Strait of Gibraltar and the benefits that the fixed link across the Strait would offer regarding terms of trade. Work carried out under the Governments of Morocco and Spain in 1987 and 1988 confirmed the seriousness with which the two countries regarded the fixed link. As in the past, the ECA and ECE secretariats wanted the Economic and Social Council to underscore the project's international nature and encourage the United Nations to participate more actively in its related studies. It was also hoped that the project's financing would also reflect its international character.

ECONOMIC AND SOCIAL COUNCIL ACTION

On 28 July 1989, the Economic and Social Council, on the recommendation of its First Committee, adopted **resolution 1989/119** without vote.

Europe-Africa permanent link through the Strait of Gibraltar

The Economic and Social Council,

Recalling its resolutions 1982/57 of 30 July 1982, 1983/62 of 29 July 1983, 1984/75 of 27 July 1984, 1985/70 of 26 July 1985 and 1987/69 of 8 July 1987,

Having considered the conclusions contained in the interim report prepared in compliance with Council resolution 1987/69 by the Executive Secretaries of the Economic Commission for Africa and the Economic Commission for Europe on the progress being made in the studies relating to the project for a Europe-Africa permanent link through the Strait of Gibraltar,

Bearing in mind the new dynamism being brought to the region owing, in particular, to the proclamation of the Maghreb Arab Union and to the greatly expanding land transport infrastructure leading to the Strait of Gibraltar,

Noting the resolution adopted on 1 February 1989 by the Parliamentary Assembly of the Council of Europe regarding measures to encourage the construction of a major traffic artery in south-western Europe and to study thoroughly the possibility of a permanent link between Europe and Africa across the Strait of Gibraltar,

Also noting the resolution adopted by the Conference of African Ministers of Transport, Communications and Planning at its sixth meeting, held at Kinshasa in March 1988, concerning the establishment of an entity for the development of transport in the North Africa region,

Aware that the studies on the permanent link have contributed to other regional projects, such as the connection of the electricity grids of Morocco and Spain and the Maghreb-Europe gas pipeline,

Welcoming the co-operation between the Economic Commission for Africa, the Economic Commission for Europe, the Governments of Morocco and Spain and the Transport Study Centre for the Western Mediterranean,

Conscious of the importance of the project for the development of transport in the region, the consolidation of North-South relations and the promotion of scientific and technological research at the international level,

1. *Invites* interested Governments and the enterprises and institutions concerned, as well as other competent organizations, to participate in the international symposium on the permanent link to be held at Marrakesh from 16 to 18 May 1990 with a view to the implementation of the project;

2. *Also invites* the countries concerned to co-operate with the Economic Commission for Africa and the Economic Commission for Europe in accelerating the creation of transport networks leading to the Strait of Gibraltar and in harmonizing transport regulations with a view to facilitating the transport of goods and merchandise between the two areas;

3. *Requests* the Executive Secretaries of the Economic Commission for Africa and the Economic Commission for Europe:

(*a*) To submit, at the Marrakesh symposium, a global evaluation of the studies and work relating to the project based on the reports of the Executive Secretaries transmitted by the Secretary-General to the Economic and Social Council;

(*b*) To allocate as far as possible the resources necessary for the evaluation of the studies and work relating to the project and of the results and recommendations of the Marrakesh symposium;

(*c*) To submit an interim report on the project to the Economic and Social Council at its second regular session of 1991.

Economic and Social Council resolution 1989/119
28 July 1989   Meeting 37   Adopted without vote

Approved by First Committee (E/1989/142) without vote, 20 July (meeting 24); 2-nation draft (E/1989/C.1/L.3); agenda item 6.
Sponsors: Morocco, Spain.

Trade and finance

During 1989, ECA carried out activities under subprogrammes for domestic, intra-African and non-African trade; international financial and monetary policies; and activities of transnational corporations.

The Conference of African Ministers of Trade, at their tenth meeting (Addis Ababa, 13-18 November),[4] postponed adoption of the draft of "The Addis Ababa Strategies for Revitalizing Africa's Trade Recovery and Growth in the 1990s"[23] to the first half of 1990 to allow more consideration at the national level. The Strategies aim to make operational the trade-related measures contained in the 1980 Lagos Plan of Action for the Implementation of the Monrovia Strategy for the Economic Development of Africa[24] with a view to restructuring and expanding Africa's trade in the next decade.

The Ministerial Conference reviewed a report on the Intra-African trade situation, its problems and prospects. Publications in 1989 included a manual on standardization of intra-African trade documentation and procedures, a volume of the *African Trade Bulletin,* and the *African Trade Directory* 1989. A second regional symposium was organized in Port Louis, Mauritius, in October involving the African State Trading Organizations, the International Association of State Trading Organizations, and the Mauritius State Trading Corporation.

Reports were issued on trade with non-African countries, including trends in interregional trade between Africa and other developing countries; implementation of the Global System of Trade Preferences among developing countries; recent developments in the situation of trade relations between Africa and China; and implementation of the Integrated Programme for Commodities.

Domestic trade reports were submitted on alternative patterns of domestic trade structures and mechanisms for the establishment of more rational distribution channels and on mechanisms of integrating women in trade and commerce. A technical publication concerned consumer goods and marketing channels to promote domestic production and trade in African countries.

Regarding international monetary and financial policies, the third session of the Conference of African Ministers of Finance was held in Blantyre from 6 to 8 March.[4] Participants discussed resource management including external debt, reviewed the establishment of the African Monetary Fund, and adopted the Blantyre Statement of African Ministers of Finance on the Alternative Framework for Structural Adjustment Programmes.[25]

In April, the ECA Conference of Ministers adopted a resolution on the establishment of the African Monetary Fund,[26] regretting the considerable delay in establishing the Fund and deciding to reactivate and expand the *ad hoc* Committee of Ministers, known as the Committee of Libreville, which was to examine all outstanding issues and take all necessary measures to speedily establish the Fund. The first meeting of the Enlarged Ministerial Committee of Libreville (Addis Ababa, 11-12 April) decided to hold an *ad hoc* meeting of experts (Addis Ababa, 27 November–1 December) to review the revised study on the Fund.

A meeting in Abidjan, Côte d'Ivoire, of representatives of OAU, ECA and the African Development Bank was held to seek agreement on modalities for implementing decisions on the African common position on Africa's external debt crisis. Its results were reviewed at an international seminar on the African common position held in Cairo from 28 to 30 August.

Industrial development

The General Assembly, on the recommendation of the Economic and Social Council, in 1989 proclaimed (**resolution 44/237**) the period 1991-2000 as the Second Industrial Development Decade for Africa (see below). Implementation of the programme for the first Industrial Development Decade for Africa (IDDA) and UNPAAERD continued to be undertaken under ECA subprogrammes of policy development, planning and institution building; development of basis industries; development of agro- and forest-based industries; and development of small-scale industries.

The ECA jointly organized the ninth meeting (Harare, 29-31 May) of the Conference of African Ministers of Industry, in co-operation with the Government of Zimbabwe and OAU, to review progress made towards African industrialization. Documents under review included eight progress reports by the secretariats of ECA, OAU and the UN Industrial Development Organization (UNIDO); and a progress report on promotion of the African Industrial Development Fund. Other reports concerned measures to strengthen the African Regional Centre for Engineering Design and Manufacturing (ARCEDEM); programmes and activities in the context of UNPAAERD; implementation of UNPAAERD regarding food processing industries; pulp and paper industries and projects in Africa; and prospects for the rationalization and development of pulp and paper industry in Africa.

Ten annual reports on implementation of IDDA projects in the chemical, engineering, metal and agro-based industries were presented to MULPOC meetings during the first quarter of 1989. The ninth meeting of the OAU, ECA and UNIDO secretariats on implementation of the programme for IDDA within the framework of the 1980 Lagos Plan of Action was held in Addis Ababa from 8 to 10 February.

ECONOMIC AND SOCIAL COUNCIL ACTION

On 28 July 1989, the Economic and Social Council, on the recommendation of its First Committee, adopted **resolution 1989/115** without vote.

Proclamation of a second industrial development decade for Africa

The Economic and Social Council,

Recalling its resolution 1987/70 of 8 July 1987, in which it recommended that, after appropriate evaluation of the Industrial Development Decade for Africa, the proclamation of a second decade should be considered in order to accelerate further the industrialization of Africa,

Noting resolution CM/RES.1188(XLIX) of the Council of Ministers of the Organization of African Unity, in which the Council of Ministers urged the Industrial Development Board of the United Nations Industrial Development Organization to adopt an appropriate decision with a view to the proclamation by the General Assembly at its forty-fourth session of a second industrial development for Africa,

Noting also Industrial Development Board decision IDB.5/Dec.7 of 6 July 1989, in which the Board recommended that the General Conference of the United Nations Industrial Development Organization request the General Assembly to proclaim, at its forty-fourth session, a second industrial development decade for Africa,

Recalling also Economic and Social Council resolution 1989/84 of 24 May 1989 on guidelines for international decades in economic and social fields,

Noting that an independent evaluation of the implementation of the Industrial Development Decade for Africa has been completed by a team of experts,

Taking note of resolution 656(XXIV) of 7 April 1989 of the Conference of Ministers of the Economic Commission for Africa,

Noting that the Conference of Ministers invited the Conference of African Ministers of Industry at its ninth meeting to examine the report on the evaluation of the implementation of the Decade and present its views on the modalities of launching a second decade for submission to the General Assembly at its forty-fourth session through the Economic and Social Council and the Industrial Development Board,

Having heard the statement made by the Executive Secretary of the Economic Commission for Africa on 10 July 1989,

1. *Recommends* that the General Assembly at its forty-fourth session consider proclaiming the period 1991-2000 the second industrial development decade for Africa;

2. *Requests* the Secretary-General, in consultation with the Director-General of the United Nations Industrial Development Organization, to submit to the General Assembly at its forty-fourth session proposals, with cost estimates, for the preparation of the programme for the second industrial development decade

for Africa, taking into account resolution 2(IX) of 31 May 1989 of the Conference of African Ministers of Industry.

Economic and Social Council resolution 1989/115
28 July 1989   Meeting 37   Adopted without vote

Approved by First Committee (E/1989/142) without vote, 20 July (meeting 24); draft by Ethiopia for ECA Conference of Ministers (E/1989/C.1/L.4), based on recommendation in report of Secretary-General (E/1989/96) and orally revised; agenda item 6.

Report of the Secretary-General. As requested by Economic and Social Council **resolution 1989/115**, on 29 November the Secretary-General submitted a report[27] of cost estimates for the preparation of the programme for the second industrial development decade for Africa to the General Assembly, including a timetable for the preparatory phase and detailed activities.

GENERAL ASSEMBLY ACTION

On 22 December 1989, on the recommendation of the Second (Economic and Financial) Committee, the General Assembly adopted **resolution 44/237** without vote.

Second Industrial Development Decade for Africa

The General Assembly,

Recalling its resolution 35/66 B of 5 December 1980 on the Industrial Development Decade for Africa,

Recalling Economic and Social Council resolution 1987/70 of 8 July 1987, in which the Council recommended that, after appropriate evaluation of the Industrial Development Decade for Africa, the proclamation of a second decade should be considered in order to accelerate further the industrialization of Africa,

Recalling also resolution AHG/Res.180(XXV), adopted by the Assembly of Heads of State and Government of the Organization of African Unity at its twenty-fifth ordinary session, held at Addis Ababa from 24 to 26 July 1989, on the proclamation of a second industrial development decade for Africa and on an Africa industrialization day,

Taking note of Economic and Social Council resolution 1989/115 of 28 July 1989 on the proclamation of a second industrial development decade for Africa,

Welcoming Industrial Development Board decision IDB.5/Dec.7 of 6 July 1989 on the Industrial Development Decade for Africa, in which the Board recommended that the General Conference of the United Nations Industrial Development Organization should request the General Assembly to proclaim a second industrial development decade for Africa,

Welcoming also resolution GC.3/10 of 23 November 1989 of the General Conference of the United Nations Industrial Development Organization on the second industrial development decade for Africa,

Having considered the report of the Secretary-General on the preparation for the second industrial development decade for Africa (1991-2000), containing proposals for the preparation of the programme for the second decade,

1. *Proclaims* the period 1991-2000 the Second Industrial Development Decade for Africa;

2. *Also proclaims* 20 November Africa Industrialization Day, for the purpose of mobilizing the commitment

of the international community to the industrialization of Africa;

3. *Endorses* the proposals of the Secretary-General, as contained in his report, on the participation of the United Nations, through the Economic Commission for Africa, in the preparation of the programme for the Second Industrial Development Decade for Africa;

4. *Requests* the Secretary-General of the United Nations, in consultation with the Director-General of the United Nations Industrial Development Organization, the Secretary-General of the Organization of African Unity, the relevant subregional and regional economic groupings in Africa and the United Nations bodies concerned, to make the necessary preparations for the Second Industrial Development Decade for Africa and to submit to the General Assembly at its forty-fifth session, through the Economic and Social Council, a report on those preparations.

General Assembly resolution 44/237

22 December 1989   Meeting 85   Adopted without vote

Approved by Second Committee (A/44/832/Add.1) without vote, 11 December (meeting 49); draft by Vice-Chairman (A/C.2/44/L.74), based on informal consultations on draft by Kenya for African States (A/C.2/44/L.46); agenda item 12.
Financial implications. 5th Committee, A/44/885; S-G, A/C.2/44/L.77, A/C.5/44/49.
Meeting numbers. GA 44th session: 2nd Committee 15-17, 19, 20, 25, 29, 31, 34, 41, 44, 46, 48, 49; 5th Committee 53, 57, 58; plenary 85.

Public administration and finance

During 1989, ECA assisted member States in developing and implementing programmes in public administration and management and in development of budgetary and taxation systems.

The ECA secretariat advised the African Centre for Applied Research and Training in Social Development in Tripoli, Libyan Arab Jamahiriya, on changes in its organization structure; collaborated with the Government of Uganda in reviewing problems of decentralization and in developing training programmes for staff of decentralized units of government; and assisted the Ministry of Local Government in the Gambia in reorganizing its local government structures. It assisted the Management Services and Training Department of the Federal Civil Service Commission in Nigeria to organize a national conference on human resources development and utilization policy. ECA also organized a series of training programmes and issued a number of technical documents on public administration and management as well as on development of budgetary and taxation systems.

Social development

ECA social development subprogrammes covered integrated rural development; youth and social welfare; and integration of women in development. The fifth Conference of African Ministers of Social Affairs and its Intergovernmental Expert Group both met at Arusha from 23 to 28 October[4]. Two working documents covered social development activities between April 1985 and September 1989 and summarized social trends and major social development problems in Africa. A report on the impact of rural youth employment programmes on rural development was presented, as was a report on juvenile delinquency, crime and justice in the light of socio-economic conditions in Africa.[23]

The Conference of Ministers adopted a resolution on strengthening the capabilities of subregional and regional structures for the integration of women in development.[28] The inaugural meeting of the Governing Council of the United Nations African Institute for the Prevention of Crime and the Treatment of Offenders (UNAFRI) was held in Kampala, Uganda, on 14 and 15 June.

The tenth meeting (Addis Ababa, 23-25 March) of the Africa Regional Co-ordinating Committee for the Integration of Women in Development reviewed regional perspectives for the advancement of women. The fourth Regional Conference on the Integration of Women in Development (Abuja, Nigeria, 6-10 November) resulted in publication of "The Abuja Declaration on Participatory Development: the Role of Women in Africa in the 1990s", a document highlighting the extent to which the 1984 Arusha strategies for women[29] had been implemented.

Information

The Regional Technical Committee for the Pan-African Documentation and Information System (PADIS), at its fourth meeting (Addis Ababa, 23-25 March),[30] considered issues related to user needs and to harmonization and standardization of documentation and information systems at ECA-sponsored regional and subregional institutions. It discussed the proposed establishment of the Eastern and Southern African Documentation and Information System (ESADIS) at Lusaka and the Central African Documentation and Information System (CADIS) at Kinshasa, Zaire, and decided to change the System's title to the Pan-African Development Information System.

In a 7 April resolution,[31] the Conference of Ministers endorsed the Committee's recommendations, called for financial support to PADIS and requested the Executive Secretary to develop a subprogramme on development information systems in Africa in the ECA medium-term plan for 1992-1997, including development and maintenance of data bases and a network promoting the exchange of information among member States for balanced and self-reliant African development.

PADIS activities included delivery of training, advisory services and other forms of technical cooperation for ECA member States on information management and development; data base development and network building; provision of user services; studies and publications; and servicing of legislative and other meetings including expert groups.

Administrative questions

On 7 April 1989, the ECA Conference of Ministers endorsed a proposed programme of work and priorities for the biennium 1990-1991[32] including additions emanating from the MULPOC meetings and the Conference of Ministers.

In a resolution on a draft medium-term plan,[33] the Conference decided to establish an open-ended *ad hoc* committee empowered to examine the Executive Secretary's draft proposals and to make recommendations to the Secretary-General on the Commission's behalf.

The Economic and Social Council adopted **decision 1989/184**, accepting the offer of the Government of the Libyan Arab Jamahiriya to host the twenty-fifth session of ECA and the sixteenth meeting of the Conference of Ministers in 1990 in Tripoli.

The General Assembly endorsed the Committee for Programme and Co-ordination recommendations[34] on ECA, asking the Secretary-General to prepare for the forty-fifth Assembly a plan to reduce the current high vacancy rate in the Commission.

GENERAL ASSEMBLY ACTION

On 21 December, on the recommendation of the Fifth (Administrative and Budgetary) Committee, the Assembly adopted **resolution 44/201 B, section VIII**, without vote.

Section 13.   Economic Commission for Africa

[*The General Assembly . . .*]

1. *Endorses* the recommendations contained in paragraphs 181 to 183 of the report of the Committee for Programme and Co-ordination and requests the Secretary-General to review the adequacy of resources for the United Nations Programme of Action for African Economic Recovery and Development 1986-1990, and to intensify his efforts to reduce the currently high vacancy rate in the Economic Commission for Africa, including the preparation of a specific plan to that end, and to report thereon to the General Assembly at its forty-fifth session;

2. *Requests* the Secretary-General to review the translation and interpretation services for all official languages in the Economic Commission for Africa, including the question of the retention of trained personnel and the possibility of restoration of the Training Centre, and to report on the results of this review to the General Assembly at its forty-fifth session;

3. *Decides* that the post proposed by the Secretary-General for a Chief, Office Automation, in the Economic Commission for Africa should be an established post in the programme budget for the biennium 1990-1991, and that the post of evaluation officer should be restored on a non-recurrent basis, subject to renewal;

4. *Requests* the Secretary-General to review the question of the resources for the evaluation function in the regional commissions, prior to the preparation of the proposed programme budget for the biennium 1992-1993;

. . .

General Assembly resolution 44/201 B, section VIII

21 December 1989   Meeting 84   Adopted without vote

Approved by Fifth Committee (A/44/905) without vote, 19 December (meeting 59); draft by Vice-Chairman (A/C.5/44/L.25); agenda item 123.

Meeting numbers. GA 44th session: 5th Committee 11-18, 27, 28, 59; plenary 84.

Co-operation with SADCC

In an August 1989 report on co-operation between the United Nations and SADCC,[35] requested by a 1987 General Assembly resolution,[36] the Secretary-General reported a remarkable increase in activities in all SADCC project sectors except manpower development, with overall total project costs of nearly $7.2 million as at August 1988, representing an increase of almost 13 per cent. However, the gap in funding for those costs was still very substantial—about 50 per cent.

At the 1989 SADCC Annual Consultative Conference (Luanda, Angola, February), discussions concentrated on reviewing the guidelines on organization governing the relations between SADCC and the UN system. It was agreed that the role of women in the SADCC Programme of Action should be enhanced and that while efforts should continue to expand emergency assistance to front-line States, such fundraising should not adversely affect contributions to the SADCC Programme of Action that addressed the long-term development needs of member States.

GENERAL ASSEMBLY ACTION

On 22 December 1989, on the recommendation of the Second Committee, the General Assembly adopted **resolution 44/221** without vote.

Co-operation between the United Nations and the Southern African Development Co-ordination Conference

The General Assembly,

Recalling its resolutions 37/248 of 21 December 1982, 38/160 of 19 December 1983, 39/215 of 18 December 1984, 40/195 of 17 December 1985 and 42/181 of 11 December 1987, in which it, *inter alia*, requested the Secretary-General to promote co-operation between the organs, organizations and bodies of the United Nations system and the Southern African Development Co-ordination Conference and urged intensification of contacts in order to accelerate the achievement of the objectives of the Lusaka Declaration of 1 April 1980, by which the Conference was established,

Having considered the report of the Secretary-General on co-operation between the United Nations and the Conference,

Recalling the significant progress made by the Conference in formulating concrete development programmes and in implementing them under its Programme of Action,

Reaffirming its recognition that successful implementation of these development programmes can be achieved only if the Conference has adequate resources at its disposal,

Concerned that the gap that still exists between the needs and the resources available to the Conference continues to widen,

Deeply concerned about the critical economic and security situation in southern Africa and the particularly difficult environment for regional co-operation caused by acts of destabilization committed by South Africa,

Reaffirming that increased self-reliance by States members of the Conference would contribute to the struggle against the *apartheid* policies of South Africa,

Noting the progress made by some organs, organizations and bodies of the United Nations system in working out mechanisms for formulating and executing co-operation programmes with the Conference,

1. *Takes note* of the report of the Secretary-General, which describes the progress made in the implementation of the resolutions of the General Assembly dealing with co-operation between the United Nations and the Southern African Development Co-ordination Conference;

2. *Commends* the Member States and organs, organizations and bodies of the United Nations system that have extended concrete assistance to the Conference and expresses appreciation to those which have established contacts and relationships with it;

3. *Calls upon* the Member States and organs, organizations and bodies of the United Nations system that have not yet established contact and relationships with the Conference to explore the possibility of doing so;

4. *Commends* the Conference for the considerable achievements it has made since its founding in implementing projects covering all the major sectors of co-operation, in spite of difficulties due to destabilization policies of the South African régime and its acts of aggression against the States members of the Conference;

5. *Renews its appeal* to the international community to increase substantially its financial, technical and material support to the Conference in order to enable it to implement fully its expanding programmes;

6. *Appeals* to the specialized agencies and other organs and organizations of the United Nations system to continue to co-operate fully in the development programmes of the Conference;

7. *Welcomes* the impending independence of Namibia, which will bring additional possibilities for expanded economic co-operation in southern Africa;

8. *Also welcomes* the ongoing peace initiatives by the Governments of Angola and Mozambique to end violence in these two Member States, and urges the international community to assist in the reconstruction of their economies;

9. *Invites* the donor community and other co-operating partners to participate at a high level in the Southern African Development Co-ordination Conference Annual Consultative Conference, to be held at Lusaka from 31 January to 2 February 1990;

10. *Requests* the Secretary-General, in consultation with the Executive Secretary of the Southern African Development Co-ordination Conference, to continue to intensify contacts aimed at promoting and harmonizing co-operation between the United Nations and the Conference;

11. *Also requests* the Secretary-General to report to the General Assembly at its forty-sixth session on the implementation of the present resolution.

General Assembly resolution 44/221

22 December 1989   Meeting 85   Adopted without vote

Approved by Second Committee (A/44/746/Add.6) without vote, 11 December (meeting 49); 28-nation draft (A/C.2/44/L.56), orally revised; agenda item 82 *(e)*.
Meeting numbers. GA 44th session: 2nd Committee 43, 44, 46, 49; plenary 85.

REFERENCES

[1]E/1989/35. [2]YUN 1986, p. 446, GA res. S-13/2, annex, 1 June 1986. [3]E/ECA/CM.15/47. [4]E/ECA/CM.16/2. [5]E/1990/53. [6]E/1989/35 (res. 668 (XXIV)). [7]*Ibid.* (res. 671(XXIV)). [8]YUN 1988, p. 269. [9]YUN 1988, p. 319, GA res. 43/182, 20 Dec. 1988. [10]A/44/315. [11]YUN 1988, p. 279, GA res. 43/27, 18 Nov. 1988. [12]E/1989/35 (res. 669(XXIV)). [13]YUN 1987, p. 392, GA res. 42/177, 11 Dec. 1987. [14]YUN 1979, p. 636. [15]YUN 1987, p. 661, GA res. 42/186, 11 Dec. 1987. [16]*Ibid.* p. 679, GA res. 42/187, 11 Dec. 1987. [17]E/ECA/TCD/66. [18]YUN 1988, p. 273. [19]YUN 1988, p. 276, GA res. 43/179, 20 Dec. 1988. [20]A/44/255-E/1989/62. [21]E/1989/58. [22]YUN 1987, p. 520, ESC res. 1987/69, 8 July 1987. [23]E/1990/42. [24]YUN 1980, p. 548. [25]E/ECA/CM.15/21. [26]E/1989/35 (res. 670(XXIV)). [27]A/44/812. [28]E/1989/35 (res. 666(XXIV)). [29]YUN 1984, p. 618. [30]E/ECA/CM.15/25. [31]E/1989/35 (res. 658(XXIV)). [32]*Ibid.* (res. 675(XXIV)). [33]*Ibid.* (res. 674(XXIV)). [34]A/44/16. [35]A/44/374. [36]YUN 1987, p. 531, GA res. 42/181, 11 Dec. 1987.

Asia and the Pacific

The forty-fifth session of the Economic and Social Commission for Asia and the Pacific (ESCAP), meeting in Bangkok, Thailand, from 27 March to 5 April, had as its theme, "Restructuring the developing economies of Asia and the Pacific in the 1990s". Five resolutions were adopted.[1]

A resolution on regional social development strategy towards the year 2000 and beyond[2] urged the ESCAP Executive Secretary to incorporate the themes of distributive justice, poverty eradication and popular participation in the strategy. Careful consideration was asked for the topics of the family in development and of drug abuse in implementation of the 1988 Jakarta Plan of Action on Human Resources Development in the ESCAP region.[3] The Commission also requested its Executive Secretary to pursue, within existing resources, establishment of a depository centre for UN human rights materials[4] and welcomed designation of the ESCAP Social Development Division as a regional focal point on human rights. In another resolution, on regional support for International Literacy Year,[5] all members and associate members were urged to participate actively in the World Conference on Education for All—Meeting Basic Learning Needs, planned for Bangkok in 1990.

Regarding an integrated programme on rural development,[6] ESCAP stressed the need to allocate resources for rural poverty alleviation. Members and associates were invited to accord priority also to natural disaster reduction and mitigation in their national development plans.[7]

In a message to ESCAP, the UN Secretary-General declared that improved growth performance of the industrial nations during 1988 had helped to stimulate the general economic recovery and improve the performance of most developing countries of the Asian and Pacific region. But, for many, the debt burden continued to impede development efforts and a number of countries, particularly the least developed and Pacific island countries, had not registered significant economic growth, continuing to require special support measures and assistance. He considered the Commission's discussion on restructuring the developing ESCAP economies in the 1990s most timely; implementation of the Jakarta Plan of Action and the Tokyo Programme on Technology for Development in Asia and the Pacific[8] was of particular significance, he added.

In a policy statement, the ESCAP Executive Secretary said that while the region's average growth had increased to 8 per cent in 1988, there had been insufficient recognition of the growth disparity between the dynamic and the less resilient developing member countries, causing exaggeration of overall regional progress. Although he was optimistic about the region's future, absolute poverty still affected 600 million people, and about 85 per cent of the developing region's population had very low average per capita incomes. Although the Substantial New Programme of Action for the 1980s for the Least Developed Countries had been adopted as an international rescue effort, the extremely low living conditions in most member least developed countries had sunk even lower during the disappointing decade. With the threatened collapse of the Uruguay Round[9] of multilateral trade negotiations because of disputes between the industrial nations, developing member countries, especially those more export-oriented, should consider asserting their economic rights and responsibilities more forcefully. At the same time, the region should look more to itself for sources of growth. He pointed to the potential benefits of growing regional complementarities and interdependence to augment export earnings and fuel growth impulses. It was advisable, however, to supplement existing regional credit and marketing mechanisms.

Economic and social trends

Although the regional growth of developing economies was notably less dependent upon the growth of industrial countries at the end of the 1980s, the slow-down of the world economy in 1989 considerably affected the overall growth rate, which had fallen to 6.1 per cent in 1989, compared with 9.2 per cent in 1988, it was reported in the *Economic and Social Survey of Asia and the Pacific 1989*[10] and a later summary.[11] This was largely explained, it went on, by the weakening of the stimulus that developing economies of the region had received in the second half of the 1980s: the previously declining United States dollar strengthened in 1989, international interest rates rose instead of falling, and oil prices firmed up.

Deceleration of growth rates was more marked in the economies of East and South Asia than in those of South-East Asia, where growth rates remained close to the high rates of the previous two years. China and the newly industrializing economies of East Asia sharply decelerated in 1989 from double-digit growth rates in previous years, with China's rate standing at 6.5 per cent compared to 11.4 per cent in 1988. Hong Kong's economy, the growth rate of which had already in 1988 fallen to 7.4 per cent from 13.8 per cent in 1987, further decelerated in 1989 to 5 per cent. The growth rate of the Republic of Korea decelerated to 6.5 per cent from 11.3 per cent in 1988.

In South-East Asia, Indonesia's growth performance improved from 5.7 per cent in 1988 to 6.2 per cent in 1989, as a result of the continued successful economic diversification to reduce oil and gas dependency. Malaysia sustained a rate close to the 7.8 per cent of 1988. In Thailand, rapid growth in manufacturing exports and an investment boom supported by large foreign direct investment inflows were major factors in its being one of the region's fastest growing economies in 1989, although the growth rate was expected to be about 1 per cent below the 11 per cent growth of 1988. The economies of the Philippines and Singapore decelerated somewhat in 1989, the former's growth rate falling to 5.7 per cent from 6.3 per cent in 1988. Viet Nam's economy improved considerably in 1988, with national income growing at 5.9 per cent compared to 2.1 per cent in 1987, an apparent response to the Government's recent liberalization policies.

In South Asia, India's rate of economic growth declined to an estimated 4.5 per cent from 10.6 per cent in 1988. Pakistan's growth decelerated to 5.1 per cent from 6.2 per cent in 1988. It had had an average rate of 6.8 per cent between 1985 and 1988 as a result of efforts to contain high fiscal and balance-of-payments deficits. In Sri Lanka, continued political problems, a decline in foreign assistance and worsening terms of foreign trade had resulted in the slowed growth since 1987, but in 1989 a 3.2 per cent expansion was expected, compared with 2.7 per cent the year before.

Among the region's least developed countries, Afghanistan's gross domestic product (GDP) declined 6.8 per cent in 1988 owing to sharp falls in agricultural and industrial production. In Bangladesh, the real GDP growth rate declined from a 4.3 per cent average in 1986-1987 to 2.6 per cent in 1988 and an estimated 2.4 per cent in 1989 due to devastating floods in 1987 and 1988.

Bhutan and Maldives were the two least developed countries which had achieved relatively high rates of growth in recent years, the former at an 8.7 per cent compound rate of real economic growth between 1980 and 1987. Spurred by significant growth in fishery and tourism, the Maldives GDP grew 13.9 per cent in 1987, moderating to 8.7 per cent in 1988. Myanmar's GDP grew 3.2 per cent in 1988, improving on 2.3 per cent in 1987. Nepal suffered a deceleration in GDP growth to 1.5 per cent in 1989, compared with 9.7 per cent in 1988.

Many South Pacific economies performed well in 1989, with Fiji anticipating a double-digit growth rate. However, Papua New Guinea, the largest island country of the region, stagnated after its mineral production was disrupted by closure of its largest mining complex in Bougainville. The Solomon Islands achieved a 5 per cent growth rate in 1988, reversing a weather-related decline of 3 per cent in 1987.

Agriculture remained the prime sector in most of the region's developing economies. The sharp drop in agricultural growth—to around 2.8 per cent in 1989 from about 7.3 per cent in 1988—was due to weather-related uncertainties, price changes in the world market and policy-induced changes, and was a major factor in moderating overall economic growth.

The region's industrial progress was significant by the end of the 1980s, with many countries attempting, through restructuring and policy reforms, to consolidate and sustain their momentum. There was considerable diversity, however, in industrial growth rates. China exercised government restraints to bring its industrial growth rate down to around 10 per cent in 1989 from 20.7 per cent in 1988, in order to maintain price stability and consolidate growth. In the Republic of Korea, from an annual rate of 16.8 per cent during 1985-89, manufacturing output growth fell drastically in 1989 due to frequent work stoppages, rapid wage increases and appreciation of the currency. The least developed countries of the region, with their narrow industrial base, remained weak. Manufacturing contributed only 8 percent to the GDP of Bangladesh and grew at an average 4 per cent during the 1980s. Nepal's industry, mainly light manufacturing, had stagnated since 1988.

Foreign trade in the region's developing economies slowed after two years of rapid growth, with, as in 1988, many countries' imports increasing faster than exports. In those countries, this widened the trade deficit; though in a few countries, such as the Republic of Korea, it reduced the surplus. The least developed and small island economies continued to face relatively large deficits in their trade and payment balances, although in some cases improvements had been achieved in 1988 largely through moderate import growth.

Administrative controls on production, trade and investment activities were being liberalized in many of the region's developing countries. Fiscal and monetary policies and measures tended to assume greater importance in economic management and stabilization as well as in developmental functions of resource mobilization, investment stimulation and resource allocation. Their role remained important in serving social objectives, such as greater distributional equity.

Total government expenditure as a proportion of GDP varied widely, the survey said, from 12 per cent in Hong Kong to 34 per cent in Sri Lanka. No major changes had occurred in recent years in government shares of GDP. Revenue shares were generally lower than expenditure shares, although in some cases the share of expenditures had tended to decline, reflecting policies intended to limit the Government's role in the economy and reduce budgetary deficits. Many economies made successful efforts in the 1980s to attain fiscal system adjustment through public expenditure rationalization and tax structure reform.

Least developed and island economies

The least developed and Pacific islands countries shared several basic common denominators of underdevelopment, setting them apart from the mainstream of the development process in the ESCAP developing region. Those included: low per capita income; the predominant share of subsistence activities and limited contribution of industrial output to GDP or net material product (NMP); high unemployment or disguised unemployment; and generally poor indicators of life quality (infant mortality, adult literacy, nutritional levels, health care, access to safe water, housing standards, among others). Historical factors and significant inflows of capital and remittances largely accounted for improved performance of some Pacific island countries.

A combination of highly difficult development conditions and constraints impacted adversely on the pace and patterns of economic growth and structural transformation. With few exceptions other than Bhutan and Maldives, the increase in aggregate production and income was very slow relative to consumption and investment needs, particularly in the larger economies of the Asian least developed and the Pacific island subregions.

Average growth rates in GDP/NMP, ranging mostly from 2 per cent to 6 per cent annually during the 1970s and the 1980s, were inadequate to produce noticeable improvement in local living standards. Economic growth in the Pacific islands slowed considerably in the 1980s, causing a deterioration or stagnation in personal income over a large part of the subregion.

The Commission reviewed implementation of the 1981 Substantial New Programme of Action for the 1980s for the Least Developed Countries,[12] noting that most of them had launched extensive development programmes. However, lack of resources hindered them from achieving their goals, and it was considered urgent that an appropriate action programme for the 1990s be formulated.

Social development

The urbanization process and its problems brought sharply into focus many of the region's pressing social issues. Pushed by rural poverty and pulled by urban opportunities and amenities, urban populations were experiencing a projected threefold increase over 40 years—from 360 million in 1960 to more than 1.2 billion by 2000. A large portion of all city dwellers were concentrated in a small number of large-sized cities, with Bangkok, Bombay, Calcutta, Dhaka, Jakarta, Karachi, Madras, Manila, New Delhi, Seoul and Shanghai developing into "mega-cities". Most had more than 5 million people by 1980, and were expected to contain between 10 and 16 million by the turn of the century.

Health and nutrition improvements had resulted in most countries meeting the average minimum calorie requirement, lowering infant mortality rates, increasing life expectancy and improving health services. But prevailing standards were still far below those in some other regions.

An expert group meeting and a meeting of senior officials on human resources development in the region were held in Bangkok in January.

ESCAP activities in 1989

ESCAP continued activities in a wide variety of areas, including food and agriculture, the environment, human settlements, trade and finance, technology, shipping, transport and communications, population and natural disasters.

Three Committees held their first sessions, all in Bangkok: the Committee on Development Planning and Statistics (24-28 July); the Committee on Industry, Technology and Human Settlements (11-15 September); and the Committee on Agriculture, Rural Development and the Environment (13-17 November). The Committee on Natural Resources also met, in its fifteenth session, at Bangkok (9-13 October).

Agriculture and rural development

Commission activities focused on improvement of agricultural policies, planning and information systems; increasing production and improving supply, distribution, marketing and use of critical farm inputs through the services of the Fertilizer Advisory, Development and Information Network for Asia and the Pacific and the agricultural requisites scheme for Asia and the Pacific; and integrated rural development, with emphasis on the alleviation of poverty. The Commission adopted a resolution[6] on an integrated programme on rural development, asking for a report in 1991 on strengthening and implementing an inter-agency co-ordinated plan of action and for the holding of periodic consultations with member countries to assess their needs for their poverty alleviation programmes for disadvantaged groups.

Meetings, training courses and seminars were held, covering such subjects as: fertilizer use in Viet Nam's southern region; integrated rural development; port handling of mineral fertilizers; chemical fertilizers import management; satellite crop monitoring; the impact of international agricultural price stability on primary producers; South Pacific fertilizer sector development; and socio-economic constraints on rural area use of new and renewable energy technologies.

Environment

Work continued on ways to achieve environmentally sound and sustainable development. In accord with a 1988 Commission resolution,[13] workshops, seminars and meetings took place on: soil conservation and soil salinity control; strengthening a regional network of research and training centres on desertification control in Asia and the Pacific; environment integration into development; "greening" the development process; strengthening the conservation and management of critical ecosystems; environmentally sound and sustainable development in Asia; and desertification control.

Human settlements

ESCAP's programme for human settlements concentrated in three major areas: integrated settlements policies and planning; development of shelter, infrastructure and land; and stimulation of institutional capabilities and public participation. Priority was accorded to technical co-operation among developing countries (TCDC) activities in settlement planning and development; strengthening institutional capabilities through technical co-operation; and promotion of public participation in human settlements financing and development. Encouragement and assistance were given for the formulation of shelter strategies towards the year 2000, as requested by the Commission in 1988.[13]

Training courses, meetings and workshops were organized in: appropriate building materials and construction technology; management of human settlements; housing development and management; development building components industries through application of updated modular co-ordination rules; innovative community-based housing finance and credit systems for low-income households; urban transport in Asia; housing and settlement improvement; local housing programmes focusing on partnership between city authorities and people; low-income housing policy and appropriate technology; and women's initiatives for participatory development.

International trade

Activities in the area of international trade centred on its expansion, promotion and development, development of commodities of regional interest, and promotion of subregional, regional and interregional trade co-operation. Technical and training assistance in trade facilitation was extended to developing countries in collaboration with UNCTAD and the Customs Co-operation Council. Special assistance to Pacific island countries in trade facilitation was provided partly through publication of the Pacific Harmonized Customs Tariff Schedule. Emphasis continued on effective utilization of trade information for trade expansion through a programme of activities drawn up for the development of the Regional Trade Information Network (TISNET). Highly sought-after publications, including trade information guides and a series of country specific traders' manuals, were produced.

Other activities included meetings, workshops and seminars, such as those on: sericulture; trade promotion with Eastern European socialist countries; small and medium enterprise exports; and one for women executives on export marketing. The fourth session of the Intergovernmental Consultative Forum of Developing Tropical Timber Producing/Exporting Countries was held in Manila, Philippines, in October.

Technology for development

Some ESCAP activities in 1989 were aimed at strengthening and establishing an institutional infrastructure for science and technology, strengthening the technological capabilities of members and associates, and monitoring major breakthroughs in science and technology. Those included a TCDC exchange of study visits between China and Thailand (March, April and May) on planning, development and evaluation of policies in science and technological development; a work-

shop in Minsk, USSR, in May-June on advanced materials technology and development; and an *ad hoc* expert group meeting in Bangkok in September on integration of women into technological development. The Governing Board of the Asian and Pacific Centre for Transfer of Technology (APCTT) held its fourth session in Bangkok in November. The Governing Body of the Regional Network for Agricultural Machinery held its twelfth session in Khatmandu, Nepal, in December. Other seminars, meetings and workshops dealt with electrical conservation in commercial and domestic subsectors and with technological rehabilitation of small foundry industries.

The Commission expressed general satisfaction with the progress of implementation of the Tokyo Programme on Technology for Development in Asia and the Pacific, noting the heightened awareness among policy planners and decision makers of development based on science and technology. It commended the contribution of APCTT to implementing the Tokyo Programme and the financial support provided by UNDP.

Transnational corporations

A seminar on transnational corporations from developing Asian countries was held in Bangkok in February. An expert group meeting on environmental management of transnational corporations in pollution-intensive industries in the ESCAP region met, also in Bangkok, in May. Several publications were completed by the ESCAP/UNCTC Joint Unit on Transnational Corporations, including the *Asia-Pacific TNC Review 1989* and *The Socio-economic Impact of Transnational Corporations in the Fast Food Industry*. The Joint Unit completed its research project on environmental management in pollution-intensive industries.

Shipping, transport and communications

National efforts towards an integrated approach to medium- and long-term planning of the transport and communications sector were supported by ESCAP in 1989. The subjects of meetings, seminars and workshops included: demonstration of cost-effective railway signalling and telecommunication system; integrated transport planning; modern methods of telecommunication planning; transport energy conservation and substitution; computerized wagon control systems; and how to speed up metre gauge lines in developing countries. An Asian and Pacific Railway Co-operation Group Meeting met in New Delhi, India, in November. The sixth session of the Intergovernmental Railway Group Meeting took place in Bangkok in November and December.

Training courses dealt with identifying railway derailment causes in China; optimal standards for design, construction and maintenance of rural roads in humid areas; and optimal standards for design, construction and maintenance of rural roads in arid and semi-arid areas.

Population

The Commission sought greater awareness concerning population aging, through generating primary data in four countries in the region and developing policy and programme recommendations on aging. Investigations were launched on inter-relationships between urbanization, economic structure and the role of migrant workers, particularly women. An analytical study was begun on implications of changes in the demographic situation for the various aspects of human resources development.

The topics covered by some ESCAP-sponsored meetings, seminars and workshops included: interaction between clients and grassroots family-planning workers; accessibility of contraceptive methods; consequences of population changes in Asia; urbanization and socio-economic development in the region; data communications and microcomputers for population programme managers and policy makers; and family planning service statistics analysis and interpretation using microcomputers. Fellowships assisted countries with limited or no training facilities to develop a cadre of manpower trained in demography.

Statistics

Significant progress was made towards strengthening national statistical capabilities. ESCAP activities in that area included seminars and training courses on: employment and unemployment statistics; social statistics and indicators for children and women; sampling and household survey methodology; computer-assisted coding; transport statistics; projections for social and economic planning; and managing national statistics services in the 1990s.

Natural disasters

The Commission, in the context of the designation of the 1990's as the International Decade for Natural Disaster Reduction,[14] adopted a resolution[7] urging Governments to designate appropriate mechanisms to implement, co-ordinate and monitor activities related to reduction of natural disasters such as cyclones, typhoons, floods, droughts, locust infestations, tsunamis, earthquakes, landslides and volcanic eruptions. The Executive Secretary of ESCAP was to set up appropriate arrangements to ensure that the intersectoral character of natural disaster reduction was reflected in all relevant programme activities. Preparation of a practical and intersectoral programme of action for the Decade at the country

level was requested, as was a report to the Commission at its forty-sixth session in 1990.

Organizational questions

On 28 July, the Economic and Social Council, in **resolution 1989/183**, decided that the Commission's forty-sixth session should be held at Kuala Lumpur, Malaysia in 1990.

REFERENCES

[1]E/1989/33. [2]*Ibid.* (res. 45/1). [3]YUN 1988, p. 282. [4]E/1989/33 (res.45/2). [5]*Ibid.* (res. 45/3). [6]*Ibid.* (res. 45/4). [7]*Ibid.* (res. 45/5). [8]YUN 1988, p. 286. [9]YUN 1986, p. 1210. [10]*Economic and Social Survey of Asia and the Pacific 1989,* Sales No. E.90.II.F4. [11]E/1990/52. [12]YUN 1981, p. 406. [13]YUN 1988, p. 282. [14]YUN 1987, p. 459, GA res. 42/169, 11 Dec. 1987.

Europe

The forty-fourth session of the Economic Commission for Europe (Geneva, 11-21 April 1989)[1] took place as the nations of eastern Europe and the Soviet Union moved at varying speeds towards pluralistic forms of governance and decentralized market economies. The ongoing economic reform process in many centrally planned economies accelerated dramatically in 1989, together with political change, creating new opportunities for enhanced East-West regional economic co-operation. The integration processes under way in Europe and North America at regional and sub-regional levels also promised improved economic relationships in the 1990s.

During the session, some ECE members expressed concern that integration processes, such as movement towards a single market within the European Community and free trade in North America, could divert trade away from current external trading partners. Problems persisted in such areas as protectionism in world trade, barriers to trade in advanced technology products, indebtedness, and imbalance in current accounts of the major industrial countries.

Environmental issues were considered to be increasingly important. More than ever, international co-operation was seen as essential to avert and repair environmental damage and to effectively confront global problems resulting from climate change, ozone depletion, nuclear and industrial accidents, and disposal of hazardous waste. The adoption[2] by ECE of the Charter on Ground-Water Management[3] was considered noteworthy.

In April, the Commission adopted one resolution, on its work as a whole and its future activities, again calling on member Governments to take full advantage of the Commission's potential as an instrument for dialogue, for strengthening economic relations and for multilateral regional co-operation.[4] In a decision brought to the Economic and Social Council's attention, the Commission recommended that electronic data interchange be used to facilitate international trade through world-wide application of UN/EDIFACT.[5]

Among other decisions adopted were those on: climate change;[6] statistics;[7] energy co-operation[8]; earthquake prediction;[9] Report of the World Commission on Environment and Development;[10] follow-up of the World Conference to Review and Appraise the Achievements of the United Nations Decade for Women;[11] environmental protection and water resources co-operation;[12] air pollution;[13] evolution in dimensions of loading units;[14] transport co-operation;[15] economic co-operation in the Mediterranean in the light of the Final Act of the Conference on Security and Co-operation in Europe;[16] standardization and related activities;[17] engineering industries and automation;[18] and analysis of economic growth conditions: medium- and long-term economic prospects and issues.[19]

Economic trends

According to the summary of the economic survey of Europe, 1989-1990,[20] economic performance of ECA market economies remained quite favourable, although average expansion tended to be moderate. In centrally planned economies, economic activity substantially slowed, turning to recession in several countries. While political change was often quite rapid, economic adjustment was generally slower and the economic performance of Eastern European countries worsened in 1989. Aggregate growth for the five reporting Eastern European countries was only half of 1 per cent. Apart from Czechoslovakia and the German Democratic Republic, output in Eastern Europe fell or stagnated, contracting in absolute terms in at least two countries. In the Soviet Union, output rose by less than 2.5 per cent, down from 4.5 per cent in 1988.

Eastern European economic problems were partly responsible for, and compounded by, social unrest, ranging from strikes to large-scale emigration. Policy-makers were preoccupied with restoring social stability and implementing economic stabilization programmes, which were expected to impose heavy burdens on the population for the immediate future. However, with an emerging social consensus, formal economic stabilization programmes were being put in place. For the first time, Western market economy countries stated their willingness to support the reform process.

Output growth slowed in North America and remained broadly unchanged in Western Europe. Total output in market economies averaged a growth rate of 3.5 per cent, compared with more than 4 per cent in 1988. Business investment continued to be the major driving force of domestic demand, but private consumption remained strong. Domestic demand stimulated international trade, making for considerable export and import growth. Western Europe's employment growth was about 1 per cent; unemployment fell from 8.5 per cent in 1988 to a still high 8 per cent. The employment rate in the United States grew by 2 per cent and, despite an economic slow-down, unemployment fell to 5 per cent, the lowest rate since 1973. Consumer prices rose somewhat faster than in 1988, although the average increase in 1989 of 4.5 per cent concealed a stabilization, or even deceleration, in the second half of the year, helped by the easing of non-oil commodity prices and a restrictive monetary policy.

East-West trade showed a decrease in exports for Eastern Europe and an increase in imports. In some countries, notably Czechoslovakia and Hungary, trade régime changes appeared to favour export growth. Overall, exports slowed by some 3 per cent in the first nine months of 1989 and were expected to be lower still as political events affected the supply of exportables. Imports from the West rose by 13 per cent in the first nine months of 1989, mainly reflecting trade liberalization in Hungary and Poland. Import growth appeared to slow towards year's end, reflecting efforts to improve current accounts or hold down the growth of foreign debt, which rose by an aggregate net of $1.5 billion in 1989.

In the Soviet Union, export growth slowed substantially, in part due to supply difficulties regarding fuels and transport. Terms of trade with the West improved, owing to higher world fuel prices. There was nonetheless a reported sharp widening in the Soviet trade deficit with the West—from some $3 billion in 1988 to $6.5 billion. The current account deficit continued to worsen, increasing from $26.5 billion to $36.5 billion, in nominal terms.

The ECE secretariat examined the question of whether a new "Marshall Plan"—the United States aid programme to assist war-ravaged Europe after the Second World War—would be appropriate now to assist Eastern Europe. Despite some similarities in problems facing post-war Western Europe and those of Eastern Europe in 1989, the differences in the basic economic structure of the two economic systems, particularly their capacity to absorb foreign financial aid, were seen as being so wide that it was concluded that a programme patterned after the Marshall Plan would be inappropriate at present. In fact, whereas

Marshall Plan aid had consisted mostly of grant aid, with a relatively small proportion of technical assistance, that proportion might more usefully be reversed with regard to Eastern European countries, given the nature of their structural problems—a lack of institutional infrastructure appropriate to a market economy. Also, the time required for Eastern programmes was seen as having to be much longer than the estimated four years for which Marshall aid was originally committed.

A proposal was also made to create, similar to the Marshall Plan, a Central European Payments Union to promote mutual convertibility and thus facilitate the transition of Eastern European countries to a system of free trade and multilateral settlements. Close monitoring and review of both the Western programmes and the Eastern reform process were considered especially important given the prevailing uncertainties.

Activities in 1989

Regional economic co-operation

The Senior Economic Advisers to ECE Governments (twenty-fifth session, Geneva, 13-17 February)[21] exchanged information on medium- and long-term economic development in the ECE region. The Executive Secretary of ECE, addressing the meeting, underlined three complex issues: reforms in the USSR and most centrally planned economies; integration processes in countries of Western Europe, North America and the Council for Mutual Economic Assistance; and co-ordination of national economic policies. Generally agreed were the necessity of structural adjustments in market economies and, in centrally planned economies, reforms to modernize planning and management systems. The Senior Economic Advisers agreed that the secretariat's work on a data base and macro-economic models should be continued as a long-term effort. Special attention was given to analysis of growth conditions for 1991-1995.

Co-operation among Mediterranean countries

By an April decision,[16] the Executive Secretary was asked to continue co-operation with the Executive Secretaries of ECA and the Economic and Social Commission for Western Asia (ESCWA) and other relevant UN bodies and to pursue contacts with non-ECE Mediterranean countries on subjects of common interest within ECE's competence. Non-ECE Mediterranean countries participated in ECE meetings on agriculture, electric power, gas, steel, timber, trade and transport. The Executive Secretary was to report on possible co-operation in environmental protection.

International trade

The Committee on the Development of Trade (thirty-eighth session, Geneva, 4-8 December)[22] continued to review recent and prospective trends, policies and problems affecting interregional and intraregional trade, particularly in the context of economic and political changes taking place in many countries of the region. It examined East-West trade in services, analysing developments and prospective trends, and requested information on efforts required by ECE member countries to extend and improve the existing data base on East-West service transactions. In a decision on statistics,[7] the Committee suggested a joint meeting of experts with the Conference of European Statisticians to discuss East-West trade statistics disparities and to suggest means to improve international comparability. On compensation trade, the Committee decided to convene a special meeting of experts in 1990, on both governmental and non-governmental levels, to consider countertrade effects on small- and medium-sized enterprises.

A seminar on industrial equipment leasing in East-West trade was held in September, which issued a report on development of market information and techniques and improved business contacts.[23]

Taking into consideration the successful Meeting of Experts on East-West Joint Ventures held in Genoa, Italy, in March, the Committee asked for an ECE study on conditions for promoting foreign direct investment, including special economic zones, joint ventures and other forms of industrial co-operation in the region.

The Working Party on International Contract Practices in Industry met in June and November and had before it drafts for a guide on legal aspects of new forms of industrial co-operation. It approved portions concerning international counter-purchase contracts; considered a draft text dealing with international buyback contracts; and decided that its next topic would be "legal aspects of financing the new and developing forms of East-West trade".

The Working Party on Facilitation of International Trade Procedures met in March and September and adopted, for trial use, a number of UN/EDIFACT messages related to customs operations. The Working Party planned to continue to develop standard messages, to update its recommendations whenever necessary, and to promote practical implementation world wide. (See above, Economic and Social Council **resolution 1989/118**.)

Transport

The Inland Transport Committee held its fiftieth regular session (Geneva, 30 January–3 February)[24] and a special fifty-first session (2-10 October).[25] During its regular session it discussed measures to simplify international transport and increase efficiency. Analysis of traffic flows on traffic corridors aimed at establishing an intermodal approach to transport within an international context was considered in light of economic and political developments in Eastern Europe. The application and possible undating of all international instruments prepared under the Committee's auspices was examined. The body endorsed the decision to organize the first "ECE Road Safety Week" in 1990 as an effort to reduce traffic accidents. It entrusted subordinate bodies with questions concerning environmental problems.[24]

Given the constant increase in transport of dangerous goods, the Committee decided to devote a special session to discussion of a draft convention on civil liability for damage caused during carriage of dangerous goods by road, rail and inland navigation vessels,[26] as a basis for adequate and rapid compensation to victims of damage caused during the transport of such goods internationally.

Industry

The twenty-second session of the Chemical Industry Committee (Geneva, 4-6 October)[27] completed its study on membrane technology in the chemical industry.[28] It endorsed reports from meetings on aromatic hydrocarbons, olefins, the periodic survey, the rational use of water in the chemical industry, and substitutes for tripolyphosphate in detergents. Two new studies were authorized: on engineering plastics and on recycling of plastics in ECE member countries. Seminars were held on the use of electrical energy in the chemical industry and on the role of the chemical industry in environmental protection.

The Working Party on Engineering Industries and Automation (ninth session, Geneva, 20-23 February)[29] endorsed reports on food-processing machinery, including packaging techniques; statistics concerning engineering industries and automation; and new means for air protection in engineering industries. Information from a seminar on computer-integrated manufacturing was considered. In April, the Commission approved the Committee's work programme for 1989-1993,[18] authorizing continued work in low-waste processing, the rehabilitation of engineering, and new materials and their application in engineering industries.

The fifty-seventh session of the Steel Committee (Geneva, 25-27 October)[30] reviewed reports on short- and medium-term trends in the steel market and relevant industry statistical data. It discussed and endorsed the reports of meetings on the steel market and steel statistics, technical and economic aspects of coated steel products

manufacture and application, recuperation and economic utilization of iron and steel industry by-products, and iron and steel industry importance for the economic activities of member countries. Work continued on the Annual Bulletin of European Steel Statistics and the Bulletin of Statistics of World Steel Trade. A seminar was held on economic and technical aspects of iron and steel industry modernization in Poland in May. The Committee, in adopting its 1990-1994 work programme, was to continue work on seminars on technical and economic aspects of coated steel product manufacture and application and on users' metallurgical requirements in the welding of steel products, as well as a study on steel product quality and maximum utilization of scrap.

Energy resources

Following a decision taken by the Senior Advisers to ECE Governments on Energy at their sixth (1988) session,[31] a Preparatory Meeting for the Study on the Interrelationship between Environmental and Energy Policies took place in May 1989.[32] The Symposium on the Optimum Use of Primary Resources in Meeting Final Heat Demand was held in June in Prague. A Preparatory Meeting for a Symposium on Energy Efficiency Measures in Industry was held in November.

The Coal Committee held its eighty-fifth session from 30 October to 2 November,[33] focusing on the region's general energy problems. Work commenced on a uniform code of practices for draught survey techniques and equipment specifications for determining the weight of bulk coal carriers. The meeting also reviewed the recommendations of a symposium on forecasting and prevention of rockbursts and sudden outbursts of coal, rock and gas.

The forty-seventh session of the Committee on Electric Power (Geneva, 6-9 February)[34] examined problems of planning and operating large power systems, the relationship between electricity and the environment, implications of climatic change, and East-West and Balkan electric power interconnections. A seminar on new developments in geothermal energy was held in May in Turkey. Preparations continued for a 1990 seminar in Iassi-Moldavia, Romania, on the rational use of electricity.

The thirty-fifth session of the Committee on Gas (Geneva, 16-19 January)[35] examined general energy problems in the region, as well as medium- and long-term prospects, and reviewed expert-level work on gas statistics, resources, production, use and distribution. A symposium on current developments and trends in underground storage of natural gas and liquid petroleum gas was held in Paris (29 May–2 June). Preparations were made for a symposium on the use of computers in the gas industry. Plans were made for a symposium, in co-operation with ESCWA and ECA, on long-term prospects of gas market developments in the respective regions and another on use of isotopes in natural gas prospecting.

Water

In April, ECE adopted the Charter on Ground-Water Management[2] on the recommendation of the Senior Advisers. The Charter underlined that ground water should be recognized as a commodity with economic and ecological value. Governments were called on to formulate and implement long-term policies to protect ground water as a natural resource by preventing pollution and over-use both at national and international levels. Ground-water policies should co-ordinate legal, administrative, regulatory and economic instruments with the best available technologies and education, and public information should be made available to increase awareness of inherent ground-water problems and strengthen international co-operation, the Charter stated.

The ECE Senior Advisers also continued work on a code of conduct on accidental pollution of transboundary inland waters and formulated recommendations on waste-water treatment, liability in case of accidental pollution and an ecosystems approach to water management. They analyzed current and future prospects for water resources utilization and pollution control in the region, and established a task force on the application of environmental impact assessment principles to policies, plans and programmes, producing a final report with draft recommendations.

The Advisers endorsed recommendations to ECE Governments on dam safety, with an emphasis on small dams,[36] and held a joint symposium, with the Committee on Agricultural Problems, on improving irrigation practices to preserve and protect water resources and increase crop yields.

Agriculture and timber

The fortieth session of the Committee on Agricultural Problems (Geneva, 6-10 March)[37] reviewed reports on trade and commodities; European trade in agricultural products; and the market situation for grains, livestock and meat, dairy products and eggs. It adopted its 1989-1993 work programme, relaunching work on agriculture output and inputs allowing for common presentation of country data irrespective of socio-economic differences. Meetings were held to consider standardization of porcine and bovine meat, new and non-conventional feeds in ruminant nutrition, and improved irrigation practices to preserve and protect water resources and increase

crop yields. A technical draft report was prepared on modern possibilities of genetic engineering for the selection of agriculture plants.

The forty-seventh session of the Timber Committee (Geneva, 9-13 October)[38] completed studies on long-term developments in the USSR and in North America. Preparations were going ahead for the fifth in the same series of studies, on European timber trends and prospects to the year 2000 and beyond. The 1990-1994 work programme was approved. A study, sponsored by the Committee and the International Tropical Timber Organization (ITTO), was published on European trade and markets for tropical hardwoods.

Seminars were held in Finland on training professional forest workers; in Belgium on soil impact of forest operations mechanization; and in Turkey on mechanization of mountain-terrain harvesting operations. A joint FAO/ECE Working Party on Forest Economics and Statistics held its biennial meeting in December, completing preparations for the temperate-zone part of the Global Forest Resource Assessment 1990, with FAO dealing with tropical-zone issues.

Science and technology

The Senior Advisers to ECE Governments on Science and Technology held their seventeenth session in Geneva (18-22 September).[39] They exchanged views on the transition from an industrial and technological society to one that was scientific and informational. Consideration was given to possible directions of international scientific and technological co-operation in the region, including promoting contacts among young scientists; ways and means to increase innovation work of small- and medium-sized enterprises; and follow-up action to the report of the World Commission on Environment and Development.

The Senior Advisers continued collecting information for the inventory of existing safety guidelines in biotechnology. They reviewed the results of seminars on evaluation in the management of research and development and on earthquake prediction and initiated follow-up action. Preparations began for a seminar on the role of long-term forecasting in the formulation of science and technology policies, to be held in Prague in April 1990.

Environment

The Senior Advisers to UN/ECE Governments on Environmental and Water Problems, at their second session (Geneva, 28 February–3 March)[40] made progress on a regional agreement on environmental impact assessment in a transboundary context. Consultations of experts on flora, fauna and their habitats were held in La Laguna, Spain, in January and Troya, Portugal, in

October/November. The group drafted a European Red List of Threatened Animals and Plants for consideration by the Senior Advisers. A seminar on the economic implications of low-waste technology (The Hague, Netherlands, October) prepared draft recommendations, focusing on legal, administrative and economic instruments to promote the development and application of such technology, its benefits for industry and society, and problems encountered in its implementation. Work continued on evaluating the cost-effectiveness of energy- and resource-saving technologies and on recovery, recycling and re-utilization of industrial wastes. The Working Party on Low- and Non-waste Technology recommended elaboration of a regional strategy on integrated waste management.

Transboundary air pollution

Under the Executive Body for the Convention on Long-range Transboundary Air Pollution (seventh session, Geneva, 21-24 November),[41] two new subsidiary bodies began work in 1989: the Working Group on Abatement Strategies, to develop internationally agreed target loads; and the Working Group on Volatile Organic Compounds, to develop a draft protocol to control emissions of such compounds. Three new task forces were established on the exchange of technology, mapping of critical levels and loads, and emissions of heavy metals.

International co-operative programmes were developed on air pollution effects on freshwaters, forests, materials, agriculture and terrestrial ecosystems. The Executive Body began arrangements for revision of existing, or preparations of new, protocols to its Convention on Long-Range Transboundary Air Pollution for further reduction of sulphur emissions after 1993. It also considered measures to promote an exchange of technology, information and experts to effectively reduce air pollutant emissions.

In April, ECE[13] appealed to member Governments to intensify efforts to protect and improve the environment, giving high priority to air pollutant control and reduction, such as sulphur dioxide and nitrogen oxide emissions.

Human settlements

The fiftieth session of the Committee on Housing, Building and Planning (Geneva, 12-15 September)[42] discussed how to adapt experiences derived from ECE activities to assist developing countries in implementing the Global Strategy for Shelter to the Year 2000. A seminar on the effectiveness of settlement planning (London, October) adopted conclusions on government policy, recommending that the Committee pursue further work on human settlements aspects of sustainable development. Plans were made for a seminar on comprehensive policies for renewal and modernization of settlements, to be held in the USSR in May 1991, and for a symposium on international tourism, to be held in the early 1990s. Studies on rent policy and research were completed, as were the final chapters of the Compendium of Model Provisions for Building Regulations. The Committee considered a draft action-plan on promotion of international trade in construction products, including a draft framework agreement on uniform rules for approval and certification of construction products. A second joint meeting on human settlements statistics, held in March in co-operation with the Conference of European Statisticians, stressed the importance of developing statistics on modernization, land-use, housing distribution and quality aspects.

Statistics

The thirty-seventh plenary session of the Conference of European Statisticians (Geneva, 12-16 June)[43] discussed co-ordination of the statistical activities of European intergovernmental organizations and regional statistical co-operation, and continued to provide methodological assistance to member countries on economic, social, demographic, energy and environmental statistics. It endorsed the importance of developing international standards for electronic data interchange of statistical information within the framework of UN/EDIFACT. General agreement was reached on enhancing the informative role of statistics through comprehensive analysis and interpretation of data. Substantive discussions were also held on the use of micro-computers in statistical services. Work in economic statistics continued to focus on revising and integrating the two systems of national accounting and comparing macro-economic data and purchasing power parities. Increased attention was given to new areas, such as statistics of services, and subjects on which international guidelines had not yet been found to work, such as income distribution statistics.

Standardization

In April,[44] ECE decided that in the first half of 1990 it would convene the eleventh Meeting of Government Officials Responsible for Standardization Policies. The Experts on Standardization Policies met in Geneva in May and agreed on preparatory work to be done. Co-ordinators and rapporteurs met (September, Washington, D.C.) to advance that work and to visit standards bodies. Preparations commenced for a one-day seminar on international standards for environmental protection, to be held around the eleventh Meeting.

Women

In April,[11] the Commission noted the Executive Secretary's report[45] on the Commission's contribution to follow-up of the World Conference to Review and Appraise the Achievements of the UN Decade for Women and asked for a further report.

In November, the Conference of European Statisticians convened a Joint Meeting with the International Research and Training Institute for the Advancement of Women on statistics of women.[46]

REFERENCES

[1]E/1989/34. [2]*Ibid.* (dec. E(44)). [3]E/ECE/1197. [4]E/1989/34 (res. 1(44)). [5]*Ibid.* (dec. L(44)). [6]*Ibid.* (dec. B(44)). [7]*Ibid.* (dec. C(44)). [8]*Ibid.* (dec. D(44)). [9]*Ibid.* (dec. F(44)). [10]*Ibid.* (dec. G(44)). [11]*Ibid.* (dec. H(44)). [12]*Ibid.* (dec. I(44)). [13]*Ibid.* (dec. J(44)). [14]*Ibid.* (dec. K(44)). [15]*Ibid.* (dec. M(44)). [16]*Ibid.* (dec. N(44)). [17]*Ibid.* (dec. O(44)). [18]*Ibid.* (dec. P(44)). [19]*Ibid.* (dec. Q(44)). [20]E/1990/51. [21]ECE/EC.AD/34. [22]E/ECE/1199. [23]ECE/TRADE/SEM.9/2. [24]ECE/TRANS/74 & Add.1. [25]ECE/TRANS/78. [26]ECE/TRANS/79. [27]ECE/CHEM/74 & Corr.1. [28]ECE/CHEM/72. [29]ECE/ENG.AUT/38. [30]ECE/STEEL/67. [31]YUN 1988, p. 291. [32]ECE/ENERGY/AC.10/4. [33]ECE/COAL/119. [34]ECE/EP/78. [35]ECE/GAS/94. [36]ENVWA/SEM.1/3. [37]ECE/AGRI/101. [38]ECE/TIM/49. [39]ECE/SC.TECH/37. [40]ECE/ENVWA/9. [41]ECE/EB.AIR/20. [42]ECE/HBP/76. [43]ECE/CES/34. [44]ECE/STAND/31. [45]E/ECE/1181. [46]E/ECE/1212.

Latin America and the Caribbean

The Economic Commission for Latin America and the Caribbean (ECLAC) Committee of the Whole held its twentieth session[1] in New York on 30 and 31 March. The Committee of High-Level Government Experts also took place in New York from 27 to 29 March and again from 22 to 24 May. Its biennial report covered the period 28 April 1988–11 May 1990.[2] Both Committee agendas focused on two substantive items: preparations for the new fourth International Development Decade, and economic evolution of the region since 1987. The region's economy in 1988 saw a prolongation of the decade's economic stagnation, with the debt crisis a prime cause.

The Committee of the Whole adopted resolutions on preparing an international development strategy for the fourth UN Development Decade and on support to Nicaragua for reconstruction following Hurricane Joan.

Economic trends

As the 1980s drew to a close, most countries of Latin America and the Caribbean continued to struggle with inflation and stabilization efforts, despite favourable results in boosting exports, according to a summary[3] of the *Economic Survey of Latin America and the Caribbean, 1989.*[4] Stagnation and high inflation resulted largely from transfer of resources abroad, through debt servicing in 1989 amounting to $26 billion. After eight years of attempting to attain adjustment, stabilization, growth and production restructuring, most countries swayed under the burden of external debt and, with little access to fresh external finance, continued to display a complex syndrome of structural imbalance, fiscal deficit and low levels of investment, frequently accompanied by high inflation and serious deterioration in real wages.

The average GDP did increase by 1.1 per cent in 1989, a little more than the year before, but still less than population growth. Thus the average per capita product declined for the second year running, falling to 1977-1978 levels. Overall, the average per capita product was 8 per cent lower than it had been in 1980, and total investment had plummeted, the huge social costs of which were considered at least partly the reason for serious outbreaks of violence in 1989 in some countries.

Significant per capita growth—more than 2 per cent—was registered only in Barbados, Costa Rica, Paraguay and, most of all, Chile, where the per capita product rose by almost 7 per cent. The slight improvement in the region's average product came principally from a modest 3 per cent growth rate in Brazil and Mexico, the economies of which accounted for almost two thirds of the economy of the region.

Average regional inflation surged for the third successive year, for the first time reaching almost 1,000 per cent. New records were set in Argentina (5,000 per cent), Peru and Brazil. Ecuador, Uruguay and Venezuela ranged between 50 and 100 per cent. Some countries contained inflation rates; in others, there were significant reductions. Nicaragua's rate of 30,000 per cent in 1988 was brought down to 3,500 per cent after a drastic stabilization programme. Mexico experienced the most striking progress, due to severe controls of the fiscal sector and price/wage reconciliation policies; its rate went down, from 52 per cent in 1988 to less than 20 per cent a year later. Overall, there was a marked decline in the number of countries still immune to inflation, especially in Central America. Only Barbados, Haiti and Panama remained free of significant inflation problems, registering price increases of less than 10 per cent a year. The main inflationary pressure was the inability of fiscal systems to discharge essential functions while maintaining external debt payments. Cases of extraordinarily high inflation stemmed from the inability to control the public deficit, sometimes combined with a growing financial burden of high real interest rates on domestic debt, uncertain future economic trends, and runs on foreign exchange.

There was a generally modest increase in export value and contraction in imports. Yet, despite a considerable surplus, the number of countries in arrears with external debt service increased, along with the number of them obliged to give up fully servicing external debts, including, for the first time together, three of the four biggest debtors—Argentina, Brazil and Venezuela. Only 5 of 19 countries for which up-to-date information was available had fully serviced their debt on time.

Although the value of exports rose by 9 per cent, that rate was significantly down from 1987 and 1988. Due to international interest-rate increases, regional interest and profits payments increased by nearly $4 billion. Oil countries' export growth—$5.4 billion—was considered sufficient, not only to cover their $1.7 billion increase in factor service payments but also to leave a substantial surplus (equivalent to 10 per cent of imports), to be used for import increase or augmenting international reserves. In non-oil-exporting countries, however, the $2.5 billion interest increase on debt wiped out most of the modest export growth.

General labour market trends in 1989 were similar to 1988, the Economic Survey reported. Severe recession in several countries led to increased underemployment. Rates of urban unemployment rose considerably in Argentina, Nicaragua, Panama, Peru and Venezuela. In Chile, Costa Rica, and Guatemala, whose economies experienced steady growth or became over-heated through an excessive expansion of demand, that rate fell notably. Unemployment tended to decrease even in countries which had slow or near zero growth rates, such as Brazil, Colombia, Honduras, Mexico and Uruguay. A continued rise in already high rates of open unemployment was seen only in Bolivia and Ecuador.

Activities in 1989

Development policy and regional economic co-operation

The Committee as a Whole of ECLAC reviewed documents on preparations for a new international development strategy[5] and recent economic trends in Latin America and the Caribbean.[6] These were considered together to lay a foundation for a regional position. The Committee decided to ask the ECLAC secretariat to follow carefully the strategy's entire preparatory process, in close consultation with Governments of member States. The Committee of High-level Experts wanted continued discussions on a common position. A working group was set up to discuss a document[7] adopted by the Experts: "Basic guidelines of the Latin American and Caribbean countries for the process of formulation of the international development strategy for the fourth United Nations development decade".

The eighth meeting[8] of the Latin American and Caribbean Institute for Economic and Social Development (ILPES) Regional Council for Planning (Montevideo, Uruguay, 9 May) adopted a report on its 1988 activities and its 1989 draft work programme. The Institute continued work in public policy planning and co-ordination in the economic and social fields, including advisory assistance, training and applied research.

The Caribbean Development and Co-operation Committee (CDCC) held its technical meeting 4-6 December and the twelfth session of its ministerial meeting on 7-8 December in Curaçao, Netherlands Antilles.[9] Resolutions were adopted on co-operation between CDCC and regional and international organizations and specialized agencies, establishing a working group on non-independent Caribbean countries, support of the removal of language barriers, and co-ordination between CDCC and the secretariat of the Caribbean Community (CARICOM) in relation to non-CARICOM member countries.

In the biennial period, seven technical reports were published on such topics as an accounting framework for evaluating fiscal policy in Latin America, fiscal policy in the 1980s, the measurement and breakdown of the public deficit in Latin America and the results of four national case-studies. National seminars were held to discuss the results of the case-studies, and a regional meeting on methodologies for measuring the public deficit and evaluating fiscal policy also took place. Regarding stabilization, adjustment and external debt, ECLAC subregional headquarters in Mexico made progress in modernizing debt recording in the Central American countries. ECLAC provided technical assistance to ministers responsible for following up the Special Plan of Economic Co-operation for Central America. In co-ordination with the secretariat of the General Treaty on Central American Economic Integration, the Central American Research Institute for Industry and UNDP, work continued on drafting a document on assessing Central American industrial reconversion needs.

The Commission continued monitoring international economic trends, especially economic changes in the industrialized countries, to ascertain effects on regional development. ECLAC jointly organized a high-level seminar (Santiago, Chile, 4-6 April) with the Deutsche Gesellschaft für Technische Zusammenarbeit (German Agency for Technical Co-operation) and the Economic Development Institute of the World Bank on adjustment with growth and on public finances in Latin America. Meetings and seminars were held on obstacles to the anti-poverty strategy in Central

America; trade policy; and adjustment policies and integration in Central America.

Industrial, scientific and technological development

The main industrial development activities of ECLAC continued to focus on industrial restructuring at the international level and in Latin America, support for small and medium-scale industry, and the capital goods industry. A high-level meeting was held (Santiago, Chile, 26-27 January) in preparation for an ECLAC/UNDP project on designing policies to strengthen the capacity for technological innovation and increase the international competitiveness of Latin American industry. Seminars were held on industrial restructuring and international competitiveness using Italy as one example.

As for science and technology, ECLAC activities focused on technological development and challenges related to the current world-wide revolution in the field. Case-studies were carried out on technological innovation and international competitiveness in Argentina, Brazil, Colombia, Costa Rica and Mexico. A methodological approach was developed to study links between international trade and technology transfer. An interregional meeting (Feldafing, Federal Republic of Germany, 22-26 February) on international co-operation in science and technology for development and a regional meeting (San Jose, Costa Rica, 8-14 April) on the progress of science and technology for regional development were organized by the United Nations Centre for Science and Technology for Development.

International trade and development finance

The International Trade and Development Division focused on three main areas: Latin America and the proposed new international economic order; economic relations between Latin America and other regions; and economic integration and co-operation.

In a follow-up to the multilateral trade negotiations within the General Agreement on Tariffs and Trade (GATT), known as the Uruguay Round, reports identifying the strategic interest pursued by Latin American countries were prepared and analyzed in collaboration with UNCTAD. The growing role of commodity exchanges, especially futures markets, in the pricing of commodities were considered in special studies of the London Metal Exchange, the Chicago grain market and the New York tropical commodities market. The impact of the latest forms of technological progress on market prospects for some commodities and on global examination of the current status of Latin America's export commodities were considered.

Meetings took place on financial and monetary co-operation in connection with regional trade; the status and prospects of commodities exported by Latin America; and technological options and development opportunities regarding regional aluminium and tin industries. A fourth meeting of Officials Responsible for the External Trade of the Member Countries of the Latin American Integration Association (ALADI) took place in Santiago on 11-12 September.

Natural resources and energy

Promotion and support of regional co-operation in water resources management, development and conservation of high-altitude river basins, co-operation in mineral exploitation and assistance in elaborating national policies concerning the oceans were the focus of the work of the Natural Resources and Energy Division. Other areas of concern were: energy forecasting, energy prices and their impact on world energy markets, and updating the ECLAC energy data bank.

Training courses and meetings were held on training in the management of water resource projects and systems; water resources management; international drinking water supply and sanitation; the mining/metallurgical sector in regional development; economic benefits of meterological services; and electrical interconnections.

The Joint Meeting of the River Lempa Executive Commission/Electrical Interconnection System for Central America was held in San Salvador.

Transport

During 1989, three major projects were carried out in the area of transport on: regional economic co-operation in establishing interior cargo terminals; technical co-operation among Latin American countries on export transport, distribution, marketing, and competitiveness; and impact of subsidies and differing control and organization on urban public transport systems.

Other meetings and seminars dealt with: containerization on the South American east coast and its role in export stimulation; the chain of distribution and the competitiveness of Latin American exports regarding Chilean fruit; and the quality of regional urban collective transport.

Social development

Major studies during the year from the ECLAC Social Development Division concerned: a broad policy outline of regional human resources development; positions of different social and institutional agents regarding incorporation of new production technologies, based on field work in

Argentina, Bolivia, Chile and Ecuador; principal institutional problems regarding social policy with special reference to health problems, based on national experiences of Argentina, Brazil and Peru; existing problems and potentialities in implementing social policies at the local level within the framework of decentralization, based on work done in Colombia, Costa Rica and Guatemala; living conditions and prospects for youth and the elderly; and the deterioration of social conditions as a result of the current economic crisis and prospects for future social trends resulting from the region's new structural conditions.

A seminar was held in Santiago (29-31 May) on the experience of Sweden and Latin America regarding development, democracy and equity, in collaboration with the International Centre of the Swedish Workers' Movement.

Population

Work of the Latin American Demographic Centre (CELADE), complementing that of ECLAC, aimed at furthering regional economic and social development through a work programme addressing problems relating specifically to population and development. Seminars were held on infant mortality in Costa Rica; demographic effects of development projects; and the elderly.

Integration of women

The Presiding Officers elected at the fourth Regional Conference on the Integration of Women into the Economic and Social Development of Latin America and the Caribbean held their ninth meeting (Panajachel, Guatemala, 26-27 September). They considered: substantive documents prepared since the fourth Regional Conference, the next regular Regional Conference, and guidelines for the preparatory meeting for the 1995 World Conference on Women.

Environment

Activities carried out by the Joint ECLAC/UNEP Development and Environment Unit aimed at strengthening the environmental dimension in ECLAC's work and at promoting regional action regarding strategies and policies for environmentally sustainable development.

Seminars were held on: priorities for sustainable regional environmental development; environmental impact assessment as an instrument of environmental management; the sustainable development strategy for southern Honduras; pollution from the Esmeraldas State Refinery in Ecuador in the Esmeraldas and Teaone Rivers; rehabilitation of terraces and other traditional technologies; methods used in constructing the Magallanes natural heritage accounts; and natural heritage

inventories and accounts in the state of Morelos, Mexico.

Human settlements

The human settlements programme, carried out jointly by ECLAC and the UN Centre for Human Settlements, strengthened research and development activities, especially regarding functioning of metropolitan centres, strengthening of local government capacity to manage human settlements and housing policy formulation within national development strategies. The unit also did preliminary work on the role of non-governmental and community organizations in managing the habitat.

A seminar on medium-sized cities was held in Santiago (15-16 June), organized by "SUR Profesionales," an NGO, ECLAC and the Latin American Council for the Social Sciences.

Food and agriculture

Significant progress was made in collaboration with FAO on a study on potentials for agricultural and rural development in Latin America and the Caribbean and also in improving methodologies used to process quantitative information for prospective agricultural analysis.

The seventh Conference of Ministers and Heads of Planning of Latin America and the Caribbean was held in Montevideo from 8 to 10 May. The Ministers of Agriculture of the Countries of the Andean Group met in Lima in August/September. Other ECLAC-sponsored meetings dealt with: trade and macroeconomic policies and their impact on agriculture in the structural adjustment context; regional agroindustrial development policies; and regional agricultural and rural development.

Statistics and economic projections

Development of the ECLAC statistics programme for the biennium focused on: expansion of data banks; technical co-operation; and dissemination of information, technological innovations and international standards.

The Directors of Statistics of the Americas held a meeting in Santiago from 26 to 29 September. Four seminars were held on: field personnel training for on-site activities; economic censuses and registers of establishments; data bases and computerized data transmission; and statistics of international trade in services.

Transnational corporations

The joint ECLAC/Centre on Transnational Corporations (TNCs) unit focused on two areas: identifying the contribution and impact of TNCs on regional development, and studies of particular issues in individual countries and sectors. A report was issued on the performance of transnational banks and the international external debt crisis. Elaboration of a regional directory of foreign investment continued. In 1989, the joint unit participated in the fifteenth session (New York, 5-14 April) of the Commission on TNCs.

Co-operation between the UN and the Latin American Economic System

In compliance with a 1988 Assembly resolution[10], the Secretary-General reported[11] in October that since the 1975 establishment of the Latin American Economic System (SELA), considerable co-operation had taken place between it and the United Nations, particularly with ECLAC, but also with other UN organizations, agencies and programmes.

Co-operation was highly diversified, he said, and a natural, close and fruitful co-operation had continued to develop between ECLAC and SELA. In many cases, the co-operation had become more permanent through various agreements and conventions. Some UN entities that were not carrying out activities with SELA had expressed their desire to explore joint activities. ECLAC participated in the third informal meeting of organizations working in areas related to services (Caracas, 19 May). Joint ECLAC/SELA meetings were planned on five service sectors: telecommunications, financial services, air transport, construction and engineering, and audiovisual materials, in order to define regional interests more clearly with regard to the trade of those services within the Uruguay Rounds and in the regional and subregional context.

The Latin American Council, at its 15th meeting (Cartagena, 25 July–1 August), adopted a resolution on co-operation between the Latin American economic system and the United Nations, giving high priority to the development of close co-operation with ECLAC in promoting a truly regional system of co-operation. It also expressed the need to deepen co-operation with UNDP and noted with satisfaction the relations of co-operation with UNESCO, UNICEF, UNCTAD, UNIDO and WIPO.

GENERAL ASSEMBLY ACTION

On 17 October 1989, the General Assembly adopted **resolution 44/4** without vote.

Co-operation between the United Nations and the Latin American Economic System

The General Assembly,

Recalling its resolution 43/5 of 17 October 1988 on co-operation between the United Nations and the Latin American Economic System,

Having considered the report of the Secretary-General on co-operation between the United Nations and the Latin American Economic System,

Taking into account decision 289 of 1 August 1989 on co-operation between the United Nations and the Latin American Economic System, adopted at the fifteenth regular session of the Latin American Council,

Considering that the Economic Commission for Latin America and the Caribbean has developed close ties of co-operation with the Latin American Economic System and that efforts have been successfully made to co-ordinate their activities,

Bearing in mind that the Permanent Secretariat of the Latin American Economic System has carried out various programmes with the support of the United Nations Development Programme in areas that are considered of priority for the economic development of the region,

Considering also that the Latin American Economic System is developing joint activities with the specialized agencies and other bodies and programmes of the United Nations system, such as the United Nations Conference on Trade and Development, the United Nations Educational, Scientific and Cultural Organization, the United Nations Industrial Development Organization, the World Meteorological Organization, the World Health Organization, the World Intellectual Property Organization, the United Nations Environment Programme, the United Nations Centre on Transnational Corporations, the Office of the United Nations Disaster Relief Co-ordinator, the United Nations Institute for Training and Research and the International Telecommunication Union,

1. *Takes note with satisfaction* of the report of the Secretary-General;

2. *Expresses satisfaction* with decision 289 of the Latin American Council of the Latin American Economic System;

3. *Urges* the Economic Commission for Latin America and the Caribbean to broaden and deepen its co-ordination and mutual support activities with the Latin American Economic System;

4. *Urges* the United Nations Development Programme to strengthen and broaden its support to the programmes that the Permanent Secretariat of the Latin American Economic System is carrying out;

5. *Urges* the specialized agencies and other organizations and programmes of the United Nations system to continue and intensify their support for and co-operation with the activities of the Latin American Economic System;

6. *Requests* the Secretary-General of the United Nations to promote, in close collaboration with the Permanent Secretary of the Latin American Economic System, the holding of a meeting in 1990 between their respective secretariats, with the aim of identifying those areas in which it will be possible to broaden co-operation between the United Nations system and the Latin American Economic System;

7. *Requests* both the Secretary-General of the United Nations and the Permanent Secretary of the Latin American Economic System to initiate consultations for the purpose of drafting an agreement of co-operation between the United Nations and the Latin American Economic System;

8. *Also requests* the Secretary-General to submit to the General Assembly at its forty-fifth session a report on the implementation of the present resolution.

General Assembly resolution 44/4

17 October 1989   Meeting 32   Adopted without vote

26-nation draft (A/44/L.8); agenda item 24.

Special plan of economic co-operation for Central America

In pursuance of May and December 1988 Assembly resolutions,[12] the Secretary-General reported[13] in October on the Special Plan of Economic Co-operation for Central America, which the Assembly had decided to review and evaluate in 1989. The Secretary-General recalled that the Special Plan had been launched in September 1988 when the Vice-Presidents of Costa Rica, El Salvador, Guatemala, Honduras and Nicaragua had approved a mechanism for implementation. By August, 21 projects totalling some $11,224,000 had been approved or were in final stages of approval.

The first meeting of Central American governments with co-operating Governments and institutions was held from 4 to 6 July in Geneva, providing the opportunity for a collective dialogue on priorities. It was attended by 27 Governments, 29 UN organizations and 15 subregional Central American integration organizations, as well as representatives of the European Economic Community, the Organization of American States and the Inter-American Development Bank.

The Secretary-General stated that forecasts suggested that economic recovery for the subregion could not regain the levels of economic welfare of the 1970's before the end of the century. However, broad-based sustainable economic development would be possible provided, among other things, that the international community strongly supported the reconstruction efforts and that lasting peace and democratization was achieved.

He said that the Special Plan provided a framework and established priorities for international development co-operation for the subregion as a whole. A Programme in Favour of Displaced Persons, Refugees and Returnees became operative with a $115 million contribution from Italy. Some 136,500 people in the five Central American countries and Belize would benefit directly and nearly half a million indirectly. UNDP was primarily responsible for the Programme's implementation. The International Conference on Central American Refugees[14] was held in Guatemala City (29-31 May), which, the Secretary-General stated, successfully made the international community realize that displaced persons required just as much assistance, including international support, as refugees.

The Central American Governments and the World Food Programme (WFP) assessed immedi-

ate food needs at some $104 million.[17] In energy, international co-operation was urgently required in maintaining hydroelectric plants and an electrical interconnection. By 1989 the subregion's external debt had risen to $19 billion, with debt servicing equivalent to nearly half of all export earnings. UNDP had financed a project to establish a computerized information system for debt monitoring and follow-up in each Central American country. A draft proposal to restructure the Central American Monetary Stabilization Fund under a UNDP project was finalized in June. Other UNDP projects under way included an industrial reconversion assessment; creation of a portfolio of organizational development projects available for investment; formulation of telecommunication projects with the International Telecommunication Union; and strengthening the Central American Bank for Economic Integration. UNCTAD was executing a project to automate customs clearance procedures. UNICEF was considering a pilot project to treat children affected by violence in the region. UNIDO was executing a project to market handicrafts. Work also continued in the areas of nutrition, drinking water and sanitation. In January, a technical assistance project for the agricultural development of Central America was initiated with a $4.4 million budget, executed by the World Bank and financed by UNDP, the International Fund for Agricultural Development and the Government of Japan.

By **resolution 44/182** of 19 December, the General Assembly emphasized the urgent need to provide the Central American countries with financial resources.

(For further details regarding Central America, see PART TWO, Chapter II, and on refugees, PART THREE, Chapter XV.)

REFERENCES
[1]LC/G.1556(PLEN.20/5). [2]E/1990/43. [3]E/1990/54. [4]*Economic Survey of Latin America and the Caribbean, 1989*, Sales No. E.90.II.G.2. [5]LC/L.494 (PLEN.20/4). [6]LC/L.492(CEG.15/3). [7]LC/G.1569(CEG.16/2). [8]LC/IP/R.78. [9]LC/G.1610. [10]YUN 1988, p. 305, GA res. 43/5, 17 Oct. 1988. [11]A/44/550. [12]YUN 1988, pp. 307 & 308, GA res. 42/231 & 43/210, 12 May & 20 Dec. 1988. [13]A/44/519. [14]A/44/527 & Corr.1,2.

Western Asia

The Economic and Social Commission for Western Asia held its fifteenth session at the ministerial level at Baghdad, Iraq, on 17 and 18 May.[1] It was preceded by meetings of the Technical Committee's sixth session (13-15 May).[2]

The ESCWA Executive Secretary reported[3] economic growth, after years of recession, assisted by oil revenue improvements and recovery in other economic sectors, particularly industry, construction and services. Despite the cease-fire between Iran and Iraq, which had had a positive effect on ESCWA activities and programmes, there remained a number of potential flashpoints in Western Asia constituting possible impediments to development. Two events occurred in the region which were considered promising: establishment of the Arab Co-operation Council comprising Egypt, Iraq, Jordan and Yemen, with 27 agreements regulating all aspects of co-operation and co-ordination; and the final stages of unification of the Yemen Arab Republic and Democratic Yemen, giving new impetus to economic and social development to those two LDCs.

ESCWA adopted 14 resolutions, including those on: environment and regional development;[4] financial assistance to existing industries;[5] regional co-operation in peaceful nuclear energy uses;[6] projects for regional and sub-regional co-operation on new and renewable energy sources;[7] the regional household survey project;[8] the Transport and Communications Decade in Western Asia (1985-1994);[9] economic and social conditions of the Palestinian Arab people;[10] strengthening the Commission's role and performance;[11] international assistance to flood-stricken areas of Democratic Yemen;[12] and international development strategy for the fourth United Nations development decade.[13]

To strengthen ESCWA's role and performance,[11] the Commission created an advisory body, composed of the heads of Commission members' diplomatic missions in Iraq and a representative of the Iraqi Ministry of Foreign Affairs, to assist the Executive Secretary in studying problems connected with the Commission's work. The first meeting took place on 2 October, and the body was to meet normally every four months.

Economic and social trends

Overall economic performance improved in 1989 according to the summary of the survey of economic and social developments in the ESCWA region in 1989.[14] The regional GDP grew by 3.4 per cent, following several years of economic slow-down; however, per capita, there was virtually no increase, given the region's 3 per cent population growth rate.

Economic growth reflected strong international oil demand accompanied by a production decline of countries not members of the Organization of Petroleum Exporting Countries (OPEC), particularly the United States and Soviet Union. The ESCWA region increased its output 7.2 per cent while at the same time benefiting from an approximate 17.7 per cent rise in the average price of its crude oil. Higher revenues of regional oil-

exporting countries then had a spillover effect favouring non-oil countries.

In the countries of the Gulf Co-operation Council (GCC) subregion (Bahrain, Kuwait, Oman, Qatar, Saudi Arabia and the United Arab Emirates), after several years of stagnation or decline, higher oil revenues and adjustment policies contributed to a 3.52 per cent GDP growth rate in 1989. In other countries, economic growth was constrained by persistent balance-of-trade deficits and heavy debt-servicing burdens.

Most economic sectors performed better in 1989 than the previous year, except for agriculture, which after exceptional growth in 1988 (4.8 per cent), declined by 2.3 per cent in 1989. Manufacturing performed well in most countries due to diversification. Particular successes included the petrochemical industry in Saudi Arabia; the aluminium industry in Bahrain and the United Arab Emirates; and the textile and leather products and aluminium industries in Egypt. Light industry performed well in Jordan, Lebanon and the Syrian Arab Republic, in part because of national currency depreciation; import restrictions in Jordan and the Syrian Arab Republic also had their effect. Improvement continued in the service sector, particularly banking and tourism, and in international trade, which increased by 2.1 per cent in nominal terms in 1989, after a 1988 decline of 17 per cent. Inflationary pressures intensified in the more diversified economies in 1989, conservative estimates indicating rates exceeding 20 per cent in Egypt, Iraq, Jordan and the Syrian Arab Republic. In GCC countries, inflation remained more modest, with the highest rates estimated at 6 per cent in the United Arab Emirates and 3.5 per cent in Kuwait. Rates in other GCC countries ranged between 0.9 per cent and 3 per cent.

Unemployment problems were such that the labour-sending countries of Democratic Yemen, Egypt, Jordan, Lebanon, the Syrian Arab Republic and Yemen faced declining remittances due to repatriation of their nationals, as well as difficulties regarding housing, infrastructure, education, health facilities and balance of payments.

External debt continued to hamper economic growth and development, with the major indebted countries—Egypt, Iraq, Jordan and the Syrian Arab Republic—estimated to have collective external debts exceeding $150 million.

Though health conditions in the ESCWA region had improved because of systematic national health programmes, it was noted that patient-doctor ratios and infant mortality rates varied widely. Access to medical services was often very limited for some populations, particularly in rural areas. The regional literacy rate had reached 50 per cent and the gross enrolment rate in primary education was nearly 85 per cent, with close to 100 per cent in Bahrain, Iraq, Jordan, Oman, Qatar, Saudi Arabia, the Syrian Arab Republic and West Bank and Gaza. The figure in other ESCWA countries was significantly lower, mainly because of the low enrolment of girls. There was urgent need to promote adult education, as illiteracy was high among the elderly, particularly elderly women.

Overall, economic progress was seen as being closely linked to resolving the debt problem; reaching a permanent settlement in the Iran-Iraq conflict; breaking the deadlock with respect to the Palestinian issue; and ending the conflict in Lebanon. If those objectives were achieved, defence expenditures, among the highest in the world per capita, should fall, and badly needed resources could be channelled to economic development and growth.

Activities in 1989

Transport and communications

The transport and communications programme for the 1988-1989 biennium focused on project appraisal methods in the transport sector and development of multimodal transport, as well as development strategy formulation and policies in the maritime transport sector and studies on road construction techniques and on container traffic in Western Asia. Many of those activities pertained as well to the Transport and Communications Decade for Asia and the Pacific (1985-1994).[15]

A report on transport policy and planning, prepared after an *ad hoc* expert group meeting on the subject held in May, was reviewed by the Commission.[16] Another report, as well as a technical publication, were completed on multimodal transport, as was a study on regional road construction techniques[17] and on regional strategies and policies for the development of maritime transport.[18]

Energy

Under the energy programme, several reports and surveys were published in 1989. A survey and assessment of energy-related activities in the region covered the electricity sector,[19] including a comprehensive review of progress in national grid expansion and improvement and regional co-operation for electricity grids interconnection.

A meeting on the impact of changing oil market conditions on regional energy policies was held in Amman, Jordan, from 20 to 23 November. The entire region still depended heavily on oil, whether as the major energy source or the greatest material wealth source, and a technical publication on the subject[20] was completed.

A report was prepared on progress in the promotion of regional and international co-operation

in peaceful nuclear energy use and on such activities at the national and regional levels. A major component of the energy programme was completion of a report on latest technologies in new and renewable energy.[21]

Food and agriculture

Two issues of the recurrent publication *Agriculture and Development in Western Asia* (nos. 11 & 12) presented an assessment of recent regional agricultural development, analysing some emerging trends and tackling some critical agricultural problems at national and regional levels. Two training workshops, one regional and one national, were held on economics of resource conservation, combating desertification and land use planning. A report was made on training in agricultural planning and project analysis.[22]

Population

The ESCWA population programme produced and disseminated reliable data on a large number of demographic and related socio-economic variables necessary for development planning and policy-making that resulted in the publication of *Demographic and Related Socio-Economic Data Sheets of the Economic and Social Commission for Western Asia*, issue no. 6, and two studies: one on infant mortality patterns and trends in Bahrain, Egypt, Jordan, Kuwait, the Syrian Arab Republic and the United Arab Emirates; the other on socio-economic differentials of child mortality in Jordan. The *Population Bulletin of ESCWA* and the *Trilingual Demographic Dictionary* were published. An advanced training workshop for member States on organizing and administrating population and housing censuses was organized, and a fully computerized labour data base was established.

A seminar in Amman from 4 to 9 December was jointly organized with the International Labour Organisation, the Arab Labour Organization and the University of Jordan, entitled "Demographic and socio-economic implications of international migration in the Arab world with special reference to return migration." Four technical studies were launched, one on working women in Western Asia and the others on international migration.

Industry

The establishment of GCC in the early 1980s, and what it accomplished to integrate the economies of its members and co-ordinate their policies, and the setting up of the Arab Co-operation Council (ACC) and the Union of the Arab Maghreb towards the end of the 1980s, in both of which the economic dimension was fundamental, were steps which furthered Arab economic integration, strengthened Arab development efforts and put the region in a better position to deal with global economic blocs, the Executive Secretary stated in his report to the Commission.[3]

One of the technical publications issued in the "Industrial Development Series", on the role of regional co-operation, recommended adjustment measures to strengthen industrial co-ordination at the level of the GCC countries and proposed co-operation through ACC. Another technical publication[23] dealt with a resource-based programme of industrial development for the least developed countries of the ESCWA region—Yemen and Democratic Yemen—identifying industrial projects viable for joint implementation.

A report was made on assistance to existing industries in ESCWA countries.[24] Other publications concerned: selected agro-food industries in the ESCWA region;[25] identification of development issues related to genetic engineering and biotechnology;[26] and requirements for an expandable computerized Arabic dictionary.

Science and technology

Technical publications included those on the end-of-decade review[27] of the implementation of the 1979 Vienna Programme of Action on Science and Technology for Development;[28] promotion of regional co-operation in science and technology; and the role and impact of public enterprises in acquisition, adaptation and utilization of technology in selected ESCWA countries.[29]

In a meeting on specialized financial institutions and development of endogenous scientific and technological capabilities, held in 1989, a distinction was made for the first time between the requirements of industrial development and the requirements of industrial technological development. A number of areas were identified for scientific co-operation together with concrete proposals and plans of action. A thorough micro-analysis of technical changes and their causes in the public sector was conducted.

Development issues

A technical publication was prepared on the region's medium-term development prospects, analyzing economic performance since 1970, especially developments in the oil sector and development strategies and adjustment policies adopted by member countries.

A comprehensive review and analysis of national, regional and subregional performance was issued in the *Survey of Economic and Social Developments in the ESCWA Region*, the 1989 issue of which covered the entire decade. Special assessment was made of the prospects of Democratic Yemen and Yemen and obstacles impeding their efforts to promote development and economic transformation.

Two studies[30] were completed on review and assessment of the implementation of the 1981 Substantial New Programme of Action for the 1980s for the Least Developed Countries.[31]

Social development

A major contribution of ESCWA's social welfare and development subprogramme was organization of the Conference on the Capabilities and Needs of Disabled Persons in the ESCWA Region, held in November in Amman, with the co-operation of the Ministry of Social Development, Jordan, the UN Centre for Social Development and Humanitarian Affairs, the regional bureau of the Middle East Committee of the Welfare of the Blind, OPEC and the Arab Gulf Programme for United Nations Development Organizations.

Regional social statistics and indicators were developed, as were two studies on social aspects of rural development and on co-operative movements.[32] A technical publication was issued on the employment of women in the informal sector.[33] The 1989 issue of a directory of Arab professional women active in technical co-operation among developing countries was postponed to the 1990-1991 biennium. Proceedings of an expert group meeting on socio-cultural changes among women were issued, along with two reports[34] on support to technical projects for the development of women, through skills, identification of women's needs, and participation of women in industry.

Human settlements

The ESCWA human settlements programme was integrated into the social development and population programmes. A technical publication was issued on alternative approaches to city management, with special reference to human settlements,[35] as well as a report on assessment of alternative building materials and architectural design and a technical publication on proceedings of an expert group meeting on appropriate building materials.

International trade

Technical publications were issued on: external trade and payments situation of countries of Western Asia; new export products from Western Asia;[36] analysis of problems and policies affecting export performance; and terms of trade index numbers.

Statistics

The third meeting of Heads of Central Statistical Organizations in the ESCWA region was convened in 1989. The statistics programme undertook a number of joint activities with regional

Arab organizations, including the League of Arab States, the Arab Fund for Economic and Social Development and the Arab Institute for Training and Research in Statistics. Training activities were carried out in a workshop on management and administration of population and housing censuses held in Amman in June. Publications included two issues of the Statistical Abstract of the Region of the Economic and Social Commission for Western Asia, the External Trade Bulletin of the ESCWA region and the second issue of the *United Arab Statistical Abstract* (April 1989).

Programme, organizational and administrative questions

By a note[37] of 26 April, the Secretary-General transmitted a report of the Joint Inspection Unit (JIU) on ESCWA to the General Assembly and the Economic and Social Council, with comments in a separate addendum on 24 May.[38]

By a note of 3 April, the Secretary-General transmitted a report[39] of the JIU to the Economic and Social Council and the governing bodies of UNDP and the UN Environment Programme on the contribution of the UN system to the preservation and management of cultural and natural heritage in Western Asia. On 14 November,[40] in a separate addendum, he transmitted the comments of the Administrative Committee on Co-ordination on the report.

By **decision 1989/182**, on 28 July, the Economic and Social Council noted a summary[41] of the survey of economic and social developments in the ESCWA region during the Third United Nations Development Decade.[42]

By **decision 44/423** of 8 December, and by **resolution 44/201 A, section I**, of 21 December, the General Assembly took note of the JIU report on ESCWA and the Secretary-General's comments.

ESCWA work programme

The Commission adopted three resolutions concerning its work programme. On the basis of recommendations of its Technical Committee, the Commission modified its work and priorities for the biennium 1988-1989.[43] It approved, in principle, the draft medium-term plan for the period 1992-1997, having considered the need to pay more attention to the two least developed countries in the region,[44] and it adopted a programme of work and priorities for the biennium 1990-1991.[45]

REFERENCES

[1]E/1989/36.　[2]E/ESCWA/15/5.　[3]E/ESCWA/1990/1. [4]E/1989/36 (res. 165(XV)).　[5]*Ibid.* (res. 166(XV)).　[6]*Ibid.* (res. 167(XV)).　[7]*Ibid.* (res. 168(XV)).　[8]*Ibid.* (res. 169(XV)). [9]*Ibid.* (res. 170(XV)).　[10]*Ibid.* (res. 172(XV)).　[11]*Ibid.* (res. 175(XV)).　[12]*Ibid.* (res. 176(XV)).　[13]*Ibid.* (res. 177(XV)). [14]*Survey of Economic and Social Developments in the ESCWA Region, 1989*, Sales No. E.92.II.L2 (summary E/1990/56).　[15]YUN 1984, p. 623.　[16]E/ESCWA/TCD/89/7.　[17]E/ESCWA/TCD/89/9. [18]E/ESCWA/TCD/89/8.　[19]E/ESCWA/NR/89/12/Rev.1. [20]E/ESCWA/NR/89/21.　[21]E/ESCWA/NR/89/24.　[22]E/ESCWA/AGR/89/4.　[23]E/ESCWA/ID/89/12.　[24]E/ESCWA/NR/89/14.　[25]E/ESCWA/ID/89/2, E/ESCWA/ID/89/13.　[26]E/ESCWA/ID/89/15.　[27]E/ESCWA/NR/88/WG.2/3/Rev.1.　[28]YUN 1979, p. 636.　[29]E/ESCWA/NR/89/20.　[30]E/ESCWA/DPD/88/4, E/ESCWA/DPD/89/6.　[31]YUN 1981, p. 406.　[32]E/ESCWA/SDP/89/8, E/ESCWA/SDP/89/7.　[33]E/ESCWA/SDP/89/2. [34]E/ESCWA/SD/89/11.　[35]E/ESCWA/HS/89/1.　[36]E/ESCWA/DPD/89/9.　[37]A/44/206-E/1989/69 & Corr.1.　[38]A/44/206-E/1989/69/Add.1.　[39]E/1989/54.　[40]E/1989/54/Add.1.　[41]E/1989/67.　[42]YUN 1980, p. 503, GA res. 35/56, 5 Dec. 1980. [43]E/1989/36 (res. 174(XV)).　[44]*Ibid.* (res. 173(XV)).　[45]*Ibid.* (res. 174(XV)).

PART THREE

Economic and social questions

Chapter I

Development policy and international economic co-operation

As the 1980s drew to a close, epoch-making political changes occurred that had far-reaching implications for the world economy. Economic growth decelerated in all major groups of economies in 1989, but unevenly; differences in growth rates were particularly large among developing countries. Per capita output increased rapidly in Asia, but in Africa and Latin America the average level of income continued to fall as it had throughout the decade.

In March, the General Assembly decided to convene in 1990 a special session devoted to international economic co-operation, in particular to the revitalization of economic growth and development in the developing countries (decision 43/460). It established a preparatory committee, which held an organizational session in March and its first session in May/June.

In the *Ad Hoc* Committee established for the purpose in 1988, preparations continued for an international development strategy for the fourth United Nations development decade (1991-2000). In December, the Assembly (resolution 44/169) recommended an outline to the Committee as the basis for the new strategy.

Preparations were also under way for the Second United Nations Conference on the Least Developed Countries (LDCs), to be held in 1990. No new countries were added to the list of officially designated LDCs, which remained at 42.

Following consideration of a report on the problems of land-locked developing countries, the Assembly adopted a December resolution (44/214), in which it urged the international community to provide land-locked and transit developing countries with financial and technical assistance for the construction, maintenance and improvement of their transport, storage and transit infrastructures and facilities, including alternative routes.

In other action concerning economic development issues, the Assembly considered implementation of the Charter of Economic Rights and Duties of States and called on all States to take concrete steps to implement the Charter fully (44/170). With regard to international co-operation for economic security, it emphasized that a universal, constructive and comprehensive dialogue aimed at revitalizing economic growth and development was essential if effective and co-operative approaches to international economic issues were to be found (44/231). As to economic measures as

a means of political and economic coercion against developing countries, the Assembly called on the international community to adopt measures to eliminate the use of coercive measures against developing countries, which had been increasing and had taken new forms (44/215).

International economic relations

Development and economic co-operation

During 1989, various aspects of development and economic co-operation were discussed in United Nations bodies, including the General Assembly, the Economic and Social Council and the Committee for Development Planning (CDP).

CDP activities. At its twenty-fifth session (New York, 9-12 May),[1] CDP analysed the economic performance of the world's regions in the 1980s and discussed development challenges for the 1990s. It observed that, during the 1980s, some countries, especially in Asia, grew rapidly; others in the developed and socialist world grew more slowly; while many developing countries, especially in Africa and Latin America, suffered severe losses in real per capita income. In general terms, it appeared that successful countries gave priority to human development, maintained a high rate of investment and financed that investment largely through domestic savings.

Economic and Social Council general discussion. At its July 1989 session,[2] the Economic and Social Council held a general discussion of international economic and social policy, including regional and sectoral developments. It focused, as decided on 5 May (**decision 1989/105**), on structural changes and imbalances in the world economy and their impact on international economic co-operation, particularly with the developing countries.

It also discussed: international trade and the Uruguay Round of multilateral trade negotiations; multilateralism and the management of independence; human rights and popular participation; environment and development; new initiatives to strengthen the global economic dialogue; the international development strategy for the 1990s; human resources development; operational activities; and the role of the United Nations and prospects for revitalizing the Council.

The Council had before it the *World Economic Survey 1989*,[3] which discussed the state of the world economy and global economic trends and prospects. It also addressed questions of international trade, finance and debt (see PART THREE, Chapter IV), the international energy situation, economic reform and integration of centrally planned economies, interest rates in the 1980s and economic adjustment and the net transfer of resources from developing countries.

ECONOMIC AND SOCIAL COUNCIL ACTION

On 28 July, the Economic and Social Council adopted **resolution 1989/110** without vote.

International economic co-operation towards common approaches to development

The Economic and Social Council,

Taking into account the need for shared responsibility for the sound development of the world economy,

Considering the growing trend towards a new international consensus on growth and development through revived multilateral dialogue aimed at enhancing economic co-operation in recognition of growing global interdependence and in conformity with the interests of the international community,

Convinced that efforts to secure a more supportive economic environment conducive to sustained growth and development, in particular in the developing countries, are essential,

Conscious of the role of the United Nations in promoting continued co-operative efforts towards the revitalization of development within a multilateral framework involving all States and in stimulating common approaches to international economic issues, as exemplified by the results of the seventh session of the United Nations Conference on Trade and Development,

Expecting that such approaches will be generated when the General Assembly, at its special session in 1990, establishes guidelines for international economic relations in the 1990s and beyond,

1. *Notes with deep concern* that external indebtedness and persistent poverty continue to affect the majority of the developing countries;

2. *Also notes* that in certain developing countries the economic situation has been exacerbated, *inter alia,* by natural disasters affecting hundreds of millions of people and that in other developing countries encouraging rates of economic growth have been achieved;

3. *Appeals* to Governments to continue to utilize the United Nations system to strengthen further the spirit of solidarity necessary for the resolution of key development problems;

4. *Requests* the Secretary-General to keep these matters under review and to report, as appropriate, to the General Assembly on the progress achieved.

Economic and Social Council resolution 1989/110

28 July 1988   Meeting 37   Adopted without vote

Draft by Vice-President (E/1989/L.43), based on informal consultations on draft by Poland (E/1989/L.33); agenda item 2.
Meeting numbers. ESC 32, 35, 37.

Also on 28 July, the Council adopted **resolution 1989/111** without vote.

Strengthening multilateral co-operation in international economic affairs

The Economic and Social Council,

Firmly rejecting trends towards unilateralism and discrimination in world economic affairs,

Seriously concerned at the effect of such trends on the multilateral trading system based on the principles of the General Agreement on Tariffs and Trade, in particular the fundamental principle of non-discrimination, and on the achievement of the objectives of the Uruguay Round of multilateral trade negotiations,

Concerned also at the persistence of structural imbalances in the world economy and stressing the need to reduce them so as to provide an international economic environment more supportive of renewed and sustained growth and development,

Bearing in mind the co-ordinating functions of the Economic and Social Council in relation to all the organs, organizations and bodies of the United Nations system, in accordance with Articles 62 and 63 of the Charter of the United Nations,

1. *Acknowledges* the need to continue to strengthen multilateralism as the foundation for international economic co-operation in order to create a supportive international economic environment for sustained growth and development world wide;

2. *Affirms* the need for in-depth discussion, in the appropriate international institutions, of questions relating to the co-ordination of macro-economic policies;

3. *Requests* the Secretary-General to include in his report to the Preparatory Committee of the Whole for the Special Session of the General Assembly Devoted to International Economic Co-operation, in Particular to the Revitalization of Economic Growth and Development of the Developing Countries, a comprehensive analysis of ways and means of strengthening multilateral co-operation in international economic relations, including the role of the United Nations, taking into account, *inter alia,* the views expressed at the second regular session of 1989 of the Economic and Social Council on changes and imbalances in the world economy and their impact on international economic co-operation, and to report thereon to the Council at its second regular session of 1990 in the light of the outcome of the special session of the General Assembly.

Economic and Social Council resolution 1989/111

28 July 1988   Meeting 37   Adopted without vote

Draft by Vice-President (E/1989/L.44), based on informal consultations on draft by Malaysia for Group of 77 (E/1989/L.30); agenda item 2.
Meeting numbers. ESC 32, 35, 37.

By **decision 1989/182** of 28 July, the Council took note of a number of documents considered by it in connection with its general discussion of international economic and social policy, including the *World Economic Survey 1989*.[3]

GENERAL ASSEMBLY ACTION

The Second (Economic and Financial) Committee devoted a major part of its work during the General Assembly's 1989 regular session to development and international economic co-operation, making recommendations on a number of topics (see APPENDIX IV, agenda item 82). A list of pertinent documents was included in part I of the Committee's report on that item,[4] which the Assembly took note of on 19 December by **decision 44/436**.

By **decision 44/459** of 22 December, the Assembly decided to include in its 1990 agenda an item on launching global negotiations on international economic co-operation for development.

Preparations for special session (1990)

As decided in 1988,[5] the General Assembly's Second Committee reconvened on 27 February and 2 March 1989 to consider convening a special session of the Assembly in 1990 devoted to international economic co-operation, in particular to the revitalization of economic growth and development in the developing countries.

GENERAL ASSEMBLY ACTION

In March, on the recommendation of the Second Committee, the General Assembly adopted **decision 43/460** by recorded vote.

Special session of the General Assembly devoted to international economic co-operation, in particular to the revitalization of economic growth and development of the developing countries, to be held in 1990

At its 90th plenary meeting, on 7 March 1989, the General Assembly, on the recommendation of the Second Committee, decided to convene from 23 to 27 April 1990, on the basis of the provisions set out in the annex to the present decision, a special session devoted to international economic co-operation, in particular to the revitalization of economic growth and development of the developing countries, and to include in the provisional agenda of its forty-fourth session an item entitled "Preparations for the special session of the General Assembly in 1990".

ANNEX
Special session of the General Assembly to be held in 1990

I. Purpose

1. In a rapidly changing and increasingly interdependent world, it is in the common interest of all members of the international community to take stock of the significance of the transformation of the world economy, to consider in greater depth ways and means of meeting the challenges and opportunities ahead, particularly those of the developing countries, and to provide more effective means of multilateral co-operation in the economic field. Concerted efforts will benefit all countries and will help ensure sustained growth in the world economy and particularly the recovery and restoration of economic growth and development in developing countries. A special session of the General Assembly is the appropriate forum for this purpose.

II. Focus

2. With a view to attaining the above-stated purpose, the special session will be a forum for dialogue, discussion and deliberation, focusing on enhanced international and regional economic co-operation, improved policy co-ordination and the formulation of policy recommendations. The General Assembly will review problems facing the world economy, consider the pressing priority issues in international economic relations, including the need for recovery and revitalization of growth and development in developing countries, and address those problems and issues taking into account their interrelationships. In this regard, the respective spheres of competence of the specialized institutions are recognized.

III. Linkage

3. The nature and importance of the issues merit a special session with the full and highest possible level of participation of all delegations. The session will be able to provide appropriate policy guidance and recommendations for the activities of the international community and the relevant bodies within the United Nations system. It could also provide useful guidelines for an international development strategy for the 1990s, as well as for other relevant United Nations plans and programmes of action for development.

IV. Outcome

4. The outcome should be a document reflecting a common understanding on appropriate policy guidance and recommendations and providing more effective means of multilateral co-operation in the economic field. The final document should be based on constructive dialogue, embody new approaches and reflect a new spirit in international co-operation. It should also help to generate and sharpen public awareness.

V. Preparations

5. The special session shall take place at United Nations Headquarters, from 23 to 27 April 1990.

6. The President of the General Assembly is invited to participate actively in the preparations for the session.

7. An intergovernmental preparatory committee of the whole shall be established to make the necessary preparations for the special session. The preparatory committee shall prepare the provisional agenda and submit a draft final document to the General Assembly at the special session.

8. In the light of paragraphs 1 to 4 above, the Secretary-General shall submit to the preparatory committee a comprehensive report on the state of international economic co-operation, in particular on effective ways and means of revitalizing the economic growth and development of the developing countries. The Secretary-General, in consultation with the President of the General Assembly, is requested to carry out appropriate high-level consultations, including consultations with eminent personalities, in the preparation of his report, in order to contribute to the success of the special session.

9. The preparatory committee shall hold an organizational session in early March 1989 to elect its Bureau. The preparatory committee shall hold a brief session in June 1989 to consider the preliminary outline of the report of the Secretary-General and shall also hold two other sessions of one week each, as and when required.

10.   The Chairman of the preparatory committee shall report to the Economic and Social Council at its second regular session of 1989 on the work of the committee. The preparatory committee shall report to the General Assembly at its forty-fourth session on the progress of work.

11.   In the light of paragraph 3 above, it is stressed that the preparatory process for the special session and for the international development strategy for the fourth United Nations development decade, as well as for other plans and programmes of the United Nations in the field of development and international economic co-operation, should be complementary and mutually supportive.

General Assembly decision 43/460

123-1 (recorded vote)

Approved by Second Committee (A/43/915/Add.9) by recorded vote (97-1), 2 March (meeting 52); draft by Chairman (A/C.2/43/L.86), based on informal consultations on draft by Tunisia for Group of 77 (A/C.2/43/L.39), orally revised; agenda item 82.
Financial implications. S-G, A/C.2/43/L.87.
Meeting numbers. GA 43rd session: 2nd Committee 51, 52; plenary 90.

Recorded vote in Assembly as follows:

In favour: Afghanistan, Albania, Algeria, Angola, Argentina, Australia, Austria, Bahamas, Bahrain, Bangladesh, Barbados, Belgium, Bolivia, Brazil, Bulgaria, Burkina Faso, Burma, Burundi, Byelorussian SSR, Cameroon, Canada, Cape Verde, Chad, Chile, China, Colombia, Costa Rica, Côte d'Ivoire, Cuba, Cyprus, Czechoslovakia, Democratic Yemen, Denmark, Djibouti, Ecuador, Egypt, Ethiopia, Finland, France, Gabon, German Democratic Republic, Germany, Federal Republic of, Ghana, Greece, Guinea, Guinea-Bissau, Guyana, Hungary, Iceland, India, Indonesia, Iraq, Ireland, Italy, Jamaica, Japan, Jordan, Kenya, Kuwait, Lao People's Democratic Republic, Lebanon, Lesotho, Liberia, Libya, Madagascar, Malawi, Malaysia, Maldives, Mali, Mauritania, Mauritius, Mexico, Mongolia, Morocco, Mozambique, Nepal, Netherlands, New Zealand, Nigeria, Norway, Pakistan, Panama, Paraguay, Peru, Philippines, Poland, Portugal, Qatar, Rwanda, Saint Vincent and the Grenadines, Samoa, Sao Tome and Principe, Saudi Arabia, Senegal, Seychelles, Sierra Leone, Singapore, Solomon Islands, Spain, Sri Lanka, Sudan, Suriname, Sweden, Swaziland, Syrian Arab Republic, Thailand, Togo, Trinidad and Tobago, Tunisia, Turkey, Uganda, Ukrainian SSR, USSR, United Kingdom, United Republic of Tanzania, Uruguay, Venezuela, Viet Nam, Yemen, Yugoslavia, Zaire, Zambia, Zimbabwe.

Against: United States.

Work of the preparatory committee. The Preparatory Committee of the Whole for the Special Session of the General Assembly Devoted to International Economic Co-operation, in particular to the Revitalization of Economic Growth and Development of the Developing Countries, to take place in 1990, held its organizational and first sessions in 1989, both in New York.[6] The organizational session (13 and 16 March) considered the Committee's programme of work.

The first session (31 May–2 June) had before it the preliminary outline of the comprehensive report of the Secretary-General on the state of international economic co-operation, in particular on effective ways and means of revitalizing the economic growth and development of the developing countries.[7] The final report was to be presented to the Assembly's special session.

The outline considered the status of the world economy and its prospects, and indicated measures that could revitalize economic growth, especially in the developing countries, by addressing the need to strengthen international economic co-

operation; reinstate the development objective; overcome the debt crisis; enhance financial flows to developing countries; stabilize the international monetary system; open markets and strengthen the global trading system and commodity earnings; encourage regional and subregional co-operation among developing countries, particularly in Africa; assure sustained development without compromising the global environment; and use the United Nations system to co-ordinate development activities so that short-term exigencies could be seen in the perspective of longer-term economic and social goals.

On 24 July, the Economic and Social Council, by **decision 1989/166**, took note of an oral report on the Preparatory Committee's work, made by its Chairman.

GENERAL ASSEMBLY ACTION

On 22 December, the General Assembly, on the recommendation of the Second Committee, adopted **decision 44/444** without vote.

Preparations for the special session of the General Assembly devoted to international economic co-operation, in particular to the revitalization of economic growth and development of the developing countries

At its 85th plenary meeting, on 22 December 1989, the General Assembly, on the recommendation of the Second Committee, decided:

(a)   To take note with appreciation of the report of the Preparatory Committee of the Whole for the Special Session of the General Assembly Devoted to International Economic Co-operation, in particular to the Revitalization of Economic Growth and Development of the Developing Countries and of the views expressed by delegations on the preliminary outline of the comprehensive report of the Secretary-General submitted to the Preparatory Committee at its first session;

(b)   To take note also of the statement made by the Chairman of the Preparatory Committee before the Second Committee on 24 November 1989;

(c)   To request the Preparatory Committee to continue its work on the basis of General Assembly decision 43/460 of 7 March 1989;

(d)   To recommend that the Preparatory Committee bear in mind, in its preparations for the special session of the General Assembly devoted to international economic co-operation, in particular to the revitalization of economic growth and development of the developing countries, the views expressed by delegations at the forty-fourth session of the General Assembly;

(e)   To recommend to the Preparatory Committee that it consider at its second substantive session the following outline:

(i)   Main developments in the 1980s and the challenges of the 1990s and an assessment of obstacles and impediments to growth and development;

(ii)   The reactivation of economic growth and development in developing countries;

(iii) Strengthening and enhancing international economic co-operation and multilateralism in international economic relations;

(f) To transmit the text of the Chairman of the Preparatory Committee, annexed to the present decision, to the Preparatory Committee for consideration at its second substantive session.

ANNEX

1. The purpose of the present text—while recalling General Assembly decision 43/460 of 7 March 1989—is to provide further impetus and guidance to the work of the Preparatory Committee of the Whole for the Special Session of the General Assembly Devoted to International Economic Co-operation, in particular to the Revitalization of Economic Growth and Development of the Developing Countries and to facilitate an agreement on common approaches, efforts and actions to ensure, through international economic co-operation, sustained growth in the world economy, in particular, the revitalization of economic growth and development in the developing countries. The reactivation of economic growth and development in developing countries must be at the top of the international economic agenda.

2. International economic co-operation, in particular the revitalization of economic growth and development of the developing countries, could be greatly facilitated by the ongoing relaxation of political tensions. This relaxation should facilitate political commitment towards durable growth and development and agreement on ways and means of stimulating the world economy and of revitalizing international economic co-operation, in particular the growth and development of the developing countries, through, *inter alia*, the strengthening of the effectiveness of the United Nations.

3. The main developments in the 1980s are characterized by growing interdependence among nations and by different situations or conditions that exist among countries. Deep and rapid transformations in the global economy and in international economic relations are leading to changes in perceptions and policies. Special attention should be given to an assessment of developments and changes in the world economy in the 1980s and to the obstacles impeding growth and development in the developing countries.

4. The special session should bring to the attention of the international community the challenges of the 1990s. It should endeavour to reach agreement on addressing adequately the pressing interrelated problems and issues facing the world, in particular those affecting developing countries. Unless those problems and issues are solved, in particular those pressing interrelated problems that include problems arising from the excessive external indebtedness of developing countries, the prospects are ominous and we might witness an era of economic decline, social and political upheaval, and turmoil.

5. With the increased interdependence in the world, the interaction of national and international policies has become more important in bringing about a more stable and favourable international economic environment, in particular one that is supportive of growth and development of developing countries. Rapidly changing external circumstances require the strengthening of the capacity of national economies in order to render them more responsive to growth impulses and emerging opportunities for modernization, taking into account that the more significant a country is in terms of economic weight, the greater the impact of its policies on the international economic environment.

6. The special session should focus on the reactivation of economic growth and development of the developing countries. In this context, it is necessary to overcome the external debt crisis, provide adequate financial flows to developing countries, strengthen the international trading system, enlarge market access for exports of developing countries, address the problems faced by developing countries in the area of commodities, promote regional economic co-operation and integration, and facilitate the creation, transfer and absorption of new and emerging technologies. The attainment of such goals should enable developing countries to achieve the central objective of sustained, durable and equitable growth and development, with a new perspective that should contribute, through, *inter alia*, human resources development, to the expansion and modernization of their economies, in order to improve the living standards of their populations and effectively eradicate poverty. Attention should be paid to national efforts in all countries and to international co-operation in the 1990s.

7. Recalling Assembly decision 43/460, the special session should also focus on enhanced international and regional economic co-operation and improved policy coordination. Common approaches should be sought to ensure that the international monetary and financial system is stable and more supportive of global growth and development, particularly growth and development of developing countries, and to integrate better all countries in the world economy and the international trading system, taking into account existing asymmetries, the special and differential treatment accorded to developing countries and the ongoing process of the Uruguay Round of multilateral trade negotiations.

8. Sustained and sustainable development and the protection and enhancement of the global environment are also recognized as a common concern and should be addressed. In-depth consideration should be given to this concern in the framework of the preparations for a United Nations conference on environment and development, noting that the largest part of the current emission of pollutants into the environment, including toxic and hazardous wastes, originates in developed countries and, therefore, recognizing that those countries have the main responsibility for combating such pollution.

9. In addressing its objectives, the special session should pay due attention to the human resources dimension. It should stress the importance of international co-operation in supporting and strengthening the development of human resources in developing countries, the inextricable link between education, acquisition of skills and technical training, and economic growth and sustained development. There is also a need for human resources development strategies to include all members of society and to encompass supportive measures in such vital and related areas as health, nutrition, employment and population.

10. The special session should consider appropriate guidance for strengthening and enhancing international economic co-operation and multilateralism in international economic relations, including co-ordination of macro-economic policies and the compatibility of those

policies with the objectives of development, as well as strengthening the unique role of the United Nations system as a universal forum for economic dialogue and co-operation.

11.   The special session should complement and be supportive of the international development strategy for the 1990s, as well as other relevant United Nations plans and programmes of action for development, and should give an impetus to the Second United Nations Conference on the Least Developed Countries.

General Assembly decision 44/444

Adopted without vote

Approved by Second Committee (A/44/859) without vote, 15 December (meeting 50); draft by Chairman (A/C.2/44/L.85), based on informal consultations on draft by Malaysia for Group of 77 (A/C.2/44/L.70); agenda item 83.

Meeting numbers. GA 44th session: 2nd Committee 44, 45, 48, 50; plenary 85.

Preparations for a strategy for the fourth UN development decade

Ad Hoc **Committee of the Whole.** The *Ad Hoc* Committee of the Whole for the Preparation of the International Development Strategy for the Fourth United Nations Development Decade (1991-2000), established by the General Assembly in 1988,[8] held its organizational, first and second sessions during 1989, all in New York.[9] At the organizational session (15-17 March), the Committee elected its officers, adopted its agenda and made arrangements for future sessions.

At its first session (5-9 June), the Committee had before it the Secretary-General's May report on the preparation of an international development strategy for the fourth United Nations development decade.[10] The report summarized action taken by the Administrative Committee on Co-ordination (ACC) and CDP (see below), discussed some recent developments that would affect an assessment of the problems of the world economy in the 1990s, drew attention to a 1988 report on socio-economic perspectives for the 1990s[11] and analysed some discussions about the content and thrust of a new strategy that had taken place in the United Nations system.

The report concluded that, in order to address the problems of future international co-operation, the strategy should: reflect and respond to rapid changes in international economic realities; aim at accelerating socio-economic progress on a wide front and seek to ensure that present obstacles to development were removed; promote resolution of the debt problems of developing countries, enhance their access to markets and increase financial flows for development; emphasize human resources development and recognize that children and the young were the agents of development, that half of the people of the world were women, and that education, health, employment and food security were the cornerstones of development; and respond forcefully to signs of environmental dis-

tress of all kinds. Annexed to the report was the proposed summary outline of a strategy.

Also before the first session was a note by the Secretariat[12] transmitting an extract of the proceedings of the Trade and Development Board (TDB) of the United Nations Conference on Trade and Development (UNCTAD) covering the Board's discussion of preparations for the strategy (see below).

On 7 July, the Chairman of the *Ad Hoc* Committee reported to the Economic and Social Council on the Committee's work. The Council took note of that report by **decision 1989/169** of 26 July.

At its second session (11-15 September), the Committee had before it a note by the Secretariat[13] suggesting, in the light of discussions at the first session, a possible structure for a new strategy that could cover the subject in five main sections. Those were, in sum, perspectives: the experience of the 1980s, salient and novel features of the world economy and prospects for the 1990s; main purpose and goals which Governments wished to articulate in a strategy; international and national policies called for to reach the agreed goals and identification of issues on which consensus seemed necessary for a strategy to be meaningful; the role of targets and indicators in the formulation, implementation and monitoring of the strategy; and the role of the United Nations system in the strategy's implementation.

The Committee also had before it position papers by a number of countries and groups of countries.

ACC action. In accordance with a 1988 ACC decision,[14] the ACC Task Force on Long-term Development Objectives (seventeenth session, Geneva, 28-31 March)[15] continued the process of inter-agency consultation on the preparation of a new international development strategy. The Task Force noted discussions on the new strategy that had been held throughout the United Nations system since its 1988 meeting[14] and considered the report of its Technical Working Group (Geneva, 24-26 January), which had discussed economic and social indicators in a new strategy.

At its first regular session of 1989 (Geneva, 19-21 April),[16] ACC decided to transmit to the Economic and Social Council the Task Force's report on its March session. By **decision 1989/168** of 26 July, the Council took note of the Task Force's report, which was circulated in a note by the Secretary-General.[17]

At its eighteenth session (New York, 18-20 September),[18] the Task Force continued its review of the state of preparations for the strategy, noting that progress had been made towards an agreed structure within which the substantive themes of primary concern to various groups of countries could be accommodated.

UNCTAD action. In accordance with agreed conclusions adopted on 22 March,[19] the UNCTAD Trade and Development Board (TDB) included the question of UNCTAD's contribution to the preparations for the international development strategy in its agenda. Also pursuant to that decision, the UNCTAD Secretary-General held special consultations on 16 May to consider the question.

On 31 October,[20] TDB decided to transmit to the *Ad Hoc* Committee of the Whole for the Preparation of the International Development Strategy a report by the UNCTAD secretariat on UNCTAD's contribution. It also decided that, under the chairmanship of the UNCTAD Secretary-General, consultations would take place in 1990 to decide on subsequent action to contribute to the preparatory process of the strategy.

CDP action. CDP discussed key elements of an international development strategy for the 1990s at its May 1989 session[1] and concluded that they were: accelerated economic growth, greater concern for human development, an absolute reduction in the number of people suffering from severe poverty and deprivation, and restraining the deterioriation in the physical environment. Those four elements were not separate issues but strands of a coherent approach to development policy in the next decade.

UNDP action. On 30 June,[21] the United Nations Development Programme (UNDP) Governing Council requested the Administrator to make a presentation to the *Ad Hoc* Committee of the Whole for the Preparation of the International Development Strategy as his contribution to the preparation of the strategy, bearing in mind the views expressed during the Council's session on UNDP's role in the 1990s (see next chapter).

CPC/ACC Joint Meetings. The Committee for Programme and Co-ordination (CPC) and ACC held Joint Meetings in New York from 16 to 18 October.[22] Following discussions on the preparation of the international development strategy, the Joint Meetings stated that ACC should assess the experience gained in strengthening co-ordination within the United Nations system relating to implementation of the Strategy for the Third United Nations Development Decade (the 1980s) with a view to identifying measures for enhanced co-ordination and co-operation during the 1990s, and should present suggestions and recommendations to the *Ad Hoc* Committee of the Whole. The executive heads of United Nations organizations and agencies should bring to the attention of their governing bodies the relevant parts of the new strategy with a view to adopting policies and programmes to facilitate its implementation. It was reaffirmed that Member States had the overall responsibility for the elaboration of the new international development strategy; United Nations organs, organizations and bodies would provide inputs in order to contribute to intergovernmental deliberations.

ECONOMIC AND SOCIAL COUNCIL ACTION

On 24 May, on the recommendation of its Second (Social) Committee and based on a draft by the Commission for Social Development,[23] the Economic and Social Council adopted **resolution 1989/55**.

The social dimension of the international development strategy for the fourth United Nations development decade

The Economic and Social Council,

Recalling General Assembly resolution 43/182 of 20 December 1988 on the preparation of an international development strategy for the fourth United Nations development decade,

Reaffirming the fundamental importance of social goals in the development process,

Recognizing that social and economic policy measures are complementary in the achievement of development objectives,

Recognizing also the importance for all countries of increasing and strengthening national and international, as well as public and private, co-operation in both the social and economic spheres,

Noting that the *Ad Hoc* Committee of the Whole for the Preparation of the International Development Strategy for the Fourth United Nations Development Decade, established by the General Assembly in its resolution 43/182, will submit a progress report to the Assembly at its forty-fourth session, with a view to finalizing the strategy in time for its adoption in 1990,

1. *Recommends* that the *Ad Hoc* Committee of the Whole, in preparing the international development strategy for the fourth United Nations development decade, take into consideration the proposals of the Commission for Social Development contained in the annex to the present resolution;

2. *Decides* that the Commission for Social Development should consider the implementation of social components of the strategy at its thirty-second session.

ANNEX
Proposals of the Commission for Social Development on the social dimension of the international development strategy for the fourth United Nations development decade

The Commission for Social Development proposes that the international development strategy for the fourth United Nations development decade should:

(*a*) Emphasize the interaction of social and economic policies, in particular the idea that social policies and programmes should be linked to both short-term and long-term economic development efforts;

(*b*) Emphasize the need to improve the social situation, in particular of developing countries, highlighting poverty in all its forms as an issue requiring urgent action by all;

(c) Be action-oriented and promote international action to create an appropriate global environment for social development;

(d) Take into account the roles of both the public and private sectors;

(e) Support the advancement of women as a global concern;

(f) Promote the social integration of all segments of society and specific population groups;

(g) Propose measures to strengthen the capacity of countries, particularly developing countries, for coordinating social policy.

Economic and Social Council resolution 1989/55

24 May 1989   Meeting 15   Adopted without vote

Approved by Second Committee (E/1989/91) without vote, 11 May (meeting 12); draft by Commission for Social Development (E/1989/25); agenda item 11.

In other action, the Council, in **resolution 1989/90** of 26 July, recommended that the General Assembly give due weight to the role of population and the importance of population policies and activities and integrate them into the goals and objectives of the strategy.

GENERAL ASSEMBLY ACTION

On 19 December, on the recommendation of the Second Committee, the General Assembly adopted **resolution 44/169** without vote.

Preparation of the international development strategy for the fourth United Nations development decade

The General Assembly,

Recalling its resolutions 42/193 of 11 December 1987 and 43/182 of 20 December 1988,

1. *Takes note* of the report of the *Ad Hoc* Committee of the Whole for the Preparation of the International Development Strategy for the Fourth United Nations Development Decade;

2. *Recommends* that the *Ad Hoc* Committee adopt the outline contained in the annex to the present resolution as the basis for the elaboration of the international development strategy for the fourth United Nations development decade.

ANNEX
Outline for the elaboration of the international development strategy for the fourth United Nations development decade

I. Preamble

Review of the 1980s and prospects for the 1990s, with a view to adopting a flexible economic framework for growth and development for the 1990s, taking into account the results of the special session of the General Assembly devoted to international economic co-operation, in particular to the revitalization of economic growth and development of the developing countries.

II. Goals and objectives

To promote the development of developing countries in the context of the strengthening of global development.

III. Policies and measures

The strategy should focus on national efforts in all countries and on international co-operation for the 1990s.

The strategy should address, *inter alia*:

(a) Reactivation and acceleration of broad durable economic growth and development, including:

(i) External debt;

(ii) International trade and commodities;

(iii) Technology;

(iv) Industrial policies; food and agricultural policies;

(v) Economic policy frameworks;

(b) Priority aspects of development:

(i) Eradication of poverty and hunger;

(ii) Human resources and institutional development;

(iii) Population;

(iv) Environment;

(v) Food and agriculture;

(c) The need to take account of different requirements, situations and problems, including those of the least developed countries;

(d) Development financing.

IV. Role of United Nations organs

V. Review and appraisal

General Assembly resolution 44/169

19 December 1989   Meeting 83   Adopted without vote

Approved by Second Committee (A/44/746/Add.1) without vote, 15 November (meeting 34); draft by Chairman (A/C.2/44/L.11); agenda item 82 *(a)*.

Charter of Economic Rights and Duties of States

In response to a 1985 General Assembly request,[24] the Secretary-General submitted a May report, with later addenda,[25] on the implementation of the Charter of Economic Rights and Duties of States, adopted by the Assembly in 1974.[26] The report concluded that, although the Charter remained unimplemented, there were grounds for cautious optimism. The easing of international tensions had created a climate in which further progress could be foreseen; specifically, there had been a renewal of interest in multilateral approaches and a recognition of the usefulness and indispensability of the United Nations. The Charter's true significance lay not so much in its precise formulations as in its intent and its overall conception of the movement of history and, from that perspective, the Charter could be seen to have been remarkably prescient. In the emerging complex and interdependent world of the future, new levels of global co-operation would be required to safeguard the security of the planet. The design and management of the régimes and institutions that would be devised for managing interdependence had to involve the participation of the developing world. The Charter clearly foresaw the need for those elements, and its principles and goals would remain a source of inspiration as future challenges were confronted.

The Secretary-General provided summaries of replies from nine Member States to a questionnaire distributed by the Secretary-General in response to a 1986 Assembly request.[27]

In **decision 1989/182** of 28 July, the Economic and Social Council took note of the Secretary-General's report.

GENERAL ASSEMBLY ACTION

On 19 December, the General Assembly, on the recommendation of the Second Committee, adopted **resolution 44/170** by recorded vote.

Charter of Economic Rights and Duties of States
The General Assembly,

Recalling its resolutions 3201(S-VI) and 3202(S-VI) of 1 May 1974, containing the Declaration and the Programme of Action on the Establishment of a New International Economic Order, 3281(XXIX) of 12 December 1974, containing the Charter of Economic Rights and Duties of States, and 3362(S-VII) of 16 September 1975 on development and international economic co-operation, which laid the foundations of the new international economic order,

Taking note of the report of the Secretary-General on the implementation of the Charter of Economic Rights and Duties of States,

Deeply concerned that, since the adoption of the Charter of Economic Rights and Duties of States, the economic situation of the developing countries has continuously worsened and the economic, social, scientific and technological disparities between the developed and the developing countries have continued to widen,

Emphasizing that the aggravation of global economic problems, which affect in particular the developing countries, necessitates more concerted international action in order to facilitate the establishment of just and equitable economic relations and the promotion of international social justice,

1. *Calls upon* all States to take concrete steps and measures to implement fully the Charter of Economic Rights and Duties of States, thus contributing to the effective restructuring of the international economic system and to the reactivation of the economic growth and development of the developing countries;

2. *Reaffirms* the right of every country to adopt without external interference the economic and social system that it deems most appropriate for its own development;

3. *Requests* the Secretary-General to submit to the General Assembly at its forty-ninth session an analytical report on the progress achieved in compliance with the Charter of Economic Rights and Duties of States and its impact on the solution of the main economic problems confronting the developing countries and the reactivation of their economic growth and development.

General Assembly resolution 44/170

19 December 1989   Meeting 83   131-1-23 (recorded vote)

Approved by Second Committee (A/44/746/Add.3) by recorded vote (103-0-23), 3 November (meeting 30); draft by Malaysia for Group of 77 (A/C.2/44/L.9); agenda item 82 *(c)*.
Meeting numbers. GA 44th session: 2nd Committee 16, 30; plenary 83.

Recorded vote in Assembly as follows:

In favour: Afghanistan, Albania, Algeria, Angola, Antigua and Barbuda, Argentina, Bahamas, Bahrain, Bangladesh, Barbados, Benin, Bhutan, Bolivia, Botswana, Brazil, Brunei Darussalam, Bulgaria, Burkina Faso, Burundi, Byelorussian SSR, Cameroon, Cape Verde, Central African Repub-

lic, Chad, Chile, China, Colombia, Comoros, Congo, Costa Rica, Cote d'Ivoire, Cuba, Cyprus, Czechoslovakia, Democratic Kampuchea, Democratic Yemen, Djibouti, Dominica, Dominican Republic, Ecuador, Egypt, El Salvador, Equatorial Guinea, Ethiopia, Fiji, Gabon, Gambia, German Democratic Republic, Ghana, Grenada, Guatemala, Guinea, Guinea-Bissau, Guyana, Haiti, Honduras, Hungary, India, Indonesia, Iran, Iraq, Jamaica, Jordan, Kenya, Kuwait, Lao People's Democratic Republic, Lebanon, Lesotho, Liberia, Libyan Arab Jamahiriya, Madagascar, Malawi, Malaysia, Maldives, Mali, Mauritania, Mauritius, Mexico, Mongolia, Morocco, Mozambique, Myanmar, Nepal, Nicaragua, Niger, Nigeria, Oman, Pakistan, Panama, Papua New Guinea, Paraguay, Peru, Philippines, Poland, Qatar, Romania, Rwanda, Saint Lucia, Saint Vincent and the Grenadines, Samoa, Sao Tome and Principe, Saudi Arabia, Senegal, Seychelles, Sierra Leone, Singapore, Solomon Islands, Somalia, Sri Lanka, Sudan, Suriname, Swaziland, Syrian Arab Republic, Thailand, Togo, Trinidad and Tobago, Tunisia, Uganda, Ukrainian SSR, USSR, United Arab Emirates, United Republic of Tanzania, Uruguay, Vanuatu, Venezuela, Viet Nam, Yemen, Yugoslavia, Zaire, Zambia, Zimbabwe.
Against: United States.
Abstaining: Australia, Austria, Belgium, Canada, Denmark, Finland, France, Germany, Federal Republic of, Greece, Iceland, Ireland, Israel, Italy, Japan, Luxembourg, Netherlands, New Zealand, Norway, Portugal, Spain, Sweden, Turkey, United Kingdom.

International co-operation for economic security

In response to a 1987 General Assembly request,[28] the Secretary-General submitted an April 1989 report on international economic security.[29] He analysed responses received from eminent persons from all regions, as requested by the Assembly, covering the concept of international economic security, policies to maintain and enhance it, and the role of the United Nations. The Secretary-General stated that the objective of international economic security was to ensure that a global normative and institutional framework was in place within which the goal of security for all could be achieved by enhancing the stability, predictability and reliability of international economic relations. Areas in which the United Nations could make positive contributions to enhanced economic security included: debt reduction; a successful conclusion of the Uruguay Round of multilateral trade negotiations; environmental protection; and increased food production levels. Another area was in the early identification, analysis and monitoring of world economic and social developments.

By **decision 1989/182** of 28 July, the Economic and Social Council took note of the Secretary-General's report.

GENERAL ASSEMBLY ACTION

On 22 December, the General Assembly, on the recommendation of the Second Committee, adopted **resolution 44/231** without vote.

Report of the Secretary-General submitted pursuant to General Assembly resolution 42/165
The General Assembly,

Recalling its resolution 42/165 of 11 December 1987, as adopted, on international economic security,

Taking note of the report of the Secretary-General on the question,

Emphasizing the role of the United Nations and the interest of its Member States in strengthening international co-operation for ensuring sustained development, particularly in the developing countries, and balanced growth in the world economy,

1. *Notes with appreciation* the work undertaken by the Secretary-General on the subject;

2. *Recognizes* that the discussions that have taken place on the subject have contributed to a growing common understanding of economic interdependence and have played a useful role in the continuing efforts to increase the efficiency and effectiveness of activities of the United Nations in the economic field and strengthen multilateral co-operation in international economic affairs to the benefit of all countries, especially developing countries;

3. *Emphasizes* that a universal, constructive and comprehensive dialogue aimed at revitalizing economic growth and development, in particular the development of developing countries, is essential if effective and co-operative approaches to international economic issues are to be found;

4. *Invites* the concerned organs and organizations of the United Nations system, in accordance with their respective mandates, to consider in their current activities the conclusions and recommendations contained in the report of the Secretary-General;

5. *Requests* the Secretary-General to take the present resolution into account when preparing his report for the special session of the General Assembly devoted to international economic co-operation, in particular to the revitalization of economic growth and development of the developing countries.

General Assembly resolution 44/231

22 December 1989   Meeting 85   Adopted without vote

Approved by Second Committee (A/44/832) by consensus, 15 November (meeting 34); draft by Vice-Chairman (A/C.2/44/L.39), based on informal consultations on draft by USSR (A/C.2/44/L.14); agenda item 12.
Meeting numbers. GA 44th session: 2nd Committee 15-17, 19, 20, 25, 34; plenary 85.

Eradication of poverty

In response to a 1988 General Assembly request,[30] the Secretary-General submitted a September report on international co-operation for the eradication of poverty in developing countries.[31] The report described the extent and intensity of poverty in those countries. The poor constituted close to half of the population of the developing countries as a whole (not including China). It also discussed the impact of the economic crisis of the 1980s on poverty, the capacity of the poor to cope, and international co-operation to facilitate poverty eradication.

The report examined three programme areas that had been used in poverty reduction: development of small enterprises; investment in urban infrastructure; and integrated rural development. It also set out policy and operational considerations with regard to earnings enhancement, security enhancement, poverty targeting and institutional aspects.

The report concluded that the economic crisis of the 1980s had had a generally adverse impact on poverty in Africa and brought to a halt the amelioration of the conditions of the poor achieved in Latin America during previous years. International co-operation was essential if progress was to be made towards achieving the goal of eradicating poverty on an urgent, lasting and comprehensive basis.

A variety of approaches—ranging from short-run welfare measures to long-term human capital formation, and from small-scale, targeted activities to macro-economic policies—could contribute to poverty eradication in important ways. The formulation and implementation of policies that aimed to increase the earnings capacity of the poor and make them less vulnerable to future crises remained a major and urgent challenge to policy makers and multilateral agencies.

GENERAL ASSEMBLY ACTION

On 22 December, on the recommendation of the Second Committee, the General Assembly adopted **resolution 44/212** without vote.

International co-operation for the eradication of poverty in developing countries

The General Assembly,

Recalling its resolutions 3201(S-VI) and 3202(S-VI) of 1 May 1974, containing the Declaration and the Programme of Action on the Establishment of a New International Economic Order, 3281(XXIX) of 12 December 1974, containing the Charter of Economic Rights and Duties of States, and 3362(S-VII) of 16 September 1975 on development and international economic co-operation,

Recalling also its resolution 43/195 of 20 December 1988 and Economic and Social Council resolution 1988/47 of 27 May 1988, and taking note of Commission on Human Rights resolution 1989/10 of 2 March 1989 concerning extreme poverty,

Realizing that insufficient attention has been paid to the human phenomenon of extreme poverty in developing countries, which frequently eludes international and intergovernmental action and current statistical analysis,

Realizing also that poverty, while not a new human phenomenon, has increased sharply, reaching alarming proportions in developing countries, threatening the very socio-political fabric of those countries and undermining peace and harmony,

Deeply concerned that more than one billion people throughout the world, mostly in developing countries, are still living in abject poverty and misery, with hunger, malnutrition, disease, illiteracy and the prospect of premature death as an integral part of their lives,

Deeply concerned also about the sharp decline in living standards, income and employment levels, and health, nutritional and educational standards that has aggravated widespread poverty in both the urban and rural areas of most developing countries,

Noting that the eradication of poverty in developing countries is one of the most important development objectives shared by both developing and developed countries and that it requires national and international action,

Noting also that the eradication of poverty, as a national objective, has merited the highest priority in domestic policies and national development efforts of developing countries and that specific programmes are needed to solve this problem,

Aware that the difficult economic situation of developing countries, exacerbated by specific aspects of international economic conditions which have adverse consequences, has hindered the development process in those countries and their capacity to undertake social and economic programmes for the eradication of poverty,

Aware also that the eradication of poverty is made more difficult by a range of factors in the international economic environment which impede growth and development in developing countries, *inter alia*, the worsening in the terms of trade, the persistence of protectionism, a sharp decline in financial and capital flows, high real interest rates, depressed prices for many commodities and the heavy burden of external debt,

Stressing that in developing countries there is a strong relationship between poverty, development and the environment and that concerted action is required, at all levels, to ensure comprehensive and effective solutions aimed at the eradication of poverty,

Emphasizing that the very large number of people living in poverty in developing countries is a challenge to the international community and, at the same time, a potential resource which, through new and imaginative approaches to the eradication of poverty in developing countries, could be integrated into the development process and become an engine for growth and development in those countries,

1. *Takes note* of the report of the Secretary-General on the subject;

2. *Recognizes* that a supportive international economic environment, together with a growth-oriented development approach, is crucial to the success of efforts of developing countries to eradicate poverty;

3. *Calls upon* the international community to intensify, on a priority basis, its development of action-oriented programmes with short-term, medium-term and long-term approaches for the eradication of poverty in support of the efforts of the developing countries themselves;

4. *Invites* the international community to adopt specific measures designed to increase financial flows to developing countries, including official development assistance, in order to strengthen the efforts of those countries to eradicate poverty;

5. *Requests* the Secretary-General to co-ordinate urgent appropriate actions for the formulation, in co-operation with intergovernmental and non-governmental organizations and other multilateral bodies, of improved and enhanced action-oriented technical co-operation programmes for the eradication of poverty within the framework of the organizations of the United Nations system, in accordance with the policies, priorities and strategies of those countries;

6. *Invites* Governments to include in the preparations for the proposed United Nations conference on environment and development to be held in 1992, and in the conference itself, the vital issue of the eradication of poverty, integrated with relevant environmental issues and with a view to strengthening international co-operation in environment and development;

7. *Requests* the Committee for Development Planning, taking into account the fact that the question of the eradication of poverty has been included as one of the priority aspects of development in the recommended outline for the elaboration of the international development strategy for the fourth United Nations development decade, to submit to the *Ad Hoc* Committee of the Whole for the Preparation of the International Development Strategy for the Fourth United Nations Development Decade, at its session to be held from 4 to 15 June 1990, in the light of the present resolution, concrete proposals for action for the eradication of poverty in developing countries;

8. *Requests* the Secretary-General, with the assistance of the regional commissions, to submit to the General Assembly at its forty-fifth session a progress report and at its forty-sixth session a comprehensive report containing, *inter alia*:

(*a*) An analysis of the diversified impact of adverse international economic conditions on the intensification of poverty in developing countries;

(*b*) A summary of the experience of developing countries concerning the eradication of poverty;

(*c*) Specific recommendations for effective policy measures for the urgent and permanent eradication of poverty, in accordance with the present resolution;

(*d*) An account of the implementation of the present resolution;

9. *Decides* to include in the provisional agenda of its forty-fifth and forty-sixth sessions an item entitled "International co-operation for the eradication of poverty in developing countries".

General Assembly resolution 44/212

22 December 1989   Meeting   85 Adopted without vote

Approved by Second Committee (A/44/746/Add.11) without vote, 15 December (meeting 50); draft by Vice-Chairman (A/C.2/44/L.84), based on informal consultations on draft by Malaysia for Group of 77 (A/C.2/44/L.48); agenda item 82.

Meeting numbers. GA 44th session: 2nd Committee 44, 46, 49, 50; plenary 85.

Rural development

The ACC Task Force on Rural Development (seventeenth meeting, Vienna, 31 May–2 June)[(32)] considered a progress report by the lead agency in rural development, the Food and Agriculture Organization of the United Nations (FAO), which included an overview of activities in certain areas of rural development undertaken by members of the Task Force during 1988. Also discussed were: people's participation in rural development; monitoring and evaluation; co-ordination and collaboration on rural development and agrarian reform activities and programmes proposed for the 1988-1989 biennium; the evaluation of United Nations rural development activities in three African least developed countries (LDCs) being carried out by the Joint Inspection Unit; implementation for rural women of the Nairobi Forward-looking Strategies for the Advancement of Women (see PART THREE, Chapter XIII); the impact of national macro-economic policies on the rural poor; and the Task Force's programme of work and timeframe for 1989/90.

Coercive economic measures

In response to a 1987 General Assembly request,[33] the Secretary-General submitted an October report[34] summarizing the views of 14 Governments and 8 organizations of the United Nations system on coercive economic measures against developing countries.

Attached to the report were the views of a group of experts, which met at Geneva from 1 to 3 May, to consider effective approaches to the elimination of the use of coercive measures against developing countries.

GENERAL ASSEMBLY ACTION

On 22 December, on the recommendation of the Second Committee, the General Assembly adopted **resolution 44/215** by recorded vote.

Economic measures as a means of political and economic coercion against developing countries

The General Assembly,

Recalling the relevant principles set forth in the Charter of the United Nations,

Recalling also its resolutions 2625(XXV) of 24 October 1970, containing the Declaration on Principles of International Law concerning Friendly Relations and Co-operation among States in accordance with the Charter of the United Nations, 3201(S-VI) and 3202(S-VI) of 1 May 1974, containing the Declaration and the Programme of Action on the Establishment of a New International Economic Order, and 3281(XXIX) of 12 December 1974, containing the Charter of Economic Rights and Duties of States,

Reaffirming article 32 of the Charter of Economic Rights and Duties of States, which declares that no State may use or encourage the use of economic, political or any other type of measures to coerce another State in order to obtain from it the subordination of the exercise of its sovereign rights,

Bearing in mind the general principles governing international trade and trade policies for development contained in its resolution 1995(XIX) of 30 December 1964, United Nations Conference on Trade and Development resolution 152(VI) of 2 July 1983 on rejection of coercive economic measures, and the principles and rules of the General Agreement on Tariffs and Trade and paragraph 7 (iii) of the Ministerial Declaration adopted on 29 November 1982 by the Contracting Parties to the General Agreement at their thirty-eighth session,

Reaffirming its resolutions 38/197 of 20 December 1983, 39/210 of 18 December 1984, 40/185 of 17 December 1985, 41/165 of 5 December 1986 and 42/173 of 11 December 1987, and considering that further work needs to be undertaken in order to implement them,

Gravely concerned that the use of coercive measures adversely affects the economies and development efforts of developing countries and that, in some cases, those measures have worsened, creating a negative impact on international economic co-operation,

1. *Takes note with appreciation* of the report of the Secretary-General on economic measures as a means of political and economic coercion against developing countries;

2. *Calls upon* the international community to adopt urgent and effective measures in order to eliminate the use of coercive measures against developing countries, which have been increasing and have taken new forms;

3. *Deplores* the fact that some developed countries continue to apply and, in some cases, have increased the scope and magnitude of economic measures that have the purpose of exerting, directly or indirectly, coercion on the sovereign decisions of developing countries subject to those measures;

4. *Calls upon* the developed countries to refrain from exercising political coercion through the application of economic instruments with the purpose of inducing changes in the economic or social systems, as well as in the domestic or foreign policies, of other countries;

5. *Reaffirms* that developed countries should refrain from threatening or applying trade and financial restrictions, blockades, embargoes and other economic sanctions, incompatible with the provisions of the Charter of the United Nations and in violation of undertakings contracted multilaterally and bilaterally, against developing countries as a form of political and economic coercion that affects their political, economic and social development;

6. *Requests* the Secretary-General to designate an identifiable unit within the Office of the Director-General for Development and International Economic Co-operation to collect pertinent information on economic measures taken by developed countries as a means of coercion against developing countries, which unit should receive and assess such information and produce a periodic report with recommendations for consideration by the General Assembly;

7. *Also requests* the Secretary-General to report to the General Assembly at its forty-sixth session on the implementation of the present resolution.

General Assembly resolution 44/215

22 December 1989   Meeting 85   118-23-2 (recorded vote)

Approved by Second Committee (A/44/746/Add.2) by recorded vote (89-22-3), 4 December (meeting 48); draft by Malaysia for Group of 77 (A/C.2/44/L.49); agenda item 82 *(b)*.

Meeting numbers. GA 44th session: 2nd Committee 44, 48; plenary 85.

Recorded vote in Assembly as follows:

In favour: Afghanistan, Albania, Algeria, Antigua and Barbuda, Argentina, Bahamas, Bahrain, Bangladesh, Barbados, Benin, Bhutan, Bolivia, Botswana, Brazil, Brunei Darussalam, Bulgaria, Burkina Faso, Burundi, Byelorussian SSR, Cameroon, Cape Verde, Central African Republic, Chad, Chile, China, Colombia, Congo, Costa Rica, Cote d'Ivoire, Cuba, Czechoslovakia, Democratic Kampuchea, Democratic Yemen, Djibouti, Dominica, Dominican Republic, Ecuador, Egypt, El Salvador, Ethiopia, Fiji, Gabon, Gambia, German Democratic Republic, Ghana, Guatemala, Guinea, Guinea-Bissau, Guyana, Haiti, Honduras, Indonesia, Iran, Iraq, Jamaica, Jordan, Kenya, Kuwait, Lao People's Democratic Republic, Lesotho, Liberia, Libyan Arab Jamahiriya, Madagascar, Malawi, Malaysia, Maldives, Mali, Mauritania, Mauritius, Mexico, Mongolia, Morocco, Mozambique, Myanmar, Nepal, Nicaragua, Niger, Nigeria, Oman, Pakistan, Papua New Guinea, Peru, Philippines, Qatar, Romania, Rwanda, Saint Lucia, Saint Vincent and the Grenadines, Sao Tome and Principe, Saudi Arabia, Senegal, Sierra Leone, Singapore, Solomon Islands, Somalia, Sri Lanka, Sudan, Suriname, Syrian Arab Republic, Thailand, Togo, Trinidad and Tobago, Tunisia, Uganda, Ukrainian SSR, USSR, United Arab Emirates, United Republic of Tanzania, Uruguay, Vanuatu, Venezuela, Viet Nam, Yemen, Yugoslavia, Zaire, Zambia, Zimbabwe.

Against: Australia, Austria, Belgium, Canada, Denmark, Finland, France, Germany, Federal Republic of, Iceland, Ireland, Israel, Italy, Japan, Luxembourg, Netherlands, New Zealand, Norway, Portugal, Spain, Sweden, Turkey, United Kingdom, United States.

Abstaining: Greece, Malta.

Economic co-operation among developing countries

During 1989, the United Nations continued to promote economic co-operation among developing countries (ECDC), mainly through UNCTAD. Technical co-operation among developing countries received the support of UNDP (see next chapter).

The first session of the Meeting of Heads of Secretariats of Economic Co-operation and Integration Groupings of Developing Countries was held at Geneva from 15 to 17 March.[35] The meeting discussed strengthening the link between national economic development planning and the subregional/regional economic integration process; debt problems and structural adjustment policies of developing countries and their relation to economic integration; and measures needed to revitalize integration schemes of developing countries and strengthen co-operation between different schemes. The meeting adopted a series of measures and actions for revitalizing the integration process among developing countries in the following areas: the link between national policies and integration objectives; strengthening of payment and financial underpinnings of the integration process; co-operation among integration groupings at the regional and international levels; expanding the role of enterprises (public and private) in the integration process; production co-operation; and services.

The UNCTAD Committee on Economic Co-operation among Developing Countries held its fifth session at Geneva from 1 to 12 June.[36] In a 12 June resolution,[37] the Committee stressed the need for developing countries to strengthen their national efforts to promote ECDC and noted that, given the magnitude of macro-economic problems, a more supportive and stable external environment was needed to enhance the abilities of developing countries to achieve the objectives of ECDC. It called on the UNCTAD Secretary-General to implement further measures to support ECDC, including in the following areas: a project for UNDP financing aimed at promoting co-operation among economic integration groupings of developing countries to follow up on the recommendations of the Meeting of Heads of Secretariats; the support of activities promoting increased investment flows and transfer of technology between enterprises of developing countries; dissemination of information on investment laws and regulations of developing countries; support of existing subregional and regional business information promotion centres and establishment of new computer-based regional and interregional investment information and promotion activities; and assistance to developing countries in monetary and financial co-operation among developing countries as an integral activity for effective trade expansion and promotion.

The Committee underlined the need to further promote co-ordination between work in ECDC and other UNCTAD activities and stressed the importance of technical assistance in ECDC. The UNCTAD Secretary-General was requested to continue efforts to raise additional extrabudgetary resources for ECDC activities and to give particular attention to support for African countries.

In **resolution 1989/21** of 24 May, the Economic and Social Council affirmed the need to enlarge the role of the United Nations Centre on Transnational Corporations in promoting new forms of ECDC.

REFERENCES

[1]E/1989/29. [2]A/44/3/Rev.1. [3]*World Economic Survey 1989: Current Trends and Policies in the World Economy* (E/1989/45 & Corr.1), Sales No. E.89.II.C.1 & corrigendum. [4]A/44/746. [5]YUN 1988, p. 324, GA dec. 43/443, 20 Dec. 1988. [6]A/44/45. [7]A/AC.233/3. [8]YUN 1988, p. 319, GA res. 43/182, 20 Dec. 1988. [9]A/44/41. [10]A/AC.232/3. [11]YUN 1988, p. 323. [12]A/AC.232/L.1. [13]A/AC.232/5. [14]YUN 1988, p. 319. [15]ACC/1989/9. [16]ACC/1989/DEC/1-20 (dec. 1989/1). [17]E/1989/80. [18]ACC/1989/16. [19]A/44/15, vol. I (dec. 371(XXXV)). [20]A/44/15, vol. II (dec. 373(XXXVI)). [21]E/1989/32 (dec. 89/62). [22]E/1990/4. [23]E/1989/25. [24]YUN 1985, p. 425, GA res. 40/182, 17 Dec. 1985. [25]A/44/266-E/1989/65 & Add.1,2. [26]YUN 1974, p. 402, GA res. 3281(XXIX), 12 Dec. 1974. [27]YUN 1986, p. 399, GA dec. 41/440, 5 Dec. 1986. [28]YUN 1987, p. 379, GA res. 42/165, 11 Dec. 1987. [29]A/44/217-E/1989/56. [30]YUN 1988, p. 322, GA res. 43/195, 20 Dec. 1988. [31]A/44/467. [32]ACC/1989/PG/5. [33]YUN 1987, p. 381, GA res. 42/173, 11 Dec. 1987. [34]A/44/510. [35]TD/B/C.7/94. [36]TD/B/1217. [37]*Ibid.* (res. 4(V)).

Economic and social trends and policy

Economic surveys and trends

The *World Economic Survey 1989*[1] stated that the output of the world economy grew by some 4.3 per cent in 1988 and world trade increased by 8.3 per cent, the highest growth rate since the early 1970s. That rapid expansion was likely to give way to more moderate increases in world output and trade in 1989 as measures had been taken to contain inflationary pressures in the industrialized countries in late 1988 and early 1989, and more cautious attitudes on the part of investors and consumers in the big industrial countries were slowing the growth of aggregate demand.

As was the case throughout the 1980s, the fastest growing economies were in Asia, where a great many countries, including China and India, showed per capita growth rates considerably higher than those in the old industrialized countries.

However, in much of Africa and Latin America, per capita income was declining instead of growing and the gap between the poorest countries and the richest was widening. The most probable short-term scenario for 1989 and 1990 was one of a modest slow-down in output and a gradual deceleration of inflation in major industrial countries. However, there was a risk that a sudden change in expectations in international financial markets could put an even heavier burden on monetary policy to counteract destabilizing price or exchange rate movements, which could make for an abrupt contraction.

In response to a 1988 Economic and Social Council request,[2] the *Survey* devoted a separate section to the socio-economic attainment of women. In response to another 1988 Council request,[3] a separate section discussed the early identification, analysis and monitoring of world economic developments. A further section presented selected demographic indications in tabular form.

In a note giving an update of the world economy at the end of 1989,[4] the Secretary-General said that world production and trade continued to expand in 1989, but more slowly than in 1988. Preliminary estimates indicated that world output increased by some 3 per cent and international trade grew by around 6.5 per cent. The developed market economies continued to grow in 1989, the seventh year of uninterrupted expansion. However, the rate of growth slowed to just over 3 per cent from 4.2 per cent in 1988. Among the large economies, the sharpest slow-down was in Canada and the United States. Estimated growth in the United States was around 2.7 per cent for 1989, or less than two thirds of the 4.4 per cent growth in 1988. Canada's deceleration was similar. Most other major economies grew almost as fast as in 1988 or even faster.

South and East Asia continued to be the most rapidly expanding region in the world, but even that region did not maintain the rapid pace of the previous year. Several export-oriented economies were adversely affected by the deceleration in some of the developed market economies and China and, in some cases, by earlier revaluations of their currencies and increasing unit labour costs. In some of those countries, the deterioriation in export prospects was being offset by a boom in private domestic consumption brought about by several years of steady growth.

In Latin America, output increased modestly after a decrease in 1988. The improvement was due almost entirely to a turn-around in Brazil, although Mexico also improved its growth performance. The rate of growth of the other countries in the region was less than in 1988, and growth in the region as a whole was insufficient to avoid a fall in per capita output for the second consecutive year.

Growth in Africa in 1989 was estimated to have been only slightly higher than in 1988, meaning a further decline in per capita output. Regional wars and civil unrest continued to be a major impediment to economic and social progress in several countries.

In 1989, oil prices were some 20 per cent higher than in 1988, and the energy-exporting countries of West Asia benefited accordingly. Nevertheless, those economies were still adjusting to the lower oil prices that had prevailed since 1986. That adjustment also had a major influence on neighbouring countries through three main channels: a decrease in energy-exporting countries' imports from them; a collapse in workers' remittances; and a reduction in development assistance flows.

China's growth slowed to about 5 per cent in 1989, one of its lowest levels in the 1980s. Industrial output increased by about 7 per cent, compared with almost 18 per cent in 1988, and agricultural output probably increased by some 4 per cent. The economy, which had been expanding rapidly in the 1980s, grew by 11 per cent in 1988. Such growth was becoming unsustainable, with serious imbalances developing. The rate of inflation rose to an unprecedented 25 per cent in the first half of 1989, and the economic slow-down that took place was mainly due to contractionary measures taken.

With regard to Eastern Europe and the USSR, it was noted that, due to political upheavals and political and economic reforms, output grew by only 2.5 per cent in 1989, a modest rate even in comparison with the average rate of the 1980s. The growth of industrial production slowed considerably, especially in Bulgaria, the German Democratic Republic, Poland and the USSR, and agricultural production in most of Eastern Europe probably increased by only about 2 per cent.

The *Trade and Development Report, 1989*[5] stated that the division of the world economy into high-growth and low-growth areas could not be explained primarily by differences in growth potential or in the quality of policy-making. Depression, disorder and debt formed a vicious and tenacious circle. Breaking out of the circle would require a new level of solidarity within and among countries. There was a need for consensus on how best to share the burdens and fruits of adjustment and for foreign creditors to lift the weight of debt from developing nations.

The *Report* devoted a section to the least developed countries (see below).

ECONOMIC AND SOCIAL COUNCIL ACTION

On 28 July, the Economic and Social Council adopted **resolution 1989/113** without vote.

Relationship between economic and social factors in development

The Economic and Social Council,

Recalling General Assembly resolution 40/179 of 17 December 1985 on patterns of consumption,

Having considered the *World Economic Survey, 1989* and the views expressed during the general discussion of international economic and social policy, including regional and sectoral developments, at its second regular session of 1989,

Concerned at the worsening economic situation of many developing countries, which includes a significant decline in living conditions, the persistence and increase of widespread poverty in a large number of countries and the decrease of the main economic and social indicators in those countries,

Aware of the close relationship between economic and social factors in the development process, and convinced of the need for an integrated approach to development,

1. *Decides* that at its organizational session for 1990 the Council shall recommend the modalities by which it will address the relationship between economic and social factors in the growth and development process, taking into account the balanced treatment that should be given to those factors;

2. *Requests* the Secretary-General, drawing upon the expertise of the competent organs, organizations and bodies of the United Nations system, to include in the *World Economic Survey* a separate chapter containing an in-depth review of the relationship between economic and social factors and an analysis of the impact of the world economic situation, including external indebtedness and other important problems in the areas of trade, finance and income, on the social situation of the developing countries.

Economic and Social Council resolution 1989/113

28 July 1989   Meeting 37   Adopted without vote

Draft by Vice-President (E/1989/L.47), based on informal consultations on draft by Brazil, Cuba, Jamaica, Mauritania, Mexico, Poland, Tunisia, Venezuela and Yugoslavia (E/1989/L.34); agenda item 2.
Meeting numbers. ESC 32, 37.

On 26 July, the Council adopted **resolution 1989/85** without vote.

Role of the United Nations in the early identification, analysis and monitoring of world economic developments

The Economic and Social Council,

Recalling its resolution 1988/75 of 29 July 1988,

Emphasizing the role of the United Nations and the common interest in strengthening international co-operation in the economic and social fields for the purpose of ensuring balanced and sustained growth and development of the world economy,

Acknowledging the importance of short-term macroeconomic forecasting and of longer-term projections of world socio-economic development,

Acknowledging also that the early identification of macroeconomic disturbances is an important element in averting their potentially negative effects at both the national and the international level,

Recognizing that each country must be able to provide and obtain timely information on developments, trends and processes affecting all countries,

Recognizing the special requirements of developing countries which may have deficiencies in their infrastructures for gathering and analysing socio-economic information on global trends and emerging problems affecting the development process,

Noting that, in view of the world-wide repercussions that sudden economic shocks can have, the international system's capacity for early identification of potential trouble-spots should be improved,

1. *Highly commends* the Secretary-General for the survey of the mechanisms and means currently available within the United Nations system for early identification, analysis and monitoring of world economic developments;

2. *Acknowledges* that for the early identification of emerging problems the United Nations should aim at improving its analytical and forecasting activities on a co-ordinated basis and should:

(a) Strengthen information links within the United Nations;

(b) Improve existing mechanisms and means of providing socio-economic data available in the United Nations in a comprehensive and readily accessible form for the use of policy makers and others;

(c) Further develop links and increase the flow of information between the United Nations and national research and information centres, wherever feasible;

(d) Expand the analysis of options and possible actions that might be taken in connection with emerging problems in the world economy, with a view to encouraging Member States to improve their own analytical work and forecasting activities;

3. *Requests* the Secretary-General to present to the Economic and Social Council at its second regular session of 1990 proposals that could be implemented within existing resources to improve the work of the United Nations on the early identification, analysis and monitoring of emerging problems in the world economy in accordance with the present resolution.

Economic and Social Council resolution 1989/85

26 July 1989   Meeting 35   Adopted without vote

Draft by Vice-President (E/1989/L.41) based on informal consultations on draft by USSR (E/1989/L.31); agenda item 2.
Meeting numbers. ESC 32, 35.

REFERENCES

[1] *World Economic Survey 1989: Current Trends and Policies in the World Economy* (E/1989/45 & Corr.1), Sales No. E.89.II.C.1 & corrigendum. [2] YUN 1988, p. 627, ESC res. 1988/49, 26 July 1988. [3] *Ibid.*, p. 325, ESC res. 1988/75, 29 July 1988. [4] E/1990/INF/1. [5] *Trade and Development Report, 1989* (UNCTAD/TDR/9), Sales No. E.89.II.D.14.

Development planning and public administration

Development planning

At its twenty-fifth session (New York, 9-12 May),[1] the Committee for Development Planning discussed the world economy in the 1980s, elements of a strategy for the 1990s (see above) and water (see PART THREE, Chapter VI). The Committee also discussed the question of identification of the least developed among the developing countries (see below).

In the 1980s, CDP noted, some countries, especially in Asia, grew rapidly, while many developing countries, especially in Africa and Latin America, suffered severe losses in real per capita income. It appeared that successful countries gave priority to human development, including the creation of a well-trained and educated labour force, maintained a high rate of investment, often through trade policies oriented towards greater openness, and financed that investment largely through domestic savings.

While performance records diverged in the 1980s, policy attitudes appeared to converge. There was a new political openness characterized by reduced ideological conflict and the prospect of reduced expenditure in armaments in both the industrialized countries and the third world. In many countries, a better understanding of difficult economic realities had contributed to a new pragmatism in economic policy thinking and formulation.

Those changes in circumstances and policy choices created a potentially unprecedented opportunity for accelerating growth to benefit the low-growth countries and reduce disparities in performance. CDP believed that that opportunity called for an international development strategy for the 1990s, emphasizing accelerated economic growth through increased levels and efficiency of domestic investment, with special emphasis on human resource development, and encouraging a more supportive international economic environment. Such a policy would seek both to preserve trading opportunities for small countries and provide adequate debt relief for countries implementing policy reform.

In **decision 1989/182** of 28 July, the Economic and Social Council took note of the report on CDP's twenty-fifth session.[1]

Technical co-operation

The United Nations Department of Technical Co-operation for Development (DTCD) executed 168 projects in development issues and policies in 1989 with delivery of $37.1 million, compared with $33.2 million in 1988.[2]

The importance of development planning was highlighted as developing countries sought to maximize benefits from resources available to them and to mitigate the social costs of economic difficulties, structural adjustment and retrenchment of government budgets and services. DTCD, therefore, strengthened its expertise in directly applicable areas of planning such as public-sector investment programming and international techni-

cal and financial assistance co-ordination, including development of computerized information systems to improve monitoring and management of those areas and strengthened linkages between financial and overall macro-economic planning and management.

Public administration

The Ninth Meeting of Experts on the United Nations Programme in Public Administration and Finance (New York, 14-23 March)[3] reviewed major current issues facing public administration and finance systems in developing countries and identified a number of policy and programme actions to be undertaken at the national level to improve the effectiveness of public-sector management in the national development process. Its recommendations addressed: policy analysis and development of policy alternatives; human resources development and management development; management of public money; issues in government financial management; public enterprises; and development and management of government information systems. The Meeting also recommended several specific activities to be undertaken at the international level, particularly under the United Nations central programme in public administration and finance.

With regard to the 1991-1997 medium-term plan of the United Nations programme in public administration and finance, the Meeting suggested two additional subprogramme areas: ethics in public services and the relationship between citizens and administration. It stressed the need for UNDP to mobilize adequate funds for the Special Action Programme in Public Administration and Management for Africa (SAPAM) and recommended that SAPAM receive assistance from UNDP's new Management Development Programme.

The Meeting noted that the Declaration on Local Self-Government, considered by it in 1987,[4] stressed the importance of local government in national development. It was not possible to carry out a comprehensive review of the Declaration since only 11 Governments had submitted comments to the Secretary-General on it. The Meeting recommended that the Secretary-General request Governments that had not done so to submit comments as soon as possible.

In a 19 April report,[5] the Secretary-General commented on the Ninth Meeting's recommendations, noting that they were sound and reflected the interests and pressing needs of developing countries in public administration and finance.

ECONOMIC AND SOCIAL COUNCIL ACTION

In May, the Economic and Social Council, on the recommendation of its First (Economic) Committee, adopted **decision 1989/114** without vote.

Tenth Meeting of Experts on the United Nations Programme in Public Administration and Finance

At its 12th plenary meeting, on 22 May 1989, the Economic and Social Council, taking note of the report of the Ninth Meeting of Experts on the United Nations Programme in Public Administration and Finance, held at New York from 14 to 23 March 1989, and the report of the Secretary-General thereon, decided:

(a) To request the Secretary-General to convene the Tenth Meeting of Experts on the United Nations Programme in Public Administration and Finance in 1991; the Meeting should review the programme of work in public administration and finance, especially in the context of the medium-term plan for the period 1992-1997, the progress made in the Special Action Programme in Public Administration and Management for Africa and the technical co-operation activities of the United Nations in public administration and finance, in particular the development of specific programmes and proposals for technical co-operation among developing countries;

(b) That the Meeting should also focus on current issues in public administration and finance with a view to providing timely technical advice to developing countries and should accord special attention, *inter alia*:

(i) To assisting Governments, as requested, in strengthening policy formulation processes by improving, in particular, government budgeting and accounting systems;

(ii) To developing ways of identifying specific needs for training programmes for promoting human resources development in the public sector.

Economic and Social Council decision 1989/114

Adopted without vote

Approved by First Committee (E/1989/84) without vote, 16 May (meeting 6); draft by Lesotho and China (E/1989/C.1/L.1), orally revised; agenda item 5.

Technical co-operation

During 1989, DTCD implemented 119 projects in public administration and finance, with a delivery of $20.8 million, compared with an $18.6 million delivery in 1988.[2] Interregional advisers undertook 47 missions in tax administration and resource mobilization; management development and training; government budgeting and financial management, including accounting and auditing; public enterprise; and administrative reform.

REFERENCES

[1]E/1989/29. [2]DP/1990/56/Add.1. [3]E/1989/43/Add.1. [4]YUN 1987, p. 387. [5]E/1989/43.

Developing countries

Least developed countries

The special problems of the officially designated LDCs were considered in several United Nations forums during 1989. No new countries were added to the list, which stood at 42: Afghanistan, Bangladesh, Benin, Bhutan, Botswana, Burkina Faso, Burma, Burundi, Cape Verde, Central African Republic, Chad, Comoros, Democratic Yemen, Djibouti, Equatorial Guinea, Ethiopia, Gambia, Guinea, Guinea-Bissau, Haiti, Kiribati, Lao People's Democratic Republic, Lesotho, Malawi, Maldives, Mali, Mauritania, Mozambique, Nepal, Niger, Rwanda, Samoa, Sao Tome and Principe, Sierra Leone, Somalia, Sudan, Togo, Tuvalu, Uganda, United Republic of Tanzania, Vanuatu, Yemen.

In a section devoted to LDCs, the UNCTAD *Trade and Development Report, 1989*[1] stated that LDCs were characterized by low levels of income, literacy and industrialization. Their per capita income in 1986 was only a quarter of that in other developing countries, adult literacy rates were only half, and the share of manufacturing in total gross domestic product (GDP) was less than half.

In addition to discussing the economic, infrastructural and social, gender-related, geographical and environmental differences of LDCs, the *Report* also discussed structural adjustment programmes and the experience of eight individual LDCs with adjustment.

ECONOMIC AND SOCIAL COUNCIL ACTION

In **resolution 1989/23** of 24 May, the Economic and Social Council emphasized the need for the United Nations Centre on Transnational Corporations (TNCs) to assist Governments of LDCs to strengthen their capabilities in dealing with TNCs. In **resolution 1989/89** of 26 July, the Council decided that special attention should be accorded, in the activities of the United Nations system, to the population situation in LDCs.

Identification of LDCs

At its 1989 session,[2] CDP discussed criteria that might supplement or replace some of those used to designate countries as least developed. The Committee made observations on the need for periodic review of the list of LDCs, the need for the qualifying criteria (per capita GDP, share of manufacturing output in GDP, and adult literacy rate) to be reviewed continually in the light of changing circumstances, and the possible use of other indicators, such as a "quality of life" index. It also expressed the view that the economic and social implication of governmental policies should be taken into account. The importance of locational vulnerabilities was stressed by some Committee members. CDP asked the Secretariat to continue its analysis of the criteria and to report to it in 1990.

*Preparations for the
Second UN Conference on LDCs*

In response to a 1988 General Assembly request,[3] the Secretary-General submitted an August 1989 report on the state of preparations for the Second (1990) United Nations Conference on LDCs.[4] The first conference on LDCs, held in 1981,[5] adopted the Substantial New Programme of Action (SNPA) for the 1980s for LDCs, which was endorsed by the General Assembly later that year.[6]

The Secretary-General noted that the first of two preparatory meetings convened by the Assembly, the Meeting of Governmental Experts of Donor Countries and Multilateral and Bilateral Financial and Technical Assistance Institutions with Representatives of LDCs (Donor/Recipient Meeting), was held at Geneva from 22 to 31 May 1989.[7] The Meeting had assessed progress in the socio-economic situation of LDCs during the 1980s and considered measures to accelerate their development process during the 1990s. Another preparatory meeting would be held in March/April 1990 and the Conference itself was scheduled to be held in Paris from 3 to 14 September 1990.

Other preparatory activities in 1989 included a high-level meeting of experts on the role of the enterprise sector in the development of LDCs (Helsinki, Finland, 4-6 April)[8] and a meeting on the role of non-governmental organizations in the development of LDCs (Kathmandu, Nepal, 8-10 November).[9] Meetings were also organized within the Economic Commission for Africa and the Economic and Social Commission for Asia and the Pacific.

With regard to preparations at the national level, Governments of LDCs, at the invitation of the UNCTAD Secretary-General, were preparing country presentations. The UNDP Administrator made extrabudgetary resources available to UNCTAD, from the Special Measures Fund for LDCs, to assist LDCs in preparing for the Conference.

UNDP action. In response to a 1988 Governing Council request,[10] the UNDP Administrator submitted a report to the Council's special session (21-24 February 1989) on UNDP's participation in the preparations for the Second United Nations Conference on LDCs.[11] The Administrator described UNDP's role in implementing SNPA for the 1980s and the assistance it was providing to LDCs in their preparations for the 1990 Conference.

On 24 February,[12] the Council requested the Administrator to inform it in 1990 of further developments regarding UNDP's role in support of the Conference preparations and invited donor countries to make special contributions, through the Special Measures Fund for LDCs, for the Conference's preparations, and, in particular, towards ensuring full participation of the delegations of LDCs.

ACC action. The ninth inter-agency consultation on the follow-up of SNPA for the 1980s for LDCs (Geneva, 19 and 20 September)[13] was devoted to preparations for the 1990 Conference on LDCs. The consultation reviewed the preparatory work for the Conference and discussed substantive contributions of United Nations organizations in the light of the Donor/Recipient Meeting.

GENERAL ASSEMBLY ACTION

On 22 December, the General Assembly, on the recommendation of the Second Committee, adopted **resolution 44/220** without vote.

Second United Nations Conference on the Least Developed Countries

The General Assembly,

Recalling its resolution 42/177 of 11 December 1987, in which it decided to convene the Second United Nations Conference on the Least Developed Countries at a high level in Paris in September 1990, as well as its resolution 43/186 of 20 December 1988,

Taking note of the outcome of the Meeting of Governmental Experts of Donor Countries and Multilateral and Bilateral Financial and Technical Assistance Institutions with Representatives of the Least Developed Countries, held at Geneva from 22 to 31 May 1989, in co-operation with the United Nations Conference on Trade and Development, and of other preparatory meetings held so far,

Recalling its decision to convene early in 1990 one session of the Intergovernmental Group on the Least Developed Countries, as Preparatory Committee for the Second United Nations Conference on the Least Developed Countries, in order to prepare for the Conference,

Reiterating its request to the Secretary-General to obtain extrabudgetary resources to finance the travel expenses of at least two representatives from each least developed country to attend the meeting of the Intergovernmental Group in order to ensure the effective participation of the representatives of those countries,

Recalling decision 88/30 of 1 July 1988 of the Governing Council of the United Nations Development Programme, in which the Governing Council requested the Administrator of the United Nations Development Programme, in close consultation with the Secretary-General of the United Nations Conference on Trade and Development, to assist the least developed countries to ensure that they are able to participate fully in the preparations for the Conference, including preparatory meetings, and in the Conference itself,

Taking note of the report of the Secretary-General on the Second United Nations Conference on the Least Developed Countries,

Expressing deep concern at the continuing deterioration in the overall socio-economic situation of the least developed countries,

1. *Emphasizes* the crucial importance of adequate preparation for the Second United Nations Conference

on the Least Developed Countries, taking into account the priorities to be put forward by the least developed countries themselves;

2. *Calls upon* all Governments, intergovernmental and multilateral institutions and others concerned to take appropriate steps to ensure that adequate preparations are made for the Conference and to participate effectively in the forthcoming session of the Intergovernmental Group on the Least Developed Countries, as well as in the Conference itself, and to support the least developed countries in making their own preparations;

3. *Reiterates its request* to all concerned organs, organizations and bodies of the United Nations system to submit, if they have not already done so, reports containing a review of the implementation of the Substantial New Programme of Action for the 1980s for the Least Developed Countries within their fields of competence and proposals for further action, as input to the preparations for the Conference;

4. *Notes* the steps being taken by the Secretary-General of the United Nations, with the assistance of the Director-General for Development and International Economic Co-operation and the Secretary-General of the United Nations Conference on Trade and Development, and urges them to ensure the full mobilization and co-ordination of all organs, organizations and bodies of the United Nations system in the preparations for the Conference and in the Conference itself;

5. *Encourages* the United Nations Development Programme to pursue its specific efforts to facilitate the preparations for the Conference by the least developed countries themselves and, pursuant to decision 89/12 of 24 February 1989 of the Governing Council of the United Nations Development Programme, invites all Governments to make special voluntary contributions, through the Special Measures Fund for the Least Developed Countries or as otherwise appropriate, for the preparations for the Conference, including the preparatory meetings, and in particular towards ensuring the full participation of the representatives of the least developed countries in the Conference;

6. *Requests* the Secretary-General to obtain additional extrabudgetary resources, in line with past practice, to provide for travel expenses and subsistence allowances for a third representative from each least developed country to the Conference, as noted in his report;

7. *Also requests* the Secretary-General, with the assistance of concerned organizations and bodies of the United Nations, including the Department of Public Information of the Secretariat, to take the necessary measures to intensify public information efforts and other relevant initiatives to enhance public awareness in favour of the Conference, its objectives and its significance;

8. *Further requests* the Secretary-General to submit to the General Assembly at its forty-fifth session a report on the outcome of the Second United Nations Conference on the Least Developed Countries.

General Assembly resolution 44/220

22 December 1989   Meeting 85   Adopted without vote

Approved by Second Committee (A/44/746/Add.2) without vote, 11 December (meeting 49); draft by Malaysia for Group of 77 (A/C.2/44/L.54), orally revised; agenda item 82 *(b)*.

Meeting numbers. GA 44th session: 2nd Committee 44, 49; plenary 85.

Land-locked developing countries

By an October note,[14] the Secretary-General transmitted to the General Assembly a report of the UNCTAD Secretary-General on progress in implementing specific action related to the particular needs and problems of land-locked developing countries, prepared in response to a 1987 Assembly request.[15] The report described the transit-transport situation of land-locked developing countries and discussed geographical constraints and their impact on trade and growth. It also contained summaries of replies received from individual countries and international and intergovernmental organizations to the UNCTAD Secretary-General's request for information on progress made in implementing action related to the needs and problems of the land-locked developing countries.

The report concluded that the weak economic performance of most land-locked developing countries over the previous 30 years reflected the direct and indirect impact of geographic situation in key macro-economic variables. Through trade and development policy, land-locked countries could modify the price and income effects of inaccessibility to international trade, but their room for manoeuvre in distributing the costs and risks of transit-transport among their producers and consumers was limited by the need to achieve balance between foreign-exchange requirements and foreign-exchange availability, and between public expenditure requirements and non-inflationary means of raising revenue.

Supply-side measures to rehabilitate, maintain and improve investment in transit corridor infrastructure, promote bilateral and subregional transit agreements, train transit managers and establish transit-transport information systems had to be complemented by longer-term development strategies that would transform the structure of land-locked national economies in a way that would reduce the adverse consequences of their geographical situation.

In planning structural change, land-locked countries should pay attention to: expanding regional exports through identifying and developing sectors of regional comparative advantage; promoting high-value, low-bulk exports and reducing the extent to which export production depended on imported inputs; and import substitution in both agriculture and manufacturing to take account of domestic resource costs of local production. Those structural changes would require a degree of regional co-operation, which would be easier to achieve for land-locked developing countries and their coastal neighbours if it were seen as a process of policy harmonization in specific sectors (such as transport, energy and particular industries), rather than an attempt to achieve total economic integration.

A strategy that attempted to solve persistent balance-of-payments deficits by exclusive focus on overseas exports and intensified export production in sectors of traditional comparative advantage was likely to increase the vulnerability of land-locked countries to transit-transport problems. Such a strategy would rather have to be broadened and modified to enable land-locked countries to benefit fully from opportunities offered by well-conceived and effectively implemented subregional and regional arrangements in key areas of trade and development. Only such a balanced long-term approach would ensure the gradual disentanglement of the land-locked developing countries from the vicious circle of depressive underdevelopment.

GENERAL ASSEMBLY ACTION

On 22 December, on the recommendation of the Second Committee, the General Assembly adopted **resolution 44/214** by recorded vote.

Specific action related to the particular needs and problems of land-locked developing countries

The General Assembly,

Recalling the provisions of its resolutions 31/157 of 21 December 1976, 32/191 of 19 December 1977, 33/150 of 20 December 1978, 34/198 of 19 December 1979, 35/58 of 5 December 1980, 36/175 of 17 December 1981, 39/209 of 18 December 1984, 40/183 of 17 December 1985 and 42/174 of 11 December 1987 and other resolutions of the United Nations relating to the particular needs and problems of land-locked developing countries,

Reiterating the importance of the specific actions related to the particular needs of the land-locked developing countries set out in United Nations Conference on Trade and Development resolutions 63(III) of 19 May 1972, 98(IV) of 31 May 1976, 123(V) of 3 June 1979, and 137(VI) of 2 July 1983 and Trade and Development Board resolution 319(XXXI) of 27 September 1985,

Recognizing that most land-locked developing countries are among the very poorest of the developing countries, and noting that, of the twenty-one land-locked developing countries, fifteen are also classified by the United Nations as least developed countries,

Recognizing also that the lack of territorial access to the sea, aggravated by remoteness and isolation from world markets, and prohibitive transit, transport and transshipment costs and risks impose serious constraints on export earnings, private capital inflow and domestic resource mobilization of the land-locked developing countries and therefore adversely affect their growth and socio-economic development,

Recognizing further that the geographical situation of land-locked developing countries is an added constraint on their overall ability to cope with the challenges of development,

Recalling the relevant provisions of the Final Act adopted by the United Nations Conference on Trade and Development at its seventh session, held at Geneva from 9 July to 3 August 1987,

Recalling also the United Nations Convention on the Law of the Sea, adopted on 10 December 1982,

Noting that bilateral, subregional and regional cooperative arrangements could make a contribution to improving the transit-transport systems in land-locked and transit developing countries,

Recognizing that most transit countries are themselves developing countries facing serious economic problems, including the lack of adequate infrastructure in the transport sector,

Recognizing also that the implementation of accepted international conventions on transit trade would contribute to the elimination of some of the bottle-necks that are currently restricting subregional and regional transit traffic,

Noting with concern that the international support measures taken thus far have not adequately addressed the problems of land-locked developing countries,

1.   *Reaffirms* the right of access of land-locked countries to and from the sea and freedom of transit through the territory of transit States by all means of transport, in accordance with international law;

2.   *Appeals* to all States, international organizations and financial institutions to implement, as a matter of urgency and priority, the specific actions related to the particular needs and problems of land-locked developing countries envisaged in United Nations Conference on Trade and Development resolutions 63(III), 98(IV), 123(V) and 137(VI) and the Final Act adopted by the Conference at its seventh session, in General Assembly resolutions 39/209, 40/183 and 42/174, in the International Development Strategy for the Third United Nations Development Decade, in the Substantial New Programme of Action for the 1980s for the Least Developed Countries and in other relevant resolutions of the United Nations;

3.   *Agrees* that measures to deal with the transit problems of land-locked developing countries require effective co-operation and collaboration between those countries and the neighbouring transit States;

4.   *Urges* the international community, in particular donor countries and multilateral financial and development organizations, to provide land-locked and transit developing countries with appropriate financial and technical assistance in the form of grants or concessional loans for the construction, maintenance and improvement of their transport, storage and transit infrastructures and facilities, including alternative routes;

5.   *Emphasizes* that assistance for the improvement of transport and transit facilities and services should be integrated into the overall economic development strategy of the land-locked developing countries and that donor assistance should consequently take into account the requirement for long-term restructuring of the economies of the land-locked developing countries, including, as appropriate, the promotion of import-substituting industries producing high-bulk, low-value goods and developing high-value, low-bulk goods for export;

6.   *Invites* transit countries and the land-locked developing countries to continue to co-operate effectively in the fields, *inter alia*, of transport and communications;

7.   *Calls upon* the appropriate multilateral and bilateral international and technical assistance institutions to take into account such co-operative arrangements between the land-locked developing countries and the neighbouring transit States;

8.   *Invites* Member States to ratify and implement, as appropriate, the relevant provisions of the international conventions on transit trade;

9.   *Invites* land-locked and transit developing countries to promote bilateral, subregional and regional arrangements, as appropriate and in their mutual interest, designed to facilitate transit traffic;

10.   *Appeals* to the international community to make available to all transit and land-locked developing countries, as required and on appropriate terms, including, *inter alia*, concessional arrangements, new scientific and technological know-how relating to specific transit-transport and communications problems;

11.   *Appeals also* to the international community and, in particular donor countries, multilateral financial and development institutions, the United Nations Conference on Trade and Development and the regional commissions, to extend all possible support to land-locked developing countries in their efforts to undertake economic measures and policies designed to promote a pattern of growth that renders their economies less vulnerable to adverse consequences of their land-locked situation;

12.   *Urges* the international development bodies, in particular the United Nations Development Programme, the United Nations Conference on Trade and Development and the regional commissions, to expand further their support to the land-locked developing countries, including technical assistance programmes in the transport and communications sectors of those countries;

13.   *Requests* the Secretary-General of the United Nations Conference on Trade and Development to continue to carry out and intensify further the technical co-operation activities of the secretariat of the Conference in the area of transit and transport, in accordance with paragraph 9 of Conference resolution 137(VI) and paragraph 10 of Trade and Development Board resolution 319(XXXI);

14.   *Also requests* the Secretary-General of the United Nations Conference on Trade and Development, for the purpose referred to in paragraph 12 of the present resolution, to continue to seek adequate resources and voluntary contributions to enable him, if requested by the Governments concerned, to assist land-locked and transit developing countries in those efforts;

15.   *Invites* the Secretary-General of the United Nations Conference on Trade and Development to make recommendations, in the context of the preparations for the Second United Nations Conference on the Least Developed Countries, on the problems of the land-locked developing countries, with a view to rendering their economies less vulnerable to the adverse consequences of their land-locked situation;

16.   *Welcomes* the report of the Secretary-General of the United Nations Conference on Trade and Development on progress in the implementation of specific action related to the particular needs and problems of land-locked developing countries, submitted pursuant to resolution 42/174, and requests him to prepare another report, taking into account the provisions of the present resolution, for submission to the General Assembly at its forty-sixth session.

General Assembly resolution 44/214

22 December 1989   Meeting 85   144-0-5 (recorded vote)

Approved by Second Committee (A/44/746/Add.2) by recorded vote (110-0-4), 17 December (meeting 51); 22-nation draft (A/C.2/44/L.42/Rev.1); agenda item 82 *(b)*.
Meeting numbers. GA 44th session: 2nd Committee 44, 48, 49, 51; plenary 85.

Recorded vote in Assembly as follows:

In favour: Afghanistan, Albania, Algeria, Antigua and Barbuda, Argentina, Australia, Austria, Bahamas, Bahrain, Bangladesh, Barbados, Belgium, Benin, Bhutan, Bolivia, Botswana, Brazil, Brunei Darussalam, Bulgaria, Burkina Faso, Burundi, Byelorussian SSR, Cameroon, Canada, Cape Verde, Central African Republic, Chad, Chile, China, Colombia, Congo, Costa Rica, Cote d'Ivoire, Cuba, Cyprus, Czechoslovakia, Democratic Kampuchea, Democratic Yemen, Denmark, Djibouti, Dominica, Dominican Republic, Ecuador, Egypt, El Salvador, Ethiopia, Fiji, Finland, France, Gabon, Gambia, German Democratic Republic, Germany, Federal Republic of, Ghana, Greece, Guatemala, Guinea, Guinea-Bissau, Guyana, Haiti, Honduras, Hungary, Iceland, Indonesia, Iraq, Ireland, Israel, Italy, Jamaica, Japan, Jordan, Kenya, Kuwait, Lao People's Democratic Republic, Lebanon, Lesotho, Liberia, Libyan Arab Jamahiriya, Luxembourg, Madagascar, Malawi, Malaysia, Maldives, Mali, Malta, Mauritania, Mauritius, Mexico, Mongolia, Morocco, Mozambique, Myanmar, Nepal, Netherlands, New Zealand, Nicaragua, Niger, Nigeria, Norway, Oman, Papua New Guinea, Peru, Philippines, Poland, Portugal, Qatar, Romania, Rwanda, Saint Lucia, Saint Vincent and the Grenadines, Samoa, Sao Tome and Principe, Saudi Arabia, Senegal, Sierra Leone, Singapore, Solomon Islands, Somalia, Spain, Sri Lanka, Sudan, Suriname, Sweden, Syrian Arab Republic, Thailand, Togo, Trinidad and Tobago, Tunisia, Turkey, Uganda, Ukrainian SSR, USSR, United Arab Emirates, United Kingdom, United Republic of Tanzania, Uruguay, Vanuatu, Venezuela, Viet Nam, Yemen, Yugoslavia, Zaire, Zambia, Zimbabwe.

Against: None.

Abstaining: Angola, India, Iran, Pakistan, United States.

REFERENCES

[1]*Trade and Development Report, 1989* (UNCTAD/TDR/9), Sales No. E.89.II.D.14. [2]E/1989/29. [3]YUN 1988, p. 329, GA res. 43/186, 20 Dec. 1988. [4]A/44/437. [5]YUN 1981, p. 406. [6]*Ibid.*, p. 410, GA res. 36/194, 17 Dec. 1981. [7]A/CONF.147/PC/2. [8]UNCLDC II/2. [9]UNCLDC II/3. [10]YUN 1988, p. 329. [11]DP/1989/9. [12]E/1989/32 (dec. 89/12). [13]ACC/1989/19. [14]A/44/588. [15]YUN 1987, p. 394, GA res. 42/174, 11 Dec. 1987.

Chapter II

Operational activities for development

In 1989, some $6.6 billion in concessional loans and grants was made available to developing countries through the United Nations system, a decrease of $0.4 billion, or 6 per cent, as compared with 1988. That amount represented less than 13 per cent of total official development assistance to those countries from all sources during the year. Following its consideration of the annual report of the Director-General for Development and International Economic Co-operation on United Nations operational activities, the General Assembly, in December, called upon the international community, in particular donor countries, to make a real and significant increase in resources for operational activities for development on a continuous, predictable and assured basis and urged all countries to increase their voluntary contributions for operational activities for development.

The United Nations Development Programme (UNDP)—the UN funding body for technical assistance to developing countries—registered another record year in 1989 with total income of $1.3 billion, a 5 per cent increase over 1988. Expenditures during the year from UNDP central resources totalled $1.2 billion, of which $892 million was spent on field programme activities. As four decades had passed since the United Nations programme of technical co-operation was started, the UNDP Administrator in his annual report considered the role of UNDP in the 1990s in the face of rapidly changing global conditions and in the light of lessons learned over the past 40 years. He remarked upon the inadequacy of the earlier straightforward supply approach by a one-way transfer of technology, superseded by that of development agencies and partner countries working together and learning from each other. This had led to the current evolving concept of a more integrated approach, bringing together the global, regional, national and local contexts, adopting multisectoral approaches and co-ordinating economic and technological strategies with other considerations such as human and environmental factors. The General Assembly subsequently designated 24 October 1990 as the day to commemorate the fortieth anniversary of multilateral technical co-operation for development within the UN system.

The United Nations Department of Technical Co-operation for Development (DTCD) executed a programme with total delivery of $162 million in 1989, a growth of $13 million, or nearly 9 per cent from 1988. Nearly two-thirds of the DTCD programme was funded by UNDP.

The United Nations Volunteers Programme expanded in 1989 with an estimated 1,801 volunteers in service at the end of the year, supported by the Special Voluntary Fund.

In 1989, project expenditures by the United Nations Capital Development Fund totalled about $45 million. Project approvals reached nearly $78 million in 1989, which was expected to lead to expenditures in future years substantially higher than in 1989.

General aspects

In his report providing statistical data on United Nations operational activities for development covering 1989,[1] the Director-General for Development and International Economic Co-operation (DIEC) stated that some $6.6 billion in concessional resources (grants and loans) was made available to developing countries through the United Nations system, representing somewhat less than 13 per cent of the total official development assistance (ODA) developing countries received from all sources in 1989 ($51.3 billion). Compared to 1988, those concessional resources had decreased by $0.4 billion or 6 per cent in dollar terms, mainly attributable to the decline of net disbursements from the International Development Association (IDA) and the International Fund for Agricultural Development (IFAD). However, as had been underlined in previous years by the governing bodies of many United Nations organizations, United Nations system assistance to developing countries went beyond its quantitative value in view of its multilateral, non-political and impartial character.

Total expenditures on operational activities overall by the system, excluding non-concessional loans but including humanitarian assistance, amounted to $7.5 billion in 1989 as against $7.8 billion in 1988. That total comprised: development grants, $3.4 billion; concessional loans, $3.2 billion; and grant-financed refugee, humanitarian, special economic and disaster relief activities, $4.9 billion.

Grant assistance through UNDP and UNDP-administered funds totalled $981 million in 1989;

through the World Food Programme (WFP), $761.3 million; through the United Nations Children's Fund (UNICEF), $501.1 million; and through the United Nations Population Fund (UNFPA), $157.2 million. Grant assistance through specialized agencies during the year totalled $797.8 million.

Net transfers from IDA decreased by 14 per cent from $3,506 million in 1988 to $3,009 million in 1989, representing a sharp drop compared to rises of 7 and 16 per cent in 1988 and 1987, respectively. Net transfers of non-concessional loans (not ODA) from the World Bank marked an improvement in their negative balances from $4,580 million in 1988 to $3,745 million in 1989. In turn, that improvement brought the overall expenditures on operational activities for development of the system to an increase of some 22 per cent in dollar terms, from $2,781 million in 1988 to $3,384 million in 1989. As a result, the declining trend of the overall expenditures in operational activities, which began in 1985, was reversed.

Triennial policy review

The Secretary-General submitted to the General Assembly a June report[2] of the Director-General for DIEC on the triennial policy review of the operational activities for development of the United Nations system, as requested by the Assembly in 1986,[3] 1987[4] and 1988.[5] Operational activities and co-ordination at the country level had improved over the past year. Also, as requested by the Assembly, the Director-General outlined interrelationships among problems and factors in the triennial policy review, for which he had organized a series of integrated country reviews for submission to the Assembly.

Discussing the major challenges for the 1990s, the Director-General noted that, in a rapidly changing international environment, innovative approaches would be required.

He pointed out that the world economy in the 1980s had grown more slowly and shown greater disparities in national performance than over the previous two decades. Per capita income grew at only 1.2 per cent per annum, just over half the rate for the 1970s and only a third of that of the 1960s. The developing countries had borne the brunt of the decline in growth, with the result that the income gap between the developed and developing countries had continued to widen. Worsening economic conditions, deteriorating social services and, in some cases, the erosion of political stability had affected most countries in Africa, Latin America and several parts of Asia. Diverse economic growth trends in the developing countries had emerged during a period of growing integration of the global market economy. The interdependence of

national economies had increased as borders opened to financial flows and, to a lesser extent, to the movement of goods, services and persons, and as various forms of communication expanded. Those negative trends were expected to continue. The challenge to the United Nations system would be to forge a new consensus, he said.

ACC action. In his report, the Director-General noted that the Administrative Committee on Co-ordination (ACC), acting on the conclusions of its subsidiary body, the Consultative Committee on Substantive Questions (Operational Activities) (CCSQ (OPS)), had adopted a decision in April,[6] outlining an overall declaration of principles concerning the role and functioning of the United Nations system in the 1990s. Noting the changes in the development scene and affirming the resolve of its members to adapt to the new circumstances, ACC called[7] for strengthening the links between the operational activities of the system and strategies for the 1990s, as well as for a continuing focus on efforts to strengthen governmental capacities, and to tailor responses to the unique circumstances of each country.

Among suggestions for making the UN system more effective, the Director-General stressed the need for the mobilization of resources, as well as a review of how funds could be channelled to best fulfil country needs to deal with the growing volume and complexity of demand for operational activities. Another possible improvement was in the programming process of individual organizations, and country-specific work organized under the resident co-ordinator. Other areas of reform included provision of technical advice better suited to individual countries, simplification and harmonization of rules and procedures, and review of field office premises.

Economic and Social Council. The Economic and Social Council considered the report at its second regular session of 1989.

ECONOMIC AND SOCIAL COUNCIL ACTION

On 28 July, the Economic and Social Council recommended in **decision 1989/185** that the General Assembly complete at its 1989 session the 1989 triennial comprehensive policy review of operational activities for development.

The Council, in **decision 1989/189** of 28 July, took note of the DIEC Director-General's report on the comprehensive policy review of operational activities for development.[2]

In **decision 1989/186** of the same day, the Council decided to consider at its 1990 organizational session arrangements to ensure its annual consideration of operational activities for development in a focused and co-ordinated manner and to request its President to hold informal consultations to that end prior to the 1990 organizational session.

Director-General's reports. During the Economic and Social Council's consideration of operational activities, the DIEC Director-General stated he would submit to the General Assembly recommendations on improving the effectiveness of operational activities based on the Council's debate, consultations with organizations, annual reports from 80 resident co-ordinators and findings from the integrated country reviews. In October 1989,[8] he submitted a report on integrated country reviews on the functioning of the operational activities for development of the United Nations system, which was based on the findings of seven country reviews undertaken in July and August. Those countries, Colombia, Egypt, Ethiopia, India, Jamaica, Niger and Uganda, were selected to reflect the diversity of size, current conditions and capacities of developing countries. The review teams found that the United Nations, in its 40 years of operational activities, had demonstrated sound and steady development co-operation work, but was now challenged to do better and to face unresolved problems.

Among the proposals cited in the report were: more project execution by national capacities rather than by external agencies; better design of projects and fewer top-heavy rules and procedures; more realistic timetables; more consideration of alternative sources of international expertise and back-stopping rather than relying solely on United Nations expertise; more flexible and more individually tailored training components in projects; maintaining support to institutions after projects were concluded; better use of exchange of technical expertise among developing countries; and better co-ordination of country programmes within the United Nations system and with the country concerned.

In an October 1988 report, the DIEC Director-General submitted recommendations for action to improve the effectiveness of operational activities, as a supplement to his report on the triennial policy review. Those recommendations focused on several major themes and specific recommendations about objectives for operational activities; strengthening and integrating developing country capacities; technical co-operation among developing countries; diversification of procurement; resource mobilization; programming of operational activities; simplification and harmonization of rules and procedures; provision of technical advice; rationalization of country-level procedures, including common premises; the role and effectiveness of the resident co-ordinator system; decentralization towards national execution and capacity-building; and governance and guidance of operational activities.

In another report,[9] submitted in response to a 1988 Assembly request,[10] the DIEC Director-General submitted information on the fulfilment of the target for official development assistance, including the responses of 20 countries to a request to provide information on their official assistance to developing countries over an 18-year period.

Further DIEC reports, issued in July and October 1989, presented statistical data for the years 1987[11] and 1988.[12] The latter provided an overview of resources channelled through United Nations organizations as well as forecasts of resources for the main funding organizations.

GENERAL ASSEMBLY ACTION

On 22 December 1989, on the recommendation of the Second (Economic and Financial) Committee, the General Assembly adopted **resolution 44/211** without vote.

Comprehensive triennial policy review of operational activities for development of the United Nations system

The General Assembly,

Recalling its resolutions 2688(XXV) of 11 December 1970, 32/197 of 20 December 1977, 41/171 of 5 December 1986, 42/196 of 11 December 1987 and 43/199 of 20 December 1988,

Taking note of the report prepared by the United Nations Population Fund on the review and assessment of population programme experience, pursuant to the request contained in resolution 43/199,

Reaffirming the exclusive responsibility of the Government of the recipient country for formulating its national development plan, priorities or objectives, as set out in the consensus of 1970 contained in the annex to its resolution 2688(XXV), and emphasizing that the integration of the operational activities for development of the United Nations system with national plans and objectives would enhance the impact and relevance of those activities,

Reaffirming also that national plans and priorities constitute the only viable frame of reference for the national programming of operational activities for development of the United Nations system,

Reaffirming further that the fundamental characteristics of the operational activities for development of the United Nations system should be, *inter alia*, their universality, their voluntary and grant nature, their neutrality and multilateralism, and their ability to respond to the needs of the developing countries in a flexible manner, and that the operational activities of the United Nations system are carried out for the benefit of the developing countries, at the request of those countries and in accordance with their own policies and priorities for development,

Recognizing the different and complex situations and conditions that exist in developing countries and the consequent need for the activities of the United Nations development system to respond effectively to them,

Recognizing also the urgent and specific needs of the least developed countries,

Aware of the acute problems of island and land-locked developing countries and their particular needs for development to overcome their economic difficulties,

Recalling the United Nations Programme of Action for African Economic Recovery and Development 1986-1990,

Recalling also its resolution 42/231 of 12 May 1988 on the Special Plan of Economic Co-operation for Central America,

Concerned about the worsening economic and social situation of many developing countries,

Stressing the need for a significant increase in real terms in the overall resources available for development co-operation, taking into account the economic problems of developing countries, the economic capacities of developed countries and recent developments in international relations, which may have an impact on resources available for development, and emphasizing in this respect the need to increase the grant element of development co-operation resources,

Concerned that the resources available for operational activities are insufficient in relation to the requirements of developing countries,

Stressing the consequent need for a substantial increase in resources for operational activities for development on a predictable, continuous and assured basis, commensurate with the increasing needs of developing countries, and emphasizing the special needs of the least developed countries,

Recalling the role of the United Nations Development Programme as the central funding mechanism for the United Nations system of technical co-operation, the full potential of which has not yet been realized,

Recognizing the need to reorient operational activities in order to strengthen and utilize fully national capacities in all aspects of the programme and project cycle,

Stressing that co-ordination in funding arrangements and procedures of the operational activities for development of the United Nations system should minimize the administrative and financial burden on recipient Governments in their endeavours effectively to monitor and co-ordinate programmes and projects and should maximize their complementarities and avoid duplication, so as to increase the positive impact of such activities on the development of developing countries,

Stressing also that government/national execution and full utilization of national capacities would contribute to ensuring that programmes and projects are managed in an integrated manner and to promoting their long-term sustainability and wider impact on the development process,

Emphasizing the need to increase and strengthen the promotion and implementation of technical co-operation among developing countries on a priority basis, through the rapid and full implementation of the Buenos Aires Plan of Action for Promoting and Implementing Technical Co-operation among Developing Countries, in order to enhance the capacities and collective self-reliance of developing countries,

Emphasizing also the need to further decentralize capacity and authority in the United Nations system to the country level in order to increase responsiveness to the needs of developing countries, enhance coherent and efficient programming and resource utilization, achieve the objectives of programmes and projects, and strengthen and utilize national capacity,

Emphasizing further that the range and quantity of skills and expertise assembled by the United Nations system at the country level, under the team leadership of the resident co-ordinator, should correspond to the multisectoral and sectoral technical backstopping needs and requirements of developing countries and should be within the framework of the respective government programme of co-operation of the United Nations system, rather than to the institutional structure of the United Nations system,

Reaffirming the need to promote the full integration of women in all aspects of the development process in accordance with the Nairobi Forward-looking Strategies for the Advancement of Women,

Affirming the need to promote the survival, protection and development of children and youth and the full integration of their concerns in the development process of the developing countries,

Recognizing the importance of regional, interregional and global co-operation for solving common problems in the light of current concern for global, regional and subregional problems,

Affirming the responsibility of the Director-General for Development and International Economic Co-operation for leadership in promoting the coherence, co-ordination and effectiveness of the operational activities for development of the United Nations system,

Welcoming the positive reaction of the governing bodies of the organizations of the United Nations development system to the conclusions and recommendations contained in the report on the case studies undertaken in 1987 and in General Assembly resolution 42/196 adopted subsequently,

Taking note with appreciation of the decision adopted by the Administrative Committee on Co-ordination in April 1989 concerning the role and functioning of the United Nations development system in the 1990s, particularly the unequivocal resolve of its members to continue to adapt, both individually and collectively, to present needs, evolving circumstances and challenges, in the developing countries,

1. *Takes note with interest* of the report of the Director-General for Development and International Economic Co-operation on the comprehensive triennial policy review of operational activities for development of the United Nations system, including the report on the integrated country reviews on the functioning of the operational activities for development of the United Nations system;

2. *Reaffirms* that the recipient Governments have the sole responsibility for the co-ordination of external assistance and the principal responsibility for its design and management and that the exercise of those responsibilities is crucial to the optimal use of external assistance and to the strengthening and utilization of national capacity;

3. *Stresses* that, in order to attain the goal of self-reliance in the developing countries through the strengthening of national capacities, the operational activities of the United Nations system should emphasize the human dimension of development, in particular through education, training and the development of human resources, should emphasize the need to reach the poorest and most vulnerable sections of societies and should have a positive impact on the overall quality of life and development;

4. *Reaffirms* the need for priority allocation of scarce grant resources to programmes and projects in low-income countries, particularly the least developed countries;

5. *Requests* the Secretary-General to include in his report on international co-operation for the eradication of poverty in developing countries a section analysing the role that operational activities for development could play in that area;

6. *Stresses* the need for maximum participation of populations, local communities and organizations, including national non-governmental organizations, in the development process, and encourages, when Governments so request, promotion of participation at the grass-roots level and of the productive sectors in the operational activities of the United Nations system;

7. *Reaffirms* the importance of the integration of women in United Nations development programmes as participants in all aspects of the development process, and calls upon the funding, technical and specialized agencies to intensify efforts to increase the participation of women, particularly those from developing countries;

8. *Emphasizes* the protection and support of children as integral to the development process, and recognizes the need for education and the promotion of opportunities for youth and the need to reflect the concerns of children and youth in development co-operation programmes of the United Nations system;

9. *Calls upon* the international community, in particular donor countries, to make a real and significant increase in resources for operational activities for development on a continuous, predictable and assured basis, and urges all countries to increase their voluntary contributions for operational activities for development;

10. *Urges* developed countries, in particular those countries whose overall performance is not commensurate with their capacity, taking into account established official development assistance targets and present levels of contribution, to increase their official development assistance substantially, including contributions to operational activities of the United Nations system;

11. *Emphasizes* the primary importance of funding through core resources in operational activities for development, and, at the same time, recognizes the value of special-purpose grant resources, provided that they are designed as a means to ensure additional resource flows and that their projects are coherently and effectively integrated in the technical co-operation programmes of the United Nations system, in conformity with each country's national development plan and programme and in accordance with the respective mandates of United Nations programmes and organizations;

12. *Stresses* the value of the concept of central funding of technical co-operation through the United Nations Development Programme in order to promote co-ordination and responsiveness to national priorities through the country programming system, and urges all Governments to channel the maximum possible share of resources available for multilateral technical co-operation through the Programme;

13. *Emphasizes* the need for full utilization of national capacities in all aspects of the programming processes and project cycles of operational activities;

14. *Stresses* the need, in this context, to improve the operational activities of the United Nations system, in particular with respect to programming, simplification and harmonization of rules and procedures governing the programming processes and project cycles, decentralization of authority, role of the country office struc-

tures and reorientation of execution modalities, in order to enable the recipient Governments to exercise their management and co-ordination responsibilities and strengthen their national capacities;

15. *Emphasizes* that the United Nations system at the country level should be structured and composed in such a way that it corresponds to ongoing and projected co-operation programmes rather than to the institutional structure of the United Nations system and, to this end, decides:

(*a*) That the country offices and the resident co-ordinators should effectively provide ongoing multidisciplinary technical advice and support to the Government in its programming and executing responsibilities;

(*b*) To reinforce the team-leadership capacity of the resident co-ordinator within the United Nations system at the country level for the integration of the sectoral inputs of the system and for the effective and coherent co-ordination of the response of the United Nations system to the national programme framework, through, *inter alia*:

(i) A clarified and strengthened mandate from the Administrative Committee on Co-ordination, in accordance with General Assembly resolutions 32/197, 41/171 and 42/196;

(ii) The effective co-ordination of technical advice and input from the United Nations system;

(iii) Closer co-operation of the field representation of the United Nations system at the country level with the resident co-ordinator;

(*c*) To request the Director-General for Development and International Economic Co-operation to include in his annual report on operational activities for development, in 1991, an analysis of possible ways and means of providing multidisciplinary technical advice from the United Nations system at the country level, including the concept of multidisciplinary teams and their ability to provide effective and flexible assistance, taking into account the need to maximize the utilization of the capacities of the country offices and field representations of the United Nations system and the varied situations and needs of the developing countries;

(*d*) To request all organs, organizations and bodies of the United Nations system to make, without delay, the necessary arrangements, in co-operation with host Governments and without additional cost to developing countries, to establish common premises at the country level, and to request the Director-General to include in his annual reports on operational activities information on progress made in that area;

16. *Recognizes* the urgent need to improve the field representation of the United Nations system in accordance with the functions set out in the present resolution, and requests the Director-General to present a report containing comprehensive information, drawing on all relevant reports on the field representation of the United Nations system, and to make specific recommendations for improvement and increased effectiveness in line with the objectives of the present resolution to the General Assembly at its forty-sixth session, and requests the executive heads of all the organizations concerned to co-operate fully in the preparation of that report by providing the relevant information;

17. *Calls* for more integrated and co-ordinated programming of United Nations system co-operation, in which programming processes would be based on an

overall national programme framework for operational activities for development to be prepared by the recipient Government, with a view to submitting it to the organizations of the United Nations system for their support and funding, whose response would be co-ordinated by the resident co-ordinator, and decides that:

(a) Governments should formulate, in accordance with their own development plans and priorities, integrated national programme frameworks setting out co-operation requirements of the organizations of the United Nations system, which would enable the system to support more effectively the development priorities of developing countries and to be more country-focused and would facilitate the development of a programme approach, through the clear definition of national objectives and systematic analysis of development problems and constraints;

(b) The organizations of the United Nations system should adapt their programming processes to base them upon those national programme frameworks and the needs and practices of recipient Governments;

(c) Programme cycles of all funding agencies of the United Nations system should be harmonized with and adapted to the planning periods of national Governments, and further consideration should be given to the introduction of budgetary cycles on a rolling-cycle basis;

(d) The need for a shift from a project approach to a programme approach implies that all relevant governing bodies, in particular the Governing Council of the United Nations Development Programme, should develop more programme-oriented mechanisms for the provision of technical co-operation, with a view to allowing more flexible and effective support of national programmes;

(e) Non-emergency food aid channelled through the organizations of the United Nations system should be programmed coherently so as to ensure its full integration with the development programmes of the Government;

(f) Organizations participating in programming should be invited to increase their efforts directed towards integrated programming under the leadership of Governments;

(g) The Director-General for Development and International Economic Co-operation should be requested to conduct an independent study aimed at developing, among other possible ways to improve the co-ordination of the United Nations system at the country level, the concept of a document containing the integrated operational response of the United Nations system at the country level to the national programme framework of the recipient Government for operational activities for development, which would give greater coherence to existing programming instruments, and to submit this study to the General Assembly at its forty-fifth session, through the Economic and Social Council, including an analysis containing his views on the impact of this approach, in particular on the role of the resident co-ordinator, on the leadership role of the United Nations Development Programme, and on the relationship and relevance of such an approach to the existing co-ordinating mechanisms of the organizations of the United Nations system at the country level, such as National Technical Co-operation Assessment and Programmes, round tables and consultative groups, and possible ways to implement the relevant elements contained therein;

18. *Decides* that, in order fully to enable Governments to assume the execution of programmes and projects funded by the United Nations system for development, the following changes should be undertaken:

(a) The present rules and procedures for government/national execution should be adapted, as appropriate, to promote and maximize the utilization and strengthening of national capacities, while enabling Governments to make effective use of the expertise available within the United Nations system in the implementation of programmes and projects;

(b) Procedures pertaining to programme and project formulation, design, appraisal, implementation, procurement, reporting, monitoring and evaluation should be simplified and harmonized, taking into account costs involved for recipient Governments and the United Nations system, at both the country and headquarters levels, and on the basis of consultation with recipient Governments;

(c) Governing bodies should review existing budget, audit and other relevant practices, with a view to taking specific decisions on measures designed to promote and maximize the utilization of national capacities through government/national execution, a more programme-oriented approach and the improved provision of technical advice and backstopping;

19. *Considers* that, in the context of the application of the system of government/national execution of programmes and projects, as set out in paragraph 18 of the present resolution, the participation of specialized agencies and technical entities of the United Nations system in operational activities should be redefined towards, in particular, the provision of technical support to Governments on a multisectoral and sectoral basis, as well as a supportive technical role in the project cycle, as requested by Governments;

20. *Requests* all organs and organizations of the United Nations system to improve their ability to provide Governments at the country level with information on the capacities and needs of other developing countries, in the required detail, so as to enable greater integration in programme and project formulation and implementation of technical co-operation among developing countries, with a view to strengthening the capacities of developing countries;

21. *Stresses* the need to attach high priority to substantially increasing procurement from developing countries, in order to promote collective self-reliance, while paying due respect to the principles of international competitive bidding, and, in this regard, emphasizes the importance for all parts of the United Nations system of setting specific goals for increasing procurement from developing countries;

22. *Acknowledges* the commitment to procurement from under-utilized major donor countries and recommends the implementation of the relevant proposals of the Director-General in accordance with the principles of international competitive bidding;

23. *Recommends*, within the framework of a more decentralized and strengthened capacity of the United Nations system at the country level, the delegation of authority from the headquarters to the country level by the organs and organizations of the United Nations system in order to develop a country-focused approach and to ensure maximum utilization and strengthening of national capacities and, in this regard, calls upon those

organs and organizations to introduce the following changes:

(a) Within the broad multi-year programmes and projects approved by governing bodies, approval authority for specific programmes and projects should, to the maximum extent possible, be delegated to the country level, in support of improvement of programme and project appraisal capacity, and field offices should fully exercise that approval authority with a view to improving speed, quality and efficiency of implementation;

(b) During implementation of the overall programmes approved by governing bodies, country offices should have the flexibility to make budgetary revisions of projects during implementation;

24. *Reaffirms* the established principles of accountability within the operational activities for development and, while maintaining the ultimate accountability of the executive heads of the funding organizations, stresses the need to redefine and adapt working mechanisms for ensuring full accountability, in the light of the reorientation of the United Nations development system towards, in particular, government/national project execution, decentralization, delegation of authority and adoption of a more programme-oriented approach, as noted in paragraphs 15, 17, 18 and 23 of the present resolution, and for this purpose recommends the following:

(a) The executive heads of the funding organizations of the United Nations system should make specific proposals to their governing bodies on ways and means of ensuring accountability through rationalizing and streamlining their existing systems, in the context of harmonization and simplification of procedures, including the possibility of conferring on the country offices a greater role in ensuring accountability;

(b) Recipient Governments should take the necessary steps to improve their capacity to satisfy the accountability requirements of their executing role, including financial reporting and the audit function, for operational activities for development, and, in this regard, the funding organizations should provide appropriate technical support;

(c) All specialized and technical agencies, in the context of the review of their budget, audit and other relevant practices referred to in paragraph 18 *(c)* of the present resolution, should take specific measures to achieve a greater degree of accountability and transparency in the use of funds for operational activities;

(d) Governing bodies of the relevant organizations should improve their working mechanisms so that they may exercise their overview function more effectively;

25. *Encourages* the Governing Council of the United Nations Development Programme to continue to consider the question of successor arrangements for agency support costs from the standpoint of how best to meet the needs of developing countries and to foster co-ordination and coherence within the United Nations system, taking into account the need to ensure maximum utilization of national capacity through, in particular, government/national execution of projects, a more programme-oriented approach and regular and timely provision of technical advice and backstopping by agencies at the country level, as stated in paragraphs 17, 18 and 19 of the present resolution;

26. *Requests* the executive heads of the United Nations funding and technical agencies to re-examine their organizational structures and staff deployment in support of the requirements of decentralization to the country offices, with a view in particular to redeploying personnel and effecting economies at headquarters;

27. *Stresses* the vital importance of the full, co-ordinated and timely implementation of all modifications required of the organs, organizations and bodies of the United Nations system, as mentioned in the present resolution;

28. *Decides* that the implementation of the present resolution by the United Nations system in all the areas mentioned in the resolution should be accomplished as early as possible, and requests the Director-General to submit a proposed three-year schedule for the implementation of the resolution by all the organs, organizations and bodies of the United Nations system to the Economic and Social Council at its second regular session of 1990 and to draw attention to recommendations on which he considers additional guidance is required, particularly those facilitating the full implementation of the present resolution, and make available his report containing recommendations for the comprehensive triennial policy review of operational activities for development of the United Nations system;

29. *Requests* the Director-General to submit, for the next three years, annual reports on the implementation of the present resolution, on a consolidated system-wide basis, to the Economic and Social Council at its second regular session;

30. *Calls upon* States members of the governing bodies of all organs, organizations and bodies of the United Nations system consistently to ensure full implementation of the provisions contained in the present resolution;

31. *Also calls upon* the governing bodies of the organs, organizations and bodies of the United Nations system to make the adjustments required to implement the provisions of paragraphs 15, 17, 18 and 20 through 24 of the present resolution and to prepare information on the measures taken, to be included, starting in 1991, in the annual reports of the Director-General submitted through the Economic and Social Council to the General Assembly;

32. *Requests* the executive heads of the organs, organizations and bodies of the United Nations system to co-operate fully with the Director-General in the implementation of the present resolution, including, in particular, the preparation and implementation of the schedule referred to in paragraph 28 of the resolution;

33. *Reaffirms* the provision contained in General Assembly resolution 32/197 concerning the representation of developing countries at the executive management and other central decision-making levels of secretariat structures in the area of operational activities for development of the United Nations system, and requests the Director-General to include, in his annual report to be submitted to the Economic and Social Council at its second regular session of 1990, a section on the implementation of this provision;

34. *Requests* the Director-General to submit to the General Assembly at its forty-seventh session, in the context of the triennial policy review, a comprehensive analysis of the implementation of the present resolution and to make appropriate recommendations.

General Assembly resolution 44/211

22 December 1989   Meeting 85   Adopted without vote

Approved by Second Committee (A/44/863) by consensus, 19 December (meeting 52); draft by Vice-Chairman (A/C.2/44/L.87/Rev.1), based on informal consultations on draft by Canada, Denmark, France, Federal Republic of Germany, Italy, Japan, Netherlands, Norway and Sweden (A/C.2/44/L.65) and on draft by Malaysia for the Group of 77 (A/C.2/44/L.68) and orally revised; agenda item 86.

Meeting numbers. GA 44th session: 2nd Committee 2-10, 30, 37-43, 47, 49, 50, 52; plenary 85.

Financing of operational activities

Expenditures

In his report on 1989 operational activities,[1] the Director-General for DIEC stated that net transfers made available to developing countries through the United Nations system amounted to $6.6 billion, a six per cent decrease from the 1988 figure of $7.0 billion. Expenditures overall on operational activities, including humanitarian assistance by the United Nations system, totalled $7.5 billion in 1989 ($7.8 billion in 1988). Of that, development grants accounted for $3.4 billion ($3.3 billion in 1988), concessional loans, $3.2 billion ($3.7 billion in 1988), and grants for refugees, humanitarian, special economic and disaster relief activities, $0.9 billion ($0.8 billion in 1988). Total grant expenditures made by the United Nations system grew by about 3 per cent in 1989, as compared with an overall rise of 16 per cent in 1988.

United Nations operational activities (including technical assistance expenditures on training and consultants under World Bank loans and IDA credits, but excluding WFP budgetary and extra-budgetary expenditures) totalled $3.6 billion ($3.4 billion in 1988), representing an increase of about 6 per cent.

Total expenditure of member organizations of the Joint Consultative Group on Policy member organizations (UNDP, UNICEF, UNFPA, WFP and IFAD) was $2.76 billion ($2.78 billion in 1988).

Contributions

Governmental and other sources of contributions for United Nations system operational activities for development in 1989 increased in dollar terms by only some 3 per cent over the previous year, to $8.6 billion from $8.3 billion in 1988, while they had increased by about 8 per cent and 12 per cent in 1987 and 1988. All those increases were affected by movements in exchange rates, particularly the movements of the United States dollar against currencies of other major donor countries.

Contributions to UNDP, UNDP-administered funds and trust funds, UNFPA, UNICEF, WFP and other United Nations funds and programmes totalled $3.1 billion ($3 billion in 1988). Contributions to core programmes of UNDP and its ad-ministered trust funds stagnated in 1989, remaining at $1.2 billion as in 1988. Those to UNICEF, amounting to $586.6 million, decreased by 2 per cent and those to WFP, at $856.6 million, also remained virtually the same. Contributions to UNFPA rose by 4 per cent in 1989 to $203.7 million, but that was still less than the 1988 increase of 12 per cent.

In 1989, extrabudgetary resources made available to specialized agencies and WFP for operational activities rose 14 and 54 per cent respectively, a continuation of the previous year's sharp increases of 29 and 36 per cent.

UN Pledging Conference for Development Activities

The 1989 United Nations Pledging Conference for Development Activities was held in New York on 30 and 31 October to receive government pledges for 1990 to United Nations funds and programmes concerned with development and related assistance.

In a September note to the General Assembly,[13] the Secretary-General listed contributions paid or pledged at the 1988 Conference for 1989, as at 30 June 1989. At that time, contributions or pledges had been received from 138 countries for 22 funds and programmes, totalling approximately $1,442 million, of which $862.2 million was designated for UNDP.

GENERAL ASSEMBLY ACTION

On 22 December 1989, on the recommendation of the Second Committee, the General Assembly adopted **resolution 44/208** without vote.

United Nations Pledging Conference for Development Activities

The General Assembly,

Noting the importance of the United Nations Pledging Conference for Development Activities,

Bearing in mind the need for the Conference, the principal occasion for Member States and others to announce their contributions to the operational activities of the United Nations system, to continue to be managed as effectively as possible,

Requests the Secretary-General to examine the modalities of the United Nations Pledging Conference for Development Activities and to make recommendations on future administrative arrangements for the Conference to the Economic and Social Council at its second regular session of 1990, for transmission to the 1990 Conference and to the General Assembly at its forty-fifth session, as appropriate, including the following arrangements:

(a) Sessional arrangements for the Conference, including the possibility of shortening it, and its timing, bearing in mind the budgetary cycles of Governments;

(b) Procedures for making pledges, including the greater use of written pledges, as appropriate;

(c) Formalization of and rationalization of procedures for the Final Act of the Conference.

General Assembly resolution 44/208

22 December 1989   Meeting 85   Adopted without vote

Approved by Second Committee (A/44/863) by consensus, 11 December
(meeting 49); draft by Vice-Chairman (A/C.2/44/L.75), based on informal consultations on draft by United Kingdom (A/C.2/44/L.66); agenda
item 86.
Meeting numbers. GA 44th session: 2nd Committee 2-10, 30, 37-43, 47,
49; plenary 85.

Inter-agency co-operation

Inter-agency co-operation regarding developmental operational activities, and, in particular,
the role and functioning of the United Nations development system in the 1990s, was discussed in
1989 at two meetings of ACC's Consultative Committee on Substantive Questions (Operational Activities). The first session was held at Geneva (3-6
April)[14] and the second in New York (2-4 October).[15] They discussed the role and effectiveness of the resident co-ordinator system; goals and
strategies for the 1990s; programming of the operational activities of the United Nations system; and
global, regional and country development goals
and strategies. The Committee recognized that an
essential prerequisite for enhanced co-ordination
and coherence as regards the programming of development assistance was confirmation that it was
a government-led effort, supported, at the request
of the Government concerned, by the United Nations system. Those subjects were reviewed by
ACC[7] in its 1989 overview report.

In May,[16] ACC reported to the Economic and
Social Council that it had published the first edition of the *Register of Development Activities of the United
Nations*,[17] compiled under the auspices of the Advisory Committee for Co-ordination of Information Services (ACCIS). Such a register had been
first requested by the Council in 1982.[18] Subsequently, ACC set up ACCIS, which proposed a format, established a technical panel and defined
specifications for data provisions. Based on data
collection for the year 1987, the register recorded
20,740 development activities. It covered not only
technical co-operation projects funded by UNDP
but also continuing or occasional activities funded
from assessed budgets and loans, credits, grants
and equity investments provided by the World
Bank and IFAD.

The Economic and Social Council took note of
the report by **decision 1989/180** of 27 July.

REFERENCES

[1]A/45/273/Add.4-E/1990/85/Add.4. [2]A/44/324-E/1989/106.
[3]YUN 1986, p. 414, GA res. 41/171, 5 Dec. 1986. [4]YUN 1987,
p. 401, GA res. 42/196, 11 Dec. 1987. [5]YUN 1988, p. 335,
GA res. 43/199, 20 Dec. 1988. [6]ACC/1989/DEC/1-20 (dec.
1989/4). [7]E/1990/18. [8]A/44/324/Add.2-E/1989/106/Add.2.
[9]A/44/324/Add.3-E/1989/106/Add.3. [10]YUN 1988, p. 320, GA
res. 43/197, 20 Dec. 1988. [11]A/44/324/Add.1-E/1989/106/Add.1.
[12]A/44/324/Add.4-E/1989/106/Add.4. [13]A/CONF.145/2 &
Corr.1. [14]ACC/1989/10. [15]ACC/1989/17. [16]E/1989/74.
[17]*Register of Development Activities of the United Nations System, 1987,*

Sales No. GV.E.88.0.4. [18]YUN 1982, p. 1506, ESC res. 1982/71,
10 Nov. 1982.

Technical co-operation through UNDP

Forty-year review. In the light of what was now
four decades of experience of the United Nations
programme of technical co-operation, the UNDP
Administrator, in his 1989 annual report,[1]
projected the Programme's role in the 1990s in the
face of rapidly changing global conditions and in
the light of lessons learned in the last 40 years.
Fundamental to UNDP's credibility, he said, was
its firm commitment to universality and neutrality.

While the 1990s held out bright prospects, the
considerable difficulties facing the developing
world had first to be addressed. Those included
increasing curtailment of resources by rising debt
and falling commodity prices, and the consequences of the structural adjustment process,
resulting in public spending reduction and added
pressure on external assistance sources.

UNDP was participating in fundamental
changes in the whole nature of technical co-
operation, replacing the inadequate approach of
one-way technology transfer. Efforts were being
made to develop and improve means of technical
co-operation by enhancing self-reliance of countries receiving UNDP technical co-operation, improving cost-effectiveness, providing a more sensitive response to developing countries' needs and
achieving more durable solutions, with development agencies and partner countries working together and learning from each other to bring about
sustainable development. The concept of development itself was evolving towards a more integrated
approach, bringing together global, regional, national and local contexts, adopting multi-sectoral
approaches and co-ordinating economic and technological strategies with other considerations such
as human and environmental factors.

UNDP's multilateral programmes played a leading role in addressing problems transcending national boundaries, such as those of the environment. Such programmes also brought about
exchanges of knowledge and skills and shared technological research that most countries could not
afford on their own. UNDP thus helped to build
self-sustaining international networks for information exchange.

A major UNDP achievement in 1989 was the
publication of the *Human Development Report, 1990,*
designed to be updated annually, giving what the
Administrator described as an uncompromising
look at the state of human development around
the world over the past 30 years. The report went
beyond the usual focus on gross national product

(GNP) and other economic indicators to explore factors making some nations healthy, well-educated and productive, and leaving others far behind. Three indices—life expectancy at birth, adult literacy rates and purchasing power—were combined to create a "human development index" and countries were ranked accordingly. The report showed that, while economic growth was vital to improved living conditions, growth alone was no guarantee of human development. The difference of index ratings of developing countries indicated the degree to which scarce resources were directed successfully towards human development. UNDP, therefore, stood ready to assist Governments wishing to review options for accelerated human development, and could bring together the full gamut of its multidisciplinary experience with the expertise of other relevant United Nations bodies in such fields as education, health, child care, nutrition, employment, industrial development, trade unions and agriculture.

The Governing Council, on 30 June,[(2)] noting that 1990 would be the fortieth anniversary of the General Assembly's establishment of the Expanded Programme of Technical Assistance,[(3)] leading eventually to UNDP's establishment in 1966,[(4)] decided that the fortieth anniversary should be commemorated in an appropriate manner at the highest possible level and recommended that the General Assembly allocate a specific period during its forty-fifth (1990) session to this commemoration.

ECONOMIC AND SOCIAL COUNCIL ACTION

On 28 July, by **decision 1989/187**, the Economic and Social Council endorsed the Governing Council's recommendation.

GENERAL ASSEMBLY ACTION

On 22 December 1989, on the recommendation of the Second Committee, the General Assembly adopted **resolution 44/209**, without vote.

Fortieth anniversary of multilateral technical co-operation for development within the United Nations system

The General Assembly,

Noting that 1990 will be the fortieth anniversary of multilateral technical co-operation for development within the United Nations system, which commenced with the establishment of the Expanded Programme of Technical Assistance and the Special Fund, the two programmes later consolidated into the United Nations Development Programme,

Taking note of decisions 89/68 of 30 June 1989 of the Governing Council of the United Nations Development Programme and 1989/187 of 28 July 1989 of the Economic and Social Council,

1. *Decides* to observe, during its forty-fifth session, the fortieth anniversary of multilateral technical co-operation for development within the United Nations

system in a manner benefiting the role and achievements of such co-operation, and also decides that Wednesday, 24 October 1990, United Nations Day, shall be the day for the commemoration of this anniversary;

2. *Invites* the Secretary-General, in close co-operation with the Administrator of the United Nations Development Programme, to make the necessary preparations for the celebration of the anniversary, and also invites all organs, organizations and bodies of the United Nations system engaged in technical co-operation to contribute to the preparations.

General Assembly resolution 44/209

22 December 1989   Meeting 85   Adopted without vote

Approved by Second Committee (A/44/863) by consensus, 11 December (meeting 49); draft by Vice-Chairman (A/C.2/44/L.76), based on informal consultations on draft by Malaysia for Group of 77 (A/C.2/44/L.69); agenda item 86.

Meeting numbers. GA 44th session: 2nd Committee 2-10, 30, 37-43, 47, 49; plenary 85.

1989 activities. The UNDP Administrator, in his annual report for 1989,[(1)] stated that the Programme was endeavouring to increase the capacity of partner countries to manage their own development and was encouraging those countries to take an increasing share of the responsibility for programming and implementation. Accordingly, UNDP was accelerating the movement towards national execution of projects, promoting decentralization to the field and encouraging recipients to put forward programme initiatives. Recently Governments had shown a growing tendency to increase participation of the private sector in development activities. UNDP continued to broaden its contribution to private-sector initiatives and the promotion of entrepreneurship.

In 1989, UNDP income was some $1.2 billion, another record year. Of the 1989 total, $932.6 million came from Government contributions ($931.0 million in 1988). Other major sources included cost-sharing contributions by recipient Governments ($118.4 million) and special trust funds established by the Administrator ($24.7 million).

UNDP administered another eight funds which provided an additional $1.2 billion for 1989. The funds were the United Nations Capital Development Fund (UNCDF) (see below), the United Nations Revolving Fund for Natural Resources Exploration (see PART THREE, Chapter VI), the United Nations Sudano-Sahelian Office (UNSO) (see PART THREE, Chapter III), the United Nations Volunteers (UNV) (see below), the United Nations Fund for Science and Technology for Development (UNFSTD) (see PART THREE, Chapter VII), the United Nations Development Fund for Women (UNIFEM) (see PART THREE, Chapter XIII), the UNDP Energy Account and the UNDP Study Programme.

At the joint United Nations Pledging Conference in October 1989, pledges and estimates of contributions to all funds administered by UNDP amounted to a record $1.3 billion, an 8 per cent increase over 1988 pledges. (See below, under "Contributions".)

Field programme expenditures in 1989 amounted to $891.6 million. That included $723.8 million delivered under indicative planning figure (IPF) resources; $107.6 million under cost-sharing arrangements; $34.0 million under Special Programme Resources (SPR); $3.2 million under Special Industrial Services; $12.1 million under the Special Measures Fund for the Least Developed Countries (SMF/LDCs); and $9.8 million in government cash counterpart contributions. Of the total field programme expenditures, 48.4 per cent was spent on project personnel and experts, 20 per cent on equipment, 13.4 per cent on sub-contracts, and another 13.4 per cent on training and fellowships.

The executing agencies of the United Nations system, together with developing country Governments, recruited the project personnel, specified and purchased the equipment, awarded the fellowships and issued the sub-contracts which constituted UNDP project delivery. The estimated number of nationally recruited project personnel assigned to UNDP-assisted projects remained relatively stable at 9,734 in 1989 after a sharp rise from 4,893 to 9,877 between 1987 and 1988. The number of experts recruited internationally decreased from 8,664 in 1988 to an estimated 7,835 in 1989.

On a regional basis, expenditures in Africa accounted for the largest portion, at 37.6 per cent. Asia and the Pacific followed at 32.8 per cent, Latin America and the Caribbean at 14.8 per cent, the Arab States at 9.4 per cent, and Europe at 1.9 per cent. Global and interregional projects accounted for 3.5 per cent of the total.

The value of new projects approved in 1989 was $589.6 million, while the number was 1,437 ($708.5 million and 1,794 in 1988). The sectors with the most new approvals were the same as in 1988: a general category including trade and finance, health, employment, culture, and science and technology; development strategies, policies and planning; and agriculture, forestry and fisheries.

Except for the Asia region, which remained buoyant, economic growth in the developing world was slow. Per capita income fell in many countries and foreign indebtedness remained a serious problem. UNDP continued to emphasize more efficient economic management and more co-ordinated planning in technical co-operation.

On 30 June,[5] the UNDP Governing Council, taking note of the Administrator's report for 1988, requested him to provide in his next annual report an assessment of the impact of measures taken since 1985 to improve programme and project quality. In an annex to that decision, it supported continued co-ordination between the World Bank and UNDP on projects and programmes. It requested a report on the UNDP technical assistance studies submitted to the Consultative Group and on the Group's work; noted with satisfaction UNDP's positive response to Governments undertaking structural adjustment programmes by supporting their efforts to improve budget and debt management, liberalize markets and pricing policies, increase public sector efficiency, strengthen entrepreneurial and export programmes and address the social aspects of structural adjustment; commended the Administrator's initiatives in support of the environment and sustainable development; and emphasized the need to give adequate attention to the relationship between the environment and sustainable development in the formulation and appraisal of all projects. It noted that UNDP had been a catalyst for discussion involving the private sector in national development efforts and had been urged to train managers and entrepreneurs and to provide technical assistance in the development of capital markets.

The Council, in another decision of 30 June,[6] stressed its role in providing guidance to the Department of Technical Co-operation for Development (DTCD) in its operational activities funded by UNDP.

On 15 June,[7] the Governing Council expressed appreciation of the work of George Arthur Brown, Associate Administrator of UNDP from 1978 to 1989, on his retirement, congratulating him on his outstanding contribution to the United Nations development system as a whole, an expression of appreciation in which the Economic and Social Council joined, in **decision 1989/188**, on 28 July.

UNDP Governing Council

In 1989, the UNDP Governing Council held a series of meetings in New York: organizational meetings on 21 and 24 February; a special session to consider pending issues from 21 to 24 February; and its thirty-sixth regular session from 5 to 30 June. At the organizational meeting, the Council adopted decisions on its schedule of meetings in 1989 and other organizational matters,[8] on the election of the members of the Working Group of the Committee of the Whole,[9] and on a review of the Working Group's role.[10]

At its special session, the Council adopted thirteen decisions. Those not covered in this chapter were on the Transport and Communications Decade in Africa; the Transport and Communications Decade in Asia and the Pacific; UNDP participation in preparation for the Second United Nations Conference on the Least Developed Countries; the United Nations Population Fund; and desert locust control.

Fifty-two decisions were adopted at the June session. Those not covered in this chapter dealt with women in development, the environment, assistance to national liberation movements recognized by the Organization of African Unity, African Economic Recovery and Development Programmes, assistance to the Palestinian people, Transport and Communications Decade in Asia and the Pacific, Transport and Communications Decade in Africa, the International Initiative against Avoidable Disablement, the United Nations Population Fund and other population aspects, the United Nations Fund for Science and Technology for Development and the Energy Account, the United Nations Revolving Fund for Natural Resources Exploration, the United Nations Sudano-Sahelian Office, the fourth United Nations development decade, and the Special Plan for Economic Co-operation for Central America.

On 5 June,[11] the Council approved the agenda and organization of work at its thirty-sixth session. Decisions were taken on future Council sessions[12] and the provisional agenda for 1990.[13] The Council took note of several reports and other documents.[14] Regarding the Working Group of the Whole, the Council on 30 June[15] (subsequent to its decision at its organizational meeting, above) decided to extend the Working Group, on an experimental basis, until June 1990, with its membership to be comprised of all Governing Council members, and, after expressing concern that the Group had not always adhered to its mandate, reaffirmed that the Group needed to avoid any discussion of a policy nature, but should discuss only operational and technical matters.

The Economic and Social Council, by **decision 1989/189** of 28 July, took note of the UNDP Governing Council's report on its 1989 organizational meeting, special session and thirty-sixth session.

UNDP operational activities

Policy review

In response to a 1988 Governing Council decision,[16] the Administrator submitted a report on UNDP and world development by the year 2000.[17] He concluded that the world of the 1990s would be one in which developing countries faced tremendous challenges, which many of them would not have the resources to meet. Debt, poverty, environmental degradation and rapid urbanization were only some of the serious problems which Governments would continue to face in their pursuit of growth with equity, sustainable development and self-reliance. There did, however, appear to be a growing preparedness by the world community to act in a concerted manner to overcome obstacles to development. With sustained effort, that preparedness could result in increased

global co-operation and more concentrated efforts to mobilize potential development resources.

The Administrator saw UNDP in the 1990s as a facilitator and catalyst for member countries, enabling them to mobilize the system's technical resources to help developing countries improve the quality of life of their citizens. The most effective way to attain that goal was to focus on enabling the developing countries to take the lead; therefore UNDP's basic tenet of providing assistance to sovereign Governments should be reaffirmed in any approach to improving United Nations system capacity to respond to future challenges. UNDP's aim was to help developing countries to accelerate the process of capacity-building, both within the Government itself and within the nation as a whole. The vision of the future UNDP was one where it was able to provide Governments with United Nations system support for comprehensive, integrated approaches to development issues.

UNDP should remain a universal agency to which all developing countries could turn for specific support required in building capacity to manage their development process. UNDP success would be demonstrated in programme quality— the ability to focus assistance on critical areas and achievement of set objectives—rather than financial delivery. A flexible array of technical co-operation approaches directed towards the two goals of national capacity-building and human development was required. UNDP staff should be highly qualified development management professionals, helping Governments to draw on a global data base of advice and information through a network of closely linked offices.

Reaffirming that approach, the Governing Council, on 30 June 1989, adopted a decision on the role of UNDP in the 1990s,[18] setting out main programme directions for UNDP support and organizational issues, outlining a UNDP funding strategy, and enumerating guidelines for co-ordination and a consultation process on Council working methods.

In the main programme directives, the Council requested the Administrator to make proposals to the Council's 1990 session for designing indicators to assess progress in strengthening of national capacity for self-reliant development, and to report to the 1990 session on strengthening UNDP's capacity, primarily at field level, of services relating to co-financing and management services. He was also encouraged to increase decentralization of authority to the Resident Representative with a view to improving efficiency and effectiveness.

Regarding a funding strategy, the Council considered the Administrator's proposal for a funding goal whereby the Programme's 1996 core income would be double that of 1991, representing a 16 per cent annual growth, and called on developed countries, and others in a position to do so, to increase their voluntary contributions, keeping in mind the Administrator's goal. The Administrator was requested to propose elements for a funding strategy by June 1990.

Concerning co-ordination, the Council decided that UNDP's main task was to contribute, in accordance with the priorities and requirements of developing countries, to strengthening their capacity to co-ordinate external assistance. As to the consultation process, the President of the Governing Council was invited to hold consultations on improving the Council's working methods and to report to the 1990 session. An *ad hoc* group was set up, open to all Council members and other interested parties, to consider the future role of UNDP in the 1990s.

ACC considered the role and functioning of the United Nations development system in the 1990s[19] in the light of major changes in the development scene in recent years, which, ACC said, called for a continuing focus to further strengthen governmental capacities and to tailor responses by the United Nations to the unique circumstances of each country. The Economic and Social Council, by **decision 1989/189** of 28 July, took note of the ACC statement.

In other action regarding the Administrator's report on UNDP and World Development by the Year 2000, the Council referred to the 1990 session consideration of his proposal for a new special fund of micro-capital grants below $200,000.[20]

Country and intercountry programmes

At the February special session, in view of the fact that the mid-term review of country, regional, interregional and global programmes for the fourth programming cycle (1987-1991) would take place over approximately two years, the UNDP Governing Council decided[21] to consider the review on three occasions over the next 18 months— at the 1989 session, the February 1990 organizational meeting and the 1990 session. For each of those occasions, the Administrator was invited to submit an overview of all country programme mid-term reviews carried out before that particular session or meeting, all mid-term review reports of country programmes which had undergone major changes or which the Administrator was explicitly requested to resubmit, and a representative selection of six country mid-term review reports, as well as all reports on the mid-term review of regional, interregional and global programmes carried out before the particular Council session or meeting.

Accordingly, the Administrator submitted to the June Council session a report[22] on country and intercountry programmes and projects as well as selected country programmes in the Africa region,[23] the Arab States and European region,[24] the Asia and Pacific region,[25] and the Latin America and Caribbean region.[26] Subsequently, the Council requested[27] the Administrator to continue such reporting. It approved[28] the global and interregional projects placed before the Council (research and training in tropical diseases, sustainable rice farming and research on diarrhoeal diseases control) and the country programme for Iran.

In response to a 1988 Council request,[29] the Administrator submitted a note[30] providing background on UNDP assistance to Lebanon, noting that, due to lack of current and accurate information, the provisional IPF for Lebanon was based on an estimate for 1983 per capita GNP. Total provisional resources of $13.9 million were available during the fourth cycle. The $2.9 million committed under the IPF in 1987 and 1988 were currently funding 12 projects in agriculture, human resources development and vocational training, telecommunications and postal services despite operational difficulties in the prevailing situation in Lebanon. New project proposals for UNDP technical co-operation amounting to $10 million had been identified in close collaboration with national authorities and non-governmental organizations (NGOs) in crucial areas such as primary health care, water supply, technical education for women, handicrafts, agricultural research and production, environment quality control and vocational training. Actual implementation would depend on the operational situation within the country. The Council took note[14] of that report on 30 June.

In a section of his annual report for 1989[1] on project results of global and interregional programmes, the Administrator said that the global programme supported research into development issues of world-wide importance, focusing mainly on sustainable agricultural production and health problems, while the interregional programme disseminated and applied the research results in such sectors as fisheries, health, water supply and sanitation, urban management, human resources and energy. The interregional programme also promoted co-operation among developing countries in sharing research and exchanging knowledge and skills. Both programmes received support from bilateral donors and international organizations, as well as UNDP core resources.

The mid-term review of global and interregional activities in the fourth planning cycle concluded that while most programmes were being carried out as foreseen, the Division for Global and Interregional Programmes (DGIP) of UNDP had also responded well to problems not clearly anticipated when fourth cycle plans were formulated, such as the AIDS epidemic, debt management and environmental degradation.

Nearly three quarters of the global programme resources were devoted to agricultural research, aimed primarily at increasing food production. In 1989, UNDP supported 12 projects carried out through a network of international agricultural research centres, which DGIP helped establish by providing $10.5 million for that purpose, combined with $240 million contributed by other donors. Research by the centres included testing of improved varieties of sorghum, millet, rice, maize and wheat in different ecosystems. UNDP assistance to the International Centre for Maize and Wheat Improvement in Mexico over the past 13 years had contributed to a major breakthrough in plant breeding and genetics with the development of a quality protein maize, tested in 38 locations around the world, that was now ready for wide-scale dissemination. With $22 million in UNDP support, the International Centre of Insect Physiology and Ecology at Nairobi had developed an effective technique for controlling African trypanosomiasis, a disease carried by the tsetse fly, which had killed thousands of livestock in a third of Africa.

UNDP was also investing $5 million in a new three-year global research project, launched in 1989, to develop environmentally acceptable desert locust control (see next chapter).

Under the banner of the International Drinking Water Supply and Sanitation Decade, 1981-1990, UNDP and partner United Nations organizations and agencies were engaged in a campaign to provide the developing world with clean drinking water and adequate sanitation (see also PART THREE, Chapter VI). By the end of 1989, UNDP had committed a record $375 million to water and sanitation activities. The UNDP programme Promotion of the Role of Women in Water and Environmental Sanitation Services, designed to involve communities, especially women, in the design and implementation of systems, had extended its operations to 20 developing countries in four regions from 13 in 1988.

More than 130 countries received support through the DGIP/WHO Global Programme on AIDS, begun in 1987, to which UNDP contributed over $20 million in 1987-1990. Responding to sharp increases in the infection rate, UNDP, in 1989, approved $2.4 million to be applied to three regional projects—in Africa, the Arab States and Asia and the Pacific—to develop national anti-AIDS strategies and assist in training and education. UNDP and WHO also co-operated in research projects to control diarrhoeal diseases, mainly through vaccines and oral rehydration salts.

Other development programmes supported by UNDP in 1989 involved fisheries, human resources, trade finance and investment, and environment.

Country programmes by region

Africa

In Africa, economic performance in some countries improved in 1989 but was not sufficiently even and widespread to reverse the persistent decline in living standards on the continent, with average income still falling (by 0.3 per cent) as population growth rose faster than the 2.9 per cent rise in GDP. As reported by the Administrator in his 1989 annual report,[1] UNDP's Regional Bureau for Africa organized an historic first meeting in April 1989 at Addis Ababa between the African Ministers for Planning and UNDP resident representatives in Africa, where the ministers affirmed the need for UNDP support in such areas as management of structural adjustment, improvement of aid co-ordination and exchange of dialogue on planning and development. The ministers endorsed the ongoing UNDP project, Social Dimensions of Adjustments, and its two other new initiatives, Structural Adjustment Advisory Teams for Africa and the Planning Approaches project. A trust fund was created for Namibia's emergence as the forty-third independent self-governing country in the sub-Saharan region.

In reporting on the implementation of selected country programmes in the Africa region during 1989,[31] the Administrator stated that technical co-operation remained in line with the priority areas identified in the United Nations Programme of Action for African Economic Recovery and Development, 1986-1990. Areas of primary focus included agricultural development, alleviation of external debt, reduction of unemployment, private sector development, environmental management, women in development, encouragement of NGOs and, most importantly, the development of human resources, which UNDP saw as a major component of its programmes in Africa for the next decade.

At the regional level, UNDP organized a series of cluster meetings of African planning ministers to build consensus on development policy, leading to a continent-wide meeting of ministers and resident representatives in Addis Ababa in April 1989. It was agreed that such continent-wide meetings should be held every two years. UNDP continued to organize round-table discussions and sectoral follow-up meetings for several least developed countries in the region, in which major donors were invited to participate.

Roughly three quarters of the African countries had embarked on some economic and institutional structural adjustment, with UNDP assisting countries to make the transition with minimum hardship. Structural Adjustment Advisory Teams for Africa, established in July 1989 as a regional project, provided for training national staff, particularly in finance ministries, to handle the complex analyses and negotiation of structural adjustment packages. A complementary project, which was rapidly expanding, helped sustain social services during structural adjustment.

As an example of UNDP support of development projects, the African Management Services Company was founded in 1989 to promote improved management of African enterprises.

One of the most important events for the region in 1989 was Namibia's independence. A UNDP office was opened in Windhoek, and a country programme was to be decided upon by the new Government by mid-1990. In the meantime, UNDP had established a trust fund for development activities to mobilize resources for preparatory activities and for contingency plans during the transition period, as called for by the Governing Council.[32] The Administrator had taken the initiative to send a fact-finding mission aimed at providing the Government of an independent Namibia with as much information as could be assembled to enable it to take important decisions for carrying on essential services immediately after independence and drafting a development programme for its further growth in the economic and social fields.[33] That initiative was welcomed by the Council in June. The Administrator was asked to report to the Council at its 1990 session on the results of necessary studies to establish a fourth cycle IPF for Namibia.[32] The Council requested[34] the Administrator to review the programme of UNDP assistance to national liberation movements recognized in its area by the Organization of African Unity, of which the South West Africa People's Organization of Namibia had been the beneficiary, so that funding could be transferred to the new Government.

Problems of acute hardship and disruption (refugees, displaced persons, famine, desertification and plagues of locusts and migratory birds) were addressed by UNDP in various countries. At the request of the Ethiopian Government, UNDP continued to co-ordinate operations within the Emergency Prevention and Preparedness Group to alleviate the effects of war and famine.

Through a specially designed package of seven projects, costing $14.4 million and involving at least 17 countries, new ways of raising the productivity of women in key development sectors were being tested. The projects focused on agriculture, drinking water supply and sanitation, energy and the informal sector, as well as women's access to credit and scientific and technical education. The purpose was to experiment with participatory grass-roots approaches and to communicate the results to government officials and donors on the front line of decision-making.

A high priority in Africa remained the building of national management and planning capac-

ity. Other project areas included: labour-intensive schemes which not only provided needed employment sources but saved on foreign exchange costs by eliminating imported heavy machinery; identification of viable small-scale enterprises for first-time entrepreneurs among youths and school drop-outs; support for national consultants by developing national consulting industries, with special focus planned for enhancing opportunities for women professionals; environmental management, including prevention of desertification; promotion of the partnership between UNDP and the UNV programme, which had been of great benefit to Africa; upgrading urban facilities where, in many parts of Africa, inadequate urban infrastructures and heavy migration had led to poor and unhygienic living conditions; and cultural heritage preservation, an area tending to be given a lower priority than economic development, but which could be of importance in terms of national identity and tourism revenues.

Arab States and Europe

The unprecedented social and political changes affecting most countries of Eastern Europe during 1989 led the Regional Bureau for Arab States and Europe to develop a new area strategy, based on mobilization of additional resources in Eastern Europe without diversion of resources intended for use elsewhere.[1] That involved technical co-operation and institution-building to assist new Governments in the transition from planned to open market economies. The Bureau organized a meeting of regional resident representatives, which included the first UNDP Workshop on the Environment (Malta, 28-29 March). One of the main results of the workshop was the Malta Declaration of the UNDP Regional Bureau for Arab States and Europe on the Environment and Sustainable Development, setting out guidelines for environmentally sensitive development.

Food security continued to be a major thrust of UNDP's work in the Arab region, where only 13 per cent of the total land surface was arable and agricultural production consistently lagged behind population growth.[31] Closely related efforts were made to optimize land and water resources use and environmental protection. Emphasis was also given to educating and training large numbers of men and women for jobs ranging from handicrafts production to operation of state-of-the-art communications technologies. Programmes for economic diversification also received support.

Transfer of technology was the dominant theme in the 10 European countries UNDP supported. High-level consultants, equipment and fellowships provided in such fields as agriculture, medicine, informatics and remote sensing enabled the countries to apply advanced techniques while saving scarce foreign currency. In keeping with political changes in the region, support was given to several Eastern European countries in their moves towards more market-oriented economies.

Arab and European Governments and institutions developed many fruitful linkages, with that collaboration given a boost in 1989 through UNDP-supported seminars and projects to promote a sharing of experience in photovoltaic energy systems, women in development and aquaculture.

Specific schemes in the Arab region included supporting agricultural development and new settlers in desert development areas of Egypt; training agricultural personnel to develop arable land and water resources; cutting post-harvest losses in Democratic Yemen; protecting soil from erosion in Tunisia; investigating deep ground-water sources and developing techniques for that purpose in Morocco; upgrading technical education in such areas as vehicle mechanics, construction, engineering and other skills in Somalia; and equipping and training the disabled as well as assisting in training personnel for the disabled in Jordan.

In Eastern Europe, programmes included computer education in Bulgaria and promoting entrepreneurship within new market economies. UNDP and UNIDO sponsored an International Forum of Small and Medium-scale Enterprises and a seminar on photovoltaic energy, attracting planners and policy makers from 13 Arab and eight European countries. Under certain circumstances, photovoltaic systems, generating electricity directly from the sun's rays, could be economically used in both Arab and European regions to provide electricity for rural health clinics, water pumps, village lighting and water desalination. As a result of that seminar, participants set up a steering group to pave the way for a network of Arab and European institutions and experts to exchange data in that field.

Asia and the Pacific

Most developing countries in Asia and the Pacific, although having a slow-down in economic growth to 6 per cent in 1989, from 8 per cent in 1988, showed per capita growth rates for 1989 considerably higher than those of the industrialized Western countries.[31] One contributing factor was an increase in agricultural production, due largely to improved weather conditions. Overall, however, there was a sharp increase in exports, owing to economic diversification and a governmental tendency to open countries to new foreign investments. Against such a background, UNDP's aim was to work towards improving productivity in the region through promotion of new skills and technologies.

There was a significant shift in assistance project resources in 1989 towards the development of industry, services and technology, though agricul-

ture remained the largest sector. While the provision of expertise was the largest component of UNDP assistance, training assumed growing significance in relation to the declining share for equipment. Several special themes were emphasized in 1989: women's role in development; promotion of public-private sector partnership for national development; management of the environment; development management; and aid co-ordination.

One objective of the UNDP-operated regional programmes was to maintain the Asian export growth momentum and to encourage its spread. A project under that programme helped establish joint ventures between Asian enterprises and developed-world counterparts by drawing up and distributing company profiles, arranging contracts between potential partners and organizing workshops. Participating Asian countries were India, Malaysia, the Philippines, Sri Lanka and Thailand. Another regional project provided consultants on marketing strategies and export development to assist leather manufacturers, furniture businesses and printing services in China, Indonesia, Malaysia, Pakistan, the Philippines and Sri Lanka.

Several Asian developing countries sought UNDP assistance in coping with disaster relief and rehabilitation, as did China, Indonesia and Myanmar. Man-made disasters also continued to present challenges. A vital feature of the Pakistan programme was an Afghanistan cross-border operation consisting of eight projects administered from Pakistan implemented by non-governmental organizations with UNDP funding of $4.15 million. Of that, approximately $500,000 was from the Afghanistan IPF, while the remaining $3.65 million was contributed by the United Nations Coordinator's Trust Fund for Afghanistan. UNDP-supported activities in Afghanistan in 1989 included: wheat seed distribution; repair of roads, bridges, culverts, drinking water facilities, irrigation and houses; mine clearing; launching of a crop protection programme in the north; and implementation of small, community-scale projects such as primary school and health clinic reconstruction, livestock vaccination and poultry breeding.

Other UNDP-supported projects in the region included combating illiteracy by such activities as training teachers, revising curricula and developing better textbooks; AIDS prevention and control; wildlife management; use of marine resources in a seafarming project and in strengthening marine science; integrating rural development by assisting new agriculture and forestry enterprises, providing transport, damming, surveying, health, veterinary services and water supplies; development of the handicrafts industry and upgrading by a systematic design programme; use of United Nations Volunteers; training in hydroelectric technology; and rain-water conservation projects.

Latin America and the Caribbean

The economies of Latin America and the Caribbean continued in 1989 to bear the impact of the economic crisis which had persisted unabated since the early 1980s, with the region's average per capita income declining for the second consecutive year (by 1 per cent) and an unprecedented 1,000 per cent average inflation rate.[1] The most serious problem continued to be in the region's external debt. The majority of countries remained in a state of continuous crisis management to the detriment of medium-term and long-term planning. Against that background, UNDP continued to provide technical co-operation in priority areas identified by Governments: alleviation of critical poverty; agricultural diversification; investment promotion; development planning; environmental issues; formulation of structural adjustment programmes; and interregional technical co-operation.

The region, beset by burdens of drug trafficking, civil conflict and pressures for environmental conservation as well as external debt and extreme poverty, took steps in 1989 to unite in facing those problems, with UNDP playing a significant role.[31] In Central America, UNDP began to implement the Special Plan of Economic Co-operation for Central America (see PART TWO, Chapter V), approving 21 regional projects at a cost of $11.2 million.

In November, the President of Costa Rica and a group of prominent regional politicians, economic and scientific leaders met in New York to draw up a common approach to the vital issues of balancing environmental needs and conservation of natural resources with the region's development needs. The Commission for Latin America and the Caribbean on Development and the Environment was formed, sponsored by UNDP and the Inter-American Development Bank, to seek major financial contributions from industrialized countries and rapid and growing technology transfer. The meeting also called for an early North-South summit to discuss a common agenda of mutual self-interest for the region.

UNDP provided emergency assistance for hurricane relief to Dominica, Jamaica and Saint Kitts and Nevis as well as the British Virgin Islands and Montserrat. Other assistance to the Caribbean in 1989 included assistance to the Pan Caribbean Disaster Preparedness and Prevention Project, and to the Caribbean Project Development Facility, which provided financial assistance to entrepreneurs in construction, furniture manufacture, agriculture and ship-building. Other projects

included harnessing geothermal energy in Saint Lucia; promotion of food security in the Dominican Republic; strengthening the technical and managerial capacity of Guyana; fostering grassroots enterprises including those for women in Brazil, Guatemala and Paraguay; provision of low-cost, self-help housing in Costa Rica; and volcano monitoring in Saint Vincent.

Indicative planning figures

The Governing Council, having earlier deferred consideration of the issue of net contributor status regarding IPFs,[35] examined at its 1989 session a report by the Administrator[36] which summarized the outstanding issues and updated IPF programme expenditures and local office cost obligations to be paid by each country covered by a multicountry office for 1987 and 1988, as well as actual contributions made by individual net contributor countries for those two years. The report also summarized the latest round of consultations with individual countries as to their acceptance of net contributor obligations.

The Administrator proposed certain arrangements applicable from 1989 onwards for all countries which either had not formally accepted their net contribution obligations or had accepted those obligations but had not made contributions to the programme for 1987-1988 equal to the cost of delivering the IPF expenditures for those years. He suggested a formula for assessing the IPFs of the countries concerned, including the setting of ceilings.

The Governing Council on 24 February approved[37] the Administrator's proposed arrangements in that regard, and invited him to develop possible economic, social, geographic, ecological and other criteria for defining and applying net contributor obligations for the fifth programming cycle. The Administrator was authorized to defer net contributor obligations for those countries facing a serious decline in economic conditions. The Council deferred all other issues regarding net contributor status to the thirty-sixth and thirty-seventh sessions, for consideration within the context of discussions both on the future of UNDP and as part of the preparation for the fifth programming cycle.

On 30 June, the Council, as part of its decision on arrangements for the fifth programming cycle,[38] invited the Administrator to submit proposals relating to the net contributor countries for consideration by the Council at its February 1990 special session, with a view to enabling the Council to take a final decision during its thirty-seventh (1990) session.

By another decision of 24 February,[39] the Council approved a revised IPF for the Trust Territory of the Pacific Islands (administered by the United States) of $3.034 million, it being understood that this increase of $1.807 million would be financed from funds set aside as unallocated.

Programme planning and management

In 1989, UNDP began planning for its fifth programming cycle which would commence on 1 January 1992 and run through 1996. In January 1989,[26] the Administrator put forward a suggested timetable for planned actions and activities in conjunction with the preparations for the fifth programming cycle covering the next 18 months. The timetable was subsequently approved by the Governing Council,[40] which requested the Administrator to submit a conceptual paper for the overall planning of UNDP resources for 1992-1996.

In response, the Administrator, in a May report,[41] raised some policy and conceptual issues for the Council to consider. Those issues related to the duration of the programming cycle, the resource scenarios to be considered for the cycle (such as variation in growth rates in voluntary contributions and carry-forward and/or borrowing of IPF entitlements) and the various principles and criteria to be used for the allocation of resources. The principles, which formed the basis on which the overall allocation for country IPFs was determined, included such issues as distribution of total IPF resources among specific categories of countries in accordance with their per capita GNP, per capita GNP and population, and ratio of basic IPF to supplementary IPF.

Having considered the report, the Council in June[42] invited the Administrator to prepare proposals and a limited number of simulations, including resource scenarios, illustrating the consequences of the various options the Council was considering for the utilization of resources in the fifth programming cycle. He was also requested to report on options aimed at calculating UNDP financial resources and the resulting IPFs.

Further deliberation on the fifth programme cycle was scheduled for 1990, when a final policy paper with a limited number of options and recommendations on resource levels and individual allocations would be submitted by the Administrator. In the interim, the Administrator was requested to continue informal consultations with UNDP members to determine the resources likely to be available for 1992-1996, as well as their distribution.

Mid-term country programme reviews

In addition to arrangements for the fifth programme cycle, UNDP considered mid-term reviews of fourth-cycle country programmes in 1989.

In accordance with a 1988 decision,[43] the Administrator provided the Council with informa-tion[44] on the mid-term review of country, regional, interregional and global programmes in respect of aggregate data, an analysis of main findings and a timetable for mid-term reviews and measures taken to carry out such reviews.

The Administrator pointed out that the country programme process was primarily the responsibility of the Government, and that the primary purpose of the mid-term review of a country programme was to assess the progress made during the first half of the programme in achieving the set objectives, measured by both activities launched and results achieved. It gave the Government an opportunity to restructure in the light of unforeseen economic and political changes or natural calamities. The review also provided an opportunity to allocate available unprogrammed funds. UNDP regarded programme reviews as key management tools.

A mid-term review of the regional programme for Africa was tentatively set for the last quarter of 1989. The regional programme for Asia and the Pacific remained under continuous review on a project-by-project basis. Meetings of aid coordinators for the regional programme for Asia and the Pacific which permitted the direct participation of Governments in intercountry programmes had been held regularly since 1981, with the fourth in March/April 1989 covering a second fully fledged mid-term review. The fourth cycle regional programme for the Arab States started in 1988 and it was too early to detail measures for a mid-term review. The mid-term review of the regional programme for Europe was scheduled for June 1989 and for Latin America and the Caribbean for May 1989. Reports would be submitted to the Council in 1990 except those from the Arab States, which would be submitted in 1991.

The Administrator asked the Council for guidance on whether reporting could be done on a selective basis to make tasks realistic and feasible. The timetable called for reviews of some 80 country programmes and four regional programmes through the third quarter of 1989, with UNDP reporting in 1990. Another 40 country programmes and one regional programme were scheduled for review in the fourth quarter of 1989, or later, with UNDP reporting in 1991.

In February 1989, the Council decided[21] to consider the question of mid-term review at the thirty-sixth session (1989), the February 1990 organizational meeting and the thirty-seventh (1990) session and invited the Administrator to submit on each occasion an overview of all country programme mid-term reviews carried out before the particular Council session or meeting; all country mid-term reviews undergoing major changes or for which reports were explicitly requested; a representative selection of six country reviews; and all regional, interregional and global programmes carried out before the particular session or meeting. The Administrator was also asked to submit to the 1990 session a report requested in a 1988 decision on the evaluation of the mid-term review process.[45]

The Administrator, as requested by the Council in February, submitted to the Council a May report on mid-term reviews with nine addenda[22] for its consideration at the thirty-sixth session. The report included an overview, summaries of eight selected country programme mid-term reviews (Chile, China, Ethiopia, India, Indonesia, Liberia, Peru and Saudi Arabia), a review of the intercountry programme for Asia and the Pacific, and annual progress reports on implementation of country programmes by region (Africa, Arab States and Europe, Asia and the Pacific, Latin America and the Caribbean). There had been no significant changes in economic policy or priorities in the countries concerned and none had shown a need for major changes in the programmes for their remaining durations. For some of the countries, recommendations were made on adjusting or improving the implementation of the programme. In each case, the report mentioned the main objectives of the country programme, financing and principal areas selected for co-operation with national organizations. The Administrator estimated that about 90 mid-term reviews of country programmes and two mid-term reviews of intercountry programmes would be conducted during 1989 in time for reporting to the Council in 1990.

Having considered the mid-term reviews, the Council, in a June decision,[27] requested the Administrator to provide further mid-term reviews as it had requested in February. The Council also asked him to notify its members of mid-term reviews to be presented in 1990, any changes in the schedule of mid-term reviews, and the completion of all mid-term reviews.

Agency accountability

In response to a 1988 Governing Council request,[46] the Administrator submitted in 1989 a report on agency accountability,[47] elaborating his efforts to reach agreement with those executing agencies that had not signed the Standard Basic Executing Agency Agreement (SBEAA) with UNDP. He stated that 11 of the 31 organizations that were executing agencies for UNDP had signed such an agreement and four regional commissions and the United Nations Centre for Human Settlements had agreed in an exchange of letters to be guided by its terms. Fifteen executing agencies, including many of the larger ones, had not signed an SBEAA. However, 11 of the larger agencies had signed earlier agreements with the Special Fund, UNDP's predecessor. Thus, four agencies were not

covered either by a UNDP standard basic agreement or by a Special Fund executing agency agreement. The UNDP standard basic agreement, drawn up in 1975, differed from earlier Special Fund Agreements (SFAs) in seeking to reflect the respective roles of UNDP and the executing agencies by recognizing UNDP's leadership role within the United Nations system in the administration of central technical co-operation funds; establishing recognition of the UNDP Resident Representatives as the central co-ordinating authority for all United Nations technical co-operation programmes; and setting out the status of the executing agency as an independent contractor who was accountable to UNDP for the execution of such activities. The major agencies that did not accept SBEAA, although they had signed an SFA, wished to hold discussions with UNDP, but after three years there had been little progress. Consequently UNDP decided that SBEAA would be used for new executing agencies.

The legal reasoning by which UNDP had decided not to pursue the matter with those larger agencies that had refused to accept the SBEAA provisions was that the concept of accountability became binding on all agencies when they signed UNDP project documents. However, the issue of how accountability was to be discharged in practice remained unresolved, although it was being addressed by the expert group on successor arrangements to agency support costs. On the basis of its findings, UNDP would consider reviewing SBEAA.

On 30 June,[48] the Council, while recalling that successor arrangements for the present support-cost system would not come into force before 1992, stated that the issue of agency accountability needed to be urgently addressed. It stressed that the Standard Basic Agreement provided a sounder basis than current arrangements for co-operation between UNDP and the executing agencies, serving, among other things, the pursuance of project quality and rationalization of expenditures. The Council welcomed the expressed willingness of executing agencies to discuss the signing of the Standard Basic Agreement and requested the Administrator to enter into negotiations with those agencies that had not yet signed such an agreement with a view to finalizing it before the end of 1989. The Administrator was asked to report the results of those efforts to the Council at its 1990 session, and he and the executing agencies and Member States were urged to pay greater attention to the issue of agency accountability.

Evaluation

In March 1989,[49] the UNDP Administrator reported on arrangements for evaluation of UNDP. He described steps taken to obtain and apply improved assessment of the quality of the Programme, summarized the results of programme analysis undertaken by the Central Evaluation Office, as well as steps taken to assist Governments to strengthen evaluation capacity, and laid down the proposed work plan for the Office for 1989-1990.

The report concluded that the benefits attained and the experience gained by a strengthened evaluation process had value only if continuously translated into operational use. Such use needed to meet the dual requirements of effective management and effective contribution to development. Therefore, the work of the Office had shifted in focus from system development to generating lessons and facilitating their use in the development of quality projects and programmes. They also involved identifying action that could be taken for aid effectiveness, sustainability and impact. This shift meant that UNDP and the executing agencies would take greater responsibility for the quality and usage of the monitoring system.

On 30 June,[50] the Governing Council took note of the Administrator's concern, as reflected in his report, for the use of evaluation through effective feedback of evaluation findings into programme development and implementation; noted with approval the steps taken to strengthen the evaluation capacity of Governments; and requested the Administrator to inform the Council in 1990 of his efforts to rationalize both the management of the resources devoted to, and the usage made of, evaluation work at all levels in the system. It expressed agreement that UNDP evaluation should move beyond aid management concerns to aid effectiveness, and encouraged UNDP to strengthen programme evaluation and project impact, and to further integrate it into thematic evaluation, taking into account the views of national experts when evaluating. The Administrator was requested to present to the 1990 Council session proposals regarding organization of evaluation activities in UNDP-administered funds.

Promotion of national capacity

On 30 June,[51] the Governing Council requested the Administrator to submit a report to its 1990 session outlining possible options, based on UNDP experience, to enable recipient countries to respond better to the serious difficulties faced by some of the poorer countries in attracting and retaining highly qualified national staff to serve in government positions dealing with economic development matters, and to promote national capacity.

Procurement

In April 1989,[52] the Administrator, in response to two 1988 Governing Council decisions,[46] sub-mitted a report on procurement from developing and under-utilized donor countries, describing activities taken and planned to increase procurement from them, and containing recommendations for the 1990-1991 biennium for strengthening the Inter-Agency Procurement Services Unit (IAPSU). A major problem with statistical reporting was that a number of agencies remained unable to report both country of procurement and country of origin statistics, compounded by the fact that projects under government execution were not reported and included in the statistics. The Director-General for Development and International Economic Co-operation was arranging a consultant mission to take a fresh look at the entire procurement process, and the Administrator had arranged for UNDP participation in the mission.

IAPSU was moving its headquarters from Geneva to Copenhagen by June 1989, hoping to expand the scope of procurement sources and enhance competition among suppliers world wide. The move was expected to save UNDP $200,000 annually in operating costs.

On 30 June,[53] the Council, noting that procurement by some United Nations system organizations from developing countries diminished in 1988, expressed concern about continuing difficulties in obtaining procurement information within the United Nations development system and urged agencies in the system to provide such information regularly through IAPSU. It reaffirmed the need to take concrete measures towards achieving equitable geographical distribution of procurement, giving preferential treatment to suppliers from developing countries. It welcomed the decision of the Inter-Agency Procurement Working Group to hold its 1990 session in Tunisia and took note of the Working Group's intention to consider holding subsequent meetings in other developing country regions.

The Council supported a number of steps the Administrator was proposing, including: requiring project documents to identify inputs which could be procured in developing countries and to stipulate that project personnel ensure maximum inputs from developing countries; adequate briefings of project experts on increased procurement from developing countries; strengthening efforts in the field to identify local sources for programme needs; use of subsidiaries in developing countries of international suppliers; and use of local procurement of imported goods when purchase of indigenous goods was not practical. The Administrator was asked to report to the 1990 Council session on IAPSU's progress in increasing procurement from developing and under-utilized donor countries, the impact of its relocation, and the status of decisions to give suppliers from developing countries preferential treatment.

Co-operation with NGOs and grass-roots organizations

In a February 1989 report,[54] the Administrator described UNDP efforts to encourage grass-roots approaches to development and to expand in-country co-operation among developing countries' Governments, UNDP field offices and NGOs. In 1988, UNDP had launched the Partners in Development Programme whereby Resident Representatives in 40 countries were enabled to grant awards totalling $25,000 per country in direct support of NGO grass-roots activities to strengthen indigenous NGOs, a programme enthusiastically supported by field offices, Governments and NGOs. Steps taken in 1988 to establish the Africa 2000 Network, a programme linking Africa-based grass-roots organizations and NGOs in a continent-wide effort to combat environmental degradation and promote ecologically sustainable development, included a consultation in Nairobi, missions to eight African countries and preparation of a document for the initial five-year programme.

On 30 June,[55] the Council requested the Administrator to expand activities supporting Governments' interests in dialogue and co-operation with grass-roots organizations and NGOs and urged him to provide information to interested Governments on the potential and capacities of NGOs for grass-roots approaches when undertaking national technical co-operation assessments and programmes and round-table meetings, and in preparation and review of country programmes. It called on him to assist Governments in exploring mechanisms for enhancing participation at the grass-roots level in development programmes and projects so as to attune to people's real needs as reflected in national plans and priorities. The Council recommended that UNDP pay increased attention to the informal sector's role and micro-enterprises in providing employment and income opportunities for the poorest population sectors, taking into account the need to collaborate with Governments. The Administrator was asked to explore the potential of the Domestic Development Services activities of UNV and UNV specialists in developing countries concerned, as a means of Technical Co-operation among Developing Countries, with a view to initiating new activities of that kind and to report to the 1990 Council session. He was also asked to report to that session on contributions to the Partners in Development Programme and Africa 2000 Network Programme to which the Council invited contributions.

Management Development Programme

After the 1988 establishment of the Management Development Programme by the Governing Council to assist developing countries in setting up long-term, sectoral or multi-sectoral programmes of management development and related institution-building,[43] the UNDP Administrator submitted preliminary guidelines for implementing the Programme.[56] He reported that UNDP had started to develop a network of experts and institutions to assist developing countries in the field of public sector management, and hoped to involve local consultants as much as possible. The guidelines were considered by the Council at the 1989 special session, which then requested him to present to the thirty-sixth (1989) session revised preliminary guidelines, and to report to the thirty-seventh (June 1990) session on progress in carrying out the Management Development Programme.[57] Those revised guidelines[58] were submitted to the Council at the 1989 session, which took note of them, and, taking into account views expressed by delegations during the session, repeated the request for a report on implementation of the Programme to the 1990 session.[59]

Short-term advisory services

In March, the Administrator submitted a report to the Governing Council evaluating the focal point for short-term advisory services,[60] as the Council had requested in 1985[61] when it established the UNDP short-term advisory services (STAS) programme to help developing countries meet their needs for top-level technical and managerial advice on specific issues. The STAS activities were aimed at matching demand for short-term problem-specific assistance with the supply of expertise available from the private and parastatal sectors of developed and developing countries. In addition, it provided ''on the job'' training to ensure the durability of the advice long after the adviser's departure. Initially set up for a two-year trial period, STAS operations had been renewed. Located at UNDP headquarters in New York with a staff of three, STAS utilized the resources of 112 UNDP field offices, UNIDO senior industrial development field advisers assigned to UNDP field offices, and the skill banks of its 31 co-operating organizations. As at 31 December 1988, it had received 275 requests from 64 countries and one regional body and had completed 129 assignments in 45 countries.

Stating that the demand for STAS-type services was expected to increase through 1991 to an estimated 200 annually, the Administrator recommended that STAS be made an operational part of UNDP beginning on 1 January 1990 and that its financial requirements be made part of the UNDP administrative budget from that date.

Having considered the report, the Governing Council in June[62] noted progress made by the STAS programme as well as the imbalances in the list of countries of origin and placement, which it requested the Administrator to redress so as to ensure adequate geographic distribution. The Council also requested the Administrator to report to the Council in 1990 on the STAS evaluation with a recommendation on the establishment of a focal point for STAS as an operational part of UNDP. The Council decided to continue the operation of the focal point on STAS through 1991 under the current organizational arrangements, subject to the Council's decision in 1990.

Financing

In his review of the financial situation in 1989,[63] the Administrator stated that total UNDP income in 1989 amounted to $1,153.9 million with total expenditures of $1,206.2 million, thus giving a net deficit of income over expenditure of $52.3 million. As a result of the deficit of main programme income over expenditure, there was a decrease in UNDP's general resources from $580.9 million at December 1988 to $523.2 million at 31 December 1989 (or $476 million if accumulated non-convertible currencies were excluded). Total income was $71.7 million less than forecast. Income received from voluntary contributions alone totalled $938.2 million. After applying the accounting linkage for local office costs, income amounted to $932.6 million, lower than forecast by $51.4 million. The lower than forecast income resulted primarily from exchange rate impact on the value of pledges for 1989, with pledge value in national currencies, in dollar terms, decreasing by $58.6 million between 31 December 1988 and the date paid, and the value of UNDP-held assets in various currencies decreasing, in dollar terms, by $37.5 million. The exchange rate fluctuations in 1989 resulted in a minimal increase in the value of pledges over those received in 1988, 0.2 per cent, as opposed to an increase of 9.8 per cent from 1987 to 1988 and a departure from the trend of substantial increases in pledges for the previous three years.[64]

Field programme expenditures in 1989 amounted to $897.6 million, of which $728.9 million represented expenditures against IPF (including $1.2 million of expenditure in respect of add-on funds), $60.8 million against supplementary programmes in the UNDP account and $107.9 million against cost-sharing. IPF expenditure in 1989 of $728.9 million, although $31.1 million less than forecast, represented an increase of 7.5 per cent over 1988 ($678 million and itself an increase of almost 15 per cent over 1987). The increase in delivery, achieved for the fifth year in a row, reflected a gradually ascending, planned expenditure pattern, confirming, the Administrator reported, an effective programme build-up yielding the desired results. This continuing build-up thus

reaffirmed the principles underlying the present programme strategy of the need to utilize all liquid resources available to UNDP in a sustainable and organized manner. However, the 4.1 per cent shortfall in the IPF delivery compared with a target of $760 million could mainly be attributed to, firstly, a late revision of the 1989 expenditure target, with the time allowed for build-up possibly insufficient for expenditures to reach new targets and, secondly, new two-year budgetary procedures and some tightening up of procedures for recording unliquidated obligations. Nevertheless, delivery at $728.9 million continued the planned trend of gradually increasing IPF expenditures, with an expected continuation at least into 1990 and 1991.

In forecasting programme financing for 1990 and 1991, the Administrator stated that in the light of the 1989 results it would appear quite difficult for UNDP to meet an expenditure budget of $840 million, the intended target of the Administrator, which was $111 million (15 per cent) higher than 1989 expenditure. The original $815 million target, before the Administrator's suggested increase, now seemed more realistic, permitting a 1991 expenditure target of $860 million.

Such a continuing gradual build-up of programme expenditure would lead to a reduction in the liquid resources being held by UNDP. At the end of 1989, UNDP resources available for programming amounted to $523.2 million, with an expected further substantial decrease by the end of 1990 to $397.9 million and in 1991 to $215 million.

In 1989, project expenditures by the Office for Project Services (OPS) increased by about 20 per cent[65] over 1988, more than $200 million, itself a 29 per cent increase over 1987.[66] In particular, activities undertaken on behalf of IFAD intensified, bringing the OPS portfolio to 52 ongoing loan projects, valued at more than $400 million, for which loan administration and project supervision services were being rendered.

The audited financial statements for UNDP for 1989[67] showed that the total unexpended UNDP resources decreased from $773.2 million at the end of 1988 to $721.0 million as at 31 December 1989.

Contributions. The audited financial statements for 1989[66] showed that the total income from contributions to the UNDP account was $1,075.7 million. That included contributions from Governments and other sources as follows: voluntary contributions $932.5 million ($938.1 million, less transfers to government local office costs of $5.6 million); voluntary contributions to SMF/LDC, $15.2 million; cost-sharing contributions, $118.4 million; and cash counterpart contributions for projects, $9.6 million. Exchange adjustments on the collection of contributions of $500,000 were deducted to derive the total.

As at 31 December 1989, pledges made in 1989 to the UNDP account for use in 1990 amounted to $551.6 million; pledges for 1990 for SMF/LDC amounted to $1.7 million. The financial statements gave a breakdown of contributions by Government in 1989 and of pledges for 1990.

In his annual report,[65] the UNDP Administrator stated that during 1989 four donor countries (Austria, Finland, Iceland, Spain) raised their contributions by 8 per cent or more in United States dollar terms, and among recipient countries nine each pledged $1 million or more (Brazil, China, Colombia, Cuba, India, Indonesia, Pakistan, Republic of Korea, Thailand). Sweden, with its multi-year system of pledging, remained the second largest donor to UNDP, close behind the United States. The other top 10 donor countries included Canada, Denmark, the Federal Republic of Germany, Italy, Japan, the Netherlands, Norway and Switzerland.

Budgets

Revised 1988-1989 budget and 1990-1991 estimates

Revised budget estimates of the UNDP core budget for the biennium 1988-1989[67] amounted to $347.1 million (gross) or $317.8 million (net), with no volume change proposed for the biennium. The $2.0 million increase in gross terms was attributable to cost and inflation increases, partly offset by a currency release. For UNDP as a whole, revised budget estimates amounted to $429.6 million (gross) and $340.5 million (net). The 3 per cent increase in gross estimates was attributable to a $10.2 million volume increase in respect of OPS, reflecting an increase in staffing by 21 Professionals and 31 General Service posts. A further $0.8 million volume increase in respect of UNV reflected an increase in its staffing by 2 Professionals and 7 General Service posts. Both the OPS and UNV increases reflected increases in work-loads.

Original gross appropriations estimates in 1987 had been $394.1 million, revised to $416.2 million in 1988, while net estimates had been $331.7 million and $351.9 respectively.

Budget estimates for 1990-1991 for the UNDP core budget amounted to $438.2 million (gross) or $405.9 million (net). In real terms, that represented a volume increase of 8.8 per cent. The volume increase in the field included an additional 106 Professional posts, including a further 73 national officer posts, as well as 171 local staff. The volume increase at headquarters included 22 Professional and 47 General Service posts.

Budget estimates for UNDP as a whole for 1990-1991 amounted to $567.6 million (gross) or $433.5 million (net). The volume increase overall was 14.7 per cent.

In presenting the 1990-1991 budget estimates, the Administrator said he had proceeded from the view that some strengthening of UNDP was required both in the field and at headquarters, and thus, for the first time since 1981 (with the notable exception of Africa operations, strengthened in the 1986-1987 and 1988-1989 bienniums), he was not presenting a zero-growth budget. Instead, he proposed some selective strengthening, with the bulk of the strengthened field office network falling in the Asia and Pacific region, which also received a substantial increase in core programmable resources.

Further explaining the budget estimates, the Administrator provided an overall review of UNDP senior management structure, as requested by the Governing Council in 1988.[68] He stated that the inner core of UNDP was not really amenable to major structural change. On the other hand, he believed the Council should periodically re-examine the validity and viability of retaining each of the satellite funds as independently administered units.

The Administrator proposed, as a separate element in the 1990-1991 estimates, a wholly new dimension to the field office network—the Development Support Service, intended to give Resident Representatives access to locally available specialized expertise. The proposal would provide for 275 Development Support Officers and $11.4 million of consultancy funds. The officers would be technical specialists with 15 or more years of practical experience in the country, who would be resident in the field office for one to three years, while the consultants would serve short terms of less than 12 months and would normally be nationals of the country concerned. Specializations of both groups would be at the discretion of the Resident Representative, and therefore vary from country to country, but envisaged areas included macroeconomic policy, social policy, environmental issues, human resource development, rural development, industrial development and development management. The underlying rationale for the proposal was the evident need for UNDP field offices to participate more fully in the policy aspects of the development process.

While the proposal was presented in the context of the biennial budget, the Administrator did not believe the funding should be classified as part of that budget, but should be charged to a new line in UNDP financial statements, titled "Development Support Services" and classified alongside programme support costs paid to agencies and UNDP sectoral support costs.

The Administrator also proposed a selective strengthening of the UNDP non-core units, IAPSU, UNCDF and UNSO, involving respectively one Professional and three General Service posts; three

Professionals and three General Service posts; and two Professional posts and three national officers in the field.

On 30 June, the Governing Council approved[69] revised appropriations of $431,869,000 (gross) to finance the 1988-1989 biennial budget and resolved that the income estimates of $48,284,700 be used to offset the gross appropriations, resulting in net appropriations of $383,584,300. It also approved the revised budget estimates for OPS, excluding the proposed post reclassifications.

On the same day, in a decision[70] covering many aspects of the 1990-1991 budget estimates, the Governing Council noted the substantial volume increase proposed in the core biennial budget for 1990-1991, and stated that this was at a time when the prospect for significant real growth in voluntary contributions was uncertain. It therefore decided to confine the overall volume increase to 4.6 per cent (plus the balance of the Africa strengthening package approved in 1988[71]), comprising a volume increase in respect of headquarters of $6,430,800 and a volume increase of field office activities of $13,196,600. The Administrator was requested to report to the thirty-seventh (1990) session on how he had utilized those volume increases. The Council deferred all proposed post reclassifications at headquarters and invited the Administrator to resubmit his proposals in the context of the revised 1990-1991 budget estimates at the Council's 1990 session.

Regarding the Development Support Services proposal, the Council decided to establish in the 1990-1991 budget a separate appropriation of $5 million for the introduction of such services in the UNDP field offices and requested the Administrator to provide a detailed report on utilization of the new facility to the thirty-eighth (1991) session in the context of the 1992-1993 budget proposals.

The Administrator was requested to prepare a comprehensive review of the UNDP senior management structure no later than the 1990 Council session, including the responsibilities of all posts at the D-2 level and above, with justification, the desirability of merging or consolidating core units performing similar or related functions, the possibility of management integration of the smaller funds and opportunities for reducing the total number of posts at D-2 level and above.

The Council approved proposed appropriations of $528,658,200 (gross) and resolved that income estimates of $53,514,000 be used to offset the appropriations, resulting in net appropriations of $475,144,200.

Review of 1988 financial situation

In a May 1989 report,[72] the Administrator provided a comprehensive financial review of activities financed from the UNDP account during 1988 (excluding trust funds) and the financial position at the end of that year. It included estimates of anticipated resources and expenditures for 1989 and 1990, as well as information on cost-sharing activities, the status of SMF/LDC and of SPR, the placement of UNDP funds, the Operational Reserve, utilization of accumulated non-convertible currencies, agency support cost arrangements, the status of the Reserve for Field Accommodation, management and other support services and the Senior Industrial Field Advisory Programme (see below under Sectoral Support). Total income in 1988 amounted to $1,163.7 million and total expenditure to $1,109.3 million, resulting in a surplus of income over expenditure of $54.3 million, which was attributable to individual funds of the UNDP account.

On 30 June, the Governing Council, taking note[73] of the 1988 annual review of the financial situation, urged the Administrator to continue to seek the co-operation of other United Nations organizations and specialized agencies to share common premises in the field for greater co-ordination and economies, and to report annually on the results of his consultations. It authorized overcommitment of the Reserve for Field Accommodation of up to $10 million to June 1990; requested continued reporting on problems related to utilizing non-convertible currencies; and requested the Administrator to establish expenditure targets over the balance of the fourth cycle providing for a continuous increase in the rate of IPF delivery. He was asked to report on the most desirable expenditure targets for the balance of the fourth cycle at the 1990 special and regular sessions. The Administrator was also requested to report to the 1990 special session on his recommendation on the release of the final 25 per cent of the supplementary IPFs and Special Programme Resources and the resulting final IPFs and Special Programme Resources authorized for the fourth cycle, and to review and report to the 1990 special session on prospects financed from the Special Measures Fund for Least Developed Countries.

Mid-term resource situation

As part of the mid-term review of the fourth programming cycle, the Administrator reported in April 1989 on the mid-term resource situation for the programming cycle and revised earmarkings and allocations for SPR activities (see below).[74] The report was made in response to a 1988 Governing Council decision,[45] in which it authorized an additional amount of $676 million for the fourth programming cycle, of which $490 million was allocated for country and intercountry IPFs. The allocations were to be disbursed in a staggered manner: 50 per cent in 1988, 25 per cent in 1989 and the other 25 per cent in 1990, pending an annual assessment by the Administrator.

Based on resource forecasts, the Administrator released the 1989 allotment in January, bringing the total of additional resources released for commitments authorized in 1988 to 75 per cent. In February,[75] the Council agreed with the Administrator's proposal to release the entire Project Development Facility earmarking for the fourth cycle in 1989 (or 100 per cent of the increase authorized by the Council's 1 July 1988 decision), provided that the overall SPR commitment during the year did not exceed the amount authorized in 1988. The April report provided details on the January 1989 resource forecast which served as a basis for the release of the 25 per cent of the additional resources. For the purpose of planning, it assumed for the years 1989 through 1991 an average annual growth rate of voluntary contributions in local currencies of at least 5 per cent, and an annual appreciation of the United States dollar of 5 per cent for those three years.

Having considered the Administrator's report on the mid-term resource situation, the Council on 30 June approved[76] as an interim measure use of funds available from reimbursements under the initial Project Development Facility allocations of a total of $2 million for future Project Development Facility missions on a non-reimbursable basis, while requesting a complete report on the operations of the Facility for the Council's 1990 session. The Council requested the Administrator, in the context of the review of the possible release of the 25 per cent of the supplementary IPFs and SPR to be undertaken in 1990, to submit proposals for possible funding of activities.

After considering the mid-term resource situation, the Governing Council, on 30 June 1989,[77] taking into account Economic and Social Council **resolution 1989/1** of 10 May 1989, regarding emergency assistance to Democratic Yemen for rehabilitation and reconstruction after the March-April torrential rain and floods, requested the Administrator to consider additional assistance to Democratic Yemen from SPR beyond the normally authorized amount. The Administrator was asked to report to the 1990 session on his efforts in that regard.

Special Programme Resources

Following the Council's 1988 approval[43] of an allocation of $110 million to augment SPR for the remainder of the fourth cycle, the Administrator submitted a report providing details on the earmarkings and allocation of resources for activities previously agreed by the Council and traditionally financed by SPR.[78] In particular, he suggested increasing SPR earmarkings for assistance for disaster relief and programme development, particularly the Project Development Facility (PDF). New SPR activities for which he proposed new allocations included the Management Development Programme (see above).

On 24 February 1989 the Governing Council requested[75] the Administrator to provide the Council's 1989 regular session with a detailed review of commitments made under the various SPR components and invited him to submit proposals on possibilities for accommodating increased amounts for Technical Co-operation among Developing Countries (TCDC) (at least $1 million) and an additional amount for disaster-related activities, while ensuring that adequate resources were allocated to SPR components which were devoted to aid co-ordination and programme quality. It agreed with the Administrator's proposal to release the entire PDF earmarking for the fourth cycle in 1989 (see above).

The Administrator, in his April report on the mid-term resource situation,[74] made proposals as suggested by the Council on increased allocations by reducing the amount of unearmarked resources from $1.7 million to $0.7 million. and by cancelling the fourth cycle earmarking for pre-investment activities. The Administrator considered that an additional amount of at least $2 million was required so that it could be effectively used by June 1990.

On 30 June 1989, the Council, after considering the Administrator's report on the mid-term resource situation, authorized[76] the additional fourth cycle earmarkings under SPR of $1 million each for TCDC and for disaster-related activities funded by corresponding reductions in non-earmarked SPR as well as the cancellation of the fourth cycle earmarking of $1 million for pre-investment activities.

UNDP-administered funds

Five new trust funds established[79] in 1989 by the Administrator on behalf of UNDP were to finance: emergency humanitarian assistance to Angola; support for priority areas during Namibia's transition period and immediately after independence; promotion of the conservation and management of the cultural and natural inheritance of Latin America and the Caribbean; the UNDP/Norway Trust Fund for the Special Plan of Economic Co-operation for Central America; and assistance for developing countries in complying with the 1987 Montreal Protocol on Substances that Deplete the Ozone Layer. Contributions to those funds received during the year amounted to some $2.8 million out of a total 1989 income of $28.2 million for all 50 trust funds. Actual expenditure on the 50 trust funds in 1989 was $19.2 million. A trust fund was also established on behalf of UNCDF; five on behalf of UNSO; two on behalf of UNFSTD; and two on behalf of UNV.

On 30 June, the Governing Council, after considering the Administrator's report on trust funds established by him in 1988,[80] the ACABQ report thereon,[81] as well as the Administrator's report on all trust funds administered by him since 1981,[82] urged[83] donor Governments to ensure that funds were received in advance of trust fund activities and requested the Administrator to provide, in future reports on trust funds established since 1981, a brief narrative text on the scope and nature of such activities.

Agency support costs

Concerning additional reimbursement of programme support costs for 1987 to executing agencies based in Europe in the light of depreciation of the United States dollar against the national currencies of the headquarters locations concerned, the Governing Council, responding to an ACC request, had in 1988 approved[84] an exceptional measure and asked[71] the Administrator to have ACC inform the executing agencies of the Council's intention to examine successor arrangements for agency support costs from 1992.

The Administrator reported[85] to the Council's February 1989 special session on subsequent developments, stating that CCSQ (OPS), a subsidiary body of ACC, had created a task force to elaborate agency views on the matter. That task force had met several times and had kept the UNDP Administrator fully informed of its discussions.

The Administrator prepared a paper[86] concerning the terms of reference for UNDP's expert group study of issues connected with agency support costs. In that paper, he outlined the group's proposed terms of reference, including its composition, working methods and timetables for study, as well as the main issues for study, including the tripartite nature of technical co-operation (UNDP, the executing agency and the Government concerned), the role of the agency involved, the UNDP central funding role, arrangements for project execution, and appropriate compensation arrangements. The Administrator proposed that experts prepare a paper for submission to the Council's February 1990 meeting, reviewing existing relationships and procedures of operational activities of the United Nations system in the light of present and future needs of developing countries and giving detailed consideration to the main issues he had mentioned.

On 23 February 1989,[87] the Council approved the Administrator's proposed terms of reference and endorsed his proposal to hire four experts to conduct the study.

Sectoral support

The Governing Council, having agreed[84] in 1988 to review the classification of Senior Industrial Development Field Advisers (SIDFAs) provided to developing countries in co-operation with UNIDO, and having considered proposals made by the Administrator in his annual review of the UNDP financial situation,[72] decided[73] on 30 June 1989 that SIDFA posts could be classified in a range from the P-4 or L-4 level to the D-1 or L-6 level.

World Maritime University

Having considered the mid-term resource situation, the Governing Council, on 30 June 1989,[88] maintained UNDP financial support for the World Maritime University at $1.2 million a year for 1990-1991, while requesting the Administrator to try to secure long-term financing.

Accounts and auditing

The financial statements of UNDP for the year ended 31 December 1988, together with the report of the Board of Auditors, were submitted to the General Assembly in July 1989.[89] The statement also covered UNDP-administered trust funds. ACABQ, in October,[90] commented on the Board's findings.

By **resolution 44/183**, the Assembly accepted the financial reports and audited financial statements and the audit opinions and reports of the Board of Auditors regarding UNDP, among others, and requested UNDP to take action to improve conditions as suggested by the Board.

Audit reports for 1987

In May 1989, the Administrator submitted to the Governing Council the audited accounts and audit reports of participating and executing agencies relating to funds allocated to them by UNDP as at 31 December 1987.[91] He included comments on substantive observations of the auditors and further information on follow-up action in response to a 1988 Council decision[92] and a 1988 General Assembly resolution[93] on preparation of audit reports.

On 30 June 1989, the Council noted[94] with concern that the Board of Auditors' opinion on the 1987 accounts was qualified on several counts, though some were of a technical nature, and noted with satisfaction that the Administrator had taken, or was taking, the necessary steps within his competence to correct the conditions that gave rise to those qualifications. It recognized that the audit opinion on UNDP accounts would remain qualified as long as audit confirmation of programme expenditure by United Nations organizations adopting biennial auditing procedures had not been received by the Board of Auditors at the time it issued opinions on UNDP accounts. The Administrator was asked, in order to resolve that problem, to submit to the 1990 session appropriate amendments to UNDP Financial Regulations providing for audited financial statements on a biennial basis, beginning with the 1990-1991 biennium, and that the Board of Auditors report, beginning in 1990, on an audit examination carried out in respect of the first year of each biennium. The Administrator was urged to continue efforts to obtain adequate audit coverage of funds disbursed by Governments as UNDP executing agencies, reporting on that to the 1990 session. The Administrator was requested to invite a representative of the Board of Auditors to future Council sessions. The Council requested the Board of Auditors to review current UNDP project budgetary procedures, in particular the impact of procedures introduced for a three-year experimental period (beginning 1 July 1987), relating to the concept of a two-year project budget cycle, and the administrations of the executing agencies were invited to involve their external auditors in the process.

The Council recommended that the General Assembly request the Administrator, in co-operation with the executing agencies, to report to the Council on specific corrective actions taken by the executing agencies to implement recommendations resulting from the external audit reports on UNDP-financed activities executed by them.

Administrative questions

In-house technical expertise

Responding to a 1988 Governing Council request,[95] the Administrator in March reported[96] on the role and need for in-house technical expertise in UNDP, including the appropriate role of the Technical Advisory Division, in the programme and project cycle. The Administrator made suggestions regarding those matters, including periodically bringing together technical professionals in the field to share experiences and identify problems or approaches which could then be pursued either in-house or through consultants. The Council on 30 June took note[14] of the report.

Actions by other organs of the UN system

In response to a Governing Council request in 1988,[95] the Administrator in February 1989[97] submitted a report on action which UNDP had taken or intended to take in response to 1988 decisions of other organs of the United Nations system, which followed up on an earlier report[98] drawing the Council's attention to 1988 General Assembly resolutions and decisions requiring Council consideration. The Administrator had proposed, for the future, to make a brief presentation to the Council's organizational meeting on issues of immediate and direct concern to UNDP arising from actions taken by other United Nations organs the previous year and to prepare a substantive report, for each June Council session, on steps taken or planned by UNDP on those matters. On 30 June, the Council took note[14] of the Administrator's February report.

Change of Council's name and venue

The General Assembly in 1988 invited[99] the Governing Council to consider the possibility of changing its name to "Governing Council of the United Nations Development Programme and the United Nations Population Fund" as well as of holding its future sessions at United Nations Headquarters. On 30 June,[100] the Governing Council decided to inform the Assembly that it wished to retain its name and venue.

Appointment of UNDP Administrator

After consulting the members of the Governing Council, the Secretary-General, on 17 October, transmitted a note[101] to the General Assembly proposing that the appointment of William H. Draper III as Administrator of UNDP, whose term of office had begun on 1 May 1986, and would expire on 31 December 1989, be extended for a four-year term until 31 December 1993. That appointment was confirmed by the General Assembly by **decision 44/307** of 1 November 1989.

REFERENCES

[1]DP/1990/17 & Add.1-6. [2]E/1989/32 (dec. 89/68). [3]YUN 1948-49, p. 452, GA res. 304(IV), 16 Nov 1949. [4]YUN 1965, p. 273, GA res. 2029(XX), 22 Nov 1965. [5]E/1989/32 (dec. 89/23). [6]Ibid. (dec. 89/50). [7]Ibid. (dec. 89/19). [8]Ibid. (dec. 89/1). [9]Ibid. (dec. 89/2). [10]Ibid. (dec. 89/3). [11]Ibid. (dec. 89/17). [12]Ibid. (dec. 89/66). [13]Ibid. (dec. 89/67). [14]Ibid. (dec. 89/65). [15]Ibid. (dec. 89/25). [16]YUN 1988, p. 338. [17]DP/1989/14 & Add.1. [18]E/1989/32 (dec. 89/20). [19]E/1989/108. [20]E/1989/32 (dec. 89/21). [21]Ibid. (dec. 89/11). [22]DP/1989/73 & Add.1-9. [23]DP/1989/28. [24]DP/1989/29. [25]DP/1989/30. [26]DP/1989/31. [27]E/1989/32 (dec. 89/40). [28]Ibid. (dec. 89/41). [29]YUN 1988, p. 341. [30]DP/1989/27. [31]DP/1990/17/Add.2 (Part I). [32]E/1989/32 (dec. 89/38). [33]DP/1989/53. [34]E/1989/32 (dec. 89/30). [35]YUN 1988, p. 343. [36]DP/1989/5. [37]E/1989/32 (dec. 89/5). [38]Ibid. (dec. 89/45). [39]Ibid. (dec. 89/9). [40]Ibid. (dec. 89/15). [41]DP/1989/74. [42]E/1989/32 (dec. 89/45). [43]YUN 1988, p. 349. [44]DP/1989/8. [45]YUN 1988, p. 344. [46]Ibid., p. 346. [47]DP/1989/17. [48]E/1989/32 (dec. 89/24). [49]DP/1989/71. [50]E/1989/32 (dec. 89/35). [51]Ibid. (dec. 89/22). [52]DP/1989/18. [53]E/1989/32 (dec. 89/29). [54]DP/1989/23. [55]E/1989/32 (dec. 89/26). [56]DP/1989/4. [57]E/1989/32 (dec. 89/4). [58]DP/1989/59. [59]E/1989/32 (dec. 89/39). [60]DP/1989/47. [61]YUN 1985, p. 474. [62]E/1989/32 (dec. 89/51). [63]DP/1990/64 & Add.1. [64]YUN 1988, p. 348. [65]DP/1990/17. [66]A/45/5/Add.1. [67]DP/1989/55 (vols. I & II). [68]YUN 1988, p. 350. [69]E/1989/32 (dec. 89/58). [70]Ibid. (dec. 89/59). [71]YUN 1988, p. 351. [72]DP/1989/54 & Add.1,2. [73]E/1989/32 (dec. 89/57). [74]DP/1989/26.

(75)E/1989/32 (dec. 89/6). (76)*Ibid.* (dec. 89/36). (77)*Ibid.* (dec. 89/37). (78)DP/1989/64. (79)DP/1990/68 & Add.1. (80)DP/1989/57. (81)DP/1989/56. (82)DP/1989/57/Add.1. (83)E/1989/32 (dec. 89/60). (84)YUN 1988, p. 352. (85)DP/1989/7. (86)DP/1989/6 & Add.1,2. (87)E/1989/32 (dec. 89/10). (88)E/1989/32 (dec. 89/44). (89)A/44/5/Add.1. (90)A/44/543. (91)DP/1989/58 & Add.1,2. (92)YUN 1988, p. 353. (93)*Ibid.* p. 867, GA res. 43/216, 21 Dec. 1988. (94)E/1989/32 (dec. 89/61). (95)YUN 1988, p. 354. (96)DP/1989/15. (97)DP/1989/61 & Add.1. (98)DP/1989/10. (99)YUN 1988, p. 335, GA res. 43/199, 20 Dec. 1988. (100)E/1989/32 (dec. 89/63). (101)A/44/108.

Other technical co-operation

UN Programmes

In 1989, the United Nations, mainly through DTCD, continued to provide technical assistance to developing countries. In a report[1] to the UNDP Governing Council, the Secretary-General addressed various policy issues and described DTCD's technical co-operation programme and those of other United Nations entities, reporting that, as it advanced into the closing decade of the twentieth century, DTCD had delivered the largest programme in its history.

The United Nations delivered in 1989 a technical co-operation programme of $250 million, compared to $222 million in 1988, an increase of 13 per cent in project expenditures. Of that amount, DTCD executed a programme of $162.2 million. UNDP-financed projects represented $104.3 million; projects financed by UNFPA accounted for $26.9 million; $21.0 million was financed by trust funds; and $10.0 million was expended under the United Nations regular programme for technical co-operation. In comparison with 1988, budgets increased by $27.7 million (15 per cent) in 1989 to $210.5 million, and the delivery of $162.2 million was up 9 per cent. The implementation rate was 77 per cent.

DTCD activities

In his report on technical co-operation activities,[1] the Secretary-General stated that in 1989 DTCD had projects under execution with a total delivery of $162.2 million against a budget of $210.5 million. The volume of expenditure for UNDP-financed projects increased by $7.1 million and accounted for 64 per cent of total expenditures, compared to 65 per cent in 1988. A high rate of growth in funding by UNFPA was maintained in 1989 with an increase of approximately $6 million, or more than 29 per cent over 1988, thereby offsetting a drop in UN trust funds. There was a reversal of the previous decline in UNDP trust funds which rose by nearly $1 million. Growth in delivery persisted for the second year in a row, amounting to $13 mil-

lion or nearly 9 per cent in 1989, in comparison to 1988.

By sector, natural resources and energy represented 36.9 per cent of total expenditures or $59.9 million. Development planning was 19.4 per cent or $31.5 million; statistics $28.2 million (17.4 per cent); public administration and finance $20.9 million (12.9 per cent); population $9.6 million (5.9 per cent); social development $6.9 million (4.2 per cent); United Nations Educational and Training Programme for Southern Africa $2.4 million (1.5 per cent); and others $2.8 million (1.6 per cent).

By geographic area, the DTCD-executed programme included expenditures of $67.4 million for Africa, $46.2 million for Asia and the Pacific, $35.1 million for the Middle East, Mediterranean, Europe and interregional projects, and $13.5 million for the Americas. The largest growth was in Asia, where the programme increased by $7.4 million. Project delivery in Africa remained the largest but its share of the total delivery again decreased somewhat, from 45 per cent to 42 per cent (47 per cent in 1987).

Highlights of the work of DTCD in 1989 included the first large-scale project funded by the United Nations Fund for Drug Abuse Control in integrated rural development (including crop substitution and diversification of employment opportunities) to facilitate elimination of opium poppy cultivation; statistical work in Namibia to obtain preliminary estimates of population and GDP, as a basis for establishing a tentative IPF; collaboration with the Southern African Development Co-ordination Conference to assist countries in the region in evaluating their potential for certain key minerals and related products; development of a rigorous and recognized methodology for assessing the size and cost of the civil service throughout Africa; assistance in financial planning and management to requesting African countries, as part of a co-ordinated package of technical co-operation in macro-economic planning and management; technical advisory services for a development planning and management information system for the public sector; build-up of investment advisory services; establishment of a focal point for environment within DTCD; authorization to undertake management services if requested; support for LDCs in their preparation of national economic data for the 1990 Second United Nations Conference on LDCs; stepped-up preparations in 71 countries for the 1990 round of population and housing censuses; an interregional meeting on corruption in Government, which called for significant administrative reform of a structural nature in the public service.

Developments in Eastern Europe in 1988 prompted DTCD and other United Nations bodies to review on-going programmes in Bulgaria, Hungary, Poland and Romania, in order to estimate the level of possible technical co-operation requirements in coming years.

Human resources development—institution-building, training, transfer of technology—remained the centrepiece of nearly all DTCD activities in 15 substantive fields, aimed at strengthening the national capacities of developing countries. In 1989, there was a noticeable increase in government requests for support related to utilization of loans financed by the International Bank for Reconstruction and Development. Financial planning and management became an important element of the programme, as developing countries wrestled with problems of foreign debt and balance of payments.

A global campaign to rehabilitate out-dated electric power stations was initiated in 1989 and an interregional training centre for energy planning and management was inaugurated in co-operation with the Latin American Energy Organization. In all sectors, data collection and information management systems were essential components of the projects. Ecological and environmental considerations became more common features of projects executed by DTCD.

UNDP Council action. On 30 June, the Governing Council stressed[2] its role in providing guidance to DTCD in its operational activities funded by UNDP and the importance of the Department's projects to the UNDP-funded assistance. It welcomed DTCD's increase in 1988 project implementation and reiterated the importance of intensifying co-operation between UNDP and DTCD in preparation of round-table meetings, national technical co-operation and assessments programmes and assistance activities of the Management Development Programme. DTCD was urged to continue to intensify its support for projects carried out by Governments, focusing on helping to strengthen national capacities for management and development. The Department's steps to establish a data bank of project results and evaluation reports were welcomed and the Department was encouraged to strengthen further its evaluation activities by establishing a self-evaluation system for all projects which it implemented. The Council welcomed DTCD's efforts to emphasize training activities, including promotion of integration of women in development at all stages of the project cycle, in particular the planning, design and execution phase. UNDP and DTCD were urged to develop a more effective division of labour in which their comparative strengths and capacities were used to maximum advantage.

Technical co-operation among developing countries

In a March report[3] to the sixth session of the High Level Committee on the Review of TCDC, covering the period 1 November 1986 to 31 Oc-

tober 1988, the UNDP Administrator recorded progress made by the United Nations development system in implementing the 1978 Buenos Aires Plan of Action for Promoting and Implementing TCDC.[4] The Administrator stated that progress had been made for facilitating and implementing TCDC and that the use of developing countries' capacities continued to expand, but many organizations continued to report difficulties in quantifying their support in financial terms. Progress continued in varying degrees, but most organizations had not succeeded in overcoming their internal procedural constraints that would enable them to document progress in financial and statistical terms, which was partly due to difficulties in defining TCDC activities and recording statistical and financial information. He suggested institution of procedures whereby at the time of approval of a development project any TCDC activities forming part of a project would be clearly identified, both in the narrative and in the budget of the document, and that ACC develop revised and more comprehensive guidelines on the subject. Despite the many constraints and difficulties still besetting implementation of TCDC activities, the Administrator found that 10 years after adoption of the Buenos Aires Plan of Action, TCDC had established itself as an integral part of the development process, with good progress continuing in utilizing developing countries' capacities in technical co-operation activities.

The report contained available statistical information on TCDC support by 23 of the 35 organizations of the United Nations development system invited to submit information. The response, the Administrator said, clearly demonstrated their strong commitment to TCDC and illustrated the steady growth in volume of their respective TCDC activities.

As requested by the High-level Committee, the Administrator reported in March[5] on strengthening and improving intergovernmental programming exercises for TCDC. UNDP's Special Unit for TCDC was specifically responsible for promoting and supporting TCDC outside as well as within the framework of UNDP programming. An important part of the Special Unit's work in recent years had been assisting developing countries in carrying out a series of structured TCDC programming exercises, and the Administrator described that work in his report. The Special Unit headed efforts to assist countries in organizing TCDC programming, as well as mobilizing catalytic funding for emerging projects.

In discharge of its lead organizational role for promoting and supporting TCDC in the United Nations development system, the UNDP Governing Council had since 1979 approved a total of $11.75 million from Special Programme Resources (in addition to IPFs) for promotion of action-oriented TCDC activities, including information support. Estimated UNDP expenditures for TCDC for the country, regional, interregional and global IPF's in the biennium 1987-1988 amounted to $104.9 million as against $55.7 million in the biennium 1985-1986, an increase of 88.3 per cent. Those represented 7.3 per cent of all IPF expenditures in 1987-1988, which were $1,443.4 million.

As another way of improving TCDC, UNDP had developed a TCDC information referral system, INRES-South, from a directory into a computerized service containing more than 40,000 items of information on the training and expertise capabilities of some 3,500 institutions in more than 100 developing countries. It was being continuously updated and linked with other data banks in and outside the United Nations system. Use of INRES-South continued to increase. Inquiries, which had almost tripled in 1987 to about 100 a month, reached 120 a month in 1988.

In a statement[6] to the High-level Committee, the Administrator, as convenor of the Committee and representative of the United Nations development system as a whole, said that a significant stimulus that the United Nations system had given TCDC was its help to Governments in organizing TCDC programming activities. Those "TCDC markets" had now occurred within and among all the regions of the developing world and had generated hundreds of TCDC exchanges. More importantly, they had opened the way to broader and lasting technical co-operation among institutions, organizations and enterprises of developing countries, where, in many cases, no contact had existed before. While initiative and action rested primarily with Governments, the United Nations system, spearheaded by the UNDP Special Unit, had played an important catalytic and supportive role.

Also addressing the Committee, the Director-General for DIEC said that the challenge remained for the United Nations development system to mobilize the capacities, skills and experiences available through TCDC in the context of all development activities, fully involving its field office network and organizations covering every possible sector. UN system organizations should selectively assemble information on innovative solutions and on capacities and then ensure that such information was effectively utilized in relevant programmes in other developing countries.

The President of the High-level Committee said the review had shown considerable progress compared with the situation that existed at the time of the adoption of the Buenos Aires Plan of Action, with TCDC taking hold as a significant and potentially pervasive element of the total endeavours in international economic and social development. Further strengthening of the capaci-

ties of national focal points was required. Actions were needed for further TCDC programming activities with a focus on priority areas of development and with more innovative methods conceived and developed from experience, as well as for fostering the role of regional and interregional organizations in promoting TCDC. Intensified efforts were expected by United Nations organizations to improve the role of women in TCDC. The Committee would also expect a revitalized momentum in the role of the Special Unit for TCDC in co-ordinating and supporting TCDC in the United Nations organizations.

As requested by the High-level Committee in 1987,[7] the Administrator submitted a report[8] on progress attained by Governments in their TCDC activities in the ten years since the Buenos Aires Plan of Action was adopted. It gave an overview of submissions made by 51 Governments and 20 intergovernmental organizations, followed by the Administrator's comments and recommendations. He said the information suggested TCDC had made substantial progress over the past decade, with clear signs of increasing momentum over the past two or three years, with multiplier effects of modest initial bilateral TCDC arrangements between countries expanding into a growing web of regional and interregional activities, both within particular geographical regions and across regions. The Administrator suggested Governments continue to strengthen national focal points, establishing appropriate links with sectoral departments responsible for development activities, with the Special Unit for TCDC assisting Governments, at their request, in strengthening internal TCDC co-ordination mechanisms. He suggested that Governments consider organizing workshops on a regional basis during 1989 and 1990 to exchange information on how countries had effectively dealt with issues relating to strengthening national focal points, programming and financing TCDC, information collection, etc., and to develop specific recommendations and action plans for further strengthening TCDC.

In March,[9] the Administrator reported on the Second Meeting of the TCDC Focal Points of the Organizations of the United Nations development system which he had convened (New York, 25-26 February 1988) in response to the High-level Committee's decision[7] and which was attended by the TCDC focal points of 16 organizations. Recommendations were made in such areas as TCDC integration in United Nations system–funded projects using TCDC as a modality for project implementation; utilization of developing countries' capacities and technical co-operation programmes and activities of United Nations organizations; active involvement of the organizations in TCDC programming exercises and absorption of activities into country IPF or Trust Funds financed projects; collaboration in improving the INRES-South data base; co-ordinated publicizing of TCDC activities and experiences; and stepped-up staff training regarding TCDC.

Responding to a further Committee request,[10] the Administrator submitted a report[5] on strengthening and improving intergovernmental programming exercises for TCDC. Proposals for future inter-country TCDC programming included use of a developing country's international airline as the prime mover of an exchange of experience, expertise and training with and between participatory countries in various aspects of civil aviation while, in another region, the development of ports would be the subject of inter-country programming. Several countries were interested in exchanging expertise and experience in aquaculture, with the Special Unit assisting in organizing a first round of regional projects for about 10 Latin American countries. The Unit was collaborating with the International Co-operative Alliance in organizing the first of a series of regional meetings of representatives of national co-operative authorities at which TCDC activities would be programmed. The Unit supported specialized single-sector seminars such as that in Argentina with selected African countries in agricultural technology, as well as an arrangement enabling Nicaragua, with an abnormal number of amputees, to study development in India of relatively low-cost artificial limbs, a project which could have major implications for Afghanistan. Pakistan's sectoral TCDC programming exercise of September 1988 concentrating on industry and science resulted in the Special Unit assisting in sending programming missions to 20 other developing countries, with 160 TCDC project agreements ultimately being concluded. More systematic training programmes were urgently required for UNDP field offices regarding TCDC and were being developed by the Special Unit.

In a March report on the role of women in TCDC,[11] the Administrator concluded that a great deal remained to be done by United Nations organizations in promoting the role of women in development. There remained scope for needs identification and programming missions to include women's concerns in their terms of reference. He recommended that United Nations organizations exchange guidelines on women, development, gender-specific statistics and rosters, with UNDP, UNIFEM and the United Nations International Research and Training Institute for the Advancement of Women co-operating in compiling and preparing methodologies of assistance on the question.

Action by the High-level Committee on TCDC. The sixth session of the High-level Committee on the Review of TCDC was held in New York, from 18 to 22 and 29 September.

In its report to the General Assembly,[6] the High-Level Committee included a draft resolution on the tenth anniversary of the Buenos Aires Plan of Action which it recommended to the Assembly for its adoption (see below).[12] In another decision, the Committee expressed concern over the lack of detailed information from many Governments of developing countries concerning their activities for TCDC and deep concern over the failure of many international organizations to supply such information to the Committee. Both the Governments and organizations concerned were urged to rectify that position.[13]

In a decision[14] on its review of TCDC activities within the United Nations system, the Committee reiterated the need for more human and financial resources for the promotion and implementation of TCDC. The Committee expressed concern about the difficulties in overcoming obstacles raised by the procedures followed by the United Nations technical co-operation bodies, as those procedures had impeded introduction of any relevant component for TCDC into the UNDP programming process at the identification, design, elaboration, evaluation or implementation stage. The Committee reiterated that the Buenos Aires Plan of Action should constitute a framework for countries, agencies in the United Nations system and international organizations in implementing TCDC. Concern was expressed over the slow promotion and implementation of TCDC activities within the United Nations system. The High-level Committee reiterated its recommendation that the UNDP Governing Council consider allocating at least 25 per cent of funds for programmes under regional, interregional and global IPFs to activities for TCDC. The UNDP Administrator was requested to organize a meeting of technical co-operation experts of interested countries to identify impediments to TCDC and changes to be introduced, so as to enable the incorporation of TCDC into all programmes and projects financed by the United Nations system. The Committee requested the Administrator to submit to the 1990 Governing Council a report based on the conclusions of that proposed meeting of experts.

Regarding strengthening TCDC, the Committee said[15] it was appropriate for developing countries to earmark a percentage of their IPF for TCDC and therefore suggested measures to be considered by Governments, including elaborating directories of supply and demand for TCDC, specifying priority areas; updating information on needs and capabilities for TCDC; ensuring access to national data banks; developing registries and methodologies for transfer of knowledge and technologies; opportunities for technical and financial support;

training opportunities; use of national experts and local equipment; information on United Nations–system programmes; regional focal points; and involvement of the private sector.

In respect of programming exercises, the Committee requested[16] UNDP to continue its support for such exercises and urged it to include projects emerging from such experience in its regional, interregional and global programming. Subregional, regional and international financial institutions were invited to offer financial support for TCDC, in particular projects and activities resulting from the meeting and programming exercises. The Committee requested the UNDP Administrator to evaluate concluded programming exercises, and invited the developing countries to identify priority themes for regional programming of TCDC activities.

As to the role of women in TCDC, the Committee requested[17] the UNDP Administrator and heads of organs of the United Nations development system to develop and improve guidelines to ensure full access and participation of women, stressing the need for UNDP-sponsored exercises to facilitate full participation of women. The Administrator was asked to report on those matters at the Committee's next session.

The Committee, in a decision[18] calling for strengthening UNDP's Special Unit for TCDC, urged the Governing Council to consider giving it greater financial and personnel support.

GENERAL ASSEMBLY ACTION

By **decision 44/412** of 20 November, the General Assembly decided, on an exceptional basis, to consider directly the report of the High-level Committee.

In **decision 44/450** of 22 December on further strengthening and improving intergovernmental programming exercises for TCDC, the Assembly took note of documents the Secretary-General and Administrator had submitted to the High-level Committee on this matter and expressed appreciation of UN system organizations' efforts in this regard.

The Assembly adopted two resolutions on TCDC.

On 22 December, on the recommendation of the Second Committee, the General Assembly adopted **resolution 44/222** without vote. **Resolution 44/223** was adopted on the same day in the same manner.

Economic and technical co-operation among developing countries

The General Assembly,

Recalling its resolutions 33/134 of 19 December 1978, in which it endorsed the Buenos Aires Plan of Action for Promoting and Implementing Technical Co-operation among Developing Countries, and 42/180 of

11 December 1987, as well as other relevant resolutions of the General Assembly,

Emphasizing the important role that technical co-operation among developing countries plays in the growth and development of those countries,

Reaffirming that developing countries have the primary responsibility for promoting technical co-operation among themselves, that developed countries and the United Nations system should assist and support such activities, and that, in addition, the United Nations system should play a prominent role as promoter and catalyst of technical co-operation among developing countries, in accordance with the Buenos Aires Plan of Action,

1. *Reaffirms* the continued validity of all the recommendations of the Buenos Aires Plan of Action for Promoting and Implementing Technical Co-operation among Developing Countries and the importance of technical co-operation among developing countries;

2. *Reaffirms also* the continued importance of the High-level Committee on the Review of Technical Co-operation among Developing Countries as the principal forum in which representatives of all the States Members of the United Nations and other relevant bodies of the United Nations system review and promote technical co-operation among developing countries;

3. *Endorses* the decisions adopted by the High-level Committee at its sixth session, taking into account the intergovernmental arrangements envisaged in recommendation 37 of the Buenos Aires Plan of Action;

4. *Urges* all Member States, the United Nations Development Programme and other relevant organs, organizations and bodies of the United Nations system to give high priority in their particular fields of activity to the support and promotion of activities in technical co-operation among developing countries;

5. *Requests* the Secretary-General to report to the General Assembly at its forty-sixth session on the implementation of the present resolution.

General Assembly resolution 44/222

22 December 1989   Meeting 85   Adopted without vote

Approved by Second Committee (A/44/746/Add.6) without vote, 11 December (meeting 49); draft by Vice-Chairman (A/C.2/44/L.73), based on informal consultations on draft by Malaysia for Group of 77 (A/C.2/44/L.62); agenda item 82 (e).

Meeting numbers. GA 44th session: 2nd Committee 43, 44, 46, 49; plenary 85.

Tenth anniversary of the adoption of the Buenos Aires Plan of Action for Promoting and Implementing Technical Co-operation among Developing Countries

The General Assembly,

Considering the importance of the tenth anniversary of the adoption of the Buenos Aires Plan of Action for Promoting and Implementing Technical Co-operation among Developing Countries,

Concerned that the economic situation of developing countries, which has been aggravated over the past decade, has had an impact generally on international co-operation for development and on the implementation of the Buenos Aires Plan of Action,

Recognizing, however, that developing countries have achieved significant progress in implementing the recommendations contained in the Buenos Aires Plan of Action, and that technical co-operation among developing countries has gradually become a means through which they contribute to development,

1. *Reaffirms* the continued validity and importance of the Buenos Aires Plan of Action for Promoting and Implementing Technical Co-operation among Developing Countries;

2. *Emphasizes* the imperative need to strengthen the implementation of activities and projects for technical co-operation among developing countries through the increased allocation and utilization of financial resources, as appropriate, for the promotion and implementation of projects for technical co-operation among developing countries;

3. *Requests* the various parties participating in the promotion and implementation of technical co-operation among developing countries, particularly within the United Nations system, including the United Nations Development Programme, the specialized agencies and the regional commissions, to give the necessary priority to the support, encouragement and implementation of specific activities and projects, so that such co-operation will become a basic component of their policies for development;

4. *Urges* the international community, including governmental and non-governmental organizations, to be favourably disposed to the requests for technical and financial support presented to them for the implementation of specific activities and projects of technical co-operation among developing countries;

5. *Reiterates* the need for developed countries and their international co-operation agencies to lend their firm support to technical co-operation among developing countries, in accordance with recommendations 35 and 36 of the Buenos Aires Plan of Action and in the context of recommendation 38 thereof.

General Assembly resolution 44/223

22 December 1989   Meeting 85   Adopted without vote

Approved by Second Committee (A/44/746/Add.6) without vote, 11 December (meeting 49); draft by High-level Committee on Review of Technical Co-operation among Developing Countries (A/44/39); agenda item 82 *(e)*.
Meeting numbers. GA 44th session: 2nd Committee 43, 44, 46, 49; plenary 85.

United Nations Volunteers

In his biennial report on the UNV programme for 1988-1989,[19] the UNDP Administrator stated that UNV, as the only multilateral volunteer-sending agency, was the largest such programme providing opportunities for volunteers from developing countries (1,600 out of its 1,800 total) to serve abroad. Serving in 108 developing countries, the majority of UNV specialists (58 per cent) worked in the fields of public health, education and training, and agricultural development, and 63 per cent served in LDCs, with about half in Africa. Asia and the Pacific region accounted for 17 per cent of the UNV total, the Arab States 13 per cent, and 7 per cent were in the Latin America and Caribbean region. The largest number of UNV specialists still came from the developing countries of Asia and Africa and were mostly male (83 per cent).

The actual profile of volunteer development workers had changed dramatically over the last quarter of the century, yet the popular image, continuing to influence decision makers from Governments and aid agencies, remained wedded to the notion of inexperienced, relatively young volunteers, often generally dedicated and enthusiastic, but with relatively few technical skills to offer. Most current volunteers were specialists in a wide range of disciplines, aged in their thirties, who had several years of professional experience as well as solid academic training; the average programme participant was 38 years old, had 10 years professional experience, and held a master's degree.

The typical annual cost of a volunteer assignment remained at about one-fifth that of regular technical co-operation personnel. Even more important was the perceived appropriateness of volunteer personnel as willing performers in difficult circumstances, who were near enough to the concerns of the local personnel to be viewed as responsible partners, thereby enhancing their potential to act as on-the-job trainers and to contribute to capacity-building and sustainability. However, there was a risk that long-term volunteers could create dependence, so volunteer-sending agencies were trying to move away from counterpart models to ones where the volunteer was part of a local team comprising different levels of skills and responsibilities, thus allowing for mutual learning.

The biennium had seen a steady growth in demand for UNV services, partly due to greater UNV participation in the LDCs of the Arab States region, and, to a lesser extent, in Latin America, a region which previously had not made extensive use of UNV specialists. At the grass-roots level, a marked expansion in the exchange of community fieldworkers had taken place in the Africa and Pacific regions, in addition to the ongoing programme in Asia, through the Domestic Development Services projects of the UNV Participatory Development Programme (PDP/DDS). By the end of 1989, some 250 PDP/DDS fieldworkers were strengthening local rural community self-help initiatives in 26 countries in the three regions. Preparations for similar activities in the Arab States and in the Caribbean were well under way.

UNV specialists served in more than 140 professional categories, and while traditional sectors of UNV activity continued to account for the majority, their weight in the total was declining, demonstrating a wider spread of demand. There was no longer any narrowly defined niche for the UNV role in development.

Responding to a specific concern of the Governing Council that the UNV Programme should reflect diversity of the volunteers' countries of origin,[20] the Administrator stated that measures to attract candidates from industrialized countries had been put in place, and the number of rostered candidates from them had risen from 460 in September 1987 to 660 on 31 December 1989. The number of fully funded UNV posts from those countries had risen from 16 in 1987 to 47 during 1989. Special efforts were made to contact women's and senior citizens' organizations. In December 1989 there were 894 female candidates on the UNV roster compared to 480 in 1987, and 270 older candidates (more than 55 years of age) compared to 200 a year earlier.

In response to other 1988 Governing Council decisions regarding support structures, a cadre of 40 UNV Programme Officers to support UNDP offices managing substantial numbers of UNV specialists became fully operational in 1989, becoming the cornerstone of the UNV field support system.

Estimated 1989 expenditures for the UNV programme amounted to $36.8 million, of which $20.2 million was allocated to projects executed by UNV, and an estimated $15 million to finance in-country costs of UNV specialists on projects executed by United Nations agencies and $1.8 million for their external costs funded from the Special Voluntary Fund (SVF). Funds for those expenditures included the following sources: $30.6 million from UNDP; $3.8 million from SVF for external costs of UNV specialists and pilot and experimental projects; and $1.2 million from funds in trust.

About 85 per cent of UNV specialists served within projects funded from IPFs. About half served in projects by United Nations specialized agencies. The other half served in projects executed by UNV or Governments.

Based on past and current trends, the number of serving UNV specialists was expected to increase to 2,400 by the end of 1991, with costs rising to $48 million, based on an estimated average annual cost of $20,000 for each specialist.

The Administrator pointed out that the UNV programme would mark its 20th anniversary in 1991 and stated that an inter-governmental meeting on volunteers and development might be held at that time to provide for a long-term, forward-looking perspective on multilateral volunteer contributions to technical co-operation and development. Among his suggestions was a special contingency fund, preferably under trust fund arrangements, to respond to urgent requests for specialists to support Governments in implementing emergency rehabilitation and reconstruction programmes and other relief efforts.

REFERENCES

[1]DP/1990/56 & Add.1-3. [2]E/1989/32 (dec. 89/50). [3]TCDC/6/2 & Corr.1,2 & Add.1,2,3 & Add.2/Corr.1 & Add.3/Corr.1. [4]YUN 1978, p. 467. [5]TCDC/6/4. [6]A/44/39. [7]YUN 1987, p. 429. [8]TCDC/6/3. [9]TCDC/6/5. [10]YUN 1987, p. 430. [11]TCDC/6/7. [12]A/44/39 (dec. 6/1). [13]*Ibid.* (dec. 6/2). [14]*Ibid.* (dec. 6/3). [15]*Ibid.* (dec. 6/4). [16]*Ibid.* (dec. 6/5). [17]*Ibid.* (dec. 6/6). [18]*Ibid.* (dec. 6/8). [19]DP/1990/57 & Add.1. [20]YUN 1988, p. 358.

UN Capital Development Fund

In his annual report for 1989,[1] the UNDP Administrator said that UNCDF, which provided capital assistance for small-scale investment projects, primarily in LDCs, received pledges for 1989 of $36.7 million and had 237 ongoing projects totalling about $445 million in value.

The Administrator, in his biennial report for 1989-1990 on the Fund,[2] said the period reflected the consolidation of achievements after a period of continued expansion. A record high volume of operations accompanied by expenditures of between $45 million and $50 million was reported. With pledges on the rise, the partial funding formula revised in 1987 had allowed project approvals to rise to $77.9 million in 1989, of which $2.3 million came from donor co-financing. Fund expenditures for 1989 rose to $49.1 million, of which $47.6 million came from general resources and $1.5 million from co-financing.

The Fund's programme was sharply focused on poverty reduction with 58 per cent of new commitments devoted to food production for lower-income groups. In the agriculture sector, the Fund gave special attention to development of small irrigation schemes as an alternative concept to the larger ventures of the past and as a means to secure food self-sufficiency with full involvement of the farmers. Since the Fund was permitted to apply a partial funding formula enabling approval levels well above current pledges, it was foreseen that increases in new projects would lead to increased expenditures and reduce the liquidity accumulated in the past under full funding conditions. This occurred in 1989 when expenditures from general resources were more than $47 million and, since funds exceeded income, UNCDF drew down accumulated financial resources by more than $6 million. Project approvals reached $77.9 million in 1989 which were expected to lead to expenditures in future years substantially higher than 1989.

On 30 June,[3] the UNDP Governing Council, which had before it the Administrator's report on Fund activities in 1987 and 1988,[4] decided to review in 1991 the partial funding system for UNCDF and its liquidity position. It urged the forthcoming (1990) Second United Nations Conference on Least Developed Countries to make appropriate recommendations about an increase in the Fund's resources and invited the Administrator to make the Fund better known to existing and potential donors.

REFERENCES

[1]DP/1990/17 & Add.1-6. [2]DP/1991/43. [3]E/1989/32 (dec. 89/56). [4]DP/1989/52.

Chapter III

Economic assistance, disasters and emergency relief

During 1989, the United Nations continued to provide special assistance to countries facing severe economic hardship. Several nations received aid for reconstruction, rehabilitation and development following natural or man-made disasters. In December, the General Assembly, by resolution 44/236, proclaimed the 1990s the International Decade for Natural Disaster Reduction, and adopted an international framework of policy measures, co-operation and action to mitigate the effects of disasters.

Another significant development was the creation in October of Operation Lifeline Sudan (44/12) which, the Secretary-General reported, set an important and historic precedent for complex relief operations. For the first time, in an area of civil war, the two warring parties agreed to a common, large-scale plan of action for relief assistance to civilians on both sides of the conflict.

The critical economic and social situation in Africa remained a major concern of the United Nations during 1989. In May, the Economic and Social Council (1989/26) invited the home countries of transnational corporations to encourage corporate investment in developing countries, particularly those in Africa, and asked the Secretary-General to increase support for technical assistance to them. In November (44/24), the Assembly invited the international community to consider the African Alternative Framework for Structural Adjustment Programmes for Socio-economic Recovery and Transformation, adopted by the Economic Commission for Africa in April. In December, it appealed for international support for economic rehabilitation and assistance programmes in Angola (44/168), Chad (44/176) and the front-line States (44/181) and other neighbouring States that had suffered from the *apartheid* policies of South Africa. The Assembly also requested continued assistance for Lebanon (44/180) and support for the Special Plan of Economic Co-operation for Central America (44/182).

The UN system, and the Office of the United Nations Disaster Relief Co-ordinator in particular, continued to provide assistance to countries stricken by natural disasters. Heavy flooding in Democratic Yemen and Djibouti during March and April prompted the Assembly (resolutions 44/179 and 44/177) and the Council (resolutions 1989/1 and 1989/2) to call for intensified relief operations and rehabilitation and reconstruction.

The Assembly (44/3) also urged international emergency assistance for Antigua and Barbuda, the British Virgin Islands, Dominica, Montserrat and Saint Kitts and Nevis after they were struck by Hurricane Hugo.

The Economic and Social Council (1989/103) recommended that desertification and drought be given priority within international assistance programmes, and also called for continued international support for efforts to control locusts and grasshoppers (1989/98). Those resolutions were subsequently endorsed by the Assembly in December (decisions 44/437 and 44/438).

With regard to man-made disasters, in May the Council (decision 1989/111) called for international support to meet urgent humanitarian needs in Somalia, particularly its northern provinces, where attacks by bandits had produced widespread destruction and large numbers of displaced persons. The Assembly echoed that request in December (resolution 44/178), and also urged States (44/239) to offer emergency humanitarian assistance to Romania.

Economic assistance

In 1989, the United Nations continued to provide economic assistance to a number of countries with severe economic problems. Some of the programmes were in support of national reconstruction following natural disasters. The United Nations responded to the increase in such disasters and a growing focus on disaster prevention and preparedness. Other programmes sought to overcome development obstacles posed by weak infrastructure and political and economic circumstances, including the negative socio-economic effects of past structural adjustment programmes. Some of the countries that received assistance faced both man-made and environmental threats.

Critical situation in Africa

In accordance with a 1987 request of the Economic and Social Council,[1] the Secretary-General in February submitted a comprehensive report on the critical social situation in Africa, as an annex to the 1989 Report on the World Social Situation.[2] It outlined the many obstacles in achieving the objectives of the 1969 Declaration on Social Progress and Development,[3] as well as the impact of economic policies on the African social situation. Most of the gains made in health, education, employment and social integration in the decade and a half following independence were either lost or seriously diminished in the African countries during the 1980s. At the root of Africa's economic and social crisis were structural economic imbalances and weaknesses, such as the dominance of export-oriented agriculture, and mining and other extractive industries. Dependence on external sources of capital, equipment and expertise, a global economic recession, and the unprecedented drought emergency from 1983 to 1985 were among the factors that led to a precipitous decline in living standards throughout the region. Per capita incomes fell by an annual average rate of 3.4 per cent between 1980 and 1986, to levels between 15 and 25 per cent lower than in 1970. In the 1970s, gross domestic product (GDP) averaged 3.3 per cent growth a year, but fell to 1 per cent in 1986 and 0.8 per cent in 1987. Inflation, a decline in real wages and shortages of essential goods and services pushed prices beyond the reach of most workers. Other factors contributing to the crisis included the collapse of commodity prices, debt and debt-servicing burdens, diminishing resource flows, and measures by African Governments to reduce their expenditures and control imports by cutting social spending. Environmental and demographic trends, such as desertification and high rates of population growth and urbanization, further aggravated the situation.

Most African countries undertook financial stabilization and macro-economic structural adjustment programmes during the 1980s to counter the economic decline, the majority of them under the influence of the International Monetary Fund (IMF) and the World Bank. The IMF and World Bank programmes took a narrowly economic approach, focused on improving the external economic position and exports. Available data and emerging evidence strongly indicated that the programmes had devastating social consequences, particularly in the areas of employment, incomes, food, nutrition, health and education. The health and nutritional status of the poorest Africans in particular was worsened by the removal of subsidies on imported food and the introduction of cost recovery for health care and other social services. Hiring freezes and retrenchment of government jobs eliminated hundreds of thousands of employment opportunities. Overall, structural adjustment programmes created a vicious circle: some measure of economic growth was achieved, but countries became more indebted and dependent on external financial resources, and were less capable of delivering the social benefits that should follow that growth.

The impact of the contracting economy was felt most severely by workers in agriculture, manufacturing and the construction industry. Particularly hard hit by unemployment were African youth and women, and, increasingly, educated Africans, who began to emigrate to other regions. Total employment in sub-Saharan Africa increased by 2 per cent a year in the 1970s, but fell by some 16 per cent between 1980 and 1987.

During the 1980s, 50 to 75 of every 100 Africans were living in poverty according to some estimates, with rates for absolute poverty in rural areas running between 50 and 90 per cent. The severely hungry and undernourished numbered 80 million in 1972-1974, but the number had risen to more than 150 million by 1984. In the early 1980s, on average, 43 per cent of children under 5 years of age suffered from moderate to severe malnutrition. Most child deaths were caused by preventable diseases, diarrhoea and malnutrition. Maternal mortality was caused mostly by ignorance, poverty and lack of access to essential services.

The economic crisis and structural adjustment requirements retarded and in some cases reversed the momentum of educational reform. Annual growth in the total number of students fell from 8.1 per cent in 1970-1980 to 3.9 per cent in 1980-1987, with the sharpest decline at the primary school level. Drop-out rates increased, especially among girls, and repetition rates were also high.

The African social situation was further aggravated by political conflicts and tensions caused by the tenuous state of both democracy and sociocultural homogeneity within States, and by disputes over boundaries between States. Regional conflicts and attendant military expenditures diverted scarce financial resources at the expense of health, education and other social services. Military engagements disrupted food production and destroyed settlements. *Apartheid* and the destabilization policies of the South African Government turned southern Africa into an especially vulnerable conflict zone.

The annex concluded that the intolerable social situation in Africa required immediate attention by all African Governments and the international community. Whereas IMF and World Bank programmes had been highly sectoral, both in analysing development malfunctions and in prescribing solutions, the report recommended a holistic approach with people as its focus. While short-term measures would be necessary to relieve immediate hardships, what needed to be restructured were the basic patterns and relations of production, distribution and consumption, with a long-term and transformational perspective aimed at ending the externally oriented and dependent economic status of African countries.

ECONOMIC AND SOCIAL COUNCIL ACTION

On 24 May, the Economic and Social Council, on the recommendation of the Second (Social) Committee, adopted **resolution 1989/46** without vote.

Critical social situation in Africa

The Economic and Social Council,

Recalling General Assembly resolution 2542(XXIV) of 11 December 1969 containing the Declaration on Social Progress and Development, which provides the framework for international co-operation in the field of social development,

Recalling also General Assembly resolutions 39/29 of 3 December 1984 and 40/40 of 2 December 1985, which led to the convening of the thirteenth special session of the General Assembly, devoted to the critical economic situation in Africa, at which the Assembly adopted by consensus resolution S-13/2 of 1 June 1986, to which is annexed the United Nations Programme of Action for African Economic Recovery and Development 1986-1990,

Alarmed at the acceleration in the deterioration of social conditions in most African countries,

Noting with concern the gravity of the situation in the southern part of Africa due to the continued policy of *apartheid* of the racist régime of South Africa,

Noting that in Africa's Priority Programme for Economic Recovery 1986-1990, the Governments of African States reaffirmed their primary responsibility for the economic and social development of their countries, identified areas for priority action, and undertook to mobilize and utilize domestic resources for the achievement of their priority objectives,

Emphasizing that the African social and economic crisis is a development crisis that concerns the international community as a whole and that greater realization of the rich physical and human potential of the continent is an integral part of a common strategy to promote the economic and social advancement of all peoples,

Recognizing the efforts being made by African Governments to redress some of the acute social problems confronting the African continent,

Noting that the prospects for concerted implementation of Africa's Priority Programme for Economic Recovery 1986-1990 are being affected by an unfavourable external economic environment, debt-servicing obligations and the rate of flow of development finance, particularly that of a concessionary nature,

1. *Takes note* of the 1989 report on the world social situation, including the annex thereto on the critical social situation in Africa;

2. *Appeals* to the international community, the States members of the specialized agencies and non-governmental organizations to increase their co-operation and assistance to enhance the efforts made by the African countries to establish or improve their infrastructure, through the creation of a favourable economic environment;

3. *Requests* the Secretary-General, in consultation with the Organization of African Unity, the Economic Commission for Africa and the African Development Bank, to prepare a report providing an in-depth evaluation of the critical social situation in Africa, paying particular attention to the obstacles to the implementation of the United Nations Programme of Action for African Economic Recovery and Development 1986-1990, including the impact of structural adjustment policies on the social situation in Africa, for submission to the Commission for Social Development at its thirty-second session;

4. *Decides* that the Commission should consider at its thirty-second session the report requested in paragraph 3 above, in the context of its review of the world social situation.

Economic and Social Council resolution 1989/46

24 May 1989   Meeting 15   Adopted without vote

Approved by Second Committee (E/1989/91) without vote, 11 May (meeting 12); draft by Commission for Social Development (E/1989/25); agenda item 11.

UNPAAERD activities

UNDP consideration. In response to a 1988 decision of the Governing Council of the United Nations Development Programme (UNDP),[4] the UNDP Administrator submitted a report[5] in April 1989 on UNDP's efforts to increase its role in implementing the United Nations Programme of Action for African Economic Recovery and Development 1986-1990 (UNPAAERD). Updating his 1988 report,[6] the Administrator noted an increase in the scope of UNDP's activities to deal with the economic and social crisis in Africa, including increases in staff. The report outlined UNDP's efforts to intensify its co-operation with the Economic Commission for Africa (ECA), the Organization of African Unity (OAU), and all major regional and subregional intergovernmental organizations in Africa to implement UNPAAERD. In 1989, 18 new projects were approved under the Special Measures Fund for the Least Developed Countries. The report also described UNDP measures to increase African assistance, speed up project approval, mobilize additional resources, develop innovative approaches to technical co-operation, participate in subregional meetings, and involve women in its development projects.

On 30 June,[7] the Governing Council called on the Administrator to intensify efforts to mobilize additional resources for UNPAAERD, and asked him to continue to provide the necessary support to ECA and OAU in implementing UNPAAERD. It urged even closer collaboration between UNDP, ECA, OAU, the African Development Bank and African subregional economic organizations. He was asked to reinvigorate initiatives to improve national planning capacity and external co-operation management, to expand training in UNDP procedures for government officials, to increase UNDP support for technical co-operation and the exchange of development experiences among African countries, and to intensify efforts to make greater use of African expertise, sub-contractors and equipment. The Administrator was asked to report to the Council in 1990.

UNCTAD action. In a July 1989 progress report[8] to the Trade and Development Board of the United Nations Conference on Trade and Development (UNCTAD), the UNCTAD secretariat stated that it had provided substantive support to UNPAAERD through assistance to the Secretary-General's Expert Group on African Commodity Problems, participated in meetings dealing with debt rescheduling for African countries, and had prepared an inventory of African investment laws and regulations[9] to provide potential investors and African financial institutions with an analytical tool for investment in joint ventures. The secretariat also prepared reports for the Second United Nations Conference on the Least Developed Countries.

In March/April, UNCTAD sent a special needs appraisal mission to Angola, Malawi, Mozambique, Rwanda and Swaziland to identify possibilities for technical co-operation. A preparatory programming mission went to Nigeria in April in response to a Nigerian request for technical assistance in several areas. UNCTAD also provided technical assistance on the generalized system of preferences through seminars and advisory missions. UNCTAD continued to help African countries strengthen their negotiating capabilities and participation in the Uruguay Round negotiations. It also continued to work with UNDP and other agencies on a project to improve economic and technical co-operation between Africa and Latin America. To increase capacity to manage external debt, UNCTAD was working towards the installation of computerized Debt Management and Financial Analysis Systems in eight African countries, and also made progress with three transport and transit projects in southern Africa, West-Central Africa and East-Central Africa.

On 5 October,[10] the Trade and Development Board asked UNCTAD's secretariat for more detailed reporting on its contributions to UNPAAERD and appealed to developed countries and multilateral institutions for more support for the implementation of UNPAAERD.

ECONOMIC AND SOCIAL COUNCIL ACTION

On 24 May, the Economic and Social Council, on the recommendation of its First (Economic) Committee, adopted **resolution 1989/26** without vote.

Contribution of the United Nations Centre on Transnational Corporations to the implementation of the United Nations Programme of Action for African Economic Recovery and Development 1986-1990

The Economic and Social Council,

Recalling General Assembly resolution S-13/2 of 1 June 1986 on the United Nations Programme of Action for African Economic Recovery and Development 1986-1990,

Recalling its resolution 1988/1 of 5 February 1988 and its decision 1988/161 of 27 July 1988,

Taking note of the report of the Secretary-General on investment of transnational corporations in Africa, submitted to the General Assembly at its forty-third session in the context of the mid-term review of the implementation of the Programme of Action,

Bearing in mind the fact that transnational corporations can contribute to Africa's economic recovery and development through increased direct investment in productive sectors of African economies,

Recognizing that investment by transnational corporations in Africa would constitute a significant source of non-debt-creating resource flows to Africa,

Noting with concern that the share of investments made by transnational corporations in developing countries has been substantially declining in general and in Africa in particular,

1. *Requests* the Secretary-General to prepare a report containing, *inter alia*, recommendations on alternative strategies that would create a mutually beneficial framework and lead to concrete measures to encourage transnational corporations to respond positively to improvements in the investment climate in Africa and thereby promote economic growth and self-sustaining socio-economic development, in accordance with the United Nations Programme of Action for African Economic Recovery and Development 1986-1990 and the Lagos Plan of Action for the Implementation of the Monrovia Strategy for the Economic Development of Africa, adopted in 1980, especially in those sectors in which transnational corporations can make a major contribution through capital mobilization, technical expertise, transfer of technology and market access;

2. *Invites* the home countries of transnational corporations, as a complement to measures taken by developing countries themselves, to encourage investment by such corporations in all developing countries, particularly those in Africa, and, to that end, to consider providing, *inter alia*, financial and fiscal incentives, including tax-sparing;

3. *Requests* the Secretary-General to continue to mobilize resources for increased support of technical assistance requirements of African countries, at the national, subregional and regional levels, to enable them to increase their capacities to deal with transnational corporations, so as to take advantage of investment opportunities through transnational corporations;

4. *Requests* the Secretary-General to upgrade the report prepared for the mid-term review of the implementation of the Programme of Action, to provide detailed and comprehensive coverage of foreign direct investment in Africa on a sector-by-sector basis and to report thereon to the Commission on Transnational Corporations at its sixteenth session.

Economic and Social Council resolution 1989/26

24 May 1989   Meeting 15   Adopted without vote

Approved by First Committee (E/1989/87) without vote, 19 May (meeting 8); draft by Commission on TNCs (E/1989/28/Rev.1); agenda item 8.

By **decision 44/411** of 17 November, the General Assembly decided that support of UNPAAERD should be continued pending the final review and appraisal of the Programme of Action, to be undertaken by the Assembly at its forty-sixth session.

Other action. In **resolution 1989/116** of 28 July, the Economic and Social Council took note with interest of the African Alternative Framework for Structural Adjustment Programmes for Socio-economic Recovery and Transformation[11] adopted by the Conference of Ministers of the Economic Commission for Africa in April 1989[12] and asked the General Assembly to consider taking action. It also called on the international community, especially developed countries and multilateral institutions, to consider support for country programmes prepared by African countries.

In **resolution 44/24** of 17 November, the Assembly took note with interest of the Alternative Framework and invited the international community, including multilateral financial and development institutions, to consider it as a basis for dialogue and consultation.

Angola

In a note verbale[13] to the President of the General Assembly on 1 December, Angola requested that an agenda item regarding international assistance for its economic rehabilitation be included in the 1989 Assembly agenda. An explanatory memorandum described the damage suffered by Angola in its 14-year military conflict with South Africa. Damage to the Angolan economy from the destruction of infrastructure was estimated at more than $16 billion, with 1988 losses at $4.5 billion, or 90 per cent of GDP. The country was further strained by the presence of an estimated 600,000 displaced persons, and another 50,000 disabled by the war.

GENERAL ASSEMBLY ACTION

On 15 December, the General Assembly adopted **resolution 44/168** by recorded vote.

International assistance for the economic rehabilitation of Angola

The General Assembly,

Having considered the item entitled "International assistance for the economic rehabilitation of Angola",

Noting with great concern the serious consequences of the acts of aggression and destabilization perpetrated by South Africa that adversely affect the economy of Angola,

Deeply concerned about the human suffering and the destruction of property resulting from the effects of South Africa's acts of aggression and destabilization,

Noting the efforts undertaken by the Government of Angola to cope with the economic and social problems confronting the country through a concerted programme of economic and financial readjustment,

Conscious of the urgent need for the international community to assist Angola in its economic rehabilitation,

Mindful of Security Council resolutions 387(1976) of 31 March 1976, 428(1978) of 6 May 1978, 447(1979) of 28 March 1979, 454(1979) of 2 November 1979, 475(1980) of 27 June 1980, 545(1983) of 20 December

1983, 546(1984) of 6 January 1984, 567(1985) of 20 June 1985, 571(1985) of 20 September 1985, 574(1985) of 7 October 1985, 577(1985) of 6 December 1985, 602(1987) of 25 November 1987, 606(1987) of 23 December 1987 and 628(1989) of 16 January 1989, in which the Council, *inter alia*, requested the international community to render assistance to Angola and considered that Angola is entitled to appropriate redress for any material damage it has suffered,

1. *Expresses* its solidarity with and support for the efforts of Angola to lessen the adverse effects caused by the acts of aggression and destabilization and to cope with the economic and social problems;

2. *Appeals* to the international community to render the substantial financial, material and technical assistance necessary for the economic rehabilitation of Angola;

3. *Requests* the Secretary-General to enter into consultation with the Government of Angola for the purpose of determining the level of assistance required by Angola and to report to Member States and the relevant United Nations bodies on the results of those consultations;

4. *Also requests* the Secretary-General to report to the General Assembly at its forty-fifth session on the implementation of the present resolution;

5. *Decides* to include in the provisional agenda of its forty-fifth session the item entitled "International assistance for the economic rehabilitation of Angola".

General Assembly resolution 44/168

15 December 1989   Meeting 82   150-0-2 (recorded vote)

56-nation draft (A/44/L.60/Rev.1); agenda item 160.

Sponsors: Afghanistan, Angola, Antigua and Barbuda, Argentina, Benin, Bolivia, Botswana, Brazil, Burkina Faso, Burundi, Cameroon, Cape Verde, Central African Republic, Chad, China, Colombia, Congo, Cuba, Czechoslovakia, Democratic Yemen, Egypt, Equatorial Guinea, Ethiopia, Gabon, Gambia, Ghana, Guinea, Guinea-Bissau, Kenya, Lesotho, Liberia, Libyan Arab Jamahiriya, Madagascar, Malawi, Mali, Mauritania, Mexico, Mozambique, Nepal, Nicaragua, Nigeria, Romania, Rwanda, Sao Tome and Principe, Senegal, Togo, Tunisia, Uganda, United Republic of Tanzania, Vanuatu, Venezuela, Viet Nam, Yugoslavia, Zaire, Zambia, Zimbabwe.

Recorded vote in Assembly as follows:

In favour: Afghanistan, Albania, Algeria, Angola, Antigua and Barbuda, Argentina, Australia, Austria, Bahamas, Bahrain, Bangladesh, Barbados, Belgium, Benin, Bhutan, Bolivia, Botswana, Brazil, Brunei Darussalam, Bulgaria, Burkina Faso, Burundi, Byelorussian SSR, Cameroon, Canada, Cape Verde, Central African Republic, Chad, Chile, China, Colombia, Congo, Costa Rica, Côte d'Ivoire, Cuba, Cyprus, Czechoslovakia, Democratic Kampuchea, Democratic Yemen, Denmark, Djibouti, Dominica, Dominican Republic, Ecuador, Egypt, Ethiopia, Fiji, Finland, France, Gabon, Gambia, German Democratic Republic, Federal Republic of Germany, Ghana, Greece, Grenada, Guatemala, Guinea, Guinea-Bissau, Guyana, Haiti, Honduras, Hungary, Iceland, India, Indonesia, Iran, Iraq, Ireland, Italy, Jamaica, Japan, Jordan, Kenya, Kuwait, Lao People's Democratic Republic, Lebanon, Lesotho, Liberia, Libyan Arab Jamahiriya, Luxembourg, Madagascar, Malawi, Malaysia, Maldives, Mali, Malta, Mauritania, Mauritius, Mexico, Mongolia, Morocco, Mozambique, Myanmar, Nepal, Netherlands, New Zealand, Nicaragua, Niger, Nigeria, Norway, Oman, Pakistan, Panama, Paraguay, Peru, Philippines, Poland, Portugal, Qatar, Romania, Rwanda, Saint Kitts and Nevis, Saint Lucia, Saint Vincent and the Grenadines, Samoa, Sao Tome and Principe, Saudi Arabia, Senegal, Seychelles, Sierra Leone, Singapore, Solomon Islands, Somalia, Spain, Sri Lanka, Sudan, Suriname, Swaziland, Sweden, Syrian Arab Republic, Thailand, Togo, Trinidad and Tobago, Tunisia, Turkey, Uganda, Ukrainian SSR, USSR, United Arab Emirates, United Kingdom, United Republic of Tanzania, Uruguay, Vanuatu, Venezuela, Viet Nam, Yugoslavia, Zaire, Zambia, Zimbabwe.

Against: None.

Abstaining: Israel, United States.

Benin

The Secretary-General reported[14] that Benin's financial crisis peaked in 1989, with fiscal revenues falling by a third from the levels of the previous year. This decline was caused by tax base erosion, the collapse of the banking system, strikes that lowered productivity in the revenue services, and the poor regional economic situation. External assistance reduced the payment lag for civil servants' salaries from three months to one by December, but 1988 arrears remained. The crisis slowed the country's development programme; as arrears on external debt accumulated, development funding was blocked. Lack of financial resources was felt most strongly in the social sector. On the positive side, agricultural production recovered from a poor 1987 performance, allowing Benin to remain self-sufficient in foodstuffs, except for wheat and rice.

In June, the Government, supported by IMF and the World Bank, adopted a structural adjustment programme for 1989-1992. It sought to create a sustainable 3 per cent growth rate in GDP, contain inflation, improve the country's debt status, and radically change Benin's development strategy by reducing the role of the public sector while promoting the private sector and restructuring the banking system. The programme would require $732 million in external assistance. In December, the Government decided to abandon Marxism-Leninism, but the new transitional Government remained committed to the programme.

Central African Republic

The Secretary-General reported[14] that the Central African Republic's public debt amounted to nearly $600 million at the beginning of 1989, and that debt servicing consumed 16 per cent of export revenues. An evaluation of the national structural adjustment programme's second phase indicated that there had been a measure of economic recovery in 1989, and that inflation had moderated. Still, the public deficit for the year equalled 13 per cent of GDP, compared with the programme's objective of 11 per cent. There was also some progress with restructuring and privatizing public enterprises.

UNDP was working to strengthen the national capacity in macro-economic analysis and programming to ameliorate the effects of the structural adjustment process on the population. In June, consultations took place on rural development. UNDP provided support for national planning and socio-economic management, and consulted with the Government and the donor community on ways to improve technical cooperation.

Chad

In response to a 1988 request of the General Assembly,[15] the Secretary-General in an August 1989 report[16] noted that although the effects of war, natural calamities and disasters had compromised Chad's efforts for reconstruction and development, favourable rainfall in 1987/88 resulted in a striking recovery of agricultural output in 1989. Food crop production was 50 per cent higher than in 1987/88. Chad continued to rely heavily on external assistance to finance its investment budget. Beginning 1 January, however, the Government undertook to pay the salaries of civil servants in full and lifted a moratorium on bank deposits, which had been introduced in 1983.

These and other developments suggested that Chad had reached a better position from which to proceed with a true restructuring of the economy. UNDP was funding a project under which the World Bank was assisting the Government with the preparation of a new 1989-1992 development plan. Development assistance for Chad for 1987-1991 from UNDP and other UN bodies amounted to $179.3 million.

In a later report,[14] the Secretary-General noted that Chad's GDP rose by 1.2 per cent in 1989, and food crop production continued its favourable trend. A 1989-1993 government programme included plans to rehabilitate the communications infrastructure, and a plan to reform the fiscal system was finalized under the aegis of IMF. Still under discussion was a planned $24 million social development programme to create jobs, improve sanitation and health, and strengthen social planning, with the support of the World Bank and other donors. In December, a new planning document identified three major objectives for Chad: increasing agricultural production through modernization, improving the population's well-being, and restoring financial equilibrium.

A programme to rehabilitate the depressed Borkou-Ennedi-Tibesti prefecture in northern Chad had yet to be fully implemented; by the end of 1989, only 38 per cent of the programme's $43 million budget had been secured.

GENERAL ASSEMBLY ACTION

On 19 December, on the recommendation of the Second (Economic and Financial) Committee, the General Assembly adopted **resolution 44/176** without vote.

Special economic assistance to Chad
The General Assembly,

Recalling its resolution 43/205 of 20 December 1988 and its previous resolutions on assistance in the reconstruction, rehabilitation and development of Chad and on special economic assistance to that country,

Recalling the round table on assistance to Chad, convened by the United Nations Development Programme at Geneva on 4 and 5 December 1985 in accordance with the arrangements agreed upon at the International Conference on Assistance to Chad, held in November 1982,

Having considered the report of the Secretary-General on special economic assistance to Chad dealing with, *inter alia*, the economic and financial situation of Chad, the status of assistance provided for the rehabilitation and reconstruction of the country and the progress made in organizing and executing the programme of assistance for that country,

Considering that the effects of war, natural calamities and disasters are compromising all the reconstruction and development efforts of the Government of Chad,

Recalling that a donor round table on assistance in the rehabilitation and reconstruction of northern Chad was convened by the Government of Chad, in collaboration with the United Nations Development Programme, on 14, 15 and 16 December 1988,

Noting that round tables on education and the development of human resources and on public health and family welfare will be convened by the Government of Chad, in collaboration with the United Nations Development Programme, in 1990,

Noting with satisfaction that the term of the interim plan for 1986-1988 is now drawing to an end and that a development plan for 1990-1994 will be submitted to all contributors in 1990,

1. *Expresses its gratitude* to the States and intergovernmental and non-governmental organizations that responded and are continuing to respond generously to the appeals of the Government of Chad and of the Secretary-General by furnishing assistance to Chad;

2. *Expresses its appreciation* to the Secretary-General for his efforts to make the international community aware of the difficulties of Chad and to mobilize assistance for that country;

3. *Renews the request* made to all States, competent United Nations organizations and programmes and international economic and financial institutions to continue to contribute to the rehabilitation and development of Chad;

4. *Notes with satisfaction* that the donor round table on assistance in the rehabilitation and reconstruction of northern Chad was held at N'Djamena on 14, 15 and 16 December 1988;

5. *Requests* the Secretary-General to continue to assess, in close collaboration with the humanitarian agencies concerned, the humanitarian needs, particularly in the area of health, of the displaced populations;

6. *Invites* all States and competent United Nations organizations and programmes to participate actively:

(a) In the contributors' round table on the implementation of the five-year development plan for Chad for 1990-1994, scheduled to be held in 1990 at Geneva;

(b) In the round tables on education and the development of human resources and on public health and family welfare, scheduled to be held in 1990 at N'Djamena;

7. *Calls upon* the Secretary-General to keep the situation in Chad under review and to report thereon to the General Assembly at its forty-fifth session.

General Assembly resolution 44/176

19 December 1989   Meeting 83   Adopted without vote

Approved by Second Committee (A/44/864) by consensus, 15 November (meeting 34); 29-nation draft (A/C.2/44/L.17), orally revised; agenda item 88.

Sponsors: Algeria, Argentina, Burkina Faso, Burundi, Cameroon, Cape Verde, Central African Republic, Chad, Chile, China, Colombia, Comoros, Congo,

Côte D'Ivoire, Egypt, France, Gabon, Guinea, Guinea-Bissau, Japan, Mali, Mauritania, Morocco, Niger, Senegal, Togo, Tunisia, United Kingdom, Zaire.
Meeting numbers. GA 44th session: 2nd Committee 19, 20, 25, 29-31, 34; plenary 83.

Djibouti

The Secretary-General, reporting[14] on the situation in Djibouti, noted that the country's budget deficit was substantially reduced between 1986 and 1989 by government efforts to limit expenditures and increase revenues, and budget balance had been achieved mainly through external financial assistance. Total external debt in 1989 was approximately $140 million. Debt-service payments, at $14.1 million, represented about 6 per cent of GNP. About one half of a $470 million public investment programme planned for 1983-1989 had been completed.

For information on UN emergency relief to Djibouti for flood relief, see below.

Madagascar

The Secretary-General reported[14] that Madagascar's economic growth accelerated in 1989 as a result of good performance in agriculture, trade, tourism and the informal sector. Rice production was up 17.6 per cent, while overall agricultural output was 3.5 per cent greater than in 1988. The inflation rate fell from 26 per cent in 1988 to 9.4 per cent in 1989. External debt, however, remained a major development constraint: in 1989, debt-servicing obligations were estimated at nearly 169 per cent of export earnings. The structural adjustment programme produced improvements in macro-economic balances, but social welfare investment remained unsatisfactory by comparison with spending for other sectors. Consultations with donors to correct this imbalance were scheduled for 1990.

Mozambique

In accordance with a 1988 General Assembly resolution,[17] a representative of the Under-Secretary-General for Special Political Questions, Regional Co-operation, Decolonization and Trusteeship reported on 12 July[18] to the Economic and Social Council on the programme of assistance to Mozambique. In 1988, the Government and the United Nations had appealed for international support for the period 1988-1989, taking into account previous problems in the areas of logistics, security, the Government's emergency relief capacity, scarcity of currency, kinds of donor support and delays in aid delivery. It was noted that government military operations had liberated many population centres and virtually all district capitals, and that a large number of affected and displaced persons could now be reached.

In April 1989, the Secretary-General launched an international appeal for emergency aid for 4.5

million affected and displaced persons, costing approximately $380 million for the biennium 1989-1990. At a donors' meeting held at UN Headquarters, pledges of some $350 million were announced, but subsequent analysis showed that the actual sums pledged amounted to $252 million, and as of mid-July, only $119 million had been allocated by donors to specific activities. Less than one third of the required food commodities had been pledged, raising the threat of severe shortages. The need for road, air and sea transport to deliver relief supplies was emphasized in the report. Inadequate support for health, water, education and agricultural programmes made the implementation of certain projects in the appeal impossible.

By **decision 1989/176** of 26 July 1989, the Economic and Social Council took note of the report by the representative of the Under-Secretary-General.

Front-line and other bordering States

In response to a 1988 General Assembly request,[19] the Secretary-General submitted a report[20] in July describing special assistance to the front-line States of Angola, Botswana, Mozambique, the United Republic of Tanzania, Zambia and Zimbabwe, as well as to other bordering States adversely affected by economic measures taken either by South Africa or by the international community against South Africa. Assistance continued to flow through direct bilateral agreements, regional networks, and UN bodies such as the World Bank, the United Nations Children's Fund (UNICEF) and the World Food Programme (WFP). Details of financial, technical, developmental and humanitarian assistance from Argentina, Brazil, Denmark, Egypt, Finland, the German Democratic Republic, the Federal Republic of Germany, New Zealand, Nigeria, Spain and Turkey were included, as well as action taken by UN bodies. Two addenda to the report contained replies from Austria, Canada, the Ukrainian SSR, UNICEF and IMF describing assistance that had been rendered.

GENERAL ASSEMBLY ACTION

On 19 December, on the recommendation of the Second Committee, the General Assembly adopted **resolution 44/181** by recorded vote.

Special assistance to the front-line States

The General Assembly,

Recalling its resolutions 41/199 of 8 December 1986, 42/201 of 11 December 1987 and 43/209 of 20 December 1988,

Having considered the report of the Secretary-General,

Deeply concerned about the adverse effects of South Africa's acts of aggression and destabilization against the front-line States and other neighbouring States,

Aware that the continuing existence of the *apartheid* system in South Africa aggravates the economic and social problems confronting the front-line States and other neighbouring States,

Conscious of the urgent need and responsibility of the international community to address the problems affecting the region,

Commending the concerted and determined efforts of the countries of the region to cope with the prevailing adverse conditions by strengthening their economic co-operation and lessening their dependence on South Africa, particularly in the areas of transportation, communications and related sectors,

Reaffirming the importance of close co-operation between the United Nations system and the front-line States,

Mindful of Security Council resolutions 568(1985) of 21 June 1985, 571(1985) of 20 September 1985 and 581(1986) of 13 February 1986, in which the Council, *inter alia*, requested the international community to render assistance to the front-line States,

1. *Expresses its appreciation* to the Secretary-General for his efforts regarding assistance to the front-line States;

2. *Notes with appreciation* the assistance being rendered to the front-line States by donor countries, intergovernmental organizations and non-governmental organizations;

3. *Strongly urges* the international community to continue to provide in a timely and effective manner the financial, material and technical assistance necessary to enhance the individual and collective capacity of the front-line States and other neighbouring States to withstand the effects of economic measures taken by South Africa, or by the international community against South Africa, in accordance with their national and regional plans and strategies;

4. *Requests* the Secretary-General and organizations and bodies of the United Nations system to respond to such requests for assistance as might be forthcoming from individual States or the appropriate subregional organizations, and further urges all States, intergovernmental organizations and non-governmental organizations to respond favourably to such requests;

5. *Appeals* to all States and appropriate intergovernmental and non-governmental organizations to support the national and collective emergency programmes prepared by the front-line States and other neighbouring States to overcome the critical problems arising from the situation in South Africa;

6. *Requests* the Secretary-General to report to the General Assembly at its forty-fifth session on the progress made in the implementation of the present resolution.

General Assembly resolution 44/181

19 December 1989   Meeting 83   154-0-1 (recorded vote)

Approved by Second Committee (A/44/864) by recorded vote (132-0-1), 21 November (meeting 41); 21-nation draft (A/C.2/44/L.27), orally revised; agenda item 88.

Sponsors: Algeria, Angola, Austria, Barbados, Botswana, Cuba, Denmark, Egypt, Finland, German Democratic Republic, Iceland, Mali, Mongolia, Mozambique, New Zealand, Nigeria, Norway, Sweden, United Republic of Tanzania, Zambia, Zimbabwe.

Meeting numbers. GA 44th session: 2nd Committee 2-10, 19, 20, 25, 29-31, 34, 41; plenary 83.

Recorded vote in Assembly as follows:

In favour: Afghanistan, Albania, Algeria, Angola, Antigua and Barbuda, Argentina, Australia, Austria, Bahamas, Bahrain, Bangladesh, Barbados,

Belgium, Benin, Bhutan, Bolivia, Botswana, Brazil, Brunei Darussalam, Bulgaria, Burkina Faso, Burundi, Byelorussian SSR, Cameroon, Canada, Cape Verde, Central African Republic, Chad, Chile, China, Colombia, Comoros, Congo, Costa Rica, Côte d'Ivoire, Cuba, Cyprus, Czechoslovakia, Democratic Kampuchea, Democratic Yemen, Denmark, Djibouti, Dominica, Dominican Republic, Ecuador, Egypt, El Salvador, Equatorial Guinea, Ethiopia, Fiji, Finland, France, Gabon, Gambia, German Democratic Republic, Germany, Federal Republic of, Ghana, Greece, Grenada, Guatemala, Guinea, Guinea-Bissau, Guyana, Haiti, Honduras, Hungary, Iceland, India, Indonesia, Iran, Iraq, Ireland, Italy, Jamaica, Japan, Jordan, Kenya, Kuwait, Lao People's Democratic Republic, Lebanon, Lesotho, Liberia, Libyan Arab Jamahiriya, Luxembourg, Madagascar, Malawi, Malaysia, Maldives, Mali, Malta, Mauritania, Mauritius, Mexico, Mongolia, Morocco, Mozambique, Myanmar, Nepal, Netherlands, New Zealand, Nicaragua, Niger, Nigeria, Norway, Oman, Pakistan, Panama, Papua New Guinea, Paraguay, Peru, Philippines, Poland, Portugal, Qatar, Romania, Rwanda, Saint Lucia, Saint Vincent and the Grenadines, Samoa, Sao Tome and Principe, Saudi Arabia, Senegal, Seychelles, Sierra Leone, Singapore, Solomon Islands, Somalia, Spain, Sri Lanka, Sudan, Suriname, Swaziland, Sweden, Syrian Arab Republic, Thailand, Togo, Trinidad and Tobago, Tunisia, Turkey, Uganda, Ukrainian SSR, USSR, United Arab Emirates, United Kingdom, United Republic of Tanzania, Uruguay, Vanuatu, Venezuela, Viet Nam, Yemen, Yugoslavia, Zaire, Zambia, Zimbabwe.
Against: None.
Abstaining: United States.

Other assistance

Central America

Pursuant to two General Assembly resolutions of 1988,[21] the Secretary-General submitted a report[22] in October on the Special Plan of Economic Co-operation for Central America.[23] The Plan, launched in September 1988, was being implemented through a mechanism that included the five Central American Governments, the United Nations and other international and regional organizations, as well as donor Governments.

The Central American economies deteriorated significantly during the 1980s. The average rate of growth in GDP was 3.6 per cent during 1981-1988—barely one third the rate of Latin America during the same period. On a per capita basis, the growth rate was minus 17 per cent. These conditions resulted from a persistent decline in the terms of trade and failure of export volumes to compensate for the fall in international prices; political unrest and civil strife, which discouraged private investments; foreign debt service; and natural disasters.

At the preparatory meeting of the Support Committee, held in New York in November 1988, it was decided that meetings with the Central American Vice-Ministers responsible for the Special Plan would include the Permanent Secretary of the General Treaty of Central American Economic Integration (SIECA) and UNDP. The first of those meetings took place in January 1989.

To facilitate aid co-ordination, a UNDP-financed computerized information system became operational in September 1989. Donors were encouraged to work directly with the recipient countries on the identification, formulation and implementation of projects, with UN assistance if requested. As of 1 August 1989, 21 projects with a total cost of $11,224,000 had been approved or

were in the final stages of approval. The Programme in Favour of Displaced Persons, Refugees and Returnees was the first result of successful resource mobilization within the framework of the Special Plan, receiving $115 million from Italy. The Programme, to be implemented by UNDP, would benefit 136,500 persons directly and 245,900 persons indirectly in the five Central American countries and Belize, by helping to establish infrastructure to meet basic needs in health, water and sanitation, food and nutrition, education and housing for targeted populations in well-defined geographical areas.

Other UN efforts regarding the Special Plan included action to meet immediate food and energy needs, and to alleviate the external debt crisis. A technical co-operation project, to be executed by UNCTAD, was formulated to help reactivate intraregional trade. UNDP was financing a project entitled Strengthening of the Central American Monetary Stabilization Fund. A draft proposal to restructure the Fund was finalized in June 1989.

The first meeting of Central American Governments with co-operating Governments and institutions was held in Geneva from 4 to 6 July, and was attended by representatives of 27 Governments, 29 organizations of the United Nations and 15 subregional Central American integration organizations.

UNDP consideration. On 30 June 1989,[24] the Governing Council of UNDP urged the co-operating community to support the funding needs of the United Nations Special Plan of Economic Co-operation for Central America. It also invited the community, intergovernmental agencies, financial institutions and UN bodies to participate in the first meeting of the Central American Governments with co-operating Governments and institutions in Geneva in July, to review the Special Plan's implementation.

GENERAL ASSEMBLY ACTION

On 19 December, on the recommendation of the Second Committee, the General Assembly adopted **resolution 44/182** without vote.

Special Plan of Economic Co-operation for Central America

The General Assembly,

Recalling its resolutions 42/1 of 7 October 1987, 42/204 of 11 December 1987, 43/24 of 15 November 1988 and 44/10 of 23 October 1989, as well as decisions 88/31 A of 1 July 1988 and 89/64 of 30 June 1989 of the Governing Council of the United Nations Development Programme,

Recalling in particular its resolutions 42/231 of 12 May 1988 and 43/210 of 20 December 1988, in which it urged the international community and international organizations to increase their technical, economic and financial co-operation with the Central American countries within the framework of the Special Plan of Economic Co-operation for Central America,

Reiterating the importance of the commitments made by the Central American Presidents in the agreement signed at Guatemala City at the Esquipulas II Summit Meeting, the declarations adopted at Alajuela, Costa Rica, and Costa del Sol, El Salvador, and, in particular, the agreements reached at Tela, Honduras, which represented concrete progress and strengthened the peace process in the region,

Welcoming with satisfaction the convening of the first meeting between the Governments of the countries of Central America and co-operating Governments and institutions, held at Geneva from 4 to 6 July 1989, to review the evolution of the regional development process with regard to assistance and co-operation requirements and to discuss programmes and projects that could be implemented in accordance with resolution 43/210,

Stressing the need to encourage the convening of sectoral meetings for the purpose of mobilizing resources for the implementation of programmes and projects within the framework of the Special Plan,

Having considered the reports of the Secretary-General on the situation in Central America and on the work done to promote the Special Plan and, in particular, his report on the work of the Organization, in which he states that "the time has now come to buttress the emerging peace by providing the massive support that the region needs to overcome its age-old problems",

Deeply concerned about the emergency situation in Central America and alarmed at the seriousness of the economic and social crisis that the region faces,

Reaffirming its conviction that peace, development and democracy are inseparable,

1. *Expresses its appreciation* to the Secretary-General for his reports on the situation in Central America and for the efforts that he has made to promote the Special Plan of Economic Co-operation for Central America;

2. *Welcomes with satisfaction* the Joint Political Declaration and the Joint Economic Communiqué of the San Pedro Sula Ministerial Conference on Political Dialogue and Economic Co-operation between the European Community and its member States and the countries of Central America and the Contadora Group, held at San Pedro Sula, Honduras, on 27 and 28 February 1989, in which they reaffirmed their commitment to and interest in continuing to participate in specific activities and in the reactivation and economic development of the region in accordance with the priorities established in the Special Plan;

3. *Welcomes* the Declaration and Concerted Plan of Action in Favour of Central American Refugees, Returnees and Displaced Persons adopted by the International Conference on Central American Refugees, held at Guatemala City from 29 to 31 May 1989;

4. *Welcomes with satisfaction* the convening of the first meeting between the Governments of Central America and co-operating Governments and institutions, at which the evolution of the regional development process, including the region's assistance and co-operation requirements, were reviewed within the framework of the Special Plan;

5. *Recommends* the convening of sectoral meetings during 1990, in continuation of the process already begun between the Governments of the countries of Central America and the co-operating Governments and in-

stitutions, to examine the possibility of mobilizing additional resources for the early implementation of programmes and projects within the framework of the Special Plan;

6. *Urges* Member States and observers, intergovernmental organizations, international financial institutions, the organs, organizations and bodies of the United Nations system and regional and subregional organs and agencies, taking into account the emergency situation faced by the Central American countries, to participate actively and to adopt immediate measures for the implementation of the activities in support of the goals and objectives of the Special Plan;

7. *Emphasizes* the urgent need to provide the Central American countries with financial resources on concessional and favourable terms, in addition to those which they are already receiving from the international community;

8. *Requests* the Secretary-General to submit a report to the General Assembly at its forty-fifth session on the progress made in the implementation of the Special Plan;

9. *Decides* to review and evaluate the progress in the implementation of the Special Plan at its forty-fifth session.

General Assembly resolution 44/182

19 December 1989   Meeting 83   Adopted without vote

Approved by Second Committee (A/44/864) by consensus, 15 November (meeting 34); 44-nation draft (A/C.2/44/L.32); agenda item 88.

Sponsors: Algeria, Argentina, Austria, Bangladesh, Belgium, Bolivia, Brazil, Canada, Colombia, Congo, Costa Rica, Cuba, Denmark, Dominican Republic, Ecuador, El Salvador, Finland, France, Germany, Federal Republic of, Greece, Guatemala, Honduras, India, Ireland, Italy, Japan, Luxembourg, Mauritania, Mexico, Morocco, Netherlands, Nicaragua, Norway, Paraguay, Peru, Philippines, Portugal, Spain, Suriname, Sweden, Tunisia, Uruguay, Venezuela, Yugoslavia.

Meeting numbers. GA 44th session: 2nd Committee 2-10, 19, 20, 25, 29-31, 34; plenary 83.

Ecuador

Reporting on economic assistance to Ecuador,[14] the Secretary-General noted that many aspects of Ecuador's economy showed improvement in 1989, largely as a result of economic policies put in place in the third quarter of 1988. Inflation had slowed to 54.2 per cent in December 1989, down from 85.7 per cent a year earlier. The budget deficit represented 1 per cent of GDP in 1989, compared with 2.7 per cent in 1988. GDP rose by 0.5 per cent, an improvement over the negative performance of previous years. The Government made substantial efforts to enhance social development, and remained concerned about inflation, stagnant wages, inequalities in national income distribution, insufficient productivity, increased social sector needs and continuing external debt.

Lebanon

In accordance with a 1988 General Assembly resolution,[25] the Secretary-General submitted a report in October[26] describing assistance programmes to Lebanon. The report stated that unprecedented violence had erupted in Lebanon, with almost uninterrupted shelling in and around Beirut. Lebanese government and social institutions continued to disintegrate, and the effect on the overall economic and social situation had been devastating. Approximately 75 per cent of Beirut's population had fled to other areas of Lebanon. United Nations and other relief operations were severely affected by the closure of the ports, and the movement of personnel and relief items were hindered by an unpredictable security situation. The economy was collapsing and the consumer price index increased by 28.5 per cent during the first half of 1989. Political instability and increasing violence made it extremely difficult for the UN system to carry out its reconstruction and development programme. The ongoing destruction meant that the organization's activities inevitably had to focus on emergency relief aid and maintenance of essential services, such as health care and water supplies.

The Secretary-General sent a high-level inter-agency mission to Lebanon from 16 to 26 January 1989 to reassess emergency relief needs, led by the Special Representative of the Secretary-General and composed of senior representatives of several UN agencies. The mission reported that the Secretary-General's 1987 appeal for $85 million had been answered, and that total relief assistance for Lebanon from contributions to the United Nations and from other sources was more than $116 million for 1988. Total requirements for relief and urgent rehabilitation for the following year were estimated at about $87.3 million, of which slightly less than half was for food aid. Following a discussion of UN assistance to Lebanon with the heads of UN programmes and specialized agencies at the Administrative Committee on Co-ordination meeting at Geneva, the Secretary-General on 21 April appealed to the international community for urgent humanitarian assistance for those most seriously affected by the crisis. To improve the United Nations ability to implement emergency relief assistance, the Special Representative established co-ordination meetings between UN representatives, government officials and donor officials, and a similar co-ordination mechanism for non-governmental organizations.

Individual reports were included on relief provided by the following bodies: UNICEF, UNDP, the Office of the United Nations Disaster Relief Co-ordinator, the United Nations High Commissioner for Refugees, the United Nations Relief and Works Agency for Palestine Refugees in the Near East, WFP, the Food and Agriculture Organization of the United Nations (FAO), the International Labour Organisation, the United Nations Educational, Scientific and Cultural Organization and the World Health Organization (WHO). The United Nations Interim Force in Lebanon (UNIFIL) continued to provide humanitarian assistance on an *ad hoc* basis. The report concluded that international relief assistance in response to the Secretary-General's appeals had significantly alleviated the suffering of the Lebanese people.

ECONOMIC AND SOCIAL COUNCIL ACTION

On 26 July, the Economic and Social Council, on the recommendation of its Third (Programme and Co-ordination) Committee, adopted **resolution 1989/100** without vote.

Assistance for the reconstruction and development of Lebanon

The Economic and Social Council,

Recalling General Assembly resolution 43/207 of 20 December 1988 and previous resolutions of the General Assembly on international assistance for the reconstruction of Lebanon, in which the Assembly requested the specialized agencies and other organizations and bodies of the United Nations system to expand and intensify their programmes of assistance in response to the needs of Lebanon,

Aware of the deteriorating socio-economic conditions of the people of Lebanon and the magnitude of their unmet needs,

Noting with great concern the unprecedented inflation in Lebanon during the past five years and the catastrophic erosion of the value of the country's currency,

Appeals to all Member States and all organizations of the United Nations system to continue and intensify their efforts to mobilize all possible assistance for the Government of Lebanon in its reconstruction and development efforts, in accordance with the relevant resolutions and decisions of the General Assembly and the Economic and Social Council.

Economic and Social Council resolution 1989/100

26 July 1989   Meeting 35   Adopted without vote

Approved by Third Committee (E/1989/131) without vote, 17 July (meeting 11); 23-nation draft (E/1989/C.3/L.4); agenda item 13.

Sponsors: Algeria, Brazil, Egypt, France, Ghana, Greece, Iraq, Italy, Japan, Jordan, Lebanon, Libyan Arab Jamahiriya, Malaysia, Morocco, Oman, Saudi Arabia, Somalia, Sudan, Syrian Arab Republic, Tunisia, USSR, Uruguay, Yugoslavia.

GENERAL ASSEMBLY ACTION

On 19 December, on the recommendation of the Second Committee, the General Assembly adopted **resolution 44/180** without vote.

Assistance for the reconstruction and development of Lebanon

The General Assembly,

Recalling its resolution 43/207 of 20 December 1988 and its previous resolutions on assistance for the reconstruction and development of Lebanon,

Taking note of Economic and Social Council resolution 1989/100 of 26 July 1989 and recalling the previous relevant resolutions and decisions of the Council,

Noting with deep concern the grave deterioration of the economic situation in Lebanon, compounded recently by the extensive damage to the basic infrastructure of the country and to its utilities,

Reaffirming the urgent need for further international action to assist the Government of Lebanon in its continuing efforts for reconstruction and development,

Taking note of the report of the Secretary-General on assistance for the reconstruction and development of Lebanon, and of the statement made by the Special Representative of the Secretary-General for the Reconstruction and Development of Lebanon,

1. *Expresses its appreciation* to the Secretary-General for his report and for the steps he has taken to mobilize assistance to Lebanon;

2. *Commends* the Under-Secretary-General for Political and General Assembly Affairs and Secretariat Services for his co-ordination of system-wide assistance to Lebanon;

3. *Requests* the Secretary-General to continue and intensify his efforts to mobilize all possible assistance within the United Nations system to help Lebanon in its reconstruction and development efforts;

4. *Calls upon* the organs, organizations and bodies of the United Nations system to intensify their programmes of assistance and to expand them in response to the pressing needs of Lebanon, and to take the necessary steps to ensure that their offices in Beirut are operational and adequately staffed at the senior level;

5. *Requests* the Secretary-General to report to the General Assembly at its forty-fifth session on the progress made in the implementation of the present resolution.

General Assembly resolution 44/180

19 December 1989   Meeting 83   Adopted without vote

Approved by Second Committee (A/44/864) by consensus, 15 November (meeting 34); 10-nation draft (A/C.2/44/L.21); agenda item 88.
Sponsors: Bahrain, Egypt, France, Italy, Jordan, Lebanon, Mauritania, Spain, Tunisia, United Kingdom.
Meeting numbers. GA 44th session: 2nd Committee 2-10, 19, 20, 25, 29-31, 34; plenary 83.

Vanuatu

Reporting on assistance to Vanuatu,[14] the Secretary-General noted that the island developing country continued to experience severe constraints on its economic and social development because of declining export prices, deteriorating terms of trade, and a high population growth rate coupled with a shortage of skilled manpower. In April 1989, cyclone Devi brought heavy rains, exacerbating difficulties caused by cyclones in previous years. Exports of copra, the main crop, declined from 42,300 tons in 1986 to 23,620 tons in 1989, but were offset by increases in other exports. Vanuatu's tourist industry made a significant contribution to foreign exchange earnings and employment, but the number of cruise ship visitors was down in the first half of 1989.

The international community had provided substantial assistance for reconstruction and rehabilitation following cyclone Uma in February 1987 and much of that work had been completed. Further relief aid was received following 1988 cyclones, but the infrastructure in rural areas would not be restored to former levels for some years. Almost all of Vanuatu's public sector capital and development expenditure in 1989 was funded by donors or lenders.

REFERENCES

[1]YUN 1987, p. 440, ESC res. 1987/39, 28 May 1987. [2]E/CN.5/1989/2. [3]YUN 1969, p. 423, GA res. 2542(XXIV), 11 Dec. 1969. [4]YUN 1988, p. 363. [5]DP/1989/22. [6]YUN 1988, p. 363. [7]E/1989/32 (dec. 89/31). [8]TD/B/1222. [9]UNCTAD/ST/ECDC/30 & Add.1. [10]A/44/15, vol. II (dec. 372(XXXVI)). [11]A/44/315. [12]E/1989/35 (dec. 676(XXIV)). [13]A/44/248. [14]A/45/358. [15]YUN 1988, p. 376, GA res. 43/205, 20 Dec. 1988. [16]A/44/418. [17]YUN 1988, p. 399, GA res. 43/208, 20 Dec. 1988. [18]E/1989/SR.27. [19]YUN 1988, p. 380, GA res. 43/209, 20 Dec. 1988. [20]A/44/373 & Add.1,2. [21]YUN 1988, pp. 307 & 308, GA res. 42/231, 12 May 1988 & GA res. 43/210, 20 Dec. 1988. [22]A/44/519. [23]A/42/949. [24]E/1989/32 (dec. 89/64) [25]YUN 1988, p. 398, GA res. 43/207, 20 Dec. 1988. [26]A/44/559.

Disasters

In 1989, the Office of the United Nations Disaster Relief Co-ordinator (UNDRO) continued to act as the focal point for disaster management within the UN system, in accordance with its mandate, covering all aspects of disaster relief and mitigation. Disaster prevention and preparedness continued to grow in importance and UNDRO moved to increase communication and co-operation. UNDRO also assisted Governments with pre-disaster planning. The rise in both the number of disasters and public interest in them posed new challenges. The number of requests from developing countries to strengthen their emergency relief capabilities also grew.

Office of the UN Disaster Relief Co-ordinator

During 1989, UNDRO—the specialized office of the United Nations for all disaster-related matters—was deeply involved in preparatory work for the International Decade for Natural Disaster Reduction, 1990-2000 (see below), and in strengthening its collaborative relationship with UNDP. In his report[1] on UNDRO activities in 1988-1989, the Secretary-General stated that the traditional division between natural and man-made disasters had increasingly lost relevance, while the distinction between sudden disasters and slow-onset emergencies had become more significant. He also reported that UNDRO's limited resources for disaster relief co-ordination had been put under great strain. With the increased vulnerability of communities to natural hazards and other emergencies, the number of disasters and their human and economic cost had grown.

Because the need for donor Governments, intergovernmental, non-governmental and UN organizations to receive reliable and immediate information from UNDRO for decision-making in emergencies was more compelling than ever, UNDRO's data management and communication capacities needed to be improved during the 1988-1989 biennium. UNDRO's information network, the United Nations International Emergency Network, completed its pilot phase at the end of 1989, and the Office planned an international conference on disaster telecommunications for early 1990.

In response to recommendations made by the Administrative Management Service in February, UNDRO's organizational structure was adjusted to reflect new requirements, which were identified by the Secretary-General in an October 1987 report[2] and later endorsed by the General Assembly.[3] UNDRO activities relating to public information, communications and electronic data-processing support, and registry and reference library functions were regrouped under the information and disaster data systems management. Two substantive branches, renamed the Relief Co-ordination Branch and the Disaster Mitigation Branch, were relieved of general office support functions to allow them to focus on their specific mandates. To strengthen further its co-operation with non-governmental organizations, in October UNDRO convened a third meeting of officials in charge of national emergency relief services on enhancing international co-operation in response to the needs of disaster victims. The emergency transport and warehousing facility at Pisa, Italy, was considerably developed, in order to increase UNDRO's efficiency and effectiveness.

Donor meetings continued to be valuable forums for presenting emergency appeals for assistance to the international donor community. In 1989, UNDRO organized or participated in such meetings for Angola, Bangladesh and Mozambique.

Contributions channelled directly through UNDRO for disaster relief totalled $40 million during 1988-1989, compared to $22 million for the preceding biennium. A total of 117 disasters, both natural and man-made, were addressed. On average, UNDRO was called upon to deal with a new emergency situation every week, issuing a minimum of four information/situation reports weekly.

Major disasters that elicited an UNDRO response included earthquakes in Algeria, Nepal and the Soviet Socialist Republics of Tajikistan and Armenia; floods in Bangladesh, Brazil, China, Democratic Yemen, Djibouti, Paraguay, the Sudan, Tunisia and Zambia; Hurricanes Hugo, Gilbert and Joan in the Caribbean and Latin America; drought in Ethiopia; civil strife in Angola, Lebanon, Mozambique and Romania; returnees in Mauritania and Senegal; and displaced persons in Mali and the Niger. UNDRO mounted large airlift and air-drop operations for emergency relief in Ethiopia and Mozambique.

UNDRO financing

UNDRO activities continued to be financed mainly from the UN regular budget and voluntary contributions to a number of trust funds administered by the Co-ordinator. Appropriations by the General Assembly for the 1988-1989 biennium were $6,944,800.[4]

Disaster relief efforts

Drought-stricken areas

Sudano-Sahelian region

In 1989, the United Nations Sudano-Sahelian Office (UNSO) continued, under UNDP supervision, to assist countries in drought preparedness, recovery and rehabilitation, medium- to long-term development, and in implementation of the 1977 Plan of Action to Combat Desertification (see also PART THREE, Chapter VIII).

In a report[5] to the UNDP Governing Council on UNSO activities during 1989, the UNDP Administrator noted that although the Sudano-Sahelian region experienced above-average rainfall compared to the deficit of the previous 17 years, outbreaks of desert locusts and flooding following the rainy seasons continued to threaten the region's physical condition. The natural resource base continued to deteriorate despite efforts to halt ecological degradation. Climatic variations and human activities, such as overexploitation of land and water, overgrazing of rangelands and deforestation, remained driving forces behind the ecological deterioration of the region.

The report summarized UNSO activities in the 22 Sudano-Sahelian countries in such areas as deforestation control, range and water management, soil and sand dune stabilization, international planning and co-ordination, ecological monitoring, funding mobilization and development, and the promotion of public awareness of drought and desertification issues. UNSO's collaborative and co-operative activities with other agencies were described, as well as measures against drought and desertification taken by other entities within UNDP. By the end of 1989, ongoing UNSO projects were valued at approximately $100 million. The total amount of resources mobilized through the UNSO Trust Fund was $37.5 million, an increase of more than 37 per cent over 1988. UNSO was designated as the UN focal point for a new initiative, the "Observatory of the Sahara and the Sahel", undertaken by France. The programme, intended for 20 countries, aimed to complete and reinforce existing anti-drought and anti-desertification programmes for northern, western and eastern Africa.

UNDP Council action. On 30 June,[6] the UNDP Governing Council, having considered the

Administrator's report on UNSO's 1988 activities,[7] noted with satisfaction UNSO's renewed efforts to combat drought and desertification and encouraged it to contribute actively to major initiatives for the protection of the environment, by promoting measures to control desertification and by ensuring their co-ordination with other development activities. The Council renewed its appeal to Governments, organizations and individuals to contribute to UNSO's general resources and particular projects, and to make use of its services.

Report of the Secretary-General. In response to a 1987 General Assembly request,[8] in May the Secretary-General submitted a report[9] on African countries stricken by desertification and drought. He noted UNSO's steps to assist the 22 countries of the Sudano-Sahelian region in controlling desertification and drought, to strengthen contacts with the Intergovernmental Authority for Drought and Development (IGADD) and the Permanent Inter-State Committee on Drought Control in the Sahel (CILSS), and its establishment of a regional office in East Africa to deal with IGADD. The report said UNSO had increased direct support to Governments in planning, co-ordination and monitoring at the country level.

The Secretary-General drew the Council's attention to the report of the UNDP Administrator on UNSO activities,[7] as well as the report of the Governing Council of the United Nations Environment Programme (UNEP) on the implementation of the Plan of Action to Contain Desertification 1987-1988,[10] which included sections on implementing the Plan of Action in the Sudano-Sahelian region and its financing.

ECONOMIC AND SOCIAL COUNCIL ACTION

On 27 July, the Economic and Social Council, on the recommendation of its First Committee, adopted **resolution 1989/103** without vote.

Countries stricken by desertification and drought in Africa

The Economic and Social Council,

Recalling General Assembly resolutions 39/208 of 17 December 1984, 40/175 of 17 December 1985 and 42/188 of 11 December 1987, as well as Economic and Social Council resolution 1986/44 of 21 July 1986,

Recalling also General Assembly resolution 40/209 of 17 December 1985, in which the Assembly rationalized its consideration of desertification and drought issues,

Deeply alarmed by studies indicating that major climatic changes have taken place in Africa, making the present situation very critical, and by the disturbing assessment that emerged from the Scientific Round Table on the Climatic Situation and Drought in Africa, held at Addis Ababa in February 1984,

Greatly concerned at the tragic consequences of the accelerating desertification, which has resulted in a substantial decline in agricultural output and contributed in particular to the worsening of the current economic crisis in Africa,

Taking note of the interest shown at the summit meeting of the seven main industrialized countries held in Paris in July 1989 in matters relating to the control of desertification and, in particular, in the plan to establish a Sahel observatory,

Recalling that, pursuant to the United Nations Programme of Action for African Economic Recovery and Development 1986-1990, African Governments have undertaken to strengthen measures to combat desertification and drought, and bearing in mind the active support and commitment to action expressed forcefully by the international community, including the United Nations system, in General Assembly resolution 43/27 of 18 November 1988 on the mid-term review and appraisal of the implementation of the Programme of Action,

Taking note of the report of the Secretary-General on countries stricken by desertification and drought,

Taking note of the work of the Governing Council of the United Nations Environment Programme on this question and its decision 15/23 of 25 May 1989,

Welcoming the results and resolutions of the Ministerial Conference for a joint policy to combat desertification in the countries of the Permanent Inter-State Committee on Drought Control in the Sahel and the Economic Community of West African States, in the Maghreb countries, in Egypt and in the Sudan, held at Dakar in July 1984 and November 1985 and at Algiers in October 1988,

Welcoming also the renewed efforts of the United Nations Sudano-Sahelian Office to increase support to the countries and organizations concerned and to co-operate with them, in particular with the Permanent Inter-State Committee on Drought Control in the Sahel and the Intergovernmental Authority on Drought and Development,

Having considered the report of the Administrator of the United Nations Development Programme on the activities of the United Nations Sudano-Sahelian Office,

Acknowledging that, in view of the scale and gravity of desertification and drought, programmes to combat those scourges require financial and human resources beyond the means of the countries concerned,

1. *Recognizes* the sustained and praiseworthy efforts made by the Permanent Inter-State Committee on Drought Control in the Sahel to combat desertification and drought, and welcomes its fruitful co-operation with Governments and United Nations organs and bodies;

2. *Appeals urgently* to the international community, particularly donor countries, while maintaining their support for the United Nations Programme of Action for African Economic Recovery and Development 1986-1990, to continue to support the Permanent Inter-State Committee on Drought Control in the Sahel, the Intergovernmental Authority on Drought and Development and the Ministerial Conference for a joint policy to combat desertification;

3. *Welcomes with satisfaction* the progress made by the International Fund for Agricultural Development through its Special Programme for Sub-Saharan African Countries Affected by Drought and Desertification;

4. *Stresses* the fundamental importance of South-South co-operation in executing programmes to combat desertification and drought and of the necessary support of the international community for such co-operation;

5. *Notes with satisfaction* the generosity and solidarity with which the international community has responded to the assistance needs resulting from the emergency in Africa, particularly with regard to food aid, emergency medical assistance and the fight against grasshoppers and locusts;

6. *Recommends* that, within the framework of bilateral and multilateral development assistance programmes, the fight against desertification and drought be given priority attention in keeping with the scope of those problems;

7. *Urges* the United Nations Sudano-Sahelian Office to assist the Sudano-Sahelian countries with regard to preparations for the United Nations conference on the environment and development and the follow-up actions resulting from the conference;

8. *Requests* the Secretary-General to place greater emphasis in the World Economic Survey on the situation and prospects of countries stricken by desertification and drought;

9. *Further requests* the Secretary-General to report to the General Assembly at its forty-sixth session, through the Economic and Social Council, on the situation in countries stricken by desertification and drought and to prepare, as necessary, specific and co-ordinated proposals for action.

Economic and Social Council resolution 1989/103

27 July 1989	Meeting 36	Adopted without vote

Approved by First Committee (E/1989/140) without vote, 21 July (meeting 25); 22-nation draft (E/1989/C.1/L.14), orally revised; agenda item 7 *(g)*.
Sponsors: Cameroon, Canada, Denmark, Egypt, Ethiopia, France, Germany, Federal Republic of, Guinea, Malaysia, Mauritania, Morocco, Netherlands, Niger, Norway, Rwanda, Senegal, Somalia, Sweden, Syrian Arab Republic, Tunisia, Yugoslavia, Zambia.

Storms and floods

Harsh weather battered several areas of the world in 1989, causing many deaths, rendering thousands homeless and leaving vast structural damage. Severe flooding in Djibouti in April affected some 250,000 people, including 150,000 who were left homeless, while 260,000 people were affected by March floods in Democratic Yemen. Hurricane Hugo struck the eastern Caribbean in mid-September with winds in excess of 150 miles per hour, causing extensive damage and leaving thousands homeless.

Hurricane Hugo

On 27 September,[11] Antigua and Barbuda requested the General Assembly to include an additional item on the agenda of the forty-fourth session, entitled "Emergency assistance to Antigua and Barbuda, Dominica and Saint Kitts and Nevis". The request stated that these islands had been devastated by hurricane Hugo on 16 September. Assistance to the British Virgin Islands and Montserrat was subsequently included in the item on the proposal of the United Kingdom and with the recommendation of the General Committee.

UNDRO entrusted the Manager of its Pan-Caribbean Disaster Preparedness and Prevention Project with monitoring the situation and activating regional and national response systems. Overall co-ordination of the disaster relief operation was provided by the Project, which co-operated closely with UNDP and other agencies. Through its direct links with the Caribbean Community Disaster Relief Unit, UNDRO was able to secure the requests from and pledges for the stricken countries in good time. UNDRO issued situation reports on damage and relief needs and, together with UNDP, provided emergency grants for the purchase of relief materials totalling $200,000. Contributions reported to UNDRO exceeded $11 million.

GENERAL ASSEMBLY ACTION

On 12 October, the General Assembly adopted **resolution 44/3** without vote.

Emergency assistance to Antigua and Barbuda, the British Virgin Islands, Dominica, Montserrat and Saint Kitts and Nevis

The General Assembly,

Recalling its resolution 43/202 of 20 December 1988 on the International Decade for Natural Disaster Reduction and its resolution 35/56 of 5 December 1980, the annex to which contains the International Development Strategy for the Third United Nations Development Decade,

Deeply distressed by the large number of afflicted persons and the destruction wrought by hurricane Hugo, which, on 16 September 1989, devastated Antigua and Barbuda, the British Virgin Islands, Dominica, Montserrat and Saint Kitts and Nevis,

Conscious of the efforts of the Governments and peoples of Antigua and Barbuda, the British Virgin Islands, Dominica, Montserrat and Saint Kitts and Nevis to save lives and alleviate the sufferings of the victims of hurricane Hugo,

Noting the enormous effort that will be required to alleviate the grave situation caused by this natural disaster,

Conscious also of the prompt response being made by Governments, the bodies and agencies of the United Nations system, international and regional agencies, non-governmental organizations and private individuals to provide relief,

Recognizing that the magnitude of the disaster and its medium-term and long-term effects will require, as a complement to the efforts being made by the peoples and Governments of Antigua and Barbuda, the British Virgin Islands, Dominica, Montserrat and Saint Kitts and Nevis, a demonstration of international solidarity and humanitarian concern to ensure broad multilateral co-operation in order to meet the immediate emergency situation in the affected areas and to initiate the process of reconstruction,

1. *Expresses its solidarity and support* to the Governments and peoples of Antigua and Barbuda, the British Virgin Islands, Dominica, Montserrat and Saint Kitts and Nevis;

2. *Expresses its appreciation* to all States of the international community, international agencies and non-governmental organizations that are providing emergency relief to the affected countries;

3. *Urges* all States of the international community, as a matter of urgency, to contribute generously to the relief, rehabilitation and reconstruction efforts in the affected countries;

4. *Requests* the Secretary-General, in collaboration with the international financial institutions and the bodies and agencies of the United Nations system, to assist the Governments of Antigua and Barbuda, the British Virgin Islands, Dominica, Montserrat and

Saint Kitts and Nevis in identifying the medium-term and long-term needs and in mobilizing resources, as well as to help with the task of reconstruction of the affected countries undertaken by their respective Governments.

General Assembly resolution 44/3

12 October 1989   Meeting 31   Adopted without vote

33-nation draft (A/44/L.3 & Add.1); agenda item 156.
Sponsors: Antigua and Barbuda, Bahamas, Barbados, Belize, Colombia, Cuba, Dominica, Dominican Republic, Ecuador, Grenada, Guatemala, Guyana, Haiti, Honduras, Jamaica, Malta, Mauritius, Netherlands, Nicaragua, Peru, Philippines, Portugal, Saint Kitts and Nevis, Saint Lucia, Saint Vincent and the Grenadines, Samoa, Singapore, Suriname, Trinidad and Tobago, United Kingdom, Uruguay, Vanuatu, Venezuela.

Following adoption of resolution 44/3, the Secretary-General reported[1] direct losses estimated at $365 million.

Floods in Democratic Yemen

In an October report,[12] the Secretary-General noted that, following heavy rains that started on 19 March and continued for more than a week, Democratic Yemen was struck by severe floods in its central and eastern regions. Twenty-five people were killed, 80,000 were left homeless, and crop losses alone reached $5.8 million.

On 26 March, the Government asked UNDRO to launch an appeal for international assistance, and UNDRO responded the same day with the first of five situation reports alerting the international community to the disaster and urging donors to extend emergency assistance. As of 31 August, UNDRO's efforts had helped secure about $2.9 million from Governments, intergovernmental and non-governmental organizations, private firms, individuals and UN agencies. Medical assistance was provided by UNICEF and WHO; UNDP provided $50,000 for food assistance; and WFP approved a three-month food-for-work programme valued at $1 million. UNDP subsequently approved additional funding of $1.1 million for a technical assistance project to supervise reconstruction of 25 schools and, in co-operation with the International Development Association, made available $2 million for construction materials. In a later report,[13] the Secretary-General noted that national damage and reconstruction costs were estimated at $72 million.

ECONOMIC AND SOCIAL COUNCIL ACTION

On 10 May, the Economic and Social Council adopted **resolution 1989/1** without vote.

Emergency assistance to Democratic Yemen

The Economic and Social Council,

Deeply concerned at the extensive and unprecedented damage and devastation in Democratic Yemen caused by torrential rain and floods in March and April 1989,

Extremely concerned about the destruction of thousands of dwellings and the widespread damage to or disruption of the country's infrastructure, in particular roads,

water supplies, electricity supplies, communication systems, health centres, schools and other public services,

Considering that many thousands of hectares of cultivated land were inundated and hundreds of villages have completely disappeared, leaving tens of thousands of people without shelter or food,

Noting that a detailed assessment of the extent and nature of the damage is being prepared by the Government of Democratic Yemen with the assistance of the Office of the United Nations Disaster Relief Co-ordinator,

Noting the efforts made by the Government of Democratic Yemen to provide adequate food and shelter promptly for those affected by the floods and to undertake rehabilitation and reconstruction programmes in response to the devastation caused by the floods,

Considering that Democratic Yemen, as one of the least developed countries, is unable to sustain the mounting burden of providing adequate food and shelter for the large number of people who need them,

Reaffirming the need for the international community to respond fully to requests for emergency humanitarian assistance and rehabilitation and reconstruction assistance for Democratic Yemen,

Noting with appreciation the support provided by various countries and intergovernmental and non-governmental organizations to emergency relief operations,

1. *Expresses its solidarity* with the Government and the people of Democratic Yemen in facing the devastation caused by the rain and floods;

2. *Expresses its gratitude* to the States and intergovernmental and non-governmental organizations that have rendered support and assistance to the Government of Democratic Yemen in its relief and rehabilitation efforts;

3. *Expresses its appreciation* to the Secretary-General for the steps he has taken to co-ordinate and mobilize relief and rehabilitation assistance for Democratic Yemen;

4. *Calls upon* all States to contribute generously and respond effectively to meet the urgent needs of relief operations and rehabilitation and reconstruction programmes;

5. *Requests* the Secretary-General, in close co-operation with the Government of Democratic Yemen, to co-ordinate the efforts of the United Nations system to help Democratic Yemen in its emergency, rehabilitation and reconstruction programmes, to mobilize resources for their implementation and to keep the international community informed of the needs of that country;

6. *Also requests* the Secretary-General to apprise the Economic and Social Council at its second regular session of 1989 of his efforts and to report to the General Assembly at its forty-fourth session on the implementation of the present resolution.

Economic and Social Council resolution 1989/1

10 May 1989   Meeting 8   Adopted without vote

30-nation draft (E/1989/L.14); agenda item 1.
Sponsors: Bangladesh, Brazil, Bulgaria, China, Colombia, Costa Rica, Cuba, Czechoslovakia, Egypt, France, Ghana, India, Indonesia, Iraq, Japan, Jordan, Libyan Arab Jamahiriya, Nicaragua, Oman, Saudi Arabia, Somalia, Sri Lanka, Sudan, Thailand, Tunisia, USSR, United Kingdom, Uruguay, Venezuela, Yugoslavia.

UNDP Council action. On 30 June,[14] the UNDP Governing Council, having considered Economic and Social Council resolution 1989/1, and asserting that Democratic Yemen was unable to sustain the mounting burden for the rehabilitation and reconstruction, requested the UNDP Administrator to consider the provision of additional assistance from Special Programme Resources. The Council asked the Administrator to report to it in 1990 on his efforts to implement the resolution.

GENERAL ASSEMBLY ACTION

On 19 December, on the recommendation of the Second Committee, the General Assembly adopted **resolution 44/179** without vote.

Assistance to Democratic Yemen

The General Assembly,

Deeply concerned at the extensive and unprecedented damage and devastation in Democratic Yemen caused by torrential rain and floods twice in the present decade, in March 1982 and in March and April 1989,

Extremely concerned about the destruction of the country's infrastructure, in particular roads, health centres and schools, as well as water supplies, electricity supplies, communication systems and other public utilities, and concerned that tens of thousands of hectares of cultivated land were inundated and that hundreds of villages have completely disappeared, leaving tens of thousands of persons without shelter or food,

Considering that Democratic Yemen, being one of the least developed countries, is unable to sustain rehabilitation and reconstruction programmes in spite of the efforts made by its Government,

Recalling the resolutions on assistance to Democratic Yemen that it has adopted since 1982 and taking note of Economic and Social Council resolution 1989/1 of 10 May 1989, resolution 176(XV) of 18 May 1989 adopted by the Economic and Social Commission for Western Asia at its fifteenth session and decision 89/37 of 30 June 1989 adopted by the Governing Council of the United Nations Development Programme at its thirty-sixth session,

Noting with appreciation the support provided by various States and intergovernmental and non-governmental organizations to emergency relief operations,

1. *Expresses its solidarity* with the Government and people of Democratic Yemen in facing the devastating consequences of the torrential rain and floods;

2. *Expresses its gratitude* to the States and intergovernmental and non-governmental organizations that have rendered support and assistance to the Government of Democratic Yemen in its relief and rehabilitation efforts;

3. *Expresses its appreciation* to the Secretary-General for the steps he has taken to mobilize and co-ordinate relief and rehabilitation assistance for Democratic Yemen;

4. *Calls upon* all States to contribute generously and to respond urgently and effectively to the rehabilitation and reconstruction needs of the country;

5. *Requests* the Secretary-General to co-ordinate, in close co-operation with the Government of Democratic Yemen, the efforts of the United Nations system to help Democratic Yemen to mobilize resources for the implementation of its rehabilitation and reconstruction pro-

grammes and to keep the international community informed of its needs;

6. *Also requests* the Secretary-General to report to the General Assembly at its forty-fifth session, through the Economic and Social Council at its second regular session of 1990, on the implementation of the present resolution.

General Assembly resolution 44/179

19 December 1989   Meeting 83   Adopted without vote

Approved by Second Committee (A/44/864) by consensus, 15 November (meeting 34); 38-nation draft (A/C.2/44/L.20); agenda item 88.

Sponsors: Algeria, Argentina, Bahrain, Bangladesh, Brazil, China, Colombia, Cuba, Democratic Yemen, Djibouti, Ecuador, Egypt, France, German Democratic Republic, India, Iraq, Jamaica, Japan, Jordan, Kuwait, Libyan Arab Jamahiriya, Malaysia, Mauritania, Mongolia, Morocco, Nicaragua, Oman, Peru, Qatar, Romania, Saudi Arabia, Somalia, Sudan, Tunisia, Turkey, Uruguay, Yemen, Yugoslavia.

Meeting numbers. GA 44th session: 2nd Committee 19, 20, 25, 29-31, 34; plenary 83.

Floods in Djibouti

In an October report,[15] the Secretary-General stated that in early April more than 500 millimetres (mm) of rain in three days had caused severe flooding and destroyed a major portion of the nation's social and economic infrastructure. The damage was a severe set-back to development efforts, which were already burdened by the presence of thousands of refugees and displaced persons. On 10 April, UNDRO appealed for international assistance; 11 Governments responded immediately with relief materials, food, medical supplies and equipment. Material support was also provided by the Food and Agriculture Organization of the United Nations, UNICEF, the United Nations High Commissioner for Refugees and WFP, as well as non-governmental and other relief organizations. Some Governments also provided specialized personnel for relief operations. UNDP, the Red Cross of Canada and several Governments made cash grants for emergency operations.

On 25 April, rains again flooded the town of Djibouti, worsening the precarious condition of the population. UNDRO chartered an aircraft to bring in water-pumping equipment and emergency relief supplies for the worst-affected population, and also collaborated with WHO in a nationwide anti-malaria spraying operation. UNDRO recorded total contributions and pledges of over $4.2 million for immediate relief supplies.

ECONOMIC AND SOCIAL COUNCIL ACTION

On 12 May, the Economic and Social Council adopted **resolution 1989/2** without vote.

Emergency assistance to Djibouti

The Economic and Social Council,

Deeply concerned at the extensive damage and devastation in Djibouti caused by unprecedented torrential rain and floods in April 1989,

Extremely concerned that thousands of dwellings were destroyed, especially in populated areas, and that a major portion of the nation's infrastructure has been affected, in particular roads, water supplies, health centres, hospitals, schools and other public services,

Considering the severe damage sustained by the limited agricultural resources of Djibouti, including the destruction of its livestock,

Noting that these serious problems have compounded the already existing burden created by the presence of thousands of refugees and displaced persons in the country,

Aware of the efforts made by the Government and the people of Djibouti to save lives and alleviate the sufferings of the 150,000 disaster victims,

Noting the enormous effort that will be required by Djibouti, which is a least developed country, to alleviate the grave situation caused by this natural calamity and to promote lasting and permanent solutions, such as programmes for rehabilitation and reconstruction, particularly those pertaining to the urban development works of the city of Djibouti,

Noting with gratitude the support provided to emergency relief operations by several countries and inter-governmental and non-governmental organizations,

1. *Expresses its solidarity* with the Government and the people of Djibouti in facing the devastating consequences of the torrential rains and floods;

2. *Expresses its gratitude* to the States and international institutions and non-governmental organizations that have rendered emergency relief assistance to the country;

3. *Calls upon* all States to contribute generously to the relief, rehabilitation and reconstruction efforts in Djibouti;

4. *Requests* the Secretary-General, in co-operation with international financial institutions and organizations of the United Nations system, not only to help the Government of Djibouti to strengthen its capacity to assess, predict and mitigate natural disasters, but also to assist in identifying and meeting its medium- and long-term needs, particularly with regard to its plans and programmes for rehabilitation and reconstruction;

5. *Also requests* the Secretary-General to apprise the Economic and Social Council at its second regular session of 1989 of his efforts and to report to the General Assembly at its forty-fourth session on the implementation of the present resolution.

Economic and Social Council resolution 1989/2

12 May 1989   Meeting 9   Adopted without vote

29-nation draft (E/1989/L.15); agenda item 1.

Sponsors: Bolivia, Brazil, China, Colombia, Costa Rica, Côte d'Ivoire, Djibouti, Egypt, France, Ghana, India, Iraq, Italy, Japan, Jordan, Libyan Arab Jamahiriya, Nigeria, Oman, Saudi Arabia, Somalia, Sri Lanka, Sudan, Thailand, Tunisia, United Kingdom, Viet Nam, Yugoslavia, Zaire, Zimbabwe.

GENERAL ASSEMBLY ACTION

On 19 December, on the recommendation of the Second Committee, the General Assembly adopted **resolution 44/177** without vote.

Assistance for the reconstruction and development of Djibouti

The General Assembly,

Taking note of Economic and Social Council resolution 1989/2 of 12 May 1989 and recalling the previous resolutions of the General Assembly on economic assistance to Djibouti,

Deeply concerned by the extensive damage and devastation in Djibouti caused by the unprecedented torrential rains and floods in April 1989,

Noting with concern the destruction of thousands of dwellings, particularly in working-class areas, and the damage to major sectors of the national infrastructure, particularly the road network, the water supply, health centres and hospitals, educational establishments and other public services,

Considering the severe damage to the scarce agricultural resources of Djibouti, including the destruction of its livestock,

Noting that the economic and social development efforts of Djibouti, which is included in the list of least developed countries, are thwarted by the negative consequences of the torrential rains and floods that periodically devastate that vulnerable country, and that the implementation of reconstruction and development programmes requires the deployment of considerable resources which exceed the real capacities of the country,

Taking note of the reports of the Secretary-General to the Economic and Social Council at its second regular session of 1989 and to the General Assembly at its forty-fourth session,

Noting with gratitude the support provided to emergency relief operations by various countries and intergovernmental and non-governmental organizations,

1. *Expresses its solidarity* with the Government and people of Djibouti in facing the devastating consequences of the torrential rains and floods;

2. *Expresses its gratitude* to the States, international institutions and non-governmental organizations that have provided emergency relief to that country and, in that connection, notes with satisfaction that the Office of the United Nations Disaster Relief Co-ordinator has undertaken a mission to strengthen the capacity of the Government of Djibouti with respect to disaster prevention and preparedness;

3. *Calls upon* the Secretary-General, in co-operation with the concerned organs and organizations of the United Nations system and in close collaboration with the Government authorities, to carry out an evaluation of the requirements of Djibouti with a view to drawing up an urgent programme of rehabilitation and reconstruction following the damage to the infrastructure of the country;

4. *Also calls upon* the Secretary-General to ensure that the international community is informed of those requirements in order that it may respond favourably to them;

5. *Requests* the Secretary-General to continue and intensify his efforts to mobilize all possible assistance within the United Nations system to help the Government of Djibouti in its reconstruction and development efforts;

6. *Encourages* the specialized agencies, organizations and programmes of the United Nations system to intensify their programmes of assistance and to expand them in response to the needs of Djibouti;

7. *Requests* the Secretary-General to report to the General Assembly at its forty-fifth session, through the Economic and Social Council at its second regular session of 1990, on the progress made in the implementation of the present resolution.

General Assembly resolution 44/177

19 December 1989   Meeting 83   Adopted without vote

Approved by Second Committee (A/44/864) by consensus, 15 November (meeting 34); 41-nation draft (A/C.2/44/L.18), orally revised; agenda item 88.

Sponsors: Algeria, Argentina, Bahrain, Bangladesh, Brazil, Burkina Faso, Burundi, Cameroon, Central African Republic, Chad, China, Colombia, Côte d'Ivoire, Democratic Yemen, Djibouti, Ecuador, Egypt, France, Guinea, Guinea-Bissau, India, Indonesia, Iraq, Italy, Japan, Jordan, Lebanon, Libyan Arab Jamahiriya, Madagascar, Mauritania, Morocco, Pakistan, Qatar, Saudi Arabia, Singapore, Sudan, Tunisia, Turkey, United Arab Emirates, Yemen, Yugoslavia.

Meeting numbers. GA 44th session: 2nd Committee 19, 20, 25, 29-31, 34; plenary 83.

Emergencies in China

Earthquakes, a hailstorm, typhoons, floods and landslides struck several provinces of China in 1988-1989. In his report[1] on UNDRO activities, the Secretary-General noted that UNDRO had been involved in 12 major events affecting more than 100 million people, including earthquakes and a hailstorm in Sichuan province in April 1989, a typhoon in Guangdong province in June of the same year, floods and landslides in Sichuan province in July, a typhoon in Zhejiang and Jiangsu provinces in September, and earthquakes in Shanxi province in October. UNDRO promptly provided $50,000 in cash grants to meet immediate needs until other assistance arrived. Australia, Canada and the Netherlands channelled their contributions through UNDRO and UNDP. Contributions for relief for China reported to UNDRO in 1989 totalled $4.9 million.

Other disasters

Earthquake in Algeria

The Secretary-General reported[1] that, on 29 October 1989, an earthquake measuring 6.0 on the Richter scale shook the northern provinces of Algeria, causing more than 30 deaths and injuring 700 persons. UNDRO organized an immediate air lift of 80 metric tons of relief supplies, valued at $500,000, which were distributed among 2,000 homeless families. On 17 November, winter tents and blankets were also airlifted to Algeria.

Earthquake in the Soviet Socialist Republic of Tajikistan

The Secretary-General reported[1] that, on 23 January 1989, an earthquake measuring 5.8 on the Richter scale struck the Soviet Socialist Republic of Tajikistan, triggering a massive mudflow of more than 10 million cubic metres that affected an area 1 kilometre (km) wide and 8 km long. Deposits in one area were 25 metres high. Some 200 lives were lost and more than 50,000 people were left homeless. UNDRO's supply depot in Pisa had been depleted by relief operations following the December 1988 Armenian earthquake but a $484,000 contribution from the United Kingdom allowed UNDRO to purchase winter tents, diesel heaters, blankets and boots, and to establish shelters in Tajikistan. Later in the year, UNDRO and the USSR organized a training seminar on the management of mudflows and landslides caused by earthquakes.

Locust and grasshopper infestation in Africa

UNDP action. In a January 1989 report[16] on alternative strategies for desert locust control, the UNDP Administrator stated that, despite international efforts, a major desert locust outbreak had occurred since 1985, and could affect as many as 60 countries. The Administrator had taken the initiative in early 1988 to investigate whether alternatives to synthetic pesticides might be developed, and UNDP convened a meeting on the development of environmentally acceptable alternatives for desert locust control in Cairo in December 1988, which was attended by representatives of Governments, international organizations and scientists.

On 24 February 1989,[17] the Governing Council noted the Administrator's proposals for research on alternative approaches to desert locust control, and agreed that he should continue consultations with a view towards presenting more specific proposals to the Council.

In a June decision,[18] the Governing Council approved the global project for the development of environmentally acceptable alternative strategies for desert locust control,[19] including the establishment of a scientific advisory panel, to be jointly selected by UNDP and FAO as programme co-sponsors. The decision stated that consideration would be given to the need to involve African-based scientists and institutions, and that progress reports would be submitted to the panel and to FAO's Desert Locust Control Commission.

Report of the Secretary-General. In accordance with a 1988 General Assembly resolution,[20] the Secretary-General submitted a June report[21] on the international strategy for the fight against locust and grasshopper infestation, particularly in Africa. The report said that, whereas recent scientific evidence suggested that the current locust and grasshopper plague might be diminishing, May rains had produced new infestations and discouraged optimism. In early June, therefore, the Secretary-General had called the attention of heads of relevant UN organizations to the continued risk of new outbreaks, and urged them to maintain their vigilance and their assistance to affected countries.

Donor countries had been extremely responsive to the 1988 Assembly resolution, and the United Nations Environment Programme (UNEP) and the World Meteorological Organization had contributed their expertise. In January, the Secretary-General organized a United Nations task force, under the chairmanship of the Director-General for Development and International Economic Co-operation, to ensure co-ordination and support for the efforts of FAO against locust and grasshopper infestations. The task force was composed of executive and department heads of UNDP, ECA, UNDRO, UNEP, the Department for Special Political Questions, Regional Co-operation, Decolonization and Trusteeship, and the Department of Technical Co-operation for Development. Members of the task force participated in meetings on locust and grasshopper control held in Rome, Italy, and in Rabat, Morocco. The report noted that between 1986 and 1989, UNDP provided approximately $2.4 million in financial assistance to national programmes for desert locust control.

FAO report. In response to a 1988 General Assembly resolution,[20] the Secretary-General submitted in June a report[22] by the Director-General of FAO on the international strategy for the fight against the locust and grasshopper infestation, particularly in Africa. The report stated that there had been a dramatic decline in the desert locust plague in Africa and the Near East in late 1988 and early 1989. Large-scale ground and aerial control operations had eliminated the great majority of high-density populations, while a massive westward movement of adult locusts from West Africa in October 1988 had drowned a tremendous number in the Atlantic. The virtual failure of the winter rains in countries bordering the Red Sea caused further reductions. But because low-density populations and a few swarms remained in the region, the threat persisted of a rapid recrudescence of the plague, depending on the duration and intensity of summer rains.

In a later report[23] the Director-General stated that during the second half of 1989, no major incidents of desert locust infestation were reported in Africa and the Near East, though there was a small outbreak in India and Pakistan. Infestations of Moroccan locusts in north-western Afghanistan, however, caused heavy damage to the wheat crop. Grasshoppers caused heavy local damage to millet and sorghum in most Sahelian countries. In a note attached to the report, the Secretary-General stated that two meetings of donors were held during the year, under the joint chairmanship of UNDP and FAO, to develop a consensus for the formation of a Consultative Group for Locust Control Research (CGLR). Composed primarily of donors and representatives from locust-affected countries, CGLR was expected to co-ordinate support for desert locust research and to review recent technical progress. An external Scientific Advisory Committee (SAC) was nominated to advise CGLR on its work. Donors provided more than $66.5 million in assistance for locust and grasshopper control in 1989.

ECONOMIC AND SOCIAL COUNCIL ACTION

On 26 July, the Economic and Social Council, on the recommendation of its Third Committee, adopted **resolution 1989/98** without vote.

International strategy for the fight against locust and grasshopper infestation, particularly in Africa
The Economic and Social Council,

Recalling General Assembly resolutions 41/185 of 8 December 1986 and 43/203 of 20 December 1988, Economic and Social Council resolutions 1988/2 of 5 February 1988 and 1988/3 of 24 May 1988 and resolution 660(XXIV) of 7 April 1989 of the Conference of Ministers of the Economic Commission for Africa,

Bearing in mind Economic and Social Council resolution 1989/99 of 26 July 1989 on the International Decade for Natural Disaster Reduction, and aware that the Decade will cover locust and grasshopper infestations,

Noting with satisfaction the almost general decline of locust and grasshopper infestations, owing to the determined efforts of the affected countries and the generous assistance of the international community,

Noting also the results of the Conference of Heads of State of the countries members of the Joint Anti-Locust and Anti-Avarian Organization held at Dakar in February 1989,

Conscious of the risk of a rapid resurgence of the locust and grasshopper infestation and of the possible reappearance of swarms as a result of widespread and abundant rainfall in the Saharan region and in other regions of the world,

Noting that small to medium-sized swarms of desert locusts have been reported or are anticipated in several Saharan countries between June and mid-August 1989 by the Emergency Centre for Locust Operations of the Food and Agriculture Organization of the United Nations,

Considering that a number of countries, particularly the poorest countries, have still to overcome the complex and harmful effects of the recent disastrous locust and grasshopper infestation,

1. *Takes note with interest* of the report of the Secretary-General and of that of the Director-General of the Food and Agriculture Organization of the United Nations on the implementation of the international strategy for the fight against locust and grasshopper infestation, particularly in Africa;

2. *Welcomes* the creation of the International Desert Locust Task Force under the technical and operational responsibility of the Food and Agriculture Organization of the United Nations for the purpose of providing direct support to the countries affected, particularly seriously infested or relatively inaccessible regions;

3. *Also welcomes* the generous and effective co-operation that exists in this regard among the States members of the Maghreb Arab Union;

4. *Further welcomes* the appeal of the Conference of Heads of State of the countries members of the Joint Anti-Locust and Anti-Avarian Organization to the international community to support the organization strongly in the rigorous implementation of the plan of action in the short, medium and long terms to combat locusts, adopted by the Council of Ministers of the organization at its twenty-fourth session, held at N'Djamena from 10 to 16 December 1988;

5. *Expresses its support* for the long-term research initiatives of the Food and Agriculture Organization of the United Nations, the United Nations Development Programme and a number of Governments aimed at further developing more effective, economical and environmentally sound control methods along with short-term activities and medium-term programmes for prevention and environmentally acceptable alternative long-term strategies for locust and grasshopper control;

6. *Invites* the Food and Agriculture Organization of the United Nations to continue to play its role as lead agency in locust control and related research activities, in close collaboration with other competent organizations and institutions, and to ensure that the proposals and plans of the International Desert Locust Task Force are implemented and fully complement the activities of national and regional authorities and donor activities;

7. *Notes* that, although the present desert locust plague appears to have receded, continued vigilance will be required on the part of all concerned with regard to the locust population still present and the new swarms reported in several Saharan countries;

8. *Expresses its appreciation* to the international community for the assistance provided to the affected countries, and calls for continued support for short-term, medium-term and long-term efforts to control locusts and grasshoppers;

9. *Appeals* to the international community, particularly the developed countries, to make the necessary resources available to the Food and Agriculture Organization of the United Nations and to co-operate with it in further developing remote-sensing techniques, training, the testing and evaluation of pesticides, the collection and dissemination of information, prevention, co-ordination and funding, and in establishing or strengthening national and regional early-warning systems in order to improve the ability of affected or vulnerable countries to cope with future threats;

10. *Endorses* the appeal made by the Secretary-General to the executive heads of other organizations of the United Nations system to remain vigilant and not to lose the expertise acquired in the past two years in controlling locust and grasshopper infestations, and requests the Director-General of the Food and Agriculture Organization of the United Nations to submit to the Economic and Social Council at its second regular session of 1990 an up-to-date report on the implementation of the international strategy for the fight against locust and grasshopper infestation, particularly in Africa.

Economic and Social Council resolution 1989/98

26 July 1989   Meeting 35   Adopted without vote

Approved by Third Committee (E/1989/130) without vote, 20 July (meeting 15); 5-nation draft (E/1989/C.3/L.6/Rev.1); agenda item 12.
Sponsors: Cameroon, Mauritania, Niger, Poland, Somalia.

GENERAL ASSEMBLY ACTION

On 19 December, the General Assembly, by **decision 44/438**, endorsed Economic and Social Council resolution 1989/98.

Disaster prevention and preparedness

In his report[1] on UNDRO activities during 1988 and 1989, the Secretary-General stated that disaster mitigation fell into two broad categories: technical and preventive measures, and logistical planning or preparedness activities. The comprehensive disaster mitigation programmes recommended by UNDRO, which were implemented with UNDRO assistance in a number of countries, involved a series of five steps, namely: to determine the hazards; to assess the vulnerability of people and property; to identify and implement the most cost-effective measures for reducing vulnerability; to develop logistical plans for responding to imminent disaster threats and providing post-disaster assistance; and to ensure that such plans were properly understood by local officials and the general population. In recent years, the Secretary-General reported, the United Nations had undertaken regional and national disaster mitigation projects in Africa, Asia, Latin America and the Caribbean, the Mediterranean and the South Pacific. During the biennium, UNDRO organized or participated in regional and national seminars and training programmes. An international training seminar on lessons learned from the management of recent earthquakes was held in October 1989 in Moscow.

International Decade for Natural Disaster Reduction

In accordance with 1987[24] and 1988[25] resolutions, the Secretary-General submitted a report in June 1989[26] on natural disasters and responses to them, and preparations for the International Decade for Natural Disaster Reduction in the 1990s. During the previous two decades, he said, natural disasters had resulted in about 3 million deaths and had adversely affected at least 800 million people, causing immediate damages in the hundreds of billions of dollars. The Secretary-General reported that the impact of disasters, particularly severe in developing countries, could be reduced through improved risk assessment and disaster preparedness.

The International *Ad Hoc* Group of Experts, appointed by the Secretary-General in 1988, met at Rabat, Morocco, in January 1989 and in Tokyo in April 1989. On the recommendation of the United Nations, several Governments created national committees for the Decade, or designated a national focal point. The Secretary-General outlined those organizations and institutions he believed should play a major role in implementing the Decade, and described the four categories of activities that the Group had suggested as a basis for national programmes: hazard prediction, risk assessment, disaster preparedness and disaster management. The Secretary-General supported the Group's view that the most important efforts to mitigate the impacts of disasters must be undertaken at national and local levels.

An annex to the report contained the Tokyo Declaration on the International Decade for Natural Disaster Reduction, adopted by the Group on 11 April 1989. It called for global support for the Decade, described the role of national committees, and suggested that the United Nations create a mechanism to fund and support the Decade.

ECONOMIC AND SOCIAL COUNCIL ACTION

By **resolution 1989/99** of 26 July, the Economic and Social Council, taking note of the Secretary-General's report, expressed its appreciation for the work of the International *Ad Hoc* Group of Experts, and recommended that the General Assembly take action to develop an appropriate framework for international co-operation to attain the Decade's goals. The Council asked that the Group's full report be submitted to the Assembly.

Report of the International *Ad Hoc* Group of Experts. In response to the Economic and Social Council's request, the Secretary-General submitted to the General Assembly the full report[27] of the International *Ad Hoc* Group of Experts on the International Decade for Natural Disaster Reduction. It stated that the Decade represented an opportunity for the world community to use existing scientific and technical knowledge to reduce the damage done by natural disasters, but that the implementation of an effective disaster prevention programme might require organization and education far exceeding the economic capacity and organizational ability of a single nation. Consequently, regionally integrated programmes would be needed.

The elements of an integrated approach to disaster management and the types of natural disaster to be covered by the Decade were outlined, as well as impediments to disaster reduction. The Group described the Decade as an opportunity to link ongoing activities and to apply scientific and technological breakthroughs. A plan of action for implementing the goals of the Decade would have to set targets for activities in widely differing regions and at various levels, establish procedures for allocating resources and suggest structures for co-ordinating activities.

The benefits of natural disaster warning systems, integrated disaster management, hazard modification and locust research were noted. The main bodies the Group considered important to co-ordinated action during the Decade included representatives of UN organizations, individual countries, regional groups, scientific organizations, research institutions, insurance and financial institutions, the media, civil protection organizations and donors. Organizational criteria for the Decade's successful implementation were given, and included the establishment of a board of trustees,

a committee, a secretariat and a trust fund. International and regional forums and an international day for disaster preparedness were among the activities proposed for the Decade's initial phase.

In an addendum,[28] the Secretary-General provided details of various projects proposed for global and regional application during the Decade. A common characteristic of the projects was that they were based on readily available technology and thus did not require significant basic research, and could yield rapid results. They also showed a shift from post-disaster relief to pre-disaster preparedness and had potential for regional application. Planning for several of the projects had already started in the respective UN entities proposing them.

GENERAL ASSEMBLY ACTION

On 22 December, the General Assembly, on the recommendation of the Second Committee, adopted **resolution 44/236** without vote.

International Decade for Natural Disaster Reduction
The General Assembly,

Recalling its resolution 42/169 of 11 December 1987, in which it decided to designate the 1990s as a decade in which the international community, under the auspices of the United Nations, would pay special attention to fostering international co-operation in the field of natural disaster reduction,

Bearing in mind the relevant provisions of its resolution 42/169 and its resolution 43/202 of 20 December 1988, and taking note of Economic and Social Council resolution 1989/99 of 26 July 1989, in which the Council recommended that the General Assembly take action to develop an appropriate framework for international co-operation to attain the objective and goals of the International Decade for Natural Disaster Reduction,

Considering that natural disasters have adversely affected the lives of a great number of people and caused considerable damage to infrastructure and property world wide, especially in developing countries,

Recognizing the importance of environmental protection for the prevention and mitigation of natural disasters,

Considering that the international community as a whole has now improved its capacity to confront this problem and that fatalism about natural disasters is no longer justified,

Recognizing the necessity for the international community to demonstrate the strong political determination required to mobilize and use existing scientific and technical knowledge to mitigate natural disasters, bearing in mind in particular the needs of developing countries,

Recognizing also the important responsibility of the United Nations system as a whole for promoting international co-operation in order to mitigate natural disasters, provide assistance and co-ordinate disaster relief, preparedness and prevention,

Recalling the specific responsibilities and functions in the field of disaster prevention and preparedness entrusted to the Office of the United Nations Disaster Relief Co-ordinator, as set out in its resolution 2816(XXVI) of 14 December 1971,

Bearing in mind the crucial role of professional and other non-governmental organizations, particularly scientific and technological societies, humanitarian groups and investment institutions, the participation of which in the implementation of specific programmes planned for the Decade is highly desirable,

Also bearing in mind the need for the United Nations system to pay special attention to the least developed, land-locked and island developing countries in that regard,

Emphasizing that appropriate emergency planning for natural disasters and its integration in national development plans could also be very helpful in preventing other kinds of disasters, such as those of an industrial or technological nature,

Taking note with appreciation of the report of the Secretary-General,

Expressing its appreciation for the work done by the International *Ad Hoc* Group of Experts on the International Decade for Natural Disaster Reduction, which submitted its report to the Secretary-General,

Bearing in mind the common position on natural disasters of the Ninth Conference of Heads of State or Government of Non-Aligned Countries, held at Belgrade from 4 to 7 September 1989,

1. *Proclaims* the International Decade for Natural Disaster Reduction, beginning on 1 January 1990;

2. *Decides* to designate the second Wednesday of October International Day for Natural Disaster Reduction, to be observed annually during the Decade by the international community in a manner befitting the objective and goals of the Decade;

3. *Adopts* the International Framework of Action for the International Decade for Natural Disaster Reduction contained in the annex to the present resolution;

4. *Requests* the Secretary-General to submit to the General Assembly at its forty-fifth session a progress report on the implementation of the present resolution, including the organizational arrangements made for the Decade, and on the status of existing international protocols and conventions for mutual assistance in cases of disaster;

5. *Also requests* the Secretary-General to bring the present resolution to the attention of all Governments, intergovernmental organizations, appropriate non-governmental organizations in consultative status with the Economic and Social Council and competent scientific institutions in the field of disaster mitigation;

6. *Decides* to include in the provisional agenda of its forty-sixth session an item entitled "International Decade for Natural Disaster Reduction".

ANNEX
International Framework of Action for the International Decade for Natural Disaster Reduction

A. Objective and goals

1. The objective of the International Decade for Natural Disaster Reduction is to reduce through concerted international action, especially in developing countries, the loss of life, property damage and social and economic disruption caused by natural disasters such as earthquakes, windstorms, tsunamis, floods, landslides, volcanic eruptions, wildfires, grasshopper and locust infestations, drought and desertification and other calamities of natural origin.

2. The goals of the Decade are:

(*a*) To improve the capacity of each country to mitigate the effects of natural disasters expeditiously and effectively, paying special attention to assisting developing countries in the assessment of disaster damage potential and in the establishment of early-warning systems and disaster-resistant structures when and where needed;

(*b*) To devise appropriate guidelines and strategies for applying existing scientific and technical knowledge, taking into account the cultural and economic diversity among nations;

(*c*) To foster scientific and engineering endeavours aimed at closing critical gaps in knowledge in order to reduce loss of life and property;

(*d*) To disseminate existing and new technical information related to measures for the assessment, prediction and mitigation of natural disasters;

(*e*) To develop measures for the assessment, prediction, prevention and mitigation of natural disasters through programmes of technical assistance and technology transfer, demonstration projects, and education and training, tailored to specific disasters and locations, and to evaluate the effectiveness of those programmes.

B. Policy measures to be taken at the national level

3. All Governments are called upon:

(*a*) To formulate national disaster-mitigation programmes, as well as economic, land-use and insurance policies for disaster prevention, and, particularly in developing countries, to integrate them fully into their national development programmes;

(*b*) To participate during the Decade in concerted international action for the reduction of natural disasters and, as appropriate, establish national committees in co-operation with the relevant scientific and technological communities and other concerned sectors with a view to attaining the objective and goals of the Decade;

(*c*) To encourage their local administrations to take appropriate steps to mobilize the necessary support from the public and private sectors and to contribute to the achievement of the purposes of the Decade;

(*d*) To keep the Secretary-General informed of the plans of their countries and of assistance that can be provided so that the United Nations may become an international centre for the exchange of information and the co-ordination of international efforts concerning activities in support of the objective and goals of the Decade, thus enabling each State to benefit from the experience of other countries;

(*e*) To take measures, as appropriate, to increase public awareness of damage risk probabilities and of the significance of preparedness, prevention, relief and short-term recovery activities with respect to natural disasters and to enhance community preparedness through education, training and other means, taking into account the specific role of the news media;

(*f*) To pay due attention to the impact of natural disasters on health care, particularly to activities to reduce the vulnerability of hospitals and health centres, as well as the impact on food storage facilities, human shelter and other social and economic infrastructures;

(*g*) To improve the early international availability of appropriate emergency supplies through the storage or earmarking of such supplies in disaster-prone areas.

4. Scientific and technological institutions, financial institutions, including banks and insurance companies, and industrial enterprises, foundations and other related non-governmental organizations are encouraged to support and participate fully in the programmes and activities of the Decade prepared and implemented by the international community, including Governments, international organizations and non-governmental organizations.

C. Action to be taken by the United Nations system

5. The organs, organizations and bodies of the United Nations system are urged to accord priority, as appropriate and in a concerted manner, to natural disaster preparedness, prevention, relief and short-term recovery, including economic damage risk assessment, in their operational activities; the Secretary-General is requested, in this regard, to ensure that adequate means are made available to the Office of the United Nations Disaster Relief Co-ordinator so that it may diligently discharge its specific role and responsibilities in the field of disaster mitigation and response in conformity with its mandate, as contained in General Assembly resolution 2816(XXVI).

6. The Secretary-General is requested, in close association with the relevant organizations of the United Nations system, in particular through the Department of Public Information of the Secretariat, as well as national information authorities, to assist in the formulation and implementation during the Decade of public information programmes aimed at raising public awareness of disaster prevention.

7. The United Nations resident co-ordinators and the field representatives of the United Nations system are requested to work closely and in a co-ordinated manner with Governments to achieve the objective and goals of the Decade.

8. The regional commissions are urged to play an active role in implementing the activities of the Decade, considering that natural disasters often transcend national boundaries.

9. The Secretary-General is requested to designate the Director-General for Development and International Economic Co-operation, in accordance with his mandate as set out in General Assembly resolution 32/197 of 20 December 1977, as the focal point for overview and co-ordination of the programmes and activities of the United Nations system referred to in the present resolution, in close co-operation with the Office of the United Nations Disaster Relief Co-ordinator and, as appropriate, in consultation with the Director of the secretariat of the Decade, mentioned in paragraph 14 of the present annex.

10. The Secretary-General is requested to report biennially to the General Assembly, through the Economic and Social Council, on the activities of the Decade.

D. Organizational arrangements during the Decade

1. Special high-level council

11. The Secretary-General is requested to establish, with due regard to equitable geographical representation, a special high-level council, consisting of a limited number of internationally prominent persons, which would provide him with general advice with respect to the Decade, take appropriate action to promote public awareness and mobilize the necessary support from the public and private sectors.

2. Scientific and technical committee on the International Decade for Natural Disaster Reduction

12. The Secretary-General is requested to establish, with due regard to equitable geographical representation and covering the diversity of disaster-mitigation issues, a scientific and technical committee on the International Decade for Natural Disaster Reduction, consisting of twenty to twenty-five scientific and technical experts selected in consultation with their Governments on the basis of their personal capacities and qualifications, including experts from the organs, organizations and bodies of the United Nations system.

13. The role of the committee shall be to develop overall programmes to be taken into account in bilateral and multilateral co-operation for the Decade, paying attention to priorities and gaps in technical knowledge identified at the national level, in particular by national committees, as well as to assess and evaluate the activities carried out in the course of the Decade and to make recommendations on the overall programmes in an annual report to the Secretary-General.

3. Secretariat

14. The Secretary-General is requested to establish a small secretariat, to be funded by extrabudgetary resources, as follows:

(a) The secretariat shall be established at the United Nations Office at Geneva, in close association with the Office of the United Nations Disaster Relief Co-ordinator, with its members drawn, as appropriate, from the international community of disaster reduction experts and other relevant experts seconded, *inter alia*, from competent United Nations organizations, Governments and non-governmental organizations;

(b) The secretariat shall be responsible for the day-to-day co-ordination of Decade activities and shall provide substantive and secretarial support to the special high-level council and the scientific and technical committee, as well as for other related activities.

E. Financial arrangements

15. It is recommended that extrabudgetary resources be provided for implementation of the activities of the Decade and, therefore, that voluntary contributions from Governments, international organizations and other sources, including the private sector, be strongly encouraged; to this end, a trust fund shall be established by the Secretary-General, who will be entrusted with its administration.

F. Review

16. The Economic and Social Council, during its second regular session of 1994, will carry out a mid-term review of the implementation of the International Framework of Action for the International Decade for Natural Disaster Reduction and report its findings to the General Assembly.

General Assembly resolution 44/236

22 December 1989   Meeting 85   Adopted without vote

Approved by Second Committee (A/44/832/Add.1) without vote, 11 December (meeting 49); draft by Albania, Austria, Belgium, Bulgaria, Byelorussian SSR, Canada, China, Czechoslovakia, Finland, France, German Democratic Republic, Greece, Hungary, Iceland, Ireland, Italy, Japan, Luxembourg, Malaysia for Group of 77, New Zealand, Norway, Poland, Portugal, Spain, Turkey, Ukrainian SSR, USSR, United States (A/C.2/44/L.31/Rev.2), orally revised; agenda item 12.

Financial implications. 5th Committee, A/44/884; S-G, A/C.2/44/L.37/Rev.1, A/C.5/44/48.
Meeting numbers. GA 44th session: 2nd Committee 15-17, 19, 20, 25, 29, 31, 34, 41, 44, 46, 48, 49; 5th Committee 53, 57, 58; plenary 85.

Solutions to natural disasters in Bangladesh

In accordance with a 1988 General Assembly resolution[29] which appealed to the international community to help strengthen the disaster mitigation capacity of Bangladesh, the Secretary-General submitted a report[30] in October on short-, medium- and long-term solutions to the problem of natural disasters in that country. Three great rivers have their confluence in Bangladesh, which is plagued by damaging floods.

Recent efforts by the Government to step up its disaster response capacity included the creation of a 1.4 million-ton stockpile of food supplies, stored at strategic locations throughout the country, and the establishment of a National Disaster Prevention Council. Several UN bodies had provided assistance to Bangladesh, including the Secretariat's Department of Technical Co-operation for Development, UNICEF, UNDP, the United Nations Population Fund, WFP, the International Labour Organisation, the Food and Agriculture Organization of the United Nations, the World Health Organization, the United Nations Industrial Development Organization, the World Meteorological Organization and the International Development Association. In September 1989, UNDRO launched an appeal for international assistance on behalf of the Government, which brought donations of more than $100 million within six weeks. United Nations efforts towards a long-term solution to Bangladesh flooding should be one of the major activities of the International Decade for Natural Disaster Reduction, according to the report, which also recommended that the Government organize pre- and post-disaster activities under a co-ordinated national disaster preparedness and relief strategy. Disaster mitigation in Bangladesh should not be seen as a separate activity, but as a part of all development planning.

In **decision 44/443** of 22 December 1989, the General Assembly took note of the report.

Disasters and nutrition

Nutrition in Times of Disaster (27-30 September 1988), organized by WHO and UNHCR, encouraged donors and disaster-affected countries to ensure that food rations for victims were nutritionally adequate and proposed a minimum daily standard (see also PART THREE, Chapter XI). In a note[31] to the Economic and Social Council, the Secretary-General drew attention to a decision of ACC, which noted with concern the prospect of a continuing need for food relief for some 20 million displaced persons, endorsed the statement of

the Conference and brought it to the attention of the Council. The Council took note of the ACC decision in its **decision 1989/175** of 26 July.

REFERENCES

[1]A/45/271. [2]YUN 1987, p. 451. [3]*Ibid.*, p. 452, GA dec. 42/433, 11 Dec. 1987. [4]YUN 1988, p. 384, GA res. 43/218 A, 21 Dec. 1988. [5]DP/1990/61. [6]E/1989/32 (dec. 89/54). [7]DP/1989/50. [8]YUN 1987, p. 702, GA res. 42/188, 11 Dec. 1987. [9]A/44/296. [10]UNEP/GC.15/9/Add.4. [11]A/44/243. [12]A/44/627. [13]A/45/358/Add.1. [14]E/1989/32 (dec. 89/37). [15]A/44/629. [16]DP/1989/66. [17]E/1989/32 (dec. 89/14). [18]*Ibid.* (dec. 89/42). [19]DP/PROJECTS/REL/23. [20]YUN 1988, p. 392, GA res. 43/203, 20 Dec. 1988. [21]A/44/314. [22]A/44/314/Add.1. [23]E/1990/59. [24]YUN 1987, p. 459, GA res. 42/169, 11 Dec. 1987. [25]YUN 1988, p. 394, GA res. 43/202, 20 Dec. 1988. [26]A/44/322. [27]A/44/322/Add.1. [28]A/44/322/Add.2. [29]YUN 1988, p. 387, GA res. 43/9, 18 Oct. 1988. [30]A/44/434. [31]E/1989/101.

Emergency relief and assistance

Afghanistan

The Office of the United Nations Co-ordinator for Humanitarian and Economic Assistance Programmes Relating to Afghanistan (UNOCA) issued its second consolidated report on Afghanistan[1] in October 1989. Hopes for peace had not been realized, and the overall refugee situation remained largely unchanged; however, the capacity of the United Nations and its operational partners to cope effectively inside Afghanistan with a massive refugee return had improved significantly. Much of the country had been visited by UN assessment missions. Offices and sub-offices for UNOCA's Operation Salam were established, from which aid commodities could be delivered. Scores of UN-funded assistance projects were initiated inside the country, while large-scale pre-positioning of aid commodities had been accomplished in bordering areas. By September 1989, UNDP, UNICEF, UNHCR, the United Nations Fund for Drug Abuse Control, the United Nations Volunteers, FAO, WFP and WHO were all engaged in a concerted effort to implement a broad range of projects, while additional programmes prepared by ILO and UNESCO awaited funding.

The United Nations Plan of Action 1989, prepared in March 1989 through inter-agency consultation, provided a framework for economic and humanitarian assistance for the year. Under the plan, projects were being implemented in agriculture, food aid, public health, mother and child care, public works, mine clearance, emergency aid to disadvantaged groups, crop substitution, rural reconstruction, vocational training, educational rehabilitation and the promotion of an institutional capacity for recovery and rehabilitation. Funding was inadequate, and, according to the report, some activities (such as road repair, anti-narcotics programmes, education and help for the disabled) would make little progress unless additional contributions were received. Given the unlikely prospect of early military or political solutions to the conflict, massive UN-system–managed multilateral economic and humanitarian assistance through the "humanitarian encirclement" of Afghanistan offered the best prospect of stability.

By September 1989, the UNDP/UNOCA NGO support and rural works programme, designed to assist small, grass-roots-level activities, had financed 20 projects, with more in planning. The report noted that there was a limit to what the United Nations could ask of non-governmental organizations (NGOs) and that Afghan partners who could meet the financial and reporting requirements of UN agencies would have to be identified—a far-from-easy task given conflicting groups and interests. Above all, the lack of funding remained a serious problem. Although total donor contributions of $991.5 million had been reported by September 1989, $694.3 million were contributions in kind, by far the greater part of which had not yet been received. Actual cash received by the Co-ordinator in the Afghanistan Emergency Trust Fund as at 31 August totalled $157.8 million, of which $90.5 million was earmarked for specific agencies. In addition, approximately $102 million had been paid by donors directly to UN agencies and other organizations.

Between September 1988 and July 1989, seven fact-finding missions visited Afghanistan to help the Co-ordinator formulate relief and rehabilitation strategies and programmes. Salam Mobile Units (SMUs) established a more durable presence inside the country, undertook more in-depth analyses, created working relationships with local partners and delivered aid. The report also chronicled the work of field monitoring missions, progress in data collection, and population movements and responses to them by UN agencies, particularly UNHCR. Agricultural and food assistance was outlined, as was the mine-clearance programme and UN efforts towards the reconstruction of Afghanistan's roads, shelters, irrigation and water supplies, power plants, and telecommunication and health services. Other aspects addressed in the report included establishment of field offices in Afghanistan and neighbouring countries; delivery of medical supplies; a health manpower training programme and several other health-related activities; assistance with education and training; and the establishment of a logistics and transport operation named UNILOG, based in Pakistan. Summaries of the situation in, and assistance for, each of Afghanistan's 28 provinces were given.

Romania

On 27 December, Romania[2] requested the inclusion of an additional item in the General Assembly agenda entitled "Emergency humanitarian assistance to Romania", for priority consideration. An explanatory memorandum stated that as a result of recent events in Romania there had been a tremendous loss of life, and humanitarian assistance was urgently needed for a large number of other persons who were suffering.

In his report on the 1989 work and activities of UNDRO,[3] the Secretary-General noted that, following civil strife in late 1989, the UNDRO appeal for relief assistance on 22 December met with a massive but unco-ordinated international response. That situation created logistical problems, and on 28 December Romania accepted an UNDRO offer of help. A relief co-ordination officer travelled to Bucharest, met with Romania's new leaders, assisted with the co-ordination of international emergency assistance, and helped establish a National Committee for the Co-ordination of Humanitarian Aid. The Committee and UNDRO also co-ordinated the mobilization of a Romanian trucking fleet and refrigerated trains to collect relief supplies from European donation points.

GENERAL ASSEMBLY ACTION

On 28 December, the General Assembly adopted **resolution 44/239** without vote.

Emergency humanitarian assistance to Romania
The General Assembly,
Expressing its concern at the loss of human lives and at the large number of afflicted persons in Romania,
Noting the need for emergency humanitarian assistance to the people of Romania,
Urges all States, international financial institutions and organizations and programmes of the United Nations system, as a matter of urgency, to offer generous emergency humanitarian assistance to Romania.

General Assembly resolution 44/239

28 December 1989   Meeting 86   Adopted without vote

43-nation draft (A/44/L.64); agenda item 161.
Sponsors: Algeria, Argentina, Australia, Austria, Belgium, Bulgaria, Canada, Colombia, Costa Rica, Cyprus, Czechoslovakia, Democratic Yemen, Denmark, Finland, France, German Democratic Republic, Germany, Federal Republic of, Greece, Guatemala, Hungary, Iceland, Iran, Ireland, Italy, Japan, Libyan Arab Jamahiriya, Luxembourg, Morocco, Netherlands, Norway, Poland, Portugal, Romania, Spain, Sudan, Sweden, Tunisia, Turkey, USSR, United Kingdom, United States, Venezuela, Yugoslavia.

Somalia

The Secretary-General, in accordance with a 1988 General Assembly resolution,[4] submitted a May 1989 report[5] on emergency assistance to Somalia. Unrest in northern Somalia in 1988 had led to armed conflict in the north-west, with devastating consequences for populations in the region. In addition to deaths and disablement, the region suffered destruction of property and facilities, and disruption of civil administration, education, banking, livestock movements and trade. Massive population movements took place both within Somalia and across borders into neighbouring countries, with some northern urban cities becoming "ghost cities". Security in urban centres continued to be of great concern, and refugee camps had come under repeated attack.

Following consultations with Somali authorities, the Secretary-General dispatched a UN inter-agency mission to Somalia on 25 February to assess urgent humanitarian and rehabilitation needs. It completed its field work on 12 March, and recommended an immediate emergency assistance programme of $19.4 million, with an additional rehabilitation programme to follow as refugees returned. It also recommended reactivation of WFP development projects, the creation of a national emergency preparedness and response policy and a monitoring system for epidemics and other health emergencies, rehabilitation of national health facilities, preparation of an environmental health plan and improvement of the water supply and sanitation. Specific proposals regarding the water situation in the regions of Berbera, Borama, Burao, Hargeisa and Las Anod were given. Action was also recommended for the agricultural sector, livestock and fisheries.

The mission urged the creation of a government crisis-management entity, and noted that the special three-man committee established on 5 March 1989 to bring about a normalization of conditions could fulfil this role. It was recommended that similar UN bodies be established in both New York and Mogadishu. The office of the Special Co-ordinator for Emergency Relief Operations in Somalia needed to have adequate resources, and UN personnel operating in Somalia required a secure working environment. In a later report,[6] the Secretary-General detailed ongoing actions by several UN agencies to deal with the emergency.

At the end of August, UNHCR and WFP informed the Government that poor security in north-west Somalia gave them no option but to suspend assistance temporarily. Subsequently, the Secretary-General approached the International Committee of the Red Cross (ICRC) about formulating a humanitarian assistance programme for the north-west, and ICRC agreed to expand its presence there, provided that its normal conditions for operating were upheld. UNHCR and WFP responded favourably to the Secretary-General's request to participate in the Extraordinary Interim Emergency Programme on a "good offices" basis. The Secretary-General designated the United Nations Special Co-ordinator for Emergency Relief Operations as his special representative on all matters concerning the programme, and a task force consisting of UNDP, UNHCR, WFP and ELU/CARE was established.

ECONOMIC AND SOCIAL COUNCIL ACTION

The Economic and Social Council in May adopted **decision 1989/111** without vote.

Emergency assistance to Somalia

At its 12th plenary meeting, on 22 May 1989, the Economic and Social Council, taking note of General Assembly resolution 43/206 of 20 December 1988 and the message addressed to the Secretary-General by the Head of State of Somalia, in which he drew attention to the grave humanitarian situation that has developed in the northern provinces of Somalia as a result of attacks by armed bandits on towns and villages and on public installations and appealed for emergency assistance to help the Government cope with the large numbers of displaced persons and the repair, rehabilitation and reconstruction of vital public facilities and installations; extremely concerned at the displacement of the population in the affected provinces of northern Somalia as a result of the attacks, at the extensive damage and destruction caused to dwellings and the widespread damage to or disruption of the country's infrastructure, in particular bridges, water supplies, electricity supplies, communication systems, health centres, schools and other public services; and taking note of the statements made before the Council by the representative of the Secretary-General and the representative of Somalia concerning emergency assistance to Somalia, decided:

(a) To express its appreciation to the Secretary-General for the efforts he is making to mobilize international resources to assist the Government and people of Somalia in coping with the emergency situation in the affected provinces of northern Somalia;

(b) To call upon all States and the competent intergovernmental and non-governmental organizations to contribute generously to meet the urgent needs identified by the United Nations inter-agency mission to Somalia;

(c) To request the Secretary-General to continue to co-ordinate the efforts of the United Nations system to help Somalia in its emergency and rehabilitation programme;

(d) To request the Secretary-General to apprise the Economic and Social Council at its second regular session of 1989 of his efforts and to report to the General Assembly at its forty-fourth session on the implementation of the present decision.

Economic and Social Council decision 1989/111

Adopted without vote

Draft by Somalia (E/1989/L.17); agenda item 1.
Meeting numbers. ESC 6, 11, 12.

By **decision 1989/176** of 26 July, the Council took note of two reports made to it on 7 July: one on emergency assistance to Somalia made on behalf of the Secretary-General by a representative of the Under-Secretary-General for Special Political Questions, Regional Co-operation, Decolonization and Trusteeship, and another by a UNDP representative on assistance to refugees in Somalia.

GENERAL ASSEMBLY ACTION

On 19 December, the General Assembly, on the recommendation of the Second Committee, adopted **resolution 44/178** without vote.

Emergency assistance to Somalia

The General Assembly,

Having considered the question of emergency assistance to Somalia,

Recalling its resolution 43/206 of 20 December 1988 and taking note of Economic and Social Council decision 1989/111 of 22 May 1989,

Noting that in humanitarian terms a grave situation has developed in the northern regions of Somalia as a result of attacks by armed bandits on rural and urban centres,

Extremely concerned at the displacement of the population in the affected regions of northern Somalia as a result of the attacks, at the extensive damage and destruction caused to dwellings and at the widespread damage to the country's infrastructure, in particular bridges, water supplies, electricity supplies, communication systems, health centres, schools and other public services,

Taking note with satisfaction of the measures taken by the Secretary-General to obtain an assessment of the emergency and rehabilitation needs of the displaced population,

Reaffirming the need for the international community to respond fully to requests for emergency humanitarian and rehabilitation assistance for Somalia,

Considering that Somalia, as one of the least developed countries, is unable to cope with the mounting burden of providing adequate food, medicine and shelter for the large number of displaced people,

1. *Expresses its appreciation* to the Secretary-General for the efforts he is making to mobilize international resources to assist the Government and people of Somalia in coping with the emergency situation in the affected regions of northern Somalia;

2. *Takes note* of the interim report of the United Nations inter-agency mission that visited Somalia from 25 February to 12 March 1989;

3. *Once again appeals* to all States and the competent intergovernmental and non-governmental organizations to contribute generously and urgently to meet the needs identified by the United Nations inter-agency mission to Somalia;

4. *Requests* the Secretary-General to continue to coordinate the efforts of the United Nations system to help Somalia in its emergency and rehabilitation programme;

5. *Also requests* the Secretary-General to apprise the Economic and Social Council at its first regular session of 1990 of his efforts and to report to the General Assembly at its forty-fifth session on the implementation of the present resolution.

General Assembly resolution 44/178

19 December 1989   Meeting 83   Adopted without vote

Approved by Second Committee (A/44/864) by consensus, 15 November (meeting 34); draft by Bahrain, Bangladesh, Cameroon, Chile, Democratic Yemen, Ecuador, Jamaica, Kenya for the African States, Kuwait, Malaysia, Pakistan, Romania, Qatar, Saudi Arabia, Singapore and Thailand (A/C.2/44/L.19); item 88.

Meeting numbers. GA 44th session: 2nd Committee 19, 20, 25, 29-31, 34; plenary 83.

Operation Lifeline Sudan

In accordance with two 1988 General Assembly resolutions,[7] the Secretary-General issued a September report[8] on emergency assistance to the Sudan. The report noted that whereas progress had been made on implementing the resolution (43/8) requesting the Secretary-General to co-ordinate UN emergency assistance in the Sudan, unforeseen political developments in the country had prevented the convening of the follow-up meeting outlined in the second resolution (43/52) between donors and pertinent organizations, intended to mobilize resources for relief to displaced persons. Some 3 million people were displaced between 1986 and 1988, and more than 400,000 had died from disease and starvation. Administrative, financial and operational constraints, as well as disruptions resulting from civil strife, caused difficulties in transporting food and other relief supplies. By January 1989, it was clear that implementation of the emergency programme then in place would not alone be sufficient. Unless adequate food aid and other emergency items were transported to the south without delay, it appeared that there could be a repetition of the large-scale human tragedy of the previous two years.

At the Secretary-General's suggestion, a high-level meeting between Sudan's main aid partners, the Government and the United Nations was held in Khartoum on 8 and 9 March to devise a crash-delivery programme that would move in-country food stocks to areas where they would be needed during the rainy season. Donors were asked to support major airlifts, to provide funding for convoys and non-food emergency supplies, and to provide advisory personnel and storage facilities. Estimated total cost of the relief operations was $133 million, of which $78 million had already been committed in response to the Secretary-General's October 1988 appeal.

All participants accepted the proposed plan of action and welcomed the participation of non-governmental organizations in relief activities. It was agreed that the United Nations would provide logistical and field advisers to ensure that relief was delivered according to the plan. Immediately following the Khartoum meeting, talks between UNICEF and the Sudanese People's Liberation Army (SPLA) led to agreement on the concept of eight "corridors of tranquillity" along which supplies could be transported without interference. UNICEF was selected as the UN lead agency in SPLA-controlled areas in the south, with WFP and the UNDP Emergency Unit in Khartoum also co-ordinating relief operations in specific areas. On 23 March, the Secretary-General appointed James P. Grant, Executive Director of UNICEF, as his Personal Representative for the operation, to work closely with the Special Co-ordinator from the UNDP Emergency Unit in Khartoum.

"Operation Lifeline Sudan" (OLS) was launched in the first week of April, with bases in Khartoum and Nairobi. It succeeded in linking and strengthening a number of programmes carried out by the

Government and various organizations, through the sharing of information, transport, infrastructure, commodities and staff, thus enhancing efficiency and impact. Through OLS, medication was supplied for 250,000 people for three months in SPLA-controlled areas, and more than 51,000 children were vaccinated against childhood diseases. By the end of August, more than 97,000 tons of food and non-food supplies had been delivered. The donor community had almost covered the outstanding $55 million needed to fund OLS, but increased costs arising from newly identified needs resulted in a new outstanding balance of $37 million at the end of August.

The Secretary-General stated that OLS had set an important and historic precedent among complex relief operations: for the first time the two major parties to what was essentially a civil war had agreed to a common large-scale plan of action for civilian relief assistance on both sides of the conflict, and had allowed unescorted relief convoys to operate in "corridors of tranquillity". One of the lessons of OLS, he said, was that humanitarian programmes undertaken by neutral and impartial parties could be catalysts for peace.

In a subsequent report,[9] the Secretary-General noted that renewed armed conflict in the Sudan intensified in October, following a six-month cease-fire. Drought and late rainfall seriously affected crops and livestock, causing significant numbers of people to migrate towards Ethiopia because of food shortages. To contain the situation, efforts were made under OLS to accelerate the movement of relief food, seeds and fishing equipment to the south, and to improve cattle vaccination, basic health care and immunization programmes for children and pregnant women.

ECONOMIC AND SOCIAL COUNCIL ACTION

On 22 May, by **decision 1989/112**, the Economic and Social Council took note of a 5 May statement by the Director of the Office for Emergencies in Africa, representing the Secretary-General, on relief efforts for the Sudan.

On 26 July, by **decision 1989/176**, the Council took note of a 7 July report made on behalf of the Secretary-General by the Under-Secretary-General for Special Political Questions, Regional Co-operation, Decolonization and Trusteeship.

GENERAL ASSEMBLY ACTION

On 24 October, the General Assembly adopted **resolution 44/12** without vote.

Operation Lifeline Sudan

The General Assembly,

Recalling its resolutions 43/8 of 18 October 1988 and 43/52 of 6 December 1988 on assistance to the Sudan, in which it called upon the international community to contribute generously and respond urgently and effec-

tively to the country's emergency, rehabilitation and reconstruction needs, in particular the urgent requirements of displaced persons and other affected Sudanese nationals,

Recalling also the Substantial New Programme of Action for the 1980s for the Least Developed Countries, in particular the section concerning emergency relief and rehabilitation assistance for least developed countries,

Noting with deep concern that the Sudan has continued to suffer from the cumulative and negative impact of persistent natural disasters and civil strife, which have resulted in the widespread destruction of its socio-economic infrastructure and large numbers of displaced persons,

Noting that large areas of the Sudan have been struck again by drought, with resulting crop failures and consequent food shortages,

Recognizing that the Sudan continues to face a complex emergency and humanitarian situation and that the magnitude of the disaster and its long-term effect will require, as a complement to the efforts being made by the Government and people of the Sudan, a continuation of international solidarity and humanitarian concern, in order to meet the urgent requirements for relief, rehabilitation and reconstruction,

Noting with appreciation that the Khartoum plan of action for Operation Lifeline Sudan endorsed by the high-level meeting organized jointly by the Government of the Sudan and the United Nations, which was held at Khartoum on 8 and 9 March 1989, has been successfully and fully implemented,

Noting the consultations currently under way at Khartoum between the representatives of the Government, the donor community and the United Nations system for the preparation of a plan to cover the second phase of Operation Lifeline Sudan in order to meet the relief and rehabilitation requirements of the displaced population in the Sudan,

Taking note of the report of the Secretary-General on Operation Lifeline Sudan,

1. *Expresses its solidarity* with the Government and the people of the Sudan in facing a complex humanitarian situation;

2. *Expresses its deep gratitude and appreciation* to the States and intergovernmental and non-governmental organizations that rendered support and assistance to the Government of the Sudan in its relief and rehabilitation efforts;

3. *Expresses its particular appreciation* to the Secretary-General for his outstanding leadership role and vigorous efforts in the effective mobilization and successful co-ordination of Operation Lifeline Sudan, thereby guaranteeing its remarkable success in averting a critical disaster situation;

4. *Reaffirms* the need for the international community to continue to respond fully and effectively to requests for relief, rehabilitation and reconstruction during the forthcoming phase of Operation Lifeline Sudan to enable displaced persons to become self-reliant;

5. *Calls upon* all States to continue to contribute generously to the relief and rehabilitation requirements of displaced persons;

6. *Requests* the Secretary-General to continue to mobilize support and to co-ordinate the efforts of the international community, to intensify rehabilitation ac-

tivities and to monitor and keep those activities under constant review;

7. *Also requests* the Secretary-General to report, through the Economic and Social Council, to the General Assembly at its forty-fifth session on the implementation of the present resolution.

General Assembly resolution 44/12

24 October 1989   Meeting 37   Adopted without vote

32-nation draft (A/44/L.11/Rev.1 & Add.1); agenda item 154.

Sponsors: Algeria, Bahrain, Costa Rica, Democratic Yemen, Djibouti, Egypt, Ethiopia, France, Iraq, Jordan, Kenya, Kuwait, Lebanon, Libyan Arab Jamahiriya, Madagascar, Malaysia, Mali, Mauritania, Morocco, Nicaragua, Oman, Pakistan, Philippines, Qatar, Saudi Arabia, Somalia, Sri Lanka, Syrian Arab Republic, Tunisia, Uganda, United Arab Emirates, Yemen.

By **decision 44/447** of 22 December, the General Assembly took note of the Secretary-General's report on emergency assistance to the Sudan.

REFERENCES

[1]UNOCA/1989/1. [2]A/44/909. [3]A/45/271. [4]YUN 1988, p. 400, GA res. 43/206, 20 Dec. 1988. [5]A/44/261. [6]A/45/483. [7]YUN 1988, pp. 389 & 401, GA res. 43/8, 18 Oct. 1988 & GA res. 43/52, 6 Dec. 1988. [8]A/44/571 & Corr.1. [9]A/45/547.

Chapter IV

International trade, finance and transport

International trade and global output continued to grow in 1989 following rapid expansion in 1988. However, the picture of an international economy in apparent good health contained a double image. Although some areas of the world, particularly the developed market economies and several developing countries of East Asia, were enjoying boom conditions, others—Africa and Latin America— were in the grip of depression and disorder.

The Trade and Development Board of the United Nations Conference on Trade and Development (UNCTAD), at both its 1989 sessions, discussed the interdependence of problems of trade, development finance and the international monetary system and the external debt problems of developing countries. In December, the General Assembly expressed its appreciation for the constructive spirit of the Board's deliberations and invited all parties to give effect to its resolutions and decisions. In other action, the Assembly stressed that deterioration in the economic situation of debtor developing countries constituted a major obstacle to their growth and could be a threat to their economic, social and political stability.

There was a major advance in the commodities area in 1989, with the coming into force in June of the 1980 Agreement Establishing the Common Fund for Commodities, a mechanism intended to stabilize the commodities market by helping to finance buffer stocks of specific commodities as well as commodity development activities such as research and marketing. Another commodity-related development was the establishment of the International Agreement on Jute and Jute Products, 1989. The Agreement, which contained no price or supply stabilization measures, was primarily in support of research and development in agriculture, industry and market promotion.

The volume of international sea-borne trade increased for the fourth consecutive year in 1989, reaching over 3.9 billion tons. However, although 47.6 per cent of world trade originated in developing countries, the effective control of 67.5 per cent of the world merchant fleet remained concentrated in the developed market-economy and open-registry countries.

At its October session, the Trade and Development Board devoted a special meeting to commemorating the twenty-fifth anniversary of the establishment of UNCTAD. It also agreed that the eighth session of UNCTAD should be held in 1991 in Latin America.

UNCTAD VII follow-up

At the second part of its thirty-fifth session (Geneva, 6-17 March, 22 March and 19 May),[1] the Trade and Development Board (TDB) discussed the respective roles of national policies and the external environment in promoting social and economic development in the context of the Final Act of the seventh (1987) session of the Conference (UNCTAD VII).[2]

Summarizing the debate on the issue, the TDB President stated that there was a striking degree of consensus on the importance of a number of elements of domestic reform programmes that had been successfully applied in some developed and developing countries. However, it was noted that much remained to be done by all countries to respond fully to the broad understanding contained in the Final Act (paragraphs 25-32), on the basis of shared responsibility, with each country contributing in accordance with its capacities and weight in the world economy. The importance of complementarity of national policies and the external environment had been stressed—national policies to foster long-term sustainable growth would have little chance of succeeding without a supportive external environment nurtured by all countries.

It was suggested that in the pursuit of UNCTAD's mandate in various sectors of activity, the UNCTAD intergovernmental bodies and the secretariat should emphasize further the interaction between national policies and the external environment.

REFERENCES
[1]A/44/15, vol. I. [2]YUN 1987, p. 465.

International trade

The volume of world trade expanded by over 9 per cent in 1988, well above the annual rate of 3 per cent which had prevailed in the 1980s, said the *Trade and Development Report, 1989*.[1] Buoyant economic activity in the developed market-economy countries, particularly as regards investment, and strong growth in several developing countries of South-East Asia were important factors contributing to their strong expansion. Exports from the developed market economies rose by some 7 per cent in 1988, compared with 5.8 per cent in 1987. The import markets for capital goods which expanded fastest were those of Japan, the South-East Asian developing economies exporters of manufactures and the countries of Western Europe. The United States experienced a strong recovery in its exports due to the accelerated growth of demand in other developed market-economy countries and the earlier realignment of the dollar exchange rate. However, United States exports lost much of their momentum in the second half of 1988. In Japan, where total imports rose by some 16 per cent in 1988, there was only a modest expansion of exports during the year. Most other developed market economies experienced a rapid acceleration of exports.

Exports from developing countries increased by some 13 per cent in volume in 1988. While the exporters of manufactures fared best, primary commodity exporters also benefited from the enhanced demand, although there were some important exceptions. Compared with other regions, Africa was handicapped by the product composition of its exports. The non-oil-exporting Asian and Latin American countries generally benefited from the buoyant trading environment, particularly with respect to manufactures.

The *World Economic Survey 1989*[(2)] observed that the improvement in the growth of world trade in 1988 was accompanied by an unexpected 4.3 per cent growth in world output, the best since 1984. The growth of trade, which was twice as fast as that of output, could be partly explained by large shifts in export and import demand resulting from the realignment of major currencies. Another significant factor was the continued fast growth of the newly industrializing countries, which had a large income elasticity of trade.

Although rising incomes probably accounted for a large part of the growth of trade, other factors were difficult to explain. Revolutionary changes in technology that greatly reduced the costs of transport and communication, quickened the response to changes or new information, introduced new products and led to an integration of world financial markets could be contributing forces.

GENERAL ASSEMBLY ACTION

On 22 December, the General Assembly, on the recommendation of the Second (Economic and Financial) Committee, adopted **resolution 44/219** without vote.

Report of the Trade and Development Board

The General Assembly,

Recalling its resolution 1995(XIX) of 30 December 1964, as amended, on the establishment of the United Nations Conference on Trade and Development and the Final Act adopted by the Conference at its seventh session, held at Geneva from 9 July to 3 August 1987,

Recalling also its resolution 43/188 of 20 December 1988 on the report of the Trade and Development Board,

Noting that the *Trade and Development Report, 1989* has made a constructive contribution to the consideration by the Trade and Development Board, at the first part of its thirty-sixth session, of the interdependence of problems of trade, development finance and the international monetary system, as well as to the Board's consideration of the debt and development problems of the developing countries,

1. *Takes note* of the report of the Trade and Development Board on the second part of its thirty-fifth session and the first part of its thirty-sixth session, expresses its appreciation for the constructive spirit permeating recent deliberations of the Board, and invites all parties to give effect to its resolutions and decisions;

2. *Welcomes* the efforts made by Governments and the secretariat of the United Nations Conference on Trade and Development to strengthen the debates of the Trade and Development Board on the interdependence of problems of trade, development finance and the international monetary system, and also welcomes Board resolution 374(XXXVI) of 13 October 1989 on that topic;

3. *Welcomes* the significant contribution made by the United Nations Conference on Trade and Development to the search for durable solutions to the problem of external indebtedness of developing countries, and also welcomes Trade and Development Board resolution 375(XXXVI) of 13 October 1989, on debt and development problems of developing countries;

4. *Welcomes* Trade and Development Board decision 367(XXXV) of 17 March 1989 on protectionism and structural adjustment, and urges the Governments concerned to fulfil their commitments to halt and reverse protectionism and to take expeditious and concrete structural adjustment measures conducive, in particular, to the widening of markets for exports of products in which the developing countries have or may develop a comparative advantage;

5. *Also welcomes* Trade and Development Board decision 368(XXXV) of 17 March 1989 on trade relations among countries having different economic and social systems and all trade flows resulting therefrom, and invites the Board to develop a programme for further promotion of trade and economic co-operation among those countries, in particular East-South trade, based on an analysis and evaluation undertaken by an intergovernmental group of experts of the existing and evolving trends and potential factors related to inter-system trade;

6. *Notes* that the Trade and Development Board has decided to consider, at a future session, the implications of bilateral arrangements and regional economic integration, especially those which have a major

impact on global trade, in particular on the trade and development of developing countries, and agrees on the need to ensure that such schemes impart dynamism to global trade and enhance trade and development possibilities for the developing countries;

7. *Stresses* that in the Uruguay Round of multilateral trade negotiations commensurate attention should be given to all areas of negotiation, especially those of particular relevance to the trade and development of developing countries;

8. *Invites* the Trade and Development Board to continue to follow closely developments and issues in the Uruguay Round that are of particular concern to the developing countries;

9. *Notes* that the Agreement Establishing the Common Fund for Commodities has entered into force and that the Common Fund has started operations, welcomes the decisions taken by the Governing Council of the Common Fund at its first annual meeting and invites States members of the Common Fund to provide full support for its operations;

10. *Takes note* of Trade and Development Board decision 377(XXXVI) of 13 October 1989 on arrangements and preparations for the eighth session of the United Nations Conference on Trade and Development, to be held in 1991, including the agreement to hold consultations on its location in Latin America.

General Assembly resolution 44/219

22 December 1989   Meeting 85   Adopted without vote

Approved by Second Committee (A/44/746/Add.2) without vote, 11 December (meeting 49); draft by Malaysia for Group of 77 (A/C.2/44/L.53/Rev.1); agenda item 82 *(b)*.
Meeting numbers. GA 44th session: 2nd Committee 38, 44, 48, 49; plenary 85.

In **resolution 1989/118** of 28 July, the Economic and Social Council invited the UN regional commissions to formulate, jointly with UNCTAD, a draft proposal for interregional co-operation for facilitation of international trade.

Trade policy

The *Trade and Development Report, 1989*[1] stated that, despite assertions from North America and Western Europe of undiminished support for the open, multilateral trading system, resort to protectionist measures, evident since the mid-1970s, had intensified. Recent developments had done much to generate fresh concern about the protectionist drift in trade policies: a 1988 United States law required bilateral negotiations for improved market access abroad and, if unsuccessful, restriction of foreign access to United States markets; the countries of the European Economic Community (EEC) had decided to unify their markets by 1992; the United States and Canada had created a free trade area; and trade between Japan and South-East Asian countries had grown. That combination had promoted fears that the world trading system might be fragmenting into three major trading blocs.

The trade policies of both EEC and the United States were at a difficult and dangerous juncture

as opposing forces struggled for ascendancy, stated the *Report*. On the hopeful side was the fact that the mid-term review of the Uruguay Round of multilateral trade negotiations had taken place in 1988[3] and the negotiating phase had begun (see PART SEVEN, Chapter XVIII). If the negotiations were to result in an effective standstill and roll-back of non-tariff measures, the incorporation of agricultural trade and textiles into the General Agreement on Tariffs and Trade (GATT) and the restoration of an adequate multilateral safeguards discipline, developing countries could look forward to a more promising trading environment in the 1990s.

Protectionism and structural adjustment

In March, TDB conducted its annual review of protectionism and structural adjustment. It had before it an UNCTAD secretariat report[4] covering restrictions on trade and structural adjustment issues in the world economy. An addendum[5] provided statistics and other information. The UNCTAD secretariat also reproduced information received from member States on their experience with regard to structural adjustment.[6]

By a 17 March decision,[7] TDB urged Governments to implement fully the commitments to halt and reverse protectionism as agreed in the Final Act of UNCTAD VII.[8] It recommended that Governments consider, as part of their fight against protectionism, concrete actions to establish transparent mechanisms at the national level, as indicated in the Final Act. The Board decided to consider at a future session the implications of bilateral arrangements and regional economic integration, especially those having a major impact on global trade, particularly on the trade and development of developing countries. The UNCTAD secretariat was asked to carry out a study of the costs and consequences of non-tariff measures, particularly those adversely affecting the exports of developing countries. The Board recommended that the special problems of the least developed countries (LDCs) be kept in view while undertaking measures to improve market access.

GENERAL ASSEMBLY ACTION

The Second Committee had before it a draft resolution[9] on protectionism and structural adjustment, consideration of which had been postponed annually by the Assembly since 1980. By the draft, the Assembly would have urged developed countries to refrain from introducing new tariff and non-tariff barriers affecting the exports of developing countries, eliminate existing barriers, and provide market access for the products of those countries.

On 17 December, Malaysia, on behalf of the Group of 77 developing countries, withdrew the draft.

In **resolution 44/219**, the Assembly welcomed the TDB decision on protectionism and structural adjustment[7] and urged Governments to take expeditious and concrete structural adjustment measures conducive to the widening of markets for exports of products in which the developing countries had or could develop a comparative advantage.

Services

For its discussion of trade in services, TDB had before it in March an UNCTAD secretariat report[10] which noted that no generally accepted definition of trade in services existed, although such trade was generally considered to include payments for transportation, travel and other services. The question of definition was being negotiated in the Uruguay Round. Trade in services, particularly tourism, had provided developing countries with an important source of foreign exchange, as well as remittances by service professionals and workers abroad. On the whole, however, developing countries ran deficits in service trade, which reflected the weakness of their domestic service sectors in terms of their support to production and trade in other sectors. A key factor in development was the strengthening of a "knowledge-based" service sector supportive of production and export in other areas of the economy and the competitiveness of national firms.

Many proposals to expand service trade seemed designed to enable firms possessing a strong competitive position in services internationally to penetrate world markets more effectively and to operate more efficiently on a global basis by facilitating their ability to locate abroad, transfer information within their global networks and compete with local suppliers. Such initiatives aimed at reducing regulation of services, which would not necessarily benefit developing countries as, to a large extent, firms there lacked the means to develop services to foreign markets. Much of the service export earnings of developing countries was linked to the movement of persons abroad. In addition, corporate policies could be such as to frustrate the efforts of developing countries to strengthen their domestic service industries and to penetrate world markets.

Trade in services could be directly supportive of development if it took place within a policy framework ensuring its consistency with overall development objectives. Expanded services trade could enhance developing countries' ability to further objectives such as upgrading human capital, transfer of technology and development of indigenous technological capacities and knowledge-intensive services, more equitable redistribution of incomes, strengthened infrastructures, increased foreign exchange earnings from goods and service exports, and others.

Trade preferences

Generalized system of preferences

TDB's Special Committee on Preferences held its sixteenth session at Geneva from 24 April to 3 May 1989.[11]

It had before it the UNCTAD secretariat's twelfth general report on implementing the generalized system of preferences (GSP),[12] which updated and highlighted changes and improvements in the various schemes that had taken place since the Committee's 1988 session.[13] Statistics relating to the value of dutiable products excluded from the schemes of EEC, Japan and the United States indicated that developing countries, particularly the least developed, could benefit from an extension of the product coverage to such products without any significant domestic impact on preference-giving countries.

Also before the Committee was a review of GSP,[14] prepared in response to an UNCTAD VII request,[15] which analysed the extent to which the multilaterally agreed principles relating to the generalized, non-discriminatory and non-reciprocal character of GSP had been complied with in the improvements of the autonomous GSP schemes since their inception. It concluded that most of the schemes had been improved as regards product coverage, depth of tariff cuts and, to some extent, the rules of origin. However, it indicated that, despite those improvements, there had been significant deviations from the multilaterally agreed principles.

By a 28 April decision,[16] the Committee agreed that preference-giving countries should strictly comply with the multilaterally agreed principles relating to their generalized, non-discriminatory and non-reciprocal character. Those countries were invited to consider improving their autonomous GSP schemes by simplification, greater transparency and stability. The Committee recommended that special consideration be given to products of export interest to LDCs while undertaking measures in the field of GSP, including those in respect of technical co-operation activities. It noted with appreciation that a number of preference-giving and preference-receiving countries had provided resources in support of technical co-operation in connection with GSP and called on countries to consider providing resources in support of technical co-operation activities. The UNCTAD secretariat should undertake an evaluation of the effectiveness of technical assistance activities and report to the Committee in 1991. The secretariat was also asked to study the feasibility and usefulness for exporters and importers of consolidating information on GSP and to report in 1990.

For the first time, the rules of origin, normally considered in the working group on the subject, were dealt with by a Sessional Committee of the Whole, which had before it an UNCTAD secretariat report[17] that attempted to prioritize initiatives. The highest priority was accorded to initiatives which appeared to present the least difficulties for implementation. The report provided information emerging from seminars held under the auspices of the UNCTAD Technical Co-operation Programme on GSP from 1986 to 1988 and reviewed the special transitory arrangements that had been made for the introduction in January 1988 of the process criterion origin rules based on the Harmonized Commodity Description and Coding System.

In agreed conclusions,[18] the Committee recognized that the approach and possible initiatives in the secretariat report provided a suitable basis for discussion with a view to improving the GSP rules of origin in regard to their harmonization, simplification and liberalization. It agreed that the main elements of the report should be carried forward for detailed consideration at its 1990 session.

Trade among countries having different economic and social systems

In a 17 March decision,[19] TDB stated that the consultations of the UNCTAD Secretary-General with Governments on the potential for increased inter-systems trade, as called for by UNCTAD VII[20] and by the Board in 1988,[21] should be carried out as soon as possible. The UNCTAD Secretary-General was asked to report on those consultations in 1990. The Board established the terms of reference of an intergovernmental group of experts on further promotion of inter-systems trade, outlined work to be carried out by the UNCTAD secretariat on the subject, and indicated action to be taken by the secretariat in providing technical assistance to developing countries in order to promote and expand trade with the socialist countries of Eastern Europe. Annexed to the decision was the outline of the approach by the Group D (centrally planned economies) countries to the elaboration of a programme for the further promotion of trade and economic co-operation among countries having different systems, in particular East-South trade, referred to in the Final Act of UNCTAD VII.[20]

The meeting of the Intergovernmental Group of Experts on Further Promotion of Inter-Systems Trade took place at Geneva from 27 November to 1 December.[22] The Group carried out an analysis and evaluation of the existing and evolving trends and potential factors related to inter-systems trade, with a view to identifying the problems and constraints, as well as the potential areas and necessary conditions for further expansion of that trade, including preference schemes, financing of inter-systems trade and economic co-operation, including payment arrangements and joint ventures. It also discussed the elements of a draft programme for further promotion of trade and economic co-operation among countries having different systems, in particular East-South trade, and recommendations to be made to TDB as to the orientations of the research work of the secretariat, proposals for technical assistance activities and the treatment of specific issues to be included in the programme. The Group of Experts received proposals for draft elements for the elaboration of a programme on the promotion of inter-systems trade from the Group of 77 developing countries and for a programme on the promotion of East-West-South trade from participating States members of Group D (except Hungary).

Trade promotion and facilitation

During 1989, UN bodies continued to assist developing countries to promote their exports and facilitate the movement of goods in international commerce. The International Trade Centre (ITC) continued to play a leading role in the delivery of technical co-operation projects.

International Trade Centre

In 1989, ITC, under the joint sponsorship of UNCTAD and GATT, continued to serve as a focal point for UN assistance to developing countries in formulating and implementing trade promotion programmes.

During the year, ITC's expenditures on technical co-operation activities increased by 12 per cent (nearly $3.3 million) over the previous year's delivery, reaching an estimated record level of $29.6 million, stated the annual report covering ITC's activities in 1989.[23]

For the second time in its history, the volume of ITC activities financed by the United Nations Development Programme (UNDP)—52 per cent —overtook that financed by trust fund contributions, which stood at 48 per cent. Delivery of UNDP-funded projects increased by 18 per cent, or nearly $2.4 million, reaching a record level of almost $15.4 million, while that of trust fund–financed projects increased by 7 per cent, or $0.9 million, thus reaching, again, a record level of some $14.3 million.

ITC assistance with regard to institutional infrastructure for trade promotion at the national level was geared to improving the overall institutional framework by encouraging optimal reallocation of functions, development of clearer and better strategies for export development, and improving the co-ordination mechanism between Governments and business organizations active in this field. Under the subprogramme, ITC projects were under implementation in all geographical areas during 1989. An important activity was a major interregional project on trade development support for structural adjustment, the objective of which was to identify why some policy-level measures did not have their desired impact at the operational level and to recommend remedial measures.

The export market development subprogramme had three elements: trade information, product and market development (for agro-based products, manufactured products and technical consultancy services) and export development of commodities. All three elements were backed by research and development activities.

The specialized national trade promotion services subprogramme was giving increased emphasis to the enterprise approach. ITC continued to provide assistance to improve administrative and technical skills in export packaging, export financing, costing and pricing for export, trade promotion communications, quality control for export, national commercial representation overseas, legal aspects of foreign trade, export co-operation schemes for small and medium-sized enterprises and export-oriented joint ventures, and international physical distribution for exports and imports.

Other ITC technical assistance subprogrammes dealt with commodity promotion, which focused mainly on jute products; human resource development for trade promotion, which continued to emphasize direct training in specialized areas to meet short-term needs, complemented by a comprehensive approach to the strengthening of training institutions; import operations and techniques; the special programme of technical co-operation with LDCs; and technical co-operation with chambers of commerce and other business organizations.

The Centre also carried out work on trade between developing countries and the socialist countries of Eastern Europe, technical and economic co-operation among developing countries and the participation of women in trade promotion activities.

The special programme of technical co-operation with LDCs continued to play a catalytic role in ITC's overall technical co-operation programme, with over 30 per cent of the Centre's delivery of technical co-operation going to those countries. Within the special programme, ITC gave special attention to commodities and to activities in the product and market development of processed and semi-processed commodities. It carried out sectoral surveys on tropical beverages, conducted market promotion activities for selected

jute products in Japan and Western Europe, implemented training workshops and in-service training activities, and prepared trainers' manuals on coffee and coffee promotion and on cotton trading. During the year, eight ITC projects were evaluated—three interregional, two in Latin America, two in Asia and one in Africa; five were financed from trust funds and three by UNDP.

As evidenced in some of the evaluations, ITC's enterprise approach was showing results, with better results occurring where in-depth assistance was given to a limited number of enterprises, rather than where resources were thinly spread over a whole sector. To maximize the impact of project activities, a number of the evaluations recommended assistance in even greater depth.

JAG action. The Joint Advisory Group (JAG) on ITC held its twenty-second session at Geneva from 10 to 14 April 1989.[24] It had before it the annual report on ITC activities during 1988,[21] a report of the technical meeting on the ITC 1988 programme evaluation and on ITC's medium-term plan[25] and a report on the evaluation of the ITC programme elements National Trade Representation, and Trade Fairs and Commercial Publicity.[26]

In general recommendations, JAG suggested that future annual reports should reflect more systematically the measures taken to follow up on its recommendations; ITC should pursue with its trust-fund donors and with UNDP initiatives to obtain increased financing for its technical co-operation programme; current ITC efforts to reinforce its co-operation with other international agencies should be continued and expanded; project design, evaluation and technical backstopping, and appropriate selection of experts should continue to be given utmost attention in order to help safeguard the qualitative aspects of the ITC programme at a time of rapid quantitative expansion; and ITC's regular resources should be increased to keep pace with the expansion of its programme.

In reviewing ITC activities by subprogramme, JAG recommended that ITC should continue to expand its trade information services, with emphasis on modern methods for speedy access to, and dissemination of, trade information and on upgrading technical capabilities in trade information at national and regional levels; it should strengthen its technical backstopping capabilities for its enterprise-oriented export development projects, as they were effective channels for providing result-oriented product and market development assistance; it should continue to assist in the export development of non-traditional products (including technical consultancy services), emphasizing new products whenever appropriate; increased trust-fund and UNDP support should be sought for ITC activities in commodity promotion, in particular those of special relevance to the rural development programmes of developing countries; the Centre should proceed with its efforts to secure financing for the project proposal to assist developing countries to organize export support exhibitions; it should continue to strengthen its technical assistance in the field of joint ventures for export, in co-ordination with the United Nations Industrial Development Organization and other agencies; it should examine with its parent bodies the type of assistance that it could provide to developing countries for the export of services traded internationally; and increased attention should be given to providing expanded training support to developing countries, with emphasis on strengthening training institutions, refining and adapting training methodologies, providing direct training in new fields, and long-term training for LDCs, supported by on-the-job training. JAG also recommended that, in implementing the subprogramme on import operations and techniques, ITC should maintain its emphasis on result orientation while stressing the provision of information on sources of supply and the application of innovative management methods. The Centre should maintain its strong support for LDCs and continue to enlist the co-operation of its trust-fund donors; it should strengthen its efforts to assist developing countries to take advantage of expanding trade opportunities in the socialist countries of Eastern Europe; and it should proceed with a strategy to strengthen the role of women in trade promotion.

Restrictive business practices

The UNCTAD Intergovernmental Group of Experts on Restrictive Business Practices held its seventh session from 27 February to 8 March[27] and its eighth session from 23 to 27 October,[28] both at Geneva.

At its seventh session, the Group had before it information from States[29] on steps taken by them to meet their commitments to the 1980 Set of Multilaterally Agreed Equitable Principles and Rules for the Control of Restrictive Business Practices (known as the Set).[30] Other reports before the Group dealt with legislative and other developments in developed and developing countries in the control of restrictive business practices (1985-1988);[31] the work programme on restrictive business practices;[32] replies from States on the use of the consultation procedures on restrictive business practices;[33] the proposed handbook on restrictive business practices legislation;[34] a revised study on tied purchasing practices;[35] and activities relating to specific provisions of the Set.[36] The Group also considered a communication from the European Com-

munities concerning EEC participation in the Group's work.[37]

The Group annexed to its report draft decisions submitted by the Group of 77, Group B (the developed market economies) and Group D. It decided that the question of EEC participation in its work should be referred to TDB for action.

By a 15 March decision,[38] TDB accorded intergovernmental organizations having competence in the area of restrictive business practices the same participation rights in the Group of Experts as those accorded to States, except for the right of vote.

At its eighth session, the Group considered its annual report for 1989 on legislative and other developments in developed and developing countries in the control of restrictive business practices;[39] an UNCTAD secretariat note on the handbook on restrictive business practices legislation;[40] a secretariat report on activities relating to specific provisions of the Set;[41] and replies by States and regional groupings on steps taken to meet their commitment to the Set.[42]

In its agreed decisions and conclusions, the Group expressed concern at the continued existence of restrictive business practices adversely affecting international trade, particularly the trade and development of developing countries, took note of efforts by a number of States to introduce, improve or effectively use their national restrictive business practices control systems in accordance with the Set, and underlined the importance of the adequate implementation of all provisions of the Set by all States. Recognizing the importance of adequate preparations for the United Nations Conference to Review All Aspects of the Set, to be held in 1990, the Group requested the UNCTAD secretariat to prepare the necessary documentation in order to assist the Group at its ninth (1990) session in preparing for the review of all aspects of the Set, including making proposals for the Conference. The secretariat was also asked to prepare for the ninth session, as well as for the Conference, a further compilation of the handbook on restrictive business practices legislation, to continue its work on the study of the concentration of market power through mergers, take-overs, joint ventures and other acquisitions of control and to continue its work on the model law or laws on restrictive business practices. The Group invited all countries, particularly the developed ones, to continue to make voluntary financial and other contributions, with a view to strengthening and broadening the technical assistance programme of the UNCTAD secretariat in the field of restrictive business practices, while expressing appreciation to France, the Federal Republic of Germany, Norway and Sweden for their efforts to support technical assistance activities.

Commodities

The *World Economic Survey 1989*[2] noted that, for a large number of developing countries, the prices of their primary commodity exports rose significantly in 1988, the first such increase since a mild upturn in 1983-1984, which was followed by an almost continuous decline. By December 1988, the overall index of dollar prices of non-fuel primary commodities exported by developing countries was only 5 per cent below its 1979-1981 average. For the year as a whole, it was about 18 per cent higher than in 1987. The significant improvement in world growth during 1987-1988 was an important factor behind the increase in commodity prices and, in some cases, reduced supply resulting from elimination of excess capacity also contributed to the rise.

Of the 40 commodity prices in the UNCTAD price index, 37 increased, many of them sharply. Prices of food and beverages, which accounted for over 50 per cent of the value of exports of primary products from the developing countries, increased by about 12 per cent over their average 1987 level. Wheat and rice prices rose sharply from the low levels of the mid-1980s, with weather-related supply factors, especially drought in the United States and some Asian countries, and low stocks contributing to the increase. Sugar prices recovered from the low levels of the mid-1980s but there were only marginal increases in prices of tropical beverages, which accounted for over half of the value of exports in the group. Coffee prices rose following a 1987 agreement on export quotas. Cocoa prices, however, reached record low levels in 1988 as the largest producers continued to increase production in the face of stagnant demand. Tea prices, which had remained weak since 1984 as supply increased, rose modestly in 1988 in dollar terms. Prices of agricultural raw materials, which accounted for about 20 per cent of non-fuel primary exports of the developing countries, rose by some 8 per cent in 1988 following a significant increase in 1987. Prices of oil and oilseeds increased by 30 per cent on the average.

The sharpest increase in prices—34 per cent over 1987 levels—occurred in minerals and metals, which accounted for a fifth of the exports of primary products of developing countries. Increased demand from world manufacturing activities and a decline in capacity over the years of low prices were contributing factors. Copper, the most important in the group, was about 45 per cent higher in 1988 than in 1987. There were also large increases in aluminium and nickel. Among the major metals, tin showed only a modest increase.

Prices of primary commodities appeared to have already peaked by the end of 1988 and a slower projected growth of world output in 1989 and improved supply of a number of commodities in response to high prices suggested that commodity prices could be somewhat lower in 1989 than in 1988 and fall again in 1990.

Inter-agency consideration. At an inter-agency meeting on commodities held at Geneva from 1 to 3 May,[43] the situation and prospects with regard to commodities and related policy aspects were discussed by experts of the organizations of the UN system. It was noted that, although there had been an upward movement in nominal prices for most non-fuel commodities since 1987, the overall price index was still about 10 per cent below its average level for 1979-1981, which was a period of relatively high prices. The short-term prospects for international commodity markets were influenced by an expected slower rate of economic growth in the industrialized countries, continued abundance of supplies of tropical beverages and a continuing relatively tight supply situation for basic food commodities. The prices of metals and minerals were expected to decline substantially over the next two years. In real terms, the overall price index for commodities was expected to decline by 10 per cent in 1989-1990. In the longer term, real prices were expected to remain depressed during the period 1990-2000, since only a modest improvement was projected in non-fuel commodity prices.

Diversification, processing, marketing and distribution. The Working Party on Diversification, Processing, Marketing and Distribution, including Transportation, held its second session at Geneva from 18 to 22 September.[44] In agreed conclusions, the Working Party noted that, while one third of the 86 developing countries examined by the UNCTAD secretariat had achieved some degree of diversification in terms of their dependence on commodities in export earnings during the period 1967 to 1986, two thirds still remained heavily commodity-dependent and half of those had even experienced an increased reliance on one or two major commodities in their export earnings. The Working Party considered market access conditions and other factors and conditions pertinent to the development of viable diversification programmes, identification of sectors offering opportunities for diversification and increased participation of developing countries in processing, marketing and distribution, and technical assistance for implementing those programmes. It agreed that, at its next session, it would consider the improvement of information flows to aid investment decisions and adequate financial resources for diversification.

Common Fund for Commodities

On 19 June 1989, the 1980 Agreement Establishing the Common Fund for Commodities[45] entered into force, following a decision taken at a meeting of ratifying countries in New York. The Fund comprised two separate accounts. The First Account was intended as a source of finances for international commodity organizations established under international commodity agreements that contained buffer-stocking provisions. The Second Account would help to finance commodity measures other than stocking, such as research and development, quality and productivity improvement, and market development.

The first annual meeting of the Governing Council of the Common Fund took place at Geneva from 10 to 21 July.

During 1989, the Agreement Establishing the Common Fund was ratified by Portugal, bringing the number of parties to 104.[(46)]

GENERAL ASSEMBLY ACTION

On 22 December, the General Assembly, on the recommendation of the Second Committee, adopted **resolution 44/218** by recorded vote.

Commodities

The General Assembly,

Recalling its resolution 1995(XIX) of 30 December 1964, as amended, on the establishment of the United Nations Conference on Trade and Development, Conference resolutions 93(IV) of 30 May 1976 on the Integrated Programme for Commodities, 124(V) of 3 June 1979, 155(VI), 156(VI) and 157(VI) of 2 July 1983, and the Final Act adopted by the Conference at its seventh session, held at Geneva from 9 July to 3 August 1987,

Recognizing the need for better functioning of commodity markets and the desirability of stable and more predictable conditions in commodity trade, of avoiding excessive price fluctuations and of searching for long-term solutions to commodity problems,

Bearing in mind that commodity exports continue to play a key role in the economies of developing countries as a whole, in particular by making a crucial contribution to their export revenues and investments and to the re-activation of their growth and development,

Expressing concern at the difficult situation faced by developing countries in the area of commodities,

Bearing in mind that developing countries, in particular the least developed and commodity-dependent developing countries, have felt the most severe impact of the commodity price situation,

Welcoming the entry into force on 19 June 1989 of the Agreement Establishing the Common Fund for Commodities and expressing the hope that the establishment of the Common Fund, in full compliance with the provisions of the Agreement, will provide a positive impetus towards long-term solutions to the commodity problems of developing countries,

1. *Stresses* the urgent need for appropriate and early action to address the present world situation in the area of commodities;

2. *Expresses its concern* at the negative effects of the long-term downward trend of commodity prices on the economic development of the developing countries, which hinders their efforts to improve the living conditions of their peoples and to redress increasing poverty;

3. *Stresses* the need for all countries, according to their economic capacity and their weight in the world economy, international organizations, multilateral financial institutions and other relevant organizations to undertake measures for the diversification of the commodity economy of developing countries and to ensure greater participation of those countries in the processing, marketing and distribution, including transportation, of commodities, and, in this context, stresses the importance of market access for commodities from developing countries and of improved market transparency;

4. *Recognizes* that decisions on diversification are primarily the responsibility of developing countries, emphasizes, in that context, the need for continued implementation of their diversification programmes, bearing in mind, *inter alia*, the long-term evolution of market conditions and the linkage between diversification efforts and market access, and invites developed countries, international financial institutions and other relevant organizations to extend financial support to such diversification programmes;

5. *Notes with concern* that a further decline in commodity prices and commodity export earnings, as well as the long-term deterioration in the terms of trade of developing countries, in particular the least developed and the commodity-dependent among them, would hinder any prospect of sustained growth and development for those countries;

6. *Expresses its conviction* that more stable market conditions for commodities would be conducive to the social and economic development of developing countries and could, *inter alia*, contribute to the international campaign against illicit production of, trafficking in and abuse of narcotic drugs, thus supporting the efforts undertaken by countries to combat such illicit activities;

7. *Recognizes* the need for a better functioning of commodity markets as well as the desirability of achieving stable and more predictable conditions in commodity trade and of avoiding excessive fluctuations of prices, and urges co-operation between producers and consumers, with a view to improving the functioning of existing international commodity agreements or arrangements and/or, as appropriate, negotiating other commodity agreements or arrangements, in line with the relevant provisions of the Final Act adopted by the United Nations Conference on Trade and Development at its seventh session;

8. *Urges* all parties involved to meet agreed commitments and work for a balanced approach to the multilateral trade negotiations within the Uruguay Round of multilateral trade negotiations, launched during the Special Session of the Contracting Parties to the General Agreement on Tariffs and Trade, held at Punta del Este, Uruguay, from 15 to 20 September 1986, so as to ensure that their successful conclusion brings about further expansion and liberalization in trade in commodities, taking into account the special and differential treatment for developing countries, as well as all other principles contained in the Ministerial Declaration on the Uruguay Round;

9. *Recognizes* the urgent need to address the grave problem of shortfalls in export earnings in the commodities of developing countries and, in this regard, notes that a special session of the Trade and Development Board will be devoted to compensatory financing of these shortfalls;

10. *Calls upon* those countries which have ratified the Agreement Establishing the Common Fund for Commodities to contribute to making both accounts of the Common Fund fully operational as soon as possible, in full compliance with the provisions of the Agreement and, in this connection, welcomes the significant voluntary contributions made to the second account of the Common Fund and expresses the hope that further contributions will be forthcoming;

11. *Invites* all countries, particularly major exporters and consumers of commodities that have not yet ratified the Agreement, to do so as soon as possible, thereby contributing to the improvement of market conditions to the benefit of both producers and consumers;

12. *Requests* the Secretary-General of the United Nations Conference on Trade and Development to submit to the General Assembly at its forty-fifth session a report on world commodity trends and prospects, with particular reference to the situation of the commodity-dependent developing countries;

13. *Decides* to include the question of commodities in the provisional agenda of its forty-fifth session.

General Assembly resolution 44/218

22 December 1989   Meeting 85   146-0-2 (recorded vote)

Approved by Second Committee (A/44/746/Add.2) by recorded vote (113-0-2), 17 December (meeting 51); draft by Malaysia for Group of 77 (A/C.2/44/L.52/Rev.1); agenda item 82 *(b)*.

Meeting numbers. GA 44th session: 2nd Committee 44, 48, 49, 51; plenary 85.

Recorded vote in Assembly as follows:

In favour: Afghanistan, Albania, Algeria, Angola, Antigua and Barbuda, Argentina, Australia, Austria, Bahamas, Bahrain, Bangladesh, Barbados, Belgium, Benin, Bhutan, Bolivia, Botswana, Brazil, Brunei Darussalam, Bulgaria, Burkina Faso, Burundi, Byelorussian SSR, Cameroon, Canada, Cape Verde, Central African Republic, Chad, Chile, China, Colombia, Congo, Costa Rica, Côte d'Ivoire, Cuba, Cyprus, Czechoslovakia, Democratic Kampuchea, Democratic Yemen, Denmark, Djibouti, Dominica, Dominican Republic, Ecuador, Egypt, Ethiopia, Fiji, Finland, France, Gabon, Gambia, German Democratic Republic, Germany, Federal Republic of, Ghana, Greece, Guatemala, Guinea, Guinea-Bissau, Guyana, Haiti, Honduras, Hungary, Iceland, India, Indonesia, Iran, Iraq, Ireland, Israel, Italy, Jamaica, Japan, Jordan, Kenya, Kuwait, Lao People's Democratic Republic, Lebanon, Lesotho, Liberia, Libyan Arab Jamahiriya, Luxembourg, Madagascar, Malawi, Malaysia, Maldives, Mali, Malta, Mauritania, Mauritius, Mexico, Mongolia, Morocco, Mozambique, Myanmar, Nepal, Netherlands, New Zealand, Nicaragua, Niger, Nigeria, Norway, Oman, Pakistan, Papua New Guinea, Peru, Philippines, Poland, Portugal, Qatar, Romania, Rwanda, Saint Lucia, Saint Vincent and the Grenadines, Samoa, Sao Tome and Principe, Saudi Arabia, Senegal, Sierra Leone, Singapore, Solomon Islands, Somalia, Spain, Sri Lanka, Sudan, Suriname, Sweden, Syrian Arab Republic, Thailand, Togo, Trinidad and Tobago, Tunisia, Turkey, Uganda, Ukrainian SSR, USSR, United Arab Emirates, United Republic of Tanzania, Uruguay, Vanuatu, Venezuela, Viet Nam, Yemen, Yugoslavia, Zaire, Zambia, Zimbabwe.

Against: None.

Abstaining: United Kingdom, United States.

Individual commodities

Agricultural commodities

Coffee. On 3 July, the International Coffee Council decided to extend for two years to 30 September 1991 the International Coffee Agreement, 1983, which was due to expire on 30 September 1989; the extension entered into force on 1 October. The Council suspended the quotas under the Agreement as from 4 July 1989. At its October session, the Council decided to prepare the way for resumption of negotiations for a new agreement.

Jute and jute products. On 3 November, the United Nations Conference on Jute and Jute Products, 1989 (Geneva, 30 October–3 November), established the International Agreement on Jute and Jute Products, 1989.[47] The new Agreement—a successor to the International Agreement on Jute and Jute Products, 1982,[48] which was due to expire on 8 January 1991—would come into force on 1 January 1991, if by that time required conditions had been fulfilled. Those conditions were that the Agreement should be signed or ratified by three Governments accounting for at least 85 per cent of net world exports and 20 Governments representing at least 65 per cent of net world imports. The new Agreement would be valid for five years, with a possibility of two extensions of two years each.

As was the case with the 1982 Agreement, the new Agreement did not contain price or supply stabilization measures; its orientation remained primarily in support of research and development in the fields of agriculture and industry, as well as projects in the area of market promotion.

The International Jute Organization, established under the 1982 Agreement and based in Dhaka, Bangladesh, would continue to administer the provisions and supervise the operation of the new Agreement.

Minerals and metals

Iron ore. The Intergovernmental Group of Experts on Iron Ore held its third session at Geneva from 16 to 19 October.[49] The Group recommended to TDB that UNCTAD's work on iron ore should be maintained and that regular intergovernmental meetings of experts should be convened, with the participation of industry advisers, to exchange views on the iron ore situation and to review and enhance iron ore statistics.

Tin. The United Nations Tin Conference, 1988, held the second part of its session from 29 March to 7 April 1989, when it established the Terms of Reference of the International Tin Study Group.[50] As at 31 December,[46] the Terms of Reference had been accepted by Malaysia and Nigeria.

Tungsten. At its twenty-first session from 4 to 8 December,[51] the Committee on Tungsten assessed the current market situation and its short-term outlook. The Committee examined factors that had resulted in only a limited market improvement for tungsten despite the upturn in demand. These were an over-abundant supply, competition for market share between tungsten concentrates and intermediate products and the uncertainty created by increased protectionism and stockpile releases. The Committee requested the UNCTAD secretariat to prepare a paper containing the different definitions and methodologies used in major tungsten-producing countries and to review existing research and development programmes to promote new applications for tungsten. It requested the UNCTAD Secretary-General to approach the Common Fund for Commodities informally for its view on the eligibility of the Committee to be an international commodity body.

Manufactures

The UNCTAD Committee on Manufactures held its twelfth session at Geneva from 9 to 17 November 1989,[52] the eleventh having been held in 1986.[53] The Committee had before it UNCTAD secretariat reports reviewing the trade in manufactures and semi-manufactures of developing countries and territories in 1989,[54] on factors affecting exports of manufactures and semi-manufactures from developing countries,[55] and on the Committee's work programme.[56]

The Committee adopted a decision,[57] in which it underscored the crucial importance of improved access to markets for the manufactured and semi-manufactured products of export interest to developing countries. While noting that some developing countries had upgraded and diversified their exports of manufactures, it expressed concern that developing countries as a whole had a low share of world exports of manufactures and a narrow product base, and emphasized the need for a substantial increase in the participation of developing countries in world trade in manufactures.

The Committee recognized that, although the primary responsibility for adopting policies conducive to improving the export supply capability of developing countries lay with the countries themselves, a supporting and stable international economic environment would play a key role.

The Committee established the main elements of its future programme of work.

REFERENCES

[1]*Trade and Development Report, 1989* (UNCTAD/TDR/9), Sales No. E.89.II.D.14. [2]*World Economic Survey 1989: Current Trends and Policies in the World Economy* (E/1989/45), Sales No. E.89.II.C.1. [3]YUN 1988, p. 982. [4]TD/B/1196. [5]TD/B/1196/Add.1 & Corr.1. [6]TD/B/1200 & Add.1,2. [7]A/44/15, vol. I (dec. 367(XXXV)). [8]YUN 1987, p. 465. [9]A/C.2/44/L.5. [10]TD/B/1197. [11]TD/B/1219. [12]TD/B/C.5/122 & Add.1. [13]YUN 1988, p. 406. [14]TD/B/C.5/121 & Corr.1. [15]YUN 1987, p. 473. [16]TD/B/1219 (dec. 9(XVI)). [17]TD/B/C.5/120. [18]TD/B/1219 (agreed conclusions 10(XVI)). [19]A/44/15, vol. I (dec. 368(XXXV)). [20]YUN 1987, p. 475. [21]YUN 1988, p. 408. [22]TD/B/1244. [23]ITC/AG(XXIII)/119. [24]ITC/AG(XXII)/116. [25]ITC/AG(XXII)/113/Add.1. [26]ITC/AG(XXII)/113. [27]TD/B/1210. [28]TD/B/1236. [29]TD/B/RBP/47 & Add.1,2. [30]YUN 1980, p. 626. [31]TD/B/RBP/51. [32]TD/B/RBP/50. [33]TD/B/RBP/52. [34]TD/B/RBP/49. [35]YUN 1988, p. 406. [36]TD/B/RBP/18/Rev.2. [37]TD/B/RBP/48. [38]A/44/15, vol. I (dec. 366(XXXV)). [39]TD/B/RBP/61. [40]TD/B/RBP/58 & Add.1. [41]TD/B/RBP/60. [42]TD/B/RBP/59. [43]ACC/1989/12. [44]TD/B/C.1/305. [45]YUN 1980, p. 621. [46]*Multilateral Treaties Deposited with the Secretary-General:*

Status as at 31 December 1989 (ST/LEG/SER.E/8), Sales No. E.90.V.6. [47]TD/JUTE.2/6. [48]YUN 1982, p. 737. [49]TD/B/1235. [50]TD/TIN.7/13. [51]TD/B/C.1/307. [52]TD/B/1238. [53]YUN 1986, p. 505. [54]TD/B/C.2/228 & Add.1. [55]TD/B/C.2/229. [56]TD/B/C.2/230. [57]TD/B/1238 (dec. 14(XII)).

Finance

Financial policy

The *World Economic Survey 1989*[1] noted that two related issues of international finance were key global policy concerns. With regard to the first—foreign indebtedness—the developing countries that were in protracted debt crisis had necessarily been a major focus of world attention, as had certain centrally planned economies. However, the country with the largest absolute amount of foreign debt was the United States. Although it was not experiencing debt-servicing difficulties, concern had been raised about the sustainability of the growth of its net foreign debtor position.

The second area of broad concern to policy makers was the availability of financing, with developing countries striving to obtain external financing to support economic adjustment and development, centrally planned economies experimenting with ways that countries with non-market economic structures might better draw on private international financing, and developed countries focusing on changing capital flows and their impact on exchange rates and on official financial movements made in response to changing private international flows.

The *Trade and Development Report, 1989*[2] observed that international capital markets during the 1980s had been notable for the difference between their overall dynamism on the one hand, and the contraction in their role as a source of financing for developing countries on the other. Recent financial innovations had served various objectives, such as the facilitation of risk transfer, liquidity enhancement, and increases in the supply of credit and equity financing. Participants in the international capital markets from the private sector had primarily benefited from those innovations, although Governments and public enterprises of countries of the Organisation for Economic Co-operation and Development had also deployed them in their international borrowing. As to developing countries, financial innovation had been manifest mainly in techniques for reducing their external debt or exchanging it for other financial instruments. The innovations had had a much more limited impact on Governments and other economic actors from those countries. For example, developing countries' share of underwritten Euronote facilities during 1984-1988 was less than 10 per cent, and their share of non-underwritten facilities during 1985-1988 was below 2 per cent. Several causes had contributed to the small role of developing countries in the markets for new financial instruments, including controls and regulations in their domestic capital markets, costs and other problems associated with establishing the required networks of communications and computer facilities and, for countries experiencing difficulties over debt service, shortages of foreign exchange.

International monetary issues

In response to a 1988 General Assembly request,[3] the Secretary-General submitted a November 1989 report on current international monetary issues.[4] The report discussed recent developments in the international monetary system (trends in monetary variables and international payments, and exchange-rate management and international policy co-ordination), monetary issues in developing countries (exchange rates and inflation, and fiscal and monetary management) and the questions of the convertibility of the Soviet rouble and the liberalization of Soviet external payments.

The report noted that, since the stock market crash of 1987, there had been increased volatility of the exchange rates of the major currencies; reduced use of monetary policy for exchange-rate management; an upward trend in interest rates; and an absence of a steady decline in the trade imbalances of the major market economies. The instability in exchange rates appeared to have stemmed more from uncertainty regarding the course of monetary policy in the United States than from the evolution of trade imbalances and differences in interest rates.

Intervention in currency markets increased significantly following the meeting of the Group of Seven major industrialized countries in September 1989, helping to push the dollar down to levels more conducive to trade adjustment. However, the report stated, the magnitude of trade imbalances could make it very difficult to manage inflation, growth and exchange rates with monetary policy alone; fiscal policy had therefore to become more flexible.

Developing countries continued to experience balance-of-payments difficulties in 1989. The report noted that those countries were suffering the effects of devaluing their currencies in order to adjust to declines in export prices, rises in interest rates and cut-back in lending. The effect of such devaluation, especially in countries with debt overhang, had been extremely destabilizing. Because the adjustment process also led to a sharp fall in investment in capacity expansion, continued depreciations designed to switch current output

from domestic to foreign markets had been needed, resulting in distributional conflicts, since total resource availability itself had declined because of the collapse of growth and sharp decline in external resource transfers. Depreciations had also destabilized demand and added to budget deficits by raising the cost of debt service and of imports for public investment. The report noted that those effects had often outweighed the revenue-increasing effect of depreciation. It was essential for those countries to reduce reliance on depreciations and achieve external adjustment by lifting investment, particularly in the tradable goods industries.

The report noted that the restructuring of the USSR economy and its integration with the international trading and financial systems were closely related to the question of the rouble's convertibility and the liberalization of Soviet external payments. Convertibility required that the rouble be given more command over domestically produced goods and services than had proved possible under the régime of comprehensive central planning. The report cautioned that there was a danger that premature liberalization of exchange and payments arrangements could generate acute difficulties, such as increasing substitution of convertible currencies for the rouble in the domestic market.

An annex to the report contained a summary of recent proposals for convening an international conference on international monetary and financial issues.

By **decision 44/449** of 22 December, the General Assembly took note of the Secretary-General's report.

Net transfer of resources

In response to a 1988 Economic and Social Council request,[5] a chapter of the *World Economic Survey 1989*[1] was devoted to economic adjustment and the net transfer of resources from developing to developed countries. The *Survey* noted that at the level of the aggregate of the capital-importing developing countries, 1989 would mark the seventh consecutive year of such negative transfers of financial resources. Those transfers were not everywhere related to economic distress; in rapidly growing economies such as the Republic of Korea, they were a sign of growing economic maturity and success. But in most cases, the negative transfer was due to adverse changes in credit-related flows that were intimately related to the developing country debt crises of the 1980s. Viewing the net transfer as the net capital flow minus the net payment of investment income, the group of countries that had not had debt-servicing problems had continuously registered a net financial resource inflow, whereas the aggregate of the debt-problem group of countries had last received a net resource inflow in 1982.

There was clearly a close relationship between net financial transfer and the adjustment problem: not a single developing country that experienced serious debt-servicing difficulties in the early 1980s and was adjusting by mid-decade had been able to recover sufficiently to restore the confidence of its international creditors and regain normal access to international finance. The solution to the adjustment problem was not merely to return financial transfers to their previous levels but to find the appropriate mix of policy reforms and to determine how much international finance to supply in support of reform.

Having reviewed five country experiences of adjustment (Bolivia, Ghana, Jamaica, Mexico, Philippines), the *Survey* concluded that, in addition to ensuring the availability of an adequate supply of investment resources, it was essential that those resources be applied most effectively. That involved both export diversification, particularly into products with high income elasticities of demand and efficient import substitution. It also involved an oversight function of economic policy-making that scanned the economy for possibilities of increasing inter-industry and intersectoral supply, as well as surveying emerging technologies that could have application to small-scale entrepreneurs as well as large ones. Also, some activities that might once have been seen as belonging to the domain of large-scale public or private initiatives could also be redesigned to capitalize on the untapped energies of the people.

ECONOMIC AND SOCIAL COUNCIL ACTION

On 28 July, the Economic and Social Council adopted **resolution 1989/112** by vote.

Net transfer of resources from developing countries and its impact on their economic growth and development

The Economic and Social Council,

Deeply concerned about difficult economic conditions confronting developing countries which undermine their development potential and about the sharp decline in the standard of living of a large number of people,

Concerned that difficult financial situations in developing countries, including net transfers of resources, are limiting them in the utilization of their own resources for investment, for much needed social programmes and for the reactivation of their per capita economic growth and development,

Emphasizing that the efforts being undertaken by developing countries to foster sustained economic growth, though important, cannot succeed in reactivating growth and development without a favourable international economic environment,

Requests the Secretary-General to include in the *World Economic Survey, 1990* a more comprehensive analysis of the transfer of resources to and from developing countries, the main factors affecting such transfers and their impact on the growth and development of developing countries, presenting alternative hypotheses on the future evolution of this issue, taking into account recent developments in the world economy and distinguishing between both gross and net resource transfers and financial transfers, and to present a preliminary oral report to the General Assembly at its forty-fourth session.

Economic and Social Council resolution 1989/112

28 July 1989   Meeting 37   47-1 (unrecorded vote)

Draft by Norway (E/1989/L.45), based on informal consultations on draft by Malaysia for Group of 77 (E/1989/L.29); agenda item 2.
Meeting numbers. ESC 32, 37.

GENERAL ASSEMBLY ACTION

On 22 December, on the recommendation of the Second Committee, the General Assembly adopted **resolution 44/232** by recorded vote.

Trends in the transfer of resources to and from the developing countries and their impact on the economic growth and sustained development of those countries

The General Assembly,

Recalling its resolutions 41/202 of 8 December 1986 on strengthened international economic co-operation aimed at resolving the external debt problems of developing countries, 42/198 of 11 December 1987 on furthering international co-operation regarding the external debt problems and 43/198 of 20 December 1988 on external debt crisis and development and the search for a durable solution of the debt problems,

Recalling also its resolution 43/197 of 20 December 1988 on fulfilment of the target for official development assistance,

Recalling Economic and Social Council decision 1988/160 of 27 July 1988 on the net transfer of resources from developing to developed countries, and taking note of Council resolution 1989/112 of 28 July 1989 on the net transfer of resources from developing countries and its impact on their economic growth and development,

Aware that the pronounced decline in the flow of resources, severe external indebtedness, the deterioration in terms of trade, the long-term downward trend of commodity prices, continued protectionism and other trade measures have resulted in a net transfer of resources from developing countries,

Deeply concerned that such a phenomenon is still contributing to the deprivation of the developing countries affected of resources needed for economic growth and sustained development and may threaten their social and political stability,

Bearing in mind that, owing to the persistent structural imbalances of the world economy, the developing countries continue to face major problems in the areas of money, finance, resource flows, trade, commodities and external debt,

Gravely concerned about the trend in the net flow of resources, and believing that there is an urgent need for all countries to act in a concerted way to address this problem in order to ensure the reactivation of economic growth and sustained development of the developing countries,

1. *Urges* the international community to take concrete measures to ensure adequate resources for the reactivation of economic growth and sustained development in developing countries, taking into account the following recommendations:

(*a*) The Governments of developed countries should promote an adequate flow of resources to developing countries, and donor countries should bring up the official development assistance rate as quickly as possible to internationally agreed targets;

(*b*) Where appropriate, national economic measures should be taken that are conducive to capital formation in developing countries with insufficient savings and flow of external resources;

(*c*) In order to overcome the longstanding external indebtedness of developing countries, there should be, *inter alia* and as appropriate, a reduction in the stock and service of debt that is large enough to contribute to the attainment of the objective of the resumption of vigorous growth and sustained development in indebted developing countries;

(*d*) The Governments of countries members of multilateral financial institutions should ensure that these institutions have an adequate level of resources for the full discharge of their mandates in order to contribute to meeting the needs and requirements of the economic and social programmes of developing countries in the context of an approach consistent with the socio-economic objectives and growth and development priorities of those countries;

(*e*) Intensified efforts should be made by industrial countries to continue structural adjustment, maintain the vigour of their expansion while reducing and/or containing inflation, and work towards a mix of fiscal and monetary policies that would allow interest rates to come down, and hence induce a more favourable international economic climate;

(*f*) All Governments should work towards a more open international trading system that improves access, especially for the export products of developing countries, particularly in the context of the Uruguay Round of multilateral trade negotiations, launched during the Special Session of the Contracting Parties to the General Agreement on Tariffs and Trade, held at Punta del Este, Uruguay, from 15 to 20 September 1986;

2. *Recommends* that the Trade and Development Board give in-depth consideration at its thirty-seventh session to the transfer of resources to and from developing countries;

3. *Invites* the Joint Ministerial Committee of the Board of Governors of the World Bank and the International Monetary Fund on the Transfer of Real Resources to Developing Countries to continue its work and to give in-depth consideration to the transfer of resources to and from developing countries;

4. *Requests* the Secretary-General to report to the General Assembly at its forty-fifth session on the implementation of the recommendations contained in paragraph 1 of the present resolution.

General Assembly resolution 44/232

22 December 1989   Meeting 85   147-1 (recorded vote)

Approved by Second Committee (A/44/832/Add.1) by recorded vote (113-1), 17 December (meeting 51); draft by Malaysia for Group of 77 (A/C.2/44/L.12/Rev.1), orally revised; agenda item 12.
Meeting numbers. GA 44th session: 2nd Committee 15-17, 19, 20, 25, 29, 31, 34, 41, 44, 46, 48, 49, 51; plenary 85.

Recorded vote in Assembly as follows:

In favour: Afghanistan, Albania, Algeria, Angola, Antigua and Barbuda, Argentina, Australia, Austria, Bahamas, Bahrain, Bangladesh, Barbados, Belgium, Belize, Benin, Bhutan, Bolivia, Botswana, Brazil, Brunei Darussalam, Bulgaria, Burkina Faso, Burundi, Byelorussian SSR, Cameroon, Canada, Cape Verde, Central African Republic, Chad, Chile, China, Colombia, Congo, Costa Rica, Côte d'Ivoire, Cuba, Cyprus, Czechoslovakia, Democratic Kampuchea, Democratic Yemen, Denmark, Djibouti, Dominica, Dominican Republic, Ecuador, Egypt, El Salvador, Ethiopia, Fiji, Finland, France, Gabon, Gambia, German Democratic Republic, Germany, Federal Republic of, Ghana, Greece, Guatemala, Guinea, Guinea-Bissau, Guyana, Haiti, Honduras, Hungary, Iceland, India, Indonesia, Iran, Iraq, Ireland, Israel, Italy, Jamaica, Japan, Jordan, Kuwait, Lao People's Democratic Republic, Lebanon, Lesotho, Liberia, Libyan Arab Jamahiriya, Luxembourg, Madagascar, Malawi, Malaysia, Maldives, Mali, Malta, Mauritania, Mauritius, Mexico, Mongolia, Morocco, Mozambique, Myanmar, Nepal, Netherlands, New Zealand, Nicaragua, Niger, Nigeria, Norway, Oman, Pakistan, Papua New Guinea, Peru, Philippines, Poland, Portugal, Qatar, Romania, Rwanda, Saint Lucia, Saint Vincent and the Grenadines, Samoa, Sao Tome and Principe, Saudi Arabia, Senegal, Sierra Leone, Singapore, Solomon Islands, Somalia, Spain, Sri Lanka, Sudan, Suriname, Sweden, Syrian Arab Republic, Thailand, Togo, Trinidad and Tobago, Tunisia, Turkey, Uganda, Ukrainian SSR, USSR, United Arab Emirates, United Kingdom, United Republic of Tanzania, Uruguay, Vanuatu, Venezuela, Viet Nam, Yemen, Zaire, Zambia, Zimbabwe.

Against: United States.

Debt problems of developing countries

TDB action. At its October session, TDB held an integrated discussion on the interdependence of problems of trade, development finance and the international monetary system and the debt and development problems of developing countries. It had before it the *Trade and Development Report, 1989,*[2] which observed that decisive improvement in the debt situation of developing countries had remained elusive in 1988. The ratio of debt to exports had improved somewhat for some developing countries (but not for those of sub-Saharan Africa), but was still generally higher than in 1982-1984. Furthermore, rising interest rates since the second half of 1988 had exerted upward pressure on the ratio of payments to exports, and lending from capital markets remained depressed. Because of its adverse impact on the availability and cost of traditional financing and payment arrangements, the debt crisis had generated increased interest in alternative mechanisms, such as countertrade and regional clearing and payments arrangements. In practice, however, both had proved for various reasons to be subject to limitations.

There had been enhanced efforts to provide relief to the developing countries on official bilateral debt, the main initiative being action to implement the agreement reached at the 1988 Toronto economic summit of the Group of Seven.[6] Thirteen countries had benefited from concessional debt relief within the framework of the Paris Club (a group of creditor Governments) since October 1988. However, all of the countries benefiting from the measures belonged to the group included in the World Bank's Special Programme of Assistance to sub-Saharan Africa. Thus, most debt-distressed developing countries, including a number of low-income countries, had been excluded. A number of donor countries had applied more generous measures to official development assistance (ODA) debt of poorer developing countries by converting them into grants. The USSR had indicated its readiness to grant debt write-offs or 100-year moratoria to LDCs. France had announced its intention to cancel $2.5 billion equivalent of ODA debt owed by 35 African countries and the United States had decided to write off up to $1.3 billion of ODA loans made to sub-Saharan African countries implementing adjustment programmes.

While the new thinking on debt represented significant and irreversible progress, more was required in terms of action, said the *Report*. Creditor Governments needed to widen their role and enlarge the scale of debt and debt-service reduction by providing further inducements and/or imposing sanctions. In addition, the conditionality on adjustment programmes had to adapt to take full account of the difficulty and complexity of overcoming disorder which had become entrenched, as well as the limits to which countries could engage in debt equity swaps and privatization without jeopardizing their public finances.

By a 13 October resolution,[7] TDB agreed that the highest priority needed to be given to making rapid and effective use of the improved and strengthened debt strategy, in conjunction with appropriate economic policies and an improved international environment. That would require: the negotiation of financing packages adequate to support growth-oriented adjustment programmes, including debt reduction, debt-service reduction, new lending and other techniques, so that the financial obligations and payment capacity of individual debtor countries could be made more compatible; the formulation and implementation by debtor countries of appropriate programmes of growth and development-oriented macro-economic stabilization and structural adjustment and reform; review by creditor Governments of tax, regulatory and accounting practices in order to remove unnecessary obstacles with respect to new lending to developing countries and debt reduction and debt-service reduction; intensified efforts by industrial countries to pay special attention to the need for an increase in the exports of heavily indebted countries, to undertake structural adjustment measures, to maintain the vigour of their expansion while reducing and/or containing inflation, and to work towards a mix of fiscal and monetary policies that would allow interest rates to come down; that all those elements be brought together in a way that would bolster confidence in the economic and financial prospects of individual debtor countries and in the strategy itself; and that all involved should take into account the above requirements in working towards a growth-oriented solution to the problems of external indebtedness of all middle-income countries with serious debt-servicing problems, including those whose debt was mainly to official creditors or multilateral institutions.

The Board underscored the importance of ongoing discussions to endow the international monetary and financial institutions with the resources required to meet the needs of all their members. It urged developed donor countries to implement the 1978 TDB resolution[8] regarding adjustment of the terms on past ODA debt and urged creditor countries to implement fully the measures with respect to Paris Club debts called for by the Board in 1988.[6]

In a 13 October resolution on the interdependence of problems of trade, development finance and the international monetary system,[9] TDB recommended that Governments design and implement effective national and international policies and adopt measures to promote balanced and more evenly spread economic growth and development for the benefit of all countries. Governments should also engage in a more comprehensive, sustained and productive dialogue towards that end.

ACC consideration. In the annual overview report of the Administrative Committee on Coordination (ACC) for 1989,[10] it was stated that, given the pervasive nature of the debt problem and its widespread consequences, ACC had discussed the debt issue in various contexts at both of its regular sessions. It summarized a number of main points that had been made during the discussions as they pertained to global aspects, the international economic environment, adjustment programmes, the social costs of such programmes, resources for multilateral financial institutions and the future of the debt strategy.

Report of the Secretary-General. In response to a 1988 General Assembly request,[11] the Secretary-General submitted an October 1989 update[12] to his 1988 report on the subject.[13] He discussed the debt and development issue, outlined recent initiatives in debt policy and, based on extensive consultations with heads of State and Government, foreign ministers and diplomatic representatives of a large number of Member States, described the state of international opinion on the debt crisis.

Despite strenuous efforts by all concerned, the economic difficulties of most debt-troubled countries had worsened. Growth in Africa remained stagnant, and in Latin America it had deteriorated sharply. The negative net transfer of financial resources, which resulted directly from the crisis, rose sharply in 1988, reaching an unprecedented $33 billion compared with $26 billion in 1987. The large budget deficit in a key industrialized country and the imbalances among industrialized countries had led to uncertainty and high real interest rates; those rates had, in turn, helped to attract large amounts of resources from the rest of the world. Against that background, said the report, there had been reluctant acceptance of the need for significant debt reduction and there were reasons to fear that the amount of debt reduction produced by recently adopted arrangements would be insufficient to improve adequately the net resource transfer situation of countries affected by slow growth, financial disorder and debt overhang.

The international community had sought to contain the debt crisis and cautiously manage the sensitive economic and financial adjustments of debtors and creditors. Although progress had been significant, it remained insufficient for many highly indebted countries. More needed to be done if the debt problem was to be mastered and conditions established that were conducive to the resumption of development.

First among areas that merited particular attention was that negotiation of debt-reduction schemes—which could take eight months or more—was much too slow and cumbersome. The process would benefit from a clarification of the positions of concerned Governments and their commitment to a firm framework for debt negotiation that would be widely regarded as adequate to resolve the debt problem once and for all, rather than merely manage it through a recurring cycle of debt negotiations. Part of that framework had to be an understanding that adequate financial resources would be made available to support the debt-reduction and financing needs of each debtor country participating in the process. If the available resources—estimated at around $30 billion— were spread over a large number of countries, it would only partially reduce the debt overhang.

It was also necessary to focus on debt owed to Governments since, in many cases, reduction of bank debt would not be sufficient to reach a sustainable debt-servicing burden. Thus, creditor Governments had to be more forthcoming in reducing Paris Club debt.

A more general concern was that the debt-rescheduling negotiations did not necessarily result in the financing appropriate to the adjustment programmes negotiated in other forums, nor was the burden-sharing among different types of creditors or debtors distributed according to any clear principle. The Paris Club accorded its most favourable terms to low-income countries, while commercial bank rescheduling committees afforded their best terms to middle-income debtors.

Numerous proposals had been made for an international facility for debt reconsolidation, which would buy up or collateralize bank debt at an appropriate discount and treat banks and debtor countries in a consistent way, but they had been coolly received. A World Institute for Development Economics Research study group saw the merit of such a facility, but concluded that its negotiation and establishment would take too long. If a new facility was not created, the functions intended for it would have to be carried out by the international financial institutions. The study group saw the International Monetary Fund (IMF) as the lead agency, negotiating in the first instance an agreed debt reduction with the debtor country and providing the funds. If no agreement was reached between the debtor and the banks, the banks would face arrears to which IMF should not object and which it should not make into a reason for discontinuing its services to the debtor country. That would provide the leverage to bring the parties to the table. Whatever the precise mechanism, adequate debt reduction would require a much more active involvement of creditor Governments—directly or through international organizations.

The large debts of some Latin American countries commanded most of the attention in the media and in the financial community. However, debt burdens weighed heavily on many African countries and the servicing of debts of Eastern European countries put additional strains on the economic reforms they were undertaking. In Africa, official creditors played a larger role, whereas elsewhere private banks accounted for most of the claims. However, debt cancellation called for strict burden-sharing, as no creditor was anxious to help to pay off another creditor. That was an argument in favour of allocating responsibility for the management of the international debt crisis to an internationally trusted agency.

Debt reduction was no substitute for policies to restore internal and external balance to manageable proportions, but it had become a condition for such policies to succeed. Sometimes it was necessary to write off debts that owed their origins to assumptions about the future that turned out to be mistaken. Such debts could make it impossible to build a new relationship that was more profitable to all parties. Since banks were unable or unwilling to act on that recognition, said the report, the time had come for Governments to do so.

GENERAL ASSEMBLY ACTION

On 22 December, the General Assembly, on the recommendation of the Second Committee, adopted **resolution 44/205** by recorded vote.

Towards a durable solution of external debt problems

The General Assembly,

Recalling its resolutions 41/202 of 8 December 1986, 42/198 of 11 December 1987 and 43/198 of 20 December 1988,

Recalling also Trade and Development Board resolutions 165(S-IX) of 11 March 1978, 222(XXI) of 27 September 1980 and 358(XXXV) of 5 October 1988 and taking note of Board resolution 375(XXXVI) of 13 October 1989,

Concerned that a large number of developing countries experiencing debt difficulties, with serious social consequences, have recorded unsatisfactory rates of growth of output and development for many years, and that overall prospects for these countries are for a continuing unsatisfactory performance in 1989,

Recognizing that such weak growth, aggravated by the external debt crisis, can pose a threat to their social and political stability,

Convinced that, in this context, overcoming the long-standing external indebtedness of developing countries would require, *inter alia* and as appropriate, a reduction in the stock and service of debt large enough to contribute to the attainment of the objective of the resumption of vigorous growth and sustained development in debtor developing countries,

Recognizing that a number of recent initiatives aimed at a reduction of the stock and service of debt of developing countries, as well as debt relief measures, represent a conceptual advance and an important contribution to the efforts aimed at dealing with the debt crisis and that, in this regard, those initiatives need to be rapidly implemented to enhance their impact on the resolution of the debt crisis of developing countries,

Noting the close interrelationship between money, finance, resource flows, trade, commodities, development and external debt, and recognizing in this regard the important policy implications of this interrelationship for a durable solution to the debt problems,

Concerned at the decline of external resources available to developing countries for development, due, *inter alia*, to severe external indebtedness,

Recognizing that overcoming the debt problems and ensuring that financial flows are fully and effectively utilized require continuing adjustment efforts on the part of all countries, collectively and individually, each country contributing to the common objective in accordance with its capacities and weight in the world economy,

Emphasizing that the efforts being undertaken by developing countries to foster sustained economic growth, although important, cannot succeed in reactivating growth and development without a favourable international economic environment,

Recognizing that such a favourable international economic environment requires, *inter alia*, adjustment in the economies of the industrialized countries having a major impact on the world economy, including appropriate fiscal, monetary and trade policies, in order to eliminate the major imbalances in the world economy,

Welcoming the recognition of the need to continue efforts by all parties concerned to resolve the severe debt crisis and to forestall its proliferation and prevent its further aggravation,

Noting with deep concern the changes that have continued to occur in the destination and pattern of flow of external resources and the decline in the flow of those resources to developing countries, which have made the economic recovery and sustained development of developing countries more difficult,

1. *Takes note* of the report of the Secretary-General on the external debt crisis and development;

2. *Welcomes* the contributions of the United Nations Conference on Trade and Development to the international search for a solution to the external debt crisis of developing countries and, in this regard, recalls Trade and Development Board resolutions 165(S-IX) and 375(XXXVI) on debt and development problems of developing countries;

3. *Expresses its appreciation* to the Secretary-General for his efforts to find a solution to the debt problems of developing countries and encourages him to continue his efforts;

4. *Recognizes* the role of the international financial institutions in dealing with the debt problems of developing countries;

5. *Urges* all parties concerned to continue their efforts in pursuit of a durable, equitable and mutually agreed growth-oriented and development-oriented solution to the debt problems of developing countries, which requires concerted international action;

6. *Stresses* that the deterioration in the economic situation of the debtor developing countries constitutes a major obstacle to their economic growth and sustained development and can be a threat to their economic, social and political stability;

7. *Welcomes* the increasing acceptance by creditor countries of the need for writing off and/or reducing the stock and service of debt of developing countries and also welcomes the contributions that the recent initiatives aimed at the reduction of the stock and service of debt of the developing countries can make;

8. *Stresses* that a supportive international economic environment, together with a growth-oriented development approach, is needed for supporting the efforts of debtor developing countries to deal with their external indebtedness and alleviate the political and social costs of structural adjustment programmes and adjustment fatigue, thus contributing to the restoration of their economic growth, development and credit-worthiness;

9. *Expresses deep concern* that the overall indebtedness of the debtor developing countries has persisted and often increased, that their growth and development are severely limited and that their economic and social prospects continue to be a cause of serious concern;

10. *Stresses* the urgent need for the broadest implementation of the recent initiatives;

11. *Emphasizes* that in order to ensure that the recent initiatives, in particular those for debt reduction, in conjunction with appropriate economic policies and a favourable international environment, have an effective and comprehensive impact on the reactivation of economic growth and sustained development in the developing countries, the following measures would be required:

(*a*) Financial packages should be negotiated that are adequate to support growth-oriented adjustment programmes, including, as appropriate, debt reduction, debt-service reduction, new lending and other measures, so that the financial obligations and payment capacity of individual debtor countries are made more compatible; the combination of these elements should lead to the release of sufficient resources to generate higher levels of investment, the resumption of vigorous growth and development and the satisfaction of the needs of the populations;

(*b*) Creditor Governments should review tax, regulatory and accounting practices in order to remove unnecessary obstacles with respect to new lending to developing countries and to debt reduction and debt-service reduction in order to ensure that a supportive policy environment is achieved and maintained;

(c) The medium-term and long-term perspective of the rescheduling process should be enhanced by ensuring that it takes fully into account the policies and programmes oriented towards development and adjustment with growth that are formulated by each country concerned; in this context, consideration should be given, where appropriate, to rescheduling agreements on a multi-year basis;

(d) The Governments of member countries of the International Monetary Fund, the World Bank and other multilateral financial institutions should ensure that these institutions have adequate resources for the full discharge of their mandates, including, where appropriate, their role in the implementation of recent initiatives;

(e) Serious consideration should continue to be given to mutually agreed ways and means of assisting debtor developing countries faced with large and bunched debts to the multilateral financial institutions;

(f) The parties concerned should continue to exercise increased flexibility in the development of innovative approaches, including those devised by banks and debtors, to take advantage of discounts prevailing in secondary markets;

(g) All those involved should take into account the above, as appropriate, in working towards a growth-oriented solution to the problems of external indebtedness of developing countries that are facing serious debt-servicing problems, including those whose debt is mainly to official creditors or multilateral institutions;

12. *Stresses* that a durable solution to the debt problems and the revival of growth and sustained development in the developing countries require, *inter alia*, the following:

(a) All Governments should work towards a more open international trading system that improves access, especially for the export products of developing countries, particularly in the context of the Uruguay Round of multilateral trade negotiations, launched during the Special Session of the Contracting Parties to the General Agreement on Tariffs and Trade, held at Punta del Este, Uruguay, from 15 to 20 September 1986;

(b) Increased efforts should be directed to the diversification of exports of developing countries in order to enable them to achieve more stable earnings; strengthened existing compensatory financing arrangements for shortfalls in export earnings from commodities can facilitate this process;

(c) External resources should be increased to complement domestic measures conducive to capital formation in developing countries with insufficient savings and inadequate flow of resources from abroad;

(d) Industrialized countries should intensify efforts to continue structural adjustment, maintain the vigour of their expansion while reducing and/or containing inflation, and work towards a mix of fiscal and monetary policies that would allow interest rates to come down, and hence induce a more favourable international economic climate;

(e) It is essential for debtor developing countries to pursue and intensify their efforts to raise savings and investment, reduce inflation and improve efficiency, taking into account their own individual characteristics and the vulnerability of the poorer strata of their populations;

(f) Coherent and co-ordinated policies should be developed on the part of the industrialized countries, including multilateral surveillance, aimed at addressing the imbalances in the world economy;

13. *Recognizes* that the external indebtedness of some other countries with serious debt-servicing problems also gives rise to considerable concern and invites all those involved to take into account, as appropriate, the provisions of the present resolution in addressing those problems and in working towards a growth-oriented solution to the external debt problems;

14. *Requests* the Secretary-General to report to the General Assembly at its forty-fifth session on the implementation of the present resolution, including an assessment of the impact of the external debt crisis on the availability of resources for the growth and socio-economic development of developing countries.

General Assembly resolution 44/205

22 December 1989   Meeting 85   139-1 (recorded vote)

Approved by Second Committee (A/44/861) by recorded vote (120-1), 15 December (meeting 50); draft by Malaysia for Group of 77 (A/C.2/44/L.47/Rev.1), orally revised; agenda item 84.

Meeting numbers. GA 44th session: 2nd Committee 26-31, 41, 50; plenary 85.

Recorded vote in Assembly as follows:

In favour: Afghanistan, Albania, Algeria, Angola, Antigua and Barbuda, Argentina, Australia, Austria, Bahamas, Bahrain, Bangladesh, Barbados, Belgium, Bhutan, Bolivia, Botswana, Brazil, Brunei Darussalam, Bulgaria, Burkina Faso, Burundi, Byelorussian SSR, Cameroon, Canada, Cape Verde, Chad, Chile, China, Colombia, Congo, Costa Rica, Côte d'Ivoire, Cuba, Cyprus, Czechoslovakia, Democratic Kampuchea, Democratic Yemen, Denmark, Djibouti, Dominica, Dominican Republic, Ecuador, Egypt, El Salvador, Ethiopia, Fiji, Finland, France, Gabon, Gambia, German Democratic Republic, Germany, Federal Republic of, Ghana, Greece, Guatemala, Guinea-Bissau, Guyana, Haiti, Honduras, Hungary, Iceland, India, Indonesia, Iran, Iraq, Ireland, Israel, Italy, Jamaica, Japan, Jordan, Kenya, Kuwait, Lao People's Democratic Republic, Lesotho, Libyan Arab Jamahiriya, Luxembourg, Madagascar, Malawi, Malaysia, Maldives, Malta, Mauritania, Mauritius, Mexico, Mongolia, Morocco, Mozambique, Myanmar, Nepal, Netherlands, New Zealand, Nicaragua, Niger, Nigeria, Norway, Oman, Pakistan, Papua New Guinea, Peru, Philippines, Poland, Portugal, Qatar, Rwanda, Saint Lucia, Saint Vincent and the Grenadines, Samoa, Sao Tome and Principe, Saudi Arabia, Senegal, Sierra Leone, Singapore, Solomon Islands, Somalia, Spain, Sri Lanka, Sudan, Suriname, Sweden, Syrian Arab Republic, Thailand, Trinidad and Tobago, Tunisia, Turkey, Uganda, Ukrainian SSR, USSR, United Arab Emirates, United Kingdom, United Republic of Tanzania, Uruguay, Vanuatu, Venezuela, Viet Nam, Yemen, Yugoslavia, Zambia, Zimbabwe.

Against: United States.

By **decision 44/445** of 22 December, the Assembly deferred to its 1990 session consideration of a draft decision on the establishment of an advisory commission on debt and development.[14] By that draft, which had also been deferred in 1988,[15] the Assembly would have established an advisory commission to develop innovative approaches and evolve specific proposals related to all types of debt.

Development finance

By an October note,[16] the Secretariat transmitted to the General Assembly the text of a draft resolution, deferred from 1988,[17] by which the Assembly would have requested the Secretary-General to undertake consultations with a view to convening an intergovernmental committee to start the preparatory process for an international conference on money and finance for development. By **decision 44/448** of 22 December, the Assembly deferred consideration of the draft text until its 1990 session.

Trade-related finance

Export earnings

The Intergovernmental Group of Experts on the Compensatory Financing of Export Earnings Shortfalls held its resumed second session at Geneva from 10 to 18 April 1989,[18] the first part of the session having been held in 1987.[19] Having continued its analysis of the need for a new facility on compensatory financing of export earnings shortfalls, the Group of Experts adopted agreed conclusions and recommendations to TDB. It noted that the IMF Executive Board had established in 1988 a new facility called the Compensatory and Contingency Financing Facility, which was based on a balance-of-payments approach and not a commodity-specific one. The Group recognized that compensatory financing could be commodity-related, addressing some aspects of the instability problems in the commodity sector, an approach that could also contribute to rehabilitation and diversification in the area of commodities. It recommended that the problem of commodity export earnings shortfalls of developing countries arising from export earnings instability, as well as actions taken or required in the area of compensatory financing of export earnings shortfalls, should be kept under continuous review in UNCTAD. It that regard, the Group requested the UNCTAD secretariat to follow developments in various compensatory financing schemes and their implications for the development of developing countries.

The Group suggested that, in accordance with a 1985 TDB decision,[20] the Board's special session be convened as soon as possible to decide on follow-up action with regard to the Group's work.

Taxation

The *Ad Hoc* Group of Experts on International Co-operation in Tax Matters held its fifth meeting at Geneva from 6 to 12 December.[21]

The Group discussed the mutual consultation procedure; monitoring the impact of the United Nations Model Double Taxation Convention between Developed and Developing Countries, adopted by a predecessor group in 1979;[22] tax sparing relief; and other topics, including a possible increase in the Group's membership to include experts from the centrally planned economies.

The Group directed a set of recommendations to the international tax administrations of developed and developing countries that would enable them to enhance the formulation and application of double taxation treaties, maximize tax compliance, improve tax equity, decrease and/or eliminate tax evasion and avoidance, and promote international co-operation in tax matters.

The Group recommended that tax authorities endeavour to obviate the need for invoking the mutual consultation procedure by publicizing their tax rules and practices. In addition, it recommended that competent authorities exchange information, publish changes in their tax laws and be flexible within the law to ensure that the taxpayer was treated according to procedure.

The Secretariat was of the view that the Group's future work should include: problems arising from tax treaties in connection with the taxation of the earnings of migrant workers; and the problems arising out of transfer pricing, the exchange of information, the relationship of withholding tax on gross sums and the credit relief applicable to the net profit component, comparison and contrast of national procedures for the assessment and collection of tax, comparison of national tax laws and practices and the prevention of tax evasion, treaty shopping and the countering of avoidance.

REFERENCES

[1] *World Economic Survey 1989: Current Trends and Policies in the World Economy* (E/1989/45), Sales No. E.89.II.C.1. [2] *Trade and Development Report, 1989* (UNCTAD/TDR/9), Sales No. E.89.II.D.14. [3] YUN 1988, p. 414, GA res. 43/187, 20 Dec. 1988. [4] A/44/631. [5] YUN 1988, p. 415, ESC dec. 1988/160, 27 July 1988. [6] *Ibid.*, p. 416. [7] A/44/15, vol. II (res. 375(XXXVI)). [8] YUN 1978, p. 429. [9] A/44/15, vol. II (res. 374(XXXVI)). [10] E/1990/18 & Add.1. [11] YUN 1988, p. 418, GA res. 43/198, 20 Dec. 1988. [12] A/44/628. [13] YUN 1988, p. 417. [14] A/C.2/44/L.8. [15] YUN 1988, p. 419, GA dec. 43/444, 20 Dec. 1988. [16] A/C.2/44/L.4. [17] YUN 1988, p. 415, GA dec. 43/442, 20 Dec. 1988. [18] TD/B/1216. [19] YUN 1987, p. 494. [20] YUN 1985, p. 579. [21] E/1990/49. [22] YUN 1980, p. 531.

Transport and tourism

Maritime transport

In 1989, the total volume of international seaborne trade increased for the fourth consecutive year, reaching over 3.9 billion tons—a 5.5 per cent increase over 1988—said the *Review of Maritime Transport*.[1] The *Review* explained that the underlying factors driving the increase had been the size and growth of the economies of developed market-economy countries. Developed market economies generated 44.6 per cent of all goods loaded and were the destination of 67.1 per cent of goods unloaded in 1989. The developing countries expanded slightly in the goods-loaded category to 47.6 per cent and experienced a 0.1 per cent decrease in goods unloaded to 26.4 per cent. Oil cargoes accounted for most of the changes in both loaded and unloaded categories.

The year saw an upturn in deadweight tonnage, with the world total mid-year figures reaching 638 million deadweight tons (dwt). While the 10.1 million dwt increase over the 1988 mid-year figure was well below the average annual growth of 16.4 per cent for the 1970-1989 period, it indicated a reversal of the annual decline in world deadweight tonnage that occurred during 1987 and 1988. The effective control of 67.5 per cent of the world merchant fleet remained concentrated in the developed market-economy and open-registry countries. The developing countries' share was 21.1 per cent, of which almost 70 per cent was concentrated in 10 countries or territories. Conversely, 47.6 per cent of world trade originated in developing countries, which had to make disproportionate freight payments. The ratio of freight to c.i.f. (cost, insurance and freight) value of imports for developing countries in Africa and Oceania was almost three times greater than that for developed countries.

Shipping

The Group of Experts on Economic Co-operation among Developing Countries in Shipping, Ports and Multimodal Transport (Geneva, 26-30 June)[2] identified a number of areas in which developing countries could intensify co-operation to achieve their shipping-policy objectives. They included: operational activities, such as central freight booking, pooling of cargoes and shipping space, joint ventures, information exchange, multinational companies, research and development, establishment of multimodal transport operators, co-operation in manning, joint financing, determination of base ports/trans-shipment ports, ship repair and building up of computer systems; training; policy formulation; and the creation or maintenance of institutional structures necessary to implement co-operation programmes at the subregional, regional and interregional levels.

Multimodal and container transport

The *Review of Maritime Transport 1989*[1] noted that statistics on the development of multimodal transport operators (MTOs) remained scarce. However, according to information from Japan, the number of non-vessel-operating MTOs operating in that country increased from 123 in 1987 to 153 in 1989, a 29 per cent increase. While a similar situation might not exist in all developed countries, the general impression was that of an overall increase in MTOs.

Maritime liens and mortgages

The Joint Intergovernmental Group of Experts on Maritime Liens and Mortgages and Related Subjects, established by UNCTAD and the International Maritime Organization (IMO), held its sixth and final session in London from 25 to 29 September.[3] It carried out the final reading of the draft articles for a convention on maritime liens and mortgages and considered the scope of the revision of the 1952 International Convention relating to the Arrest of Seagoing Ships.

Having completed the final reading of the draft articles, the Group decided that the draft convention was sufficiently developed for submission to a diplomatic conference for adoption, and recommended that TDB and the IMO Council suggest the convening of such a conference to the relevant UN bodies.

The Group also adopted its final report[4] covering its work since 1986.[5]

Transport of dangerous goods

The Committee of Experts on the Transport of Dangerous Goods did not meet in 1989.

The Economic and Social Council had before it a report[6] of the Secretary-General covering the work of the Committee and its subsidiary bodies during the 1987-1988 biennium.

ECONOMIC AND SOCIAL COUNCIL ACTION

On 27 July, the Economic and Social Council, on the recommendation of its First (Economic) Committee, adopted **resolution 1989/104** without vote.

Work of the Committee of Experts on the Transport of Dangerous Goods

The Economic and Social Council,

Recalling its resolutions 1983/7 of 26 May 1983, 1985/9 of 28 May 1985, 1986/66 of 23 July 1986 and 1987/54 of 28 May 1987,

Noting the ever-increasing volume of dangerous goods in world-wide commerce and the rapid expansion of technology and innovation,

Bearing in mind the continuing need to meet the growing concern for the protection of life and property through the safe transport of dangerous goods while facilitating trade,

Aware that, in order to achieve internationally harmonized laws, the specialized agencies and other international organizations and interested Member States are committed to taking the recommendations of the Committee of Experts on the Transport of Dangerous Goods as a basis for the formulation of their requirements and regulations and therefore rely on the work of the Committee,

Reaffirming the desirability of widening the decision-making base of the Committee by encouraging the participation of developing countries and other non-member countries in its future work,

1. *Takes note* of the report of the Secretary-General on the work of the Committee of Experts on the Transport of Dangerous Goods in the biennium 1987-1988 and of the new and amended recommendations approved by the Committee for inclusion in its existing recommendations;

2. *Welcomes and approves,* in principle, the request of the Government of India to become a full member of the Committee of Experts on the Transport of Dangerous Goods as a suitable step towards widening its decision-making base;

3. *Requests* the Secretary-General:

(a) To incorporate in the existing recommendations of the Committee of Experts on the Transport of Dangerous Goods all the new and amended recommendations approved by the Committee at its fifteenth session;

(b) To publish the new and amended recommendations in all the official languages of the United Nations, in the most cost-effective manner, not later than the end of 1989;

(c) To circulate the new and amended recommendations immediately after their publication to the Governments of Member States, the specialized agencies, the International Atomic Energy Agency and the other international organizations concerned;

4. *Invites* all Governments, the specialized agencies, the International Atomic Energy Agency and the other international organizations concerned to transmit to the Secretary-General their views on the Committee's work, together with any comments they may wish to make on the amended recommendations;

5. *Invites* all interested Governments and the international organizations concerned, when developing appropriate codes and regulations, to take full account of the recommendations of the Committee;

6. *Endorses* the decision of the Committee, aimed at increasing efficiency, to combine its two subsidiary bodies, the Group of Rapporteurs and the Group of Experts on Explosives, into a single Sub-Committee of Experts on the Transport of Dangerous Goods, adequate time to be allocated during the sessions of the Sub-Committee to the discussion of matters relating to the transport of explosives;

7. *Recommends* that adequate funding be provided to support the work of the Committee as indicated in the report of the Committee in its fifteenth session, if possible by setting up a special fund;

8. *Reiterates* its request to the Secretary-General to make available, within existing resources, the staff necessary for the adequate servicing of the Committee, namely one Professional and one General Service post, and regrets that the requests made in its resolutions 1983/7, 1985/9, 1986/66 and 1987/54 have not yet been met;

9. *Requests* the Secretary-General to submit a report to the Council in 1991 on the implementation of the present resolution.

Economic and Social Council resolution 1989/104

27 July 1989   Meeting 36   Adopted without vote

Approved by First Committee (E/1989/140) without vote, 24 July (meeting 26); draft by Committee of Experts (E/1989/63), orally amended following informal consultations; agenda item 7 (h).

Tourism

As requested by the General Assembly in 1987,[7] the Secretary-General of the World Tourism Organization (WTO) reported[8] on progress made in implementing the 1980 Manila Declaration on World Tourism[9] and the 1982 Acapulco Document on World Tourism.[10]

The report stated that international tourist arrivals, which totalled 390 million in 1988, were an estimated 37 per cent higher than in 1980. Receipts from international tourism, totalling an estimated $195 billion in 1988, represented an increase of 90 per cent over 1980. The annual turnover of world tourism, including domestic tourism, was estimated at some $1,400 billion, accounting for 12 per cent of the world's gross national product. The report discussed the image of tourism; tourism and the environment; the facilitation of travel and tourist stays; tourist protection and security; human resources development; and WTO technical assistance to developing countries to increase their share of the benefits of tourism.

Annexed to the report was the Hague Declaration on Tourism, adopted by the Inter-Parliamentary Conference on Tourism (The Hague, Netherlands, 10-14 April 1989).

By **decision 1989/180** of 27 July, the Economic and Social Council took note of the WTO report, as did the General Assembly by **decision 44/455** of 22 December.

REFERENCES

[1]*Review of Maritime Transport 1989* (TD/B/C.4/334 & Corr.1), Sales No. E.90.II.D.7. [2]TD/B/C.4/321. [3]TD/B/C.4/326. [4]TD/B/C.4/327. [5]YUN 1986, p. 520. [6]E/1989/63. [7]YUN 1987, p. 505, GA res. 42/167, 11 Dec. 1987. [8]A/44/273-E/1989/77. [9]YUN 1981, p. 573. [10]YUN 1983, p. 577.

Programme and finances of UNCTAD

The Trade and Development Board—the executive body of UNCTAD—held two sessions in 1989, in Geneva. The second part of its thirty-fifth session was held from 6 to 17 March, on 22 March and on 19 May;[1] the first part of its thirty-sixth session was held from 2 to 13 October and on 18 October.[2]

The Board adopted four resolutions and 10 decisions during 1989. In March, it adopted a resolution on UNCTAD's twenty-fifth anniversary (see below) and decisions on the rules of procedure of the Intergovernmental Group of Experts on Restrictive Business Practices, protectionism and structural adjustment and trade relations among countries having different economic and social systems (see above); on its calendar of meetings (see below); on UNCTAD's contribution to sustainable development; and on UNCTAD's contribution to preparations for the international development strategy for the fourth UN development decade (see PART THREE, Chapter I). In October, resolutions were adopted on the twenty-fifth anniversary (see below) and on the interdependence of problems of trade, development finance and the international monetary system and on debt and development problems of developing countries (see above). Decisions were adopted on UNCTAD's contribution to the implementation of the United Nations Programme of Action for African Economic Recovery and Development (see preceding chapter); on its contribution to preparations for the international development strategy for the fourth development decade (see PART THREE, Chapter I); and on arrangements for UNCTAD VIII and the Board's calendar of meetings (see below).

By **decision 1989/167** of 26 July, the Economic and Social Council took note of the report of TDB on the second part of its thirty-fifth session.

The General Assembly, in **resolution 44/219**, took note of the reports of TDB on its two 1989 sessions and invited all parties to give effect to its resolutions and decisions.

Programme policy

The TDB Working Party on the Medium-term Plan and the Programme Budget held its seventeenth (8-12 May)[3] and eighteenth (30 October–8 November)[4] sessions in 1989, both at Geneva.

Programme budget (1990-1991)

At its May session,[3] the Working Party reviewed the UNCTAD section of the proposed UN programme budget for the biennium 1990-1991.[5]

In agreed conclusions, the Working Party stated that programme budgets should clearly reflect the work to be carried out by the secretariat and differentiate between final and intermediate outputs. The secretariat should ensure that posts allocated to various programmes were staffed and were located within the appropriate programmes. Secretariat activities based on intergovernmental mandates should have priority over *ad hoc* requests without such mandate. The distinction between actions to be taken by Governments and by the secretariat should be taken into consideration in preparing the programme budget document. The Working Party stressed the importance of using consultants for tasks of a specialized nature that were not expected to be performed by the regular staff. It expressed the hope that the secretariat would further develop its own expertise in the various areas covered by UNCTAD's mandate. Recognizing the indicative nature of items concerning *ad hoc* expert groups, the Working Party considered that their work should be related to areas of special interest in the work of the intergovernmental machinery. The UNCTAD Secretary-General was invited to allow for interactions between experts participating in those groups and delegations. *Ad hoc* expert groups in areas where intergovernmental groups of experts had been convened should be avoided.

The Working Party agreed to amendments to the proposed programme budget and to their transmittal to the appropriate bodies in New York.

In **resolution 44/202 A** of 21 December, the General Assembly established the programme budget for the 1990-1991 biennium, allocating $73,107,600 for the UNCTAD programme.

Medium-term plan (1992-1997)

At its October/November session,[4] the Working Party reviewed the draft UNCTAD sections of the UN medium-term plan for 1992-1997.[6]

In agreed conclusions, the Working Party, noting that a number of major events that would take place in the forthcoming period would have implications for the UNCTAD sections of the medium-term plan, stressed the importance of taking into account the results of those events in revising the plan. It approved a text[7] reflecting the outcome of its review for transmission to the appropriate authorities in New York.

Technical co-operation

In a report to the UNDP Governing Council,[8] the UN Secretary-General stated that, in 1989, expenditure under UNCTAD technical co-operation activities reached the record level of about $19 million, an increase of some 50 per cent over 1988. The objectives of the programme remained the strengthening of national capacities for formulating and implementing national and international policies, strategies, measures and instruments for developing international trade, promoting a better functioning of the international economic system in support of national development and enhancing economic co-operation among developing countries.

Within the international trade programmes, UNCTAD assisted developing countries to participate effectively in the Uruguay Round of multilateral trade negotiations through studies and seminars/workshops on the issues involved. Developing countries were also assisted, through advisory services and regional and national seminars, to take advantage of various schemes offered under GSP. UNCTAD responded to increasing requests from developing countries for assistance in studying and developing the service sector of their economies. As regards technical co-operation with interested developing countries to expand their trade with socialist countries in Eastern Europe, seminars and workshops in 1989 addressed the implications of the new reforms in the foreign trade systems and external economic relations of those countries.

Technical co-operation in data management expanded rapidly in 1989. Activities continued to improve and disseminate the data base on trade control measures and to support simplification of trade procedures. Progress was made in software development and in implementing the automatic customs data system.

Under the resources for development programmes, assistance was provided within the framework of the debt-management and financial analysis system. An improved software of that system was introduced in 1989. Increased attention was given to supporting government efforts to strengthen the administrative and institutional environment in offices dealing with national debt.

As regards commodities, contributions from Italy and Switzerland provided an impetus to UNCTAD assistance to food-importing developing countries to improve their import management and policies in the context of national food plans and to reduce the foreign exchange costs of food imports.

A main focus of the UNCTAD technical co-operation programme continued to be maritime and multimodal transport, which covered interlinked activities related to the management and operations of ports, shipping, multimodal transport, maritime legislation and training in maritime issues.

Organizational questions

Twenty-fifth anniversary of UNCTAD

On 14 March,[9] TDB decided to devote one meeting at the first part of its thirty-sixth session to marking UNCTAD's twenty-fifth anniversary and invited the UNCTAD Secretary-General to undertake the necessary preparations.

On 5 October, TDB held a special meeting to commemorate the twenty-fifth anniversary. On 13 October,[10] the Board, acknowledging with appreciation statements and messages delivered on that occasion, adopted a declaration stating that the main substantive challenge facing UNCTAD was to bring fresh thinking to bear on long-standing problems and new areas of concern with a view to promoting innovative policy measures. It should do so taking full account of the interdependence of economies and of policy areas, of long-term structural changes in the world economy, as well as of the need for a more supportive and predictable international economic environment for trade and development, particularly of developing countries. Member States pledged themselves to enhance their political support for the organization and to make it a more effective and responsive instrument of international co-operation for trade, growth and development.

GENERAL ASSEMBLY ACTION

On 14 November, the General Assembly adopted **resolution 44/19** without vote.

Twenty-fifth anniversary of the establishment of the United Nations Conference on Trade and Development

The General Assembly,

Recalling its resolution 1995(XIX) of 30 December 1964 by which the United Nations Conference on Trade and Development (UNCTAD) was established,

Recalling also its resolution 43/183 of 20 December 1988,

Noting that 1989 marks the twenty-fifth anniversary of the establishment of UNCTAD,

Noting with appreciation the valuable contribution that UNCTAD as a whole has made to the promotion of international economic co-operation and development,

Recognizing that important policy advances and agreements have been achieved through intergovernmental negotiation and deliberation, conceptual innovation and implementation, and recognizing also the influence of the work of UNCTAD on the thinking and decisions of Governments and of other international forums,

1. *Congratulates* the United Nations Conference on Trade and Development (UNCTAD) on the twenty-fifth anniversary of its establishment;

2. *Reaffirms* the role of UNCTAD as set out in resolutions of the General Assembly and the United Nations Conference on Trade and Development and in the Final Act of the seventh session of the Conference;

3. *Invites* UNCTAD to continue its efforts to bring fresh thinking to bear on long-standing problems and new areas of concern, with a view to promoting effective and innovative policy measures;

4. *Invites* the member States of UNCTAD to enhance their political support for that organization and to make it a more effective and responsive instrument of international co-operation for trade, growth and development, particularly of developing countries;

5. *Endorses* the Declaration on the twenty-fifth anniversary of UNCTAD adopted by the Trade and Development Board at the first part of its thirty-sixth session.

General Assembly resolution 44/19

14 November 1989   Meeting 54   Adopted without vote

Draft by Malaysia (A/44/L.39); agenda item 82 *(b)*.

Other matters

On 13 October,[11] TDB agreed that the eighth session of UNCTAD should be held in 1991, and requested consultations on a location in Latin America and an agenda.

On 17 March,[12] TDB approved a calendar of meetings for the remainder of 1989 and noted draft calendars for 1990 and 1991. On 13 October,[13] it approved the calendar of meetings for the remainder of 1989 and 1990 and noted the tentative calendar for 1991.

REFERENCES

[1]A/44/15, vol. I. [2]A/44/15, vol. II. [3]TD/B/1218. [4]TD/B/1237. [5]A/44/6 (sect. 15). [6]TD/B/WP/65 & Add.1-3. [7]UNCTAD/PSM/CAS/141-143. [8]DP/1990/56/Add.2. [9]A/44/15, vol. I (res. 365(XXXV)). [10]A/44/15, vol. II (res. 376(XXXVI)). [11]*Ibid.* (dec. 377(XXXVI)). [12]A/44/15, vol. I (dec. 369 (XXXV)). [13]A/44/15, vol. II (dec. 378 (XXXVI)).

Chapter V

Transnational corporations

The impact of transnational corporations (TNCs) on international development, trade and global investment flows continued to attract the attention of the international community in 1989.

The Commission on Transnational Corporations (fifteenth session, New York, 5-14 April) considered, among other things, the draft code of conduct on TNCs, the role of TNCs in South Africa and Namibia, TNCs and international economic relations, the role of TNCs in services and transborder data flows, and the work of the Centre on Transnational Corporations. At the seventh session of the Commission's Intergovernmental Working Group of Experts (New York, 5-14 April), international standards of accounting and reporting were discussed.

In May, the Economic and Social Council requested the Secretary-General to conduct a study of joint ventures among national corporations from various developing countries and their contributions to the development process (resolution 1989/21). It also requested the Secretary-General to submit a report on trends concerning TNCs and international economic relations (1989/22), and to study the impact of development assistance to least developed countries on flows of foreign direct investment to them (1989/23).

The Council further requested the Secretary-General to conduct a study of the main sectors of TNC activity that had an adverse impact on the environment (1989/25) and to prepare a report on the activities of transnational banks in relation to the external indebtedness of developing countries (1989/28). It condemned TNCs that continued to collaborate with the racist minority régime in South Africa (1989/27), and requested the Chairman of the Commission's special session to intensify consultations on the code of conduct (1989/24).

Draft code of conduct

The Commission on TNCs, at its fifteenth session,[1] continued its work towards a draft code of conduct on TNCs. In a February report,[2] the Secretary-General reviewed the status of code negotiations, as well as recent developments in the international economic situation of relevance to the code. The report mentioned the transnation-

alization of economic activity, the ongoing round of multilateral trade negotiations aimed at establishing an international régime on foreign direct investment measures and a framework for liberalization of trade in services, and the development of joint ventures between the socialist countries of Eastern Europe and foreign private investors relevant to the code of conduct.

In April,[1] the Commission noted the report and requested the Secretary-General to report again on the subject in 1990.

International arrangements related to TNCs

The Secretary-General, in his report[3] on international arrangements and agreements related to TNCs, considered trends and developments in international economic co-operation in areas that touched upon foreign direct investment. The report reviewed relevant discussions in the context of the Uruguay Round of multilateral trade negotiations[4] and current developments in the Multilateral Investment Guarantee Agency. International standards to be observed by TNCs and Governments in protection of intellectual property rights, labour relations and environment were also reviewed. It was noted that a new trend was emerging towards a greater linkage of national and international policies and measures relating to economic issues.

In April,[1] the Commission took note of the report and requested the Secretary-General to update it for its 1990 session.

ECONOMIC AND SOCIAL COUNCIL ACTION

On 24 May, on the recommendation of its First (Economic) Committee, the Economic and Social Council adopted **resolution 1989/24** without vote.

Code of conduct on transnational corporations

The Economic and Social Council,

Taking note of the reports of the Secretary-General on a code of conduct on transnational corporations and on international arrangements and agreements related to transnational corporations,

Reiterating that the Commission on Transnational Corporations, meeting in special session, continues to be the competent and authoritative body of the United Nations for negotiating the code of conduct on transnational corporations,

Reaffirming the need to finalize the code of conduct on transnational corporations as soon as possible,

Taking into account the comments on the subject made by delegations during the fifteenth session of the Commission,

Requests the Chairman presiding at the special session of the Commission on Transnational Corporations, in co-ordination with the Executive Director of the United Nations Centre on Transnational Corporations, to intensify consultations on the code of conduct on transnational corporations, with a view to resuming negotiations on the code in the context of the special session of the Commission on Transnational Corporations, if possible no later than the end of 1990.

Economic and Social Council resolution 1989/24

24 May 1989   Meeting 15   Adopted without vote

Approved by First Committee (E/1989/87) without vote, 19 May (meeting 8); draft by Commission on TNCs (E/1989/28/Rev.1); agenda item 8.

REFERENCES

[1]E/1989/28/Rev.1. [2]E/C.10/1989/4. [3]E/C.10/1989/5. [4]YUN 1986, p. 1210.

Standards of accounting and reporting

The seventh session of the Intergovernmental Working Group of Experts on International Standards of Accounting and Reporting was held in New York from 5 to 14 April 1989.[1] The Group had before it two reports of the Secretary-General on current developments in the field of accounting and reporting by TNCs, viewed at a global[2] and at a national level.[3] It also reviewed the Secretary-General's reports on accounting for inflation and changing prices and market and historical values of assets and liabilities,[4] appropriate measures to give effect to the work of the Group,[5] information disclosure requirements concerning the annual reports of boards of directors,[6] the special case of Africa in developing ways to improve education, research and practical training in the field of accounting and reporting in Member States,[7] objectives and concepts underlying financial statements,[8] and data on foreign direct investment.[9]

The Group recognized the usefulness of the review of important current developments in accounting and reporting at both a global and a national level and suggested that a short questionnaire accompany the note verbale to promote a more structured format in replies from Governments.

With regard to accounting for inflation, changing prices, and market and historical values of assets and liabilities, the Group concluded that "hyperinflation" described an environment where inflation had reached a very high or excessive rate, and agreed to several descriptions of accounting problems that arise during periods of hyperinflation.

In considering the question of information disclosure requirements concerning the annual reports of boards of directors, the Group identified a number of subjects for discussion and analysis that could be included in the directors' reports.

The Group discussed the feasibility of the Centre's offering technical assistance in Africa in the fields of accounting education, research and practical training, and agreed that a survey should first be conducted to collect information on local needs and practices in all countries in Africa.

Regarding measures to give effect to its work, the Group requested the Centre to complete a promotional brochure, including a cover design with a logo by which the Group could be identified. It also asked that items already in the agreed conclusions be deleted from the list of accounting and reporting issues, and that an explanatory paragraph be provided for each remaining item. The Group also suggested that a trust fund be created to defray the cost of participation by developing countries in the Group's sessions.

With regard to objectives and concepts underlying financial statements, the Group agreed that the report[8] could be issued as a companion publication to *Conclusions on Accounting and Reporting by Transnational Corporations*, published in 1988.

The Commission on TNCs adopted[10] the Group's recommendation on the following three measures to be taken by the Centre to give effect to the work of the Group: publishing the objectives and concepts underlying financial statements as a companion volume to the *Conclusions*, completing and publishing the work on the promotional brochure, and establishing a trust fund.

The Commission also approved the report of the Group and the provisional agenda for its eighth (1990) session.[11]

REFERENCES

[1]E/C.10/1989/7. [2]E/C.10/AC.3/1989/2. [3]E/C.10/AC.3/1989/3. [4]E/C.10/AC.3/1989/4. [5]E/C.10/AC.3/1989/5. [6]E/C.10/AC.3/1989/6. [7]E/C.10/AC.3/1989/7. [8]E/C.10/AC.3/1989/8. [9]E/C.10/AC.3/1989/9. [10]E/1989/28/Rev.1 (dec. 1989/2). [11]*ibid.* (dec. 1989/1).

Commission on TNCs

The Commission on TNCs held its fifteenth session in New York from 5 to 14 April 1989.[1] Among the subjects discussed were recent developments related to TNCs and international economic relations, activities of the Centre on TNCs, work related to the code of conduct on TNCs, international standards of accounting and reporting (see above), TNCs in South Africa and Namibia, strengthening of the negotiating capacity of developing countries in their dealings with TNCs, the role of TNCs in services (including transborder data flows), the Centre's development of a comprehensive information system, and the provisional agenda for the Commission's sixteenth (1990) session.

On 24 May, the Economic and Social Council took note of the report of the Commission on its fifteenth session (**decision 1989/125**) and approved the provisional agenda and documentation for its sixteenth session (**decision 1989/124**).

TNCs in South Africa and Namibia

The Commission on TNCs, at its April session,[1] had before it three reports by the Secretary-General related to the activities of TNCs in South Africa and Namibia. The first[2] examined their collaboration with the racist minority régime in that area and reviewed the state of the South African economy, its main trading partners and changes in foreign direct investment. It also examined the potential impact of a cessation in foreign trade and disinvestment, and the cutting off of new loans and trade credits on South Africa's economy. The report showed that while a number of countries had reduced their trade with South Africa, pulled out investments and cut off loans, there was evidence that other countries had filled part of that gap. It also suggested that curtailing foreign trade and loans would have more immediate impact on the South African economy than changes in foreign direct investment, because of the tendency of departing firms to maintain non-equity arrangements which allowed for continued technology transfers.

Another report[3] discussed the responsibilities of the home countries of TNCs that operated in South Africa and Namibia in violation of United Nations resolutions and decisions. The report concluded that differences in the content, scope, nature and approach of national measures pursuant to resolutions against *apartheid* tended to create opportunities for avoiding sanctions. The various economic measures applied were illustrated with a view to standardizing measures and devising co-ordinated action to strengthen the sanctions.

A third report[4] followed up the recommendations of the Panel of Eminent Persons,[5] which was established to conduct public hearings on the activities of TNCs in South Africa and Namibia. The report listed those TNCs that had disposed of their equity interests, as well as those with continuing interests in South Africa and Namibia. The Commission took note of the reports and approved the information programme for public hearings in 1989 on the role of TNCs in both countries. It condemned TNCs that continued to collaborate with the racist minority régime in South Africa in defiance of UN resolutions and called on the Governments of home countries of TNCs to consider adopting further measures to prohibit all forms of collaboration.

Public hearings

The Panel of Eminent Persons, established by the Secretary-General in accordance with a 1988 Economic and Social Council request,[6] conducted the second public hearings on the activities of TNCs in South Africa and Namibia at the United Nations Office at Geneva from 4 to 6 September 1989. In its report,[7] the Panel examined the current situation in South Africa, finding that economic and political changes were under way due to the domestic and international pressures on the Government and the business community to dismantle the *apartheid* system. The Panel reviewed the impact, efficacy and monitoring of sanctions, and considered the importance of training and educating black South Africans for a post-*apartheid* era. It recommended that the General Assembly appoint an independent group to prepare a detailed report on Governments' and TNCs' circumvention of sanctions in many areas, including trade in arms, oil and technology, and noted that the arms and oil embargoes should be strengthened. The Panel also made specific recommendations on financial, investment and trade sanctions, and the monitoring system of the sanctions, and recommended that a comprehensive study of a future training programme for black South Africans be conducted. (See also PART TWO, Chapter I.)

In connection with the public hearings, six background papers were prepared by the Centre on TNCs on: an overview of the activities of TNCs in South Africa;[8] the activities of TNCs in Namibia;[9] the South African economy and TNCs;[10] the role of transnational banks in South Africa;[11] sanctions against South Africa;[12] and the list of TNCs with interests in South Africa and Namibia.[13] The papers concluded that the immediate effect of sanctions and disinvestment on South Africa had been felt by all segments of the economy, including black workers who had lost benefits and employment as a result of disinvestment by TNCs, but that the world economy was too fluid for any set of measures to be fully effective. Loopholes and explicit sanctions-busting actions had weakened the impact of the measures and of disinvestment by TNCs. Although disinvestment had not prevented the transfer of technology essential to the functioning of South Africa's economy, the evidence indicated that sanctions and disinvestment had imposed economic costs on South Africa. The falling due in 1990 of foreign debt of about $8 billion was expected to increase further the country's vulnerability to international pressure.

On 24 May, on the recommendation of its First Committee, the Economic and Social Council adopted **resolution 1989/27** by recorded vote.

Activities of transnational corporations in South Africa and Namibia

The Economic and Social Council,

Recalling its previous resolutions on the activities of transnational corporations in South Africa and Namibia, in particular resolution 1988/56 of 27 July 1988, in which it urged all transnational corporations to stop immediately all forms of collaboration with the racist minority régime in South Africa and called for specific actions by Member States and transnational corporations to end such collaboration,

Noting with grave concern the brutal perpetuation of the inhuman system of *apartheid* in South Africa and the continued denial of the civil and political rights of the majority of the population in that country,

Bearing in mind the fact that continued investments, trade, technological co-operation and other covert or overt activities by transnational corporations inside and outside South Africa provide sustenance to *apartheid*,

Noting the current efforts to implement Security Council resolution 435(1978) of 29 September 1978 and attain the independence of Namibia,

Having examined the reports of the Secretary-General on the activities of transnational corporations in South Africa and Namibia and collaboration of such corporations with the racist minority régime in that area and on the responsibilities of home countries with respect to the transnational corporations operating in South Africa and Namibia in violation of the relevant resolutions and decisions of the United Nations,

1. *Reiterates* its abhorrence of *apartheid*, which is a crime against humanity, and condemns the South African régime for its perpetuation of *apartheid*, for its continued oppression of the majority of the people of South Africa and for its acts of military and economic destabilization against the neighbouring independent States;

2. *Condemns* those transnational corporations that continue to collaborate with the racist minority régime in South Africa in defiance of United Nations resolutions and international public opinion and, in many cases, in violation of measures adopted by their home countries;

3. *Welcomes* as an initial step the measures taken by some Governments to impose restrictions on investments, bank loans and other economic activities in South Africa, as well as the divestment by some transnational corporations of their equity investments in South Africa;

4. *Deeply regrets* that the measures taken so far fall short of the comprehensive and mandatory sanctions against the racist régime in South Africa called for in relevant resolutions of the General Assembly;

5. *Calls upon* the Governments of home countries of transnational corporations to implement fully the provisions of Economic and Social Council resolution 1988/56, and to consider adopting further measures to prohibit all forms of collaboration by transnational corporations with the racist minority régime in South Africa, including not only direct investments, but also services, non-equity forms of business arrangements,

technology licensing, distribution and franchising agreements and other such activities;

6. *Urges* all transnational corporations to stop immediately any operations in South Africa and all forms of trade and economic links with the racist minority régime;

7. *Calls upon* all multilateral financial and development institutions to cease immediately any kind of support or other form of collaboration with the racist régime in South Africa;

8. *Requests* the Secretary-General to expedite the implementation of paragraph 9 of Council resolution 1988/56 and to report on the results thereof to the Commission on Transnational Corporations at its sixteenth session;

9. *Also requests* the Secretary-General:

(a) To continue the useful work of collecting and disseminating information on the activities of transnational corporations in South Africa and in Namibia until the attainment of its independence, including the compiling of a list of transnational corporations still conducting operations there;

(b) To prepare studies on the level and forms of operations by transnational corporations in South Africa and in Namibia until the attainment of its independence, including their non-equity business arrangements and their involvement in particular sectors of the South African and Namibian economies, and an updated study on the responsibilities of home countries with respect to the transnational corporations operating in South Africa and Namibia in violation of the relevant resolutions and decisions of the United Nations;

(c) To report annually to the Commission on Transnational Corporations, the Economic and Social Council, the General Assembly and the Security Council on the implementation of the present resolution.

Economic and Social Council resolution 1989/27

24 May 1989   Meeting 15   45-2-7 (recorded vote)

Approved by First Committee (E/1989/87) by roll-call vote (34-2-7), 19 May (meeting 8); draft by Commission on TNCs (E/1989/28/Rev.1); agenda item 8.

Recorded vote in Council as follows:

In favour: Bahamas, Belize, Bolivia, Brazil, Bulgaria, Cameroon, China, Colombia, Cuba, Czechoslovakia, Denmark, Ghana, Greece, Guinea, India, Indonesia, Iran, Iraq, Italy, Jordan, Kenya, Lesotho, Liberia, Libyan Arab Jamahiriya, New Zealand, Nicaragua, Niger, Norway, Oman, Poland, Rwanda, Saudi Arabia, Somalia, Sri Lanka, Sudan, Thailand, Trinidad and Tobago, Tunisia, Ukrainian SSR, USSR, Uruguay, Venezuela, Yugoslavia, Zaire, Zambia.

Against: United Kingdom

Abstaining: Canada, France, Germany, Federal Republic of, Ireland, Japan, Netherlands, Portugal.

TNCs and international economic relations

In February, the Secretary-General issued a report[14] on recent developments related to TNCs and international economic relations. While total world-wide outflows of foreign direct investment had trebled from the end of 1983 through 1987, with average annual outflows during that period reaching $81 billion, the developing countries' share had declined from 27 per cent of the total in the period 1981-1983 to 21 per cent in 1984-1987. Developed countries, especially France, the Federal Republic of Germany, Japan, the United Kingdom and the United States, increased their share of both foreign direct investment inflows and outflows. Services as a share of foreign direct investment outflows continued to grow, representing more than half of total outflows. The report concluded that the creation of a single market within the European Economic Community by the end of 1992 was already stimulating greater activities within the Community by both Community- and non-Community-based TNCs, but that the implications for developing countries remained uncertain.

ECONOMIC AND SOCIAL COUNCIL ACTION

On 24 May, on the recommendation of its First Committee, the Economic and Social Council adopted **resolution 1989/22** without vote.

Recent trends concerning transnational corporations and international economic relations

The Economic and Social Council,

Reaffirming its resolutions 1908(LVII) of 2 August 1974 and 1913(LVII) of 5 December 1974 on the impact of transnational corporations on the development process and on international relations,

Reaffirming also its resolution 1988/58 of 27 July 1988 on strengthening the role of the Commission on Transnational Corporations and the activities of the United Nations Centre on Transnational Corporations in support of developing countries,

Taking note with appreciation of the reports of the Secretary-General on recent developments related to transnational corporations and international economic relations and on the role of transnational corporations in the least developed countries,

Aware that structural imbalances in the economies of major actors in the world economy have an impact on investment flows, including those to developing countries,

Noting that developed market economy countries increasingly attract foreign direct investment in a situation in which developing countries increasingly face limitations on financial and technological resources that could contribute to their economic and social development,

1. *Requests* the Secretary-General to submit to the Commission on Transnational Corporations at its sixteenth session, in 1990, a report analysing those trends and to recommend ways and means of increasing the operations of transnational corporations in developing countries in order to contribute to their economic, social and technological development;

2. *Also requests* the Secretary-General to include in that report an assessment of the potential impact of the regional economic integration processes taking place among developed countries on the future operations of transnational corporations, particularly in developing countries, and, in turn, the impact on regional economic integration processes in developing countries.

Economic and Social Council resolution 1989/22

24 May 1989   Meeting 15   Adopted without vote

Approved by First Committee (E/1989/87) without vote, 19 May (meeting 8); draft by Commission on TNCs (E/1989/28/Rev.1); agenda item 8.

Role of TNCs in the least developed countries

Pursuant to a 1988 request by the Commission on TNCs, in February the Secretary-General issued a report[15] on the role of TNCs in the least developed countries. The report stated that there were a number of areas in which TNCs could help to accelerate development in those countries, but that they had so far played an insignificant role. The report suggested actions that could be taken by host countries, home countries of TNCs and international organizations to accelerate the flow of foreign direct investment to the least developed countries and to improve its qualitative contribution to their economies.

ECONOMIC AND SOCIAL COUNCIL ACTION

On 24 May, on the recommendation of its First Committee, the Economic and Social Council adopted **resolution 1989/23** without vote.

Role of transnational corporations in the least developed countries

The Economic and Social Council,

Mindful of the role that transnational corporations can play in the development of the least developed countries, and concerned that transnational corporations have largely bypassed those countries,

Stressing the need for appropriate policies and measures, including those instituted by Governments of home countries of transnational corporations, and for international action, including action by the United Nations Centre on Transnational Corporations, to enhance the contribution of transnational corporations in the least developed countries,

Mindful of the development objectives and priorities of the least developed countries,

Taking note with appreciation of the report of the Secretary-General on the role of transnational corporations in the least developed countries,

1. *Emphasizes* the crucial need for the United Nations Centre on Transnational Corporations to provide assistance to the Governments of the least developed countries, at their request, in various areas pertaining to foreign direct investment by transnational corporations, as outlined in the report of the Secretary-General, with a view to strengthening their capabilities in dealing with transnational corporations, as well as to devise innovative and action-oriented approaches in that regard, aimed at substantially increasing the contribution of transnational corporations in the least developed countries;

2. *Requests* the Secretary-General to conduct a study on home-country legislation on investment by transnational corporations in the least developed countries;

3. *Invites* the Secretary-General to study further the impact of levels of official development assistance, balance-of-payment support, technical assistance and other forms of assistance to the least developed countries on flows of foreign direct investment to those countries;

4. *Requests* the United Nations Centre on Transnational Corporations to participate actively in the Sec-

ond United Nations Conference on the Least Developed Countries, to be held in 1990, and in the preparatory meetings for that Conference;

5. *Requests* the Secretary-General to submit a report to the Commission on Transnational Corporations at its sixteenth session on the implementation of the present resolution.

Economic and Social Council resolution 1989/23

24 May 1989   Meeting 15   Adopted without vote

Approved by First Committee (E/1989/87) without vote, 19 May (meeting 8); draft by Commission on TNCs (E/1989/28/Rev.1); agenda item 8.

TNCs and the environment

Pursuant to a 1988 request by the Commission on TNCs, the Secretary-General, in February, issued a report[16] on TNCs and issues related to the environment, which identified ways in which TNCs could contribute to long-term development and sustainable growth. At the macro-economic level, TNCs could make investment changes to reduce their negative impact on the global environment. The report stated that, at a more immediate and practical level, TNCs could adopt environmentally sensitive policy directives and management techniques, improve their methods for examining the environmental consequences of high-risk technologies, disseminate more complete information on their environmental practices, and change their procedures for handling toxic wastes. The report also identified some general management principles for sustainable development, namely, that TNCs take more fully into account the social and environmental costs of production; use natural resources efficiently; employ longer time horizons in decision-making; develop and transfer technologies that were environmentally and socially appropriate to each particular region; and invest more in production in poorer countries.

ECONOMIC AND SOCIAL COUNCIL ACTION

On 24 May, on the recommendation of its First Committee, the Economic and Social Council adopted **resolution 1989/25** by recorded vote.

Transnational corporations and environmental protection in developing countries

The Economic and Social Council,

Recalling General Assembly resolutions 42/186 of 11 December 1987 on the Environmental Perspective to the Year 2000 and Beyond, 42/187 of 11 December 1987 on the report of the World Commission on Environment and Development and 43/196 of 20 December 1988 on a United Nations conference on environment and development,

Aware that large industrial enterprises, including transnational corporations, are frequently the repositories of scarce technical skills for the preservation of the environment, and conduct activities in sectors that have an impact on the environment and, to that extent, have a specific responsibility,

Recognizing the role that the United Nations Centre on Transnational Corporations can play in analysing the activities and strategies of transnational corporations in the context of environmental protection and preservation,

Expressing concern that pollution-intensive processes which disrupt the ecological balance and use technology that poses a high risk for the environment have been transferred to developing countries through the operations of transnational corporations,

Expressing concern about the illegal traffic in and dumping of toxic and other hazardous wastes and products in many countries, particularly developing countries,

Noting with satisfaction the recent adoption of the Basel Convention on the Control of Transboundary Movements of Hazardous Wastes and Their Disposal,

Emphasizing the need for all transnational corporations to develop further technologies that are not pollution-intensive or environmentally hazardous and to apply them wherever they operate,

Aware of the co-ordinating role of the United Nations Environment Programme in the field of the environment,

1. *Takes note* of the report of the Secretary-General on transnational corporations and issues relating to the environment;

2. *Requests* the Secretary-General, in consultation with leading experts in this field, transnational corporations and appropriate international organizations, to conduct an analytical study of the main sectors of activity that have adverse effects on environmental preservation and the factors that determine the allocation of activities between developed and developing countries;

3. *Requests* the Secretary-General, in view of the specific responsibilities in this field of large industrial enterprises, including transnational corporations, to continue to develop ways and means of strengthening the participation of those enterprises in efforts to preserve and protect the environment, including, in particular, the elaboration of a set of criteria and operational principles;

4. *Requests* the Secretary-General to gather data on existing sources of information on technologies that are environmentally hazardous and on the availability of alternative technologies, and to make recommendations on ways and means of increasing and facilitating the effective transfer of alternative technologies to developing countries;

5. *Requests* the Secretary-General to identify ways in which developing countries in particular might benefit from the experience of other countries in their efforts to protect the environment in relation to the activities of industrial enterprises, including transnational corporations;

6. *Requests* the Secretary-General, in consultation with Governments and other interested parties, to examine, within the context of overall efforts for the preservation of the environment, in particular for strengthening the role of transnational corporations, the feasibility of establishing a fund financed by voluntary contributions from transnational corporations and devoted to supporting the efforts of developing countries to protect the environment;

7. *Requests* the Secretary-General to submit to the Commission on Transnational Corporations at its six-

teenth session a report on the implementation of the present resolution.

Economic and Social Council resolution 1989/25

24 May 1989   Meeting 15   53-1 (recorded vote)

Approved by First Committee (E/1989/87) by roll-call vote (34-1-0), 19 May (meeting 8); draft by Commission on TNCs (E/1989/28/Rev.1); agenda item 8.

Recorded vote in Council as follows:

In favour: Bahamas, Belize, Bolivia, Brazil, Bulgaria, Cameroon, Canada, China, Colombia, Cuba, Czechoslovakia, Denmark, France, Germany, Federal Republic of, Ghana, Greece, Guinea, India, Indonesia, Iran, Iraq, Ireland, Italy, Japan, Jordan, Kenya, Lesotho, Liberia, Libyan Arab Jamahiriya, Netherlands, New Zealand, Nicaragua, Niger, Norway, Oman, Poland, Portugal, Rwanda, Saudi Arabia, Somalia, Sri Lanka, Sudan, Thailand, Trinidad and Tobago, Tunisia, Ukrainian SSR, USSR, United Kingdom, Uruguay, Venezuela, Yugoslavia, Zaire, Zambia.

Against: United States.

Transnational services

In February,[17] the Secretary-General issued a report on the role of TNCs in services other than banking. It focused on the approaches and policies of developing countries towards transnational service corporations and on the possible contributions such corporations could make to development. It found that developing countries had, in general, not been left out of the global shift in foreign direct investment towards services, but that regulations for foreign direct investment in services in developing countries tended to be more restrictive than for manufacturing.

In March,[18] the Secretary-General issued a report on the role of transnational banks in developing countries, noting that lending to those countries peaked in 1974-1982 and was followed by a sharp reduction, which, when combined with debt service on the previous loans, led to a sizeable reverse transfer of resources during the period 1983-1986. The report stated that new initiatives were needed to integrate proposals for debt relief into a coherent strategy. One suggestion was that debt problems should be treated as if an international law of bankruptcy were in effect. The report also suggested policy measures to improve the contribution of transnational banks to development through on-shore operations.

ECONOMIC AND SOCIAL COUNCIL ACTION

On 24 May, on the recommendation of its First Committee, the Economic and Social Council adopted **resolution 1989/28** by recorded vote.

Role of transnational banks in developing countries

The Economic and Social Council,

Recalling General Assembly resolution 43/198 of 20 December 1988 entitled ''External debt crisis and development: towards a durable solution of the debt problems'',

Recalling its resolution 1988/58 of 27 July 1988 on strengthening the role of the Commission on Transnational Corporations and the activities of the United Nations Centre on Transnational Corporations in support of developing countries,

Reaffirming the importance of continuing the consideration by the Commission on Transnational Corporations of issues related to the activities of transnational banks,

Taking into account the linkage existing between the activities of transnational banks on the one hand, and the financial flow of resources to, and the external indebtedness of, the developing countries on the other,

Taking into account also the role of the United Nations Centre on Transnational Corporations in the context of the interrelatedness of the activities and policies of all relevant actors in the field of external indebtedness,

Taking into account further the contribution transnational banks can make to a solution of the external debt problems of developing countries and certain other countries with serious debt-servicing problems,

Requests the Secretary-General to prepare for submission to the Commission on Transnational Corporations at its sixteenth session a report on the present and potential activities of transnational banks related to the external indebtedness of developing countries and certain other countries with serious debt-servicing problems, taking into account the recent proposals that emphasize, *inter alia*, reduction of the stock and service of commercial debt.

Economic and Social Council resolution 1989/28

24 May 1989   Meeting 15   52-1-1 (recorded vote)

Approved by First Committee (E/1989/87) by roll-call vote (43-1-1), 19 May (meeting 8); draft by Commission on TNCs (E/1989/28/Rev.1); agenda item 8.

Recorded vote in Council as follows:

In favour: Bahamas, Belize, Bolivia, Brazil, Bulgaria, Cameroon, China, Colombia, Cuba, Czechoslovakia, Denmark, France, Germany, Federal Republic of, Ghana, Greece, Guinea, India, Indonesia, Iran, Iraq, Ireland, Italy, Japan, Jordan, Kenya, Lesotho, Liberia, Libyan Arab Jamahiriya, Netherlands, New Zealand, Nicaragua, Niger, Norway, Oman, Poland, Portugal, Rwanda, Saudi Arabia, Somalia, Sri Lanka, Sudan, Thailand, Trinidad and Tobago, Tunisia, Ukrainian SSR, USSR, United Kingdom, Uruguay, Venezuela, Yugoslavia, Zaire, Zambia.

Against: United States.

Abstaining: Canada.

REFERENCES

[1]E/1989/28/Rev.1 [2]E/C.10/1989/8. [3]E/C.10/1989/9. [4]E/1989/17. [5]YUN 1986, p. 526. [6]YUN 1988, p. 429, ESC res. 1988/56, 27 July 1988. [7]A/44/576-S/20867. [8]E/C.10/AC.4/1989/3. [9]E/C.10/AC.4/1989/7. [10]E/C.10/AC.4/1989/5. [11]E/C.10/AC.4/1989/6. [12]E/C.10/AC.4/1989/4 & Corr.1. [13]E/C.10/AC.4/1989/8. [14]E/C.10/1989/2. [15]E/C.10/1989/6. [16]E/C.10/1989/12. [17]E/C.10/1989/14. [18]E/C.10/1989/13.

Centre on TNCs

In 1989, the UN Centre on TNCs continued to develop an information system, to conduct research and to carry out technical co-operation activities. It also acted as the secretariat to the Commission on TNCs and the Intergovernmental Working Group of Experts on International Standards of Accounting and Reporting.

The Secretary-General submitted a report on activities of the Centre and the joint units established with the regional commissions.[1] It summarized the Centre's work on securing an effective code of conduct and other international arrangements and agreements relating to TNCs. It also described the Centre's activities aimed at minimizing the negative effects of TNCs and enhancing their contribution to development, as well as strengthening the capacities of host developing countries in dealing with matters relating to TNCs.

ECONOMIC AND SOCIAL COUNCIL ACTION

On 24 May, on the recommendation of its First Committee, the Economic and Social Council adopted **resolution 1989/21** without vote.

Activities of the United Nations Centre on Transnational Corporations related to economic co-operation among developing countries

The Economic and Social Council,

Recalling General Assembly resolutions 3241(XXIX) of 29 November 1974, 32/182 of 19 December 1977, 33/134 of 19 December 1978 and 39/216 of 18 December 1984 concerning economic co-operation among developing countries,

Reaffirming the important role that economic co-operation among developing countries can play in promoting the development of developing countries,

Recognizing the competence of the United Nations Centre on Transnational Corporations in the areas of transnational corporations in general and of joint ventures and other alternative and new forms of international economic co-operation among national corporations from different developing countries,

Encouraged by the fact that a sizeable portion of the foreign investment in the least developed among the developing countries is received from developing countries,

1. *Affirms* the need to enlarge the role of the United Nations Centre on Transnational Corporations in promoting new forms of economic co-operation among developing countries within its mandate and in technical co-operation and assistance for interested developing countries;

2. *Requests* the Secretary-General to conduct a study of the experience of joint ventures among national corporations from different developing countries and their contribution to the development process in developing countries, including an analysis of the possibilities and potentialities offered in this field by regional economic integration and co-operation among developing countries;

3. *Invites* the Centre to explore the possibilities for further increasing the co-operation between the least developed countries and other developing countries in the field of foreign investment;

4. *Requests* the Secretary-General to include in the study referred to in paragraph 2 above specific proposals on ways and means of promoting that form of co-operation and to report on the matter to the Commission on Transnational Corporations at its sixteenth session.

Economic and Social Council resolution 1989/21

24 May 1989   Meeting 15   Adopted without vote

Approved by First Committee (E/1989/87) without vote, 19 May (meeting 8); draft by Commission on TNCs (E/1989/28/Rev.1); agenda item 8.

Information system

The Centre has developed a system for the exchange of textual information and statistical data on TNCs and foreign direct investment. In response to the need for information on TNCs in developing countries, the Centre compiled a data-base on international standards to facilitate integration into national data-bases. Other activities to develop the information system included compiling statistics on foreign direct investment, economic and financial data on the world's largest TNCs in the manufacturing and extractive sectors and information on policies, laws and regulations. The Centre added to its collection of contracts and agreements negotiated between developing countries and TNCs, and provided information on information sources. It continued its work on a directory and data-base of the world's 500 largest service firms and began a feasibility study on creating a UN information dissemination system on hazardous technologies.

During the year, work continued on a manual on information needs and sources.[2] Intended to meet the requirements of developing countries when making decisions on involving TNCs in their economies, the manual would address the kinds of information pertinent to the decision-making process, as well as the sources, tools and technologies useful in that process. The second part of the manual would concern information system development.

The Centre continued to respond to requests from government institutions for assistance in developing and refining national information systems on TNCs, with a view to increasing the effectiveness of those systems.

During 1989, requests from Governments, trade unions, business organizations, academic institutions and the media and public interest groups increased. The information system received 2,019 requests for which the responses required research, as well as an additional 2,415 short queries.

Joint units with regional commissions

Joint units of the Centre and the UN regional commissions continued to operate in 1989 in Africa, Asia and the Pacific, Europe, Latin America and the Caribbean, and Western Asia.[1]

The joint unit with the Economic Commission for Africa (ECA) focused its efforts on research on TNCs within the context of the United Nations Programme of Action for African Economic Recovery and Development 1986-1990,[3] emphasizing the role of foreign private investment in African development and the role of institutional mechanisms in promoting foreign direct investment. Studies were also conducted on the role of TNCs in the development of information technology in Africa and on regional co-operation in arrangements and agreements relating to foreign direct investment in the ECA region. The unit collected data on foreign direct investment and the main TNC operations in the African region for the directory to be issued by the Centre, and assisted in workshops and training programmes. A number of advisory missions were undertaken to selected countries to assess the role of TNCs in development financing in Africa, as well as to review the development of national information systems on TNCs, regional arrangements related to TNCs, and the role of TNCs in the development of information technology in Africa.

The joint unit with the Economic Commission for Europe (ECE) undertook research projects on international co-operation agreements and international take-overs/mergers, the establishment of Japanese TNCs in Europe, foreign direct investment and TNCs in services, and public development finance corporations as a means to enhance foreign direct investment in developing countries. The unit also assisted in seminars and meetings, represented the Centre in intergovernmental conferences held in Geneva, supported the European Documentation Centre on TNCs, and maintained liaison with other international organizations and governmental agencies in Europe.

The joint unit with the Economic and Social Commission for Asia and the Pacific (ESCAP) researched the impact of TNCs in the trade of selected primary commodities in the ESCAP region and the subject of transnational technology towards the year 2000. The unit also conducted preparatory data collection and literature review for its project on TNCs and selected service industries of Asian and Pacific developing countries. During the year, an expert group meeting on environmental management of TNCs in pollution-intensive industries in the ESCAP region (Bangkok, Thailand, 10-12 May) and a workshop on transnational investments in Malaysia (Kuala Lumpur, 13-17 November) were organized. The unit also provided advisory services in China, Hong Kong, India, Indonesia, Malaysia, Papua New Guinea, the Philippines, the Republic of Korea and Singapore.

The joint unit established with the Economic Commission for Latin America and the Caribbean continued to help prepare the *World TNC Yearbook* by gathering information from national sources, developing a regional network of focal points, identifying methodologies and working definitions in each country, and supplementing local reports with additional information available to the unit. The first phase of the project, to be completed in 1990, would include 11 country reports (Argentina, Bolivia, Brazil, Chile, Colombia, Ecuador, Mexico, Paraguay, Peru, Uruguay, Venezuela). Research was undertaken on policy alternatives towards foreign investment, USSR–Latin American joint ventures, the impact of TNCs on industrial restructuring in Latin America and the Carib-

bean, transnational banks and national financing sectors, and transnational banks and the debt crisis.

The joint unit established with the Economic and Social Commission for Western Asia (ESCWA) prepared a report on the status of the negotiations on the draft code of conduct relating to TNCs and other relevant regional and international agreements. It assisted in an intergovernmental meeting on trade in services and development in the ESCWA region (Baghdad, Iraq, 17-19 January) and a pan-arab intergovernmental meeting on UN efforts towards the international harmonization of accounting and reporting by TNCs (Baghdad, 19 and 20 November). The unit and the Centre co-sponsored a workshop, organized by ESCWA and the United Nations Industrial Development Organization, on negotiating and contracting for the acquisition of technology, equipment and materials (Muscat, Oman, 18-28 October). A research project was begun on Arab petrochemicals and rising protectionism in the developed market economies, particularly the European Community, and would be completed during 1990 with the cooperation of the joint unit with ECE.

On 24 May, the Economic and Social Council, by **resolution 1989/26**, requested the Secretary-General to prepare a report containing, *inter alia*, recommendations on alternative strategies to encourage TNCs to respond positively to improvements in the investment climate in Africa, thereby promoting economic growth and self-sustaining development, in accordance with the UN Programme of Action for African Economic Recovery and Development 1986-1990.

Research

In February, the Secretary-General issued a report[4] on continuing and future research programmes of the Centre, focusing on the impact of new technologies on the activities of TNCs and the transfer of such technologies to developing countries. It stated that although new technologies could create many opportunities for developing countries, there were also potential problems. The principal areas likely to be affected by the new technologies were the competitiveness of exports of minerals, commodities and traditional processed products from developing countries; the structure and strategies of TNCs; the location of enterprises based on the utilization of new technologies; and employment and earnings as a result of the above factors. The report emphasized the need for constant review and re-evaluation of policies on TNCs and the transfer of new technologies to developing countries.

During 1989, the Centre published two issues of the *CTC Reporter* and four issues of *Transnationals*, a new quarterly newsletter.

In co-operation with the International Development Research Centre of Canada, a paper on small and medium-sized enterprises in foreign direct investment was prepared.

The Centre started a research project on intellectual property rights and foreign direct investment, particularly in relation to computer software, semiconductor layouts and data-bases. Another study, on the adverse effects of energy-producing and energy-consuming TNCs on global climate change, was also begun.

The Centre continued its research in response to a growing interest in services resulting from the progress of the Uruguay Round of multilateral trade negotiations, and published *Transnational Service Corporations and Developing Countries: Impact and Policy Issues*[5] and *Transnational Corporations in the Construction and Design Engineering Industry*.[6]

Technical co-operation

In 1989,[1] host developing countries continued to seek the Centre's assistance in devising investment policies, structuring régimes for investments in specific sectors, and drafting model contracts and agreements in order to attract more appropriate investments and much-needed technologies.

During the year, the Centre completed or initiated 120 advisory and information projects, the majority of which concerned the formulation of foreign investment régimes and model contracts and agreements, and the streamlining of institutional mechanisms and administrative procedure for promoting and monitoring foreign investment. Of the Centre's projects, 30 were on general issues, 20 on hard-rock mining, 16 on tourism and other services, and 20 on petroleum. The rest dealt with such other issues as technology transfer, manufacturing, forestry, agriculture and fisheries. By region, 65 projects were in Africa, 42 in Asia and the Pacific and 13 in Latin America and the Caribbean. The Centre implemented 30 training projects, consisting of 20 workshops and 10 study tours and fellowships. Syllabuses in economics, business administration and law on TNCs developed by the Centre were used in a number of universities in Asia and the Pacific. The programme was introduced in Africa and would later be applied in Latin America and the Caribbean.

Countries that newly entered the foreign investment arena involved the Centre in their formulation of liberalized investment laws and regulations. Programmes were designed for seven countries to assist them in establishing legal, fiscal and financial régimes, and to develop the skills of public and private-sector officials in implementing them.

The Centre organized a seminar in the USSR to promote the understanding of accounting practices used in joint ventures and to identify areas for future training. It received a number of requests for assistance and began to set up a task force on the Nakhodka (Soviet Far East) zone of joint entrepreneurship.

The Centre initiated a programme for the Association of South-East Asian Nations (ASEAN) to train ASEAN officials on financial policy and institutional management for better access to external resources from TNCs and transnational banks. Preparations were made for national studies on the financial systems of the ASEAN countries. The Centre also assisted the Pacific Forum secretariat in negotiating with a TNC on the establishment of a regional satellite telecommunications system.

With regard to natural resources, the Centre provided a number of developing countries with assistance in establishing an appropriate fiscal and legal framework for natural resource projects and in strengthening their capacity to handle negotiations with TNCs, particularly in the mining and petroleum sectors.

In a report[7] on experience gained in technical co-operation activities with respect to policies of developing countries for the acquisition of foreign technology, the Secretary-General described the evolution of technology policies, examined some factors that determined an appropriate technology policy, and analysed the critical issues relevant to licensing agreements between TNCs and local enterprises in host countries.

Financing

The Centre's technical co-operation programme continued to be financed mainly by extra-budgetary resources from the Centre's Trust Fund and from allocation from the United Nations Development Programme (UNDP).[1] Total extra-budgetary resources in 1989 amounted to $4,752,061. Contributions to the Trust Fund totalled $2,883,974. The Fund's opening balance was $1,845,222 and interest income amounted to $150,000. Resources made available by UNDP totalled $1,696,465. Total disbursements in 1989 amounted to $4,180,594, with workshops and other training activities accounting for $1,820,868 and advisory projects for $1,155,582.

REFERENCES

[1]E/C.10/1990/16. [2]E/C.10/1989/15. [3]YUN 1986, p. 446, GA res. S-13/2, annex, 1 June 1986. [4]E/C.10/1989/11. [5]*Transnational Service Corporations and Developing Countries: Impact and Policy Issues*, Sales No. E.89.II.A.14. [6]*Transnational Corporations in the Construction and Design Engineering Industry*, Sales No. E.89.II.A.6. [7]E/C.10/1989/10.

Chapter VI

Natural resources, energy and cartography

The development of natural resources, problems of energy resources, and cartographic issues continued to be dealt with by several UN bodies in 1989.

The United Nations Revolving Fund for Natural Resources Exploration entered a new phase with its ongoing efforts to assist developing countries in the exploration and exploitation of their mineral and geothermal energy resources. The Economic and Social Council requested the Administrator of the United Nations Development Programme to outline a programme for the implementation of new techniques, including remote sensing, by which developing countries could enhance their technical capacity for identifying, exploring for and assessing natural resources (resolution 1989/9).

At its eleventh session, the Committee on Natural Resources considered the report of the Secretary-General on trends and salient issues in energy resources. By resolution 1989/5, the Council requested the Secretary-General to continue to conduct studies on prospects for small-scale mining and to explore ways and means of strengthening technical co-operation and possible sources of financing for small-scale mining initiatives.

In May, the Economic and Social Council called for an outline for a programme on energy-saving devices to overcome the lack of electrical power in developing countries (1989/6).

Concerns for the diminishing stock of the world's scarce water resources continued to engage the attention of the United Nations and its related bodies. The Council (1989/7) requested the Secretary-General to submit a comprehensive report on strategies and measures to continue implementation of the 1977 Mar del Plata Action Plan on the development and conservation of water resources.

In October, the General Assembly affirmed its confidence in the role of the International Atomic Energy Agency in the application of nuclear energy for peaceful purposes (44/13). All nations were urged to strive for effective and harmonious international co-operation in carrying out the work of the Agency and to ensure the effectiveness and efficiency of the Agency's safeguards system for nuclear installations.

UN work in the area of cartography continued in 1989. The Fourth UN Regional Conference for the Americas was held in New York in January. The UN Group of Experts on Geographical Names met in Geneva in May.

Natural resources

Committee on Natural Resources

The Committee on Natural Resources, at its eleventh session (New York, 27 March–5 April 1989),[1] discussed mineral, water and energy resources; new techniques for identifying, exploring for and assessing natural resources; activities of the UN Revolving Fund for Natural Resources Exploration; permanent sovereignty over natural resources; co-ordination of programmes within the UN system; and programme questions. The Committee recommended eight draft resolutions and one draft decision for adoption by the Economic and Social Council. It also decided[2] to include in its 1990 agenda an item entitled "Disaster prevention and mitigation in developing and utilizing natural resources".

On 22 May, the Economic and Social Council, by **decision 1989/117**, noted the Committee's report, approved the provisional agenda and documentation for its 1990 session, and decided that priority should be given to the question of energy resources.

Exploration

**UN Revolving Fund for
Natural Resources Exploration**

In 1989, the UN Revolving Fund for Natural Resources Exploration continued to assist developing countries in natural resources exploration and development. It also pursued the two long-term goals of more equitable geographic distribution of its projects and greater diversity in the type of minerals being sought.[3]

The Fund signed its first replenishment agreement with the Government of the Philippines, covering deposits of metallurgical chromite ore on the island of Dinagat. The deposits, an estimated 2 million tons with a potential ground value as high as $200 million, were to be extracted by small-scale miners under licence from the Government. The Fund completed a gold exploration operation in Peru which identified 250 million cubic metres of gold-bearing gravel. In Honduras, drilling in the Yuscarán area was completed, confirming the existence of gold and silver deposits with an estimated value of $150 million. Another drilling programme was completed in Ghana, and a report was being prepared on the feasibility of extensions to dormant gold-mines.

New projects began during the year. A pyrophyllite project was started in Fujian Province, China, with financial support from Italy; in Bolivia, a gold exploration project was initiated.

The Fund also negotiated for heavy mineral exploration in Sri Lanka, for gold drilling in the United Republic of Tanzania and in Zimbabwe, and for chromite exploration in Madagascar. El Salvador, Guatemala and Honduras agreed to seek financing for Fund mineral projects in the Trifinio region, which incorporates part of each of the three countries.

In the field of geothermal energy, the Fund submitted a final report for its first geothermal project in St. Lucia and continued to assist the Government in attracting investment for it. Work on geothermal exploration continued in China and in Nicaragua.

UNDP action. On 30 June 1989, the Governing Council of the United Nations Development Programme (UNDP) took note[4] of the Administrator's report on Fund activities for 1987-1988.[5] It noted his approval of supplementary short-term financing for the geothermal exploration project in St. Lucia, and approved exploration for pyrophyllite in China, chromite in the Philippines, and precious and base metals in Guatemala. The Administrator was asked to explore alternative ways of securing the Fund's activities, in view of the continuing low levels of financial contributions.

Financing

In 1989, Fund project expenditures totalled $1.2 million, compared to $6.9 million in 1988. Total income was $3.5 million, including voluntary contributions of $2.5 million from seven Governments. At year's end, the Fund's balance stood at $4.5 million.

ECONOMIC AND SOCIAL COUNCIL ACTION

On 22 May, the Economic and Social Council, on the recommendation of its First (Economic) Committee, adopted **resolution 1989/9** without vote.

United Nations Revolving Fund for Natural Resources Exploration

The Economic and Social Council,

Recalling General Assembly resolution 3167(XXVIII) of 17 December 1973 and Economic and Social Council resolution 1762(LIV) of 18 May 1973, concerning the establishment of the United Nations Revolving Fund for Natural Resources Exploration,

Recalling also General Assembly resolution 33/194 of 29 January 1979 on multilateral development assistance for the exploration of natural resources,

Recognizing the important role of the Fund in providing assistance to developing countries in the development of their natural resources,

Recognizing also the need for the developing countries to enhance their technical capacity for identifying, exploring for and assessing natural resources,

Noting the low level of the general financial resources of the Fund, and the consequent limitations on its ability to fulfil its mandate,

1. *Notes with appreciation* the achievements of the United Nations Revolving Fund for Natural Resources Exploration and its ongoing efforts to assist developing countries in the exploration of their mineral and geothermal energy resources;

2. *Welcomes* the further efforts made by the Fund to promote pre-investment follow-up of successful mineral discoveries, in close co-operation with recipient Governments;

3. *Notes* the interest shown by an increasing number of Governments in co-financing specific projects of the Fund;

4. *Notes also* the efforts of the Fund to expand the geographical distribution of its projects and to promote exploration for a greater variety of minerals;

5. *Requests* that projects implemented by the Fund incorporate, where appropriate and within the existing mandate of the Fund, new techniques, including remote sensing, and provide appropriate opportunities by which developing countries can enhance their technical capacity for identifying, exploring for and assessing natural resources;

6. *Requests* the Fund to expand the use of locally available goods and services in the implementation of its projects;

7. *Recognizes* the urgent need to increase financial support for the Fund by means of voluntary contributions so that it may continue to fulfil its mandate;

8. *Requests* the Administrator of the United Nations Development Programme to submit to the Committee on Natural Resources at its twelfth session a report on the implementation of the present resolution.

Economic and Social Council resolution 1989/9

22 May 1989   Meeting 12   Adopted without vote

Approved by First Committee (E/1989/86) without vote, 17 May (meeting 7); draft by Committee on Natural Resources (E/1989/26); agenda item 7.

On 28 July, the Council, by **decision 1989/189**, took note of the report of the Administrator on the Fund's activities for 1987-1988.

New techniques for exploration and assessment

In 1989, at its eleventh session,[1] the Committee on Natural Resources considered new techniques for identifying, exploring for and assessing natural resources. It had before it a report[6] of the Secretary-General on the feasibility of establishing an information referral system on satellite remote-sensing data.

The report described the major sources of satellite remote-sensing data and discussed selected existing commercial satellite remote-sensing referral systems that provide data on global coverage.

Due to financial constraints, an alternative to the establishment of an information referral system within the Secretariat was proposed, by which existing data banks and referral systems would be used, with the United Nations performing a clearing-house function.

ECONOMIC AND SOCIAL COUNCIL ACTION

On 22 May, the Economic and Social Council, on the recommendation of its First Committee, adopted **resolution 1989/8** without vote.

New techniques, including remote sensing, for identifying, exploring for and assessing natural resources

The Economic and Social Council,

Recalling General Assembly resolution 41/65 of 3 December 1986 on principles relating to remote sensing of the Earth from outer space,

Recalling also its resolution 1987/9 of 26 May 1987,

Having considered the report of the Secretary-General on an information referral system on satellite remote-sensing data,

Considering that developing countries need to be apprised of the limitations and opportunities of commercial and non-commercial hardware and software systems for digital processing of remote-sensing data and of procedures for obtaining access to such systems,

Bearing in mind the important role of remote-sensing data in the process of identifying, exploring for and assessing natural resources,

Recognizing the need for developing countries to have access to the information obtained by remote sensing in order to optimize the utilization of their natural resources,

1. *Takes note* of the two options proposed in the report of the Secretary-General and requests the Secretary-General to submit an updated version of that report to the Committee on Natural Resources at its twelfth session;

2. *Calls upon* the developed countries to expand the sharing of their technical capacity in remote sensing with the developing countries;

3. *Requests* the Secretary-General to explore appropriate ways and means by which the developing countries can gain easier and increased access to remote-sensing systems in order to optimize the exploration and exploitation of their natural resources;

4. *Calls upon* the developed countries to contribute to the efforts of the Secretary-General aimed at identifying approaches and modalities that would facilitate the transfer of new and emerging remote-sensing technologies to the developing countries;

5. *Requests* the Secretary-General to intensify his efforts, within existing resources, in the dissemination of available remote-sensing software packages, in both the commercial and the public sectors, for the exploration, exploitation, management and development of natural resources through application-oriented workshops, seminars and training courses to be organized at the regional or the country level in developing countries;

6. *Also requests* the Secretary-General to submit to the Committee on Natural Resources at its twelfth session a report on the implementation of the present resolution.

Economic and Social Council resolution 1989/8

22 May 1989   Meeting 12   Adopted without vote

Approved by First Committee (E/1989/86) without vote, 17 May (meeting 7); draft by Committee on Natural Resources (E/1989/26); agenda item 7.

Application of microcomputers

In response to a 1987 Economic and Social Council request,[7] the Secretary-General reported[8] to the Committee on Natural Resources on the application of microcomputer technology to resource development in developing countries. He reviewed new techniques and innovations, recent activities of the Department of Technical Co-operation for Development (DTCD), and activities of other UN organizations in the energy and natural resources sectors. DTCD had embarked on the establishment of a microcomputer software reference library, which was to contain software developed for the natural resource sectors relating to energy, minerals and water.

The Secretary-General emphasized, in the light of the importance of microcomputer-based information systems for the planning and development of energy, mineral and water resources, the need for seminars and workshops for the training of developing country nationals.

Permanent sovereignty over natural resources

In a report[9] submitted in accordance with a 1987 request[10] by the Economic and Social Council, the Secretary-General discussed developments related to the exercise of permanent sovereignty over natural resources, particularly in the non-fuel minerals industry. The report considered the relationship between mineral-producing developing countries and the international economic system. It also reviewed public-sector activities in mineral and petroleum development; mineral development policy and permanent sovereignty; the relationship of mineral financing and national debt; mineral taxation; and developments in the hydrocarbon sector, including natural gas exploitation and cross-border petroleum development.

The ability of mineral-producing countries to sell commodities in an open world market had been hampered by such measures as tariffs, non-tariff trade barriers, production subsidies which distorted or restricted trade, and government regulations protecting domestic mineral production at prices far above competitive world market prices. The report concluded that resource protectionism and distortion of free trade were in the interest of neither producing nor consuming countries, and that free access to consuming markets was a condition for the success of mineral development.

ECONOMIC AND SOCIAL COUNCIL ACTION

On 22 May, the Economic and Social Council, on the recommendation of its First Committee, adopted **resolution 1989/10** without vote.

Permanent sovereignty over natural resources

The Economic and Social Council,

Recalling its resolution 1987/12 of 26 May 1987,

Recognizing the problems that the present international economic situation causes all countries, in particular the developing countries,

Noting that it is important for all countries, in particular the developing countries, to make optimum economic use of their natural resources in order to strengthen their economic development,

Taking note of the report of the Secretary-General on permanent sovereignty over natural resources,

Taking into account the work done by other organs and organizations of the United Nations system regarding permanent sovereignty over natural resources,

1. *Reaffirms* the importance of the principle of permanent sovereignty over natural resources;

2. *Also reaffirms* the importance of the ongoing work of the Commission on Transnational Corporations on a code of conduct on transnational corporations, as it relates to natural resources;

3. *Requests* the Secretary-General to submit to the Committee on Natural Resources at its twelfth session a concise, updated report on permanent sovereignty over natural resources.

Economic and Social Council resolution 1989/10

22 May 1989   Meeting 12   Adopted without vote

Approved by First Committee (E/1989/86) without vote, 17 May (meeting 7); draft by Committee on Natural Resources (E/1989/26); agenda item 7.

Mineral resources

In 1989, total delivery for mineral resources projects executed by DTCD was $15.2 million, up from $12.5 million in 1988,[11] with most expenditures in Africa and Asia. DTCD conducted 120 advisory missions; requests for advisory services were mainly in mineral sector planning, programming, mineral exploration and processing, organizational strengthening, investment promotion and fields requiring highly specialized expertise.

Two seminars took place in 1989. A seminar held in co-operation with the International Chamber of Commerce of Minas Gerais and with UNDP support (Belo Horizonte, Brazil, 28-29 September) trained executives in joint-ventures negotiations under new legislation, while an interregional seminar (Yamoussoukro, Côte d'Ivoire, 11-15 December) addressed the mining exploration and investment potential of West Africa and was organized by DTCD and the Ministry of Mines of Côte d'Ivoire with UNDP support.

In a report[12] on mineral resources, the Secretary-General discussed trends in the international mineral sector, in particular consumption, trade and supply patterns, stocks and prices, short-term prospects for metal markets, technology and long-term consumption trends, new cost-saving technologies, and development of non-metallic minerals. He concluded that the current high prices for major metals and continuing fluctuations of mineral commodity prices were likely to induce

consuming sectors to seek alternatives to raw metallic materials. The mining industry, Governments and companies would be well advised to strengthen efforts to develop new applications and make natural raw materials more efficient in current applications. Market development activities would also be necessary in other sectors, in particular copper, lead, zinc and tin, if more substitution of metals was to be avoided.

In another report,[13] the Secretary-General discussed small-scale mining prospects in developing countries. These types of operations included artisanal mining, involving individuals, families and *ad hoc* groups; co-operatives; and partly mechanized, centrally managed quarrying and mining activities with limited technical and managerial know-how. The report described the growing interest in small-scale mining; its significance and characteristics; socio-economic conditions and national policies; and technical co-operation activities of DTCD.

The report stated that problems of small-scale mining—including a lack of technical and managerial expertise and mechanized equipment, an uncertain legal environment, social hardships and difficult access to markets—must be dealt with at the national level. It suggested such measures as the creation of legal, fiscal and administrative conditions favourable to an active small-scale mining sector; introduction and maintenance of a reasonable foreign exchange régime combined with easy access to marketing channels; and realistic pricing of mineral products in accordance with world market conditions. Noting a need for regional and international programmes to assist developing countries, it also suggested, as possible future activities of DTCD, basic data gathering and dissemination of information; formulation of policies and legislation; human resources development; technical advice; and the supply of essential equipment.

ECONOMIC AND SOCIAL COUNCIL ACTION

On 22 May, the Economic and Social Council, on the recommendation of its First Committee, adopted **resolution 1989/5** without vote.

Trends and salient issues in the development of mineral resources, especially small-scale mining

The Economic and Social Council,

Recalling its resolutions 1985/47 of 25 July 1985 and 1987/8 of 26 May 1987, in which the effective contribution of small-scale mining to the economic and social development of some countries was recognized, in particular as a source of employment and regional development,

Considering that small-scale mines are often characterized by high labour intensity and low labour productivity and that working conditions are often hazardous and related legal protection is often inadequate,

Noting that the International Labour Organisation will hold the Fifth Tripartite Technical Meeting for Mines

Other than Coal Mines at Geneva in 1990, at which labour and social issues in the sector will be discussed,

Aware of the need to balance small-scale mining operations with the improvement of social working conditions and benefits and the consideration of health hazards and safety,

1. *Takes note* of the reports of the Secretary-General on small-scale mining prospects in developing countries and on trends and salient issues in mineral resources;

2. *Recommends* that in the elaboration of the international development strategy for the fourth United Nations development decade, in regard to issues relating to mineral resources, special attention should be given to training in the development of new approaches, including methods, in small-scale mining, in accordance with national development plans and priorities;

3. *Requests* the Secretary-General to continue to conduct studies on prospects for small-scale mining, to evaluate the experience gained through technical co-operation endeavours and to explore ways and means of strengthening technical co-operation and possible sources of financing for small-scale mining initiatives;

4. *Also requests* the Secretary-General to ensure the assistance of the United Nations system in providing adequate facilities for seminars and symposia, to promote local dissemination of information on small-scale mining and to establish policies and programmes, according to the priorities of Member States, for the support and promotion of small-scale mining projects;

5. *Further requests* the Secretary-General to submit to the Committee on Natural Resources at its twelfth session an updated report on trends and salient issues in the development of mineral resources, especially small-scale mining, including the outcome of the Fifth Tripartite Technical Meeting for Mines Other than Coal Mines, to be convened by the International Labour Organisation at Geneva in 1990, particularly with regard to issues relating to working conditions and occupational safety and health hazards in small-scale mining.

Economic and Social Council resolution 1989/5

22 May 1989   Meeting 12   Adopted without vote

Approved by First Committee (E/1989/86) without vote, 17 May (meeting 7); draft by Committee on Natural Resources (E/1989/26); agenda item 7.

Water resources

Implementation of the 1977 Mar del Plata Action Plan

In 1989, the Committee on Natural Resources considered the Secretary-General's report[14] on improved efficiency in the management of water resources and developments in co-operative action in the field of shared water resources, as well as his report[15] on progress achieved and problems foreseen in the implementation by Governments of the 1977 Mar del Plata Action Plan.[16]

The first report presented the views of 28 Governments in response to the report of the Interregional Symposium on Improved Efficiency in the Management of Water Resources: Follow-up to the Mar del Plata Action Plan.[17] The major problems identified were a lack of financial resources and insufficient trained manpower. The improvement of water quality was cited as a primary goal. The report found that since the adoption of the Action Plan, more emphasis had been placed on legislation, institution-building, human resources, training and community participation. As for co-operative action in shared water resources, the report discussed the exchange of data and information on meteorological, hydrological and climatological phenomena; common efforts against land degradation, desertification and floods; and prevention and control of transboundary pollution of water. Significant progress was noted in the development of data bases, data exchange, flood and erosion alleviation studies and measures, and prevention and control of transboundary pollution.

The second report reviewed progress in implementation of the Action Plan by region, and considered the formulation of a strategy for the 1990s. It expressed concern over the serious situation regarding water resources assessment, drinking-water supply and sanitation, agriculture, urban growth and pollution, water management and legislation, and financing of water resources development. As demand grew, efficient water use became more necessary. It concluded that these issues needed to be worked out in more detail for the implementation of the Action Plan.

In March, a panel of experts, financed by UNDP and hosted by the World Health Organization, met (Challes Les Eaux, France, 8-10 March) to formulate a strategy. It recommended the establishment of benchmarks against which progress could be gauged, and that assessments should take into account the principles of sustainable development and the effects of population dynamics. Other areas recommended for particular attention were water resources assessment and management, mobilization of financial resources, water resources technology and human resources management.

ECONOMIC AND SOCIAL COUNCIL ACTION

On 22 May, the Economic and Social Council, on the recommendation of its First Committee, adopted **resolution 1989/7** without vote.

Water resources and progress in the implementation of the Mar del Plata Action Plan

The Economic and Social Council,

Recalling General Assembly resolution 32/158 of 19 December 1977,

Recalling also General Assembly resolution 34/191 of 18 December 1979, in which the Assembly requested the Committee on Natural Resources to review during the 1980s the progress made by Governments in the implementation of the Mar del Plata Action Plan and provide guidance to the supporting water-related activities undertaken by the organizations of the United Nations system,

Recalling further its resolutions 1979/67, 1979/68 and 1979/70 of 3 August 1979, 1981/80 and 1981/81 of 24 July

1981, 1983/57 of 28 July 1983, 1985/49 of 25 July 1985 and 1987/7 of 26 May 1987 concerning the implementation of the Mar del Plata Action Plan,

Aware that some of the major obstacles confronting developing countries in their endeavours to implement the Mar del Plata Action Plan are lack of financial and technical resources and insufficient expertise in water resources management,

Considering the need to give high priority to strengthening the capacity of the developing countries to assess their water resources through the collection, analysis and dissemination of hydrological and hydrogeological data,

Having considered the reports of the Secretary-General on improved efficiency in the management of water resources and developments in co-operative action in the field of shared water resources and on progress achieved and foreseen in the implementation by Governments of the Mar del Plata Action Plan,

Bearing in mind the oral report on the work of the panel of experts, carried out under the auspices of the United Nations Development Programme in March 1989, regarding issues to be incorporated in the proposals for a comprehensive strategy to implement the Mar del Plata Action Plan, made before the Committee on Natural Resources at its 204th meeting, on 30 March 1989, by the representative of the United Nations Secretariat,

1. *Expresses* its deep concern regarding the obstacles that make it difficult for the developing countries to prevent natural disasters, such as flooding, which endanger the lives of a large number of their inhabitants and have negative effects on the process of development, especially of agriculture;

2. *Takes note* of the report of the Secretary-General on improved efficiency in the management of water resources and developments in co-operative action in the field of shared water resources, part one of which contains the views of Governments on the report of the Interregional Symposium on Improved Efficiency in the Management of Water Resources: Follow-up to the Mar del Plata Action Plan, held in New York from 5 to 9 January 1987, and includes possible solutions to the problems facing countries, particularly developing countries, in dealing with water resources management;

3. *Urges* the organizations of the United Nations system to intensify their efforts and increase their activities in water resources management, including recycling of waste water, with a view to strengthening the capacities of developing countries in water resources development through, *inter alia*, the assessment, analysis and dissemination of hydrological and hydrogeological data;

4. *Requests* the Secretary-General to submit to the Committee on Natural Resources at its twelfth session a comprehensive report on strategies and measures necessary for the implementation of the Mar del Plata Action Plan, as requested in Economic and Social Council resolution 1987/7.

Economic and Social Council resolution 1989/7

22 May 1989   Meeting 12   Adopted without vote

Approved by First Committee (E/1989/86) without vote, 17 May (meeting 7); draft by Committee on Natural Resources (E/1989/26); agenda item 7.

Inter-agency co-ordination

The Intersecretariat Group for Water Resources of the Administrative Committee on Co-ordination (ACC), at its tenth session (New York,

25-27 October),[18] discussed progress on a proposed strategy to implement the Mar del Plata Action Plan in the 1990s. Other topics considered included the water situation in Africa; collection and dissemination of hydrogeological information by UN organizations; issues pertaining to the International Drinking Water Supply and Sanitation Decade (1981-1990)[19] and environmental aspects of water resources.

Technical co-operation

In 1989, water resources projects executed by DTCD were valued at $24.2 million, as compared to $19.2 million in 1988.[11] UNDP financed 117 projects, and 35 interregional advisory missions were sponsored under the UN Regular Programme for Technical Co-operation, covering fields such as water legislation, water-well drilling, computerized data management and hydrogeology.

DTCD's activities concentrated on improving rural water-supply conditions through exploration and development of ground water, maintaining reserve water points for emergency use in water-short areas of developing countries, and strengthening water resources planning at the national and river basin levels. In the area of water supply, the earlier concentration on borehole drilling had evolved to broader water resources planning and management, including training, operation and maintenance, and monitoring.

Due to an increasing demand for the transfer of high technology, DTCD was developing computer software and holding training seminars and workshops. Computers were used in almost all DTCD water projects, which involved storing and analysing data on such factors as rainfall, run-off river flows, lake levels and aquifer characteristics, as well as for modelling. For Bermuda and Nepal, DTCD was developing hydrogeological software consisting of 10 packages and programs sufficient for most normal hydrogeological studies.

Some projects aimed to preserve the environment in parallel with water resources development. In Brazil, a project was under way to restore polluted Lake Paranoa, both by reducing the pollution load from the city of Brasilia and by studying inexpensive pollution control methods. In Qatar, the relationship between overpumping and sea-water intrusion into ground-water aquifers was examined.

During the year, DTCD convened four interregional seminars on various subjects: water resources management techniques for small island countries (Suva, Fiji, 26 June–1 July); water quality management in developing countries (Warsaw, Poland, 18-22 September); water resources planning and management in arid areas (Tashkent, USSR, 17-25 October); and water resources management in drought-prone areas (New Delhi, India, 27 November–1 December).

Co-ordination of UN activities

In a report[20] to the Committee on Natural Resources, the Secretary-General presented an overview of the objectives, priorities and activities of the UN system for the biennium 1988-1989 in water, mineral and energy resources. The review showed that the activities had been carried out in accordance with the guidelines established by the Committee and elaborated upon in the Mar del Plata Action Plan[16] and in the Nairobi Programme of Action on the Development and Utilization of New and Renewable Sources of Energy.[21] No duplication was revealed in the activities of the varous units, but it was suggested that further consideration should be given to strengthening the co-ordination of the activities in minerals and energy resources, particularly at the programming stage. Co-ordination of activities was facilitated by the Intersecretariat Group for Water Resources and the Inter-Agency Group on New and Renewable Sources of Energy, both of the ACC, in their respective fields.

ECONOMIC AND SOCIAL COUNCIL ACTION

On 22 May, the Economic and Social Council, on the recommendation of its First Committee, adopted **resolution 1989/12** without vote.

**Co-ordination of programmes within the
United Nations system in the
field of natural resources**
The Economic and Social Council,
Taking note of the report of the Secretary-General on the activities of the United Nations system in water, mineral and energy resources,
Bearing in mind the broad range of activities proposed for the United Nations in preparation of the medium-term plan for the period 1992-1997,
Convinced of the need to increase the effectiveness and relevance of the work of the United Nations system,
Concerned that the documentation relating to the co-ordination of programmes within the United Nations system in the field of natural resources, prepared for the eleventh session of the Committee on Natural Resources, was not provided sufficiently in advance of the session to allow the Committee to give guidance on the programming and implementation of activities in the United Nations system for the development of natural resources, as called for in its terms of reference,
1. *Requests* the Secretary-General to submit to the Committee on Natural Resources at its twelfth session an updated report containing an overview of the activities of the United Nations system in water, mineral and energy resources, identifying the organizations or units within the United Nations system mandated to carry out work in those fields and assessing the extent to which the guidelines provided by the Committee have been followed;

2. *Also requests* the Secretary-General to implement fully the measures to improve the work of the Committee identified at its tenth session, and to submit documentation at least three months in advance of the Committee's sessions;
3. *Further requests* the Secretary-General to identify, in the report referred to in paragraph 1 above, the existing priorities and objectives for the work of the United Nations system in the field of natural resources.

Economic and Social Council resolution 1989/12

22 May 1989   Meeting 12   Adopted without vote

Approved by First Committee (E/1989/86) without vote, 17 May (meeting 7); draft by Committee on Natural Resources (E/1989/26); agenda item 7.

Also on 22 May, the Economic and Social Council, on the recommendation of its First Committee, adopted **resolution 1989/11** without vote.

**Impact of financial constraints on the
development, conservation and maintenance
of the natural resources and related
infrastructure in developing countries**
The Economic and Social Council,
Recognizing that the financial constraints facing developing countries have reduced their ability to develop, conserve and maintain their natural resources and related infrastructures,
Bearing in mind the detrimental consequences of those problems, which have affected the long-term development prospects of developing countries,
Calls upon the Secretary-General to include in the report requested in paragraph 1 of Council resolution 1989/12 a section on the activities of the organizations of the United Nations system relating to the impact of financial constraints on developing countries in the development, conservation and maintenance of their natural resources.

Economic and Social Council resolution 1989/11

22 May 1989   Meeting 12   Adopted without vote

Approved by First Committee (E/1989/86) without vote, 17 May (meeting 7); draft by Committee on Natural Resources (E/1989/26); agenda item 7.

REFERENCES
[1]E/1989/26. [2]*Ibid.* (dec. 11/1). [3]DP/1990/17/Add.2 (Part II). [4]E/1989/32 (dec. 89/53). [5]YUN 1988, p. 436. [6]E/C.7/1989/2. [7]YUN 1987, p. 566, ESC res. 1987/10, 26 May 1987. [8]E/C.7/1989/3. [9]E/C.7/1989/5. [10]YUN 1987, p. 568, ESC res. 1987/12, 26 May 1987. [11]DP/1990/56/Add.1. [12]E/C.7/1989/7. [13]E/C.7/1989/4 & Add.1. [14]E/C.7/1989/6. [15]E/C.7/1989/8. [16]YUN 1977, p. 553. [17]YUN 1987, p. 571. [18]ACC/1989/PG/9. [19]YUN 1980, p. 702, GA res. 35/18, 10 November 1980. [20]E/C.7/1989/9. [21]YUN 1981, p. 691, GA res. 36/193, 17 December 1981.

Energy

Energy resources development

In 1989, the Committee on Natural Resources had before it a report[1] by the Secretary-General on salient issues in energy resources.

It described trends in the institutional and technological underpinnings of the energy market, including reintegration in the oil industry, movement towards a single European energy market, new electric power technology and advances in super-conductive materials. Energy supply and demand scenarios for the remainder of the century were given separately for developed market economies, developing countries and centrally planned economies.

The report concluded that vigorous policy measures to enhance energy efficiency and spur energy production in forms appropriate to specific locales could not only favourably shape the evolution of the energy sector but also augment the rate of economic growth over the rest of the century.

ECONOMIC AND SOCIAL COUNCIL ACTION

On 22 May, the Economic and Social Council, on the recommendation of its First Committee, adopted **resolution 1989/6** without vote.

Development of energy resources and efficient use of energy production and utilization infrastructures

The Economic and Social Council,

Recalling General Assembly resolution 40/208 of 17 December 1985 on the development of the energy resources of developing countries,

Recalling also General Assembly resolution 43/193 of 20 December 1988, in which the Assembly requested the Secretary-General to outline a programme of action aimed at accelerating the exploration and development of the energy resources of developing countries,

Recalling further its resolution 1987/10 of 26 May 1987 on the application of microcomputer technology in the assessment and development of natural resources and energy,

Considering that the Committee on Natural Resources at its tenth and eleventh sessions focused on water and mineral resources, respectively, and that the practice of giving priority consideration to a particular subject at each session has improved the work of the Committee,

1. *Decides* that the Committee on Natural Resources at its twelfth session shall give priority consideration to energy resources, emphasizing the need to intensify technical co-operation programmes aimed at the exploration, development and efficient utilization of the energy resources of the developing countries, and requests the Secretary-General to submit to the Committee at that session a report on the question of technical co-operation programmes in energy resources;

2. *Reaffirms* the need for the United Nations system to intensify its efforts to promote the international exchange of experience and knowledge and the flow of efficient technologies, especially new and emerging ones and particularly to developing countries, for use in the exploration and exploitation of energy resources, and to pursue actively the establishment of computer-based national information systems on energy technologies and projects, as well as other information for energy policy analysis and energy sector management;

3. *Welcomes* the report of the Secretary-General on trends and salient issues in energy resources and requests

him to submit to the Committee on Natural Resources at its twelfth session a report on trends and salient issues in energy, including the potential of development and utilization of the natural gas, heavy crude, tar sand, oil shale and geothermal resources available in the developing countries, as well as prospects for subregional, regional and interregional co-operation in that area;

4. *Requests* the Secretary-General to submit to the Committee on Natural Resources at its twelfth session a report on energy-saving strategies and measures to improve the efficient utilization of the electricity system, on power-loss reduction and on the upgrading of electricity generation plants, including the level of investment required, as well as other possible options, such as small hydropower stations, to overcome the lack of electrical power in the developing countries.

Economic and Social Council resolution 1989/6

22 May 1989   Meeting 12   Adopted without vote

Approved by First Committee (E/1989/86) without vote, 17 May (meeting 7); draft by Committee on Natural Resources (E/1989/26); agenda item 7.

Technical co-operation

During 1989,[2] DTCD undertook 33 advisory missions, which provided advice on energy policy, resource evaluation and exploration and project design. Feasibility studies were also conducted, in the areas of petroleum, coal, natural gas, electric power, energy planning and conservation, geothermal, solar, wind and multi-source renewable energy packages, computerized data banks and microcomputer-based energy analysis.

Under an interregional project executed in co-operation with the Latin American Energy Organization (OLADE), a training centre equipped with microcomputers, projection systems and course material in Spanish, English and French was established. Several DTCD projects aimed at reducing environmental problems in developing countries, such as geothermal fluid production in Bolivia and China (Tibet); reduction of power losses in Bangladesh; and the efficiency of industrial, transport and residential/commercial sector operations in India, Peru and Zambia. Other projects assisted energy-deficient countries in developing indigenous energy sources. New petroleum development technologies were introduced in China, and pilot programmes were designed for the application in India of enhanced oil recovery techniques.

Under the DTCD global large-scale power plant modernization and rehabilitation programme, projects were under way in Angola, China, Guinea-Bissau and Viet Nam.

Meetings were held to explore new fields of technical co-operation in developing countries, namely petroleum geology and geochemistry (Kiev, Ukrainian SSR, 31 May–6 June); power plant operation, maintenance, rehabilitation and distribution in the Arab region (Amman, Jordan, 3-8 June); wind energy (Roskilde, Denmark, 20-27 August); energy conservation (Stockholm, Sweden, 3-9 September); policy and management of petroleum resources (Oslo, Norway, 25-30 September); solar energy applications (Lanshou, China, 23-29 October); and a marine engineering geological survey for petroleum exploration (Guangzhou, China, 30 November–6 December).

New and renewable energy sources

The ACC Inter-Agency Group on New and Renewable Sources of Energy, at its eighth session (Geneva, 9 and 10 March),[3] considered the follow-up to the Castel Gandolfo Colloquium of High-level Experts on New and Renewable Sources of Energy.[4] It also analysed the report of the fourth (1988) session of the Committee on the Development and Utilization of New and Renewable Sources of Energy.[5] Individual entities of the Group presented their current and planned activities. The Group affirmed the need to look at new and renewable sources of energy in relation to the environment and sustainable development, and also agreed that women's needs should be taken into account and their full participation assured in the planning and implementation of projects.

As a follow-up to proposals made at the Castel Gandolfo Colloquium, the first meeting of the Consultative Group of High-level Experts on New and Renewable Sources of Energy (Rome, 27 and 28 April) provided guidance regarding the feasibility of an international network of research centres in this field. Types of mission and suitable geographical locations for the centres, as well as the networking scheme, were discussed. It was agreed that three or four centres should act as focal points for the creation of networks; Group members would verify, with their respective Governments, their willingness to undertake start-up actions to create the first centres.

Nuclear energy

IAEA report

Total installed nuclear-power-generating capacity in the world amounted to 318 gigawatts in 1989. Nuclear power plants accounted for about 16.8 per cent of the world's electricity generation. During the year, 12 nuclear power plants came on line, in the German Democratic Republic, the Federal Republic of Germany, India, Japan, the Republic of Korea, Mexico, the USSR, the United Kingdom and the United States, bringing the world's total number of operating reactors to 426. In addition, construction began on five reactors in Japan, the Republic of Korea and the USSR.

In August, the Secretary-General transmitted[6] to the General Assembly the 1988 report of the International Atomic Energy Agency (IAEA).[7] In presenting an update of the report to the General Assembly on 25 October,[8] the IAEA

Director General discussed Agency work in such areas as nuclear safeguards (see PART ONE, Chapter II) and nuclear power and the environment. He expressed optimism that the risks associated with nuclear energy could be reduced. Although the advent of nuclear power had been greeted by unbounded optimism and was followed by rapid expansion, the pace of construction had levelled off. He noted that the World Commission on Environment and Development[9] had recognized the need for energy to achieve growth, but had expressed concern over both the severe damage inflicted on the environment by the use of fossil fuels and questions of nuclear waste, accidents and proliferation.

The Director General also said that, as the UN system did not have any agency that covered all energy systems, the IAEA was co-operating with other international organizations, including UNEP, the World Health Organization, the World Meteorological Organization, the World Bank, OECD and the World Energy Conference, in arranging a symposium in which senior experts would examine the consequences for life, health and the environment of different ways of generating electricity.

In 1989, IAEA organized two regional workshops, in China and in Cyprus, to promote the exchange of experience in the use of IAEA methodologies for energy, electricity and nuclear power planning. Agency support was provided to Iran in the review of its Bushehr nuclear power project, and to Romania in the preparation of commissioning procedures for a reactor cooling system. An advisory mission to Indonesia assisted its National Atomic Energy Agency in drawing up terms of reference for a feasibility study on the introduction of nuclear power plants. Quality assurance assistance was provided through 15 technical co-operation projects. The Agency also completed the preparatory work for establishing a regional co-operative agreement for Member States in Africa.

IAEA also participated in the work of the Intergovernmental Panel on Climate Change, providing factual information on the potential role of nuclear power in avoiding carbon dioxide emissions and on issues of nuclear safety. (See PART SEVEN, Chapter I, for further information on activities of IAEA.)

GENERAL ASSEMBLY ACTION

On 25 October 1989, the General Assembly adopted **resolution 44/13** without vote.

Report of the International Atomic Energy Agency
The General Assembly,
Having received the report of the International Atomic Energy Agency to the General Assembly for the year 1988,

Taking note of the statement of the Director General of the International Atomic Energy Agency of 25 October 1989, which provides additional information on the main developments in the Agency's activities during 1989,

Recognizing the importance of the work of the Agency to promote further the application of atomic energy for peaceful purposes, as envisaged in its statute,

Also recognizing the special needs of the developing countries for technical assistance by the Agency in order to benefit effectively from the application of nuclear technology for peaceful purposes as well as from the contribution of nuclear energy to their economic development,

Conscious of the importance of the work of the Agency in the implementation of safeguards provisions of the Treaty on the Non-Proliferation of Nuclear Weapons and other international treaties, conventions and agreements designed to achieve similar objectives, as well as in ensuring, as far as it is able, that the assistance provided by the Agency or at its request or under its supervision or control is not used in such a way as to further any military purpose, as stated in article II of its statute,

Further recognizing the importance of the work of the Agency on nuclear power, nuclear safety, radiological protection and radioactive waste management, including its work directed towards assisting developing countries in planning for the introduction of nuclear power in accordance with their needs,

Again stressing the need for the highest standards of safety in the design and operation of nuclear plants so as to minimize risks to life, health and the environment,

Taking note with appreciation of the report of the Agency on its programme activities with a view to achieving the objectives of sustainable and environmentally sound development,

Noting that the General Conference of the Agency at its thirty-third regular session approved the reappointment by the Board of Governors of the Agency of Mr. Hans Blix as Director General of the Agency for a further term of four years, commencing on 1 December 1989,

Bearing in mind resolutions GC(XXXIII)/RES/506 on Israeli nuclear capabilities and threat, GC(XXXIII)/RES/508 on measures to strengthen international co-operation in matters relating to nuclear safety and radiological protection, GC(XXXIII)/RES/509 on dumping of nuclear wastes, GC(XXXIII)/RES/510 on the Convention on the Physical Protection of Nuclear Material, GC(XXXIII)/RES/511 on the Convention on Early Notification of a Nuclear Accident and the Convention on Assistance in the Case of a Nuclear Accident or Radiological Emergency, GC(XXXIII)/RES/515 on the plan for the production of low-cost potable water and GC(XXXIII)/RES/524 on South Africa's nuclear capabilities, adopted on 29 September 1989 by the General Conference of the Agency at its thirty-third regular session,

1. *Takes note* of the report of the International Atomic Energy Agency;

2. *Affirms* its confidence in the role of the Agency in the application of nuclear energy for peaceful purposes;

3. *Urges* all States to strive for effective and harmonious international co-operation in carrying out the work of the Agency, pursuant to its statute; in promoting the use of nuclear energy and the application of the necessary measures to strengthen further the safety of nuclear installations and to minimize risks to life, health and the environment; in strengthening technical assistance and co-operation for developing countries; and in ensuring the effectiveness and efficiency of the Agency's safeguards system;

4. *Requests* the Secretary-General to transmit to the Director General of the Agency the records of the forty-fourth session of the General Assembly relating to the Agency's activities.

General Assembly resolution 44/13

25 October 1989   Meeting 40   Adopted without vote

3-nation draft (A/44/L.18); agenda item 14.
Sponsors: Czechoslovakia, Japan, Venezuela.

Conventions

Following the nuclear power plant disaster at Chernobyl, Ukrainian SSR, in April 1986, two international conventions were adopted in September of the same year by the IAEA General Conference: one on early notification of a nuclear accident, and the second on assistance in the case of a nuclear accident or radiological emergency.[10] The question of UN accession to these instruments was considered in 1987[11] and again in 1988.[12] On 22 December 1989, by **decision 44/452**, the General Assembly, on the recommendation of its Second Committee, deferred action on the question.

REFERENCES

[1]E/C.7/1989/10. [2]DP/1990/56/Add.1. [3]ACC/1989/PG/1. [4]YUN 1987, p. 579. [5]YUN 1988, p. 441. [6]A/44/450. [7]GC(XXXIII)/873. [8]A/44/PV.39. [9]YUN 1987, p. 679. [10]YUN 1986, p. 1101. [11]YUN 1987, p. 581, GA dec. 42/443, 11 Dec. 1987. [12]YUN 1988, p. 444, GA res. 43/441, 20 Dec. 1988.

Cartography

During 1989, UN projects in cartography in developing countries continued. Technical co-operation projects addressed institution-building, transfer of technical expertise to national cartographic and hydrographic institutions and provision of training and equipment. Fellowships and grants were awarded to candidates from all regions for studies in data processing, photogrammetry, cartography and map compilation, cadastral and land information systems, geographical information systems, integrated digital mapping, geodetic science, map reproduction and map printing.

Fourth UN Regional
Cartographic Conference for the Americas

In March 1989, the Secretary-General submitted a report[1] on the Fourth United Nations Regional Cartographic Conference for the Americas (New York, 23-27 January). Participants recognized the value of holding such conferences in the region and called for a more active involvement of the countries concerned. The latest technology in cartographic data gathering and processing was also reviewed, with special emphasis on potential applications in developing countries. Other topics included the latest developments related to policies and management of national mapping and charting programmes, matters of technical assistance, transfer of appropriate and affordable technology, and future UN regional cartographic conferences. Among the 17 resolutions adopted by the Conference were those concerning technical assistance related to national mapping standards; geographical names of undersea features; training courses in toponymy; hydrographic surveying and nautical charting; development of a world-wide digital cartographic data base; remote sensing for cartography; and the Fifth United Nations Cartographic Conference for the Americas.

On 22 May, the Economic and Social Council, by **decision 1989/116**, noted the Secretary-General's report on the Conference and endorsed the recommendation to convene the Fifth Conference in 1993. The Council also requested the Secretary-General to take measures, where appropriate, to implement the other recommendations made by the Conference.

Standardization of geographical names

In 1989, the United Nations Group of Experts on Geographical Names, at its fourteenth session (Geneva, 17-26 May), considered progress in the standardization of geographical names since its thirteenth session the previous year. The Group reviewed the latest technology related to the standardization of geographical names and its relationship to policy, economy and development in the fields of cartographic data acquisition, manipulation and depiction. It also considered matters of technical assistance and transfer of technology in these areas.

REFERENCE

[1]E/1989/44 & Add.1.

Chapter VII

Science and technology

The year 1989 marked the tenth anniversary of the adoption of the Vienna Programme of Action on Science and Technology for Development, the cornerstone of United Nations activities in that field. An end-of-decade review provided an opportunity for UN bodies dealing with science and technology issues to evaluate progress made through the Vienna Programme of Action and suggest improvements. The General Assembly reaffirmed the Programme's basic goals and validity and expressed concern regarding its implementation.

The activities of UN bodies concerned with science and technology continued to focus on strengthening the scientific and technological activities of developing countries, mobilizing financial resources and upgrading institutional arrangements. The UN Centre for Science and Technology for Development continued to make policy recommendations for action. The Assembly called on UN organizations to devote increased attention to national capacity-building in science and technology and entrusted the Centre, through the Advance Technology Alert System, to serve as the focal point for technological assessment within the UN system.

The Assembly recommended that the UN Fund for Science and Technology for Development give priority to pilot projects on the endogenous capacity-building of developing countries, activities related to new and emerging areas of science and technology, and projects aimed at fostering co-operation among developing countries. It also called upon the Fund and other UN organizations to enhance co-ordination and harmonization at the country level.

Consultations on an international code of conduct on the transfer of technology continued. The Assembly invited the Secretary-General of the UN Conference on Trade and Development to submit a complete report on the outcome of those consultations.

The Intergovernmental Committee on Science and Technology for Development, the main directing and policy-making body for that area, held its tenth session in August/September, focusing on the end-of-decade review of the Vienna Programme of Action. The Advisory Committee on Science and Technology for Development, which provides policy and planning advice to the Intergovernmental Committee, held its eighth session in September.

Implementation of the Vienna Programme

The year marked the tenth anniversary of the Vienna Programme of Action on Science and Technology for Development, adopted in August 1979.[1] Pursuant to a 1987 General Assembly resolution,[2] the tenth session of the Intergovernmental Committee on Science and Technology for Development was devoted to the substantive theme of the end-of-decade review of the Programme.

Strengthening capacities of developing countries

In 1989, the Centre for Science and Technology for Development continued to manage a series of pilot projects, originally launched in 1987, to assist developing countries in developing endogenous capacity in science and technology.[3] Dialogue meetings were held in Nepal and Jordan, the first two countries to undertake such projects. Other projects were slated for the United Republic of Tanzania, as well as for another African country where the impact of simple technologies on women in rural areas was to be assessed.

In April,[4] the Administrative Committee on Co-ordination (ACC) stated that the emphasis in this area might in the future be placed on promoting endogenous capacity-building through involving all segments of society concerned with the development process in order to identify prioritized activities in science and technology. Emphasis should also be placed on assistance to Member States in developing their technology assessment capacity to enable them to evolve policy issues and options in technological development, and enhancing the collective contribution of the UN system to endogenous capacity-building of developing countries through technical co-operation activities, including joint inter-agency missions. ACC recognized that the future focus of the UN system could be on emerging science and technologies and on medium- and small-scale industries.

Drought and desertification

On the basis of the Intergovernmental Committee recommendations made in 1987,[5] the Centre for Science and Technology for Development was to organize, in Lanzhou, China, an international seminar on desertification processes of contiguous areas: science and technology policy issues and options. The Centre reported that while understanding of drought and desertification had been greatly enhanced, the individual situations in affected countries did not seem to have improved much.[3] The problem seemed to lie in the fact that past approaches addressed global conditions; what was needed now was development of an interdisciplinary approach more specific to variable local conditions.

GENERAL ASSEMBLY ACTION

On 26 October, the General Assembly adopted **resolution 44/14 B** without vote.

Endogenous capacity-building in science and technology

The General Assembly,

Recalling the relevant parts of the Vienna Programme of Action on Science and Technology for Development,

Stressing that the endogenous capacity of developing countries in science and technology lies, *inter alia*, in their capacity to choose, acquire, adapt, utilize and innovate technologies, including new ones, through institutional mechanisms for technology assessment in the areas of priority action,

Emphasizing that the building by developing countries of endogenous capacity for science and technology is of major concern to the United Nations system,

Recalling also resolutions 4(VIII) of 6 June 1986 and 1(IX) of 7 August 1987 of the Intergovernmental Committee on Science and Technology for Development, in which the Committee recommended that the Centre for Science and Technology for Development of the Secretariat should carry out studies on helping interested Member States to identify priority activities in science and technology for development, in accordance with national development plans and objectives, so as to lead to the strengthening of their endogenous capacities,

Taking note with appreciation of the work of the Centre in initiating pilot studies on endogenous capacity-building in some selected countries and welcoming the close co-operation between the Centre and the United Nations Fund for Science and Technology for Development in undertaking the studies and in planning additional studies in the future,

Recalling further the sections of resolution 1(IX) of the Intergovernmental Committee on the problems and requirements of the least developed countries in the field of science and technology, and emphasizing in that regard the need to enhance the level of commitment and support for the special needs of the least developed countries in that area,

Stressing the importance of the continued integration of women in the development process, particularly in developing countries, and, in that context, recalling resolution 2, adopted on 31 August 1979 by the United Nations Conference on Science and Technology for Development, and the relevant parts of the Nairobi Forward-looking Strategies for the Advancement of Women in the field of science and technology,

1. *Calls upon* the organizations of the United Nations system to devote increased attention to national capacity-building in science and technology, in accordance with the development objectives, priorities and plans of developing countries, and to enable them to take effective measures to build better and more sustainable institutions, strengthen human resource capacities and develop and adapt technology;

2. *Stresses* that international co-operation to foster the endogenous capacity-building of developing countries, in accordance with their autonomous decision-making in science and technology, must also be oriented to demand-driven priorities in order to support the efforts of developing countries in economic growth and development;

3. *Emphasizes* that international co-operation to foster endogenous capacity-building should give particular attention to management of technology in order to cope with technological change and promote technological innovation;

4. *Calls upon* the United Nations system to provide sustained support to the process of building the endogenous capacities of developing countries in science and technology, including their capacity for assessment of technology;

5. *Urges* the Centre for Science and Technology for Development of the Secretariat and the United Nations Fund for Science and Technology for Development, in co-operation with other bodies of the United Nations system, to continue to implement further pilot studies;

6. *Also urges* the United Nations Development Programme and other interested bodies of the United Nations system, as well as major donor countries, to support the implementation of those studies;

7. *Invites* the Advisory Committee on Science and Technology for Development to provide expert advice and support for that endeavour;

8. *Requests* the Secretary-General to submit an interim progress report on the implementation of the present resolution to the Intergovernmental Committee on Science and Technology for Development at its eleventh session.

General Assembly resolution 44/14 B

26 October 1989   Meeting 42   Adopted without vote

Draft by Intergovernmental Committee on Science and Technology for Development (A/44/37); agenda item 82 *(i)*.

End-of-decade review

In a July report on the end-of-decade review of the implementation of the Vienna Programme of Action,[6] the Secretary-General summarized the achievements of and gaps in the Programme in relation to goals set out at the 1979 Vienna Conference on Science and Technology for Development. Despite a high level of societal awareness of the importance of science and technology for development, he said, accomplishments during the 1980s fell far short of the Vienna Programme's objectives, except in a limited number of countries. That slow-down could be partly attributed to the difficult economic environment world wide during the decade. More important was the inertia which had delayed the drastic changes needed in conceptual and institutional approaches to fulfil the three basic goals of the Programme—strengthening the endogenous capacity of developing countries; restructuring international scientific and technological relations; and strengthening the role of the UN system.

The concept of endogenous capacity-building should be interpreted as a demand-driven process, since conventional supply-oriented processes, such as building policy-making bodies, were not sufficient to enable science and technology to play an effective role in mainstream national efforts. Ways to determine areas of priority attention had to be sought, as top-down centralized formulation of science and technology programmes had generally failed. Development efforts should be redirected to reduce disparities, as well as to achieve increased levels of production.

Systems of development assistance required major rethinking to achieve the following goals: greater coherence and effectiveness of development support; a balanced approach to priority demands among different problem areas; complementarity in support from bilateral and multilateral agencies; and reinforcement for endogenous capacity-building as a process leading to autonomous decision-making ability, in addition to encompassing equipment supply, infrastructure and expertise for isolated projects.

The potential of UN institutions dealing with science and technology had not been realized to the extent anticipated. Nevertheless, an analysis of their role over the last 10 years had reinforced the validity of the assumptions in creating those institutions. What was needed was a redefinition of their scope and functions. They should primarily undertake specific activities to: promote the endogenous capacity in arriving at portfolios of priority actions through national policy dialogues among stakeholders, policy analysis and technology assessments; assess the implications of change in technological environments on specific themes of socio-economic interest to the General Assembly; and catalyse the participatory linkages in the UN system, development co-operation agencies, the science and technology community and other concerned stakeholders.

Pursuant to a 1987 Intergovernmental Committee resolution,[7] the Centre for Science and Technology for Development addressed a questionnaire to all national focal points asking Member States to report on their experiences and constraints in implementing the Vienna Programme. Responses were detailed in a July report.[3] Some developing countries indicated that limited financial resources earmarked for science and technology constituted a major obstacle to implementation of the Vienna Programme. Still, many developing countries said they had established science and technology structures and policies. Most UN entities affirmed that the Vienna Programme had positively affected their activities in the area of science and technology. Analytical studies by the UN in four regions of the developing world clearly indicated different perspectives concerning the use of science and technology to meet specific priority needs of development.

Based on those studies, the Centre for Science and Technology had organized four regional meetings and one interregional meeting. One consensus that had emerged from those meetings was that the results of the Vienna Programme had lagged considerably behind the expectations of developing Member States, in particular with regard to mobilization of additional resources for promoting science and technology for development. The gap between developed and developing countries in science and technology remained and was widening, including among groups of developing countries. There was a need for new approaches in implementing the Vienna Programme of Action and for international co-operation in science and technology, it was felt.

GENERAL ASSEMBLY ACTION

On 26 October 1989, the General Assembly adopted **resolution 44/14 A** without vote.

End-of-decade review of the Vienna Programme of Action on Science and Technology for Development and its revitalization

The General Assembly,

Recalling its resolution 34/218 of 19 December 1979, in which it endorsed the Vienna Programme of Action on Science and Technology for Development,

Stressing the increasing importance of science and technology for development in the context of the rapidly changing international economic environment,

Noting with great concern that the effect of increasing disparities in scientific and technological capabilities between the industrialized countries and the developing countries as a whole has been to contribute to a widening of the economic gap between them,

Stressing also the central role that science and technology play as vital instruments for the improvement of the quality of life and the eradication of poverty in the context of the promotion of economic growth and sustained development in developing countries,

Expressing concern that the absence of a favourable external economic environment has adversely affected the capacity of developing countries to foster and finance their activities concerning science and technology for development,

Emphasizing the need to enhance human resources development in order to promote the endogenous capacity in science and technology of developing countries, in particular to face the challenges of development and accelerated technological change posed by the present scientific and technological revolution,

Taking note of the report of the Secretary-General on the end-of-decade review of the implementation of the Vienna Programme of Action,

1. *Reaffirms* the validity of the Vienna Programme of Action on Science and Technology for Development and its basic goals, and expresses concern regarding its implementation;

2. *Considers* that science and technology should be one of the major components in the deliberations of the special session of the General Assembly in 1990 devoted to international economic co-operation, in particular to the revitalization of economic growth and development of the developing countries, the *Ad Hoc* Committee of the Whole for the Preparation of the International Development Strategy for the Fourth United Nations Development Decade, the Second United Nations Conference on the Least Developed Countries and the proposed United Nations conference on environment and development.

General Assembly resolution 44/14 A

26 October 1989   Meeting 42   Adopted without vote

Draft by Intergovernmental Committee on Science and Technology for Development (A/44/37); agenda item 82 *(i)*.

Co-ordination and harmonization

The framework for formulating policy guidelines for harmonizing activities of UN organizations in the area of science and technology for development had been set out in 1987 by the Intergovernmental Committee.[8] In July 1989, the Secretary-General reported[3] on the activities of the Centre for Science and Technology for Development, discussing guidelines and progress made in harmonizing science and technology activities. Nine guidelines were proposed, including the following: that science and technology for development might be included as a major programme in medium-term plans of UN organizations and agencies; that the future focus of co-ordination in science and technology for development should be at the country level; that co-ordination of science and technology for development required the enhanced involvement and co-operation of other intergovernmental policy-making bodies; and that harmonization of UN policies in this area could be greatly stimulated if policies of individual countries were fully in consonance with each other. The Secretary-General concluded that the co-operation between the Centre and the Fund for Science and Technology for Development had in the past two years brought about a close and interactive relationship.

GENERAL ASSEMBLY ACTION

On 26 October 1989, the General Assembly adopted **resolution 44/14 C** without vote.

Co-ordination and harmonization of activities in the field of science and technology

The General Assembly,

Recalling the parts of the Vienna Programme of Action on Science and Technology for Development relating to co-ordinated implementation of the Programme by the United Nations system and the formulation of policy guidelines for the harmonization of policies of the organs, organizations and bodies of the United Nations system in regard to activities in the field of science and technology,

Also recalling resolution 4(IX) of 7 August 1987 of the Intergovernmental Committee on Science and Technology for Development, which provided the framework for the formulation of policy guidelines for the harmonization of activities of the organizations of the United Nations system in science and technology for development,

Having considered the report of the Secretary-General on the activities of the Centre for Science and Technology for Development of the Secretariat, which, *inter alia*, analysed and provided information on harmonization of science and technology activities within the United Nations system,

Reaffirming the leadership role assigned to resident co-ordinators of the United Nations system to harmonize the efforts of the different organizations of the system, in accordance with the priorities of each Government,

Taking note of the guidelines suggested in paragraph 66 of the report of the Secretary-General,

1. *Calls upon* the governing bodies of the organizations of the United Nations system, including the United Nations Fund for Science and Technology for Development, to enhance co-ordination and harmonization at the country level, including the inter-agency missions, at the request of interested developing countries, through the office of the resident co-ordinator, in order to increase coherence and efficiency in responding adequately to the priorities in science and technology established by each developing country;

2. *Requests* the Director-General for Development and International Economic Co-operation to ensure close monitoring and follow-up of the mandated programmes and activities of the United Nations system in the areas of science and technology for development for the successful implementation of the Vienna Programme of Action on Science and Technology for Development and to report thereon regularly to the Intergovernmental Committee on Science and Technology for Development.

General Assembly resolution 44/14 C

26 October 1989   Meeting 42   Adopted without vote

Draft by Intergovernmental Committee on Science and Technology for Development (A/44/37); agenda item 82 *(i)*.

REFERENCES

[1]YUN 1979, p. 636. [2]YUN 1987, p. 595, GA res. 42/192, 11 Dec. 1987. [3]A/CN.11/88. [4]ACC/1989/DEC/1-20 (dec. 1989/7). [5]YUN 1987, p. 594. [6]A/CN.11/89. [7]YUN 1987, p. 596. [8]YUN 1987, p. 597.

Financial resources for science and technology

UN Fund for Science and Technology for Development

The UN Fund for Science and Technology for Development (UNFSTD) continued during 1989 to strengthen national technical capacities through strategic funding, project design and implementation, and advisory services to enhance project effectiveness. The UNDP Administrator, in April,[1] reviewed activities of short-term advisory services (STAS) and the Transfer of Knowledge through Expatriate Nationals (TOKTEN) programmes, which had been managed by the Fund since 1987, and of the Energy Account, which had become a separate sub-account of UNFSTD in 1988.

UNFSTD resources had been used in two ways: to initiate activities from core resources to prepare the ground for larger-scale projects, and to help develop projects for co-financing arrangements with bilateral and multilateral partners. Fifty-two new and ongoing projects were being implemented by the Fund, which had responded to 132 requests for advice from UNDP regional bureaux and field offices in 1987 and 1988.

The UNDP Administrator stated that the integration of UNFSTD with UNDP in 1987 had helped alleviate the Fund's financial situation. UNFSTD expenditures for 1987-1988 under core and co-financing arrangements had been over $17 million. Total expenditures for 1989 were estimated at $10.23 million and for 1990 at $13.9 million. Voluntary contributions amounting to $250,000 were received by the Fund in early 1988; in November of that year, 32 countries had pledged $1.4 million. UNFSTD administrative expenses were met wholly from its own core/non-core resources. The UNDP Administrator noted that the Fund had made vigorous efforts to reduce its administrative expenses, which represented about 11 per cent of the Fund's overall expenditure and which could drop as its operations increased.

The UNDP Administrator stated that the Fund had given UNDP greater operational flexibility, better opportunities for unified country programming, and the capacity to move rapidly in innovative directions and in specialized fields. High-risk activities had been initiated with seed money provided by the Fund, which then could be followed up through the use of UNDP and bilateral resources. Every dollar provided by the Fund had attracted three dollars through co-financing arrangements, it was stated.

On 30 June,[2] the UNDP Governing Council welcomed UNFSTD's revitalized close co-operation with the UN Centre for Science and Technology for Development and expressed its appreciation for the efforts of the UNDP Administrator to reduce the Fund's administrative expenses. The Council stated that arrangements for co-financing had been diversified and had helped to maintain the Fund's overall resource base, but noted with concern that, without a substantial increase in its core resources, it would be difficult to maintain the Fund as an identifiable entity within UNDP. The UNDP Administrator was asked to explore ways to strengthen Fund activities and to report on that issue for consideration by the Council in 1990.

GENERAL ASSEMBLY ACTION

On 26 October 1989, the General Assembly adopted **resolution 44/14 D** without vote.

Financing of science and technology for development

The General Assembly,

Recalling the relevant parts of the Vienna Programme of Action on Science and Technology for Development,

Concerned at the continued inadequacy of resources devoted to fostering science and technology for development,

Recalling its resolution 41/183 of 8 December 1986 on the United Nations Financing System for Science and Technology for Development,

Recalling also resolution 5(IX) of 7 August 1987 of the Intergovernmental Committee on Science and Technology for Development,

Recalling further decision 89/52 of 30 June 1989 of the Governing Council of the United Nations Development Programme,

1. *Reaffirms* the need for adequate resources on a continuous and assured basis to foster science and technology for development in accordance with the priorities of developing countries;

2. *Requests* the Secretary-General to explore the possibility of organizing a more effective coalition of resources within the United Nations development system, multilateral financial institutions, regional development banks and bilateral funding agencies to strengthen the endogenous capacity-building of developing countries in science and technology;

3. *Stresses* the importance of the work of the United Nations Fund for Science and Technology for Development as an identifiable entity with the present size of staff and mode of operation;

4. *Requests* the Intergovernmental Committee on Science and Technology for Development to continue to provide policy guidance and set priorities for activities of the Fund within the framework of the Vienna Programme of Action on Science and Technology for Development;

5. *Calls upon* the Administrator of the United Nations Development Programme to continue to ensure close and interactive co-operation between the Fund and the Centre for Science and Technology for Development of the Secretariat on a programmatic and substantive basis, particularly in implementing decisions emanating from the end-of-the-decade review of the Vienna Programme of Action;

6. *Recommends* that the Fund, at the request of the interested developing countries, accord priority in support of:

(*a*) Pilot projects on the endogenous capacity-building of developing countries;

(*b*) Activities directly related to the follow-up of substantive themes such as new and emerging areas of science and technology considered by the Intergovernmental Committee;

(*c*) Projects and programmes aimed at fostering co-operation among developing countries;

7. *Emphasizes* the important function played by the Fund as the focal point within the United Nations Development Programme for endogenous capacity-building in developing countries and networking with the international science and technology community;

8. *Takes note* of the decision of the Intergovernmental Committee to include an item entitled "Financing science and technology for development" in the agenda of its eleventh session and to request the Secretary-General to submit a comprehensive report to it on the question.

General Assembly resolution 44/14 D

26 October 1989   Meeting 42   Adopted without vote

Draft by Intergovernmental Committee on Science and Technology for Development (A/44/37); agenda item 82 *(i)*.

Operational activities

UNFSTD continued to help developing countries to assess national needs and to devise policies and structures with regard to science, technology and energy. It continued to provide assistance to five projects: in Burundi, Cyprus, Ethiopia and Jordan and in the member States of the Gulf Co-operation Council.

Several projects continued in the field of initiating new technologies and upgrading traditional technologies. The woodstove development programme in West Africa continued, as did research on using the soapberry plant in East Africa as an agent in the fight against schistosomiasis. The Fund assisted in assessing the potential use of Zambia's abundant raw materials and agricultural waste products to be put to use through bio-technology-based methods. The UNFSTD-funded Computer Science Division at the Asian Institute of Technology in Bangkok, Thailand, was considered a success by an evaluation mission. Projects in remote-sensing training and the development of drip irrigation techniques in semi-arid environments in China continued. Several countries benefited from projects in non-conventional energy, such as Costa Rica and Djibouti (geothermal energy,) Cape Verde (biogas) and Seychelles, Maldives and Mauritius (photovoltaic technology).

Ten new countries were expected to participate in the technological information pilot system, an information exchange among over 2,000 users in Africa, the Arab States, Asia and Latin America. Preparations were made to establish a technology expert knowledge system—a computer-based technical and scientific information network of UNDP offices around the world.

UNFSTD conducted a major programme on technological innovation and entrepreneurship, including efforts to establish business incubators in developing countries to enhance the viability of small technology-based firms. One feasibility exercise examined the possibility of setting up such incubators in China; a conference was held in Gabon in March/April 1988 on business incuba-tors for West African States. INNOTECH, a technology incubator in Trinidad and Tobago, was launched in February 1989. The third Beijing international conference on technological innovation and entrepreneurship was held in September 1989.

In the area of quality control and maintenance, the UNFSTD-supported National Food Technology and Quality Control Research Centre in China, inaugurated in September 1988, worked on soybean-derived proteins and national standards for quality control. The problem of lack of maintenance of scientific instruments in Africa was addressed, using Fund resources. The training of technicians in Latin America in the use of ultra high-frequency sound waves, lasers and other techniques continued.

The TOKTEN programme completed 449 projects in 1988, the most productive year in its 10-year history, attaining a cumulative total of 2,270. Its basic strength was considered to be the concept of fielding skilled third world professionals living in industrialized countries to provide voluntary consultancy services to their countries of origin. The STAS programme completed 70 assignments in 1988, with experts from developed and developing countries helping to solve technical and managerial problems in private and parastatal enterprises. Since STAS began operations in 1985, 131 assignments had been completed. The linking of STAS and TOKTEN under UNFSTD was seen as mutually beneficial.

REFERENCES
[1]DP/1989/48. [2]E/1989/32 (dec. 89/52).

Institutional arrangements

Intergovernmental Committee

The Intergovernmental Committee on Science and Technology for Development, at its tenth session (New York, 21 August–1 September), adopted one resolution and one decision.[1] The resolution dealt with the activities of the UN system in science and technology, including those of the Centre, the Advisory Committee and the Fund for Science and Technology for Development.

The Intergovernmental Committee decided to continue holding its sessions on a biennial basis.

Advisory Committee

The Advisory Committee on Science and Technology for Development was established to provide policy and planning advice to the Intergovernmental Committee. At its eighth session in 1988,[2] it had focused on endogenous capacity-building and technological innovation, including human resources and information systems, and on financial resources for science and technology. Its ninth session, at Vienna, was held from 4 to 12 September 1989.

A declaration[3] to mark the tenth anniversary of the Vienna Programme of Action was issued by current and former Committee members in July. In September, the Intergovernmental Committee invited[4] the Advisory Committee to hold sessions, to the extent possible, in developing countries, in order to provide opportunities for interaction between Committee members and the host countries' science and technology communities. It encouraged the Advisory Committee to provide a substantive contribution to the _Ad Hoc_ Committee of the Whole for the Preparation of the International Development Strategy for the Fourth United Nations Development Decade.

Centre for Science and Technology

Serving as the secretariat for the Intergovernmental Committee, the Advisory Committee and the ACC Task Force, the Centre for Science and Technology for Development continued in 1989 to provide support for implementing the Vienna Programme of Action.

In a March report,[5] the Secretary-General described the Centre's activities, which, pursuant to a 1987 Intergovernmental Committee request,[6] concentrated on: endogenous capacity-building; development of the Advanced Technology Alert System (ATAS); harmonization of science and technology activities within the UN system; and issues dealing with science and technology information. These priorities and programmes were to continue to be the principal focus for the Centre during 1990 and 1991. The Centre's work in 1989 focused on the theme of the tenth session of the Intergovernmental Committee: the end-of-decade review of the implementation of the Vienna Programme of Action.

The Intergovernmental Committee, at its August/ September session,[4] requested the Centre to report, in line with the Committee's substantive theme for its eleventh session, on ensuring the participation of developing countries in international co-operation for development of environmentally sound technology. The Centre was to continue pilot studies on building endogenous capacities, employ subregional approaches to endogenous capacity-building in the area of science and technology, and examine possibilities of co-ordinating efforts to improve the infrastructure of institutions of higher learning in the field of science and technology in developing countries, particularly in Africa. The Centre was also to report on the contribution of the UN system to endogenous

capacity-building, and on planning and management of science and technology policy to promote science and technology in developing countries. The Intergovernmental Committee requested the Centre to enhance its efforts to promote science and technology in the least developed countries and to submit concrete proposals on that issue through the Preparatory Committee for the Second UN Conference on the Least Developed Countries. Reports were also requested on: progress made in involving women in activities in the field of science and technology, and the question of financing science and technology for development. The Committee approved the draft programme in science and technology of the UN medium-term plan for the period 1992-1997 in the light of the end-of-decade review of the Vienna Programme of Action.

Advance Technology Alert System

The Secretary-General, in May, reported[7] on the ATAS pilot project, which had ended in 1987. An evaluation had been made at a workshop of international experts held in the German Democratic Republic in August 1988. Participants recommended that the Centre, through ATAS and in co-operation with other UN organizations, be the focal point for technology assessment within the UN system.

GENERAL ASSEMBLY ACTION

On 26 October, the General Assembly adopted **resolution 44/14 E** without vote.

Assessment of technology
The General Assembly,

Recalling decision 7(V) of 20 June 1983, in which the Intergovernmental Committee on Science and Technology for Development established the Advance Technology Alert System and called for a review of the project, and the Committee's resolution 4(VIII) of 6 June 1986,

Taking note with appreciation of the report of the Secretary-General on the evaluation by the international group of experts of the Advance Technology Alert System,

Recognizing that, because of the complexity and the global implications of new and emerging areas of science and technology, careful assessment of technology is required to take full advantage of such emerging technologies and to avoid negative repercussions for developing countries,

1. _Resolves_ that, in pursuance of the substantive theme approach, the Intergovernmental Committee on Science and Technology for Development shall choose subjects of particular significance with major science and technology dimensions with a view to providing an assessment of technology and related policy analysis in order to facilitate the debate of the question in the General Assembly;

2. _Decides_:

_(a)_ To continue and to improve further the Advance Technology Alert System as an important and effective means of applying technology assessment to endogenous capacity-building in developing countries;

(b) To continue also to publish the *ATAS Bulletin* within existing resources, focusing on the risks and benefits of new and emerging technology to development, especially in developing countries, and on diverse practices of technological assessment being used by Member States and international organizations;

(c) To entrust the Centre for Science and Technology for Development of the Secretariat, through the Advance Technology Alert System and in co-operation with other United Nations bodies, to serve as the focal point for technological assessment within the United Nations system and, where possible, for relations with Governments and non-governmental organizations concerning technological assessment activities in Member States;

3. *Takes note* of the decision of the Intergovernmental Committee to choose as the substantive theme for its eleventh session "Ways and means of ensuring the participation of developing countries in international co-operation for research on and development of environmentally sound technologies, and the rapid and effective transfer of such technologies to those countries";

4. *Requests* the Centre to study ways and means of assisting developing countries in enhancing their capacity to assess new technologies, and recommends that a study be undertaken regarding new materials and the processing of raw materials, making use of the results of the Centre's ongoing programme on materials technology, and requests the Secretary-General to report thereon to the Intergovernmental Committee at its eleventh session.

General Assembly resolution 44/14 E

26 October 1989   Meeting 42   Adopted without vote

Draft by Intergovernmental Committee on Science and Technology for Development (A/44/37); agenda item 82 (i).

Co-ordination in the UN system

ACC Task Force

The Task Force on Science and Technology for Development, established by ACC to promote closer co-operation among UN bodies, in 1989 held its tenth session (Vienna, 13-16 March).[8] It concentrated on three subjects: impact studies and inter-agency missions to selected countries; closer inter-institutional co-operation on assessment of new technologies; and review of the implementation during the 1980s of the Vienna Programme of Action. The Task Force considered that there was currently no need for additional joint activities in the field of new and emerging areas of science and technology.

REFERENCES

[1]A/44/37. [2]YUN 1988, p. 447. [3]A/CN.11/91/Add.1/Rev.1. [4]A/44/37 (res. 2(X)). [5]A/CN.11/88. [6]YUN 1987, p. 602. [7]A/CN.11/90. [8]ACC/1989/PG/4.

Technology transfer

Draft code of conduct

Pursuant to a 1988 General Assembly request,[1] the United Nations Conference on Trade and Development (UNCTAD) Secretary-General reported on progress made in the negotiations on an international code of conduct on the transfer of technology.[2] The draft consisted of a preamble and nine chapters on: definitions and scope of application; objectives and principles; national regulation of transfer-of-technology transactions; restrictive practices; responsibilities and obligations of parties to transfer-of-technology transactions; special treatment for developing countries; international collaboration; international institutional machinery; and applicable law and settlement of disputes. The UNCTAD Secretary-General stated that, despite all efforts, no concrete results enjoying general consensus had so far emerged. Most issues still outstanding in the code concerned restrictive practices and applicable law and settlement of disputes.

The President of the UN Conference on an International Code of Conduct on the Transfer of Technology and the UNCTAD Secretary-General in 1989 continued consultations with regional groups and interested Governments (23 January–2 February). Subsequently, the UNCTAD secretariat informed all UNCTAD member States that the UNCTAD secretariat might study the relevance to the draft code of conduct of recent policy and legislative developments in the area of technology, particularly issues outstanding in the negotiations. The UNCTAD Secretary-General would then report to the General Assembly in 1990 on the study's outcome.

GENERAL ASSEMBLY ACTION

On 22 December, the General Assembly, on the recommendation of the Second (Economic and Financial) Committee, adopted **resolution 44/216** without vote.

International code of conduct on the transfer of technology

The General Assembly,

Recalling its resolutions 40/184 of 17 December 1985, 41/166 of 5 December 1986 and 42/172 of 11 December 1987 and its decision 43/439 of 20 December 1988 on an international code of conduct on the transfer of technology,

1. *Takes note* of the report of the Secretary-General of the United Nations Conference on Trade and Development on the consultations carried out in 1989 relating to the negotiations on an international code of conduct on the transfer of technology;

2. *Invites* the Secretary-General of the United Nations Conference on Trade and Development to submit to the General Assembly at its forty-fifth session a complete report, based on the outcome of consultations, so as to enable the Assembly to take appropriate action on the negotiations on the draft code of conduct.

General Assembly resolution 44/216

22 December 1989   Meeting 85   Adopted without vote

Approved by Second Committee (A/44/746/Add.2) without vote, 4 December (meeting 48); draft by Malaysia for Group of 77 (A/C.2/44/L.50); agenda item 82 *(b)*.

Meeting numbers. GA 44th session: 2nd Committee 38, 44, 48; plenary 85.

REFERENCES

[1]YUN 1988, p. 450, GA dec. 43/439, 20 Dec. 1988.
[2]A/44/554.

Other questions

Social welfare

On 24 May, the Economic and Social Council adopted **resolution 1989/47**, calling upon all States to encourage co-operation to ensure scientific and technological progress for the welfare and social and economic development of their peoples. The Council requested the Secretary-General, in the next report on the world social situation, to take due account of the effects of science and technology on processes of social welfare and development. It also requested the Secretary-General to consider convening in the near future a seminar of experts on the effects of science and technology on social welfare and development.

In December, by **resolution 44/54**, the General Assembly endorsed the Council's recommendations.

Education

Pursuant to a 1987 General Assembly resolution,[1] the Secretary-General, in January 1989, reported[2] on national experiences in achieving far-reaching social and economic changes for the purpose of social progress, including the promotion of education, science and technology. The report also provided information on science and technology policies submitted by six developing countries and four countries with centrally planned or developed market economies. Developing countries emphasized ways to make best use of their limited resources and to overcome organizational constraints. In developed countries, stress was laid on policies aimed at concentrating research efforts on those spheres considered most important for future progress.

International security

In response to a 1988 General Assembly request,[3] the Secretary-General reported in September on scientific and technological developments and their impact on international security,[4] based on information received from Governments.

GENERAL ASSEMBLY ACTION

By **resolution 44/118 A**, the General Assembly requested the Secretary-General to conclude his work on the issue and report to the Assembly in 1990. The Assembly also decided, by **resolution 44/118 B**, to include in its 1990 provisional agenda an item entitled "Science and technology for disarmament".

Informatics

A decision by the Executive Board of the United Nations Educational, Scientific and Cultural Organization (UNESCO), contained in a note by the Secretary-General,[5] invited the UNESCO Director-General to ensure that UNESCO made its specific contribution to international co-operation in the field of informatics, in close collaboration with the Economic and Social Council, the United Nations Industrial Development Organization, the International Telecommunication Union and relevant non-governmental organizations, fostering the use and promotion of informatics as an instrument of development.

ECONOMIC AND SOCIAL COUNCIL ACTION

In **decision 1989/179**, the Economic and Social Council decided to consider, at its organizational session for 1990, the inclusion of a separate item on international co-operation in the field of informatics in its 1990 programme of work.

REFERENCES

[1]YUN 1987, p. 612, GA res. 42/50, 30 Nov. 1987. [2]A/44/86. [3]YUN 1988, p. 43, GA res. 43/77 A, 7 Dec. 1988. [4]A/44/487 & Add.1,2. [5]E/1989/L.28.

Chapter VIII

Environment

The year 1989 witnessed a heightened interest in the environment, both internationally and regionally, as the world's political leadership made environmental issues, particularly the relationship between environment and development, a major priority. In January, the Montreal Protocol on Substances that Deplete the Ozone Layer entered into force, and in March the Basel Convention on the Control of Transboundary Movements of Hazardous Wastes and their Disposal was adopted and signed at an international conference in Switzerland, organized by the United Nations Environment Programme (UNEP). During the year, environmental concerns were discussed at major regional and international conferences and meetings. In December 1989, the General Assembly decided to convene in Brazil in 1992 the United Nations Conference on Environment and Development, and established a preparatory committee for the Conference. The Assembly also urged Governments to prepare a framework convention and associated protocols on climate change.

The Economic and Social Council concluded that increasing attention needed to be paid to the provision of new and additional financial resources to address the environmental concerns of the developing countries and that such provision should be kept under continuous review.

In 1989, UNEP acted to strengthen its role and effectiveness as the central catalysing, co-ordinating and stimulating body in the field of the environment within the UN system. The UNEP Governing Council in May, meeting at Nairobi, Kenya, adopted a record number of decisions on the environment. The Programme continued its various activities to conserve biological diversity and protected areas, control soil erosion and forest loss, protect the marine environment and collect information on such topics as air and water quality, food contamination and ozone depletion.

General aspects

International co-operation

In an introductory report[1] to the UNEP Governing Council, the Executive Director pointed to the dramatic increase in concern for the environ-

ment over the past two years, as well as the relationship between environmental matters and their management and national and international security. He identified as key issues those concerning the atmosphere, fresh water, oceans and coastal areas, land degradation, impoverishment of biological diversity, and hazardous wastes and toxic chemicals. The Executive Director outlined the nature of UNEP's role and immediate measures to enhance its effectiveness, and discussed preparations for the United Nations Conference on Environment and Development (see below), environmentally sound and sustainable development and the financial resources of the Environment Fund.

On 25 May, the Governing Council reaffirmed[2] the role of UNEP as the central catalysing, co-ordinating and stimulating body in the field of the environment within the UN system, and stressed the need to further develop and strengthen that role and make the Governing Council a more effective and efficient mechanism. The Council urged Governments to establish UNEP national committees, and requested the Executive Director to support their establishment and to ensure the flow of information and views between them and UNEP. It decided on areas of focus for UNEP efforts and calls upon the international community, including protection of the atmosphere by combating climate change and global warming, depletion of the ozone layer and transboundary air pollution; protection of the quality of freshwater resources, oceans and coastal areas and resources and land resources by combating deforestation and desertification; conservation of biological diversity; and environmentally sound management of biotechnology, and minimization of hazardous wastes and toxic chemicals. The Governing Council agreed to set a target of $100 million for contributions to the Environment Fund by 1992, and called on Governments to increase their contributions by at least 35 per cent per annum from 1 January 1989 levels.

GENERAL ASSEMBLY ACTION

The General Assembly, by **decision 44/453**, of 22 December, on the recommendation of the Second (Economic and Financial) Committee,[3] decided to consider the draft resolution[4] entitled "International co-operation in the field of the environment", as orally revised, and to take appropriate action at the current session.

On the same date, the Assembly adopted **resolution 44/229** without vote.

International co-operation in the field of the environment

The General Assembly,

Deeply concerned at the increasing degradation of the environment, which, if allowed to continue, could endanger not only economic and social development but the very basis of life itself,

Noting the increased political interest in solving environmental problems and intensified international co-operation to that effect,

Welcoming the fact that there have been encouraging developments in some important areas of environmental co-operation,

Reaffirming that there is a direct interrelationship between environment and development, and recognizing that a favourable international economic climate conducive to sustained economic growth and development, particularly in developing countries, is of major importance for sound management of the environment,

Reaffirming also the importance of integrating environmental concerns and considerations into policies and programmes in all countries without introducing a new form of conditionality in aid or development financing or constituting a pretext for unjustified barriers to trade,

Noting the fact that the largest part of the current emission of pollutants into the environment, including toxic and hazardous wastes, originates in developed countries, and recognizing that those countries therefore have the main responsibility for combating such pollution,

Recognizing that serious environmental problems are arising for all countries and that those problems must be progressively addressed through preventive measures at their sources by national efforts and international co-operation,

Reaffirming the need for developed countries and appropriate international organs and organizations to strengthen technical co-operation with developing countries, increase the transfer of technology and provide additional resources to enhance the capacity of developing countries to solve their environmental problems,

Recognizing that the United Nations Conference on Environment and Development, to be held in 1992, is a unique opportunity for all nations to address environmental and development issues in an integrated manner and to mobilize their political will to solve environmental problems through international co-operation,

Recalling decision 14/10 of 18 June 1987 of the Governing Council of the United Nations Environment Programme on the environmental impact of *apartheid* on black agriculture in South Africa,

Having considered the report of the Governing Council of the United Nations Environment Programme on the work of its fifteenth session,

1. *Endorses* the work of the United Nations Environment Programme, welcomes the report of the Governing Council on the work of its fifteenth session and takes note with appreciation of the decisions therein, as adopted, in the light of the present resolution;

2. *Reaffirms* the mandate of the Programme as defined in General Assembly resolution 2997(XXVII) of 15 December 1972, and supports further strengthening of the role of the Programme as the central catalysing,

co-ordinating and stimulating body in the field of the environment within the United Nations system;

3. *Welcomes* the measures adopted by the Governing Council, in its decision 15/1 of 25 May 1989, to improve its own effectiveness and efficiency;

4. *Reaffirms* that, owing to its universal character, the United Nations system, through the General Assembly, is the appropriate forum for concerted political action on global environmental problems;

5. *Considers,* in this regard, that the structure of the United Nations and its responsiveness in dealing with major environmental issues should be reviewed in order to strengthen its capacity to deal with these matters in an integrated, coherent and effective way, and requests the Secretary-General to prepare a report on this issue, taking into account the views expressed by Governments, to be considered in the preparatory process for the United Nations Conference on Environment and Development;

6. *Takes note* of the areas of concentration for the international community set out by the Governing Council in section IV of its decision 15/1 and the list of issues within those areas, which are not listed in any particular order of priority, to which the Programme should give special attention;

7. *Takes note* of Governing Council decision 15/4 of 26 May 1989 and supports the decision of the Council to hold a special session in 1990 of three days' duration at the same location as, and in conjunction with, the first substantive session of the Preparatory Committee for the United Nations Conference on Environment and Development, which, at its organizational session, should bear this issue in mind with a view to achieving an effective preparatory process for the Conference; this special session should deal with the elaboration of and the process of making and implementing decisions on priority environmental issues, in particular ways and means of enhancing the role of the Programme within the United Nations system in addressing those issues;

8. *Reaffirms* the need to provide new and additional financial resources to support developing countries in identifying, analysing, monitoring, preventing and managing environmental problems primarily at their source, in accordance with their national development goals, objectives and plans, so as to ensure that their development priorities are not adversely affected;

9. *Stresses* the need for new and additional financial resources for measures aimed at solving major environmental problems of global concern, and especially to support those countries, in particular developing countries, for whom the implementation of such measures would entail a special or abnormal burden, due, in particular, to their lack of financial resources, expertise and/or technical capacity;

10. *Expresses its satisfaction* at indications that the flow of resources to the Environment Fund is increasing in real terms, and endorses the annual target of a minimum of one hundred million United States dollars in contributions by the year 1992, taking into account the increasing tasks of the Programme, and calls upon all Governments to contribute or increase their contributions to the Fund by at least 35 per cent per annum from the 1 January 1989 level to enable that target to be met by 1992;

11. *Endorses* the views and suggestions of the Governing Council as expressed in its decision 15/2 of 26 May

1989 on the implementation of General Assembly resolutions 42/186 and 42/187 of 11 December 1987 as a positive step towards a better understanding of the concept of sustainable and environmentally sound development by all countries;

12. *Takes note* of the recommendation made by the Governing Council in its decision 15/5 of 25 May 1989 and stresses that sustainable and environmentally sound development in all countries should become one of the central guiding principles in the international development strategy being elaborated for the fourth United Nations development decade;

13. *Concurs* with Governing Council decision 15/14 of 25 May 1989 on the clearing-house function, in which it is considered that the Programme should play a more vigorous role in supporting developing countries, upon their request:

(*a*) To establish and strengthen their institutions and professional capacities to integrate environmental considerations into their development policies and planning;

(*b*) To formulate and initiate programmes and activities for dealing with their most serious environmental problems;

(*c*) To formulate and participate in action plans for the common management of ecosystems and critical environmental problems at the national, regional and global levels;

14. *Stresses* that sustainable and environmentally sound development requires changes in the unsustainable pattern of production and consumption, particularly in industrialized countries, and the development of environmentally sound technologies, and, in this context, stresses also the need to examine, with a view to making recommendations, effective modalities for favourable access to, and transfer of, environmentally sound technologies, in particular to the developing countries, including on concessional and preferential terms, and modalities for supporting all countries in their efforts to create and develop their endogenous technological capacities in the field of scientific research and development, as well as in the acquisition of relevant information, and, in this context, stresses further the need to explore the concept of assured access for developing countries to environmentally sound technologies, in its relation to proprietary rights, with a view to developing effective responses to the needs of developing countries in this area;

15. *Takes note* of Governing Council decision 15/24 of 25 May 1989 on sustainable agriculture, and calls upon the Governing Council to pay special attention to the implementation thereof;

16. *Reaffirms* the urgent need for Governments, multilateral organizations and governmental and non-governmental financial institutions to take into account in their policies, decision-making processes and financial mechanisms the relationship between the foreign debt and the ability of developing countries to strengthen their capacity to address the critical environmental issues fundamental to development and protection of the environment;

17. *Urges* the Intergovernmental Panel on Climate Change to take the necessary steps to ensure the participation of developing countries in scientific and policy aspects of its work, and calls upon the international community, in particular the developed countries, to consider contributing generously to the Intergovernmen-

tal Panel on Climate Change Trust Fund with a view to financing the participation of experts designated by Governments of the developing countries in all the meetings of the Intergovernmental Panel, including those of its working groups and sub-groups;

18. *Supports* the request made by the Governing Council, in its decision 15/36 of 25 May 1989, that the Executive Director of the United Nations Environment Programme, in co-operation with the Secretary-General of the World Meteorological Organization, begin preparations for negotiations on a framework convention on climate, taking into account the work of the Intergovernmental Panel and its interim report, as well as the results achieved at international meetings on the subject, including the Second World Climate Conference, and recommends that such negotiations begin as soon as possible after the adoption of the interim report of the Intergovernmental Panel and that the General Assembly at an early date during its forty-fifth session take a decision recommending ways and means and modalities for further pursuing these negotiations, taking into account the work of the Preparatory Committee for the United Nations Conference on Environment and Development, to be held in 1992;

19. *Notes with satisfaction* the progress made in the protection of the ozone layer and urges all States to co-operate with the Executive Director of the United Nations Environment Programme in the process of strengthening the Montreal Protocol on Substances that Deplete the Ozone Layer, adopted on 16 September 1987, in the light of the Helsinki Declaration on the Protection of the Ozone Layer, adopted on 2 May 1989, and emphasizes the importance of taking into account the special needs and requirements of developing countries and developing appropriate funding mechanisms in order to enable all countries, in particular developing countries, to participate effectively in the revised Protocol;

20. *Notes* the adoption, on 22 March 1989, of the Basel Convention on the Control of Transboundary Movements of Hazardous Wastes and their Disposal, and calls upon all States to consider signing the Convention without prejudice to the final position to be adopted by regional organizations in this regard and to strengthen their co-operation in problem areas within the scope of the Convention;

21. *Supports* Governing Council decision 15/23 of 25 May 1989 on desertification, in which the Council, *inter alia*, invites donor Governments and intergovernmental bodies to accord high priority in their bilateral and multilateral assistance activities to national programmes for combating desertification and for the rehabilitation of land resources;

22. *Considers* the conservation and utilization of biological diversity to be a priority issue, an important element of ecological balance and a source of benefit to mankind, and welcomes Governing Council decision 15/34 of 25 May 1989;

23. *Notes* the consideration given by the Governing Council in its decision 15/10 of 25 May 1989 to the proposed establishment of a United Nations centre for urgent environmental assistance and takes note of the information provided by the Executive Director of the United Nations Environment Programme on the preliminary results of his consultations regarding the views expressed by Governments and organizations on

this matter, bearing in mind the mandates of the Programme, the Office of the United Nations Disaster Relief Co-ordinator, the World Meteorological Organization, the International Maritime Organization and the International Atomic Energy Agency, as well as other relevant United Nations specialized agencies and bodies;

24. *Expresses its satisfaction* at the impetus given to addressing environmental concerns through meetings at the regional level, and calls on the Programme and other relevant organizations to continue to play an effective role in this regard.

General Assembly resolution 44/229

22 December 1989   Meeting 85   Adopted without vote

5-nation draft (A/C.2/44/L.63/Rev.1), orally revised; agenda item 82 *(f)*.
Sponsors: Bangladesh, Egypt, Finland, Iran, New Zealand.
Meeting numbers. GA 44th session: 2nd Committee 46, 49-52; plenary 85.

International conventions

The UNEP Executive Director reported[5] in February on international conventions and protocols in the field of the environment. The report contained information on changes in the status of existing conventions and information describing the reported intentions of Governments to take action with regard to multilateral legal instruments. The 1987 Montreal Protocol on Substances that Deplete the Ozone Layer[6] entered into force on 1 January 1989, and the Convention Concerning Safety in the Use of Asbestos entered into force on 16 June.

On 25 May, the Governing Council asked[7] the Executive Director to transmit his report to the General Assembly at its 1989 session, and called on States and regional intergovernmental organizations in a position to do so and that had not already done so to sign, ratify, approve, accede to or accept and implement multilateral legal instruments in the field of the environment.

On 22 December, by **decision 44/454**, the General Assembly took note of the Executive Director's report.

Biological diversity

The Executive Director, in a February report[8] on programme matters requiring policy guidance from the UNEP Governing Council, outlined the decisions of the *Ad Hoc* Working Group of Experts on biological diversity, endorsing the view that a new global legal instrument and additional measures were required for the conservation of biological diversity. He proposed that the UNEP Governing Council decide on the process and procedures to that end.

On 25 May, the Governing Council agreed[9] that the full implications of the new biotechnologies should be taken into account in any international legal instrument on the conservation of the biological diversity of the planet. It urged the Executive Director to promote co-operation in the implementation of existing international instru-

ments and agreements, and to convene, in co-operation with other appropriate international organizations, additional sessions of the *Ad Hoc* Working Group of Experts to consider the technical content within a broad socio-economic context of a suitable new international legal instrument and other measures for the conservation of the biological diversity of the planet. It authorized him, on the basis of the final report of the *Ad Hoc* Working Group of Experts on biological diversity, to convene an *ad hoc* working group of legal and technical experts with a mandate to negotiate an international legal instrument for the conservation of biological diversity. The Council called on Governments to provide financial and technical resources for the functioning of the Working Group and, in particular, the participation of the developing countries. It requested the Executive Director to expedite the work of the *Ad Hoc* Working Group with the aim of having the proposed new international legal instrument ready for adoption as soon as possible, and to submit a progress report to the first session of the preparatory committee for the 1992 Conference on Environment and Development and to the 1990 session of the Governing Council.

Transboundary movements of hazardous wastes

The UNEP Executive Director, in a May progress report,[10] informed the Governing Council that the Basel Convention on the Control of Transboundary Movements of Hazardous Wastes and their Disposal had been adopted on 22 March by the 116 States participating in the Conference of Plenipotentiaries on the Global Convention on the Control of Transboundary Movements of Hazardous Wastes, held at Basel, Switzerland. Thirty-five States had signed the Convention, which was to enter into force upon ratification by 20 States. As of 31 December 1989,[11] 40 States and the European Community had ratified the Convention and Jordan had approved it.

The Convention provided for the orderly control of imports and exports of hazardous wastes, and called for international co-operation to assist countries lacking the technical, legal and administrative capacity to manage and dispose of wastes in an environmentally sound manner, and emphasized the importance of assisting developing countries in that regard. It authorized the establishment of a secretariat to process and disseminate information provided by the parties to the Convention, to ensure co-operation between parties and to assist them in implementing the Convention. UNEP would function as the interim secretariat, pending the first meeting of the parties to the Convention after its entry into force.

On 25 May, the Governing Council requested[12] the Executive Director to assist in implementing the Basel Convention and the resolutions of the Final Act of the Conference of Plenipotentaries on the Global Convention on the Control of Transboundary Movements of Hazardous Wastes. It called on Governments that were in a position to do so to sign and ratify the Convention, and to consider voluntary contributions towards the operating costs of the interim secretariat. The Council asked the Executive Director to develop programmes for assisting developing countries and to submit them to donors for financing, and to avoid duplication between the work of the International Register of Potentially Toxic Chemicals (see below) and that of the interim secretariat.

In December, the General Assembly considered the Secretary-General's report[13] on developments in regard to a global convention on the control of the transboundary movement of hazardous wastes, which it took note of by **decision 44/454** of 22 December.

Also on the same date, the Assembly, in **resolution 44/229**, noted the adoption of the Basel Convention on the Control of Transboundary Movements of Hazardous Wastes and their Disposal and called upon all States to consider signing the Convention, without prejudice to the final position to be adopted by regional organizations in that regard, and to strengthen their co-operation in problem areas within the scope of the Convention.

Regional and other efforts

Latin America and the Caribbean Environmental Conference

The Sixth Ministerial Meeting on the Environment in Latin America and the Caribbean (Brasilia, 30-31 March)[14] focused attention on the urgent need to find a balance between socio-economic development and the protection and conservation of the environment through the proper utilization of natural resources and control of the environmental impacts. The Ministers adopted the Declaration of Brasilia, in which they recognized the inextricable relationship between environmental concerns and socio-economic development, as well as the obligation to ensure the rational use of resources for the benefit of present and future generations. The Ministers urged the international financing agencies to ensure, through specific institutional facilities, availability of sufficient additional resources, on concessional terms, to fund environmental protection projects in developing countries. They argued that international co-operation for environmental protection should include free access to scientific information and the transfer—at cost—to the developing countries of non-polluting technologies and of technologies intended for environmental conservation. Access

to new environmental technologies, they said, could not be subject to purely commercial interests. The countries of the region, in addition to their internal efforts to design and implement national plans for the protection and conservation of the environment, expressed commitment to strengthening their co-operation and to requesting technical and financial co-operation from extra-regional countries and international organizations.

On 25 May, the Governing Council requested[15] the UNEP Executive Director to transmit the Declaration of Brasilia, which was annexed to its decision, to Governments and international governmental and non-governmental organizations (NGOs), and also to inform other interested entities. It invited Governments, international multilateral credit organizations and NGOs to take into account the Declaration as a frame of reference for international co-operation with developing countries.

In other action, the Council requested[16] the Executive Director to support the plans and programmes already being implemented in the Latin American and Caribbean region, and to initiate, in consultation with the Governments of the region, the formulation of an Action Plan for the Environment for Latin America and the Caribbean. It urged him to initiate the programmes selected for priority at the Sixth Ministerial Meeting on the Environment in Latin America and the Caribbean.

Co-operation with the Council of Arab Ministers

On 25 May, the Governing Council requested[17] the Executive Director to provide technical and financial assistance to the priority programmes in the work plan of the Council of Arab Ministers Responsible for the Environment, particularly in the areas of desertification control and expansion of the area suitable for cultivation in the Arab world, the control of industrial pollution and environmental education and awareness. It also requested him to support the technical secretariat of the Council of Arab Ministers Responsible for the Environment through the provision of technical advice, particularly in the initial years of its activities.

UNDP activities

The UNDP Administrator, in a May report,[18] outlined the UNDP strategy at country, regional and international levels for responding to increasing demands from Governments for technical co-operation in the integration of environmental considerations into development planning and macro-economic management. The strategy envisaged expanded collaboration among relevant agencies of the UN system, especially UNEP, the World Meteorological Organization (WMO), the United Nations Educational, Scientific and Cultural Organization (UNESCO), multilateral financial institutions, regional commissions and the Administrative Committee on Co-ordination (ACC). It also focused on strengthening the technical capacity of developing countries to participate effectively in the international dialogue on the biosphere's systems; education and human resources development; communications; community and NGO participation; and the role of women.

On 30 June, the UNDP Governing Council endorsed[19] expanded collaboration among UN agencies, and requested the Administrator to implement activities outlined in his report and to report thereon to the Council in 1990.

REFERENCES

[1]UNEP/GC.15/5. [2]A/44/25 (dec. 15/1). [3]A/44/746/Add.7. [4]A/C.2/44/L.63/Rev.1. [5]UNEP/GC.15/9/Add.5. [6]YUN 1987, p. 700. [7]A/44/25 (dec. 15/31). [8]UNEP/GC.15/9/Add.2 & Corr.1. [9]A/44/25 (dec. 15/34). [10]UNEP/GC.15/9/Add.7. [11]*Multilateral Treaties Deposited with the Secretary-General: Status as at 31 December 1989*, ST/LEG/SER.E/8, Sales No. E.90.V.6. [12]A/44/25 (dec. 15/33). [13]A/44/479. [14]A/44/683. [15]A/44/25 (dec. 15/16). [16]*Ibid.* (dec. 15/17). [17]*Ibid.* (dec. 15/7). [18]DP/1989/63. [19]E/1989/32 (dec. 89/28).

Environment and development

UN conference preparations

The Secretary-General, in response to a 1988 General Assembly request,[1] in May submitted a report,[2] with later addenda, containing the views of Governments, UN organs, organizations and programmes, intergovernmental organizations and NGOs on the convening of a UN conference on environment and development. Those views related to the scope, objectives and content, conference title, preparatory process, time and place, and other modalities. All responses cited the importance and timeliness of such a conference, and there was general agreement that an intergovernmental preparatory committee would be required and that NGOs should take an active role in preparations. The conference should be held for two weeks in 1992 at the highest political level, it was stated.

The report also addressed the financial implications of preparing and convening the conference, including a proposal that the Assembly establish a trust fund to receive voluntary contributions for special projects, media events and publicity and other activities. The comments of the USSR were contained in a 15 May letter[3] addressed to the Secretary-General. In November, France submitted the views of the European Community.[4]

The UNEP Executive Director, in a May note,[5] transmitted to the UNEP Governing Council the Secretary-General's report.

On 25 May, the Governing Council recommended[6] that the Assembly, when taking a decision on the exact scope, title, venue and date of a UN conference on environment and development, to be held no later than 1992, and on the modalities and financial implications of holding such a conference, should consider the elements annexed to the Council's decision on the subject.

ECONOMIC AND SOCIAL COUNCIL ACTION

On 26 July, the Economic and Social Council adopted **resolution 1989/87** without vote.

Convening of a United Nations conference on environment and development

The Economic and Social Council,

Recalling General Assembly resolution 43/196 of 20 December 1988,

Taking note of the report of the Secretary-General on the question of the convening of a United Nations conference on environment and development,

Taking note also of decision 15/3 adopted by the Governing Council of the United Nations Environment Programme on 25 May 1989,

Decides to transmit decision 15/3 of the Governing Council of the United Nations Environment Programme, together with the views on the convening of a United Nations conference on environment and development expressed under items 2 and 7 (*f*) of the agenda of the second regular session of 1989 of the Economic and Social Council, to the General Assembly at its forty-fourth session for consideration and appropriate action.

Economic and Social Council resolution 1989/87

26 July 1989   Meeting 35   Adopted without vote

Draft by Austria, Canada, Denmark, Finland, Germany, Federal Republic of, Malaysia for the Group of 77, New Zealand, Norway, Poland, Sweden and Switzerland (E/1989/L.36); agenda item 7 (*f*).
Meeting numbers. ESC 28, 33, 35.

GENERAL ASSEMBLY ACTION

On 22 December, on the recommendation of the Second Committee, the Assembly adopted **resolution 44/228** without vote.

United Nations Conference on Environment and Development

The General Assembly,

Recalling its resolution 43/196 of 20 December 1988 on a United Nations conference on environment and development,

Taking note of decision 15/3 of 25 May 1989 of the Governing Council of the United Nations Environment Programme on a United Nations conference on environment and development,

Taking note also of Economic and Social Council resolution 1989/87 of 26 July 1989 on the convening of a United Nations conference on environment and development,

Taking note further of Economic and Social Council resolution 1989/101 of 27 July 1989 on strengthening international co-operation on environment through the provision of additional financial resources to developing countries,

Recalling its resolutions 42/186 of 11 December 1987 on the Environmental Perspective to the Year 2000 and Beyond and 42/187 of 11 December 1987 on the report of the World Commission on Environment and Development,

Taking note of the report of the Secretary-General on the question of the convening of a United Nations conference on environment and development,

Mindful of the views expressed by Governments in the debate at its forty-fourth session on the convening of a United Nations conference on environment and development,

Recalling the Declaration of the United Nations Conference on the Human Environment,

Deeply concerned by the continuing deterioration of the state of the environment and the serious degradation of the global life-support systems, as well as by trends that, if allowed to continue, could disrupt the global ecological balance, jeopardize the life-sustaining qualities of the Earth and lead to an ecological catastrophe, and recognizing that decisive, urgent and global action is vital to protecting the ecological balance of the Earth,

Recognizing the importance for all countries of the protection and enhancement of the environment,

Recognizing also that the global character of environmental problems, including climate change, depletion of the ozone layer, transboundary air and water pollution, the contamination of the oceans and seas and degradation of land resources, including drought and desertification, necessitates action at all levels, including the global, regional and national levels, and the commitment and participation of all countries,

Gravely concerned that the major cause of the continuing deterioration of the global environment is the unsustainable pattern of production and consumption, particularly in industrialized countries,

Stressing that poverty and environmental degradation are closely interrelated and that environmental protection in developing countries must, in this context, be viewed as an integral part of the development process and cannot be considered in isolation from it,

Recognizing that measures to be undertaken at the international level for the protection and enhancement of the environment must take fully into account the current imbalances in global patterns of production and consumption,

Affirming that the responsibility for containing, reducing and eliminating global environmental damage must be borne by the countries causing such damage, must be in relation to the damage caused and must be in accordance with their respective capabilities and responsibilities,

Recognizing the environmental impact of material remnants of war and the need for further international co-operation for their removal,

Stressing the importance for all countries of taking effective measures for the protection, restoration and enhancement of the environment in accordance, *inter alia*, with their respective capabilities, while at the same time acknowledging the efforts being made in all countries in this regard, including international co-operation between developed and developing countries,

Stressing the need for effective international co-operation in the areas of research, development and application of environmentally sound technologies,

Conscious of the crucial role of science and technology in the field of environmental protection and of the need of developing countries, in particular, for favourable access to environmentally sound technologies, processes, equipment and related research and expertise through international co-operation designed to further global efforts for environmental protection, including the use of innovative and effective means,

Recognizing that new and additional financial resources will have to be channelled to developing countries in order to ensure their full participation in global efforts for environmental protection,

I

1. *Decides* to convene the United Nations Conference on Environment and Development, which shall be of two weeks' duration and shall have the highest possible level of participation, to coincide with World Environment Day, on 5 June 1992;

2. *Accepts with deep appreciation* the generous offer of the Government of Brazil to act as host to the Conference;

3. *Affirms* that the Conference should elaborate strategies and measures to halt and reverse the effects of environmental degradation in the context of increased national and international efforts to promote sustainable and environmentally sound development in all countries;

4. *Affirms also* that the protection and enhancement of the environment are major issues that affect the well-being of peoples and economic development throughout the world;

5. *Affirms further* that the promotion of economic growth in developing countries is essential to address problems of environmental degradation;

6. *Affirms* the importance of a supportive international economic climate conducive to sustained economic growth and development in all countries for the protection and sound management of the environment;

7. *Reaffirms* that, in accordance with the Charter of the United Nations and the applicable principles of international law, States have the sovereign right to exploit their own resources pursuant to their environmental policies, and also reaffirms their responsibility to ensure that activities within their jurisdiction or control do not cause damage to the environment of other States or of areas beyond the limits of national jurisdiction and to play their due role in preserving and protecting the global and regional environment in accordance with their capacities and specific responsibilities;

8. *Affirms* the responsibility of States, in accordance with national legislation and applicable international law, for the damage to the environment and natural resources caused by activities within their jurisdiction or control through transboundary interference;

9. *Notes* that the largest part of the current emission of pollutants into the environment, including toxic and hazardous wastes, originates in developed countries, and therefore recognizes that those countries have the main responsibility for combating such pollution;

10. *Stresses* that large industrial enterprises, including transnational corporations, are frequently the repositories of scarce technical skills for the preservation and

enhancement of the environment, that they conduct activities in sectors that have an impact on the environment and, to that extent, have specific responsibilities and that, in this context, efforts need to be encouraged and mobilized to protect and enhance the environment in all countries;

11. *Reaffirms* that the serious external indebtedness of developing countries and other countries with serious debt-servicing problems has to be addressed in an efficient and urgent manner in order to enable those countries to contribute fully and in accordance with their capacities and responsibilities to global efforts to protect and enhance the environment;

12. *Affirms* that, in the light of the foregoing, the following environmental issues, which are not listed in any particular order of priority, are among those of major concern in maintaining the quality of the Earth's environment and especially in achieving environmentally sound and sustainable development in all countries:

(a) Protection of the atmosphere by combating climate change, depletion of the ozone layer and transboundary air pollution;

(b) Protection of the quality and supply of freshwater resources;

(c) Protection of the oceans and all kinds of seas, including enclosed and semi-enclosed seas, and coastal areas and the protection, rational use and development of their living resources;

(d) Protection and management of land resources by, *inter alia*, combating deforestation, desertification and drought;

(e) Conservation of biological diversity;

(f) Environmentally sound management of biotechnology;

(g) Environmentally sound management of wastes, particularly hazardous wastes, and of toxic chemicals, as well as prevention of illegal international traffic in toxic and dangerous products and wastes;

(h) Improvement of the living and working environment of the poor in urban slums and rural areas, through the eradication of poverty by, *inter alia*, implementing integrated rural and urban development programmes, as well as taking other appropriate measures at all levels necessary to stem the degradation of the environment;

(i) Protection of human health conditions and improvement of the quality of life;

13. *Emphasizes* the need to strengthen international co-operation for the management of the environment to ensure its protection and enhancement and the need to explore the issue of benefits derived from activities, including research and development, related to the protection and development of biological diversity;

14. *Reaffirms* the need to strengthen international co-operation, particularly between developed and developing countries, in research and development and the utilization of environmentally sound technologies;

15. *Decides* that the Conference, in addressing environmental issues in the developmental context, should have the following objectives:

(a) To examine the state of the environment and changes that have occurred since the United Nations Conference on the Human Environment, held in 1972, and since the adoption of such international agreements as the Plan of Action to Combat Desertification, the Vienna Convention for the Protection of the Ozone Layer, adopted on 22 March 1985, and the Montreal Protocol on Substances that Deplete the Ozone Layer, adopted on 16 September 1987, taking into account the actions taken by all countries and intergovernmental organizations to protect and enhance the environment;

(b) To identify strategies to be co-ordinated regionally and globally, as appropriate, for concerted action to deal with major environmental issues in the socio-economic development processes of all countries within a particular time-frame;

(c) To recommend measures to be taken at the national and international levels to protect and enhance the environment, taking into account the specific needs of developing countries, through the development and implementation of policies for sustainable and environmentally sound development with special emphasis on incorporating environmental concerns in the economic and social development process and of various sectoral policies and through, *inter alia*, preventive action at the sources of environmental degradation, clearly identifying the sources of such degradation and appropriate remedial measures, in all countries;

(d) To promote the further development of international environmental law, taking into account the Declaration of the United Nations Conference on the Human Environment, as well as the special needs and concerns of the developing countries, and to examine in this context the feasibility of elaborating general rights and obligations of States, as appropriate, in the field of the environment, and taking into account relevant existing international legal instruments;

(e) To examine ways and means further to improve co-operation in the field of protection and enhancement of the environment between neighbouring countries, with a view to eliminating adverse environmental effects;

(f) To examine strategies for national and international action with a view to arriving at specific agreements and commitments by Governments for defined activities to deal with major environmental issues in order to restore the global ecological balance and to prevent further deterioration of the environment, taking into account the fact that the largest part of the current emission of pollutants into the environment, including toxic and hazardous wastes, originates in developed countries, and therefore recognizing that those countries have the main responsibility for combating such pollution;

(g) To accord high priority to drought and desertification control and to consider all means necessary, including financial, scientific and technological resources, to halt and reverse the process of desertification with a view to preserving the ecological balance of the planet;

(h) To examine the relationship between environmental degradation and the international economic environment, with a view to ensuring a more integrated approach to problems of environment and development in relevant international forums without introducing new forms of conditionality;

(i) To examine strategies for national and international action with a view to arriving at specific agreements and commitments by Governments and by intergovernmental organizations for defined activities to promote a supportive international economic climate conducive to sustained and environmentally sound development in all countries, with a view to combating poverty and improving the quality of life, and bearing in mind that the incorporation of environmental concerns and considerations in development planning and policies should not be used to introduce new forms of conditionality in aid or in development financing and should not serve as a pretext for creating unjustified barriers to trade;

(j) To identify ways and means of providing new and additional financial resources, particularly to developing countries, for environmentally sound development programmes and projects in accordance with national development objectives, priorities and plans and to consider ways of effectively monitoring the provision of such new and additional financial resources, particularly to developing countries, so as to enable the international community to take further appropriate action on the basis of accurate and reliable data;

(k) To identify ways and means of providing additional financial resources for measures directed towards solving major environmental problems of global concern and especially of supporting those countries, in particular developing countries, for which the implementation of such measures would entail a special or abnormal burden, owing, in particular, to their lack of financial resources, expertise or technical capacity;

(l) To consider various funding mechanisms, including voluntary ones, and to examine the possibility of a special international fund and other innovative approaches, with a view to ensuring, on a favourable basis, the most effective and expeditious transfer of environmentally sound technologies to developing countries;

(m) To examine, with a view to making recommendations, effective modalities for favourable access to, and transfer of, environmentally sound technologies, in particular to the developing countries, including on concessional and preferential terms, and modalities for supporting all countries in their efforts to create and develop their endogenous technological capacities in the field of scientific research and development, as well as in the acquisition of relevant information, and, in this context, to explore the concept of assured access for developing countries to environmentally sound technologies, in its relation to proprietary rights, with a view to developing effective responses to the needs of developing countries in this area;

(n) To promote the development of human resources, particularly in developing countries, for the protection and enhancement of the environment;

(o) To recommend measures to Governments and the relevant bodies of the United Nations system, with a view to strengthening technical co-operation with the developing countries to enable them to develop and strengthen their capacity for identifying, analysing, monitoring, managing or preventing environmental problems in accordance with their national development plans, objectives and priorities;

(p) To promote open and timely exchange of information on national environmental policies, situations and accidents;

(q) To review and examine the role of the United Nations system in dealing with the environment and possible ways of improving it;

(r) To promote the development or strengthening of appropriate institutions at the national, regional and global levels to deal with environmental matters in the context of the socio-economic development processes of all countries;

(s) To promote environmental education, especially of the younger generation, as well as other measures to increase awareness of the value of the environment;

(t) To promote international co-operation within the United Nations system in monitoring, assessing and anticipating environmental threats and in rendering assistance in cases of environmental emergency;

(u) To specify the respective responsibilities of and support to be given by the organs, organizations and programmes of the United Nations system for the implementation of the recommendations of the Conference;

(v) To quantify the financial requirements for the successful implementation of Conference decisions and recommendations and to identify possible sources, including innovative ones, of additional resources;

(w) To assess the capacity of the United Nations system to assist in the prevention and settlement of disputes in the environmental sphere and to recommend measures in this field, while respecting existing bilateral and international agreements that provide for the settlement of such disputes;

II

1. *Decides* to establish the Preparatory Committee for the United Nations Conference on Environment and Development, which shall be open to all States Members of the United Nations or members of the specialized agencies, with the participation of observers, in accordance with the established practice of the General Assembly;

2. *Decides* that the Preparatory Committee shall hold an organizational session of two weeks' duration in March 1990 and a final session, both at United Nations Headquarters, as well as three additional substantive sessions, the first at Nairobi and the following two at Geneva, the timing and duration of which shall be determined by the Preparatory Committee at its organizational session;

3. *Decides* that the Preparatory Committee, at its organizational session, shall elect, with due regard to equitable geographic representation, a chairman and other members of its Bureau, comprising a substantial number of vice-chairmen and a rapporteur;

4. *Decides* that the host country of the Conference, Brazil, shall be *ex officio* a member of the Bureau;

5. *Requests* the Secretary-General, following the organizational session of the Preparatory Committee, to establish an appropriate *ad hoc* secretariat at the United Nations Office at Geneva, with a unit in New York and another unit in Nairobi, taking into account the decisions to be made by the Preparatory Committee regarding the preparatory process for the Conference and based on the principle of equitable geographic distribution;

6. *Decides* that the *ad hoc* secretariat will be headed by the Secretary-General of the United Nations Conference on Environment and Development, who will be appointed by the Secretary-General of the United Nations;

7. *Requests* the Secretary-General of the United Nations to prepare a report for the organizational session of the Preparatory Committee containing recommendations on an adequate preparatory process, taking into account the provisions of the present resolution and the

views expressed by Governments in the debate at the forty-fourth session of the General Assembly;

8. *Decides* that the Preparatory Committee shall:

(a) Draft the provisional agenda of the Conference, in accordance with the provisions of the present resolution;

(b) Adopt guidelines to enable States to take a harmonized approach in their preparations and reporting;

(c) Prepare draft decisions for the Conference and submit them to the Conference for consideration and adoption;

9. *Requests* the United Nations Environment Programme, as the main organ dealing with environmental issues, and other organs, organizations and programmes of the United Nations system, as well as other relevant intergovernmental organizations, to contribute fully to the preparations for the Conference on the basis of guidelines and requirements to be established by the Preparatory Committee;

10. *Requests* the Secretary-General to ensure the coordination of contributions from the United Nations system through the Administrative Committee on Coordination;

11. *Invites* all States to take an active part in the preparations for the Conference, to prepare national reports, as appropriate, to be submitted to the Preparatory Committee in a timely manner, and to promote international co-operation and broad-based national preparatory processes involving the scientific community, industry, trade unions and concerned non-governmental organizations;

12. *Requests* relevant non-governmental organizations in consultative status with the Economic and Social Council to contribute to the Conference, as appropriate;

13. *Stresses* the importance of holding regional conferences on environment and development with the full co-operation of the regional commissions, and recommends that the results of such regional conferences be introduced into the preparatory process for the Conference, bearing in mind that regional conferences should make important substantive contributions to the Conference;

14. *Decides* that the preparatory process and the Conference itself should be funded through the regular budget of the United Nations without adversely affecting other ongoing activities and without prejudice to the provision of sources of extrabudgetary resources;

15. *Decides* to establish a voluntary fund for the purpose of assisting developing countries, in particular the least developed among them, to participate fully and effectively in the Conference and in its preparatory process, and invites Governments to contribute to the fund;

16. *Requests* the Chairman of the Preparatory Committee to report to the General Assembly at its forty-fifth and forty-sixth sessions on the progress of work of the Committee;

17. *Decides* to include in the provisional agenda of its forty-fifth and forty-sixth sessions an item entitled "United Nations Conference on Environment and Development".

General Assembly resolution 44/228

22 December 1989   Meeting 85   Adopted without vote

Approved by Second Committee (A/44/746/Add.7) without vote, 19 December (meeting 52); draft by Chairman (A/C.2/44/L.86), based on informal consultations on drafts by Malaysia for Group of 77 (A/C.2/44/L.55) and by France for European Community (A/C.2/44/L.58) and on draft decision by UNEP Governing Council (A/C.2/44/L.7); agenda item 82 *(f)*.
Financial implications. 5th Committee, A/44/903; S-G, A/C.2/44/L.88, A/C.5/44/53.
Meeting numbers. GA 44th session: 2nd Committee 31, 32, 40, 44, 46, 49-52; 5th Committee 60; plenary 85.

On 21 December, the General Assembly, on the recommendation of the Fifth Committee, adopted **section IX** of **resolution 44/201 B** without vote.

Section 18.   United Nations Environment Programme

[*The General Assembly . . .*]

Invites the Secretary-General to ensure that all efforts are made in the United Nations system for the preparations for the United Nations Conference on Environment and Development, to be held in 1992, and the implementation of other new mandates, including provisions for adequate resources for effective coordination in the secretariat of the United Nations Environment Programme;

. . .

General Assembly resolution 44/201 B, section IX

21 December 1989   Meeting 84   Adopted without vote

Approved by Fifth Committee (A/44/905) without vote, 19 December (meeting 59); draft by Vice-Chairman (A/C.5/44/L.25); agenda item 123.
Meeting numbers. GA 44th session: 5th Committee 37, 39, 59; plenary 84.

Other issues

Resolutions 42/186 and 42/187

In a March note,[7] the UNEP Executive Director submitted proposed comments of the Governing Council on the responses received from Governments on the implementation of 1987 General Assembly resolutions 42/186 and 42/187, respectively, on the Environmental Perspective to the Year 2000 and Beyond,[8] and on the report of the World Commission on Environment and Development.[9] Annexed to the note was material for the consolidated report of the Secretary-General on the implementation of the two resolutions.

On 14 May, the Governing Council requested[10] the Executive Director to arrange for the views and suggestions of the Council to be incorporated in the draft report of the Secretary-General on the implementation of General Assembly resolutions 42/186 and 42/187, so that the amended report could be submitted through the Economic and Social Council to the Assembly in 1990. It invited the attention of the Assembly to the understanding of the UNEP Governing Council with regard to the concept of sustainable development, and requested the Executive Director to pursue full implementation and follow-up to the relevant resolutions and decisions of the Assembly and the Economic and Social Council.

Report of the Secretary-General. The Secretary-General in July submitted to the Economic and Social Council and the General Assembly a report[11] on the implementation of Assembly resolutions 42/186 and 42/187 on the

Environmental Perspective to the Year 2000 and Beyond[8] and on the report of the World Commission on Environment and Development,[9] respectively. The report contained the views of the UNEP Governing Council on efforts towards sustainable and environmentally sound development, as well as information received from Governments and the European Community and from governing bodies of UN organizations, bodies and programmes on action and activities undertaken to achieve such development. The Council also offered suggestions on long-term strategies and new environmental concerns. The data confirmed that long-standing environmental priorities continued to require attention and effort by Governments and the UN system in their ongoing programmes. Further reports[12] on progress made towards sustainable, environmentally sound development were submitted by the United Nations Conference on Trade and Development, the World Health Organization (WHO), UNESCO, the Food and Agriculture Organization of the United Nations (FAO), the International Labour Organisation (ILO), the World Food Programme, WMO, the United Nations Centre for Human Settlements (Habitat), the United Nations Industrial Development Organization, the International Maritime Organization (IMO) and the International Atomic Energy Agency (IAEA).

The Economic and Social Council, by **decision 1989/177** of 27 July, took note of the report of the Secretary-General on the implementation of General Assembly resolutions 42/186 and 42/187 and of the reports of governing bodies of UN organs, organizations and programmes on progress made towards sustainable and environmentally sound development.

The General Assembly, by **decision 44/454** of 22 December, also noted the Secretary-General's report.

GENERAL ASSEMBLY ACTION

On 22 December, on the recommendation of the Second Committee, the General Assembly adopted **resolution 44/227** without vote.

Implementation of General Assembly resolutions 42/186 and 42/187

The General Assembly,

Recalling its resolution 42/186 of 11 December 1987 on the Environmental Perspective to the Year 2000 and Beyond, in which it adopted the Environmental Perspective as a broad framework to guide national action and international co-operation on policies and programmes aimed at achieving sustainable and environmentally sound development in all countries,

Recalling also its resolution 42/187 of 11 December 1987 on the report of the World Commission on Environment and Development, in which it welcomed the report and, *inter alia*, invited Governments and organizations of the

United Nations system to take account of the analysis and recommendations contained in the report in determining their policies and programmes,

Recalling further its resolution 43/196 of 20 December 1988 on a United Nations conference on environment and development,

Having considered the report of the Secretary-General, containing information on action taken by Governments and organizations of the United Nations system to pursue sustainable and environmentally sound development in all countries, and taking note of decision 15/2 of 26 May 1989 of the Governing Council of the United Nations Environment Programme,

1. *Takes note* of the report of the Secretary-General;

2. *Notes with appreciation* the efforts made by Governments and intergovernmental and non-governmental organizations to promote sustainable and environmentally sound development in all countries;

3. *Expresses its concern*, none the less, that much more needs to be done in translating the increased understanding of the need for sustainable and environmentally sound development into concrete action in all countries;

4. *Notes with satisfaction* the regional activities that have taken place or are being planned with a view to promoting sustainable and environmentally sound development, including the First African Regional Conference on Environment and Sustainable Development, organized by the Economic Commission for Africa and the United Nations Environment Programme and held at Kampala from 12 to 16 June 1989, as well as similar conferences in the other regions planned to take place in 1990;

5. *Invites* Governments and the governing bodies of the organizations and programmes of the United Nations system, as well as other intergovernmental and non-governmental organizations, to intensify further their efforts towards promoting and achieving sustainable and environmentally sound development by integrating environmental concerns and considerations into policies and programmes in all areas;

6. *Notes with appreciation* the efforts made by the Secretary-General in reviewing, co-ordinating and strengthening the activities of the United Nations system for the promotion of sustainable and environmentally sound development;

7. *Notes* that serious environmental problems are arising for all countries and that those problems must be progressively addressed through preventive measures at their sources by national efforts and international co-operation;

8. *Reaffirms* that there is a direct interrelationship between environment and development, and recognizes that a supportive international economic climate conducive to sustained economic growth and development, particularly in developing countries, is of major importance for sound management of the environment;

9. *Reaffirms also* that environment issues are closely related to development policies and practices and that, consequently, environmental goals and actions need to be defined in relation to development objectives and policies;

10. *Notes* that the critical objectives for environment and development policies that follow from the need for sustainable and environmentally sound development must include creating a healthy, clean and safe environ-

ment in all countries, reviving overall economic growth, particularly in developing countries, and improving its quality, eradicating poverty and satisfying human needs by raising the standard of living and improving the quality of life, addressing the issues of sound management and enhancement of the resource base, furthering the promotion, accelerated development and transfer of environmentally sound technology, minimizing environmental dangers and merging environment and economics in decision-making in all countries, as well as taking cognizance of the interrelationship between people, resources, environment and development;

11. *Stresses* that sustainable and environmentally sound development requires changes in the unsustainable pattern of production and consumption, particularly in industrialized countries, and the development of environmentally sound technologies, and, in this context, stresses also the need to examine, with a view to making recommendations on effective modalities for favourable access to, and transfer of, environmentally sound technologies, in particular to the developing countries, including on concessional and preferential terms, and on modalities for supporting all countries in their efforts to create and develop their endogenous technological capacities in the field of scientific research and development, as well as in the acquisition of relevant information, and, in this context, stresses further the need to explore the concept of assured access for developing countries to environmentally sound technologies, in its relation to proprietary rights, with a view to developing effective responses to the needs of developing countries in this area;

12. *Endorses* the views and suggestions of the Governing Council of the United Nations Environment Programme at its fifteenth session on the implementation of General Assembly resolutions 42/186 and 42/187, contained in the report of the Secretary-General, regards Governing Council decision 15/2 as a positive step towards a better understanding of the concept of sustainable and environmentally sound development and of the implications of the implementation of the concept for all countries, and invites Governments and the governing bodies of the organizations and programmes of the United Nations system as well as other intergovernmental and non-governmental organizations to take them into account in their further efforts towards promoting and achieving sustainable and environmentally sound development in all countries;

13. *Reaffirms* the need to provide new and additional financial resources to support developing countries in measures, *inter alia*, to identify, analyse, monitor, prevent and manage environmental problems, primarily at their sources, in accordance with their national development goals, objectives and plans, so as to ensure that their development priorities are not adversely affected;

14. *Stresses* the need for new and additional financial resources for measures aimed at solving major environmental problems of global concern, and especially to support those countries, in particular developing countries, for which the implementation of such measures would entail a special or abnormal burden, due, in particular, to their lack of financial resources, expertise and/or technical capacity;

15. *Reaffirms* the need for developed countries and relevant organs, organizations and bodies of the United Nations system to strengthen technical co-operation with the developing countries to assist them to develop and strengthen their endogenous capacity for identifying, analysing, monitoring, preventing and managing environmental problems in accordance with their national development plans, priorities and objectives;

16. *Reaffirms also* that, in accordance with the Charter of the United Nations and the principles of international law, States have the sovereign right to exploit their own resources pursuant to their environmental policies, and reaffirms further their responsibility to ensure that activities within their jurisdiction or control do not cause damage to the environment of other States or of areas beyond the limits of national jurisdiction and to play their due role in preserving and protecting the global and regional environment in accordance with their capacities and specific responsibilities;

17. *Considers* that the regional follow-up conferences should contribute to a better understanding and a more concrete definition of the concept of sustainable and environmentally sound development and of the implications of the implementation of the concept, and should make important substantive contributions to the United Nations conference on environment and development in 1992;

18. *Invites* the preparatory committee for the conference to take duly into account the recommendations contained in the Environmental Perspective to the Year 2000 and Beyond and the report of the World Commission on Environment and Development in the preparatory process for the conference, as well as recommendations for action by the General Assembly and the Economic and Social Council and the views and suggestions expressed by the Governing Council of the United Nations Environment Programme and other organs, organizations and bodies of the United Nations system on those matters;

19. *Requests* the Secretary-General to prepare for submission to the preparatory committee for the conference, and to the General Assembly at its forty-sixth session, through the Governing Council of the United Nations Environment Programme and the Economic and Social Council, a progress report on the implementation of the present resolution;

20. *Also requests* the Secretary-General to prepare, for submission to the conference and to the General Assembly at its forty-seventh session, through the Governing Council of the United Nations Environment Programme and the Economic and Social Council, a new consolidated report on further substantive follow-up to General Assembly resolutions 42/186 and 42/187 by Governments and organizations of the United Nations system.

General Assembly resolution 44/227

22 December 1989   Meeting 85   Adopted without vote

Approved by Second Committee (A/44/746/Add.7) by consensus, 19 December (meeting 52); 30-nation draft (A/C.2/44/L.64/Rev.1), orally revised; agenda item 82 *(f)*.
Meeting numbers. GA 44th session: 2nd Committee 31, 32, 40, 44, 46, 49-52; plenary 85.

Sustainable agriculture

The UNEP Governing Council, on 25 May, recommended[13] convening a joint FAO and UNEP meeting on sustainable agriculture, within the framework of the preparation of the proposed 1992 United Nations conference on environment and development, with a view to reviewing the mechanism for integrating agricultural production and environmental policies world wide; elaborating a world strategy for sustainable agriculture to guide agricultural policies at national and international levels, in order to ensure that such policies encouraged farmers to adopt practices that were ecologically sustainable and that led, *inter alia*, to improving the quality of life of rural people; and formulating recommendations for practical action that might be taken by UNEP, FAO and other international organizations within the context of their ongoing activities to promote sustainable agriculture. It requested the Executive Director to forward its recommendation to the Director-General of FAO, for consideration by the FAO Council.

International development strategy

On 25 May, the UNEP Governing Council recommended[14] to the General Assembly that sustainable and environmentally sound development should become a central guiding principle in the international development strategy for the fourth United Nations development decade (see PART THREE, Chapter I). It invited the *Ad Hoc* Committee of the Whole for the Preparation of the International Development Strategy for the Fourth United Nations Development Decade to recognize, in view of the global character of some major environmental problems, the common interest of all countries in pursuing policies aimed at the equitable and sustainable use of global resources, and to reflect that fully in the international development strategy under preparation. It also invited the *Ad Hoc* Committee to reaffirm, in the context of the international development strategy, that the critical objectives for environment and development policies that followed from the need for sustainable and environmentally sound development must include creating a healthy, clean and safe environment, reviving growth and improving its quality, remedying the problems of poverty and the satisfaction of human needs by raising the standard of living and the quality of life, addressing the issues of population and of conserving and enhancing the resource base, reorienting technology and managing risk, and merging environment and economics in decision-making. It called on the Executive Director to contribute to the preparatory process for the strategy and to keep the Governing Council and its Committee of Permanent Representatives informed of developments.

Environmental aspects of political, economic and other issues

Israeli-occupied territories

In 1989, the Governing Council had before it the Executive Director's report on the environmental situation in the occupied Palestinian and other Arab territories.[15] UNEP and WHO were taking part in a 25-month project beginning in February 1989 entitled "Training course on water supply, sanitation and health for environmental health officers working with the Palestinian people". The project would facilitate training in pollution control and environmentally sound management of environmentally related diseases in refugee camps and settlements. Although there was general improvement in the environmental situation in the occupied territories, great public awareness and additional funding were needed for water treatment, refuse and conservation measures and other environmental improvements. There was also a need, the report said, for specific studies and collaborative efforts among UNDP, Israel and local authorities and other public and private entities to undertake environmentally sound development programmes and projects. The Executive Director recommended that an apolitical joint professional programme of environmentally sound development projects and other specific scientific, legal, economic and ecological efforts related to the territories should be considered.

On 25 May,[16] the Council noted that the Executive Director's report did not include reference to the environmental situation in the Palestinian refugee camps in their occupied homeland or in the Syrian and Lebanese territories occupied by Israel. It considered the Executive Director's report to be inadequate and said that it should be updated and the information it contained corroborated. It further considered that the formation of a group of consultants specialized in environmental problems was required, with a mandate to prepare a comprehensive report on the environmental situation in the occupied Palestinian and other territories, making use of the relevant data and information from sources provided by the population of those territories and by the States and regional and international organizations concerned. The Council requested the Executive Director to submit in 1991 a comprehensive report based on findings of that group.

Economic crisis, foreign debt and the environment

On 25 May, the UNEP Governing Council expressed concern[17] that the deterioration of the economic situation of developing countries, exacerbated by the debt crisis, had contributed to a significant and dangerous diminution in the capacity of those countries to protect and preserve the environment. It decided to bring to the attention of Governments, multilateral organizations, and governmental and non-governmental financial institutions the urgent need to change the existing conditions and treatment of the foreign debt of developing countries, in order to strengthen their capacity to address the critical environmental issues fundamental to development and protection of the environment.

Transnational corporations and environmental protection

The Secretary-General submitted to the Economic and Social Council a February report[18] on ongoing and future research relating to transnational corporations (TNCs) and issues relating to the environment. The report examined TNCs and aspects of sustainable development, including their role in environmental restructuring, international corporate environmental management, technology assessment, environmental information disclosures and international waste disposal. It also identified criteria for sustainable development management of TNCs.

The Council, in **resolution 1989/25** of 24 May, requested the Secretary-General to conduct a study of the main sectors of activities that had adverse effects on environmental preservation and the factors that determined the allocation of activities between developed and developing countries and to continue to strengthen the participation of TNCs (see PART THREE, Chapter V) in efforts to preserve and protect the environment, including the elaboration of a set of criteria and operating principles.

Chemical and other weapons of mass destruction

On 25 May,[19] the UNEP Governing Council expressed its concern at the devastating effects of chemical and other weapons of mass destruction on mankind and the environment, and recognized the need for international scientific and technical co-operation in order to protect mankind and the environment from such weapons. The Council requested the Executive Director to prepare a comprehensive report on the devastating effects of chemical weapons on human health and the environment, for submission in 1991.

Human settlements

The Governing Council had before it a February report[20] by the Executive Directors of UNEP and the United Nations Centre for Human Settlements (Habitat) on co-operation between the two organizations, particularly in assessment of environmental conditions in human settlements; environmental aspects of policies, planning and management of both rural and urban human settlements; environmentally sound and appropriate human settlements technology; and research, training and the dissemination of information on environmentally sound human settlements planning and management.

On 25 May,[21] the Governing Council requested the UNEP Executive Director, in consul-

tation with the Executive Director of Habitat, to increase co-operation between the two organizations, particularly with respect to the application of Environmental Guidelines for Settlements Planning and Management in selected metropolitan areas and, *inter alia*, the special needs of coastal human settlements likely to be affected by global climate change.

Transfer of environmental protection technology

On 25 May,[22] the Governing Council urged UNEP to continue its catalytic role to promote, with Governments, industry, research organizations and other relevant institutions, the establishment of a network for information sharing in environmental protection technology. It invited Governments to find bilateral and multilateral arrangements for financial support for exports of environmental protection technology, taking into account the needs of developing countries; and to promote the holding of symposia, exhibitions and training courses in support of a more effective dissemination of information about environmental protection technology and knowledge.

Cultural and natural heritage in Western Asia

On 25 May,[23] the Governing Council took note of the report[24] of the Joint Inspection Unit concerning the UN contribution to the preservation and management of cultural and natural heritage in Western Asia, and of the comments by the Executive Director thereon.

REFERENCES

[1]YUN 1988, p. 456, GA res. 43/196, 20 Dec. 1988. [2]A/44/256-E/1989/66 and Corr.1 & Add.1,2. [3]A/44/278-E/1989/92. [4]A/C.2/44/3. [5]UNEP/GC.15/6/Add.4. [6]A/44/25 (dec. 15/3). [7]UNEP/GC.15/6/Add.2. [8]YUN 1987, p. 661, GA res. 42/186, 11 Dec. 1987. [9]*Ibid.*, p. 679, GA res. 42/187, 11 Dec. 1987. [10]A/44/25 (dec. 15/2). [11]A/44/350-E/1989/99. [12]A/44/339-E/1989/119 & Add.1-11. [13]A/44/25 (dec. 15/24). [14]*Ibid.* (dec. 15/5). [15]UNEP/GC.15/5/Add.2. [16]A/44/25 (dec. 15/8). [17]*Ibid.* (dec. 15/6). [18]E/C.10/1989/12. [19]A/44/25 (dec. 15/9). [20]UNEP/GC.15/8/Add.1. [21]A/44/25 (dec. 15/18). [22]*Ibid.* (dec. 15/37). [23]*Ibid.* (dec. 15/19). [24]JIU/REP/88/5.

Environmental activities

Monitoring and assessment

In 1989, Earthwatch, the environmental assessment arm of UNEP, was composed of three units—the Global Environmental Monitoring System (GEMS), the International Environmental Information System (INFOTERRA) and the International Register of Potentially Toxic Chemicals (IRPTC).[1] Earthwatch gathered information on the state of and trends in the environment and fed the processed information back to managers and decision makers.

Global Environmental Monitoring System

In 1989, GEMS continued to co-ordinate environmental data collection and the production of relevant and timely information for those responsible for managing natural resources and the environment. Due to the growing demand for good environmental information and assessments, consideration was given to reshaping the monitoring assessment machinery of GEMS.

During the year, officials of the GEMS Programme Activity Centre visited several African countries to ascertain their needs in resource monitoring and assessment capabilities. Specific proposals were formulated for Guinea and Mali. Efforts were also made to establish a network of subregional and national geographic information system centres across Africa which would be the nucleus for national environmental monitoring and assessment centres. UNEP, in collaboration with other organizations, universities and research centres, was developing a satellite-based technology to support global forest assessments, particularly in Africa and Amazonia. The GEMS/WATER programme was revised to facilitate the setting up of a select global network of strategically sited monitoring stations in the major basins of the world. Under the GEMS/AIR programme, a systematic collection of national and regional data on urban air pollution and other related factors was initiated to provide a wider basis for interpreting urban air-quality assessments.

Global Resource Information Data Base

During 1989, the Global Resource Information Data Base (GRID), the principal data management programme within GEMS, grew significantly. In addition to GRID-Nairobi and GRID-Geneva, a new GRID-Bangkok facility was established within the Asian Institute of Technology. In August, the first self-financed GRID node in a developed country was opened in Norway, which was intended to provide the system with data from Nordic and polar regions and with special technical and environmental assessment support. GRID's global and regional data holdings rose to nearly 100 data sets. A project was initiated to develop a global landcover data set, using landcover classifications detectable from space and verifiable on the ground. GRID would also take a lead role in providing a data management service for the International Biosphere-Geosphere Programme. The GRID-Nairobi laboratory was used by the International Laboratory for Research and Animal Diseases to model the areas of Africa at risk from tick-borne disease and East Coast fever. GRID also

provided technical support to developing countries in the form of training, data sets and analyst time. Some 40 experts from 30 developing countries were trained in GRID technology.

INFOTERRA

In 1989, INFOTERRA, the UNEP environmental information system, placed greater emphasis on providing substantive and quality data. During the year, more than 16,000 inquiries were received from some 95 countries; more than half came from developing countries. The number of INFOTERRA national focal points grew to 137, and the regional service centres increased to 9. INFOTERRA Special Sectoral Sources grew to 28.

The Executive Director, in co-operation with the Government of the USSR, convened a World Conference on Environmental Information Exchange in the 1990s (INFOTERRA 3) in Moscow (13-18 March).[2] The Conference, attended by representatives of 120 countries and UN agencies and organizations, reviewed all aspects of INFOTERRA activities. Thirty-two recommendations were approved, covering such areas as network development, operations, new technology and promotional activities, and constituting a strategy for the further development of INFOTERRA. The revision of the *INFOTERRA Thesaurus for Environmental Terms* was completed, and the second volume in the INFOTERRA Exchange of Environmental Experiences series—*Drylands, Wetlands, Croplands: Turning Liabilities into Assets*—and the fifth volumes of the INFOTERRA *International Directory* and the *Index* were published. Efforts were also made to strengthen the information infrastructure in less developed countries by associating national focal points from those countries with those from developed countries.

In May, the Governing Council called upon[3] Governments to make full use of INFOTERRA services and to strengthen their INFOTERRA national focal points. It requested the Executive Director to strengthen INFOTERRA, taking into account the recommendations of the World Conference on Environmental Information Exchange, and to provide technical and operational assistance to developing countries to afford them more effective participation in the international exchange of environmental information and experience.

Environmental impact assessment

In February, the Executive Director reported[4] that UNEP was providing information, guidance, advice and assistance to countries in the application of environmental impact assessment (EIA), including the use of the goals and principles of EIA adopted by the Governing Council in 1987.[5] The application of EIA was promoted from sectoral, methodological, legal and procedural standpoints, and included training of personnel from developing countries, providing guidance on EIA techniques and procedures for developing project design and for appraising, and systematizing the inclusion of environmental objectives in the development process. The report also included the opinions of States and relevant international organizations on measures to further international co-operation and agreement in the field, including the application of EIA to development projects with possible transboundary effects.

On 25 May, the Governing Council reaffirmed[6] that EIA was a valuable means of promoting and integrating environmental issues into planning and programme implementation and that it helped to identify potential adverse impacts and the additional resources required to avoid them. The Council called upon Governments to identify the use of the goals and principles of EIA and authorized the UNEP Executive Director to continue to seek the views of Governments and relevant international organizations on modes of further development in EIA.

Harmonization of environmental measurements

The UNEP Executive Director reported[4] in April that, in accordance with the recommendation of a meeting of experts in Munich, Federal Republic of Germany (9-11 March 1987), on improving and harmonizing environmental measurements, the GEMS/Harmonization of Environmental Measurement project was established in Munich, with financial support from the Federal Republic of Germany. Additional funds were being sought from other interested countries. The objectives of the project included establishing and updating inventories of environmentally harmonized techniques and practices of environmental measurement; establishing a system to determine the quality and compatibility of environmental data; and preparing a priority list of areas where data compatibility should be increased.

On 25 May, the Governing Council requested[7] the Executive Director to follow up on contacts with interested countries in seeking support for the project. It appealed to Governments and international organizations to assist the project by participating and by providing financial resources and seconding staff. The Council also requested the Executive Director to report in 1990 on the project.

Control of harmful products, chemicals and wastes

Consolidated List of Products

In a 30 May report[8] on products harmful to health and the environment, the Secretary-General, pursuant to a 1984 General Assembly request,[9] reviewed the Consolidated List of Products Whose Consumption and/or Sale Have Been Banned, Withdrawn, Severely Restricted or Not Approved by Governments,[10] and examined it in relation to protection against products harmful to health and the environment. The review covered arrangements for the production of the List, its coverage and scope, utilization, format, publication in language versions, questions of direct computer access and the public health context. It also considered the issue of protection against products harmful to health and the environment, including new initiatives on prior informed consent and technical assistance. The report concluded that the noxious effect on human health and the environment of hazardous products was gaining increased international recognition. It recommended that production of the List by WHO and UNEP/IRPTC would be improved if a data-base system was established that would be usable by the three organizations, and if the List was made available every year in English. The List should continue to refer to all the technical work being accomplished within the system and ensure that for each product entry, reference was made to the relevant complementary publications and conventions.

The Economic and Social Council, in **decision 1989/177** of 27 July, took note of the Secretary-General's report.

International Register of Potentially Toxic Chemicals

In 1989, the computerized central files of the International Register of Potentially Toxic Chemicals (IRPTC) continued to be updated and expanded.[1] Complete data profiles existed for more than 600 chemicals of international concern. Priorities for further development were based on the needs identified in the implementation of the amended London Guidelines for the Exchange of Information on Chemicals in International Trade.[11] During the year, IRPTC focused on the collection of data on chemicals and their toxicity to mammals and aquatic organisms, and on legal information. The incorporation of all the evaluations of more than 600 chemicals carried out by the International Agency for Research on Cancer was completed, and efforts were initiated to incorporate the relevant health and environmental risk appraisals for chemicals evaluated by the International Programme on Chemical Safety. Co-operation continued with network partners from Canada, the Federal Republic of Germany, Japan and the Netherlands in the exchange and management of toxicity, and legal and other data on specific priority chemicals. IRPTC, with the support of the Netherlands, initiated an expanded three-year effort to establish national registers of potentially toxic chemicals.

In March, the Executive Director reported[12] to the Governing Council that IRPTC required additional human and financial resources to meet its expanding responsibilities. While longer-term resource needs could be met from extrabudgetary sources, an immediate increase in UNEP funding was required to stabilize IRPTC and to enable the programme to attract external funding for its additional tasks, particularly in the light of the major responsibilities emanating from the 1989 Basel Convention on the Control of Transboundary Movements of Hazardous Wastes and their Disposal. The Executive Director also proposed, on the basis of recommendations of a 1988 expert consultation,[13] a number of amendments to the objectives and strategies for IRPTC.

On 25 May, the Governing Council requested[14] the Executive Director to give high priority to the work of the Register through full and flexible utilization of the resources of the Fund, additional sources of income and coordination with other related budget subprogrammes; to solicit extrabudgetary resources from Governments to cover the resource needs of the Register and prepare package programmes for the different activities; and to submit the programmes to potential donors for financing. It approved the revised objectives and strategies of the Register to reflect its expanded responsibilities, as contained in the annex to its decision. The Council invited the Executive Director to assist developing countries in the legal and institutional arrangements for the management of chemicals at the national level and to organize training activities.

List of harmful chemical substances

Responding to a 1987 Governing Council request,[15] the Executive Director reported[2] in April that he had kept the list of selected environmentally harmful chemical substances, processes and phenomena of global significance under continuous review by collecting and screening new scientific, technical and legal information on the subjects listed. He planned to refer the report on the list to Governments, relevant international institutions, industries and NGOs for further study and action by the end of the year, and to invite them to respond to the report, including measures adopted and planned to prevent serious impacts of the environmentally harmful chemical substances, processes and phenomena cited. Based on the responses, he would prepare an updated report for submission to the Governing Council in 1991, containing sections on cadmium, lead, mercury, carbon dioxide, nitrogen oxides and photochemical oxidants, sulphur dioxide and derivatives, production and use of coal and other fossil fuels, injudicious use of pesticides, oil pollution and eutrophication. The Executive Director would also decide whether other chemical substances, processes and phenomena should be added to the list.

On 25 May, the Governing Council noted[16] the Executive Director's report.

Amended London Guidelines on chemicals

The second session of the *Ad Hoc* Working Group of Experts[2] on Prior Consent and Other Modalities to Supplement the London Guidelines for the Exchange of Information on Chemicals in International Trade[11] was held in New York from 13 to 16 February. The Working Group reached consensus on a prior informed consent procedure and on a measure for incorporating it into the London Guidelines. A list of chemicals that had been banned or severely restricted by 10 or more countries would be circulated to Governments participating in the London Guidelines for their decision regarding future importation; a list of chemicals banned or severely restricted by five or more countries would be circulated and decisions sought. Whenever a country banned or severely restricted a chemical that had previously not been the subject of a control action, participating countries would be notified and provided with guidance documents for a decision regarding future importation. An expert group would consider the problem of acutely hazardous pesticide formulations of concern to developing countries, to determine whether there should be a list of such products. The Working Group also developed proposed amendments to the Guidelines.

On 25 May, the Governing Council adopted[17] the amended London Guidelines for the Exchange of Information on Chemicals in International Trade, and recommended: that the Expert Group to be established keep the issue of acutely hazardous pesticides formulations under review with a view to formulating recommendations for additional action; that UNEP and FAO develop an information exchange system to ensure that designated national authorities of importing and exporting countries had a single contact point for obtaining information and communicating decisions on chemicals subject to the prior informed consent procedure; and that the operational responsibility be shared for implementation of the prior informed consent procedure and that common elements be jointly managed and implemented, including the selection of chemicals to be included in the prior informed consent procedure, preparation of prior informed consent decision guidance documents, mechanisms for environmental information-sharing and creation of data bases. It called on FAO to adopt procedures equally protective for man and the environment for pesticides subject to the prior informed consent procedure.

The Council requested the Executive Director to reconvene the *Ad Hoc* Working Group to monitor the implementation of the amended Guidelines, with particular attention to the prior informed consent procedure and the technical assistance provisions of part III of the Guidelines; review other activities related to the production and use of chemicals in States; and report on further steps needed to supplement the amended London Guidelines, including possibility of a convention, for submission to the Governing Council in 1990. It urged Governments to take steps for the early implementation of the London Guidelines.

Illegal traffic in toxic products and wastes

Responding to a 1987 General Assembly request,[18] the Secretary-General in July reported[19] on illegal traffic in toxic and dangerous products and wastes. The report contained an assessment, by region of origin and of destination of illegal traffic, and a classification of types of toxic and dangerous products; and examined the relation of the 1989 Basel Convention on the Control of Transboundary Movements of Hazardous Wastes and their Disposal (see above), as well as the relation of the amended London Guidelines for the Exchange of Information on Chemicals in International Trade, with efforts to eliminate or reduce illegal traffic in toxic and dangerous products and wastes. Replies from countries and organizations to the Secretary-General's request for information on the instances and impact of illegal traffic were also summarized. The report concluded that the threat of illegal traffic in toxic and dangerous products and wastes would continue to grow as landfill-area capacity decreased and disposal prices increased. The quantity of such products and wastes would likely increase as the global economy continued to expand. It recommended that efforts be made to achieve the earliest entry into force of the Basel Convention and world-wide participation in it, as well as the prior informed consent procedures of the amended London Guidelines. Through the auspices of UNEP, a technical working group of experts should begin developing waste minimization and disposal technology and guidelines. Funding should be provided for technical legal assistance to developing countries for the development of national legislation dealing with hazardous and other wastes and participation in the prior informed consent procedure of the amended London rules. All countries should comply with the notification provisions of the Basel Convention and the London Guidelines, and maintain an inventory of imports and exports, which could be used to control and monitor the transboundary movement of wastes. Efforts should be made to prevent the avoidance of waste designation as hazardous by sham recycling schemes.

GENERAL ASSEMBLY ACTION

On 22 December, the General Assembly, on the recommendation of the Second Committee, adopted **resolution 44/226** without vote.

Traffic in and disposal, control and transboundary movements of toxic and dangerous products and wastes

The General Assembly,

Recalling its resolutions 37/137 of 17 December 1982, 38/149 of 19 December 1983 and 39/229 of 18 December 1984, as well as its decision 41/450 of 8 December 1986,

Recalling also its resolution 42/183 of 11 December 1987 on traffic in toxic and dangerous products and wastes,

Recalling further its resolution 43/212 of 20 December 1988 entitled "Responsibility of States for the protection of the environment: prevention of the illegal international traffic in, and the dumping and resulting accumulation of, toxic and dangerous products and wastes affecting the developing countries in particular",

Recalling Economic and Social Council resolutions 1988/70 and 1988/71 of 28 July 1988 and taking note of Council resolution 1989/104 of 27 July 1989,

Taking note of the report of the Secretary-General on products harmful to health and the environment and Economic and Social Council decision 1989/177 of 27 July 1989,

Taking note also of decisions 15/28 and 15/30 of 25 May 1989 of the Governing Council of the United Nations Environment Programme,

Welcoming the report of the Secretary-General on illegal traffic in toxic and dangerous products and wastes,

Taking note of the conclusion of the Basel Convention on the Control of Transboundary Movements of Hazardous Wastes and their Disposal,

Inviting all States to consider signing the Basel Convention without prejudice to the final positions to be taken by regional intergovernmental organizations in this regard,

Mindful of the growing threat to the environment and to human health and safety posed by the improper management and the increased generation, complexity and transboundary movement of hazardous wastes,

Convinced that illegal traffic in toxic and dangerous products and wastes poses a severe threat to the environment and to human health and safety,

Also convinced that these problems cannot be resolved without adequate co-operation among members of the international community,

Deeply concerned by the fact that cases of illegal transboundary movement and dumping of dangerous products and wastes particularly harmful for the environment and human health continue to occur, affecting, in particular, developing countries,

Convinced of the need to assist all countries, particularly developing countries, in obtaining all appropriate information concerning toxic and dangerous products and wastes and in reinforcing their capacity to detect and halt any illegal attempt to introduce toxic and dangerous products and wastes into the territory of any State in contravention of national legislation and relevant international legal instruments, as well as traffic not carried out in compliance with internationally accepted guidelines and principles in this field,

I

Traffic in toxic and dangerous products and wastes

1. *Requests* each regional commission, within existing resources, to contribute to the prevention of the illegal traffic in toxic and dangerous products and wastes by monitoring and making regional assessments of this illegal traffic and its environmental and health implications, on a continuing basis, in each region, and, in this context, in co-operation with and relying upon expert support and advice from the United Nations Environment Programme and other relevant bodies of the United Nations, including the International Register of Potentially Toxic Chemicals, the *Ad Hoc* Working Group of Experts on Prior Informed Consent and Other Modalities to Supplement the London Guidelines for the Exchange of Information on Chemicals in International Trade, and the Interim Secretariat of the Basel Convention on the Control of Transboundary Movements of Hazardous Wastes and their Disposal, without prejudice to the final position to be taken by regional intergovernmental organizations on the Convention, and to report to the Economic and Social Council at its second regular session starting in 1990;

2. *Also requests* the regional commissions to interact among themselves and co-operate with the United Nations Environment Programme, with a view to maintaining efficient and co-ordinated monitoring and assessment of the illegal traffic in toxic and dangerous products and wastes;

3. *Requests* the Economic and Social Council to submit recommendations to the General Assembly on the findings and conclusions of the regional commissions, in their consideration of environmental issues;

4. *Calls upon* all countries to co-operate with their respective regional commissions with the aim of preventing the illegal traffic in toxic and dangerous products and wastes;

II

Protection against products harmful to health and the environment

1. *Expresses its appreciation* to the Secretary-General for his report on products harmful to health and the environment, which contains a review of the Consolidated List of Products Whose Consumption and/or Sale Have Been Banned, Withdrawn, Severely Restricted or Not Approved by Governments;

2. *Notes with appreciation* the co-operative relationship established between the United Nations, the World Health Organization and the United Nations Environment Programme International Register of Potentially Toxic Chemicals for the preparation of the Consolidated List;

3. *Notes,* in this context, the need to utilize also the work being done by the Working Group on Export of Domestically Prohibited Goods and Other Hazardous Substances established by the General Agreement on Tariffs and Trade and those activities which are currently under way within the framework of the United Nations Environment Programme and the Food and Agriculture Organization of the United Nations in connection with implementation of prior informed consent schemes for chemicals and pesticides in international trade and which implement the system of information exchange envisaged by the developers of the Consolidated List, as well as the work being done under international agreements and conventions in related areas;

4. *Expresses its appreciation* for the growing co-operation by Governments in the preparation of the Consolidated List, and urges all Governments that have not yet done so to provide the necessary information for inclusion in updated versions of the Consolidated List;

5. *Requests* the Secretary-General to ensure, within existing resources, publication of the Consolidated List in English, French and Spanish, in accordance with demand, bearing in mind its resolution 39/229;

6. *Also requests* the Secretary-General to undertake a special effort to ensure effective and wider dissemination of the Consolidated List in all appropriate circles;

7. *Further requests* the Secretary-General, in this context, to consider ways and means of ensuring more effective involvement of non-governmental organizations in promoting the dissemination and utilization of the Consolidated List;

8. *Requests* the Secretary-General, in the context of the preparation of his next scheduled report on the question:

(a) To make specific suggestions on ways and means of providing technical co-operation, including through appropriate United Nations organizations, to countries, in particular developing countries, to create and strengthen their capacity to utilize the Consolidated List;

(b) To study all the pending issues, such as sustainable alternatives to banned and severely restricted products and unregistered pesticides, with a focus on improving the usefulness of the Consolidated List;

III

Control of transboundary movements of hazardous wastes and their disposal

1. *Recognizes* the necessity of developing rules of international law, as early as practicable, on liability and compensation for damage resulting from the transboundary movement and disposal of hazardous wastes;

2. *Requests* the Executive Director of the United Nations Environment Programme, in accordance with the resolutions adopted at the Conference of Plenipotentiaries on the Global Convention on the Control of Transboundary Movements of Hazardous Wastes, held at Basel, Switzerland, from 20 to 22 March 1989, to establish, on the basis of equitable geographical representation and in consultation with Governments, an *ad hoc* working group of legal and technical experts to develop, as early as practicable, elements that might be included in a protocol on liability and compensation for damage resulting from the transboundary movement and disposal of hazardous wastes and to report to the preparatory committee of the United Nations conference on environment and development and to the Governing Council of the United Nations Environment Programme, in accordance with its mandate in this regard;

3. *Invites* the Executive Director of the United Nations Environment Programme and the Secretary-General of the International Maritime Organization, in consultation, as appropriate, with other relevant international organizations, to review the existing rules, regulations and practices with respect to the disposal of

hazardous wastes at sea, in order to harmonize the provisions of the relevant conventions as adopted in this regard;

4. *Requests* the Secretary-General, in co-operation with the Executive Director of the United Nations Environment Programme, to report to the General Assembly at its forty-sixth session, through the Economic and Social Council, on the progress achieved in the implementation of the provisions of the Basel Convention on the Control of Transboundary Movements of Hazardous Wastes and their Disposal and of the present resolution.

General Assembly resolution 44/226

22 December 1989   Meeting 85   Adopted without vote

Approved by Second Committee (A/44/746/Add.7) without vote, 17 December (meeting 51); draft by Vice-Chairman (A/C.2/44/L.80), based on informal consultations on draft by Malaysia for Group of 77 (A/C.2/44/L.43/Rev.1); agenda item 82 *(f)*.

Meeting numbers. GA 44th session: 2nd Committee 31, 32, 40, 44, 46, 49-51; plenary 85.

Dumping of nuclear wastes

By a May note,[20] the UNEP Executive Director, in response to a 1988 Economic and Social Council request,[21] submitted to the Governing Council the Secretary-General's report on the effects on the environment of dumping of nuclear wastes. The report, prepared by IAEA, examined national and international standards and procedures for waste disposal, the environmental impacts of the dumping of radioactive wastes, the transboundary movements of such wastes, future international co-operation in radioactive waste management and its impact on the transboundary movement of wastes, the issue of alleged dumping of radioactive wastes, and the code of practice for international transactions involving nuclear wastes. The report distinguished between disposal performed under regulatory control and illicit dumping. The consequences of dumping, it said, could vary from negligible to the exposure of whole population groups to significant hazards. There was, however, no evidence to date that any transboundary dumping of nuclear wastes had occurred; international transactions involving nuclear waste were based on bilateral agreements and took place under strict regulatory supervision. IAEA, in accordance with a 1988 resolution of its General Conference,[22] invited a group of experts to meet in Vienna, Austria, from 22 to 26 May to elaborate an internationally agreed code of practice for international transactions involving nuclear wastes. It was expected that the group of experts would complete its task in time for consideration by the IAEA General Conference in 1990.

On 25 May, the Governing Council took note[23] of the efforts of IAEA to elaborate an internationally agreed code of practice for international transactions involving nuclear wastes and requested the Executive Director to participate fully in its preparation.

The Secretary-General's report[24] was also submitted to the General Assembly, which took note of the report by **decision 44/454** of 22 December.

Other risks

In March, the Executive Director submitted a report[25] on emerging environmental issues, which focused on health risks from diesel vehicles, acid fog, environmental issues in new technologies, algal blooms in the sea, and the need to develop an Antarctic conservation strategy and conventions for the environmental protection and management of the region's various ecosystems.

On 23 May, the Governing Council took note[26] of the Executive Director's report and of the reservations of various delegations with regard to the issue of Antarctica. It requested him to provide in 1991 a detailed elaboration of the issue of new technologies and a brief description of issues on municipal waste, plastics and the ecological situation in the Arctic.

Environmental emergencies

International co-operation

On 22 December, the General Assembly, on the recommendation of the Second Committee, adopted **resolution 44/224** without vote.

International co-operation in the monitoring, assessment and anticipation of environmental threats and in assistance in cases of environmental emergency

The General Assembly,

Convinced that one of the main global problems facing the world today is the deterioration of the environment,

Recalling its resolution 43/196 of 20 December 1988 on a United Nations conference on environment and development,

Aware that increasing environmental degradation caused by human activities has led in some cases to irreversible changes in the environment that threaten life-sustaining ecosystems and undermine the health, well-being, development prospects and very survival of life on the planet,

Also aware that potential environmental disasters, whether natural, accidental or caused by human beings, as well as accidents, could pose serious and immediate dangers to populations and to the economic development and environment of the affected countries and regions,

Convinced that through monitoring, assessment, anticipation and prompt multilateral response upon request, in particular on the part of the United Nations system, environmental threats could be minimized or even prevented,

Also convinced that early warning of emerging environmental threats and degradation would help Governments to take preventive action,

Noting with appreciation the work undertaken by the United Nations Environment Programme to develop criteria for the identification of environmental threats at the national, regional and global levels,

Stressing the need for close co-operation between all countries, in particular through a broad exchange of information, scientific knowledge and experience as well as transfer of technology, in monitoring, assessing and anticipating environmental threats, dealing with environmental emergencies and rendering timely assistance, at the request of Governments, in accordance with respective national laws, regulations and policies and taking into account the particular needs and requirements of the developing countries,

Affirming the need, in this context, for closer co-operation between the United Nations Environment Programme, the Office of the United Nations Disaster Relief Co-ordinator, the World Health Organization and the World Meteorological Organization, as well as other competent organs, programmes and agencies of the United Nations system, bearing in mind the co-ordinating role of the United Nations Environment Programme in environmental matters in the United Nations system,

Noting that other proposals have been made on strengthening and improving the effectiveness within the United Nations system of international co-operation in monitoring, assessing and anticipating environmental threats and the rendering of timely assistance in cases of environmental emergency,

1. *Recognizes* the need to strengthen international co-operation in monitoring, assessing and anticipating environmental threats and rendering assistance in cases of environmental emergency;

2. *Reaffirms* that, owing to its universal character, the United Nations system, through the General Assembly, is the appropriate forum for concerted political action on global environmental problems;

3. *Underlines* the importance of broader participation in Earthwatch, established by the United Nations Conference on the Human Environment and operated by the United Nations Environment Programme, in order to strengthen its capacity to make authoritative assessments, to anticipate environmental degradation and to issue early warnings to the international community;

4. *Reaffirms* that, in accordance with the Charter of the United Nations and the principles of international law, States have the sovereign right to exploit their own resources in accordance with their environmental policies, and also reaffirms their responsibility to ensure that activities within their jurisdiction or control do not cause damage to the environment of other States or of areas beyond the limits of national jurisdiction as well as to play their due role in preserving and protecting the global and regional environment in accordance with their capacities and specific responsibilities;

5. *Requests* the Secretary-General, assisted by the Executive Director of the United Nations Environment Programme, to prepare a report, on the basis of the views of Member States and existing national and international legislation in this field, containing proposals and recommendations on possible ways and means to strengthen the capacity of the United Nations:

(*a*) To monitor, assess and anticipate environmental threats;

(*b*) To define criteria for determining when environmental degradation undermines health, well-being, development prospects and the very survival of life on the planet to such an extent that international co-operation may be required, if requested;

(*c*) To issue early warnings to the international community when such degradation becomes imminent;

(*d*) To facilitate intergovernmental co-operation in monitoring, assessing and anticipating environmental threats;

(*e*) To assist Governments facing environmental emergencies, at their request;

(*f*) To mobilize financial resources and technical co-operation to fulfil the tasks listed in paragraphs 5 (*a*) to (*e*) of the present resolution, taking into account the needs of the countries concerned, particularly the developing countries;

6. *Also requests* the Secretary-General to submit to the Governing Council of the United Nations Environment Programme the report called for in paragraph 5 of the present resolution for consideration during the preparatory process for the United Nations conference on environment and development;

7. *Invites* the Governing Council of the United Nations Environment Programme to consider that report and to present its views thereon to the General Assembly at its forty-sixth session, through the Economic and Social Council.

General Assembly resolution 44/224

22 December 1989   Meeting 85   Adopted without vote

Approved by Second Committee (A/44/746/Add.7) without vote, 27 November (meeting 46); draft by Vice-Chairman (A/C.2/44/L.60), based on informal consultations on 15-nation draft (A.C.2/44/L.29/Rev.1), subsequently withdrawn; agenda item 82 *(f)*.
Meeting numbers. GA 44th session: 2nd Committee 18, 21-24, 26, 31, 32, 35, 38, 40, 44, 46; plenary 85.

A 1988 draft resolution on the same subject,[27] the consideration of which had been deferred by the General Assembly,[28] was also withdrawn.

Proposed centre for urgent environmental assistance

In a 2 May letter[29] to the Secretary-General, the Soviet Union transmitted a 30 April letter outlining proposals concerning the establishment of a UN centre for emergency environmental assistance, and its objectives and functions.

On 25 May, the Governing Council requested[30] the Executive Director to invite Governments, UN bodies and specialized agencies and competent regional organizations to express their views regarding the need for and the objectives, scope and functions of the proposed centre; to assess the contribution of such a centre to existing UNEP activities, WMO's Global Telecommunications System, the Office of the United Nations Disaster Relief Co-ordinator, IMO, IAEA and other relevant UN bodies and specialized agencies, and the advisability and financial implications of establishing such a centre; to inform the Assembly at its forty-fourth session of the preliminary results of that assessment and consultation; and to report to the Council in 1990.

The General Assembly, in **resolution 44/229** of 22 December, noted the Governing Council's consideration of the proposed centre and information from the Executive Director on his consultations regarding the views of Governments and organizations on the matter.

Industrial accidents

On 25 May, the Governing Council noted[31] the activities of the Executive Director in the field of industrial accidents.[2] It called upon the United Nations and its specialized agencies, in particular the United Nations Industrial Development Organization, and NGOs and world industry to support the APELL (awareness and preparedness for industrial accidents at the local level) process. It requested the Executive Director to set up a network of organizations and experts to facilitate the exchange of information and technology for the prevention of industrial accidents, to assist in the case of emergencies, and to report to the Council on those efforts in 1990.

REFERENCES

[1]UNEP/GC.16/2. [2]UNEP/GC.15/9/Add.2/Suppl.3 & Corr.1. [3]A/44/25 (dec. 15/40). [4]UNEP/GC.15/9/Add.2 & Corr.1. [5]YUN 1987, p. 696. [6]A/44/25 (dec. 15/41). [7]A/44/25 (dec. 15/38). [8]A/44/276-E/1989/78. [9]YUN 1984, p. 752, GA res. 39/229, 18 Dec. 1984. [10]*Consolidated List of Products Whose Consumption and/or Sale Have Been Banned, Withdrawn, Severely Restricted or Not Approved by Governments,* Sales No. E.87.IV.1. [11]YUN 1987, p. 697. [12]UNEP/GC.15/9/Add.2/Suppl.1. [13]YUN 1988, p. 460. [14]A/44/25 (dec. 15/28). [15]YUN 1987, p. 698. [16]A/44/25 (dec. 15/29). [17]*Ibid.* (dec. 15/30). [18]YUN 1987, p. 699, GA res. 42/183, 11 Dec. 1987. [19]A/44/362. [20]UNEP/GC.15/9/Add.6. [21]YUN 1988, p. 462, ESC res. 1988/174, 28 July 1988. [22]*Ibid.,* p. 81. [23]A/44/25 (dec. 15/22). [24]A/44/480. [25]UNEP/GC.7/Add.3. [26]A/44/25 (dec. 15/13 B). [27]A/C.2/44/L.6. [28]YUN 1988, p. 458, GA dec. 43/440, 20 Dec. 1988. [29]A/44/264-E/1989/73. [30]A/44/25 (dec. 15/10). [31]*Ibid.* (dec. 15/39).

Major areas of concern

Global climate change

The Intergovernmental Panel on Climate Change (IPCC), whose establishment in 1988 by UNEP and WMO was endorsed[1] by the General Assembly, continued to be the major forum for examining the issue of climate change within the framework of its three main working groups. The Group on the Scientific Aspects of Climate Change, at its first session (Nuneham Park, United Kingdom, 24-26 January), agreed on its terms of reference and on the format and authorship of its report. The Group on Environmental and Socio-economic Impacts resulting from Climate Change held two sessions during the year. At the first (Moscow, 2 and 3 February), the Group agreed on the principal focus of its work and established corresponding subgroups and a steering committee to co-ordinate and facilitate liaison with other

IPCC working groups. At its second session (Geneva, 31 October and 1 November), the Group reviewed the progress made by the different subgroups in compiling their reports. The first session of the Response Strategies Working Group (Washington, D.C., 30 January–1 February) established four subgroups and identified the basis of a multidisciplinary approach to the implementation of strategies in response to climate change. The Group's second session was held in Geneva from 2 to 6 October.

At its first session (6 and 7 February), the IPCC Bureau reviewed work plans, proposed the structure of the three working groups, made recommendations on the structure of IPCC's first assessment report, and endorsed the budget for the secretariat. It established an *ad hoc* group to examine and report on the low level of participation of developing countries in IPCC activities. At its second session (Nairobi, 28-30 June), the Bureau endorsed progress reports of the working groups and of the *ad hoc* group on developing countries' participation. IPCC established a trust fund to finance its activities and set a target of $1 million to support the participation of developing countries. A target date of 1990 was set for the completion of the first assessment report on climate change, which would consist of the reports of the three working groups. It also agreed to establish the elements for a future convention on climate change and decided that the first assessment report of the work of IPCC should form the starting-point for negotiations on a framework convention on climate change.

In March, the Executive Director submitted to the Governing Council a report on global climate change.[2] In September, the Secretary-General, in response to a 1988 General Assembly resolution,[1] submitted to the Assembly a report[3] on protection of global climate for present and future generations. He reported that he had brought that resolution to the attention of concerned parties, but had received only a small number of replies, mainly from international organizations.

On 25 May, the Governing Council requested[4] the Executive Director, in collaboration with the WMO Secretary-General, to consult with IPCC on the determination of its internal organization and procedures, its budget and financing, and authorized him to support the work of IPCC. It urged UN Member States, specialized agencies and international organizations, including IAEA, and relevant intergovernmental and non-governmental organizations to support and participate in the work of IPCC. It also urged IPCC to ensure the scientific and policy participation of developing countries in its work, and recommended that the international community provide assistance in that respect. The Council requested the Executive Director, in co-operation with the WMO Secretary-General, to begin preparations for negotiations on a framework convention on climate, taking into account the outcome of recent and forthcoming international meetings on the subject. Such negotiations should be initiated as soon as possible after the adoption of the interim report of IPCC. Governments and competent regional integration economic organizations should consider options for averting the potentially damaging impacts of climate change, for removing its causes and for developing programmes more appropriate to national needs. The Council also recommended the institution of programmes and measures of assistance, including technology transfer, that would make it possible for developing countries to avoid global climate risks. Governments should also increase their activities in support of the UNEP World Climate Programme and International Geosphere-Biosphere Programme, including the monitoring of atmospheric composition and climate conditions, and the international community should support efforts by developing countries to participate in those scientific activities.

GENERAL ASSEMBLY ACTION

On 22 December, the General Assembly, on the recommendation of the Second Committee, adopted **resolution 44/207** without vote.

Protection of global climate for present and future generations of mankind

The General Assembly,

Recalling its resolution 43/53 of 6 December 1988, in which it recognized climate change as a common concern of mankind,

Taking note of decision 15/36 of 25 May 1989 of the Governing Council of the United Nations Environment Programme on global climate change,

Taking note of the message of the Chairman of the Conference on Saving the Ozone Layer, held in London from 5 to 7 March 1989, the Declaration of The Hague endorsed by 24 heads of State or Government or their representatives at The Hague 11 March 1989, the Helsinki Declaration on the Protection of the Ozone Layer adopted on 2 May 1989, the relevant parts of the Langkawi Declaration on Environment issued by the Commonwealth Heads of Government Meeting on 21 October 1989, the Declaration adopted at Noordwijk, the Netherlands, by the Ministerial Conference on Atmospheric Pollution and Climate Change, held on 6 and 7 November 1989, and relevant parts of the Caracas Declaration adopted at the special ministerial meeting of the Group of Seventy-seven, held at Caracas from 21 to 23 June 1989,

Taking note of the relevant declarations and decisions adopted at intergovernmental regional meetings during 1989, including the Amazon Declaration, adopted by the Presidents of the States parties to the Treaty for Amazonian Co-operation at Manaus, Brazil, on 6 May 1989, the Declaration of Brasilia, issued at the Sixth Ministerial Meeting on the Environment in Latin America and the Caribbean, held at Brasilia on 30 and 31 March 1989, and the relevant parts of the Final Communiqué of the Twentieth South Pacific Forum, held at Tarawa, Kiribati, on 10 and 11 July 1989,

Noting that, in the Economic Declaration adopted in Paris on 16 July 1989, at the Summit of the seven major industrial nations, the heads of State or Government of those countries and the President of the Commission of the European Communities supported the decision of the World Meteorological Organization to establish a global reference network to detect climate change, agreed that a framework convention on climate was urgently required and recognized that specific protocols with commitments could develop within this framework,

Taking note of the final documents of the Ninth Conference of Heads of State or Government of Non-Aligned Countries, held at Belgrade from 4 to 7 September 1989, which, *inter alia*, emphasized that necessary and timely action should be taken to deal with climate changes and their consequences within a global framework and, in this context, called for the preparation and adoption of a framework convention on climate on an urgent basis in conformity with General Assembly resolution 43/53,

Recognizing the need for additional research and scientific studies into all sources, causes and effects of climate change,

Noting the fact that the largest part of the current emission of pollutants into the environment originates in developed countries, and recognizing therefore that those countries have the main responsibility for combating such pollution,

Recognizing the need for international collaboration with a view to adopting effective measures on the question of climate change, within a global framework and taking into account the particular needs and development priorities of developing countries,

Concerned that the participation of the developing countries in the Intergovernmental Panel on Climate Change remains limited, and stressing the need for the Intergovernmental Panel, in view of its intergovernmental nature, to do all that it can to ensure adequate participation and governmental involvement in its activities in accordance with United Nations practice,

1. *Emphasizes* the need to address with urgency the question of climate change as reflected in the conclusions of various important international meetings;

2. *Recommends* that Governments, with due consideration for the need for increased scientific knowledge of the sources, causes and impact of climate change and of global, regional and local climates, continue and, wherever possible, increase their activities in support of the World Climate Programme and the International Geosphere-Biosphere Programme, including the monitoring of atmospheric composition and climate conditions, and also recommends that the international community support efforts by developing countries to participate in these scientific activities;

3. *Urges* Governments, in keeping with their national policies, priorities and regulations, and intergovernmental organizations to collaborate in making every possible effort to limit, reduce and prevent activities that could adversely affect climate, and calls upon non-governmental organizations, industry and other productive sectors to play their due role;

4. *Reaffirms* that, in accordance with the Charter of the United Nations and the principles of international

law, States have the sovereign right to exploit their own resources in accordance with their environmental policies, and also reaffirms their responsibility to ensure that activities within their jurisdiction or control do not cause damage to the environment of other States or of areas beyond the limits of national jurisdiction and to play their due role in preserving and protecting the global and regional environment in accordance with their capacities and specific responsibilities;

5. *Reaffirms* that, owing to its universal character, the United Nations system, through the General Assembly, is the appropriate forum for concerted political action on global environmental problems;

6. *Welcomes* the joint efforts of the World Meteorological Organization and the United Nations Environment Programme in providing support to the urgent work being undertaken by the Intergovernmental Panel on Climate Change and its three working groups established to assess scientific information on, and the social and economic impact of, climate change and to formulate response strategies;

7. *Invites* all Governments, as well as relevant intergovernmental and non-governmental organizations, to support fully and participate actively in the work of the Intergovernmental Panel;

8. *Welcomes* the establishment of the Intergovernmental Panel on Climate Change Trust Fund and the contributions made to it;

9. *Urges* the Intergovernmental Panel to take the necessary steps to ensure the participation of developing countries in scientific and policy aspects of its work, and calls upon the international community, in particular the developed countries, to consider contributing generously to the Trust Fund, with a view to financing the participation of experts designated by Governments of developing countries in all the meetings of the Intergovernmental Panel, including its working groups and subgroups;

10. *Supports* the request made by the Governing Council of the United Nations Environment Programme, in its decision 15/36, that the Executive Director of the Programme, in co-operation with the Secretary-General of the World Meteorological Organization, begin preparations for negotiations on a framework convention on climate, taking into account the work of the Intergovernmental Panel on Climate Change, as well as the results achieved at international meetings on the subject, including the Second World Climate Conference, and recommends that such negotiations begin as soon as possible after the adoption of the interim report of the Intergovernmental Panel and that the General Assembly, at an early date during its forty-fifth session, take a decision recommending ways and means and modalities for pursuing these negotiations further, taking into account the work of the preparatory committee for the United Nations conference on environment and development to be held in 1992;

11. *Requests* the Secretary-General to circulate for the information of delegations the reports of the third and fourth plenary meetings of the Intergovernmental Panel, as well as its interim report, as official documents of the forty-fifth session of the General Assembly;

12. *Urges* Governments, intergovernmental and non-governmental organizations and scientific institutions to collaborate in efforts to prepare, as a matter of ur-

gency, a framework convention on climate and associated protocols containing concrete commitments in the light of priorities that may be authoritatively identified on the basis of sound scientific knowledge, and taking into account the specific development needs of developing countries;

13. *Recommends* that Governments and competent intergovernmental organizations consider, while awaiting the outcome of the negotiations, the range of possible options for averting the potentially damaging impact of climate change, for removing the causes of the phenomenon and for developing programmes for implementing those options which respond more appropriately to national needs as outlined in paragraphs 11 *(a)* to *(f)* of decision 15/36 of the Governing Council;

14. *Encourages* Governments and relevant international organizations to further the development of international funding mechanisms, taking account of proposals for a climate fund and other innovative ideas and bearing in mind the need to provide new and additional financial resources to support developing countries in identifying, analysing, monitoring, preventing and managing environmental problems, primarily at their source, in accordance with national development goals, objectives and plans, so as to ensure that development priorities are not adversely affected;

15. *Decides* that the concept of assured access for developing countries to environmentally sound technologies and assured transfer of those technologies to developing countries on favourable terms and the relation of that concept to intellectual property rights should be explored in the context of the elaboration of a framework convention on climate, with a view to developing effective responses to the needs of developing countries in this area;

16. *Requests* the Secretary-General, in the context of ongoing intergovernmental and other efforts in this field, to continue his support for the formulation and implementation of strategies to respond to climate change;

17. *Also requests* the Secretary-General to bring the present resolution to the attention of all Governments, as well as intergovernmental organizations, non-governmental organizations in consultative status with the Economic and Social Council and scientific institutions with expertise in matters concerning climate;

18. *Further requests* the Secretary-General to report to the General Assembly at its forty-fifth session on the progress achieved in the implementation of the present resolution;

19. *Decides* to include this question in the provisional agenda of its forty-fifth session, without prejudice to the application of the principle of biennialization.

General Assembly resolution 44/207

22 December 1989   Meeting 85   Adopted without vote

Approved by Second Committee (A/44/862) without vote, 17 December (meeting 51); 51-nation draft (A/C.2/44/L.40/Rev.1); agenda item 85.
Meeting numbers. GA 46th session: 2nd Committee 18, 21-24, 33, 35, 40, 45, 48, 51; plenary 85.

The Assembly, by **decision 44/446** of the same date, took note of the Secretary-General's report on the protection of global climate for present and future generations of mankind.[3]

Protection of the ozone layer

In 1989, UNEP continued to work on implementation of the 1985 Vienna Convention for the Protection of the Ozone Layer[5] and the 1987 Montreal Protocol on Substances that Deplete the Ozone Layer.[6] Four panels were established to review the scientific, environmental, technical and economic information required so that the parties to the Montreal Protocol could undertake a review of control measures. The scientific review found that man-made chemicals containing halogens were primarily responsible for the springtime loss of Antarctic ozone; the same potentially ozone-destroying processes for the Antarctic ozone hole had been identified in the Arctic stratosphere, and the possibility of future significant ozone destruction could not be ruled out; there had been a downward trend in ozone concentrations in the northern hemisphere of 3 to 5 per cent from 1969 to 1988, which could not be attributed to natural processes; and there was continuing uncertainty about the predictive capability of current models, particularly with regard to future ozone changes at high altitudes. Those findings had had important implications for the parties to the Montreal Protocol with regard to the decision to amend the existing control measures for ozone-depleting substances.

An international meeting, "Saving the Ozone Layer Conference", convened in London in March by the United Nations with the support of UNEP, underscored the importance of protecting the ozone shield. There was a consensus among representatives from 120 countries that all countries should aim at ending the production and consumption of chlorofluorocarbons by the end of the century.

On 25 May, the Governing Council noted[7] the entry into force of the Montreal Protocol on 1 January 1989 (see above, under "International conventions"), and urged all countries that had not done so to become parties to it and to the Vienna Convention. It also noted the offer of Finland to make available some 8.6 million markkaa to facilitate activities of developing countries within the scope of the Vienna Convention and the Montreal Protocol. The Council welcomed the proposal by Norway to set aside 0.1 per cent of its annual gross national income towards an international climate fund, provided other industrialized countries did likewise. It requested the Executive Director to support activities as approved by the parties to the Vienna Convention and the Montreal Protocol, until the establishment of the trust fund and the permanent secretariat.

In a June note,[8] the Secretary-General submitted to the Economic and Social Council and the General Assembly the report of the UNEP Executive Director, pursuant to a 1987 Assembly request,[9] in which he reported on decisions adopted by the first meeting of the Conference of the Parties to the 1985 Vienna Convention and the first meeting of the parties to the Montreal Protocol, which were held at Helsinki, Finland, from 26 to 28 April and from 2 to 5 May, respectively.

The General Assembly, by **decision 44/454** of 22 December, took note of the Secretary-General's report.

Sea-level rise

In a 20 November letter[10] to the Secretary-General, Maldives transmitted the text of the Malé Declaration on Global Warming and Sea Level Rise, adopted by the Small States Conference on Sea Level Rise, held at Malé, Maldives, from 14 to 18 November. Conference participants decided to adopt a programme of action for co-operation and exchange of information on strategies and policies relating to climate change, global warming and sea-level rise, to establish an action group to oversee implementation of Conference recommendations, and a climate and sea-level programme and a monitoring network, and to apply to UN agencies, particularly WMO, UNEP and UNESCO, for assistance.

GENERAL ASSEMBLY ACTION

On 22 December, the General Assembly, on the recommendation of the Second Committee, adopted **resolution 44/206** without vote.

Possible adverse effects of sea-level rise on islands and coastal areas, particularly low-lying coastal areas

The General Assembly,

Recalling its resolutions 42/202 of 11 December 1987 and 43/53 of 6 December 1988,

Aware of the potential global problem of sea-level rise, which could adversely affect islands and coastal areas, particularly low-lying coastal areas,

Recognizing the need for further scientific study of climate change, including the possibility of sea-level rise induced by global warming,

Noting the ongoing work within the United Nations system, in particular within the United Nations Environment Programme, the World Meteorological Organization and the Intergovernmental Panel on Climate Change, on the potential global problem of sea-level rise, and taking note, in this connection, of decision 15/36 of 25 May 1989 of the Governing Council of the United Nations Environment Programme on global climate change,

Noting also the concern expressed in the Final Communiqué of the Twentieth South Pacific Forum, held at Tarawa, Kiribati, on 10 and 11 July 1989, at the possible effects on island countries of rising sea levels resulting from global warming,

Noting further the support expressed in the Langkawi Declaration on Environment, adopted by the Commonwealth Heads of Government Meeting on 21 October 1989, for low-lying and island countries in their efforts to protect themselves and their vulnerable natural marine ecosystems from the effects of sea-level rise,

Taking note of the Malé Declaration on Global Warming and Sea Level Rise, adopted by the Small States Conference on Sea Level Rise, held at Malé, Maldives, from 14 to 18 November 1989, in which the participants declared their intent to work, collaborate and seek international co-operation to protect the low-lying small coastal and island States of the world from the dangers posed by climate change, global warming and sea-level rise,

Expressing concern that sea-level rise resulting from global climate change could lead, *inter alia*, to abnormally high tides, which could intensify flooding and the erosion of coastal areas and damage infrastructure on islands and in low-lying coastal areas,

1. *Welcomes* the growing attention being given worldwide to the potentially serious effects on islands and coastal areas, particularly low-lying coastal areas, of sea-level rise resulting from climate change;

2. *Urges* the international community to provide effective and timely support to countries affected by sea-level rise, particularly developing countries, in their efforts to develop and implement strategies to protect themselves and their vulnerable natural marine ecosystems from the particular threats of sea-level rise caused by climate change;

3. *Requests* the Secretary-General to invite the United Nations Environment Programme, the World Meteorological Organization and, through them, the Intergovernmental Panel on Climate Change to take account in their work of the particular situation of islands and coastal areas, particularly low-lying coastal areas, by undertaking further scientific studies and by seeking ways to address the problems of sea-level rise, *inter alia*, by providing expertise, as requested, in accordance with their specific mandates, for improved management of coastal zones;

4. *Recommends* that the vulnerability of affected countries and their marine ecosystems to sea-level rise be considered during discussions of a draft framework convention on climate as well as within the framework of the United Nations conference on environment and development to be held in 1992 and during the preparatory process for the conference;

5. *Requests* the Secretary-General to report on the implementation of the present resolution to the General Assembly at its forty-sixth session, through the Economic and Social Council and the Governing Council of the United Nations Environment Programme.

General Assembly resolution 44/206

22 December 1989   Meeting 85   Adopted without vote

Approved by Second Committee (A/44/862) without vote, 4 December (meeting 48); 46-nation draft (A/C.2/44/L.38/Rev.1); agenda item 85.
Meeting numbers. GA 46th session: 2nd Committee 18, 21-24, 33, 35, 40, 45, 48; plenary 85.

Terrestrial ecosystems

Desertification

In 1989, UNEP continued to implement the 1977 Plan of Action to Combat Desertification.[11] It focused its efforts on engaging countries affected by desertification and donors to search for effective

institutional mechanisms to integrate desertification control programmes into national development plans and priorities. In that regard, it held consultations with Argentina, Mali, Mauritania, the Sudan, the Syrian Arab Republic and Yemen. UNEP also initiated action for the development and assessment of simple technologies for application in regions prone to desertification, and assisted selected countries in the identification and development of methodologies to assess and map desertification. Other activities related to reinforcing regional networking, subregional projects and development of a global data base.

The Inter-Agency Working Group on Desertification (IAWGD) supported and co-ordinated a number of regional networks of training and research institutions dealing with sand-dune stabilization and afforestation and supported NGOs in Africa, Asia and Latin America. UNEP assisted NGOs in Asia to administer national forums, with a view to setting up a regional network for NGOs. UNEP also established the Desertification Information System to deal with information related to drylands development and desertification processes.

In February, the Executive Director submitted to the Governing Council a report[12] on the Plan of Action to Combat Desertification, which discussed the Special Account to finance the implementation of the Plan and additional financing measures; ways of enhancing the efficiency of the Consultative Group for Desertification Control; and measures to enhance the work of IAWGD and implementation of the Plan of Action, particularly in the Sudano-Sahelian region.

On 25 May, the Council invited[13] affected countries to prepare national programmes to combat desertification within the framework of national plans for development of natural resources and rehabilitation of impaired ecosystems; provide appropriate resources for the implementation of the programme for combating desertification; and establish or strengthen machineries to mobilize national resources for implementing the national programme and for monitoring progress. It invited donor Governments and intergovernmental bodies, including aid agencies and NGOs, to accord high priority in their bilateral and multilateral activities to national programmes for combating desertification and for the rehabilitation of degraded land resources, and to take into account the promotion of long-term ecological and social rehabilitation programmes in areas prone to desertification. The Council requested IAWGD to implement measures to enhance its work. The Executive Director was asked to assist countries to develop programmes for combating desertification and to include in UNEP's proposed programme budget for 1990-1991 activities on pastoral nomadism and to invite other UN agencies and donors to support such activities. It further requested an external evaluation of the Plan of Action, with its results to be presented in time for the 1992 UN conference on environment and development, but not later than the 1991 session of the Governing Council.

In related action, the Council recommended[14] the abolition of the United Nations Special Account to finance the implementation of the Plan of Action. It asked that the Consultative Group for Desertification Control hold sessions every two years (in even-numbered years starting from 1990), to review the status of the Plan of Action and to exchange information on scientific research, national programmes and the implementation of the Plan of Action, as well as to advise on further action against desertification. It invited the international community to create the necessary economic and financial conditions to enable countries prone to desertification to appropriate part of their resources to combat that phenomenon.

The Assembly, in **resolution 44/172 A** of 19 December, approved the Council's recommendations relating to the Special Account and additional measures for financing the Plan of Action.

Reports of the Secretary-General. The Secretary-General, in response to a 1987 General Assembly request,[15] submitted a May report[16] on African countries stricken by desertification and drought. He drew attention to various other reports on the subjects of desertification and drought and to the activities of the specialized agencies.

In a July report[17] on the implementation of three 1987 Assembly resolutions,[18] the Secretary-General submitted to the Economic and Social Council and the Assembly a report[12] of the UNEP Governing Council on the Special Account.

On 27 July, the Economic and Social Council, on the recommendation of its First (Economic) Committee, adopted **resolution 1989/102** without vote.

Plan of Action to Combat Desertification

The Economic and Social Council,

Recalling General Assembly resolution 42/189 of 11 December 1987 concerning the implementation and financing of the Plan of Action to Combat Desertification, in particular resolution 42/189 B concerning the implementation of the Plan in the Sudano-Sahelian region,

Taking note with interest of the report of the Administrator of the United Nations Development Programme on the activities of the United Nations Sudano-Sahelian Office,

Taking note also of the report of the Secretary-General on the implementation of General Assembly resolutions 42/189 A, B and C,

Noting that the delay in the availability of documentation prevented the Council from giving full consideration to this question,

Decides to transmit to the General Assembly at its forty-fourth session, for in-depth consideration and appropriate action, the reports of the Secretary-General and of the Administrator of the United Nations Development Programme and decision 15/23 of 25 May 1989 of the Governing Council of the United Nations Environment Programme, as well as the draft resolution contained in the annex to decision 15/23 D, together with the views and comments expressed at the second regular session of 1989 of the Economic and Social Council.

Economic and Social Council resolution 1989/102

27 July 1989   Meeting 36   Adopted without vote

Approved by First Committee (E/1989/140) without vote, 20 July (meeting 24); draft by Mauritania (E/1989/C.1/L.13), orally revised; agenda item 7 *(g)*.

On the same date, the Council, in **resolution 1989/103** on countries stricken by desertification and drought in Africa, appealed to the international community, particularly donor countries, while maintaining their support for the United Nations Programme of Action for African Economic Recovery and Development 1986-1990, to continue to support the Permanent Inter-State Committee on Drought Control in the Sahel, the Intergovernmental Authority on Drought and Development and the Ministerial Conference for a joint policy to combat desertification.

The General Assembly, in **decision 44/437** of 19 December, endorsed Council resolution 1989/103.

On 19 December, the General Assembly, on the recommendation of the Second Committee, adopted **resolution 44/172 A** without vote.

Implementation of the Plan of Action to Combat Desertification

The General Assembly,

Recalling its resolution 32/172 of 19 December 1977, by which it approved the Plan of Action to Combat Desertification, and all its subsequent resolutions on the subject,

Recalling also its resolution S-13/2 of 1 June 1986, by which it adopted the United Nations Programme of Action for African Economic Recovery and Development 1986-1990, which identified measures to combat desertification as a priority,

Bearing in mind the draft resolution to be adopted at the present session, concerning the United Nations conference on environment and development, to be held in 1992, fifteen years after the adoption of the Plan of Action to Combat Desertification,

Deeply concerned that the problem of desertification, which has a global impact, is still on the fringe of the growing awareness on the part of the international community that it is imperative to combat environmental deterioration effectively within the framework of the interdependence of nations,

Gravely concerned by the continuing spread and intensification of desertification in developing countries, particularly in Africa, and the indescribable human suffering, economic and financial losses and social disruption caused by that scourge,

Aware that drought and desertification place a considerable burden on the economic and financial capacities of the developing countries affected and that the negative effects of the international economic environment impede their efforts to undertake effective and sustained programmes to combat desertification, for which they bear primary responsibility,

1. *Takes note* of the report of the Secretary-General on the implementation of General Assembly resolutions 42/189 A, B and C of 11 December 1987 and of the relevant section of the report of the Governing Council of the United Nations Environment Programme;

2. *Expresses its deep concern* about the inadequacy of financial resources for the implementation of the Plan of Action to Combat Desertification;

3. *Urges* Governments, in particular those of the developed countries, United Nations organizations and other intergovernmental bodies to increase and intensify their efforts to combat desertification and to accord the highest priority to the recommendations contained in the Plan of Action;

4. *Invites* the Executive Director of the United Nations Environment Programme to consult the principal international organizations, private foundations, individuals and the major media enterprises that finance or promote environmental protection activities in order to draw their attention to the compelling need to consider desertification control on an equal footing with other current environmental issues;

5. *Invites* the United Nations conference on environment and development, to be held in 1992, to accord high priority to desertification control and to deploy all means necessary, including financial, scientific and technological resources, to halt and reverse the process of desertification with a view to preserving the ecological balance of the planet;

6. *Invites* the Governing Council of the United Nations Environment Programme to contribute substantially to the discussion on desertification at the conference, *inter alia*, by undertaking a general evaluation, sufficiently in advance of the conference, of the progress achieved in implementing the Plan of Action;

7. *Requests* the Secretary-General, in consultation with the Executive Director of the United Nations Environment Programme, to submit to the conference, through its preparatory committee, a report containing relevant expert studies on, *inter alia*, the following:

(a) Relevant suggestions and proposals formulated within the United Nations system on the possibility of utilizing new methods to finance the programmes of multilateral organizations at the global level, over and above regular budgets and conventional extrabudgetary resources;

(b) The state of implementation of the Plan of Action and objectives and courses of action to further the struggle against desertification, including an evaluation of the additional resources needed in order to attain the minimum objectives of the struggle against desertification;

(c) Ways and means of promoting, in particular in the developing countries, research into and development of existing and potential technology to combat deser-

tification and procedures for the transfer of such technology on favourable terms, in particular to developing countries;

(d) Possibilities for obtaining loans on concessional terms, from Governments and other sources, to finance the struggle against desertification;

(e) Possibilities for reducing the impact of desertification, including reafforestation, with the help of mechanisms involving the cancellation or reduction of external debt;

(f) Possibilities for strengthening and co-ordinating the activities of funds established for that purpose in various international institutions;

(g) Ways of encouraging the active participation of non-governmental organizations, foundations and individuals in the financing of training and scientific research programmes to combat desertification, including reafforestation programmes;

8. *Decides* to close the Special Account to finance the implementation of the Plan of Action to Combat Desertification, and requests the Executive Director of the United Nations Environment Programme to take the necessary steps to do so;

9. *Also decides* that the Consultative Group for Desertification Control will meet every year until the conference on environment and development is held in 1992 and every two years thereafter, and reaffirms its mandate as contained in resolutions 32/172 of 19 December 1977 and 39/168 of 17 December 1984;

10. *Calls upon* the Consultative Group, in co-operation with the Executive Director of the United Nations Environment Programme, to contribute to the enhancement of awareness of environmental issues and to intensify its efforts to mobilize additional resources, to exchange information on scientific research, national programmes and the implementation of the Plan of Action and to give its opinions on the actions to be undertaken in the battle against desertification;

11. *Urges* the Governments of countries affected by desertification to accord high priority, in their national development plans, to medium-term and long-term strategies and programmes for desertification control;

12. *Requests* the Secretary-General, together with the Executive Director of the United Nations Environment Programme and the Administrator of the United Nations Development Programme, to submit a report to the General Assembly at its forty-sixth session, through the Economic and Social Council, on the various provisions of the present resolution, and to ensure that it is submitted, immediately after publication, to the preparatory committee for the United Nations conference on environment and development.

General Assembly resolution 44/172 A

19 December 1989   Meeting 83   Adopted without vote

Approved by Second Committee (A/44/746/Add.8) without vote, 11 December (meeting 49); draft by Vice-Chairman (A/C.2/44/L.72), based on informal consultations on 13-nation draft (A/C.2/44/L.33); agenda item 82 (g).

Meeting numbers. GA 44th session: 2nd Committee 29, 32, 34, 49; plenary 83.

Sudano-Sahelian region

In 1989, the United Nations Sudano-Sahelian Office (UNSO), which was responsible for implementing the Plan of Action in the region, focused on the protection and rehabilitation of natural productive resources and the promotion of sustainable development in 22 Sudano-Sahelian countries. It continued to assist Governments in the planning and co-ordination of anti-desertification activities. Its strategy entailed close co-operation with Governments in formulating strategic policy frameworks and programmes to protect the productive capacity of the natural resources of each country. In the United Republic of Tanzania, UNSO helped to establish a Drought and Desertification Control Unit within the National Environment Council, and assisted in preparing a national plan to combat desertification, establishing a data base and mapping areas threatened by desertification. In Kenya, it supported the planning and formulation of desertification control policies and programmes, and assisted Mali in improving its operational and institutional capacities to monitor and co-ordinate its desertification control efforts. Activities in planning and co-ordination also took place in Chad, Guinea-Bissau and Mauritania.

In 1989, UNSO's ongoing projects focusing on deforestation control, rangeland management and water resources development, soil protection and sand-dune stabilization and integrated land management reached a value of some $100 million. Total resources mobilized through the UNSO Trust Fund were $37.5 million, an increase of more than 37 per cent over 1988.

In April, the UNDP Administrator presented to the UNDP Governing Council a report[19] on UNSO activities in 1988.

On 25 May, the UNEP Governing Council requested[20] UNSO to consider the Council's recommendations on implementation of the Plan of Action and authorized the Executive Director to continue to support the Office as a joint venture with UNDP. It invited him and the UNDP Administrator to intensify efforts to mobilize resources for continued assistance to the countries served by the Office.

GENERAL ASSEMBLY ACTION

On 19 December, the General Assembly, on the recommendation of the Second Committee, adopted **resolution 44/172 B** without vote.

Implementation in the Sudano-Sahelian region of the Plan of Action to Combat Desertification

The General Assembly,

Recalling its resolutions 32/170 of 19 December 1977, 33/88 of 15 December 1978, 34/187 of 18 December 1979, 35/72 of 5 December 1980, 36/190 of 17 December 1981, 37/216 of 20 December 1982, 38/164 of 19 December 1983, 39/168 B and 39/206 of 17 December 1984, 40/198 B of 17 December 1985, S-13/2 of 1 June 1986 and 42/189 B of 11 December 1987,

Bearing in mind the particularly serious nature of the problem of desertification in the Sudano-Sahelian region and of the critical situations it creates, which impede the economic and social development of the region and have tragic implications for the living conditions of the population,

1. *Takes note with appreciation* of the report of the Administrator of the United Nations Development Programme on the activities of the United Nations Sudano-Sahelian Office, as well as the relevant section of the report of the Governing Council of the United Nations Environment Programme;

2. *Stresses with deep concern:*

(a) That desertification in the countries of the Sudano-Sahelian region has worsened and that it has spread to other regions of Africa;

(b) That the chronic insufficiency of financial resources continues to pose obstacles to desertification control;

(c) That the struggle against desertification requires financial and technical resources beyond the means of the affected countries;

3. *Urges* the affected countries that have not yet done so to include projects to combat desertification and drought in their national development plans and to accord high priority to them;

4. *Also urges* the affected countries to use all appropriate mechanisms, including the round-table meetings of the United Nations Development Programme and the consultative groups of the World Bank, to mobilize resources for the implementation of programmes to combat desertification, and appeals to donor countries to provide substantial additional resources for the financing of such programmes;

5. *Notes with satisfaction* that the United Nations Sudano-Sahelian Office has endorsed the concept of sustainable development in adopting a global approach to the question of the management and conservation of natural resources and to environmental issues and in emphasizing the importance of the incorporation of desertification control activities in national development plans;

6. *Urges* the United Nations Sudano-Sahelian Office to assist the countries of the region with their preparations for the United Nations conference on environment and development, to be held in 1992, and with the resulting follow-up activities;

7. *Notes with appreciation* the interest displayed at the Summit of the seven major industrial nations, held in Paris from 14 to 16 July 1989, in aspects of the struggle against desertification and, specifically, in the planned observatory for the Sahara and the Sahel;

8. *Expresses its gratitude* to those Governments which contribute to the United Nations Trust Fund for Sudano-Sahelian Activities, and renews its urgent appeal to all members of the donor community to contribute substantially to the Trust Fund in order to enable the United Nations Sudano-Sahelian Office to respond more effectively to the pressing needs of the African countries stricken by desertification;

9. *Requests* the Executive Director of the United Nations Environment Programme and the Administrator of the United Nations Development Programme to strengthen their common undertaking to support the United Nations Sudano-Sahelian Office;

10. _Invites_ the United Nations Sudano-Sahelian Office:

_(a)_ To intensify its efforts to mobilize additional resources to support the efforts of the countries covered under its mandate and of the relevant regional organizations, in particular the Intergovernmental Authority for Drought and Development and the Permanent Inter-State Committee on Drought Control in the Sahel;

_(b)_ To continue to support the Ministerial Conference for a joint policy to combat desertification in the countries of the Permanent Inter-State Committee on Drought Control in the Sahel and the Economic Community of West African States, in the Maghreb countries, in Egypt and in the Sudan (COMIDES) and, in this context, to co-operate with the Southern African Development Co-ordination Conference and with the Arab Maghreb Union.

General Assembly resolution 44/172 B

19 December 1989   Meeting 83   Adopted without vote

Approved by Second Committee (A/44/746/Add.8) without vote, 11 December (meeting 49); draft by Vice-Chairman (A/C.2/44/L.72), based on informal consultations on 13-nation draft (A/C.2/44/L.33); agenda item 82 (g).

Meeting numbers. GA 44th session: 2nd Committee 29, 32, 34, 49; plenary 83.

Marine ecosystems

Protection of the marine environment

Work continued under the direction of the Group of Experts on the Scientific Aspects of Marine Pollution (GESAMP) on a major global review of the state of the marine environment. Based in part on 14 regional reports prepared with UNEP support, a GESAMP working group of the world's leading specialists analysed and prepared a summary of the health of the oceans.

In the light of the growing concern about the possibilities of a major climate change and sea-level rise as a result of the greenhouse effect, a significant effort was made, through a series of UNEP-supported regional teams, to determine the potential effects of the changes on coastal and marine areas, with particular emphasis on vulnerable islands. Two new task teams were formed, for eastern and western Africa, and the first regional intergovernmental meeting was held to present the results to government planners and policy makers.

Planning continued for the development of a globally co-ordinated marine pollution monitoring system. Under the general supervision of UNEP's Oceans and Coastal Areas Programme Activity Centre (OCA/PAC), work continued on the standard set of reference methods for marine pollution studies. Those methods, prepared through the collaboration of several international agencies, were designed to ensure the high quality and comparability of data from all regions of the world.

On 25 May, the Governing Council recommended[21] that Governments adopt the "principle of precautionary action" as the basis of their policies with regard to the prevention and elimi-

nation of marine pollution. It urged all eligible Governments that had not done so to become contracting parties to all relevant conventions. The international community was to work towards the complete elimination of the practice of dumping of pollutants liable to endanger the marine environment.

In a decision on pollution of the Red Sea, the Council emphasized[22] the need to combat pollution by oil and other harmful substances and to mobilize resources beyond those available in the area. It requested the Executive Director to prepare, in co-operation with IMO and relevant organizations, an inventory of available equipment and expertise for combating, surveying and containing pollution, as well as for shore clean-up, in cases of pollution by oil and other harmful substances, which could be made available for immediate response in any affected regional sea. It also requested that regional and subregional arrangements be developed where such arrangements did not exist so as to facilitate immediate response on either a reciprocal or a payment basis, and that Governments participating in the UNEP regional seas programme, in co-operation with IMO, facilitate the preparation of the inventory and develop customs procedures to promote the mobility of equipment.

Offshore mining

In a February report,[23] the Executive Director updated information on environmental co-operation concerning natural resources shared by two or more States. The report was based on replies received from Governments and international organizations in response to requests for information on the implementation of the principles of conduct in the field of the environment for the guidance of States in the conservation and harmonious utilization of shared natural resources,[24] as well as the conclusions of a 1981 study on the legal aspects concerning the environment related to offshore mining and drilling within the limits of national jurisdiction.[25] On 25 May, the Governing Council noted[26] the Executive Director's report, and called on Governments and international organizations to take further action to implement the principles of conduct and the conclusions of the study.

"Extraterritorial spaces"

In an 11 August letter[27] to the Secretary-General, Malta requested the inclusion in the agenda of the General Assembly under item 82, "Development and international economic co-operation", a supplementary sub-item entitled "Environmental protection of extraterritorial spaces for present and future generations". Malta explained that the environmental protection of "extraterritorial spaces", such as the high seas, was vital to safeguard the global environment, and proposed that the Assembly request the Secretary-General to establish, through the Executive Director of UNEP, a group of eminent persons to prepare a study and make recommendations on how the effective and comprehensive environmental protection of such spaces could best be achieved.

On 20 November, Malta submitted a draft resolution[28] also on behalf of Maldives, Mali, Morocco, Paraguay, Togo and Vanuatu, entitled "Environmental protection of extraterritorial spaces for present and future generations", by which the Assembly would have requested the Secretary-General to establish such a group.

By **decision 44/451** of 22 December, the General Assembly decided to take no action on the draft resolution.

Driftnet fishing

In a 28 November letter[29] to the Secretary-General, New Zealand, also on behalf of Australia, Fiji, Papua New Guinea, Samoa, Solomon Islands and Vanuatu, transmitted a press communiqué issued by the South Pacific Driftnet Fishing Conference (Wellington, New Zealand, 21-24 November). The Conference adopted the Convention on the Prohibition of Driftnet Fishing in the South Pacific, which called for an immediate ban on the practice of driftnet fishing in the South Pacific Commission region.

GENERAL ASSEMBLY ACTION

On 22 December, the General Assembly, on the recommendation of the Second Committee, adopted **resolution 44/225** without vote.

Large-scale pelagic driftnet fishing and its impact on the living marine resources of the world's oceans and seas

The General Assembly,

Noting that many countries are disturbed by the increase in the use of large-scale pelagic driftnets, which can reach or exceed 30 miles (48 kilometres) in total length, to catch living marine resources on the high seas of the world's oceans and seas,

Mindful that large-scale pelagic driftnet fishing, a method of fishing with a net or a combination of nets intended to be held in a more or less vertical position by floats and weights, the purpose of which is to enmesh fish by drifting on the surface of or in the water, can be a highly indiscriminate and wasteful fishing method that is widely considered to threaten the effective conservation of living marine resources, such as highly migratory and anadromous species of fish, birds and marine mammals,

Drawing attention to the fact that the present resolution does not address the question of small-scale driftnet fishing traditionally conducted in coastal waters, especially by developing countries, which provides an important contribution to their subsistence and economic development,

Expressing concern that, in addition to targeted species of fish, non-targeted fish, marine mammals, seabirds and other living marine resources of the world's oceans and seas can become entangled in large-scale pelagic driftnets, either in those in active use or in those that are lost or discarded, and as a result of such entanglement are often either injured or killed,

Recognizing that more than one thousand fishing vessels use large-scale pelagic driftnets in the Pacific, Atlantic and Indian Oceans and in other areas of the high seas,

Recognizing also that any regulatory measure to be taken for the conservation and management of living marine resources should take account of the best available scientific data and analysis,

Recalling the relevant principles elaborated in the United Nations Convention on the Law of the Sea,

Affirming that, in accordance with the relevant articles of the Convention, all members of the international community have a duty to co-operate globally and regionally in the conservation and management of living resources on the high seas, and a duty to take, or to co-operate with others in taking, such measures for their nationals as may be necessary for the conservation of those resources,

Recalling that, in accordance with the relevant articles of the Convention, it is the responsibility of all members of the international community to ensure the conservation and management of living marine resources and the protection and preservation of the living marine environment within their exclusive economic zones,

Noting the serious concern, particularly among coastal States and States with fishing interests, that the overexploitation of living marine resources of the high seas adjacent to the exclusive economic zones of coastal States is likely to have an adverse impact on the same resources within such zones, and noting also, in this regard, the responsibility for co-operation in accordance with the relevant articles of the Convention,

Noting also that the countries of the South Pacific Forum and the South Pacific Commission, in recognition of the importance of living marine resources to the people of the South Pacific region, have called for a cessation of such fishing in the South Pacific and the implementation of effective management programmes,

Taking note of the adoption of the Tarawa Declaration on this subject by the Twentieth South Pacific Forum at Tarawa, Kiribati, on 11 July 1989 and the adoption by South Pacific States and territories of the Convention on the Prohibition of Driftnet Fishing in the South Pacific, at Wellington on 24 November 1989,

Noting that some members of the international community have entered into co-operative enforcement and monitoring programmes for the immediate evaluation of the impact of large-scale pelagic driftnet fishing,

Recognizing that some members of the international community have taken steps to reduce their driftnet operations in some regions in response to regional concerns,

1. *Calls upon* all members of the international community, particularly those with fishing interests, to strengthen their co-operation in the conservation and management of living marine resources;

2. *Calls upon* all those involved in large-scale pelagic driftnet fishing to co-operate fully with the international community, and especially with coastal States and the

relevant international and regional organizations, in the enhanced collection and sharing of statistically sound scientific data in order to continue to assess the impact of such fishing methods and to secure conservation of the world's living marine resources;

3. *Recommends* that all interested members of the international community, particularly within regional organizations, continue to consider and, no later than 30 June 1991, review the best available scientific data on the impact of large-scale pelagic driftnet fishing, and agree upon further co-operative regulation and monitoring measures, as needed;

4. *Also recommends* that all members of the international community, bearing in mind the special role of regional organizations and regional and bilateral co-operation in the conservation and management of living marine resources as reflected in the relevant articles of the United Nations Convention on the Law of the Sea, agree to the following measures:

(a) Moratoria on all large-scale pelagic driftnet fishing on the high seas by 30 June 1992, with the understanding that such a measure will not be imposed in a region or, if implemented, can be lifted, should effective conservation and management measures be taken based upon statistically sound analysis to be jointly made by concerned parties of the international community with an interest in the fishery resources of the region, to prevent the unacceptable impact of such fishing practices on that region and to ensure the conservation of the living marine resources of that region;

(b) Immediate action to reduce progressively large-scale pelagic driftnet fishing activities in the South Pacific region leading to the cessation of such activities by 1 July 1991, as an interim measure, until appropriate conservation and management arrangements for South Pacific albacore tuna resources are entered into by the parties concerned;

(c) Immediate cessation of further expansion of large-scale pelagic driftnet fishing on the high seas of the North Pacific and all the other high seas outside the Pacific Ocean, with the understanding that this measure will be reviewed subject to the conditions in paragraph 4 *(a)* of the present resolution;

5. *Encourages* those coastal countries which have exclusive economic zones adjacent to the high seas to take appropriate measures and to co-operate in the collection and submission of scientific information on driftnet fishing in their own exclusive economic zones, taking into account the measures taken for the conservation of living marine resources of the high seas;

6. *Requests* specialized agencies, particularly the Food and Agriculture Organization of the United Nations, and other appropriate organs, organizations and programmes of the United Nations system, as well as the various regional and subregional fisheries organizations, urgently to study large-scale pelagic driftnet fishing and its impact on living marine resources and to report their views to the Secretary-General;

7. *Requests* the Secretary-General to bring the present resolution to the attention of all members of the international community, intergovernmental organizations, non-governmental organizations in consultative status with the Economic and Social Council, and well-established scientific institutions with expertise in relation to living marine resources;

8. *Also requests* the Secretary-General to submit to the General Assembly at its forty-fifth session a report on the implementation of the present resolution.

General Assembly resolution 44/225

22 December 1989   Meeting 85   Adopted without vote

Approved by Second Committee (A/44/746/Add.7) without vote, 15 December (meeting 50); draft by Vice-Chairman (A/C.2/44/L.81), based on informal consultations on draft by Japan (A/C.2/44/L.28/Rev.1) and on 18-nation draft (A/C.2/44/L.30/Rev.1); agenda item 82 *(f)*.
Meeting numbers. GA 44th session: 2nd Committee 31, 32, 40, 44, 46, 49-50; plenary 85.

Freshwater issues

UNEP's efforts related to fresh water focused on the management of lake and river basins, particularly the implementation of the Zambezi Action Plan.[30] In co-operation with the International Institute for Applied System Analysis, a computer-oriented programme for the Zambezi decision support system was developed and tested. In July, a training seminar was organized in Kariba, Zimbabwe, to demonstrate the system to professionals from the countries participating in the Zambezi Action Plan.

At the second meeting of the African Ministerial Conference on the Environment (AMCEN) Committee on River and Lake Basins, which was held in Harare, Zimbabwe, in April, priorities were established for subregional activities in Africa. Following a decision of AMCEN to support the Lake Chad Basin Commission to halt the drying-up of Lake Chad and to use its waters and ecosystems rationally during 1988-1989, the programme for environmentally sound management of inland waters focused on the Lake Chad basin. A diagnostic study for an action plan on the national management of the Lake Chad basin was completed. In August and September, a training course for specialists from the Lake Chad basin was organized in co-operation with the USSR Commission for UNEP (UNEPCOM). In the Mekong Delta, UNEP, jointly with the Mekong Delta Commission and UNEPCOM, supported activities to increase food production through the improvement of water and land management and the reclamation of acid sulphate soils.

An International Conference on Climate and Water was convened by WHO in Helsinki, Finland, in September. In co-operation with the Water Research Centre and the Ministry of Public Works and Water Resources of Egypt, UNEP supported an international seminar on climatic fluctuations and water management in Cairo in December, at which the impacts of climate change in developing countries were studied. The seminar reviewed policy, management and operational implications of climate fluctuations on water development. Seminar recommendations were subsequently submitted to the International Conference on Climate, held in Cairo in December.

In co-operation with the International Training Centre for Water Resources Management, UNEP organized training courses in environmentally sound water management. It also supported an international conference entitled ''Industrial Wastewaters '89'', organized by the International Association on Water Pollution Research and the University of Tampere in Nairobi, Kenya, to discuss the problems of wastewaters in Africa.

REFERENCES

(1)YUN 1988, p. 463, GA res. 43/53, 6 Dec. 1988.
(2)UNEP/GC.15/9/Add.2/Suppl.2. (3)A/44/484. (4)A/44/25 (dec. 15/36). (5)YUN 1985, p. 804. (6)YUN 1987, p. 700.
(7)A/44/25 (dec. 15/35).(8)A/44/349-E/1989/102. (9)YUN 1987, p. 700, GA res. 42/182, 11 Dec. 1987. (10)A/C.2/44/7. (11)YUN 1977, p. 509. (12)UNEP/GC.15/9/Add.4. (13)A/44/25 (dec. 15/23 A). (14)*Ibid.* (dec. 15/23 B). (15)YUN 1987, p. 702, GA res. 42/188, 11 Dec. 1987. (16)A/44/296-E/1989/81.
(17)A/44/351-E/1989/122. (18)YUN 1987, pp. 703, 705 & 707, GA res. 42/189 A-C, 11 Dec. 1987. (19)DP/1989/50. (20)A/44/25 (dec. 15/23 C). (21)A/44/25 (dec. 15/27). (22)*Ibid.* (dec. 15/25).
(23)UNEP/GC.15/9/Add.2. (24)YUN 1979, p. 692. (25)YUN 1981, p. 832. (26)A/44/25 (dec. 15/32). (27)A/44/193. (28)A/C.2/44/L.41.
(29)A/44/807. (30)YUN 1987, p. 710.

Role of UNEP

Programme and other issues

UNEP Council

At its fifteenth session, held in Nairobi (15-26 May), the UNEP Governing Council adopted decisions on environmental and administrative matters.[1]

On 25 May,[2] the Governing Council stressed the need to: make the Council a more effective and efficient mechanism in order to promote international co-operation and to recommend policies to that end; provide policy guidance for the direction and co-ordination of environmental programmes within the UN system; keep under review the world environmental situation to ensure that emerging environmental problems of international significance received adequate consideration by Governments; promote the contribution of relevant scientific and other professional communities to the acquisition, assessment and exchange of environmental knowledge and information; and review the impact of national and international environmental policies and measures on developing countries, as well as the problem of additional costs to developing countries incurred in implementing environmental programmes and projects.

The organization of the Governing Council's regular sessions would be restructured, with the first week devoted to work on programme, Fund, finance and administrative questions, and the second week to discussion in plenary, at the ministerial or equivalent level, of major policy issues.

On an experimental basis, the Bureau of the fifteenth session was to meet with bureaux of counterpart organs of specialized agencies and other UN organs to develop more collaborative relationships, and the Executive Director was invited to put forward proposals for a standing committee, including its membership, functions and financial implications, for consideration by the Council in 1991.

The Council also took a decision[3] to hold a three-day special session in 1990, immediately preceding, and at the same location as, the first meeting of the preparatory committee for the 1992 UN conference on environment and development. The session would deal with the elaboration and implementation of decisions on priority environmental issues, particularly ways of enhancing the role of UNEP within the UN system in addressing those issues, with the understanding that regular programme and budget matters would be discussed at the Council's 1991 session, the agenda of which was approved.

By **decision 1989/177**, the Economic and Social Council took note of the report of the UNEP Governing Council.

Provision of language facilities

In a December note[4] to the Governing Council, the Executive Director provided information on language services for the meetings of the Committee of Permanent Representatives to UNEP. On 25 May, the Governing Council decided[5] to recognize the requirements for full language services for the meetings of the Committee of Permanent Representatives and to provide them as soon as funding could be provided.

State of the environment

On 23 May, the UNEP Governing Council took note[6] of the Executive Director's 1988 state-of-the-environment report on the public and environment,[7] his report on the state of the world environment for 1989[8] and the outline of the 1990 state-of-the-environment report on children and the environment.[9] The Council drew the attention of Governments and relevant intergovernmental organizations to salient findings in the 1988 and 1989 reports, and requested the Executive Director to accord high priority to enhancing the role and active participation of women in environmental protection and to supporting global, regional, national and local training programmes on environmental awareness directed at media personnel. With regard to the 1989 report, the Executive Director was asked to give priority to activities related to the control of global emissions of substances that depleted the ozone layer, possible climate change and limitation of emissions of greenhouse gases and management of hazardous wastes.

The Council also requested the Executive Director to proceed, in consultation with UNICEF, with preparing, for submission to the Council at its sixteenth session, the 1990 state-of-the-environment report on children and the environment, including sections on female children, drugs and smoking, and institutional structures for enhancing children's environment. The Executive Director should continue to produce, in odd years, reports on the state of the environment along the lines of the 1989 report; prepare, for presentation at the 1992 UN conference on environment and development, a brief analytical report on changes in the state of the world environment since 1972; and prepare a comprehensive report on the state of the environment, covering the decade since the Council's 1982 special session in Nairobi, for submission to the Council in 1993.

On the same day, the Council took note[6] of the Executive Director's report[10] on activities since its eleventh session to implement Council decisions related to the annual state-of-the-environment reports, and requested him to report on the follow-up and implementation of decisions related to the annual state-of-the-environment reports.

System-wide medium-term programme

The Executive Director submitted to the Governing Council a January note[11] on guidelines for the revision of the system-wide medium-term environment programme for 1990-1995 (SWMTEP), which had been approved by the Council in 1988.[12] He reported that he had received only 27 responses to his request to Governments for their views on possible changes to SWMTEP, and, of those, only 14 had made suggestions for its revision. Suggestions related to general recommendations, amendments to specific paragraphs or sections of the document, and inclusion of new subjects or rearrangement of the structure of the document. The report also referred to the timetable for the Council's consideration of SWMTEP, the UNEP medium-term plan and programme budget documents, and raised the difficulties faced by the UNEP secretariat and UN bodies that participated in the monitoring, evaluation and revision process of SWMTEP. The Executive Director recommended that SWMTEP II be revised only once, preferably on the basis of the mid-term review of the plan, which could then be presented to the Council in 1993, together with the results of the mid-term review.

On 25 May, the Governing Council decided[13] that, while the system-wide medium-term environment programme for 1990-1995 should not be subject to a formal revision at the present time, its development and implementation should continue

in the course of ongoing joint programming, resulting, *inter alia*, in forthcoming biennial environment programmes of UNEP and other UN bodies reflecting more closely the structure and recommendations of the Environmental Perspective to the Year 2000 and Beyond[14] and taking into account the report of the World Commission on Environment and Development[15] so as to orient the programmes towards an anticipatory and preventive approach. No further evaluation of the system-wide medium-term environment programme was needed for the period 1984-1989, and the medium-term review for 1990-1995 should be carried out in accordance with paragraph 411 of the programme. In 1991, the Governing Council would provide the Administrative Committee on Co-ordination (ACC) with its views as policy guidance for the preparation of the 1996-2001 programme.

Environmental education and training

The International Environmental Education Programme (IEEP), developed jointly by UNEP and UNESCO, remained the only major world-wide programme for environmental education. In 1989, four issues of the IEEP journal *Connect* were produced in six languages. International, regional and national training courses, workshops and seminars on environmental education were organized for teachers, teacher trainers, administrators, professionals and other groups in 20 countries, providing direct training to 640 cadres and, through them, indirect training to thousands of others. In the area of environmental training, UNEP's policy and activities promoted the acceptance of the concept of sustainable development. Under a joint project, UNEP, UNIDO, the USSR and the Tampere University of Technology (Finland) organized a five-week training course on environment management for industrial managers and engineers from Asia and the Pacific (11 October–15 November). The thirteenth annual international post-graduate course conducted by UNEP and UNESCO, with the new title of post-graduate course in environmental management and a completely revised curriculum, took place at the Technical University of Dresden, German Democratic Republic. UNEP helped several universities to set up undergraduate or master's degree courses in environmental science or studies.

Public information

During 1989, UNEP reported that media and public interest in the environment continued to surge. On 5 June, World Environment Day ceremonies in Brussels focused on global warming—an appeal for global action to cope with the greenhouse effect. UNEP presented the Global 500 Awards to 114 individuals and organizations in 1989 for outstanding achievements in protecting and improving the environment.

Media coverage of various environmental issues helped the public to understand better the scope of the challenge and helped UNEP to fulfil its role as a catalyst through the dissemination of information on crucial environmental issues. UNEP was able to win support from all segments of society for its outreach activities. UNEP's audio-visual activities increased, with radio productions, travelling exhibits, television and film productions and an expanded video library. A new 12-panel photo exhibit was produced on the subject of the marine environment, and five exhibits were assembled for various meetings and conferences in Nairobi and abroad. The UNEP video presentation ''View from UNEP'', produced in collaboration with the Television Trust for the Environment, was distributed world wide through United Nations information centres and UNEP regional offices.

UNEP also strengthened its relationships with NGOs and community groups, giving special attention to youth groups. More than 3,000 students participated in a global youth forum on the environment, organized by UNEP in May. UNEP continued to publish a wide range of books, brochures, periodicals and other materials. Of particular interest was *A Coast in Common*, about the Eastern African Action Plan, and *Our Planet*, a new quarterly that replaced *UNEP News*. Efforts were concentrated on joint publications requiring minimal funding, such as *The Economics of Dryland Management*, *Action on the Environment: the Role of the United Nations*, published in association with the National Centre for Atmospheric Research. UNEP's promotional booklet *UNEP Profile* appeared in Chinese and Japanese.

Finances

UNEP Fund

On 18 May, the UNEP Governing Council reconfirmed[16] the appropriation of $25,846,300 previously authorized for 1988-1989 with the revised distribution by programme and object of expenditure proposed by the Executive Director. It also approved for 1990-1991 an appropriation of $29,087,000 for the programme and support costs budget and requested the Executive Director to report to its sixteenth session on implementation of the programme and programme support costs budget during the first year of the 1990-1991 biennium.

The Council appealed[17] to Governments to pledge contributions for the 1992-1993 biennium at an increasing rate to provide the Executive Director with a firm basis on which to plan future programmes, as well as to pay their contributions either before the end of the year preceding that to which their contributions related or as near as possible to the beginning of that year. The Council approved an appropriation of $68 million for Fund programme activities for 1990-1991 and an appropriation of $4 million to the Fund programme reserve for the same period. Core activities approved by the Governing Council should be afforded first priority in implementation. The Executive Director was to enter into commitments not exceeding $16 million for Fund programme activities in 1992-1993.

In other action,[2] the Council confirmed that the programme of activities within the appropriation for Fund programme activities for 1990-1991 did not cover all the urgent environmental activities for the next biennium, and decided that the additional tasks enumerated by the Executive Director in his supplementary programme should be implemented as soon as resources were available. For the supplementary programme, it approved an appropriation of $35 million.

The Council also took note[18] of the comments of the Executive Director on the report of the Board of Auditors and the observations of ACABQ.[19]

Additional funding sources

The Executive Director, in a February report,[20] described steps taken to secure additional funding to the Environment Fund, and identified possibilities for expanding the funding base, including additional sources from Governments for specific projects that governmental agencies might wish to support; non-governmental funding from industry and foundations; and resources for projects that appealed to special audiences.

On 19 May, the UNEP Governing Council requested[21] Governments to increase their support in the form of funds for the employment of UNEP additional staff, including staff in developing countries, and for specific activities within the programme. It requested the Executive Director to secure additional support from Governments, intergovernmental organizations, regional banks, NGOs and private corporations; and to ensure that all fund-raising activities were self-financed and would generally have no financial or other implications for the regular budget or the Environment Fund.

The Secretary-General, responding to a 1988 Economic and Social Council request,[22] submitted in June[23] to the Council and the General Assembly the report of the UNEP Executive Director on the provision of additional resources to developing countries. The report summarized information from six States and the European Community and from five UN organizations. The Executive Director stated that the information received was not an adequate basis for the review requested by the Assembly in 1972[24] and considered that a further request for information would be required, as well as the convening of a small, geographically balanced group including experts and financing institutions of the UN system.

ECONOMIC AND SOCIAL COUNCIL ACTION

On 27 July, on the recommendation of its First Committee, the Economic and Social Council adopted **resolution 1989/101** without vote.

Strengthening international co-operation on the environment: provision of additional financial resources to developing countries

The Economic and Social Council,

Recalling General Assembly resolution 2997(XXVII) of 15 December 1972 on institutional and financial arrangements for international environmental co-operation, in particular, section III, paragraph 4, thereof,

Recalling also Economic and Social Council resolution 1988/69 of 28 July 1988,

Taking note of the report of the Executive Director of the United Nations Environment Programme,

1. *Concludes* that increasing attention needs to be paid to the provision of new and additional financial resources to developing countries for environmental programmes and projects, so as to ensure that their development priorities are not adversely affected, and that such provision should be kept under more effective and continuous review;

2. *Recommends* that, during the preparatory process for the proposed United Nations conference on environment and development and at the conference itself, careful consideration should be given to this question with a view to enabling the conference to establish modalities for effective monitoring or review, in order to provide a factual basis for promoting appropriate action.

Economic and Social Council resolution 1989/101

27 July 1989   Meeting 36   Adopted without vote

Approved by First Committee (E/1989/140) without vote, 24 July (meeting 26); draft by Malaysia for Group of 77 (E/1989/C.1/L.12), orally revised; agenda item 7 (f).

The General Assembly, in **resolution 44/229**, reaffirmed the need for new and additional financial resources to support developing countries in dealing with environmental problems to ensure that their development priorities were not adversely affected, as well as to support measures to solve major environmental problems of global concern and to support those countries, especially developing countries, for which implementation of such measures would entail a special or abnormal burden.

Trust funds

On 19 May, the UNEP Governing Council urged[25] Governments to pay their contributions to the trust funds before the beginning of the year.

It approved the extension of six general trust funds and approved the establishment of four new general trust funds: the Trust Fund for Environmental Training Network in Latin America and the Caribbean, from 1 July 1989 to 31 December 1991; the Trust Fund for the Vienna Convention for the Protection of the Ozone Layer,[26] from 1 October 1989 to 31 March 1993; the Trust Fund for the Montreal Protocol on Substances that Deplete the Ozone Layer,[27] from 1 October 1989 to 31 March 1993; and the Trust Fund for the Conference on the Global Environment and Human Response towards Sustainable Development, from 1 March 1989 to 28 February 1990. It also approved, on a contingency basis, the Trust Fund for the Basel Convention on the Control of Transboundary Movements of Hazardous Wastes and their Disposal (see above) for two years, effective on the first day of the month after the Convention came into force. The Council also noted with approval the extension by the Executive Director of six technical co-operation trust funds and the establishment of six new ones.

Regional office system

In March, the Executive Director reported[28] on UNEP's regional office system, reviewing the role of the system and making suggestions for strengthening it, as well as related financial considerations. The report indicated that the regional office system was essential to the effective discharge of UNEP's mandate, but its staff and resources were insufficient to meet the environmental challenges of the 1990s. He proposed to strengthen it through the creation of new regions by the subdivision of existing ones and by the establishment of a regional relations section at UNEP headquarters. Costs for implementing the proposals should be met through arrangements with donor Governments.

On 25 May, the Governing Council welcomed[29] the Executive Director's intention to strengthen relationships between the regional offices of UNEP and the relevant offices of UNDP, the World Bank and the regional development banks in order to enhance immediate and sustainable development; develop closer working relationships with the UN regional commissions; and improve the management and administration of the regional offices. It approved his proposal to reduce the charges to the programme and the programme support costs budget by 11.4 per cent by increasing the proportion of the cost of the existing regional offices charged as Fund programme activities by approximately 24 per cent in 1990-1991; and requested him to consult with concerned Governments about the establishment of subregional offices, taking into account that Africa and Latin America and the Caribbean should each be served by one office with subregional offices as appropriate.

The Council noted the Executive Director's intention to establish a regional relations unit at headquarters to serve the regional offices, requested him to support, through the regional office for Africa, the Cairo Programme for African Co-operation[30] and invited the governing bodies of UNDP, the World Bank and the regional development banks to support the development of stronger relationships among the relevant field offices of those organizations to enhance immediate and sustainable development. Regional economic and social commissions were to play a more active role in the activities of the designated officials for environmental matters.

UNEP clearing-house mechanism

UNEP's clearing-house mechanism, established as a bridge between developing countries and potential donors, supported its co-ordinating and catalytic role in assisting those countries to deal with environmental problems and to help secure the needed financial and technical resources.

The Executive Director reported to the UNEP Governing Council on the results of the external evaluation[31] of UNEP's clearing-house function. The Executive Director's summary of the evaluation discussed the achievements of the clearinghouse during the period 1982-1988, the efficiency and catalytic impact of the mechanism, its relevance to sustainable development policy in relation to the UNEP mandate, causes of successes and failures, and recommendations of the external evaluation team. That team recommended that the distribution of tasks between the clearing-house and other UNEP entities concerned, and the Office of the Environment Programme in particular, should be revised so as to leave to the clearinghouse unit the tasks of internal co-ordination, presentation of activities to donors and fundraising. Other, more substantive tasks pertaining to the clearing-house function should be entrusted to other UNEP entities. UNEP should prepare a long- and medium-term clearing-house fundraising plan for presentation to donors, including activities of a global nature and activities addressed to the problems of developing countries. The report also contained the comments of the Executive Director on the report of the evaluators.

On 25 May, the Governing Council reaffirmed[32] that the clearing-house function was an essential aspect of the co-ordinating and catalytic role of UNEP. It should enable developing countries to: establish and strengthen their policies, institutions and professional capacity to integrate environmental considerations into their development policies; initiate programmes and activities for dealing with their most serious environmental problems; and formulate and participate in action plans for the common management of ecosystems and critical environmental problems. The Council stressed that UNEP should play an active role in providing and mobilizing assistance to developing countries and expressed concern that UNEP had not attracted sufficient additional resources in that respect. The Council reiterated its call to Governments and other donors to consider favourably requests by UNEP for additional resources as well as direct requests from developing countries. It requested the Executive Director to revise the terminology with regard to the clearing-house function in order to make it clearer and to continue his efforts to obtain additional resources to manage and implement its activities. He should ensure that clearing-house activities were made more widely known to all sources of development assistance. The Executive Director was requested to study and implement organizational arrangements to make UNEP more efficient in assisting developing countries, to clarify the responsibilities of its various departments and to strengthen the execution of the clearing-house function.

By **resolution 44/229** of 22 December, the General Assembly concurred with the Governing Council decision on the clearing-house function.

REFERENCES

[1]A/44/25. [2]*Ibid.* (dec. 15/1). [3]*Ibid.* (dec. 15/4). [4]UNEP/GC.15/11. [5]A/44/25 (dec. 15/12). [6]*Ibid.* (dec. 15/13). [7]YUN 1988, p. 459. [8]UNEP/GC.15/7/Add.2. [9]UNEP/GC.15/7/Add.4. [10]UNEP/GC.15/7/Add.5. [11]UNEP/GC.15/8/Add.4. [12]YUN 1988, p. 453. [13]A/44/25 (dec. 15/21). [14]YUN 1987, p. 661, GA res. 42/186, 11 Dec. 1987. [15]*Ibid.*, p. 679, GA res. 42/187, 11 Dec. 1987. [16]A/44/25 (dec. 15/45). [17]*Ibid.* (dec. 15/46). [18]*Ibid.* (dec. 15/44). [19]A/43/5/Add.6. [20]UNEP/GC.15/10/Add.5 & Corr.1. [21]A/44/25 (dec. 15/42). [22]YUN 1988, p. 452, ESC res. 1988/69, 28 July 1988. [23]A/44/332. [24]YUN 1972, p. 331, GA res. 2997(XXVII), 15 Dec. 1972. [25]A/44/25 (dec. 15/43). [26]YUN 1985, p. 804. [27]YUN 1987, p. 700. [28]UNEP/GC.15/5/Add.3. [29]A/44/25 (dec. 15/15). [30]YUN 1985, p. 793. [31]UNEP/GC.15/5/Add.1 & Corr.1 & Suppl.1. [32]A/44/25 (dec. 15/14).

Chapter IX

Population and human settlements

In 1989, the United Nations Population Fund assisted more than 3,500 country and intercountry projects and completed upwards of 200 projects. Major activities of the Fund focused on maternal/child health care and family planning; information, education and communication; basic data collection; utilization of population data and research for policy formulation and development planning; and issues related to women, population and development. Special programmes largely concentrated on AIDS-related activities.

After a third review of the 1974 World Population Plan of Action, several recommendations were proposed for its further implementation, which were subsequently adopted by the Economic and Social Council. The Council also decided to convene in 1994 an international meeting on population in order to assess the progress made in carrying out the Plan and provide guidance for the treatment of population issues for the next decade. The International Forum on Population in the Twenty-first Century, held in November, adopted the Amsterdam Declaration, recommending specific population goals to be achieved by the year 2000.

The Commission on Human Settlements considered as its major themes the implementation, monitoring and financing of the Global Strategy for Shelter to the Year 2000; opportunities for co-operation between governmental and non-governmental sectors in human settlements; and maintenance of buildings and infrastructure. It adopted its first report to the General Assembly on implementation of the first phase of the Global Strategy.

The UN Centre for Human Settlements, also known as Habitat, was designated the lead agency in implementing the Global Strategy. In addition, Habitat continued to assist developing countries in human settlements activities, including technical co-operation, research and development and information dissemination.

Population

Third review of World Population Plan

The third review and appraisal of the World Population Plan of Action, adopted at the 1974 World Population Conference,[1] covered progress made towards achieving the goals of the Plan in the period 1984-1989.

A report by the Secretary-General[2] on action by the United Nations to implement that Plan focused on 31 selected population issues in the fields of: socio-economic development, the environment and population; the role and status of women; development of population policies; population trends, prospects, goals and policies; promotion of knowledge and policy; the role of national Governments and the international community; and monitoring, review and appraisal. It concluded that the Plan continued to provide a policy framework for carrying out population activities at the national, regional and global levels. The Plan's implementation was judged to have been satisfactory, and 11 recommendations were proposed for its further implementation. Governments and organizations were urged to reiterate their support for the principles and provisions of the Plan, to pay special attention to recommendations of the World Commission on Environment and Development, and to strengthen programmes to improve the role and status of women. Other recommendations dealt with halting the spread of the acquired immunodeficiency syndrome (AIDS) pandemic, evaluating biotechnologies affecting human reproduction, assisting refugee populations, improving population data collection, and giving priority to assisting population programmes in the least developed countries, in particular those in sub-Saharan Africa.

ECONOMIC AND SOCIAL COUNCIL ACTION

On 26 July, on the recommendation of its First (Economic) Committee, the Economic and Social Council adopted **resolution 1989/92** without vote.

Strengthening actions concerned with the fulfilment of the World Population Plan of Action

The Economic and Social Council,

Recalling General Assembly resolutions 3344(XXIX) of 17 December 1974 on the United Nations World Population Conference and 39/228 of 18 December 1984 on the International Conference on Population,

Recalling also Economic and Social Council resolutions 1985/4 of 28 May 1985, 1986/7 of 21 May 1986 and 1987/72 of 8 July 1987 on follow-up to the recommendations of the International Conference on Population,

Having considered and approved the findings of the third quinquennial review and appraisal of progress made towards achieving the goals of the World Population Plan of Action which was called for in paragraph 108 of the Plan of Action and recommendation 88 of the International Conference on Population,

Expressing its appreciation of the action taken by many States, organizations of the United Nations system and intergovernmental and non-governmental organizations pursuant to the provisions of the World Population Plan of Action,

Concerned about certain population issues that have emerged during the past five years and the need to reinforce previous recommendations that urgently call for new action,

1. *Urges* all Member States and regional and international bodies to continue their advocacy of the principles and objectives of the World Population Plan of Action and the recommendations for its further implementation adopted by the International Conference on Population and in particular to provide special support for the implementation of the recommendations contained in the annex to the present resolution;

2. *Urges* governmental, intergovernmental and non-governmental organizations and organizations of the United Nations system that provide technical and financial assistance in the area of population to increase their efforts to implement the World Population Plan of Action through their programmes of work and to give special attention to the recommendations contained in the annex to the present resolution.

ANNEX
Conclusions and recommendations of the third review and appraisal of progress made towards the implementation of the World Population Plan of Action

A. *Overall assessment*

1. The World Population Plan of Action and the recommendations for its further implementation continue to provide a policy framework for carrying out population activities at the national, regional and global levels. Governments have found the provisions useful for formulating, implementing and evaluating their population policies. The international community has made them the analytical basis for the provision of financial and technical assistance to developing countries.

2. During the recent discussions on the efficiency of the United Nations and on its intergovernmental structure and functions in the economic and social fields, the field of population was singled out as one in which the work of the United Nations had been relatively effective. In spite of the inherently controversial nature of the subject, population is one of the main fields of work of the United Nations and other international organizations and is considered a programmable sector by many Governments. Today, there is a set of reliable population indicators for virtually every country in the world. Population is one of the better co-ordinated sectors of international assistance. Furthermore, the World Population Plan of Action is an international instrument that serves as a standard reference and continues to rest firmly on a global consensus. Although there are many reasons for such achievements, it is important to emphasize the benefits that result from bringing together the political will of Governments and the scientific and programming skills of many units of the United Nations and of numerous academic centres and professional associations and other non-governmental organizations.

3. It can be concluded that the main findings of the third review and appraisal of the implementation of the Plan have been judged satisfactory, although a number of issues remain unresolved and others have emerged only recently. Further implementation of the Plan requires the serious consideration of certain critical issues. On the basis of the findings of the current assessment, the following recommendations have been adopted to address, in particular, the new issues that have emerged during the past five years and, in a few cases, to reinforce previous recommendations that urgently require new action.

B. *Recommendations*

Recommendation 1

Governments, intergovernmental and non-governmental organizations, parliamentarians and the public in general are urged to reaffirm their support for the principles, objectives and provisions of the World Population Plan of Action and the recommendations for its further implementation.

Recommendation 2

Governments and intergovernmental and non-governmental organizations are urged to attach high priority to co-operative efforts to alleviate problems arising from the difficult economic situation faced by developing countries, including the problem of external indebtedness, in order to overcome major obstacles to the economic and social development of developing countries, and to the fulfilment of the objectives of the World Population Plan of Action.

Recommendation 3

Governments and intergovernmental and non-governmental organizations are invited to pay special attention to the conclusions and recommendations of the Environmental Perspective to the Year 2000 and Beyond and the report of the World Commission on Environment and Development, particularly on matters pertaining to population issues.

Recommendation 4

Governments and international organizations are encouraged to give the support needed to strengthen programmes to improve the role and status of women. In those programmes particular attention should be paid to the needs of young women and the importance of the active involvement of men in all areas of family responsibility, including family planning and child care.

Recommendation 5

Governments are urged to give full attention to all aspects of population in the formulation of their social and economic development plans and programmes, both within and outside the context of formal development planning, and the international community should assign high priority to supporting them in that respect. The concept of integrating population factors into development plans and programmes needs to be more clearly defined, as do the approaches to be used. The definitions must cover the institutional and human resources needed for effective integration.

Recommendation 6

Governments and international organizations are urged to strengthen their efforts to achieve the targets established by the International Conference on Population for mortality in general and child and maternal mortality in particular.

Recommendation 7

A continuous assessment of the demographic, economic and social consequences of the acquired immunodeficiency syndrome (AIDS) pandemic should be made at the national, regional and global levels, and the results should be conveyed to Governments and international organizations. Special attention should be given to the spread of AIDS among the working-age population and among children, protection of the human rights of persons infected with AIDS, the devastating consequences for the families of persons infected with AIDS and the possible adverse effects on resource allocations to general health and development programmes. Governments are urged to encourage patterns of behaviour and promote the development and use of barrier contraceptive methods that would deter the spread of AIDS and other sexually transmitted diseases.

Recommendation 8

In view of the rapid development and growing availability of new biotechnologies affecting human reproduction, Governments should evaluate their multiple consequences, both with respect to universally recognized ethical values and human rights and with respect to their possible demographic impact.

Recommendation 9

Considering that the new area of assistance called "refugee aid and development" is aimed at assisting not only refugees but also host communities, Governments and local and international organizations are urged to collaborate with the United Nations High Commissioner for Refugees in providing full support for the design and implementation of programmes in that area.

Recommendation 10

Governments are invited to design a balanced programme of data collection, analysis and dissemination that includes gathering population data through civil registration systems, population censuses and national sample survey programmes. To that end, international organizations are invited to provide support and assistance. Special emphasis should be given to data on the education and socio-economic integration of women and special population groups, such as indigenous communities, disabled persons, youth and the elderly.

Recommendation 11

Governments and the international community should strengthen the institutional base required to carry out the theoretical, methodological and applied research needed to support population programmes and policies and to fill gaps in knowledge. While biomedical research should continue to receive support, more intensive policy-oriented research is needed on the socio-cultural factors affecting human behaviour in relation not only to reproduction but also to morbidity, mortality, migration and urbanization.

Recommendation 12

Governments and intergovernmental and non-governmental organizations are urged to give high pri-

ority to the managerial aspects of population programmes and to ensure the availability of trained specialists in that area. Increased efforts will be needed to establish monitoring, evaluation and research activities and make use of them in formulating and implementing population programmes. Family planning programmes should receive increased support in order to guarantee higher standards and meet the demand for services.

Recommendation 13

The Governments concerned and the international community should give the highest priority to assisting the population programmes of the least developed countries that have large populations and high rates of population growth, in particular those in sub-Saharan Africa.

Economic and Social Council resolution 1989/92

26 July 1989   Meeting 35   Adopted without vote

Approved by First Committee (E/1989/139) without vote, 21 July (meeting 25); draft by Population Commission (E/1989/24); agenda item 7 *(d)*.

Follow-up to the 1984 Conference

As a follow-up to the 1984 International Conference on Population,[3] the Secretary-General submitted three reports to the Economic and Social Council and/or the Population Commission: on the activities of the United Nations system in the field of population;[4] on the work of intergovernmental and non-governmental organizations in the implementation of the World Population Plan of Action;[5] and on monitoring of multilateral population assistance (see below).[6]

UNFPA activities. As requested by the Economic and Social Council in 1987,[7] the Executive Director of the UN Population Fund (UNFPA) reported to the Population Commission on the Fund's activities.[8] The report reviewed the mandate of the Fund, re-examined its recent realignment and decentralization of authority and responsibility, surveyed the financial scope of its activities and examined its programme of work.

The Executive Director noted that 1989 marked the twentieth anniversary of UNPFA, and stated that it would continue to concentrate on enhanced programme delivery and on improving the quality and effectiveness of its programmes. The Fund's goals would be better data for programme and operational use; better integration of population with other development programmes; safe, acceptable, cheap and easy-to-use means of contraception; better delivery systems; more self-reliance and commitment of national resources; and improved co-ordination within and outside the United Nations system.

Proposed international meeting on population (1994)

In January, the Secretary-General submitted a report[9] to the Population Commission on options for convening an intergovernmental conference on population in 1994. It provided factual information to enable the Commission to consider and advise the Economic and Social Council on the possibilities for such a conference and suggested five options: an intergovernmental conference; a special session of the General Assembly; a special session of the Economic and Social Council; a special session of the Population Commission; and a joint meeting of the Population Commission and the Governing Council of the United Nations Development Programme (UNDP).

ECONOMIC AND SOCIAL COUNCIL ACTION

On 26 July, on the recommendation of its First Committee, the Economic and Social Council adopted **resolution 1989/91** without vote.

Convening of an international meeting on population in 1994

The Economic and Social Council,

Recalling General Assembly resolutions 3344(XXIX) of 17 December 1974 on the United Nations World Population Conference and 39/228 of 18 December 1984 on the International Conference on Population,

Recalling also Economic and Social Council resolutions 1985/4 of 28 May 1985, 1986/7 of 21 May 1986 and 1987/72 of 8 July 1987 on follow-up to the recommendations of the International Conference on Population,

Recognizing the full validity of the principles and objectives of the World Population Plan of Action, adopted by the United Nations World Population Conference in 1974,

Having considered the findings of the third review and appraisal of progress made towards achieving the goals and objectives of the World Population Plan of Action,

Noting with appreciation the efforts and achievements of many States, organizations of the United Nations system and intergovernmental and non-governmental organizations pursuant to the provisions of the World Population Plan of Action, the recommendations for the further implementation of the Plan adopted by the International Conference on Population in 1984 and the Mexico City Declaration on Population and Development,

Concerned about the magnitude and growing urgency of population issues in the next decade,

Aware of the evolving diversity of population issues, including the regional variations in demographic trends and population problems, as indicated in the report of the Secretary-General on the monitoring of world population trends and policies,

Stressing the need for continued attention to be given to population issues at a high policy level in order to ensure that population concerns are integrated into policies, priorities and programmes for social and economic development, and, in that context, recognizing the usefulness of convening periodic international meetings at a high level to address population issues,

1. *Decides*, in principle, to convene in 1994, under the auspices of the United Nations, an international meeting on population that would bring together high-level governmental authorities and population experts and be open to all States as full participants, the specialized agencies and other relevant organizations, in order to:

(a) Assess the progress made and identify the obstacles encountered in carrying out the World Population Plan of Action and the recommendations for its further implementation;

(b) Increase the level of awareness of population issues on the international agenda;

(c) Provide guidance at the global, regional and national levels on the treatment of population issues of the highest priority for the next decade;

(d) Adopt a consolidated and updated set of recommendations;

2. *Decides further* that the international meeting on population should be conducted effectively and efficiently and that its size, duration and other cost factors should be determined with due regard for economy;

3. *Decides*, in the light of paragraph 1 of the present resolution, to designate the Population Commission, meeting in open-ended session, with the participation of any Member of the United Nations that is not a member of the Commission and of any other State, as the preparatory committee for the international meeting on population, and for that purpose decides that rule 11 of the rules of procedure of the functional commissions of the Economic and Social Council and rule 1 *(d)* of the rules governing payment of travel expenses and subsistence allowances in respect of members of organs or subsidiary organs of the United Nations shall be waived;

4. *Requests* the Secretary-General to ensure that the regional commissions, the specialized agencies, other bodies of the United Nations system and other international organizations make a substantive contribution to the international meeting on population;

5. *Requests* the Population Commission, utilizing, *inter alia*, the reports of the Secretary-General and in consultation with appropriate organs, organizations and bodies of the United Nations system and relevant intergovernmental and non-governmental organizations, to consider at its twenty-sixth session and to submit recommendations to the Council on:

(a) The further elaboration and refinement of the objectives of the international meeting on population as set out in paragraph 1 of the present resolution;

(b) The issues to be discussed at the meeting;

(c) The nature of the preparatory work for the meeting, including the possibility of holding regional intergovernmental meetings;

(d) The assignment of responsibilities for the preparation of the meeting to organizations and bodies of the United Nations system and relevant intergovernmental and non-governmental organizations;

6. *Requests* the Secretary-General to make the necessary organizational arrangements for the preparation of the international meeting on population, including the appointment of principal officers, and to submit to the Council, through the Population Commission at its twenty-sixth session, a detailed report on the state of the preparations for the meeting, including:

(a) The financial implications of alternative preparatory options, bearing in mind paragraph 2 of the present resolution;

(b) Measures proposed to ensure the participation and co-ordination of the relevant organizations and bodies of the United Nations system;

7. *Requests* the Secretary-General to take appropriate measures to obtain resources for the international meeting on population, to report on progress to the Council at its second regular session of 1990 and to report on the results obtained to the Council, through the Population Commission at its twenty-sixth session, in 1991.

Economic and Social Council resolution 1989/91

26 July 1989   Meeting 35   Adopted without vote

Approved by First Committee (E/1989/139) without vote, 24 July (meeting 26); draft by Population Commission (E/1989/24); agenda item 7 (d).

UN Population Fund

UNFPA activities

The largest share of UNFPA assistance in 1989 was directed to maternal and child health care and family planning (MCH/FP) activities, followed by communication and education programmes, population dynamics programmes, basic data collection, and formulation and evaluation of population policies. Work also proceeded on special programme interests, including those related to youth, aging and AIDS.

Total UNFPA income in 1989 was $184.9 million. The number of donors was 98, including two first-time donors—Equatorial Guinea and Vanuatu. The Fund's ongoing efforts to secure multibilateral and other arrangements generated an additional $6.4 million during 1989 for projects with allocations totalling $10.1 million at year's end. Project allocations amounted to $194.2 million, while expenditures were close to $204 million, including $109.8 million for country programmes, $47.7 million for intercountry (regional, interregional and global) programmes, $32.1 million in administrative and programme support services, and $11.6 million in field office costs. Agency support costs amounted to $14.1 million.

At the end of 1989, UNFPA was assisting 3,538 projects: 2,596 country and 942 regional and intercountry projects. Some 229 projects were completed during the year, bringing to 3,173 the cumulative total of all projects completed until the end of 1989.

Assistance to MCH/FP programmes totalled $89.8 million, 46.3 per cent of total allocations. UNFPA supported more than 500 country and intercountry family planning projects, approximately two thirds of which were in the Africa and Asia and Pacific regions.

A highlight of UNFPA technical assistance was the transformation of the Tunisian national training programme in family planning into an international programme, with the establishment in Tunis of an international training centre for family planning for French-speaking countries, particularly those in Africa. UNFPA developed a diagnostic instrument covering management information inputs, outputs, quality and impact during the year, and used it to diagnose management information systems in countries in the Africa, Asia and Pacific, and Latin America and Caribbean regions. It also examined the MCH/FP logistics systems of 18 sub-Saharan African countries.

The Fund continued to support the improvement of contraceptive technologies. It organized an in-house seminar for headquarters staff on community-based MCH/FP programmes in rural areas. On 30 June, the UNDP Governing Council requested[10] the UNFPA Executive Director to submit in 1991 a report detailing the Fund's current expenditures for contraceptives and its estimate of the contraceptive requirements of developing countries in the 1990s.

UNFPA assistance for information, education and communication totalled $32.7 million, 16.8 per cent of total programme allocations. The Fund helped to develop strategies in that field for country programming exercises, to clarify national population objectives, identify key target groups, select appropriate communications channels, and design information and education messages. Other projects included: using modern communications technology, such as videotape and computer graphics, to reach groups with low levels of literacy; educating adolescents as to how to deal with reproductive health issues and AIDS prevention; examining educational approaches to reach newly married couples; and integrating the safe-motherhood concept into population education programmes. UNFPA assessed training institutions in both developed and developing countries and contributed to an action plan to assess communication needs to support development in Africa in the 1990s. The Fund expanded activities related to non-formal education in order to reach the large number of school drop-outs and unschooled youth, and provided support for national sex-education programmes.

Basic data collection received $21.1 million, 10.9 per cent of total allocations. Some 74 country projects under the 1990 round of population censuses were supported, the majority in Africa. Assistance was provided for population sample surveys, to establish or strengthen civil registration and vital statistics systems, and for demographic analysis and training.

UNFPA allocated $37.6 million, 19.3 per cent of its assistance, to programmes on population dynamics, formulation and evaluation of population policies, and implementation of policies. This aid aimed at developing suitable methodological techniques for policy formulation and development planning, strengthening national technical capacities, and setting up institutional arrangements for population policies. Activities included studies on the social and economic consequences of population trends; the interrelationship between population, environment, resources and development; the formulation and evaluation of development policies; and the integration of population factors into national development plans.

Assistance for women, population and development activities amounted to $5.9 million, 3.1 per cent of total allocations. The Fund continued to strengthen its capacity to deal with those issues. The UNFPA Advisory Panel on Women, Population and Development (New York, February) made recommendations regarding implementation of the UNFPA strategy, the 1989 *State of World Population* report, and background documents for the International Forum on Population in the Twenty-first Century (see below). Following a mid-term review, the UNFPA Executive Director, in reporting on implementation of the strategy,[11] stated that the Fund would continue to focus attention on training activities to ensure that all international staff, as well as other policy makers, acquired skills for incorporating women's concerns and needs into all population and development activities.

On 30 June, the UNDP Governing Council requested[10] the UNFPA Executive Director to report in 1991 on the final two years of the implementation of the strategy to strengthen the Fund's capacity to deal with issues concerning women, population and development.

Training workshops on issues of special importance in the area of women, population and development were organized in the Asia and Pacific and Latin America and Caribbean regions. In-depth evaluations of UNFPA-supported programmes underscored the need for: sharpening the focus on the women's dimension in the terms of reference for evaluation missions; requiring that the women's dimension be included in evaluation reports; identifying shortcomings in evaluated programmes; and providing practical and concrete approaches to reflect women's concerns more effectively in the programmes.

Special programme interests—youth, aging and AIDS—received $1.6 million in assistance, 0.8 per cent of allocations. UNFPA-supported projects aimed at youth focused on the areas of population and family life education, communication and family planning. Projects in the field of aging sought to increase the awareness of policy makers and strengthen the capability of developing countries to understand the causes and implications of population aging and its interrelationship with socio-economic development. UNFPA special components on AIDS were integrated into MCH/FP and information and education projects in several countries. Collaborative work continued under the Global Programme on AIDS of the World Health Organization (WHO), and with other organizations, notably the UN Children's Fund.

Review and assessment of population experience

The findings of a two-year review and assessment of accumulated population experience by UNFPA were discussed in an April report to the UNDP Governing Council by the UNFPA Executive Director.[12] He recommended that the Council endorse the strengthening of population interventions by developing countries in the 1990s, as well as future population goals.

On 30 June, the Council expressed concern[13] at the high rate of population growth and its social, economic and environmental implications for the 1990s and beyond. It endorsed the general population goals and approaches contained in the UNFPA report and requested the development of financial resource requirements for international population assistance.

International Forum on Population

The International Forum on Population in the Twenty-first Century (Amsterdam, Netherlands, 6-9 November), organized by UNFPA in co-operation with the Government of the Netherlands, brought together some 250 senior government officials and population experts from around the world to discuss the most important population questions of the 1990s and beyond. Participants discussed ways to implement population policies and programmes more effectively, and recommended strategies for mobilizing resources to support future population activities.

The Forum issued a declaration entitled "A Better Life for Future Generations", recommending specific population goals and objectives to be achieved by the year 2000, including: an increase in family planning user couples from 326 million to 535 million; a substantial reduction in very early marriage and in teenage pregnancy; a reduction of infant mortality rates to, at most, 50 per 1,000 live births and of maternal mortality rates by at least 50 per cent; and an increase in life expectancy at birth to 62 years or more for men and women in countries with high mortality.

The Amsterdam Declaration called on all countries to increase their commitment to population policies and programmes, as well as to contribute to the development of comprehensive population objectives and goals. All countries should make every effort to provide the financial resources necessary to reach the UN medium variant population projection by the year 2000, estimated at $9 billion a year by that time, approximately double the current level of such resources.

GENERAL ASSEMBLY ACTION

On 22 December, on the recommendation of the Second (Economic and Financial) Committee, the

General Assembly adopted **resolution 44/210** without vote.

Future needs in the field of population, including the development of resource requirements for international population assistance

The General Assembly,

Reaffirming the principles and objectives of the World Population Plan of Action, which were affirmed and expanded at the International Conference on Population,

Recalling decision 87/30 of 18 June 1987 of the Governing Council of the United Nations Development Programme, in which the Governing Council welcomed the intention of the United Nations Population Fund to conduct a wide-ranging review and assessment of accumulated population experience in key areas within its mandate,

Recalling also its resolution 43/199 of 20 December 1988, in which it welcomed the review and assessment being conducted by the United Nations Population Fund of its experience in the field of population and requested that an appropriate summary of the main findings, conclusions and recommendations be submitted to the General Assembly at its forty-fourth session,

Mindful of the diversity in culture and traditions and in social, economic and political conditions among countries, and respectful of the national sovereignty of all countries with regard to the formulation, promotion and implementation of their own population policies,

1. *Takes note* of the report prepared by the United Nations Population Fund containing the findings, conclusions and recommendations resulting from its review and assessment of population programme experience;

2. *Takes note with appreciation* of the Amsterdam Declaration on A Better Life for Future Generations, adopted by the International Forum on Population in the Twenty-first Century, held at Amsterdam from 6 to 9 November 1989;

3. *Stresses* the importance of taking duly into account the outcome of the International Forum in the preparations for and deliberations on relevant forthcoming United Nations conferences, particularly the proposed international meeting on population in 1994, and in the preparation of the international development strategy for the fourth United Nations development decade;

4. *Requests* the Executive Director of the United Nations Population Fund:

(*a*) To bring the results of the International Forum to the attention of Governments, United Nations organizations and non-governmental organizations;

(*b*) To examine in particular the implications of the Amsterdam Declaration for population programmes and to develop further the analysis of resource requirements for international population assistance;

(*c*) To submit a report thereon to the General Assembly at its forty-fifth session, through the Governing Council of the United Nations Development Programme and the Economic and Social Council.

General Assembly resolution 44/210

22 December 1989   Meeting 85   Adopted without vote

Approved by Second Committee (A/44/863) by consensus, 15 December (meeting 50); draft by Vice-Chairman (A/C.2/44/L.79), based on informal consultations on 19-nation draft (A/C.2/44/L.67); agenda item 86.
Meeting numbers. GA 44th session: 2nd Committee 30, 37-43, 47, 49, 50; plenary 85.

Population and the environment

In March, the UNFPA Executive Director reported[14] on the Fund's programmes and projects aimed at sustainable development. Efforts to incorporate environmental and resource concerns into population activities were examined and an overview given of current activities in the area of population, environment and sustainable development. The report also contained suggestions on how to ensure the integration of environmental concerns into population activities.

On 30 June,[10] the UNDP Governing Council encouraged the Fund to continue to develop insight into the relationship between population, environment and development.

Country and intercountry programmes

In 1989, UNFPA focused on the needs of 56 priority countries, 31 of which were in Africa, 16 in Asia and the Pacific, 6 among the Arab States and 3 in Latin America and the Caribbean. Of total resources allocated in 1989 to country programmes and projects, 74.6 per cent was allocated to those priority countries. Allocations for intercountry activities (regional, interregional and global) totalled $52.7 million, 27.1 per cent of allocations.

In May, the UNFPA Executive Director reported[15] on implementation of the Fund's 1988-1991 intercountry programme. It was noted that improvement was needed in the areas of technical backstopping and research, and that the lack of timely recruitment reduced the effectiveness of technical backstopping and thus affected the pace of project implementation.

On 30 June, the UNDP Governing Council requested[16] the Executive Director to include information on the status of the Fund's intercountry programme in his report for 1989. The Council also approved country programmes for Algeria, the Central African Republic, Chad, China, the Comoros, El Salvador, Mauritius, Nicaragua, Panama, the Philippines, Sao Tome and Principe, Togo and Zimbabwe.

Also on 30 June, the Council requested[17] that the Executive Director provide information on the number, cost and placement by agency of regional and interregional advisory services. He was also to review periodically the adequacy of existing arrangements for providing advisory services with a view to ensuring requisite standards of quality, cost and effectiveness. The Council invited UN entities with UNFPA-funded advisory posts to integrate population posts into their regular budgets.

In April, the UNFPA Executive Director reported[18] on the status of the strategy for the Fund's assistance to sub-Saharan Africa. She stated that UNFPA had made significant strides towards achieving the objectives set forth in the strategy in the previous two years, and that the

Fund would intensify efforts at both country and regional levels to improve implementation of approved country programmes in sub-Saharan Africa. On 30 June, the UNDP Governing Council requested[10] the Executive Director to report in 1991 on the status of support for the establishment of a regional information, education and communication clearing-house and regional training centres on population, education, communication and MCH/FP. She was also to report on issues surrounding the financing of technical assistance provided to demographic centres in the African countries, including the question of increasing such financing.

Work programmes,
planning and evaluation, financing

In an April report[19] on the work plan for 1990-1993, the UNFPA Executive Director provided information on the Fund's resource situation and utilization, and distribution of programmable resources between country and intercountry activities. It also provided information on allocations and utilization of resources in 1988. Another report[20] gave the status of financial implementation of UNDP Governing Council–approved UNFPA programmes and projects.

On 30 June, the Governing Council, on the basis of the UNFPA report,[19] endorsed[21] the use of the following estimates for new programmable resources for 1991-1993: $172.8 million for 1991, $191.1 million for 1992 and $211.3 million for 1993. The Council approved the revised programme ceiling for 1989 of $191.6 million and the request for programme expenditure authority in the amount of $156.2 million for 1990.

Evaluation activities of UNFPA, intensified in 1988-1989, as well as the independent, in-depth evaluations undertaken during that period, were outlined in a March report by the UNFPA Executive Director.[22] Evaluation activities were seen as a useful management tool, with their focus shifted from individual projects to country and intercountry programmes and to technical areas and issues in a global comparative perspective. The Fund introduced in 1989 the Programme Review and Strategy Development exercise, combining evaluation, needs assessment and strategy development, which took the place of separate country programme evaluations.

Evaluations were undertaken in Indonesia, Nicaragua and Zimbabwe in 1988, and in Nigeria and Zaire in 1989. Also evaluated were the intercountry programmes of the Food and Agriculture Organization of the United Nations and the International Labour Organisation and those of the WHO Regional Offices for Africa and for the Eastern Mediterranean. UNFPA conducted a series of diagnostic exercises of MCH/FP management information systems in 27 sub-Saharan African, 5 Asian and 8 Latin American and Caribbean countries in 1989. It also studied five approaches being carried out in Indonesia, Mexico and the Philippines in the area of family planning education and services for newly-weds.

In 1989, the UNDP Governing Council had before it budget estimates for UNFPA administrative and programme support services for the 1990-1991 biennium.[23] The total biennial budget amounted to $84.2 million, compared to $63.2 million for 1988-1989.

On 30 June, the Council approved[24] gross appropriations of $83,492,500 to finance the 1990-1991 biennial budget for administrative and programme support services.

Other population activities

Population Commission

The Population Commission, at its twenty-fifth session (New York, 21 February–2 March),[25] reviewed action taken by the United Nations to implement the recommendations of the 1974 World Population Conference,[1] programme implementation, the proposed programme of work for the biennium 1990-1991, the medium-term plan for 1992-1997, and follow-up to the recommendations of the 1984 International Conference on Population.[3]

On 26 July, the Economic and Social Council, by **decision 1989/170**, approved the provisional agenda and documentation for the Commission's twenty-sixth (1991) session. Also on that date, by **decision 1989/171**, the Council noted the report of the Commission on its 1989 session[25] and reports by the Secretary-General and the UNDP Governing Council relating to population issues.

Population work programme

In response to Economic and Social Council requests of 1986[26] and 1987,[7] the Secretary-General submitted to the Council, through the Population Commission, an overview[4] of the main activities in the field of population carried out by the various organizations of the UN system.

The overview covered socio-economic development, the environment and population; the role and status of women; development of population policies; population goals and policies; and promotion of knowledge and policy. The institutional framework, resources and co-ordination of population activities in the UN system were also described.

In a report on monitoring multilateral population assistance,[6] the Secretary-General concluded that the concept of population programmes was taking root in the developing countries. He stated that population policy formulation within the context of development would become increasingly important and would thus require greater attention by the multilateral system in the future. While that sentiment was widely accepted, multilateral assistance was quite inadequate compared to the demand and need for population programmes in developing countries.

The Secretary-General also submitted two reports on the progress of recent work of the UN Secretariat in the field of population. One report[27] described the work in the areas of world demographic analysis, demographic projections, population policies, population and development, monitoring and review and appraisal, factors affecting patterns of reproduction and dissemination of population information. The other[28] detailed technical co-operation activities during the period 1 July 1987 to 30 June 1988, particularly support for projects in training in demography and population, evaluation and analysis of basic population and demographic data, and population policy planning and development; and analysis and evaluation of technical co-operation activities in population.

ECONOMIC AND SOCIAL COUNCIL ACTION

On 26 July, on the recommendation of its First Committee, the Economic and Social Council adopted **resolution 1989/94** without vote.

United Nations support for African countries in the field of population

The Economic and Social Council,

Recalling General Assembly resolutions S-13/2 of 1 June 1986, the annex to which contains the United Nations Programme of Action for African Economic Recovery and Development 1986-1990, and 43/27 of 18 November 1988 on the mid-term review and appraisal of the implementation of the Programme,

Recalling also the Kilimanjaro Programme of Action for African Population and Self-Reliant Development adopted by the Second African Population Conference and endorsed by the Economic Commission for Africa,

Noting with satisfaction the activities carried out in the field of population by the organizations of the United Nations system, as reported by the Secretary-General, and especially the priority given by the United Nations Population Fund to African countries in view of the serious economic and social problems they face,

Reaffirming the need for technical assistance and financial resources for training additional personnel in African countries so as to ensure that those countries are able to effectively implement policies to harmonize population growth with economic and environmental capacities,

1. *Welcomes* the proposed programme of work for the biennium 1990-1991 in technical co-operation in the field of population;

2. *Requests* the Secretary-General to ensure the continued availability of funds for technical co-operation in the field of population, particularly for fellowships for training at the United Nations–supported Cairo Demographic Centre, the Regional Institute for Population Studies at Accra, the Institut de formation et de recherche démographiques at Yaoundé and other United Nations demographic centres and programmes serving African countries;

3. *Requests* the organizations of the United Nations system to give priority to population needs and problems in Africa in accordance with the United Nations Programme of Action for African Economic Recovery and Development 1986-1990.

Economic and Social Council resolution 1989/94

26 July 1989   Meeting 35   Adopted without vote

Approved by First Committee (E/1989/139) without vote, 21 July (meeting 25); draft by Population Commission (E/1989/24); agenda item 7 *(d)*.

1990-1991 work programme

In January, the Secretary-General, reporting[29] on the proposed UN work programme for the 1990-1991 biennium in the area of population, said it was designed to carry out research of the highest priority, to disseminate research findings in an effective manner and to provide support for technical co-operation projects in the field of population.

ECONOMIC AND SOCIAL COUNCIL ACTION

On 26 July, on the recommendation of its First Committee, the Economic and Social Council adopted **resolution 1989/93** without vote.

Work programme in the field of population

The Economic and Social Council,

Recalling General Assembly resolutions 3344(XXIX) and 3345(XXIX) of 17 December 1974, concerning the recommendations of the United Nations World Population Conference, and 39/228 of 18 December 1984 on the International Conference on Population,

Recalling also Economic and Social Council resolutions 1981/28 of 6 May 1981 on the strengthening of actions concerned with the fulfilment of the World Population Plan of Action, 1985/3 on population structure, 1985/4 on the implications of the recommendations of the International Conference on Population and 1985/6 on the status and role of women and population, all of 28 May 1985, 1986/7 of 21 May 1986 on population questions and 1987/71 of 8 July 1987 on the work programme in the field of population,

Stressing the supportive role of the work programmes of the United Nations system in the field of population in the attainment of the goals and objectives of the international development strategy for the fourth United Nations development decade and the pursuit of economic co-operation,

Recalling the preamble, the section on peace, security and population, and the other sections of the recommendations for the further implementation of the World Population Plan of Action adopted by the International Conference on Population, at which it was reaffirmed that the principles and objectives of the World Population Plan of Action remained fully valid and that creating conditions for international peace and security was of great importance for the achievement of the goals of population policies and economic and social development and at which emphasis was placed on a number of issues in the field of population that should continue to be included in the work programme, as appropriate,

Reaffirming the important role of the Population Commission as the advisory body of the Economic and Social Council on population matters,

Taking note of the report of the Population Commission on its twenty-fifth session and the views expressed therein on the progress of work in the field of population and the proposed work programme,

1. *Notes with satisfaction* the progress made in implementing the work programme for the biennium 1988-1989 and the medium-term plan for the period 1984-1991 in the field of population;

2. *Requests* the Secretary-General, in formulating the medium-term plan for the period 1992-1997, to take into account, as appropriate, the views expressed at the twenty-fifth session of the Population Commission and the guidelines for the work programmes of the United Nations Secretariat set out in paragraphs 3 and 4 of the present resolution;

3. *Also requests* the Secretary-General:

(*a*) To continue to give high priority to the monitoring of world population trends and policies, including in-depth consideration of special topics;

(*b*) To continue work on the following:

(i) Studies on the interrelationships between population, resources, environment and development, with particular attention to studies to promote the integration of population factors into development planning;

(ii) Studies on the interrelationship between population and the status and role of women;

(iii) Comparative analysis of population policies;

(iv) Periodic revision of estimates and projections of population and its structure and of urbanization;

(v) Analysis of mortality, in particular infant and child mortality;

(vi) Studies on reproductive behaviour and on family planning and its demographic impact;

(vii) Studies on internal and international migration and on comparative patterns of urbanization and population distribution;

(viii) Dissemination of population information and further development of the Population Information Network at the regional and global levels;

(*c*) To start substantive preparatory work for the international meeting on population in 1994, as appropriate;

(*d*) To continue to work closely with Member States, organizations of the United Nations system, other intergovernmental organizations and non-governmental organizations, as appropriate, in the implementation of programmes;

(*e*) To further improve communication and co-ordination between the Population Division of the United Nations Secretariat, the regional commissions and Governments, particularly in order to prepare the most accurate and widely accepted population estimates and projections possible, an activity in which the Population Division should play a leading role;

4. *Further requests* the Secretary-General:

(*a*) To continue and strengthen interdisciplinary technical co-operation activities in the field of population, including technical co-operation among developing countries, as appropriate, in the following areas:

(i) Training in demography and matters related to population and development, including courses to upgrade knowledge and skills, particularly in the use of microcomputer software;

(ii) Evaluation and analysis of basic population data, particularly from the 1990 round of population censuses, dissemination and utilization of the results and use of computer technology, ensuring technical co-ordination at the national level in the process;

(iii) Formulation and implementation of population policies and programmes in the context of national development plans, with special attention to cultural and socio-economic conditions at the subnational level;

(*b*) To continue to evaluate and analyse experience with technical co-operation activities in the field of population and publish studies thereon;

(*c*) To prepare for the Population Commission at its twenty-sixth session a report on requirements for population specialists in national institutions and international organizations;

5. *Re-emphasizes* the importance of maintaining the scope, effectiveness and efficiency of the global population programme and of continuing to strengthen co-ordination and collaboration among the Department of International Economic and Social Affairs, the Department of Technical Co-operation for Development, the regional commissions, the United Nations Population Fund and other organizations and bodies of the United Nations system in the planning and execution of their population programmes, as well as the need for organizations of the United Nations system to strengthen co-ordination and collaboration with Member States, other intergovernmental organizations and non-governmental and national organizations, as appropriate.

Economic and Social Council resolution 1989/93

26 July 1989   Meeting 35   Adopted without vote

Approved by First Committee (E/1989/139) without vote, 21 July (meeting 25); draft by Population Commission (E/1989/24); agenda item 7 *(d)*.

Population trends and policies

In January, the Secretary-General submitted a report[30] to the Economic and Social Council on monitoring world population trends and policies, with special emphasis on the population situation in the least developed countries. Trends included population growth, structure, mortality, fertility, population distribution, and international migration in all countries.

ECONOMIC AND SOCIAL COUNCIL ACTION

On 26 July, on the recommendation of its First Committee, the Economic and Social Council adopted **resolution 1989/89** without vote.

Population situation in the least developed countries

The Economic and Social Council,

Recalling General Assembly resolutions 42/177 of 11 December 1987 and 43/186 of 20 December 1988 on the

Second United Nations Conference on the Least Developed Countries, to be held in September 1990,

Reaffirming the close relationship between population and social and economic development,

Expressing serious concern at the fact that the least developed countries, which are economically the weakest members of the international community, face serious demographic challenges, in particular high levels of mortality, fertility and population growth,

Recognizing also the need for special attention to be given to the population situation in the least developed countries,

Expressing appreciation for the report of the Secretary-General on the monitoring of world population trends and policies, with special emphasis on the population situation in the least developed countries,

1. *Decides* that special attention shall be accorded, in the activities of the United Nations system, to the population situation in the least developed countries;

2. *Recommends* that population issues be incorporated in the policies and measures to be adopted by the Second United Nations Conference on the Least Developed Countries to accelerate the development process of the least developed countries during the 1990s;

3. *Requests* the Secretary-General of the Conference to address appropriately population issues and their relationship to the socio-economic development of the least developed countries in the preparations for the Conference;

4. *Requests* the Secretary-General to prepare for the Conference a report on the population situation in the least developed countries, with specific recommendations for action at the national, regional and international levels, taking into account the findings regarding the situation in the least developed countries contained in his report on the monitoring of world population trends and policies, in particular the high levels of mortality, fertility and population growth in those countries;

5. *Also requests* the Secretary-General to include a separate analysis on the population situation in the least developed countries in his reports on the monitoring of world population trends and policies;

6. *Calls upon* the organizations of the United Nations system to incorporate population issues in their programmes and activities relating to the least developed countries, with a view to strengthening the ability of those countries to address population issues in an effective manner.

Economic and Social Council resolution 1989/89

26 July 1989   Meeting 35   Adopted without vote

Approved by First Committee (E/1989/139) without vote, 21 July (meeting 25); draft by Population Commission (E/1989/24); agenda item 7 *(d)*.

Also on 26 July and on the recommendation of its First Committee, the Council adopted **resolution 1989/90** without vote.

Incorporating population factors in the international development strategy for the fourth United Nations development decade

The Economic and Social Council,

Recalling General Assembly resolution 43/182 of 20 December 1988, in which the Assembly decided to establish an *Ad Hoc* Committee of the Whole for the Preparation of the International Development Strategy for the Fourth United Nations Development Decade,

Recalling also the recommendations of the United Nations World Population Conference, in particular those contained in the World Population Plan of Action, in which it is stated, *inter alia*, that the explicit aim of the Plan is to help co-ordinate trends in population and trends in economic and social development and that population measures should be integrated into comprehensive social and economic plans and programmes,

Recalling the section on population of the Environmental Perspective to the Year 2000 and Beyond, contained in the annex to General Assembly resolution 42/186 of 11 December 1987,

Recalling its own resolution 1979/32 of 9 May 1979 and the annex thereto, in particular section C, paragraph 2, in which it urged that the results of periodic monitoring, review and appraisal, regional consultations on population and development and associated activities of appropriate agencies of the United Nations should be fully taken into account in the formulation of any new international development strategy,

Recalling also the recommendations of the International Conference on Population, in particular recommendation 1, which states that social and economic development is a central factor in the solution of population and interrelated problems, that population factors are very important in development plans and strategies and have a major impact on the attainment of development objectives and that international development strategies should therefore be formulated on the basis of an integrated approach that takes into account the interrelationships between population, resources, environment and development,

Noting with satisfaction the recognition of the role of population factors in the International Development Strategy for the Third United Nations Development Decade, in paragraph 166 of which it is stated that population policies will be considered an integral part of overall development policies and that all countries will continue to integrate their population measures and programmes into their social and economic goals and strategies,

1. *Urges* all States, in formulating the international development strategy for the fourth United Nations development decade, to give full consideration to the interrelationships between population factors, social, economic, cultural and political development and protection of the environment;

2. *Calls upon* organs, organizations and bodies of the United Nations system, in contributing to the preparation of the international development strategy for the fourth United Nations development decade, to give appropriate recognition to the interrelationships between population factors, social, economic, cultural and political development and the protection of the environment, taking into account the section on population of the Environmental Perspective to the Year 2000 and Beyond;

3. *Requests* the Secretary-General to ensure that the contributions of the secretariats of the organizations of the United Nations system to the preparation of the international development strategy take due account of the World Population Plan of Action and the recommendations for its further implementation adopted by the International Conference on Population;

4. *Recommends* that the General Assembly, in considering the international development strategy for the fourth United Nations development decade, give due weight to the role of population and the importance of population policies and activities and duly integrate them into the goals and objectives and the policy measures of the strategy.

Economic and Social Council resolution 1989/90

26 July 1989   Meeting 35   Adopted without vote

Approved by First Committee (E/1989/139) without vote, 21 July (meeting 25); draft by Population Commission (E/1989/24); agenda item 7 *(d)*.

UN Population Award

In June, the Secretary-General presented the 1989 United Nations Population Award to President Soeharto of Indonesia and the Programme national de bien-être familial of Togo.[31]

The Award, presented annually by the Committee for the United Nations Population Award to individuals or institutions for the most outstanding contribution to the awareness of population questions or to their solutions, consists of a diploma, a gold medal and a monetary prize.

REFERENCES
[1]YUN 1974, p. 550. [2]E/CN.9/1989/2. [3]YUN 1984, p. 714. [4]E/1989/11. [5]E/CN.9/1989/7. [6]E/1989/12. [7]YUN 1987, p. 632, ESC res. 1987/72, 8 July 1987. [8]E/CN.9/1989/6. [9]E/CN.9/1989/3. [10]E/1989/32 (dec. 89/46 A). [11]DP/1989/36. [12]DP/1989/37. [13]E/1989/32 (dec. 89/48). [14]DP/1989/39. [15]DP/1989/70. [16]E/1989/32 (dec. 89/46 C). [17]*Ibid.* (dec. 89/47). [18]DP/1989/38. [19]DP/1989/34. [20]DP/1989/35. [21]E/1989/32 (dec. 89/46 B). [22]DP/1990/49. [23]DP/1989/41 & Corr.1. [24]E/1989/32 (dec. 89/49). [25]E/1989/24. [26]YUN 1986, p. 627, ESC res. 1986/7, 21 May 1986. [27]E/CN.9/1989/4. [28]E/CN.9/1989/4/Add.1. [29]E/CN.9/1989/5. [30]E/1989/10. [31]A/45/278.

Human settlements

Commission on Human Settlements

At its twelfth session (Cartagena de Indias, Colombia, 24 April–3 May 1989),[1] the Commission on Human Settlements adopted its first report[2] to the General Assembly on the implementation of the Global Strategy for Shelter to the Year 2000, adopted in 1988.[3] It decided to establish a Latin American and Caribbean Centre for the Exchange and Promotion of Human Settlements Technologies as a contribution to the fulfilment of the objectives of the Global Strategy.[4]

Other topics dealt with by the Commission included: assistance to the Namibian people and victims of *apartheid* in Africa, conditions of human settlements in Lebanon, promotion of low-cost shelter construction, adoption of a strategy and mechanism for the early mobilization of human settlements project sites, housing conditions of the Palestinian people in the occupied territories, a programme for the eradication of poor housing conditions and for the urban rehabilitation of historic centres, and the contribution of the Commission to the preparations for a UN conference on environment and development in 1992.

ECONOMIC AND SOCIAL COUNCIL ACTION

On 26 July, the Economic and Social Council, by **decision 1989/172**, noted the report[1] of the Commission on Human Settlements on its twelfth session and on the implementation of the Global Strategy for Shelter to the Year 2000. By the same decision, the Council took note of the Secretary-General's note on the living conditions of the Palestinian people in the occupied Palestinian territories (see PART TWO, Chapter IV).

1991 session

On 2 May, the Commission, recalling its 1988 decision regarding the selection of two themes for its thirteenth (1991) session and having considered the report by the Executive Director of the UN Centre for Human Settlements (UNCHS) on themes for consideration,[5] requested[6] the Executive Director to prepare two papers for that session: one on the significance of human settlements and the Global Strategy for Shelter to the year 2000 for the concept of sustainable development, and another on the use of energy by households, in construction and in production of building materials, with emphasis on renewable, non-polluting energy sources. It also decided to consider in 1991 the inclusion of two of the following themes in the agenda of its 1993 session: the improvement of metropolitan and municipal management; land policies with emphasis on access and affordability to low-income groups; and natural disaster reduction and its effect on the construction and maintenance of buildings.

Human settlements activities

Global Strategy for Shelter to the Year 2000

In 1988, the General Assembly had adopted[3] the Global Strategy for Shelter to the Year 2000, to facilitate the provision of shelter for all by then, and requested the Commission to report biennially on progress made.

In February, the UNCHS Executive Director issued a report,[7] proposing a series of activities for the Centre in support of the Strategy's first phase (1989-1991). Those activities covered: technical assistance in the formulation of national shelter strategies; support to lead countries in the establishment of Strategy monitoring and evaluation capabilities; development of shelter-sector training capacities; and promotion of awareness of the Global Strategy among policy makers and professionals in developing countries. A budget was suggested for which donors might make contributions to a special Global Strategy account under the UN Habitat and Human Settlements Foundation. The report also suggested guidelines for the monitoring of national shelter strategies by Governments. A series of indicators were identified, by which progress in the implementation of the Strategy could be measured.

Pursuant to a 1988 General Assembly request,[3] the Commission submitted in June the first biennial report on the implementation of the Global Strategy,[8] covering the period between its formulation in April 1988 and the review of progress at the Commission's twelfth session in May 1989. The report outlined the general framework and timetable for the Global Strategy as follows: formulation of national shelter strategies, design of new institutional arrangements and implementation of national programmes (1989-1991); introduction of new institutional arrangements and strengthening of existing national programmes (1992-1994); and the full-scale operation of national programmes and progressive strengthening of institutions beyond the year 2000 (1995-2000). The main principles of the Strategy were summarized as follows: enabling policies should be at the heart of national and international efforts; the important links between shelter and economic development had to be recognized in policy-making; sustainable management of the environment should be an important factor in designing programmes; and the role of women, as income-earners, home-makers and heads of households, should be fully recognized. Annexed to the report was the 1989-1991 Plan of Action for the Strategy.

The Consultative Committee on Substantive Questions (Programme Matters) of the Administrative Committee on Co-ordination, in considering the implementation of the Global Strategy, noted that UNCHS would be designated as the lead agency for implementation and would exercise a certain degree of flexibility with regard to the modality for inter-agency co-operation in that area.[9]

On 3 May, the Commission adopted[10] its first report on the implementation of the Global Strategy,[8] and urged Governments to prepare annual progress reports on national shelter strategies. It requested the UNCHS Executive Director to use the Global Strategy as an overall guide for all Centre activities, and to report to the Commission in 1991 on implementation of the first phase of the Strategy.

On 2 May, the Commission urged[11] the international community to: establish conditions that favoured the generation of investments in developing countries, which would include an essential factor in attaining the objectives of the Global Strategy; assume their responsibilities in the allocation of resources required for the implementation of the Strategy; and consider shelter as an investment in a social asset. The Commission also appealed to all Governments and relevant institutions and organizations to ensure that appropriate consideration was given to the needs and requirements for low-income groups in the implementation of the Strategy.[12]

The Commission recommended that the UNCHS Executive Director prepare a study on the possibilities of formulating a strategy and mechanism to ensure early mobilization of human settlements project sites for implementation within the Global Strategy, and requested him to incorporate the results of that study in a 1993 report on land policy.[13]

Governmental and non-governmental sectors

In a report on the roles, responsibilities and capabilities of governmental and non-governmental sectors in the field of human settlements,[14] the Executive Director identified recent policy and institutional innovations in the management of human settlements, and outlined policy options available to Governments in deepening the involvement of different sectors in that area. Considering that report, as well as a report on 49 case-studies of recent policy initiatives in decentralization and non-governmental sector participation in the field of human settlements,[15] the Commission requested the Executive Director, in the development of the Global Strategy, to develop the relations between government and the private and community sectors in areas such as the supply of urban services, housing and land, and to encourage effective community participation at all levels in human settlements programmes.[16] The Commission also requested Governments to take steps to help shelter organizations to increase their co-operation with their respective partners abroad, and requested them and the Executive Director to report on those aspects of the Global Strategy.

Maintenance of buildings

In a report on the maintenance of buildings and infrastructure,[17] the Executive Director proposed national and international action to improve maintenance practices. In another report,[18] he reviewed the funding practices of local authorities concerned with the maintenance of buildings and infrastructure and examined strategies to improve revenue generation, accounting and budgeting procedures. On 2 May, the Commission urged[19] Governments to reflect the significance of the maintenance of buildings and infrastructure in their national development programmes and budgets as a contribution towards the implementation of the Global Strategy. It requested the Executive Director to incorporate in the work programme of UNCHS the issues of building maintenance and actively encourage international co-operation.

Aid for human settlements

In considering the Global Strategy, the Commission considered the Executive Director's report on financial and other assistance for developing countries for human settlements.[20] Noting that a low priority had been accorded to aid for human settlements, the report outlined remedies for that problem, including increasing the scale of aid, setting new priorities for aid and utilizing new channels to meet poor groups' basic needs. From 1980 to 1987, less than 2 per cent of all bilateral and multilateral aid programmes had gone to "shelter" projects; in 1985 and 1986, less than 6 per cent of bilateral aid from members of the Organisation for Economic Co-operation and Development was directed to water supply and less than 6 per cent to health and population.

GENERAL ASSEMBLY ACTION

On 19 December, on the recommendation of the Second Committee, the General Assembly adopted **resolution 44/173** without vote.

Global Strategy for Shelter to the Year 2000
The General Assembly,

Recalling its resolution 43/181 of 20 December 1988, in which it designated the Commission on Human Settlements as the United Nations intergovernmental body responsible for co-ordinating, evaluating and monitoring the Global Strategy for Shelter to the Year 2000, the core of which consists of integrated national shelter strategies,

Also recalling its request, contained in paragraph 7 of resolution 43/181, that the Commission on Human Settlements, as the body designated to co-ordinate implementation of the Global Strategy, report biennially to the General Assembly on progress made in its implementation,

Recognizing that the Global Strategy is the most ambitious programme that the international community has so far adopted in the human settlements sector and, as such, requires the concerted efforts of all Member States, United Nations bodies and donor agencies, as well as the entire attention of the United Nations Centre for Human Settlements (Habitat),

Convinced that, while integrating the most effective and efficient policy tools in all action areas, national shelter strategies can be crucial instruments of enablement leading to the full mobilization of all types of resources on a sustainable basis and thereby facilitating adequate shelter for all by the year 2000,

Paying special attention to the need to ensure equal access to available resources by all population groups, while recognizing the critical role that women should play in the implementation of the Global Strategy, as well as the need to remove obstacles that some population groups, such as households headed by women, may face in this respect,

Concerned about the economic constraints many countries face in their development efforts, but at the same time encouraged by the positive impact which enabling shelter strategies have on economic development,

Emphasizing that the objective of facilitating shelter for all can be promoted by a national strategy which is recognized and supported at the highest possible political level, adjusted to the macro-economic need of consolidating the national resource base and minimizing the import content, based on nationally and individually affordable standards, flexible in terms of the diversity of shelter priorities and specific in terms of institutional arrangements for partnership between various sectors of implementation,

Having considered the first report of the Commission on Human Settlements on the implementation of the Global Strategy for Shelter to the Year 2000,

Noting with satisfaction the support given to the Plan of Action of the Global Strategy by donor Governments and international bodies and agencies in assisting Governments in the formulation of their national shelter strategies,

Cognizant of the importance of sustaining and expanding national and international support to this crucial phase of the Plan of Action,

Noting that, when considering future voluntary contributions to the United Nations Habitat and Human Settlements Foundation, donors will be influenced by the degree of emphasis of the work programme of the United Nations Centre for Human Settlements (Habitat) on the Global Strategy and by the priorities within the Global Strategy reflected in that programme,

1. *Commends* Governments which are reviewing, revising and consolidating their national shelter strategies, as well as implementing them with great determination, and urges all other Governments to do the same;

2. *Recommends* that all Governments gradually set in place the monitoring system to be proposed by the Executive Director of the United Nations Centre for Human Settlements (Habitat), following the guidelines to be prepared by the Executive Director;

3. *Invites* Governments to make voluntary contributions whenever possible to the United Nations Habitat and Human Settlements Foundation, in cash or in kind, in order to facilitate the implementation of the Global Strategy for Shelter to the Year 2000;

4. *Urges* the organizations of the United Nations system, particularly the United Nations Development Programme, and other multilateral and bilateral agencies to provide financial and other support to the implementation of the Plan of Action of the Global Strategy.

General Assembly resolution 44/173

19 December 1989   Meeting 83   Adopted without vote

Approved by Second Committee (A/44/746/Add.9) without vote, 3 November (meeting 30); draft by Commission on Human Settlements (A/44/8); agenda item 82 *(h)*.
Meeting numbers. GA 44th session: 2nd Committee 10-13, 29, 30; plenary 83.

Human settlements and political, economic and social issues

Assistance to Africa

On 2 May, the Commission strongly condemned[21] South Africa for its acts of aggression and destabilization against neighbouring States and for its continuous forced removal of the African population from their homes. It called on the international community to extend political and material support to the front-line States and to provide material assistance to the displaced and homeless victims in southern Africa. It requested the Executive Director to intensify his efforts for the provision of increased assistance to victims of *apartheid* and to continue assisting the national liberation movements in obtaining approval of their human settlements project proposals within a reasonable time.

Also on 2 May, the Commission requested[22] the Executive Director to prepare a short-term shelter strategy for the resettlement of returning refugees in Namibia, as well as a proposal for a long-term comprehensive national shelter strategy. He was also requested to identify and implement specific projects to facilitate an orderly and effective resettlement of the returning refugees, to continue the implementation of an intensive training programme to ensure that Namibia would possess a core of skilled construction labour at the time of independence, and to report to the Commission in 1991 on the implementation of its requests.

Aid for Palestinians

In February, the Executive Director reported[23] on the results of a study on the reconstruction needed in Palestinian camps in Lebanon, concluding that detailed studies were needed to prepare comprehensive reconstruction, improvement and development plans. In a report on the housing requirements of the Palestinian people in the occupied territories,[24] the Executive Director described difficulties in communications and those related to the hiring of a consultant, due to the situation in the occupied territories.

Annexed to an October note by the Secretary-General[25] was a report from UNCHS, outlining steps taken to implement the development of the programme of economic and social assistance to the Palestinian people. The report identified 30 specific project proposals to be prepared by experts. Annexed to another October note by the Secretary-General[26] was a study on transport infrastructure in the occupied Palestinian territories, which included a description of the current transportation system and proposals for a future one.

By 30 votes to 1, with 10 abstentions,[27] the Commission called on the Israeli authorities to cease their malpractices against Palestinian people in the occupied territories, particularly the destruction of Palestinian homes, and to open the houses sealed by military order. The Secretary-General was asked to establish an international fund to rebuild homes and other structures demolished by the Israeli occupation authorities. The Commission condemned Israel's alteration of the demographic character of the occupied territories by establishing exclusively Jewish colonies on the Palestinian homeland. It called on the UNCHS Executive Director to dispatch a fact-finding mission to the occupied territories to investigate the question of denial of housing rights to and the destruction of housing of the Palestinian people, and to devise a national housing development strategy for the year 2000 for the Palestinian people based on the Global Strategy for Shelter to the Year 2000.

The Commission also called for an end to the continuous destruction of human settlements in Lebanon and appealed to the world community to assist in the reunification and rebuilding of that country.[28]

Environmental aspects of human settlements

Pursuant to 1987 General Assembly requests,[29] the Executive Director submitted in February a report on human settlements and sustainable development.[30] It contained a narrative, based on the Global Strategy for Shelter to the Year 2000, to show how the medium-term plan and the Centre's biennial work programme had been oriented to contribute to the international efforts towards sustainable development.

On 2 May, the Commission requested[31] the Executive Director to give due consideration to the issues raised in his report,[30] as well as to issues such as the production and use of energy with regard to human settlements and shelter, recycling of building materials, sanitation and sewage facilities, and avoidance of the production and use of hazardous and unhealthy building materials. It recommended to the General Assembly that the critical role and contribution of human settlements and urbanization to sustainable development and their impact on the environment should be among the issues to be addressed within the context of a UN conference on environment and development.

In January, the Executive Directors of UNCHS and the United Nations Environment Programme (UNEP) submitted a joint progress report[32] on co-operation between the two bodies. Four subject areas were highlighted: assessment of environmental conditions in human settlements; environmental aspects of policies, planning and management of human settlements; environmentally sound human settlements technology; and research, training and the dissemination of information on environmentally sound human settlements planning and management. On 2 May, the Commission requested[33] the UNCHS Executive Director, in consultation with the UNEP Executive Director, to continue and increase co-operation between the Centre and UNEP.

Rehabilitation of historic centres

On 2 May, the Commission adopted a resolution[34] urging international organizations and interested countries to bear in mind the fact that, in many countries, the inner cities, which represented a valuable historical and cultural heritage, had become slum areas that constituted a serious social problem demanding solutions. It urged them to mobilize resources to address both the social problem and the conservation of the historical and cultural heritage, and requested the Executive Director to co-ordinate with the United Nations Educational, Scientific and Cultural Organization and other organizations and Governments the technical and financial assistance required for such rehabilitation programmes.

Other issues

On 2 May, the Commission invited[35] the Statistical Commission to include the item "Human settlements statistics" on the agenda of its next session.

In February, the Executive Director submitted a report[36] on low-cost alternatives to intersessional consultations with Governments after 1989, including: establishment of a formal intersessional programme committee; formal meetings of the Bureau of the Commission or of an enlarged Bureau; a special *ad hoc* group of experts designated by Governments; and a full-fledged intersessional informal consultation meeting with Governments, perhaps through their permanent representatives in Nairobi. The Commission decided that the informal Committee of Permanent Representatives to UNCHS and/or Government-designated officials should continue to ensure liaison between Governments and the Executive Director between Commission sessions.[37]

UN Centre for Human Settlements

Activities

The 1988-1989 UNCHS work programme[38] had eight subprogrammes: policies and strategies, settlement planning, shelter and community services, the indigenous construction sector, low-cost infrastructure, land, mobilization of finance, and institutions and management.

Under the first subprogramme, an executive summary of the *Global Report on Human Settlements, 1986* was issued and a publication entitled *A New Agenda for Human Settlements* was widely distributed. An illustrated summary of the Global Strategy for Shelter to the Year 2000 was also made widely available.

Under the settlement planning subprogramme, research on rural settlements development continued and a technical publication reviewing national rural settlement programmes in developing countries was prepared. Three volumes of *Environmental Guidelines for Settlements Planning and Management* were published.

As for shelter and community services, the UNCHS community participation training programme, being implemented in Bolivia, Sri Lanka and Zambia, continued to offer support services to national and local authorities in strengthening their capacity to work with low-income communities to improve their shelter and environmental conditions. Two training manuals on affordable shelter projects were produced, one in English and one in Arabic. Workshops on housing in development were held in Bangkok, Thailand, and Nairobi, Kenya. Research continued on public sector strategies for the consolidation of stability in inner-city areas.

With regard to the indigenous construction sector, three technical papers were prepared on soil construction technology, selected local building materials, and development of the construction industry for delivery of low-income shelter and infrastructure. A bibliography on earth construction technology and the first volume of a journal for African countries on local building materials technology were also made available. Workshops on standards and specifications for local building materials were held in Ghana and Malawi. Missions were sent to Malawi and Zambia in connection with the establishment of pilot plants for selected building materials.

Concerning low-cost infrastructure, reports and publications were prepared on new and renewable sources of energy, improvement of sanitation and the design and manufacture of low-cost motorized vehicles. Missions were undertaken to Bangladesh, to assist in formulating rural housing programmes, and to Brazil, on alternative technologies for housing and sanitation.

The subprogramme on land continued to assess organizational and technical requirements for setting up and operating low-technology land-registration systems through local governments. A workshop to review basic issues and research on land management was held, and a technical publication on land for housing was issued.

In the area of human settlements financing, case-studies were prepared on employment-generation activities in low-income human settlements development programmes in Chile, India, Nigeria, the Philippines, Sri Lanka and Zambia. A draft report was prepared on that subject. Research on human settlements finance focused on mobilization of public and private resources, and the adequate and efficient channelling of resources of human settlements development activities. A technical publication on mechanisms to mobilize and channel resources was completed, a trainers' manual on urban finance and management was published, and a manual on housing finance was prepared.

The subprogramme on institutions and management continued to formulate guidelines and proposals for the introduction of appropriate legislative, institutional and management procedures for human settlements, and to design, implement and evaluate training courses in human settlements management for national and local officials. Advisory services in the evaluation and design of training courses were provided to Cameroon, Côte d'Ivoire, India, Kenya, Rwanda, Senegal and Thailand.

UNCHS information activities included the production of issues of the *Shelter Bulletin*, which had replaced the former *IYSH Bulletin*, *UNCHS (Habitat) News*, information kits, posters and photographic exhibitions, as well as two supplements on seminars on women in human settlements development and management, radio programmes and video programmes. An update of the *Habitat Directory* was begun.

Work programme

On 3 May, the Commission, after considering the Executive Director's report on the draft 1990-1991 work programme of UNCHS,[39] and noting that it reflected the principles and orientations of the Global Strategy for Shelter to the Year 2000, adopted[40] the draft work programme. It decided on a higher-priority designation for the programme elements on land policies and procedures and on shelter co-operatives. The element on global conditions and trends was to receive a lowest-priority designation. The Executive Director was requested to maintain a high level of research and information activities on low-cost water supply and sanitation.

Medium-term plan

On 3 May, the Commission endorsed[41] the draft medium-term plan for human settlements proposed by the UNCHS Executive Director, as translated into his report on the draft programme of the medium-term plan for the period 1992-1997.[42] It confirmed that the number of subprogrammes in the draft plan could not be reduced and reaffirmed that the Global Strategy for Shelter to the Year 2000 and its enabling approach should guide the implementation of the subprogrammes.

Co-ordination

On 2 May, the Commission, having reviewed the Executive Director's report on co-ordination and co-operation within the United Nations sys-

tem,[43] welcomed[44] the synoptic table of activities of the United Nations system in the area of human settlements, as included in that report. It decided that co-ordination in the area of human settlements should focus on the following priority areas: national policies and strategies, including land policies; settlements management, with particular emphasis on urban management; and infrastructure.

The Commission emphasized[45] the importance of human settlements development as a means of revitalizing the economies of developing countries, and recommended that Governments give priority to the promotion of indigenous building materials and construction techniques and to meeting shelter needs. It requested the UNCHS Executive Director to bring its resolution to the attention of the *ad hoc* committee of the whole for the preparation of the international development strategy for the fourth UN development decade.

The Commission invited the Executive Director to ensure that the Commission and UNCHS participated fully in the activities of the International Decade for Natural Disaster Reduction (the 1990s), and requested him to report on those activities.[46]

Global parliamentarians on Habitat

The Committee of Global Parliamentarians on Habitat, which held its third meeting in Cartagena de Indias, Colombia, in conjunction with the twelfth session of the Commission, decided to hold a conference in Japan in 1990 to discuss, among other things, the role of parliamentarians in the implementation of the Global Strategy for Shelter to the Year 2000.

The Commission on 2 May noted[47] the meeting's decisions and recommendations, which were annexed to the Commission's resolution.

Financing

During the 1988-1989 biennium, the UNCHS work programme was financed from the United Nations regular budget and from extrabudgetary resources. Programme support income from the execution of projects financed by UNDP and trust funds amounted to $4.3 million, while income for the UN Habitat and Human Settlements Foundation was $12.7 million.

UNCHS project delivery amounted in 1988-1989 to $48.3 million, including projects financed by UNDP ($34.3 million), the Foundation ($7.6 million) and other sources ($6.4 million).

UN Habitat and Human Settlements Foundation

In February, the Executive Director reported[48] on the proposed budget of the UN Habitat and Human Settlements Foundation for the biennium 1990-1991, which also contained revised estimates of income and expenditure of the Foundation in the biennium 1988-1989. Expected contributions and pledges for 1990-1991 were $8.5 million; total resource availability was about $13.2 million. The estimated programme expenditure and project commitments for the period amounted to some $11.2 million.

The status of voluntary contributions to the Foundation, as at 1 March 1989,[49] consisted of unpaid pledges of $553,638 and pledges for 1989 of $2.86 million.

On 3 May, the Commission approved[50] the revised estimates for the biennium 1988-1989 and the budget proposals for the biennium 1990-1991.

REFERENCES

[1]A/44/8 & Add.1. [2]HS/C/12/3/Add.1. [3]YUN 1988, p. 478, GA res. 43/181, 20 Dec. 1988. [4]A/44/8 (res. 12/13). [5]HS/C/12/13. [6]A/44/8 (res. 12/21). [7]HS/C/12/3. [8]A/44/8/Add.1. [9]E/1989/18. [10]A/44/8 (res. 12/1). [11]*Ibid.* (res. 12/12). [12]*Ibid.* (res. 12/9). [13]*Ibid.* (res. 12/10). [14]HS/C/12/5. [15]HS/C/12/5/Add.1. [16]A/44/8 (res. 12/14). [17]HS/C/12/6. [18]HS/C/12/6/Add.1. [19]A/44/8 (res. 12/15). [20]HS/C/12/4/Add.1. [21]A/44/8 (res. 12/3). [22]*Ibid.* (res. 12/2). [23]HS/C/12/2/Add.3. [24]HS/C/12/2/Add.2. [25]A/44/637. [26]A/44/534. [27]A/44/8 (res. 12/11). [28]*Ibid.* (res. 12/4). [29]YUN 1987, pp. 661 & 679, GA res. 42/186 & 42/187, 11 Dec. 1987. [30]HS/C/12/10/Add.1. [31]A/44/8 (res. 12/18). [32]HS/C/12/10. [33]A/44/8 (res. 12/20). [34]*Ibid.* (res. 12/16). [35]*Ibid.* (res. 12/6). [36]HS/C/12/2/Add.1. [37]A/44/8 (res. 12/8). [38]HS/C/12/2. [39]HS/C/12/7. [40]A/44/8 (dec. 12/23). [41]*Ibid.* (res. 12/22). [42]HS/C/12/8. [43]HS/C/12/11. [44]A/44/8 (res. 12/19). [45]*Ibid.* (res. 12/7). [46]*Ibid.* (res. 12/17). [47]*Ibid.* (res. 12/5). [48]HS/C/12/9. [49]HS/C/12/INF.5. [50]A/44/8 (dec. 12/24).

Chapter X

Human rights

In 1989, the United Nations continued its efforts to promote human rights and fundamental freedoms and to curtail their violations.

Progress continued to be made on a number of international instruments. In November, the General Assembly adopted and opened for signature the Convention on the Rights of the Child, and called on States to consider ratifying or acceding to the Convention as a matter of priority (resolution 44/25). In December, the Assembly adopted the Second Optional Protocol to the International Covenant on Civil and Political Rights, aimed at abolishing the death penalty (resolution 44/128).

The Working Group on Indigenous Populations reviewed developments pertaining to the promotion and protection of human rights and fundamental freedoms of indigenous peoples. It considered the first revised text of the draft Universal Declaration on the Rights of Indigenous Peoples prepared by the Group's Chairman/Rapporteur. The Working Group on the Drafting of an International Convention on the Protection of the Rights of All Migrant Workers and Their Families discussed the provisions of the draft convention still pending during the second reading. As in the past, the Commission on Human Rights set up an informal open-ended working group to elaborate a draft declaration on the rights of persons belonging to national, ethnic, religious and linguistic minorities. The Working Group on Detention discussed a new draft declaration on the protection of all persons from enforced or involuntary disappearance.

In economic and social matters, the Working Group of Governmental Experts on the Right to Development considered the implementation of the 1986 Declaration on the Right to Development. The Committee on Economic, Social and Cultural Rights examined reports submitted by countries on their implementation of the 1966 International Covenant on Economic, Social and Cultural Rights. The Committee's day of general discussion focused on the right of each person to an adequate standard of living for self and family.

The Commission on Human Rights at its forty-fifth session, held in January-March, reviewed activities under the UN programme of advisory services in the field of human rights and the programme of the World Public Information Campaign for Human Rights, and considered the implications of scientific and technological developments for human rights as well as other issues relating to the promotion and protection of human rights. It examined situations involving alleged human rights violations on a large scale in several countries. The Commission adopted 75 resolutions and 14 decisions. Its Sub-Commission on Prevention of Discrimination and Protection of Minorities at its forty-first session, held in August/September, adopted 47 resolutions and 13 decisions.

Discrimination

Racial discrimination

Second Decade to Combat Racism and Racial Discrimination (1983-1993)

Implementation of the Programme for the Decade

In 1989, United Nations efforts to implement the Programme of Action for the Second Decade to Combat Racism and Racial Discrimination continued under the plan of activities for 1985-1989 put forward in 1984.[1] In 1988,[2] the General Assembly affirmed again the need for implementing the plan of activities for the remainder of the Decade (1990-1993).

Reports of the Secretary-General. As requested by the Economic and Social Council in 1988,[3] the Secretary-General submitted in April his annual report[4] summarizing activities carried out or planned within the UN system to achieve the Decade's objectives. In later addenda,[5] the Secretary-General presented information from Governments and intergovernmental and non-governmental organizations (NGOs) and information relating to the review and appraisal of Decade activities and the formulation of suggestions and recommendations.

The Secretary-General submitted a September report[6] informing the Assembly that he was proceeding with the publication of the global compilation of national legislation against racial discrimination, in accordance with a 1985 Assembly resolution.[7]

Also in September, the Secretary-General submitted to the Assembly a report[8] containing the views of three Governments, two specialized agencies and two NGOs on his 1986 report[9] on the role of private group action to combat racism and racial discrimination.

Pursuant to a 1988 Assembly request,[2] the Secretary-General submitted, in October, a report[10] on the implementation of the Programme of Action. It described actions taken by UN bodies, national legislation to combat racism, seminars and training courses, the Trust Fund for the Programme for the Decade, and the plans of activities for both halves of the Second Decade. He noted that the global consultation on racism and racial discrimination had taken place in 1988 (Geneva, 3-6 October), as authorized by the Assembly in 1987,[11] and set out its conclusions and recommendations, which were annexed to a March note.[12]

On 24 May, the Economic and Social Council by **decision 1989/159** took note of the Secretary-General's note on the global consultation.

Human Rights Commission action. On 23 February,[13] the Commission noted with concern that despite the efforts of the international community, the principal objectives of the first Decade for Action to Combat Racism and Racial Discrimination (1973-1983) had not been attained, and that millions continued to be victims of varied forms of racism, racial discrimination and *apartheid*. It appealed to those States that had not yet done so to take steps to ratify, accede to and implement the international instruments relevant to the Decade. The Commission decided to give thematic consideration each year to a selected topic within the plan of activities for 1990-1993, as listed in the annex to a 1987 Assembly resolution,[11] and requested the Secretary-General to envisage organizing a seminar on the political, historical, economic, social and cultural factors that contribute to racism, racial discrimination and *apartheid*. The Commission decided that the topic of the global consultation for 1991 would be ways and means of denying support to racist régimes with a view to making them change their policies. It appealed to Governments, organizations and individuals in a position to do so to contribute generously to the Trust Fund for the Programme for the Decade. The Secretary-General was asked to prepare and finalize a handbook of recourse procedures for victims of racism and racial discrimination, to ensure that sufficient resources were included in the proposed programme budgets for the 1990-1991 and 1992-1993 bienniums to provide for implementation of the activities of the Second Decade and to organize in 1990 a meeting of representatives of national institutions and organizations promoting tolerance and harmony and combating racism and racial discrimination.

Report of the Special Rapporteur. In a July report and later addendum,[14] Special Rappor-

teur Asbjorn Eide (Norway) submitted his final report on the achievements made and obstacles encountered during the first and Second Decades.

Sub-Commission action. On 31 August,[15] the Sub-Commission on Prevention of Discrimination and Protection of Minorities decided to refer the final report of Special Rapporteur Eide to the Commission for further consideration and recommended to the Commission that the report be published and distributed as widely as possible.

Other action. At its thirty-seventh session (Geneva, 7 August–1 September),[16] the Committee on the Elimination of Racial Discrimination (CERD) considered revisions proposed for its study[17] on progress made towards achieving the objectives of the International Convention on the Elimination of All Forms of Racial Discrimination, which it had prepared in 1978 for the World Conference to Combat Racism and Racial Discrimination.[18] The Convention was adopted by the General Assembly in 1965[19] and had been in force since 1969.[20] The Committee agreed that the revised draft should be prepared by the Secretariat, in consultation with designated members, for approval by the Committee in 1990. CERD endorsed the conclusions and suggestions that had emerged from the 1988 global consultation on racism and racial discrimination.[12] The Committee also agreed on arrangements to commemorate in 1990 its twentieth year of activities.

In 1989, the Commission on Human Rights had before it the annual reports on racial discrimination submitted by the International Labour Organisation (ILO)[21] and the United Nations Educational, Scientific and Cultural Organization (UNESCO).[22]

ECONOMIC AND SOCIAL COUNCIL ACTION

On 24 May, the Economic and Social Council adopted **resolution 1989/83** without vote.

Implementation of the Programme of Action for the Second Decade to Combat Racism and Racial Discrimination

The Economic and Social Council,

Reaffirming the purpose set forth in the Charter of the United Nations of achieving international co-operation in solving international problems of an economic, social, cultural or humanitarian character, and in promoting and encouraging respect for human rights and fundamental freedoms for all without distinction as to race, sex, language or religion,

Recalling the proclamation by the General Assembly, in its resolution 38/14 of 22 November 1983, of the Second Decade to Combat Racism and Racial Discrimination,

Recalling also the Programme of Action for the Second Decade to Combat Racism and Racial Discrimination, approved by the General Assembly in its resolution 38/14 to which it is annexed, to achieve the objectives of the Second Decade,

Reaffirming the plan of activities for the periods 1985-1989 and 1990-1993, to be implemented by the Secretary-General in accordance with General Assembly resolutions 39/16 of 23 November 1984 and 42/47 of 30 November 1987,

Conscious of the responsibility conferred upon it by the General Assembly for co-ordinating and, in particular, evaluating the activities undertaken in the implementation of the Programme of Action for the Second Decade,

Bearing in mind, in particular, its mandate under General Assembly resolution 41/94 of 4 December 1986 to submit to the Assembly, during the period of the Second Decade, annual reports on the activities undertaken or contemplated to achieve the objectives of the Second Decade,

Having examined the report of the Secretary-General on the implementation of the Programme of Action for the Second Decade,

Noting that, despite the efforts of the international community, the principal objectives of the first Decade for Action to Combat Racism and Racial Discrimination and the first years of the Second Decade have not been attained, and that millions of human beings continue to be victims of varied forms of racism, racial discrimination and *apartheid*,

Stressing the need to continue the co-ordination of activities undertaken by various United Nations bodies and specialized agencies for the purpose of implementing the Programme of Action for the Second Decade,

1. *Reaffirms* the importance of achieving the objectives of the Second Decade to Combat Racism and Racial Discrimination;

2. *Takes note with appreciation* of the report of the Secretary-General on the implementation of the Programme of Action for the Second Decade, in particular the recommendations contained therein;

3. *Welcomes* the results of the global consultation on racism and racial discrimination organized by the Secretary-General and held at Geneva from 3 to 6 October 1988;

4. *Reaffirms* the need for continued co-ordination of the full range of programmes being implemented by the United Nations system as they relate to the objectives of the Second Decade;

5. *Requests* the Secretary-General to ensure the effective and immediate implementation of those activities proposed for the first half of the Second Decade that have not yet been undertaken, in particular the 1989 seminar on cultural dialogue between the countries of origin and the host countries of migrant workers;

6. *Invites* the Secretary-General to proceed with the implementation of the activities for the period 1990-1993 listed in the annex to General Assembly resolution 42/47, and requests him, in this context, to accord the highest priority to measures to combat *apartheid;*

7. *Also invites* all Governments to take or continue to take all necessary measures to combat all forms of racism and racial discrimination and to support the work of the Second Decade by making contributions to the Trust Fund for the Programme for the Decade for Action to Combat Racism and Racial Discrimination, in order to ensure further implementation of activities for the Second Decade;

8. *Decides*, as a matter of priority, to give particular attention to the specific activities of the Programme of Action for the Second Decade that are directed towards the elimination of *apartheid*, in view of the explosive situation in southern Africa;

9. *Requests* the Secretary-General, in his reports, to continue to pay special attention to the situation of migrant workers and their families;

10. *Emphasizes* the importance of public information activities in combating racism and racial discrimination and in mobilizing public support for the objectives of the Second Decade, and, in this context, commends the efforts of the Co-ordinator for the Second Decade to Combat Racism and Racial Discrimination;

11. *Decides* to continue to accord the highest priority each year to the agenda item entitled ''Implementation of the Programme of Action for the Second Decade to Combat Racism and Racial Discrimination''.

Economic and Social Council resolution 1989/83

24 May 1989   Meeting 16   Adopted without vote

Draft by Burkina Faso (E/1989/L.18) on behalf of the African States; agenda item 2.

GENERAL ASSEMBLY ACTION

On 8 December, on the recommendation of the Third (Social, Humanitarian and Cultural) Committee, the General Assembly adopted **resolution 44/52** without vote.

Second Decade to Combat Racism and Racial Discrimination

The General Assembly,

Reaffirming its objective set forth in the Charter of the United Nations to achieve international co-operation in solving international problems of an economic, social, cultural or humanitarian character and in promoting and encouraging respect for human rights and fundamental freedoms for all without distinction as to race, sex, language or religion,

Reaffirming also its firm determination and its commitment to eradicate totally and unconditionally racism in all its forms, racial discrimination and *apartheid*,

Recalling the Universal Declaration of Human Rights, the International Convention on the Elimination of All Forms of Racial Discrimination, the International Convention on the Suppression and Punishment of the Crime of *Apartheid*, the International Convention against *Apartheid* in Sports and the Convention against Discrimination in Education adopted by the United Nations Educational, Scientific and Cultural Organization on 14 December 1960,

Recalling also its resolution 3057(XXVIII) of 2 November 1973, on the first Decade for Action to Combat Racism and Racial Discrimination, and its resolution 38/14 of 22 November 1983, on the Second Decade to Combat Racism and Racial Discrimination,

Recalling further the two World Conferences to Combat Racism and Racial Discrimination, held at Geneva in 1978 and 1983,

Bearing in mind the *Report of the Second World Conference to Combat Racism and Racial Discrimination,*

Convinced that the Second World Conference represented a positive contribution by the international community towards attaining the objectives of the Decade, through its adoption of a Declaration and an operational Programme of Action for the Second Decade to Combat Racism and Racial Discrimination,

Noting with concern that, despite the efforts of the international community, the principal objectives of the first Decade for Action to Combat Racism and Racial Discrimination were not attained and that millions of human beings continue to this day to be the victims of varied forms of racism, racial discrimination and *apartheid*,

Recalling its resolutions 39/16 of 23 November 1984, 42/47 of 30 November 1987 and 43/91 of 8 December 1988,

Emphasizing once again the necessity of attaining the objectives of the Second Decade to Combat Racism and Racial Discrimination,

Having considered the note by the Secretary-General and his reports submitted within the framework of the implementation of the Programme of Action for the Second Decade,

Convinced of the need to take more effective and sustained international measures for the elimination of all forms of racism and racial discrimination and the total eradication of *apartheid* in South Africa,

Aware that certain activities of the Second Decade scheduled for the period 1985-1989 have not been implemented owing to a lack of financial resources,

Aware also of the importance and the magnitude of the phenomenon of migrant workers, as well as the efforts undertaken by the international community to improve the protection of the human rights of migrant workers and their families,

Taking note of the conclusions and suggestions of the global consultation on racism and racial discrimination held at Geneva from 3 to 6 October 1988, the conclusions and recommendations of the seminar on the effects of racism and racial discrimination on the social and economic relations between indigenous peoples and States, held at Geneva from 16 to 20 January 1989, and the conclusions and recommendations of the seminar on cultural dialogue between the countries of origin and the host countries of migrant workers, held at Athens from 18 to 26 September 1989,

1. *Declares once again* that all forms of racism and racial discrimination, particularly in their institutionalized form, such as *apartheid*, or resulting from official doctrines of racial superiority or exclusivity, are among the most serious violations of human rights in the contemporary world and must be combated by all available means;

2. *Decides* that the international community, in general, and the United Nations, in particular, should continue to give the highest priority to programmes for combating racism, racial discrimination and *apartheid* and intensify their efforts, during the Second Decade to Combat Racism and Racial Discrimination, to provide assistance and relief to the victims of racism and all forms of racial discrimination and *apartheid*, especially in South Africa and Namibia and in occupied territories and territories under alien domination;

3. *Appeals* to all Governments and to international and non-governmental organizations to increase and intensify their activities to combat racism, racial discrimination and *apartheid* and to provide relief and assistance to the victims of these evils;

4. *Takes note* of the reports submitted by the Secretary-General containing information on the activities of Governments, specialized agencies, regional intergovernmental organizations and non-governmental organizations, as well as United Nations organs, to give effect to the Programme of Action for the Second Decade to Combat Racism and Racial Discrimination;

5. *Notes and commends* the efforts made to co-ordinate all the programmes currently under implementation by the United Nations system that relate to the objectives of the Second Decade and encourages the Co-ordinator for the Second Decade to Combat Racism and Racial Discrimination to continue his efforts;

6. *Notes with satisfaction* the holding of the seminar on the effects of racism and racial discrimination on the social and economic relations between indigenous peoples and States and the seminar on cultural dialogue between the countries of origin and the host countries of migrant workers and requests the Secretary-General to give the reports on the seminars wide distribution among Governments, competent United Nations bodies, specialized agencies, other intergovernmental organizations and non-governmental organizations;

7. *Notes* that the publication of the global compilation of national legislation against racial discrimination is proceeding, and requests the Secretary-General to transmit it to Governments as soon as possible;

8. *Requests* the Secretary-General to continue the study on the effects of racial discrimination on the children of minorities, in particular those of migrant workers, in the field of education, training and employment, and to submit, *inter alia*, specific recommendations for the implementation of measures to combat the effects of that discrimination;

9. *Takes note* of the reports of the Secretary-General on the study on the role of private group action to combat racism and racial discrimination;

10. *Requests* the Secretary-General to prepare and issue as soon as possible a collection of model legislation for the guidance of Governments in the enactment of further legislation against racial discrimination;

11. *Renews its invitation* to the United Nations Educational, Scientific and Cultural Organization to expedite the preparation of teaching materials and teaching aids to promote teaching, training and educational activities on human rights and against racism and racial discrimination, with particular emphasis on activities at the primary and secondary levels of education;

12. *Welcomes* the completion and the submission to the Sub-Commission on Prevention of Discrimination and Protection of Minorities of the study of the results achieved and the obstacles encountered during the first Decade for Action to Combat Racism and Racial Discrimination and the first half of the Second Decade, and requests the Commission on Human Rights to transmit this study to the General Assembly at its forty-fifth session;

13. *Emphasizes again* the importance of adequate recourse procedures for victims of racism and racial discrimination, and therefore once again requests the Secretary-General, in the light of the results of the seminars held on this topic, to prepare and finalize, with the assistance of experts in this field, a handbook of recourse procedures;

14. *Considers* that all the parts of the Programme of Action for the Second Decade to Combat Racism and Racial Discrimination should receive equal attention in order to attain the objectives of the Second Decade;

15. *Invites* the Secretary-General to implement immediately those activities scheduled for the period 1985-

1989 not yet carried out and to proceed with the implementation of the activities scheduled for the biennium 1990-1991;

16. *Affirms once again* the need for the implementation of the plan of activities proposed for the period 1990-1993 contained in the annex to General Assembly resolution 42/47;

17. *Requests* the Secretary-General to continue to accord the highest priority, in executing the plan of activities, to measures for combating *apartheid;*

18. *Also requests* the Secretary-General, pursuant to General Assembly resolution 42/47, to ensure that sufficient additional resources are included in the proposed programme budgets for the bienniums 1990-1991 and 1992-1993 to provide for the implementation of the activities of the Second Decade, and requests him to inform the Assembly of the steps taken in that regard;

19. *Further requests* the Secretary-General to continue to accord special attention to the situation of migrant workers and their families and to include regularly in his reports all information on such workers;

20. *Invites* all Governments, United Nations bodies, the specialized agencies and other intergovernmental organizations, as well as interested non-governmental organizations in consultative status with the Economic and Social Council, to participate fully in the implementation of the plans of activities for the periods 1985-1989 and 1990-1993 by intensifying and broadening their efforts to bring about the speedy elimination of *apartheid* and all forms of racism and racial discrimination;

21. *Considers* that voluntary contributions to the Trust Fund for the Programme for the Decade for Action to Combat Racism and Racial Discrimination are indispensable for the implementation of the above-mentioned programmes;

22. *Notes once again with regret* that the present situation of the Trust Fund is not encouraging;

23. *Strongly appeals,* therefore, to all Governments, organizations and individuals in a position to do so to contribute generously to the Trust Fund and, to this end, requests the Secretary-General to continue to undertake appropriate contacts and initiatives to encourage contributions;

24. *Takes note* of the reports on the activities of the Second Decade, and reiterates its request to the Economic and Social Council, throughout the Decade, to submit annually to the General Assembly a report containing, *inter alia:*

(a) An enumeration of the activities undertaken or contemplated to achieve the objectives of the Second Decade, including the activities of Governments, United Nations bodies, the specialized agencies and other international and regional organizations, as well as nongovernmental organizations;

(b) A review and appraisal of those activities;

(c) Its suggestions and recommendations;

25. *Requests* the Secretary-General to report to the General Assembly at its forty-fifth session on the implementation of the present resolution;

26. *Decides* to keep the item entitled "Implementation of the Programme of Action for the Second Decade to Combat Racism and Racial Discrimination" on its agenda throughout the Second Decade and to consider it as a matter of the highest priority at its forty-fifth session.

General Assembly resolution 44/52

8 December 1989   Meeting 78   Adopted without vote

Approved by Third Committee (A/44/715) without vote, 27 October (meeting 21); draft by Kenya (A/C.3/44/L.6) on behalf of the Group of African States, orally revised; agenda item 89.

Meeting numbers. GA 43rd session: 3rd Committee 3-11, 15, 21; plenary 78.

Convention on the Elimination of Racial Discrimination

Accessions and ratifications

As at 31 December 1989,[23] there were 128 parties to the International Convention on the Elimination of All Forms of Racial Discrimination, adopted by the General Assembly in 1965[19] and in force since 1969.[20] Yemen became a party in 1989.

Implementation of the Convention

The Committee on the Elimination of Racial Discrimination (CERD), set up under article 8 of the Convention, held only one extended session in 1989 (Geneva, 7 August-1 September).[16] Due to non-payment of contributions by a number of States parties, the Committee was unable to hold its spring session. Normally it held two 3-week sessions annually.

Most of CERD's work was devoted to examining reports submitted by States parties on measures taken to implement the Convention's provisions. It considered 49 reports submitted by 28 States parties under article 9 of the Convention. The report summarized the views of Committee members on each country report and the statements made by the States parties concerned.

CERD also considered, in conformity with article 14 of the Convention, communications from individuals or groups of individuals claiming violation of their rights under the Convention by a State party recognizing CERD competence to receive and consider such communications. Twelve States parties—Costa Rica, Denmark, Ecuador, France, Iceland, Italy, the Netherlands, Norway, Peru, Senegal, Sweden and Uruguay—had declared such recognition.

Under article 15 of the Convention, the Secretary-General transmitted to CERD documents related to Trust and Non-Self-Governing Territories. CERD observed that it found it impossible to fulfil its function under article 15 as the documents did not include copies of petitions and did not contain valid information concerning legislative, judicial, administrative or other measures directly related to the Convention's principles and objectives. The Committee asked that appropriate information be furnished.

As to its critical financial situation, the Committee adopted a decision containing a draft resolution by which the General Assembly would have authorized the Secretary-General to ensure, on a temporary basis, the financing of the expenses of the members of the Committee from the UN regular budget until a more permanent solution was found. In an October report,[24] the Secretary-General stated that as at 1 September 1989, the total of outstanding assessments and arrears amounted to $168,758.

GENERAL ASSEMBLY ACTION

On 8 December, the General Assembly, on the recommendation of the Third Committee, adopted **resolution 44/68** without vote.

Report of the Committee on the Elimination of Racial Discrimination

The General Assembly,

Recalling its previous resolutions concerning the reports of the Committee on the Elimination of Racial Discrimination and resolution 43/95 of 8 December 1988 on the status of the International Convention on the Elimination of All Forms of Racial Discrimination, as well as its other relevant resolutions on the implementation of the Programme of Action for the Second Decade to Combat Racism and Racial Discrimination,

Reiterating the importance of the International Convention on the Elimination of All Forms of Racial Discrimination, which is the most widely accepted human rights instrument adopted under the auspices of the United Nations,

Aware of the importance of the contributions of the Committee to the efforts of the United Nations to combat racism and all other forms of discrimination based on race, colour, descent or national or ethnic origin,

Welcoming the report of the Committee on the work of its thirty-seventh session,

Reiterating once again the need to intensify the struggle for the elimination of racism and racial discrimination throughout the world, especially the elimination of the system of *apartheid* in South Africa and Namibia,

Emphasizing the obligation of all States parties to the Convention to take legislative, judicial and other measures in order to secure full implementation of the provisions of the Convention,

Recalling the urgent appeals made by the Secretary-General, the General Assembly, the eleventh and twelfth meetings of States parties to the Convention and the Committee itself to the States parties to honour their financial obligations under the Convention,

Gravely concerned that, despite those appeals and other efforts, the meeting schedule of the Committee has been interrupted and the proper functioning of the Committee continues to deteriorate,

Expressing its appreciation for the efforts of the members of the Committee to explore ways and means to overcome the Committee's current financial crisis,

Having considered the report of the Secretary-General on the question of financing the expenses of the members of the Committee,

1. *Expresses its profound concern* at the fact that a number of States parties to the International Convention on the Elimination of All Forms of Racial Discrimination have still not fulfilled their financial obligations, which led to the cancellation of the February/March 1989 session of the Committee on the Elimination of Racial Discrimination;

2. *Expresses once again its concern* that such a situation led to a further delay in the discharge of the substantive obligations of the Committee under the Convention;

3. *Commends* the Committee for its work with regard to the implementation of the Convention and the Programme of Action for the Second Decade to Combat Racism and Racial Discrimination;

4. *Takes note with appreciation* of the report of the Committee on the work of its thirty-seventh session;

5. *Calls upon* States parties to fulfil their obligations under article 9, paragraph 1, of the Convention and to submit in due time their periodic reports on measures taken to implement the Convention;

6. *Endorses* the decision of the Committee to hold one of its regular sessions in New York, if resources are available, in commemoration of its twentieth year of activities under the Convention, to coincide with the International Day for the Elimination of Racial Discrimination, 21 March 1990;

7. *Strongly appeals* to all States parties, especially those in arrears, to fulfil their financial obligations under article 8, paragraph 6, of the Convention and to pay their outstanding contributions and, if possible, their contributions for 1990 before 1 February 1990, so as to enable the Committee to meet regularly;

8. *Invites* the Secretary-General to do everything possible to ensure that funds are available to meet all the costs of the meetings of the Committee in 1990, including the expenses of its members;

9. *Requests* the Secretary-General to invite those States parties which are in arrears to pay the amounts in arrears, and to report thereon to the General Assembly at its forty-fifth session;

10. *Invites* the Secretary-General to report to the States parties at their thirteenth meeting on all legal and administrative measures that the States parties and the General Assembly could take to guarantee the regular functioning of the Committee;

11. *Invites* States parties at their thirteenth meeting to decide on administrative and legal measures to improve the financial situation of the Committee;

12. *Decides* to consider at its forty-fifth session, under the item entitled "Elimination of all forms of racial discrimination", the next report of the Committee, as well as the report of the Secretary-General on the financial situation of the Committee.

General Assembly resolution 44/68

8 December 1989   Meeting 78   Adopted without vote

Approved by Third Committee (A/44/716) without vote, 27 October (meeting 21); 29-nation draft (A/C.3/44/L.7), orally revised; agenda item 100.
Financial implications. S-G, A/C.3/44/L.12.
Meeting numbers. GA 44th session: 3rd Committee 3-11, 15, 21; plenary 78.

Other aspects of discrimination

Religious intolerance

Report of the Secretary-General. As requested by the Sub-Commission on Prevention of Discrimination and Protection of Minorities in 1987,[25] the Secretary-General, in a May report,[26] presented information received from 22 Governments, 2 specialized agencies and 9 NGOs relevant to its consideration of measures that might be taken to eliminate all forms of intolerance and discrimination based on religion or belief.

Report of the Special Rapporteur. The Commission on Human Rights had before it in 1989 a report of the Special Rapporteur, Angelo Vidal d'Almeida Ribeiro (Portugal),[27] containing allegations transmitted to the Governments concerned regarding situations which seemed to be inconsistent with the provisions in the 1981 Declaration on the Elimination of All Forms of Intolerance and of Discrimination Based on Religion or Belief,[28] and a summary of the replies received. He discussed national and international guarantees for freedom of thought, conscience, religion and belief, and presented examples of some positive steps taken to implement the Declaration. The report contained an analysis of the information collected by the Special Rapporteur as evidence of the persistence of numerous infringements of the rights set out in the Declaration.

The Special Rapporteur concluded that incidents and governmental actions inconsistent with the provisions of the Declaration persisted in nearly all regions of the world, but also that genuine efforts were being made to introduce and implement measures to combat the problem. He recommended the preparation of new international norms on the elimination of intolerance and discrimination based on religion or belief and urged States to ratify the relevant international human rights instruments. Advantage should be taken, he stated, of the advisory services made available by the United Nations in the field of human rights.

Human Rights Commission action. As requested by the General Assembly in 1988,[29] the Commission continued in 1989 to consider measures to implement the Declaration. On 6 March,[30] it urged States to provide adequate constitutional and legal guarantees of freedom of thought, conscience, religion and belief; to combat intolerance; and to ensure that members of law enforcement bodies, civil servants, educators and other public officials respected different religions and beliefs. The Commission further called on them to encourage understanding, tolerance and respect for freedom of religion or belief. The Commission asked the Secretary-General to continue to accord high priority to disseminating the Declaration in all UN official languages and to make the text available for use by UN information centres (UNICs) and other interested bodies. It also asked him to invite interested NGOs to consider facilitating the text's dissemination in national and local languages.

The Commission recalled its request to the Sub-Commission to: prepare a compilation of provisions relevant to the elimination of intolerance and discrimination based on religion or belief contained in the Declaration and other international instruments; examine the issues and factors which should be considered before any drafting of a further binding international instrument on freedom of religion and belief took place; and report on those issues in 1989.

The Commission asked the Secretary-General to report to it in 1990 and to assist the Special Rapporteur to enable him to report in 1990 as well.

Sub-Commission action. On 31 August,[31] the Sub-Commission decided to submit to the Commission for consideration in 1990 Secretary-General's report[26] and a working paper[32] by Theo van Boven (Netherlands), which contained a compilation of provisions relevant to the elimination of intolerance and discrimination based on religion or belief and a discussion of issues and factors that should be taken into account before drafting a further binding international instrument on freedom of religion or belief. It brought to the Commission's attention the following issues: the Declaration should continue to serve as a basis for any further work in standard-setting and in considering measures to ensure respect for the right to freedom of thought, conscience, religion and belief; the possibility of drafting any new binding instrument should be considered along the lines of a 1986 General Assembly resolution;[33] the Secretary-General might be asked to organize within the programme of advisory services, and not later than 1991, a seminar on the interrelationship between the enjoyment of the right to freedom of thought, conscience, religion and belief and the other human rights and fundamental freedoms; and consideration might also be given to organizing, in co-operation with UNESCO, the United Nations University, other interested intergovernmental and non-governmental organizations, and academic and research institutions, a global consultation on the positions and approaches of different religions and beliefs to human rights and fundamental freedoms.

GENERAL ASSEMBLY ACTION

On 15 December, the General Assembly, on the recommendation of the Third Committee, adopted **resolution 44/131** without vote.

Elimination of all forms of religious intolerance
The General Assembly,

Conscious of the need to promote universal respect for, and observance of, human rights and fundamental freedoms for all without distinction as to race, sex, language or religion,

Reaffirming its resolution 36/55 of 25 November 1981, by which it proclaimed the Declaration on the Elimination of All Forms of Intolerance and of Discrimination Based on Religion or Belief,

Recalling its resolution 43/108 of 8 December 1988, in which it requested the Commission on Human Rights to continue its consideration of measures to implement the Declaration,

Encouraged by the efforts being made by the Commission on Human Rights and by the Sub-Commission on Prevention of Discrimination and Protection of Minorities to study relevant developments affecting the implementation of the Declaration,

Recalling Commission on Human Rights resolution 1988/55 of 8 March 1988 and Economic and Social Council decision 1988/142 of 27 May 1988, by which the mandate of the Special Rapporteur appointed to examine incidents and governmental actions in all parts of the world that are incompatible with the provisions of the Declaration and to recommend remedial measures as appropriate was extended for two years,

Emphasizing that non-governmental organizations and religious bodies and groups at every level have an important role to play in the promotion of tolerance and the protection of freedom of religion or belief by, *inter alia*, engaging in the examination of the most effective means to promote the implementation of the Declaration,

Conscious of the importance of education in ensuring tolerance of religion and belief,

Seriously concerned that intolerance and discrimination on the grounds of religion or belief continue to occur in many parts of the world,

Believing that further efforts are therefore required to promote and protect the right to freedom of thought, conscience, religion and belief and to eliminate all forms of intolerance and discrimination based on religion or belief,

1. *Reaffirms* that freedom of thought, conscience, religion and belief is a right guaranteed to all without discrimination;

2. *Urges* States, therefore, in accordance with their respective constitutional systems and with such internationally accepted instruments as the Universal Declaration of Human Rights, the International Covenant on Civil and Political Rights, and the Declaration on the Elimination of All Forms of Intolerance and of Discrimination Based on Religion or Belief, to provide, where they have not already done so, adequate constitutional and legal guarantees of freedom of thought, conscience, religion and belief, including the provision of effective remedies where there is intolerance or discrimination based on religion or belief;

3. *Urges* all States to take all appropriate measures to combat intolerance and to encourage understanding, tolerance and respect in matters relating to freedom of religion or belief and, in this context, to examine where necessary the supervision and training of their civil servants, educators and other public officials to ensure that, in the course of their official duties, they respect different religions and beliefs and do not discriminate against persons professing other religions or beliefs;

4. *Invites* the United Nations University and other academic and research institutions to undertake programmes and studies on the encouragement of understanding, tolerance and respect in matters relating to freedom of religion or belief;

5. *Considers* it desirable to enhance the promotional and public information activities of the United Nations in matters relating to freedom of religion or belief and

to ensure that appropriate measures are taken to this end in the World Public Information Campaign for Human Rights;

6. *Invites* the Secretary-General to continue to give high priority to the dissemination of the text of the Declaration on the Elimination of All Forms of Intolerance and of Discrimination Based on Religion or Belief, in all the official languages of the United Nations, and to take all appropriate measures to make the text available for use by United Nations information centres, as well as by other interested bodies;

7. *Welcomes* the efforts of non-governmental organizations to promote the implementation of the Declaration, including the Second International Conference on Ways to Promote the Declaration on the Elimination of All Forms of Intolerance and of Discrimination Based on Religion or Belief, held at Warsaw from 14 to 18 May 1989;

8. *Requests* the Secretary-General to invite interested non-governmental organizations to consider what further role they could envisage playing in the implementation of the Declaration and in its dissemination in national and local languages;

9. *Urges* all States to consider disseminating the text of the Declaration in their respective national languages and to facilitate its dissemination in national and local languages;

10. *Recalls with satisfaction* the decision of the Economic and Social Council, based on the recommendation of the Commission on Human Rights at its forty-fourth session, to renew for two years the mandate of the Special Rapporteur appointed to examine incidents and governmental actions in all parts of the world that are incompatible with the provisions of the Declaration and to recommend remedial measures as appropriate;

11. *Notes* that the Commission on Human Rights, on the basis of a report to be submitted by the Sub-Commission on Prevention of Discrimination and Protection of Minorities, intends to consider at its forty-sixth session the question of drafting a binding international instrument on freedom of religion or belief, and emphasizes, in this connection, the relevance of General Assembly resolution 41/120 of 4 December 1986, entitled ''Setting international standards in the field of human rights'';

12. *Requests* the Commission on Human Rights to continue its consideration of measures to implement the Declaration and to report, through the Economic and Social Council, to the General Assembly at its forty-fifth session;

13. *Decides* to include in the provisional agenda of its forty-fifth session the item entitled ''Elimination of all forms of religious intolerance'' and to consider the report of the Commission on Human Rights under that item.

General Assembly resolution 44/131

15 December 1989   Meeting 82   Adopted without vote

Approved by Third Committee (A/44/825) without vote, 22 November (meeting 52); 34-nation draft (A/C.3/44/L.58); agenda item 106.
Meeting numbers. GA 44th session: 3rd Committee 36-43, 50, 52; plenary 82.

Indigenous populations

Human Rights Commission action. On 6 March,[34] the Commission welcomed the Sub-

Commission's 1988 decision[35] to entrust to the Chairman/Rapporteur of the Working Group on Indigenous Populations, Erica-Irene A. Daes (Greece), the further development of a draft declaration on indigenous rights, and asked the Secretary-General to give her the assistance she needed to carry out the task. The Economic and Social Council endorsed those actions by **decision 1989/140** of 24 May. The Secretary-General was also asked to assist the Working Group in discharging its tasks and to distribute widely the report[36] on the UN seminar on the effects of racism and racial discrimination on the social and economic relations between peoples and States (Geneva, 16-20 January).

The Commission appealed to Governments, organizations and individuals to consider favourably requests for contributions to the United Nations Voluntary Fund for Indigenous Populations. It also asked the Working Group and the Sub-Commission to consider ways to broaden the scope and activities of the Fund and to transmit their recommendations thereon in 1990.

Working Group activities. At its seventh session (Geneva, 31 July–4 August),[37] the Working Group on Indigenous Populations reviewed developments pertaining to the promotion and protection of human rights and fundamental freedoms of indigenous peoples. It had before it the first revised text of the draft universal declaration on the rights of indigenous peoples[38] prepared by the Chairman/Rapporteur. Subsequent addenda[39] contained comments received on the draft declaration from Member States, specialized agencies, intergovernmental organizations and NGOs. The Working Group recommended that the Chairman/Rapporteur prepare a second revised text of the draft declaration and that the Sub-Commission strongly encourage Governments and indigenous peoples to hold joint meetings in order to present to the Group in 1990 and in future sessions agreed-upon texts.

The Group decided to consider further the possibility of establishing a United Nations Commissioner for Indigenous Peoples, to co-ordinate international action for the recognition and promotion of the rights of indigenous peoples and for the improvement of their economic, social and political conditions. It recommended that the General Assembly proclaim 1993 the International Year for Indigenous Rights.

Sub-Commission action. By a resolution of 1 September,[40] the Sub-Commission recommended that the Chairman/Rapporteur prepare a second revised text of the draft declaration and asked the Secretary-General to assist her. It also asked him to transmit the Working Group's report to Governments, indigenous peoples and intergovernmental and non-governmental organiza-

tions for comments and proposals on the revised text. The Sub-Commission further asked him to assist the Working Group in discharging its tasks and to consider ways of better publicizing the aims of the Working Group.

Also on 1 September,[41] the Sub-Commission asked the Secretary-General to encourage the global consultation on the realization of the right to development (see below, under "Economic, social and cultural rights") to take account of the rights and concerns of indigenous peoples, particularly the report of the seminar on the effects of racism and racial discrimination on the social and economic relations between indigenous peoples and States, and to consider the extent to which the same principles might be applicable to other groups. It also asked him to organize regional training courses for indigenous peoples' organizations on international human rights standards and procedures, and to facilitate their participation in the work of the Working Group and their attendance at other UN human rights organs and bodies. The United Nations Centre on Transnational Corporations was invited to assist the Working Group in compiling information on investments and operations on the lands of indigenous peoples.

On the same date,[42] the Sub-Commission entrusted Asbjorn Eide and Christy Mbonu (Nigeria) with the task of preparing a working paper on possible UN activities for an international year for indigenous rights.

In other action on that date, the Sub-Commission decided[43] to endorse the recommendations made by the Working Group on Indigenous Populations in annex I of its report on its 1989 session. It also recommended, for the Working Group's consideration, an agenda including: the scope and effective exercise of internal autonomy and self-government; fiscal and administrative relations between indigenous governments and States; effective means of planning for and implementing autonomy, including negotiated constitutional arrangements and involving both territorial and personal autonomy; and recommendations for standard-setting.

The Sub-Commission expressed its thanks to Bangladesh[44] for progress made in the treatment of its tribal populations.

Study on treaties, agreements and other constructive arrangements

On 6 March,[45] the Commission on Human Rights recommended to the Economic and Social Council a draft text regarding a study on treaties, agreements and other constructive arrangements between States and indigenous populations and the appointment of Special Rapporteur Miguel Alfonso Martínez (Cuba). The text was adopted by the Council on 24 May (see below).

On 24 May, the Economic and Social Council, on the recommendation of its Second (Social) Committee, adopted **resolution 1989/77** without vote.

Study on treaties, agreements and other constructive arrangements between States and indigenous populations

The Economic and Social Council,

Recalling its decision 1988/134 of 27 May 1988,

Taking note of Commission on Human Rights resolutions 1988/56 of 9 March 1988 and 1989/41 of 6 March 1989 and resolutions 1987/17 of 2 September 1987 and 1988/20 of 1 September 1988 of the Sub-Commission on Prevention of Discrimination and Protection of Minorities,

Taking into account the outline of the study prepared by the Special Rapporteur, Mr. Miguel Alfonso Martínez, and of the substantive debate on the topic in the Sub-Commission's Working Group on Indigenous Populations at its sixth session,

1. *Confirms* the appointment of Mr. Miguel Alfonso Martínez as Special Rapporteur of the Sub-Commission on Prevention of Discrimination and Protection of Minorities and authorizes him to carry out the study on the potential utility of treaties, agreements and other constructive arrangements between indigenous populations and Governments referred to in Commission on Human Rights resolution 1988/56;

2. *Requests* the Secretary-General to provide all necessary assistance to the Special Rapporteur in order for him to carry out the study;

3. *Requests* the Special Rapporteur to submit a progress report to the Sub-Commission at its forty-first session.

Economic and Social Council resolution 1989/77

24 May 1989   Meeting 16   Adopted without vote

Approved by Second Committee (E/1989/88) without vote, 19 May (meeting 22); draft by Commission on Human Rights (E/1989/20); agenda item 9.

On 1 September,[46] the Sub-Commission authorized the Special Rapporteur to undertake the travel necessary to prepare his preliminary report. It asked the Secretary-General to assist the Special Rapporteur and to secure the appointment of a consultant to help him during the 1990-1991 biennium.

Hopi-Navajo relocation

On 1 September,[47] the Sub-Commission expressed its appreciation to Erica-Irene Daes and John Carey for their report[48] regarding the relocation of Navajo and Hopi families in northern Arizona (United States) in accordance with the settlement of a land dispute between the two parties. It welcomed initiatives taken by the Navajo Nation and Hopi Tribe to resolve the situation by agreement.

Migrant workers

Draft convention

Human Rights Commission action. On 7 March,[49] the Commission asked the Secretary-General to inform it in 1990 of the progress made on the draft international convention on the protection of migrant workers and their families.

Working Group activities. The Working Group on the Drafting of an International Convention on the Protection of the Rights of All Migrant Workers and Their Families held its eighth inter-sessional meeting from 31 May to 9 June[50] and its tenth session from 26 September to 6 October,[51] both in New York.

At the meetings, the Group discussed the provisions of the draft convention still pending during the second reading.

On 15 December, the General Assembly, on the recommendation of the Third Committee, adopted **resolution 44/155** without vote.

Measures to improve the situation and ensure the human rights and dignity of all migrant workers

The General Assembly,

Reaffirming once more the permanent validity of the principles and standards set forth in the basic instruments regarding the international protection of human rights, in particular in the Universal Declaration of Human Rights, the International Covenants on Human Rights, the International Convention on the Elimination of All Forms of Racial Discrimination and the Convention on the Elimination of All Forms of Discrimination against Women,

Bearing in mind the principles and standards established within the framework of the International Labour Organisation and the United Nations Educational, Scientific and Cultural Organization and the importance of the task carried out in connection with migrant workers and their families in other specialized agencies and in various organs of the United Nations,

Reiterating that in spite of the existence of an already established body of principles and standards, there is a need to make further efforts to improve the situation and ensure the human rights and dignity of all migrant workers and their families,

Recalling its resolution 34/172 of 17 December 1979, in which it decided to establish a working group open to all Member States to elaborate an international convention on the protection of the rights of all migrant workers and their families,

Recalling also its resolutions 35/198 of 15 December 1980, 36/160 of 16 December 1981, 37/170 of 17 December 1982, 38/86 of 16 December 1983, 39/102 of 14 December 1984, 40/130 of 13 December 1985, 41/151 of 4 December 1986, 42/140 of 7 December 1987 and 43/146 of 8 December 1988, by which it renewed the mandate of the Working Group on the Drafting of an International Convention on the Protection of the Rights of All Migrant Workers and Their Families and requested it to continue its work,

Having examined the progress made by the Working Group at its eighth inter-sessional meeting, held from 31 May to 9 June 1989, and at the current session of the General Assembly, from 26 September to 6 October 1989, during which the Working Group continued with the second reading of the draft convention,

1. *Takes note with satisfaction* of the two most recent reports of the Working Group on the Drafting of an International Convention on the Protection of the Rights of All Migrant Workers and Their Families and, in particular, of the progress made by the Working Group on the drafting, in second reading, of the draft convention;

2. *Requests* the Secretary-General to entrust to the Centre for Human Rights of the Secretariat the technical revision of the text of the articles of the draft convention that have been approved so far by the Working Group in second reading, with a view to ensuring uniformity of terminology and gender and to harmonizing the versions in the official languages of the United Nations, bearing in mind General Assembly resolution 41/120 of 4 December 1986, and to transmit the results of this technical revision to Governments as soon as possible, and at least one month before the next meeting of the Working Group, to be held in 1990;

3. *Decides* that the Working Group shall hold a meeting of two weeks' duration in New York, immediately after the first regular session of 1990 of the Economic and Social Council, with a view to completing the remaining articles and considering the results of the technical revision of the draft convention;

4. *Invites* the Secretary-General to transmit to Governments the two most recent reports of the Working Group so as to enable the members of the Working Group to finish the drafting, in second reading, of the draft convention during the meeting referred to in paragraph 3 of the present resolution, as well as to transmit the results obtained at that meeting to the General Assembly so that it may take a decision during its forty-fifth session;

5. *Also invites* the Secretary-General to transmit the above-mentioned documents to the competent organs of the United Nations and to the international organizations concerned, for their information, so as to enable them to continue their co-operation with the Working Group;

6. *Requests* the Secretary-General to do everything possible to ensure adequate secretariat services for the Working Group during the meeting to be held immediately after the first regular session of 1990 of the Economic and Social Council, for the timely fulfilment of its mandate.

General Assembly resolution 44/155

15 December 1989   Meeting 82   Adopted without vote

Approved by Third Committee (A/44/848) without vote, 29 November (meeting 60); 25-nation draft (A/C.3/44/L.74), agenda item 12.
Financial implications. 5th Committee, A/44/854; S-G, A/C.3/44/L.92, A/C.5/44/42.
Meeting numbers. GA 44th session: 3rd Committee 48, 50-60; 5th Committee, 53; plenary 82.

Protection of minorities

The Commission on Human Rights again established an informal open-ended working group to continue work on a draft declaration on the rights of persons belonging to national, ethnic, religious or linguistic minorities. The working group considered draft articles 4 and 5 in meetings held on 8, 9, 10, 14 and 20 February and 6 March.[52]

On 8 March,[53] the Commission decided to establish another working group in 1990 to consider the draft declaration. It further decided that the group would have no fewer than four full meetings, preferably during the first two weeks of the Commission's 1990 session. The Secretary-General was asked to give the group the assistance it needed. The Commission's decisions and request to the Secretary-General were approved by the Economic and Social Council in **decision 1989/146** of 24 May.

As requested by the Sub-Commission in 1988,[54] Claire Palley (United Kingdom) submitted a July working paper[55] on possible ways and means to facilitate the peaceful and constructive resolution of situations involving racial, national, religious and linguistic minorities. On 1 September,[56] the Sub-Commission decided to entrust Asbjorn Eide with preparing a further report on national experience in that area, in accordance with the guidelines and principles set out in the working paper submitted by Claire Palley, for consideration in 1991 and asked him to present a progress report in 1990.

HIV- and AIDS-related discrimination

As requested by the Sub-Commission in 1988,[57] Luis Varela Quirós (Costa Rica) in a July report[58] submitted proposals for a study on AIDS and human rights. He discussed medical and legal aspects of AIDS and possible questions for a study on human rights and AIDS.

On 31 August,[59] the Sub-Commission decided to entrust Mr. Varela Quirós with a study of problems and causes of discrimination against HIV-infected people or people with AIDS and recommended that the Special Rapporteur take into account a resolution of the Commission on Human Rights concerning non-discrimination in the field of health[60] (see below, under ''Other human rights questions'') and the guidelines contained in the International Consultation on HIV/AIDS and Human Rights (Geneva, 26-28 July).[61] It recommended that the Special Rapporteur carry out the study in close co-operation with the World Health Organization (WHO) and asked him to make a preliminary report in 1990. It asked the Secretary-General and the WHO Global Programme on AIDS to provide the Special Rapporteur with all the assistance he needed for the task.

REFERENCES

[1]YUN 1984, p. 785. [2]YUN 1988, p. 487, GA res. 43/91, 8 Dec. 1988. [3]*Ibid.*, p. 485, ESC res. 1988/6, 24 May 1988. [4]E/1989/42. [5]E/1989/42/Add.1-4. [6]A/44/574. [7]YUN 1985, p. 837, GA res. 40/22, 29 Nov. 1985. [8]A/44/575. [9]YUN 1986, p. 682. [10]A/44/595. [11]YUN 1987, p. 730, GA res.

42/47, 30 Nov. 1987. [12]E/1989/48. [13]E/1989/20 (res. 1989/9). [14]E/CN.4/Sub.2/1989/8 & Add.1. [15]E/CN.4/Sub.2/1989/58 (res. 1989/19). [16]A/44/18. [17]*Committee on the Elimination of Racial Discrimination and the Progress Made Toward the Achievement of the Objectives of the International Convention on the Elimination of All Forms of Discrimination: Published on the Occasion of the World Conference to Combat Racism and Racial Discrimination, Geneva, 14-25 August 1978* (CERD.1), Sales No. E.79.XIV.4. [18]YUN 1978, p. 661. [19]YUN 1965, p. 440, GA res. 2106 A (XX), annex, 21 Dec. 1965. [20]YUN 1969, p. 488. [21]E/CN.4/1989/35. [22]E/CN.4/1989/36. [23]*Multilateral Treaties Deposited with the Secretary-General: Status as at 31 December 1989* (ST/LEG/SER.E/8), Sales No. E.90.V.6. [24]A/44/593. [25]YUN 1987, p. 736. [26]E/CN.4/Sub.2/1989/31 & Add.1. [27]E/CN.4/1989/44. [28]YUN 1981, p. 881, GA res. 36/55, 25 Nov. 1981. [29]YUN 1988, p. 492, GA res. 43/108, 8 Dec. 1988. [30]E/1989/20 (res. 1989/44). [31]E/CN.4/Sub.2/1989/58 (res. 1989/23). [32]E/CN.4/Sub.2/1989/32. [33]YUN 1986, p. 736, GA res. 41/120, 4 Dec. 1986. [34]E/1989/20 (res. 1989/34). [35]YUN 1988, p. 495. [36]E/CN.4/1989/22. [37]E/CN.4/Sub.2/1989/36. [38]E/CN.4/Sub.2/1989/33. [39]E/CN.4/Sub.2/1989/33/Add.1-3. [40]E/CN.4/Sub.2/1989/58 (res. 1989/34). [41]*Ibid.* (res. 1989/35). [42]*Ibid.* (res. 1989/36). [43]*Ibid.* (dec. 1989/112). [44]*Ibid.* (dec. 1989/109). [45]E/1989/20 (res. 1989/41). [46]E/CN.4/Sub.2/1989/58 (res. 1989/38). [47]*Ibid.* (res. 1989/37). [48]E/CN.4/Sub.2/1989/35, Part I & Part II & Add.1. [49]E/1989/20 (res. 1989/55). [50]A/C.3/44/1. [51]A/C.3/44/4. [52]E/CN.4/1989/38. [53]E/1989/20 (res. 1989/61). [54]YUN 1988, p. 497. [55]E/CN.4/Sub.2/1989/43. [56]E/CN.4/Sub.2/1989/58 (res. 1989/44). [57]YUN 1988, p. 497. [58]E/CN.4/Sub.2/1989/5. [59]E/CN.4/Sub.2/1989/58 (res. 1989/17). [60]E/1989/20 (res. 1989/11). [61]HR/PUB/90/2.

Civil and political rights

Covenant on Civil and Political Rights and Optional Protocols

Accessions and ratifications

As at 31 December 1989, parties to the International Covenant on Civil and Political Rights and the Optional Protocol thereto, adopted by the General Assembly in 1966[1] and in force since 1976,[2] totalled 89 and 48 States, respectively.[3] Argentina and Ireland ratified the Covenant in 1989; Algeria, Ireland, the Libyan Arab Jamahiriya, Nicaragua and the Philippines acceded to or ratified the Optional Protocol.

In August, the Secretary-General reported on the status of the Covenant as at 1 August 1989.[4]

Human Rights Commission action. On 2 March,[5] the Commission appealed to States that had not yet done so to become parties to the Covenant and Optional Protocol and to consider making the declaration provided for in article 41 of the Covenant. The Commission asked the Secretary-General to report in 1990 on the status of the Covenant and its Protocol.

Second optional protocol

Human Rights Commission action. On 6 March,[6] the Commission decided to transmit to the General Assembly, through the Economic and Social Council, the comparative analysis and the draft second optional protocol to the Covenant aimed at abolishing the death penalty prepared in 1987,[7] as well as the comments expressed thereon by the Sub-Commission in 1988 and 1989 and the Commission in 1989. It asked the Secretary-General to bring the comparative analysis to the attention of all Governments and to invite them to communicate their comments on the text of the draft. He was also requested to submit a report thereon to the General Assembly in 1989. The Commission recommended that the Assembly consider taking action on the second optional protocol.

On 24 May, the Economic and Social Council, by **resolution 1989/64**, recommended that Member States take steps to implement the safeguards and strengthen further the protection of the rights of those facing the death penalty.

ECONOMIC AND SOCIAL COUNCIL ACTION

On 19 May, the Economic and Social Council, on the recommendation of its Second Committee, adopted **decision 1989/139** by recorded vote.

Elaboration of a second optional protocol to the International Covenant on Civil and Political Rights aiming at the abolition of the death penalty

At its 16th plenary meeting, on 24 May 1989, the Economic and Social Council, taking note of Commission on Human Rights resolution 1989/25 of 6 March 1989, approved the Commission's decision to transmit to the General Assembly for suitable action the comparative analysis concerning the proposal to elaborate a second optional protocol to the International Covenant on Civil and Political Rights and the draft second optional protocol prepared by the Special Rapporteur of the Sub-Commission on Prevention of Discrimination and Protection of Minorities, as well as the comments expressed at the thirty-ninth and fortieth sessions of the Sub-Commission and the forty-fifth session of the Commission.

Economic and Social Council decision 1989/139

27-7-15 (recorded vote)

Approved by Second Committee (E/1989/88) by recorded vote (28-4-17), 19 May (meeting 22); draft by Commission on Human Rights (E/1989/20); agenda item 9.

Recorded vote in Council as follows:

In favour: Bolivia, Brazil, Bulgaria, Canada, Colombia, Czechoslovakia, Denmark, France, Germany, Federal Republic of, Greece, Ireland, Italy, Kenya, Netherlands, New Zealand, Nicaragua, Niger, Norway, Poland, Portugal, Ukrainian SSR, USSR, United Kingdom, United States, Uruguay, Venezuela, Zaire.

Against: Iran, Jordan, Libyan Arab Jamahiriya, Oman, Saudi Arabia, Somalia, Sudan.

Abstaining: Bahamas, Belize, Cameroon, Cuba, Ghana, Guinea, Indonesia, Japan, Lesotho, Liberia, Rwanda, Sri Lanka, Trinidad and Tobago, Yugoslavia, Zambia.

Reports of the Secretary-General. In October, the Secretary-General presented the views of 28 Governments on the draft text of the second optional protocol.[8]

In an October note,[9] the Secretary-General stated that pursuant to decisions of the Commission on Human Rights and the Economic and Social Council (see above), the comparative analysis and other necessary documents had been transmitted to the Assembly.

On 15 December, the General Assembly, on the recommendation of the Third Committee, adopted **resolution 44/128** by recorded vote.

Second Optional Protocol to the International Covenant on Civil and Political Rights, aiming at the abolition of the death penalty
The General Assembly,

Recalling article 3 of the Universal Declaration of Human Rights adopted in its resolution 217 A (III) of 10 December 1948,

Recalling also article 6 of the International Covenant on Civil and Political Rights contained in the annex to its resolution 2200 A (XXI) of 16 December 1966,

Mindful of its decision 35/437 of 15 December 1980, reaffirmed in its resolution 36/59 of 25 November 1981, to consider the idea of elaborating a draft of a second optional protocol to the International Covenant on Civil and Political Rights, aiming at the abolition of the death penalty,

Mindful also of its resolution 37/192 of 18 December 1982, in which it requested the Commission on Human Rights to consider the idea of elaborating a draft of a second optional protocol, and its resolution 39/137 of 14 December 1984, in which it requested the Commission and the Sub-Commission on Prevention of Discrimination and Protection of Minorities to consider the idea further,

Taking note of the comparative analysis prepared by the Special Rapporteur of the Sub-Commission on Prevention of Discrimination and Protection of Minorities,

Taking note also of the views expressed by Governments in favour of and against the death penalty and of their comments and observations regarding such a second optional protocol, as reproduced in the relevant reports of the Secretary-General,

Referring to its decision 42/421 of 7 December 1987, and to Commission on Human Rights resolution 1989/25 of 6 March 1989 and Economic and Social Council decision 1989/139 of 24 May 1989, pursuant to which the comparative analysis and the draft second optional protocol to the International Covenant on Civil and Political Rights, aiming at the abolition of the death penalty, prepared by the Special Rapporteur, were transmitted to the General Assembly for suitable action,

Wishing to give States parties to the International Covenant on Civil and Political Rights that choose to do so the opportunity to become parties to a second optional protocol to that convention,

Having considered the draft second optional protocol,

1. *Expresses its appreciation* for the work achieved by the Commission on Human Rights and the Sub-Commission on Prevention of Discrimination and Protection of Minorities;

2. *Adopts* and opens for signature, ratification and accession the Second Optional Protocol to the International Covenant on Civil and Political Rights, aiming at the abolition of the death penalty, contained in the annex to the present resolution;

3. *Calls upon* all Governments in a position to do so to consider signing and ratifying or acceding to the Second Optional Protocol.

ANNEX
Second Optional Protocol to the International Covenant on Civil and Political Rights, aiming at the abolition of the death penalty
The States Parties to the present Protocol,

Believing that abolition of the death penalty contributes to enhancement of human dignity and progressive development of human rights,

Recalling article 3 of the Universal Declaration of Human Rights, adopted on 10 December 1948, and article 6 of the International Covenant on Civil and Political Rights, adopted on 16 December 1966,

Noting that article 6 of the International Covenant on Civil and Political Rights refers to abolition of the death penalty in terms that strongly suggest that abolition is desirable,

Convinced that all measures of abolition of the death penalty should be considered as progress in the enjoyment of the right to life,

Desirous to undertake hereby an international commitment to abolish the death penalty,

Have agreed as follows:

Article 1
1. No one within the jurisdiction of a State Party to the present Protocol shall be executed.
2. Each State Party shall take all necessary measures to abolish the death penalty within its jurisdiction.

Article 2
1. No reservation is admissible to the present Protocol, except for a reservation made at the time of ratification or accession that provides for the application of the death penalty in time of war pursuant to a conviction for a most serious crime of a military nature committed during wartime.
2. The State Party making such a reservation shall at the time of ratification or accession communicate to the Secretary-General of the United Nations the relevant provisions of its national legislation applicable during wartime.
3. The State Party having made such a reservation shall notify the Secretary-General of the United Nations of any beginning or ending of a state of war applicable to its territory.

Article 3
The States Parties to the present Protocol shall include in the reports they submit to the Human Rights Committee, in accordance with article 40 of the Covenant, information on the measures that they have adopted to give effect to the present Protocol.

Article 4
With respect to the States Parties to the Covenant that have made a declaration under article 41, the competence of the Human Rights Committee to receive and consider communications when a State Party claims that another State Party is not fulfilling its obligations shall extend to the provisions of the present Protocol, unless the State Party concerned has made a statement to the contrary at the moment of ratification or accession.

Article 5

With respect to the States Parties to the first Optional Protocol to the International Covenant on Civil and Political Rights adopted on 16 December 1966, the competence of the Human Rights Committee to receive and consider communications from individuals subject to its jurisdiction shall extend to the provisions of the present Protocol, unless the State Party concerned has made a statement to the contrary at the moment of ratification or accession.

Article 6

1. The provisions of the present Protocol shall apply as additional provisions to the Covenant.

2. Without prejudice to the possibility of a reservation under article 2 of the present Protocol, the right guaranteed in article 1, paragraph 1, of the present Protocol shall not be subject to any derogation under article 4 of the Covenant.

Article 7

1. The present Protocol is open for signature by any State that has signed the Covenant.

2. The present Protocol is subject to ratification by any State that has ratified the Covenant or acceded to it. Instruments of ratification shall be deposited with the Secretary-General of the United Nations.

3. The present Protocol shall be open to accession by any State that has ratified the Covenant or acceded to it.

4. Accession shall be effected by the deposit of an instrument of accession with the Secretary-General of the United Nations.

5. The Secretary-General of the United Nations shall inform all States that have signed the present Protocol or acceded to it of the deposit of each instrument of ratification or accession.

Article 8

1. The present Protocol shall enter into force three months after the date of the deposit with the Secretary-General of the United Nations of the tenth instrument of ratification or accession.

2. For each State ratifying the present Protocol or acceding to it after the deposit of the tenth instrument of ratification or accession, the present Protocol shall enter into force three months after the date of the deposit of its own instrument of ratification or accession.

Article 9

The provisions of the present Protocol shall extend to all parts of federal States without any limitations or exceptions.

Article 10

The Secretary-General of the United Nations shall inform all States referred to in article 48, paragraph 1, of the Covenant of the following particulars:

(a) Reservations, communications and notifications under article 2 of the present Protocol;

(b) Statements made under articles 4 or 5 of the present Protocol;

(c) Signatures, ratifications and accessions under article 7 of the present Protocol;

(d) The date of the entry into force of the present Protocol under article 8 thereof.

Article 11

1. The present Protocol, of which the Arabic, Chinese, English, French, Russian and Spanish texts are equally authentic, shall be deposited in the archives of the United Nations.

2. The Secretary-General of the United Nations shall transmit certified copies of the present Protocol to all States referred to in article 48 of the Covenant.

General Assembly resolution 44/128

15 December 1989   Meeting 82   59-26-48 (recorded vote)

Approved by Third Committee (A/44/824) by recorded vote (55-28-45), 22 November (meeting 52); 36-nation draft (A/C.3/44/L.42); agenda item 98.
Meeting numbers. GA 44th session: 3rd Committee 36-43, 50, 52; plenary 82.

Recorded vote in Assembly as follows:

In favour: Argentina, Australia, Austria, Belgium, Bolivia, Brazil, Bulgaria, Byelorussian SSR, Canada, Cape Verde, Colombia, Costa Rica, Cyprus, Czechoslovakia, Democratic Kampuchea, Denmark, Dominican Republic, Ecuador, El Salvador, Finland, France, German Democratic Republic, Germany, Federal Republic of, Greece, Grenada, Guatemala, Haiti, Honduras, Hungary, Iceland, Ireland, Italy, Luxembourg, Malta, Mexico, Mongolia, Nepal, Netherlands, New Zealand, Norway, Panama, Paraguay, Peru, Philippines, Poland, Portugal, Saint Kitts and Nevis, Saint Lucia, Saint Vincent and the Grenadines,* Samoa, Spain, Sweden, Togo, Ukrainian SSR, USSR, United Kingdom, Uruguay, Venezuela, Yugoslavia.

Against: Afghanistan, Bahrain, Bangladesh, Cameroon, China, Djibouti, Egypt, Indonesia, Iran, Iraq, Japan, Jordan, Kuwait, Maldives, Morocco, Nigeria, Oman, Pakistan, Qatar, Saudi Arabia, Sierra Leone, Somalia, Syrian Arab Republic, United Republic of Tanzania, United States, Yemen.

Abstaining: Algeria, Antigua and Barbuda, Bahamas, Barbados, Bhutan, Botswana, Brunei Darussalam, Burkina Faso, Burundi, Chile, Congo, Côte d'Ivoire, Cuba, Democratic Yemen, Dominica, Ethiopia, Fiji, Gambia, Ghana, Guinea, Guyana, India, Israel, Jamaica, Kenya, Lebanon, Lesotho, Liberia, Libyan Arab Jamahiriya, Madagascar, Malawi, Mauritius, Mozambique, Myanmar, Romania, Rwanda, Senegal, Singapore, Solomon Islands, Sri Lanka, Suriname, Trinidad and Tobago, Turkey, Uganda, Vanuatu, Zambia, Zimbabwe.

*Subsequently advised the Secretariat it had intended to abstain.

Implementation

The Human Rights Committee, established under article 28 of the Covenant, held three sessions in 1989: its thirty-fifth from 20 March to 7 April in New York; and the thirty-sixth from 10 to 28 July[10] and thirty-seventh from 23 October to 10 November,[11] both in Geneva.

At those sessions, the Committee considered reports submitted under article 40 of the Covenant from 11 States—Bolivia, Cameroon, Chile, Democratic Yemen, Italy, Mauritius, New Zealand, the Philippines, Togo, the USSR and Uruguay.

In April, the Committee adopted a general comment on article 24 (the enjoyment by children of the right of special protection), which was transmitted to the Economic and Social Council. On 9 November, the Committee adopted a general comment on non-discrimination for transmission to the Economic and Social Council at its first regular session in 1990.

State of siege or emergency

Human Rights Commission action. On 6 March,[12] the Commission, noting a 1988 Sub-Commission resolution,[13] approved the Sub-Commission's request to its Special Rapporteur on the question of human rights and states of emergency to continue to update his work and to submit to the Sub-Commission in 1989 an annual report and a list updated on the basis of the information received, and to update his report to the Sub-Commission for the forty-sixth session of the Commission. It further approved the Sub-Commission's request to the Secretary-General to give the Special Rapporteur all the assistance he required.

Report of the Special Rapporteur. In June, the Special Rapporteur, Leandro Despouy (Argentina), submitted his third annual report[14] containing information on States or territories which, since 1 January 1985, had proclaimed, extended or terminated a state of emergency. The first and second annual reports were issued in 1987[15] and 1988,[16] respectively.

Sub-Commission action. On 1 September,[17] the Sub-Commission asked the Special Rapporteur to present in 1990 the next annual report and list updated on the basis of the information received and to update his present report for the Commission's consideration in 1990. It asked the Secretary-General to give consideration to the technical assistance which might be provided by the Special Rapporteur or by the Secretariat to States requesting it. The Secretary-General was also asked to assist the Special Rapporteur.

As requested by the Sub-Commission, the Special Rapporteur submitted revised and updated information on countries where measures had been taken that constituted the proclamation, introduction, extension, maintenance or termination of emergency regimes in various forms.[14]

Self-determination of peoples

By five resolutions adopted in 1989, the Commission on Human Rights reaffirmed the right to self-determination of the people of Afghanistan,[18] Kampuchea,[19] Palestine,[20] Namibia[21] and Western Sahara.[22] A sixth resolution adopted under the item on the right to self-determination pertained to mercenaries and condemned their use as a means to impede the exercise of the right of peoples to self-determination.[23]

In an October report,[24] the Secretary-General summarized action taken by the Commission and the Economic and Social Council on the right of peoples to self-determination. He also summarized replies received from 13 Governments, 4 specialized agencies, 5 intergovernmental organizations and 3 NGOs in response to his request for information for inclusion in his report. The report was prepared in response to two 1988 General Assembly resolutions.[25]

GENERAL ASSEMBLY ACTION

On 8 December 1989, the General Assembly adopted two resolutions on the right to self-determination, a right it repeatedly reaffirmed for individual Non-Self-Governing Territories (see PART FOUR, Chapter I).

On the recommendation of the Third Committee, the Assembly adopted **resolution 44/79** by recorded vote.

Importance of the universal realization of the right of peoples to self-determination and of the speedy granting of independence to colonial countries and peoples for the effective guarantee and observance of human rights

The General Assembly,

Reaffirming its faith in the importance of the implementation of the Declaration on the Granting of Independence to Colonial Countries and Peoples contained in its resolution 1514(XV) of 14 December 1960,

Reaffirming also the importance of the universal realization of the right of peoples to self-determination, national sovereignty and territorial integrity and of the speedy granting of independence to colonial countries and peoples as imperatives for the full enjoyment of all human rights,

Reaffirming further the obligation of all Member States to comply with the principles of the Charter of the United Nations and the resolutions of the United Nations regarding the exercise of the right to self-determination by peoples under colonial and foreign domination,

Recalling its resolution 1514(XV) and all relevant resolutions concerning the implementation of the Declaration on the Granting of Independence to Colonial Countries and Peoples,

Recalling also its resolutions on the question of Namibia, in particular resolutions 2145(XXI) of 27 October 1966 and S-14/1 of 20 September 1986, as well as the relevant Security Council resolutions, in particular resolutions 385(1976) of 30 January 1976, 435(1978) of 29 September 1978, 629(1989) of 16 January 1989, 632(1989) of 16 February 1989 and 640(1989) of 29 August 1989,

Recalling further the final communiqué adopted by the United Nations Council for Namibia at its ministerial meeting held at United Nations Headquarters on 2 October 1987,

Expressing its support for, and solidarity with, the people of Namibia in their demand for the removal of the racist South African military personnel from Namibia and for the total removal of former Koevoet elements from the South West Africa Police,

Bearing in mind the Declaration adopted by the World Conference on Sanctions against Racist South Africa,

Welcoming the adoption at Harare on 21 August 1989 of the Declaration of the Organization of African Unity *Ad Hoc* Committee on Southern Africa on the question of South Africa[a] and its subsequent endorsement by the Ninth Conference of Heads of State or Government of Non-Aligned Countries, held at Belgrade from 4 to 7 September 1989,[b]

Bearing in mind the outcome of the International Conference on the Alliance between South Africa and Israel, held at Vienna from 11 to 13 July 1983,

---

[a]A/44/697.

[b]A/44/551-S/20870.

Taking note of resolutions CM/Res.1206(L) on Namibia and CM/Res.1207(L) on South Africa adopted by the Council of Ministers of the Organization of African Unity at its fiftieth ordinary session, held at Addis Ababa from 17 to 22 July 1989,[c]

Reaffirming that the system of *apartheid* imposed on the South African people constitutes a violation of the fundamental rights of that people, a crime against humanity and a constant threat to international peace and security,

Reaffirming also its resolution 39/2 of 28 September 1984, and recalling Security Council resolution 554(1984) of 17 August 1984, in which the Council rejected the so-called "new constitution" as null and void, Council resolution 569(1985) of 26 July 1985 and the statement made by the President of the Security Council on 13 June 1986 on the nation-wide state of emergency in South Africa,

Alarmed by the increasing number of assassinations and abductions of members and leaders of the national liberation movements in Africa and elsewhere by hit squads deployed and paid by the racist régime,

Deeply concerned that the restrictions imposed by the Pretoria régime in 1988 on thirty-four democratic and non-violent organizations have not been lifted and that since the beginning of 1989 severe restrictions have been imposed on over six hundred political activists committed to peaceful means of struggle against *apartheid*,

Indignant at the latest ploy of the Pretoria régime aimed at legitimizing its undemocratic structures, namely, the staging on 6 September 1989 of so-called "general elections" for its tri-cameral parliamentary system, which has been overwhelmingly rejected,

Outraged by the massacre of twenty-nine peaceful demonstrators by the racist police during a non-violent protest against the so-called "general elections",

Deeply concerned about the racist régime's increased attacks on the religious community and its individual leaders, including the recent poisoning of the Secretary-General of the South African Council of Churches, as well as the spraying of poisonous substances in the church premises serving as the venue for a conference of religious leaders,

Gravely concerned about the *apartheid* régime's continued use of the death penalty against South African patriots with contemptuous disregard for appeals for clemency from the international community, including the General Assembly,

Considering the concerted campaign by the new President of the *apartheid* régime to project himself as a reformer in order to ward off the further imposition of sanctions by the international community,

Deeply concerned about the continued terrorist acts of aggression committed by the Pretoria régime against independent African States in the region, in particular the unprovoked attacks against Botswana, Mozambique, Zambia and Zimbabwe,

Deeply indignant at the persistent policy of hostility by the racist régime of South Africa against Angola, which constitutes an act of aggression against the sovereignty and territorial integrity of that country,

Reaffirming the national unity and territorial integrity of the Comoros,

Recalling the Political Declaration adopted by the first Conference of Heads of State and Government of the Organization of African Unity and the League of Arab States, held at Cairo from 7 to 9 March 1977,

Recalling also the Geneva Declaration on Palestine and the Programme of Action for the Achievement of Palestinian Rights, adopted by the International Conference on the Question of Palestine,

Considering that the denial of the inalienable rights of the Palestinian people to self-determination, sovereignty, independence and return to Palestine and the brutal suppression by the Israeli forces of the heroic uprising, the *intifadah*, of the Palestinian population in the occupied territories, as well as the repeated Israeli aggression against the population of the region, constitute a serious threat to international peace and security,

Bearing in mind Security Council resolutions 605(1987) of 22 December 1987, 607(1988) of 5 January 1988 and 608(1988) of 14 January 1988 and General Assembly resolutions 43/21 of 3 November 1988, 43/177 of 15 December 1988 and 44/2 of 6 October 1989, on the deterioration of the situation of the Palestinian people in the occupied territories,

Deeply concerned and alarmed at the deplorable consequences of Israel's continuing acts of aggression against Lebanon and recalling all the relevant resolutions of the Security Council, in particular resolutions 425(1978) of 19 March 1978, 508(1982) of 5 June 1982, 509(1982) of 6 June 1982, 520(1982) of 17 September 1982 and 521(1982) of 19 September 1982,

1. *Calls upon* all States to implement fully and faithfully all the resolutions of the United Nations regarding the exercise of the right to self-determination and independence by peoples under colonial and foreign domination;

2. *Reaffirms* the legitimacy of the struggle of peoples for independence, territorial integrity, national unity and liberation from colonial domination, *apartheid* and foreign occupation by all available means, including armed struggle;

3. *Reaffirms also* the inalienable right of the Namibian people, the Palestinian people and all peoples under foreign occupation and colonial domination to self-determination, national independence, territorial integrity, national unity and sovereignty without foreign interference;

4. *Strongly condemns* those Governments that do not recognize the right to self-determination and independence of all peoples still under colonial domination, alien subjugation and foreign occupation, notably the peoples of Africa and the Palestinian people;

5. *Calls upon* Israel to refrain from deporting any Palestinian civilians from the occupied Palestinian territories and to release immediately all Palestinian detainees;

6. *Strongly condemns* the constant and deliberate violations of the fundamental rights of the Palestinian people, as well as the expansionist activities of Israel in the Middle East, which constitute an obstacle to the achievement of self-determination and independence by the Palestinian people and a threat to peace and stability in the region;

7. *Urges* all States, the specialized agencies and organizations of the United Nations system, as well as other international organizations, to extend their support to the Palestinian people through its sole and legiti-

---

[c]A/44/603.

mate representative, the Palestine Liberation Organization, in its struggle to regain its right to self-determination and independence in accordance with the Charter of the United Nations;

8. *Welcomes* the adoption by the Security Council of resolutions 629(1989) and 632(1989), by which the Council commenced the process of implementing the United Nations plan for the independence of Namibia, contained in its resolutions 385(1976) and 435(1978);

9. *Reaffirms* that Namibia remains under the direct and legal responsibility of the United Nations until independence, and expresses full support for the inalienable rights of the Namibian people to self-determination and genuine national independence, in a united Namibia, with its territorial integrity untruncated;

10. *Expresses concern* that South Africa has persistently violated the letter and spirit of Security Council resolution 435(1978), which remains the only internationally acceptable basis for the peaceful settlement of the Namibian conflict and must be implemented in its original and definitive form;

11. *Demands* the immediate and unconditional release of all Namibians still imprisoned and detained by the Pretoria régime;

12. *Demands also* that the racist régime of Pretoria put an immediate end to the persistent denial of equal access to the State-controlled media in Namibia by all political organizations participating in the electoral process in accordance with Security Council resolution 435(1978);

13. *Urges* all States, the specialized agencies and organizations of the United Nations system, as well as other international organizations, to extend their support to the Namibian people in their struggle for self-determination and national independence in accordance with the Charter;

14. *Condemns* the policy of "bantustanization" and reiterates its support for the oppressed people of South Africa in its just and legitimate struggle against the racist minority régime of Pretoria;

15. *Reaffirms* its rejection of the so-called "new constitution" and the so-called "general elections" based on that constitution as null and void, and reiterates that peace in South Africa can be guaranteed only by the establishment of majority rule through the full and free exercise of adult suffrage by all the people in a united and undivided South Africa;

16. *Commends* the mass democratic movement in South Africa for the tremendous advances scored during the recent campaign of defiance to unjust *apartheid* laws in the ongoing struggle against *apartheid;*

17. *Strongly condemns* the holding of so-called "general elections" on 6 September 1989, which will further entrench white supremacy, and demands the calling of free and fair elections based on universal adult suffrage in a united and democratic South Africa;

18. *Also strongly condemns* the wanton killing of peaceful and defenceless demonstrators and workers on strike, as well as the arbitrary arrests of leaders and activists of the mass democratic movement, including women and young children, and demands their immediate and unconditional release, in particular that of Nelson Mandela;

19. *Further strongly condemns* South Africa for the imposition, renewal and extension of the state of emergency under its repugnant Internal Security Act and calls for the immediate lifting of the state of emergency, as well as the repeal of the Internal Security Act and all other legislation designed to circumscribe political activity;

20. *Welcomes* the unconditional release of Walter Sisulu and six other political prisoners and demands that the *apartheid* régime lift the restrictions imposed on all of the released political prisoners;

21. *Strongly urges* the *apartheid* régime to respond positively to the provisions of the Declaration of the Organization of African Unity *Ad Hoc* Committee on Southern Africa on the question of South Africa, adopted at Harare on 21 August 1989, by releasing unconditionally all political prisoners and detainees, including Nelson Mandela, by lifting all bans and restrictions on all proscribed and restricted organizations and persons, and by halting all political trials and political executions as a means of creating an environment conducive to the peaceful resolution of the South African situation;

22. *Strongly condemns* the increased attacks on the religious community and its leaders and demands that the racist Pretoria régime bring to justice those responsible for the bombing of the offices of religious bodies and for the poisoning of the Secretary-General of the South African Council of Churches and the attempts to poison other religious leaders;

23. *Also strongly condemns* the establishment and use of armed terrorist groups by South Africa with a view to pitting them against the national liberation movements and destabilizing the legitimate Governments of southern Africa;

24. *Calls once again* for the full implementation of the provisions of the Declaration adopted by the World Conference on Sanctions against Racist South Africa;

25. *Again demands* the immediate application of the mandatory arms embargo against South Africa, imposed under Security Council resolution 418(1977) of 4 November 1977, by all countries and more particularly by those countries which maintain military and nuclear co-operation with the racist Pretoria régime and continue to supply it with related *matériel;*

26. *Strongly condemns* the policy of those Western States, Israel and other States whose political, economic, military, nuclear, strategic, cultural and sports relations with the racist minority régime of South Africa encourage that régime to persist in its suppression of the aspirations of the people to self-determination and independence;

27. *Denounces* the collusion between Israel and South Africa and expresses support for the Declaration of the International Conference on the Alliance between South Africa and Israel;

28. *Strongly condemns* the persistent policy of hostility and aggression pursued by racist South Africa against the sovereignty and territorial integrity of Angola, which constitutes a violation of the New York accord of 22 December 1988;

29. *Demands* that the Pretoria régime respect the sovereignty and territorial integrity of Angola and the principle of non-interference in the internal affairs of that State, and demands the immediate payment of compensation to Angola for damages caused, in accordance with the relevant decisions and resolutions of the Security Council;

30. *Commends* the Government of Angola for its political will, diplomatic flexibility and constructive spirit

in the search for a negotiated solution to the problems of southern Africa;

31. *Strongly reaffirms* its solidarity with the independent African countries and national liberation movements that are victims of murderous acts of aggression and destabilization by the racist régime of Pretoria, and calls upon the international community to render increased assistance and support to these countries in order to enable them to strengthen their defence capacity, defend their sovereignty and territorial integrity and peacefully rebuild and develop;

32. *Strongly condemns* the racist régime of Pretoria for its acts of destabilization against Lesotho, and strongly urges the international community to continue to extend maximum assistance to Lesotho to enable it to fulfil its international humanitarian obligations towards refugees and to use its influence on the racist régime so that it desists from such acts against Lesotho;

33. *Also strongly condemns* the unprovoked and unwarranted military attacks of 14 June 1985, 19 May 1986 and 20 June 1988 on the capital of Botswana, and demands that the racist régime pay full and adequate compensation to Botswana for the loss of life and damage to property;

34. *Further strongly condemns* the escalation of massacres of defenceless people and the continuing destruction of economic and social infrastructures perpetrated against Mozambique by armed terrorists, who are an extension of the South African army of aggression;

35. *Reaffirms* all relevant resolutions adopted by the Organization of African Unity and the United Nations on the question of Western Sahara, including General Assembly resolution 43/33 of 22 November 1988, and calls upon the current Chairman of the Assembly of Heads of State and Government of the Organization of African Unity and the Secretary-General of the United Nations to continue their efforts to find a just and lasting solution to the question;

36. *Notes* the contacts between the Government of the Comoros and the Government of France in the search for a just solution to the problem of the integration of the Comorian island of Mayotte into the Comoros, in accordance with the resolutions of the Organization of African Unity and the United Nations on the question;

37. *Strongly condemns* the continued violation of the human rights of the peoples still under colonial domination and alien subjugation;

38. *Calls* for a substantial increase in all forms of assistance given by all States, United Nations organs, the specialized agencies and non-governmental organizations to the victims of racism, racial discrimination and *apartheid* through national liberation movements recognized by the Organization of African Unity;

39. *Reaffirms* that the practice of using mercenaries against sovereign States and national liberation movements constitutes a criminal act, and calls upon the Governments of all countries to enact legislation declaring the recruitment, financing and training of mercenaries in their territories and the transit of mercenaries through their territories to be punishable offences, and prohibiting their nationals from serving as mercenaries, and to report on such legislation to the Secretary-General;

40. *Demands* the immediate and unconditional release of all persons detained or imprisoned as a result of their struggle for self-determination and independence, full respect for their fundamental individual rights and compliance with article 5 of the Universal Declaration of Human Rights, under which no one shall be subjected to torture or to cruel, inhuman or degrading treatment;

41. *Expresses its appreciation* for the material and other forms of assistance that peoples under colonial rule continue to receive from Governments, organizations of the United Nations system and other intergovernmental organizations, and calls for a substantial increase in that assistance;

42. *Urges* all States, the specialized agencies and other competent organizations of the United Nations system to do their utmost to ensure the full implementation of the Declaration on the Granting of Independence to Colonial Countries and Peoples and to intensify their efforts to support peoples under colonial, foreign and racist domination in their just struggle for self-determination and independence;

43. *Requests* the Secretary-General to give maximum publicity to the Declaration on the Granting of Independence to Colonial Countries and Peoples and to give the widest possible publicity to the struggle of oppressed peoples for the achievement of their self-determination and national independence and to report periodically to the General Assembly on his activities in this regard;

44. *Decides* to consider this item at its forty-fifth session on the basis of the reports on the strengthening of assistance to colonial territories and peoples that Governments, organizations of the United Nations system, other intergovernmental organizations and non-governmental organizations have been requested to submit.

General Assembly resolution 44/79

8 December 1989   Meeting 78   123-15-16 (recorded vote)

Approved by Third Committee (A/44/717) by recorded vote (107-15-15), 30 October (meeting 23); draft by Kenya (A/C.3/44/L.8) for Group of African States, orally revised; agenda item 105.
Meeting numbers. GA 44th session: 3rd Committee 3-11, 15, 23; plenary 78.

Recorded vote in Assembly as follows:

In favour: Afghanistan, Albania, Algeria, Angola, Antigua and Barbuda, Argentina, Bahamas, Bahrain, Bangladesh, Barbados, Benin, Bhutan, Bolivia, Botswana, Brazil, Brunei Darussalam, Bulgaria, Burkina Faso, Burundi, Byelorussian SSR, Cameroon, Cape Verde, Central African Republic, Chad, China, Colombia, Comoros, Congo, Côte d'Ivoire, Cuba, Cyprus, Czechoslovakia, Democratic Kampuchea, Democratic Yemen, Djibouti, Dominica, Dominican Republic, Ecuador, Egypt, Equatorial Guinea, Ethiopia, Gabon, Gambia, German Democratic Republic, Ghana, Greenada, Guatemala, Guinea, Guinea-Bissau, Guyana, Haiti, Honduras, Hungary, India, Indonesia, Iran, Iraq, Jamaica, Jordan, Kenya, Kuwait, Lao People's Democratic Republic, Lebanon, Lesotho, Liberia, Libyan Arab Jamahiriya, Madagascar, Malaysia, Maldives, Mali, Mauritania, Mauritius, Mexico, Mongolia, Morocco, Mozambique, Myanmar, Nepal, Nicaragua, Niger, Nigeria, Oman, Pakistan, Panama, Papua New Guinea, Peru, Philippines, Poland, Qatar, Romania, Rwanda, Saint Vincent and the Grenadines, Sao Tome and Principe, Saudi Arabia, Seychelles, Sierra Leone, Singapore, Solomon Islands, Somalia, Sri Lanka, Sudan, Suriname, Swaziland, Syrian Arab Republic, Thailand, Togo, Trinidad and Tobago, Tunisia, Turkey, Uganda, Ukrainian SSR, USSR, United Arab Emirates, United Republic of Tanzania, Uruguay, Vanuatu, Venezuela, Viet Nam, Yemen, Yugoslavia, Zaire, Zambia, Zimbabwe.

Against: Belgium, Canada, Denmark, Finland, France, Germany, Federal Republic of, Iceland, Israel, Italy, Luxembourg, Netherlands, Norway, Sweden, United Kingdom, United States.

Abstaining: Australia, Austria, Chile, El Salvador, Fiji, Greece, Ireland, Japan, Malawi, Malta, New Zealand, Paraguay, Portugal, Saint Lucia, Samoa, Spain.

Also on 8 December, the Assembly adopted **resolution 44/80**, on the recommendation of the Third Committee, without vote.

Universal realization of the right of peoples to self-determination

The General Assembly,

Reaffirming the importance, for the effective guarantee and observance of human rights, of the universal realization of the right of peoples to self-determination enshrined in the Charter of the United Nations and embodied in the International Covenants on Human Rights, as well as in the Declaration on the Granting of Independence to Colonial Countries and Peoples contained in General Assembly resolution 1514(XV) of 14 December 1960,

Welcoming the progressive exercise of the right to self-determination by peoples under colonial, foreign or alien occupation and their emergence into sovereign statehood and independence,

Deeply concerned at the continuation of acts or threats of foreign military intervention and occupation that are threatening to suppress, or have already suppressed, the right to self-determination of an increasing number of sovereign peoples and nations,

Expressing grave concern that, as a consequence of the persistence of such actions, millions of people have been and are being uprooted from their homes as refugees and displaced persons, and emphasizing the urgent need for concerted international action to alleviate their condition,

Recalling the relevant resolutions regarding the violation of the right of peoples to self-determination and other human rights as a result of foreign military intervention, aggression and occupation, adopted by the Commission on Human Rights at its thirty-sixth, thirty-seventh, thirty-eighth, thirty-ninth, fortieth, forty-first, forty-second, forty-third, forty-fourth and forty-fifth sessions,

Reiterating its resolutions 35/35 B of 14 November 1980, 36/10 of 28 October 1981, 37/42 of 3 December 1982, 38/16 of 22 November 1983, 39/18 of 23 November 1984, 40/24 of 29 November 1985, 41/100 of 4 December 1986, 42/94 of 7 December 1987 and 43/105 of 8 December 1988,

Taking note of the report of the Secretary-General,

1. *Reaffirms* that the universal realization of the right of all peoples, including those under colonial, foreign and alien domination, to self-determination is a fundamental condition for the effective guarantee and observance of human rights and for the preservation and promotion of such rights;

2. *Declares its firm opposition* to acts of foreign military intervention, aggression and occupation, since these have resulted in the suppression of the right of peoples to self-determination and other human rights in certain parts of the world;

3. *Calls upon* those States responsible to cease immediately their military intervention and occupation of foreign countries and territories and all acts of repression, discrimination, exploitation and maltreatment, particularly the brutal and inhuman methods reportedly employed for the execution of these acts against the peoples concerned;

4. *Deplores* the plight of the millions of refugees and displaced persons who have been uprooted as a result of the aforementioned acts and reaffirms their right to return to their homes voluntarily in safety and honour;

5. *Requests* the Commission on Human Rights to continue to give special attention to the violation of human rights, especially the right to self-determination, resulting from foreign military intervention, aggression or occupation;

6. *Requests* the Secretary-General to report on this issue to the General Assembly at its forty-fifth session under the item entitled ''Importance of the universal realization of the right of peoples to self-determination and of the speedy granting of independence to colonial countries and peoples for the effective guarantee and observance of human rights''.

General Assembly resolution 44/80

8 December 1989   Meeting 78   Adopted without vote

Approved by Third Committee (A/44/717) without vote, 30 October (meeting 23); 25-nation draft (A/C.3/44/L.9); agenda item 105.
Meeting numbers. GA 44th session: 3rd Committee 3-11, 15, 23; plenary 78.

Afghanistan

On 6 March,[18] the Commission on Human Rights welcomed the conclusion in 1988 of the Agreements on the Settlement of the Situation Relating to Afghanistan[26] and the completion of the withdrawal of foreign troops from the country. It also welcomed the appointment of the Special Co-ordinator for Humanitarian and Economic Assistance relating to Afghanistan and called on all States to provide adequate resources to the Special Co-ordinator to repatriate and rehabilitate Afghan refugees, as well as for the economic and social reconstruction of the country. Reaffirming the right of the Afghan people to self-determination, the Commission called for the establishment of a broad-based representative government to ensure the broadest support and immediate participation of all segments of the Afghan people, thus enabling them freely to exercise that right. It called on the parties concerned to work for the urgent achievement of a comprehensive political solution and the creation of peace and normal conditions. The Secretary-General was asked to facilitate the early realization of a comprehensive political settlement.

Kampuchea

On 6 March,[19] by a roll-call vote of 35 to 7, with 1 abstention, the Commission reiterated its condemnation of persistent gross violations of human rights in Kampuchea and reaffirmed that the continued illegal occupation of the country by foreign forces deprived Kampucheans of their right to self-determination and constituted the primary human rights violation in that country. It emphasized that the withdrawal of all foreign forces, restoration of Kampuchea's independence, sovereignty and territorial integrity, recognition of the Kampucheans' right to self-determination and the commitment of all States to non-interference in the country's internal affairs were essential for a solution. The Commission reaffirmed its call for an end to hostilities and an immediate withdrawal of foreign forces. The Secretary-General was asked to continue to monitor developments in Kampuchea and to intensify efforts to bring about a comprehensive political settlement and the restoration of fundamental human rights. The Commission recommended that the Economic and Social Council continue to undertake measures to implement recommendations to achieve the full enjoyment of fundamental human rights and freedoms by the Kampuchean people.

The Economic and Social Council, by **decision 1989/156** of 24 May, also expressed its grave concern at the continued violations of fundamental human rights in Kampuchea by foreign occupying forces, in particular the shelling of civilian camps along the border, and requested the Secretary-General to report to the Council any further violations perpetrated against Kampuchean civilian refugees. It endorsed the Commission's resolution and reaffirmed its previous calls for the withdrawal of all foreign forces. The Council also took note of the announced withdrawal of occupying forces, the dialogue between the parties directly involved and other diplomatic activities; however, it expressed concern at the unresolved problem of the 350,000 Kampuchean civilians still stranded in Thailand (see also PART TWO, Chapter III).

Palestinians

On 6 March,[20] by a roll-call vote of 31 to 1, with 11 abstentions, the Commission on Human Rights adopted a resolution reaffirming the right of the Palestinian people to self-determination and calling on Israel to withdraw from the Palestinian and Arab territories. It asked the Secretary-General to make available to the Commission, prior to its 1990 session, all information pertaining to the implementation of its resolution and to transmit the resolution to Israel and to report thereon in 1990.

South Africa and Namibia

In a 6 March resolution,[21] the Commission called on States to take steps to enable the peoples of South Africa and Namibia to exercise fully and without delay their right to self-determination and independence. It reaffirmed the inalienable right of the people of Namibia to self-determination, freedom and national independence in a united Namibia, including Walvis Bay and the offshore islands. The Commission demanded that South Africa release all people detained or imprisoned as a result of their struggle for self-determination and independence and that it guarantee full respect for their fundamental rights. It also demanded that all States impose mandatory and comprehensive sanctions against South Africa in order to stop it from committing further acts of destabilization against neighbouring States.

(For human rights violations in South Africa and Namibia, see below, under "Human rights violations". For details on the situation in Namibia, see also PART TWO, Chapter II, and PART FOUR, Chapter III.)

Western Sahara

On 6 March,[22] by a roll-call vote of 24 to none, with 17 abstentions, the Commission reaffirmed that the question of Western Sahara was one of decolonization to be resolved through the exercise of the people's right to self-determination and independence. It again requested the parties to the conflict, the Kingdom of Morocco and the Frente Popular para la Liberación de Saguia el-Hamra y de Río de Oro (POLISARIO), to negotiate directly with a view to bringing about a cease-fire and creating conditions for a referendum for self-determination.

Mercenaries

Human Rights Commission action. By a resolution of 6 March,[23] adopted by a roll-call vote of 32 to 10, with 1 abstention, the Commission condemned the increased recruitment, financing, training, assembly, transit and use of mercenaries, and urged States to take measures to prohibit those and all other forms of assistance to mercenaries. Taking note of a report of the Special Rapporteur (see below), the Commission asked him, among other things, to develop further the position that mercenary acts and mercenarism in general were means of violating human rights and thwarting the self-determination of peoples. It also asked him to submit a report to the Commission in 1990 and a preliminary report to the General Assembly in 1989. The Secretary-General was asked to assist the Special Rapporteur in carrying out his duties. The Commission recommended to the Economic and Social Council that it make arrangements to ensure that the resources were provided to implement its resolution.

Reports of the Special Rapporteur. As requested by the Commission in 1988,[27] the Special Rapporteur, Enrique Bernales Ballesteros (Peru), submitted a January report[28] containing information on mercenary activities. Based on replies received in response to his request to States for information, the Special Rapporteur noted that despite repeated condemnation of mercenary activities by the United Nations, the problem continued to exist, and that the main form taken by such activities was directly related to illicit activities involving interventionism and the use of force. It also appeared from the replies that few countries had made specific provision in their national legislation to treat mercenary activities as offences. Among other things, the Special Rapporteur recommended support for the work of the *Ad Hoc* Committee on the Drafting of an International Convention against the Recruitment, Use, Financing and Training of Mercenaries. The General Assembly adopted the Convention in December 1989 by **resolution 44/34** (see PART FIVE, Chapter II).

In accordance with a 1988 request of the General Assembly,[29] the Secretary-General, by an October note,[30] transmitted a report of the Special Rapporteur which stated that the number of complaints of mercenary activities had declined appreciably, and that the world had entered a phase of significant easing of tensions.

The Special Rapporteur recommended strengthening UN principles and declarations by adding provisions aimed at eliminating all types of mercenary activities; the inclusion by States in their national legislation of sanctions against mercenary activities; and calling on States to ensure that their territory was not used for the recruitment, assembly, financing, training and transit of mercenaries or the planning of mercenary activities.

GENERAL ASSEMBLY ACTION

On 8 December, the General Assembly, on the recommendation of the Third Committee, adopted **resolution 44/81** by recorded vote.

Use of mercenaries as a means to violate human rights and to impede the exercise of the right of peoples to self-determination

The General Assembly,

Recalling the purposes and principles enshrined in the Charter of the United Nations concerning the strict observance of the principles of sovereign equality, political independence, territorial integrity of States and self-determination of peoples, as well as a scrupulous respect for the principle of the non-use or threat of use of force in international relations, as developed in the Declaration on Principles of International Law concerning Friendly Relations and Co-operation among States in accordance with the Charter of the United Nations,

Reaffirming the legitimacy of the struggle of peoples and their liberation movements for independence, territorial integrity, national unity and liberation from colonial domination, *apartheid* and foreign intervention and occupation, and that their legitimate struggle can in no way be considered as or equated to mercenary activity,

Recognizing that the use of mercenaries is a threat to international peace and security,

Deeply concerned about the menace that the activities of mercenaries represent for all States, particularly African, Central American and other developing States,

Alarmed at the emergence of new international criminal activities carried out by mercenaries in collusion with drug traffickers,

Recognizing that the activities of mercenaries are contrary to the fundamental principles of international law, such as non-interference in the internal affairs of States, territorial integrity and independence, and impede the process of the self-determination of peoples struggling

against colonialism, racism and *apartheid* and all forms of foreign domination,

Recalling all of its relevant resolutions, in which, *inter alia*, it condemned any State that permitted or tolerated the recruitment, financing, training, assembly, transit and use of mercenaries, with the objective of overthrowing the Governments of States Members of the United Nations, especially those of developing countries, or of fighting against national liberation movements, and recalling also the relevant resolutions of the Security Council and the Economic and Social Council, as well as of the Organization of African Unity,

Deeply concerned about the loss of life, the substantial damage to property and the short-term and long-term negative effects on the economy of southern African countries resulting from mercenary aggression,

Convinced that it is necessary to develop international co-operation among States for the prevention, prosecution and punishment of such offences,

1. *Expresses its appreciation* to the Special Rapporteur of the Commission on Human Rights for his report on the question of the use of mercenaries as a means to violate human rights and to impede the exercise of the right of peoples to self-determination;

2. *Condemns* the recruitment, financing, training, assembly, transit and use of mercenaries, as well as all other forms of support to mercenaries for the purpose of destabilizing and overthrowing the Governments of States in southern Africa and Central America and of other developing States and fighting against national liberation movements of peoples struggling for the exercise of their right to self-determination;

3. *Affirms* that the use as well as the recruitment, financing and training of mercenaries are offences of grave concern to all States and violate the purposes and principles enshrined in the Charter of the United Nations;

4. *Strongly condemns* the racist régime of South Africa for its use of groups of armed mercenaries against national liberation movements and for the destabilization of the Governments of southern African States;

5. *Denounces* any State that persists in the recruitment, or permits or tolerates the recruitment, of mercenaries and provides facilities to them for launching armed aggression against other States;

6. *Urges* all States to take the necessary steps and to exercise the utmost vigilance against the menace posed by the activities of mercenaries and to ensure, by both administrative and legislative measures, that the territory of those States and other territories under their control, as well as their nationals, are not used for the recruitment, assembly, financing, training and transit of mercenaries, or for the planning of activities designed to destabilize or overthrow the Government of any State and to fight the national liberation movements struggling against racism, *apartheid*, colonial domination and foreign intervention or occupation;

7. *Calls upon* all States to extend humanitarian assistance to victims of situations resulting from the use of mercenaries, as well as from colonial or alien domination or foreign occupation;

8. *Considers* that the use of channels of humanitarian and other assistance to finance, train and arm mercenaries is inadmissible;

9. *Welcomes* the provisions of Commission on Human Rights resolution 1988/7 of 22 February 1988 aimed at

giving the Special Rapporteur the full opportunity to carry out his mandate most effectively;

10. *Requests* the Secretary-General to report to the General Assembly at its forty-fifth session on the use of mercenaries.

General Assembly resolution 44/81

8 December 1989   Meeting 78   125-10-21 (recorded vote)

Approved by Third Committee (A/44/717) by recorded vote (111-10-20), 30 October (meeting 23); 41-nation draft (A/C.3/44/L.10), orally revised; agenda item 105.

Meeting numbers. GA 44th session: 3rd Committee 3-11, 15, 23; plenary 78.

Recorded vote in Assembly as follows:

In favour: Afghanistan, Albania, Algeria, Angola, Antigua and Barbuda, Argentina, Bahamas, Bahrain, Bangladesh, Barbados, Benin, Bhutan, Bolivia, Botswana, Brazil, Brunei Darussalam, Bulgaria, Burkina Faso, Burundi, Byelorussian SSR, Cameroon, Cape Verde, Central African Republic, Chad, China, Colombia, Comoros, Congo, Côte d'Ivoire, Cuba, Cyprus, Czechoslovakia, Democratic Kampuchea, Democratic Yemen, Djibouti, Dominica, Dominican Republic, Ecuador, Egypt, Equatorial Guinea, Ethiopia, Gabon, Gambia, German Democratic Republic, Ghana, Grenada, Guatemala, Guinea, Guinea-Bissau, Guyana, Haiti, Hungary, India, Indonesia, Iran, Iraq, Jamaica, Jordan, Kenya, Kuwait, Lao People's Democratic Republic, Lebanon, Lesotho, Liberia, Libyan Arab Jamahiriya, Madagascar, Malawi, Malaysia, Maldives, Mali, Mauritania, Mauritius, Mexico, Mongolia, Morocco, Mozambique, Myanmar, Nepal, Nicaragua, Niger, Nigeria, Oman, Pakistan, Panama, Papua New Guinea, Peru, Philippines, Poland, Qatar, Romania, Rwanda, Saint Lucia, Saint Vincent and the Grenadines, Samoa, Sao Tome and Principe, Saudi Arabia, Senegal, Seychelles, Sierra Leone, Singapore, Solomon Islands, Somalia, Sri Lanka, Sudan, Suriname, Swaziland, Syrian Arab Republic, Thailand, Togo, Trinidad and Tobago, Tunisia, Uganda, Ukrainian SSR, USSR, United Arab Emirates, United Republic of Tanzania, Uruguay, Vanuatu, Venezuela, Viet Nam, Yemen, Yugoslavia, Zaire, Zambia, Zimbabwe.

Against: Belgium, France, Germany, Federal Republic of, Italy, Japan, Luxembourg, Netherlands, Portugal, United Kingdom, United States.

Abstaining: Australia, Austria, Canada, Chile, Costa Rica, Denmark, El Salvador, Fiji, Finland, Greece, Honduras, Iceland, Ireland, Israel, Malta, New Zealand, Norway, Paraguay, Spain, Sweden, Turkey.

Rights of detained persons

Administration of justice

On 6 March,[31] the Commission called on Member States to provide effective legislation and other mechanisms to ensure implementation of UN standards on human rights in the administration of justice, taking into account recommendations made by the General Assembly in 1988.[32] It called on its special rapporteurs and working groups to give special attention to questions relating to the effective protection of human rights in the administration of justice and to provide specific recommendations, including proposals for concrete measures under the UN advisory services programmes. The Commission asked the Secretary-General to study the feasibility of drafting model texts for national legislative or other measures for the effective implementation of standards in the area of the administration of justice, to seek the views of Member States on the issue and to inform the Commission in 1990 of the results of his study.

Reports of the Secretary-General. In a July report,[33] the Secretary-General presented succinct information on the work of the Human Rights Committee and CERD, developments elsewhere in the human rights programme and the activities within the UN programme on crime prevention and control related to the rights of detained or imprisoned persons. In addition, he discussed extralegal, arbitrary and summary executions; capital punishment; the work of the Committee against Torture; the 1988 Body of Principles for the Protection of All Persons under Any Form of Detention or Imprisonment;[34] standard minimum rules for the treatment of prisoners; independence of the judiciary; a code of conduct for law enforcement officials; victims of crime and abuse of power; juvenile justice; computerization of the administration of justice; and advisory services and the administration of justice.

Also in July,[35] the Secretary-General presented a synopsis of material from NGOs referring to practices such as enforced disappearances, administrative detention without charge or trial, death during detention, and extrajudicial executions and other arbitrary or summary executions. Special attention was called to the issues of children in detention, the death penalty and the involvement of doctors in torture.

GENERAL ASSEMBLY ACTION

On 15 December, the General Assembly, on the recommendation of the Third Committee, adopted **resolution 44/162** without vote.

Human rights in the administration of justice

The General Assembly,

Bearing in mind the principles embodied in articles 3, 5, 9, 10 and 11 of the Universal Declaration of Human Rights and the relevant provisions of the International Covenant on Civil and Political Rights, in particular article 6, which explicitly states that no one shall be arbitrarily deprived of his life and prohibits the imposition of the death penalty for crimes committed by persons below eighteen years of age,

Bearing in mind also the relevant principles embodied in the Convention against Torture and Other Cruel, Inhuman or Degrading Treatment or Punishment and in the International Convention on the Elimination of All Forms of Racial Discrimination,

Calling attention to the Body of Principles for the Protection of All Persons under Any Form of Detention or Imprisonment, set forth in the annex to its resolution 43/173 of 9 December 1988,

Calling attention also to the Declaration of Basic Principles of Justice for Victims of Crime and Abuse of Power and the safeguards guaranteeing protection of the rights of those facing the death penalty, as well as to the Basic Principles on the Independence of the Judiciary, the Model Agreement on the Transfer of Foreign Prisoners and recommendations on the treatment of foreign prisoners, the Code of Conduct for Law Enforcement Officials and the Standard Minimum Rules for the Treatment of Prisoners,

Reaffirming in this context the importance of the principles contained in its resolution 41/120 of 4 December 1986 on standard-setting in the field of human rights,

Recognizing the important contribution of the Commission on Human Rights in the field of human rights in the administration of justice, as reflected in its resolutions 1989/24 of 6 March 1989 on human rights in the administration of justice, 1989/32 of 6 March 1989 on the independence and impartiality of the judiciary, jurors and assessors and the independence of lawyers, 1989/38 of 6 March 1989 on administrative detention without charge or trial and 1989/64 of 8 March 1989 on summary or arbitrary executions,

Recognizing also the significant work accomplished in this area under the United Nations crime prevention and criminal justice programme, including the results of the interregional and regional preparatory meetings for the Eighth United Nations Congress on the Prevention of Crime and the Treatment of Offenders,

Convinced of the need for further co-ordinated and concerted action in promoting respect for human rights in the administration of justice,

Noting with satisfaction that the Commission on Human Rights, in its resolution 1989/24, *inter alia*, stressed the desirability of providing States, at their request, with continued assistance in the field of the administration of justice and of including in such assistance the provision of model texts for national legislative or other measures for the effective implementation of standards in this field,

1. *Reaffirms* the importance of the full implementation of United Nations norms and standards on human rights in the administration of justice;

2. *Endorses* Economic and Social Council resolution 1989/63 of 24 May 1989 on the implementation of United Nations standards and norms in crime prevention and criminal justice;

3. *Also endorses* the Principles on the Effective Prevention and Investigation of Extra-legal, Arbitrary and Summary Executions set forth in the annex to Economic and Social Council resolution 1989/65 of 24 May 1989;

4. *Further endorses* Economic and Social Council resolutions 1989/57 of 24 May 1989 on the implementation of the Declaration of Basic Principles of Justice for Victims of Crime and Abuse of Power, 1989/60 of 24 May 1989 on the Procedures for the Effective Implementation of the Basic Principles on the Independence of the Judiciary, 1989/61 of 24 May 1989 on Guidelines for the Effective Implementation of the Code of Conduct for Law Enforcement Officials and 1989/64 of 24 May 1989 on the implementation of the safeguards guaranteeing protection of the rights of those facing the death penalty;

5. *Invites* Member States to pay attention to these resolutions in developing strategies for the practical implementation of United Nations norms and standards on human rights in the administration of justice, as it requested in its resolution 43/153 of 8 December 1988;

6. *Requests* the Commission on Human Rights to invite the Sub-Commission on Prevention of Discrimination and Protection of Minorities to study the practical implementation of United Nations norms and standards in this field and to recommend practical measures to the Commission;

7. *Requests* the Secretary-General in this regard:

(a) To solicit from Member States as well as from the relevant international agencies and bodies, in particular the Human Rights Committee, the Committee against Torture and the Committee for the Elimination of Racial Discrimination, comments on the implementation of these standards;

(b) To forward those comments to the Sub-Commission on Prevention of Discrimination and Protection of Minorities at its next session;

8. *Also requests* the Secretary-General:

(a) To identify general problems that may impinge on the effective implementation of standards and norms and to recommend viable solutions with action-oriented proposals;

(b) To formulate practical proposals on procedures and action at the national, regional and international levels to implement United Nations norms and standards on human rights in the administration of justice for the Eighth United Nations Congress on the Prevention of Crime and the Treatment of Offenders;

(c) To continue to assist Member States, at their request, in implementing existing international human rights standards in the administration of justice, in particular under the programme of advisory services;

(d) To continue to provide all necessary support to United Nations bodies working on standard-setting in this field;

(e) To co-ordinate the various technical advisory services provided by the Centre for Human Rights and the Centre for Social Development and Humanitarian Affairs of the Secretariat with a view to undertaking joint programmes and strengthening existing mechanisms for the protection of human rights in the administration of justice;

9. *Emphasizes* the important role of the regional commissions, specialized agencies and United Nations institutes in the area of human rights and crime prevention and criminal justice and other organizations of the United Nations system, as well as intergovernmental and non-governmental organizations, including national professional associations concerned with promoting United Nations standards in this field;

10. *Draws the attention* of the Commission on Human Rights and the Sub-Commission on Prevention of Discrimination and Protection of Minorities, as well as the Eighth United Nations Congress on the Prevention of Crime and the Treatment of Offenders and the Committee on Crime Prevention and Control, to the issues raised in the present resolution, so that priority is accorded to issues related to human rights in the administration of justice;

11. *Decides* to consider at its forty-fifth session the question of human rights in the administration of justice.

General Assembly resolution 44/162

15 December 1989   Meeting 82   Adopted without vote

Approved by Third Committee (A/44/848) without vote, 29 November (meeting 60); 21-nation draft (A/C.3/44/L.83); agenda item 12.
Meeting numbers. GA 44th session: 3rd Committee 48, 50-60; plenary 82.

Torture and cruel treatment

Report of the Special Rapporteur. In January, Special Rapporteur Peter H. Kooijmans (Netherlands) presented a report to the Commission on questions relating to torture.[36] As in previous years, the Special Rapporteur received allegations of torture from different sources. After analysing them, letters with a summarized description of the allegations were transmitted to 37 countries for clarification. The letters and replies received were summarized in the report.

The Special Rapporteur stated that the majority of allegations received referred to torture practised during incommunicado detention and recommended a formal prohibition of that form of detention. He also recommended medical inspection of persons at the time of arrest and regular inspections thereafter, with compulsory inspections whenever a detainee was transferred from one place of detention to another; identification of all persons present during an interrogation; interrogation only at official interrogation centres; the establishment of independent bodies to inspect regularly places of detention; and the right by detainees to initiate proceedings before a court on the lawfulness of their detention.

In a later report,[37] the Special Rapporteur described his visits to Guatemala (18-24 September) and Honduras (25-27 September).

Convention against torture

As at 31 December 1989,[3] 49 States had become parties to the 1984 Convention against Torture and Other Cruel, Inhuman or Degrading Treatment or Punishment,[38] 10 of them (Algeria, Australia, Brazil, Finland, Guinea, Italy, Libyan Arab Jamahiriya, New Zealand, Poland, Portugal) in 1989. The Convention entered into force in 1987.[39] The optional provisions of articles 21 and 22 (under which a party recognized the competence of the Committee against Torture to receive and consider communications to the effect that a party claimed that another was not fulfilling its obligations under the Convention, and to receive communications from or on behalf of individuals claiming to be victims of a violation of the Convention by a State party) also entered into force in 1987; 23 parties had made the required declarations.

The Secretary-General reported on the status of the Convention as at 1 August 1989.[40]

Human Rights Commission action. On 6 March,[41] the Commission requested all States to become parties to the Convention as a matter of priority. It invited all ratifying or acceding States and those States parties that had not done so to make the declaration provided for in articles 21 and 22. The Commission asked the Secretary-General to continue to submit annual reports on the Convention's status and to ensure appropriate staff and facilities for the effective functioning of the Committee against Torture.

On the same date,[42] the Commission decided to postpone until 1991 consideration of a draft optional protocol to the Convention submitted by Costa Rica in 1980 which would provide a system of periodic visits by a committee of experts to places of detention or imprisonment within the jurisdiction of States parties to the Convention.

GENERAL ASSEMBLY ACTION

On 15 December, the General Assembly, on the recommendation of the Third Committee, adopted **resolution 44/144** without vote.

Status of the Convention against Torture and Other Cruel, Inhuman or Degrading Treatment or Punishment

The General Assembly,

Recalling article 5 of the Universal Declaration of Human Rights and article 7 of the International Covenant on Civil and Political Rights, both of which provide that no one shall be subjected to torture or to cruel, inhuman or degrading treatment or punishment,

Recalling also the Declaration on the Protection of All Persons from Being Subjected to Torture and Other Cruel, Inhuman or Degrading Treatment or Punishment, adopted by the General Assembly in its resolution 3452(XXX) of 9 December 1975,

Recalling further its resolution 39/46 of 10 December 1984, by which it adopted and opened for signature, ratification and accession the Convention against Torture and Other Cruel, Inhuman or Degrading Treatment or Punishment and called upon all Governments to consider signing and ratifying the Convention as a matter of priority, as well as its resolutions 40/128 of 13 December 1985, 41/134 of 4 December 1986, 42/123 of 7 December 1987 and 43/132 of 8 December 1988 and Commission on Human Rights resolutions 1987/30 of 10 March 1987 and 1988/36 of 8 March 1988, and taking note of Commission resolution 1989/29 of 6 March 1989,

Mindful of the relevance, for the eradication of torture and other cruel, inhuman or degrading treatment or punishment, of the Code of Conduct for Law Enforcement Officials and of the Principles of Medical Ethics relevant to the role of health personnel, particularly physicians, in the protection of prisoners and detainees against torture and other cruel, inhuman or degrading treatment or punishment,

Recalling the adoption of the Body of Principles for the Protection of All Persons under Any Form of Detention or Imprisonment,

Seriously concerned about the alarming number of reported cases of torture and other cruel, inhuman or degrading treatment or punishment taking place in various parts of the world,

Determined to promote the full implementation of the prohibition, under international and national law, of the practice of torture and other cruel, inhuman or degrading treatment or punishment,

Recalling the decision of the Commission on Human Rights, in its resolution 1988/32 of 8 March 1988, to extend for two years the mandate of the Special Rapporteur to examine questions relevant to torture,

1. *Welcomes* the report of the Committee against Torture;

2. *Takes note* of the report of the Secretary-General on the status of the Convention against Torture and Other Cruel, Inhuman or Degrading Treatment or Punishment;

3. *Stresses* the importance of strict adherence by States parties to the obligations under the Convention regarding the financing of the Committee against Torture, to enable it to carry out in an effective and efficient manner all the functions entrusted to it under the Convention, and appeals to all States parties not to take any measures that might impair the financing of all the functions of the Committee under the Convention, so as to ensure the long-term viability of the Committee as an essential mechanism for overseeing the effective implementation of the provisions of the Convention;

4. *Welcomes* the attention that the Committee against Torture has given to the development of an effective system

of reporting on the implementation of the Convention by States parties, and especially its decision to revise its general guidelines for the submission of initial reports by States parties;

5. *Notes with appreciation* the adoption by the Committee against Torture of its rules of procedure;

6. *Welcomes* the exchange of views that has taken place between the Committee against Torture and the Special Rapporteur of the Commission on Human Rights on questions relating to torture, and requests that this exchange be continued;

7. *Requests* the Secretary-General to ensure the provision of appropriate staff and facilities for the effective performance of the functions of the Committee against Torture;

8. *Reiterates its request* to all States to become parties to the Convention as a matter of priority;

9. *Once again invites* all States, upon ratification of or accession to the Convention, or subsequently, to consider the possibility of making the declarations provided for in articles 21 and 22 of the Convention;

10. *Requests* the Secretary-General to submit to the Commission on Human Rights at its forty-sixth session and to the General Assembly at its forty-fifth session a report on the status of the Convention against Torture and Other Cruel, Inhuman or Degrading Treatment or Punishment;

11. *Decides* to consider the report of the Secretary-General at its forty-fifth session under the item entitled ''Torture and other cruel, inhuman or degrading treatment or punishment''.

General Assembly resolution 44/144

15 December 1989   Meeting 82   Adopted without vote

Approved by Third Committee (A/44/827) without vote, 22 November (meeting 52); 35-nation draft (A/C.3/44/L.52); agenda item 112.
Meeting numbers. GA 44th session: 3rd Committee 36-43, 50, 52; plenary 82.

Committee against Torture

The Committee against Torture, established as a monitoring body under the Convention, held its second session in Geneva from 17 to 28 April.[43] It examined reports submitted by Austria, Denmark, Egypt, Mexico, Norway, the Philippines and Sweden under article 19 of the Convention.

The Committee adopted rules of procedure pertaining to its activities under article 20, by which the Committee studied confidential information appearing to contain well-founded indications that torture was systematically practised in a State party to the Convention.

The Committee held its third session, also in Geneva, from 13 to 24 November,[44] during which it examined reports submitted by Argentina, the Byelorussian SSR, Cameroon, Canada, Chile, Colombia, France, the German Democratic Republic, Hungary, Senegal, Switzerland and the USSR. Under article 22, the Committee declared inadmissible the first three communications submitted to it by individuals claiming to be victims of violations by a State party.

Fund for victims of torture

On 6 March,[45] the Commission on Human Rights appealed to Governments, organizations and individuals to contribute to the United Nations Voluntary Fund for Victims of Torture, which was established in 1981.[46] It asked the Secretary-General to transmit to Governments its appeals for contributions, to assist the Board of Trustees in its efforts to make the Fund and its work better known and to inform the Commission annually of the Fund's operations.

In his annual report to the General Assembly on the status of the Fund,[47] the Secretary-General stated that, at its eighth session (Geneva, 24-28 April), the Fund's Board of Trustees discussed its mandate, the definition of torture and the prevention of torture with a view to making the best possible use of the finances available. It decided to make recommendations to the Secretary-General for grants of nearly $500,000. The focus of the grants was on therapy and rehabilitation projects and extended to some 36 countries in Africa, the Americas, Asia and Europe. The Secretary-General reported that during the period from 16 October 1988 to 15 October 1989, 21 States had contributed or pledged $857,859 to the Fund.

GENERAL ASSEMBLY ACTION

On 15 December, the General Assembly, on the recommendation of the Third Committee, adopted **resolution 44/145** without vote.

United Nations Voluntary Fund for Victims of Torture

The General Assembly,

Recalling article 5 of the Universal Declaration of Human Rights, which states that no one shall be subjected to torture or to cruel, inhuman or degrading treatment or punishment,

Recalling also the Declaration on the Protection of All Persons from Being Subjected to Torture and Other Cruel, Inhuman or Degrading Treatment or Punishment,

Recalling with satisfaction the entry into force on 26 June 1987 of the Convention against Torture and Other Cruel, Inhuman or Degrading Treatment or Punishment,

Recalling its resolution 36/151 of 16 December 1981, in which it noted with deep concern that acts of torture took place in various countries, recognized the need to provide assistance to the victims of torture in a purely humanitarian spirit and established the United Nations Voluntary Fund for Victims of Torture,

Convinced that the struggle to eliminate torture includes the provision of assistance in a humanitarian spirit to the victims and members of their families,

Taking note of the report of the Secretary-General,

1. *Expresses its gratitude and appreciation* to the Governments, organizations and individuals that have already contributed to the United Nations Voluntary Fund for Victims of Torture;

2. *Calls upon* all Governments, organizations and individuals in a position to do so to respond favourably to requests for initial as well as further contributions to the Fund;

3. *Invites* Governments to make contributions to the Fund, if possible on a regular basis, in order to enable the Fund to provide continuous support to projects that depend on recurrent grants;

4. *Requests* the Secretary-General to include the Fund on an annual basis among the programmes for which funds are pledged at the United Nations Pledging Conference for Development Activities;

5. *Expresses its appreciation* to the Board of Trustees of the Fund for the work it has carried out;

6. *Also expresses its appreciation* to the Secretary-General for the support given to the Board of Trustees of the Fund;

7. *Requests* the Secretary-General to make use of all existing possibilities, including the preparation, production and dissemination of information materials, to assist the Board of Trustees of the Fund in its efforts to make the Fund and its humanitarian work better known and in its appeal for contributions.

General Assembly resolution 44/145

15 December 1989   Meeting 82   Adopted without vote

Approved by Third Committee (A/44/827) without vote, 22 November (meeting 52); 21-nation draft (A/C.3/44/L.53); agenda item 112.
Meeting numbers. GA 44th session: 3rd Committee 36-43, 50, 52; plenary 82.

Torture or inhuman treatment
of detained children in South Africa and Namibia

As requested by the Commission on Human Rights in 1988,[48] the *Ad Hoc* Working Group on southern Africa, in a January report,[49] described incidents regarding allegations of torture and ill-treatment and the detention of children in South Africa and Namibia. The Group concluded that torture and other forms of inhuman and degrading treatment of children and young people continued unabated. (For further details, see below, under "Human rights violations".)

On 23 February,[50] the Commission condemned the detention, torture and inhuman treatment of children in South Africa and Namibia, and demanded their immediate and unconditional release; the immediate dismantlement of the so-called "rehabilitation camps" or "re-education centres"; the termination of the state of emergency and abrogation of all repressive and discriminatory legislation; and the immediate abolition of the *apartheid* system. It asked the *Ad Hoc* Working Group to pay special attention to the detention, torture and other inhuman treatment of children and to report in 1990. The Secretary-General was asked to assist the Working Group; to intervene with the Government of South Africa to bring an end to the detention, torture and other inhuman treatment of children in South Africa and to report in 1990; and to bring the Commission's resolution to the attention of relevant UN bodies, specialized agencies and NGOs.

In an October report,[51] the Secretary-General summarized information received from UN bodies, specialized agencies and NGOs concerning torture and inhuman treatment of children in detention in South Africa and Namibia and presented relevant excerpts from the report of the *Ad Hoc* Working Group.

GENERAL ASSEMBLY ACTION

On 15 December, the General Assembly, on the recommendation of the Third Committee, adopted **resolution 44/143** without vote.

Torture and inhuman treatment of children in detention in South Africa and Namibia

The General Assembly,

Recalling its resolution 43/134 of 8 December 1988 and taking note of Commission on Human Rights resolution 1989/4 of 23 February 1989,

Recalling also the relevant provisions of the Declaration on the Protection of All Persons from Being Subjected to Torture and Other Cruel, Inhuman or Degrading Treatment or Punishment, the Convention against Torture and Other Cruel, Inhuman or Degrading Treatment or Punishment and the Declaration on the Rights of the Child,

Taking note of the report of the Secretary-General and in particular the conclusion that torture and other forms of inhuman and degrading treatment of children and young people have continued unabated during the period under review,

1. *Expresses its profound outrage* at evidence of detention, torture and inhuman treatment of children in South Africa;

2. *Vigorously condemns* the *apartheid* racist régime for the increasing detention, torture and inhuman treatment of children in South Africa;

3. *Reiterates its demand* for the immediate and unconditional release of children held in detention by the *apartheid* régime in South Africa;

4. *Demands* the immediate dismantlement of the so-called "rehabilitation camps" and "re-education centres" in South Africa, since they only serve the racist régime's strategy of physically and mentally abusing black South African children;

5. *Reiterates its request* to all relevant United Nations bodies, specialized agencies and non-governmental organizations to intensify the world-wide campaign aimed at drawing attention to, monitoring and exposing these inhuman practices;

6. *Requests* the Commission on Human Rights to continue to pay special attention to the question of detention, torture and other inhuman treatment of children in South Africa;

7. *Also requests* the Commission on Human Rights to pay special attention to the children of Namibia who have been victims of torture, detention and other inhuman treatment by the *apartheid* régime, with a view to rehabilitating them;

8. *Requests* the Secretary-General to submit a report to the General Assembly at its forty-fifth session on the implementation of the present resolution;

9. *Decides* to consider this question at its forty-fifth session under the item entitled "Torture and other cruel, inhuman or degrading treatment or punishment".

General Assembly resolution 44/143

15 December 1989   Meeting 82   Adopted without vote

Approved by Third Committee (A/44/827) without vote, 22 November (meeting 52); 34-nation draft (A/C.3/44/L.51); agenda item 112.
Meeting numbers. GA 44th session: 3rd Committee 36-43, 50, 52; plenary 82.

Detention of juveniles

On 1 September,[52] the Sub-Commission, considering that a 1987 report of the Secretary-General[53] concerning the incarceration of children under the age of 18 with adult prisoners had not yet been discussed by the Sub-Commission, and that further information had meanwhile been made available to the Secretary-General on the issue, asked him to submit a revised version to the Sub-Commission for discussion in 1990. It decided to appoint María Concepción Bautista (Philippines) to prepare a report on the application of international standards concerning the human rights of detained juveniles, in particular the separation of juvenile children and adult offenders in penal institutions, detention pending trial, least possible use of institutionalization, and the objectives of institutional treatment. The Sub-Commission asked the Secretary-General to submit its resolution to Governments, specialized agencies and NGOs and request their comments on those issues.

Detention without charge or trial

On 6 March,[54] the Commission, taking note of an analysis of questions dealt with in a paper on administrative detention without charge or trial[55] prepared by Special Rapporteur Louis Joinet (France), asked the Sub-Commission to consider the report to be submitted by Mr. Joinet and to make any proposals necessary on the question.

In a July report on administrative detention,[56] Mr. Joinet recommended the annual submission to the Commission of a special report on the development of all forms of administrative detention throughout the world, and said that particular attention should be paid to the subject by the Special Rapporteurs on summary executions, torture and states of emergency, as well as by the Working Group on Enforced or Involuntary Disappearances and other relevant UN monitoring bodies. It was recommended that the Special Rapporteur carry out an in-depth study, with a view to submitting proposals to the Commission.

Sub-Commission action. On 1 September,[57] the Sub-Commission, expressing its appreciation for the report submitted by Mr. Joinet, regretted that it was unable to study the report properly due to lack of time, and decided to examine his proposals and his revised report in 1990 as a matter of high priority.

Working Group on Detention

The Working Group on Detention met on 9 to 11, 15, 17 and 23 August in Geneva.[58] It discussed a new draft declaration on the protection of all persons from enforced or involuntary disap-

pearance, taking into account comments and views on the draft received from Governments, specialized agencies, UN bodies, NGOs and regional organizations.[59] The Group continued to consider detention resulting from the exercise of the right to freedom of expression, reviewed developments concerning the human rights of persons subjected to any form of detention or imprisonment and discussed the privatization of prisons. On 1 September,[60] the Sub-Commission decided to ask the Group's Chairman, Miguel Alfonso Martínez (Cuba), to prepare a working paper for consideration in 1990 containing proposals on the best way for the Sub-Commission to study further the issue of privatization of prisons. In response to the Working Group's suggestion, the Sub-Commission appealed[61] to States that retained the death penalty to consider the possibility of enacting legislation prohibiting the imposition of the death penalty on those persons under 18 years of age. The Sub-Commission asked the Secretary-General to transmit its resolution to all Governments, requesting comments and information on their legislation on the subject, as well as to specialized agencies and NGOs, and to prepare a report for submission in 1990 on the basis of information received.

Hostage-taking

Human Rights Commission action. On 6 March,[62] the Commission strongly condemned hostage-taking and those responsible and demanded the immediate release of those being held. It called on States to take preventive and punitive measures to put an immediate end to causes of abduction and unlawful restraint. It asked the Secretary-General, whenever a State so requested, to use all available means to secure the immediate release of persons held hostage.

Sub-Commission action. On 1 September,[63] the Sub-Commission condemned hostage-taking and the torture and murder that frequently accompanied it. It asked that all States take steps to prevent hostage-taking and to charge and bring to trial those who might participate in hostage-taking. The Secretary-General was asked to provide, prior to the Sub-Commission's 1990 session, a complete, up-to-date list of all UN personnel held in captivity including information concerning their names and the whereabouts of the captors, if known.

Detained UN staff members

Report of the Secretary-General. In February, the Secretary-General submitted to the Commission a report[64] updating developments pertaining to the detention of international civil servants and their families. Annexed to the report was a consolidated list of staff members under arrest and detention or missing.

Human Rights Commission action. On 6 March,[65] the Commission appealed to Member States to respect and ensure respect for the rights of staff members and others acting under UN authority and their families, and urged them, in accordance with the 1988 Body of Principles for the Protection of All Persons under Any Form of Detention or Imprisonment,[34] to provide adequate and prompt information concerning their arrest or detention. It further urged Member States to allow medical teams to investigate the health of detained staff members, experts and their families and permit the necessary medical treatment. It asked the Secretary-General to continue his efforts to ensure that the human rights, privileges and immunities of UN staff members, experts and their families were fully respected, and to submit an updated report in 1990 on the situation of UN staff members, experts and their families detained, imprisoned, missing or held in a country against their will, including those cases that had been successfully settled during the last year.

Report of the Special Rapporteur. In August, María Concepción Bautista submitted a preliminary report[66] on the protection of the human rights of UN staff members, experts and their families. She discussed procedures to be followed in cases of arrest, detention or death; legal rights of the United Nations in cases of arrest or detention of staff members; relevant international instruments; and the Secretary-General's efforts to ensure respect for the privileges and immunities of UN staff members and experts.

Sub-Commission action. On 1 September,[67] the Sub-Commission asked the Secretary-General to redouble his efforts to ensure that the human rights, privileges and immunities of UN personnel, experts and their families were fully respected. It asked María Concepción Bautista, the Special Rapporteur, to continue her study and to submit an updated version of her report in 1990. Member States, the Secretary-General and the heads of the secretariats of the specialized agencies who had not yet done so were asked to communicate all information concerning cases of arrest, detention or abduction of officials of the United Nations or the specialized agencies since 1980, in order to enable the Special Rapporteur to complete her task.

Summary or arbitrary executions

Reports of the Special Rapporteur. The Commission on Human Rights considered a report[68] submitted by its Special Rapporteur on summary or arbitrary executions, S. Amos Wako (Kenya). In response to allegations of imminent or threatened summary or arbitrary executions which appeared *prima facie* relevant to his mandate, the Spe-

cial Rapporteur addressed urgent appeals to 23 Governments, and summarized the messages and replies in the report. He also sent letters to 36 Governments concerning alleged summary or arbitrary executions in their countries. Those allegations and the replies thereto were summarized in the report.

The Special Rapporteur concluded that there had been much indiscriminate killing of unarmed civilians on the part of governmental forces in conflict areas. He had also received more reports than at any prior time alleging increased use of chemical weapons. In addition, there was an increasing number of allegations to the effect that thousands of people had lost their lives at the hands of police or other enforcement officials in demonstrations. He recommended that the Centre for Human Rights should organize seminars for law enforcement officials to train them to carry out their work with due respect for the human rights of the individual, and to familiarize them with international human rights instruments related to their work.

The Special Rapporteur submitted a report[69] on his visit to Colombia (11-20 October) made at the invitation of the Government in connection with reports on summary or arbitrary executions transmitted to it by the Special Rapporteur.

Human Rights Commission action. On 8 March,[70] the Commission strongly condemned the large number of extrajudicial, summary or arbitrary executions taking place throughout the world, and appealed to Governments, UN bodies, specialized agencies, regional intergovernmental organizations and NGOs to take action to combat and eliminate them. It asked the Special Rapporteur on extrajudicial, summary or arbitrary executions to continue examining such executions and to respond effectively to information he received. The Commission asked the Secretary-General to assist the Special Rapporteur, to consider ways to publicize his work and recommendations, and to continue to use his best endeavours in cases where the minimum standard of legal safeguards provided for in articles 6, 14 and 15 of the 1966 International Covenant on Civil and Political Rights[1] appeared not to be respected.

Report of the Secretary-General. In accordance with a 1988 Sub-Commission request,[71] the Secretary-General, in July, described action by other international forums on international standards for the investigation of suspicious deaths in detention, as well as adequate autopsies.[72]

Sub-Commission action. On 1 September,[73] the Sub-Commission, emphasizing that law enforcement officials should not use force in ways which would undermine the right of everyone to peaceful assembly, recommended a draft text for adoption by the Commission on Human Rights.

On 15 December, the General Assembly, on the recommendation of the Third Committee, adopted **resolution 44/159** without vote.

Summary or arbitrary executions

The General Assembly,

Recalling the provisions of the Universal Declaration of Human Rights, in which it is stated that every human being has the right to life, liberty and security of person,

Having regard to the provisions of the International Covenant on Civil and Political Rights, in which it is stated that every human being has the inherent right to life, that this right shall be protected by law and that no one shall be arbitrarily deprived of his life,

Recalling its resolution 36/22 of 9 November 1981, in which it condemned the practice of summary or arbitrary executions, and its resolutions 37/182 of 17 December 1982, 38/96 of 16 December 1983, 39/110 of 14 December 1984, 40/143 of 13 December 1985, 41/144 of 4 December 1986, 42/141 of 7 December 1987 and 43/151 of 8 December 1988,

Deeply alarmed at the continued occurrence on a large scale of summary or arbitrary executions, including extra-legal executions,

Recalling Economic and Social Council resolution 1984/50 of 25 May 1984 and the safeguards guaranteeing protection of the rights of those facing the death penalty annexed thereto, which resolution was endorsed by the Seventh United Nations Congress on the Prevention of Crime and the Treatment of Offenders in its resolution 15,

Recalling also the close co-operation established between the Centre for Human Rights, the Crime Prevention and Criminal Justice Branch of the Centre for Social Development and Humanitarian Affairs of the Secretariat and the Committee on Crime Prevention and Control with regard to the elaboration of the principles on the effective prevention and investigation of arbitrary and summary executions, including extra-legal executions,

Welcoming the adoption by the Economic and Social Council of its resolution 1989/65 of 24 May 1989, containing the Principles on the Effective Prevention and Investigation of Extra-legal, Arbitrary and Summary Executions,

Welcoming also the adoption by the Economic and Social Council of its resolution 1989/64 of 24 May 1989, entitled "Implementation of the safeguards guaranteeing protection of the rights of those facing the death penalty" and the recommendations contained therein,

Convinced of the need for appropriate action to combat and eventually eliminate the abhorrent practice of summary or arbitrary executions, which represents a flagrant violation of the most fundamental human right, the right to life,

1. *Once again strongly condemns* the large number of summary or arbitrary executions, including extra-legal executions, that continue to take place in various parts of the world;

2. *Demands* that the practice of summary or arbitrary executions be brought to an end;

3. *Appeals urgently* to Governments, United Nations bodies, the specialized agencies, regional intergovernmental organizations and non-governmental organizations to take effective action to combat and eliminate summary or arbitrary executions, including extra-legal executions;

4. *Reaffirms* Economic and Social Council resolution 1982/35 of 7 May 1982, in which the Council decided to appoint a special rapporteur to consider the questions related to summary or arbitrary executions;

5. *Recalls with satisfaction* Economic and Social Council resolution 1988/38 of 7 May 1988, by which the Council decided to renew the mandate of the Special Rapporteur, Mr. S. Amos Wako, for two years, while maintaining the annual reporting cycle;

6. *Urges* all Governments, in particular those which have consistently not responded to communications transmitted to them by the Special Rapporteur, and all others concerned to co-operate with and assist the Special Rapporteur so that he may carry out his mandate effectively;

7. *Requests* the Special Rapporteur, in carrying out his mandate, to respond effectively to information that comes before him, in particular when a summary or arbitrary execution is imminent or threatened, or when such an execution has recently occurred, and, furthermore, to promote exchanges of views between Governments and those who provide reliable information to the Special Rapporteur, where the Special Rapporteur considers that such exchanges of information might be useful;

8. *Welcomes* the recommendations made by the Special Rapporteur in his reports to the Commission on Human Rights at its forty-fourth and forty-fifth sessions with a view to eliminating summary or arbitrary executions;

9. *Encourages* Governments, international organizations and non-governmental organizations to organize training programmes and support projects with a view to training or educating law enforcement officers in human rights issues connected with their work, and appeals to the international community to support endeavours to that end;

10. *Considers* that the Special Rapporteur, in carrying out his mandate, should continue to seek and receive information from Governments, United Nations bodies, specialized agencies, regional intergovernmental organizations and non-governmental organizations in consultative status with the Economic and Social Council, as well as medical and forensic experts;

11. *Requests* the Secretary-General to continue to provide all necessary assistance to the Special Rapporteur so that he may effectively carry out his mandate;

12. *Again requests* the Secretary-General to continue to use his best endeavours in cases where the minimum standard of legal safeguards provided for in articles 6, 14 and 15 of the International Covenant on Civil and Political Rights appear not to have been respected;

13. *Requests* the Commission on Human Rights at its forty-sixth session, on the basis of the report of the Special Rapporteur to be prepared in conformity with Economic and Social Council resolutions 1982/35, 1983/36, 1984/35, 1985/40, 1986/36, 1987/60 and 1988/38, to make recommendations concerning appropriate action to combat and eventually eliminate the abhorrent practice of summary or arbitrary executions.

General Assembly resolution 44/159

15 December 1989   Meeting 82   Adopted without vote

Approved by Third Committee (A/44/848) without vote, 29 November (meeting 60); 23-nation draft (A/C.3/44/L.80); agenda item 12.
Meeting numbers. GA 44th session: 3rd Committee 48, 50-60; plenary 82.

Disappearance of persons

Human Rights Commission action. On 6 March,[74] the Commission requested the Working Group on Enforced or Involuntary Disappearances to submit all information it deemed necessary and any specific recommendations it might have regarding the fulfilment of its task and to report to the Commission in 1990. It noted the intention of the Working Group to submit to the Sub-Commission in 1989 observations concerning the draft declaration on enforced or involuntary disappearances. The Commission asked the Secretary-General to consider ways of better publicizing the Group's work and to ensure that the Group received all necessary assistance, in particular staff and resources, especially in carrying out missions and holding sessions in countries that were prepared to receive them.

Working Group activities. The five-member Working Group on Enforced or Involuntary Disappearances, established in 1980,[75] held three sessions in 1989: its twenty-seventh in New York (17-21 April), and its twenty-eighth and twenty-ninth in Geneva (28 August-1 September, 6-15 December).[76] The Group examined information on enforced or involuntary disappearances received from Governments, NGOs and relatives of missing persons.

In 1989, the Working Group received some 2,700 reports of enforced or involuntary disappearances and transmitted some 1,650 newly reported cases to the Governments concerned; 721 of those cases were reported to have occurred in 1989, 515 were transmitted under the urgent action procedure, and 112 were clarified in the same year. The remaining cases were referred back to the sources as they lacked elements required by the Group for their transmission.

The Working Group examined the draft declaration on enforced or involuntary disappearances, which was annexed to a 1988 report of the Working Group on Detention.[77]

In its concluding observations, the Group reviewed its activities over the past 10 years. It stated that during those years it had transmitted 19,000 cases to a total of 41 Governments. It noted that advisory services would benefit countries where the problem of disappearance was endemic.

GENERAL ASSEMBLY ACTION

On 15 December, the General Assembly, on the recommendation of the Third Committee, adopted **resolution 44/160** without vote.

Question of enforced or involuntary disappearances

The General Assembly,

Recalling its resolution 33/173 of 20 December 1978 concerning disappeared persons, and its resolution 43/159 of 8 December 1988 on the question of enforced or involuntary disappearances,

Deeply concerned about the persistence, in certain cases, of the practice of enforced or involuntary disappearances, and about the fact that, in certain cases, the families of disappeared persons have been the target of intimidation and ill-treatment,

Expressing its profound emotion at the anguish and sorrow of the families concerned, who are unsure of the fate of their relatives,

Convinced of the need to continue implementing the provisions of its resolution 33/173 and of the other United Nations resolutions on the question of enforced or involuntary disappearances, with a view to finding solutions for cases of disappearances and helping to eliminate such practices,

Welcoming the progress made in the preparation of the draft declaration on enforced or involuntary disappearances,

Bearing in mind Commission on Human Rights resolution 1989/27 of 6 March 1989,

1. *Expresses its appreciation* to the Working Group on Enforced or Involuntary Disappearances for its humanitarian work and to those Governments that have cooperated with it;

2. *Recalls* the decision of the Commission on Human Rights, at its forty-fourth session, to extend for two years the term of the mandate of the Working Group, as defined in Commission resolution 20(XXXVI) of 29 February 1980, while maintaining the principle of annual reporting by the Working Group;

3. *Also recalls* the provisions made by the Commission on Human Rights in its resolution 1986/55 of 13 March 1986 to enable the Working Group to fulfil its mandate with greater efficiency;

4. *Appeals* to the Governments concerned, particularly those which have not yet replied to the communications addressed to them by the Working Group, to cooperate fully with it so as to enable it, with respect for its working methods based on discretion, to perform its strictly humanitarian role, and in particular to reply more quickly to the requests for information addressed to them;

5. *Encourages* the Governments concerned to consider the wish of the Working Group, when such a wish is expressed, to visit their countries, thus enabling it to fulfil its mandate even more effectively;

6. *Extends its warm thanks* to those Governments that have invited the Working Group and requests them to give all necessary attention to its recommendations;

7. *Appeals* to the Governments concerned to take steps to protect the families of disappeared persons against any intimidation or ill-treatment of which they may be the target;

8. *Calls upon* the Commission on Human Rights to continue to study this question as a matter of priority and to take any step it may deem necessary to the pursuit of the task of the Working Group when it considers the report to be submitted by the Working Group to the Commission at its forty-sixth session;

9. *Renews its request* to the Secretary-General to continue to provide the Working Group with all necessary facilities.

General Assembly resolution 44/160

15 December 1989   Meeting 82   Adopted without vote

Approved by Third Committee (A/44/848) without vote, 29 November (meeting 60); 24-nation draft (A/C.3/44/L.81), orally revised; agenda item 12.
Meeting numbers. GA 44th session: 3rd Committee 48, 50-60; plenary 82.

Other aspects of civil and political rights

Slavery

Human Rights Commission action. On 6 March,[78] the Commission asked the Secretary-General to invite States parties to the three slavery conventions—the 1926 Slavery Convention, the 1956 Supplementary Convention on the Abolition of Slavery, the Slave Trade, and Institutions and Practices Similar to Slavery,[79] and the 1949 Convention for the Suppression of the Traffic in Persons and of the Exploitation of the Prostitution of Others[80]—to submit regular reports to the Sub-Commission on the situation in their countries. It invited States that had not ratified the conventions to do so, or to explain in writing why they felt unable to. Relevant intergovernmental organizations, UN organizations and NGOs were asked to supply information to the Working Group on Contemporary Forms of Slavery. The Secretary-General was asked to undertake a study of ways of establishing an effective mechanism to implement the three slavery conventions; to assign a full-time professional staff member to serve the Working Group and undertake other activities relating to contemporary forms of slavery; to designate the Centre for Human Rights as the focal point for the co-ordination of activities; and to submit his final report on the sale of children to the Working Group in 1989.

Working Group activities. The Sub-Commission's five-member Working Group on Contemporary Forms of Slavery, at its fourteenth session (Geneva, 31 July–4 August and 25 August),[81] considered the status and implementation of the conventions on slavery and slavery-like practices; prevention of the sale of children, child prostitution and child pornography; and developments in other areas, including slavery and the slave trade, exploitation of child labour, debt bondage, the prevention of traffic in persons and the exploitation of the prostitution of others and slavery-like practices of *apartheid* and colonialism.

The Working Group had before it a May report[82] of the Secretary-General on ways of establishing an effective mechanism to implement the slavery conventions. He addressed the issues of amendment or modification of the slavery conventions, the establishment of a reporting procedure and strengthening the mandate, role and functioning of the Working Group on Slavery.

Sub-Commission action. On 1 September,[83] the Sub-Commission congratulated the Anti-Slavery Society, the oldest human rights organization in the world, on its one-hundred-and-fiftieth anniversary.

ECONOMIC AND SOCIAL COUNCIL ACTION

On 24 May, the Economic and Social Council, on the recommendation of its Second Committee, adopted **resolution 1989/74** without vote.

Working Group on Contemporary Forms of Slavery of the Sub-Commission on Prevention of Discrimination and Protection of Minorities

The Economic and Social Council,

Recalling Commission on Human Rights resolution 1982/20 of 10 March 1982 on the question of slavery and the slave trade in all their practices and manifestations, including the slavery-like practices of *apartheid* and colonialism,

Recalling also its resolutions 1982/20 of 4 May 1982 and 1983/30 of 26 May 1983 on the suppression of the traffic in persons and of the exploitation of the prostitution of others,

Considering that the report of its Special Rapporteur on the suppression of the traffic in persons and the exploitation of the prostitution of others still constitutes a useful basis for further action,

Recalling General Assembly resolutions 38/107 of 16 December 1983 and 40/103 of 13 December 1985 on the prevention of prostitution,

Gravely concerned that slavery, the slave trade and slavery-like practices still exist, that there are modern manifestations of those phenomena and that such practices represent some of the gravest violations of human rights,

Aware of the complexity of the issue of the suppression of the traffic in persons and the exploitation of the prostitution of others, and the need for further co-ordination and co-operation to implement the recommendations made by the Special Rapporteur and by various United Nations bodies,

1. *Reminds* States parties to the Slavery Convention of 1926, the Supplementary Convention on the Abolition of Slavery, the Slave Trade and Institutions and Practices Similar to Slavery of 1956, and the Convention for the Suppression of the Traffic in Persons and of the Exploitation of the Prostitution of Others of 1949 of their obligation to submit to the Working Group on Contemporary Forms of Slavery of the Sub-Commission on Prevention of Discrimination and Protection of Minorities regular reports on the situation in their countries, as provided for under the relevant conventions and under Council decision 16(LVI);

2. *Endorses* the request made by the Commission on Human Rights in its resolution 1989/35 of 6 March 1989 that the Secretary-General should assign a full-time professional staff member to serve the Working Group and undertake other activities relating to contemporary forms of slavery under the post which has been included in the budget of the Centre for Human Rights of the Secretariat for questions relating to slavery and slavery-like practices;

3. *Also endorses* the request made by the Commission on Human Rights in its resolution 1988/42 of 8 March 1988, that the Secretary-General should report to the Council on the steps taken by Member States, United Nations organizations and other intergovernmental organizations to implement the recommendations made in Council resolution 1983/30, and the request made by the Commission in its resolution 1989/35 that the Secretary-General should report to the Council at its first regular session of 1990 on the comments received;

4. *Further endorses* the request made by the Commission on Human Rights in its resolution 1989/35 that the Secretary-General should designate the Centre for Human Rights as the focal point for the co-ordination of United Nations activities for the suppression of contemporary forms of slavery;

5. *Decides* to consider the question of the suppression of traffic in persons at its first regular session of 1990 under the agenda item entitled "Human rights".

Economic and Social Council resolution 1989/74

24 May 1989   Meeting 16   Adopted without vote

Approved by Second Committee (E/1989/88) without vote, 19 May (meeting 22); draft by Commission on Human Rights (E/1989/20), amended by Netherlands (E/1989/C.2/L.16); agenda item 9.

Freedom of movement

Human Rights Commission action. On 6 March,[84] the Commission asked the Secretary-General to provide the necessary assistance to the Sub-Commission and the Special Rapporteur during the consideration of the Special Rapporteur's report[85] (see below, under "Discrimination") and the draft declaration on the right of everyone to leave any country, including his own, and to return to his country.

Report of the Secretary-General. In a May report and later addenda,[86] the Secretary-General presented comments on the draft declaration received from Governments, specialized agencies, intergovernmental organizations and NGOs.

Sub-Commission action. On 31 August,[87] the Sub-Commission asked the Secretary-General to prepare an analytical compilation of the comments on the draft declaration received from Governments, specialized agencies, intergovernmental organizations and NGOs and of the comments made by Sub-Commission members. It decided to establish, at its 1990 session, a sessional open-ended working group with a view to preparing a revised version of the draft declaration.

Human rights and fundamental freedoms

On 7 March,[88] the Commission expressed concern that in many parts of the world, persons were detained for seeking to exercise peacefully their human rights and fundamental freedoms, particularly the rights to freedom of expression, assembly and association. It asked Governments to release all persons deprived of their liberty for seeking peacefully to exercise those rights and freedoms or to promote and defend them and called on Governments, pending such release, to take measures to safeguard their human rights and fundamental freedoms.

Freedom of speech

Human Rights Commission action. On 6 March,[89] expressing concern at the extensive occurrence of detention of persons exercising their right to freedom of opinion and expression, the Commission appealed to States to ensure respect and support for that right. It took note of a 1988 Sub-Commission decision asking Danilo Türk (Yugoslavia) to prepare a working paper containing a proposal for carrying out a study concerning the right to freedom of opinion and expression, to serve as a basis for future Sub-Commission decisions.

Working paper. In a June working paper,[90] Mr. Türk discussed the main elements of the right to freedom of opinion and expression, permissible limitations of that right and the limitations which might jeopardize it. He recommended that the Sub-Commission appoint two of its members to work jointly on a study to be entitled "The right to freedom of opinion and expression: current problems of its realization and measures necessary for its strengthening and promotion". He stated that the priority area of the study should be the political dimension of that right.

Sub-Commission action. On 31 August,[91] the Sub-Commission, endorsing the recommendations made by Mr. Türk, decided to entrust Louis Joinet and Mr. Türk with preparing a study on the right to freedom of opinion and expression, current problems of its realization and measures necessary for its strengthening and promotion.

Conscientious objectors

Report of the Secretary-General. In 1989, the Commission on Human Rights had before it a report of the Secretary-General[92] presenting views on conscientious objection to military service of States with national military service that provided for alternatives to service in the armed forces; of States that did not, in principle, allow conscientious objection to military service but considered individual cases; of States that had no standing army or with voluntary military service; and of UN bodies and specialized agencies, intergovernmental organizations and NGOs.

Human Rights Commission action. On 8 March,[93] the Commission requested the Secretary-General to report in 1991 on conscientious objection to military service, taking into account comments provided by Governments and other information received by him.

Independence of the judicial system

On 6 March,[94] the Commission expressed its appreciation to Special Rapporteur L. M. Singhvi (India) for his 1985 study on the independence and impartiality of the judiciary[95] and the revised draft declaration on the independence and impartiality of the judiciary, jurors and assessors and the independence of lawyers.[96] It also asked Governments to take into account the principles set forth in the draft declaration in implementing the 1985 Basic Principles on the Independence of the Judiciary.[97] It asked the Sub-Commission to consider effective means to monitor the implementation of the Basic Principles and the protection of practising lawyers. The Secretary-General was asked to transmit the study and the draft declaration to the Committee on Crime Prevention and Control and to the Eighth (1990) United Nations Congress on the Prevention of Crime and the Treatment of Offenders. The Commission also urged the Committee and the Congress to take them into account in completing work on the draft basic principles on the role of lawyers (see PART THREE, Chapter XII).

The Economic and Social Council, by **resolution 1989/60** of 24 May, adopted the Procedures for the Effective Implementation of the Basic Principles on the Independence of the Judiciary (see PART THREE, Chapter XII).

Sub-Commission action. On 31 August,[98] the Sub-Commission asked Louis Joinet to prepare a working paper on ways by which the Sub-Commission could assist in ensuring respect for the independence of the judiciary and the protection of practising lawyers. It also asked the Secretary-General to assist Mr. Joinet.

Right to a fair trial

Sub-Commission action. On 1 September,[99] the Sub-Commission decided to appoint Stanislav Chernichenko (Russian Federation) and William Treat (United States) as rapporteurs to prepare a report on existing international norms and standards pertaining to the right to a fair trial. It asked them to recommend which provisions guaranteeing the right to a fair trial should be made nonderogable.

REFERENCES

[1]YUN 1966, p. 423, GA res. 2200 A (XXI), annex, 16 Dec. 1966. [2]YUN 1976, p. 609. [3]*Multilateral Treaties Deposited with the Secretary-General: Status as at 31 December 1989* (ST/LEG/SER.E/8), Sales No. E.90.V.6. [4]A/44/441. [5]E/1989/20 (res. 1989/17). [6]*Ibid.* (res. 1989/25). [7]YUN 1987, p. 760. [8]A/44/592 & Add.1. [9]A/44/662. [10]A/44/40. [11]A/45/40. [12]E/1989/20 (dec. 1989/105). [13]YUN 1988, p. 499. [14]E/CN.4/Sub.2/1989/30 & Add.1,2 & Add.2/Rev.1. [15]YUN 1987, p. 741. [16]YUN 1988, p. 499. [17]E/CN.4/Sub.2/1989/58 (res. 1989/28). [18]E/1989/20 (res. 1989/23). [19]*Ibid.* (res. 1989/20). [20]*Ibid.* (res. 1989/19). [21]*Ibid.* (res. 1989/22). [22]*Ibid.* (res. 1989/18). [23]*Ibid.* (res. 1989/21). [24]A/44/548. [25]YUN 1988, p. 499, GA res. 43/105, 8 Dec. 1988 & p. 500, GA res. 43/106, 8 Dec. 1988. [26]*Ibid.*, p. 184. [27]YUN 1988, p. 506. [28]E/CN.4/1989/14. [29]YUN 1988, p. 506, GA res. 43/107, 8 Dec. 1988. [30]A/44/526. [31]E/1989/20 (res. 1989/24). [32]YUN 1988, p. 508, GA res. 43/153, 8 Dec. 1988. [33]E/CN.4/Sub.2/1989/23. [34]YUN 1988, p. 510, GA res. 43/173, annex, 9 Dec. 1988. [35]E/CN.4/Sub.2/1989/22. [36]E/CN.4/1989/15. [37]E/CN.4/1990/17. [38]YUN 1984, p. 813, GA res. 39/46, annex, 10 Dec. 1984. [39]YUN 1987, p. 755. [40]A/44/443. [41]E/1989/20 (res. 1989/29). [42]*Ibid.* (dec. 1989/104). [43]A/44/46. [44]A/45/44 & Corr.1. [45]E/1989/20 (res. 1989/30). [46]YUN 1981, p. 906, GA res. 36/151, 16 Dec. 1981. [47]A/44/708. [48]YUN 1988, p. 516. [49]E/CN.4/1989/8. [50]E/1989/20 (res. 1989/4). [51]A/44/623. [52]E/CN.4/Sub.2/1989/58 (res. 1989/31). [53]E/CN.4/Sub.2/1987/30. [54]E/1989/20 (res. 1989/38). [55]YUN 1988, p. 518. [56]E/CN.4/Sub.2/1989/27. [57]E/CN.4/Sub.2/1989/58 (dec. 1989/111). [58]E/CN.4/Sub.2/1989/29/Rev.1. [59]E/CN.4/Sub.2/1989/24 & Add.1-3. [60]E/CN.4/Sub.2/1989/58 (dec. 1989/110). [61]*Ibid.* (res. 1989/32). [62]E/1989/20 (res. 1989/26). [63]E/CN.4/Sub.2/1989/58 (res. 1989/26). [64]E/CN.4/

1989/19. [65]E/1989/20 (res. 1989/28). [66]E/CN.4/Sub.2/1989/28. [67]E/CN.4/Sub.2/1989/58 (res. 1989/30). [68]E/CN.4/1989/25. [69]E/CN.4/1990/22/Add.1. [70]E/1989/20 (res. 1989/64). [71]YUN 1988, p. 519. [72]E/CN.4/Sub.2/1989/25. [73]E/CN.4/Sub.2/1989/58 (res. 1989/33). [74]*Ibid.* (res. 1989/27). [75]YUN 1980, p. 843. [76]E/CN.4/1990/13. [77]YUN 1988, p. 510. [78]E/1989/20 (res. 1989/35). [79]YUN 1956, p. 228. [80]YUN 1948-49, p. 613, GA res. 317(IV), annex, 2 Dec. 1949. [81]E/CN.4/Sub.2/1989/39. [82]E/CN.4/Sub.2/1989/37. [83]E/CN.4/Sub.2/1989/58 (res. 1989/40). [84]E/1989/20 (res. 1989/39). [85]E/CN.4/Sub.2/1989/35 & Add.1 & Add.1/Corr.1. [86]E/CN.4/Sub.2/1989/44 & Add.1-7. [87]E/CN.4/Sub.2/1989/58 (res. 1989/25). [88]E/1989/20 (res. 1989/56). [89]*Ibid.* (res. 1989/31). [90]E/CN.4/Sub.2/1989/26. [91]E/CN.4/Sub.2/1989/58 (dec. 1989/14). [92]E/CN.4/1989/30. [93]E/1989/20 (res. 1989/59). [94]*Ibid.* (res. 1989/32). [95]YUN 1985, p. 873. [96]YUN 1988, p. 525. [97]YUN 1985, p. 757. [98]E/CN.4/Sub.2/1989/58 (res. 1989/22). [99]*Ibid.* (res. 1989/27).

Economic, social and cultural rights

Report of the Secretary-General. The Commission on Human Rights considered a report of the Secretary-General containing replies from Governments, UN bodies, specialized agencies and NGOs on their policies regarding the implementation, promotion and protection of economic, social and cultural rights.[1]

Human Rights Commission action. On 2 March,[2] by a roll-call vote of 31 to 10, with 1 abstention, the Commission appealed to States to pursue policies for the implementation, promotion and protection of economic, social, cultural, civil and political rights and called on them to co-operate in promoting social progress and better standards of life in larger freedom. It asked the Secretary-General to provide the Special Rapporteur, Danilo Türk, appointed in 1988,[3] with any assistance he might need in preparing a study of problems, policies and progressive measures relating to a more effective realization of those rights. On the same date,[4] the Commission approved the Sub-Commission's 1988 decision[3] to entrust the Special Rapporteur with the study and its request to him to submit a preliminary report in 1989, as well as its request to the Secretary-General for assistance. The Commission's request to the Secretary-General to assist the Special Rapporteur was endorsed by the Economic and Social Council by **decision 1989/138** of 24 May.

Report of the Special Rapporteur. In a preliminary report[5] submitted in June, the Special Rapporteur discussed the possibility of a unified UN approach to economic, social and cultural rights, problems in realizing those rights at the national level, and international co-operation. He indicated a number of problem areas on which the study on the realization of economic, social and cultural rights should focus; these included further discussion of a unified approach to the interpretation and realization of the rights in question; extreme poverty and the effects of structural adjustment policies; international co-operation; and the role of UN development agencies.

Sub-Commission action. On 31 August,[6] the Sub-Commission asked the Special Rapporteur to prepare a progress report for consideration at its forty-second session and requested the Secretary-General to provide him with all the assistance he needed.

Covenant on Economic, Social and Cultural Rights

As at 31 December 1989, the International Covenant on Economic, Social and Cultural Rights, adopted by the General Assembly in 1966[7] and in force since 1976,[8] had been ratified or acceded or succeeded to by 94 States. Algeria and Ireland became parties to the Covenant in 1989.[9]

The Secretary-General provided information on the status of ratifications of or accessions and successions to the Covenant as at 1 August 1989.[10]

Implementation of the Covenant

Human Rights Commission action. On 2 March,[11] the Commission appealed to all States that had not done so to become parties to the Covenant. It encouraged the Committee on Economic, Social and Cultural Rights to strive towards the application of universally recognized criteria in implementing the Covenant and encouraged Governments to publish the Covenant in as many languages as possible and to disseminate it widely. The Commission also asked the Secretary-General to report in 1990 on the status of the Covenant.

On the same date,[12] the Commission asked the Secretary-General to consult with the Committee as to how the programme of advisory services could be used to promote enhanced respect for economic, social and cultural rights.

Committee on Economic, Social and Cultural Rights. The Committee on Economic, Social and Cultural Rights, established in 1985,[13] held its third session at Geneva from 6 to 24 February.[14] Its pre-sessional working group, a five-member group established in 1988[15] to meet for one week prior to each session, met at Geneva from 30 January to 3 February.

Concerning the rights covered by articles 6 to 9 of the Covenant (the right to work and to favourable conditions of work, trade union rights and the right to social security), the Committee examined reports from Canada,[16] the Netherlands,[17] Rwanda,[18] and Trinidad and Tobago.[19] Rights covered under articles 10 to 12 (the protection of the family, mothers and children, and the right to an adequate living standard and to physical and mental health) were examined in reports submitted by Cameroon,[20] France,[21] the Nether-

lands,[22] Poland,[23] Trinidad and Tobago,[24] Tunisia[25] and the United Kingdom.[26] As to the rights covered by articles 13 to 15 (education, including compulsory education, and cultural participation), the Committee considered reports from the Netherlands,[27] Rwanda,[28] and Trinidad and Tobago.[29] It also considered supplementary information submitted by Zaire.[30]

The Committee's day of general discussion focused on article 11, the right of everyone to an adequate standard of living for himself and his family (including adequate food, clothing and housing) and to the continuous improvement of living conditions.

In response to a 1988 Economic and Social Council request,[31] Special Rapporteur Asbjorn Eide made a presentation of his 1987 study[32] on the right to adequate food in order for the Committee to submit its observations thereon.

In 1989, the Committee began to prepare general comments based on the articles and provisions of the Covenant with a view to assisting the States parties in fulfilling their reporting obligations. Its first general comment outlined the objectives of reports submitted by States parties.

Annexed to the Committee's report was a list of States parties to the Covenant as at 24 February 1989 and provisional rules of procedure adopted by the Committee on 21 February.

The Economic and Social Council, by **decision 1989/158** of 24 May, took note of the provisional rules of procedure and decided to defer until 1990 consideration of those rules. In the interim, the Council asked the Committee to continue to use the rules of procedure of the Council.[33]

Other action. The Secretary-General transmitted to the Economic and Social Council the eleventh report of the International Labour Organisation (ILO) Committee of Experts on the Application of Conventions and Applications on progress made towards the observance of the provisions of the Covenant lying within ILO's scope of activities. The report described progress in the observance of articles 6 to 10 in 13 States.[34]

Interdependence of economic, social, cultural, civil and political rights

On 15 December, the General Assembly, on the recommendation of the Third Committee, adopted **resolution 44/130** by recorded vote.

Indivisibility and interdependence of economic, social, cultural, civil and political rights

The General Assembly,

Mindful of the obligations of States under the Charter of the United Nations to promote social progress and better standards of life in larger freedom and universal respect for, and observance of, human rights and fundamental freedoms for all without distinction as to race, sex, language or religion,

Reaffirming the Universal Declaration of Human Rights, the International Covenant on Civil and Political Rights, the International Covenant on Economic, Social and Cultural Rights and the Declaration on Social Progress and Development,

Recalling that in the preambles to the International Covenants on Human Rights, it is recognized that the ideal of free human beings enjoying freedom from fear and want can be achieved only if conditions are created whereby persons may enjoy their economic, social and cultural rights as well as their civil and political rights,

Also recalling its resolutions 40/114 of 13 December 1985, 41/117 of 4 December 1986, 42/102 of 7 December 1987 and 43/113 of 8 December 1988,

Reaffirming the provisions of its resolution 32/130 of 16 December 1977 that all human rights and fundamental freedoms are indivisible and interdependent and that the promotion and protection of one category of rights can never exempt or excuse States from the promotion and protection of the other rights,

Convinced that equal attention and urgent consideration should be given to the implementation, promotion and protection of economic, social, cultural, civil and political rights,

Desirous of removing all obstacles to the full realization of human rights, in particular mass and flagrant violations of human rights,

Reaffirming that there is a close and multidimensional relationship between disarmament and development, that progress in disarmament would considerably promote progress in development and that resources released through disarmament measures could contribute to the economic and social development and well-being of all peoples,

Recognizing that the realization of the right to development may help to promote the enjoyment of all human rights and fundamental freedoms,

Recalling Commission on Human Rights resolutions 1985/42 of 14 March 1985, 1986/15 of 10 March 1986, 1987/19 and 1987/20 of 10 March 1987, and 1988/22 and 1988/23 of 7 March 1988, and taking note of Commission resolutions 1989/12 and 1989/13 of 2 March 1989, in which it is stated that the implementation, promotion and protection of economic, social and cultural rights have not received sufficient attention within the framework of the United Nations system,

1. *Notes* the essential importance of national efforts and international co-operation to achieve the full and effective realization of all human rights recognized in the International Covenants on Human Rights and other international instruments;

2. *Appeals* to all States to pursue policies directed towards the implementation, promotion and protection of economic, social, cultural, civil and political rights recognized in the International Covenants on Human Rights and other international instruments;

3. *Requests* the Secretary-General to intensify his efforts under the programme of advisory services to States in the implementation, promotion and protection of human rights and fundamental freedoms set forth in the International Covenants on Human Rights and other international instruments;

4. *Urges* the Secretary-General to take determined steps, within existing resources, to give publicity to the

Human Rights Committee and to the Committee on Economic, Social and Cultural Rights and to ensure that they receive full administrative support in order to enable them to discharge their functions effectively;

5. *Requests* the organs of the United Nations, in co-operation with the specialized agencies, Member States and non-governmental organizations, to pay equal attention to economic, social, cultural, civil and political rights in the World Public Information Campaign for Human Rights;

6. *Decides* to consider the question of the indivisibility and interdependence of economic, social, cultural, civil and political rights at its forty-fifth session under the item entitled "International Covenants on Human Rights".

General Assembly resolution 44/130

15 December 1989   Meeting 82   124-0-23 (recorded vote)

Approved by Third Committee (A/44/824) by recorded vote (116-0-24), 22 November (meeting 52); 7-nation draft (A/C.3/44/L.48), orally revised; agenda item 98.

Sponsors: Algeria, Bulgaria, Byelorussian SSR, German Democratic Republic, Guatemala, Mongolia, Nicaragua.

Meeting numbers. GA 44th session: 3rd Committee 36-43, 50, 52; plenary 82.

Recorded vote in Assembly as follows:

In favour: Afghanistan, Algeria, Angola, Antigua and Barbuda, Argentina, Australia, Bahamas, Bahrain, Bangladesh, Barbados, Benin, Bhutan, Bolivia, Botswana, Brazil, Brunei Darussalam, Bulgaria, Burkina Faso, Burundi, Byelorussian SSR, Cameroon, Cape Verde, Central African Republic, Chad, China, Colombia, Congo, Costa Rica, Côte d'Ivoire, Cuba, Cyprus, Czechoslovakia, Democratic Yemen, Djibouti, Dominica, Dominican Republic, Ecuador, Egypt, Ethiopia, Fiji, Gabon, Gambia, German Democratic Republic, Ghana, Grenada, Guatemala, Guinea, Guinea-Bissau, Guyana, Haiti, Honduras, Hungary, India, Indonesia, Iran, Iraq, Jamaica, Jordan, Kenya, Kuwait, Lao People's Democratic Republic, Lebanon, Lesotho, Liberia, Libyan Arab Jamahiriya, Madagascar, Malawi, Malaysia, Maldives, Mali, Malta, Mauritania, Mauritius, Mongolia, Morocco, Mozambique, Myanmar, Nepal, New Zealand, Nicaragua, Niger, Nigeria, Oman, Pakistan, Panama, Paraguay, Peru, Philippines, Poland, Qatar, Romania, Rwanda, Saint Kitts and Nevis, Saint Lucia, Saint Vincent and the Grenadines, Samoa, Sao Tome and Principe, Saudi Arabia, Senegal, Seychelles, Sierra Leone, Singapore, Solomon Islands, Somalia, Sri Lanka, Sudan, Suriname, Syrian Arab Republic, Thailand, Trinidad and Tobago, Tunisia, Uganda, Ukrainian SSR, USSR, United Arab Emirates, United Republic of Tanzania, Uruguay, Vanuatu, Venezuela, Viet Nam, Yemen, Yugoslavia, Zambia, Zimbabwe.

Against: None.

Abstaining: Austria, Belgium, Canada, Chile, Denmark, Finland, France, Germany, Federal Republic of, Greece, Iceland, Ireland, Israel, Italy, Japan, Luxembourg, Netherlands, Norway, Portugal, Spain, Sweden, Turkey, United Kingdom, United States.

Right to development

Working Group activities. In 1989, the Working Group of Governmental Experts on the Right to Development held its twelfth session (Geneva, 23-27 January).[35]

Pursuant to a 1988 General Assembly resolution,[36] the 15-member Group considered an analytical compilation of comments on the implementation of the 1986 Declaration on the Right to Development[37] prepared by the Secretary-General and replies received from Governments, UN bodies and specialized agencies, governmental organizations and NGOs.[38] The Group recommended eliciting from Governments, UN organs and other bodies through a questionnaire more specific views on ways to implement the Declaration. It also advised: integrating the right to development with other human rights in the World Public Information Campaign to be launched in 1989; including the right to development in the advisory services of the Centre for Human Rights; paying special attention to vulnerable groups; inviting the Secretary-General to prepare, on a continuing basis, an analytical compendium containing provisions of national laws and administrative and judicial measures that implement the Declaration's provisions; and urging the Secretary-General to increase collaboration and co-ordination with interested NGOs. It recommended to the Commission on Human Rights that the Commission request the Secretary-General to explore possibilities of initiating consultation and an exchange of views with experts in development and human rights, and invite him to organize a global consultation on the realization of the right to development, in 1989 if possible. It reiterated its recommendation that there was a need for continuing evaluation mechanisms regarding the Declaration.

Human Rights Commission action. On 6 March,[(39)] the Commission asked the Secretary-General to circulate the Working Group's report to Governments, UN bodies and specialized agencies, governmental organizations and NGOs, drawing their attention to the analytical compilation of replies. It also asked him to transmit the Group's report to the General Assembly at its current session and to transmit a questionnaire to Governments, UN bodies and specialized agencies, governmental organizations and NGOs to elicit additional, updated and more specific views on the implementation and further enhancement of the Declaration. It further invited him to organize, in 1989, a global consultation on the realization of the right to development; to prepare background documents to assist the consultation; and to submit a report on the consultation in 1990. The Commission requested that the right to development be fully integrated with other human rights in the World Public Information Campaign for Human Rights to be launched in 1989 and that the right to development be included in the programme of activities of the advisory services of the Centre for Human Rights.

On 24 May, the Economic and Social Council, by **decision 1989/141**, approved the Commission's invitation to the Secretary-General to organize a global consultation.

The global consultation was scheduled to be held in January 1990 at Geneva.

Sub-Commission action. On 30 August,[(40)] the Sub-Commission, considering that among the reasons for the non-realization of human rights and fundamental freedoms in developing countries were economic, social and cultural problems, decided to consider, on an annual basis, the item

"The new international economic order and the promotion of human rights".

GENERAL ASSEMBLY ACTION

On 15 December, the General Assembly, on the recommendation of the Third Committee, adopted **resolution 44/62** without vote.

Right to development

The General Assembly,

Recalling the proclamation by the General Assembly at its forty-first session of the Declaration on the Right to Development,

Recalling also its resolutions and those of the Commission on Human Rights relating to the right to development, and taking note of Commission resolution 1989/45 of 6 March 1989, endorsed by the Economic and Social Council by its decision 1989/141,

Reiterating the importance of the right to development for all countries, in particular the developing countries,

Having considered the report of the Working Group of Governmental Experts on the Right to Development and all other relevant documents submitted to the General Assembly at its forty-fourth session,

Aware of the interest shown by several Member States, specialized agencies and non-governmental organizations in the work of the Working Group,

1. *Expresses the hope* that the replies of Governments, United Nations bodies and specialized agencies, and governmental and non-governmental organizations, including those active in development and human rights, to the request made by the Secretary-General, pursuant to Commission on Human Rights resolution 1989/45, will contain additional, updated and more specific views and proposals on the subject of the implementation and further enhancement of the Declaration on the Right to Development;

2. *Takes note* of the invitation of the Commission to the Secretary-General to organize, within existing resources, a global consultation on the realization of the right to development, which would involve experts with relevant experience gained at the national level and representatives of the United Nations system, including the specialized agencies, regional intergovernmental organizations and interested non-governmental organizations, including those active in development and human rights, and which would focus on the fundamental problems posed by the implementation of the Declaration, the criteria that might be used to identify progress and mechanisms for evaluating and stimulating such progress;

3. *Expresses the hope* that the results of that global consultation, the report on which is to be presented to the Commission at its forty-sixth session, will substantially contribute to the future work of the Commission on the implementation and further enhancement of the Declaration;

4. *Endorses* the view of the Commission that there is a need for a continuing evaluation mechanism to ensure the promotion, encouragement and reinforcement of the principles set forth in the Declaration;

5. *Urges* all relevant bodies of the United Nations system, particularly the specialized agencies, when planning their programmes of activities, to take due account

of the Declaration and to make efforts to contribute to its application;

6. *Requests* the Secretary-General to inform the Commission at its forty-sixth session and the General Assembly at its forty-fifth session of the activities of the organizations of the United Nations system for the implementation of the Declaration;

7. *Calls upon* the Commission to decide at its forty-sixth session on the future course of action on the question, in particular on practical measures for the implementation and enhancement of the Declaration;

8. *Invites* the Commission to report on the question to the General Assembly at its forty-fifth session, through the Economic and Social Council;

9. *Decides* to consider this question at its forty-fifth session under the item entitled ''Alternative approaches and ways and means within the United Nations system for improving the effective enjoyment of human rights and fundamental freedoms''.

General Assembly resolution 44/62

8 December 1989   Meeting 78   Adopted without vote

Approved by Third Committee (A/44/799) without vote, 20 November (meeting 49); 39-nation draft (A/C.3/44/L.38); agenda item 96 *(b)*.
Meeting numbers. GA 44th session: 3rd Committee 34, 35, 43, 49; plenary 78.

Extreme poverty

Human Rights Commission action. On 2 March,[41] the Commission drew the attention of the General Assembly and all UN bodies to the contradiction between the existence of situations of extreme poverty and exclusion of society and the duty to guarantee full enjoyment of human rights, and urged the Committee on Economic, Social and Cultural Rights to give the necessary attention to that question. It asked the Sub-Commission to pay particular attention to the question of extreme poverty and exclusion from society and to examine the feasibility of a study on the topic.

Foreign debt

Human Rights Commission action. By a roll-call vote of 30 to 6, with 6 abstentions, the Commission, on 2 March,[42] decided to include in the agenda of its 1990 session the subject of foreign debt, economic adjustment policies and their effects on the full enjoyment of human rights and, in particular, on the implementation of the Declaration on the Right to Development.

Sub-Commission action. On 31 August,[43] by a roll-call vote of 17 to 1, with 1 abstention, the Sub-Commission invited the Special Rapporteur on problems, policies and progressive measures relating to the more effective realization of economic, social and cultural rights to take those factors into account in his study. It considered it necessary to invite the developed countries and multilateral financial institutions to take particular account, in formulating their debt policies, of

social objectives and growth and development priorities.

Right to food

In a July report,[44] the Secretary-General presented information received from the Food and Agriculture Organization of the United Nations (FAO) and the International Law Association on the right to food in response to his request for a description of laws States had pertaining to the right to food.

Popular participation and human rights

Reports of the Secretary-General. The Commission had before it two reports of the Secretary-General on popular participation and human rights.

One of the reports[45] contained comments on a 1985 study on popular participation in its various forms as an important factor in development and in the full realization of all human rights[46] received from Governments, UN bodies and Secretariat departments, specialized agencies and NGOs. The other report, a study of laws and practices regarding popular participation,[47] presented the views of States on popular participation in relation to some civil and political rights, certain economic, social and cultural rights, and vulnerable or disadvantaged groups.

Human Rights Commission action. On 2 March,[48] the Commission invited Governments, UN organs, specialized agencies and NGOs that had not yet done so to comment on the study on popular participation,[45] and asked the Secretary-General to submit a report in 1990 containing comments made by them. It also asked him to prepare a study for submission in 1991 regarding the extent to which the right to participation had been established and had evolved at the national level.

GENERAL ASSEMBLY ACTION

On 8 December, the General Assembly, on the recommendation of the Third Committee, adopted **resolution 44/53** without vote.

Popular participation in its various forms as an important factor in development and in the full realization of all human rights

The General Assembly,

Recalling its resolutions 34/152 of 17 December 1979, 37/55 of 3 December 1982, 38/24 of 22 November 1983 and 40/99 of 13 December 1985,

Recalling also Economic and Social Council resolution 1983/31 of 27 May 1983 and decision 1984/131 of 24 May 1984 and taking note of Commission on Human Rights resolution 1989/14 of 2 March 1989,

Reaffirming that popular participation in all its various forms constitutes an important factor in socio-economic development and in the full realization of all human rights and the dignity of the human person,

1. *Invites* Governments, the concerned specialized agencies and other organizations of the United Nations system and the relevant non-governmental organizations that have not yet done so to transmit to the Secretary-General their comments on the study on popular participation in its various forms as an important factor in development and in the full realization of all human rights;

2. *Requests* the Commission on Human Rights to continue to consider at its forty-sixth and, if desired by the Commission, at its forty-seventh, forty-eighth and forty-ninth sessions, the question of popular participation in its various forms as an important factor in the full realization of all human rights, and to inform the General Assembly at its forty-eighth session, through the Economic and Social Council, of the results of that consideration;

3. *Decides* to continue the consideration of this question at its forty-eighth session, in the context of the item relating to the world social situation, under the sub-item entitled ''Popular participation in its various forms as an important factor in development and in the full realization of all human rights''.

General Assembly resolution 44/53

8 December 1989   Meeting 78   Adopted without vote

Approved by Third Committee (A/44/749) without vote, 9 November (meeting 37); 20-nation draft (A/C.3/44/L.13); agenda item 90 *(b)*.
Meeting numbers. GA 44th session: 3rd Committee 12-20, 30, 37; plenary 78.

REFERENCES

[1]E/CN.4/1989/9. [2]E/1989/20 (res. 1989/12). [3]YUN 1989, p. 526. [4]E/1989/20 (dec. 1989/103). [5]E/CN.4/Sub.2/1989/19. [6]E/CN.4/Sub.2/1989/58 (res. 1989/20). [7]YUN 1966, p. 419, GA res. 2200 A (XXI), annex, 16 Dec. 1966. [8]YUN 1976, p. 609. [9]*Multilateral Treaties Deposited with the Secretary-General: Status as at 31 December 1989* (ST/LEG/SER.E/8), Sales No. E.90.V.6. [10]A/44/441. [11]E/1989/20 (res. 1989/17). [12]*Ibid.* (res. 1989/13). [13]YUN 1985, p. 878, ESC res. 1985/17, 28 May 1985. [14]E/1989/22. [15]YUN 1988, p. 527, ESC res. 1988/4, 24 May 1988. [16]E/1984/7/Add.28. [17]E/1984/6/Add.20. [18]E/1984/7/Add.29. [19]E/1984/6/Add.21. [20]E/1986/3/Add.8. [21]E/1986/3/Add.10. [22]E/1986/4/Add.24. [23]E/1986/4/Add.12. [24]E/1986/3/Add.11. [25]E/1986/3/Add.9. [26]E/1986/4/Add.23. [27]E/1982/3/Add.44. [28]E/1982/3/Add.42. [29]E/1988/5/Add.1. [30]E/1989/5. [31]YUN 1988, p. 531, ESC res. 1988/33, 27 May 1988. [32]YUN 1987, p. 773. [33]E/5715/Rev.1. [34]E/1989/6. [35]E/CN.4/1989/10. [36]YUN 1988, p. 530, GA res. 43/127, 8 Dec. 1988. [37]YUN 1986, p. 717, GA res. 41/128, annex, 4 Dec. 1986. [38]E/CN.4/AC.39/1989/1. [39]E/1989/20 (res. 1989/45). [40]E/CN.4/Sub.2/1989/58 (res. 1989/1). [41]E/1989/20 (res. 1989/10). [42]*Ibid.* (res. 1989/15). [43]E/CN.4/Sub.2/1989/58 (res. 1989/21). [44]E/CN.4/Sub.2/1989/16. [45]E/CN.4/1989/11. [46]YUN 1985, p. 881. [47]E/CN.4/1989/12. [48]E/1989/20 (res. 1989/14).

Advancement of human rights

In November, in his fourth biennial progress report on international conditions and human rights[1] issued pursuant to a 1981 General Assembly request,[2] the Secretary-General submitted substantive information and views on the subject received during the year from seven Governments and four UN specialized agencies.

The Secretary-General noted that Member States had drawn attention to such issues as international peace and security and human rights; the impact of the arms race on human rights; international co-operation and human rights; elimination of racial discrimination and *apartheid;* decolonization; development and international economic conditions; legislative activity and the implementation of international human rights instruments; activities of international organizations; and measures undertaken at the national level. Specialized agencies, for their part, described activities for the promotion and protection of human rights within their areas of concern. Some Governments and organizations underlined the necessity to intensify the struggle against racism, racial discrimination and *apartheid,* stating that their eradication was central to achieving the UN objectives in maintaining world peace and securing social progress. It was emphasized that all forms of racial discrimination, besides constituting a violation of fundamental human rights, tended to jeopardize friendly relations among peoples, co-operation between nations, and international peace and security.

Noting the complex interrelationship between international conditions and human rights, the Secretary-General pointed out that human rights violations led to political consequences injurious to the long-term interests of peace and that the stability of national and international society could only rest upon a foundation of assured human rights.

GENERAL ASSEMBLY ACTION

On 8 December, the General Assembly, on the recommendation of the Third Committee, adopted **resolution 44/63** by recorded vote.

Alternative approaches and ways and means within the United Nations system for improving the effective enjoyment of human rights and fundamental freedoms

The General Assembly,

Recalling that in the Charter of the United Nations the peoples of the United Nations declared their determination to reaffirm faith in fundamental human rights, in the dignity and worth of the human person and in the equal rights of men and women and of nations large and small and to employ international machinery for the promotion of the economic and social advancement of all peoples,

Recalling also the purposes and principles of the Charter to achieve international co-operation in solving international problems of an economic, social, cultural or humanitarian character, and in promoting and encouraging respect for human rights and for fundamental freedoms for all without distinction as to race, sex, language or religion,

Emphasizing the significance and validity of the Universal Declaration of Human Rights and of the International Covenants on Human Rights in promoting respect for and observance of human rights and fundamental freedoms,

Recalling its resolution 32/130 of 16 December 1977, in which it decided that the approach to future work within the United Nations system with respect to human rights questions should take into account the concepts set forth in that resolution,

Recalling also its resolutions 34/46 of 23 November 1979, 35/174 of 15 December 1980, 36/133 of 14 December 1981, 38/124 of 16 December 1983, 39/145 of 14 December 1984, 40/124 of 13 December 1985, 41/131 and 41/133 of 4 December 1986, 42/119 of 7 December 1987 and 43/125 of 8 December 1988,

Taking into account Commission on Human Rights resolution 1985/43 of 14 March 1985,

Reiterating that the right to development is an inalienable human right and that equality of development opportunities is a prerogative both of nations and of individuals within nations,

Recognizing that the human being is the main subject of development and that everyone has the right to participate in, as well as to benefit from, the development process,

Bearing in mind that the grave economic situation facing the developing countries noticeably affects the effective promotion and full enjoyment of human rights and fundamental freedoms,

Reiterating once again that the establishment of the new international economic order is an essential element for the effective promotion and full enjoyment of human rights and fundamental freedoms for all,

Reiterating also its profound conviction that all human rights and fundamental freedoms are indivisible and interdependent and that equal attention and urgent consideration should be given to the implementation, promotion and protection of civil and political rights and of economic, social and cultural rights,

Emphasizing the need for the creation, at the national and international levels, of conditions for the promotion and full protection of the human rights of individuals and peoples,

Recognizing that international peace and security are essential elements for the full realization of human rights, including the right to development,

Convinced that the resources that would be released by disarmament could contribute significantly to the development of all States, in particular the developing countries,

Reiterating that co-operation among all nations on the basis of respect for the independence, sovereignty and territorial integrity of each State, including the right of every people to choose freely its own socio-economic and political system, is essential for the promotion of peace and development,

Convinced that the primary aim of such international co-operation must be the achievement by all human beings of a life of freedom and dignity and freedom from want,

Concerned, however, about the occurrence of violations of human rights in the world,

Reaffirming that nothing in the Universal Declaration of Human Rights or in the International Covenants on Human Rights may be interpreted as implying for any State, group or person the right to engage in any activity or perform any act aimed at destroying any of the rights and freedoms proclaimed therein,

Affirming that the ultimate aim of development is the steady improvement of the well-being of the entire population, on the basis of its full participation in the process of development and a fair distribution of the benefits therefrom,

Considering that the efforts of the developing countries for their own development should be supported by an increased flow of resources and by the adoption of appropriate and substantive measures for creating an external environment conducive to such development,

Taking into account the final documents of the Ninth Conference of Heads of State or Government of Non-Aligned Countries, held at Belgrade from 4 to 7 September 1989,[a]

Bearing in mind the stipulations of the final documents of the Ministerial Meeting of the Co-ordinating Bureau of the Movement of Non-Aligned Countries, held at Harare from 17 to 19 May 1989,[b] particularly paragraphs 10 to 13 of the Economic Declaration,

Emphasizing the special importance of the purposes and principles proclaimed in the Declaration on the Right to Development,

Taking into account Commission on Human Rights resolutions 1989/15 of 2 March 1989 and 1989/45 of 6 March 1989,

Reaffirming the importance of furthering the activities of the organs of the United Nations in the field of human rights in conformity with the principles of the Charter,

Emphasizing that Governments have the duty to ensure respect for all human rights and fundamental freedoms,

1. *Reiterates its request* that the Commission on Human Rights should continue its current work on overall analysis with a view to further promoting and strengthening human rights and fundamental freedoms, including the question of the programme and working methods of the Commission, and on the overall analysis of the alternative approaches and ways and means for improving the effective enjoyment of human rights and fundamental freedoms, in accordance with the provisions and concepts of General Assembly resolution 32/130 and other relevant texts;

2. *Affirms* that a primary aim of international co-operation in the field of human rights is a life of freedom, dignity and peace for all peoples and for every human being, that all human rights and fundamental freedoms are indivisible and interrelated and that the promotion and protection of one category of rights should never exempt or excuse States from promoting and protecting the others;

3. *Reaffirms* that equal attention and urgent consideration should be given to the implementation, promotion and protection of civil and political rights and of economic, social and cultural rights;

4. *Reaffirms also* that it is of paramount importance for the promotion of human rights and fundamental freedoms that Member States should assume specific obligations by acceding to or ratifying international instruments in this field and, consequently, that the work within the United Nations system of setting standards

---

[a] A/44/551-S/20870.
[b] A/44/409-S/20743 & Corr.1,2.

in the field of human rights and universal acceptance and implementation of the relevant international instruments should be encouraged;

5. *Reiterates once again* that the international community should accord, or continue to accord, priority to the search for solutions to mass and flagrant violations of human rights of peoples and individuals affected by situations such as those mentioned in paragraph 1 *(e)* of General Assembly resolution 32/130, paying due attention also to other situations of violations of human rights;

6. *Reaffirms* its responsibility for achieving international co-operation in promoting and encouraging respect for human rights and fundamental freedoms for all, and expresses its concern at serious violations of human rights, in particular mass and flagrant violations of those rights, wherever they occur;

7. *Expresses concern* at the present situation as regards the achievement of the objectives and goals for the establishment of the new international economic order, and at its adverse effects on the full realization of human rights, in particular the right to development;

8. *Reaffirms* that the right to development is an inalienable human right;

9. *Reaffirms also* that international peace and security are essential elements for achieving full realization of the right to development;

10. *Recognizes* that all human rights and fundamental freedoms are indivisible and interdependent;

11. *Considers it necessary* for all Member States to promote international co-operation on the basis of respect for the independence, sovereignty and territorial integrity of each State, including the right of every people to choose freely its own socio-economic and political system, with a view to solving international economic, social and humanitarian problems;

12. *Expresses concern* at the disparity existing between established norms and principles and the actual situation of all human rights and fundamental freedoms in the world;

13. *Urges* all States to co-operate with the Commission on Human Rights in the promotion and protection of human rights and fundamental freedoms;

14. *Reiterates* the need to create, at the national and international levels, conditions for the full promotion and protection of the human rights of individuals and peoples;

15. *Reaffirms once again* that, in order to facilitate the full enjoyment of all human rights without diminishing personal dignity, it is necessary to promote the rights to education, work, health and proper nourishment through the adoption of measures at the national level, including those that provide for the right of workers to participate in management, as well as the adoption of measures at the international level, including the establishment of the new international economic order;

16. *Decides* that the approach to future work within the United Nations system on human rights matters should also take into account the content of the Declaration on the Right to Development and the need for the implementation thereof;

17. *Decides* to include in the provisional agenda of its forty-fifth session the item entitled ''Alternative approaches and ways and means within the United Nations system for improving the effective enjoyment of human rights and fundamental freedoms''.

General Assembly resolution 44/63

8 December 1989   Meeting 78   129-1-25 (recorded vote)

Approved by Third Committee (A/44/799) by recorded vote (113-1-25), 20 November (meeting 49); 37-nation draft (A/C.3/44/L.39); agenda item 96.
Meeting numbers. GA 44th session: 3rd Committee 34, 35, 43, 49; plenary 78.

Recorded vote in Assembly as follows:

In favour: Afghanistan, Algeria, Angola, Antigua and Barbuda, Argentina, Bahamas, Bahrain, Bangladesh, Barbados, Benin, Bhutan, Bolivia, Botswana, Brazil, Brunei Darussalam, Bulgaria, Burkina Faso, Burundi, Byelorussian SSR, Cameroon, Cape Verde, Central African Republic, Chad, China, Colombia, Comoros, Congo, Costa Rica, Côte d'Ivoire, Cuba, Cyprus, Czechoslovakia, Democratic Kampuchea, Democratic Yemen, Djibouti, Dominica, Dominican Republic, Ecuador, Egypt, El Salvador, Equatorial Guinea, Ethiopia, Fiji, Gabon, Gambia, German Democratic Republic, Ghana, Grenada, Guatemala, Guinea, Guinea-Bissau, Guyana, Haiti, Honduras, Hungary, India, Indonesia, Iran, Iraq, Jamaica, Jordan, Kenya, Kuwait, Lao People's Democratic Republic, Lebanon, Lesotho, Liberia, Libyan Arab Jamahiriya, Madagascar, Malawi, Malaysia, Maldives, Mali, Mauritania, Mauritius, Mexico, Mongolia, Morocco, Mozambique, Myanmar, Nepal, New Zealand, Nicaragua, Niger, Nigeria, Oman, Pakistan, Panama, Papua New Guinea, Paraguay, Peru, Poland, Qatar, Romania, Rwanda, Saint Lucia, Saint Vincent and the Grenadines, Samoa, Sao Tome and Principe, Saudi Arabia, Senegal, Seychelles, Sierra Leone, Singapore, Solomon Islands, Somalia, Sri Lanka, Sudan, Suriname, Swaziland, Syrian Arab Republic, Thailand, Togo, Trinidad and Tobago, Tunisia, Uganda, Ukrainian SSR, USSR, United Arab Emirates, United Republic of Tanzania, Uruguay, Vanuatu, Venezuela, Viet Nam, Yemen, Yugoslavia, Zaire, Zambia, Zimbabwe.

Against: United States.

Abstaining: Australia, Austria, Belgium, Canada, Chile, Denmark, Finland, France, Germany, Federal Republic of, Greece, Iceland, Ireland, Israel, Italy, Japan, Luxembourg, Malta, Netherlands, Norway, Philippines, Portugal, Spain, Sweden, Turkey, United Kingdom.

National institutions for human rights protection

Report of the Secretary-General. In response to a 1987 General Assembly request,[3] the Secretary-General submitted to the Commission at its 1989 session an updated report[4] on national institutions for the promotion and protection of human rights, prepared further to his 1987 report on the subject.[5] The updated report analysed information received from seven Governments as at 15 February 1989 with regard to various models of institutions and their functioning, including legislative organs and organs established to examine the constitutionality of law, judicial organs, administrative organs and the ombudsman, as well as the role of NGOs. Annexed to the report was a list of national institutions.

Human Rights Commission action. On 7 March, the Commission reaffirmed[6] the importance of developing national institutions for the promotion and protection of human rights and of maintaining their independence and integrity. It encouraged Member States to exchange information and experience as well as to develop funding and other strategies concerning the establishment and operation of such institutions. The Commission also affirmed the role of national institutions as focal points for the dissemination of human rights materials and other public information activities under UN auspices, and requested the Secretary-General to assist Member States in that regard.

Note of the Secretary-General. In a 22 September note,[7] the Secretary-General informed the General Assembly that, pursuant to its 1987 request,[3] the Centre for Human Rights was in the process of preparing his updated report for publication as a UN handbook in the six official languages, to be distributed world wide.

On 8 December, on the recommendation of the Third Committee, the Assembly adopted **resolution 44/64** without vote.

National institutions for the protection and promotion of human rights

The General Assembly,

Recalling the relevant resolutions concerning national institutions for the protection and promotion of human rights, notably its resolution 41/129 of 4 December 1986 and Commission on Human Rights resolutions 1987/40 of 10 March 1987 and 1988/72 of 10 March 1988, and taking note of Commission resolution 1989/52 of 7 March 1989,

Emphasizing the importance of the Universal Declaration of Human Rights, the International Covenants on Human Rights and other international instruments for promoting respect for and observance of human rights and fundamental freedoms,

Affirming that priority should be accorded to the development of appropriate arrangements at the national level to ensure the effective implementation of international human rights standards,

Conscious of the significant role that institutions at the national level can play in protecting and promoting human rights and fundamental freedoms and in developing and enhancing public awareness of those rights and freedoms,

Recognizing that the United Nations can play a catalytic role in assisting the development of national institutions by acting as a clearing-house for the exchange of information and experience,

Mindful in this regard of the guidelines on the structure and functioning of national and local institutions for the protection and promotion of human rights endorsed by the General Assembly in its resolution 33/46 of 14 December 1978,

Noting the diverse approaches adopted throughout the world for the protection and promotion of human rights at the national level, and recognizing the value of such approaches,

1. *Takes note* of the note by the Secretary-General;

2. *Reaffirms* the importance of developing, in accordance with national legislation, effective national institutions for the protection and promotion of human rights and of maintaining their independence and integrity;

3. *Encourages* Member States to establish or, where they already exist, to strengthen national institutions for the protection and promotion of human rights and to incorporate those elements in national development plans;

4. *Welcomes* the increase in the number of national institutions for the protection and promotion of human rights in various countries around the world;

5. *Encourages* initiatives on the part of Governments and regional, international, intergovernmental and non-governmental organizations intended to strengthen existing national institutions and to establish such institutions where they do not exist;

6. *Notes with appreciation* the action taken by the Centre for Human Rights of the Secretariat to co-operate with regional and national institutions for the protection and promotion of human rights;

7. *Encourages* all Member States to take appropriate steps to promote the exchange of information and experience concerning the establishment and operation of such national institutions;

8. *Requests* the Secretary-General to prepare, with the assistance of experts, if necessary, and incorporating materials submitted by Governments, a report containing conceptual models of national institutions for the protection and promotion of human rights, to be submitted to the Commission on Human Rights at its forty-seventh session;

9. *Also requests* the Secretary-General to respond favourably to requests from Member States for assistance in the establishment and strengthening of national institutions as part of the programme of advisory services and technical assistance in the field of human rights;

10. *Invites* the Secretary-General to include in an updated report all the information provided by Governments and any additional information that Governments may wish to provide, giving particular emphasis to the functioning of various models of national institutions in the implementation of international standards on human rights, as well as a list of existing national institutions with contact points and a bibliography of relevant materials;

11. *Affirms* the role of national institutions as agencies for the dissemination of human rights materials and other public information activities under the auspices of the United Nations;

12. *Recognizes* the constructive role that non-governmental organizations can play in relation to national institutions;

13. *Requests* the Secretary-General to report to the General Assembly at its forty-sixth session on the implementation of the present resolution.

General Assembly resolution 44/64

8 December 1989   Meeting 78   Adopted without vote

Approved by Third Committee (A/44/799) without vote, 20 November (meeting 49); 18-nation draft (A/C.3/44/L.43); agenda item 96 *(a)*.

Meeting numbers. GA 44th session: 3rd Committee 34, 35, 43, 49; plenary 78.

UN machinery

Commission on Human Rights

The Commission on Human Rights held its forty-fifth session at Geneva from 30 January to 10 March 1989 and adopted 75 resolutions and 14 decisions. In addition, it recommended 8 draft resolutions and 20 draft decisions for adoption by the Economic and Social Council.

On 24 May, by **decision 1989/157**, the Council took note of the Commission's report on its forty-fifth session.[8]

With regard to the organization of its work, the Commission decided[9] to set up informal open-ended working groups on the question of a convention on the rights of the child; on the rights of persons belonging to national, ethnic, religious and linguistic minorities; and on the drafting of a declaration on the right and responsibility of individuals, groups and organs of society to promote and protect universally recognized human rights and fundamental freedoms.

On 6 March, the Commission, having considered a report[10] of its Sub-Commission's Chairman on the implementation of the guidelines for organizing the Sub-Commission's work set out by the Commission in 1988,[11] noted[12] the steps taken by the Sub-Commission to rationalize and streamline its work. The Sub-Commission was encouraged to continue that process, and further guidelines were recommended. The Chairman of the Sub-Commission was requested to report to the Commission on their implementation.

On 7 March, the Commission emphasized[13] the need to increase the effectiveness of its monitoring mechanisms, and requested the Secretary-General to consider convening a meeting of its special rapporteurs and representatives, and representatives of other mechanisms established by the Commission, as well as its Chairman and the Chairman and rapporteurs of the Sub-Commission, to discuss ways of improving the monitoring procedures. It decided to examine the meeting's recommendations no later than at its forty-seventh (1991) session.

Organization of work of the 1990 session

On 7 March, the Commission decided,[14] subject to the approval of the Economic and Social Council, to set up a five-member working group to examine particular human rights violations that might be referred to it at its 1990 session by the Sub-Commission under the confidential procedure governed by a 1970 Council resolution.[15]

On 24 May, by **decision 1989/144**, the Council approved the Commission's decision. By **decision 1989/155** of the same date, the Council, on the Commission's recommendation,[16] authorized 30 fully serviced additional meetings for the Commission's forty-sixth (1990) session. It noted that the Commission had requested its Chairman to make every effort to organize the session's work within the time normally allotted, with additional meetings to be held only if absolutely necessary.

Enlargement of the Commission

On 15 December, the General Assembly, on the recommendation of the Third Committee, adopted **resolution 44/167** by recorded vote.

Enlargement of the Commission on Human Rights and the further promotion of human rights and fundamental freedoms

The General Assembly,

Recalling Economic and Social Council resolutions 845(XXXII) of 3 August 1961, 1147(XLI) of 4 August 1966 and 1979/36 of 10 May 1979,

Appreciating the contribution made by the Commission on Human Rights to the cause of human rights and recognizing the need to reinforce the Commission,

Reaffirming that the Commission on Human Rights shall be guided by the standards in the field of human rights laid down in the various international instruments in that field,

Emphasizing the importance of further improving the effective functioning of the Commission on Human Rights and the participation therein by Member States at a high level,

Taking note of the relevant section of the final documents of the Ninth Conference of Heads of State or Government of Non-Aligned Countries adopted at Belgrade on 7 September 1989,[a] in which it is recognized that, in order to strengthen the role and efficiency of the United Nations and to reinforce United Nations mechanisms so as to allow for efficient co-ordination of the Organization's activities, there is an urgent need, *inter alia*, for an overall review of the current distribution of membership in the various United Nations bodies and commissions, with a view to achieving a more equitable geographical distribution,

1. *Decides* to recommend that the Economic and Social Council take the necessary steps, at its first regular session of 1990, to expand the membership of the Commission on Human Rights, on the basis of the principle of equitable geographical distribution, for the further promotion of human rights and fundamental freedoms;

2. *Calls upon* the Economic and Social Council to conclude deliberations on this question with urgency;

3. *Requests* the Commission on Human Rights to examine ways and means of making its work more effective and to submit its recommendations thereon to the Economic and Social Council.

---

[a]A/44/551-S/20870.

General Assembly resolution 44/167

15 December 1989   Meeting 82   151-2-2 (recorded vote)

Approved by Third Committee (A/44/848) by recorded vote (133-3), 29 November (meeting 62); draft by Malaysia, for Group of 77 (A/C.3/44/L.88); agenda item 12.

Meeting numbers. GA 44th session: 3rd Committee 48, 50-62; plenary 82.

Recorded vote in Assembly as follows:

In favour: Afghanistan, Albania, Algeria, Angola, Antigua and Barbuda, Argentina, Australia, Austria, Bahamas, Bahrain, Bangladesh, Barbados, Belgium, Benin, Bhutan, Bolivia, Botswana, Brazil, Brunei Darussalam, Bulgaria, Burkina Faso, Burundi, Byelorussian SSR, Cameroon, Canada, Cape Verde, Central African Republic, Chad, Chile, China, Colombia, Congo, Costa Rica, Côte d'Ivoire, Cuba, Cyprus, Czechoslovakia, Democratic Kampuchea, Democratic Yemen, Denmark, Djibouti, Dominica, Dominican Republic, Ecuador, Egypt, El Salvador, Ethiopia, Fiji, Finland, France, Gabon, Gambia, German Democratic Republic, Germany, Federal Republic of, Ghana, Greece, Grenada, Guatemala, Guinea, Guinea-Bissau, Guyana, Haiti, Honduras, Hungary, Iceland, India, Indonesia, Iran, Iraq, Ireland, Italy, Jamaica, Jordan, Kenya, Kuwait, Lao People's Democratic Republic, Lebanon, Lesotho, Liberia, Libyan Arab Jamahiriya, Luxembourg, Madagascar, Malawi, Malaysia, Maldives, Mali, Malta, Mauritania, Mauritius, Mexico, Mongolia, Morocco, Mozambique, Myanmar, Nepal, Netherlands, New Zealand, Nicaragua, Niger, Nigeria, Norway, Oman, Pakistan, Panama, Papua New Guinea, Paraguay, Peru, Philippines, Poland, Portugal, Qatar, Romania, Rwanda, Saint Kitts and Nevis, Saint Lucia, Saint Vincent and the Grenadines, Samoa, Sao Tome and Principe, Saudi Arabia, Senegal, Seychelles, Sierra Leone, Singapore, Solomon Islands, Somalia, Spain, Sri Lanka, Sudan, Suriname, Swaziland, Sweden, Syrian Arab Republic, Thailand, Togo, Trinidad and Tobago, Tunisia, Turkey, Uganda, Ukrainian SSR, USSR, United Arab Emirates, United Kingdom, United Republic of Tanzania, Uruguay, Vanuatu, Venezuela, Viet Nam, Yemen, Yugoslavia, Zambia, Zimbabwe.

Against: Israel, United States.

Abstaining: Japan, Zaire.*

*Later advised the Secretariat it had intended to vote in favour.

Sub-Commission on Prevention of Discrimination and Protection of Minorities

The Sub-Commission on Prevention of Discrimination and Protection of Minorities held its forty-first session at Geneva from 7 August to 1 September 1989;[17] it adopted 47 resolutions and 13 decisions. It also recommended 14 draft resolutions and 4 draft decisions for adoption by the Commission on Human Rights, its parent body.

On 25 August, by a roll-call vote of 14 to 6, with 4 abstentions, the Sub-Commission suspended[18] its rule of procedure concerning the method of voting, so as to allow for voting by secret ballot on decisions considered under the confidential procedure governed by a 1970 Economic and Social Council resolution.[15] By another decision,[19] adopted by a roll-call vote of 14 to 6, with 3 abstentions, the Sub-Commission provisionally suspended the same rule of procedure with regard to decisions relating to human rights violations, including policies of racial discrimination and segregation and of *apartheid*, with particular reference to colonial and other dependent countries and territories. It also decided,[20] by 15 votes to 2, with 7 abstentions, that its Working Group on Communications, acting under the 1970 Council resolution,[15] should not consider a communication unless the Government concerned had had five months to submit a reply from the day on which the communication was transmitted to the Government.

On 30 August, the Sub-Commission, noting the organizational guidelines recommended by the Commission on Human Rights in March (see above), decided[21] to examine in 1990 ways of rationalizing proposals for studies, as well as the possibility of drawing up a medium-term programme that would ensure participation of the greatest number of Sub-Commission members in this programme. The Secretary-General was requested to submit a list of the studies already undertaken and the names of those who prepared them. On the same date, the Sub-Commission decided[22] to continue the review of its work at its forty-second (1990) session and to establish at that session a five-member working group to prepare an overview of proposals for improving the Sub-Commission's functioning in dealing with human rights violations. On 1 September, the Sub-Commission approved[23] the composition of its working groups on communications, slavery, and indigenous populations, each representing five regions (Africa, Asia, Eastern Europe, Latin America, and Western Europe and others).

Strengthening the Centre for Human Rights

On 7 March, the Commission on Human Rights expressed[24] its support for the Secretary-General's efforts to enhance the role of the Centre for Human Rights as a co-ordinating unit for bodies dealing with the protection of human rights, and invited him to request Governments, UN specialized agencies and intergovernmental and non-governmental organizations to express their views on strengthening the Centre's activities.

Programme and budgetary questions

On 21 April, the Secretary-General submitted to the Committee for Programme and Co-ordination (CPC) a report[25] on the in-depth evaluation of the UN human rights programme. The report described basic characteristics of the programme, provided observations on the programme as a whole and evaluated its four subprogrammes: implementation of international standards, instruments and procedures; elimination and prevention of discrimination and protection of minorities and vulnerable groups; advisory services, technical assistance in the field of human rights and publications; and standard-setting, research and studies. It set forth 17 recommendations for the subprogrammes and for programme management, which included improving the reporting systems for human rights instruments and monitoring and response capacity; ensuring that financial problems did not hamper the functioning of the supervisory systems; enhancing co-ordination of activities to combat racism and racial discrimination and to protect and assist vulnerable groups; strengthening national capacity through enhanced advisory services and technical assistance projects; enhancing publicity, information dissemination and education; improving procedures for drafting new instruments, the use of results from research and studies, and programmatic co-ordination; rationalizing meetings of human rights bodies; and increasing the resources of the Centre for Human Rights.

In May,[26] CPC took note of the Secretary-General's report and recommended that he ensure the balanced implementation of international human rights instruments and strengthen co-ordination between the UN Secretariat's Department of Public Information (DPI) and the Centre for Human Rights. The Committee also considered the proposed programme budget in the field of human rights for the biennium 1990-1991 and recommended it for adoption by the General Assembly.

GENERAL ASSEMBLY ACTION

On 21 December, the General Assembly, on the recommendation of the Fifth (Administrative and Budgetary) Committee, adopted **resolution 44/201 B, section XI,** without vote.

[*The General Assembly . . .*]

Section 23. Human rights

1. *Decides* that additional requirements for those new mandates emanating from decisions of the Economic and Social Council which are outside the scope of the perennial activities included in section 23 are to be treated in accordance with the provisions for the use and operation of the contingency fund;

2. *Requests* the Secretary-General to include the question of the relationship between the treatment of perennial activities in the programme budget and the use of the contingency fund in the report that he is to prepare in the light of the experience gained with regard to the contingency fund during the implementation of the programme budget for the biennium 1990-1991;

. . .

General Assembly resolution 44/201 B, section XI

21 December 1989   Meeting 84   Adopted without vote

Approved by Fifth Committee (A/44/905) without vote, 19 December (meeting 59); draft by Vice-Chairman (A/C.5/44/L.25); agenda item 123.
Meeting numbers. GA 44th session: 5th Committee 31, 32, 59; plenary 84.

Public information activities

On 19 January, the Secretary-General submitted to the Commission a report[27] on the development of public information activities in the human rights field, with special emphasis on commemoration of the fortieth anniversary of the 1948 Universal Declaration of Human Rights[28] in 1988[29] as well as activities carried out by the Centre for Human Rights and DPI.

In addition, the report provided an outline of the World Public Information Campaign for Human Rights, launched by the General Assembly in 1988,[30] including its aims and scope; envisaged responsibilities of the UN system, Member States and NGOs; target audiences; co-ordination and financing; and planned activities.

Activities focused on organization of workshops and training courses on human rights issues, provision of fellowships and internships, and dissemination of information on UN activities through publications, audio-visual materials, briefings and radio and television interviews. The report paid special attention to the Human Rights Day (10 December) activities and to co-ordination and co-operation within and outside the UN system. It also noted the establishment of a new dissemination division within DPI to revise the Department's distribution methods, and the creation by the Centre for Human Rights of a consolidated computerized list of addresses for the dissemination of information.

The Secretary-General emphasized the role of the 67 UN information centres (UNICs) in the dissemination of information, and pointed out that their directors had been instructed to undertake special programmes to draw the attention of national communities to human rights observances. He further noted that DPI had continued to reprint and distribute basic reference works and UN materials for UNICs and that it had produced and distributed the Universal Declaration in some 86 languages, while the Centre for Human Rights had finalized a teaching booklet, *ABC Teaching Human Rights*, and begun worldwide distribution.

Human Rights Commission action. On 7 March, the Commission supported[31] the general thrust of the proposed programme for the World Public Information Campaign, reaffirmed the need to tailor information materials on human rights to regional and national requirements and specific target audiences, and urged the Secretariat to ensure further production and dissemination of such materials in national and local languages. It emphasized the need to harmonize UN public information activities in the human rights field with organizations such as the International Committee of the Red Cross (ICRC), the Office of the UN High Commissioner for Refugees (UNHCR) and the UN Educational, Scientific and Cultural Organization (UNESCO). It asked the Centre to co-ordinate World Campaign activities within the UN system.

The Commission encouraged Member States to publicize UN human rights activities and give priority to disseminating international instruments in their national and local languages, and urged them to include in their educational curricula materials relevant to a comprehensive understanding of human rights. The Secretary-General was requested to draw the attention of Member States to the booklet on teaching human rights, to complete the establishment of collections of basic UN information and reference materials on human rights at each UNIC by the end of 1989, to ensure adequate funding for the World Campaign and other public information activities in that field, and to report on those activities in 1990.

Report of the Secretary-General. In response to a 1988 General Assembly request,[30] the Secretary-General reported[32] on activities of the Centre for Human Rights and DPI. He noted that efforts for the promotion of human rights within the framework of the World Campaign were grouped into five major areas: preparation and dissemination of printed public information and reference materials; workshops, seminars and training courses; fellowships and internships; special human rights observances; and coverage and promotion activities (see also below, under "Advisory services").

The report noted that the Centre continued to publish its Fact Sheet series, the *Newsletter on Human Rights*, the *Bulletin on Human Rights* and a series of *ad hoc* publications on human rights issues. On 12 April, the Centre convened an inter-agency meeting to identify potential areas of co-operation in human rights information and education as well as advisory services and technical assistance.

The Department of Public Information co-sponsored a symposium on the World Campaign (New York, 19 October) and launched a comprehensive education campaign for teachers and students on global issues, including human rights issues, and UN activities. The Department ensured that UN information centres and services intensified direct and systematic communication exchange with local media, informational and educational institutions and NGOs.

UNICs promoted coverage of UN activities in the local and national press as well as on radio and television, and organized or co-sponsored numerous seminars, symposia, workshops, lectures, exhibitions, film festivals, concerts and round tables to generate public discussion on human rights issues.

Annexed to the Secretary-General's report was a list of national focal points for the World Campaign designated by Governments as at 31 August.

GENERAL ASSEMBLY ACTION

On 8 December, on the recommendation of the Third Committee, the General Assembly adopted **resolution 44/61** without vote.

Development of public information activities in the field of human rights

The General Assembly,

Reaffirming that activities to improve public knowledge in the field of human rights are essential to the fulfilment of the purposes of the United Nations set out in Article 1, paragraph 3, of the Charter of the United Nations and that carefully designed programmes of teaching, education and information are essential to the achievement of lasting respect for human rights and fundamental freedoms,

Recalling the resolutions adopted on this subject, in particular its resolution 43/128 of 8 December 1988, and taking note of Commission on Human Rights resolution 1989/53 of 7 March 1989,

Recognizing the catalytic effect of initiatives of the United Nations on national and regional public information activities in the field of human rights,

Recognizing also the valuable role that non-governmental organizations can play in those endeavours,

Believing that the World Public Information Campaign on Human Rights is a valuable complement to the activities of the United Nations further to promote and to protect human rights world-wide,

1. *Takes note* of the report of the Secretary-General on the development of public information activities in the field of human rights;

2. *Reaffirms* the need for information materials on human rights to be carefully designed in clear and accessible form, to be tailored to regional and national requirements and circumstances with specific target audiences in mind and to be effectively disseminated in national and local languages and in sufficient volume to have the desired impact, and for effective use also to be made of the mass media, in particular radio and television and audio-visual technologies, in order to reach wider audiences, with priority being given to children, other young people and the disadvantaged, including those in isolated areas;

3. *Appreciates* the measures taken by the Secretariat to update, increase stocks and extend the language versions of human rights information materials, especially those on the basic United Nations human rights instruments and institutions, and urges the Secretariat to take measures to ensure the further production and effective dissemination of such documents in national and local languages, in co-operation with regional, national and local organizations as well as with Governments, making full and effective use of the United Nations information centres;

4. *Encourages* all Member States to make special efforts to provide, facilitate and encourage publicity for the activities of the United Nations in the field of human rights and to accord priority to the dissemination, in their respective national and local languages, of the texts of the Universal Declaration of Human Rights, the International Covenants on Human Rights and other international conventions, as well as to information and education on the practical ways in which the rights and freedoms enjoyed under those instruments can be exercised;

5. *Urges* all Member States to include in their educational curricula materials relevant to a comprehensive understanding of human rights issues, and encourages all those responsible for training in law and its enforcement, the armed forces, medicine, diplomacy and other relevant fields to include appropriate human rights components in their programmes;

6. *Requests* the Secretary-General to draw the attention of Member States to the teaching booklet on human rights, which could serve as a broad and flexible framework adaptable to national circumstances for the structuring and development of the teaching of human rights;

7. *Notes* the special value, under the advisory services and technical assistance programme, of regional and national training courses and workshops, in co-operation with Governments, regional and national organizations and non-governmental organizations, in promoting practical education and awareness in the field of human rights, and welcomes the priority given to the organization of such activities by the Centre for Human Rights of the Secretariat;

8. *Requests* the Secretary-General to ensure the fullest effective deployment of the skills and resources of all concerned units of the Secretariat and to make available, within existing resources, and in particular from the budget of the Department of Public Information of the Secretariat, adequate funding for developing practical and effective human rights information activities, including those within the programme of the World Public Information Campaign for Human Rights;

9. *Calls upon* the Centre for Human Rights, which has primary responsibility within the United Nations

system in the field of human rights, to co-ordinate the substantive activities of the World Campaign pursuant to the direction of the General Assembly and the Commission on Human Rights, and to serve as liaison with Governments, regional and national institutions, non-governmental organizations and concerned individuals in the development and implementation of the activities of the World Campaign;

10. *Calls upon* the Department of Public Information, which has primary responsibility for public information activities, to co-ordinate the public information activities of the World Campaign and, in its responsibility as secretariat to the Joint United Nations Information Committee, to promote co-ordinated system-wide information activities in the field of human rights;

11. *Stresses* the need for close co-operation between the Centre for Human Rights and the Department of Public Information, *inter alia*, in the implementation of the aims established for the World Campaign and the need for the United Nations to harmonize its activities in the field of human rights with those of other organizations, including the International Committee of the Red Cross, with regard to the dissemination of information on international humanitarian law, and the United Nations Educational, Scientific and Cultural Organization, with regard to education for human rights;

12. *Requests* the Secretariat, in the implementation of the World Campaign, to take advantage, as much as possible, of the collaboration of non-governmental organizations for, *inter alia*, the dissemination of human rights materials, with a view to increasing universal awareness of human rights and fundamental freedoms;

13. *Requests* the Commission on Human Rights, at its forty-sixth session, on the basis of the report of the Secretary-General, to give priority consideration to this question with a view to providing appropriate guidance on the aims and activities of the World Campaign;

14. *Requests* the Secretary-General to submit to the General Assembly at its forty-fifth session a comprehensive report on the implementation of the present resolution for consideration under the item entitled ''Alternative approaches and ways and means within the United Nations system for improving the effective enjoyment of human rights and fundamental freedoms''.

General Assembly resolution 44/61

8 December 1989   Meeting 78   Adopted without vote

Approved by Third Committee (A/44/799) without vote, 20 November (meeting 49); 24-nation draft (A/C.3/44/L.37), orally corrected; agenda item 96 (c).
Meeting numbers. GA 44th session: 3rd Committee 34, 35, 43, 49; plenary 78.

Advisory services

In 1989, under the UN programme of advisory services and technical assistance in human rights established in 1955,[33] the Centre for Human Rights organized a seminar on the effects of racism and racial discrimination on social and economic relations between indigenous peoples and States (Geneva, 16-20 January), subregional and national workshops on human rights issues (Quito, Ecuador, 8-12 May; Manila, Philippines, 31 July–4 August), and an international seminar on cultural

dialogue between countries of origin and host countries of migrant workers (Athens, Greece, 17-26 September). Training courses were held on the application of international human rights standards (Conakry, Guinea, 17-22 April; Moscow, 27 November–1 December), human rights and the administration of justice (Rome, Italy, 11-22 September; Buenos Aires, Argentina, 9-13 October; Antigua, Guatemala, 23-27 October), and UN monitoring mechanisms, humanitarian law and national legislation (Lima, Peru, 2-6 October). The Centre assisted the African Commission on Human and Peoples' Rights of the Organization of African Unity (OAU), inaugurated on 12 June, in organizing a training course on developing national strategies and mechanisms for human rights promotion and protection in Africa (Banjul, Gambia, 24 April–2 May). It also provided assistance to the newly established Arab Institute of Human Rights in Tunis, and continued to strengthen co-operation with the Inter-American Commission on Human Rights and the Inter-American Institute of Human Rights, the Strasbourg Institute of Human Rights (France) and a number of other academic and research institutes.

Under a co-operative project to strengthen legal institutions in the Gambia, launched in 1989, a feasibility study was carried out on the establishment of an African Centre for Democracy and Human Rights Studies at Banjul, and advisory services were rendered in the revision of national laws. The Centre also continued its technical assistance programmes to Colombia and Guatemala. Most of those activities were financed by the UN Voluntary Fund for Advisory Services and Technical Assistance in the Field of Human Rights (see below).

In addition, the Centre granted training fellowships to 31 individuals and one NGO, and awarded 36 internships to outstanding graduate students. Within the UN system, the Centre co-operated, *inter alia*, with the World Health Organization (WHO) in organizing a global consultation on AIDS and human rights (Geneva, 26-28 July); with UNESCO in exploring the development of educational curricula on human rights and distribution of materials through UNESCO national channels; with the UN Children's Fund (UNICEF) in the envisaged follow-up to the adoption of the Convention on the Rights of the Child (see below, under ''Other human rights questions''); and with the Crime Prevention and Criminal Justice Branch of the UN Centre for Social Development at Vienna in considering the development of human rights training materials for African countries, strengthening of legal aid services in Latin America, organization of training workshops for the judiciary and activities related to the administration of justice.

During the year, requests for advisory services and technical assistance in human rights were received from 43 Governments.

Reports of the Secretary-General. The Secretary-General presented a report[34] to the Commission in 1989 on advisory services and technical assistance in the field of human rights, which covered 1988 activities involving country programmes and projects; training courses, workshops and seminars; expert services; and fellowships and internships. The report also described the programme development under the UN Voluntary Fund for Advisory Services and Technical Assistance, and outlined a plan of future activities.

In another report,[35] the Secretary-General communicated to the Sub-Commission an additional request from a State and a list of requests for technical assistance to strengthen legal institutions, received as at 19 June 1989 from States in response to a 1987 Sub-Commission resolution.[36]

Human Rights Commission action. On 8 March, the Commission recommended[37] that expert assistance and other activities to assist Governments in developing necessary infrastructures to meet international human rights standards should continue to increase, and requested the Secretary-General to: pursue his efforts for a medium-term plan for advisory services and technical assistance, as well as continue to facilitate the flow of bilateral assistance; explore further possibilities for co-operation between the Centre for Human Rights and the UN Development Programme (UNDP), UNHCR and other UN bodies and agencies, as well as ICRC; ensure close co-ordination between activities financed under the regular programme and by the Voluntary Fund; bring the need for further technical legal assistance to the attention of the relevant UN bodies and agencies; draw the attention of Governments, within the framework of the World Public Information Campaign for Human Rights (see above, under ''Public information activities''), to the availability of advisory services and technical assistance; and report to the Commission in 1990 on progress made in implementing the programme of advisory services.

The Commission requested its special rapporteurs and representatives, as well as the Working Group on Enforced or Involuntary Disappearances, to inform Governments of the availability of advisory services, and invited competent UN bodies to make proposals for their implementation. It also appealed to Member States to consider organizing national training courses for government personnel on the application of international human rights standards, and encouraged Governments in need of technical assistance to take advantage of the advisory services of experts in the field of human rights.

Voluntary Fund for Advisory Services

In 1989, the UN Voluntary Fund for Advisory Services and Technical Assistance in the Field of Human Rights, established pursuant to a 1987 Commission resolution[38] endorsed by the Economic and Social Council,[39] financed eight training courses and workshops, projects of assistance to the OAU African Commission on Human and Peoples' Rights, and country programmes in Colombia, Guatemala and the Gambia, including the provision of 21 fellowships and the advisory services of 17 experts. As at 31 December 1989, contributions to the Fund totalled $1,035,404, and an additional $361,730 had been pledged.

Human Rights Commission action. On 8 March, the Commission called[40] for voluntary contributions to the Fund, and recommended that activities under the Fund be directed towards expert assistance to Governments. It also recommended that the Secretary-General continue implementing through the Fund those projects that could catalyse the realization of international human rights standards, paying due attention to the needs of developing countries. It requested him to bring to the attention of Governments and competent human rights organs the availability of advisory services and technical assistance under the Fund, elaborate guidelines on the use and allocation of resources, and report annually to the Commission on the operation and administration of the Fund.

Equatorial Guinea

Human Rights Commission action. On 8 March, the Commission on Human Rights, taking note of the Secretary-General's report[41] on the situation in Equatorial Guinea, recommended[42] to the Government of that country that it consider becoming a party to the Convention against Torture and Other Cruel, Inhuman or Degrading Treatment or Punishment,[43] and requested it to consider implementing the plan of action for full restoration of human rights, proposed by the United Nations in 1981,[44] taking particular account of the recommendations and proposals submitted by the Secretary-General's appointed Expert, Fernando Volio Jiménez (Costa Rica), in 1985.[45] A report on progress in implementing the plan was requested for submission to the Commission in 1990.

On 24 May, by **decision 1989/151**, the Economic and Social Council approved the Commission's decision to consider the Expert's report on the manner in which Equatorial Guinea intended to implement the plan of action.

Further developments. On behalf of the Expert on Equatorial Guinea, Consultant Arnaldo Ortiz López (Costa Rica) visited the country from 20 to 26 November and held discussions with the President, other senior government officials and members of the judiciary. The Consultant observed that the Government had agreed to comply with and implement the UN plan of action. It undertook to establish immediately a drafting committee to prepare an up-to-date codification of fundamental laws that could be adapted to the country's ethnic and cultural composition. A media campaign was under way to increase public awareness of the importance of law and courts as well as an education programme on values and advantages of a democratic government and of harmonization with the indigenous cultural heritage. A training programme in public administration was being offered at the School of Public Administration with expert assistance from the UN Secretariat's Department of Technical Co-operation for Development, and training to encourage popular participation in electoral processes and democratic decision-making had been initiated.

The Consultant further noted that the Government was prepared to co-operate in implementing other recommendations of the plan of action, including the training of lawyers and court staff and the establishment of codification commissions to draft penal and civil codes, codes of civil and criminal procedure and a judicial power organization act. A general labour bill was already under consideration by the Government. The Consultant made a number of recommendations to the Government concerning the need to set up a Special Review Commission to monitor implementation of the plan of action; promulgate a General Associations Act for the establishment and registration of political parties other than the official party; and develop a free press, including the installation of a printing press, which the country currently lacked. He also noted the President's willingness to consider relevant constitutional amendments in accordance with the plan of action.

In December 1989, Equatorial Guinea decided to issue a decree, based on international human rights instruments, to indicate the fundamental rights and freedoms of its citizens.

Guatemala

In his report on advisory services to Guatemala,[46] submitted to the Commission on 20 January, Expert Héctor Gros Espiell (Uruguay) reviewed the legal framework and the current human rights situation in that country, summarized the results of his three visits undertaken in 1988, and described activities under the technical assistance programme to Guatemala for 1988-1989, financed by the Voluntary Fund for Advisory Services. He concluded that, while the human rights situation had generally improved, the continuing climate of violence, coupled with problems of indigenous populations and severe deficiencies regarding respect for economic, social and cultural rights, as well as other negative factors, prevented the Government from ensuring full safeguards and respect for human rights. The Expert recommended continuation of the broad programme of assistance, particularly support for courses and seminars for the judiciary, police and armed forces as well as human rights courses at all levels of education.

Human Rights Commission action. On 8 March, the Commission recognized[47] that the Government of Guatemala was committed to guaranteeing and promoting the protection of human rights, and encouraged it to continue examining the situation of its indigenous populations and to take into account their demands and proposals. At the same time, the Commission expressed its serious concern at the persistent harmful conditions which placed severe limitations on the process of improving the human rights situation in that country, and urged Guatemala to intensify efforts to ensure that all authorities and security forces respected the rights and freedoms of its citizens. The Secretary-General was requested to continue providing advisory services and other assistance to Guatemala and to renew for one year the mandate of the Expert, who was asked to report in 1990.

By **decision 1989/153** of 24 May, the Economic and Social Council approved the request to extend the Expert's mandate.

Sub-Commission action. On 31 August, the Sub-Commission encouraged[48] Guatemala to adopt measures for improving the economic, social and political conditions of its indigenous populations and to create conditions for a safe return of refugees, urged it to apply energetic measures to prevent human rights violations, and recommended that the Expert, in his forthcoming report, give particular attention to the existing obstacles to the full realization of human rights in that country, and indicate ways to remedy the situation.

Further developments. The Expert on Guatemala visited that country twice in 1989, in May and from 22 October to 3 November. He held meetings with the President and other senior government officials, the Procurator for Human Rights, and the Chairwoman of the *Ad Hoc* Committee for Aid to Returnees, as well as with members of the judiciary, the Human Rights Commission of Congress, the National Reconciliation Commission, and public figures.

Haiti

In his report on advisory services to Haiti,[49] submitted to the Commission on 6 February, Expert Philippe Texier (France) reviewed the history of events in Haiti from 7 February 1986 to 31 December 1988, described the legal framework and the current human rights situation, and summarized the results of his December 1988 visit. He concluded that, despite signs of an awareness of the need to ensure respect for human rights, the current Government—brought to power in a military take-over on 17 September 1988—had not been able to prevent human rights violations from occurring on a daily basis, nor had any measures been devised to conduct inquiries into past violations and punish the culprits. Among obstacles to the improvement of the situation were an ineffective judiciary, the militarization of rural areas, failure to separate the army and police forces, the failure to put on trial those responsible for past massacres, and the military and economic power of paramilitary forces.

The Expert asserted that the situation could not change without the firm will to ensure respect for the rule of law, which would involve the prompt entry into force of Haiti's 1987 Constitution and speedy restoration of the electoral process. He recommended that the Commission consider appointing a special rapporteur to study the human rights situation in Haiti and examine whether conditions had been met for that country to continue receiving UN advisory services. Should such assistance be maintained, the Expert recommended that efforts focus on holding free elections, strengthening and improving the judiciary, planning a general policy for development and assistance for the poorest communities, and fostering the organization of civilian police forces trained in human rights. He also recommended involving all human rights organizations in any training programmes.

Human Rights Commission action. The human rights situation in Haiti was considered by the Commission in closed session under the agenda item on the study of situations that appeared to reveal a consistent pattern of gross human rights violations. In an 8 March resolution,[50] the Commission noted with concern that the basic causes of human rights violations in Haiti had not been eradicated; urged the Haitian authorities to take measures without delay for the rapid investigation of violations that had occurred before 17 September 1988 and to ensure that the commission of inquiry was enabled to single out the culprits for arrest and trial; expressed the hope that the Haitian Government would fulfil its pledge to restore as early as possible a constitutional régime freely chosen by the people; and encouraged it to pursue contacts with democratic forces in the country so as to expedite the resumption of the electoral process.

The Commission appealed for international assistance to Haiti and requested the Secretary-General to provide advisory services and other assistance in order to encourage the régime's democratic development, with emphasis on strengthening the independence of the judiciary and promoting the organization of civilian police trained in human rights. The Secretary-General was also requested to extend the Expert's mandate for one year and to give him all necessary assistance; the Expert was asked to encourage implementation of the assistance programme, to make recommendations to the Government for the full restoration of human rights, and to report to the Commission in 1990, including in his report information on the development of the human rights situation in Haiti.

On 24 May, the Economic and Social Council, by **decision 1989/152**, approved the Commission's request that the Secretary-General extend the Expert's mandate and give him all necessary assistance.

Note of the Secretary-General. In response to a 1988 Sub-Commission request,[51] the Secretary-General submitted a note[52] on 28 April informing the Sub-Commission of the action taken by the Commission on Human Rights with regard to the situation in Haiti.

Further developments. During 1989, major developments in Haiti included the establishment of an Electoral Council, a decision to undertake a thorough reform of the justice system, and elaboration of an electoral timetable providing for municipal and legislative elections in July 1990 and presidential elections in October/November 1990. The 1987 Constitution was partially restored in March, but the nature of the reservations meant that the power of the head of State was unchanged. An attempted military take-over in April failed, and there were subsequent violent confrontations between the Presidential Guard and elements of the military. In September, an independent public body for prison administration was established. An intensification of repression and a new deterioration in the human rights situation occurred in November with the arrest of several trade union and political leaders, and the use of torture and illegal searches.

The Expert on Haiti visited the country from 25 July to 3 August to renew contact with authorities as well as with democratic forces and NGOs, to monitor developments and assess the human rights situation, and to offer special assistance to the Government concerning human rights and the electoral process.

Paraguay

On 31 August, the Sub-Commission, bearing in mind the acknowledged progress in the field of human rights in Paraguay as well as the request by the Paraguayan authorities for co-operation in that field, recommended[53] that the Commission adopt a resolution encouraging Paraguay to further democratization and advances in the field of human rights. It also requested the Secretary-General to provide advisory services and other assistance in the human rights field to Paraguay.

International human rights instruments

Human rights treaty bodies

There were six human rights treaty instruments in force in 1989, the implementation of which was monitored by expert bodies established under each treaty. Those instruments and their respective treaty bodies were: the 1965 International Convention on the Elimination of All Forms of Racial Discrimination[54] (Committee on the Elimination of Racial Discrimination); the 1966 International Covenant on Civil and Political Rights[55] (Human Rights Committee); the 1966 International Covenant on Economic, Social and Cultural Rights[55] (Committee on Economic, Social and Cultural Rights); the 1973 International Convention on the Suppression and Punishment of the Crime of *Apartheid*[56] (Group of Three); the 1979 Convention on the Elimination of All Forms of Discrimination against Women[57] (Committee on the Elimination of Discrimination against Women); and the 1984 Convention against Torture and Other Cruel, Inhuman or Degrading Treatment or Punishment[43] (Committee against Torture).

On 2 February, the Secretary-General submitted to the Commission on Human Rights a note[58] containing conclusions and recommendations of the second meeting of persons chairing the treaty bodies, held in 1988.[59]

Human Rights Commission action. On 6 March, the Commission welcomed[60] the meeting's recommendations aimed at enhancing the effectiveness of the human rights treaty bodies, acknowledged the need to ensure financing and adequate staffing resources for their operations, suggested alleviating their financial difficulties by allocating advances from the UN regular budget against contributions to be received within the same budget year, and urged States parties to the human rights instruments to meet their financial obligations under those instruments. The Secretary-General was requested to report regularly to the Commission on possible technical assistance projects identified by the treaty bodies, to entrust an independent expert with preparing a study on long-term approaches to enhancing the effectiveness of existing and prospective treaty bodies and to report on that matter to the General Assembly in 1989 and to the Commission in 1990.

On 24 May, the Economic and Social Council, by **decision 1989/143**, approved the Commission's request for the study.

Sub-Commission action. On 31 August, by 15 votes to 2, with 3 abstentions, the Sub-Commission recommended[61] that the Commission adopt a resolution emphasizing the need to enhance the effectiveness of and co-ordination between the human rights monitoring mechanisms, and requesting the Secretary-General to consider convening, not later than 1991, an international meeting of experts on issues related to international monitoring in the field of human rights.

Note of the Secretary-General. By an 8 November note,[62] the Secretary-General transmitted to the General Assembly the study called for by the Commission in March.[60] The study provided an overview of the rapidly changing environment within which the treaty bodies were functioning, reviewed reporting procedures under the human rights instruments (see below), examined financial and administrative aspects as well as substantive issues related to the functioning of treaty bodies, and considered a long-term perspective on standard-setting as well as other long-term issues. It set forth a number of recommendations, proposing, *inter alia*, to change the method of financing of treaty bodies from funding by States parties to regular budget funding temporarily, while other options were explored; to better publicize activities of treaty bodies; and to prepare an inventory of international human rights standard-setting activities, to be updated on a regular basis.

(For General Assembly action, see resolution 44/135 below.)

Reporting obligations of States parties

By a 3 February note,[63] the Secretary-General transmitted to the Assembly the report of the second meeting of persons chairing the human rights treaty bodies. The meeting made proposals for remedial action concerning harmonization and consolidation of reporting guidelines, co-ordination of reporting, measures for expediting consideration of reports, and projects for technical assistance and advisory services to help States parties fulfil their reporting obligations.

The study on enhancing the effectiveness of treaty bodies (above) noted the problem of overlapping reporting requirements under different instruments and suggested using cross-references in reports to different bodies to reduce such duplication. The question of reporting procedures was also considered in 1989 by the Committee on Economic, Social and Cultural Rights (see above, under "Economic, social and cultural rights"), which had before it the Secretary-General's report[64] on the nature and extent of overlapping under the six human rights instruments.

Human Rights Commission action. On 6 March, the Commission endorsed[60] recommendations of the second meeting aimed at streamlining, rationalizing and improving reporting procedures, and requested the Secretary-General to report to the General Assembly in 1989 and to the Commission in 1990 on progress in that regard. On the same date, it requested[65] him to appoint a task force to prepare a study on computerizing the work of the treaty bodies in relation to reporting, to give it all possible assistance and to report to the Commission in 1990 on the results.

By **decision 1989/142** of 24 May, the Economic and Social Council approved the Commission's request for establishment of the task force.

Report of the Secretary-General. In a 6 October report[66] to the Assembly, the Secretary-General reviewed specific actions as well as views and suggestions by relevant UN bodies concerning the effective implementation of international human rights instruments, including reporting obligations of States parties. He summarized activities of the newly appointed task force on computerization of work of the treaty bodies and noted that several of those bodies had already approved consolidated guidelines governing the initial part of reports of States parties and had decided to appoint individual rapporteurs or establish pre-sessional working groups to expedite consideration of reports. In addition, a detailed manual to assist States in fulfilling their reporting obligations was expected to be finalized by the end of the year.

GENERAL ASSEMBLY ACTION

On 15 December, the General Assembly, on the recommendation of the Third Committee, adopted **resolution 44/135** without vote.

Effective implementation of international instruments on human rights, including reporting obligations under international instruments on human rights

The General Assembly,

Recalling its resolution 43/115 of 8 December 1988, as well as its other relevant resolutions,

Taking note of Commission on Human Rights resolutions 1989/46 and 1989/47 of 6 March 1989,

Reaffirming that the effective implementation of United Nations instruments on human rights is of major importance to the efforts made by the Organization, pursuant to the Charter of the United Nations and to the Universal Declaration of Human Rights, to promote universal respect for and observance of human rights and fundamental freedoms,

Considering that the effective functioning of treaty bodies established pursuant to United Nations instruments on human rights is indispensable for the effective implementation of such instruments,

Reaffirming its responsibility to ensure the proper functioning of the treaty bodies established pursuant to instruments adopted by the General Assembly and, in this connection, further reaffirming the importance of:

(a) Ensuring the effective functioning of systems of periodic reporting by States parties to these instruments;

(b) Addressing the problem of securing sufficient financial resources, which continues to hamper the proper functioning of human rights treaty bodies, and of providing sufficient resources to ensure their effective functioning;

(c) Addressing the question of reporting obligations and that of financial implications whenever considering the possibility of establishing any further instruments on human rights,

Recognizing that the effective implementation of instruments on human rights, involving periodic reporting by States parties to the relevant treaty bodies and the efficient functioning of the treaty bodies themselves, not only enhances international accountability in relation to the promotion and protection of human rights, but also provides States parties with a valuable opportunity to review policies and programmes affecting the promotion and protection of human rights and to make any appropriate adjustments,

Expressing concern about the continuing and increasing backlog of reports on implementation by States parties of United Nations instruments on human rights and about delays in consideration of reports by the treaty bodies,

Taking note of the report of the Secretary-General on progress achieved in enhancing the effective functioning of the treaty bodies, pursuant, *inter alia*, to the conclusions and recommendations of the meeting of persons chairing the human rights treaty bodies, held at Geneva from 10 to 14 October 1988,

Taking note with appreciation of the study on possible long-term approaches to enhancing the effective operation of existing and prospective bodies established under United Nations instruments on human rights, prepared by an independent expert pursuant to the above-mentioned resolutions,

1. *Endorses* the recommendations of the meeting of persons chairing the human rights treaty bodies aimed at streamlining, rationalizing and otherwise improving reporting procedures, and supports the continuing efforts in this connection by the treaty bodies and the Secretary-General within their respective spheres of competence;

2. *Welcomes* the appointment by the Secretary-General of a task force to prepare a study on computerizing, as far as possible, the work of the treaty-monitoring bodies, with a view to increasing efficiency and facilitating compliance by States parties with their reporting obligations and the examination of reports by the treaty bodies;

3. *Takes note* of the report of the Secretary-General to the Committee on Economic, Social and Cultural Rights showing the extent of overlapping of issues dealt with in international instruments on human rights, which will assist efforts to reduce, as appropriate, duplication in the supervisory bodies of issues raised with respect to any given State party;

4. *Encourages* the Secretary-General to proceed with the planned finalization of the draft detailed reporting manual to assist States parties in the fulfilment of their reporting obligations, as well as with its circulation to the various treaty bodies by the end of 1989;

5. *Again urges* States parties to make every effort to meet their reporting obligations and to assist, individually and through meetings of States parties, in identifying and implementing ways of further streamlining and

improving reporting procedures as well as enhancing co-ordination and information flow between the treaty bodies and with relevant United Nations bodies, including specialized agencies;

6. *Welcomes* the emphasis placed by the meeting of persons chairing the human rights treaty bodies and by the Commission on Human Rights on the importance of technical assistance and advisory services and, therefore:

(a) Endorses the request of the Commission that the Secretary-General report regularly to it on possible technical assistance projects identified by the treaty bodies;

(b) Invites the treaty bodies to give priority attention to identifying such possibilities in the regular course of their work of reviewing the periodic reports of States parties;

7. *Endorses* the recommendations of the meeting of persons chairing the human rights treaty bodies on the need to ensure financing and adequate staffing resources for the operations of the treaty bodies and, with this in mind:

(a) Reiterates its request that the Secretary-General review the need for adequate staffing resources in regard to the various treaty bodies;

(b) Requests that he report on this question to the Commission on Human Rights at its forty-sixth session and to the General Assembly at its forty-fifth session;

8. *Calls upon* all States parties to meet fully and without delay their financial obligations under the relevant instruments on human rights, and requests the Secretary-General to consider ways and means of strengthening collection procedures and making them more effective;

9. *Requests* the Secretary-General, as a matter of priority, to consider administrative and budgetary measures to alleviate the current financial difficulties of the treaty bodies and thus guarantee their regular functioning, and to report on these measures to the Commission on Human Rights at its forty-sixth session;

10. *Emphasizes* that the adoption of such administrative and budgetary measures shall not prejudice the duty of States parties under United Nations human rights instruments to meet all their financial obligations pursuant to such instruments;

11. *Invites* the persons chairing the human rights treaty bodies to maintain communication and dialogue with each other on common issues and problems and, to this end, requests the Secretary-General, within existing resources, to convene a meeting of the persons chairing the treaty bodies in 1990;

12. *Expresses its satisfaction* with the study by the independent expert on possible long-term approaches to enhancing the effective operation of existing and prospective bodies established under United Nations instruments on human rights, which contains several recommendations on reporting and monitoring procedures, servicing and financing of supervisory bodies and long-term approaches to human rights standard-setting and implementation mechanisms, and which will be presented to the Commission on Human Rights for detailed consideration at its forty-sixth session;

13. *Decides* to give priority consideration at its forty-fifth session to the conclusions and recommendations of the independent expert, in the light of the deliberations of the Commission on Human Rights and those of the meeting of persons chairing the treaty bodies,

under an item entitled "Effective implementation of United Nations instruments on human rights and effective functioning of bodies established pursuant to such instruments".

General Assembly resolution 44/135

15 December 1989   Meeting 82   Adopted without vote

Approved by Third Committee (A/44/849) without vote, 29 November (meeting 60); 17-nation draft (A/C.3/44/L.73), orally revised; agenda item 109.
Meeting numbers. GA 44th session: 3rd Committee 48, 50-60; plenary 82.

International Covenants on Human Rights

Human Rights Commission action. On 2 March, the Commission adopted a resolution[67] on the 1966 International Covenants on Human Rights,[55] which corresponded largely to resolutions adopted by the Economic and Social Council and the General Assembly later in the year (see below). The Commission appealed for the application of uniform standards in the implementation of the Covenants, invited the Secretary-General to assist States with their ratification of or accession to those instruments, and requested him to consider ways of assisting States parties to prepare their reports. The Secretary-General was also requested to report in 1990 on the status of the Covenants and the work of the Committee on Economic, Social and Cultural Rights.

ECONOMIC AND SOCIAL COUNCIL ACTION

On 24 May, the Economic and Social Council adopted **resolution 1989/81** without vote.

International Covenants on Human Rights
The Economic and Social Council,

Bearing in mind its important responsibilities in relation to the co-ordination of activities to promote the International Covenants on Human Rights,

Mindful that the International Covenants on Human Rights constitute the first all-embracing and legally binding international treaties in the field of human rights and, together with the Universal Declaration of Human Rights, form the core of the International Bill of Human Rights,

Recalling the International Covenant on Economic, Social and Cultural Rights, the International Covenant on Civil and Political Rights, and the Optional Protocol to the International Covenant on Civil and Political Rights, and reaffirming that all human rights and fundamental freedoms are indivisible and interrelated and that the promotion and protection of one category of rights should never exempt or excuse States from the promotion and protection of the other rights,

Recognizing the important role of the Human Rights Committee and the Committee on Economic, Social and Cultural Rights in promoting and implementing the International Covenants on Human Rights,

Taking note with appreciation of the report of the Committee on Economic, Social and Cultural Rights on its third session, as well as the general comments of the Human Rights Committee on article 24 of the International Covenant on Civil and Political Rights, adopted by the Committee at its thirty-fifth session,

Emphasizing the importance of General Assembly resolution 43/128 of 8 December 1988, by which the Assembly decided to launch a World Public Information Campaign on Human Rights,

Convinced of the continuing need to promote the universal observance and enjoyment of human rights, which contributes to peaceful and friendly relations among nations,

1. *Reaffirms* the central importance of the International Covenants on Human Rights in international efforts to promote universal respect for and observance of human rights and fundamental freedoms, and recognizes these instruments as a basis for any standard setting and codification in the field of human rights, bearing in mind General Assembly resolution 41/120 of 4 December 1986;

2. *Appeals strongly* to all States that have not yet done so to become parties to the International Covenant on Economic, Social and Cultural Rights and the International Covenant on Civil and Political Rights and to consider acceding to the Optional Protocol to the International Covenant on Civil and Political Rights, so that those instruments may acquire genuine universality;

3. *Emphasizes* the importance of the strictest compliance by States parties to the Covenants with their obligations under the International Covenant on Economic, Social and Cultural Rights, the International Covenant on Civil and Political Rights and, where applicable, the Optional Protocol to the International Covenant on Civil and Political Rights;

4. *Invites* the States parties to the International Covenant on Civil and Political Rights to consider making the declaration provided for in article 41 of the Covenant;

5. *Stresses* the importance of avoiding the erosion of human rights by derogation, and the necessity for strict observance of all the agreed conditions and procedures for derogation, under article 4 of the International Covenant on Civil and Political Rights;

6. *Reaffirms* the important role of the Human Rights Committee and the Committee on Economic, Social and Cultural Rights with respect to the implementation by States parties of the International Covenants on Human Rights, and expresses its satisfaction with the serious and constructive manner in which those Committees are carrying out their functions;

7. *Welcomes* the general comments of the Human Rights Committee on article 24 of the International Covenant on Civil and Political Rights;

8. *Also welcomes* the decision of the Committee on Economic, Social and Cultural Rights to consider articles 22 and 23 of the International Covenant on Economic, Social and Cultural Rights, as well as to continue to focus on article 11, with a view to developing general comments at its fourth session, so as to encourage States parties to the Covenant to take appropriate steps to ensure the implementation of that article;

9. *Further welcomes* the relevant activities of the Commission on Human Rights in the field of effective implementation of economic, social, cultural, civil and political rights, and the promotion of universal adherence to the International Covenants on Human Rights;

10. *Urges* the Secretary-General, in conjunction with the World Public Information Campaign on Human Rights, to publicize the work of the Human Rights Committee and the Committee on Economic, Social and Cultural Rights and to ensure sufficient administrative and related support of their meetings and activities to enable them to carry out their respective functions effectively;

11. *Encourages* all Governments to publicize the texts of the International Covenant on Economic, Social and Cultural Rights, the International Covenant on Civil and Political Rights and the Optional Protocol to the International Covenant on Civil and Political Rights in as many languages as possible and to distribute them and make them known as widely as possible in their territories;

12. *Decides* to include in the agenda of its first regular session of 1990 an item entitled "International Covenants on Human Rights" and to consider under that item the general comments of the Human Rights Committee and the report of the Committee on Economic, Social and Cultural Rights on its fourth session;

13. *Also decides* to transmit the report of the Committee on Economic, Social and Cultural Rights on its third session to the General Assembly at its forty-fourth session for consideration under the agenda item entitled "International Covenants on Human Rights".

Economic and Social Council resolution 1989/81

24 May 1989   Meeting 16   Adopted without vote

Approved by Second Committee (E/1989/88) without vote, 19 May (meeting 22); 14-nation draft (E/1989/C.2/L.19); agenda item 9.

Report of the Secretary-General. In response to a 1988 Assembly request,[68] the Secretary-General reported[69] on 11 August 1989 on the status of the International Covenants as at 1 August, as well as on questions related to their implementation (see also above, under "Civil and political rights" and "Economic, social and cultural rights").

GENERAL ASSEMBLY ACTION

On 15 December, on the recommendation of the Third Committee, the General Assembly adopted **resolution 44/129** without vote.

International Covenants on Human Rights

The General Assembly,

Recalling its resolutions 33/51 of 14 December 1978, 34/45 of 23 November 1979, 35/132 of 11 December 1980, 36/58 of 25 November 1981, 37/191 of 18 December 1982, 38/116 and 38/117 of 16 December 1983, 39/136 and 39/138 of 14 December 1984, 40/115 and 40/116 of 13 December 1985, 41/32 of 3 November 1986, 41/119 and 41/121 of 4 December 1986, 42/103 and 42/105 of 7 December 1987 and 43/114 of 8 December 1988, and taking note of the general comments adopted by the Human Rights Committee at its 891st meeting, on 5 April 1989, under article 40, paragraph 4, of the International Covenant on Civil and Political Rights,

Mindful that the International Covenants on Human Rights constitute the first all-embracing and legally binding international treaties in the field of human rights and, together with the Universal Declaration of Human Rights, form the core of the International Bill of Human Rights,

Taking note of the report of the Secretary-General on the status of the International Covenant on Economic,

Social and Cultural Rights, the International Covenant on Civil and Political Rights, and the Optional Protocol to the International Covenant on Civil and Political Rights,

Recalling the International Covenant on Economic, Social and Cultural Rights and the International Covenant on Civil and Political Rights, and reaffirming that all human rights and fundamental freedoms are indivisible and interrelated and that the promotion and protection of one category of rights should never exempt or excuse States from the promotion and protection of the other,

Recognizing the important role of the Human Rights Committee in the implementation of the International Covenant on Civil and Political Rights and the Optional Protocol thereto,

Also recognizing the important role of the Committee on Economic, Social and Cultural Rights in the implementation of the International Covenant on Economic, Social and Cultural Rights,

Bearing in mind the important responsibilities of the Economic and Social Council in relation to the International Covenants on Human Rights,

Welcoming the submission to the General Assembly of the annual report of the Human Rights Committee and the report of the Committee on Economic, Social and Cultural Rights on its third session,

Considering that the effective functioning of treaty bodies established in accordance with the relevant provisions of international instruments on human rights plays a fundamental role and hence represents an important continuing concern of the United Nations,

Noting with concern the critical situation with regard to overdue reports from States parties to the International Covenants on Human Rights,

Recalling with satisfaction the results of the meeting of persons chairing human rights treaty bodies, held at Geneva from 10 to 14 October 1988,

1. *Takes note with appreciation* of the report of the Human Rights Committee on its thirty-fourth, thirty-fifth and thirty-sixth sessions, including the suggestions and recommendations of a general nature approved by the Committee;

2. *Also takes note with appreciation* of the report of the Committee on Economic, Social and Cultural Rights on its third session, including its suggestions and recommendations;

3. *Expresses its satisfaction* with the serious and constructive manner in which both Committees are carrying out their functions;

4. *Urges* States parties to the International Covenants on Human Rights to pay active attention to the protection and promotion of civil and political rights, as well as economic, social and cultural rights;

5. *Expresses its appreciation* to the States parties to the International Covenant on Civil and Political Rights that have submitted their reports to the Human Rights Committee under article 40 of the Covenant and urges States parties that have not yet done so to submit their reports as speedily as possible;

6. *Urges* those States parties to the International Covenant on Civil and Political Rights that have been requested by the Human Rights Committee to provide additional information to comply with that request;

7. *Commends* the States parties to the International Covenant on Economic, Social and Cultural Rights that

have submitted their reports under article 16 of the Covenant and urges States parties that have not yet done so to submit their reports as soon as possible;

8. *Notes with satisfaction* that the majority of States parties to the International Covenant on Civil and Political Rights and an increasing number of States parties to the International Covenant on Economic, Social and Cultural Rights have been represented by experts in the presentation of their reports, thereby assisting the respective monitoring bodies in their work, and hopes that all States parties to both Covenants will arrange such representation in the future;

9. *Again urges* all States that have not yet done so to become parties to the International Covenant on Economic, Social and Cultural Rights and the International Covenant on Civil and Political Rights, and to consider acceding to the Optional Protocol to the International Covenant on Civil and Political Rights;

10. *Invites* the States parties to the International Covenant on Civil and Political Rights to consider making the declaration provided for in article 41 of the Covenant;

11. *Emphasizes* the importance of the strictest compliance by States parties with their obligations under the International Covenant on Economic, Social and Cultural Rights and the International Covenant on Civil and Political Rights and, where applicable, the Optional Protocol to the International Covenant on Civil and Political Rights;

12. *Stresses* the importance of avoiding the erosion of human rights by derogation, and underlines the necessity of strict observance of the agreed conditions and procedures for derogation under article 4 of the International Covenant on Civil and Political Rights, bearing in mind the need for States parties to provide the fullest possible information during states of emergency, so that the justification for and appropriateness of measures taken in these circumstances can be assessed;

13. *Appeals* to States parties to the Covenants that have exercised their sovereign right to make reservations in accordance with relevant rules of international law to consider whether any such reservation should be reviewed;

14. *Urges* States parties to the International Covenant on Economic, Social and Cultural Rights, the specialized agencies and other relevant United Nations bodies to extend their full support and co-operation to the Committee on Economic, Social and Cultural Rights;

15. *Requests* the Secretary-General to keep the Human Rights Committee and the Committee on Economic, Social and Cultural Rights informed of the relevant activities of the General Assembly, the Economic and Social Council, the Commission on Human Rights, the Commission on the Status of Women, the Sub-Commission on Prevention of Discrimination and Protection of Minorities, the Committee on the Elimination of Racial Discrimination, the Committee on the Elimination of Discrimination against Women, the Committee against Torture and, where appropriate, other functional commissions of the Economic and Social Council and the specialized agencies, and also to transmit the annual reports of the Human Rights Committee and the Committee on Economic, Social and Cultural Rights to those bodies;

16. *Also requests* the Secretary-General, within existing resources, to ensure that the Human Rights Committee and the Committee on Economic, Social and Cul-

tural Rights are able to hold the necessary sessions and are provided with administrative support and summary records;

17. *Further requests* the Secretary-General to ensure that the Centre for Human Rights of the Secretariat effectively assists the Human Rights Committee and the Committee on Economic, Social and Cultural Rights in the implementation of their respective mandates;

18. *Again urges* the Secretary-General, taking into account the suggestions of the Human Rights Committee, to take determined steps, within existing resources, to give more publicity to the work of that Committee and, similarly, to the work of the Committee on Economic, Social and Cultural Rights;

19. *Encourages* all Governments to publish the texts of the International Covenant on Economic, Social and Cultural Rights, the International Covenant on Civil and Political Rights and the Optional Protocol to the International Covenant on Civil and Political Rights in as many languages as possible and to distribute them and make them known as widely as possible in their territories;

20. *Requests* the Secretary-General to submit to the General Assembly at its forty-fifth session, under the item entitled ''International Covenants on Human Rights'', a report on the status of the International Covenant on Economic, Social and Cultural Rights, the International Covenant on Civil and Political Rights and the Optional Protocol to the International Covenant on Civil and Political Rights.

General Assembly resolution 44/129

15 December 1989   Meeting 82   Adopted without vote

Approved by Third Committee (A/44/824) without vote, 22 November (meeting 52); 24-nation draft (A/C.3/44/L.46); agenda item 98.
Meeting numbers. GA 44th session: 3rd Committee 36-43, 50, 52; plenary 82.

Electoral processes

Human Rights Commission action. On 7 March, the Commission recommended,[70] through the Economic and Social Council, that the General Assembly adopt the framework for future efforts to enhance the effectiveness of the principle of periodic and genuine elections proposed by the Commission. The framework emphasized such aspects as universal and equal suffrage; the right to take part in the government of one's country, directly or through freely chosen representatives; the right to equal access to public service; the need for a secret vote or equivalent free voting procedures; freedoms of peaceful assembly, of association and of opinion and expression, including the freedom to seek, receive and impart information and ideas; the right of citizens to change their governmental system through appropriate constitutional means; equal opportunity for all citizens to become candidates for public office; and the right of candidates to put forward their political views. National institutions should ensure universal and equal suffrage and impartial administration, with particular emphasis on independent supervision, appropriate voter registration, reliable balloting

procedures and methods for preventing electoral fraud and resolving disputes. It was also stressed that the country holding elections might wish to invite observers or seek advisory services, either from regional organizations or from the UN system.

By **decision 1989/145** of 24 May, the Economic and Social Council took note of the Commission's resolution and recommended that the Assembly adopt the annexed framework for future efforts. The framework was transmitted to the Assembly by a 16 August note[71] of the Secretary-General.

GENERAL ASSEMBLY ACTION

On 15 December, the General Assembly, on the recommendation of the Third Committee, adopted **resolution 44/146** without vote.

Enhancing the effectiveness of the principle of periodic and genuine elections

The General Assembly,

Aware of its obligations under the Charter of the United Nations to develop friendly relations among nations based on respect for the principle of equal rights and self-determination of peoples and to promote and encourage respect for human rights and fundamental freedoms for all,

Reaffirming the Universal Declaration of Human Rights, which provides that everyone has the right to take part in the government of his or her country, directly or through freely chosen representatives, that everyone has the right of equal access to public service in his or her country, that the will of the people shall be the basis of the authority of government, and that this will shall be expressed in periodic and genuine elections which shall be by universal and equal suffrage and shall be held by secret vote or by equivalent free voting procedures,

Noting that the International Covenant on Civil and Political Rights provides that every citizen shall have the right and the opportunity, without distinction of any kind, such as race, colour, sex, language, religion, political or other opinion, national or social origin, property, birth or other status, to take part in the conduct of public affairs, directly or through freely chosen representatives, to vote and to be elected at genuine periodic elections which shall be by universal and equal suffrage and shall be held by secret ballot, guaranteeing the free expression of the will of the electors, and to have access, on general terms of equality, to public service in his or her country,

Condemning the system of *apartheid* and any other denial or abridgement of the right to vote on the grounds of race, colour, sex, language, religion, political or other opinion, national or social origin, property, birth or other status,

Considering that the tricameral parliament established under the system of *apartheid* is a gross violation of the principle of universal and equal suffrage and has been overwhelmingly rejected by the international community,

Recalling that all States enjoy sovereign equality and that each State has the right freely to choose and develop its political, social, economic and cultural systems,

Recognizing that there is no single political system or electoral method that is equally suited to all nations and their people,

Recalling its resolution 43/157 of 8 December 1988,

Taking note of Commission on Human Rights resolution 1989/51 of 7 March 1989,

1. *Underscores* the significance of the Universal Declaration of Human Rights and the International Covenant on Civil and Political Rights, which establish that the authority to govern shall be based on the will of the people, as expressed in periodic and genuine elections;

2. *Stresses* its conviction that periodic and genuine elections are a necessary and indispensable element of sustained efforts to protect the rights and interests of the governed and that, as a matter of practical experience, the right of everyone to take part in the government of his or her country is a crucial factor in the effective enjoyment by all of a wide range of other human rights and fundamental freedoms, embracing political, economic, social and cultural rights;

3. *Declares* that determining the will of the people requires an electoral process that provides an equal opportunity for all citizens to become candidates and put forward their political views, individually and in co-operation with others within the constitution and national legislation;

4. *Recognizes* that the efforts of the international community to enhance the effectiveness of the principle of periodic and genuine elections should not call into question each State's sovereign right freely to choose and develop its political, social, economic and cultural systems, whether or not they conform to the preferences of other States;

5. *Underscores* the duty of each member of the international community to respect the decisions taken by other States in freely choosing and developing their electoral institutions;

6. *Reaffirms* that *apartheid* must be abolished, that the systematic denial or abridgement of the right to vote on the grounds of race or colour is a gross violation of human rights and an affront to the conscience and dignity of mankind, and that the right to participate in a political system based on common and equal citizenship and universal franchise is essential for the exercise of the principle of periodic and genuine elections;

7. *Rejects* the tricameral parliament established under the system of *apartheid* as an abhorrent expression of a fundamentally oppressive and flagrantly inhuman political system;

8. *Calls upon* the Commission on Human Rights, at its forty-sixth session, to continue its consideration of appropriate ways and means of enhancing the effectiveness of the principle of periodic and genuine elections, in the context of full respect for the sovereignty of Member States, and to report to the General Assembly at its forty-fifth session, through the Economic and Social Council;

9. *Decides* to include in the provisional agenda of its forty-fifth session the item entitled ''Enhancing the effectiveness of the principle of periodic and genuine elections''.

General Assembly resolution 44/146

15 December 1989   Meeting 82   Adopted without vote

Approved by Third Committee (A/44/828 & Corr.1) without vote, 27 November (meeting 56); 25-nation draft (A/C.3/44/L.59), orally revised, and amended by 10 nations (A/C.3/44/L.72); agenda item 114.

Meeting numbers. GA 44th session: 3rd Committee 36-43, 50, 54, 56; plenary 82.

On the same date, the Assembly, also on the recommendation of the Third Committee, adopted **resolution 44/147** by recorded vote.

Respect for the principles of national sovereignty and non-interference in the internal affairs of States in their electoral processes

The General Assembly,

Reaffirming the purposes of the United Nations to develop friendly relations among nations based on respect for the principle of equal rights and self-determination of peoples and to take other appropriate measures to strengthen universal peace,

Recalling its resolution 1514(XV) of 14 December 1960, containing the Declaration on the Granting of Independence to Colonial Countries and Peoples,

Also recalling its resolution 2625(XXV) of 24 October 1970, by which it approved the Declaration on Principles of International Law concerning Friendly Relations and Co-operation among States in accordance with the Charter of the United Nations,

Further recalling the principle enshrined in Article 2, paragraph 7, of the Charter of the United Nations, which establishes that nothing contained in the Charter shall authorize the United Nations to intervene in matters which are essentially within the domestic jurisdiction of any State or shall require the Members to submit such matters to settlement under the Charter,

Reaffirming the legitimacy of the struggle of the oppressed people of South Africa for the elimination of *apartheid* and for the establishment of a society in which all the people of South Africa as a whole, irrespective of race, colour or creed, will enjoy equal and full political and other rights and participate freely in the determination of their destiny,

Also reaffirming the legitimacy of the struggle of all peoples under colonial and foreign domination, particularly the Palestinian people, for the exercise of their inalienable right to self-determination and national independence, which will enable them to decide freely on their own future,

Recognizing that the principles of national sovereignty and non-interference in the internal affairs of any State should be respected in the holding of elections,

Also recognizing that there is no single political system or single model for electoral processes equally suited to all nations and their peoples, and that political systems and electoral processes are subject to historical, political, cultural and religious factors,

1. *Reiterates* that, by virtue of the principle of equal rights and self-determination of peoples enshrined in the Charter of the United Nations, all peoples have the right, freely and without external interference, to determine their political status and to pursue their economic, social and cultural development, and that every State has the duty to respect that right in accordance with the provisions of the Charter;

2. *Affirms* that it is the concern solely of peoples to determine methods and to establish institutions regarding the electoral process, as well as to determine the ways for its implementation according to their constitution and national legislation;

3. *Also affirms* that any extraneous activities that attempt, directly or indirectly, to interfere in the free development of national electoral processes, in particular in the developing countries, or that intend to sway the

results of such processes, violate the spirit and letter of the principles established in the Charter and in the Declaration on Principles of International Law concerning Friendly Relations and Co-operation among States in accordance with the Charter of the United Nations;

4. *Urges* all States to respect the principle of non-interference in the internal affairs of States and the sovereign right of peoples to determine their political, economic and social system;

5. *Strongly appeals* to all States to abstain from financing or providing, directly or indirectly, any other form of overt or covert support for political parties or groups and from taking actions to undermine the electoral processes in any country;

6. *Condemns* any act of armed aggression or threat or use of force against peoples, their elected Governments or their legitimate leaders;

7. *Solemnly declares* that only the total eradication of *apartheid* and the establishment of a non-racial, democratic society based on majority rule, through the full and free exercise of adult suffrage by all the people in a united and non-fragmented South Africa, can lead to a just and lasting solution to the explosive situation in South Africa;

8. *Reaffirms once again* the legitimacy of the struggle of all peoples under colonial and foreign domination, particularly the Palestinian people, for the exercise of their inalienable right to self-determination and national independence, which will enable them to determine their political, economic and social system, without external interference;

9. *Calls upon* the Commission on Human Rights, at its forty-sixth session, to give priority to the review of the fundamental factors that negatively affect the observance of the principle of national sovereignty and non-interference in the internal affairs of States in their electoral processes, and to report to the General Assembly at its forty-fifth session, through the Economic and Social Council;

10. *Requests* the Secretary-General to report to the General Assembly at its forty-fifth session on the implementation of the present resolution under the item entitled ''Enhancing the effectiveness of the principle of periodic and genuine elections''.

General Assembly resolution 44/147

15 December 1989   Meeting 82   113-23-11 (recorded vote)

Approved by Third Committee (A/44/828 & Corr.1) by recorded vote (100-24-11), 27 November (meeting 56); 14-nation draft (A/C.3/44/L.60/Rev.1), orally revised; agenda item 114.

Meeting numbers. GA 44th session: 3rd Committee 36-43, 50, 54, 56; plenary 82.

Recorded vote in Assembly as follows:*

In favour: Afghanistan, Albania, Algeria, Angola, Antigua and Barbuda, Argentina, Bahamas, Bahrain, Bangladesh, Barbados, Benin, Bhutan, Bolivia, Botswana, Brazil, Bulgaria, Burkina Faso, Burundi, Byelorussian SSR, Cameroon, Cape Verde, Central African Republic, Chad, China, Colombia, Congo, Côte d'Ivoire, Cuba, Cyprus, Czechoslovakia, Democratic Kampuchea, Democratic Yemen, Dominica, Dominican Republic, Ecuador, Ethiopia, Gabon, Gambia, German Democratic Republic, Ghana, Guatemala, Guinea, Guinea-Bissau, Guyana, Haiti, Honduras, India, Indonesia, Iran, Iraq, Jamaica, Jordan, Kenya, Kuwait, Lao People's Democratic Republic, Lebanon, Lesotho, Liberia, Libyan Arab Jamahiriya, Madagascar, Malawi, Malaysia, Maldives, Mali, Mauritania, Mauritius, Mexico, Mongolia, Morocco, Mozambique, Myanmar, Nepal, Nicaragua, Niger, Nigeria, Oman, Pakistan, Panama, Peru, Philippines, Qatar, Romania, Rwanda, Saint Kitts and Nevis, Saint Lucia, Saint Vincent and the Grenadines, Sao Tome and Principe, Saudi Arabia, Senegal, Seychelles, Singapore, Solomon Islands, Somalia, Sri Lanka, Sudan, Suriname, Swaziland, Syrian Arab Republic, Thailand, Tunisia, Uganda, Ukrainian SSR, USSR,

United Arab Emirates, United Republic of Tanzania, Uruguay, Vanuatu, Venezuela, Viet Nam, Yemen, Yugoslavia, Zambia, Zimbabwe.

Against: Australia, Austria, Belgium, Canada, Denmark, Finland, France, Germany, Federal Republic of, Greece, Iceland, Ireland, Israel, Italy, Japan, Luxembourg, Netherlands, New Zealand, Norway, Portugal, Spain, Sweden, United Kingdom, United States.

Abstaining: Chile, Egypt, El Salvador, Fiji, Grenada, Hungary, Malta, Poland, Sierra Leone, Trinidad and Tobago, Turkey.

*Costa Rica announced that it was not participating in the vote.

Regional arrangements

In 1989, the Commission had before it the Secretary-General's report[72] on regional arrangements for the promotion and protection of human rights in the Asian and Pacific region, submitted pursuant to a 1988 Commission resolution.[73] As requested by the Commission, the Secretary-General continued to encourage the Executive Secretary of the Economic and Social Commission for Asia and the Pacific (ESCAP) to pursue the establishment of a depository centre for UN human rights materials at Bangkok, Thailand, to collect, process and disseminate such materials in the Asian and Pacific region. The report noted, however, that there had been no substantive change in the ESCAP mandate that would enable it to establish the centre. It also stated that UN development agencies in the region had been informed of the Commission's particular interest in promoting regional arrangements and of the Secretary-General's readiness to assist them in that regard, and had been asked to forward their comments on the matter to the Centre for Human Rights.

Human Rights Commission action. On 7 March, the Commission requested[74] the Secretary-General to continue to assist the ESCAP Executive Secretary in establishing the depository centre, to ensure a continuing flow of human rights materials to the ESCAP library for their dissemination in the region, and to report in 1990 on the progress achieved. UN development agencies in the region were encouraged to co-ordinate with ESCAP their efforts to promote the human rights dimension in their activities.

Further developments. On 23 November, the Secretary-General reported[75] to the Commission that in April ESCAP had adopted a resolution requesting its Executive Secretary to pursue the establishment of the centre, following which the ESCAP library was designated as depository centre for UN human rights materials. Its dissemination capacity, however, was limited to distribution of bibliographies, references and reading lists; for the library to become a disseminating centre would necessitate development of a clearing-house operation, which would require sufficient additional resources. The Secretary-General noted that the Centre for Human Rights had provided the ESCAP library with an initial stock of its human rights information and reference materials issued to date.

Responsibility to promote and protect human rights

Working group activities. The working group on a draft declaration on the right and responsibility of individuals, groups and organs of society to promote and protect universally recognized human rights and fundamental freedoms met at Geneva from 23 to 30 January and on 27 February.[76] It discussed various elements of chapters III and IV of the draft declaration, and provisionally adopted, at first reading, paragraph 1 of chapter IV. Annexed to the group's report was a compilation of all the texts showing the state of the whole draft declaration.

Human Rights Commission action. On 8 March, the Commission decided[77] to continue work at its 1990 session on the elaboration of the draft declaration and to make meeting time available to the working group prior to and during that session.

ECONOMIC AND SOCIAL COUNCIL ACTION

On 24 May, the Economic and Social Council, on the recommendation of its Second Committee, adopted **resolution 1989/80** without vote.

Question of a draft declaration on the right and responsibility of individuals, groups and organs of society to promote and protect universally recognized human rights and fundamental freedoms

The Economic and Social Council,

Recalling Commission on Human Rights resolution 1989/60 of 8 March 1989,

1. *Authorizes* an open-ended working group of the Commission on Human Rights to meet for a period of eight working days prior to the forty-sixth session of the Commission, in order to continue the elaboration of a draft declaration on the right and responsibility of individuals, groups and organs of society to promote and protect universally recognized human rights and fundamental freedoms;

2. *Requests* the Secretary-General to extend all facilities to the working group for its meetings prior to and during the forty-sixth session of the Commission and in order to enable it to continue its work on the elaboration of the draft declaration, to transmit the report of the working group that met prior to and during the forty-fifth session of the Commission, together with the annexes thereto, to all Member States in advance of the next meeting of the working group.

Economic and Social Council resolution 1989/80

24 May 1989   Meeting 16   Adopted without vote

Approved by Second Committee (E/1989/88) without vote, 19 May (meeting 22); draft by Commission on Human Rights (E/1989/20); agenda item 9.

International co-operation in human rights

On 7 March, the Commission called[78] on all States to implement fully the international standards for the promotion and protection of human rights, and urged them to co-operate fully with the relevant UN bodies and human rights treaty bod-

ies. It also invited Governments and international organizations to submit to the Secretary-General their comments and views on ways of strengthening international co-operation in solving international problems of a social, cultural and humanitarian character, and in promoting universal respect for, and observance of, human rights and fundamental freedoms. Governments were also invited to co-operate closely with special rapporteurs of the Commission.

World conference on human rights

On 15 December, the General Assembly, on the recommendation of the Third Committee, adopted **resolution 44/156** without vote.

World conference on human rights

The General Assembly,

Noting the progress made by the United Nations over the past twenty years towards achieving its goal of promoting respect for human rights and fundamental freedoms for all, without distinction as to race, sex, language or religion,

Noting also that there are still areas in which further progress could be made towards this goal,

Considering that, in view of the progress made and the new challenges that lie ahead, it would be appropriate to conduct a review of what has been accomplished through the human rights programme and what remains to be done,

1. *Requests* the Secretary-General to seek the views of Governments, specialized agencies, non-governmental organizations and United Nations bodies concerned with human rights on the desirability of convening a world conference on human rights for the purpose of dealing at the highest level with the crucial questions facing the United Nations in connection with the promotion and protection of human rights;

2. *Also requests* the Secretary-General to submit to the General Assembly at its forty-fifth session a report on this question;

3. *Decides* to consider the report of the Secretary-General at its forty-fifth session.

General Assembly resolution 44/156

15 December 1989   Meeting 82   Adopted without vote

Approved by Third Committee (A/44/848) without vote, 29 November (meeting 60); 43-nation draft (A/C.3/44/L.75); agenda item 12.

Meeting numbers. GA 44th session: 3rd Committee 48, 50-60; plenary 82.

Human rights based on solidarity

On 15 December, on the recommendation of the Third Committee, the Assembly adopted **resolution 44/148** without vote.

Human rights based on solidarity

The General Assembly,

Reaffirming the Universal Declaration of Human Rights, the International Covenant on Civil and Political Rights, the International Covenant on Economic, Social and Cultural Rights, and other international instruments adopted by the United Nations concerning human rights,

Stressing that respect for the inherent dignity and for the equal and inalienable rights of all members of the human family is the foundation of freedom, justice and peace in the world,

Convinced that the severe suffering of innumerable human beings throughout the world, particularly those in conditions of extreme poverty, calls for the strengthening of a common sense of human solidarity,

1. _Requests_ the Commission on Human Rights to obtain from States, the specialized agencies and organizations of the United Nations system, as well as from other international organizations, including non-governmental organizations, their views and to study the question;

2. _Decides_ to include in the provisional agenda of its forty-sixth session an item entitled "Human rights based on solidarity".

General Assembly resolution 44/148

15 December 1989   Meeting 82   Adopted without vote

Approved by Third Committee (A/44/829) without vote, 27 November (meeting 56); draft by Colombia (A/C.3/44/L.61/Rev.1); agenda item 115.
Meeting numbers. GA 44th session: 3rd Committee 36-43, 50, 54, 56; plenary 82.

REFERENCES

(1)A/44/696. (2)YUN 1981, p. 928, GA res. 36/133, 14 Dec. 1981. (3)YUN 1987, p. 780, GA res. 42/116, 7 Dec. 1987. (4)E/CN.4/1989/47 & Add.1. (5)YUN 1987, p. 780. (6)E/1989/20 (res. 1989/52). (7)A/44/525. (8)E/1989/20. (9)_Ibid._ (dec. 1989/101). (10)E/CN.4/1989/37. (11)YUN 1988, p. 537. (12)E/1989/20 (res. 1989/36). (13)_Ibid._ (res. 1989/48). (14)_Ibid._ (dec. 1989/109). (15)YUN 1970, p. 529, ESC res. 1503(XLVIII), 27 May 1970. (16)E/1989/20 (dec. 1989/114). (17)E/CN.4/Sub.2/1989/58. (18)_Ibid._ (dec. 1989/101). (19)_Ibid._ (dec. 1989/105). (20)_Ibid._ (dec. 1989/102). (21)_Ibid._ (dec. 1989/103). (22)_Ibid._ (dec. 1989/104). (23)_Ibid._ (dec. 1989/113). (24)E/1989/20 (res. 1989/54). (25)E/AC.51/1989/2. (26)A/44/16. (27)E/CN.4/1989/21. (28)YUN 1948-49, p. 535, GA res. 217 A (III), 10 Dec. 1948. (29)YUN 1988, p. 547. (30)_Ibid._, p. 538, GA res. 43/128, 8 Dec. 1988. (31)E/1989/20 (res. 1989/53). (32)A/44/660 & Add.1. (33)YUN 1955, p. 164, GA res. 926(X), 14 Dec. 1955. (34)E/CN.4/1989/42. (35)E/CN.4/Sub.2/1989/17. (36)YUN 1987, p. 791. (37)E/1989/20 (res. 1989/72). (38)YUN 1987, p. 790. (39)_Ibid._, ESC dec. 1987/147, 29 May 1987. (40)E/1989/20 (res. 1989/71). (41)E/CN.4/1989/41. (42)E/1989/20 (res. 1989/70). (43)YUN 1984, p. 813, GA res. 39/46, annex, 10 Dec. 1984. (44)YUN 1981, p. 938. (45)YUN 1985, p. 894. (46)E/CN.4/1989/39. (47)E/1989/20 (res. 1989/74). (48)E/CN.4/Sub.2/1989/58 (res. 1989/6). (49)E/CN.4/1989/40. (50)E/1989/20 (res. 1989/73). (51)YUN 1988, p. 575. (52)E/CN.4/Sub.2/1989/12. (53)E/CN.4/Sub.2/1989/58 (res. 1989/15). (54)YUN 1965, p. 440, GA res. 2106 A (XX), annex, 21 Dec. 1965. (55)YUN 1966, pp. 419 & 423, GA res. 2200 A (XXI), annex, 16 Dec. 1966. (56)YUN 1973, p. 103, GA res. 3068(XXVIII), annex, 30 Nov. 1973. (57)YUN 1979, p. 895, GA res. 34/180, annex, 18 Dec. 1979. (58)E/CN.4/1989/62. (59)YUN 1988, p. 542. (60)E/1989/20 (res. 1989/47). (61)E/CN.4/Sub.2/1989/58 (res. 1989/11). (62)A/44/668. (63)A/44/98. (64)E/C.12/1989/3. (65)E/1989/20 (res. 1989/46). (66)A/44/539. (67)E/1989/20 (res. 1989/17). (68)YUN 1988, p. 546, GA res. 43/114, 8 Dec. 1988. (69)A/44/441. (70)E/1989/20 (res. 1989/51). (71)A/44/454 & Corr.1. (72)E/CN.4/1989/20. (73)YUN 1988, p. 551. (74)E/1989/20 (res. 1989/50). (75)E/CN.4/1990/18. (76)E/CN.4/1989/45. (77)E/1989/20 (res. 1989/60). (78)_Ibid._ (res. 1989/49).

Human rights violations

In 1989, alleged violations of human rights on a large scale in several countries were examined by the General Assembly, the Economic and Social Council and the Commission on Human Rights, as well as by special bodies and appointed officials. In addition, alleged human rights violations involving the self-determination of peoples were discussed with regard to Afghanistan, Kampuchea, South Africa, Western Sahara and the Palestinian people (see above, under "Civil and political rights").

Under a procedure established by the Economic and Social Council in 1970[1] to deal with communications alleging denial or violation of human rights, the Working Group on Communications of the Sub-Commission on Prevention of Discrimination and Protection of Minorities met from 24 July to 4 August 1989. After consideration of the Working Group's confidential report, the Sub-Commission referred to the Commission for consideration situations which appeared to reveal a consistent pattern of gross human rights violations. It decided to defer action on certain communications until 1990 and to take no action on certain others.

On 7 March 1989, the Commission Chairman announced that the Commission had examined, in closed session, the human rights situations in Brunei Darussalam, Haiti, Honduras, Iraq, Paraguay, Somalia, the Syrian Arab Republic and Zaire, referred to it by the Sub-Commission at its 1988 session. He also announced that the situations in Honduras, Iraq, the Syrian Arab Republic and Zaire were no longer under consideration under the 1970 procedure.

Africa

South Africa and Namibia

Working Group activities. On 31 January, the six-member _Ad Hoc_ Working Group of Experts on southern Africa, established by the Commission on Human Rights in 1967,[2] reported[3] to the Commission on recent developments in South Africa and Namibia. It described, in particular, the results of its 1988 fact-finding mission,[4] during which the Group held 24 meetings and heard 59 witnesses.

Developments dealt with in the report concerned the right to life, physical integrity and protection from arbitrary arrest and detention; _apartheid_, including bantustanization and forced population removals; the right to education, health and freedom of expression and of movement; and the right to work and freedom of association, including the situation of black workers and trade union activities in both South Africa and Namibia. Issues relating to Namibia also included human rights violations affecting individuals, such as capital punishment, and other manifestations of policies and practices constituting a violation of human rights, as well as the situation of refugees. The report also noted that the Group had not received sufficient information during the period under review to determine the responsibilities of persons suspected of being guilty of the crime of *apartheid* or of a serious human rights violation. Annexed to the report was a list of known political detainees in South Africa from January to May 1988.

The Working Group observed that the extension of the state of emergency in South Africa continued to cause new outbreaks of violence, while the extremely broad powers granted to the police and armed forces gave rise to abuses of authority. The Group pointed to the persistence of massive repression against students and trade union members, resumption of forced population removals, new restrictions on freedom of expression, and a growing number of arrests and detentions without trial of political prisoners, as well as cases of torture and ill-treatment, in particular against children (see above, under "Civil and political rights"). Accordingly, the Working Group was of the opinion that discrimination continued to be the rule in South Africa as *apartheid* remained institutionalized, despite indications that the Government envisaged reviewing its policy. With regard to Namibia, the Group, while underscoring the continuing illegal occupation of the Territory by South Africa characterized by repression and flagrant human rights violations, noted recent efforts towards implementing the UN plan for the independence of Namibia (see PART FOUR, Chapter III).

The report set forth a number of recommendations for action by the Commission.

In pursuance of its mandate, the Group carried out a mission of inquiry to London from 14 to 18 August, to gather information on policies and practices violating human rights in South Africa and Namibia, on the situation of children and on trade union rights in South Africa. It also undertook a joint mission with the Special Rapporteur on summary and arbitrary executions (see above, under "Civil and political rights") to collect on-the-spot information concerning violations of the right to life. The Group heard 18 witnesses with respect to the situation in South Africa and 6 witnesses with respect to the situation in Namibia. On 14 August, it decided to postpone its on-the-spot investigation of living conditions in Namibia and the treatment of its people by South Africa, requested by the Commission earlier in the year (see below).

Human Rights Commission action. On 23 February, by a roll-call vote of 35 to 3, with 5 abstentions, the Commission strongly condemned[5] the escalation of human rights violations in South Africa since the imposition of the state of emer-

gency in June 1986,[6] the widespread detention and incarceration of children and pregnant women, the use of torture and other ill-treatment against political opponents and indiscriminate use of force against unarmed demonstrators. It demanded that South Africa immediately abolish the system of *apartheid* in all its forms, and denounced the policies of "bantustanization" and denationalization, the forced removals of the black population and so-called "voluntary" removals. The Commission rejected South Africa's so-called reforms, which fell short of terminating the state of emergency, abolishing *apartheid* laws, dismantling the "bantustans", lifting bans on political organizations and parties and on the return of political exiles and freedom fighters, and ensuring the unconditional release of political prisoners.

The Commission demanded that South Africa desist from its brutal repression, torture and harassment of organizations and individuals opposed to *apartheid* and from the abduction and assassination of political refugees and members of liberation movements based in neighbouring States, and called on it to respect international standards on trade union rights and to desist from harassing, intimidating, arresting and maltreating black trade union leaders. It also demanded that South Africa repeal its ban on political organizations, release unconditionally all political prisoners and ensure that all South Africans were afforded access to a unified, free educational system. It condemned South Africa for its military pressures and other destabilization policies towards the front-line States.

Urging all States to stop any assistance to South Africa, the Commission called on the Security Council to impose mandatory sanctions against the South African régime, and endorsed, pending the adoption of sanctions, other measures adopted by certain countries, including prohibition of the transfer of technology; cessation of exports, sales or transport of oil and oil products as well as of any co-operation with South Africa's oil industry; cessation of further investments, financial loans and credit guarantees or support for trade; prohibition of the sale of krugerrand and other coins minted in South Africa; prohibition of imports from South Africa; termination of visa-free entry and of the promotion of tourism to South Africa; termination of air and shipping links; cessation of academic, cultural, scientific and sports relations; suspension or abrogation of agreements and termination of double taxation agreements; and a ban on government contracts with majority-owned South African companies.

The Commission strongly recommended to the Economic and Social Council that a year be declared as Academic Year against *Apartheid* and that the subject of the evils of *apartheid* be taught in educational institutions world wide, so as to sensitize public opinion to the realities of that system. It endorsed recommendations of the *Ad Hoc* Working Group of Experts on southern Africa, renewed its mandate and decided that the Group should continue to study human rights violations in South Africa and Namibia, as well as infringements of trade union rights in South Africa. The Group was requested to continue bringing to the Commission Chairman's attention particularly serious violations and, in co-operation with the Special Committee against *Apartheid*, to continue investigating cases of torture, ill-treatment and deaths of detainees in South Africa. The Group Chairman was also authorized to participate in events connected with action against *apartheid* organized under the Special Committee's auspices.

In connection with the Group's on-the-spot investigations of living conditions in South African and Namibian prisons and the treatment of prisoners, the Commission requested South Africa to guarantee the Group free and confidential access to any current or former prisoner or detainee or any other persons, and to grant those persons immunity from any State action arising from their participation in the investigation. It also requested the Secretary-General to provide the Group with all possible assistance, and asked the Group to submit its interim report to the Commission in 1990 and its final report in 1991.

In another resolution,[7] adopted on 23 February by a roll-call vote of 32 to none, with 10 abstentions, the Commission reaffirmed the Namibian people's inalienable right to self-determination and independence under conditions determined by the Security Council in 1978,[8] which it said remained the only internationally accepted basis for a peaceful and definitive settlement of the Namibian problem, and reiterated that South Africa's illegal occupation of Namibia was an act of aggression. It condemned South Africa for the militarization of Namibia; the use of mercenaries; the recruitment and training of Namibians for tribal armies; the proclamation of a so-called security zone in Namibia; forcible displacement of Namibians from their homes; torture and brutality against the population and captured freedom fighters in particular; the military conscription of Namibians; the exploitation and depletion of Namibia's natural resources; and the use of Namibia as a supply base for armed groups based in Angola.

The Commission denounced South Africa's schemes to achieve a neo-colonial solution to the Namibian problem, as well as its attempts to separate parts of the Territory from the rest of Namibia; it urged States to reject such schemes and not to recognize any administration in Namibia that did not ensue from free elections conducted under UN auspices. It strongly urged the immediate holding of free and fair elections in Namibia, called for support to and co-operation with the UN Transition Assistance Group, appealed to the Security Council to adopt measures for implementing the UN plan for the independence of Namibia, and demanded that South Africa co-operate with the United Nations in bringing about Namibia's independence (see also above, under "Civil and political rights", and PART FOUR, Chapter III). The Commission also demanded that South Africa terminate the curfew in Namibia and release unconditionally all Namibian political prisoners; discontinue its military build-up and military conscription there as well as the torture and murder of innocent Namibians; accord prisoner-of-war status to captured freedom fighters and apply international humanitarian law to the liberation struggle in Namibia; and account for all "disappeared" Namibians. In that regard, it declared South Africa to be liable for compensating the victims, their families and the future lawful Government of an independent Namibia for losses sustained.

The Commission called for the unimpeded return of all Namibian refugees and exiles and urged international assistance in their repatriation. It requested the *Ad Hoc* Working Group of Experts to make an on-the-spot investigation in 1989 of living conditions in Namibia and the treatment of Namibians by the South African régime, to bring to the Commission Chairman's attention human rights violations in Namibia and to report to the Commission in 1990. The Secretary-General was asked to provide the Group with all necessary assistance.

By **decision 1989/136** of 24 May, the Economic and Social Council approved the Commission's decision to renew the Working Group's mandate and its request to the Secretary-General to provide the Group with all possible assistance.

Sub-Commission action. On 31 August, the Sub-Commission reaffirmed[9] that *apartheid* was a crime against humanity and demanded the immediate lifting of the state of emergency, the cessation of all acts of brutality by the South African army and security forces, and the release of all political prisoners. Urging South Africa to lift promptly the ban on anti-*apartheid* organizations, the Sub-Commission strongly condemned it for the recent imposition of capital punishment on 66 opponents of *apartheid;* the continuing acts of international terrorism and destabilization carried out against the front-line and other neighbouring States; and the decision to proceed with local government elections organized along racial lines. It reaffirmed the right of all persons to refuse service in military or police forces used to enforce *apartheid*, appealed for international pressure on South

Africa not to proceed with the execution of *apartheid* opponents, and requested the Chairman of the Commission on Human Rights to transmit that appeal urgently to the South African Government. The Sub-Commission urged States to provide assistance to the people of South Africa and Namibia, and called on them to assist the front-line States and to continue efforts towards the *apartheid* régime's total economic, cultural and political isolation.

Condemning all collaboration with South Africa and any breach or circumvention of the international sports boycott against *apartheid*, the Sub-Commission called on States, particularly Equatorial Guinea and Israel, to cut all military links with that country. It also called for immediate and complete disinvestment from South Africa and urged the foreign companies concerned to ensure that benefits that had accrued to the black labour force were fully respected.

1973 Convention against apartheid

As at 31 December 1989,[10] the number of parties to the International Convention on the Suppression and Punishment of the Crime of *Apartheid*, which was adopted by the General Assembly in 1973[11] and entered into force in 1976,[12] remained at 88. In a 9 August report[13] to the Assembly on the status of the Convention, the Secretary-General provided a list of States that had signed, ratified or acceded to it as at 1 August.

Activities of the Group of Three. The Group of Three (Ethiopia, German Democratic Republic, Mexico)—established under article IX of the Convention to consider reports by States parties on measures taken to implement the Convention's provisions—held its twelfth session at Geneva from 23 to 27 January.[14]

The Group examined, in the presence of representatives of the reporting States, an initial report from Trinidad and Tobago; the second periodic report from Romania; the third periodic reports from Peru and Rwanda; the fourth periodic report from Yugoslavia; the fifth periodic reports from Bulgaria, the German Democratic Republic and Qatar; and the sixth periodic reports from Cuba and the USSR. It agreed to postpone consideration of the report from Czechoslovakia to its 1990 session.

The Group also continued to consider whether actions of transnational corporations (TNCs) operating in South Africa and Namibia came under the definition of the crime of *apartheid*. It had before it a note[15] by the Secretary-General transmitting the views of three States parties, as well as previously expressed views of States parties, specialized agencies and NGOs. The Group reiterated its view that such TNCs exhausted South African and Namibian natural resources, exploited the region's labour force with the single aim of making larger profits, and strengthened the *apartheid* régime. It endorsed the conclusion that, by their complicity, those TNCs must be considered, in conformity with article III *(b)* of the Convention, accomplices in the crime of *apartheid* and must be prosecuted for their responsibility in continuing that crime. However, the Group was of the opinion that further examination of the extent and nature of that responsibility was needed.

Noting the recommendations of the second meeting of persons chairing the human rights treaty bodies, held in 1988[16] (see also above, under "Advancement of human rights"), the Group authorized its Chairman to request the 38 States parties that had not yet submitted their initial reports to do so for its consideration in 1990. It also recommended that the Commission on Human Rights extend the periodicity of reporting by States parties from two to four years. The Group had before it the Secretary-General's note[17] indicating the status of submission of reports; noting with concern that more than 190 reports were overdue as at 31 December 1988, the Group urged those parties to fulfil their reporting obligations. It made a further number of recommendations for action by the Commission.

Human Rights Commission action. On 23 February, by a roll-call vote of 32 to 1, with 10 abstentions, the Commission urged[18] States that had not done so to ratify or accede to the 1973 Convention against *apartheid* without delay and to ratify the 1948 Convention on the Prevention and Punishment of the Crime of Genocide[19] (see below, under "Genocide"), and requested States parties to the former Convention to submit their initial reports not later than two years after the Convention's entry into force for them, and their periodic reports at four-year intervals. It reiterated its recommendations that parties take into account the general guidelines for submission of reports, laid down by the Group of Three in 1978,[20] and that States parties be represented during the Group's consideration of their reports.

The Commission requested the Group to continue examining the extent and nature of TNCs' responsibility for the continued existence of the *apartheid* system as well as legal action that could be taken against TNCs whose operations came under the crime of *apartheid*, and to report in 1990. The Secretary-General was requested to invite the comments of States parties on that matter. He was further asked to invite States parties, specialized agencies and NGOs to provide the Commission with relevant information on the forms of the crime of *apartheid*, as described in article II, committed by TNCs operating in South Africa. The Commission decided on the time-frame for the Group's 1990 meeting and requested the

Secretary-General to provide it with all necessary assistance. He was also asked to intensify his efforts to disseminate information on the Convention and its implementation.

The Commission further called on States parties whose TNCs continued to do business with South Africa to terminate their dealings with South Africa and Namibia and to strengthen co-operation in implementing UN decisions aimed at preventing, suppressing and punishing the crime of *apartheid*. States, UN bodies, specialized agencies and NGOs were asked to step up their activities in enhancing public awareness by denouncing the crimes committed by the South African régime.

ECONOMIC AND SOCIAL COUNCIL ACTION

In May, the Economic and Social Council adopted **decision 1989/137** by vote.

Implementation of the International Convention on the Suppression and Punishment of the Crime of *Apartheid*

At its 16th plenary meeting, on 24 May 1989, the Economic and Social Council, taking note of Commission on Human Rights resolution 1989/8 of 23 February 1989, approved the Commission's decision that the Group of Three of the Commission, established in accordance with article IX of the International Convention on the Suppression and Punishment of the Crime of *Apartheid*, should meet for a period of not more than five days before the forty-sixth session of the Commission to consider the reports submitted by States parties in accordance with article VII of the Convention. The Council also approved the Commission's request to the Secretary-General to provide all necessary assistance to the Group of Three.

Economic and Social Council decision 1989/137

39-1-13 (unrecorded vote)

Approved by Second Committee (E/1989/88) by recorded vote (40-1-13), 19 May (meeting 22); draft by Commission on Human Rights (E/1989/20); agenda item 9.

GENERAL ASSEMBLY ACTION

On 8 December, on the recommendation of the Third Committee, the General Assembly adopted **resolution 44/69** by recorded vote.

Status of the International Convention on the Suppression and Punishment of the Crime of *Apartheid*

The General Assembly,

Recalling its resolutions 41/103 of 4 December 1986, 42/56 of 30 November 1987 and 43/97 of 8 December 1988,

Mindful that the International Convention on the Suppression and Punishment of the Crime of *Apartheid* constitutes an important international treaty in the field of human rights and serves to implement the ideals of the Universal Declaration of Human Rights,

Reaffirming its conviction that *apartheid* is a crime against humanity and constitutes a total negation of the purposes and principles of the Charter of the United Nations and a gross violation of human rights, seriously threatening international peace and security,

Strongly condemning the abhorrent policy and system of *apartheid* and the brutal repression it engenders, which continue to aggravate the situation in South Africa,

Emphasizing that the root cause of the conflict in southern Africa is *apartheid* and the racist régime's policy of aggression, State terrorism and destabilization against the front-line and other neighbouring States,

Condemning the continued collaboration of certain States and transnational corporations with the racist régime of South Africa in the political, economic, military and other fields as an encouragement to the intensification of its odious policy of *apartheid*,

Firmly convinced that the legitimate struggle of the oppressed peoples in southern Africa against *apartheid*, racism and colonialism and for the effective implementation of their inalienable right to self-determination and independence demands more than ever all necessary support by the international community and, in particular, further action by the Security Council in accordance with Chapter VII of the Charter,

Underlining that ratification of or accession to the Convention on a universal basis and the implementation of its provisions without any delay are necessary for its effectiveness and will therefore contribute to the eradication of the crime of *apartheid*,

1. *Takes note* of the report of the Secretary-General on the status of the International Convention on the Suppression and Punishment of the Crime of *Apartheid;*

2. *Commends* those States parties to the Convention that have submitted their reports under article VII thereof;

3. *Appeals once again* to those States that have not yet done so to ratify or to accede to the Convention without further delay, in particular those States that have jurisdiction over transnational corporations operating in South Africa and Namibia and without whose co-operation such operations could not be halted;

4. *Underlines* the importance of the universal ratification of the Convention, which would be an effective contribution to the fulfilment of the ideals of the Universal Declaration of Human Rights and other human rights instruments;

5. *Recalls with satisfaction* the report of the Group of Three of the Commission on Human Rights, which was set up under the Convention, and, in particular, the conclusions and recommendations contained in that report;

6. *Once again draws the attention* of all States to the opinion expressed by the Group of Three in its report that transnational corporations operating in South Africa and Namibia must be considered accomplices in the crime of *apartheid*, in accordance with article III (*b*) of the Convention;

7. *Calls upon* all States whose transnational corporations continue to do business with South Africa to take appropriate steps to terminate their dealings with South Africa;

8. *Requests* the Commission on Human Rights to intensify, in co-operation with the Special Committee against *Apartheid*, its efforts to compile periodically the progressive list of individuals, organizations, institutions and representatives of States deemed responsible for crimes enumerated in article II of the Convention, as

well as those against whom or which legal proceedings have been undertaken;

9. *Requests* the Secretary-General to circulate that list among all States parties to the Convention and all Member States and to bring such facts to the attention of the public by all means of mass communication;

10. *Also requests* the Secretary-General to invite the States parties to the Convention, the specialized agencies and non-governmental organizations to provide the Commission on Human Rights with relevant information concerning the forms of the crime of *apartheid*, as described in article II of the Convention, committed by transnational corporations operating in South Africa;

11. *Notes* the importance of measures to be taken by States parties in the field of teaching and education for fuller implementation of the Convention;

12. *Appeals* to all States, United Nations organs, the specialized agencies and international and national non-governmental organizations to step up their activities to enhance public awareness by denouncing the crimes committed by the racist régime of South Africa;

13. *Requests* the Secretary-General to intensify his efforts, through appropriate channels, to disseminate information on the Convention and its implementation with a view to promoting further ratification of or accession to the Convention;

14. *Also requests* the Secretary-General to include in his next annual report under General Assembly resolution 3380(XXX) of 10 November 1975 a special section concerning the implementation of the Convention.

General Assembly resolution 44/69

8 December 1989   Meeting 78   124-1-27 (recorded vote)

Approved by Third Committee (A/44/716) by recorded vote (110-1-28), 27 October (meeting 21); 33-nation draft (A/C.3/44/L.11); agenda item 100.
Meeting numbers. GA 44th session: 3rd Committee 3-11, 15, 21; plenary 78.

Recorded vote in Assembly as follows:

In favour: Afghanistan, Albania, Algeria, Angola, Antigua and Barbuda, Argentina, Bahamas, Bahrain, Bangladesh, Barbados, Benin, Bhutan, Bolivia, Botswana, Brazil, Brunei Darussalam, Bulgaria, Burkina Faso, Burundi, Byelorussian SSR, Cameroon, Cape Verde, Central African Republic, Chad, China, Colombia, Comoros, Congo, Costa Rica, Côte d'Ivoire, Cuba, Cyprus, Czechoslovakia, Democratic Kampuchea, Democratic Yemen, Djibouti, Dominica, Dominican Republic, Ecuador, Egypt, El Salvador, Equatorial Guinea, Ethiopia, Gabon, Gambia, German Democratic Republic, Ghana, Grenada, Guatemala, Guinea, Guinea-Bissau, Guyana, Haiti, Honduras, Hungary, India, Indonesia, Iran, Iraq, Jamaica, Jordan, Kenya, Kuwait, Lao People's Democratic Republic, Lebanon, Lesotho, Liberia, Libyan Arab Jamahiriya, Madagascar, Malaysia, Maldives, Mali, Mauritania, Mexico, Mongolia, Morocco, Mozambique, Myanmar, Nepal, Nicaragua, Niger, Nigeria, Pakistan, Panama, Peru, Philippines, Poland, Qatar, Romania, Rwanda, Saint Lucia, Saint Vincent and the Grenadines, Samoa, Sao Tome and Principe, Saudi Arabia, Senegal, Seychelles, Sierra Leone, Singapore, Solomon Islands, Somalia, Sri Lanka, Sudan, Suriname, Swaziland, Syrian Arab Republic, Thailand, Togo, Trinidad and Tobago, Tunisia, Uganda, Ukrainian SSR, USSR, United Arab Emirates, United Republic of Tanzania, Uruguay, Vanuatu, Venezuela, Viet Nam, Yemen, Yugoslavia, Zaire, Zambia, Zimbabwe.

Against: United States.

Abstaining: Australia, Austria, Belgium, Canada, Chile, Denmark, Fiji, Finland, France, Germany, Federal Republic of, Greece, Iceland, Ireland, Israel, Italy, Japan, Luxembourg, Malta, Netherlands, New Zealand, Norway, Paraguay, Portugal, Spain, Sweden, Turkey, United Kingdom.

Before adopting the text as a whole, the Assembly adopted paragraphs 6, 7 and 10 by recorded votes of 113 to 16, with 20 abstentions, 117 to 8, with 25 abstentions, and 120 to 15, with 15 abstentions, respectively. The Third Committee had approved the same paragraphs by recorded votes of 104 to 16, with 17 abstentions, 107 to 8, with 23 abstentions, and 106 to 15, with 16 abstentions. By a recorded vote of 115 to 15, with 19 abstentions, the Assembly retained the words ''State terrorism'' in the fifth preambular paragraph, as had the Committee by a recorded vote of 107 to 15, with 16 abstentions.

Foreign support to South Africa

Human Rights Commission action. On 23 February, by a roll-call vote of 31 to 8, with 4 abstentions, the Commission expressed its appreciation[21] to the Sub-Commission's Special Rapporteur, Ahmed Khalifa (Egypt), for his updated 1988 report[22] on the adverse consequences for the enjoyment of human rights of political, military, economic and other forms of assistance to South Africa. It vigorously condemned assistance to South Africa by major Western countries and Israel, particularly in the military field, and demanded that such assistance, which it was convinced was a hostile action against the people of South Africa, Namibia and neighbouring States, be immediately terminated. Condemning the continuing nuclear collaboration of some Western States, Israel and others with South Africa, the Commission urged them to stop supplying it with nuclear equipment and technology, and called on Governments to end technological assistance or collaboration in the manufacture of arms and military supplies in South Africa and Namibia and to cease all nuclear collaboration with South Africa.

Reaffirming the right of the South African and Namibian peoples to dispose of natural resources in their territories and to obtain reparation for the exploitation, depletion, loss or depreciation of those resources, the Commission strongly condemned foreign economic activities in Namibia and demanded that TNCs exploiting Namibian resources immediately refrain from new investments or activities there, withdraw from the Territory and end their co-operation with the South African administration. It called on States to take measures to prevent nationals and corporations under their jurisdiction from trading, manufacturing and investment in South Africa and Namibia, and appealed for intensified international efforts to force the South African régime to comply with UN resolutions and decisions. In that regard, the Commission welcomed the General Assembly's request to the Security Council to consider complete and mandatory sanctions against South Africa, in particular the prohibition of technological assistance or collaboration in the manufacture of arms and military supplies; cessation of nuclear collaboration; prohibition of loans to and investment in South Africa, and the cessation of trade; and an embargo on the supply of petroleum, petroleum products and other strategic goods.

The Commission rejected all policies that encouraged the South African régime to intensify its repression of South Africans and Namibians and to escalate its aggression against neighbouring States, and demanded that South Africa cease all acts of aggression and destabilization against those States. It appealed to States, specialized agencies and NGOs to co-operate with the recognized liberation movements of southern Africa and to intensify, along with regional intergovernmental organizations, their campaign aimed at mobilizing public opinion to enforce economic and other sanctions against South Africa. The Commission urgently requested specialized agencies, particularly the International Monetary Fund (IMF), to refrain from granting loans or financial assistance to the South African régime, and called for contributions to the Action for Resisting Invasion, Colonialism and *Apartheid* Fund, as well as for measures to facilitate implementation of the Tripartite Agreement for Namibia's independence (see PART FOUR, Chapter III).

Also on 23 February, by a roll-call vote of 32 to 7, with 4 abstentions, the Commission recommended[23] a draft resolution for adoption by the Economic and Social Council (see below).

ECONOMIC AND SOCIAL COUNCIL ACTION

On 24 May, the Economic and Social Council adopted **resolution 1989/73** by recorded vote.

Adverse consequences for the enjoyment of human rights of political, military, economic and other forms of assistance given to the racist and colonialist régime of South Africa

The Economic and Social Council,

Recalling General Assembly resolutions 39/15 of 23 November 1984 and 41/95 of 4 December 1986,

1. *Expresses its satisfaction* to the Special Rapporteur of the Sub-Commission on Prevention of Discrimination and Protection of Minorities, Mr. Ahmad Khalifa, for his updated report;

2. *Expresses its thanks* to all Governments and all organizations that have provided information to the Special Rapporteur;

3. *Invites* the Special Rapporteur:

(*a*) To continue to update, subject to annual review, the list of banks, transnational corporations and other organizations assisting the racist régime of South Africa, giving such details regarding enterprises listed as the Rapporteur may consider necessary and appropriate, including explanations of responses, if any, and to submit the updated report to the Commission on Human Rights, through the Sub-Commission on Prevention of Discrimination and Protection of Minorities;

(*b*) To use all available material from other United Nations organs, Member States, specialized agencies and other relevant sources in order to indicate the volume, nature and adverse human consequences of the assistance given to the racist régime of South Africa;

(*c*) To intensify direct contacts with the United Nations Centre on Transnational Corporations and the Centre against *Apartheid* of the Secretariat, with a view to consolidating mutual co-operation in updating his report;

4. *Calls upon* Governments:

(*a*) To co-operate with the Special Rapporteur in making the report even more accurate and informative;

(*b*) To disseminate the updated report and give its contents the widest possible publicity;

5. *Invites* the Sub-Commission to consider the updated report at its forty-first session;

6. *Requests* the Secretary-General, in accordance with General Assembly resolution 41/95, to make available to the Special Rapporteur two economists to help him to develop his work of analysis and documentation of certain specific cases of particular importance;

7. *Also requests* the Secretary-General to give the Special Rapporteur all the assistance that he may require in the exercise of his mandate, with a view to intensifying direct contacts with the United Nations Centre on Transnational Corporations and the Centre against *Apartheid;*

8. *Further requests* the Secretary-General to bring the updated report of the Special Rapporteur to the attention of Governments whose national financial institutions continue to deal with the régime of South Africa and to call upon them to provide the Special Rapporteur with any information or comments they may wish to present on the matter;

9. *Invites* the Secretary-General to continue to give the updated report of the Special Rapporteur the widest distribution and publicity as a United Nations publication;

10. *Requests* the Special Rapporteur to provide the Sub-Commission at its forty-first session with a concise note on the feasibility of consolidating the lists maintained by United Nations organs of enterprises doing business in South Africa;

11. *Also requests* the Special Rapporteur to provide the Sub-Commission at its forty-first session with a brief analysis of the partial disinvestment of foreign enterprises in South Africa, enumerating the various techniques employed to avoid total withdrawal from participation in the South African economy;

12. *Decides* that the Commission on Human Rights shall consider the updated report at its forty-sixth session under the agenda item entitled ''The adverse consequences for the enjoyment of human rights of political, military, economic and other forms of assistance given to colonial and racist régimes in southern Africa''.

Economic and Social Council resolution 1989/73

24 May 1989   Meeting 16   38-7-8 (recorded vote)

Approved by Second Committee (E/1989/88) by recorded vote (39-7-7), 19 May (meeting 22); draft by Commission on Human Rights (E/1989/20); agenda item 9.

Recorded vote in Council as follows:

In favour: Bahamas, Belize, Bolivia, Brazil, Bulgaria, Cameroon, China, Colombia, Cuba, Czechoslovakia, Ghana, Guinea, Indonesia, Iran, Iraq, Jordan, Kenya, Lesotho, Libyan Arab Jamahiriya, Nicaragua, Niger, Oman, Poland, Rwanda, Saudi Arabia, Somalia, Sri Lanka, Sudan, Thailand, Trinidad and Tobago, Tunisia, Ukrainian SSR, USSR, Uruguay, Venezuela, Yugoslavia, Zaire, Zambia.

Against: France, Germany, Federal Republic of, Italy, Netherlands, Portugal, United Kingdom, United States.

Abstaining: Canada, Denmark, Greece, Ireland, Japan, Liberia,* New Zealand, Norway.

*Later advised the Secretariat it had intended to vote in favour.

Report of the Special Rapporteur. On 11 and 12 July, the Special Rapporteur presented to the Sub-Commission an updated report and later addendum,[24] which analysed disinvestment trends in South Africa and listed TNCs, banks, insurance companies, firms and other enterprises giving direct or indirect military, economic and other assistance to that country. The report also provided comments on the subject from 12 States and 6 UN organs and specialized agencies, and noted that 3 regional intergovernmental organizations, 6 NGOs and a number of other bodies of the UN system had replied.

Sub-Commission action. On 31 August, the Sub-Commission recommended[25] that the Commission recommend to the Economic and Social Council a resolution requesting the Special Rapporteur to continue updating his report for annual review by the Sub-Commission and the Commission; calling on States to co-operate with the Rapporteur and to disseminate his report; requesting the Secretary-General to provide the Rapporteur with all necessary assistance and to bring the report to the attention of Governments concerned; and inviting him to give it wide distribution and publicity as a UN publication.

Trade union rights in South Africa

In 1989, the *Ad Hoc* Working Group of Experts on southern Africa (see above) continued to study alleged infringements of trade union rights in South Africa, as requested by the Economic and Social Council in 1988.[26] By a 3 April note,[27] the Secretary-General communicated to the Council sections of the Group's report[3] to the Commission containing its findings concerning labour legislation, freedom of association, restrictions under state-of-emergency regulations, as well as the situation of black workers, trade union activities, action against trade union movements, and sanctions and disinvestment in South Africa.

On 7 April, the Secretary-General informed[28] the Council that the International Labour Organisation (ILO) had in 1988 referred for Council consideration, in accordance with its 1950 resolution,[29] certain allegations of infringements of trade union rights in South Africa, addressed to ILO by the Congress of South African Trade Unions (COSATU). As South Africa was not a member of ILO, the Secretary-General had sought its Government's consent to having the allegations referred to the ILO Fact-Finding and Conciliation Commission on Freedom of Association. He provided a 14 February 1989 reply from South Africa, which stated that COSATU had not yet exhausted the available internal procedures to settle the complaint in question and that it would be premature to refer it to the ILO Commission.

ECONOMIC AND SOCIAL COUNCIL ACTION

On 24 May, the Economic and Social Council adopted **resolution 1989/82** without vote.

Infringements of trade union rights in South Africa

The Economic and Social Council,

Recalling its resolution 1988/41 of 27 May 1988,

Having examined the relevant section of the report of the *Ad Hoc* Working Group of Experts on southern Africa of the Commission on Human Rights and having considered the complaint made by the Congress of South African Trade Unions against the South African régime concerning the infringement of the right of freedom of association, referred to the Council in accordance with its resolution 277(X) of 17 February 1950 and contained in annex II to the note by the Secretary-General on allegations regarding infringements of trade union rights,

Noting that the reply from the Government of South Africa addressed to the Secretary-General and contained in annex III to the note by the Secretary-General predates the enactment of the legislation which constitutes the subject of the complaint,

Gravely concerned at the further deterioration of the situation as a result of the enactment of new legislation placing drastic restrictions on the exercise of trade union rights,

Noting with indignation that dehumanizing conditions imposed on black workers by the Government of South Africa and police intervention in industrial disputes, including mass arrests, banning and harassment of trade unionists, continue,

Aware of the ever-growing importance of the role of the independent black trade union movement in the struggle against *apartheid*,

1. *Takes note* of the relevant section of the report of the *Ad Hoc* Working Group of Experts on southern Africa of the Commission on Human Rights;

2. *Condemns* the increased repression of the independent black trade union movement by the Government of South Africa;

3. *Demands once again* that the persecution of trade unionists and repression of the independent black trade union movement cease;

4. *Requests once again* immediate recognition of the right of the entire population of South Africa to exercise freedom of association and to form and join trade unions without impediment or discrimination of any kind;

5. *Demands* the immediate unconditional release of all trade unionists imprisoned for exercising their legitimate trade union rights;

6. *Requests* the *Ad Hoc* Working Group of Experts to continue to study the situation and to report thereon to the Commission on Human Rights and the Council;

7. *Also requests* the *Ad Hoc* Working Group of Experts, in the discharge of its mandate, to consult with the International Labour Organisation and the Special Committee against *Apartheid*, as well as with international and African trade union confederations;

8. *Decides* to consider at its first regular session of 1990 the question of allegations regarding infringements of trade union rights in South Africa as a sub-item of the item entitled ''Human rights'';

9. *Requests* the Secretary-General to persist in his efforts to ensure referral of the complaint made by the Congress of South African Trade Unions to the Fact-finding and Conciliation Commission on Freedom of Association of the International Labour Organisation.

Economic and Social Council resolution 1989/82

24 May 1989   Meeting 16   Adopted without vote

Approved by Second Committee (E/1989/88) without vote, 19 May (meeting 22); draft by Burkina Faso, for African States (E/1989/C.2/L.20); orally amended by Lesotho in plenary; agenda item 9.

Asia and the Pacific

Afghanistan

Report of the Special Rapporteur. On 16 February 1989, Special Rapporteur Felix Ermacora (Austria) submitted to the Commission a report[30] on the human rights situation in Afghanistan. The Special Rapporteur visited that country and Pakistan in 1988, and again in 1989, from 27 January to 1 February (Pakistan) and from 2 to 5 February (Afghanistan).

He stated that the situation in Afghanistan was characterized by such factors as the decision to withdraw Soviet troops by 15 February 1989 (see PART TWO, Chapter III); efforts to establish a broad-based interim government including members of the current Government; and the continuation of the armed conflict. The human rights situation was adversely affected by government attempts to retain control over the areas formerly occupied by Soviet troops and by opposition attacks during the troop withdrawal, as well as retaliatory action, resulting in considerable civilian casualties and damage to property. At the same time, the Government accused the opposition of rejecting all its proposals to normalize the situation in the country, while the opposition claimed that the so-called policy of national reconciliation pursued by the Government had had no effect on either the return of refugees or the restoration of human rights in Afghanistan, due to continued bombing raids, arbitrary arrests and cases of torture and ill-treatment.

The Special Rapporteur continued to receive allegations concerning disappearances of persons, and was informed of cases of torture and ill-treatment which occurred during interrogation. Despite the Government's claim that only two interrogation centres existed in the country, he had obtained information that tended to confirm that other similar centres existed. He described the situation of prisoners awaiting trial as deplorable, and noted that Iranian and Pakistani prisoners had not benefited from general amnesties. He also pointed out that, whereas 16,110 prisoners had been released since 1986, 3,405 more persons were imprisoned during the same period; the official figure given for political prisoners was 3,500, but whether there were more prisoners in places other than known detention centres could not be determined.

Following the rejection by the opposition of the Government's proposal for a cease-fire, the downward trend in casualties in combat areas had reversed. It had been asserted, the Rapporteur said, that the Soviet forces used military strength to safeguard their troop withdrawal and that government troops attacked areas recently vacated by the Soviet forces. The Special Rapporteur also underscored that neither the use of prisoners of war for bargaining or exchange nor their treatment in general met the provisions laid down in the Geneva Conventions of 1949. As a result of the conflict, the food supply had decreased dramatically, which had especially negative effects on lower strata of the population and children.

The number of Afghan refugees outside the country stood at some 5.5 million, with only 185,945 having returned from Iran and Pakistan. Despite the existence of 31 ''peace guest houses'', 4 receiving points, 12 receiving camps and 8 clinics for refugees, their return was impeded by continued fighting, the presence of mines and the absence of an Islamic government or a broad-based government without members of the current ruling party demanded by most refugees. In that regard, the report noted attempts by the opposition alliance to designate a traditional consultative body, *Shura*, to hold power until general elections. It also stressed that only a portion of the population accepted the type of government provided for in the Constitution of December 1987 and that the existence of such a high number of refugees, who had not had the opportunity to express themselves on the Constitution, created a major obstacle to the full exercise of the right to self-determination.

The Special Rapporteur concluded that the human rights situation in Afghanistan remained a matter of deep concern and that all parties to the conflict were responsible for ensuring the respect for human rights in areas under their control. He recommended that all parties strictly respect provisions of humanitarian law, increase efforts to solve the conflict by peaceful means, cooperate in facilitating the return of refugees, allow humanitarian NGOs (particularly ICRC) unrestricted access to all parts of the country and transmit to them the names of all political prisoners and detained Afghan soldiers, and release prisoners of war without delay or conditions of reciprocity. It was also recommended that all military commanders provide minefield plans to facilitate mine-clearing activities, that members of the armed forces and civil servants not be subjected to arbitrary justice but stand fair trial on an individual basis, that the fate of disappeared persons be thoroughly investigated, that no ban on supplies of medicine and foodstuffs and other essential goods be declared as a means of pressure against the civilian population, and that international consensus be promoted to implement humanitarian projects in Afghanistan. The Special Rapporteur further suggested that, in implementation of those recommendations and in other respects, recourse might be had to the assistance provided under advisory services of the UN Centre for Human Rights.

Human Rights Commission action. On 8 March, the Commission noted[(31)] with grave concern the continuation of the armed conflict in Afghanistan and urged efforts for a comprehensive political solution and for the creation of a situation permitting the full enjoyment of human rights in that country. It again called on parties to the conflict to respect provisions of international humanitarian law and to co-operate with humanitarian organizations by granting them unrestricted access to all parts of the country. The parties were urged to treat all prisoners in accordance with humanitarian law and to release all prisoners of war, while the Afghan authorities were called upon to investigate thoroughly the fate of disappeared persons. The Commission expressed its concern at the large number of political prisoners, conditions of prisoners awaiting trial and reports of ill-treatment and torture during interrogation by Afghan authorities, as well as at alleged atrocities committed against Afghan soldiers, civil servants and their families. It was also concerned at the number of refugees outside Afghanistan, and urged every effort possible to facilitate their return.

The Commission requested the Working Group on Enforced or Involuntary Disappearances (see above, under ''Civil and political rights'') to examine the cases of disappeared persons, a list of whom was annexed to the Special Rapporteur's report, and took note of his recommendation regarding the possibility of assistance from the Centre for Human Rights in respect of Afghanistan. The Commission decided to extend the Special Rapporteur's mandate for one year and to have him report to the General Assembly in 1989 and to the Commission in 1990, while the Secretary-General was asked to give him all necessary assistance. In addition, all parties concerned were urged not to place any ban on supplies of medicine, food and other essential goods and to extend their co-operation to the Commission and its Special Rapporteur.

On 24 May, the Economic and Social Council, by **decision 1989/149**, approved the Commission's decision to extend for one year the Special Rapporteur's mandate and its request that the Secretary-General give him all necessary assistance.

Interim report of the Special Rapporteur. On 30 October, the Secretary-General transmitted to the Assembly an interim report[(32)] on the human rights situation in Afghanistan, prepared by the Special Rapporteur in response to the Commission's request. The report provided an evaluation of the current situation following the Special Rapporteur's visits to Pakistan from 9 to 16 September, to Afghanistan from 17 to 20 September and to Iran from 30 September to 5 October.

The Special Rapporteur reported that, in accordance with the Afghan Constitution, a state of emergency had been declared by the President of the Republic of Afghanistan on 19 February and a law was issued to that effect on 22 February. The parliament was suspended and State power concentrated in the hands of the President, who could suspend or limit by decree certain provisions of the Constitution concerning human rights; however, he had not yet used those powers. At the same time, far-reaching powers granted to the attorney for State security and a broad definition of crimes under the security law created a potential for violations of the right to freedom and security of the individual, and arrests for political activities continued. In the Special Rapporteur's opinion, prison conditions, despite some surface improvements, remained deplorable, including at the rehabilitation centre for adolescents in Dar-el-Taadib, where none of the minimum detention requirements were fulfilled. He also noted that a person sentenced to less than 10 years of imprisonment could not lodge an appeal and that an accused person could not choose his legal assistance, which contradicted international human rights standards. The Special Rapporteur pointed out that ICRC had access to convicted prisoners at Kabul and outside the capital, but regretted that no agreement had been reached on ICRC visits to prisoners awaiting trial.

The Special Rapporteur stated that the educational situation appeared to have improved and that the Government was pursuing a policy of combating illiteracy. The Special Rapporteur was informed that 400 of the 700 mosques destroyed during the past 10 years had been rebuilt. The enjoyment of economic rights was poor as a result of the war situation, and he stated that the population outside of towns could only survive with the help of the UN humanitarian programme and NGOs operating in Afghanistan (see PART THREE, Chapter III). Severe food shortages caused a reported exodus of farm families to cities in Afghanistan and Iran.

From March to August 1989, more than 7,431 war-wounded were registered at various hospitals in Afghanistan and Pakistan, while acts of terrorism committed between 15 February and 19 September caused the deaths of 2,249 civilians and wounded 5,269. The Rapporteur reiterated that the existence of minefields remained a particular cause for anxiety and fear. He further noted that the fate of Soviet prisoners of war remained un-clarified and that captured members of the oppo-sition forces were treated not as prisoners of war but as terrorists and were submitted to the courts of State security.

As for the refugee situation, the Government re-ported that the number of returnees had risen from 185,945 at the end of January to 203,943 by the end of September. The Rapporteur estimated the number of refugees outside Afghanistan at more than 5 mil-lion, including some 2.3 million in Iran, and noted that no official statistics were available concerning internally displaced persons. At the same time, the living conditions of refugees had become increas-ingly difficult as international aid to them had diminished.

The Special Rapporteur reiterated recommen-dations made in his report to the Commission[30] and added that fighters should be recognized as com-batants within the meaning of the Geneva Conven-tions of 1949; any use of weapons against the ci-vilian population must be qualified as terrorism; humanitarian assistance to refugees should be rein-forced; amnesty decrees should apply equally to for-eign detainees, the conditions of prisoners await-ing trial should be improved and the waiting period should be shortened; and the right to self-determination should also be respected by the op-position forces.

GENERAL ASSEMBLY ACTION

On 15 December, the General Assembly, on the recommendation of the Third Committee, adopted **resolution 44/161** without vote.

Situation of human rights in Afghanistan
The General Assembly,

Guided by the principles embodied in the Charter of the United Nations, the Universal Declaration of Human Rights, the International Covenants on Human Rights and the humanitarian rules set out in the Geneva Con-ventions of 12 August 1949 and the Additional Protocols thereto, of 1977,

Aware of its responsibility to promote and encourage respect for human rights and fundamental freedoms for all and resolved to remain vigilant with regard to viola-tions of human rights wherever they occur,

Reaffirming that all Member States have an obligation to promote and protect human rights and fundamental freedoms and to fulfil the obligations they have freely undertaken under the various international instruments,

Recalling Economic and Social Council resolution 1984/37 of 24 May 1984, in which the Council requested the Chair-man of the Commission on Human Rights to appoint a special rapporteur to examine the situation of human rights in Afghanistan, with a view to formulating proposals that could contribute to ensuring full protection of the human rights of the inhabitants of the country before, during and after the withdrawal of all foreign forces,

Recalling also its relevant resolutions as well as resolu-tions of the Commission on Human Rights and deci-sions of the Economic and Social Council,

Taking note in particular of Commission on Human Rights resolution 1989/67 of 8 March 1989, in which the Commission decided to extend the mandate of its Spe-cial Rapporteur for one year and requested him to re-port to the General Assembly at its forty-fourth session on the situation of human rights in Afghanistan,

Emphasizing the relevance of the Agreements on the Set-tlement of the Situation relating to Afghanistan, con-cluded at Geneva on 14 April 1988, which constitute an important step towards a comprehensive political solution,

Welcoming the completion, on 15 February 1989, of the withdrawal of Soviet troops from Afghanistan in accord-ance with the Agreements concluded at Geneva,

Welcoming also the co-operation that the Afghan authorities have extended in particular to the Co-ordinator for Hu-manitarian and Economic Assistance Programmes Relat-ing to Afghanistan, and to international organizations such as the specialized agencies, the Office of the United Nations High Commissioner for Refugees and the In-ternational Committee of the Red Cross,

Having examined the interim report of the Special Rap-porteur on the situation of human rights in Afghanistan, a situation which remains a matter of great concern even after the withdrawal of Soviet troops,

Noting with deep concern that a situation of armed con-flict persists in Afghanistan, leaving large numbers of victims and causing enormous suffering to the civilian population,

Noting with grave concern that the treatment of prisoners detained in connection with the conflict does not con-form to the internationally recognized principles of hu-manitarian law,

Noting with equal concern that more than five million refu-gees are living outside Afghanistan, that many Afghans are displaced within the country and that in both cases the numbers have increased,

Aware that the main reasons given by the refugees for not returning to Afghanistan pending the achievement of a comprehensive political solution are the continued fighting in some provinces, the use of very destructive arms in the conflict, and the minefields that have been laid in many parts of the country,

Noting with concern that acts of terrorism have signifi-cantly increased,

1. *Takes note with appreciation* of the interim report of the Special Rapporteur on the situation of human rights in Afghanistan and of the conclusions and recommen-dations contained therein;

2. *Welcomes* the co-operation of the Afghan authori-ties with the Special Rapporteur;

3. *Urges* all parties concerned to work for the achieve-ment of a comprehensive political solution based on the right of self-determination and for the creation of a sit-uation that will permit the return of refugees and the full enjoyment of human rights by all Afghans;

4. *Calls once again upon* all parties to the conflict, in order to alleviate the serious suffering of the Afghan people, strictly to respect human life and the principles and pro-visions of international humanitarian law and to co-operate fully and effectively with international humanitarian or-ganizations, especially the International Committee of the Red Cross, in particular by granting it unrestricted access to all parts of the country;

5. *Notes with grave concern* the continuation of the armed conflict, which threatens the life and security of innocent men, women and children;

6. *Urges* all parties to the conflict to respect the Geneva Conventions of 12 August 1949 and the Additional Protocols thereto, of 1977, to halt the use of weapons against the civilian population, to transmit to humanitarian organizations, in particular to the International Committee of the Red Cross, the names of all political prisoners and detained Afghan soldiers, and to allow the International Committee of the Red Cross to visit all prisoners in accordance with its established criteria;

7. *Also urges* all parties to the conflict to release all prisoners of war in accordance with the internationally recognized principles of humanitarian law;

8. *Expresses its concern* at reports that the living conditions of refugees, especially those of women and children, are becoming increasingly difficult because of the decline in international humanitarian assistance;

9. *Urgently appeals* to all Member States, humanitarian organizations and all parties concerned to co-operate fully, in co-ordination with the Office of the United Nations High Commissioner for Refugees, in order to facilitate the return of refugees and displaced persons in safety;

10. *Urgently appeals also* to all Member States and humanitarian organizations to promote the implementation of the projects envisaged by the Co-ordinator for Humanitarian and Economic Assistance Programmes Relating to Afghanistan and the programmes of the United Nations High Commissioner for Refugees;

11. *Urges* all parties to the conflict to treat all prisoners in their custody in accordance with the internationally recognized principles of humanitarian law and to protect them from all acts of reprisal and violence, including ill-treatment, torture and summary execution;

12. *Notes with concern* reports of the interrogation practices of the Afghan authorities, the large number of political prisoners and the conditions of prisoners awaiting trial;

13. *Calls upon* the Afghan authorities to investigate thoroughly the fate of persons who have disappeared, to apply amnesty decrees equally to foreign detainees, to reduce the period during which prisoners await trial, to treat all prisoners, especially those awaiting trial or those in custody in juvenile rehabilitation centres, in accordance with the Standard Minimum Rules for the Treatment of Prisoners and to allow the International Committee of the Red Cross to visit them regularly in accordance with its established criteria;

14. *Requests* the Afghan authorities strictly to apply to all convicted persons article 14, paragraphs 3 (*d*) and 5, of the International Covenant on Civil and Political Rights;

15. *Notes with concern* the allegations of atrocities committed against Afghan soldiers, civil servants and captured civilians;

16. *Urges* all parties concerned to extend their full co-operation to the Commission on Human Rights and its Special Rapporteur;

17. *Requests* the Secretary-General to give all necessary assistance to the Special Rapporteur;

18. *Decides* to keep under consideration, during its forty-fifth session, the situation of human rights in Afghanistan in order to examine it anew in the light of additional elements provided by the Commission on Human Rights and the Economic and Social Council.

General Assembly resolution 44/161

15 December 1989   Meeting 82   Adopted without vote

Approved by Third Committee (A/44/848) without vote, 29 November (meeting 60); 19-nation draft (A/C.3/44/L.82), orally revised; agenda item 12.
Meeting numbers. GA 44th session: 3rd Committee 48, 50-60; plenary 82.

Iran

Report of the Special Representative. On 26 January, Special Representative Reynaldo Galindo Pohl (El Salvador) submitted to the Commission a report[33] on the human rights situation in Iran. He summarized discussions held with Iranian government representatives in New York and Geneva in November 1988 and January 1989, as well as information provided by the Government and the statements made during informal hearings at Geneva on 11 January by eight witnesses of alleged human rights violations. The report also contained written information pertaining to alleged violations of the right to life and the situation of the Baha'i religious community.

It stated that the Special Representative continued receiving persistent reports about a wave of executions of political prisoners; it alleged that there were several thousand victims. A list containing more than 1,000 names of victims made available to the Representative was annexed to his report. He also noted that the Special Rapporteur on summary and arbitrary executions (see above, under "Civil and political rights") had, from July to December 1988, transmitted to the Iranian Government allegations regarding the summary or arbitrary execution of several hundred persons, and sent urgent appeals concerning some 150 persons facing an imminent danger of execution. It was alleged that many of those serving prison sentences in Iran had had their sentences changed to the death penalty, in contravention of international human rights instruments to which Iran was a party.

The Special Representative received information concerning the execution of two members of the Baha'i community. The number of Baha'i prisoners continued to decrease and stood at 101 as at January 1989, including four detained without charges; the sentences of some Baha'i prisoners had reportedly been reduced and detention conditions of some had improved. Yet many Baha'is continued to be denied jobs in education and government or their pensions, and there was new information on persons who lost their jobs on the grounds of belonging to the Baha'i community or whose property had been confiscated.

Reports also continued to be received of ill-treatment and torture; arrests made in an intimidatory manner; investigation, trial and serving of sentence effected under duress; and detention incommunicado or in solitary confinement as a method of obtaining confessions or information.

The Special Representative examined such aspects of Iran's legal system as punishment and the death penalty, irregularities concerning investigation and trial, and available remedies. He noted the view of the Iranian Government that its Constitution was Islamic in nature, but pointed out that the upcoming revision of Iran's Penal Code provided the Government with a unique opportunity to bring its legal system in line with international human rights standards. Among incompatibilities between the current system and the human rights treaties to which Iran was a party were corporal punishment; a broad application of the death penalty; denial of the right of defendants to call defence witnesses or examine prosecution witnesses, as well as of the right of a convicted person to present statements with respect to his or her trial and conviction during the review of the sentence by a higher tribunal; and absence of legal recourse under which persons condemned to death could seek pardon or commutation of the sentence.

In addition, the Representative pointed to a recent judicial directive approving the imprisonment or exile for up to two years of anyone with a criminal record, even without evidence of further criminal acts, and to reported practices of detaining family members of persons accused of political crimes, detaining prisoners after the expiration of their sentence, and making arrests without an explanation of reasons to the prisoner. According to both oral and written information, political detainees did not receive legal assistance, nor were they given the opportunity to prepare their defence or communicate with a legal counsel. Hearings concerning political defendants were usually held without a lawyer, family members, the public or the press. The report also stated that, whereas Iranian laws provided judicial remedies against abuses of power and human rights violations, there was no known case of punishment of a government official for abuse of power nor of compensation for arbitrary arrest.

The Special Representative concluded that acts still occurred in Iran that were inconsistent with international human rights instruments and justified international concern, study and monitoring. He set forth a number of recommendations which were acted on by the Commission on Human Rights (below). He pleaded with the Iranian Government, *inter alia*, to limit the use of the death penalty strictly to the most serious crimes, to exempt from that penalty those under 18 years of age and to replace punishments involving torture by those compatible with international standards. The Special Representative also suggested that a national commission on human rights be set up and that Iran consider establishing a programme of information on human rights for law enforcement personnel and taking advantage of the technical assistance provided by the UN Centre for Human Rights.

Human Rights Commission action. On 8 March, by a roll-call vote of 20 to 6, with 12 abstentions, the Commission expressed its deep concern[34] about allegations of grave human rights violations in Iran, including summary executions and cases of ill-treatment and torture, and endorsed the Special Representative's conclusion that those acts were inconsistent with human rights instruments and justified international concern, study and monitoring. It also endorsed his concern about apparent flaws in Iran's legal system, in particular frequent irregularities regarding fair trial, the large number of arrests and poor conditions of imprisonment, and urged the Iranian Government to investigate and report in detail on all allegations of human rights violations; to ensure fair trial; to ensure that the prison régime conformed to international standards and that prisoners were not subjected to unjustified or unnecessary hardships; to suppress ill-treatment and torture; and to ensure that a firm policy of compliance with international human rights instruments was adopted and enforced by the highest competent officials.

Taking note of an amnesty declared on 11 February 1989, the Commission nevertheless expressed its deep concern at the existence of political prisoners and at allegations that persons could be jailed on the basis of mere suspicion of misdoing or on account of their political opinions or political criticism. It called on Iran immediately to provide detailed information concerning the allegations brought to its attention, and urged it to respect and ensure to all individuals within its territory and under its jurisdiction the rights recognized in the 1966 International Covenant on Civil and Political Rights,[35] to which it was party. The Commission also urged the Iranian Government to extend full co-operation to the Special Representative and to permit him to visit that country; decided to extend his mandate for another year; requested him to report to the General Assembly in 1989 and to the Commission in 1990; and asked the Secretary-General to give him all necessary assistance.

ECONOMIC AND SOCIAL COUNCIL ACTION

In May, the Economic and Social Council adopted **decision 1989/148** by recorded vote.

Situation of human rights in the Islamic Republic of Iran

At its 16th plenary meeting, on 24 May 1989, the Economic and Social Council, taking note of Commission on Human Rights resolution 1989/66 of 8 March 1989, approved the decision of the Commission to extend the mandate of the Special Representative on the human rights situation in the Islamic Republic of Iran, as contained in Commission resolution 1984/54 of 14 March 1984, for a further year. The Council also approved the Commission's request to the Secretary-General to give all necessary assistance to the Special Representative.

Economic and Social Council decision 1989/148

22-8-16 (recorded vote)

Approved by Second Committee (E/1989/88) by recorded vote (23-8-15), 19 May (meeting 22); draft by Commission on Human Rights (E/1989/20); agenda item 9.

Recorded vote in Council as follows:

In favour: Bahamas, Canada, Colombia, Denmark, France, Germany, Federal Republic of, Greece, Iraq, Ireland, Italy, Japan, Jordan, Lesotho, Netherlands, New Zealand, Norway, Portugal, Rwanda, Trinidad and Tobago, United Kingdom, United States, Venezuela.

Against: Cuba, Indonesia, Iran, Libyan Arab Jamahiriya, Nicaragua, Oman, Sri Lanka, Sudan.

Abstaining: Belize, Bolivia, Brazil, Cameroon, Ghana, Guinea, Kenya, Liberia, Niger, Saudi Arabia, Somalia, Thailand, Tunisia, Yugoslavia, Zaire, Zambia.

Sub-Commission action. In a resolution[36] adopted by secret ballot on 31 August by 17 votes to 3, with 4 abstentions, the Sub-Commission expressed its deep concern about grave human rights violations in Iran related to the right to life and to freedom from torture and other cruel, inhuman or degrading treatment or punishment; the right to liberty and security of person; and the right to a fair trial and to freedom of thought, conscience, religion and expression. It urged Iran to cease executions, particularly those of political prisoners, and to co-operate fully with the Special Representative, including by facilitating his visits to prisons and other places of detention. The Secretary-General was requested to inform the Sub-Commission in 1990 of the Special Representative's report and of relevant reports by other special rapporteurs or human rights bodies, and of steps taken by the UN system to prevent human rights violations in Iran.

Interim report of the Special Representative. On 2 November, the Secretary-General transmitted to the General Assembly an interim report[37] of the Special Representative, prepared in accordance with the Commission's request. The report summarized communications with the Iranian Government, in which Iran pointed, *inter alia,* to 140 forged names and particulars of persons included in the Special Representative's list as allegedly executed between July and September 1988, and questioned the credibility of his sources. The report provided further oral information obtained by the Representative during informal hearings of 15 witnesses on 10, 12 and 17 July 1989, as well as written information transmitted by Iran and received from other sources. The Special Representative also informed the Assembly of his meeting with a representative of the Government at Geneva on 19 and 22 September.

He noted that on 6 March, Iran had submitted its comments and views, stating that 2,000 persons had thus far been granted amnesty. With re-

gard to the study of human rights in Iran, the Government asked that UN organs take into account the situation in the country, particularly the eight years of international war and the revolutionary process, under harassment and threats from terrorist and subversive groups. Iran repeated its complaint that countries subjected to the scrutiny of the Commission on Human Rights were determined selectively, for political reasons, and called for equal treatment of all countries in similar situations. In its view, the United Nations did not give appropriate consideration to groups and organizations responsible for human rights violations which acted separately from and even against the Government. Iran further criticized the text of Commission resolutions, saying that they attempted to confer the status of a religious minority on Baha'is, which prevented the Government from co-operating fully with the Special Representative. However, it expressed its readiness to improve such co-operation.

In the meantime, the Special Representative continued to receive allegations of human rights violations in Iran and to communicate them to the Government. The allegations related to the right to life, to liberty and security of person and to a fair trial, as well as to freedom from torture or ill-treatment and freedom of conscience and religion. The Representative stated that the Government, which had disputed 140 cases of execution contained on his most recent list, had yet to reply to previous lists as well as to other allegations, and pointed to continuing reports of torture and ill-treatment in Iranian prisons, distressing conditions for prisoners, and the lack of procedural guarantees relating to fair trial and the legality of detention. He noted that no measures had been taken to rectify the situation, and expressed his conviction that the treatment of prisoners continued to be left to the initiatives of guards and that investigators used methods at variance with humanitarian principles to extract confessions or information.

The report stated that harassment of Baha'is had decreased and that many had been released from prison; they were being admitted to primary and secondary schools and were permitted to use their cemeteries, and some Baha'i businesses had been reopened. On the other hand, 14 Baha'is were still in prison and 4 had been executed, their access to universities remained blocked, and their right to travel freely was still denied. Regarding the recent amnesty, the Special Representative noted that there had been allegations that some of those released had subsequently disappeared, and politically motivated executions had again been reported, coupled with a dramatic increase in the number of executions for ordinary offences, in particular drug trafficking. He also reported the public hanging of scores of men and women, carried out in various cities and in groups in implementation of a 21 January law making drug trafficking punishable by death.

The Special Representative concluded that the basic framework regarding human rights in Iran had not changed and that his recommendations to the Commission remained current and pertinent. He deemed it appropriate to renew the appeal to the Government for full co-operation with him, and maintained his conviction that acts committed in that country were incompatible with international human rights instruments binding on Iran and that the persistence of such acts justified both international concern and study and constant vigilance by the Assembly and the Commission.

Communication from Iran. On 24 November, Iran transmitted[38] to the Secretary-General its Government's invitation to the Special Representative to visit the country.

GENERAL ASSEMBLY ACTION

On 15 December, on the recommendation of the Third Committee, the General Assembly adopted **resolution 44/163** without vote.

Situation of human rights in the Islamic Republic of Iran

The General Assembly,

Guided by the principles embodied in the Charter of the United Nations, the Universal Declaration of Human Rights and the International Covenants on Human Rights,

1. *Takes note with appreciation* of the interim report of the Special Representative of the Commission on Human Rights;

2. *Takes note* of the view of the Special Representative that, in order to achieve full co-operation between the Government of the Islamic Republic of Iran and the Special Representative, there is a need to proceed to another stage in the discharge of his mandate;

3. *Welcomes* the invitation by the Islamic Republic of Iran to the Special Representative for him to visit that country;

4. *Requests* the Secretary-General to give all necessary assistance to the Special Representative;

5. *Decides* to continue its examination of the situation of human rights in the Islamic Republic of Iran during its forty-fifth session in the light of additional elements provided by the Commission on Human Rights and the Economic and Social Council.

General Assembly resolution 44/163

15 December 1989   Meeting 82   Adopted without vote

Approved by Third Committee (A/44/848) without vote, 28 November (meeting 58); draft by Chairman (A/C.3/44/L.84), based on informal consultations; agenda item 12.

Meeting numbers. GA 44th session: 3rd Committee 48, 50-58; plenary 82.

Kampuchea

On 6 March, by a roll-call vote of 35 to 7, with 1 abstention, the Commission, *inter alia*, reiter-

ated[39] its condemnation of persistent flagrant violations of human rights in Kampuchea and reaffirmed that the continuing illegal occupation of Kampuchea by foreign forces constituted the primary violation of human rights in that country. It deplored military attacks against civilians by occupying forces as a violation of human rights, and reaffirmed its call for the unconditional withdrawal of such forces to enable the Kampuchean people to exercise their inalienable human rights in their totality.

Europe and the Mediterranean

Albania

Communication from Albania. By an 8 February note verbale,[40] Albania transmitted to the Commission information concerning the socialist democracy, rights and freedoms enjoyed by its citizens. It listed the rights and freedoms guaranteed under the Albanian Constitution and examined the functioning of the legal system to ensure their observance. It dealt in particular with the protection of minorities and the freedom of conscience, stating that the Government decreed neither the protection of religion nor its suppression by administrative measures and had never allowed any administrative infringement on religious sensibilities of believers. At the same time, Albania condemned those who had committed criminal acts under the cover of religion and religious rites.

Human Rights Commission action. On 8 March, by a roll-call vote of 23 to 3, with 13 abstentions, the Commission, noting with regret Albania's failure to respond to allegations of human rights violations transmitted to it by the Commission's Special Rapporteur on religious discrimination, reminded[41] Albania of its obligation to co-operate with the Commission and called on it to provide information on its compliance with the provisions of the Universal Declaration of Human Rights[42] and to respond to the specific allegations concerning discrimination based on religion or belief. The Secretary-General was asked to invite the Albanian Government to provide the requested information and co-operation, and to report to the Commission in 1990.

Note and report of the Secretary-General. In a 22 June note and a later addendum,[43] the Secretary-General informed the Sub-Commission of his request for information from Albania concerning implementation of the Commission's March resolution and Albania's reply that, in its view, it had already complied with the request for co-operation with the Commission by submitting its note verbale in February (above).

He subsequently reported[44] to the Commission that Albania, on 27 July, had submitted to the Sub-Commission a document[45] containing information on the guarantee of freedoms and rights to all its citizens and, on 30 August, had replied to allegations of human rights violations.

Cyprus

Human Rights Commission action. At its 1989 session, the Commission had before it the Secretary-General's 2 February report[46] describing developments in Cyprus relating to human rights. On 7 March, the Commission decided[47] to postpone consideration of the question of human rights in Cyprus until 1990, on the understanding that action required by its previous resolutions on the subject would remain operative, including its request to the Secretary-General to report to the Commission.

Report of the Secretary-General. The Secretary-General subsequently reported[48] that the two sides in Cyprus had agreed on 29 June to complete an outline for an overall settlement; however, the Turkish Cypriot side subsequently expressed reservations about the process. He nevertheless believed that it should be possible for the two leaders to proceed expeditiously with their work on the outline. The Committee on Missing Persons held eight sessions between 1 December 1988 and 4 December 1989, while the UN Peacekeeping Force in Cyprus continued, under its mandate, to discharge humanitarian functions on behalf of the Greek Cypriots remaining in the northern part of the island, whose number stood at 611 at the beginning of December, as well as to make periodic visits to Turkish Cypriots living in the south. (See PART ONE, Chapter IV.)

Romania

On 9 March, by a roll-call vote of 21 to 7, with 10 abstentions, the Commission expressed its concern[49] at the allegations of serious human rights violations in Romania, as well as at the imposition of increasingly severe obstacles to the maintenance of cultural identity of Romania's national minorities, and noted that the Government's policy of rural systematization, which involved forcible resettlement and affected long-standing traditions, would, if implemented, lead to further human rights violations. It also noted with concern that Romanian nationals continued to seek protection and refuge in neighbouring countries for reasons related to serious violations of their human rights, and urged the Romanian Government to abide by its international obligations under human rights treaties.

The Commission requested its Chairman to appoint a special rapporteur to examine the human rights situation in Romania; authorized the Rapporteur to seek relevant information from Romania's Government, specialized agencies and inter-

governmental and non-governmental organizations; and requested him to report to it in 1990. Romania was urged to co-operate with the Commission and its Special Rapporteur, while the Secretary-General was asked to give him all necessary assistance.

In May, the Economic and Social Council adopted **decision 1989/154** by recorded vote.

Human rights situation in Romania

At its 16th plenary meeting, on 24 May 1989, the Economic and Social Council, taking note of Commission on Human Rights resolution 1989/75 of 9 March 1989, approved the decision of the Commission to request its Chairman to appoint a special rapporteur of the Commission with the mandate to examine the human rights situation in Romania. The Council also approved the Commission's request to the Secretary-General to provide all necessary assistance to the special rapporteur to enable him to carry out his mandate in the best possible conditions.

Economic and Social Council decision 1989/154

19-7-19 (recorded vote)

Approved by Second Committee (E/1989/88) by recorded vote (21-7-18), 19 May (meeting 22); draft by Commission on Human Rights (E/1989/20); agenda item 9.

Recorded vote in Council as follows:

> *In favour:* Canada, Colombia, Denmark, France, Germany, Federal Republic of, Greece, Ireland, Italy, Japan, Netherlands, New Zealand, Norway, Portugal, Trinidad and Tobago, United Kingdom, United States, Uruguay, Venezuela, Yugoslavia.
> *Against:* China, Cuba, Indonesia, Iran, Nicaragua, Somalia, Sri Lanka.
> *Abstaining:* Bahamas, Belize, Bolivia, Brazil, Cameroon, Ghana, Guinea, Iraq, Jordan, Kenya, Lesotho, Liberia, Niger, Oman, Rwanda, Sudan, Thailand, Zaire, Zambia.

Speaking prior to the vote, Romania stated that there were no ethnic or social problems in that country, where *de jure* and *de facto* equality existed among all inhabitants, and that the Commission's resolution and a draft decision before the Council amounted to attempts to sow discord among ethnic groups and dismember sovereign States. Accordingly, it rejected such attempts, as well as the methods of investigation and monitoring by "special rapporteurs", as incompatible with the principles of sovereignty of States and non-interference in their internal affairs, and considered those decisions null and void.

Activities of the Special Rapporteur. Special Rapporteur Joseph Voyame (Switzerland), appointed pursuant to the Commission's March resolution, reported[50] that he had, on 15 June, requested Romania to allow him to visit the country in implementation of his mandate. On 30 June, the Romanian authorities replied that they considered the Commission's resolution as well as any action to implement it null and void. The Rapporteur proceeded to collect information from available sources, including oral testimony from witnesses, and visited Hungary from 24 to 29 September. On 30 October, he transmitted to Romania a list of alleged human rights violations in that country as well as a list of requests for family reunification; updated versions were subsequently communicated to the Government on 11 December.

Later in December, however, revolutionary events in Romania brought about a new organization of power in that country, which was now headed by the Council of the National Salvation Front and a Government appointed by it, until elections in April 1990. On 23 December, the National Salvation Front announced the release of all political prisoners and the arrest of the President and his spouse, who were subsequently sentenced to death by a military court and executed on 25 December; on 29 December, the official name of the State was changed to "Romania"; and on 31 December, the Chairman of the Council of the National Salvation Front announced the abolition of the death penalty, introduction of a five-day work week and a programme to redistribute collectivized land to peasants. Measures were also adopted to repeal certain laws of the previous régime, to make arrangements for the distribution of food products and to set up emergency courts to try "terrorists".

Latin America and the Caribbean

Chile

Report of the Special Rapporteur (February). In a 17 February report[51] to the Commission on the human rights situation in Chile, Special Rapporteur Fernando Volio Jiménez (Costa Rica) described his fourth visit to that country (October 1988), during which he observed the presidential plebiscite held on 5 October. The Special Rapporteur noted that he had been afforded full co-operation by the Government and given complete freedom of action.

At the same time, he received oral testimony from witnesses complaining of torture and ill-treatment during detention, arbitrary incommunicado detention, unlawful searches, illegal expropriation of property, irregularities in trial proceedings, threats and intimidation against the security of individuals, persecution of recent returnees from exile, detention for political reasons, convictions for illegal entry into Chile despite the lifting of any administrative ban on entry, lack of judicial independence, and the absence of co-operation between law enforcement agencies and the judiciary. The Special Rapporteur also received written information alleging violations of the rights to life, physical and moral integrity, liberty, security, freedom of expression and information and freedom of movement.

A number of complaints were brought up by defence lawyers against military prosecutors, dealing with the misuse of legal definitions, use of extrajudicial confessions for conviction, unlawful coercion to obtain confessions, improper use of measures to make detention more difficult, unjustified extension of investigatory powers of the magistrate, extension of pre-trial detention and impediments to trial proceedings and to the right to a defence. During his meetings with government officials, the Rapporteur also expressed his concern at apparent cases of bogus confrontations, which seemed actually to have been arbitrary executions, and at the difficulty created by the existence of legal incommunicado detention up to 10 days under the Anti-Terrorism Act. He was informed that an amendment to the Code of Penal Procedure to that effect was pending.

The Special Rapporteur drew attention to a number of unresolved cases of gross human rights violations, terrorist activities and grave deficiencies of the military justice system, which, in his view, constituted a serious obstacle to the enjoyment of human rights in Chile. Despite those negative developments, he nevertheless acknowledged that important progress had been made with regard to respect for human rights, and noted that the success of the 1988 plebiscite and the scheduling of presidential and parliamentary elections for the end of 1989 gave grounds for hope for further improvements. In that regard, he recommended that the National Congress Organization Act, governing the establishment of democratic institutions, be concluded without delay, and that maximum attention be devoted to outstanding cases of human rights violations, and assistance be provided by police authorities to judicial investigators. He said that efforts should be intensified to ensure respect for human dignity of detainees; eliminate torture, unlawful coercion and other ill-treatment; amend provisions for incommunicado detention and/or repeal the Anti-Terrorism Act; establish a judicial police force; and review the legislation concerning indigenous populations, particularly the division of land, to avert expulsions and observe proper respect for their culture.

Other recommendations dealt with the investigation of specific cases such as missing detainees and judicial proceedings brought against 29 journalists, as well as with the need for a drastic change in the conduct of those responsible for military justice. The Special Rapporteur concluded that the Government and people of Chile should make every effort to ensure the establishment of democratic institutions in their country, scheduled for March 1990.

Human Rights Commission action. On 8 March, the Commission took note[52] of the Chilean Government's decision to respect the results of the 1988 referendum and of its partial response to the demands of various political and social elements in the country, and urged it to work for the re-establishment of a representative and pluralistic democracy based on the expression of popular sovereignty and on the full enjoyment of human rights. At the same time, the Commission expressed dismay at continued acts of extreme violence in Chile and concern at the persistence of serious human rights violations, and urged the Government to put an end to those situations and to continue adopting measures for the restoration of the rule of law, as well as to authorize publication of the 1966 International Covenants on Civil and Political Rights[35] and on Economic, Social and Cultural Rights.[53] The Government was particularly urged to promote reforms of the institutional framework so as to bring it into line with relevant international standards, to allow investigation of all complaints of human rights violations with a view to the trial and punishment of those responsible, to ensure the independence of the judiciary and the effectiveness of legal remedies, and to restore the full range of economic, social and cultural rights.

The Commission decided to extend the Special Rapporteur's mandate for one more year and to request him to report to the Assembly in 1989 and to the Commission in 1990, and recommended that the Economic and Social Council ensure provision of the necessary resources and staff.

On 24 May, the Council, by **decision 1989/147**, approved extension of the Special Rapporteur's mandate and the Commission's recommendation regarding appropriate financial and staff arrangements.

Note of the Secretary-General. In response to a 1988 Sub-Commission request,[54] the Secretary-General submitted a 24 July note[55] on the results of the Special Rapporteur's investigations as well as on General Assembly and Commission deliberations and resolutions. He noted in particular that the Government of Chile had informed him of its decision no longer to co-operate with *ad hoc* procedures for consideration of the human rights situation in that country, stating that its previous co-operation with the Rapporteur was not fully appreciated by UN human rights bodies, which continued to treat Chile in a discriminatory, selective and unfair manner, in contrast with the actual situation in the country. At the same time, the Government affirmed that it would continue to take part in universal and regular UN procedures to ensure fuller protection of human rights.

Report of the Special Rapporteur (October). On 17 October, the Secretary-General transmitted[56] to the General Assembly a report prepared by the Special Rapporteur in accordance with the Commission's March request.

The Special Rapporteur noted Chile's decision not to co-operate with the Commission's *ad hoc* monitoring procedures and stated that he had received no reply from the Chilean Government to his September request to visit the country. He summarized replies by the Government to previous complaints of human rights violations, communicated to him during his fourth visit, as well as a March 1989 government report on terrorist acts that had occurred in the country since October 1988. The Special Rapporteur also provided information on complaints of new human rights violations, alleged to have occurred between October 1988 and June 1989, concerning the rights to life, physical and moral integrity, liberty, security, and a fair trial and procedural guarantees. Another complaint involved allegations of ill-treatment, torture, unlawful detention and sexual abuse of minors, which had prompted government investigation.

The Rapporteur stated that the human rights situation in Chile had improved in the past six months, as manifested by constitutional reforms approved by Chileans on 30 July 1989 and aimed at ending the special powers of the President, ensuring respect for political pluralism and strengthening the rule of law and a representative political system. The movement towards representative democracy was to culminate in general elections in December 1989 and inauguration of the National Congress in March 1990. However, the democratic process could be jeopardized by certain situations which continued to have an adverse effect on the protection of basic freedoms in Chile, such as the persistence of torture, violations of the rights to life and to physical and moral integrity, irregularities concerning fair trial and procedural guarantees, and broad powers of military justice. Among other causes for concern were the lack of progress in the investigation of both new and long-standing cases of human rights violations, including disappearance; continuing judicial banishments of two trade union leaders; inadequate conditions of imprisonment and trial proceedings of those detained for offences against the security of State; the unsatisfactory situation of the indigenous population; and continuing terrorist acts. Government replies to previous complaints of human rights violations did not cover all the cases reported and were in some cases incomplete.

The Special Rapporteur reiterated the recommendations contained in his February report, emphasizing that the practice of torture must end immediately; investigations of past and recent violations, including forced disappearances, should be completed; and judicial banishments of trade union leaders should be repealed. He also recommended that the Government take measures to strengthen the civil justice system, give attention to activities of groups apparently close to the Government which threatened or violated freedoms, and make the situation of indigenous peoples consistent with the enjoyment of human rights.

GENERAL ASSEMBLY ACTION

On 15 December, on the recommendation of the Third Committee, the General Assembly adopted **resolution 44/166** by recorded vote.

Situation of human rights in Chile

The General Assembly,

Guided by the purposes and principles of the Charter of the United Nations and bearing in mind the Universal Declaration of Human Rights, the International Covenant on Economic, Social and Cultural Rights, and the International Covenant on Civil and Political Rights,

Aware of its responsibility to promote and encourage respect for human rights and fundamental freedoms, and determined to remain vigilant with regard to violations of human rights wherever they occur,

Reiterating that the Government of Chile has the obligation to respect and protect human rights in accordance with the international instruments to which Chile is a party,

Bearing in mind that the concern of the international community about the situation of human rights in Chile has been expressed by the General Assembly in a number of resolutions, particularly resolution 33/173 of 20 December 1978, on disappeared persons, and resolution 43/158 of 8 December 1988,

Bearing in mind the pertinent resolutions of the Commission on Human Rights, particularly resolution 1989/62 of 8 March 1989, in which the Commission decided, *inter alia*, to extend the mandate of the Special Rapporteur for one year, to consider the question as a matter of high priority in view of the persistence of serious violations of human rights in Chile and to determine how the item was to be dealt with on the agenda of its forty-sixth session in the light of developments in the situation,

Regretting the decision of the Government of Chile to discontinue its co-operation with the Special Rapporteur,

Regretting also that the process of restoration of civil and political rights in Chile does not yet include the amendment of numerous laws that constitute an institutional and legal framework that makes violations of human rights possible,

1. *Takes note with appreciation* of the report of the Special Rapporteur submitted in accordance with Commission on Human Rights resolution 1989/62;

2. *Congratulates* the Chilean people on their peaceful progress towards the re-establishment of a representative and pluralist democracy based on respect for human rights and fundamental freedoms, and for reaffirming their will to achieve peace and national reconciliation through the restoration of justice;

3. *Expresses its satisfaction* at the progress of the Chilean electoral process which it considers an important step towards the rapid return of democracy in that country;

4. *Welcomes*, as a positive development, the decision by the Government of Chile to heed the demands of democratic sectors of the country and of the interna-

tional community with regard to reforming certain aspects of the institutional and legal framework harmful to civil and political rights;

5. *Takes note with satisfaction* of the decision by the Government of Chile to incorporate the International Covenant on Civil and Political Rights and the International Covenant on Economic, Social and Cultural Rights into domestic law;

6. *Welcomes* the improvement of the situation of human rights in Chile noted by the Special Rapporteur during the six months covered by his report;

7. *Regrets*, nevertheless, the decision of the Government of Chile to discontinue its co-operation with the Special Rapporteur in the fulfilment of his mandate, and urges it to resume such co-operation in compliance with the resolutions of the General Assembly and the Commission on Human Rights;

8. *Urges* the Government of Chile to continue to make progress regarding respect for human rights and fundamental freedoms for all the Chilean people, including the indigenous peoples, especially by adapting the legal system to the relevant principles and provisions and refraining from making any more changes in national institutions without duly consulting the people, and to be guided by those principles and provisions in the exercise of its powers in the same way as the judiciary;

9. *Also urges* the Government of Chile for that purpose to ensure the independence of the judiciary and the effectiveness of judicial remedies, by respecting procedural guarantees, equality before the law and the right to defence in all cases;

10. *Expresses its concern* at acts of violence of any origin that continue to occur in Chile, thereby aggravating the climate of insecurity and rendering the return to democracy more difficult;

11. *Again expresses its serious concern* at the persistence of violations of human rights and fundamental freedoms in Chile involving, *inter alia*, cases of death, torture and ill-treatment, and at the Colonia Dignidad case, as described by the Special Rapporteur in his report;

12. *Urges* the Government of Chile to investigate all cases of serious violations of human rights that occurred in the past, bearing in mind the reports of special rapporteurs;

13. *Invites* the Commission on Human Rights to evaluate at its forty-sixth session the situation of human rights in Chile, bearing in mind the reports presented by special rapporteurs, to consider the mandate of the Special Rapporteur and also how the item is to be dealt with on the agenda in the light of developments in the situation, and to report to the General Assembly at its forty-fifth session.

General Assembly resolution 44/166

15 December 1989   Meeting 82   84-2-60 (recorded vote)

Approved by Third Committee (A/44/848) by recorded vote (80-2-50), 29 November (meeting 61); 14-nation draft (A/C.3/44/L.87), orally revised; agenda item 12.

Meeting numbers. GA 44th session: 3rd Committee 48, 50-61; plenary 82.

Recorded vote in Assembly as follows:

In favour: Afghanistan, Albania, Algeria, Angola, Australia, Austria, Barbados, Belgium, Bolivia, Botswana, Bulgaria, Burkina Faso, Burundi, Byelorussian SSR, Canada, Cape Verde, Congo, Costa Rica, Cuba, Cyprus, Czechoslovakia, Democratic Yemen, Denmark, Ecuador, Ethiopia, Finland, France, German Democratic Republic, Germany, Federal Republic of, Ghana, Greece, Guatemala, Guinea, Guinea-Bissau, Guyana, Hungary, Iceland, Ireland, Italy, Jamaica, Kenya, Kuwait, Lao People's Democratic

Republic, Liberia, Luxembourg, Madagascar, Mali, Malta, Mauritania, Mexico, Mongolia, Mozambique, Netherlands, New Zealand, Nicaragua, Norway, Papua New Guinea, Poland, Portugal, Rwanda, Saint Kitts and Nevis, Saint Lucia, Samoa, Seychelles, Solomon Islands, Spain, Sri Lanka, Swaziland, Sweden, Togo, Trinidad and Tobago, Tunisia, Uganda, Ukrainian SSR, USSR, United Arab Emirates,* United Kingdom, United Republic of Tanzania, Vanuatu, Venezuela, Viet Nam, Yugoslavia, Zambia, Zimbabwe.

Against: Chile, Morocco.

Abstaining: Antigua and Barbuda, Argentina, Bahamas, Bahrain, Bangladesh, Bhutan, Brazil, Brunei Darussalam, Cameroon, Central African Republic, Chad, China, Colombia, Côte d'Ivoire, Democratic Kampuchea, Djibouti, Dominica, Egypt, El Salvador, Fiji, Gambia, Grenada, Haiti, Honduras, India, Indonesia, Iraq, Israel, Japan, Jordan, Lebanon, Lesotho, Malaysia, Maldives, Mauritius, Myanmar, Nepal, Niger, Nigeria, Oman, Pakistan, Panama, Paraguay, Peru, Philippines, Qatar, Saint Vincent and the Grenadines, Saudi Arabia, Senegal, Sierra Leone, Singapore, Somalia, Sudan, Suriname, Thailand, Turkey, United States, Uruguay, Yemen, Zaire.

*Later advised the Secretariat it had intended to abstain.

El Salvador

Report of the Special Representative (February). In a 2 February report[57] to the Commission on the human rights situation in El Salvador, covering mainly the events of 1988, Special Representative José Antonio Pastor Ridruejo (Spain) noted that the situation of economic, social and cultural rights continued to deteriorate as a result of the continuing armed conflict between the government troops and guerrilla forces of the Frente Farabundo Martí para la Liberación Nacional (FMLN), the absence of conditions safeguarding private investment, FMLN attacks on the economic infrastructure, alleged corruption in the administration of public funds, the world economic crisis and the prolonged drought. He drew particular attention to the difficult living conditions of some communities in resettled areas, which he had been able to observe during his October 1988 visit to the country. The Special Representative also noted complaints alleging violations of labour rights, including arrests, and illtreatment, including summary execution and disappearance of trade union leaders, attacks on their offices and threats against them. He emphasized that FMLN's systematic attacks on the infrastructure also seriously undermined the enjoyment of economic, social and cultural rights, and provided a list of damage caused by recent violent acts.

As for civil and political rights, an alarming number of politically motivated summary executions, including mass executions, had been carried out by members of the State apparatus, particularly the armed forces, reversing the recent downward trend in such crimes. Many summary executions and other serious human rights violations were attributed to the so-called "death squads", allegedly linked to the army or security forces, while the guerrilla organizations persisted in the practice of *adjusticiamientos* of alleged collaborators with the armed forces, which was equivalent to summary execution, and revived the practice of indiscriminate urban terrorism. Cases of politically motivated disappearances also had been reported, as well as guerrilla abductions of individuals, in-

cluding young people and very young children. The Special Representative continued to report illtreatment of political detainees during interrogation, although he did not believe that practice to be widespread and to represent a government policy. At the same time, activities of the criminal justice system to investigate serious human rights violations and punish those responsible remained highly unsatisfactory, which, combined with the promulgation and application of the Amnesty Act of October 1987, reinforced a climate of impunity.

The Special Representative provided information on civilian victims of indiscriminate attacks by both the army and guerrillas, stating that the guerrilla organizations continued to cause more deaths and injuries than the army as a result of contact mines. He also reported problems with evacuation from the country of wounded guerrilla fighters in need of humanitarian treatment. Acknowledging efforts to strengthen respect for human rights in El Salvador, including activities of the Salvadorian Human Rights Commission, the Special Representative expressed his belief that the Government continued to be committed to a policy of human rights observance, although its ability to exert efficient control over all State agencies was more limited than in previous years.

He appealed to El Salvador's political powers, agencies and forces to end completely attempts on the life and physical integrity of individuals, and recommended that the Government and FMLN create conditions for an open dialogue conducive to an early peaceful settlement of the conflict. The Special Representative reiterated his previous recommendations to the country's constitutional authorities, particularly adoption of measures to ensure efficient control of all State agencies, dismissal from service of those responsible for human rights violations, investigation of such violations as early as possible and punishment of offenders, urgent attention to health and food needs of peasant populations resettled in combat zones, and the use of the advisory services offered by the UN Centre for Human Rights (see above, under "Advancement of human rights"). He further recommended that FMLN and guerrilla organizations refrain from summary executions and indiscriminate urban terrorist acts, planting of contact mines in a manner incompatible with international humanitarian law, attacks on the country's economic infrastructure and prohibition of road traffic.

Human Rights Commission action. On 8 March, the Commission emphasized[58] the significance of the Special Representative's observation that the Government of El Salvador remained committed to a policy of respect for human rights, and expressed its confidence that the fulfilment of commitments under the agreement on procedures for the establishment of a firm and lasting peace in Central America (see PART TWO, Chapter II) would lead to an improvement in the human rights situation in that country. However, the Commission expressed its deep concern at the increased number of politically motivated human rights violations in El Salvador, at continuing frequent breaches of international humanitarian law and at the unsatisfactory capacity of the judicial system to determine those responsible for human rights violations, and urged the authorities to implement reforms and measures for ensuring the efficiency of the system. It requested parties to the conflict in El Salvador to end attempts on the life and physical integrity of individuals as well as attacks on the economic infrastructure and other action constituting human rights violations; to continue applying agreements for the evacuation of those wounded or maimed in combat for medical attention; and to co-operate with humanitarian organizations concerned with alleviating the suffering of civilians.

The Commission also encouraged the parties to make all possible efforts to arrive at an early peaceful solution to the conflict, and reiterated its appeal to all States to refrain from intervening in the internal situation in El Salvador and to encourage dialogue until a just and lasting peace was achieved. Noting with satisfaction mass returns of refugees to resettle in rural areas, it urged the Salvadorian authorities to ensure assistance to returnees in meeting their basic health and food needs. The Commission repeated its request to the UN bodies and organizations to provide necessary advice and technical assistance to El Salvador in the human rights and legal fields upon its request, and decided to extend the Special Representative's mandate for another year and requested him to report to the Assembly in 1989 and to the Commission in 1990.

On 24 May, the Economic and Social Council, by **decision 1989/150**, approved extension of the Special Representative's mandate.

Note of the Secretary-General. In response to a 1988 Sub-Commission request,[59] the Secretary-General submitted on 15 June 1989 a note[60] on the results of the Special Representative's investigations as well as on General Assembly and Commission deliberations and resolutions.

Sub-Commission action. In a resolution[61] adopted by secret ballot on 31 August by 12 votes to 7, with 5 abstentions, the Sub-Commission expressed its deep concern at the continuing increase in the number of human rights violations in El Salvador and at the persistent failure to observe the fundamental norms of humanitarian law which hold that persons not participating directly in combat preserve their civilian character and must not be subjected to military attacks or prevented from receiving medical, food and material assistance.

It reminded the Government of its obligation to respect and give protection to the war-wounded and disabled, not to obstruct their evacuation by ICRC and not to punish health personnel for their medical activities. The Government was strongly urged to take measures to bring to trial those responsible for the murder of the Archbishop of San Salvador and to ensure the independence and effectiveness of the judicial system, compatibility of the Penal Code with the Universal Declaration of Human Rights[42] and respect for human rights by all military, paramilitary and police forces.

The Sub-Commission expressed the hope that parties to the conflict in El Salvador could develop a negotiation process to achieve a comprehensive political settlement and guarantee the full exercise of economic, political and social rights in the country. It repeated its request to the Special Rapporteur on human rights and disability to undertake all possible measures for the prompt and regular evacuation of the war-wounded and disabled and to report in 1990.

Report of the Special Representative (October). On 26 October, the Secretary-General transmitted[62] to the Assembly a report on the human rights situation in El Salvador, prepared by the Special Representative in accordance with the Commission's request.

The Special Representative visited El Salvador from 8 to 15 October, and reported that the armed conflict between government and guerrilla forces continued but did not prevent presidential elections from taking place on 19 March. Despite attempts by FMLN to disrupt the process, Alfredo Cristiani was elected and was inaugurated President of the Republic on 1 June. His subsequent efforts to resume dialogue with the country's various political parties culminated in talks held in September and October. At the same time, the economic situation continued to be adversely affected by the persistent climate of violence, including FMLN's systematic attacks on the infrastructure and the increasing government action against trade unions as well as peasant and other organizations, some of which the Government claimed answered to FMLN.

The Special Representative also received information regarding many cases of summary execution as well as arrests, abductions and disappearances attributed to both government forces and guerrilla organizations. There had been an increase in the number of political arrests during the first nine months of 1989, while the number of politically motivated summary executions carried out by the State apparatus was comparable to 1988. There were no reports of mass executions, however, and investigations and judicial proceedings had been instituted in some cases of summary executions.

The number of people detained for political offences had risen to 250 by 14 October 1989, much higher than the 45 political prisoners reported in October 1988, and the Representative believed that there were also more cases of torture during interrogation than in the previous year. As for the criminal justice system, the Special Representative noted that the Criminal Investigation Commission had closed investigation of 49 out of the 87 cases assigned to it between 1985 and 1989, that proceedings had been brought against some members of the armed forces accused of summary executions and that in September an army officer was sentenced for the crime of homicide. However, there had been no convictions or significant progress in the investigations of some other cases of human rights violations. The Representative concluded that the functioning of the criminal justice system remained highly unsatisfactory. He noted, however, new proposals for judicial reform by the Government and measures to improve the administration of justice, including the establishment of a National Council of the Judiciary and new criminal courts and a draft bill amending the Criminal Code.

He provided information regarding attacks by the armed forces on civilian communities and the number of civilian deaths as a result of military actions by the army and by guerrillas as well as explosion of contact mines. The Special Representative noted that civilian casualties caused by the army were not widespread and fewer than from summary executions, but stated that the army had killed medical and health personnel and patients when dismantling FMLN health facilities. No casualties from contact mines had been reported since July.

Among other important developments were a truce between parties to the conflict, agreed to on 5 March to facilitate child immunization in El Salvador; a unilateral cease-fire declared by FMLN in September; elaboration of plans for the repatriation of Salvadorian refugees in Honduras; and a special amnesty adopted on 6 October to enable the war-wounded and disabled to leave the country for medical treatment. In addition, 644 talks on human rights and international humanitarian law were reported to have been given to 32,200 members of the armed forces, which planned to establish an office for civilian affairs and human rights, and the Salvadorian Human Rights Commission continued its activities.

The Special Representative reiterated his appeal for a complete end to attempts on the life, physical integrity and dignity of individuals, and recommended that FMLN and guerrilla organizations refrain from indiscriminate urban operations and from planting contact mines, and that El Salvador's constitutional authorities ensure conformity of police interrogation of detainees to international human rights standards and to the country's 1983 Constitution and persevere with the judicial, agrarian and other structural reforms.

In November, FMLN launched a heavy general offensive throughout the country, purportedly to put pressure on the armed forces to stop opposing the negotiations; as a result, a state of emergency was declared in accordance with the Constitution, and a curfew was proclaimed. On 8 December, the Legislative Assembly extended the state of emergency for another month.

GENERAL ASSEMBLY ACTION

On 15 December, on the recommendation of the Third Committee, the General Assembly adopted **resolution 44/165** without vote.

Situation of human rights and fundamental freedoms in El Salvador

The General Assembly,

Guided by the principles of the Charter of the United Nations, the Universal Declaration of Human Rights, the International Covenant on Civil and Political Rights, the International Covenant on Economic, Social and Cultural Rights, and the humanitarian rules laid down in the Geneva Conventions of 12 August 1949 and Additional Protocol II thereto, of 1977,

Deeply alarmed that, despite the encouraging signs offered by the meetings held by the Government of El Salvador and the Frente Farabundo Martí para la Liberación Nacional, the aggravation of the conflict and the resurgence of violence have seriously affected the civilian population,

Reaffirming that it is the duty of the Governments of all Member States to promote and protect human rights and fundamental freedoms and to fulfil the obligations that they have assumed under the relevant international instruments,

Recalling that, since 1980, it has been expressing its deep concern about the situation of human rights in El Salvador, as indicated in its resolution 43/145 of 8 December 1988,

Bearing in mind Commission on Human Rights resolution 32(XXXVII) of 11 March 1981, in which the Commission decided to appoint a special representative on the situation of human rights in El Salvador, and subsequent resolutions, and taking note of Commission resolution 1989/68 of 8 March 1989, in which it decided to extend the mandate of the Special Representative for another year and requested him to report to the General Assembly at its forty-fourth session and to the Commission at its forty-sixth session,

Considering that an armed conflict of a non-international character continues in El Salvador, in which the parties involved are under an obligation to apply the minimum standards of protection of human rights and humanitarian treatment provided for in article 3 common to the Geneva Conventions of 1949 and in Additional Protocol II thereto, of 1977,

Deeply concerned that, as the Special Representative has indicated in his report on the situation of human rights in El Salvador, the number of politically motivated serious violations of human rights continues to increase and, in particular, that there has been a resurgence of torture and an increase in arrests and that summary executions, disappearances, abductions, attacks on the economic infrastructure and violations of the humanitarian rules of war have remained at disturbing levels,

Concerned that many sources continue to attribute summary executions and other serious violations of human rights to the so-called "death squads",

Deeply disturbed by the collective assassination in cold blood, on 16 November 1989, of the Rector, five professors and two members of the service staff of the Central American University,

Expressing its concern that as a consequence of the current situation, acts of intimidation and harassment have been carried out against the church hierarchy, political and trade union leaders, members of humanitarian organizations belonging to various churches and the headquarters of political parties and trade unions, as well as against relatives of members of the armed forces and against civil servants and members of their families,

Considering that there has been no progress during 1989 in the judicial case of the assassination of Monsignor Romero, which took place in 1980, and that it is a matter of urgency that those responsible for many other recent violations of human rights, including the assassination of the Minister for the Presidency and the fatal collective attacks on a trade union federation, should be identified and punished,

Convinced that the strict fulfilment of the commitments assumed by the Government of El Salvador under the agreement on "Procedures for the establishment of a firm and lasting peace in Central America" concluded at the Esquipulas II summit meeting and the joint declarations of the Central American Presidents signed in Costa Rica, El Salvador and Honduras will contribute to the promotion, respect and realization of human rights and fundamental freedoms in El Salvador,

Recognizing the importance of the fact that, in the agreements adopted at Tela, Honduras, the five Central American Presidents expressed their firm belief in the necessity of an immediate and effective end to hostilities in El Salvador and therefore strongly urged the Frente Farabundo Martí para la Liberación Nacional to carry out a constructive dialogue for the purpose of achieving a just and lasting peace and, equally strongly, urged the Government of El Salvador to arrange, with full guarantees and in the spirit of the agreement concluded at the Esquipulas II summit meeting, the integration of members of the Frente Farabundo Martí para la Liberación Nacional into peaceful and institutional life,

Considering it necessary and urgent to return to the agreements of 15 September and 18 October 1989 signed at Mexico City and at San José, respectively, by the Government of El Salvador and the Frente Farabundo Martí para la Liberación Nacional by which, *inter alia*, they undertook to maintain a process of ongoing dialogue not permitting unilateral withdrawal, in order that they might, in an effort to arrive at a negotiated understanding, manage to end the armed conflict by political means as soon as possible, promote the democratization of the country and reunify Salvadorian society and agreed on the need to create international verification mechanisms appropriate to the characteristics and realities of El Salvador to monitor the implementation of the agreements reached by them,

Considering that, under Additional Protocol II to the Geneva Conventions, the war-wounded and war-injured must be respected and protected, their evacuation by the International Committee of the Red Cross so that they may receive the medical care that they need must not be impeded and no one may be punished for carrying out medical activities compatible with medical ethics, regardless of the circumstances and the beneficiaries of such activities,

Taking note of the holding of the summit at San Isidro Coronado, Costa Rica, from 10 to 12 December 1989,

Aware that a negotiated political solution of the Salvadorian conflict can be cut short if external forces do not support the resumption of the dialogue but instead seek in different ways to spur the intensification or prolongation of the war, with ensuing grave effects on the situation of human rights and the possibilities of economic recovery in El Salvador,

1. *Commends* the Special Representative for his report on the situation of human rights in El Salvador, endorses the recommendations contained therein and requests him to update the report in the light of the serious events taking place in that country;

2. *Expresses its deepest dismay* at the aggravation of the conflict, the resurgence of violence, the bombings and the indiscriminate use of high-powered heavy weapons in densely populated areas, resulting in numerous civilian casualties and substantial material damage;

3. *Expresses its deep concern* about the systematic attacks on the country's economic infrastructure, which seriously undermine the present and future enjoyment by the Salvadorian people of important economic, social and cultural rights;

4. *Urgently appeals* to the Government of El Salvador and the Frente Farabundo Martí para la Liberación Nacional to put an immediate end to the armed conflict and to work for a resumption of the currently suspended dialogue in order to reach agreements that would lead to the definitive cessation of all hostilities within an agreed time-frame;

5. *Requests* the parties to the conflict to guarantee respect for the international standards applicable to an armed conflict of a non-international character, in particular the protection of the civilian population and the war-wounded, to make possible the immediate evacuation of the war-wounded and war-injured, whether civilians or combatants, in order that they may receive the medical care that they need and, furthermore, to co-operate with humanitarian organizations working to alleviate the suffering of the civilian population in any part of the country in which such organizations are operating, and requests that medical and health personnel shall under no circumstances be penalized for carrying out their activities;

6. *Supports fully* the expressed readiness of the Secretary-General to help bring about, as the first stage of a political solution, an immediate agreement on the cessation of the armed conflict, and his decision taken last September to accept the invitation from the Government of El Salvador and the Frente Farabundo Martí para la Liberación Nacional for him or his representatives to participate in their process of dialogue and negotiation, since all this forms part of the mission of good offices that he is performing to assist the Central American Governments in their efforts to achieve the

objectives set forth in the agreement concluded at the Esquipulas II summit meeting;

7. *Expresses its firm support* for the efforts of the Secretary-General of the Organization of American States to bring about a resumption of the political dialogue in El Salvador;

8. *Urgently appeals* to the parties to the conflict to respect and guarantee the security of the staff and official premises of international agencies;

9. *Condemns* the brutal assassination of the Rector and seven other members of the Central American University and hopes that the Government of El Salvador will fulfil its pledge to carry out an immediate investigation and to punish those responsible for such an abominable crime;

10. *Expresses its deep concern* about the persistence of and increase in politically motivated serious violations of human rights, such as summary executions, enforced disappearances, torture and abductions;

11. *Also expresses its deep concern* about the persistence of and increase in the alleged activities of the so-called "death squads", which are operating with impunity in El Salvador;

12. *Renews its appeal* to all States to refrain from intervening in the internal situation of El Salvador and, instead of seeking in different ways to spur the prolongation and intensification of the armed conflict, to stimulate dialogue until a firm and lasting peace is attained;

13. *Expresses its profound concern* at the fact that the capacity of the Salvadorian judicial system continues to be extremely unsatisfactory, despite the efforts made by the Government to determine the responsibility of the instigators of some violations of human rights, and consequently urges the competent authorities to accelerate the adoption of the measures necessary for ensuring the effectiveness of the system and its compatibility with the commitments made in the field of human rights;

14. *Renews its appeal* to the competent organs and organizations of the United Nations system that, on the basis of Commission on Human Rights resolution 1989/68 and General Assembly resolution 43/145, they provide the advice and assistance that the Government of El Salvador may request in order to enhance the promotion and protection of human rights and fundamental freedoms;

15. *Requests* the Commission on Human Rights at its forty-sixth session to consider the situation of human rights in El Salvador and the mandate of its Special Representative, taking into account the evolution of the situation of human rights in that country and the developments linked to the fulfilment of all the agreements signed by the Central American Presidents within the framework of the regional peace process and the agreements concluded by the Government of El Salvador and the Frente Farabundo Martí para la Liberación Nacional at Mexico City and San José;

16. *Urges*, in accordance with the recommendations of the Special Representative, the Government of El Salvador and all the country's political powers, agencies and forces, including the Frente Farabundo Martí para la Liberación Nacional, to adopt immediate measures to put an end to attacks on the life, integrity and dignity of persons outside, during and as a result of combat situations;

17. *Reiterates its call* to the Government of El Salvador and the Frente Farabundo Martí para la Liberación Na-

cional to continue co-operating with the Special Representative of the Commission on Human Rights;

18. *Decides* to keep under consideration, during its forty-fifth session, the situation of human rights and fundamental freedoms in El Salvador in order to re-examine this situation in the light of the information provided by the Commission on Human Rights and the Economic and Social Council.

General Assembly resolution 44/165

15 December 1989   Meeting 82   Adopted without vote

Approved by Third Committee (A/44/848) by recorded vote (96-1-34), 29 November (meeting 61); 17-nation draft (A/C.3/44/L.86/Rev.1), orally revised; revised in plenary by Mexico (A/44/L.61); agenda item 12.
Meeting numbers. GA 44th session: 3rd Committee 48, 50-61; plenary 82.

Middle East

Lebanon

Human Rights Commission action. On 8 March, by a roll-call vote of 30 to 1, with 12 abstentions, the Commission strongly condemned[63] Israel for its continued violations of human rights in southern Lebanon, manifested by forced occupation of parts of that territory, bombardment of civilian populations, their arrest and detention, destruction of their property and their expulsion from the occupied area, as well as other arbitrary practices. It called on Israel to end such practices immediately, to liberate the detained Lebanese, to return those who were expelled to their homes, to stop expelling Palestinians arbitrarily to southern Lebanon, and to implement Security Council resolutions requiring Israel's immediate, total and unconditional withdrawal from all Lebanese territory and respect for Lebanon's sovereignty, independence and territorial integrity.

The Commission also called on Governments assisting Israel to exert pressure to end its aggressive and expansionist policy in southern Lebanon. The Secretary-General was requested to bring the Commission's resolution to the attention of Israel and to invite it to provide information on its implementation, and to report to the General Assembly in 1989 and to the Commission in 1990 on the results of his efforts.

Sub-Commission action. In a resolution[64] adopted by secret ballot on 31 August by 18 votes to 2, with 3 abstentions, the Sub-Commission expressed grave concern at the escalating violence in Lebanon and extensive loss of life and called on all parties in that country to initiate confidence-building measures towards restoring peaceful democratic processes. Considering that restoration of confidence was possible only through restoration of Lebanon's sovereignty and territorial integrity, it called for implementation of the relevant Security Council resolutions. The Sub-Commission underlined that humanitarian aid should reach all the civilian population in Lebanon without discrimination, and that it must not be used selectively for political purposes. The Sub-Commission further recommended that the Commission consider in 1990 the human rights situation in Lebanon and the role of external Powers in aggravating that situation.

On 1 September, the Sub-Commission called[65] on all parties in Lebanon to release immediately and unconditionally all their detainees and hostages detained for political, religious, ethnic or other reasons inconsistent with human rights norms, and considered that a lasting solution to the tragedy of hostages in Lebanon should be sought primarily by helping that country to recover its sovereignty and legal authority and to re-establish the rule of law in its territory.

Report of the Secretary-General. In accordance with the Commission's request (above), the Secretary-General reported[66] to the Assembly in October that he had asked Israel in April for information on the implementation of the Commission's resolution; as at 6 October, he had received no reply.

Territories occupied by Israel

In 1989, the question of human rights violations in the territories occupied by Israel as a result of the 1967 hostilities in the Middle East was again considered by the Commission. Political and other aspects were considered by the General Assembly, its Special Committee to Investigate Israeli Practices Affecting the Human Rights of the Population of the Occupied Territories (Special Committee on Israeli practices), and other bodies (see PART TWO, Chapter IV).

Reports of the Secretary-General. As requested by the Commission in 1988,[67] the Secretary-General reported[68] to it on 24 January 1989 that he had brought the Commission's 1988 resolutions on human rights violations in the Israeli-occupied territories to the attention of Governments as well as General Assembly and Security Council members, the Special Committee on Israeli practices and the Committee on the Exercise of the Inalienable Rights of the Palestinian People; they had also been transmitted to the specialized agencies, the United Nations Relief and Works Agency for Palestine Refugees in the Near East, the Council of Europe, the Organization of African Unity, the Organization of American States and the League of Arab States, and had been brought to the attention of the ICRC and 24 other NGOs. Information on human rights in the Israeli-occupied territories, including relevant UN resolutions, was disseminated through UN press releases, publications, media information kits, audio-visual services, UN radio and television programmes as well as arrangements with television networks, fact-finding missions for media representatives, journalists' encounters on the question of Palestine, and special activities held in observance of relevant international days and weeks. The UN Department of Public Information published a booklet on the rights of Palestinians in Arabic, English, French and Spanish and began revising its booklet on the work of the Special Committee on Israeli practices. It also established a project manager on the question of Palestine to co-ordinate public information activities.

Also in accordance with the 1988 Commission request,[67] the Secretary-General submitted[69] on 21 January a list of all UN reports issued since 11 March 1988 on the situation of the population of the occupied Arab territories.

Human Rights Commission action. On 17 February, by a roll-call vote of 32 to 8, with 2 abstentions, the Commission affirmed[70] that occupation itself was a gross violation of human rights, that Israel's violations of the 1949 Geneva Convention relative to the Protection of Civilian Persons in Time of War (fourth Geneva Convention) constituted war crimes under international law, and that practices of the Israeli occupation authorities amounted to serious violations of the principles of international law, human rights and fundamental freedoms. It condemned Israel for the gross violation of international conventions and called on it to withdraw from the Palestinian territories occupied by force and to desist from practices such as the killing of Palestinians, breaking of bones, imposition of curfews and military siege, throwing of gas bombs into houses as well as mosques and hospitals, savage beatings and maltreatment of pregnant women, torture of Palestinian detainees, imposition of collective punishment on towns and villages, forced deportation and expulsion of Palestinians, raiding and demolition of their houses and confiscation of their property.

The Commission also condemned the expropriation of Palestinian land and the establishment of Israeli settlements, attacks against holy places and obstruction of the freedom of worship and religious practices, attacks on and closure of educational institutions and obstruction of education. It further condemned Israel for annexing Jerusalem and altering its architectural character and demographic and structural composition as well as the institutional status of the occupied Palestinian territories, and considered such measures and their consequences null and void. The Secretary-General was requested to give the resolution wide publicity and to provide the Commission with all UN reports on the situation in the occupied territories issued between Commission sessions.

Also on 17 February, by a roll-call vote of 32 to 1, with 9 abstentions, the Commission, reaffirming the applicability of the fourth Geneva Convention to the territories, including Jerusalem, strongly condemned[71] Israel for refusing to apply that Convention and for ill-treating and torturing Palestinian detainees and prisoners, urging it to grant prisoner-of-war status to all captured Palestinian fighters and to treat them accordingly. It also strongly condemned Israel for deporting Palestinians and called on it to desist from that policy and to comply with the UN resolutions demanding their return to their homeland. States parties to the fourth Geneva Convention were urged to make every effort to ensure respect for and compliance with its provisions in the occupied territories, including Jerusalem.

By another resolution,[72] adopted on the same day by a roll-call vote of 31 to 1, with 10 abstentions, the Commission strongly condemned Israel for persistently disregarding and defying UN resolutions regarding occupied Syrian Arab territory, and strongly deprecated its failure to end its occupation of and human rights violations in that territory. Demanding that Israel allow the Special Committee on Israeli practices access to the occupied Arab territories, the Commission declared once again that Israeli occupation of the Golan Heights and its 1981 decision[73] to impose its laws, jurisdiction and administration on the territory were acts of aggression, declared that decision null and void and without international legal effect as a violation of international law and the UN Charter and called on Israel to rescind it. The Commission condemned Israel's persistence in changing the Golan Heights' physical character, demographic composition, institutional structure and legal status and emphasized that evacuated persons must be allowed to return and recover their property. It further emphasized the need for Israel's total and unconditional withdrawal from the occupied Syrian and other Arab territories, including Jerusalem.

The Commission deplored the inhuman treatment, terror and other practices applied against Syrian citizens in the Golan Heights, including the imposition of Israeli citizenship and identity cards, which was a flagrant violation of international law and UN resolutions, and called on Israel to cease its acts of terrorism. It also condemned Israel for repressing educational institutions in the Golan Heights and imposing curricula promoting hatred, prejudice and religious intolerance, as well as for expropriating land in the occupied territory, establishing Israeli settlements, and depriving the Syrian Golan population of the right to export their agricultural products. The Commission called on all States to urge Israel to cease such practices and to facilitate the marketing of the Golan population's agricultural produce. It also reaffirmed its request to Member States not to recognize any jurisdiction, laws or measures established by Israel in the occupied territories, and

called on the specialized agencies and other international organizations to comply in their relations with Israel with the provisions of the Commission's resolution. The Secretary-General was requested to provide the Special Committee on Israeli practices with the resources necessary to visit the occupied territories and investigate Israeli policies and practices, and to give wide publicity to the resolution. He was also asked to report in 1990 on progress in implementing the resolutions and to bring them to the attention of Governments, UN organs and agencies, intergovernmental and international humanitarian organizations and NGOs.

Sub-Commission action. In a resolution[74] adopted by secret ballot on 31 August by 15 votes to 5, with 2 abstentions, the Sub-Commission reaffirmed that Israeli occupation constituted a gross violation of human rights in the occupied territories and that acts perpetrated by Israel that caused the death of or physical harm to Palestinians, as well as the obstruction of delivery of food and medical supplies to their cities, villages and camps, imposition of curfews and attacks on their houses, mosques and hospitals were grave violations of international law. It also affirmed the right of Palestinians to resist the occupation by all means, including the uprising, and reaffirmed their inalienable rights to return to their homeland, to self-determination and to the establishment of an independent and sovereign State, as well as the need to enable them to enjoy full sovereignty over their land without foreign interference. It reaffirmed that the fourth Geneva Convention was applicable to the occupied territories and that Israel's violations of its provisions, including torture and ill-treating Palestinian detainees, imposition of collective punishment and administrative detention, expelling and deportation of Palestinians and destruction of their properties, were crimes of war. The Sub-Commission condemned Israel for such practices and called on it to desist from them, and also to withdraw from the occupied territories. It called for the dismantlement of Israeli settlements in the occupied territories and confirmed that measures taken by Israel to alter the territories' political, cultural, religious and other characteristics were illegal, null and void.

The Sub-Commission also condemned Israel's occupation of the Golan Heights, its inhuman and terrorist practices against Syrians in that territory for their refusal of Israeli identity cards, and its 1981 decision[73] to impose its laws, jurisdiction and administration on that territory, which the Sub-Commission considered null and void. It requested States and international organizations not to recognize Israeli laws or jurisdiction in respect of the Golan Heights, and supported the call to convene an international peace conference on the Middle East to achieve a settlement in accordance with the provisions of a 1967 Security Council resolution.[75] The Secretary-General was requested to provide the Sub-Commission in 1990 with an updated list of reports, studies, statistics and other documents and UN decisions and resolutions on the question of Palestine and other Arab territories.

Pursuant to a similar request made in 1988,[76] the Secretary-General presented such a list[77] on 19 May 1989.

Other alleged human rights violations

Burma (now Myanmar)

Human Rights Commission action. On 8 March, the Commission, concerned at allegations of human rights violations in Burma in 1988, encouraged[78] the Burmese authorities to take measures to assure fundamental freedoms, and, welcoming their undertaking to organize free and fair multiparty democratic elections, urged them to implement it as early as possible. The Burmese delegation was invited to continue providing the Commission with the necessary information on the subject.

China

Sub-Commission action. In a resolution[79] adopted by secret ballot on 31 August by 15 votes to 9, the Sub-Commission, concerned about recent events in China and their consequences in the field of human rights, requested the Secretary-General to transmit to the Commission information provided by the Chinese Government and other reliable sources, and made an appeal for clemency, in particular in favour of persons deprived of their liberty as a result of those events.

Further developments. On 1 December,[80] in its reply to the Secretary-General's note verbale of 30 October, China stated that a rebellion had occurred in Beijing in June which constituted an attempt to overthrow the legitimate Government through violent means, and that the Chinese Government had taken resolute measures to quell it. China considered the matter to be its internal affair and different in nature from the human rights question and declared its firm objection to the Sub-Commission's resolution, regarding it as an interference in its internal affairs and deeming it to be illegal, null and void.

Cuba

On 21 February, a six-member group, established in accordance with a 1988 Commission decision[76] and mandated to visit Cuba to observe the human rights situation, submitted a report[81] on its activities. The report noted that the group, headed by the Commission Chairman, held a total of five meetings and undertook a mission to Cuba

from 16 to 25 September 1988. In the course of its work, the group gathered written and oral information from individuals, organizations and the Cuban Government on various aspects of the human rights situation in the country.

The report contained comments by Cuban officials on questions put by the group, as well as testimony received from other sources, concerning constitutional and legal aspects of human rights in Cuba; civil and political rights; and economic, social and cultural rights. The group sought, in particular, the Government's comments with regard to compatibility of the Cuban Constitution with the Universal Declaration of Human Rights[42] and implementation of relevant provisions, as well as replies to specific complaints relating to the administration of justice and judicial protection of rights and freedoms; limit on freedoms recognized by the Constitution; states of emergency; guarantees of the freedom of movement, opinion and expression, the press, religion, education and conscience, and association and assembly; guarantees of the rights of citizenship and of asylum and of the right to life, liberty, physical integrity, security, privacy and political participation; and labour matters and social security, health, housing, education and culture.

Human Rights Commission action. On 21 February, the Commission decided[82] to discuss the group's report under a sub-item of the agenda item on further promotion and encouragement of human rights and fundamental freedoms. On 9 March, by a roll-call vote of 32 to 1, with 10 abstentions, the Commission took note[83] of the report; thanked the Government and people of Cuba for co-operating with the mission, and the Cuban authorities for reaffirming the desire to continue co-operation in the human rights sphere and to keep the Secretary-General informed; noted the Government's willingness to analyse the mission's observations and to take into account its assessments with regard to the exercise and enjoyment of human rights in Cuba; welcomed Cuba's willingness to maintain direct contact with the Secretary-General on issues and questions contained in the report; and emphasized the spirit of multilateral co-operation which characterized the fulfilment of the mission.

East Timor

In a resolution[84] adopted by secret ballot on 31 August by 12 votes to 9, with 3 abstentions, the Sub-Commission, considering repeated allegations of gross human rights violations in East Timor, requested the Secretary-General to continue his efforts to encourage co-operation of all parties concerned in achieving a durable solution, and took note of a communication addressed to the Secretary-General which called for a referendum in East Timor (see PART FOUR, Chapter I). The Sub-Commission appreciated the Indonesian Government's new policy of openness in East Timor but regretted that more arrests, torture and summary executions were alleged to have taken place since the end of 1988, and hoped that the Government would allow representatives of human rights organizations to visit the territory. It further recommended that the Commission consider the human rights situation in East Timor at its 1990 session.

Iraq

Human Rights Commission action. On 8 March, by a roll-call vote of 17 to 13, with 9 abstentions, the Commission decided[85] not to take action on a draft resolution by which it would have expressed concern at the human rights situation in Iraq, including the reported killing of Kurdish civilians by military attacks with the use of chemical weapons, and would have urged the Government of Iraq to ensure full respect for human rights. The Commission also would have requested its Chairman to appoint a special rapporteur to study the human rights situation in that country.

Sub-Commission action. On 31 August, by secret ballot, the Sub-Commission decided,[86] by 14 votes to 10, to take no action on a draft resolution by which it would have recommended that the Commission study at its 1990 session the evolution of the human rights situation in Iraq.

Mass exoduses

Human Rights Commission action. On 8 March, the Commission invited[87] Governments and international organizations to intensify their co-operation and assistance in efforts to address the causes of mass exoduses of refugees and displaced persons and the problems resulting from them, and requested States to ensure implementation of the relevant international instruments to avert new massive flows of refugees and displaced persons. It encouraged the Secretary-General to continue discharging responsibilities pursuant to the 1986 report of the Group of Governmental Experts on International Co-operation to Avert New Flows of Refugees,[88] and looked forward to his report to the General Assembly in 1989 on developments relating to the Group's recommendations. He was also urged to consolidate the system for early-warning activities in the humanitarian area by computerizing the UN Office for Research and the Collection of Information, serving as an inter-agency focal point for situation analysis and policy response, and by strengthening co-ordination within the UN system in that respect.

Report of the Secretary-General. In response to a 1988 General Assembly request[89] and the Commission's resolution (above), the Secretary-General submitted a report[90] on 17 October 1989 on human rights and mass exoduses. The report summarized activities of the Office for Research and the Collection of Information, which continued to monitor and provide early warning of situations that had the potential to cause mass exoduses. The Office also continued its efforts to establish a computerized early-warning system, including elaboration of criteria and co-ordination measures necessary for the operation of such a system and the development of early-warning indicators and data systems. Consultations on the subject were held with specialized agencies and NGOs, and a preliminary study was begun on co-ordination of early-warning activities with regard to potential refugee outflows.

The report also provided views and information on the question of mass exoduses and related developments received from four Governments, three UN bodies and specialized agencies, and one intergovernmental organization.

On 15 December, on the recommendation of the Third Committee, the General Assembly adopted **resolution 44/164** without vote.

Human rights and mass exoduses

The General Assembly,

Mindful of its general humanitarian mandate under the Charter of the United Nations to promote and encourage respect for human rights and fundamental freedoms,

Deeply disturbed by the continuing scale and magnitude of exoduses of refugees and displacements of population in many regions of the world and by the human suffering of millions of refugees and displaced persons,

Conscious of the fact that human rights violations are one of the multiple and complex factors causing mass exoduses of refugees and displaced persons, as indicated in the study of the Special Rapporteur of the Commission on Human Rights on this subject and also in the report of the Group of Governmental Experts on International Co-operation to Avert New Flows of Refugees,

Aware of the recommendations concerning mass exoduses made by the Commission on Human Rights to its Sub-Commission on Prevention of Discrimination and Protection of Minorities and to special rapporteurs to be taken into account when violations of human rights in any part of the world are studied,

Deeply preoccupied by the increasingly heavy burden being imposed, particularly upon developing countries with limited resources of their own and upon the international community as a whole, by these sudden mass exoduses and displacements of population,

Stressing the need for international co-operation aimed at averting new massive flows of refugees while providing durable solutions to actual refugee situations,

Reaffirming its resolution 41/70 of 3 December 1986, in which it endorsed the conclusions and recommendations contained in the report of the Group of Governmental Experts on International Co-operation to Avert New Flows of Refugees,

Bearing in mind its resolution 43/154 of 8 December 1988 and Commission on Human Rights resolution 1989/63 of 8 March 1989, as well as all previous relevant resolutions of the General Assembly and the Commission on Human Rights,

Welcoming the steps taken so far by the United Nations to examine the problem of massive outflows of refugees and displaced persons in all its aspects, including its root causes,

1. *Reaffirms* its support for the recommendation of the Group of Governmental Experts on International Co-operation to Avert New Flows of Refugees that the principal organs of the United Nations should make fuller use of their respective competencies under the Charter of the United Nations for the prevention of new massive flows of refugees and displaced persons;

2. *Again invites* all Governments and intergovernmental and humanitarian organizations concerned to intensify their co-operation with and assistance to world-wide efforts to address the serious problems resulting from mass exoduses of refugees and displaced persons, and also the causes of such exoduses;

3. *Requests* all Governments to ensure the effective implementation of the relevant international instruments, in particular in the field of human rights, as this would contribute to averting new massive flows of refugees and displaced persons;

4. *Invites* the Commission on Human Rights to keep the question of human rights and mass exoduses under review with a view to supporting the early-warning arrangement instituted by the Secretary-General to avert new massive flows of refugees and displaced persons;

5. *Takes note* of the report of the Secretary-General on human rights and mass exoduses, and invites him to inform the General Assembly in future reports of the modalities of early warning activities to avert new and massive flows of refugees;

6. *Specially encourages* the Secretary-General to continue to discharge the task described in the report of the Group of Governmental Experts on International Co-operation to Avert New Flows of Refugees;

7. *Requests* the Secretary-General to continue to develop the role of the Office for Research and the Collection of Information of the Secretariat as a focal point for the operation of an effective early-warning system and the strengthening of co-ordination of information-gathering and analysis among United Nations agencies with a view to preventing new massive flows of refugees and displaced persons;

8. *Urges* the Secretary-General to use available resources to consolidate and strengthen the system for undertaking early-warning activities in the humanitarian area by, *inter alia*, early computerization of the Office for Research and the Collection of Information and strengthened co-ordination among the relevant parts of the United Nations system, especially the Office for Research and the Collection of Information, the Office of the United Nations High Commissioner for Refugees, the Centre for Human Rights of the Secretariat and the relevant specialized agencies;

9. *Requests* the Secretary-General to report to the General Assembly at its forty-fifth session on the strengthened role that he is playing with regard to early-warning activities, especially in the humanitarian area,

as well as on any further developments relating to the recommendations contained in the report of the Group of Governmental Experts on International Co-operation to Avert New Flows of Refugees;

10. *Decides* to continue consideration of the question of human rights and mass exoduses at its forty-fifth session.

General Assembly resolution 44/164

15 December 1989   Meeting 82   Adopted without vote

Approved by Third Committee (A/44/848) without vote, 29 November (meeting 60); 22-nation draft (A/C.3/44/L.85); agenda item 12.
Meeting numbers. GA 44th session: 3rd Committee 48, 50-60; plenary 82.

Genocide

On 2 March, the Commission strongly condemned[91] the crime of genocide and affirmed the necessity for international co-operation towards its elimination. It noted that many States had ratified or acceded to the 1948 Convention on the Prevention and Punishment of the Crime of Genocide[19] and urged those that had not done so to become parties without delay.

Status of the 1948 Convention

As at 31 December 1989,[10] 102 States had ratified, acceded to or succeeded to the Convention. Three States—the Democratic People's Republic of Korea, the Libyan Arab Jamahiriya and Yemen—became parties in 1989. On 8 August, the Secretary-General reported[92] to the General Assembly on the status of the Convention as at 1 August 1989.

GENERAL ASSEMBLY ACTION

On 15 December, the Assembly, on the recommendation of the Third Committee, adopted **resolution 44/158** without vote.

Status of the Convention on the Prevention and Punishment of the Crime of Genocide

The General Assembly,

Recalling its resolutions 40/142 of 13 December 1985, 41/147 of 4 December 1986, 42/133 of 7 December 1987 and 43/138 of 8 December 1988,

Recalling also Commission on Human Rights resolutions 1986/18 of 10 March 1986, 1987/25 of 10 March 1987 and 1988/28 of 7 March 1988, and taking note of Commission resolution 1989/16 of 2 March 1989,

Recalling further its resolution 260 A (III) of 9 December 1948, by which it approved and proposed for signature, ratification or accession the Convention on the Prevention and Punishment of the Crime of Genocide annexed thereto,

Reaffirming once again its conviction that genocide is a crime that violates the norms of international law and runs counter to the spirit and aims of the United Nations,

Convinced that international co-operation is necessary in order to liberate mankind from such an odious crime,

Recognizing that crimes of genocide have caused great losses to mankind,

Taking note of the report of the Secretary-General,

1. *Once again strongly condemns* the crime of genocide;

2. *Reaffirms* the necessity of international co-operation in order to liberate mankind from such an odious crime;

3. *Notes with satisfaction* that many States have ratified the Convention on the Prevention and Punishment of the Crime of Genocide or have acceded thereto;

4. *Expresses its conviction* that implementation of the provisions of the Convention by all States is necessary for the prevention and punishment of the crime of genocide;

5. *Urges* those States that have not yet become parties to the Convention to ratify it or accede thereto without further delay;

6. *Invites* the Secretary-General to submit to the General Assembly at its forty-fifth session a report on the status of the Convention.

General Assembly resolution 44/158

15 December 1989   Meeting 82   Adopted without vote

Approved by Third Committee (A/44/848) without vote, 29 November (meeting 60); 2-nation draft (A/C.3/44/L.79); agenda item 12.
Sponsors: Byelorussian SSR, Poland.
Meeting numbers. GA 44th session: 3rd Committee 48, 50-60; plenary 82.

Other aspects of human rights violations

Protection of journalists

In a resolution[93] adopted by secret ballot on 31 August by 15 votes to 6, with 2 abstentions, the Sub-Commission called on journalists and other mass media personnel to carry out their mission to expose gross human rights violations and to inform public opinion with maximum neutrality, fairness and objectivity, and requested Governments to protect their human rights and support their efforts to reveal human rights violations. It also requested Waleed Sadi (Jordan) to prepare for Sub-Commission consideration in 1990 a report on the feasibility of a study on ways of extending additional protection and assistance to journalists and mass media personnel.

Compensation for human rights violations

On 31 August, the Sub-Commission recommended[94] that the Commission recommend to the Economic and Social Council a resolution authorizing the Sub-Commission to entrust one of its members, Theo van Boven (Netherlands), with undertaking a study on the right to restitution, compensation and rehabilitation for victims of gross human rights violations, with a view to exploring the possibility of developing some basic principles and guidelines in that respect, and asking the Secretary-General to provide him with all necessary assistance. The Sub-Commission requested Theo van Boven to submit a preliminary report to it in 1990.

REFERENCES

[1]YUN 1970, p. 530, ESC res. 1503(XLVIII), 27 May 1970. [2]YUN 1967, p. 509. [3]E/CN.4/1989/8. [4]YUN 1988, p. 555. [5]E/1989/20 (res. 1989/5). [6]YUN 1986, p. 745. [7]E/1989/20 (res. 1989/3). [8]YUN 1978, pp. 915 & 916, SC res. 435(1978) & 439(1978), 29 Sep. & 13 Nov. 1978. [9]E/CN.4/Sub.2/1989/58 (res. 1989/3). [10]*Multilateral Treaties Deposited with the Secretary-General: Status as at 31 December 1989* (ST/LEG/SER.E/8), Sales No. E.90.V.6. [11]YUN 1973, p. 103, GA res. 3068(XXVIII), annex, 30 Nov. 1973. [12]YUN 1976, p. 575. [13]A/44/442. [14]E/CN.4/1989/33. [15]E/CN.4/1989/32. [16]YUN 1988, p. 542. [17]E/CN.4/1989/31. [18]E/1989/20 (res. 1989/8). [19]YUN 1948-49, p. 959, GA res. 260 A (III), annex, 9 Dec. 1948. [20]YUN 1978, p. 677. [21]E/1989/20 (res. 1989/7). [22]YUN 1988, p. 559. [23]E/1989/20 (res. 1989/6). [24]E/CN.4/Sub.2/1989/9 & Add.1. [25]E/CN.4/Sub.2/1989/58 (res. 1989/18). [26]YUN 1988, p. 562, ESC res. 1988/41, 27 May 1988. [27]E/1989/53. [28]E/1989/49. [29]YUN 1950, p. 539, ESC res. 277(X), 17 Feb. 1950. [30]E/CN.4/1989/24. [31]E/1989/20 (res. 1989/67). [32]A/44/669. [33]E/CN.4/1989/26. [34]E/1989/20 (res. 1989/66). [35]YUN 1966, p. 423, GA res. 2200 A (XXI), annex, 16 Dec. 1966. [36]E/CN.4/Sub.2/1989/58 (res. 1989/10). [37]A/44/620. [38]A/C.3/44/9. [39]E/1989/20 (res. 1989/20). [40]E/CN.4/1989/67. [41]E/1989/20 (res. 1989/69). [42]YUN 1948-49, p. 535, GA res. 217 A (III), 10 Dec. 1948. [43]E/CN.4/Sub.2/1989/14 & Add.1. [44]E/CN.4/1990/27. [45]E/CN.4/Sub.2/1989/48. [46]E/CN.4/1989/28. [47]E/1989/20 (dec. 1989/110). [48]E/CN.4/1990/21. [49]E/1989/20 (res. 1989/75). [50]E/CN.4/1990/28 & Add.1. [51]E/CN.4/1989/7. [52]E/1989/20 (res. 1989/62). [53]YUN 1966, p. 419, GA res. 2200 A (XXI), annex, 16 Dec. 1966. [54]YUN 1988, p. 570. [55]E/CN.4/Sub.2/1989/15. [56]A/44/635. [57]E/CN.4/1989/23. [58]E/1989/20 (res. 1989/68). [59]YUN 1988, p. 573. [60]E/CN.4/Sub.2/1989/13. [61]E/CN.4/Sub.2/1989/58 (res. 1989/9). [62]A/44/671. [63]E/1989/20 (res. 1989/65). [64]E/CN.4/Sub.2/1989/58 (res. 1989/8). [65]*Ibid.* (res. 1989/29). [66]A/44/573. [67]YUN 1988, p. 576. [68]E/CN.4/1989/4. [69]E/CN.4/1989/6. [70]E/1989/20 (res. 1989/2 A). [71]*Ibid.* (res. 1989/2 B). [72]*Ibid.* (res. 1989/1). [73]YUN 1981, p. 308. [74]E/CN.4/Sub.2/1989/58 (res. 1989/4). [75]YUN 1967, p. 257, SC res. 242(1967), 22 Nov. 1967. [76]YUN 1988, p. 577. [77]E/CN.4/Sub.2/1989/11. [78]E/1989/20 (dec. 1989/112). [79]E/CN.4/Sub.2/1989/58 (res. 1989/5). [80]E/CN.4/1990/52. [81]E/CN.4/1989/46 & Corr.1. [82]E/1989/20 (dec. 1989/102). [83]*Ibid.* (dec. 1989/113). [84]E/CN.4/Sub.2/1989/58 (res. 1989/7). [85]E/1989/20 (dec. 1989/111). [86]E/CN.4/Sub.2/1989/58 (dec. 1989/106). [87]E/1989/20 (res. 1989/63). [88]YUN 1986, p. 851. [89]YUN 1988, p. 578, GA res. 43/154, 8 Dec. 1988. [90]A/44/622. [91]E/1989/20 (res. 1989/16). [92]A/44/440. [93]E/CN.4/Sub.2/1989/58 (res. 1989/2). [94]*Ibid.* (res. 1989/13).

Other human rights questions

Additional Protocols I and II to the 1949 Geneva Conventions

In a September 1989 report[1] on the status of the two 1977 Protocols Additional to the Geneva Conventions of 12 August 1949 for the protection of war victims,[2] the Secretary-General informed the General Assembly that 13 States had ratified or acceded to the Protocols since his 1988 report on the subject,[3] and provided a list of all States that had ratified or acceded to the Protocols as at 20 September 1989.

As at 31 December, 91 States and the United Nations Council for Namibia had ratified or acceded to Protocol I (on protection of victims of international armed conflicts), including 14 States—Algeria, Bulgaria, Byelorussian SSR, Côte d'Ivoire, Gambia, Greece, Hungary, Liechtenstein, Luxembourg, Mali, Malta, Peru, Spain, USSR—that did so in 1989.

All except 12 of the parties also adhered to Protocol II (on protection of victims of non-international conflicts). Two States—France and the Philippines—adhered only to Protocol II.

Sub-Commission action. On 31 August, the Sub-Commission recommended[4] that the Commission on Human Rights adopt a resolution calling on Governments to give particular attention to educating members of the police and armed forces in the international law of human rights and humanitarian law applicable in armed conflicts, including, *inter alia*, the Geneva Conventions of 1949 and the two 1977 Additional Protocols, and requesting them to submit information on the scope of such education.

Rights of the child

Convention on the Rights of the Child

The open-ended working group on a draft convention on the rights of the child met from 21 to 23 February 1989[5] and adopted the draft convention at the second reading.

On 8 March, the Commission on Human Rights decided[6] to adopt the draft convention[7] as submitted by the working group and to transmit it to the General Assembly through the Economic and Social Council.

By an 11 April note,[8] the Secretariat transmitted to the Council general comments adopted by the Human Rights Committee on 5 April concerning provisions of the 1966 International Covenant on Civil and Political Rights[9] relating to the rights of the child (see also above, under "Civil and political rights"). The Committee was of the view that, in so far as article 24 of the Covenant recognized the right of every child to receive the protection required by his or her status as a minor, its implementation entailed the adoption of special measures to protect children, in addition to those required for the protection of the rights of all persons. The Committee pointed out that some other provisions of the Covenant expressly indicated that minors should be afforded greater protection than adults.

ECONOMIC AND SOCIAL COUNCIL ACTION

On 24 May, the Economic and Social Council, on the recommendation of its Second Committee, adopted **resolution 1989/79** without vote.

Question of a convention on the rights of the child
The Economic and Social Council,

Recalling General Assembly resolutions on the question of a convention on the rights of the child, in particular resolution 43/112 of 8 December 1988, in which the Assembly requested the Commission on Human Rights to submit a draft convention on the rights of the child, through the Council, to the Assembly at its forty-fourth session,

Expressing its appreciation to the Commission for having concluded the elaboration of a draft convention on the rights of the child,

Decides to submit the draft convention on the rights of the child and the report of the working group of the Commission on Human Rights to the General Assembly at its forty-fourth session, with a view to the adoption of the draft convention.

Economic and Social Council resolution 1989/79

24 May 1989   Meeting 16   Adopted without vote

Approved by Second Committee (E/1989/88) without vote, 19 May (meeting 22); draft by Commission on Human Rights (E/1989/20); agenda item 9.

By a 16 October note,[10] the Secretary-General transmitted the text of the draft convention to the Assembly.

Sub-Commission action. On 1 September, the Sub-Commission expressed[11] concern that the current formulation of article 21 of the draft convention, concerning adoption of children, was open to differing interpretations, and the belief that the article should be revised to preclude the use of adoption as a source of profit. It also expressed deep concern at the participation of children in military training and hostilities in some countries, and recognized that no effort should be spared to prevent the militarization of children, as stipulated in article 38. The Secretary-General was requested to bring the Sub-Commission's resolution to the attention of the General Assembly and to submit to the Sub-Commission in 1990 a report on the adoption of children for commercial purposes and on their recruitment into armed forces and their participation in hostilities.

GENERAL ASSEMBLY ACTION

On 20 November, the General Assembly, on the recommendation of the Third Committee, adopted **resolution 44/25** without vote.

Convention on the Rights of the Child
The General Assembly,

Recalling its previous resolutions, especially resolutions 33/166 of 20 December 1978 and 43/112 of 8 December 1988, and those of the Commission on Human Rights and the Economic and Social Council related to the question of a convention on the rights of the child,

Taking note, in particular, of Commission on Human Rights resolution 1989/57 of 8 March 1989, by which the Commission decided to transmit the draft convention on the rights of the child, through the Economic and Social Council, to the General Assembly, and Economic and Social Council resolution 1989/79 of 24 May 1989,

Reaffirming that children's rights require special protection and call for continuous improvement of the situation of children all over the world, as well as for their development and education in conditions of peace and security,

Profoundly concerned that the situation of children in many parts of the world remains critical as a result of inadequate social conditions, natural disasters, armed conflicts, exploitation, illiteracy, hunger and disability, and convinced that urgent and effective national and international action is called for,

Mindful of the important role of the United Nations Children's Fund and of that of the United Nations in promoting the well-being of children and their development,

Convinced that an international convention on the rights of the child, as a standard-setting accomplishment of the United Nations in the field of human rights, would make a positive contribution to protecting children's rights and ensuring their well-being,

Bearing in mind that 1989 marks the thirtieth anniversary of the Declaration of the Rights of the Child and the tenth anniversary of the International Year of the Child,

1. *Expresses its appreciation* to the Commission on Human Rights for having concluded the elaboration of the draft convention on the rights of the child;

2. *Adopts* and opens for signature, ratification and accession the Convention on the Rights of the Child contained in the annex to the present resolution;

3. *Calls upon* all Member States to consider signing and ratifying or acceding to the Convention as a matter of priority and expresses the hope that it will come into force at an early date;

4. *Requests* the Secretary-General to provide all the facilities and assistance necessary for dissemination of information on the Convention;

5. *Invites* United Nations agencies and organizations, as well as intergovernmental and non-governmental organizations, to intensify their efforts with a view to disseminating information on the Convention and to promoting its understanding;

6. *Requests* the Secretary-General to submit to the General Assembly at its forty-fifth session a report on the status of the Convention on the Rights of the Child;

7. *Decides* to consider the report of the Secretary-General at its forty-fifth session under an item entitled "Implementation of the Convention on the Rights of the Child".

ANNEX
Convention on the Rights of the Child

Preamble

The States Parties to the present Convention,

Considering that, in accordance with the principles proclaimed in the Charter of the United Nations, recognition of the inherent dignity and of the equal and inalienable rights of all members of the human family is the foundation of freedom, justice and peace in the world,

Bearing in mind that the peoples of the United Nations have, in the Charter, reaffirmed their faith in fundamental human rights and in the dignity and worth of the human person, and have determined to promote social progress and better standards of life in larger freedom,

Recognizing that the United Nations has, in the Universal Declaration of Human Rights and in the International Covenants on Human Rights, proclaimed and agreed that everyone is entitled to all the rights and freedoms set forth therein, without distinction of any kind, such as race, colour, sex, language, religion, political or other opinion, national or social origin, property, birth or other status,

Recalling that, in the Universal Declaration of Human Rights, the United Nations has proclaimed that childhood is entitled to special care and assistance,

Convinced that the family, as the fundamental group of society and the natural environment for the growth and well-being of all its members and particularly children, should be afforded the necessary protection and assistance so that it can fully assume its responsibilities within the community,

Recognizing that the child, for the full and harmonious development of his or her personality, should grow up in a family environment, in an atmosphere of happiness, love and understanding,

Considering that the child should be fully prepared to live an individual life in society, and brought up in the spirit of the ideals proclaimed in the Charter of the United Nations, and in particular in the spirit of peace, dignity, tolerance, freedom, equality and solidarity,

Bearing in mind that the need to extend particular care to the child has been stated in the Geneva Declaration of the Rights of the Child of 1924 and in the Declaration of the Rights of the Child adopted by the General Assembly on 20 November 1959 and recognized in the Universal Declaration of Human Rights, in the International Covenant on Civil and Political Rights (in particular in articles 23 and 24), in the International Covenant on Economic, Social and Cultural Rights (in particular in article 10) and in the statutes and relevant instruments of specialized agencies and international organizations concerned with the welfare of children,

Bearing in mind that, as indicated in the Declaration of the Rights of the Child, "the child, by reason of his physical and mental immaturity, needs special safeguards and care, including appropriate legal protection, before as well as after birth",

Recalling the provisions of the Declaration on Social and Legal Principles relating to the Protection and Welfare of Children, with Special Reference to Foster Placement and Adoption Nationally and Internationally; the United Nations Standard Minimum Rules for the Administration of Juvenile Justice (The Beijing Rules); and the Declaration on the Protection of Women and Children in Emergency and Armed Conflict,

Recognizing that, in all countries in the world, there are children living in exceptionally difficult conditions, and that such children need special consideration,

Taking due account of the importance of the traditions and cultural values of each people for the protection and harmonious development of the child,

Recognizing the importance of international cooperation for improving the living conditions of children in every country, in particular in the developing countries,

Have agreed as follows:

Part I

Article 1

For the purposes of the present Convention, a child means every human being below the age of eighteen years unless, under the law applicable to the child, majority is attained earlier.

Article 2

1. States Parties shall respect and ensure the rights set forth in the present Convention to each child within their jurisdiction without discrimination of any kind,

irrespective of the child's or his or her parent's or legal guardian's race, colour, sex, language, religion, political or other opinion, national, ethnic or social origin, property, disability, birth or other status.

2. States Parties shall take all appropriate measures to ensure that the child is protected against all forms of discrimination or punishment on the basis of the status, activities, expressed opinions, or beliefs of the child's parents, legal guardians, or family members.

Article 3

1. In all actions concerning children, whether undertaken by public or private social welfare institutions, courts of law, administrative authorities or legislative bodies, the best interests of the child shall be a primary consideration.

2. States Parties undertake to ensure the child such protection and care as is necessary for his or her wellbeing, taking into account the rights and duties of his or her parents, legal guardians, or other individuals legally responsible for him or her, and, to this end, shall take all appropriate legislative and administrative measures.

3. States Parties shall ensure that the institutions, services and facilities responsible for the care or protection of children shall conform with the standards established by competent authorities, particularly in the areas of safety, health, in the number and suitability of their staff, as well as competent supervision.

Article 4

States Parties shall undertake all appropriate legislative, administrative, and other measures for the implementation of the rights recognized in the present Convention. With regard to economic, social and cultural rights, States Parties shall undertake such measures to the maximum extent of their available resources and, where needed, within the framework of international cooperation.

Article 5

States Parties shall respect the responsibilities, rights and duties of parents or, where applicable, the members of the extended family or community as provided for by local custom, legal guardians or other persons legally responsible for the child, to provide, in a manner consistent with the evolving capacities of the child, appropriate direction and guidance in the exercise by the child of the rights recognized in the present Convention.

Article 6

1. States Parties recognize that every child has the inherent right to life.

2. States Parties shall ensure to the maximum extent possible the survival and development of the child.

Article 7

1. The child shall be registered immediately after birth and shall have the right from birth to a name, the right to acquire a nationality and, as far as possible, the right to know and be cared for by his or her parents.

2. States Parties shall ensure the implementation of these rights in accordance with their national law and their obligations under the relevant international instruments in this field, in particular where the child would otherwise be stateless.

Article 8

1. States Parties undertake to respect the right of the child to preserve his or her identity, including national-

ity, name and family relations as recognized by law without unlawful interference.

2. Where a child is illegally deprived of some or all of the elements of his or her identity, States Parties shall provide appropriate assistance and protection, with a view to speedily re-establishing his or her identity.

Article 9

1. States Parties shall ensure that a child shall not be separated from his or her parents against their will, except when competent authorities subject to judicial review determine, in accordance with applicable law and procedures, that such separation is necessary for the best interests of the child. Such determination may be necessary in a particular case such as one involving abuse or neglect of the child by the parents, or one where the parents are living separately and a decision must be made as to the child's place of residence.

2. In any proceedings pursuant to paragraph 1 of the present article, all interested parties shall be given an opportunity to participate in the proceedings and make their views known.

3. States Parties shall respect the right of the child who is separated from one or both parents to maintain personal relations and direct contact with both parents on a regular basis, except if it is contrary to the child's best interests.

4. Where such separation results from any action initiated by a State Party, such as the detention, imprisonment, exile, deportation or death (including death arising from any cause while the person is in the custody of the State) of one or both parents or of the child, that State Party shall, upon request, provide the parents, the child or, if appropriate, another member of the family with the essential information concerning the whereabouts of the absent member(s) of the family unless the provision of the information would be detrimental to the well-being of the child. States Parties shall further ensure that the submission of such a request shall of itself entail no adverse consequences for the person(s) concerned.

Article 10

1. In accordance with the obligation of States Parties under article 9, paragraph 1, applications by a child or his or her parents to enter or leave a State Party for the purpose of family reunification shall be dealt with by States Parties in a positive, humane and expeditious manner. States Parties shall further ensure that the submission of such a request shall entail no adverse consequences for the applicants and for the members of their family.

2. A child whose parents reside in different States shall have the right to maintain on a regular basis, save in exceptional circumstances, personal relations and direct contacts with both parents. Towards that end and in accordance with the obligation of States Parties under article 9, paragraph 1, States Parties shall respect the right of the child and his or her parents to leave any country, including their own, and to enter their own country. The right to leave any country shall be subject only to such restrictions as are prescribed by law and which are necessary to protect the national security, public order (ordre public), public health or morals or the rights and freedoms of others and are consistent with the other rights recognized in the present Convention.

Article 11

1. States Parties shall take measures to combat the illicit transfer and non-return of children abroad.

2. To this end, States Parties shall promote the conclusion of bilateral or multilateral agreements or accession to existing agreements.

Article 12

1. States Parties shall assure to the child who is capable of forming his or her own views the right to express those views freely in all matters affecting the child, the views of the child being given due weight in accordance with the age and maturity of the child.

2. For this purpose, the child shall in particular be provided the opportunity to be heard in any judicial and administrative proceedings affecting the child, either directly, or through a representative or an appropriate body, in a manner consistent with the procedural rules of national law.

Article 13

1. The child shall have the right to freedom of expression; this right shall include freedom to seek, receive and impart information and ideas of all kinds, regardless of frontiers, either orally, in writing or in print, in the form of art, or through any other media of the child's choice.

2. The exercise of this right may be subject to certain restrictions, but these shall only be such as are provided by law and are necessary:

(a) For respect of the rights or reputations of others; or

(b) For the protection of national security or of public order *(ordre public)*, or of public health or morals.

Article 14

1. States Parties shall respect the right of the child to freedom of thought, conscience and religion.

2. States Parties shall respect the rights and duties of the parents and, when applicable, legal guardians, to provide direction to the child in the exercise of his or her right in a manner consistent with the evolving capacities of the child.

3. Freedom to manifest one's religion or beliefs may be subject only to such limitations as are prescribed by law and are necessary to protect public safety, order, health or morals, or the fundamental rights and freedoms of others.

Article 15

1. States Parties recognize the rights of the child to freedom of association and to freedom of peaceful assembly.

2. No restrictions may be placed on the exercise of these rights other than those imposed in conformity with the law and which are necessary in a democratic society in the interests of national security or public safety, public order *(ordre public)*, the protection of public health or morals or the protection of the rights and freedoms of others.

Article 16

1. No child shall be subjected to arbitrary or unlawful interference with his or her privacy, family, home or correspondence, nor to unlawful attacks on his or her honour and reputation.

2. The child has the right to the protection of the law against such interference or attacks.

Article 17

States Parties recognize the important function performed by the mass media and shall ensure that the child has access to information and material from a diversity of national and international sources, especially those aimed at the promotion of his or her social, spiritual and moral well-being and physical and mental health. To this end, States Parties shall:

(a) Encourage the mass media to disseminate information and material of social and cultural benefit to the child and in accordance with the spirit of article 29;

(b) Encourage international co-operation in the production, exchange and dissemination of such information and material from a diversity of cultural, national and international sources;

(c) Encourage the production and dissemination of children's books;

(d) Encourage the mass media to have particular regard to the linguistic needs of the child who belongs to a minority group or who is indigenous;

(e) Encourage the development of appropriate guidelines for the protection of the child from information and material injurious to his or her well-being, bearing in mind the provisions of articles 13 and 18.

Article 18

1. States Parties shall use their best efforts to ensure recognition of the principle that both parents have common responsibilities for the upbringing and development of the child. Parents or, as the case may be, legal guardians have the primary responsibility for the upbringing and development of the child. The best interests of the child will be their basic concern.

2. For the purpose of guaranteeing and promoting the rights set forth in the present Convention, States Parties shall render appropriate assistance to parents and legal guardians in the performance of their child-rearing responsibilities and shall ensure the development of institutions, facilities and services for the care of children.

3. States Parties shall take all appropriate measures to ensure that children of working parents have the right to benefit from child-care services and facilities for which they are eligible.

Article 19

1. States Parties shall take all appropriate legislative, administrative, social and educational measures to protect the child from all forms of physical or mental violence, injury or abuse, neglect or negligent treatment, maltreatment or exploitation, including sexual abuse, while in the care of parent(s), legal guardian(s) or any other person who has the care of the child.

2. Such protective measures should, as appropriate, include effective procedures for the establishment of social programmes to provide necessary support for the child and for those who have the care of the child, as well as for other forms of prevention and for identification, reporting, referral, investigation, treatment and follow-up of instances of child maltreatment described heretofore, and, as appropriate, for judicial involvement.

Article 20

1. A child temporarily or permanently deprived of his or her family environment, or in whose own best interests cannot be allowed to remain in that environment, shall be entitled to special protection and assistance provided by the State.

2.   States Parties shall in accordance with their national laws ensure alternative care for such a child.

3.   Such care could include, *inter alia*, foster placement, *kafalah* of Islamic law, adoption or, if necessary, placement in suitable institutions for the care of children. When considering solutions, due regard shall be paid to the desirability of continuity in a child's upbringing and to the child's ethnic, religious, cultural and linguistic background.

Article 21

States Parties that recognize and/or permit the system of adoption shall ensure that the best interests of the child shall be the paramount consideration and they shall:

 (a)   Ensure that the adoption of a child is authorized only by competent authorities who determine, in accordance with applicable law and procedures and on the basis of all pertinent and reliable information, that the adoption is permissible in view of the child's status concerning parents, relatives and legal guardians and that, if required, the persons concerned have given their informed consent to the adoption on the basis of such counselling as may be necessary;

 (b)   Recognize that inter-country adoption may be considered as an alternative means of the child's care, if the child cannot be placed in a foster or an adoptive family or cannot in any suitable manner be cared for in the child's country of origin;

 (c)   Ensure that the child concerned by inter-country adoption enjoys safeguards and standards equivalent to those existing in the case of national adoption;

 (d)   Take all appropriate measures to ensure that, in inter-country adoption, the placement does not result in improper financial gain for those involved in it;

 (e)   Promote, where appropriate, the objectives of the present article by concluding bilateral or multilateral arrangements or agreements, and endeavour, within this framework, to ensure that the placement of the child in another country is carried out by competent authorities or organs.

Article 22

1.   States Parties shall take appropriate measures to ensure that a child who is seeking refugee status or who is considered a refugee in accordance with applicable international or domestic law and procedures shall, whether unaccompanied or accompanied by his or her parents or by any other person, receive appropriate protection and humanitarian assistance in the enjoyment of applicable rights set forth in the present Convention and in other international human rights or humanitarian instruments to which the said States are Parties.

2.   For this purpose, States Parties shall provide, as they consider appropriate, co-operation in any efforts by the United Nations and other competent intergovernmental organizations or non-governmental organizations co-operating with the United Nations to protect and assist such a child and to trace the parents or other members of the family of any refugee child in order to obtain information necessary for reunification with his or her family. In cases where no parents or other members of the family can be found, the child shall be accorded the same protection as any other child permanently or temporarily deprived of his or her family environment for any reason, as set forth in the present Convention.

Article 23

1.   States Parties recognize that a mentally or physically disabled child should enjoy a full and decent life, in conditions which ensure dignity, promote self-reliance and facilitate the child's active participation in the community.

2.   States Parties recognize the right of the disabled child to special care and shall encourage and ensure the extension, subject to available resources, to the eligible child and those responsible for his or her care, of assistance for which application is made and which is appropriate to the child's condition and to the circumstances of the parents or others caring for the child.

3.   Recognizing the special needs of a disabled child, assistance extended in accordance with paragraph 2 of the present article shall be provided free of charge, whenever possible, taking into account the financial resources of the parents or others caring for the child, and shall be designed to ensure that the disabled child has effective access to and receives education, training, health care services, rehabilitation services, preparation for employment and recreation opportunities in a manner conducive to the child's achieving the fullest possible social integration and individual development, including his or her cultural and spiritual development.

4.   States Parties shall promote, in the spirit of international co-operation, the exchange of appropriate information in the field of preventive health care and of medical, psychological and functional treatment of disabled children, including dissemination of and access to information concerning methods of rehabilitation, education and vocational services, with the aim of enabling States Parties to improve their capabilities and skills and to widen their experience in these areas. In this regard, particular account shall be taken of the needs of developing countries.

Article 24

1.   States Parties recognize the right of the child to the enjoyment of the highest attainable standard of health and to facilities for the treatment of illness and rehabilitation of health. States Parties shall strive to ensure that no child is deprived of his or her right of access to such health care services.

2.   States Parties shall pursue full implementation of this right and, in particular, shall take appropriate measures:

 (a)   To diminish infant and child mortality;

 (b)   To ensure the provision of necessary medical assistance and health care to all children with emphasis on the development of primary health care;

 (c)   To combat disease and malnutrition, including within the framework of primary health care, through, *inter alia*, the application of readily available technology and through the provision of adequate nutritious foods and clean drinking-water, taking into consideration the dangers and risks of environmental pollution;

 (d)   To ensure appropriate pre-natal and post-natal health care for mothers;

 (e)   To ensure that all segments of society, in particular parents and children, are informed, have access to education and are supported in the use of basic knowledge of child health and nutrition, the advantages of breast-feeding, hygiene and environmental sanitation and the prevention of accidents;

(*f*) To develop preventive health care, guidance for parents and family planning education and services.

3. States Parties shall take all effective and appropriate measures with a view to abolishing traditional practices prejudicial to the health of children.

4. States Parties undertake to promote and encourage international co-operation with a view to achieving progressively the full realization of the right recognized in the present article. In this regard, particular account shall be taken of the needs of developing countries.

Article 25

States Parties recognize the right of a child who has been placed by the competent authorities for the purposes of care, protection or treatment of his or her physical or mental health to a periodic review of the treatment provided to the child and all other circumstances relevant to his or her placement.

Article 26

1. States Parties shall recognize for every child the right to benefit from social security, including social insurance, and shall take the necessary measures to achieve the full realization of this right in accordance with their national law.

2. The benefits should, where appropriate, be granted, taking into account the resources and the circumstances of the child and persons having responsibility for the maintenance of the child, as well as any other consideration relevant to an application for benefits made by or on behalf of the child.

Article 27

1. States Parties recognize the right of every child to a standard of living adequate for the child's physical, mental, spiritual, moral and social development.

2. The parent(s) or others responsible for the child have the primary responsibility to secure, within their abilities and financial capacities, the conditions of living necessary for the child's development.

3. States Parties, in accordance with national conditions and within their means, shall take appropriate measures to assist parents and others responsible for the child to implement this right and shall in case of need provide material assistance and support programmes, particularly with regard to nutrition, clothing and housing.

4. States Parties shall take all appropriate measures to secure the recovery of maintenance for the child from the parents or other persons having financial responsibility for the child, both within the State Party and from abroad. In particular, where the person having financial responsibility for the child lives in a State different from that of the child, States Parties shall promote the accession to international agreements or the conclusion of such agreements, as well as the making of other appropriate arrangements.

Article 28

1. States Parties recognize the right of the child to education, and with a view to achieving this right progressively and on the basis of equal opportunity, they shall, in particular:

(*a*) Make primary education compulsory and available free to all;

(*b*) Encourage the development of different forms of secondary education, including general and vocational

education, make them available and accessible to every child, and take appropriate measures such as the introduction of free education and offering financial assistance in case of need;

(*c*) Make higher education accessible to all on the basis of capacity by every appropriate means;

(*d*) Make educational and vocational information and guidance available and accessible to all children;

(*e*) Take measures to encourage regular attendance at schools and the reduction of drop-out rates.

2. States Parties shall take all appropriate measures to ensure that school discipline is administered in a manner consistent with the child's human dignity and in conformity with the present Convention.

3. States Parties shall promote and encourage international co-operation in matters relating to education, in particular with a view to contributing to the elimination of ignorance and illiteracy throughout the world and facilitating access to scientific and technical knowledge and modern teaching methods. In this regard, particular account shall be taken of the needs of developing countries.

Article 29

1. States Parties agree that the education of the child shall be directed to:

(*a*) The development of the child's personality, talents and mental and physical abilities to their fullest potential;

(*b*) The development of respect for human rights and fundamental freedoms, and for the principles enshrined in the Charter of the United Nations;

(*c*) The development of respect for the child's parents, his or her own cultural identity, language and values, for the national values of the country in which the child is living, the country from which he or she may originate, and for civilizations different from his or her own;

(*d*) The preparation of the child for responsible life in a free society, in the spirit of understanding, peace, tolerance, equality of sexes, and friendship among all peoples, ethnic, national and religious groups and persons of indigenous origin;

(*e*) The development of respect for the natural environment.

2. No part of the present article or article 28 shall be construed so as to interfere with the liberty of individuals and bodies to establish and direct educational institutions, subject always to the observance of the principles set forth in paragraph 1 of the present article and to the requirements that the education given in such institutions shall conform to such minimum standards as may be laid down by the State.

Article 30

In those States in which ethnic, religious or linguistic minorities or persons of indigenous origin exist, a child belonging to such a minority or who is indigenous shall not be denied the right, in community with other members of his or her group, to enjoy his or her own culture, to profess and practise his or her own religion, or to use his or her own language.

Article 31

1. States Parties recognize the right of the child to rest and leisure, to engage in play and recreational ac-

tivities appropriate to the age of the child and to participate freely in cultural life and the arts.

2. States Parties shall respect and promote the right of the child to participate fully in cultural and artistic life and shall encourage the provision of appropriate and equal opportunities for cultural, artistic, recreational and leisure activity.

Article 32

1. States Parties recognize the right of the child to be protected from economic exploitation and from performing any work that is likely to be hazardous or to interfere with the child's education, or to be harmful to the child's health or physical, mental, spiritual, moral or social development.

2. States Parties shall take legislative, administrative, social and educational measures to ensure the implementation of the present article. To this end, and having regard to the relevant provisions of other international instruments, States Parties shall in particular:

(a) Provide for a minimum age or minimum ages for admission to employment;

(b) Provide for appropriate regulation of the hours and conditions of employment;

(c) Provide for appropriate penalties or other sanctions to ensure the effective enforcement of the present article.

Article 33

States Parties shall take all appropriate measures, including legislative, administrative, social and educational measures, to protect children from the illicit use of narcotic drugs and psychotropic substances as defined in the relevant international treaties, and to prevent the use of children in the illicit production and trafficking of such substances.

Article 34

States Parties undertake to protect the child from all forms of sexual exploitation and sexual abuse. For these purposes, States Parties shall in particular take all appropriate national, bilateral and multilateral measures to prevent:

(a) The inducement or coercion of a child to engage in any unlawful sexual activity;

(b) The exploitative use of children in prostitution or other unlawful sexual practices;

(c) The exploitative use of children in pornographic performances and materials.

Article 35

States Parties shall take all appropriate national, bilateral and multilateral measures to prevent the abduction of, the sale of or traffic in children for any purpose or in any form.

Article 36

States Parties shall protect the child against all other forms of exploitation prejudicial to any aspects of the child's welfare.

Article 37

States Parties shall ensure that:

(a) No child shall be subjected to torture or other cruel, inhuman or degrading treatment or punishment. Neither capital punishment nor life imprisonment without possibility of release shall be imposed for offences committed by persons below eighteen years of age;

(b) No child shall be deprived of his or her liberty unlawfully or arbitrarily. The arrest, detention or imprisonment of a child shall be in conformity with the law and shall be used only as a measure of last resort and for the shortest appropriate period of time;

(c) Every child deprived of liberty shall be treated with humanity and respect for the inherent dignity of the human person, and in a manner which takes into account the needs of persons of his or her age. In particular, every child deprived of liberty shall be separated from adults unless it is considered in the child's best interest not to do so and shall have the right to maintain contact with his or her family through correspondence and visits, save in exceptional circumstances;

(d) Every child deprived of his or her liberty shall have the right to prompt access to legal and other appropriate assistance, as well as the right to challenge the legality of the deprivation of his or her liberty before a court or other competent, independent and impartial authority, and to a prompt decision on any such action.

Article 38

1. States Parties undertake to respect and to ensure respect for rules of international humanitarian law applicable to them in armed conflicts which are relevant to the child.

2. States Parties shall take all feasible measures to ensure that persons who have not attained the age of fifteen years do not take a direct part in hostilities.

3. States Parties shall refrain from recruiting any person who has not attained the age of fifteen years into their armed forces. In recruiting among those persons who have attained the age of fifteen years but who have not attained the age of eighteen years, States Parties shall endeavour to give priority to those who are oldest.

4. In accordance with their obligations under international humanitarian law to protect the civilian population in armed conflicts, States Parties shall take all feasible measures to ensure protection and care of children who are affected by an armed conflict.

Article 39

States Parties shall take all appropriate measures to promote physical and psychological recovery and social reintegration of a child victim of: any form of neglect, exploitation, or abuse; torture or any other form of cruel, inhuman or degrading treatment or punishment; or armed conflicts. Such recovery and reintegration shall take place in an environment which fosters the health, self-respect and dignity of the child.

Article 40

1. States Parties recognize the right of every child alleged as, accused of, or recognized as having infringed the penal law to be treated in a manner consistent with the promotion of the child's sense of dignity and worth, which reinforces the child's respect for the human rights and fundamental freedoms of others and which takes into account the child's age and the desirability of promoting the child's reintegration and the child's assuming a constructive role in society.

2. To this end, and having regard to the relevant provisions of international instruments, States Parties shall, in particular, ensure that:

(a) No child shall be alleged as, be accused of, or recognized as having infringed the penal law by reason

of acts or omissions that were not prohibited by national or international law at the time they were committed;

(b) Every child alleged as or accused of having infringed the penal law has at least the following guarantees:

(i) To be presumed innocent until proven guilty according to law;

(ii) To be informed promptly and directly of the charges against him or her, and, if appropriate, through his or her parents or legal guardians, and to have legal or other appropriate assistance in the preparation and presentation of his or her defence;

(iii) To have the matter determined without delay by a competent, independent and impartial authority or judicial body in a fair hearing according to law, in the presence of legal or other appropriate assistance and, unless it is considered not to be in the best interest of the child, in particular, taking into account his or her age or situation, his or her parents or legal guardians;

(iv) Not to be compelled to give testimony or to confess guilt; to examine or have examined adverse witnesses and to obtain the participation and examination of witnesses on his or her behalf under conditions of equality;

(v) If considered to have infringed the penal law, to have this decision and any measures imposed in consequence thereof reviewed by a higher competent, independent and impartial authority or judicial body according to law;

(vi) To have the free assistance of an interpreter if the child cannot understand or speak the language used;

(vii) To have his or her privacy fully respected at all stages of the proceedings.

3. States Parties shall seek to promote the establishment of laws, procedures, authorities and institutions specifically applicable to children alleged as, accused of, or recognized as having infringed the penal law, and, in particular:

(a) The establishment of a minimum age below which children shall be presumed not to have the capacity to infringe the penal law;

(b) Whenever appropriate and desirable, measures for dealing with such children without resorting to judicial proceedings, providing that human rights and legal safeguards are fully respected.

4. A variety of dispositions such as care, guidance and supervision orders; counselling; probation; foster care; education and vocational training programmes and other alternatives to institutional care shall be available to ensure that children are dealt with in a manner appropriate to their well-being and proportionate both to their circumstances and the offence.

Article 41

Nothing in the present Convention shall affect any provisions which are more conducive to the realization of the rights of the child and which may be contained in:

(a) The law of a State Party; or

(b) International law in force for that State.

Part II

Article 42

States Parties undertake to make the principles and provisions of the Convention widely known, by appropriate and active means, to adults and children alike.

Article 43

1. For the purpose of examining the progress made by States Parties in achieving the realization of the obligations undertaken in the present Convention, there shall be established a Committee on the Rights of the Child, which shall carry out the functions hereinafter provided.

2. The Committee shall consist of ten experts of high moral standing and recognized competence in the field covered by this Convention. The members of the Committee shall be elected by States Parties from among their nationals and shall serve in their personal capacity, consideration being given to equitable geographical distribution, as well as to the principal legal systems.

3. The members of the Committee shall be elected by secret ballot from a list of persons nominated by States Parties. Each State Party may nominate one person from among its own nationals.

4. The initial election to the Committee shall be held no later than six months after the date of the entry into force of the present Convention and thereafter every second year. At least four months before the date of each election, the Secretary-General of the United Nations shall address a letter to States Parties inviting them to submit their nominations within two months. The Secretary-General shall subsequently prepare a list in alphabetical order of all persons thus nominated, indicating States Parties which have nominated them, and shall submit it to the States Parties to the present Convention.

5. The elections shall be held at meetings of States Parties convened by the Secretary-General at United Nations Headquarters. At those meetings, for which two thirds of States Parties shall constitute a quorum, the persons elected to the Committee shall be those who obtain the largest number of votes and an absolute majority of the votes of the representatives of States Parties present and voting.

6. The members of the Committee shall be elected for a term of four years. They shall be eligible for re-election if renominated. The term of five of the members elected at the first election shall expire at the end of two years; immediately after the first election, the names of these five members shall be chosen by lot by the Chairman of the meeting.

7. If a member of the Committee dies or resigns or declares that for any other cause he or she can no longer perform the duties of the Committee, the State Party which nominated the member shall appoint another expert from among its nationals to serve for the remainder of the term, subject to the approval of the Committee.

8. The Committee shall establish its own rules of procedure.

9. The Committee shall elect its officers for a period of two years.

10. The meetings of the Committee shall normally be held at United Nations Headquarters or at any other convenient place as determined by the Committee. The Committee shall normally meet annually. The duration of the meetings of the Committee shall be determined, and reviewed, if necessary, by a meeting of the States Parties to the present Convention, subject to the approval of the General Assembly.

11. The Secretary-General of the United Nations shall provide the necessary staff and facilities for the effective performance of the functions of the Committee under the present Convention.

12. With the approval of the General Assembly, the members of the Committee established under the present Convention shall receive emoluments from United Nations resources on such terms and conditions as the Assembly may decide.

Article 44

1. States Parties undertake to submit to the Committee, through the Secretary-General of the United Nations, reports on the measures they have adopted which give effect to the rights recognized herein and on the progress made on the enjoyment of those rights:

(a) Within two years of the entry into force of the Convention for the State Party concerned;

(b) Thereafter every five years.

2. Reports made under the present article shall indicate factors and difficulties, if any, affecting the degree of fulfilment of the obligations under the present Convention. Reports shall also contain sufficient information to provide the Committee with a comprehensive understanding of the implementation of the Convention in the country concerned.

3. A State Party which has submitted a comprehensive initial report to the Committee need not, in its subsequent reports submitted in accordance with paragraph 1 (b) of the present article, repeat basic information previously provided.

4. The Committee may request from States Parties further information relevant to the implementation of the Convention.

5. The Committee shall submit to the General Assembly, through the Economic and Social Council, every two years, reports on its activities.

6. States Parties shall make their reports widely available to the public in their own countries.

Article 45

In order to foster the effective implementation of the Convention and to encourage international co-operation in the field covered by the Convention:

(a) The specialized agencies, the United Nations Children's Fund and other United Nations organs shall be entitled to be represented at the consideration of the implementation of such provisions of the present Convention as fall within the scope of their mandate. The Committee may invite the specialized agencies, the United Nations Children's Fund and other competent bodies as it may consider appropriate to provide expert advice on the implementation of the Convention in areas falling within the scope of their respective mandates. The Committee may invite the specialized agencies, the United Nations Children's Fund and other United Nations organs to submit reports on the implementation of the Convention in areas falling within the scope of their activities;

(b) The Committee shall transmit, as it may consider appropriate, to the specialized agencies, the United Nations Children's Fund and other competent bodies any reports from States Parties that contain a request, or indicate a need, for technical advice or assistance, along with the Committee's observations and suggestions, if any, on these requests or indications;

(c) The Committee may recommend to the General Assembly that it request the Secretary-General to undertake on its behalf studies on specific issues relating to the rights of the child;

(d) The Committee may make suggestions and general recommendations based on information received pursuant to articles 44 and 45 of the present Convention. Such suggestions and general recommendations shall be transmitted to any State Party concerned and reported to the General Assembly, together with comments, if any, from States Parties.

Part III

Article 46

The present Convention shall be open for signature by all States.

Article 47

The present Convention is subject to ratification. Instruments of ratification shall be deposited with the Secretary-General of the United Nations.

Article 48

The present Convention shall remain open for accession by any State. The instruments of accession shall be deposited with the Secretary-General of the United Nations.

Article 49

1. The present Convention shall enter into force on the thirtieth day following the date of deposit with the Secretary-General of the United Nations of the twentieth instrument of ratification or accession.

2. For each State ratifying or acceding to the Convention after the deposit of the twentieth instrument of ratification or accession, the Convention shall enter into force on the thirtieth day after the deposit by such State of its instrument of ratification or accession.

Article 50

1. Any State Party may propose an amendment and file it with the Secretary-General of the United Nations. The Secretary-General shall thereupon communicate the proposed amendment to States Parties, with a request that they indicate whether they favour a conference of States Parties for the purpose of considering and voting upon the proposals. In the event that, within four months from the date of such communication, at least one third of the States Parties favour such a conference, the Secretary-General shall convene the conference under the auspices of the United Nations. Any amendment adopted by a majority of States Parties present and voting at the conference shall be submitted to the General Assembly of the United Nations for approval.

2. An amendment adopted in accordance with paragraph 1 of the present article shall enter into force when it has been approved by the General Assembly of the United Nations and accepted by a two-thirds majority of States Parties.

3. When an amendment enters into force, it shall be binding on those States Parties which have accepted it, other States Parties still being bound by the provisions of the present Convention and any earlier amendments which they have accepted.

Article 51

1. The Secretary-General of the United Nations shall receive and circulate to all States the text of reservations made by States at the time of ratification or accession.

2. A reservation incompatible with the object and purpose of the present Convention shall not be permitted.

3. Reservations may be withdrawn at any time by notification to that effect addressed to the Secretary-General of the United Nations, who shall then inform all States. Such notification shall take effect on the date on which it is received by the Secretary-General.

Article 52
A State Party may denounce the present Convention by written notification to the Secretary-General of the United Nations. Denunciation becomes effective one year after the date of receipt of the notification by the Secretary-General.

Article 53
The Secretary-General of the United Nations is designated as the depositary of the present Convention.

Article 54
The original of the present Convention, of which the Arabic, Chinese, English, French, Russian and Spanish texts are equally authentic, shall be deposited with the Secretary-General of the United Nations.

IN WITNESS WHEREOF the undersigned plenipotentiaries, being duly authorized thereto by their respective Governments, have signed the present Convention.

General Assembly resolution 44/25

20 November 1989   Meeting 61   Adopted without vote

Approved by Third Committee (A/44/736) without vote, 15 November (meeting 44); 72-nation draft (A/C.3/44/L.44); agenda item 108.

Sponsors: Argentina, Australia, Austria, Bangladesh, Bolivia, Bulgaria, Burkina Faso, Byelorussian SSR, Cameroon, Canada, China, Colombia, Congo, Costa Rica, Côte d'Ivoire, Cuba, Cyprus, Czechoslovakia, Denmark, Dominican Republic, Ecuador, Egypt, El Salvador, Ethiopia, Finland, France, German Democratic Republic, Germany, Federal Republic of, Greece, Guatemala, Guinea-Bissau, Honduras, Hungary, Iceland, India, Indonesia, Italy, Jordan, Libyan Arab Jamahiriya, Luxembourg, Madagascar, Mali, Malta, Mauritania, Mexico, Mongolia, Morocco, Nepal, New Zealand, Nicaragua, Nigeria, Norway, Pakistan, Panama, Peru, Philippines, Poland, Portugal, Romania, Samoa, Senegal, Spain, Sri Lanka, Suriname, Sweden, Tunisia, Ukrainian SSR, USSR, Uruguay, Venezuela, Viet Nam, Yugoslavia.

Financial implications. 5th Committee, A/44/743; S-G, A/C.3/44/L.47, A/C.5/44/28.

Meeting numbers. GA 44th session: 3rd Committee 36-44; 5th Committee 43; plenary 61.

Sale of children, child prostitution and child pornography

Human Rights Commission action. On 6 March, the Commission commended[12] the Sub-Commission and its Working Group on Contemporary Forms of Slavery, noting that the Group's 1989-1991 work programme concerned, *inter alia*, the prevention of the sale of children, child prostitution and child pornography, as well as the eradication of child labour and of debt bondage. It requested interested specialized agencies and NGOs to gather and communicate to the Secretary-General information on the sale of children, including their observations on ways of preventing it, and asked the Secretary-General to submit his final report on the subject in 1989. Member States were urged to take measures to protect children and promote their rights, and to enact legislation making it a crime to produce, distribute or possess pornographic material involving children.

Note of the Secretary-General. In a 12 July note[13] to the Sub-Commission, the Secretary-General stated that, pursuant to the Commission's March resolution, he had requested Governments, UN organs, specialized agencies, intergovernmental organizations and NGOs to submit information relevant to the issue of the sale of children. By 1 July, replies had been received from four States, two intergovernmental organizations and three NGOs. Most communications, however, dealt with the general question of trafficking in human beings and not specifically the sale of children. The note provided a summary of replies and reviewed other developments that had occurred since the Secretary-General's 1988 report on the subject,[14] including the 1988 activities of the Working Group on Contemporary Forms of Slavery.

The Secretary-General concluded that, in view of the paucity of replies, he was not in a position to produce a comprehensive final report on the sale of children, nor did the new communications add much to complement information previously submitted on the subject, in particular on organ transplants in the context of the sale of children. No information at all had been received on the foetus trade. He therefore suggested that the Sub-Commission consider the Working Group's recommendation that a special rapporteur be appointed to undertake an overall study of the question.

Working Group activities. The Working Group on Contemporary Forms of Slavery, at its fourteenth session[15] (see also above, under "Civil and political rights"), examined, *inter alia*, issues related to the adoption of children for commercial purposes, child prostitution and child pornography and the exploitation of child labour and debt bondage. It recommended two draft resolutions for adoption by the Sub-Commission (see below), including a draft programme of action for prevention of the sale of children, child prostitution and child pornography. The draft programme proposed action in the areas of information and education, social measures and development assistance, legal measures and law enforcement, rehabilitation and reintegration for victims of sexual exploitation, and international co-ordination. The Working Group also called on the Sub-Commission to study the possibility of drafting model laws to combat the sale of children, child prostitution and child pornography, and recommended that requests for additional information on child labour and bonded labour be sent as early as possible to Governments, relevant intergovernmental organizations and NGOs competent in that field.

Sub-Commission action. On 1 September, the Sub-Commission endorsed[16] the draft programme of action proposed by the Working Group and recommended that the Commission transmit it to Governments, specialized agencies and other intergovernmental as well as non-governmental organizations for comments, and that it examine the draft programme at its 1991 session. The Sub-Commission also recommended[17] that the Commission appoint for one year a special rapporteur on the sale of children, child prostitution and child pornography, including the adoption of children for commercial purposes, and request the rapporteur to report to it in 1991.

Youth and human rights

Note of the Secretary-General. By a 13 February note,[18] the Secretary-General informed the Commission that the Sub-Commission had, in 1988,[14] requested him to invoke the applicability of the 1946 Convention on the Privileges and Immunities of the United Nations[19] to ensure the completion of a report on human rights and youth, entrusted to Special Rapporteur Dumitru Mazilu (Romania) in 1985,[20] as the Romanian authorities had not permitted the Special Rapporteur to travel to Geneva to present his report at the 1988 session of the Sub-Commission. In case of non-concurrence by Romania with the applicability of the Convention, the matter was to be brought to the attention of the Commission on Human Rights.

Annexed to the note was an aide-mémoire transmitted by Romania to the UN Legal Counsel on 6 January 1989 and stating, _inter alia_, that Mr. Mazilu had applied for and received a disability pension due to ill health and was unable to prepare the report; that his term as a Sub-Commission member had expired at the end of 1987; that the applicability of the Convention was limited only to activities of experts while on mission, but not during their stay in the country of residence, and only to acts performed as part of that mission; and that the report should be prepared by the current Romanian expert serving on the Sub-Commission.

The Secretary-General noted that the Legal Counsel had made it clear that acceptance of the aide-mémoire for transmittal to the Commission did not mean his acceptance of its contents. The note also indicated that the Secretariat continued to collect information relating to the report and to seek Romania's assistance in establishing contact with the Special Rapporteur.

Human Rights Commission action. On 6 March, by a roll-call vote of 26 to 5, with 12 abstentions, the Commission recommended[21] a resolution for adoption by the Economic and Social Council (see below). On 8 March, the Commission reaffirmed[22] the role of youth in promoting the full and effective enjoyment of human rights and fundamental freedoms and called for legislative, administrative and other action to allow the exercise by young people of all human rights, including the right to education and the right to work, so as to create conditions for their active participation in implementation of national development programmes.

ECONOMIC AND SOCIAL COUNCIL ACTION

On 24 May, the Economic and Social Council, on the recommendation of its Second Committee, adopted **resolution 1989/75** by recorded vote.

Status of special rapporteurs
The Economic and Social Council,

Having considered resolution 1988/37 of 1 September 1988 of the Sub-Commission on Prevention of Discrimination and Protection of Minorities and Commission on Human Rights resolution 1989/37 of 6 March 1989,

1. _Concludes_ that a difference has arisen between the United Nations and the Government of Romania as to the applicability of the Convention on the Privileges and Immunities of the United Nations of 13 February 1946 to Mr. Dumitru Mazilu as Special Rapporteur of the Sub-Commission on Prevention of Discrimination and Protection of Minorities;

2. _Requests_, on a priority basis, pursuant to Article 96, paragraph 2, of the Charter of the United Nations and in accordance with General Assembly resolution 89(I) of 11 December 1946, an advisory opinion from the International Court of Justice on the legal question of the applicability of article VI, section 22, of the Convention on the Privileges and Immunities of the United Nations in the case of Mr. Dumitru Mazilu as Special Rapporteur of the Sub-Commission.

Economic and Social Council resolution 1989/75

24 May 1989   Meeting 16   24-8-19 (recorded vote)

Approved by Second Committee (E/1989/88) by recorded vote (26-9-16), 19 May (meeting 22); draft by Commission on Human Rights (E/1989/20); oral amendment by United States adopted in plenary; agenda item 9.

Recorded vote in Council as follows:

In favour: Bahamas, Belize, Bolivia, Brazil, Canada, Colombia, Denmark, France, Germany, Federal Republic of, Greece, Ireland, Italy, Japan, Kenya, Netherlands, New Zealand, Norway, Portugal, Trinidad and Tobago, United Kingdom, United States, Uruguay, Venezuela, Yugoslavia.

Against: Bulgaria, Cuba, Czechoslovakia, Iran, Libyan Arab Jamahiriya, Poland, Ukrainian SSR, USSR.

Abstaining: Cameroon, China, Ghana, Guinea, Indonesia, Iraq, Jordan, Lesotho, Liberia, Nicaragua, Niger, Oman, Rwanda, Sri Lanka, Sudan, Thailand, Tunisia, Zaire, Zambia.

Before adopting the resolution as a whole, the Council adopted, by a recorded vote of 17 to 9, with 22 abstentions, the United States oral amendment inserting the words "on a priority basis" in operative paragraph 2.

Speaking prior to the vote, Romania stated that the case in question involved incapacity for work, that it considered the efforts to transform a case of illness into a political and legal issue to be contrary to the purposes of the UN Charter, and that it did not agree that the alleged dispute should be referred to the International Court of Justice.

Report of the Special Rapporteur. In 1989, the Sub-Commission had before it a report[23] on human rights and youth, prepared by Special Rapporteur Dumitru Mazilu and transmitted to it on 10 July. In an introductory note, the Secretary-

General explained that the report was reproduced as received, as he had been unable to consult with the Special Rapporteur regarding its presentation and editing.

The report reviewed the situation of young people and the state of human rights in the world, examined the rights and freedoms of youth as an important component of human rights, and discussed the need to ensure the freedom of thought and expression and the enjoyment by youth of the right to life, education and work. It also suggested measures to be taken by Governments to ensure and promote the rights and freedoms of the younger generation, and proposed a charter of the rights and freedoms of youth. In an addendum, the Special Rapporteur discussed the situation of human rights and youth in Romania, including unprecedented aggression against the rights and freedoms of the younger generation and the destruction of their values and faith under political despotism.

The Special Rapporteur made a number of recommendations pertaining to the right of young people to life; creation of a healthy economic and social environment for youth; measures to attack the production of, demand for and use of illicit drugs; education, vocational training and employment programmes for young people; the establishment of non-exploitative working conditions; the use of science and technology to promote the rights and freedoms of youth; and the promotion of cultural exchanges and organization of seminars and conferences to stimulate public discussion of problems affecting youth.

Sub-Commission action. On 1 September, the Sub-Commission, by 12 votes to 4, with 2 abstentions, requested[24] the Special Rapporteur to update his report and invited him to present it in person to the Sub-Commission in 1990; the Secretary-General was asked to continue to provide him with information relevant to his report and to give the Special Rapporteur all necessary assistance. The Sub-Commission also expressed its deep concern at reports of the personal situation of Mr. Mazilu and his family and asked the Secretary-General to follow the matter closely. The Special Rapporteur on the human rights of UN staff members, experts and their families was requested to submit a note on the subject of Mr. Mazilu's situation to the Commission on Human Rights and to report to the Sub-Commission in 1990.

Traditional practices affecting the health of women and children

Human Rights Commission action. On 6 March, the Commission approved[25] the Sub-Commission's 1988 request[26] to Halima Embarek Warzazi (Morocco) to study recent developments with regard to traditional practices affecting the health of women and children and to report to the Sub-Commission in 1989, as well as its request to the Secretary-General to provide her with all necessary assistance.

Report of the Special Rapporteur. In a preliminary report[27] on the subject, transmitted to the Sub-Commission on 21 August, the Special Rapporteur summarized information received from 17 Governments, 3 UN bodies and 12 NGOs on traditional practices affecting health. In view of the small number of replies, she recommended the continuation of the study and measures to obtain more information and strengthen the report.

Sub-Commission action. On 31 August, the Sub-Commission recommended[28] to the Commission that the Special Rapporteur's mandate be extended for two years and that she undertake field missions, if possible to two countries where harmful traditional practices were prevalent; that seminars be held on such practices in Africa and Asia; that the Centre for Human Rights provide necessary support in preparation of the study, including a full-time professional assistant; and that the subject remain on the Sub-Commission's agenda for sustained follow-up.

Human rights and science and technology

On 15 December, on the recommendation of the Third Committee, the General Assembly adopted **resolution 44/133** without vote.

Human rights and scientific and technological developments

The General Assembly,

Noting that scientific and technological progress is one of the decisive factors in the development of human society,

Recalling the Declaration on the Use of Scientific and Technological Progress in the Interests of Peace and for the Benefit of Mankind, adopted by the General Assembly in its resolution 3384(XXX) of 10 November 1975,

Bearing in mind the relevant provisions of the Universal Declaration of Human Rights, the International Covenant on Economic, Social and Cultural Rights, the International Covenant on Civil and Political Rights and the Declaration on Social Progress and Development,

Conscious that it is only the creative genius of man that makes progress and the development of civilization possible in a peaceful environment and that human life must be recognized as supreme,

Recalling the fundamental importance of the right to life,

Convinced that in the era of modern scientific and technological progress, the resources of mankind and the activities of scientists should be used to promote the peaceful economic, social and cultural development of countries and to improve the living standards of all people,

Bearing in mind that the exchange and transfer of scientific and technological knowledge is one of the important ways to accelerate the social and economic development of the developing countries,

Recalling its relevant resolutions,

1. *Reaffirms* the value of the Declaration on the Use of Scientific and Technological Progress in the Interests of Peace and for the Benefit of Mankind in the promotion of human rights and fundamental freedoms;

2. *Calls upon* all States to make every effort to use the achievements of science and technology in order to promote peaceful social, economic and cultural development and progress;

3. *Recalls* the historic responsibility of the Governments of all countries of the world to preserve civilization and to ensure that everyone enjoys his or her inherent right to life, and calls upon them to do their utmost to assist in protecting the right to life through the adoption of appropriate measures at both the national and international levels;

4. *Calls upon* all States, appropriate United Nations bodies, the specialized agencies and intergovernmental and non-governmental organizations concerned to take the necessary measures to ensure that the results of scientific and technological progress and the material and intellectual potential of mankind are used for the benefit of mankind and for promoting and encouraging universal respect for human rights and fundamental freedoms;

5. *Requests* the Commission on Human Rights to continue to give attention, in its consideration of the item entitled "Human rights and scientific and technological developments", to the question of the implementation of the provisions of the Declaration;

6. *Invites* the Commission on Human Rights to assist the Sub-Commission on Prevention of Discrimination and Protection of Minorities in preparing the study requested by the Commission in its resolutions 1982/4 of 19 February 1982, 1984/29 of 12 March 1984, 1986/11 of 10 March 1986 and 1988/61 of 9 March 1988;

7. *Decides* to include in the provisional agenda of its forty-fifth session the item entitled "Human rights and scientific and technological developments".

General Assembly resolution 44/133

15 December 1989   Meeting 82   Adopted without vote

Approved by Third Committee (A/44/826) without vote, 22 November (meeting 52); 34-nation draft (A/C.3/44/L.55); agenda item 107.
Meeting numbers. GA 44th session: 3rd Committee 36-43, 50, 52; plenary 82.

Computerized personal files

Human Rights Commission action. On 6 March, the Commission, having considered the final report on guidelines for the regulation of computerized personal data files submitted by Special Rapporteur Louis Joinet (France) to the Sub-Commission in 1988,[29] recommended[30] a resolution for adoption by the Economic and Social Council.

ECONOMIC AND SOCIAL COUNCIL ACTION

On 24 May, on the recommendation of its Second Committee, the Council adopted **resolution 1989/78** without vote.

Guidelines on the use of computerized personal files

The Economic and Social Council,

Taking note of resolution 1988/29 of 1 September 1988 of the Sub-Commission on Prevention of Discrimination and Protection of Minorities, and Commission on Human Rights resolution 1989/43 of 6 March 1989 on guidelines on the use of computerized personal files,

1. *Expresses its appreciation* to the Special Rapporteur of the Sub-Commission on Prevention of Discrimination and Protection of Minorities, Mr. Louis Joinet, for his study on guidelines for the regulation of computerized personal data files;

2. *Decides* to transmit to the General Assembly the final report of the Special Rapporteur;

3. *Requests* the Secretary-General to draw the attention of all Governments to the final report of the Special Rapporteur and to invite them to communicate their comments to him before 1 September 1989;

4. *Requests* the Secretary-General to submit to the General Assembly at its forty-fourth session the final report of the Special Rapporteur and a report containing the views expressed thereon by Governments;

5. *Recommends* that the General Assembly consider, as a matter of priority, the adoption and publication of the guidelines on the use of computerized personal files.

Economic and Social Council resolution 1989/78

24 May 1989   Meeting 16   Adopted without vote

Approved by Second Committee (E/1989/88) without vote, 19 May (meeting 22); draft by Commission on Human Rights (E/1989/20); agenda item 9.

Report of the Secretary-General. In a 24 October report to the General Assembly and a later addendum,[31] the Secretary-General analysed replies from nine Governments containing general comments and suggestions on the draft guidelines, as well as comments and proposals for principles stating the minimum guarantees to be incorporated into national legislation.

GENERAL ASSEMBLY ACTION

On 15 December, the Assembly, on the recommendation of the Third Committee, adopted **resolution 44/132** without vote.

Guidelines for the regulation of computerized personal data files

The General Assembly,

Bearing in mind Commission on Human Rights resolution 1989/43 of 6 March 1989 and Economic and Social Council resolution 1989/78 of 24 May 1989, entitled "Guidelines on the use of computerized personal data files",

1. *Expresses its appreciation* to the Special Rapporteur of the Sub-Commission on Prevention of Discrimination and Protection of Minorities, Mr. Louis Joinet, for his report on the draft guidelines for the regulation of computerized personal data files;

2. *Conveys its thanks* to the Governments that have communicated to the Secretary-General their comments and suggestions on the draft guidelines;

3. *Invites* the Special Rapporteur to submit to the Commission on Human Rights at its forty-sixth session

a revised version of the draft guidelines, taking into account, *inter alia*, those comments and suggestions;

4. *Requests* the Commission on Human Rights to examine the revised draft guidelines and, once it has examined and, if necessary, modified them, to transmit them, through the Economic and Social Council, to the General Assembly at its forty-fifth session for final adoption.

General Assembly resolution 44/132

15 December 1989   Meeting 82   Adopted without vote

Approved by Third Committee (A/44/826) without vote, 22 November (meeting 52); 7-nation draft (A/C.3/44/L.54); agenda item 107.
Sponsors: France, Germany, Federal Republic of, Guatemala, Japan, Luxembourg, Morocco, United Kingdom.
Meeting numbers. GA 44th session: 3rd Committee 36-43, 50, 52; plenary 82.

Chemical weapons and the right to life

Report of the Secretary-General. In response to a 1988 Sub-Commission request,[32] the Secretary-General submitted a 17 August report[33] on chemical weapons and respect for the right to life. The report analysed substantive information received from 23 Governments, 3 UN bodies, and 10 NGOs and educational institutions. The information dealt with such topics as the definition of chemical weapons, their use and allegations of use, the importance and continuing validity of the Geneva Protocol of 1925 banning the use of asphyxiating, poisonous and other gases and analogous liquids as well as bacteriological weapons, and multilateral and national action to ban chemical weapons. The Secretary-General concluded that the use of chemical weapons constituted a violation of basic human rights, the right to life and to liberty and security of person, and that urgent and effective international measures should be undertaken to prevent their future use. The complete and effective prohibition of the development, production and stockpiling of all chemical weapons as well as their destruction should be pursued as a matter of continuing urgency, he said. Other conclusions dealt with the strict observance by States of the 1925 Geneva Protocol and mobilization of public opinion in favour of banning chemical weapons.

Sub-Commission action. On 1 September, the Sub-Commission took note[34] of the Secretary-General's report, called on States to abide strictly by their international obligations in that field, and decided to consider the matter further in 1990.

Human rights and the environment

On 31 August, the Sub-Commission concluded[35] that the information on human rights and the environment provided to it in 1989 by a number of NGOs and some of its members, together with the Environmental Perspective to the Year 2000 and Beyond adopted by the General Assembly in 1987,[36] justified consideration of a study of the environment and its relation to human rights. Accordingly, the Sub-Commission asked one of its members, Fatma Ksentini (Algeria), to submit in 1990 a note on methodology for such a study. The Secretary-General was requested to seek relevant information and observations from Governments, UN bodies and specialized agencies, as well as intergovernmental and non-governmental organizations.

Movement and dumping of toxic and dangerous products and waste

Human Rights Commission action. On 6 March, the Commission requested[37] States producing toxic and dangerous wastes to ban their export to countries technically incapable of their environmentally sound disposal; abrogate existing agreements for the disposal of such wastes and products with those countries; and take measures to ensure that those wastes did not imperil human health and the ecosystem in their own as well as other countries. It also requested the United Nations Environment Programme (UNEP) to expedite elaboration of a global convention on the control of transboundary movements of hazardous wastes, and asked the Secretary-General to report on the matter to the Sub-Commission in 1989.

Report of the Secretary-General. In response to the Commission's March request, the Secretary-General reported[38] to the Sub-Commission on 19 June that a conference of plenipotentiaries, convened in Basel, Switzerland, by the Executive Director of UNEP, had adopted on 22 March 1989 the Final Act of the Basel Convention on the Control of Transboundary Movements of Hazardous Wastes and Their Disposal (see PART THREE, Chapter VIII). The Final Act provided, *inter alia*, for the establishment of a technical working group to prepare draft guidelines on environmentally sound waste management aimed at minimizing the risk to human health, and urged States to take steps to stop illegal traffic in hazardous wastes, including by signing and becoming parties to the Convention. The Secretary-General informed the Sub-Commission that UNEP was in the process of finalizing a report to the General Assembly on illegal traffic of hazardous wastes, and that the Basel Convention addressed steps to prevent and respond to such traffic.

Sub-Commission action. On 31 August, the Sub-Commission recommended[39] that the Commission adopt a resolution requesting UNEP to enter into negotiations with the Organization of African Unity (OAU) to find global solutions to the problem of the transboundary movement of hazardous wastes and their disposal, and asking the Secretary-General to report on the result of the negotiations to the Sub-Commission in 1990 and to the Commission in 1991.

Human rights and health

On 2 March, the Commission on Human Rights reaffirmed[40] the right of everyone to the enjoyment of the highest attainable standard of physical and mental health, recognized the importance of non-discrimination in access to health care, and invited the Sub-Commission to consider extending the scope of a study on discrimination against persons with HIV or suffering from AIDS (see above, under "Discrimination") to other kinds of discrimination against sick or disabled persons.

Human rights of disabled persons

On 6 March, the Commission approved[41] the Sub-Commission's 1988 request[32] to Special Rapporteur Leandro Despouy (Argentina) to continue his work on the study of the relationship between human rights and disability and to submit a final report to the Sub-Commission in 1990. It also approved the request to the Secretary-General to provide the Rapporteur with all possible assistance.

Mental illness

Human Rights Commission action. On 6 March, the Commission decided[42] to establish an open-ended working group to revise the draft body of principles and guarantees for the protection of mentally ill persons and for the improvement of mental health care, adopted by the Sub-Commission in 1988,[43] and requested the working group to meet for two weeks before the Commission's 1990 session. Member States were invited, pending the adoption of a body of principles and guarantees, to adhere to the existing standards set out in international human rights instruments and to take steps to protect the rights of persons detained on grounds of mental ill-health or suffering from mental disorder. The Commission requested the Secretary-General to invite comments on the subject from Governments, specialized agencies and NGOs for consideration by the working group.

ECONOMIC AND SOCIAL COUNCIL ACTION

On 24 May, the Economic and Social Council, on the recommendation of its Second Committee, adopted **resolution 1989/76** without vote.

Principles and guarantees for the protection of persons detained on grounds of mental ill-health or suffering from mental disorder

The Economic and Social Council,

Recalling Commission on Human Rights resolution 1989/40 of 6 March 1989,

1. *Authorizes* an open-ended working group of the Commission on Human Rights to meet for a period of two weeks prior to the forty-sixth session of the Commission to examine, revise and simplify as necessary the draft body of principles and guarantees for the protec-

tion of mentally ill persons and for the improvement of mental health care submitted to the Commission by the Sub-Commission on Prevention of Discrimination and Protection of Minorities, with a view to submitting it to the Commission at its forty-sixth session;

2. *Requests* the Secretary-General to extend all facilities to the working group for its meeting to be held prior to the forty-sixth session of the Commission;

3. *Requests* the Secretary-General, on the basis of the comments received from Governments, specialized agencies and non-governmental organizations in response to paragraph 6 of Commission on Human Rights resolution 1989/40, to prepare a working paper showing the modifications that would be made to the existing draft body of principles and guarantees as a result of those comments.

Economic and Social Council resolution 1989/76

24 May 1989   Meeting 16   Adopted without vote

Approved by Second Committee (E/1989/88) without vote, 19 May (meeting 22); draft by Commission on Human Rights (E/1989/20), amended by 6 nations (E/1989/C.2/L.17); agenda item 9.
Sponsors of amendment: France, Germany, Federal Republic of, Italy, Peru, Philippines, United Kingdom.

Sub-Commission action. On 31 August, the Sub-Commission requested[44] the Secretary-General to make available to the working group and to the Commission's 1990 session copies of the study on principles, guidelines and guarantees for the protection of persons detained on the grounds of mental ill-health or suffering from mental disorder, as well as the relevant documentation containing a summary of national legislation and comments on the subject from Governments, specialized agencies, intergovernmental organizations and NGOs.[45]

GENERAL ASSEMBLY ACTION

On 15 December, on the recommendation of the Third Committee, the General Assembly adopted **resolution 44/134** without vote.

Human rights and scientific and technological developments

The General Assembly,

Recalling its resolution 33/53 of 14 December 1978, in which it requested the Commission on Human Rights to urge the Sub-Commission on Prevention of Discrimination and Protection of Minorities to undertake, as a matter of priority, a study of the question of the protection of those persons detained on the grounds of mental ill-health, with a view to formulating guidelines,

Bearing in mind the obligation of all States to promote and respect the human rights and fundamental freedoms of everyone, including disadvantaged people, such as those suffering from mental illness,

Mindful of the Principles of Medical Ethics relevant to the role of health personnel, particularly physicians, in the protection of prisoners and detainees against torture and other cruel, inhuman or degrading treatment or punishment,

Recalling also its resolution 43/109 of 8 December 1988, in which it welcomed the progress made by the Working Group of the Sub-Commission on Prevention of Discrimination and Protection of Minorities and invited the Commission on Human Rights to consider the subject at its forty-fifth session, in the light of the Sub-Commission's recommendations,

Taking note of Commission on Human Rights resolution 1989/40 of 6 March 1989 and Economic and Social Council resolution 1989/76 of 24 May 1989, by which the Council authorized an open-ended working group of the Commission to examine, revise and simplify as necessary the draft body of principles and guarantees for the protection of mentally ill persons and for the improvement of mental health care submitted by the Sub-Commission, with a view to submitting it to the Commission at its forty-sixth session,

Expressing its belief that all mentally ill persons should be treated with humanity and the respect due the inherent dignity of the human person,

Reaffirming its conviction that the misuse of psychiatry to detain persons in mental institutions on account of their political views or on other non-medical grounds, as reflected in the report of the Special Rapporteur of the Sub-Commission, is a violation of their human rights,

1. *Reiterates* the urgent need for principles and guarantees to protect persons suffering from mental disorder or detained on the grounds of mental ill-health;

2. *Welcomes* the establishment of the open-ended working group of the Commission on Human Rights, and urges that group to examine expeditiously the draft body of principles and guarantees for the protection of mentally ill persons and for the improvement of mental health care;

3. *Requests* the Commission on Human Rights to consider the subject at its forty-sixth session, in the light of the deliberations and recommendations of the open-ended working group, with a view to submitting the draft body of principles and guarantees to the General Assembly at its forty-fifth session, through the Economic and Social Council.

General Assembly resolution 44/134

15 December 1989   Meeting 82   Adopted without vote

Approved by Third Committee (A/44/826) without vote, 22 November (meeting 52); 17-nation draft (A/C.3/44/L.56); agenda item 107.
Meeting numbers. GA 44th session: 3rd Committee 36-43, 50, 52; plenary 82.

Human rights of the individual and international law

Human Rights Commission action. On 6 March, the Commission approved[46] the Sub-Commission's 1988 request[32] to Special Rapporteur Erica-Irene A. Daes (Greece) to update her study on the status of the individual and contemporary international law for submission to the Sub-Commission in 1989, and the request to the Secretary-General to give the Rapporteur all necessary assistance.

Report of the Special Rapporteur. On 26 July, the Special Rapporteur submitted her updated study[47] to the Sub-Commission. The study provided an overview of contemporary international law, reviewed institutions and concepts related to the protection of the individual and his responsibilities, discussed the individual as a subject of international duties and as a subject in contemporary international law, and considered the international procedural capacity of the individual and his position in the European Community, in the inter-American system and in the African system.

It concluded that the legal doctrine after the Second World War prevailingly recognized a world community of individuals who were subjects of international law along with States, and that the individual became the bearer of rights under the rules of international law. The study recommended greater popularization of international human rights standards and dissemination of information on the promotion, protection and restoration of those rights; creation of more effective institutions accessible to individuals for protecting their rights; new mechanisms for reviewing violations of such rights and obtaining redress, and for appeal to international procedures when domestic remedies had been exhausted; easier access for individuals to international courts and tribunals; due ratification and application as substantive law of international human rights instruments; recognition by States of the need for supranational protection and enforcement of human rights norms; and the accordance of the individual with personality under international law and with certain rights and responsibilities as a subject of such law. Other recommendations dealt with the establishment of an objective international criminal jurisdiction, adoption of international standards related specifically to the status of the individual, and proposed studies on related topics.

Sub-Commission action. On 1 September, the Sub-Commission recommended[48] to the Commission a resolution by which it would decide that the study on the status of the individual and contemporary international law should be published and widely disseminated.

Human rights and international peace

On 1 September, the Sub-Commission, convinced of the necessity to undertake a study on the negative consequences of the arms race requested by the Commission in 1982,[49] and having discussed the Secretary-General's 1988 report[26] on the interrelationship between human rights and international peace, emphasized[50] that that interrelationship required further examination and invited one of its members, Murlidhar Bhandare (India), to prepare a working paper on the subject for consideration in 1991. It also emphasized that the strengthening of international peace and security and reduction of expenditure for arms were important conditions for social and economic development and for the materialization of all human rights, particularly the right to life and the right to development. It also underlined that the realization of human rights in the whole world would contribute to achieving international peace and security.

REFERENCES

[1]A/INF/44/3. [2]YUN 1977, p. 706. [3]YUN 1988, p. 580. [4]E/CN.4/Sub.2/1989/58 (res. 1989/24). [5]E/CN.4/1989/48. [6]E/1989/20 (res. 1989/57). [7]E/CN.4/1989/29/Rev.1. [8]E/1989/57. [9]YUN 1966, p. 423, GA res. 2200 A (XXI), annex, 16 Dec. 1966. [10]A/44/616. [11]E/CN.4/Sub.2/1989/58 (res. 1989/41). [12]E/1989/20 (res. 1989/35). [13]E/CN.4/Sub.2/1989/38. [14]YUN 1988, p. 582. [15]E/CN.4/Sub.2/1989/39. [16]E/CN.4/Sub.2/1989/58 (res. 1989/43). [17]*Ibid.* (res. 1989/42). [18]E/CN.4/ 1989/69. [19]YUN 1946-47, p. 100, GA res. 22 A (I), annex, 13 Feb. 1946. [20]YUN 1985, p. 931. [21]E/1989/20 (res. 1989/37). [22]*Ibid.* (res. 1989/58). [23]E/CN.4/Sub.2/1989/41 & Add.1. [24]E/CN.4/Sub.2/1989/58 (res. 1989/45). [25]E/1989/20 (dec. 1989/107). [26]YUN 1988, p. 583. [27]E/CN.4/Sub.2/1989/42 & Add.1. [28]E/CN.4/Sub.2/1989/58 (res. 1989/16). [29]YUN 1988, p. 585. [30]E/1989/20 (res. 1989/43). [31]A/44/606 & Add.1. [32]YUN 1988, p. 586. [33]E/CN.4/Sub.2/1989/4. [34]E/CN.4/ Sub.2/1989/58 (res. 1989/39). [35]*Ibid.* (dec. 1989/108). [36]YUN 1987, p. 661, GA res. 42/186, 11 Dec. 1987. [37]E/1989/20 (res. 1989/42). [38]E/CN.4/Sub.2/1989/3. [39]E/CN.4/Sub.2/1989/58 (res. 1989/12). [40]E/1989/20 (res. 1989/11). [41]*Ibid.* (dec. 1989/ 106). [42]*Ibid.* (res. 1989/40). [43]YUN 1988, p. 517. [44]E/CN.4/ Sub.2/1989/58 (dec. 1989/107). [45]YUN 1983, p. 841. [46]E/1989/20 (dec. 1989/108). [47]E/CN.4/Sub.2/1989/40. [48]E/CN.4/Sub.2/1989/58 (res. 1989/46). [49]YUN 1982, p. 1140. [50]E/CN.4/Sub.2/1989/58 (res. 1989/47).

Chapter XI

Health, food and nutrition

In 1989, the United Nations continued to respond to international problems concerning health, food and nutrition. As the global dimension of acquired immunodeficiency syndrome (AIDS), the human immunodeficiency virus (HIV) and their extensive socio-economic and humanitarian implications became widely known, collaboration among organizations of the UN system and governmental and non-governmental organizations accelerated. The World Health Organization estimated the actual number of AIDS cases world wide to be three times higher than officially reported. In December, the General Assembly urged increased efforts to advance the global strategy against the pandemic (resolution 44/233).

Efforts continued to reactivate and strengthen national disability committees to attain the goals set in the Programme of Action concerning the United Nations Decade of Disabled Persons. The Assembly reaffirmed the validity of the Programme of Action and reiterated that for the second half of the Decade, special emphasis should be placed on the equalization of opportunities for the disabled (44/70). It also drew attention to the Tallinn Guidelines for Action on Human Resources in the Field of Disability, adopted at an International Meeting held in the USSR.

World food production rose 3.2 per cent in 1989. In per capita terms, it rose 1.4 per cent, after having fallen by a cumulative 2.5 per cent during 1986-1988. In all developing regions except East Asia, food and agricultural growth fell below the average rate of the 1980s. In May, the World Food Council adopted the Programme of Co-operative Action, calling for fundamental policy changes and a firm political commitment to eliminating hunger and poverty. In July, the Economic and Social Council urged the World Food Council to carry out activities in the areas of nutrition, food security and agricultural trade (resolution 1989/88). A sum of $1.5 billion was set by the General Assembly as the target for voluntary contributions to the World Food Programme for the period 1991-1992 (resolution 44/230).

The statement issued by the 1988 Conference on Nutrition in Times of Disaster was brought to the Economic and Social Council's attention in July.

Health

Human and environmental health

In 1989, human and environmental health questions were dealt with by several United Nations agencies and bodies such as the World Health Organization (WHO), the United Nations Environment Programme (UNEP), the United Nations Children's Fund (UNICEF) and the International Labour Organisation (ILO).

During the year,[1] WHO continued to promote human and environmental health by monitoring air, water and food; studying the potential and actual risks of modern technology to human health; and controlling adverse health effects of industrial development and energy use. It carried out a wide range of activities in community water supply and sanitation, environmental health in rural and urban development and housing, control of environmental health hazards and food safety. It co-operated with the Food and Agriculture Organization of the United Nations (FAO) on nutrition and safe use of pesticides; with the United Nations Educational, Scientific and Cultural Organization (UNESCO) on health education and AIDS; with ILO on occupational safety and health and social security schemes; and with the United Nations Industrial Development Organization on industrial aspects of the production of essential drugs and pharmaceutical supplies.

The WHO/ILO/UNEP International Programme on Chemical Safety continued to provide information on the risks to human health and the environment of potentially toxic chemicals, and guidance in the safe use of chemicals. (See also PART SEVEN, Chapter V.)

In a May report,[2] the Secretary-General reviewed the *Consolidated List of Products Whose Consumption and/or Sale Have Been Banned, Withdrawn, Severely Restricted or Not Approved by Governments*, including its scope, format and use. He recommended introducing a data-base system, an annual compilation in English and cross-referencing for each product entry.

The United Nations Scientific Committee on the Effects of Atomic Radiation, at its thirty-eighth session in May, decided[3] to undertake studies in the following fields: occupational radiation exposures; effects of radiation exposures on plants and animals in the environment; effects on the developing human brain from pre-natal radiation exposures; and mechanisms by which radiation causes cancer.

AIDS prevention and control

In May, the Secretary-General transmitted to the General Assembly, through the Economic and Social Council, a WHO Director-General's report on a global strategy for the prevention and control of AIDS,[4] and a supplementary note on AIDS-related activities by the organizations of the UN system.[5] The report, requested by the General Assembly in 1988,[6] reviewed the global epidemiological situation and WHO's collaboration with organizations of the system and non-governmental organizations (NGOs).

The number of AIDS cases reported to WHO continued to rise rapidly in 1989. As at 1 March, 141,894 cases had been reported by 145 of the 177 reporting countries and territories. This included 99,752 cases, or 70 per cent, in the Americas, 85 per cent of which were in the United States. Africa and Europe each accounted for some 15 per cent of the world total, while Asia and the Pacific (including the Eastern Mediterranean region) reported 1 per cent. However, under-recognition of AIDS cases and under-reporting to national health authorities had resulted in an underestimate of the total. The actual cumulative number of AIDS cases as at the same date was estimated to be some 450,000.

The Global Commission on AIDS, a group of eminent experts established to give guidance to the Director-General of WHO, held its first meeting (Geneva, 29-31 March) and recommended integrating activities of the Global Programme on AIDS, intensifying co-operation with the United Nations Drug Control Programme on policies on AIDS and drug use, paying attention to risk behaviours and applicable international law on human rights, and involving NGOs. The Global Programme on AIDS continued to alert countries to the serious public health problem represented by AIDS and collaborated with them to strengthen national programmes on AIDS. Its Management Committee consisted of UNICEF, the United Nations Development Programme (UNDP), UNESCO, the United Nations Population Fund and the World Bank, as well as the Commission for the European Communities, 18 donor Governments and 12 member States selected by WHO. By the end of 1989, the Global Programme had collaborated with 159 countries on a technical evaluation of the HIV/AIDS situation or in support of national programme formulation. Of those countries, 123 had a short-term plan and 95 had formulated a medium-term plan for their programme. To strengthen collaboration with NGOs, WHO supported the organizing committee for a proposed non-governmental international council of AIDS service organizations, to be launched in 1990. In addition, over $650,000 were provided to NGOs for country-level activities. In May, the WHO World Health Assembly emphasized the importance of the collaboration between WHO and NGOs; urged Member States to collaborate with WHO to increase their capacity; and requested the Director-General to ensure co-ordination between the WHO programme on the prevention and control of drug and alcohol abuse and the Global Programme on AIDS.

Co-ordination of activities of the United Nations system was facilitated through the United Nations steering committee, established by the Under-Secretary-General for International Economic and Social Affairs as the focal point at UN Headquarters for activities related to the prevention and control of AIDS, and through the Inter-Agency Advisory Group on AIDS, established by WHO in response to a 1987 General Assembly resolution.[7] The steering committee provided input to the work of the Advisory Group.

Under the auspices of the WHO/UNDP Alliance to Combat AIDS, proclaimed in 1988,[8] UNDP assisted the integration of national AIDS plans into overall development policies and priorities, supported programme development and delivery, and helped Governments minimize the impact of AIDS on social and economic development.

WHO, in collaboration with UNESCO, completed a guide for school health education to prevent AIDS and other sexually transmitted diseases, which served as a catalyst for seven projects aimed at introducing innovative approaches to AIDS education. In March, UNESCO established the AIDS School Education Resource Centre to collect, analyse and disseminate information and documentation among UNESCO member States and their partners in education for AIDS prevention.

During the year, several volumes were published in the WHO AIDS series, including: the second edition of the *Guidelines on Sterilization and Disinfection Methods Effective against Human Immunodeficiency Virus (HIV)*, *Guidelines on the Monitoring of National AIDS Prevention and Control Programmes*, and the *Guide to Planning Health Promotion for AIDS Prevention and Control*.

In December, the Population Division Task Force of the Department of International Economic and Social Affairs, in collaboration with WHO, organized a workshop on modelling the demographic impact of the AIDS epidemic in pattern II (sub-Saharan African and some Caribbean and Latin American) countries. A consultation on AIDS and human rights was organized by the

United Nations Centre for Human Rights (Geneva, 26-28 July), which discussed the need to protect the human rights and dignity of people with AIDS or HIV infection and those perceived to be at risk, and specified a number of areas for further work (see PART THREE, Chapter X).

With the Government of France, WHO organized the International Conference on the Implications of AIDS for Mothers and Children (Paris, 27-30 November). Among topics discussed were virology, HIV and pregnancy, and diagnosis. World AIDS Day was observed on 1 December with a focus on AIDS and youth.

ECONOMIC AND SOCIAL COUNCIL ACTION

On 27 July, the Economic and Social Council, on the recommendation of the Third (Programme and Co-ordination) Committee, adopted **resolution 1989/108** without vote.

Prevention and control of acquired immunodeficiency syndrome (AIDS)

The Economic and Social Council,

Recalling its resolution 1988/55 of 27 July 1988, General Assembly resolution 43/15 of 27 October 1988, World Health Assembly resolutions WHA 42.20 of 17 May 1989 and WHA 42.33 and WHA 42.34 of 19 May 1989, other relevant resolutions, the London Declaration on AIDS Prevention and the discussions at the Fifth International Conference on AIDS, held at Montreal from 4 to 9 June 1989,

Acknowledging the established leadership of the World Health Organization in directing and co-ordinating AIDS education, prevention, control and research,

Noting with appreciation the efforts of other organizations of the United Nations system, as well as national Governments and non-governmental organizations,

Welcoming, in particular, the World Health Organization/United Nations Development Programme Alliance to Combat AIDS and the role of the Alliance in facilitating the implementation at the country level of the global strategy for the prevention and control of AIDS,

Recalling the resolutions of the World Health Assembly and the General Assembly concerning the socio-economic and humanitarian aspects of the problem, including the need to respect the human rights and dignity of all people, including those infected with the human immunodeficiency virus (HIV),

Reaffirming that the struggle against AIDS should be consistent with and divert neither attention nor resources from other national public health priorities and development goals and should not divert international efforts and resources needed for overall health priorities,

Aware that AIDS can have serious economic and social consequences, particularly in countries with a high incidence of infection from the human immunodeficiency virus and limited public health services and other developmental resources,

Aware of the need to address the problem of drug abuse from the perspective of AIDS prevention and control,

Concerned that, depending upon individual and social circumstances, women and children recently appear to have developed a higher risk of infection from the human immunodeficiency virus,

1. *Takes note* of the report of the Director-General of the World Health Organization on the global strategy for the prevention and control of AIDS and the supplementary report on AIDS-related activities being carried out by the organizations of the United Nations system;

2. *Notes with appreciation and welcomes* the arrangements made by the Secretary-General, in close co-operation with the Director-General of the World Health Organization, to ensure a co-ordinated response by the United Nations system to the AIDS pandemic pursuant to Economic and Social Council resolution 1988/55 and General Assembly resolution 43/15;

3. *Requests* the Secretary-General, in view of the potentially serious implications of the AIDS pandemic for socio-economic development in some developing countries, to intensify his efforts, in close co-operation with the Director-General of the World Health Organization, to mobilize the technical and other relevant resources of the United Nations system, through co-ordinated research and programme measures, to deal with this aspect of the problem;

4. *Calls upon* Governments and non-governmental organizations to co-ordinate their efforts with the World Health Organization in implementing the global strategy for the prevention and control of AIDS;

5. *Invites* the General Assembly to consider the report of the Director-General of the World Health Organization and the response of the United Nations system to the AIDS pandemic and to take an appropriate decision on further action, taking the present resolution into account.

Economic and Social Council resolution 1989/108

27 July 1989   Meeting 36   Adopted without vote

Approved by Third Committee (E/1989/133) without vote, 21 July (meeting 16); 23-nation draft (E/1989/C.3/L.10/Rev.1); agenda item 9c.
Sponsors: Australia, Austria, Brazil, Bulgaria, Canada, Denmark, Finland, France, German Democratic Republic, Japan, Netherlands, New Zealand, Norway, Poland, Rwanda, Spain, Sweden, Thailand, USSR, United Kingdom, United States, Zambia, Zimbabwe.

GENERAL ASSEMBLY ACTION

On 22 December, the General Assembly, on the recommendation of the Second (Economic and Financial) Committee, adopted **resolution 44/233** without vote.

Prevention and control of acquired immunodeficiency syndrome (AIDS)

The General Assembly,

Recalling its resolution 43/15 of 27 October 1988, other relevant resolutions and the London Declaration on AIDS Prevention adopted by the World Summit of Ministers of Health on Programmes for AIDS Prevention on 28 January 1988 and taking note of Economic and Social Council resolution 1989/108 of 27 July 1989, World Health Assembly resolutions WHA 42.20 of 17 May 1989 and WHA 42.33 and WHA 42.34 of 19 May 1989 and the discussions of the Fifth International Conference on AIDS, held at Montreal, Canada, from 4 to 9 June 1989,

Acknowledging the established leadership of the World Health Organization in directing and co-ordinating AIDS education, prevention, control and research,

Noting with appreciation the efforts of other organizations of the United Nations system, as well as Governments, intergovernmental and non-governmental organizations and the public and private sector, in combating the spread of AIDS,

Welcoming, in particular, the World Health Organization Global Programme on AIDS, and noting that the World Health Organization/United Nations Development Programme Alliance to Combat AIDS is facilitating the implementation at the country level of the global strategy for the prevention and control of AIDS,

Recalling the resolutions of the General Assembly, the World Health Assembly and the Economic and Social Council concerning the need to respect the human rights and dignity of all people, including those affected by the human immunodeficiency virus (HIV), their families and those with whom they live,

Reaffirming that the struggle against AIDS should be consistent with and divert neither attention nor resources from other national public health priorities and development goals and should not divert international efforts and resources needed for overall health priorities,

Aware that AIDS can have serious social and economic consequences, particularly in countries with a high incidence of infection from HIV and limited public health services and other developmental resources,

Recognizing that, depending upon individual and social circumstances, women and children may be at a higher risk of infection from HIV than previously recognized and may otherwise suffer deprivation as a consequence of the indirect impact of AIDS on their families and communities,

Emphasizing the crucial importance of a supportive socio-economic environment in ensuring the effective implementation of national AIDS prevention programmes and the humane care of affected persons,

Recognizing the need for all sectors of society to contribute actively to the local, national and international efforts for HIV/AIDS prevention and control,

Noting that scientific research is making progress in the development of improved diagnostic, therapeutic and preventive technologies and pharmaceuticals, and stressing the importance of making these technologies and pharmaceuticals available as soon as possible and at an affordable cost,

1. *Takes note* of the report of the Director-General of the World Health Organization on the global strategy for the prevention and control of AIDS and the supplementary report on activities and programmes being carried out by United Nations entities on the socio-economic and humanitarian aspects of AIDS;

2. *Notes with appreciation and welcomes* the arrangements made by the Secretary-General, in close co-operation with the Director-General of the World Health Organization, to ensure a co-ordinated response by the United Nations system to the AIDS pandemic pursuant to General Assembly resolution 43/15 and Economic and Social Council resolution 1989/108;

3. *Requests* the Secretary-General, in view of the potentially serious implications of the AIDS pandemic for socio-economic development in some developing countries, to intensify his efforts, in collaboration with the Director-General of the World Health Organization, all other relevant organizations of the United Nations system, and the World Health Organization/United Nations Development Programme Alliance to Combat AIDS, to mobilize the technical and other relevant resources of the United Nations system, at all levels, in-

cluding at the regional and country levels, through co-ordinated research and programmes, to deal with this aspect of the problem;

4. *Urges* Member States to increase their efforts to combat AIDS and to encourage, support and facilitate national efforts to prevent the further spread of AIDS;

5. *Calls upon* Governments, the World Health Organization, all other relevant United Nations organizations and intergovernmental and non-governmental organizations to promote greater awareness about the transmission of the pandemic in order to avoid misconceptions as much as possible and to increase the understanding of the general public towards people affected by the human immunodeficiency virus (HIV);

6. *Calls upon* international, national and research institutions and organizations to co-ordinate their activities so as to provide input to and be supportive of the policy of national AIDS committees and the global AIDS strategy of the World Health Organization in a manner appropriate to local conditions and requirements;

7. *Requests* the Secretary-General to invite the Director-General of the World Health Organization, in close collaboration with the other organizations of the United Nations system and without prejudice to ongoing priorities and programmes, to continue to develop and advance the global strategy for the prevention and control of AIDS, and specifically:

(a) To promote the contribution of non-governmental organizations to the global strategy through support of national efforts;

(b) To collaborate, as appropriate, with the United Nations Office at Vienna, the United Nations Children's Fund and other United Nations bodies, as well as Governments and non-governmental organizations in their efforts to develop:

(i) Policies, programmes and research proposals to address the impact of AIDS, including issues affecting women, and to promote the vital role of women in preventing and controlling the pandemic;

(ii) Policies and programmes to alleviate the impact of AIDS, in all its aspects, on children;

(iii) Policies and programmes to combat the illicit traffic in and abuse of drugs, with a view to contributing to a reduction in the spread of HIV infection;

(c) To promote access of all peoples to appropriate preventive, diagnostic and therapeutic technologies and pharmaceuticals and to help make these technologies and pharmaceuticals available at an affordable cost;

(d) To promote the active participation of public and private sector enterprises, including through financial contributions, in HIV/AIDS prevention and control efforts at the local, national and international levels;

8. *Requests* the Secretary-General to invite the Director-General of the World Health Organization to report to the General Assembly at its forty-fifth session, through the Economic and Social Council, on the implementation of the present resolution.

General Assembly resolution 44/233

22 December 1989   Meeting 85   Adopted without vote

Approved by Second Committee (A/44/832/Add.1) by consensus, 21 November (meeting 41); draft by Vice-Chairman (A/C.2/44/L.34), based on informal consultations on 30-nation draft (A/C.2/44/L.22) and orally revised; agenda item 12.

Meeting numbers. GA 44th session: 2nd Committee 15, 17, 34, 35, 41; plenary 85.

Women and AIDS

In a February report[9] on the effects of AIDS on the advancement of women, submitted to the Commission on the Status of Women, the Secretary-General outlined the nature and epidemiology of AIDS, considered the particular vulnerability of women to HIV infection and dealt with effects of HIV/AIDS on women, both infected and non-infected. Women in many societies lacked equal access to education, training, health, independent incomes, and property and legal rights, which affected both their access to knowledge of AIDS and the measures to prevent transmission of HIV virus, as well as their ability to protect themselves from infection. According to WHO, at least 1.5 million women were infected with HIV world wide. Non-infected women were also affected in so far as societies and families expected women to bear the sole burden as carers for AIDS patients, and in cases where their partners on whom they were economically dependent died of the disease. The report recommended the holding of a seminar for representatives of both the national machineries and the national AIDS committees; co-operation between the United Nations and relevant NGOs to assist Governments in policy formulation and implementation; and action-oriented research on economic, social and cultural consequences for women of the AIDS pandemic in order to assist national machineries to develop their role.

By **decision 1989/127** of 24 May, the Economic and Social Council took note of the Secretary-General's report. It requested the Secretary-General to convene an expert group meeting to prepare for an international meeting of representatives of national machineries for the advancement of women and of national AIDS committees, to identify appropriate strategies and programmes at the national level and to promote co-operation between them.

Disabled persons

Implementation of the Programme of Action

Report of the Secretary-General. The Secretary-General, in a January report[10] to the Commission for Social Development, reviewed progress made in monitoring and evaluating the implementation of the 1982 World Programme of Action concerning Disabled Persons[11] for the second half of the United Nations Decade of Disabled Persons (1983-1992).[12] He noted that considerable additional resources were still needed to ensure the success of the Decade. While a global campaign in support of the Decade had been proposed, it had not been possible to raise the seed money to launch it. For its part, the Commission called for further implementation of the Programme of Action and

the consistent financial support of the Member States.

ECONOMIC AND SOCIAL COUNCIL ACTION

On 24 May, the Economic and Social Council, on the recommendation of its Second (Social) Committee, adopted **resolution 1989/52** without vote.

United Nations Decade of Disabled Persons

The Economic and Social Council,

Recalling General Assembly resolutions 37/52 of 3 December 1982, by which the Assembly adopted the World Programme of Action concerning Disabled Persons, and 37/53 of 3 December 1982, by which it proclaimed the period 1983-1992 the United Nations Decade of Disabled Persons, and other relevant General Assembly and Economic and Social Council resolutions,

Recalling also General Assembly resolution 43/98 of 8 December 1988, by which the Assembly adopted a list of priorities for global activities and programmes for the second half of the Decade and requested the Secretary-General to undertake a feasibility study on the substantive, financial and administrative implications of alternative ways of marking the end of the Decade in 1992, and to submit the study to the Assembly at its forty-fifth session,

Noting with satisfaction the strengthening of the Disabled Persons Unit of the Centre for Social Development and Humanitarian Affairs of the Secretariat through the generous financial support of some Governments,

Noting with appreciation the installation at the Centre for Social Development and Humanitarian Affairs of a Thiel Braille Printer donated by a foundation,

Noting with deep concern that many developing countries are facing enormous difficulties in dealing with increasing numbers of disabled people, and recognizing the need for developed countries and appropriate United Nations bodies to take this into account when planning bilateral and multilateral development co-operation,

Recognizing the pivotal role of the United Nations in promoting the exchange of information, experience and expertise and closer regional and interregional co-operation to advance the status and welfare of disabled persons,

Stressing that the Centre for Social Development and Humanitarian Affairs is the focal point within the United Nations system for the implementation and monitoring of the World Programme of Action concerning Disabled Persons,

Mindful that the incidence of disability rapidly increases with age, that the problems facing the aging are very often similar to those facing the disabled and that the number of aged persons affected by disability is increasing,

Mindful also of the often extremely difficult position of disabled women,

Taking note with appreciation of the report of the Secretary-General on the progress made in monitoring and evaluating the implementation of the World Programme of Action concerning Disabled Persons for the second half of the United Nations Decade of Disabled Persons,

1. *Calls upon* Member States, bodies and organizations of the United Nations system and intergovernmental and non-governmental organizations to further the

practical implementation of the World Programme of Action concerning Disabled Persons during the second half of the United Nations Decade of Disabled Persons, based on the list of priorities for global activities and programmes set forth in the annex to General Assembly resolution 43/98;

2. *Urges* Member States, bodies and organizations of the United Nations system and intergovernmental and non-governmental organizations to provide all possible support to the awareness and fund-raising campaigns to give added momentum to the Decade;

3. *Requests* the Secretary-General to strengthen the clearing-house function of the Secretariat by exploring possibilities, including the financial implications of implementing an international information system, and by encouraging Member States and organizations that have acquired experience in the disability field to inform the Centre for Social Development and Humanitarian Affairs of the Secretariat of their experience;

4. *Also requests* the Secretary-General to disseminate relevant information, on a pilot basis, within existing resources and with voluntary contributions, on the activities of the Disabled Persons Unit of the Centre for Social Development and Humanitarian Affairs in forms accessible to blind persons, in order to facilitate the Secretary-General's examination of ways of making United Nations meetings, information materials and documents accessible to disabled persons, as well as his determination of the financial implications thereof, pursuant to General Assembly resolution 43/98, paragraph 7;

5. *Further requests* the Secretary-General to determine the financial implications of the implementation of the recommendations contained in the three studies on accessibility to United Nations buildings, documents and information by persons with sensory disabilities, prepared in conjunction with the International Year of Disabled Persons 1981, pursuant to General Assembly resolution 35/133 of 11 December 1980;

6. *Requests* the Secretary-General and Member States to pay special attention during the second half of the Decade to the functioning and reactivation of national bodies for disabled persons and to the development and strengthening of powerful and influential organizations of disabled persons;

7. *Calls upon* Member States to give due consideration to the close interrelationship between aging and disability and to give attention to the application of measures aimed at avoiding or curing disabilities of aging persons, and invites Member States that have conducted research in this field to provide the Secretariat with information on the results;

8. *Also calls upon* Member States and appropriate United Nations organizations and bodies, when planning their development co-operation and similar projects, to give increased attention to the needs of disabled persons in developing countries;

9. *Invites* the Secretary-General, in connection with the preparation of the feasibility study of alternative ways to mark the end of the Decade in 1992, to convene an expert meeting in 1990, within the existing resources, *inter alia*, to advise on the best possible ways of marking the end of the Decade and of continuing the work in the disability field;

10. *Requests* the Secretary-General and Member States to give particular attention to improving the situation of vulnerable groups, as outlined in the World Programme of Action, emphasizing the need for social justice and the participation of those groups in each sector of society;

11. *Requests* the Secretary-General to ensure that contributions, in kind or cash, related to the Decade are channelled into the Voluntary Fund for the United Nations Decade of Disabled Persons, already established by the General Assembly; such contributions may be earmarked by the donors for special purposes;

12. *Also requests* the Secretary-General to report to the Commission for Social Development at its thirty-second session on the implementation of the present resolution.

Economic and Social Council resolution 1989/52

24 May 1989   Meeting 15   Adopted without vote

Approved by Second Committee (E/1989/91) without vote, 11 May (meeting 12); draft by Commission for Social Development (E/1989/25); agenda item 11.

Report of the Secretary-General. In response to a 1988 General Assembly request,[13] the Secretary-General reported[14] on the implementation of the Programme of Action concerning Disabled Persons. In reviewing the recent activities of Member States, organizations of the UN system, and intergovernmental and non-governmental organizations, he stated that progress since 1983 in attaining the goals of the Programme of Action—namely, prevention, rehabilitation and equalization of opportunities—had been slow and frustrating at all levels.

National disability committees or similar co-ordinating bodies continued to play a crucial role in the implementation of the Programme of Action. In May, the Secretary-General appealed to Member States to establish or strengthen their co-ordinating committees on disability. The Centre for Social Development and Humanitarian Affairs of the United Nations Office at Vienna prepared a study on the structure and functioning of those committees. Other activities of the Centre included disseminating information material, strengthening organizations of disabled persons, co-ordinating inter-agency collaboration in the field of disability, developing its own clearing-house capacity through a data-base system and promoting employment opportunities for disabled persons in the United Nations.

The Office of the Special Representative of the Secretary-General for the Promotion of the United Nations Decade of Disabled Persons established contacts with some 200 organizations of or for disabled persons and organized a consultative meeting with international NGOs (Vienna, 8 and 9 June).

The seventh inter-agency meeting on the United Nations Decade of Disabled Persons (Vienna, 6-8 December)[15] discussed employment and social security; statistics on disabled persons, including necessary adaptation of the International Classification of Impairment, Disability and Handicap; the second round of the monitoring and evaluation exercise on the implementation of the World Programme of Action concerning Disabled Persons; alternative ways to mark the end of the Decade in 1992; and equal employment opportunities for disabled persons in the United Nations. It made a number of recommendations to the Administrative Committee on Co-ordination (ACC).

Although progress was made in planning the global campaign to increase public awareness of the Decade and to raise funds for projects to benefit disabled people, the seed money needed to launch it had not yet been raised. The campaign was to be carried out under the auspices of the United Nations with the full participation of key international NGOs.

UNDP action. The Governing Council of UNDP, in June, requested[16] the Administrator to provide the necessary support to enhance the capacity of the International Initiative against Avoidable Disablement[17] and its network foundations to promote actions for the prevention and cure of the causes of disability. The International Initiative, established in 1983 with the joint sponsorship by UNDP, WHO and UNICEF, in collaboration with the United Nations Centre for Social Development and Humanitarian Affairs, sought to apply proven low-cost techniques for preventing and treating disabilities by incorporating them into health and other development programmes.

Human resources
in the field of disability

In 1989, the International Meeting on Human Resources in the Field of Disability was convened (Tallinn, USSR, 14-22 August) by the Centre for Social Development and Humanitarian Affairs. It considered the situation of human resources development in the field of disability, particularly in developing countries. The Meeting adopted the Tallinn Guidelines for Action on Human Resources Development in the Field of Disability (see below) to promote the participation, training and employment of disabled persons.

GENERAL ASSEMBLY ACTION

On 8 December, the General Assembly, on the recommendation of the Third (Social, Humanitarian and Cultural) Committee, adopted **resolution 44/70** without vote.

Implementation of the World Programme of Action concerning Disabled Persons and the United Nations Decade of Disabled Persons
The General Assembly,
Recalling all its relevant resolutions, including resolution 37/52 of 3 December 1982, by which it adopted the World Programme of Action concerning Disabled Persons, and resolution 37/53 of 3 December 1982, in which, *inter alia*, it proclaimed the period 1983-1992 the United Nations Decade of Disabled Persons,
Recalling also its resolution 43/98 of 8 December 1988, and reaffirming all of the relevant provisions contained

therein, in particular the list of priorities for global activities and programmes during the second half of the United Nations Decade of Disabled Persons set forth in the annex to the resolution,
Taking note of Economic and Social Council resolution 1989/52 of 24 May 1989, in which the Council, *inter alia*, urged Member States, bodies and organizations of the United Nations system and intergovernmental and non-governmental organizations to provide all possible support to the awareness and fund-raising campaigns to give added momentum to the Decade,
Noting the important work currently being undertaken by the Sub-Commission on Prevention of Discrimination and Protection of Minorities on human rights and disability, which could serve as a useful basis for the continued efforts to ensure for disabled persons the enjoyment of human rights and fundamental freedoms,
Taking into account the concrete measures already carried out by the Governments of Member States, the bodies and organizations of the United Nations system and non-governmental organizations to implement the objectives of the World Programme of Action within the framework of the Decade, and recognizing that much more should be done at all levels to improve the living conditions of persons with disabilities,
Mindful that Member States bear the ultimate responsibility for the implementation of the World Programme of Action and that national disability committees or similar co-ordinating bodies play a crucial role in this regard,
Recognizing the pivotal role of the United Nations in promoting the exchange of information, experience and expertise and closer regional and interregional co-operation towards more effective strategies and policies to advance the status and welfare of persons with disabilities,
Stressing that the Centre for Social Development and Humanitarian Affairs of the Secretariat is the focal point within the United Nations for the implementation and monitoring of the World Programme of Action,
Noting with satisfaction the strengthening of the Disabled Persons Unit of the Centre through the generous financial support of some Governments,
Concerned that the Voluntary Fund for the United Nations Decade of Disabled Persons continues to suffer from a lack of sufficient contributions and that, unless this declining trend is reversed and the resource capacities of the Fund are strengthened, many priority requests may not be met and the implementation of the World Programme of Action will be seriously affected,
Mindful that, since developing countries are experiencing difficulties in mobilizing resources, international co-operation should be encouraged to assist in national efforts to implement the World Programme of Action and the objectives of the Decade,
Noting that the International Meeting on Human Resources in the Field of Disability was held at Tallinn, Union of Soviet Socialist Republics, from 14 to 22 August 1989 and that it adopted a nine-point strategy to promote the participation, training and employment of disabled persons, especially in developing countries,
Having considered the report of the Secretary-General,
1. *Reaffirms* the validity of the World Programme of Action concerning Disabled Persons;
2. *Reiterates* that for the second half of the United Nations Decade of Disabled Persons special emphasis should be placed on the equalization of opportunities for disabled persons;

3. *Urges* Member States, intergovernmental organizations and non-governmental organizations concerned to translate into action at all levels, as appropriate, the priorities for global activities and programmes during the second half of the Decade, such as those set forth in the annex to General Assembly resolution 43/98;

4. *Renews its invitation* to all States to give high priority to projects concerning the prevention of disabilities, rehabilitation and the equalization of opportunities for disabled persons within the framework of bilateral assistance, as well as financial support to strengthen organizations of disabled persons;

5. *Invites* Governments to participate actively in the international co-operation with a view to improving the living conditions of disabled persons by encouraging professional experts, in particular disabled persons, in various aspects of rehabilitation and the equalization of opportunity, including the expertise of retired persons;

6. *Requests* the Secretary-General to assist Member States in establishing and strengthening national committees on disability issues and similar co-ordinating bodies and to promote and support the establishment of strong national organizations of disabled persons;

7. *Also requests* the Secretary-General to encourage all organs and bodies of the United Nations, including regional commissions, international organizations and specialized agencies, to take into account in their programmes and operational activities the specific needs of disabled persons;

8. *Invites* the Secretary-General, in connection with the feasibility study on the substantive, financial and administrative implications of alternative ways to mark the end of the Decade in 1992, called for by the General Assembly in its resolution 43/98, to request Member States, in consultation with organizations of disabled persons, to submit their comments to him by 28 February 1990 for inclusion in the background document to be discussed at the meeting of experts to be held at Helsinki in May 1990;

9. *Requests* the Secretary-General to strengthen the regional commissions to enable them to promote technical co-operation activities and the sharing of national resources for personnel training, the exchange of information, policy and programme development and research and the participation of disabled persons;

10. *Invites* the Secretary-General and Member States to involve disabled persons to a greater extent in United Nations programmes and activities, including the provision of employment opportunities, and to give particular attention to improving the situation of special groups as outlined in the World Programme of Action, emphasizing the need for social justice and the participation of these groups in each sector of the society;

11. *Invites* the Centre for Social Development and Humanitarian Affairs of the Secretariat to expand its close collaboration with intergovernmental and non-governmental organizations active in the field of disability, in particular organizations of disabled persons, and to consult with them on a regular and systematic basis on matters relating to the implementation of the World Programme of Action, with a view to ensuring that the results of the Decade become meaningful and lasting;

12. *Notes with satisfaction* the progress made by the office of the Special Representative for the Promotion of the United Nations Decade of Disabled Persons;

13. *Calls upon* Member States, national committees, the United Nations system and non-governmental organizations, especially organizations of disabled persons, to assist in a global information and fund-raising campaign to publicize the Decade through all appropriate means;

14. *Recognizes* the important role of non-governmental organizations, especially those representing persons with disabilities, in the effective implementation of the World Programme of Action, in raising international awareness of the concerns of persons with disabilities and in monitoring and evaluating progress achieved during the Decade;

15. *Requests* the Secretary-General to ensure that contributions, in cash or in kind, related to the Decade are channelled into the Voluntary Fund for the United Nations Decade of Disabled Persons, while giving donors the option of earmarking contributions for special purposes;

16. *Reaffirms* that the resources of the Voluntary Fund should be used to support catalytic and innovative activities in order to implement further the objectives of the World Programme of Action within the framework of the Decade, with priority given, as appropriate, to programmes and projects of the least developed countries;

17. *Invites* Governments and non-governmental organizations to continue their contributions to the Voluntary Fund, and calls upon Governments and non-governmental organizations that have not yet done so to consider contributing to the Voluntary Fund so as to enable it to respond effectively to the growing demand for assistance;

18. *Requests* the Secretary-General to bring the Tallinn Guidelines for Action on Human Resources Development in the Field of Disability, the text of which is annexed to the present resolution, to the attention of Member States, national co-ordinating mechanisms in the field of disability, organizations of the United Nations system, other intergovernmental bodies and non-governmental organizations concerned with disabilities;

19. *Requests* the Secretary-General to report to the General Assembly at its forty-fifth session on the implementation of the present resolution;

20. *Decides* to include in the provisional agenda of its forty-fifth session the item entitled ''Implementation of the World Programme of Action concerning Disabled Persons and the United Nations Decade of Disabled Persons''.

ANNEX
Tallinn Guidelines for Action on Human Resources Development in the Field of Disability

Introduction

1. The International Meeting on Human Resources in the Field of Disability, convened at Tallinn, Union of Soviet Socialist Republics, from 14 to 22 August 1989, having considered the situation of human resources development in the field of disability, particularly in developing countries, firmly believes that it is necessary to reinforce existing activities, as well as to undertake new and innovative ones, in order to promote the further development and continued progress of disabled persons.

2. Following the adoption of the World Programme of Action concerning Disabled Persons by the General

Assembly, in its resolution 37/52 of 3 December 1982, there has been a growing need for higher priority to be given to the development of the human resources of disabled persons, with specific reference to education and training, employment, and science and technology. In this connection, the General Assembly, in its resolution 37/53 of 3 December 1982, proclaimed the period 1983-1992 the United Nations Decade of Disabled Persons, encouraging Member States to utilize that period as one of the means to implement the World Programme of Action.

3. The main objectives of the World Programme of Action are to promote effective measures for the prevention of disability, for rehabilitation and for the realization of the goals of full participation and equality for persons with disabilities. To accomplish these goals, due regard must be paid to education, training and work opportunities.

4. While it is acknowledged that the living conditions of the general population in developing countries urgently need to be improved, the objectives of the World Programme of Action call for the situation of disabled persons to be given special attention during the remainder of the Decade and beyond. Effective implementation of the World Programme of Action will make an important contribution to the process of development of societies through the mobilization of more human resources.

5. While it is also acknowledged that a number of countries have already initiated or carried out activities within the framework of the World Programme of Action, further concerted efforts should be made to integrate the human resources development of disabled persons into intersectoral planning at the national level.

Guiding philosophy

6. Human resources development is a process centred on the human person that seeks to realize the full potential and capabilities of human beings. This process is fundamental to the concept of equalization of opportunities, in keeping with the goals of the World Programme of Action.

7. Through human resources development, disabled persons are able effectively to exercise their rights of full citizenship. As full citizens, they have the same rights and responsibilities as other members of society, including the right to life, as declared in international human rights instruments. They also have the same choices as other citizens in the social, cultural, economic and political life of their communities.

8. Because persons with disabilities are agents of their own destiny rather than objects of care, Governments and organizations need to reflect this perception in their policies and programmes. This means that disabled persons, as individuals and as members of organizations, should be involved in the decision-making process as equal partners.

9. The abilities of disabled persons and their families should be strengthened through community-based supplementary services provided by Governments and non-governmental organizations. These services should promote self-determination and enable disabled persons to participate in the development of society. Governments should recognize and support the role of organizations of disabled persons in enabling those persons to take charge of their own lives.

Strategies

A. *Participation of persons with disabilities*

10. A statutory basis is required to enable disabled persons to participate as full citizens in decision-making at all levels of the planning, implementation, monitoring and evaluation of policies and programmes.

11. To facilitate the full participation of disabled persons and to enable them to exercise their rights as citizens, access to information is essential. To this end, all information has to be adapted to appropriate formats. These information formats may include Braille script, large print, audio-visual media and sign-language interpretation. Information channels should include television, radio, newspapers and postal services. Governments should work with organizations of disabled persons to identify appropriate information formats and channels to reach disabled citizens.

12. Governments should adopt, enforce and fund legally binding standards and regulations to improve access for persons with disabilities, ensuring that buildings, streets, and road, sea and air transport are barrier-free, architecturally and in all other ways. Communication systems and security and safety measures should be developed and adapted to meet the needs of disabled citizens.

13. To facilitate the recruitment of disabled persons and to assist private-sector industries in hiring them, organizations at the national, regional and international levels, including the United Nations, should identify and maintain listings of qualified disabled candidates.

B. *Strengthening of grass-roots initiatives*

14. Local community initiatives should be especially promoted. Disabled persons and their families should be encouraged to form grass-roots organizations, with governmental recognition of their importance and governmental support in the form of financing and training.

15. Governmental and non-governmental organizations concerned with disability issues should allow disabled persons to participate as equal partners.

16. The efficient functioning of governmental and non-governmental organizations concerned with disability calls for training in organizational and management skills.

C. *Promotion of an integrated approach*

17. Overall national policy frameworks with supporting legislation should be developed.

18. The essence of an integrated approach is the inclusion of disability issues in all government ministries and at every level of governmental policy and planning. National co-ordination bodies, with linkages at the local, regional and interregional levels, should be established or strengthened. The membership of those bodies should include all government ministries, legislative committees and non-governmental organizations, particularly organizations of disabled persons. Those bodies should review existing policies, plans and programmes, identify existing and projected resources and monitor and evaluate the implementation of national policies.

19. National development programmes should include disability components.

20. Disabled women should be included in the existing national and regional programmes aimed at women.

21. At the level of service delivery, an integrated approach entails co-operation and referral among professionals working in organizational settings that provide educational, vocational, health and social services.

D. *Promotion of education and training*

22. The early years are critical in the overall development of a disabled child and for the fostering of positive attitudes towards the child. Specific programmes and training materials should be developed to address these needs during the formative infant and pre-school years.

23. Education at the primary, secondary and higher levels should be available to disabled persons within the regular educational system and in regular school settings, as well as in vocational training programmes. When such education is provided to deaf students, teachers and/or interpreters who are proficient in the indigenous sign language must be provided.

24. Special education programmes and schools that promote the indigenous sign language and the indigenous deaf culture must be available to deaf people. Deaf people should be employed in such programmes and schools.

25. Cost-effective alternatives to segregated school facilities should be developed and implemented by Governments at the national and local levels. These alternatives include special education teachers as consultants to regular education teachers, resource rooms with specialized personnel and materials, special classrooms in regular schools and interpreters for deaf students.

26. The education of disabled children should involve the co-operation and concerted efforts of health and social services, as well as of teachers and parents. It should provide support measures, such as technical aids, especially adapted pedagogical approaches, and incentives for teachers.

27. The content and quality of education and training should ensure the acquisition of skills that are economically viable and that provide opportunities for work. Career education and vocational training programmes should be available to ensure the transition of disabled students into the economic mainstream.

28. In addition to being offered formal skills training and education, disabled persons should be offered training in social and self-help skills to prepare them for independent living. Special efforts should be made to promote education and skills training for disabled girls and women, in both urban and rural areas.

29. General teacher-training curricula should include a course of study in skills for teaching disabled children and young persons in regular schools.

30. Each Government should have a national plan for training and employing an adequate number of health, education and vocational professionals in rehabilitation. Persons with disabilities should be recruited for such training and employment.

31. In fields such as education, labour, health and social services, law, architecture and technical development, which are often involved in the different aspects of rehabilitation, professional training should include training on the rights and needs of disabled people. Professionals in these fields should also be made aware of the resources available for disabled persons so that appropriate referrals can be made or services provided.

32. Appropriate technology should be considered essential for the utilization of available resources. This may include simple, universally available equipment, as well as computer technology.

E. *Promotion of employment*

33. Disabled persons have the right to be trained for and to work on equal terms in the regular labour force. Community-based rehabilitation programmes should be encouraged to provide better job opportunities in developing countries. Use should be made of the vocational services, guidance and training, placement, employment and related services that already exist for workers in general. On-the-job training may be more effective than conventional training.

34. General development programmes that provide loans, training and equipment for income-generating activities should include disabled persons.

35. Employment opportunities can be promoted, primarily, by measures relating to employment and salary standards that apply to all workers and, secondarily, by measures offering special support and incentives. In addition to formal employment, opportunities should be broadened to include self-employment, co-operatives and other group income-generating schemes. Where special national employment drives have been launched for youth and unemployed persons, disabled persons should be included. Disabled persons should be actively recruited, and when a disabled candidate and a non-disabled candidate are equally qualified, the disabled candidate should be chosen.

36. Organizations of employers and of workers should adopt, in co-operation with organizations of disabled persons, policies that promote the training and employment of disabled persons, including women, and non-disabled persons on an equal basis.

37. Policies for affirmative action should be formulated and implemented to increase the employment of disabled women. Governments and non-governmental organizations should support the creation of income-generating projects involving disabled women.

F. *Provisions for funding*

38. In general, funding should be allocated through regular sectoral budgeting systems. A national rehabilitation fund may be established to facilitate the employment or self-employment of disabled persons. This fund could be used to cover the costs of training, equipment and initial capital outlay.

39. Similarly, funds should be established for loans to small-scale pilot projects at the grass-roots level; such funds could be administered locally with the use of simple procedures.

G. *Promotion of community awareness*

40. To increase community understanding of the rights, needs and potentials of disabled persons, collaborative efforts with disabled persons and their organizations are required to develop and promote a flow of information using mass media, especially film, television, radio and print media. In particular, information for disabled persons and their families on all aspects of living with a disability should be as clear and uncomplicated as possible.

41. Community awareness programmes should include specific strategies for the prevention of disability. Government efforts aimed at early identification, intervention and prevention should be strengthened through community awareness and community involvement in programmes on disability.

42. Persons with mental disabilities (mental retardation or mental illness) or multiple disabilities are among the most stigmatized groups of citizens. They have the right to make choices, take risks, control their own lives and live in the community. Their adult status, abilities and aspirations must be respected and reinforced by their inclusion in decision-making, although many may need individual advocacy to be clearly understood.

43. It should be acknowledged that people with mental and multiple disabilities benefit from education, skills training and work opportunities. For many of these people, opportunities need to be individualized. Support is required to help them and their families to establish and maintain a positive life-style.

44. The World Programme of Action should be translated into all national languages, through governmental action. Braille, large print and simplified versions should also be made available by the appropriate media to ensure as wide a distribution as possible to all citizens, including disabled persons, their families and non-governmental and governmental organizations.

H. *Improving the methodology for human resources development*

45. Policies and programmes for human resources development concerning disabled persons should be based on an assessment of their needs and resources as well as on the potential of existing development programmes and services to meet those needs. The implementation of such policies and programmes should be periodically monitored, with adjustments made to ensure effective implementation.

46. Evaluation should be built into programmes at the planning stage so that their overall efficacy in fulfilling policy objectives can be assessed. Persons with disabilities should play an active role in developing the criteria for monitoring and evaluation.

47. Increased attention should be given to services for people with hearing, speech, mental, intellectual or multiple disabilities.

48. The requirements of particular groups, such as disabled children, disabled women, the disabled elderly, disabled migrants and refugees, should also be recognized and met.

49. Governmental and non-governmental organizations should utilize recent developments in education through communications media, also known as distance education, which has been found to be an appropriate methodology in human resources development in the field of disability.

50. The local use of appropriate technologies for producing such items as wheel chairs, prosthetic devices and mobility aids, as well as aids for hearing and seeing, should take into account the technical, socio-economic and cultural conditions in the particular society. Each country should have a national system for the delivery of rehabilitation aids.

I. *Regional and international co-operation*

51. Training programmes in human resources development in the field of disability should be strengthened by collaborative efforts at the regional and/or subregional levels. Such programmes should be co-ordinated through existing intergovernmental and regional organizations, including those of disabled persons.

52. International development aid projects should include a component specifically aimed at supporting

organizations of disabled persons and training their members. In addition, employment opportunities should be made available to disabled individuals within these projects.

53. All international development assistance programmes directed at macro-level planning and development, such as those in agriculture or education, should include a specific component ensuring the participation of disabled persons in such programmes.

54. At both the national and interregional levels, Governments should strongly support collaboration with non-governmental agencies in specific areas of disability, to ensure co-ordination and to prevent duplication of services.

55. Linkages between organizations of disabled persons in developed and developing countries should be strengthened. This can be done through the exchange of information, training and meetings to provide forums for disabled persons to share experiences on strategic approaches. Workshops and field studies should be organized to train trainers and the management personnel of organizations of disabled persons.

56. Implementation of these Guidelines relies on effective action at the national level. This action should be supplemented by concerted efforts at the international level, particularly on the part of the United Nations and its focal point for the implementation of the World Programme of Action concerning Disabled Persons, as well as relevant United Nations organizations and specialized agencies. National and international non-governmental organizations, in particular organizations of disabled persons, should be fully involved.

General Assembly resolution 44/70

8 December 1989   Meeting 78   Adopted without vote

Approved by Third Committee (A/44/755) without vote, 9 November (meeting 37); 35-nation draft (A/C.3/44/L.20), orally revised; agenda item 101.
Sponsors: Bangladesh, Belgium, Cameroon, Canada, China, Colombia, Costa Rica, Denmark, Dominica, Dominican Republic, Egypt, El Salvador, Finland, Germany, Federal Republic of, Greece, Guatemala, Iceland, Italy, Japan, Kenya, Libyan Arab Jamahiriya, Mauritania, Morocco, Myanmar, Norway, Peru, Philippines, Romania, Samoa, Sudan, Sweden, USSR, United States, Yugoslavia, Zimbabwe.
Meeting numbers. GA 44th session: 3rd Committee 12-20, 30, 37; plenary 78.

UN trust fund

The Voluntary Fund for the United Nations Decade of Disabled Persons since 1980 had provided over $2 million in seed money grants to 110 projects of benefit to disabled persons.[14] It received more than 70 requests for assistance in the 18-month period ending June 1989. Of those, 25 were approved for funding, involving a resource disbursement of $353,651; of those grants, 8 were in Africa, 7 in Asia and the Pacific, 2 in Latin America and the Caribbean, 1 in Western Asia, and 7 were interregional and global. Projects included training, technical exchange, data collection and applied research, support to organizations of or for disabled persons, promotional activities and technical co-operation on disability policies and programmes.

At the 1989 United Nations Pledging Conference for Development Activities (New York, 30 and 31 October), a total of $237,035 from 11 Governments was pledged or paid to the Fund for 1990.

REFERENCES

(1)A/44/339/Add.2-E/1989/119/Add.2. (2)A/44/276-E/1989/78. (3)A/44/587. (4)A/44/274-E/1989/75. (5)A/44/274/Add.1-E/1989/75/Add.1. (6)YUN 1988, p. 589, GA res. 43/15, 27 Oct. 1988. (7)YUN 1987, p. 645, GA res. 42/8, 26 Oct. 1987. (8)YUN 1988, p. 588. (9)E/CN.6/1989/6/Add.1. (10)E/CN.5/1989/6. (11)YUN 1982, p. 980. (12)_Ibid._, p. 983, GA res. 37/53, 3 Dec. 1982. (13)YUN 1988, p. 590, GA res. 43/98, 8 Dec. 1988. (14)A/44/406/Rev.1. (15)ACC/1989/PG/11. (16)E/1989/32 (dec. 89/43). (17)YUN 1983, p. 760.

Food and agriculture

Food problems

World agricultural and food production rose 3.2 per cent in 1989, exceeding the average of the 1980s by a substantial margin. This increase mainly reflected a recovery in North America after the 1988 drought and a moderate recovery in Eastern Europe and the USSR from the 1988 shortfall. Although developing countries increased agricultural and food production by 2.5 per cent, 64 of them failed to increase per capita food production. In a report to the World Food Council (WFC) on the current world food situation,(1) the Food and Agriculture Organization of the United Nations (FAO) provided an overview of the food supply, food emergencies, cereal stocks, food imports by developing countries and food aid.

In Africa, food supplies in the sub-Saharan region remained stable in most of the 45 countries, but critical shortages persisted in several countries, including Ethiopia and the Sudan. Shortfalls in food supplies requiring exceptional or emergency assistance were reported also in Afghanistan, Haiti, Lebanon, Nicaragua, Peru, Samoa and Sri Lanka.

Global cereal production reached 1,867 million tons, 123 million tons more than in 1988; however, world cereal stocks were expected to decline by 13 million tons to 293 million tons, which would represent 17 per cent of total cereal consumption, the minimum level estimated by FAO to safeguard world food security.

In the 1989/90 season, cereal imports by developing countries were expected to increase by 3.5 per cent to 121 million tons; wheat, 71.3 million tons; coarse grain, 39.5 million tons; and rice, 10.4 million tons. Food aid in cereals for the same season was estimated at 11.6 million tons, compared to 10 million tons in 1988/89. The increase reflected additional allocations, mainly to Poland and Romania, from the European Economic Community, the United States and other donors. Total shipments to low-income food-deficit countries were expected to be 8.5 million tons.

In response to a 1988 General Assembly request,(2) the Secretary-General submitted an updated comprehensive report(3) on trends in the international market for agricultural and tropical products and on the liberalization of international agricultural trade. He discussed the importance of agricultural production and trade to developing countries, global and regional trends in this area, and the current situation and short-term prospects for international agricultural markets, including food security. Suggestions were made on ways and means of increasing the share of developing countries in international agricultural trade, while avoiding the potentially adverse short-term effects on these countries, in particular those that imported food.

WFC activities

The 36-member WFC, the highest international body dealing with food problems, held its fifteenth ministerial session(4) (Cairo, Egypt, 22-25 May) in 1989, and deliberated on the implementation of the Cyprus Initiative against Hunger in the World.(5) The Council's discussions were based on its President's report,(6) comprised of a review of global hunger 15 years after the World Food Conference,(7) an assessment of the effectiveness of selected policies and programmes against hunger and malnutrition, and a proposed programme of co-operative action. The Council noted that hunger was growing and existed everywhere, including in many developed countries, despite the fact that the world was feeding more people than at the time of the World Food Conference. It stated that the elimination of hunger and poverty must be made a central objective of national policies, emphasizing the importance of supportive changes in social and cultural policies, economic reforms, employment, judicious population policies and comprehensive food strategies. The Programme of Co-operative Action was adopted as a framework for individual and collective action to combat hunger. The Council decided to refer to its conclusions and recommendations as the Cairo Declaration.

As a follow-up to the Cairo Declaration, WFC organized a regional consultation for Latin America and the Caribbean (San José, Costa Rica, 5-6 December). The meeting reviewed the hunger and poverty situation, identified priorities to improve the food security of the poor and discussed the issue of international co-operation and assistance.

ECONOMIC AND SOCIAL COUNCIL ACTION

On 26 July, the Economic and Social Council, on the recommendation of its First (Economic) Committee, adopted **resolution 1989/88** without vote.

Food and agriculture

The Economic and Social Council,

Deeply concerned that hunger, malnutrition and poverty continue to increase in large areas of the third world while the world has the capacity to provide adequate food for every human being,

Noting with concern that, although the growth of world agricultural production has to some degree slowed down, tensions concerning trade in agricultural markets remain serious, notably owing to the persistence and, in some cases, intensification of agricultural protectionism and support measures, including, among other problems, import restrictions and export subsidies in some developed countries,

Taking note of the report of the World Food Council on the work of its fifteenth session and of the report of the Secretary-General on trends in the international market for agricultural and tropical products and the liberalization of international agricultural trade,

1. *Welcomes* the renewed international commitment to fight hunger, malnutrition and poverty expressed in the Cyprus Initiative against Hunger in the World and in the Cairo Declaration of the World Food Council;

2. *Welcomes also* the Programme of Co-operative Action annexed to the Cairo Declaration, as a framework for concrete action against hunger and poverty by Governments, international organizations and non-governmental organizations;

3. *Urges* developed countries that are in a position to do so to increase their official development assistance flows and to adopt aid strategies that focus in particular on meeting the needs of the poorest countries and peoples and on improving their food production capabilities;

4. *Stresses* the urgent need for substantial progress in stimulating food production in developing countries and the importance of increasing domestic food production for stimulating national economic growth and social progress in those countries and helping to resolve the problem of hunger and malnutrition in an effective way;

5. *Calls upon* all countries to continue to respond to food emergency situations promptly and flexibly, in conformity with the provisions of General Assembly resolution 43/131 of 8 December 1988;

6. *Reaffirms* that the right to food is a human right that should be guaranteed to all people and, in that context, that, as a general principle, food should not be used as an instrument of political pressure at either the national or the international level;

7. *Stresses* that the Uruguay Round of multilateral trade negotiations presents a unique opportunity to develop a more open, viable and durable trading system, to reverse the disquieting rise in protectionism and to bring agriculture under the strengthened and more operationally effective rules and disciplines of the General Agreement on Tariffs and Trade, in accordance with the relevant parts of the Punta del Este Declaration and the mid-term review of the Uruguay Round, taking into account the need to avoid potentially adverse effects on developing countries, especially those that import food, and bearing in mind the overall benefits of trade liberalization;

8. *Urges* the World Food Council, within its mandate, to continue:

(a) To assess the overall impact of structural adjustment programmes in developing countries on the nutritional levels of their populations, especially among children and low-income groups, and to suggest remedial measures, including ways of stimulating the provision of resources to eliminate the suffering of those groups;

(b) To assess the potential impact of liberalizing international trade in agricultural and tropical products on all countries, and especially on the food security and development efforts of developing countries, and, in this context, to maintain an active interest in the progress and outcome of the Uruguay Round of multilateral trade negotiations;

(c) To promote activities related to food security and agricultural trade as well as to regional and South-South co-operation in food and agriculture, within the context of economic growth and the development needs of developing countries;

(d) To stimulate progress in and contribute more actively to the full implementation of the food policy and programme components of the United Nations Programme of Action for African Economic Recovery and Development 1986-1990;

9. *Calls upon* bilateral, multilateral and non-governmental international organizations to improve the co-ordination of their activities in support of efforts to fight hunger and poverty in developing countries;

10. *Requests* the Secretary-General, in consultation with the World Food Council, the United Nations Conference on Trade and Development and the Food and Agriculture Organization of the United Nations, to prepare for the General Assembly at its forty-fifth session an updated comprehensive report on trends in the international market for agricultural and tropical products and the liberalization of international agricultural trade.

Economic and Social Council resolution 1989/88

26 July 1989   Meeting 35   Adopted without vote

Approved by First Committee (E/1989/137) without vote, 24 July (meeting 27); draft by Malaysia for Group of 77 (E/1989/C.1/L.10), orally revised; agenda item 7 *(b)*.

Food aid

CFA activities

At its twenty-seventh session (Rome, Italy, 29 May–3 June),[8] the Committee on Food Aid Policies and Programmes (CFA)—the governing body of the World Food Programme (WFP)—conducted its fourteenth annual review of food aid policies and programmes and approved the WFP Executive Director's annual report covering 1988.[9] It approved the strong rural bias in WFP-assisted projects and urged the strengthening of agricultural and rural development assistance by improving planning and implementation and by training local personnel. CFA supported the Executive Director's proposal to increase WFP assistance on a case-by-case basis to help least developed countries bear the costs of internal transport, storage and handling of food provided by WFP, and to sell limited amounts of food, within existing authorities and guidelines, for that purpose. Endorsing the comprehensive WFP sectoral guidelines on women and development, it urged intensified support for women's access to credit, land and other factors of production, as well as investment in social services that would improve women's participation in production sectors. CFA also endorsed new funding mechanisms for protracted emergency operations for refugees and displaced persons; from 1990, $15 million would be set aside each year for sudden emergencies, while situations that had endured for more than one year would be funded from a subset of regular resources to be contributed separately by donors over and above their pledges, which could be supplemented by up to $30 million annually from regular resources.

The Committee approved 17 projects with a total cost of $300.6 million, representing a food commitment of approximately 718,600 tons, as well as budget increases for five approved projects, making a total cost of $15.8 million.

At its twenty-eighth session (Rome, 11-13 December),[10] CFA approved 14 projects with a combined cost of $225.9 million, representing a food commitment of approximately 760,000 tons. The Committee also approved the 1990 WFP operations and resources for the relief and rehabilitation of Afghan refugees and displaced persons.

The fourteenth annual report covering WFP's activities in 1988 was submitted to the Economic and Social Council in June 1989.[11] The Council, by **decision 1989/189** of 28 July, took note of the report.

WFP activities

In 1989, WFP—a joint undertaking of the United Nations and FAO—continued to provide developing countries with food aid for development and emergency relief.[12] The volume of food aid deliveries declined due to the reduction in aggregate cereal production in the major food-exporting developed countries in 1987 and 1988. Twenty-three per cent of all food aid was channelled through WFP, which delivered 1.6 million tons of cereals and 262,000 tons of non-cereals, compared to 2.4 million tons and 311,000 tons in 1988, respectively. In value terms, nearly half of the food aid, including that for development and emergency purposes, was to least developed countries.

WFP provided 8.4 million people with emergency food assistance. A record 680,000 tons of food, valued at over $157 million, was purchased using its own resources and funds provided through the Food Aid Convention (FAC), the International Emergency Food Reserve (IEFR), and on behalf of bilateral donors and other UN organizations. More than two thirds of the commodities were purchased in developing countries.

During the year, more than 3,500 government officials from 35 countries participated in WFP training programmes in the areas of project management, monitoring and evaluation, food storage and distribution.

Development assistance

At the end of 1989, WFP had 288 active development projects with a total value of $3.45 billion—193 agricultural and rural development projects valued at $2.23 billion and 95 human resources development projects valued at $1.23 billion—155 of which had environmental components.[13] WFP shipped over 1 million tons of food with a total value of $486 million to development projects; a further $575 million (representing 1.58 million tons of food) was committed for future delivery to 43 new development projects or expansions of existing projects as well as budget increases for ongoing ones.

Low-income food-deficit countries received 80 per cent of 1989 commitments for development activities. With $1.2 billion worth of ongoing projects, sub-Saharan Africa received the largest share—32 per cent—of total WFP development assistance. However, new commitments for projects in 1989 were $141 million, compared to $266 million committed in 1988. The region also received $15.4 million of non-food assistance. New development commitments in 1989 to other regions were as follows: $184 million (32 per cent) to Asia and the Pacific; $106 million (18 per cent) to Latin America and the Caribbean; and $144 million (25 per cent) to North Africa and the Middle East.

During the year, 22 projects for protracted assistance to refugees and displaced persons were approved for 1990 under new funding modalities, entailing a total commitment of 857,000 tons of food with a value of $265.6 million.

Emergency operations

Nearly 8.4 million people in 24 countries received emergency food assistance through WFP's 46 emergency operations approved in 1989. The year's commitment under those programmes of 259,000 tons of food, valued at more than $93 million, was considerably lower than in 1988. The decline was a result of the introduction of the umbrella programme for Afghan refugees and of the protracted refugee and displaced person projects, both funded under separate subsets of WFP resources. Sub-Saharan Africa received 76 per cent of the emergency resources; Europe, North Africa and the Near East, 13 per cent; Asia and the Pacific, 8 per cent; and Latin America and the Caribbean, 3 per cent.

Man-made disasters required 78 per cent of WFP's emergency resources. These disasters included new situations in El Salvador, Mauritania and Senegal, Rwanda and Burundi, Namibia, Turkey, and Uganda. Six countries (Ethiopia, Lao People's Democratic Republic, Madagascar, Tunisia, Uganda, United Republic of Tanzania) received assistance to overcome drought or crop failures.

In 1989, WFP participated in "Operation Lifeline Sudan", the relief effort launched by the United Nations, and transported some 40,000 tons of food aid to the war-devastated country. Its costs were funded by pledges from donors amounting to $21.9 million (see PART THREE, Chapter III).

WFP resources

Pledges and contributions

For the 1989-1990 biennium, combined total resources contributed or pledged to WFP regular resources, FAC, IEFR, the Afghanistan programme and other efforts reached nearly $1.4 billion, including some 3.6 million tons of food. By the end of 1989, 73 countries had pledged just over $1 billion, or 72 per cent of the target. Of that amount, 75 per cent was in the form of commodities, with 25 per cent in cash.

Contributions to IEFR for 1989 amounted to some 400,000 tons of food, worth $129 million. In addition, 188,000 tons of food for Afghan refugees was pledged, but was accounted for separately starting 1 April 1989. Twenty-three donors, including four developing countries, contributed to IEFR. Had assistance for Afghan refugees been included in the IEFR total, contributions would have exceeded the 1989 target of 500,000 tons.

CFA proposed a pledging target of $1.5 billion for the WFP regular resources for the 1991-1992 biennium, of which one third should be in cash.

ECONOMIC AND SOCIAL COUNCIL ACTION

On 28 July, the Economic and Social Council, on the recommendation of its Third Committee, adopted **resolution 1989/121** without vote.

Target for World Food Programme pledges for the period 1991-1992

The Economic and Social Council,

Noting the comments of the Committee on Food Aid Policies and Programmes of the World Food Programme concerning the minimum target for voluntary contributions to the Programme for the period 1991-1992,

Recalling General Assembly resolution 2462(XXIII) of 20 December 1968 and 2682(XXV) of 11 December 1970, in which the Assembly recognized the experience gained by the World Food Programme in the field of multilateral food aid,

1. *Recommends* to the General Assembly the adoption of the draft resolution annexed to the present resolution;

2. *Urges* States Members of the United Nations and members and associate members of the Food and Agriculture Organization of the United Nations to undertake the necessary preparations for the announcement of pledges at the Fourteenth Pledging Conference for the World Food Programme.

ANNEX
[For text, see General Assembly resolution 44/230 below.]

Economic and Social Council resolution 1989/121

28 July 1989   Meeting 37   Adopted without vote

Approved by Third Committee (E/1989/135) without vote, 24 July (meeting 17); draft by Committee on Food Aid Policies and Programmes (E/1989/107); agenda item 8.

GENERAL ASSEMBLY ACTION

On 22 December, the General Assembly, on the recommendation of the Second Committee, adopted **resolution 44/230** without vote.

Target for World Food Programme pledges for the period 1991-1992

The General Assembly,

Recalling the provisions of its resolution 2095(XX) of 20 December 1965 to the effect that the World Food Programme is to be reviewed before each pledging conference,

Recalling also the provisions of paragraph 4 of its resolution 42/164 of 11 December 1987 stipulating that, subject to the review provided for in its resolution 2095(XX), the next pledging conference, at which Governments and appropriate donor organizations should be invited to pledge contributions for 1991 and 1992, with a view to reaching such a target as may then be recommended by the General Assembly and by the Conference of the Food and Agriculture Organization of the United Nations, should be convened at the latest early in 1990,

Noting that the Programme was reviewed by the Committee on Food Aid Policies and Programmes of the World Food Programme at its twenty-seventh session and by the Economic and Social Council at its second regular session of 1989,

Having considered Economic and Social Council resolution 1989/121 of 28 July 1989, and the recommendation of the Committee on Food Aid Policies and Programmes,

Recognizing the value of and continuing need for multilateral food aid as provided by the World Food Programme, both as a form of capital investment and for meeting emergency food needs,

1. *Establishes* for the period 1991-1992 a target for voluntary contributions to the World Food Programme of 1.5 billion United States dollars, of which not less than one third should be in cash and/or services, and expresses the hope that those resources will be substantially augmented by additional contributions from other sources in view of the prospective volume of sound project requests and the capacity of the Programme to operate at a higher level;

2. *Urges* States Members of the United Nations and members and associate members of the Food and Agriculture Organization of the United Nations and appropriate donor organizations to make every effort to ensure that the target is fully attained;

3. *Requests* the Secretary-General, in co-operation with the Director-General of the Food and Agriculture

Organization of the United Nations, to convene a pledging conference for this purpose at United Nations Headquarters early in 1990.

General Assembly resolution 44/230

22 December 1989   Meeting 85   Adopted without vote

Approved by Second Committee (A/44/832) by consensus, 15 November (meeting 34); draft recommended by ESC res. 1989/121 (A/C.2/44/L.3); agenda item 12.
Meeting numbers. GA 44th session: 2nd Committee 15-17, 19, 20, 25, 34; plenary 85.

1986 Food Aid Convention

In 1989, six States (Belgium, Italy, Luxembourg, Netherlands, Portugal, United Kingdom) became parties to the Food Aid Convention, 1986, bringing the total number to 20.[14] The Food Aid Convention, together with the Wheat Trade Convention, 1986, constitutes the International Wheat Agreement, 1986.

REFERENCES

[1]WFC/1990/7. [2]YUN 1988, p. 595, GA res. 43/191, 20 Dec. 1988. [3]E/1989/97. [4]A/44/19. [5]YUN 1988, p. 594. [6]WFC/1989/2 & Add.1,2. [7]YUN 1974, p. 488. [8]WFP/CFA:27/16. [9]YUN 1988, p. 598. [10]WFP/CFA:28/8. [11]E/1989/107. [12]WFP/CFA:29/P/4 & Add.1. [13]WFP/CFA:29/10. [14]*Multilateral Treaties Deposited with the Secretary-General: Status as at 31 December 1989* (ST/LEG/SER.E/8), Sales No. E.90.V.6.

Nutrition

Advances in technology, the spread of knowledge and the adoption of effective policies over the past few decades had raised food production to a level sufficient to feed everyone on earth, yet 500 to 730 million people were still chronically deprived of food, according to the report[1] prepared by the United Nations on the world social situation. Unequal food distribution, the lack of food purchasing power and the fall in food production due to civil strife and natural disasters in a number of countries contributed to the problem. Of all those deprived of adequate food in the late 1980s, 60 per cent lived in Asia, 25 per cent in Africa, 10 per cent in Latin America and 5 per cent in West Asia.

While global per capita dietary energy supplies increased from 2,340 calories a day in 1961-1963 to 2,666 in 1983-1985, 42 developing countries experienced a decline. With regard to daily per capita consumption of dietary energy, there were 42 countries, more than half of them in Africa, where it was less than the required minimum.

Malnutrition was especially severe in developing countries owing to widespread deficiencies in the intake of vitamin A, iron and iodine. Vitamin A deficiency was the largest single cause of the estimated total of 40 million people world wide considered to be blind. Some new cases of vitamin A deficiency occur among 700,000 children every year.

Almost 50 per cent of women of reproductive age in developing countries suffered from anaemia, caused by iron deficiency. About 800 million people were at risk of iodine deficiency, most of them in Asia, with an estimated 300 million in China and 200 million in India.

In industrialized countries, both those with centrally planned and market economies, malnutrition was a problem caused by excess dietary fat, due to over-consumption of animal protein (beef, pork), saturated fat (palm oil, coconut oil) and dairy products, which scientists and epidemiologists have associated with certain illnesses. Many individuals had started to reduce their daily intake of dietary fat and adopted a more active life-style, for example, by engaging in physical exercise.

UNU activities. The alleviation of hunger and malnutrition remained a priority of the Council of the United Nations University (UNU), according to its report[2] on its 1989 activities. To that end, UNU continued its research, training and information dissemination activities in the areas of food, nutrition and biotechnology.

The first phase of the joint regional project with the Association of African Universities was under way, aimed at co-ordinating Africa's scientific and technological resources in the areas of food and nutrition. Workshops were held on the development of high protein–energy foods from grain legume sources (Ghana, 25 September–4 November) and on research planning and management for directors of food and nutrition institutions (Douala, Cameroon, 20 November–2 December).

The rapid assessment procedure (RAP) methodology, pioneered by UNU and UNICEF with WHO endorsement, operates through participant observation and focused group discussions; it had proved to be an efficient tool for producing and analysing information. A number of organizations were using RAP, and its wider distribution in the form of a video was planned. A workshop on using RAP for child survival programmes was held at Cairo, Egypt, in July for participants from North Africa and the Middle East.

ACC activities. The Sub-Committee on Nutrition and its Advisory Group on Nutrition, at its fifteenth session (New York, 27 February–3 March),[3] drew the attention of the Administrative Committee on Co-ordination (ACC) to the objectives of the fourth United Nations development decade (1990s) in the area of nutrition and proposed an international conference on nutrition. It also addressed nutrition in times of disaster (see below) and the significance of small body size in populations. A symposium on women and nutrition, held during the session, considered the nutritional status of women and their role in determining nutrition of households and societies. It recommended action for direct nutrition interventions for women as well as for the strengthening of their roles as an important step in improving nutrition for all. The Sub-Committee also examined work in various areas, such as a report updating the nutrition situation; economic adjustment and nutrition; food security in Africa; iodine, vitamin A and iron deficiencies; the International Dietary Energy Consultative Group; the International Network of Food Data Bases; and the Inter-Agency Food and Nutrition Surveillance Programme.

ACC, at its 1989 second regular session in October, welcomed the joint initiative of FAO and WHO, following the proposal of the Sub-Committee, to convene the international conference on nutrition in 1992 or 1993.[5]

Nutrition in times of disaster

Following the 1988 Conference on Nutrition in Times of Disaster (Geneva, 27-30 September 1988), convened under the auspices of the ACC Sub-Committee on Nutrition and the International Nutrition Planners Forum and organized by WHO and the United Nations High Commissioner for Refugees, ACC decided to bring to the attention of the Economic and Social Council a statement issued by the Conference.[6] The decision and the statement were transmitted to the Council by the Secretary-General.[7] The statement noted that famine and disasters in the past 15 years had resulted in unprecedented numbers of people depending for survival upon international food aid, and that the volume of emergency resources had fallen short of the escalating needs. The Conference considered that 1,900 kilocalories per person (including all essential nutrients) was a minimum daily requirement under emergency conditions. It urged donors to help the United Nations achieve that goal, to increase their emergency resource allocation and to diversify the composition of food aid to meet the nutritional standards. It also encouraged efforts to strengthen the capacity of Governments of affected countries to cope with their own disasters.

By **decision 1989/175** of 26 July, the Economic and Social Council took note of ACC's decision.

REFERENCES

[1]*1989 Report on the World Social Situation* (ST/ESA/213-E/CN.5/1989/2), Sales No. E.89.IV.1. [2]A/45/31. [3]ACC/1989/PG/2. [4]YUN 1987, p. 378. [5]ACC/1989/DEC/24-32 (dec. 1989/25). [6]ACC/1989/DEC/1-20 (dec. 1989/11). [7]E/1989/101.

Chapter XII

Human resources, social and cultural development

In 1989, the United Nations advanced efforts to promote human resources and social and cultural development, which involved work in numerous interrelated areas including literacy, the family, crime prevention and criminal justice.

In a report on the world social situation, the Secretary-General cited economic adversity as one of the most prominent features of the current social situation, noted a widespread demand for a more efficient use of resources in promoting social welfare, and suggested that the private sector and voluntary associations should play a more important role in social development. The report included for the first time a section on the impact of structural adjustment on the social development of developing countries. In addition, the report emphasized the social aspects of rural development.

The Commission for Social Development held its thirty-first session in March. It reviewed trends and strategies for social integration, popular participation, and policies for the advancement of specific social groups. On its recommendation, the Economic and Social Council adopted a series of resolutions.

Concerning crime prevention and criminal justice, efforts were made to improve the functioning of the UN work programme, to promote implementation of international standards and norms, and to increase international co-operation. The Economic and Social Council adopted resolutions recommended by the Committee on Crime Prevention and Control at its tenth (1988) session.

With respect to cultural development, the Secretary-General of the United Nations and the Director-General of the United Nations Educational, Scientific and Cultural Organization (UNESCO) conducted the first biennial review on the progress of the World Decade for Cultural Development (1988-1997).

Human resources

Human resources development

Responding to a 1987 Economic and Social Council request,[1] the Secretary-General in May submitted a report[2] on human resources devel-

opment and the activities of the UN system in that field. The concept of human resources development, which originally had been defined narrowly in terms of labour supply or the provision of skills, was now widely accepted as a process of human-centred development that sought to enhance the full capacities and capabilities of human beings, he said. Deteriorating economic conditions in many countries in the 1980s had brought about a reversal of previous positive trends in economic growth, and the adjustment process imposed on many developing countries had curbed spending on social services. A renewed interest in human resources development was partly a reaction to the set-backs that had accompanied the adjustment process in most countries; other factors included the spectre of labour redundancy resulting from new labour-saving technologies, changing global production patterns and their impact on labour markets, and problems encountered in efforts to upgrade and adapt human resources in an era of rapid change and world-wide economic instability. Although there was no commonly accepted definition of what in practice constituted human resources development, some progress was made in defining for the UN system a workable and integrative approach. Referring to recommendations made at the 1987 joint meetings of the Committee for Programme and Co-ordination and the Administrative Committee on Co-ordination,[3] the Secretary-General concluded that there seemed to be considerable scope for all UN organizations to increase their co-operation with non-governmental organizations (NGOs). The organizations of the UN system could work together to prepare joint technical advisory notes as well as an agenda of action, including country-specific support policies and programmes related to human resources development.

The Committee for Development Planning, at its twenty-fifth session (New York, 9-12 May),[4] stated that the emergence of a new pragmatism in economic policy-making called for an international development strategy for the 1990s. It identified four key elements of the strategy, including greater concern for human development, and recommended that over the next 10 years, people be placed firmly at the centre of the development process and emphasis be placed on the areas of education and training, health and nutrition, and housing.

Communications. On 15 May,[5] Ethiopia transmitted the text of the African Alternative Framework to Structural Adjustment Programmes for Socio-Economic Recovery and Transformation, adopted by the Conference of Ministers of the Economic Commission for Africa (ECA) on 10 April. The Framework set the attainment of food self-sufficiency as the very first goal towards the achievement of overall well-being for the people through a sustained improvement in their living standards. At the tenth meeting of the Conference of Heads of Government of the Caribbean Community (Grand Anse, Grenada, 3-7 July),[6] the future of the Community was considered, and it was acknowledged that countries of the region must place greater emphasis on human resources development, improved competitiveness and more active promotion of service.

Human resources in the field of disability

An international meeting was held at Tallinn, USSR, from 14 to 22 August 1989, to consider the situation of human resources development in the field of disability, particularly in developing countries. The Tallinn Guidelines for Action on Human Resources Development in the Field of Disability (see PART THREE, Chapter XI) were adopted at its conclusion.

ECONOMIC AND SOCIAL COUNCIL ACTION

On 28 July, on the recommendation of its Third (Programme and Co-ordination) Committee, the Economic and Social Council adopted **resolution 1989/120** without vote.

Development of human resources

The Economic and Social Council,

Reaffirming the crucial role of human resources in the socio-economic development process, and recognizing that the development of human resources is both an essential pre-condition for development and the ultimate aim of development,

Bearing in mind that it is the sovereign right and responsibility of each country to formulate and implement national strategies, policies, plans and programmes for human resources development as part of the overall development process and within the context of its specific national development needs and objectives,

Recognizing that the integrated and concerted strategies, policies, plans and programmes for development in the 1990s should place greater emphasis on human resources development,

Emphasizing that many developing countries are devoting a considerable share of their limited resources to the development of their human resources,

Taking into account the continuing evolution of the concept of human resources development and the consequent variety in the scope and nature of the experience and technical capacity of organs, organizations and bodies of the United Nations system in contributing to the promotion of human resources development in their respective fields of competence, and convinced of the need for greater effectiveness, clarity and co-ordination in carrying out such activities,

Aware that the development of human resources is a long-term and multidisciplinary process requiring an integrated approach,

Believing that a more common operational definition of human resources development, reflecting the views, priorities and objectives of Member States, would enhance the effectiveness and impact of activities of the United Nations system in this field,

Noting with satisfaction the contribution to the elaboration of the concept of human resources development made by the Khartoum Declaration: Towards a Human-focused Approach to Socio-economic Recovery and Development in Africa, the Jakarta Plan of Action on Human Resources Development in the ESCAP Region and the African Alternative Framework for Structural Adjustment Programmes for Socio-economic Recovery and Transformation,

Recalling Economic and Social Council resolution 1987/81 of 8 July 1987 on the development of human resources,

Also recalling decision 88/29 of 1 July 1988 of the Governing Council of the United Nations Development Programme on its experience in human resources development,

Bearing in mind that human resources development is an important area of activity for organizations of the United Nations system,

1. *Takes note* of the report of the Secretary-General on human resources development and the activities of the United Nations system in that field;

2. *Recognizes* the important work already done by relevant organs, organizations and bodies of the United Nations system, including funding bodies, in the field of human resources development, and invites them to enhance those activities;

3. *Notes* that the Administrator of the United Nations Development Programme intends to issue a report on human development, and invites him to continue to prepare the report in close co-operation with the other organizations of the United Nations system concerned;

4. *Reaffirms* the need for an integrated and multidisciplinary approach to all aspects of human resources development as an important feature of the programmes of work of the relevant mandated organs, organizations and bodies of the United Nations system that deal with economic and social development;

5. *Stresses* the continuing need to strengthen and expand the human resource base of developing countries and their capacity to face the challenges of development and accelerated technological change in order to achieve sustained development, and calls upon the international community to support the efforts of developing countries in this area, in accordance with their national priorities and plans;

6. *Invites* the organs, organizations and bodies of the United Nations system, including funding bodies, to co-operate effectively with developing countries in support of the development and implementation of their strategies, policies, plans and programmes for human resources development and to promote the effective co-ordination of the activities of the United Nations system in this field;

7. *Invites* the *Ad Hoc* Committee of the Whole for the Preparation of the International Development Strategy for the Fourth United Nations Development Decade to consider the issue of human resources development in the light of its economic and social impact on the overall process of development;

8. *Requests* the Secretary-General to enhance the efforts made in the Administrative Committee on Co-ordination to elaborate a more common operational definition of human resources development in order to strengthen the effectiveness of programmes in this field in accordance with specific national development objectives and needs;

9. *Also requests* the Secretary-General to entrust the Director-General for Development and International Economic Co-operation, within his competence and functions as set out in General Assembly resolution 32/197 of 20 December 1977, with the responsibility for overall co-ordination of the activities of relevant secretariat units of the organizations of the United Nations system in the field of human resources development;

10. *Further requests* the Secretary-General to report on the implementation of the present resolution in the context of the reports on operational activities for development and on the world social situation and to include in those reports recommendations for improving operational arrangements and focusing support, especially financial and technical support, for more commonly defined human resources development activities.

Economic and Social Council resolution 1989/120

28 July 1989   Meeting 37   Adopted without vote

Approved by Third Committee (E/1989/135) without vote, 24 July (meeting 17); 4-nation draft (E/1989/C.3/L.15/Rev.1); agenda item 8.
Sponsors: Canada, German Democratic Republic, Japan, United Kingdom.

GENERAL ASSEMBLY ACTION

On 22 December, on the recommendation of the Second (Economic and Financial) Committee, the General Assembly adopted **resolution 44/213** without vote.

Developing human resources for development

The General Assembly,

Affirming that the human being is at the centre of all development activities,

Recognizing that human resources development is a broad concept encompassing many components and requiring integrated and concerted strategies, policies, plans and programmes to ensure the development of the full potential of human beings,

Recalling resolution 40/213 of 17 December 1985 on the role of qualified national personnel in the social and economic development of developing countries,

Recalling also Economic and Social Council resolutions 1986/73 of 23 July 1986 and 1987/81 of 8 July 1987 on the development of human resources,

Emphasizing that education and the acquisition and up-grading of skills, as well as continued technical training, are inextricably linked to the economic growth and sustained development of all countries, in particular developing countries,

Stressing the importance of international co-operation in supporting and strengthening the development of human resources in developing countries and, in this context, stressing also the valuable role that technical co-operation, particularly among developing countries, can play,

Deeply concerned that the negative impact of the international economic situation of the 1980s on developing countries and the resulting adjustment measures have led to significant cuts in national expenditures, including expenditures in sectors crucial to the development of human resources, and in this regard, that prolonged reduction of investment in human resources development will have grave implications for sustained growth and development,

1. *Endorses* Economic and Social Council resolution 1989/120 of 28 July 1989 on the development of human resources;

2. *Welcomes* the contributions to the elaboration of the concept of human resources development made by the Khartoum Declaration: Towards a Human-focused Approach to Socio-economic Recovery and Development in Africa, the Jakarta Plan of Action on Human Resources Development in the Region of the Economic and Social Commission for Asia and the Pacific, the African Alternative Framework to Structural Adjustment Programmes for Socio-Economic Recovery and Transformation, and the communiqué of the tenth Meeting of the Conference of Heads of Government of the Caribbean Community, held at Grand Anse, Grenada, from 3 to 7 July 1989;

3. *Emphasizes* that efforts for human resources development should optimize all means for the overall development of human beings so that they may, individually and collectively, be capable of improving their standard of living;

4. *Also emphasizes* that it is within the context of this objective that economic growth and sustained development should be pursued, and that human resources development in itself is a specific means to achieve specific economic goals;

5. *Further emphasizes* the need to continue to strengthen and expand the human resources base of developing countries in order to enable them to face the challenges of development and accelerated technological change so as to achieve sustained development;

6. *Stresses* the need for demand-oriented strategies for human resources in order to encourage programmes aimed at inspiring people to upgrade their knowledge and skills and making it possible for them to fulfil their aspirations and, in this context, also stresses the need to pay attention to employment constraints that affect the most vulnerable groups;

7. *Further stresses* the critical importance of developing human resources at all levels and strengthening the scientific and technological capabilities of developing countries in order to overcome present economic challenges and to take advantage of the opportunities unfolding in the world economy;

8. *Reaffirms* that education and training of nationals, including the most vulnerable groups, are an integral and the most important part of human resources development, and emphasizes that the flow of resources to developing countries for these activities needs to be increased;

9. *Stresses* the need for human resources development strategies to encompass supportive measures in such vital and related areas as health, nutrition, water, sanitation, housing and population;

10. *Also stresses* that the public sector is an essential element in the growth and development of developing countries and that, therefore, in the process of making the public sector more effective, it is desirable that efforts be made to foster new and productive employment opportunities so as to minimize any adverse impact on overall employment levels;

11. *Further stresses* that policies, plans and programmes for human resources development in developing countries should focus, *inter alia*, on generating employment in all sectors, including self-employment and entrepreneurship;

12. *Emphasizes* the need, in formulating strategies and programmes for human resources development, to intensify efforts for the full integration of women in the development process and to create opportunities for them, as well as to intensify efforts for the full integration of, and to create opportunities for, youth and the poor in the development process, both as beneficiaries and as agents of development;

13. *Also emphasizes* the importance of human resources development in enhancing the endogenous capacity-building of the developing countries in the fields of science and technology;

14. *Further emphasizes* the vital importance of qualified nationals in enhancing capacity-building in developing countries and, in this context, calls upon the international community to pay due attention to the serious problem of the brain drain from developing countries;

15. *Agrees* that internationally supported structural adjustment programmes should be designed and formulated to have, *inter alia*, a positive impact on human resources development in developing countries;

16. *Calls upon* the international community, including the multilateral financial and development institutions, to support the efforts of developing countries in human resources development, taking into account the national priorities and plans of those countries, through, *inter alia*, operational activities of the United Nations system;

17. *Invites* the *Ad Hoc* Committee of the Whole for the Preparation of the International Development Strategy for the Fourth United Nations Development Decade to take the present resolution into account in the formulation of the new strategy;

18. *Requests* the Secretary-General to submit to the General Assembly at its forty-fifth session a report on human resources development, including an assessment of the negative impact of the current economic situation facing developing countries or their efforts for human resources development, recommendations for policy measures to promote human resources development in developing countries and ways and means of increasing the support of the international community, in particular developed countries, for human resources development in developing countries, taking into account, *inter alia*, the report requested by the Economic and Social Council in resolution 1989/120 and the results of the World Conference on Education for All, to be held at Bangkok in March 1990.

General Assembly resolution 44/213

22 December 1989   Meeting 85   Adopted without vote

Approved by Second Committee (A/44/746/Add.11) by consensus, 11 December (meeting 49); draft by Vice-Chairman (A/C.2/44/L.78), based on

informal consultations on draft by Malaysia for Group of 77 (A/C.2/44/L.57) and orally revised; agenda item 82.

Meeting numbers. GA 44th session: 2nd Committee 44, 46, 49; plenary 85.

Also on 22 December, the Assembly, by **decision 44/455**, took note of the Secretary-General's report.

Education and literacy

Preparations for the International Literacy Year

During 1989, various UN bodies continued, with UNESCO as the lead agency, preparations for the International Literacy Year (ILY) (1990), proclaimed by the General Assembly in 1987.[7] The Year was officially launched on 6 December 1989.

The ILY programme was formulated within the framework of the Plan of Action for the Eradication of Illiteracy by the Year 2000, approved in 1989 by the UNESCO General Conference. The Plan identified the creation of a literate world as the absolute priority of UNESCO and defined main areas of effort as: alerting world public opinion to the problems of illiteracy; rallying the international community; strengthening regional literacy programmes; and reinforcing technical co-operation with Member States. The ILY secretariat established by UNESCO prepared key documents on literacy, as well as a poster and a video for international distribution.

In Africa, the Regional Programme for the Eradication of Illiteracy called for: training in forming integrated plans for the eradication of illiteracy; fellowships to promote exchanges of ideas between key personnel from education ministries; projects on literacy and civic education of women; and intensified national efforts to develop teaching materials for literacy and post-literacy education. Under the regional programme for the Arab States, 10 studies on the status of literacy and primary education were conducted, and a manual on project identification and preparation was produced. Regional programmes were also organized for Europe and Asia and the Pacific.

To mobilize public opinion, more than 30 international and regional NGOs and other co-operating bodies formed the International Task Force on Literacy which met throughout the year, and 107 national committees were set up to plan literacy-related activities.

GENERAL ASSEMBLY ACTION

On 15 December, on the recommendation of the Third (Social, Humanitarian and Cultural) Committee, the General Assembly adopted **resolution 44/127** without vote.

International Literacy Year

The General Assembly,

Recalling its resolution 42/104 of 7 December 1987, by which it proclaimed 1990 as International Literacy Year,

Recalling also that in the Universal Declaration of Human Rights and the International Covenant on Economic, Social and Cultural Rights the inalienable right of every individual to education is recognized,

Mindful of the fact that the eradication of illiteracy is one of the paramount objectives of the International Development Strategy for the Third United Nations Development Decade and should become one of the objectives of the strategy for the fourth United Nations development decade,

Emphasizing that widespread illiteracy, especially in many developing countries, seriously hinders the process of economic and social development and the cultural and spiritual advancement of society,

Convinced that literacy, especially functional literacy and adequate education, represents an indispensable element for development and for the harnessing of science, technology and human resources for economic and social progress,

Confident that International Literacy Year will offer a unique opportunity for mobilizing efforts at the national, regional and international levels to combat illiteracy,

Welcoming the programme for International Literacy Year prepared by the United Nations Educational, Scientific and Cultural Organization,

Recognizing that the United Nations Educational, Scientific and Cultural Organization has assumed the role of lead organization for International Literacy Year,

1. *Notes with satisfaction* the commendable work done by the United Nations Educational, Scientific and Cultural Organization and its Director-General to ensure adequate preparation for International Literacy Year;

2. *Commends* those Governments that have established national committees or similar structures for International Literacy Year and have launched national programmes aimed at meeting the objectives of the Year;

3. *Expresses its appreciation* to the specialized agencies and other organizations of the United Nations system for their contribution to the preparation for International Literacy Year;

4. *Notes with satisfaction* the active involvement of many non-governmental organizations in preparatory activities for International Literacy Year and, in particular, the establishment of the International Task Force on Literacy;

5. *Welcomes* the convening of the World Conference on Education for All, to be held in Thailand in March 1990 under the joint sponsorship of the United Nations Educational, Scientific and Cultural Organization, the United Nations Development Programme, the United Nations Children's Fund and the World Bank;

6. *Invites* Member States, specialized agencies and other organizations of the United Nations system and relevant intergovernmental and non-governmental organizations to take appropriate measures with a view to achieving the objectives of International Literacy Year;

7. *Also invites* Governments that have not yet done so to establish a programme of measures for enhancing literacy and functional literacy for the period up to the year 2000 along the lines of the Plan of Action for the Eradication of Illiteracy by the Year 2000 of the United Nations Educational, Scientific and Cultural Organization;

8. *Appeals* to Governments, economic and financial organizations and institutions, both national and international, to lend financial and material support to local, national and regional initiatives to promote literacy;

9. *Requests* the Secretary-General of the United Nations and the Director-General of the United Nations Educational, Scientific and Cultural Organization to give wide publicity to the activities and measures to be undertaken during International Literacy Year;

10. *Also requests* the Secretary-General to submit to the General Assembly at its forty-sixth session, through the Economic and Social Council, a report on the implementation of the programme for International Literacy Year;

11. *Decides* to include in the provisional agenda of its forty-sixth session an item entitled "International Literacy Year".

General Assembly resolution 44/127

15 December 1989   Meeting 82   Adopted without vote

Approved by Third Committee (A/44/798) without vote, 22 November (meeting 52); 41-nation draft (A/C.3/44/L.57); agenda item 95.
Meeting numbers. GA 44th session: 3rd Committee 36-43, 50, 52; plenary 82.

Research and training

UN Institute for Training and Research

During 1989, the United Nations Institute for Training and Research (UNITAR) was restructured and reduced its staff, as requested by the General Assembly in 1987.[8] The volume of UNITAR activities, however, continued to grow. The UNITAR Executive Director reported in October 1989[9] that all resident representatives of the United Nations Development Programme (UNDP) had been requested to consult the Governments of their countries of assignment to ensure that UNITAR's 1990-1991 work programme responded as closely as possible to the desires of the countries.

UNITAR activities

In the area of international co-operation and multilateral diplomacy, UNITAR continued to organize orientation courses on the role, function and work of the United Nations for new members of permanent missions to the United Nations in New York and orientation courses on practices and procedures of organs and institutions of the UN system for new members of UN permanent missions at Geneva. Other training for members of UN permanent missions included workshops and seminars on drafting of international legal instruments; the structure, retrieval and use of UN documentation; international economics for non-economists; international development issues; and the setting, issues and techniques of multilateral economic negotiations.

During 1989, the Institute launched a new training course on the Security Council; designed training programmes for peace-making and peace-keeping; and helped organize a training course on diplomatic practices and international co-operation for French-speaking junior diplomats from developing countries. For the first time, a programme of lectures for UN staff members preparing for promotion examinations was held.

Other training exercises dealt with social development, the use of informatics in development organization and management, prospective techniques for officers of ministries of planning, planning under conditions of uncertainty, port management, and oil spill containment.

Studies were executed on the changing role of the United Nations, a new approach to arms control and disarmament, the influence of the UN Charter on the constitutions of Member States, and UN-related research in European institutions.

The first issue of the *UNITAR Newsletter*, published in June, contained a list of publications prepared by UNITAR and information on Institute activities.

UNITAR financing

In 1989, UNITAR's General Fund income—from government contributions and other sources—totalled $1,175,478, while total expenditures amounted to $1,279,454. Income of the Special Purpose Grants Fund was $2,116,852; expenditures, amounting to $2,189,710, surpassed income by $72,858.[10]

1988 accounts

In July, the UN Board of Auditors submitted to the General Assembly the financial statements of UNITAR for 1988.[11] In August,[12] the Secretary-General transmitted to the Assembly a summary of the Board's principal findings and conclusions for remedial action. The Board recommended that expenditures not be allowed to exceed allotments and that no expenditures be incurred for any special purpose projects unless allotments had been issued for that purpose. It stressed that the administration should provide in the General Fund budget for the possible losses from the undocumented accounts receivable and deferred charges and that the reconciliation of accounting records should be updated and improved. Also, special purpose grants should always be accounted for as UNITAR funds so that project support income could be derived.

Commenting on the Board's remarks, the Advisory Committee on Administrative and Budgetary Questions (ACABQ) in September[13] endorsed the Board's view that activities should not be commenced unless funds were available. The Committee, while noting that corrective action was being taken with regard to the direct receipt by a fellow of grant funds for a UNITAR project, cautioned

that that improper practice should not be allowed to happen again.

The Assembly, in **resolution 44/183** of 19 December, accepted the financial statements and the audit opinions and report of the Board of Auditors regarding UNITAR.

UNITAR restructuring

In response to a 1988 General Assembly resolution,[14] the Secretary-General submitted a report in October[15] reviewing steps taken or to be taken in regard to the restructuring of UNITAR prescribed by the Assembly in 1987.[8] The report presented an analysis of the current and projected financial situation and discussed possible measures that would enhance greater co-ordination among autonomous UN research bodies.

UNITAR in 1989 maintained the same level of training activities in international co-operation and multilateral diplomacy as in previous years, despite an overall reduction in staff. The UNITAR Board of Trustees agreed in 1989 that priority would be given to training on peace-making and peace-keeping, as well as for new members of the Security Council. Joint training projects were developed in the area of economic and social development. The Secretary-General forwarded to the General Assembly the proposal of the UNITAR Board of Trustees that the Institute be given the status of executing agency of UNDP. As the Board of Auditors noted,[11] existing arrangements under which UNITAR had to pre-finance UNDP-sponsored projects before it received reimbursement had further strained the Institute's already limited funds.

Negotiations on the sale of UNITAR headquarters, authorized in 1987[8] by the General Assembly, encountered problems, with the non-negotiable decision of the sellers of the land the building occupied to increase the selling price from $4 million (quoted in 1986) to $4.5 million requiring further consultation with ACABQ. The closing, however, took place on 22 September, with realized savings for the Organization amounting to $207,000. The sale of the entire property, however, could not be completed, thus precluding the establishment of the reserve fund endorsed by the Assembly in 1987.[8]

Regarding the conditions for appointment of full-time senior fellows, it was considered that they should undertake work within the framework of the UNITAR programme; conduct their work on a full-time basis and free of charge to the Institute, though they could receive certain honorariums; and have no concurrent outside remunerated activities without prior approval of the Secretary-General. Based on those revised criteria and procedures for appointment, eight eminent persons were appointed as full-time senior fellows for 1989.

The Institute's draft General Fund budget for 1989 was reviewed by ACABQ prior to approval by the Board of Trustees, as requested by the General Assembly in 1987.[14] ACABQ recommended that UNITAR budget submissions include narratives highlighting policy considerations and underlying assumptions and explaining proposed changes in the estimates of income and expenditures from one year to the next. It also said that future submissions should include information on the status of funding and use of UNITAR under special purpose grants, and that information should also be provided on the status of the Institute's total accumulated operating deficits from prior years, as well as on reimbursements of the advance of $886,000 approved by the General Assembly in 1983.[16] The ACABQ recommendations were endorsed by the UNITAR Board of Trustees.

The Secretary-General concluded that although efforts had been made to further strengthen the administrative, financial and programmatic reorganization of the Institute, the financial situation remained a source of grave concern. The delay of the sale of the entire property, compounded by a decline in government contributions to the General Fund, led in 1989 to a net increase in the overall liabilities of the Institute.

GENERAL ASSEMBLY ACTION

On 19 December 1989, on the recommendation of the Second Committee, the General Assembly adopted **resolution 44/175** without vote.

United Nations Institute for Training and Research

The General Assembly,

Recalling its resolutions 41/172 of 5 December 1986, 42/197 of 11 December 1987 and 43/201 of 20 December 1988,

Having considered the report of the Secretary-General and taking into account the statements made by the representative of the Secretary-General and the Executive Director of the United Nations Institute for Training and Research,

Recognizing the continuing importance and relevance of the mandate of the Institute, particularly in the field of training,

Recognizing also the need for Governments to contribute or increase their voluntary contributions, as appropriate, to the Institute,

Noting with concern the continuing lack of a sufficiently broad base of donor countries supporting the Institute,

Deeply concerned that the sale of the headquarters building of the Institute, which would enable a reserve fund for the Institute to be established, has not yet been completed,

Noting with concern that the 1989 United Nations Pledging Conference for Development Activities did not provide the General Fund of the United Nations Institute for Training and Research with the level of resources required for it to maintain a minimum training programme and institutional structure,

1. *Takes note* of the report of the Secretary-General;

2. *Reaffirms* the continuing validity and relevance of the mandate of the United Nations Institute for Training and Research, as contained in the amended statute;

3. *Commends* the Secretary-General for the measures taken to implement the provisions of resolution 43/201 and encourages him to take further steps in that direction;

4. *Takes note* of the criteria and qualifications to apply to full-time senior fellows of the Institute and of the amendment to the statute of the Institute regarding full-time senior fellows, fellows, consultants, correspondents and advisory bodies, contained in the annexes to the report of the Secretary-General;

5. *Reiterates* its request that the budgetary proposals of the Institute for 1990, as well as those for subsequent years, be submitted to the Advisory Committee on Administrative and Budgetary Questions for review and comment prior to approval by the Board of Trustees of the Institute;

6. *Authorizes* the Institute to enter into appropriate arrangements with the Administrator of the United Nations Development Programme to execute projects funded by the Programme falling within the functions of the Institute, taking into account all relevant factors, including the comments of the Board of Auditors concerning the status of the Institute as an executing agency of the United Nations Development Programme;

7. *Urges* the Secretary-General to proceed rapidly with the sale of the headquarters building of the Institute, as approved in resolutions 42/197 and 43/201;

8. *Reiterates* its approval of the recommendation of the Secretary-General that the Institute should, after the sale of the building, repay the amounts currently owed to the United Nations and use the balance to establish a reserve fund for the Institute;

9. *Agrees* with the Secretary-General that the purpose of the reserve fund to be established by the Institute is to provide greater stability, predictability and reliability in the financing of the Institute, and notes that the fund is not intended to be a substitute for voluntary contributions from Governments, either to the General Fund of the Institute or to the special projects;

10. *Requests* the Secretary-General to submit to the Board of Trustees of the Institute at its forthcoming session a complete report on his efforts to sell the headquarters building of the Institute and the land on which it is situated;

11. *Urges* all States that have not yet contributed to the General Fund of the Institute to do so and calls upon all contributing States to increase their contributions to the Institute so as to enable it to continue to fulfil its mandate and to implement fully and successfully the provisions of the present resolution and other relevant resolutions;

12. *Appeals* to all States to provide appropriate special-purpose grants to enable the Institute to implement the training and research programmes that cannot be financed from its General Fund, and calls upon appropriate intergovernmental and non-governmental organizations to contribute to the Institute;

13. *Emphasizes* the urgent need for broad-based financing for the Institute and invites the traditional donors, in implementation of resolutions 42/197 and 43/201 and the present resolution, to resume or continue, as appropriate, their voluntary contributions to the Institute;

14. *Requests* the Secretary-General to report to the General Assembly at its forty-fifth session, through the Board of Trustees of the Institute, on the longer-term issues related to the financing of the Institute;

15. *Encourages* the Secretary-General to continue to explore new modalities for greater interfacing among United Nations research bodies, endorses the proposals of the Secretary-General and requests the Director-General for Development and International Economic Co-operation to organize a meeting of United Nations research institutes with a view to enhancing practical co-operation among them, particularly in regard to the formulation and implementation of their programmes and plans;

16. *Requests* the Secretary-General to report to the General Assembly at its forty-fifth session on the implementation of the present resolution.

General Assembly resolution 44/175

19 December 1989   Meeting 83   Adopted without vote

Approved by Second Committee (A/44/833) without vote, 15 November (meeting 34); draft by Vice-Chairman based on informal consultations (A/C.2/44/L.36), orally revised; agenda item 87.
Meeting numbers. GA 44th session: 2nd Committee 2-10, 25, 30, 34; plenary 83.

United Nations University

Activities and financing

In 1989,[17] the United Nations University (UNU), an autonomous academic institution within the UN system, carried out research, training and dissemination projects in eight programme areas: peace, culture and governance; global economy and development; global life-support systems; alternative rural-urban configurations; science, technology and society; food, nutrition and biotechnology; human and social development; and global learning and informatics. Most of the programmatic and operational developments were part of preparations for start-up of the second medium-term perspective for 1990-1995. The restructuring of the University was completed by the end of 1989 as part of overall institutional development of the University.

A series of workshops were held in 1989 dealing with the human dimensions of environmental issues: global environmental change (Moscow, USSR); carbon dioxide emission reduction strategies (Budapest, Hungary); understanding global environmental change (Worcester, Massachusetts, United States); and global modelling (Moscow). Also, three regional workshops were organized in Africa, Latin America and Asia, to review research and training activities.

UNU continued to make progress in establishing its own research and training centres. In September, formal negotiations commenced with

Macau to establish the Institute for Software Technology. A feasibility study was under way on a proposed institute on culture and development at Fukuoka, Japan. A pre-feasibility study, consisting of a survey on the establishment of an international network of centres of excellence on new and renewable resources of energy, was being carried out in collaboration with the Office of the Director-General for International Economic Co-operation of the UN Secretariat and the Nuclear and Alternative Energy Commission of Italy, with a grant from the Government of Italy. The Government of Japan initiated construction of the University's headquarters building, to be completed in 1991.

The University Centre published 25 new books in 1989, bringing the number published to date to well over 250. Twenty issues of the University's four journals were published: *Abstracts of Selected Solar Energy Technology* (*ASSET*) (eight issues), *Journal of Food Composition and Analysis* (quarterly) *Food and Nutrition Bulletin* (quarterly) and *Mountain Research and Development* (quarterly).

During the year, 40 UNU fellows completed their training, bringing to 988 the total trained since 1976 by the University under the regular fellowship programme. In addition, the University sponsored other training activities involving some 700 short-term trainees. Forty-one regular fellows commenced training.

Total UNU income in 1988-1989 was $65.9 million, while expenditures amounted to $41.6 million.[18] Unpaid pledges as at 31 December 1989 amounted to $19 million, with $26.2 million collected during the year.

Council activities

The UNU Council met twice in 1989, holding its thirty-third session at Budapest, Hungary, from 3 to 8 July and its thirty-fourth session at Tokyo from 4 to 8 December.

At the July session, during which a symposium on global challenges and international responses in the 1990s was held, the Council focused mainly on the University's ongoing and future programmes and the need to broaden its approach to achieve a more interrelated overall programme. It endorsed the report on a feasibility study on the proposed establishment at Macau of a research and training centre on computer software technology, and authorized the Rector to proceed with negotiations for a host country agreement and a memorandum of agreement.

The Council took action to defend the Endowment Fund from further erosion. It decided to reinvest a portion of the interest income each year in the Fund and to establish an independently managed portfolio that would provide a greater degree of flexibility for investments in the international financial markets. In December, the Council approved the programme and budget for the biennium 1990-1991.

By **decision 1989/113** of 22 May 1989, the Economic and Social Council noted the report of the UNU Council on the work of the University in 1988.[19]

REFERENCES

[1]YUN 1987, p. 652, ESC res. 1987/81, 8 July 1987. [2]A/44/229-E/1989/60. [3]YUN 1987, p. 652. [4]E/1989/29. [5]A/44/315. [6]A/44/477. [7]YUN 1987, p. 654, GA res. 42/104, 7 Dec. 1987. [8]*Ibid.*, p. 656, GA res. 42/197, 11 Dec. 1987. [9]A/C.2/44/SR.25. [10]A/45/5/Add.4. [11]A/44/5/Add.4. [12]A/44/356. [13]A/44/543. [14]YUN 1988, p. 604, GA res. 43/201, 20 Dec. 1988. [15]A/44/611. [16]YUN 1983, p. 763, GA res. 38/177, 19 Dec. 1983. [17]A/45/31. [18]A/45/5. [19]E/1989/37.

Social and cultural development

Social aspects of development

World social situation

The *1989 Report on the World Social Situation*,[1] prepared in accordance with guidelines set forth by the General Assembly[2] in 1985 and by the Economic and Social Council[3] in 1987, was the twelfth in a series issued by the United Nations since 1952.

Responding to a 1987 Council resolution,[4] the *Report* assessed the impact of structural adjustment, discussed consequences for the social situation and social development, and emphasized the social aspects of rural development. It included, as requested by the Council,[5] a section on recent views and trends concerning the family. Pursuant to another Council request,[6] information on the critical social situation in Africa was provided in the annex.

The *Report* noted that the 1980s had been a period of profound change. On the political front, international tensions had eased considerably and regional conflicts had subsided. The decade also witnessed a resumption of economic growth in developed market economies, a process of reform in most industrialized socialist countries, and some improvements in food and industrial production in Asia. In Africa and Latin America, however, socio-economic conditions had worsened perceptibly.

Changes had occurred in the structure and function of the family, largely depending upon the level of national economic development and diversification, the *Report* stated. The number of single-parent families was on the rise, creating legal and social problems. Developed countries achieved considerable progress in increasing the participation of women in the labour force, but wages and responsibilities remained very different for men and women. In developing countries, women still did not have equal access to education in all forms. Hunger and malnutrition continued to be worldwide problems owing to unequal distribution of food. The disparity in per capita incomes between developed and developing countries continued to widen in absolute as well as relative terms. Recent advances in electronics, biotechnology and materials development had had a major impact on social life in the advanced industrial countries and, to some extent, on the world community as a whole, becoming more closely integrated because of new instant communication facilities. Although there was world-wide concern over the environment, adjustments involving structural change often met opposition, because of loss of jobs and displacement of those who did not have the skills required for new jobs. The *Report* also discussed social development and disarmament; international co-operation against drug abuse, terrorism and AIDS; migrants and refugees; and changing perceptions regarding social development issues.

Commission action. The Commission for Social Development, at its thirty-first session in March,[7] had before it a mimeographed version of the *Report*.[8] On 22 March,[9] the Commission noted the *Report*, recommending that the quality of social conditions be addressed in the next issue.

ECONOMIC AND SOCIAL COUNCIL ACTION

On 24 May 1989, on the recommendation of its Second (Social) Committee, the Economic and Social Council adopted **resolution 1989/72** by recorded vote.

World social situation

The Economic and Social Council,

Recalling General Assembly resolution 40/100 of 13 December 1985 and Council resolutions 1987/40 and 1987/52 of 28 May 1987,

Bearing in mind the importance of the report on the world social situation for increasing awareness of the advances made towards the goals of social progress and better standards of living, established in the Charter of the United Nations, and of the obstacles to further progress,

Deeply concerned at the low levels of per capita income and overall reductions in the standards of living and the main indicators of social well-being in a great number of the developing countries during the 1980s,

Reaffirming the common goal of realizing, through national and international efforts, the well-being of the world's population, especially with regard to the basic indicators of social development—food, employment, housing, education and health care,

Considering that there is a need for greater efforts to study and disseminate data on the existing world social situation, particularly the situation in developing countries,

Bearing in mind the importance of the report on the world social situation for the preparation of the international development strategy for the fourth United Nations development decade,

Stressing the need for a comprehensive and integrated view of the interrelationships between economic and social problems,

1. *Reaffirms* that, pursuant to General Assembly resolution 40/100 and Council resolutions 1987/40 and 1987/52, the 1989 report on the world social situation will be submitted to the Assembly at its forty-fourth session;

2. *Requests* the Secretary-General to submit to the General Assembly at its forty-fifth session, through the Council at its first regular session of 1990, an expanded version of the 1989 report on the world social situation, which should include:

(a) A special chapter devoted to a comprehensive overview of the general trends in the main indicators of the social situation and standards of living world wide, particularly in developing countries, giving special attention to those cases, at the national and regional levels, in which there have been negative trends and low levels of per capita income during the 1980s;

(b) A special chapter on an analysis of the relationship between trends in the world economy and trends in the social situation, including projections to the year 2000, with special attention to the developing countries;

(c) A chapter which, in full implementation of Council resolution 1987/40, studies the impact of structural adjustments and the external indebtedness of developing countries on the social situation;

(d) A chapter in which the individual conclusions of chapters dealing with specific social problems are integrated and placed in the overall context of the world economic and social situations;

3. *Also requests* the Secretary-General to submit a report to the General Assembly at its forty-sixth session, through the Council, on the work being done within the United Nations system to improve and further develop quantitative and qualitative indicators that measure accurately the social condition and the standards of living of the world's population, particularly in developing countries;

4. *Further requests* the Secretary-General, in preparing the next report on the world social situation, to give high priority to an analysis of the main indicators of social progress and standards of living, and to make a comprehensive analysis of the main causes and circumstances that explain negative trends in those indicators; chapters devoted to the study of specific social problems must be related to the global economic and social situations, taking into account both national and international conditions.

Economic and Social Council resolution 1989/72

24 May 1989   Meeting 15   39-1-13 (recorded vote)

Approved by Second Committee (E/1989/91/Add.1) by recorded vote (40-1-13), 19 May (meeting 22); draft by Malaysia for Group of 77 (E/1989/C.2/L.9/Rev.1), orally revised; agenda item 11.

Recorded vote in Council as follows:

In favour: Bahamas, Belize, Bolivia, Brazil, Bulgaria, Cameroon, China, Colombia, Cuba, Czechoslovakia, Ghana, Guinea, Indonesia, Iran, Iraq, Jordan, Kenya, Lesotho, Liberia, Libyan Arab Jamahiriya, Nicaragua, Niger, Oman, Poland, Rwanda, Saudi Arabia, Somalia, Sri Lanka, Sudan, Thailand, Trinidad and Tobago, Tunisia, Ukrainian SSR, USSR, Uruguay, Venezuela, Yugoslavia, Zaire, Zambia.

Against: United States.

Abstaining: Canada, Denmark, France, Germany, Federal Republic of, Greece, Ireland, Italy, Japan, Netherlands, New Zealand, Norway, Portugal, United Kingdom.

GENERAL ASSEMBLY ACTION

On 8 December 1989, on the recommendation of the Third Committee, the General Assembly adopted **resolution 44/56** by recorded vote.

World social situation

The General Assembly,

Recalling its resolutions 1392(XIV) of 20 November 1959, 2542(XXIV) of 11 December 1969, 40/98 and 40/100 of 13 December 1985, 42/49 of 30 November 1987 and 43/113 of 8 December 1988 and Economic and Social Council resolutions 1987/39, 1987/40, 1987/46 and 1987/52 of 28 May 1987, and taking note of Council resolution 1989/72 of 24 May 1989 and Council decision 1989/113 of 28 July 1989,

Bearing in mind the objective of improving the well-being of the world's population on the basis of the full participation of all members of society in the process of development and the fair distribution to them of the benefits therefrom, and recognizing that the pace of development in the developing countries should be accelerated substantially in order to enable them to achieve this objective, especially to meet the basic needs for food, housing, education, employment and health care,

Concerned about the worsening economic situation in the developing countries, particularly in the least developed countries, as evidenced by, *inter alia*, a significant decline in living conditions, the persistence and increase of widespread poverty in a large number of countries and the decrease of the main social and economic indicators of those countries,

Conscious that each country has the sovereign right freely to adopt the economic and social system that it deems the most appropriate and that each Government has the primary role of ensuring the social progress and well-being of the people,

Convinced of the urgent need to eradicate policies and practices that hinder social progress, including racism and racial discrimination, in particular *apartheid*,

Convinced also of the crucial need to eradicate dangerous trends and habits that debilitate individuals and incapacitate society, in particular drug abuse and illicit trafficking,

Bearing in mind the importance of the *1989 Report on the World Social Situation* for increasing awareness of the advances made towards the goals of social progress and better standards of living, established in the Charter of the United Nations, and of the obstacles to further progress,

Believing that there is a need for greater efforts by the United Nations system to study and disseminate data on the existing world social situation, in particular in the developing countries,

Bearing in mind the important contribution of the *1989 Report on the World Social Situation* to the preparation of an international development strategy for the fourth United Nations development decade,

Taking note of the deliberations on the question of the world social situation by the Commission for Social Development at its thirty-first session and by the Economic and Social Council at its first regular session of 1989,

Having considered the *1989 Report on the World Social Situation,*

Concerned about certain shortcomings in the *1989 Report on the World Social Situation,*

1. *Takes note* of the *1989 Report on the World Social Situation,* including the information on the critical social situation in Africa provided in the annex thereto;

2. *Urges* the timely issue of future reports on the world social situation in order to enable the Commission for Social Development to consider them;

3. *Notes with deep concern* the continuing deterioration of the economic and social situation in the developing countries, in particular in the least developed countries, as well as in the low-income countries;

4. *Notes also with deep concern* that the situation faced by the developing countries has been worsened by sharp fluctuations in exchange rates, high real rates of interest, fluctuations in commodity prices, a serious deterioration in the terms of trade of developing countries, increased protectionist pressures, the net transfer of resources from developing countries, crushing debt burdens, the restrictive adjustment process demanded by financial and development institutions, the decline in official development assistance in real terms and the severe inadequacy of resources experienced by multilateral development and financial institutions;

5. *Notes further with deep concern* the critical social situation in Africa resulting from structural imbalances and weaknesses of the African economy and a hostile international economic environment, in spite of the efforts of the Governments of African countries to undertake measures, with the support of the international community, to stabilize and adjust their economies;

6. *Reaffirms* the principles and objectives of the Declaration on Social Progress and Development and calls for their effective realization as a means of attaining a more equitable world social situation;

7. *Calls upon* all Member States to promote economic development and social progress by the formulation and implementation of an interrelated set of policy measures to achieve the goals and objectives established within the framework of national plans and priorities for employment, education, health, nutrition, housing facilities, crime prevention, the well-being of children, equal opportunities for the disabled and the aging, full participation of youth in the development process and full integration and participation of women in development;

8. *Calls upon* the relevant organs, organizations and bodies of the United Nations system to mobilize the necessary resources to undertake measures aimed at improving social conditions world wide;

9. *Endorses* the request made by the Economic and Social Council in paragraph 2 of its resolution 1989/72 that the Secretary-General should submit an expanded version of the *1989 Report on the World Social Situation* to the Council at its first regular session of 1990, as well as the other requests made of him in paragraphs 3 and 4 of the same resolution;

10. *Requests* the Secretary-General to continue monitoring the world social situation in depth on a regular basis and to submit the next full report on the world social situation, through the Economic and Social Council, to the General Assembly in 1993, for consideration at its forty-eighth session, and also requests the Secretary-General to submit an interim report to the

Assembly in 1991, through the Commission for Social Development and the Economic and Social Council;

11. *Also requests* the Secretary-General to make the necessary arrangements for the wider dissemination of the reports on the world social situation;

12. *Invites* the organs, organizations and bodies of the United Nations system to co-operate fully with the Secretary-General in the preparation of future reports by making available all relevant information pertaining to their respective areas of competence;

13. *Decides* to include the item entitled "World social situation" in the provisional agenda of its forty-fifth session for the purpose of considering the expanded version of the *1989 Report on the World Social Situation,* in that of its forty-sixth session for the purpose of considering the interim report, and in that of its forty-eighth session for the purpose of considering the next full report in 1993.

General Assembly resolution 44/56

8 December 1989   Meeting 78   131-1-23 (recorded vote)

Approved by Third Committee (A/44/749) by recorded vote (114-1-2), 9 November (meeting 37); draft by Malaysia for Group of 77 (A/C.3/44/L.24); agenda item 90 *(a).*
Meeting numbers. GA 44th session: 3rd Committee 12-20, 30, 37; plenary 78.

Recorded vote in Assembly as follows:

In favour: Afghanistan, Albania, Algeria, Angola, Antigua and Barbuda, Argentina, Bahamas, Bahrain, Bangladesh, Barbados, Benin, Bhutan, Bolivia, Botswana, Brazil, Brunei Darussalam, Bulgaria, Burkina Faso, Burundi, Byelorussian SSR, Cameroon, Cape Verde, Central African Republic, Chad, Chile, China, Colombia, Comoros, Congo, Costa Rica, Côte d'Ivoire, Cuba, Cyprus, Czechoslovakia, Democratic Kampuchea, Democratic Yemen, Djibouti, Dominica, Dominican Republic, Ecuador, Egypt, El Salvador, Equatorial Guinea, Ethiopia, Fiji, Gabon, Gambia, German Democratic Republic, Ghana, Grenada, Guatemala, Guinea, Guinea-Bissau, Guyana, Haiti, Honduras, Hungary, India, Indonesia, Iran, Iraq, Jamaica, Jordan, Kenya, Kuwait, Lao People's Democratic Republic, Lebanon, Lesotho, Liberia, Libyan Arab Jamahiriya, Madagascar, Malawi, Malaysia, Maldives, Mali, Mauritania, Mauritius, Mexico, Mongolia, Morocco, Mozambique, Myanmar, Nepal, Nicaragua, Niger, Nigeria, Oman, Pakistan, Panama, Papua New Guinea, Paraguay, Peru, Philippines, Poland, Qatar, Romania, Rwanda, Saint Lucia, Saint Vincent and the Grenadines, Samoa, Sao Tome and Principe, Saudi Arabia, Senegal, Seychelles, Sierra Leone, Singapore, Solomon Islands, Somalia, Sri Lanka, Sudan, Suriname, Swaziland, Syrian Arab Republic, Thailand, Togo, Trinidad and Tobago, Tunisia, Uganda, Ukrainian SSR, USSR, United Arab Emirates, United Republic of Tanzania, Uruguay, Vanuatu, Venezuela, Viet Nam, Yemen, Yugoslavia, Zaire, Zambia, Zimbabwe.
Against: United States.
Abstaining: Australia, Austria, Belgium, Canada, Denmark, Finland, France, Germany, Federal Republic of, Greece, Iceland, Ireland, Israel, Italy, Japan, Luxembourg, Netherlands, New Zealand, Norway, Portugal, Spain, Sweden, Turkey, United Kingdom.

Critical social situation in Africa

The Commission for Social Development and the Economic and Social Council considered the critical social situation in Africa, detailed in an annex to the *1989 Report on the World Social Situation.*[1] The annex reviewed and analysed economic crisis and social deterioration, particularly in the areas of employment, income, food, nutrition, health and education. It also dealt with the pervasive social effects of *apartheid* and destabilization on the peoples and States of southern Africa, and considered other regional conflicts.

The Council adopted **resolution 1989/46** on 24 May, in which it appealed to members of the international community to increase their co-operation and assistance to enhance efforts of African countries to establish or improve their infrastructure through the creation of a favourable economic environment (see PART THREE, Chapter III).

Social progress and development

Implementation of the 1969 Declaration

Pursuant to a 1986 General Assembly resolution,[10] the Secretary-General reported[11] in February on the implementation of the 1969 Declaration on Social Progress and Development.[12] He also provided, as requested by the Assembly in 1987,[13] a summary of responses received from Member States on the subject.

The report contained a historical review of how the UN system had promoted economic and social advancement and a summary of activities undertaken by UN bodies since the adoption of the Declaration in the areas of trade, finance and environment. It also described contributions of the UN system to national efforts in food security, poverty alleviation, employment, health, illiteracy and education, housing and human settlements, human rights, the status of women and protection of vulnerable groups, and dissemination of information on UN activities.

The Secretary-General concluded that the goals of the 1969 Declaration remained valid. The United Nations had stressed the provision of services to Member countries and mobilization of international support for national efforts in such fields as eradication of mass diseases, development of human resources, and norm-setting in transportation and development finance. There was a growing perception that multilateral institutions played an important role in ensuring a favourable international environment and that they were necessary to bring about a fair distribution of the benefits of international economic relations and to support economic forces working towards social progress. The Secretary-General noted that the preparation of a new international development strategy for the fourth United Nations development decade[14] (1991-2000) would be an opportunity for the international community to incorporate a wide array of economic and social issues into a comprehensive framework.

On 22 March,[15] the Commission for Social Development noted the report, as did the General Assembly by **decision 44/421** of 8 December.

Twentieth anniversary of the Declaration

ECONOMIC AND SOCIAL COUNCIL ACTION

On 24 May 1989, on the recommendation of its Second Committee, the Economic and Social Council adopted **resolution 1989/48** without vote.

Twentieth anniversary of the Declaration on Social Progress and Development

The Economic and Social Council

Recommends to the General Assembly the adoption of the following draft resolution:

[For text, see General Assembly resolution 44/57 below.]

Economic and Social Council resolution 1989/48

24 May 1989   Meeting 15   Adopted without vote

Approved by Second Committee (E/1989/91) without vote, 11 May (meeting 12); draft by Commission for Social Development (E/1989/25), orally amended by Bulgaria; agenda item 11.

GENERAL ASSEMBLY ACTION

On 8 December 1989, on the recommendation of the Third Committee, the General Assembly adopted **resolution 44/57** without vote.

Twentieth anniversary of the Declaration on Social Progress and Development

The General Assembly,

Recalling its resolution 2542(XXIV) of 11 December 1969, by which it solemnly proclaimed the Declaration on Social Progress and Development, and resolutions 2543(XXIV) of 11 December 1969, 32/117 of 16 December 1977, 34/59 of 29 November 1979 and 41/142 of 4 December 1986 on the implementation of the Declaration,

Reaffirming, on the occasion of the twentieth anniversary of its proclamation, the importance of the Declaration as a source of inspiration for national and international efforts for the promotion of social progress and development,

Recalling its resolutions 40/98 of 13 December 1985 on the improvement of the role of the United Nations in the field of social development, 42/49 of 30 November 1987 on the achievement of social justice, and 43/113 of 8 December 1988 on the indivisibility and interdependence of economic, social, cultural, civil and political rights,

Recalling also that in its resolution 42/48 of 30 November 1987 it decided to observe in 1989 the twentieth anniversary of the Declaration,

Desirous of achieving effective application of the provisions of the Declaration,

Noting the continuing validity and importance of the principles and objectives proclaimed in the Declaration,

1. *Invites* all Governments to take into consideration the provisions of the Declaration on Social Progress and Development in their developmental policies, plans and programmes, as well as in their bilateral and multilateral co-operation;

2. *Recommends* that the Declaration be taken into account in the formulation of the international development strategy for the fourth United Nations development decade and in the implementation of programmes of international action to be carried out during the decade;

3. *Recommends also* that the international organizations concerned with development continue to use the provisions of the Declaration, which is an important United Nations document, in formulating strategies, programmes and international instruments aimed at social progress and development;

4. *Urges* the Secretary-General to carry out the activities indicated in the annex to its resolution 42/48 in

order to ensure the successful observance of the twentieth anniversary of the Declaration;

5. *Reiterates its invitation* to all States that have not yet done so to transmit to the Secretary-General their views and comments pursuant to paragraphs 4 and 5 of its resolution 42/48;

6. *Requests* the Secretary-General to include in the next report on the world social situation a special section dealing with the activities carried out in pursuance of the present resolution;

7. *Decides* to include in the provisional agenda of its forty-ninth session an item entitled "Twenty-fifth anniversary of the Declaration on Social Progress and Development".

General Assembly resolution 44/57

8 December 1989   Meeting 78   Adopted without vote

Approved by Third Committee (A/44/750) without vote, 9 November (meeting 37); draft recommended by ESC res. 1989/48 (A/C.3/44/L.4); agenda item 91.
Meeting numbers. GA 44th session: 3rd Committee 12-13, 15-20, 37; plenary 78.

Social progress

In connection with the preparation of the international development strategy for the fourth UN development decade,[14] the Commission for Social Development in March[7] put forward proposals on the social dimension of the strategy. It was proposed that the strategy emphasize the interaction of social and economic policies and the need to improve the social situation; consider the roles of both the public and private sectors; support the advancement of women; and propose measures to strengthen the capacity of countries for co-ordinating social policy.

On 24 May, the Economic and Social Council adopted **resolution 1989/55** recommending that the *Ad Hoc* Committee of the Whole for the Preparation of the International Development Strategy for the Fourth UN Development Decade take into consideration the proposals of the Commission, and also deciding that the Commission should consider the implementation of social components of the strategy at its thirty-second (1990) session.

National experience in social progress and co-operation

Responding to a 1987 General Assembly request,[16] the Secretary-General reported[17] in January on national experience in achieving far-reaching social and economic changes for social progress.

The report, a summary of replies from 29 Member States to a questionnaire on the subject, described accounts of achievements in social development in the areas of employment, social welfare and income distribution; education, science and technology; the environment; capital formation; and rural development.

Approaches to social and economic issues, the Secretary-General said, had been subject to a searching re-examination in most parts of the world. The problems of resource mobilization and lack of revenue had forced many Governments to seek new avenues towards social progress, less dependent on redistribution and more reliant on incentives and self-help. The provision of productive and remunerative work to all those seeking employment, particularly the young, remained a high priority. At the same time, there was increased concern that training be geared to adapting the skills of those employed to the changing demands of the workplace. Significant achievements had been made with regard to assistance to handicapped and vulnerable groups, incorporation of women, minorities and the rural population into the mainstream of economic and social life, and the preservation of the environment; still, social conditions for nearly 1 billion people continued to deteriorate drastically, mostly in Africa and Latin America.

The Economic and Social Council, in **decision 1989/135** of 24 May, took note of the report. On 8 December, the General Assembly, in **decision 44/422**, also noted the report.

Monitoring of information in the social field

GENERAL ASSEMBLY ACTION

On 8 December, the General Assembly, on the recommendation of the Third Committee, adopted **resolution 44/66** without vote.

Monitoring of information on effective measures and alternative methods of implementing the plans, strategies and programmes of action in the social field at the national level

The General Assembly,

Having considered the *1989 Report on the World Social Situation,*

Recalling its resolutions 37/51 of 3 December 1982, in which it endorsed the International Plan of Action on Aging, 37/52 of 3 December 1982, in which it adopted the World Programme of Action concerning Disabled Persons, 40/14 of 18 November 1985, in which it endorsed the guidelines for further planning and suitable follow-up in the field of youth, 40/32 of 29 November 1985, in which it approved the Milan Plan of Action, and 40/108 of 13 December 1985, in which it endorsed the Nairobi Forward-looking Strategies for the Advancement of Women,

Recalling also its resolution 42/125 of 7 December 1987, in which it endorsed the Guiding Principles for Developmental Social Welfare Policies and Programmes in the Near Future,

Aware that much remains to be done at the national level to achieve the full realization of the principles and objectives contained in those major documents adopted at the international level,

Convinced of the need to study effective measures and alternative methods of implementing the above-mentioned plans, strategies and programmes of action,

Recognizing that, in addition to material and technical assistance, both committed leadership and self-reliance of people for effective popular participation are required for mobilization to action in the social field,

Considering that sustained co-operation and regular dialogue are necessary between leaders and people and among citizens themselves in order to foster social change,

1. *Recognizes* the need for Member States to select their own specific social priorities;

2. *Emphasizes* that national leaders need commitment and political will in order to realize in concrete terms, at the national, local and grass-roots levels, the provisions of the plans, strategies and programmes of action approved by the General Assembly in its resolutions 37/51, 37/52, 40/14, 40/32 and 40/108;

3. *Reaffirms* that non-governmental organizations and individual citizens require the qualities of self-reliance and initiative in order to undertake their own programmes and projects;

4. *Recognizes* the need for Governments, non-governmental organizations and citizens to co-operate effectively with each other in undertaking social development programmes, notably with regard to social welfare policies, youth, the elderly, the advancement of women and disabled persons, as well as crime prevention and criminal justice;

5. *Stresses* the need to formulate at the national level innovative, effective and viable measures for social development in the face of limited budgetary allocations for social issues and diminishing natural resources;

6. *Requests* the Secretary-General and the Centre for Social Development and Humanitarian Affairs of the Secretariat, in particular, to include on a regular basis in their reports on social issues more information on ways and means of fully implementing the above-mentioned plans, strategies and programmes of action at the national, local and grass-roots levels, stressing, *inter alia*, the attitudes and values that leaders and citizens need to adopt in order to achieve social goals despite limited resources, effective methods that can be used on a larger scale at the national level and adopted in other countries, and methods of co-operation and networking at the international level aimed at assistance in the implementation of plans of action at the national level.

General Assembly resolution 44/66

8 December 1989   Meeting 78   Adopted without vote

Approved by Third Committee (A/44/753) without vote, 9 November (meeting 37); 10-nation draft (A/C.3/44/L.21); agenda item 97.
Sponsors: Costa Rica, Dominican Republic, El Salvador, Malaysia, Morocco, Myanmar, Paraguay, Philippines, Poland, Thailand.
Meeting numbers. GA 44th session: 3rd Committee 12, 15-18, 30, 37; plenary 78.

Social justice

ECONOMIC AND SOCIAL COUNCIL ACTION

On 24 May, the Economic and Social Council, on the recommendation of its Second Committee, adopted **resolution 1989/71** without vote.

Achievement of social justice

The Economic and Social Council,

Recalling General Assembly resolution 42/49 of 30 November 1987 and Council resolution 1988/46 of 27 May 1988,

Considering the pledge made by States Members of the United Nations in the Charter to take joint and separate action to promote higher standards of living, full employment and conditions of economic and social progress and development,

Bearing in mind that, in accordance with the Declaration on Social Progress and Development, social progress and development shall be founded on respect for the dignity and value of the human person and shall ensure the promotion of human rights and social justice,

Convinced that more extensive international and regional co-operation is important for promoting social progress at the national level,

Mindful of the Guiding Principles for Developmental Social Welfare Policies and Programmes in the Near Future,

Persuaded of the importance of taking measures to ensure co-ordination within the United Nations system in order to develop a comprehensive approach to developmental social welfare, including integrated and mutually supportive economic and social development policies, focused on the achievement of social justice,

1. *Recognizes* that social justice is one of the most important goals of social progress;

2. *Calls upon* States to take concepts of social justice as a basis for the preparation of their national development plans and programmes, giving priority to endeavouring to solve problems relating to employment, education, health care, nutrition, housing, social welfare and the raising of standards of living;

3. *Recommends* that the appropriate United Nations bodies and specialized agencies take into account the need to achieve social justice for all when considering social development issues and the observance of human rights;

4. *Requests* the Secretary-General, in his studies and reports concerning international social development issues, including the reports on the world social situation, to devote attention to social justice issues and, in particular, to ways of achieving the objective in question;

5. *Requests* the Commission for Social Development at its thirty-second session, when monitoring the implementation of international plans and programmes of action, specifically the Guiding Principles for Developmental Social Welfare Policies and Programmes in the Near Future, to consider ways and means of developing approaches to the achievement of social justice.

Economic and Social Council resolution 1989/71

24 May 1989   Meeting 15   Adopted without vote

Approved by Second Committee (E/1989/91) without vote, 12 May (meeting 14); 2-nation draft (E/1989/C.2/L.10/Rev.1); agenda item 11.
Sponsors: Poland, Ukrainian SSR.

GENERAL ASSEMBLY ACTION

The General Assembly, on the recommendation of the Third Committee, adopted **resolution 44/55** without vote on 8 December.

Achievement of social justice

The General Assembly,

Recalling its resolution 42/49 of 30 November 1987 and Economic and Social Council resolution 1988/46 of 27 May 1988, and taking note of Council resolution 1989/71 of 24 May 1989,

Bearing in mind that, in accordance with the Declaration on Social Progress and Development, social progress and development shall be founded on respect for the dignity and value of the human person and shall ensure the promotion of human rights and social justice,

Convinced that more extensive international and regional co-operation is important for promoting social progress at the national level,

Mindful of the Guiding Principles for Developmental Social Welfare Policies and Programmes in the Near Future,

Persuaded of the importance of taking measures to ensure co-ordination within the United Nations system in order to develop a comprehensive approach to developmental social welfare, including better integrated and mutually supportive economic and social development policies, aimed at the achievement of social justice,

1. *Considers* that the common purpose of the international community must be to forge from varied economic, social and political conditions a global environment of sustained development, full enjoyment of human rights and fundamental freedoms, and social justice and peace;

2. *Recognizes* that social justice is one of the most important goals of social progress;

3. *Reaffirms* the importance of co-operation among countries in promoting a climate conducive to the achievement by individual countries of the goals of development and social justice and progress;

4. *Considers* that such co-operation should continue to be a major focus of activities of the United Nations, in accordance with the principles of the Charter of the United Nations;

5. *Calls upon* Member States, in elaborating their national policy in the field of social development, to take into consideration the importance of achieving social justice for all;

6. *Recommends* that the Secretary-General, in preparing studies and reports on social problems and, in particular, the report on the world social situation, should examine questions concerning the achievement of social justice and ways in which it could be realized;

7. *Requests* the Commission for Social Development, at its next regular session, to continue to consider the question of achieving social justice.

General Assembly resolution 44/55

8 December 1989   Meeting 78   Adopted without vote

Approved by Third Committee (A/44/749) without vote, 9 November (meeting 37); 2-nation draft (A/C.3/44/L.16); agenda item 90.
Sponsors: Poland, Ukrainian SSR.
Meeting numbers. GA 44th session: 3rd Committee 12-20, 30, 37; plenary 78.

Social welfare, development and science and technology

ECONOMIC AND SOCIAL COUNCIL ACTION

On 24 May, the Economic and Social Council adopted **resolution 1989/47**, concerning social welfare, development and science and technology (see General Assembly resolution 44/54 below).

GENERAL ASSEMBLY ACTION

On 8 December, the General Assembly, on the recommendation of the Third Committee, adopted **resolution 44/54** without vote.

Social welfare, development and science and technology

The General Assembly,

Noting that scientific and technological progress is an important factor in the social and economic development of society,

Reaffirming the Declaration on Social Progress and Development, which was proclaimed by the General Assembly by its resolution 2542(XXIV) of 11 December 1969, in which States were called upon to share equitably scientific and technological advances, to intensify international co-operation in the field and to use science and technology for the benefit of the social development of society,

Reaffirming also the Declaration on the Use of Scientific and Technological Progress in the Interests of Peace and for the Benefit of Mankind, which was proclaimed by the General Assembly in its resolution 3384(XXX) of 10 November 1975, in which all States were called upon to promote international co-operation to ensure that the results of scientific and technological developments were used in the interests of strengthening international peace and security, freedom and independence, and also for the purpose of the economic and social development of peoples and the realization of human rights and freedoms in accordance with the Charter of the United Nations,

Considering that implementation of those Declarations will contribute to the social and economic development of peoples and international co-operation in the interests of scientific and technological progress, as well as to the strengthening of peace,

Emphasizing that international co-operation among States for the promotion of scientific and technological progress is in the interest of the social and economic development of all peoples,

Convinced that, in a time of rapid scientific and technological progress, the resources of mankind and the work of scientists make an important contribution to the peaceful economic and social development of nations and to the improvement of the living standards of all peoples,

Aware that technical co-operation, including the possibility of transfer of technology, is one of the ways of achieving better social progress in developing countries,

1. *Calls upon* all States to encourage co-operation to ensure scientific and technological progress for the welfare and social and economic development of their peoples, as well as of all human beings, and to contribute to the promotion of economic development and the elimination of grave social problems in the world;

2. *Stresses* the necessity of using scientific and technological progress as a major aspect of the process of fully implementing fundamental civil and political, economic, social and cultural human rights, as laid down in the International Covenants on Human Rights;

3. *Calls upon* all Governments to make every effort to use scientific and technological achievements for the promotion of peaceful social and economic development and to prevent their misuse to the disadvantage of human beings;

4. *Invites* the Commission for Social Development, in its discussion of the world social situation, to pay in-

creasing attention to the effects of science and technology on the processes of social welfare and development;

5. *Requests* the Secretary-General, when elaborating the next report on the world social situation, to take due account of the effects of science and technology on processes of social welfare and development on the basis of information available from Governments and from organizations of the United Nations system;

6. *Requests* the Secretary-General or interested Governments to consider convening in the near future, within existing resources, a seminar of experts on the effects of science and technology on social welfare and development.

General Assembly resolution 44/54

8 December 1989   Meeting 78   Adopted without vote

Approved by Third Committee (A/44/749) without vote, 9 November (meeting 37); 13-nation draft (A/C.3/44/L.14), orally revised; agenda item 90.

Meeting numbers. GA 44th session: 3rd Committee 12-20, 30, 37; plenary 78.

Social welfare

Guiding Principles for Social Welfare Policies and Programmes

The Commission for Social Development, at its thirty-first session in March,[7] reviewed the results of the 1987 Interregional Consultation on Developmental Social Welfare Policies and Programmes,[18] as requested by the Economic and Social Council in 1987.[19] The Secretary-General reported[20] on activities initiated in line with the suggestions for follow-up, contained in the Guiding Principles for Developmental Social Welfare Policies and Programmes in the Near Future.[18] Initially, highest priority was given to the widest possible dissemination of the documents of the Interregional Consultation and the Guiding Principles. A European expert meeting (Bonn, 25-27 January) was held as the first regional follow-up to the Consultation.

Alcohol use

On 24 May, the Economic and Social Council, on the recommendation of its Second Committee, adopted **resolution 1989/49** without vote.

Follow-up to the Guiding Principles for Developmental Social Welfare Policies and Programmes in the Near Future

The Economic and Social Council,

Recalling its resolution 1987/48 of 28 May 1987 on the Interregional Consultation on Developmental Social Welfare Policies and Programmes,

Recalling also General Assembly resolution 42/125 of 7 December 1987, in which the Assembly, *inter alia*, endorsed the Guiding Principles for Developmental Social Welfare Policies and Programmes in the Near Future, adopted by the Interregional Consultation,

Taking note of the recommendation made to the Interregional Consultation by the Conference of European Ministers Responsible for Social Affairs, held at Warsaw in April 1987, that the United Nations should look into ways in which the international community could in the future deal with pressing problems related to alcohol use,

Guided by the recommendations set out in the Guiding Principles for action at the national, regional and interregional levels to identify social measures that may appropriately be taken to meet the challenges posed to social structures, values, traditions and attitudes by, *inter alia*, the negative social consequences of alcohol use,

Mindful of the important contribution made by the World Health Organization in highlighting the negative health aspects of alcohol use,

1. *Requests* the Secretary-General to consider ways of following up the recommendations of the Interregional Consultation on Developmental Social Welfare Policies and Programmes by, *inter alia*, carrying out a study on the negative social consequences of alcohol use, based on the report of an expert meeting to be convened in 1990 under the auspices of the United Nations;

2. *Takes note with appreciation* of the offer of the Government of Norway to act as host to the expert meeting on the negative social consequences of alcohol use;

3. *Requests* the Secretary-General, within existing resources and drawing on support from interested Governments and appropriate intergovernmental and non-governmental organizations, to make the necessary preparations for the expert meeting;

4. *Also requests* the Secretary-General to consult with Member States on the nomination of experts to attend the meeting and to invite Member States to participate in the preparatory work by, *inter alia*, contributing national reports on relevant aspects of the questions deemed of particular importance;

5. *Further requests* the Secretary-General to report to the Commission for Social Development at its thirty-second session on the outcome of the expert meeting and to distribute the report of the meeting to Member States, inviting their comments on the recommendations contained therein.

Economic and Social Council resolution 1989/49

24 May 1989   Meeting 15   Adopted without vote

Approved by Second Committee (E/1989/91) without vote, 11 May (meeting 12); draft by Commission for Social Development (E/1989/25); agenda item 11.

Follow-up measures

The Council also adopted on 24 May, on the recommendation of the Second Committee, **resolution 1989/53** without vote.

Guiding Principles for Developmental Social Welfare Policies and Programmes in the Near Future and follow-up to the Interregional Consultation on Developmental Social Welfare Policies and Programmes

The Economic and Social Council

Recommends to the General Assembly the adoption of the following draft resolution:

[For text, see General Assembly resolution 44/65 below.]

Economic and Social Council resolution 1989/53
24 May 1989   Meeting 15   Adopted without vote

Approved by Second Committee (E/1989/91) without vote, 11 May (meeting 12); draft by Commission for Social Development (E/1989/25); agenda item 11.

In a 7 July note[21] responding to a 1987 General Assembly request,[22] the Secretary-General outlined steps taken pursuant to Economic and Social Council resolution 1989/53 (see above). A special task force was established within UNOV to provide input on social policy to the new international development strategy for the fourth United Nations development decade.[14] The focus was on integrated family- and community-oriented cost-effective innovations in social welfare, planning a data base and expert meetings and preparing a policy manual. A study was also being carried out on co-operation in social matters among the countries of Africa, Asia and Latin America.

GENERAL ASSEMBLY ACTION

On 8 December, the General Assembly, on the recommendation of the Third Committee, adopted **resolution 44/65** without vote.

Guiding Principles for Developmental Social Welfare Policies and Programmes in the Near Future and follow-up action to the Interregional Consultation on Developmental Social Welfare Policies and Programmes

The General Assembly,

Recalling the Universal Declaration of Human Rights proclaimed by the General Assembly in its resolution 217 A (III) of 10 December 1948, the International Covenant on Economic, Social and Cultural Rights and the International Covenant on Civil and Political Rights, contained in the annex to its resolution 2200 A (XXI) of 16 December 1966, and the Declaration on Social Progress and Development proclaimed by the Assembly in its resolution 2542(XXIV) of 11 December 1969, as well as other relevant international instruments,

Reaffirming the importance and value of strategies and plans of action concerning the situation of women, aging, youth, the disabled, crime prevention and drug abuse,

Recalling its resolution 42/125 of 7 December 1987, in which, *inter alia*, it endorsed the Guiding Principles for Developmental Social Welfare Policies and Programmes in the Near Future and requested the Secretary-General to take the necessary steps to ensure follow-up action to the Guiding Principles,

Stressing the importance of Economic and Social Council resolution 1987/48 of 28 May 1987, in which the Council requested the Secretary-General to redeploy resources to ensure appropriate follow-up action to the Interregional Consultation on Developmental Social Welfare Policies and Programmes,

Mindful of the critical importance of practical social welfare questions and the need to provide adequate resources to deal with them,

Concerned about the lack of follow-up action in the regions of Asia and the Pacific, Latin America and the Caribbean, Africa and Western Asia,

1.   *Reaffirms* the validity of the Guiding Principles for Developmental Social Welfare Policies and Programmes in the Near Future as an appropriate framework for future action in the field of social welfare and development;

2.   *Calls upon* Governments to make use of the Guiding Principles, to apply the recommendations contained therein, as appropriate, in accordance with their national structures, needs and objectives, to inform the Secretary-General of problems of implementation at the national level, and to accelerate the follow-up action to the Interregional Consultation on Developmental Social Welfare Policies and Programmes;

3.   *Requests* the executive secretaries of the regional commissions to give particular attention to the recommendations for action at the regional level contained in the Guiding Principles;

4.   *Urges* the Secretary-General and all organizations of the United Nations system concerned to include the implementation of the Guiding Principles in their respective programmes of work and to assist Governments, particularly those of the developing countries, in formulating appropriate social welfare policies and in setting up effective programmes according to their needs;

5.   *Requests* the Secretary-General to strengthen the follow-up action to the Interregional Consultation, focusing, *inter alia*, on integrated, family-oriented and community-oriented cost-effective innovations in the design of social welfare policies and programmes;

6.   *Also requests* the Secretary-General to strengthen co-operation and technical support for Governments, especially those of developing countries, focusing on the policy, planning, administration and training aspects of developmental social welfare;

7.   *Reiterates its request* to the Secretary-General to redeploy resources for taking measures to follow up the Interregional Consultation;

8.   *Recommends* the organization of additional regional expert group meetings devoted to issues raised in the Guiding Principles, such as the first regional follow-up international expert meeting, held at Bonn in January 1989;

9.   *Also recommends* that the efforts to reinforce the functioning of United Nations intergovernmental machinery in the social field should continue in line with the view expressed in paragraph 95 of the report of the Interregional Consultation;

10.   *Decides* that social issues as conceived in the Guiding Principles should become a major part of the international development strategy for the fourth United Nations development decade;

11.   *Welcomes* the report of the Secretary-General on the results of and follow-up action to the Interregional Consultation;

12.   *Notes* the progress made so far in strengthening the United Nations Office at Vienna as the nucleus for all issues and reports relating to social policy and development;

13.   *Invites* funding agencies within the United Nations system to consider a readjustment and an appropriate increase of their input of resources in the field of social development in order to reflect fully the changing world situation and actual requirements;

14. *Requests* the Secretary-General:

(*a*) To enhance the monitoring functions of and within the United Nations Office at Vienna and to maintain effective co-ordination between its individual units;

(*b*) To prepare, maintain and publicize an overview of social components and internationally accepted norms of the many international plans, covenants, declarations and strategies in the social field;

(*c*) To ensure that all bodies of the United Nations system concerned with developmental programmes and projects consult the Centre for Social Development and Humanitarian Affairs of the Secretariat on the social components of those programmes and projects;

(*d*) To reflect appropriately the recommendations of the Guiding Principles in the medium-term plan for the period 1992-1997 and in the programme budget for the biennium 1990-1991;

(*e*) To report to the General Assembly at its forty-sixth session on the progress achieved in implementing and following up the Guiding Principles and the present resolution;

15. *Decides* to include in the provisional agenda of its forty-sixth session an item entitled "Implementation of the Guiding Principles for Developmental Social Welfare Policies and Programmes in the Near Future".

General Assembly resolution 44/65

8 December 1989   Meeting 78   Adopted without vote

Approved by Third Committee (A/44/753) without vote, 9 November (meeting 37); draft recommended by ESC res. 1989/53 (A/C.3/44/L.5); agenda item 97.

Meeting numbers. GA 44th session: 3rd Committee 12, 15-18, 30, 37; plenary 78.

Co-operatives

In accordance with a 1987 Economic and Social Council resolution,[23] the Secretary-General reported on national experience in promoting the co-operative movement in developing countries.[24] Based on information received from 28 Member States, 3 specialized agencies and 3 international NGOs, he discussed the participation of all population groups, but particularly peasants, and including women, youth, disabled persons and the aging, in co-operatives. The role of government support and other programmes in promoting co-operatives was also discussed.

Co-operatives had become an integral part of the development process, demonstrating their ability to enable the poor to band together in successful self-help ventures, he stated. The majority of all co-operatives in developing countries were active in agriculture (53 per cent) and in finance (29 per cent); they were the most widespread form of organization of rural people. Their potential, however, for meeting the needs of poor peasants, the landless and nomadic populations had not been fully used. Urban co-operatives were facing challenges to improve management and financing in order to increase financial resources. While there was continuous growth of informal, pre-co-operative women's groups, little attention had been paid to the needs of youth, the aging and disabled persons. There

was a compelling need for co-operatives to adopt new technologies to increase productivity and ensure improved levels of marketing in the agricultural, commercial and industrial spheres.

The Secretary-General recommended that Governments encourage greater citizen participation; adopt legislation governing the status, membership and administrative procedures of all types of co-operative organizations; and strengthen co-operative organizations at the national level to enable them to function as full partners to government in all areas of common concern.

On 24 May, the Economic and Social Council, by **decision 1989/135**, took note of the report.

On 8 December, the General Assembly, on the recommendation of the Third Committee, adopted **resolution 44/58** without vote.

National experience in promoting the co-operative movement

The General Assembly,

Recalling its resolutions 2459(XXIII) of 20 December 1968, 3273(XXIX) of 10 December 1974, 31/37 of 30 November 1976, 33/47 of 14 December 1978 and 36/18 of 9 November 1981, as well as Economic and Social Council resolutions 1983/15 of 26 May 1983, 1985/22 of 29 May 1985 and 1987/47 of 28 May 1987,

Aware of the ongoing work to elaborate the international development strategy for the fourth United Nations development decade,

Bearing in mind that co-operatives in their different forms are becoming an indispensable factor of economic and social development in all countries, especially the developing countries,

Noting that co-operatives are called upon to help to ensure the fullest possible participation in the development process of all population groups, including women, youth, disabled persons and the aging, and to contribute to the implementation of the Guiding Principles for Developmental Social Welfare Policies and Programmes in the Near Future,

Having in mind the recent widespread reassessment by Governments of the status of co-operatives and their role in enhancing economic and social development,

Convinced that the sharing among countries of national experience relating to the active involvement of co-operatives in the development process is acquiring increasing importance in the light of new trends in the approach to co-operatives,

1. *Commends* the report of the Secretary-General on national experience in promoting the co-operative movement;

2. *Invites* all States, the regional commissions and the specialized agencies concerned to make further efforts with a view to promoting the co-operative movement as an important instrument of economic and social development, thus contributing to the implementation of the Guiding Principles for Developmental Social Welfare Policies and Programmes in the Near Future;

3. *Requests* the Secretary-General to follow closely national experience in promoting co-operatives and to

encourage all forms of international co-operation, in collaboration with interested Governments, governmental and non-governmental organizations, as an important part of the social development strategy;

4. *Also requests* the Secretary-General, in consultation with Member States and relevant organizations of the United Nations system, to prepare a report on the status and role of co-operatives in the light of new economic and social trends and to submit it, through the Economic and Social Council, to the General Assembly at its forty-seventh session;

5. *Decides* to consider a question entitled "Co-operatives and new trends in socio-economic development" at its forty-seventh session as a sub-item of the item entitled "National experience in achieving far-reaching social and economic changes for the purpose of social progress".

General Assembly resolution 44/58

8 December 1989   Meeting 78   Adopted without vote

Approved by Third Committee (A/44/751) without vote, 9 November (meeting 37); 14-nation draft (A/C.3/44/L.23), orally revised; agenda item 92.
Meeting numbers. GA 44th session: 3rd Committee 12-13, 15-20, 30, 37; plenary 78.

The family

International co-operation to protect and assist the family

In compliance with a 1987 Economic and Social Council resolution,[5] the Secretary-General reported on the social situation of families,[25] describing results of a survey of national policies for families received from 48 Governments.

According to replies, the single-parent family was most likely to receive attention from the Government, owing to its high incidence of poverty and dependence on the State and the heavy responsibilities falling on the woman who headed such a family. Specific concerns were expressed regarding children, women, youth, the aging and the disabled. The services and benefits mentioned by Governments covered such sectors as health, education, housing and welfare.

It was observed that Governments often designed policies and programmes aimed at specific target groups, such as children and the aging. Such an approach might not support the family as a unit. At the same time, family policy was often framed with a particular family model in mind, which did not reflect the rich variety of family forms in each country. The survey also showed that in many cases families were supported in their attempts to meet their needs, not by governmental intervention, but by private charities and other organizations providing services to people in need.

ECONOMIC AND SOCIAL COUNCIL ACTION

On 24 May, the Economic and Social Council, on the recommendation of its Second Committee, adopted **resolution 1989/54** without vote.

Need to enhance international co-operation in the field of protection and assistance to the family

The Economic and Social Council,

Recalling General Assembly resolution 43/135 of 8 December 1988,

1. *Takes note with appreciation* of the report of the Secretary-General entitled "Social situation of families: results of the survey of national policies for families", prepared in accordance with its resolution 1987/46 of 28 May 1987;

2. *Requests* the Secretary-General, Member States, organizations and bodies of the United Nations system and intergovernmental and non-governmental organizations, as appropriate, to implement fully General Assembly resolution 43/135.

Economic and Social Council resolution 1989/54

24 May 1989   Meeting 15   Adopted without vote

Approved by Second Committee (E/1989/91) without vote, 11 May (meeting 12); draft by Commission for Social Development (E/1989/25); agenda item 11.

International year of the family

Pursuant to a 1988 General Assembly request,[26] the Secretary-General reported on preparations for an international year of the family.[27] An annex dealt with issues that might be addressed during such an international year.

The Secretary-General recommended that the year 1994 be proclaimed "International Family Year", with the theme "Family: resources and responsibilities in a changing world", and that the UN system and all organizations intending to participate undertake specially focused activities. The international year would aim to increase awareness of family issues among Governments, as well as in the private sector; strengthen national institutions to implement family-related policies and to respond to family-related problems; enhance local efforts and improve collaboration among NGOs; and build on results of international activities concerning women, children, youth, the aging and the disabled. A number of fundamental principles were also recommended as a foundation for all activities for the international year.

GENERAL ASSEMBLY ACTION

On 8 December, the General Assembly, on the recommendation of the Third Committee, adopted **resolution 44/82** without vote.

International Year of the Family

The General Assembly,

Guided by the resolve of the peoples of the United Nations to promote social progress and better standards of life in larger freedom, with a view to the creation of conditions of stability and well-being, which are necessary for peaceful and friendly relations between nations,

Guided also by the relevant provisions of the Universal Declaration of Human Rights, the International Covenant on Economic, Social and Cultural Rights and the Declaration on Social Progress and Development, according to which the widest possible protection and assistance should be accorded to the family,

Bearing in mind its resolution 42/49 of 30 November 1987 and Economic and Social Council resolutions 1988/46 of 27 May 1988 and 1989/71 of 24 May 1989 entitled "Achievement of social justice",

Bearing in mind also the Nairobi Forward-looking Strategies for the Advancement of Women and recalling that by its resolution 42/125 of 7 December 1987 it endorsed for action the Guiding Principles for Developmental Social Welfare Policies and Programmes in the Near Future, which called for social welfare policies to give greater attention to the family,

Recognizing the efforts of Governments at the local, regional and national levels in carrying out specific programmes concerning the family, in which the United Nations may have an important role to play, and in raising awareness, increasing understanding and promoting policies that improve the position and well-being of the family,

Recalling its resolutions 42/134 of 7 December 1987 and 43/135 of 8 December 1988 on the need to enhance international co-operation in the field of the protection of and assistance to the family, as well as Economic and Social Council resolutions 1983/23 of 26 May 1983 and 1985/29 of 29 May 1985, and taking note of Council resolution 1989/54 of 24 May 1989,

Taking into account its decision 35/424 of 5 December 1980 and Economic and Social Council resolution 1980/67 of 25 July 1980 concerning guidelines for international years and anniversaries,

Taking note with interest and appreciation of the report of the Secretary-General prepared in pursuance of its resolution 43/135,

1. *Proclaims* 1994 as International Year of the Family;

2. *Decides* that the major activities for the observance of the Year should be concentrated at the local, regional and national levels and assisted by the United Nations and its system of organizations, with a view to creating among Governments, policy-makers and the public a greater awareness of the family as the natural and fundamental unit of society;

3. *Endorses* the main recommendations, objectives and principles for the observance of the Year, as contained in the comprehensive outline of a possible programme for the Year;

4. *Invites* all Governments, specialized agencies, intergovernmental and non-governmental organizations concerned, as well as interested national organizations, to exert all possible efforts in the preparation for and observance of the Year and to co-operate with the Secretary-General in achieving the objectives of the Year;

5. *Requests* the Secretary-General to prepare, on the basis of his report and in consultation with Member States, concerned specialized agencies and interested intergovernmental and non-governmental organizations, a draft programme for the preparation for and observance of the Year and to submit a progress report thereon to the General Assembly at its forty-fifth session;

6. *Also requests* the Secretary-General to take specific measures, through all the communication media at his disposal, to give widespread publicity to the activities of the United Nations system in the area of family issues and to increase the dissemination of information on this subject;

7. *Designates* the Commission for Social Development as the preparatory body and the Economic and Social Council as the co-ordinating body for the International Year of the Family;

8. *Decides* to consider the report of the Secretary-General at its forty-fifth session under an item entitled "International Year of the Family".

General Assembly resolution 44/82

8 December 1989   Meeting 78   Adopted without vote

Approved by Third Committee (A/44/757) without vote, 9 November (meeting 37); 21-nation draft (A/C.3/44/L.18); agenda item 113.

Meeting numbers. GA 44th session: 3rd Committee 12, 14-18, 20, 30, 37; plenary 78.

Migrant workers

The situation of migrant workers was dealt with in the *1989 Report on the World Social Situation*.[1] Economic and social inequalities as well as man-made and natural disasters motivated people to migrate to other countries in search of better economic opportunities and freedom from persecution and discrimination, the report stated. The increasing number of migrants gave rise to sensitive and difficult issues for an international community in which States had come to consider it natural to control immigration, emigration, or both.

In a report on the social situation of migrant workers and their families[28] submitted pursuant to a 1985 Economic and Social Council request,[29] the Secretary-General discussed problems and needs of second-generation migrants, with particular reference to developed market economies. He also described the principal features of contract migration in western Asia and southern Africa, referring to the social situation of both migrant workers and the families left behind in the home country.

Restrictive measures on immigration taken by Governments during the 1970s had, ironically, encouraged a large number of migrant workers to settle permanently in receiving countries and to bring their families and relatives to live with them. With their relatively high birth rates, the numbers of young people were increasing within total foreign populations. In France, the Federal Republic of Germany, Luxembourg, Norway, Sweden and Switzerland, the proportion of those under 24 years was between 35 and 40 per cent, and in Belgium and the Netherlands, around 50 per cent. They often constituted a disproportionately high number of the long-term unemployed, school drop-outs, and juvenile delinquents, in spite of their best efforts and special programmes designed to help them. The report pointed out that second-generation migrants were socially integrated but in a subordinate position, as a result of the cultural structure, diffused or disguised discrimination or rigid educational systems in receiving countries. It suggested that social integration of migrants was more a matter of helping societies adapt their individuals, and of offering equal opportunities to all, native and migrant.

Contract-migration workers, living and working in segregated compounds, had very little control over their living and working conditions and were often exploited. Their lengthy absences from home might cause family problems and have negative economic consequences in the sending countries. The report suggested guiding principles for establishing social services for second-generation and contract migrants.

In March,[30] the Commission for Social Development took note of the report.

Poverty

The *1989 Report on the World Social Situation*[1] discussed inequality in world incomes. Inequalities of income distribution among countries were extremely large, and trends in inequality, employment and poverty diverged markedly among the developing regions. In Asia as a whole, there was continued progress in providing employment and reducing poverty. In sub-Saharan Africa, on the other hand, significant set-backs were experienced in those areas. In Latin America, the situation had sharply deteriorated and eventually had stabilized at a new, lower level. Income distribution had not changed markedly in Asia, whereas it worsened in the heavily indebted countries of Latin America. The difference between the relative income shares of urban and rural populations narrowed in the poorer countries of sub-Saharan Africa.

In March, the Commission for Social Development considered the problem of extreme poverty, in accordance with a 1988 Economic and Social Council request.[31] It was generally agreed that the fight against extreme poverty remained an international challenge that required full international co-operation and, within countries, further intensification of efforts involving state agencies, civic associations and humanitarian organizations.

Institutional machinery

Commission for Social Development

At its thirty-first session (Vienna, 13-22 March),[7] the Commission for Social Development adopted three resolutions and five decisions. The draft resolutions covered social welfare, development and science and technology (Council resolution 1989/47); twentieth anniversary of the Declaration on Social Progress and Development (1989/48); the Guiding Principles for Developmental Social Welfare Policies and Programmes in the Near Future (1989/53) and its follow-up (1989/49); international co-operation in the field of protection and assistance to the family (1989/54); the so-

cial dimension of the international development strategy for the fourth United Nations development decade (1989/55); the critical social situation in Africa (see PART THREE, Chapter III); the second review and appraisal of the implementation of the International Plan of Action on Aging; youth in the contemporary world (see PART THREE, Chapter XIV); and the United Nations Decade of Disabled Persons (see PART THREE, Chapter XI).

The Commission also recommended to the Economic and Social Council the adoption of another 10 draft resolutions and one draft decision.

On 24 May, the Council, by **decision 1989/131**, noted the Commission's report and approved the provisional agenda and documentation for the thirty-second (1991) session.

Improvement of work

At its thirty-first session, the Commission for Social Development considered a note by the Secretary-General summarizing suggestions for improvement of its work.[32] These suggestions covered the agenda, advance selection of specific topics for in-depth consideration, inter-sessional expert group meetings, in-session, open-ended working groups, organization of the work of future sessions, draft resolutions for adoption by the Economic and Social Council, Commission membership and the frequency and duration of sessions.

Having considered the note, the Commission reaffirmed[33] that it would organize its substantive work under three agenda items and decided to select specific subjects for in-depth consideration at each session. For the thirty-second session, it selected the integration of young people into society and the social impact of the critical economic environment on developing countries; and for the thirty-third session, either disability matters or family issues would be given such consideration. The Commission encouraged Governments to host expert group meetings which would prepare for in-depth consideration of priority subjects. No consensus was reached on membership or the frequency of sessions.

Programme of work

In a report[34] submitted to the Commission for Social Development, the Secretary-General summarized the programme of work for the period 1988-1989 in the field of social development of the Centre for Social Development and Humanitarian Affairs (CSDHA) at the UN Office at Vienna, and the UN Department of International Economic and Social Affairs. The report also summarized social welfare and social development activities by the regional commissions.

In March, the Commission noted[35] the report.

UN Research Institute for Social Development

In 1989, the United Nations Research Institute for Social Development (UNRISD) began a new research programme, approved by its Board in 1988.[36]

In preparation for the programme dealing with crisis, adjustment and social change, UNRISD organized, in co-operation with the Institute of Social and Economic Research of the University of the West Indies, a conference on economic crisis in the third world: impact and response (Kingston, 3-6 April), and successfully secured funding by the Netherlands for the research phase of the programme. Under a programme on food pricing and marketing reform, a seminar was held (Geneva, 20-22 November) to facilitate dialogue among researchers. In February, the Institute began preparing an annotated bibliography and a review monograph on the social, economic and political consequences of illicit trade in cocaine, heroin, marijuana and hashish. Following a workshop on economic reform and social participation (Geneva, September) attended by European scholars, a preliminary research phase was launched in central and eastern Europe and the USSR, involving an overview of the economic and political reforms introduced in the 1980s, with an assessment of implications for different social groups and probable changes in forms of participation. Other ongoing research activities involved the environment, sustainable development and social changes; ethnic conflict and development; patterns of consumption; political violence and social movements; and refugees, returnees and local society.

UNRISD continued to disseminate its research results in a variety of publications. Several reports were co-published in Latin America and a number of English-language monographs were issued.

Institute assets prior to expenditures in 1989 totalled $3,716,459. Of this amount, $200,000 represented the legal operating reserve, and an additional $1,259,741 was tied income or otherwise unavailable for expenditure in 1989. The amount available for expenditure in 1989 therefore totalled $2,256,718. Expenditures in 1989 amounted to $1,775,861.

On 22 March, the Commission for Social Development considered[37] a report of the UNRISD Board,[38] covering Institute activities in 1987 and 1988. Governments were invited to make or increase financial contributions to the Institute. The Commission also decided[39] to increase the number of nominated members of the UNRISD Board from 7 to 10, and that the nomination and confirmation of the 3 additional members would take place at the first regular session in 1989 of the Economic and Social Council. By **decision 1989/132** of 24 May, the Council endorsed the increase in members, but deferred the nomination and confirmation issue to its second regular session of 1989. On 6 July, the Council, in **decision 1989/181**, confirmed the nomination of the three candidates. (For members, see APPENDIX III.)

Crime prevention and criminal justice

In 1989, the United Nations continued to focus its activities in crime prevention and criminal justice on the implementation of the 1985 Milan Plan of Action, adopted by the Seventh UN Congress on the Prevention of Crime and the Treatment of Offenders,[40] and the preparation for the Eighth Congress, to be held in 1990.

Report of the Secretary-General. Pursuant to a 1988 General Assembly resolution,[41] the Secretary-General in August reported[42] on progress achieved by Governments and relevant entities of the UN system in implementing the Milan Plan of Action. A total of 14 Governments provided information on activities to implement the Plan, international co-operation in crime prevention and criminal justice, measures against the most serious forms of crime, and human rights in the administration of justice. They indicated that measures to strengthen international co-operation and harmonize national policies in line with the Milan Plan of Action and other recommendations of the Seventh Congress were either already fully implemented in national legislation and policies or efforts were being made towards that end. Organized crime and illicit drug trafficking were of great concern to many Member States.

Other topics dealt with included preparations for the Eighth Congress and technical co-operation in crime prevention and criminal justice (see below).

GENERAL ASSEMBLY ACTION

On 8 December, the General Assembly, on the recommendation of the Third Committee, adopted **resolution 44/72** without vote.

Crime prevention and criminal justice
The General Assembly,

Bearing in mind the responsibilities assumed by the United Nations in the field of crime prevention and criminal justice under Economic and Social Council resolution 155 C (VII) of 13 August 1948 and General Assembly resolution 415(V) of 1 December 1950, as well as its pivotal role in the promotion of international co-operation in this field, in accordance with Assembly resolutions 3021(XXVII) of 18 December 1972, 32/59 and 32/60 of 8 December 1977 and 35/171 of 15 December 1980,

Emphasizing the importance of its resolution 40/32 of 29 November 1985, in which it approved the Milan Plan of Action, adopted by consensus by the Seventh United Nations Congress on the Prevention of Crime and the Treatment of Offenders, as a useful and effective means of strengthening international co-operation in the field of crime prevention and criminal justice,

Recalling its resolution 41/107 of 4 December 1986, in which it invited Member States and the Secretary-General to ensure timely preparations for the Eighth United Nations Congress on the Prevention of Crime and the Treatment of Offenders, its resolution 42/59 of 30 November 1987, in which, *inter alia*, it welcomed the results of the comprehensive review of the functioning and programme of work of the United Nations in the field of crime prevention and criminal justice conducted by the Secretary-General and approved the recommendations contained in Economic and Social Council resolutions 1986/11 of 21 May 1986 and 1987/53 of 28 May 1987, and its resolution 43/99 of 8 December 1988, in which it stressed the necessity for Member States to continue to make concerted and systematic efforts to strengthen international co-operation in crime prevention and criminal justice,

Recalling also Economic and Social Council resolution 1987/49 of 28 May 1987, in which the Council approved the provisional agenda for the Eighth Congress, and taking note of Council resolutions 1989/68 of 24 May 1989 on the review of the functioning and programme of work of the United Nations in crime prevention and criminal justice and 1989/69 of 24 May 1989 on the continuation of preparations for the Eighth Congress,

Taking note of Economic and Social Council resolutions 1989/56 of 24 May 1989, the annex to which contains the statute of the United Nations Interregional Crime and Justice Research Institute, 1989/59 of 24 May 1989 concerning the establishment of the African Institute for the Prevention of Crime and the Treatment of Offenders, 1989/62 of 24 May 1989 on concerted international action against the forms of crime identified in the Milan Plan of Action and 1989/67 of 24 May 1989 on domestic violence,

Taking note also of Economic and Social Council decision 1989/134 of 24 May 1989 by which the Council accepted the invitation of the Government of Cuba to hold the Eighth Congress at Havana from 27 August to 7 September 1990,

Conscious that the convening of such a global meeting demonstrates the continuing interest and capacity of Member States, intergovernmental and non-governmental organizations, scholars and experts to react to the challenge posed by the new forms and dimensions of criminality, both nationally and internationally,

Acknowledging that the United Nations congresses, as major intergovernmental forums, have influenced national policies and practices by facilitating the exchange of views and experiences, mobilizing public opinion and recommending policy options at the national, regional and international levels, thus making a significant contribution to progress and the promotion of international co-operation in this field,

Appreciative of the success of all the preparatory activities for the Eighth Congress, which have been carried out in a spirit of mutual understanding, productive consensus and professional competence,

Mindful of the main objectives of the United Nations in the field of crime prevention and criminal justice,

which include the promotion of a more effective administration of justice, the strengthening of international co-operation in the fight against transnational crime, the observance of human rights and the pursuance of the highest standards of fairness, efficiency, humanity and professional conduct,

Aware that transnational criminality, particularly in its violent and organized forms, constitutes a serious threat to the development and security of nations,

Concerned about the increase in the incidence and seriousness of crime, both conventional and non-conventional, as well as juvenile delinquency, in many parts of the world, and its negative effects on the quality of life and the enjoyment of human rights and fundamental freedoms,

Also concerned about the level of the human and financial resources available to the United Nations in this field, taking into account the increased responsibilities and expanded mandates of the Organization,

Recognizing that constraints of an economic and technical nature impede many countries in their fight against crime, and that technological advances may not only entail dangers to the human environment but may also be utilized in the perpetration of sophisticated forms of crime, against which criminal law can serve a useful function, including the penal protection of the environment,

Convinced of the urgent need to strengthen international co-operation and co-ordination at all levels in order to meet the challenge posed by contemporary crime,

Determined to improve joint action to achieve further progress in combating crime, particularly in its new forms and transnational dimensions, and in ensuring respect for the rule of law, as well as to increase the usefulness and impact of the Eighth Congress through the discussion and adoption of new important international instruments and heightened public awareness of the results of the Congress,

1. *Takes note* of the report of the Secretary-General on the implementation of its resolution 43/99, in which, *inter alia*, the recommendations of the regional preparatory meetings for the Eighth United Nations Congress on the Prevention of Crime and the Treatment of Offenders are summarized;

2. *Reaffirms* the continued validity of the Milan Plan of Action and the importance of its goals, which include the strengthening of international co-operation and the enhancement of the United Nations role in this field;

3. *Urges* the international community to implement the recommendations contained in the Milan Plan of Action, together with the resolutions adopted by the Seventh United Nations Congress on the Prevention of Crime and the Treatment of Offenders, and invites those Governments that have not yet done so to provide relevant information to the Secretary-General on the progress made in this regard;

4. *Expresses the hope* that the Eighth Congress will make a major contribution to the solution of problems related to crime prevention and criminal justice;

5. *Approves* the recommendations contained in Economic and Social Council resolutions 1989/68 and 1989/69, and requests the Secretary-General to take appropriate measures to translate them into action;

6. *Acknowledges* the crucial functions of the Committee on Crime Prevention and Control, which the Economic and Social Council has entrusted with develop-

ing practical crime prevention and criminal justice policies and monitoring the implementation of United Nations standards and norms in this field and which is also the preparatory body for the United Nations congresses on the prevention of crime and the treatment of offenders;

7. *Welcomes* the establishment by the Committee of a sub-committee charged with the task of providing an overview of the problem of crime and assessing the most efficient means of stimulating practical international action in support of Member States, as well as the establishment of a pre-sessional working group to oversee the process of implementing existing standards;

8. *Also welcomes* the adoption of the statute of the United Nations Interregional Crime and Justice Research Institute and the formal establishment, at Kampala, of the African Institute for the Prevention of Crime and the Treatment of Offenders;

9. *Invites* the Committee on Crime Prevention and Control, at its eleventh session, to give priority attention to the conclusions and recommendations of its sub-committee and to consider appropriate follow-up thereto by the Eighth Congress;

10. *Stresses* the importance of the programme of work of the United Nations in crime prevention and criminal justice and the necessity of strengthening it in order to make it more responsive to the needs and expectations of Member States, whose stability and social peace, as well as law enforcement and judicial structures, may be undermined by the growing level and impact of criminality;

11. *Requests* the Secretary-General to ensure that the level of human and financial resources of the Crime Prevention and Criminal Justice Branch of the Centre for Social Development and Humanitarian Affairs of the Secretariat is sufficient for it to carry out its multiple tasks mandated by United Nations policy-making bodies, including the promotion of collaborative action by Governments on problems of mutual concern, evaluation research, the collection and dissemination of information, the preparation of reports and studies, and technical co-operation activities, and to ensure that the specialized nature of the programme of work of the Branch is fully reflected in its management and staffing;

12. *Takes note* of the efforts made by the Secretariat towards the establishment of a global crime prevention and criminal justice information network, urges governmental agencies concerned and criminal justice institutions to join the network, in view of its value, and requests the Secretary-General to secure adequate resources for its full development and functioning;

13. *Invites* the Economic and Social Council, at its first regular session of 1990, to give priority consideration to the report of the Committee on Crime Prevention and Control on the work of its eleventh session, paying attention also to the operational aspects of the programme of work in crime prevention, with a view to assisting interested countries in developing self-reliant and adequate law enforcement and judicial structures through human resources development, the reinforcement of national machinery, the promotion of human rights, the organization of joint training activities and the development of pilot and demonstration projects, and urges the World Bank, the United Nations Development Programme, the Department of Technical Co-operation for Development of the Secretariat and other funding agencies to continue to provide financial support and assistance for technical co-operation activities;

14. *Encourages* Governments and intergovernmental and non-governmental organizations, in co-operation with the Secretariat, to play an active role in the formulation and implementation of technical co-operation projects in crime prevention and criminal justice, to allocate adequate resources and expertise for technical assistance activities and to increase their support to the interregional and regional institutes for the prevention of crime and the treatment of offenders;

15. *Reiterates its invitation* to Governments to participate actively in the preparations for the Eighth Congress, particularly through the involvement of national correspondents in the field of crime prevention and control, the submission of national position papers on the different agenda items, the establishment, as appropriate, of national committees and focal points and the encouragement of contributions from the academic community and relevant scientific institutions;

16. *Urges* Member States to contribute to the two research workshops to be held during the Eighth Congress on the computerization of criminal justice information and alternatives to imprisonment by preparing research and technical papers and other information that would make possible a substantive and fruitful exchange of national experiences in these areas;

17. *Calls upon* the specialized agencies, in particular the International Labour Organisation, the United Nations Educational, Scientific and Cultural Organization, the World Health Organization, the International Civil Aviation Organization and the International Maritime Organization, and other intergovernmental organizations and non-governmental organizations to participate actively in the Eighth Congress and to give the necessary attention and priority to national, regional and international measures aimed at preventing crime and improving the quality of the administration of justice;

18. *Requests* the Eighth Congress, under item 3 of its provisional agenda, to give urgent attention to strengthening international co-operation in crime prevention and criminal justice, in pursuance of the recommendations of the preparatory meetings and of the Committee on Crime Prevention and Control, which also emphasized, *inter alia*, the role of criminal law in environmental protection;

19. *Also requests* the Eighth Congress, under item 5 of its provisional agenda, to pay particular attention to the linkages between illicit drug trafficking, organized crime and terrorist criminal activities, and to propose viable control measures;

20. *Encourages* Member States to contribute to the United Nations Trust Fund for Social Defence in order to enable the Fund to undertake activities of assistance to countries requesting it;

21. *Requests* the Secretary-General to ensure, with a strengthened information programme, that the substantive and organizational work of the Eighth Congress is fully adequate for the successful outcome of the Congress, and to provide the required resources;

22. *Also requests* the Secretary-General to submit to the Eighth Congress and to the General Assembly at its forty-fifth session a report on the implementation of the recommendations of the Seventh Congress, to be prepared in pursuance of resolution 22 of the Seventh Congress and of Economic and Social Council resolution 1987/49, with a view to assessing the progress achieved and ensuring continuity between the congresses;

23. *Further requests* the Secretary-General to submit to the General Assembly at its forty-fifth session his views and recommendations on the implementation of the conclusions of the Eighth Congress;

24. *Decides* to include in the provisional agenda of its forty-fifth session the item entitled "Crime prevention and criminal justice".

General Assembly resolution 44/72

8 December 1989   Meeting 78   Adopted without vote

Approved by Third Committee (A/44/756) without vote, 9 November (meeting 37); 22-nation draft (A/C.3/44/L.22); agenda item 102.
Meeting numbers. GA 44th session: 3rd Committee 12-20, 30, 37; plenary 78.

Review of UN crime programme

In response to a 1988 Economic and Social Council resolution,[43] the Secretary-General reported[44] on the review of the functioning and programme of work of the United Nations in crime prevention and criminal justice. He also drew attention to recommendations made by the Committee on Crime Prevention and Control at its 1988 session.[45] Other topics discussed included preparations for the Eighth Congress (see below) and regional and international collaboration and activities.

The Sub-Committee of the Committee on Crime Prevention and Control (Riyadh, 18-19 January)[46] discussed the world-wide problem of crime, the need for international co-operation and assistance, the inadequacy of the present co-operation and assistance, and development of an effective international crime and justice programme. It concluded that existing mechanisms for collective action and assistance were seriously deficient in both concept and capacity; therefore, national Governments should develop and subscribe to a broad UN convention on crime to provide a foundation for a genuinely effective international programme of crime prevention and control. It suggested that a new convention could be submitted to the Ninth UN Congress on the Prevention of Crime and the Treatment of Offenders.

To deal with its increasing activities in this area, the Secretariat had attempted to make operational activities more cost-effective and to better integrate them with criminological and legal research, policy analysis, monitoring of global trends and implementation of existing standards. The Secretary-General pointed out that human and financial resources available to the United Nations programme for crime prevention were shrinking while legislative mandates were multiplying.

ECONOMIC AND SOCIAL COUNCIL ACTION

On 24 May, the Economic and Social Council, on the recommendation of its Second Committee, adopted **resolution 1989/68** without vote.

Review of the functioning and programme of work of the United Nations in crime prevention and criminal justice

The Economic and Social Council,

Recalling the responsibility assumed by the United Nations in the field of crime prevention and criminal justice in pursuance of Council resolution 155 C (VII) of 13 August 1948 and General Assembly resolution 415(V) of 1 December 1950,

Recalling also its resolutions 1986/11 of 21 May 1986, 1987/53 of 28 May 1987 and 1988/44 of 27 May 1988, and General Assembly resolutions 40/32 of 29 November 1985, 41/107 of 4 December 1986 and 42/59 of 30 November 1987,

Alarmed at the increase both in the incidence and seriousness of crime, both conventional and non-conventional, in many parts of the world, which undermines the development process, impairs the quality of life and threatens human rights and fundamental freedoms,

Bearing in mind the fact that crime has assumed a transnational character, which calls for a concerted international response,

Convinced of the urgent need to strengthen international co-operation in order to face the challenge posed by contemporary forms of crime,

Determined to improve regional, interregional and international co-operation to achieve further progress in combating crime, particularly in its new forms and dimensions,

Recognizing the pivotal role of the Committee on Crime Prevention and Control in providing guidance in this field through the elaboration of draft instruments, model agreements and guidelines in crime prevention and criminal justice, the preparation of United Nations congresses and the co-ordination of United Nations activities,

Recalling that 1988 is the fortieth anniversary of the establishment of the programme of the United Nations in the field of crime prevention and criminal justice,

Determined to make further progress in the implementation of the conclusions and recommendations of the Seventh United Nations Congress on the Prevention of Crime and the Treatment of Offenders and the relevant Economic and Social Council and General Assembly resolutions on the review of the functioning and programme of work of the United Nations in crime prevention and criminal justice,

Aware of the constraints the Secretary-General faces in allocating to particular programmes the resources available to the United Nations,

Noting with alarm that the present capacity and the status of the Crime Prevention and Criminal Justice Branch of the Centre for Social Development and Humanitarian Affairs of the Secretariat are not commensurate with its enlarged responsibilities and expanded programme mandates,

1. *Welcomes* the report of the Secretary-General concerning the progress made in the implementation of the conclusions of the review of the functioning and programme of work of the United Nations in crime prevention and criminal justice;

2. *Reaffirms* its conviction of the importance of the programme of the United Nations in the field of crime prevention and criminal justice and the necessity of strengthening it in order to make it more fully responsive to the needs and expectations of Member States;

3. *Reaffirms also* the value of the quinquennial United Nations congresses on the prevention of crime and the treatment of offenders in fostering the exchange of information and experiences and recommends that the congresses focus on priority issues for in-depth examination and expand the number of workshops on specific topics involving the regional and interregional institutes, the Arab Security Studies and Training Centre at Riyadh, non-governmental organizations and relevant professional associations;

4. *Notes* that, while serious efforts have been made to implement recommendations related to the substantive aspects of the programme, more attention should be paid to the existing structure and level of management of the Crime Prevention and Criminal Justice Branch of the Centre for Social Development and Humanitarian Affairs of the Secretariat in pursuance of Council resolutions 1986/11 and 1987/53 and General Assembly resolution 42/59;

5. *Requests* the Secretary-General to take steps to implement paragraph 3 *(a)* of its resolution 1987/53, in which he was requested to develop the Crime Prevention and Criminal Justice Branch as a specialized body in the field of crime and justice;

6. *Notes with concern* the shortage of staff of the Crime Prevention and Criminal Justice Branch needed to carry out the multiple tasks mandated by the policy-making bodies, including action-oriented research, collection and dissemination of information, preparation of reports and technical co-operation, and reiterates its request to the Secretary-General to increase the number of regular posts assigned to the Branch, at least to the former level;

7. *Requests* the Secretary-General, in preparing his proposals for the medium-term plan for the period 1992-1995, to incorporate a separate programme on crime and justice and to include in the proposed programme budget for the biennium 1990-1991 sufficient resources for the Crime Prevention and Criminal Justice Branch to enable it to implement fully its programme activities;

8. *Also requests* the Secretary-General and the organizations concerned to take appropriate measures for the full implementation of the conclusions and recommendations adopted as a result of the programme review, as contained in Council resolutions 1986/11, 1987/53 and 1988/44 and General Assembly resolution 42/59;

9. *Calls upon* Member States to contribute more generously to the United Nations Trust Fund for Social Defence so as to enable the Crime Prevention and Criminal Justice Branch and the regional and interregional institutes to intensify technical co-operation activities and organize training courses and regional seminars on more effective crime prevention and criminal justice policies and strategies in the context of development;

10. *Takes note* of the efforts made towards the establishment of a global crime prevention and criminal justice information network and requests the Secretary-General to secure adequate resources for its full realization, including:

(a) Designing the specifications for the system;

(b) Recruiting a specialist to implement it, ensuring access to all potential users and taking advantage of existing information networks;

11. *Urges* Governments in the process of improving the management of criminal justice to consider the use of suitable information technology, including electronic data processing, and requests the Secretary-General, within existing resources, to develop guidelines and training materials on the use of information technology in the management of criminal justice for interested Member States, and to seek additional extrabudgetary resources to expand that work;

12. *Requests* the Secretary-General to continue his efforts to improve the efficiency of the implementation of the United Nations crime prevention and criminal justice programme;

13. *Also requests* the Secretary-General to continue making the necessary provisions for the optimal functioning of the Committee on Crime Prevention and Control, pursuant to Council resolutions 1986/11 and 1987/53;

14. *Determines* that, in view of the crucial role of the Committee on Crime Prevention and Control as the preparatory body for the Eighth United Nations Congress on the Prevention of Crime and the Treatment of Offenders and in view of the various draft instruments and widely ranging recommendations stemming from the preparatory meetings, the eleventh session of the Committee, to be held in 1990 before the Congress, should be extended by two days;

15. *Decides* to authorize the Chairman of the Committee on Crime Prevention and Control to convene, whenever necessary, inter-sessional working groups in co-operation with the Secretariat and to designate special rapporteurs, in pursuance of Council resolution 1986/11, to consider priority issues of concern to Member States and prepare recommendations thereon, subject to the availability of extrabudgetary resources;

16. *Requests* the Secretary-General, in co-operation with the regional and interregional institutes, the regional commissions and relevant agencies, to intensify the operational aspects of the United Nations programme in crime prevention and criminal justice, *inter alia*, through the formulation and implementation of technical assistance projects on specific crime prevention and criminal justice issues;

17. *Also requests* the Secretary-General to strengthen the professional capacity of the Crime Prevention and Criminal Justice Branch in order to support interregional advisory services and follow up the recommendations made at the country level;

18. *Urges* the Secretary-General to seek increased support for the critically needed interregional advisory services in the field of crime prevention and criminal justice, to expand such services and to provide additional interregional and regional advisers as soon as budgetary and extrabudgetary resources permit;

19. *Invites* the United Nations funding agencies, in particular the United Nations Development Programme and the Department of Technical Co-operation for Development of the Secretariat, to continue to provide financial support to the United Nations regional and interregional institutes for crime prevention and criminal justice so as to assist them in carrying out their technical co-operation programmes, and invites other United Nations entities, such as the World Bank, the United Nations Population Fund, the United Nations Fund for Drug Abuse Control and the United Nations Children's Fund, to support projects in this field relating to their areas of concern;

20. *Invites* the regional commissions to increase their involvement in activities related to crime prevention and

criminal justice by establishing closer collaborative ties with the regional institutes, and to designate focal points to co-ordinate technical co-operation activities undertaken at the regional and national levels, and requests the Secretary-General to provide the necessary resources;

21. *Expresses its appreciation* to the Arab Security Studies and Training Centre for organizing annual meetings on the co-ordination of activities of the regional and interregional institutes, which helped strengthen existing collaborative arrangements between the Secretariat and the institutes, and requests the Secretary-General to ensure appropriate follow-up of agreed programmes;

22. *Requests* the Secretary-General to ensure the full co-ordination of activities relating to crime prevention and criminal justice in the United Nations system, paying particular attention to the strengthening of collaboration with the United Nations drug control bodies and the Centre for Human Rights of the Secretariat;

23. *Urges* the Secretary-General to promote joint initiatives involving the Secretariat, intergovernmental and non-governmental organizations and the professional community, to support the full realization of the project on the establishment of an advisory council of scholars and scientific organizations, and to inform the Committee on Crime Prevention and Control of progress made in that regard;

24. *Requests* the Secretary-General to submit to the Council, at its first regular session of 1990, a progress report on the implementation of the present resolution, paying particular attention to Council resolution 1986/11, paragraph 4, Council resolution 1987/53, paragraphs 3 *(a)* and 4, and General Assembly resolution 42/59, paragraph 5.

Economic and Social Council resolution 1989/68

24 May 1989   Meeting 15   Adopted without vote

Approved by Second Committee (E/1989/91) without vote, 11 May (meeting 12); draft by Committee on Crime Prevention and Control (E/1988/20); agenda item 11.

On the same date, the Council, by **decision 1989/133**, took note of the report of the Committee on Crime Prevention and Control on its tenth (1988) session and approved the provisional agenda and documentation for its eleventh (1990) session.

Preparations for the Eighth (1990) Congress

During 1989, five regional preparatory meetings for the Eighth UN Congress on the Prevention of Crime and the Treatment of Offenders were convened, bringing together more than 600 participants from 129 Member States, as well as a large number of intergovernmental and non-governmental organizations, in Bangkok (10-14 April), Helsinki (24-28 April), San José, Costa Rica (8-12 May), Cairo (27-31 May) and Addis Ababa (5-9 June). Resolutions were adopted on the UN crime prevention and criminal justice programme, international co-operation and international instruments, among other subjects.

The International Commission of Jurists, under UN auspices, organized a conference (Caracas, 16-18 January) on the independence of judges and lawyers, adopting the Caracas Plan of Action in support of the UN programme aimed at strengthening the independence and impartiality of the judiciary and enhancing the role of lawyers. The seventh joint colloquium of the International Association of Penal Law, the International Society for Criminology, the International Society of Social Defence and the International Penal and Penitentiary Foundation (Bellagio, Italy, 4-7 May) submitted a statement[47] to the Economic and Social Council, calling on the United Nations to intensify relations with NGOs. An international seminar on corruption in government, organized by the Netherlands Ministry of Foreign Affairs and the UN Department of Technical Co-operation for Development, reviewed major causes and forms of corruption in government, exchanged experiences, and evaluated measures taken by Governments to combat corruption. It also considered a draft manual on practical measures against corruption, for submission to the Eighth Congress.

In March, the Secretary-General reported[44] that conference facilities, hotel accommodation and other facilities in Havana, Cuba, had been found satisfactory, and urged the Economic and Social Council to decide on the venue of the Congress urgently in view of time constraints and the need for advance planning.

ECONOMIC AND SOCIAL COUNCIL ACTION

On 24 May, on the recommendation of its Second Committee, the Economic and Social Council adopted **resolution 1989/69** without vote.

Continuation of preparations for the Eighth United Nations Congress on the Prevention of Crime and the Treatment of Offenders

The Economic and Social Council,

Recalling General Assembly resolutions 415(V) of 1 December 1950, 32/60 of 8 December 1977, 41/107 of 4 December 1986 and 42/59 of 30 November 1987,

Recalling its resolutions 1986/11 of 21 May 1986, 1987/49 and 1987/53 of 28 May 1987 and 1988/44 of 27 May 1988,

Recalling also its decision 1988/146 of 27 May 1988, by which it took note with appreciation of the offer of the Government of Cuba to act as host to the Eighth United Nations Congress on the Prevention of Crime and Treatment of Offenders,

Noting that many members of the Committee on Crime Prevention and Control, at its tenth session, expressed support for the invitation and gratitude to the Government of Cuba for its generous offer,

Bearing in mind that the General Assembly and the Council have reaffirmed in numerous resolutions the importance of the United Nations congresses on the prevention of crime and the treatment of offenders,

Acknowledging that the United Nations congresses, as global events, have influenced national policies and practices by facilitating the exchange of views and experiences, by mobilizing public opinion and by recommending policy options at the national, regional and international levels, thus making a significant contribution to the promotion of international and technical co-operation in this field,

Emphasizing the importance of undertaking all preparatory activities for the Eighth Congress in a timely and concerted manner,

Conscious of the need to increase the relevance and impact of the results of the Eighth Congress through heightened public awareness of those results,

Bearing in mind General Assembly resolution 42/59, in which the Secretary-General was requested to take immediate steps to ensure the successful and cost-effective preparation of the Eighth Congress, including the appropriate scheduling of interregional and regional preparatory meetings and the timely finalization and circulation of the required documentation through the provision of the necessary resources, including temporary assistance,

Aware that the resources so far allocated for the preparation of the Eighth Congress are considerably less than the funds usually provided for the consultants, temporary staff, travel and public information activities for major conferences,

Also aware of the important work to be accomplished by the regional preparatory meetings and by the Secretariat in preparing the relevant documentation,

Having considered the report of the Secretary-General relating to preparations for the Eighth Congress,

1. *Takes note with satisfaction* of the work so far accomplished by the United Nations Secretariat in the preparations for the Eighth United Nations Congress on the Prevention of Crime and the Treatment of Offenders, in pursuance of Council resolution 1987/49 and following the directives of the Committee on Crime Prevention and Control;

2. *Notes with appreciation* the interest shown and the support given to the Secretariat in the preparations for the Eighth Congress by many Governments and non-governmental organizations and the professional and scientific community;

3. *Takes note* of the Discussion guide for the interregional and regional preparatory meetings for the Eighth United Nations Congress on the Prevention of Crime and the Treatment of Offenders which provides general guidelines for the discussion at interregional meetings of the substantive topics of the Congress, and of the reports of the interregional preparatory meetings;

4. *Take note also* of the various documents prepared by the Secretariat on the substantive items considered by the Seventh United Nations Congress on the Prevention of Crime and the Treatment of Offenders, and requests the Secretary-General to update them for submission to the Eighth Congress under the relevant agenda items;

5. *Endorses* the recommendations contained in the reports of the interregional preparatory meetings for the Eighth Congress and requests the Secretary-General to transmit those reports to the regional preparatory meetings, to be organized in 1989, with the observations, amendments and specific comments made on the occasion of the tenth session of the Committee on Crime Prevention and Control, as contained in annex IV to the report of the Committee on its tenth session;

6. *Recommends* that the regional preparatory meetings consider in depth the recommendations of the in-

terregional preparatory meetings and make specific comments on the draft instruments contained in the reports;

7. *Approves* the documentation for the Eighth Congress as contained in annex III to the report of the Committee on its tenth session, pending further review by the Committee at its eleventh session;

8. *Decides* that item 3 of the provisional agenda for the Eighth Congress should serve as an umbrella topic, under which Governments and intergovernmental and non-governmental organizations could exchange experiences and examine problems encountered and successes achieved in international co-operation in the field of crime prevention and criminal justice;

9. *Recommends* that a research workshop on alternatives to imprisonment, consisting of at least two sessions with full conference support services, be held within the framework of item 4 of the provisional agenda for the Eighth Congress and that the report adopted be submitted to the committee dealing with that item;

10. *Also recommends* that work should continue on the development of guidelines for the computerization of the administration of criminal justice and that a workshop for the discussion of national experiences be held within the framework of item 4 of the provisional agenda for the Eighth Congress, the report of which should be submitted to the committee dealing with that item;

11. *Further recommends* that the Eighth Congress finalize the United Nations draft Standard Minimum Rules for Non-custodial Measures (the Tokyo Rules), the draft Bilateral Model Treaty on Mutual Assistance in Criminal Matters, the United Nations draft Guidelines for the Prevention of Juvenile Delinquency (the Guidelines of Riyadh), the United Nations draft Rules for the Protection of Juveniles Deprived of their Liberty, the draft Basic Principles on the Use of Force and Firearms by Law Enforcement Officials, the draft Basic Principles on the Role of Lawyers, the draft Model Agreement on Transfer of Proceedings in Criminal Matters and the draft Model Agreement on Transfer of Supervision of Foreign Offenders Who Have Been Conditionally Sentenced or Conditionally Released, and make every effort to secure their adoption for the strengthening of regional and international co-operation in the fight against crime;

12. *Decides* that the Eighth Congress should be held from 27 August to 7 September 1990, with the necessary pre-Congress consultations;

13. *Also decides* that the theme for the Eighth Congress should be "International co-operation in crime prevention and criminal justice for the twenty-first century";

14. *Approves* the rules of procedure for the United Nations congresses on the prevention of crime and the treatment of offenders adopted by the Seventh Congress, on the understanding that the Eighth Congress should make every effort to reach a consensus on all substantive matters;

15. *Requests* the Secretary-General, in his preparation of the proposed programme budget for the biennium 1990-1991, to allocate the necessary resources for the organization of the Eighth Congress, in accordance with past practice and the existing guidelines for the organization of major United Nations conferences;

16. *Also requests* the Secretary-General to continue the practice of inviting twenty-five consultants to participate in the congresses at the expense of the Organiza-

tion so as to ensure that adequate expertise is provided to the Eighth Congress by each region for each substantive item of the provisional agenda;

17. *Calls on* Governments to make preparations for the Eighth Congress by all appropriate means, with a view to formulating national position papers;

18. *Urges* the regional commissions, regional and interregional institutes in the field of crime prevention and the treatment of offenders, specialized agencies and other entities within the United Nations system, other intergovernmental organizations concerned, and non-governmental organizations in consultative status with the Council to become actively involved in the preparations for the Eighth Congress;

19. *Invites* representatives of the Committee on Crime Prevention and Control attending the regional preparatory meetings for the Eighth Congress to assist Government representatives in their substantive deliberations on the topics to be considered by the Congress and provide adequate follow-up of the recommendations made by the interregional preparatory meetings;

20. *Also invites* the Committee, at its eleventh session, to accord priority attention to the preparations for the Eighth Congress and to ensure that all necessary organizational and substantive arrangements are made in good time;

21. *Requests* the Secretary-General, in his report to the General Assembly, to stress the urgency of providing the necessary additional resources, including temporary assistance and travel for the Secretary-General of the Eighth Congress and additional staff members of the Secretariat, to service the regional preparatory meetings in 1989 and to engage in relevant consultations with Member States so as to enable the Secretariat to undertake, in an effective and timely manner, all the preparatory activities for the Congress;

22. *Also requests* the Secretary-General to strengthen the information programme related to the Eighth Congress in order to create awareness among experts and the general public of the significance of the work of the United Nations in the field of crime prevention and criminal justice.

Economic and Social Council resolution 1989/69

24 May 1989   Meeting 15   Adopted without vote

Approved by Second Committee (E/1989/91) without vote, 11 May (meeting 12); draft by Committee on Crime Prevention and Control (E/1988/20); agenda item 11.

Also on 24 May and on the recommendation of its Second Committee, the Council adopted **decision 1989/134** by recorded vote.

Eighth United Nations Congress on the Prevention of Crime and the Treatment of Offenders

At its 15th plenary meeting, on 24 May 1989, the Economic and Social Council, recalling its decision 1988/146 of 27 May 1988, in which it took note with appreciation of the offer of the Government of Cuba to act as host, in accordance with General Assembly resolution 40/243 of 18 December 1985, to the Eighth United Nations Congress on the Prevention of Crime and the Treatment of Offenders at Havana in 1990, and taking note of the report of the Secretary-General on crime prevention and criminal justice, which indicated that a first planning mission visited Havana and concluded

that the conference facilities were satisfactory, and that, in view of time constraints and the need to make preparations, a decision by the Council on the venue of the Congress was urgently required, accepted with gratitude the kind offer of the Government of Cuba to act as host to the Eighth Congress.

Economic and Social Council decision 1989/134

24 May 1989   Meeting 15   51-1 (recorded vote)

Approved by Second Committee (E/1989/91) by recorded vote (43-2), 12 May (meeting 14); 15-nation draft (E/1989/C.2/L.7); agenda item 11.

Recorded vote in Council as follows:

In favour: Bahamas, Belize, Bolivia, Brazil, Bulgaria, Cameroon, Canada, China, Colombia, Cuba, Czechoslovakia, Denmark, France, Germany, Federal Republic of, Ghana, Greece, Guinea, Indonesia, Iran, Iraq, Ireland, Italy, Japan, Jordan, Kenya, Lesotho, Liberia, Libyan Arab Jamahiriya, Netherlands, New Zealand, Nicaragua, Niger, Norway, Oman, Poland, Portugal, Rwanda, Somalia, Sri Lanka, Sudan, Thailand, Trinidad and Tobago, Tunisia, Ukrainian SSR, USSR, United Kingdom, Uruguay, Venezuela, Yugoslavia, Zaire, Zambia.

Against: United States.

Concerted action against crime

On 24 May 1989, the Economic and Social Council, on the recommendation of the Second Committee, adopted **resolution 1989/62** without vote.

Concerted international action against the forms of crime identified in the Milan Plan of Action

The Economic and Social Council,

Recalling the Milan Plan of Action, unanimously adopted by the Seventh United Nations Congress on the Prevention of Crime and the Treatment of Offenders, and resolutions 1 on organized crime, 2 on the struggle against illicit drug trafficking, 22 on crime prevention in the context of development, and 23 on criminal acts of a terrorist character, also unanimously adopted by the Seventh Congress,

Recalling also its resolution 1986/10, section I, of 21 May 1986, in which the Secretary-General was urged to accord priority to the development of specific proposals for concerted international action against the forms of crime identified in the Milan Plan of Action,

Recalling further General Assembly resolutions 41/107 of 4 December 1986 and 42/59 of 30 November 1987, in which the Assembly called for priority attention to be accorded to the forms of crime identified in the Milan Plan of Action,

Alarmed by the marked increase in the transnational dimensions of grave forms of crime and by the comparative impunity enjoyed by the perpetrators of such forms of crime,

Noting with dismay the shortcomings of existing international co-operation arrangements and instruments for the prevention of transnational forms of crime,

Gravely concerned at the growing tendency of some Governments and transnational corporations to facilitate the dumping of toxic nuclear and industrial waste in developing countries,

Deeply preoccupied with the devastating damage to the environment which is the direct outcome of harmful and illicit practices, such as the dumping of toxic waste, the thoughtless depletion of non-renewable resources, the extermination of animal species, the massive use of herbicides and defoliants and the release into the atmosphere of harmful gases and radioactive substances,

Concerned about the sustained pillage of archaeological sites and the illicit international trade in objects belonging to the cultural heritage of nations, and the ensuing damage to the national identity of peoples,

Aware of the necessity of revising existing international instruments so as to make them more responsive to the new realities of transnational forms of crime,

Conscious of the indispensability of international co-operation and concerted action for the effective control of transnational forms of crime,

1. *Takes note with appreciation* of the report of the Secretary-General on proposals for concerted international action against the forms of crime identified in the Milan Plan of Action;

2. *Invites* Governments, international organizations, concerned non-governmental organizations in consultative status with the Economic and Social Council and other decision-making bodies to examine favourably the recommendations contained in that report, with a view to implementing them, taking into account the social, political and economic characteristics of each country;

3. *Urges* Governments to examine existing domestic legislation with a view to enacting provisions, including penal provisions, to protect the natural environment, in cases where such legislation is non-existent or insufficiently developed, and to establish adequate compensation for the victims of such practices;

4. *Reiterates* the need for the international community to make a concerted effort to prevent, combat and monitor all actions leading to the dumping of toxic nuclear and industrial waste in developing countries, in close co-operation with the United Nations Environment Programme and the International Atomic Energy Agency;

5. *Invites* Governments to exercise stricter and more effective control over the industrial sector or other sectors that could be involved in such conduct;

6. *Decides* that the topics of transnational crimes against the environment and against the cultural patrimony of countries should be considered under item 3 of the provisional agenda for the Eighth United Nations Congress on the Prevention of Crime and the Treatment of Offenders, in order to explore the possibilities of formulating comprehensive policies of international co-operation for the prevention of such offences, including the imposition of sanctions;

7. *Requests* the Secretary-General, in the light of the present resolution, to expand his report on proposals for concerted international action against the forms of crime identified in the Milan Plan of Action, for submission to the Eighth Congress.

Economic and Social Council resolution 1989/62

24 May 1989   Meeting 15   Adopted without vote

Approved by Second Committee (E/1989/91) without vote, 11 May (meeting 12); draft by Committee on Crime Prevention and Control (E/1988/20); agenda item 11.

Organized crime

On 24 May, the Economic and Social Council, on the recommendation of its Second Committee, adopted **resolution 1989/70** without vote.

International co-operation in combating organized crime
The Economic and Social Council,

Recalling the responsibility assumed by the United Nations in the field of crime prevention and criminal justice,

Concerned that organized crime has increased in many parts of the world and has become more transnational in character, leading, in particular, to the spread of such negative phenomena as violence, terrorism, corruption, illegal trade in narcotic drugs and, in general, undermining the development process, impairing the quality of life and threatening human rights and fundamental freedoms,

Taking into account the decisions of the Seventh United Nations Congress on the Prevention of Crime and the Treatment of Offenders relating to organized crime, as well as views expressed on the matter by members of the Committee on Crime Prevention and Control,

Convinced of the need to strengthen international co-operation in combating organized crime,

Recognizing the pivotal role of the Committee in providing guidance and the co-ordinating role to be played by the Centre for Social Development and Humanitarian Affairs of the Secretariat, especially by the Crime Prevention and Criminal Justice Branch, in strengthening international co-operation in crime prevention and criminal justice,

1. *Invites* the Committee on Crime Prevention and Control to give special attention in its work to promoting international co-operation in combating organized crime;

2. *Calls upon* Governments, international organizations and interested non-governmental organizations to co-operate to that end with the Committee and to submit to the Committee, through the Secretary-General, their proposals on strengthening international co-operation in combating organized crime;

3. *Requests* the Committee to consider ways of strengthening international co-operation in combating organized crime, taking due account of the opinions of Governments, international organizations and non-governmental organizations, and to submit its views to the Council at its first regular session of 1992.

Economic and Social Council resolution 1989/70

24 May 1989   Meeting 15   Adopted without vote

Approved by Second Committee (E/1989/91) without vote, 12 May (meeting 14); 12-nation draft; agenda item 11.

Sponsors: Belgium, Bulgaria, Canada, Colombia, France, German Democratic Republic, Germany, Federal Republic of, Italy, Poland, USSR, United Kingdom, United States.

GENERAL ASSEMBLY ACTION

On 8 December, the General Assembly, on the recommendation of the Third Committee, adopted **resolution 44/71** without vote.

International co-operation in combating organized crime
The General Assembly,

Recalling the responsibility assumed by the United Nations in the field of crime prevention and criminal justice,

Concerned that organized crime has increased in many parts of the world and has become more transnational in character, leading, in particular, to the spread of such negative phenomena as violence, terrorism, corruption and illegal trade in narcotic drugs and, in general, undermining the development process, impairing the quality of life and threatening human rights and fundamental freedoms,

Taking into account the decisions of the Seventh United Nations Congress on the Prevention of Crime and the Treatment of Offenders relating to organized crime, as well as the views expressed on the matter by members of the Committee on Crime Prevention and Control,

Taking note of Economic and Social Council resolution 1989/70 of 24 May 1989,

Convinced of the need to strengthen international co-operation in combating organized crime,

Convinced also that the Eighth United Nations Congress on the Prevention of Crime and the Treatment of Offenders will, *inter alia,* explore the possibilities and ways of strengthening further international co-operation in combating organized crime,

Recognizing the pivotal role of the Committee on Crime Prevention and Control in providing guidance and the co-ordinating role to be played by the Centre for Social Development and Humanitarian Affairs of the Secretariat, especially by the Crime Prevention and Criminal Justice Branch, in strengthening international co-operation in crime prevention and criminal justice,

1. *Invites* the Economic and Social Council to request the Committee on Crime Prevention and Control, at its eleventh session, to give special attention in its work to promoting international co-operation in combating organized crime;

2. *Calls upon* Governments, international organizations and interested non-governmental organizations to co-operate to that end with the Committee and to submit to the Committee, through the Secretary-General, their proposals on strengthening international co-operation in combating organized crime;

3. *Requests* the Committee to consider ways of strengthening international co-operation in combating organized crime, taking due account of the opinions of Governments, international organizations and non-governmental organizations, as well as opinions expressed at and decisions taken by the Eighth United Nations Congress on the Prevention of Crime and the Treatment of Offenders, and to submit its views, through the Economic and Social Council, to the General Assembly at its forty-seventh session.

General Assembly resolution 44/71

8 December 1989   Meeting 78   Adopted without vote

Approved by Third Committee (A/44/756) without vote, 9 November (meeting 37); 26-nation draft (A/C.3/44/L.19), orally revised; agenda item 102.
Sponsors: Australia, Austria, Belgium, Bulgaria, Canada, Colombia, Costa Rica, Czechoslovakia, Denmark, El Salvador, France, German Democratic Republic, Germany, Federal Republic of, Greece, Hungary, Italy, Morocco, Netherlands, Norway, Poland, Trinidad and Tobago, Turkey, USSR, United Kingdom, United States, Yugoslavia.
Meeting numbers. GA 44th session: 3rd Committee 12-20, 30, 37; plenary 78.

Domestic violence

ECONOMIC AND SOCIAL COUNCIL ACTION

On 24 May, the Economic and Social Council, on the recommendation of the Third Committee, adopted **resolution 1989/67** without vote.

Domestic violence

The Economic and Social Council,

Recalling General Assembly resolution 40/36 of 29 November 1985,

Recalling also its resolution 1986/10, section IV, of 21 May 1986,

Bearing in mind the significance for victims of domestic violence of the Declaration of Basic Principles of Justice for Victims of Crime and Abuse of Power,

Aware of the need for measures to be taken on behalf of victims of crime and abuse of power,

Taking into account its resolution 1988/27 of 26 May 1988 on efforts to eradicate violence against women within the family and society, in which, *inter alia,* it requested the Secretary-General to bring to the attention of the Committee on Crime Prevention and Control at its tenth session the relevant recommendations of the Expert Group Meeting on Violence in the Family with Special Emphasis on its Effects on Women, held at Vienna from 8 to 12 December 1986, in order for the Committee to review them and provide guidance on their implementation, and to submit appropriate documentation thereon to the Eighth United Nations Congress on the Prevention of Crime and the Treatment of Offenders,

Concerned about the fact that domestic violence against spouses, children and the elderly cuts across all cultures and socio-economic classes,

Mindful of the need for different legal and social systems, at all levels, to provide a more effective and concerted response to domestic violence and to ensure the fair treatment of victims by justice and social assistance systems,

Bearing in mind that the question of domestic violence should be considered under item 6 of the provisional agenda for the Eighth Congress, entitled "Prevention of delinquency, juvenile justice and the protection of the young: policy approaches and directions",

1. *Takes note with satisfaction* of the note by the Secretary-General on progress achieved with respect to the implementation of General Assembly resolution 40/36 on domestic violence;

2. *Takes note* of the recommendations of the Expert Group Meeting on Violence in the Family with Special Emphasis on its Effects on Women;

3. *Requests* the Secretary-General to continue to pursue actively the implementation of General Assembly resolution 40/36;

4. *Also requests* the Secretary-General to undertake further comparative research, studies and reports on developments in the phenomenon of domestic violence against spouses, children and the elderly, from the perspective of criminal justice, criminal law and procedure, taking into account the recommendations of the Expert Group Meeting, especially the role of crisis intervention and protection and of social and other service delivery systems;

5. *Further requests* the Secretary-General to prepare a report on domestic violence for consideration under item 6 of the provisional agenda for the Eighth United Nations Congress on the Prevention of Crime and the Treatment of Offenders.

Economic and Social Council resolution 1989/67

24 May 1989   Meeting 15   Adopted without vote

Approved by Second Committee (E/1989/91) without vote, 11 May (meeting 12); draft by Committee on Crime Prevention and Control (E/1988/20); agenda item 11.

Rights of those facing death penalty

On 24 May, on the recommendation of its Second Committee, the Economic and Social Council adopted **resolution 1989/64** without vote.

Implementation of the safeguards guaranteeing protection of the rights of those facing the death penalty

The Economic and Social Council,

Recalling its resolution 1984/50 of 25 May 1984, in which it approved the safeguards guaranteeing protection of the rights of those facing the death penalty,

Recalling also resolution 15 of the Seventh United Nations Congress on the Prevention of Crime and the Treatment of Offenders,

Recalling further section X of its resolution 1986/10 of 21 May 1986, in which it requested a study on the question of the death penalty and new contributions of the criminal sciences to the matter,

Taking note of the report of the Secretary-General on the implementation of the United Nations safeguards guaranteeing protection of the rights of those facing the death penalty,

Noting with satisfaction that a large number of Member States have provided the Secretary-General with information on the implementation of the safeguards and have made contributions,

Noting with appreciation the study on the question of the death penalty and the new contributions of the criminal sciences to the matter,

Alarmed at the continued occurrence of practices incompatible with the safeguards guaranteeing protection of the rights of those facing the death penalty,

Aware that effective implementation of those safeguards requires a review of relevant national legislation and the improved dissemination of the text to all persons and entities concerned with them, as specified in resolution 15 of the Seventh Congress,

Convinced that further progress should be achieved towards more effective implementation of the safeguards at the national level on the understanding that they shall not be invoked to delay or to prevent the abolition of capital punishment,

Acknowledging the need for comprehensive and accurate information and additional research about the implementation of the safeguards and the death penalty in general in every region of the world,

1. *Recommends* that Member States take steps to implement the safeguards and strengthen further the protection of the rights of those facing the death penalty, where applicable, by:

(*a*) Affording special protection to persons facing charges for which the death penalty is provided by allowing time and facilities for the preparation of their defence, including the adequate assistance of counsel at every stage of the proceedings, above and beyond the protection afforded in non-capital cases;

(*b*) Providing for mandatory appeals or review with provisions for clemency or pardon in all cases of capital offence;

(*c*) Establishing a maximum age beyond which a person may not be sentenced to death or executed;

(*d*) Eliminating the death penalty for persons suffering from mental retardation or extremely limited mental competence, whether at the stage of sentence or execution;

2. *Invites* Member States to co-operate with specialized bodies, non-governmental organizations, academic institutions and specialists in the field in efforts to conduct research on the use of the death penalty in every region of the world;

3. *Also invites* Member States to facilitate the efforts of the Secretary-General to gather comprehensive, timely and accurate information about the implementation of the safeguards and the death penalty in general;

4. *Further invites* Member States that have not yet done so to review the extent to which their legislation provides for the safeguards guaranteeing protection of the rights of those facing the death penalty as set out in the annex to Council resolution 1984/50;

5. *Urges* Member States to publish, for each category of offence for which the death penalty is authorized, and if possible on an annual basis, information on the use of the death penalty, including the number of persons sentenced to death, the number of executions actually carried out, the number of persons under sentence of death, the number of death sentences reversed or commuted on appeal and the number of instances in which clemency has been granted, and to include information on the extent to which the safeguards referred to above are incorporated in national law;

6. *Recommends* that the report of the Secretary-General on the question of capital punishment, to be submitted to the Council in 1990, in pursuance of its resolution 1745(LIV) of 16 May 1973, should henceforth cover the implementation of the safeguards as well as the use of capital punishment;

7. *Requests* the Secretary-General to publish the study on the question of the death penalty and the new contributions of the criminal sciences to the matter, prepared pursuant to Council resolution 1986/10, section X, and to make it available, with other relevant documentation, to the Eighth United Nations Congress on the Prevention of Crime and the Treatment of Offenders.

Economic and Social Council resolution 1989/64

24 May 1989   Meeting 15   Adopted without vote

Approved by Second Committee (E/1989/91) without vote, 11 May (meeting 12); draft by Committee on Crime Prevention and Control (E/1988/20); agenda item 11.

Juvenile justice

ECONOMIC AND SOCIAL COUNCIL ACTION

On 24 May, the Economic and Social Council, on the recommendation of its Second Committee, adopted **resolution 1989/66** without vote.

United Nations Standard Minimum Rules for the Administration of Juvenile Justice (The Beijing Rules)

The Economic and Social Council,

Recalling General Assembly resolution 40/33 of 29 November 1985, to which is annexed the United Nations Standard Minimum Rules for the Administration of Juvenile Justice (The Beijing Rules),

Recalling also section II of its resolution 1986/10 of 21 May 1986, entitled "Juvenile justice and the prevention of juvenile delinquency",

Aware of the exemplary role of the Beijing Rules in promoting the development, improvement and reform of juvenile justice systems world wide,

Emphasizing the need to promote continued progress and reform in the administration of juvenile justice and to ensure universal and effective recognition of, and respect for, the legitimate rights and interests of juveniles in conflict with the law,

1. *Expresses its satisfaction* with the report of the Secretary-General concerning the implementation of General Assembly resolution 40/33 and other resolutions on juvenile justice;

2. *Expresses its appreciation* of the efforts of Member States, specialized agencies, United Nations regional commissions and institutes, intergovernmental and non-governmental organizations, experts, policy makers and practitioners, as well as the Secretariat, to promote the principles of the Beijing Rules;

3. *Calls upon* Member States that have not yet done so to apply the Beijing Rules and to submit information thereon to the Secretary-General;

4. *Invites* Member States to exchange views and information on their experiences and progress in implementing the Beijing Rules and to undertake multifaceted co-operation;

5. *Urges* Member States to provide funds for model projects which promote the principles of the Beijing Rules at the national, regional and interregional levels;

6. *Requests* the Secretary-General:

   (*a*) To continue to promote concerted regional and international action and co-operation in connection with the Beijing Rules;

   (*b*) To continue to disseminate the Beijing Rules widely in all official languages of the United Nations and to assist those countries that have not yet done so in translating the text of the Rules into their national languages and in disseminating them for the benefit of those working in the field of juvenile justice;

   (*c*) To promote the letter and spirit of the Beijing Rules wherever possible, especially in all United Nations programmes relating to young persons;

   (*d*) To ensure effective programme interlinkages within the United Nations system between juvenile justice, within the framework of the Beijing Rules, and situations of "social risk", especially youthful drug abuse, child abuse, child sale and trafficking, child prostitution and street children;

   (*e*) To conduct collaborative research on various aspects of the administration of juvenile justice, with emphasis on innovative and effective programming, and to develop training programmes, material and curricula for juvenile justice personnel;

   (*f*) To provide the necessary technical assistance to Member States, particularly the developing countries, in implementing the Beijing Rules, developing projects and evaluating achievements;

   (*g*) To allocate the necessary funds for activities relating to the Beijing Rules, especially pilot projects;

7. *Invites* the International Labour Organisation, the World Health Organization, the United Nations Educational, Scientific and Cultural Organization, the United Nations Children's Fund and the Office of the United Nations High Commissioner for Refugees to promote and apply the principles of the Beijing Rules in all activities and programmes of relevance to young persons;

8. *Calls upon* the Department of Technical Co-operation for Development of the Secretariat and the United Nations Development Programme to support projects of technical assistance, to co-operate in promoting activities in the field of juvenile justice, and to invite other funding agencies within and outside the United Nations system to provide financial support for programmes relating to the administration of juvenile justice;

9. *Requests* the United Nations regional commissions and institutes for the prevention of crime and the treatment of offenders to intensify efforts to promote the Beijing Rules, both in their work programmes and their project and advisory activities;

10. *Decides* that the Eighth United Nations Congress on the Prevention of Crime and the Treatment of Offenders should consider the progress achieved in the implementation of the Beijing Rules, and that the Secretary-General should submit an updated report thereon for consideration under item 6 of the provisional agenda for the Congress.

Economic and Social Council resolution 1989/66

24 May 1989   Meeting 15   Adopted without vote

Approved by Second Committee (E/1989/91) without vote, 11 May (meeting 12); draft by Committee on Crime Prevention and Control (E/1988/20); agenda item 11.
Financial implications. E/1989/C.2/L.13.

Arbitrary and summary executions

On 24 May, on the recommendation of its Second Committee, the Economic and Social Council adopted **resolution 1989/65** without vote.

Effective prevention and investigation of extra-legal, arbitrary and summary executions

The Economic and Social Council,

Recalling that article 3 of the Universal Declaration of Human Rights proclaims that everyone has the right to life, liberty and security of person,

Bearing in mind that paragraph 1 of article 6 of the International Covenant on Civil and Political Rights states that every human being has an inherent right to life, that that right shall be protected by law and that no one shall be arbitrarily deprived of his or her life,

Also bearing in mind the general comments of the Human Rights Committee on the right to life as enunciated in article 6 of the International Covenant on Civil and Political Rights,

Stressing that the extra-legal, arbitrary and summary executions contravene the human rights and fundamental freedoms proclaimed in the Universal Declaration of Human Rights,

Mindful that the Seventh United Nations Congress on the Prevention of Crime and the Treatment of Offenders, in resolution 11 on extra-legal, arbitrary and summary executions, called upon all Governments to take urgent and incisive action to investigate such acts, wherever they may occur, to punish those found guilty and to take all other measures necessary to prevent those practices,

Mindful also that in its resolution 1986/10, section VI, of 21 May 1986, it requested the Committee on Crime Prevention and Control to consider at its tenth session the question of extra-legal, arbitrary and summary executions with a view to elaborating principles on the effective prevention and investigation of such practices,

Recalling that the General Assembly in its resolution 33/173 of 20 December 1978 expressed its deep concern about reports from various parts of the world relating to enforced or involuntary disappearances and called upon Governments, in the event of such reports, to take appropriate measures to search for such persons and to undertake speedy and impartial investigations,

Noting with appreciation the efforts of non-governmental organizations to develop standards for investigations,

Emphasizing that the General Assembly, in its resolution 42/141 of 7 December 1987, strongly condemned once again the large number of summary or arbitrary executions, including extra-legal executions, that continued to take place in various parts of the world,

Noting that in the same resolution the General Assembly recognized the need for closer co-operation between the Centre for Human Rights and the Crime Prevention and Criminal Justice Branch of the Centre for Social Development and Humanitarian Affairs of the Secretariat and the Committee on Crime Prevention and Control in efforts to bring to an end summary or arbitrary executions,

Aware that effective prevention and investigation of extra-legal, arbitrary and summary executions requires the provision of adequate financial and technical resources,

1. *Recommends* that the Principles on the Effective Prevention and Investigation of Extra-legal, Arbitrary and Summary Executions annexed to the present resolution should be taken into account and respected by Governments within the framework of their national legislation and practices, and should be brought to the attention of law enforcement and criminal justice officials, military personnel, lawyers, members of the executive and legislative bodies of the Governments and the public in general;

2. *Requests* the Committee on Crime Prevention and Control to keep the above recommendations under constant review, taking into account the various socio-economic, political and cultural circumstances in which extra-legal, arbitrary and summary executions occur;

3. *Invites* Member States that have not yet ratified or acceded to international instruments that prohibit extra-legal, arbitrary and summary executions, including the International Covenant on Civil and Political Rights, the Optional Protocol to the International Covenant on Civil and Political Rights and the Convention against Torture and Other Cruel, Inhuman or Degrading Treatment or Punishment, to become parties to these instruments;

4. *Requests* the Secretary-General to include the Principles in the United Nations publication entitled *Human Rights: A Compilation of International Instruments;*

5. *Requests* the United Nations regional and interregional institutes for the prevention of crime and the treatment of offenders to give special attention in their research and training programmes to the Principles, and to the International Covenant on Civil and Political Rights, the provisions of the Convention against Torture and Other Cruel, Inhuman or Degrading

Treatment or Punishment, the Code of Conduct for Law Enforcement Officials, the Declaration of Basic Principles of Justice for Victims of Crime and Abuse of Power and other international instruments relevant to the question of extra-legal, arbitrary and summary executions.

ANNEX
Principles on the Effective Prevention and Investigation of Extra-legal, Arbitrary and Summary Executions

Prevention

1. Governments shall prohibit by law all extra-legal, arbitrary and summary executions and shall ensure that any such executions are recognized as offences under their criminal laws, and are punishable by appropriate penalties which take into account the seriousness of such offences. Exceptional circumstances including a state of war or threat of war, internal political instability or any other public emergency may not be invoked as a justification of such executions. Such executions shall not be carried out under any circumstances including, but not limited to, situations of internal armed conflict, excessive or illegal use of force by a public official or other person acting in an official capacity or by a person acting at the instigation, or with the consent or acquiescence of such person, and situations in which deaths occur in custody. This prohibition shall prevail over decrees issued by governmental authority.

2. In order to prevent extra-legal, arbitrary and summary executions, Governments shall ensure strict control, including a clear chain of command over all officials responsible for apprehension, arrest, detention, custody and imprisonment, as well as those officials authorized by law to use force and firearms.

3. Governments shall prohibit orders from superior officers or public authorities authorizing or inciting other persons to carry out any such extra-legal, arbitrary or summary executions. All persons shall have the right and the duty to defy such orders. Training of law enforcement officials shall emphasize the above provisions.

4. Effective protection through judicial or other means shall be guaranteed to individuals and groups who are in danger of extra-legal, arbitrary or summary executions, including those who receive death threats.

5. No one shall be involuntarily returned or extradited to a country where there are substantial grounds for believing that he or she may become a victim of extra-legal, arbitrary or summary execution in that country.

6. Governments shall ensure that persons deprived of their liberty are held in officially recognized places of custody, and that accurate information on their custody and whereabouts, including transfers, is made promptly available to their relatives and lawyer or other persons of confidence.

7. Qualified inspectors, including medical personnel, or an equivalent independent authority, shall conduct inspections in places of custody on a regular basis, and be empowered to undertake unannounced inspections on their own initiative, with full guarantees of independence in the exercise of this function. The inspectors shall have unrestricted access to all

persons in such places of custody, as well as to all their records.

8. Governments shall make every effort to prevent extra-legal, arbitrary and summary executions through measures such as diplomatic intercession, improved access of complainants to intergovernmental and judicial bodies, and public denunciation. Intergovernmental mechanisms shall be used to investigate reports of any such executions and to take effective action against such practices. Governments, including those of countries where extra-legal, arbitrary and summary executions are reasonably suspected to occur, shall co-operate fully in international investigations on the subject.

Investigation

9. There shall be a thorough, prompt and impartial investigation of all suspected cases of extra-legal, arbitrary and summary executions, including cases where complaints by relatives or other reliable reports suggest unnatural death in the above circumstances. Governments shall maintain investigative offices and procedures to undertake such inquiries. The purpose of the investigation shall be to determine the cause, manner and time of death, the person responsible, and any pattern or practice which may have brought about that death. It shall include an adequate autopsy, collection and analysis of all physical and documentary evidence, and statements from witnesses. The investigation shall distinguish between natural death, accidental death, suicide and homicide.

10. The investigative authority shall have the power to obtain all the information necessary to the inquiry. Those persons conducting the investigation shall have at their disposal all the necessary budgetary and technical resources for effective investigation. They shall also have the authority to oblige officials allegedly involved in any such executions to appear and testify. The same shall apply to any witness. To this end, they shall be entitled to issue summonses to witnesses, including the officials allegedly involved, and to demand the production of evidence.

11. In cases in which the established investigative procedures are inadequate because of lack of expertise or impartiality, because of the importance of the matter or because of the apparent existence of a pattern of abuse, and in cases where there are complaints from the family of the victim about these inadequacies or other substantial reasons, Governments shall pursue investigations through an independent commission of inquiry or similar procedure. Members of such a commission shall be chosen for their recognized impartiality, competence and independence as individuals. In particular, they shall be independent of any institution, agency or person that may be the subject of the inquiry. The commission shall have the authority to obtain all information necessary to the inquiry and shall conduct the inquiry as provided for under these Principles.

12. The body of the deceased person shall not be disposed of until an adequate autopsy is conducted by a physician, who shall, if possible, be an expert in forensic pathology. Those conducting the autopsy shall have the right of access to all investigative data, to the place where the body was discovered, and to the place where the death is thought to have occurred. If the body has been buried and it later appears that an investigation is required, the body shall be promptly and competently exhumed for an autopsy. If skeletal remains are discovered, they should be carefully exhumed and studied according to systematic anthropological techniques.

13. The body of the deceased shall be available to those conducting the autopsy for a sufficient amount of time to enable a thorough investigation to be carried out. The autopsy shall, at a minimum, attempt to establish the identity of the deceased and the cause and manner of death. The time and place of death shall also be determined to the extent possible. Detailed colour photographs of the deceased shall be included in the autopsy report in order to document and support the findings of the investigation. The autopsy report must describe any and all injuries to the deceased including any evidence of torture.

14. In order to ensure objective results, those conducting the autopsy must be able to function impartially and independently of any potentially implicated persons or organizations or entities.

15. Complainants, witnesses, those conducting the investigation and their families shall be protected from violence, threats of violence or any other form of intimidation. Those potentially implicated in extra-legal, arbitrary or summary executions shall be removed from any position of control or power, whether direct or indirect, over complainants, witnesses and their families, as well as over those conducting investigations.

16. Families of the deceased and their legal representatives shall be informed of, and have access to, any hearing as well as to all information relevant to the investigation, and shall be entitled to present other evidence. The family of the deceased shall have the right to insist that a medical or other qualified representative be present at the autopsy. When the identity of a deceased person has been determined, a notification of death shall be posted, and the family or relatives of the deceased immediately informed. The body of the deceased shall be returned to them upon completion of the investigation.

17. A written report shall be made within a reasonable period of time on the methods and findings of such investigations. The report shall be made public immediately and shall include the scope of the inquiry, procedures and methods used to evaluate evidence as well as conclusions and recommendations based on findings of fact and on applicable law. The report shall also describe in detail specific events that were found to have occurred and the evidence upon which such findings were based, and list the names of witnesses who testified, with the exception of those whose identities have been withheld for their own protection. The Government shall, within a reasonable period of time, either reply to the report of the investigation, or indicate the steps to be taken in response to it.

Legal proceedings

18. Governments shall ensure that persons identified by the investigation as having participated in extra-legal, arbitrary or summary executions in any territory under their jurisdiction are brought to justice. Governments shall either bring such persons to justice or co-operate to extradite any such persons to other countries wishing to exercise jurisdiction. This principle shall apply irrespective of who and where the perpetrators or the victims are, their nationalities or where the offence was committed.

19. Without prejudice to principle 3 above, an order from a superior officer or a public authority may not be invoked as a justification for extra-legal, arbitrary or summary executions. Superiors, officers or other public officials may be held responsible for acts committed by officials under their authority if they had a reasonable opportunity to prevent such acts. In no circumstances, including a state of war, siege or other public emergency, shall blanket immunity from prosecution be granted to any person allegedly involved in extra-legal, arbitrary or summary executions.

20. The families and dependants of victims of extra-legal, arbitrary or summary executions shall be entitled to fair and adequate compensation within a reasonable period of time.

Economic and Social Council resolution 1989/65

24 May 1989   Meeting 15   Adopted without vote

Approved by Second Committee (E/1989/91) without vote, 11 May (meeting 12); draft by Committee on Crime Prevention and Control (E/1988/20); agenda item 11.

UN crime prevention and criminal justice programmes

During 1989, the Economic and Social Council adopted five resolutions aimed at strengthening international co-operation and implementing internationally applicable principles of criminal justice.

Network of national correspondents

On 24 May, the Economic and Social Council, on the recommendation of its Second Committee, adopted **resolution 1989/58** without vote.

United Nations network of government-appointed national correspondents in the field of crime prevention and control

The Economic and Social Council,

Reaffirming General Assembly resolution 415(V) of 1 December 1950, by which the Assembly established a system of national correspondents appointed by Governments to co-operate with the Secretariat in all matters concerning crime prevention and control,

Reaffirming also its resolution 357(XII) of 13 March 1951, in which it emphasized that the appointment of national correspondents should be made on the basis of their expert qualifications or experience, professional or scientific, in the field of crime prevention and control,

Recognizing the important role of national correspondents, the valuable contributions they have made and the work they have accomplished in the promotion and implementation of the United Nations programme of work in the field of crime prevention and control, including that of the United Nations institutes, the United Nations quinquennial congresses on the prevention of crime and the treatment of offenders, and the Committee on Crime Prevention and Control,

Recognizing also the role the network has played in achieving a consensus and promoting co-operation, at the regional, interregional and international levels, on questions of criminal policy,

Bearing in mind the various legislative directives which have, over the years, called upon the national correspondent network to undertake an increasing number of activities of a technical and scientific nature, such as the conducting of research, participation in the implementation of major regional and global surveys, preparation of analytical reports on developments in crime and juvenile delinquency and criminal justice operations,

Also bearing in mind the fact that the role, functions and contributions of the network have substantially increased over the years, both in level and scope,

Taking into account the recommendations of the first general meeting of national correspondents, held on the occasion of the Seventh United Nations Congress on the Prevention of Crime and the Treatment of Offenders,

1. *Expresses satisfaction* with the work and efforts of the Secretariat in bringing about an expansion of the national correspondents network to cover nearly all countries of the world;

2. *Invites* those Member States that have not yet done so to appoint one or more national correspondents and to inform the Secretary-General accordingly;

3. *Also invites* Member States:

(*a*) To appoint national correspondents from among experts, practitioners and policy makers in the field of crime prevention and control, and when appointing more than one national correspondent, to designate a chief national correspondent as national co-ordinator, as is already the case in numerous countries;

(*b*) To facilitate and support the work of national correspondents, recognizing their role and functions and according appropriate official status at the national level, thus promoting more effective collaboration with the United Nations in the field of crime prevention and control;

(*c*) To enhance the representation and involvement of national correspondents in technical meetings of the United Nations by, *inter alia,* including them in governmental delegations to United Nations quinquennial congresses on the prevention of crime and the treatment of offenders and relevant preparatory meetings;

4. *Requests* the Secretary-General to make every effort to strengthen the functional capacity of the network and to co-ordinate and mobilize it by, *inter alia:*

(*a*) Fostering more systematic involvement in the United Nations programme of work;

(*b*) Ensuring a more effective flow of information and closer collaboration;

(*c*) Taking more fully into account the views of national correspondents on key questions of criminal policy to ensure their reflection in the work of the United Nations, facilitating consensus building, and ensuring that the programme of work responds to the technical needs and problems of various regions;

(*d*) Convening general meetings of national correspondents attending United Nations quinquennial congresses;

(*e*) Exploring ways and means of establishing strong, permanent, ongoing links between the network and the United Nations Secretariat, the Committee on Crime Prevention and Control, the United Nations Development Programme and United Nations institutes, as well as justice agencies, scientific institutions and other organizations world wide;

(*f*) Continuing to publish, at regular intervals, information circulars to keep national correspondents abreast of developments in the work programme of the United Nations in the field of crime prevention and control;

(g) Encouraging the organization of international advisory groups and meetings of national correspondents, to review, in particular, the implementation of relevant resolutions;

5. *Requests* the United Nations Development Programme to provide liaison services between national correspondents and the Secretariat;

6. *Requests* the United Nations institutes to involve national correspondents more fully in their activities;

7. *Requests* the Secretary-General to report on the implementation of the present resolution to the Committee on Crime Prevention and Control at its eleventh session;

8. *Recommends* that the Secretary-General transmit the present resolution to the Governments of Member States.

Economic and Social Council resolution 1989/58

24 May 1989   Meeting 15   Adopted without vote

Approved by Second Committee (E/1989/91) without vote, 11 May (meeting 12); draft by Committee on Crime Prevention and Control (E/1988/20); agenda item 11.
Financial implications. E/1989/C.2/L.13.

UN principles, standards and norms

Principles of justice for victims

On 24 May, the Economic and Social Council, on the recommendation of the Second Committee, adopted **resolution 1989/57** without vote.

Implementation of the Declaration of Basic Principles of Justice for Victims of Crime and Abuse of Power

The Economic and Social Council,

Bearing in mind that the General Assembly, in its resolution 40/34 of 29 November 1985, adopted the Declaration of Basic Principles of Justice for Victims of Crime and Abuse of Power, set forth in the annex to the resolution, which had been approved by the Seventh United Nations Congress on the Prevention of Crime and the Treatment of Offenders,

Recalling the request made to Member States to take the necessary steps to give effect to the provisions of the Declaration so as to secure for victims of crime and abuse of power the rights due to them,

Taking into account section III of its resolution 1986/10 of 21 May 1986, in which it recommended that continued attention be given to the implementation of the Declaration with a view to developing the co-operation of Governments, intergovernmental and non-governmental organizations and the public in securing justice for victims and in promoting integrated action on behalf of victims at the national, regional and international levels,

Noting that the first report of the Secretary-General concerning measures taken to implement the Declaration indicates a number of areas which require further attention,

Noting with satisfaction the adoption of the European Convention on the Compensation of Victims of Violent Crimes by the Council of Europe on 24 November 1983 and of the recommendation on assistance to victims and the prevention of victimization by the Council of Europe on 17 September 1987, as well as the creation by some Member States of national funds for the compensation of victims of intentional and non-intentional offences,

Recognizing that effective implementation of the provisions of the Declaration in respect of victims of abuse of power is sometimes hampered by problems of jurisdiction and by difficulties in identifying and halting such abuses, owing, *inter alia*, to the transnational nature of the victimization,

Noting with appreciation the significant efforts made since the Seventh United Nations Congress on the Prevention of Crime and the Treatment of Offenders to follow up and give effect to the Declaration, including the report prepared by an *ad hoc* committee of experts at the International Institute of Higher Studies in Criminal Sciences at Syracuse, Italy, in May 1986, as revised at a colloquium of leading non-governmental organizations active in crime prevention, criminal justice and the treatment of offenders and victims, held at Milan, Italy, in November and December 1987,

1. *Recommends* that the Secretary-General consider, subject to the provision of extrabudgetary funds and consideration by the Committee on Crime Prevention and Control, the preparation, publication and dissemination of a guide for criminal justice practitioners and others engaged in similar activities, taking into account the work already done on the subject;

2. *Also recommends* that Member States take the necessary steps to give effect to the provisions contained in the Declaration of Basic Principles of Justice for Victims of Crime and Abuse of Power, through:

(a) The adoption and implementation of the provisions contained in the Declaration in their national justice systems in accordance with their constitutional process and domestic practice;

(b) The introduction of legislation to simplify access by victims to the justice system in order to obtain compensation and restitution;

(c) The examination of methods of assisting victims, including adequate redress for the actual harm or damage inflicted, identifying limitations and exploring ways by which these may be overcome, to ensure that they meet effectively the needs of victims;

(d) The establishment of measures to protect victims from abuse, calumny or intimidation in the course or as a result of any criminal or other proceedings related to the crime, including effective remedies, should such abuses occur;

3. *Further recommends* that Member States, in collaboration with relevant services, agencies and organizations, endeavour:

(a) To encourage the provision of assistance and support services to victims of crime, with due regard to different social, cultural and legal systems, taking into account the experience of different models and methods of service delivery and the current state of knowledge concerning victimization, including its emotional impact, and the consequent need for service organizations to extend offers of assistance to victims;

(b) To develop suitable training for all who provide services to victims to enable them to develop the skills and understanding needed to help victims cope with the emotional impact of crime and overcome bias, where it may exist, and to provide factual information;

(c) To establish effective channels of communication between all those who are involved with victims, organize courses and meetings and disseminate information to enable them to prevent further victimization as a result of the workings of the system;

(d) To ensure that victims are kept informed of their rights and opportunities with respect to redress from the offender, from third parties or from the State, as well as of the progress of the relevant criminal proceedings and of any opportunities that may be involved;

(e) Where informal mechanisms for the resolution of disputes exist, or have been newly introduced, to ensure, if possible and with due consideration to established legal principles, that the wishes and sensibilities of victims are fully taken into consideration and that the outcome is at least as beneficial for the victims as would have been the case if the formal system had been used;

(f) To establish a monitoring and research programme to keep the needs of victims and the effectiveness of services provided to them under constant review; such a programme might include the organization of regular meetings and conferences of representatives of relevant sectors of the criminal justice system and other bodies concerned with the needs of victims, in order to examine the extent to which existing law, practice and victim services are responsive to the needs of victims;

(g) To undertake studies to identify the needs of victims in cases of unreported crime and make the appropriate services available to them;

4. *Recommends* that, at the national, regional and international levels, all appropriate steps be taken to develop international co-operation in criminal matters, *inter alia*, to ensure that those who suffer victimization in another State receive effective help, both immediately following the crime and on their return to their own country of residence or nationality, in protecting their interests and obtaining adequate restitution or compensation and support services, as necessary;

5. *Recognizes* the need to work out in greater detail part B of the Declaration and to develop international means for preventing the abuse of power and for providing redress for victims of such abuse where national channels may be insufficient, and recommends that appropriate steps be taken to this effect;

6. *Requests* the Secretary-General to organize, subject to the availability of extrabudgetary funds, a meeting of experts to formulate specific proposals for the implementation of General Assembly resolution 40/34 and the Declaration of Basic Principles of Justice for Victims of Crime and the Abuse of Power, in so far as those documents apply to the abuse of power, in time for the proposals to be submitted to the Committee on Crime Prevention and Control at its eleventh session and for consideration by the Eighth United Nations Congress on the Prevention of Crime and the Treatment of Offenders.

Economic and Social Council resolution 1989/57

24 May 1989   Meeting 15   Adopted without vote

Approved by Second Committee (E/1989/91) without vote, 11 May (meeting 12); draft by Committee on Crime Prevention and Control (E/1988/20); agenda item 11.
Financial implications. E/1989/C.2/L.13.

Principles on the independence of the judiciary

On 24 May, the Economic and Social Council, on the recommendation of its Second Committee, adopted **resolution 1989/60** without vote.

Procedures for the effective implementation of the Basic Principles on the Independence of the Judiciary

The Economic and Social Council,

Recalling the Basic Principles on the Independence of the Judiciary, adopted by the Seventh United Nations Congress on the Prevention of Crime and the Treatment of Offenders and endorsed by the General Assembly in its resolutions 40/32 of 29 November 1985 and 40/146 of 13 December 1985,

Recalling also that the Congress, in its resolution on the Basic Principles, recommended them for national, regional and interregional action and called upon the Committee on Crime Prevention and Control to consider, as a matter of priority, the effective implementation of that resolution,

Bearing in mind its resolution 1986/10, section V, of 21 May 1986, by which Member States were invited to inform the Secretary-General every five years, beginning in 1988, of the progress achieved in the implementation of the Basic Principles, including their dissemination, their incorporation into national legislation, the problems faced in their implementation at the national level and assistance that might be needed from the international community,

Also bearing in mind General Assembly resolution 41/149 of 4 December 1986, in which the recommendations made by the Council were welcomed,

Having considered the report of the Committee on Crime Prevention and Control on its tenth session,

Guided by the desire to promote the independence and impartiality of the judiciary,

1. *Adopts* the Procedures for the Effective Implementation of the Basic Principles on the Independence of the Judiciary, recommended by the Committee on Crime Prevention and Control and annexed to the present resolution;

2. *Invites* the Eighth United Nations Congress on the Prevention of Crime and the Treatment of Offenders and its preparatory body to accord priority to ways and means of stimulating adherence to the Procedures.

ANNEX
Procedures for the effective implementation of the Basic Principles on the Independence of the Judiciary

Procedure 1

All States shall adopt and implement in their justice systems the Basic Principles on the Independence of the Judiciary in accordance with their constitutional process and domestic practice.

Procedure 2

No judge shall be appointed or elected for purposes, or be required to perform services, that are inconsistent with the Basic Principles. No judge shall accept judicial office on the basis of an appointment or election, or perform services, that are inconsistent with the Basic Principles.

Procedure 3

The Basic Principles shall apply to all judges, including, as appropriate, lay judges, where they exist.

Procedure 4

States shall ensure that the Basic Principles are widely publicized in at least the main or official language or languages of the respective State. Judges, lawyers, members of the executive, the legislature, and the public in general, shall be informed in the most appropriate manner of the content and the importance of the Basic Principles so that they may promote their application within the framework of the justice system. In particular, States shall make the text of the Basic Principles available to all members of the judiciary.

Procedure 5

In implementing principles 7 and 11 of the Basic Principles, States shall pay particular attention to the need for adequate resources for the functioning of the judicial system, including appointing a sufficient number of judges in relation to case-loads, providing the courts with necessary support staff and equipment, and offering judges appropriate personal security, remuneration and emoluments.

Procedure 6

States shall promote or encourage seminars and courses at the national and regional levels on the role of the judiciary in society and the necessity for its independence.

Procedure 7

In accordance with Economic and Social Council resolution 1986/10, section V, Member States shall inform the Secretary-General every five years, beginning in 1988, of the progress achieved in the implementation of the Basic Principles, including their dissemination, their incorporation into national legislation, the problems faced and difficulties or obstacles encountered in their implementation at the national level and the assistance that might be needed from the international community.

Procedure 8

The Secretary-General shall prepare independent quinquennial reports to the Committee on Crime Prevention and Control on progress made with respect to the implementation of the Basic Principles, on the basis of the information received from Governments under procedure 7, as well as other information available within the United Nations system, including information on the technical co-operation and training provided by institutes, experts and regional and interregional advisers. In the preparation of those reports the Secretary-General shall also enlist the co-operation of specialized agencies and the relevant intergovernmental organizations and non-governmental organizations, in particular professional associations of judges and lawyers, in consultative status with the Economic and Social Council, and take into account the information provided by such agencies and organizations.

Procedure 9

The Secretary-General shall disseminate the Basic Principles, the present implementing procedures and the periodic reports on their implementation referred to in procedures 7 and 8, in as many languages as possible, and make them available to all States and intergovern-mental and non-governmental organizations concerned, in order to ensure the widest circulation of those documents.

Procedure 10

The Secretary-General shall ensure the widest possible reference to and use of the text of the Basic Principles and the present implementing procedures by the United Nations in all its relevant programmes and the inclusion of the Basic Principles as soon as possible in the United Nations publication entitled *Human Rights: A Compilation of International Instruments*, in accordance with Economic and Social Council resolution 1986/10, section V.

Procedure 11

As part of its technical co-operation programme, the United Nations, in particular the Department of Technical Co-operation for Development of the Secretariat and the United Nations Development Programme, shall:

(a) Assist Governments, at their request, in setting up and strengthening independent and effective judicial systems;

(b) Make available to Governments requesting them the services of experts and regional and interregional advisers on judicial matters to assist in implementing the Basic Principles;

(c) Enhance research concerning effective measures for implementing the Basic Principles, with emphasis on new developments in that area;

(d) Promote national and regional seminars, as well as other meetings at the professional and non-professional levels, on the role of the judiciary in society, the necessity for its independence, and the importance of implementing the Basic Principles to further those goals;

(e) Strengthen substantive support for the United Nations regional and interregional research and training institutes for crime prevention and criminal justice, as well as other entities within the United Nations system concerned with implementing the Basic Principles.

Procedure 12

The United Nations regional and interregional research and training institutes for crime prevention and criminal justice as well as other concerned entities within the United Nations system shall assist in the implementation process. They shall pay special attention to ways and means of enhancing the application of the Basic Principles in their research and training programmes, and to providing technical assistance upon the request of Member States. For this purpose, the United Nations institutes, in co-operation with national institutions and intergovernmental and non-governmental organizations concerned, shall develop curricula and training materials based on the Basic Principles and the present implementing procedures, which are suitable for use in legal education programmes at all levels as well as in specialized courses on human rights and related subjects.

Procedure 13

The regional commissions, the specialized agencies and other entities within the United Nations system as well as other concerned intergovernmental organizations shall become actively involved in the implementation process. They shall inform the Secretary-General of the efforts made to disseminate the Basic Principles, the measures taken to give effect to them and any obstacles and shortcomings encountered. The Secretary-General shall also take steps to ensure that non-governmental organizations in consultative status with the Economic and Social Council become actively involved in the implementation process and the related reporting procedures.

Procedure 14

The Committee on Crime Prevention and Control shall assist the General Assembly and the Economic and Social Council in following up the present implementing procedures, including periodic reporting under procedures 7 and 8 above. To this end, the Committee shall identify existing obstacles to, or shortcomings in, the implementation of the Basic Principles and the reasons for them. The Committee shall make specific recommendations, as appropriate, to the Assembly and the Council and any other relevant United Nations human rights bodies on further action required for the effective implementation of the Basic Principles.

Procedure 15

The Committee on Crime Prevention and Control shall assist the General Assembly, the Economic and Social Council and any other relevant United Nations human rights bodies, as appropriate, with recommendations relating to reports of *ad hoc* inquiry commissions or bodies, with respect to matters pertaining to the application and implementation of the Basic Principles.

Economic and Social Council resolution 1989/60

24 May 1989   Meeting 15   Adopted without vote

Approved by Second Committee (E/1989/91) without vote, 11 May (meeting 12); draft by Committee on Crime Prevention and Control (E/1988/20); agenda item 11.

Code of Conduct for Law Enforcement Officials

On 24 May, the Economic and Social Council, on the recommendation of its Second Committee, adopted **resolution 1989/61** without vote.

Guidelines for the effective implementation of the Code of Conduct for Law Enforcement Officials

The Economic and Social Council,

Recalling General Assembly resolution 34/169 of 17 December 1979, by which the Assembly adopted the Code of Conduct for Law Enforcement Officials set forth in the annex to the resolution,

Recalling also resolution 14 of the Seventh United Nations Congress on the Prevention of Crime and the Treatment of Offenders, in which the Congress, *inter alia*, called attention to the guidelines for the more effective implementation of the Code formulated at the Interregional Preparatory Meeting for the Seventh Congress on the topic "Formulation and application of United Nations standards and norms in criminal justice", held at Varenna, Italy, in 1984,

Bearing in mind its resolution 1986/10, section IX, of 21 May 1986, in which it requested the Committee on Crime Prevention and Control, at its tenth session, to consider measures for the more effective implementation of the Code, in the light of the guidance provided by the Seventh Congress,

Having considered the report of the Committee on Crime Prevention and Control on its tenth session,

Guided by the desire to promote the implementation of the Code,

1. *Adopts* the Guidelines for the Effective Implementation of the Code of Conduct for Law Enforcement Officials, recommended by the Committee on Crime Prevention and Control and annexed to the present resolution;

2. *Invites* the Eighth United Nations Congress on the Prevention of Crime and the Treatment of Offenders and its preparatory meetings to explore ways and means of stimulating adherence to the Guidelines.

ANNEX
Guidelines for the Effective Implementation of the Code of Conduct for Law Enforcement Officials

I. *Application of the Code*

A. *General principles*

1. The principles embodied in the Code shall be reflected in national legislation and practice.

2. In order to achieve the aims and objectives set out in article 1 of the Code and its Commentary, the definition of "law enforcement officials" shall be given the widest possible interpretation.

3. The Code shall be made applicable to all law enforcement officials, regardless of their jurisdiction.

4. Governments shall adopt the necessary measures to instruct, in basic training and all subsequent training and refresher courses, law enforcement officials in the provisions of national legislation connected with the Code as well as other basic texts on the issue of human rights.

B. *Specific issues*

1. *Selection, education and training.* The selection, education and training of law enforcement officials shall be given prime importance. Governments shall also promote education and training through a fruitful exchange of ideas at the regional and interregional levels.

2. *Salary and working conditions.* All law enforcement officials shall be adequately remunerated and shall be provided with appropriate working conditions.

3. *Discipline and supervision.* Effective mechanisms shall be established to ensure the internal discipline and external control as well as the supervision of law enforcement officials.

4. *Complaints by members of the public.* Particular provisions shall be made, within the mechanisms mentioned under paragraph 3 above, for the receipt and processing of complaints against law enforcement officials made by members of the public, and the existence of these provisions shall be made known to the public.

II. *Implementation of the Code*

A. *At the national level*

1. The Code shall be made available to all law enforcement officials and competent authorities in their own language.

2. Governments shall disseminate the Code and all domestic laws giving effect to it so as to ensure that the principles and rights contained therein become known to the public in general.

3. In considering measures to promote the application of the Code, Governments shall organize symposia on the role and functions of law enforcement officials in the protection of human rights and the prevention of crime.

B. *At the international level*

1. Governments shall inform the Secretary-General at appropriate intervals of at least five years on the extent of the implementation of the Code.

2. The Secretary-General shall prepare periodic reports on progress made with respect to the implementation of the Code, drawing also on observations and on the co-operation of specialized agencies and relevant intergovernmental organizations and non-governmental organizations in consultative status with the Economic and Social Council.

3. As part of the reports mentioned above, Governments shall provide to the Secretary-General copies of abstracts of laws, regulations and administrative measures concerning the application of the Code, any other relevant information on its implementation, as well as information on possible difficulties in its application.

4. The Secretary-General shall submit the above-mentioned reports to the Committee on Crime Prevention and Control for consideration and further action, as appropriate.

5. The Secretary-General shall make available the Code and the present guidelines to all States and intergovernmental and non-governmental organizations concerned, in all official languages of the United Nations.

6. The United Nations, as part of its advisory services and technical co-operation and development programmes, shall:

(a) Make available to Governments requesting them the services of experts and regional and interregional advisers to assist in implementing the provisions of the Code;

(b) Promote national and regional training seminars and other meetings on the Code and on the role and functions of law enforcement officials in the protection of human rights and the prevention of crime.

7. The United Nations regional institutes shall be encouraged to organize seminars and training courses on the Code and to carry out research on the extent to which the Code is implemented in the countries of the region as well as the difficulties encountered.

Economic and Social Council resolution 1989/61

24 May 1989   Meeting 15   Adopted without vote

Approved by Second Committee (E/1989/91) without vote, 11 May (meeting 12); draft by Committee on Crime Prevention and Control (E/1988/20); agenda item 11.

UN standards and norms

The Economic and Social Council, on the recommendation of its Second Committee, adopted **resolution 1989/63** on 24 May without vote.

Implementation of United Nations standards and norms in crime prevention and criminal justice

The Economic and Social Council,

Calling attention to the Milan Plan of Action and the Guiding Principles for Crime Prevention and Criminal Justice in the Context of Development and a New International Economic Order, adopted by the Seventh United Nations Congress on the Prevention of Crime and the Treatment of Offenders,

Recalling the Declaration of Basic Principles of Justice for Victims of Crime and Abuse of Power, the Safeguards guaranteeing protection of the rights of those facing the death penalty, the Code of Conduct for Law Enforce-

ment Officials, the Basic Principles on the Independence of the Judiciary, the Standard Minimum Rules for the Treatment of Prisoners, the United Nations Standard Minimum Rules for the Administration of Juvenile Justice (The Beijing Rules) and the Model Agreement on the Transfer of Foreign Prisoners,

Recognizing the important role the United Nations has played in the development of those standards and norms in crime prevention and criminal justice through its quinquennial congresses on the prevention of crime and the treatment of offenders and the Committee on Crime Prevention and Control,

Acknowledging the valuable contribution the United Nations has made to those endeavours through its activities in the field of human rights, based on the Universal Declaration of Human Rights, the International Covenant on Economic, Social and Cultural Rights, the International Covenant on Civil and Political Rights and other instruments,

Recalling General Assembly resolutions 40/146 of 13 December 1985, 41/149 of 4 December 1986 and 42/143 of 7 December 1987 on human rights in the administration of justice,

Recalling also its resolution 1987/53 of 28 May 1987 on the review of the functioning and programme of work of the United Nations in crime prevention and criminal justice,

Commending the steps initiated by the Crime Prevention and Criminal Justice Branch of the Centre for Social Development and Humanitarian Affairs and the Centre for Human Rights of the Secretariat to ensure even closer co-operation, including preparations for the Eighth United Nations Congress on the Prevention of Crime and the Treatment of Offenders, which were noted with appreciation by the General Assembly in its resolution 42/143,

Welcoming in particular the fact that focal points have been created within the Crime Prevention and Criminal Justice Branch of the Centre for Social Development and Humanitarian Affairs and the Centre for Human Rights to monitor the human rights aspects of the administration of justice within various programmes and to provide, as appropriate, advice on co-ordination and other relevant issues,

Convinced of the need for further co-ordinated and concerted action by the Centre for Social Development and Humanitarian Affairs and the Centre for Human Rights, as called for, *inter alia*, in Commission on Human Rights resolutions 1988/33 of 8 March 1988 on human rights in the administration of justice, 1988/40 of 8 March 1988 on the independence and impartiality of the judiciary, jurors and assessors and the independence of lawyers, 1988/45 of 8 March 1988 on administrative detention without charge or trial, and 1988/68 of 10 March 1988 on summary or arbitrary executions,

Noting with appreciation the report of the Interregional Preparatory Meeting for the Eighth United Nations Congress on the Prevention of Crime and the Treatment of Offenders on the topic "United Nations norms and guidelines in crime prevention and criminal justice: implementation and priorities for further standard setting",

1. *Invites* Governments:

(a) To adopt in national legislation and practice and to implement fully United Nations standards and guidelines on crime prevention and criminal justice, making them available to all persons concerned;

(b) To design realistic and effective mechanisms for implementing the standards and guidelines;

(c) To increase, as far as possible, the level of support provided to technical co-operation and advisory services at all levels for the more effective implementation of standards and norms, either directly or through such international funding agencies as the United Nations Development Programme, particularly when developing countries include specific projects in their country programmes;

(d) To devise measures to promote the observance of the principles embodied in United Nations instruments, including educational and promotional activities, the support of the mass media and increased community involvement;

2. *Requests* the Secretary-General:

(a) To prepare a compilation of all existing United Nations standards and norms in crime prevention and criminal justice and publish them in a form similar to that of the United Nations publication entitled *Human Rights: A Compilation of International Instruments*;

(b) To formulate practical proposals for the Eighth United Nations Congress on the Prevention of Crime and the Treatment of Offenders on procedures and actions at national, regional and international levels to implement United Nations norms and standards in crime prevention and criminal justice;

3. *Encourages* the continuing development of strategies for the practical implementation of United Nations standards and guidelines in crime prevention and criminal justice and of measures to assist Member States, at their request, in their implementation, as well as in evaluating their impact and effectiveness, in particular through the advisory services of the Department of Technical Co-operation for Development, the Centre for Human Rights and the Crime Prevention and Criminal Justice Branch of the Centre for Social Development and Humanitarian Affairs of the Secretariat;

4. *Also encourages* intensified co-operation between the United Nations and its regional and interregional institutes in crime prevention and criminal justice, and requests that special attention be paid, *inter alia*, to:

(a) The strengthening, as far as possible, of substantive support to the institutes;

(b) The application of United Nations instruments by the institutes in their research and training programmes, including the development of appropriate curricula and training materials based on those instruments;

(c) The provision of technical assistance to Member States upon request;

5. *Emphasizes* the need to strengthen the role of the Committee on Crime Prevention and Control in overseeing, evaluating and following up the implementation process, including:

(a) Keeping under review the application of existing standards;

(b) Assisting the General Assembly, the Economic and Social Council and other United Nations bodies and related entities, as appropriate, with reports and recommendations relating to their work;

(c) Fostering more active inter-sessional involvement of Committee members, *inter alia*, by designating them as resource persons on priority topics;

6. *Requests* the Secretary-General to take appropriate action to establish pre-sessional working groups of the Committee on Crime Prevention and Control which would:

(a) Prepare certain items for discussion by the Committee;

(b) Oversee the elaboration of questionnaires to be used for the reporting system;

(c) Examine in-depth replies, data and reports received from Governments and other relevant sources, including non-governmental organizations;

(d) Identify general problems that may impinge on the effective implementation of standards and norms and recommend viable solutions with action-oriented proposals based on the principles of international co-operation and solidarity;

7. *Notes with appreciation* that the United Nations continues to give special attention to standard-setting work in priority areas, in pursuance of the mandates of the Seventh United Nations Congress on the Prevention of Crime and the Treatment of Offenders;

8. *Recognizes* the importance of developing diversified funding strategies, including recourse to voluntary and mixed multilateral and bilateral contributions for specific projects, and of strengthening the involvement of United Nations development agencies, including the World Bank and the United Nations Development Programme;

9. *Acknowledges* the significant role of the United Nations regional and interregional institutes and the regional commissions, the specialized agencies and other organizations of the United Nations system, as well as intergovernmental and non-governmental organizations, including professional associations concerned with promoting United Nations standards and norms in crime prevention and criminal justice;

10. *Decides* to draw the attention of the regional preparatory meetings for the Eighth Congress and of the Congress itself to the issues raised in the present resolution;

11. *Requests* the Secretary-General to implement the provisions of the present resolution and to report thereon to the Eighth Congress.

Economic and Social Council resolution 1989/63

24 May 1989　　　　Meeting 15　　　　Adopted without vote

Approved by Second Committee (E/1989/91) without vote, 11 May (meeting 12); draft by Committee on Crime Prevention and Control (E/1988/20); agenda item 11.
Financial implications. E/1989/C.2/L.13.

Technical co-operation

During 1989, the Interregional Advisor in Crime Prevention and Criminal Justice carried out missions to a number of countries. Advisory services were provided on a range of subjects, including legal reform; the establishment of crime prevention councils or other mechanisms; improving access to justice, especially for the poor or marginalized segments of society; reduction of prison overcrowding and other correctional reforms, with emphasis on non-institutional alternatives and staff training; and upgrading the capability of law enforcement and criminal justice personnel to deal with sophisticated new forms of transnational crime, especially drug trafficking. Preventive and protective strategies and improved juvenile justice were given special attention in advisory services. The Interregional Advisor also visited Italy, Japan, Spain and the United States to obtain financial support for projects in developing countries.

The UN Secretariat consulted with both developing and potential donor countries in order to expand technical co-operation. Through the good offices of the Secretariat, Italy provided advisory assistance to the Latin American Institute for the Prevention of Crime and the Treatment of Offenders, and to Jamaica for the computerization of criminal justice and improvement of prison conditions. The United Kingdom provided advice to Malawi and Zambia on probation and prison reforms. Several possible projects were identified, following consultations with officials of Member States; they included the establishment of a senior police officers' school for Ghana, the prevention of juvenile delinquency in Botswana, an assessment of crime trends in Mauritius, a criminal statistics project in Ethiopia, treatment of drug addicts in prison in Malaysia, and training of judges in Bolivia.

In October, a memorandum of understanding on co-operation in crime prevention and criminal justice was signed in Moscow by the United Nations Office at Vienna and the Minister of the Interior of the USSR. It would provide for collaborative activities between the Ministry, the Crime Prevention and Criminal Justice Branch of the Centre for Social Development and Humanitarian Affairs, the UN Interregional Crime and Justice Research Institute in Rome and the UN-affiliated Helsinki Institute for Crime Prevention and Control. Among envisaged activities were a research workshop on the prevention of organized crime and a training course on computer technology and police work.

Information network

During 1989, the UN Crime Prevention and Criminal Justice Information Network, established with the co-operation of the State University of New York at Albany, became operational. It was developed to facilitate information exchange and linkages between policy makers, planners, practitioners, scholars and other experts, as well as national correspondents and research institutions, and to ensure better use of the data base of world crime surveys. Electronic bulletins on special subjects were also provided.

Crime prevention institutes

The regional and interregional UN institutes for the prevention of crime and the treatment of offenders continued wide-ranging activities, including research and dissemination of informa-

tion. Increasingly, they provided direct advisory assistance on criminal law reform, alternatives to imprisonment, application of modern management techniques to criminal justice systems, juvenile justice and implementation of human rights standards. Their Fifth Annual Joint Meeting on Programme Co-ordination (Riyadh, Saudi Arabia, 18 January) examined modalities of closer co-operation, co-ordination and joint work, and discussed priority areas for further action, including the Third UN Survey of Crime Trends, Operations of Criminal Justice Systems and Crime Prevention Strategies[48] and practical implementation of UN standards in crime prevention and criminal justice.

African Institute for the Prevention of Crime and the Treatment of Offenders

Since the adoption of the statute of the UN African Institute for the Prevention of Crime and the Treatment of Offenders by the Conference of African Ministers in 1988, 23 countries had signed the statute, including Uganda, the Institute's host country. At the inaugural meeting of the Institute's Governing Board at Kampala on 14 and 15 June 1989, the Board approved the Institute's proposed 1989-1993 work programme and considered the financing of the Institute and responsibilities of participating States. In August, the Board appointed the Director and the Deputy Director of the Institute. The Institute was to concentrate its activities on training, research and collection and dissemination of information, with major emphasis on the study of juvenile delinquency, economic and commercial crimes, corruption and bribery, violence against persons, and drug abuse and trafficking.

ECONOMIC AND SOCIAL COUNCIL ACTION

On 24 May, the Economic and Social Council, on the recommendation of its Second Committee, adopted **resolution 1989/59** without vote.

African Institute for the Prevention of Crime and the Treatment of Offenders

The Economic and Social Council,

Recalling its resolution 1984/51 of 25 May 1984, by which it urged the Secretary-General and all the organizations and agencies involved in the establishment of the African Institute for the Prevention of Crime and the Treatment of Offenders to take steps to ensure its prompt creation and appealed to Governments in the African region to co-operate fully and act expeditiously in this respect,

Affirming the usefulness of regional co-operation in crime prevention and criminal justice as fostered by the United Nations regional and interregional institutes for the prevention of crime and the treatment of offenders, which have played pivotal roles in assisting the Member States of their respective regions,

Bearing in mind that the Conference of Ministers of the Economic Commission for Africa, by its resolution 642(XXIII) of 15 April 1988, adopted the statute of the Institute and decided that its headquarters should be located at Kampala,

Acknowledging with satisfaction the activities so far undertaken during the initial phase of the operation of the Institute and the efforts made by the Economic Commission for Africa, in co-operation with the Organization of African Unity and the Crime Prevention and Criminal Justice Branch of the Centre for Social Development and Humanitarian Affairs of the Secretariat, towards the full realization of the project,

Noting with appreciation the responsiveness of the United Nations Development Programme in earmarking the necessary funds for the initial phase of the operation of the Institute,

Firmly convinced that the Institute should undertake its activities on a continuous basis, so as to respond promptly and efficiently to the needs and concerns of the African States, meet their training and research requirements in the field of crime prevention and criminal justice, and contribute to existing regional and international efforts directed towards the prevention of crime and the treatment of offenders,

1. *Expresses its appreciation* to the Secretary-General for the steps taken to establish the African Institute for the Prevention of Crime and the Treatment of Offenders;

2. *Requests* the Secretary-General to continue making every effort to ensure adequate support for the Institute, through the Crime Prevention and Criminal Justice Branch of the Centre for Social Development and Humanitarian Affairs of the Secretariat, and to explore other means of ensuring the effective operation of the Institute;

3. *Urges* the Secretary-General and all the organizations and agencies involved in the establishment of the Institute to make every effort to assist the host country in arrangements necessary for the effective operation of the Institute;

4. *Invites* Member States in the African region and other interested States to contribute generously to the activities of the Institute to enable it to formulate and implement technical co-operation projects;

5. *Invites* the international community, including governmental and non-governmental organizations, to respond positively to the need for assistance and support, which would enable the Institute to fulfil its mandates effectively;

6. *Urges* the United Nations Development Programme to continue providing the necessary financial support to the Institute, and appeals to other funding agencies to do likewise;

7. *Requests* the Secretary-General to issue special postage stamps on the occasion of the Eighth United Nations Congress on the Prevention of Crime and the Treatment of Offenders, to be held in 1990, and to place the revenue earned at the disposal of the Institute for the formulation and implementation of specific technical assistance projects in the African region;

8. *Invites* the United Nations regional and interregional institutes for the prevention of crime and the treatment of offenders to strengthen existing collaboration with the Institute, promote a regular exchange of information and experience and implement joint activities of mutual interest;

9. *Requests* the Secretary-General to submit a report on the implementation of the present resolution to the Council at its first regular session of 1990.

Economic and Social Council resolution 1989/59

24 May 1989   Meeting 15   Adopted without vote

Approved by Second Committee (E/1989/91) without vote, 11 May (meeting 12); draft by Committee on Crime Prevention and Control (E/1988/20); agenda item 11.
Financial implications. E/1989/C.2/L.13.

United Nations Interregional Crime and Justice Research Institute

In 1989, the United Nations Social Defence Research Institute was transformed into the United Nations Interregional Crime and Justice Research Institute.

ECONOMIC AND SOCIAL COUNCIL ACTION

On 24 May, the Economic and Social Council, on the recommendation of its Second Committee, adopted **resolution 1989/56** without vote.

Statute of the United Nations Interregional Crime and Justice Research Institute

The Economic and Social Council,

Recalling its resolution 1086 B (XXXIX) of 30 July 1965, in which it requested the Secretary-General to proceed to the establishment of a funds-in-trust account to be administered by the United Nations for the purpose of strengthening the capacity of the Organization to carry out its responsibilities in the social defence field,

Recalling also the establishment in 1968 at Rome of the United Nations Social Defence Research Institute within the framework of its resolution 1086 B (XXXIX),

Recalling further resolution 20 of the Seventh United Nations Congress on the Prevention of Crime and the Treatment of Offenders, in which the Congress noted with satisfaction the invaluable contribution made, *inter alia*, by the Institute to the growing international and national recognition of the central importance of action-oriented research as an effective instrument for the formulation and implementation of policies for crime prevention and control,

Noting with satisfaction that the activities of the Institute have been positively reviewed by the Committee on Crime Prevention and Control on a periodic basis and that the Institute's work programme has evolved and expanded in response to the needs of the international community, particularly in the developing regions of the world,

Noting especially the diversification of the Institute's activities in terms of extension of research results through training and field activities aimed at assisting developing countries and in terms of an enhanced contribution to the United Nations crime prevention and criminal justice programme,

Bearing in mind that the Milan Plan of Action, adopted by the Seventh United Nations Congress on the Prevention of Crime and the Treatment of Offenders, called for the strengthening of the United Nations regional and interregional institutes in the field of crime prevention and criminal justice,

Mindful of the importance of updating the terms of reference and the *modus operandi* of the United Nations Social Defence Research Institute to bring them into line with current thinking in the field of crime prevention and criminal justice, in particular in respect of the needs of developing countries,

Mindful also of the importance of making more permanent arrangements for the governance of the Institute,

1. *Adopts* the statute of the United Nations Interregional Crime and Justice Research Institute set forth in the annex to the present resolution;

2. *Requests* the Secretary-General to take steps, in consultation with the Director of the Institute, to implement the statute and to report thereon to the Committee on Crime Prevention and Control at its eleventh session.

ANNEX
Statute of the United Nations Interregional Crime and Justice Research Institute

Article I

Establishment of the Institute

The United Nations Social Defence Research Institute (UNSDRI) is hereby established as the United Nations Interregional Crime and Justice Research Institute (UNICRI).

Article II

Objectives and functions

1. The objective of the Institute shall be to contribute, through research, training, field activities and the collection, exchange and dissemination of information, to the formulation and implementation of improved policies in the field of crime prevention and control, due regard being paid to the integration of such policies within broader policies for socio-economic change and development, and to the protection of human rights. The Institute shall assist intergovernmental, governmental and non-governmental organizations in their efforts in this regard. Accordingly, the principal functions of the Institute shall be the following:

(a) To promote, conduct, co-ordinate and support research and, in collaboration with the countries concerned, to organize and support field activities with a view to:

(i) Establishing a reliable base of knowledge and information on social problems involving juvenile delinquency and adult criminality, special attention being given to the new, frequently transnational forms of the phenomena;

(ii) Identifying appropriate strategies, policies and instruments for the prevention and control of the phenomena so as to contribute to socio-economic development and to promote the protection of human rights;

(iii) Designing practical models and systems aimed at providing support for policy formulation, implementation and evaluation;

(b) To provide action-oriented research and training relating to the United Nations programme on crime prevention and criminal justice;

(c) To design and carry out training activities at the interregional level and, at the request of interested countries, at the national level;

(d) To promote the exchange of information by, *inter alia*, maintaining an international documentation centre on criminology and related disciplines to enable the Institute to respond to the need of the international community for the dissemination of information world-wide and to serve the needs of the United Nations and of scholars and other experts requiring such facilities.

2. In the pursuit of its objectives, the Institute shall carry out its activities in close collaboration and co-ordination with institutes and other bodies within and outside the United Nations system, especially with the United Nations regional institutes on the prevention of crime.

Article III

Status, organization and location of the Institute

1. The Institute shall be a United Nations entity and thus form part of the United Nations system.

2. The Institute shall have its own Board of Trustees and a Director and supporting staff. It shall be subject to the Financial Regulations and Staff Regulations of the United Nations, except as may be provided otherwise by the General Assembly. It shall also be subject to the Financial Rules, the Staff Rules and all other administrative issuances of the Secretary-General, except as may be otherwise decided by the Secretary-General.

3. The Headquarters of the Institute shall be located at Rome. The Institute may, with the approval of the Board of Trustees and of the Secretary-General, establish such other offices as it deems necessary.

Article IV

Board of Trustees

1. The Institute and its work shall be governed by a Board of Trustees (hereinafter referred to as "the Board") under the overall guidance of the Committee on Crime Prevention and Control.

2. The Board shall be composed of the following:

(a) Seven members selected by the Committee on Crime Prevention and Control upon nomination by the Secretary-General and endorsed by the Economic and Social Council, with due regard to the fact that the Institute and its work are funded from voluntary contributions and to the principle of equitable geographical distribution. The members shall be chosen from among eminent persons who possess the necessary qualifications and expertise. They shall serve in their individual capacity for a term of five years from the date of the first Board meeting in which they are invited to participate. They shall be eligible for reappointment by the Committee on Crime Prevention and Control with the endorsement of the Economic and Social Council for not more than one additional term. Members shall retire by rotation; for this purpose, when the members are first appointed, three shall serve for five years, two for four years and two for three years. The members to serve these initial terms shall be determined by the Board at its first session by the drawing of lots;

(b) A representative of the Secretary-General, who shall normally be the Head of the Crime Prevention and Criminal Justice Branch of the Centre for Social Development and Humanitarian Affairs of the Secretariat, a representative of the Administrator of the United Nations Development Programme, a representative of the host country and the Director of the Institute shall serve as *ex officio* members of the Board.

3. The Board, under the guidance of the Committee on Crime Prevention and Control, shall:

(a) Formulate principles, policies and guidelines for the activities of the Institute;

(b) Consider and approve the work programme and budget proposals of the Institute on the basis of recommendations submitted to it by the Director of the Institute;

(c) Evaluate the Institute's completed and ongoing activities on the basis of periodic reports submitted to it by the Director of the Institute;

(d) Make the recommendations necessary or desirable for the operation of the Institute;

(e) Report periodically to the Economic and Social Council through the Committee on Crime Prevention and Control.

4. The Board shall meet at least once every two years. It shall adopt its own rules of procedure. It shall elect its own officers, including its President, in accordance with the adopted rules of procedure. It shall take its decisions in the manner provided in its rules of procedure.

5. The Board shall consider methods for enhancing the financial resources of the Institute with a view to ensuring the effectiveness of its operations and their continuity within the overall framework of the United Nations programme on crime prevention and criminal justice.

6. Members of the Board, in furtherance of the principles and policies of the Institute, may be invited to help in achieving the goals of the Institute by attending meetings on behalf of the Institute, raising funds for the Institute's operations and helping to establish national support teams, if possible, in their respective countries for the attainment of the objectives of the Institute.

7. Organizations of the United Nations system and other institutions may be represented as appropriate at meetings of the Board in respect of activities of interest to them under the conditions outlined in the rules of procedure of the Board.

Article V

Director and staff

1. The Director shall be appointed by the Secretary-General of the United Nations after consultation with the Board.

2. The Director shall have overall responsibility for the organization, direction and administration of the Institute in accordance with general directives issued by the Board and within the terms of the authority delegated to the Director by the Secretary-General. The Director shall, *inter alia:*

(a) Submit the work programmes and the budget estimates of the Institute to the Board for its consideration and adoption;

(b) Oversee the execution of the work programmes and make the expenditures envisaged in the budget of the Institute as adopted by the Board;

(c) Submit to the Board annual and *ad hoc* reports on the activities of the Institute and the execution of its work programmes;

(d) Submit to the Committee on Crime Prevention and Control the reports approved by the Board;

(e) Appoint and direct the staff of the Institute on behalf of the Secretary-General;

(f) Co-ordinate the work of the Institute with that of other organs and bodies of the United Nations, the specialized agencies and international, national and regional institutions engaged in similar fields;

(g) Negotiate arrangements with Governments and intergovernmental organizations, as well as non-governmental organizations and academic and philanthropic institutions, with a view to offering and receiving services related to the activities of the Institute;

(h) Actively seek appropriate funding for the implementation of the work programme of the Institute;

(i) Accept, subject to the provisions of article VII, voluntary contributions to the Institute;

(j) Make the necessary arrangements for securing established and continuous contact with, and support from, United Nations Headquarters;

(k) Undertake other assignments or activities as may be determined by the Board or requested by the Secretary-General, provided that any such requests are consistent with the programme budget approved by the Board.

3. The staff of the Institute shall be appointed by the Director under letters of appointment signed by him or her in the name of the Secretary-General and limited to service with the Institute. The staff shall be responsible to the Director in the exercise of their functions.

4. The terms and conditions of service of the Director and the staff shall be those provided in the Staff Regulations and Staff Rules of the United Nations, subject to such arrangements for special rules or terms of appointment as may be proposed by the Director and approved by the Secretary-General.

5. The Director and the staff of the Institute shall not seek or receive instructions from any Government or from any authority external to the United Nations. They shall refrain from any action that might reflect on their position as international officials responsible only to the Organization.

6. The Director and the staff of the Institute shall be officials of the United Nations and therefore shall be covered by Article 105 of the Charter of the United Nations, and by other international agreements and United Nations resolutions defining the status of such officials.

Article VI

Fellows and consultants

1. The Director may designate a limited number of well-qualified persons to serve as senior fellows of the Institute. Senior fellows shall be permitted to pursue their research at the Institute and shall be expected to provide advice and assistance in matters related to the work programme of the Institute.

2. The Director may also designate junior fellows as part of the training programme of the Institute. Junior fellows shall be expected to provide assistance in matters concerning the work programme of the Institute.

3. The Institute shall establish a restricted network of national fellows specialized in the field of criminological research to assist the activities of the Institute by advising on studies, research and training.

4. Fellows shall be designated in accordance with criteria established by the Board and procedures formulated by the Secretary-General and shall not be considered to be members of the staff of the Institute.

5. The Director may arrange for the services of consultants for special assignments in connection with the work programme of the Institute. Such consultants shall be engaged in accordance with policies established by the Secretary-General.

Article VII

Financial resources and rules governing the financial management of the Institute

The activities of the Institute shall be funded by voluntary contributions from States. The Institute may derive further resources in cash or in kind from the United Nations, its specialized agencies, other intergovernmental and governmental organizations and institutions, and non-governmental organizations. Acceptance by the Institute of offers of such further assistance shall, in every case, be subject to the decision of the President of the Board, in consultation with the Director of the Institute, in accordance with the basic aims of the Institute and the relevant provisions of the rules governing the financial management of the Institute. The President of the Board shall report on the matter to the Board at its following session.

Article VIII

Administrative and other support

The Secretary-General of the United Nations shall provide the Institute with appropriate administrative and other support in accordance with the Financial Regulations and Rules of the United Nations. The Institute shall reimburse the United Nations the cost of such support, as determined by the Controller of the United Nations after consultation with the Director.

Article IX

Relations with the Centre for Social Development and Humanitarian Affairs of the Secretariat, and other United Nations bodies, specialized agencies and international organizations

1. The Institute shall establish and maintain a close consultative, co-operative and working relationship with the Centre for Social Development and Humanitarian Affairs of the Secretariat, including in particular the Crime Prevention and Criminal Justice Branch.

2. The Institute may also establish and maintain such relations as it considers appropriate with other United Nations bodies, specialized agencies and international organizations.

Economic and Social Council resolution 1989/56

24 May 1989   Meeting 15   Adopted without vote

Approved by Second Committee (E/1989/91) without vote, 11 May (meeting 12); draft by Committee on Crime Prevention and Control (E/1988/20); agenda item 11.

UN Trust Fund for Social Defence

As at 31 December 1989, the Fund's balance stood at $2,727,395, with income totalling $3,787,797. Expenditures were $2,821,034 during the year.

Cultural development

World Decade for Cultural Development

In response to a 1986 General Assembly resolution,[49] the Secretary-General and the UNESCO Director-General in May submitted the first biennial report[50] on the progress of the World Decade for Cultural Development (1988-1997).

The report described efforts towards the four objectives of the Decade: acknowledging the cultural dimension of development; affirming and enriching cultural identities; broadening participation in culture; and promoting international cultural co-operation. It reviewed activities undertaken by Member States, by UN organizations (including UNESCO, the lead agency) and by intergovernmental and non-governmental organizations. During 1988 and 1989, several regional meetings were held by national commissions for UNESCO to identify activities. Although it was still too early to draw a conclusion, the report stated that activities carried out by parties concerned during the first year of the Decade had not been as significant as might have been wished. The slow pace of implementation of the Plan of Action by Member States was attributed to the need felt by government officials to interpret Decade objectives in the contexts of their own economic and social development strategies before envisaging specific Decade activities. In most cases, there was more attention to traditional cultural activities involving artistic and literary fields than to activities taking into account cultural factors in development strategies. The report recommended that Member States that had not yet done so establish national committees for the Decade and resolutely envisage activities and projects in an innovative spirit of development, thereby expanding their efforts to optimize human resources, achieve economic recovery and make structural adjustments.

UN organizations were encouraged to step up their efforts to devise activities by appointing Decade co-ordinators and by periodically reporting on developments in implementing Decade activities. They also were to ensure the interlinking of the aims of the Decade and the new International Strategy for the Fourth United Nations Development Decade (1991-2000).[14] The report emphasized the importance of disseminating information on the cultural Decade and its purposes in order to involve the public at large.

ECONOMIC AND SOCIAL COUNCIL ACTION

On 27 July, on the recommendation of its Third Committee, the Economic and Social Council adopted **resolution 1989/107** without vote.

World Decade for Cultural Development
The Economic and Social Council,

Recalling General Assembly resolution 41/187 of 8 December 1986, in which the Assembly proclaimed the period 1988-1997 the World Decade for Cultural Development, to be observed under the auspices of the United Nations and the United Nations Educational, Scientific and Cultural Organization,

Noting that, in addition to the regional meetings listed in the report of the Secretary-General of the United Nations and the Director-General of the United Nations

Educational, Scientific and Cultural Organization, the National Commissions for the United Nations Educational, Scientific and Cultural Organization in the Arab States met at Nouakchott in June 1989 to co-ordinate their efforts to implement the Decade,

1. *Takes note* of the report of the Secretary-General of the United Nations and the Director-General of the United Nations Educational, Scientific and Cultural Organization on the progress of the World Decade for Cultural Development during the period 1988-1989;

2. *Invites* Member States, intergovernmental organizations and non-governmental organizations to strengthen their efforts, as appropriate, in the implementation of the Plan of Action for the World Decade for Cultural Development;

3. *Requests* the Secretary-General, in co-operation with the Director-General of the United Nations Educational, Scientific and Cultural Organization, to take the measures necessary to reinforce the co-ordination of the activities undertaken by the organizations of the United Nations system in support of the Decade through the Administrative Committee on Co-ordination; such measures might include the establishment of a steering committee, if appropriate.

Economic and Social Council resolution 1989/107

27 July 1989   Meeting 36   Adopted without vote

Approved by Third Committee (E/1989/133) without vote, 18 July (meeting 13); draft by Mauritania (E/1989/C.3/L.5), orally revised; agenda item 9.

GENERAL ASSEMBLY ACTION

On 22 December, on the recommendation of its Second Committee, the General Assembly adopted **resolution 44/238** without vote.

World Decade for Cultural Development

The General Assembly,

Recalling its resolution 41/187 of 8 December 1986, in which it proclaimed the period 1988-1997 the World Decade for Cultural Development, to be observed under the auspices of the United Nations and the United Nations Educational, Scientific and Cultural Organization,

Taking note of Economic and Social Council resolution 1989/107 of 27 July 1989,

Recognizing the importance of cultural development based on the affirmation and enrichment of the cultural identities of all countries and its close relationship to overall development,

Welcoming the progress made by Member States and by non-governmental organizations in developing activities within the framework of the Decade,

1. *Takes note* of the report of the Secretary-General and of the Director-General of the United Nations Educational, Scientific and Cultural Organization on the progress of the World Decade for Cultural Development during the period 1988-1989;

2. *Invites* Member States that have not yet done so to establish national committees for the Decade and otherwise to strengthen their efforts to implement the Plan of Action for the Decade;

3. *Expresses its appreciation* to those countries that have provided voluntary contributions in the form of consultant services to the secretariat of the Decade, and encourages other countries, international organizations and other organizations to make voluntary contributions in support of the Decade;

4. *Invites* the organizations and programmes of the United Nations system to continue their efforts to develop activities within the framework of the Decade, in accordance with directives of the Administrative Committee on Co-ordination;

5. *Requests* the Secretary-General, in co-operation with the Director-General of the United Nations Educational, Scientific and Cultural Organization, to strengthen co-ordination of the activities undertaken by the organizations and programmes of the United Nations system in support of the Decade;

6. *Emphasizes* the importance of taking the cultural dimension of development into account in the elaboration of the international development strategy for the fourth United Nations development decade and in the working documents for the special session of the General Assembly devoted to international economic co-operation, in particular the revitalization of economic growth and development of the developing countries, to be held in 1990;

7. *Reaffirms* its support for the recommendations of the Nairobi Forward-looking Strategies for the Advancement of Women aimed at promoting women's participation in the World Decade for Cultural Development, in particular those relating to better integration and promotion of women in the objectives of the Decade;

8. *Requests* the Secretary-General, with the assistance of the Director-General of the United Nations Educational, Scientific and Cultural Organization, to obtain the views of Governments, appropriate organs and organizations of the United Nations system and relevant intergovernmental and non-governmental organizations on the objectives and scope of the global review for the purpose of evaluation, as recommended in paragraph 92 of the report of the Secretary-General and the Director-General on the Decade, and to submit those views to the General Assembly at its forty-fifth session, through the Economic and Social Council;

9. *Expresses its support* for the recommendation in paragraph 92 of the report of the Secretary-General and the Director-General for the conduct of an evaluation at the mid-point of the Decade, in 1993, under the auspices of the United Nations and the United Nations Educational, Scientific and Cultural Organization, in order to evaluate the implementation of the Plan of Action for the Decade;

10. *Requests* the Secretary-General and the Director-General of the United Nations Educational, Scientific and Cultural Organization to submit to the General Assembly at its forty-sixth session a report on the progress of the Decade for the period 1990-1991.

General Assembly resolution 44/238

22 December 1989   Meeting 85   Adopted without vote

Approved by Second Committee (A/44/832/Add.1) by consensus, 4 December (meeting 48); draft by Ecuador (A/C.2/44/L.59); agenda item 12.
Meeting numbers. GA 44th session: 2nd Committee 17, 46, 48; plenary 85.

Restitution of cultural property

Pursuant to a 1987 General Assembly request,[51] the Secretary-General transmitted a report[52] of the UNESCO Director-General on return or restitution of cultural property to countries of origin.

The Director-General described UNESCO efforts to implement the 1987 recommendations of the Intergovernmental Committee for Promoting the Return of Cultural Property to Its Countries of Origin or Its Restitution in Case of Illicit Appropriation,[53] including measures to promote bilateral negotiations for the return or restitution of cultural property, international technical co-operation, and steps to curb illicit traffic in cultural property and public information. The recommendations adopted by the Intergovernmental Committee at its sixth session (Paris, 24-27 April 1989) were appended to the report.

The Committee, welcoming the International Council of Museums' Code of Professional Ethics and the International Confederation of Art Dealers' Code of Practice, expressed the hope that they would serve as a standard for acquisitions by private as well as public collectors. It recommended that countries subject to clandestine excavations consider regional arrangements for the certification of excavated cultural property where its locality, but not its State of origin, could be traced. Member States were urged to ensure the widest possible dissemination of notices by the International Criminal Police Organization of stolen cultural objects, not only to police and customs authorities but also to museums and dealers. The Committee appealed to mass media and cultural and educational institutions to accord greater attention to issues of return or restitution, and urged UNESCO to step up efforts to inform and educate both specialized and general audiences about the problems posed and progress achieved in the areas within the Committee mandate.

GENERAL ASSEMBLY ACTION

On 6 November 1989, the General Assembly adopted **resolution 44/18** by recorded vote.

Return or restitution of cultural property to the countries of origin

The General Assembly,

Recalling its resolutions 3026 A (XXVII) of 18 December 1972, 3148(XXVIII) of 14 December 1973, 3187(XXVIII) of 18 December 1973, 3391(XXX) of 19 November 1975, 31/40 of 30 November 1976, 32/18 of 11 November 1977, 33/50 of 14 December 1978, 34/64 of 29 November 1979, 35/127 and 35/128 of 11 December 1980, 36/64 of 27 November 1981, 38/34 of 25 November 1983, 40/19 of 21 November 1985 and 42/7 of 7 October 1987,

Recalling also the Convention on the Means of Prohibiting and Preventing the Illicit Import, Export and Transfer of Ownership of Cultural Property adopted on 14 November 1970 by the General Conference of the United Nations Educational, Scientific and Cultural Organization,

Taking note with satisfaction of the report of the Secretary-General submitted in co-operation with the Director-General of the United Nations Educational, Scientific and Cultural Organization,

Noting with satisfaction that, following its appeal, other Member States have become parties to the Convention on the Means of Prohibiting and Preventing the Illicit Import, Export and Transfer of Ownership of Cultural Property,

Aware of the importance attached by the countries of origin to the return of cultural property which is of fundamental spiritual and cultural value to them, so that they may constitute collections representative of their cultural heritage,

Reaffirming the importance of inventories as an essential tool for the understanding and protection of cultural property and for the identification of dispersed heritage and as a contribution to the advancement of scientific and artistic knowledge and intercultural communication,

Deeply concerned at the clandestine excavations and the illicit traffic in cultural property that continue to impoverish the cultural heritage of all peoples,

Again supporting the solemn appeal made on 7 June 1978 by the Director-General of the United Nations Educational, Scientific and Cultural Organization for the return of irreplaceable cultural heritage to those who created it,

1. *Commends* the United Nations Educational, Scientific and Cultural Organization and the Intergovernmental Committee for Promoting the Return of Cultural Property to Its Countries of Origin or Its Restitution in Case of Illicit Appropriation on the work they have accomplished, in particular through the promotion of bilateral negotiations, for the return or restitution of cultural property, the preparation of inventories of movable cultural property, the reduction of illicit traffic in cultural property and the dissemination of information to the public;

2. *Reaffirms* that the restitution to a country of its *objets d'art*, monuments, museum pieces, archives, manuscripts, documents and any other cultural or artistic treasures contributes to the strengthening of international co-operation and to the preservation and flowering of universal cultural values through fruitful co-operation between developed and developing countries;

3. *Recommends* that Member States adopt or strengthen the necessary protective legislation with regard to their own heritage and that of other peoples;

4. *Requests* Member States to study the possibility of including in permits for excavations a clause requiring archaeologists and palaeontologists to provide the national authorities with photographic documentation of each object brought to light during the excavations immediately after its discovery;

5. *Invites* Member States to continue drawing up, in co-operation with the United Nations Educational, Scientific and Cultural Organization, systematic inventories of cultural property existing in their territory and of their cultural property abroad;

6. *Also recommends* that Member States should ensure that inventories of museum collections include not only the items on display but also those in storage, and that they comprise all necessary documentation, particularly photographs of each item;

7. *Also invites* Member States engaged in seeking the recovery of cultural and artistic treasures from the seabed, in accordance with international law, to facilitate by mutually acceptable conditions the participation of States having a historical and cultural link with those treasures;

8. *Appeals* to Member States to co-operate closely with the Intergovernmental Committee for Promoting the Return of Cultural Property to Its Countries of Origin or Its Restitution in Case of Illicit Appropriation and to conclude bilateral agreements for this purpose;

9. *Also appeals* to Member States to encourage the mass information media and educational and cultural institutions to strive to arouse a greater and more general awareness with regard to the return or restitution of cultural property to its country of origin;

10. *Requests* States parties to the Convention on the Means of Prohibiting and Preventing the Illicit Import, Export and Transfer of Ownership of Cultural Property to keep the Secretary-General of the United Nations and the Director-General of the United Nations Educational, Scientific and Cultural Organization fully informed of the measures taken to ensure implementation of the Convention at the national level;

11. *Welcomes* the steady increase in the number of States parties to the Convention;

12. *Invites once again* those Member States that have not yet done so to sign and ratify the Convention;

13. *Requests* the Secretary-General, in co-operation with the Director-General of the United Nations Educational, Scientific and Cultural Organization, to submit to the General Assembly at its forty-sixth session a report on the implementation of the present resolution;

14. *Decides* to include in the provisional agenda of its forty-sixth session the item entitled "Return or restitution of cultural property to the countries of origin".

General Assembly resolution 44/18

6 November 1989   Meeting 45   139-0-16 (recorded vote)

32-nation draft (A/44/L.22 & Add.1); agenda item 20.
Sponsors: Angola, Bolivia, Burkina Faso, Burundi, Central African Republic, Chad, Colombia, Comoros, Congo, Costa Rica, Côte d'Ivoire, Ecuador, Egypt, Gabon, Ghana, Greece, Guatemala, Guinea-Bissau, Haiti, Libyan Arab Jamahiriya, Madagascar, Malawi, Mali, Mauritania, Mauritius, Mexico, Nepal, Niger, Peru, Rwanda, Yugoslavia, Zaire.

Recorded vote in Assembly as follows:

In favour: Afghanistan, Albania, Algeria, Angola, Antigua and Barbuda, Argentina, Australia, Bahamas, Bahrain, Bangladesh, Barbados, Belize, Benin, Bhutan, Bolivia, Botswana, Brazil, Brunei Darussalam, Burkina Faso, Burundi, Byelorussian SSR, Cameroon, Canada, Cape Verde, Central African Republic, Chad, Chile, China, Colombia, Comoros, Congo, Costa Rica, Côte d'Ivoire, Cuba, Cyprus, Czechoslovakia, Democratic Kampuchea, Democratic Yemen, Djibouti, Dominica, Dominican Republic, Ecuador, Egypt, El Salvador, Equatorial Guinea, Ethiopia, Fiji, Finland, Gabon, Gambia, German Democratic Republic, Ghana, Greece, Grenada, Guatemala, Guinea-Bissau, Guyana, Honduras, Hungary, Iceland, India, Indonesia, Iran, Iraq, Jamaica, Jordan, Kenya, Kuwait, Lao People's Democratic Republic, Lebanon, Lesotho, Liberia, Libyan Arab Jamahiriya, Madagascar, Malawi, Malaysia, Maldives, Mali, Malta, Mauritania, Mauritius, Mexico, Mongolia, Morocco, Mozambique, Myanmar, Nepal, New Zealand, Nicaragua, Niger, Nigeria, Norway, Oman, Pakistan, Panama, Papua New Guinea, Paraguay, Peru, Philippines, Poland, Qatar, Romania, Rwanda, Saint Lucia, Saint Vincent and the Grenadines, Samoa, Sao Tome and Principe, Saudi Arabia, Senegal, Seychelles, Sierra Leone, Singapore, Solomon Islands, Somalia, Sri Lanka, Sudan, Suriname, Swaziland, Syrian Arab Republic, Thailand, Togo, Trinidad and Tobago, Tunisia, Turkey, Uganda, Ukrainian SSR, USSR, United Arab Emirates, United Republic of Tanzania, Uruguay, Vanuatu, Venezuela, Viet Nam, Yemen, Yugoslavia, Zaire, Zambia, Zimbabwe.

Against: None.

Abstaining: Austria, Belgium, Denmark, France, Germany, Federal Republic of, Ireland, Israel, Italy, Japan, Luxembourg, Netherlands, Portugal, Spain, Sweden, United Kingdom, United States.

Speaking in explanation of its vote, the United Kingdom said it could not accept the principle that cultural property legitimately acquired should be returned to the country of origin; however, it condemned illicit trafficking in such property and was willing to discuss specific cultural property questions bilaterally with other Governments. The second paragraph of the resolution ran counter to its belief that the great international collections of art constituted a unique resource for the benefit of both the public and the international academic community, the United Kingdom said.

REFERENCES

[1]*1989 Report on the World Social Situation* (ST/ESA/213), Sales No. E.89.IV.1. [2]YUN 1985, p. 723, GA res. 40/100, 13 Dec. 1985. [3]YUN 1987, p. 607, ESC res. 1987/52, 28 May 1987. [4]*Ibid.*, p. 609, ESC res. 1987/40, 28 May 1987. [5]*Ibid.*, p. 618, ESC res. 1987/46, 28 May 1987. [6]*Ibid.*, p. 609, ESC res. 1987/39, 28 May 1987. [7]E/1989/25. [8]E/CN.5/1989/2. [9]E/1989/25 (res. 31/1). [10]YUN 1986, p. 609, GA res. 41/142, 4 Dec. 1986. [11]A/44/116-E/1989/15 & Corr.1 & Add.1. [12]YUN 1969, p. 433, GA res. 2542(XXIV), 11 Dec. 1969. [13]YUN 1987, p. 610, GA res. 42/48, 30 Nov. 1987. [14]*Ibid.*, p. 378, GA res. 42/193, 11 Dec. 1987. [15]E/1989/25 (dec. 31/103). [16]YUN 1987, p. 612, GA res. 42/50, 30 Nov. 1987. [17]A/44/86-E/1989/14. [18]YUN 1987, p. 616. [19]*Ibid.*, p. 615, ESC res. 1987/48, 28 May 1987. [20]E/CN.5/1989/3. [21]A/44/343. [22]YUN 1987, p. 616, GA res. 42/125, 7 Dec. 1987. [23]*Ibid.*, p. 620, ESC res. 1987/47, 28 May 1987. [24]A/44/79-E/1989/8. [25]E/CN.5/1989/4. [26]YUN 1988, p. 607, GA res. 43/135, 8 Dec. 1988. [27]A/44/407. [28]E/CN.5/1989/5. [29]YUN 1985, p. 734, ESC res. 1985/24, 29 May 1985. [30]E/1989/25 (dec. 31/104). [31]YUN 1988, p. 608, ESC res. 1988/47, 27 May 1988. [32]E/CN.5/1989/11. [33]E/1989/25 (res. 31/3). [34]E/CN.5/1989/8. [35]E/1989/25 (dec. 31/105). [36]YUN 1988, p. 609. [37]E/1989/25 (res. 31/2). [38]E/CN.5/1989/9 & Corr.1. [39]E/1989/25 (dec. 31/102). [40]YUN 1985, p. 738. [41]YUN 1988, p. 610, GA res. 43/99, 8 Dec. 1988. [42]A/44/400. [43]YUN 1988, p. 612, ESC res. 1988/44, 27 May 1988. [44]E/1989/47. [45]YUN 1988, p. 613. [46]E/AC.57/1990/6. [47]E/1989/NGO/5. [48]YUN 1986, p. 621. [49]*Ibid.*, p. 624, GA res. 41/187, 8 Dec. 1986. [50]A/44/284-E/1989/109. [51]YUN 1987, p. 629, GA res. 42/7, 22 Oct. 1987. [52]A/44/485. [53]YUN 1987, p. 628.

Chapter XIII

Women

In 1989, the United Nations continued to take steps to implement the Nairobi Forward-looking Strategies for the Advancement of Women, adopted in 1985 to overcome continuing obstacles to the goals and objectives of the United Nations Decade for Women (1976-1985). Key activities centred around preparations for the review and appraisal of progress in implementing the Forward-looking Strategies, to be undertaken by the Commission on the Status of Women in 1990. The Commission held its thirty-third session in Vienna from 29 March to 7 April 1989.

The first regular update of the *World Survey on the Role of Women in Development* was submitted in 1989 to the forty-fourth session of the General Assembly. The *Survey*, primarily a study of women's economic role in development, suggested that three issues were of particular relevance for future analyses: women's participation in economic decision-making, the relationship between women's economic role and the support functions provided in the family, and women's involvement in crucial issues related to the environment. The 1989 *Survey*, compiled by the Division for the Advancement of Women of the Centre for Social Development and Humanitarian Affairs, updated information contained in the original *Survey* published in 1985.

The General Assembly in 1989 acted to improve the situation of rural women based on a comprehensive report by the Secretary-General and on the results of an International Seminar on Women and Rural Development, convened in May. In addition, the Assembly addressed matters concerning elderly women, the integration of women into development, and the status of various bodies and instruments to advance the status of women and ensure their equality. The Assembly also took action to improve the status of women in the UN Secretariat.

The Economic and Social Council, acting on the recommendations of the Commission on the Status of Women, decided to increase the membership of the Commission, beginning in 1990, and to convene in 1991 a high-level interregional consultation on women in public life. The Council considered questions relating to women and development, including the impact of AIDS and women living in absolute poverty, as well as the situations of women in Latin America and the Caribbean, and in Central America, Palestinian women and those living under *apartheid*.

The Committee on the Elimination of Discrimination against Women considered reports of States parties to the 1979 Convention on the Elimination of All Forms of Discrimination against Women. On 18 December, the tenth anniversary of the treaty's adoption by the General Assembly, Chile became the one hundredth country to ratify the Convention.

Advancement of women

Implementation of the Nairobi Strategies

In response to a 1988 request of the General Assembly,[1] the Secretary-General in October submitted a report[2] on implementation of the Nairobi Forward-looking Strategies for the Advancement of Women, adopted in 1985 by the World Conference to Review and Appraise the Achievements of the United Nations Decade for Women.[3] The report provided an overview of actions taken by organizations of the UN system to implement the Strategies, including a comprehensive reporting system for its monitoring, review and appraisal and contributions to the work of the Commission on the Status of Women. It described activities related to the situation of disabled women; new targets for the percentage of women in UN Professional and decision-making positions; more effective public information programmes related to the advancement of women; and plans for a consultation on women in public life and a seminar on women and rural development (see below). The report also detailed issues related to the three priority themes to be considered by the Commission at its 1990 session: equality (closing the gap between discrimination in law and discrimination in practice); development (integrating women fully into the development process and involving them in efforts to protect the environment as part of development); and peace (ensuring women's participation in politics and decision-making).

In March, pursuant to the Forward-looking Strategies and a 1988 request of the Economic and Social Council,[4] the Secretary-General reported on statistical indicators for monitoring implementation of the Strategies.[5] The report provided basic indicators on the situation of women in 178 countries from the *Compendium of Statistics and Indicators on the Situation of Women—1986.*[6] The indicators covered by the report related to population, households and families; women in public affairs; women and crime and justice; economic activity, agriculture and national product; women and education; and health, water, sanitation and housing.

GENERAL ASSEMBLY ACTION

On 8 December, on the recommendation of the Third (Social, Humanitarian and Cultural) Committee, the General Assembly adopted **resolution 44/77** without vote.

Implementation of the Nairobi Forward-looking Strategies for the Advancement of Women

The General Assembly,

Recalling all its relevant resolutions, in particular resolutions 40/108 of 13 December 1985, 42/62 of 30 November 1987 and 43/101 of 8 December 1988, in which, *inter alia,* it endorsed and reaffirmed the importance of the Nairobi Forward-looking Strategies for the Advancement of Women for the period up to the year 2000 and set out measures for their immediate implementation and for the overall achievement of the interrelated goals and objectives of the United Nations Decade for Women: Equality, Development and Peace,

Taking into consideration the resolutions adopted by the Economic and Social Council on issues relating to women since its resolution 1987/18 of 26 May 1987,

Reaffirming its resolution 40/30 of 29 November 1985, in which it emphasized that the elderly must be considered an important and necessary element in the development process at all levels within a given society, and that, consequently, elderly women should be considered contributors to as well as beneficiaries of development,

Reaffirming also its determination to encourage the full participation of women in economic, social, cultural, civil and political affairs and to promote development, co-operation and international peace,

Conscious of the important and constructive contribution to the improvement of the status of women made by the Commission on the Status of Women, the specialized agencies, the regional commissions and other organizations and bodies of the United Nations system and non-governmental organizations concerned,

Emphasizing once again the priority of the implementation, monitoring, review and appraisal of the Forward-looking Strategies,

Recognizing the advancement of women as one of the priorities of the Organization for the biennium 1990-1991,

Recalling that the Commission will hold in 1990 a session of extended duration to review and appraise progress in the implementation of the Forward-looking Strategies,

1. *Takes note* of the report of the Secretary-General;

2. *Reaffirms* the importance of resolutions 1, 2 and 4 adopted by the Commission on the Status of Women at its special session in 1987, in particular its recommendation that the implementation of the Forward-looking Strategies and the status of women in general should be incorporated as one of the priorities in the introduc-

tion to the medium-term plan of the Organization for the period 1992-1997;

3. *Reaffirms* the urgent need for the Forward-looking Strategies to be translated immediately into concrete action by Governments, within the framework of overall national priorities, as well as by the organizations and bodies of the United Nations system, the specialized agencies and intergovernmental and non-governmental organizations;

4. *Calls upon* Member States to give priority to policies and programmes relating to the subtheme "Employment, Health and Education", in particular to literacy, for the empowerment of women, especially those in the rural areas, to meet their own needs through self-reliance and the mobilization of indigenous resources, as well as to issues relating to the role of women in economic and political decision-making, population, the environment and information;

5. *Reaffirms* the central role of the Commission in matters related to the advancement of women, and calls upon it to promote the implementation of the Forward-looking Strategies to the year 2000 based on the goals of the United Nations Decade for Women: Equality, Development and Peace and the subtheme "Employment, Health and Education", and urges all organizations of the United Nations system to co-operate effectively with the Commission in this task;

6. *Notes* the preparations for the session of the Commission in 1990 to review and appraise progress in the implementation of the Forward-looking Strategies;

7. *Requests* the Commission during its session in 1990 to consider the role of women in and their contribution to development so as to ensure adequate attention to issues concerning women in the process of preparing for the special session of the General Assembly devoted to international economic co-operation, in particular to the revitalization of economic growth and development of the developing countries and the international development strategy for the fourth United Nations development decade;

8. *Also requests* the Commission to consider at its session in 1990 the question of holding in 1995 a world conference on women, at the lowest possible cost, and to report thereon to the General Assembly at its forty-fifth session;

9. *Requests* the relevant United Nations bodies to continue to provide action-oriented input when reporting to the Commission on the priority themes;

10. *Emphasizes,* in the framework of the Forward-looking Strategies, the importance of the total integration of women in the development process, bearing in mind the specific and urgent needs of the developing countries, and calls upon Member States to establish specific targets at each level in order to increase the participation of women in professional, management and decision-making positions in their countries;

11. *Also emphasizes* the need to give urgent attention to redressing socio-economic inequities at the national and international levels as a necessary step towards the full realization of the goals and objectives of the Forward-looking Strategies;

12. *Urges* that particular attention be given by the United Nations and Governments to the situation of disabled women and that Governments take steps to ensure the equalization of opportunities for these women in the economic, social and political fields;

13. *Endorses* the convening in 1991 of a high-level interregional consultation on women in public life, to be financed within existing resources and from voluntary and other contributions;

14. *Takes note with interest* of the conclusions and recommendations of the International Seminar on Women and Rural Development: Programmes and Projects, held at Vienna from 22 to 26 May 1989;

15. *Requests* the Secretary-General, in formulating the system-wide medium-term plan for the advancement of women for the period 1996-2001, and in integrating the Forward-looking Strategies into activities mandated by the General Assembly, to pay particular attention to the strengthening of national machineries for the advancement of women and to specific sectoral themes that cut across the three objectives, equality, development and peace, and include, in particular, literacy, education, health, population, the environment and the full participation of women in decision-making;

16. *Also requests* the Secretary-General to continue updating the *World Survey on the Role of Women in Development*, bearing in mind its importance, placing particular emphasis on the adverse impact of the difficult economic situation affecting the majority of developing countries, in particular on the condition of women, and giving special attention to worsening conditions for the incorporation of women into the labour force as well as to the impact of reduced expenditures for social services on women's opportunities for education, health and child care, and to submit a preliminary version of the updated *World Survey on the Role of Women in Development* to the Economic and Social Council, through the Commission, in 1993 and a final version in 1994;

17. *Requests* Governments, when presenting candidatures for vacancies in the Secretariat, in particular at the decision-making level, to give priority to women's candidatures when the required qualifications exist, and requests the Secretary-General in reviewing these candidatures to give special consideration to candidates from underrepresented and unrepresented countries;

18. *Once again calls upon* the Secretary-General and the executive heads of the specialized agencies and other United Nations bodies to establish five-year targets at each level for the percentage of women in Professional and decision-making positions, taking into account the principle of equitable geographical distribution, in order that a definite upward trend in the implementation of General Assembly resolution 41/206 D of 11 December 1986 may be registered with regard to the number of Professional and decision-making positions held by women by 1990, and to set additional targets every five years;

19. *Requests* the Secretary-General to invite Governments, organizations of the United Nations system, including the regional commissions and the specialized agencies, and intergovernmental and non-governmental organizations to report periodically to the Economic and Social Council, through the Commission, on activities undertaken at all levels to implement the Forward-looking Strategies;

20. *Also requests* the Secretary-General to continue to provide for the existing weekly radio programmes on women in the regular budget of the United Nations, making adequate provisions for broadcasts in different languages, and to develop the focal point for issues relating to women in the Department of Public Information

of the Secretariat, which, in concert with the Centre for Social Development and Humanitarian Affairs of the Secretariat, should provide a more effective public information programme relating to the advancement of women;

21. *Further requests* the Secretary-General to include in his report on the implementation of the Forward-looking Strategies, to be submitted to the General Assembly at its forty-fifth session, an assessment of recent developments that are relevant to the priority themes to be considered at the subsequent session of the Commission and to transmit to the Commission a summary of relevant views expressed by delegations during the debate in the Assembly;

22. *Requests* the Secretary-General to report to the General Assembly at its forty-fifth session on measures taken to implement the present resolution;

23. *Decides* to consider these questions further at its forty-fifth session under the item entitled ''Forward-looking Strategies for the advancement of women to the year 2000''.

General Assembly resolution 44/77

8 December 1989   Meeting 78   Adopted without vote

Approved by Third Committee (A/44/803 & Corr.1) without vote, 20 November (meeting 49); draft by Malaysia, for Group of 77 (A/C.3/44/L.30), orally revised; agenda item 104 (a).
Meeting numbers. GA 44th session: 3rd Committee 21-28, 36, 49; plenary 78.

Monitoring, review and appraisal

In February 1989, the Secretary-General submitted a note[7] regarding the convening of a world conference to review and appraise progress in the implementation of the Forward-looking Strategies. He pointed out that, because of differences in composition, level of participation and public visibility, regular sessions of the Commission on the Status of Women might not be as effective a forum for review and appraisal as the three world conferences convened by the United Nations in 1975,[8] 1980[9] and 1985.[3] One matter of concern was the lack of response by Member States to his request for information on the implementation of the Strategies, as requested by the Economic and Social Council in 1988.[4] By 31 January 1989, only 16 Member States had replied, whereas for the 1985 Nairobi Conference information had been received from 127 Member States. The Secretary-General further noted that a number of delegations, in statements to the General Assembly, had suggested that 1995 would be an appropriate date for a new world conference, in line with the schedule of review and appraisal already adopted.

1990 Commission session

In 1988, the Economic and Social Council had decided[10] to extend the duration of the thirty-fourth (1990) session of the Commission on the Status of Women to 10 days, so that the Commission could review and appraise progress made by Governments, international organizations and non-governmental organizations (NGOs) in implementing the Forward-looking Strategies. Pursuant to that decision, the Secretary-General in February 1989 submitted a note[11] describing preparations for the 1990 review, including regional preparatory meetings, conference servicing preparations and consolidated views of NGOs in consultative status with the Council on their contribution to the 1990 session.

ECONOMIC AND SOCIAL COUNCIL ACTION

On 24 May, the Economic and Social Council, on the recommendation of its Second (Social) Committee, adopted without vote **resolution 1989/32**.

Preparations for the session of the Commission on the Status of Women in 1990 to review and appraise progress in the implementation of the Nairobi Forward-looking Strategies for the Advancement of Women

The Economic and Social Council,

Recalling its resolution 1988/19 of 26 May 1988, in which it decided to extend the duration of the thirty-fourth session of the Commission on the Status of Women, to be held in 1990, in order that the Commission might review and appraise progress made in the implementation of the Nairobi Forward-looking Strategies for the Advancement of Women,

Concerned about the urgent need to implement the above-mentioned resolution, taking into account the provisional agenda outlined in the annex to the resolution,

Emphasizing the importance of a successful review and appraisal in order to increase the pace of implementation of the Nairobi Forward-looking Strategies,

1. *Decides* that a comprehensive report on the progress achieved and obstacles encountered in implementing the Nairobi Forward-looking Strategies for the Advancement of Women in the first five years should be submitted to the Commission on the Status of Women at its extended session in 1990;

2. *Further decides* that draft conclusions and recommendations arising from the review and appraisal should also be submitted and that they should include measures to overcome the obstacles that should be addressed immediately if the pace of implementation of the Nairobi Forward-looking Strategies is to be increased;

3. *Recommends* that the Secretary-General, in order to obtain guidance in the formulation of draft conclusions and recommendations, make available information on the preliminary results of the review and appraisal, which will ultimately be included in the comprehensive report, to an open-ended group of Member States meeting on an informal basis in New York during the forty-fourth session of the General Assembly at the time of the debate on the advancement of women;

4. *Requests* the Secretary-General, in preparing the comprehensive report and draft conclusions and recommendations, to use the documents listed in the annex to Council resolution 1988/22 of 26 May 1988, especially the first regular update of the *World Survey on the Role of Women in Development;*

5. *Urges* the Secretary-General to contact national machineries for the advancement of women that have not yet responded to the questionnaire and exhort them to do so immediately, in order to obtain representative responses to the questionnaire and, if possible, to arrange for diagnostic missions to be sent on request to selected countries to provide assistance in the preparation of responses;

6. *Requests* the Commission on the Status of Women to consider the documentation prepared by the Secretary-General in plenary meeting and to convene a committee of the whole to provide the final text of the recommendations.

Economic and Social Council resolution 1989/32

24 May 1989   Meeting 15   Adopted without vote

Approved by Second Committee (E/1989/90) without vote, 16 May (meeting 16); draft by Commission on women (E/1989/27/Rev.1); agenda item 10.

Programme planning

In March 1989, pursuant to a 1988 request of the Economic and Social Council,[12] the Secretary-General reported[13] on the future of the Trust Fund for the Preparatory Activities for the 1985 World Conference to Review and Appraise the Achievements of the UN Decade for Women. In 1988,[12] the Council had approved continuation of the Fund through the biennium 1988-1989 for the monitoring and review and appraisal of the Nairobi Forward-looking Strategies. The Secretary-General asserted that long-term extra-budgetary financing was essential for full programme delivery of legislative mandates and suggested that a possible long-term arrangement should be explored with the UN Development Fund for Women. In the mean time, the Trust Fund should be continued to the end of the 1990-1991 biennium.

In April, the Commission on the Status of Women recommended[14] that the Secretary-General explore ways of supplementing the information contained in his overall report on the programme performance of the United Nations with subprogramme-specific information on activities related to the advancement of women, including the following elements: a qualitative assessment of output produced; a quantitative scale differentiating output by scope and scale; and a correlation between output achieved and original objectives, as set out in the biennial programmes of work, medium-term plans and ultimately the Nairobi Forward-looking Strategies. The Commission endorsed the proposed work programme of the Division for the Advancement of Women for the biennium 1990-1991.[15]

ECONOMIC AND SOCIAL COUNCIL ACTION

On 24 May, on the recommendation of its Second Committee, the Economic and Social Council adopted **resolution 1989/30** without vote.

Programme planning and activities to advance the status of women

The Economic and Social Council,

Reaffirming the high priority that Member States attach to activities to advance the status of women and the important role played by the Commission on the Status of Women in achieving that objective,

Stressing the need to ensure that, in the allocation of budgetary resources, activities for the advancement of women do not suffer disproportionately from the impact of restructuring and retrenchment measures,

Taking note of the reports of the Secretary-General concerning programme planning matters,

Recalling previous resolutions on programme planning and activities to advance the status of women, including resolution 32/3 of 23 March 1988 of the Commission on the Status of Women, and, in particular, Council resolution 1988/18 of 26 May 1988,

Concerned that not all elements of the recommendations contained in Council resolution 1988/18 have been fully implemented, particularly those contained in section I, paragraph 1, and section II, paragraph 1,

Stressing that in subsuming the programme on the advancement of women under a major programme entitled "International co-operation for social development" of the proposed medium-term plan for the period 1992-1997, women's issues should not be limited to the rubric of social issues,

1. *Welcomes* the decision of the Secretary-General to include a separate programme on the advancement of women in his draft proposal for the medium-term plan for the period 1992-1997, as recommended by the Economic and Social Council in its resolution 1988/18 and by the Commission on the Status of Women in its resolution 32/3;

2. *Decides* that the inclusion of paragraph 65 in the draft introduction to the medium-term plan beginning 1992 is not an adequate response to the recommendation contained in Council resolution 1988/18, section I, paragraph 1;

3. *Reiterates* that the implementation of the Nairobi Forward-looking Strategies for the Advancement of Women and the status of women in general should be identified as a global priority in the introduction to the medium-term plan;

4. *Urges* the Secretary-General to ensure that women's issues are not marginalized under the rubric of social issues and that they are reflected in particular in the economic programmes of the medium-term plan, as well as in other programmes;

5. *Endorses* the view expressed by the Secretary-General that the proposed subprogramme entitled "Monitoring, review and appraisal of the implementation of the Nairobi Forward-looking Strategies" should be given high priority, and urges that the highest priority be accorded to addressing the fundamental needs of women in developing countries, particularly in such areas as literacy, education, employment, health and population, with a view to ensuring their full integration in the development process and full participation in decision-making;

6. *Decides* that the proposed subprogramme entitled "Development" should be reoriented to focus on the fundamental needs of women in developing countries, particularly the least developed countries;

7. *Reaffirms* the decision contained in its resolution 1988/18, section II, paragraph 1, that the proposed programme budget for the biennium 1990-1991 and subsequent programme budgets should provide for full funding from the regular budget for the implementation of all aspects of legislative mandates for the advancement of women;

8. *Decides* that the Trust Fund for the Preparatory Activities for the 1985 World Conference to Review and Appraise the Achievements of the United Nations Decade for Women, established by the Secretary-General pursuant to Council decision 1983/132 of 26 May 1983, should be continued for the biennium 1990-1991 under the terms of reference set out in Council resolution 1988/18, section II, paragraph 2, as indicated in the proposed programme of work for the Division for the Advancement of Women of the Centre for Social Development and Humanitarian Affairs of the Secretariat for the biennium 1990-1991;

9. *Urges* the Secretary-General, in carrying out this decision, to improve collaboration with the specialized agencies and the United Nations Development Fund for Women in consultation with their respective governing bodies, as required;

10. *Requests* the Secretary-General to submit a report on the future of the Trust Fund to the Commission on the Status of Women at its thirty-fifth session.

Economic and Social Council resolution 1989/30

24 May 1989   Meeting 15   Adopted without vote

Approved by Second Committee (E/1989/90) without vote, 16 May (meeting 16); draft by Commission on women (E/1989/27/Rev.1); agenda item 10.

System-wide co-ordination

In March, in accordance with a 1988 Council request,[16] the Secretary-General proposed a timetable for the preparation of a system-wide medium-term plan for the advancement of women for 1996-2001,[17] which would be directed towards the objectives of equality, development and peace. He proposed submission of the proposed plan to the Council in 1993, with a preliminary report outlining the proposed framework of the plan to be submitted in 1992 through the Commission on the Status of Women and the Committee for Programme and Co-ordination. The proposed timetable would make it possible to take into account in the system-wide plan the views and inputs of governing bodies of the other organizations of the UN system.

The thirteenth *ad hoc* inter-agency meeting on women was held in Vienna on 10 April[18] to consider activities by UN organizations related to implementation of the Forward-looking Strategies and to discuss the system-wide medium-term plan for women and development (see below). Recommendations were adopted on implementation of the Strategies, which were brought to the attention of the Administrative Committee on Co-ordination (ACC). In October, ACC adopted a statement[19] on the review and appraisal of the Strategies, in which the organizations of the UN system recommitted themselves to the full implementation of their responsibilities under the Strategies: in programmes, in policies, in institutional arrangements and in personnel practices.

ECONOMIC AND SOCIAL COUNCIL ACTION

On 24 May 1989, by **decision 1989/126**, the Economic and Social Council deferred action until its second regular session of 1989 on a draft resolution entitled "System-wide co-ordination of activities to advance the status of women and to integrate women into development", recommended by the Commission on the Status of Women.[20]

On 27 July, the Council, on a recommendation of its First (Economic) Committee, adopted **resolution 1989/105** without vote.

System-wide co-ordination of activities to advance the status of women and to integrate women in development

The Economic and Social Council,

Reaffirming its essential role in reviewing and co-ordinating all activities of the United Nations system relevant to women's issues,

Recalling all relevant resolutions on co-ordination matters pertaining to the status of women, particularly Economic and Social Council resolutions 1985/46 of 31 May 1985, 1986/71 of 23 July 1986, 1987/65 of 8 July 1987, 1987/86 of 8 July 1987, 1988/22 of 26 May 1988, 1988/59 of 27 July 1988 and 1988/60 of 27 July 1988 and decision 1987/182 of 8 July 1987,

Noting, in particular, the report of the Administrative Committee on Co-ordination on plans and programmes of the organizations of the United Nations system to implement the system-wide medium-term plan for women and development for the period 1990-1995, the report of the Secretary-General on the preparation of a system-wide medium-term plan for the advancement of women for the period 1996-2001 and the report of the Secretary-General on the scope and general approach of the cross-organizational programme analysis on the activities of the United Nations system related to the advancement of women,

Recalling the system-wide medium-term plan for women and development for the period 1990-1995, accepted by the Economic and Social Council in resolution 1987/86,

Considering the central role of the Commission on the Status of Women in promoting international co-operation to integrate women fully in economic development programmes and activities,

Recalling General Assembly resolutions 42/193 of 11 December 1987 and 43/182 of 20 December 1988 on the preparation of an international development strategy for the fourth United Nations development decade,

1. *Decides* to continue to include the question of the system-wide co-ordination of activities to advance the status of women and to integrate women in development in its programme of work under the item on co-ordination in order to monitor the implementation of the system-wide medium-term plan for women and development in the programmes and programme budgets of the organizations of the United Nations system;

2. *Requests* the Secretary-General, in his capacity as Chairman of the Administrative Committee on Co-ordination, to report to the Committee for Programme and Co-ordination and the Economic and Social Council, biennially in odd-numbered years beginning in 1991, on the extent to which the system-wide medium-term plan is incorporated into the programmes and programme budgets of the organizations of the United Nations system, using as a baseline indicator the cross-organizational programme analysis of the activities of the United Nations system for the advancement of women;

3. *Requests* the Secretary-General to integrate the parts of the reports of the Committee for Programme and Co-ordination and the Council on the programme budget aspects of the implementation of the system-wide medium-term plan into his biennial report on monitoring the progress made by the organizations of the United Nations system in implementing the Nairobi Forward-looking Strategies for the Advancement of Women, prepared under Council resolution 1988/22;

4. *Recommends* that all substantive reporting to the Commission on the Status of Women on the implementation of the system-wide medium-term plan be consolidated in a concise, detailed and analytical way in the biennial report on monitoring the progress made by the organizations of the United Nations system;

5. *Requests* the Secretary-General, to the extent possible, to subsume under the comprehensive reporting system established by Council resolution 1988/22 the existing reporting obligations to the Commission on the Status of Women not otherwise provided for in the present resolution regarding the implementation of the Forward-looking Strategies;

6. *Requests* the Secretary-General to make available to the Commission on the Status of Women at its thirty-fourth session documents related to the cross-organizational programme analysis of the activities of the United Nations system for the advancement of women, including the analysis itself and the relevant portions of the report of the Committee for Programme and Co-ordination on the work of its twenty-ninth session, as well as the report of the Secretary-General on the effective mobilization and integration of women in development and the report of the Secretary-General to the General Assembly on the implementation of the Nairobi Forward-looking Strategies for the Advancement of Women;

7. *Urges* all United Nations bodies, including the regional commissions, and the specialized agencies that have not yet done so to adopt and implement comprehensive policies for the advancement of women, on the basis of the system-wide medium-term plan for women and development, and to incorporate them in their organization's medium-term plans, statements of objectives, programmes and other major policy statements;

8. *Endorses* the timetable proposed by the Secretary-General for the preparation of a system-wide medium-term plan for the advancement of women for the period 1996-2001;

9. *Requests* the Secretary-General, in formulating the system-wide medium-term plan for the advancement of women for the period 1996-2001, to pay particular attention to the strengthening of national machinery for the advancement of women and to specific sectoral themes that cut across the three objectives—equality,

development and peace—of the Forward-looking Strategies, such as literacy, education, population, health and the full participation of women in decision-making;

10. *Requests* the Secretary-General to continue to take the necessary measures to ensure that specific action is taken to integrate the Forward-looking Strategies into related activities mandated by the General Assembly, in particular those mandated in the following resolutions: 42/104 of 7 December 1987 on the International Literacy Year, 42/186 of 11 December 1987 on the Environmental Perspective to the Year 2000 and Beyond, 42/193 of 11 December 1987 and 43/182 of 20 December 1988 on the preparation of an international development strategy for the fourth United Nations development decade, 43/15 of 27 October 1988 on the prevention and control of acquired immunodeficiency syndrome (AIDS) and 43/181 of 20 December 1988 on the Global Strategy for Shelter to the Year 2000;

11. *Requests* the *Ad Hoc* Committee of the Whole for the Preparation of the International Development Strategy for the Fourth United Nations Development Decade to attach high priority to issues related to the full integration of women in the development process, particularly by focusing on such prerequisites as literacy, education, employment, child care, population, health and participation in decision-making, and to stress the importance of the improvement of the situation of women for the fulfilment of such prerequisites.

Economic and Social Council resolution 1989/105

27 July 1989   Meeting 36   Adopted without vote

Approved by First Committee (E/1989/141) without vote, 21 July (meeting 25); draft by Commission on women (E/1989/27/Rev.1), orally amended by Canada; agenda item 7 *(i)*.

Research and Training Institute for the Advancement of Women

The Board of Trustees of the International Research and Training Institute for the Advancement of Women (INSTRAW) held its ninth session at the Institute's headquarters in Santo Domingo, Dominican Republic, from 20 to 24 February 1989.[21] Among the decisions brought to the attention of the Economic and Social Council was one by which the Board endorsed the Institute's medium-term plan for the period 1990-1995, taking into account the system-wide medium-term plan for women and development covering the same period. The main objectives of the INSTRAW plan aimed at strengthening the national capability of developing countries in the area of research, training and information for the advancement of women, and concentrated on network-building for co-operation with INSTRAW.

The Board agreed that INSTRAW mandates in research, training and information on women and development had been further strengthened during 1988. It recommended that the Institute explore the possibility of formulating concrete programmes on communication support for women and development activities in co-operation with other UN bodies and organizations.

After examining, for the first time, the publication policy of INSTRAW, the Board endorsed the different types of its publications and recommended continuation of the policy related to their content and mode of production.

The Board reviewed the report of the first consultative meeting of the regional commissions (Santo Domingo, 16-17 February) and welcomed their suggestions for possible future long-term co-operation with INSTRAW. It also considered ways to strengthen co-operation with the regional commissions in terms of network-building and strengthening of focal points, which it said continued to be crucial to the Institute's mode of operation. Three new focal points for co-operation with INSTRAW at the national level were approved.

The Board also expressed satisfaction with the holding in 1988 of an international consultative meeting on communications for women in development.[22] The meeting's guidelines could provide the basis for formulating concrete programmes on communication support for women and development activities in co-operation with UN bodies and agencies.

The Board invited the regional commissions, INSTRAW focal points, NGOs and others to participate in celebrating the tenth anniversary of INSTRAW in 1990 at the regional and national levels.

ECONOMIC AND SOCIAL COUNCIL ACTION

On 24 May, on the recommendation of its Second Committee, the Economic and Social Council adopted **resolution 1989/43** without vote.

International Research and Training Institute for the Advancement of Women

The Economic and Social Council,

Recalling its resolution 1988/31 of 26 May 1988,

Having considered the report of the Board of Trustees of the International Research and Training Institute for the Advancement of Women on its ninth session,

Convinced of the importance of research, training and information, the three main functions of the Institute, in questions relating to women and development, for bringing about mainstream developmental changes benefiting women and society,

Welcoming the fact that the Institute has intensified its training activities and is elaborating training methodologies, materials and programmes for defined target groups,

1. *Takes note with appreciation* of the report of the Board of Trustees of the International Research and Training Institute for the Advancement of Women on its ninth session and the decisions contained therein;

2. *Expresses its satisfaction* at the fact that networking, the mode of operation of the Institute, has been strengthened by such activities as the consultative meeting between the regional commissions and the Institute, which contributed to programme development;

3. *Recommends* that the Institute give priority to co-operation with the regional commissions, other United

Nations bodies and the specialized agencies in future programming of joint activities;

4. *Notes with interest* the International Consultative Meeting on Communications for Women in Development organized by the Institute in co-operation with other organizations of the United Nations system, and endorses the recommendation of the Board that the report of the meeting be circulated widely;

5. *Affirms* that the role of the Institute in the implementation of the system-wide medium-term plan for women and development, which places emphasis on analysis of the interrelationship of factors affecting women and development, is important for the implementation of the Nairobi Forward-looking Strategies for the Advancement of Women;

6. *Notes* that in 1990 the Institute will observe the tenth anniversary of its establishment;

7. *Renews its appeal* to Governments, intergovernmental and non-governmental organizations and other potential donors to contribute, to the extent possible, to the United Nations Trust Fund for the International Research and Training Institute for the Advancement of Women;

8. *Expresses its appreciation* to those Governments and organizations that have contributed to the Trust Fund, thus ensuring the continuity of research, training and information programmes crucial for improved methodological approaches relating to women and development.

Economic and Social Council resolution 1989/43

24 May 1989   Meeting 15   Adopted without vote

Approved by Second Committee (E/1989/90) without vote, 17 May (meeting 19); 44-nation draft (E/1989/C.2/L.14); agenda item 10.

INSTRAW activities

In accordance with a General Assembly request of 1987,[23] the Secretary, in August 1989, transmitted a report on the activities of INSTRAW.[24] The report presented the major highlights and results of the INSTRAW programme of activities during the 1988-1989 biennium. It noted that, since the last report of INSTRAW to the Assembly in 1987,[25] the work of the Institute had expanded, with priority given to the launching of a long-term research programme on evaluation methodologies for women and development projects, intensifying training and strengthening the communication component of the programme. In the context of the medium-term plan for the period 1990-1995, which emphasized networking and co-operation with the UN system, INSTRAW had given particular attention to the strengthening of co-operation with the regional commissions and the experimental network of INSTRAW focal points established at the national level.

During the 1988-1989 biennium, INSTRAW launched a new long-term research programme related to monitoring and evaluation methodologies for programmes and projects on women and development, as mandated by the Economic and Social Council in 1987.[26] In July, INSTRAW organized a regional seminar on women in development at its headquarters in Santo Domingo.

The Institute expanded the scope of action of its long-term research programme on improving concepts and methods for data collection on women. Its training activities in statistics and indicators on women were intensified. In 1989, INSTRAW jointly organized with the Economic Commission for Europe the second meeting on statistics on women (Geneva, 14-16 November). One subregional training workshop (in Costa Rica for the Central American countries) and five more at the national level (in China, Ecuador, Greece, India and Senegal) were held during the year.

The Institute emphasized its public information component by producing material that would reach both the general public and the development community. Its newsletter, *INSTRAW News*, continued to be published biannually in English, French and Spanish.

In February, the Institute met with representatives of the five regional commissions to co-ordinate strategies within the system-wide medium-term plan for women and development for 1990-1995 (see below) and within the Institute's medium-term plan for the same period.

Voluntary contributions pledged to the INSTRAW Trust Fund increased from $488,457 in 1987 to $828,285 in 1989.

GENERAL ASSEMBLY ACTION

On 8 December, on the recommendation of the Third Committee, the General Assembly adopted **resolution 44/60** without vote.

International Research and Training Institute for the Advancement of Women

The General Assembly,

Recalling its resolution 42/65 of 30 November 1987 and taking note of Economic and Social Council resolution 1989/43 of 24 May 1989,

Taking note with satisfaction of the report of the International Research and Training Institute for the Advancement of Women on its activities,

Recognizing that research, training and information activities relating to women and development, the three main components of the programme of work of the Institute, have been further strengthened, thus reflecting the current trends with regard to mainstream developmental changes benefiting women and society,

Convinced that networking, the mode of operation of the Institute, has been consolidated by co-operative arrangements with organizations within and outside the United Nations system and that this could strengthen interaction between regions and countries with a view to integrating the participation and needs of women into mainstream development,

1. *Expresses its satisfaction* at the significance and scope of the activities of the International Research and Training Institute for the Advancement of Women and at the special importance attached to research, training, information, documentation and communication activities relating to women and development in order to contribute to the design of mainstream developmental policy;

2. *Notes with appreciation* that the Institute, in consultation with bodies and organizations of the United Nations system, has launched a new research programme for the elaboration of special methodologies for the monitoring and evaluation of programmes and projects for women, as requested in resolution 42/65;

3. *Requests* the Institute to continue its research on the contribution of women to development, including the work of women in the informal sector of the economy, and the elaboration of special methodologies for the monitoring and evaluation of programmes and projects for women, and to intensify its efforts to apply innovative training strategies with a view to strengthening national training capabilities, particularly in developing countries;

4. *Commends* the Institute for the priority that it has assigned to co-operation with the bodies and organizations of the United Nations system, and welcomes the ongoing consultations between the regional commissions and the Institute with a view to launching parallel activities relating to women and development;

5. *Notes* that in 1990 the Institute will observe the tenth anniversary of its establishment;

6. *Expresses its appreciation* to those Governments and organizations that have contributed to or supported the activities of the Institute, thus expanding the scope of its research, training and information programmes relating to women and development;

7. *Renews its invitation* to States as well as intergovernmental and non-governmental organizations to contribute to the United Nations Trust Fund for the International Research and Training Institute for the Advancement of Women, so as to ensure that the Institute has the necessary resources to continue its research, training and information programmes, which are still of vital importance for the elaboration of improved methodological criteria relating to women and development;

8. *Requests* the Secretary-General to submit to the General Assembly at its forty-sixth session a report on the activities of the Institute;

9. *Decides* to include in the provisional agenda of its forty-sixth session the item entitled "International Research and Training Institute for the Advancement of Women".

General Assembly resolution 44/60

8 December 1989   Meeting 78   Adopted without vote

Approved by Third Committee (A/44/801 & Corr.1) without vote, 20 November (meeting 49); 52-nation draft (A/C.3/44/L.25); agenda item 94.
Meeting numbers. GA 44th session: 3rd Committee 21-28, 36, 49; plenary 78.

REFERENCES

(1)YUN 1988, p. 615, GA res. 43/101, 8 Dec. 1988. (2)A/44/511. (3)YUN 1985, p. 937. (4)YUN 1988, p. 617, ESC res. 1988/22, 26 May 1988. (5)E/CN.6/1989/2. (6)*Compendium of Statistics and Indicators on the Situation of Women—1986*, Sales No. E/F.88.XVII.6. (7)E/CN.6/1989/9 & Corr.1. (8)YUN 1975, p. 645. (9)YUN 1980, p. 886. (10)YUN 1988, p. 619, ESC res. 1988/19, 26 May 1988. (11)E/CN.6/1989/8. (12)YUN 1988, p. 620, ESC res. 1988/18, 26 May 1988. (13)E/CN.6.1989/10. (14)E/1989/27/Rev.1 (res. 33/1). (15)E/CN.6/1989/CRP.1. (16)YUN 1988, p. 628, ESC res. 1988/59, 27 July 1988. (17)E/1989/9. (18)ACC/1989/PG/3. (19)ACC/1989/DEC/24-32 (dec. 1989/28). (20)E/1989/27/Rev.1. (21)E/1989/46. (22)YUN 1988, p. 624. (23)YUN 1987, p. 835, GA res. 42/65, 30 Nov. 1987. (24)A/44/416. (25)YUN 1987, p. 834. (26)*Ibid.*, p. 835, ESC res. 1987/25, 26 May 1987.

Women and development

As part of its consideration of the priority theme of development, the Commission on the Status of Women, at its March/April 1989 session, reviewed a January report of the Secretary-General[1] examining issues concerning education, eradication of illiteracy, employment, health and other social services in terms of their common function as social support measures, enabling women to contribute to, and benefit from, development. The report also examined the role of social support as a prerequisite for progress in education, employment and health.

According to the report, social, economic and demographic changes were weakening the family or household as the normal source of social support at a time when women were having to work outside the home and were therefore in greater need of such services. Steps needed to strengthen the structure of social support included greater sharing of domestic and family responsibilities by men and women, improved education and training, better attention to health and family planning, and adoption of legislation and programmes by Governments and NGOs covering child care, among other matters.

On the basis of the results of an Expert Group on Social Support Measures for the Advancement of Women, which met in Vienna in November 1988, wide-ranging recommendations were made as to steps that could and should be taken nationally and internationally to heighten the support given to women by the family, the community and society as a whole.

ECONOMIC AND SOCIAL COUNCIL ACTION

On 24 May, on the recommendation of its Second Committee, the Economic and Social Council adopted **resolution 1989/37** without vote.

Measures to facilitate the participation of women in development

The Economic and Social Council,

Recognizing that women must have education and training to enter the labour market, take part in it on an equal footing with men, and be able to exercise their rights and participate in political and social life,

Considering that women should be able to enter employment without having to sacrifice their right to equality or their reproductive function, and that they therefore require social support measures, especially child care,

Affirming the importance of women's access to health programmes, including nutrition and family planning, for promoting their advancement and equality,

Affirming also that only the advancement of women on an equal basis with men permits the strengthening and revitalization of the family,

Having considered the recommendations of the Expert Group on Social Support Measures for the Advancement of Women which met at Vienna, from 14 to 18 November 1988,

Taking note of the report of the Secretary-General,

1. *Endorses* the recommendations of the Expert Group on Social Support Measures for the Advancement of Women;

2. *Invites* Governments to give high priority to programmes to promote the participation of women in education, assuring them equal access to and the availability of literacy programmes;

3. *Urges* Governments to endeavour to meet the relevant provisions of the conventions of the International Labour Organisation, especially those relating to equal pay and working conditions, thus ensuring women's awareness of their rights in all sectors of the economy, both formal and informal;

4. *Invites* Governments, in co-operation with the World Health Organization and other agencies, to strive to achieve the goal of the World Health Organization of health for all, by ensuring that all women are provided with primary health care services and related information, and that women are involved in the design of these services and in decision-making;

5. *Recommends* the establishment of programmes of social support for working women, especially comprehensive child-care systems;

6. *Invites* Governments to design adequate policies to reduce the need for caring for disabled persons by providing them with opportunities to develop their potential and contribute to society and the family, and to pay particular attention to the special needs of women;

7. *Recommends* that the United Nations Educational, Scientific and Cultural Organization and other organizations that have mandates in education and training give, in their activities, especially those related to the International Literacy Year, proclaimed by the General Assembly in its resolution 42/104 of 7 December 1987, higher priority to women in programmes and campaigns intended to eliminate illiteracy in all countries, especially in developing countries;

8. *Recommends also* that the International Labour Organisation undertake campaigns to disseminate the conventions approved by Governments, especially those in which women's rights as workers are referred to, and promote the role of labour unions and employers in providing social support to working women;

9. *Requests* the Secretary-General, bearing in mind General Assembly resolution 43/98, paragraph 7, of 8 December 1988, to promote and support the establishment of strong national organizations of disabled persons and, on that basis, provide assistance in the formation of networks of disabled women and reinforce the movement for self-help by these women, making use of the appropriate non-governmental organizations;

10. *Urges* United Nations bodies, including the International Research and Training Institute for the Advancement of Women and the Statistical Office of the Secretariat, and intergovernmental and non-governmental organizations to continue their efforts to elaborate sufficient and adequate indicators on women in development, especially in terms of education, employment and health, and to improve data collection at all levels so as to enable realistic policy formulation;

11. *Calls on* Member States and organizations of the United Nations system, within the framework of the Nairobi Forward-looking Strategies for the Advancement of Women, to increase the participation of women in professional and decision-making positions;

12. *Recommends* that all plans, programmes and activities relating to the family should be considered by the Commission for Social Development and the Commission on the Status of Women in order to ensure harmonious co-ordination and effectiveness in achieving results;

13. *Requests* the Secretary-General to report on the implementation of the present resolution to the Commission on the Status of Women at its thirty-fourth session.

Economic and Social Council resolution 1989/37

24 May 1989   Meeting 15   Adopted without vote

Approved by Second Committee (E/1989/90) without vote, 16 May (meeting 16); draft by Commission on women (E/1989/27/Rev.1); agenda item 10.

Also on 24 May and on the recommendation of its Second Committee, the Council adopted **resolution 1989/41** by recorded vote.

Women and development

The Economic and Social Council,

Recalling its resolution 1987/24 of 26 May 1987, by which it endorsed the long-term programme of work of the Commission on the Status of Women,

Recognizing that developing countries are suffering the most severe economic and social crisis of recent decades and consequently a grave deterioration in their social situation, which has disproportionately affected women,

Considering, in particular, the severe effects of servicing external debt and the effects of ongoing structural adjustment programmes on the economies and economic development of the developing countries, which have led to a deterioration in the quality of life of large sections of the population, especially of women and children,

Emphasizing the vital importance of economic growth and development for the effective mobilization and integration of women in the economy,

Noting the link between education, employment and health, and also the negative impact that the lack of adequate social support measures has on the integration of women in development,

Taking note of the report of the Secretary-General entitled "Women and education, eradication of illiteracy, employment, health and social services, including population issues and child care: the need for social support measures",

1. *Urges* Governments to accord higher priority to programmes to promote the participation of women in the labour force and their access to education, health and social services, and to allow women access to decision-making on the design and implementation of such programmes;

2. *Requests* the Secretary-General, in collaboration with regional commissions, to include in the report to be submitted to the Commission on the Status of Women at its thirty-fourth session an evaluation of the effects of the debt crisis, including the effects of the structural adjustment programmes, on the implementation of the Nairobi Forward-looking Strategies for the Advancement of Women;

3. *Requests* the organizations of the United Nations system concerned with development, when designing

their relevant programmes, to pay special attention to the role of women, especially rural women and poor women, in the development process, particularly in the fields of education, health, employment, agriculture and social services;

4. *Requests* the organizations of the United Nations system to maintain and strengthen their institutional support structures for women in developing countries;

5. *Requests* the Secretary-General to report on the implementation of the present resolution to the Commission on the Status of Women at its thirty-fourth session.

Economic and Social Council resolution 1989/41

24 May 1989   Meeting 15   40-1-13 (recorded vote)

Approved by Second Committee (E/1989/90) by recorded vote (32-1-14), 16 May (meeting 16); draft by Commission on women (E/1989/27/Rev.1); agenda item 10.

Recorded vote in Council as follows:

In favour: Bahamas, Belize, Bolivia, Brazil, Bulgaria, Cameroon, China, Colombia, Cuba, Czechoslovakia, Ghana, Guinea, India, Indonesia, Iran, Iraq, Jordan, Kenya, Lesotho, Liberia, Libyan Arab Jamahiriya, Nicaragua, Niger, Oman, Poland, Rwanda, Saudi Arabia, Somalia, Sri Lanka, Sudan, Thailand, Trinidad and Tobago, Tunisia, Ukrainian SSR, USSR, Uruguay, Venezuela, Yugoslavia, Zaire, Zambia.

Against: United States.

Abstaining: Canada, Denmark, France, Germany, Federal Republic of, Greece, Ireland, Italy, Japan, Netherlands, New Zealand, Norway, Portugal, United Kingdom.

Women and AIDS

In connection with its consideration of the priority theme of development, the Commission had before it a report on the effects of the acquired immunodeficiency syndrome (AIDS) on the advancement of women,[2] prepared pursuant to a 1988 General Assembly resolution,[3] by which the UN system was urged to support the world-wide struggle against AIDS under the leadership of the World Health Organization (WHO). Prepared by the UN Secretariat in co-operation with WHO, the report outlined the effects of AIDS on women and its relationship to the objectives of the Nairobi Forward-looking Strategies for the Advancement of Women. It concluded that the advancement of women was affected not only by the adverse effect of AIDS on the health of women, but also by its social and economic consequences. It suggested that the multidisciplinary and cross-organizational mandate of the Commission offered it an opportunity to play a key role in activating a world-wide effort to advance the status of women while contributing to the global fight against AIDS. The Commission was asked to encourage all relevant bodies to consider the consequences of the AIDS pandemic on women in development.

ECONOMIC AND SOCIAL COUNCIL ACTION

On 24 May, the Economic and Social Council, by **decision 1989/127**, took note of the report on the effects of AIDS on women. It also requested that the Secretary-General, in close collaboration with WHO, convene an expert group meeting to prepare for an international meeting of representatives of units of national machinery for the advancement of women and of national AIDS committees to identify issues relating to women raised by the AIDS pandemic and appropriate strategies and programmes for possible adoption at the national level, and to promote co-operation between such national units.

Women living in absolute poverty

On 24 May, on the recommendation of its Second Committee, the Economic and Social Council adopted **resolution 1989/40** without vote.

Women living in absolute poverty

The Economic and Social Council,

Recalling General Assembly resolution 43/195 of 20 December 1988 on international co-operation for the eradication of poverty in developing countries,

Recalling also its resolution 1988/47 of 27 May 1988 on extreme poverty,

Noting with great concern the information on the population living in poverty in developing countries and on women's participation in the labour force contained in the 1989 report on the world social situation,

Convinced that absolute poverty limits the advancement of women in the social, political and economic development of their countries,

1. *Requests* the Secretary-General to take into account, in the report to be prepared in accordance with General Assembly resolution 43/195, the impact of absolute poverty on women;

2. *Draws the attention* of the Commission for Social Development to the need to discuss in depth, at its thirty-second and subsequent sessions, the subject of absolute poverty and women, when considering reports of the Secretary-General concerning the world social situation;

3. *Urges* the Commission on the Status of Women to give due consideration to the subject of absolute poverty when considering its priority themes of equality, development and peace;

4. *Appeals* to all Member States to make efforts to overcome absolute poverty by increasing the level of integration of women in the economic and social development of their countries.

Economic and Social Council resolution 1989/40

24 May 1989   Meeting 15   Adopted without vote

Approved by Second Committee (E/1989/90) without vote, 16 May (meeting 16); draft by Commission on women (E/1989/27/Rev.1); agenda item 10.

Integration of women in economic development

Pursuant to a 1987 request of the General Assembly,[4] the Secretary-General in June 1989 reported on a variety of steps taken to encourage the effective mobilization of women in development.[5] The report described action taken by various intergovernmental bodies to address the integration of women in development, especially economic development, both in policies and in operational activities. It proposed several measures to enhance co-ordination at the intergovernmental level, including use of the biennial monitoring reports on the implementation of the Nairobi

Forward-looking Strategies for the Advancement of Women to keep a record of intergovernmental resolutions and decisions. It also proposed more co-ordinated examination of the advancement of women within the work of the Economic and Social Council as part of the implementation of a 1988 Council resolution on its revitalization.[6] The report described action taken by the secretariats of the organizations of the UN system related to the integration of women in development, especially in terms of major surveys and in operational activities and their co-ordination.

On 27 July, by **decision 1989/178**, the Economic and Social Council took note of the Secretary-General's report.

The Governing Council of the United Nations Development Programme (UNDP) also considered the question of women in development. It reviewed a report of the Administrator,[7] who noted initial experiences in country programmes and proposed possible approaches for women-in-development-responsive country programming (see PART THREE, Chapter II).

World Survey

The final draft of the first regular update of the *World Survey on the Role of Women in Development* was reviewed at an expert group meeting convened in Vienna from 13 to 17 February. The meeting adopted as the central theme of the *1989 World Survey* a statement stressing that the 1980s had been a period of uneven economic conditions and responses to them. While growth continued or was restored in developed countries and a number of developing countries in Asia, economic decline prevailed in Africa and Latin America. One major shortcoming of development strategies had been the failure to take into account the role and potential of women. The facts suggested that that shortcoming had to be remedied if development strategies of the 1990s were to succeed.

The experts, on the basis of the analysis of economic and social changes affecting women over the past years, stated that, despite economic progress measured in growth rates, economic progress for women had virtually stopped, social progress had slowed and social well-being in many cases had deteriorated. They recommended that the *World Survey* be updated again for consideration in 1994, as an input to the quinquennial review of the Nairobi Forward-looking Strategies. The *1994 World Survey* would also constitute a basic document for the fourth world conference on women, which was recommended to take place in 1995.

In June, the Secretary-General circulated chapter I of the *1989 World Survey*.[8] The original *Survey*—prepared for the 1985 World Conference to Review and Appraise the Achievements of the UN Decade for Women[9]—emphasized material that

clearly demonstrated the important role played by women in the world economy. The *1989 World Survey*[10] centred on the more complex questions of how women played that role, factors that enhanced or impeded them, and the type of issues that had to be addressed if women's full and equal participation in the economy was to be achieved. That approach, more analytical than descriptive, had been made possible by the dramatic increase of research on economic variables taking gender into account.

On 27 July, by **decision 1989/178**, the Economic and Social Council took note of chapter I.

The 390-page *1989 World Survey* was released in October and submitted to the General Assembly. It included material provided by the Food and Agriculture Organization of the United Nations, the UN Industrial Development Organization, the UN Conference on Trade and Development, the International Labour Organisation, the UN Centre for Science and Technology for Development, the UN Educational, Scientific and Cultural Organization and the UN Statistical Office.

The *1989 World Survey* dealt with women, debt and adjustment; development of key economic sectors, including agriculture, industry, services and the informal sector; and certain policy issues such as equal employment, technology, culture and the economic role of women. One chapter explored the interrelationships between equality, development and peace.

Main trends reviewed in the *Survey* indicated that, while no complete estimate could be made of the direct impact of the economic crisis of the 1980s on the advancement of women, there was no doubt that there had been a differential effect on women. Beyond the effects caused by a reduction in expenditures on public services, with its consequences for education and health, and the documented need for more women to enter the labour force in order to maintain acceptable levels of household income, there were less obvious effects on the fabric of women's lives, reflected in the increase of female-headed households which, in many countries, was becoming a major factor in increasing poverty.

ECONOMIC AND SOCIAL COUNCIL ACTION

On 27 July, on the recommendation of its First Committee, the Economic and Social Council adopted **resolution 1989/106** without vote.

Effective mobilization and integration of women in development

The Economic and Social Council,

Recalling its resolution 1988/49 of 26 July 1988,

Noting the section of the *World Economic Survey, 1989* on the socio-economic attainment of women,

Noting also that the first update of the *World Survey on the Role of Women in Development* will be submitted to the General Assembly at its forty-fourth session,

1. *Welcomes* the section on the socio-economic attainment of women contained in the *World Economic Survey, 1989;*

2. *Requests* the Secretary-General to maintain that section in the *World Economic Survey* and to incorporate, *inter alia,* statistical indicators on income distribution, health, nutrition, fertility and education;

3. *Also requests* the Secretary-General to focus, in the next edition of the *World Survey on the Role of Women in Development,* on socio-economic aspects, *inter alia,* of emerging trends with respect to women and education, health, population, income distribution, employment and environment issues, as well as the participation of women in decision-making, and to submit a draft text to the Economic and Social Council at its second regular session of 1994 for comment;

4. *Further requests* the Secretary-General to invite the regional commissions, within their terms of reference, to provide relevant input for the section of the *World Economic Survey* on the socio-economic attainment of women and for the *World Survey on the Role of Women in Development;*

5. *Recommends* that the Statistical Office of the United Nations Secretariat play a central role in the intensified co-ordination of statistical data within the United Nations system on women in development and that United Nations sectoral studies be planned and published in a mutually supportive manner.

Economic and Social Council resolution 1989/106

27 July 1989	Meeting 36	Adopted without vote

Approved by First Committee (E/1989/141) without vote, 21 July (meeting 25); 18-nation draft (E/1989/C.1/L.15), orally revised; agenda item 7 *(i).*

GENERAL ASSEMBLY ACTION

On 19 December, the General Assembly, on the recommendation of the Second (Economic and Financial) Committee, adopted without vote **resolution 44/171.**

Integration of women in development

The General Assembly,

Recalling its resolution 40/204 of 17 December 1985 on the effective mobilization and integration of women in development, in which it requested the Secretary-General to update the *World Survey on the Role of Women in Development* on a regular basis,

Recalling also Economic and Social Council resolution 1986/64 of 23 July 1986 concerning the approach to be taken in updating the world survey and General Assembly resolution 42/178 of 11 December 1987, and taking note of Council resolutions 1989/106 of 27 July 1989 on the effective mobilization and integration of women in development and 1989/105 of 27 July 1989 on system-wide co-ordination of activities to advance the status of women and to integrate women in development,

Stressing the need for the operational activities for development of the United Nations system to take fully into account the position of women, and recognizing the catalytic role played by the United Nations Development Fund for Women,

Recalling the Nairobi Forward-looking Strategies for the Advancement of Women and stressing that activities for the integration of women in development should take into account the relevant recommendations contained therein,

Taking note of the *1989 World Survey on the Role of Women in Development* and the report of the Secretary-General

on the effective mobilization and integration of women in development,

Recognizing the contribution of new concepts and methods in collection of statistics on women, which enhance the depth and coverage of the analysis,

Bearing in mind that the world survey, as a fundamental assessment of the progress or lack of progress in the advancement of women, should constitute the basic documentation for the world conference on women envisaged in the Nairobi Forward-looking Strategies for the Advancement of Women,

Recognizing that for many women, particularly in developing countries, the evolution of the economic and social situation during the 1980s has not resulted in the benefits anticipated at the beginning of the decade,

Recognizing also the significant contribution women make to economic activity and the major force they represent for change and development in all sectors of the economy, especially in key areas such as agriculture, industry and services, and convinced that the development process should seek to improve and facilitate their participation in all areas of the economy,

1. *Requests* the Secretary-General to distribute the *1989 World Survey on the Role of Women in Development,* especially to national machineries for the advancement of women, ministries concerned with economic policy and universities;

2. *Invites* Governments to take into account, as appropriate, the recommendations contained in the *1989 World Survey on the Role Of Women in Development* in designing national policies for development, adjustment and economic reform;

3. *Considers* that the economic role and potential of women should be taken into account fully in the international development strategy for the fourth United Nations development decade;

4. *Requests* the Secretary-General to submit to the General Assembly at its forty-eighth session an annotated outline of the next regular update of the world survey and requests that the completed update be submitted to the Assembly at its forty-ninth session, through the Economic and Social Council and in co-operation with the organizations of the United Nations system, in a timely manner in order to allow its proper consideration;

5. *Requests* that the next edition of the world survey, taking into account the recommendations contained in the *1989 World Survey on the Role of Women in Development,* address the impact on women of the prevailing economic conditions in developing countries and identify obstacles to women's economic role in key areas of development, with particular focus on the socio-economic aspects of emerging trends with respect to women and education, health, population, income distribution, employment and the environment, as well as the participation of women in economic and political decision-making and their economic role at the national, regional and international levels, and that it contain proposals for concerted national, regional and international action to enhance the role of women as development agents and beneficiaries;

6. *Requests* the Secretary-General, in updating the world survey, to ensure that its preparation is co-ordinated with that of the *World Economic Survey,* the medium-term plan and the system-wide medium-term plan for women and development;

7. *Also requests* the Secretary-General to continue to develop gender disaggregated data and indicators con-

cerning the role of women in development, including regular updates of the United Nations Women's Indicators and Statistics Data Base, at two-year intervals; in this context, particular attention should be given to economic statistics that take into account the remunerated and unremunerated contribution of women to development and to including the informal sector in the new systems of national accounts and balances to reflect adequately women's activities and ensuring that relevant studies and documents produced by the United Nations system contain such data;

8. *Calls upon* the organizations of the United Nations system to assist Governments, at their request, in monitoring the implementation of the Nairobi Forward-looking Strategies for the Advancement of Women;

9. *Calls upon* the United Nations system, under its operational activities for development, to ensure that it will collect and report gender disaggregated data covering national and international project personnel, including consultants, as well as beneficiaries of its programmes;

10. *Requests* the Director-General for Development and International Economic Co-operation to include in his 1991 report on operational activities for development of the United Nations system a separate chapter on United Nations efforts to integrate women in development, both as a mainstream and specific activity of the United Nations system, and with particular attention to literacy, education, health, population, environment, employment and participation in decision-making;

11. *Requests* the Commission on the Status of Women to take the present resolution into account when reviewing, at its extended session in 1990, progress made in implementing the Nairobi Forward-looking Strategies.

General Assembly resolution 44/171

19 December 1989   Meeting 83   Adopted without vote

Approved by Second Committee (A/44/746/Add.4) without vote, 21 November (meeting 41); draft by Vice-Chairman (A/C.2/44/L.45), based on informal consultations on 21-nation draft (A/C.2/44/L.10); agenda item 82 *(d)*.
Meeting numbers. GA 44th session: 2nd Committee 10-13, 16, 35, 41, 42; plenary 83.

Medium-term plan

Pursuant to Economic and Social Council resolutions of 1987[11] and 1988,[12] ACC reported in March on plans and programmes of the organizations of the UN system to implement the system-wide medium-term plan for women and development for the period 1990-1995.[13] The report provided information on how the plan was reflected in the programmes of the UN system related to: elimination of legal and attitudinal forms of discrimination; access to productive resources, income and employment; access to services; decision-making; improving means of international action; and comprehensive approaches to women and development. An annex to the report contained a list of organizations that had agreed to implement the system-wide medium-term plan.

Report of the Secretary-General. In April, pursuant to recommendations of the Economic and Social Council, most recently in 1987,[11] the Secretary-General submitted a cross-organizational

programme analysis of the activities of the UN system for the advancement of women,[14] which was to serve as a baseline for monitoring progress of the system-wide medium-term plan for women and development for the period 1990-1995. The analysis examined policy aims and approaches of the participating organizations, noted identifiable trends and presented recommendations on legislative structures, policy orientation, programme activities, co-ordination and monitoring the system-wide plan.

On 27 July, by **decision 1989/178**, the Economic and Social Council took note of the reports of ACC and the Secretary-General.

Technical co-operation

In March, the UNDP Administrator submitted a report[15] to the High-level Committee on the Review of Technical Co-operation among Developing Countries (see PART THREE, Chapter II) on actions taken and proposed by the organizations of the UN development system to increase the participation and enlarge the role of women in development through technical co-operation among developing countries (TCDC).

In September, the Committee requested[16] the Administrator and the heads of all UN development organs to develop and improve guidelines to ensure full access and participation of women in TCDC activities, stressing the need for UNDP-sponsored exercises to encourage women's participation and to take account of the need to integrate women in the identification, design and implementation of projects adopted as a result of those exercises.

Rural women

In April, the Secretary-General noted[17] that, in accordance with a 1988 Economic and Social Council resolution,[18] a seminar on women and rural development would be convened in Vienna from 22 to 26 May 1989. The seminar would emphasize development assistance strategies, project formulation and execution, monitoring and evaluation. In order that its major findings could be taken into account in his report on national experience relating to rural women (see below), he proposed that that report be submitted directly to the Assembly.

On 24 May, the Council, by **decision 1989/130**, took note of the note of the Secretary-General and authorized him to submit directly to the Assembly in 1989 a comprehensive report on the improvement of the situation of rural women.

Report of the Secretary-General. In October, pursuant to a 1985 request of the General Assembly,[19] the Secretary-General submitted his report,[20] prepared in consultation with Member States, on national experience relating to the improvement of the situation of women in rural areas.

Reviewing the status and prospects for improving the situation of rural women, the report paid special attention to: the participation of rural women in socio-economic and political life; the exercise by rural women of their rights; the role of agricultural co-operatives in improving the situation of women; agrarian reform; elimination of illiteracy and upgrading education levels among rural women; and assistance to rural women.

The Secretary-General made recommendations on women and sustainable rural development, integrating women into mainstream development policies, programmes and projects, and the role of the international community.

Regarding major issues and policy options for rural women, the Secretary-General summed up the lessons learned from the 1980s and suggested that emerging issues of greatest relevance for rural women in the 1990s comprised three areas: environment, rural employment and empowerment.

Annexed to the report were the conclusions and recommendations of the International Seminar on Women and Rural Development: Programmes and Projects.

GENERAL ASSEMBLY ACTION

On 8 December, the General Assembly, on the recommendation of the Third Committee, adopted **resolution 44/78** without vote.

Improvement of the situation of women in rural areas

The General Assembly,

Recalling its resolution 34/14 of 9 November 1979, in which it endorsed the Declaration of Principles and the Programme of Action as adopted by the World Conference on Agrarian Reform and Rural Development, and other relevant resolutions,

Recalling also the importance given to the problems of rural women in the Nairobi Forward-looking Strategies for the Advancement of Women,

Bearing in mind Economic and Social Council resolution 1988/29 of 26 May 1988, in which the Council urged Governments and development agencies of the United Nations system to pay particular attention to the role of women in rural development,

Taking note with satisfaction of the results of the International Seminar on Women and Rural Development: Programmes and Projects, held at Vienna from 22 to 26 May 1989,

Recognizing that the economic and financial crises in many developing countries have severely affected the socio-economic status of women, especially in rural areas,

Recognizing also the urgent need to take appropriate measures aimed at improving further the situation of women in rural areas,

1. *Commends* the report of the Secretary-General on national experience relating to the improvement of the situation of women in rural areas;

2. *Calls upon* Member States to make use of the report and the main conclusions and recommendations

of the International Seminar on Women and Rural Development: Programmes and Projects, contained in the annex to the report, and to endeavour to reflect them, as appropriate, in national development strategies, paying special attention, *inter alia*, to:

(a) Setting up or strengthening national machineries for the advancement of women in order to ensure effective execution, monitoring and evaluation of national strategies in the field of rural development and, in particular, to strengthen liaison with agricultural and rural development institutions;

(b) Identifying and formulating more comprehensive priority development projects aimed at improving the situation of rural women and integrating them into national development plans at all levels;

(c) Taking measures designed to give rural women broader access to material and financial resources, that is, the provision of land, credit and loans, to promote the establishment and strengthening of rural women's associations and to encourage the development of women's co-operatives and other small enterprises;

3. *Requests* the organizations and funds of the United Nations system, donor organizations and countries to promote the realization of programmes and projects aimed at the improvement of the situation of rural women, and to provide, on request, training opportunities for national machineries in order to increase their effectiveness;

4. *Requests* the Secretary-General to prepare, in consultation with Member States, a report on the implementation of the present resolution and to submit it to the General Assembly at its forty-eighth session, through the Economic and Social Council.

General Assembly resolution 44/78

8 December 1989   Meeting 78   Adopted without vote

Approved by Third Committee (A/44/803 & Corr.1) without vote, 20 November (meeting 49); 41-nation draft (A/C.3/44/L.31), orally revised; agenda item 104 *(e)*.

Meeting numbers. GA 44th session: 3rd Committee 21-28, 36, 49; plenary 78.

Economic situation of women in Latin America and the Caribbean

On 24 May, on the recommendation of its Second Committee, the Economic and Social Council adopted **resolution 1989/42** without vote.

Economic situation of women in Latin America and the Caribbean

The Economic and Social Council,

Taking account of the fact that the debtor countries of Latin America and the Caribbean are undergoing an economic crisis manifested, *inter alia*, by the stagnation of their economies and the unprecedented drop in their per capita income,

Considering the negative effect of the economic crisis on social indicators, particularly those relating to the status of women,

Taking account of the analysis of the difficult situation of Latin American and Caribbean women prepared by the Fourth Regional Conference on the Integration of Women into the Economic and Social Development of Latin America and the Caribbean, held under the auspices of the Economic Commission for Latin America and the Caribbean,

Taking account also of the need to face, at the national, regional and international levels, the problems in the debtor countries that are hampering the implementation of the Nairobi Forward-looking Strategies for the Advancement of Women,

Recommends that:

(a) The organizations of the United Nations system, in their programmes for the improvement of the status of women, take account of the problems facing women in the debtor countries of Latin America and the Caribbean;

(b) Documentation on priority themes of the Commission on the Status of Women prepared by the Secretary-General for submission to the Commission identify the differences between the various national and regional situations and highlight the specific problems affecting women in the context of the economic crisis in Latin America and the Caribbean;

(c) In his report on the review and appraisal of the implementation of the Nairobi Forward-looking Strategies for the Advancement of Women, to be submitted to the Commission on the Status of Women at its thirty-fourth session, the Secretary-General pay special attention to the obstacles originating in the economic stagnation caused, *inter alia*, by the burden of the external debt;

(d) The recommendations put forward by the Commission on the Status of Women for future action at the national and international levels include an appeal to the appropriate parties in the debtor and creditor countries to create better conditions for the effective implementation of the Nairobi Forward-looking Strategies.

Economic and Social Council resolution 1989/42

24 May 1989   Meeting 15   Adopted without vote

Approved by Second Committee (E/1989/90) without vote, 16 May (meeting 16); draft by Commission on women (E/1989/27/Rev1); agenda item 10.

UN Development Fund for Women

The Consultative Committee on the UN Development Fund for Women (UNIFEM), at its twenty-fifth and twenty-sixth sessions (3-19 April and 28 August–1 September 1989), reviewed the scope of UNIFEM activities, fund-raising and strategic objectives for the Fund in the 1990s, as well as project implementation and financing arrangements.

In 1989, UNIFEM initiated an ongoing process of strategic planning, which included setting strategic objectives for UNIFEM's work in the areas of programme focus, management systems, and financial and human resources. Two strategic planning workshops were held, resulting in a "mission statement" setting out UNIFEM objectives and philosophy, together with a strategic plan to achieve those objectives.

The Fund continued the development of global programmes, including those dealing with women and food-cycle technologies and the credit support system. It also worked closely with other UN agencies in system-wide efforts to help women participate in and benefit from development initiatives.

At the regional level, UNIFEM approved 12 new projects for implementation in Africa, focusing on food and agriculture; energy and environment; micro-enterprise development, trade and commerce; and human resources development.

It approved 11 new projects for the Asia, Pacific and Western Asia region, where an "impact points" strategy was developed, identifying four points of intervention that could have significant impact on large numbers of poor women. The four impact points were macro-policies, data and statistics, gender-sensitizing training, and institution strengthening.

In Latin America and the Caribbean, 10 new projects were approved for implementation, stressing a grass-roots approach to assisting poor rural and urban women, and increasing the capacity of existing institutions to serve women.

The Fund's total income during 1989 was approximately $11.78 million, representing an overall increase of 35 per cent over the total income of 1988. Estimated total expenditures for the year were $9.39 million.

In July, the Secretary-General transmitted to the General Assembly the report of the UNDP Administrator on the 1988 activities of UNIFEM.[21]

GENERAL ASSEMBLY ACTION

On 8 December, on the recommendation of the Third Committee, the General Assembly adopted **resolution 44/74** without vote.

United Nations Development Fund for Women

The General Assembly,

Reaffirming the decisions contained in its resolution 39/125 of 14 December 1984,

Emphasizing the catalytic role of the United Nations Development Fund for Women in the United Nations system as well as with governmental and non-governmental organizations and financial institutions and its support for innovative and experimental activities directly benefiting women in line with national and regional priorities,

Reaffirming those dual priorities of the Fund, which would better position women for more effective participation in the development of their countries,

Recognizing the mainstream initiatives of the Fund to assist national machineries on women, ministries concerned with planning and other relevant ministries and intergovernmental organizations to integrate the concerns of women and to ensure their involvement in development programmes at all levels,

Noting the focused and proactive interventions of the Fund within its regional priority frameworks and its overall strategic objectives through investments in tested and documented models and approaches for women and development,

1. *Takes note* of the note by the Secretary-General transmitting the report of the Administrator of the United Nations Development Programme on the activities of the United Nations Development Fund for Women;

2. *Notes* the Fund's continued co-operation with units concerned with issues relating to women and development throughout the United Nations system and with planning and sectoral ministries and national machineries on women in the development of developing countries;

3. *Stresses* the importance of strengthening the technical and financial capacities of the Fund to enable it to preserve and augment its flexibility and to facilitate its

own implementation of the governmental and non-governmental projects and programmes that it supports at the national, regional and global levels;

4. *Expresses its appreciation* to Governments, non-governmental organizations and individuals that have pledged and contributed to the Fund;

5. *Commends* national committees for the Fund and non-governmental organizations for their initiatives in the development of education and public awareness programmes and resource mobilization on behalf of the Fund;

6. *Notes with concern* that the Fund's resources are still insufficient to enable it to implement fully its programmes and to preserve and augment its flexible approaches to supporting activities at the national, regional and global levels;

7. *Invites* Governments, non-governmental organizations and others to make substantial contributions to the Fund;

8. *Requests* the Secretary-General to transmit to the General Assembly at its forty-fifth session the report of the Administrator of the United Nations Development Programme on the activities of the Fund to be submitted pursuant to Assembly resolution 39/125.

General Assembly resolution 44/74

8 December 1989   Meeting 78   Adopted without vote

Approved by Third Committee (A/44/803) without vote, 20 November (meeting 49); 5-nation draft (A/C.3/44/L.26); agenda item 104 *(b)*.
Sponsors: German Democratic Republic, India, Mexico, Netherlands, Senegal.
Meeting numbers. GA 44th session: 3rd Committee 21-28, 36, 49; plenary 78.

REFERENCES
[1]E/CN.6/1989/6. [2]E/CN.6/1989/6/Add.1. [3]YUN 1988, p. 589, GA res. 43/15, 27 Oct. 1988. [4]YUN 1987, p. 837, GA res. 42/178, 11 Dec. 1987. [5]A/44/290-E/1989/105. [6]YUN 1988, p. 705, ESC res. 1988/77, 29 July 1988. [7]DP/1989/24. [8]E/1989/L.23. [9]YUN 1985, p. 937. [10]*1989 World Survey on the Role of Women in Development*, Sales No. E.89.IV.2. [11]YUN 1987, p. 840, ESC res. 1987/86, 8 July 1987. [12]YUN 1988, p. 628, ESC res. 1988/59, 27 July 1988. [13]E/1989/16 & Corr.1. [14]E/1989/19 & Corr.1. [15]TCDC/6/7. [16]A/44/39 (dec. 6/6). [17]E/1989/70. [18]YUN 1988, p. 625, ESC res. 1988/29, 26 May 1988. [19]YUN 1985, p. 947, GA res. 40/106, 13 Dec. 1985. [20]A/44/516. [21]A/44/389.

Status of women

Commission on the Status of Women

The Commission on the Status of Women, at its thirty-third session (Vienna, 29 March–7 April 1989),[1] focused debate on ways to revive the pace of improvements in the struggle for equality of women with men by the year 2000 and considered three priority themes related to equality, development and peace: equality in economic and social participation; women and education, eradication of illiteracy, employment, health and social services, including population issues and child care; and full participation of women in the construction of their countries and in the creation of just social and political systems. As requested by the Economic

and Social Council in 1988,[2] the Commission also discussed enlarging its membership.

The Commission adopted six resolutions and recommended 15 draft resolutions and two draft decisions for adoption by the Council. Among the issues dealt with were: improvement of the status of women in the Secretariat (see PART SIX, Chapter II); programme planning and system-wide co-ordination to advance the status of women and integrate them in development; equality in economic and social participation; and the status of women in various countries and situations. It also prepared for and recommended Council action on its 1990 session to review and appraise progress in the implementation of the 1985 Nairobi Forward-looking Strategies for the Advancement of Women.

ECONOMIC AND SOCIAL COUNCIL ACTION

On 24 May, on the recommendation of its Second Committee, the Economic and Social Council adopted **resolution 1989/45** by recorded vote.

Enlargement of the Commission on the Status of Women

The Economic and Social Council,

Recalling its resolution 1987/23 of 26 May 1987, in which it accepted, in principle, the need for an increase in the membership of the Commission on the Status of Women and decided that the Commission, at its thirty-second session, should discuss the matter and submit proposals to the Council at its first regular session of 1988,

Bearing in mind the increase in membership of the United Nations from 120 Member States in 1966 to 159 Member States in 1988, which provides the basis for a proportionate enlargement of the Commission, and taking into consideration the principle of equitable geographical distribution for the allocation of seats,

Recalling its decision 1988/125 of 27 May 1988, in which it invited the Commission to offer its views on the question of its enlargement,

Taking note of the discussions held on this matter by the Commission at its thirty-third session,

Considering that issues relating to women have grown more complex and numerous, particularly in the developing countries,

Recalling that the Commission is to hold in 1990 a session of extended duration to review and appraise progress in the implementation of the Nairobi Forward-looking Strategies for the Advancement of Women,

1. *Decides* that the membership of the Commission on the Status of Women should be increased to forty-five and that the seats should be allocated on the basis of the principle of equitable geographical distribution according to the following pattern:

(*a*)   Thirteen members from African States;

(*b*)   Eleven members from Asian States;

(*c*)   Four members from Eastern European States;

(*d*)   Nine members from Latin American and Caribbean States;

(*e*)   Eight members from Western European and other States;

2. *Also decides* that the enlargement of the Commission should take effect from the beginning of 1990 before the convening of the extended session of the Commission to review and appraise progress in the implementation of the Nairobi Forward-looking Strategies for the Advancement of Women;

3. *Further decides* that the additional seats resulting from the increase in the membership of the Commission should be filled at the organizational session for 1990 of the Council.

Economic and Social Council resolution 1989/45

24 May 1989   Meeting 15   35-19 (recorded vote)

Approved by Second Committee (E/1989/90/Add.1) by recorded vote (34-19), 19 May (meeting 23); draft by Malaysia, for Group of 77 (E/1989/C.2/L.5/Rev.1); agenda item 10.
Financial implications. S-G, E/1989/C.2/L.12.

Recorded vote in Council as follows:

In favour: Bahamas, Belize, Bolivia, Brazil, Cameroon, China, Colombia, Cuba, Ghana, Guinea, India, Indonesia, Iran, Iraq, Jordan, Kenya, Lesotho, Liberia, Libyan Arab Jamahiriya, Nicaragua, Niger, Oman, Rwanda, Saudi Arabia, Somalia, Sri Lanka, Sudan, Thailand, Trinidad and Tobago, Tunisia, Uruguay, Venezuela, Yugoslavia, Zaire, Zambia.

Against: Bulgaria, Canada, Czechoslovakia, Denmark, France, Germany, Federal Republic of, Greece, Ireland, Italy, Japan, Netherlands, New Zealand, Norway, Poland, Portugal, Ukrainian SSR, USSR, United Kingdom, United States.

1990 session

On 24 May, by **decision 1989/128**, the Economic and Social Council took note of the Commission's report on its thirty-third session and approved the provisional agenda and documentation for the thirty-fourth session in 1990.

Equality in economic and social participation

During consideration of the priority theme of equality, the Commission on the Status of Women had before it a February report of the Secretary-General[3] on equality in economic and social participation. The report contained information on women's economic participation in the formal and informal sectors, on their access to credit and on their participation in co-operatives. The section on social participation covered women's participation in education and leisure activities.

The information available showed that, while progress might have been made in the *de jure* situation of women, corresponding legal provisions had not been implemented so that the *de facto* situation had not improved during the previous decade. The Secretary-General suggested that the pace of progress towards equality might be slowing and that, unless special efforts were taken over the next decade, the objective of equality in economic and social participation set at Nairobi in 1985[4] might be at risk.

In April, the Commission recommended[5] that a report on statistics and indicators to be considered at its thirty-fifth (1991) session make suggestions for including in the gross national product the economic value of work carried out by women in informal sectors. It asked that existing activities to that end be covered in the report on the monitoring of the Nairobi Forward-looking Strategies, to be submitted in 1990.

ECONOMIC AND SOCIAL COUNCIL ACTION

On 24 May, the Economic and Social Council, on the recommendation of its Second Committee, adopted **resolution 1989/36** without vote.

Equality in economic and social participation

The Economic and Social Council,

Recalling General Assembly resolution 40/108 of 13 December 1985, in which the Assembly endorsed the Nairobi Forward-looking Strategies for the Advancement of Women,

Noting that progress in achieving *de jure* equality between women and men has been steady,

Welcoming the clear improvement in some indicators of equality in social participation in most regions, but concerned that progress in other regions is slowing,

Gravely concerned that the pace of achieving *de facto* equality, particularly equality in economic participation, has evidently been slowing in most countries over the past decade,

Bearing in mind the important economic contributions of women to their communities,

Recognizing that equality for women is closely linked to their economic independence,

Recalling the Plan of Action on equality of opportunity and treatment of men and women in employment of the International Labour Organisation,

Noting that various affirmative action policies can accelerate the elimination of discrimination against women,

1. *Urges* Governments to give high priority to measures and temporary affirmative action programmes that will more rapidly bring about equality in women's economic participation, in particular to programmes that will ensure the following:

(*a*) Women's access to the labour market and to education and training;

(*b*) Elimination of sex segregation in the labour market and in education;

(*c*) Women's participation in trade unions;

(*d*) Equal pay for equal work;

(*e*) Equal access to economic resources, including credit and membership in co-operatives;

(*f*) Improved conditions in the informal sector including, where desirable, the application of labour standards, and the development or improvement of sex-disaggregated statistics that accurately reflect women's work in the informal economic sector;

2. *Also urges* Governments that have not yet done so to ratify conventions of the International Labour Organisation on equal pay and working conditions;

3. *Requests* the Commission on the Status of Women at its thirty-fourth session, in carrying our its review and appraisal of the implementation of the Nairobi Forward-looking Strategies for the Advancement of Women to consider measures to accelerate the pace of achieving equality in economic and social participation, including the definition and compilation of bench-mark statistical indicators that could be used for national, regional and international reporting, as well as affirmative action programmes;

4. *Requests* the Secretary-General to present to the Commission on the Status of Women at its thirty-fourth

session examples of affirmative action programmes that would be effective for the achievement of equality in economic and social participation;

5. *Also requests* the Secretary-General to submit to the Commission on the Status of Women at its thirty-fourth session proposals for the definition and compilation of bench-mark statistical indicators of equality in economic and social participation.

Economic and Social Council resolution 1989/36

24 May 1989   Meeting 15   Adopted without vote

Approved by Second Committee (E/1989/90) without vote, 16 May (meeting 16); draft by Commission on women (E/1989/27/Rev.1); agenda item 10.

Women in public life

Under the priority theme of peace, the Commission on the Status of Women had before it a January report of the Secretary-General[6] on the full participation of women in the construction of their countries and in the creation of just social and political systems. The report concentrated on the active and organized participation of women collectively. In most countries where elections were held, it said, legal impediments to women's participation as voters had been removed and women were a significant part of the electorate. Women had also played major roles in independence struggles and reconstruction after armed conflict; that participation was not reflected in the proportion of women in parliaments, however, which raised questions as to why more women candidates were not selected and about the participation of women in political parties, trade unions, national liberation movements and NGOs. The Secretary-General offered a number of solutions, including affirmative action, to increase the participation of women in political life.

In April,[7] the Commission urged Governments to give priority to affirmative action programmes and temporary measures to ensure increased participation of women in parliaments, Governments and other decision-making bodies; equal participation of women in political parties and trade unions; and equal participation in all peace-related activities at the governmental level, particularly in the diplomatic service, in governmental delegations and in peace negotiations. It asked the Secretary-General to organize an exchange of experience on the subject and to report thereon to the Commission.

The Commission also recommended[8] that the Economic and Social Council convene in 1991 a high-level interregional consultation on women in public life. The consultation, to convene for not more than three days, should discuss issues such as a more equal sharing of responsibilities between women and men at all decision-making levels in political, economic and social fields; factors facilitating or inhibiting the entry of women into public life; and changing roles of women and men and their impact on participation in policy formulation.

ECONOMIC AND SOCIAL COUNCIL ACTION

On 24 May, the Economic and Social Council, by **decision 1989/129**, endorsed the Commission's recommendation that it convene in 1991 a high-level interregional consultation on women in public life, to be financed from voluntary and other contributions.

Refugee and displaced women

In April, the Commission on the Status of Women called for a concerted international response to the needs of refugee and displaced women, along with intensified co-operation to ensure that they received full protection and assistance.[9] It called on Governments receiving refugees to take into account the special situation of refugee women in formulating, within available resources, national policies for refugees. It decided that the Secretary-General's report on women in areas affected by armed conflicts, foreign intervention, alien and colonial domination, foreign occupation and threats to peace—to be submitted to the Commission in 1990—should be prepared in co-operation with the Office of the UN High Commissioner for Refugees (UNHCR) and the UN Relief and Works Agency for Palestine Refugees in the Near East (UNRWA), taking into account the importance of the legal protection of refugee women.

Elderly women

On 24 May, on the recommendation of its Second Committee, the Economic and Social Council adopted **resolution 1989/38** without vote.

Elderly women

The Economic and Social Council,

Aware that women constitute the majority of the older population and that in the years to come the number of elderly women will increase more rapidly in the developing countries than in the developed ones,

Recognizing the important contribution that these women have made, paid or unpaid, throughout their lives, in particular during their older years, to social, economic and cultural activities,

Concerned that, as they age, women are increasingly exposed to marginalization or to poverty,

Bearing in mind the need for the Commission on the Status of Women to give particular attention to the specific problems faced by elderly women,

1. *Recommends* that concerted efforts be undertaken or strengthened at the national, regional and international levels in order to enable women to meet the challenges they face during their lives, in particular during their older years;

2. *Recommends* that, within existing budgetary resources or, where necessary, with the help of extrabudgetary or voluntary resources, the organizations of the United Nations system concerned provide to the bodies responsible for the advancement of women information that would enable them to undertake a precise and in-depth analysis of the situation of elderly women, developing, if necessary, specific new methods for data collection;

3. *Requests* the Secretary-General to organize a seminar, within available budgetary resources, to study questions arising from the above-mentioned analysis and to transmit the results of the study to the Commission on the Status of Women;

4. *Encourages* Governments to ensure that women increase their participation in social and economic progress throughout their lives;

5. *Urges* Governments, in co-operation with the non-governmental organizations concerned, to strengthen activities for the benefit of elderly women, taking better account of their specific needs;

6. *Requests* the Commission on the Status of Women, in carrying out its review and appraisal of the implementation of the Nairobi Forward-looking Strategies for the Advancement of Women, to devote particular attention to the current and future situation of elderly women throughout the world.

Economic and Social Council resolution 1989/38

24 May 1989   Meeting 15   Adopted without vote

Approved by Second Committee (E/1989/90) without vote, 16 May (meeting 16); draft by Commission on women (E/1989/27/Rev.1); agenda item 10.

GENERAL ASSEMBLY ACTION

On 8 December, on the recommendation of the Third Committee, the General Assembly adopted **resolution 44/76** without vote.

Elderly women

The General Assembly,

Taking note of Economic and Social Council resolution 1989/38 of 24 May 1989, in which the Council requested the Commission on the Status of Women to devote particular attention to the current and future situation of elderly women in the world,

Recalling its resolution 40/30 of 29 November 1985, in which it was emphasized that the elderly must be considered an important and necessary element in the development process at all levels within a given society,

Aware that age segregation, in addition to sex stereotyping, makes the social and economic problems of elderly women even more acute, and that they are often viewed only as beneficiaries and not as contributors to development,

Also aware that statistics are an essential ingredient of planning and policy evaluation and that few statistics are available on the situation of elderly women,

1. *Recommends* that the United Nations and the specialized agencies take the lead in recognizing the important contributions made by older women and their potential to participate in and shape the future of their societies;

2. *Reaffirms* Economic and Social Council resolution 1989/38, in which the Council requested the Secretary-General to organize a seminar, within available budgetary resources, to study questions arising from an in-depth analysis of the situation of women as they age, and to transmit the results of the study to the Commission on the Status of Women, under the priority theme of development, at its session in 1992, at which the tenth anniversary of the adoption of the International Plan of Action on Aging will also be observed;

3. *Invites* the International Research and Training Institute for the Advancement of Women and the Statistical

Office of the Secretariat, in co-operation with the regional commissions, to pay specific attention to older women in their efforts to improve methodology for data-gathering on women;

4. *Notes with appreciation* the valuable contributions that non-governmental organizations have made in calling attention to the specific needs of elderly women and encourages them to continue to co-operate with the international community on behalf of these women;

5. *Appeals* to the United Nations system to pay due attention in relevant activities to the importance of the role of elderly women, in all its interrelated aspects, as participants in political, economic, social and cultural development;

6. *Requests* the Secretary-General to report to the General Assembly at its forty-fifth session on the implementation of the present resolution.

General Assembly resolution 44/76

8 December 1989   Meeting 78   Adopted without vote

Approved by Third Committee (A/44/803 & Corr.1) without vote, 20 November (meeting 49); 14-nation draft (A/C.3/44/L.28), orally revised; agenda item 104.

Meeting numbers. GA 44th session: 3rd Committee 21-28, 36, 49; plenary 78.

Palestinian women

The Secretary-General reported in February[10] on the situation of Palestinian women, as requested by the Economic and Social Council in 1988.[11] The report described the situation of Palestinian women and children living inside and outside the occupied Palestinian territories in the period from 15 October 1987 to 1 November 1988.

UNRWA continued to provide both regular and emergency programmes to the refugee population. The UN Children's Fund provided immunization and vaccinations, technical assistance for training and improvement of infrastructure, and assistance to reduce water-related diseases. The International Labour Organisation identified for financing several UNDP projects in vocational training for women. The United Nations Educational, Scientific and Cultural Organization, WHO and the UN Population Fund provided assistance to women and children in primary health care, environmental health and the training and education of health personnel.

ECONOMIC AND SOCIAL COUNCIL ACTION

On 24 May, on the recommendation of its Second Committee, the Economic and Social Council adopted **resolution 1989/34** by recorded vote.

Situation of Palestinian women

The Economic and Social Council,

Having considered the report of the Secretary-General,

Mindful of the humanitarian principles and provisions of the Geneva Convention relative to the Protection of Civilian Persons in Time of War of 12 August 1949,

Recalling the Nairobi Forward-looking Strategies for the Advancement of Women, in particular paragraph 260 thereof,

Recalling also its resolution 1988/25 of 26 May 1988,

Taking into account the _intifadah_ of the Palestinian people in the occupied Palestinian territories against the Israeli occupation and the oppressive practices of Israel against the Palestinian people, including women and children,

1. _Requests_ the Secretary-General to prepare a comprehensive report on the situation of Palestinian women, making use of all available information, including United Nations reports, information from Governments, non-governmental organizations and missions undertaken by United Nations bodies and specialized agencies to the occupied territories, and reports of meetings and seminars, as appropriate, and to submit the report to the Commission on the Status of Women at its thirty-fourth session;

2. _Requests_ the specialized agencies, in sending missions to the occupied Palestinian territories, to include an expert on women's issues to assess the situation of the Palestinian women and to elaborate specific projects of assistance;

3. _Strongly condemns_ the continuation of the "iron-fist" policy practised by Israel, the occupying Power, against Palestinian women and their families in the occupied Palestinian territories;

4. _Reaffirms_ that the Geneva Convention relative to the Protection of Civilian Persons in Time of War of 12 August 1949 is applicable to the territories occupied by Israel since 1967, including Jerusalem;

5. _Again requests_ the Secretary-General to send a mission composed of experts on the status of women to investigate the condition of Palestinian women and children, in the light of the drastic deteriorating situation in the occupied Palestinian territories;

6. _Requests_ the Commission on the Status of Women to monitor the implementation of the Nairobi Forward-looking Strategies for the Advancement of Women, in particular the provisions of paragraph 260 thereof concerning assistance to Palestinian women and children inside and outside the occupied Palestinian territories;

7. _Reaffirms_ that Palestinian women, as an integral part of a nation whose people are prevented from exercising their basic human and political rights, cannot fully participate in the attainment of the objectives of the Forward-looking Strategies, namely, equality, development and peace, without the realization of their inalienable right to return to their homes, their right to self-determination and their right to establish an independent State in accordance with the relevant United Nations resolutions.

Economic and Social Council resolution 1989/34

24 May 1989   Meeting 15   38-1-15 (recorded vote)

Approved by Second Committee (E/1989/90) by recorded vote (32-1-14), 16 May (meeting 16); draft by Commission on women (E/1989/27/Rev.1); agenda item 10.

Recorded vote in Council as follows:

In favour: Bahamas, Belize, Bolivia, Brazil, Bulgaria, Cameroon, China, Colombia, Cuba, Czechoslovakia, Ghana, Greece, Guinea, India, Indonesia, Iran, Iraq, Jordan, Liberia, Libyan Arab Jamahiriya, Nicaragua, Niger, Oman, Poland, Rwanda, Saudi Arabia, Somalia, Sri Lanka, Sudan, Thailand, Trinidad and Tobago, Tunisia, Ukrainian SSR, USSR, Uruguay, Venezuela, Yugoslavia, Zambia.

Against: United States.

Abstaining: Canada, Denmark, France, Germany, Federal Republic of, Ireland, Italy, Japan, Kenya, Lesotho, Netherlands, New Zealand, Norway, Portugal, United Kingdom, Zaire.

Women and children under _apartheid_

In accordance with 1988 requests of the Economic and Social Council,[12] the Secretary-General submitted in January 1989 a summary of major developments from 1 October 1987 to 30 November 1988 concerning the situation of women living under _apartheid_ in South Africa and Namibia.[13] The report outlined new developments in the political, social and economic spheres and described measures of assistance undertaken by UN organizations and the international community. It also examined current economic and social conditions that could affect the pace of women's advancement after the independence of Namibia.

ECONOMIC AND SOCIAL COUNCIL ACTION

On 24 May, on the recommendation of its Second Committee, the Economic and Social Council adopted **resolution 1989/31** without vote.

Women and children in Namibia
The Economic and Social Council,

Welcoming the full implementation of Security Council resolution 435(1978) of 29 September 1978, concerning the independence of Namibia,

Recalling its resolution 1988/24 of 26 May 1988, in which it expressed deep concern at the suffering of Namibian women under South African occupation,

Recalling also the Nairobi Forward-looking Strategies for the Advancement of Women, in particular paragraph 259, which calls for the speedy and effective implementation of Security Council resolution 435(1978),

Recognizing that the agreement recently reached on Namibian independence under Security Council resolution 435(1978) provides a historic opportunity for the Namibian people to realize their right to self-determination following 104 years of colonial domination,

Noting that with the implementation of Security Council resolution 435(1978) on 1 April 1989, Namibia faces a crucial transitional period, with an election campaign commencing on 1 July 1989 and the election scheduled for early November 1989, and that it is incumbent upon the international community to take immediate action to ensure that the elections render the justice and freedom to which the Namibian people have the right,

Bearing in mind that the repatriation of Namibian refugees from neighbouring States, which is scheduled to take place from 15 May to 30 June 1989, poses special problems that require massive humanitarian assistance,

1. _Urges_ Governments and intergovernmental and non-governmental organizations to make resources available to assist in making the repatriation process as smooth as possible and to continue material and financial support to Namibian women and children during the transitional period;

2. _Urges_ all parties to respect the process of implementing Security Council resolution 435(1978), in order to ensure independence for Namibia;

3. _Invites_ the Commission on the Status of Women to help raise international consciousness of the special circumstances and concerns of Namibian women;

4. _Requests_ the Secretary-General to encourage and give special attention to the full and equal participation of Namibian women, in both registration and voting;

5. *Also requests* the Secretary-General to submit to the Commission on the Status of Women at its thirty-fourth session a comprehensive report on the implementation and monitoring of the Nairobi Forward-looking Strategies for the Advancement of Women regarding women and children in Namibia.

Economic and Social Council resolution 1989/31

24 May 1989   Meeting 15   Adopted without vote

Approved by Second Committee (E/1989/90) without vote, 16 May (meeting 16); draft by Commission on women (E/1989/27/Rev.1); agenda item 10.

On the same date and on the Second Committee's recommendation, the Council adopted **resolution 1989/33** by recorded vote.

Women and children under *apartheid*

The Economic and Social Council,

Recalling its resolution 1988/23 of 26 May 1988,

Noting the concern of women throughout the world about the continuing degradation and abuse to which African women and children are subjected daily by the white minority régime of South Africa,

Recalling that this concern was expressed in the Nairobi Forward-looking Strategies for the Advancement of Women, which also contain proposals for various forms of assistance to be rendered to women and children inside South Africa and to those who have become refugees,

Recognizing that the inhuman exploitation and dispossession of the African people by the white minority régime is directly responsible for the appalling conditions in which African women and children live,

Also recognizing that the equality of women cannot be achieved without the success of the struggle for national liberation and self-determination of the people of South Africa against the racist régime of Pretoria,

Having considered the report of the Secretary-General on new developments concerning the situation of women under *apartheid* in South Africa and Namibia and measures of assistance to women in South Africa and Namibia,

1. *Commends* the tenacity and bravery of those women both inside and outside South Africa who have resisted oppression, who have been detained, tortured or killed, and of those whose husbands, children and relatives have been detained, tortured or killed and who, despite this, have remained steadfast in their opposition to the racist régime;

2. *Acknowledges* the efforts of those Governments, intergovernmental and non-governmental organizations and individuals that have campaigned for and applied sanctions against the racist régime;

3. *Condemns unequivocally* the South African régime for the imposition of the state of emergency, the forcible separation of black families, the detention and imprisonment of women and children and the restrictions on non-violent anti-*apartheid* democratic organizations and individuals;

4. *Urges* the South African régime to accord prisoner-of-war status to captured freedom fighters, in accordance with the Geneva Conventions of 12 August 1949 and the Protocol Additional to the Geneva Conventions of 12 August 1949 relating to the protection of victims of international armed conflicts (Protocol I), adopted in 1977, to accord all political prisoners sentenced to death, among whom are women, a fair trial based on international legal standards, and to stop the execution of political prisoners;

5. *Demands* the immediate and unconditional release of all political prisoners and detainees, among whom are an increasing number of women and children;

6. *Again calls upon* Governments, in view of the deterioration of the situation in South Africa, to impose, as a matter of urgency, comprehensive sanctions in accordance with the resolutions of the Security Council and the Nairobi Forward-looking Strategies for the Advancement of Women;

7. *Appeals* to all countries to support educational, health and social welfare programmes for women and children under *apartheid;*

8. *Also appeals* to the international community for increased assistance for women and children refugees in southern Africa;

9. *Urges* the international community to look into the newly developing situation of refugees and displaced persons, with a view to providing material assistance for them;

10. *Urges* Member States and United Nations bodies, in consultation with liberation movements, to give effect forthwith to the Nairobi Forward-looking Strategies that deal with women and children under *apartheid*, giving particular attention to education, health, vocational training and employment opportunities and to the strengthening of the women's sections of the liberation movements;

11. *Requests* the Commission on the Status of Women to work closely with women in the liberation movements in order to disseminate information and to ensure a proper assessment of the needs and aspirations of the women and children living under *apartheid;*

12. *Requests* the Secretary-General to submit to the Commission on the Status of Women at its thirty-fourth session a comprehensive report on the implementation and monitoring of the Nairobi Forward-looking Strategies in regard to women and children under *apartheid*.

Economic and Social Council resolution 1989/33

24 May 1989   Meeting 15   44-2-8 (recorded vote)

Approved by Second Committee (E/1989/90) by recorded vote (37-2-9), 16 May (meeting 16); draft by Commission on women (E/1989/27/Rev1); agenda item 10.

Recorded vote in Council as follows:

In favour: Bahamas, Belize, Bolivia, Brazil, Bulgaria, Cameroon, China, Colombia, Cuba, Czechoslovakia, Denmark, Ghana, Greece, Guinea, India, Indonesia, Iran, Iraq, Jordan, Kenya, Lesotho, Liberia, Libyan Arab Jamahiriya, New Zealand, Nicaragua, Niger, Norway, Oman, Poland, Rwanda, Saudi Arabia, Somalia, Sri Lanka, Sudan, Thailand, Trinidad and Tobago, Tunisia, Ukrainian SSR, USSR, Uruguay, Venezuela, Yugoslavia, Zaire, Zambia.

Against: United Kingdom, United States.

Abstaining: Canada, France, Germany, Federal Republic of, Ireland, Italy, Japan, Netherlands, Portugal.

Women in Central America

The Economic and Social Council, on the recommendation of its Second Committee, on 24 May adopted **resolution 1989/35** without vote.

Women and peace in Central America

The Economic and Social Council,

Recalling that, in adopting the Nairobi Forward-looking Strategies for the Advancement of Women, the World Conference to Review and Appraise the Achievements of the United Nations Decade for Women: Equality, Development and Peace recognized that women should participate fully in all efforts to strengthen and maintain international peace and security and to promote international co-operation,

Recalling also that the World Conference also recognized that the violence and destabilization in Central America hindered the fulfilment of the Nairobi Forward-looking Strategies, essential for the advancement of women,

Recalling further the agreement on "Procedures for the establishment of a firm and lasting peace in Central America", signed at the Esquipulas II summit meeting at Guatemala City, on 7 August 1987, by the Presidents of Costa Rica, El Salvador, Guatemala, Honduras and Nicaragua, and noting the subsequent meetings of the Presidents in 1988 and February 1989,

Recognizing the valuable contribution of the Contadora Group and its Support Group to the process of bringing peace to Central America,

Recognizing also the valuable efforts put forth by the Secretary-General and the international community to secure peace and development in Central America,

Convinced of the exceptional importance to the peoples of Central America, particularly the women, of the achievement of peace, reconciliation, development and social justice in the region, as well as the recognition of their economic, social, cultural, civil and political rights,

Considering that the General Assembly, in its resolution 42/1 of 7 October 1987, requested the Secretary-General to promote a special plan of co-operation for Central America,

Desiring to encourage the active participation of women in the promotion of peace and development in Central America,

1. *Expresses its satisfaction* at the will to achieve peace manifested by the Presidents of the Central American countries in their signing of the agreement on "Procedures for the establishment of a firm and lasting peace in Central America" and at their efforts for the implementation thereof;

2. *Again calls upon* the Presidents of the Central American countries to continue their joint efforts to achieve peace in Central America, particularly the efforts to establish the Central American Parliament, in order to ensure conditions favourable for the attainment in the region of the objectives of the Nairobi Forward-looking Strategies for the Advancement of Women, and requests the international community to support those efforts;

3. *Urges* all States to support the peace efforts, fully respecting the principles of self-determination of peoples and non-intervention;

4. *Also urges* the international community to ensure that programmes of technical, economic and financial co-operation for the region take account of the particular needs and interests of women in Central America;

5. *Recommends* to the Secretary-General that the special plan of co-operation for Central America include specific activities supporting the advancement of women in the region;

6. *Exhorts* the Governments of the Central American countries and of the countries of the Contadora Group and its Support Group to encourage and ensure the full participation of women at all levels in the search for peace, pluralism, democracy and overall development in the Central American region;

7. *Urges* national and international, governmental and non-governmental women's organizations to participate in and support actively the processes of democratization, peace and development in Central America.

Economic and Social Council resolution 1989/35

24 May 1989   Meeting 15   Adopted without vote

Approved by Second Committee (E/1989/90) without vote, 16 May (meeting 16); draft by Commission on women (E/1989/27/Rev.1); agenda item 10.

Also on the recommendation of its Second Committee and on the same date, the Council adopted **resolution 1989/39** without vote.

Women, human rights and development in Central America

The Economic and Social Council,

Considering the economic, social and political crisis in the Central American region, which involves various forms of discrimination and violence affecting women in particular,

Taking note of the report of the Secretary-General on the full participation of women in the construction of their countries and in the creation of just social and political systems,

Considering that in recent years various women's organizations have been formed in the region and that they are fighting and calling for the defence of human rights in general and women's rights in particular,

Recognizing the efforts that the Governments and peoples of Central America are making to achieve a political solution to the conflicts,

Recognizing also the need to unite and strengthen further the efforts of Governments, United Nations bodies and non-governmental organizations aimed at achieving a new international economic and social order, so as to make real and effective the development to which the peoples of Central America aspire,

1. *Urges* Governments, United Nations bodies and non-governmental organizations to support:

(a) Programmes to strengthen women's organizations that are demanding that women be granted their full rights as citizens;

(b) Activities or forums to broaden and deepen discussion of the problems of Central American women and solutions thereto, in which all social, political and cultural sectors of the countries of Central America may participate;

(c) Research to analyse the problems of Central American women in all their dimensions and to propose viable alternative solutions based on the opinions of all the women's sectors concerned;

(d) Publications and information and documentation systems relative to the results of the proposals for integration or practical action that will permit women's organizations in the Central American region to advance within the general context of society;

2. *Urges* the international community to publicize, and to support through international solidarity, the need for greater participation of women in the processes of change and in the bodies involved in negotiations and dialogue, which are designed to bring about a political solution to the problems and conflicts of the Central American region;

3. *Urges* national and international women's associations, both governmental and non-governmental, to develop education, training and self-help programmes aimed at improving the living conditions and the social and political participation of Central American women;

4. *Requests* the Secretary-General and the specialized agencies to pay particular attention to the implementa-

tion of the Nairobi Forward-looking Strategies for the Advancement of Women and to the human rights of women in Central America, as a prerequisite for ensuring women's full participation in the building of their countries and in the creation of social and political systems that are just.

Economic and Social Council resolution 1989/39

24 May 1989   Meeting 15   Adopted without vote

Approved by Second Committee (E/1989/90) without vote, 16 May (meeting 16); draft by Commission on women (E/1989/27/Rev.1); agenda item 10.

REFERENCES

[1]E/1989/27/Rev.1. [2]YUN 1988, p. 631, ESC dec. 1988/125, 27 May 1988. [3]E/CN.6/1989/5. [4]YUN 1985, p. 937. [5]E/1989/27/Rev.1 (res.33/5). [6]E/CN.6/1989/7. [7]E/1989/27/Rev.1 (res.33/4). [8]*Ibid.* (res. 33/2). [9]*Ibid.* (res. 33/6). [10]E/CN.6/1989/4 & Corr.1. [11]YUN 1988, p. 634, ESC res. 1988/25, 26 May 1988. [12]*Ibid.*, pp. 153 & 784, ESC res. 1988/23 & 1988/24, 26 May 1988. [13]E/CN.6/1989/3.

Discrimination against women

Convention on elimination of discrimination against women

The Committee on the Elimination of Discrimination against Women (CEDAW), established under the 1979 Convention on the Elimination of All Forms of Discrimination against Women[1] held its eighth session in Vienna from 20 February to 3 March 1989.[2]

The 23-member expert Committee was set up to monitor implementation of the Convention and progress made by States parties to ensure equality. Its members meet annually to review periodic country reports, traditionally alternating sessions between New York and Vienna. In 1989, CEDAW considered six initial reports of States parties (Belgium, Equatorial Guinea, Finland, Gabon, Ireland, Nicaragua) and three second periodic reports (Byelorussian SSR, German Democratic Republic, USSR) on legislative, judicial, administrative and other measures they had adopted to give effect to the Convention.

Noting that 1989 marked the tenth anniversary of the Convention's adoption, CEDAW, in a general recommendation, asked that countries undertake conferences and seminars to publicize the Convention and invited national women's organizations to participate in publicity campaigns. The Secretary-General was asked to assist in the commemoration by publishing and disseminating materials and preparing television documentaries about the Convention. He was also asked to make the necessary resources available to the Division for the Advancement of Women to prepare an analysis of the information provided by States parties.

Another general recommendation stated that States parties should ensure that their reports to CEDAW included information on statistical data to help clarify the situation of women in particular sectors. A third general recommendation stated that States parties should encourage, support and co-operate in projects for technical advisory services, including training seminars, to assist in reporting obligations. A fourth called for information to be included on legislation in force to protect women against all kinds of violence in everyday life; measures adopted to eradicate violence; support services for women who were the victims of abuse; and statistical data on the incidence of violence of all kinds against women and on women who were victims of violence.

A final general recommendation called for the study, development and adoption of job evaluation systems based on gender-neutral criteria. The Committee recommended support, as far as practicable, for the creation of implementation machinery to ensure the application of the principle of equal remuneration for work of equal value.

CEDAW also discussed recommendations to improve the functioning of the human rights treaty-monitoring bodies within the UN system. It suggested that the Secretary-General accord higher priority to the strengthening of the secretariat services of the Committee to ensure its effective operation.

Annexed to the Committee's report were a list of States parties to the Convention, CEDAW membership and the status of submission of reports by States parties under article 18 of the Convention as at 3 March 1989.

Tenth anniversary

In April, the Commission on the Status of Women adopted a resolution[3] on the tenth anniversary of the Convention. It strongly supported the view of CEDAW that the Secretary-General should accord higher priority within existing resources to strengthening support for CEDAW. It urged States parties to submit their periodic reports in accordance with the Convention and recognized the special relevance of those reports to efforts of the Commission to review and appraise implementation of the Nairobi Forward-looking Strategies for the Advancement of Women.

ECONOMIC AND SOCIAL COUNCIL ACTION

On 24 May, the Economic and Social Council, on the recommendation of its Second Committee, adopted **resolution 1989/44** without vote.

Elimination of discrimination against women in accordance with the aims of the Convention on the Elimination of All Forms of Discrimination against Women

The Economic and Social Council,

Bearing in mind that one of the purposes of the United Nations, as stated in Articles 1 and 55 of the Charter, is to promote universal respect for human rights and fundamental freedoms for all without distinction of any kind, including distinction as to sex,

Affirming that women and men should participate equally in social, economic and political development, should contribute equally to such development and should share equally in improved conditions of life,

Recalling General Assembly resolution 43/100 of 8 December 1988 and Council resolution 1988/26 of 26 May 1988,

Taking note of resolution 33/3 of 6 April 1989 of the Commission on the Status of Women,

Aware of the important contribution that the implementation of the Nairobi Forward-looking Strategies for the Advancement of Women can make to the elimination of all forms of discrimination against women and to the achievement of legal and *de facto* equality of women and men,

Bearing in mind that 18 December 1989 marks the tenth anniversary of the adoption of the Convention on the Elimination of All Forms of Discrimination against Women,

Having considered the report of the Committee on the Elimination of Discrimination against Women on its eighth session,

Noting that the Committee agreed, in examining reports, to take due account of the different cultural and socio-economic systems of States parties to the Convention,

1. *Welcomes* the ratification of or accession to the Convention on the Elimination of All Forms of Discrimination against Women by an increasing number of Member States;

2. *Urges* all States that have not yet ratified or acceded to the Convention to do so as soon as possible;

3. *Urges* States parties to the Convention to make all possible efforts to submit their initial reports on its implementation, as well as their second and subsequent periodic reports, in accordance with article 18 of the Convention and the guidelines provided by the Committee on the Elimination of Discrimination against Women, and to co-operate fully with the Committee in the presentation of their reports;

4. *Strongly supports* the view of the Committee that the Secretary-General should accord higher priority within existing resources to strengthening support for the Committee;

5. *Requests* the Secretary-General, in preparing the proposed programme budget for the biennium 1990-1991, to take due account of article 17, paragraph 9, of the Convention and provide the Committee with the staff and facilities necessary for the effective performance of its functions, so that it may carry out its mandate as efficiently as other human rights treaty bodies;

6. *Welcomes* the efforts made by the Committee to rationalize its procedures and expedite the consideration of periodic reports and to develop procedures and guidelines for the consideration of second and subsequent periodic reports, and strongly encourages the Committee to continue those efforts;

7. *Supports* the proposal made by the Committee to convene a working group to meet for three to five days prior to the ninth session of the Committee to prepare issues and questions relating to the second and subsequent periodic reports of the States parties, to be considered at that session of the Committee, and invites the General Assembly to take the necessary action;

8. *Recognizes* the special relevance of the periodic reports of States parties to the Convention to the efforts of the Commission on the Status of Women to review and appraise the implementation of the Nairobi Forward-looking Strategies for the Advancement of Women in those countries;

9. *Requests* the Secretary-General, in view of the tenth anniversary of the adoption of the Convention on 18 December 1989, to provide for, facilitate and encourage, within existing resources, the dissemination of information relating to the Committee and the Convention, taking into account all the relevant general recommendations made by the Committee at its eighth session, in particular general recommendation 10;

10. *Recommends* that sessions of the Committee on the Elimination of Discrimination against Women be scheduled, whenever possible, to allow for the timely transmission of the results of its work to the Commission on the Status of Women, for information, the same year.

Economic and Social Council resolution 1989/44

24 May 1989   Meeting 15   Adopted without vote

Approved by Second Committee (E/1989/90) without vote, 17 May (meeting 19); 18-nation draft (E/1989/C.2/L.15); agenda item 10.

GENERAL ASSEMBLY ACTION

On 8 December, the General Assembly, on the recommendation of the Third Committee, adopted **resolution 44/73** without vote.

Convention on the Elimination of All Forms of Discrimination against Women

The General Assembly,

Bearing in mind that one of the purposes of the United Nations, as stated in Articles 1 and 55 of the Charter, is to promote universal respect for human rights and fundamental freedoms for all without distinction of any kind, including distinction as to sex,

Affirming that women and men should participate equally in social, economic and political development, should contribute equally to such development and should share equally in improved conditions of life,

Recalling its resolution 34/180 of 18 December 1979, by which it adopted the Convention on the Elimination of All Forms of Discrimination against Women,

Recalling also its previous resolutions on the Convention, in particular resolution 43/100 of 8 December 1988, and taking note of Economic and Social Council resolution 1989/44 of 24 May 1989,

Recalling further the decisions taken on 7 and 8 March 1988 at the Fourth Meeting of States Parties to the Convention,

Aware of the important contribution that the implementation of the Nairobi Forward-looking Strategies for the Advancement of Women can make to eliminating all forms of discrimination against women and to achieving legal and *de facto* equality between women and men,

Noting the emphasis placed by the World Conference to Review and Appraise the Achievements of the United Nations Decade for Women: Equality, Development and Peace on ratification of and accession to the Convention,

Bearing in mind that 18 December 1989 marks the tenth anniversary of the adoption of the Convention,

Having considered the report of the Committee on the Elimination of Discrimination against Women on its eighth session,

Noting that the Committee agreed, in examining reports, to take due account of the different cultural and socio-economic systems of States parties to the Convention,

1. *Welcomes* the ratification of or accession to the Convention on the Elimination of All Forms of Discrimination against Women by an increasing number of Member States;

2. *Urges* all States that have not yet ratified or acceded to the Convention to do so as soon as possible;

3. *Emphasizes* the importance of the strictest compliance by States parties with their obligations under the Convention;

4. *Takes note* of the report of the Secretary-General and requests him to submit annually to the General Assembly a report on the status of the Convention;

5. *Takes note also* of the report of the Committee on the Elimination of Discrimination against Women on its eighth session;

6. *Endorses* general recommendation No. 10 of the Committee, made at its eighth session, on activities to commemorate the tenth anniversary of the adoption of the Convention, including the request that its report on the achievements of States parties and obstacles encountered by them in implementing the Convention be regularly updated, and requests that sufficient resources be provided for that purpose;

7. *Urges* States parties to the Convention to make all possible efforts to submit their initial as well as second and subsequent reports on the implementation of the Convention, in accordance with article 18 thereof and with the guidelines of the Committee, and to co-operate fully with the Committee in the presentation of the reports;

8. *Recognizes* the special relevance of the periodic reports of States parties to the Convention to the efforts of the Commission on the Status of Women to review and appraise the implementation of the Nairobi Forward-looking Strategies for the Advancement of Women in those countries;

9. *Strongly supports* the view of the Committee that the Secretary-General should accord higher priority to strengthening support for the Committee;

10. *Endorses* the proposal made by the Committee that a working group be convened to meet for three to five days prior to the ninth session of the Committee to prepare issues and questions relating to the second and subsequent periodic reports of the States parties to be considered at the ninth session of the Committee, and invites the Secretary-General to take the necessary action towards that end;

11. *Strongly encourages* the Committee to enhance its efforts to rationalize its procedures and expedite the consideration of periodic reports and to develop procedures and guidelines for the consideration of second reports;

12. *Takes note* of the proposals of the Secretary-General for full funding of the Committee and requests that the programme budget for 1990-1991 provide for attendance at all the Committee's meetings by relevant professional staff from the Division for the Advancement of Women of the Centre for Social Development and Humanitarian Affairs of the Secretariat, legal staff expert in human rights treaty implementation and adequate secretarial staff, and for the necessary facilities for the effective functioning of the Committee in order to enable it to carry out its mandate as efficiently as other human rights treaty bodies;

13. *Welcomes* the steps already taken by the Secretary-General and requests him, in view of the observance of the tenth anniversary of the adoption of the Convention on 18 December 1989, to facilitate and encourage, within existing resources, the dissemination of information relating to the Convention and the Committee, taking into account all the relevant general recommendations made by the Committee at its eighth session, in particular general recommendation No. 10;

14. *Requests* the Secretary-General to transmit the report of the Committee to the Commission on the Status of Women for information;

15. *Also requests* the Secretary-General to submit to the General Assembly at its forty-fifth session a report on the implementation of the present resolution, and to transmit the report to the Commission on the Status of Women at its thirty-fifth session.

General Assembly resolution 44/73

8 December 1989   Meeting 78   Adopted without vote

Approved by Third Committee (A/44/802) without vote, 20 November (meeting 49); 36-nation draft (A/C.3/44/L.29); agenda item 103.
Financial implications. S-G, A/C.3/44/L.40.
Meeting numbers. GA 44th session: 3rd Committee 21-28, 36, 49; plenary 78.

Ratifications, accessions and signatures

As at 31 December 1989, the Convention on the Elimination of All Forms of Discrimination against Women had 100 States parties. During the year, Antigua and Barbuda, Chile, the Libyan Arab Jamahiriya, Luxembourg and Madagascar became parties.[4]

In his annual report to the General Assembly on the status of the Convention,[5] the Secretary-General provided a list of States that had signed, ratified or acceded to the Convention as at 1 August 1989 and information on reservations and objections made between 1 September 1988 and 1 August 1989.

REFERENCES

[1]YUN 1979, p. 895, GA res. 34/180, annex, 18 Dec. 1979. [2]A/44/38. [3]E/1989/27/Rev.1 (res. 33/3). [4]*Multilateral Treaties Deposited with the Secretary-General: Status as at 31 December 1989* (ST/LEG/SER.E/8), Sales No. E.90.V.6. [5]A/44/457.

Chapter XIV

Children, youth and aging persons

During 1989, the United Nations Children's Fund (UNICEF) continued to make efforts to reduce infant and child mortality and improve the quality of life for children. Despite the world-wide economic set-backs, 42 countries had achieved universal child immunization by December, and many countries started linking immunization programmes with the basic maternal, child and primary health care systems. Emergency activities were continued in conflict-affected countries. UNICEF actively participated in Operation Lifeline Sudan, launched in April to assist 2.25 million people affected by recurring natural and man-made disasters, civil war and famine. In April, James P. Grant was reappointed as Executive Director of UNICEF for a further term of five years from 1 January 1990.

The education and unemployment problems facing young people were considered by the General Assembly, which, in December, requested the Secretary-General to promote and monitor intensively the inclusion of youth-related projects and activities in the programmes of UN bodies and specialized agencies, specifically in the areas of communication, health, housing, culture, youth employment and education, drug abuse and the environment.

The second review and appraisal of the implementation of the International Plan of Action on Aging was conducted during the year. Taking note with interest of the priorities identified and recommendations made therein, the Assembly endorsed the draft programme of UN activities relating to the tenth anniversary of the adoption of the Plan of Action, in 1992.

Children

UN Children's Fund

As in previous years, programmes for children were primarily carried out by UNICEF, which provided assistance for child survival and development, basic services and social mobilization.

In 1989, UNICEF co-operated in programmes in 128 countries and territories, the majority of which were in Africa (44), followed by Latin America and the Caribbean (35), Asia (34) and the Middle East and North Africa (15).

Programme expenditures totalled $501 million, of which $203 million was spent on child health; $76 million on water supply and sanitation; $74 million on planning and project preparation and programme support services; $48 million on emergency relief; $37 million on education; $35 million on community- and family-based services; and $28 million on child nutrition.

In his report on 1989 activities,[1] the UNICEF Executive Director noted that UNICEF programme performance reflected a mixture of continuity and innovation. Immunization coverage was continuing to expand. Some 112 countries, comprising about 99 per cent of developing country populations, had operational control of diarrhoeal diseases programmes, and 60 per cent of children under the age of five had access to trained providers of oral rehydration salts. UNICEF-supported drinking water supply programmes were reaching increasing numbers of developing country populations, especially in rural areas. From literacy to income-generation to food security, the focus had been on integrating women's concerns in all programme development. As a result, programme expenditures for women increased to 29 per cent of total expenditures in 1989, from 23 per cent in 1987. The Executive Director stated that the adoption of the Convention on the Rights of the Child in November (see below) was a major milestone in advocacy for children and set an appropriate stage for the new decade, in which the World Summit for Children, to be held in 1990, would provide new impetus for ratification of the Convention and promotion of attention to children.

Programme policy

Medium-term plan

At its 1989 regular session, the Executive Board endorsed[2] the programme objectives of the medium-term plan for the period 1988-1992,[3] and also approved[4] the medium-term plan as a framework of financial projections for 1989-1992, including the preparation of up to $248 million in programme expenditures from general resources. The medium-term plan consisted of five major sections related to planning environment and goals; major programme thrusts for the period; regional strategies; strengthening UNICEF capacity for supportive actions; and the financial plan for 1988-1992. It outlined as basic goals the reduction of maternal, infant and child mortality through the improvement of maternal and child health; the protection and improvement of children's well-being, their family and physical environment through sustainable development actions; the improvement of the well-being, situation and environment of women as well as their role in development; and the promotion of appropriate child-spacing to protect the health of the mother and child.

Strategies for children in the 1990s

In February, the Executive Director presented[5] to the UNICEF Executive Board views on how the needs of children should be addressed in an international development strategy for the fourth United Nations development decade (the 1990s), and proposed goals for child survival, development and protection by the year 2000. Those included reduction of the maternal and infant mortality rates by 50 per cent; virtual elimination of severe malnutrition; universal access to safe drinking water and eradication of guinea worm by 1995; universal access to sanitary means of excreta disposal; universal basic education for children and accelerated adult literacy programmes, especially for women; and improved protection of children in difficult circumstances. Also proposed were goals in specific and sectoral areas (maternal health, child health, nutrition, safe water supply and environmental sanitation, basic education, children in especially difficult circumstances) and for children in industrialized countries. Stating that those proposals were ambitious but feasible, the Executive Director suggested strategies to meet them, including the setting up of country- and region-specific targets.

In April, the Board authorized[6] the Executive Director to prepare an operational strategy for UNICEF to guide its activities and to help implement the national strategies, and to consult with Governments and other partners in development. It encouraged him to use the views and proposals presented as a basis for the global strategy for the well-being of children, as well as to serve as UNICEF input into the formulation of the international development strategy for the fourth United Nations development decade. It also invited[7] the Executive Director to explore ways to reach the poorest groups and to bring about their participation in the basic services and actions for development.

Policy reviews

The Executive Board considered, among other matters: children and environment; the implementation of UNICEF policy on women in development; UNICEF activities in the prevention of ac-

quired immunodeficiency syndrome (AIDS); and UNICEF external relations policies and function.

The policy review of children and environment[8] discussed the impact of environmental degradation on the health and well-being of children and women, and reviewed how environmental considerations were reflected in ongoing UNICEF-assisted programmes. Recommendations were made to address explicitly environmental concerns in the situation analysis, country programming and evaluation, as well as to add or strengthen environmental components in programmes. The Board approved[9] the recommendations as the broad policy framework for UNICEF action, and invited[10] the Economic and Social Council to take into account the ideas and expertise of UNICEF on the issue in its future preparatory work for the UN conference on environment and development.

The report on UNICEF policy on women in development[11] analysed the extent to which UNICEF assistance reflected the new policy on women in development and suggested areas requiring further attention, including needs of and services available to young girls, support to women farmers and special measures for women living in countries experiencing political crisis and economic adjustment.

The Board reviewed progress in UNICEF's AIDS-prevention activities in 1988.[12] The effect of AIDS on women and children worsened dramatically as heterosexual transmission spread human immunodeficiency virus (HIV) infection to increasing numbers of women, who passed the virus to their unborn children. In response, UNICEF would develop projects focusing on information, education and communication, training and the socio-economic impact of AIDS on women and children, and would also address new areas of impact on children, such as orphans of AIDS victims.

In response to a 1988 Executive Board request,[13] the Executive Director submitted a comprehensive review of UNICEF external relations policies and function.[14] Summarizing UNICEF advocacy activities on behalf of children, the review concluded that it had started contributing significantly to shaping the development process, rather than simply making a technical contribution to its advancement, and the full resources of the organization had been mobilized in synergistic, co-ordinated, sustained programme information efforts. The Board requested[15] the Executive Director to analyse and evaluate further the effectiveness of current external relations policies, functions, guidelines and activities.

UNICEF Maurice Pate Award

In March 1989, the Executive Director submitted to the Board a recommendation[16] to amend the process of nomination and selection of the recipient of the UNICEF Maurice Pate Award, established in 1966[17] to commemorate the first UNICEF Executive Director. Under the proposed changes, solicitation of nominations would be expanded to ensure a broad range of nominations and would stipulate a deadline of 31 July of the year preceding the presentation of the Award. The Executive Director would prepare a recommendation for review by the Bureau of the Board at its autumn meeting and the review would be based on the biographical data of all formally submitted nominations. At its April session, the Board endorsed[18] the proposed amendment.

The 1989 Award was presented to Suzanne Mubarak, the First Lady of Egypt, for, among other contributions, her role in establishing the National Council for Childhood and Motherhood in Egypt; her work in creating libraries and child development centres in Egypt; and the critical role she had played as Vice-President in shaping the direction of the Arab Council for Childhood and in mobilizing pan-Arab support for child development in the Arab world.

Adjustment with a human face

Faced with the tremendous social costs of adjustment programmes and the economic set-backs of the 1980s, international financial institutions, as well as many Governments of both developed and developing countries, were increasingly recognizing the need to protect vulnerable groups in the course of adjustment and to restore their long-term economic growth. In support of alternative economic adjustment policies, UNICEF frequently held consultations with the World Bank and the International Monetary Fund and was active in the dialogue between the World Bank and the Economic Commission for Africa on the African alternative adjustment programme. An informal group had been formed with the International Labour Organisation (ILO) and the World Food Programme to co-ordinate agency activities on problems of adjustment and food policy.

Activities related to structural adjustment continued in Argentina, Bolivia, Ecuador, the Gambia, Ghana, Guinea, Guyana, Kenya, Madagascar, Mozambique, the Philippines, Somalia and the United Republic of Tanzania. Programmes of action to mitigate the social consequences of adjustment were under way, with UNICEF support, in Ghana and Madagascar. In many countries, UNICEF offices actively supported interministerial task forces on priority-setting in social and economic programmes in collaboration with other UN agencies and non-governmental organizations (NGOs).

In April, the Executive Board, welcoming UNICEF's efforts to support countries interested in pursuing debt relief for promoting child survival, protection and development, encouraged[19] the Executive Director to explore with regional banks possibilities for voluntary debt-reduction schemes and to invite all private and official creditors to explore expanded application of debt-relief schemes for child survival, protection and development.

UNICEF programmes by region

Africa

The deleterious impact of structural adjustment programmes, external debt, a decrease in foreign aid flows, warfare and civil conflicts, domestic policy failures, natural disasters and AIDS continued to affect the quality of life and survival prospects of millions of African children in 1989. Countries in the sub-Saharan region continued to experience widespread decline in standards of child health and nutrition. As a result of the ongoing economic crisis and the accelerated pace of urbanization, African society was undergoing profound changes that affected the social and organizational behaviour of its populations. Strategies of Governments and organizations were passive, whereas societies were in a state of rapid transformation. Total expenditures for UNICEF's programmes in Africa in 1989 amounted to $170 million.

The West and Central Africa region continued to make progress towards immunization goals of 75 per cent of children under one year of age by the end of the 1990s: Cape Verde and the Gambia succeeded in sustaining universal child immunization (UCI); the Congo, Gabon, Guinea-Bissau and Togo reached over 60 per cent; and the Central African Republic, Mali, the Niger and particularly Nigeria, which accounted for more than half of the region's population, doubled their coverage rates. Multisectoral primary health care/Bamako Initiative planning committees, often including donor agencies, had been established in most countries of the region. Coverage under Bamako Initiative activities was still generally limited, but good progress had been achieved in Benin, Guinea, Nigeria and Sierra Leone. Various community-financing schemes were tested, all of which had as a major objective raising at least enough funds to ensure the continuous replenishment of 30 to 40 basic essential drugs. Oral rehydration therapy (ORT) was used to treat only 19 per cent of child diarrhoea cases, with 13 countries in West and Central Africa having rates at or below 10 per cent. Much assistance was provided for the training of health personnel and volunteers on correct diagnosis and proper use of ORT.

The number of AIDS cases progressively increased in West and Central Africa. With technical assistance from the World Health Organization (WHO), most countries were finalizing or implementing medium-term plans for AIDS control that included priority activities such as strengthening epidemiological surveillance and adopting measures to reduce the risks of sexual, blood and transplacental HIV transmission. UNICEF co-sponsored and participated in the International Symposium on AIDS Education held in Yaoundé, Cameroon.

With regard to water supply and environmental sanitation, strategies were being revised to achieve more systematic participation of the population. Communities were required to prove first that they were capable of maintenance and repair before new water and sanitation services were installed. Sanitation programmes were increasingly sustained by community mobilization, with schools, parents and political leaders becoming involved. Projects benefiting women had been firmly integrated into all UNICEF-assisted programmes in the region. Literacy and social mobilization were especially targeted towards women in Benin, Burkina Faso, Cape Verde, Côte d'Ivoire, Mali and Senegal.

In the Eastern and Southern Africa region, immunization activities continued to be the major thrust of UNICEF activities with Governments. As morbidity and mortality from immunizable diseases decreased, mortality from dehydration, acute respiratory infections, malaria and malnutrition had attracted greater attention as major causes of death among infants and young children. Many countries undertook coverage studies to develop strategies and actions for achieving UCI by 1990 or for sustaining the successes already achieved, and were working on strategies to increase the tetanus toxoid coverage of women of child-bearing age. Access to vaccination against tuberculosis was over 80 per cent, except in Angola, Ethiopia, Madagascar, Mozambique, Namibia, Somalia and Uganda. While the costs of the expanded programme on immunization (EPI) were borne by external funds in almost every country, and some countries still depended heavily on expatriate technical support for programme management, measures were being sought for gradual take-over by Governments. To fight against the persistently high incidence of diarrhoea stemming from unsafe water, poor environmental and personal hygiene and AIDS, UNICEF input to country programmes consisted of supplying oral rehydration salts (ORS), training, and equipment and raw materials for local ORS production.

In those countries with a high prevalence of AIDS (Burundi, Kenya, Rwanda, Uganda, United Republic of Tanzania, Zambia), an increase in deaths caused directly by paediatric AIDS and in-

directly by maternal AIDS was of great concern. Paediatric AIDS transmitted via the placenta was the most common route for HIV infection in children under five years of age. All countries in the region had medium-term plans for national AIDS control programmes, formulated with technical assistance from WHO. UNICEF assistance included mainly information, education and communication programmes, supplies (syringes, needles, sterilizers and protective materials), training, and studies on behavioural changes.

The countries in the region were in various phases of planning and/or implementing the Bamako Initiative. The principal focus of UNICEF support was, therefore, to strengthen national capacity. At headquarters, the Bamako Initiative Management Unit continued its central role in developing the conceptual framework of the Initiative into a broad-based maternal and child health/primary health care revitalization effort. Although challenges remained on such issues as the rational use of drugs, cost recovery problems, equity of access to primary health care, and essential drugs supply, provisional data from 44 health centres in Benin, for example, showed an overall increase of service utilization of 144 per cent since the introduction of the Initiative in February 1988. Breast-feeding was promoted through health education by nurses and the mass media. More than 70 per cent of children were breast-fed up to 12 months and 24 months of age in Botswana and Lesotho, respectively.

Good progress was made in 1989 towards the development of a systematic approach to gender-responsive planning and programming. Guidelines for undertaking studies and situation analyses of women and children had been adjusted so as to reflect gender concerns more effectively.

In order to assess the magnitude and severity of the problem of internally displaced children, a region-wide study was under way covering Angola, Ethiopia, Mozambique, Somalia, the Sudan and Uganda, and UNICEF responded to their emergency needs. In Namibia, UNICEF organized immunization, provided women farmers with tools and seeds, and supplied school materials.

The Economic and Social Council, in **resolution 1989/33** of 24 May, appealed to the international community for increased assistance for women and children refugees in southern Africa, and urged Member States and UN bodies to give particular attention to women and children under *apartheid* in their education, health, vocational training and employment opportunities.

Latin America and the Caribbean

The economic decline of the 1980s deeply affected all countries in the Latin American and Caribbean region. The region's 1989 gross domestic product was almost 10 per cent below that of 1980 and external debt amounted to $426 billion. It had approximately 103 million poor people under the age of 18. The economic crisis not only eroded the strength and credibility of democratic Governments but also was complicated by war and violence in some countries. Total expenditures in 1989 for UNICEF's programmes in the region amounted to $52 million.

All countries in the region adopted vaccination strategies which reinforced surveillance activities and routine vaccination at all government and non-government health facilities, created national vaccination days featuring application of all antigens, including tetanus toxoid for women of child-bearing age, and executed a house-to-house vaccination campaign in polio-infected communities. By October 1989, the incidence of polio had declined to 105 confirmed cases, concentrated in less than 2 per cent of municipalities. A regional inter-agency committee, composed of the Pan American Health Organization (PAHO)/WHO, UNICEF and the United States Agency for International Development (USAID), set guidelines for the preparation of five-year regional and national plans on the control of diarrhoeal diseases (CDD).

Low-cost water supply systems were developed in Bolivia, Cuba, Guatemala, Haiti, Honduras and Mexico, featuring community participation, social mobilization, health education, and training of counterparts and community personnel in maintenance operations. Educational coverage and access were expanded; Bolivia established multi-grade primary education covering 60,000 children in 1,700 schools and promoted intercultural bilingual education, while Colombia included the theme of child survival at all levels of education. Flexible learning systems, church alliances and the use of communication media were promoted in Brazil, El Salvador and Haiti. Initiatives in early child development continued to take place mostly through low-cost family-based approaches. New strategies were developed in the English-speaking Caribbean countries with emphasis on information and social mobilization. A development-oriented approach for women emphasized basic services, income-generating activities, organization of women and institutionalization. By the end of the 1980s, the number of programmes featuring actions for women, either as separate activities or a part of all projects, reached 20. Projects for children in especially difficult circumstances focused on health, education, nutrition, occupational training, family and community reintegration and psycho-social adjustment. There had been a clear change of attitude regarding those children, and a regional movement on their behalf was under way.

UNICEF, together with several Governments, addressed the problems of the urban poor by supporting basic service programmes, with emphasis on com-

munity participation. Successful experiences in pioneer countries such as Brazil, Colombia, Ecuador and Peru had contributed to the development of similar programmes in Argentina, Belize, Central America, Haiti, Jamaica, Mexico and Panama. The Mexico programme developed a methodology for primary health care delivery and a local health information system. Emphasis was on nutrition and income-generating activities for women through a community kitchen project in marginal areas of Mexico City, benefiting 3,000 families.

In April, with a view to ensuring the achievement of development targets, the Executive Board decided[20] to consider, in the light of the Executive Director's 1990 report, an allocation of resources to the Special Adjustment Fund for Latin America and the Caribbean.

Asia

While a number of Asian countries reported economic growth in 1989, others experienced high inflation and economic stagnation. High population growth, environmental degradation, inequity in access to services, ethnic unrests, and an overall increase in the number of families below the poverty line remained challenges for the near future. Programme expenditure in Asia amounted to $204 million, or 41 per cent of the Fund's global programme budget.

In the East Asia and Pakistan region and China, progress towards UCI continued to be rapid, with the Marshall Islands, the Philippines, the Republic of Korea and Thailand virtually achieving it. Indonesia, Malaysia and Pakistan were likely to achieve UCI by 1990. Many countries had CDD policies with ORT training, but implementation still remained low. Sanitation coverage improved throughout the region, as in the case of Bangladesh where it increased by 50 per cent in 1988-1989, although remaining at a very low 5 per cent. In Myanmar, 30 per cent of rural and 35 per cent of urban households had latrines and, in Indonesia, 22 per cent of the population had access to latrines and satisfactory waste disposal. UNICEF's nutritional activities concentrated on growth monitoring, the promotion of breast-feeding, food and nutrition surveillance and family food production. Control activities for iodine deficiency disorders improved in the region, with an increased production of iodated salt. The problem of vitamin A deficiency was pursued through the administration of high-dose vitamin A in Bangladesh, Indonesia, Myanmar, Pakistan and Viet Nam. The number of persons infected with AIDS increased significantly in 1989, with 9,473 cases reported by August. The majority (9,027) were recorded in Thailand.

UNICEF continued to support programmes benefiting women, such as training, literacy, income-generating activities and research studies on women.

Thailand trained 400 women from 20 cities in income-generating skills and formulated a model for granting credit facilities to women's groups. In Kampuchea, the Women's Association produced and distributed booklets for neo-literate women on child survival, women's health and income-generating activities. Activities in China focused on enhancing women's status, role and participation in development. They included the training of women cadres, assistance to teacher training and curriculum development for community-run pre-schools promoted by the All China Women's Federation, and the training of women community extension workers in Tibet. The provision of co-ordinated services for the children of the urban poor in Asia proved to be particularly difficult. However, in Pakistan, the Philippines and Thailand, UNICEF supported urban community organization by training community-level workers and volunteers.

In Bangladesh, UNICEF supported an experimental pilot scheme of "satellite schools" aimed at providing the rural poor and females with access to education. Kampuchea, the Lao People's Democratic Republic and Viet Nam reached almost full primary enrolment. In Solomon Islands, a comprehensive four-year plan of action was developed to integrate nutrition into the non-formal education curriculum.

In May, a regional consultation on strategies for development in Asia urged UNICEF to encourage countries to assess the need for the social education of children; to monitor the safety and wellbeing of children in armed conflicts or other serious violent situations; to assist with the collection, analysis and dissemination of social indicators; to advocate that Governments allocate more prime broadcast time to child survival and development and women's development issues; and to ensure the selection of well-qualified staff.

In South Central Asia, where about one half of the world's absolute poor lived, the population growth rate was well above the planned level and the gap between the haves and the have-nots continued to widen. A combination of inadequate nutrition, sanitation and education aggravated the health problems. However, there was a continually increasing attention to child-related issues at the policy and planning levels, especially in the area of primary health care.

The UNICEF immunization programme in Afghanistan continued in 14 provinces. In Bhutan, the establishment of more than 300 EPI outreach clinics had brought some 80 per cent of the population into contact with health workers. This led to the introduction of a more comprehensive series of services, including antenatal care, growth monitoring, the treatment of diarrhoea, deworming and concerns for water and sanitation. The phased implementation of the UCI programme in India reached all of India's 436 districts. Immunization coverage rates reached more than 60 per cent generally and over 80 per cent in some parts of the country. Although coverage for measles lagged behind, tetanus toxoid coverage might be one of the highest in the world with a verified 76 per cent coverage throughout the country. Through a mobile team approach, Maldives achieved UCI in 1989, and expanded functions of that team covered a wide array of primary health care activities.

In Mongolia, immunization coverage, supported and completely managed by the Government, exceeded 80 per cent for each antigen. UNICEF focused on the Ministry of Health diarrhoea management programme that included training of health workers in ORT. A public information programme using the press, radio and television resulted in the reduction in diarrhoea morbidity and mortality levels. Encouraging results had been obtained in Nepal with regard to EPI, the control of iodine deficiency disorders, the training of traditional birth attendants and the essential drugs programme. In the community water and sanitation programme, 62 per cent of the planned targets were achieved, although the sanitation component continued to be weak. Despite terrible set-backs due to civil unrest, Sri Lanka achieved UCI in 1989 and formed a task force to monitor and investigate maternal deaths.

Middle East and North Africa

The Middle East and North Africa region, with the possible exceptions of Lebanon and the Israeli-occupied territories, continued to experience a rapid decline in infant mortality. The resumption of diplomatic relations between Egypt and neighbouring Arab countries helped to make Egypt's leading performance in EPI and CDD a more widely accepted model for other Arab countries. UNICEF programme expenditures for the Middle East and North Africa in 1989 amounted to $61 million, 12 per cent of the global budget.

UCI by 1990 came within reach for all but three countries (Democratic Yemen, Sudan, Yemen) in 1989. To reach the target, Democratic Yemen and the Sudan decided to launch immunization thrusts in 1990 and Yemen would continue its decentralization programme. The Maghreb Arab Union and UNICEF co-operated to accelerate coverage through a simultaneous immunization thrust in all five member countries (Algeria, Libyan Arab Jamahiriya, Mauritania, Morocco, Tunisia). After the Union's collaborative acceleration day on 14 October, Libya announced its first internationally recognized coverage figures for children under one year old: 100 per cent for anti-tuberculosis vaccine; 84 per cent for three doses of oral polio vaccine

and three doses of combined diphtheria/pertus-
sis/tetanus vaccine; and 79 per cent for measles
vaccine. For 1989, all countries in the region set
a new common purpose of reducing child mortality from diarrhoeal diseases at an accelerated rate.

Sponsored by the United Nations, NGOs and
the Government of the Sudan, Operation Lifeline
Sudan, a six-month, $209 million famine-relief
programme, was launched in April (see below).
In the occupied territories, on the other hand, the
toll of injuries and deaths among Palestinian children took a sharp upturn.

UNICEF programmes by sector

Child survival and development

UNICEF, together with WHO, the World Bank,
the United Nations Development Programme
(UNDP) and the Rockefeller Foundation, continued to support the Task Force for Child Survival,
which was responsible for sponsoring an international meeting in Bangkok, Thailand, in 1990 to
promote final efforts to achieve the 1990 UCI goal
and to develop an international consensus on
strategies for achieving child survival goals for the
1990s.

Immunization

Globally, immunization coverage continued to
rise, leading to a significant reduction in disease
morbidity and mortality, and preventing an estimated 2 million deaths during 1989. Some 68 per
cent of children in developing countries had
received three doses each of combined diphthe-
ria/pertussis/tetanus vaccine and polio vaccine by
their first birthday. Coverage for anti-tuberculosis
vaccine had reached 75 per cent and measles had
reached 60 per cent. The immunization of pregnant women with tetanus toxoid also showed a
substantial increase.

To reach the more difficult areas and population groups, many countries carried out coverage
surveys to evaluate the comprehensiveness and
reliability of routinely collected data. UNICEF
worked together with WHO and Governments to
unify data bases to facilitate the assessment of UCI
achievement at the end of 1990.

Control of diarrhoeal diseases

Some 112 countries had operational CDD programmes, covering an estimated 99 per cent of the
total population in developing countries. It was estimated that nearly 60 per cent of children under
five years of age had access to trained and regularly supplied providers of ORS, although that access varied widely by region, from about 25 per
cent in Africa to over 75 per cent in Asia.

By the end of 1989, more than one in three epi-
sodes of diarrhoea in children under five were
treated with ORT, either in health facilities or at
home. UNICEF support included improving and
refining national plans of action and/or national
treatment guidelines; improving distribution and
availability of ORS; establishing diarrhoea training units and ORT corners to train health workers;
and reducing the inappropriate use of antibiotics
and anti-diarrhoeal drugs. UNICEF also provided
assistance for a wide variety of communications
activities, including the development of materials
for face-to-face communication between health
workers and mothers.

Primary health care

There was a greater recognition of the need for
community financing of primary health care, not
merely to assist Governments with severe budget
constraints, but also as a means of increasing community involvement in health. Attention had been
on sustaining the significant achievements in immunization; the decentralization of health services;
the strengthening of district management systems;
and the integration of primary health care, health
information, logistics and referral services. Many
countries started linking immunization programmes with the basic maternal and child
health/primary health care systems and other
health interventions such as malaria and CDD. In
many countries in Africa, where chloroquine resistance continued to increase, and in South-East
Asia, where resistance had spread to various
antimalarials, malaria control activities were integrated with maternal and child health care activities.

In collaboration with WHO, USAID and NGOs,
UNICEF developed appropriate low-cost technology in the field of maternal and child health and
immunization, such as a solar-powered electronic
scale and self-destruct syringes and needles. A
technology introduction panel was formed in 1989
to institutionalize the co-operation of agencies in
that area.

UNICEF support to national efforts on acute
respiratory infections (ARI) included the development of diagnosis and treatment protocols, training, communication activities and information-
gathering. UNICEF also supported preventive
measures. The impact of smoke-free stoves on the
incidence and severity of ARI was being tested in
Bhutan and Papua New Guinea, and immunization was promoted in the Sudan.

Bamako Initiative

In 1989, the Bamako Initiative made considerable progress in gaining acceptance for its ideas,
in developing programmes of action in 24 African countries and in demonstrating further progress in those countries which were already implementing programmes. The Initiative's basic

aim was to reinforce primary health care at the district level, including the rehabilitation of health care services at the periphery.

During the year, Benin expanded its primary health care project to 300 subdistricts in 70 districts of a total 517 subdistricts in 86 districts. Guinea's community-based strategy integrated the various components of primary health care, including immunization and essential drugs; the Government's decentralization policy allowed the district level to plan its development and manage local resources for health. Kenya introduced cost-sharing at all levels of the public health system and fees for out-patient services throughout the referral chain. A UNICEF-supported study on the willingness and ability of community members to pay for health care provided the basis for establishing affordability. An innovative approach in Burundi allowed families to pay for health cards in advance. It was estimated that $4.70 per family per year would cover the costs of essential drugs. Angola, Côte d'Ivoire, Malawi and Senegal were in the initial stages of planning on the Bamako Initiative.

In April, the Executive Board called on[21] UNICEF further to integrate education and communication components into the Initiative. It also urged UNICEF to seek supplementary funding for support to individual country programmes.

Acquired immunodeficiency syndrome

It was well-recognized that AIDS-related mortality in children under five years of age would impede the child mortality reduction that had been achieved in the past 20 years. The pandemic nature of the disease was producing a large group of orphans, who had lost one or both parents to AIDS.

UNICEF, in collaboration with WHO, had been assisting national AIDS-control programmes by teaching people to avoid behaviour and practices that could spread the AIDS virus. In Kenya, UNICEF supported a national women's organization and the Christian Health Association of Kenya in training health workers and community and church leaders in HIV/AIDS awareness. School health-education programmes which included AIDS prevention were supported in Burundi, Kenya, Rwanda, Uganda and other African countries. In addition, Governments were assisted in understanding the socio-economic impact of HIV/AIDS in order to find solutions to the problems of care for those suffering directly and indirectly from HIV/AIDS.

Nutrition and food security

UNICEF support for nutrition and food security reflected the general recognition that the nutritional status of children was primarily influenced by health care and a healthy environment; mater-nal and child care, including proper feeding practices; and food security.

During 1989, food and nutrition surveillance activities were expanded in co-operation with the Food and Agriculture Organization of the United Nations and WHO and supported by the Netherlands and Switzerland. Country projects became operational in China, Madagascar, the United Republic of Tanzania, Venezuela, Viet Nam and Zambia. Regional activities included the development of a training programme in food and nutrition surveillance for the Americas, in close co-operation with PAHO.

To reverse the declining trend in breast-feeding, a wide range of activities was carried out, including training of health workers, use of the mass media, and integrating breast-feeding promotion in maternal and child care programmes. Over 35,000 copies of the joint WHO/UNICEF statement on the topic were distributed.

Support was provided for food production at the household level. The United Republic of Tanzania mobilized communities to plant nearly 100,000 acres of food crops. As a result, many households produced far in excess of their consumption needs, thus contributing to increased levels of household income. In several Sahelian countries, assistance was provided for food production, dry-season gardening activities and community-based cereal banks.

UNICEF support to vitamin A deficiency control programmes more than doubled in 1989 over the levels of the previous two years, and supplies of high-dose vitamin A capsules reached a record 105 million. The distributions of the supplements in Bangladesh and India were built on the successful outreach of their immunization programmes. As for the control of iodine-deficiency disorders, support in 24 countries included advocacy, programme development, implementation, monitoring and evaluation.

The Joint Nutrition Support Programme (JNSP), started by WHO and UNICEF in 1983,[22] was evaluated in 1989. Findings indicated that there was no predetermined set of interventions that resulted in improved nutrition and that a programme to improve nutrition was more likely to succeed if it had a community-based approach. It was agreed that country-level activities would be supported through normal agency channels after JNSP ended in December 1989.

Childhood disability

In 1989, UNICEF assisted early detection and rehabilitation services of childhood disability in 27 countries. Egypt, Kenya and Pakistan reported national commitment at the highest level to programmes for disabled children. In Central America, through an innovative grass-roots approach involving parents and low-cost technology, the programme developed methodologies for providing care for disabled children, often allowing them to be "mainstreamed" in the regular educational systems. In China, there were programmes for the early identification of and intervention for children with special needs and for mentally retarded pre-school children. Brazil emphasized the training of special education teachers in disability prevention and early detection. In Mauritius, where it was estimated that 12 per cent of children suffered from some kind of impairment, UNICEF assistance focused on the design of a system for early identification and intervention in pre-schools and on a widespread sensitization campaign in the community to integrate disabled children in schools and to train teachers.

A systematic situation analysis regarding disabled children was conducted in each country as part of the subregional situation analysis. This new subregional programme included components related to community-based prevention and early detection and treatment of childhood disabilities. In August, UNICEF co-sponsored an international conference on the current state and future trends of rehabilitation of disabled children, held in Tallinn, Estonia, USSR.

Water supply and sanitation

In an increasing number of countries, UNICEF-supported CDD programmes were linked to water and sanitation programmes. Evaluation in some of those countries showed that integrated water, sanitation and hygiene education programmes could reduce the incidence of diarrhoea among children by 20 to 25 per cent. In Benin and Nigeria, the UNICEF water supply projects were linked to the eradication of guinea worm.

In the area of water and sanitation, UNICEF activities included rainwater harvesting via roof and rock catchment in a number of countries; the experimental use of solar pumps in Benin, the Gambia and Myanmar; the rehabilitation of old and non-functional water and sanitation systems simultaneously with the construction of new systems; linking water and sanitation programmes with environmental concerns; and material and equipment development.

In April, the Executive Board called on[23] all endemic States to intensify measures towards the elimination of guinea-worm disease in the 1990s and authorized the Executive Director to support them in the active case-search of the disease and in the formulation of national plans of action. It approved $1.55 million for the period 1989-1990 for country studies and services.

Basic education

In many countries, the number of primary-school students had decreased, the disparity between the enrolment of boys and girls had widened and both the quality and relevance of education had declined. About 100 million children had no access to education. However, UNICEF programme co-operation in education remained modest.

Support for primary education, adult literacy and training, special education for disabled children and education facilities for children in difficult circumstances had been of a catalytic nature. UNICEF co-operated in curriculum reform, teacher training and the production or supply of teaching materials. Lessons on health, nutrition, sanitation and other aspects of child and maternal health had been incorporated in most basic education programmes at the pre-school, primary and adult literacy levels. Linking women's literacy programmes with some income-generating activities had reduced high drop-out rates and motivated poor, illiterate women to become literate.

In April, the Executive Board recommended[24] that, in order to protect children, youth and the unborn child, UNICEF should be more actively involved in control of tobacco-use programmes in public, maternal and school education.

Urban basic services

As the economic situation deteriorated and war or internal strife continued in many countries, their urban centres were strained in trying to cope with the needs of new migrants.

The urban basic services programme in India had reached 118 cities, supporting community development efforts in city governments, community organizations and basic services, including primary health care, immunization, early childhood development, and water and basic sanitation. In Thailand, urban programmes had reached all major and secondary cities, and in Bangkok the programme was extended to include a working- and street-children project. In Latin America, urban basic services achieved solid results in Guatemala, Honduras and Nicaragua. Colombia was expanding the programme to other poor areas and approaching sustainability. Programmes were being developed in Kenya, Liberia, Nigeria and the Sudan.

Women in development

UNICEF country programme initiatives in 1989 showed growing application of the policy on women, which was to incorporate the needs and concerns of girls and women into the mainstream programmes. In child and maternal health interventions, women and women's organizations contributed to the successes of large-scale immunization and water services in several countries. The provision of community water services in UNICEF-assisted countries had helped to reduce the time and energy spent by women in the task of water collection.

Major initiatives were being undertaken on the education, health and overall well-being of girls, and non-formal education and literacy programmes for women and adolescents continued to be strengthened and integrated with health education, vocational training and economic activities for women. Strategic objectives identifying women's participation, income generation, access to credit, employment, work-load reduction, non-formal education and the provision of child-care facilities for working women were specified in the programmes of Brazil, Burkina Faso, Colombia, Democratic Yemen, Mauritius, Mexico, Nepal, Sierra Leone, the United Republic of Tanzania and Venezuela. Regarding programme design, many countries utilized the area-based approach to target poor women and enhance their participation, permitting the integration of gender concerns in sectoral programmes such as health, education, water and sanitation, nutrition and household food security. The area-based strategy in Mozambique reached women in their communities, identified their needs and successfully involved them in implementing integrated projects covering household food security, health, child care, adult education and training.

Women were the principal mobilizers and agents in health and water and sanitation sectors in Bolivia, India, Indonesia, Iraq, Nigeria, Peru, Somalia and the Sudan. Women participated in the management and maintenance of water systems in Ethiopia, India, Morocco, Pakistan, the Sudan and Zimbabwe. Some 14,200 women mechanics and caretakers in India had been trained with UNICEF assistance.

Emergency relief and rehabilitation

In 1989, emergency relief assistance to 15 countries hit by natural disasters, epidemics and man-made crises was authorized from the Executive Director's Emergency Reserve Fund in the amount of more than $2.6 million for unforeseen and unmet survival and rehabilitation needs of children and women. In addition, a total of $481,000 was diverted from regular programme funds to provide a rapid response to emergency situations in 16 countries, and cash contributions were received for emergency relief operations in 21 countries amounting to $51.3 million. A total of $54.3 million was received from all sources of funding for emergency operations in 39 countries.

In response to outbreaks of meningococcal meningitis in Benin, Ethiopia, the Gambia, Morocco, the Sudan and the Syrian Arab Republic, and of measles in El Salvador and Guatemala, UNICEF carried out massive vaccination campaigns. The bulk of emergency assistance to vic-

tims of typhoons and floods in Angola, the Caribbean, the Comoros, Democratic Yemen, Djibouti, Malawi, Mali, Mauritius, Somalia, Sri Lanka, the United Republic of Tanzania, Viet Nam and Zambia was directed to the rehabilitation of essential services damaged during the disaster.

Emergency and rehabilitation assistance continued in conflict-affected countries, including Afghanistan, Angola, Ethiopia, Iran, Iraq, Lebanon, Mozambique, Namibia and the Sudan. UNICEF's emergency appeals for those countries made within the UN system-wide appeal or launched independently received a total of $107.8 million, with a total unfunded balance of $88 million. In the West Bank and Gaza, UNICEF implemented a physiotherapy project jointly with the UN Relief and Works Agency for Palestine Refugees in the Near East in order to provide medical care for injured children with the threat of life-long disabilities from limb fractures as a result of the Palestinian uprising.

As part of 17 UNICEF-supported projects inside Afghanistan, 45 immunization teams reached 400,000 children and mothers, and female health workers were trained. A general survey of childhood disability of all Afghan children was being conducted with a view to establishing community-based rehabilitation services.

Increasingly, UNICEF field offices began to participate in the development of national early-warning and preparedness efforts. In support of those initiatives in Angola, Bangladesh, Ethiopia, Mozambique, the Sudan and Zimbabwe, UNICEF provided programme and operational assistance to the Governments' co-ordinating mechanisms and personnel training. UNICEF's own preparedness was enhanced through staff training in emergency management.

Operation Lifeline Sudan

In view of the grave situation in the Sudan, where recurring natural and man-made disasters, civil war and famine had led to more than 250,000 deaths since 1988, "Operation Lifeline Sudan" was launched in April 1989. The food and non-food supplies required to meet the needs of the affected 2.25 million people were estimated at 120,000 metric tons and the total costs at $133 million.

As the UN Secretary-General's Personal Representative for Operation Lifeline Sudan, the UNICEF Executive Director contacted Governments and international organizations at the highest level to mobilize support and to serve as a point of contact with the central Government of the Sudan and the Sudan People's Liberation Movement/Sudan People's Liberation Army. In addition to its role as the UN lead agency for relief activities co-ordination, UNICEF supported immunization, essential drugs and other health-related matters, supplementary feeding, water supply, general relief provisions and school materials. To ensure the immediate start of UNICEF activities, the Executive Director authorized the provisional release of $2.9 million from the Emergency Fund, prior to the receipt of contributions. An appeal launched within the framework of the plan of action resulted in the contribution of more than $17 million as at 25 December 1989.

By the end of September 1989, total deliveries of food and non-food items amounted to some 106,424 metric tons, representing 88 per cent of the total needs. The Operation officially ended on 31 October 1989. However, it was to be followed by a second phase that would provide a similar level of food and non-food support to the target population.

On 24 October, the General Assembly, in **resolution 44/12**, reaffirmed the need to continue responding to requests for relief, rehabilitation and reconstruction during the forthcoming phase of the Operation.

Children in difficult circumstances

UNICEF remained involved in activities for children in armed conflict and for working and street children. In the Sudan, it created "corridors of peace" to allow relief supplies to be distributed, carrying out the concept of "children as a zone of peace". In Lebanon, over 100 summer camps were organized for specific educational activities to promote peace and mutual understanding among youth from conflicting factions. Action research on the psycho-social effects of armed conflict was under way in Central America and Mozambique.

Ongoing co-operation with ILO to combat child labour exploitation included UNICEF support for a tripartite meeting on child labour in Africa (Cairo, Egypt, September). In Egypt, the Philippines, Thailand and several Latin American countries, programmes were started to provide protection and services for working children. Programmes for street children expanded rapidly in Latin America and were being initiated in Africa and Asia. UNICEF continued to expand its co-operation with national and international NGOs to raise public awareness and concern about child abuse and neglect.

Drug abuse among children

In April, the Executive Board, recognizing the rapid growth of drug abuse among children, especially those living in extreme poverty and in difficult circumstances, requested[25] the Executive Director to co-operate with interested Govern-

ments in the planning of an assessment of the causes and magnitude of the problem.

On 22 May, by **decision 1989/123**, the Economic and Social Council, recalling a 1988 General Assembly resolution[26] in which the Assembly strongly condemned drug trafficking in all its forms, particularly those criminal activities that involved children in the use, production and illicit sale of narcotic drugs, appealed to the United Nations Fund for Drug Abuse Control to assign high priority to support for programmes to rehabilitate drug-addicted minors.

UNICEF finances

UNICEF income in 1989 totalled $667 million, comprising $423 million in general resources and $244 million in supplementary funds, including $57 million in emergency contributions. Contributions from Governments and intergovernmental organizations accounted for 75 per cent of the total income. Expenditures in 1989 totalled $633 million.

In April, the Executive Board approved[27] new allocations for programme co-operation and the replenishment of the Emergency Reserve Fund of $242,906,000 for general resources funding and $326,924,000 for programmes for supplementary funding. In view of the proposed goals and strategies for children in the 1990s (see above), the Board requested[28] the Executive Director to analyse the criteria used for the allocation of UNICEF resources to support country programme priorities. The Board also approved[29] the revised expenditure estimates and income estimates for the bienniums 1988-1989 and 1990-1991.

Organizational questions

UNICEF Executive Board

During 1989, the UNICEF Executive Board held at UN Headquarters its regular session from 17 to 28 April,[30] two organizational sessions on 12 June[31] and 20 December,[32] respectively, and a special session from 18 to 22 December.[33] The Board elected, at its June organizational session, its officers for the period 1 August 1989 to 31 July 1990 (see APPENDIX III). At its December organizational session, representatives were elected to the United Nations Educational, Scientific and Cultural Organization (UNESCO)/UNICEF Joint Committee on Education Policy. The special session was devoted to the planning of the proposed World Summit for Children.

At its 1989 regular session, the Executive Board streamlined[34] its procedures on time allotment, draft proposals for adoption and documentation. The Board also amended[35] the UNICEF Rules of Procedure and established[36] a working group responsible for making recommendations to the Board in 1990 regarding the continuation of the updating of the Rules of Procedure.

The Economic and Social Council, in **decision 1989/189** of 28 July, took note of the Board's report on its regular session.

Greeting Card Operation

In 1989, the mandate of the Greeting Card Operation was enlarged to encompass activities in the areas of product sales, exhibits and promotion, private sector fund-raising support to national committees and field offices, and special fund-raising events and new initiatives. In the 1988/89 season, the sale of 139 million cards brought in revenues of $98.9 million and the Operation contributed $43.2 million to UNICEF general resources.

In the area of sales, new product lines were tested and adapted to new markets, the retail store programme in Europe was expanded and cost controls were implemented to move towards the goal of 50 per cent profitability. The Danny Kaye Visitors Centre at UNICEF House hosted numerous groups of schoolchildren, volunteers and other visitors, and a teacher's guide for the exhibit was produced in co-operation with the United States Committee for UNICEF. The Operation also provided a number of direct mail packages that had been adapted to specific countries and used by national committees to raise funds.

In April, the Executive Board approved[37] budgeted expenditures of $34.8 million to $36.7 million and budgeted income of $76.2 million to $90.6 million, for the fiscal year 1 May 1989 to 30 April 1990.

International Child Development Centre

The Executive Director, pursuant to a 1988 Executive Board request,[38] reported[39] on the International Child Development Centre in Florence, Italy, updating the Centre's staffing and financing status and the use of facilities.

The Centre's work concentrated on four major programme areas: national capacity-building for child survival and development; economic policies and the mobilization of resources for children; the rights of the child; and the needs of the urban child. The first of the new series of global "Innocenti Seminars" was held in Florence in June on the subject of early childhood development.

Inter-agency co-operation

During 1989, UNICEF collaborated with a widening range of partners, including agencies of the UN system, to focus attention on development issues related to children. Major work was carried out in co-operation with the Centre for Human

Rights and the Department of Public Information of the UN Secretariat related to the draft Convention on the Rights of the Child (see below); with WHO on a series of health measures, especially in immunization, malaria, essential drugs and health education; with WHO, UNDP, the World Bank and the Rockefeller Foundation in the Task Force for Child Survival; and with WHO and UNDP on guinea-worm eradication efforts. The Task Force for Child Survival was organizing a meeting in Bangkok, Thailand, in 1990, to provide support for the final push to reach the UCI goal and for activities to enable countries to reach additional goals set for the 1990s.

In April, the Executive Board requested[40] the Executive Director to participate fully in the operational activities for development of the UN system and in the forthcoming triennial policy review on them.

UNICEF/WHO Joint Committee on Health Policy

At its twenty-seventh session (Geneva, 23-25 January),[41] the UNICEF/WHO Joint Committee on Health Policy considered the impact of the world economic crisis on health and health services, a strategy for improved nutrition of mothers and children in the developing world, and common goals for the health of women and children by the year 2000. It also reviewed progress made in EPI, the Bamako Initiative, diarrhoeal diseases control, the Safe Motherhood Initiative and the Global Programme on AIDS.

In April, the UNICEF Executive Board invited[42] the Executive Director to use the goals for the health of women and children by the year 2000 as the basis for part of UNICEF's contribution to the preparation of the international development strategy for the fourth UN development decade.

UNESCO/UNICEF Joint Committee on Education Policy

In April, the Executive Director recommended the establishment of the UNESCO/UNICEF Joint Committee on Education Policy to facilitate a high-level exchange of views on policy and approaches in areas of mutual interest and to strengthen co-operation at the country level.

The establishment of the Joint Committee was approved[43] by the UNICEF Executive Board in April and by the UNESCO Executive Board in June.

Draft Convention on the Rights of the Child

At its 1989 regular session, the Executive Board requested[44] UNICEF to continue its efforts to facilitate the final adoption by the General Assembly of the draft Convention on the Rights of the Child. UNICEF organized several meetings, involving the Inter-Parliamentary Union (Budapest,

Hungary, March); the Maghreb nations (Tunis, Tunisia, June); the heads of States members of the Organization of African Unity (Kampala, Uganda, July); the First Ladies of several Central American countries (El Salvador, September); and the Commonwealth parliamentarians (Barbados, October). Field offices and national committees also organized meetings to support the Convention, through which key constituency groups and the media were mobilized.

On 24 May, the Economic and Social Council, by **resolution 1989/79**, submitted to the General Assembly the draft Convention prepared by the Commission on Human Rights. The Assembly, by **resolution 44/25** of 20 November, adopted the Convention and opened it for signature, ratification and accession.

World Summit for Children (1990)

The Executive Board held a special session (New York, 18-22 December)[33] to consider secretariat support for the 1990 World Summit for Children, initiated by six Governments (Canada, Egypt, Mali, Mexico, Pakistan, Sweden). The Summit had originally been proposed in *The State of the World's Children, 1989*, in order to bring attention and promote commitment, at the highest political level, to goals and strategies for ensuring the survival, protection and development of children as key elements in the socio-economic development of all countries. The Executive Director recommended that UNICEF take advantage of the opportunity presented by the Summit to promote public awareness and stimulate programme mobilization among Governments, NGOs, the media, professional organizations and public leaders.

Welcoming the initiative of the six Governments, the Board agreed[45] that UNICEF should provide secretariat support for the preparation of the Summit. It noted the initiators' establishment of an *ad hoc* planning committee and requested that its membership include other Governments. The Executive Director was authorized to enter into necessary committal expenditures for the preparation of the Summit up to an amount of $700,000; he was requested to establish a special account for the preparation of the Summit and a special account for mobilization activities related to the Summit.

REFERENCES

[1]E/ICEF/1990/2 & Add.1. [2]E/1989/31 (dec. 1989/4). [3]E/ICEF/1989/3. [4]E/1989/31 (dec. 1989/26).[5]E/ICEF/1989/L.5. [6]E/1989/31 (dec. 1989/5). [7]*Ibid.* (dec. 1989/8). [8]E/ICEF/1989/L.6. [9]E/1989/31 (dec. 1989/18). [10]*Ibid.* (dec. 1989/6). [11]E/ICEF/1989/L.1. [12]E/ICEF/1989/L.7. [13]YUN 1988, p. 648. [14]E/ICEF/1989/L.4. [15]E/1989/31 (dec. 1989/11). [16]E/ICEF/1989/L.14. [17]YUN 1966, p. 385. [18]E/1989/31 (dec. 1989/22). [19]*Ibid.* (dec. 1989/9). [20]*Ibid.*

(dec. 1989/13). [21]*Ibid.* (dec. 1989/15). [22]YUN 1983, p. 932. [23]E/1989/31 (dec. 1989/7). [24]*Ibid.* (dec. 1989/19). [25]*Ibid.* (dec. 1989/16). [26]YUN 1988, p. 691, GA res. 43/121, 8 Dec. 1988. [27]E/1989/31 (dec. 1989/20). [28]*Ibid.* (dec. 1989/23). [29]*Ibid.* (dec. 1989/27). [30]E/1989/31. [31]E/ICEF/1989/13. [32]E/ICEF/1989/16. [33]E/ICEF/1989/17. [34]E/1989/31 (dec. 1989/1). [35]*Ibid.* (dec. 1989/2). [36]*Ibid.* (dec. 1989/3). [37]*Ibid.* (dec. 1989/30). [38]YUN 1988, p. 649. [39]E/ICEF/1990/L.9. [40]E/1989/31 (dec. 1989/14). [41]E/ICEF/1989/L.11. [42]E/1989/31 (dec. 1989/12). [43]*Ibid.* (dec. 1989/17). [44]*Ibid.* (dec. 1989/10). [45]E/ICEF/1989/17 (dec. 1989/31).

Youth

During 1989, the Centre for Social Development and Humanitarian Affairs (CSDHA) of the UN Secretariat, at Vienna, as the focal point for youth matters within the UN system, continued to play an important role in highlighting main issues and problems of youth, as well as their possible solutions. It also continued to enhance national capacities in developing comprehensive youth policies and programmes through the provision of policy guidance and information, advisory services and direct operational support.

Follow-up to International Youth Year (1985)

CSDHA co-ordinated global efforts to achieve the objectives of the International Youth Year (IYY).[1] Despite the financial and human resource constraints, it carried out research and analysis to identify youth issues and trends at the national level. It also initiated a global exchange of information on youth issues by disseminating the trimesterly *Youth Information Bulletin*, the quarterly *IYY Follow-up Newsletter* and directories pertaining to youth research centres and to international youth organizations.

CSDHA, in co-operation with the Department of Technical Co-operation for Development of the UN Secretariat, continued to provide the services of the Interregional Adviser on Youth Policies and Programmes to assist requesting Governments in developing long-term integrated youth policies and programmes. From January 1988 to June 1989, the Interregional Adviser undertook missions to 14 countries. CSDHA was developing training programmes and material for juvenile justice personnel and providing advisory services in juvenile justice administration. Greater emphasis was placed on delinquency prevention and dealing with young people "at risk", such as school-leavers, unemployed youth, street children and drug abusers.

Implementation of the guidelines in the field of youth

Pursuant to a 1987 Economic and Social Council request,[2] the Secretary-General submitted to the Commission for Social Development, at its thirty-first session (Vienna, 13-22 March),[3] a report[4] on the implementation of the guidelines for further planning and suitable follow-up in the field of youth. The guidelines, endorsed by the General Assembly in 1985,[5] provided both an internationally agreed framework of strategies for future work and a basis for concerted follow-up activities to IYY. The report presented a review of national activities for the implementation of the guidelines, paying particular attention to efforts aimed at developing integrated national youth policies.

The Secretary-General noted that there had been increased recognition of the need to formulate and implement comprehensive youth policies within the context of integrated development planning. Many Governments had made progress in developing institutional arrangements and setting up mechanisms for that purpose. Priority had been accorded to such areas as improving educational attainment and skills training; non-formal education for out-of-school youth; facilitating the transition from school to work; training schemes leading to employment; health; social services; and recreational programmes. However, a number of obstacles remained, including lack of adequate data on youth, a paucity of financial resources and trained personnel, and insufficient inter-institutional co-ordination.

The Secretary-General recommended that political commitment be strengthened and the national youth policy integrated into the overall national development policy. He also recommended that NGOs and young people should be represented in all relevant decision-making bodies and more attention should be paid to young people in marginal situations, including women, migrants and refugees.

The Commission decided[6] to consider at its thirty-second (1991) session, as a priority subject, the problem of the integration of young people into society.

ECONOMIC AND SOCIAL COUNCIL ACTION

On 24 May, the Economic and Social Council, on the recommendation of its Second (Social) Committee, adopted **resolution 1989/51** without vote.

Youth in the contemporary world

The Economic and Social Council,

Recalling its resolutions 1985/23 of 29 May 1985 and 1987/45 of 28 May 1987,

Recalling also General Assembly resolution 40/14 of 18 November 1985 entitled "International Youth Year: Participation, Development, Peace", in which the Assembly requested the Commission for Social Development to examine, on a regular basis, specific youth issues, and resolution 43/94 of 8 December 1988, in which the Assembly called upon all States, all United Nations bodies, in particular the Economic and Social Council through its Commission for Social Development, the specialized agencies and the intergovernmental and non-governmental organizations concerned, in particular youth organizations, to continue to exert all possible efforts for the implementation of the guidelines for further planning and suitable follow-up in the field of youth, in accordance with their experience, conditions and priorities,

Recognizing the necessity of adopting effective measures, particularly in the fields of education, above all, teaching, culture and information, in order to strengthen the efforts for the promotion of understanding, mutual respect and friendship among nations and, primarily, among young people, for the creation of an international climate free from mistrust and discord,

Convinced that it is necessary to ensure full enjoyment by youth of all the rights stipulated in the Universal Declaration of Human Rights, adopted by the General Assembly in resolution 217 A (III) of 10 December 1948, and the International Covenant on Economic, Social and Cultural Rights and the International Covenant on Civil and Political Rights, adopted by the Assembly in resolution 2200 A (XXI) of 16 December 1966,

1. *Takes note* of the report of the Secretary-General on the implementation of the guidelines for further planning and suitable follow-up in the field of youth;

2. *Recognizes* that the guidelines provide a constructive framework for a long-term strategy in the field of youth;

3. *Expresses its concern* that the lack of financial and human resources within the Centre for Social Development and Humanitarian Affairs of the Secretariat has hindered the effective implementation of the guidelines, especially in developing countries;

4. *Calls upon* all States, all governmental, intergovernmental and non-governmental organizations and the United Nations system, in particular the Economic and Social Council through its Commission for Social Development, to continue to give appropriate attention to proper follow-up and implementation of the guidelines;

5. *Urges* the Secretary-General to strengthen the efforts aimed at proposing and monitoring action-oriented programmes to promote the process of implementation of the guidelines, *inter alia*, focusing on the promotion of regional and international co-operation;

6. *Invites* Governments and intergovernmental and non-governmental organizations to contribute generously, according to their ability, to the United Nations Youth Fund, taking into account the specific recommendations included in the guidelines;

7. *Requests* the Secretary-General to submit to the Commission for Social Development at its thirty-second session a report on the implementation of the guidelines;

8. *Requests* the Commission for Social Development at its thirty-third session to prepare a draft programme of action to mark the tenth anniversary of the International Youth Year: Participation, Development, Peace, for implementation at the international level, and to identify future strategies in the field of youth, and requests the Secretary-General to report thereon to the General Assembly at its forty-eighth session.

Economic and Social Council resolution 1989/51
24 May 1989   Meeting 15   Adopted without vote

Approved by Second Committee (E/1989/91) without vote, 11 May (meeting 12); draft by Commission for Social Development (E/1989/25); agenda item 11.

Policies and programmes involving young people

Responding to a 1988 General Assembly request,[7] the Secretary-General reported[8] in September 1989 on policies and programmes involving young people, in which he summarized activities undertaken by Member States concerning the implementation of the guidelines for further planning and suitable follow-up in the field of youth, and activities carried out by CSDHA (see above). He also outlined activities of intergovernmental organizations and of the Institute of HOPE '87 (Hundreds of Original Projects for Employment), established by the Government of Austria to promote youth employment by encouraging vocational training and educational programmes.

UN bodies and organizations, including the regional commissions, continued to promote the objectives originally established for the observance of IYY. They undertook a wide range of youth-related activities, including technical assistance to Governments to formulate, implement and evaluate national youth policies and programmes, preparation of reports and studies on the situation and needs of young people, organization of meetings, seminars and workshops on youth-related topics, strengthening channels of communication to promote youth involvement in policy formulation and implementation, and strengthening system-wide co-operation through the informal inter-agency technical working group.

In addition to traditional problem areas—development, education and training, employment, family life, health and housing—new issues such as AIDS and other sexually transmitted diseases, the abuse of narcotic drugs and psychotropic substances, and the degradation of the environment seriously affected youth. The Secretary-General suggested that the Assembly provide new directives and mandates, as appropriate, in support of the Secretariat units or specialized agencies to tackle those emerging issues.

The Secretary-General recommended, among other things, that Governments establish appropriate national co-ordination mechanisms in order to secure the effective integration of youth policy into national development planning, and that concerned UN agencies and bodies, including the regional commissions, take measures to assist Governments in that regard.

Strengthening communication between youth organizations and the United Nations

Since 1985, youth-related NGOs had continued to facilitate the global exchange of ideas, information, experience and partnership among their constituencies. Numerous NGOs had motivated Governments to accept the concept of a youth policy by providing them with relevant information, training experiences and research findings, and made a valuable contribution to the work of the United Nations by drawing attention to issues and disseminating information to promote an informed understanding about its aims and activities. However, the Secretary-General reported[8] that the maintenance of effective channels of communication had become more difficult owing to the decrease in publicity and momentum following the conclusion of IYY and resource constraints of CSDHA. In addition, the emphasis on improving channels for youth organizations excluded the vast majority of young people who did not participate in youth organizations.

He proposed the evaluation of functions, objectives and effectiveness of channels, the targeting of "unorganized youth", greater efforts to disseminate publications among youth, and the conduct of a survey to understand the perceptions of youth towards the United Nations.

UN Youth Fund

The United Nations Youth Fund continued to provide seed-money grants for post-IYY activities. In accordance with the Fund's terms of reference, special attention was paid to strengthening national capacities and institutions for youth-related concerns in developing countries.

Since 1984, the Fund had received over 300 requests for assistance and had provided nearly $350,000 as at 30 June 1989 for 46 innovative and catalytic youth projects. Income-generating activities and data collection and research accounted for nearly two thirds of disbursed grants. From January 1988 to June 1989, the Fund approved 10 projects for funding, involving a disbursement of $65,700.

Co-ordination

The informal inter-agency working group at the technical level of the Administrative Committee on Co-ordination (ACC), at its seventh meeting (Vienna, 4-5 December),[9] reviewed progress achieved in the implementation of the guidelines for further planning and suitable follow-up in the field of youth, and considered ways and means of strengthening national co-ordination mechanisms for youth and co-operation with NGOs for the development of youth activities. It endorsed the recommendations of the Consultative Meeting on Interregional, Regional and National Co-ordination for Integrated Youth Policies and Programmes (Pattaya, Thailand, 2-5 November), which pertained to: organization of informal intersectoral consultative meetings at the regional level; exchange, between CSDHA and other regional organizations, of their work programmes in order to facilitate collaboration and co-ordination of activities; exchange of information on their respective technical assistance activities by international and regional organizations; preparation of action-oriented studies on emergency trends and issues confronting youth in the coming decade; and the creation of a central data bank on youth-related issues under the responsibility of CSDHA.

The working group recommended that appropriate activities be undertaken in the field of youth to enlarge and reinforce East-West co-operation; resolutions on youth emanating from the governing bodies of the member agencies be analysed with a view to determining the priorities set up by the member States; and CSDHA reinforce its role as a co-ordinating body. It also recommended that the next meeting of the working group consider the strengthening of co-operation with NGOs. The Department of Public Information of the UN Secretariat was requested to investigate, through the Joint UN Information Committee, possible inter-agency projects to raise awareness about the question of youth and the need to improve communications with young people.

GENERAL ASSEMBLY ACTION

On 8 December, the General Assembly, on the recommendation of the Third (Social, Humanitarian and Cultural) Committee, adopted **resolution 44/59** without vote.

Policies and programmes involving youth
The General Assembly,

Recalling its resolution 43/94 of 8 December 1988,

Recalling also its resolution 40/14 entitled "International Youth Year: Participation, Development, Peace", adopted on 18 November 1985 by the General Assembly acting as the United Nations World Conference for the International Youth Year, by which the guidelines for further planning and suitable follow-up in the field of youth were endorsed, and its other relevant resolutions,

Recalling further its resolutions 32/135 of 16 December 1977 and 36/17 of 9 November 1981, by which it adopted guidelines for the improvement of the channels of communication between the United Nations and youth and youth organizations, and its other relevant resolutions,

Recalling its resolution 40/16 of 18 November 1985 entitled "Opportunities for youth" and its other relevant resolutions,

Recalling also its resolution 36/29 of 13 November 1981 and its subsequent resolutions in which it, *inter alia*, recognized the need to adopt appropriate measures for securing the implementation and the enjoyment by youth of human rights, particularly the right to education and to work,

Having considered the report of the Secretary-General submitted in accordance with resolution 43/94,

Recognizing that the guidelines for further planning and suitable follow-up in the field of youth provide a constructive framework for a long-term strategy in the field of youth,

Expressing its serious interest in systematically consolidating and building further on the results of the International Youth Year in order to contribute to the increasingly active participation of young people in the political and socio-economic life of their countries,

Convinced of the importance of making the channels of communication between the United Nations and youth and youth organizations more effective and efficient as a means of providing adequate information on young people and of encouraging their active participation in the United Nations system at the national, regional and international levels,

Recognizing that in many countries the majority of young people, under prevailing critical social and economic conditions, are facing serious problems in the exercise of their right to education and to work and that insufficient education and unemployment of young people limit their ability to participate effectively in the development process and impede their full integration into society,

Emphasizing that the suitable education of young people, which equips them with proper and up-to-date skills and qualifications, prepares them for entering the labour market at a level commensurate with their skills,

Noting that the year 1990 will mark the twenty-fifth anniversary of the proclamation by the General Assembly, in its resolution 2037(XX) of 7 December 1965, of the Declaration on the Promotion among Youth of the Ideals of Peace, Mutual Respect and Understanding between Peoples,

1. *Calls upon* all States, all United Nations bodies, in particular the Economic and Social Council through the Commission for Social Development, the specialized agencies and intergovernmental and non-governmental organizations concerned, in particular youth organizations, to continue to exert all possible efforts for the implementation of the guidelines for further planning and suitable follow-up in the field of youth;

2. *Appeals* to all States to adopt effective measures, in accordance with their legislations, particularly in the fields of teaching and education, culture, and information, in order to strengthen and promote among nations and, primarily, among youth understanding, mutual respect and friendship, for further progress towards an international climate free of mistrust and discord;

3. *Requests* the Secretary-General to promote and monitor intensively, by using the Centre for Social Development and Humanitarian Affairs of the Secretariat as a focal point, the inclusion of youth-related projects and activities in the programmes of United Nations bodies and the specialized agencies, specifically on such themes as communication, health, housing, culture, youth employment and education, drug abuse and the environment;

4. *Calls upon* Member States, United Nations bodies, the specialized agencies and other governmental and intergovernmental organizations to implement fully the guidelines relating to the channels of communication adopted by the General Assembly in its resolutions 32/135 and 36/17;

5. *Requests* the Secretary-General to organize a meeting, from extrabudgetary resources if necessary, between

United Nations bodies and the specialized agencies concerned and non-governmental youth organizations to discuss the problems of existing channels of communication between the United Nations system and youth organizations with a view to improving those channels and establishing effective structures of communication and co-operation between youth and the United Nations;

6. *Also requests* the Secretary-General to develop methods that indicate specifically how the channels of communication could efficiently be attuned to youth-related projects and activities of the United Nations organs and of the specialized agencies, and to include in a report on the implementation of the present resolution, to be submitted to the General Assembly at its forty-fifth session, concrete suggestions for co-operation between the United Nations system and the non-governmental youth organizations;

7. *Calls upon* youth mechanisms that have been set up by youth and youth organizations at the national, regional and international levels to continue to act as channels of communication between the United Nations and youth and youth organizations by putting forward their proposals for co-operation with the United Nations system and, where such mechanisms do not exist, recommends that national co-ordinating committees of the International Youth Year should continue to act as channels of communication;

8. *Calls upon* all States, all governmental and non-governmental organizations, interested United Nations bodies, in particular the Economic and Social Council through the Commission for Social Development, and specialized agencies to continue to give priority to the formulation and implementation of effective measures for securing the exercise by youth of the right to education and to work, with a view to resolving the problem of unemployment among youth;

9. *Calls upon* Member States to enable young people to obtain a proper and up-to-date education and to pay increased attention to the promotion of the employment of youth in all sectors of the economy, thereby facilitating their integration into social and professional life;

10. *Stresses* the importance for youth and youth organizations of freedom of association, in accordance with the relevant national legislation, the Universal Declaration of Human Rights, the International Covenant on Civil and Political Rights and other relevant international human rights instruments, that would enable their active and direct participation at all stages of implementation of the policies, projects and activities organized at the local, national, regional and international levels in the field of youth;

11. *Emphasizes* that providing education and employment to each young person is a worthy goal for all States and should serve the full development of the human being, which can best be ensured by countries that respect the fundamental rights and freedoms of everyone;

12. *Requests* the Secretary-General to continue to explore the possibilities for a linkage between the Centre for Social Development and Humanitarian Affairs and the Institute of HOPE '87, referred to in his report, taking into account the importance of that Institute for promoting, technically and financially, income-generating youth employment projects;

13. *Again invites* Governments to include youth representatives in their national delegations to the General Assembly and other relevant United Nations meetings and international conferences dealing with youth-related issues, thus enhancing and strengthening the channels of communication through the discussion of such issues, with a view to finding solutions to the problems confronting youth in the contemporary world;

14. *Invites* Governments and intergovernmental and non-governmental organizations to contribute generously to the United Nations Youth Fund, in order to enable it to continue its mandated role and to contribute effectively to the needs of developing countries in the field of youth;

15. *Requests* the Secretary-General to continue to include the United Nations Youth Fund among the programmes for which funds are pledged at the United Nations Pledging Conference for Development Activities;

16. *Also requests* the Secretary-General to prepare a report on the implementation of the guidelines for further planning and suitable follow-up in the field of youth and to include therein a draft programme of action to mark the tenth anniversary of the International Youth Year and to submit the report to the General Assembly at its forty-eighth session, through the Commission for Social Development and the Economic and Social Council;

17. *Decides* to consider the item entitled "Policies and programmes involving youth" at its forty-fifth session on the basis of the report of the Secretary-General on the implementation of the present resolution.

General Assembly resolution 44/59

8 December 1989   Meeting 78   Adopted without vote

Approved by Third Committee (A/44/752) without vote, 9 November (meeting 37); 5-nation draft (A/C.3/44/L.17), orally revised; agenda item 93.
Sponsors: Austria, Czechoslovakia, Egypt, Netherlands, Romania.
Meeting numbers. GA 44th session: 3rd Committee 12-20, 30, 37; plenary 78.

REFERENCES

[1]YUN 1985, p. 978. [2]YUN 1987, p. 864, ESC res. 1987/45, 28 May 1987. [3]E/1989/25. [4]E/CN.5/1989/7. [5]YUN 1985, p. 979, GA res. 40/14, 18 Nov. 1985. [6]E/1989/25 (res. 31/3, annex). [7]YUN 1988, p. 651, GA res. 43/94, 8 Dec. 1988. [8]A/44/387. [9]ACC/1989/PG/12.

Aging persons

The United Nations continued in 1989 to consider the question of persons aged 60 and over in the context of the International Plan of Action on Aging, adopted in 1982 by the World Assembly on Aging[1] and endorsed later that year by the General Assembly.[2] The Plan's primary aim was to assist States in strengthening their capacities to deal with aging populations.

Plan of Action on Aging

Second review of implementation

The Commission for Social Development, at its thirty-first session (Vienna, 13-22 March),[3] conducted the second quadrennial review and appraisal of the implementation of the International Plan of Action on Aging, on the basis of a report[(4)] of the Secretary-General on the subject. The report, prepared on the basis of 59 replies to a questionnaire sent to Member States, bodies of the UN system and intergovernmental and nongovernmental organizations and other information available to the UN Secretariat, presented a demographic analysis of the aging of the world's population, an assessment of the policy implications of that process, and implementation of the Plan of Action at the national, regional and international levels.

According to the projection, between 1950 and 2025 the elderly population of the world would have grown by a factor of six, while the total world population, by a factor of little more than three. The trends showed that the world's elderly would be concentrated in developing regions; a contracting working population would have to support an expanding dependent population; the 80 plus age group would grow twice as fast as the 60 plus age group; and there would be a greater increase in the number of older women than that of older men.

The Secretary-General noted that, in spite of the growing awareness that the world's population continued to age with increasing rapidity, responsive policies and programmes had not kept pace. There were 84 national co-ordination machineries for aging (51 in developing countries and 33 in developed ones), but few developing countries had detailed demographic profiles or projections of their elderly populations. A majority of programmes aimed at the elderly were in the areas of economic matters, health questions, living arrangements and personal social services. With regard to care-giving, the major policy trend, in developed as well as developing countries, was to support family care-giving and the maintenance of the elderly in their own communities. While a majority of responding Member States had an educational policy which reflected the principle of the elderly having a right to education, only a minority had programmes to educate the general public about the process of aging. In developing countries, income security for the elderly remained confined to selected segments of the aging population. The Secretary-General proposed a set of priorities and made recommendations to supplement the Plan of Action and encourage its implementation. In addition, he set forth a draft programme of activities to mark the tenth anniversary in 1992 of the adoption of the Plan of Action.

ECONOMIC AND SOCIAL COUNCIL ACTION

On 24 May, the Economic and Social Council, on the recommendation of its Second Committee, adopted **resolution 1989/50** without vote.

Second review and appraisal of the implementation of the International Plan of Action on Aging

The Economic and Social Council,

Having considered the report of the Secretary-General on the second review and appraisal of the implementation of the International Plan of Action on Aging, conducted by the Commission for Social Development in accordance with General Assembly resolution 37/51 of 3 December 1982,

1. *Expresses its appreciation* to the Secretary-General for his comprehensive report on the second review and appraisal of the implementation of the International Plan of Action on Aging;

2. *Decides* to adopt the set of priorities and recommendations to encourage further implementation of the Plan of Action contained in annex I to the present resolution;

3. *Endorses* the draft programme of United Nations activities relating to the tenth anniversary of the adoption of the Plan of Action, in 1992, contained in annex II to the present resolution;

4. *Reaffirms* the recommendation made in the Plan of Action that the Centre for Social Development and Humanitarian Affairs of the Secretariat should serve as the focal point in the United Nations system for activities related to aging and that, to that end, the Secretary-General, within the existing global resources of the United Nations, should give due consideration to the provision of appropriate increased resources for the implementation of the Plan of Action;

5. *Recommends* the establishment of an open-ended *ad hoc* working group of the Third Committee of the General Assembly at the forty-fourth session of the Assembly to focus on the conclusions of the second review and appraisal;

6. *Decides* to establish an open-ended *ad hoc* working group of the Economic and Social Council to monitor the preparatory activities for the tenth anniversary of the adoption of the Plan of Action, in 1992;

7. *Recommends* the convening of an *ad hoc* working group of the Commission for Social Development at its thirty-second session to monitor the activities for the tenth anniversary of the adoption of the Plan of Action;

8. *Decides* that the Centre for Social Development and Humanitarian Affairs should co-ordinate, within existing resources or with extrabudgetary resources, activities to mark the tenth anniversary of the adoption of the Plan of Action, as suggested in paragraph 103 of the report of the Secretary-General;

9. *Urges* the Aging Unit of the Centre for Social Development and Humanitarian Affairs to place special emphasis on developing expertise in, and providing technical assistance to, Member States on social and economic developmental issues related to aging;

10. *Urges* the Commission on the Status of Women to give particular attention to the specific problems faced by elderly women;

11. *Urges* Governments and the United Nations to involve non-governmental organizations in consultative status with the Economic and Social Council to a greater extent than previously in the implementation of the Plan of Action so that their expertise and well-known contributions in the field may be used more effectively;

12. *Notes with appreciation* the activities, plans and programmes of the International Institute on Aging recently established in Malta, particularly in the area of training;

13.　*Recommends* that the Secretary-General take into consideration a feasibility study, conducted at the request of the Government of Yugoslavia, recommending the establishment of a United Nations–affiliated international institute on aging at Belgrade;

14.　*Welcomes* the progress made at the preparatory meeting to establish an African society of gerontology held at Dakar from 17 to 22 December 1988, pursuant to General Assembly resolution 43/93 of 8 December 1988, at which a draft statute, draft rules of procedure and a draft work programme were elaborated;

15.　*Also welcomes* the initiative of the Government of Argentina in establishing a subregional South American centre on aging;

16.　*Calls upon* the Centre for Social Development and Humanitarian Affairs, as the focal point in the United Nations system for activities related to aging, to coordinate the activities of such institutes or centres, in particular to avoid duplication;

17.　*Reiterates* that the existence of these and any other such institutes or centres would not preclude the establishment in other countries or regions of the world of other institutes or centres affiliated with the United Nations and financed by voluntary contributions;

18.　*Decides* to include the question of aging in the agenda of the thirty-second session of the Commission for Social Development.

ANNEX I
Second review and appraisal of the implementation of the International Plan of Action on Aging: priorities and recommendations

1.　As their populations age, most countries are simultaneously confronted by economic constraints. In such a climate, aging is often low on the list of priorities. Yet, as noted in the report of the Secretary-General on the second review and appraisal of the implementation of the International Plan of Action on Aging, policy interventions are necessary now. In these circumstances, the expanded awareness of aging issues must be tapped, specific priorities must be identified and resources must be marshalled. If specific measures based on existing structures and activities are instituted, and collaborative efforts encompassing Governments and intergovernmental and non-governmental organizations are intensified, the synergy will achieve more, even with limited resources.

2.　The Plan of Action contains broad recommendations dealing with different facets of aging. It would serve no useful purpose to repeat or reformulate them. Set forth below, to supplement the Plan of Action and encourage its implementation, are specific recommendations that emerge from the second review and appraisal.

3.　In considering those recommendations, Member States might wish to bear in mind the following priorities:

(a)　The provision of basic services for all—food, water, shelter, health protection and education—must form the corner-stone of any national or community-based group-specific programme;

(b)　Specific policies and programmes focusing on the elderly must recognize both the humanitarian needs and the human resource potential of the aged;

(c)　Policies to promote the developmental and humanitarian needs of the aged must focus on the family and community as indivisible social units;

(d)　The use of the elderly as a societal resource must be predicated upon their involvement and participation in the development of policies and programmes affecting them;

(e)　Expanding economic opportunities for the elderly must not be seen to imply contracting opportunities for the young; policies and programmes directed at either end of the age spectrum of the labour force can be mutually reinforcing;

(f)　Policies and programmes for and by the elderly must grow upon quality baseline information that reflects the demographic, epidemiological, biological, social and economic aspects of aging.

4.　The following recommendations are emphasized for the consideration of Member States:

(a)　National machinery should be established or strengthened to ensure that the humanitarian needs and developmental potential of the aged are appropriately addressed within the context of each country and culture;

(b)　The United Nations should continue to provide support, particularly to developing countries, in the development of the national, local and voluntary institutional capacities necessary to respond appropriately to population aging;

(c)　International development agencies, both governmental and non-governmental, are strongly encouraged to assist Governments, particularly those of developing countries, in developing or expanding their institutional capacities for responding appropriately to population aging;

(d)　The expansion of research focusing on the demographic, epidemiological, biological, social and economic aspects of aging, particularly in developing countries, should be supported;

(e)　Bilateral and multilateral co-operative research arrangements, particularly between developing and developed countries, should be encouraged in order to understand and respond better to global-specific and country-specific aging issues;

(f)　The establishment or expansion of community-based or institutional care systems that provide the necessary health and social services for the frail elderly who have limited or no family support should be encouraged;

(g)　The ability of families to care for their frail elderly should be supported and strengthened by the development or expansion of community-based health and social services that foster home care;

(h)　Family support for the aged should be promoted by policies and programmes that provide economic and psychosocial incentives for families that care for their older members;

(i)　To ensure their dignity and support, elderly women should be given special attention in appropriate policies and programmes;

(j)　In countries where institutions are used to shelter and provide services for the frail elderly, policies that ensure active quality control and community integration should be promoted;

(k)　Self-help initiatives on the part of the elderly should be encouraged and supported;

(l)　Organizations and associations of the elderly that ensure their active involvement in policy and programme development should be encouraged and promoted;

(m) Intergenerational service programmes and educational opportunities should be supported to maintain intergenerational cohesion;

(n) Training in gerontology and geriatrics should be offered by the expansion of international institutes, as well as by individual country institutes and training centres, to ensure that policy-makers, researchers and practitioners have an adequate knowledge of aging issues;

(o) Bilateral and multilateral co-operation between Governments and non-governmental organizations to provide training for specialists in aging, particularly specialists from developing countries, should be encouraged and supported;

(p) Laws and practices that support age discrimination should be discouraged;

(q) Income security programmes, including those related to pensions, employment opportunities and family assistance, should be supported to ensure dignity and opportunity in old age;

(r) Income security should be enhanced, where necessary, by the development and support of income-generating projects for and by the elderly.

ANNEX II
Draft programme of United Nations activities relating to the tenth anniversary of the adoption of the International Plan of Action on Aging

1. A draft programme of organizational and substantive activities to mark the tenth anniversary of the adoption of the International Plan of Action on Aging is given below, in accordance with General Assembly resolution 43/93 of 8 December 1988. The substantive focus reflects priority needs identified in the report of the Secretary-General on the second review and appraisal of the implementation of the Plan of Action.

2. The draft programme aims at stimulating interest, research and responsive policies and programmes, and at promoting the celebration of aging as a significant phenomenon and achievement of the twentieth century. When implemented, the draft programme's substantive focus and organizational arrangements would vary among the entities concerned and from country to country.

3. The Centre for Social Development and Humanitarian Affairs of the Secretariat, as the focal point within the United Nations system for activities on aging, will co-ordinate the programmes of the anniversary year. Working within existing resources, it will endeavour:

(a) To mobilize national machinery on aging to launch national consciousness-raising events;

(b) To use the expertise of the organizations of the United Nations system for action-oriented programmes on aging in their respective areas of concern;

(c) To co-operate with non-governmental organizations in the production and distribution of specialized and general information for wide distribution within their respective networks;

(d) To ensure that the general public is informed of the year and its follow-up activities by increasing channels of communication between the Centre for Social Development and Humanitarian Affairs and United Nations information centres around the world;

(e) To raise extrabudgetary resources for supplementing those activities.

4. Issues selected for special attention during the year and in the course of the follow-up activities will include, in accordance with the findings of the second review and appraisal, policies and programmes relating to the following:

(a) Income security and income-generating activities;
(b) Health-care delivery and its financing in aging societies;
(c) Community-based activities for and with the elderly;
(d) Organizations of the elderly;
(e) Training.

5. In addition to Governments, groups to be targeted during the year and in the course of the follow-up activities will include middle-aged and elderly persons, trade unions and employers' organizations, women's and youth organizations, schools and universities, and research and training institutions.

6. If extrabudgetary resources become available, the following specific activities will be undertaken to prepare for and mark the tenth anniversary:

1989 International meeting of non-governmental organizations to assist in the development and organization of concrete programmes and activities for 1992 and beyond;

1990 Regional meetings of developing countries, in co-operation with regional commissions and national machinery on aging, to promote the development of country-specific profiles and the preparation of national agenda on aging for the decade 1992-2001;

1991 Publication of a graphic and succinct status report entitled "Aging: highlights from the twentieth century, forecasts for the twenty-first century";

1992 Activities marking the tenth anniversary of the adoption of the International Plan of Action on Aging, including:

(a) A public information campaign focusing on selected aging issues to stimulate the necessary preparation for or response to aging;

(b) An international art and literature campaign (including a poster competition) to enlist the general public, artists and writers in celebrating aging;

(c) The issue of United Nations stamps to commemorate the occasion;

(d) Publication of an agenda for the decade, entitled "Selected priorities for action on aging: 1992-2001". This would complement the broad-based Plan of Action, and priorities would be selected on the basis of national profiles and experience in implementing the Plan of Action at various levels. It would be for use by decision makers, practitioners and non-governmental organizations;

(e) An information packet containing technical reports, news features, human interest items and so forth for use by schools, universities, the media and non-governmental organizations.

7. After 1992, substantive activities might focus on several specific issues within the general context of the aging of populations, with a view to ensuring that exchanges of knowledge and expertise can actually be operationalized. Four clusters of activities are suggested below, each one to begin with a draft paper prepared

by the Centre for Social Development and Humanitarian Affairs, in consultation with the appropriate specialized agencies; the draft papers will be refined at regional meetings, in co-operation with the regional commissions, and finally published as technical manuals or monographs. The clusters of activities suggested are:

(a) Establishment of community-based organizations of the aged;

(b) Income security and income generation for and by the aged;

(c) Health-care delivery and financing in aging societies;

(d) Intersectoral co-operation on aging.

8. Information on the activities undertaken on the occasion of the tenth anniversary of the adoption of the Plan of Action and the follow-up activities proposed for the decade 1992-2001 will be made available to the General Assembly at its forty-seventh session when, in accordance with its Assembly resolution 43/93, the occasion will be commemorated in the plenary Assembly.

Economic and Social Council resolution 1989/50

24 May 1989   Meeting 15   Adopted without vote

Approved by Second Committee (E/1989/91) without vote, 11 May (meeting 12); draft by Commission for Social Development (E/1989/25); agenda item 11.

Implementation of the Plan of Action

Pursuant to a 1988 General Assembly request,[5] the Secretary-General submitted a report,[6] in which he discussed new initiatives on aging, UN activities and co-operation, and development co-operation.

As the traditional social support structure of family and community changed and, on the whole, weakened, new structures such as national machineries on aging, organizations of the elderly, gerontological societies, training institutes on aging, WHO's special programme for research on aging and a world foundation on aging (see below) were emerging.

CSDHA, as the UN system-wide focal point on aging, served as the substantive secretariat on aging for the UN legislative bodies concerned and ensured that the Plan of Action was considered in the context of broad social policy and development. In addition, CSDHA enjoyed the co-operation of six networks, including NGOs, each devoted to a specific function such as policy, research, training, advocacy, technical co-operation and participation strategies. At the XIVth International Congress of Gerontology (Acapulco, Mexico, 18-23 June), CSDHA supported expansion of the international dialogue on aging and promoted awareness of the Plan of Action among the experts. It also held talks with organizations on developing and expanding a technical co-operation network with special focus on small self-help projects throughout the world.

The International Institute on Aging in Malta completed a global survey of service delivery systems to the elderly in developing countries as a basis for assessing training needs. The Institute convened a number of expert group meetings to assist in developing long- and short-term training programmes. The local costs of the Institute were funded by the Government of Malta. In response to a request of Yugoslavia, the Department of Technical Co-operation for Development of the UN Secretariat supported a feasibility study on establishing an international institute on aging in Belgrade. Another feasibility study on establishing a subregional centre on aging in Buenos Aires was being considered at the request of Argentina.

The Secretary-General, in order to further the implementation of the Plan of Action, suggested that the various networks on aging identify and disseminate successful models of contributions by the elderly to society; effective care of the elderly as well as of their informal care-givers; integrated community development, encompassing participation and care strategies as well as intergenerational and intersectoral co-operation; government support to the elderly, their families and communities, to encourage self-reliance and sharing; and census and other information-gathering and -processing for use in policy and programme formulation on aging. He also suggested that the major international NGOs and donor countries, together with the UN system, could establish a technical co-operation network, which would design and support implementation of a series of self-help projects by the elderly.

Inter-agency co-ordination. The third *ad hoc* inter-agency meeting on aging (Vienna, 30 November–1 December)[7] reviewed activities of the United Nations and the specialized agencies in the field of aging; considered the implications for the UN system of the results of the second review and appraisal of the implementation of the Plan of Action (see above); followed up on the action taken by ACC regarding the system-wide approach to the implementation of the Plan of Action; and considered specific inter-agency projects in further implementation of the Plan. The meeting also addressed itself to future inter-agency co-operation in the context of the preparation of the report on the world aging situation, the elaboration of a system-wide medium-term plan on aging and the 1992 programme for the tenth anniversary of the adoption of the Plan of Action.

It recommended, among other things, that in connection with the 1992 survey for the third quadrennial review and appraisal of the implementation of the Plan of Action, CSDHA, together with specialized agencies and bodies of the UN system, should initiate for the General Assembly the preparation of a global strategy, with targets, indicators and a timetable, for translating the Plan of Action into concrete programmes.

Funding of policies and programmes

The Secretary-General convened a meeting of eminent persons in New York on 18 and 19 September[8] to develop an international fund-raising strategy for policies and programmes on population aging, established in the Plan of Action. It was co-sponsored by the American Association of Retired Persons, HelpAge International, the International Association of Gerontology and the International Federation on Ageing. The meeting noted that, since the aging of individuals and populations had opened up a growing market, private-sector financing was available, but developing that potential source of funding required flexible organization.

The meeting agreed on the desirability and urgency of establishing an independent international foundation on aging under the patronage of the United Nations, appointed a task force to prepare a blueprint for the foundation, and requested it to present an initial proposal no later than March 1990 to be considered by a further meeting of eminent persons.

Trust funds

Since 1982, the United Nations Trust Fund for Aging had disbursed over $900,000 in seed-money grants to 35 projects. During the period January 1988 to June 1989, the Fund received some 30 project proposals and inquiries; one third of them were approved for funding, involving a resource disbursement of $196,100. The largest sum, $59,300, was for exchange of technical expertise, followed by $57,500 for support to organizations of or for the elderly. The Fund also supported an international seminar on aging and development (Kuala Lumpur, Malaysia, 17-21 July) and enabled scientists from developing countries to participate in the XIVth International Congress of Gerontology. The Fund not only provided direct substantive and financial support, but also acted as a catalyst for resource mobilization; its grants of $196,100 mobilized over $1 million in additional resources for aging-related projects.

For the biennium 1988-1989, the Fund's total income was $302,696, while its expenditure was $410,442. The resource base created during the initial years of the Fund had been gradually eroded and several worthwhile projects in developing countries could not be funded.

With the concurrence of the two contributors to the Trust Fund for the Promotion of the United Nations Programme for the Aging—the Government of the Dominican Republic and the American Association of Retired Persons—the Fund's resources, set at $18,000, were used for the meeting of eminent persons (see above).

On 8 December, the General Assembly, on the recommendation of the Third Committee, adopted **resolution 44/67** without vote.

Implementation of the International Plan of Action on Aging and related activities

The General Assembly,

Recalling its resolution 43/93 of 8 December 1988,

Having considered the report of the Secretary-General on the second review and appraisal of the implementation of the International Plan of Action on Aging conducted by the Commission for Social Development at its thirty-first session,

Taking note with interest of the priorities identified and recommendations made in the second review and appraisal of the implementation of the Plan of Action,

Noting with appreciation the renewed momentum of the United Nations programme on aging but deeply regretting the proposed cut in the resources under section 8, subprogramme 7 (Aging), of the proposed programme budget for the biennium 1990-1991,

Aware of the need of the developing countries for technical assistance and expert advice in the field of aging,

Reiterating the appeal made to the Secretary-General in its resolution 43/93 to maintain and strengthen the existing programmes on aging and to strengthen the United Nations system-wide co-ordination of policies and programmes on aging, with the Centre for Social Development and Humanitarian Affairs of the Secretariat continuing in its role as focal point in the United Nations system for activities relating to aging,

1. *Takes note* of the report of the Secretary-General on the question of aging;

2. *Endorses* Economic and Social Council resolution 1989/50 of 24 May 1989;

3. *Also endorses* the draft programme of United Nations activities relating to the tenth anniversary of the adoption of the International Plan of Action on Aging, in 1992, as contained in annex II to Economic and Social Council resolution 1989/50;

4. *Notes with interest* that aging is being considered as a priority theme of the international development strategy for the fourth United Nations development decade and the medium-term plan for the period 1992-1997;

5. *Calls upon* Member States, the specialized agencies and non-governmental organizations to assist the Centre for Social Development and Humanitarian Affairs of the Secretariat in elaborating for the consideration of the General Assembly at its forty-fifth session a detailed global programme of activities for 1992 on the basis of the draft programme endorsed by the Economic and Social Council, which would simultaneously serve as a guide for parallel national and regional programmes;

6. *Also calls upon* Member States that have special expertise or an interest in aging to consider giving direct staff or extrabudgetary support to the Centre in its preparatory activities for 1992;

7. *Decides* that the priorities identified and recommendations made in the second review and appraisal of the implementation of the Plan of Action should be included as an annex in future publications of the Plan of Action;

8. *Requests* the Secretary-General to consider the feasibility of preparing a system-wide medium-term plan on aging in order to ensure that all concerned organizations of the United Nations system address the question of aging in a coherent and effective manner, bearing in mind that the Centre is the duly mandated focal point in all matters related to aging;

9. *Invites* the Statistical Office of the Secretariat to increase the availability and use of national statistics on aging for the formulation and implementation of national policies and programmes and to consider the possibility of dedicating the 1992 *Demographic Yearbook* to the question of aging;

10. *Invites* the major international non-governmental organizations and donor countries to join the United Nations system in establishing a technical co-operation network that would design and support the implementation of a series of straightforward self-help projects by the elderly in order to bridge the gap between major funding entities and local self-help initiatives, as well as the gap between globally espoused standards and the real living conditions of the elderly;

11. *Requests* the Commission on the Status of Women to pay particular attention to the specific problems faced by elderly women and to the discrimination suffered by these women because of their gender and age;

12. *Urges* all the relevant agencies of the United Nations system dealing with refugees to pay special attention to the plight of all elderly refugees;

13. *Urges* the Department of Public Information of the Secretariat to co-operate with the Centre in the preparation of a report on the status and highlights of the global aging of populations for distribution to the media and the general public in 1992;

14. *Calls upon* the United Nations Population Fund to consider seconding a demographer to the Centre to assist in producing demographic profiles of the global, regional and selected national aging populations;

15. *Calls upon* the United Nations Postal Administration to produce in 1992 commemorative United Nations stamps to mark the tenth anniversary of the adoption of the Plan of Action;

16. *Recommends* that in view of the rapid expansion of activities and infrastructure for aging, the participants in the United Nations programme on aging give careful attention to its mandate with a view to avoiding duplication of the activities of other programmes and continuing in the 1990s the unified approach to implementing the Plan of Action that has been a distinguishing mark of the programme to date;

17. *Takes note with appreciation* of the progress report submitted by the Secretary-General on the training programmes and activities of the International Institute on Aging in Malta, welcomes the unique contribution of the Institute to the implementation of the Plan of Action and requests the Secretary-General, in reporting on the question of aging to the General Assembly at its forty-fifth session, to inform the Assembly of the activities, plans and programmes of the Institute;

18. *Notes with appreciation* the establishment, with the assistance of the United Nations Office at Vienna, of an African Society of Gerontology at Dakar;

19. *Notes with satisfaction* the offer of the Governments of Yugoslavia and Argentina to establish institutes on aging at Belgrade and Buenos Aires, respectively;

20. *Also notes with satisfaction* the convening of the meeting of eminent persons to develop an international fund-raising strategy for policies and programmes on population aging, at United Nations Headquarters on 18 and 19 September 1989, takes note of the adoption at that meeting of a declaration on the desirability and urgency of establishing an independent international foundation on aging under the patronage of the United Nations that would encourage the public and private sectors as well as non-governmental organizations to support the work of the United Nations system in the field of aging, and in this regard invites Member States, non-governmental organizations and the private sector to support this initiative;

21. *Further notes with satisfaction* the success achieved at the XIVth International Congress of Gerontology, held at Acapulco, Mexico, from 18 to 23 June 1989;

22. *Strongly appeals* to Governments and intergovernmental and non-governmental organizations to contribute generously to the United Nations Trust Fund for Aging, bearing in mind that the Fund is particularly well placed to act as a catalyst for resource mobilization;

23. *Requests* the Secretary-General to report to the General Assembly at its forty-fifth session on the implementation of the present resolution;

24. *Decides* to include in the provisional agenda of its forty-fifth session the item entitled "Question of aging".

General Assembly resolution 44/67

8 December 1989   Meeting 78   Adopted without vote

Approved by Third Committee (A/44/754) without vote, 9 November (meeting 37); 3-nation draft (A/C.3/44/L.15/Rev.1), orally revised; agenda item 101.
Sponsors: Austria, Dominican Republic, Malta.
Meeting numbers. GA 44th session: 3rd Committee 12-20, 30, 37; plenary 78.

Elderly women

By **resolution 1989/38** of 24 May, the Economic and Social Council recommended that the organizations of the UN system concerned provide the bodies responsible for the advancement of women with information that would enable them to undertake a precise and in-depth analysis of the situation of elderly women, developing, if necessary, specific new methods for data collection. It requested the Commission on the Status of Women to devote particular attention to the current and future situation of elderly women throughout the world.

The General Assembly, by **resolution 44/76** of 8 December, recommended that the United Nations and the specialized agencies take the lead in recognizing the important contributions made by older women and their potential to participate in and shape the future of their societies. It invited the International Research and Training Institute for the Advancement of Women and the Statistical Office of the Secretariat to pay specific attention to older women in their efforts to improve methodology for data-gathering on women.

REFERENCES
[1]YUN 1982, p. 1184. [2]*Ibid.*, p. 1186, GA res. 37/51, 3 Dec. 1982. [3]E/1989/25. [4]E/1989/13. [5]YUN 1988, p. 655, GA res. 43/93, 8 Dec. 1988. [6]A/44/420. [7]ACC/1989/PG/10. [8]A/44/420/Add.1.

Chapter XV

Refugees and displaced persons

During 1989, despite continuing and widespread refugee problems in the world, there were encouraging developments in relation to certain long-standing situations. The single most notable of these was in Namibia; the emergence there of an independent State was preceded by the successful repatriation of more than 43,000 Namibians. The International Conference on Central American Refugees formulated in May a special plan of action to facilitate the return and rehabilitation of refugees and displaced persons and to benefit local populations as well. The Comprehensive Plan of Action, adopted at the International Conference on Indo-Chinese Refugees in June, set out measures to deal with asylum-seekers in the South-East Asian region.

However, the repatriation of more than 3 million Afghan refugees in Pakistan and another 2.5 million in Iran remained stalled by an intractable political situation in Afghanistan. Similarly, prospects for peace in Kampuchea did not materialize, preventing the repatriation of hundreds of thousands of Kampuchean refugees and displaced persons.

Faced with the most difficult financial crisis ever in its 40-year history, the Office of the United Nations High Commissioner for Refugees in 1989 undertook repeated cuts in programmed and assessed needs, with serious negative consequences for refugees and the Office's ability to protect and find durable solutions for them.

The Nansen Medal, awarded since 1954 in honour of Fridtjof Nansen, the first League of Nations High Commissioner for Refugees, was not awarded in 1989.

Jean-Pierre Hocké resigned as High Commissioner with effect from 1 November. The General Assembly on 20 November elected Thorvald Stoltenberg of Norway as his successor for a four-year term beginning on 1 January 1990 (decision 44/312).

UNHCR programme and finances

Programme policy

Executive Committee action. At its fortieth session (Geneva, 5-13 October 1989), the Executive Committee of the Programme of the UN High Commissioner for Refugees[1] reiterated the primary nature and fundamental importance of the High Commissioner's protection responsibilities. In expressing deep concern about the financial situation of the Office of the UN High Commissioner for Refugees (UNHCR), it called on UNHCR, States, governmental and non-governmental organizations and the international community at large to give the necessary priority to protection activities and to ensure their efficiency and effectiveness. The Committee also expressed concern over the lack of adequate international protection for various groups of refugees, including a large number of Palestinians, and hoped that efforts would continue within the UN system to address their protection needs (for more information on Palestinian refugees, see PART TWO, Chapter IV). States were urged to abide by international prohibitions against expulsion and *refoulement*, or forcible return of refugees, and were called upon to ensure the protection of refugees from arbitrary detention and violence. In welcoming resettlement opportunities offered by several African States, the Committee invited all States to make places available to respond to urgent or emergency protection situations facing individual refugees.

The Committee welcomed the outcome of the Round Table on Solutions to the Problem of Refugees and the Protection of Refugees (San Remo, Italy, 12-14 July) and called on the High Commissioner to convene, in consultation with the Chairman of the Committee, an open-ended working group of Committee members to examine protection problems and solutions in a coherent and comprehensive manner.

With regard to the promotion and dissemination of refugee law, the Committee encouraged the High Commissioner actively to promote further the universal applicability of the 1951 Convention relating to the Status of Refugees[2] and the 1967 Protocol thereto[3] and to continue organizing protection training courses for government and other concerned officials. States were asked to adopt appropriate legislative and/or administrative measures for the effective implementation of those international instruments.

The Committee considered the phenomenon of refugees and asylum-seekers who moved in an irregular manner from a country in which they had already found protection or who wilfully destroyed or disposed of their documentation in order to mislead the authorities of the country of arrival. While it recognized that there might be exceptional cases to justify the former, it considered the latter unacceptable and concluded that appropriate arrangements should be made to deal with the problem.

Progress was made towards promoting the participation of refugee women as agents, as well as beneficiaries, in the planning and implementation of protection and assistance programmes. The Committee urged the High Commissioner to develop a methodology for systematically addressing gender issues in refugee programmes and encouraged additional efforts to raise public awareness of the specific situation of refugee women. As regards refugee children, the High Commissioner was requested to give special attention to the needs of unaccompanied minors, particularly with regard to forced recruitment into armed forces and to the risks associated with irregular adoption.

With regard to Central American refugees, the Committee welcomed the commitments of Belize, Costa Rica, El Salvador, Guatemala, Honduras, Mexico and Nicaragua in the implementation of the Concerted Plan of Action, adopted in May at the International Conference on Central American Refugees (see below). It also welcomed the adoption in June of the Declaration and Comprehensive Plan of Action on Indo-Chinese Refugees (see below).

To help implement development projects relating to refugees, returnees and the areas hosting them, the Committee requested the High Commissioner to establish a close working relationship with relevant agencies of the UN system, including the UN Development Programme (UNDP), so as to examine the conditions and modalities of an appropriate implementing mechanism. It further requested UNHCR to give priority to and identify with development agencies and Governments of host countries appropriate projects and initiatives that might be presented to development agencies for implementation and funding in refugee/returnee areas of developing countries.

The Committee approved the allocation under General Programmes amounting to $389.4 million (including the $10 million Emergency Fund) for 1989 and $414.4 million for 1990.

ECONOMIC AND SOCIAL COUNCIL ACTION

By **decision 1989/164** of 5 July, the Economic and Social Council transmitted the report of the UN High Commissioner for Refugees[4] to the General Assembly at its forty-fourth (1989) session.

GENERAL ASSEMBLY ACTION

On 15 December, the General Assembly, on the recommendation of the Third (Social, Humani-

tarian and Cultural) Committee, adopted **resolution 44/137** without vote.

Office of the United Nations High Commissioner for Refugees

The General Assembly,

Having considered the report of the United Nations High Commissioner for Refugees on the activities of his Office, as well as the report of the Executive Committee of the Programme of the High Commissioner on the work of its fortieth session, and having heard the statements made by the Officer-in-Charge of the Office of the High Commissioner on 15 and 17 November 1989,

Recalling its resolution 43/117 of 8 December 1988,

Reaffirming the purely humanitarian and non-political character of the activities of the Office of the High Commissioner, as well as the fundamental importance of the High Commissioner's protection function and the need for States to co-operate with the High Commissioner in the exercise of this primary and essential function,

Noting with satisfaction that, following recent accessions, one hundred and six States are now parties to the 1951 Convention and the 1967 Protocol relating to the Status of Refugees,

Noting with concern that, despite developments that offer hope for solutions to refugee problems, refugees and displaced persons of concern to the Office of the High Commissioner continue to face, in certain situations, distressingly serious problems, including problems of protection as a result of expulsion and *refoulement* of refugees, their unjustified detention and measures that do not recognize their special situation,

Particularly concerned that in various regions the safety and welfare of refugees and asylum-seekers are seriously undermined on account of military or armed attacks, forced recruitment of refugees into armed forces and other forms of violence, and noting that further efforts should be made to ensure rescue and disembarkation of asylum-seekers in distress at sea and, in this context, noting also the problems relating to stowaway asylum-seekers,

Noting the efforts of the Office of the High Commissioner to continue to address the special problems and needs of refugee and displaced women and children, who in many cases are exposed to a variety of difficult situations affecting their physical and legal protection as well as their psychological and material well-being,

Emphasizing the need for States to assist, on as wide a basis as possible, the efforts of the Office of the High Commissioner in its search for durable and timely solutions to the problems of refugees based on new approaches that meet current realities and at the same time respect the basic principles and concerns of protection,

Realizing in this context that voluntary repatriation or return remains the most desirable solution to the problems facing refugees and displaced persons of concern to the Office of the High Commissioner, and welcoming the fact that it has been possible for significant numbers of them to return voluntarily to their country of origin,

Recognizing that the promotion of fundamental human rights is essential to the achievement of self-sufficiency and family security for refugees, as well as to the process of re-establishing the dignity of the human person and realizing durable solutions to refugee problems,

Deeply concerned about the unprecedented financial crisis that the Office of the High Commissioner is currently facing,

Aware that the application of the principle of international solidarity and the search for durable solutions imply a better sharing of responsibilities and arrangements among all the agencies of the United Nations system and other concerned organizations, both governmental and non-governmental, for the implementation and the financing of related activities,

Recognizing that durable solutions for refugees in developing countries can, in many cases, be achieved through a development-oriented approach and that the heavy burden placed on a host country as a result of growing influxes of refugees requires sufficient resources to redress the negative impact and the strain on its socio-economic infrastructure in rural and urban areas, and emphasizing the need to ensure the compatibility of refugee aid and national development plans of developing countries of asylum,

Welcoming the conclusions and decisions on refugee aid and development adopted by the Executive Committee of the Programme of the High Commissioner at its fortieth session, in particular the request to the Office of the High Commissioner to continue its catalytic role in the area of refugee aid and development,

Commending those States which, despite severe economic and development problems of their own, continue to admit large numbers of refugees and displaced persons of concern to the Office of the High Commissioner into their territories, and emphasizing the need to share the burden of these States to the maximum extent possible through international assistance,

Emphasizing the need for close co-operation between the Office of the High Commissioner and relevant agencies of the United Nations system and other international organizations, both intergovernmental and non-governmental, in devising and implementing specific elements of development assistance for solving problems of refugees and returnees and of areas hosting them,

Stressing the need for the international community to continue to provide adequate resettlement opportunities for those refugees for whom no other durable solution may be in sight, with particular attention being paid to those refugees who have spent an inordinately long period of time in camps and to individuals facing urgent or emergency protection situations,

Welcoming the valuable support extended by Governments to the Office of the High Commissioner in the peformance of its humanitarian tasks, and recognizing the need for continuing and increasing co-operation between the Office of the High Commissioner and other bodies of the United Nations system and with intergovernmental and non-governmental organizations,

Noting the efforts of the Office of the High Commissioner, in co-operation with the Executive Committee of the Programme of the High Commissioner, including the establishment of a Working Group, to improve the efficiency and effectiveness of the Office, and the need to further strengthen field activities and responsibilities,

Commending the Office of the High Commissioner and its staff for the dedicated manner in which they discharge their responsibilities, and paying tribute to those staff members who have endangered their lives in the course of their duties,

1. *Strongly reaffirms* the fundamental nature of the function of the United Nations High Commissioner for Refugees to provide international protection and the need for States to co-operate fully with his Office in the fulfilment of this function, in particular by acceding to and fully and effectively implementing the relevant international and regional refugee instruments;

2. *Endorses* the conclusions on the implementation of the 1951 Convention and the 1967 Protocol relating to the Status of Refugees, adopted by the Executive Committee of the Programme of the High Commissioner at its fortieth session;

3. *Calls upon* all States to refrain from measures that jeopardize the institution of asylum, in particular the return or expulsion of refugees and asylum-seekers contrary to fundamental prohibitions against these practices, and urges States to continue to admit and receive refugees pending identification of their status and appropriate solutions to their plight;

4. *Urges* all States to establish quick and effective procedures for determining refugee status and granting asylum in accordance with internationally accepted criteria and appropriate legal guarantees, in order to deal expeditiously with manifestly unfounded claims and to protect refugees and asylum-seekers from unjustified or unduly prolonged detention or stay in camps;

5. *Notes with deep concern*, in this context, that large numbers of refugees and asylum-seekers in different areas of the world are currently subject to detention or similar restrictive measures by reason of their illegal entry or presence in search of asylum, pending resolution of their situation, and reiterates the conclusions on detention adopted by the Executive Committee of the Programme of the High Commissioner at its thirty-seventh session, which set out the grounds for detention of such persons;

6. *Condemns* violations of the rights and safety of refugees and asylum-seekers, in particular those perpetrated by military or armed attacks against refugee camps and settlements, forced recruitment into armed forces and other forms of violence;

7. *Notes* the accomplishments of the Office of the High Commissioner in the promotion and dissemination of refugee law, including, in particular, the organization of training courses on protection directed towards government and other concerned officials, and urges the Office to pursue its activities in this regard, making every effort to ensure that such protection training courses continue on a significant scale;

8. *Endorses* the conclusions on refugee children adopted by the Executive Committee of the Programme of the High Commissioner at its fortieth session, in particular on the development and dissemination of the ''Guidelines on Refugee Children'' and the implementation of a work plan concerning refugee children that requires the active co-operation and collaboration of Governments, United Nations bodies, among them the United Nations Children's Fund, and non-governmental organizations with the Office of the High Commissioner;

9. *Endorses* the conclusions on refugee women adopted by the Executive Committee of the Programme of the High Commissioner at its fortieth session, in which, in particular, the Executive Committee recognized the need to facilitate the participatory role of refugee women and the need for a policy framework and organizational work plan for the implementation of the

next stages of bringing issues concerning refugee women into the mainstream of the activities of the Office of the High Commissioner;

10. *Endorses* the conclusions on durable solutions and refugee protection adopted by the Executive Committee of the Programme of the High Commissioner at its fortieth session, in which the Executive Committee recognized the need for the active promotion of solutions by the international community and by countries of origin, asylum and resettlement, in accordance with their respective obligations and responsibilities and the desirability of prevention through, *inter alia*, the observance of human rights, as the best solution;

11. *Recognizes* the importance of attaining durable solutions to refugee problems and, in particular, the need to address in this process the root causes of refugee movements in order to avert new flows of refugees and to facilitate the solution of existing problems;

12. *Approves* the decision entitled "Sharing of responsibilities for operational activities relating to refugees", adopted by the Executive Committee of the Programme of the High Commissioner at its fortieth session, and invites the agencies of the United Nations system as well as all other relevant international organizations, both governmental and non-governmental, to establish as soon as possible specific mechanisms of co-operation to assure an agreed division of responsibilities and arrangements for the financing of these activities, while preserving the specific mandate of the High Commissioner to provide protection;

13. *Urges* the member States of relevant bodies to ensure that their delegates to such bodies as the Development Assistance Committee of the Organisation for Economic Co-operation and Development, the World Bank and regional development banks, and multilateral agencies such as the United Nations Development Programme and the International Fund for Agricultural Development are made aware of the refugee-related conclusions of the Executive Committee of the Programme of the High Commissioner at its fortieth session and urges them to use their good offices to ensure the adoption of policies and the establishment of mechanisms, both institutional and financial, that will provide for co-ordinated and expeditious implementation of development initiatives related to refugees and returnees;

14. *Notes with appreciation* the ongoing work being done by the Office of the High Commissioner to put into practice the concept of development-oriented assistance to refugees and returnees, as initiated at the Second International Conference on Assistance to Refugees in Africa and reaffirmed in the Oslo Declaration and Plan of Action adopted by the International Conference on the Plight of Refugees, Returnees and Displaced Persons in Southern Africa, as well as in the Declaration and Concerted Plan of Action in favour of Central American Refugees, Returnees and Displaced Persons adopted by the International Conference on Central American Refugees, held at Guatemala City from 29 to 31 May 1989, urges the Office to continue that process wherever appropriate, in full co-operation with appropriate international agencies, and urges Governments to support these efforts, being fully aware of the catalytic role of the Office of the High Commissioner;

15. *Recognizes* the importance of the International Conference on Indo-Chinese Refugees, held at Geneva on 13 and 14 June 1989, and the Comprehensive Plan

of Action adopted at that Conference, as well as the International Conference on Central American Refugees and the Concerted Plan of Action in favour of Central American Refugees, Returnees and Displaced Persons;

16. *Urges* all States to support the Office of the High Commissioner in its search for durable solutions to the problem of refugees and displaced persons of concern to the Office, primarily through voluntary repatriation or return, with assistance to returnees as appropriate, and, wherever appropriate, through integration into countries of asylum or through resettlement in third countries;

17. *Expresses its deep appreciation* for the valuable material and humanitarian response of receiving countries, in particular those developing countries which, despite limited resources, continue to admit, on a permanent or temporary basis, large numbers of refugees and asylum-seekers;

18. *Urges* the international community, in accordance with the principle of international solidarity and in the spirit of burden-sharing, to assist the countries referred to in paragraph 17 of the present resolution in order to enable them to cope with the additional burden that the care for refugees and asylum-seekers represents;

19. *Endorses* the conclusions and decisions on assistance activities adopted by the Executive Committee of the Programme of the High Commissioner at its fortieth session, which reflect the gravity of the financial crisis that the Office of the High Commissioner is facing at present;

20. *Calls upon* all Governments to contribute to the High Commissioner's programmes and, taking into account the need to achieve greater burden-sharing among donors, to assist the High Commissioner in securing additional income from traditional governmental sources, other Governments and the private sector in order to ensure that the needs of refugees, returnees and displaced persons of concern to the Office of the High Commissioner are met.

General Assembly resolution 44/137

15 December 1989   Meeting 82   Adopted without vote

Approved by Third Committee (A/44/823) without vote, 27 November (meeting 56); 31-nation draft (A/C.3/44/L.67), orally revised; agenda item 110.
Meeting numbers. GA 44th session: 3rd Committee 44-47, 49, 56; plenary 82.

Financial and administrative questions

The year 1989 was a particularly difficult year for UNHCR in financial terms. Total voluntary funds expenditure amounted to $570.3 million,[5] reflecting a marked increase compared to $545.5 million in 1988. Of the 1989 total, $386.6 million was spent on General Programmes and $183.7 million went to Special Programmes and other accounts. Total income for 1989 amounted to $533.6 million, compared to $529.1 million in 1988.

Severe funding problems, started by a negative carry-over of some $6.8 million from 1988 in General Programmes, were compounded by a reduction in secondary income while overall requirements continued to increase. The initial General Programmes target had been $429 million. In addition, UNHCR had had to address new situations in Ethiopia, Central America, South-East Asia and Hong Kong, with costs totalling some $42.4 million. Drastic reassessment of priorities had brought about savings of some $34 million. Due to limited levels of contributions, further reductions were made in programmes for all regions. In July, operational projects were cut and austerity measures imposed, for further savings of some $35 million. Thus, the final revised General Programmes target was $389.4 million.

In view of funding difficulties, the Executive Committee in October[1] authorized an exceptional carry-over of a maximum of $40 million into 1990 in order to cover the anticipated shortfall for the year. It also decided to hold an extraordinary session in mid-1990 to address the content of the General Programmes and other assistance activities, with a view to examining the effective use of funds and administration of programmes and projects. The Committee endorsed the recommendation of the Board of Auditors[5] that UNHCR should intensify its efforts to extend fund-raising activities to non-traditional sources, including the private sector.

Contributions

Contributions in cash and in kind in 1989 totalled $505.9 million, compared to $482.7 million in 1988. Paid cash contributions amounted to $407.6 million in 1989; outstanding cash pledges amounted to $55.2 million. Contributions in kind amounted to $10.7 million, with an additional $32.4 million outstanding. Seventy-two Governments made contributions totalling $459 million, while 30 non-governmental and intergovernmental organizations made contributions in cash and kind valued at some $47 million. Donor support continued to be strong in absolute terms, with an increase of 5.6 per cent from the total contributions income figure of $480 million in 1988.

In October, the Executive Committee of UNHCR, noting the shortfall in funds in relation to requirements, appealed to Governments that had already contributed to consider making additional contributions and requested those Governments that had not previously contributed to provide financial support.

Government pledges of $166 million were announced at a meeting on 20 November of the *Ad Hoc* Committee of the General Assembly for the Announcement of Voluntary Contributions to the 1990 Programme of UNHCR.

1988 accounts

The audited financial statements on funds administered by UNHCR for the year ended 31 December 1988[5] showed total expenditures of $545.5 million and total income of $529.1 million. In October 1989, the Executive Committee took note[1] of the report of the Advisory Committee on Administrative and Budgetary Questions (ACABQ).[6]

On 19 December, in **resolution 44/183**, the General Assembly accepted the financial reports and audited financial statements of UNHCR and endorsed the observations and recommendations of the Board of Auditors and ACABQ.

Administrative and personnel issues

The Executive Committee of UNHCR in October approved the transfer in 1990 of up to $800,000 from the General Programme Reserve to the Fund for Staff Housing and Basic Amenities, bringing the ceiling of the Fund from $5.1 million to $5.9 million.

The Committee urged the High Commissioner to reduce in 1990 the average grade level at headquarters and to raise the average grade level in the field, *inter alia*, through the reallocation of senior management posts from headquarters to the field.

REFERENCES

[1]A/44/12/Add.1. [2]YUN 1951, p. 520. [3]YUN 1967, p. 769. [4]A/44/12. [5]A/44/5/Add.5. [6]A/AC.96/732.

Refugee assistance and protection

Assistance

During 1989,[1] UNHCR continued to cooperate with concerned Governments and the international community in efforts to meet the humanitarian needs of refugees throughout the world and to direct programmes towards durable solutions through either voluntary repatriation or local integration in the country of first asylum, or, where those were not possible, resettlement in another country.

More than $255 million was obligated in 1989 to promote durable solutions, including $71 million spent under Special Programmes to facilitate voluntary repatriation and the rehabilitation of returnees in their countries of origin. UNHCR continued to emphasize that States must create the necessary conditions in concerned countries of origin to make voluntary repatriation a viable option and, in that connection, advocated the establishment of tripartite commissions to promote and facilitate voluntary return whenever possible.

In Africa, the voluntary repatriation of more than 43,000 Namibians, mainly from Angola and Zambia, was successfully completed as called for in a 1978 Security Council resolution.[2] In Angola and Zaire, a two-way repatriation began in September 1989. In Latin America, some 9,000 persons were repatriated, mainly from Honduras to El Salvador, and another 5,000 persons from Honduras and Costa Rica to Nicaragua. Also, some 1,800 Chileans were repatriated under UNHCR auspices. Where voluntary repatriation was unlikely and where the host Government was agreeable, UNHCR assisted refugees in settling within the host country. In China, Mexico, Somalia, the Sudan, Swaziland, Uganda, the United Republic of Tanzania, Viet Nam, Zaire and Zambia, rural settlement projects enabled refugees to resume a more normal life and become self-sufficient. Education, vocational training, counselling services, housing facilities and social amenities were provided to refugees in urban and semi-urban areas. An upward trend in resettlement continued in 1989, with a total of 124,244 refugees resettled in third countries under UNHCR auspices. That increase was composed essentially of Indo-Chinese and contrasted with slightly fewer refugees resettled from most other areas, as compared with 1988. Only Africa showed an increase of some 26 per cent, with 4,563 persons resettled.

UNHCR also responded to requests for emergency assistance in 1989. Almost all of the $10 million in the UNHCR Emergency Fund was needed for urgent intervention in Angola ($1.05 million), Ethiopia ($0.6 million), Malaysia ($0.5 million), Mauritania ($0.48 million), Pakistan ($0.73 million), Senegal ($2.7 million), Uganda ($2.6 million) and Zaire ($0.95 million). In October, UNHCR introduced a new Refugee Contingency Plan format. It was complemented in high-priority locations by the UNHCR emergency preparedness profile, containing infrastructural and institutional resource data to facilitate emergency preparedness planning. New emergency measures, including a central emergency stockpile, an emergency staffing roster, an emergency registration kit and a field-level emergency alert system, were being prepared.

UNHCR developed a training course to enable project planners and implementers to conduct a thorough analysis of the situation of women in any refugee population through examination of the gender-based division of socio-economic roles. In July, a Senior Co-ordinator for Refugee Women was appointed to co-ordinate and monitor the integration of women's issues into all UN activities.

Implementation of the UNHCR *Guidelines on Refugee Children*[3] was delayed in several areas due to the continued financial difficulties of the Office. Refugee children continued to face serious problems with respect to protection and general welfare. To identify the most appropriate durable solutions for unaccompanied minors, UNHCR issued draft guidelines for interviewing unaccompanied refugee children and adolescents and for preparing social histories.

During 1989, some $3.5 million was spent on public information activities to create international awareness and understanding of the plight of refugees and the goals and activities of UNHCR. The Office continued to publish the magazine *Refugees* monthly in English, French and Spanish, bi-monthly in German and Japanese, quarterly in Italian and twice yearly in Greek. Some 200,000 copies were distributed free of charge in over 100 countries. With television networks, UNHCR co-produced programmes on refugee children in Ethiopia, victims of torture, Vietnamese "boat people", Afghan refugees in Pakistan and refugee women.

Refugee aid and development

UNHCR co-operated in 1989 with development agencies to implement projects reinforcing ongoing assistance or facilitating the phasing-out of such assistance. It worked with the World Bank in the "Second Income-generating Project for Refugee Areas in Pakistan" and agreed to a third phase in 1991-1992, pending the voluntary repatriation of refugees to Afghanistan. In Somalia, a joint World Bank/UNHCR/UNDP/European Economic Community mission made initial assessments for a "refugee-affected area project", to help refugees who might opt to remain in Somalia when the majority repatriated. UNHCR undertook project-preparation work with the International Fund for Agricultural Development in Mexico for Guatemalan refugees and in Ethiopia for returnees. Projects in the Sudan and Iran awaited the necessary funding.

In a report[4] to the Executive Committee, the High Commissioner delineated the role and mandate of UNHCR with regard to other agencies working to resolve and alleviate refugee and returnee problems through developmental initiatives, and addressed the character and operational aspects of a proposed Project Planning Fund for Refugee Aid and Development and financial resources allocated to developing asylum countries. Observing that appropriately targeted development assistance could play an important role in reversing or at least attenuating the root causes leading to refugee outflows, he concluded that the concept of refugee aid and development could contribute to a more cost-effective and co-ordinated approach by UNHCR in its search for durable solutions. He proposed: strengthening co-ordination between national refugee administration authorities and planning and technical departments; advancing refugee-related concerns in policy bodies of international development organizations; and introducing multi-year programme planning into the UNHCR programme.

In October, the Executive Committee requested[5] the High Commissioner to continue his catalytic role in the area of refugee aid and development and to give priority to and identify appropriate projects and initiatives with development agencies and Governments of host countries. Member States were asked to respond favourably to refugee aid and development appeals for projects to be undertaken by UNHCR in partnership with refugee-hosting Governments and development agencies.

Also in October, on a related subject on sharing responsibilities for operational activities relating to refugees, the Committee requested the High Commissioner to enter into consultations as soon as possible with UNDP and other development agencies of the UN system, so as to examine the condition and modalities of an appropriate implementing mechanism for development projects relating to refugees, returnees and the areas that received them.

Africa

The overall number of refugees in Africa increased during 1989. Refugees continued to flee from Mozambique into Malawi and from the Sudan into south-western Ethiopia. Events in Mauritania and Senegal in May, and in Liberia at the end of the year, necessitated new emergency operations in a part of Africa that had been relatively free of large-scale refugee movements. African Governments continued to offer generous asylum to refugees, but their increased burden brought greater difficulties in maintaining past liberal practices.

During the year, expenditures in Africa under UNHCR voluntary funds totalled $257.8 million, of which $176.7 million was obligated under General Programmes, the greater part for care and maintenance operations, and $78 million under Special Programmes, the greater part for repatriation operations and the needs of newly arrived refugees.

ECONOMIC AND SOCIAL COUNCIL ACTION

On 26 July, the Economic and Social Council, by **decision 1989/176**, noted the oral reports made on behalf of the Secretary-General by the High Commissioner on the situation of refugees in the Sudan and refugees and displaced persons in Djibouti and Malawi, assistance to refugees in Somalia, assistance to refugees and returnees in Ethiopia, and assistance to student refugees in southern Africa, as well as an oral report on behalf of the Secretary-General by a UNDP representative on assistance to refugees in Somalia.

Southern Africa

During 1989, assistance continued to more than 120,000 Mozambicans in Swaziland, Zambia and Zimbabwe. A two-way repatriation between Angola and Zaire began by air in September and

some 6,500 Angolans and 3,000 Zairians were repatriated. The number of South African refugees reported to have found asylum in southern Africa remained stable at some 35,000, over half of whom received UNHCR assistance.

In discharging responsibilities assigned to UNHCR in a 1978 Security Council resolution,[2] and within the framework of the activities of the United Nations Transition Assistance Group, a total of 43,387 Namibians were repatriated. Of that number, 35,553 returned from Angola, 3,841 from Zambia and 3,993 from 40 other countries (see PART FOUR, Chapter III).

Mozambican refugees in Malawi

In response to a 1988 General Assembly request,[6] the Secretary-General in July 1989 reported[7] on assistance to refugees and displaced persons in Malawi. There were 646,864 refugees in Malawi, mainly from Mozambique, as at 1 April 1989.

The continued influx of refugees over the years had resulted in the Government's policy to discourage refugee settlements among the local Malawian population. Although the Government regularly opened new sites for refugees to keep up with the rate of the arrivals, land shortages remained a serious problem. In addition, government services had to support both national and refugee populations, often to the detriment of the Malawian citizens, he said.

The original target—to provide one potable water point per 1,000 persons—had been achieved by the end of 1988; a new objective of one water point for every 750 was set. As for education, some 206 classrooms were completed, with 60,000 Mozambican children enrolled in primary education programmes following the Mozambican curriculum. Some 20 handicapped refugees received training in carpentry, sewing, shoemaking and tinsmithing. The World Food Programme (WFP) co-ordinated the supply of most basic food items, with UNHCR purchasing additional basic commodities and supplementary and therapeutic food.

Following the establishment of a tripartite commission in December 1988, the Governments of Malawi and Mozambique, together with UNHCR, held two meetings during 1989 on voluntary repatriation.

GENERAL ASSEMBLY ACTION

On 15 December, the General Assembly, on the recommendation of the Third Committee, adopted **resolution 44/149** without vote.

Assistance to refugees and displaced persons in Malawi
The General Assembly,

Recalling its resolutions 42/132 of 7 December 1987 and 43/148 of 8 December 1988 on assistance to refugees and displaced persons in Malawi,

Having considered the report of the Secretary-General,

Having examined that part of the report of the United Nations High Commissioner for Refugees that deals with the situation of refugees and displaced persons in Malawi,

Gravely concerned about the continuing serious social and economic impact of the massive presence of refugees and displaced persons, as well as its far-reaching consequences for the country's long-term development process,

Appreciating the important measures that the Government of Malawi is taking in order to provide shelter, protection, food, education and health and other humanitarian services to thousands of refugees and displaced persons,

Recognizing the heavy burden placed on the people and Government of Malawi and the sacrifices they are making in caring for the refugees and displaced persons, given the country's limited social services and infrastructure, and the need for adequate international assistance to enable them to continue their efforts to provide assistance to the refugees and displaced persons,

Expressing its appreciation for the assistance rendered by Member States, the various organizations of the United Nations system, the Office of the United Nations High Commissioner for Refugees and other international, intergovernmental and non-governmental organizations in support of the refugee programme in Malawi,

Bearing in mind the findings and recommendations of the inter-agency mission to Malawi, particularly on the need to strengthen the country's socio-economic infrastructure in order to enable it to provide for the immediate humanitarian relief requirements of the refugees and displaced persons, as well as the long-term national development needs of the country,

Recognizing the need to view refugee-related development projects within local and national development plans,

1. *Takes note* of the report of the Secretary-General;

2. *Commends* the measures that the Government of Malawi is taking to provide material and humanitarian assistance to refugees and displaced persons, in spite of the serious economic situation it faces, and stresses the need for additional resources to lessen the impact of the presence of refugees and displaced persons on the country's long-term development process;

3. *Expresses its appreciation* to the Secretary-General, the United Nations High Commissioner for Refugees, donor countries and intergovernmental and non-governmental organizations for their efforts to assist the refugees and displaced persons in Malawi;

4. *Expresses grave concern* at the serious and far-reaching consequences of the massive presence of refugees and displaced persons in the country and its implications for the long-term socio-economic development of the whole country;

5. *Appeals* to Member States, the appropriate organs, organizations and bodies of the United Nations system, intergovernmental and non-governmental organizations and the international financial institutions to continue providing the Government of Malawi with the necessary resources for the implementation of development assistance projects in regions affected by the presence of refugees and displaced persons, as well as for the development programmes now being implemented;

6. *Requests* the Secretary-General to continue his efforts to mobilize the necessary financial and material assistance for the full implementation of ongoing projects in the areas affected by the presence of refugees and displaced persons and for programmes now being implemented;

7. *Requests* the High Commissioner to continue coordination with the appropriate specialized agencies in order to consolidate and ensure the continuation of essential services to the refugees and displaced persons in their settlements;

8. *Requests* the Secretary-General to report to the General Assembly at its forty-fifth session, through the Economic and Social Council, on the implementation of the present resolution.

General Assembly resolution 44/149

15 December 1989   Meeting 82   Adopted without vote

Approved by Third Committee (A/44/848) without vote, 29 November (meeting 60); 27-nation draft (A/C.3/44/L.62); agenda item 12.
Meeting numbers. GA 44th session: 3rd Committee 48, 50-60; plenary 82.

Student refugees

In July, the Secretary-General reported[8] on assistance to student refugees in southern Africa. Assistance was provided by UNHCR to equip student refugees with skills to make them productive and self-reliant in their countries of asylum, and also to prepare them to assume leadership roles in various fields of competence upon their return to their countries of origin. Appropriations for 1989 amounted to $489,000. Higher education for Namibian and South African refugees was funded by the UN Educational and Training Programme for Southern Africa.

The Secretary-General reported that during the 1987/88 academic year, some 708 South African and Namibian students were assisted to study at the lower secondary school level, both in and outside the region.

GENERAL ASSEMBLY ACTION

On 15 December, the General Assembly, on the recommendation of the Third Committee, adopted **resolution 44/157** without vote.

Assistance to student refugees in southern Africa
The General Assembly,

Recalling its resolution 43/149 of 8 December 1988, in which it, *inter alia*, requested the United Nations High Commissioner for Refugees, in co-operation with the Secretary-General, to continue to organize and implement an effective programme of educational and other appropriate assistance for student refugees from South Africa and Namibia who had been granted asylum in Botswana, Lesotho, Swaziland and Zambia,

Having considered the report of the Secretary-General,

Noting with appreciation that some of the projects recommended in the report continue to be successfully implemented,

Noting with concern that the discriminatory and repressive policies that continue to be applied in South Africa cause a continued and increasing influx of student refugees into Botswana, Lesotho, Swaziland and Zambia,

Conscious of the burden placed on the limited financial, material and administrative resources of the host countries by the increasing number of student refugees,

Appreciating the efforts of the host countries to deal with their student refugee populations, with the assistance of the international community,

1. *Takes note with satisfaction* of the report of the Secretary-General;

2. *Expresses its appreciation* to the Governments of Botswana, Lesotho, Swaziland and Zambia for granting asylum and making educational and other facilities available to the student refugees, in spite of the pressure that the continuing influx of those refugees exerts on facilities in their countries;

3. *Also expresses its appreciation* to the Governments of Botswana, Lesotho, Swaziland and Zambia for the co-operation that they have extended to the United Nations High Commissioner for Refugees on matters concerning the welfare of the refugees;

4. *Notes with appreciation* the financial and material support provided for the student refugees by Member States, the Office of the United Nations High Commissioner for Refugees, other bodies of the United Nations system and intergovernmental and non-governmental organizations;

5. *Requests* the High Commissioner, in co-operation with the Secretary-General, to continue to organize and implement an effective programme of educational and other appropriate assistance for student refugees from South Africa and Namibia who have been granted asylum in Botswana, Lesotho, Swaziland and Zambia;

6. *Urges* all Member States and intergovernmental and non-governmental organizations to continue contributing generously to the assistance programme for student refugees, through financial support of the regular programmes of the High Commissioner and of the projects and programmes, including unfunded projects, which were submitted to the Second International Conference on Assistance to Refugees in Africa, held at Geneva from 9 to 11 July 1984;

7. *Also urges* all Member States and all intergovernmental and non-governmental organizations to assist the countries of asylum materially and otherwise to enable them to continue to discharge their humanitarian obligations towards refugees;

8. *Appeals* to the Office of the United Nations High Commissioner for Refugees, the United Nations Development Programme and all other competent United Nations bodies, as well as other international and non-governmental organizations, to continue providing humanitarian and development assistance so as to facilitate and expedite the settlement of student refugees from South Africa who have been granted asylum in Botswana, Lesotho, Swaziland and Zambia;

9. *Calls upon* agencies and programmes of the United Nations system to continue co-operating with the Secretary-General and the High Commissioner in the implementation of humanitarian programmes of assistance for the student refugees in southern Africa;

10. *Requests* the High Commissioner, in co-operation with the Secretary-General, to continue to keep the matter under review, to apprise the Economic and Social Council, at its second regular session of 1990, of the current status of the programmes and to report to the General Assembly at its forty-fifth session on the implementation of the present resolution.

General Assembly resolution 44/157

15 December 1989   Meeting 82   Adopted without vote

Approved by Third Committee (A/44/848) without vote, 29 November (meeting 60); 49-nation draft (A/C.3/44/L.78); agenda item 12.

Meeting numbers. GA 44th session: 3rd Committee 48, 50-60; plenary 82.

Follow-up to the 1988
Conference on refugees in southern Africa

In response to a 1988 General Assembly resolution,[9] the Secretary-General reported[10] in September 1989 on follow-up to the 1988 International Conference on the Plight of Refugees, Returnees and Displaced Persons in Southern Africa. He summarized activities of UN bodies and Member States in implementing the Oslo Declaration and Plan of Action,[11] adopted at the Conference, which were designed to promote emergency preparedness, needs assessment and delivery of assistance, recovery and development, and mobilization of resources.

The Secretary-General also considered the nature of the problem of internally displaced persons and UN mechanisms to deal with that problem. He noted that since internally displaced persons remained within their own territory, they fell under the jurisdiction of their own national Governments, and that there was no formal mechanism within the UN system to deal specifically with that problem. Referring to the arrangements in place at the headquarters and at the field level, in the case of Africa, he concluded that it was not appropriate to establish a new mechanism but, rather, necessary to strengthen existing arrangements so as to enhance accessibility and effectiveness. He suggested that the UNDP resident representative/UN resident co-ordinator should play the key role whenever an emergency situation involving displaced persons evolved, including early warning.

GENERAL ASSEMBLY ACTION

On 15 December, on the recommendation of the Third Committee, the General Assembly adopted **resolution 44/136** without vote.

**International Conference on the Plight
of Refugees, Returnees and
Displaced Persons in Southern Africa**

The General Assembly,

Recalling its resolution 43/116 of 8 December 1988 on the International Conference on the Plight of Refugees, Returnees and Displaced Persons in Southern Africa,

Gravely concerned about the constant deterioration of the situation in southern Africa arising from the domination and oppression of the people of South Africa by the minority racist régime of South Africa,

Having considered the report of the Secretary-General on the International Conference on the Plight of Refugees, Returnees and Displaced Persons in Southern Africa, held at Oslo from 22 to 24 August 1988,

Conscious of its responsibility to provide economic, material and humanitarian assistance to independent States in southern Africa in order to assist them in coping with the situation resulting from the acts of aggression and destabilization committed by the *apartheid* régime of South Africa,

Taking note with appreciation of the consultations undertaken by the Secretary-General to establish within the United Nations system a mechanism to ensure the implementation and overall co-ordination of relief programmes for internally displaced persons,

Noting with indignation that South Africa's policy of *apartheid* and its direct and indirect acts of aggression, intimidation and destabilization through armed terrorists continue to be the main causes of refugee flows and increasing displacement of persons in southern Africa,

Convinced that there is an urgent need for the international community to extend maximum and concerted assistance to southern African countries sheltering refugees, returnees and displaced persons and also to highlight the plight of these persons,

1. *Takes note with satisfaction* of the report of the Secretary-General on the International Conference on the Plight of Refugees, Returnees and Displaced Persons in Southern Africa;

2. *Reaffirms* the need to continue the implementation of the Oslo Declaration and Plan of Action on the Plight of Refugees, Returnees and Displaced Persons in Southern Africa adopted by the Conference;

3. *Expresses its gratitude* to the countries and organizations that have given assistance to the countries in southern Africa to enable them to cope with the situation of refugees, returnees and displaced persons in their countries;

4. *Calls upon* the international community to provide increased assistance to the countries of southern Africa to enable them to strengthen their capacity to provide the necessary facilities and services for the care and well-being of the refugees, returnees and displaced persons in their countries;

5. *Reiterates its appreciation* to the Secretary-General for his efforts, on behalf of the international community, to organize and mobilize special programmes of economic assistance for the front-line and other neighbouring States to help them withstand the effects of the acts of aggression and destabilization committed by the *apartheid* régime of South Africa;

6. *Takes note with appreciation* of the efforts made by the Secretary-General, the Office of the United Nations High Commissioner for Refugees and the Administrator of the United Nations Development Programme to implement those specific tasks and responsibilities assigned to them in the Oslo Declaration and Plan of Action, and encourages them to continue their efforts;

7. *Endorses* the recommendation of the Secretary-General aimed at assigning to the United Nations resident co-ordinators the function of co-ordinating assistance for internally displaced persons, in close co-operation with Governments, local representatives of donor countries and United Nations agencies in the field;

8. *Once again urges* all Member States, organizations of the United Nations system and governmental and non-governmental organizations to undertake the measures as required of them under the Oslo Declaration and Plan of Action;

9. *Decides* to consider this question at its forty-fifth session on the basis of a report to be submitted by the Secretary-General.

General Assembly resolution 44/136

15 December 1989   Meeting 82   Adopted without vote

Approved by Third Committee (A/44/823) without vote, 27 November (meeting 56); draft by Lesotho, for African Group (A/C.3/44/L.63); agenda item 110 *(a)*.

Meeting numbers. GA 44th session: 3rd Committee 44-47, 49, 56; plenary 82.

Other African countries

Chad

In response to a 1988 General Assembly request,[12] the Secretary-General reported[13] in October 1989 on emergency assistance to voluntary returnees and displaced persons in Chad. UNHCR's special programme, which was extended several times until 31 March 1989, provided assistance to returnees in the country. At the end of 1988, approximately 103,000 returnees had benefited from the programme, which included provision of food, blankets, household utensils, seeds and agricultural tools, as well as transportation costs. When the programme closed in March, $2.25 million had been spent. Limited repatriation continued in 1989, particularly from Cameroon, the Central African Republic and Nigeria.

GENERAL ASSEMBLY ACTION

The General Assembly, on the recommendation of the Third Committee, adopted **resolution 44/153** on 15 December without vote.

Assistance to voluntary returnees and displaced persons in Chad

The General Assembly,

Recalling its resolution 43/143 of 8 December 1988 on emergency assistance to voluntary returnees and displaced persons in Chad, as well as all its previous resolutions on this question,

Taking note of the report of the Secretary-General,

Deeply concerned about the persistence of the harmful effects of the natural calamities that are compounding the already precarious food and health situation in Chad,

Considering that the large number of voluntary returnees poses serious social and economic problems for the Government of Chad,

Considering also that the return of displaced persons in the northern region poses serious resettlement problems for the Government of Chad,

Bearing in mind the many appeals made by the Government of Chad for international assistance to the voluntary returnees and displaced persons in Chad,

1. *Endorses* the appeals made by the Government of Chad for humanitarian assistance to the voluntary returnees and displaced persons in Chad;

2. *Reiterates its appeal* to all States and intergovernmental and non-governmental organizations to support, by generous contributions, the efforts being made by the Government of Chad to assist and resettle the voluntary returnees and displaced persons;

3. *Notes with satisfaction* the action taken by the various organizations of the United Nations system and the specialized agencies with a view to mobilizing humani-

tarian assistance to the voluntary returnees and displaced persons in Chad;

4. *Again requests* the United Nations High Commissioner for Refugees and the United Nations Disaster Relief Co-ordinator to mobilize humanitarian assistance to the voluntary returnees and displaced persons in Chad;

5. *Calls upon:*

(a) The Secretary-General to continue his efforts to mobilize special humanitarian assistance for the resettlement of displaced persons in the northern region of Chad;

(b) The international community to support the efforts made by the Government of Chad to implement the programmes for repatriating and resettling the voluntary returnees and displaced persons in Chad;

6. *Requests* the Secretary-General, in co-operation with the United Nations High Commissioner for Refugees and the United Nations Disaster Relief Co-ordinator, to report to the General Assembly at its forty-fifth session on the implementation of the present resolution.

General Assembly resolution 44/153

15 December 1989   Meeting 82   Adopted without vote

Approved by Third Committee (A/44/848) without vote, 29 November (meeting 60); 36-nation draft (A/C.3/44/L.70); agenda item 12.
Meeting numbers. GA 44th session: 3rd Committee 48, 50-60; plenary 82.

Djibouti

In response to a 1988 General Assembly request,[14] the Secretary-General in July 1989 reported[15] on humanitarian assistance to refugees in Djibouti. With full co-operation from the Government, UNHCR had mobilized resources throughout 1988 and the first half of 1989, successfully determining a durable solution for the majority of some 13,000 refugees living in Djibouti-Ville and at the Dikhil camp. Following the departure of 6,455 Djibouti nationals in 1988 from the Dikhil camp, who settled elsewhere in the country, 5,671 Ethiopian refugees, by 14 February 1989, had voluntarily repatriated. As a result, the camp closed by the end of March. The remaining 1,500 refugees in Djibouti, all Ethiopians, received supplementary aid and counselling, educational and medical services from UNHCR. In addition, some 35,000 Somalis fled to Djibouti as a result of armed conflict in north-west Somalia.

GENERAL ASSEMBLY ACTION

On 15 December, the General Assembly, on the recommendation of the Third Committee, adopted **resolution 44/150** without vote.

Humanitarian assistance to refugees and displaced persons in Djibouti

The General Assembly,

Recalling its resolutions 42/126 of 7 December 1987 and 43/142 of 8 December 1988 on humanitarian assistance to refugees in Djibouti, as well as all its previous resolutions on this question,

Having considered the report of the Secretary-General on humanitarian assistance to refugees in Djibouti,

Deeply concerned about the recent inflow of over thirty-five thousand externally displaced persons, which has added considerably to the burden already being carried by Djibouti in respect of refugees in the country,

Noting that Djibouti is considered one of the least developed countries and that the recent inflow of large numbers of externally displaced persons and the continued presence of refugees have severely strained the already inadequate social and economic infrastructure,

Noting also that the present situation has required the diversion of scarce resources from development to emergency relief and precautionary measures,

Appreciating the determined and sustained efforts made by the Government of Djibouti to cope with the growing needs of refugees and externally displaced persons,

Noting with appreciation the steps taken by the Government of Djibouti, in close co-operation with the United Nations High Commissioner for Refugees, to implement appropriate and lasting solutions with respect to the refugees and externally displaced persons in Djibouti,

Noting with satisfaction that over six thousand refugees have been settled and integrated in Djibouti, despite the physical, social and economic obstacles that the country faces,

Appreciating the assistance provided by Member States, the specialized agencies, intergovernmental and non-governmental organizations and voluntary agencies to the ongoing relief and rehabilitation programmes for the refugees and externally displaced persons in Djibouti,

1. *Takes note* of the report of the Secretary-General on humanitarian assistance to refugees in Djibouti and appreciates the efforts of the United Nations High Commissioner for Refugees to keep the situation under constant review;

2. *Welcomes* the steps taken by the Government of Djibouti, in close co-operation with the High Commissioner, to implement appropriate and lasting solutions with respect to the refugees and externally displaced persons in Djibouti;

3. *Expresses its appreciation* to Member States, the specialized agencies, intergovernmental and non-governmental organizations and voluntary agencies for their assistance to the relief and rehabilitation programmes for the refugees and externally displaced persons in Djibouti;

4. *Urges* the High Commissioner to intensify his efforts to mobilize, on an emergency basis, the resources necessary to implement lasting solutions with respect to the refugees in Djibouti and the increasing inflow of externally displaced persons;

5. *Calls upon* all Member States, the specialized agencies and other organizations of the United Nations system, and intergovernmental and non-governmental organizations to continue to support the determined and sustained efforts made by the Government of Djibouti to cope with the urgent needs of refugees and externally displaced persons and to implement lasting solutions as regards their situation;

6. *Requests* the Secretary-General to report to the General Assembly at its forty-fifth session, through the Economic and Social Council, on the implementation of the present resolution.

General Assembly resolution 44/150

15 December 1989   Meeting 82   Adopted without vote

Approved by Third Committee (A/44/848) without vote, 29 November (meeting 60); 82-nation draft (A/C.3/44/L.64); agenda item 12.
Meeting numbers. GA 44th session: 3rd Committee 48, 50-60; plenary 82.

Ethiopia

In response to a 1988 General Assembly request,[16] the Secretary-General reported[17] in September on assistance to refugees and returnees in Ethiopia.

The influx of Sudanese refugees into southwestern Ethiopia continued at an average of 4,400 persons per month. By the end of 1989, the total refugee population was 384,989. UNHCR spent $26.8 million to assist them, 76 per cent of that amount for transport. All refugee shelters were sprayed twice a year with insecticide to control malaria outbreaks and adequate numbers of refuse disposal pits had been constructed. The morbidity and mortality rate dropped considerably as a result of strengthened primary care activities. Some 90 refugees were undergoing training as community health agents and traditional birth attendants.

Throughout 1989, a steady influx of Somali refugees into eastern Ethiopia continued. In August, the five camps hosting Somali refugees were occupied by 324,808 persons. In late 1989, a new camp was established for 10,000 new Somali refugees. Following completion of geological surveys, exploratory drilling was taking place in the Jerrer Valley for a proposed piped water supply system. WFP contributed 63,452 metric tons of food, worth $16.5 million, for Somali refugees. UNHCR provided $34.2 million to assist refugees, with $6.2 million worth of food contributions to augment WFP food aid.

Repatriation of Ethiopian refugees from Somalia and Djibouti continued. Some 4,704 returnees from Somalia, reintegrated in southern Ethiopia during 1989, received cash grants, water, food and shelters. In May, a UNHCR technical mission launched studies aimed at increasing the receiving capacity in southern Ethiopia and to prepare for a possible large-scale repatriation of Ethiopian refugees from Somalia. By the end of February 1989, some 5,600 refugees had voluntarily repatriated from Djibouti.

UNHCR's total expenditures in Ethiopia during 1989 amounted to $89.5 million.

GENERAL ASSEMBLY ACTION

On 15 December, the General Assembly, on the recommendation of the Third Committee, adopted **resolution 44/154** without vote.

Assistance to refugees and returnees in Ethiopia
The General Assembly,

Recalling all its resolutions, in particular resolution 43/144 of 8 December 1988, as well as all those of the Economic and Social Council, on assistance to displaced persons in Ethiopia,

Taking note of the report of the Secretary-General,

Having considered the report of the United Nations High Commissioner for Refugees,

Recognizing the increasing number of refugees and voluntary returnees in Ethiopia,

Deeply concerned about the massive flow of refugees and voluntary returnees into the country and the enormous burden this has placed on the country's infrastructure and meagre resources,

Deeply concerned also about the grave consequences this has entailed for the country's capability to grapple with the effects of the prolonged drought,

Aware of the heavy burden placed on the Government of Ethiopia and of the need for adequate assistance to refugees, voluntary returnees and victims of natural disasters,

1. *Commends* the Office of the United Nations High Commissioner for Refugees and intergovernmental organizations and voluntary agencies for their assistance in mitigating the plight of the large number of refugees and voluntary returnees in Ethiopia;

2. *Appeals* to Member States and to international organizations and voluntary agencies to provide adequate material, financial and technical assistance for relief and rehabilitation programmes for the large number of refugees and voluntary returnees in Ethiopia;

3. *Requests* the United Nations High Commissioner for Refugees to continue his efforts to mobilize humanitarian assistance for the relief, rehabilitation and resettlement of voluntary returnees and the large number of refugees in Ethiopia;

4. *Requests* the Secretary-General, in co-operation with the High Commissioner, to apprise the Economic and Social Council, at its second regular session of 1990, of the implementation of the present resolution and to report thereon to the General Assembly at its forty-fifth session.

General Assembly resolution 44/154

15 December 1989   Meeting 82   Adopted without vote

Approved by Third Committee (A/44/848) without vote, 29 November (meeting 60); 71-nation draft (A/C.3/44/L.71); agenda item 12.
Meeting numbers. GA 44th session: 3rd Committee 48, 50-60; plenary 82.

Somalia

In response to a 1988 General Assembly request,[18] the Secretary-General in August reported[19] on assistance to refugees in Somalia.

In February/March, a UN inter-agency mission to Somalia assessed urgent humanitarian requirements and recommended that measures be taken to ensure both the safety of refugees and the civilian nature of those assisted.[20] The mission was dispatched after Somalia requested assistance to cope with the country's emergency situation caused by armed conflict (see PART THREE, Chapter III).

Refugees hosted in Somalia, all of Ethiopian origin, numbered 600,000 in 1989. At high-level negotiations between UNHCR and Somalia (Geneva, 17-25 May; Mogadishu, 12-14 June), agreement was reached on general principles and implementation modalities of the refugee programme. It dealt with voluntary repatriation, spontaneous local integration and assistance to refugees. Later, a tripartite commission, consisting of representatives of Ethiopia, Somalia and UNHCR, was established.

An organized voluntary repatriation programme for the Gedo region continued, with 4,700 repatriated in 1989. Total operational expenditures for voluntary repatriation in 1989 amounted to $1.59 million. While UNHCR, WFP and Somalia agreed to continue food rations for a fixed period, during which civilians in the camps would be re-registered and assisted to relocate to selected sites outside conflict zones, relocation proved not to be feasible. In August, UNHCR and WFP suspended assistance in north-western Somalia due to security problems. In December, a joint mission to Somalia by UNHCR, the European Community, the World Bank and UNDP outlined projects for the refugee-affected areas.

GENERAL ASSEMBLY ACTION

On 15 December, the General Assembly, on the recommendation of the Third Committee, adopted **resolution 44/152** without vote.

Assistance to refugees in Somalia

The General Assembly,

Recalling its resolutions 35/180 of 15 December 1980, 36/153 of 16 December 1981, 37/174 of 17 December 1982, 38/88 of 16 December 1983, 39/104 of 14 November 1984, 40/132 of 13 December 1985, 41/138 of 4 December 1986, 42/127 of 7 December 1987 and 43/147 of 8 December 1988 on assistance to refugees in Somalia,

Having considered the report of the Secretary-General,

Deeply concerned about the heavy burden that has been placed on the fragile economy of Somalia by the continuing presence of large numbers of refugees,

Noting the circumstances that have made it necessary for the Office of the United Nations High Commissioner for Refugees and the World Food Programme to suspend temporarily their food and other humanitarian assistance programmes for refugees in the north-west districts of Somalia,

Gravely concerned about the resultant serious food shortages that have occurred in the refugee settlements in the north-west districts of Somalia,

Conscious of the fact that Somalia, as a least developed country, does not possess the economic or financial capacity to fill the gap created by the temporary suspension of humanitarian assistance programmes for refugees in the north-west districts of Somalia,

Aware of the fact that Somalia does not have the capacity to provide humanitarian assistance from its limited resources,

Noting with concern the deleterious effect of the presence of refugees on the environment, which has resulted in widespread deforestation, soil erosion and the threat of destruction to an already fragile ecological balance,

1. *Takes note* of the report of the Secretary-General;

2. *Commends* the measures that the Government of Somalia is taking to provide material and humanitarian assistance to refugees, in spite of its own limited resources and fragile economy;

3. *Expresses its appreciation* to the Secretary-General, the United Nations High Commissioner for Refugees,

donor countries and intergovernmental and non-governmental organizations for their efforts to assist the refugees in Somalia;

4. *Calls upon* the Office of the United Nations High Commissioner for Refugees and the World Food Programme to resume their assistance programmes for the refugees in the north-west districts of Somalia as soon as possible;

5. *Requests* the Secretary-General, in close co-operation with the Office of the High Commissioner, the World Food Programme and the donor community, to launch an interim assistance programme that would ensure that essential food and other humanitarian supplies continue to reach the refugee settlements in the north-west districts of Somalia until such time as a more permanent arrangement can be made;

6. *Appeals* to Member States, international organizations and voluntary agencies to give full support to the Secretary-General in the launching of the proposed interim assistance programme;

7. *Also appeals* to Member States, international organizations and voluntary agencies to render maximum and timely material, financial and technical assistance to enable the Government of Somalia to implement the projects and activities identified in the report of the 1987 inter-agency mission annexed to the report submitted by the Secretary-General to the General Assembly at its forty-second session as the basis for a comprehensive programme of action relating to both the humanitarian and the developmental needs of refugees;

8. *Requests* the pertinent organizations of the United Nations system, namely the Food and Agriculture Organization of the United Nations, the International Labour Organisation, the World Health Organization, the United Nations Educational, Scientific and Cultural Organization and the United Nations Children's Fund, as well as the United Nations Environment Programme and the World Food Programme, to prepare, in consultation with the Government of Somalia, detailed project documentation for the implementation of those projects and activities identified in the report of the Secretary-General as priority endeavours for a comprehensive programme of action;

9. *Calls upon* the United Nations Development Programme, the United Nations Environment Programme, the United Nations Sudano-Sahelian Office and the Food and Agriculture Organization of the United Nations to continue and expand their activities in Somalia, in co-operation with the Government of Somalia, and to protect and rehabilitate its damaged environment;

10. *Recognizes* the important role that non-governmental organizations are playing with regard to programmes for the care, maintenance and rehabilitation of refugees, particularly in activities related to small-scale development projects, and in the fields of health and agriculture;

11. *Requests* the United Nations High Commissioner for Refugees and the Administrator of the United Nations Development Programme to apprise the Economic and Social Council at its second regular session of 1990 of the progress made in their respective fields of responsibility with regard to those provisions of the present resolution which concern them;

12. *Requests* the Secretary-General, in consultation with the High Commissioner and the United Nations

Development Programme, to submit to the General Assembly at its forty-fifth session a report on the progress achieved in the implementation of the present resolution.

General Assembly resolution 44/152

15 December 1989   Meeting 82   Adopted without vote

Approved by Third Committee (A/44/848) without vote, 29 November (meeting 60); 47-nation draft (A/C.3/44/L.66), orally revised; agenda item 12.
Meeting numbers. GA 44th session: 3rd Committee 48, 50-60; plenary 82.

Sudan

In response to a 1988 General Assembly resolution,[21] the Secretary-General reported[22] in August on the situation of refugees in the Sudan.

Of an estimated 745,000 refugees in the country, UNHCR assisted 380,000, about 350,000 of whom were from Ethiopia. With the Ugandan returnee operation completed, and a reduced caseload of Chadian refugees in the west, UNHCR focused its efforts on the large Ethiopian refugee population in eastern Sudan. UNHCR worked with the World Bank to prepare an agricultural development project to benefit small farmers, including refugees in settlements. It also co-operated with UNDP in following up recommendations of a 1987 inter-agency mission to the Sudan.[23] Four technical missions, dispatched in March/April 1989, subsequently proposed 33 projects requiring a total of $167 million in donor support in the areas of agriculture ($21.6 million), heat and water ($59.4 million), income generation ($11.3 million) and education ($74.4 million).

In March, a revolving fund for small-scale ventures, employment promotion and income generation for women, particularly refugees in the Sudan, with a total allocation of $268,300 was approved. It was financed by funds from the 1984 Second International Conference on Assistance to Refugees in Africa.[24]

GENERAL ASSEMBLY ACTION

On 15 December, the General Assembly, on the recommendation of the Third Committee, adopted **resolution 44/151** without vote.

Situation of refugees in the Sudan

The General Assembly,

Recalling its resolution 43/141 of 8 December 1988 and its other previous resolutions on the situation of refugees in the Sudan,

Having considered the report of the Secretary-General on the implementation of resolution 43/141 and the report of the United Nations High Commissioner for Refugees,

Expressing its appreciation for the efforts made by the Government of the Sudan for the reception of the refugees and the provision of protection, shelter, food, education and health and other humanitarian services to the ever increasing number of refugees who have been crossing the borders into the Sudan since the early 1960s,

Recognizing the heavy burden shouldered by the people and the Government of the Sudan and the sacrifices they are making to host more than one million refugees,

who constitute approximately 7.5 per cent of the total population of the country,

Deeply concerned that the great majority of the refugees have settled of their own accord in various urban and rural communities throughout the country and are thus sharing with the indigenous population the already meagre resources and services,

Expressing grave concern at the devastating and far-reaching effects of the successive calamities, ranging from the drought in 1984 to the torrential rains and floods and locust infestations in 1988, that have afflicted the country, thus exacerbating the already deteriorating situation resulting from the presence of this great number of refugees,

Gravely concerned also that the Government of the Sudan, besides dealing with the difficult prevailing economic and social problems, has the additional task of taking care of more than 1.5 million persons displaced by successive calamities and civil strife in the south,

Recognizing the efforts undertaken by the Government of the Sudan to initiate a wide-ranging rehabilitation programme to redress the damages incurred by the natural disasters,

Considering those serious circumstances, which render the Government of the Sudan less prepared than ever to meet its obligations to its own people, and the more serious consequences, which affect the capacity of the Government of the Sudan to receive and grant asylum to additional numbers of refugees,

Expressing its appreciation for the assistance rendered by Member States and intergovernmental and non-governmental organizations in support of the refugee programme in the Sudan,

1. *Takes note* of the report of the Secretary-General;

2. *Takes note also* of the report of the United Nations High Commissioner for Refugees and, in particular, of the new trends identified in the area of refugee aid and development;

3. *Expresses its appreciation* to the Secretary-General, the High Commissioner, donor countries and intergovernmental and non-governmental organizations for their efforts to assist the refugees in the Sudan;

4. *Expresses grave concern* at the serious and far-reaching consequences of the presence of massive numbers of refugees on the security and stability of the country and the overall negative impact on its basic infrastructure and socio-economic development;

5. *Also expresses grave concern* at the shrinking resources available for refugee programmes in the Sudan and the serious consequences of this situation on the country's ability to continue to host and assist refugees;

6. *Appeals* to Member States, the appropriate organs, organizations and bodies of the United Nations system, intergovernmental and non-governmental organizations and the international financial institutions to provide the Government of the Sudan with the necessary resources for the implementation of development assistance projects, in particular those prepared by the United Nations Development Programme, in the regions affected by the presence of refugees;

7. *Requests* the Secretary-General to mobilize the necessary financial and material assistance for the full implementation of ongoing projects in the areas affected by the presence of refugees;

8. *Requests* the High Commissioner to continue co-ordination with the appropriate specialized agencies in

order to consolidate and ensure the continuation of essential services to the refugees in their settlements and to explore ways and means to extend assistance to refugees who have settled of their own accord elsewhere;

9. *Requests* the Secretary-General to report to the General Assembly at its forty-fifth session, through the Economic and Social Council, on the implementation of the present resolution.

General Assembly resolution 44/151

15 December 1989   Meeting 82   Adopted without vote

Approved by Third Committee (A/44/848) without vote, 29 November (meeting 60); 45-nation draft (A/C.3/44/L.65); agenda item 12.
Meeting numbers. GA 44th session: 3rd Committee 48, 50-60; plenary 82.

Asia and Oceania

In China, UNHCR implemented 42 projects related to water supply, crop production, forestry, education, animal husbandry, health and income generation to benefit the younger generation among some 280,000 Vietnamese refugees. As a result, some 6,000 jobs were created, some 400 children and youths were admitted to primary schools and a vocational training centre, and some 700 families were provided with housing and drinkable water. UNHCR's financial contribution to these projects totalled $4 million.

As lead agency for repatriation of some 300,000 Kampuchean refugees and displaced persons, UNHCR, following a debate on repatriation at the International Conference on Cambodia (Paris, July/August), prepared draft proposals for a repatriation plan (see PART TWO, Chapter III).

The organized repatriation of Sri Lankan Tamils from south India, which began in 1987, ended in April 1989. At the beginning of 1989, there were 9,549 registered refugees in India comprising some 8,322 Afghans and 1,010 Iranians. Assistance was provided in the form of care and maintenance, including education and vocational training. A total of 1,231 refugees departed for resettlement in third countries; 33 Afghans and 19 Iranians voluntarily repatriated.

During 1989, UNHCR expenditures in the region stood at $67.5 million under General Programmes and $41.4 million under Special Programmes.

Indo-China

The rising spiral of arrivals of Vietnamese asylum-seekers continued during 1989, bringing the overall number of Indo-Chinese asylum-seekers in the UNHCR-assisted camps to more than 195,000. Of those, approximately 100,000 persons were in Thailand and 56,000 in Hong Kong, with the rest spread throughout the countries of the Association of South-East Asian Nations (ASEAN) and Japan. The number of registered asylum-seekers rose by 33 per cent compared to the pre-

vious year. On the other hand, close to 45,000 refugees left various countries of first asylum for resettlement in third countries, and over 43,000 persons left Viet Nam under the Orderly Departure Programme.

Regarding Vietnamese and Lao asylum-seekers, the Comprehensive Plan of Action adopted at the International Conference on Indo-Chinese Refugees (see below) presented measures to rechannel departures through legal means, while limiting resettlement to recognized refugees. In 1989, more than 900 Vietnamese and close to 2,000 Lao asylum-seekers returned home voluntarily. However, no consensus could be reached on the problem of return, other than voluntary, to Viet Nam of those persons determined not to be bona fide refugees. In December, the Hong Kong authorities deported some 51 screened-out Vietnamese. Another problem was partial denial of asylum to "boat people", practised in the form of redirecting arriving boats to neighbouring countries.

International Conference on Indo-Chinese Refugees

The International Conference on Indo-Chinese Refugees was held in Geneva on 13 and 14 June 1989 to deal with problems posed by the continuing presence in South-East Asia of large numbers of refugees and asylum-seekers from Viet Nam and the Lao People's Democratic Republic and by their continuing exodus into the region. As requested by the General Assembly,[25] which in 1988 had welcomed the call by ASEAN for the convening of the Conference, the Secretary-General reported[26] on the Conference in September.

The Conference adopted both a Declaration and a Comprehensive Plan of Action, which set out measures regarding organized clandestine departures, regular departure programmes, refugee status, and implementation and review procedures. The Conference established a Steering Committee consisting of 15 "core group" countries (Australia, Austria, Canada, France, Japan, Lao People's Democratic Republic, Malaysia, Netherlands, Norway, Philippines, Switzerland, Thailand, United Kingdom, United States, Viet Nam) to review the Plan's implementation.

In October, the UNHCR Executive Committee reaffirmed[5] that the Comprehensive Plan of Action was an important and sound basis for a balanced, humanitarian and durable solution to the problem of Indo-Chinese refugees.

ECONOMIC AND SOCIAL COUNCIL ACTION

On 26 July, the Economic and Social Council, by **decision 1989/176**, noted an oral report made on behalf of the Secretary-General by the High Commissioner on the International Conference on Indo-Chinese Refugees.

On 15 December, the General Assembly, on the recommendation of the Third Committee, adopted **resolution 44/138** without vote.

International Conference on Indo-Chinese Refugees

The General Assembly,

Recalling its resolution 43/119 of 8 December 1988,

Having considered the report of the Secretary-General on the International Conference on Indo-Chinese Refugees, held at Geneva on 13 and 14 June 1989, and the Declaration and Comprehensive Plan of Action adopted by the Conference,

Noting with satisfaction the active participation of Member States, specialized agencies and regional, intergovernmental and non-governmental organizations in the Conference,

Taking note of the decision on the Conference adopted by the Executive Committee of the Programme of the United Nations High Commissioner for Refugees at its fortieth session,

1. *Welcomes* the successful conclusion of the International Conference on Indo-Chinese Refugees, which was convened by the Secretary-General, under the presidency of the Minister for Foreign Affairs of Malaysia;

2. *Takes note with satisfaction* of the report of the Secretary-General on the Conference;

3. *Expresses its appreciation* to the Secretary-General for convening the Conference and to the United Nations High Commissioner for Refugees for his valuable assistance and contribution in organizing the Conference;

4. *Welcomes* the adoption by the Conference of the Declaration and Comprehensive Plan of Action and affirms its belief that the Plan of Action is an important and sound basis for a balanced, humanitarian and durable solution to the problems addressed by the Conference;

5. *Stresses* that the measures stipulated in the Comprehensive Plan of Action are interrelated and mutually reinforcing and should be implemented in their totality by all States concerned, within the context of national laws and regulations and of international standards;

6. *Notes* the progress on the implementation of the Comprehensive Plan of Action at the various bilateral and multilateral meetings among the parties concerned, especially those held within the context of the Steering Committee established by the Conference;

7. *Calls upon* all States concerned and the relevant specialized agencies and regional, intergovernmental and non-governmental organizations to undertake the various measures required of them within the framework and letter of the Comprehensive Plan of Action;

8. *Appeals* to all States and regional, intergovernmental and non-governmental organizations to provide resources for the General and Special Programmes of the Office of the United Nations High Commissioner for Refugees to enable it to carry out the tasks prescribed in the Comprehensive Plan of Action;

9. *Stresses* that the solution of the problem of those seeking refuge in the South-East Asian region could contribute positively towards a climate of peace, harmony and good-neighbourliness among States in the region;

10. *Requests* the Secretary-General to continue to monitor closely the progress towards implementation of the Comprehensive Plan of Action and to report thereon to the General Assembly at its forty-fifth session.

General Assembly resolution 44/138

15 December 1989   Meeting 82   Adopted without vote

Approved by Third Committee (A/44/823) without vote, 27 November (meeting 56); 17-nation draft (A/C.3/44/L.68/Rev.1); agenda item 110 *(c)*.
Meeting numbers. GA 44th session: 3rd Committee 44-47, 49, 56; plenary 82.

Europe and North America

In Western Europe, the number of asylum-seekers from outside the region continued to increase in 1989, reaching approximately 320,000, as compared to 290,000 in 1988. The influx created a large backlog of undecided applications, leading to a serious strain on reception facilities and increased expenditures on public relief and assistance. Consultations on multilateral solutions to the new asylum situation were held by 14 European and North American Governments and UNHCR.

In December, the High Commissioner appealed to the international community for funds for a shelter project to improve the living conditions of some 13,500 Iraqi nationals in south-east Turkey. The Government of Turkey assisted 30,000 Iraqi nationals living in the country.

During the year, 24,623 refugees were resettled in Canada and 94,000 in the United States. Also, approximately 22,000 persons requested asylum in Canada and 102,000 persons in the United States.

Following the Hungarian Government's accession to the 1951 Convention relating to the Status of Refugees[27] and its 1967 Protocol,[28] UNHCR opened an office in Budapest. UNHCR elaborated a programme to help the Government to establish adequate infrastructure for asylum-seekers in Hungary; an appeal for $5.2 million was launched for that purpose.

In 1989, UNHCR's voluntary funds expenditures in Europe and North America totalled $24.1 million, of which $18.8 million was obligated under General Programmes and $5.3 million under Special Programmes.

Latin America and the Caribbean

The estimated refugee population in southern Latin America at the end of 1989 was 22,700, of whom 6,437 were receiving UNHCR assistance. In Mexico, where 41,500 Guatemalan refugees lived, UNHCR commenced a multi-year plan aimed at achieving self-sufficiency in the states of Campeche and Quintana Roo and elaborated a project for the promotion of income-generating activities in Chiapas.

UNHCR opened sub-offices in French Guiana and Suriname in 1989. Efforts to facilitate the voluntary repatriation of Surinamese refugees in French Guiana were strengthened within the framework of a tripartite commission composed of representatives of France, Suriname and UNHCR. The voluntary repatriation of Chilean refugees increased considerably. Some 1,720 refugees returned from Argentina, Cuba and Eastern European countries. From the Dominican Republic, 492 Haitian refugees repatriated.

During 1989, UNHCR voluntary funds expenditures in Latin America and the Caribbean totalled $39.6 million, of which $32.8 million was under General Programmes and $6.8 million under Special Programmes.

Central America

By the end of 1989, about 122,000 Central American refugees were receiving UNHCR assistance. There was a considerable increase in the number of returnees, with significant movements taking place from Honduras. UNHCR continued to assess the welfare of returnees in El Salvador, Guatemala and Nicaragua.

At a summit meeting (Tela, Honduras, 5-7 August),[29] the five Central American Presidents (Costa Rica, El Salvador, Guatemala, Honduras, Nicaragua) adopted a joint plan for the voluntary demobilization, repatriation or relocation of the members of the Nicaraguan resistance and their families. Following repatriation, beneficiaries would be integrated into the development process in their country of origin, according to the plan. The Secretaries-General of the United Nations and of the Organization of American States, as requested by the five Presidents, set up an International Support and Verification Commission to implement the plan. The number of beneficiaries of the plan was estimated at 90,000 persons, with financial requirements of $48 million. (See also PART TWO, Chapter II.)

Conference on Central American Refugees

The International Conference on Central American Refugees was held in Guatemala City from 29 to 31 May.[30] It adopted a Concerted Plan of Action in favour of Central American Refugees, Returnees and Displaced Persons, which described an overall strategy and follow-up and promotion mechanisms. Objectives of the Plan of Action included identification of durable solutions, within the possibilities of the affected countries, including voluntary repatriation, local integration and resettlement in third countries. The Plan also set out a three-year regional programme consisting of 32 projects, valued at $380 million.

In October, the Executive Committee of UNHCR, welcoming the commitments given by the affected countries, urged[5] the international community to ensure that the support expressed during the Conference became concrete commitments of collaboration with the affected countries for implementation of the Plan.

ECONOMIC AND SOCIAL COUNCIL ACTION

On 26 July, the Economic and Social Council, by **decision 1989/176**, noted the oral report made on behalf of the Secretary-General by the UN High Commissioner on the International Conference on Central American Refugees.

GENERAL ASSEMBLY ACTION

On 15 December, the General Assembly, on the recommendation of the Third Committee, adopted **resolution 44/139** without vote.

International Conference on Central American Refugees
The General Assembly,

Recalling its resolutions 42/1 of 7 October 1987, 42/110 of 7 December 1987, 42/204 of 11 December 1987, 42/231 of 12 May 1988 and 43/118 of 8 December 1988,

Taking note of the report of the Secretary-General,

Also taking note of the report of the United Nations High Commissioner for Refugees,

Welcoming the Declaration and Concerted Plan of Action in favour of Central American Refugees, Returnees and Displaced Persons adopted by the International Conference on Central American Refugees, held at Guatemala City from 29 to 31 May 1989,

Bearing in mind that a concerted effort in favour of lasting solutions to the problems of refugees, returnees and displaced persons requires the support, co-operation and co-ordination of the affected and interested Governments and of the various international organizations involved, in particular the Office of the United Nations High Commissioner for Refugees and the United Nations Development Programme,

Noting the establishment of the machinery for follow-up and co-ordination at the national level in pursuance of the Concerted Plan of Action and the establishment of priority and design of projects within the framework of the strategies defined by each Government,

Noting with interest that meetings for co-ordination, management and execution have begun with the co-operating countries and the non-governmental organizations interested in participating in the programmes and projects to assist the returnees, displaced persons and refugees in Central America,

Aware of the need to deal with the serious problem of the refugees in Central America who have found asylum in a number of Central American countries, including Belize, and Mexico, and wishing to contribute to the search for lasting solutions that would benefit the countries and communities of asylum and origin,

Recognizing the need to incorporate in the plans of assistance to refugees, returnees and displaced persons measures to restore the ecological balance and the rational utilization of the natural resources in the areas of the countries affected,

Bearing in mind that, as stated in point 8 of the agreement on "Procedures for the establishment of a firm and lasting peace in Central America", concluded at the Esquipulas II summit meeting, the Central American countries have undertaken, as a matter of urgency, to address the problem of refugees, including their repatriation and relocation through bilateral and multilateral processes,

Reiterating its determination to continue its efforts and contributions in the context of the peace agreements, and welcoming the agreements adopted at Tela, Honduras, on 7 August 1989, which include aspects of voluntary repatriation and relocation,

Emphasizing that, among the possible solutions, voluntary repatriation is the most appropriate means of solving the problems caused by the massive presence of refugees in the countries and communities of asylum,

Once again reiterating the paramount importance of humanitarian and apolitical considerations, both in dealing with and in solving the problems of refugees, returnees and displaced persons, and the need to ensure that this approach is strictly observed by the countries of origin and of asylum and other interested parties,

Recognizing the work carried out by the Office of the United Nations High Commissioner for Refugees and by the United Nations Development Programme with the Governments of the affected countries in the preparation and convening of the Conference and in the meetings of the Follow-Up Committee of the International Conference on Central American Refugees,

Aware of the reductions in the budget of the Office of the High Commissioner in the region, which seriously affect the beneficiary populations and the policies for a solution put forward in the context of the agreement concluded at the Esquipulas II summit meeting and at the International Conference on Central American Refugees,

Taking into consideration the priority assigned to that section of the emergency programme of the Special Plan of Economic Co-operation for Central America that is intended to promote activities for solving the problem of refugees, displaced persons and returnees,

Recognizing that the search for solutions goes beyond emergency activities and is linked to aspects of the development of the region and assistance for the displaced populations in the countries of origin and asylum that are directly affected by the massive presence of refugees,

Recognizing also that the tripartite commissions, composed of representatives of the countries of asylum, the country of origin and the Office of the High Commissioner, constitute an ongoing mechanism for solving the problem of refugees and that they require support in order to continue the current voluntary repatriation programmes in conditions of personal and material security,

Recognizing further that solutions to the problems of refugees, returnees and displaced persons form an integral part of the efforts for peace, democratization and development being made in the region by each Government,

1. *Expresses its profound satisfaction* with the success of the International Conference on Central American Refugees, as well as with the adoption by acclamation of the Declaration and Concerted Plan of Action in favour of Central American Refugees, Returnees and Displaced Persons;

2. *Welcomes* the guidelines, goals and objectives of the Concerted Plan of Action as a promising initial basis for future activities, and therefore reaffirms its commitment to contribute to the achievement of a firm and lasting peace in Central America;

3. *Welcomes* the establishment of the machinery for follow-up and co-ordination at the national level, in pursuance of the Concerted Plan of Action, and the establishment of priority and design of projects within the framework of the strategies defined by each Government;

4. *Requests* the United Nations High Commissioner for Refugees to support, in close collaboration with the Governments of the affected countries and the Follow-Up Committee of the International Conference on Central American Refugees, together with the United Nations Development Programme and the organs, specialized agencies and other organizations of the United Nations system, the holding of meetings for follow-up to the Concerted Plan of Action, so that they may be held at the earliest possible time;

5. *Notes with interest* that the Follow-Up Committee will hold its first meeting during the first week of March 1990, and urges the co-operating countries to respond positively to the assistance projects submitted by the Central American countries, including Belize, and Mexico;

6. *Urges* Member States and organs, specialized agencies and other organizations of the United Nations system, as well as the regional and subregional, intergovernmental and non-governmental organizations engaged in the humanitarian task of helping Central American refugees, to continue to provide and to increase their assistance and support to the affected countries in order to implement and follow up the guidelines, goals and objectives of the Concerted Plan of Action;

7. *Calls upon* the co-operating countries and the relevant agencies of the United Nations system to assist in restoring the ecological balance of the areas in the countries of asylum affected by the massive presence of refugees, in order to provide the populations of those areas with the conditions conducive to development;

8. *Appeals* to the international community to ensure that the co-operation extended in the solution of the problem of refugees takes into account both the sacrifice borne by the countries of asylum in receiving massive flows of refugees and the effort exerted by the countries of origin to create the conditions that would facilitate the return of their nationals;

9. *Also appeals* to the international community to increase its assistance to the countries of asylum and of origin of Central American refugees in order to strengthen their capacity to provide the means and services necessary for the solution of the problem of refugees, returnees and displaced persons, in accordance with national development programmes;

10. *Expresses its appreciation* to the Secretary-General, the Office of the United Nations High Commissioner for Refugees and the United Nations Development Programme for the assistance rendered for the holding of the Conference;

11. *Expresses its concern* at the reductions in the budget of the Office of the High Commissioner in the region, which seriously affect the beneficiary populations and the policies for a solution formulated at the Conference and by each Government, and urges that the budget previously allocated be restored;

12. *Expresses its gratitude* to the people and Government of Guatemala for the hospitality extended for the holding of the Conference;

13. *Requests* the Secretary-General, in co-operation with the High Commissioner, to report on the implementation of the present resolution to the Economic and Social Council at its second regular session of 1990 and to the General Assembly at its forty-fifth session.

General Assembly resolution 44/139

15 December 1989   Meeting 82   Adopted without vote

Approved by Third Committee (A/44/823) without vote, 27 November (meeting 56); 30-nation draft (A/C.3/44/L.69), orally revised; agenda item 110 *(b)*.

Meeting numbers. GA 44th session: 3rd Committee 44-47, 49, 56; plenary 82.

South-West Asia, North Africa and the Middle East

An estimated 100,000 Afghan refugees were reported to have returned, mainly from Pakistan, to their places of origin in the south-western and northern provinces of Afghanistan, but continued fighting in 1989 in certain provinces created new waves of refugees to Pakistan. UNHCR continued to fund cross-border projects implemented by non-governmental organizations in areas of Afghanistan from which high numbers of refugees originated. Of total 1989 disbursements of some $24.8 million, $14.2 million was for activities inside Afghanistan, and the remainder was disbursed for activities in Iran and Pakistan.

In Iran, there were more than 2 million Afghan refugees and 500,000 others, mainly Iraqis. UNHCR's assistance to the Afghan refugees was aimed at extending the rural health delivery infrastructure, water and sanitation systems, access roads, educational facilities and some income-generating activities. About 90,000 Iraqi refugees in Iran received assistance in the areas of health, sanitation and housing facilities.

The UNHCR regional office for the Middle East in Bahrain continued to assist refugees and asylum-seekers in Middle Eastern countries, including cases of *refoulement*, deportation and expulsion. Due to the prevailing security situation in Lebanon, UNHCR was not able to maintain an international presence in Beirut.

In Algeria, of an estimated 165,000 Sahrawi refugees living in camps around Tindouf, 80,000 persons received assistance from UNHCR, including food, education, health and water. Most were women, children, handicapped and elderly persons. Beginning in April, a group of about 22,000 Senegalese refugees found refuge in Mauritania. A multi-sectoral emergency programme was implemented.

During 1989, UNHCR voluntary funds expenditure in South-West Asia, North Africa and the Middle East totalled $104.2 million, of which $60.2 million was under General Programmes and $44 million under Special Programmes.

Refugee protection

Protection involved using law and principles to secure the rights, security and welfare of refugees. During 1989, continued and improved consultations took place between States and UNHCR on region-specific concerns. Governments increasingly addressed refugee problems in a comprehensive manner with a view to developing broad strategies to respond positively to those problems.

In October, the UNHCR Executive Committee expressed[5] deep concern that refugee protection was seriously jeopardized in some States by expulsion and *refoulement* of refugees or by measures that did not recognize the special situation of refugees. It called on all States to refrain from taking such measures. The Committee called on the High Commissioner to convene an open-ended working group to examine protection and solutions in a comprehensive manner.

Refugee law

International instruments

As at 31 December 1989, the 1951 Convention relating to the Status of Refugees[27] had been ratified or acceded to by 102 States as a result of the 1989 accession by Hungary. The 1967 Protocol to the Convention[28] had 103 States parties as a result of the 1989 accession by Hungary and Mozambique.[31] While the majority were parties to both instruments, some were parties to only one; the number of parties to one or both instruments, therefore, totalled 103.

Other intergovernmental legal instruments benefiting refugees included the 1957 Agreement relating to Refugee Seamen and its 1973 Protocol, the 1959 European Agreement on the Abolition of Visas for Refugees, the 1969 Convention governing the Specific Aspects of Refugee Problems in Africa, the 1969 American Convention on Human Rights, Pact of San José, Costa Rica, and the 1980 European Agreement on Transfer of Responsibility for Refugees.

As at 31 December 1989, there were 36 States parties to the 1954 Convention relating to the Status of Stateless Persons[32] (Madagascar had acceded to the Convention in 1962, but denounced it in 1965) and 15 States parties to the 1961 Convention on the Reduction of Statelessness.[33]

In many countries, the High Commissioner reported that implementation of these instruments was satisfactory, particularly where specific legislative and/or administrative measures to implement them had been adopted, and where they were known and understood by the concerned officials. There were even countries where such laws and measures went beyond the minimum standards of the instruments. At the same time, however, a number of obstacles of a socio-economic, legal, policy or practical nature impeded the full and proper implementation of the instruments in the territory of many contracting States.

In October, the UNHCR Executive Committee requested[5] the UN High Commissioner to prepare a detailed report on implementation of the 1951 Convention and the 1967 Protocol.

Promotion and dissemination of refugee law

In 1989, despite severely limited financial resources, UNHCR pursued its traditional promotion and dissemination activities with respect to refugee law and protection principles. The Centre for Documentation on Refugees continued to strengthen and systematize information and documentation policies. It published the quarterly *Refugee Abstracts* and the *International Journal of Refugee Law*, and helped develop the publication by the International Refugee Documentation Network of an international thesaurus on refugee terminology.

UNHCR continued to advise and train government officials and others on how to determine refugee status. It also assisted all receiving countries in South-East Asia in establishing procedures for determination of refugee status.

In October, the Executive Committee of UNHCR urged[5] the High Commissioner to ensure that protection training courses continued on a significant scale.

Rights of refugees

The granting of admission and asylum and protection from *refoulement* were indispensable components of the international system for the protection of refugees, according to UNHCR. Many States continued to respect their commitments in that field and the vast majority of the world's refugees were admitted into the territory of States, granted at least temporary asylum and protected from *refoulement*. However, in a number of instances, admission and asylum were denied on various grounds. These included the refusal of States to examine asylum requests based on a strict application of the notion of "country of first asylum", even where the persons concerned were not permitted to re-enter or remain in the country from which they had last come or where it was far from clear that they would receive humane treatment.

In October, the Executive Committee of UNHCR adopted[5] a conclusion on the problem of refugees and asylum-seekers who moved in an irregular manner from a country in which they had already found protection. The Committee recognized that return to a country in which individuals had already found protection might take place only if the persons concerned were protected there against *refoulement* and permitted to remain there and be treated in accordance with recognized basic human standards until a durable solution was found. It also drew attention to problems posed by false documents or lack of documents, which were often compounded by the application by certain States of immigration measures restricting the number of persons who could seek admission and

asylum. Another growing practice was the restrictive interpretation of various elements of the refugee definition contained in the 1951 Convention relating to the Status of Refugees and its 1967 Protocol, coupled with the demand that applicants for refugee status satisfy an excessively stringent burden and standard of proof. In addition, a few countries limited or discontinued their previous practice of granting asylum to persons who were compelled to leave their countries of origin as a result of generalized violence, foreign aggression, internal conflicts, massive violation of human rights or other circumstances that seriously disturbed public order.

Other violations of rights of refugees reported during the year included *refoulement*, unjustified detention of refugees, military and armed attacks on refugee camps and settlements, and forced recruitment of refugees into armed forces.

Protection of refugee women and children

Although there had been a gradual increase in recent years in the general awareness of the protection problems of refugee women, serious violations of their safety and well-being continued, according to UNHCR. An evaluation of the impact of the UNHCR guidelines on refugee women indicated that, while identification of the problems of refugee women and formulation of necessary remedies had improved considerably, the guidelines had to be expanded if the objectives for which they were issued were to be fully met. Refugee children continued to be exposed to physical violence, detention, sexual abuse and forced recruitment into armed forces. The number of unaccompanied minors also increased.

In October, the UNHCR Executive Committee called[5] for the reinforcement of preventive measures and for States and concerned agencies to strengthen their support of the protection activities of UNHCR relating to refugee women by providing resettlement places for women at risk. It requested the UN High Commissioner to prepare a revised and expanded version of the internal guidelines relating to the international protection of refugee women.

Also in October, the Committee, noting the increasing incidence of nutritional problems among refugee children dependent on food aid, called on UNHCR to initiate formal discussions with relevant UN bodies, donors and other humanitarian organizations to develop strategies for alleviating the problems. It requested the High Commissioner to continue to give special attention to the needs of unaccompanied minors.

REFERENCES

(1)A/45/12. (2)YUN 1978, p. 915, SC res. 435(1978), 29 Sep. 1978. (3)YUN 1988, p. 663. (4)A/AC.96/736.

(5)A/44/12/Add.1. (6)YUN 1988, p. 664, GA res. 43/148, 8 Dec. 1988. (7)A/44/403. (8)A/44/404. (9)YUN 1988, p. 666, GA res. 43/116, 8 Dec. 1988. (10)A/44/520. (11)YUN 1988, p. 665. (12)*Ibid.*, p. 668, GA res. 43/143, 8 Dec. 1988. (13)A/44/657. (14)YUN 1988, p. 668, GA res. 43/142, 8 Dec. 1988. (15)A/44/402. (16)YUN 1988, p. 669, GA res. 43/144, 8 Dec. 1988. (17)A/44/482. (18)YUN 1988, p. 670, GA res. 43/147, 8 Dec. 1988. (19)A/44/462. (20)A/44/261. (21)YUN 1988, p. 672, GA res. 43/141, 8 Dec. 1988. (22)A/44/426. (23)YUN 1987, p. 893. (24)YUN 1984, p. 943. (25)YUN 1988, p. 673, GA res. 43/119, 8 Dec. 1988. (26)A/44/523. (27)YUN 1951, p. 520. (28)YUN 1967, p. 769. (29)A/44/451-S/20778. (30)A/44/527 & Corr.1,2. (31)*Multilateral Treaties Deposited with the Secretary-General: Status as at 31 December 1989* (ST/LEG/SER.E/8), Sales No. E.90.V.6. (32)YUN 1954, p. 416. (33)YUN 1961, p. 533.

Chapter XVI

Drugs of abuse

The global situation regarding illicit drug trafficking and abuse reached a new and dangerous stage in 1989, with heavily armed and well-financed drug trafficking organizations threatening political institutions in some countries. In its annual report, the International Narcotics Control Board (INCB) stated that the illegal production of narcotic drugs had increased and had spread to more countries. The environment of some countries continued to be damaged by the illicit cultivation of the opium poppy and coca bush. The increasing spread of AIDS through intravenous drug abuse was viewed with growing alarm.

The United Nations continued to seek ways to aid the international fight against drug abuse. Many States and organizations took action in response to the 1988 Convention against Illegal Traffic in Narcotic Drugs and Psychotropic Substances. INCB continued to supervise drug control activities, and the UN Fund for Drug Abuse Control expanded and intensified its activities, providing financial and technical assistance to drug control projects in 49 countries. The General Assembly and the Economic and Social Council adopted a number of resolutions dealing with drug abuse control, some on the recommendation of the Council's Commission on Narcotic Drugs, the principal UN policy-making body on drug control issues. Because of the alarming state of global drug trafficking and abuse, the General Assembly decided to hold a special session to address the problem.

Convention against illicit traffic

Pursuant to a 1988 General Assembly resolution,[1] the Secretary-General submitted in September a report[2] focusing on the conclusions of the 1988 UN Conference for the Adoption of a Convention against Illicit Traffic in Narcotic Drugs and Psychotropic Substances.[3] The Conference adopted by acclamation the text of the UN Convention against Illicit Traffic in Narcotic Drugs and Psychotropic Substances, which addresses such issues as offences and sanctions, jurisdiction, extradition, co-operation between States and law-enforcement agencies, and measures to eradicate illicit cultivation of narcotic plants and to eliminate illicit demand for narcotic drugs and psychotropic substances.

The Secretary-General outlined in the report his actions to implement the 1988 Convention stating that he had assisted States in establishing the legislative and administrative measures necessary for the application of the Convention, and had calculated the resources required by the UN Division of Narcotic Drugs and the INCB secretariat for implementation measures.

ECONOMIC AND SOCIAL COUNCIL ACTION

On 22 May, on the recommendation of its Second (Social) Committee, the Economic and Social Council adopted three resolutions. **Resolution 1989/20** was adopted without vote.

International Conference on Drug Abuse and Illicit Trafficking

The Economic and Social Council,

Recalling its resolution 1988/9 of 25 May 1988,

Recalling General Assembly resolution 43/122 of 8 December 1988, in which the Assembly, *inter alia*, recalled with satisfaction the successful conclusion of the International Conference on Drug Abuse and Illicit Trafficking, in particular the adoption of the Declaration, as an expression of the political will of nations to combat the drug menace, and the Comprehensive Multidisciplinary Outline of Future Activities in Drug Abuse Control, a compendium of recommendations for implementation,

Taking note of the report of the Commission on Narcotic Drugs on its thirty-third session, in particular chapter VI thereof,

Recognizing the important contributions of the United Nations drug control bodies and their distinct mandates and responsibilities, and welcoming the efforts of the Secretary-General to increase co-ordination of activities related to drug control and to implement the recommendations of the Comprehensive Multidisciplinary Outline,

Bearing in mind the need to ensure the implementation of the courses of action recommended in the Comprehensive Multidisciplinary Outline, particularly in the areas of education and public information, with regard to the abuse of narcotic drugs and psychotropic substances,

1. *Urges* Governments and organizations to adhere to the principles set forth in the Declaration of the International Conference on Drug Abuse and Illicit Trafficking and to utilize the recommendations of the Comprehensive Multidisciplinary Outline of Future Activities in Drug Abuse Control in developing national and regional strategies, particularly to promote bilateral, regional and international co-operative arrangements;

2. *Urges* Governments to provide additional resources to the United Nations Fund for Drug Abuse Control in order to enable it to strengthen its co-operation with the developing countries in their efforts to implement drug control programmes;

3. *Invites* intergovernmental and regional and international non-governmental organizations that are referred to under the particular targets of the Comprehensive Multidisciplinary Outline to continue to inform the Commission on Narcotic Drugs about activities undertaken in pursuit of those targets;

4. *Invites* the Secretary-General to support, within available resources, the activities of the non-governmental organizations concerned and, in recognition of the experience and expertise of those organizations, to co-ordinate United Nations activities in drug abuse control with them;

5. *Requests* the Secretary-General to ensure continued inter-agency co-operation in drug abuse control activities, which will enhance efforts of the Commission on Narcotic Drugs to implement activities in follow-up to the Conference;

6. *Calls upon* the Commission on Narcotic Drugs to keep under review action taken with respect to the Declaration and the Comprehensive Multidisciplinary Outline.

Economic and Social Council resolution 1989/20

22 May 1989   Meeting 12   Adopted without vote

Approved by Second Committee (E/1989/76) without vote, 5 May (meeting 6); 16-nation draft (E/1989/C.2/L.3; agenda item 12.
Sponsors: Australia, Bahamas, Bolivia, Brunei Darussalam, China, Colombia, Costa Rica, India, Indonesia, Malaysia, Nicaragua, Peru, Philippines, Singapore, Thailand, United Kingdom.

Resolution 1989/19 was also adopted without vote.

Provisional application of the United Nations Convention against Illicit Traffic in Narcotic Drugs and Psychotropic Substances

The Economic and Social Council,

Recalling the Final Act of the United Nations Conference for the Adoption of a Convention against Illicit Traffic in Narcotic Drugs and Psychotropic Substances, adopted at Vienna on 19 December 1988,

Recalling also resolution 2 of the Conference contained in the Final Act, the purpose of which was to seek early ratification of the United Nations Convention against Illicit Traffic in Narcotic Drugs and Psychotropic Substances, so that its implementation by States parties might begin at the earliest possible time,

Taking into account the urgency for States to employ all legal means available to them in the effort to curb drug trafficking, including the measures defined in the new Convention,

1. *Urges* States, to the extent that they are able to do so, to accelerate steps to ratify the United Nations Convention against Illicit Traffic in Narcotic Drugs and Psychotropic Substances so that it may enter into force as soon as possible;

2. *Invites* States, to the extent that they are able to do so, to apply provisionally the measures set out in the Convention pending its entry into force for each of them;

3. *Requests* the Secretary-General to transmit the present resolution to all Governments.

Economic and Social Council resolution 1989/19

22 May 1989   Meeting 12   Adopted without vote

Approved by Second Committee (E/1989/76) without vote, 5 May (meeting 6); 32-nation draft (E/1989/C.2/L.2); agenda item 12.
Sponsors: Australia, Bahamas, Bangladesh, Belgium, Bolivia, China, Colombia, Costa Rica, Denmark, Dominican Republic, Ecuador, Finland, France,

Germany, Federal Republic of, Greece, Hungary, Italy, Malaysia, Mexico, Norway, Peru, Poland, Portugal, Spain, Sweden, Thailand, Turkey, USSR, United Kingdom, United States, Venezuela, Yugoslavia.

The Council adopted **resolution 1989/13** without vote.

Implementation of the United Nations Convention against Illicit Traffic in Narcotic Drugs and Psychotropic Substances

The Economic and Social Council,

Recalling the many resolutions adopted by the General Assembly, the Economic and Social Council and the Commission on Narcotic Drugs, as well as the many political declarations such as the Quito Declaration against Traffic in Narcotic Drugs of 11 August 1984, the New York Declaration against Drug Trafficking and the Illicit Use of Drugs of 1 October 1984, the Lima Declaration of 29 July 1985 and, in particular, the Declaration of the International Conference on Drug Abuse and Illicit Trafficking, all of which called for the urgent preparation of a draft convention against illicit trafficking,

Noting that those resolutions and declarations led to the adoption on 19 December 1988 of the United Nations Convention against Illicit Traffic in Narcotic Drugs and Psychotropic Substances by a conference of plenipotentiaries convened by the United Nations at Vienna from 25 November to 20 December 1988,

Reaffirming the importance of the Convention for improving international co-operation in this field, and noting that the Convention will add to the existing instruments for the control of narcotic drugs and psychotropic substances,

Taking into account General Assembly resolution 43/214 of 21 December 1988 and the Regulations and Rules Governing Programme Planning, the Programme Aspects of the Budget, the Monitoring of Implementation and the Methods of Evaluation, as well as resolution 3 of the United Nations Conference for the Adoption of a Convention against Illicit Traffic in Narcotic Drugs and Psychotropic Substances,

Noting the priority assigned by the Committee for Programme and Co-ordination at its twenty-eighth session to matters relating to narcotic drugs and psychotropic substances,

1. *Expresses its appreciation* to the Secretary-General for the excellent preparation of the working document on the draft convention, which was circulated to States for consideration at the conference of plenipotentiaries;

2. *Expresses its thanks* to States that participated in the development and adoption of the United Nations Convention against Illicit Traffic in Narcotic Drugs and Psychotropic Substances;

3. *Urges* States to proceed with the signing and ratification of the Convention, so that it may enter into force as early as possible;

4. *Also urges* States to take the requisite legislative and administrative measures and to devote the necessary resources at the national level so that the Convention may be implemented effectively;

5. *Invites* States, to the extent that they are able to do so, to apply provisionally the measures set out in the Convention pending its entry into force for each of them;

6. *Requests* the Secretary-General to modify the section of the annual reports questionnaire regarding the implementation of international treaties so that the

Commission on Narcotic Drugs, at its regular and special sessions, may review the steps that States have taken to ratify, accept, approve or formally confirm the Convention;

7. *Also requests* the Secretary-General to provide assistance to States, at their request, to enable them to establish the legislative and administrative measures necessary for the application of the Convention;

8. *Urges* all Member States to take appropriate steps in the General Assembly and its financial organs to assign the appropriate priority and approve the budgetary appropriations necessary to enable the Division of Narcotic Drugs of the Secretariat and the secretariat of the International Narcotics Control Board to carry out their additional responsibilities under the Convention;

9. *Invites* the Secretary-General to identify the financial, technical and human resources required by those bodies to carry out their additional responsibilities under the Convention and, within existing resources, to make every effort to assign the necessary resources to the drug control units for the biennium 1990-1991.

Economic and Social Council resolution 1989/13

22 May 1989   Meeting 12   Adopted without vote

Approved by Second Committee (E/1989/76) without vote, 4 May (meeting 5); draft by Commission on Narcotic Drugs (E/1989/23); agenda item 12.

GENERAL ASSEMBLY ACTION

On 15 December, on the recommendation of the Third (Social, Humanitarian and Cultural) Committee, the General Assembly adopted **resolution 44/140** without vote.

Implementation of the United Nations Convention against Illicit Traffic in Narcotic Drugs and Psychotropic Substances

The General Assembly,

Recalling its resolutions 33/168 of 20 December 1978, 35/195 of 15 December 1980, 36/132 of 14 December 1981, 36/168 of 16 December 1981, 37/168 of 17 December 1982, 37/198 of 18 December 1982, 38/93 and 38/122 of 16 December 1983, 39/141 and 39/143 of 14 December 1984, 40/120, 40/121 and 40/122 of 13 December 1985, 41/125, 41/126 and 41/127 of 4 December 1986, 42/111, 42/112 and 42/113 of 7 December 1987 and 43/120 of 8 December 1988 and other relevant provisions,

Noting that these resolutions led to the adoption on 19 December 1988 of the United Nations Convention against Illicit Traffic in Narcotic Drugs and Psychotropic Substances by a conference of plenipotentiaries convened by the United Nations at Vienna from 25 November to 20 December 1988,

Reaffirming the importance of the Convention for improving international co-operation in that field and further strengthening the existing international instruments for the control of narcotic drugs and psychotropic substances, namely, the Single Convention on Narcotic Drugs of 1961, as amended by the 1972 Protocol Amending the Single Convention on Narcotic Drugs of 1961, and the Convention on Psychotropic Substances of 1971,

Noting with satisfaction the broad support granted to the Convention, including signature and ratification,

Encouraging the Commission on Narcotic Drugs to begin consideration of measures that could be recommended to Governments for the implementation of the Convention,

Having considered the report of the Secretary-General on the conclusions of the conference of plenipotentiaries,

1. *Expresses its appreciation* to the Secretary-General for the report on the conclusions of the conference of plenipotentiaries that adopted the United Nations Convention against Illicit Traffic in Narcotic Drugs and Psychotropic Substances at Vienna;

2. *Also expresses its appreciation* to the States that participated in the preparation and adoption of the Convention;

3. *Urges* States that have not yet done so to proceed rapidly to sign and to ratify the Convention, so that it may enter into force as early as possible;

4. *Also urges* States to establish the necessary legislative and administrative measures so that their internal juridical regulations may be compatible with the spirit and scope of the Convention;

5. *Invites* States, to the extent that they are able to do so, to apply provisionally the measures set forth in the Convention, pending its entry into force for each of them;

6. *Requests* the Secretary-General to modify the section of the annual reports questionnaire regarding the implementation of international treaties so that the Commission on Narcotic Drugs, at its regular and special sessions, may review the steps that States have taken to ratify, accept, approve or formally confirm the Convention;

7. *Invites* the Commission on Narcotic Drugs, as the principal United Nations policy-making body on the subject, to identify suitable measures to be taken prior to the entry into force of the Convention;

8. *Requests* the Secretary-General to assign the appropriate priority to providing the Division of Narcotic Drugs of the Secretariat and the secretariat of the International Narcotics Control Board with the necessary financial, technical and human resources that would enable them to carry out the additional responsibilities under the Convention for the biennium 1990-1991;

9. *Urges* the Secretary-General to provide assistance to States, at their request, to enable them to establish the legislative and administrative measures necessary for the implementation of the Convention;

10. *Once again urges* all States that have not yet done so to ratify or to accede to the Single Convention on Narcotic Drugs of 1961, as amended by the 1972 Protocol Amending the Single Convention on Narcotic Drugs of 1961, and the Convention on Psychotropic Substances of 1971;

11. *Requests* the Secretary-General, within existing resources and drawing, in particular, on funds available to the Department of Public Information of the Secretariat, to provide for, facilitate and encourage public information activities relating to the Convention and also to disseminate the text of the Convention in the official languages of the United Nations;

12. *Also requests* the Secretary-General to report to the General Assembly at its forty-fifth session on the implementation of the present resolution.

General Assembly resolution 44/140

15 December 1989   Meeting 82   Adopted without vote

Approved by Third Committee (A/44/850) without vote, 2 November (meeting 60); 64-nation draft (A/C.3/44/L.33), orally revised; agenda item 111 *(a)*.

Sponsors: Angola, Argentina, Australia, Bahamas, Bangladesh, Barbados, Belgium, Bolivia, Brazil, Canada, Chile, China, Colombia, Costa Rica, Côte d'Ivoire, Cuba, Cyprus, Denmark, Dominican Republic, Ecuador, Egypt, El Salvador, Fiji, Finland, France, German Democratic Republic, Germany, Federal Republic of, Ghana, Greece, Guatemala, Honduras, Hungary, India, Indonesia, Ireland, Italy, Jamaica, Japan, Luxembourg, Madagascar, Malaysia, Mexico, Morocco, Netherlands, Nicaragua, Norway, Pakistan, Panama, Paraguay, Peru, Philippines, Poland, Portugal, Senegal, Spain, Suriname, Sweden, Trinidad and Tobago, Turkey, United Kingdom, United States, Venezuela, Yugoslavia, Zambia.
Meeting numbers. GA 44th session: 3rd Committee 29-34, 43, 58, 60; plenary 82.

Drug abuse and international control

The 1989 INCB report[4] provided a global overview of drug abuse and trafficking, and summarized the actions of the international drug control system to combat the production, sale and use of illicit drugs. It warned of the growing power of drug trafficking organizations, stating that the traffickers' victory in a single country would endanger the security and integrity of all countries. INCB cited the conclusion of the 1988 Convention against Illicit Traffic in Narcotic Drugs and Psychotropic Substances as a milestone and a valuable new tool in the fight against illegal drug trafficking.

Pursuant to a 1988 General Assembly resolution,[5] the Secretary-General issued a report[6] in October on the actions taken by the Commission on Narcotic Drugs, the Economic and Social Council and the Secretary-General in the international campaign against drug abuse and illicit trafficking.

GENERAL ASSEMBLY ACTION

On 15 December, on the recommendation of the Third Committee, the General Assembly adopted **resolution 44/142** without vote.

International action to combat drug abuse and illicit trafficking

The General Assembly,

Deeply concerned that the illicit demand for, production of, traffic in and use of narcotic drugs and psychotropic substances has become one of the most serious dangers to the health and welfare of populations, adversely affecting the political, economic, social and cultural structure of all societies,

Recognizing that the criminal activities of drug trafficking and its marketing network destabilize economies, adversely affect the development of many countries and pose a threat to the stability, national security and sovereignty of States,

Alarmed by the growing connection between drug trafficking and terrorism,

Reaffirming the principle of collective responsibility of the international community in combating drug abuse and illicit trafficking,

Recognizing the serious efforts being made by the Governments of some countries in their programmes for crop substitution, integrated rural development and interdiction, and that international economic and technical co-operation has so far proved inadequate to the task at hand and therefore should be substantially stepped up,

Considering that the necessary steps must be taken to preclude the illicit cultivation of plants containing narcotic drugs and psychotropic substances, such as the opium poppy, coca bush and cannabis plant, together with the manufacture of psychotropic substances not used for industrial, scientific or traditional purposes,

Recalling that the International Conference on Drug Abuse and Illicit Trafficking adopted unanimously the Declaration and the Comprehensive Multidisciplinary Outline of Future Activities in Drug Abuse Control, which represent the proper framework for international co-operation in drug control,

Welcoming the efforts made by those countries that produce narcotic drugs for scientific, medicinal and therapeutic uses to prevent the channelling of such substances to illicit markets and to maintain production at a level consistent with licit demand,

Reiterating that the transit routes used by drug traffickers change constantly and that an ever-growing number of countries in all regions of the world, and even entire regions, are particularly vulnerable to illicit transit traffic on account, *inter alia*, of their geographical location,

Recognizing the need for greater international co-operation which would facilitate the marketing of crop substitution products and the control of chemical substances used to process illicit drugs and psychotropic substances, as well as the impact of the social and economic consequences of drug-money transfers and conversion, which have an adverse effect on national economic systems,

Recognizing also the commendable work carried out by the United Nations in controlling narcotic drugs and psychotropic substances, which is being seriously impeded by a lack of human and financial resources,

Recalling its resolution 43/122 of 8 December 1988 and resolution 3 of the United Nations Conference for the Adoption of a Convention against Illicit Traffic in Narcotic Drugs and Psychotropic Substances, held at Vienna from 25 November to 20 December 1988, which, *inter alia*, recognized the urgent need for additional resources, both human and financial, for the Division of Narcotic Drugs of the Secretariat and the secretariat of the International Narcotics Control Board,

Recalling also its resolution 43/121 of 8 December 1988, in which, *inter alia*, it strongly condemned the criminal activities that involved children in the use, production and illicit sale of narcotic drugs and psychotropic substances and appealed to the competent international agencies and the United Nations Fund for Drug Abuse Control to assign high priority to the study of proposals designed to tackle the problem,

Having regard to its resolution 44/16 of 1 November 1989, by which it decided to convene a special session to consider the question of closer international co-operation to combat drug abuse and illicit trafficking,

1. *Strongly condemns* the crime of drug trafficking in all its forms and urges all States to remain steadfast in their political commitment to the concerted international struggle to put an end to it;

2. *Endorses* Economic and Social Council resolution 1989/20 of 22 May 1989 and urges Governments and organizations to adhere to the principles set forth in the Declaration of the International Conference on Drug Abuse and Illicit Trafficking and to apply, as appropriate, the recommendations of the Comprehensive Multidisciplinary Outline of Future Activities in Drug Abuse Control;

3.   *Emphasizes* that the international struggle against drug trafficking and the abuse and sale of, and illicit traffic in, narcotic drugs and psychotropic substances is a collective responsibility and that the eradication of the problem requires efficient and co-ordinated international co-operation, in keeping with the principle of respect for national sovereignty and the cultural identity of States;

4.   *Emphasizes* the connection between the illicit production and supply of, demand for, sale of and traffic in narcotic drugs and psychotropic substances, and the economic, social and cultural conditions of the countries affected;

5.   *Recognizes* that the international community, in seeking solutions to the problem of illicit production of, demand for and trade, transit or traffic in narcotic drugs and psychotropic substances, must take into account the differences and diversity of the problem in each country;

6.   *Calls upon* the international community to provide increased international economic and technical co-operation to Governments, at their request, in support of programmes for the substitution of illicit crops by means of integrated rural development programmes that respect fully the jurisdiction and sovereignty of countries and the cultural traditions of peoples;

7.   *Recognizes* the importance of international co-operation in facilitating trade flows in support of integrated rural development programmes leading to economically viable alternatives to illicit cultivation, taking into account factors such as access to markets for crop substitution products;

8.   *Requests* countries that produce the chemical substances necessary for the manufacture of narcotic drugs and psychotropic substances to take the initiative in adopting measures which ensure effective control of the export of such substances;

9.   *Requests* the Secretary-General to undertake as soon as possible, with the assistance of a group of inter-governmental experts, a study on the economic and social consequences of illicit traffic in drugs, with a view to analysing, *inter alia*, the following elements:

(a)   The magnitude and characteristics of economic transactions related to drug trafficking in all its stages, including production of, traffic in and distribution of illicit drugs, in order to determine the impact of drug-related money transfers and conversion on national economic systems;

(b)   Mechanisms which would prevent the use of the banking system and the international financial system in this activity;

10.   *Also requests* the Secretary-General to ask Member States for their views on the scope and context of such a study, taking into account the elements set forth in paragraph 9 of the present resolution, and to transmit such views to the group of experts;

11.   *Considers* that a system should be established to identify the methods and routes used for the illicit transit traffic in narcotic drugs and psychotropic substances, to enhance the interdiction capability of those States along such routes;

12.   *Strongly condemns* the illicit arms trade that is arming drug traffickers, causing political destabilization and loss of human lives;

13.   *Calls upon* all States, particularly those with high rates of use of narcotic drugs and psychotropic substances, to take prevention and rehabilitation measures

and also increasingly stringent political and legal measures to eliminate the demand for narcotic drugs and psychotropic substances, and calls upon the United Nations and other relevant international organizations to devote greater attention to this aspect of the problem;

14.   *Takes note with satisfaction* of the proposal by the Government of the United Kingdom of Great Britain and Northern Ireland to convene an international conference on drug demand reduction;

15.   *Recognizes* that the publication and dissemination of materials which encourage or stimulate the production of and demand for narcotic drugs and psychotropic substances do not contribute positively to the international action to combat drug abuse and illicit trafficking;

16.   *Requests* the Secretary-General to report to the General Assembly at its forty-fifth session on the implementation of its resolution 43/121 and of Economic and Social Council decision 1989/123 of 22 May 1989;

17.   *Calls upon* Member States substantially to increase their contributions to the United Nations Fund for Drug Abuse Control, so that it can expand its programmes;

18.   *Endorses* Economic and Social Council resolution 1989/18 of 22 May 1989;

19.   *Expresses its serious concern* at the considerable reduction in the budget and staff of the Division of Narcotic Drugs of the Secretariat and the secretariat of the International Narcotics Control Board, which threatens their ability to carry out adequately any additional responsibilities deriving from the activities which the United Nations must undertake to tackle the new dimension of the problem of drug abuse and illicit trafficking;

20.   *Recommends* that the Secretary-General take urgent steps to ensure the increase of allocations to the Division of Narcotic Drugs and the secretariat of the International Narcotics Control Board;

21.   *Takes note with satisfaction* of the results of the Second Interregional Meeting of Heads of National Drug Law Enforcement Agencies;

22.   *Takes note* of the reports of the Secretary-General and requests him to report to the General Assembly at its forty-fifth session on the implementation of the present resolution and also to prepare on a yearly basis a detailed report on international drug-control activities reflecting the work done by the United Nations system to implement the recommendations of the Comprehensive Multidisciplinary Outline of Future Activities in Drug Abuse Control;

23.   *Decides* to include in the provisional agenda of its forty-fifth session an item entitled ''International action to combat drug abuse and illicit trafficking''.

General Assembly resolution 44/142

15 December 1989   Meeting 82   Adopted without vote

Approved by Third Committee (A/44/850) without vote, 29 November (meeting 61); 47-nation draft (A/C.3/44/L.41/Rev.2), orally revised; agenda item 111 *(b)*.

Sponsors: Argentina, Bahamas, Bangladesh, Bolivia, Botswana, Chile, Colombia, Costa Rica, Côte d'Ivoire, Cuba, Cyprus, Dominican Republic, Ecuador, Egypt, El Salvador, Fiji, France, Gabon, Germany, Federal Republic of, Ghana, Greece, Guatemala, Guinea, Honduras, India, Indonesia, Iraq, Italy, Jamaica, Malaysia, Mexico, Morocco, Nicaragua, Pakistan, Panama, Paraguay, Peru, Philippines, Senegal, Singapore, Spain, Sweden, Thailand, Togo, United States, Venezuela, Yugoslavia.

Financial implications. 5th Committee, A/44/852; S-G, A/C.3/44/L.90, A/C.5/44/40.

Meeting numbers. GA 44th session: 3rd Committee 29-34, 43, 58, 60, 61; 5th Committee 53; plenary 82.

Pursuant to a 1979 General Assembly resolution,[7] the Secretary-General submitted in October a report[8] on international co-operation in drug abuse control, outlining the progress made by specialized agencies and UN bodies with respect to the recommendations of the 1987 International Conference on Drug Abuse and Illicit Trafficking[9] and the Comprehensive Multidisciplinary Outline of Future Activities in Drug Abuse Control.[10]

Division of Narcotic Drugs. During 1989, the Division of Narcotic Drugs continued to implement its responsibilities under drug control treaties and intergovernmental mandates. The Division provided assistance and legal and technical advice to Member States, continued to service the Commission on Narcotic Drugs and its various bodies, and conducted follow-up work arising from the 1987 International Conference. It continued to publish, but with reduced frequency, the *Bulletin on Narcotics* (including a double issue on drug abuse assessment) and an *Information Letter*.

Regional workshops on the utilization of community resources for the prevention and reduction of drug abuse were held in La Paz (Bolivia), Nairobi (Kenya) and Vigo (Spain). An expert group meeting was held in Banjul, Gambia, in March, which established international curricula for training in the analysis of controlled drugs in biological material. The Division also developed a network of collaborating national training institutions with relevant experience in forensic toxicology.

In the area of supply, the Division's Laboratory made efforts to monitor and control new trends in the licit movement of chemicals and equipment used in the manufacture of illicit drugs. A manual on the clandestine manufacture of substances under international control was being updated. A project was developed to collect and evaluate available data on eradication methods for the three major narcotic plants—the cannabis plant, the coca bush and the opium poppy. The Division continued to advise Governments on the formulation of national legislation related to drug abuse control and to provide relevant examples of existing national legislation.

The twenty-fourth session of the Sub-Commission on Illicit Drug Traffic and Related Matters in the Near and Middle East was held in Vienna in February, and the twenty-fifth session in Ankara, Turkey, in October. The Economic and Social Council, by decision 1989/120 of 22 May, noted the report of the Sub-Commission on its twenty-fourth session, and approved applications for membership from Kuwait, Lebanon, Oman, Saudi Arabia, the United Arab Emirates and Yemen.

In the area of suppression of illicit trafficking, a workshop on the use of drug-scenting dogs was organized by the Division in April in Vienna and in Budapest, Hungary. An expert group meeting on the development of a new UN drug law enforcement training manual was held in Riyadh, Saudi Arabia, in November. The Division's Laboratory undertook the development or strengthening of laboratories in Bangladesh, Bolivia, Ghana, Sri Lanka, Uruguay and Yemen. Four laboratories were started in 1989, in Benin, Kenya, Sierra Leone and the United Republic of Tanzania, and the regional training laboratories in Bangkok and Buenos Aires were further strengthened. The Division published manuals on the analysis of methaqualone/mecloqualone, benzodiazepine derivatives and LSD, and continued the production and provision of UN drug identification kits.

On 17 February,[11] the Commission on Narcotic Drugs requested that States members and observers of the Commission review the usefulness of the publications and documentation of the Division of Narcotic Drugs, and submit their findings to the Division for review by the Commission at its thirty-fourth session.

UNDP activities. UNDP continued to support drug abuse control in 1989, including collaborative projects with the UN Fund for Drug Abuse Control (UNFDAC). UNDP's Office for Project Services (OPS), formerly the Office for Projects Execution, implemented projects financed by the Fund. The Fund programme executed by OPS amounted to $132 million. Regional programme activities in drug abuse control continued to be concentrated in Asia and the Pacific and in Latin America and the Caribbean.

UNDP activities in the field of drug abuse control were detailed in a March report[12] by the UNDP Administrator.

WHO activities. The activities of the World Health Organization (WHO) to reduce the harm caused by psycho-active substances were greatly strengthened by the adoption by the World Health Assembly in May 1989 of a far-reaching resolution on the prevention and control of drug and alcohol abuse. A major review of preventive strategies was published in 1989, with special emphasis on techniques for the reduction of drug demand, bringing together much of the work undertaken by WHO in this area in the previous five years. As part of its overall responsibility to monitor health trends, WHO continued to gather data on drug-related mortality and morbidity.

In the area of supply control, WHO continued to implement its guidelines for review of dependence-producing psycho-active substances, and began preparing a revised version of these guidelines. It also convened a Programme Planning Working Group and an Expert Committee on Drug Dependence. The Director-General addressed letters to ministers of health in 33 countries, where methaqualone was legally available, to stop production, sale and use of that drug, since it had created a drug abuse problem in nearly every country in the world. WHO also promoted the rational use of psycho-active drugs in the health-care industry through its educational efforts.

ILO activities. The Governing Body of the International Labour Organisation (ILO) intensified its activity in the area of drug abuse control in 1989, and endorsed a series of new proposals in February. ILO continued to promote drug abuse prevention in the workplace in three major ways: preparation of training materials and training of personnel; promotion of plant-level, union-based or community-based action programmes; and research and analyses of programmes and needs in specific industries and professions. A multi-media kit, "Responses to drug and alcohol problems in the workplace", and the Conditions of Work Digest on "Alcohol and drugs: Programmes of assistance for workers" were disseminated widely, as was a monograph, "Rehabilitation approaches to drug and alcohol dependence".

Other activities. The Council of the International Civil Aviation Organization (ICAO) referred the issue of drug abuse in "sensitive occupations" to the ICAO Air Navigation Commission, an advisory body of independent experts, in view of its relevance to many occupations in the air transport industry. The Commission concluded that current regulatory provisions in the ICAO Standards and Recommended Practices represented a sufficient safeguard against drug abuse by flight crew members and air traffic controllers, and that there was no evidence of a problem of drug abuse in those occupations.

The International Maritime Organization (IMO) devoted substantial efforts to preventing illicit carriage of drugs on ships. The comprehensive Multidisciplinary Outline was examined with a view to its application to shipping, and guidelines for shipowners and masters were circulated.

The Crime Prevention and Criminal Justice Branch of the Centre for Social Development and Humanitarian Affairs maintained close collaboration with UNFDAC in order to draw up a blueprint for drug abuse prevention in Latin America. Technical co-operation projects were prepared for Argentina, Ghana and Uganda, covering such areas as special training for law enforcement officials and criminal justice personnel to fight organized crime and drug trafficking, policy formulation on drug abuse, improvement of the capacity of forensic laboratories in screening techniques for seized drugs and research and community programmes. A study of AIDS in prison was being conducted in close co-operation with WHO.

The United Nations Educational, Scientific and Cultural Organization (UNESCO) organized

South-South exchanges of experts in the context of education projects designed to combat drug abuse. It also conducted several projects to promote health and prevent drug abuse in developing countries. With regard to the role of the media, UNESCO organized a meeting of experts in Ottawa, Canada, in September to consider the efficacy of media campaigns to combat drug abuse.

The Executive Board of the United Nations Children's Fund (UNICEF) adopted a resolution on drug abuse among children. It requested the Executive Director to give immediate attention to the planning of an objective assessment of the causes and magnitude of the problem, especially among those children from social groups living in extreme poverty in developing countries.

The Economic and Social Commission for Asia and the Pacific (ESCAP) expressed concern over the growing problem of drug abuse in the region at its forty-fifth session (Bangkok, Thailand, 27 March–5 April). Five country studies were initiated in 1988-1989 with the collaboration of country drug abuse focal points, with the studies in Australia and Sri Lanka still under way. Drug abuse demand reduction was introduced into ESCAP youth activities where appropriate, and the ESCAP/WHO project on drug abuse rehabilitation in Asia and the Pacific continued.

The Economic and Social Commission for Western Asia (ESCWA) incorporated the drug abuse issue into its ongoing regional study on social indicators and trends in the region. A regional study entitled "The impact of drug abuse among youth in the ESCWA region: approaches to social reintegration" was planned, as was a comprehensive study on national policies on crime prevention.

Activities related to drug control were also carried out by the Economic Commission for Europe, the UN Research Institute for Social Development, the World Food Programme, the International Fund for Agricultural Development (IFAD) and the UN Industrial Development Organization (UNIDO).

GENERAL ASSEMBLY ACTION

On 15 December, on the recommendation of the Third Committee, the General Assembly adopted **resolution 44/141** without vote.

Global programme of action against illicit narcotic drugs

The General Assembly,

Alarmed by the dramatic increase in drug abuse and illicit production and trafficking in narcotics, which is threatening the health and well-being of millions of people, in particular youth, in the majority of countries of the world,

Deeply concerned that the evolving drug problem is assuming new dimensions and is threatening the economic, social and political structures of affected countries, through acts of violence perpetrated against their democratic institutions and the extensive economic power of illicit drug organizations,

Commending the determined efforts of the Government of Colombia to stop drug trafficking and recognizing the importance of support for such efforts by the international community,

Welcoming the increasing international attention to these issues and the unflinching commitment demonstrated at the highest levels by heads of Government and State to increase their efforts and resources to achieve co-ordinated action in the international fight against production, trafficking and abuse of narcotic drugs,

Recognizing that the collective responsibility of States for the campaign against the demand for, production of and trafficking in illicit drugs requires intensified international co-operation and joint action, including the capability to provide, in appropriate forms, necessary support and assistance, if requested by affected States, in order to strengthen their capacity to deal with the problem in all its aspects,

Noting with appreciation the work carried out within the United Nations in the field of drug abuse control and the valuable knowledge and experience represented there,

Recognizing the important contributions made to the international campaign against drug abuse and illicit trafficking by the International Conference on Drug Abuse and Illicit Trafficking, held at Vienna from 17 to 26 June 1987, and, in particular, by its adoption of the Declaration and the Comprehensive Multidisciplinary Outline of Future Activities in Drug Abuse Control, as well as by the conference of plenipotentiaries, held at Vienna from 25 November to 20 December 1988, which adopted the United Nations Convention against Illicit Traffic in Narcotic Drugs and Psychotropic Substances,

Deeply concerned that, owing to a lack of resources, it has not been possible for the United Nations organs concerned to execute several of the important steps and measures that were mandated for the biennium 1988-1989,

Acknowledging the recommendations made by the Administrative Committee on Co-ordination and the Committee for Programme and Co-ordination at their twenty-fourth series of Joint Meetings, at which they concluded, *inter alia*, that the Administrative Committee on Co-ordination should prepare a system-wide action plan leading to specific activities to be undertaken by organizations of the United Nations system, individually and collectively, and that consideration could be given to the need for the establishment of additional mechanisms to enhance the effectiveness of the United Nations system in the field of drug abuse control,

Recognizing that the new dimensions taken on by the drug menace will necessitate a more comprehensive approach to international drug control and a more efficient and co-ordinated structure in this field in order to enable the United Nations to play the central and greatly increased role necessary for countering this threat,

Bearing in mind its decision, in resolution 44/16 of 1 November 1989, to hold a special session to consider the question of international co-operation against illicit production, supply, demand, trafficking and distribution of narcotic drugs, with a view to expanding the scope and increasing the effectiveness of such co-operation, and stressing the importance of this special session and of the need for Member States to make the fullest possible contributions to its preparatory work,

1. *Resolves* that action against drug abuse and illicit production and trafficking in narcotics should, as a collective responsibility, be accorded the highest possible priority by the international community and that the United Nations should be the main focus for concerted action against illicit drugs;

2. *Agrees* to strengthen the capability of the United Nations in order to achieve more efficient and co-ordinated co-operation at the international, regional and national levels against the threats posed by illicit narcotic drugs and psychotropic substances;

3. *Requests* the Secretary-General, in his capacity as Chairman of the Administrative Committee on Co-ordination, to co-ordinate at the inter-agency level, the development of a United Nations system-wide action plan on drug abuse control aimed at the full implementation of all existing mandates and subsequent decisions of intergovernmental bodies throughout the United Nations system, using as a guide the Declaration of the International Conference on Drug Abuse and Illicit Trafficking and the recommendations in the Comprehensive Multidisciplinary Outline of Future Activities in Drug Abuse Control, and for the attainment of this purpose:

(*a*) Calls upon the Division of Narcotic Drugs of the Secretariat, the International Narcotics Control Board and its secretariat, as well as the United Nations Fund for Drug Abuse Control, to consult closely with and contribute their expertise to the other agencies represented on the Administrative Committee on Co-ordination in developing the action plan;

(*b*) Requests the Administrative Committee on Co-ordination to include in the action plan, *inter alia*:

(i) A statement of purposes that defines the overall goal and denotes specific objectives;

(ii) An outline of concrete activities that each agency should undertake, within its mandate, ensuring that there is no duplication or overlap;

(iii) A reasonable time-frame for implementation of each portion of the action plan;

(iv) A realistic cost estimate for implementing the action plan, being mindful that resources are limited and that it would be necessary for agencies to focus priorities, review deployment of resources or obtain, if necessary, from their governing bodies the authority needed to fulfil their part of the plan;

(*c*) Requests the Administrative Committee on Co-ordination to present the action plan to all Member States no later than 31 March 1990, in order to permit discussion by the Committee for Programme and Co-ordination at its thirtieth session and by the Economic and Social Council at its next regular session of 1990;

(*d*) Requests that the executive heads of United Nations bodies report annually to the Administrative Committee on Co-ordination on the progress made in implementing the action plan and that the Administrative Committee include the same information in its annual report, so as to enable the Committee for Programme and Co-ordination and the Economic and Social Council to consider it, within their respective mandates, and to make appropriate recommendations to the General Assembly;

(e) Requests the Administrative Committee on Co-ordination to make the necessary adjustments to the action plan annually and to ensure that each agency brings up to date and revises its related activities annually in order to meet changing circumstances;

4. *Requests* the Secretary-General to select a limited number of experts from developed and developing countries to advise and assist him for a maximum period of one year, in full co-operation with United Nations officials, in order to enhance the efficiency of the United Nations structure for drug abuse control, taking into account the ability of the United Nations to perform its increasing tasks in the light of existing mandates and of decisions adopted by the General Assembly at its special session, and to report to the Assembly at its forty-fifth session;

5. *Requests* States, without prejudice to the basic criteria that the General Assembly shall adopt at its special session, to consider in the preparatory work for that session, *inter alia*, the following areas, with the purpose of ensuring that all aspects of the problem are adequately addressed in the elaboration of a global programme of action against illicit narcotic drugs for adoption at the special session:

(a) Giving increased attention to curbing the rising demand for narcotic drugs by intensified rehabilitative, legal and preventive measures, including public information and education;

(b) The possibility of declaring a United Nations decade against drug abuse, with the purpose of raising public awareness through a world-wide campaign against drug abuse;

(c) The expansion of the scope of international co-operation in support of rural development programmes and other economic development and technical assistance programmes aimed at reducing illicit production and drug trafficking through the strengthening of economic, judicial and legal systems;

(d) The full involvement of international, regional and national financial institutions within their respective areas of competence in the elaboration of measures to counteract the negative economic and social consequences of the drug problem in all its aspects, paying special attention to the characteristics and magnitude of the conversion and transference of drug-related monies in the economic systems of countries;

(e) The development of mechanisms to prevent the use of the banking system and other financial institutions for the processing or laundering of drug-related money;

(f) An examination of recommendations to enhance the efficiency of the United Nations structure for drug abuse control in the most appropriate way to enable the United Nations to perform its increasing tasks in the most effective and co-ordinated manner;

(g) The development of recommendations for generating increased financial resources to the United Nations drug effort and for ensuring sufficient regular budget resources for the United Nations drug bodies to carry out their mandates;

(h) The co-ordination of an expanded programme of training for national narcotics agents in investigative methods, interdiction and narcotics intelligence;

(i) The feasibility of establishing a reserve pool of experienced narcotics agents and experts pledged by other States, whose services States may request for specified periods of time;

(j) The establishment under the United Nations of a facility to gather and collate information on the financial flow from drug-related funds, to be made available to States at their request;

(k) The feasibility of a United Nations capability that, at the request of States, would provide training and equipment for the anti-drug operations of the States to inhibit the use, interdict the supply and eliminate the illicit trafficking of drugs;

(l) The elaboration of any other appropriate measures whereby the United Nations can contribute further to concerted international action against illicit narcotic drugs;

6. *Invites* States, at the special session of the General Assembly, to consider requesting the Secretary-General to appoint a limited number of experts, representing the various aspects of the drug problem with regard to both developed and developing countries, to develop further the global programme of action as adopted at the special session;

7. *Requests* the Secretary-General to give priority to narcotics control activities in his proposals for the medium-term plan for the period beginning in 1992;

8. *Urges* States to contribute to the United Nations Fund for Drug Abuse Control;

9. *Also urges* States to consider giving financial or other support to enhance the efficiency of the United Nations structure for drug abuse control and to assist and promote a truly comprehensive global programme of action;

10. *Requests* the Secretary-General to transmit the present resolution to the Preparatory Committee of the Whole for the Seventeenth Special Session of the General Assembly, which the Assembly established by its decision 44/410 of 14 November 1989.

General Assembly resolution 44/141

15 December 1989   Meeting 82   Adopted without vote

Approved by Third Committee (A/44/850 & Corr.1) without vote, 29 November (meeting 61); 49-nation draft (A/C.3/44/L.36/Rev.2), orally revised; agenda item 111 *(b)*.

Sponsors: Antigua and Barbuda, Bahamas, Barbados, Belgium, Belize, Bolivia, Colombia, Costa Rica, Cyprus, Denmark, Dominica, Dominican Republic, Egypt, El Salvador, Fiji, Finland, France, Gabon, Germany, Federal Republic of, Grenada, Guyana, Haiti, Honduras, Iceland, Ireland, Italy, Jamaica, Japan, Luxembourg, Malaysia, Nigeria, Norway, Pakistan, Papua New Guinea, Peru, Philippines, Portugal, Saint Kitts and Nevis, Saint Lucia, Saint Vincent and the Grenadines, Senegal, Spain, Suriname, Sweden, Trinidad and Tobago, Ukrainian SSR, United Kingdom, United States, Yugoslavia.

Financial implications. 5th Committee, A/44/853; S-G, A/C.3/44/L.91, A/C.5/44/41.

Meeting numbers. GA 44th session: 3rd Committee 29-34, 43, 58, 60, 61; 5th Committee 53; plenary 82.

UN Fund for Drug Abuse Control

The activities of UNFDAC were expanded during 1989. A budget of $62.5 million for 1989 enabled the planning of financial and technical assistance to 49 countries through 114 drug control projects. Also included in UNFDAC's budget were

38 regional and global projects involving such drug control activities as special training, research, conferences and workshops. Efforts were made to improve programme management and evaluation, for example through the recruitment of experts on law enforcement and psychotropic drugs, the extension of the network of field advisers, and the increase of administrative and support services received from UNDP.

Of the total 1989 budget, 34 per cent was allocated to reducing the supply of illicit drugs; 34 per cent to reducing illicit demand; 25 per cent to strengthening control measures; 4 per cent to staffing and procurement for field offices in a working arrangement with UNDP; 2 per cent to administration and programme evaluation; and 1 per cent to research.

Among UNFDAC's activities in 1989 in Latin America and the Caribbean were: rural development programmes to help eradicate coca cultivation in Bolivia; support for an anti-narcotics unit, education and drug treatment in Brazil; prevention programmes in Chile and Costa Rica; and rural development projects in Mexico and Peru. A $20 million master plan for urban prevention projects and rural development programmes in Colombia was finalized. An UNFDAC Interpol telecommunications network in the Caribbean came into operation in 1989.

Several projects were undertaken in Asia and the Pacific. A $20 million programme was begun in 1989 in India to reduce illicit traffic and demand, while also controlling leakages of licit opium production into the illicit trade. A rural development project was launched in the Lao People's Democratic Republic for opium poppy-growing zones. Other programmes continued in China, Malaysia, Myanmar, Sri Lanka and Thailand.

In the Near and Middle East, UNFDAC actively participated in the work of the Coordinator for UN humanitarian and economic assistance programmes in Afghanistan. In view of the prospect of a resettlement programme in opium poppy-growing parts of the country, a $1.4 million rural rehabilitation and reconstruction programme was approved. Law enforcement projects in Cyprus and Jordan were completed, and others were developed for Turkey and the eastern Mediterranean. A rural development programme in Pakistan was enhanced.

In Africa, programmes were under way in 25 countries. A multisectoral project was started in Morocco, and new programmes in Ghana and Nigeria were planned. Drug control projects became operational in Kenya, Malawi, the United Republic of Tanzania and Zambia. UNFDAC opened an office for a Regional Field Adviser in Nairobi.

ECONOMIC AND SOCIAL COUNCIL ACTION

On 22 May, on the recommendation of its Second Committee, the Economic and Social Council adopted **resolution 1989/16** without vote.

Contribution of the United Nations Fund for Drug Abuse Control to the fight against illicit traffic in and abuse of drugs

The Economic and Social Council,

Recognizing the strategic role of the United Nations Fund for Drug Abuse Control in the multilateral effort to eliminate the drug problem,

Expressing appreciation to the Executive Director of the United Nations Fund for Drug Abuse Control and his staff for their efforts to develop programmes that meet the needs of countries and address the major aspects of the drug problem,

Noting the significant role in guiding the multilateral narcotics control programme played by the Single Convention on Narcotic Drugs of 1961, as amended by the 1972 Protocol Amending the Single Convention on Narcotic Drugs of 1961, and by the Convention on Psychotropic Substances of 1971, and noting also the adoption on 19 December 1988 of the United Nations Convention against Illicit Traffic in Narcotic Drugs and Psychotropic Substances by the conference of plenipotentiaries held at Vienna from 25 November to 20 December 1988,

Recognizing the benefits that will emanate from the entry into force of the United Nations Convention against Illicit Traffic in Narcotic Drugs and Psychotropic Substances for the strengthening of the international narcotics control effort, particularly those activities designed to enhance co-operation between legal, judicial and law enforcement entities,

1. *Urges* the United Nations Fund for Drug Abuse Control to continue to develop programmes that will address the multifaceted drug problem;

2. *Also urges* the Fund to continue to use the Single Convention on Narcotic Drugs of 1961, as amended by the 1972 Protocol Amending the Single Convention on Narcotic Drugs of 1961 and the Convention on Psychotropic Substances of 1971, and to use the United Nations Convention against Illicit Traffic in Narcotic Drugs and Psychotropic Substances, as guiding tools;

3. *Affirms* that the United Nations Convention against Illicit Traffic in Narcotic Drugs and Psychotropic Substances shall not derogate from earlier treaty rights and obligations;

4. *Encourages* the International Narcotics Control Board, the Division of Narcotic Drugs of the Secretariat and the United Nations Fund for Drug Abuse Control to continue to strengthen their co-operation and take whatever measures may be necessary to achieve the aims of the international conventions in accordance with the advice and suggestions of the Commission on Narcotic Drugs and in accordance with the policy directives received from the United Nations legislative bodies;

5. *Expresses its appreciation* to the Secretary-General and the Executive Director of the United Nations Fund for Drug Abuse Control for the initiative and leadership that have characterized the development of the Fund;

6. *Urges* Governments to consider continuing and increasing substantially their voluntary contributions to the Fund.

Economic and Social Council resolution 1989/16
22 May 1989   Meeting 12   Adopted without vote

Approved by Second Committee (E/1989/76) without vote, 4 May (meeting
5); draft by Commission on Narcotic Drugs (E/1989/23); agenda item 12.

Special session of General Assembly

On 1 November, the General Assembly adopted **resolution 44/16** without vote.

Special session of the General Assembly to consider the question of international co-operation against illicit production, supply, demand, trafficking and distribution of narcotic drugs, with a view to expanding the scope and increasing the effectiveness of such co-operation

The General Assembly,

Deeply concerned about the serious problem of the illicit production, supply, demand, trafficking and distribution of narcotic drugs and about the devastating effect of drug abuse on individuals and society,

Bearing in mind statements delivered before the Assembly in plenary meeting during its forty-fourth session, including the address given by the President of the Republic of Colombia on 29 September 1989 and, in particular, his call for a special session of the General Assembly,

1. *Decides* to hold a special session, at a high political level, to consider as a matter of urgency the question of international co-operation against illicit production, supply, demand, trafficking and distribution of narcotic drugs, with a view to expanding the scope and increasing the effectiveness of such co-operation;

2. *Requests* the Secretary-General to make the necessary administrative arrangements for the convening of the special session.

General Assembly resolution 44/16

1 November 1989   Meeting 43   Adopted without vote

121-nation draft (A/44/L.12 & Add.1); agenda item 157.
Sponsors: Afghanistan, Algeria, Antigua and Barbuda, Argentina, Australia, Austria, Bahamas, Bahrain, Bangladesh, Barbados, Belgium, Benin, Bolivia, Brazil, Brunei Darussalam, Bulgaria, Burundi, Canada, Cape Verde, Chad, Chile, China, Colombia, Comoros, Congo, Costa Rica, Côte D'Ivoire, Cuba, Cyprus, Czechoslovakia, Democratic Yemen, Denmark, Djibouti, Dominica, Dominican Republic, Ecuador, Egypt, El Salvador, Ethiopia, Finland, France, Gabon, Gambia, German Democratic Republic, Germany, Federal Republic of, Ghana, Greece, Grenada, Guatemala, Guinea, Guinea-Bissau, Guyana, Haiti, Honduras, Iceland, India, Indonesia, Iran, Ireland, Italy, Jamaica, Japan, Jordan, Kuwait, Lebanon, Liberia, Libyan Arab Jamahiriya, Luxembourg, Madagascar, Malawi, Malaysia, Malta, Mauritania, Mauritius, Mexico, Morocco, Nepal, Netherlands, New Zealand, Nicaragua, Nigeria, Norway, Oman, Pakistan, Panama, Paraguay, Peru, Philippines, Portugal, Qatar, Romania, Saint Lucia, Saint Vincent and the Grenadines, Samoa, Sao Tome and Principe, Saudi Arabia, Senegal, Seychelles, Sierra Leone, Singapore, Spain, Sri Lanka, Suriname, Swaziland, Sweden, Thailand, Trinidad and Tobago, Togo, Tunisia, Turkey, Ukrainian SSR, USSR, United Kingdom, United States, Uruguay, Vanuatu, Venezuela, Yugoslavia, Zaire, Zambia, Zimbabwe.
Financial implications. 5th Committee, A/44/695; S-G, A/C.5/44/19.
Meeting numbers. GA 44th session: 5th Committee 26; plenary 43.

On 14 November, by **decision 44/410**, the General Assembly decided that the special session on the question of international co-operation against illicit trafficking in narcotic drugs should take place at United Nations Headquarters from 20 to 23 February 1990. The Assembly also requested the Commission on Narcotic Drugs to consider the question of the enhancement of the role of the United Nations in the fight against il-

licit drugs at its eleventh special session, and invited it and other UN bodies to submit their views on matters related to the special session of the General Assembly. The Secretary-General was requested to submit a report on the development of a UN plan of action on drug abuse control, and on progress towards the allocation of sufficient resources to deal with the issue of narcotic drugs.

International court for drug trafficking crimes

On 4 December, by **resolution 44/39**, the General Assembly requested the International Law Commission to address the question of establishing an international criminal court or other international criminal trial mechanism whose jurisdiction would include the illicit trafficking of narcotic drugs across national frontiers.

New title for agenda item

On 15 December, by **decision 44/434**, the General Assembly decided, considering the increased magnitude of the problem of drug abuse and illicit trafficking, to change the title of agenda item 111 to read "International action to combat drug abuse and illicit trafficking".

Supply and demand

Demand reduction

In a report[13] on drug abuse and measures to reduce illicit demand, the Secretary-General outlined trends in abuse by region and activities by Governments, non-governmental organizations, civic and educational institutions and companies to reduce demand. The report stated that more countries than ever before appeared to be applying a broader range of measures aimed at both prevention and treatment. Most reporting countries had carried out some prevention programmes, usually targeted at youth but also at parents and other persons dealing with youths. Most countries provided behavioural and psychiatric treatment, with the best results achieved when rehabilitation, after-care, social reintegration and treatment were combined in a multidisciplinary approach to ensure the reintegration of an individual into normal community life. A number of countries were reconsidering their drug abuse prevention and treatment policies and programmes in response to the AIDS pandemic, recognizing that intravenous drug abusers were a major vector in the spread of HIV.

ECONOMIC AND SOCIAL COUNCIL ACTION

On 22 May, on the recommendation of its Second Committee, the Economic and Social Council adopted **resolution 1989/14** without vote.

Intensification and co-ordination of measures for reduction of the illicit demand for narcotic drugs and psychotropic substances

The Economic and Social Council,

Recalling that the General Assembly, in its resolution 42/112 of 7 December 1987, welcomed the successful conclusion of the International Conference on Drug Abuse and Illicit Trafficking, in particular, the adoption of the Declaration and the Comprehensive Multidisciplinary Outline of Future Activities in Drug Abuse Control,

Noting that the General Assembly, in the same resolution, requested the Commission on Narcotic Drugs, as the principal United Nations policy-making body on drug control, to identify suitable measures for follow-up to the International Conference on Drug Abuse and Illicit Trafficking,

Seriously concerned at the increasing availability of illicit drugs and the world-wide upward trend in drug abuse, which is causing widespread human suffering, loss of life and social disruption,

Recognizing that measures of prevention, public awareness, early intervention, treatment, rehabilitation and social reintegration are essential factors in curbing drug abuse,

Recalling that, by its resolution 1988/16 of 25 May 1988, it urged Governments to improve measures for demand reduction,

Noting that article 14 of the United Nations Convention against Illicit Traffic in Narcotic Drugs and Psychotropic Substances, adopted on 19 December 1988 at Vienna, requires parties to adopt measures aimed at eliminating or reducing illicit demand for narcotic drugs and psychotropic substances,

Acknowledging that the specialized agencies concerned with demand reduction initiatives have responded positively to General Assembly resolution 38/93 of 16 December 1983 and the Declaration of the International Conference on Drug Abuse and Illicit Trafficking in intensifying their drug control activities,

Recognizing the important role that international non-governmental organizations play in all aspects of demand reduction,

Mindful of the fundamental need for action at the national, regional and international levels to achieve a balanced programme of reduction of the supply of and demand for illicit drugs,

Aware that the achievement of this goal requires continuous attention, in-depth analysis, monitoring, co-ordination, follow-up and extensive collaboration,

Noting with satisfaction that the Commission on Narcotic Drugs has included in the provisional agenda of its thirty-fourth session an item concerning the prevention and reduction of the illicit demand for narcotic drugs and psychotropic substances,

1. *Requests* the Secretary-General, in order to assess the level of national and international progress in implementing the seven targets set out in chapter I of the Comprehensive Multidisciplinary Outline of Future Activities in Drug Abuse Control, adopted by the International Conference on Drug Abuse and Illicit Trafficking:

(*a*) To issue a succinct questionnaire, by 31 December 1989, to all Governments and regional intergovernmental organizations, requesting details of action taken at the national and regional levels in implementing the seven targets, together with details of any practical difficulties they have experienced in meeting them;

(*b*) To prepare, in collaboration with the International Labour Organisation, the United Nations Educational, Scientific and Cultural Organization and the World Health Organization, a report, to be issued by 30 November 1990, analysing the information submitted and assessing, in particular, how best to provide help to States in furthering demand reduction strategies and the extent to which each of the seven targets continues to be relevant, for consideration by the Commission on Narcotic Drugs at its thirty-fourth session;

2. *Urges* all Governments and regional intergovernmental organizations to co-operate fully in the preparation of the above-mentioned report by providing the information requested in the questionnaire in good time;

3. *Urges* all Governments to continue to give higher priority to demand reduction in their national strategies to combat drug abuse through the necessary policy and legislative adjustments, including the allocation of appropriate resources and services for prevention, treatment, rehabilitation and social reintegration;

4. *Calls upon* the International Labour Organisation, the United Nations Educational, Scientific and Cultural Organization and the World Health Organization and other appropriate intergovernmental organizations to intensify relevant activities and accord them higher priority, and to collaborate closely with international non-governmental organizations;

5. *Calls upon* international non-governmental organizations to extend and co-ordinate their activities for developing and executing demand reduction programmes through their contacts with the community at the grass-roots level, in close co-operation with the Division of Narcotic Drugs of the Secretariat and appropriate United Nations organizations and agencies, with the aim of effectively complementing and supplementing their work;

6. *Encourages* the United Nations Fund for Drug Abuse Control in the further development of its master plans to give due attention to demand reduction activities and the provision of greater resources for related intervention programmes;

7. *Urges* all Member States to take appropriate steps in the General Assembly and its financial organs to assign the appropriate priority and, within the proposed programme budget outline for the biennium 1990-1991 approved by the General Assembly by its resolution 43/214 of 21 December 1988, to approve the budgetary appropriations necessary to enable the Division of Narcotic Drugs to carry out the tasks referred to in paragraph 1 above;

8. *Invites* the Secretary-General to identify the financial, technical and human resources required by the Division of Narcotic Drugs to carry out the above-mentioned tasks and to make recommendations, taking into account General Assembly resolution 43/214 and the Regulations and Rules Governing Programme Planning, the Programme Aspects of the Budget, the Monitoring of Implementation and the Methods of Evaluation;

9. *Requests* the Secretary-General to transmit the present resolution to all Governments, specialized agencies and the international non-governmental organizations concerned for consideration and implementation as appropriate.

Economic and Social Council resolution 1989/14
22 May 1989   Meeting 12   Adopted without vote
Approved by Second Committee (E/1989/76) without vote, 4 May (meeting
    5); draft by Commission on Narcotic Drugs (E/1989/23); agenda item 12.

Narcotic raw materials for licit use

Under the 1961 Single Convention on Narcotic Drugs,[14] countries were allowed to make reservations regarding traditional, non-medical use of some drugs for a limited time period. The Convention specified that all non-medical use of opium should be suppressed by 12 December 1979, and non-medical use of coca leaf, cannabis and cannabis resin was to be suppressed by 12 December 1989.

In its annual report for 1989,[4] INCB stated that the objective of the 1961 Convention of suppressing the officially sanctioned non-medical use of drugs had been achieved with regard to non-medical use of opium, cannabis and cannabis resin, with the possible exception of Bangladesh. Coca leaf use continued, however, in Bolivia and Peru, and INCB called for assistance to those countries to enable them to comply with their treaty obligations. The report noted that the time periods of the transitional reservations had elapsed; six countries (Argentina, Bangladesh, India, Myanmar, Nepal and Pakistan) had made such reservations.

INCB observed that the diversion of psychotropic substances from licit use into illicit traffic had been controlled, but that traffickers had switched to less regulated substances: amphetamines had been replaced in part by fenetylline, which was being replaced by anorectics and pemoline, and barbiturates and benzodiazepines were now being used as substitutes for methaqualone. The demand for and supply of opiates for medical and scientific needs were the subject of a special study[15] by INCB.

ECONOMIC AND SOCIAL COUNCIL ACTION

On 22 May, on the recommendation of its Second Committee, the Economic and Social Council adopted **resolution 1989/15** without vote.

Demand and supply of opiates for medical and scientific purposes

The Economic and Social Council,

Recalling its resolutions 1979/8 of 9 May 1979, 1980/20 of 30 April 1980, 1981/8 of 6 May 1981, 1982/12 of 30 April 1982, 1983/3 of 24 May 1983, 1984/21 of 24 May 1984, 1985/16 of 28 May 1985, 1986/9 of 21 May 1986, 1987/31 of 26 May 1987 and 1988/10 of 25 May 1988,

Emphasizing once again the central role of the Single Convention on Narcotic Drugs of 1961 as amended by the 1972 Protocol Amending the Single Convention on Narcotic Drugs of 1961 in the control of the production of and trade in opiates,

Reaffirming the need to maintain a balance between the supply of and demand for opiate raw materials for medical and scientific purposes, which is an important element in the international strategy and policy on drug abuse control,

Concerned that the traditional supplier countries continue to face financial and other burdens as a result of their large stocks of opiate raw materials,

Emphasizing once again the fundamental need for international co-operation and solidarity to overcome the problem of excess stocks,

Having considered the section of the report of the International Narcotics Control Board for 1988 on the demand for and supply of opiates for medical and scientific needs,

1. *Urges* all Governments to give serious consideration to ways of resolving the problem of excess stocks and bringing about rapid improvement;

2. *Commends* the International Narcotics Control Board for its efforts and requests it to pursue the early finalization and implementation of the project, referred to in paragraph 40 of its report, which would assess legitimate needs for opiates in various regions of the world, hitherto unmet because of insufficient health care, difficult economic situations or other conditions;

3. *Requests* the Secretary-General to transmit the present resolution to all Governments and appropriate international agencies for consideration and implementation.

Economic and Social Council resolution 1989/15
22 May 1989   Meeting 12   Adopted without vote
Approved by Second Committee (E/1989/76) without vote, 4 May (meeting
    5); draft by Commission on Narcotic Drugs (E/1989/23); agenda item 12.

Illicit traffic

In a February report,[16] the Secretary-General reviewed the world situation and trends in illicit traffic in drugs. There was some evidence that demand for opium and opiates in traditional consuming areas could be reduced through preventive measures and that some countries had made encouraging progress in that direction. On the other hand, traffickers were finding new markets for heroin in other countries, and the relatively low cost of cocaine in major consuming areas seemed to have aroused the interest of traffickers and drug cartels in revitalizing and expanding heroin distribution through illicit trafficking.

ECONOMIC AND SOCIAL COUNCIL ACTION

On 22 May, on the recommendation of its Second Committee, the Economic and Social Council adopted **resolution 1989/18** without vote.

Allocation of appropriate resources and priority to the international drug control programme

The Economic and Social Council,

Recalling that the General Assembly, in its resolution 43/122, of 8 December 1988, endorsed Commission on Narcotic Drugs resolution 4(S-X) of 12 February 1988, considering that its implementation was essential for the adequate functioning of the Division of Narcotic Drugs of the Secretariat and the secretariat of the International Narcotics Control Board,

Recalling also that, in its resolution 1987/29 of 26 May 1987, it requested the Secretary-General to give the sector of international drug control priority, as a matter of urgency, in the allocation of available United Nations resources,

Noting that the General Assembly, in its resolution 42/113 of 7 December 1987, requested the Secretary-General to take steps to provide, within existing resources, appropriate support for strengthening the Division of Narcotic Drugs and the secretariat of the International Narcotics Control Board, *inter alia*, through redeployment,

Considering that both the International Conference on Drug Abuse and Illicit Trafficking and the United Nations Convention against Illicit Traffic in Narcotic Drugs and Psychotropic Substances, which was adopted on 19 December 1988, have called for new activities to be undertaken by the Division of Narcotic Drugs as secretariat of the Commission and on behalf of the Secretary-General, as well as by the International Narcotics Control Board and its secretariat,

Recalling the recommendation of the Committee for Programme and Co-ordination, with regard to the programme budget for the biennium 1988-1989, that the Secretary-General, in implementing General Assembly resolution 41/213 of 19 December 1986, in which he was requested to reduce the number of posts in the Secretariat by 15 per cent, should keep in mind the concerns expressed by Member States regarding the proposed reductions in posts in smaller offices, including those concerned with narcotics affairs,

Deeply concerned that the proposed cuts envisaged for the international drug control programme would adversely affect programmes which the Commission considers to be of priority,

Having considered the proposed programme budget for the biennium 1990-1991 for the Division of Narcotic Drugs,

1. *Endorses* the recommendations on priorities made by the Commission on Narcotic Drugs at its thirty-third session on the various programme elements contained in the programme of work of the Division of Narcotic Drugs Secretariat for the biennium 1990-1991;

2. *Draws to the attention* of Member States, in the light of resource reductions and in spite of the identification of priorities, the fact that without additional resources implementation of many important programme elements will be seriously impaired or prevented;

3. *Urges* States to implement resolution 3 of the United Nations Conference for the Adoption of a Convention against Illicit Traffic in Narcotic Drugs and Psychotropic Substances by taking appropriate steps in the General Assembly as well as in the financial organs of the Assembly to assign the appropriate priority and approve the necessary budgetary appropriations with a view to providing the Division of Narcotic Drugs and the secretariat of the International Narcotics Control Board with the necessary resources to discharge fully the tasks entrusted to them;

4. *Invites* the Secretary-General to take the necessary measures in conformity with General Assembly resolution 42/113.

Economic and Social Council resolution 1989/18

22 May 1989   Meeting 12   Adopted without vote

Approved by Second Committee (E/1989/76) without vote, 4 May (meeting 5); draft by Commission on Narcotic Drugs (E/1989/23); agenda item 12.

Drug addiction among children

On 22 May, by **decision 1989/123**, the Economic and Social Council recalled a 1988 General Assembly resolution,[17] in which the Assembly strongly condemned drug trafficking in all its forms, particularly those criminal activities that involved children in the use, production and illicit sale of narcotic drugs, and appealed to UNFDAC and relevant international agencies to assign high priority to support for programmes to rehabilitate drug-addicted minors. The Council requested the Secretary-General to submit to the Assembly at its 1989 session a report on the implementation of the resolution.

Regional concerns

Africa

In its 1989 report,[4] INCB noted a rapid expansion of illicit drug trafficking in Africa. It stated that the demonstration of firm political will by Governments to take the necessary action to permit effective control was of primary importance. To that end, the enactment of comprehensive laws and administrative regulations and the establishment of implementing agencies were essential first steps. A number of countries had adopted stronger measures to suppress illicit traffic, including the imposition of more severe penalties for trafficking and the establishment of closer co-operation with enforcement agencies in other countries. Efforts to combat drug trafficking were also accompanied by increased bilateral or multilateral cooperation during 1989.

Abuse of cannabis, grown clandestinely in many African countries, remained widespread. Heroin, principally from south-west Asia, was trafficked in increased quantities through Africa to destinations in Europe or North America. Cocaine abuse had not attained alarming proportions in countries of the continent, INCB reported, but cases of abuse were steadily increasing as a result of the use of Africa as a transit point by traffickers.

On 17 February,[18] the Commission on Narcotic Drugs recommended that the creation of three drug law enforcement training centres in the African region be considered, and requested UNFDAC to consider favourably financial requests for the organization of the centres. It also recommended technical aid for the establishment of drug laboratories to countries that lacked such facilities, and invited the Division of Narcotic Drugs, the International Criminal Police Organization, the Customs Co-operation Council and all other interested national and international bodies to consider co-ordinating law enforcement training and resources in the region to enhance their efficiency.

On the same date, the Commission recommended[19] that all African States develop systems for the exchange of information, obtain drug detection and identification equipment, undertake studies of the extent of illicit drug traffic and abuse and enact laws to combat it, and establish special administrations to apply the provisions of international drug control treaties.

Asia

East and South-East Asia. The INCB reported that opium production had increased in 1989 in the region. In the Lao People's Democratic Republic, favourable weather conditions raised harvests. In Myanmar, insurgent groups engaged in illicit drug trafficking took advantage of the prevailing internal situation in that country to increase production. In Thailand, the opium crop was estimated at some 30 tonnes, an increase of 10 per cent over 1988. Some 1,800 of approximately 5,000 hectares devoted to illicit poppy cultivation that had been detected were destroyed. Thai authorities were concerned at the increase in the use of violence and particularly firearms by traffickers. The growing AIDS epidemic in Thailand also had produced a notable increase in the number of HIV-positive heroin addicts.

In China, the trend towards increased drug trafficking on the borders of the Yunnan province continued during 1989. In April, China hosted in Beijing an INCB training seminar for national drug control administrators.

South Asia. The impact of the large illicit opium crop produced in South-East Asia was felt in Bangladesh, where abuse and illicit traffic increased in 1989. Illicit traffic also increased on India's eastern border. India was the only exporter of licit opium for medical and scientific requirements, and its poppy cultivation areas were limited to approximately 15,000 hectares in order to reduce stocks. The Indo-Pakistan Committee to combat drug trafficking met in New Delhi in May, and reached an agreement on several measures to increase co-operation and exchange information.

Europe

Abuse of narcotic drugs, mainly diverted from local sources, continued to be a problem in Eastern European countries. These nations were also confronted with the problem of transit traffic, especially the USSR and the countries along the so-called Balkan route. In June 1989, an expert group meeting convened in Belgrade to discuss ways to combat drug trafficking and organized crime. The participants were Albania, Bulgaria, Greece, Romania, Turkey and Yugoslavia. Over a period of two years, USSR customs officials had seized more than 10 tonnes of drugs, such as heroin or cannabis, and which were being smuggled to Western Europe. The USSR customs service had also

developed co-operative arrangements with more than 25 Western countries.

In Western Europe, the increase in drug-related deaths of recent years continued. Drug-related crime was rising more quickly than any other type of criminal offence, and seizures of heroin, cocaine, cannabis and amphetamines reached record levels in most countries. A number of political declarations were made at an Extraordinary Ministerial Conference held in London in May concerning the cocaine threat, the confiscation of proceeds of drug trafficking and the relationship between AIDS and drug addiction. Although less strict controls had been imposed at borders between certain countries of the European Economic Community, authorities found that drug seizures increased substantially, even though fewer persons were checked.

The Second Interregional Meeting of Heads of National Drug Law Enforcement Agencies (HONLEA) was held in Vienna from 11 to 15 September.[20]

Near and Middle East

Widespread illicit opium production continued in Afghanistan, although its actual extent and the amount of drug abuse remained unclear due to the unstable situation in many parts of the country. During the 1988/89 crop season in Pakistan, approximately 150 tonnes of opium had been produced, a figure comparable to that of the previous year. Eradication of poppy cultivation by aerial means was continued, but no significant results were achieved. Opiates continued to enter Iran, where there was a high incidence of abuse. No opium was produced in Turkey, but transit traffic in cannabis resin, heroin and morphine through the eastern frontier continued. In 1989, Turkey made formal agreements with Greece and Iran relating to co-operation in suppressing illegal trafficking.

On 17 February,[21] the Commission on Narcotic Drugs requested Governments to consider making contributions to UNFDAC to be used specifically for the development of a region-wide drug law enforcement training programme for the Near and Middle East, or other regions expressing similar interest. It also requested the Secretary-General, with the International Criminal Police Organization, the Customs Co-operation Council, the Arab Security Studies and Training Centre and other interested intergovernmental organizations, to identify drug law enforcement training requirements in the region and to make proposals to the Commission at its thirty-fourth session.

North America

In the United States, a survey indicated that the total number of "current" drug users had dropped 37 per cent since 1985, but the number of "frequent'' cocaine abusers had doubled. Intravenous drug abuse accounted for 31 per cent of all adult AIDS cases, and was the largest source of new AIDS cases in the United States. A new Director of National Drug Control Policy, with the overall responsibility for co-ordinating drug policy, took office in 1989, and the Federal Government intensified its war on drugs by significantly increasing the budgets of most federal drug-control agencies. A new federal law, which entered into force in 1989, allowed the Federal Government to track and claim ownership of laundered drug money. On the international level, the United States began or continued its co-operation with a number of countries in combating drug abuse, including the Andean countries, Mexico and the Bahamas.

Mexico increased significantly the material and human resources it allocated to the battle against drug trafficking. Some 25 per cent of its armed forces had been assigned to fight illicit drug trafficking, and the budget for drug control activities was increased by 174 per cent. Between December 1988 and August 1989, the authorities destroyed 2,900 hectares of opium poppy and 2,400 hectares of cannabis.

In Canada, cocaine abuse was rising at a faster rate than previously. In 1989, changes in Canadian law went into effect that provided the courts with increased powers to seize the assets of drug criminals.

Latin America and the Caribbean

Drug abuse was reported to be spreading throughout Latin America, adding to the continuing problem of drug trafficking, which had already become a dominant public issue. Heavily armed drug cartels with enormous financial resources continued to undermine political institutions, disrupt national economies and murder officials and private citizens. In addition to the production of cocaine and cannabis, a new threat emerged involving opium-poppy cultivation and heroin processing.

Following a mission to Bolivia, INCB urged that a new drug control law be resolutely applied and that a programme of eradicating the coca bush be pursued rigorously. The Brazilian variety of coca was being increasingly cultivated by Brazilian Indian tribes at the instigation of Colombian traffickers.

In Colombia, escalating violence directed against Government institutions and individuals combating drug trafficking led the authorities to declare an all-out war against the traffickers. Measures decreed by the President included the seizure of traffickers' assets and increased protection for judges. During the first half of 1989, Colombian authorities conducted successful operations in the middle Magdalena region, an area where drug traffickers and guerrilla groups were operating.

In Ecuador, eradication operations between 1984 and 1989 appeared to have decimated coca-bush cultivation. In Peru, efforts to eradicate illicit coca-bush cultivation continued, despite terrorist acts and armed violence by insurgent groups.

Traffickers continued to expand operations in Central America in reaction to stricter controls and enforcement in several South American countries. A sharp increase in illicit opium-poppy cultivation was reported in Guatemala, despite eradication efforts that included the manual destruction of some 1,300 hectares. A programme to track essential chemicals and precursors used in the manufacture of cocaine and heroin—the first of its kind in Central America—was also established.

Stricter measures against drug trafficking in the Bahamas had a major impact on the pattern of illicit traffic. In Cuba, four high-level officials were executed and several others sentenced to prison in 1989 as a result of their involvement with Colombian drug cartels. In Jamaica, authorities continued the cannabis eradication campaign, which had yielded significant results.

Oceania

In Australia, a three-year national campaign against drug abuse was extended for another three years, a reflection of the Government's continued commitment to drug abuse control. More heroin was seized in 1989 than during the previous year. A large seizure of heroin destined for Australia was made in Vanuatu.

Organizational questions

Commission on Narcotic Drugs

The Commission on Narcotic Drugs held its thirty-third session in Vienna from 6 to 17 February 1989.[22] It decided that it would hold a special session in 1990 to consider further measures to facilitate the entry into force of the 1988 Convention against Illegal Traffic in Narcotic Drugs and Psychotropic Substances, as well as action to improve regional co-operation in drug law enforcement.

ECONOMIC AND SOCIAL COUNCIL ACTION

On 22 May, on the recommendation of its Second Committee, the Economic and Social Council adopted **resolution 1989/17** without vote.

Special session of the Commission on Narcotic Drugs

The Economic and Social Council,

Recalling its resolution 2001(LX) of 12 May 1976,

Recognizing that the complex health, legal, social and human problems associated with drug abuse require the continuous attention of the Commission on Narcotic Drugs,

Aware of the need for the Commission to consider urgently further measures that may be required to facilitate the entry into force of the 1988 United Nations Convention against Illicit Traffic in Narcotic Drugs and Psychotropic Substances or, if the Convention has entered into force in the interim, the measures required to ensure implementation of its provisions; to consider any urgent questions relating to the possible scheduling of substances under the provisions of the international drug control treaties, following receipt of recommendations to that effect from the World Health Organization; and to consider appropriate action to improve regional co-operation in drug law enforcement,

Decides that the Commission on Narcotic Drugs shall hold a special session of five working days in 1990 at a time when it will not overlap with other meetings and within existing United Nations resources, for the following purposes:

(a) To consider urgently further measures that may be required to facilitate the entry into force of the 1988 United Nations Convention against Illicit Traffic in Narcotic Drugs and Psychotropic Substances or, if the Convention has entered into force in the interim, the measures required to ensure implementation of its provisions;

(b) To consider any urgent questions relating to the possible scheduling of substances under the provisions of the international drug control treaties, following receipt of recommendations to that effect from the World Health Organization;

(c) To consider appropriate action to improve regional co-operation in drug law enforcement;

(d) To consider the report of the International Narcotics Control Board for 1989, an interim report from the United Nations Fund for Drug Abuse Control, and other relevant matters requiring urgent attention.

Economic and Social Council resolution 1989/17
22 May 1989   Meeting 12   Adopted without vote

Approved by Second Committee (E/1989/76) without vote, 4 May (meeting 5); draft by Commission on Narcotic Drugs (E/1989/23); agenda item 12.

Also on 22 May, the Council approved the provisional agenda and documentation of the Commission's eleventh special session (**decision 1989/119**), took note of the report on its thirty-third session (**decision 1989/122**) and approved the provisional agenda and documentation for its thirty-fourth session (**decision 1989/118**).

International Narcotics Control Board

By **decision 1989/121** of 22 May 1989, the Economic and Social Council took note of the Board's 1988 report.[23] On 10 February, by **decision 1989/102**, the Council decided to discontinue the practice of constituting a Committee on Candidatures to select candidates for election to INCB.

REFERENCES

[1]YUN 1988, p. 689, GA res. 43/120, 8 Dec. 1988. [2]A/44/572. [3]YUN 1988, p. 690. [4]E/INCB/1989/1. [5]YUN 1988, p. 683, GA res. 43/122, 8 Dec. 1988. [6]A/44/601. [7]YUN 1979, p. 933, GA res. 34/177, 17 Dec. 1979. [8]A/44/600 & Corr.1. [9]YUN 1987, p. 900. [10]Ibid., p. 901. [11]E/1989/23 (res.4(XXXIII)). [12]DP/1989/19. [13]E/CN.7/1989/16. [14]YUN 1961, p. 382. [15]E/INCB/1989/1/Supp. [16]E/CN.7/1989/8 & Corr.1. [17]YUN 1988, p. 691, GA res. 43/121, 8 Dec. 1988. [18]E/1989/23 (res. 1(XXXIII)). [19]Ibid., (res. 2(XXXIII)). [20]E/CN.7/1990/2. [21]E/1989/23 (res. 3(XXXIII)). [22]E/1989/23. [23]*Report of the International Narcotics Control Board for 1988* (E/INCB/1988/1), Sales No. E.88.XI.4.

Chapter XVII

Statistics

The United Nations Statistical Commission in 1989 adopted two major economic classifications: the third revision of the International Standard Industrial Classification of All Economic Activities and the provisional Central Product Classification. Their adoption represented the culmination of more than a decade of effort by both the Statistical Office of the UN Secretariat and the Commission, in co-operation with the European Economic Community and other international organizations. The Economic and Social Council recommended that Member States adopt the revised Industrial Classification and make use of the Central Product Classification.

The importance of development indicators in evaluating progress achieved was discussed by the Economic and Social Council and the General Assembly. The Council, in May, strongly supported the work of the UN Statistical Office, the UN Research Institute for Social Development and the World Bank in producing development indicators. In December, the Assembly requested the Office and the Institute to pursue actively their co-operation with the other relevant bodies of the UN system.

With regard to the revised System of National Accounts, a recommendation to defer its adoption until 1993, owing to insufficient time for the completion of the full draft, was made by the Inter-Secretariat Working Group on National Accounts.

UN statistical bodies

Statistical Commission

The Statistical Commission held its twenty-fifth session in New York from 6 to 15 February 1989.[1] It discussed and made recommendations in connection with three special issues: co-ordination of international statistical activities; recruitment and selection of professional staff for work in national statistical offices and statistical services of the United Nations; and recurrent UN statistical publications. Other recommendations concerned: the System of National Accounts (SNA); the System of Balances of the National Economy (MPS); links between SNA and MPS; service statistics; the International Standard Industrial Classification of All Economic Activities and the Central Product Classification; the International Classification of Status in Employment; price statistics; population and housing censuses; social statistics and indicators; environment statistics; patterns of consumption; general devel-

opment and integration of methodological work; technical co-operation in statistics; the current state of statistics and statistical development in developing countries; the National Household Survey Capability Programme; World Bank initiatives in the design of permanent integrated household surveys; co-ordination and integration of international statistical programmes; and programme questions.

On 22 May, by **decision 1989/115**, the Economic and Social Council took note of the Commission's report on its twenty-fifth session and approved the provisional agenda and documentation for its twenty-sixth (1991) session.

Working Group on Statistical Programmes and Co-ordination

The Statistical Commission examined a report on the twelfth (1987) session[2] of its Working Group on International Statistical Programmes and Co-ordination. It noted that the Working Group had set out its views on co-ordination of *ad hoc* requests to Member States for statistics from non-statistical units of the United Nations and other international organizations; co-ordination of recurrent statistical data collection, processing and sharing among international organizations; representation of regional intergovernmental statistical bodies in the Statistical Commission; and co-ordination of international statistical activities as a special topic. The Commission also noted that the Working Group had expressed views on special topics to be taken up by the Commission at future sessions, and that it had reviewed progress and plans on the revision of SNA and environment statistics.

At its thirteenth session (Geneva, 11-14 September 1989),[3] the Working Group reviewed progress and plans on the revision of SNA and on the International Comparison Programme (ICP), and finalized the provisional agenda for the twenty-sixth session of the Commission. It also considered ways to accelerate statistical development while ensuring co-ordination in selected fields of statistics.

ACC Sub-Committee

The Sub-Committee on Statistical Activities of the Administrative Committee on Co-ordination (ACC) held its twenty-third session in 1989 (Geneva, 19-23 June).[4] It considered a survey of work plans, follow-up to 1989 decisions of the Statistical Commission, processing and dissemination of trade statistics, publication and dissemination policy, including co-ordination of statistical data bases, external debt statistics, environment statistics, revision of SNA, service statistics, general price statistics and ICP, population and housing censuses, civil registration and vital statistics, social statistics and indicators, indicative patterns of consumption, tourism and migration statistics, and status in employment classification.

The Sub-Committee also considered statistical implications of the single market of the European Economic Community (EEC), co-ordination of technical co-operation in statistics, monitoring achievement of social goals in the 1990s, the National Household Survey Capability Programme, the Living Standards Measurement Study and the Social Dimensions of Adjustment project, and review of the base year for international statistics.

The Sub-Committee recommended that its next session be held in Geneva from 18 to 22 June 1990.

Economic statistics

Environment statistics

After considering a report[5] on environment statistics, the Statistical Commission reaffirmed the high priority attached to that subject and commended the joint efforts of the United Nations Environment Programme, the Statistical Office, the World Bank and other organizations on the linkage of environmental accounting to SNA by means of satellite accounts. It endorsed the preparation of a handbook on environmental accounting, and recommended that a group of specialists from interested countries be established to assist the Statistical Office in developing and implementing the environment statistics programme. The Commission stressed the need for securing extra-budgetary resources or otherwise mobilizing external support for rapid implementation of the environment statistics programme of the Statistical Office and the regional commissions.

National accounts and balances

A progress report[6] on the revision of the System of National Accounts was submitted in 1989 to the Statistical Commission.

The Commission reaffirmed the original objectives of the SNA revision—simplification and clarification, harmonization and updating the system to fit new circumstances; it assigned the highest priority to work on the SNA review, and specified that handbooks should be prepared as soon as possible, with the active involvement of developing countries.

During 1989, the Expert Group on SNA Co-ordination met in January in Luxembourg, and in July and September in New York, to discuss outstanding issues and to review the first draft chapters of the revised SNA.

At a meeting of the Inter-Secretariat Working Group on National Accounts (New York, 20 September), widespread concern was expressed over the insufficient time before the twenty-sixth (1991) session of the Commission to resolve outstanding methodological issues, to complete and review the full draft of the revised SNA, and to ensure that it took into account all comments received. Accordingly, the Working Group recommended that the draft be submitted in 1991 for information and comments only, and be considered for adoption in 1993.

The Commission also had before it a note of the Secretary-General[6] transmitting a report of the secretariat of the Council for Mutual Economic Assistance (CMEA), containing information on developments in MPS. Noting that most countries with centrally planned economies intended to continue work to bring SNA and MPS closer, and the increased number of co-operation projects between countries using MPS and those using SNA, the Commission urged further elaboration of MPS. The Commission welcomed the new orientation of the work on links between SNA and MPS, with a view to making the two systems more applicable to countries with different social and economic systems. It endorsed the continuation of work on the linkages by the Statistical Office, particularly in conjunction with CMEA, with the aim of their integration.

An expert group meeting on the reconciliation of SNA/MPS standards of national accounting (Moscow, 4-9 December)[7] examined the ways to improve harmonization between SNA and MPS and how the two systems could be further integrated, both in theory and in practice. It was recognized that there was a problem in converting data from national currencies into a common unit for international comparisons of levels of aggregates. For that purpose, the calculation of purchasing power parity was strongly recommended. Other recommendations dealt with the design of an integrated framework to permit the derivation of major aggregates of both SNA and MPS from the same coherent system of balances; guidance on variations in institutional arrangements; and identification of non-material services.

Price statistics

The Statistical Commission in 1989 considered a report[6] of the Secretary-General on the International Comparison Programme. Work on phase V of ICP, with 1985 as reference year, was welcomed. Results for EEC, the Organisation for Economic Co-operation and Development (OECD) and the European Comparison Programme had already been published; computations had been finalized for the African comparison; and nearly final results were available for the Asia and the Pacific comparison. A partial and preliminary world comparison covering 57 countries had been compiled jointly by the Statistical Office of the European Communities (EUROSTAT) and the UN Statistical Office. It was noted that in phase VI (1990), ICP would likely consist of regional comparisons only, with some possible links among them, owing to the problems of core comparisons and funding of central co-ordination.

The Inter-Secretariat Working Group on ICP convened in New York on 10 and 11 July to review organizational and other arrangements for phase VI and to expedite the preparation and dissemination of technical documents connected with ICP methodology and use of ICP data, particularly the handbook on ICP methods.

An expert group meeting (Paris, 12-16 June), convened jointly by OECD, EUROSTAT and the UN Statistical Office, dealt with outstanding methodological issues and financing of ICP.

Service statistics

A report[6] of the Secretary-General on plans for the further development of service statistics, including international trade in services, was considered by the Statistical Commission in February.

The Commission noted the progress achieved by the Voorburg Group on Service Statistics, a co-operative effort among volunteer national and international statistical agencies to address problems related to data gaps and conceptual issues in service statistics. It welcomed the intention of volunteer countries, in association with participating international organizations, to continue efforts to promote methodology and international comparability in the field of service statistics. It also noted with satisfaction that the work programme of the Voorburg Group was entirely in accord with its own priorities. With regard to priorities for further work on the methodological development of service statistics, the most support was expressed for work on the guidelines on the statistics of financial, business and information services.

The Commission endorsed the continuation of work on service statistics, including trade in services, in appropriate co-ordination with other international organizations. The Secretary-General was requested to seek, in co-operation with international organizations, extrabudgetary funding to support a comprehensive programme involving methodological development, data compilation and technical co-operation to advance work in the important new field of service statistics.

In August, the Statistical Office and the International Monetary Fund finalized their joint inquiry into national practices and selected methodological problems in trade-in-services statistics. The

Voorburg Group held its fourth meeting (Ottawa, Canada, October), which covered classification systems in service statistics, price and quantity in services, trade in services, and services that would, among other things, test the application of international standards of services classification according to product and activity. The Group also decided to undertake a survey of its participants' priorities in service statistics in order to facilitate the focus of the Group's future discussions.

International economic classifications

At its February session, the Statistical Commission considered a report[8] on the revision and harmonization of international economic classifications. It also had before it the final draft of the International Standard Industrial Classification of All Economic Activities (ISIC), Revision 3, and the final draft of the Central Product Classification (CPC). The Commission approved the final draft of ISIC, Rev. 3, and the provisional CPC, both modified to take into account comments by the Commission. The Secretary-General was requested: to prepare a publication on ISIC, Rev. 3, together with indexes and correlation tables between the Classification, the Harmonized Commodity Description and Coding System, the Standard International Trade Classification, Revision 3, and the provisional CPC; to prepare a publication on CPC, with explanatory notes, for the services part of the classification, as a provisional document; and to publish and circulate ISIC, Rev. 3, and CPC, and to draw them to the attention of UN Member States or members of the specialized agencies.

The Commission recommended that UN Member States adopt ISIC, Rev. 3, or use it in reporting data according to kind of economic activity for the purpose of international comparison, and make use of CPC as a provisional classification in order to gain experience in obtaining international comparability for data according to goods and services. It also recommended that the Statistical Office provide guidance to countries in implementing the recommendations, including the provision of necessary technical co-operation and supplementary documentation.

With regard to the International Classification of Status in Employment (ICSE), the Commission strongly endorsed its proposed revision[9] by the International Labour Office, in collaboration with the UN Statistical Office, and supported the strategy of establishing networks and informal groups for that work. It recommended detailed examination of the classifications of status in employment currently used by countries and of the problems experienced in their application, prior to any revision. The International Labour Office was to report in 1991 on the progress of work on ICSE.

On 22 May, the Economic and Social Council, on the recommendation of its First (Economic) Committee, adopted **resolution 1989/3** without vote.

International economic classifications

The Economic and Social Council,

Recalling resolution 4(XV) adopted by the Statistical Commission at its fifteenth session, in 1968,

Considering:

(a) The need for implementation of the programme on harmonization of international economic classifications developed by different international organizations,

(b) The importance of international data comparability for various statistics classified according to kind of economic activity or goods and services,

(c) The need to maintain co-ordination among the International Standard Industrial Classification of All Economic Activities (ISIC), the General Industrial Classification of Economic Activities within the European Communities (NACE) and the Classification of Branches of the National Economy (CBNE) of the Council for Mutual Economic Assistance, as well as among the Harmonized Commodity Description and Coding System (HS) of the Customs Co-operation Council, the Standard International Trade Classification (SITC) and the new Central Product Classification (CPC),

(d) The desirability of integrating different types of international economic classifications developed by different international organizations and ensuring their consistency with the revised System of National Accounts and the System of Balances of the National Economy,

(e) The action taken by the Joint Working Group on World Level Classifications of the Statistical Office of the United Nations Secretariat and the Statistical Office of the European Communities, by the United Nations Expert Group on Harmonization of Economic Classifications and by the Voorburg Group on Service Statistics to resolve the outstanding issues related to the third revision of the International Standard Industrial Classification of All Economic Activities and the development of the Central Product Classification,

(f) The proposed revision of the International Standard Industrial Classification of All Economic Activities, Revision 2, as described in the report of the Secretary-General on the revision and harmonization of international economic classifications, to be known as the International Standard Industrial Classification of All Economic Activities, Revision 3,

(g) The proposed new Central Product Classification, as described in the report of the Secretary-General, to be known as the provisional Central Product Classification,

1. *Recommends* that Member States:

(a) Adopt, as soon as possible, the International Standard Industrial Classification of All Economic Activities, Revision 3, with such modifications as may be necessary to meet national requirements, without disturbing the framework of the classification, or use, for purposes of international comparison, the International Standard Industrial Classification of All Economic Activities, Revision 3, in reporting data classified according to kind of economic activity;

(b) Make use of the provisional Central Product Classification in order to gain experience in obtaining international comparability for data classified according to goods and services;

2. *Requests* the Secretary-General:

(a) To prepare a publication on the International Standard Industrial Classification of All Economic Activities, Revision 3, together with indexes and correlation tables between that Classification, the Harmonized Commodity Description and Coding System, the Standard International Trade Classification, Revision 3, and the provisional Central Product Classification, based on the provisional text before the Statistical Commission at its twenty-fifth session and in the light of the conclusions of the Commission;

(b) To prepare a publication on the provisional Central Product Classification, together with the explanatory notes for the services part of the classification, based on the provisional text before the Statistical Commission at its twenty-fifth session and in the light of the conclusions of the Commission;

(c) To publish and circulate the International Standard Industrial Classification of All Economic Activities, Revision 3, and the provisional Central Product Classification and to bring them to the attention of States Members of the United Nations and members of the specialized agencies for adoption.

Economic and Social Council resolution 1989/3

22 May 1989   Meeting 12   Adopted without vote

Approved by First Committee (E/1989/85) without vote, 17 May (meeting 7); draft by Statistical Commission (E/1989/21); agenda item 6*(a)*.

Social and demographic statistics

Social indicators

The Statistical Commission in 1989 considered reports of the Secretary-General on international co-ordination of social statistics and indicators and development of statistics and indicators on special population groups[8] and on the development of guidelines on national accounts for women's contribution to development.[8] The Commission noted that there had been an increasing awareness of the need for social statistics and indicators in both developed and developing countries in order to assess socio-economic trends and problems and provide relevant inputs for policy formulation and programme management. It discussed the importance of using population and housing censuses as a basic source of social and related indicators; the development of social data bases on microcomputers; the need for statistics on poverty; the importance of understanding and documenting the underlying methodology in each subject field in order to avoid misinterpretation and misuse of indicators; the usefulness of international comparability; and the importance of creating broad, general support for social statistics.

The Commission endorsed the programmes of the Statistical Office in co-ordinating international work on social statistics, including the new emphasis on the measurement of poverty, and on the development of statistics on women, children, youth, the elderly, the disabled and other special population groups. It recommended that further work in the Statistical Office focus on the development of a co-ordinated UN system data base for selected social statistics and indicators of common interest at the national and international levels. It recommended that national and international statistical services collect social statistics and indicators essential for reliable monitoring of human factors and social impacts of development, and disseminate them in non-technical form on a frequent and timely basis and in a comparable form.

Population and housing censuses

The Statistical Commission had before it a report[9] on the general development and integration of methodological work in population and housing censuses. The Commission noted that, while a range of national and regional activities were taking place relating to the 1990 round of population and housing censuses, many developing countries would require assistance to supplement their own resources. In that connection, the United Nations Population Fund and other multilateral agencies were urged to continue their support to developing countries to enable them to meet national and subnational needs in carrying out population and housing censuses. The Commission strongly supported technical co-operation activities to improve training in census management, sampling, quality control procedures, data processing and analysis, and endorsed the recommendations of the 1988 Cairo International Conference on Dissemination and Use of Census Data for the development of videotape training materials and an expert system in census taking. The Commission recommended that post-enumeration surveys be carried out, and that work be undertaken to establish data bases of census results and to integrate data on special population groups with related socio-economic data.

Patterns of consumption

In 1989, the Statistical Commission considered a report[9] of the Secretary-General and the United Nations Research Institute for Social Development (UNRISD) on qualitative aspects of the development of indicators on patterns of consumption. The Commission agreed that there was an urgent need for methodological work on such indicators to assess qualitative aspects of development in the long term, and in connection with the preparations for the fourth UN development decade (the 1990s). Ongoing case-studies of UNRISD

would be valuable in identifying data sources and gaps relative to the needed indicators.

The Commission urged interested donors to provide extrabudgetary funds for UNRISD to increase the number of its case-studies to ensure representation from as many geographical regions as possible and to include developing countries at various levels of development. It emphasized that the whole issue of development should be dealt with, including its social, economic, technological and environmental aspects, and that it be treated in the light of their interrelationship. The Secretary-General and UNRISD were requested to prepare a final report on the case-studies and qualitative aspects of development, for consideration by the Commission in 1991.

In connection with Morocco's proposal that it host a meeting of a group of high-level experts, the Commission requested UNRISD to make the necessary contacts with that Government and with interested organizations, including the World Bank and the UN Statistical Office, in order to convene such a meeting to review the progress made on development indicators and to explore the availability of extrabudgetary resources.

ECONOMIC AND SOCIAL COUNCIL ACTION

On 22 May, on the recommendation of its First Committee, the Economic and Social Council adopted **resolution 1989/4** without vote.

Patterns of consumption and qualitative indicators of development

The Economic and Social Council,

Recalling General Assembly resolution 40/179 of 17 December 1985 and Economic and Social Council resolution 1987/6 of 26 May 1987,

Recalling also the report of the Statistical Commission on its twenty-fourth session, in particular, the section on development indicators,

Recognizing that the subject of patterns of consumption and related socio-economic indicators is of considerable importance and priority for developing countries,

Reaffirming that the choice of indicators is a critical matter if structural shifts and trends in the development process are to be accurately assessed,

Stressing that the development of indicators tailored to the fundamental economic and socio-cultural needs of the population in the fields identified in General Assembly resolution 40/179 would help to orient national development and support international co-operation by helping Governments to formulate and follow policies better geared to the well-being of the population,

Stressing also that in order for the international development strategy for the fourth United Nations development decade to be successful, there must be a range of indicators relating to economic and social progress, the application of concerted objectives and early-warning systems,

Having examined the report of the Secretary-General and the United Nations Research Institute for Social Development entitled "Development of indicators on patterns of consumption: qualitative aspects of development'',

1. *Strongly supports* the work of the Statistical Office of the Secretariat, the United Nations Research Institute for Social Development and the World Bank, which have made considerable progress in producing development indicators, and encourages the United Nations Children's Fund, the United Nations Environment Programme, the Food and Agriculture Organization of the United Nations, the United Nations Educational, Scientific and Cultural Organization, the World Health Organization and the regional commissions to continue their work on indicators tailored to the needs identified by the General Assembly in its resolution 40/179;

2. *Affirms* the need to identify, as a phase in the development process, patterns of consumption tailored to the well-being of populations and defined as a series of numerical indicative objectives to permit the evaluation, for the use of countries, of the adequate level of satisfaction of fundamental economic and socio-cultural needs in regard to food, housing, clothing, education, health care and necessary social services;

3. *Considers* that this requires a reliable measuring instrument consisting of a set of indicators related to living conditions, employment and the circumstances underlying them;

4. *Encourages* countries, in this regard, to improve their basic statistical programmes and capabilities and to make efforts to develop the collection, processing, analysis and dissemination of data relating to patterns of consumption, and invites the international community to strengthen the national capabilities of the developing countries with respect to the collection of integrated socio-economic data and their processing, in particular by microcomputer, with a view to having better and more up-to-date data;

5. *Agrees* that the *Handbook on Social Indicators* prepared by the Statistical Office of the Secretariat and the Living Standards Measurement Study and other conceptual work undertaken by the World Bank should contain guidelines for the selection and compilation of indicators in the precise fields referred to in General Assembly resolution 40/179;

6. *Recommends* that different ways of developing new indicators be explored and that advantage be taken in particular of the household survey mechanisms available at the national level so as to include therein appropriate modules relating to patterns of consumption and the qualitative aspects of development, while making wide use of conventional survey techniques as well as of new methods of collecting and processing data;

7. *Requests* the United Nations Research Institute for Social Development and the Statistical Office of the Secretariat to continue their collaboration on the in-depth analysis of the views of Governments, in particular those of the developing countries, and on the timely completion of the national case-studies, of which there should be a greater number, endeavouring to ensure their methodological coherence and the representation of all the developing regions and taking into consideration the economic, technological, social and environmental aspects of development;

8. *Welcomes* the offer made by the Government of Morocco to act as host, in 1990, in co-operation with the United Nations Research Institute for Social Development and any other interested organizations, in-

cluding the World Bank and the Statistical Office of the Secretariat, to an international conference of high-level experts, open to the participation of the members of the Statistical Commission, for the purpose of examining methodological questions and the conceptual aspects of the qualitative indicators of development and of consolidating the various research projects and studies currently under way on that subject;

9. *Agrees* that the conference would be preceded by a preparatory working group meeting to be convened at Geneva as soon as possible, under the auspices of the United Nations Research Institute for Social Development and with the participation of appropriate international organizations, including the Food and Agriculture Organization of the United Nations, the United Nations Educational, Scientific and Cultural Organization and the World Bank, with a view to drawing up, *inter alia*, a common conceptual framework with a relevant set of core indicators;

10. *Recommends* that appropriate extrabudgetary resources be allocated for the preparation of the case-studies referred to in paragraph 7 above, and invites interested donor countries, the relevant international organizations and other bodies and institutions wishing to participate in the research work on patterns of consumption and qualitative indicators of development to make voluntary contributions for that purpose to the United Nations Research Institute for Social Development;

11. *Requests* the Secretary-General to ensure the proper dissemination of the present resolution and to take it into consideration in the future work programme of the Statistical Office of the Secretariat, and requests the Secretary-General and the United Nations Research Institute for Social Development to submit a final report, containing recommendations, to the Statistical Commission at its twenty-sixth session.

Economic and Social Council resolution 1989/4

22 May 1989   Meeting 12   Adopted without vote

Approved by First Committee (E/1989/85) without vote, 17 May (meeting 7); draft by Statistical Commission (E/1989/21); agenda item 6(a)).

GENERAL ASSEMBLY ACTION

On 22 December, on the recommendation of the Second (Economic and Financial) Committee, the General Assembly adopted **resolution 44/234** without vote.

Patterns of consumption and qualitative indicators of development

The General Assembly,

Recalling its resolution 40/179 of 17 December 1985, Economic and Social Council resolution 1987/6 of 26 May 1987 and the reports of the Statistical Commission on its twenty-fourth and twenty-fifth sessions, in particular the sections on development indicators, and taking note of Council resolution 1989/4 of 22 May 1989,

Reiterating that the subject of patterns of consumption and related socio-economic indicators is of considerable importance and high priority for developing countries,

Reaffirming that, in order for the international development strategy for the fourth United Nations development decade to be successful, there must be a range of indicators relating to economic and social progress, the application of concerted objectives and early-warning systems, with due regard for the economic, technological, social and environmental aspects of development,

1. *Endorses* Economic and Social Council resolution 1989/4, and requests the Statistical Office of the Secretariat and the United Nations Research Institute for Social Development to pursue actively their co-operation with the other relevant bodies of the United Nations system, with a view to achieving the objectives set out in paragraphs 2 and 3 of Council resolution 1989/4;

2. *Recognizes* that the identification of indicative patterns of consumption and the development of qualitative indicators of development would be extremely useful in the evaluation of the progress achieved in the implementation of the international development strategy and would make a substantial contribution to the work of a United Nations conference on environment and development;

3. *Invites* interested donor countries, the relevant international organizations and other bodies and institutions wishing to participate in the research work on patterns of consumption and qualitative indicators of development to make voluntary contributions for that purpose to the United Nations Research Institute for Social Development with a view to the holding in good time of the preparatory meeting and the international conference of high-level experts referred to in paragraphs 8 and 9 of Economic and Social Council resolution 1989/4;

4. *Requests* the Secretary-General to invite the United Nations Research Institute for Social Development to submit a preliminary progress report to the General Assembly at its forty-fifth session on the implementation of the present resolution and of Economic and Social Council resolution 1989/4.

General Assembly resolution 44/234

22 December 1989   Meeting 85   Adopted without vote

Approved by Second Committee (A/44/832/Add.1) by consensus, 21 November (meeting 41); draft by Malaysia for Group of 77 (A/C.2/44/L.23/Rev.1); agenda item 12.
Meeting numbers. GA 44th session: 2nd Committee 15-17, 19, 20, 25, 29, 31, 34, 41; plenary 85.

National Household Survey Capability Programme

In February, the Statistical Commission considered a report[9] on the long-range future of the National Household Survey Capability Programme (NHSCP). In operation in 30 developing countries, the Programme had generated world-wide interest in the role of household surveys as a means of collecting much-needed information on the demographic, social and socio-economic aspects of household populations, and was well set to meet the target coverage of 45 countries by 1991, the report stated. The Commission emphasized the need for effective co-ordination with other household survey programmes.

World Bank household survey initiatives

The Statistical Commission had before it a World Bank report[9] on its initiatives in the design of permanent integrated household surveys: the Living Standards Measurement Study (LSMS) and Social Dimensions of Adjustment (SDA) programmes.

The LSMS programme, launched in 1980 as a research project, had a threefold objective: collection of policy-relevant high-quality data, rapid processing of results, and appropriate policy-oriented analysis of data. It had moved into an operational phase, and several countries had either taken up or proposed to take up integrated multi-subject surveys of the LSMS type on a continuous basis. The Commission endorsed the World Bank's effort to continue to document in detail and disseminate widely the experiences of LSMS.

The SDA programme, designed to assist in minimizing the impact of macro-economic adjustment measures on sub-Saharan Africa, was endorsed by the Commission as an important, unique initiative in capability-building in Africa directed at data gathering and use in the formulation of national policies for structural adjustment. The World Bank was invited to report on the progress of LSMS and SDA, including fuller details of the survey methodology proposed for the SDA programme, for submission to the Commission in 1991.

Special issues

Considering the issue of co-ordination of international statistical activities, the Commission was of the opinion that the existing institutional structures for promoting co-ordination and statistical development were appropriate and effective. The structures included the Commission itself, regional intergovernmental bodies, the Commission's Working Group on International Statistical Programmes and Co-ordination, and the ACC Sub-Committee on Statistical Activities. Some areas requiring additional development and co-ordination, including standardization of definitions, classifications and practices, were environment statistics, indicators for development, productivity statistics and statistics on illiteracy. The Commission, recognizing that considerable success had been achieved in co-ordination in a number of areas, requested international organizations to investigate ways to facilitate the translation of international methodological publications into local languages and to help promote implementation of international guidelines. It requested the Statistical Office to investigate the possibility of developing additional mechanisms for the exchange of country experiences in statistical development and standardization.

With regard to recruitment and selection of professional staff for work in national statistical offices and UN statistical services, the Commission recognized the importance of recruiting technically qualified professional staff in national and international statistical services, including the need for a variety of skills and subject-matter specializations to cover the wide range of responsibilities that statistical offices were to meet. It requested more national statistical offices providing specialized and general training courses for their staff to consider the possibility of opening those programmes to participants from other countries and statistical staff from international organizations. The Statistical Office was to consider the feasibility of collecting information on training curricula and sharing it with national statistical services.

As for recurrent UN statistical publications, the Commission emphasized that those prepared by the Statistical Office were unique and especially useful to Governments, universities and research centres. Particularly for developing countries, those publications were the basic source of information in the economic and social area. The Commission endorsed the continuation of the Office's statistical publications programme, and requested the Office to continue the ongoing review of recurrent publications in order to assess current usefulness and relevance in relation to user needs and to improve timeliness and quality. Alternative methods of disseminating statistical information should also be explored.

Other statistical activities

Technical co-operation

The Statistical Commission had before it a report[9] of the Secretary-General, in which he summarized the technical co-operation programmes in statistics for the period 1985-1988. The Commission, endorsing the technical co-operation activities in statistics carried out by the UN Department of Technical Co-operation for Development (DTCD), recommended that DTCD take the lead, in co-operation with the Statistical Office, in promoting capacities in data systems and informatics technology. The Statistical Office was urged to play a leading role in the area of co-ordination in multilateral and bilateral technical co-operation statistical activities. The Commission supported new initiatives in technical co-operation related to the generation of trade statistics, educational video cassettes, civil registration and vital statistics, and statistics on women and disabled persons.

In a later report,[10] the Secretary-General said that the main activities of DTCD included work related to the promotion of NHSCP, and assistance in demographic statistics and population censuses. The total cost of the support provided by the UN technical co-operation programme for the formulation and execution of country, regional and interregional projects was $33.6 million for 1989. Workshops and seminars organized by DTCD during 1989

dealt with: disability statistics, national accounts development and training, external trade, planning organization and administration for large-scale demographic and social data-collection activities, population data bases and related topics, and civil registration. On-the-job and international training and technical expert services were also provided to national statistical offices during the year.

Statistics in developing countries

The Statistical Commission in 1989 considered a report[11] on the current state of statistics and statistical development in developing countries. The Commission noted that the report would have been more useful if references to quality, timeliness and coverage, and topics such as debt and financial transactions and health had been included. It endorsed strategies proposed in the report as useful guides for multilateral and bilateral technical co-operation in statistics. These related to identification of the value of statistics; a balanced approach to technical co-operation; statistical training; data processing; technical advice to countries; statistical organization and management; co-ordination of technical co-operation activities; and the needs of the statistically least developed countries.

Programme questions

In February, the Statistical Commission reviewed the statistical work of international organizations for the period 1986 to June 1988. It approved the UN Statistical Office 1990-1991 work programme, giving highest priority to further development of SNA and linkage with MPS. It urged mobilization of the necessary extrabudgetary resources or development of other approaches, along the lines of the Voorburg Group model, to ensure continuation of methodological work, on the understanding that any such experiments would preserve the roles of the Statistical Commission and the Statistical Office. The Commission expressed general support for the proposed objectives and strategies of the medium-term plan for the period 1992-1997.

REFERENCES

[1]E/1989/21. [2]YUN 1987, p. 921. [3]E/CN.3/1991/2. [4]ACC/1989/PG/6. [5]YUN 1988, p. 698. [6]*Ibid.*, p. 699. [7]E/CN.3/1991/11. [8]YUN 1988, p. 700. [9]*Ibid.*, p. 701. [10]E/CN.3/1991/25. [11]YUN 1988, p. 702.

PUBLICATIONS

1987 International Trade Statistics Yearbook, vols. I and II (STAT/SER.G/36), Sales No. E.89.XVII.2. *Basic Methodological Principles Governing the Compilation of the System of Statistical Balances* (STAT/SER.F.17/Rev.1 (vol. II)), Sales No. E.89.XVII.3. *Classification by Broad Economic Categories—Defined in Terms of SITC, Revision 3* (STAT/SER.M/53/Rev.3), Sales No. E.89.XVII.4. *Basic Methodological Principles Governing the Compilation of the System of Statistical Balances* (STAT/SER.F/17/Rev.1 (vol. I)), Sales No. E.89.XVII.5. *Handbook on Social Indicators* (STAT/SER.F/49), Sales No. E.89.XVII.6. *Handbook for National Statistical Data Bases on Women* (STAT/SER.K/6), Sales No. E.89.XVII.9. *Customs Areas of the World* (STAT/SER.M/30/Rev.2), Sales No. E.89.XVII.12.

Chapter XVIII

Institutional arrangements

The Economic and Social Council continued during 1989 to review its structure and functioning. In July, it adopted measures with regard to major policy themes and thematic analyses, documentation, organization of work and substantive support, the purpose of which was to revitalize the Council in its efforts to carry out its responsibilities.

Following the January/February session of the Committee on Non-Governmental Organizations (NGOs), the Council in May granted consultative status to 33 NGOs, added 17 to the Roster, and reclassified certain others.

The Administrative Committee on Co-ordination (ACC), at its two regular sessions in 1989, gave priority attention to debt and development, an international development strategy for the fourth United Nations development decade, international drug abuse control and the environment. It also held a special session devoted to the conditions of service of the Professional and higher categories of staff.

The Committee for Programme and Co-ordination (CPC) continued efforts to harmonize system-wide activities and work programmes.

Restructuring questions

Revitalization of the Economic and Social Council

In response to a 1988 Economic and Social Council request,[1] the Secretary-General submitted a June report[2] on the revitalization of the Council. The report described action taken to implement a set of interrelated measures, prepared by the Council, which aimed at improving its ability to carry out effectively its responsibilities under the Charter of the United Nations. The Secretary-General gave detailed comments on implementing each paragraph of the 1988 Council resolution[1] and made suggestions for further follow-up.

Among the suggestions were: (1) each year, the President of the Council, in consultation with Member States, should attempt to summarize the major conclusions of the Council's general discussion of economic and social policy, which could serve as a policy statement of the Council; (2) a multi-year programme should be drawn up of major policy themes for in-depth discussion; (3) the Secretary-General should draw the Council's attention to urgent and emerging issues through mechanisms within the UN system for the early identification, analysis and monitoring of world economic developments; (4) the Secretary-General could draw attention to policies and priorities needing Council monitoring and make proposals on how the monitoring should be carried out, including through a periodic progress review of the implementation of the International Development Strategy and specific modalities for monitoring resolutions; (5) there was an urgent need for a thorough review of all documentation prepared for the Council to avoid duplication and excessive documentation; and (6) the specialized agencies should be invited to suggest major policy themes for Council discussion. In conclusion, the Secretary-General stated that political will and attitudinal change on the part of Member States were essential if the Council was to regain its credibility and prestige, for, without such change, efforts to improve the Council's functioning would be ineffective and would not contribute to meaningful revitalization.

In a statement annexed to the Secretary-General's report, the Administrative Committee on Co-ordination (ACC) welcomed the efforts to revitalize the Council. Suggestions for further revitalization included the allocation of one to two days of the Council's annual general discussion to an exchange of views between the executive heads of the UN system, or their senior representatives, with Council members. Co-ordination was a two-way process of dialogue, ACC stated, in which due weight had to be given to the overall policy and co-ordination concerns of the Council on the one hand, and the mandates, policies and experiences of the various organizations of the system on the other. ACC welcomed the Council's establishment of a multi-year work programme and would assist the Council in identifying and discussing annual in-depth reviews of previously identified major policy themes.

On 28 July 1989, the Economic and Social Council adopted **resolution 1989/114** without vote.

Further measures for the implementation of Economic and Social Council resolution 1988/77 on the revitalization of the Council

The Economic and Social Council,

Recalling General Assembly resolutions 41/213 of 19 December 1986, 42/170 of 11 December 1987, 42/211 of 21 December 1987, 43/174 of 9 December 1988 and 43/213 of 21 December 1988, concerning the review of the efficiency of the administrative and financial functioning of the United Nations,

Aware that the reform of the economic and social sectors of the United Nations is a continuing process aimed at strengthening the effectiveness of the United Nations in dealing with economic and social issues and requires further attention,

Reaffirming its resolution 1988/77 of 29 July 1988 on the revitalization of the Economic and Social Council, endorsed by the General Assembly in decision 43/432 of 20 December 1988,

Taking note of the report of the Secretary-General on the revitalization of the Economic and Social Council,

Concerned that some of the provisions of Council resolution 1988/77 have not been implemented,

Concerned also that the documentation submitted to the Council in 1989 was distributed with considerable delay, contravening rule 13 of the rules of procedure of the Council, which states, *inter alia*, that documentation relating to an item of the agenda shall be circulated six weeks before the opening of the regular session,

1. *Notes* that the organs, organizations and bodies of the United Nations system have expressed their readiness to contribute fully to the revitalization of the Economic and Social Council;

2. *Requests* the Secretary-General to intensify his efforts towards the full implementation of all relevant provisions of Council resolution 1988/77 and also to implement fully the present resolution;

I. Major policy themes and thematic analyses

3. *Decides* to consider at its organizational session for 1990 the establishment, on a provisional basis, of a multi-year work programme identifying major policy themes for in-depth consideration each year in accordance with paragraphs 2 *(a)* (ii), 2 *(a)* (iii) and 2 *(e)* (iii) of Council resolution 1988/77, in order to enable the Council, under the authority of the General Assembly, to exercise effectively its functions and powers as set out in the Charter of the United Nations and relevant resolutions of the Assembly and the Council; the multi-year work programme should be updated and adjusted as and when necessary;

4. *Decides* that the thematic analyses referred to in paragraphs 2 *(a)* (ii) and 2 *(e)* (iii) of Council resolution 1988/77, which shall replace the present cross-organizational programme analyses as from 1991, should be made available to the Council in all official languages at least eight weeks in advance of a session;

5. *Further decides* that the thematic analyses should review existing activities and be forward-looking in identifying policy options; they should also:

(a) Describe the issue and the relationships between fields, sectors and activities of the bodies of the United Nations system concerned;

(b) Provide information on recent conclusions and recommendations of the intergovernmental bodies of the United Nations system concerned;

(c) Review relevant policy decisions and recent, ongoing and planned programmatic activities relating to the theme and their system-wide implementation, highlighting practical problems encountered;

(d) Identify emerging problems and the potential need for action by the United Nations system;

(e) Draw attention, as appropriate, to both social and economic aspects of the selected policy theme;

(f) Recommend substantive and programmatic steps to promote complementarities, co-operation and joint activities, fill gaps and reduce duplication in the United Nations system;

(g) Propose co-ordinated measures to translate legislative mandates and overall guidelines into programmes, taking into account the structure of the United Nations system and the respective areas of competence of its organizations;

(h) Propose monitoring arrangements;

6. *Decides,* in the context of its consideration of major policy themes, to review the functioning of the relevant subsidiary bodies with a view to developing common approaches to co-ordination, monitoring and follow-up;

7. *Invites* Member States to be represented in the discussions on major policy themes at an appropriately high level, with a view to the effective consideration of each theme;

8. *Invites* the executive heads of organs, organizations and bodies of the United Nations system to participate actively in the in-depth discussions on major policy themes and to co-operate closely with the Secretary-General in the preparation of the thematic analyses;

II. Documentation

9. *Notes* that it is important to improve the quality and reduce the length of documents submitted to the Council and subsidiary bodies in the economic, social and related fields and to avoid overwhelming the Council with excessive documentation;

10. *Decides* that the President of the Council and other members of the Bureau should continually monitor, with the assistance of the Secretariat, the status of the preparation of documentation, taking into account relevant decisions on documentation, and should propose appropriate measures to the Council, after having held informal meetings to be convened at least eight weeks before each regular session of the Council, bearing in mind the need to adhere to rule 13 of the rules of procedure of the Council and other relevant rules and regulations;

11. *Invites* all organs, organizations and bodies of the United Nations system to provide the Council with all the necessary input and support, particularly material required for the preparation of thematic analyses and consolidated reports, and requests the specialized agencies to continue to submit annually to the Council executive summaries of their activities;

12. *Requests* its subsidiary bodies to highlight policy recommendations and decisions resulting from their deliberations for consideration and appropriate action by the Council, and recommends that the General Assembly request its subsidiary bodies reporting through the Council to do the same;

13. *Emphasizes* that all reports submitted to the Council should be prefaced by a summary outlining the main issues addressed and the conclusions and recommendations;

14. *Urges* its subsidiary bodies to implement fully Council resolution 1979/41 of 10 May 1979 in submitting to the Council for consideration their provisional agendas together with the lists of requested documentation, with a view to ensuring greater consistency in requests for documentation and improving reporting procedures, and recommends that the General Assembly request its subsidiary bodies reporting through the Council to do the same;

15. *Requests* the Secretary-General, when introducing new information technologies, to take into account the need to improve the availability of documentation and to reduce the quantity of paper stored and distributed to the Council;

16. *Takes note with appreciation* of the report made orally by the Chairman of the open-ended task force on documentation established by the Council in its decision 1989/105 of 5 May 1989, and requests the task force to continue its work with a view to submitting concrete recommendations to the Council at its organizational session for 1990, taking duly into account the relevant provisions of the present resolution;

17. *Decides* to consider at its organizational session for 1990 the proposed format of the report of the Economic and Social Council to the General Assembly;

III. Organization of Work

18. *Recommends* that the General Assembly at its forty-fourth session request its subsidiary bodies reporting through the Council to make proposals that will provide adequate time for their reports to be considered by the Council;

19. *Requests* the General Assembly, with the assistance of the Committee on Conferences, to approve and adjust the calendar of conferences and meetings for 1990 and 1991, bearing in mind the recommendation in paragraph 18 above;

20. *Decides* that, in order to ensure that it is fully effective and substantive, the general discussion on international economic and social policy, including regional and sectoral developments, should not exceed four days and that statements made should not exceed fifteen minutes;

21. *Affirms* that the President of the Council may prepare a summary of the major conclusions of the general discussion;

22. *Decides* that, after the conclusion of all the statements in the general discussion, one day should be devoted to an informal exchange of views among members of the Council, with the active participation of the executive heads of the organs, organizations and bodies of the United Nations system concerned;

23. *Decides* that the sessional committees shall not begin their substantive work until the conclusion of the general discussion and that, to the extent possible, those committees should devote more time to a constructive dialogue on the agenda items under consideration, with the active participation of representatives of the organizations of the United Nations system concerned, and decides to consider at its organizational session for 1990 modalities for implementing these arrangements, taking into account the need to ensure that its sessions are not prolonged;

24. *Requests* the Secretary-General to submit to the Council in sufficient time for consideration at its organizational session for 1990 proposals for:

(a) A draft six-year work programme on major policy themes in the economic and social sectors as referred to in paragraph 2 (e) (iii) of Council resolution 1988/77;

(b) A biennial programme of work, with the adjustments in agenda and documentation necessary for the full implementation of Council resolution 1988/77 and the present resolution;

(c) Modalities for the in-depth discussions on major policy themes, possibly in a high-level segment of the Council;

IV. Substantive support

25. *Requests* the Committee for Programme and Co-ordination, in accordance with its mandate and acting as a subsidiary body of the Council, to continue to assist the Council in formulating appropriate recommendations relating to the programmatic and co-ordination aspects of relevant activities of the Council.

26. *Requests* the Secretary-General, in order to implement fully and effectively Council resolution 1988/77 and the present resolution, to take the following points into consideration in providing secretariat support for the Council, as referred to in paragraph 2 (g) of Council resolution 1988/77:

(a) There should be an organizationally distinct and identifiable secretariat structure for providing substantive support in regard to the preparation of thematic analyses and consolidated reports;

(b) The expertise of other organizations of the United Nations system should be drawn upon, as appropriate;

(c) Such secretariat support should be provided, as appropriate, *inter alia*, within existing resources through redeployment of staff and the use of extrabudgetary resources.

Economic and Social Council resolution 1989/114
28 July 1989   Meeting 37   Adopted without vote

Draft by Vice-President (E/1989/L.46), based on informal consultations on drafts by Malaysia for Group of 77 (E/1989/L.39) and by France for EEC (E/1989/L.40); agenda item 4.
Meeting numbers. ESC 31, 34, 37.

In **decision 1989/182** of 28 July, the Council took note of a note by the Secretariat[3] on reports submitted by specialized agencies on economic, social and related matters falling within their mandates.

Restructuring of economic and social sectors

Note of the Secretary-General. Responding to a 1988 General Assembly request,[4] the Secretary-General transmitted a November note[5] regarding the UN intergovernmental structure and functions in the economic and social fields. As requested by the Assembly, the Secretary-General had sought the views of all Member States on ways to achieve a balanced and effective implementation of recommendations 2 and 8 of the Group of High-level Intergovernmental Experts to Review the Efficiency of the Administrative and Financial Functioning of the United Nations (Group of 18), which had reported to the Assembly in 1986.[6] Recommendations 2 and 8 dealt with enhancing the effectiveness of the intergovernmental structure and its secretariat support structures, and with programme delivery in the economic and social fields. The Secretary-General reported that he had received responses from 20 countries, as well as one on behalf of the 12 members of the European Economic Community. The responses were summarized in an annex to his note.

The Secretary-General said the fundamental concern was to ensure the capacity to respond effectively to the requirements of Member States, with one of the important elements being the ability of the Organization to adapt itself to respond effectively to new and emerging issues.

Major intergovernmental deliberations were scheduled that were expected to develop new approaches, to identify priority concerns and to indicate the manner in which the United Nations could best respond to them. For example, two General Assembly special sessions were to be held in 1990 to consider international co-operation against illicit narcotic drug activities, as well as international economic co-operation, particularly the revitalization of economic growth and development in developing countries. In addition, preparatory work was being undertaken on the elaboration of an international development strategy for the fourth UN development decade, expected to be adopted by the Assembly in 1990 (see PART THREE, Chapter I). The widening gap between developed and developing countries was expected to be addressed by the Second United Nations Conference on Least Developed Countries, also scheduled for 1990. As for the environment and its relationship to development, the 1989 Assembly was expected to decide on preparatory arrangements for a major conference on environment and development, to be held in 1992. Preparations were also under way regarding the eighth session of the United Nations Conference on Trade and Development (UNCTAD), also to be held in 1992. The forty-fourth Assembly's comprehensive policy review of operational activities for development would be likely to have an important bearing (see PART THREE, Chapter II), and both intergovernmental and secretariat work would be affected by the 1992-1997 medium-term plan, scheduled to be adopted by the Assembly in 1990.

Because those deliberations would have critical implications for the UN intergovernmental structure and functions, the Secretary-General believed it would be appropriate to await their results and integrate them into his restructuring recommendations. In the same spirit, he suggested that the Economic and Social Council might also consider scheduling, at an appropriate time, a comprehensive review of the UN intergovernmental structure in the light of the outcome of the various discussions. In the meantime, the Secretary-General had

assigned to the Director-General for Development and International Economic Co-operation (DIEC) responsibility for providing various reports, notably thematic analyses and issue-oriented consolidated reports, as well as substantive support for the Council in the form of a separate and identifiable secretariat, as requested by the Council in 1988.[1]

JIU report. In August, the Secretary-General transmitted to the General Assembly the concluding report[7] of the Joint Inspection Unit (JIU) on implementation of a 1977 Assembly resolution[8] concerning the restructuring of the economic and social sectors of the UN system. The report contained recommendations regarding the functioning of the Economic and Social Council, including the allocation of three, rather than five, days to general debate; the reduction of documentation submitted for the general debate; and identification of major items and urgent questions requiring Council decisions. With regard to more effective inter-agency co-ordination, JIU recommended streamlining Council debates on co-ordination; making greater use of the DIEC Director-General; and ensuring flexibility of co-ordination mechanisms. As to making full use of available programming instruments, it was recommended that the Secretariat should prepare and distribute preliminary drafts or provisional versions of planning and programming documents in order to overcome delays. A more operational division of labour between the Department of Technical Co-operation for Development (DTCD), the Department of International Economic and Social Affairs (DIESA), the Centre for Social Development and Humanitarian Affairs (CSDHA) and the Statistical Office, based on the clustering of distinct sectors in each entity, was recommended, as was clarification and formalization of the Director-General's functions, with the Director-General preparing an annual work plan, indicating his priority activities and the contributions anticipated from UN system entities.

In November comments on the JIU report,[9] the Secretary-General pointed out that the Council had in 1989 taken a number of decisions regarding its work, including that the general debate should not exceed four days, with statements limited to 15 minutes. It had also begun to consider establishing a multi-year work programme, identifying main policy themes for in-depth discussion each year. In comments on particular recommendations, the Secretary-General concurred with the proposal that greater use be made of the DIEC Director-General in co-ordination; stated that he had taken steps to submit the draft introduction to the medium-term plan to Member States for wide consultations; and reported his intention to refer later, after the Assembly's completion of its review of the intergovernmental structure, to changes in the secretariat structure, while stating that he did not share the view that DTCD, DIESA and CSDHA should be restructured along sectoral lines. Although he agreed with certain proposals on clarifying the Director-General's role, he pointed out that they needed to be defined within the terms of specific Assembly resolutions on the subject. He agreed that the Director-General could prepare an annual work plan, indicating priorities and contributions expected from other UN entities.

GENERAL ASSEMBLY ACTION

On 11 December, the General Assembly adopted **resolution 44/103** without vote.

Restructuring and revitalization of the United Nations in the economic and social fields

The General Assembly,

Recalling its resolutions 32/197 of 20 December 1977, 41/213 of 19 December 1986, 42/170 of 11 December 1987, 43/174 of 9 December 1988 and 43/213 of 21 December 1988 and its decision 43/432 of 20 December 1988,

Recalling also Economic and Social Council resolution 1988/77 of 29 July 1988 on the revitalization of the Council and endorsing Council resolution 1989/114 of 28 July 1989 on further measures for its implementation,

Desiring to strengthen further the role and effectiveness of the United Nations as a whole through enhanced multilateral co-operation in the economic, social and related fields in accordance with the purposes and principles of the Charter of the United Nations,

Reaffirming that Member States must honour, promptly and in full, their financial obligations as set out in the Charter, and emphasizing that the financial stability of the Organization will facilitate its effective functioning in the economic, social and related fields,

Emphasizing the need for more effective and efficient functioning of the intergovernmental structure of the United Nations and its secretariat support structure in the economic, social and related fields in order to enhance international co-operation and efforts to promote the development of the developing countries,

Affirming that the goal of restructuring and revitalization of the United Nations in the economic and social fields is to ensure effective and efficient use of resources in support of the objectives determined by Member States and not to make financial savings,

Conscious of the new demands that are likely to emerge in the economic, social and related fields from major intergovernmental deliberations scheduled to take place in the early 1990s and the consequent need to adapt the intergovernmental system to these demands,

Emphasizing the need to strengthen co-operation and enhance understanding between the United Nations and the other organizations of the United Nations system as a whole in order to enable the General Assembly and the Economic and Social Council to carry out their responsibilities for promoting international economic and social co-operation in accordance with the relevant articles of the Charter,

Reaffirming the central role assigned to the Economic and Social Council in co-ordinating the activities of the agencies of the United Nations system, as set out in Article 63 of the Charter,

Conscious of the special responsibilities assigned to the Economic and Social Council in chapters IX and X of the Charter,

Emphasizing that a high level of commitment and political support on the part of Member States will be necessary if measures agreed upon to improve the functioning of the intergovernmental system in the economic and social sectors are to be effectively implemented and truly realized,

1. *Stresses* the common interest of all countries in the effective functioning of the United Nations in the economic and social fields so that it is more responsive not only to current issues but also to emerging problems and issues, particularly those relating to the development of the developing countries;

2. *Takes note* of the note of the Secretary-General on the review of the efficiency of the administrative and financial functioning of the United Nations and the view expressed therein that more time is required before submission to the Assembly of the detailed report requested in resolution 43/174;

3. *Decides* to review the efficiency of the administrative and financial functioning of the United Nations in the economic, social and related fields, including the secretariat support structure, taking into account the major intergovernmental conferences scheduled to take place in the early 1990s, including the special session of the General Assembly to consider the question of international co-operation against illicit production, supply, demand, trafficking and distribution of narcotic drugs, with a view to expanding the scope and increasing the effectiveness of such co-operation, the special session of the Assembly devoted to international economic co-operation, in particular to the revitalization of economic growth and development of the developing countries, the Second United Nations Conference on the Least Developed Countries, the eighth session of the United Nations Conference on Trade and Development and the United Nations Conference on Environment and Development, as well as the elaboration of the international development strategy for the fourth United Nations development decade;

4. *Stresses* the need for the full implementation of Economic and Social Council resolutions 1988/77 and 1989/114, including the provisions related to the secretariat support structure of the Council, and requests the Secretary-General to submit a report on the implementation of those resolutions to the Economic and Social Council so that the Council can review the question at its second regular session of 1990;

5. *Requests* the Secretary-General to report to the General Assembly at its forty-fifth session on the follow-up and implementation of the present resolution;

6. *Decides* to review the question at its forty-fifth session.

General Assembly resolution 44/103

11 December 1989   Meeting 80   Adopted without vote

Draft by Bolivia (A/44/L.58); agenda item 38.

REFERENCES

[1]YUN 1988, p. 705, ESC res. 1988/77, 29 July 1988.
[2]E/1989/95. [3]E/1989/INF/8. [4]YUN 1988, p. 704, GA
res. 43/174, 9 Dec. 1988. [5]A/44/747. [6]YUN 1986, p. 1021.
[7]A/44/486. [8]YUN 1977, p. 438, GA res. 32/197, 20
Dec. 1977. [9]A/44/486/Add.1.

Economic and Social Council

The Economic and Social Council in 1989 held
its organizational session in New York on 19 January and on 9 and 10 February. Its first regular session, which was also held in New York, was from
2 to 24 May; its second regular session took place
in Geneva from 5 to 28 July.

Co-operation with other organizations

Non-governmental organizations

The Committee on Non-Governmental Organizations met in New York from 23 January to 3
February,[1] when it heard requests from NGOs to
be granted consultative status with the Economic
and Social Council and requests for reclassification. The Committee recommended that 11 NGOs
be heard by the Council or its committees in connection with items on the agenda.[2]

In May 1989, the number of NGOs in consultative status with the Council totalled 893.[3]
They were divided into three groups: category I—
organizations representative of major population
segments in a large number of countries, involved
with the economic and social life of the areas they
represented; category II—international organizations having special competence in a few of the
Council's areas of activity; and the Roster—
organizations considered able to make occasional
and useful contributions to the Council's work.

The Committee submitted three draft decisions
calling for Council action: by the first, it recommended that consultative status be granted to 51
NGOs that had applied and that six NGOs be
reclassified; in the second, it recommended approval of the provisional agenda and documentation for its 1991 session; and in the third, it requested that three NGOs be reclassified for failure
to provide additional information requested by the
Committee in 1987, and that one be reclassified
for failure to provide satisfactory additional information. The Committee further recommended
that the Council consider a question entitled
"Charter of housing rights", as proposed by an
NGO, at its second regular session of 1989, under
the item "Development and international economic co-operation: human settlements".

By **decision 1989/106** of 10 May, the Economic
and Social Council granted category II consultative status to 33 NGOs and placed 17 NGOs on the
Roster. It reclassified one organization from category II to category I and five organizations from
the Roster to category II.

By **decision 1989/108** of the same date, the
Council reclassified three NGOs from category II
to the Roster for failure to provide additional information requested in 1987 and requested those
organizations to submit in 1991 a detailed report
on their 1986-1989 activities, on the understanding that failure to do so would cause withdrawal
of consultative status. It further decided that the
Union of International Fairs be reclassified from
category II to the Roster, since additional information provided by it was not satisfactory.

Also on 10 May, the Council decided to consider the question "Charter of housing rights" at
its second regular session of 1989 (**decision
1989/109**), took note of the report of the Committee on NGOs on its 1989 session (**decision
1989/110**) and approved the provisional agenda
and documentation for the 1991 session (**decision
1989/107**).

Intergovernmental organizations

During the year, 34 intergovernmental organizations were designated by the Economic and
Social Council under rule 79[a] of the rules of
procedure for participation in the Council's
deliberations on questions within the scope of their
activities. Of these, 25 were participating on a continuing basis and 9 on an *ad hoc* basis.[4]

By **decision 1989/165** of 24 July, the Council
decided that the Arab Security Studies and Training Center and the Customs Co-operation Council could participate on an *ad hoc* basis, without the
right to vote, in the Council's deliberations on
questions within the scope of their activities.

Work programme

At its 1989 organizational session, the Economic
and Social Council considered its draft basic programme of work for 1989 and 1990, as submitted
by the Secretary-General;[5] on 10 February it
adopted **decision 1989/101**.

In section I of the decision, the Council approved the list of items for consideration in 1989—

---

[a]Rule 79 of the Council's rules of procedure states: "Representatives of intergovernmental organizations accorded permanent observer
status by the General Assembly and of other intergovernmental organizations designated on an *ad hoc* or a continuing basis by the Council
on the recommendation of the Bureau may participate, without the right
to vote, in the deliberations of the Council on questions within the scope
of the activities of the organizations."

14 items for the first regular session and 13 for the second regular session—and allocated the items to its sessional committees and plenary meetings. Subject to the decision to be taken by the General Assembly at its resumed forty-third session (see PART THREE, Chapter I), the Council would consider the inclusion in the agenda of an item relating to the General Assembly's 1990 special session on international economic co-operation, in particular the revitalization of economic growth and development in the developing countries. It also decided to take note of a request from the United Nations Educational, Scientific and Cultural Organization[(6)] for inclusion in the agenda of an item on co-operation in the field of informatics. The question of interregional co-operation in international trade facilitation was to be considered at the second regular session, under the item on regional co-operation. That session would also consider the report of the UNCTAD Trade and Development Board on the second part of its thirty-fifth session, the Secretary-General being authorized to transmit the report of the first part of its thirty-sixth session directly to the General Assembly. An in-depth review of the report of the World Food Council on the work of its fifteenth session was allocated to the second regular session, at which recommendations would be made for submission to the Assembly. The Chairman of the *Ad Hoc* Committee of the Whole for the Preparation of the International Development Strategy for the Fourth United Nations Development Decade was invited to make an oral report to the Council at the second regular session. The Council decided, when reviewing the report of the Commission on Human Settlements, to limit consideration to specific proposals requiring Council action or relating to the co-ordination aspect of the Commission's work. One plenary meeting of the second regular session was to be devoted to the question of convening a UN conference on environment and development.

The Council also decided: to authorize the Secretary-General to transmit directly to the Assembly the report of the Intergovernmental Committee on Science and Technology for Development on its tenth session; to carry out at its second regular session the triennial comprehensive policy review of operational activities for development; and to request the Secretary-General to make available the revisions to the medium-term plan for 1984-1989 in the economic, social and human rights fields.

By section II of the decision, the Council took note of the list of questions for inclusion in its 1990 work programme.

Agenda of 1989 sessions

On 9 February, the Economic and Social Council adopted a five-item agenda for its organiza-

tional session. The annotated provisional agenda for the first regular session[(7)] was adopted on 2 May in **decision 1989/161**. The Council also added several items to that agenda.

By **decision 1989/162** of 24 May, the Council approved the draft provisional agenda and the draft programme of work for its second regular session, as orally revised.[(8)] It decided, by **decision 1989/105** of 5 May, to focus, in its general discussion of international economic and social policy, on the question of structural changes and imbalances in the world economy and their impact on international economic co-operation, particularly with developing countries. It further decided to select major policy themes with a view to adoption of action-oriented recommendations, pending approval of a multi-year work programme. Those items were: a comprehensive policy review of operational activities for development of the UN system; environment and development; revitalization of the Council; national disaster reduction; and the interrelated issue of money, finance, trade, external debt and development. An open-ended task force, to be convened by the Council President, would consider what Council documentation might be redundant, had lost its usefulness or could be issued less frequently.

By **decision 1989/163**, the Council, on 5 July, adopted the agenda and approved the organization of work for its second regular session.[(9)]

For the agenda lists, see APPENDIX IV.

Calendar of meetings

By **decision 1989/190** of 28 July, the Economic and Social Council approved the calendar of conferences and meetings for 1990 and 1991,[(10)] as orally revised.

Limitation of documentation

On 26 July, by **decision 1989/174**, the Council decided to discontinue for a further two years, from 1990, summary records for its three sessional committees and for 11 subsidiary bodies.

Report for 1989

The work of the Economic and Social Council during 1989 was summarized in its annual report to the General Assembly.[(4)] Parts of the report were considered by the plenary Assembly and others by the Second (Economic and Financial) and Fifth (Administrative and Budgetary) Committees.

On 21 December, by **decision 44/441**, the Assembly took note of the parts of the Council's report considered by the Fifth Committee. By **decision 44/457** of 22 December, it took note of those parts considered in the plenary. Also on 22 December, on the recommendation of the Second Committee, the Assembly took note of a number of documents relating to the Council's report (**decision 44/455**).

REFERENCES

(1)E/1989/40 & Corr.1. (2)E/1989/71. (3)E/1989/INF/11. (4)A/44/3/Rev.1. (5)E/1989/1 & Add.1. (6)E/1989/39. (7)E/1989/30. (8)E/1989/L.16. (9)E/1989/100. (10)E/1989/L.20 & Corr.1.

Co-ordination in the UN system

ACC activities

The Administrative Committee on Co-ordination held three sessions in 1989,[1] two regular sessions (Geneva, 19-21 April; New York, 19-20 October) and one special session (Geneva, 5 July).

During the year, ACC gave priority attention to four substantive issues: debt and development; preparation of the international development strategy for the fourth UN development decade; international drug abuse control; and questions related to the environment. ACC also considered appropriate system-wide responses to a number of other issues, ranging from the prevention and control of AIDS to nutrition, recognizing the need to further strengthen inter-agency co-operation to meet the challenges of the 1990s. It recognized that the pervasive nature of the debt problem was crippling growth in a large number of developing countries, particularly in Africa and Latin America. The social and human aspects of adjustment programmes were reviewed and discussed, as was the impact of the current debt strategy, with acknowledgement that a strengthened debt strategy and debt reduction needed to be quickly implemented in a larger number of countries.

ACC proposed for consideration by the Economic and Social Council its suggestions regarding the content of the new international development strategy for the fourth UN development decade (see PART THREE, Chapter I). It also submitted a statement to the Council on the need to accelerate the international fight against drug abuse and commenced work on a system-wide plan of action for international drug abuse control, as called for by the General Assembly in **resolution 44/141**. ACC welcomed the increased emphasis on environmentally sound and sustainable development, believing that the UN Conference on Environment and Development, to be held in 1992, could lead to a strengthening of the capacities of developing countries, as well as the organizations of the UN system, to carry out concrete measures and identify the requisite resources.

ACC carried out a review of policy formulation and management of operational activities for development. It adopted a statement to the Economic and Social Council on the role and functioning of the UN development system in the 1990s (see PART THREE, Chapter II), which reaffirmed its unequivocal resolve to continue to adapt to major changes that had taken place on the development scene and recognized the importance of further strengthening the links between the operational activities of the system and the goals and strategies of the 1990s.

With regard to financial, administrative and personnel issues, ACC continued to be concerned with the financial difficulties faced by the UN system. Noting that the system was the scene of renewed and revitalized interest on the part of Member States, ACC concluded that the plans, programmes and budgets developed to meet the priorities of Member States could be translated into effective action through the system only with solid financial support. Member States were called on to pay promptly and in full their contributions to the organizations of the system. As to personnel policies and practices, ACC was of the view that more needed to be done to improve the conditions of service in order to maintain an international civil service of the highest quality.

At its special session, which was devoted to a comprehensive review of conditions of service of the Professional and higher categories of staff, ACC adopted a statement expressing grave concern that the conditions of employment and the purchasing power of UN common system staff had been and continued to be significantly eroded throughout the world (see PART SIX, Chapter II).

ACC's principal subsidiary bodies met as follows:

Organizational Committee (New York, 15-17 February, 9-11 October; Geneva, 10-12 and 21 April, 3 and 5 July); Consultative Committee on Administrative Questions (CCAQ) (Personnel and General Administrative Questions) (special session, New York, 15-18 January; seventieth session, Vienna, 2-17 March; second special session, Geneva, 29-30 June; seventy-first session, New York, 24 July-4 August); CCAQ (Operational Activities) (first regular session, Geneva, 3-6 April; second regular session, New York, 2-4 October); CCAQ (Financial and Budgetary Questions) (seventieth session, Copenhagen, Denmark, 6-10 March; seventy-first session, New York, 11-15 September).

Bodies on specific subjects met as follows:

Technical working group of the Task Force on Long-term Development Objectives (Geneva, 24-26 January); *ad hoc* inter-agency meeting on co-ordination in matters of international drug abuse control (Vienna, 11 February; Paris, 4-6 September); Sub-Committee on Nutrition (fifteenth session, New York, 22 February-3 March); Inter-Agency Group on New and Renewable Sources of Energy (Geneva, 9-10 March); Task Force on Science and Technology for Development (tenth session, Vienna, 13-16 March); Task Force on Long-term Development Objectives (seventeenth session, New York, 28-31 March; eighteenth session, New York, 18-21 September); thirteenth *ad hoc* inter-agency meeting on women (Vienna, 10-11 April); *ad hoc* inter-agency meeting on commodities (Geneva, 1-3 May); Task Force on Rural Development (17th meeting, Vienna, 31 May-2 June); Sub-Committee on Statistical Activities (twenty-third session, Geneva, 19-23 June); Advisory Committee for the Co-ordination of Information Systems (fifth session, Geneva, 18-21 September); ninth inter-agency consultation on the follow-up to the Substantial New Programme of Action for the 1980s for the Least Developed Countries (Geneva, 19-20 September); *ad hoc* inter-agency meeting on outer space activities (Geneva, 27-29 September).

Report for 1988

The ACC annual overview report for 1988[2] was considered by the Committee for Programme and Co-ordination (CPC) at its May/June session.[3] The Committee felt that more emphasis should be given to system-wide co-ordination in specific sectors of activity, identifying problems and suggesting remedial measures. It recommended examination of possible substantial modifications of the report so that it would be more forward-looking and analytical and would provide inter-governmental bodies with alternative suggestions on policy measures for major programmes. The Committee recommended that ACC take action to make its role more effective, to review its working methods and to make its work more visible and transparent. It recommended that the Economic and Social Council and the General Assembly consider the ACC report in more detail.

By **decision 1989/180** of 27 July, the Council took note of the 1988 ACC report.

CPC activities

In 1989, CPC met in New York for an organizational meeting on 10 April and for its twenty-ninth session from 8 May to 5 June.[3]

In reviewing the efficiency of the administrative and financial functioning of the United Nations, the Committee considered the Secretary-General's report[4] on the implementation of a 1986 General Assembly resolution on the matter,[5] which had approved the 1986 recommendations of the Group of High-level Intergovernmental Experts to Review the Efficiency of the Administrative and Financial Functioning of the United Nations (Group of 18).[6] CPC noted that the Secretary-General's report did not cover the entire three-year period required by the Assembly and therefore could not be considered a final report. In general, it found that significant progress had been achieved due to the joint efforts of Member States, the Secretary-General and staff of the Organization, but the recommendations of the Group of 18 had not been implemented in a

balanced manner. Concrete progress had been achieved in political affairs and administration and management, but results were uneven in carrying out recommendations addressed to intergovernmental bodies and Member States, particularly in the economic and social sectors. There was a need to strengthen the Secretary-General's role regarding co-ordination within the UN system, as well as the role of Member States through intergovernmental bodies. The Committee noted that while the financial situation had improved somewhat recently, it had not been conducive to a co-ordinated implementation of reforms. It stressed the importance for Member States to monitor closely the financial situation and to fulfil strictly their financial obligations under the Charter. To carry out successfully the process of reform and restructuring, it was essential that the current financial uncertainties be dispelled. The Committee recommended that the Secretary-General submit to the Assembly in 1990 an update on implementation of the Assembly's 1986 resolution, and suggested a structure for that report.

The Committee discussed the introduction to and overview of the proposed programme budget for the biennium 1990-1991, referring, in pursuance of established practice, to the Advisory Committee on Administrative and Budgetary Questions all non-programmatic sections of the budget. After commenting and making recommendations on various aspects of the programme budget, the Committee recommended that the Assembly approve the budget's programme narratives and sections. The Committee considered a report of the Secretary-General on all aspects of priority-setting in future outlines of the proposed programme budget,[7] concluding that it was a first step in the direction of re-examining priority-setting. Since the Committee did not have sufficient time to consider fully that very complex issue, it referred the report to the Economic and Social Council and to the Assembly for further consideration (see PART SIX, Chapter I).

ECONOMIC AND SOCIAL COUNCIL ACTION

On 27 July, the Economic and Social Council, on the recommendation of its Third (Programme and Co-ordination) Committee, adopted **resolution 1989/109** without vote.

Report of the Committee for Programme and Co-ordination

The Economic and Social Council,

Having considered the report of the Committee for Programme and Co-ordination on the work of its twenty-ninth session,

Recalling the provisions of Chapters IX and X of the Charter of the United Nations and, in particular, the role of the Economic and Social Council in co-ordination in the economic and social fields within the United Nations system,

Reaffirming the importance of the programming and co-ordinating functions carried out by the Committee for Programme and Co-ordination as the main subsidiary organ of the Economic and Social Council and the General Assembly for planning, programming and co-ordination,

Recognizing that programme performance reports, programme evaluations, system-wide programme analyses and other relevant co-ordination instruments should be significant tools for promoting effectiveness and better integration, as appropriate, of the programming and co-ordination processes and for enabling the United Nations to fulfil its role and functions,

1. *Takes note* of the report of the Committee for Programme and Co-ordination on the work of its twenty-ninth session and endorses the conclusions and recommendations contained therein;

2. *Requests* the Committee for Programme and Co-ordination to intensify its efforts on such important matters as priority-setting, evaluation methodologies, the format and presentation of the medium-term plan, and relevant co-ordination instruments;

3. *Affirms* that the implementation of the present resolution shall take into account relevant decisions of the Council on revitalization of the Economic and Social Council.

Economic and Social Council resolution 1989/109

| 27 July 1989 | Meeting 36 | Adopted without vote |

Approved by Third Committee (E/1989/133) without vote, 21 July (meeting 16); draft by Chairman (E/1989/C.3/L.12/Rev.1); agenda item 9.

On 26 July, the Council, also on the recommendation of its Third Committee, adopted **resolution 1989/97** without vote.

Programme questions

The Economic and Social Council,

Recalling rule 31 of the rules of procedure of the Economic and Social Council,

Noting the importance of the additional responsibilities in the budget process assigned to the Committee for Programme and Co-ordination by the General Assembly in its resolution 41/213 of 19 December 1986,

Recalling Economic and Social Council resolution 1988/77 of 29 July 1988, in which the Council decided that it would, *inter alia*, examine in depth the relevant sections of the proposed programme budget of the United Nations in the light of the recommendations of the Committee for Programme and Co-ordination, with a view to submitting appropriate recommendations to the General Assembly on the overall and programme priorities of the United Nations in the economic, social and related fields,

Having considered the report of the Secretary-General on all aspects of priority-setting in future outlines of the proposed programme budget,

Emphasizing the importance of priority-setting in the planning and budget process,

Having considered the relevant sections of the report of the Committee for Programme and Co-ordination on the work of its twenty-ninth session,

Recalling General Assembly resolution 42/211 of 21 December 1987, in which the Assembly decided that the date for submission of the outline of the programme budget should be 15 August of the off-budget year,

1. *Endorses* the conclusions and recommendations of the Committee for Programme and Co-ordination on programme questions, in particular on sections 4 to 24 of the proposed programme budget for the biennium 1990-1991;

2. *Stresses* the need for the sectoral, functional and regional intergovernmental bodies to consider in a timely manner the draft programmes of work within their areas of responsibility, in order that their recommendations may be taken into account by the Secretary-General when he prepares his proposed programme budget;

3. *Endorses* the conclusions and recommendations of the Committee for Programme and Co-ordination regarding priority-setting;

4. *Notes* that the thirtieth session of the Committee for Programme and Co-ordination, which will be of six weeks' duration, in accordance with paragraph 8 of the annex to Economic and Social Council resolution 2008(LX) of 14 May 1976, will be held in two parts and that the second part will be devoted to consideration of the outline of the programme budget for the biennium 1992-1993;

5. *Endorses* the recommendation of the Committee for Programme and Co-ordination that the General Assembly consider the possibility of adjusting the calendar of meetings so that the sessions of the Committee would start later in May.

Economic and Social Council resolution 1989/97

| 26 July 1989 | Meeting 35 | Adopted without vote |

Approved by Third Committee (E/1989/134) without vote, 20 July (meeting 15); draft by Chairman (E/1989/C.3/L.13); agenda item 11 *(a)*.

Joint Meetings of CPC and ACC

The twenty-fourth series of Joint Meetings of CPC and ACC was held in New York from 16 to 18 October 1989.[8] By **decision 1989/103** of 10 February, the Economic and Social Council had set the dates and venue of the Meetings and requested CPC, in consultation with ACC, to agree on a topic. The topics agreed on were drug abuse control and the international development strategy for the fourth UN development decade (see PART THREE, Chapter I).

In general conclusions and recommendations, the Joint Meetings stated that ACC's annual report should be strengthened to realize its potential as an effective instrument to provide Member States with an overview of system-wide activities, plans and resource allocations. The Meetings provided a unique instrument for Member States and organizations of the system to exchange views and formulate recommendations on issues of relevance for improved co-ordination. The Meetings should take place annually in New York, it was stated.

Cross-organizational programme analyses

In response to a 1988 CPC request,[9] the Secretary-General submitted a March note[10] concerning a 1988 Economic and Social Council resolution,[11] in which it was proposed that cross-organizational programme analyses (COPAs) be replaced in their current form by brief analyses or major priority themes in the medium-term plan. The Secretary-General would submit to the Council draft proposals on a multi-year programme for analyses immediately after the General Assembly's adoption of the medium-term plan in 1990. He also reported on the scope and general approach of the COPA on industrial development,[12] to be considered in 1990, and the COPA on the advancement of women.[13]

CPC stated[3] that there was still a need for programme analyses across the system. It suggested that the Council consider the topic of human resources development as a future subject for a COPA. As to the industrial development topic, CPC reiterated that the analysis should reflect the central co-ordinating role of the United Nations Industrial Development Organization (UNIDO). Noting that UNIDO was currently experiencing financial difficulties, it recommended that financial questions be taken into account in the proposed analysis. It also recommended in-depth examination of what had been done within the system regarding industrialization in developing countries, particularly the least developed countries, and a review of progress in implementing the Industrial Development Decade for Africa (1980-1990) and of the role of women in industrialization.

With regard to the COPA related to the advancement of women, CPC considered that the Secretary-General's report would serve as an indicator of the system-wide effort to implement the 1985 Nairobi Forward-looking Strategies for the Advancement of Women,[14] serving as a benchmark against which progress and results of the system-wide medium-term plan for women could be measured.

REFERENCES
[1]E/1990/18. [2]E/1989/18. [3]A/44/16. [4]A/44/222 & Corr.1. [5]YUN 1986, p. 1024, GA res. 41/213, 19 Dec. 1986. [6]*Ibid.*, p. 1021. [7]A/44/272. [8]E/1990/4. [9]YUN 1988, p. 714. [10]E/AC.51/1989/10. [11]YUN 1988, p. 705, ESC res. 1988/77, 29 July 1988. [12]E/AC.51/1989/9. [13]E/1989/19. [14]YUN 1985, p. 937.

Other institutional arrangements

Work programmes of Assembly's Second and Third Committees

Second Committee

By **decision 43/461** of 7 March, the General Assembly approved the biennial programme of work for its Second (Economic and Financial) Committee for 1989-1990.

By **decision 44/456** of 22 December, the Assembly approved the Committee's biennial programme of work for 1990-1991.

Third Committee

The Third (Social, Humanitarian and Cultural) Committee had before it a note by the Secretariat[1] transmitting a draft decision concerning its programme of work. Originally submitted in 1986, consideration of the draft had been deferred three times—until 1987, then until 1988, when it was deferred until 1989.[2]

As originally submitted, the draft would have had the Assembly decide to consider the following items every two years, beginning at its 1986 session: the question of aging; implementation of the World Programme of Action concerning Disabled Persons and the United Nations Decade of Disabled Persons; elimination of all forms of religious tolerance; human rights and scientific and technological developments; and alternative approaches and ways and means within the UN system for improving the effective enjoyment of human rights and fundamental freedoms (with the exception of the question related to the right to development).

By **decision 44/435** of 15 December, the Assembly deferred consideration of the draft until 1990.

International decades

In accordance with a 1988 General Assembly decision,[3] the Economic and Social Council considered further the guidelines for international decades, which it had recommended to the Assembly for adoption in 1988.[4]

ECONOMIC AND SOCIAL COUNCIL ACTION

On 24 May, the Council adopted **resolution 1989/84** without vote.

Guidelines for international decades in economic and social fields

The Economic and Social Council,

Recalling its resolution 1980/67 of 25 July 1980, in which it adopted guidelines for international years and anniversaries,

Recalling also General Assembly resolution 42/171 of 11 December 1987, in which the Assembly requested the Council to submit recommendations on guidelines for the designation of future international decades,

Recalling further its resolution 1988/63 of 27 July 1988, in which it recommended guidelines for international decades for adoption by the General Assembly,

Taking note of General Assembly decision 43/434 of 20 December 1988, in which the Assembly decided to refer the issue to the Council in 1989 for further consideration as appropriate, with a view to enabling the Assembly at its forty-fourth session to consider and take appropriate action on guidelines for international decades,

Recommends that the General Assembly consider further and take appropriate action on the revised guidelines for international decades contained in the annex to the present resolution, on the understanding that these guidelines are not intended to apply to United Nations development decades.

ANNEX
Guidelines for international decades in economic and social fields

A. Selection of subjects for and timing of international decades

1. The subject proposed for a decade should be consistent with the purposes and principles of the United Nations, as stated in the Charter. It should be of priority concern in the economic, social, cultural, humanitarian or human rights field and should require long-term action at the international or regional level and at the national level. Action on the subject should contribute to the strengthening of international peace and to the development of international co-operation towards the proclaimed objectives of the decade.

2. In areas where effective programmes already exist, international decades may be proclaimed provided that the decade can be expected to advance the implementation of the objectives of those programmes.

3. While taking exceptions into account, in general decades should not overlap. A new international decade may be initiated provided it is clear that the United Nations system has the substantive, administrative and financial capacity to play an effective role in the implementation of a programme for the decade.

4. Before a new decade is proposed, consideration should be given to the possibility of an observance for a shorter period of time.

B. Requirements for the proclamation of international decades

5. Proposals for international decades should include a draft programme of action with well-defined objectives and activities to be carried out at the international, regional and national levels. The activities should be directed towards clearly defined objectives. The draft programme of action should indicate the proposed organizational arrangements and modalities for financing, from both budgetary and extrabudgetary sources, as well as procedures for monitoring implementation. Provision should also be made for public information activities and, where appropriate, for advisory services upon request from Governments.

6. The draft programme of action should indicate a lead agency or agencies for the decade and the mechanisms to be used for co-ordinating the activities of the organizations of the United Nations system, as well as those of the other intergovernmental and non-governmental organizations concerned.

7. At the national level, the programme of action should provide for the establishment of national committees or other mechanisms to mobilize public support and carry out activities connected with the decade.

C. Procedures for the proclamation of international decades

8. Proposals for international decades should be submitted to the Economic and Social Council so that it may review the purpose and timing, drawing on the views of the Committee for Programme and Co-ordination and other intergovernmental bodies concerned.

9. The General Assembly should proclaim an international decade after the proposal has been thoroughly reviewed by the intergovernmental bodies concerned and the views of all Member States and of the non-governmental organizations concerned have been taken into consideration. For this purpose, while taking exceptions into account, in general there should be an interval of two years between the introduction of the proposal in the Economic and Social Council and the proclamation of the decade by the General Assembly.

10. There should be sufficient time between the proclamation of the decade by the General Assembly and the start of the decade to allow for preparatory work at the international, regional and national levels.

11. When a subsequent decade on a particular subject is proposed, the following should be taken into consideration, on the understanding that exceptions may be possible:

(a) There should be a two-year preparatory period between the end of a decade and the start of the subsequent decade for drafting the programme of action for the subsequent decade;

(b) Steps should be taken to ensure that the expertise and experience acquired during a decade are retained in order to ensure the prompt implementation of activities once a subsequent decade is launched;

(c) The mid-term and end-term reviews of a decade should be used as a baseline for the programme of action for the subsequent decade;

(d) A subsequent decade should be proclaimed in accordance with the provisions of paragraph 2 of the present guidelines, provided that the objectives of the first decade have not been fully attained, particularly in cases where projects or programmes of the first decade have reached an advanced stage of implementation.

D. Review and appraisal of the implementation of the programme of action for the decade

12. The implementation of the programme of action for the decade should normally be reviewed by an appropriate intergovernmental body at the mid-point and end of the decade. When a world conference on the subject of an international decade is convened within the period of the decade, such a conference should serve, *inter alia*, as an instrument for the review and appraisal of the implementation of the programme of action for the decade.

Economic and Social Council resolution 1989/84

24 May 1989   Meeting 16   Adopted without vote

Draft by Vice-Chairman of Second Committee (E/1989/L.19); agenda item 1.
Meeting numbers. ESC 8, 16.

REFERENCES
[1]A/C.3/44/L.2. [2]YUN 1988, p. 714, GA dec. 43/426, 8 Dec. 1988. [3]*Ibid.*, p. 716, GA dec. 43/434, 20 Dec. 1988. [4]*Ibid.*, p. 715, ESC res. 1988/63, 27 July 1988.

PART FOUR

Trusteeship and decolonization

Chapter I

Questions relating to decolonization

Decolonization remained a concern of the United Nations in 1989. The main body dealing with the issue, the General Assembly's Special Committee on the Situation with regard to the Implementation of the 1960 Declaration on the Granting of Independence to Colonial Countries and Peoples (Special Committee on decolonization), continued to consider decolonization questions in general, as well as the individual situations of Non-Self Governing Territories (NSGTs), including 13 small territories. The Committee also considered the Trust Territory of the Pacific Islands (see next chapter) and Namibia (see Chapter III of this Part).

The Assembly endorsed a Programme of Activities in Observance of the Thirtieth Anniversary of the 1960 Declaration (resolution 44/100). Having declared the 1990s the Decade for the Eradication of Colonialism, the Assembly recommended that the Secretary-General again solicit suggestions from States for incorporation into a final report to be submitted at the forty-fifth (1990) session which would enable the Assembly to adopt an action plan for the elimination of colonialism (44/429).

In relation to specific Territories, the Assembly deferred consideration of the question of the Falkland Islands (Malvinas) to its forty-fifth (1990) session (44/406), after receiving letters from Argentina and the United Kingdom stating that all hostilities between the two countries had ceased and that substantive talks had taken place. The Assembly welcomed talks on the question of Western Sahara between His Majesty King Hassan II of Morocco and a high-level delegation from the Frente Popular para la Liberación de Saguia el-Hamra y de Río de Oro (POLISARIO Front) (44/88).

1960 Declaration on decolonization

During 1989, the United Nations continued to focus its decolonization efforts on implementation of the 1960 Declaration on the Granting of Independence to Colonial Countries and Peoples.[1] The Special Committee on decolonization held two sessions in 1989, both in New York—the first on 2 February, at which it considered organizational questions, and the second from 1 to 16 August.[2]

Its Sub-Committee on Petitions, Information and Assistance held meetings between 14 March and 27 May, and the Sub-Committee on Small Territories met between 10 March and 20 June. On their recommendations, the Committee took action on the implementation of the Declaration by international organizations, on the dissemination of information on decolonization and on reports on the Territories supplied by the administering Powers and by the Committee's visiting missions.

Implementation of the Declaration

On 11 December, the General Assembly adopted **resolution 44/101** by recorded vote.

Implementation of the Declaration on the Granting of Independence to Colonial Countries and Peoples

The General Assembly,

Having examined the report of the Special Committee on the Situation with regard to the Implementation of the Declaration on the Granting of Independence to Colonial Countries and Peoples,

Recalling its resolutions 1514(XV) of 14 December 1960, containing the Declaration on the Granting of Independence to Colonial Countries and Peoples, 2621(XXV) of 12 October 1970, containing the programme of action for the full implementation of the Declaration, and 35/118 of 11 December 1980, the annex to which contains the Plan of Action for the Full Implementation of the Declaration, as well as 40/56 of 2 December 1985, on the twenty-fifth anniversary of the Declaration,

Also recalling all its previous resolutions concerning the implementation of the Declaration, in particular resolution 43/45 of 22 November 1988, as well as the relevant resolutions of the Security Council,

Deeply conscious of the urgent need to take all necessary measures to eliminate forthwith the last vestiges of colonialism, and, in that respect, recalling its resolution 43/47 of 22 November 1988,

Reiterating its conviction that the total eradication of racial discrimination, *apartheid* and violations of the basic human rights of the peoples of colonial Territories will be achieved most expeditiously by the faithful and complete implementation of the Declaration,

Conscious that the success of national liberation struggles and the resultant international situation have provided the international community with a unique opportunity to make a decisive contribution towards the total elimination of colonialism in all its forms and manifestations in Africa,

Welcoming the successful conclusion of the elections in Namibia under the supervision and control of the United Nations and the establishment of a Constituent Assembly as an embodiment of the sovereign will of the people of Namibia, and in this regard expressing the hope for the early emergence of Namibia as an independent State,

Noting with satisfaction the work accomplished by the Special Committee with a view to securing the effective and complete implementation of the Declaration contained in General Assembly resolution 1514(XV) and other relevant resolutions of the United Nations,

Noting also with satisfaction the co-operation and active participation of the administering Powers concerned in the relevant work of the Special Committee, as well as their continued readiness to receive United Nations visiting missions in the Territories under their administration,

Stressing the importance of the participation of the administering Powers in the work of the Special Committee and noting with concern the negative impact which the non-participation of certain administering Powers has had on the work of the Special Committee, depriving it of an important source of information on the Territories under their administration,

Keenly aware of the pressing need of the newly independent and emerging States for assistance from the United Nations and its system of organizations in the economic, social and other fields,

Mindful that the year 1990 will mark the thirtieth anniversary of the Declaration,

1. *Reaffirms* its resolution 1514(XV) and all other resolutions on decolonization and calls upon the administering Powers, in accordance with those resolutions, to take all necessary steps to enable the dependent peoples of the Territories concerned to exercise fully and without further delay their inalienable right to self-determination and independence;

2. *Affirms once again* that the continuation of colonialism in all its forms and manifestations—including racism, *apartheid*, those activities of foreign economic and other interests contrary to the Charter of the United Nations and the Declaration on the Granting of Independence to Colonial Countries and Peoples, as well as the violations of the right to self-determination and basic human rights of the peoples of colonial Territories and continuous policies and practices to suppress legitimate national liberation movements—is incompatible with the Charter, the Universal Declaration of Human Rights and the Declaration on the Granting of Independence to Colonial Countries and Peoples and poses a serious threat to international peace and security;

3. *Reaffirms its determination* to take all necessary steps with a view to the complete and speedy eradication of colonialism and to the faithful and strict observance by all States of the relevant provisions of the Charter, the Declaration on the Granting of Independence to Colonial Countries and Peoples and the guiding principles of the Universal Declaration of Human Rights;

4. *Affirms once again* its recognition of the legitimacy of the struggle of the peoples under colonial and alien domination to exercise their right to self-determination and independence by all the necessary means at their disposal;

5. *Approves* the report of the Special Committee on the Situation with regard to the Implementation of the Declaration on the Granting of Independence to Colonial Countries and Peoples covering its work during 1989, including the programme of work envisaged for 1990;

6. *Calls upon* all States, in particular the administering Powers, as well as the specialized agencies and other organizations of the United Nations system within their respective spheres of competence, to give effect to the recommendations contained in the report of the Special Committee for the speedy implementation of the Declaration contained in General Assembly resolution 1514(XV) and other relevant resolutions of the United Nations;

7. *Condemns* the activities of foreign economic and other interests which are impeding the implementation of the Declaration with respect to the colonial Territories;

8. *Strongly condemns* all collaboration, particularly in the nuclear and military fields, with the Government of South Africa and calls upon the States concerned to cease forthwith all such collaboration;

9. *Calls upon* the colonial Powers to withdraw immediately and unconditionally their military bases and installations from colonial Territories, to refrain from establishing new ones and not to involve those Territories in any offensive acts or interference against other States;

10. *Urges* all States, directly and through their action in the specialized agencies and other organizations of the United Nations system, to provide all moral and material assistance to the people of Namibia, both during the transitional period and after independence, and, in respect of the other Territories, requests the administering Powers, in consultation with the Governments of the Territories under their administration, to take steps to enlist and make effective use of all possible assistance, on both a bilateral and a multilateral basis, in the strengthening of the economies of those Territories;

11. *Requests* the Special Committee to continue to seek suitable means for the immediate and full implementation of General Assembly resolution 1514(XV) in all Territories that have not yet attained independence and, in particular:

(*a*) To formulate specific proposals for the elimination of the remaining manifestations of colonialism and to report thereon to the General Assembly at its forty-fifth session;

(*b*) To make concrete suggestions which could assist the Security Council in considering appropriate measures under the Charter with regard to developments in colonial Territories that are likely to threaten international peace and security;

(*c*) To continue to examine the compliance of Member States with resolution 1514(XV) and other relevant resolutions on decolonization;

(*d*) To continue to pay special attention to the small Territories, in particular through the dispatch of visiting missions to those Territories whenever the Special Committee deems it appropriate, and to recommend to the General Assembly the most suitable steps to be taken to enable the populations of those Territories to exercise their right to self-determination and independence;

(*e*) To take all necessary steps to enlist world-wide support among Governments, as well as national and international organizations having a special interest in decolonization, for the achievement of the objectives of the Declaration and the implementation of the relevant resolutions of the United Nations;

12. *Calls upon* the administering Powers to continue to co-operate with the Special Committee in the discharge of its mandate and to permit the access of visit-

ing missions to the Territories to secure first-hand information and ascertain the wishes and aspirations of their inhabitants, and urges, in particular, those administering Powers which do not participate in the work of the Special Committee to do so at its 1990 session;

13. *Requests* the Secretary-General and the specialized agencies and other organizations of the United Nations system to provide or continue to provide to the newly independent and emerging States all possible assistance in the economic, social and other fields;

14. *Requests* the Secretary-General to provide the Special Committee with the facilities and services required for the implementation of the present resolution, as well as of the various resolutions and decisions on decolonization adopted by the General Assembly and the Special Committee.

General Assembly resolution 44/101

11 December 1989   Meeting 80   142-2-8 (recorded vote)

38-nation draft (A/44/L.55 & Add.1); agenda item 18.

Sponsors: Afghanistan, Algeria, Angola, Benin, Bulgaria, Burkina Faso, Byelorussian SSR, Congo, Cuba, Cyprus, Czechoslovakia, Democratic Yemen, Ethiopia, German Democratic Republic, China, India, Iran, Lao People's Democratic Republic, Libyan Arab Jamahiriya, Madagascar, Mali, Mongolia, Nicaragua, Pakistan, Papua New Guinea, Philippines, Sierra Leone, Solomon Islands, Sudan, Syrian Arab Republic, Tunisia, Ukranian SSR, United Republic of Tanzania, Vanuatu, Venezuela, Viet Nam, Yugoslavia, Zambia.

Financial implications. 5th Committee, A/44/860; S-G, A/C.5/44/46.

Meeting numbers. GA 44th session: 5th Committee 54; plenary 74, 75, 80.

Recorded vote in Assembly as follows:

In favour: Afghanistan, Albania, Algeria, Angola, Antigua and Barbuda, Argentina, Australia, Austria, Bahamas, Bahrain, Bangladesh, Barbados, Benin, Bhutan, Bolivia, Botswana, Brazil, Brunei Darussalam, Bulgaria, Burkina Faso, Burundi, Byelorussian SSR, Cameroon, Cape Verde, Central African Republic, Chad, Chile, China, Colombia, Comoros, Congo, Costa Rica, Côte d'Ivoire, Cuba, Cyprus, Czechoslovakia, Democratic Kampuchea, Democratic Yemen, Denmark, Djibouti, Dominica, Dominican Republic, Ecuador, Egypt, El Salvador, Equatorial Guinea, Ethiopia, Fiji, Finland, Gabon, Gambia, German Democratic Republic, Ghana, Greece, Grenada, Guatemala, Guinea, Guinea-Bissau, Guyana, Haiti, Honduras, Hungary, Iceland, India, Indonesia, Iran, Iraq, Ireland, Jamaica, Japan, Jordan, Kenya, Kuwait, Lao People's Democratic Republic, Lebanon, Lesotho, Liberia, Libyan Arab Jamahiriya, Madagascar, Malawi, Malaysia, Maldives, Mali, Malta, Mauritania, Mauritius, Mexico, Mongolia, Morocco, Myanmar, Nepal, New Zealand, Nicaragua, Niger, Nigeria, Norway, Oman, Pakistan, Panama, Papua New Guinea, Peru, Philippines, Poland, Portugal, Qatar, Romania, Rwanda, Saint Kitts and Nevis, Saint Lucia, Saint Vincent and the Grenadines, Samoa, Sao Tome and Principe, Saudi Arabia, Senegal, Seychelles, Sierra Leone, Singapore, Solomon Islands, Somalia, Spain, Sri Lanka, Suriname, Swaziland, Sweden, Syrian Arab Republic, Thailand, Togo, Trinidad and Tobago, Tunisia, Turkey, Uganda, Ukrainian SSR, USSR, United Arab Emirates, United Republic of Tanzania, Uruguay, Vanuatu, Venezuela, Viet Nam, Yemen, Yugoslavia, Zaire.

Against: United Kingdom, United States.

Abstaining: Belgium, Canada, France, Federal Republic of Germany, Israel, Italy, Luxembourg, Netherlands.

The Assembly took related action in **resolution 44/79,** by which it affirmed that the universal realization of the right of all peoples to self-determination was a fundamental condition for the guarantee of human rights (see PART THREE, Chapter X).

Implementation of Declaration by UN organizations

In response to a 1988 request of the General Assembly,[3] the Secretary-General in 1989 invited 25 specialized agencies and other international organizations to provide information on their activities aimed at implementing the 1960 Declaration,

and submitted a report[4] summarizing the responses received from 18 of the organizations.

In response to a 1988 request of the Economic and Social Council,[5] the Council's President and the Chairman of the Special Committee on decolonization reported[6] on consultations they had held on the implementation of the 1960 Declaration by specialized agencies and international institutions associated with the United Nations. They noted that some bodies had extended or formulated programmes of assistance to NSGTs, in addition to acting as executing agencies for projects funded by the United Nations Development Programme (UNDP). While they noted with satisfaction the close co-operation with Governments of front-line States and newly independent countries, they felt that these organizations must intensify their assistance to those countries.

The Special Committee on decolonization considered the issue and adopted a resolution[7] which formed the basis of a draft forwarded to the Assembly for consideration.

ECONOMIC AND SOCIAL COUNCIL ACTION

In **resolution 1989/95** adopted by recorded vote on 26 July, the Economic and Social Council recommended that all States intensify their efforts in the specialized agencies and other organizations of the UN system to ensure the full and effective implementation of the Declaration and other related UN resolutions.

GENERAL ASSEMBLY ACTION

On 11 December, on the recommendation of the Fourth (Special Political) Committee, the General Assembly adopted **resolution 44/85** by recorded vote.

Implementation of the Declaration on the Granting of Independence to Colonial Countries and Peoples by the specialized agencies and the international institutions associated with the United Nations

The General Assembly,

Having considered the item entitled "Implementation of the Declaration on the Granting of Independence to Colonial Countries and Peoples by the specialized agencies and the international institutions associated with the United Nations",

Having considered the reports submitted on the item by the Secretary-General and the Chairman of the Special Committee on the Situation with regard to the Implementation of the Declaration on the Granting of Independence to Colonial Countries and Peoples,

Bearing in mind the relevant provisions of the final documents of the successive Conferences of Heads of State or Government of Non-Aligned Countries and of the resolutions adopted by the Assembly of Heads of State and Government of the Organization of African Unity,

Welcoming the emplacement on 1 April 1989 of the United Nations Transition Assistance Group in Namibia and encouraged by the beginning of the independence process under the terms of Security Council resolution 435(1978) of 29 September 1978,

Deeply conscious of the continuing critical need of the people of Namibia, particularly during the period of transition to independence and immediately after the attainment of independence, for concrete assistance from the specialized agencies and the international institutions associated with the United Nations,

Noting the assistance extended thus far to colonial Territories by certain specialized agencies and other organizations of the United Nations system, in particular the United Nations Development Programme, and considering that such assistance should be expanded further, commensurate with the pressing needs of the peoples concerned for external assistance,

Stressing the importance of securing additional resources for funding expanding programmes of assistance for the peoples concerned and the need to enlist the support of the major funding institutions within the United Nations system in that regard,

Noting with deep concern that South Africa's practice of *apartheid* and acts of destabilization against the frontline and neighbouring States continue to present a serious threat to international peace and security,

Reaffirming the responsibility of the specialized agencies and other organizations of the United Nations system to take all the necessary measures, within their respective spheres of competence, to ensure the full and speedy implementation of General Assembly resolution 1514(XV) of 14 December 1960 and other relevant resolutions of the United Nations, particularly those relating to the extension of assistance to the peoples of the colonial Territories,

Expressing its appreciation to the General Secretariat of the Organization of African Unity for the continued co-operation and assistance it has extended to the specialized agencies and other organizations of the United Nations system in connection with the implementation of the relevant resolutions of the United Nations, and convinced that closer contacts and consultations between the specialized agencies and other organizations of the United Nations system and regional organizations help to facilitate the effective formulation of assistance programmes to the peoples concerned,

Expressing its appreciation to the Governments of the front-line States for the consistent support extended to the people of Namibia in their quest for independence and aware of the particular needs of those Governments for international assistance,

Considering that the retention of any links with the racist régime of South Africa is tantamount to support for, or endorsement of, the repressive policy and practice of *apartheid* pursued by that régime against the people of South Africa and its policy of destabilization against the neighbouring African States,

Bearing in mind the importance of the activities of non-governmental organizations aimed at putting an end to the assistance which is still being rendered to South Africa by some specialized agencies,

Mindful of the imperative need to keep under continuous review the activities of the specialized agencies and other organizations of the United Nations system in the implementation of the various United Nations decisions relating to decolonization,

1. *Approves* the chapter of the report of the Special Committee on the Situation with regard to the Implementation of the Declaration on the Granting of Independence to Colonial Countries and Peoples relating to the item;

2. *Reaffirms* that the specialized agencies and other organizations and institutions of the United Nations system should continue to be guided by the relevant resolutions of the United Nations in their efforts to contribute, within their spheres of competence, to the full and speedy implementation of the Declaration on the Granting of Independence to Colonial Countries and Peoples;

3. *Reaffirms also* that the recognition by the General Assembly, the Security Council and other United Nations organs of the legitimacy of the struggle of colonial peoples to exercise their right to self-determination and independence entails, as a corollary, the extension by the specialized agencies and other organizations of the United Nations system of all the necessary moral and material assistance to those peoples and their national liberation movements;

4. *Expresses its appreciation* to those specialized agencies and other organizations of the United Nations system that have continued to co-operate in varying degrees with the United Nations and the Organization of African Unity in the implementation of General Assembly resolution 1514(XV) and other relevant resolutions of the United Nations, and urges all the specialized agencies and other organizations of the United Nations system to accelerate the full and speedy implementation of the relevant provisions of those resolutions;

5. *Requests* the specialized agencies and other organizations of the United Nations system to render or continue to render, as a matter of urgency, all possible moral and material assistance to the colonial peoples, bearing in mind that such assistance should not only meet their immediate needs but also create conditions for development after they have exercised their right to self-determination and independence;

6. *Also requests* all specialized agencies and other organizations of the United Nations system to render concrete assistance to the people of Namibia, in particular during the period of transition to independence and immediately after the attainment of independence;

7. *Once again requests* the specialized agencies and other organizations of the United Nations system to continue to provide all moral and material assistance to the newly independent and emerging States so as to enable them to achieve genuine economic independence;

8. *Reiterates its recommendation* that the specialized agencies and other organizations of the United Nations system should initiate or broaden contacts and co-operation with the colonial peoples and the administering Powers concerned, directly or, where appropriate, through regional organizations, in order to intensify programmes of assistance and to facilitate and accelerate the implementation of General Assembly resolution 1514(XV);

9. *Urges* the executive heads of the specialized agencies and other organizations of the United Nations system, in co-operation with the regional and other organizations where appropriate, to submit to their governing and legislative organs concrete proposals for the full implementation of the relevant United Nations decisions, particularly specific programmes of assistance to the peoples of the colonial Territories and their national liberation movements;

10. *Once again urges* the executive heads of the World Bank and the International Monetary Fund to draw the attention of their governing bodies to the present resolution and urges them to introduce flexible procedures to prepare specific programmes for the peoples of the colonial Territories;

11. *Urges* the specialized agencies and other organizations of the United Nations system that have not already done so to include in the agenda of the regular meetings of their governing bodies a separate item on the progress they have made in the implementation of resolution 1514(XV) and other relevant resolutions of the United Nations;

12. *Also urges* the specialized agencies and other organizations and institutions of the United Nations system to extend substantial material assistance to the Governments of the front-line States in order to enable them to resist the acts of the destabilization being perpetrated by the racist régime of South Africa;

13. *Requests* the specialized agencies and other organizations of the United Nations system to continue to take, in accordance with the relevant resolutions of the General Assembly and the Security Council, all necessary measures to withhold any financial, economic, technical or other assistance from the Government of South Africa and to refrain from taking any action that might imply support for, or endorsement of, the repressive policy and practice of *apartheid* pursued by the racist régime against the people of South Africa and its policy of destabilization against the neighbouring African States;

14. *Invites* the specialized agencies and other organizations of the United Nations system to co-operate with the Action for Resisting Invasion, Colonialism and *Apartheid* Fund, established by the non-aligned countries, with the common objective of providing emergency assistance to the front-line States and national liberation movements in southern Africa in their struggle against the *apartheid* régime;

15. *Recommends* that all Governments should intensify their efforts in the specialized agencies and other organizations of the United Nations system of which they are members to ensure the full and effective implementation of resolution 1514(XV) and other relevant resolutions of the United Nations and, in that connection, should accord priority to the question of providing assistance on an emergency basis to the peoples of the colonial Territories;

16. *Requests* the Secretary-General to continue to assist the specialized agencies and other organizations of the United Nations system in working out appropriate measures for implementing the relevant resolutions of the United Nations and to prepare for submission to the relevant bodies, with the assistance of those agencies and organizations, a report on the action taken in implementation of the relevant resolutions, including the present resolution, since the circulation of his previous report;

17. *Requests* the Economic and Social Council to continue, as appropriate, to consider, in consultation with the Special Committee on the Situation with regard to the Implementation of the Declaration on the Granting of Independence to Colonial Countries and Peoples, appropriate measures for co-ordination of the policies and activities of the specialized agencies and other organizations of the United Nations system in implementing the relevant resolutions of the General Assembly;

18. *Requests* the specialized agencies to report periodically to the Secretary-General on their implementation of the present resolution;

19. *Requests* the Special Committee to continue to examine the question and to report thereon to the General Assembly at its forty-fifth session.

General Assembly resolution 44/85

11 December 1989   Meeting 80   142-2-10 (recorded vote)

Approved by Fourth Committee (A/44/740) by recorded vote (134-2-10), 25 October (meeting 16); draft by Special Committee on decolonization (A/44/23); agenda items 118 & 12.

Meeting numbers. GA 44th session: 4th Committee 5, 9-16; plenary 80.

Recorded vote in Assembly as follows:

In favour: Afghanistan, Albania, Algeria, Angola, Antigua and Barbuda, Argentina, Austria, Bahamas, Bahrain, Bangladesh, Barbados, Benin, Bhutan, Bolivia, Botswana, Brazil, Brunei Darussalam, Bulgaria, Burkina Faso, Burundi, Byelorussian SSR, Cameroon, Canada, Cape Verde, Central African Republic, Chad, Chile, China, Colombia, Comoros, Congo, Costa Rica, Côte d'Ivoire, Cuba, Cyprus, Czechoslovakia, Democratic Kampuchea, Democratic Yemen, Denmark, Djibouti, Dominica, Dominican Republic, Ecuador, Egypt, El Salvador, Equatorial Guinea, Ethiopia, Fiji, Finland, Gabon, Gambia, German Democratic Republic, Ghana, Grenada, Greece, Guatemala, Guinea, Guinea-Bissau, Guyana, Haiti, Honduras, Hungary, Iceland, India, Indonesia, Iran, Iraq, Ireland, Jamaica, Jordan, Kenya, Kuwait, Lao People's Democratic Republic, Lebanon, Lesotho, Liberia, Libyan Arab Jamahiriya, Madagascar, Malawi, Malaysia, Maldives, Mali, Malta, Mauritania, Mauritius, Mexico, Mongolia, Morocco, Mozambique, Myanmar, Nepal, New Zealand, Nicaragua, Niger, Nigeria, Norway, Oman, Pakistan, Panama, Papua New Guinea, Paraguay, Peru, Philippines, Poland, Qatar, Romania, Rwanda, Saint Kitts and Nevis, Saint Lucia, Saint Vincent and the Grenadines, Samoa, Sao Tome and Principe, Saudi Arabia, Senegal, Seychelles, Sierra Leone, Singapore, Solomon Islands, Somalia, Spain, Sri Lanka, Suriname, Swaziland, Sweden, Syrian Arab Republic, Thailand, Togo, Trinidad and Tobago, Tunisia, Turkey, Uganda, Ukrainian SSR, USSR, United Arab Emirates, United Republic of Tanzania, Uruguay, Vanuatu, Venezuela, Viet Nam, Yemen, Yugoslavia, Zaire.

Against: United Kingdom, United States.

Abstaining: Australia, Belgium, France, Germany, Federal Republic of, Israel, Italy, Japan, Luxembourg, Netherlands, Portugal.

Thirtieth anniversary of Declaration

In response to a 1988 request of the General Assembly,[8] the Special Committee on decolonization, in February 1989, addressed the programme of activities for the thirtieth anniversary of the Declaration and referred it to its working group for consideration and recommendations. The Committee approved[2] without objection the recommendations made by the working group, which contained the Programme of Activities in Observance of the Thirtieth Anniversary of the Declaration on the Granting of Independence to Colonial Countries and Peoples. It also decided that the motto for the anniversary should be "Complete decolonization—objective 2000".

GENERAL ASSEMBLY ACTION

On 11 December, the General Assembly adopted **resolution 44/100** by recorded vote.

Programme of Activities in Observance of the Thirtieth Anniversary of the Declaration on the Granting of Independence to Colonial Countries and Peoples

The General Assembly,

Having considered the relevant chapter of the report of the Special Committee on the Situation with regard to the Implementation of the Declaration on the

Granting of Independence to Colonial Countries and Peoples,

Bearing in mind that the year 1990 will mark the thirtieth anniversary of the Declaration on the Granting of Independence to Colonial Countries and Peoples,

Emphasizing the importance of the occasion to evaluate the progress achieved during the period in the process of decolonization, in particular in the implementation of the Declaration during the past thirty years, as well as the role played by the United Nations and its system of organizations in that regard, and to formulate specific measures for the elimination of all remnants of colonialism in all its forms and manifestations in various areas of the world,

1. *Approves* the relevant chapter of the report of the Special Committee on the Situation with regard to the Implementation of the Declaration on the Granting of Independence to Colonial Countries and Peoples and endorses the Programme of Activities in Observance of the Thirtieth Anniversary of the Declaration on the Granting of Independence to Colonial Countries and Peoples set out in the annex to the present resolution;

2. *Commends* the Programme, for appropriate action, to all States, the United Nations bodies concerned, the specialized agencies and other organizations of the United Nations system and the non-governmental organizations active in the field of decolonization;

3. *Requests* the Secretary-General to assist in the implementation of the present resolution and, in particular, to make adequate resources available for undertaking the measures envisaged in the Programme;

4. *Requests* the Special Committee to follow closely the implementation of the Programme and to report to the General Assembly at its forty-fifth session on the implementation of the present resolution.

ANNEX
Programme of Activities in Observance of the Thirtieth Anniversary of the Declaration on the Granting of Independence to Colonial Countries and Peoples

1. The commemoration of the thirtieth anniversary of the Declaration on the Granting of Independence to Colonial Countries and Peoples would be an appropriate occasion to evaluate the progress achieved during the past thirty years in the implementation of the Declaration, as well as the role played by the United Nations and its system of organizations in that regard. It would also, in the light of General Assembly resolution 43/47, of 22 November 1988, on the International Decade for the Eradication of Colonialism, provide the opportunity to formulate specific measures for the elimination of all remnants of colonialism in all its forms and manifestations in various areas of the world. To this end, the following special programme of activities is envisaged.

A. Activities at the international level

Commemorative meeting of the General Assembly

2. The General Assembly shall hold a special commemorative meeting in observance of the thirtieth anniversary of the Declaration, it being understood that the specific modalities and procedures for the commemoration (recognition of contributions made by individuals) would be the subject of subsequent consultations between the President of the General Assembly and the Chairman of the Special Committee on the Situation

with regard to the Implementation of the Declaration on the Granting of Independence to Colonial Countries and Peoples.

(a) The meeting shall be held at United Nations Headquarters in early October 1990 when a number of heads of State or Government are present.

(b) Statements might be made by the President of the General Assembly, the Secretary-General, the Chairman of the Special Committee and the Chairman of the Special Committee against *Apartheid*, and by the representatives of the regional groups.

Commemorative declaration to be adopted by the General Assembly

3. The Special Committee shall prepare the draft text of a commemorative declaration to be submitted to the General Assembly at its forty-fifth session. The declaration would not only highlight the work accomplished during the past thirty years but would also take into account the plan of action for the International Decade for the Eradication of Colonialism to be submitted to the General Assembly at its forty-fifth session.

Seminars to be held by the Special Committee
Regional seminars

4. The Special Committee shall hold in 1990 two regional seminars on the subject of decolonization.

5. Those seminars would be an appropriate occasion for the participants to reflect upon the specific concerns and problems of the small dependent islands. In that connection, the following themes might be considered:

(a) Self-determination and economic and social development: the case of small islands;

(b) Heightening of awareness of options concerning future political status;

(c) Colonialism and racial discrimination;

(d) Self-determination: the constraints faced by small Territories—prospects and challenges for the future;

(e) Self-determination and regional integration of small islands;

(f) Advantages and disadvantages of foreign economic interests and/or activities in the small Territories: the views of the populations concerned;

(g) Consequences of the military use of small islands;

(h) Environmental problems affecting small islands;

(i) Protection of land for island populations and dangers of foreign exploitation;

(j) Protection of natural resources, particularly marine resources, for the benefit of the populations of small islands and Territories.

6. The working papers prepared by the Secretariat on specific Territories for the 1990 session of the Special Committee could serve as a basis for discussions. Participants will also be asked to submit papers on the above themes.

7. The seminars will be held in the Caribbean and the Asia/Pacific regions at the appropriate time prior to the session of the Special Committee to be held in July/August 1990.

8. Seminars may be attended by the following:

(a) Up to five members of the Special Committee, one from each region;

(b) The representative of the Secretary-General;

(c) The Chairman of the Special Committee against *Apartheid*;

(d) Representatives of the host Government;

(e) Representatives of the administering Powers;

(f) Representatives of specialized agencies and other organizations within the United Nations system;

(g) Representatives of the Non-Self-Governing Territories in the regions concerned—at least one per Territory—should be invited to participate in those seminars (the modalities for their participation to be determined in consultation with the administering Powers concerned);

(h) Up to 30 representatives of non-governmental organizations based in the region;

(i) Up to three eminent personalities in the field of decolonization.

Seminar at United Nations Headquarters

9. The Special Committee shall organize, in close consultation with the Department of Public Information of the Secretariat, a seminar on dissemination of information on decolonization to be held at United Nations Headquarters. Participants would include journalists accredited to the United Nations and representatives of non-governmental organizations, universities and other educational and research institutions, etc.

Activities by the specialized agencies and other organizations of the United Nations system, other international organizations and the non-governmental organizations concerned

10. The organizations concerned are requested to undertake various activities in commemoration of the anniversary during 1990. These activities may include the preparation of special publications and studies and the holding of exhibits, seminars and symposia. An account of activities related to decolonization would be highlighted with a view to enhancing the assistance of those organizations to the ongoing decolonization process.

11. The organizations concerned are requested to draw up concrete programmes of assistance to the peoples of colonial Territories.

Dissemination of information on decolonization

12. The Secretary-General is requested to take concrete measures to give widespread and intensified publicity to the situation in the Territories concerned and to the work of the United Nations in the field of decolonization. In particular, the Department of Public Information and the Department for Special Political Questions, Regional Co-operation, Decolonization and Trusteeship, in consultation with the Special Committee, should:

(a) Prepare special publications devoted to the thirtieth anniversary of the Declaration, including special issues of the *Decolonization* bulletin and *Objective: Justice*;

(b) Hold public screenings of films concerning the process of decolonization;

(c) Prepare and distribute audio-visual materials on decolonization to national radio and television stations;

(d) Hold exhibitions of photographs and publications related to decolonization, both at United Nations Headquarters and at various United Nations information centres;

(e) Organize special briefings of non-governmental organizations and other interested groups on the subject of decolonization.

Other activities

13. The motto for the anniversary shall be: "Complete decolonization—objective 2000".

14. The Secretary-General is requested to arrange, through the United Nations Postal Administration, for a special postal cancellation to mark the thirtieth anniversary of the Declaration.

B. Activities at the regional level

15. Intergovernmental regional organizations are requested to intensify their activities to help eliminate the last manifestations of colonialism and, to that end, to increase their collaboration with one another. They are also encouraged to hold commemorative meetings and seminars, prepare special studies on various aspects of colonial questions and adopt measures to increase moral and material assistance to the peoples concerned.

C. Activities at the national level

16. Heads of State and Government, high-ranking officials and representatives of political movements, religious organizations, trade unions and other national organizations are called upon to issue special messages on the occasion of the anniversary.

17. Governments may be invited to establish, in co-operation with national United Nations associations, national committees for the commemoration of the anniversary to plan and co-ordinate various activities to be undertaken in 1990, such as publicizing the work of the United Nations on decolonization through publications, educational programmes in schools and universities, special studies, seminars and radio-television programmes, including the widest possible dissemination in their national languages of the Declaration and the various resolutions and decisions of the United Nations on decolonization, and through the issuance of a commemorative postage stamp and other activities.

18. In undertaking the above activities, particular attention shall be devoted to the various manifestations of colonialism, including racial discrimination and *apartheid*.

General Assembly resolution 44/100

11 December 1989   Meeting 80   137-2-14 (recorded vote)

Draft by Special Committee on decolonization (A/44/23); agenda item 18.
Financial implications. 5th Committee, A/44/860; S-G, A/C.5/44/46.
Meeting numbers. GA 44th session: 5th Committee 54; plenary 74, 75, 80.

Recorded vote in Assembly as follows:

In favour: Afghanistan, Albania, Algeria, Angola, Antigua and Barbuda, Argentina, Australia, Austria, Bahamas, Bahrain, Bangladesh, Barbados, Benin, Bhutan, Bolivia, Botswana, Brazil, Brunei Darussalam, Bulgaria, Burkina Faso, Burundi, Byelorussian SSR, Cameroon, Cape Verde, Central African Republic, Chad, Chile, China, Colombia, Comoros, Congo, Costa Rica, Côte d'Ivoire, Cuba, Cyprus, Czechoslovakia, Democratic Kampuchea, Democratic Yemen, Djibouti, Dominica, Dominican Republic, Ecuador, Egypt, El Salvador, Equatorial Guinea, Ethiopia, Fiji, Gabon, Gambia, German Democratic Republic, Ghana, Greece, Grenada, Guatemala, Guinea, Guinea-Bissau, Guyana, Haiti, Honduras, Hungary, India, Indonesia, Iran, Iraq, Ireland, Jamaica, Jordan, Kenya, Kuwait, Lao People's Democratic Republic, Lebanon, Lesotho, Liberia, Libyan Arab Jamahiriya, Madagascar, Malawi, Malaysia, Maldives, Mali, Malta, Mauritania, Mauritius, Mexico, Mongolia, Morocco, Myanmar, Nepal, New Zealand, Nicaragua, Niger, Nigeria, Norway, Oman, Pakistan, Panama, Papua New Guinea, Paraguay, Peru, Philippines, Poland, Qatar, Romania, Rwanda, Saint Kitts and Nevis, Saint Lucia, Saint Vincent and the Grenadines, Samoa, Sao Tome and Principe, Saudi Arabia, Senegal, Seychelles, Sierra Leone, Singapore, Solomon Islands, Somalia, Spain, Sri Lanka, Suriname, Swaziland, Syrian Arab Republic, Thailand, Togo, Trinidad and Tobago, Tunisia, Turkey, Uganda, Ukrainian SSR, USSR, United Arab Emirates, United Republic of Tanzania, Uruguay, Vanuatu, Venezuela, Viet Nam, Yemen, Yugoslavia, Zaire.

Against: United Kingdom, United States.

Abstaining: Belgium, Canada, Denmark, Finland, France, Germany, Federal Republic of, Iceland, Israel, Italy, Japan, Luxembourg, Netherlands, Portugal, Sweden.

Military activities in Territories

Pursuant to a 1988 request of the General Assembly,[9] the Special Committee on decolonization continued to consider the issue of military activities and bases in colonial countries. On 15 August, it adopted a decision[10] which became the basis of a draft recommendation to the Assembly. On 18 August,[11] the Committee's Chairman transmitted the decision to the Security Council, drawing attention to a paragraph in which the Committee urged the Council to make the arms embargo against South Africa more effective and comprehensive.

GENERAL ASSEMBLY ACTION

On 11 December, the General Assembly adopted **decision 44/425** by recorded vote.

Military activities and arrangements by colonial Powers in Territories under their administration which might be impeding the implementation of the Declaration on the Granting of Independence to Colonial Countries and Peoples

At its 80th plenary meeting, on 11 December 1989, the General Assembly, on the recommendation of the Fourth Committee, adopted the following text:

"1. The General Assembly, having considered the chapter of the report of the Special Committee on the Situation with regard to the Implementation of the Declaration on the Granting of Independence to Colonial Countries and Peoples relating to an item on the agenda of the Special Committee entitled 'Military activities and arrangements by colonial Powers in Territories under their administration which might be impeding the implementation of the Declaration on the Granting of Independence to Colonial Countries and Peoples', and recalling its decision 43/410 of 22 November 1988 on the question, deplores the fact that the colonial Powers concerned have taken no steps to implement the request that the Assembly has repeatedly addressed to them, most recently in paragraph 10 of its resolution 43/45 of 22 November 1988, to withdraw immediately and unconditionally their military bases and installations from colonial Territories and to refrain from establishing new ones.

"2. In recalling its resolution 1514(XV) of 14 December 1960 and all other resolutions and decisions of the United Nations relating to military bases and installations in colonial and Non-Self-Governing Territories, the General Assembly reaffirms its strong conviction that the presence of military bases and installations in the colonial and Non-Self-Governing Territories could constitute a major obstacle to the implementation of the Declaration on the Granting of Independence to Colonial Countries and Peoples and that it is the responsibility of the administering Powers to ensure that the existence of such bases and installations does not hinder the populations of the Territories from exercising their right to self-determination and independence in conformity with the purposes and principles of the Charter of the United Nations and the Declaration. Furthermore, aware of the

presence of military bases and installations of the administering Powers concerned and other countries in those Territories, the Assembly urges the administering Powers concerned to continue to take all necessary measures not to involve those Territories in any offensive acts or interference against other States and to comply fully with the purposes and principles of the Charter, the Declaration and the resolutions and decisions of the United Nations relating to military activities and arrangements by colonial Powers in Territories under their administration.

"3. The General Assembly reiterates its condemnation of all military activities and arrangements by colonial Powers in Territories under their administration that are detrimental to the rights and interests of the colonial peoples concerned, especially their right to self-determination and independence. The Assembly once again calls upon the colonial Powers concerned to terminate immediately and unconditionally such activities and to eliminate such military bases in compliance with the relevant resolutions of the Assembly, in particular with paragraph 9 of the Plan of Action for the Full Implementation of the Declaration on the Granting of Independence to Colonial Countries and Peoples, contained in the annex to Assembly resolution 35/118 of 11 December 1980.

"4. The General Assembly reiterates that the colonial Territories and areas adjacent thereto should not be used for nuclear testing, dumping of nuclear wastes or deployment of nuclear and other weapons of mass destruction.

"5. The General Assembly notes with serious concern that, in southern Africa in general, a critical situation continues to prevail as a result of South Africa's inhuman repression of the people of South Africa. The Assembly declares that the policy of *apartheid* and destabilization pursued by Pretoria not only undermines the peace and stability of the southern African region but also constitutes a threat to international peace and security.

"6. The General Assembly condemns the continued military, nuclear and intelligence collaboration between South Africa and certain countries, which constitutes a violation of the arms embargo imposed against South Africa by the Security Council in its resolution 418(1977) of 4 November 1977 and poses a threat to international peace and security. The Assembly urges the Council to consider, as a matter of urgency, the report of the Committee established under its resolution 421(1977) of 9 December 1977 and adopt further measures to widen the scope of resolution 418(1977) in order to make it more effective and comprehensive. The Assembly also calls for the scrupulous observance of Security Council resolution 558(1984) of 13 December 1984 enjoining all States to refrain from importing armaments from South Africa. The Assembly is particularly mindful in that regard of a series of resolutions adopted by the Security Council, the General Assembly, the Special Committee on the Situation with regard to the Implementation of the Declaration on the Granting of Independence to Colonial Countries and Peoples, the Special Committee against *Apartheid* and the United Nations Council for Namibia, as well as the Movement of Non-Aligned Countries, the Organization of African Unity, the

Commonwealth and a number of intergovernmental and regional organizations.

"7. The General Assembly reaffirms the legitimacy of the struggle of the people of Namibia to achieve their freedom and independence and appeals to all States to render sustained assistance in all fields in support of the faithful implementation of Security Council resolution 435(1978) of 29 September 1978.

"8. The General Assembly considers that the acquisition of nuclear-weapon capability by the racist régime of South Africa, with its infamous record of violence and aggression, constitutes a further effort on its part to terrorize and intimidate independent States in the region into submission while also posing a threat to all mankind. The Assembly condemns the continuing support to the racist régime of South Africa in the military and nuclear fields. In this context, the Assembly expresses its concern at the grave consequences for international peace and security of the collaboration between the racist régime of South Africa and certain Western Powers, Israel and other countries in the military and nuclear fields. It calls upon the States concerned to end all such collaboration and, in particular, to halt the supply to South Africa of equipment, technology, nuclear materials and related training, which increases its nuclear capability.

"9. The General Assembly strongly condemns the continuing collaboration of certain countries with the racist régime in the political, economic, military and nuclear fields and expresses its conviction that such collaboration is in contravention of the arms embargo imposed against South Africa under Security Council resolution 418(1977) and undermines international solidarity against the *apartheid* régime. The Assembly thus calls for the termination forthwith of all such collaboration.

"10. The General Assembly urges all Governments, the specialized agencies and other intergovernmental organizations to provide increased material assistance to the thousands of refugees who have been forced by the *apartheid* régime's oppressive policies in South Africa to flee into the neighbouring States.

"11. The General Assembly deprecates the continued alienation of land in colonial Territories for military installations. The large-scale utilization of local economic and manpower resources for this purpose diverts resources that could be more beneficially utilized in promoting the economic development of the Territories concerned and is thus contrary to the interests of their populations.

"12. The General Assembly requests the Secretary-General to continue, through the Department of Public Information of the Secretariat, an intensified campaign of publicity with a view to informing world public opinion of the facts concerning the military activities and arrangements in colonial Territories which are impeding the implementation of the Declaration on the Granting of Independence to Colonial Countries and Peoples, contained in Assembly resolution 1514(XV).

"13. The General Assembly requests the Special Committee on the Situation with regard to the Implementation of the Declaration on the Granting of Independence to Colonial Countries and Peoples to continue to examine this question and to report thereon to the Assembly at its forty-fifth session."

General Assembly decision 44/425

125-12-13 (recorded vote)

Approved by Fourth Committee (A/44/664) by recorded vote (86-12-12), 10 October (meeting 6); draft by Special Committee on decolonization (A/44/23); agenda item 117.

Meeting numbers. GA 44th session: 4th Committee 2-6; plenary 80.

Recorded vote in Assembly as follows:

In favour: Afghanistan, Albania, Algeria, Angola, Antigua and Barbuda, Argentina, Bahamas, Bahrain, Bangladesh, Barbados, Benin, Bhutan, Bolivia, Botswana, Brazil, Brunei Darussalam, Burkina Faso, Burundi, Byelorussian SSR, Cameroon, Cape Verde, Central African Republic, Chad, China, Colombia, Comoros, Congo, Costa Rica, Côte d'Ivoire, Cuba, Cyprus, Czechoslovakia, Democratic Kampuchea, Democratic Yemen, Djibouti, Dominica, Dominican Republic, Ecuador, Egypt, El Salvador, Equatorial Guinea, Ethiopia, Fiji, Gabon, Gambia, German Democratic Republic, Ghana, Grenada, Guatemala, Guinea, Guinea-Bissau, Guyana, Haiti, Honduras, Hungary, India, Indonesia, Iran, Iraq, Jamaica, Jordan, Kenya, Kuwait, Lao People's Democratic Republic, Lebanon, Lesotho, Liberia, Libyan Arab Jamahiriya, Madagascar, Malaysia, Maldives, Mali, Mauritania, Mauritius, Mexico, Mongolia, Morocco, Mozambique, Myanmar, Nepal, Nicaragua, Niger, Nigeria, Oman, Pakistan, Panama, Papua New Guinea, Peru, Philippines, Poland, Qatar, Romania, Rwanda, Saint Kitts and Nevis, Saint Lucia, Saint Vincent and the Grenadines, Samoa, Sao Tome and Principe, Saudi Arabia, Senegal, Seychelles, Sierra Leone, Singapore, Solomon Islands, Somalia, Sri Lanka, Suriname, Swaziland, Syrian Arab Republic, Thailand, Togo, Trinidad and Tobago, Tunisia, Uganda, Ukrainian SSR, USSR, United Arab Emirates, United Republic of Tanzania, Uruguay, Vanuatu, Venezuela, Viet Nam, Yemen, Yugoslavia, Zaire.

Against: Belgium, Canada, France, Germany, Federal Republic of, Israel, Italy, Japan, Luxembourg, Netherlands, Portugal, United Kingdom, United States.

Abstaining: Australia, Austria, Denmark, Finland, Greece, Iceland, Ireland, Malta, New Zealand, Norway, Spain, Sweden, Turkey.

Information dissemination

The Special Committee on decolonization considered[2] the question of disseminating information on decolonization. In its deliberations on the subject, it examined reports of the Sub-Committee on Petitions, Information and Assistance on its consultations with the United Nations Secretariat,[12] as well as with non-governmental organizations (NGOs),[13] and with the Organization of African Unity (OAU) and various national liberation movements.[14] The Committee endorsed the conclusions and recommendations of the Sub-Committee with the understanding that consultations would be held in connection with the implementation of specific recommendations as necessary, and that the reservations expressed by members would be reflected in the record of the meeting. The Committee also paid due regard to information supplied by representatives of the African National Congress of South Africa, the Pan Africanist Congress of Azania, and NGOs.

Among the recommendations and conclusions of the Committee were requests to the relevant UN departments to intensify publicity efforts regarding decolonization; to disseminate information on the remaining colonial Territories more widely; to provide NGOs with more information; and to increase press coverage of the situation in southern

Africa to counter the destructive and hostile propaganda campaign being waged against the national liberation movements.

GENERAL ASSEMBLY ACTION

On 11 December, the General Assembly adopted **resolution 44/102** by recorded vote.

Dissemination of information on decolonization

The General Assembly,

Having examined the chapter of the report of the Special Committee on the Situation with regard to the Implementation of the Declaration on the Granting of Independence to Colonial Countries and Peoples relating to the dissemination of information on decolonization and publicity for the work of the United Nations in the field of decolonization,

Recalling its resolution 1514(XV) of 14 December 1960, containing the Declaration on the Granting of Independence to Colonial Countries and Peoples, and all other resolutions and decisions of the United Nations concerning the dissemination of information on decolonization, in particular General Assembly resolution 43/46 of 22 November 1988,

Reiterating the importance of publicity as an instrument for furthering the aims and purposes of the Declaration and mindful of the continuing pressing need to take all possible steps to acquaint world public opinion with all aspects of the problems of decolonization with a view to assisting effectively the peoples of the colonial Territories in achieving self-determination, freedom and independence,

Noting with deep concern the measures of censorship imposed by the racist régime of South Africa upon the local and international media with respect to the policies and practices of *apartheid,*

Aware of the increasingly important role being played in the widespread dissemination of relevant information by a number of non-governmental organizations having a special interest in decolonization, and noting with satisfaction the intensified efforts of the Special Committee in enlisting the support of those organizations in that regard,

1. *Approves* the chapter of the report of the Special Committee on the Situation with regard to the Implementation of the Declaration on the Granting of Independence to Colonial Countries and Peoples relating to the dissemination of information on decolonization and publicity for the work of the United Nations in the field of decolonization;

2. *Considers* it incumbent upon the United Nations to continue to play an active role in the process of self-determination and independence and to intensify its efforts for the widest possible dissemination of information on decolonization, with a view to the further mobilization of international public opinion in support of complete decolonization;

3. *Requests* the Secretary-General, having regard to the suggestions of the Special Committee, to continue to take concrete measures through all the media at his disposal, including publications, radio and television, to give widespread and continuous publicity to the work of the United Nations in the field of decolonization, and, *inter alia:*

(a) To continue, in consultation with the Special Committee, to collect, prepare and disseminate basic material, studies and articles relating to the problems of decolonization and, in particular, to continue to publish the periodical *Objective: Justice* and other publications, special articles and studies, including the *Decolonization* series, and to select from them appropriate material for wider dissemination by means of reprints in various languages;

(b) To seek the full co-operation of the administering Powers concerned in the discharge of the tasks referred to above;

(c) To intensify the activities of all United Nations information centres;

(d) To maintain a close working relationship with the Organization of African Unity by holding periodic consultations and by systematically exchanging relevant information with that organization;

(e) To enlist, with the close co-operation of United Nations information centres, the support of non-governmental organizations having a special interest in decolonization in the dissemination of the relevant information;

(f) To continue to provide full press release coverage for all meetings of the Special Committee and its subsidiary bodies;

(g) To ensure the availability of the necessary facilities and services to that end;

(h) To report to the Special Committee on the measures taken in implementation of the present resolution;

4. *Requests* all States, in particular the administering Powers, the specialized agencies and other organizations of the United Nations system and non-governmental organizations having a special interest in decolonization, to undertake or intensify, in co-operation with the Secretary-General and within their respective spheres of competence, the large-scale dissemination of the information referred to in paragraph 2 above;

5. *Requests* the Special Committee to follow the implementation of the present resolution and to report thereon to the General Assembly at its forty-fifth session.

General Assembly resolution 44/102

11 December 1989   Meeting 80   143-2-7 (recorded vote)

37-nation draft (A/44/L.56 & Add.1); agenda item 18.
Sponsors: Afghanistan, Algeria, Angola, Benin, Burkina Faso, Byelorussian SSR, Congo, Cuba, Cyprus, Czechoslovakia, Democratic Yemen, Ethiopia, German Democratic Republic, Ghana, India, Iran, Lao People's Democratic Republic, Libyan Arab Jamahiriya, Madagascar, Mali, Mongolia, Nicaragua, Pakistan, Papua New Guinea, Philippines, Sierra Leone, Solomon Islands, Sudan, Syrian Arab Republic, Tunisia, Ukrainian SSR, United Republic of Tanzania, Vanuatu, Venezuela, Viet Nam, Zambia.
Financial implications. 5th Committee, A/44/860; S-G, A/C.5/44/46.
Meeting numbers. GA 44th session: 5th Committee 54; plenary 74, 75, 80.

Recorded vote in Assembly as follows:

In favour: Afghanistan, Albania, Algeria, Angola, Antigua and Barbuda, Argentina, Australia, Austria, Bahamas, Bahrain, Bangladesh, Barbados, Benin, Bhutan, Bolivia, Botswana, Brazil, Brunei Darussalam, Bulgaria, Burkina Faso, Burundi, Byelorussian SSR, Cameroon, Canada, Cape Verde, Central African Republic, Chad, Chile, China, Colombia, Comoros, Congo, Costa Rica, Côte d'Ivoire, Cuba, Cyprus, Czechoslovakia, Democratic Kampuchea, Democratic Yemen, Denmark, Djibouti, Dominica, Dominican Republic, Ecuador, Egypt, El Salvador, Equatorial Guinea, Ethiopia, Fiji, Finland, Gabon, Gambia, German Democratic Republic, Ghana, Greece, Grenada, Guatemala, Guinea, Guinea-Bissau, Guyana, Haiti, Honduras, Hungary, Iceland, India, Indonesia, Iran, Iraq, Ireland, Jamaica, Japan, Jordan, Kenya, Kuwait, Lao People's Democratic Republic, Lebanon, Lesotho, Liberia, Libyan Arab Jamahiriya, Madagascar, Malawi, Malaysia, Maldives, Mali, Malta, Mauritania, Mauritius, Mexico, Mongolia, Morocco, Myanmar, Nepal, New Zealand, Nicaragua, Niger, Nigeria, Norway, Oman, Pakistan, Panama, Papua New Guinea, Peru, Philippines, Poland, Portugal, Qatar, Romania, Rwanda, Saint Kitts and Nevis, Saint Lucia, Saint Vincent and the Grenadines, Samoa, Sao Tome and Principe, Saudi Arabia, Senegal, Seychelles, Sierra Leone, Singapore, Solomon Islands, Somalia, Spain, Sri Lanka, Suriname, Swaziland, Sweden, Syrian Arab Republic, Thailand, Togo, Trinidad and Tobago, Tunisia, Turkey, Uganda, Ukrainian SSR, USSR, United Arab Emirates, United Republic of Tanzania, Uruguay, Vanuatu, Venezuela, Viet Nam, Yemen, Yugoslavia, Zaire.

Against: United Kingdom, United States.

Abstaining: Belgium, France, Germany, Federal Republic of, Israel, Italy, Luxembourg, Netherlands.

Week of solidarity with the peoples of Namibia and other colonial Territories

In 1989, the UN Secretariat undertook a series of public information activities assisted by UN information centres throughout the world, in observance of the Week of Solidarity with the Peoples of Namibia and All Other Colonial Territories, as well as Those in South Africa, Fighting for Freedom, Independence and Human Rights (22-26 May). In commemoration of the Week, the Chairman of the Special Committee on decolonization issued a statement on 22 May. He reviewed developments regarding decolonization, particularly in southern Africa, and appealed to Member States and the UN system, as well as NGOs, to mobilize material and moral support for colonial peoples.

Role of NGOs

The Sub-Committee on Petitions, Information and Assistance held consultations in 1989 with a number of NGOs with regard to the implementation of the Declaration on the Granting of Independence to Colonial Countries and Peoples. In its conclusions and recommendations,[13] the Sub-Committee stated that NGOs played an important role in the decolonization process, particularly by disseminating information and by assisting colonial peoples and liberation movements. It encouraged NGOs to intensify their efforts and suggested that they be assisted in disseminating information.

In **resolution 44/102** (see above), the General Assembly requested the Secretary-General to publicize the work of the United Nations on decolonization and to enlist the support of NGOs.

International Decade for the Eradication of Colonialism

In accordance with a 1988 General Assembly resolution[15] declaring the period 1990-2000 as the International Decade for the Eradication of Colonialism, the Secretary-General invited all States and organizations of the UN system to submit suggestions for the preparation of an action plan aimed at ushering a world free of colonialism in the twenty-first century. An interim report,[16] submitted in November 1989, reproduced the replies received from 16 Member States, one from a non-Member State and three from organizations within the UN system. He noted that at the Ninth Conference of Heads of State or Govern-

ments of Non-Aligned Countries (Belgrade, Yugoslavia, 4-7 September), members created a working group to contribute to the UN plan of action for the Decade. In addition, members of the Organization of American States had recently adopted a resolution committing their organization to full participation in UN activities for the Decade.

GENERAL ASSEMBLY ACTION

On 11 December, the General Assembly adopted **decision 44/429** by recorded vote.

International Decade for the Eradication of Colonialism

At its 80th plenary meeting, on 11 December 1989, the General Assembly took note of the interim report of the Secretary-General on the International Decade for the Eradication of Colonialism and recommended that the Secretary-General should request those States and organizations of the United Nations system that have not yet done so to reply not later than 1 April 1990 to his communication of 31 January 1989, and that he should invite them once again to submit suggestions so that they may be taken into account in the final report which would be submitted to the Assembly at its forty-fifth session and which would enable the Assembly to consider and adopt an action plan aimed at ushering in, in the twenty-first century, a world free from colonialism.

General Assembly decision 44/429

130-0-22 (recorded vote)

Draft by Yugoslavia (A/44/L.57); agenda item 18.
Meeting numbers. GA 44th session: plenary 74, 75, 80.

Recorded vote in Assembly as follows:

In favour: Afghanistan, Albania, Algeria, Angola, Antigua and Barbuda, Argentina, Australia, Bahamas, Bahrain, Bangladesh, Barbados, Benin, Bhutan, Bolivia, Botswana, Brazil, Brunei Darussalam, Bulgaria, Burkina Faso, Burundi, Byelorussian SSR, Cameroon, Cape Verde, Central African Republic, Chad, Chile, China, Colombia, Comoros, Congo, Costa Rica, Côte d'Ivoire, Cuba, Cyprus, Czechoslovakia, Democratic Kampuchea, Democratic Yemen, Djibouti, Dominican Republic, Ecuador, Egypt, El Salvador, Equatorial Guinea, Ethiopia, Fiji, Gabon, Gambia, German Democratic Republic, Ghana, Grenada, Guatemala, Guinea, Guinea-Bissau, Guyana, Haiti, Honduras, Hungary, India, Indonesia, Iran, Iraq, Jamaica, Jordan, Kenya, Kuwait, Lao People's Democratic Republic, Lebanon, Lesotho, Liberia, Libyan Arab Jamahiriya, Madagascar, Malawi, Malaysia, Maldives, Mali, Malta, Mauritania, Mauritius, Mexico, Mongolia, Morocco, Myanmar, Nepal, New Zealand, Nicaragua, Niger, Nigeria, Oman, Pakistan, Panama, Papua New Guinea, Peru, Philippines, Poland, Qatar, Romania, Rwanda, Saint Kitts and Nevis, Saint Lucia, Saint Vincent and the Grenadines, Samoa, Sao Tome and Principe, Saudi Arabia, Senegal, Seychelles, Sierra Leone, Singapore, Solomon Islands, Somalia, Sri Lanka, Suriname, Swaziland, Syrian Arab Republic, Thailand, Togo, Trinidad and Tobago, Tunisia, Turkey, Uganda, Ukrainian SSR, USSR, United Arab Emirates, United Republic of Tanzania, Uruguay, Vanuatu, Venezuela, Viet Nam, Yemen, Yugoslavia, Zaire.

Against: None.

Abstaining: Austria, Belgium, Canada, Denmark, Dominica, Finland, France, Germany, Federal Republic of, Greece, Iceland, Ireland, Israel, Italy, Japan, Luxembourg, Netherlands, Norway, Portugal, Spain, Sweden, United Kingdom, United States.

Puerto Rico

In August 1989, the Special Committee on decolonization considered, as a separate item, its 1988 decision[17] on Puerto Rico. The Committee heard statements by representatives of 57 organizations and on 17 August, adopted a resolution[18] by 9 votes to 2, with 11 abstentions, reaffirming the inalienable right of the people of Puerto Rico to self-determination and independence, and expressing the hope that the people of Puerto Rico might exercise that right without hindrance. The text of the resolution was transmitted to the United States.

REFERENCES

[1]YUN 1960, p. 49, GA res. 1514(XV), 14 Dec. 1960. [2]A/44/23. [3]YUN 1988, p. 724, GA res. 43/30, 22 Nov. 1988. [4]A/44/297 & Add.1,2. [5]YUN 1988, p. 722, ESC res. 1988/53, 26 July 1988. [6]E/1989/112 & Add.1. [7]A/44/23 (A/AC.109/1010). [8]YUN 1988, p. 719, GA res. 43/45, 22 Nov. 1988. [9]Ibid., p. 731, GA dec. 43/410, 17 Nov. 1988. [10]A/44/23 (A/AC.109/1011). [11]S/20796. [12]A/AC.109/L.1685. [13]A/AC.109/1687. [14]A/AC.109/L.1688. [15]YUN 1988, p. 734, GA res. 43/47, 22 Nov. 1988. [16]A/44/800. [17]YUN 1988, p. 735. [18]A/44/23 (A/AC.109/1013).

General matters

Scholarships

In accordance with a 1988 General Assembly request,[1] the Secretary-General reported[2] on offers made by Member States to provide study and training facilities for inhabitants of non-self-governing territories (NSGTs). The report listed the 42 Member States which had over the years offered scholarships: Australia, Austria, Brazil, Bulgaria, Canada, Cuba, Cyprus, Czechoslovakia, Egypt, Gabon, German Democratic Republic, Germany, Federal Republic of, Ghana, Greece, Hungary, India, Iran, Ireland, Israel, Italy, Libyan Arab Jamahiriya, Malawi, Malta, Mexico, New Zealand, Pakistan, Philippines, Poland, Romania, Sri Lanka, Sudan, Syrian Arab Republic, Tunisia, Turkey, Uganda, Ukrainian SSR, USSR, United Arab Emirates, United Kingdom, United States, Uruguay, and Yugoslavia. Information on those offers was included in the twenty-fifth edition of the handbook *Study Abroad*, published by the United Nations Educational, Scientific and Cultural Organization. The scholarships were for study and training of university standard as well as for post-primary, technical, and vocational training. Applications for scholarships received by the United Nations Secretariat from inhabitants of NSGTs were transmitted to the offering States for consideration and to the administering Powers for information. Applications from Namibian students were referred to the Office of the United Nations Commissioner for Namibia and to the United Nations Educational and Training Programme for Southern Africa, as well as to offering Governments.

Australia reported that it had 5 subsidized students from New Caledonia and 10 from the Trust Territory of the Pacific Islands; Canada had offered 12 awards to residents of Anguilla, Bermuda, the British Virgin Islands, the Cayman Islands, the Falkland Islands (Malvinas), Gibraltar, Montserrat, St. Helena, and the Turks and Caicos Islands; and Cuba informed the Secretary-General that 1,714 Namibian and 1,559 Saharawi students were studying in Cuba. Cyprus offered one two-year scholarship, Czechoslovakia offered 20 scholarships, and Egypt granted 139 scholarships. The Federal Republic of Germany offered 78 scholarships for professional training in that country for Namibians and a further 163 in Africa. Scholarships to NSGT students were also offered by New Zealand, Poland, Sudan and Turkey. The Ukrainian SSR informed the Secretary-General that, during the academic year 1988/1989, 20 NSGT students had received training; 220 had received training in the USSR; and in the United Kingdom, 176 students from British Dependent Territories had benefited from assistance in 1988 plus 67 from Namibia.

GENERAL ASSEMBLY ACTION

On 11 December, the General Assembly, on the recommendation of the Fourth Committee, adopted **resolution 44/87** without vote.

Offers by Member States of study and training facilities for inhabitants of Non-Self-Governing Territories

The General Assembly,

Recalling its resolution 43/32 of 22 November 1988,

Having examined the report of the Secretary-General on offers by Member States of study and training facilities for inhabitants of Non-Self-Governing Territories, prepared pursuant to General Assembly resolution 845(IX) of 22 November 1954,

Conscious of the importance of promoting the educational advancement of the inhabitants of Non-Self-Governing Territories,

Strongly convinced that the continuation and expansion of offers of scholarships is essential in order to meet the increasing need of students from Non-Self-Governing Territories for educational and training assistance, and considering that students in those Territories should be encouraged to avail themselves of such offers,

1. *Takes note* of the report of the Secretary-General;

2. *Expresses its appreciation* to those Member States that have made scholarships available to the inhabitants of Non-Self-Governing Territories;

3. *Invites* all States to make or continue to make generous offers of study and training facilities to the inhabitants of those Territories that have not yet attained self-government or independence and, wherever possible, to provide travel funds to prospective students;

4. *Urges* the administering Powers to take effective measures to ensure the widespread and continuous dissemination in the Territories under their administration of information relating to offers of study and training

facilities made by States and to provide all the necessary facilities to enable students to avail themselves of such offers;

5. *Requests* the Secretary-General to report to the General Assembly at its forty-fifth session on the implementation of the present resolution;

6. *Draws the attention* of the Special Committee on the Situation with regard to the Implementation of the Declaration on the Granting of Independence to Colonial Countries and Peoples to the present resolution.

General Assembly resolution 44/87

11 December 1989   Meeting 80   Adopted without vote

Approved by Fourth Committee (A/44/742) without vote, 25 October (meeting 16); 41-nation draft (A/C.4/44/L.4); agenda item 120.

Sponsors: Algeria, Argentina, Australia, Bahamas, Barbados, Brazil, Bulgaria, Burundi, Cameroon, China, Colombia, Congo, Costa Rica, Cyprus, Fiji, Ghana, Guinea, India, Indonesia, Jamaica, Liberia, Madagascar, Mali, New Zealand, Nicaragua, Pakistan, Papua New Guinea, Philippines, Samoa, Sri Lanka, Sudan, Sweden, Thailand, Trinidad and Tobago, Tunisia, Turkey, United States, Vanuatu, Venezuela, Yugoslavia.

Meeting numbers. GA 44th session: 4th Committee 5, 9-16; plenary 80.

Information on conditions in Territories

States responsible for the administration of NSGTs continued to be required, under Article 73 *e* of the United Nations Charter, to transmit regularly to the Secretary-General information on the Territories' economic, social and educational conditions. In 1988, the General Assembly had requested[3] the fullest possible information on political and constitutional developments in the Territories. In a September 1989 report,[4] the Secretary-General stated that he had received information on NSGTs from administering countries as follows:

New Zealand: Tokelau

United Kingdom: Anguilla, Cayman Islands, Falkland Islands (Malvinas), Gibraltar, Pitcairn, Turks and Caicos Islands

United States: American Samoa, Guam

On 24 April 1989,[5] Portugal informed the Secretary-General that it had nothing to add to the information it had provided in 1979[6] when it had stated that conditions in East Timor had prevented it from assuming its responsibilities for the Territory's administration.

The Special Committee on decolonization considered the question of information from NSGTs and, on 9 August, adopted a resolution[7] that became the basis of a draft recommendation to the General Assembly.

GENERAL ASSEMBLY ACTION

On 11 December, the General Assembly, on the recommendation of the Fourth Committee, adopted **resolution 44/83** by recorded vote.

Information from Non-Self-Governing Territories transmitted under Article 73 *e* of the Charter of the United Nations

The General Assembly,

Having examined the chapter of the report of the Special Committee on the Situation with regard to the Implementation of the Declaration on the Granting of

Independence to Colonial Countries and Peoples relating to the information from Non-Self-Governing Territories transmitted under Article 73 *e* of the Charter of the United Nations and the action taken by the Special Committee in respect of that information,

Having also examined the report of the Secretary-General on this item,

Recalling its resolution 1970(XVIII) of 16 December 1963, in which it requested the Special Committee to study the information transmitted to the Secretary-General in accordance with Article 73 *e* of the Charter and to take such information fully into account in examining the situation with regard to the implementation of the Declaration on the Granting of Independence to Colonial Countries and Peoples, contained in General Assembly resolution 1514(XV) of 14 December 1960,

Recalling also its resolution 43/28 of 22 November 1988, in which it requested the Special Committee to continue to discharge the functions entrusted to it under resolution 1970(XVIII),

Stressing the importance of timely transmission by the administering Powers of adequate information under Article 73 *e* of the Charter, in particular in relation to the preparation by the Secretariat of the working papers on the Territories concerned,

1. *Approves* the chapter of the report of the Special Committee on the Situation with regard to the Implementation of the Declaration on the Granting of Independence to Colonial Countries and Peoples relating to the information from Non-Self-Governing Territories transmitted under Article 73 *e* of the Charter of the United Nations;

2. *Reaffirms* that, in the absence of a decision by the General Assembly itself that a Non-Self-Governing Territory has attained a full measure of self-government in terms of Chapter XI of the Charter, the administering Power concerned should continue to transmit information under Article 73 *e* of the Charter with respect to that Territory;

3. *Requests* the administering Powers concerned to transmit or continue to transmit to the Secretary-General the information prescribed in Article 73 *e* of the Charter, as well as the fullest possible information on political and constitutional developments in the Territories concerned, within a maximum period of six months following the expiration of the administrative year in those Territories;

4. *Requests* the Secretary-General, in connection with the preparation of the working papers relating to the Territories concerned, to continue to ensure that adequate information is drawn from all available published sources;

5. *Requests* the Special Committee to continue to discharge the functions entrusted to it under General Assembly resolution 1970(XVIII), in accordance with established procedures, and to report thereon to the Assembly at its forty-fifth session.

General Assembly resolution 44/83

11 December 1989   Meeting 80   150-0-3 (recorded vote)

Approved by Fourth Committee (A/44/739) by recorded vote (141-0-3), 25 October (meeting 16); draft by Special Committee on decolonization (A/44/23); agenda item 116.

Meeting numbers. GA 44th session: 4th Committee 5, 9-16; plenary 80.

Recorded vote in Assembly as follows:

In favour: Afghanistan, Albania, Algeria, Angola, Antigua and Barbuda, Argentina, Australia, Austria, Bahamas, Bahrain, Bangladesh, Barbados,

Belgium, Benin, Bhutan, Bolivia, Botswana, Brazil, Brunei Darussalam, Bulgaria, Burkina Faso, Burundi, Byelorussian SSR, Cameroon, Canada, Cape Verde, Central African Republic, Chad, Chile, China, Colombia, Congo, Costa Rica, Côte d'Ivoire, Cuba, Cyprus, Czechoslovakia, Democratic Kampuchea, Democratic Yemen, Denmark, Djibouti, Dominica, Dominican Republic, Ecuador, Egypt, El Salvador, Equatorial Guinea, Ethiopia, Fiji, Finland, Gabon, Gambia, German Democratic Republic, Germany, Federal Republic of, Ghana, Greece, Grenada, Guatemala, Guinea, Guinea-Bissau, Guyana, Haiti, Honduras, Hungary, Iceland, India, Indonesia, Iran, Iraq, Ireland, Israel, Italy, Jamaica, Japan, Jordan, Kenya, Kuwait, Lao People's Democratic Republic, Lebanon, Lesotho, Liberia, Libyan Arab Jamahiriya, Luxembourg, Madagascar, Malawi, Malaysia, Maldives, Mali, Malta, Mauritania, Mauritius, Mexico, Mongolia, Morocco, Mozambique, Myanmar, Nepal, Netherlands, New Zealand, Nicaragua, Niger, Nigeria, Norway, Oman, Pakistan, Panama, Papua New Guinea, Paraguay, Peru, Philippines, Poland, Portugal, Qatar, Romania, Rwanda, Saint Kitts and Nevis, Saint Lucia, Saint Vincent and the Grenadines, Samoa, Sao Tome and Principe, Saudi Arabia, Senegal, Seychelles, Sierra Leone, Singapore, Solomon Islands, Somalia, Spain, Sri Lanka, Suriname, Swaziland, Sweden, Syrian Arab Republic, Thailand, Togo, Trinidad and Tobago, Tunisia, Turkey, Uganda, Ukrainian SSR, USSR, United Arab Emirates, United Republic of Tanzania, Uruguay, Vanuatu, Venezuela, Viet Nam, Yemen, Yugoslavia, Zaire.

Against: None.

Abstaining: France, United Kingdom, United States.

Visiting Missions

In 1989, the Chairman of the Special Committee on decolonization, as requested by the Committee, continued to consult with the administering Powers of NSGTs on the question of permitting access of visiting missions to the Territories. In an August report[8], he stated that New Zealand and the United States had reiterated their readiness to continue to provide the Committee with all relevant information on the Territories under their administration, to participate in the work of the Committee and to receive visiting missions. Noting the decision of the United Kingdom not to take part in the related work of the Committee, and that the United Kingdom had permitted visiting missions to its Territories in the past, the Chairman expressed the hope that the Committee would again receive invitations from that country in the near future.

On 9 August, the Committee adopted a resolution[9] in which it stressed the need to periodically dispatch visiting missions to colonial Territories and called on administering Powers to co-operate with the United Nations in that regard. It also urged the United Kingdom to reconsider its decision not to participate in the work of the Committee and to permit the access of visiting missions to the Territories under its administration.

In **resolution 44/101** (see above), the General Assembly called on administering Powers to co-operate with the Committee and to permit the access of visiting missions to the Territories for the purpose of securing first-hand information and ascertaining the wishes and aspirations of the inhabitants. Those administering Powers that did not participate in the work of the Committee were urged to do so in 1990. The Assembly also addressed this topic in resolutions on individual Territories (see below).

REFERENCES
[1]YUN 1988, p. 736, GA res. 43/32, 22 Nov. 1988. [2]A/44/613 & Add.1. [3]YUN 1988, p. 736, GA res. 43/28, 22 Nov. 1988. [4]A/44/553. [5]A/44/262. [6]YUN 1979, p. 1117. [7]A/44/23 (A/AC.109/1005). [8]A/AC.109/L.1707. [9]A/44/23 (A/AC.109/1006).

Territories under review

In 1989, the Special Committee on decolonization continued to consider the peaceful settlement of the dispute over the Falkland Islands (Malvinas), the conflict in Western Sahara, the questions of New Caledonia and East Timor, and the situation in a number of other small colonial Territories. It also considered the Trust Territory of the Pacific Islands (see next chapter) and Namibia (see Chapter III of this Part).

Falkland Islands (Malvinas)

Committee action. The Falkland Islands (Malvinas) question was considered by the Special Committee on decolonization at its August session,[1] during which it heard statements by Argentina, Cuba, two representatives of the Falkland Islands Legislative Council and two other petitioners. It also had before it a Secretariat working paper on political, economic and social developments in the Territory.[2] The United Kingdom, the administering Power, did not participate.

In a resolution[3] of 15 August, the Committee reiterated its position that the way to end the special and particular colonial situation of the Falklands was through a negotiated settlement. Regretting that the implementation of the General Assembly resolutions on this question had not yet started, it urged Argentina and the United Kingdom to resume negotiations, and restated its support for the renewed good offices mission of the Secretary-General.

Report of the Secretary-General. In October, the Secretary-General submitted a report[4] on developments regarding the question of the Falkland Islands (Malvinas). In accordance with the agreement reached between the representatives of the Governments of Argentina and the United Kingdom in August,[5] a meeting took place in Madrid from 17 to 19 October,[6] at which the two Governments agreed to a formula protecting the position of each side with regard to sovereignty or territorial and maritime jurisdiction over the Falkland Islands (Malvinas), South Georgia and the South Sandwich Islands and surrounding maritime areas. They also noted that all hostilities between them had ceased and agreed to re-establish consular relations.

In welcoming the improvement in bilateral relations between the two Governments, the Secretary-General expressed his continued willingness to assist in any manner in accordance with the mandate entrusted to him by the General Assembly.

By **decision 44/406** of 1 November, the General Assembly decided to defer consideration of the Falkland Islands (Malvinas) question and to include it in the provisional agenda of its forty-fifth (1990) session.

Western Sahara

Action by the Commission on Human Rights. The Commission on Human Rights, on 6 March,[7] reaffirmed that the issue of Western Sahara was one of decolonization and again requested the parties to the conflict, Morocco and the POLISARIO Front, to negotiate a cease-fire and create the necessary conditions for a referendum for self-determination. The Commission welcomed the efforts of the Secretary-General and the Chairman of OAU's Assembly of Heads of State and Government to promote a solution, and decided to consider the situation in 1990 as a high-priority matter.

Committee consideration. The Special Committee on decolonization considered the question of Western Sahara at its August session,[1] during which it heard a statement by a representative of the POLISARIO Front. The Committee also had before it a working paper by the Secretariat on political and military developments in the Territory.[8] Following a meeting in Marrakech on 4 January between a high-level delegation of the POLISARIO Front and King Hassan of Morocco, the Secretary-General of the POLISARIO Front, on 27 January, announced that his forces would observe a cease-fire throughout February to encourage dialogue and the search for peace; a Moroccan Foreign Ministry spokesman said that Morocco saw the cease-fire as proof of POLISARIO's goodwill. At the end of the month, however, a second meeting had not taken place and POLISARIO resumed its operations against Morocco on 1 March.

Report of the Secretary-General. The Secretary-General, pursuant to a 1988 General Assembly resolution,[9] submitted a report[10] in October 1989 on the results of meetings he, his representatives and the OAU Chairman had held between October 1988 and September 1989 with Morocco and the POLISARIO Front. Significant developments included the appointment of the Secretary-General's Special Representative for Western Sahara, the meeting in January 1989 between King Hassan II and the POLISARIO Front,

and the Secretary-General's June visit to the area and meetings with both sides. Progress was also made in processing the data contained in the 1974 Spanish census of Western Sahara, which was to serve as the basis of a voters' list for the proposed referendum.

The Secretary-General held discussions with African leaders during the Assembly of Heads of State and Government of OAU at its twenty-seventh ordinary session (Addis Ababa, 23-26 July). The Ninth Conference of Heads of State or Government of Non-Aligned Countries (Belgrade, 4-7 September) urged the Secretary-General and the OAU Chairman to intensify their efforts to resolve the remaining problems. Following the acceptance by the two parties in August 1988 of the Settlement Proposals for resolving the question of Western Sahara,[11] the effort of the OAU Chairman and the Secretary-General had been directed towards clarifying specific matters raised by the parties on some aspects of the Proposals. On 30 June, the Secretary-General established the Technical Commission under his chairmanship, to facilitate and accelerate the implementation of the Settlement Proposals. He reported that concerns expressed by the parties included in the case of Morocco, the question of security and peace in the Territory during the referendum, and in the case of the POLISARIO Front, assurances for a free and fair referendum.

On 11 December, the General Assembly, on the recommendation of the Fourth Committee, adopted **resolution 44/88** without vote.

Question of Western Sahara

The General Assembly,

Having considered in depth the question of Western Sahara,

Recalling the inalienable right of all peoples to self-determination and independence, in accordance with the principles set forth in the Charter of the United Nations and in General Assembly resolution 1514(XV) of 14 December 1960, containing the Declaration on the Granting of Independence to Colonial Countries and Peoples,

Recalling its resolution 43/33 of 22 November 1988 on the question of Western Sahara,

Recalling resolution AHG/Res.104(XIX) on Western Sahara, adopted by the Assembly of Heads of State and Government of the Organization of African Unity at its nineteenth ordinary session, held at Addis Ababa from 6 to 12 June 1983,

Taking note with appreciation of the final document on Western Sahara adopted by the Ninth Conference of Heads of State or Government of Non-Aligned Countries, held at Belgrade from 4 to 7 September 1989,

Recalling Security Council resolution 621(1988) of 20 September 1988 concerning the question of Western Sahara,

Having examined the relevant chapter of the report of the Special Committee on the Situation with regard to the Implementation of the Declaration on the Granting of Independence to Colonial Countries and Peoples,

Having examined the report of the Secretary-General on the question of Western Sahara,

Reiterating its support for the joint good offices process initiated in New York on 9 April 1986 by the current Chairman of the Assembly of Heads of State and Government of the Organization of African Unity and the Secretary-General of the United Nations with a view to promoting a just and definitive solution of the question of Western Sahara, in accordance with resolution AHG/Res.104(XIX) and General Assembly resolution 40/50 of 2 December 1985,

1. *Takes note with appreciation* of the report of the Secretary-General on the question of Western Sahara;

2. *Reaffirms* that the question of Western Sahara is a question of decolonization which remains to be completed on the basis of the exercise by the people of Western Sahara of their inalienable right to self-determination and independence;

3. *Stresses* the importance of the agreement in principle given on 30 August 1988 by the Kingdom of Morocco and the Frente Popular para la Liberación de Saguia el-Hamra y de Río de Oro to the joint proposals of the current Chairman of the Assembly of Heads of State and Government of the Organization of African Unity and the Secretary-General of the United Nations with a view to the holding of a referendum for self-determination of the people of Western Sahara, organized and supervised by the United Nations in cooperation with the Organization of African Unity;

4. *Welcomes* the efforts of the current Chairman of the Assembly of Heads of State and Government of the Organization of African Unity and the Secretary-General of the United Nations to promote a just and definitive solution of the question of Western Sahara, in accordance with General Assembly resolution 40/50;

5. *Also welcomes* the progress achieved by the joint good offices process and urges the current Chairman of the Assembly of Heads of State and Government of the Organization of African Unity and the Secretary-General of the United Nations to continue and intensify their efforts with a view to resolving the remaining problems, and thus to fulfil the necessary conditions for the holding of a referendum for self-determination of the people of Western Sahara, without any administrative or military constraints, organized and supervised by the United Nations in co-operation with the Organization of African Unity;

6. *Takes note with appreciation* of the establishment of a technical commission to assist the current Chairman of the Assembly of Heads of State and Government of the Organization of African Unity and the Secretary-General of the United Nations in their joint good offices with a view to resolving the question of Western Sahara;

7. *Welcomes* the talks in Marrakech between His Majesty King Hassan II of Morocco and a high-level delegation from the Frente Popular para la Liberación de Saguia el-Hamra y de Río de Oro, and endorses the hope of the Secretary-General of the United Nations and the current Chairman of the Assembly of Heads of State and Government of the Organization of African Unity that there will be further meetings of this nature to improve the prospects for the success of the peace process;

8. *Expresses its conviction* that the continuation of direct dialogue between the two parties to the conflict could contribute to the completion of the joint good offices process of the current Chairman of the Assembly of Heads of State and Government of the Organization of African Unity and the Secretary-General of the United Nations, to the restoration of peace in Western Sahara and to stability and security in the whole region;

9. *Appeals once again* to the Kingdom of Morocco and the Frente Popular para la Liberación de Saguia el-Hamra y de Río de Oro to display the co-operation and the political goodwill necessary for the success of the joint good offices process of the current Chairman of the Assembly of Heads of State and Government of the Organization of African Unity and the Secretary-General of the United Nations;

10. *Requests* the Special Committee on the Situation with regard to the Implementation of the Declaration on the Granting of Independence to Colonial Countries and Peoples to continue to consider the situation in Western Sahara as a matter of priority and to report thereon to the General Assembly at its forty-fifth session;

11. *Invites* the Secretary-General of the Organization of African Unity to keep the Secretary-General of the United Nations informed of the progress achieved in the implementation of the decisions of the Organization of African Unity relating to Western Sahara;

12. *Invites* the Secretary-General to follow the situation in Western Sahara closely with a view to the implementation of the present resolution and to report thereon to the General Assembly at its forty-fifth session.

General Assembly resolution 44/88

11 December 1989　　　　Meeting 80　　　　Adopted without vote

Approved by Fourth Committee (A/44/738) without vote, 25 October (meeting 16); 43-nation draft (A/C.4/44/L.5), orally revised; agenda item 18.
Meeting numbers. GA 44th session: 4th Committee 5, 7-16; plenary 80.
Sponsors: Afghanistan, Albania, Algeria, Antigua and Barbuda, Barbados, Belize, Benin, Botswana, Burkina Faso, Burundi, Colombia, Congo, Cuba, Cyprus, Democratic Yemen, Ethiopia, Ghana, Guyana, India, Iran, Lao People's Democratic Republic, Lesotho, Madagascar, Malawi, Mali, Mauritania, Mexico, Mozambique, Nicaragua, Nigeria, Panama, Papua New Guinea, Rwanda, Seychelles, Suriname, Swaziland, Uganda, United Republic of Tanzania, Vanuatu, Viet Nam, Yugoslavia, Zambia, Zimbabwe.

New Caledonia

The General Assembly had determined in 1986[12] that New Caledonia was an NSGT within the meaning of the United Nations Charter and affirmed the right of its people to self-determination and independence in accordance with the 1960 Declaration on decolonization;[13] however, France (the administering Power) did not consider New Caledonia an NSGT. It had organized a referendum on 13 September 1987 in which, it maintained, the people of the Territory had had the opportunity to express their views and had favoured remaining with France.[14]

In July 1989, a Secretariat working paper[15] reported that despite the assassinations of the head of the six-party coalition Front de libération nationale kanak socialiste (FLNKS) and his deputy in May, elections were held on 11 June for three new provincial assemblies. Voter turn-out was almost 70 per cent, in an electorate of 92,000. According to official results, FLNKS won 19 seats and the Rassemblement pour la Calédonie dans la République (RPCR) won 27 seats, out of the total of 54 seats. Front uni de libération Kanak (FULK), a dissident party of the FLNKS coalition, had reportedly stated that it would intensify its campaign to speed up the independence process for New Caledonia; FULK refused to meet with French authorities in June, on the grounds that the Government was not prepared to discuss redrafting previous agreements on the status of New Caledonia.

Committee action. The Special Committee on decolonization considered the question of New Caledonia at four meetings in August 1989.[1] It had before it the Secretariat working paper[15] and heard statements by FULK and FLNKS, among others.

On 15 August, the Committee adopted a resolution[16] in which it urged all the parties involved to maintain their dialogue and to refrain from acts of violence, and which formed the basis for a draft forwarded to the Assembly. The text of the resolution was transmitted to France for its attention.

GENERAL ASSEMBLY ACTION

On 11 December, the General Assembly, on the recommendation of the Fourth Committee, adopted **resolution 44/89** without vote.

Question of New Caledonia

The General Assembly,

Having considered the question of New Caledonia,

Having examined the chapter of the report of the Special Committee on the Situation with regard to the Implementation of the Declaration on the Granting of Independence to Colonial Countries and Peoples relating to New Caledonia,

Recalling its resolutions 1514(XV) of 14 December 1960 and 1541(XV) of 15 December 1960,

Noting the positive measures being pursued in New Caledonia by the French authorities, in co-operation with all sectors of the population, to promote political, economic and social development in the Territory, in order to provide a framework for its peaceful progress to self-determination,

1. *Approves* the chapter of the report of the Special Committee on the Situation with regard to the Implementation of the Declaration on the Granting of Independence to Colonial Countries and Peoples relating to New Caledonia;

2. *Urges* all the parties involved, in the interest of all the people of New Caledonia, to maintain their dialogue and, in the spirit of harmony, to refrain from acts of violence;

3. *Invites* all the parties involved to continue promoting a framework for the peaceful progress of the Territory towards an act of self-determination in which all options are open and which would safeguard the rights of all New Caledonians;

4. *Requests* the Special Committee to continue the examination of this question at its next session and to report thereon to the General Assembly at its forty-fifth session.

General Assembly resolution 44/89

11 December 1989   Meeting 80   Adopted without vote

Approved by Fourth Committee (A/44/738) without vote, 25 October (meeting 16); draft by Special Committee on decolonization (A/44/23); agenda item 18.
Meeting numbers. GA 44th session: 4th Committee 5, 7-16; plenary 80.

East Timor

The General Assembly, on 22 September, decided to defer the consideration of the question of East Timor until 1990. The Secretary-General, however, continued substantive, high-level talks with Portugal—considered to be the legal administering Power by the United Nations—and Indonesia, which had maintained that decolonization in East Timor was complete and that its people had chosen independence through integration with Indonesia.

Committee consideration. The Special Committee on decolonization considered the East Timor question at three meetings between 7 and 14 August,[1] and heard statements by Indonesia and Portugal, as well as by a representative of the Frente Revolucionária de Timor Leste Independente (FRETILIN) and NGOs. The Committee had before it a Secretariat working paper[17] on political developments, human rights and economic and social conditions in East Timor. The paper mentioned reports of frequent small-scale clashes between FRETILIN and the Indonesian military, and the killing of 37 Indonesian troops by FRETILIN fighters in the Laline region in January. It also cited a report of the United States which stated that, over the past years, the Indonesian Government had sought to win over FRETILIN rebels through more peaceful means; authorities had encouraged East Timorese with contacts within FRETILIN to advertise the benefits that Indonesian development had brought to East Timor, particularly in social services. In addition, the Indonesian Government had continued its amnesty programme, under which FRETILIN rebels who surrendered were permitted to settle, under the guardianship of the local church and authorities.

Communications. Indonesia and Portugal, in letters to the Secretary-General, expressed their positions on the issue of East Timor. On 24 Jaunary[18] and 28 March,[19] Indonesia categorically rejected allegations that the people of East Timor were being denied the exercise of self-determination and human rights.

On 24 April,[20] Portugal informed the Secretary-General that it had nothing to add to the information it had provided in 1979[21] as required by Article 73 *e* of the Charter, at which time it had stated that conditions in East Timor had prevented it from assuming its responsibilities for the Territory's administration.

In letters of 4 and 14 August to the Chairman of the Special Committee on decolonization,[22] Indonesia stated that the decolonization process of East Timor had been carried out in conformity with the provisions of the Charter and Assembly resolutions on decolonization, and that East Timor had been formally integrated into Indonesia in 1976. It reiterated its view that consideration of the question of East Timor by the Committee was therefore inappropriate and would constitute interference in a sovereign State's internal affairs, and expressed strong opposition to the participation of the petitioners in the deliberation of the Committee.

In a letter of 28 November,[(23)] Portugal strongly protested the announcement of the creation of a "zone of co-operation in an area between the Indonesian province of East Timor and Northern Australia (Timor Gap)" by Australia and Indonesia, stating that Indonesia lacked the legitimacy to undertake any commitments regarding East Timor. It said that the two countries planned to exploit petroleum resources in the maritime area between Australia and the NSGT of East Timor.

Report of the Secretary-General. In a September progress report,[(24)] the Secretary-General stated that during the preceding year he had consulted on several occasions with the Presidents and Foreign Ministers of Indonesia and Portugal, and had obtained a reaffirmation from both sides of their commitment to achieving a comprehensive and internationally acceptable solution to the question of East Timor. The Secretary-General was present when the substantive talks between Indonesia and Portugal were formally resumed at a meeting held on 9 May. Although he said the pace of progress had not been constant, he was encouraged by the increased frequency of discussions between the two sides in recent months. The Secretary-General expressed hope at the possibility of a proposed visit to the territory by a delegation from the Portuguese Parliament. He believed such a visit could help create a conducive atmosphere for achieving a solution.

Small territories

American Samoa

The Special Committee on decolonization considered the question of American Samoa on 7 August and had before it a working paper by the Secretariat on developments in the Territory.[(25)] The text of the Committee's conclusions and recommendations was transmitted to the United States for its attention.

GENERAL ASSEMBLY ACTION

On 11 December, on the recommendation of the Fourth Committee, the General Assembly adopted **resolution 44/97** without vote.

Question of American Samoa

The General Assembly,

Having considered the question of American Samoa,

Having examined the relevant chapters of the report of the Special Committee on the Situation with regard to the Implementation of the Declaration on the Granting of Independence to Colonial Countries and Peoples,

Recalling its resolution 1514(XV) of 14 December 1960, containing the Declaration on the Granting of Independence to Colonial Countries and Peoples, and all resolutions and decisions of the United Nations relating to American Samoa, in particular General Assembly resolution 43/43 of 22 November 1988,

Conscious of the need to promote progress towards the full implementation of the Declaration in respect of American Samoa,

Having heard the statement of the representative of the United States of America, as the administering Power,

Aware of the special circumstances of the geographical location and economic conditions of the Territory and bearing in mind the necessity of diversifying and strengthening further its economy as a matter of priority in order to promote economic stability,

Noting that the current Chief Justice of the Territory is the first indigenous American Samoan appointed to that position,

Recalling the dispatch in 1981 of a United Nations visiting mission to the Territory,

Mindful that United Nations visiting missions provide an effective means of ascertaining the situation in the small Territories and reaffirming the value of sending, at an appropriate time, a further visiting mission to American Samoa,

1. *Approves* the chapter of the report of the Special Committee on the Situation with regard to the Implementation of the Declaration on the Granting of Independence to Colonial Countries and Peoples relating to American Samoa;

2. *Reaffirms* the inalienable right of the people of American Samoa to self-determination and independence in conformity with the Declaration on the Granting of Independence to Colonial Countries and Peoples;

3. *Reiterates the view* that such factors as territorial size, geographical location, size of population and limited natural resources should in no way delay the speedy exercise by the people of the Territory of their inalienable right to self-determination and independence in conformity with the Declaration, which fully applies to American Samoa;

4. *Calls upon* the Government of the United States of America, as the administering Power, to take all necessary steps, bearing in mind the rights, interests and wishes of the people of American Samoa as expressed freely in any act of self-determination, to expedite the process of decolonization of the Territory in accordance with the relevant provisions of the Charter of the United Nations and the Declaration and reaffirms the importance of fostering an awareness among the people of American Samoa of the possibilities open to them in the exercise of their right to self-determination and independence;

5. *Reaffirms* the responsibility of the administering Power, under the Charter, to promote the economic and social development of American Samoa and calls upon the administering Power to intensify its efforts to strengthen and diversify the economy of the Territory;

6. *Urges* the administering Power, in co-operation with the territorial Government, to take effective meas-

ures to safeguard and guarantee the inalienable right of the people of American Samoa to own and dispose of the natural resources of the Territory, including marine resources, and to establish and maintain control over the future development of those resources;

7. *Reiterates its appeal* to the administering Power to consider favourably the expressed request of the people of the Territory to appoint the Chief Justice and other members of the Territory's judiciary themselves;

8. *Also urges* the administering Power to continue to foster close relations between the Territory and other island communities in the region and promote co-operation between the territorial Government and regional institutions, as well as the specialized agencies and other organizations of the United Nations system;

9. *Requests* the Special Committee to continue the examination of this question at its next session, including the possible dispatch of a further visiting mission to American Samoa at an appropriate time and in consultation with the administering Power, taking into account, in particular, the wishes of the people of the Territory, and to report thereon to the General Assembly at its forty-fifth session.

General Assembly resolution 44/97

11 December 1989   Meeting 80   Adopted without vote

Approved by Fourth Committee (A/44/738) without vote, 25 October (meeting 16); draft by Special Committee on decolonization (A/44/23); agenda item 18.
Meeting numbers. GA 44th session: 4th Committee 5, 7-16; plenary 80.

Anguilla

The Special Committee on decolonization considered the question of Anguilla on 7 August and had before it working papers prepared by the Secretariat on developments in the Territory[26] and on foreign economic and other interests.[27]

GENERAL ASSEMBLY ACTION

On 11 December, on the recommendation of the Fourth Committee, the General Assembly adopted **resolution 44/94** without vote.

Question of Anguilla

The General Assembly,

Having considered the question of Anguilla,

Having examined the relevant chapters of the report of the Special Committee on the Situation with regard to the Implementation of the Declaration on the Granting of Independence to Colonial Countries and Peoples,

Recalling its resolution 1514(XV) of 14 December 1960, containing the Declaration on the Granting of Independence to Colonial Countries and Peoples, and all resolutions and decisions of the United Nations relating to Anguilla, including in particular General Assembly resolution 43/36 of 22 November 1988,

Conscious of the need to ensure the full and speedy implementation of the Declaration in respect of the Territory,

Having heard the statement of the representative of the United Kingdom of Great Britain and Northern Ireland, as the administering Power,

Noting that the revision of the laws of Anguilla remains a priority of the Government of the Territory,

Taking note of the results of the general elections of February 1989 and the statement of the Chief Minister that

the Government of Anguilla had no intention of moving towards independence during its current term of office,

Noting the stated policy of the Government of the United Kingdom, the administering Power, that it remains ready to respond positively to the express wish of the people of the Territory on the question of independence,

Noting that the decisions of the House of Assembly on the report of the Constitutional Review Committee were released in August 1988 for public review, discussion and consent and that the report would be considered by the United Kingdom Secretary of State for Foreign and Commonwealth Affairs,

Aware of the special circumstances of the geographical location and economic conditions of the Territory and bearing in mind the necessity of diversifying and strengthening further its economy as a matter of priority in order to promote economic stability,

Reaffirming the responsibility of the administering Power to promote the economic and social development of the Territory, and noting the continued growth of the economy of the Territory in 1988 as a result of the expansion of tourism,

Expressing its concern at the continued illegal operation of foreign fishing vessels within the territorial waters of Anguilla and welcoming the measures taken by the territorial Government to protect and conserve marine resources and to control the activities of foreign fishermen operating illegally in the area,

Stressing the importance of an efficient and effective civil service and noting the measures being taken by the territorial Government aimed at alleviating the problem of unemployment and providing increased job opportunities,

Noting with concern the vulnerability of the Territory to drug trafficking and related activities,

Noting the contribution to the development of the Territory by specialized agencies and other organizations of the United Nations system, in particular the United Nations Development Programme,

Recalling that in 1987 Anguilla became a member of the Eastern Caribbean Central Bank and that it continues to participate and maintain an active interest in the related activities of other regional organizations,

Recalling also the dispatch in 1984 of a United Nations visiting mission to the Territory,

Mindful that United Nations visiting missions provide an effective means of ascertaining the situation in the small Territories and considering that the possibility of sending a further visiting mission to Anguilla at an appropriate time should be kept under review,

1. *Approves* the chapter of the report of the Special Committee on the Situation with regard to the Implementation of the Declaration on the Granting of Independence to Colonial Countries and Peoples relating to Anguilla;

2. *Reaffirms* the inalienable right of the people of Anguilla to self-determination and independence in conformity with the Declaration on the Granting of Independence to Colonial Countries and Peoples;

3. *Reiterates the view* that such factors as territorial size, geographical location, size of population and limited natural resources should in no way delay the speedy exercise by the people of the Territory of their inalienable right to self-determination and independence in conformity with the Declaration, which fully applies to Anguilla;

4. *Reiterates* that it is the responsibility of the United Kingdom of Great Britain and Northern Ireland, as the administering Power, to create such conditions in Anguilla as will enable its people to exercise freely and without interference, from a well-informed standpoint as to the available options, their inalienable right to self-determination and independence in accordance with resolution 1514(XV) and all other relevant resolutions of the General Assembly;

5. *Reaffirms* that it is ultimately for the people of Anguilla themselves to determine freely their future political status in accordance with the relevant provisions of the Charter of the United Nations and the Declaration and, in that connection, reaffirms the importance of fostering an awareness among the people of the Territory of the possibilities open to them in the exercise of their right to self-determination and independence;

6. *Calls upon* the administering Power to continue, in co-operation with the territorial Government, to strengthen the economy and to increase its assistance to programmes of diversification;

7. *Urges* the administering Power, in co-operation with the territorial Government, to continue the assistance necessary to increase employment of the local population in the civil service and other sectors of the economy;

8. *Also urges* the administering Power, in co-operation with the territorial Government, to take effective measures to safeguard and guarantee the inalienable right of the people of Anguilla to own and dispose of the natural resources of the Territory, including marine resources, and to establish and maintain control over the future development of those resources;

9. *Calls upon* the administering Power to continue to take all necessary measures, in co-operation with the territorial Government, to counter problems related to drug trafficking;

10. *Reiterates its request* to the administering Power to continue to enlist the assistance of the specialized agencies and other organizations of the United Nations system, as well as other international and regional bodies, in the development and strengthening of the economy of Anguilla;

11. *Also reiterates its request* to the administering Power to continue to make every effort to facilitate and encourage the participation of the Territory in regional and international organizations;

12. *Requests* the Special Committee to continue the examination of this question at its next session, including the possible dispatch of a further visiting mission to Anguilla at an appropriate time and in consultation with the administering Power, and to report thereon to the General Assembly at its forty-fifth session.

General Assembly resolution 44/94

11 December 1989   Meeting 80   Adopted without vote

Approved by Fourth Committee (A/44/738) without vote, 25 October (meeting 16); draft by Committee on colonial countries (A/44/23); agenda item 18.
Meeting numbers. GA 44th session: 4th Committee 5, 7-16; plenary 80.

Bermuda

The Special Committee on decolonization considered the question of Bermuda on 7 August, at which time it had before it working papers prepared by the Secretariat on developments in the Territory[28], on foreign economic and other interests,[29] and on military activities.[30]

GENERAL ASSEMBLY ACTION

On 11 December, on the recommendation of the Fourth Committee, the General Assembly adopted **resolution 44/92** without vote.

Question of Bermuda

The General Assembly,

Having considered the question of Bermuda,

Having examined the relevant chapters of the report of the Special Committee on the Situation with regard to the Implementation of the Declaration on the Granting of Independence to Colonial Countries and Peoples,

Recalling its resolution 1514(XV) of 14 December 1960, containing the Declaration on the Granting of Independence to Colonial Countries and Peoples, and all resolutions and decisions of the United Nations relating to Bermuda, in particular General Assembly resolution 43/39 of 22 November 1988,

Conscious of the need to ensure the full and speedy implementation of the Declaration in respect of the Territory,

Having heard the statement of the representative of the United Kingdom of Great Britain and Northern Ireland, as the administering Power,

Noting the stated policy of the Government of the United Kingdom, the administering Power, that it remains ready to respond positively to the express wish of the people of the Territory on the question of independence,

Noting the active discussions in the Territory, both within and outside the territorial Government, on the future status of Bermuda,

Aware of the special circumstances of the geographical location and economic conditions of the Territory and bearing in mind the necessity of diversifying and strengthening further its economy as a matter of priority in order to promote economic stability,

Noting with concern the vulnerability of the Territory to drug trafficking and related activities,

Noting with appreciation the assistance extended to the Territory by the United Nations Development Programme,

Mindful that United Nations visiting missions provide an effective means of ascertaining the situation in the small Territories and considering that the possibility of sending a visiting mission to Bermuda at an appropriate time should be kept under review,

1. *Approves* the chapter of the report of the Special Committee on the Situation with regard to the Implementation of the Declaration on the Granting of Independence to Colonial Countries and Peoples relating to Bermuda;

2. *Reaffirms* the inalienable right of the people of Bermuda to self-determination and independence in conformity with the Declaration on the Granting of Independence to Colonial Countries and Peoples;

3. *Reiterates the view* that such factors as territorial size, geographical location, size of population and limited natural resources should in no way delay the speedy exercise by the people of the Territory of their inalienable right to self-determination and independence in conformity with the Declaration, which fully applies to Bermuda;

4. *Reiterates* that it is the responsibility of the United Kingdom of Great Britain and Northern Ireland, as the administering Power, to create such conditions in the Territory as will enable the people of Bermuda to exer-

cise freely and without interference their inalienable right to self-determination and independence in accordance with General Assembly resolution 1514(XV) and, in that connection, reaffirms the importance of fostering an awareness among the people of Bermuda of the possibilities open to them in the exercise of that right;

5. *Reaffirms* that it is ultimately for the people of Bermuda themselves to determine their own future political status in accordance with the relevant provisions of the Charter of the United Nations and the Declaration;

6. *Reaffirms its strong conviction* that the presence of military bases and installations in the Territory could constitute a major obstacle to the implementation of the Declaration and that it is the responsibility of the administering Power to ensure that the existence of such bases and installations does not hinder the population of the Territory from exercising its right to self-determination and independence in conformity with the purposes and principles of the Charter;

7. *Urges* the administering Power to continue to take all necessary measures not to involve Bermuda in any offensive acts or interference directed against other States and to comply fully with the purposes and principles of the Charter, the Declaration and the resolutions and decisions of the General Assembly relating to military activities and arrangements by colonial Powers in Territories under their administration;

8. *Also urges* the administering Power, in co-operation with the territorial Government, to take effective measures to safeguard and guarantee the inalienable right of the people of Bermuda to own and dispose of the natural resources of the Territory, including marine resources, and to establish and maintain control over the future development of those resources;

9. *Calls upon* the administering Power to continue to take all necessary measures, in co-operation with the territorial Government, to counter problems related to drug trafficking;

10. *Invites* the specialized agencies and other organizations of the United Nations system to continue to provide assistance for the development needs of Bermuda;

11. *Reaffirms* the value of sending a visiting mission to the Territory and requests the administering Power to facilitate the dispatch of such a mission at the earliest possible opportunity;

12. *Requests* the Special Committee to continue the examination of this question at its next session, including the possible dispatch of a visiting mission to Bermuda at an appropriate time and in consultation with the administering Power, and to report thereon to the General Assembly at its forty-fifth session.

General Assembly resolution 44/92

11 December 1989   Meeting 80   Adopted without vote

Approved by Fourth Committee (A/44/738) without vote, 25 October (meeting 16); draft by Special Committee on decolonization (A/44/23); agenda item 18.
Meeting numbers. GA 44th session: 4th Committee 5, 7-16; plenary 80.

British Virgin Islands

The Special Committee on decolonization considered the question of the British Virgin Islands on 7 August and had before it a working paper prepared by the Secretariat on developments in the Territory.[31]

On 11 December, on the recommendation of the Fourth Committee, the General Assembly adopted **resolution 44/95** without vote.

Question of the British Virgin Islands

The General Assembly,

Having considered the question of the British Virgin Islands,

Having examined the relevant chapters of the report of the Special Committee on the Situation with regard to the Implementation of the Declaration on the Granting of Independence to Colonial Countries and Peoples,

Recalling its resolution 1514(XV) of 14 December 1960, containing the Declaration on the Granting of Independence to Colonial Countries and Peoples, and all resolutions and decisions of the United Nations relating to the British Virgin Islands, including in particular General Assembly resolution 43/41 of 22 November 1988,

Conscious of the need to ensure the full and speedy implementation of the Declaration in respect of the Territory,

Having heard the statement of the representative of the United Kingdom of Great Britain and Northern Ireland, as the administering Power,

Noting the stated policy of the Government of the United Kingdom, the administering Power, that it remains ready to respond positively to the express wish of the people of the Territory on the question of independence,

Aware of the special circumstances of the geographical location and economic conditions of the Territory and bearing in mind the necessity of diversifying and strengthening further its economy as a matter of priority in order to promote economic stability,

Reaffirming that it is the responsibility of the administering Power to promote the economic and social development of the Territory and noting that while economic growth was recorded in tourism, other economic sectors continued to play a minor role in the Territory's economy,

Expressing its concern over the continued illegal operations of foreign fishermen and stressing that this uncontrolled exploitation could deplete current fish stocks and adversely affect future yields,

Noting the critical need for the cadre training of nationals in all fields and noting with satisfaction the measures being taken by the territorial Government in that connection,

Noting with concern the vulnerability of the Territory to drug trafficking and related activities,

Welcoming the contribution to the development of the Territory by the specialized agencies and other organizations of the United Nations system, particularly the United Nations Development Programme, as well as by regional organizations,

Noting the continued participation of the Territory in regional and other international organizations,

Expressing its sympathy to the people of the British Virgin Islands for the extensive damage caused by hurricane Hugo in September 1989,

Recalling the dispatch in 1976 of a United Nations visiting mission to the Territory,

Mindful that United Nations visiting missions provide an effective means of ascertaining the situation in the small Territories and considering that the possibility of sending a further visiting mission to the British Virgin Islands at an appropriate time should be kept under review,

1. *Approves* the chapter of the report of the Special Committee on the Situation with regard to the Implementation of the Declaration on the Granting of Independence to Colonial Countries and Peoples relating to the British Virgin Islands;

2. *Reaffirms* the inalienable right of the people of the British Virgin Islands to self-determination and independence in conformity with the Declaration on the Granting of Independence to Colonial Countries and Peoples;

3. *Reiterates the view* that such factors as territorial size, geographical location, size of population and limited natural resources should in no way delay the speedy exercise by the people of the Territory of their inalienable right to self-determination and independence in conformity with the Declaration, which fully applies to the British Virgin Islands;

4. *Reiterates* that it is the responsibility of the United Kingdom of Great Britain and Northern Ireland, as the administering Power, to create such conditions in the Territory as will enable the people of the British Virgin Islands to exercise freely and without interference their inalienable right to self-determination and independence in accordance with resolution 1514(XV) and all other relevant resolutions of the General Assembly;

5. *Reaffirms* that it is ultimately for the people of the British Virgin Islands themselves to determine freely their future political status in accordance with the relevant provisions of the Charter of the United Nations and the Declaration and, in that connection, reaffirms the importance of fostering an awareness among the people of the Territory of the possibilities open to them in the exercise of their right to self-determination;

6. *Calls upon* the administering Power to continue, in co-operation with the territorial Government, to take measures with a view to strengthening and diversifying the Territory's economy;

7. *Urges* the administering Power, in co-operation with the territorial Government, to take effective measures to safeguard and guarantee the inalienable right of the people of the British Virgin Islands to own and dispose of the natural resources of the Territory, including marine resources, and to establish and maintain control over the future development of those resources;

8. *Calls upon* the administering Power, in co-operation with the territorial Government, to take further measures in the cadre training of nationals so as to facilitate their wider participation in the decision-making process in all sectors;

9. *Also calls upon* the administering Power to continue to take all necessary measures, in co-operation with the territorial Government, to counter problems related to drug trafficking;

10. *Reiterates its appeal* to the administering Power to continue to facilitate the participation of the British Virgin Islands in various international and regional organizations and in other organizations of the United Nations system;

11. *Urges* the specialized agencies and other organizations of the United Nations system, as well as the regional organizations concerned, to intensify measures to accelerate progress in the social and economic development of the Territory;

12. *Urges* Member States and specialized agencies and other organizations of the United Nations system to extend all possible assistance with a view to rehabilitating and reconstructing the Territory, devastated by hurricane Hugo;

13. *Requests* the Special Committee to continue the examination of this question at its next session, including the possible dispatch of a further visiting mission to the British Virgin Islands at an appropriate time and in consultation with the administering Power, and to report thereon to the General Assembly at its forty-fifth session.

General Assembly resolution 44/95

11 December 1989   Meeting 80   Adopted without vote

Approved by Fourth Committee (A/44/738) without vote, 25 October (meeting 16); draft by Special Committee on decolonization (A/44/23); agenda item 18.

Meeting numbers. GA 44th session: 4th Committee 5, 7-16; plenary 80.

Cayman Islands

The Special Committee on decolonization considered the question of the Cayman Islands on 7 August and had before it working papers prepared by the Secretariat on political developments and economic conditions in the Territory[32] and on foreign economic and other interests.[33]

GENERAL ASSEMBLY ACTION

On 11 December, on the recommendation of the Fourth Committee, the General Assembly adopted **resolution 44/91** without vote.

Question of the Cayman Islands

The General Assembly,

Having considered the question of the Cayman Islands,

Having examined the relevant chapters of the report of the Special Committee on the Situation with regard to the Implementation of the Declaration on the Granting of Independence to Colonial Countries and Peoples,

Recalling its resolution 1514(XV) of 14 December 1960, containing the Declaration on the Granting of Independence to Colonial Countries and Peoples, and all resolutions and decisions of the United Nations relating to the Cayman Islands, in particular General Assembly resolution 43/37 of 22 November 1988,

Conscious of the need to ensure the full and speedy implementation of the Declaration in respect of the Territory,

Having heard the statement of the representative of the United Kingdom of Great Britain and Northern Ireland, as the administering Power,

Noting the stated policy of the Government of the United Kingdom, the administering Power, that it remains ready to respond positively to the express wish of the people of the Territory on the question of independence,

Aware of the special circumstances of the geographical location and economic conditions of the Territory and bearing in mind the necessity of diversifying and strengthening further its economy as a matter of priority in order to promote economic stability,

Noting the measures being taken by the territorial Government to promote agricultural production with a view to reducing the Territory's dependence on imported provisions,

Expressing its concern that property and land continue to be owned and developed largely by investors from abroad,

Noting that a large proportion of the labour force of the Territory consists of expatriates,

Noting with concern the vulnerability of the Territory to drug trafficking and related activities,

Noting with appreciation the continued contribution of the United Nations Development Programme, as well as regional institutions, to the development of the Territory,

Recalling the dispatch in 1977 of a United Nations visiting mission to the Territory,

Mindful that United Nations visiting missions provide an effective means of ascertaining the situation in the small Territories and considering that the possibility of sending a further visiting mission to the Cayman Islands at an appropriate time should be kept under review,

1. *Approves* the chapter of the report of the Special Committee on the Situation with regard to the Implementation of the Declaration on the Granting of Independence to Colonial Countries and Peoples relating to the Cayman Islands;

2. *Reaffirms* the inalienable right of the people of the Cayman Islands to self-determination and independence in conformity with the Declaration on the Granting of Independence to Colonial Countries and Peoples;

3. *Reiterates the view* that such factors as territorial size, geographical location, size of population and limited natural resources should in no way delay the speedy exercise by the people of the Territory of their inalienable right to self-determination and independence in conformity with the Declaration, which fully applies to the Cayman Islands;

4. *Reiterates* that it is the responsibility of the United Kingdom of Great Britain and Northern Ireland, as the administering Power, to create such conditions in the Territory as will enable the people of the Cayman Islands to exercise freely and without interference their inalienable right to self-determination and independence in accordance with resolution 1514(XV) and all other relevant resolutions of the General Assembly;

5. *Reaffirms* that it is ultimately for the people of the Cayman Islands themselves to determine their future political status in accordance with the relevant provisions of the Charter of the United Nations and the Declaration and, in that connection, reaffirms the importance of fostering an awareness among the people of the Territory of the possibilities open to them in the exercise of their right to self-determination and independence;

6. *Calls upon* the administering Power, in consultation with the territorial Government, to facilitate and promote increased participation by the local population in the decision-making process in the affairs of the Territory;

7. *Reaffirms* the responsibility of the administering Power to promote the economic and social development of the Territory and recommends that priority should continue to be given to the diversification of the Territory's economy;

8. *Urges* the administering Power, in co-operation with the territorial Government, to take effective measures to safeguard and guarantee the inalienable right of the people of the Cayman Islands to own and dispose of the natural resources of the Territory, including marine resources, and to establish and maintain control over the future development of those resources;

9. *Calls upon* the administering Power to continue to take all necessary measures, in co-operation with the territorial Government, to counter problems related to drug trafficking;

10. *Invites* the specialized agencies and other organizations of the United Nations system, as well as other international and regional institutions, to continue to take all necessary measures to accelerate progress in the social and economic life of the Territory;

11. *Requests* the Special Committee to continue the examination of this question at its next session, including the possible dispatch of a further visiting mission to the Cayman Islands at an appropriate time and in consultation with the administering Power, and to report thereon to the General Assembly at its forty-fifth session.

General Assembly resolution 44/91

11 December 1989   Meeting 80   Adopted without vote

Approved by Fourth Committee (A/44/738) without vote, 25 October (meeting 16); draft by Special Committee on decolonization (A/44/23); agenda item 18.
Meeting numbers. GA 44th session: 4th Committee 5, 7-16; plenary 80.

Gibraltar

The Special Committee on decolonization considered the question of Gibraltar on 15 August and had before it a working paper prepared by the Secretariat on recent developments and current conditions in the Territory.[34] The Committee decided to continue consideration of Gibraltar at its next session subject to any General Assembly directives.

GENERAL ASSEMBLY ACTION

On 11 December, the General Assembly adopted **decision 44/426** without vote.

Question of Gibraltar

At its 80th plenary meeting, on 11 December 1989, the General Assembly, on the recommendation of the Fourth Committee, adopted the following text as representing the consensus of the members of the Assembly:

"The General Assembly, recalling its decision 43/411 of 22 November 1988 and recalling at the same time that the statement agreed to by the Governments of Spain and the United Kingdom of Great Britain and Northern Ireland at Brussels on 27 November 1984 stipulates, *inter alia*, the following:

" 'The establishment of a negotiating process aimed at overcoming all the differences between them over Gibraltar and at promoting co-operation on a mutually beneficial basis on economic, cultural, touristic, aviation, military and environmental matters. Both sides accept that the issues of sovereignty will be discussed in that process. The British Government will fully maintain its commitment to honour the wishes of the people of Gibraltar as set out in the preamble of the 1969 Constitution' ",

takes note of the fact that, as part of this process, the Ministers for Foreign Affairs have held annual meetings alternatively in each capital, and urges both Governments to continue their negotiations with the object of reaching a definitive solution to the problem of Gibraltar in the light of relevant resolutions of the General Assembly and in the spirit of the Charter of the United Nations.''

General Assembly decision 44/426

Adopted without vote

Approved by Fourth Committee (A/44/738) without vote, 25 October (meeting 16); draft consensus (A/C.4/44/L.2); agenda item 18.
Meeting numbers. GA 44th session: 4th Committee 5, 7-16; plenary 80.

Guam

The Special Committee on decolonization considered the question of Guam on 7 August, and had before it working papers prepared by the Secretariat on political developments and economic conditions in the Territory[35] and on military activities.[36]

GENERAL ASSEMBLY ACTION

On 11 December, on the recommendation of the Fourth Committee, the General Assembly adopted **resolution 44/98** without vote.

Question of Guam

The General Assembly,

Having considered the question of Guam,

Having examined the relevant chapters of the report of the Special Committee on the Situation with regard to the Implementation of the Declaration on the Granting of Independence to Colonial Countries and Peoples,

Recalling its resolution 1514(XV) of 14 December 1960, containing the Declaration on the Granting of Independence to Colonial Countries and Peoples, and all resolutions and decisions of the United Nations relating to Guam, in particular General Assembly resolution 43/42 of 22 November 1988,

Conscious of the need to ensure the full and speedy implementation of the Declaration in respect of the Territory, *Having heard* the statement of the representative of the United States of America, as the administering Power,

Recalling the approval, in referendums held in Guam in 1987, of a draft Commonwealth Act, which, upon its enactment by the United States Congress, would reaffirm the right of the people of Guam to draft their own Constitution and to govern themselves,

Noting that the draft Commonwealth Act provides that the Congress of the United States would recognize the inalienable right to self-determination of the Chamorro people, for which provisions would be made in the Guam Constitution,

Aware of the special circumstances of the geographical location and economic conditions of the Territory and bearing in mind the necessity of diversifying and strengthening further its economy as a matter of priority in order to promote economic stability,

Taking note of the statement of the representative of the administering Power that legislation had been introduced in the United States Congress to release 1,431 hectares of land no longer required by the Department of Defense and that the 100th Congress of the United States had considered the issue, and noting that a decision has yet to be taken on the matter,

Noting the potential for diversifying and developing the economy of Guam through commercial fishing and agriculture,

Taking note of the statement of the representative of the administering Power concerning the growth in tourism and the desire of the Government of Guam for balanced economic growth,

Taking note also of the statement of the representative of the administering Power that the cultural identity of the Chamorro people, the indigenous inhabitants of Guam, would be recognized,

Recalling the dispatch in 1979 of a United Nations visiting mission to the Territory,

Mindful that United Nations visiting missions provide an effective means of ascertaining the situation in the small Territories and reiterating that the possibility of sending a further visiting mission to Guam at an appropriate time should be kept under review,

1. *Approves* the chapter of the report of the Special Committee on the Situation with regard to the Implementation of the Declaration on the Granting of Independence to Colonial Countries and Peoples relating to Guam;

2. *Reaffirms* the inalienable right of the people of Guam to self-determination and independence in conformity with the Declaration on the Granting of Independence to Colonial Countries and Peoples;

3. *Reaffirms its conviction* that such factors as territorial size, geographical location, size of population and limited natural resources should in no way delay the implementation of the Declaration, which fully applies to Guam;

4. *Reaffirms* the importance of fostering an awareness among the people of Guam of the possibilities open to them with regard to their right to self-determination and calls upon the United States of America, as the administering Power, in co-operation with the territorial Government, to expedite the process of decolonization strictly in accordance with the expressed wishes of the people of the Territory;

5. *Reaffirms its strong conviction* that the presence of military bases and installations in the Territory could constitute a major obstacle to the implementation of the Declaration and that it is the responsibility of the administering Power to ensure that the existence of such bases and installations does not hinder the population of the Territory from exercising its right to self-determination and independence in conformity with the purposes and principles of the Charter of the United Nations;

6. *Urges* the administering Power to continue to take all necessary measures not to involve the Territory in any offensive acts or interference against other States and to comply fully with the purposes and principles of the Charter, the Declaration and the resolutions and decisions of the General Assembly relating to military activities and arrangements by colonial Powers in Territories under their administration;

7. *Reaffirms* the responsibility of the administering Power, under the Charter, to promote the economic and social development of Guam and, in that connection, calls upon the administering Power to take further steps to strengthen and diversify the economy of the Territory, with a view to reducing its economic dependence on the administering Power;

8. *Reiterates* that one of the obstacles to economic growth in Guam is the holding of large tracts of land by the United States federal authorities, and calls upon the administering Power, in co-operation with the territorial Government,

to expedite the transfer of land to the people of the Territory and to take the necessary steps to safeguard their property rights;

9. *Urges* the administering Power, in co-operation with the territorial Government, to take effective measures to safeguard and guarantee the inalienable right of the people of Guam to own and dispose of the natural resources of the Territory, including marine resources, and to establish and maintain control over the future development of those resources, as well as to support measures by the territorial Government aimed at removing constraints to growth in commercial fishing and agriculture;

10. *Reaffirms* the importance of continued efforts by the territorial Government, with the support of the administering Power, to promote and develop Guam's unique cultural identity;

11. *Urges* the administering Power to give full recognition to the status and rights of the Chamorro people;

12. *Requests* the Special Committee to continue the examination of this question at its next session, including the possible dispatch of a further visiting mission to Guam at an appropriate time and in consultation with the administering Power, and to report thereon to the General Assembly at its forty-fifth session.

General Assembly resolution 44/98

11 December 1989   Meeting 80   Adopted without vote

Approved by Fourth Committee (A/44/738) without vote, 25 October (meeting 16); draft by Special Committee on decolonization (A/44/23); agenda item 18.
Meeting numbers. GA 44th session: 4th Committee 5, 7-16; plenary 80.

Montserrat

The Special Committee on decolonization considered the question of Montserrat on 7 August. It had before it working papers prepared by the Secretariat on developments in the Territory[37] and on foreign economic and other interests.[38]

GENERAL ASSSEMBLY ACTION

On 11 December, on the recommendation of the Fourth Committee, the General Assembly adopted **resolution 44/96** without vote.

Question of Montserrat

The General Assembly,

Having considered the question of Montserrat,

Having examined the relevant chapters of the report of the Special Committee on the Situation with regard to the Implementation of the Declaration on the Granting of Independence to Colonial Countries and Peoples,

Recalling its resolution 1514(XV) of 14 December 1960, containing the Declaration on the Granting of Independence to Colonial Countries and Peoples, and all resolutions and decisions of the United Nations relating to Montserrat, including in particular General Assembly resolution 43/38 of 22 November 1988,

Conscious of the need to ensure the full and speedy implementation of the Declaration in respect of the Territory,

Having heard the statement of the representative of the United Kingdom of Great Britain and Northern Ireland, as the administering Power,

Noting the stated policy of the Government of the United Kingdom, the administering Power, that it remains ready

to respond positively to the express wish of the people of the Territory on the question of independence,

Recalling the discussions held between an adviser to the Foreign and Commonwealth Office of the United Kingdom and the Executive Council of Montserrat in May 1988 and the wish expressed by the Chief Minister of Montserrat to transfer some of the reserved powers of the Governor to the elected Government,

Taking note of the statement by the Chief Minister that a referendum should precede any move towards political independence and that his Government favoured both independence and participation in the political union among the countries of the Organization of Eastern Caribbean States,

Aware of the special circumstances of the geographical location and economic conditions of the Territory and bearing in mind the necessity of diversifying and strengthening further its economy as a matter of priority in order to promote economic stability,

Noting the measures being taken by the territorial Government to improve the efficiency of the civil service, the priority it places on cadre training and the strengthening of the educational system and its efforts to promote the integration of women in all phases of national development, and drawing attention to the need to associate the Territory in the related work of the United Nations bodies concerned in that regard,

Welcoming the contribution to the development of the Territory by the specialized agencies and other organizations of the United Nations system operating in Montserrat, in particular the United Nations Development Programme and the United Nations Children's Fund,

Noting with concern the continued dissociation of the Territory from the activities of the United Nations Educational, Scientific and Cultural Organization since the withdrawal by the administering Power of the associate membership of Montserrat from that organization in 1983, and aware of the active interest of the Government of Montserrat in the readmission of the Territory as an associate member of the agency,

Expressing its sympathy to the people of Montserrat for the extensive damage caused by hurricane Hugo in September 1989,

Recalling the dispatch in 1975 and 1982 of United Nations visiting missions to the Territory,

Mindful that United Nations visiting missions provide an effective means of ascertaining the situation in the small Territories and considering that the possibility of sending a further visiting mission to Montserrat at an appropriate time should be kept under review,

1. *Approves* the chapter of the report of the Special Committee on the Situation with regard to the Implementation of the Declaration on the Granting of Independence to Colonial Countries and Peoples relating to Montserrat;

2. *Reaffirms* the inalienable right of the people of Montserrat to self-determination and independence in conformity with the Declaration on the Granting of Independence to Colonial Countries and Peoples;

3. *Reiterates the view* that such factors as territorial size, geographical location, size of population and limited natural resources should in no way delay the speedy exercise by the people of the Territory of their inalienable right to self-determination and independence in conformity with the Declaration, which fully applies to Montserrat;

4. *Reiterates* that it is the responsibility of the United Kingdom of Great Britain and Northern Ireland, as the administering Power, to create such conditions in the Territory as will enable the people of Montserrat to exercise freely and without interference their inalienable right to self-determination and independence in accordance with resolution 1514(XV) and all other relevant resolutions of the General Assembly;

5. *Reaffirms* that it is ultimately for the people of Montserrat themselves to determine their future political status in accordance with the relevant provisions of the Charter of the United Nations and the Declaration, and reiterates its call upon the administering Power to launch programmes, in co-operation with the territorial Government, to foster an awareness among the people of Montserrat of the possibilities available to them in the exercise of their right to self-determination and independence;

6. *Reaffirms* the responsibility of the administering Power to promote the economic and social development of Montserrat and calls upon the administering Power to continue, in co-operation with the territorial Government, to strengthen the economy of the Territory and to increase its assistance to programmes of diversification;

7. *Urges* the administering Power, in co-operation with the territorial Government, to take effective measures to safeguard and guarantee the inalienable right of the people of Montserrat to own and dispose of the natural resources of the Territory, including marine resources, and to establish and maintain control over the future development of those resources;

8. *Urges* the administering Power, in co-operation with the territorial Government, to overcome shortages in human resources by providing appropriate incentives to assist nationals in finding better opportunities at home and to attract qualified nationals from abroad;

9. *Invites* the specialized agencies and other organizations of the United Nations system, as well as other international and regional organizations, to intensify their efforts to accelerate progress in the economic and social life of the Territory;

10. *Urges* Member States and specialized agencies and other organizations of the United Nations system to extend all possible assistance with a view to rehabilitating and reconstructing the Territory devastated by hurricane Hugo;

11. *Calls upon* the administering Power, in co-operation with the territorial Government, to take urgent steps to facilitate the readmission of Montserrat as an associate member of the United Nations Educational, Scientific and Cultural Organization;

12. *Requests* the Special Committee to continue the examination of this question at its next session, including the possible dispatch of a further visiting mission to Montserrat at an appropriate time and in consultation with the administering Power, and to report thereon to the General Assembly at its forty-fifth session.

General Assembly resolution 44/96

11 December 1989   Meeting 80   Adopted without vote

Approved by Fourth Committee (A/44/738) without vote, 25 October (meeting 16); draft by Special Committee on decolonization (A/44/23); agenda item 18.
Meeting numbers. GA 44th session: 4th Committee 5, 7-16; plenary 80.

Pitcairn

The Special Committee on decolonization considered the question of Pitcairn on 7 August, at which time it had before it a working paper prepared by the Secretariat on political developments and social and economic conditions in the Territory.[39]

GENERAL ASSEMBLY ACTION

On 11 December, the General Assembly adopted **decision 44/427** without vote.

Question of Pitcairn

At its 80th plenary meeting, on 11 December 1989, the General Assembly, on the recommendation of the Fourth Committee, adopted the following text as representing the consensus of the members of the Assembly:

"The General Assembly, having examined the relevant chapter of the report of the Special Committee on the Situation with regard to the Implementation of the Declaration on the Granting of Independence to Colonial Countries and Peoples, reaffirms the inalienable right of the people of Pitcairn to self-determination in conformity with the Declaration on the Granting of Independence to Colonial Countries and Peoples, which fully applies to the Territory. The Assembly further reaffirms the responsibility of the administering Power to promote the economic and social development of the Territory. The Assembly urges the administering Power to continue to respect the very individual life-style that the people of the Territory have chosen and to preserve, promote and protect it. The Assembly requests the Special Committee to continue to examine the question at its next session and to report thereon to the Assembly at its forty-fifth session."

General Assembly decision 44/427

Adopted without vote

Approved by Fourth Committee (A/44/738) without vote, 25 October (meeting 16); draft by Special Committee on decolonization (A/44/23); agenda item 18.
Meeting numbers. GA 44th session: 4th Committee 5, 7-16; plenary 80.

St. Helena

The Special Committee on decolonization considered the question of St. Helena on 7 August, and had before it a working paper prepared by the Secretariat on political and other developments in the Territory.[40]

GENERAL ASSEMBLY ACTION

On 11 December, the General Assembly adopted **decision 44/428** by recorded vote.

Question of St. Helena

At its 80th plenary meeting, on 11 December 1989, the General Assembly, on the recommendation of the Fourth Committee, having examined the relevant chapters of the report of the Special Committee on the Situation with regard to the Implementation of the Declaration on the Granting of Independence to Colonial Countries and Peoples, reaffirmed the inalienable right of the people of St. Helena to self-determination and independence in conformity with the Declaration on the Granting of Independence to Colonial Countries and Peoples, contained in Assembly resolution 1514(XV) of 14 December 1960. The Assembly urged the administering Power, in consultation with the Legislative Council and other representatives of the people of St. Helena, to continue to take all necessary steps to ensure the speedy implementation of the Declaration in respect of the Territory and, in that connection, reaffirmed the importance of promoting an awareness among the people of St. Helena of the possibilities open to them in the exercise of their right to self-determination. The Assembly expressed the view that the administering Power should continue to implement infrastructure and community development projects aimed at improving the general welfare of the community, including the unemployment situation, and to encourage local initiative and enterprise, particularly in the areas of fisheries development, forestry, handicrafts and agriculture. The Assembly, in view of the serious developments in South Africa, noted with concern the trade and transportation dependency of the Territory on South Africa. The Assembly reaffirmed that continued development assistance from the administering Power, together with any assistance that the international community might be able to provide, constituted an important means of developing the economic potential of the Territory and of enhancing the capacity of its people to realize fully the goals set forth in the relevant provisions of the Charter of the United Nations. The Assembly, in that connection, welcomed the assistance rendered by the United Nations Development Programme and invited other organizations of the United Nations system to assist in the development of the Territory. The Assembly noted with deep concern the continued presence of military facilities on the dependency of Ascension Island and, in that regard, recalled all the United Nations resolutions and decisions concerning military bases and installations in colonial and Non-Self-Governing Territories. The Assembly urged the administering Power to take all the necessary measures not to involve the Territory in any offensive acts or interference against neighbouring States by the racist régime of South Africa. The Assembly considered that the possibility of dispatching a United Nations visiting mission to St. Helena at an appropriate time should be kept under review, and requested the Special Committee to continue to examine the question of St. Helena at its next session and to report thereon to the Assembly at its forty-fifth session.

General Assembly decision 44/428

122-2-27 (recorded vote)

Approved by Fourth Committee (A/44/738) by recorded vote (109-2-28), 25 October (meeting 16); draft by Special Committee on decolonization (A/44/23); agenda item 18.

Meeting numbers. GA 44th session: 4th Committee 5, 7-16; plenary 80.

Recorded vote in Assembly as follows:

In favour: Afghanistan, Albania, Algeria, Angola, Antigua and Barbuda, Argentina, Bahamas, Bahrain, Bangladesh, Barbados, Benin, Bhutan, Bolivia, Botswana, Brazil, Brunei Darussalam, Bulgaria, Burkina Faso, Burundi, Byelorussian SSR, Cape Verde, Central African Republic, Chad, China, Colombia, Comoros, Congo, Costa Rica, Côte d'Ivoire, Cuba, Cyprus, Czechoslovakia, Democratic Kampuchea, Democratic Yemen, Djibouti, Dominican Republic, Ecuador, Egypt, El Salvador, Equatorial Guinea, Ethiopia, Gabon, Gambia, German Democratic Republic, Ghana, Grenada, Guatemala, Guinea, Guinea-Bissau, Guyana, Haiti, Honduras, Hungary, India, Indonesia, Iran, Iraq, Jamaica, Jordan, Kenya, Kuwait, Lao People's Democratic Republic, Lesotho, Liberia, Libyan Arab Jamahiriya, Madagascar, Malawi, Malaysia, Maldives, Mali, Mauritania, Mauritius, Mexico, Mongolia, Morocco, Mozambique, Myanmar, Nepal, Nicaragua, Niger, Nigeria, Oman, Pakistan, Panama,

Papua New Guinea, Paraguay, Peru, Philippines, Poland, Qatar, Romania, Rwanda, Saint Kitts and Nevis, Saint Lucia, Saint Vincent and the Grenadines, Sao Tome and Principe, Saudi Arabia, Senegal, Seychelles, Sierra Leone, Singapore, Solomon Islands, Somalia, Sri Lanka, Suriname, Swaziland, Syrian Arab Republic, Thailand, Togo, Tunisia, Uganda, Ukrainian SSR, USSR, United Arab Emirates, United Republic of Tanzania, Uruguay, Vanuatu, Venezuela, Viet Nam, Yemen, Yugoslavia, Zaire.

Against: United Kingdom, United States.

Abstaining: Australia, Austria, Belgium, Canada, Denmark, Dominica, Fiji, Finland, France, Germany, Federal Republic of, Greece, Iceland, Ireland, Israel, Italy, Japan, Luxembourg, Malta, Netherlands, New Zealand, Norway, Portugal, Samoa, Spain, Sweden, Trinidad and Tobago*, Turkey.

Later advised the Secretariat that it had intended to vote in favour.

Tokelau

The Special Committee on decolonization considered the question of Tokelau on 7 August. It had before it a working paper prepared by the Secretariat on political and economic developments in the Territory.[41]

GENERAL ASSEMBLY ACTION

On 11 December, on the recommendation of the Fourth Committee, the General Assembly adopted **resolution 44/90** without vote.

Question of Tokelau

The General Assembly,

Having considered the question of Tokelau,

Having examined the relevant chapters of the report of the Special Committee on the Situation with regard to the Implementation of the Declaration on the Granting of Independence to Colonial Countries and Peoples,

Recalling its resolution 1514(XV) of 14 December 1960, containing the Declaration on the Granting of Independence to Colonial Countries and Peoples, and all resolutions and decisions of the United Nations relating to Tokelau, in particular General Assembly resolution 43/35 of 22 November 1988,

Having heard the statement of the representative of New Zealand, the administering Power,

Noting the continuing devolution of power to the local authority, the General *Fono* (Council), and mindful that the cultural heritage and traditions of the people of Tokelau should be taken fully into account in the evolution of Tokelau's political institutions,

Noting with satisfaction the continued progress in the preparation of a legal code to conform with the traditional laws and cultural values of Tokelau and noting the express wish that the General *Fono* share additional responsibility in the process of law-making,

Aware of the special circumstances of the geographical location and economic conditions of the Territory and bearing in mind the necessity of diversifying and strengthening further its economy as a matter of priority in order to promote economic stability,

Noting the inspection of the Tokelau Public Service and its staff at Apia undertaken by the New Zealand State Services Commission in early 1989, and expressing the hope that the completion of this inspection will contribute to the development of the Public Service of the Territory,

Reaffirming the responsibility of the administering Power to promote the economic and social development of the Territory and noting the measures being taken by the Government of New Zealand in that regard,

Recalling the decision of the General *Fono* to include Tokelau in a fisheries treaty between countries in the region and stressing the importance of safeguarding the right of the people of Tokelau to the full enjoyment of their marine resources,

Noting the strong opposition expressed by the people of Tokelau to nuclear testing in the Pacific region and their concern that those tests constitute a grave threat to the natural resources of the Territory and its social and economic development,

Recalling with appreciation the assistance extended to Tokelau by the administering Power, other States Members of the United Nations and organizations of the United Nations system, in particular by the United Nations Development Programme, for the rehabilitation and reconstruction of the islands following the natural disasters in 1987,

Welcoming the reports that new telecommunications equipment has been installed on Fakaofo and is fully operational,

Recalling the dispatch in 1976, 1981 and 1986 of United Nations visiting missions to the Territory,

Mindful that United Nations visiting missions provide an effective means of ascertaining the situation in the small Territories and considering that the possibility of sending a further visiting mission to Tokelau at an appropriate time should be kept under review,

1. *Approves* the chapter of the report of the Special Committee on the Situation with regard to the Implementation of the Declaration on the Granting of Independence to Colonial Countries and Peoples relating to Tokelau;

2. *Reaffirms* the inalienable right of the people of Tokelau to self-determination and independence in accordance with the Declaration on the Granting of Independence to Colonial Countries and Peoples;

3. *Reiterates the view* that such factors as territorial size, geographical location, size of population and limited natural resources should in no way delay the implementation of the Declaration, which fully applies to Tokelau;

4. *Urges* the Government of New Zealand, the administering Power, to continue to respect fully the wishes of the people of Tokelau in carrying out the Territory's political and economic development, in order to preserve their social, cultural and traditional heritage;

5. *Calls upon* the administering Power, in consultation with the General Fono (Council) of Tokelau, to continue to expand its development assistance to Tokelau;

6. *Urges* the administering Power, other Member States and organizations of the United Nations system to continue to extend to Tokelau the maximum assistance possible for the rehabilitation and reconstruction of the islands in order to overcome the losses incurred in natural disasters in 1987;

7. *Invites* the specialized agencies and other organizations of the United Nations system, as well as other international and regional institutions, to extend or continue to extend all possible assistance to Tokelau, in consultation with the administering Power and the people of Tokelau;

8. *Requests* the Special Committee to continue the examination of this question at its next session, including the possible dispatch of a further visiting mission to Tokelau at an appropriate time and in consultation with the administering Power, and to report thereon to the General Assembly at its forty-fifth session.

General Assembly resolution 44/90
11 December 1989   Meeting 80   Adopted without vote

Approved by Fourth Committee (A/44/738) without vote, 25 October (meeting 16); draft by Special Committee on decolonization (A/44/23); agenda item 18.
Meeting numbers. GA 44th session: 4th Committee 5, 7-16; plenary 80.

Turks and Caicos Islands

The Special Committee on decolonization considered the question of Turks and Caicos Islands on 7 August, and had before it working papers prepared by the Secretariat on political developments and economic and social conditions in the Territory[42] and on foreign economic and other interests.[43]

GENERAL ASSEMBLY ACITON

On 11 December, on the recommendation of the Fourth Committee, the General Assembly adopted **resolution 44/93** without vote.

Question of the Turks and Caicos Islands

The General Assembly,

Having considered the question of the Turks and Caicos Islands,

Having examined the relevant chapters of the report of the Special Committee on the Situation with regard to the Implementation of the Declaration on the Granting of Independence to Colonial Countries and Peoples,

Recalling its resolution 1514(XV) of 14 December 1960, containing the Declaration on the Granting of Independence to Colonial Countries and Peoples, and all resolutions and decisions of the United Nations relating to the Turks and Caicos Islands, including in particular General Assembly resolution 43/40 of 22 November 1988,

Conscious of the nee d to ensure the full and speedy implementation of the Declaration in respect of the Territory, *Having heard* the statement of the representative of the United Kingdom of Great Britain and Northern Ireland, as the administering Power,

Noting the stated policy of the Government of the United Kingdom, the administering Power, that it remains ready to respond positively to the express wish of the people of the Territory on the question of independence,

Noting that the efforts of the administering Power to resolve the 1986 constitutional crisis in the Territory resulted in the drafting of a new Constitution by the administering Power and the subsequent holding of general elections in March 1988,

Aware of the special circumstances of the geographical location and economic conditions of the Turks and Caicos Islands and bearing in mind the necessity of diversifying and strengthening further its economy as a matter of priority in order to promote economic stability and develop a wider economic base for the Territory,

Noting with concern the vulnerability of the Territory to drug trafficking and related activities,

Noting the continuing contribution of the United Nations Development Programme to the economic and social development of the Territory,

Recalling the dispatch in 1980 of two United Nations visiting missions to the Territory,

Mindful that United Nations visiting missions provide an effective means of ascertaining the situation in the small Territories and considering that the possibility of sending a further visiting mission to the Turks and Caicos Islands at an appropriate time should be kept under review,

1. *Approves* the chapter of the report of the Special Committee on the Situation with regard to the Implementation of the Declaration on the Granting of Independence to Colonial Countries and Peoples relating to the Turks and Caicos Islands;

2. *Reaffirms* the inalienable right of the people of the Turks and Caicos Islands to self-determination and independence in conformity with the Declaration on the Granting of Independence to Colonial Countries and Peoples;

3. *Reiterates the view* that such factors as territorial size, geographical location, size of population and limited natural resources should in no way delay the speedy exercise by the people of the Territory of their inalienable right to self-determination and independence in conformity with the Declaration, which fully applies to the Turks and Caicos Islands;

4. *Reiterates* that it is the obligation of the United Kingdom of Great Britain and Northern Ireland, as the administering Power, to create such conditions in the Territory as will enable the people of the Turks and Caicos Islands to exercise freely and without interference their inalienable right to self-determination and independence in accordance with resolution 1514(XV) and all other relevant resolutions of the General Assembly;

5. *Reaffirms* that it is ultimately for the people of the Turks and Caicos Islands themselves to determine freely their future political status in accordance with the relevant provisions of the Charter of the United Nations and the Declaration and, in that connection, reaffirms the importance of fostering an awareness among the people of the Territory of the possibilities open to them in the exercise of their right to self-determination and independence;

6. *Reaffirms* that it is the responsibility of the administering Power under the Charter to develop its dependent Territories economically and socially and urges the administering Power, in consultation with the Government of the Turks and Caicos Islands, to take the necessary measures to promote the economic and social development of the Territory;

7. *Urges* the administering Power, in co-operation with the territorial Government, to take effective measures to safeguard and guarantee the inalienable right of the people of the Turks and Caicos Islands to own and dispose of the natural resources of the Territory, including marine resources, and to establish and maintain control over the future development of those resources;

8. *Also urges* the administering Power, in consultation with the territorial Government, to continue to provide the necessary assistance for the localization of the civil service at all levels and for the training of local personnel;

9. *Calls upon* the administering Power to continue to take all necessary measures, in co-operation with the territorial Government, to counter problems related to drug trafficking;

10. *Invites* the specialized agencies and other organizations of the United Nations system, as well as the regional institutions concerned, to continue to pay special attention to the development needs of the Turks and Caicos Islands;

11. *Requests* the Special Committee to continue the examination of this question at its next session, including the possible dispatch of a further visiting mission to the Turks and Caicos Islands at an appropriate time and in consultation with the administering Power, and to report thereon to the General Assembly at its forty-fifth session.

General Assembly resolution 44/93

11 December 1989   Meeting 80   Adopted without vote

Approved by Fourth Committee (A/44/738) without vote, 25 October (meeting 16); draft by Special Committee on decolonization (A/44/23); agenda item 18.

Meeting numbers. GA 44th session: 4th Committee 5, 7-16; plenary 80.

United States Virgin Islands

The Special Committee on decolonization considered the question of the United States Virgin Islands on 7 August. It had before it working papers prepared by the Secretariat on developments in the Territory,[44] on foreign economic and other interests[45] and on military activities.[46]

GENERAL ASSEMBLY ACTION

On 11 December, on the recommendation of the Fourth Committee, the General Assembly adopted **resolution 44/99** without vote.

Question of the United States Virgin Islands

The General Assembly,

Having considered the question of the United States Virgin Islands,

Having examined the relevant chapters of the report of the Special Committee on the Situation with regard to the Implementation of the Declaration on the Granting of Independence to Colonial Countries and Peoples,

Recalling its resolution 1514(XV) of 14 December 1960, containing the Declaration on the Granting of Independence to Colonial Countries and Peoples, and all resolutions and decisions of the United Nations relating to the United States Virgin Islands, including in particular General Assembly resolution 43/44 of 22 November 1988,

Conscious of the need to ensure the full and speedy implementation of the Declaration in respect of the Territory,

Having heard the statement of the representative of the United States of America, as the administering Power,

Recalling the statement of the representative of the administering Power that the participation of the people of the Territory in the electoral process demonstrated that they exercised responsibility for local government and local political affairs and recalling also that the representative of the administering Power re-emphasized the policy of her Government to respond to the wishes of the people regarding their future political status whenever they indicated the direction in which they wished to proceed,

Noting with satisfaction that the territorial Commission on Status and Federal Relations started its work in September 1988 in preparation for the referendum on the Territory's future political status that had been scheduled to be held on 14 November 1989,

Noting, however, that the devastation to the Territory caused by hurricane Hugo resulted in an indefinite postponement of the referendum,

Noting also that legislation of July 1988 would lengthen from 30 to 90 days the residency requirement for voting in general elections and that a ruling of the United States Supreme Court could render the new law inoperative before it is due to take effect at the general elections to be held in the Territory in 1990,

Aware of the special circumstances of the geographical location and economic conditions of the Territory and bearing in mind the necessity of diversifying and strengthening further its economy as a matter of priority in order to promote economic stability,

Noting the measures being taken by the territorial Government with a view to strengthening the Territory's financial viability and facilitating its economic development,

Taking note of the statement of the representative of the Territory that his Government shares the concern of other Caribbean countries over the rapid depletion of the region's marine resources due to massive overfishing, mostly by large extraregional vessels, and bearing in mind the measures taken by the territorial Government and the administering Power to address this problem,

Noting the stated position of the Government of the United States Virgin Islands on the disposition of Water Island as well as the need for the Territory to exercise control over its own resources,

Noting also the continued concern expressed by a petitioner at the reclamation and development of submerged land at Long Bay in the Charlotte Amalie Harbour, and taking note of the statement of the representative of the administering Power that the issue had been settled by litigation and that those activities were subject to the regulatory powers of the Government of the Territory,

Noting with concern the vulnerability of the Territory to drug trafficking and related activities,

Noting the active interest of the Government of the United States Virgin Islands in participating in the related work of the international and regional organizations concerned,

Expressing its sympathy to the people of the United States Virgin Islands for the extensive damage caused by hurricane Hugo in September 1989,

Recalling the dispatch in 1977 of a United Nations visiting mission to the Territory,

Mindful that United Nations visiting missions provide an effective means of ascertaining the situation in the small Territories, and considering that the possibility of sending a further visiting mission to the United States Virgin Islands at an appropriate time should be kept under review,

1. *Approves* the chapter of the report of the Special Committee on the Situation with regard to the Implementation of the Declaration on the Granting of Independence to Colonial Countries and Peoples relating to the United States Virgin Islands;

2. *Reaffirms* the inalienable right of the people of the United States Virgin Islands to self-determination and independence in conformity with the Declaration on the Granting of Independence to Colonial Countries and Peoples;

3. *Reiterates the view* that such factors as territorial size, geographical location, size of population and limited natural resources should in no way delay the speedy exercise by the people of the Territory of their inalienable right to self-determination and independence in conformity with the Declaration, which fully applies to the United States Virgin Islands;

4. *Reiterates* that it is the responsibility of the United States of America, as the administering Power, to continue to create such conditions in the United States Virgin Islands as will enable the people of the Territory to exercise freely and without interference their inalienable right to self-determination and independence in conformity with resolution 1514(XV);

5. *Reaffirms* that it is ultimately for the people of the United States Virgin Islands themselves to determine their future political status in accordance with the relevant provisions of the Charter of the United Nations, the Declaration and the relevant resolutions of the General Assembly and, in that connection, calls upon the administering Power, in co-operation with the territorial Government, to facilitate programmes of political education in the Territory in order to foster an awareness among the people of the possibilities open to them in the exercise of their right to self-determination;

6. *Reaffirms* the responsibility of the administering Power under the Charter to continue to promote the economic and social development of the United States Virgin Islands, and urges the administering Power, in co-operation with the territorial Government, to continue to take measures with a view to strengthening and diversifying the Territory's economy;

7. *Urges* the administering Power, in co-operation with the territorial Government, to take effective measures to safeguard and guarantee the inalienable right of the people of the United States Virgin Islands to own and dispose of the natural resources of the Territory, including marine resources, and to establish and maintain control over the future development of those resources;

8. *Expresses its concern* about the continued depletion of the Territory's marine resources and urges the administering Power, in consultation with the territorial Government, to take the necessary steps to reverse this trend;

9. *Calls upon* the administering Power to continue to take all necessary measures, in co-operation with the territorial Government, to counter problems related to drug trafficking;

10. *Urges* the administering Power to facilitate the participation of the United States Virgin Islands in various international and regional organizations;

11. *Urges* Member States and specialized age ncies and other organizations of the United Nations system to extend all possible assistance with a view to rehabilitating and reconstructing the Territory devastated by hurricane Hugo;

12. *Urges* the administering Power to continue to take all necessary measures to comply fully with the purposes and principles of the Charter, the Declaration and the relevant resolutions and decisions of the General Assembly relating to military activities and arrangements by colonial Powers in Territories under their administration;

13. *Requests* the Special Committee to continue the examination of this question at its next session, including the possible dispatch of a further visiting mission to the United States Virgin Islands at an appropriate time and in consultation with the administering Power, particularly in the light of the referendum referred to in the seventh and eighth preambular paragraphs of the present resolution, and to report thereon to the General Assembly at its forty-fifth session.

General Assembly resolution 44/99

11 December 1989   Meeting 80   Adopted without vote

Approved by Fourth Committee (A/44/738) without vote, 25 October (meeting 16); draft by Special Committee on decolonization (A/44/23); agenda item 18.
Meeting numbers. GA 44th session: 4th Committee 5, 7-16; plenary 80.

REFERENCES

[1]A/44/23. [2]A/AC.109/1004. [3]A/44/23 (A/AC.109/1008). [4]A/44/692. [5]A/44/490-S/20818. [6]A/44/678-S/20915. [7]E/1989/20 (res. 1989/18). [8]A/AC.109/999/Rev.1. [9]YUN 1988, p. 741, GA res. 43/33, 22 Nov. 1988. [10]A/44/634 & Corr.1. [11]YUN 1988, p. 740. [12]YUN 1986, p. 913, GA res. 41/41 A, 2 Dec. 1986. [13]YUN 1960, p. 49, GA res. 1514(XV), 14 Dec. 1960. [14]YUN 1987, p. 1030. [15]A/AC.109/1000. [16]A/44/23 (A/AC.109/1012). [17]A/AC.109/1001. [18]A/44/94-S/20421. [19]A/44/201-S/20546 & Corr.1. [20]A/44/262. [21]YUN 1979, p. 1117. [22]A/AC.109/1002 & Add.1. [23]A/45/57-S/21022. [24]A/44/524. [25]A/AC.109/988. [26]A/AC.109/975 & Add.1. [27]A/AC.109/976. [28]A/AC.109/995. [29]A/AC.109/997. [30]A/AC.109/996. [31]A/AC.109/983. [32]A/AC.109/982. [33]A/AC.109/989. [34]A/AC.109/1007 & Corr.1. [35]A/AC.109/992. [36]A/AC.109/993. [37]A/AC.109/980. [38]A/AC.109/994. [39]A/AC.109/977. [40]A/AC.109/978. [41]A/AC.109/979 & Add.1. [42]A/AC.109/985. [43]A/AC.109/984. [44]A/AC.109/986. [45]A/AC.109/990. [46]A/AC.109/987.

Chapter II

International Trusteeship System

During the year, the Trusteeship Council continued to monitor the status of Palau, the single remaining entity of the Trust Territory of the Pacific Islands, which had not completed the process of self-determination. In 1989, the Trust Territory was the last still under the International Trusteeship System.

In April, a Visiting Mission was dispatched to Palau. The Council in June invited the United States, the Administering Authority, to take into account the Mission's recommendations.

The five-member Trusteeship Council—China, France, the USSR, the United Kingdom and the United States—held its nineteenth special session in New York on 16 and 17 March, and its fifty-sixth session, also in New York, from 15 May to 1 August. The Council considered the Administering Authority's annual report, heard 10 petitioners and examined 125 written petitions and 14 communications regarding the Territory.

Trust Territory of the Pacific Islands

The Trust Territory of the Pacific Islands, designated as a strategic area and administered by the United States in accordance with the Trusteeship Agreement approved by the Security Council in 1947,[1] consists of more than 2,100 islands and atolls scattered over an area of some 7.8 million square kilometres of the western Pacific Ocean, north of the Equator. It had 168,431 inhabitants in 1986 and was composed of four constitutional Governments: the Federated States of Micronesia, Marshall Islands, Northern Mariana Islands and Palau.

In 1986, the United States signed legislation enacting a Commonwealth Covenant with the Northern Mariana Islands, and Compacts of Free Association with the Marshall Islands and with the Federated States of Micronesia, which entered into force the same year.[2]

With regard to Palau, a Compact of Free Association was favoured by 73 per cent of Palauans in an August 1987 plebiscite.[3] A group of Palauan citizens, however, challenged the plebiscite on the grounds that the Constitution had been improperly amended, when a law passed by the Palau National Congress altered the majority required for approval of the Compact from 75 per cent to a simple majority. The Palau Supreme Court found for the plaintiffs and handed down a verdict declaring the plebiscite null and void.

In February 1989, the Government of Palau established a Commission on Future Palau/United States Relations, with a mandate to improve the provisions of the Compact of Free Association before it was again put to the voters in an eventual referendum. Negotiations were conducted with the United States authorities on a number of proposals for revision of the Compact, particularly regarding capital improvement projects and land compensation. In May, the representatives of Palau and the United States announced that they had signed an Agreement concerning Special Programs Relating to the Entry into Force of the Compact of Free Association. In December, the United States passed the Implementation Act to authorize the entry into force of the Compact of Free Association with Palau.

Conditions in the Trust Territory

In a working paper submitted to the Trusteeship Council in May,[4] the Secretariat provided an outline of conditions in the Trust Territory covering political, economic, social and educational advancement. An updated report[5] described constitutional developments and progress towards self-government (see above), and summarized the structure of the four constitutional Governments, including the legislature, executive, state and municipal governments, and the civil service. Under the 1987 status arrangements, the Marshall Islands and the Federated States of Micronesia were defined as "sovereign and self-governing" and the Northern Mariana Islands as "self-governing".

Funding for government operations in the Trust Territory was derived mainly from an annual grant provided by the U.S. Department of the Interior. The second and third largest sources of income were federal grants and revenues locally collected from taxation. Total revenues during fiscal year 1988/89 amounted to $45.7 million, which balanced annual expenditures ($45.7 million) for the same period. For 1988/89, the grant from the Administering Authority to the Trust Territory totalled approximately $36 million, of which $14.7 million represented funds from the Department of the Interior, $9.7 million was federal grants and $12.4 million was Capital Improvement Program funds. Local revenues amounted to $9 million, derived from taxes and reimbursements for the use of public utilities.

Palau's total revenue for 1988/89 amounted to approximately $23 million, of which approximately $14.7 million was derived from the Department of the Interior and $8.8 million from taxes and payments for utilities. During the same period, expenditures amounted to approximately $23.2 million, leaving a budgetary deficit of approximately $469,000. The total accumulated value of Palauan government property at the end of 1988/89 was estimated at $13 million, while personal property, exclusive of the value of land and improvements, was estimated at $13.4 million.

War damage claims by the inhabitants of the Trust Territory fell into two categories, namely claims against the Governments of the United States and Japan, mainly for damages sustained by the indigenous inhabitants during the Second World War (Title I claims), and post-war claims against the Government of the United States (Title II claims). All claims under Title II (a total of $32.6 million) had already been settled. As regards Title I claims (a total of $34.3 million), the remaining balance due (about $10 million) was appropriated in the fiscal year 1989 budget and combined with the fiscal year 1988 appropriation.

Subsistence farming is the main agricultural activity in the Trust Territory. Local production of agricultural commodities in Palau increased in 1989, as did the number of private businesses, mostly in construction, transportation and services.

Trusteeship Council consideration. The Trusteeship Council held its fifty-sixth session in New York from 15 May to 1 August.[6] It had before it the most recent annual report[7] of the Administering Authority and a working paper prepared by the Secretariat.[4] By a note of 10 May,[8] the Secretary-General transmitted the Administering Authority's report to the Security Council.

On 1 June,[6] the Trusteeship Council adopted a set of conclusions and recommendations regarding the Trust Territory by 4 votes to 1. It noted the formation in Palau in February 1989 of the Commission on Future Palau/United States Relations to address certain concerns with regard to the proposed future relationship between the United States and Palau, and it welcomed the fact that the negotiations between representatives of the Commission and U.S. authorities had resulted in the signing, on 26 May, of an agreement between the two sides. The Council expressed its hope that the agreement would help to achieve an early completion of the process of approval of the Compact of Free Association, in accordance with the wishes of the people of Palau.

In its conclusions, the Council also: noted that the peoples of the Trust Territory had elected to assume full responsibility for administration in the economic, social and educational fields; considered that any difficulties over the interpretation of the new status agreements should be resolved bilaterally by the parties concerned; noted the particular concern of the Government of Palau about poaching by foreign fishing vessels; and noted with satisfaction the assurances given by the Administering Authority that it would continue to fulfil its responsibilities under the Charter of the United Nations and under the Trusteeship Agreement.

On 1 August,[6] the Council adopted, by 4 votes to 1, its report to the Security Council covering the period 20 July 1988 to 1 August 1989.

Consideration by Special Committee on decolonization. The General Assembly's Special Committee on the Situation with regard to the Implementation of the Declaration on the Granting of Independence to Colonial Countries and Peoples (Special Committee on decolonization)[9] considered the question of the Trust Territory on 7 August and endorsed the conclusions and recommendations made by its Sub-Committee on Small Territories. In considering the question, the Committee had before it a Secretariat working paper on developments in the Territory.[10]

The Committee reaffirmed the inalienable right of the people of the Territory to self-determination and independence in conformity with the UN Charter and the 1960 Declaration on the Granting of Independence to Colonial Countries and Peoples.[11] It reiterated its appeal to the Administering Authority to reconsider its non-participation in the work of the Sub-Committee during its consideration of the Territory, and to resume its participation in the work of the Committee. Recognizing that it was ultimately for the people of the Trust Territory to decide their political destiny, the Committee called upon the Administering Authority not to fragment the Territory or take any action against the wishes of the people as expressed in any genuine act of self-determination. It urged the Authority to continue to take measures not to involve the Territory in any offensive acts or interference against other States, and to take measures to safeguard the right of the people of the Territory to own and dispose of the natural resources of the Territory.

The text of the conclusions and recommendations was transmitted on 30 August to the President of the Security Council[12] and to the President of the Trusteeship Council.[13] The Committee also recommended to the General

Assembly for its adoption a draft resolution on the question of the Trust Territory of the Pacific Islands.

GENERAL ASSEMBLY CONSIDERATION

On 25 October, the Chairman of the General Assembly's Fourth Committee, following consultations with the Chairman of the Special Committee on decolonization and with delegations concerned, suggested that no action be taken on a draft resolution submitted by the latter Committee. The suggestion was adopted without objection.[14]

Visiting mission

By letters dated 1 March[15] and 3 March 1989,[16] the United States invited the Trusteeship Council to send at its earliest convenience a visiting mission to observe current conditions in Palau, and requested that a special session of the Council be convened to consider that invitation. Having received the support of the majority of delegations, the nineteenth special session was held in New York on 16 and 17 March.[6]

TRUSTEESHIP COUNCIL ACTION

On 17 March, the Trusteeship Council adopted **resolution 2190(S-XIX)** by vote.

Arrangements for the dispatch of a visiting mission to observe current conditions in Palau, Trust Territory of the Pacific Islands

The Trusteeship Council,

Recalling its resolution 2183(LIII) in which, *inter alia*, it expressed the view that the United States of America, as the Administering Authority, had satisfactorily discharged its obligations under the terms of the Trusteeship Agreement,

Aware that the proposed Compact of Free Association between the United States and Palau has not yet come into effect,

Having been invited by the Administering Authority to dispatch a mission to observe current conditions in Palau,

1. *Decides* to dispatch a visiting mission to Palau, Trust Territory of the Pacific Islands, in April 1989 for approximately two weeks;

2. *Further decides* that the Visiting Mission should be composed of members of the Council wishing to participate, except the Administering Authority, which may provide an escort officer;

3. *Directs* the Visiting Mission to observe the steps being taken in Palau towards bringing into effect the proposed Compact of Free Association;

4. *Directs* the Visiting Mission, as may be appropriate in the light of discussions in the Trusteeship Council and of resolutions adopted by it, to obtain first-hand information concerning political, economic and social developments in Palau;

5. *Directs* the Visiting Mission to receive petitions, without prejudice to its action in accordance with the rules of procedure of the Council, and to examine on the spot such of the petitions as, in its opinion, warrant special examination;

6. *Requests* the Visiting Mission to submit to the Council as soon as practicable a report on its visit containing its findings, with such observations, conclusions and recommendations as it may wish to make;

7. *Requests* the Secretary-General to provide the necessary staff and facilities to assist the Visiting Mission in the performance of its functions.

Trusteeship Council resolution 2190(S-XIX)
17 March 1989   Meeting 1660   3-1

Draft by United Kingdom (T/L.1267); agenda item 3.
Meeting members. TC 1659, 1660

In a statement after the vote, the USSR said that the draft resolution had been put to a vote and adopted by the majority without taking the views of its delegation into account. The USSR had on many occasions drawn attention to the arbitrary, illegal and unilateral actions by the United States to alter the Trust Territory status of the Territory, in violation of the Charter, the 1947 Trusteeship Agreement and the Declaration on the Granting of Independence to Colonial Countries and Peoples. The resolution totally ignored those facts, and the USSR had voted against it.

The United Kingdom, in response to the statement by the USSR, noted the suggestion that it should have engaged in more dialogue on the draft resolution with a view to reaching a consensus, but said there had been no evidence of new thinking; it had heard the same charges and accusations year after year. The United Kingdom could not accept the view that there was a violation of the Charter if the people of a Trust Territory were allowed to determine their own future.

Report of the Visiting Mission. The Trusteeship Council's 1989 Visiting Mission to Palau,[17] composed of one representative each from France and the United Kingdom, began its visit at Koror, Palau, on 10 April and ended it on 17 April. The Mission was to observe the steps taken towards bringing into effect the proposed Compact of Free Association, to obtain first-hand information on political, economic and social developments in Palau, and to receive petitions.

In its conclusions and recommendations, the Mission stated that very few of those to whom it talked questioned the status of free association as the basis for future relations between Palau and the Administering Authority. The Mission therefore concluded that free association with the United States remained the preferred future status option of the overwhelming majority of the people of Palau. Nevertheless, some Palauans seemed to view the end of the Trusteeship with anxiety as a step into the unknown, and concern was also expressed that the Trusteeship might be terminated prematurely, i.e., before the Compact of Free Association had entered into force. The Mission drew attention to assurances given by the Administering Authority that it would continue to fulfil its responsibilities under the Charter of the United Nations and the Trusteeship Agreement, and assured those to whom it talked that the Trusteeship Council would continue to carry out its responsibilities as long as the Trusteeship Agreement remained in force.

The Mission felt that the United Nations should be able to provide more effective assistance to the economic planning process than at present. It recommended that, following the resolution of the question of Palau's future political status, consideration be given to the assignment of a full-fledged expert or the dispatch of an interregional adviser from the Department of Technical Co-operation for Development to review the Government's need for UN assistance.

TRUSTEESHIP COUNCIL ACTION

On 1 June,[6] at its fifty-sixth session, the Trusteeship Council adopted **resolution 2191(LVI)** by 4 votes in favour to 1 against, by which it took note of the report of the Visiting Mission, and expressed its appreciation of the work it had accomplished. It decided that it would continue to take the recommendations of the Visiting Mission into account in future examination of matters relating to the Trust Territory, and invited the Administering Authority to consider them also, as well as the comments made thereon by members of the Trusteeship Council.

Hearings, petitions and communications

On 16 and 17 May, the Trusteeship Council heard 10 petitioners on issues concerning the conditions in and status of the Trust Territory.[6]

At its meetings between 19 and 23 May, the Council considered 14 communications and 125 petitions. On 22 May, it took note of those communications, and with respect to 118 petitions, it decided to draw the attention of the petitioners to the observations made during the session by the Administering Authority and members of the Council.

REFERENCES
(1)YUN 1946-47, p. 398. (2)YUN 1986, p. 917. (3)YUN 1987, p. 978. (4)T/L.1269. (5)T/L.1274. (6)S/20843. (7)T/1934. (8)S/20624. (9)A/44/23 (Part VI). (10)A/AC.109/998. (11)YUN 1960, p. 49, GA res. 1514(XV), 14 Dec. 1960. (12)S/20827. (13)T/1939. (14)A/44/738. (15)T/1928. (16)T/1929. (17)T/1935.

Other aspects of the International Trusteeship System

Fellowships and scholarships

Under a scholarship programme launched in 1952,[1] 11 Member States had in the past made scholarships available for students from Trust Ter-

ritories: Czechoslovakia, Hungary, Indonesia, Italy, Mexico, Pakistan, Philippines, Poland, Tunisia, the USSR and Yugoslavia. In a report to the Trusteeship Council covering the period from 18 May 1988 to 19 May 1989,[2] the Secretary-General stated that he had received information from one offering State, the USSR, which said that during the academic year 1988/89 no inhabitants from the Trust Territory of the Pacific Islands were studying in the country.

On 23 May,[3] the Council took note of the Secretary-General's report.

Information dissemination

A May report[4] by the Secretary-General covering the period from 1 May 1988 to 30 April 1989 described the dissemination by the United Nations Department of Public Information (DPI) of UN documents and information materials, including taped radio and video programmes, in the Trust Territory of the Pacific Islands. Those activities, primarily carried out through the United Nations Information Centre (UNIC) at Tokyo, were aimed at keeping the people of the Territory aware of UN activities, particularly with respect to the Trusteeship System. Other departments, including the secretariat of the Trusteeship Council, assisted in the distribution of information.

Information materials provided by DPI consisted of press releases in English and French dealing with the Trusteeship Council and photo coverage of the proceedings of the Council. DPI also prepared for the *UN Chronicle* a report on the Council's deliberations.

In the Trusteeship Council, the USSR expressed regret that a control file on materials sent to the Territory was not available to the Council, and called for details of taped radio and video programmes distributed by DPI. The representative of DPI stated that he had noted the request of the USSR and that the Department had assembled a list of materials distributed, which was annexed to the Secretary-General's report on the dissemination of information. To maintain a separate file for each item for each place of distribution would, however, be cumbersome. He also stated that it was difficult to obtain systematic evaluation of the effectiveness of the materials, to identify target audiences and to see if the materials were useful.

On 18 May,[3] the Council took note of the Secretary-General's report.

Co-operation with Special Committee on decolonization

In 1989,[3] the Trusteeship Council considered jointly two items of its agenda: the attainment of self-government and independence by the Trust

Territory, and co-operation with the Special Committee on the Situation with regard to the Implementation of the Declaration on the Granting of Independence to Colonial Countries and Peoples.

During the discussion in the Council, the USSR stated that under the Administering Authority's policy, which promoted the fragmentation of a single Trust Territory and imposed on each of them unequal agreements, the Micronesian people had no real opportunity to enjoy their right to self-determination and independence. Referring to the regret expressed by the Committee over the Authority's failure to participate in its work and its lack of co-operation with the Trusteeship Council, he said that the Committee's appeal to the Administering Authority to resume its participation deserved the Council's very real consideration.

On 1 June,[3] the Trusteeship Council drew the Security Council's attention to the conclusions and recommendations it had adopted at its fifty-sixth session concerning the attainment of self-government or independence by the Trust Territory, and to the statements made by Trusteeship Council members on those questions.

Co-operation with CERD and the Decade against racial discrimination

In 1989, the Trusteeship Council decided to consider jointly the question of co-operation with the Committee on the Elimination of Racial Discrimination (CERD) and the matter of the Second Decade to Combat Racism and Racial Discrimination.

During the discussion in the Council, the USSR stated that, as a result of the position of the Administering Authority of the Trust Territory of the Pacific Islands, supported by some Council members, the Trusteeship Council was on the sidelines of the UN measures being taken regarding the Second Decade for Action to Combat Racism and Racial Discrimination (1983-1993).[5] In the USSR's view, the Council should invite representatives of CERD to attend meetings of the Council, and should provide CERD full documentation on the situation with regard to the civil, social, economic, political and cultural rights of the people of the Territory, as well as information on developments in the constitutional process, which had often been requested by the Committee.

On 25 May, the Council took note of the statement by the USSR.

REFERENCES

[1]YUN 1951, p. 788, GA res. 557(VI), 18 Jan. 1952. [2]T/1937. [3]S/20843. [4]T/1936. [5]YUN 1983, p. 806, GA res. 38/14, 22 Nov. 1983.

Chapter III

Namibia

The year 1989 saw the beginning of the end of colonialism in Africa, as Namibia—the largest Territory with a colonial background anywhere in the world—began an irreversible march to independence. As a pre–First World War German colony known as South West Africa, it was the only one of seven African Territories once held under the League of Nations Mandate System that was not placed under the United Nations Trusteeship System, due to the fact that South Africa refused to accept UN competence, and despite Security Council and General Assembly resolutions and opinions of the International Court of Justice asserting the Organization's primary role in the Territory.[a] As early as 1969, the Security Council called on South Africa to withdraw its illegal administration,[b] and in 1976 it demanded that South Africa accept elections for the Territory under UN supervision and control.[c] The Territory was then renamed Namibia, rather than South West Africa, under a 1968 General Assembly resolution[d] stating that that was the name desired by the people. In 1976, the Assembly decided[e] that any independence talks must include the South West Africa People's Organization (SWAPO), which the Assembly recognized as the sole and authentic representative of the Namibian people. In 1978, at a special session, the General Assembly expressed support for the armed liberation struggle of the Namibian people, stating that any settlement must be arrived at with SWAPO's agreement and within the framework of UN resolutions.[f]

The United Nations Transition Assistance Group (UNTAG), the fundamental role of which was decolonization, moved into place in the Territory on 1 April 1989, mandated through 31 March 1990. South Africa, which had administered the Territory for some 70 years, thereafter began its withdrawal, though renewed fighting between its forces and the national liberation movement, SWAPO, during the first few days of April briefly threatened to derail the UNTAG operation. Once the cease-fire was reinstated and forces of both parties had returned to agreed bases and positions, UNTAG began to focus on creating conditions for elections to a Constituent Assembly, which was to draw up a constitution for an independent Namibia, scheduled to come into existence in early 1990.

While elections eventually took place without incident in November 1989, under UN supervision and control, and were subsequently certified free and fair by the Secretary-General's Special Representative—a validation accepted by the parties—the Security Council had to take actions earlier in the year to ensure that the UN operation was able to fulfil its mandate. In August, it acted regarding Koevoet, the South African counter-insurgency group, as well as regarding election procedures (resolution 640(1989)), followed by a further resolution on the same issues in October (643(1989)). In a statement in November, the Council deplored what it found to be false allegations by South Africa about concentrations of SWAPO combatants in southern Angola. For its part, the General Assembly approved UNTAG financing (resolution 44/191), and adopted other resolutions on activities of transnational corporations in Namibia (44/84) and on torture and inhuman treatment of children in detention in South Africa and Namibia (44/143). Preparing for the post-independence period, other United Nations bodies, particularly the Council for Namibia, launched assistance programmes, while continuing to oversee programmes already in operation.

UN Transition Assistance Group

Pre-operational aspects (January-April 1989)

By resolution 435(1978),[1] the Security Council endorsed a plan for Namibian independence, based on a proposal submitted by Canada, France, the Federal Republic of Germany, the United Kingdom and the United States—the Western members of the Council of that year—and authorized the establishment of UNTAG. In 1980, South Africa accepted the proposal of the five Western Powers, and in 1981[2] it participated in a pre-

[a]YUN 1966, p. 598.
[b]YUN 1969, p. 696, SC res. 264(1969), 20 Mar. 1969.
[c]YUN 1976, p. 782, SC res. 385(1976), 30 Jan. 1976.
[d]YUN 1968, p. 787, GA res. 2372(XXII), 12 June 1968.
[e]YUN 1976, p. 784, GA res. 31/146, 20 Dec. 1976.
[f]YUN 1978, p. 912, GA res. S-9/2, 3 May 1978.

implementation meeting in Geneva. However, South Africa ultimately set out new conditions, in particular one linking Namibian independence with the withdrawal of Cuban troops from Angola. It was not until December 1988[3] that the latter issue was resolved, when a tripartite agreement between Angola, Cuba and South Africa, mediated by the United States, was signed at UN Headquarters, and a UN observer mission, the United Nations Angola Verification Mission, was created.[4] South Africa then undertook to co-operate with the Secretary-General to ensure Namibia's independence through free and fair elections, and SWAPO agreed to the cessation of all hostile acts. The starting date for implementation of the independence plan was set for 1 April 1989, after the Security Council had launched the much-delayed UN decolonization operation by adopting two resolutions in January.

Following the December 1988 signing of the tripartite[3] and bilateral[5] agreements regarding Angola and Namibia, the Security Council unanimously adopted **resolution 628(1989)** on 16 January 1989.

The Security Council,

Recalling its resolution 626(1988) of 20 December 1988,

Taking note of the agreement between the People's Republic of Angola, the Republic of Cuba and the Republic of South Africa, signed on 22 December 1988,

Taking note also of the agreement between the People's Republic of Angola and the Republic of Cuba, signed on 22 December 1988,

Emphasizing the importance of these two agreements in strengthening international peace and security,

1. *Welcomes* the signature of the agreement between the People's Republic of Angola, the Republic of Cuba and the Republic of South Africa on the one hand, and of the agreement between the People's Republic of Angola and the Republic of Cuba on the other hand;

2. *Expresses* its full support for these agreements, and to that effect decides to follow closely the developments in their implementation;

3. *Calls upon* all parties concerned, as well as all Member States, to co-operate in the implementation of these agreements;

4. *Requests* the Secretary-General to keep the Security Council fully informed on the implementation of this resolution.

Security Council resolution 628(1989)

16 January 1989   Meeting 2842   Adopted unanimously

Draft prepared in consultations among Council members (S/20399).

Also on 16 January, the Council unanimously adopted **resolution 629(1989)**.

The Security Council,

Reaffirming its relevant resolutions, in particular, resolutions 431(1978) of 27 July 1978 and 435(1978) of 29 September 1978,

Taking note of its resolution 628(1989) of 16 January 1989,

Noting that the parties to the Protocol of Brazzaville agreed to recommend to the Secretary-General that 1 April 1989 be established as the date for the implementation of resolution 435(1978),

Recognizing the progress in the south-western Africa peace process,

Expressing its concern at the increase in the police and paramilitary forces and the establishment of the South-West Africa Territorial Force since 1978, and stressing the need to ensure conditions under which the Namibian people will be able to participate in free and fair elections under the supervision and control of the United Nations,

Noting also that these developments make appropriate a re-examination of the requirements for the United Nations Transition Assistance Group effectively to fulfil its mandate which include, *inter alia*, keeping borders under surveillance, preventing infiltration, preventing intimidation and ensuring the safe return of refugees and their free participation in the electoral process,

Recalling the approval by the Security Council of the Secretary-General's statement on 29 September 1978 to the Council,

Emphasizing its determination to ensure the early independence of Namibia through free and fair elections under the supervision and control of the United Nations, in accordance with its resolution 435(1978),

Reaffirming the legal responsibility of the United Nations over Namibia,

1. *Decides* that 1 April 1989 shall be the date on which implementation of resolution 435(1978) will begin;

2. *Requests* the Secretary-General to proceed to arrange a formal cease-fire between the South West Africa People's Organization and South Africa;

3. *Calls upon* South Africa to reduce immediately and substantially the existing police forces in Namibia with a view to achieving reasonable balance between these forces and the United Nations Transition Assistance Group so as to ensure effective monitoring by the latter;

4. *Reaffirms* the responsibility of all concerned to co-operate to ensure the impartial implementation of the settlement plan in accordance with resolution 435(1978);

5. *Requests* the Secretary-General to prepare at the earliest possible date a report to the Council on the implementation of resolution 435(1978), taking into account all relevant developments since the adoption of that resolution;

6. *Also requests* the Secretary-General, in preparing his report, to re-examine requirements necessary for the Group in order to identify wherever possible tangible cost-saving measures without prejudice to his ability fully to carry out the mandate as established in 1978, namely, to ensure the early independence of Namibia through free and fair elections under the supervision and control of the United Nations;

7. *Calls upon* Members of the United Nations to consider, in co-ordination with the Secretary-General, how they might provide economic and financial assistance to the Namibian people, both during the transitional period and after independence.

Security Council resolution 629(1989)

16 January 1989   Meeting 2842   Adopted unanimously

Draft prepared in consultations among Council members (S/20400).

Report of the Secretary-General (January). A week after the adoption of the two Council resolutions, the Secretary-General submitted a further report,[6] dated 23 January, in his series concerning the implementation of the 1978 UN plan for Namibia's independence.[1]

Before detailing his own concept for UNTAG operations, the Secretary-General described the different views of the five permanent members of the Security Council and of the Movement of Non-Aligned Countries. The permanent Council members, pointing out they would be paying 57 per cent of the operation's cost, said they believed it would be possible to achieve a maximum reduction of costs by considering a reduction in the envisaged military component, given positive developments in the south-western Africa peace process. On the other hand, the Non-Aligned Movement, together with SWAPO, believed the circumstances, including consolidation of the South African military, police and administrative presence, required an increase in the UNTAG military component, if free and fair elections were to ensue.

The Secretary-General commented that, in his contacts with both groups, he had consistently stressed that the 1978 Security Council plan had called for a certain level of resources. If the Council wished fewer resources to be made available, he said it should indicate which tasks in the settlement proposal were no longer required. Since the 1 April date for launching implementation of the plan should not be jeopardized, he would submit to the Council a concept of operations which might not be wholly satisfactory to either side, nor to the Secretary-General, but which would offer the best available prospect for fulfilling his mandate of ensuring Namibia's early independence through free and fair elections under UN supervision and control, while at the same time enjoying the necessary financial support of the Members of the Organization.

His concepts were based on the settlement proposal of the then Secretary-General of 29 August 1978,[7] which called for every adult Namibian, without discrimination or fear of intimidation from any source, to be eligible to vote, campaign and stand for election to the Constituent Assembly. Provision was made for secret ballot and full freedom of speech, assembly, movement and the press. Electoral machinery must ensure that all political parties, without regard to their political views, had a full and fair opportunity to organize and participate in the electoral process. The proposal urged the repeal of all remaining discriminatory or restrictive measures which might abridge the objective of free and fair elections and the release of all political prisoners or detainees so that they could fully and freely participate in the electoral process, without fear of arrest, detention, intimidation or imprisonment. The proposal also provided for the peaceful return of all Namibians in exile, so that they too might fully and freely participate in the elections. It stipulated that all Namibians should be given a full and voluntary choice whether to return. The Secretary-General declared that those criteria would be his guiding principle in the Namibian peace process and would be scrupulously ensured by his Special Representative and his staff.

Continuing, he said that the civilian component of UNTAG would consist of two elements: electoral and civil police. As regards the electoral element, the Secretary-General proposed that about 800 electoral supervisors be provided. Civil police duties would include taking measures against any intimidation or interference with the electoral process. The primary responsibility for maintaining law and order during the transition period would rest with existing police forces. The Secretary-General recommended that the organizational and deployment format of UNTAG police monitors follow that of existing police forces. They should come under the authority of the Special Representative of the Secretary-General from his headquarters in Windhoek, and should operate through a number of district headquarters situated throughout Namibia. The stations would be so located as to enable the police monitors to visit all existing police stations in the Territory. The Secretary-General proposed that the number of police monitors should be 500, an increase from the original 1978 proposal of 360, since the South African police force in 1989 would be substantially greater than those present in the Territory in 1978, amounting to about 6,000.

Military aspects

In his January report,[6] the Secretary-General said that, under the existing plan, the military component would account for more than 75 per cent of UNTAG costs. Its tasks would include the monitoring of: cessation of hostile acts by all parties; the restriction of South African Defence Force (SADF) troops to base, and their subsequent reduction to the agreed strength of 1,500 men, who would be restricted to certain agreed locations; such SADF personnel as continued to perform civilian functions during the transitional period; the dismantling of the command structures of citizen forces, commando units and ethnic forces, the withdrawal of all SADF personnel attached to those forces and the confinement of all arms and ammunition of such forces to agreed locations; and the restriction of SWAPO troops to base in Angola and Zambia. It would also keep the borders under surveillance, prevent infiltration, ensure that all military installations along the northern border were deactivated or placed under UN supervision, and provide security for vital installations in the northern border area. Lieutenant-General Dewan Prem Chand (India) was appointed Force Commander.

The Secretary-General recommended the following concept of operations: (1) the Force Commander would concentrate on the tasks of monitoring the disbandment of the citizen forces, commando units and ethnic units, including the South-West Africa Territorial Force (SWATF), monitoring SADF forces in Namibia, as well as SWAPO forces in neighbouring countries, and supervising and securing installations in the northern border area; (2) the authorized upper limit for the military component of UNTAG would remain at 7,500; (3) three enlarged infantry battalions, each averaging 850 all ranks, would be deployed initially, with other battalions held in reserve (that would provide as many operational troops as five battalions of the size envisaged in the earlier deployment plan, but with the overall numbers being reduced because of the regrouping of the operational troops, and the consequent elimination of some headquarters and administrative elements); (4) the military observer element would be increased from 200 to 300 officers to permit the transfer of certain tasks from infantry to military observers; (5) the logistic elements deployed initially would total about 1,700 all ranks and would be appropriate for a force of three enlarged infantry battalions and 300 military observers, taking into account also the need for military logistic elements to support the civilian component. The total number involved in the military component was envisaged at about 4,650. Should it become apparent during the operation that a military component of that size was insufficient, the Secretary-General would inform the Security Council and, if there was no objection, the reserve battalions would be deployed as necessary and urgent financial support sought from the General Assembly. Preliminary costs of the civilian and military components of UNTAG were estimated at $416 million. A special appeal would be launched by the Secretary-General for funds needed by the Office of the United Nations High Commissioner for Refugees (UNHCR) for the return of Namibians currently in exile.

Regarding a cease-fire between South Africa and SWAPO, envisaged to begin under the 1978 plan at the beginning of the plan's implementation, the Secretary-General had asked that both South Africa and SWAPO agree to the *de facto* cessation of hostilities, with effect from 10 August 1988, as provided for in the Geneva Protocol of 5 August 1988.[8] The Secretary-General also proposed to send identical letters to South Africa and SWAPO, setting out a specific date and hour for a formal cease-fire to begin, and requesting that they inform him in writing of their agendas.

In an explanatory statement of 9 February,[9] the Secretary-General, commenting on his further consultations, confirmed his proposals of 23 January, stating that no tasks had been eliminated, and that final and definitive decisions concerning functional priorities and deployment could be taken only in the light of circumstances prevalent at the time of implementation. He said he had been assured by all Council members, including the permanent members, that they would respond promptly to any need for additional military personnel, up to the authorized upper limit of 7,500. Following representations from a number of delegations, the Secretary-General had decided to make an exception to the standard peace-keeping practice of military observers not carrying weapons, and had given the UNTAG Force Commander discretion to authorize their carrying defensive weapons. With those clarifications, he hoped the Security Council could approve his report and make its final determination for UNTAG's emplacement in Namibia by 1 April, in accordance with the decision it had already taken.

SECURITY COUNCIL ACTION (February)

On 16 February, the Security Council unanimously adopted **resolution 632(1989)**.

The Security Council,

Reaffirming its relevant resolutions, in particular, resolutions 431(1978) of 27 July 1978, 435(1978) of 29 September 1978 and also 629(1989) of 16 January 1989,

Reaffirming also that the United Nations plan contained in its resolution 435(1978) remains the only internationally accepted basis for the peaceful settlement of the Namibian question,

Confirming its decision contained in paragraph 1 of resolution 629(1989) that 1 April 1989 shall be the date on which implementation of resolution 435(1978) will begin,

Having considered the report of 23 January 1989 submitted by the Secretary-General and his explanatory statement of 9 February 1989,

Taking into account the assurances given to the Secretary-General by all the members of the Council as contained in paragraph 5 of his explanatory statement,

Reaffirming the legal responsibility of the United Nations over Namibia until independence,

1. *Approves* the report of the Secretary-General and his explanatory statement concerning the implementation of the United Nations plan for Namibia;

2. *Decides* to implement its resolution 435(1978) in its original and definitive form to ensure conditions in Namibia which will allow the Namibian people to participate freely and without intimidation in the electoral process under the supervision and control of the United Nations leading to early independence of the Territory;

3. *Expresses its full support* for and pledges its cooperation with the Secretary-General in carrying out the mandate entrusted to him by the Security Council under resolution 435(1978);

4. *Calls upon* all parties concerned to honour their commitments to the United Nations plan and to co-

operate fully with the Secretary-General in the implementation of the present resolution;

5. *Requests* the Secretary-General to keep the Security Council fully informed on the implementation of the present resolution.

Security Council resolution 632(1989)

16 February 1989   Meeting 2848   Adopted unanimously

Draft prepared in consultations among Council members (S/20466).

UNTAG composition

In a letter[10] dated 21 February 1989, the Secretary-General proposed to the Security Council that the various units in the military component of UNTAG be contributed by the following countries: Bangladesh, Finland, Kenya, Malaysia, Togo, Venezuela, Yugoslavia (*infantry battalions*); Bangladesh, Czechoslovakia, Finland, India, Ireland, Kenya, Malaysia, Pakistan, Panama, Peru, Poland, Sudan, Togo, Yugoslavia (*military observers*); Australia, Canada, Denmark, Italy, Poland, Spain, United Kingdom (*logistic units*). In addition, the logistic units would include civilian elements contributed by the Federal Republic of Germany and Switzerland. On 23 February, the President of the Council informed[11] the Secretary-General that the Council agreed with those proposals.

Financing

On 16 February, the Secretary-General requested[12] the inclusion in the agenda of the General Assembly's forty-third session of an additional item on the financing of UNTAG.

On 1 March, the Assembly, following consideration of the report of the Secretary-General[13] and the recommendations of the Advisory Committee on Administrative and Budgetary Questions (ACABQ),[14] adopted **resolution 43/232**, on the recommendation of the Fifth (Administrative and Budgetary) Committee, without vote.

Financing of the United Nations Transition Assistance Group

The General Assembly,

Reaffirming the direct and legal responsibility of the United Nations for Namibia until independence, as indicated in its resolution 2145(XXI) of 27 October 1966 and its subsequent relevant resolutions on the question of Namibia,

Bearing in mind Security Council resolution 435(1978) of 29 September 1978, by which the Council established the United Nations Transition Assistance Group for a period of up to twelve months, as well as Council resolutions 629(1989) of 16 January 1989 and 632(1989) of 16 February 1989,

Having considered the report of the Secretary-General on the financing of the United Nations Transition Assistance Group and the related report of the Advisory Committee on Administrative and Budgetary Questions,

Noting, as indicated in paragraph 5 of the explanatory statement of the Secretary-General of 9 February 1989 approved by the Security Council in its resolution 632(1989), that the mandate of the military component of the United Nations Transition Assistance Group, as approved by the Council in its resolution 435(1978), remains unchanged,

Considering that, in the light of paragraphs 11 and 14 of the report of the Secretary-General and of the report of the Advisory Committee on Administrative and Budgetary Questions, in particular paragraphs 6, 8, 9 and 42 of that report, and taking into account that the number of troops to be deployed initially would be 4,650 all ranks while at the same time the figure of 7,500 would be maintained as the upper limit, additional resources may be required for the implementation of Security Council resolution 435(1978) in its original and definitive form,

Recognizing that the costs of the United Nations Transition Assistance Group are expenses of the Organization to be borne by Member States in accordance with Article 17, paragraph 2, of the Charter of the United Nations,

Mindful of the fact that it is essential to provide the United Nations Transition Assistance Group with the necessary financial resources to enable it to fulfil its responsibilities under the relevant resolutions of the Security Council,

Urging all Member States to make every possible effort to ensure payment of their assessed contributions to the United Nations Transition Assistance Group in full and on time, especially in view of the urgent need for and the magnitude of the start-up costs required for the Group,

Recognizing that, in order to meet the expenditures caused by the United Nations Transition Assistance Group, a different procedure is required from the one applied to meet expenditures of the regular budget of the United Nations,

Taking into account the fact that the economically more developed countries are in a position to make relatively larger contributions and that the economically less developed countries have a relatively limited capacity to contribute towards such an operation,

Bearing in mind the special responsibilities of the States permanent members of the Security Council, as indicated in General Assembly resolution 1874(S-IV) of 27 June 1963, in the financing of the United Nations Transition Assistance Group,

Noting with appreciation that voluntary contributions have been made to the United Nations Transition Assistance Group,

1. *Concurs* with the observations, recommendations and conclusions contained in the report of the Advisory Committee on Administrative and Budgetary Questions;

2. *Decides* to appropriate an amount of 416,162,000 United States dollars, inclusive of the amount of 450,000 dollars authorized by the Secretary-General for pre-implementation expenses and of the amount of 10 million dollars authorized with the concurrence of the Advisory Committee on Administrative and Budgetary Questions, under the terms of General Assembly resolution 42/227 of 21 December 1987, for the operation of the United Nations Transition Assistance Group for its mandate period beginning on 1 April 1989 as authorized by the Security Council, bearing in mind that this amount corresponds, in part, to the deployment of 4,650 troops all ranks of the authorized upper limit of 7,500 troops all ranks, and requests the Secretary-General to establish a special account for the Group;

3. *Decides*, as an *ad hoc* arrangement, to apportion:

(a) An amount of 240,083,840 dollars for the above-mentioned period among the States permanent members of the Security Council in the proportions determined by the scale of assessments for the years 1989, 1990 and 1991;

(b) An amount of 165,091,465 dollars for the above-mentioned period among the economically developed Member States that are not permanent members of the Security Council in the proportions determined by the scale of assessments for the years 1989, 1990 and 1991;

(c) An amount of 10,786,919 dollars for the above-mentioned period among the economically less developed Member States in the proportions determined by the scale of assessments for the years 1989, 1990 and 1991;

(d) An amount of 199,776 dollars for the above-mentioned period to the following of the economically less developed Member States in the proportions determined by the scale of assessments for the years 1989, 1990 and 1991: Afghanistan, Angola, Antigua and Barbuda, Bangladesh, Belize, Benin, Bhutan, Botswana, Burkina Faso, Burundi, Cape Verde, Chad, Comoros, Democratic Yemen, Djibouti, Dominica, Ethiopia, Grenada, Guinea, Guinea-Bissau, Haiti, Lao People's Democratic Republic, Lesotho, Malawi, Maldives, Mali, Mozambique, Nepal, Niger, Papua New Guinea, Rwanda, Saint Kitts and Nevis, Saint Lucia, Saint Vincent and the Grenadines, Samoa, Sao Tome and Principe, Senegal, Seychelles, Soloman Islands, Somalia, Sudan, Suriname, Uganda, United Republic of Tanzania, Vanuatu, Yemen and Zimbabwe;

4. *Decides* that, for the purpose of the present resolution, the term "economically less developed Member States" in paragraph 3 *(c)* above shall mean all Member States except Australia, Austria, Belgium, the Byelorussian Soviet Socialist Republic, Canada, Czechoslovakia, Denmark, Finland, the German Democratic Republic, Germany, Federal Republic of, Iceland, Ireland, Italy, Japan, Luxembourg, the Netherlands, New Zealand, Norway, Poland, South Africa, Sweden, the Ukranian Soviet Socialist Republic and the Member States referred to in paragraphs 3 *(a)* and *(d)* above;

5. *Decides* that, in accordance with the provisions of its resolution 973(X) of 15 December 1955, there shall be set off against the apportionment among Member States, as provided for in paragraph 3 above, their respective share in the Tax Equalization Fund of the estimated staff assessment income of 9,541,000 dollars approved for the above-mentioned period;

6. *Invites* voluntary contributions to the United Nations Transition Assistance Group both in cash and in the form of services and supplies acceptable to the Secretary-General, to be administered, as appropriate, in accordance with the procedure established by the General Assembly in section II of its resolution 43/230 of 21 December 1988;

7. *Requests* the Secretary-General to make every effort to avail himself of the widest possible sources of procurement, consistent with the requirements of the mandate and with economy and efficiency, taking into account the relevant resolutions and decisions of the General Assembly and the Security Council;

8. *Also requests* the Secretary-General to proceed without delay with the necessary arrangements for the funding of the programme of repatriation of refugees and exiles, which is to be carried out by the Office of the United Nations High Commissioner for Refugees, as indicated in paragraph 42 of the report of the Advisory Committee on Administrative and Budgetary Questions, taking into account that the repatriation programme is an integral part of the United Nations Transition Assistance Group operation;

9. *Recognizes* that follow-up activities to the repatriation programme, including assistance in the resettlement of refugees and exiles, are to be carried out by United Nations bodies, including, *inter alia*, the Office of the United Nations High Commissioner for Refugees, the United Nations Development Programme, the United Nations Children's Fund, the World Food Programme and the World Health Organization, and will continue past the end of the mandate of the United Nations Transition Assistance Group;

10. *Requests* the Secretary-General to take all necessary action to ensure that the United Nations Transition Assistance Group is administered with the maximum of efficiency and economy, bearing in mind the relevant observations contained in the report of the Advisory Committee on Administrative and Budgetary Questions;

11. *Decides* to include in the provisional agenda of its forty-fourth session the item entitled "Financing of the United Nations Transition Assistance Group",

12. *Requests* the Secretary-General to submit to the General Assembly, at its forty-fourth and forty-fifth sessions, detailed performance reports on the budget of the United Nations Transition Assistance Group, as recommended by the Advisory Committee on Administrative and Budgetary Questions in paragraph 45 of its report.

General Assembly resolution 43/232

1 March 1989   Meeting 89   Adopted without vote

Approved by Fifth Committee (A/43/998) without vote, 28 February (meeting 58); draft by Chairman (A/C.5/43/L.24), following informal consultations; agenda item 154.
Meeting numbers. GA 43rd session: 5th Committee 54-58; plenary 89.

Political aspects

On 16 March, the Secretary-General transmitted to the Security Council the text of a 10 March agreement[15] between the United Nations and South Africa concerning the status of UNTAG in Namibia. It stated that UNTAG members should refrain from any activity of a political nature in the Territory and from any action or activity incompatible with the impartial and international nature of their duties, or inconsistent with the spirit of the arrangements in the agreement, while South Africa undertook to respect the exclusively international nature of UNTAG. Specific provisions covered tax exemptions; display of UN flags and vehicular markings; communications; freedom of movement; imports, exports and local purchases; privileges and immunities; visa exemptions; carrying of arms; discrepancy jurisdiction; and settlement of disputes.

Pursuant to Council resolutions 629(1989) and 632(1989) (see above), the Secretary-General's Special Representative, Martti Ahtisaari, arrived in Windhoek on 31 March 1989, mandated with the supervision and control of free and fair elections in Namibia on the basis of Council resolution 435(1978).

On 30 March, the Secretary-General informed[16] the Security Council that South Africa and SWAPO had confirmed their agreement to abide by the formal cease-fire to begin at 0400 hours Greenwich mean time on 1 April 1989.

REFERENCES
[1]YUN 1978, p. 915, SC res. 435(1978), 29 Sep. 1978. [2]YUN 1981, p. 1126. [3]YUN 1988, p. 772. [4]*Ibid.*, p. 160, SC res. 626(1988), 20 Dec. 1988. [5]*Ibid.*, p. 773. [6]S/20412. [7]YUN 1978, p. 892. [8]*Ibid.*, p. 771. [9]S/20457. [10]S/20479. [11]S/20480. [12]A/43/997. [13]A/43/997/Add.1. [14]A/43/997/Add.2. [15]S/20412/Add.1. [16]S/20412/Add.2.

Operational aspects

April clashes

On 2 April 1989, the Minister for Foreign Affairs of South Africa, in a letter[1] to the Secretary-General, stated that a grave situation had arisen on the northern border of South West Africa/Namibia as a result of continued and escalating violations by SWAPO of the agreements signed in New York on 22 December 1988 by Angola, Cuba and South Africa. He said that the incontrovertible facts were that during the night of 31 March and on 1 April 1989, an estimated 600 to 800 SWAPO elements crossed the border from Angola to Namibia, and the figure could be as high as 1,000. They were heavily armed, with AK-47 semi-automatic rifles, mortars and ground-to-air missiles, and had entered the Territory in uniform. On the basis of information from those captured, they had been ordered to cross the border in order to establish bases in Namibia. Reliable information indicated between 4,000 and 5,000 SWAPO elements below latitude 16° S, even though SWAPO under the agreements was required by 1 April to have all personnel confined to bases north of that latitude. The Foreign Minister said that SWAPO's leadership would have to account for the unnecessary carnage of SWAPO elements, the callous disregard for human life and contempt for international agreements. Since UNTAG should, under the agreements, be monitoring SWAPO bases, he asked the Secretary-General if it was, in fact, doing so. He trusted that the Secretary-General and the Security Council would make it possible for South Africa to continue to co-operate and fulfil its commitments in terms of the agreements, and he appealed to them to take a firm and clear stand on the act of defiance by SWAPO.

In a further letter[2] of 4 April, the Foreign Minister said that more than 1,000 SWAPO forces had infiltrated into Namibia. Unless action and effective measures were taken to stem the rapid

deterioration of the situation, the whole peace process in Namibia was in danger of collapse. South Africa could not be expected to implement its undertakings under the agreements while SWAPO continued to act in flagrant violation of them with the acquiescence, tacit or otherwise, of the Security Council. Under the circumstances, South Africa had the undoubted right to suspend compliance with its obligations.

On 4 April, South Africa also circulated as a Security Council document[3] the Protocol of Geneva, signed on 5 August 1988 by Angola, Cuba and South Africa, which covered South Africa's withdrawal of forces from Angola and SWAPO's deployment of forces north of the 16th parallel.

On 5 April, in a letter[4] to the Secretary-General, the Foreign Minister said his Government felt encouraged by the firm and positive reaction of various Governments in endorsing the provisions of the Geneva Protocol, including the SWAPO obligation to remain north of the 16th parallel. He repeated his urgent appeal to the Secretary-General to bring influence to bear on the SWAPO leadership to cease its senseless course. He said a further 300 SWAPO armed personnel crossed the border from Angola on 4 April, having received radioed orders that day. The South African Government had requested its Administrator-General in Namibia to broadcast an appeal to the infiltrators to surrender and to lay down their arms or to withdraw northwards to Angola. SWAPO members laying down their arms in peace would be given safe conduct to assembly points under UNTAG supervision, from where they could be transported safely to suitable points north of latitude 16° S, with the co-operation of the Angolan authorities. SWAPO members wishing to return northwards into Angola would not be pursued.

In a communiqué issued in New York on 6 April,[5] the Co-ordinating Bureau of the Movement of Non-Aligned Countries expressed shock and dismay at the campaign of the illegal occupation régime of South Africa against the Namibian people at a time when the process of bringing genuine independence to Namibia was already under way. The Bureau was scandalized to learn that UNTAG was wholly unprepared to assume its responsibilities by 1 April, the designated date for commencement of the implementation of Security Council resolution 435(1978).[6] The Bureau reaffirmed that the SWAPO combatants who, it was well known, had always been operating on the ground inside Namibia since the beginning of their liberation struggle, had a legitimate right to remain in their country and to be assigned to bases of confinement. It called on the Secretary-General to confine the South African forces to their bases without delay and to effect the immediate full deployment of the 7,500 personnel of the UNTAG military component in Namibia.

In a letter[7] of 7 April to the Secretary-General, the South African Foreign Minister stated that there were continued orchestrated SWAPO incursions. He invited the Security Council to dispatch a fact-finding mission. SWAPO had had no military bases in Namibia on 1 April. He noted that a meeting of the Joint Commission (created under the Angola/Namibia agreements), comprising representatives of Angola, Cuba and South Africa, with observers from the United States and the USSR, would take place in Namibia on 8 April.

On 17 April, the Secretary-General circulated, at the request of the Joint Commission, its Mount Etjo (Namibia) Declaration, adopted on 9 April.[8] It reaffirmed the obligations of the 22 December 1988 accord and urged the Secretary-General urgently to adopt all necessary measures for the most rapid and complete deployment of UNTAG. It set out a withdrawal procedure aimed at restoring the situation in existence on 31 March. A period would be established during which SWAPO forces would be granted free passage to border assembly points in a procedure executed under UNTAG supervision. Angola committed itself to receive on its territory SWAPO forces leaving Namibia and to ensure that those and other forces on its territory were confined north of latitude 16° S under UNTAG supervision. As of 9 April, SWAPO troops still in Namibia should present themselves to border assembly points or to established assembly points south of the border. All assembly points would be under UNTAG supervision. At the border assembly points, joint border control posts manned by forces of Angola and South Africa would be established with the presence of UNTAG to guarantee the control of the crossing of SWAPO forces. SWAPO forces turning themselves over to UNTAG custody were to lay down their weapons with UNTAG. SWAPO members presenting themselves to assembly points would be transferred to bases north of latitude 16° S under UNTAG supervision. By 15 April, SWAPO would inform the Special Representative about the conclusion of the removal of its forces from Namibia.

Cahama Minute

At a meeting of representatives of Angola, Cuba and South Africa on 15 and 19 May, the three reached an agreement known as the Cahama Minute,[9] noting in particular UNTAG information that SWAPO armed elements were confined to base under UNTAG monitoring, north of the 16th parallel. Both the United Nations Special Representative and the Administrator-General confirmed that South African forces were again confined to

bases under UNTAG monitoring, and that a *de facto* cessation of hostilities had been re-established in northern Namibia. The South African Government, in transmitting the Cahama Minute, reiterated that responsibility for the administration of Namibia during the transitional period rested with its own Administrator-General, including responsibility for maintaining law and order. Particularly in the light of the incursions as from 31 March, and to avoid any misunderstanding in the future, the South African Government made clear that the Administrator-General had the right to use such measures and means he would deem appropriate to counter activities of an aggressive, violent or intimidating nature, emanating from whatever quarter.

In a letter[10] of 24 May to the South African Foreign Minister, the Secretary-General said he could not accept any implication that the South African Government, or any other party to the delicate process, could unilaterally resort to any measures or means not provided for in the UN plan, as approved by the Security Council.

On 23 May,[11] the Secretary-General wrote to the President of Zimbabwe, Chairman of the Movement of Non-Aligned Countries, regarding comments made by the Movement on the April events. He stated that it was prolonged disagreement among Member States over the UNTAG military component that had led to the unfortunate delay in intergovernmental decisions necessary for the timely establishment and deployment of the Group. Moreover, had the cease-fire arrangements and related undertakings been scrupulously observed, as required by the UN plan, the tragic events that occurred in April could well have been avoided. In that connection, he reiterated that UNTAG did not have powers of enforcement. To be successful, it had to rely on the full co-operation of all parties, who must fulfil their obligations to adhere strictly to the agreements and understandings to which they had committed themselves.

Report of the Secretary-General. In an October report,[12] the Secretary-General detailed developments since UNTAG had first become operational.

Immediately preceding implementation of the UN plan on 1 April 1989, the strength of South African security forces in Namibia had been 30,743, composed of 9,895 SADF, of which 1,015 were serving with citizen forces, commando units and ethnic forces; 5,450 citizen forces; 6,128 commando units; and 9,270 ethnic forces. Included in the above was a counter-insurgency unit known as "Koevoet".

Restriction to base of SADF personnel by UNTAG came into effect at the beginning of implementation on 1 April. However, following the outbreak of hostilities later that day between SWAPO and the

South African security forces, some SADF personnel had moved out of their bases, and full confinement was not restored until 13 May. Thereafter, the withdrawal of the bulk of SADF personnel from Namibia was rapidly implemented, and their strength was reduced to just under 1,500 by 24 June, in accordance with the UN plan. The remaining personnel, known as the Merlyn Force, were confined to base, under close monitoring of UNTAG, at Grootfontein and Oshivello, as provided for in the plan. About 800 SADF personnel also remained to perform certain essential civilian functions, with 495 running four airfields and the others performing medical, teaching, veterinary and other services. All were unarmed, in civilian clothes and closely monitored by UNTAG. Discussions were under way to substitute civilians for these SADF personnel, and an International Civil Aviation Organization (ICAO) mission was advising on arrangements for the four airfields. Some 156 other SADF personnel provided bimonthly payments to the demobilized ethnic forces. Early reduction in numbers and rank level had been requested. The citizen forces and commandos were demobilized by 31 March, immediately before the beginning of implementation of the UN plan, and their arms, military equipment and ammunition were thereafter deposited in drill halls, where they remained guarded by the military component of UNTAG. The demobilization of the ethnic forces known as SWATF was completed by 27 May, with the exception of two bushmen battalions.

The bushmen battalions, numbering 1,351 soldiers, were not demobilized because their personnel had become completely alienated from their traditional way of life. Their families lived with them in the camps, and they would have no other means of livelihood if sent away from the camps. They were closely monitored by UNTAG to ensure that they did not leave the camps or undertake military activities. Command structure had, in the view of the UNTAG Force Commander, been dismantled.

As for the counter-insurgency unit "Koevoet", the Secretary-General reported that, after its disbandment, it had been absorbed into the South-West Africa Police (SWAPOL). After the clashes which occurred in early April, the South African authorities reconstituted Koevoet as a unit, on the grounds that SWAPO combatants had crossed the border from Angola into Namibia. In mid-May, the South African authorities stated that Koevoet had again been disbanded, but some 3,000 of its personnel, estimated at two thirds of its total, had again been reabsorbed into SWAPOL, an arrangement inconsistent with the UN plan. Although ostensibly members of SWAPOL, many ex-Koevoet personnel continued to operate in the same manner as they had before the disbandment of Koevoet, including use of "Casspir" armoured personnel carriers mounted with heavy machine-guns. That activity was also inconsistent with the UN plan, which specified that police forces would be limited to the carrying of small arms in the normal performance of their duties. It became clear that many ex-Koevoet personnel had not fulfilled the condition of suitability for continued employment in the police forces during the transition period. The Secretary-General took the position that all ex-Koevoet personnel should be removed immediately from SWAPOL and any other security-related duties. UNTAG received many complaints of intimidation and other unacceptable conduct by ex-Koevoet personnel, and UNTAG police monitors were themselves, on a number of occasions, witnesses of such behaviour.

SECURITY COUNCIL ACTION

On 10 August, the Co-ordinating Bureau of the Movement of Non-Aligned Countries met in New York to consider the situation in Namibia, hearing a statement from a representative of SWAPO regarding continuing serious irregularities in the implementation of the independence plan. He said that South Africa had refused to comply with some key aspects of resolution 435(1978), and asked the Security Council to take action.

At the request of the Chairman of the Group of African States[13] and of the Chairman of the Co-ordinating Bureau,[14] the Security Council convened between 16 and 29 August to consider the deteriorating situation in Namibia.

At the opening meeting, the Chairman of the African Group assessed the situation in Namibia, expressing serious concern over what he described as the continued presence and violent activities of Koevoet; loopholes in the Voter Registration Proclamation which would allow South African nationals to register and vote in the elections; the draft proclamations issued by the Administrator-General, which attempted to exclude a substantial number of SWAPO members, especially its leadership, from registering and voting in the elections, as well as from being qualified to be elected; and the excessive power that the various proclamations vested in the Administrator-General.

After meetings on 16, 17, 18, 21 and 22 August, the Security Council unanimously adopted **resolution 640(1989)** on 29 August.

The Security Council,
Having critically reviewed the implementation process of resolution 435(1978) of 29 September 1978 since its commencement and noting with concern that all its provisions are not being fully complied with,
Concerned at reports of widespread intimidation and harassment of the civilian population, in particular by Koevoet elements in the South-West Africa Police,

Recognizing the efforts being exerted by the United Nations Transition Assistance Group to carry out its responsibilities in spite of obstacles thus placed in its way,

Recalling and reaffirming all its resolutions on the question of Namibia, particularly 435(1978), 629(1989) of 16 January 1989 and 632(1989) of 16 February 1989,

Reiterating that resolution 435(1978) must be implemented in its original and definitive form to ensure conditions in Namibia which will allow the Namibian people to participate freely and without intimidation in the electoral process, under the supervision and control of the United Nations, leading to early independence of the Territory,

Recalling and reaffirming its firm commitment to the decolonization of Namibia through the holding of free and fair elections under the supervision and control of the United Nations and in which the Namibian people will participate without intimidation or interference,

1. *Demands* strict compliance by all parties concerned, especially South Africa, with the terms of resolutions 435(1978) and 632(1989);

2. *Also demands* the disbandment of all paramilitary and ethnic forces and commando units, in particular Koevoet, as well as the dismantling of their command structures as required by resolution 435(1978);

3. *Calls upon* the Secretary-General to review the actual situation on the ground with a view to determining the adequacy of the military component of the United Nations Transition Assistance Group in relation to its ability to carry out its responsibilities as authorized under resolutions 435(1978) and 632(1989) and to inform the Security Council;

4. *Invites* the Secretary-General to review the adequacy of the number of police monitors in order to undertake the process for any appropriate increase that he may deem necessary for the effective fulfilment of the Group's responsibilities;

5. *Requests* the Secretary-General, in his supervision and control of the electoral process, to ensure that all legislation concerning the electoral process is in conformity with the provisions of the settlement plan;

6. *Also requests* the Secretary-General to ensure that all proclamations conform with internationally accepted norms for the conduct of free and fair elections and, in particular, that the proclamation on the Constituent Assembly also respects the sovereign will of the people of Namibia;

7. *Further requests* the Secretary-General to ensure the observance of strict impartiality in the provision of media facilities, especially on radio and television, to all parties for the dissemination of information concerning the election;

8. *Appeals* to all the parties concerned to co-operate fully with the Secretary-General in the implementation of the settlement plan;

9. *Expresses its full support* for the Secretary-General in his efforts to ensure that resolution 435(1978) is implemented in its original and definitive form and requests him to report to the Council before the end of September on the implementation of the present resolution;

10. *Decides* to remain seized of the matter.

Security Council resolution 640(1989)

29 August 1989   Meeting 2882   Adopted unanimously

7-nation draft (S/20808/Rev.1).
Sponsors: Algeria, Colombia, Ethiopia, Malaysia, Nepal, Senegal, Yugoslavia.
Meeting numbers. SC 2876-2882.

In his October report[12], the Secretary-General took the position that all ex-Koevoet personnel should be immediately removed from SWAPOL and other security-related duties. In September, some 1,200 ex-Koevoet members of SWAPOL, or approximately 45 per cent of SWAPOL personnel in the Oshakati district (Ovamboland, in the north), were being demobilized. UNTAG closely monitored the situation, while the Secretary-General continued to press for demobilization of the remaining ex-Koevoet personnel and for an end to payments which the South African authorities continued to make, both to them and to the demobilized personnel of SWATF, payments the South African authorities intended to pay until after the elections.

Demobilization of 1,207 ex-Koevoet members was completed on 28 October, and of a further 418 on 30 October.[15]

UNTAG military aspects

In his October report,[12] the Secretary-General stated that the strength of the UNTAG military component had been sufficient to enable it to carry out its tasks. UNTAG military monitors had monitored the restriction of SADF troops to base, the withdrawal of most of those troops to South Africa and the restriction of the remaining 1,500 (Merlyn Force) to base at Grootfontein and Oshivello. In addition, UNTAG personnel had monitored the demobilization of citizen forces, commando units and ethnic forces, the dismantling of their command structures and the confinement of their arms and ammunition to drill halls guarded by UNTAG. The infantry battalions had also guarded bases and other installations, including the reception centres set up by UNHCR. UNTAG also established a detachment of military monitors in Lubango, Angola, with a liaison office in Luanda, to verify confinement to base by the Angolan Armed Forces of SWAPO combatants remaining in Angola. In that aspect UNTAG had encountered problems, particularly at the start of its mandate in April (see above). The great majority of SWAPO combatants had, however, by October returned to Namibia as unarmed civilians under the UNHCR repatriation programme, with fewer than 300 of them remaining in Angola in the vicinity of Lubango.

The UNTAG military component had also been able to play an important role in monitoring the cessation of hostile acts by all parties, keeping the borders under surveillance and preventing infiltration. All crossing points from South Africa and Walvis Bay were monitored by means of permanently manned check-points established by military monitors of UNTAG, who also patrolled along the borders. In the north, the Finnish and Malaysian battalions of UNTAG mounted as many daily patrols as their strength permitted. That work was shared with UNTAG police monitors, who accompanied the SWAPOL border patrols. Experience had shown that the military component could make a further contribution to creation of conditions for free and fair elections by regularly patrolling populated areas in order to strengthen confidence by advertising UNTAG's presence.

UNTAG financing

Report of the Secretary-General. (For approval of the budget, see above, under ''Pre-operational aspects''.) In a December report,[16] the Secretary-General stated that assessments totalling $409,555,646 had been apportioned among Member States. Of that amount, contributions of $314,945,088 had been received as at 30 November. Contributions in the amount of $94,610,558 remained outstanding. The following donated voluntary contributions in cash and in kind: Federal Republic of Germany ($4.2 million), Greece ($350,000), Japan ($13 million), Switzerland ($1.6 million) and the United States ($4 million). The Secretary-General estimated the total requirements through 31 March 1990 at $366,890,000 (gross), which was $49,272,000 (gross) less than the original estimates; that figure included estimated liquidation costs of $6,469,000.

The Secretary-General recommended that the General Assembly defer until 1990 action as might be called for in consequence of the outstanding contributions of Member States. He requested Assembly approval of proposals regarding the disposition of UNTAG property upon completion of the mandate. Where suitable, equipment would be kept in reserve for other peace-keeping operations while other equipment would be made available to UN agencies in the process of establishing a presence in Namibia. Surplus equipment would be contributed to the duly recognized Government of Namibia.

ACABQ report. ACABQ, in a December report,[17] noted that voluntary contributions in cash totalled $13,050,000 and the valuation of contributions in kind amounted to $10,103,109. It recommended that the costs associated with the liquidation and the closing of the accounts be met from the appropriations approved by the Assembly in **resolution 43/232**. It supported the Secretary-General's proposal to defer action concerning the outstanding contributions and agreed in principle to his proposed course regarding disposition of UNTAG property.

GENERAL ASSEMBLY ACTION

On 21 December, on the recommendation of the Fifth Committee, the General Assembly adopted **resolution 44/191** without vote.

Financing of the United Nations Transition Assistance Group

The General Assembly,

Recalling its resolution 43/232 of 1 March 1989,

Reaffirming the direct and legal responsibility of the United Nations for Namibia until independence, as indicated in its resolution 2145(XXI) of 27 October 1966 and its subsequent relevant resolutions on the question of Namibia,

Bearing in mind Security Council resolution 435(1978) of 29 September 1978, by which the Council established the United Nations Transition Assistance Group for a period of up to twelve months, as well as Council resolutions 629(1989) of 16 January 1989 and 632(1989) of 16 February 1989,

Having considered the report of the Secretary-General on the financing of the Group and the related report of the Advisory Committee on Administrative and Budgetary Questions,

Taking note, in particular, of paragraphs 9 and 10 of the report of the Secretary-General and paragraphs 10, 12 and 13 of the report of the Advisory Committee,

Recognizing that the costs of the Group are expenses of the Organization to be borne by Member States in accordance with Article 17, paragraph 2, of the Charter of the United Nations,

Taking into account the fact that the economically more developed countries are in a position to make relatively larger contributions and that the economically less developed countries have a relatively limited capacity to contribute towards such an operation,

Bearing in mind the special responsibilities of the States permanent members of the Security Council, as indicated in General Assembly resolution 1874(S-IV) of 27 June 1963, in the financing of the Group,

Mindful of the fact that it is essential to provide the Group with the necessary financial resources to enable it to fulfil its responsibilities under the relevant resolutions of the Security Council,

Concerned that, as mentioned in paragraph 7 of the report of the Secretary-General, assessments totalling approximately 94.6 million United States dollars remain uncollected,

Noting with appreciation that voluntary contributions have been made to the Group,

1. *Concurs* with the observations, recommendations and conclusions contained in the report of the Advisory Committee on Administrative and Budgetary Questions;

2. *Urges* all Member States to pay their assessed contributions to the United Nations Transition Assistance Group in full and on time;

3. *Approves* the request of the Secretary-General that he proceed with the disposition of the property of the Group upon completion of its mandate in the manner set out in annex III, paragraph 4, to his report and paragraph 10 of the report of the Advisory Committee;

4. *Decides* that the costs associated with the liquidation of the Group and the closing of the accounts, amounting to 6,469,000 dollars gross (5,625,000 dollars net), shall be met from the appropriations made available by the General Assembly in its resolution 43/232;

5. *Also decides,* taking into account the outstanding assessed contributions due to the Special Account of the United Nations Transition Assistance Group, to defer any action on the estimated unencumbered balance of the appropriations as may be called for until its forty-fifth session;

6. *Requests* the Secretary-General to take all necessary action to ensure that the Group is administered with the maximum of efficiency and economy, bearing in

mind the relevant observations contained in the report of the Advisory Committee;

7. *Decides* to include in the provisional agenda of its forty-fifth session the item entitled "Financing of the United Nations Transition Assistance Group";

8. *Requests* the Secretary-General to submit to the General Assembly, at its forty-fifth session, a detailed performance report on the budget of the Group, in accordance with the observations made by the Advisory Committee in its report, in particular those made in paragraphs 7 and 8 thereof.

General Assembly resolution 44/191

21 December 1989   Meeting 84   Adopted without vote

Approved by Fifth Committee (A/44/891) without vote, 18 December (meeting 58); draft by Chairman (A/C.5/44/L.13); agenda item 136.
Meeting numbers. GA 44th session: 5th Committee 56, 58; plenary 84.

Civilian police monitors

In January, the Secretary-General recommended that the number of civilian police monitors (CIVPOL) be increased from the 360 previously envisaged to 500, because of the substantial increase in SWAPOL numbers since 1978.[18]

In a 24 May letter[19] to the President of the Security Council, the Secretary-General recalled that, in consultations of 11 May, he had informed the Council that he had accepted in principle his Special Representative's recommendation that CIVPOL be further increased to 1,000. He was undertaking urgent consultations on the matter, including notification to ACABQ of the cost implications, following which he intended to dispatch an additional 500 CIVPOL to Namibia, starting in mid-June. On 26 May,[20] the Council President informed the Secretary-General that the Council agreed to his proposal. Subsequently, experience on the ground led the Special Representative to recommend a further increase of 500 officers,[21] and the Council approved that increase on 28 September.[22]

The Secretary-General noted in an October report[12] that the UN plan entrusted to the South African Administrator-General the primary responsibility for the maintenance of law and order, for which he was to use existing police forces—SWAPOL. It had always been clear that SWAPOL's conduct would be one of the factors determining whether conditions existed for free and fair elections. Experience had confirmed the necessity of monitoring SWAPOL very closely. In that regard, the Secretary-General referred to the Koevoet issue (see above) and the misconduct of such personnel, who did not appear to understand or appreciate the role of civilian police officers. Wherever possible, CIVPOL accompanied SWAPOL on its patrols; it also conducted independent patrols of its own, on foot and by vehicle, including using mine-resistant vehicles in the north. In September, nearly 5,000 patrols were undertaken,

1,967 jointly with SWAPOL. The organizational and deployment format of UNTAG police monitors followed that of the existing police forces. They came under the authority of the Special Representative of the Secretary-General from his headquarters at Windhoek, and operated through a number of district headquarters situated throughout the Territory. Each district had several sub-stations or posts at strategic locations.

At the time of the October report, police monitors were contributed by the following 26 Member States: Austria, Bangladesh, Barbados, Belgium, Cameroon, Canada, Egypt, Germany, Federal Republic of, Fiji, German Democratic Republic, Ghana, Guyana, Hungary, India, Indonesia, Ireland, Jamaica, Kenya, Netherlands, New Zealand, Nigeria, Norway, Pakistan, Singapore, Sweden, Tunisia.

The Secretary-General stated that CIVPOL had encountered a certain lack of co-operation by SWAPOL in some crucial areas of its operations. It had not been possible to reach agreement on the right of CIVPOL to visit detainees in the custody of SWAPOL stations. CIVPOL had been prevented by SWAPOL from being present when statements were taken from SWAPOL members accused of offences. In some instances, SWAPOL failed to inform CIVPOL accurately of patrol scheduling, making it difficult to ensure that all SWAPOL patrols were monitored, a particular problem when ex-Koevoet personnel were involved. SWAPOL did not always share with UNTAG information relevant to the security situation in Namibia, although it had itself made unsubstantiated allegations of imminent infiltration of SWAPO combatants from southern Angola. The SWAPOL investigations of complaints from Namibians were closely monitored by CIVPOL, but in many cases they proceeded very slowly, so that several, including some serious cases of homicide, would not be completed within the transition period. CIVPOL also played an important role in the electoral process, attending and monitoring political gatherings, at which it had a calming effect, the Secretary-General stated. During the registration of voters, CIVPOL deployed monitors at all registration centres. During the elections, CIVPOL would be present at all polling stations.

In a November report,[15] the Secretary-General stated that the 1,500 police monitors would be adequate to enable CIVPOL to carry out its functions in current conditions. There had been an improvement in co-operation between SWAPOL and CIVPOL. Of the 1,500, some 1,100 would be deployed to specific duties relating to the election, including monitoring polling stations, round-the-clock guarding of ballot boxes (together with SWAPOL), and being present at the counting of votes, among other things. Their number was adequate to carry out their principal function of comprehensive monitoring of SWAPOL activities.

Amnesty and exile repatriation

The Secretary-General noted in an October report[12] that, in accordance with the UN plan, granting of full and unqualified amnesty to all Namibian exiles was considered an essential prerequisite for their voluntary repatriation under UNHCR auspices. The draft Amnesty Proclamation proposed by the South African Administrator-General had made a distinction between political crimes and common law/statutory crimes, a distinction unacceptable to the Secretary-General. Protracted discussions between the Secretary-General and the South African authorities, in both Windhoek and New York, eventually led to agreement on an unqualified amnesty for all Namibian exiles. That was promulgated on 6 June 1989 and permitted the beginning of the repatriation operation, which had been delayed for several weeks pending agreement on the amnesty. The operation was entrusted to UNHCR, which established three air and three land entry points and five reception centres in central and northern Namibia to receive, register and materially assist the returnees. By 29 September, more than 41,000 Namibians from 46 countries had returned home, and all but 579 had resettled into their former communities. The cost had been $39.1 million (compared with the original estimate of $38.5 million). So far, $30.2 million had been pledged by the donor community, leaving $8.9 million still to be raised.

The return of so many exiles had created a reintegration problem. In order to address that situation, an inter-agency mission—comprising representatives from the Food and Agriculture Organization of the United Nations (FAO), the United Nations Educational, Scientific and Cultural Organization (UNESCO), the United Nations Children's Fund (UNICEF), UNHCR and the World Health Organization (WHO), in consultation with the World Food Programme—visited Namibia in July/August and formulated proposals for an emergency rehabilitation programme of some $20 million regarding shelter, agriculture, health, education, water, income generation and family support.

Political prisoners and detainees

In an October report,[12] the Secretary-General noted that the UN plan required the release of all Namibian political prisoners or political detainees. On 24 May, UNTAG military observers stationed in Angola were enabled to interview 201 former detainees who had been released by SWAPO. On 4 July, 153 ex-detainees, including 18 children, were repatriated to Namibia from Angola, followed by two further groups of 63 and 16, on 29 July and 8 August, respectively. On 20 July, 25 Namibian political prisoners were released by the South African authorities from the central prison in Windhoek. In the case of both the South African authorities and SWAPO, it was alleged that additional persons remained in detention and were yet to be released. Regarding South Africa, the Administrator-General had replied that persons on the lists submitted to him in 1989 had either been released or were unknown to the South African authorities. As for SWAPO, it had stated that it no longer held any detainees and it had invited the international community to investigate allegations that a number of people were still in SWAPO detention in Angola and Zambia or were otherwise unaccounted for.

A UN mission on detainees was sent to Angola and Zambia in September to ascertain whether any Namibians were still detained by SWAPO. The mission visited virtually all sites where people had reportedly been detained, and concluded[23] that there were no detainees in any of the alleged detention centres and other places which it had visited; that most locations, particularly in Angola, where detainees were allegedly held, had been evacuated and abandoned several weeks previously and were incapable of being used for detention purposes; that the vast majority of SWAPO members in both countries had already been repatriated; and that many of those remaining behind in the refugee settlements had already been to Namibia, registered for the elections and returned either to Angola or Zambia.

Repeal of laws

In his October report,[12] the Secretary-General noted that, in accordance with the UN plan, two Repeal Proclamations had been enacted regarding laws which might abridge or inhibit the holding of free and fair elections. The first was widely considered to have repealed the bulk of the discriminatory laws. At the request of the Special Representative, that Proclamation made provision for further repeals at the request of the public, while not prejudicing the Special Representative's right himself to call for further repeals. No member of the public had taken advantage of the provision. The Secretary-General and his Special Representative had, however, drawn the Administrator-General's attention on several occasions to the continued existence of the system of ethnic administration, whose repeal had been requested by the great majority of political parties in Namibia. The Administrator-General had so far taken the position that repeal of that system was outside the scope of the UN plan, as it did not abridge or inhibit the holding of free and fair elections. The Secretary-General continued to believe that the spirit, if not the letter, of the plan required the repeal of the legislation in question (Proclamation AG 8).

Media impartiality

In his October report,[12] the Secretary-General observed that the South West African Broadcasting Corporation (SWABC), for whose activities the Administrator-General had ultimate responsibility, was, in effect, the last essentially political body that had not been dissolved following agreement on the UN plan's implementation. Given SWABC's monopoly and the high degree of dependence on it by a society with a high illiteracy rate, there was a need to achieve total impartiality and even-handedness. Substantial reform was especially necessitated by the rapid change taking place in Namibia as a result of the long-delayed implementation of the transition to independence. In response to the Special Representative's repeated representations regarding equal access by the political parties to SWABC broadcasting facilities, the Administrator-General informed him on 15 September that registered parties would have equal access to set periods of air time, on both radio and television. The parties also agreed on the manner in which SWABC would give coverage to political meetings, news conferences and media releases. They also agreed to establish a standing consultative committee at which they would regularly meet with SWABC management. To ensure impartial editorial decision-making, the Special Representative was insisting that a management or editorial committee be created.

The Secretary-General reported that a full and integrated UNTAG information operation was under way, with daily radio broadcasts transmitted in all the main languages of the country since 12 June 1989, dealing with all aspects of the UNTAG mandate. Texts were regularly carried by the local news agencies and newspapers. Programmes were focused on familiarizing the electorate with all aspects of the electoral process, emphasizing such basic themes as the secrecy of the voting process. Since July, a weekly television slot had also been available to UNTAG at a peak viewing hour. Those programmes, and other materials produced by UNTAG, were also made available to the UNTAG regional and district offices. The offices played an important role in providing prompt and accurate information about the election to the people in their area. UNTAG civilian personnel had addressed countless meetings in every part of the country, the Secretary-General stated, and had made early and continuing contacts with community, party and other opinion-leaders. Many UNTAG offices had become established as the principal sources of objective and reliable information.

In his November report,[15] the Secretary-General reported that the Governing Board of SWABC had been pronounced to be in recess until further notice, with its position to be reconsidered after the election. The problem of editorial impartiality, however, remained unresolved. The Secretary-General said he would continue to press for essential reforms.

REFERENCES

[1]S/20557. [2]S/20565. [3]S/20566. [4]S/20567. [5]A/44/231-S/20595. [6]YUN 1978, p. 915, SC res. 435(1978), 29 Sep. 1978. [7]S/20576. [8]S/20579. [9]S/20647. [10]S/20655. [11]A/44/521. [12]S/20883. [13]S/20779. [14]S/20782. [15]S/20943. [16]A/44/856. [17]A/44/875. [18]S/20412. [19]S/20657. [20]S/20658. [21]S/20871. [22]S/20872. [23]S/20883/Add.1.

Elections

Pre-election activities

Electoral legislation

The basic objectives of Security Council resolution 435(1978)[1] were the withdrawal of South Africa's illegal administration from Namibia and transfer of power to the people of the Territory through free and fair elections under UN supervision. In accordance with the resolution, voters were to exercise their inalienable right to self-determination by choosing their representatives to a Constituent Assembly charged with drafting a constitution for an independent Namibia. The elections, to be held in November 1989, were to be supervised and controlled by UNTAG.

In an October report,[2] the Secretary-General stated that prolonged and difficult negotiations had been required to obtain agreement on amendments necessary to the Administrator-General's 21 July draft to make the Election (Constituent Assembly) Proclamation acceptable to the Secretary-General and his Special Representative. The negotiations were concluded on 6 October and published in an extraordinary *Official Gazette* on 13 October after being finalized by the Secretary-General's Special Representative and the Administrator-General.

The Secretary-General stated that because of the slow progress of the negotiations, it had been necessary to take earlier, separate action on the registration of political parties for the election, and an agreed Registration of Political Organization (Constituent Assembly) Proclamation was promulgated on 4 September. The polling period was set from Tuesday, 7 November, to Saturday, 11 November. In Windhoek, 11 political parties submitted applications to the Registration Court on or before its first sitting on 12 September. Of those, nine were immediately considered qualified, with the requisite 2,000 signatures of registered voters, and a further party qualified later, so that 10 parties were eligible to participate in the election.

In July, the Secretary-General convened at UNTAG headquarters in Windhoek a meeting of leaders of all the major political parties, at which he suggested they should have regular meetings with his Special Representative. Those took place fortnightly thereafter, and, as a result, with the Special Representative as witness, nine of the parties signed a code of conduct on 12 September, mutually agreeing to regulate their electoral behaviour. The code contained 16 articles, dealing with such questions as intimidation; carrying of weapons; regulation and non-disruption of meetings and rallies; use of violent or inflammatory language; secrecy of the ballot; non-destruction of others' campaign materials; access to all voters; systems of communications and liaison; and self-policing and self-enforcement. Most importantly, the parties also undertook to accept and respect the outcome of the elections if certified as free and fair by the Special Representative. Meetings of all parties, similar to those held in Windhoek, took place throughout the Territory at virtually all UNTAG regional and district offices, chaired by the UNTAG regional director or district head, to discuss matters of common concern arising from the electoral process.

The Secretary-General reported[3] that registration of voters began on 3 July and ended on 23 September. He said the process took place in an orderly way, without serious incident and under the close supervision and control of UNTAG. More than 701,000 voters were registered, with only 593 applications rejected in the 23 electoral districts. Some 350 polling stations were to be established, with the possibility of 15 more in the most populated areas. An issue of concern had been the presence among the registrants of approximately 10,000 persons normally resident in South Africa, who were made eligible to vote under the applicable legislation.[4]

In a letter to the Security Council[5] dated 10 October, the Secretary-General stated that the estimated number of electoral supervisors was too low; some 1,395 would be required to supervise the voting. The Security Council agreed to that proposal on 17 October.[6] Subsequently, in November, the Secretary-General reported[3] that 1,695 electoral personnel were in Namibia, their training was complete and they had been deployed to their electoral regions. Besides UN and agency staff, those included 885 electoral personnel made available by 27 Governments.

Obstacles

On 18 October, Kenya, on behalf of the African Group, requested[7] an urgent meeting of the Security Council regarding the grave situation prevailing in Namibia. Also on 18 October, Kenya transmitted to the Secretary-General a statement[8] issued by the African Group on his October report,[2] which the Group said had exposed some serious continuing obstacles to implementing the UN plan. It confirmed that South Africa had not fully complied with the plan's letter and spirit; the Group said that raised serious concerns as to whether conditions existed for the holding of free and fair elections. In particular, the Group commented on the failure to demobilize two bushmen battalions; Koevoet elements in SWAPOL; the late issuance of the Electoral Proclamation; non-issuance of legislation on the Constituent Assembly; non-repeal of the system of ethnic administration; and registration of South Africans to vote.

South Africa transmitted to the Secretary-General the text of a communiqué[9] issued on 18 October following a further meeting of the Joint Commission of Angola, Cuba and South Africa. Among other things, the Commission called for an urgent solution to the Koevoet issue, to which South Africa undertook to provide a timely response, and took measures to confirm, on the spot, the demobilization of the bushmen battalions.

SECURITY COUNCIL ACTION (October)

On 31 October, the Security Council unanimously adopted **resolution 643(1989)**.

The Security Council,

Reaffirming all its relevant resolutions on the question of Namibia, in particular resolutions 435(1978) of 29 September 1978, 629(1989) of 16 January 1989, 632(1989) of 16 February 1989 and 640(1989) of 29 August 1989,

Reaffirming also that the United Nations plan for the independence of Namibia, contained in resolution 435(1978), remains the only internationally accepted basis for the peaceful settlement of the Namibia question,

Having considered the report of the Secretary-General of 6 October 1989 and the addendum thereto of 16 October 1989,

Noting with deep concern that, one week before the scheduled elections in Namibia, all the provisions of resolution 435(1978) are not being fully complied with,

Noting the progress made so far in the implementation of the settlement plan and the remaining obstacles placed in its way as well as the efforts being exerted by the United Nations Transition Assistance Group to carry out its responsibilities,

Reaffirming the continuing legal responsibility of the United Nations over Namibia until the full attainment by the Namibian people of national independence,

1. *Welcomes* the report of the Secretary-General and the addendum thereto;

2. *Expresses its full support* for the Secretary-General in his efforts to ensure that resolution 435(1978) is fully implemented in its original and definitive form;

3. *Expresses its firm determination* to implement resolution 435(1978) in its original and definitive form in order to ensure holding of free and fair elections in Namibia under the supervision and control of the United Nations;

4. *Reaffirms* its commitment in carrying out the continuing legal responsibility over Namibia until its independence to ensure the unfettered and effective exercise by the people of Namibia of their inalienable rights to self-determination and genuine national independence in accordance with resolutions 435(1978) and 640(1989);

5. *Demands* immediate, full and strict compliance by all parties concerned, in particular South Africa, with the terms of resolutions 435(1978), 632(1989) and 640(1989);

6. *Reiterates* its demand for the complete disbandment of all remaining paramilitary and ethnic forces and commando units, in particular the Koevoet and the South-West Africa Territorial Force as well as the complete dismantling of their command structures, and other defence-related institutions as required by resolutions 435(1978) and 640(1989);

7. *Requests* the Secretary-General to pursue his efforts to ensure the immediate replacement of the remaining South African Defence Force personnel in accordance with resolution 435(1978);

8. *Demands* the immediate repeal of such remaining restrictive and discriminatory laws and regulations as inhibit the holding of free and fair elections and that no such new laws be introduced and endorses the position of the Secretary-General as expressed in his report that Proclamation AG 8 should be repealed;

9. *Invites* the Secretary-General to keep under constant review the adequacy of the number of police monitors in order to undertake the process for any appropriate increase that he may deem necessary for the effective fulfilment of the United Nations Transition Assistance Group's responsibilities;

10. *Demands* that the South-West Africa Police extend full co-operation to the Group civil police in carrying out the tasks entrusted to it under the settlement plan;

11. *Mandates* the Secretary-General to ensure that all necessary arrangements are made in accordance with the settlement plan to safeguard the territorial integrity and security of Namibia in order to ensure a peaceful transition to national independence, and to assist the Constituent Assembly in the discharge of responsibilities entrusted to it under the settlement plan;

12. *Requests* the Secretary-General to prepare appropriate plans for mobilizing all forms of assistance, including technical, material and financial resources, for the people of Namibia during the period following the elections for the Constituent Assembly until the accession to independence;

13. *Urgently appeals* to Member States, United Nations agencies and intergovernmental and non-governmental organizations to extend, in co-ordination with the Secretary-General, generous financial, material and technical support to the Namibian people, both during the transitional period and after independence;

14. *Decides* that, if the pertinent provisions of the present resolution are complied with, the Security Council shall convene as required before the elections to review the situation and consider appropriate action;

15. *Requests* the Secretary-General to report on the implementation of the present resolution as soon as possible;

16. *Decides* to remain seized of the matter.

Security Council resolution 643(1989)

31 October 1989   Meeting 2886   Adopted unanimously

7-nation draft (S/20923/Rev.1).

Sponsors: Algeria, Colombia, Ethiopia, Malaysia, Nepal, Senegal, Yugoslavia.

Report of the Secretary-General (November). In a 3 November report,[3] the Secretary-General stated that in the past month the situation in Namibia had remained calm. However, UNTAG had received numerous allegations from South Africa that concentrations of SWAPO combatants were present in parts of southern Angola, allegations denied by Sam Nujoma, President of SWAPO, who said the entire People's Liberation Army of Namibia had been demobilized and that virtually all its personnel had returned, unarmed, to Namibia. Moreover, the entire SWAPO leadership had returned to the Territory. Patrols conducted by UNTAG and the Angolan Armed Forces had found no evidence of the concentrations alleged by South Africa. The most recent South African allegation was made on 1 November, claiming that intercepted internal UNTAG messages had reported an imminent incursion into Namibia from Angola by SWAPO combatants. The Secretary-General stated that he had established that the messages were fraudulent, not emanating from any UNTAG source.

SECURITY COUNCIL ACTION (November)

On 3 November, following consultations, the President of the Security Council issued a statement[10] deploring South Africa's false alarm of 1 November and calling on South Africa to desist from any such further actions. The Council expressed profound concern about the incident, as well as the political implications for the elections of the initial South African reaction.

Election results

Report of the Secretary-General. In a post-election report,[11] the Secretary-General said elections for a Constituent Assembly of 72 members were held from 7 to 11 November. Some 358 polling stations were established in Namibia for the voting, comprising 215 fixed locations and 143 mobile polling stations. The Special Representative was assisted in the process by some 1,700 electoral supervisors drawn from the UN system, including the military component of UNTAG, and from 27 Member States of the United Nations. Additionally, 1,023 police monitors participated in the exercise. UNTAG electoral personnel supervised some 2,500 counterparts appointed by the Administrator-General in connection with the poll. UNTAG electoral supervisors were trained in their functions of supervision and control of the electoral process at four training centres in the Territory over a four-day period.

In accordance with the provisions of the UN plan, the elections were organized and conducted by the Administrator-General under the supervision and control of the UN Special Representative. More than 96 per cent of the electorate was estimated to have participated in the elections. After the poll and prior to commencement of the count, the Special Representative announced that, while there had been a few minor incidents, he was satisfied that the process had gone smoothly and that it had been free and fair, and in accordance with the provisions of Security Council resolution 435(1978).[1] The counting of the votes began on 13 November and was completed early on 14 November. The elections resulted in the following distribution of seats (based on proportional representation) in the Constituent Assembly: SWAPO, 41 (57.3 per cent of vote); Democratic Turnhalle Alliance (DTA), 21 (28.5 per cent); United Democratic Front, 4 (5.6 per cent); Aksie Christelik Nasionaal, 3 (3.5 per cent); National Patriotic Front of Namibia, 1 (1.6 per cent); Federal Convention of Namibia, 1 (1.6 per cent); and Namibia National Front, 1 (0.8 per cent). The Christian Democratic Action for Social Justice, Namibia National Democratic Party and South West Africa People's Organization—Democrats did not obtain sufficient votes to obtain an Assembly seat.

On 14 November, after full scrutiny of the procedures, and after contacting the Secretary-General, the Special Representative certified that the electoral process, at every stage, had been free and fair and conducted to his satisfaction.

SECURITY COUNCIL ACTION

On 20 November, following consultations, the President of the Security Council issued a statement[12] on behalf of the Council members, in which they welcomed with satisfaction the successful conclusion of the elections in Namibia, paving the way for the convening of the Constituent Assembly and Namibia's early independence, at a date to be determined by the Assembly.

Constituent Assembly

Report of the Secretary-General. In a further November report,[13] the Secretary-General stated that the Constituent Assembly held its first meeting on 23 November at the Tinten Palast, Windhoek, presided over by Sam Nujoma, President of SWAPO, the majority party, as provided for in the Constituent Assembly Proclamation. In a secret ballot for the office of Chairman of the Assembly, Hage Geingob (SWAPO) was elected over A. Matjila (DTA). The Assembly endorsed by acclamation that the 1982 principles concerning the Constituent Assembly and the Constitution for an independent Namibia[14] would serve as the framework

for the drafting of the Constitution. On 28 November, the Assembly adopted its rules of procedure. Discussions on the draft Constitution continued through the remainder of the year.

Special Committee mission

The Special Committee on the Situation with regard to the Implementation of the Declaration on the Granting of Independence to Colonial Countries and Peoples decided in August to send a visiting mission to Namibia to monitor the decolonization process, in particular to observe the preparations for the elections and the elections themselves. The mission visited Namibia from 29 October to 17 November. In a December report[4] to the General Assembly, it reviewed the situation in Namibia before and during the elections and concluded that the elections had been held in conformity with established UN standards of decolonization. The people of Namibia had freely chosen representatives to determine their political future, the mission stated.

REFERENCES

[1]YUN 1978, p. 915, SC res. 435(1978), 29 Sep. 1978. [2]S/20883. [3]S/20943. [4]A/44/23. [5]S/20905. [6]S/20906. [7]S/20908. [8]A/44/656-S/20909. [9]S/20910. [10]S/20946. [11]S/20967. [12]S/20974. [13]S/20967/Add.1. [14]YUN 1982, p. 1292.

Economic and social issues

Transnational corporations

The Commission on Transnational Corporations (TNCs) held its fifteenth session in New York in April[1] (see PART THREE, Chapter V). In regard to Namibia, it had before it three reports of the Secretary-General: a February report,[2] in response to a 1980 Economic and Social Council resolution,[3] regarding the responsibilities of home countries with respect to TNCs operating in Namibia in violation of UN resolutions and decisions; another February report[4] on activities of TNCs in Namibia and collaboration of such corporations with the racist minority régime; and a March report[5] on follow-up to the recommendations of the Panel of Eminent Persons that had conducted public hearings on TNCs in Namibia in 1985.[6]

In a July report,[7] the United Nations Centre on TNCs gave an overview of the Namibian economy, especially the activities of TNCs in Namibia, and future prospects for foreign investments after independence. Stating that the Namibian economy had evolved as an appendage of the South African economy and reflected the latter's *apartheid* structure, the report stressed that the new Namibian Government would need to take urgent policy decisions on the role of TNCs.

In an August report,[8] the Centre stated that TNCs in Namibia had contributed little to its economic development, and those operating in mining and fishing had operated at levels that depleted scarce resources. The high profits had been repatriated, usually to South Africa, with little or no new investment. As a result, net investment had been negative for some time. In addition, TNCs had made no attempt to educate the local labour force, the report stated.

The Commission on TNCs, after detailed discussions, took note[1] of the three reports of the Secretary-General. It also approved an information programme for the public hearings on the role of TNCs in South Africa and Namibia, to be held in September (see PART TWO, Chapter I).

GENERAL ASSEMBLY ACTION

On 11 December, on the recommendation of the Fourth Committee, the General Assembly adopted **resolution 44/84** by recorded vote.

Activities of foreign economic and other interests which are impeding the implementation of the Declaration on the Granting of Independence to Colonial Countries and Peoples in Namibia and in all other Territories under colonial domination and efforts to eliminate colonialism, *apartheid* and racial discrimination in southern Africa

The General Assembly,

Having considered the item entitled "Activities of foreign economic and other interests which are impeding the implementation of the Declaration on the Granting of Independence to Colonial Countries and Peoples in Namibia and in all other Territories under colonial domination and efforts to eliminate colonialism, *apartheid* and racial discrimination in southern Africa",

Having examined the chapter of the report of the Special Committee on the Situation with regard to the Implementation of the Declaration on the Granting of Independence to Colonial Countries and Peoples relating to the item,

Recalling its resolutions 1514(XV) of 14 December 1960, containing the Declaration on the Granting of Independence to Colonial Countries and Peoples, 2621(XXV) of 12 October 1970, containing the programme of action for the full implementation of the Declaration, 35/118 of 11 December 1980, the annex to which contains the Plan of Action for the Full Implementation of the Declaration, and 40/56 of 2 December 1985 on the twenty-fifth anniversary of the Declaration, as well as all other resolutions of the United Nations relating to the item,

Reaffirming the solemn obligation of the administering Powers under the Charter of the United Nations to promote the political, economic, social and educational advancement of the inhabitants of the Territories under their administration and to protect the human and natural resources of those Territories against abuses,

Reaffirming also that any economic or other activity that impedes the implementation of the Declaration on the Granting of Independence to Colonial Countries and Peoples and obstructs efforts aimed at the elimination of colonialism, *apartheid* and racial discrimination in southern Africa and other colonial Territories is in direct violation of the rights of the inhabitants and of the principles of the Charter and all relevant resolutions of the United Nations,

Reaffirming further that the natural resources of all Territories under colonial and racist domination are the heritage of the peoples of those Territories and that the depletive exploitation of those resources by foreign economic interests constitutes a direct violation of the rights of the peoples and of the principles of the Charter and all relevant resolutions of the United Nations,

Bearing in mind the relevant provisions of the final documents of the successive Conferences of Heads of State or Government of Non-Aligned Countries and of the resolutions adopted by the Assembly of Heads of State and Government of the Organization of African Unity,

Condemning the intensified activities of those foreign economic, financial and other interests that continue to exploit the natural and human resources of the colonial Territories and to accumulate and repatriate huge profits to the detriment of the interests of the inhabitants, thereby impeding the realization by the peoples of the Territories of their legitimate aspirations for self-determination and independence,

Strongly condemning the investment of foreign capital in the production of uranium and the collaboration by certain Western and other countries with the racist minority régime of South Africa in the nuclear field which, by providing that régime with nuclear equipment and technology, enable it to develop nuclear and military capabilities and to become a nuclear Power, thereby strengthening its abhorrent system of *apartheid*,

Concerned about any foreign economic, financial and other activities which continue to deprive the indigenous populations of colonial Territories, including certain Territories in the Caribbean and the Pacific Ocean regions, of their rights over the wealth of their countries, and concerned that the inhabitants of those Territories continue to suffer from a loss of land ownership as a result of the failure of the administering Powers concerned to restrict the sale of land to foreigners, despite the repeated appeals of the General Assembly,

Conscious of the continuing need to mobilize world public opinion against the involvement of foreign economic, financial and other interests in the exploitation of natural and human resources, which impedes the independence of colonial Territories and the elimination of racism, particularly in South Africa, and emphasizing the importance of action by local authorities, trade unions, religious bodies, academic institutions, mass media, solidarity movements and other non-governmental organizations, as well as individuals, in applying pressure on transnational corporations to refrain from any investment or activity in South Africa, in encouraging a policy of systematic divestment of any financial or other interest in corporations doing business with South Africa and in counteracting all forms of collaboration with the *apartheid* régime,

1. *Reaffirms* the inalienable right of the peoples of dependent Territories to self-determination and independence and to the enjoyment of the natural resources of

their Territories, as well as their right to dispose of those resources in their best interests;

2. *Reiterates* that any administering or occupying Power that deprives the colonial peoples of the exercise of their legitimate rights over their natural resources or subordinates the rights and interests of those peoples to foreign economic and financial interests violates the solemn obligations it has assumed under the Charter of the United Nations;

3. *Reaffirms* that, by their depletive exploitation of natural resources, the continued accumulation and repatriation of huge profits and the use of those profits for the enrichment of foreign settlers and the perpetuation of colonial domination and racial discrimination in the Territories, the activities of foreign economic, financial and other interests operating at present in the colonial Territories constitute a major obstacle to political independence and racial equality, as well as to the enjoyment of the natural resources of those Territories by the indigenous inhabitants;

4. *Condemns* those activities of foreign economic and other interests in the colonial Territories that are impeding the implementation of the Declaration on the Granting of Independence to Colonial Countries and Peoples and the efforts to eliminate colonialism, *apartheid* and racial discrimination;

5. *Strongly condemns* the collaboration of the Governments of certain Western Powers, Israel and other countries with the racist minority régime of South Africa in the nuclear field and calls upon those and all other Governments concerned to refrain from supplying that régime, directly or indirectly, with installations, equipment or material that might enable it to produce uranium, plutonium and other nuclear materials, reactors or military equipment;

6. *Strongly condemns* the collaboration with the racist minority régime of South Africa of the Governments of certain Western and other countries as well as transnational corporations that continue to make new investments in South Africa and supply the régime with armaments, nuclear technology and all other materials that are likely to buttress it and thus aggravate the threat to world peace;

7. *Calls upon* all States, in particular certain Western and other States, to take urgent, effective measures to terminate all collaboration with the racist régime of South Africa in the political, economic, trade, military and nuclear fields and to refrain from entering into other relations with that régime in violation of the relevant resolutions of the United Nations and of the Organization of African Unity;

8. *Calls once again upon* all Governments that have not yet done so to take, in accordance with the relevant provisions of its resolutions 2621(XXV) of 12 October 1970 and 43/29 of 22 November 1988, legislative, administrative or other measures in respect of their nationals and the bodies corporate under their jurisdiction that own and operate enterprises in colonial Territories that are detrimental to the interests of the inhabitants of those Territories, in order to put an end to such enterprises and to prevent new investments that run counter to the interests of the inhabitants of those Territories;

9. *Calls upon* those oil-producing and oil-exporting countries that have not yet done so to take effective measures against the oil companies concerned so as to ter-

minate the supply of crude oil and petroleum products to the racist régime of South Africa;

10. *Reiterates* that the exploitation and plundering of the marine and other natural resources of colonial Territories by foreign economic interests, including the activities of those transnational corporations that are engaged in the exploitation and export of the natural resources of the Territories, in violation of the relevant resolutions of the General Assembly and the Security Council, are illegal and are a grave threat to the integrity and prosperity of those Territories;

11. *Reiterates its request* to all States, pending the imposition of comprehensive mandatory sanctions against South Africa, to take legislative, administrative and other measures, individually or collectively, as appropriate, in order effectively to isolate South Africa politically, economically, militarily and culturally, in accordance with the relevant resolutions of the General Assembly, and encourages those Governments that have recently taken certain unilateral sanction measures against the South African régime to take further measures;

12. *Invites* all Governments and organizations of the United Nations system, having regard to the relevant provisions of the Declaration on the Establishment of a New International Economic Order, contained in General Assembly resolution 3201(S-VI) of 1 May 1974, and of the Charter of Economic Rights and Duties of States, contained in Assembly resolution 3281(XXIX) of 12 December 1974, to ensure, in particular, that the permanent sovereignty of the colonial Territories over their natural resources is fully respected and safeguarded;

13. *Urges* the administering Powers concerned to take effective measures to safeguard and guarantee the inalienable right of the peoples of the colonial Territories to their natural resources, as well as their right to establish and maintain control over the future development of those natural resources, and requests the administering Powers to take all necessary steps to protect the property rights of the peoples of those Territories;

14. *Calls upon* the administering Powers concerned to abolish all discriminatory and unjust wage systems and working conditions prevailing in the Territories under their administration and to apply in each Territory a uniform system of wages to all the inhabitants without any discrimination;

15. *Requests* the Secretary-General to undertake, through the Department of Public Information of the Secretariat, a sustained and broad campaign with a view to informing world public opinion of the facts concerning the pillaging of natural resources in colonial Territories and the exploitation of their indigenous populations by foreign economic interests;

16. *Appeals* to mass media, trade unions and non-governmental organizations, as well as individuals, to co-ordinate and intensify their efforts to mobilize international public opinion against the policy of the *apartheid* régime of South Africa and to work for the enforcement of economic and other sanctions against that régime and for encouraging a policy of systematic and genuine divestment from corporations doing business in South Africa;

17. *Decides* to continue to monitor closely the situation in the remaining colonial Territories so as to ensure that all economic activities in those Territories are aimed at strengthening and diversifying their economies

in the interests of the indigenous peoples, at promoting the economic and financial viability of those Territories and at speeding their accession to independence and, in that connection, requests the administering Powers concerned to ensure that the peoples of the Territories under their administration are not exploited for political, military and other purposes detrimental to their interests;

18. *Requests* the Special Committee on the Situation with regard to the Implementation of the Declaration on the Granting of Independence to Colonial Countries and Peoples to continue to examine this question and to report thereon to the General Assembly at its forty-fifth session.

General Assembly resolution 44/84

11 December 1989   Meeting 80   125-10-17 (recorded vote)

Approved by Fourth Committee (A/44/664) by recorded vote (84-10-16), 10 October (meeting 6); draft by Special Committee on decolonization (A/44/23 (Part III)); agenda item 117.

Meeting numbers. GA 44th session: 4th Committee 2-6; plenary 80.

Recorded vote in Assembly as follows:

In favour: Afghanistan, Albania, Algeria, Angola, Antigua and Barbuda, Argentina, Bahamas, Bahrain, Bangladesh, Barbados, Benin, Bhutan, Bolivia, Botswana, Brazil, Brunei Darussalam, Bulgaria, Burkina Faso, Burundi, Byelorussian SSR, Cameroon, Cape Verde, Central African Republic, Chad, Chile, China, Colombia, Comoros, Congo, Costa Rica, Cuba, Cyprus, Czechoslovakia, Democratic Kampuchea, Democratic Yemen, Djibouti, Dominica, Dominican Republic, Ecuador, Egypt, El Salvador, Equatorial Guinea, Ethiopia, Fiji, Gabon, Gambia, German Democratic Republic, Ghana, Grenada, Guatemala, Guinea, Guinea-Bissau, Guyana, Haiti, Honduras, India, Indonesia, Iran, Iraq, Jamaica, Jordan, Kenya, Kuwait, Lao People's Democratic Republic, Lebanon, Lesotho, Liberia, Libyan Arab Jamahiriya, Madagascar, Malaysia, Maldives, Mali, Mauritania, Mauritius, Mexico, Mongolia, Morocco, Mozambique, Myanmar, Nepal, Nicaragua, Niger, Nigeria, Oman, Pakistan, Panama, Papua New Guinea, Peru, Philippines, Poland, Qatar, Romania, Rwanda, Saint Kitts and Nevis, Saint Lucia, Saint Vincent and the Grenadines, Samoa, Sao Tome and Principe, Saudi Arabia, Senegal, Seychelles, Sierra Leone, Singapore, Solomon Islands, Somalia, Sri Lanka, Suriname, Swaziland, Syrian Arab Republic, Thailand, Togo, Trinidad and Tobago, Tunisia, Uganda, Ukrainian SSR, USSR, United Arab Emirates, United Republic of Tanzania, Uruguay, Vanuatu, Venezuela, Viet Nam, Yemen, Yugoslavia, Zaire.

Against: Belgium, France, Germany, Federal Republic of, Israel, Italy, Luxembourg, Netherlands, Portugal, United Kingdom, United States.

Abstaining: Australia, Austria, Canada, Côte d'Ivoire, Denmark, Finland, Greece, Hungary, Iceland, Ireland, Japan, Malta, New Zealand, Norway, Spain, Sweden, Turkey.

Women and children

The Commission on the Status of Women, at its thirty-third session (29 March–7 April)[9] (see PART THREE, Chapter XIII), following consideration of a report by the Secretary-General on developments in the situation of women and children in Namibia[10] (see also PART TWO, Chapter I), recommended a resolution for adoption by the Economic and Social Council.

ECONOMIC AND SOCIAL COUNCIL ACTION

On 24 May, on the recommendation of its Second (Social) Committee, the Economic and Social Council adopted **resolution 1989/31** without vote.

Women and children in Namibia

The Economic and Social Council,

Welcoming the full implementation of Security Council resolution 435(1978) of 29 September 1978, concerning the independence of Namibia,

Recalling its resolution 1988/24 of 26 May 1988, in which it expressed deep concern at the suffering of Namibian women under South African occupation,

Recalling also the Nairobi Forward-looking Strategies for the Advancement of Women, in particular paragraph 259, which calls for the speedy and effective implementation of Security Council resolution 435(1978),

Recognizing that the agreement recently reached on Namibian independence under Security Council resolution 435(1978) provides a historic opportunity for the Namibian people to realize their right to self-determination following 104 years of colonial domination,

Noting that with the implementation of Security Council resolution 435(1978) on 1 April 1989, Namibia faces a crucial transitional period, with an election campaign commencing on 1 July 1989 and the election scheduled for early November 1989, and that it is incumbent upon the international community to take immediate action to ensure that the elections render the justice and freedom to which the Namibian people have the right,

Bearing in mind that the repatriation of Namibian refugees from neighbouring States, which is scheduled to take place from 15 May to 30 June 1989, poses special problems that require massive humanitarian assistance,

1. *Urges* Governments and intergovernmental and non-governmental organizations to make resources available to assist in making the repatriation process as smooth as possible and to continue material and financial support to Namibian women and children during the transitional period;

2. *Urges* all parties to respect the process of implementing Security Council resolution 435(1978), in order to ensure independence for Namibia;

3. *Invites* the Commission on the Status of Women to help raise international consciousness of the special circumstances and concerns of Namibian women;

4. *Requests* the Secretary-General to encourage and give special attention to the full and equal participation of Namibian women, in both registration and voting;

5. *Also requests* the Secretary-General to submit to the Commission on the Status of Women at its thirty-fourth session a comprehensive report on the implementation and monitoring of the Nairobi Forward-looking Strategies for the Advancement of Women regarding women and children in Namibia.

Economic and Social Council resolution 1989/31

24 May 1989   Meeting 15   Adopted without vote

Approved by Second Committee (E/1989/90) without vote, 16 May (meeting 16); draft by Commission on women (E/1989/27/Rev.1); agenda item 10.

Human Rights Commission action. By a resolution[11] of 23 February 1989, the Commission on Human Rights reiterated its condemnation of the detention, torture and inhuman treatment of children in South Africa and Namibia; appealed to the international community to adopt concrete and effective measures to bring pressure to bear against the Government of South Africa until it dismantled *apartheid*; and requested the *Ad Hoc* Working Group of Experts on southern Africa to pay special attention to the question of detention, torture and other inhuman treatment of children in South Africa and Namibia.

On 15 December 1989, the General Assembly adopted **resolution 44/143**, on torture and inhuman treatment of children in detention in South Africa and Namibia, in which the Commission on Human Rights was requested to pay special attention to the children of Namibia who had been victims of torture, detention and other inhuman treatment by the *apartheid* régime, with a view to rehabilitating them.

REFERENCES
[1]E/1989/28/Rev.1. [2]E/C.10/1989/9. [3]YUN 1988, p. 429, ESC res. 1988/56, 27 July 1988. [4]E/C.10/1989/8 & Corr.1. [5]E/1989/17. [6]YUN 1985, p. 149. [7]E/C.10/AC.4/1989/7. [8]E/C.10/AC.4/1989/3. [9]E/1989/27/Rev.1. [10]E/CN.6/1989/3. [11]E/1989/20 (res. 1989/4).

Other UN activities

Council for Namibia

In its annual report to the General Assembly,[1] the United Nations Council for Namibia made an assessment of the political situation in the Territory, stating that a convergence of factors had pushed the South African régime towards a political settlement. One factor was the escalating cost of its continued military occupation of Namibia, estimated at $1.5 million a day in 1984 and reported to have risen to $1 billion annually by 1988. At the same time, South Africa had sustained heavy losses in men and equipment during its 1988 incursions into Angola, and high casualties among white soldiers had made the war increasingly unpopular among white segments of the population.

While the Council continued to carry out its mandate as legal Administering Authority for Namibia until independence, in view of the commencement on 1 April 1989 of the implementation of resolution 435(1978) (see above, under "UN Transition Assistance Group"), it adjusted its work programme to focus on mobilization of development assistance to Namibia. During the year, it organized three major seminars—on contingency planning for technical assistance to Namibia during the transition to independence (Vienna, 24-28 July);[2] on the integration of Namibia into the regional structures for economic co-operation and development in southern Africa (Harare, Zimbabwe, 23-27 October);[3] and on the role of the United Nations regarding technical assistance for an independent Namibia (Rio de Janeiro, Brazil, 4-8 December).[4]

The purpose of the Vienna seminar was to survey Namibia's technical assistance requirements, with special emphasis on human resources, during the transition to independence and the immediate post-independence period; to draw up proposals for sectoral contingency plans which would ensure the functioning of essential services during that time; and to consider the co-operation and assistance of donors, international agencies and other organizations during the same period. It was attended by 50 participants, including 12 Namibian experts, representatives of specialized agencies, other UN organizations and national and international aid agencies and non-governmental organizations (NGOs). The seminar noted that, in a number of areas, appropriate channels for assistance in the immediate term already existed via Namibian NGOs, such as the Council of Churches in Namibia and other church groups, but there was still a need to provide assistance to maintain certain crucial services currently being provided by territorial government units responsible to the South African Administrator-General. In its final document, the seminar made specific recommendations for immediate technical assistance in the 10 socio-economic sectors under consideration.

The purpose of the Harare seminar was to assess areas of Namibia's economic dependence on South Africa, to develop plans and programmes intended to reduce such dependence in the context of the Southern African Development Co-ordination Conference and other regional structures for economic co-operation and development in southern Africa, and to define and assess priority areas of international assistance in the implementation of those measures and programmes. The overall conclusion was that Namibia's economic dependence on South Africa was almost total. The seminar concluded that the integration of its economy into that of South Africa was unparalleled in southern Africa. The reduction of economic dependence on South Africa would be difficult and a long-term exercise, but prospects were good because there was no natural dependence. The seminar made recommendations regarding the mining sector; agricultural and food security; fisheries; industrial development; energy; transport and communications; manpower development; trade development; water resources development; and the financial and monetary system.

The purpose of the Rio de Janeiro seminar was to assess the development and technical assistance needs of an independent Namibia, to increase understanding and support for those needs in the international community, and to consider the role of the UN system in mobilizing resources to meet them. Participants included representatives of the United Nations, specialized agencies, other intergovernmental and regional organizations, the Brazilian Agency for Co-operation, and a delegation of Namibians who were expected to assume important policy-making technical positions in Namibia after independence. In its final document, the seminar made recommendations in all areas concerning economic and social development in Namibia, divided into sections on agriculture, rural development and fisheries; trade and industry; utilities, transport and communications; health, shelter, education, labour and human resources development; and monetary and fiscal matters.

UN Commissioner for Namibia

The annual report[1] of the Council for Namibia summarized the work of the United Nations Commissioner for Namibia, stating that in 1989 the Commissioner, acting through his offices in New York, Gaborone (Botswana), Luanda (Angola) and Lusaka (Zambia), continued to protect Namibian interests through the issuance of travel documents and through efforts to ensure implementation of the 1974 Decree No. 1 for the Protection of the Natural Resources of Namibia.[5] The Commissioner was also engaged in the provision of assistance to Namibians and the mobilization of international support for the Namibian cause. His Office administered assistance programmes under the United Nations Fund for Namibia (see below).

The Luanda Office of the Commissioner, where SWAPO maintained its provisional headquarters and in a country where over 90 per cent of Namibians in exile were based, continued to play an active role in the co-ordination of assistance to Namibians and the monitoring of political developments in Namibia. Under the field attachment programme, the Office helped place Namibians in various training fields. It co-operated in the crash-course training in the United Republic of Tanzania of 400 Namibian students as immigration, customs and excise officers. Following agreements on resolving the conflicts in south-western Africa, which resulted in the commencement of the implementation of Security Council resolution 435(1978), the Luanda Office collaborated with the UNHCR in the registration and repatriation of 35,000 Namibian exiles to Namibia to enable them to participate in the independence process. It also issued 500 travel documents of the Council for Namibia to Namibians.

UN Fund for Namibia

The Council for Namibia, in its annual report,[1] summarized the international assistance programmes of the UN Fund for Namibia. The Fund, for which voluntary contributions were the major financial source, continued to serve in the first half of 1989 as the main instrument through

which the Council for Namibia, acting as its trustee, channelled assistance to the Namibians. The Fund had three main programmes with special accounts: the Nationhood Programme for Namibia; the United Nations Institute for Namibia; and educational, social and relief assistance (General Account). Fund expenditures for the three programmes totalled $5,590,765 from January to June 1989 as follows: Nationhood Programme, $787,221; Institute, $1,529,849; and General Account, $3,273,695.

The Nationhood Programme consisted of two major components: manpower training programmes, and surveys and analyses of Namibian economic and social sectors, including identification of development tasks and policy options. Under manpower training, hundreds of Namibians continued their training at various institutions, mostly in African countries. They were trained in a variety of professions, trades and crafts, including land use and human settlements development, food distribution, labour administration, radio programming, rural development, agriculture, truck mechanics, cartography, cargo handling, port management, fish processing, air traffic control, health services, mining, railway operations and leatherwork. The UN Vocational Training Centre at Cuacra, Angola, continued to operate during 1989 at full capacity. It offered six trades: auto mechanics, machine shop and fitting, electrical installations, plumbing, carpentry, and building and construction. During 1989, a transitional plan for the gradual phasing out of the Centre in Angola and the transfer of activities to an independent Namibia was prepared.

The UN Institute for Namibia, located in Lusaka, continued to train middle-level skilled manpower for an independent Namibia and carried out applied research in various sectors of the Namibian economy. In 1989, the tenth graduating group, comprising 123 students, was awarded diplomas in management and development studies, bringing the total number of Institute graduates in that field to 888. The Institute's diploma was underwritten by the University of Zambia. In addition, 29 students were awarded teaching diplomas in basic education, and 36 students received certificates in secretarial training programmes, bringing the Institute's total number of graduates from its various programmes since its inception to 1,266.

In January 1989, the Senate Research Committee, created to guide all Institute research, adopted a transitional plan for the gradual transfer of the Institute's activities to an independent Namibia. In accordance with the plan, no new intake of students was accepted for 1989. The Namibian Extension Unit, established in 1981, continued during the first half of 1989 to expand its distance education programme for Namibians who had been denied education by the South African administration in Namibia. It continued to serve several thousand Namibian adults and youths in Zambia and Angola, and plans were drawn up for the transfer of its activities to an independent Namibia. The total expenditure of the Institute during the first six months of 1989 was $1,529,849.

Educational, social and relief assistance, especially in the form of scholarships, was the main activity financed by the Fund's General Account in 1989. It was also used to finance vocational and technical training; provide assistance in health and medical care, nutrition and social welfare; acquire books and periodicals for Namibian refugee camps and SWAPO offices; and facilitate the attendance of Namibian representatives at international seminars, meetings and conferences. During 1989, the demand for scholarships continued to increase. As at 30 June, 255 Namibians were being sponsored under the scholarship programme.

In the first half of the year, 38 countries contributed more than $8 million to the Fund: $2,023,706 to the Nationhood Programme, $5,090,394 to the Institute, and $1,246,853 to the General Account. In addition, the Fund received financing from the UN regular budget; for 1989, the General Assembly allocated $1.5 million from the regular budget. Funding was also provided by the United Nations Development Programme (UNDP): in 1988,[6] the UNDP Governing Council had increased the indicative planning figure for Namibia for the 1987-1991 programming cycle to $10.6 million.

UN Educational and Training Programme

In a report to the General Assembly,[7] the Secretary-General stated that the United Nations Educational and Training Programme for Southern Africa, between 1 September 1988 and 31 August 1989, granted 11 new scholarships to Namibians and extended 431, in addition to those financed by the UN Fund for Namibia.

System-wide activities

UNDP

By a 30 June 1989 decision,[8] the Governing Council of UNDP urged the Administrator to establish a trust fund for Namibia to mobilize resources for preparatory activities and the preparation of contingency plans during the transitional period leading to independence. The UNDP Trust Fund for Namibia was established on 18 September and became operational on 23 November, fol-

lowing the approval of the first project to be financed from the Fund's resources.[9] Representatives of the UN Department of Technical Cooperation for Development, in collaboration with the UN Statistical Office, undertook a mission to Namibia from 22 October to 10 November to prepare population estimates and estimates of gross domestic product.

Other agencies

The Secretary-General reported[10] to the General Assembly on agency assistance to Namibia in 1989. UNESCO contributed to the education of Namibian refugees in southern Africa and, after the start of the repatriation, within Namibia by: providing teaching material and educational equipment; paying for support staff for SWAPO education centres; executing UNDP-financed education projects, providing training for candidates sponsored by SWAPO; and training teachers for SWAPO education centres. UNESCO assistance was also designated to provide a basis for planning a post-*apartheid* society. The International Labour Organisation (ILO) actively collaborated with the UN Commissioner for Namibia, especially in programmes of technical assistance within the framework of the Nationhood Programme. ILO activities covered vocational training, rehabilitation, employment planning and creation, rural development, migrant workers and fellowship schemes. ICAO provided advice to the Commissioner for Namibia regarding placement of trained personnel in the civil aviation departments and airlines of other African countries to obtain practical experience.

The International Monetary Fund (IMF) indicated its readiness to help Namibia in areas of IMF competence, as and when asked by the Secretary-General. WHO organized a joint mission composed of staff of WHO Headquarters and the African Regional Office to Namibia during 1989. FAO assisted SWAPO with emergency food and carried out surveys and analyses of policy options on various aspects of Namibia's agriculture. Projects included contingency plans for fisheries, formulation of plans for the protection of food supplies and nutrition, preparation of agrarian reform and settlement programmes, formulation of programmes for agricultural education and an assessment of land suitability for various types of agricultural activity.

REFERENCES
[1]A/44/24. [2]A/AC.131/VIE/1/Rev.1. [3]A/AC.131/318. [4]A/AC.131/319. [5]YUN 1974, p. 152. [6]YUN 1988, p. 786. [7]A/44/557. [8]E/1989/32 (dec. 89/38). [9]DP/1990/37. [10]A/44/297 & Add.1,2.

PART FIVE

Legal questions

Chapter I

International Court of Justice

In 1989, the International Court of Justice (ICJ) continued to deal with five contentious cases. Three new disputes were referred to it, and a request for an advisory opinion was received. During the year, the Court delivered one Judgment, one advisory opinion and 10 Orders.

The General Assembly and the Security Council independently held elections in April to fill a vacancy created by the death in 1988 of Judge Nagendra Singh. In December, the Court, following the death of one of the *ad hoc* judges in one of the Chambers, issued an Order on the composition of that Chamber.

On 8 February and 7 August, Zaire and Guinea-Bissau, respectively, deposited with the Secretary-General a declaration recognizing as compulsory the jurisdiction of the Court, as contemplated by Article 36 of the ICJ Statute.

In November, the General Assembly declared 1990-1999 to be the United Nations Decade of International Law. In December, for the fourth time the Assembly called for full and immediate compliance with the Court's 1986 Judgment in the case concerning *Military and paramilitary activities in and against Nicaragua (Nicaragua v. United States)*.

Judicial work of the Court

In 1989, at the request of the Economic and Social Council, the Court delivered an advisory opinion in the case of the *Applicability of Article VI, Section 22, of the Convention on the Privileges and Immunities of the United Nations*. A Chamber of the Court gave a Judgment in the case concerning *Elettronica Sicula S.p.A. (ELSI) (United States v. Italy)*.

The 1989 activities of ICJ were described in two reports to the General Assembly, covering the periods 1 August 1988 to 31 July 1989[1] and 1 August 1989 to 31 July 1990.[2] By **decision 44/405** of 1 November 1989, the Assembly took note of the 1988/89 report.

Military and paramilitary activities in and against Nicaragua (Nicaragua v. United States)

The question of responsibility for military and paramilitary activities in Nicaragua had been before ICJ since 1984.[3] In its Judgment of 27 June 1986[4] on the merits of the case, the Court had found, *inter alia*, that the United States was under

an obligation to make reparation to Nicaragua for all injury caused by certain breaches of obligations under international law committed by the United States. It had further decided that the form and amount of such reparation, failing agreement between the Parties, would be settled by the Court in the subsequent procedure of the case. After a 1987 Court Order[5] had fixed specific time-limits for written proceedings on the form and amount of reparation, Nicaragua duly filed its Memorial on 29 March 1988,[6] but the United States did not file a Counter-Memorial within the prescribed time-limit. No further developments took place.

GENERAL ASSEMBLY ACTION

On 7 December 1989, the General Assembly adopted **resolution 44/43** by recorded vote.

Judgment of the International Court of Justice of 27 June 1986 concerning military and paramilitary activities in and against Nicaragua: need for immediate compliance

The General Assembly,

Recalling Security Council resolutions 530(1983) of 19 May 1983 and 562(1985) of 10 May 1985, and General Assembly resolutions 41/31 of 3 November 1986, 42/18 of 12 November 1987 and 43/11 of 25 October 1988,

Aware that, under the Charter of the United Nations, the International Court of Justice is the principal judicial organ of the United Nations and that each Member undertakes to comply with the decision of the Court in any case to which it is a party,

Considering that Article 36, paragraph 6, of the Statute of the Court provides that "in the event of a dispute as to whether the Court has jurisdiction, the matter shall be settled by the decision of the Court",

Recalling the Judgment of the International Court of Justice of 27 June 1986 in the case of "Military and Paramilitary Activities in and against Nicaragua",

Having considered the events that have taken place in and against Nicaragua since the Judgment was rendered, in particular the continued financing by the United States of America of military and other activities in and against Nicaragua,

Emphasizing the obligation of States, under customary international law, not to intervene in the internal affairs of other States,

1. *Reiterates once again its urgent call* for full and immediate compliance with the Judgment of the International Court of Justice of 27 June 1986 in the case of "Military and Paramilitary Activities in and against Nicaragua" in conformity with the relevant provisions of the Charter of the United Nations;

2. *Requests* the Secretary-General to keep the General Assembly informed on the implementation of the present resolution;

3. *Decides* to include in the provisional agenda of its forty-fifth session the item entitled "Judgment of the International Court of Justice of 27 June 1986 concerning military and paramilitary activities in and against Nicaragua: need for immediate compliance".

General Assembly resolution 44/43

7 December 1989   Meeting 77   91-2-41 (recorded vote)

Draft by Nicaragua (A/44/L.52); agenda item 26.

Recorded vote in Assembly as follows:

In favour: Afghanistan, Albania, Algeria, Angola, Argentina, Australia, Austria, Bahamas, Barbados, Bolivia, Botswana, Brazil, Bulgaria, Burkina Faso, Burundi, Byelorussian SSR, Canada, Cape Verde, China, Colombia, Congo, Cuba, Cyprus, Czechoslovakia, Denmark, Ecuador, Ethiopia, Fiji, Finland, German Democratic Republic, Ghana, Greece, Guinea, Guinea-Bissau, Guyana, Hungary, Iceland, India, Indonesia, Iran, Iraq, Ireland, Kenya, Kuwait, Lao People's Democratic Republic, Lesotho, Libyan Arab Jamahiriya, Madagascar, Malawi, Maldives, Mali, Mexico, Mongolia, Myanmar, Nepal, New Zealand, Nicaragua, Nigeria, Norway, Pakistan, Panama, Peru, Philippines, Poland, Qatar, Romania, Saint Kitts and Nevis, Saint Lucia, Saint Vincent and the Grenadines, Sao Tome and Principe, Saudi Arabia, Seychelles, Solomon Islands, Spain, Suriname, Swaziland, Sweden, Syrian Arab Republic, Trinidad and Tobago, Uganda, Ukrainian SSR, USSR, United Arab Emirates, United Republic of Tanzania, Uruguay, Vanuatu, Venezuela, Viet Nam, Yugoslavia, Zambia, Zimbabwe.

Against: Israel, United States.

Abstaining: Antigua and Barbuda, Bahrain, Belgium, Brunei Darussalam, Central African Republic, Chad, Costa Rica, Côte d'Ivoire, Dominica, Dominican Republic, Egypt, France, Gambia, Germany, Federal Republic of, Grenada, Guatemala, Honduras, Italy, Jamaica, Japan, Jordan, Liberia, Luxembourg, Malaysia, Malta, Mauritius, Morocco, Netherlands, Oman, Portugal, Rwanda, Samoa, Senegal, Sierra Leone, Sri Lanka, Sudan, Togo, Tunisia, Turkey, United Kingdom, Yemen.

Border and transborder armed actions (Nicaragua v. Honduras)

Nicaragua had instituted proceedings on 28 July 1986[7] alleging border and transborder armed actions, military attacks and threats of force from Honduras against it. In its Judgment of 20 December 1988,[8] the Court had found that it had jurisdiction to entertain the Nicaraguan Application and that the latter was admissible. By an Order of 21 April 1989,[9] the President of the Court fixed 19 September 1989 as the time-limit for the Memorial of Nicaragua and 19 February 1990 for the Counter-Memorial of Honduras. In an Order of 31 August,[10] the President of the Court extended the time-limit for the Memorial to 8 December 1989 and reserved the question of extension of the time-limit for the Counter-Memorial. The Nicaraguan Memorial was filed within the prescribed time-limit.

On 13 December, the Agents of both Parties transmitted to the Court the text of an agreement[11] between the Presidents of the Central American countries, which included an agreement between the Presidents of Nicaragua and Honduras to seek an extra-judicial settlement of the dispute, and requesting the postponement of the date for fixing the time-limit for the Honduran Counter-Memorial until 11 June 1990. It was decided by a Court Order of 14 December 1989,[12] that the time-limit would be extended to a date to be fixed by a subsequent Order after 11 June 1990.

Maritime delimitations in the area between Greenland and Jan Mayen (Denmark v. Norway)

On 16 August 1988, Denmark had instituted proceedings against Norway, requesting the Court to decide where a boundary should be drawn between Denmark's and Norway's fishing zones and continental shelf areas in the waters between the east coast of Greenland and the Norwegian island of Jan Mayen. In October 1988,[13] the Court set time-limits for written proceedings. The Memorial of Denmark was duly filed on 1 August 1989.

Aerial incident of 3 July 1988 (Iran v. United States)

On 17 May 1989, Iran filed an Application instituting proceedings against the United States over the destruction of an Iranian aircraft and its 290 passengers and crew in Iranian airspace on 3 July 1988 by missiles launched from the guided-missile cruiser USS *Vincennes*. Iran contended that the United States had violated certain provisions of the 1944 Chicago Convention on International Civil Aviation and the 1971 Montreal Convention for the Suppression of Unlawful Acts Against the Safety of Civil Aviation and was responsible to pay compensation to Iran.

By an Order of 13 December 1989,[14] the Court fixed 12 June 1990 as the time-limit for the filing of the Iranian Memorial and 10 December 1990 for the Counter-Memorial of the United States. Judge Oda appended a declaration to the Order of the Court; Judges Schwebel and Shahabuddeen appended separate opinions.

Certain phosphate lands in Nauru (Nauru v. Australia)

On 19 May 1989, the Republic of Nauru filed an Application instituting proceedings against Australia in a dispute concerning the rehabilitation of certain phosphate lands mined under Australian administration before Nauruan independence. Nauru claimed that Australia had breached the trusteeship obligations it had accepted under the Charter of the United Nations and the 1947 Trusteeship Agreement for Nauru.

On 18 July, the Court issued an Order[15] fixing 20 April 1990 as the time-limit for the Memorial of Nauru and 21 January 1991 for the Counter-Memorial of Australia.

Arbitral award of 31 July 1989 (Guinea-Bissau v. Senegal)

On 23 August 1989, Guinea-Bissau filed an Application instituting proceedings against Senegal in a dispute concerning the validity of the Arbitral Award of 31 July 1989 by the Arbitration Tribunal formed to determine the maritime boundary between the two States. In its Application, Guinea-Bissau claimed that the Tribunal's decision, though supposed to serve as an award, did not in fact amount to one, and asked the Court to declare the decision inexistent, null and void, and that Senegal was not justified in seeking to require Guinea-Bissau to apply it. Guinea-Bissau chose Hubert Thierry as judge *ad hoc*.

By an Order of 1 November 1989,[16] the Court fixed 2 May 1990 as the time-limit for the Memorial of Guinea-Bissau and 31 October 1990 for the Counter-Memorial of Senegal.

Land, island and maritime frontier dispute (El Salvador/Honduras)

In 1986,[17] El Salvador and Honduras had submitted to the Court a Special Agreement requesting the formation of a Chamber to deal with their frontier dispute. The Court had acceded to the request in 1987,[18] and fixed 1 June 1988 as the time-limit for the filing of Memorials. Both Parties complied with the prescribed time-limit.

Following a joint request by El Salvador and Honduras, the President of the Chamber extended the time-limits for Counter-Memorials and Replies to 10 February 1989 and 12 January 1990, respectively, by Orders made on 12 January 1989[19] and 13 December 1989.[20] Each Party duly filed its Counter-Memorial.

On 17 November, Nicaragua made an Application for permission to intervene in the case, stating as its object the protection of the legal rights of Nicaragua in the Gulf of Fonseca and adjacent maritime areas. Nicaragua further expressed the view that its request for permission to intervene was a matter exclusively within the procedural mandate of the full Court. On 14 December, the Court invited the Parties to the case to submit their observations on whether the Nicaraguan Application should be decided by the full Court or by the Chamber.

In an Order of 13 December 1989,[21] the Court took note of the death of Judge *ad hoc* Virally and of the nomination by Honduras of Santiago Torres Bernárdez to replace him. Judge Shahabuddeen appended a separate opinion to the Order.

Case concerning Elettronica Sicula S.p.A. (ELSI) (United States v. Italy)

In 1987,[22] the United States had instituted proceedings against Italy in a dispute concerning the requisition by Italy of the plant and assets of Elettronica Sicula S.p.A. (ELSI), an Italian company stated to have been 100 per cent owned by two United States corporations. The Court decided to accede to the request by both Parties for the constitution of a Chamber and the Parties filed their initial pleadings within the prescribed time-limits in 1987. In 1988, the United States

Reply and the Italian Rejoinder were filed within the time-limits set by the Court.

Oral proceedings took place from 13 February to 2 March 1989. On 20 July, at a public sitting, the Chamber delivered its Judgment,[23] the operative paragraph of which read as follows:

> *The Chamber,*
>
> (1) Unanimously,
>
> *Rejects* the objection presented by the Italian Republic to the admissibility of the Application filed in this case by the United States of America on 6 February 1987;
>
> (2) By four votes to one,
>
> *Finds* that the Italian Republic has not committed any of the breaches, alleged in the said Application, of the Treaty of Friendship, Commerce and Navigation between the Parties signed at Rome on 2 February 1948, or of the Agreement Supplementing that Treaty signed by the Parties at Washington on 26 September 1951.
>
> *In favour:* President Ruda; Judges Oda, Ago and Sir Robert Jennings;
>
> *Against:* Judge Schwebel.
>
> (3) By four votes to one,
>
> *Rejects*, accordingly, the claim for reparation made against the Republic of Italy by the United States of America.
>
> *In favour:* President Ruda; Judges Oda, Ago and Sir Robert Jennings;
>
> *Against:* Judge Schwebel.

Judge Oda appended a separate opinion and Judge Schwebel a dissenting opinion to the Judgment.

Applicability of article VI, section 22, of the Convention on UN privileges and immunities

On 24 May 1989, the Economic and Social Council, by **resolution 1989/75**, requested the Court to give, on a priority basis, an advisory opinion on the applicability of article VI, section 22, of the Convention on Privileges and Immunities of the United Nations in the case of Dumitru Mazilu as a special rapporteur of the Sub-Commission on Prevention of Discrimination and Protection of Minorities. The letter from the Secretary-General transmitting the request was received in the Registry of the Court on 13 June 1989.

By an Order of 14 June,[24] the President of the Court found that the United Nations and States that were parties to the Convention were likely to be able to provide information on the matter. The Order fixed 31 July 1989 as the time-limit for written statements and 31 August 1989 for subsequent comments on those statements. The United Nations, Canada, the Federal Republic of Germany, Romania and the United States filed their statements within the fixed time-limit, and the

Secretary-General submitted to the Court a dossier of documents pertaining to the matter.

Public sittings were held on 4 and 5 October. On 15 December, the Court delivered an advisory opinion,[25] the operative paragraph of which read as follows:

> *The Court,*
>
> Unanimously,
>
> *Is of the opinion* that Article VI, Section 22, of the Convention on the Privileges and Immunities of the United Nations is applicable in the case of Mr. Dumitru Mazilu as a special rapporteur of the Sub-Commission on Prevention of Discrimination and Protection of Minorities.

Judges Oda, Evensen and Shahabuddeen appended separate opinions to the advisory opinion.

Other questions

Two international conferences held in the Hague in 1989 called for an expanded role for ICJ. In its declaration of 11 March,[26] the conference on global warming and the deterioration of the ozone layer emphasized the need for a UN environmental authority whose decisions would be subject to the control of the Court. The Hague Declaration adopted by the ministerial meeting of the Movement of Non-Aligned Countries on peace and the rule of law in international affairs (26-29 June)[27] called for the enhancement of the Court's role in the peaceful settlement of disputes. It emphasized the supremacy of international law in the preservation of peace and the promotion of justice, and requested the General Assembly to declare a decade of international law. On 17 November, the Assembly acted on the request in its **resolution 44/23**, declaring 1990-1999 the United Nations Decade of International Law, the main purposes of which were to promote methods for the peaceful settlement of disputes between States, including resort to ICJ, as well as respect for, development and dissemination of international law.

On 28 February,[28] the USSR informed the Assembly that it had, as of 10 February 1989, withdrawn its previous reservations and accepted the compulsory jurisdiction of the Court with respect to the following international treaties: the 1948 Convention on the Prevention and Punishment of the Crime of Genocide; the 1949 Convention for the Suppression of the Traffic in Persons and of the Exploitation of the Prostitution of Others; the 1952 Convention on the Political Rights of Women; the 1965 International Convention on the Elimination of All Forms of Racial Discrimination; the 1979 Convention on the Elimination of All Forms of Discrimination against Women; and the 1984 Convention against Torture and Other Cruel, Inhuman or Degrading Treatment or Punishment.

On 11 April,[29] the Byelorussian SSR recognized the compulsory jurisdiction of the Court over the same treaties.

Organizational questions

Vacancy in the Court

The Secretary-General, on 20 December 1988,[30] informed the Security Council of the death, on 11 December, of Judge Nagendra Singh, and of the resulting vacancy in the Court. The procedure for nominating and electing a candidate in the General Assembly and the Security Council was outlined in the Secretary-General's memorandum[31] of 12 April 1989. On 6 April, the Secretary-General, in accordance with the Statute of the Court, submitted to the Assembly and the Council a list of candidates[32] for the vacancy nominated by national groups, along with their curricula vitae.[33] The list was subsequently expanded on 17 April[34] and revised on 18 April.[35]

Elections to the Court

On 9 January 1989, the Security Council unanimously adopted **resolution 627(1989)**.

> *The Security Council,*
>
> *Noting with regret* the death of Judge Nagendra Singh on 11 December 1988,
>
> *Noting further* that a vacancy in the International Court of Justice for the remainder of the term of office of the deceased judge has thus occurred and must be filled in accordance with the terms of the Statute of the Court,
>
> *Noting* that, in accordance with Article 14 of the Statute, the date of the election to fill the vacancy shall be fixed by the Security Council,
>
> *Decides* that the election to fill the vacancy shall take place on 18 April 1989 at a meeting of the Security Council and at a meeting of the forty-third session of the General Assembly.

Security Council resolution 627(1989)

9 January 1989   Meeting 2838   Adopted unanimously

Draft prepared in consultations among Council members (S/20374)

By a Security Council decision of 18 April 1989, and by General Assembly **decision 43/327** of the same date, Raghunandan Swarup Pathak was elected to fill the vacancy on the Court.

Trust Fund to assist in the settlement of disputes

At a meeting of the General Assembly on 1 November 1989,[36] the Secretary-General announced the establishment of his Trust Fund to assist States in the settlement of disputes through ICJ, which was intended to provide financial assistance to States for expenses incurred in a dispute submitted to the Court by way of a Special Agreement, or in the execution of a Judgment resulting from such an Agreement. The Secretary-General appealed to all parties concerned to make financial contributions to the Fund. The United Kingdom and Senegal formally supported the announcement, and the Court took note of it in its 1989/90 report.[2]

Publications of the Court

In November 1987, the General Assembly's Fifth (Administrative and Budgetary) Committee considered a 1986 Joint Inspection Unit (JIU) report on the possibility of publishing the Court's judgments and advisory opinions in UN official languages other than English and French (the official languages of the Court) at no additional cost.[37] Pursuant to a 1987 resolution of the Assembly,[38] the Secretary-General submitted, on 23 October 1989, the Court's and his comments[39] on the matter.

The Court stated its agreement with the proposal, to publish its judgments in other languages, given proper means and available resources. It opposed, however, some of the recommendations contained in the JIU report, such as the omission of separate or dissenting opinions, limiting the number of copies to be published, and other changes to the existing system, which ICJ considered detrimental. Consequently, the Secretary-General expressed his intention not to implement the JIU recommendations. In December, the General Assembly took note of the Secretary-General's comments in its **resolution 44/201 A, section II**.

REFERENCES

[1]A/44/4. [2]A/45/4. [3]YUN 1984, p. 1084. [4]YUN 1986, p. 981. [5]YUN 1987, p. 1047. [6]YUN 1988, p. 793. [7]YUN 1986, p. 983. [8]YUN 1988, p. 794. [9]*Case concerning Border and Transborder Armed Actions (Nicaragua v. Honduras), Order of 21 April 1989*, I.C.J. Sales No. 550. [10]*Ibid., Order of 31 August 1989*, I.C.J. Sales No. 564. [11]A/44/872-S/21019. [12]*Case concerning Border and Transborder Armed Actions (Nicaragua v. Honduras), Order of 14 December 1989*, I.C.J. Sales No. 572. [13]YUN 1988, p. 795. [14]*Case concerning the Aerial Incident of 3 July 1988 (Islamic Republic of Iran v. United States of America), Order of 13 December 1989*, I.C.J. Sales No. 570. [15]*Case concerning Certain Phosphate Lands in Nauru (Nauru v. Australia), Order of 18 July 1989*, I.C.J. Sales No. 561. [16]*Case concerning the Arbitral Award of 31 July 1989 (Guinea-Bissau v. Senegal), Order of 1 November 1989*, I.C.J. Sales No. 566. [17]YUN 1986, p. 984. [18]YUN 1987, p. 1048. [19]*Case concerning the Land, Island and Maritime Frontier Dispute (El Salvador/Honduras), Order of 12 January 1989*, I.C.J. Sales No. 549. [20]*Ibid., Order of 13 December 1989*, I.C.J. Sales No. 569. [21]*Ibid., Composition of Chamber, Order of 13 December 1989*, I.C.J. Sales No. 571. [22]YUN 1987, p. 1048. [23]*Case concerning Elettronica Sicula S.p.A. (ELSI)(United States of America v. Italy), Judgment of 20 July 1989*, I.C.J. Sales No. 562. [24]*Case concerning the Applicability of Article VI, Section 22, of the Convention on the Privileges and Immunities of the United Nations, Order of 14 June 1989*, I.C.J. Sales No. 552. [25]*Ibid., Advisory Opinion of 15 June 1989*, I.C.J. Sales No. 573. [26]A/44/340-E/1989/120. [27]A/44/191. [28]A/44/171. [29]A/44/238 & Corr.1. [30]S/20340. [31]A/43/1001-S/20551. [32]A/43/1002-S/20552. [33]A/43/1003-S/20553. [34]A/43/1006-S/20593. [35]A/43/1002/Rev.1-S/20552/Rev.1. [36]A/44/PV.43. [37]YUN 1987, p. 1050. [38]*Ibid.*, GA res. 42/225, sect.IV, 21 Dec. 1987. [39]A/C.5/44/13.

OTHER PUBLICATIONS

International Court of Justice: Reports of Judgments, Advisory Opinions and Orders, Index 1989, I.C.J. Sales No. 586. *International Court of Justice Yearbook 1988-1989*, No. 43, I.C.J. Sales No. 568. *Bibliography of the International Court of Justice*, No. 43, 1989, I.C.J. Sales No. 583.

Chapter II

Legal aspects of international political relations

Continuing its efforts to develop legal measures for promoting friendly international political relations, the General Assembly in December 1989 again urged States to observe and promote the 1982 Manila Declaration on the Peaceful Settlement of International Disputes and stressed the need to settle such disputes through progressive development and codification of international law and through enhancing the effectiveness of the United Nations in this field. The Assembly commended the Special Committee on the Charter of the United Nations and on the Strengthening of the Role of the Organization for completion of the draft on resort to a commission of good offices, mediation or conciliation within the United Nations, and decided that it should be brought to the attention of States. Also in December, the Assembly invited the International Law Commission (ILC) to continue its elaboration of the draft Code of Crimes against the Peace and Security of Mankind, including the elaboration of a list of crimes.

The Assembly adopted and opened for signature and ratification or accession the International Convention against the Recruitment, Use, Financing and Training of Mercenaries. It condemned all acts of terrorism, called on States to fulfil their obligations under international law to refrain from participating in terrorist acts and urged them to take effective measures for the elimination of international terrorism. It further called for the release of all hostages and abducted persons and called on States to use their political influence, in accordance with the Charter of the United Nations and international law, to secure their release.

In July, the Security Council had likewise condemned all acts of hostage-taking and abduction and demanded the immediate safe release of all hostages and abducted persons. The Council also condemned all acts of unlawful interference against the security of civil aviation and called upon States to cooperate in devising and implementing measures to prevent acts of terrorism, including those involving explosives. It urged the International Civil Aviation Organization to intensify its work on devising an international régime for the marking of plastic or sheet explosives for the purpose of detection.

ILC continued in 1989 to consider draft articles on the law of the non-navigational uses of international watercourses.

Maintenance of international peace and security

In accordance with a General Assembly resolution of 1988,[1] the Special Committee on the Charter of the United Nations and on the Strengthening of the Role of the Organization met in New York from 27 March to 14 April 1989[2] and accorded priority to the question of the maintenance of international peace and security. It additionally devoted attention to the rationalization of procedures of the United Nations (see PART FIVE, Chapter V). The Committee further examined the peaceful settlement of disputes between States and the progress report of the Secretary-General on the elaboration of the draft handbook on the peaceful settlement of disputes between States.

Peaceful settlement of disputes between States

The General Assembly considered again in 1989 the peaceful settlement of disputes. In December, it urged States to observe the provisions of the 1982 Manila Declaration on the Peaceful Settlement of International Disputes.[3] The Assembly commended the Special Committee on the Charter of the United Nations and on the Strengthening of the Role of the Organization for completion of the draft on the resort to a commission of good offices, mediation or conciliation within the United Nations.

Special Committee consideration. The Special Committee on the Charter of the United Nations and on the Strengthening of the Role of the Organization, at its March/April 1989 session,[2] continued work on the peaceful settlement of disputes. Its open-ended Working Group considered a proposal contained in a working paper[4] on the resort to a commission of good offices, mediation or conciliation within the United Nations. First introduced in 1983 by Nigeria, the Philippines and Romania and revised by Romania in 1987[5] and 1988,[6] the proposal for a commission[7] had been under Committee consideration each year since 1983.

As a result of the 1989 meetings and consultations, the Special Committee completed its consideration of the proposal. There was general agreement that the discussions had contributed to a better understanding of the importance and usefulness of good offices, mediation or conciliation as means for the settlement of disputes. The Committee was of the opinion that States should consider the proposal as useful guidance and recommended that the General Assembly bring it to the attention of States.

The Committee further examined the progress report of the Secretary-General on preparation of a draft handbook on the peaceful settlement of disputes between States.[(8)] The report, introduced by the Legal Counsel on 3 April, gave information on a 1988 meeting under his chairmanship of the Consultative Group composed of competent individuals from among permanent missions of States Members of the United Nations, where a further portion of the draft handbook dealing with arbitration, prepared by the Secretariat, was reviewed.

Report of the Secretary-General. The Secretary-General, as requested by the General Assembly in 1988,[(9)] submitted in August 1989 a report with a later addendum[(10)] containing replies received from nine Member States, eight international intergovernmental organizations and a communication from the International Law Association on the implementation of the Manila Declaration on the Peaceful Settlement of International Disputes and on ways and means of increasing its effectiveness.

GENERAL ASSEMBLY ACTION

On 4 December 1989, the General Assembly, on the recommendation of the Sixth Committee, adopted **resolution 44/31** by recorded vote.

Peaceful settlement of disputes between States

The General Assembly,

Having examined the item entitled "Peaceful settlement of disputes between States",

Recalling its resolution 37/10 of 15 November 1982, by which it approved the Manila Declaration on the Peaceful Settlement of International Disputes, annexed thereto,

Recalling also its resolutions 38/131 of 19 December 1983, 39/79 of 13 December 1984, 40/68 of 11 December 1985, 41/74 of 3 December 1986, 42/150 of 7 December 1987 and 43/163 of 9 December 1988,

Recalling further its resolution 43/51 of 5 December 1988, by which it approved the Declaration on the Prevention and Removal of Disputes and Situations Which May Threaten International Peace and Security and on the Role of the United Nations in this Field, annexed thereto,

Considering that the world political climate has improved and that, although sources of disputes and tension in international relations still remain, including the use of force and the threat thereof, encouraging progress has been made towards finding peaceful solutions to regional and global problems,

Taking into account the need to exert the utmost effort in order to settle any situations and disputes between States on the basis of sovereign equality and exclusively by peaceful means, in conformity with the Charter of the United Nations, and to avoid any military actions and hostilities against other States, which can only make more difficult the solution of existing problems,

Considering that the question of the peaceful settlement of disputes should represent one of the central concerns for States and for the United Nations and that efforts for strengthening the process of peaceful settlement of disputes should be continued,

Emphasizing the responsibility of every State for the promotion of a policy of respect for the national independence and sovereignty of other States, non-interference in internal affairs, and good understanding and co-operation, which is a basic requirement for reducing tension and for establishing a climate of peace and mutual confidence in the world,

Bearing in mind the decision in its resolution 44/23 of 17 November 1989 to proclaim the period 1990-1999 the United Nations Decade of International Law, which will contribute to the strengthening of all means of peaceful settlement of disputes between States,

Taking note with interest of the report of the Secretary-General, submitted in accordance with its resolution 43/163, which contains useful opinions, proposals and considerations for a broader implementation of the Manila Declaration,

1. *Again urges* all States to observe and promote in good faith the provisions of the Manila Declaration on the Peaceful Settlement of International Disputes in the settlement of their international disputes;

2. *Stresses* the need to continue efforts to strengthen the process of the peaceful settlement of disputes through progressive development and codification of international law and through enhancing the effectiveness of the United Nations in this field;

3. *Calls upon* Member States to make full use, in accordance with the Charter of the United Nations, of the framework provided by the United Nations for the peaceful settlement of disputes and international problems;

4. *Requests* the Secretary-General to submit to the General Assembly at its forty-fifth session a further report containing the replies of Member States, relevant United Nations bodies and specialized agencies, regional intergovernmental organizations and interested international legal bodies on the implementation of the Manila Declaration and on ways and means of increasing the effectiveness of this instrument;

5. *Decides* that the question of the peaceful settlement of disputes between States shall be considered at its forty-fifth session as a separate agenda item, in conjunction with the item of the provisional agenda entitled "Report of the Special Committee on the Charter of the United Nations and on the Strengthening of the Role of the Organization".

General Assembly resolution 44/31

4 December 1989   Meeting 72   131-0-21 (recorded vote)

Approved by Sixth Committee (A/44/764) by recorded vote (103-0-21), 22 November (meeting 46); 59-nation draft (A/C.6/44/L.7), orally revised; agenda item 141.

Sponsors: Afghanistan, Albania, Angola, Bahrain, Bangladesh, Barbados, Benin, Bolivia, Botswana, Burkina Faso, Burundi, Cameroon, Cape Verde, Central African Republic, Colombia, Congo, Costa Rica, Cuba, Cyprus, Democratic Yemen, Ecuador, Ghana, Guatemala, Guinea, Guyana, Haiti, Honduras, India, Indonesia, Lesotho, Liberia, Libyan Arab Jamahiriya, Madagascar, Malaysia, Mali, Mauritius, Mozambique, Myanmar, Nepal, Nicaragua, Niger, Nigeria, Pakistan, Panama, Paraguay, Philippines, Romania, Rwanda, Saint Lucia, Sierra Leone, Somalia, Sri Lanka, Sudan, Suriname, Swaziland, Togo, Trinidad and Tobago, Uganda, Uruguay.

Meeting numbers. GA 44th session: 6th Committee 7-15, 44, 46; plenary 72.

Recorded vote in Assembly as follows:

In favour: Afghanistan, Albania, Algeria, Angola, Antigua and Barbuda, Argentina, Austria, Bahamas, Bahrain, Bangladesh, Barbados, Benin, Bhutan, Bolivia, Botswana, Brazil, Brunei Darussalam, Bulgaria, Burkina Faso, Burundi, Byelorussian SSR, Cameroon, Cape Verde, Central African Republic, Chad, Chile, China, Colombia, Congo, Costa Rica, Côte d'Ivoire, Cuba, Cyprus, Czechoslovakia, Democratic Kampuchea, Democratic Yemen, Djibouti, Dominican Republic, Ecuador, Egypt, Equatorial Guinea, Ethiopia, Fiji, Gabon, Gambia, German Democratic Republic, Ghana, Greece, Grenada, Guatemala, Guinea, Guinea-Bissau, Guyana, Haiti, India, Indonesia, Iran, Iraq, Ireland, Jamaica, Jordan, Kenya, Kuwait, Lao People's Democratic Republic, Lebanon, Lesotho, Liberia, Libyan Arab Jamahiriya, Madagascar, Malawi, Malaysia, Maldives, Mali, Malta, Mauritania, Mauritius, Mexico, Mongolia, Morocco, Mozambique, Myanmar, Nepal, New Zealand, Nicaragua, Niger, Nigeria, Oman, Pakistan, Panama, Papua New Guinea, Paraguay, Peru, Philippines, Poland, Qatar, Romania, Rwanda, Saint Lucia, Saint Vincent and the Grenadines, Samoa, Sao Tome and Principe, Saudi Arabia, Senegal, Seychelles, Sierra Leone, Singapore, Solomon Islands, Somalia, Sri Lanka, Sudan, Suriname, Swaziland, Syrian Arab Republic, Thailand, Togo, Trinidad and Tobago, Tunisia, Uganda, Ukrainian SSR, USSR, United Arab Emirates, United Republic of Tanzania, Uruguay, Vanuatu, Venezuela, Viet Nam, Yemen, Yugoslavia, Zaire, Zambia, Zimbabwe.

Against: None.

Abstaining: Australia, Belgium, Canada, Denmark, Finland, France, Germany, Federal Republic of, Hungary, Iceland, Israel, Italy, Japan, Luxembourg, Netherlands, Norway, Portugal, Spain, Sweden, Turkey, United Kingdom, United States.

Amendments[11] to the draft resolution were rejected by recorded votes in the Sixth Committee.[12] Introduced by Denmark and sponsored by Australia, Belgium, Canada, Denmark, Finland, France, the Federal Republic of Germany, Hungary, Iceland, Italy, Japan, the Netherlands, Norway, Portugal, Spain, Sweden and the United Kingdom, the amendments would have replaced the fifth preambular paragraph by ''*Welcoming* the growing tendency to settle regional conflicts by peaceful means,''; deleted operative paragraph 4; and replaced operative paragraph 5 by a new operative paragraph 4. The new operative paragraph 4 would have read as follows: ''4. *Decides,* in view of General Assembly resolution 44/23 of 17 November 1989, that the question of the peaceful settlement of disputes between States will be examined in the framework of the United Nations Decade of International Law''.

Explaining its vote in the Assembly, Finland, on behalf of the five Nordic countries—Denmark, Iceland, Norway, Sweden and Finland—stated that they abstained in the voting on the draft resolution because of voting results on its co-sponsored amendments in the Sixth Committee. Since the amendments could not be adopted, they consequently abstained in the voting on the draft as a whole.

GENERAL ASSEMBLY ACTION

On 4 December, on the recommendation of the Sixth Committee, the General Assembly adopted **decision 44/415** without vote.

Resort to a commission of good offices, mediation or conciliation within the United Nations

At its 72nd plenary meeting, on 4 December 1989, the General Assembly, on the recommendation of the Sixth

Committee, commended the Special Committee on the Charter of the United Nations and on the Strengthening of the Role of the Organization for the completion of the work on the draft document on resort to a commission of good offices, mediation or conciliation within the United Nations, and decided that the present decision, to which that document is annexed, should be brought to the attention of States so that it might become generally known.

ANNEX
Resort to a commission of good offices, mediation or conciliation within the United Nations

States parties to disputes may wish to avail themselves of the possibility to resort to third-party assistance in the form of a commission of good offices, mediation or conciliation in order to settle their disputes by peaceful means. In doing so, they may be guided by the following:

1. Resort to a commission of good offices, mediation or conciliation within the United Nations may be considered by States as a procedure at their disposal for the peaceful settlement of international disputes in accordance with the provisions of the Charter of the United Nations.

2. Such a commission may be established for each particular case, in accordance with modalities described below, through the agreement of the States parties to a dispute, or, with their agreement, on the basis of a recommendation of the Security Council, or of the General Assembly or following the contacts of the States parties to a dispute with the Secretary-General. Other modalities and conditions may also be agreed upon by the States parties to a dispute for the establishment of such a commission.

3. When the States parties to a dispute accept to resort to a commission of good offices, mediation or conciliation as described in paragraph 2 above, the designation of members of the commission is proceeded with.

4. For each particular case the commission of good offices, mediation or conciliation may be constituted of persons nominated by up to three States, which are not parties to the dispute concerned.

Such States will be designated by the States parties to the dispute or, with their agreement, as the case may be, by the President of the Security Council or by the President of the General Assembly or by the Secretary-General.

5. Each designated State will appoint, upon approval by the States parties to the dispute, a highly qualified person, with adequate experience, who will act in the commission in his individual capacity.

The chairman of the commission will be selected from among its members by the States parties to the dispute. They may also agree in a particular case that the chairman be appointed by the Secretary-General.

6. The proceedings of the commission may take place at United Nations Headquarters in New York, or in any other place agreed upon by the States parties to the dispute.

7. After taking note of the elements of the respective dispute, on the basis of submissions made by the States parties and, as appropriate, of information provided by the Secretary-General, the commission in performing its good offices functions will seek to bring the parties to enter immediately into direct negotiations for the settlement of the dispute, or to resume such

negotiations or to resort to another means of peaceful settlement.

If the States parties to the dispute so request, the commission will seek to establish the aspects on which the States parties agree, as well as their differences of opinion and perception, and to elucidate the elements related to the dispute with a view to making suggestions for the beginning or the resuming of negotiations, including their framework and stages, as well as problems to solve.

8. If the States parties to the dispute request the commission, at any time, to mediate, the commission will offer to the parties proposals which it deems adequate for facilitating the negotiations and seeking through mediation to bring closer their positions until an agreement is reached.

9. The States parties to the dispute may agree at any moment of the procedure to entrust the commission with functions of conciliation. The States parties to the dispute determine the legal basis on which the commission should perform its functions. If such a basis is not determined, the commission should be guided mainly by the rights and duties of States resulting from the Charter and by the applicable principles of international law. In performing its functions, the commission formulates the terms which it deems adequate for the amicable settlement of the dispute and submits them to the parties.

The States parties to the dispute will be requested to pronounce themselves on these terms within a period of time established by the commission, which may be prolonged if the States parties to the dispute deem it necessary.

10. A period of time during which the commission should discharge its mission may be established by the States parties to the dispute or, where appropriate, following their contacts with the Secretary-General.

11. The States parties to the dispute may wish that the commission work in confidentiality. As long as the commission continues its efforts, no statement will be made public on its activity without the agreement of the States parties to the dispute.

12. The States parties to the dispute may wish that, upon conclusion of the commission's activity, the commission prepare a report and communicate it to them. The States parties to the dispute will decide if the report is to be made public.

Where appropriate, the commission may submit a report to the United Nations organ concerned in the form accepted by the States parties to the dispute.

13. Unless otherwise provided, any expenses of the commission shall be borne by the States parties to the dispute. They may request the Secretary-General to provide the commission with reasonable assistance and facilities as it may require.

14. The States parties to the dispute, as well as other States, shall act in accordance with the purposes and principles of the Charter and shall refrain from any action whatsoever which may aggravate the situation, endanger the maintenance of international peace and security or make more difficult or impede the peaceful settlement of the dispute.

15. Nothing in the present document shall be construed as prejudicing in any manner the provisions of the Charter, in particular those relating to the peaceful settlement of disputes.

General Assembly decision 44/415

Adopted without vote

Approved by Sixth Committee (A/44/768) without vote, 21 November (meeting 44); draft by Chairman (A/C.6/44/L.15); agenda item 146.
Meeting numbers. GA 44th session: 6th Committee 7-15, 44; plenary 72.

Draft code of crimes against peace and security

In 1989, at its forty-first session from 2 May to 21 July,[13] the International Law Commission (ILC) continued examining the draft Code of Crimes against the Peace and Security of Mankind. ILC in 1982 had resumed work on the topic,[14] whose title in English had been amended by the Assembly in 1987,[15] replacing the word "offences" by "crimes". The draft Code, originally prepared by ILC in 1954[16] in response to a 1947 Assembly request,[17] defined crimes under international law for which the responsible individual was to be punished.

ILC consideration. ILC discussed in 1989 the seventh report by its Special Rapporteur on the draft Code, Doudou Thiam (Senegal).[18] The report contained in particular two draft articles respectively entitled "War crimes" and "Crimes against humanity". The Commission referred both articles to its Drafting Committee. ILC provisionally adopted, on the recommendation of the Drafting Committee, three new articles on the topic, with commentaries thereto for inclusion in part II of the draft devoted to crimes against peace, namely article 13, "Threat of aggression"; article 14, "Intervention"; and article 15, "Colonial domination and other forms of alien domination".

The three articles provisionally adopted in 1989 were transmitted to the General Assembly by the Secretary-General.[19]

In **resolution 44/35** on the work of ILC, the Assembly recommended that, taking into account the comments of Governments, ILC should continue its work on the topic.

Report of the Secretary-General. The Secretary-General submitted to the General Assembly in August 1989 a report[20] containing replies from four Governments in response to the Assembly's 1988 invitation[21] for views on the 1983 conclusions of ILC.[22]

GENERAL ASSEMBLY ACTION

On 4 December, on the recommendation of the Sixth Committee, the General Assembly adopted **resolution 44/32** by recorded vote.

Draft Code of Crimes against the Peace and Security of Mankind

The General Assembly,

Mindful of Article 13, paragraph 1 *a*, of the Charter of the United Nations, which provides that the General Assembly shall initiate studies and make recommendations for the purpose of encouraging the progressive development of international law and its codification,

Recalling its resolution 177(II) of 21 November 1947, by which it directed the International Law Commission to prepare a draft code of offences against the peace and security of mankind,

Having considered the draft Code of Offences against the Peace and Security of Mankind prepared by the Commission and submitted to the General Assembly in 1954,

Reaffirming its belief that the elaboration of a code of offences against the peace and security of mankind could contribute to strengthening international peace and security and thus to promoting and implementing the purposes and principles set forth in the Charter,

Recalling also its resolution 36/106 of 10 December 1981, in which it invited the Commission to resume its work with a view to elaborating the draft Code and to examine it with the required priority in order to review it, taking into account the results achieved by the process of the progressive development of international law,

Bearing in mind that the Commission should fulfil its task on the basis of early elaboration of draft articles thereof,

Having considered chapter III of the report of the Commission on the work of its forty-first session,

Taking note of the report of the Secretary-General on the subject,

Taking into account the views expressed during the debate on this item at its forty-fourth session,

Recognizing the importance and urgency of the subject,

1. *Invites* the International Law Commission to continue its work on the elaboration of the draft Code of Crimes against the Peace and Security of Mankind, including the elaboration of a list of crimes, taking into account the progress made at its forty-first session, as well as the views expressed during the forty-fourth session of the General Assembly;

2. *Notes* the approach currently envisaged by the Commission in dealing with the judicial authority to be assigned for the implementation of the provisions of the draft Code, and encourages the Commission to explore further all possible alternatives on the question;

3. *Requests* the Secretary-General to continue to seek the views of Member States regarding the conclusions contained in paragraph 69 *(c)* (i) of the Commission's report on the work of its thirty-fifth session;

4. *Also requests* the Secretary-General to include the views received from Member States in accordance with paragraph 3 of the present resolution in a report to be submitted to the General Assembly at its forty-fifth session;

5. *Decides* to include in the provisional agenda of its forty-fifth session the item entitled "Draft Code of Crimes against the Peace and Security of Mankind", to be considered in conjunction with the examination of the report of the Commission.

General Assembly resolution 44/32

4 December 1989   Meeting 72   133-5-14 (recorded vote)

Approved by Sixth Committee (A/44/765) by recorded vote (95-5-13), 21 November (meeting 45); 25-nation draft (A/C.6/44/L.11); agenda item 142.
Sponsors: Algeria, Angola, Bulgaria, Cameroon, Cape Verde, Chad, Cuba, Cyprus, Czechoslovakia, Ethiopia, German Democratic Republic, Ghana, Guinea, Jamaica, Kenya, Madagascar, Mali, Mongolia, Philippines, Poland, Romania, Rwanda, Senegal, Tunisia, Viet Nam.
Meeting numbers. GA 44th session: 6th Committee 24-38, 45; plenary 72.

Recorded vote in Assembly as follows:

In favour: Afghanistan, Albania, Algeria, Angola, Antigua and Barbuda, Argentina, Australia, Austria, Bahamas, Bahrain, Bangladesh, Barbados, Benin, Bhutan, Bolivia, Botswana, Brazil, Brunei Darussalam, Bulgaria, Burkina Faso, Burundi, Byelorussian SSR, Cameroon, Cape Verde, Central African Republic, Chad, Chile, China, Colombia, Congo, Costa Rica, Côte d'Ivoire, Cuba, Cyprus, Czechoslovakia, Democratic Kampuchea, Democratic Yemen, Djibouti, Dominican Republic, Ecuador, Egypt, Equatorial Guinea, Ethiopia, Fiji, Gabon, Gambia, German Democratic Republic, Ghana, Greece, Grenada, Guatemala, Guinea, Guinea-Bissau, Guyana, Haiti, Hungary, India, Indonesia, Iran, Iraq, Ireland, Jamaica, Jordan, Kenya, Kuwait, Lao People's Democratic Republic, Lebanon, Lesotho, Liberia, Libyan Arab Jamahiriya, Madagascar, Malawi, Malaysia, Maldives, Mali, Malta, Mauritania, Mauritius, Mexico, Mongolia, Morocco, Mozambique, Myanmar, Nepal, New Zealand, Nicaragua, Niger, Nigeria, Oman, Pakistan, Panama, Papua New Guinea, Paraguay, Peru, Philippines, Poland, Qatar, Romania, Rwanda, Saint Lucia, Saint Vincent and the Grenadines, Samoa, Sao Tome and Principe, Saudi Arabia, Senegal, Seychelles, Sierra Leone, Singapore, Solomon Islands, Somalia, Sri Lanka, Sudan, Suriname, Swaziland, Syrian Arab Republic, Thailand, Togo, Trinidad and Tobago, Tunisia, Uganda, Ukrainian SSR, USSR, United Arab Emirates, United Republic of Tanzania, Uruguay, Vanuatu, Venezuela, Viet Nam, Yemen, Yugoslavia, Zaire, Zambia, Zimbabwe.

Against: France, Germany, Federal Republic of, Israel, United Kingdom, United States.

Abstaining: Belgium, Canada, Denmark, Finland, Iceland, Italy, Japan, Luxembourg, Netherlands, Norway, Portugal, Spain, Sweden, Turkey.

Draft convention against mercenaries

The General Assembly, in 1989, adopted and opened for signature and ratification or accession the International Convention against the Recruitment, Use, Financing and Training of Mercenaries, which was annexed to resolution 44/34. The question of the use of mercenaries as a means of impeding the exercise of the right of peoples to self-determination was also considered in a report[23] by the Special Rapporteur of the Commission on the question of mercenaries. The report, having examined, among other things, the situation in Angola, the Maldives and in Central America, recommended that United Nations principles and declarations on mercenary practices must be maintained and strengthened by the addition of provisions that may help to eliminate all types of such activity. It recommended that States include in their national legislation adequate sanctions against mercenary activities. States should be called upon to exercise the utmost vigilance and ensure that their territory and others under their control, as well as their nationals, were not used for the recruitment, assembly, financing, training and transit of mercenaries (see PART THREE, Chapter X).

Ad Hoc **Committee consideration.** The *Ad Hoc* Committee on the Drafting of an International Convention against the Recruitment, Use, Financing and Training of Mercenaries was convened in 1989 in accordance with a General Assembly resolution of 1988,[24] and met in New York from 30 January to 17 February.[25] Its Drafting Group, established in 1989, held 10 meetings between 31 January and 17 February and approved a set of draft articles for an international convention against the recruitment, use, financing and training of mercenaries.

On 4 December 1989, the General Assembly, on the recommendation of the Sixth Committee, adopted **resolution 44/34** without vote.

International Convention against the Recruitment, Use, Financing and Training of Mercenaries

The General Assembly,

Considering that the progressive development of international law and its codification contribute to the implementation of the purposes and principles set forth in Articles 1 and 2 of the Charter of the United Nations,

Mindful of the need to conclude, under the auspices of the United Nations, an international convention against the recruitment, use, financing and training of mercenaries,

Recalling its resolution 35/48 of 4 December 1980, by which it established the *Ad Hoc* Committee on the Drafting of an International Convention against the Recruitment, Use, Financing and Training of Mercenaries and requested it to elaborate at the earliest possible date an international convention to prohibit the recruitment, use, financing and training of mercenaries,

Having considered the draft convention prepared by the *Ad Hoc* Committee in pursuance of the above-mentioned resolution and finalized by the Working Group on the Drafting of an International Convention against the Recruitment, Use, Financing and Training of Mercenaries, which met during the forty-fourth session of the General Assembly,

Adopts and opens for signature and ratification or for accession the International Convention against the Recruitment, Use, Financing and Training of Mercenaries, the text of which is annexed to the present resolution.

ANNEX
International Convention against the Recruitment, Use, Financing and Training of Mercenaries

The States Parties to the present Convention,

Reaffirming the purposes and principles enshrined in the Charter of the United Nations and in the Declaration on Principles of International Law concerning Friendly Relations and Co-operation among States in accordance with the Charter of the United Nations,

Being aware of the recruitment, use, financing and training of mercenaries for activities which violate principles of international law, such as those of sovereign equality, political independence, territorial integrity of States and self-determination of peoples,

Affirming that the recruitment, use, financing and training of mercenaries should be considered as offences of grave concern to all States and that any person committing any of these offences should be either prosecuted or extradited,

Convinced of the necessity to develop and enhance international co-operation among States for the prevention, prosecution and punishment of such offences,

Expressing concern at new unlawful international activities linking drug traffickers and mercenaries in the perpetration of violent actions which undermine the constitutional order of States,

Also convinced that the adoption of a convention against the recruitment, use, financing and training of merce-

naries would contribute to the eradication of these nefarious activities and thereby to the observance of the purposes and principles enshrined in the Charter,

Cognizant that matters not regulated by such a convention continue to be governed by the rules and principles of international law,

Have agreed as follows:

Article 1

For the purposes of the present Convention,

1. A mercenary is any person who:

(a) Is specially recruited locally or abroad in order to fight in an armed conflict;

(b) Is motivated to take part in the hostilities essentially by the desire for private gain and, in fact, is promised, by or on behalf of a party to the conflict, material compensation substantially in excess of that promised or paid to combatants of similar rank and functions in the armed forces of that party;

(c) Is neither a national of a party to the conflict nor a resident of territory controlled by a party to the conflict;

(d) Is not a member of the armed forces of a party to the conflict; and

(e) Has not been sent by a State which is not a party to the conflict on official duty as a member of its armed forces.

2. A mercenary is also any person who, in any other situation:

(a) Is specially recruited locally or abroad for the purpose of participating in a concerted act of violence aimed at:

(i) Overthrowing a Government or otherwise undermining the constitutional order of a State; or

(ii) Undermining the territorial integrity of a State;

(b) Is motivated to take part therein essentially by the desire for significant private gain and is prompted by the promise or payment of material compensation;

(c) Is neither a national nor a resident of the State against which such an act is directed;

(d) Has not been sent by a State on official duty; and

(e) Is not a member of the armed forces of the State on whose territory the act is undertaken.

Article 2

Any person who recruits, uses, finances or trains mercenaries, as defined in article 1 of the present Convention, commits an offence for the purposes of the Convention.

Article 3

1. A mercenary, as defined in article 1 of the present Convention, who participates directly in hostilities or in a concerted act of violence, as the case may be, commits an offence for the purposes of the Convention.

2. Nothing in this article limits the scope of application of article 4 of the present Convention.

Article 4

An offence is committed by any person who:

(a) Attempts to commit one of the offences set forth in the present Convention;

(b) Is the accomplice of a person who commits or attempts to commit any of the offences set forth in the present Convention.

Article 5

1. States Parties shall not recruit, use, finance or train mercenaries and shall prohibit such activities in

accordance with the provisions of the present Convention.

2. States Parties shall not recruit, use, finance or train mercenaries for the purpose of opposing the legitimate exercise of the inalienable right of peoples to self-determination, as recognized by international law, and shall take, in conformity with international law, the appropriate measures to prevent the recruitment, use, financing or training of mercenaries for that purpose.

3. They shall make the offences set forth in the present Convention punishable by appropriate penalties which take into account the grave nature of those offences.

Article 6

States Parties shall co-operate in the prevention of the offences set forth in the present Convention, particularly by:

(*a*) Taking all practicable measures to prevent preparations in their respective territories for the commission of those offences within or outside their territories, including the prohibition of illegal activities of persons, groups and organizations that encourage, instigate, organize or engage in the perpetration of such offences;

(*b*) Co-ordinating the taking of administrative and other measures as appropriate to prevent the commission of those offences.

Article 7

States Parties shall co-operate in taking the necessary measures for the implementation of the present Convention.

Article 8

Any State Party having reason to believe that one of the offences set forth in the present Convention has been, is being or will be committed shall, in accordance with its national law, communicate the relevant information, as soon as it comes to its knowledge, directly or through the Secretary-General of the United Nations, to the States Parties affected.

Article 9

1. Each State Party shall take such measures as may be necessary to establish its jurisdiction over any of the offences set forth in the present Convention which are committed:

(*a*) In its territory or on board a ship or aircraft registered in that State;

(*b*) By any of its nationals or, if that State considers it appropriate, by those stateless persons who have their habitual residence in that territory.

2. Each State Party shall likewise take such measures as may be necessary to establish its jurisdiction over the offences set forth in articles 2, 3 and 4 of the present Convention in cases where the alleged offender is present in its territory and it does not extradite him to any of the States mentioned in paragraph 1 of this article.

3. The present Convention does not exclude any criminal jurisdiction exercised in accordance with national law.

Article 10

1. Upon being satisfied that the circumstances so warrant, any State Party in whose territory the alleged offender is present shall, in accordance with its laws, take him into custody or take such other measures to ensure his presence for such time as is necessary to ena-ble any criminal or extradition proceedings to be instituted. The State Party shall immediately make a preliminary inquiry into the facts.

2. When a State Party, pursuant to this article, has taken a person into custody or has taken such other measures referred to in paragraph 1 of this article, it shall notify without delay either directly or through the Secretary-General of the United Nations:

(*a*) The State Party where the offence was committed;

(*b*) The State Party against which the offence has been directed or attempted;

(*c*) The State Party of which the natural or juridical person against whom the offence has been directed or attempted is a national;

(*d*) The State Party of which the alleged offender is a national or, if he is a stateless person, in whose territory he has his habitual residence;

(*e*) Any other interested State Party which it considers it appropriate to notify.

3. Any person regarding whom the measures referred to in paragraph 1 of this article are being taken shall be entitled:

(*a*) To communicate without delay with the nearest appropriate representative of the State of which he is a national or which is otherwise entitled to protect his rights or, if he is a stateless person, the State in whose territory he has his habitual residence;

(*b*) To be visited by a representative of that State.

4. The provisions of paragraph 3 of this article shall be without prejudice to the right of any State Party having a claim to jurisdiction in accordance with article 9, paragraph 1 (*b*), to invite the International Committee of the Red Cross to communicate with and visit the alleged offender.

5. The State which makes the preliminary inquiry contemplated in paragraph 1 of this article shall promptly report its findings to the States referred to in paragraph 2 of this article and indicate whether it intends to exercise jurisdiction.

Article 11

Any person regarding whom proceedings are being carried out in connection with any of the offences set forth in the present Convention shall be guaranteed at all stages of the proceedings fair treatment and all the rights and guarantees provided for in the law of the State in question. Applicable norms of international law should be taken into account.

Article 12

The State Party in whose territory the alleged offender is found shall, if it does not extradite him, be obliged, without exception whatsoever and whether or not the offence was committed in its territory, to submit the case to its competent authorities for the purpose of prosecution, through proceedings in accordance with the laws of that State. Those authorities shall take their decision in the same manner as in the case of any other offence of a grave nature under the law of that State.

Article 13

1. States Parties shall afford one another the greatest measure of assistance in connection with criminal proceedings brought in respect of the offences set forth in the present Convention, including the supply of all evidence at their disposal necessary for the proceedings.

The law of the State whose assistance is requested shall apply in all cases.

2.   The provisions of paragraph 1 of this article shall not affect obligations concerning mutual judicial assistance embodied in any other treaty.

Article 14

The State Party where the alleged offender is prosecuted shall in accordance with its laws communicate the final outcome of the proceedings to the Secretary-General of the United Nations, who shall transmit the information to the other States concerned.

Article 15

1.   The offences set forth in articles 2, 3 and 4 of the present Convention shall be deemed to be included as extraditable offences in any extradition treaty existing between States Parties. States Parties undertake to include such offences as extraditable offences in every extradition treaty to be concluded between them.

2.   If a State Party which makes extradition conditional on the existence of a treaty receives a request for extradition from another State Party with which it has no extradition treaty, it may at its option consider the present Convention as the legal basis for extradition in respect of those offences. Extradition shall be subject to the other conditions provided by the law of the requested State.

3.   States Parties which do not make extradition conditional on the existence of a treaty shall recognize those offences as extraditable offences between themselves, subject to the conditions provided by the law of the requested State.

4.   The offences shall be treated, for the purpose of extradition between States Parties, as if they had been committed not only in the place in which they occurred but also in the territories of the States required to establish their jurisdiction in accordance with article 9 of the present Convention.

Article 16

The present Convention shall be applied without prejudice to:

(*a*)   The rules relating to the international responsibility of States;

(*b*)   The law of armed conflict and international humanitarian law, including the provisions relating to the status of combatant or of prisoner of war.

Article 17

1.   Any dispute between two or more States Parties concerning the interpretation or application of the present Convention which is not settled by negotiation shall, at the request of one of them, be submitted to arbitration. If, within six months from the date of the request for arbitration, the parties are unable to agree on the organization of the arbitration, any one of those parties may refer the dispute to the International Court of Justice by a request in conformity with the Statute of the Court.

2.   Each State may, at the time of signature or ratification of the present Convention or accession thereto, declare that it does not consider itself bound by paragraph 1 of this article. The other States Parties shall not be bound by paragraph 1 of this article with respect to any State Party which has made such a reservation.

3.   Any State Party which has made a reservation in accordance with paragraph 2 of this article may at any time withdraw that reservation by notification to the Secretary-General of the United Nations.

Article 18

1.   The present Convention shall be open for signature by all States until 31 December 1990 at United Nations Headquarters in New York.

2.   The present Convention shall be subject to ratification. The instruments of ratification shall be deposited with the Secretary-General of the United Nations.

3.   The present Convention shall remain open for accession by any State. The instruments of accession shall be deposited with the Secretary-General of the United Nations.

Article 19

1.   The present Convention shall enter into force on the thirtieth day following the date of deposit of the twenty-second instrument of ratification or accession with the Secretary-General of the United Nations.

2.   For each State ratifying or acceding to the Convention after the deposit of the twenty-second instrument of ratification or accession, the Convention shall enter into force on the thirtieth day after deposit by such State of its instrument of ratification or accession.

Article 20

1.   Any State Party may denounce the present Convention by written notification to the Secretary-General of the United Nations.

2.   Denunciation shall take effect one year after the date on which the notification is received by the Secretary-General of the United Nations.

Article 21

The original of the present Convention, of which the Arabic, Chinese, English, French, Russian and Spanish texts are equally authentic, shall be deposited with the Secretary-General of the United Nations, who shall send certified copies thereof to all States.

IN WITNESS WHEREOF the undersigned, being duly authorized thereto by their respective Governments, have signed the present Convention.

General Assembly resolution 44/34

4 December 1989   Meeting 72   Adopted without vote

Approved by Sixth Committee (A/44/766) without vote, 21 November (meeting 44); 5-nation draft (A/C.6/44/L.10); agenda item 144.
Sponsors: Democratic Yemen, Ethiopia, Italy, Suriname, Ukrainian SSR.
Meeting numbers. GA 44th session: 6th Committee 41, 42, 44; plenary 72.

In explanation of its position on the draft resolution, Nicaragua believed that the definition of mercenaries should not be confined to non-nationals of any given country. It was public knowledge that the world had seen a marked trend towards nationals of a country being contracted in large numbers by other countries to carry out mercenary activities from outside against their country of origin. Consequently, Nicaragua felt that the fact that the definition of mercenaries in the Convention did not include nationals whose very existence and activities depended on a foreign Power was a serious deficiency.

On 8 December, the Assembly adopted **resolution 44/81** on the use of mercenaries as a means to violate human rights and to impede the exercise of the right of peoples to self-determination.

Prevention of terrorism

The prevention of terrorism in all its aspects continued to be a concern of the United Nations in 1989. In December, the Assembly condemned all acts of terrorism and urged States to take effective measures for the elimination of international terrorism. It further called for the release of all hostages and abducted persons. The Security Council in July condemned all acts of hostage-taking and abduction and demanded the immediate safe release of those persons. It also condemned acts of unlawful interference against the security of civil aviation and called upon States to prevent acts of terrorism, including those involving explosives. The Council urged the International Civil Aviation Organization (ICAO) to intensify work on devising an international régime for the marking of plastic or sheet explosives for the purpose of detection.

Report of the Secretary-General. The Secretary-General submitted to the Assembly in August a report with a later addendum,[26] containing replies received from 13 Member States and six intergovernmental organizations in response to invitations in 1988 by the Secretary-General and the Legal Counsel, and as requested by the General Assembly in 1987.[27]

Annexed to the report was information, as at 15 August, on the state of signatures of, and ratifications of or accessions to, a number of international conventions relating to terrorism, including two adopted by the General Assembly for which the Secretary-General performed depositary functions: the 1973 Convention on the Prevention and Punishment of Crimes against Internationally Protected Persons, including Diplomatic Agents,[28] and the 1979 International Convention against the Taking of Hostages.[29] In 1989, the 1973 Convention was acceded to by Bhutan and Kuwait. The 1979 Convention was ratified by Haiti and acceded to by Côte d'Ivoire, Kuwait and Turkey. As at 31 December 1989, the two instruments had 76 and 70 parties, respectively.[30]

GENERAL ASSEMBLY ACTION

On 4 December, on the recommendation of the Sixth Committee, the General Assembly adopted **resolution 44/29** without vote.

Measures to prevent international terrorism which endangers or takes innocent human lives or jeopardizes fundamental freedoms and study of the underlying causes of those forms of terrorism and acts of violence which lie in misery, frustration, grievance and despair and which cause some people to sacrifice human lives, including their own, in an attempt to effect radical changes:
(a) **Report of the Secretary-General;**
(b) **Convening, under the auspices of the United Nations, of an international conference to define terrorism and to differentiate it from the struggle of peoples for national liberation**

The General Assembly,

Recalling its resolutions 3034(XXVII) of 18 December 1972, 31/102 of 15 December 1976, 32/147 of 16 December 1977, 34/145 of 17 December 1979, 36/109 of 10 December 1981, 38/130 of 19 December 1983, 40/61 of 9 December 1985 and 42/159 of 7 December 1987,

Recalling also the recommendations of the *Ad Hoc* Committee on International Terrorism contained in its report to the General Assembly at its thirty-fourth session,

Recalling further the Declaration on Principles of International Law concerning Friendly Relations and Co-operation among States in accordance with the Charter of the United Nations, the Declaration on the Strengthening of International Security, the Definition of Aggression and relevant instruments on international humanitarian law applicable in armed conflict,

Recalling moreover the existing international conventions relating to various aspects of the problem of international terrorism, *inter alia*, the Convention on Offences and Certain Other Acts Committed on Board Aircraft, signed at Tokyo on 14 September 1963, the Convention for the Suppression of Unlawful Seizure of Aircraft, signed at The Hague on 16 December 1970, the Convention for the Suppression of Unlawful Acts against the Safety of Civil Aviation, concluded at Montreal on 23 September 1971, the Convention on the Prevention and Punishment of Crimes against Internationally Protected Persons, including Diplomatic Agents, adopted in New York on 14 December 1973, the International Convention against the Taking of Hostages, adopted in New York on 17 December 1979, the Convention on the Physical Protection of Nuclear Material, adopted at Vienna on 3 March 1980, the Protocol for the Suppression of Unlawful Acts of Violence at Airports Serving International Civil Aviation, supplementary to the Convention for the Suppression of Unlawful Acts against the Safety of Civil Aviation, signed at Montreal on 24 February 1988, the Convention for the Suppression of Unlawful Acts against the Safety of Maritime Navigation, done at Rome on 10 March 1988, and the Protocol for the Suppression of Unlawful Acts against the Safety of Fixed Platforms located on the Continental Shelf, done at Rome on 10 March 1988,

Convinced that a policy of firmness and effective measures should be taken in accordance with international law in order that all acts, methods and practices of international terrorism may be brought to an end,

Noting the ongoing work within the International Civil Aviation Organization regarding research as to the detection of plastic or sheet explosives and the devising of an international régime for the marking of such explosives for the purposes of detection, and taking note of Security Council resolution 635(1989) of 14 June 1989 relating thereto,

Taking note of Security Council resolution 638(1989) of 31 July 1989 on the taking of hostages,

Deeply disturbed by the world-wide persistence of acts of international terrorism in all its forms, including those in which States are directly or indirectly involved, which endanger or take innocent lives, have a deleterious effect on international relations and may jeopardize the territorial integrity and security of States,

Calling attention to the growing connection between terrorist groups and drug traffickers,

Convinced of the importance of the observance by States of their obligations under the relevant international conventions to ensure that appropriate law-enforcement measures are taken in connection with the offences addressed in those conventions,

Convinced also of the importance of expanding and improving international co-operation among States, on a bilateral, regional and multilateral basis, which will contribute to the elimination of acts of international terrorism and their underlying causes and to the prevention and elimination of this criminal scourge,

Convinced further that international co-operation in combating and preventing terrorism will contribute to the strengthening of confidence among States, reduce tensions and create a better climate among them,

Mindful of the need to enhance the role of the United Nations and the relevant specialized agencies in combating international terrorism,

Mindful also of the necessity of maintaining and protecting the basic rights of, and guarantees for, the individual in accordance with the relevant international human rights instruments and generally accepted international standards,

Reaffirming the principle of self-determination of peoples as enshrined in the Charter of the United Nations,

Reaffirming also the inalienable right to self-determination and independence of all peoples under colonial and racist régimes and other forms of alien domination and foreign occupation, and upholding the legitimacy of their struggle, in particular the struggle of national liberation movements, in accordance with the purposes and principles of the Charter and the Declaration on Principles of International Law concerning Friendly Relations and Co-operation among States in accordance with the Charter of the United Nations,

Noting the efforts and important achievements of the International Civil Aviation Organization and the International Maritime Organization in promoting the security of international air and sea transport against acts of terrorism,

Recognizing that the effectiveness of the struggle against terrorism could be enhanced by the establishment of a generally agreed definition of international terrorism,

Taking into account the proposal made at its forty-second session to hold an international conference on international terrorism, as referred to in agenda item 139 (*b*) of the forty-fourth session,

Taking note of the report of the Secretary-General,

1. *Once again unequivocally condemns*, as criminal and unjustifiable, all acts, methods and practices of terrorism wherever and by whomever committed, including those which jeopardize friendly relations among States and their security;

2. *Deeply deplores* the loss of human lives which results from such acts of terrorism, as well as the pernicious impact of these acts on relations of co-operation among States;

3. *Calls upon* all States to fulfil their obligations under international law to refrain from organizing, instigating, assisting or participating in terrorist acts in other States, or acquiescing in or encouraging activities within their territory directed towards the commission of such acts;

4. *Urges* all States to fulfil their obligations under international law and take effective and resolute measures for the speedy and final elimination of international terrorism and to that end, in particular:

(*a*) To prevent the preparation and organization in their respective territories, for commission within or outside their territories, of terrorist and subversive acts directed against other States and their citizens;

(*b*) To ensure the apprehension and prosecution or extradition of perpetrators of terrorist acts;

(*c*) To endeavour to conclude special agreements to that effect on a bilateral, regional and multilateral basis;

(*d*) To co-operate with one another in exchanging relevant information concerning the prevention and combating of terrorism;

(*e*) To take promptly all steps necessary to implement the existing international conventions on this subject to which they are parties, including the harmonization of their domestic legislation with those conventions;

5. *Appeals* to all States that have not yet done so to consider becoming party to the international conventions relating to various aspects of international terrorism referred to in the preamble to the present resolution;

6. *Urges* all States, unilaterally and in co-operation with other States, as well as relevant United Nations organs, to contribute to the progressive elimination of the causes underlying international terrorism and to pay special attention to all situations, including colonialism, racism and situations involving mass and flagrant violations of human rights and fundamental freedoms and those involving alien domination and foreign occupation, that may give rise to international terrorism and may endanger international peace and security;

7. *Firmly calls* for the immediate and safe release of all hostages and abducted persons, wherever and by whomever they are being held;

8. *Calls upon* all States to use their political influence in accordance with the Charter of the United Nations and the principles of international law to secure the safe release of all hostages and abducted persons and to prevent the commission of acts of hostage-taking and abduction;

9. *Expresses concern* at the growing and dangerous links between terrorist groups, drug traffickers and their paramilitary gangs, which have resorted to all types of violence, thus endangering the constitutional order of States and violating basic human rights;

10. *Welcomes* the efforts undertaken by the International Civil Aviation Organization aimed at promoting universal acceptance of, and strict compliance with, international air-security conventions, and welcomes its recent adoption of the Protocol for the Suppression of

Unlawful Acts of Violence at Airports Serving International Civil Aviation;

11. *Also welcomes* the adoption by the International Maritime Organization of the Convention for the Suppression of Unlawful Acts against the Safety of Maritime Navigation and the Protocol for the Suppression of Unlawful Acts against the Safety of Fixed Platforms located on the Continental Shelf;

12. *Urges* the International Civil Aviation Organization to intensify its work on devising an international régime for the marking of plastic or sheet explosives for the purposes of detection;

13. *Requests* the other relevant specialized agencies and intergovernmental organizations, in particular the Universal Postal Union, the World Tourism Organization and the International Atomic Energy Agency, within their respective spheres of competence, to consider what further measures can usefully be taken to combat and eliminate terrorism;

14. *Requests* the Secretary-General to continue seeking the views of Member States on international terrorism in all its aspects and on ways and means of combating it, including the convening, under the auspices of the United Nations, of an international conference to deal with international terrorism in the light of the proposal referred to in the penultimate preambular paragraph of the present resolution;

15. *Also requests* the Secretary-General to seek the views of Member States on the ways and means of enhancing the role of the United Nations and the relevant specialized agencies in combating international terrorism, as well as on proposals made during the debate on this item in the Sixth Committee at the forty-fourth session of the General Assembly;

16. *Further requests* the Secretary-General to follow up, as appropriate, the implementation of the present resolution and to submit a report in this respect to the General Assembly at its forty-sixth session;

17. *Considers* that nothing in the present resolution could in any way prejudice the right to self-determination, freedom and independence, as derived from the Charter of the United Nations, of peoples forcibly deprived of that right referred to in the Declaration on Principles of International Law concerning Friendly Relations and Co-operation among States in accordance with the Charter of the United Nations, particularly peoples under colonial and racist régimes or other forms of alien domination, or the right of these peoples to struggle legitimately to this end and to seek and receive support in accordance with the principles of the Charter, the above-mentioned Declaration and the relevant General Assembly resolutions, including the present resolution;

18. *Decides* to include the item in the provisional agenda of its forty-sixth session.

General Assembly resolution 44/29

4 December 1989   Meeting 72   Adopted without vote

Approved by Sixth Committee (A/44/762) without vote, 1 December (meeting 48); draft by Chairman (A/C.6/44/L.22); agenda item 139.
Meeting numbers. GA 44th session: 6th Committee 17-23, 48; plenary 72.

Explaining its position on the draft resolution in the Assembly, Ghana said it had reservations on the insertion of the phrase ''and not justifiable'' in paragraph 1, because it could only lead to confusion in the absence of an agreed definition of who was a terrorist. It also reserved its position on the insertion of the word ''legitimately'' in the language of paragraph 17, which it considered inconsistent with the import of that paragraph. Ghana's intention was to draw a line between terrorist activities and the just fight of peoples under colonial domination for self-determination, freedom and independence.

Question of hostage-taking and abduction

The Security Council on 31 July considered the question of hostage-taking and abduction. The Council President made a statement, pointing out that the meeting took place under the shadow of recent events and the cruel reports that Lieutenant-Colonel Higgins, who served the United Nations on a peace-keeping mission in Lebanon, may have been murdered that day. This illustrated with the utmost clarity the necessity for effective international action on the subject of hostage-taking and abduction.

SECURITY COUNCIL ACTION

The Council, on the same day, unanimously adopted **resolution 638(1989)**.

The Security Council,

Deeply disturbed by the prevalence of incidents of hostage-taking and abduction, and the continued protracted incarceration of many of those held hostage,

Considering that the taking of hostages and abductions are offences of grave concern to all States and serious violations of international humanitarian law, having severe adverse consequences for the human rights of the victims and their families and for the promotion of friendly relations and co-operation among States,

Recalling its resolutions 579(1985) of 18 December 1985 and 618(1988) of 29 July 1988 condemning all acts of hostage-taking and abduction,

Bearing in mind the International Convention against the Taking of Hostages, adopted on 17 December 1979, the Convention on the Prevention and Punishment of Crimes against Internationally Protected Persons, including Diplomatic Agents, adopted on 14 December 1973, the Convention for the Suppression of Unlawful Acts against the Safety of Civil Aviation, signed on 23 September 1971, the Convention for the Suppression of Unlawful Seizure of Aircraft, signed on 16 December 1970, and other relevant conventions,

1. *Condemns unequivocally* all acts of hostage-taking and abduction;

2. *Demands* the immediate safe release of all hostages and abducted persons, wherever and by whomever they are being held;

3. *Calls upon* all States to use their political influence in accordance with the Charter of the United Nations and the principles of international law to secure the safe release of all hostages and abducted persons and to prevent the commission of acts of hostage-taking and abduction;

4.   *Expresses appreciation* for the efforts of the Secretary-General in seeking the release of all hostages and abducted persons and invites him to continue such efforts whenever so requested by a State;

5.   *Appeals* to all States that have not yet done so to consider becoming parties to the International Convention against the Taking of Hostages, the Convention on the Prevention and Punishment of Crimes against Internationally Protected Persons, including Diplomatic Agents, the Convention for the Suppression of Unlawful Acts against the Safety of Civil Aviation, the Convention for the Suppression of Unlawful Seizure of Aircraft and other relevant conventions;

6.   *Urges* the further development of international co-operation among States in devising and adopting effective measures which are in accordance with the rules of international law to facilitate the prevention, prosecution and punishment of all acts of hostage-taking and abduction as manifestations of terrorism.

Security Council resolution 638(1989)

31 July 1989   Meeting 2872   Adopted unanimously

2-nation draft (S/20757).
Sponsors: Canada, Finland.

Marking of plastic or sheet explosives for the purpose of detection

The Security Council on 14 June met to discuss the marking of plastic or sheet explosives for the purpose of detection.

SECURITY COUNCIL ACTION

The Council, on the same day, unanimously adopted **resolution 635(1989)**.

The Security Council,

Conscious of the implications of acts of terrorism for international security,

Deeply concerned by all acts of unlawful interference against international civil aviation,

Mindful of the important role of the United Nations in supporting and encouraging efforts by all States and intergovernmental organizations in preventing and eliminating all acts of terrorism, including those involving the use of explosives,

Determined to encourage the promotion of effective measures to prevent acts of terrorism,

Concerned about the ease with which plastic or sheet explosives can be used in acts of terrorism with little risk of detection,

Taking note of the International Civil Aviation Organization Council resolution of 16 February 1989, in which it urged its member States to expedite current research and development on detection of explosives and on security equipment,

1.   *Condemns* all acts of unlawful interference against the security of civil aviation;

2.   *Calls upon* all States to co-operate in devising and implementing measures to prevent all acts of terrorism, including those involving explosives;

3.   *Welcomes* the work already undertaken by the International Civil Aviation Organization, and by other international organizations, aimed at preventing and eliminating all acts of terrorism, in particular in the field of aviation security;

4.   *Urges* the International Civil Aviation Organization to intensify its work aimed at preventing all acts of terrorism against international civil aviation, and in particular its work on devising an international régime for the marking of plastic or sheet explosives for the purpose of detection;

5.   *Urges* all States, and in particular the producers of plastic or sheet explosives, to intensify research into means of making such explosives more easily detectable, and to co-operate in this endeavour;

6.   *Calls upon* all States to share the results of such research and co-operation with a view to devising, in the International Civil Aviation Organization and other competent international organizations, an international régime for the marking of plastic or sheet explosives for the purpose of detection.

Security Council resolution 635(1989)

14 June 1989   Meeting 2869   Adopted unanimously

Draft prepared in consultations among Council members (S/20690).

Draft articles on non-navigational uses of international watercourses

In 1989, ILC continued work on the law of the non-navigational uses of international watercourses,[13] as recommended by the General Assembly in 1988.[31] It discussed the matter on the basis of the fifth report by its Special Rapporteur, Stephen C. McCaffrey (United States),[32] which contained in particular two draft articles[33] respectively entitled "Water-related hazards, harmful conditions and other adverse effects" and "Water-related dangers and emergency situations". At the conclusion of its discussion, the Commission heard a presentation by the Special Rapporteur of the concluding section of his fifth report,[34] containing in particular two draft articles respectively entitled "Relationship between navigational and non-navigational uses; absence of priority among uses" and "Regulation of international watercourses". That section of the report was not discussed by the Commission for lack of time.

REFERENCES

(1) YUN 1988, p. 820, GA res. 43/170, 9 Dec. 1988. (2)A/44/33. (3)YUN 1982, p. 1372, GA res. 37/10, annex, 15 Nov. 1982. (4)A/AC.182/L.52/Rev.2. (5)YUN 1987, p. 1051. (6)YUN 1988, p. 798. (7)YUN 1983, p. 1106. (8)A/AC.182/L.61. (9)YUN 1988, p. 799, GA res. 43/163, 9 Dec. 1988. (10)A/44/460 & Add.1. (11)A/C.6/44/L.17. (12)A/44/764. (13)A/44/10. (14)YUN 1982, p. 1375. (15)YUN 1987, p. 1058, GA res. 42/151, 7 Dec. 1987. (16)YUN 1954, p. 411. (17)YUN 1947-48, p. 215, GA res. 177(II), 21 Nov. 1947. (18)A/CN.4/419 & Corr.1 & Add.1. (19)A/44/475. (20)A/44/465. (21)YUN 1988, p. 802, GA res. 43/164, 9 Dec. 1988. (22)YUN 1983, p. 1110, GA res. 38/132, 19 Dec. 1983. (23)A/44/526. (24)YUN 1988, p. 803, GA res. 43/168, 9 Dec. 1988. (25)A/44/43. (26)A/44/456 & Add.1. (27)YUN 1987, p. 1063, GA res. 42/159, 7 Dec. 1987. (28)YUN 1973, p. 775, GA res. 3166(XXVIII), annex, 14 Dec. 1973. (29)YUN 1979, p. 1144, GA res. 34/146, annex, 17 Dec. 1979. (30)*Multilateral Treaties Deposited with the Secretary-General: Status as at 31 December 1989* (ST/LEG/SER.E/8), Sales No. E.90.V.6. (31)YUN 1988, p. 832, GA res. 43/169, 9 Dec. 1988. (32)A/CN.4/421. (33)A/CN.4/421/Add.1. (34)A/CN.4/421/Add.2.

Chapter III

States and international law

In 1989, the United Nations continued to be involved in the promotion and development of international law governing States, as well as their international treaties and agreements.

The Secretary-General in November reported on measures to protect diplomatic and consular missions and representatives. The International Law Commission (ILC) continued its work on the status of the diplomatic courier and the diplomatic bag not accompanied by diplomatic courier. In December, the General Assembly expressed its appreciation to the Commission for its work and decided to hold consultations at its forty-fifth session to study draft articles on the matter (resolution 44/36). ILC also examined state responsibility, international liability for injurious consequences arising out of acts not prohibited by international law, jurisdictional immunities of States and their property, and relations between States and international organizations.

The Secretariat continued its depositary functions for agreements, conventions, and treaties deposited with the Secretary-General.

Diplomatic relations

Protection of diplomats

As at 31 December 1989, the number of parties to the various international instruments relating to the protection of diplomats and diplomatic and consular relations[1] was as follows: 153 States were parties to the 1961 Vienna Convention on Diplomatic Relations,[2] with South Africa ratifying in 1989; 42 States were parties to the Optional Protocol concerning acquisition of nationality;[3] and 54 States were parties to the Optional Protocol concerning the compulsory settlement of disputes,[3] with Bulgaria and Hungary having acceded in 1989.

The 1963 Vienna Convention on Consular Relations[4] had 126 parties, with the Byelorussian SSR, Bulgaria, Mongolia, South Africa, the Ukrainian SSR and the USSR acceding in 1989; 35 States were parties to the Optional Protocol concerning the acquisition of nationality,[5] with Bulgaria acceding in 1989, and 42 States were parties to the Optional Protocol concerning the com-

pulsory settlement of disputes,[5] with Bulgaria and Hungary acceding in 1989.

The 1973 Convention on the Prevention and Punishment of Crimes against Internationally Protected Persons, including Diplomatic Agents,[6] had 76 States parties, with Bhutan and Kuwait having acceded in 1989.

Report of the Secretary-General. Pursuant to General Assembly resolutions of 1987[7] and 1988,[8] the Secretary-General requested States to submit information on serious violations of the protection, security and safety of diplomatic and consular missions and representatives, as well as to inform him of their views on any measures needed to enhance such protection and safety. In November, the Secretary-General submitted a report[9] to the Assembly which contained the reports and views received from States, as well as a list of States parties, as at 1 October 1989, to the relevant conventions (see above).

Austria reported that, on 28 March 1989, demonstrators in front of the Embassy of Iraq at Vienna physically attacked an Embassy employee and threw stones, damaging the building. Five to ten persons forcibly entered the Embassy and shots were fired inside the building. Sixty-five persons of Kurdish origin from Turkey and Iran were arrested and temporarily detained. Bolivia informed the Secretary-General of the 6 December 1988 slaying of the Naval Attaché of the Peruvian Embassy. Bulgaria reported that, on 28 May 1989, during a demonstration in front of the Consulate General of Bulgaria at Istanbul, Turkey, shots were fired and stones were thrown at the building and the residence accommodating families of the consular staff, inflicting considerable damage. Participants in the demonstration tried to break into the Consulate premises and called upon the crowd to commit acts of violence against members of the Consulate General.

Chile drew attention to a 30 September 1988 attempt to occupy its Consulate General at Amsterdam, Netherlands, by a group of some 30 Chileans and Netherlanders, and an attempt to occupy its Consulate General at Montreal, Canada, by approximately 20 persons on 13 October 1988. Denmark provided information on the 20 May attack against the Embassy of Belgium at Copenhagen by approximately 15 persons, who threw stones and glasses filled with paint through windows of the building. Demonstrations in front of South Africa's new Consulate General building at Copenhagen led to some incidents and caused damage to the building.

Finland reported that, on 30 August 1989, Iraq's Embassy at Helsinki was attacked by two Finnish persons with an automatic weapon, who fired shots and inflicted damage to the Embassy. Police arrested the offenders. Iran provided information on a 7 February attack by 50 persons against its Embassy at The Hague, Netherlands, that caused considerable damage to the premises. On 14 December, six persons forced their way into Iran's Consulate General at Geneva, Switzerland. They behaved violently, threatened the personnel and caused considerable damage to the building. According to a note verbale of Israel on 16 January, its Embassy in London received a letter bomb addressed to the Ambassador. The device was dismantled safely and there were no injuries. On 23 August, a bomb exploded at Israel's Consulate General at Istanbul, causing considerable damage to the building. The Netherlands reported that, on 16 February, the Second Secretary at the Netherlands Embassy at Bogotá, Colombia, surprised burglars breaking into his residence. A fight ensued but the Secretary was unharmed.

Status of diplomatic bags and couriers

In 1989, the International Law Commission, at its forty-first session,[10] continued work on the status of the diplomatic courier and the diplomatic bag not accompanied by diplomatic courier. In response to a 1987 General Assembly request,[11] the Commission received in 1989 an additional reply,[12] from the United States, on a set of draft articles on the topic. ILC provisionally adopted the articles in 1986.[13]

In 1989, ILC completed a second reading of that set of 32 draft articles. The Commission had before it the eighth report[14] of its Special Rapporteur, Alexander Yankov (Bulgaria), which contained an analytical survey of comments and observations presented by Governments on the 1986 articles, as well as revised texts prepared by the Special Rapporteur. ILC, on the recommendation of its Drafting Committee, adopted the draft articles on the status of the diplomatic courier and diplomatic bag not accompanied by diplomatic courier, as well as two draft optional protocols devoted, respectively, to the courier and bag of special missions and to the courier and bag of international organizations of a universal character. It recommended to the General Assembly that it convene a conference to study the three drafts and to conclude a convention on the subject.

The 32 articles as well as the draft optional protocols adopted in 1989 were transmitted to the General Assembly by the Secretary-General.[15]

GENERAL ASSEMBLY ACTION

On 4 December, the General Assembly, on the recommendation of the Sixth (Legal) Committee, adopted **resolution 44/36** without vote.

Consideration of the draft articles on the status of the diplomatic courier and the diplomatic bag not accompanied by diplomatic courier and of the draft optional protocols thereto

The General Assembly,

Noting that the International Law Commission, taking into account the written comments of Governments and views expressed in debates in the Assembly, completed at its forty-first session the second reading of the draft articles on the status of the diplomatic courier and the diplomatic bag not accompanied by diplomatic courier and also prepared a draft optional protocol on the status of the courier and the bag of special missions and a draft optional protocol on the status of the courier and the bag of international organizations of a universal character,

Taking note of the recommendation of the International Law Commission that the General Assembly should convene an international conference of plenipotentiaries to study the draft articles concerned and the draft optional protocols thereto and to conclude a convention on the subject,

1. *Expresses its appreciation* to the International Law Commission for its valuable work on the status of the diplomatic courier and the diplomatic bag not accompanied by diplomatic courier and to the Special Rapporteur on the topic for his contribution to this work;

2. *Decides* to hold informal consultations at the forty-fifth session of the General Assembly to study the draft articles on the status of the diplomatic courier and the diplomatic bag not accompanied by diplomatic courier and the draft optional protocols thereto, as well as the question of how to deal further with these draft instruments with a view to facilitating the reaching of a generally acceptable decision in the latter respect;

3. *Also decides* to include in the provisional agenda of its forty-fifth session an item entitled "Consideration of the draft articles on the status of the diplomatic courier and the diplomatic bag not accompanied by diplomatic courier and of the draft optional protocols thereto".

General Assembly resolution 44/36

4 December 1989   Meeting 72   Adopted without vote

Approved by Sixth Committee (A/44/767) without vote, 21 November (meeting 44); 22-nation draft (A/C.6/44/L.14); agenda item 145.

Sponsors: Argentina, Austria, Brazil, Bulgaria, Chile, China, Cyprus, Czechoslovakia, Gabon, German Democratic Republic, Germany, Federal Republic of, India, Ireland, Jamaica, Mali, Mexico, Peru, Poland, Spain, USSR, Venezuela, Viet Nam.

Meeting numbers. GA 44th session: 6th Committee 24-38, 44; plenary 72.

REFERENCES

[1]*Multilateral Treaties Deposited with the Secretary-General: Status as at 31 December 1989* (ST/LEG/SER.E/8), Sales No. E.90.V.6. [2]YUN 1961, p. 512. [3]*Ibid.*, p. 516. [4]YUN 1963, p. 510. [5]*Ibid.*, p. 512. [6]YUN 1973, p. 775, GA res. 3166(XXVIII), annex, 14 Dec. 1973. [7]YUN 1987, p. 1068, GA res. 42/154, 7 Dec. 1987. [8]YUN 1988, p. 807, GA res. 43/167, 9 Dec. 1988. [9]A/INF/44/5. [10]A/44/10. [11]YUN 1987, p. 1086, GA res. 42/156, 7 Dec. 1987. [12]A/CN.4/420. [13]YUN 1986, p. 996. [14]A/CN.4/417/Add.1 & Corr.1,2. [15]A/44/475.

State responsibility, liability, immunities and relations

In response to a 1988 General Assembly resolution,[1] ILC, at its 1989 session,[2] continued its work on four aspects of international law concerning States: State responsibility, international liability for injurious consequences arising out of acts not prohibited by international law, jurisdictional immunities of States and their property, and relations between States and international organizations.

In December, the Assembly recommended that, taking into account Government comments, ILC should continue its work on those and other topics (**resolution 44/35**).

Draft articles on State responsibility

In 1989, ILC [2] considered the preliminary report[3] of its Special Rapporteur, Gaetano Arangio-Ruiz (Italy) on State responsibility. The report contained in particular two draft articles entitled "Cessation of an internationally wrongful act of a continuing character" and "Restitution in kind". Both articles were referred to the Drafting Committee. The second report[4] of the Special Rapporteur was not considered for lack of time.

Draft articles on State liability

In 1989, ILC[2] continued its consideration of draft articles on international liability for injurious consequences arising out of acts not prohibited by international law. It examined the fifth report[5] of its Special Rapporteur on the topic, Julio Barboza (Argentina). The report contained a revised text for the 10 articles of chapters I and II, which had been referred to the Drafting Committee in 1988,[6] and eight new articles for Chapter III (notification, information and warning by the affected State). The first 9 articles were referred to the Drafting Committee. The new articles were: assessment, notification and information (article 10); procedure for protecting national security or industrial secrets (11); warning by the presumed affected State (12); period for reply to notification; obligation of the State of origin (13); reply to notification (14); absence of reply to notification (15); obligation to negotiate (16); and absence of reply to the notification under article 12 (17).

Draft articles on State immunities

At its 1989 session, ILC considered jurisdictional immunities of States and their property, basing its discussion on a set of 28 draft articles adopted on first reading by the Commission in 1986,[7] and the preliminary report[8] and second report[9] of its Special Rapporteur on the issue, Motoo Ogiso (Japan). The reports contained an analytical survey of comments and observations presented by Governments on the draft articles adopted in 1986, as well as revised texts prepared by the Special Rapporteur for consideration by the Commission on its second reading. After discussion, ILC referred to the Drafting Committee articles 1 to 11 *bis* and agreed to examine articles 12 to 28 at its next session.

Draft articles on State relations

ILC resumed consideration of relations between States and international organizations (second part of the topic). Its Special Rapporteur, Leonardo Díaz-González (Venezuela), presented his fourth report,[10] which contained in particular 11 draft articles concerning general provisions, legal personality and property, and funds and assets. The report was not discussed for lack of time.

REFERENCES

[1]YUN 1988, p. 832, GA res. 43/169, 9 Dec. 1988. [2]A/44/10. [3]A/CN.4/416 & Corr.1,2 & Add.1 & Corr.1,2. [4]A/CN.4/425 & Corr.1 & Add.1 & Corr.1. [5]A/CN.4/423 & Corr.1,2. [6]YUN 1988, p. 808. [7]YUN 1986, p. 997. [8]A/CN.4/415 & Corr.1,2. [9]A/CN.4/422 & Corr.1 & Add.1 & Corr.1. [10]A/CN.4/424 & Corr.1.

Treaties and agreements

In 1989, the Secretariat continued to act as depositary for bilateral and multilateral agreements deposited with the Secretary-General.

Treaties involving international organizations

The 1986 Vienna Convention on the Law of Treaties between States and International Organizations or between International Organizations,[1] which was not in force, had 6 parties as at 31 December 1989.[2]

Registration and publication of treaties by the United Nations

During 1989, some 729 international agreements and 349 subsequent actions were received by the Secretariat for registration or filing and recording. In addition, there were 352 registrations of formalities concerning agreements for which the Secretary-General performs depositary functions.

The texts of international agreements registered or filed and recorded are published in the United Nations *Treaties Series* in the original languages, with translations into English and French where necessary. In 1989, the following volumes of the *Treaty*

Series covering treaties registered or filed in 1978, 1979, 1980 and 1981 were issued:

1044, 1107, 1122, 1128, 1131, 1141, 1142, 1146, 1150, 1151, 1154, 1157, 1161, 1165, 1171, 1172, 1178, 1180, 1194, 1195, 1201, 1209, 1210, 1215, 1240.

Multilateral treaties

New multilateral treaties concluded under United Nations auspices

The following treaties, concluded under United Nations auspices, were deposited with the Secretary-General during 1989:[2]

Convention on the Rights of the Child, adopted by the General Assembly of the United Nations on 20 November 1989
Second Optional Protocol to the International Covenant on Civil and Political Rights aiming at the abolition of the death penalty, adopted by the General Assembly of the United Nations on 15 December 1989
Convention on Civil Liability for Damage caused during Carriage of Dangerous Goods by Road, Rail and Inland Navigation Vessels (CRTD), done at Geneva on 10 October 1989
International Convention against the Recruitment, Use, Financing and Training of Mercenaries, adopted by the General Assembly of the United Nations on 4 December 1989
International Agreement on Jute and Jute Products, 1989, concluded at Geneva on 3 November 1989
Basel Convention on the Control of Transboundary Movements of Hazardous Wastes and their Disposal, concluded at Basel on 22 March 1989

Multilateral treaties deposited with the Secretary-General

The number of multilateral treaties for which the Secretary-General performed depositary functions stood at 399 at the end of 1989. During the year, 92 signatures were affixed to treaties for which the Secretary-General performed depositary functions and 374 instruments of ratification, accession or acceptance and approval or notifications were transmitted to him. In addition, he received 182 communications from States expressing ob-

servations or declarations and reservations made at the time of signature, ratification or accession.

The following multilateral treaties for which the Secretary-General acts as depositary came into force during 1989:[2]

Regulations of the *Agreement concerning the Adoption of Uniform Conditions of Approval and Reciprocal Recognition of Approval for Motor Vehicle Equipment and Parts*, done at Geneva on 20 March 1958:
Regulation No. 80: Uniform provisions concerning the approval of seats of large passenger vehicles and of these vehicles with regard to the strength of the seats and their anchorages; Regulation No. 81: Uniform provisions concerning the approval of rear-view mirrors, and of two-wheeled power-driven vehicles with or without side car with regard to the installation of rear-view mirrors on handlebars;
Regulation No. 82: Uniform provisions concerning the approval of moped headlamps equipped with filament halogen lamps (HS2);
Regulation No. 83: Uniform provisions concerning the approval of vehicles with regard to the emission of gaseous pollutants by the engine according to the engine fuel requirements
European Agreement on Main International Railway Lines, concluded at Geneva on 31 May 1985
International Natural Rubber Agreement, 1987, concluded at Geneva on 20 March 1987
Montreal Protocol on Substances that Deplete the Ozone Layer, concluded at Montreal on 16 September 1987
Agreement establishing the Common Fund for Commodities, concluded at Geneva on 27 June 1980
Extension of the International Coffee Agreement, 1983, with modifications, approved by the International Coffee Council in resolution No. 347 of 3 July 1989
International Coffee Agreement, 1983, adopted by the International Coffee Council on 16 September 1982, as modified and extended by resolution No. 347 of 3 July 1989

REFERENCES

[1]YUN 1986, p. 1006. [2]*Multilateral Treaties deposited with the Secretary-General: Status as at 31 December 1989* (ST/LEG/SER.E/8), Sales No. E.90.V.6.

OTHER PUBLICATION

Statement of Treaties and International Agreements, registered or filed and recorded with the Secretariat during 1989, ST/LEG/SER.A/503-514 (monthly).

Chapter IV

Law of the sea

The 1982 United Nations Convention on the Law of the Sea continued in 1989 to set the legal standards for the use of the world's seas and oceans, exerting a dominant influence on the maritime practices of States even before the entry into force of the Convention. In the light of the significant change in the international political climate, the Secretary-General expressed renewed hope for universal participation in the Convention and urged recognition of its importance in environmental issues.

The Preparatory Commission for the International Sea-bed Authority and for the International Tribunal for the Law of the Sea, at its seventh session, continued to examine issues related to the implementation of the obligations of the four registered pioneer investors in the international sea-bed "Area" (the sea-bed beyond national jurisdiction), and to prepare draft agreements, rules, regulations and procedures for the Authority.

In November, the General Assembly called on all States that had not done so to consider ratifying or acceding to the Convention and to observe its provisions when enacting national legislation. It requested the competent international organizations to intensify financial, technological, organizational and managerial assistance to the developing countries in their efforts to realize the benefits of the régime established by the Convention.

UN Convention on the Law of the Sea

Signatures and ratifications

During 1989, five States (Antigua and Barbuda, Kenya, Oman, Somalia and Zaire) ratified the United Nations Convention on the Law of the Sea, bringing the number of ratifications to 42.[1] The Convention was to enter into force 12 months after receipt of the sixtieth instrument of ratification or accession.

The Convention was adopted by the Third United Nations Conference on the Law of the Sea in 1982.[2] When the period for signature closed in 1984, it had received 159 signatures.[3]

Developments relating to the Convention

In response to a 1988 General Assembly resolution,[4] the Secretary-General reported in November 1989[5] on developments relating to the

Convention and on the implementation of that resolution. The report brought the Assembly up to date on the status of the Convention and outlined the Convention's impact on State practice and national policy, the settlement of conflicts and disputes, peace and security issues, maritime law, and protection and preservation of the marine environment. It also reviewed marine scientific research, fisheries management and the work of the Preparatory Commission for the International Sea-bed Authority and for the International Tribunal for the Law of the Sea, and described the activities of the Office for Ocean Affairs and the Law of the Sea, including assistance to the Preparatory Commission and Member States, monitoring of developments and dissemination of relevant information, and co-operation within the United Nations system.

According to the report, the Convention continued to influence the maritime practices of States, particularly the delimitation of maritime jurisdictional zones. By November 1989, 107 States had established territorial seas not exceeding 12 nautical miles, 18 States had a territorial sea claim over 12 nautical miles, 74 States had proclaimed exclusive economic zones and 18 States had claims to exclusive fishing zones. The report emphasized an increasing number of negotiated agreements between States on the issue of maritime boundaries and provided recent examples of such agreements. It was noted that, in compliance with the Convention, some States had referred their boundary disputes and other disputes pertaining to the law of the sea to the International Court of Justice (see PART FIVE, Chapter I). The report also pointed out an agreement between Australia and Indonesia, providing for the establishment of a joint development zone for exploitation of petroleum resources in the Timor Sea.

Another area that received growing attention of the international community was the integrated management of coastal and ocean resources. A number of initiatives and projects were undertaken in this field by some countries in an effort to combine into a single plan the management of both coastal and wider marine areas under national jurisdiction.

The report further outlined efforts to enhance safety at sea and to prevent pollution of the marine environment, including protocols adopted at the end of 1988 amending the 1974 International

Convention for the Safety of Life at Sea[6] that aimed to establish a Global Maritime Distress and Safety System and a new harmonized system of survey and certification for ships. Those protocols were expected to enter into force on 1 February 1992. It also indicated considerable support for the development of a multilateral agreement on the prevention of incidents at sea beyond the territorial sea, based on the existing bilateral arrangements and taking into account instruments such as the International Maritime Organization 1972 Convention on Regulations for Preventing Collisions at Sea.[7]

An International Convention on Salvage was adopted in London on 25 April 1989 in order to update decades-old international rules on salvage operations at sea. The Convention recognized the major contribution of timely salvage to the safety of vessels and environmental protection and provided guarantees of special compensation to the salvor if the work performed had prevented or minimized damage to the environment.

Issues pertaining to the protection and preservation of the marine environment, including oil pollution, special and particularly sensitive sea areas, ocean dumping, transboundary movement of hazardous wastes and radioactive waste disposal continued to be addressed by the UN and its specialized agencies, and received a detailed consideration in the Secretary-General's special report to the Assembly (see below).

The Intergovernmental Oceanographic Commission (IOC) and the Inter-secretariat Committee on Scientific Programmes Relating to Oceanography (ICSPRO) remained engaged in matters related to marine scientific research and ocean services, promoting international co-operation through the framework known as the Long-term and Expanded Programme of Oceanic Research. The framework set out priority areas for international co-ordination in research on the oceans, the "last frontier", including global climate research programmes, research and monitoring of marine pollution, study of the marine environment and accelerated development of ocean services.

The report also described the state of world fisheries, their management and development, and paid special attention to the issue of driftnet fishing, noting an agreement made in September 1989 between the Soviet Union and the United States to co-operate in monitoring driftnet operations by some Pacific countries, with particular concern for the declining numbers of salmon, and the adoption of the Tarawa Declaration by the Twentieth South Pacific Forum (Tarawa, Kiribati, 10-11 July),[8] which had affirmed that driftnet fishing was not consistent with international legal requirements for high seas fisheries conservation and management. Pursuant to that Declaration, the South Pacific Driftnet Conference (Wellington, New Zealand, 21-24 November)[9] adopted a convention banning driftnet operations in the region.

Marine environment

In response to a 1988 General Assembly request,[4] the Secretary-General reported in September 1989[10] on developments related to the protection and preservation of the marine environment in the light of the relevant provisions of the Convention on the Law of the Sea. The report gave an overview of the Convention as a global framework for new environmental law, analysed its relevant provisions and related multilateral treaties, assessed the current state of the marine environment and identified major areas for future actions.

The Convention struck an important balance between the protection of the marine environment and the use of ocean resources and was an instrument for environmentally sustainable development, incorporating new or emerging principles and concepts regarding the global environment that could serve as a model for future international law. The Convention placed States under the responsibility to protect and preserve the marine environment and, for that purpose, to prevent, reduce and control all sources of marine pollution. It paid special attention to transboundary effects of pollution and formulated three major obligations of States: to co-operate in the implementation of international environmental law; to provide assistance to developing countries; and to establish rules, standards and recommended procedures as part of the pollution control system. The Convention also addressed the conservation of the marine living resources in the exclusive economic zone and the high seas, laying down States' duties regarding the protection of marine biodiversity.

The report described the provisions on major pollution sources and certain enforcement measures contained in the Convention, and outlined the framework for the settlement of disputes relating to the subject. The Convention specifically did not prejudice the duties assumed by States under other international agreements, but those obligations were to be carried out in a manner consistent with the Convention's principles and objectives.

According to the assessment based on the work of the Joint Group of Experts on the Scientific Aspects of Marine Pollution (GESAMP), contamination of ocean resources and sea litter resulting from coastal development, sewage disposal and near-shore activities caused serious concern and could have long-term environmental effects. The report stated that, although there was a large body of existing international law on the marine environment, additional regulations were needed on land-based and atmospheric pollution, dumping at sea and pollution from sea-bed activities and oil spills, as well as on the issue of liability and enforcement of existing laws.

The necessity of new environmental agreements in the framework of the Convention was also emphasized at the *ad hoc* inter-agency meeting convened by the Special Representative of the Secretary-General for the Law of the Sea in July 1989.

Preparatory Commission

The Preparatory Commission for the International Sea-bed Authority and for the International Tribunal for the Law of the Sea met twice in 1989: it held its seventh session at Kingston, Jamaica (27 February–23 March), and a summer meeting in New York (14 August–1 September).[5] Major issues considered were the preparation of draft agreements, rules, regulations and procedures for the Authority and the implementation of resolution II,[11] adopted in 1982 by the Third United Nations Conference on the Law of the Sea, regarding obligations of the registered pioneer investors in deep sea-bed mining (France, India, Japan and the Soviet Union).[12]

In need of technical assistance, the Commission mandated a meeting[13] of its Group of Technical Experts (New York, 7-16 August), which submitted to the General Committee a two-stage exploration plan and a report identifying the priority disciplines for personnel training, required skills and areas of training. It was decided to resume the consultations on the pioneer investors' obligations at the Commission's eighth session.

Concerning the preparation of draft agreements, rules, regulations and procedures for the International Sea-bed Authority, the Commission completed in 1989 the first reading of the draft Agreement between the Authority and Jamaica regarding the Authority headquarters, provisionally approved a substantial number of articles, and decided to complete the consideration of the Agreement at the Commission's eighth session. The Commission also discussed a proposal on the voting rights of international organizations, submitted by the European Economic Community, and identified some procedural issues for further consideration. With regard to the establishment of a finance committee to provide assistance and advisory expertise to the Assembly and the Council of the Authority, the issues discussed both in the plenary and during an informal consultation included the Committee's composition, functions and decision-making.

The Commission approved a long-term plan of work for the plenary, providing for the examination in 1990 of the draft rules of the finance committee, the draft protocol on the privileges and immunities of the Authority and the draft staff rules and regulations, as well as consideration in 1991 of the draft Agreement on relations between the Authority and the United Nations, and the draft financial rules and regulations. The Commission's activities were described in its Chairman's statements in March[14] and August.[15]

Special Commissions

The Preparatory Commission's four Special Commissions continued to work in accordance with their respective mandates.

Developing land-based producer States

Special Commission 1, mandated to study ways to minimize the difficulties of developing land-based producer States whose economies might be affected by sea-bed mineral production, began its first reading of 66 provisional conclusions[16] on which to base its recommendations to the Authority. They covered: projection of production from the sea-bed area beyond territorial seas ("the Area"); relationship between production from the Area and existing land-based production; identification, definition and measurement of effects on developing land-based producer States; determination of the problems of those affected; and formulation of measures to minimize their difficulties. At the recommendation of its Bureau, the Special Commission added to the list five new topics dealing with production and trading of copper, nickel, cobalt and manganese. The Commission considered 17 provisional conclusions and decided to continue the discussion at its next session.

The *Ad Hoc* Working Group of the Special Commission continued its deliberations on the criteria for identifying developing land-based producer States actually or likely to be affected by sea-bed production, and on a system of compensation and assistance to the States affected. The Group accepted, with two modifications and one exception, suggestions formulated by its Chairman both on the criteria[17] and on three stages of remedial measures[18] involving assistance through international, regional and subregional organizations, bilateral arrangements between the affected States and sea-bed miners, and the Authority's own compensation fund. The Group was to continue discussions on unresolved issues in 1990. The Chairman of Special Commission 1 reported in March[19] and August[20] on the progress of its work.

The Enterprise

Special Commission 2, charged with preparing for the establishment of the Enterprise—the operational arm of the Authority—completed, in 1989, an article-by-article review of the provisions of the United Nations Convention on the Law of the Sea relating to the structure and organization of the Enterprise. According to March[21] and August[22] reports of its Chairman, the Special Commission identified a number of provisions where annotations to the Convention were called for. Those included: qualifications of nominees to the Governing Board of the Enterprise; the relationship between the Governing Board and the Director-General and between the Council of the Authority and the Governing Board; the Board's auditing and decision-making powers; the confidentiality issue; and the initial fund of the Enterprise.

The Chairman's Advisory Group on Assumptions continued to monitor metal price movements, long-term projections and technological developments relating to sea-bed mining. It reported an escalation of nickel, copper and manganese prices and concluded that, although deep mining of those metals was not economically viable yet, the price increase might reach a level at which it would become feasible.

The Commission's *Ad Hoc* Working Group on Training, set up to prepare draft principles, guidelines and procedures for the training programme, completed its work in March 1989. In August, the Preparatory Commission adopted the Training Programme for the Enterprise,[23] submitted by the Chairman of Special Commission 2. In a statement[24] accompanying the Programme, the Chairman noted that its adoption represented the first concrete preparatory measure taken by the signatories to the Convention with regard to the future Enterprise of the Authority.

The Special Commission's plan of work for 1990 included the implementation of the Training Programme, discussion of transitional arrangements for the Enterprise and matters dealing with exploration.

Sea-bed mining code

Special Commission 3, established to prepare the rules, regulations and procedures for the exploration and exploitation of the deep sea-bed, completed its first reading of the draft regulations on technology transfer until 10 years after the commencement of commercial production by the Enterprise. The issues discussed included limitations on undertakings, scope of the regulations and the procedure for obtaining technology.

In August, the Commission began its preliminary first reading of the draft regulations on production authorizations, taking into consideration a working paper by the Special Representative of the Secretary-General for Ocean Affairs and the Law of the Sea, which, taking into account the production policies and production control formula contained in the Convention, elaborated upon the two-step procedure in the authorization system based on that formula. During the exami-

nation of the draft regulations, particular attention was paid to the articles dealing with authorization for commercial production, the time-limit for submission of applications and their consideration by the Legal and Technical Commission, and the setting of a production ceiling. The Special Commission hoped to finish with the full first reading in 1990.

On 15 and 17 August, Special Commission 3 held a seminar on production policies, which examined the Convention's provisions on the authorization system and discussed matters relating to the "floor", ceiling and safeguard clauses of production policy. The activities of Special Commission 3 were described in its Chairman's reports in March[25] and August.[26]

International Tribunal

Special Commission 4, set up to recommend practical arrangements for the establishment of the International Tribunal for the Law of the Sea, completed its examination of the draft Protocol on the Privileges and Immunities of the Tribunal and requested the secretariat to revise it in the light of the suggestions made. It then began to consider principles governing relationship agreements between the Tribunal and the United Nations, its specialized agencies with relevant competences, the Authority, the International Court of Justice and other international organizations.

The Commission's Chairman continued informal consultations with the Chairman of the Group of 77 and interested delegations on matters relating to the seat of the Tribunal, some important elements of which required further consideration. Consultations were also completed on the prompt release of vessels and crews, and the Commission decided that redrafts of two articles of the draft rules should be incorporated into the revised draft rules of the Tribunal.

The agenda recommended by the Bureau to the Special Commission for its next session included consideration of the institutional structure and initial staffing needs of the Tribunal and continued examination of the main content of relationship agreements to be concluded with other bodies. The Special Commission's Acting Chairman reported in March[27] and its Chairman reported in August[28] on progress made.

Functions of the Secretary-General

Office for Ocean Affairs and the Law of the Sea

The Office for Ocean Affairs and the Law of the Sea, in conformity with a 1988 resolution of the General Assembly,[4] provided services to the Preparatory Commission, Member States and intergovernmental and other organizations in preparing for the entry into force of the Convention and for the commencement of the functioning of the International Sea-bed Authority and the International Tribunal for the Law of the Sea. In 1989, it provided information, advice and assistance to States as well as to global, regional and subregional organizations, academic institutions, scholars and others on various aspects of the Convention and its implementation. It also monitored and reported on marine-related developments, including a special report on the protection and preservation of the marine environment (see above) and another on economic and technical aspects of marine affairs,[29] and prepared studies and analyses to facilitate a better understanding by States of the Convention and its effect on their rights and duties.

As the focal point for marine affairs within the United Nations, the Office continued to participate in and support inter-agency programmes and activities such as a meeting of experts sponsored by the United Nations Industrial Development Organization (Vienna, 21 April), which discussed the establishment of a Mediterranean regional centre for research and development in marine industrial technology. A seminar of the Economic and Social Commission for Asia and the Pacific (Bangkok, Thailand, 6-10 February) focused on offshore installations and structures in exclusive economic zones. A Meeting of Experts for the Co-operation on Ocean Mining and Uses of the Sea (Quito, Ecuador, 12-16 June) considered scientific, technical, legal, environmental and planning components of the question. In February and in April, the Office participated in, respectively, the third session of the joint Intergovernmental Oceanographic Commission and the twenty-fifth session of the Inter-secretariat Committee on Scientific Programmes Relating to Oceanography and was represented at the nineteenth session of GESAMP in May. It assisted the Economic Commission for Latin America and the Caribbean in preparing guidelines and recommendations on sea-use planning and coastal management for the States of the region and provided support to the ongoing activities of the Conference on Indian Ocean Marine Affairs Co-operation and the Zone of Peace and Co-operation of the South Atlantic. In the formulation and conduct of the annual training programme by the World Maritime University (Malmö, Sweden, 20-26 August), the Office examined various aspects relating to the exclusive economic zone. It continued its support and assistance to the Marine Affairs Institute in Trinidad and Tobago, as well as to the United Nations Educational, Scientific and Cultural Organization on the establishment of an oceanographic institute in Yemen.

To facilitate research and study on the law of the sea, its implementation and related marine af-

fairs, the Office offered annually the Hamilton Shirley Amerasinghe Memorial Fellowship on the Law of the Sea, established in 1981[30] in honor of the first President of the Third United Nations Conference on the Law of the Sea. The fourth annual fellowship, providing post-graduate research and study and a subsequent internship with the Office, was awarded to Patricia Sobion of the Ministry of Legal Affairs of Trinidad and Tobago.

The Office in 1989 published, completed or was preparing for publication a number of legislative histories concerning navigation on the high seas;[31] archipelagic States; exclusive economic zones; artificial islands; offshore installations and structures; and passage through straits. The first two volumes (1985-1987)[32] of the *Annual Review of Ocean Affairs: law and policy, main documents* were published, providing a comprehensive compilation of documents on current developments in legal and policy matters relating to ocean affairs and the law of the sea.

As to State practice, work was completed on three volumes dealing with maritime jurisdiction and the regime applicable to it,[33] national legislation on the continental shelf[34] and marine scientific research in areas under national jurisdiction (legislation, regulations and supplementary documents).[35] Two issues of the *Law of the Sea Bulletin* appeared in English, French and Spanish (Nos. 13 and 14).

Analytical studies on economic and technical aspects of marine affairs, prepared by the Office, dealt with prevention and resolution of conflicts in sea-use planning, a simulation exercise for such planning, sea-bed mineral development, and the practical implementation of the régime for marine scientific research in areas under national jurisdiction. A 1988 study on baselines and relevant provisions of the Convention[36] was reissued in 1989 for technical reasons.

The Law of the Sea Information System (LOSIS) was further developed in 1989. The system, composed of a group of databases, each containing information on different aspects of the law of the sea, was being supplemented by the collection of additional marine-related data. The Country Marine Profile Database had 98 categories of information for more than 240 countries and entities. References to legislation and regulations had been coded into the National Marine Legislation Database, comprising 3,641 entries. The Minerals Database contained 25 categories of information on copper, nickel, manganese and cobalt, by country and globally, covering production, consumption, import and export of the minerals in various forms at varous prices for the period 1971-1986. To assess the impact of data changes in the assumptions of future mineral situations, two new databases had been developed: PRODAUTH, concerning provisions of the Convention dealing with the production ceiling for sea-bed mining; and FIN-TERM, for financial terms applicable for sea-bed mining contractors.

The Office also continued to support the development of the Aquatic Sciences and Fisheries Information System (ASFIS) as an international coordinating input centre for the Aquatic Sciences and Fisheries Abstracts, a major information module for ASFIS.

By **decision 1989/180** of 27 July, the Economic and Social Council took note of the Secretary-General's report on economic and technical aspects of marine affairs.[29] By the same decision, it also took note of an IOC report on its long-term and expanded programme of oceanographic research.[37]

GENERAL ASSEMBLY ACTION

On 20 November 1989, the General Assembly adopted **resolution 44/26** by recorded vote.

Law of the sea

The General Assembly,

Recalling its resolutions 37/66 of 3 December 1982, 38/59 A of 14 December 1983, 39/73 of 13 December 1984, 40/63 of 10 December 1985, 41/34 of 5 November 1986, 42/20 of 18 November 1987 and 43/18 of 1 November 1988, regarding the law of the sea,

Recognizing that, as stated in the third preambular paragraph of the United Nations Convention on the Law of the Sea, the problems of ocean space are closely interrelated and need to be considered as a whole,

Convinced that it is important to safeguard the unified character of the Convention and related resolutions adopted therewith and to apply them in a manner consistent with that character and with their object and purpose,

Emphasizing the need for States to ensure consistent application of the Convention, as well as the need for harmonization of national legislation with the provisions of the Convention,

Considering that, in its resolution 2749(XXV) of 17 December 1970, it proclaimed that the sea-bed and ocean floor, and the subsoil thereof, beyond the limits of national jurisdiction (hereinafter referred to as "the Area"), as well as the resources of the Area, are the common heritage of mankind,

Recalling that the Convention provides the régime to be applied to the Area and its resources,

Welcoming the expressions of willingness to explore all possibilities of addressing issues, as referred to in the statements made at the end of the meeting of the Preparatory Commission for the International Sea-Bed Authority and for the International Tribunal for the Law of the Sea, held in New York from 14 August to 1 September 1989, in order to secure universal participation in the Convention,

Recognizing the need for co-operation in the early and effective implementation by the Preparatory Commission of resolution II of the Third United Nations Conference on the Law of the Sea,

Noting with satisfaction the progress made in the Preparatory Commission since its inception, including the registration in 1987 as pioneer investors of the Institut français de recherche pour l'exploitation de la mer (IFREMER), the Government of India, Deep Ocean Resources Development Co., Ltd. (DORD) and Yuzhmorgeologiya, whose applications were submitted by the Governments of France, India, Japan and the Union of Soviet Socialist Republics, respectively, bearing in mind that such registration entails both rights and obligations,

Noting also with satisfaction the designation by the Preparatory Commission of reserved areas for the Authority from the application areas submitted by the pioneer investors pursuant to resolution II,

Noting that the Preparatory Commission has decided to hold its eighth regular session at Kingston from 5 to 30 March 1990 and to hold a summer meeting in New York in 1990,

Noting also the increasing needs of countries, especially developing countries, for information, advice and assistance in the implementation of the Convention and in their developmental process for the full realization of the benefits of the comprehensive legal régime established by the Convention,

Concerned that the developing countries are as yet unable to take effective measures for the full realization of these benefits owing to the lack of resources and of the necessary scientific and technological capabilities,

Recognizing the need to enhance and supplement the efforts of States and competent international organizations to enable developing countries to acquire such capabilities,

Recognizing also that the Convention encompasses all uses and resources of the sea and that all related activities within the United Nations system need to be implemented in a manner consistent with it,

Noting with appreciation the important initiative of the Secretary-General in convening inter-agency consultations on international and regional developments in ocean affairs and the law of the sea,

Deeply concerned at the current state of the marine environment,

Mindful of the importance of the Convention for the protection of the marine environment,

Noting with concern the use of fishing methods and practices that can have an adverse impact on the conservation and management of marine living resources,

Taking special note of the report of the Secretary-General on the protection and preservation of the marine environment prepared in pursuance of paragraph 15 of General Assembly resolution 43/18,

Conscious of the urgent need to increase the scientific knowledge of the marine environment,

Taking note of activities carried out in 1989 under the major programme on marine affairs, set forth in chapter 25 of the medium-term plan for the period 1984-1989, in accordance with the report of the Secretary-General, as approved in General Assembly resolution 38/59 A, and the report of the Secretary-General,

Recalling its approval of the financing of the expenses of the Preparatory Commission from the regular budget of the United Nations,

Taking special note of the report of the Secretary-General prepared in pursuance of paragraph 14 of General Assembly resolution 43/18,

1. *Recalls* the historic significance of the United Nations Convention on the Law of the Sea as an important contribution to the maintenance of peace, justice and progress for all peoples of the world;

2. *Expresses its satisfaction* at the increasing and overwhelming support for the Convention, as evidenced, *inter alia*, by the one hundred and fifty-nine signatures and forty-two of the sixty ratifications or accessions required for entry into force of the Convention;

3. *Invites* all States to make renewed efforts to facilitate universal participation in the Convention;

4. *Calls upon* all States that have not done so to consider ratifying or acceding to the Convention at the earliest possible date to allow the effective entry into force of the new legal régime for the uses of the sea and its resources;

5. *Calls upon* all States to safeguard the unified character of the Convention and related resolutions adopted therewith and to apply them in a manner consistent with that character and with their object and purpose;

6. *Also calls upon* States to observe the provisions of the Convention when enacting their national legislation;

7. *Notes* the progress being made by the Preparatory Commission for the International Sea-Bed Authority and for the International Tribunal for the Law of the Sea in all areas of its work;

8. *Reiterates its conviction* that the early, satisfactory and successful conclusion of the current consultations in the Preparatory Commission on the implementation of the obligations of the registered pioneer investors and the certifying States would constitute an important contribution to the overall progress in the work of the Commission;

9. *Expresses its appreciation* to the Secretary-General for his efforts in support of the Convention and for the effective execution of the major programme on marine affairs set forth in chapter 25 of the medium-term plan for the period 1984-1989 and requests him to take into account the prospective entry into force of the Convention and the increased needs of States for assistance in the implementation of the Convention in the medium-term plan for the period 1992-1997;

10. *Also expresses its appreciation* for the report of the Secretary-General prepared in pursuance of paragraph 14 of General Assembly resolution 43/18 and requests him to carry out the activities outlined therein, as well as those aimed at the strengthening of the legal régime of the sea, special emphasis being placed on the work of the Preparatory Commission, including the implementation of resolution II of the Third United Nations Conference on the Law of the Sea;

11. *Calls upon* the Secretary-General to continue to assist States in the implementation of the Convention and in the development of a consistent and uniform approach to the legal régime thereunder, as well as in their national, subregional and regional efforts towards the full realization of the benefits therefrom, and invites the organs and organizations of the United Nations system to co-operate and lend assistance in these endeavours;

12. *Requests* the competent international organizations, in accordance with their respective policies, to intensify financial, technological, organizational and managerial assistance to the developing countries in their efforts to realize the benefits of the comprehensive legal régime established by the Convention and to examine means of strengthening co-operation among themselves and with donor States in the provision of such assistance;

13. *Requests* the Secretary-General to present to the General Assembly at its forty-fifth and forty-sixth sessions a report identifying the needs of States in regard to the development and management of ocean resources and the measures currently taken by States and by the competent international organizations in responding to those needs, and to suggest methods and mechanisms for maximizing opportunities for the early realization for all States, during the decade beginning in 1990, of the benefits of the comprehensive legal régime established by the Convention;

14. *Approves* the decision of the Preparatory Commission to hold its eighth regular session at Kingston from 5 to 30 March 1990 and to hold a summer meeting in New York in 1990;

15. *Recognizes* that the protection of the marine environment will be significantly enhanced by the implementation of applicable provisions of the Convention;

16. *Expresses its appreciation* to the Secretary-General for his report on the protection and preservation of the marine environment and requests him to make the report available to the intergovernmental meetings to be held in preparation of the proposed 1992 United Nations conference on environment and development;

17. *Requests* the Secretary-General to prepare an updated and expanded report on the protection and preservation of the marine environment as a contribution to the proposed 1992 conference, taking into account, *inter alia*, the comments thereon;

18. *Calls upon* States and other members of the international community to strengthen their co-operation in the conservation of marine living resources, including the prevention of the use of fishing methods and practices that can have an adverse impact on the conservation and management of marine living resources;

19. *Also requests* the Secretary-General to prepare for the General Assembly at its forty-fifth session a study on marine scientific research in the light of the provisions of the United Nations Convention on the Law of the Sea;

20. *Further requests* the Secretary-General to report to the General Assembly at its forty-fifth session on developments pertaining to the Convention and all related activities and on the implementation of the present resolution;

21. *Decides* to include in the provisional agenda of its forty-fifth session the item entitled "Law of the sea".

General Assembly resolution 44/26

20 November 1989   Meeting 62   138-2-6 (recorded vote)

47-nation draft (A/44/L.42 & Add.1); agenda item 30.

Sponsors: Australia, Austria, Bahrain, Bangladesh, Byelorussian SSR, Cameroon, Canada, Cape Verde, Chile, China, Cyprus, Denmark, Fiji, Finland, German Democratic Republic, Guinea-Bissau, Iceland, Indonesia, Ireland, Jamaica, Liberia, Madagascar, Malaysia, Mauritania, Mexico, Myanmar, Nepal, New Zealand, Norway, Oman, Pakistan, Papua New Guinea, Philippines, Portugal, Romania, Saint Lucia, Samoa, Senegal, Singapore, Sri Lanka, Sweden, Trinidad and Tobago, Ukrainian SSR, United Republic of Tanzania, Uruguay, Vanuatu and Zambia.

Recorded vote in Assembly as follows:

In favour: Algeria, Angola, Antigua and Barbuda, Argentina, Australia, Austria, Bahamas, Bahrain, Bangladesh, Barbados, Belgium, Belize, Benin, Bhutan, Bolivia, Botswana, Brazil, Brunei Darussalam, Bulgaria, Burkina Faso, Burundi, Byelorussian SSR, Cameroon, Canada, Cape Verde, Central African Republic, Chad, Chile, China, Colombia, Comoros, Congo, Costa Rica, Côte d'Ivoire, Cuba, Cyprus, Czechoslovakia, Democratic Kampuchea, Democratic Yemen, Denmark, Djibouti, Dominican Republic, Egypt, Ethiopia, Fiji, Finland, France, Gabon, Gambia, German Democratic Republic, Ghana, Greece, Guatemala, Guinea, Guinea-Bissau, Guyana, Haiti, Honduras, Hungary, Iceland, India, Indonesia, Iran, Iraq, Italy, Jamaica, Japan, Jordan, Kenya, Kuwait, Lao People's Democratic Republic, Lesotho, Liberia, Libyan Arab Jamahiriya, Luxembourg, Madagascar,

Malawi, Malaysia, Maldives, Mali, Malta, Mauritania, Mauritius, Mexico, Mongolia, Morocco, Myanmar, Nepal, Netherlands, New Zealand, Nicaragua, Niger, Nigeria, Norway, Oman, Pakistan, Panama, Papua New Guinea, Paraguay, Philippines, Poland, Portugal, Qatar, Romania, Rwanda, Saint Lucia, Saint Vincent and the Grenadines, Samoa, Sao Tome and Principe, Saudi Arabia, Senegal, Seychelles, Sierra Leone, Singapore, Solomon Islands, Somalia, Spain, Sri Lanka, Sudan, Suriname, Swaziland, Sweden, Thailand, Togo, Trinidad and Tobago, Tunisia, Uganda, Ukrainian SSR, USSR, United Arab Emirates, United Republic of Tanzania, Uruguay, Vanuatu, Viet Nam, Yemen, Yugoslavia, Zaire.

Against: Turkey, United States.

Abstaining: Ecuador, Germany, Federal Republic of, Israel, Peru, United Kingdom, Venezuela.

REFERENCES

[1]*Multilateral Treaties Deposited with the Secretary-General: Status as at 31 December 1989* (ST/LEG/SER.E/8), Sales No. E.90.V.6. [2]YUN 1982, p. 178. [3]YUN 1984, p. 108. [4]YUN 1988, p. 816, GA res. 43/18, 1 Nov. 1988. [5]A/44/650 & Corr.1. [6]YUN 1974, p. 1030. [7]YUN 1972, p. 813. [8]A/44/463, annex. [9]A/44/807, annex. [10]A/44/461 & Corr.1. [11]YUN 1982, p. 216. [12]YUN 1987, p. 109. [13]LOS/PCN/108. [14]LOS/PCN/L.72. [15]LOS/PCN/L.77. [16]LOS/PCN/SCN.1/1989/CRP.16. [17]LOS/PCN/SCN.1/1989/CRP.18/Rev.4. [18]LOS/PCN/SCN.1/1989/CRP.19/Rev.3. [19]LOS/PCN/L.68. [20]LOS/PCN/L.73. [21]LOS/PCN/L.70. [22]LOS/PCN/L.75. [23]LOS/PCN/SCN.2/L.6/Rev.1. [24]LOS/PCN/L.75/Add.1. [25]LOS/PCN/L.69. [26]LOS/PCN/L.74. [27]LOS/PCN/L.71 & Corr.1. [28]LOS/PCN/L.76. [29]E/1989/110. [30]YUN 1981, p. 139. [31]*The Law of the Sea: Navigation on the High Seas*, Sales No. E.89.V.2. [32]*Annual Review of Ocean Affairs: law and policy, main documents*, UNIFO Publishers, Ltd. (United States of America), 1989. [33]*The Law of the Sea: Current Developments in State Practice*, Sales No. E.89.V.7. [34]*The Law of the Sea: National Legislation on the Continental Shelf*, Sales No. E.89.V.5. [35]*The Law of the Sea: National Legislation, Regulations and Supplementary Documents on Marine Scientific Research in Areas under National Jurisdiction*, Sales No. E.89.V.9. [36]*The Law of the Sea: Baselines—An Examination of the Relevant Provisions of the United Nations Convention on the Law of the Sea*, Sales No. E.88.V.5. [37]E/1989/111.

OTHER PUBLICATION

The Law of the Sea: A Select Bibliography—1988, Sales No. E.89.V.3.

Chapter V

Other legal questions

In 1989, the United Nations continued its work on various aspects of international law and international economic law.

In December, the General Assembly took note of the report of the Special Committee on the Charter of the United Nations and on the Strengthening of the Role of the Organization and requested it to accord priority, at its 1990 session, to the maintenance of international peace and security in all its aspects in order to strengthen the role of the United Nations, and to continue work on the peaceful settlement of disputes between States. It requested the Secretary-General to continue the preparation of a draft handbook on the peaceful settlement of disputes (resolution 44/37).

The Committee on Relations with the Host Country continued to consider in 1989 the relations between the UN diplomatic community and the United States, its host country. In December, the Assembly urged the host country, in the light of travel regulations issued by the United States, to continue to bear in mind its obligations to facilitate the functioning of the United Nations and its missions, and stressed the importance of a positive perception of the United Nations and its role in the strengthening of international peace and security (44/38).

In November, the Assembly declared the period 1990-1999 as the United Nations Decade of International Law, the main purposes of which would be to promote acceptance of and respect for international law; promote means for the peaceful settlement of disputes between States, including resort to and full respect for the International Court of Justice (ICJ); encourage the progressive development of international law and its codification; and encourage its teaching, study, dissemination and wider appreciation (44/23).

The International Law Commission (ILC) continued to elaborate on the progressive development and codification of international law. At its forty-first session (Geneva, 2 May–21 July 1989), ILC adopted 32 draft articles and 2 draft optional protocols on the status of the diplomatic courier and the diplomatic bag not accompanied by diplomatic courier. It recommended to the Assembly that it convene a conference to study the three drafts and conclude a convention on the subject. The Commission also provisionally adopted

three new articles of the Draft Code of Crimes against the Peace and Security of Mankind. In December, the Assembly took note of the report of the Commission (44/35).

The twenty-fifth session of the International Law Seminar was held at Geneva from 12 to 30 June and was attended by 22 participants of different nationalities, mostly from developing countries. The Assembly requested States and interested organizations to make voluntary contributions towards the financing of the United Nations Programme of Assistance in the Teaching, Study, Dissemination and Wider Appreciation of International Law (44/28). The Assembly requested ILC to address, at its forty-second session, the question of establishing an international criminal court or other international criminal trial mechanism with jurisdiction over persons alleged to have committed crimes that may be covered under a draft Code of Crimes against the Peace and Security of Mankind, including persons engaged in illicit trafficking in narcotic drugs across national frontiers (44/39).

Legal aspects of international economic law and the new international economic order continued to be considered by the United Nations Commission on International Trade Law (UNCITRAL) and by the General Assembly's Sixth (Legal) Committee. At its twenty-fourth session, UNCITRAL dealt primarily with a Draft Convention on the Liability of Operators of Transport Terminals in International Trade, which was adopted by its Working Group on International Contract Practices. The Assembly decided that an international conference of plenipotentiaries should be convened at Vienna in 1991 to consider the draft convention prepared by the Commission and to embody the results of its work in a convention on the subject. It repeated its invitation to States that had not yet done so to sign, ratify or accede to the conventions elaborated under the auspices of the Commission (44/33).

The Assembly also requested the Secretary-General to seek proposals of Member States concerning the most appropriate procedures to be adopted with regard to the codification and progressive development of the principles and norms of international law relating to the new international economic order (44/30).

International organizations and international law

Strengthening the role of the United Nations

The Secretary-General, in his annual report to the General Assembly on the work of the Organization (see p. 3), stated that no realistic view of human experience from 1945 to the present could ignore the transformation of the world scene reflected by the presence of the United Nations. It was under the auspices of the Organization that an international agenda encompassing all matters of common concern to nations had taken shape and a massive change in international life had been effected and, by and large, peacefully absorbed.

The Secretary-General said, however, that the cold war had left the United Nations in the position of waiting until common sense and the dynamics of the world situation would induce a return to the manner of handling international affairs outlined in its Charter. He noted that it had not yet been two years since the United Nations had begun to witness signs of such a return. The two major power blocs had started an assiduous search for bases of stable peace between them. In addition, a growing determination to work together by the permanent members of the Security Council had facilitated purposeful diplomatic efforts towards the resolution of some long-standing disputes. In an increasing number of cases, the role of the United Nations was being looked upon as pivotal in the settlement of problems that not too long before had appeared intractable. The assistance of the Organization was being sought more than ever before in its history. There was recognition that around the world lasting solutions to international problems must be based on universally accepted principles as laid down in the Charter. The Secretary-General cited progress towards independence for Namibia as a special example of international co-operation.

Regarding the new demand and enthusiasm for peace-keeping operations, the Secretary-General stated that it was imperative to keep this situation under constant scrutiny so that the best could be made of the Organization's peace-keeping capacity, and also so that it could be developed in a positive and constructive way. Three main areas needed to be kept under constant review: function, capacity and performance, and support. The question of enhancing the credibility and authority of peace-keeping operations needed to be examined at the United Nations by Member States, he said, and especially by members of the Security Council. The degree of training for peace-keeping in national armies needed to be enhanced as a measure of readiness for United Nations peace-keeping duties. The Secretary-General hoped that Member States would address the financial problems of peace-keeping urgently and with imagination. A promising possibility would be the establishment of a special reserve fund for peace-keeping, supported by all Member States. Such a fund would vastly facilitate the timely launching of operations mandated by the Security Council. The Secretary-General noted that peace-keeping had been operated on a shoe-string, and nowhere had the inadequacy of present arrangements been more evident than in the area of logistical support, which needed to be made more reliable and responsive. Here again the new political climate, he said, should allow a much freer exchange and more co-operation. In particular, he hoped that countries with large and far-ranging military establishments would work together to establish a more dependable and responsive logistical framework. For the longer term, the United Nations needed to consider where peace-keeping fitted into the underlying effort to build the international rule of law and a reliable system for the maintenance of international peace and security.

The United Nations, the Secretary-General said, needed to demonstrate its capacity to function as the guardian of the world's security. What was needed was an improvement of existing mechanisms and capabilities in the light of the demands of the unfolding international situation, rather than any changes in the Organization's structure. In order to activate the potential of the United Nations for averting wars, earlier discussion of potentially explosive situations was needed, for which timely, accurate and unbiased information was a prerequisite. The current pool of material available to the Secretary-General, consisting of information provided by government representatives supplemented by the collection and analyses of published reports and comments, was manifestly insufficient in cases where more than anticipatory diplomacy was required. The Secretary-General needed to have at his disposal information that was dependable *prima facie*. Only then could he be in a position to assess whether an issue needed to be brought to the attention of the Security Council under Article 99 of the Charter. Arrangements could be made to receive information from space-based and other technical surveillance systems.

The Secretary-General said that he wanted the United Nations to play a key role, as envisaged in the Charter, in promoting social progress and better standards of life for people throughout the world. There was an opportunity to extend to the economic and social spheres the same spirit of co-operation as had recently emerged in the political field. Discussions were continuing over the restructuring of the intergovernmental machinery in the economic and social sectors, including the revitalization of the Economic and Social Council. Although the Council had made progress in enhancing its effectiveness, what was required above all was an increased commitment by Member States to utilize and support the Organization in its economic and social activities. Only thus could the full potential of the United Nations in this sphere be realized.

The Secretary-General concluded by noting that the capabilities of the United Nations would be best employed if the Organization as a whole was used more purposefully by its Member States than in the recent past. The decision-making process on political matters had vastly improved with the emergence of a collegial spirit among permanent Security Council members and with daily cooperation between the Council as a whole and the Secretary-General. But more was demanded: agreement among the major Powers must carry with it the support of a majority of Member States if it was to make the desired impact on the world situation.

Activities of the Special Committee

The Special Committee on the Charter of the United Nations and on the Strengthening of the Role of the Organization met in New York from 27 March to 14 April 1989. It reported[1] on its discussion of proposals on the maintenance of international peace and security, in addition to the rationalization of existing UN procedures and the peaceful settlement of disputes between States (see PART FIVE, Chapter II) as requested by the General Assembly in 1988.[2]

The Committee's Working Group discussed a working paper[3] submitted by Belgium, the Federal Republic of Germany, Italy, Japan, New Zealand and Spain on fact-finding by the United Nations to assist in the maintenance of international peace and security. It also examined a document[4] submitted by Czechoslovakia and the German Democratic Republic devoted to the same issue. Careful note of all comments on each document was taken by the co-sponsors, who planned to work on the revision of the documents for the future work of the Committee.

The Working Group had before it a working paper[5] submitted by France and the United Kingdom and a conference room paper by the USSR pertaining to the rationalization of procedures of the United Nations. The Working Group called upon the sponsors of both papers and other interested delegations to conduct informal consultations under the chairmanship of the Committee's chairman. After an extensive round of consultations, France and the United Kingdom indicated that they would submit a revised version of their working paper at the Committee's next session.

GENERAL ASSEMBLY ACTION

On 4 December 1989, the General Assembly, on the recommendation of the Sixth Committee, adopted **resolution 44/37** without vote.

Report of the Special Committee on the Charter of the United Nations and on the Strengthening of the Role of the Organization

The General Assembly,

Recalling its resolution 3499(XXX) of 15 December 1975, by which it established the Special Committee on the Charter of the United Nations and on the Strengthening of the Role of the Organization, and its relevant resolutions adopted at subsequent sessions,

Taking note of the reports of the Secretary-General on the work of the Organization submitted to the General Assembly at its thirty-seventh, thirty-ninth, fortieth, forty-first, forty-second, forty-third and forty-fourth sessions, as well as the views and comments expressed on them by Member States,

Having considered the report of the Special Committee on the Charter of the United Nations and on the Strengthening of the Role of the Organization on the work of its session held in 1989,

Expressing its satisfaction at the completion of the work on the draft document on the resort to a commission of good offices, mediation or conciliation within the United Nations and at the recommendation of the Special Committee that it should be annexed to a decision to be adopted by the General Assembly at its present session,

Mindful of the desirability of further work being done by the Special Committee in the field of the peaceful settlement of disputes between States,

Noting with appreciation the progress achieved in the elaboration of the draft handbook on the peaceful settlement of disputes between States,

1. *Takes note* of the report of the Special Committee on the Charter of the United Nations and on the Strengthening of the Role of the Organization;

2. *Decides* that the Special Committee shall hold its next session from 12 February to 2 March 1990;

3. *Requests* the Special Committee, at its session in 1990, in accordance with the provisions of paragraph 5 below:

   (*a*) To accord priority to the question of the maintenance of international peace and security in all its aspects in order to strengthen the role of the United Nations and, in this context, to consider:

      (i) Primarily, the question of fact-finding activities by the United Nations on the basis of proposals and suggestions before it;

      (ii) Other proposals relating to the maintenance of international peace and security that might be submitted to the Special Committee at its session in 1990;

   (*b*) To continue its work on the question of the peaceful settlement of disputes between States and, in this context:

      (i) To consider proposals relating to this question that might be submitted to the Special Committee;

(ii) To examine the progress report of the Secretary-General on the elaboration of the draft handbook on the peaceful settlement of disputes between States;

4. *Requests* the Special Committee to keep the question of the rationalization of the procedures of the United Nations under active review;

5. *Also requests* the Special Committee to be mindful of the importance of reaching general agreement whenever that has significance for the outcome of its work;

6. *Decides* that the Special Committee shall accept the participation of observers of Member States in its meetings, including those of its working group;

7. *Requests* the Secretary-General to continue, on a priority basis, the preparation of the draft handbook on the peaceful settlement of disputes between States, on the basis of the outline elaborated by the Special Committee and in the light of the views expressed in the course of the discussions in the Sixth Committee and in the Special Committee, and to report to the Special Committee at its session in 1990 on the progress of work, before submitting to it the draft handbook in its final form, with a view to its approval at a later stage;

8. *Requests* the Special Committee to submit a report on its work to the General Assembly at its forty-fifth session;

9. *Decides* to include in the provisional agenda of its forty-fifth session the item entitled ''Report of the Special Committee on the Charter of the United Nations and on the Strengthening of the Role of the Organization''.

General Assembly resolution 44/37

4 December 1989   Meeting 72   Adopted without vote

Approved by Sixth Committee (A/44/768) without vote, 21 November (meeting 44); 26-nation draft (A/C.6/44/L.12); agenda item 146.
Sponsors: Argentina, Belgium, Colombia, Cyprus, Czechoslovakia, Ecuador, Egypt, Gabon, German Democratic Republic, Germany, Federal Republic of, Ghana, Indonesia, Italy, Japan, Libyan Arab Jamahiriya, Morocco, New Zealand, Oman, Philippines, Poland, Romania, Senegal, Spain, Venezuela, Yugoslavia, Zambia.
Financial implications. 5th Committee, A/44/830; S-G, A/C.5/44/38, A/C.6/44/L.19.
Meeting numbers. GA 44th session: 5th Committee 50; 6th Committee 7-15, 44; plenary 72.

In **resolution 44/21** of 15 November, the Assembly called upon States to intensify their practical efforts to ensure international peace and security in all its aspects through co-operative means in accordance with the Charter of the United Nations. It also reaffirmed its support of the validity and relevance of the Charter and urged all States to abide by it (see PART ONE, Chapter I).

Host country relations

In 1989, the Committee on Relations with the Host Country continued to consider relations between the United Nations diplomatic community and the United States, its host country, as requested by the General Assembly in 1988.[6] The Committee's annual report to the Assembly[7] contained summaries of discussions held at five meetings between March and November, and of communications from Member States on the security of their missions and the safety of their per-

sonnel. In May, the Committee set up a Working Group to explore the possibility of establishing a commissary at UN headquarters to assist diplomatic personnel and staff. The Committee also organized, in co-operation with the Secretariat and the United States mission, a talk on matters relating to the use of motor vehicles, including parking problems.

Topics dealt with by the Committee included travel regulations, acceleration of immigration and customs procedures, exemption from taxes, transportation and other matters. On 19 January, the United States advised the Secretary-General that all Chinese employees of the United Nations assigned to New York would be required to submit written notification for non-official travel in the United States. China objected to the travel restrictions and limitations imposed by the United States, characterizing them as illegal and unfair. Bulgaria, the USSR and Czechoslovakia also described the restrictions as discriminatory. The United States asserted that travel regulations had been adopted by the host country for national security reasons, which, in no way however, affected official travel nor created impediments in travelling to or from the Headquarters district. The legal position of the United Nations with respect to the new regulations was that they constituted an unjustified and unmotivated measure which discriminated against staff members of the Secretariat solely on the basis of their nationality.

On 10 November, the Committee urged the host country to take all measures necessary to prevent any interference with the functioning of missions; took note of positions of affected Member States, the Secretary-General and the host country regarding travel regulations; called upon missions to co-operate fully with the United States authorities in cases affecting the security of missions and their personnel; and appealed to the host country to review the measures relating to diplomatic vehicles with a view to responding to the needs of the diplomatic community. The Committee stressed the importance of a positive perception of the increasingly important work of the United Nations, and urged that efforts be continued to build public awareness of the vital role played by the United Nations and missions in the solution of global and regional problems and in the strengthening of international peace and security.

GENERAL ASSEMBLY ACTION

On 4 December 1989, the General Assembly, on the recommendation of the Sixth Committee, adopted **resolution 44/38** without vote.

Report of the Committee on Relations with the Host Country

The General Assembly,

Having considered the report of the Committee on Relations with the Host Country,

Recalling Article 105 of the Charter of the United Nations, the Convention on the Privileges and Immunities of the United Nations and the Agreement between the United Nations and the United States of America regarding the Headquarters of the United Nations,

Recalling also that any problems related to the privileges and immunities of all missions accredited to the United Nations, the security of the missions and the safety of their personnel are of great importance and concern to Member States, as well as the primary responsibility of the host country,

Recognizing that effective measures should continue to be taken by the competent authorities of the host country, in particular to prevent any acts violating the security of missions and the safety of their personnel,

Conscious of the increased interest shown by Member States in participating in the work of the Committee,

1. *Endorses* the recommendations and conclusions of the Committee on Relations with the Host Country contained in paragraph 45 of its report;

2. *Considers* that the maintenance of appropriate conditions for the normal work of the delegations and the missions accredited to the United Nations is in the interest of the United Nations and all Member States and urges the host country to continue to take all measures necessary to prevent any interference with the functioning of missions;

3. *Expresses its appreciation* for the efforts made by the host country and hopes that outstanding problems raised at the meetings of the Committee will be duly settled in a spirit of co-operation and in accordance with international law;

4. *Urges* the host country, in the light of the consideration by the Committee of travel regulations issued by the host country, to continue to bear in mind its obligations to facilitate the functioning of the United Nations and the missions accredited to it;

5. *Stresses* the importance of a positive perception of the work of the United Nations, and urges that efforts be continued to build up public awareness by explaining, through all available means, the importance of the role played by the United Nations and the missions accredited to it in the strengthening of international peace and security;

6. *Requests* the Secretary-General to remain actively engaged in all aspects of the relations of the United Nations with the host country;

7. *Requests* the Committee to continue its work, in conformity with General Assembly resolution 2819(XXVI) of 15 December 1971;

8. *Decides* to include in the provisional agenda of its forty-fifth session the item entitled "Report of the Committee on Relations with the Host Country".

General Assembly resolution 44/38

4 December 1989   Meeting 72   Adopted without vote

Approved by Sixth Committee (A/44/769) without vote, 27 November (meeting 47); draft by Cyprus (A/C.6/44/L.20); agenda item 147.
Meeting numbers. GA 44th session: 6th Committee 44, 47; plenary 72.

United Nations Decade of International Law

In 1989, Zimbabwe, on behalf of the Movement of Non-Aligned Countries, requested[8] the General Assembly to include on its agenda an item concerning a United Nations Decade of International Law.

On 17 November 1989, the General Assembly adopted **resolution 44/23** without vote.

United Nations Decade of International Law
The General Assembly,

Recognizing that one of the purposes of the United Nations is to maintain international peace and security, and to that end to bring about by peaceful means, and in conformity with the principles of justice and international law, adjustment or settlement of international disputes or situations which might lead to a breach of the peace,

Recalling the Declaration on Principles of International Law concerning Friendly Relations and Co-operation among States in accordance with the Charter of the United Nations and the Manila Declaration on the Peaceful Settlement of International Disputes,

Recognizing the role of the United Nations in promoting greater acceptance of and respect for the principles of international law and in encouraging the progressive development of international law and its codification,

Convinced of the need to strengthen the rule of law in international relations,

Stressing the need to promote the teaching, study, dissemination and wider appreciation of international law,

Noting that, in the remaining decade of the twentieth century, important anniversaries will be celebrated that are related to the adoption of international legal documents, such as the centenary of the first International Peace Conference, held at The Hague in 1899, which adopted the Convention for the Pacific Settlement of International Disputes and created the Permanent Court of Arbitration, the fiftieth anniversary of the signing of the Charter of the United Nations and the twenty-fifth anniversary of the adoption of the Declaration on Principles of International Law concerning Friendly Relations and Co-operation among States in accordance with the Charter of the United Nations,

1. *Declares* the period 1990-1999 as the United Nations Decade of International Law;

2. *Considers* that the main purposes of the Decade should be, *inter alia:*

(*a*) To promote acceptance of and respect for the principles of international law;

(*b*) To promote means and methods for the peaceful settlement of disputes between States, including resort to and full respect for the International Court of Justice;

(*c*) To encourage the progressive development of international law and its codification;

(*d*) To encourage the teaching, study, dissemination and wider appreciation of international law;

3. *Requests* the Secretary-General to seek the views of Member States and appropriate international bodies, as well as of non-governmental organizations working in the field, on the programme for the Decade and on appropriate action to be taken during the Decade, including the possibility of holding a third international peace conference or other suitable international conference at the end of the Decade, and to submit a report thereon to the Assembly at its forty-fifth session;

4. *Decides* to consider this question at its forty-fifth session in a working group of the Sixth Committee with a view to preparing generally acceptable recommendations for the Decade;

5. *Also decides* to include in the provisional agenda of its forty-fifth session the item entitled "United Nations Decade of International Law".

General Assembly resolution 44/23

17 November 1989   Meeting 60   Adopted without vote

72-nation draft (A/44/L.41 & Add.1); agenda item 149.

Sponsors: Afghanistan, Algeria, Angola, Argentina, Austria, Belgium, Bulgaria, Canada, Cape Verde, China, Colombia, Costa Rica, Cuba, Cyprus, Czechoslovakia, Denmark, Ecuador, Egypt, Ethiopia, Finland, France, German Democratic Republic, Germany, Federal Republic of, Ghana, Guyana, Greece, Guatemala, Iceland, India, Iran, Ireland, Italy, Jamaica, Jordan, Liberia, Libyan Arab Jamahiriya, Luxembourg, Madagascar, Malaysia, Mali, Malta, Mauritania, Mexico, Mongolia, Morocco, Nepal, Netherlands, Nicaragua, Nigeria, Norway, Pakistan, Panama, Peru, Philippines, Poland, Portugal, Romania, Senegal, Spain, Sri Lanka, Suriname, Sweden, Tunisia, USSR, United Kingdom, United Republic of Tanzania, United States, Venezuela, Viet Nam, Yugoslavia, Zambia, Zimbabwe.

REFERENCES

[1]A/44/33. [2]YUN 1988, p. 820, GA res. 43/170, 9 Dec. 1988. [3]A/AC.182/L.60. [4]A/AC.182/L.62. [5]A/AC.182/L.43/Rev.3,4. [6]YUN 1988, p. 821, GA res. 43/172, 9 Dec. 1988. [7]A/44/26. [8]A/44/191.

International Law Commission

In its report[1] on its forty-first session (Geneva, 2 May–21 July), ILC described its work on the progressive development and codification of international law.

In 1989 it adopted a set of 32 draft articles and 2 draft optional protocols on the status of the diplomatic courier and the diplomatic bag not accompanied by diplomatic courier, and recommended to the Assembly that it convene a conference to study the drafts and conclude a convention on the subject (see PART FIVE, Chapter III). The Commission also provisionally adopted three new articles of the Draft Code of Crimes against the Peace and Security of Mankind (see PART FIVE, Chapter II). The draft articles adopted by ILC in 1989 were subsequently transmitted by the Secretary-General to the General Assembly.[2]

The Commission also considered the issues of State responsibility, international liability for injurious consequences arising out of acts not prohibited by international law, jurisdictional immunities of States and their property, relations between States and international organizations (see PART FIVE, Chapter III), and the law of non-navigational uses of international watercourses (see PART FIVE, Chapter II).

The Commission held 54 public meetings. In addition, its Drafting Committee held 36 meetings, the Enlarged Bureau of the Commission, 3 meetings, and the Bureau's Planning Group, 9 meetings. Based on their recommendations regarding its programme, procedures and working methods and efforts to improve the ways in which the Commission's report was considered in the Sixth Committee, ILC adopted on 18 July paragraphs on its present and future programme of work; the role of the Drafting Committee; the relationship of the Commission with the General Assembly; the duration of the session and other matters. The Secretariat prepared for ILC's attention a topical summary[3] of the Assembly's Sixth Committee's discussion in 1989 on the ILC report for the previous year.

ILC continued to co-operate in 1989 with the Asian-African Legal Consultative Committee, the European Committee on Legal Co-operation and the Inter-American Juridical Committee.

GENERAL ASSEMBLY ACTION

On 4 December 1989, the General Assembly, on the recommendation of the Sixth Committee, adopted **resolution 44/35** without vote.

Report of the International Law Commission on the work of its forty-first session

The General Assembly,

Having considered the report of the International Law Commission on the work of its forty-first session,

Emphasizing the need for the progressive development of international law and its codification in order to make it a more effective means of implementing the purposes and principles set forth in the Charter of the United Nations and in the Declaration on Principles of International Law concerning Friendly Relations and Co-operation among States in accordance with the Charter of the United Nations and to give increased importance to its role in relations among States,

Recognizing the importance of referring legal and drafting questions to the Sixth Committee, including topics that might be submitted to the International Law Commission, and of enabling the Sixth Committee and the Commission further to enhance their contributions to the progressive development of international law and its codification,

Recalling the need to keep under review those topics of international law which, given their new or renewed interest for the international community, may be suitable for the progressive development and codification of international law and therefore may be included in the future programme of work of the International Law Commission,

Considering that experience has demonstrated the usefulness of structuring the debate on the report of the International Law Commission in the Sixth Committee in such a manner that conditions are provided for concentrated attention on each of the main topics dealt with in the report, and that this process is facilitated when the Commission indicates specific issues on which expressions of views by Governments are of particular interest for the continuation of its work,

1. *Takes note* of the report of the International Law Commission on the work of its forty-first session;

2. *Recommends* that, taking into account the comments of Governments, whether in writing or expressed orally in debates in the General Assembly, the International Law Commission should continue its work on the topics in its current programme, listed as items 2, 3 and 5 to 8 in paragraph 7 of its report;

3. *Expresses its appreciation* for the efforts of the International Law Commission to improve its procedures and

methods of work and to formulate proposals on its future programme of work;

4. *Requests* the International Law Commission:

(a) To keep under review the planning of its activities for the term of office of its members, bearing in mind the desirability of achieving as much progress as possible in the preparation of draft articles on specific topics;

(b) To consider further its methods of work in all their aspects, bearing in mind that the staggering of the consideration of some topics might contribute, *inter alia*, to a more effective consideration of its report in the Sixth Committee;

(c) To pay special attention to indicating in its annual report, for each topic, those specific issues on which expressions of views by Governments, either in the Sixth Committee or in written form, would be of particular interest for the continuation of its work;

5. *Invites* the International Law Commission, when circumstances so warrant, to request a special rapporteur to attend the session of the General Assembly during the discussion of the topic for which that special rapporteur is responsible and requests the Secretary-General to make the necessary arrangements within existing resources;

6. *Recommends* the continuation of efforts to improve the ways in which the report of the International Law Commission is considered in the Sixth Committee, with a view to providing effective guidance for the Commission in its work;

7. *Decides* that the Sixth Committee, in structuring its debate on the report of the International Law Commission at the forty-fifth session of the General Assembly, should continue to bear in mind the possibility of reserving time for informal exchanges of views on matters relating to the work of the Commission;

8. *Recommends* that the debate on the report of the International Law Commission at the forty-fifth session of the General Assembly commence on 29 October 1990;

9. *Takes note* of the comments of the International Law Commission on the question of the duration of its session, as presented in paragraph 743 of its report, and expresses the view that the requirements of the work for the progressive development of international law and its codification and the magnitude and complexity of the subjects on the agenda of the Commission make it desirable that the usual duration of its sessions be maintained;

10. *Reaffirms* its previous decisions concerning the increased role of the Codification Division of the Office of Legal Affairs of the Secretariat and those concerning the summary records and other documentation of the International Law Commission;

11. *Urges* Governments and, as appropriate, international organizations to respond in writing as fully and expeditiously as possible to the requests of the International Law Commission for comments, observations and replies to questionnaires and for materials on topics in its programme of work;

12. *Reaffirms its wish* that the International Law Commission continue to enhance its co-operation with intergovernmental legal bodies whose work is of interest for the progressive development of international law and its codification;

13. *Once again expresses the wish* that seminars will continue to be held in conjunction with the sessions of the International Law Commission and that an increasing number of participants from developing countries will be given the opportunity to attend those seminars, appeals to States that can do so to make the voluntary contributions that are urgently needed for the holding of the seminars and expresses the hope that every effort will continue to be made by the Secretary-General, within existing resources, to provide the seminars with adequate services, including interpretation, as required;

14. *Requests* the Secretary-General to forward to the International Law Commission, for its attention, the records of the debate on the report of the Commission at the forty-fourth session of the General Assembly, together with such written statements as delegations may circulate in conjunction with their oral statements, and to prepare and distribute a topical summary of the debate.

General Assembly resolution 44/35

4 December 1989   Meeting 72   Adopted without vote

Approved by Sixth Committee (A/44/767) without vote, 21 November (meeting 44); 42-nation draft (A/C.6/44/L.13); agenda item 145.

Sponsors: Algeria, Argentina, Australia, Austria, Brazil, Bulgaria, Canada, Chile, China, Cyprus, Czechoslovakia, Denmark, Egypt, Ethiopia, Finland, France, German Democratic Republic, Germany, Federal Republic of, Greece, Guinea, Iceland, India, Ireland, Italy, Jamaica, Japan, Mexico, Morocco, New Zealand, Norway, Peru, Romania, Senegal, Spain, Sweden, Tunisia, Turkey, USSR, United Kingdom, Venezuela, Viet Nam, Yugoslavia.

Meeting numbers. GA 44th session: 6th Committee 24-38, 44; plenary 72.

UN Programme for the teaching and study of international law

International Law Seminar

Pursuant to a 1988 General Assembly resolution,[4] the twenty-fifth session of the International Law Seminar was held at Geneva, 12-30 June 1989. For post-graduate students of international law and young professors or government officials dealing with international law, the seminar took place during the ILC 1989 session. Twenty-two participants of different nationalities, mostly from developing countries, and three United Nations Institute for Training and Research (UNITAR) fellows participated, attending ILC meetings as well as lectures specifically organized for them. Austria, Finland, the Federal Republic of Germany, Ireland, Mexico, Sweden and Switzerland made voluntary financial contributions making possible 12 full fellowships and four partial fellowships for participants in 1989. Since the first seminar in 1964, fellowships had been awarded to 280 of 558 participants representing 124 nationalities.

The General Assembly appealed for voluntary contributions to the seminars in **resolutions 44/35 and 44/28**.

Other activities

A number of additional training courses were offered in 1989 as part of the United Nations Programme of Assistance in the Teaching, Study, Dissemination and Wider Appreciation of International Law.[5] Under the annual joint United

Nations–UNITAR Fellowship Programme and as authorized by the General Assembly in 1987,[6] 16 middle-grade governmental legal officers and young teachers of international law from developing countries attended courses for six weeks at The Hague Academy of International Law (Netherlands), as well as special lectures and seminars organized by UNITAR. Some fellows also participated in the International Law Seminar in Geneva (see above), and others received practical training at legal offices of the United Nations and related organizations. Because of lack of funds, UNITAR did not implement the regional training and refresher course in international law which had been scheduled in 1989 for the African region.

In response to a 1987 General Assembly request,[6] the Secretary-General recommended that, for the biennium 1990-1991, the programme should continue to be conducted by the Secretariat along the same lines as in the past, leaving room for new initiatives.

GENERAL ASSEMBLY ACTION

On 4 December 1989, the General Assembly, on the recommendation of the Sixth Committee, adopted **resolution 44/28** without vote.

United Nations Programme of Assistance in the Teaching, Study, Dissemination and Wider Appreciation of International Law

The General Assembly,

Taking note with appreciation of the report of the Secretary-General on the implementation of the United Nations Programme of Assistance in the Teaching, Study, Dissemination and Wider Appreciation of International Law and the recommendations made by the Secretary-General and adopted by the Advisory Committee on the United Nations Programme of Assistance in the Teaching, Study, Dissemination and Wider Appreciation of International Law, which are contained in that report,

Considering that international law should occupy an appropriate place in the teaching of legal disciplines at all universities,

Bearing in mind the objectives of the United Nations Decade of International Law,

Noting with appreciation the efforts made by States at the bilateral level to provide assistance in the teaching and study of international law,

Convinced, nevertheless, that States and international organizations and institutions should be encouraged to give further support to the Programme and to increase their activities to promote the teaching, study, dissemination and wider appreciation of international law, in particular those activities which are of special benefit to persons from developing countries,

Reaffirming its resolutions 2464(XXIII) of 20 December 1968, 2550(XXIV) of 12 December 1969, 2838(XXVI) of 18 December 1971, 3106(XXVIII) of 12 December 1973, 3502(XXX) of 15 December 1975, 32/146 of 16 December 1977, 36/108 of 10 December 1981 and 38/129 of 19 December 1983, in which it stated that

in the conduct of the Programme it was desirable to use as far as possible the resources and facilities made available by Member States, international organizations and others, as well as its resolutions 34/144 of 17 December 1979, 40/66 of 11 December 1985 and 42/148 of 7 December 1987, in which it also expressed the hope that, in appointing lecturers for the seminars to be held within the framework of the fellowship programme in international law sponsored jointly by the United Nations and the United Nations Institute for Training and Research, account would be taken of the need to secure representation of major legal systems and balance among various geographical regions,

Noting that the publication of the *United Nations Juridical Yearbook* in languages other than French and English contributes to the wider dissemination, study and teaching of international law,

Recalling the provisions of Article 39 of the Statute of the International Court of Justice,

Taking into account the circumstances surrounding the recommendations made by the Joint Inspection Unit to publish in languages other than French and English the judgments of the International Court of Justice and, in particular, the difficulties to which the Court has drawn attention,

1. *Approves* the recommendations of the Secretary-General contained in section III of his report on the implementation of the United Nations Programme of Assistance in the Teaching, Study, Dissemination and Wider Appreciation of International Law, in particular those designed to achieve the best possible results in the administration of the Programme within a policy of maximum financial restraint;

2. *Authorizes* the Secretary-General to carry out in 1990 and 1991 the activities specified in his report, including the provision of:

(*a*) A minimum of fifteen fellowships each in 1990 and 1991, at the request of Governments of developing countries;

(*b*) A minimum of one scholarship each in 1990 and 1991 under the Hamilton Shirley Amerasinghe Memorial Fellowship on the Law of the Sea, subject to the availability of new voluntary contributions made specifically to the fellowship fund;

(*c*) Assistance in the form of a travel grant for one participant from each developing country who will be invited to the regional courses to be organized in 1990 and 1991;

and to finance the above activities from provisions in the regular budget, when appropriate, as well as from voluntary financial contributions earmarked for each of the activities concerned, which would be received as a result of the requests set out in paragraphs 10, 11 and 12 of the present resolution;

3. *Expresses its appreciation* to the Secretary-General for his constructive efforts to promote training and assistance in international law within the framework of the Programme in 1988 and 1989, in particular for the organization of the twenty-fourth and twenty-fifth sessions of the International Law Seminar, held at Geneva from 6 to 24 June 1988 and 12 to 30 June 1989, respectively, and for the participation of the Office of Legal Affairs of the Secretariat and its Codification Division in the conduct of the fellowship programme in international law sponsored jointly by the United Nations and the United Nations Institute for Training and Research,

as well as for the activities related to the award of the Hamilton Shirley Amerasinghe Memorial Fellowship on the Law of the Sea;

4. *Expresses its appreciation* to the United Nations Institute for Training and Research for its participation in the Programme, particularly for its efforts in the organization of regional courses and in the administration and organization of the fellowship programme in international law jointly sponsored and conducted by the United Nations and the Institute;

5. *Expresses its appreciation* to the United Nations Educational, Scientific and Cultural Organization for its participation in the Programme, in particular for the efforts it has made to support the teaching of international law;

6. *Also expresses its appreciation* to the Government of Brazil for its willingness to co-sponsor the regional training and refresher course for Latin American and Caribbean countries, held at Brasília from 21 November to 1 December 1988, and for acting as host to the course;

7. *Further expresses its appreciation* to the Hague Academy of International Law for the valuable contributions it has made to the Programme by enabling international law fellows under the sponsorship of the United Nations and the United Nations Institute for Training and Research to attend its annual international law courses and by providing facilities for seminars organized under the fellowship programme in international law in conjunction with the Academy courses, and for its constructive efforts in organizing the regional training and refresher courses held at Dakar in 1988 and at Bogotá in 1989;

8. *Notes with appreciation* the contributions made by the Hague Academy of International Law to the teaching, study, dissemination and wider appreciation of international law, and calls upon Member States and interested organizations to give favourable consideration to the appeal of the Academy for a continuation of, and, if possible, an increase in their financial contributions in order to enable the Academy to carry on with the above-mentioned activities;

9. *Urges* all Governments to encourage the inclusion of courses on international law in the programmes of legal studies offered at institutions of higher learning;

10. *Requests* the Secretary-General to continue to publicize the Programme and periodically to invite Member States, universities, philanthropic foundations and other interested national and international institutions and organizations, as well as individuals, to make voluntary contributions towards the financing of the Programme or otherwise to assist in its implementation and possible expansion;

11. *Reiterates its request* to Member States and to interested organizations and individuals to make voluntary contributions towards the financing of the Programme, in particular for the Hamilton Shirley Amerasinghe Memorial Fellowship on the Law of the Sea, for the International Law Seminar and for the fellowship programme in international law sponsored jointly by the United Nations and the United Nations Institute for Training and Research, and expresses its appreciation to those Member States, institutions and individuals that have made voluntary contributions for this purpose;

12. *Urges* in particular all Governments to make voluntary contributions with a view to covering the amount needed for the financing of the daily subsistence

allowance for up to twenty-five participants in each regional course organized by the United Nations Institute for Training and Research, thus alleviating the burden on prospective host countries and making it possible for the Institute to continue to organize the regional courses;

13. *Requests* the Secretary-General to report to the General Assembly at its forty-sixth session on the implementation of the Programme during 1990 and 1991 and, following consultations with the Advisory Committee on the United Nations Programme of Assistance in the Teaching, Study, Dissemination and Wider Appreciation of International Law, to submit recommendations regarding the execution of the Programme in subsequent years;

14. *Also requests* the Secretary-General to study alternative means of making the publications of the International Court of Justice available in all the other official languages in addition to French and English within existing appropriations in a way which meets the concerns expressed by the Court and to present the result of his considerations to the General Assembly;

15. *Decides* to include in the provisional agenda of its forty-sixth session the item entitled "United Nations Programme of Assistance in the Teaching, Study, Dissemination and Wider Appreciation of International Law".

General Assembly resolution 44/28

4 December 1989   Meeting 72   Adopted without vote

Approved by Sixth Committee (A/44/761) without vote, 27 November (meeting 47); 15-nation draft (A/C.6/44/L.16), amended by 12 nations (A/C.6/44/L.21), orally revised; agenda item 138.

Sponsors: Bolivia, Cyprus, Gabon, Ghana, Kenya, Lesotho, Libyan Arab Jamahiriya, Madagascar, Malawi, Netherlands, Romania, Turkey, Uganda, Uruguay, Venezuela.

Sponsors of amendment: Bolivia, Chile, Colombia, Costa Rica, Ecuador, Guatemala, Kuwait, Mexico, Nicaragua, Panama, Spain, Uruguay.

Meeting numbers. GA 44th session: 6th Committee 43, 44, 46, 47; plenary 72.

Establishment of an international criminal court on drug trafficking

In 1989, Trinidad and Tobago requested[7] the General Assembly to include on its agenda the question of international criminal responsibility of individuals and entities engaged in illicit trafficking in narcotic drugs and other transnational criminal activities, and the establishment of an international criminal court with jurisdiction over such crimes.

GENERAL ASSEMBLY ACTION

On 4 December 1989, the General Assembly, on the recommendation of the Sixth Committee, adopted **resolution 44/39** without vote.

International criminal responsibility of individuals and entities engaged in illicit trafficking in narcotic drugs across national frontiers and other transnational criminal activities: establishment of an international criminal court with jurisdiction over such crimes

The General Assembly,

Mindful that, in accordance with Article 13, paragraph 1, of the Charter of the United Nations, the General Assembly is called upon to initiate studies and make recommendations for the purpose of encouraging the progressive development of international law and its codification,

Recognizing that there is an established link between illicit trafficking in narcotic drugs and other organized criminal activities which endanger the constitutional order of States and violate basic human rights,

Mindful of the adoption on 19 December 1988 of the United Nations Convention against Illicit Traffic in Narcotic Drugs and Psychotropic Substances, which recognizes that illicit trafficking in narcotic drugs is an international criminal activity,

Bearing in mind the need to keep under review those topics of international law which, given their new or renewed interest for the international community, may be suitable for the progressive development of international law and its codification,

1. *Requests* the International Law Commission, when considering at its forty-second session the item entitled "Draft Code of Crimes against the Peace and Security of Mankind", to address the question of establishing an international criminal court or other international criminal trial mechanism with jurisdiction over persons alleged to have committed crimes which may be covered under such a code, including persons engaged in illicit trafficking in narcotic drugs across national frontiers, and to devote particular attention to that question in its report on that session;

2. *Requests* the Secretary-General to transmit to the International Law Commission any views expressed by Member States pursuant to paragraph 3 of resolution 44/32 of 4 December 1989, as well as the summary records of the debate on the present agenda item during the forty-fourth session of the General Assembly;

3. *Decides* to consider the question of establishing an international criminal court or other international criminal trial mechanism at its forty-fifth session when examining the report of the International Law Commission.

General Assembly resolution 44/39

4 December 1989   Meeting 72   Adopted without vote

Approved by Sixth Committee (A/44/770) without vote, 22 November (meeting 46); 17-nation draft (A/C.6/44/L.18); agenda item 152.

Sponsors: Antigua and Barbuda, Bahamas, Barbados, Belize, Comoros, Costa Rica, Grenada, Guyana, Jamaica, Libyan Arab Jamahiriya, Papua New Guinea, Saint Kitts and Nevis, Saint Lucia, Saint Vincent and the Grenadines, Suriname, Trinidad and Tobago, Vanuatu.

Meeting numbers. GA 44th session: 6th Committee 38-41, 46; plenary 72.

REFERENCES

[1]A/44/10. [2]A/44/475. [3]A/CN.4/L.431. [4]YUN 1988, p. 832, GA res. 43/169, 9 Dec. 1988. [5]A/44/712. [6]YUN 1987, p. 1087, GA res. 42/148, 7 Dec. 1987. [7]A/44/195.

International economic law

In 1989, aspects of international economic law continued to be considered by the United Nations Commission on International Trade Law (UNCITRAL) and by the Sixth Committee of the General Assembly.

International trade law

Report of UNCITRAL

In its report[1] on its twenty-second session (Vienna, 16 May–2 June 1989), UNCITRAL summarized its deliberations over the Draft Convention on the Liability of Operators of Transport Terminals in International Trade. The session also addressed international payments, the new international economic order, guarantees and stand-by letters of credit, international countertrade, status of conventions, training and assistance, and relevant General Assembly resolutions and other matters (see below). UNCITRAL's report was forwarded for comments to UNCTAD.

In response to a 1987 General Assembly request,[2] the Secretary-General submitted a report[3] containing replies by Governments concerning their intention to become party to conventions relating to international trade. Such information was received from Australia, Austria, Burkina Faso, Canada, Cuba, Czechoslovakia, Denmark, Finland, the Federal Republic of Germany, Greece, Japan, Kenya, Mexico, the Netherlands, the Philippines, Sweden, Switzerland and the United Kingdom.

Unification of trade law

Draft Convention on the Liability of Operators of Transport Terminals in International Trade

At its twenty-second session, the Commission had before it the text of the draft Convention,[4] as well as two reports by the Secretary-General, one being a compilation of comments by Governments and international organizations on the draft Convention,[5] and the other containing draft final clauses for the Convention.[6]

The Commission established a drafting group and requested it to incorporate into the text of the draft Convention the decisions taken by the Commission and to review the draft articles to ensure linguistic consistency within each language version and correspondence among them. The draft articles, as modified and submitted by the drafting group, were subsequently reviewed by the Commission. On 2 June, the Commission decided to submit the draft Convention to the General Assembly and recommended that the Assembly convene an international conference of plenipotentiaries in 1991 to conclude a Convention on the Liability of Operators of Transport Terminals in International Trade.

GENERAL ASSEMBLY ACTION

On 4 December 1989, the General Assembly, on the recommendation of the Sixth Committee, adopted **resolution 44/33** without a vote.

Report of the United Nations Commission on International Trade Law on the work of its twenty-second session

The General Assembly,

Recalling its resolution 2205(XXI) of 17 December 1966, by which it created the United Nations Commission on International Trade Law with a mandate to further the progressive harmonization and unification of the law of international trade and in that respect to bear in mind the interests of all peoples, in particular those of developing countries, in the extensive development of international trade, as well as its resolution 43/166 of 9 December 1988,

Reaffirming its conviction that the progressive harmonization and unification of international trade law, in reducing or removing legal obstacles to the flow of international trade, especially those affecting the developing countries, would significantly contribute to universal economic co-operation among all States on a basis of equality, equity and common interest and to the elimination of discrimination in international trade and, thereby, to the well-being of all peoples,

Having considered the report of the United Nations Commission on International Trade Law on the work of its twenty-second session,

Noting that the Commission adopted a draft convention on the liability of operators of transport terminals in international trade and recommended in the decision in paragraph 225 of its report that the General Assembly should convene an international conference of plenipotentiaries for a duration of three weeks in 1991 to conclude, on the basis of the draft convention, a convention on the liability of operators of transport terminals in international trade,

Recognizing the need for the Commission to have adequate sources of funding for its programme of training and assistance in international trade law,

1. *Takes note with appreciation* of the report of the United Nations Commission on International Trade Law on the work of its twenty-second session;

2. *Reaffirms* the mandate of the Commission, as the core legal body within the United Nations system in the field of international trade law, to co-ordinate legal activities in this field in order to avoid duplication of effort and to promote efficiency, consistency and coherence in the unification and harmonization of international trade law and, in this connection, recommends that the Commission, through its secretariat, should continue to maintain close co-operation with the other international organs and organizations, including regional organizations, active in the field of international trade law;

3. *Calls upon* the Commission to continue to take account of the relevant provisions of the resolutions concerning the new international economic order, as adopted by the General Assembly at its sixth and seventh special sessions;

4. *Expresses its appreciation* to the Commission for the valuable work done in preparing a draft convention on the liability of operators of transport terminals in international trade;

5. *Decides* that an international conference of plenipotentiaries shall be convened at Vienna from 2 to 19 April 1991 to consider the draft convention prepared by the Commission and to embody the results of its work in a convention on the liability of operators of transport terminals in international trade;

6. *Requests* the Secretary-General:

(a) To invite all States to participate in the conference;

(b) To invite representatives of organizations that have received a standing invitation from the General Assembly to participate in the sessions and the work of all international conferences convened under its auspices in the capacity of observers to participate in the conference in that capacity, in accordance with Assembly resolutions 3237(XXIX) of 22 November 1974 and 31/152 of 20 December 1976;

(c) To invite representatives of the national liberation movements recognized by the Organization of African Unity in its region to participate in the conference in the capacity of observers in accordance with General Assembly resolution 3280(XXIX) of 10 December 1974;

(d) To invite the specialized agencies and the International Atomic Energy Agency, as well as interested organs of the United Nations and interested international organizations, to be represented at the conference by observers;

7. *Reaffirms* the importance, in particular for developing countries, of the work of the Commission concerned with training and assistance in the field of international trade law and the desirability for it to sponsor seminars and symposia, in particular those organized on a regional basis, to promote such training and assistance, and, in this connection:

(a) Expresses its appreciation to the Commission for organizing the symposium on international trade law held in conjunction with the twenty-second session of the Commission and to the Governments whose contributions enabled the symposium to take place;

(b) Invites Governments, the relevant United Nations organs, organizations, institutions and individuals to make voluntary contributions to the United Nations Commission on International Trade Law symposia and, where appropriate, to the financing of special projects, and otherwise to assist the secretariat of the Commission in financing and organizing seminars and symposia, in particular in developing countries, and in the award of fellowships to candidates from developing countries to enable them to participate in such seminars and symposia;

8. *Repeats its invitation* to those States that have not yet done so to consider signing, ratifying or acceding to the conventions elaborated under the auspices of the Commission;

9. *Approves* the initiative of the Commission to have prepared an official Arabic language version of the Convention on the Limitation Period in the International Sale of Goods, of 14 June 1974, as amended by the Protocol of 11 April 1980.

General Assembly resolution 44/33

4 December 1989   Meeting 72   Adopted without vote

Approved by Sixth Committee (A/44/723) without vote, 10 November (meeting 38); 26-nation draft (A/C.6/44/L.5); agenda item 143.

Sponsors: Argentina, Austria, Brazil, Byelorussian SSR, Canada, Cyprus, Czechoslovakia, Denmark, Egypt, Finland, France, German Democratic Republic, Germany, Federal Republic of, Guyana, Hungary, Italy, Kenya, Lesotho, Libyan Arab Jamahiriya, Morocco, Netherlands, Poland, Spain, Sweden, Turkey, Yugoslavia.

Financial implications. 5th Committee, A/44/809; SG, A/C.5/44/26.

Meeting numbers. GA 44th session: 5th Committee 48; 6th Committee 4-6, 38; plenary 72.

International payments

The Commission in 1989 had before it the reports of the seventeenth[7] and eighteenth[8] sessions of the Working Group on International Payments, which had decided that provisions should be prepared in the form of a model law, and that the scope of application should be limited to those credit transfers that were international in nature. It specified, however, that the model law should apply to all international credit transfers, whether they were in electronic or paper-based form, and decided that the draft provisions should be entitled draft Model Law on International Credit Transfers.

The Commission recommended that the Working Group continue its efforts with a view to presenting a text to UNCITRAL for consideration at its twenty-fourth session.

Guarantees and stand-by letters of credit

The Commission had before it the report[9] of its Working Group on International Contract Practices from its twelfth session. It noted that the Working Group had reviewed the International Chamber of Commerce (ICC) draft Uniform Rules for Guarantees, and had discussed the desirability and feasibility of achieving greater uniformity at the statutory level. UNCITRAL noted the recommendation of the Working Group that the preparation of a uniform law, whether in the form of a model law or a convention, be initiated. The Commission decided that the work on a uniform law should be undertaken by the Working Group, and requested the Secretariat to prepare the necessary documentation.

International countertrade

The Commission considered a report[10] on a draft outline of a legal guide on drawing up international countertrade contracts. UNCITRAL considered whether it should continue work in the area. The prevailing view was that such a guide should be prepared by UNCITRAL, and that, because it was a specialized legal body including States at different levels of economic development, its work would not duplicate that of other bodies. The Commission requested the Secretariat to prepare for its next session draft chapters of the legal guide. It considered that the draft outline of the possible content and structure of such a guide already prepared by the Secretariat provided a good basis for the commencement of its future work.

Co-ordination of work

The Commission reviewed a report[11] of the Secretary-General on current activities of international organizations related to the harmonization and unification of international trade law. The report dealt with international commercial contracts, commodities, industrialization, transnational corporations, transfer of technology, industrial and intellectual property law, international payments, international transport, international commercial arbitration, private international law, trade facilitation, and other topics of international trade law, congresses and publications.

The Secretary of the Commission noted that, while it had been the practice to submit a report on the current activities of international organizations every three years, the Secretariat intended in the future to submit them on a more frequent basis.

Training and assistance

In 1989, the Commission had before it a note[12] by the Secretariat describing training and assistance carried out during the prior year, as well as possible future activities. The note indicated that the Secretariat had endeavoured to plan a more extensive programme of activities than previously; in doing so, it had kept in mind the 1981 decision by UNCITRAL that a major purpose of training and assistance activities should be the promotion of texts that had been prepared by the Commission.

UNCITRAL continued to co-operate and participate in seminars and symposia on international trade law. It held a symposium on UNCITRAL activities during its 1989 session. Funds were made available for 32 scholarships covering travel expenses of participants from developing countries, and an additional 48 individuals participated in the symposium without financial support. A seminar was held at New Delhi, India (12-16 October) and was conducted jointly with the Asian-African Legal Consultative Committee (AALCC). UNCTAD and the International Institute for the Unification of Private Law (UNIDROIT) also sponsored the seminar, which was intended to promote awareness in the Asian States members of AALCC of the conventions and other legal texts prepared by the sponsoring organizations. The majority of participants were from the embassies of the respective States at New Delhi. It was also attended by members of the Indian Council of Arbitration.

In **resolution 44/33** of 4 December 1989, the General Assembly reaffirmed the importance of such training and assistance, particularly for developing countries, and called for contributions to the trust fund for UNCITRAL to finance seminars and symposia.

Legal aspects of the new international economic order

In 1989, legal aspects of the new international economic order (NIEO) continued to be dealt with by UNCITRAL and the Sixth Committee of the General Assembly.

UNCITRAL consideration. In 1989, the Commission had before it a report[13] of the Working Group on the New International Economic Order. The Working Group had engaged in an examination of major issues arising in connection with procurement and had discussed ways in which those issues might be treated. It had decided to begin preparing a model procurement law to assist countries in restructuring or improving their procurement laws and procedures, or to help them establish sound procurement laws in cases where none currently existed.

The Commission endorsed the Working Group's view of the desirability of greater participation by developing countries in the Working Group, and requested it to proceed with its work on NIEO expeditiously.

Report of the Secretary-General. In August,[14] a report was submitted by the Secretary-General in response to a 1988 General Assembly resolution[15] regarding NIEO. The report contained views and comments received from seven Member States on a 1984 UNITAR study[16] on the codification and progressive development of the principles and norms of international law relating to NIEO.

GENERAL ASSEMBLY ACTION

On 4 December 1989, the General Assembly, on the recommendation of the Sixth Committee, adopted **resolution 44/30** by recorded vote.

Progressive development of the principles and norms of international law relating to the new international economic order

The General Assembly,

Bearing in mind that, in accordance with the Charter of the United Nations, the General Assembly is called upon to initiate studies and make recommendations for the purpose of encouraging the progressive development of international law and its codification,

Recalling its resolutions 3201(S-VI) and 3202(S-VI) of 1 May 1974, containing the Declaration and the Programme of Action on the Establishment of a New International Economic Order, 3281(XXIX) of 12 December 1974, containing the Charter of Economic Rights and Duties of States, 3362(S-VII) of 16 September 1975 on development and international economic cooperation and 35/56 of 5 December 1980, the annex to which contains the International Development Strategy for the Third United Nations Development Decade,

Recalling also its resolutions 34/150 of 17 December 1979 and 35/166 of 15 December 1980, entitled "Consolidation and progressive development of the principles and norms of international economic law relating in particular to the legal aspects of the new international economic order", and its resolutions 36/107 of 10 December 1981, 37/103 of 16 December 1982, 38/128 of 19 December 1983, 39/75 of 13 December 1984, 40/67 of 11 December 1985, 41/73 of 3 December 1986, 42/149

of 7 December 1987 and 43/162 of 9 December 1988, entitled "Progressive development of the principles and norms of international law relating to the new international economic order",

Bearing in mind the urgent need to adopt measures to reactivate the process of international economic cooperation and the negotiations undertaken for that purpose, particularly in view of the economic difficulties encountered by the developing countries,

Considering the close link between the establishment of a just and equitable international economic order and the existence of an appropriate legal framework,

Recognizing the need for the codification and progressive development of the principles and norms of international law relating to the new international economic order,

Recalling the analytical study submitted to the General Assembly at its thirty-ninth session by the United Nations Institute for Training and Research,

1. *Notes with appreciation* the views and comments submitted by Governments pursuant to resolutions 40/67, 41/73, 42/149 and 43/162;

2. *Requests* the Secretary-General:

(a) To continue to seek proposals of Member States concerning the most appropriate procedures to be adopted with regard to the consideration of the analytical study, as well as the codification and progressive development of the principles and norms of international law relating to the new international economic order;

(b) To include the proposals received in accordance with paragraph 2 *(a)* of the present resolution in a report to be submitted to the General Assembly at its forty-sixth session;

3. *Recommends* that the Sixth Committee should consider making a final decision at the forty-sixth session of the General Assembly on the question of the appropriate forum within its framework which would undertake the task of completing the elaboration of the process of codification and progressive development of the principles and norms of international law relating to the new international economic order, taking into account the proposals and suggestions which have been or will be submitted by Member States on the matter;

4. *Decides* to include in the provisional agenda of its forty-sixth session the item entitled "Progressive development of the principles and norms of international law relating to the new international economic order".

General Assembly resolution 44/30

4 December 1989   Meeting 72   126-1-24 (recorded vote)

Approved by Sixth Committee (A/44/763) by recorded vote (102-0-25), 21 November (meeting 44); 38-nation draft (A/C.6/44/L.6); agenda item 140.

Sponsors: Angola, Bangladesh, Burkina Faso, Burundi, Cameroon, Cape Verde, Chile, China, Colombia, Congo, Cuba, Democratic Yemen, Ecuador, Equatorial Guinea, Ethiopia, Gabon, Ghana, Guatemala, Guinea, Jamaica, Lao People's Democratic Republic, Mali, Mexico, Nicaragua, Niger, Nigeria, Pakistan, Panama, Peru, Philippines, Romania, Rwanda, Suriname, Uganda, United Republic of Tanzania, Venezuela, Viet Nam, Zambia.

Meeting numbers. GA 44th session: 6th Committee 15, 16, 44; plenary 72.

Recorded vote in Assembly as follows:

In favour: Afghanistan, Albania, Algeria, Angola, Antigua and Barbuda, Argentina, Bahamas, Bahrain, Bangladesh, Barbados, Benin, Bhutan, Bolivia, Botswana, Brazil, Brunei Darussalam, Bulgaria, Burkina Faso, Burundi, Byelorussian SSR, Cameroon, Cape Verde, Central African Republic, Chad, Chile, China, Colombia, Congo, Costa Rica, Côte d'Ivoire, Cuba, Cyprus, Czechoslovakia, Democratic Kampuchea, Democratic Yemen, Djibouti, Ecuador, Egypt, Equatorial Guinea, Ethiopia, Fiji, Gabon, Gambia, German Democratic Republic, Ghana, Grenada, Guatemala, Guinea, Guinea-Bissau, Guyana, Haiti, India, Indonesia, Iran, Iraq, Jamaica, Jordan, Kenya, Kuwait, Lao People's Democratic Republic, Lebanon, Lesotho, Liberia, Libyan Arab Jamahiriya, Madagascar, Malawi, Malaysia, Maldives, Mali, Malta, Mauritania, Mauritius, Mexico, Mongolia, Morocco, Mozambique, Myanmar, Nepal, Nicaragua, Niger, Nigeria, Oman, Pakistan, Panama, Papua New Guinea, Paraguay, Peru, Philippines, Poland, Qatar, Romania, Rwanda, Saint Lucia, Saint Vincent and the Grenadines, Samoa, Sao Tome and Principe, Saudi Arabia, Senegal, Seychelles, Sierra Leone, Singapore, Solomon Islands, Somalia, Sri Lanka, Sudan, Suriname, Swaziland, Syrian Arab Republic, Thailand, Togo, Trinidad and Tobago, Tunisia, Uganda, Ukrainian SSR, USSR, United Arab Emirates, United Republic of Tanzania, Uruguay, Vanuatu, Venezuela, Viet Nam, Yemen, Yugoslavia, Zaire, Zambia, Zimbabwe.

Against: Luxembourg.*

Abstaining: Australia, Austria, Belgium, Canada, Denmark, Finland, France, Germany, Federal Republic of, Greece, Hungary, Iceland, Ireland, Israel, Italy, Japan, Netherlands, New Zealand, Norway, Portugal, Spain, Sweden, Turkey, United Kingdom, United States.

*Later advised the Secretariat it had intended to abstain.

REFERENCES

[1]A/44/17. [2]YUN 1987, p. 1079, GA res. 42/152, 7 Dec. 1987. [3]A/44/453 & Add.1. [4]A/CN.9/298. [5]A/CN.9/319 & Add.1-5. [6]A/CN.9/321. [7]A/CN.9/317. [8]A/CN.9/318. [9]A/CN.9/316. [10]A/CN.9/322. [11]A/CN.9/324. [12]A/CN.9/323. [13]A/CN.9/315. [14]A/44/455 & Add.1. [15]YUN 1988, p. 850, GA res. 43/162, 9 Dec. 1988. [16]YUN 1984, p. 1115.

PUBLICATION

United Nations Commission on International Trade Law: Yearbook, vol. XX: *1989*, Sales No. E.90.V.9.

PART SIX

Administrative and budgetary questions

Chapter I

United Nations financing and programming

The Secretary-General reported to the General Assembly at the close of the year that the Organization had very narrowly avoided bankruptcy during 1989 and prospects were very grim indeed. The only real solution to the continuing financial crisis (resulting from the withholding of assessed contributions to the Organization's regular budget and for peace-keeping operations) was the payment by all Member States of their assessed contributions in full and on time. Unless and until that basic legal obligation under the Charter was honoured by all Member States without exception, the threat of financial collapse would continue to haunt the United Nations.

As at 8 December, more than a third of the 1989 regular budget assessment remained unpaid; total assessed contributions outstanding, including for prior years, were $529.2 million, of which $430.1 million, including about $213.9 million of past arrears, was owed by one Member State. On the basis of present assumptions, all reserves would be exhausted and cash depletion would occur in the last quarter of 1990.

To maintain the United Nation's financial viability, according to the Secretary-General, it was essential to at least double the Working Capital Fund from its present level for the biennium 1990-1991, and for the membership to assume collective responsibility and authorize the necessary assessments on all Member States. However, on the recommendation of the Advisory Committee on Administrative and Budgetary Questions this proposal was deferred to 1990.

The financial crisis was not restricted to the United Nations itself but extended to the UN system as a whole. Unpaid assessments by mid-year amounted to $1,034 million, or more than 51 per cent of total 1989 assessment. In addition, some $618 million in arrears due to prior years, corresponding to nearly 31 per cent of total 1989 assessments, remained outstanding.

The Secretary-General submitted his final report on the administrative and financial reforms recommended by the Group of High-level Intergovernmental Experts to Review the Efficiency of the Administrative and Financial Functioning of the United Nations (Group of 18) covering reforms since 1 January 1987. Proposed post reduction for the biennium 1990-1991 included 11 posts at the Under-Secretary-General and Assistant Secretary-General level, while the overall post reduction be-

tween the programme budget for the biennium 1988-1989 and then for 1990-1991 was 1,368 posts, a reduction of about 12 per cent (from 11,422 posts to 10,054).

Final budget appropriations for the biennium 1988-1989 were decreased by $16.4 million from the $1,788.7 million appropriated in 1988. The Secretary-General submitted a proposed programme budget for 1990-1991 of $1,983,863,400 which he stated represented a negative real growth rate of 0.4 per cent. Actual appropriations approved by the General Assembly amounted to $1,974,634,000. ACABQ calculated that the grand total of UN expenditures for the biennium, including the net estimate for the regular budget, support services, substantive activities and operational projects, to be about $4.2 billion. The Advisory Committee also calculated that the regular budgets (or budget estimates) of the United Nations, the specialized agencies (excluding the International Fund for Agricultural Development and the International Atomic Energy Agency (IAEA) for 1990 would amount to $2,306,839,721, of which $2,178,378,229 would be covered by assessed contributions. Further assessed contributions for the United Nations were likely to arise in 1990 for peace-keeping operations, ACABQ said; 1989 assessments totalled $720.7 million. Regarding the established posts for 1990 authorized or requested against the regular budget, ACABQ noted a decrease of 1,132 compared to the 1989 total. ACABQ also calculated that as at 30 September 1989 contributions of $609.6 million were outstanding to the United Nations and $675.2 million to the specialized agencies and IAEA, representing 63.45 per cent of total net contributions of Member States actually payable in respect of 1989, as compared to a corresponding figure of 58.01 per cent as at 30 September 1988.

The General Assembly also adopted resolutions on the scale of assessments (44/197 A), assessment procedures for non-member States (44/197 B), financial reports, audited financial statements and reports of the Board of Auditors (44/183), programme planning (44/194), and the Joint Inspection Unit (44/184).

United Nations financing

Financial crisis
Reports of the Secretary-General. On 29 November, the Secretary-General submitted a report[1]

analyzing the UN's financial emergency, in response to a 1988 General Assembly request.[2] He noted that the origin and nature of the financial difficulties had been discussed year after year, and every year since 1965, the Assembly had included an item entitled "Financial emergency of the United Nations" on its agenda. Nevertheless, fundamental solutions had not been found and the situation continued to be precarious.

The level of unpaid assessed contributions, the Secretary-General reported, had risen from $83.4 million at the end of 1978 to $394.9 million at the end of 1988—far exceeding the $255.5 million then available from the Working Capital Fund. The Secretary-General believed it was essential to increase the Working Capital Fund from its present level of $100 million to not less than $200 million for the biennium 1990-1991. He recalled that the Working Capital Fund had been established in 1946 for the purpose of providing sufficient liquidity to enable the Secretary-General to advance from it such sums as might be necessary to finance budgetary appropriations pending receipt of contributions. It had been based on a percentage of authorized appropriations, but whereas it had reflected 43.1 per cent of the annual budget in 1963, with the growth of appropriations for peace-keeping operations, the current level of the Fund as a percentage of the combined regular budget and peace-keeping operations for 1989 was 6 per cent.

The Secretary-General listed four options for financing the proposed Working Capital Fund increase: apportionment among all Member States as part of their assessments; assessing the increase over several years rather than at one time; financing through voluntary contributions; and crediting to the Fund all or part of the amounts realized from suspension of financial regulation provisions in respect of surpluses under the regular budget.

Regarding peace-keeping operations, outstanding contributions as at 31 October 1989 to the five peace-keeping operations from assessed contributions totalled $569.9 million. The dramatic increase in the number of peace-keeping operations had also focused attention on the problem of start-up financing for such operations—funds needed in advance of General Assembly approval of financing for an operation. The Working Capital Fund was now insufficient for the purpose.

In December, the Secretary-General submitted to the General Assembly a report[3] on the current financial crisis and funding prospects. As of 8 December, $261.9 million or 33.7 per cent of 1989's total regular budget assessments of $777 million remained unpaid. Together with arrears of $267.3 million for prior years, total assessed contributions outstanding amounted to $529.2 million. Cash reserves were replenished only during the first four months of the year and had been drawn down since to meet current operating requirements. The pattern of membership payment as a whole was much less encouraging in 1989 than in previous years despite the efforts of some Member States. By 8 December, only 72 Member States had fully paid their assessed contributions to the regular budget, in contrast to 79 at the same time in 1988. Of the 87 Member States still in arrears, 44 owed more than their 1989 assessments, and 19 owed an amount equal to their 1989 assessment. At the same date, 22 Member States had made no payment at all, compared to 14 at the same time the previous year.

The Organization had managed to avoid insolvency so far only by repeated use of its reserves, together with lower expenditures than expected, resulting primarily from currency fluctuations and consistently high vacancy rates. If actual receipts followed the projected pattern—an element heavily dependent on one Member State—at the end of 1989 the Organization's reserves (the Working Capital Fund and the Special Account) would be replenished only by $48.1 million, leaving a deficit in the reserves of $166.4 million. Unpaid assessed contributions at that point would stand at the unprecedented level of $456.1 million.

The Secretary-General recalled that he had indicated to the General Assembly the previous year that expanding responsibilities for peacemaking and peace-keeping had placed new strains on the Organization's already precarious financial situation. If Member States did not meet their legal obligations in 1990 to pay all assessed contributions in full and on time, the Organization would be even more likely to face insolvency in 1990. With income for 1990 expected to be $772.9 million and disbursements amounting to $849.5 million, a shortfall of $76.6 million would result.

The Secretary-General concluded that the fragility of the Organization's financial situation would continue so long as its reserves were not fully funded. The financial situation could deteriorate even more rapidly and dramatically should additional demands arise from existing or new peace-keeping operations, or through the negative effect of acute currency fluctuations or inflation. So long as the Organization's reserves were not fully re-established, he would continue to seek agreement of Member States to a substantial increase in the level of the Working Capital Fund. He paid tribute to all Member States that had paid their 1989 assessments in full and in a timely manner, as well as to the one Member State which, by advancing the payment of its 1989 regular budget assessment to December 1988, had helped bridge the 1988 cash problem. He again requested those Member States able to do so to make advance payment in December 1989 on their estimated 1990 assessments and urged all Member States to pay their 1990 regular budget assessment in January 1990 or as early as possible. He again appealed to those Member States in arrears, especially the major contributor, to meet their legal obligations so that the Organization's reserves could be restored. The Secretary-General urged the General Assembly to address the cash and the reserve aspects of the financial crisis in concrete terms during its current session.

ACC Consideration. In October, the Administrative Committee on Co-ordination (ACC), at its second regular session of 1989, adopted a decision[5] stating that the financial difficulties from which the UN system was now suffering had one common cause: the failure of a number of Member States to pay, promptly and in full, their contributions. The international co-operation of which UN organizations were instruments was jeopardized by a lack of resources, and contributions owed had reached record levels. A common feature of measures taken by the UN organizations to deal with the cash shortage was the curtailment of programmes and activities, which had inflicted serious damage on the infrastructure of international, political, economic and social co-operation.

ACABQ action. On 13 December, the Advisory Committee on Administrative and Budgetary Questions (ACABQ), having considered the two reports of the Secretary-General, stated[4] that the reports did not provide sufficient basis for ACABQ to formulate and submit definitive recommendations concerning increasing the level of the Working Capital Fund and modalities for financing such an increase. It recommended deferral of consideration of the Secretary-General's proposal to increase the Fund's level until 1990. The Advisory Committee would then return to the matter on a priority basis at its spring 1990 session, with a view to preparing a comprehensive report attempting to address all major aspects of the issue and submitting definitive recommendations.

GENERAL ASSEMBLY ACTION

On 21 December, on the recommendation of the Fifth (Administrative and Budgetary) Committee, the General Assembly adopted together **resolutions 44/195 A** and **B** without vote.

Current financial crisis and financial emergency of the United Nations

A

The General Assembly,

Recalling the purposes and principles of the Charter of the United Nations and, in particular, Article 17,

Recalling also its resolutions 41/213 of 19 December 1986, 42/211 and 42/212 of 21 December 1987 and 43/215 of 21 December 1988,

Deeply concerned that the current financial crisis threatens the financial solvency, stability and work of the Organization,

Reaffirming the need for a durable, reliable and lasting financial foundation for the Organization, in accordance with the Charter,

Taking note of the report of the Secretary-General on the current financial crisis of the United Nations and of the related report of the Advisory Committee on Administrative and Budgetary Questions,

Taking note also of the views expressed by Member States in the Fifth Committee on the financial situation, especially the current financial crisis of the United Nations,

1. *Reaffirms* the legal obligation of all Member States, under the Charter of the United Nations, to finance the expenses of the Organization as apportioned by the General Assembly;

2. *Urges* all Member States to pay their assessed contributions in full and in a timely manner in accordance with regulation 5.4 of the Financial Regulations of the United Nations;

3. *Requests* those Member States which are in arrears to make every effort to pay their outstanding contributions;

4. *Requests* the Secretary-General to continue to monitor the financial situation of the United Nations and to keep the President of the General Assembly and the chairmen of the regional groups informed so as to facilitate consideration by Member States if the situation so requires;

5. *Also requests* the Secretary-General to communicate to all Member States the latest information on the current financial crisis facing the Organization and to submit a report thereon in a timely and comprehensive manner to the General Assembly at its forty-fifth session.

B

The General Assembly,

Recalling its resolution 43/220 of 21 December 1988 and all previous relevant resolutions,

Noting the increased importance of the role of the Organization in peace-keeping and other related activities,

Mindful of the report of the Negotiating Committee on the Financial Emergency of the United Nations and of the views expressed by Member States in the Fifth Committee at the thirty-second session of the General Assembly,

Having considered the report of the Secretary-General on the analysis of the financial situation of the United Nations, and the related report of the Advisory Committee on Administrative and Budgetary Questions,

Noting with concern that the short-term deficit of the Organization, although marginally reduced during the year, is expected to reach approximately 315 million United States dollars as at 31 December 1989,

Concerned at the precarious financial situation of all peace-keeping operations and noting that troop-contributing Member States, including the developing-country troop contributors of past and present peace-keeping operations, have borne most of the burden of the deficit,

Noting with concern long delays in and partial payments and non-payment of assessed contributions to past and current peace-keeping operations,

Reiterating earlier appeals to Member States, without prejudice to their position of principle, to make voluntary contributions to the Special Account referred to in annex VI to the report of the Secretary-General on the analysis of the financial situation of the United Nations,

Taking note of the proposal of the Secretary-General in paragraph 29 of his report on the analysis of the financial situation of the United Nations to increase the level of the Working Capital Fund,

Taking into account the views expressed by Member States in the Fifth Committee during the forty-fourth session,

1. *Reaffirms* its commitment to seek a comprehensive and generally acceptable solution to the financial problems of the United Nations, based on the principle of the collective financial responsibility of Member States and in strict compliance with the Charter of the United Nations;

2. *Urges* all Member States to meet their financial obligations under the Charter by paying promptly and in full all assessed contributions and advances to the Working Capital Fund;

3. *Requests* the Secretary-General, in addition to sending his official communications to the permanent representatives of Member States, to approach, as and when appropriate, the Governments of Member States for the purpose of encouraging expeditious payment in full of all outstanding assessed contributions to all peace-keeping operations, as well as seeking further voluntary contributions for peace-keeping operations;

4. *Expresses its appreciation* to all Member States that pay their assessed contributions in full within thirty days of the receipt of the Secretary-General's communication, in accordance with regulation 5.4 of the Financial Regulations of the United Nations;

5. *Requests* the Negotiating Committee on the Financial Emergency of the United Nations to keep the financial situation of the Organization under review and to report, as and when appropriate, to the General Assembly;

6. *Concurs* with the recommendation of the Advisory Committee on Administrative and Budgetary Questions in paragraph 12 of its report;

7. *Requests* the Secretary-General to submit a report on the financial emergency of the United Nations to the General Assembly at its forty-fifth session by 10 October 1990, including therein a comprehensive analysis of the financial situation of the United Nations and results of his efforts in implementation of paragraph 3 of the present resolution.

General Assembly resolutions 44/195 A and B

21 December 1989   Meeting 84   Adopted without vote

Approved by Fifth Committee (A/44/899 & A/44/900) without vote, 19 December (meeting 59); draft by Chairman following informal consultations (A/C.5/44/L.21, part A); agenda items 40 & 125.
Meeting numbers. GA 44th session: 5th Committee 56-59; plenary 84.

Also on 21 December, on the recommendation of the Fifth Committee, the General Assembly adopted **resolution 44/204** without vote.

Working Capital Fund for the biennium 1990-1991

The General Assembly,

Resolves that:

1. The Working Capital Fund shall be established for the biennium 1990-1991 in the amount of 100 million United States dollars;

2. Member States shall make advances to the Working Capital Fund in accordance with the scale adopted by the General Assembly for contributions of Member States to the budget for the year 1990;

3. There shall be set off against this allocation of advances:

(*a*) Credits to Member States resulting from transfers made in 1959 and 1960 from surplus account to the Working Capital Fund in an adjusted amount of 1,025,092 dollars;

(*b*) Cash advances paid by Member States to the Working Capital Fund for the biennium 1988-1989 under General Assembly resolution 42/228 of 21 December 1987;

4. Should the credits and advances paid by any Member State to the Working Capital Fund for the biennium 1988-1989 exceed the amount of that Member State's advance under the provisions of paragraph 2 of the present resolution, the excess shall be set off against the amount of the contributions payable by the Member State in respect of the biennium 1990-1991;

5. The Secretary-General is authorized to advance from the Working Capital Fund:

(*a*) Such sums as may be necessary to finance budgetary appropriations pending the receipt of contributions; sums so advanced shall be reimbursed as soon as receipts from contributions are available for the purpose;

(*b*) Such sums as may be necessary to finance commitments which may be duly authorized under the provisions of the resolutions adopted by the General Assembly, in particular resolution 44/203 of 21 December 1989 relating to unforeseen and extraordinary expenses; the Secretary-General shall make provision in the budget estimates for reimbursing the Working Capital Fund;

(*c*) Such sums as may be necessary to continue the revolving fund to finance miscellaneous self-liquidating purchases and activities, which, together with net sums outstanding for the same purpose, do not exceed 200,000 dollars; advances in excess of the total of 200,000 dollars may be made with the prior concurrence of the Advisory Committee on Administrative and Budgetary Questions;

(*d*) With the prior concurrence of the Advisory Committee on Administrative and Budgetary Questions, such sums as may be required to finance payments of advance insurance premiums where the period of insurance extends beyond the end of the biennium in which payment is made; the Secretary-General shall make provision in the budget estimates of each biennium, during the life of the related policies, to cover the charges applicable to each biennium;

(*e*) Such sums as may be necessary to enable the Tax Equalization Fund to meet current commitments pending the accumulation of credits; such advances shall be repaid as soon as credits are available in the Tax Equalization Fund;

6. Should the provision in paragraph 1 of the present resolution prove inadequate to meet the purposes normally related to the Working Capital Fund, the Secretary-General is authorized to utilize, in the biennium 1990-1991, cash from special funds and accounts in his custody, under the conditions approved by the General Assembly in its resolution 1341(XIII) of 13 December 1958, or the proceeds of loans authorized by the Assembly.

General Assembly resolution 44/204

21 December 1989   Meeting 84   Adopted without vote

Approved by Fifth Committee (A/44/905) without vote, 20 December (meeting 61); agenda item 123.
Meeting numbers. GA 44th session: 5th Committee 11-18, 19, 23-32, 34, 36, 37, 39, 45, 46, 48, 61; plenary 84.

Reform efforts

Report of the Secretary-General. In April 1989, the Secretary-General submitted his final report[6] on the implementation of a 1986 General Assembly resolution[7] on the review of UN efficiency and functioning that had endorsed the recommendations of the Group of 18. Earlier progress reports had been submitted, in 1987[8] and 1988.[9] The final report was requested by the Assembly in 1988.[10]

The report presented a factual review of all actions taken by the Secretary-General since 1 January 1987 to implement the 1986 resolution, as well as actions taken by the Assembly itself on a number of related issues. The Secretary-General noted that, at the same time that it embarked on an unprecedented reform programme, the Secretariat continued to face one of its most serious financial crises, which required measures in 1986 and 1987 that hampered his efforts to implement the 1986 resolution.[7] Considerable effort had to be devoted to crisis management rather than to structural reform. Reductions in staff resulted less from planned implementation of post reduction than from financial restrictions, since posts were often left vacant that were never intended for abolition but could be filled neither through staff redeployment nor recruitment, owing to lack of funds.

Despite these circumstances, a substantial number of recommendations of the Group of 18 had been implemented. The Secretary-General discussed progress regarding recommendations pertaining to the intergovernmental machinery and its functioning, structure of the Secretariat, personnel monitoring, evaluation and inspection, and planning and budget procedure.

The Group of 18, noting the expansion of the UN agenda and corresponding growth in intergovernmental machinery, had felt that there was ample room for reduction in the volume of meetings and documentation. The Secretary-General reported that the expected reductions had not been achieved, but a number of intergovernmental bodies were still considering aspects of the recommendations. He also stated that a more effective use of the time and conference facilities by the General Assembly and its subsidiary organs was contingent primarily upon the co-operation of Member States.

The restructuring of the Secretariat's political sector was now completed but that of the economic and social sectors was still pending. Delays were attributed to the fact that the Secretariat's structure and work programme was closely linked to the structure of the intergovernmental machinery and also to Assembly instructions to the Secretary-General to take into account decisions by the intergovernmental machinery when proceeding with reforms. The Secretary-General therefore believed that the reform period for the economic and social sectors should be extended. Major reorganization had occurred in the political, administrative and information areas, though the Secretariat's review had revealed that there was little real duplication.

The Secretary-General noted that he had presented his proposals for post reduction to the General Assembly through the Committee for Programme and Coordination (CPC) and ACABQ, and the Assembly had decided[10] that 12.1 per cent of posts funded by the regular budget should be abolished by the end of 1989, with a 10 per cent reduction in conference service staffing in New York and Geneva. Regarding the 25 per cent reduction in posts at the Assistant Secretary-General and Under-Secretary-General level,[11] the Secretary-General proposed abolition of two posts at the Under-Secretary-General level and 8 at the Assistant Secretary-General level, to be reflected in the proposed 1990-1991 programme budget.[12]

The Secretary-General concluded that while resolution 41/213 envisaged implementation of the various recommendations over three years, some recommendations could not be implemented within a fixed period, but were of an ongoing nature, particularly in the area of human resources management. Furthermore, actions by the Secretary-General had to be based on decisions yet to be taken by Member States in the General Assembly or its subsidiary bodies. He therefore viewed implementation of the 1986 resolution not as a finite process but as one that would continue to contribute to a more effective and efficient Secretariat.

An October report[13] of the Secretary-General related to the establishment and operation of a reserve fund. The General Assembly had requested formulation of a set of procedures for such a fund in 1988.[14] The Secretary-General said the purpose of a reserve fund seemed to be to minimize, during any given biennium, changes in the level of the programme budget resulting from variations in the forecast included in the programme budget in respect of currency fluctuation, inflation in non-staff costs and statutory cost increases for staff. There were two alternatives for a reserve: a separate fund outside the programme budget, or a section within the programme budget, with either being funded through assessed contributions. The Secretary-General concluded that the second approach was to be preferred, and suggested guidelines for its operation.

ACABQ reported in November[15] that it had a number of difficulties with the Secretary-General's suggestions. For example, the idea of financing the fund from the outset through assessment, even before the need for recourse to it had been identified, presented Member States with an unnecessary additional burden. It said that further thought needed to be given to the question and recommended consideration be deferred to 1991.

In 1988, the General Assembly had established[14] the contingency fund at a level of $15 million, based on preliminary estimates, for the biennium 1990-1991. By **resolution 44/201 A, Section IX**, the Assembly, on 21 December, noted that a balance of $13,120,500 remained in the contingency fund.

GENERAL ASSEMBLY ACTION

On 21 December, on the recommendation of the Fifth Committee, the General Assembly adopted **resolutions 44/200 A** and **B** without vote.

Implementation of General Assembly resolution 41/213

A

The General Assembly,

Recalling its resolution 41/213 of 19 December 1986 on the review of the efficiency of the administrative and financial functioning of the United Nations and its resolutions 42/211 of 21 December 1987 and 43/213 of 21 December 1988 on the implementation of General Assembly resolution 41/213,

Reaffirming that measures to improve the efficiency of the administrative and financial functioning of the United Nations and to improve the planning, programming and budgeting process should aim at and contribute to strengthening the effectiveness of the Organization in dealing with political, economic and social issues in order better to achieve the purposes of and respect for the principles set out in the Charter of the United Nations,

Emphasizing that this process requires careful monitoring and the continuing support of Member States, including in financial terms, so as to permit its orderly and balanced implementation and to avoid negative impact on programmes,

Recognizing that the process of implementation of its resolution 41/213 has taken place in a situation of persistent financial crisis,

Reaffirming that all Member States must honour, promptly and in full, their financial obligations as set out in the Charter,

Reiterating its support for the Secretary-General in the fulfilment of his responsibilities as chief administrative officer of the Organization,

Noting the progress made in the implementation of its resolution 41/213, including in the new budgetary process,

Noting also that further efforts are required in implementing, in a balanced manner, the various recommen-

dations approved in its resolution 41/213, including those related to personnel issues,

Recognizing that the implementation of certain recommendations approved in its resolution 41/213 depends upon further review by intergovernmental bodies,

Recalling its request contained in its resolution 43/213 for the Secretary-General to submit to the General Assembly at its forty-fifth session an analytical report on the implementation of resolution 41/213,

Having considered the relevant reports of the Secretary-General and noting that the report of the Secretary-General on the implementation of resolution 41/213 did not cover the entire three-year period foreseen in recommendation 71 of the Group of High-level Intergovernmental Experts to Review the Efficiency of the Administrative and Financial Functioning of the United Nations,

Having considered also the relevant parts of the report of the Committee for Programme and Co-ordination on the work of its twenty-ninth session, and of the report of the Advisory Committee on Administrative and Budgetary Questions,

Taking into account the views expressed by Member States during the consideration of this item at its forty-fourth session,

1. *Renews its appeal* to Member States to demonstrate their commitment to the United Nations by, *inter alia*, meeting their financial obligations on time and in full, in accordance with the Charter and the Financial Regulations of the United Nations;

2. *Stresses* that, in order to carry out successfully the process of reform and restructuring, it is essential that the present financial uncertainties be dispelled;

3. *Encourages* the Secretary-General and Member States to intensify their efforts with respect to implementation of the provisions of its resolution 41/213 that fall within their respective purviews, particularly those aspects which have not been implemented;

4. *Stresses* that implementation of its resolution 41/213 must not have a negative impact on mandated programmes and activities;

5. *Emphasizes* in this respect that, in accordance with the existing regulations and rules, while output revisions in programme budgets may be proposed in order to comply more efficiently with the objectives of those programmes and activities, outputs specifically requested in mandates should be fully delivered;

6. *Reiterates* that further implementation of its resolution 41/213 should be carried out in a balanced way and with flexibility, so as to improve, *inter alia*, the structure and composition of the Secretariat;

7. *Decides*, with regard to recommendation 15 of the Group of High-level Intergovernmental Experts to Review the Efficiency of the Administrative and Financial Functioning of the United Nations:

(*a*) To recognize the progress achieved to date in the implementation of the overall post reduction mandated by the General Assembly in resolution 43/213;

(*b*) To acknowledge that the Secretary-General is not in a position at the present stage to propose further post reductions;

(*c*) To consider, in the light of the analytical report to be submitted to the General Assembly at its forty-fifth session, proposals that may be put forward by the Secretary-General for further implementation of recommendation 15 as approved by the Assembly in resolution 41/213;

8. *Invites* the Secretary-General to implement recommendation 37 of the Group of High-level Intergovernmental Experts in accordance with the recommendations of the Committee for Programme and Co-ordination at its twenty-ninth session, as contained in paragraph 19 of its report;

9. *Concurs* with the observations of the Committee for Programme and Co-ordination, in paragraph 21 of its report, regarding the provision of conference services;

10. *Reiterates its request* that, in implementation of recommendation 5 of the Group of High-level Intergovernmental Experts, the Secretary-General should ensure close adherence to the schedule outlined in his report to the General Assembly at its forty-third session;

11. *Stresses* the need for greater transparency and coherence in personnel management, especially in the Staff Regulations and Rules of the United Nations, as set out in paragraph 18 of the report of the Committee for Programme and Co-ordination;

12. *Also stresses* the need to strengthen the role of the Secretary-General with respect to co-ordination within the United Nations system, as well as the role of Member States through the relevant intergovernmental bodies throughout the United Nations system;

13. *Requests* the Secretary-General, in his capacity as Chairman of the Administrative Committee on Co-ordination, to consider appropriate organizational arrangements for the secretariat of the Committee with a view to ensuring its adequacy in addressing the increasing responsibilities of the Committee;

14. *Requests* the Secretary-General to provide to the General Assembly at its forty-fifth session a compendium of mandates of subsidiary administrative and budgetary bodies of the Assembly, together with information on relevant reviews carried out over the past five years, on the understanding that the decisions of the Assembly relating to those mandates remain valid;

15. *Renews its request* to the Secretary-General to submit to the General Assembly at its forty-fifth session an analytical report assessing the effect of the implementation of its resolution 41/213 on the Organization and its activities, as a whole, and the way in which it has enhanced the efficiency of its administrative and financial functioning;

16. *Recommends* that the report should be structured along the following lines:

(a) The first part should be an exhaustive presentation of recommendations fully implemented, partially implemented and not implemented, as well as those which, in the view of the Secretary-General, could not be implemented;

(b) The second part of the report should provide explanations with regard to such implementation and an assessment of its impact on programmes, giving particular emphasis to those programmes which have been terminated or completed;

(c) The final part should provide a general critical assessment of the implementation of its resolution 41/213 in the light of the objective of that resolution, namely, the enhancement of the administrative and financial functioning of the Organization.

B

The General Assembly,

Recognizing the need for improvement in the format and methodology of the programme budget and its outline, including the question of comparability of estimates in those two instruments,

Mindful of the fact that the operation and use of the contingency fund is still at an experimental stage and that statements of programme budget implications play an important role in the budget process,

Recognizing the need for a comprehensive solution to the problem of all additional expenditures, including those deriving from inflation and currency fluctuation,

Recognizing also the growing level of extrabudgetary resources available to the United Nations and the need to define more precisely their impact on the activities and programmes of the Organization,

1. *Endorses* the relevant conclusions and recommendations of the Committee for Programme and Co-ordination and the relevant observations and recommendations of the Advisory Committee on Administrative and Budgetary Questions;

2. *Requests* the Secretary-General to take into account the relevant comments and recommendations of the Committee for Programme and Co-ordination and the Advisory Committee on Administrative and Budgetary Questions on the format and methodology of the programme budget and its outline, when submitting the outline and the proposed programme budget for the biennium 1992-1993;

3. *Also requests* the Secretary-General to extend progressively, in accordance with paragraph 28 of his report on statements of programme budget implications and in so far as feasible, the provision of statements of programme budget implications to all subsidiary bodies of the General Assembly and the Economic and Social Council, in order to facilitate their decision-making process, and to keep under review the format and content of statements of programme budget implications in the context of the new budgetary process;

4. *Further requests* the Secretary-General to submit to the General Assembly at its forty-sixth session, through the Advisory Committee on Administrative and Budgetary Questions and the Committee for Programme and Co-ordination, and in the light of the experience gained during the implementation of the programme budget for the biennium 1990-1991, a single report on the review of the procedures for the provision of statements of programme budget implications and for the use and operation of the contingency fund;

5. *Decides,* given the shortcomings of the present system, to keep under review the question of a comprehensive solution to the problem of all additional expenditures, including those deriving from inflation and currency fluctuation, and to consider it again at its forty-sixth session;

6. *Requests* the Secretary-General to take fully into account the conclusions, recommendations and observations of the Committee for Programme and Co-ordination and the Advisory Committee on Administrative and Budgetary Questions on the treatment of extrabudgetary resources when preparing and presenting the outline and the proposed programme budget for the biennium 1992-1993.

General Assembly resolutions 44/200 A and B

21 December 1989   Meeting 84   Adopted without vote

Approved by Fifth Committee (A/44/901) without vote, 19 December (meeting 59); draft by Vice-Chairman following informal consultations (A/C.5/44/L.24, parts A and B); agenda item 38.

Meeting numbers. GA 44th session: 5th Committee 11-16, 18, 46, 49, 59; plenary 84.

UN budget

Budget for 1988-1989

Final appropriations

In December, the Secretary-General submitted his second programme budget performance report[16] on the 1988-1989 budget. Taking into account actual expenditures so far and projections to the end of the 1988-1989 biennium, the Secretary-General reported a net increase of $3,165,200 compared with the net amount approved by the General Assembly in 1988.[17]

In a 14 December report,[18] ACABQ pointed out that, because of the repayment provisions of a loan by the United Nations to the United Nations Industrial Development Organization (UNIDO),[19] the Secretary-General was ultimately reporting a net decrease of $12,834,800 in expenditure requirements for the biennium 1988-1989. ACABQ recommended that the General Assembly approve the Secretary-General's revised estimates.

GENERAL ASSEMBLY ACTION

On 21 December, on the recommendation of the Fifth Committee, the General Assembly adopted together **resolutions 44/193 A** and **B** without vote.

A
Final budget appropriations for the biennium 1988-1989

The General Assembly

Resolves that for the biennium 1988-1989:

1.   The amount of 1,788,746,300 United States dollars appropriated by its resolution 43/218 A of 21 December 1988 shall be decreased by 16,432,600 dollars as follows:

Section	Amount appropriated by resolution 43/218 A	Increase or (decrease) (US dollars)	Final appropriation
PART I. *Overall policy-making, direction and co-ordination*			
1. Overall policy-making, direction and co-ordination	50,213,700	(1,787,400)	48,426,300
Total, PART I	50,213,700	(1,787,400)	48,426,300
PART II. *Political and Security Council affairs; peace-keeping activities*			
2A. Political and Security Council affairs; peace-keeping activities	99,259,000	716,300	99,975,300
2B. Disarmament affairs activities	10,247,600	251,600	10,499,200
Total, PART II	109,506,600	967,900	110,474 500
PART III. *Political affairs, trusteeship and decolonization*			
3. Political affairs, trusteeship and decolonization	33,419,300	(5,454,500)	27,964,800
Total, PART III	33,419,300	(5,454,500)	27,964,800

Section	Amount appropriated by resolution 43/218 A	Increase or (decrease) (US dollars)	Final appropriation
PART IV. *Economic, social and humanitarian activities*			
4. Policy-making organs (economic and social activities)	1,982,400	(134,700)	1,847,700
5A. Office of the Director-General for Development and International Economic Co-operation	4,072,800	305,500	4,378,300
5B. Regional Commissions Liaison Office	755,900	24,900	780,800
6A. Department of International Economic and Social Affairs	42,236,700	(1,814,600)	40,422,100
6B. Activities on global social development issues	10,261,900	(45,200)	10,216,700
7. Department of Technical Co-operation for Development	21,917,100	(35,600)	21,881,500
9. Transnational corporations	9,878,700	544,400	10,423,100
10. Economic Commission for Europe	34,619,000	(2,991,100)	31,627,900
11. Economic and Social Commission for Asia and the Pacific	35,848,000	(952,900)	34,895,100
12. Economic Commission for Latin America and the Caribbean	42,811,000	(2,114,200)	40,696,800
13. Economic Commission for Africa	51,207,200	(3,126,200)	48,081,000
14. Economic and Social Commission for Western Asia	36,766,200	(2,510,400)	34,255,800
15. United Nations Conference on Trade and Development	76,958,200	(3,897,300)	73,060,900
16. International Trade Centre	13,409,100	(955,900)	12,453,200
17. Centre for Science and Technology for Development	3,824,000	70,800	3,894,800
18. United Nations Environment Programme	10,591,300	(376,400)	10,214,900
19. United Nations Centre for Human Settlements (Habitat)	8,722,500	(1,198,600)	7,523,900
20. International drug control	7,433,600	462,400	7,896,000
21. Office of the United Nations High Commissioner for Refugees	35,932,000	1,110,900	37,042,900
22. Office of the United Nations Disaster Relief Co-ordinator	6,944,800	338,800	7,283,600
23. Human rights	16,937,200	(824,700)	16,112,500
24. Regular programme of technical co-operation	32,418,400	340,600	32,759,000
Total, PART IV	505,528,000	(17,779,500)	487,748,500
PART V. *International justice and law*			
25. International Court of Justice	13,250,800	(193,900)	13,056,900
26. Legal activities	16,634,000	(571,600)	16,062,400
Total, PART V	29,884,800	(765,500)	29,119,300
PART VI. *Public information*			
27. Public information	78,255,800	(1,031,100)	77,224,700
Total, PART VI	78,255,800	(1,031,100)	77,224,700

Section	Amount appropriated by resolution 43/218 A	Increase or (decrease) (US dollars)	Final appropriation
PART VII. *Common support services*			
28. Administration and management	371,150,800	9,894,500	381,045,300
29. Conference and library services	324,950,400	7,078,500	332,028,900
Total, PART VII	696,101,200	16,973,000	713,074,200
PART VIII. *Special expenses*			
30. United Nations bond issue	3,520,800	2,600	3,523,400
Total, PART VIII	3,520,800	2,600	3,523,400
PART IX. *Staff assessment*			
31. Staff assessment	263,220,100	(7,401,800)	255,818,300
Total, PART IX	263,220,100	(7,401,800)	255,818,300
PART X. *Capital expenditures*			
32. Construction, alteration, improvement and major maintenance of premises	19,096,000	(156,300)	18,939,700
Total, PART X	19,096,000	(156,300)	18,939,700
GRAND TOTAL	1,788,746,300	(16,432,600)	1,772,313,700

2. The Secretary-General shall be authorized to transfer credits between sections of the budget, with the concurrence of the Advisory Committee on Administrative and Budgetary Questions;

3. The total net provision made under the various sections of the budget for contractual printing shall be administered as a unit under the direction of the United Nations Publications Board;

4. The appropriations for the regular programme of technical co-operation under part IV, section 24, shall be administered in accordance with the Financial Regulations of the United Nations, except that the definition of obligations and the period of validity of obligations shall be subject to the following procedures:

(*a*) Obligations for personal services established in the current biennium shall be valid for the succeeding biennium, provided that appointments of the experts concerned are effected by the end of the current biennium and that the total period to be covered by obligations established for these purposes against the resources of the current biennium shall not exceed twenty-four work-months;

(*b*) Obligations established in the current biennium for fellowships shall remain valid until liquidated, provided that the fellow has been nominated by the requesting Government and accepted by the Organization and that a formal letter of award has been issued to the requesting Governments;

(*c*) Obligations in respect of contracts or purchase orders for supplies or equipment recorded in the current biennium shall remain valid until payment is ef-

fected to the contractor or vendor, unless they are cancelled;

5. In addition to the appropriations voted under paragraph 1 of the present resolution, an amount of 29,500 dollars is appropriated for each year of the biennium 1988-1989 from the accumulated income of the Library Endowment Fund for the purchase of books, periodicals, maps and library equipment and for such other expenses of the Library at the Palais des Nations as are in accordance with the objects and provisions of the endowment.

B

Final income estimates for the biennium 1988-1989

The General Assembly

Resolves that for the biennium 1988-1989:

1. The estimates of income in the amount of 344,443,300 United States dollars approved by its resolution 43/218 B of 21 December 1988 shall be decreased by 19,597,800 dollars as follows:

	Amount approved by resolution 43/218 B	Increase or (decrease) (United States dollars)	Final approved estimates
PART I. *Income from staff assessment*			
1. Income from staff assessment	267,581,500	(7,772,500)	259,809,000
Total, PART I	267,581,500	(7,772,500)	259,809,000
PART II. *Other income*			
2. General income	63,035,200	(7,800,200)	55,235,000
3. Revenue-producing activities	13,826,600	(4,025,100)	9,801,500
Total, PART II	76,861,800	(11,825,300)	65,036,500
GRAND TOTAL	344,443,300	(19,597,800)	324,845,500

2. The income from staff assessment shall be credited to the Tax Equalization Fund in accordance with the provisions of General Assembly resolution 973(X) of 15 December 1955;

3. Direct expenses of the United Nations Postal Administration, services to visitors, catering and related services, garage operations, television services and the sale of publications, not provided for under the budget appropriations, shall be charged against the income derived from those activities.

General Assembly resolutions 44/193 A and B

21 December 1989   Meeting 84   Adopted without vote

Approved by Fifth Committee (A/44/894) without vote, 18 December (meeting 58); agenda item 122.

Meeting numbers. GA 44th session: 5th Committee 47, 58; plenary 84.

Budget for 1990-1991

In submitting his proposed programme budget for 1990-1991,[20] the Secretary-General noted that this was the first budget prepared in accordance with the budgetary procedures established by the General Assembly in 1986,[7] which had been a major step in the reform process begun with the establishment of the Group of 18.

The proposed budget, at $1,983,863,400, reflected an increase of $195,117,100 over the revised appropriation of $1,788,746,300 for the biennium 1988-1989 and a negative real growth rate of 0.4 per cent. Inflation in 1990-1991 was calculated at 7.2 per cent. The level of resources for the proposed programme budget showed an increase of $1,339,700 over the preliminary estimate of $1,982,523,700 approved for the programme budget outline in 1988,[14] an increase attributable to the impossibility of fully absorbing the costs of posts restored under another 1988 resolution.[10]

Regarding the $80.8 million requested for non-recurrent items, $58 million related to construction and major maintenance, $8.5 million to modernization of administrative systems and $3.5 million to conference services, including for acquisition and installation of office automation and reproduction equipment. The remaining $10.8 million was distributed among other activities not expected to continue beyond 1991. Proposed recurrent growth, showing a decrease of $7,700,800, was accounted for partly by discontinuation of the provision for repayment of the UN bond issue—a reduction of $3,500,000—and partly by the net effect of increases and reduction under a variety of expenditures. The programme budget reflected the medium-term plan, which had been extended to 1991; it contained 153 programmes and 472 subprogrammes, representing a large element of programme continuity, both in distribution of resources and in the objectives pursued in response to legislative mandates.

Compared with the budget for the biennium 1988-1989, the proposed programme budget for 1990-1991, with 10,054 posts (of which 28 were temporary), showed a difference of 1,368 posts or a reduction of about 12 per cent.

In May, CPC considered the Secretary-General's proposed budget for the biennium 1990-1991 at its 1989 session. In its recommendations, CPC recalled that the new budgetary procedure established by the General Assembly in 1986[7] aimed at a more intense participation by Member States in preparation of the programme budget, the widest possible agreement on the budget, and an increase in management efficiency. It made a number of recommendations to improve presentation of future programme budgets. Regarding the negative growth rate of 0.4 per cent, the Committee stressed the relative magnitude of that growth rate, given the methodology used and the lack of clarity on the relationship between such growth and the programmatic content of the budget. It therefore recommended refining the methodology with a more thorough analysis of the relationship between rate of growth in the programme budget and its impact upon the activities of the Organization. It stressed the necessity of avoiding nega-

tive effects of the proposed rate of real growth on programme implementation. CPC noted that there was unevenness in the presentation of outputs and priorities in different sections of the budget. It recommended that, in the context of consideration of the proposed programme budget, the Secretary-General submit proposals for priorities.

ACABQ, in its first report[22] to the Assembly on the proposed programme budget for 1990-1991, said there was still much to be done before arriving at an acceptable methodology and procedure for the preparation and consideration of the budget outline. Indeed, the whole budget process was still in its formative steps, with contingency fund procedures yet to be tested and formulation of reserve fund procedures still to be agreed upon. The Committee said the grand total of the budget, including the net estimate for the regular budget, was $4,179,105,300. ACABQ recommended total reductions of $6,898,000 in the expenditure estimate (of which $1.5 million was provisional) and an increase of $6,200 in the income estimate. In later addenda,[23] ACABQ took account of the Secretary-General's revised estimates, which responded to measures taken by the Economic and Social Council and other matters.

GENERAL ASSEMBLY ACTION

On 21 December, on the recommendation of the Fifth Committee, the General Assembly adopted **resolution 44/201 B, sections II, V, VI, VII** and **X** without vote.

Questions relating to the proposed programme budget for the biennium 1990-1991

B

The General Assembly . . .

II
Functions and posts related to global social development issues in sections 6 and 8 of the proposed programme budget for the biennium 1990-1991

1. *Decides* that the activities related to global social development issues identified in paragraphs 6.14 and 8.2 of the proposed programme budget for the biennium 1990-1991 and the corresponding resources shall be in section 6 of the programme budget;

2. *Requests* the Secretary-General to review the functions and administrative support of the departments having mandates relating to global social development issues, bearing in mind the need for an integrated approach to development;

3. *Also requests* the Secretary-General to submit proposals, as appropriate, to the General Assembly at its forty-fifth session for the strengthening of the United Nations Office at Vienna; . . .

V
Section 3. Political affairs, trusteeship and decolonization

1. *Accepts* the estimate and proposal of the Secretary-General for section 3C (Namibia) of the proposed pro-

gramme budget for the biennium 1990-1991, as endorsed by the Committee for Programme and Co-ordination and the Advisory Committee on Administrative and Budgetary Questions, notes that the Secretary-General will submit revised estimates for that section and requests him to do so no later than at the forty-fifth session of the General Assembly;

2. *Requests* the Secretary-General, taking full account of the priority attached by the General Assembly to activities against *apartheid* and of the views expressed by Member States at the forty-fourth session, to ensure optimum utilization of resources within section 3, including the possibility of redeployment of staff resources, when submitting revised estimates and priorities for section 3 to the General Assembly at its forty-fifth session;

VI

Section 5A. Office of the Director-General for Development and International Economic Co-operation

Notes that the reference to ''peace-keeping'' in section 5A of the proposed programme budget for the biennium 1990-1991 refers only to humanitarian assistance activities related to peace-keeping operations;

VII

Section 6. Department of International Economic and Social Affairs: programmatic content of programme B.3 (analysis of the world population)

Requests the Secretary-General to implement programme B.3 (Analysis of the world population) of section 6 of the proposed programme budget for the biennium 1990-1991, within the framework of the recommendations of the International Conference on Population, 1984, and the World Population Plan of Action, and in this context to give special attention to the question of the relationship between population and development, taking into account paragraph 6.9 and noting that the word ''sustainable'' should not be part of paragraph 6.42; . . .

X

Section 20. International drug control

Endorses the observations and recommendations contained in paragraphs 20.4 and 20.7 to 20.9 of the report of the Advisory Committee on Administrative and Budgetary Questions and the conclusions and recommendations contained in paragraph 217 of the report of the Committee for Programme and Co-ordination; . . .   .

General Assembly resolution 44/201 B

21 December 1989   Meeting 84   Adopted without vote

Approved by Fifth Committee (A/44/905) without vote, 19 December (meeting 59); draft by Vice-Chairman (A/C.5/44/L.25); agenda item 123.
Meeting numbers. GA 44th session: 5th Committee 37, 39, 59; plenary 84.

GENERAL ASSEMBLY ACTION

On 21 December, at the recommendation of the Fifth Committee, the General Assembly adopted together **resolutions 44/202A-C** without vote.

A

Budget appropriations for the biennium 1990-1991

The General Assembly

Resolves that for the biennium 1990-1991:

1. Appropriations totalling 1,974,634,000 United States dollars are hereby approved for the following purposes:

Section	(US dollars)
PART I. *Overall policy-making, direction and co-ordination*	
1. Overall policy-making direction and co-ordination	59,705,000
Total, PART I	59,705,000
PART II. *Political and Security Council affairs; peace-keeping activities*	
2A. Political and Security Council affairs; peace-keeping activities	88,089,300
2B. Disarmament affairs activities	11,184,500
2C. Office for Ocean Affairs and the Law of the Sea	8,196,900
Total, PART II	107,470,700
PART III. *Political affairs, trusteeship and decolonization*	
3. Political affairs, trusteeship and decolonization	35,988,200
Total, PART III	35,988,200
PART IV. *Economic, social and humanitarian activities*	
4. Policy-making organs (economic and social activities)	2,163,100
5A. Office of the Director-General for Development and International Economic Co-operation	4,670,800
5B. Regional Commissions New York Office	855,300
6. Department of International Economic and Social Affairs	46,814,800
7. Department of Technical Co-operation for Development	23,853,200
8. Activities on global social development issues	9,985,700
9. Transnational corporations	10,919,200
10. Economic Commission for Europe	33,089,300
11. Economic and Social Commission for Asia and the Pacific	39,791,400
12. Economic Commission for Latin America and the Caribbean	49,010,700
13. Economic Commission for Africa	57,725,700
14. Economic and Social Commission for Western Asia	38,595,400
15. United Nations Conference on Trade and Development	73,107,600
16. International Trade Centre	15,400,800
17. Centre for Science and Technology for Development	4,298,800
18. United Nations Environment Programme	11,195,600
19. United Nations Centre for Human Settlements (Habitat)	9,937,800
20. International drug control	8,333,600
21. Office of the United Nations High Commissioner for Refugees	34,180,100
22. Office of the United Nations Disaster Relief Co-ordinator	6,481,200
23. Human rights	16,105,700
24. Regular programme of technical co-operation	36,163,200
Total, PART IV	532,679,000
PART V. *International justice and law*	
25. International Court of Justice	13,333,000
26. Legal activities	18,766,500
Total, PART V	32,099,500
PART VI. *Public information*	
27. Public information	87,225,400
Total, PART VI	87,225,400
PART VII. *Common support services*	
28. Administration and management	397 759 500
29. Conference and library services	352,777,600
Total, PART VII	750,537,100
PART VIII. *Special expenses*	
30. United Nations bond issue	—
Total, PART VIII	—
PART IX. *Staff assessment*	
31. Staff assessment	298,390,400
Total, PART IX	298,390,400
PART X. *Capital expenditures*	
32. Construction, alteration, improvement and major maintenance of premises	70,538,700
Total, PART X	70,538,700
GRAND TOTAL	1,974,634,000

2. The Secretary-General shall be authorized to transfer credits between sections of the budget with the concurrence of the Advisory Committee on Administrative and Budgetary Questions;

3. The total net provision made under the various sections of the budget for contractual printing shall be administered as a unit under the direction of the United Nations Publications Board;

4. The appropriations for the regular programme of technical co-operation under part IV, section 24, shall be administered in accordance with the Financial Regulations of the United Nations, except that the definition of obligations and the period of validity of obligations shall be subject to the following procedures:

(a) Obligations for personal services established in the current biennium shall be valid for the succeeding biennium, provided that appointments of the experts concerned are effected by the end of the current biennium, and that the total period to be covered by obligations established for these purposes against the resources of the current biennium shall not exceed twenty-four work-months;

(b) Obligations established in the current biennium for fellowships shall remain valid until liquidated, provided that the fellow has been nominated by the requesting Government and accepted by the Organization, and that a formal letter of award has been issued to the requesting Government;

(c) Obligations in respect of contracts or purchase orders for supplies or equipment recorded in the current biennium shall remain valid until payment is effected to the contractor or vendor, unless they are cancelled;

5. In addition to the appropriations approved under paragraph 1 of the present resolution, an amount of 19,000 dollars is appropriated for each year of the biennium 1990-1991 from accumulated income of the Library Endowment Fund for the purchase of books, periodicals, maps and library equipment and for such other expenses of the Library at the Palais des Nations as are in accordance with the objects and provisions of the endowment.

B
Income estimates for the biennium 1990-1991
The General Assembly

Resolves that for the biennium 1990-1991:

1. Estimates of income other than assessments on Member States totalling 367,226,200 United States dollars are approved as follows:

Income section	*(US dollars)*
PART I. *Income from staff assessment*	
1. Income from staff assessment	303,040,800
Total, PART I	303,040,800
PART II. *Other income*	
2. General income	54,524,200
3. Revenue-producing activities	9,661,200
Total, PART II	64,185,400
GRAND TOTAL	367,226,200

2. The income from staff assessment shall be credited to the Tax Equalization Fund in accordance with the provisions of General Assembly resolution 973(X) of 15 December 1955;

3. Direct expenses of the United Nations Postal Administration, services to visitors, catering and related services, garage operations, television services and the sale of publications, not provided for under the budget appropriations, shall be charged against the income derived from those activities.

C
Financing of appropriations for the year 1990
The General Assembly

Resolves that for the year 1990:

1. Budget appropriations in a total amount of 970,884,400 United States dollars, consisting of 987,317,000 dollars, being half of the appropriations approved for the biennium 1990-1991 by the General Assembly under paragraph 1 of resolution A above, less 16,432,600 dollars, being the decrease in revised appropriations for the biennium 1988-1989 approved by the General Assembly in its resolution 44/193 A of 21 December 1989, shall be financed in accordance with regulations 5.1 and 5.2 of the Financial Regulations of the United Nations as follows:

(a) 32,092,700 dollars, being half the estimated income other than staff assessment approved for the biennium 1990-1991 under resolution B above;

(b) 4,174,700 dollars, being the increase in estimated income other than staff assessment for the biennium 1988-1989 approved by the General Assembly in its resolution 44/193 B of 21 December 1989, excluding the decrease of 16 million dollars in income section 2 pertaining to the repayment of the loan to the United Nations Industrial Development Organization;

(c) 934,617,000 dollars, being the assessment on Member States in accordance with General Assembly resolution 43/223 A of 21 December 1988 on the scale of assessments for the years 1989, 1990 and 1991;

2. There shall be set off against the assessment on Member States, in accordance with the provisions of General Assembly resolution 973(X) of 15 December 1955, their respective share in the Tax Equalization Fund in the total amount of 143,747,900 dollars consisting of:

(a) 151,520,400 dollars, being half of the estimated staff assessment income approved for the biennium 1990-1991 under resolution B above;

(b) Less 7,772,500 dollars, being the decrease in the revised income from staff assessment for the biennium 1988-1989 approved by the General Assembly in its resolution 44/193 B.

General Assembly resolutions 44/202 A-C

21 December 1989   Meeting 84   Adopted without vote

Approved by Fifth Committee (A/44/905) without vote, 20 December (meeting 61); agenda item 123.
Meeting numbers. GA 44th session: 5th Committee 11-18, 19, 23-32, 34, 36, 37, 39, 45, 46, 48, 61; plenary 84.

Also on 21 December, the General Assembly, on the recommendation of the Fifth Committee, adopted **resolution 44/203** without vote.

Unforeseen and extraordinary expenses for the biennium 1990-1991
The General Assembly

1. *Authorizes* the Secretary-General, with the prior concurrence of the Advisory Committee on Administrative and Budgetary Questions and subject to the Financial Regulations of the United Nations and the provisions of paragraph 3 of the present resolution, to enter into

commitments in the biennium 1990-1991 to meet unforeseen and extraordinary expenses arising either during or subsequent to that biennium, provided that the concurrence of the Advisory Committee shall not be necessary for:

(a) Such commitments, not exceeding a total of 3 million United States dollars in any one year of the biennium 1990-1991, as the Secretary-General certifies relate to the maintenance of peace and security;

(b) Such commitments as the President of the International Court of Justice certifies relate to expenses occasioned by:

(i) The designation of *ad hoc* judges (Statute of the Court, Article 31), not exceeding a total of 250,000 dollars;

(ii) The appointment of assessors (Statute, Article 30), or the calling of witnesses and the appointment of experts (Statute, Article 50), not exceeding a total of 75,000 dollars;

(iii) The holding of sessions of the Court away from The Hague (Statute, Article 22), not exceeding a total of 100,000 dollars;

(c) Such commitments, in an amount not exceeding 300,000 dollars, in the biennium 1990-1991, as the Secretary-General certifies are required for interorganizational security measures pursuant to section IV of General Assembly resolution 36/235 of 18 December 1981;

2. *Resolves* that the Secretary-General shall report to the Advisory Committee on Administrative and Budgetary Questions and to the General Assembly at its forty-fifth and forty-sixth sessions all commitments made under the provisions of the present resolution, together with the circumstances relating thereto, and shall submit supplementary estimates to the Assembly in respect of such commitments;

3. *Decides* that, for the biennium 1990-1991, if a decision of the Security Council results in the need for the Secretary-General to enter into commitments relating to the maintenance of peace and security in an amount exceeding 10 million dollars in respect of that decision, the matter shall be brought to the General Assembly or, if the Assembly is suspended or not in session, a resumed or special session of the Assembly shall be convened by the Secretary-General to consider the matter.

General Assembly resolution 44/203

21 December 1989   Meeting 84   Adopted without vote

Approved by Fifth Committee (A/44/905) without vote, 20 December (meeting 61); agenda item 123.
Meeting numbers. GA 44th session: 5th Committee 11-18, 19, 23-32, 34, 36, 37, 39, 45, 46, 48, 61; plenary 84.

REFERENCES

(1)A/C.5/44/27. (2)YUN 1988, p. 855, GA res. 43/220, 21 Dec. 1988. (3)A/44/857 & Corr.1. (4)A/44/873. (5)ACC/1989/DEC/24-32 (dec 1989/26). (6)A/44/222 & Corr.1. (7)YUN 1986, p. 1024, GA res. 41/213, 19 Dec. 1986. (8)YUN 1987, p. 1097. (9)YUN 1988, p. 856. (10)*Ibid.*, GA res. 43/213, 21 Dec. 1988. (11)YUN 1988 p. 879. (12)A/44/6. (13)A/44/665. (14)YUN 1988, p 862, GA res. 43/214, 21 Dec. 1988. (15)A/44/729. (16)A/C.5/44/35 & Adds.1-35. (17)YUN 1988, p. 858, GA res. 43/218 A and B, 21 Dec. 1988. (18)A/44/876. (19)YUN 1988, p. 860. (20)A/44/6. (21)A/44/16 & Add.1. (22)A/44/7. (23)A/44/7/Adds.1-8. (24)A/C.5/44/5.

Assessed contributions

The Committee on Contributions, at its forty-ninth session (New York, 5-28 June 1989),[1] considered such matters as assessments scale methodology, *ad hoc* adjustments (mitigation), representations by Member States, collection of contributions, payments of contributions in currencies other than United States dollars and assessments of non-member States.

In response to a 1988 General Assembly resolution,[2] the Committee began a comprehensive review of all aspects of the existing methodology of the determination of the scale of assessments, which is used to transform national income into assessable income for the determination of individual assessment rates. A summary of the evolution of the scale methodology was included.

The Committee considered representations made by India, the Islamic Republic of Iran and the Libyan Arab Jamahiriya regarding their assessments.

GENERAL ASSEMBLY ACTION

On 21 December, on the recommendation of the Fifth Committee, the General Assembly adopted **resolution 44/197 A** without vote.

Scale of assessments for the apportionment of the expenses of the United Nations

A

The General Assembly,

Recalling all its previous resolutions on the scale of assessments, in particular resolutions 39/247 B of 12 April 1985, 42/208 of 11 December 1987 and 43/223 B of 21 December 1988,

Having considered the report of the Committee on Contributions, and noting the efforts of the Committee, particularly in the context of the difficulties it encountered in performing its tasks,

Taking into account the views expressed in the Fifth Committee during the forty-fourth session,

1. *Reaffirms* that:

(a) The capacity to pay is the fundamental criterion for determining the scale of assessments;

(b) The scale of assessments should be determined on the basis of reliable, verifiable and comparable data;

(c) The methodology for determining the scale of assessments should be simplified as far as possible with a view to making it more transparent and stable over time;

2. *Takes note* of the possible areas for adjustments to the existing methodology identified in the report of the Committee on Contributions;

3. *Requests* the Committee on Contributions:

(a) To continue its work on the following elements of the existing methodology:

(i) The statistical base period;

(ii) The debt adjustment factor;

(iii) The per capita income limit;

(iv) The scheme to avoid excessive variations of individual rates of assessment between successive scales;

(b) As a means further to improve the current methodology:

(i) To examine fully the use of other factors, including the situation of countries having the economic characteristics outlined in resolution 43/223 B, paragraph 3;

(ii) To continue its work on the price-adjusted rates of exchange methodology;

(c) To continue, in conformity with the mandate set out in resolution 43/223 B, paragraph 2 *(e)*, its consideration of *ad hoc* adjustments to the machine scale, which should be uniformly applied, based on broad, objective, rational and transparent criteria, including those mentioned in paragraph 38 of the report of the Committee on Contributions, and which should be limited in scope and made on a voluntary and multilateral basis;

4. *Also requests* the Committee on Contributions to submit to the General Assembly, at its forty-fifth session, recommendations on adjustments, if necessary and where appropriate, to the elements and factors referred to in paragraph 3 of the present resolution;

5. *Invites* the Committee on Contributions, in conducting the work mentioned in paragraph 3 of the present resolution, to continue to examine the interrelationship of each of the elements and factors as a part of the overall methodology;

6. *Requests* the Committee on Contributions to proceed with the further exploration of alternative income concepts and to report thereon to the General Assembly at its forty-fifth session;

7. *Also requests* the Committee on Contributions to consider excluding the allocation of any additional points, as a result of the application of the scheme of limits, to those Member States having a very low per capita income, and to report thereon to the General Assembly at its forty-fifth session;

8. *Further requests* the Committee on Contributions to include in its report to the General Assembly at its forty-fifth session illustrative examples, consistent with the statistical annexes to its report to the Assembly at its forty-fourth session, of the implications of using the elements and factors mentioned in the present resolution, including different alternatives for ceiling and floor amounts.

General Assembly resolution 44/197 A

21 December 1989   Meeting 84   Adopted without vote

Approved by Fifth Committee (A/44/896) without vote, 19 December (meeting 59); draft by Chairman following informal consultations (A/C.5/44/L.18, part A); agenda item 129.
Meeting numbers. GA 44th session: 5th Committee 13, 17, 18, 20-23, 25, 59; plenary 84.

On the same date, the Assembly adopted **resolution 44/197 C**, also without vote.

C

The General Assembly,

Recalling rule 160 of the rules of procedure of the General Assembly,

1. *Requests* the Committee on Contributions to examine the question of providing access of Member States to information on how the Committee, being an expert body, arrives at its decisions on the scale of assessments,

and to submit specific recommendations to the General Assembly at its forty-fifth session on how to establish an effective mechanism of communication between Member States and the Committee, in particular by holding information meetings at its regular sessions before the preparation of a new scale and during the consideration of *ad hoc* adjustments, to enable interested Member States to convey their views and request the Committee to take those views into account in the preparation of the new scale;

2. *Decides* to continue at its forty-fifth session its consideration of the functioning of the Committee on Contributions on the basis of the views to be expressed by that Committee in its report.

General Assembly resolution 44/197 C

21 December 1989   Meeting 84   Adopted without vote

Approved by Fifth Committee (A/44/896) without vote, 19 December (meeting 59); draft by Chairman following informal consultations (A/C.5/44/L.18, part C); agenda item 129.
Meeting numbers. GA 44th session: 5th Committee 13, 17, 18, 20-23, 25, 59; plenary 84.

Status of contributions

On 6 December, the Secretary-General reported[3] on the status of contributions. Of the almost $1,171.5 million in contributions to the UN regular budget payable as of 1 January 1989 (including for prior years), $642.2 million had been collected as at 30 November, leaving some $529.2 million outstanding.

By a 14 February letter, the Secretary-General informed[4] the President of the General Assembly that 10 Member States—Benin, Central African Republic, Congo, Dominican Republic, El Salvador, Equatorial Guinea, Nicaragua, Romania, Sao Tome and Principe, South Africa—were more than two years in arrears in the payment of their budget contributions. In subsequent letters,[5] the Secretary-General reported that Benin, the Central African Republic, the Congo, the Dominican Republic, El Salvador, Equatorial Guinea, Nicaragua, Romania and Sao Tome Principe had made the necessary payments to reduce their arrears below the two-year limit to maintain voting privileges, as specified in Article 19 of the UN Charter. On 11 December 1989,[6] he stated that South Africa remained $35,184,200 in arrears.

Contributions from non-member States

In 1989, the Committee on Contributions recommended[1] to the General Assembly that it endorse a sliding scale of flat annual fee rates and periodic review procedures for the Democratic People's Republic of Korea, the Holy See, Liechtenstein, Monaco, Nauru, the Republic of Korea, San Marino, Switzerland and Tonga. Participation levels of non-member States would be reviewed every five years on the basis of self-reporting by non-member States in response to a survey by the UN Secretariat. The sliding scale of flat annual fee rates would be adjusted as required.

On 21 December, by resolution 44/197 B, the General Assembly endorsed the Committee's recommendations.

REFERENCES

(1)A/44/11 & Add.1 & Add.1/Corr.1. (2)YUN 1988, p. 863, GA res. 43/223 A, 21 Dec. 1988. (3)ST/ADM/SER.B/323. (4)A/43/995. (5)A/43/995/Add.1-4 & A/44/535/Add.1-3. (6)A/S-16/3.

Board of Auditors

In August, the Secretary-General transmitted[1] to the General Assembly a summary of the principal findings and conclusions and recommendations for remedial action of the Board of Auditors based on the audit of accounts for the financial period ended 31 December 1988, which had been prepared in response to a 1988 resolution.[2] Among other things, the auditors found continued weaknesses in United Nations Development Programme (UNDP) budgetary control, with 35 field offices out of 114 exceeding their 1988 allotments, compared to 23 in 1987. Regarding the United Nations Institute for Training and Research (UNITAR), the Board found that both UNITAR funds had exceeded their allotments and some projects had incurred expenditures even though no allotments had been issued. Also, UNITAR was to incur substantial losses for long outstanding receivables and deferred charges for which no records were available to determine their nature. The United Nations Relief and Works Agency for Palestine Refugees in the Near East (UNRWA) operations pertaining to the school voluntary assistance fund were not accounted for in compliance with regular procedures and the amounts shown in the fund statements could not be ascertained. In the Office of the United Nations High Commissioner for Refugees (UNHCR), the Board recommended that action be taken to correct the wrong recording of an outstanding contribution of some $6 million, and that appropriate action be initiated for its collection. Gross financial mismanagement of a project by an implementing agency was found in UNHCR, while a number of UNHCR field offices were operating *ad hoc* and informal arrangements with host countries. Basic cash management guidelines remained lacking at the United Nations Population Fund (UNFPA). The Board of Auditors recommended specific remedial action for these and other cases.

In September, the Secretary-General reported[3] on implementation of recommendations of the Board of Auditors and ACABQ. He noted that, during the period under review, the normal practice of issuing allotment advices on an annual basis had been temporarily suspended; measures to deal with the financial crisis had been instituted and allotments issued to cover shorter periods, as availability of funds permitted. These measures resulted in savings of some $125 million. He regretted that in a few cases expenditures had temporarily exceeded allotments, but noted that allotments were once again being issued on an annual basis and frequent reviews of expenditure reports were being undertaken. The Secretary-General also addressed questions related to unliquidated obligations, International Narcotics Control Board (INCB), multinational programming and operational centres (MULPOCs), utilization of programme support funds, programme performance reports, payroll procedures, dependency allowances, reviews of appointment status, staff training, payment of benefits and allowances at offices away from Headquarters, the Pan-African Documentation and Information System, procurement at Headquarters and offices away from Headquarters, computer operations, the UN Postal Administration, expendable and non-expendable property, project implementation and progress performance reporting, and establishment and management of trust funds.

Also in September, the Secretary-General submitted a report[4] on the preservation and format of financial statements and accounting policies of all audited organizations and programmes. He concluded that the framework within which financial statements were prepared and prescribed, while not completely standard, was generally harmonized, and the form of presentation was, to a large extent, comparable. However, he said, the General Assembly might wish to request such statements be fully comprehensive, beginning with financial statements for the current year or biennium. The Board of Auditors could be invited to keep each organization's accounting policies under review and to draw the Assembly's attention to any specific area in which it considered a comparative review of such policies to be required.

GENERAL ASSEMBLY ACTION

On 19 December, on the recommendation of the Fifth Committee, the General Assembly adopted **resolution 44/183** without vote.

Financial reports and audited financial statements, and reports of the Board of Auditors

The General Assembly,

Having considered the financial reports and audited financial statements for the period ended 31 December 1988 of the United Nations Development Programme, the United Nations Relief and Works Agency for Palestine Refugees in the Near East, the United Nations Institute for Training and Research, the voluntary funds administered by the United Nations High Commissioner for Refugees, and the United Nations Population Fund, the reports and audit opinions of the Board of Auditors, the report of the Advisory Committee on Administrative and Budgetary Questions, the concise summary of the principal findings, conclusions and recommendations of common interest contained in the reports of the Board of Auditors, the report on the presentation and format of financial statements and accounting policies of all audited organizations and programmes and the reports submitted in accordance with paragraphs 6 and 7 of General Assembly resolution 43/216 of 21 December 1988,

Noting with concern that the Board of Auditors, for the reasons stated in its reports, issued qualified audit opinions on the financial statements of the United Nations Development Programme and the United Nations Population Fund, and also issued a qualified audit opinion on compliance with the Financial Regulations of the United Nations and with legislative authority in the transactions of the United Nations Institute for Training and Research,

Noting also with concern the delay in the issuance of some reports related to this item for consideration by the General Assembly at its forty-fourth session,

Noting the efforts by a number of United Nations organizations and programmes to improve the presentation and format of financial statements and the accounting policies followed,

Taking into consideration the views expressed by delegations, by the Board of Auditors and by the Advisory Committee on Administrative and Budgetary Questions during the debate in the Fifth Committee on this item, and the widely expressed support for measures to improve the efficiency, effectiveness, management, financial accountability, budgetary control and standardization of the presentation of financial statements and accounting policies, and the accounting practices and procedures of the United Nations organizations and programmes concerned,

Stressing the need to standardize the presentation and format of financial statements and accounting policies among United Nations organizations and programmes,

Stressing also the importance of an effective internal audit function in those organizations and programmes on which the Board of Auditors reports,

1. *Accepts* the financial reports and audited financial statements and the audit opinions and reports of the Board of Auditors regarding the aforementioned organizations;

2. *Requests* the governing bodies of the United Nations Development Programme, the United Nations Population Fund and the United Nations Institute for Training and Research to require the executive heads concerned to take immediate steps within their competence to correct or improve the conditions that gave rise to the qualification of audit opinions of the Board of Auditors;

3. *Urges* the administrations and governing bodies of the executing agencies and other relevant parties concerned to solve the technical problems identified by the Board of Auditors with regard to the certification of programme expenditures and programme support costs in co-operation with the United Nations Development Programme and with the United Nations Population Fund;

4. *Endorses* the observations and recommendations of the Board of Auditors and the Advisory Committee on Administrative and Budgetary Questions as contained in their respective reports;

5. *Requests* the competent governing bodies to ensure that the executive heads concerned take necessary steps to implement the recommendations of the Board of Auditors and the Advisory Committee on Administrative and Budgetary Questions as contained in their respective reports, and to report thereon to the General Assembly at its forty-fifth session;

6. *Requests* the Secretary-General and the executive heads of United Nations organizations and programmes concerned to take without delay appropriate measures within their competence and in the light of the comments, observations and recommendations of the Board of Auditors and the Advisory Committee on Administrative and Budgetary Questions, as endorsed in the present resolution, in particular those relating to accounts and financial reporting, programme expenditure, assets and liabilities, including unliquidated obligations, budgetary controls, cash management, trust funds accounts and management issues such as hiring of consultants, award of contracts and project formulation, and to report to the General Assembly at its forty-fifth session, through the governing bodies of those organizations and programmes;

7. *Also requests* the Secretary-General and the executive heads of United Nations organizations and programmes concerned to report to the General Assembly at its forty-fifth session, through the Board of Auditors and the Advisory Committee on Administrative and Budgetary Questions, on specific measures taken to implement the recommendations of the Board, and to explain if any of those recommendations have not yet been implemented, and requests the Board and the Advisory Committee to evaluate the efficacy of those measures and to report thereon to the Assembly at its forty-fifth session;

8. *Recommends* that all future reports of the Board of Auditors continue to include separate sections that summarize recommendations for corrective action to be taken by the organizations and programmes concerned, with an indication of relative urgency;

9. *Also recommends* that the Board of Auditors continue to submit to the General Assembly a concise document summarizing its principal findings, conclusions and recommendations of common interest, classified by audit area and, where appropriate, identifying the audited organization;

10. *Approves* the changes in the financial procedures of the United Nations Development Programme, as recommended by the Governing Council of the Programme in its decision 89/61, and the United Nations Population Fund, as recommended by the Governing Council of the Programme in its decision 89/49;

11. *Requests* the governing bodies of those audited organizations and programmes which are on biennial budget cycles to review at their next session the question of the periodicity of audit reports, bearing in mind the desirability of annual reporting on management issues;

12. *Requests* the Board of Auditors and the Advisory Committee on Administrative and Budgetary Questions to continue to cover in their reviews of the organizations and programmes, including peace-keeping oper-

ations, the areas relating to the efficiency and effectiveness of the financial procedures and controls, the accounting system and related administrative and management areas, in accordance with regulation 12.5 of the Financial Regulations of the United Nations, and to recommend measures, as appropriate, to strengthen financial and management controls;

13. *Also requests* the Board of Auditors to continue to study the desirability and feasibility of conducting its reviews as stipulated in regulation 12.5 of the Financial Regulations of the United Nations in a more comprehensive manner and to report thereon to the General Assembly at its forty-fifth session;

14. *Requests* the Secretary-General and the executive heads of United Nations organizations and programmes concerned, in consultation with the Board of Auditors, to develop further, with a view to prompt completion, the general accounting framework within which financial statements may be prepared, having regard to the relevant financial regulations and rules and also to generally accepted accounting principles, and to report thereon to the General Assembly at its forty-fifth session;

15. *Invites* the Board of Auditors to keep under review the stated accounting policies of each organization and programme and to draw the attention of the General Assembly to specific areas in which it considers that there are differences in accounting policies, having regard to the respective mandates of each entity and with a view to greater harmonization;

16. *Requests* all administrations and governing bodies concerned, in co-operation with the Board of Auditors, to complete the review and clarification of their accounting policies with respect to the recording of unliquidated obligations, taking into account generally accepted accounting principles and regulations 4.3 and 4.4 of the Financial Regulations of the United Nations;

17. *Invites* Governments that are represented on the governing bodies of organizations and programmes for which audited financial statements have been considered by the General Assembly to ensure that full consideration is given to the reports of the Board of Auditors and the Advisory Committee on Administrative and Budgetary Questions and the comments made thereon in the Fifth Committee;

18. *Encourages* all governing bodies of organizations and programmes to invite a representative of the Board of Auditors to be present at their meetings when considering the reports of the Board;

19. *Requests* the Secretary-General and the executive heads of United Nations organizations and programmes concerned to ensure that their respective internal audit units carry out follow-up audit work to assess the corrective action taken by the administrations in response to the main recommendations of the Board of Auditors;

20. *Requests* the administrations concerned and the Board of Auditors to ensure that comments of the administrations on the observations of the Board are available to the Board prior to the finalization of its reports;

21. *Requests* the executive heads of the organizations and programmes concerned to apply existing controls and procedures in order to ensure that expenditures do not exceed the level of funds provided under allotments in accordance with financial rules and to enforce existing disciplinary measures with a view to enhanced accountability and budgetary discipline;

22. *Requests* the Board of Auditors and the Advisory Committee on Administrative and Budgetary Questions to review the liquidity position held by all United Nations organizations and to report thereon to the General Assembly at its forty-fifth session;

23. *Also requests* the Board of Auditors to carry out an audit examination of substantive matters, including management issues, for the United Nations Children's Fund in respect of the first year of each biennium and to submit a report on its findings and recommendations, through the Advisory Committee on Administrative and Budgetary Questions, to the General Assembly and to the Executive Board of the Fund;

24. *Further requests* the Board of Auditors to review the administrative instructions issued in implementation of the Financial Regulations and Rules of the United Nations, in particular rule 114.1, and to report on their adequacy and efficacy to the General Assembly at its forty-fifth session.

General Assembly resolution 44/183

19 December 1989   Meeting 83   Adopted without vote

Approved by Fifth Committee (A/44/674) without vote, 17 October (meeting 13); draft by Vice-Chairman following informal consultations (A/C.5/44/L.3), orally revised; agenda item 121.
Meeting numbers. GA 44th session: 5th Committee 3-7, 12, 13; plenary 83.

REFERENCES

(1)A/44/356. (2)YUN 1988, p. 867, GA res. 43/216, 21 Dec. 1988. (3)A/44/541. (4)A/44/537.

UN programmes

Programme planning, performance and evaluation

Reports of the Secretary-General. In April, the Secretary-General reported,[1] in response to a 1988 General Assembly resolution,[2] on monitoring, evaluation and management information. The report addressed the need to improve the monitoring and evaluation functions in the United Nations so as to provide adequate feedback for the formulation of the medium-term plan and programme budgets; to ensure the effective implementation of programmes; and to provide Member States with a basis for more informed decision-making. It covered such matters as self-evaluation and training; refinement of evaluation methodologies; monitoring and programme performance reporting; and management improvement and information.

Also in April, the Secretary-General submitted a report[3] regarding statements of programme budget implications of draft resolutions and decisions as requested by the General Assembly in 1988.[2] He concluded that there was a need to replace the perception that the statements be prepared to justify the need for additional resources with a conviction that legislative bodies ought to be better informed on the programmatic consequences of draft resolutions and decisions. The time allowed for preparation of the statements should be extended to 72 hours, he said. The statements should indicate whether revisions of the medium-term plan were required, and the provision of statements should be progressively extended to all General Assembly and Economic and Social Council subsidiary bodies.

In July, the Secretary-General submitted a report[4] on all aspects of priority-setting in future outlines of the proposed programme budget, as requested by the General Assembly in 1988.[5] The Secretary-General proposed a modification of the current system of priority-setting, with the aim of starting a dialogue between Member States and the Secretariat. The primary focus of priority-setting would be the medium term plan. The Secretary-General suggested that the modified system of priorities be implemented for a trial period and that CPC and ACABQ review the results after completion of the programme budget for the biennium 1992-1993.

In its first report on the proposed programme budget for 1990-1991,[6] ACABQ agreed with the Secretary-General's suggestion that the medium-term plan be the point of departure for the establishment of priorities in the programme budget outline, but said that much had to be done to improve the form and content of the medium-term plan itself.

CPC consideration. CPC considered the question of planning and evaluation at its twenty-ninth session (New York, 8 May–5 June) and made recommendations on the consultation procedures for preparation of the programme budget, priority setting in future outlines of the budget, evaluation and co-ordination. CPC recommended that the Assembly request relevant intergovernmental bodies to hold meetings in accordance with a calendar that would enable the Secretary-General to take into account their recommendations in the preparation of the proposed programme budget. Its conclusions and recommendations dealt with such topics as political affairs and peace-keeping, policy-making organs for economic and social activities, activities on global social development issues, decisions regarding functioning of MULPOCs, the evaluation report on the disarmament programme, the human rights programme, public information, international protection and assistance to refugees, the review of the programme on development issues and policies and the activities of various UN entities. CPC also addressed co-ordination questions and the rationalization of co-ordination instruments.

Regarding joint meetings of CPC and ACC, CPC recommended that the topic to be considered for 1989 be the preparation of the international development strategy for the fourth United Nations development decade and drug abuse control; for 1990, natural disaster reduction and improvement of co-ordination in the UN system; and for 1991, implementation of the international development strategy for the fourth United Nations development decade and another topic to be decided, possibly environment.

GENERAL ASSEMBLY ACTION

On 21 December, on the recommendation of the Fifth Committee, the General Assembly adopted **resolution 44/194** without vote.

Programme planning

The General Assembly,

Recalling its resolutions 31/93 of 14 December 1976, 32/197 of 20 December 1977, 37/234 of 21 December 1982, 38/227 A and B of 20 December 1983, 41/213 of 19 December 1986, 42/215 of 21 December 1987 and 43/219 of 21 December 1988,

Recalling also Economic and Social Council resolutions 2008(LX) of 14 May 1976 and 1988/77 of 29 July 1988 and taking note of Council resolutions 1989/97 of 26 July 1989, 1989/109 of 27 July 1989 and 1989/114 of 28 July 1989,

Having considered the report of the Committee for Programme and Co-ordination on the work of its twenty-ninth session and the relevant parts of the report of the Economic and Social Council for 1989,

Having considered also the reports of the Advisory Committee on Administrative and Budgetary Questions,

Having considered further the reports of the Secretary-General on all aspects of priority-setting in future outlines of the proposed programme budget, on statements of programme budget implications, and on monitoring, evaluation and management information,

Reaffirming the importance of an appropriate consultation procedure of functional, sectoral and regional bodies on the planning, programming and budgeting process,

Reaffirming also the importance of priority-setting as an integral part of the planning, programming and budgeting process,

Emphasizing the importance of a reliable methodology for monitoring programme performance,

Stressing the importance of evaluation for the systematic and objective determination of the relevance, efficiency, effectiveness and impact of programmes and activities in relation to their objectives,

Recognizing that co-ordination should aim at greater compatibility and mutual complementarity of the activities and programmes of the United Nations system,

Recognizing also the co-ordinating role of the Economic and Social Council in the economic and social sectors,

Reaffirming the importance of the programming and co-ordinating functions within the United Nations carried out by the Committee for Programme and Co-ordination, as the main subsidiary organ of the General Assembly and the Economic and Social Council for planning, programming and co-ordination,

Noting the co-ordinating role of the Administrative Committee on Co-ordination at the secretariat level,

Reaffirming, in this regard, the role of the Secretary-General of the United Nations as the Chairman of the

Administrative Committee on Co-ordination in co-ordinating the activities of the United Nations system,

Taking into account the comments and observations made in the Fifth Committee concerning programme planning,

I
Role of intergovernmental bodies

1. *Approves* the recommendations of the Committee for Programme and Co-ordination on the consultation procedure for the preparation of the proposed programme budget;

2. *Takes note* of the observations of the Advisory Committee on Administrative and Budgetary Questions on the extent of involvement of specialized bodies in the planning and programming process;

3. *Invites* the Committee for Programme and Co-ordination and the Committee on Conferences to take appropriate action, within their respective mandates, with a view to assisting the functional, sectoral and regional bodies in playing a more effective role in the planning, programming and budgeting process in accordance with the relevant resolutions of the General Assembly;

4. *Invites also* the functional, sectoral and regional intergovernmental bodies to consider, in a timely manner, the draft medium-term plan and programme budget proposals within their areas of responsibility, in order that their recommendations may be taken into account by the Secretary-General when he prepares the proposed medium-term plan and the proposed programme budget;

5. *Requests* the Secretary-General to provide the necessary advice to the organs and bodies mentioned in paragraphs 3 and 4 of the present section, in order to enable them effectively to carry out the tasks entrusted to them in the present resolution;

II
Priorities

1. *Approves* the conclusions and recommendations of the Committee for Programme and Co-ordination on priority-setting in future outlines of the proposed programme budget;

2. *Takes note* of the relevant comments of the Advisory Committee on Administrative and Budgetary Questions;

3. *Requests* all relevant entities and bodies to continue to make every effort to set and apply priorities in accordance with the Regulations and Rules Governing Programme Planning, the Programme Aspects of the Budget, the Monitoring of Implementation and the Methods of Evaluation;

4. *Requests* the Committee for Programme and Co-ordination to complete at its thirtieth session consideration of the report of the Secretary-General on all aspects of priority-setting in future outlines of the proposed programme budget, including the relationship between priorities and extrabudgetary resources and taking into account the pertinent observations of the Advisory Committee on Administrative and Budgetary Questions, and to make recommendations thereon to the General Assembly at its forty-fifth session;

III
Programme performance monitoring

1. *Requests* the Secretary-General to continue to improve the methodology for monitoring and reporting on programme performance so that implementation rates may more meaningfully reflect programme performance and that a better comparison may be made between actual delivery of final output and commitments set out in the programme narratives of the approved programme budget;

2. *Also requests* the Secretary-General to develop a methodology for the harmonization of programme performance and budget performance reporting;

IV
Evaluation

1. *Approves* the conclusions and recommendations of the Committee for Programme and Co-ordination on evaluation;

2. *Welcomes* the efforts made by the Secretariat to refine the methodology for evaluation, stresses the need for further improvements, and urges the Secretariat to adopt a more qualitative approach in its evaluation analyses wherever justified by programmatic considerations;

3. *Stresses* the importance of self-evaluation in relation to the preparation and implementation of the medium-term plan and of the programmatic content of the programme budget;

4. *Renews its request* to the Secretary-General, made in section III, paragraph 8, of its resolution 43/219, that programme performance and evaluation reports, together with the conclusions and recommendations of the Committee for Programme and Co-ordination thereon, as endorsed by the General Assembly, should be submitted to the relevant intergovernmental and expert bodies to ensure follow-up action;

V
Co-ordination questions

1. *Approves* the conclusions and recommendations of the Committee for Programme and Co-ordination on co-ordination;

2. *Requests* the Administrative Committee on Co-ordination to modify substantially the format and content of its annual overview report in accordance with the relevant conclusions and recommendations of the Committee for Programme and Co-ordination;

3. *Invites* the Economic and Social Council and the Committee for Programme and Co-ordination to consider in greater detail the annual overview report of the Administrative Committee on Co-ordination, in accordance with their respective mandates;

4. *Requests* the Secretary-General to submit the annual overview report of the Administrative Committee on Co-ordination for 1989 to the Committee for Programme and Co-ordination at its thirtieth session and to the Economic and Social Council at its second regular session of 1990 and subsequently to make it available to the General Assembly at its forty-fifth session, together with the relevant conclusions and recommendations of those bodies on the report in accordance with existing practice;

5. *Invites* the Committee for Programme and Co-ordination and the Administrative Committee on Co-ordination, at their joint meeting in 1990, to discuss, in a thorough manner, all measures for improving the efficacy of the joint meetings, including their structure and level of participation;

VI
Implementation
Requests the Secretary-General to ensure the full implementation of all aspects of the Regulations and Rules Governing Programme Planning, the Programme Aspects of the Budget, the Monitoring of Implementation and the Methods of Evaluation;

VII
Other conclusions and recommendations
Approves those other conclusions and recommendations of the Committee for Programme and Co-ordination at its twenty-ninth session which have not otherwise been approved by the General Assembly at its forty-fourth session.

General Assembly resolution 44/194

21 December 1989   Meeting 84   Adopted without vote

Approved by Fifth Committee (A/44/902) without vote, 19 December (meeting 59); draft by Vice-Chairman following informal consultations (A/C.5/44/L.23); agenda item 124.
Meeting numbers. GA 44th session: 5th Committee 11-16, 18, 19, 23-32, 34, 36, 37, 39, 45, 46, 48, 59; plenary 84.

Joint Inspection Unit

In August, JIU reported[8] on progress in its 1989 work programme, and summarized inspection, review or evaluation of selected UN programmes carried out between 1 July 1988 and 30 June 1989.

JIU noted that Member States had supported its efforts to improve its functioning and the quality and effectiveness of its reports, in accordance with a 1988 General Assembly resolution.[9] JIU had taken a more contemplative approach to the formulation of its work programmes and had limited the 1990-1991 nucleus to five studies, compared with eight in the previous work programme. It had been unable to implement completely the recommendation to give greater attention to management, budgetary and administrative issues because of the short interval between the adoption of the resolution[9] and the formulation of the work programme; JIU noted, however, that 60 per cent of the studies inscribed in the work programme dealt with management, budgetary and administrative matters.

JIU summarized its previous reports on such matters as the evaluation systems for technical co-operation projects, the representation of UN organizations at conferences and meetings, UN public information activities and the reorganization of the Department of Public Information, evaluations of certain rural development and regional projects and its concluding report on the implementation of a 1977 General Assembly resolution[10] on the restructuring of the economic and social sectors of the UN system.

Reports of the Secretary-General. In February, the Secretary-General transmitted[11] JIU's 1989 work programme and the nucleus of the 1990-1991 work programme to the General Assem-

bly. In September, the Secretary-General reported[12] on the implementation of the recommendations contained in six JIU reports. The recommendations dealt with the role of UNHCR, drug abuse control activities, UN support for technical co-operation among developing countries, technical co-operation in Central America and the Caribbean and field representation of UN organizations.

CPC consideration. In June, CPC considered[7] selected JIU reports. It decided to transmit the reports to the General Assembly and to consider at its 1990 session the possibility of a better means of considering the Unit's reports.

GENERAL ASSEMBLY ACTION

On 19 December, on the recommendation of the Fifth Committee, the General Assembly adopted **resolution 44/184** without vote.

Joint Inspection Unit
The General Assembly,

Recalling its resolutions 40/259 of 18 December 1985, 41/213 of 19 December 1986, 42/218 of 21 December 1987 and 43/221 of 21 December 1988,

Having considered the report of the Joint Inspection Unit on its activities during the period 1 July 1988 to 30 June 1989, the work programme of the Unit for 1989 and the nucleus of its work programme for 1990-1991, and the report of the Secretary-General on the implementation of the recommendations of the Unit,

Welcoming the continuing reform measures employed by the Joint Inspection Unit to enhance the quality and effectiveness of its work in all respects, as described in section VI of its report,

Reiterating the importance of a detailed and timely consideration of the report of the Joint Inspection Unit, particularly by Member States and the organizations concerned,

1.	*Takes note* of the report of the Joint Inspection Unit and of its work programme for 1989, as well as of the detailed information contained in the report of the Secretary-General on the implementation of the recommendations of the Unit;

2.	*Requests* the Joint Inspection Unit, in the development of its work programme, to give even greater attention to management, budgetary and administrative issues relevant to the agendas of the governing bodies of its participating organizations and to their main and common concerns;

3.	*Requests* the Secretary-General to standardize the format of his reports relating to the work and recommendations of the Joint Inspection Unit in order to include therein the recommendations of the Unit and any decisions of the General Assembly and other governing bodies before making his comments;

4.	*Urges* the Secretary-General, in preparing his report on the implementation of the recommendations of the Joint Inspection Unit, and the Unit, in preparing its annual report, to co-ordinate their efforts in order to submit to the General Assembly the maximum possible information on the implementation of the recommendations of the Unit;

5. *Invites* the Joint Inspection Unit to continue to make every possible effort to issue its reports well in advance of meetings of the governing bodies of its participating organizations, in particular the General Assembly, and of the relevant subsidiary bodies, to ensure that the comments of the Secretary-General and those of the Administrative Committee on Co-ordination, where pertinent, are issued in accordance with existing regulations for the timely receipt of documentation;

6. *Requests* the Joint Inspection Unit to make every effort to shorten its reports, using comparative tables and graphics whenever appropriate, and to include therein an executive summary of its recommendations in order to facilitate the consideration of its reports;

7. *Also requests* the Joint Inspection Unit to take into account the guidelines outlined in the present resolution in finalizing its work programme for 1990-1991;

8. *Requests* the Secretary-General to bring the present resolution to the attention of the executive heads of the participating organizations of the Joint Inspection Unit.

General Assembly resolution 44/184

19 December 1989   Meeting 83   Adopted without vote

Approved by Fifth Committee (A/44/675) without vote, 19 October (meeting 14); draft by Vice-Chairman following informal consultations (A/C.5/44/L.4); agenda item 127.

Meeting numbers. GA 44th session: 5th Committee 4, 5, 7, 13, 14; plenary 83.

Financing of peace-keeping

In October, the Secretary-General reported[13] on administrative and budgetary aspects of the financing of UN peace-keeping operations (see PART ONE, Chapter I). A subsequent report[14] dealt with voluntary contributions of supplies and services for peace-keeping operations, whether as a loan, advance or outright grant. The report included draft technical guidelines concerning the nature and purpose, acceptability, basis for valuation and budgetary treatment and accounting of such contributions. Another report[15] considered the rates of reimbursement to troop-contributing States. The Secretary-General discussed possible revision of the standardized rates in the light of absorption factors (that part of the costs to troop contributors that is not compensated for by the standard rates and hence must be absorbed by the respective Member State). He concluded that because usable data from 5 of the 13 contributors was absent, a further, more comprehensive review was needed.

In November, ACABQ considered[16] the Secretary-General's reports, bearing in mind its own visits to a number of peace-keeping operations during its spring 1989 session. ACABQ addressed such questions as economies of scale in procurement; the use of civilian personnel in peace-keeping operations, which was growing rapidly; start-up problems of operations; rates of reimbursement; and voluntary contributions. The Advisory Committee recommended that a study

be made of the feasibility of establishing a Secretariat planning and monitoring group to address the need for greater co-ordination among the various units involved in the preparation for and management of peace-keeping operations.

On 21 December, on the recommendation of the Fifth Committee, the General Assembly adopted **resolutions 44/192 A-C** without vote.

Administrative and budgetary aspects of the financing of the United Nations peace-keeping operations
A

The General Assembly,

Recalling its resolution 43/230 of 21 December 1988 on the financing of the United Nations Iran-Iraq Military Observer Group and its decision 43/455 of 21 December 1988 on the administrative and budgetary aspects of the financing of the United Nations peace-keeping operations,

Recalling also its resolution 44/49 of 8 December 1989 on the comprehensive review of the whole question of peace-keeping operations in all their aspects,

Recognizing the mutual relevance of the work of the Special Committee on Peace-keeping Operations and the work done by the Fifth Committee in connection with matters relating to peace-keeping operations,

Having considered with appreciation the reports of the Secretary-General on the administrative and budgetary aspects of the financing of the United Nations peace-keeping operations, on the review of the background and development of reimbursement to Member States contributing troops to peace-keeping operations and on voluntary contributions of supplies and services, and the related report of the Advisory Committee on Administrative and Budgetary Questions,

Bearing in mind the views expressed by Member States on those reports at the forty-fourth session,

Recognizing that each peace-keeping operation has special characteristics, which thus calls for flexibility in addressing the administrative requirements of each operation,

Recognizing also that all necessary action should be taken to ensure that peace-keeping operations are administered with a maximum of efficiency and economy,

Bearing in mind the significant increase in United Nations peace-keeping activities and the resulting increased demands on the human, material and financial resources of the Organization and of Member States,

Noting that, as a result of the recent expansion in peace-keeping activities, an absorptive capacity in respect of trained and experienced United Nations staff members with the technical skills required in peace-keeping operations is no longer available,

Taking into account the observations of the Advisory Committee on the need for greater co-ordination among the various Secretariat units involved in preparing and managing peace-keeping operations,

Mindful of the fact that it is essential to provide peace-keeping operations with the necessary financial resources, especially those essential for the start-up of such operations, to enable them to fulfil their mandates in accordance with the relevant resolutions of the Security Council,

Aware of the extremely difficult financial situation of the existing peace-keeping operations and of the heavy burden on troop-contributing States,

Emphasizing the need to ensure a secure and sound financial basis for peace-keeping operations,

1. *Urges* all Member States to make every possible effort to ensure payment of their assessed contributions to peace-keeping operations in full and on time, in accordance with their obligations under the Charter of the United Nations;

2. *Takes note* of the observations and proposals made by the Secretary-General on economies of scale, start-up problems and the establishment of a reserve stock of equipment and supply items, and endorses the relevant recommendations of the Advisory Committee on Administrative and Budgetary Questions;

3. *Also takes note* of the observations and proposals of the Secretary-General on the criteria and procedures by which Governments may offer the services of civilian personnel for peace-keeping operations, concurs with the recommendations of the Advisory Committee, in particular that standard administrative procedures to govern the provision of such personnel should be established, consistent with existing rules and practices and taking into consideration the practical and legal concerns and the experience gained in the newly established peace-keeping operations, and requests the Secretary-General to submit those standard administrative procedures to the Advisory Committee at its spring session in 1990;

4. *Invites* States willing to participate in peace-keeping operations to submit to the Secretary-General, with his assistance, detailed inventories of specialized civilian individuals or units, including numbers of personnel and equipment, that they would be prepared to provide for those tasks and services identified by the Secretary-General in his report and in the manner outlined therein, consistent with General Assembly resolution 44/49, paragraphs 2 and 3;

5. *Takes note* of the observations and proposals of the Secretary-General on the technical guidelines relating to the treatment and valuation of voluntary contributions in the form of supplies and services, and endorses the observations of the Advisory Committee;

6. *Also takes note* of the proposals of the Advisory Committee on the need for greater co-ordination among the various Secretariat units involved in preparing and managing peace-keeping operations and, in this respect, welcomes the intention of the Secretary-General to establish a planning and monitoring group on the basis described in his report;

7. *Further takes note* of the proposals of the Secretary-General to establish an account for programme support of peace-making and peace-keeping operations, and endorses the views of the Advisory Committee in that respect;

8. *Requests* the Secretary-General to submit a report to the General Assembly at its forty-fifth session on the measures taken in accordance with the observations and recommendations of the Advisory Committee contained in its reports and to provide further information covering, *inter alia*:

(a) Economies of scale;

(b) Start-up problems;

(c) The establishment of a reserve stock of equipment and supply items;

(d) The use of civilian personnel in peace-keeping operations;

(e) Problems related to overload posts and the proposed establishment of a support account for peace-keeping operations;

9. *Also requests* the Secretary-General to keep under review the format of his reports on the financing of United Nations peace-keeping operations and the amount of information that should be included therein, in order to assist Member States in the scrutiny and evaluation of those reports;

10. *Decides* to include in the provisional agenda of its forty-fifth session the item entitled "Administrative and budgetary aspects of the financing of the United Nations peace-keeping operations".

B

The General Assembly,

Having considered the report of the Secretary-General on the composition of the existing groups of Member States for the apportionment of the costs of peace-keeping operations financed through assessed contributions,

Recalling its resolution 3101(XXVIII) of 11 December 1973 and its subsequent resolutions relating to the composition of the existing groups, the latest of which is resolution 43/232 of 1 March 1989 on the financing of the United Nations Transition Assistance Group,

Recalling also paragraph 3 of resolution 44/44 of 7 December 1989 on the financing of the United Nations Observer Group in Central America, in which it, *inter alia*, refers to the decision to be taken, at its forty-fourth session, on the composition of groups "a", "b", "c" and "d" of Member States,

Welcoming the proposal made by the Government of Spain to reclassify Spain from group "c" to group "b",

Having considered the requests of Poland for reclassification from group "b" to group "c" and of the Central African Republic, Equatorial Guinea, the Gambia, Myanmar, Sierra Leone and Togo for reclassification from group "c" to group "d",

Having identified grounds for anomalies on the basis of the information contained in the report of the Secretary-General, particularly concerning the least developed countries,

Decides, as an *ad hoc* arrangement:

(a) To accept the proposal made by the Government of Spain and to place Spain among the Member States referred to in paragraph 3 (b) of resolution 43/232 and, in accordance with that proposal, to apportion its share of the costs of peace-keeping operations financed through assessed contributions on the basis of the proportion determined by the scale of assessments in the following manner: 50 per cent in 1990, 80 per cent in 1991 and 100 per cent in 1992 and subsequent years;

(b) To place Poland among the Member States referred to in paragraph 3 (c) of resolution 43/232;

(c) To place the Central African Republic, Equatorial Guinea, the Gambia, Mauritania, Myanmar, Sierra Leone and Togo among the Member States referred to in paragraph 3 (d) of resolution 43/232.

C

The General Assembly,

Recalling its resolution 42/224 of 21 December 1987,

Having considered the report of the Secretary-General on the review of the rates of reimbursement to the Governments of troop-contributing States, submitted pursuant to General Assembly resolution 42/224, as well as the related report of the Advisory Committee on Administrative and Budgetary Questions,

Noting with concern the delay by some Member States in submitting the data requested by the Secretary-General, thus preventing him from making a substantive recommendation on the revision of the current rates of reimbursement,

1. *Urges* all those troop-contributing States which the Secretary-General requested to provide data and which have not yet done so to provide complete data as soon as possible and at the latest by 1 February 1990;

2. *Notes with concern* that, in consequence of the shortfall of financial contributions, troop-contributing States are not being reimbursed to the full extent of the established rates for some operations, thus bearing considerably larger portions of the costs for their troops serving in the United Nations peace-keeping forces than those indicated by the Secretary-General in his report;

3. *Requests* the Secretary-General, to the extent possible, to make the payment of arrears due to current and former troop-contributing States;

4. *Also requests* the Secretary-General to complete the review of the rates of reimbursement on receipt of the outstanding information and to submit, through the Advisory Committee on Administrative and Budgetary Questions, his report for the consideration of the General Assembly at its forty-fifth session;

5. *Further requests* the Secretary-General to include in each of his reports on the financing of the United Nations peace-keeping operations relevant information on the status of reimbursement to the troop-contributing States.

General Assembly resolutions 44/192 A-C

21 December 1989   Meeting 84   Adopted without vote

Approved by Fifth Committee (A/44/892) without vote, 18 December (meeting 58); draft by Chairman following informal consultations (A/C.5/44/L.17, part A); agenda item 137.
Meeting numbers. GA 44th session: 5th Committee 43, 45-49, 56-58; plenary 84.

REFERENCES
[1]A/44/233. [2]YUN 1988, p. 871, GA res. 43/219, 21 Dec. 1988. [3]A/44/234. [4]A/44/272. [5]YUN 1988, p. 862, GA res. 43/214, 21 Dec. 1988. [6]A/44/7. [7]A/44/16 & Add.1. [8]A/44/34. [9]YUN 1988, p. 874, GA res. 43/221, 21 Dec. 1988. [10]YUN 1977, p. 438, GA res. 32/197, 20 Dec. 1977. [11]A/44/129. [12]A/44/488. [13]A/44/605 & Add.1,2. [14]A/44/624. [15]A/44/500. [16]A/44/725.

Administrative and budgetary co-ordination in UN system

The administrative and budgetary co-ordination of the United Nations with the specialized agencies and International Atomic Energy Agency (IAEA) was the subject of a report submitted to the General Assembly on 7 November 1989 by ACABQ.[1] In accordance with its terms of reference, ACABQ met with the executive heads (or their senior representatives) of 10 organizations, and received the required data by correspondence

from 3 others, whose agreements with the United Nations provided for transmittal of their budgets for review by the General Assembly.

These organizations were ILO, FAO, UNESCO, ICAO, UPU, WHO, ITU, WMO, IMO, WIPO, IFAD, UNIDO and IAEA.

The regular budgets (or budget estimates) of the United Nations and the specialized agencies (excluding IFAD) and IAEA for 1990 would total $2,306.8 million, of which $2,178.4 million would be covered by assessed contributions. In addition, further assessed contributions for the United Nations were likely to arise in 1990 for peace-keeping operations; 1989 assessments for peace-keeping totalled $720.7 million. The total number of established posts authorized or requested under the regular budgets of the specialized agencies (excluding IFAD) and IAEA for 1990 was 13,230, 33 more than the 1989 total of 13,197 (excluding IFAD). Since the number of established posts authorized or requested under the UN regular budget for 1990 was 10,004, a grand total of 23,234 established posts for 1990 had been authorized or requested, a decrease of 1,132 posts compared to the 1989 total of 24,366 (excluding IFAD).

Total outstanding contributions as at 30 September 1989 equalled 63.45 per cent of total net contributions of Member States actually payable in respect of 1989, compared to 58.01 per cent as at 30 September 1988. Of the total, $609.6 million was owed to the UN and $675.2 million to the specialized agencies and IAEA.

According to the report, cash payments received by the UN system from voluntary contributions (extrabudgetary funds) totalled $2,911.3 million in 1987 and $3,360.8 million in 1988, of which Member States contributed $2,730.6 million in 1987 and $3,180.5 million in 1988. Some $97.2 million was contributed by non-members in 1988, compared to $91.5 million in 1987. Extrabudgetary fund expenditures totalled $3,657.3 million in 1987 and $4,386.8 million in 1988.

GENERAL ASSEMBLY ACTION

By **decision 44/414** of 22 November, the General Assembly took note with appreciation of the Advisory Committee's report and decided to support its intention to revert to its former practice of in-depth studies of individual agencies of the United Nations system every other year with a view to making appropriate recommendations whenever required. It also invited the Advisory Committee to consider conducting in-depth studies of administrative and budgetary aspects of topics of system-wide concern.

REFERENCES
[1]A/44/711 & Add 1.

Chapter II

UN staff matters

In 1989, the Secretary-General submitted a final report on implementation of the 1986 General Assembly–approved recommendations for restructuring. However, after considering it, the Committee for Programme and Co-ordination (CPC) recommended a further report to the 1990 Assembly, in order to assess the impact of the administrative and financial reforms.

During the year, the International Civil Service Commission (ICSC) submitted a report on its comprehensive review of the conditions of service of staff in the Professional and higher categories, while the Administrative Committee on Co-ordination (ACC) called for at least a 5 per cent remuneration increase for all staff, as a beginning step towards restoration of the margin envisaged in the Noblemaire principle of UN staff remuneration, in comparison to the highest-paid national civil service.

The General Assembly, in acting on the ICSC report, noted with concern that it had not been possible for the Commission to recommend the introduction of a revised remuneration structure and urged it to submit final and complete conclusions to the Assembly in 1990. In regard to the Secretary-General's report on implementation of the recommendations of the Group of High-level Intergovernmental Experts to Review the Efficiency of the Administrative and Financial Functioning of the United Nations (Group of 18), the Assembly stressed that in order to successfully carry out the process of reform and restructuring, it was essential that the present financial uncertainties facing the Organization be dispelled. It recognized the progress achieved so far in implementing overall post reduction, while acknowledging that the Secretary-General was not in a position at present to propose further reductions. It renewed its request to the Secretary-General to submit to the Assembly in 1990 an analytical report assessing the effect of the reforms, and made recommendations for the structure of that report.

Also in 1989, the Secretary-General reported on the establishment of a fully revised internal justice system; changes were made in the UN pension scheme to re-establish actuarial viability; and the General Assembly agreed to increase the mandatory retirement age of staff from 60 to 62 years in respect of new staff members.

There were continued disturbing reports about officials of the UN system who had been arrested and detained or who had disappeared in various places throughout the world, a situation given tragic emphasis by the apparent murder of a senior United Nations Truce Supervision Operation (UNTSO) officer serving with the United Nations Interim Force in Lebanon (UNIFIL).

Conditions of service

International Civil Service Commission

In 1989, the International Civil Service Commission (ICSC) held its second special session in New York (16-19 January), its twenty-ninth session in Vienna (6-23 March) and its thirtieth session in New York (31 July–25 August). The Commission examined issues derived from General Assembly decisions as well as from its own Statute. In its fifteenth annual report to the Assembly,[1] ICSC focused attention on a comprehensive review of service conditions of Professional and higher salary staff, conducted by a Working Group of ICSC members and its secretariat as well as representatives of both the Organization and staff, which was the subject of the second volume of the report. The financial implications resulting from the Commission's 1989 decisions and recommendations for the United Nations common system totalled approximately $90 million a year.

The Commission reported that it had adopted guidelines to supplement the working methods approved at its twenty-seventh and twenty-eighth sessions.[2] It decided to examine facts and alternatives in open, as opposed to executive, sessions; to limit executive sessions to the taking of decisions; and to continue to monitor progress and to review its rules of procedure as appropriate. Because of the unique requirements of the comprehensive review, representatives of organizations and the staff could attend Commission meetings at which substantive determinations were made regarding decisions on the comprehensive review.

Noblemaire principle

The Noblemaire principle, first adopted under the League of Nations, provides that the salaries of Professional and higher category staff should be adequate to attract staff from all countries, including the country with the highest-compensated civil service, known as the comparator.

In 1989, the Commission continued to review the relationship between the levels of net remuneration of the United Nations and the United States federal civil service (the current comparator) under the Noblemaire principle. In 1988, the General Assembly had stated[3] that the Noblemaire principle should continue to serve as the basis for comparison between UN emoluments and those of the highest-paying civil service. Based on the margin between the net remuneration of the United States federal civil service and the UN system, ICSC decided to implement a class 10 post adjustment for New York effective in May 1989.

Remuneration issues

A change in methodology for adjustments to the pensionable remuneration of staff in the Professional and higher categories was recommended to the General Assembly, in view of the fact that UN pensionable remuneration had been adjusted by 9.3 percentage points beyond the adjustment applied to the comparator's scale. The Commission decided thenceforth to consider pensionable remuneration annually. It also recommended that the mandatory age of separation for new staff members appointed after 1 January 1990 be raised from 60 to 62, and decided to continue to monitor the situation.

By **resolution 44/185 D** of 19 December, the General Assembly approved the amendment of the staff regulations to raise the mandatory separation age to 62 and asked the Secretary-General to report to the Assembly in 1990 on the implications of the change for staff recruitment, mobility, career development and promotion, staffing structure, representation of Member States in the Secretariat and long-term staff expenditures.

Supplementary payments and deductions

The Commission in 1989 continued to study the issue of supplementary payments to and deductions from the remuneration of common system staff by certain Member States. In 1987,[4] the General Assembly had requested all Member States and common system organizations to provide ICSC with information on the subject. In 1988,[3] the Assembly asked the Commission to continue its review of the matter.

The Commission deplored that, after repeated requests, 64 Member States had still not responded to the Chairman's latest inquiry, and noted that the non-responding States included four permanent members of the Security Council. It reviewed further information provided by three Member States that made supplementary payments, and decided to continue to pursue its inquiry into the

matter. It reiterated its position that supplementary payments and deductions by Member States contravened the Organization's staff regulations; recalled its previous request to the General Assembly to take appropriate action to discourage those practices; and requested the Secretary-General, together with other executive heads, to contact Member States, if necessary at the highest level, to eliminate such practices.

Comprehensive review

The Commission addressed six major areas in the context of the comprehensive review of the conditions of service of staff in the Professional and higher categories, requested by the General Assembly in 1987[4] in order to provide a sound and stable methodological basis for staff remuneration. The Commission considered various alternatives to the current remuneration system, but stated that further testing was needed before definite conclusions could be reached.

The six major areas were: competitiveness of the current UN salary system related to recruitment and retention needs; matters relating to the comparator and the margin; the post adjustment system; mobility and hardship; motivation and productivity; and allowances. The effective date for implementation of decisions taken on the comprehensive review would be 1 July 1990.

Regarding competitiveness, the Commission recommended the establishment of new base salary levels and a 5 per cent general increase in remuneration for staff in Professional and higher categories, the cost of which would total some $61 million.

As to the comparator and margin, the Commission confirmed that in the application of the Noblemaire principle as the basis for determining the conditions of service of UN staff in the Professional and higher categories, the comparator should continue to be the highest-paid national civil service. A check should be made every five years to ensure that the current comparator was still the highest-paid national civil service. The current margin range should continue to apply, and should be allowed to fluctuate freely within the range; corrective measures would be recommended by the Commission if the margin dropped below the lower limit or exceeded the top of the range. The existing cumulative margin procedure and the four-month waiting period between the granting of successive classes of post adjustment for New York should be discontinued. Comparisons would be based on the net remuneration of UN officials in grades P-1 through D-2 in New York and that of their comparator counterparts in Washington, D.C.; the cost-of-living differential between New York and Washington should continue to be taken into account; average salaries at each grade should be used on both sides of the comparison; and bonuses and performance awards not considered to be included in base salary should be excluded from comparisons.

Regarding the post adjustment system, the Commission made a range of recommendations relating to various operational aspects of the system, including simplification through the elimination of special measures for high inflation, for abrupt or continuous devaluation and for duty stations with a low or negative post adjustment classification.

The Commission recommended a new mobility and hardship scheme incorporating incentives and payments for hardship, mobility and the existing assignment allowance. The scheme provided for a number of other measures related to the assignment grant (formerly the installation grant), removal entitlements, home leave and boarding costs for educational facilities. Time off for medical/dental check-ups was recommended to be discontinued.

In respect of motivation and productivity, the Commission recommended structural improvements to the salary scale for staff in the Professional and higher categories. The Commission reiterated earlier recommendations regarding cash awards for outstanding performance, non-monetary awards such as pins, plaques and certificates, and environmental motivators in areas of security, health, education and briefing and other work-related conditions. Regarding allowances, the Commission made recommendations in three areas—the education grant, dependency allowances and separation payments—with the Commission reaffirming that the education grant was to remain solely an expatriate benefit. Existing dependency allowances remained unchanged, with the exception of the children's allowance for a disabled child, which was set at double the amount of the children's allowance. The existing scale of separation payments should be abolished and, with the exception of the commutation of unused annual leave, all separation payments were to be calculated in the future using the base/floor amount for the remuneration system. Unused annual leave was to be calculated on the basis of net remuneration at the duty station where the staff member had served prior to separation.

ACC consideration. In April, the Administrative Committee on Co-ordination adopted a statement[5] for submission to ICSC, in which it said that in comparison with expatriate staff of the comparator civil service, especially those in the field, the conditions of common system staff were highly unfavourable. Similar comparisons with staff of bilateral or other multilateral financial and aid agencies revealed that employment conditions of

the common system were less than adequate. Conditions of service in the system were no longer competitive or attractive, ACC stated; in many instances, they acted as a disincentive to continuing in service. It was increasingly difficult to find qualified and experienced staff to fill vacancies, which was a very real day-to-day problem. It was expected that the outcome of the ICSC review would be the restoration of the competitiveness of the UN system as an employer. ACC identified the key elements in an improved remuneration system as more responsive treatment of the housing component; a more meaningful mobility and hardship allowance; more flexibility in managing and operating the margin; establishment of a more meaningful floor remuneration level; and appropriate incentives to motivate staff and improve productivity. The building up of the integrated package of proposals should not be unduly affected by cost considerations, ACC said.

In another decision,[6] regarding staffing levels, ACC recommended that the secretariat of ICSC should be reduced by one P-4, two P-3 and two General Service posts.

On 5 July, ACC convened a special session at which it adopted a further statement[7] for submission to ICSC. It repeated its grave concern that conditions of employment and the purchasing power of UN common system staff continued to be eroded and that good staff were leaving. ICSC was requested to give the closest attention in proposing a revised system to several factors, including substantially improved remuneration for all staff at all duty stations, starting with at least a 5 per cent across-the-board increase, with a mechanism of continuing yearly increases until the competitive level of take-home pay was restored.

GENERAL ASSEMBLY ACTION

On 21 December 1989, on the recommendation of the Fifth (Administrative and Budgetary) Committee, the General Assembly adopted **resolution 44/198** without vote.

United Nations common system: report of the International Civil Service Commission

The General Assembly,

Having considered the fifteenth annual report of the International Civil Service Commission and other related reports,

I

Comprehensive review of the conditions of service of the staff in the Professional and higher categories

Recalling that, in section III of its resolution 42/221 of 21 December 1987, it requested the International Civil Service Commission to undertake a comprehensive review of the conditions of service of the staff in the Professional and higher categories,

Recalling also the guidance it provided on this comprehensive review in section III of its resolution 42/221 and in section I of its resolution 43/226 of 21 December 1988,

Recalling further, in respect of the request contained in section I, paragraph 4 *(c)*, of resolution 43/226, that the overall costs of all the elements of the solutions proposed in the comprehensive review should, as far as possible, be comparable to the costs of the current remuneration system,

Noting that only upon completion of the comprehensive review in all its aspects can the decisions covered in section I of the present resolution be considered final,

1. *Requests* the Secretary-General to make all necessary efforts to absorb in 1991 and subsequent years a significant portion of the additional costs arising in respect of the regular budget of the United Nations as a result of the adoption of the present resolution;

2. *Also requests* the Secretary-General, in his capacity as Chairman of the Administrative Committee on Co-ordination, to emphasize to the executive heads of the specialized agencies the importance of assisting the respective governing bodies in taking parallel measures to the same effect;

A. *Remuneration structure*

Noting with concern that it has not been possible for the Commission to recommend the introduction of a revised remuneration structure,

1. *Takes note* of the views of the Commission with regard to the proposal that housing should be treated separately from the rest of the remuneration package and of the decision of the Commission, relating to undertaking further work on remuneration structures, contained in paragraph 196 of volume II of its report;

2. *Urges* the Commission to complete its consideration of all issues related to the introduction of a revised remuneration structure for the United Nations common system, including its impact on margin consideration and on the housing needs of staff in hardship duty stations, and to submit its final and complete conclusions to the General Assembly at its forty-fifth session;

B. *Comparator*

1. *Reaffirms* that the Noblemaire principle should continue to serve as the basis of comparison between United Nations emoluments and those of the highest-paying civil service—currently the United States federal civil service—which, by its size and structure, lends itself to such comparison;

2. *Endorses* the recommendation of the Commission to conduct periodic checks, every five years, to determine which is the highest-paying civil service, and consequently requests the Commission to propose to the General Assembly at its forty-sixth session a methodology for carrying out such checks;

C. *Margin considerations*

Recalling that, in section I, paragraph 2, of its resolution 40/244 of 18 December 1985, it approved a range of 110 to 120 with a desirable mid-point of 115, for the margin between the net remuneration of officials in the Professional and higher categories of the United Nations in New York and that of officials in comparable positions in the United States federal civil service, on the understanding that the margin would be maintained at a level around the desirable mid-point of 115 over a period of time,

1. *Confirms* that the current concept of the margin should continue to apply;

2. *Also confirms* that the current margin range of 110 to 120 should continue to apply;

3. *Endorses* the methodological approach, as outlined in paragraph 173 *(d)* of volume II of the report of the Commission, for the calculation of the net remuneration margin;

4. *Requests* the Commission to continue to report the net remuneration margin on an annual basis;

5. *Also requests* the Commission to monitor the annual net remuneration margin over the five-year period beginning in the calendar year 1990 with a view to ensuring, to the extent possible, that by the end of that period the average of the successive annual margins is around the desirable mid-point of 115, and to report to the General Assembly at its forty-ninth session on the experience gained and, in the mean time, to submit to the Assembly at its forty-seventh session an interim report on the net remuneration margin for the period 1990-1991;

D. *Post adjustment*

1. *Requests* the Commission to reconsider the decision contained in paragraph 250 *(a)* of volume II of its report relating to the granting of post adjustment increases due to cost of living;

2. *Takes note* of all other decisions taken by the Commission in respect of the operation of the post adjustment system as reflected in chapter VI of volume II of its report;

3. *Endorses*, with effect from 1 July 1990, the recommendations contained in paragraph 261 of volume II of the report of the Commission regarding the removal of regressivity from the post adjustment system and the inclusion of pension contributions as a separate item in the post adjustment index, on the understanding that, as indicated in paragraph 262, the current remuneration correction factor and floor protection measures will be discontinued;

4. *Instructs* the Commission to complete as soon as possible, and preferably by the end of 1991, a round of place-to-place surveys using the methodology outlined in chapter VI of volume II of its report, on the understanding that the surveys at the seven headquarters duty stations and at other duty stations with more than 150 Professional staff members will be finalized by the end of 1990 and that, at duty stations with small numbers of staff members, every effort will be made to utilize to the maximum the external data sources as outlined in paragraph 235 of volume II of the report of the Commission;

5. *Requests* the executive heads and the staff to co-operate with the Commission during the place-to-place survey process;

6. *Requests* the Commission to devise appropriate measures to deal with those duty stations where, upon implementation of a place-to-place survey, there exists a significant difference between the post adjustment index and the actual multiplier;

7. *Confirms* that, following the introduction of the revised salary scale referred to in section I.H, paragraph 3, of the present resolution and pending the outcome of the respective place-to-place surveys in those locations where the index reflected in the post adjustment multipliers exceeds the post adjustment index, net remuneration will continue to be adjusted only to reflect currency fluctuations until the post adjustment index

surpasses the index reflected by the post adjustment multipliers;

E. *Mobility and hardship*

1. *Approves*, with effect from 1 July 1990, the introduction of a mobility and hardship allowance as outlined in paragraphs 313 to 322 and 328 of volume II of the report of the Commission, an assignment grant as outlined in paragraphs 323 to 327 and the provisions relating to the reimbursement of boarding costs contained in paragraph 329, on the understanding that the amounts indicated in the matrix for staff serving at Headquarters or in North American and European duty stations and similar designated locations will be payable from their fourth assignment only if they have served in at least two field duty stations;

2. *Requests* the Commission to report to the General Assembly at its forty-seventh session on the operation of the mobility and hardship allowance and the assignment grant;

F. *Motivation and productivity*

1. *Endorses*, with effect from 1 July 1990, the recommendations contained in paragraph 356 of volume II of the report of the Commission concerning structural improvements to the salary scale, which should be appropriately reflected in the scale of pensionable remuneration, and also endorses the recommendation contained in paragraph 357 *(a)* relating to the modification of promotion policy;

2. *Invites* the organizations of the United Nations common system to take appropriate steps to introduce the Commission's recommendations as outlined in paragraphs 357 *(d)* and *(e)* in respect of non-monetary awards and environmental motivators;

3. *Invites* the Commission again to review performance evaluation systems in all organizations of the United Nations common system with a view to:

(a) Ensuring that such systems are objective and transparent;

(b) Tying within-grade step increments and promotions to merit, as indicated in the performance evaluation reports, rather than primarily to longevity;

G. *Allowances*

1. *Endorses*, with effect from 1 July 1990, the recommendations contained in chapter IX of volume II of the report of the Commission and the consequential amendment to the Staff Regulations of the United Nations, with respect to:

(a) The children's allowance in respect of disabled children, as outlined in paragraph 429 *(e)*;

(b) The calculation of the commutation of unused annual leave, as outlined in paragraph 453 *(d)*;

(c) The scale of separation payments, as outlined in paragraph 453 *(g)*;

2. *Takes note* of the conclusions of the Commission reflected in paragraphs 406 and 453 *(a)*, *(e)* and *(f)* and confirms, with respect to paragraph 453 *(b)* and *(c)*, that the terms and conditions of payment of the repatriation grant should remain unchanged in all respects;

3. *Requests* the Commission to collect the necessary information on the practices of the organizations of the United Nations common system regarding the granting of expatriate entitlements to staff members living in their home countries while stationed at duty stations located in another country in order to assess the feasibility of harmonizing practices among organizations, and to report thereon to the General Assembly at its forty-fifth session;

4. *Also requests* the Commission to reconsider the methodology for the determination of dependency allowances in the light of the tax practices of the comparator and to report thereon to the General Assembly at its forty-fifth session;

5. *Further requests* the Commission to provide an overview of the package of common system allowances, including the level, rationale and procedure for review of each allowance, *inter alia*, by reference to the package of allowances provided by the comparator, and to report thereon to the General Assembly at its forty-fifth session;

H. *Base salary scale*

1. *Approves*, with effect from 1 July 1990, the establishment of a floor net salary level for staff in the Professional and higher categories by reference to the corresponding base net salary levels of officials in comparable positions serving at the base city of the comparator civil service;

2. *Also approves*, with effect from 1 July 1990, revised rates of staff assessment for staff members with neither a dependent spouse nor a dependent child, to be used in conjunction with gross base salaries and gross amounts of separation payments and, consequently, approves as at the same date an amendment to the Staff Regulations of the United Nations as set forth in annex I to the present resolution, to replace, for staff in the Professional and higher categories, the present scale of staff assessment for staff with neither a dependent spouse nor a dependent child;

3. *Further approves*, with effect from 1 July 1990, the revised scale of gross and net salaries for staff in the Professional and higher categories contained in annex II to the present resolution, and the consequential amendment to the Staff Regulations of the United Nations, together with the procedures for its construction and implementation that are reflected in annex III to the present resolution;

II
Functioning of the International
Civil Service Commission

Recalling that, in section VIII of its resolution 42/221, it requested the International Civil Service Commission to undertake a study of its functioning with a view to enhancing its work,

Recalling also its request to the Commission in section II of its resolution 43/226 to expand the review of its functioning in consultation with the organizations of the United Nations common system and staff representatives and to submit proposals thereon to the General Assembly at its forty-fifth session,

Noting that the action of the Commission has been limited so far to considering the format of its annual report and to agreeing to practical arrangements for the conduct of its work during its sessions,

1. *Requests* the Secretary-General, together with his colleagues in the Administrative Committee on Coordination and after consultations with the representatives of staff participating in the International Civil Service Commission, to review the functioning of the Commission and to submit to the General Assembly at its forty-sixth session a report on the matter together with

the views of the Commission thereon and, in the mean time, requests the Commission to maintain, in connection with matters related to comprehensive reviews of conditions of service of staff, the arrangements established in response to the invitation expressed by the Assembly in section I, paragraph 2, of its resolution 43/226;

2. *Requests* the Commission to continue to seek improvements in the presentation of its report;

III
Other questions

A

Recognizing the changing demographic pattern of the work-force of the United Nations common system, as well as the increasing trend in some Member States towards extending the length of service of its work-force, and noting that in a number of Member States the normal retirement age and the corresponding mandatory age of separation are higher than they are at present in the United Nations common system,

Commends to the attention of the governing bodies of the organizations of the United Nations common system the recommendation of the International Civil Service Commission to increase the mandatory age of separation to 62 for staff members entering into service on or after 1 January 1990;

B

Recalling its request made in section III.C of its resolution 43/226 that the Commission report to the General Assembly at its forty-fifth session on progress made by the organizations of the United Nations common system in connection with the introduction of special measures for the recruitment of women,

Urges the organizations of the United Nations common system to provide the fullest information to the Commission on the introduction of special measures for the recruitment of women so as to enable the Commission to analyse appropriately the progress achieved and to report thereon to the General Assembly at its forty-fifth session;

C

Recalling section II of its resolution 37/126 of 17 December 1982 and section VII of its resolution 42/221 concerning the practice of some Member States of making supplementary payments or deductions with respect to their nationals,

Recalling also its request made in section III.C of its resolution 43/226 that the Commission report on these practices to the General Assembly at its forty-fourth session,

Noting the limited response to the inquiries of the Commission on the matter,

Taking note of the decisions of the Commission contained in paragraph 90 of volume I of its report, including its decision to report further to the General Assembly at its forty-fifth session on this matter,

1. *Requests* the Secretary-General to contact those Member States that have not so far provided information on supplementary payments and deductions to seek their co-operation in providing such information forthwith in order for the Commission to complete its study, which should also include a review of the impact of the introduction of the revised remuneration package on practices currently in effect;

2. *Requests* the Secretary-General and the executive heads of the specialized agencies to take appropriate steps to bring an end to these practices.

ANNEX I
Amendment to the Staff Regulations of the United Nations
Regulation 3.3

Replace the last column of the table under assessment in paragraph *(b)* (i) by the following:

"Assessment
(In percentages)

Total assessable payments (US dollars)	Staff assessment rates used in conjunction with gross base salaries and the gross amounts of separation payments — Staff member with neither a dependent spouse nor a dependent child
First $15,000 per year	17.7
Next $5,000 per year	34.3
Next $5,000 per year	38.6
Next $5,000 per year	41.9
Next $5,000 per year	43.9
Next $10,000 per year	46.3
Next $10,000 per year	48.4
Next $10,000 per year	50.4
Next $15,000 per year	51.3
Next $20,000 per year	54.1
Remaining assessable payments	59.0''

ANNEX II
Salary scale for the Professional and higher categories
showing annual gross salaries and net equivalents
after application of staff assessment
(Effective 1 July 1990)
(In United States dollars)

							Steps								
Level	*I*	*II*	*III*	*IV*	*V*	*VI*	*VII*	*VIII*	*IX*	*X*	*XI*	*XII*	*XIII*	*XIV*	*XV*
Under-Secretary-General															
USG Gross 121,635															
Net D 73,050															
Net S 65,255															
Assistant Secretary-General															
ASG Gross 110,000															
Net D 67,000															
Net S 60,485															

Level								*Steps*							
	I	*II*	*III*	*IV*	*V*	*VI*	*VII*	*VIII*	*IX*	*X*	*XI*	*XII*	*XIII*	*XIV*	*XV*
Director															
D-2 Gross	89,189	91,251	93,313	95,375	97,438	99,500									
Net D	56,070	57,163	58,256	59,349	60,442	61,535									
Net S	51,423	52,369	53,316	54,262	55,209	56,156									
Principal Officer															
D-1 Gross	78,333	80,068	81,834	83,600	85,366	87,132	88,898	90,664	92,430						
Net D	50,300	51,236	52,172	53,108	54,044	54,980	55,916	56,852	57,788						
Net S	46,393	47,236	48,047	48,857	49,668	50,479	51,289	52,100	52,910						
Senior Officer															
P-5 Gross	68,611	70,180	71,748	73,317	74,885	76,454	78,022	79,591	81,181	82,779	84,377	85,975	87,574		
Net D	45,050	45,897	46,744	47,591	48,438	49,285	50,132	50,979	51,826	52,673	53,520	54,367	55,214		
Net S	41,659	42,423	43,186	43,950	44,714	45,478	46,242	47,006	47,747	48,481	49,214	49,948	50,681		
First Officer															
P-4 Gross	55,818	57,320	58,822	60,324	61,825	63,327	64,829	66,356	67,885	69,415	70,944	72,474	74,004	75,533	77,063
Net D	38,050	38,876	39,702	40,528	41,354	42,180	43,006	43,832	44,658	45,484	46,310	47,136	47,962	48,788	49,614
Net S	35,346	36,091	36,836	37,581	38,325	39,070	39,815	40,560	41,305	42,050	42,795	43,540	44,285	45,030	45,775
Second Officer															
P-3 Gross	45,088	46,449	47,811	49,172	50,533	51,895	53,256	54,618	56,015	57,425	58,836	60,247	61,658	63,069	64,480
Net D	31,950	32,726	33,502	34,278	35,054	35,830	36,606	37,382	38,158	38,934	39,710	40,486	41,262	42,038	42,814
Net S	29,825	30,528	31,230	31,933	32,635	33,338	34,040	34,743	35,443	36,143	36,843	37,543	38,242	38,942	39,642
Associate Officer															
P-2 Gross	35,831	37,007	38,183	39,359	40,536	41,712	42,888	44,064	45,249	46,467	47,684	48,902			
Net D	26,490	27,184	27,878	28,572	29,266	29,960	30,654	31,348	32,042	32,736	33,430	34,124			
Net S	24,856	25,488	26,119	26,751	27,383	28,014	28,646	29,277	29,908	30,537	31,165	31,793			
Assistant Officer															
P-1 Gross	26,857	27,916	28,975	30,034	31,128	32,221	33,315	34,408	35,519	36,649					
Net D	20,970	21,637	22,304	22,971	23,638	24,305	24,972	25,639	26,306	26,973					
Net S	19,779	20,394	21,009	21,624	22,238	22,851	23,465	24,078	24,689	25,296					

D = Rate applicable to staff members with a dependent spouse or child.
S = Rate applicable to staff members with no dependent spouse or child.

ANNEX III

A. Construction of the salary scale

The salary scale in annex II to the present resolution has been derived from the current net base salary scale applicable to staff with a dependent spouse or child through a combination of the following:

(*a*) Consolidation of 12 multiplier points of post adjustment on a no gain/no loss basis on the basis of the existing methodology for such consolidation;

(*b*) Elimination of regressivity in accordance with section I.D, paragraph 3, of the present resolution;

(*c*) Introduction of structural changes in accordance with section I.F, paragraph 1, of the present resolution;

(*d*) Inclusion, on an overall average basis, of the remuneration adjustment recommended by the International Civil Service Commission in paragraph 125 of volume II of its report;

(*e*) Determination of gross salary through reverse application of the current staff assessment rates for staff with a dependent spouse or child;

(*f*) Determination of net salary for staff with neither a dependent spouse nor a dependent child through the application of the revised staff assessment rates contained in annex I to the present resolution.

B. Implementation measures

1. Upon implementation, on 1 July 1990, of the salary scale contained in annex II to the present resolution, a revised post adjustment multiplier and a revised post adjustment index will be established at each duty station.

2. At the base of the system, New York, the revised post adjustment multiplier applicable on 1 July 1990 will be determined, using if necessary partial classes of post adjustment, so as to arrive at total net emoluments, which, when compared with the corresponding net

emoluments that would have been applicable on 1 July 1990 on the basis of the current system, on an overall average basis, represent the percentage adjustment recommended by the Commission in paragraph 125 of volume II of its report.

3. At all other duty stations, the revised post adjustment multipliers applicable on 1 July 1990 will be determined, using if necessary partial classes of post adjustment, so as to arrive at total net emoluments, which, when compared to the net emoluments that would have been applicable on 1 July 1990 at that duty station on the basis of the current system, represent an adjustment equivalent in amount to that applicable at the base of the system.

4. After 1 July 1990, at each duty station, the first change in the post adjustment classification resulting from cost-of-living movement will take place when the post adjustment index applicable prior to the introduction of the new salary scale reaches the level that would have triggered the next full class of post adjustment under the operation of the post adjustment system. Thereafter, changes will be effected on the basis of the movement of the revised post adjustment index.

General Assembly resolution 44/198

21 December 1989   Meeting 84   Adopted without vote

Approved by Fifth Committee (A/44/898) without vote, 19 December (meeting 59); draft by Chairman following informal consultations (A/C.5/44/L.19); agenda item 131.
Meeting numbers. GA 44th session: 5th Committee 28, 31, 33, 35, 38, 44, 59; plenary 84.

By **resolution 44/201 A, section VII**, of 21 December, relating to the proposed budget for the biennium 1990-1991, the General Assembly decided on rates for the emoluments of members of the Committee on the Rights of the Child.

REFERENCES

(1)A/44/30, vols. I & II. (2)YUN 1988, p. 883. (3)*Ibid.*, GA res. 43/226, 21 Dec. 1988. (4)YUN 1987, p. 1144, GA res. 42/221, 21 Dec. 1987. (5)ACC/1989/DEC/1-20 (dec. 1989/8). (6)*Ibid.* (dec. 1989/12). (7)ACC/1989/DEC/21-23 (dec. 1989/21).

Other staff issues

Effects of restructuring

Report of the Secretary-General. The Secretary-General's final report[1] on the implementation of a 1986 Assembly resolution[2] endorsing recommendations made by the Group of 18 to further improve the efficiency of the administrative and financial functioning of the United Nations was transmitted to the Assembly in April (see PART SIX, Chapter I).

The Secretary-General noted that some recommendations, particularly in the area of human resources management, were of an ongoing nature. The report illustrated the progress accomplished in a number of areas, many of them affecting personnel. Staff reductions resulting from financial considerations and pressures often left posts vacant that were never intended for abolition but could be filled neither through redeployment of staff nor through recruitment. There was now, however, a clearer distribution of responsibilities in a number of organizational entities, such as the political, social and common service area. Some actions, such as the establishment of an integrated information system in the administrative area, would not yield results immediately, but would improve the functioning of the Organization in the long run.

The Secretary-General reported on specific measures to implement the Group of 18 recommendations regarding personnel management,[3] which had held that the organizational structure was too complex and top-heavy. He proposed abolition of two Under-Secretary-General posts and eight Assistant Secretary-General posts. The recommendation to fill entry-level posts at the P-1 and P-2 levels through competitive examinations, either internal or external, had been fully implemented; so far, 33 Member States had participated in national competitive examinations. P-3 examinations had to be postponed until the biennium 1990-1991 owing partly to a lack of resources. As recommended, the proportion of appointments at the P-1 to P-3 levels (55 per cent) was higher than at the other levels of the Professional category. Regarding the recommendation that no post should be considered the exclusive preserve of any Member State or group of States,

the report stated that that was being taken into account when posts became vacant.

On 21 December, by **resolution 44/200 A**, the General Assembly recognized that the implementation of the Group of 18's approved recommendations took place against a background of financial crisis, and noted that further efforts were needed to implement, in a balanced manner, the various recommendations, including those related to personnel issues. It stressed the need for greater transparency and coherence in personnel management, and recognized progress in post reduction while acknowledging that the Secretary-General was not then in a position to recommend further reductions. The Assembly encouraged the Secretary-General and Member States to intensify their efforts to implement the recommendations.

On the same date, by **resolution 44/201 B, section I**, the Assembly requested the Secretary-General to continue his efforts, as soon as possible in the course of the biennium 1990-1991, to identify four further high-level posts for reduction. In **section XIII** of the same resolution, concerning the Office of General Services at Headquarters, the General Assembly requested the Secretary-General to devise a more satisfactory system for the reimbursement to the regular budget of the cost of accommodation for posts related to extrabudgetary activities and to report thereon to the next Assembly.

Staff composition

In October, the Secretary-General presented to the General Assembly his annual report[4] on the composition of the UN Secretariat by nationality, sex and type of appointment, for the period 1 July 1988 to 30 June 1989. The total number of staff of the Secretariat as at 30 June 1989 was 13,561, of whom 9,155 were paid from the regular budget. Staff in the Professional category and above numbered 3,749; staff in the General Service and related categories, 8,816; and project personnel, 996.

During the reporting period, 134 appointments were made to Professional posts subject to geographical distribution.

On 30 June, there were 11 unrepresented Member States, as compared to 10 at the beginning of the reporting period. There were 26 underrepresented Member States, compared to 27 the previous year. Changes in the representation of Member States resulted not only from staff appointments and separations, but also from changes in the status of some staff members, reduced recruitment activities, and adjustments to the desirable ranges based on assessed contributions.

During the reporting period, 36 women were appointed to posts subject to geographical distribution, representing 26.8 per cent of the appointments made. This compared with 28.8 per cent during the previous reporting period.

GENERAL ASSEMBLY ACTION

On 19 December, on the recommendation of the Fifth Committee, the General Assembly adopted **resolution 44/185 A** without vote.

Composition of the Secretariat

The General Assembly,

Recalling Articles 100 and 101 of the Charter of the United Nations,

Reaffirming its resolutions 33/143 of 20 December 1978, 35/210 of 17 December 1980, 41/213 of 19 December 1986, 42/220 A of 21 December 1987 and 43/224 A of 21 December 1988,

Emphasizing the independent international status of the staff of the Secretariat,

Having considered the report of the Secretary-General on the composition of the Secretariat,

Noting the progress among nationals of some Member States who have served primarily on fixed-term contracts in accepting long-term and permanent contracts for service with the Secretariat,

Noting with satisfaction the positive results derived from holding national competitive examinations as a recruitment tool for nationals of unrepresented and underrepresented Member States,

Noting that there continues to be some unevenness between the number of appointments made to posts subject to geographical distribution of nationals of unrepresented and underrepresented Member States and those of Member States within range or overrepresented,

Noting also the efforts made and still required to fill posts in organizational units with high vacancy rates, particularly in the regional commissions,

Bearing in mind the views on personnel questions expressed by Member States in the Fifth Committee during the forty-fourth session,

1. *Reiterates* its full support for the Secretary-General as chief administrative officer of the Organization and his prerogatives and responsibilities under the Charter of the United Nations;

2. *Urges* the Secretary-General, whenever making appointments to posts subject to geographical distribution, to make every effort to recruit nationals of unrepresented and underrepresented Member States, including candidates successful in the national competitive examinations, taking also into consideration paragraph 4 of resolution 41/206 A of 11 December 1986, in order to ensure that all such countries come closer to the midpoint of their desirable ranges;

3. *Requests* the Secretary-General to take every available measure to ensure, at the senior and policy formulating levels of the Secretariat, the equitable representation of Member States, in particular of developing countries and other Member States with inadequate representation at those levels, in accordance with the relevant resolutions of the General Assembly, and to report thereon to the Assembly at its forty-fifth session, bearing in mind that no post should be considered the exclusive preserve of any Member State or group of States and with due regard to the principle of equitable geographical distribution;

4. *Also requests* the Secretary-General to continue his efforts aimed at improving the composition of the Secretariat by ensuring a wide and equitable geographical distribution of staff in the Professional and higher categories in all main departments and offices, bearing in mind that paramount consideration shall be the necessity of securing the highest standards of efficiency, competence and integrity;

5. *Further requests* the Secretary-General to monitor closely the effects of the reduction of posts on geographical distribution, particularly at the senior levels, and to take appropriate measures to redress any imbalances;

6. *Requests* the Secretary-General to endeavour to complete the work on the development of a methodology for holding national competitive examinations for posts at the P-3 level in all Member States and to submit a progress report thereon to the General Assembly at its forty-fifth session;

7. *Also requests* the Secretary-General to complete his efforts towards the development of a comprehensive career development plan for all staff that allows for fair and transparent post-bidding throughout the Secretariat by integrating the vacancy management programme, ensures adequate, equitable and transparent promotion procedures and recognizes merit through a rational performance evaluation and reporting system;

8. *Further requests* the Secretary-General to report to the General Assembly at its forty-fifth session on:

(*a*) The review of rules, regulations and criteria used for the promotion of staff;

(*b*) Efforts to ensure transparency in the work of the appointment and promotion bodies;

(*c*) The inclusion of effective and expeditious appeal and recourse mechanisms in the vacancy management programme;

9. *Requests* the Secretary-General to develop a personnel policy to increase the mobility of staff, keeping in view the functional requirements of the Organization, and to report to the General Assembly at its forty-fifth session on the measures proposed;

10. *Also requests* the Secretary-General to prepare proposals for groupings of Member States in presenting tables in his report to the General Assembly at its forty-fifth session on the composition of the Secretariat, taking into account the views expressed by Member States;

11. *Further requests* the Secretary-General to report to the General Assembly at its forty-fifth session on the implementation of the present resolution.

General Assembly resolution 44/185 A

19 December 1989   Meeting 83   Adopted without vote

Approved by Fifth Committee (A/44/880) without vote, 14 December (meeting 56); draft by Vice-Chairman following informal consultations (A/C.5/44/L.10), orally revised; agenda item 130 *(a)*.

Meeting numbers. GA 44th session: 5th Committee 28, 37, 39-42, 44, 55, 56; plenary 83.

Status of women in the Secretariat

In his final report[1] on the implementation of the approved 1986 recommendations of the Group of High-level Intergovernmental Experts (see above), the Secretary-General said that the proportion of women successful in national competitive examinations to fill entry-level posts at the

P-1 and P-2 levels had increased in recent years, reaching 44 per cent in 1987. The Secretary-General had so far approved 51 special measures to improve the status of women, based on the action programme and the recommendations of a high-level steering committee established by the Secretary-General in 1985.[5] As a consequence, the proportion of women in posts subject to geographical distribution had risen from 23.1 per cent as at 30 June 1985 to 26.5 per cent as at 31 January 1989. The number of women promoted to decision- and policy-making levels had increased substantially; the number of women at the D-2 level had increased from 3 to 7 in the past four years.

At the highest levels, it was recorded in the Secretary-General's report on the composition of the Secretariat[4] that women held two (8.3 per cent) of 24 Under-Secretary-General positions; none of 17 Assistant Secretary-General positions; 7 of 85 D-2 positions (8.2 per cent); and 15 of 235 D-1 positions (6.4 per cent).

In October, the Secretary-General issued the fifth report[6] in a series dealing with the status of women in the Secretariat. He stated that despite retrenchment and the 12 per cent reduction in the total number of posts, the number of women in the Secretariat had increased slightly. The most noteworthy increase was at the D-2 level. The 30 per cent target for promotions of women set by the vacancy management system had been exceeded. The Secretary-General noted that the system appeared to be an effective tool for the advancement of women into management positions. He also recalled that on 8 March, a senior woman had been selected at the D-1 level to act as the focal point for questions relating to women in the Secretariat.

ECONOMIC AND SOCIAL COUNCIL ACTION

On 24 May, the Economic and Social Council adopted **resolution 1989/29**.

Improvement of the status of women in the Secretariat

The Economic and Social Council,

Welcoming the decision of the Secretary-General to deploy on a full-time basis a senior-level officer, preferably a woman, within existing resources, in a position designated as the focal point within the Office of Human Resources Management of the Secretariat to monitor and facilitate the improvement of the status of women in the Secretariat,

Noting the absence of the progress report requested by the General Assembly in resolution 43/224 C of 21 December 1988,

Recalling General Assembly resolutions 43/101 of 8 December 1988 on the implementation of the Nairobi Forward-looking Strategies for the Advancement of Women, 43/103 of 8 December 1988 and 43/224 C of 21 December 1988 on the improvement of the status of women in the Secretariat, and 43/226 of 21 December

1988 on the United Nations common system, and all of their relevant provisions, as well as other related resolutions and decisions and their relevant provisions,

Recalling also the priorities identified by the Steering Committee for the Improvement of the Status of Women in the Secretariat in its fourth report,

1. *Requests* the Secretary-General to continue his efforts and to consider additional measures to increase the number of women in posts subject to geographical distribution, particularly in senior policy-making and decision-making posts, with a view to achieving an overall participation rate of 30 per cent of the total by 1990;

2. *Also requests* that such additional measures meet the goal of ensuring equitable representation of women from developing countries;

3. *Reiterates* the request to all Member States to continue to support the efforts of the United Nations and its specialized agencies to increase the proportion of women in the Professional category and above by, *inter alia*, nominating more women candidates and encouraging women to apply for vacant posts and to participate in national competitive examinations;

4. *Urges* the Secretary-General to take note of the view of the Commission on the Status of Women that budgetary constraints should not interfere with the important goal, in accordance with the action programme for the improvement of the status of women in the Secretariat, of rectifying the underrepresentation of women in the Secretariat and, in particular, of recruiting and promoting women to senior policy-making and decision-making positions;

5. *Requests* the Commission on the Status of Women to continue monitoring the improvement of the status of women in the Secretariat and within the United Nations system;

6. *Requests* the Secretary-General to report on the progress achieved in the continued implementation of the action programme for the improvement of the status of women in the Secretariat to the Economic and Social Council and to the General Assembly at its forty-fourth session, as well as to the Commission on the Status of Women at its thirty-fourth session.

Economic and Social Council resolution 1989/29

24 May 1989   Meeting 15   Adopted without vote

Approved by Second Committee (E/1989/90) without vote, 16 May (meeting 16); draft by Commission on women (E/1989/27); agenda item 10.

GENERAL ASSEMBLY ACTION

On 8 December, the General Assembly adopted **resolution 44/75** without vote.

Improvement of the status of women in the Secretariat

The General Assembly,

Recalling the relevant paragraphs of the Nairobi Forward-looking Strategies for the Advancement of Women, in which importance is attached to the appointment of women at senior decision-making and managerial levels,

Noting the deployment of a senior-level officer in a position designated as the focal point for women in the office of the Assistant Secretary-General for Human Resources Management, to be responsible for all aspects of the action programme for the improvement of the status of women in the Secretariat,

Recalling its resolutions 43/101 of 8 December 1988 on the implementation of the Nairobi Forward-looking Strategies, 43/103 of 8 December 1988 and 43/224 C of 21 December 1988 on the improvement of the status of women in the Secretariat, and 43/226 of 21 December 1988 on the United Nations common system, and taking note of Economic and Social Council resolution 1989/29 of 24 May 1989 on the improvement of the status of women in the Secretariat, as well as other related resolutions and decisions,

Recalling also the recommendations for action contained in the fourth report of the Steering Committee for the Improvement of the Status of Women in the Secretariat of 30 June 1988,

Taking note of the report of the Secretary-General of 16 October 1989 on the composition of the Secretariat, in which it is stated that of the twenty-four Under-Secretary-General positions, twenty-two are held by men and only two are held by women (8.3 per cent), that seventeen Assistant Secretary-General positions are held by men and none by women, that of the eighty-five D-2 positions, seventy-eight are held by men and seven by women (8.2 per cent), and that of the two hundred and thirty-five D-1 positions, two hundred and twenty are held by men and fifteen by women (6.4 per cent),

1.   *Requests* the Secretary-General, in full conformity with Articles 8, 97 and 101 of the Charter of the United Nations, to intensify his efforts to increase the number of women employed throughout the United Nations system, particularly in senior policy-level and decision-making posts, in order to achieve an overall rate of participation by women of 30 per cent by 1990, in accordance with paragraph 3 of its resolution 40/258 B of 18 December 1985;

2.   *Requests* that renewed efforts be made to ensure more equitable representation of women from developing countries in posts subject to geographical distribution, subject to Article 101 of the Charter;

3.   *Urges* the Secretary-General to take note of the view of the Commission on the Status of Women and the Economic and Social Council that, within budgetary constraints, the achievement of the goal of rectifying the underrepresentation of women in the Secretariat, in particular at the policy-making levels, as well as the career development of women already in the Secretariat, in accordance with the action programme for the improvement of the status of women in the Secretariat, should not be impeded;

4.   *Reiterates its request* to Member States to continue to support efforts of the United Nations and its specialized agencies to increase the proportions of women in the Professional categories and above by, *inter alia*, nominating more women candidates and encouraging women to apply for vacant posts;

5.   *Requests* the Secretary-General to submit to the General Assembly at its forty-fifth session through the appropriate bodies, including the Commission on the Status of Women at its thirty-fourth session, an outline of a programme for the improvement of the status of women in the Secretariat for the period 1991-1995, based on specific goals and appropriate monitoring to ensure a substantially higher rate of participation by women from all geographic regions, especially in senior-level posts, by 1995;

6.   *Also requests* the Secretary-General to ensure that his annual report on progress achieved and future strategies to implement action programmes on the status of women in the Secretariat and the relevant mandates adopted by the General Assembly and the Economic and Social Council is submitted to the Commission on the Status of Women and to the General Assembly for consideration by the Third Committee, under the item on the implementation of the Nairobi Forward-looking Strategies for the Advancement of Women.

General Assembly resolution 44/75

8 December 1989   Meeting 78   Adopted without vote

Approved by Third Committee (A/44/803) without vote, 20 November (meeting 49); 45-nation draft (A/C.3/44/L.27), orally revised; agenda item 104 *(c)*.

Sponsors: Australia, Austria, Bahamas, Bangladesh, Byelorussian SSR, Cameroon, Chile, Costa Rica, Côte d'Ivoire, Denmark, Dominican Republic, Ecuador, El Salvador, Finland, Gabon, Greece, Guatemala, Iceland, Indonesia, Ireland, Jamaica, Kenya, Malawi, Malaysia, Mexico, Myanmar, New Zealand, Nigeria, Norway, Pakistan, Peru, Philippines, Samoa, Senegal, Singapore, Suriname, Sweden, Thailand, Turkey, USSR, United States, Uruguay, Vanuatu, Venezuela, Yugoslavia.

Meeting numbers. GA 44th session: 3rd Committee 21-28, 36, 49; plenary 78.

On 19 December, the Assembly adopted **resolution 44/185 C** without vote.

Improvement of the status of women in the Secretariat

The General Assembly,

Recalling Articles 8, 100 and 101 of the Charter of the United Nations,

Recalling also all relevant resolutions on the improvement of the status of women in the Secretariat, and the relevant paragraphs of the Nairobi Forward-looking Strategies for the Advancement of Women, in particular paragraphs 315, 356 and 358,

Noting with satisfaction that the question of the improvement of the status of women in the secretariats of the United Nations system continues to be a standing item on the agenda of the Administrative Committee on Coordination,

Reaffirming the goal of increasing by 1990 the number of women in posts subject to geographical distribution to 30 per cent of the total,

Noting, however, the inadequate increase in the number of women in posts subject to geographical distribution and in the appointment of women to the senior and policy-formulating levels, particularly with regard to women from developing countries, keeping in view that recruitment overall has been affected by the implementation of recommendation 15 of the Group of High-level Intergovernmental Experts to Review the Efficiency of the Administrative and Financial Functioning of the United Nations during the period 1987-1989,

Taking note of the report of the Secretary-General on the improvement of the status of women in the Secretariat, and of section II.E of the report of the Secretary-General on the composition of the Secretariat,

1.   *Reiterates* its full support for the Secretary-General as the chief administrative officer of the Organization and his prerogatives and responsibilities under the Charter of the United Nations;

2.   *Urges* the Secretary-General to strengthen his efforts to increase the number of women in posts subject to geographical distribution, in particular at the senior and policy-formulating levels, with a view to achieving

to the extent possible an overall participation rate of 30 per cent of the total by 1990, taking into account the principle that the paramount consideration shall be the necessity of securing the highest standards of efficiency, competence and integrity and with full respect for the principle of equitable geographical distribution;

3. *Requests* the Secretary-General to increase the representation of women from developing countries, including at the senior and policy-formulating levels, in view of the small proportion of women from those countries;

4. *Reiterates its request* to all Member States to support the efforts of the Secretary-General referred to in paragraphs 2 and 3 of the present resolution by nominating more women candidates and encouraging more women to apply for posts subject to geographical distribution, in particular those at the senior and policy-formulating levels;

5. *Requests* the Secretary-General, in seeking to achieve more tangible progress for women in the Secretariat, not to lose sight of equality of opportunity for all staff in the Secretariat;

6. *Also requests* the Secretary-General to report in the future on all aspects of the status of women in the Secretariat in one single document, taking into account the importance of comprehensiveness, transparency and analysis in the presentation;

7. *Further requests* the Secretary-General to include in his report to the General Assembly at its forty-fifth session information on, *inter alia*:

(*a*) The implementation of the action programme for the improvement of the status of women in the Secretariat;

(*b*) The implementation of the recommendations made by the Steering Committee for the Improvement of the Status of Women in the Secretariat, as well as all relevant resolutions on that subject;

(*c*) The recruitment of women from developing countries to posts subject to geographical distribution;

(*d*) The appointment of women to posts at the senior and policy-formulating levels;

(*e*) The respective roles of the focal point in the office of the Assistant Secretary-General for Human Resources Management and of the Steering Committee;

(*f*) Recommendations for further action, including his approach to the setting of new targets for the period 1991-1995;

8. *Requests* the Secretary-General to make available the information referred to in paragraph 7 of the present resolution to all relevant bodies, as set out in General Assembly resolutions and paragraph 358 of the Nairobi Forward-looking Strategies for the Advancement of Women.

General Assembly resolution 44/185 C

19 December 1989   Meeting 83   Adopted without vote

Approved by Fifth Committee (A/44/880) without vote, 14 December (meeting 56); draft by Vice-Chairman following informal consultations (A/C.5/44/L.10), orally revised; agenda item 130 *(c)*.
Meeting numbers. GA 44th session: 5th Committee 28, 37, 39-42, 44, 55, 56; plenary 83.

Staff rules

In September 1989, the Secretary-General submitted to the General Assembly his annual report[7] containing the texts of provisional amend-

ments made to the staff rules since his previous report in 1988.[8] The changes concerned hours of work, official holidays, inter-agency loans of staff, non-acceptance of external honoraria or remuneration, salaries and related allowances, staff assessments, education grants, mission salary and allowances, assignment allowances, annual leave, special leave, home leave, sick leave, maternity leave, travel and removal expenses, expenses connected with assignment and separation, and disciplinary measures and procedures. Many changes were a consequence of the recommendations of the Group of 18 approved in 1986.[2]

On 19 December, the General Assembly, by **decision 44/439**, took note of the Secretary-General's report.

Staff representation

By a 3 November note,[9] the Secretary-General transmitted to the Fifth Committee a document submitted by the staff unions and associations of the UN Secretariat, pursuant to a 1980 General Assembly resolution.[10] In the document, the staff representative stated that the financial crisis, the Group of 18 report and the retrenchment process had presented a serious challenge to UN staff. The document said that there had been an unstated but clear implication that the staff was somehow to blame for UN problems. The staff had been sensitive to the unstated message that if there were fewer staff members, or if they did their work better or more cheaply, somehow the problems would disappear. The entire process had neither improved morale nor increased efficiency. Ironically, the dénouement of retrenchment came at a time when demands on the United Nations and its staff were at their peak. Yet no significant effort had been made to address the staffing needs or the efficiency of the Organization.

The report covered staff views on retrenchment and "reform"; vacancy management and mobility; career development; the need for a unified personnel structure; disappointing progress in advancing the status of women; staff management allocations; security and independence of the international civil service; and administration of justice.

Privileges and immunities

In response to a 1988 General Assembly resolution,[11] the Secretary-General submitted to the Fifth Committee, on behalf of and with the approval of the Administrative Committee on Co-ordination (ACC), a 2 November report[12] on respect for the privileges and immunities of officials of the UN system during the period 1 July 1988 to 30 June 1989.

The period had been marked by one particularly disturbing development: the report of the brutal murder of Lieutenant Colonel William Richard Higgins, a United States officer serving as chief of a group of military observers assigned to the United Nations Interim Force in Lebanon (UNIFIL). He was abducted on 17 February 1988, and on 13 July 1989 an announcement at Beirut by his captors stated that he had been killed. The Secretary-General said that while he would continue to try to establish that fact, he had regretfully concluded that it was almost certain that Colonel Higgins was dead. If his fears were confirmed he would try to recover the body (for Security Council action, see PART TWO, Chapter IV).

The Middle East, with the most cases of arrest, detention and abduction of officials, continued to be an area of prime concern, the Secretary-General said. Efforts to improve the situation had not produced encouraging results. The number of cases of arrest and detention without charge or trial of staff members of the United Nations Relief and Works Agency for Palestine Refugees in the Near East (UNRWA) remained very high. Elsewhere, also, to the Secretary-General's great regret and disappointment, the number of cases of arrest, detention or disappearance of officials for which the Organization had not been able fully to exercise their rights had increased substantially in the reporting period.

The Secretary-General reported that 157 UNRWA staff had been arrested or detained, an increase over the 151 cases reported in the period 1 July 1987 to 30 June 1988. There had been a decrease in the number of staff detained by one or another of the militia groups in Lebanon, from 24 in the last reporting period to 11 in the current one. In no case had UNRWA received adequate and timely information on the reason for arrest and detention, despite requests to the authorities. Several staff were being held in prisons in Israel, having been transferred there from the occupied West Bank and Gaza Strip.

While he was able to report the release of some staff in Chad, Egypt, Ethiopia, the Gaza Strip and the West Bank, Jordan, Lebanon and the Syrian Arab Republic, the Secretary-General regretted to report the death in prison of an UNRWA staff member detained in Lebanon by Syrian armed forces. There had been no resolution regarding the arrest and expulsion of staff members in Mauritania.

The Secretary-General also reported on restrictions on official and private travel of United Nations and other officials, including the difficulties of UNRWA as to staff movement into and out of the West Bank and Gaza Strip and restrictions, due to United States regulations, on travel beyond a 25-mile radius of Columbus Circle in New York City by staff members and their dependants who were citizens of particular countries, and unauthorized taxation of officials by some States, including Burundi, Egypt and Switzerland.

As to the case of Dumitru Mazilu, a former member of the Sub-Commission on Prevention of Discrimination and Protection of Minorities, charged by the Sub-Commission in 1985 with preparing a report on human rights and youth, the Secretary-General reported that Romanian authorities had not permitted Mr. Mazilu to travel to Geneva to present his report. (See PART THREE, Chapter X.)

An appendix to the document[9] submitted by the staff unions and associations of the United Nations Secretariat listed staff members whose basic rights were stated to have been violated in Afghanistan, Argentina, Chad, Chile, Egypt, Ethiopia, Guatemala, Jordan, Kenya, Lebanon (by either Syrian armed forces or members of unknown elements), Mauritania, Nepal, Pakistan, Rwanda, Somalia, the Syrian Arab Republic, Zambia, and by Israeli authorities in the Gaza Strip and West Bank.

GENERAL ASSEMBLY ACTION

On 19 December, by **decision 44/440**, the General Assembly, on the recommendation of the Fifth Committee, requested the Secretary-General to intensify efforts to make his report on respect for the privileges and immunities of United Nations and other officials available to Member States well in advance of the subject's consideration.

Also on 19 December, on the recommendation of the Fifth Committee, the General Assembly adopted **resolution 44/186**.

Respect for the privileges and immunities of officials of the United Nations and the specialized agencies and related organizations

The General Assembly,

Recalling, under Article 100 of the Charter of the United Nations, that each Member of the United Nations undertakes to respect the exclusively international character of the responsibilities of the Secretary-General and the staff and not to seek to influence them in the discharge of their responsibilities and that the Secretary-General and the staff shall refrain from any action which might reflect on their position as international officials responsible only to the Organization,

Recalling that, under Article 105 of the Charter, all officials of the Organization shall enjoy in the territory of each of its Member States such privileges and immunities as are necessary for the independent exercise of their functions in connection with the Organization,

Recalling the Convention on the Privileges and Immunities of the United Nations, the Convention on the Privileges and Immunities of the Specialized Agencies, the Agreement on the Privileges and Immunities of the International Atomic Energy Agency and the United Nations Development Programme Standard Basic Assistance Agreements,

Recalling also its resolution 76(I) of 7 December 1946, in which it approved the granting of the privileges and immunities referred to in articles V and VII of the Convention on the Privileges and Immunities of the United Nations to all members of the staff of the United Nations,

Recalling further its resolution 43/173 of 9 December 1988, the annex to which contains the Body of Principles for the Protection of All Persons under Any Form of Detention or Imprisonment, including the principle that all persons under arrest or detention shall be provided whenever necessary with medical care and treatment,

Reiterating the obligation of all officials of the Organization in the conduct of their duties to observe fully both the laws and regulations of Member States and their duties and responsibilities to the Organization,

Mindful of the responsibilities of the Secretary-General to safeguard the functional immunity of all United Nations officials,

Mindful also of the importance in this respect of the provision by Member States of adequate and timely information concerning the arrest and detention of staff members and, more particularly, their granting of access to them,

Bearing in mind the considerations of the Secretary-General to guarantee minimum standards of justice and due process to United Nations officials,

Reaffirming its previous resolutions, in particular resolutions 42/219 of 21 December 1987 and 43/225 of 21 December 1988,

1. *Takes note with grave concern* of the report submitted by the Secretary-General, on behalf of the Administrative Committee on Co-ordination, and of the developments indicated therein, in particular the reported case of abduction and killing, as well as the, once again, very high number of new cases of arrest and detention and the very negative developments in respect of various previously reported cases under this category;

2. *Deplores* the increase in the number of cases in which the safety, functioning and well-being of officials have been placed in jeopardy;

3. *Also deplores* the substantially increased number of cases of arrest or detention of officials for which the organizations of the United Nations system have not been able fully to exercise their rights during the reporting period;

4. *Calls upon* all Member States scrupulously to respect the privileges and immunities of all officials of the United Nations and the specialized agencies and related organizations and to refrain from any acts that would impede such officials in the performance of their functions, thereby seriously affecting the proper functioning of the organizations;

5. *Urges* those Member States holding under arrest or detention officials of the United Nations and the specialized agencies and related organizations to enable the Secretary-General or the executive head of the organization concerned fully to exercise the right of functional protection inherent in the relevant multilateral conventions and bilateral agreements, particularly with respect to immediate access to detained staff members;

6. *Calls upon* all Member States otherwise impeding officials of the United Nations and the specialized agencies and related organizations in the proper discharge of their duties to review the cases mentioned in the report of the Secretary-General and to co-ordinate efforts with the Secretary-General or the executive head of the organization concerned to resolve every case with all due speed;

7. *Calls upon* the Secretary-General to take the necessary measures in order to promote knowledge of and compliance with the Body of Principles for the Protection of All Persons under Any Form of Detention or Imprisonment, including the principle that all persons under arrest or detention shall be provided whenever necessary with medical care and treatment;

8. *Calls upon* the staff of the United Nations and the specialized agencies and related organizations fully to comply with the provisions of Article 100 of the Charter of the United Nations and with the obligations resulting from the Staff Regulations and Rules of the United Nations, in particular regulation 1.8, and from the equivalent provisions governing the staff of the other agencies;

9. *Welcomes* the efforts undertaken by the Secretary-General that have led to the release of many staff members who were previously reported as being under arrest or detention;

10. *Also welcomes* the Secretary-General's determination to continue to work together with the respective executive heads and with the authorities of Governments concerned to ensure strict implementation of the international agreements concerning privileges and immunities of international organizations and their officials;

11. *Calls upon* the Secretary-General to intensify his efforts to bring about an expeditious solution of the cases still pending, which were referred to in his report;

12. *Notes with concern* the restrictions on duty travel of officials as indicated in the report of the Secretary-General;

13. *Takes note with concern* of the information in the report of the Secretary-General related to taxation on salaries and emoluments as well as the status, privileges and immunities of officials;

14. *Calls upon* the Secretary-General, as chief administrative officer of the United Nations, to continue personally to act as the focal point in promoting and ensuring the observance of the privileges and immunities of officials of the United Nations and the specialized agencies and related organizations by using all such means as are available to him;

15. *Urges* the Secretary-General promptly to follow up all cases of arrest, detention and any matters relating to the security and proper functioning of officials of the United Nations and the specialized agencies and related organizations;

16. *Requests* the Secretary-General, as Chairman of the Administrative Committee on Co-ordination, to review and appraise the measures already taken to enhance the proper functioning, safety and protection of international civil servants.

General Assembly resolution 44/186

19 December 1989   Meeting 83   Adopted without vote

Approved by Fifth Committee (A/44/880) without vote, 14 December (meeting 56); draft by Chairman following informal consultations (A/C.5/44/L.7); agenda item 130 *(b)*.

Meeting numbers. GA 44th session: 5th Committee 28, 37, 39-42, 44, 55, 56; plenary 83.

Pensions

According to the report[13] of the United Nations Joint Staff Pension Board to the General Assembly, during 1989 the number of participants in the United Nations Joint Staff Pension Fund had increased from 54,006 to 56,222. As at 31 December, there were 29,566 periodic benefits in award: 9,888 retirement benefits, 5,024 early retirement benefits, 5,232 deferred retirement benefits, 3,775 widows' and widowers' benefits, 5,019 children's benefits, 581 disability benefits and 47 secondary dependants' benefits. In the course of the year, 3,020 lump-sum withdrawals and other settlements were paid. The principal of the Fund increased from $6,810,774,123 to $7,579,591,411. Investment income totalled $735,093,188, comprising $457,822,273 in interest and dividends and $277,270,915 in net profit on sales of investments. After deductions of investment management costs of $8,787,091, net investment income was $726,306,097.

Over the previous 39 years, the total book value of the portfolio had risen from $13 million to $6,813 million, a compound increase of 17.4 per cent a year. During the 1988 calendar year, investment income from interest and dividends amounted to $395.6 million, an increase of 11.6 per cent over 1987. Total new funds that became available for investment amounted to $396 million (contributions plus investment income, minus benefit payments and investment expenses). Realized capital gains amounted to $302 million.

As at 1 January 1989, the Joint Staff Pension Board consisted of 33 members, an increase from 21, mandated by a 1987 General Assembly resolution.[14] The Board held its thirty-eighth session (12-21 July, New York),[15] and dealt with actuarial valuation of the Fund as at 31 December 1988; a study of measures to restore over the long term the actuarial balance of the Fund; arrangements for a comprehensive review of the methodology for determination of the scale of pensionable remuneration of staff in the Professional and higher categories; evolution of the pensionable remuneration of such staff since the last comprehensive review in 1986; and preliminary examination of the methodology for determining pension remuneration and consequent staff pensions in the General Service and other locally recruited categories.

ACABQ submitted its comments[16] on the 1989 report of the Board and the report of the Secretary-General on Fund investments (see below). It recommended approval of $30,573,400 for expenses chargeable to the Fund for the biennium 1990-1991. It also recommended approval of new posts and resources for data processing, and said that the staffing situation of the Fund should be carefully monitored.

Pension Fund investments

The annual report[17] of the Secretary-General for the year ended 31 March 1989 on the investments of the United Nations Joint Staff Pension Fund was submitted to the Assembly in October.

The market value of the Fund's assets had increased to $7,632 million from $7,229 million a year earlier, an increase of 5.57 per cent and $819 million above book value. Total investment return for the year ending 31 March 1989 was 5.9 per cent which, after adjusting for inflation, represented a "real" rate of return of 0.9 per cent. The Fund remained one of the most diversified pension funds in the world. Investments were held in 29 currencies and 44 countries; 50 per cent of the assets were invested in currencies other than the United States dollar, the Fund's unit of account. The appreciation in the relative value of the United States dollar during the year under review had influenced market values of investments outside the United States when expressed in dollars, and had consequently also had an impact on positive rates of return in local currencies when expressed in dollar terms. Equities constituted 42 per cent of the assets as at 31 March, down from 43 per cent in the previous year. Bonds accounted for 34 per cent, the same as in the previous year, while real estate-related securities amounted to 12 per cent, compared to 11 per cent in 1988.

Considering the volatility of the major financial markets and fluctuations of exchange rates, the Secretary-General regarded the 5.9 per cent investment return for the financial year as satisfactory. He considered the policy of diversification and careful selection of investments, including active investigation of opportunities in developing countries, to be the best way to achieve the goal of preserving the principal and enhancing the Fund's investment return over the medium and long term.

Actuarial balance

The Board stated[15] its strong belief that measures were required to restore the Fund's actuarial balance. It therefore recommended the increase of the normal retirement age under the Fund's Regulations from age 60 to 62 for new participants; elimination of cost-of-living adjustments for future deferred retirement benefits until the separated participants reached ages 55, rather than 50; increasing the reduction factor to 6 per cent a year for early retirement at age 55 and 56 for new participants; and the increase of the contribution rate from 22.5 per cent to 23.7 per cent of pensionable remuneration. The package would constitute actuarial savings (percentage of pensionable remuneration) of 3.54 per cent. Implementation should be as soon as possible, the

Board said, preferably at 1 January 1990 but not later than 1 January 1991.

Administrative expenses

By **resolution 44/199** (see below), the General Assembly approved expenses chargeable to the Fund totalling $30,573,400 (net) for the biennium 1990-1991 for administration of the Fund. This comprised $10,259,400 for administrative costs and $20,314,000 for investment costs.

GENERAL ASSEMBLY ACTION

On 21 December, on the recommendation of the Fifth Committee, the General Assembly adopted **resolution 44/199** without vote.

United Nations pension system

The General Assembly,

Recalling its resolution 43/227 of 21 December 1988,

Having considered the report of the United Nations Joint Staff Pension Board for 1989 to the General Assembly and to the member organizations of the United Nations Joint Staff Pension Fund, chapter III of volume I of the report of the International Civil Service Commission, the report of the Secretary-General on the investments of the Fund and the related report of the Advisory Committee on Administrative and Budgetary Questions,

I

Measures to restore the actuarial balance of the United Nations Joint Staff Pension Fund

Recalling section I, paragraph 2, of its resolution 42/222 of 21 December 1987 and section I, paragraph 2, of its resolution 43/227, in which the United Nations Joint Staff Pension Board was requested to complete the study of all possible measures to restore the actuarial balance of the United Nations Joint Staff Pension Fund over the long term for presentation to the General Assembly at its forty-fourth session, together with the results of the twentieth actuarial valuation of the Fund as at 31 December 1988,

Recalling also its resolutions 37/131 of 17 December 1982, 38/233 of 20 December 1983 and 39/246 of 18 December 1984, in which it indicated that a co-operative effort by member organizations, participants and beneficiaries is required if the actuarial imbalance is to be reduced or eliminated, thereby securing an adequate level of benefits under the Fund,

Noting the continuing actuarial imbalance of the Fund as revealed by the valuation as at 31 December 1988,

Taking note of the proposals made by the Board to restore the actuarial balance of the Fund over the long term,

Approves, without retroactive effect, the following measures, including the necessary amendments to articles 1, 25 and 29 of the Regulations of the United Nations Joint Staff Pension Fund, and changes in the pension adjustment system, as set out in annexes I and II to the present resolution:

(*a*) For participants who enter or re-enter the Fund on or after 1 January 1990, the normal retirement age shall be 62;

(*b*) For participants who enter or re-enter the Fund on or after 1 January 1990, and who take early retire-

ment before reaching age 57, the reduction factors applicable for ages 55 and 56 shall be 6 per cent for each year;

(*c*) For participants who separate from service on or after 31 December 1989 and who elect a deferred retirement benefit, adjustments of the benefit, in accordance with the pension adjustment system, shall commence only when the separated participant reaches age 55;

(*d*) The rate of contribution shall be increased, with effect from 1 January 1990, from 22.5 to 23.7 per cent of pensionable remuneration, of which the employing member organization shall pay 15.8 per cent and the participant 7.9 per cent;

II

Pensionable remuneration of staff in the Professional and higher categories

Recalling its request in section I, paragraph 6, of its resolution 41/208 of 11 December 1986 that the International Civil Service Commission undertake, in full co-operation with the United Nations Joint Staff Pension Board, a further comprehensive review of the methodology for the determination of the scale of pensionable remuneration of staff in the Professional and higher categories, for monitoring the level of the scale and for its adjustment in between comprehensive reviews, and submit its recommendations thereon to the General Assembly at its forty-fifth session,

Recalling also that in section I, paragraph 2, of its resolution 41/208 the General Assembly approved the procedure for adjusting the scale of pensionable remuneration in between comprehensive reviews,

1. *Takes note* of the arrangements agreed upon by the International Civil Service Commission, as set out in paragraphs 50 and 51 of volume I of its report, and by the United Nations Joint Staff Pension Board, as set out in paragraphs 82 and 83 of its report, to ensure full co-operation in the conduct of the comprehensive review;

2. *Requests* the Commission, in undertaking, in full co-operation with the Board, the comprehensive review of the pensionable remuneration of staff in the Professional and higher categories, to take into account:

(*a*) The relevant recommendations on the remuneration structure;

(*b*) The considerations set out in paragraphs 34 to 41 of volume I of the report of the Commission and paragraphs 84 to 95 of the report of the Board in studying the desirability of establishing a margin range between the pensionable remuneration of staff in the United Nations common system and staff in comparable grades in the comparator civil service;

and to submit its report thereon to the General Assembly at its forty-fifth session;

3. *Approves*, pending the completion of the comprehensive review, the modification of the procedure for adjusting pensionable remuneration as recommended by the Commission in paragraph 42 of volume I of its report;

4. *Amends* accordingly, with effect from 1 January 1990, article 54 of the Regulations of the United Nations Joint Staff Pension Fund as set out in annex I to the present resolution;

III
Other amendments to the Regulations of the United Nations Joint Staff Pension Fund

Approves, with effect from 1 January 1990, an amendment to article 36 of the Regulations of the United Nations Joint Staff Pension Fund, as set out in annex I to the present resolution, to provide for commencement of the payment of a disabled child's benefit at the same time as an early retirement benefit;

IV
Proposal of the International Telecommunication Union to establish a Pension Purchasing Power Protection Fund

Taking note of the information provided in paragraphs 106 to 116 of the report of the United Nations Joint Staff Pension Board on the proposal of the International Telecommunication Union to establish a Pension Purchasing Power Protection Fund for its staff in the Professional and higher categories,

Reaffirming the strong concern expressed by the General Assembly in section IV of its resolution 38/233 about the need to maintain the unity, cohesion and integrity of the United Nations joint staff pension system and to avoid any action which may have an adverse effect on that system,

Endorses the conclusions of the United Nations Joint Staff Pension Board as set out in paragraphs 115 and 116 of its report, that the proposal of the International Telecommunication Union should be studied, within the context of the comprehensive review of pensionable remuneration, as one possible long-term approach to the adjustment of pensions in local currency terms and that the International Telecommunication Union should not proceed with the implementation of its proposal as that would weaken the United Nations common system;

V
Application for membership of the World Tourism Organization

Notes the suspension of the application of the World Tourism Organization for membership in the United Nations Joint Staff Pension Fund;

VI
Emergency Fund

Authorizes the United Nations Joint Staff Pension Fund to supplement the voluntary contributions to the Emergency Fund, for the biennium 1990-1991, by an amount not exceeding 200,000 United States dollars;

VII
Administrative expenses

Approves expenses, chargeable directly to the United Nations Joint Staff Pension Fund, totalling 30,573,400 United States dollars (net) for the biennium 1990-1991, and a reduction in expenses of 295,000 dollars (net) for the biennium 1988-1989, for the administration of the Fund;

VIII
Other questions

Takes note of the other questions considered in the report of the United Nations Joint Staff Pension Board;

IX
Investments of the United Nations Joint Staff Pension Fund

Takes note with appreciation of the report of the Secretary-General on the investments of the United Nations Joint Staff Pension Fund.

ANNEX I
Amendments to the Regulations of the United Nations Joint Staff Pension Fund

Article 1
Definitions

1. Add a new paragraph *(n)* to read as follows:

"(n) 'Normal retirement age' shall mean age 60, except that it shall mean age 62 for a participant whose participation commences or recommences on or after 1 January 1990.''

2. Reletter existing paragraphs *(n)* to *(v)* as *(o)* to *(w)*.

Article 25
Contributions

Replace paragraph *(a)* by the following text:

"(a) Contributions by the participant and by the employing member organization shall be payable to the Fund concurrently with the accrual of contributory service under article 22 *(a)* at the percentage rates of pensionable remuneration specified below:

A	B	C
		Employing member
For periods of	*Participants*	*organizations*
contributory service	*(percentage)*	*(percentage)*
Before 1984	7.00	14.00
As from 1 January 1984 to 30 June 1988	7.25	14.50
As from 1 July 1988 to 30 June 1989	7.40	14.80
As from 1 July 1989 to 31 December 1989	7.50	15.00
As from 1 January 1990	7.90	15.80.''

Article 29
Early retirement benefit

Replace paragraphs *(a)* and *(b)* by the following text:

"(a) An early retirement benefit shall be payable to a participant whose age on separation is at least 55 but less than the normal retirement age and whose contributory service was five years or longer.

"(b) The benefit shall be payable at the standard annual rate for a retirement benefit, reduced for each year or part thereof by which the age of the participant on separation was less than the normal retirement age, at the rate of 6 per cent a year, except that:

"(i) If the contributory service of the participant was 25 years or longer but less than 30 years, 2 per cent a year in respect of the period of contributory service performed before 1 January 1985, and 3 per cent a year in respect of the period of such service performed as from 1 January 1985; or

"(ii) If the contributory service of the participant was 30 years or longer, 1 per cent a year, provided, however, that the rate in (i) or (ii) above shall apply to no more than five years.''

Article 36
Child's benefit

Replace paragraph *(c)* by the following text:

"*(c)* A child's benefit shall, notwithstanding *(a)* above, not become payable if the participant has chosen an early retirement benefit until he dies or reaches the normal retirement age, except to a child under the age of twenty-one, found by the Board to be disabled."

Article 54
Pensionable remuneration

Replace paragraph *(b)* by the following text:

"*(b)* In the case of participants in the Professional and higher categories, the scale of pensionable remuneration effective 1 May 1989, set out in the appendix hereto, shall be adjusted on the same date as the net remuneration amounts of officials in the Professional and higher categories in New York are adjusted. Such adjustment shall be by a uniform percentage equal to the weighted average percentage variation in the net remuneration amounts, as determined by the International Civil Service Commission, except that:

"(i)   The amount of the first adjustment due after 1 January 1990 shall be reduced by 2.8 percentage points;

"(ii)   The scale of pensionable remuneration determined by the International Civil Service Commission as corresponding to the revised salary structure entering into effect on 1 July 1990 shall become effective on the same date."

APPENDIX

Scale of pensionable remuneration for Professional and higher categories
(In United States dollars)
(Effective 1 May 1989)

Level	Steps												
	I	*II*	*III*	*IV*	*V*	*VI*	*VII*	*VIII*	*IX*	*X*	*XI*	*XII*	*XIII*
Under-Secretary-General													
USG	122,580												
Assistant Secretary-General													
ASG	113,342												
Director													
D-2	94,506	96,927	99,242	101,662									
Principal Officer													
D-1	82,499	84,581	86,653	88,735	90,817	92,889	94,855						
Senior Officer													
P-5	74,286	76,030	77,637	79,264	80,987	82,499	84,222	85,839	87,583	89,190			
First Officer													
P-4	60,196	61,930	63,663	65,270	67,130	68,747	70,364	71,865	73,588	75,449	77,182	78,905	
Second Officer													
P-3	49,214	50,947	52,575	54,076	55,683	57,300	59,033	60,661	61,930	63,547	65,048	66,432	67,933
Associate Officer													
P-2	39,859	41,244	42,523	43,897	45,292	46,561	47,946	49,214	50,715	52,110	53,495		
Assistant Officer													
P-1	31,308	32,471	33,507	34,553	35,705	36,741	38,010	39,289	40,557	41,709			

ANNEX II
Changes in the pension adjustment system

J.   Deferred retirement benefit

Replace paragraph 27 by the following text:

"27.   *(a)*   For participants whose date of separation was before 31 December 1989, no adjustment will be applied to deferred retirement benefits prior to the beneficiary's reaching age 50. Commencing at age 50 or the date of separation, if later, the dollar base pension under paragraph 5 *(a)* above is adjusted by the United States CPI in accordance with section H above without retroactive effect. The two-track system will become operative on the date of commencement of the payment of the periodic benefit. At that time a local currency base amount will be established by applying to the adjusted dollar amount the average exchange rate over 36 consecutive months up to and including the month of first payment.

"*(b)*   For participants separating on or after 31 December 1989, no adjustment shall be applied to deferred retirement benefits prior to the beneficiary's reaching age 55. Commencing at age 55 or the date of separation, if later, the adjustment procedures set out in *(a)* above will be applied to the deferred retirement benefits of such beneficiaries."

General Assembly resolution 44/199

21 December 1989   Meeting 84   Adopted without vote

Approved by Fifth Committee (A/44/897) without vote, 19 December (meeting 59); draft by Chairman following informal consultations (A/C.5/44/L.20); agenda item 132.
Meeting numbers. GA 44th session: 5th Committee 28, 31, 33, 35, 38, 44, 59; plenary 84.

By **resolution 44/201 B, section XIV**, of 21 December, the Assembly requested the Secretary-General to submit to the 1990 Assembly, through ACABQ, a comprehensive review of the after-service health insurance programme.

Travel-related matters

In 1989, the Secretary-General continued to keep under review the travel and related entitlements of representatives of Member States attending United Nations meetings, as requested by the General Assembly in 1987.[18] He submitted a report[19] in October on standards of accommodation for air travel, listing the cost of first-class travel for heads of delegations of least developed countries to regular and special sessions of the Assembly from 1 July 1988 to 30 June 1989 ($246,707); exceptions to the non-first-class travel practice for medical conditions and advanced age ($13,184); for immediate aides or security officers accompanying the Secretary-General ($15,836); cases when no lower-class seat was available ($7,495); eminent persons and entertainers donating services free of charge ($12,306); consecutive overnight flights on long trips without a rest day ($9,055); and other exceptions.

ACABQ noted[20] that during the period 1 July 1988 to 30 June 1989, 58 exceptions were granted to the rules on standards of accommodation for air travel as set forth by the Assembly in 1987,[18] at an additional cost of $61,197. This compared with 42 exceptions in the period from 1 January 1988 to 30 June 1989. The Advisory Committee recommended that, in the future, the Secretary-General should submit his annual report on the question directly to the Committee, with the Committee then reporting to the Assembly as necessary.

On 21 December, the General Assembly, on the recommendation of the Fifth Committee, took note of the Secretary-General's report by **decision 44/442**.

Administration of justice

In October, the Secretary-General reported[21] to the General Assembly on implementation of a 1988 resolution[22] requesting him to establish by 1989 a fully revised internal justice system, pursuant to the recommendations of the Group of 18, approved in 1986,[2] and to finish putting into place improved disciplinary rules and procedures at the earliest stage, as well as revised appellate procedures. In 1988, ACABQ had also recommended that the Secretary-General submit a proposal for possible revision of the Staff Regulations and/or Rules in the disciplinary area, addressed in the Secretary-General's proposed revisions[7] in 1989 (see above).

The Secretary-General noted that the steady increase in the number of pending cases before the Headquarters Joint Advisory Board (JAB) had been a matter of serious concern, placing a critical strain on the management of the administrative justice system. In 1989, Headquarters JAB had succeeded in reducing the number of pending appeals to 30, and had virtually eliminated its backlog of cases pending for more than one year. Average age of pending cases was now four-and-a-half months, as compared to two or more years previously. No further action was envisaged beyond ensuring the smooth operation of the streamlined system and optimum utilization of resources. The Secretary-General's policy of accepting unani-

mous JAB reports, except where a major question of law or principle was involved, continued to be applied. During 1989, the Secretary-General took decisions on some 50 reports from various JABs, accepting the recommendations in full regarding 32 cases and in part in 4 cases, and rejecting them in 5. He took note of 9 reports where the Board decided it was not competent to address the matter.

While staff representatives had stated they would wish further consultations regarding revised disciplinary rules to replace Chapter X of the Staff Rules, intended to be promulgated on 1 January 1990, the Secretary-General was of the view that adequate consultations had already taken place since 1987, and to delay implementation of reform any further would constitute failure to comply with the General Assembly's specific directions.

The principal changes in the disciplinary process resulting from the Staff Rules revisions were: a description of unsatisfactory conduct; staff charged with misconduct would be entitled to have their cases considered by a Joint Disciplinary Committee; flexibility would allow cases to be referred to a JDC at a different duty station; provision for creating *ad hoc* JDCs to hear cases at duty stations not having a standing JDC; regulation of the use of appeals provisions against summary dismissals; greater flexibility in the range of disciplinary measures and specification of actions available to the Secretary-General including recovery of monies; clarification of suspension circumstances; elimination of the separation of staff-elected members of JDC into salary groups; enlargement of access to counsel to include returned staff members; and introduction of the concept of the Presiding Officer with an outline of his powers. Work had begun on devising rules of procedure of JDCs.

In 1989, the number of members of the Panel of Counsel was 86. During the first eight months of the year, the Co-ordinator of the Panel of Counsel received 112 cases. As to grievance panels, the Secretary-General had established panels to investigate allegations of discriminatory treatment at Headquarters, at Geneva and in various agencies. These informal procedures were designed to supplement, rather than replace, the formal ones of JAB, the Administrative Tribunal and specialized appeal bodies. Since their establishment, grievance panels had handled about 100 cases a year, the Secretary-General said.

The first phase of reform reported to the 1988 General Assembly[23] had focused on the appellate area. The current phase dealt mainly with the disciplinary area, and the third phase would focus on improvement of informal procedures for amicable resolution of staff grievances. The Secretary-General said promulgation of revised rules and procedures in a specific area of administration of justice did not mark the end of the process in that area; assessment of their effectiveness would take place in consultations with members of the joint advisory bodies, the Panel of Counsel and the staff representatives. Accordingly, the subject of administration of justice had been inscribed on the agenda of the forthcoming Staff Management Coordination Committee meeting as a standing agenda item.

On 19 December, on the recommendation of the Fifth Committee, the General Assembly adopted **resolution 44/185 B** without vote.

Administration of justice in the Secretariat

The General Assembly,

Noting the importance of a just and efficient internal justice system in the Secretariat,

Having considered the report of the Secretary-General on the administration of justice in the Secretariat,

Welcoming the further improvements in the internal justice system and the progress achieved during the current year, including the reduction of the backlog of pending cases, largely due to the introduction of procedural improvements, and the completion of work on the revision of disciplinary rules to be promulgated effective January 1990,

1. *Endorses* the report of the Secretary-General on the administration of justice in the Secretariat;

2. *Requests* the Secretary-General to proceed without delay with the promulgation of the revised set of disciplinary rules effective 1 January 1990 and to report to the General Assembly at its forty-fifth session on the operation of the new system;

3. *Also requests* the Secretary-General to continue with the reforms in the administration of justice in the Secretariat, in particular with regard to improving the informal procedures for amicable settlements of staff grievances, and to report thereon to the General Assembly at its forty-fifth session.

General Assembly resolution 44/185 B

19 December 1989   Meeting 83   Adopted without vote

Approved by Fifth Committee (A/44/880) without vote, 14 December (meeting 56); draft by Vice-Chairman following informal consultations (A/C.5/44/L.10); agenda item 130 *(c)*.

Meeting numbers. GA 44th session: 5th Committee 28, 37, 39-42, 44, 55, 56; plenary 83.

Single administrative tribunal

In 1989, the Secretary-General reported[24] on responses from Member States to a 1988 Assembly decision[25] inviting them to submit written comments on proposals set out by the Secretary-General to harmonize the statutes, rules and practices of the administrative tribunals of the International Labour Organisation (ILO) and the United Nations.

As of 19 September, the Secretary-General had received substantive comments from eight Member States.

On 22 November by **decision 44/413**, the General Assembly, on the recommendation of the Fifth Committee, decided, pending further consideration, to retain the existing statute of the Administrative Tribunal of the United Nations. The Secretary-General was requested to revert to the matter, when appropriate, taking into account the views of Member States.

REFERENCES

[1]A/44/222 & Corr.1. [2]YUN 1986, p. 1024, GA res. 41/213, 19 Dec. 1986. [3]YUN 1986, p. 1050. [4]A/44/604. [5]YUN 1985, p. 1238. [6]A/C.5/44/17. [7]A/C.5/44/2. [8]YUN 1988, p. 883. [9]A/C.5/44/21. [10]YUN 1980, p. 1196, GA res. 35/213, 17 Dec. 1980. [11]YUN 1988, p. 886, GA res. 43/225, 21 Dec. 1988. [12]A/C.5/44/11. [13]A/45/9. [14]YUN 1987, p. 1158, GA res. 42/222, 21 Dec. 1987. [15]A/44/9. [16]A/44/682. [17]A/C.5/44/6. [18]YUN 1987, p. 1166, GA res. 42/225, section VI, 21 Dec. 1987. [19]A/C.5/44/12. [20]A/44/730. [21]A/C.5/44/9. [22]YUN 1988, p. 891, GA res. 43/224 B, 21 Dec. 1988. [23]YUN 1988, p. 891. [24]A/C.5/44/1 & Add.1. [25]YUN 1988, p. 892, GA dec. 43/452, 21 Dec. 1988.

Chapter III

Other administrative and management questions

In 1989, the Committee on Conferences continued to examine ways in which conference resources within the UN system could be used more effectively. In December, the General Assembly requested the Committee to review the methodology of conference-servicing utilization rates in order to provide, if possible, a more accurate assessment of the overall use of conference resources, so that optimum use could be made of those services (resolution 44/196 A). It also asked the Secretary-General to analyze the printing requirements of the Organization and to recommend proposals to maximize the cost-effectiveness of external and internal printing (resolution 44/196 B). The Assembly endorsed the Secretary-General's view that a single conference-servicing facility at the Vienna International Centre would represent the ideal solution for servicing the UN system there, and requested him to expedite consultations within the system to that end (resolution 44/201 A). An in-depth review of the operation of common services at Vienna was also requested (resolution 44/201 B). The Assembly expressed deep concern at the delay in completion of reports on work-load statistics and standards regarding conference and library services, as earlier requested by the Advisory Committee on Administrative and Budgetary Questions (ACABQ). It also requested that the Secretary-General begin implementing an optical disc system for storage and retrieval of digital material and to submit to the Assembly in 1990 a report providing a comprehensive plan for full implementation of that system, including by regional commissions and at other duty stations.

Regarding the general introduction of electronic data processing and new technologies in the United Nations, the Assembly asked for a report in 1990 assessing results and outlining future plans (resolution 44/200 C).

Conferences and meetings

In 1989, the Committee on Conferences approved the draft calendar of conferences and meetings for the biennium 1990-1991.[1] It also considered improved utilization of conference-servicing resources; the draft calendar of the subsidiary organs of the Economic and Social Council for the biennium; control and limitation of documentation; UN publication policy; the possibility of central planning and co-ordination of all organizational aspects of conference servicing; programme performance of the Department of Conference Services for the biennium 1986-1987; the medium-term plan of Conference and Library Services for 1992-1997; meetings of organs of programmes not funded by the regular budget of the United Nations; and the application of new technology to conference services.

In 1988, the General Assembly had decided[2] to retain the Committee on Conferences as a permanent subsidiary body, to be composed of 21 members, with one third of the membership retiring annually. Retiring members were eligible for reappointment. The composition of the Committee was to be six members from African States, five from Asian States, four from Latin American and Caribbean States, two from Eastern European States, and four from Western European and other States. As a transitional arrangement, the Committee decided at its 1 March organizational meeting to appoint one third of the membership for a one-year term, one third for two years and one third for three years. By a communication of 3 January 1989, the President of the General Assembly informed the Secretary-General of the composition of the Committee. The Committee also decided that, in principle, the chairmanship would rotate annually among regional groups.

The Committee met on 8 June to discuss the draft calendar of conferences and meetings of the Economic and Social Council, and held its substantive session in New York from 21 to 25 August. In its report, the Committee submitted three draft resolutions which served as the basis for Assembly resolutions.

Calendar of meetings

In February 1989, the Secretariat circulated a note[3] containing as an annex the calendar of UN conferences and meetings for 1989, as adopted by the General Assembly in 1988[4] and amended by subsequent Assembly resolutions and decisions. The note also contained the calendar of conferences and meetings of the principal organs of the specialized agencies and the International Atomic Energy Agency (IAEA). An earlier note[5] circulated a list of meetings scheduled to be held in 1989 by intergovernmental and expert bodies in the economic, social and related fields.

At its organizational meeting on 1 March, the Committee agreed that proposed changes in the calendar that did not have programme budgetary implications could continue to be dealt with by the Secretariat, in consultation with the Committee Bureau. The Committee was advised of a number of such changes during 1989.

Calendar for 1990-1991

In introducing the draft calendar of conferences and meetings for the biennium 1990-1991,[1] a representative of the Secretariat informed the General Assembly that it had been drawn up in accordance with the Committee's terms of reference,[2] and with a 1988 Committee decision[6] relating to the need to be as up to date as possible regarding Economic and Social Council decisions. The Committee approved the draft calendar as amended and submitted it to the Assembly for adoption.

Regarding the draft calendar of conferences and meetings of Economic and Social Council subsidiary organs for 1990-1991, the Committee noted steps taken by the Council on the biennialization of its subsidiary bodies, and encouraged the Council to continue consideration of the question.

Conference and meeting services

The Committee on Conferences considered a March report[7] on the utilization of conference-servicing resources by certain UN bodies meeting in New York, Geneva and Vienna in 1988. The report indicated that the bodies in the sample had consistently improved their performance between 1980 and 1987, with utilization rising collectively from 58 per cent to 77 per cent, thus exceeding the 1983 benchmark (75 per cent) set by the Committee as a minimum standard of efficiency. In 1988, however, despite marked improvements in the ratings of a number of individual bodies and a continuing strong performance by others, the rate of utilization of the sample as a whole fell slightly from the 1987 level. Of the two complementary methods used to calculate the utilization factor, one put it at 76 per cent, and the other at 74 per cent. Pursuant to a Committee request in 1988, the Secretariat also provided reports showing the meeting statistics of bodies related to the United Nations Conference on Trade and Development (UNCTAD) and of the principal organs of the United Nations. In 1988,[6] the Committee Chairman had sent letters to the Chairmen of bodies failing to make adequate use of conference resources, and that communication, together with replies received, was also before the Committee.[8]

The Committee agreed on a refined methodology which would include information on the holding of informal meetings, together with information on time lost owing to late starting or early ending of meetings. While noting with appreciation the improved utilization by a number of UN organs, it again recommended that the General Assembly urge those UN organs failing to make adequate use of the conference services allocated to them to consider reducing their request for such services. The Chairman was again asked to write letters to organs utilizing less than 75 per cent of their conference-servicing resources. The Committee decided to remain seized of the matter on the basis of further reports of the Secretary-General.

GENERAL ASSEMBLY ACTION

On 21 December, on the recommendation of the Fifth (Administrative and Budgetary) Committee, the Assembly adopted **resolution 44/196 A** without vote.

Report of the Committee on Conferences

The General Assembly,

Recalling all its relevant resolutions,

Having considered the report of the Committee on Conferences,

1. *Approves* the draft calendar of conferences and meetings of the United Nations for the biennium 1990-1991 as submitted by the Committee on Conferences;

2. *Authorizes* the Committee on Conferences to make any adjustments in the calendar of conferences and meetings for the biennium 1990-1991 that may become necessary as a result of action and decisions taken by the General Assembly at its forty-fourth session;

3. *Notes with appreciation* the efforts made by a number of United Nations organs to improve the utilization of conference-servicing resources;

4. *Requests* the Committee on Conferences to review the methodology on conference-servicing utilization rates in order to provide, if possible, a more accurate assessment of the overall use of conference resources with a view to enabling United Nations bodies to make the optimum use of conference services and to facilitate, where necessary, continued rationalization of their meeting requirements;

5. *Urges* all United Nations organs to intensify their efforts to improve their utilization of conference-servicing resources, taking into account the need to reduce costs without adversely affecting their efficiency;

6. *Requests* the Chairman of the Committee on Conferences and the Secretary-General to maintain their contacts with United Nations organs that have failed to make adequate use of the conference-servicing resources provided to them in order to assist those organs in making better use of those resources;

7. *Recommends* that the Chairmen of those organs bring the concerns about the utilization of conference-servicing resources to the attention of the organs concerned;

8. *Requests* the Committee on Conferences to remain seized of the matter on the basis of further reports from the Secretary-General;

9.   *Welcomes* the intention of the Committee on Conferences to consider further the draft chapter of the medium-term plan for the period 1992-1997 on conference and library services, bearing in mind that this strategy should have, *inter alia*, the objective of utilizing to the optimum and in the most cost-effective manner, the conference services, resources and facilities world wide, in accordance with relevant General Assembly resolutions and the rules and principles governing conference planning;

10.   *Takes note* of the intention of the Committee on Conferences to play a role in the review of the Department of Conference Services envisaged by the Secretary-General, on the understanding that the role to be determined by the Committee at its 1990 session will be in full accordance with its mandate and in conformity with resolution 43/222 B of 21 December 1988, as adopted by the General Assembly;

11.   *Invites* the Committee on Conferences to adopt a more comprehensive programme of work, taking into account its responsibilities as established by the General Assembly.

General Assembly resolution 44/196 A

21 December 1989   Meeting 84   Adopted without vote

Approved by Fifth Committee (A/44/895) without vote, 19 December (meeting 59); draft by Vice-Chairman (A/C.5/44/L.22) following informal consultations, orally revised; agenda item 128.
Meeting numbers. GA 44th session: 5th Committee 5, 8-10, 59; plenary 84.

Language and interpretation services

The Secretary-General in September 1989 reported[9] on the implementation of a 1987 Assembly resolution,[10] reaffirmed by the 1988 Assembly,[11] requesting the Secretary-General to provide adequate conference-servicing personnel to ensure equal treatment of all official languages of the United Nations (Arabic, Chinese, English, French, Russian and Spanish). In response to the need to maintain adequate conference-servicing resources, the General Assembly in 1988,[12] *inter alia*, approved adjusted staffing of conference services within the appropriations for the 1988-1989 biennium, which was reflected by the Secretary-General in section 29 of the proposed programme budget for the biennium 1990-1991.[13]

Regarding implementation of a 1981 Assembly resolution[14] on simultaneous distribution of UN documents in all applicable languages, the Secretary-General reported that since adoption of the resolution, no exception had been permitted to that requirement without an express request from the body concerned, and the number of such requests had been very small.

The Committee on Conferences took note[1] of the Secretary-General's report, stressing the importance of the item and agreeing to follow the item closely and to return to it at an appropriate time on the basis of further reports by the Secretary-General.

On 21 December, the General Assembly, by **resolution 44/196 C**, requested the Secretary-General to continue to implement its 1987 resolution[10] and decided to remain seized of the matter.

Representation at conferences

In February, the Secretary-General transmitted[15] to the Assembly a report of the Joint Inspection Unit (JIU) regarding specialized agency representation at conferences and meetings. It was the second part of a JIU report on its examination of the effectiveness of participation by Secretariat staff members in meetings, together with recommendations on increasing efficiency and reducing the costs involved. The first part,[16] on UN participation, was submitted in 1988.

In the report on specialized agencies, JIU recommended that executive heads of organizations assure periodic reviews on overall representational activity, particularly from the point of view of effectiveness and costs. To achieve substantial savings and better utilization of human resources, attendance at international meetings should be limited, as a general policy rule, to one representative, and only to the period of discussions of the agenda item of direct interest to the organization. Consideration should be given to use of new technologies such as teleconferencing in representation situations.

The Secretary-General, in an April note,[17] commented on the JIU report on UN representation at conferences and meetings,[18] which the Secretary-General welcomed as timely and relevant to his own efforts to ensure maximum restraint in official travel in the light of the serious financial situation of the Organization. In regard to technological innovations, he said limited experiments were already under way. The use of facsimile machines to permit control and translation of documents at Headquarters for meetings at locations away from Headquarters, as well as other forms of off-site conference-support services, had so far proved more immediately useful than vanguard techniques, teleconferencing in particular, but the Secretary-General would continue to explore its potential.

REFERENCES

[1]A/44/32 & Corr.1,2. [2]YUN 1988, p. 895, GA res. 43/222 B, 21 Dec. 1988. [3]A/AC.172/130. [4]YUN 1988, p. 897, GA res. 43/222 A, 21 Dec. 1988. [5]E/1989/INF/3. [6]YUN 1988, p. 897. [7]A/AC.172/88/Add.7. [8]A/AC.172/96/Add.5,6. [9]A/44/502. [10]YUN 1987, p. 1173, GA res. 42/207 C, 11 Dec. 1987. [11]YUN 1988, p. 898, GA res. 43/222 E, 21 Dec. 1988. [12]*Ibid.*, p. 856, GA res. 43/213, 21 Dec 1988. [13]A/44/6/Rev.1. [14]YUN 1981, p. 1376, GA res. 36/117 B, 10 Dec. 1981. [15]A/44/135 & Add.1. [16]YUN 1988, p. 898. [17]A/44/221. [18]A/44/586.

Documents and publications

Documents limitation

In May, the Secretary-General published an updated version of a note[1] setting forth the policies laid down by the General Assembly regarding the control and limitation of documentation, as requested by the General Assembly in 1969,[2] and taking into account policies adopted by the Assembly up to the end of 1988. The note was distributed to all Member States. The policies applied, for the most part, to the documentation of the Assembly and its subsidiary bodies, although other UN organs, in particular the Economic and Social Council, and bodies such as the UNCTAD Trade and Development Board, had been invited to apply the same policies.

The document set out specific recommendations for the control of meeting records, statements, reports and studies, annexes and supplements to official records, documentation for treaty bodies, and statements of programme budget implications. Annexes to the note contained a list of meeting record entitlements and revised guidelines for the format and content of reports of Assembly subsidiary organs, as well as guidelines for the control and limitation of documentation for special conferences of the United Nations.

In accordance with a decision taken at its organizational meeting on 1 March 1989, the Committee on Conferences deferred discussion of the control and limitation of certain documents until 1990.

GENERAL ASSEMBLY ACTION

On 21 December, on the recommendation of the Fifth Committee, the Assembly adopted **resolution 44/196 B** without vote.

Control and limitation of documentation

The General Assembly,

Recalling its resolutions 2292(XXII) of 8 December 1967, 2538(XXIV) of 11 December 1969, 3415(XXX) of 8 December 1975, 34/50 of 23 November 1979, 35/10 B of 3 November 1980, 36/117 of 10 December 1981, 37/14 C of 16 November 1982, 38/32 E of 25 November 1983, 40/243, section III, of 18 December 1985, 41/177 D of 5 December 1986, 42/207 of 11 December 1987 and 43/222 C of 21 December 1988,

1. *Decides* to extend for a further year the experimental period established under its resolution 37/14 C, during which no subsidiary organ of the General Assembly shall be entitled to summary records, with the exception of the following:

(*a*) *Ad Hoc* Committee on the Indian Ocean;

(*b*) Committee on the Exercise of the Inalienable Rights of the Palestinian People;

(*c*) International Law Commission;

(*d*) Legal Sub-Committee of the Committee on the Peaceful Uses of Outer Space;

(*e*) Special Committee against *Apartheid*;

(*f*) United Nations Commission on International Trade Law;

(*g*) United Nations Council for Namibia;

2. *Takes note* of the decision of the Board of Trustees of the United Nations Institute for Training and Research to discontinue its request for summary records;

3. *Takes note also* of the decision of the Committee on Conferences to review the issue of control and limitation of documentation in more detail at its 1990 substantive session;

4. *Requests* the Secretary-General to analyse the printing requirements of the Organization and recommend proposals to maximize the cost-effectiveness of external and internal printing, through the Committee on Conferences and the Advisory Committee on Administrative and Budgetary Questions, to the General Assembly at its forty-fifth session.

General Assembly resolution 44/196 B

21 December 1989   Meeting 84   Adopted without vote

Approved by Fifth Committee (A/44/895) without vote, 19 December (meeting 59); draft by Vice-Chairman (A/C.5/44/L.22) following informal consultations; agenda item 128.

Meeting numbers. GA 44th session: 5th Committee 5, 8-10, 59; plenary 84.

Recurrent publications

In June, the Secretary-General submitted to the Committee on Conferences a report[3] on recurrent publications of the United Nations. A total of 233 publications were subject to review. The Committee decided[4] to consider the matter in more detail at its 1990 session, on the basis of further Secretariat reports.

REFERENCES

[1]A/INF/44/1. [2]YUN 1969, p. 830, GA res. 2538(XXIV), 11 Dec. 1969. [3]A/AC.172/131. [4]A/44/32.

UN premises

Conference facilities

Addis Ababa and Bangkok

An October report of the Secretary-General[1] on the construction of conference facilities at Addis Ababa, Ethiopia, and Bangkok, Thailand, reviewed progress since 1988 and contained updated timetables for construction and related financial considerations, as approved by the General Assembly in 1984.[2] Activities in 1989 related to the expansion of conference facilities of the Economic Commission for Africa (ECA) at Addis Ababa included the signing of contracts with the quantity surveyor and the architect/engineers; completion of the schematic design and preparation of detailed design drawings; and completion of a detailed topographical survey of the construction site.

Up-to-date project estimates were prepared by the quantity surveyor and a projection was made of the necessary financial commitments to be entered into during construction. While the need for further geotechnical investigation necessitated some revision of the project timetable, completion of the main construction by the second half of 1993 was still envisaged. While in September 1988 a composite annual inflation rate of 4.5 per cent had been projected, it was now considered that, for the balance of the project, the rate should be increased to 5.5 per cent compounded. Construction costs, including furniture and equipment, estimated at $54.4 million in 1988, were now estimated at $60.7 million. The overall cost estimate of $73,501,000 was now revised to $93,889,500.

Regarding the conference facilities of the Economic and Social Commission for Asia and the Pacific (ESCAP) at Bangkok, activities in 1989 included the receipt of 8 tenders from the 11 contractors/consortia representing firms from six countries who had been invited to submit them, and the subsequent signing, in April 1989, of a construction contract with the lowest bidder of the eight tenders received. Construction began in May and was scheduled to take 30 months, with main construction to be completed by December 1991. The construction contract was for 955 million baht ($37.6 million, at the April 1989 exchange rate), which, because of inflation, represented a sizeable increase from the previous estimate of $36.8 million. The current estimate for construction, furnishings and equipment was slightly more than $39 million; however, on the assumption that no major change in the current situation occurred, the total project cost of $44,177,700 already approved by the Assembly was considered to be sufficient.

On 21 December, the Assembly, by **resolution 44/201 A, section V**, took note of the Secretary-General's report and requested him to proceed as recommended by ACABQ.[3]

Vienna

In November 1989, the Secretary-General reported[3] on conference services for UN meetings held in Vienna, Austria. He said that, after several years of experience of the operation of common services at Vienna, including conference services, an in-depth review of such services was needed during the coming biennium. Regarding conference services, the Secretary-General remained convinced that, as proposed in 1985,[4] a single conference-servicing facility at the Vienna International Centre would represent the ideal solution from the standpoint of cost efficiency and that, in view of its mandate to provide a full range of servicing operations for its deliberative bodies, the United Nations was best suited to assume the responsibility of providing conference services to all organizations at the Centre. Since the language and documentation requirements of the United Nations and the Vienna-based United Nations Industrial Development Organization (UNIDO) were similar, and many substantive matters were dealt with by both organizations, the language staff recruited and trained by the United Nations would be able to meet UNIDO requirements as well, and the United Na-

tions could draw upon its world-wide resources to meet the needs of both organizations at Vienna.

In November, ACABQ issued a report[5] in which it agreed with the Secretary-General's views regarding unified conference services at Vienna, and stated that the time had come for urgent action in that regard. It recommended that the Assembly request the Secretary-General to take early action to reopen consultations with all interested parties on the subject, with a view to arriving at practical arrangements for the establishment of unified conference services at Vienna at the earliest possible date. The Secretary-General should submit a report on the outcome of the consultations to the General Assembly, at the latest by its 1990 session, ACABQ said.

On 21 December, by **resolution 44/201 A, section VIII**, the Assembly endorsed the view that a single conference-servicing facility represented the ideal solution from the standpoint of cost efficiency and that a unified service operated by the United Nations was best equipped for this purpose. The Secretary-General was requested to expedite consultations with UNIDO and other interested parties as recommended by ACABQ. On the same date, by **resolution 44/201 B, section XV**, the Assembly concurred with the Secretary-General's view regarding the need for an in-depth review of the operation of common services at Vienna and requested him to report at the most appropriate time on the progress of consultations regarding necessary improvements.

Venue of sessions

By **resolution 44/201 B, section III**, the Assembly requested the Human Rights Committee and the Legal Sub-Committee of the Committee on the Peaceful Uses of Outer Space to take fully into account the recommendations of ACABQ,[6] including the need for optimum use of resources, when deciding on the venue of their future sessions, and to report to the Assembly at its forty-fifth session.

REFERENCES

[1]A/C.5/44/7 & Add.1,2. [2]YUN 1984, pp. 620 & 628, GA res. 39/236, sections III & XI, 18 Dec. 1984. [3]A/C.5/44/24. [4]YUN 1985, p. 1260. [5] A/44/7/Add.4. [6]A/44/7 & Corr.1,2.

Information systems and computers

Technological innovations

Integrated management information system (IMIS)

In October, the Secretary-General submitted a progress report[1] on the integrated management information system (IMIS), approved by the Assembly in 1988.[2] A project team had been established and, to ensure involvement from the outset of major duty stations away from UN Headquarters, a network of central focal points for the project had been established at each major duty station. An initial work plan had been developed for Phase I of the project, as well as a preliminary timetable for system development between October 1989 and October 1992. A consulting firm was to be selected in October 1989 to begin the user requirement study early in November, at which point a meeting of focal points would be held at Headquarters. A cost-benefit analysis would be available in 1990 so that a detailed report could be given to the Assembly that year.

The Assembly, on 21 December, by **resolution 44/201 A, section IV**, took note of the Secretary-General's progress report. By **section III**, it approved budget estimates for 1990 of $11,260,400 for the International Computing Centre.

Optical disc system

In October 1989, the Secretary-General transmitted to the Assembly the JIU report[3] regarding the optical disc pilot project of the United Nations Office at Geneva (UNOG), begun in April 1988, which the Inspectors judged a success, and endorsing the UNOG Interdepartmental Working Group's recommendation that the 1990-1991 budget fund it on an operational basis in Geneva. The Inspectors were particularly struck by the implications of the project, above all by the convenience and savings it promised to the missions of Member States. For very little expenditure, each mission could receive and print in its own office whatever conference documents were available in the system. Major savings and improvements in efficiency were certain to accrue when all conference documents, from the beginning of the Organization, were entered on optical discs (at an estimated contractual cost of about $5 million). Other implications included extension of the system beyond missions to the specialized agencies, capitals of Member States, educational institutions, libraries and UN system field offices.

In commenting on the JIU recommendations, the Secretary-General said it did not seem appropriate at this stage to install a fully operational optical disc system for storage and retrieval of recent and future documentation in the UN Secretariat. He believed a more measured development was required in order to resolve the problems inevitably encountered when introducing a new system. Based on experience of that phase, proposals regarding the system would be included in the proposed programme budget for the biennium 1992-1993, rather than 1990-1991 as suggested by JIU.

In a December report,[4] ACABQ said it fully shared the JIU conclusion and that of the Secretary-General that optical disc technology held great promise for the Organization and should be utilized. It approved establishment of an optical disc system in the UN Secretariat, but believed it should be implemented on a phased basis, taking into account the availability of funds and in the light of technological developments. The Committee did not believe there was a need for an additional appropriation in the biennium 1990-1991 for that purpose. Requirements estimated at $1.2 million should be financed from redeployment of resources and other savings. The Secretary-General should explore further the possibility of voluntary contributions in cash and/or in kind towards the optical disc system. Resource requirements for the system in the biennium 1992-1993 should be proposed by the Secretary-General in the context of his proposed programme budget outline for that biennium.

On 21 December, the Assembly, by **resolution 44/201 B, section XVI**, requested the Secretary-General to implement the optical disc system in accordance with the ACABQ recommendation and to submit a comprehensive plan on full implementation of the system to the 1990 Assembly.

GENERAL ASSEMBLY ACTION

On 21 December, on the recommendation of the Fifth Committee, the Assembly adopted **resolution 44/200 C** without vote.

The General Assembly,

Recognizing the importance of technological innovations in relation to the search for efficiency in the Organization,

Requests the Secretary-General to prepare, for submission to the General Assembly at its forty-fifth session, a report on the status of the introduction of electronic data-processing and new technologies in the United Nations, which should include:

(a) A review and assessment of current policies and processes;

(b) A review and assessment of co-ordinating mechanisms, including those between the Department of Conference Services of the Secretariat and other units within the United Nations system;

(c) A preliminary assessment of the results obtained with the introduction of technological innovations, including cost-benefit analyses, utilization capacity and budgeting and accounting practices;

(d) An outline of future plans and anticipated results for the efficiency of the Organization.

General Assembly resolution 44/200 C

21 December 1989   Meeting 84   Adopted without vote

Approved by Fifth Committee (A/44/901) without vote, 19 December (meeting 59); draft by Vice-Chairman (A/C.5/44/L.24), following informal consultations; agenda item 38.
Meeting numbers. GA 44th session: 5th Committee 11-16, 18, 46, 49, 59; plenary 84.

Co-ordination of information systems

The Administrative Committee on Co-ordination (ACC) issued a report in December[5] on the fifth session of its Advisory Committee for the Co-ordination of Information Systems (Geneva, 18-21 September). The Advisory Committee considered the use of the United Nations Telecommunications Network by the specialized agencies, welcoming the decision by the International Telecommunication Union (ITU) to allow such use as a landmark decision, 37 years after the proposal had first been made. It decided to establish a technical panel to advise and assist the United Nations in discharge of its mandate to enhance the UN telecommunications network. It drew the attention of ACC to the far-reaching consequences of the shift from a paper environment to an electronic one, giving its opinion that close co-operation between records management, data administration and communications management would be required to tackle the problem.

REFERENCES

[1]A/C.5/44/8. [2]YUN 1988, p. 901, res. 43/217, section XII, 21 Dec. 1988. [3]A/44/684 & Add.1. [4]A/44/7/Add.6. [5]ACC/1989/21.

UN Postal Administration

In 1989, gross revenue of the United Nations Postal Administration (UNPA) from the sale of philatelic items at United Nations Headquarters and at overseas offices totalled more than $15.8 million, up from about $12.6 million in 1988. Revenue from the sale of stamps for philatelic purposes was retained by the United Nations. Under the terms of an agreement between the United Nations and the United States, revenue from the sale of United States dollar–denominated stamps used for postage from Headquarters was reimbursed to the United States Postal Service. Similarly, postal agreements between the United Nations and the Governments of Switzerland and Austria required that revenue derived from the sale of Swiss franc– and Austrian schilling–denominated stamps for postage use be reimbursed to the Swiss and Austrian postal authorities, respectively.

Six commemorative stamps issues, one definitive stamp, two souvenir cards and 13 pieces of postal stationery were released by UNPA during the year.

On 27 January, a set of six commemorative stamps in denominations of 25 and 45 United States cents, 0.80 and 1.40 Swiss francs (SwF) and 5.50 and 8 Austrian schillings (S) were issued on the theme of "World Bank". A souvenir card accompanied the issue.

Stamps commemorating "Nobel Peace Prize 1988—United Nations Peace-keeping Forces" were issued on 17 March, together with 13 pieces of postal stationery. The stamps, in denominations of 25 cents, SwF 0.90 and S 6, remained on sale for an additional one year in recognition of that special award. A 45-cent definitive stamp was issued on the same date.

The "World Weather Watch" was commemorated by a set of six stamps in denominations of 25 cents, 36 cents, SwF 0.90 and 1.10, and S 4 and 9.50, which were issued on 21 April. A souvenir card accompanied the issue.

On 23 August, the "United Nations Office at Vienna—10th Anniversary" was marked by the release of six commemorative stamps carrying denominations of 25 cents, 90 cents, SwF 0.50 and 2.00, and S 5 and 7.50.

The tenth group of 16 stamps in the commemorative "Flag Series" was released on 22 September. Each stamp was denominated 25 cents.

The human rights commemorative stamp series was inaugurated on 17 November with the release of the first six stamps illustrating articles 1 to 6 of the 1948 Universal Declaration of Human Rights.[1] The denominations of the stamps were 25 cents, 45 cents, SwF 0.35 and 0.80, and S 4 and S 6.

In 1989, a total of 61,337,000 stamps were printed for UNPA. In the same year, a total of 2,615,766 envelopes received first day of issue cancellations.

REFERENCE

[1]YUN 1948-49, p. 535, GA res. 217 A (III), 10 Dec. 1948.

PART SEVEN

Intergovernmental organizations
related to the United Nations

Chapter I

International Atomic Energy Agency (IAEA)

The International Atomic Energy Agency (IAEA), established in 1957 to foster the peaceful uses of nuclear energy, continued in 1989 to promote the exchange of scientific and technical information, to establish and administer safeguards and health and safety standards, and to provide technical assistance to its members.

The thirty-third session of the IAEA General Conference (Vienna, 25-29 September) adopted resolutions relating to Israeli nuclear capabilities and threat; measures to strengthen international cooperation in matters of nuclear safety and radiological protection; the dumping of nuclear wastes; the 1987 Convention on the Physical Protection of Nuclear Material;[a] production of low-cost potable water using nuclear heat reactors in sea-water desalination; and the nuclear capabilities of South Africa.

The IAEA Board of Governors held five meetings in 1989, in February, June, September, October and December.

IAEA membership remained at 113 in 1989. In September, the General Conference resolved to take a decision at its 1990 session on the suspension of South Africa from the exercise of the privileges and rights of membership of IAEA.

Nuclear safety

During 1989, IAEA continued to emphasize nuclear safety and radiation protection, with activities that focused on advancing the operational safety of nuclear plants, safety assessment techniques, defining safety requirements for nuclear installations and improving public understanding of radiation risk. At the request of the USSR, arrangements began for a team of international experts under IAEA auspices to carry out an assessment of the concept of enabling the population to live safely in areas affected by radioactive contamination following the 1986 Chernobyl (Ukrainian SSR) accident and evaluate the effectiveness of steps taken to safeguard the health of the population.

In June, the Agency signed a memorandum of understanding with the recently established World Association of Nuclear Operators. The aim of the Association, which held its inaugural meeting in Moscow in May, was to improve plant operational safety by strengthening existing links and co-operation among operators of the world's nuclear electricity plants.

The Operational Safety Review Team (OSART) conducted 11 missions in 1989, 3 of which were pre-operational missions to China, Poland and the USSR. The Assessment of Safety Significant Events Team (ASSET) visited nuclear power plants in Pakistan and the USSR, systematically analysing the root causes of safety-related events and the effectiveness of steps taken to prevent their recurrence. In late 1989, there was a significant increase in requests from the countries of Eastern Europe for OSART, ASSET and other missions to assess and upgrade water-cooled and moderated reactor nuclear plant operational safety, and work began on ways to meet the demand. Radiation Protection Advisory Teams conducted 10 missions to member States; they recommended long-term strategies for assistance and co-operation in the use and control of ionizing radiation.

The Incident Reporting System received 189 reports of nuclear power incidents and malfunctions during 1989, bringing to more than 800 the number of reports in the data base. In October, IAEA sponsored a meeting with the Organisation for Economic Co-operation and Development to define a common severity scale for use when communicating nuclear events to the public. A draft scale was expected to be ready by mid-1990 for trial use. Through the Integrated Safety Assessments of Research Reactors programme, missions visited reactors in Hungary and Viet Nam.

Under the radiation protection programme, IAEA set up the 24-hour Emergency Response System to meet its obligations under the 1986 Convention on the Early Notification of a Nuclear Accident[b] and under the 1987 Convention on Assistance in the Case of a Nuclear Accident or Radiological Emergency.[a] In November, some 250 experts participated in an IAEA symposium, which reviewed world-wide experience of recovery operations following a major nuclear accident or a radiological emergency. The accidents at Three Mile Island (United States, 1979) and Chernobyl served as starting-points for reviewing the lessons learned about recovery operations.

---

[a]YUN 1987, p. 1187.
[b]YUN 1986, p. 585.

Nuclear power

The total installed nuclear power-generating capacity in the world increased by about 3 per cent, reaching 318 gigawatts (electrical) by the end of 1989. Five countries—Belgium, France, Hungary, the Republic of Korea and Sweden—generated close to half or more of their total electricity using nuclear power and 13 countries relied on nuclear power plants to supply at least one fourth of their total electricity needs. The 426 nuclear power plants in operation accounted for some 16.8 per cent of the world's electrical generation, representing an accumulated operating experience of about 5,200 reactor-years.

During the year, 12 nuclear power plants came on line, in the German Democratic Republic, the Federal Republic of Germany, India, Japan, Mexico (the first in that country), the Republic of Korea, the USSR, the United Kingdom and the United States. Construction work started on five plants in Japan, the Republic of Korea and the USSR. Five reactors, with a total capacity of 1,370 megawatts, permanently shut down in the USSR, the United Kingdom and the United States.

IAEA continued to provide assistance to member States through 15 technical support projects in quality assurance in Bangladesh, Bulgaria, China, Czechoslovakia, Egypt, Hungary, Indonesia, Pakistan, Poland, the Republic of Korea and Yugoslavia. In addition, 28 training courses and seminars covering such topics as quality assurance, inspections and safety systems for nuclear power plants were conducted in several countries. In March, the Agency's Power Reactor Information System (PRIS) opened for on-line access to member States. The System contained information on 426 power reactors with an accumulated 4,645 reactor-years of experience at the end of the year. In mid-year, the micro-PRIS project began; the objective was to make PRIS data available through personal computers.

Nuclear fuel cycle

In 1989, in addition to publishing an array of reports and guidebooks, including the *Red Book* containing statistical data on uranium resources, IAEA conducted a comprehensive analysis of the dominant trends in the world nuclear fuel cycle and Agency projects in that area. With the continued downward trend in uranium spot market prices, a number of uranium producers ceased production during the year. IAEA sponsored 34 technical co-operation projects on uranium exploration and resources development in 33 countries, as well as 10 studies on nuclear fuel fabrication, materials, development and related topics in eight countries.

Since spent fuel storage was of crucial importance to many countries, IAEA paid special attention to the improved technology of storage with emphasis on safety and reliability. As part of the programme, it finalized the *Guidebook on Spent Fuel Storage*, to be used for critical comparison of existing approaches and for justification of national solutions.

Radioactive waste management

The 18-member International Radioactive Waste Management Advisory Committee was established in 1989 to provide guidance on the scope, content and direction of the waste management programme, including technical, safety, environmental and regulatory aspects. The Committee held its first meeting in April and strongly endorsed proposals to establish a new series of Radioactive Waste Safety Standards publications to facilitate international harmonization of safety-related activities in waste management.

During the year, the Board of Governors approved the issuance of safety standards, reflecting for the first time an international consensus on criteria for the safe underground disposal of high-level wastes. The Agency conducted expert missions to eight developing countries, providing assistance on the establishment and implementation of national radioactive waste management programmes. It also helped to sponsor a symposium in Paris on the safety assessment of radioactive waste repositories.

Food and agriculture

The Joint Food and Agriculture Organization of the United Nations (FAO)/IAEA Division of Nuclear Technology in Food and Agriculture continued to assist member States to improve agriculture and food production. During the year, 39 co-ordinated research programmes and 12 regional and interregional training courses were in progress, and technical supervision was provided for 233 technical co-operation projects in 67 countries.

The Joint Division developed and introduced radiotracer-aided research methods for evaluating local agricultural practices, identifying problems related to pesticide use and monitoring pesticide residues. In 1989, there were 317 research reactors in 56 countries, which were also producing radioisotopes for use in industry, agriculture and medicine.

In October, an FAO/IAEA/United Nations Environment Programme (UNEP)/World Health Organization (WHO) International Symposium on Environmental Effects Following a Major Nuclear Accident (Vienna) reviewed the extent and magnitude of environmental contamination that would arise after a large injection of radioactive materials, and considered methods to monitor, assess and limit the short- and long-term effects on the environment, agriculture and human health.

Programmes in the area of animal production and health focused on indigenous breeds and types of animals kept by smallholder farmers in tropical and subtropical countries, and included studies on camelids in Latin America and water buffaloes in Asia. Radioimmunoassay methods, used to measure reproductive performance in indigenous ruminant livestock, continued to be successfully employed in several developing countries. Using the sterile-insect technique, several North African States initiated a regional co-operation programme to determine the feasibility of Mediterranean fruit fly (medfly) eradication, and IAEA joined FAO in developing plans to eradicate the New World screwworm, which had become established in the Libyan Arab Jamahiriya. Other activities supported by the joint IAEA/FAO efforts included studies related to biofertilizers, plant breeding and irradiation as a means of food preservation.

Nuclear medicine

IAEA continued to provide support in areas of nuclear medicine, applied radiation biology and radiotherapy, dosimetry, and nutritional and health-related environmental studies. Scientific and other support was provided to 52 new technical co-operation projects in the area of nuclear medicine. Research support focused on quality control procedures for nuclear medicine instruments in Asia and Latin America; radioaerosol inhalation for the diagnosis of respiratory diseases in developing countries; immunodiagnosis of tuberculosis; immunodiagnostic techniques for human schistosomiasis; and the monitoring of malaria vectors.

A new set of procedures was developed to improve quality control of radiation sterilization and a revised code of practice for the radiation sterilization of disposable medical supplies. Other projects focused on the use of radiation to improve fermentation, sewage recycling and cancer treatment.

During 1989, the number of calibrations performed by the IAEA network of Secondary Standard Dosimetry Laboratories increased significantly and the biannual intercomparison service showed improved accuracy of the dosimeters used.

Nuclear and isotopic techniques continued to play an important role in human nutrition studies. In October, the results of an IAEA study on human daily dietary intakes of nutritionally important trace elements as measured by nuclear and other techniques—the first international study of its kind—was presented at the first WHO/FAO/IAEA Expert Consultation on Trace Elements in Human Nutrition.

The Marine Environmental Studies Laboratory of the International Laboratory of Marine Radio-activity in Monaco organized world-wide inter-calibration exercises for trace metals and chlorinated hydrocarbons (pesticides) with the participation of 143 laboratories from 57 member States. As part of an ongoing co-operative programme with UNEP, the Laboratory continued to co-ordinate the development, testing and revision of reference methods and guidelines for marine pollution measurements.

Physical and earth sciences

IAEA continued to promote the exchange of information in the physical and earth sciences and to assist States with the application of nuclear technologies in environmental studies, ore processing, hydrology, analytical and applied chemistry, radiation chemistry, radiation processing, biomedicine and bioengineering and industry.

In the area of isotope hydrology, the Agency supported 44 technical co-operation projects in 34 member States, participated in three regional projects in Africa, the Middle East and Latin America, and executed 69 research contracts in 30 countries. Isotope hydrology was used to locate leakages from hydraulic structures, study the movement of sediments in rivers and harbours, determine the economic viability of ports and guard against erosion.

The Agency fulfilled more than 820 requests from 64 member States for experimental and evaluative data, data-processing computer codes and publications on the subject of nuclear measurements and instrumentation. An interregional project involving 23 nuclear analytical laboratories in 14 developing countries reflected deficiencies in instrumentation and proper utilization of techniques.

Some 4,100 scientists took part in the activities of the International Centre for Theoretical Physics in Trieste, Italy, and in the programme for training at Italian laboratories. The Centre, which celebrated its twenty-fifth anniversary in October, was operated jointly with the United Nations Educational, Scientific and Cultural Organization. Main fields of research and training at the Centre in 1989 included fundamental, condensed matter, atomic and molecular physics; mathematics; physics and energy; physics and the environment; physics of space; applied physics and high technology; and science, high technology and development.

Technical co-operation

In 1989, the IAEA annual programming cycle for technical co-operation activities was replaced with a two-year cycle. A total of 165 projects were completed and 191 new projects approved during the year. In addition, some 2,144 expert assignments were undertaken, training programmes were devised for 924 fellows and visiting scientists, and 106 regional and interregional training courses for 1,265 participants were organized. New resources for technical co-operation totalled $50.1 million, a 10 per cent increase over 1988.

Agency safeguards responsibilities

During 1989, 2,196 safeguards inspections were performed by IAEA, which concluded that the nuclear material under its safeguards remained in peaceful nuclear activities or was otherwise adequately accounted for. As at 31 December, 172 safeguards agreements were in force with 101 States, compared to 168 agreements with 98 States and Taiwan at the end of 1988.

Safeguards were applied in 43 States and Taiwan under agreements pursuant to the 1968 Treaty on the Non-Proliferation of Nuclear Weapons (NPT)[c] and/or the 1967 Treaty for the Prohibition of Nuclear Weapons in Latin America (Treaty of Tlatelolco).[d] Safeguards agreements were in force with 82 States pursuant to NPT. Of 51 non-nuclear-weapon States party to NPT which did not have safeguards agreements in force, safeguards were being applied in three of them, the only ones with significant nuclear activities. Safeguards agreements had been concluded with 10 of the 11 signatories of the 1985 South Pacific Nuclear Free Zone Treaty (Rarotonga Treaty),[e] and safeguards were applied in one of those States. Safeguards agreements had been concluded with 19 of the 23 States parties to the Treaty of Tlatelolco, 16 of which were in force; two States with territories in the zone of application of the Tlatelolco Treaty had concluded similar agreements.

As at 31 December 1989, 515 nuclear facilities were under safeguards or contained safeguarded material; 10 of them were in nuclear-weapon States. A further 405 locations outside nuclear facilities contained small amounts of safeguarded material and there were two safeguarded non-nuclear installations.

Nuclear information

Mongolia joined the International Nuclear Information System in 1989, bringing its membership to 79 IAEA member States and 15 international organizations. During the year, the System's Advisory Committee approved changes in the subject scope of the literature to be covered, the most significant being the exclusion of cosmology and astrophysics and the inclusion of economic and environmental aspects of all energy sources, nuclear and non-nuclear. By the end of the year, the bibliographic data base of nuclear literature contained 1,352,356 records.

Secretariat

At the end of 1989, the number of staff members of the IAEA secretariat totalled 2,171—825 in the Professional and higher categories, 1,202 in the General Service category and 144 in the Maintenance and Operatives Service category.

Budget

The regular budget for 1989 was $152,520,000, of which $143,749,000 was to be financed from contributions by member States on the basis of the 1989 scale of assessment, $5,045,000 from income from work for others and $3,726,000 from other miscellaneous income. Actual expenditures amounted to $147,831,764, resulting in an unencumbered balance of $4,688,236.

The target for voluntary contributions to the Technical Assistance and Co-operation Fund in 1989 was established at $42 million, of which $35,680,915 had been pledged by member States by the end of the year.

NOTE: For further information, see *The Annual Report for 1989*, published by IAEA.

[c]YUN 1968, p. 17, GA res. 2373(XXII), annex, 12 June 1968.
[d]YUN 1967, p. 13.
[e]YUN 1985, p. 58.

HEADQUARTERS AND OTHER OFFICES

HEADQUARTERS
International Atomic Energy Agency
Wagramerstrasse 5
(P.O. Box 100, Vienna International Centre)
A-1400 Vienna, Austria
  Cable address: INATOM VIENNA
  Telephone: (43) (1) 20600
  Fax: (43) (1) 20607
  Telex: 1–2645 ATOM A
  Internet: http://www.iaea.or.at/worldatom

LIAISON OFFICE
International Atomic Energy Agency Liaison Office at the
  United Nations
1 United Nations Plaza, Room 1155
New York, N.Y. 10017, United States
  Telephone: (1) (212) 963-6010, 6011, 6012
  Fax: (1) (212) 751-4117
  Telex: 42 05 44 UNH

Chapter II

International Labour Organisation (ILO)

During the year, the International Labour Organisation (ILO), established in 1919 as an autonomous institution associated with the League of Nations, continued its standard-setting, technical co-operation, research and publishing activities in six major areas of work: promoting policies to create employment and satisfy basic human needs; developing human resources; improving working conditions and environment; promoting social security; strengthening industrial relations and tripartite (government/employer/worker) co-operation; and advancing human rights in the social and labour fields.

ILO membership in 1989 remained at 150.

Meetings

The seventy-sixth session of the ILO Conference, held at ILO headquarters (Geneva, 7-28 June), adopted a revised convention on indigenous and tribal peoples and began a two-year process of setting new safety standards for the use of chemicals and night work. The International Labour Conference also considered the annual reports of the ILO Governing Body and of the Director-General, which focused on economic recovery and employment, and a special report on the effect of *apartheid* on labour and employment in South Africa. The Conference monitored the application of ILO standards in all regions and adopted conclusions on the application of the ILO Declaration concerning Action against *Apartheid* in South Africa and Namibia. The Conference also adopted a draft protocol to revise the Convention on night work for women in industry. A tripartite (government/employer/worker) committee again examined the application of ILO conventions and recommendations by member States and reviewed the application of ILO standards concerning social security.

The first of a planned series of meetings to follow up the 1987 High-level Meeting on Employment and Structural Adjustment was held—a tripartite symposium (Nairobi, Kenya, 16-19 October) on structural adjustment and employment in Africa. Attended by representatives of 12 Governments and employers' and workers' organizations, the meeting proposed policy guidelines for sustainable development.

The ninth session of the Committee of Work on Plantations (Geneva, 12-20 April) adopted conclusions on conditions of employment and work on plantations and the role of that sector in rural development. The first session of the Hotel, Catering and Tourism Committee (Geneva, 6-14 December) adopted conclusions aimed at improving conditions of work and stepping up productivity and training.

International standards

During the year, priority was given to promoting wider observance of international labour standards and fuller respect for those human rights falling within the ILO mandate.

With that objective, advisory missions concerning various Conventions visited Brazil, the Central African Republic, Ecuador, Liberia and Zambia. In addition, regional advisers and ILO officials visited 33 countries to promote international standards. Courses and seminars were held to familiarize national labour administrations and workers' and employers' representatives with the obligations and ILO procedures relating to Conventions and Recommendations. Officials from 22 countries participated in training at ILO headquarters. Numerous regional and subregional meetings and seminars were held during the year. National tripartite seminars on labour standards took place in Bolivia, Equatorial Guinea and Guinea, and ILO also took part in other meetings on national and international standards in over 20 countries.

A number of activities were undertaken on links between international labour standards and technical co-operation, including publication of a brochure entitled *International Labour Standards for Development and Social Justice* and workshops in Barbados, Indonesia, the Philippines, Thailand, and Trinidad and Tobago. In order to enhance the impact of international labour standards, emphasis was placed on assisting ILO constituents, particularly in developing countries, to participate more actively in their elaboration and implementation. At its November session, the ILO Governing Body discussed the inclusion of flexibility devices in Conventions, taking into account differences between countries and levels of development.

Standard-setting

At its 1989 session, the General Conference adopted the revised Indigenous and Tribal Peoples Convention to help improve the situation and status of those people in the light of developments which had taken place since the adoption of the Indigenous and Tribal Populations Convention (No. 107) in 1957.

The Conference also continued consideration of proposals for a new Convention on safety in the use of chemicals at work and for a new Convention and Recommendation concerning night work as well as a Protocol revising the Night Work (Women) Convention (Revised), 1948.

During the year, 62 ratifications of ILO Conventions on basic human rights and tripartism by 26 member States were registered, bringing total ratifications at the end of 1989 to 5,463. There were also three denunciations unaccompanied by the ratification of a revised Convention.

Supervision of standards

At its annual meeting in March, the Committee of Experts on the Application of Conventions and Recommendations dealt with 1,547 reports from Governments regarding compliance with the ILO Constitution and international labour standards, as well as 154 observations from workers' and employers' organizations. The Committee examined the application of Conventions in export processing zones and enterprises and of the Employment Policy Convention (No. 122), 1964, and surveyed national law and practice in ILO member States as to the Social Security (Minimum Standards) Convention (No. 102), 1952, and the Invalidity, Old-Age and Survivors' Benefits Convention (No. 128) and Recommendation (No. 131), 1967, with regard to old-age benefits.

The Governing Body dealt with a number of representations and complaints as provided for under the ILO Constitution. Its Committee on Freedom of Association met three times in 1989 to consider eight reports on 77 cases of complaints of violations of freedom of association.

Following the General Conference's consideration of the special report of the Director-General on the application of the Declaration concerning Action against *Apartheid* in South Africa and Namibia, and adoption of the report of the Committee on Action against *Apartheid*, a new expert group to monitor sanctions and other actions against *apartheid* throughout the world held its first meeting in New York in October. The group established its programme for 1990, emphasizing studies of an embargo on South African coal, effective financial sanctions and severance of air links with South Africa.

Employment and development

To ensure close co-ordination in following up on the conclusions of the 1987 High-level Meeting on Employment and Structural Adjustment, an interdepartmental Task Force on Structural Adjustment, Employment and Training was established in early 1989 and met four times during the year. ILO also undertook a variety of studies, training workshops, preparatory assistance missions and other advisory services in several countries as part of an ongoing effort to strengthen the capacity of member States to design and implement labour market policies and employment plans. Additional activities in 1989 addressed rural development and employment; technology, employment and development; and international migration for employment.

Working environment

Under its international programme for the improvement of working conditions and employment, ILO continued to assist countries in promoting occupational safety and health and improving general working conditions. Consultations and fellowships were provided in 14 developing countries, and projects carried out in about a dozen countries during 1989 dealt with the promotion of occupational safety and health, mine safety, major hazard control, and training in occupational safety and health. Services provided by the International Occupational Safety and Health Information Centre (CIS) were expanded, while co-operation continued with the World Health Organization and the United Nations Environment Programme within the International Programme on Chemical Safety and with the International Atomic Energy Agency on radiation protection.

Draft codes of practice on major hazard control, on safety and health in construction and on opencast mines were prepared, as were a guide to safety and health in the use of agrochemicals and a training manual on the use of chemicals at work. In addition to a number of specific studies, ILO published a special issue of 1,800 annotated references entitled *Laws, Regulations and Directives* and the CIS bimonthly bulletin *Safety and Health at Work*.

Technical co-operation activities aimed at improving working conditions and productivity in small and medium-sized enterprises included training for small entrepreneurs, programmes on abolition of child labour and a project on welfare facilities for women workers. In addition to a meeting of experts on special protective measures for women and equality of opportunity and treatment (Geneva, 10-17 October), several tripartite seminars were held at subregional and regional levels on equality of opportunity. Studies were in progress on policy aspects of female participation in the labour force, access of rural women to land, women's involvement in afforestation, the role of women in small enterprise development, working conditions of women in the informal sector, and self-employment schemes for female-headed households.

Field activities

The volume of ILO operational activities increased significantly during the year, in terms of both annual expenditure and new project approvals. Operational activities expenditures in 1989 rose for the fifth consecutive year, to $143.4 million, or 14 per cent more than 1988. Of the total, $16.1 million was funded from the regular budget of ILO, while the United Nations Development Programme continued to provide the bulk of external funding ($64.1 million) and the rest came from trust funds, multi- and bilateral arrangements and the United Nations Population Fund.

As in previous years, Africa remained the leading region in terms of operational expenditure, receiving 53.7 per cent of the total. The share of least developed countries, most of them in Africa, in overall programme expenditure increased to 37.3 per cent. Employment promotion, human resources development and sectoral activities remained the main fields of ILO activity, accounting for 80 per cent of all expenditure. Operational activities in support of employers' and workers' organizations increased by some 30 per cent. Regular budget for technical co-operation resources amounting to some $16 million continued to be especially significant in supporting activities directly benefiting workers' and employers' organizations and ILO regional projects and centres in the fields of employment, training and labour administration.

Special emphasis was placed on raising the capability of field offices to promote more links between international labour standards and operational activities.

The profile of ILO experts changed during the year, with nearly 38 per cent of all experts on duty being nationals of developing countries and the number of national professional personnel increasing.

Training and research

In 1989, ILO training concentrated on assisting member States to define and implement an effective approach to entrepreneurship, small enterprises and management development, and strengthening national, regional and interregional institutions. Its vocational training programme aimed at increasing, particularly in the urban informal sector and the rural sectors, the efficiency of national training systems and the availability of skilled manpower. Efforts were made to promote greater self-reliance through trade and development training and increased training opportunities for specific groups, particularly women and out-of-school youth. ILO's vocational rehabilitation programme was geared towards furthering equal training and employment opportunities for disabled persons. Over 60 countries received technical assistance or advice and the number of advisers, experts, UN volunteers and external collaborators involved increased to over 100.

Emphasis was placed on assisting countries through advisory services, the regional vocational training centres in Africa, Asia and Latin America, and technical co-ordination with other international agencies and institutions. Projects included strengthening African training institutions focused on the development of marketing strategies and client-based market policies for francophone institutions, and skills development in eight Arab countries to enhance their response to changing manpower needs in the public and private sectors. The diversification of women's training and employment was the theme of major technical co-operation programmes in Africa and Asia.

The International Centre for Advanced Technical and Vocational Training (Turin, Italy) provided group training and fellowships as well as teaching materials, publications and advisory services, with a major focus on educational technology and higher management training. In 1989, the Centre organized 75 courses and seminars for 1,391 participants, 23 per cent of whom were women, mainly from developing countries. A large number of courses, seminars and advisory services took place in the field, in an effort to strengthen national technical skills. The number of fellowships rose to 850. During the year, the Centre took further steps to strengthen collaboration with Governments, the European Community and the UN system.

The International Institute for Labour Studies at Geneva, the ILO centre for education and research, held its twenty-fourth international internship course on active labour policy development (Geneva, 10 May–9 June), which focused on tripartism and the role of workers' and employers' organizations, as well as on ILO's standard-setting activities and supervisory machinery. The Institute also collaborated in organizing a national seminar in Rwanda on human resources and a tripartite subregional seminar in Senegal on the role of co-operatives in economic and social development. Under its new industrial organization programme, the Institute addressed trends in industrial restructuring and the reorganization of enterprises. The promotion of regional networks of researchers remained a priority within the labour market programme. Several activities were aimed at developing further labour market analysis techniques. One of the Institute's main educational activities was a pilot project for training labour market specialists from francophone Africa. A two-volume reference book on workers' participation was being prepared for publication.

Publications

During the year, ILO published the fourth volume of the *World Labour Report*, which surveyed the employment conditions of public service employees and reviewed recent employment and labour income trends. In addition to at least 17 new volumes on a variety of issues related to its work, ILO also continued to produce the bimonthly *International Labour Review*, the quarterly *Social and Labour Bulletin* and the biannual *Legislative Series*.

Secretariat

As at 31 December 1989, full-time staff under permanent, fixed-term and short-term appoint-ments at ILO headquarters and elsewhere numbered 3,148, including 1,427 in the Professional and higher categories, and 1,721 in the General Service or Maintenance categories. Of the Professional staff, 688 were assigned to technical co-operation projects.

Budget

The International Labour Conference in June adopted a budget of $330.4 million for the 1990-1991 biennium.

NOTE: for further information on ILO, see *Report of the Director-General: Activities of the ILO, 1989.*

HEADQUARTERS, LIAISON AND OTHER OFFICES

HEADQUARTERS
International Labour Office
4 Route des Morillons
CH-1211 Geneva 22
Switzerland
   Cable address: INTERLAB GENEVE
   Telephone: (41) (22) 799-6111
   Fax: (41) (22) 798-8686
   Telex: 415647 ILO CH

LIAISON OFFICE
International Labour Organization
Liaison Office with the United Nations
Suite 3101
220 East 42nd Street
New York, N.Y. 10017, United States
   Telephone: (1) (212) 697-0150
   Fax: (1) (212) 883-0844
   Telex: 422716

ILO maintained regional offices at Abidjan, Côte d'Ivoire; Bangkok, Thailand; Geneva, Switzerland; and Lima, Peru; as well as other liaison offices with the European Community at Brussels, Belgium; and with the Economic Commission for Latin America and the Caribbean at Santiago, Chile.

Chapter III

Food and Agriculture Organization of the United Nations (FAO)

In 1989, the Food and Agriculture Organization of the United Nations (FAO) continued to assist farmers, fishermen and foresters to improve their standards of living and produce more foods using techniques that did not degrade the environment. Established in 1945 to raise levels of nutrition, improve agricultural productivity and better the condition of the rural poor, FAO's main objective remained the achievement of global food security, where everyone would have access at all times to the food needed for an active and healthy life. The organization also continued to monitor food supply conditions world wide and provide emergency relief.

The FAO Conference, the organization's governing body, held its twenty-fifth biennial session at FAO headquarters (Rome, Italy, 11-29 November). It approved the organization's programme of work and budget for 1990-1991 and adopted resolutions on various aspects of food, agriculture and rural development. The Conference noted that global food and agricultural production had been at exceptionally low levels in 1987 and 1988 and that, despite an increase in production in 1989, cereal production was expected to be below consumption for the third consecutive year. It also noted that per capita staple food production had declined in many developing countries, especially in Africa, and that developing countries required differential treatment in the light of their economic problems and falling prices for certain agricultural commodities, notably coffee and cocoa.

The Conference approved the conclusions of a two-year review of certain aspects of the organization's goals and operations, carried out by the FAO Programme and Finance Committees, with the assistance of an independent panel of experts, at the request of the 1987 Conference. The review recommended, among other things, strengthening FAO's field operations, including the creation of a project identification and formulation facility, and improved co-ordination and co-operation with other UN bodies, particularly the World Bank group.

As part of FAO's activities to promote environmentally sound practices in agriculture, the Conference approved a Prior Informed Consent clause to the International Code of Conduct on the Distribution and Use of Pesticides, adopted in 1985, which called for participating countries to be notified when a pesticide was banned or severely restricted in the country of origin or by other importing countries.

The Conference unanimously endorsed a Plan of Action for the Integration of Women in Agricultural and Rural Development, designed to ensure that rural women were accorded equal rights and opportunities and increased access to land, credit, extension services, rural organizations, decision-making and improved technology. Aiming to increase acceptance of the International Undertaking on Plant Genetic Resources, adopted in 1983, the Conference endorsed an agreed interpretation of the Undertaking, which recognized the rights of both plant breeders and farmers in relation to the exploration, development and conservation of plant germplasm. It also established an International Fund for Plant Genetic Resources.

The Conference also decided to move the FAO Regional Office for the Near East from headquarters back to its old premises in Cairo, Egypt, to improve the quality and impact of its activities.

During the year, FAO membership remained unchanged at 158 countries.

More than 140 countries observed World Food Day on 16 October.

World food situation

World food production rose by 3.2 per cent in 1989 to nearly 3,600 million tonnes, a growth rate well above the average of the 1980s, reflecting mainly a sharp recovery in crop production in North America, as well as significant increases in Eastern Europe and the USSR. Despite the better overall performance of global agriculture, which appeared to recover from the stagnation of 1987 and 1988, set-backs were recorded in many developing countries. In all the developing regions except the Far East, the 1989 agricultural growth rate fell below the 1980s average. Per capita production fell in 75 per cent of African countries, two thirds of countries in the Near East, and more than a third of the countries in the Far East, while population growth exceeded production in 64 of 108 developing countries, compared to only 56 in 1988.

Global cereal production rose by 7 per cent in 1989 to 1,865 million tonnes, but global cereal stocks remained at a record low, with their volume standing at 17 per cent of consumption, the minimum FAO considered necessary to safeguard world food security. Among other major food commodities, growth in animal products was slow, especially in developed countries. While sugar and coffee output showed little improvement, cocoa production rose 9 per cent and oilseed output was well above 1988 levels following good harvests in North and Latin America.

Activities in 1989

Emergency assistance

While food supply conditions in Africa as a whole improved during 1988-1989, FAO reported that grave difficulties persisted in several countries, particularly in Mozambique and southern Sudan. Exceptional food emergencies were also declared in Angola, Malawi, Sierra Leone and Somalia. Harvests in 1989 were down sharply in Botswana, Lesotho and Zimbabwe, and the food situation was deemed precarious in 10 other African countries. A UN emergency programme, Operation Lifeline Sudan, launched in April 1989 (see PART THREE, Chapter III), brought some relief to strife-torn southern Sudan. By August, some 108,000 tonnes of food had been delivered with the help of the World Food Programme. In Mozambique, food shortages were severe with starvation-related deaths widely reported, especially in inaccessible areas. At the end of the year, the FAO Director-General warned of famine threats in parts of Africa and called for special assistance to Ethiopia to avert widespread loss of life from famine.

In other regions, serious food supply problems were reported in several populous Asian countries—Afghanistan, Bangladesh, the Lao People's Democratic Republic and Sri Lanka—as well as in Haiti, Lebanon, Nicaragua and Peru.

FAO estimated food-aid shipments in 1989/90 at about 11.6 million tonnes, compared to 10 million tonnes in the previous year. Twenty-two countries—including four developing ones—contributed some 424,000 tonnes of cereals and other food commodities to the multilateral International Emergency Food Reserve during 1989. A further 188,000 tonnes was channelled through UN relief and rehabilitation programmes to the Afghan people.

Northern Africa, which had suffered in 1988 its worst desert locust plague since the 1950s, did not experience an expected upsurge of desert locusts in 1989 due to an FAO-led spraying campaign, as well as a massive locust migration into the Atlantic Ocean and a failure to breed around the Red Sea in winter. However, by mid-1989, grasshopper infestations affected some 9.2 million hectares in Sahelian countries, causing severe damage to crops in Chad, Mali and the Niger before being controlled by a $60 million chemical spraying operation co-ordinated by FAO.

During the year, FAO spearheaded a campaign in North Africa to halt an invasion of the New World screwworm, a lethal insect pest of livestock. Some 1.7 million insecticide and wound-treatment kits were distributed in the Libyan Arab Jamahiriya and experts were sent to investigate the possible use of the sterile-insect technique, which had successfully eradicated the New World screwworm from North America.

Field programme

During 1989, FAO provided developing countries with technical advice in all areas of food and agriculture, fisheries, forestry and rural development. In 1989, 2,583 field projects were under way for a total annual expenditure of $358 million, financed through contributions from the United Nations Development Programme ($164.3 million or 45.9 per cent), trust funds from Governments and international funding sources ($163.8 million or 45.7 per cent) and from FAO's regular budget ($29.9 million or 8.4 per cent). During the year, international financing institutions approved some $2,309 million in funding for agricultural and rural development projects that were prepared with the assistance of FAO's Investment Centre.

Rural development

Following a 1988 decision to expand the scope of its food security assistance, FAO set up task forces to assist Chad, the Niger, the United Republic of Tanzania and Zambia in drawing up comprehensive national food security programmes. The task forces, which consisted of FAO experts familiar with each country, were to help government counterparts design a long-term food security policy framework and formulate projects for its implementation.

Through FAO's People's Participation Programme, under way in 10 countries, some 14,000 poor farmers were assisted in forming small groups and pooling their efforts to receive training, access to credit and other farm inputs. Through its Rural Energy Planning Programme, FAO continued to promote a strategy to improve access to both conventional and renewable sources of energy. In 1989, the strategy, which stressed closer co-ordination between energy authorities and agricultural ministries, was presented to a meeting in Beijing of staff from agricultural and energy ministries of 13 Asian countries. Similar activities were planned for Africa and Latin America and the Caribbean.

Crops

Many FAO projects in 1989 contributed to improving crop production. The organization set up an integrated data base on agrometeorology to assess the effect of rainfall and other weather factors on crop growing conditions world-wide. Among projects in developing countries was a strategy for soil conservation in Lesotho, where every year some 39 million tonnes of soil were swept away from farmland. The strategy focused on improving farming practices rather than controlling the run-off. FAO and the European Space Agency were developing a satellite communications system to transmit information from FAO's environmental monitoring system on crop and vegetation conditions to receiving stations in Africa.

To help introduce higher yielding and more resistant varieties of crop plants, FAO continued to sponsor the exchange and storage of breeding materials between crop research centres. In 1989, it promoted the cultivation of improved sesame and safflower seeds—important sources of edible oil in the developing world—by collecting samples of safflower hybrids from donors in China, India, Israel, Mexico and the United States and distributing them to eight countries in Asia and Africa. Samples of sesame varieties, donated by four countries, were sent to breeders in Guatemala, India, Iran, Kenya and Pakistan.

The FAO Prevention of Food Losses (PFL) Programme sent an expert to find new potato-processing methods for women farmers in isolated areas of north-west Cameroon. During the year, some 35 PFL projects were implemented in developing countries. In Indonesia, for example, farmers helped design processing equipment for soybeans, maize, ground-nuts and cassava.

Livestock

One focus of FAO activities related to livestock during 1989 was the development and promotion of dairy farming. Milk production in 13 districts in western Kenya, for example, was increased by an average of 70 per cent through an FAO project that introduced high-yielding fodder grasses and legumes.

A variety of other activities were carried out to strengthen animal production and health. A pilot project eliminated the tsetse fly—a major obstacle to livestock production in large areas of Africa—from a 500–square–kilometre area in southern Ethiopia, using cloth screens impregnated with insecticide. Another project helped strengthen poultry-meat quality control and food testing in Thailand after its agricultural exports suffered a set-back when Japan found unacceptable levels of pesticide in a shipment of frozen chicken. FAO tested a programme to use sugar cane as feed for livestock in several Caribbean countries and helped Caribbean island States to control the spread of tropical bont tick, the cause

of the cattle disease heartwater, through improved veterinary services and animal handling services, stricter quarantine procedures and regular treatment of livestock and dogs.

Other areas of FAO activity included veterinary services development; parasitic and vector-borne disease; non-infectious disease and reproductive diseases; tropical animal feeds; animal breed preservation and development; improved animal husbandry and animal product processing; and the production of the *Animal Health Yearbook* (a reference book on more than 135 infectious diseases).

Fisheries

FAO expanded activities in aquaculture and inland fisheries during the year, starting programmes on fish diseases, fish nutrition and fishery genetics. Increasing emphasis was placed on integrating fish culture into general agricultural practices, with the organization's fisheries department undertaking many activities in tandem with other departments to facilitate the introduction of fish into farming.

Activities under way in 1989 as part of FAO's $7.7 million Bay of Bengal project—launched in 1987 to improve techniques and the incomes of small-scale fishing communities in seven countries—included a radio programme for fisherfolk in Sri Lanka, seaweed farming trials in India, oyster growing in peninsular Malaysia, and testing of fish-hauling equipment in Maldives.

In Africa, highly productive cropping systems for rain-fed swamp rice were introduced in Sierra Leone and other countries, combining rice cultivation with vegetable and fish farming, and plans were made to extend a successful credit scheme for poor fishermen on Lake Tanganyika to fishing communities throughout the United Republic of Tanzania.

In addition to providing fishery statistics and data bases, FAO in 1989 launched the Fishery Project Information Service to collect and disseminate information on externally assisted fishery and aquaculture projects in developing countries. FAO's Legal Office prepared a study of the legal and institutional aspects of managing estuaries and deltas, considered an overlooked area of fisheries law.

Forestry

FAO continued activities to integrate trees and forests with other land uses, particularly in arid lands and mountainous watersheds, and to promote self-sustained forestry programmes and appropriate forest-based industries. In Nepal, for example, it helped plant hundreds of thousands of trees during 1989 to protect the severely eroded Shivapuri watershed serving the Kathmandu valley. The project reduced pressure on forests in the watershed that were being destroyed by local farmers for fuelwood and fodder. Farmers were also encouraged to increase their incomes through beekeeping, horticulture and mushroom cultivation.

The Tropical Forestry Action Plan, launched in 1986, continued to be a major focus of FAO efforts to conserve and regenerate the world's tropical forest resources and to help 60 countries make maximum sustainable use of them. Activities included preparation of national, subregional and regional plans. In 1989, FAO drew up a five-year plan for Bolivia after studies found that forest destruction and soil erosion were most intense in the country's highly populated altiplano, while lumbering and ranching had destroyed valuable forest stands in low-lying areas. Some 75 projects were developed for fuelwood plantations, erosion control, forest industry development, conservation of forest ecosystems and the strengthening of forestry institutions.

During the year, FAO data services were expanded to provide global resource assessments for both tropical and temperate forests. The organization launched a project to assess changes in forest cover and set up a global forest-monitoring system. Vegetation maps were completed for Africa and Asia and the Pacific, and a data base was prepared for Latin America as part of the FAO Geographic Information System. Projects were also carried out for collecting, conserving, evaluating and exchanging genetic materials guided by recommendations of the FAO Panel of Experts on Forest Gene Resources.

Environment

In 1989, FAO's work on environment and sustainable development was co-ordinated through an Interdepartmental Working Group on Environment and Energy, which oversaw the work of subgroups in such areas as policy and planning, biological diversity, climate change, desertification control, integrated coastal area management and energy, with the aim of seeking solutions to environmental problems in different agro-ecological zones of the developing world.

The theme of World Food Day 1989 was food and the environment. During the year, FAO finalized an international scheme for the conservation and rehabilitation of Africa's forests, pastures and croplands, which provided a framework for formulating national plans, co-ordinating regional programmes and enlisting international support for land restoration; the

scheme was to be reviewed at the FAO Regional Conference for Africa in 1990.

The conservation and use of plant and animal genetic resources received renewed support from the FAO Conference in November, which also called for strengthening FAO programmes for environmental protection and sustainable development. Work began on setting up a global programme for the preservation of the world's threatened livestock breeds. An updated FAO–United Nations Educational, Scientific and Cultural Organization Soil Map of the World was published, which included several changes in diagnostic principles, soil units and nomenclature.

Nuclear techniques

In 1989, the Joint FAO–International Atomic Energy Agency Division, which celebrated its twenty-fifth anniversary, undertook a wide range of activities in soil fertility, plant production, pest control, animal production, agrochemicals and food irradiation. Among its achievements during the year, the Division enhanced efforts to control the Mediterranean fruit fly by developing methods of determining its sex by colour.

The Division undertook soil studies, using radioactive and stable isotopes to measure nutrients, in the search for techniques to reduce reliance on costly fertilizers. It carried out *in vitro* experiments for breeding several species of tropical crop plants, including bananas, plantains yams and cassava. Other activities included evaluating tropical fodder species, distributing diagnostic kits for livestock diseases and to measure animal fertility, and testing controlled-release agrochemicals in efforts to reduce the amounts required of pesticides and herbicides. In addition, the Division sponsored hundreds of seminars and exchange programmes for scientists from developing countries.

Information

Hundreds of information booklets, technical papers and reference materials were compiled and published by FAO in 1989. Major periodicals included *Ceres* (general topic, bimonthly, a review of agriculture and development), *Unasylva* (forestry, quarterly), *World Animal Review* (quarterly), *State of Food and Agriculture* (annual), *Quarterly Bulletin of Statistics*, *FAO Production Yearbook*, *Commodity Review and Outlook*, *Plant Protection Bulletin* (quarterly) and FAO's yearbooks on trade, fertilizers, forest products, fishery statistics and animal health.

Grass-roots publications, training manuals, film strips and radio and video programmes were produced, covering a wide array of topics, from improved farming techniques to animal husbandry, aquaculture and soil conservation. To reach the millions of small farmers and extension workers who could not use the organization's official languages (Arabic, Chinese, English, French, Spanish), FAO encouraged the adaptation, translation and distribution of its publications in local languages. It also published a series of handbooks on farm systems management for seven developing countries and helped publish the first complete review in English of livestock breeds in the USSR.

Secretariat

At the end of 1989, the number of staff employed at FAO headquarters was 3,175, including 1,175 in the Professional and higher categories. Field project personnel and those in regional and country offices numbered 3,052, including 1,302 in the Professional and higher categories and 1,750 in the General Service category. There were also 70 Associate Experts working at headquarters and 311 at regional and country offices or in the field.

Budget

The FAO regular programme budget was financed by the organization's 158 member States according to a scale of contributions set by the FAO Conference. The Conference in 1989 approved a total working budget for 1990-1991 of $568.8 million, an increase of $76.4 million over the previous biennium, mostly to cover rising costs. Unpaid arrears amounted to some $175 million.

NOTE: For further details on FAO activities in 1989, see the annual report, *FAO in 1989.*

HEADQUARTERS AND OTHER OFFICES

HEADQUARTERS
Food and Agriculture Organization of the United Nations
Viale delle Termi di Caracalla
00100 Rome, Italy
Telephone: (39) (6) 52251
Fax: (39) (6) 5225 3152
Telex: 6585 FAO I
E-mail: telex-room@fao.org
Internet sites: www.fao.org and gopher.fao.org

NEW YORK LIAISON OFFICE
Food and Agriculture Organization Liaison Office with the United Nations
1 United Nations Plaza, Room 1125
New York, N.Y. 10017, United States
Cable address: FOODAGRI NEW YORK
Telephone: (1) (212) 963-6036
Fax: (1) (212) 888-6188
E-mail: FAO-LONY@field.fao.org

FAO also maintained liaison offices in Washington, D.C., Geneva, Brussels and Tokyo; regional offices in Accra, Ghana; Bangkok, Thailand; Cairo, Egypt; Santiago, Chile; and subregional offices in Harare, Zimbabwe; Apia, Samoa; Budapest, Hungary; and Bridgetown, Barbados.

Chapter IV

United Nations Educational, Scientific and Cultural Organization (UNESCO)

The United Nations Educational, Scientific and Cultural Organization (UNESCO) continued throughout 1989 to promote co-operation among nations in education, natural and social sciences, culture and communication. To pave the way for the future, particular attention was given during the year to increasing the efficiency of UNESCO, bringing its work more into the public eye, enhancing its credibility and developing its operational capabilities.

The twenty-fifth session of the UNESCO General Conference, which convened at the organization's headquarters in Paris (17 October–16 November), adopted the Convention on Technical and Vocational Education and approved the medium-term plan for 1990-1995, as well as the programme and budget for 1990-1991. The third medium-term plan set out priorities for future action in the organization's spheres of competence, striking a balance between continuity and innovation, with a view to responding more effectively to the changing needs of the world community, particularly the developing countries and disadvantaged groups.

Membership of UNESCO increased in 1989 to 161 States (plus three associate members) with the admission of the Cook Islands, Djibouti and Kiribati.

Education

During the year, UNESCO educational programmes focused on fighting illiteracy, expanding primary education and formulating new education policies to meet the demands of the twenty-first century. The organization continued as lead agency in preparations for the International Literacy Year (ILY) (see PART THREE, Chapter XII) and for the World Conference on Education for All in 1990, the latter in co-ordination with the World Bank, the United Nations Development Programme (UNDP) and the United Nations Children's Fund (UNICEF). The programme for ILY was launched at a ceremony at UN Headquarters on 6 December. UNESCO also undertook a wide range of projects and publications aimed at improving child and adult education; modernizing science, mathematics and technology teaching; promoting educational equality for girls and women; facilitating access to schooling for rural populations; and promoting the right to education

for marginalized groups, such as disabled persons, refugees and migrant workers.

UNESCO co-operated in framing national, regional and international strategies and plans for the eradication of illiteracy by the year 2000 and conducted several national and regional workshops for the training of key literacy personnel. During the year, the organization awarded four literacy prizes: the Nadezhda K. Krupskaya Prize to the Jamaican Movement for the Advancement of Literacy; the International Reading Association Literacy Award to the Adult Education Department of the University of Ibadan, Nigeria; the Noma Prize to the Directorate of Community Education of the Ministry of Education and Culture of Indonesia; and the Iraq Literacy Prize to the Secretariat of State for Literacy and Religious Education in Mauritania.

The forty-first session of the International Conference on Education (Geneva, 9-17 January) focused on the diversification of post-secondary education in the light of the employment situation. An international congress on education and informatics (Paris, 12-21 April), attended by some 500 participants from 90 member States and by 30 international and non-governmental organizations, highlighted ways of making better use of informatics to develop and improve educational processes and systems.

Natural sciences and environment

UNESCO continued to promote co-operation in science and technology for development through training and research courses, workshops and seminars for specialists, most of them from developing countries, on biology, biotechnology, chemistry, mathematics and physics.

The intergovernmental programme on Man and the Biosphere (MAB) continued to advance interdisciplinary research on and training in land resource management through a series of international research networks and 293 biosphere reserves in 74 countries, to which seven new reserves were added. The organization issued the first publications in the newly launched MAB Book Series and MAB Digest Series and continued publishing its quarterly review *Nature and Resources*.

The Intergovernmental Oceanographic Commission implemented programmes covering ocean sciences and services, education and mutual assistance. It promoted research on ocean dynamics and climate, living and non-living resources, marine pollution and ocean mapping. Under the Integrated Global Ocean Services System, ocean data were collected jointly with the World Meteorological Organization through drifting buoys and about 300 observation ships from 26 nations. Some 550 scientists and technicians were trained through courses and workshops in Africa, Asia and Central and Latin America on data and information management, marine geology, physical oceanography, marine pollution research and monitoring, fish recruitment estimations and sea-level measurement. Thirty grants were awarded for shipboard training and study at oceanographic institutions.

The International Hydrological Programme completed its third phase (1984-1989), with the combined efforts of 145 co-operating member States, 9 participating international scientific and non-governmental organizations, more than 30 national and international organizations and several hundred individual water experts.

UNESCO trained some 300 engineering staff in curriculum design and innovative teaching methodology, educated 40 students, mostly from the Mediterranean and the Middle East, in earthquake engineering and took steps towards the creation of a first UNESCO masters degree course in energy engineering.

As part of its human settlements programme, UNESCO continued working on the rehabilitation of the Barrio Rio Salado, a squatter settlement of 4,500-5,000 people in La Romana, Dominican Republic. A water supply and sewage system was installed as a first step towards creating necessary infrastructures and socio-cultural facilities. The organization contributed to similar rehabilitation projects in Córdoba, Argentina, and Caracas, Venezuela.

With 90 established national committees, the International Geological Correlation Programme, undertaken jointly with the International Union of Geological Sciences, continued to stimulate international collaboration in the earth sciences through 51 research projects in which scientists from 122 countries were involved. Geological maps of Africa and Asia were completed and work continued on the geological maps of Europe and a geological map of the world.

In environmental education, emphasis was placed on improving and disseminating environmental information, innovation in content and methods of such education, and drawing greater attention to environmental issues in national educational policies, plans and programmes. UNESCO-supported studies and pilot projects focused on issues such as incorporating environmental education into agricultural education, the concept and development of environmental ethics, and, within the framework of the World Decade for Cultural Development (1988-1997), the role of ecomuseums and the natural and cultural heritage in the promotion of environmental education.

Social and human sciences

The International Congress on Peace in the Minds of Men (Yamoussoukro, Côte d'Ivoire, 26 June–1 July), organized by UNESCO in co-operation with the Houphouët-Boigny International Foundation for Peace, adopted the Yamoussoukro Declaration, which defined peace positively—not as the mere absence of war—and called for development of a "peace culture" based on justice among human beings and a harmonious partnership of humankind with the environment. The UNESCO Prize for Peace Education was awarded to the International Peace Research Association and to Robert Muller (France), Chancellor of the United Nations University for Peace in Costa Rica.

UNESCO organized or co-operated in training sessions, seminars and workshops on human rights in a number of countries in 1989. An international meeting of experts (Ottawa, Canada, December) discussed implementation in UNESCO's fields of competence of the two 1966 International Covenants on Human Rights. In co-operation with the World Federation of Modern Language Associations, an international symposium was held on languages and human rights (Paris, 25 April). To study the concept of the rights of peoples and the relationship of those rights with human rights, UNESCO organized an international meeting of experts (Paris, 27-30 November).

As part of its programme dedicated to eliminating prejudice, intolerance and racism, UNESCO emphasized teacher training and commissioned a study on discriminatory stereotypes in school textbooks and children's books. It also undertook a variety of activities to support the struggle against *apartheid* in South Africa and supported a wide variety of projects relating to women, including the contribution of women to development, as well as literacy and civic education for women in five countries in Africa, the Arab States and Asia. Co-operation with international youth organizations was stepped up and activities aimed at associating young people with development were carried out. An interregional group and several studies addressed the effects of structural adjustment policies and highlighted proposals that could mitigate their negative impact on socio-cultural life. Also in 1989, a new framework of co-operation was negotiated between UNESCO and the World Bank, which resulted in collaboration that extended beyond education to sectors such as the sciences and technology, the environment, statistics and the development of human resources.

Culture

UNESCO functioned as lead agency for the World Decade for Cultural Development (1988-1997) (see PART THREE, Chapter XII). It designated 231 of 300 submitted projects as Decade activities, while 48 new projects in the arts, crafts, documentation, the collection and safeguarding of cultural traditions, and the media were financed by the International Fund for the Promotion of Culture.

The World Heritage Committee, established under the 1972 Convention concerning the Protection of the World Cultural and Natural Heritage, held its thirteenth session (Paris, 11-15 December). Seven sites were added to the World Heritage List, bringing to 322 the number of cultural and natural properties in 69 countries protected by the Convention, to which 111 States were parties in 1989. Within the framework of its programme for training young creative and performing artists, UNESCO awarded short-term travel scholarships to candidates from different geocultural regions and working in different disciplines.

During the year, two new campaigns for the safeguarding of cultural heritage were launched, raising the number of such campaigns in progress to 24. Advisory services were provided for preservation projects in 20 countries and for museological projects in seven countries. UNESCO continued efforts to preserve cultural identities through the publication of histories of Africa, Latin America, the Caribbean and Central Asian civilizations, as well as its work on Islamic culture. Seventeen titles were produced on cassette and compact disc as part of the UNESCO collection of traditional music.

Mexican and Bengal poetry anthologies were issued as the first two volumes in the new UNESCO Library of World Poetry series. Among its regular publications, the magazines *Copyright Bulletin* and *Museum* continued to be published quarterly.

Communication

Focusing on the socio-cultural impact of new communication technologies, UNESCO supported a variety of studies and research projects. The *World Communication Report* was published, comprising basic information on communication statistics worldwide, training and research institutions, and new technology. The UNESCO *Mass Communication Thesaurus* was revised and updated. An international survey of some 500 communication training institutions was completed. At UNESCO's initiative, the Arab Network of Documentation Centres on Communication Research and Policies was strengthened.

In its efforts to develop communication worldwide, UNESCO gave assistance to nine communication training institutions in all regions and trained more than 2,000 communication specialists in 30 workshops and courses. The 35-member Intergovernmental Council of the International Programme for the Development of Communication (IPDC), at its tenth session (Paris, 7-13 March), allocated some $1.6 million to 18 projects. The IPDC-UNESCO prize for rural communication, awarded every two years in recognition of innovative activity in communication in rural communities of developing countries, was awarded in 1989 to the Asociación Nacional de Agricultores Pequeños of Cuba and the Acción Cultural Popular of Colombia.

UNESCO's General Information Programme continued to assist countries, particularly in the developing world, to increase their capacity to gather, organize, diffuse and utilize scientific information. UNESCO supported 11 national and subregional meetings on the formulation and implementation of information policies in developing countries, including those in Bangladesh, Jordan, Senegal and Uruguay. A *Handbook on the Formulation, Approval, Implementation and Operation of National Information Policies* was published. The Programme helped to strengthen co-operation between regional information networks by initiating pilot projects on community information services, issuing guidelines for the use of environmental information, and training some 75 decision makers and key scientists. Two international symposia were held on the revival of the Library of Alexandria, Egypt.

Secretariat

As at 31 December 1989, UNESCO had a full-time staff of 2,727, of which 1,045, drawn from 128 nationalities, were in the Professional or higher categories and 1,682 in the General Service category.

Budget

Regular budget expenditures in 1988-1989 totalled $336.4 million, or $14.4 million less than the budgeted amount of $350.8 million. Extrabudgetary expenditures totalled $155.5 million, of which $92.1 million was financed through UNDP, the United Nations Population Fund and other UN sources, and $63.4 million from other extrabudgetary sources. The General Conference in 1989 approved regular budget appropriations of $378.8 million for the 1990-1991 biennium.

NOTE: For further details of UNESCO's activities in 1989, see *Report of the Director-General, 1988-1989.*

HEADQUARTERS AND OTHER OFFICES

HEADQUARTERS
UNESCO House
7 Place de Fontenoy
75352 Paris 07-SP, France
  Cable address: UNESCO PARIS
  Telephone: (33) (1) 45-68-10-00
  Fax: (33) (1) 45-67-16-90
  Telex: 204461 PARIS
      270602 PARIS

NEW YORK LIAISON OFFICE
United Nations Educational, Scientific and Cultural
  Organization
2 United Nations Plaza, Room 900
New York, N.Y. 10017, United States
  Cable address: UNESCORG NEWYORK
  Telephone: (1) (212) 963-5995
  Fax: (1) (212) 355-5627

UNESCO also maintained liaison offices in Geneva and Vienna.

Chapter V

World Health Organization (WHO)

The World Health Organization (WHO), established in 1948, continued during 1989 to serve as the directing and co-ordinating authority on international health. The World Health Assembly, the governing body of WHO, at its forty-second session (Geneva, 8-19 May), endorsed proposals related to the work of the organization in the following areas: strengthening the basic infrastructure of health systems based on primary health care; improving management, information support and research capabilities; ensuring the development and transfer of appropriate technology to countries; developing and reorienting human resources in line with new strategies; and mobilizing and making best use of all possible financial and material resources for sustainable development. The Assembly also adopted a plan of action to eradicate poliomyelitis, as well as vigorous measures against malaria, dracunculiasis, acquired immunodeficiency syndrome (AIDS), and the abuse of tobacco, alcohol and drugs. It approved a budget of $653.7 million for the 1990-1991 biennium.

During 1989, the membership of WHO remained at 166, with one associate member.

Strategy for health for all

The Assembly endorsed the second report on monitoring progress in implementing strategies for health for all and urged action on five critical challenges to the health sector: sustained political commitments to the principles of primary health care and the reduction of social inequity; intensification of efforts to strengthen managerial capacities; strengthening health infrastructure, particularly on the district and community levels; strengthening health research and development for the implementation of national health strategies; and increased support to the least developed countries, especially those with high infant mortality.

As part of the organization's continuing support of education for health-for-all leaders, during 1989 some 200 senior officials from approximately 35 countries participated in interregional, inter-country and national colloquiums and training workshops in Guyana, India, Indonesia, Thailand, the United Republic of Tanzania and Zimbabwe.

Health policy and infrastructure

The International Conference for the Tenth Revision of the International Classification of Diseases (Geneva, 26 September–2 October) proposed a new coding system that would allow for the coding of almost twice as many conditions in classifying morbidity for hospital inpatients and general medical practice. The Conference also considered proposals to facilitate trend assessments and projection studies and the comparison of health information between countries.

To provide a link between the producers and users of health systems research and clinical epidemiology, a new international newsletter, *Bridge*, began publication in 1989 in collaboration with the International Clinical Epidemiology Network and the Foundation for Health Services Research, and with the support of the Rockefeller Foundation.

The third meeting of the Consultative Group on the Organization of Health Systems Based on Primary Health Care was held in Manila, Philippines, in March to review the recommendations of the Riga (Latvia) meeting of the previous year, with particular emphasis on health financing and management, primary health care in urban areas, quality assurance in health systems, and health in public policy.

Also during the year, in collaboration with other international organizations and Governments, WHO participated in a variety of intersectoral initiatives related to primary health care systems, including a study on the effects of development policies on health status and training courses on equipment maintenance management.

The organization also worked to redefine co-operation in the area of human resources development, revising policy and refining the guidance given in manuals, reports of expert committees and study groups. The 1989 report of the Expert Committee on Management of Human Resources for Health stressed opportunities to improve motivation and productivity through the application of sound managerial principles and techniques. An interregional seminar on financing human resources for health was held in Bangkok, Thailand, in March and an interregional workshop on nursing leadership development was conducted in Copenhagen, Denmark, in August.

Following the 1988 World Conference on Medical Education, ministerial meetings in 1989 (in July in Abuja, Nigeria, for the African region and in October in Jakarta, Indonesia, for South-East Asia) discussed the establishment of a regional task force on medical education in order to monitor progress in curriculum reorientation.

In relation to national drug policies, more than 100 countries had adopted or adapted the WHO Model List of Essential Drugs by the end of the year. WHO continued to promote the scientific evaluation of traditional remedies to ensure that the selection of medicinal plants in health systems balanced efficacy and side-effects. The fifth International Conference of Drug Regulatory Authorities (Paris, October) discussed ways to develop and introduce appropriate national policies, regulations and control measures to ensure the safety of remedies. The organization also adopted a standard acupuncture nomenclature for international use.

Public information and education for health

In addition to celebrating World Health Day—under the theme ''Let's Talk Health'' in 1989—WHO continued to support a No-Tobacco Day on 31 May and a World AIDS Day on 1 December. Growing international awareness of the need for measures to make health education more effective led to a Conference on Effectiveness of Health Education in Rotterdam, Netherlands, which stressed the importance of evaluation.

Through inter-country workshops in several regions, WHO continued to emphasize the role of young people by involving them in the promotional aspects of health development. In Europe, for example, it collaborated on a project to promote the health of young people, underlining the importance of integrating AIDS-related education programmes for young people and school-age children.

WHO also published a manual on training in the community for people with disabilities, developed guidelines and training material for intermediate-level personnel for specific countries and encouraged modifications in the training of rehabilitation specialists.

Health protection and promotion

A WHO Interregional Workshop on Leadership and Participation of Women in Maternal and Child Health and Family Planning (Mauritius, December), held with the support of the United Nations Population Fund (UNFPA), discussed the involvement of women and women's organizations in programmes and policies to enable them to regulate their own fertility as a means of both improving the health of mothers and children and enabling women to participate fully in social and overall development. In July, WHO convened a consultation in Geneva on emerging needs in family health for the 1990s, in the broad context of reproductive health and child growth and development. Workshops and seminars facilitated by WHO focused on the benefits of improved water supply and sanitation facilities for women (Kupang, Indonesia), the control of iodine deficiency disorders (New Delhi, India), community safety programme planning (Indonesia, March), epidemiology and prevention of burn injuries (Cyprus), and improvement of emergency medical services (Seoul, Republic of Korea).

In the area of food and nutrition, WHO participated in a symposium on women and nutrition during the fifteenth session of the Administrative Committee on Co-ordination's Sub-Committee on Nutrition (New York, February/March), which considered as closely related issues the role of women in determining nutrition of households and societies and the nutritional status of women.

The First World Conference on Accident and Injury Prevention (Stockholm, Sweden, September), co-sponsored by WHO, discussed experiences in community safety and adopted a manifesto on the essential principles for a global policy for safety in communities. A meeting of representatives of ministries of health of five African countries convened in Brazzaville, Congo, in April to prepare policy for the health sector in road safety as WHO's contribution to the Second African Road Safety Congress organized by the Economic Commission for Africa (Addis Ababa, Ethiopia, October).

As to the protection and promotion of mental health, the eighth meeting of the Global Co-ordinating Group for the WHO Mental Health Programme in October emphasized the need to maintain a broadly defined mental health programme dealing with human behaviour in health and ill-health, as well as with specific problems, such as those linked to alcohol and drug abuse, and with the prevention and treatment of mental and neurological disorders. As part of a programme undertaken with the Office of the United Nations High Commissioner for Refugees to produce training manuals on mental health services in refugee camps, WHO made visits to camps of displaced Khmer populations on the Thai border under the jurisdiction of the UN Border Relief Operations to assess mental health and psycho-social problems and to recommend preventive and remedial measures. In October, WHO finalized the first of three instruments to permit standardized assessment of mental disorders. During the year, the organization convened experts from its network of collaborating centres on biological psychiatry and psychopharmacology to produce consensus statements on the pharmacology of depressive disorders, the pharmacology of schizophrenia and pharmacotherapy in old age.

Health of specific populations

WHO continued its advocacy of safe motherhood, sponsoring workshops and training in midwifery and essential obstetric care with the financial support and collaboration of other UN agencies and organizations and publishing a monograph on preventing maternal deaths.

The Global Programme on Health of the Elderly was moved in 1989 to WHO headquarters in order to respond with an integrated approach to the growing problems associated with the aging. The Programme continued to focus on community-based health care for the elderly, with particular attention on information, research and ways to preserve and encourage care in the family.

Also during the year, a joint WHO/UNFPA/UNICEF statement was published on objectives for improved adolescent reproductive health, and the tenth meeting of the Joint International Labour Organisation (ILO)/WHO Committee on Occupational Health published its report on the epidemiology of work-related diseases and accidents.

Environment, health and development

In 1989, the WHO Director-General expressed his intention to redefine and restructure the organization's approach to environmental health and proposed the convening of a high-level technical expert commission on health and the environment to review current knowledge of the impact of environmental factors on health. The commission's finding would form the basis of the WHO contribution to the UN Conference on Environment and Development in 1992.

During the year, WHO collaborated with the United Nations Environment Programme (UNEP), the World Bank and the Food and Agriculture Organization of the United Nations in formulating health and technical guidelines for waste-water reuse in agriculture and aquaculture. The joint WHO/ILO/UNEP International Programme on Chemical Safety continued to provide information on the risks of potentially toxic chemicals to human health and the environment, and guidance in the safe use of chemicals. The FAO/International Atomic Energy Agency (IAEA)/WHO International Consultative Group on Food Irradiation, which had a membership of 30 countries, sponsored a consultation (Geneva, May/June) to propose microbiological criteria for foods to be further processed by methods including irradiation. The first phase of the Human Exposure Assessment Location Project was completed. An interregional training course in nuclear medicine for developing countries (Berlin, September/October) was held in collaboration with IAEA. In addition,

WHO conducted seminars and workshops in several regions on health and housing and on urbanization and health.

Disease prevention and control

Throughout the year, the global number of AIDS cases continued to rise rapidly. By 31 December 1989, 203,559 cases had been reported for 152 of 177 countries and areas. However, taking into account under-reporting and delays in reporting, the actual number was estimated at about 600,000 cases by the end of the year. In June, the annual International Conference on AIDS was held in Montreal, Canada. In November, an international conference in Paris issued the Paris Declaration on Women, Children and AIDS. The Global Commission on AIDS, established in 1989 to provide the WHO Director-General with broad policy and scientific guidance, held its first and second meetings in Geneva in May and in Brazzaville, Congo, in November. WHO continued to assert its directing and co-ordinating role by further developing its global strategy for the prevention and control of AIDS. Under the Global Programme on AIDS, WHO consultants undertook more than 1,300 missions, and 75 posts were established in national programmes. At the end of the year, 120 countries had short-term AIDS programmes and 95 countries had formulated a medium-term plan for their national AIDS programmes

The organization's cancer control programme remained based on three main priorities: prevention; early detection followed by efficient therapy; and palliative care, including cancer pain relief. In July, an expert committee recommended expansion of the cancer pain relief programme and established guidelines for the control of other cancer symptoms and the training of health care professionals. WHO sponsored workshops on national cancer control plans in China, Indonesia and the United Arab Emirates. It also received requests for assistance with national cancer control programmes from Cameroon, Cuba and Spain.

Prevention continued to be the main objective of WHO's cardiovascular diseases programme. In September, the third international WHO MONICA (multinational monitoring of trends and determinants in cardiovascular diseases) congress was held in Nice, France, in conjunction with the eleventh European Congress on Cardiology. A MONICA session also took place at the second International Conference on Preventive Cardiology in Washington, D.C., in June.

The WHO Diarrhoeal Diseases Control Programme collaborated with more than 100 countries in the implementation of national programmes and related research. Some 200 diarrhoeal diseases control training units had been established in 76 countries since 1980. In addition, more than 2,500 participants from some 140 countries had attended programme managers' courses and training courses for national health staff. During the year, WHO, in collaboration with UNICEF, initiated local production of oral rehydration salts (ORS) in three countries, bringing the total number of producing countries to 61. The number of packets of ORS or similar products produced in 1989 was estimated at 350 million litre equivalents, of which more than 75 per cent were manufactured in developing countries.

Through its Expanded Programme on Immunization, WHO continued its efforts to reduce morbidity resulting from diphtheria, pertussis, tetanus, measles, poliomyelitis and tuberculosis. Figures issued in 1989 indicated that at least one of the vaccines under the Programme reached some 73 per cent of the developing world. However, differences in the success of the immunization programmes between the WHO regions generally reflected their levels of socio-economic development. In Africa, for example, success ranged from 12 per cent in Guinea to 99 per cent in Botswana. Following its call in 1988 for the eradication of poliomyelitis by the year 2000, the World Health Assembly endorsed two additional goals for the Expanded Programme on Immunization to be achieved by 1995: the elimination of neonatal tetanus and the reduction of measles incidence by 90 per cent.

The number of registered cases of leprosy decreased to 3.85 million in 1989 from 5.4 million in 1985, a 28.7 per cent drop within a four-year period. In South-East Asia, which had 71.4 per cent of the world's registered leprosy cases, improvement of case-finding and holding and expansion of coverage with multidrug therapy produced a decline from 3.7 million cases in 1985 to 2.75 million in 1989. In Africa, which had 470,000 registered cases, Governments participating in the WHO interregional conference on leprosy control (Brazzaville, Congo, November) affirmed their commitment to multidrug therapy. In the western Pacific region, the number of cases decreased from 250,000 to 190,000 cases between 1982 and 1989. A number of countries in the South Pacific reported that very few cases remained.

A report published in 1989 on the world malaria situation, 1986-1987, indicated that about 30 per cent of the world population lived in areas where successful malaria eradication was being maintained, while 34 per cent lived in endemic areas where malaria transmission had returned and the situation was unstable or deteriorating and 9 per cent lived in areas where no national antimalarial programme had been implemented, mainly in tropical Africa. In November, the nineteenth meeting of the WHO Expert Committee on Malaria provided practical guidance for malaria-endemic countries on diagnosis and treatment, epidemiological indicators, criteria for selecting areas where specific vector control might be introduced and the management of malaria epidemics.

Secretariat

As at 31 December 1989, WHO employed a total of 4,453 full-time staff on permanent and fixed-term contracts. Of those, 1,468 staff members from 130 nationalities were in the Professional and higher categories and 2,985 were in the General Service category.

Budget

The WHO working budget for the 1988-1989 biennium, as revised by the Director-General in 1988, was $609 million. The forty-second World Health Assembly approved an effective working budget of $653.7 million for the 1990-1991 biennium.

NOTE: For further details of WHO activities, see *The Work of WHO, 1988-1989, Biennial Report of the Director-General.*

HEADQUARTERS AND OTHER OFFICES

HEADQUARTERS
World Health Organization
20 Avenue Appia
CH-1211 Geneva 27, Switzerland
  Cable address: UNISANTE GENEVA
  Telephone: (41) (22) 791-21-11
  Fax: (41) (22) 791-07-46
  Telex: 415416

WHO OFFICE AT THE UNITED NATIONS
2 United Nations Plaza
New York, N.Y. 10017, United States
  Cable address: UNISANTE NEW YORK
  Telephone: (1) (212) 963-6001
  Fax: (1) (212) 223-2920
  Telex: 234292

WHO also maintained regional offices in Alexandria, Egypt; Brazzaville, Congo; Copenhagen, Denmark; Manila, Philippines; New Delhi, India; and Washington, D.C.

Chapter VI

International Bank for Reconstruction and Development (World Bank)

The International Bank for Reconstruction and Development (World Bank) continued during 1989 to assist developing countries to progress economically and socially by providing loans and other assistance. Lending commitments by the Bank totalled $16.4 billion for the fiscal year ending 30 June 1989, an 11 per cent increase over fiscal 1988. During the year, the Bank sought to strengthen its efforts in several key policy areas, including reducing poverty in the developing world; increasing assistance to highly indebted middle-income countries undertaking adjustment measures; integrating environmental considerations into its policy and operational work; and launching an action programme to provide an increased role for the private sector in the Bank's developing member countries.

Membership in the Bank rose to 152 in 1989 with the admission of Angola.

Lending operations

In the fiscal year ending 30 June 1989, the World Bank made a total of 119 loans to 38 countries, amounting to $16,433,200,000. This brought the cumulative total of loan commitments by the Bank since it began operations in 1946 to $171,482 million.

In the agriculture and rural development sector, the Bank made 24 loans to 17 countries, totalling $2,066.1 million; major borrowers included Algeria, India, Morocco and Turkey. Nine loans totalling $2,223 million were made to strengthen development finance companies in seven countries, including China, Mexico, the Philippines and Venezuela. Another nine loans totalling $441.6 million were extended by the Bank to education projects in nine countries, including Colombia, Morocco and Tunisia. The Bank extended $3,408 million in loans to 11 countries for energy projects; the largest recipients included India, Indonesia and Mexico. Those three countries were also among nine countries receiving $1,858 million in loans for the industrial sector. Ten non-project loans totalling $2,692 million were granted during fiscal 1989.

For population, health and nutrition projects, the Bank granted loans totalling $399.5 million to seven countries, including Brazil, Jordan and Turkey. Five countries, including Colombia, Indonesia and Nigeria, received loans totalling $585 million to support small-scale enterprises. The Bank made two loans to Argentina and one to Uruguay, totalling $41 million for technical assistance, and two loans totalling $53.1 million were granted to Ecuador and Fiji for telecommunications projects. Ten countries received 13 loans amounting to $1,137.7 million for the development of their transportation systems and seven urban projects totalling $959 million were approved for six countries. The Bank also granted $569.2 million in loans for water supply and sewerage programmes in five countries.

Economic Development Institute

Fiscal year 1989 marked the final year of a five-year plan instituted by the Economic Development Institute (EDI) in 1984. During that period, EDI activities, which focused on the transfer of knowledge rather than of funds, shifted towards policy-related training in the form of senior policy seminars and of macroeconomic and sector-management seminars. Some 44 per cent of EDI's training and assistance activities focused on sub-Saharan Africa in fiscal 1989, compared with 30 per cent in fiscal 1984.

The Institute's work programme in fiscal 1989 was strongly oriented towards structural-adjustment policy and implementation issues at the macro-economic level, including the social costs of adjustment. At the sectoral level, increased attention was given to issues in the financial sector, health, natural-resource management and public-expenditure planning. External sources of support for EDI programmes in developing countries continued to expand. While UNDP continued to be the largest external contributor to EDI, bilateral aid agencies, the World Health Organization and the UN Commission on Human Settlements were important collaborators with the Institute.

Co-financing

The total volume of co-financing anticipated in support of World Bank–assisted operations reached $9.9 billion in fiscal 1989. The Bank contributed some $9.3 billion for 131 co-financed projects, an increase of about $5.5 billion over fiscal 1988. For the first time, more than half of all Bank-assisted projects and programmes attracted some form of co-financing. The largest source of co-financing continued to be official bilateral aid agencies and multilateral development institutions, which, together, accounted for $5.7 billion. Export-credit flows increased, reaching an estimated $3.2 billion, while commercial bank co-financing accounted for $1.1 billion.

Fiscal 1989 was the second year of a three-year, multi-donor special programme of assistance (SPA) in support of adjustment programmes in sub-Saharan Africa. In addition to $2.3 billion in co-financing to the African region as a whole, some $1.1 billion in co-ordinated financing (quick-disbursing financing administered by donors) was provided to the group of 22 countries eligible for SPA funding.

Financing activities

During fiscal 1989, the Bank raised an equivalent of $9.3 billion through medium- and long-term borrowings in 17 currencies. About 99 per cent of its borrowings, after swaps, were in United States dollars, Japanese yen, deutsche mark and Swiss francs.

Of the 710 new borrowing operations that the Bank conducted during the year, 703 were in the private sector, accounting for 84 per cent ($7.8 bil-lion) of total new funds borrowed. The Bank's outstanding debt, net of discounts and premia, decreased by $4.2 billion to $80.3 billion as at 30 June 1989. Those obligations were denominated in 23 different currencies and currency units.

Capitalization

As at 30 June 1989, the subscribed capital of the Bank totalled $115.7 billion, an increase of $24.2 billion over fiscal 1988.

Income, expenditures and reserves

The Bank's gross revenues totalled $8.3 billion in fiscal 1989, down $275 million, or 3.2 per cent, from the previous year. Net income was $1.1 billion, $263 million less than it should have been, owing to interest income not accrued for countries that were six months or more in arrears on debt service to the Bank. Expenses decreased by 5 per cent to $7.1 billion; administrative costs totalled $462 million.

Secretariat

As at 30 June 1989, the World Bank staff totalled 5,695, of whom 3,648 were in the Professional or higher categories, drawn from 116 countries.

NOTE: For further details regarding the Bank's activities, see *The World Bank Annual Report 1989*.

HEADQUARTERS AND OTHER OFFICE

The World Bank
1818 H Street, N.W.
Washington, D.C. 20433, United States
Cable address: INTBAFRAD WASHINGTONDC
Telephone: (1) (202) 477-1234
Fax: (1) (202) 477-6391
Telex: MCI 64145 WORLDBANK
　　　MCI 248423 WORLDBANK
World Wide Web: HTTP://WWW.WORLDBANK.ORG
E-mail: BOOKS@WORLDBANK.ORG

The World Bank Mission to the United Nations
809 United Nations Plaza, Suite 900
New York, N.Y. 10017, United States
Cable address: INTBAFRAD NEWYORK
Telephone: (1) (212) 963-6008
Fax: (1) (212) 697-7020

Chapter VII

International Finance Corporation (IFC)

Established in 1956 as an independent affiliate of the International Bank for Reconstruction and Development (World Bank), the International Finance Corporation (IFC) continued in 1989 to further economic growth in developing member countries by promoting productive private investment. IFC provided long-term loans and risk capital without government guarantees to private sector enterprises. It also continued to provide the technical assistance and advisory services needed to make good use of investment opportunities in developing countries and to encourage the flow of private capital to them.

During fiscal year 1989 (1 July 1988–30 June 1989), IFC membership remained at 133.

Financial and advisory services

During fiscal 1989, IFC approved 90 investments in 37 countries with a total value of $1,709 million and overall project costs of $9,694 million. It mobilized $8,403 million in funds from other investors and lenders for its projects, up from $3,971 million in fiscal 1988. Disbursements for IFC's own account increased to $870 million, 14 per cent more than in fiscal 1988.

During IFC's latest five-year programme, which ended in 1989, the volume of investment approvals grew by an average of 28 per cent per year. In fiscal 1989, the Corporation approved $1,291 million in investments of all types for its own account, compared with $391 million in fiscal 1984. The IFC-disbursed portfolio also grew during the five-year programme, from $1,447 million in fiscal 1984 to $2,793 million at the end of fiscal 1989. IFC disbursed $749 million in loans and $121 million in equity in fiscal 1989, compared with $212 million in loans and $26 million in equity in 1984. Funds mobilized by IFC through joint financings, syndications and underwritings increased by some 37 per cent per year to $8,403 million, compared with $2,092 million in fiscal 1984.

During fiscal 1989, IFC established a Corporate Finance Services Group to strengthen its capacity to provide advisory services in two areas: the restructuring of potentially viable enterprises needing assistance in coping with a difficult economic environment and the privatization of public sector enterprises, as developing member countries sought to increase the role of the private sector in their economies. The Corporation also established

a new International Securities Group within the Capital Markets Department to assist corporations in developing countries to raise capital on international markets.

A new IFC office was opened in Casablanca, Morocco, to serve the Maghreb countries, and the Caribbean Project Development Facility opened an office in Barbados to make its services more accessible to entrepreneurs in the eastern Caribbean.

Regional projects

The 90 new projects approved by IFC in fiscal 1989 included one regional project and one of international scope. Of the total approvals, 38, accounting for $418 million, were located in low-income developing countries with per capita incomes of $835 or less.

Sub-Saharan Africa remained one of the Corporation's priority areas. The Africa Project Development Facility, launched in 1986 in co-operation with the UN Development Programme and the African Development Bank, provided assistance to small and medium-sized enterprises in Africa. In fiscal 1989, IFC launched the African Management Services Company to address the need for better management in Africa by seconding senior executives to African enterprises for fixed terms and providing management training to local staff. Loans and equity financing totalling some $282 million were approved for 19 projects in Africa in 1989, including capital markets projects. IFC concentrated on promising sectors, such as mining, fishing, agribusiness, food processing and shipping. At the end of the fiscal year, IFC had committed investments of $624 million in 123 companies in 33 countries in Africa, consisting of $550 million in loans and $74 million in equity.

IFC investment in Asia focused on infrastructure projects, funding of small and medium-sized companies and advisory services. Infrastructure financing involved the use of both the build-operate-transfer (BOT) concept and the support of a few private companies already active in their respective fields. The Corporation's advisory work in the region included providing advice on privatization and BOT possibilities in Indonesia, Malaysia, Nepal, Pakistan and the Philippines, as well as undertaking a feasibility study in Thailand. During fiscal 1989, total financing of $321 million in loans and equity investments was approved for 25 projects in Asia, including capital markets projects. At the end of the fiscal year, IFC had committed investments of $729 million in 109 companies in 12 countries in Asia—$566 million in loans and $163 million in equity.

In Europe and the Middle East, IFC initiatives concentrated on expanding private sector participation in the manufacturing and service sectors. The majority of projects in the region were in Turkey and the Eastern European countries. During fiscal year 1989, IFC approved $259 million in loans and equity investments for 15 projects, including capital markets projects. At the end of the fiscal year, the Corporation had committed investments of $756 million in 74 companies in 12 countries in Europe and the Middle East—$685 million in loans and $71 million in equity.

Investment in Latin America and the Caribbean focused on the exploration for and development of natural resources, such as the mining, petrochemical and pulp industries. Total IFC financing in the region during fiscal 1989 amounted to $842 million for 30 projects, including capital markets projects. At the end of the fiscal year, the Corporation had committed investments of $1.9 billion in 160 companies in 22 countries in the region—$1.7 billion in loans and $236 million in equity.

Financial performance

In fiscal year 1989, IFC's net income reached $196.5 million, a 95 per cent increase over fiscal 1988. The increase was due in large part to the performance of the equity portfolio, which yielded capital gains of $118.6 million, compared with $32.9 million the previous year. The Corporation collected dividends of $30.8 million, compared with $15.5 million in fiscal 1988, and fees from investment and advisory services totalled $25.3 million, compared with $11.8 million in fiscal 1988.

Capital and retained earnings

The Corporation's net worth as at 30 June 1989 was $1,583 million, up from $1,288 million at the end of fiscal 1988. Paid-in capital totalled $948 million and retained earnings, including the fiscal year net income, amounted to $635 million. Some $165 million of IFC's subscribed capital had not been paid in at the end of fiscal 1989.

Secretariat

As at 30 June 1989, IFC's staff totalled 541 from 74 countries, including from 56 developing countries.

NOTE: For further details of IFC's activities, see *International Finance Corporation Annual Report 1989*, published by the Corporation.

HEADQUARTERS AND OTHER OFFICE

HEADQUARTERS
International Finance Corporation
1850 I Street, N.W.
Washington, D.C. 20433, United States
Telephone: (1) (202) 473-7711
Fax: (1) (202) 676-0365
E-mail: information @ifc.org
Library: library@ifc.org.

NEW YORK OFFICE
International Finance Corporation
809 United Nations Plaza, Suite 900
New York, N.Y. 10017, United States
Cable address: CORINTFIN NEWYORK
Telephone: (1) (212) 963-6008
Fax: (1) (212) 697-7020

Chapter VIII

International Development Association (IDA)

The International Development Association (IDA), which was established in 1960 as an affiliate of the International Bank for Reconstruction and Development (World Bank), continued to provide concessionary assistance, primarily to low-income countries and on easier terms than the Bank. During fiscal year 1989 (1 July 1988–30 June 1989), IDA concentrated on the very poor countries—those with an annual per capita gross national product of less than $480 (in 1987 United States dollars).

IDA resources, called credits to distinguish them from World Bank loans, were derived mostly from subscriptions in convertible currencies from members; general replenishments from its more industrialized members; and transfers from the Bank's net earnings. Credits were made only to Governments and had 35- to 40-year maturities, including a 10-year grace period, and were interest-free.

Negotiations for the ninth replenishment of IDA resources (IDA-9) were launched in February 1989 at a meeting of IDA deputies in Washington, D.C. The deputies then met in London on 17 and 18 May to consider issues related to allocation, eligibility and the size of the ninth replenishment. Further meetings were scheduled for the remainder of calendar year 1989 in Copenhagen, Denmark, Washington, D.C., and Kyoto, Japan.

As at 30 June 1989, cumulative IDA commitments totalled $52 billion. During fiscal 1989, IDA approved 115 credits totalling $4.93 billion to 43 developing countries. The majority of funding went to Africa, $2.3 billion to 28 countries, and Asia, $2.2 billion to nine countries. India was the largest borrower, with six credits amounting to $900.3 million, followed by China, with five credits totalling $515 million, and Bangladesh, with four credits totalling $423.1 million. Credits financed projects primarily in the agriculture and rural development, education, energy, industry, transportation, and population, health and nutrition sectors.

During the year, a total of 21 countries received 30 credits totalling $1.4 billion for agriculture and rural development. IDA granted credits totalling $141.7 million to assist development finance companies in eight countries. It also granted credits totalling $134.3 million to eight countries for technical assistance, five credits totalling $229.5 million for urban development, five credits totalling $222 million for water supply and sewerage projects, and 18 non-project credits totalling $726.5 million to assist 16 countries with economic recovery, structural adjustment and financial reform programmes. In addition, 10 countries received credits totalling $449.1 million for the education sector; eight received $455.6 million for the energy sector; four received $124.5 million for the industrial sector; five received $107.9 million for the telecommunications sector; 10 received $693.1 million for the transportation sector; and six received $223.5 million for projects related to population, health and nutrition.

IDA membership increased to 138 in 1989, with the admission of Angola.

Secretariat

Though legally and financially distinct from the World Bank, the staffing and headquarters of IDA are the same as those of the Bank.

NOTE: For further details regarding IDA activities, see *The World Bank Annual Report 1989.*

HEADQUARTERS AND OTHER OFFICE

HEADQUARTERS
International Development Association
1818 H Street, N.W.
Washington, D.C. 20433, U.S.A.

For cable address, telephone, fax and telex numbers, and World Wide Web address, see World Bank, p. 935.

NEW YORK OFFICE
International Development Association
809 United Nations Plaza, Suite 900
New York, N.Y. 10017, United States
  Cable address: INDEVAS NEW YORK
  Telephone: (1) (212) 963-6008
  Fax: (1) (212) 697-7020

Chapter IX

International Monetary Fund (IMF)

The International Monetary Fund (IMF) in 1989 continued to serve as a permanent forum for the discussion of global monetary issues and related economic matters, to assist its members to develop sound economic policies and to promote conditions conducive to a healthy world economy. The Fund's primary activities included advising on economic and financial policies; providing information and technical assistance; and making loans to members undertaking economic reforms to overcome balance-of-payments difficulties. Each member contributed to IMF's pool of financial resources—measured in special drawing rights (SDRs)—and the amount of its contribution determined each member's voting power and how much it could borrow from the Fund.

In 1989, IMF membership increased to 152, with the admission of Angola.

IMF facilities and policies

During fiscal year 1989, which covered the period 1 May 1988 to 30 April 1989, the Fund's Interim Committee of the Board of Governors encouraged the Executive Board—the Fund's permanent decision-making body—to strengthen surveillance in the areas of economic indicators and structural policies in order to improve the appropriateness, consistency and timely implementation of policies adopted by the industrial countries. IMF continued to monitor the international monetary system and to promote an adequate supply of international liquidity.

The Fund conducted consultations with member States annually or at intervals of up to 24 months to gather up-to-date economic and financial information, review economic policies and developments, examine members' fiscal, monetary and balance-of-payments accounts, and assess the impact of policies on exchange rates and external accounts. The Fund completed 99 full consultations in 1989—the fourth successive annual decline in the number of such consultations.

IMF's provision of financial resources to member States was contingent on certain conditions designed to encourage appropriate economic adjustment and ensure that the use of Fund credit was temporary and otherwise consistent with the Fund's purposes. Generally, the Fund provided direct financial support in the way of stand-by arrangements, covering adjustment programmes lasting one to two years, or extended arrangements, covering programmes of three years, with a possible one-year extension.

Low-income countries obtained concessional financial assistance under the structural adjustment facility (SAF), established in 1986, and the extended structural adjustment facility (ESAF), which became operational in 1988. At the end of fiscal year 1989, 62 countries were eligible to borrow under SAF and ESAF. As at 30 April 1989, commitments under SAF and ESAF totalled SDR 2.5 billion, up from SDR 1.4 billion a year earlier.

The Fund's compensatory and contingency financing facility was designed to help stabilize the earnings of countries exporting primary commodities. Under the facility's contingency mechanism, the Fund provided additional financing to countries whose structural adjustment programmes might be threatened by external disruptions that could cause economic variables to deviate from those originally forecast.

The Fund also provided emergency assistance to member countries to meet payments problems arising from sudden and unforeseen natural disasters. During fiscal 1989, emergency assistance was approved for Bangladesh for SDR 71.8 million and Jamaica for SDR 36.2 million.

Financial assistance

Commitments of Fund resources increased substantially during fiscal 1989. Amounts approved under stand-by, extended Fund facility, SAF and ESAF arrangements increased by about 50 per cent in fiscal 1989 to SDR 4.6 billion. The bulk of the 46 Fund arrangements in effect at the end of the fiscal year entailed relatively strict conditions, corresponding to drawings in the upper credit tranches.

While commitments of Fund resources increased, actual drawings in the General Department declined from SDR 4.1 billion in fiscal 1988 to SDR 2.1 billion in fiscal 1989. The Fund's concessional lending under SAF and ESAF increased from SDR 445 million to SDR 554 million, reflecting progress made by low-income member States in adopting structural adjustment programmes.

Repurchases and repayments in fiscal 1989 totalled SDR 6.7 billion, including advance repurchases by a number of countries whose external positions had improved. Outstanding Fund credit declined from SDR 29.5 billion as at 30 April 1988 to SDR 25.5 billion as at 30 April 1989.

During the fiscal year, 12 stand-by arrangements (Brazil, Cameroon, Guatemala, Hungary, Jamaica, Madagascar, Mali, Morocco, Nigeria, Pakistan, Trinidad and Tobago, Yugoslavia), one extended arrangement (Tunisia), four SAF arrangements (Equatorial Guinea, Lesotho, Mali, Pakistan) and seven ESAF arrangements (Bolivia, Gambia, Ghana, Malawi, Niger, Senegal, Uganda) came into effect. This resulted in a total of 14 stand-by arrangements, two extended arrangements, 23 SAF arrangements and seven ESAF arrangements in effect at the end of fiscal 1989.

Liquidity

The Fund's liquid resources consisted of usable currencies, SDRs and borrowed resources. As at 30 April 1989, the Fund's usable ordinary resources totalled SDR 42.9 billion, compared with SDR 41 billion a year earlier. The increase resulted from the inflow of repurchases in the General Resources Account, partially offset by the use of ordinary resources to repay SDR 0.8 billion of short-term borrowing.

IMF borrowed from official sources to supplement its resources and to finance members' purchases under the enlarged access policy. At the end of fiscal 1989, available borrowed resources amounted to SDR 3.3 billion, representing a decline of SDR 2 billion over the year before. The use of borrowed resources also declined. The Fund's liquid liabilities, comprising reserve tranche positions and loan claims, declined from SDR 31.3 billion at the end of fiscal 1988 to SDR 27.3 billion in 1989.

SDR activity

The overall level of SDR activity decreased in fiscal 1989 from the record high in 1988, but was nevertheless higher than in any other year except fiscal 1984. The number of institutions prescribed by IMF as eligible to accept, hold and use SDRs remained unchanged at 16 during the year. Holdings of SDRs by participants declined to SDR 19.9 billion from SDR 20.6 billion in 1988.

Almost half of all transfers of SDRs in fiscal 1989 took place between participants and the Fund. Receipts of SDRs by the General Resources Account declined to SDR 4.26 billion from SDR 4.61 billion in 1988. Transfers from the General Resources Account to participants fell by 30 per cent to SDR 4.05 billion. Participants and prescribed holders also used SDRs for a swap, settlement of financial obligations and Fund-related transfers other than those involving the General Resources Account. In addi-

tion, SDRs were used in other operations involving SAF, ESAF and Trust Fund loans, including their repayment and interest payments, payment of special charges and subsidy payments to members.

Policy on arrears

Overdue financial obligations remained a serious problem in 1989. The amount of overdue obligations at the end of the fiscal year totalled SDR 2.9 billion, while the amount in arrears by six months or more increased to SDR 2.8 billion due from 11 members, compared with SDR 1.9 billion due from nine members at the end of fiscal 1988. During the fiscal year, IMF declared one member ineligible to use the general resources of the Fund in the light of its overdue obligations. Earlier declarations of ineligibility with respect to seven members remained in effect.

To help eliminate overdue obligations, the IMF Board of Governors developed, and in some cases implemented, a strategy involving the prevention of new arrears, intensified collaboration to resolve existing cases of protracted arrears and remedial action to be taken if a country with protracted arrears failed to collaborate with the Fund.

Technical assistance and training

IMF provided technical assistance related to general economic policy, balance-of-payments adjustment programmes, legal matters, debt management, problems arising from inflation, exchange and trade systems, public finance issues, financial sector issues, accounting, statistics and data processing. During fiscal 1989, training through the IMF Institute in Washington, D.C., included 15 courses and three high-level seminars, attended by 559 participants. In addition, the Institute organized 27 briefings at IMF headquarters for 232 visiting officials.

During the year, the Fiscal Affairs Department assisted authorities in 57 countries through 34 staff missions and advice from 61 fiscal panel members. The Central Banking Department undertook 31 advisory missions and participated in five joint World Bank–Fund missions for 51 countries and four regional organizations. The Bureau of Statistics participated in 58 technical assistance missions to 34 countries and provided training at headquarters to officials from nine member States.

IMF–World Bank collaboration

IMF and the World Bank agreed in 1989 to define better the responsibilities stemming from the Articles of each institution and to build on previous agreements by adopting additional administrative and procedural steps. During the year, collaboration between the two institutions included joint participation in missions, attendance at each other's Executive Board meetings and participation in conferences and seminars. In addition, Fund staff attended a number of aid coordination meetings held under World Bank auspices and provided background documents for some of those meetings.

Secretariat

As at 31 December 1989, the total full-time staff of IMF, including permanent and fixed-term employees, was 1,864, drawn from 107 countries.

NOTE: For details of IMF activities for the 1989 fiscal year, see *International Monetary Fund, Annual Report of the Executive Board for the Financial Year Ended April 30, 1989.*

HEADQUARTERS AND OTHER OFFICE

HEADQUARTERS
International Monetary Fund
700 19th Street, N.W.
Washington, D.C. 20431, United States
Cable address: INTERFUND WASHINGTONDC
Telephone: (1) (202) 623-7000
Fax: (1) (202) 623-4661
Telex: 248331 IMF UR

IMF OFFICE, UNITED NATIONS, NEW YORK
International Monetary Fund
1 United Nations Plaza, Room 1140
New York, N.Y. 10017, United States
Cable address: INTERFUND NEW YORK
Telephone: (1) (212) 963-6009
Fax: (1) (212) 319-9040

Chapter X

International Civil Aviation Organization (ICAO)

The International Civil Aviation Organization (ICAO), an intergovernmental regulatory body whose objectives were set down in annexes to the 1944 Convention on International Civil Aviation, continued in 1989 to prescribe standards for and facilitate the safety and efficiency of civil air transport.

In 1989, traffic on the world's scheduled airlines increased by 5.4 per cent over 1988, to 224 billion tonne-kilometres. The airlines carried about 1.1 billion passengers, an increase of almost 2 per cent over 1988. As the number of seats offered increased at the same rate as passengers carried, the estimated passenger load factor remained at 68 per cent. Air freight increased by more than 7 per cent, to some 57 billion tonne-kilometres. Airmail traffic increased by 5 per cent.

The ICAO Assembly held its twenty-seventh session in Montreal, Canada, from 19 September to 6 October. It elected a new Council, reviewed ICAO's activities and approved a work programme.

The ICAO Council held three regular sessions in 1989. Concerned with acts of unlawful interference with international civil aviation, especially the destruction over Lockerbie, Scotland, of Pan American flight 103 in December 1988, the Council decided, in June, to include as a priority in the general work programme of the Legal Committee preparation of a new legal instrument regarding the marking of explosives for detectability.

In 1989, ICAO membership increased to 162 with the admission of Bhutan and Mongolia.

Activities in 1989

Air navigation

ICAO efforts during 1989 in the field of air navigation were mainly directed towards updating and implementing specifications, guidance materials and regional plans. Air navigation meetings covered a wide range of subjects and recommended changes to ICAO specifications contained in three annexes to the Convention on International Civil Aviation and one annex to the Procedures for Air Navigation Services. Revisions were made to regional plans setting forth air navigation facilities and services required in the nine ICAO regions. ICAO regional offices continued to assist States with implementation of regional plans.

During the year, special attention was given to technical projects dealing with accident investigation and prevention; aerodromes; aeronautical in-

formation services; airworthiness; audio-visual training aids; aviation medicine; flight safety and human factors; illicit transport of drugs; meteorology; obstacle clearance; personnel licensing and training; rules of the air and air traffic services; future air navigation systems; and telecommunications.

Air transport

ICAO continued its programmes of regulatory and economic studies; economic research, analysis and forecasting; air carrier tariffs; collection and publication of air transport statistics; airport and route facility management; and the promotion of greater facilitation in international air transport. Meeting in April, the Statistics Division reviewed all aspects of the ICAO statistics programme. An airport economics panel met twice in 1989 and worked on the development of an airport economics manual. A panel on fares and rates completed an extensive review of the organization's policy and guidance in that area and reached agreement on a detailed text of models of bilateral tariff clauses. In December, a technical advisory group undertook a preliminary review of specifications for machine-readable visas.

Legal matters

In November, the ICAO Council approved the inclusion of the subject of preparation of a new international instrument regarding the marking of explosives for detectability in the Legal Committee's work programme and decided to convene a special Legal Sub-Committee to consider the matter in Montreal in January 1990.

During the year, the following ratifications, adherences or successions to conventions and protocols on international air law concluded under ICAO auspices were received:

Convention for the Unification of Certain Rules relating to International Carriage by Air (Warsaw, 1929)
   Mauritius
Protocol to Amend the Convention for the Unification of Certain Rules relating to International Carriage by Air Signed at Warsaw on 12 October 1929 (The Hague, 1955)
   Mauritius
Convention on Offences and Certain Other Acts Committed on Board Aircraft (Tokyo, 1963)
   Bhutan, Bulgaria, Cape Verde, German Democratic Republic, Marshall Islands, Vanuatu, Zimbabwe

Convention for the Suppression of Unlawful Seizure of Aircraft (The Hague, 1970)
Lao People's Democratic Republic, Marshall Islands, Vanuatu, Zimbabwe

Protocol to Amend the Convention for the Unification of Certain Rules relating to International Carriage by Air Signed at Warsaw on 12 October 1929 as Amended by the Protocol Done at The Hague on 28 September 1955 (Guatemala City, 1971) (not in force)
Greece

Convention for the Suppression of Unlawful Acts against the Safety of Civil Aviation (Montreal, 1971)
Lao People's Democratic Republic, Marshall Islands, Vanuatu, Zimbabwe

Additional Protocol No. 1 to Amend the Convention for the Unification of Certain Rules relating to International Carriage by Air Signed at Warsaw on 12 October 1929 (Montreal, 1975) (not in force)
Ireland

Additional Protocol No. 2 to Amend the Convention for the Unification of Certain Rules relating to International Carriage by Air Signed at Warsaw on 12 October 1929 as Amended by the Protocol Done at The Hague on 28 September 1955 (Montreal, 1975)
Ireland

Additional Protocol No. 3 to Amend the Convention for the Unification of Certain Rules relating to International Carriage by Air Signed at Warsaw on 12 October 1929 as Amended by the Protocols Done at The Hague on 28 September 1955 and at Guatemala City on 8 March 1971 (Montreal, 1975) (not in force)
Ireland, Spain

Montreal Protocol No. 4 to Amend the Convention for the Unification of Certain Rules relating to International Carriage by Air Signed at Warsaw on 12 October 1929 as Amended by the Protocol Done at The Hague on 28 September 1955 (Montreal, 1975) (not in force)
Ireland

Protocol for the Suppression of Unlawful Acts of Violence at Airports Serving International Civil Aviation, Supplementary to the Convention for the Suppression of Unlawful Acts against the Safety of Civil Aviation, Done at Montreal on 23 September 1971 (Montreal, 1988)
Austria, Byelorussian SSR, Chile, Denmark, France, German Democratic Republic, Hungary, Kuwait, Marshall Islands, Mauritius, Peru, Saudi Arabia, Turkey, USSR, United Arab Emirates, Yugoslavia

Technical assistance

During 1989, ICAO provided technical assistance to 141 countries in the form of resident missions in 52 of those countries during all or part of the year. The organization employed 459 experts from 51 countries, with 345 on assignment to the United Nations Development Programme (UNDP) and 114 on Trust Fund projects. The total number of experts in the field at the end of 1989 was 191, compared with 200 at the end of 1988.

UNDP-funded country projects decreased slightly in 1989; expenditures on inter-country and inter-regional projects increased to $9,715,145 from $7,835,960 in 1988, while those on country projects fell to $26,529,022 from $30,302,277. During the year, country projects comprised 73 per cent of total UNDP expenditures.

Equipment purchases and sub-contracts continued to represent a substantial proportion of the technical co-operation programme. In addition to UNDP and Trust Fund projects, 57 Governments or organizations had registered with ICAO under its Civil Aviation Purchasing Service. Commitments for equipment and sub-contracts in 1989 totalled $19.02 million.

During the year, 1,456 fellowships were awarded; the average duration of a fellowship was 2.2 months and the average cost was $6,600.

Secretariat

As at 31 December 1989, the total number of staff members employed in the ICAO secretariat stood at 897, comprising 379 in the Professional and higher categories and 518 in the General Service and related categories.

Budget

Appropriations for the ICAO budget for 1989 totalled $34,108,000, as modified by the ICAO Council; actual obligations for the year amounted to $33,996,083.

NOTE: For further details on the activities of ICAO in 1989, see *Annual Report of the Council—1989.*

HEADQUARTERS

International Civil Aviation Organization
1000 Sherbrook Street West
Montreal, Quebec
Canada, H3A 2R2
Cable address: ICAO MONTREAL
Telephone: (1) (514) 954-8219
Fax: (1) (514) 954-4772
Telex: 05-24513
E-mail: icaohq@icao.org

Chapter XI

Universal Postal Union (UPU)

The Universal Postal Union (UPU), established at Berne, Switzerland, in 1874, continued during 1989 to promote the organization and improvement of postal services and to develop international collaboration. At the request of its members, UPU also participated in various forms of postal technical assistance.

In 1989, UPU membership increased to 170, with the admission of Samoa.

Activities of UPU organs

Universal Postal Congress

The Universal Postal Congress, the supreme legislative authority of UPU, composed of all member States, held its twentieth session in 1989 (Washington, D.C., United States, 13 November–14 December). The twentieth Congress adopted the Washington General Action Plan, a blueprint outlining commercial and operational strategies for the bodies of the Union and for postal administrations during 1990-1994. It also adopted several decisions on postal services, including a new terminal dues remuneration system, measures to give more freedom to postal administrations with regard to rate-fixing, updated postal financial services agreements, the structure of the Acts of UPU and technical co-operation.

Executive Council

The UPU Executive Council carries out the work of the Union between sessions of the Congress, held at five-year intervals, by maintaining close contact with postal administrations, exercising control over the International Bureau, promoting technical assistance and working with the United Nations and other organizations. The Council, at its 1989 session (Berne, 10-28 April), considered a variety of administrative matters and examined studies concerning international mail referred to it by the 1984 Congress.

The twentieth Congress elected a new Executive Council, which met for the first time in Washington, D.C. (11-12 December). Among its tasks were implementation of the Washington General Action Plan, postal service quality control at world level, the permanent project to modernize and enhance the quality of the international postal service, the second phase of the transfer to the Council of part of the legislative functions of the Congress and the structure of the technical Acts of the Union.

Consultative Council for Postal Studies (CCPS)

The Consultative Council for Postal Studies (CCPS), elected by the twentieth Congress, met in Washington, D.C. (12-13 December). Its 1989-1994 work programme adopted by the Congress comprised 17 studies and a number of sub-studies. A review of CCPS activities during the five-year period from 1984 to 1989 reflected a focus on issues such as competition, product marketing, responding to customer needs, monitoring the quality of service and development of new products and services.

Prior to the Congress, a meeting of CCPS/Electronic Transmission Standards Group was held (Berne, September) to study, among other issues, the consideration of proposals on telematics and bar codes to be submitted to the Congress, examination of the work of the International Air Transport Association/UPU Operations Working Group and future collaboration with the International Standards Organization.

International Bureau

The International Bureau, which functions as the UPU secretariat, continued to serve the postal administrations of member States as an organ for liaison, information and consultation. During the year, the Bureau collected, co-ordinated, published and disseminated international postal service information; conducted inquiries at the request of postal administrations; and acted as a clearing-house for settling certain accounts between members.

As at 31 December 1989, the UPU Bureau employed 143 permanent and temporary staff members, 59 of whom were in the Professional and higher categories and 84 in the General Service category. Also, as French remained the sole official UPU language, the Union employed 14 officials in the Arabic, English, Portuguese, Russian and Spanish translation services.

Technical co-operation

UPU technical assistance totalled about $3.9 million in 1989, of which some $2.5 million was financed by the United Nations Development Programme. Assistance was also provided through the

UPU regular budget and its special fund, consisting of voluntary contributions in cash and kind from member States.

During the year, 101 expert and consultant missions were carried out and 311 training fellowships were granted, with the emphasis placed on the quality of postal services, primarily to the benefit of African countries.

The twentieth Congress decided to strengthen and develop technical assistance so as to help postal administrations implement the Washington General Action Plan. With a view to enhancing UPU's technical assistance, the Congress adopted six resolutions dealing with technical co-operation, focusing on UPU's technical assistance priorities and principles; financing technical assistance; technical co-operation among developing countries; an increased UPU presence in the field with regard to technical assistance; UPU action on behalf of the least developed countries; and guidelines to be emphasized in UPU technical assistance activities. The Congress also adopted a document on human resources and training.

Budget

Under the Union's self-financing system, contributions are payable in advance by member States based on the following year's budget. The budget approved for 1989 amounted to 22,205,265 Swiss francs net expenditure.

In 1989, the Executive Council approved the 1990 budget at a total of 24,389,550 Swiss francs net expenditure.

NOTE: For details of UPU activities, see *Report of the Work of the Union, 1989*, published by UPU.

HEADQUARTERS

Universal Postal Union
Weltpoststrasse 4
Berne, Switzerland
   Postal address: Union postale universelle
      Case postale
      3000 Berne 15, Switzerland
   Cable address: UPU BERNE
   Telephone: (41) (31) 350 31 11
   Fax: (41) (31) 350 31 10
   Telex: 912761 UPU CH
   E-mail: lb.info@ub.upu.org
   World Wide Web site: http://ibis.ib.upu.org/

Chapter XII

International Telecommunication Union (ITU)

The International Telecommunication Union (ITU), which was founded in 1865 as the International Telegraph Union, became a specialized agency of the United Nations in 1947 to promote the development and efficient operation of telecommunications facilities world-wide. In 1989, ITU also continued to offer technical assistance in its areas of expertise and to encourage adoption of a global approach to telecommunications.

The ITU Plenipotentiary Conference at its thirteenth session (Nice, France, 23 May–30 June) adopted a new constitution and convention to supersede the convention adopted at Nairobi, Kenya, in 1982.

The ITU Administrative Council held its forty-fourth session (Geneva, 30 January–3 February; Nice, 24 May) and opened its forty-fifth session (Nice, 30 June), reviewing financial and administrative matters and approving the ITU budget for 1990. It also examined the report of the Advisory Board of the Centre for Telecommunications Development. At an extraordinary session (Geneva, November), convened in accordance with a decision of the Plenipotentiary Conference, the Council established a high-level committee to review the structure and functioning of ITU and decided to continue its forty-fifth ordinary session in Geneva from 11 to 22 June 1990.

ITU membership remained at 166 in 1989, with no new admissions during the year.

Conferences

The 1989 ITU Plenipotentiary Conference decided to hold two World Administrative Radio Conferences (WARC): the first in Spain in 1992 to deal with specific allocation issues, including mobile and mobile-satellite services and broadcasting, and a high-frequency broadcasting planning conference in 1993.

The second session of the Regional Administrative Conference for the planning of VHF/UHF (very high frequency/ultra high frequency) television broadcasting in the African Broadcasting Area and neighbouring countries (AFBC-2) (Geneva, 8-13 November) aimed to establish an agreement for television broadcasting in the various frequency bands. The session adopted Final Acts comprising an Agreement and an associated Plan containing the frequency assignments of

10,285 television stations in Africa, an appendix containing the assignments of 118 stations and annexes with technical data. The Agreement was to enter into force on 1 July 1992. In December 1989, African members of ITU agreed that the new Plan would replace the 1963 agreement for the African Broadcasting Area.

Radio and telecommunication activities

The final study group of the International Radio Consultative Committee (CCIR) prepared in 1989 171 new and revised recommendations for CCIR's seventeenth plenary assembly (scheduled for 1990), representing significant progress in the areas of television and sound broadcasting, fixed and mobile satellite systems and mobile communications. CCIR continued to provide technical services and advice for all administrative radio conferences. It assisted in two training courses, on telecommunication science and on theoretical and experimental radio propagation physics (Trieste, Italy, January/February), organized especially for developing countries. The CCIR secretariat published in the ITU *Telecommunication Journal* information pertaining to computer programs for radio frequency management submitted by Czechoslovakia, Japan, Poland, Sweden and the United States. Important modifications were made to the VHF and UHF broadcasting antenna system to permit calculations of more complex systems with up to 60 individual radiators.

The activities of the International Telegraph and Telephone Consultative Committee (CCITT) in 1989 focused mainly on preparing an 18,500-page blue book containing recommendations pertaining to its scope of work. Publication of the book, originally planned for 1989, was delayed due to the large volume of recommendations. CCITT study groups established working parties, designated rapporteurs and laid down guidelines for the study of questions assigned to them; in addition, they followed up on the work carried out before the 1988 CCITT plenary assembly and drew up nine draft recommendations which were transmitted to the members for approval. Three questions were approved for study. CCITT also helped select experts for technical co-operation projects.

At the end of the year, 229 private operating agencies and scientific or industrial organizations, as well as 37 international organizations, were registered as participants in the work of CCITT, in addition to the ITU member administrations.

Following the closure of its laboratory, the CCITT secretariat was restructured slightly.

Major activities of the ITU International Frequency Registration Board (IFRB) during 1989 included follow-up action on decisions of the May Plenipotentiary Conference, as well as various radio conferences of previous years. The Board also undertook activities related to implementation of further modules for the IFRB Frequency Management System (FMS) and continuing development of the system with a view to improving and rationalizing services.

Telecommunication training and development

During the year, 582 ITU expert missions were carried out under various technical co-operation programmes. In addition, 686 fellows were undergoing training abroad and equipment valued at $9,786,755 was delivered, mainly to telecommunication training centres. Total assistance amounted to $32.47 million for 189 projects in 70 countries. Of those, 150 were country projects, while 37 were regional and 2 were interregional projects. Expenditures by region were as follows: $12.9 million for 70 projects in Africa, $7.7 million for 41 projects in the Americas, $7.2 million for 48 projects in Asia and the Pacific, $2.9 million for 17 projects in the Middle East, $0.4 million for 11 projects in Europe, and $1.3 million for interregional projects.

A main goal of ITU technical co-operation continued to be developing regional communications networks and their integration into the world-wide telecommunication system, in accordance with objectives established by ITU's World and Regional Plan Committees. For example, the pan-African telecommunication network (PANAFTEL), aimed at interconnecting the countries of Africa without the need for extra-continental transit, continued to make steady progress, except in the Central African subregion. Of the 45 countries south of the Sahara, 41 had satellite earth stations, as well as overland and/or submarine cable networks. Additional funds were needed to bridge some 7,600 kilometres of land links, 7 international switching centres and 4 earth stations.

Other objectives of ITU technical co-operation included strengthening the telecommunication technical and administrative services in developing countries and developing human resources required for telecommunications. Particular focus was placed on efforts to strengthen national telecommunications technical and administrative services.

By the end of the year, 630 training courses were available through the ITU sharing system and 244 more were being developed. The computerized data base of training opportunities was updated, reaching a total of 589 openings for trainees. Regional training meetings, symposia and seminars were held for Europe and the Arab States (Darmstadt, Federal Republic of Germany, September), for eastern and southern Africa (Nairobi, Kenya, November), for the countries of the EUROTELDEV project (Zruc, Czechoslovakia, September), and for the least developed countries (Geneva, September). In addition, some 430 participants took part in ITU training workshops, and nine missions to assist and advise on training matters were carried out in Cape Verde, Colombia, Ecuador, Guinea-Bissau, the Lao People's Democratic Republic, the Libyan Arab Jamahiriya, Swaziland and Viet Nam.

The ITU Centre for Telecommunications Development, which became operational in 1987, completed five projects during 1989 on: rural/urban network planning in Egypt; provincial/rural telecommunications in the Gambia; telecommunication feasibility and development in Nepal; rural telecommunications development in the United Republic of Tanzania; and establishment of a nucleus for the training centre in Democratic Yemen. Missions were undertaken to the Gambia, Malta, Mozambique, the United Republic of Tanzania and Uruguay.

Secretariat

As at 31 December 1989, the total number of ITU staff at headquarters or in the field (excluding staff on short-term contracts and project staff) was 745. Of those, 9 were elected officials, 589 had permanent contracts and 147 had fixed-term contracts; 74 nationalities were represented in those posts subject to geographical distribution.

Budget

The ITU budget for 1989 totalled 138,839,800 Swiss francs (SwF), including SwF 112,269,200 for ordinary budget expenditures, SwF 1,802,900 for regional administrative conferences, SwF 9,667,700 for technical co-operation and SwF 15,100,000 for publications. Total expenditures were offset by the equal amount of income, of which SwF 114,072,100 came from contributions by member States and private operating agencies, SwF 9,667,700 from the United Nations Development Programme and funds-in-trust for technical co-operation, and SwF 15,100,000 from the sale of publications.

NOTE: For further details regarding ITU's activities, see *Report on the Activities of the International Telecommunication Union in 1989*, published by the Union.

HEADQUARTERS

International Telecommunication Union
Place des Nations
CH-1211, Geneva 20, Switzerland
  Cable address: BURINTERNA GENEVA
  Telephone: (41) (22) 730-5111
  Fax: (41) (22) 733-7256
  Telex: 45 421000
  Internet address: itumail@itu.int

Chapter XIII

World Meteorological Organization (WMO)

The World Meteorological Organization (WMO), established in 1950 to facilitate world-wide co-operation related to meteorological information and the application of meteorology to aviation, shipping, agriculture and other human activities, continued during 1989 to implement its scientific and technical programmes along the lines indicated by its highest body, the World Meteorological Congress, in May 1987.

The forty-first session of the 36-member Executive Council (Geneva, 5-16 June) made several important decisions related to climate change and protecting the global atmosphere, including establishment of the Global Atmosphere Watch early warning system. On 8 September, WMO and the Government of Japan signed an agreement designating the Japan Meteorological Agency as the WMO World Data Centre for Greenhouse Gases, to commence operations in 1990.

WMO was also involved in planning the International Decade for Natural Disaster Reduction whose aim was, during the 1990s, to reduce the impact of extreme natural calamities through co-ordinated global action.

As at 31 December 1989, WMO membership had increased to 161—156 States and 5 territories—with the admission of Antigua and Barbuda.

World Weather Watch

As the core programme of WMO, the World Weather Watch (WWW) Programme continued to co-ordinate observations, data processing and the exchange of data, weather analyses and forecasts between meteorological centres. The WWW essential elements were the Global Observing System (GOS), the Global Telecommunication System (GTS) and the Global Data-processing System.

On 21 April, the UN Postal Administration issued a set of six stamps to commemorate the twenty-fifth anniversary of WWW.

Operational WWW Systems Evaluations (OWSEs) were continued to ensure the smooth incorporation of new technologies and procedures into WWW and the efficient transfer of knowledge and technology to developing countries. Following the successful OWSE for the North Atlantic, planning for OWSE-Africa, aimed at improving the telecommunication system over the continent,

began. During 1989, equipment was installed in Ethiopia, Kenya and the Sudan, with further installations scheduled for the early part of 1990.

The activities of GOS continued under its two subsystems, one surface-based and the other space-based. In 1989, there were some 10,000 stations on land, 7,000 ships and buoys at sea, 3,000 aircraft and a system of four polar-orbiting and five geostationary satellites. GOS provided member States with quantitative information, derived from instrument measurements, such as atmospheric pressure, humidity, air temperature and wind velocity, and qualitative information on the state of the sky, forms of clouds and types of precipitation.

Several new satellites were added to GOS in 1989, including METEOSAT-4, the first of a new series of three satellites operated by the European Organisation for the Exploitation of Meteorological Satellites, which was launched on 6 March, and the Geostationary Meteorological Satellite (Japan) (GMS-4), which was launched on 6 September.

GTS, consisting of 245 circuits interconnecting 188 meteorological centres, was further developed in 1989 by the implementation of new satellite circuits, upgrading of the data-signalling rate on several circuits (up to 64 kbit/s) and the introduction of advanced communication protocols. The support of GTS for exchanging data related to other international programmes was maintained or enhanced, including, in particular, the exchange of data related to the early notification of a nuclear accident (International Atomic Energy Agency) and exchange of seismic data contributing to the large-scale experiment organized by the Conference on Disarmament.

WWW Data Management

WWW Data Management provided support functions for the overall management of meteorological data and products of the whole WWW system, for the most economical use of resources and for the monitoring of data and products both in respect of availability and quality.

A scheme for real-time monitoring of the quality and availability of data and verification of products was established and lead centres were nominated to provide regular feedback to members. A WMO-European Centre for Medium-Range Weather Forecasts (ECMWF) workshop on data quality control procedures was held (Reading, United Kingdom, 6-10 March) to exchange views and recommend procedures for real-time quality control and monitoring.

One of the most important Data Management projects was the introduction and refinement of binary formats for the representation of meteorological data and data fields, as they allowed for faster transmission and processing by computer and reduced storage requirements. A number of refinements to those formats were proposed by the Subgroup on Data Representation, which met in May. Standards for the representation and presentation of meteorological data were the subject of a WMO/ECMWF workshop held in December.

The concept of distributed data bases was developed in October at a meeting of experts, which defined principles and proposed appropriate strategies for their implementation.

WWW Operational Information Service

As in the previous year, the WWW Operational Information Service continued to collect from and distribute to WMO members and WWW centres detailed information on available facilities, services, data and products. In view of the progressive automation of WWW centres, it was becoming increasingly important that basic directories of fixed and mobile stations, composition of bulletins, telecommunication arrangements, lists of stations for global and regional exchange, etc., were kept constantly up to date.

Instruments and methods of observation

The Commission for Instruments and Methods of Observation (tenth session, Brussels, Belgium, 11-22 September) considered the preparation of standard algorithms for surface and upper-air measurements, and publications in the Instruments and Observing Methods Series. It also addressed preparation of the sixth edition of the WMO *Guide to Meteorological Instruments and Methods of Observation*.

Tropical Cyclone Programme and cyclone research

Under the general component of the Tropical Cyclone Programme (TCP), major emphasis in 1989 was placed on the acceleration of technology transfer and on training, through the provision of expert services, training workshops, publications, exchange programmes and other arrangements for technical co-operation among developing countries.

Under the regional component of TCP, activities were carried out through five regional tropical cyclone bodies for the mitigation of damage resulting from tropical cyclones and associated floods and storm surges. Major accomplishments included a complete review and revision of implementation plans by four of the regional bodies in the light of the objectives of the WMO second long-term plan for the years 1988-1997. Agreement was reached on the establishment of tropical cyclone advisory centres in each of the areas of the five regional tropical cyclone bodies.

With the assistance of the United Nations Development Programme (UNDP), the WMO Voluntary Co-operation Programme and/or bilateral arrangements, activities were continued to improve warning systems through the rehabilitation of weather radars, the upgrading of telecommunications, the transplantation of software in regional computer network projects and relevant training. For the south-west Indian Ocean, which had so far had to rely on national efforts alone, further steps were taken to obtain external (regional) assistance.

The second WMO international workshop on tropical cyclones (Manila, Philippines, 27 November–8 December) considered ways of using research results to alleviate damage caused by hazardous weather in the tropical regions. Among meetings organized under TCP during 1989 were the sixteenth session of the Economic and Social Commission for Asia and the Pacific (ESCAP)/WMO panel on tropical cyclones (New Delhi, India, 21-27 February); a meeting on hurricanes (San Andrés, Colombia, 11-17 April); a workshop on hurricane analysis, forecasting and warning (Miami, Florida, United States, 19-28 April); the ninth session of the Tropical Cyclone Committee for the South-West Indian Ocean (Harare, Zimbabwe, 9-14 October); and the twenty-second session of the ESCAP/WMO Typhoon Committee (Tokyo, Japan, 30 October–6 November).

World Climate Programme

The Commission for Climatology, which played the leading role in organizing the World Climate Data Programme and the World Climate Applications Programme, at its tenth session (Cascais, Portugal, 3–14 April), emphasized that it would contribute to the study of climate change by improving and enlarging the data base for research, assisting in the regional-scale interpretation of climate model predictions and investigating the impacts of climate changes on human life and activities in different parts of the world.

During the year, climate computing (CLICOM) systems were installed in 32 countries, bringing the total number of members having such systems to 84. CLICOM training seminars were held in Barbados, Mali, the Philippines and Portugal, in addition to 26 installation training sessions in other countries. INFOCLIMA, a world climate data and information referral service, provided information on the availability of climate data at various data centres around the globe.

World Climate Impact Studies Programme

The World Climate Impact Studies Programme, organized by the United Nations Environment Programme (UNEP) in co-operation with WMO, continued to develop methods for assessing the economic and social impacts of climate variations, with special regard to agricultural planning, water-resources management and the development of appropriate energy policies. In 1989, UNEP continued to update an inventory on climate impact activities on a global scale and encourage the development of national climate impact programmes and their co-ordination in an international network. Under the programme, a regional seminar on climate impact assessment techniques was organized in Cairo, Egypt, as were workshops on drought forecasting and early warning systems in Ethiopia and Kenya.

World Climate Research Programme

Strong emphasis was placed in 1989 on reinforcing activities under the World Climate Research Programme (WCRP)—a joint undertaking of WMO and the International Council of Scientific Unions—aimed at improving predictions of climate change and monitoring the Earth's climate system. Progress was made in the global energy and water cycle experiment, whose objectives were to observe and model the hydrological cycle and energy fluxes in the atmosphere and at the Earth's surface. The WCRP international satellite cloud climatology project, which assembled cloud and radiance data, was extended until 1995.

Progress was made in implementing the global precipitation climatology project, aimed at providing the first climatological record of monthly mean rainfall totals over the whole Earth (including the oceans) by combining rainfall estimates from satellite observations of clouds with rain-gauge measurements; all the participating centres achieved operational status during 1989 and the first year's data were being processed. The Joint Scientific Committee for WCRP, at its tenth session (Villefranche, France, 13-18 March), decided to constitute a working group on modelling of greenhouse gases.

Three working groups of the WMO/UNEP Intergovernmental Panel on Climate Change were charged with assessing information on climate change; assessing the environmental and socio-economic impacts of such change; and formulating response options to address such change. At its second session (Nairobi, Kenya, 28-30 June), the Panel established a committee to promote more effective participation of developing countries in its activities.

Research and development

In response to demonstrated concerns of Governments about the atmospheric pollution arising from human activities, the WMO Executive Council approved measures for strengthening the organization's role in the scientific aspects of that global problem. WMO continued to monitor the global atmosphere using the Background Air Pollution Monitoring Network and the Global Ozone Observing System. The success of those systems motivated WMO to develop a new Global Atmosphere Watch (GAW), which was established by the Executive Council in June to provide atmospheric composition information to complement the weather and climate information provided by WWW. Some members were already providing vital, centralized data-collection points and services for GAW.

Among the meetings organized by WMO during 1989 were the fifth WMO scientific conference on weather modification and applied cloud physics (Beijing, China, 8-12 May); a conference on mountain meteorology and alpine experiments (Garmisch-Partenkirchen, Federal Republic of Germany, 5-8 June); a conference on measurements and analysis of carbon dioxide data (Hinterzarten, Federal Republic of Germany, 16-21 October); and a technical conference on the monitoring and assessment of the troposphere (Sofia, Bulgaria, 23-27 October).

Applications of meteorology

Agricultural meteorology

The Agricultural Meteorology Programme assisted members in developing sustainable agricultural systems and in improving productivity, quality, cost-effectiveness and efficiency in the use of water, labour and energy, conserving natural resources and reducing pollution caused by agricultural chemicals.

A symposium on the agrometeorology of rainfed, barley-based farming systems (Tunis, Tunisia, 6-10 March) recommended several new activities to help agricultural research and development planning. Seminars on the use of agrometeorological data and information to assess potential primary production of natural pastures in the rainy season (Syrian Arab Republic, January; Lesotho, November; Botswana, December) helped to estimate the optimum animal-carrying capacity during the dry season. Participants from eastern and southern Africa attended a drought preparedness and management training seminar organized by WMO in co-operation with the United States

National Oceanic and Atmospheric Administration (Gabarone, Botswana, 25-29 September). WMO, together with other organizations, pursued the recommendations of a locust-control workshop to combat the worst locust plague in 30 years affecting many countries in Africa.

WMO promoted the use of the INSTAT software package in many developing countries in Africa, Asia and Latin America for analysing agrometeorological data using hand-held computers.

Marine meteorology

The Marine Meteorology and Associated Oceanographic Activities Programme continued to provide services in support of marine users. During the year, a global ocean-observing system was established, based on a proposal approved by the WMO Executive Council and the Intergovernmental Oceanographic Commission Assembly.

The Commission for Marine Meteorology (tenth session, Paris, 6-17 February) considered such topics as ocean waves, marine pollution emergency response operations, the potential impact of data obtained from the next generation of oceanographic satellites, training facilities and reorganizing the broadcast of high seas forecasts and warnings to be compatible with the International Maritime Organization's global maritime distress and safety system.

Aeronautical meteorology

WMO co-sponsored with the American Meteorological Society the third international conference on the aviation weather system (Anaheim, California, United States, 29 January–3 February). Meteorologists from 24 countries participated in a seminar on aeronautical meteorology with emphasis on satellite applications (Tallahassee, Florida, United States, 16-27 October), organized by WMO and the United States National Oceanic and Atmospheric Administration. A meeting attended by WMO, the International Civil Aviation Organization and aviation user groups (Geneva, 2-6 October) suggested that the aeronautical meteorological codes, which had come into force some 20 years earlier, were outdated and needed to be changed.

Hydrology and water resources

In 1989, there were nearly 50 hydrometeorological services among the 161 WMO members, while, among the remainder, where there were separate meteorological and hydrological services, a large proportion of the meteorological products were provided for hydrology and water resources purposes. The Advisory Working Group of the Commission for Hydrology and its three working groups met during the year, addressing the principal parts of WMO's Hydrology and Water Resources Programme: data acquisition and processing systems; hydrological forecasting and applications for water management; and operational hydrology, climate and the environment.

A conference on climate and water (Helsinki, Finland, 11-15 September) examined the impact of climate change on water supply, flood potential, irrigation and drainage, water pollution, navigation, health and the hydrological consequences of sea-level rise. Following a meeting on hydrological aspects of accidental pollution of water bodies (Kiev, Ukrainian SSR, 24-28 April), a practical guide was being prepared for the use of hydrological services and water-supply authorities in the event of nuclear or chemical accidents.

Throughout the year, the Global Run-off Data Centre (Koblenz, Federal Republic of Germany), established in 1988, continued to collect run-off data from the world's hydrological services. At the end of 1989, the data base contained records for 2,268 stations from 120 countries which could be used for studying the world water balance and chemicals discharged into the oceans. During the year, WMO executed some 20 UNDP-funded hydrology technical assistance projects and 20 other projects combining meteorology and hydrology.

Two projects were initiated to improve and update hydrological instrument networks—a basic hydrological network assessment project, and an intercomparison of operational hydrological network design techniques—whose results were to be presented at a workshop in 1991 in order to update WMO guidance on network design. A WMO co-sponsored meeting on intercomparison of methods and models for estimation of areal evapotranspiration (Zurich, Switzerland, 24-27 October) discussed plans for a comparison of some 44 methods for assessing areal evapotranspiration using data from at least 20 countries.

Education and training

The Executive Council in June endorsed the recommendations presented by its panel of experts on education and training (thirteenth session, Cairo, 5-9 February) relating to training and fellowships. A second global survey of members' training requirements was undertaken. During the year, 428 people participated in 14 WMO training events in 12 countries, and another 20 training events were co-sponsored or supported by WMO. A computerized data base was being developed to incorporate information on training facilities and programmes in approximately 100 countries. UNDP and other organizations assisted WMO in granting 238 training fellowships.

Technical cooperation

During 1989, the technical co-operation programme of WMO—financed by UNDP (56 per cent), the WMO Voluntary Co-operation Programme (VCP) (25 per cent), trust funds (16 per cent) and the WMO regular budget (3 per cent)—provided assistance totalling $30 million to 130 member States. With UNDP financing, advisory missions to 33 countries were undertaken. Twelve new projects, supported by UNDP, were approved. Under the WMO regular budget, 90 countries received assistance and 24 fellowships were granted. As at 31 December 1989, 143 VCP projects were being implemented in 67 countries. The estimated value of contributions in the form of equipment, services and fellowships during the year amounted to some $7.9 million.

Secretariat

As at 31 December 1989, the total number of full-time staff employed by WMO (excluding 48 professionals on technical assistance projects) on permanent and fixed-term contracts stood at 290. Of those, 134 representing 50 nationalities were in the Professional and higher categories and 156 in the General Service and related categories.

Budget

The year 1989 was the second year of the first biennium of the tenth financial period (1988-1991), for which the 1987 WMO Congress had established a maximum expenditure of 170 million Swiss francs (SwF). It had authorized additional expenditures for increases in salaries and allowances. Additional expenditures of no more than SwF 800,000 were authorized to meet urgent, unforeseen programme activities.

The regular budget for 1988-1989 was SwF 82,634,400, including supplementary estimates. Actual expenditure amounted to SwF 79,121,366. Unpaid contributions in respect of assessments for the biennium amounted to SwF 19,269,593 as at 31 December 1989. The 1989 budget for technical co-operation activities, financed from overhead allocations and other extrabudgetary sources, was SwF 3,111,100.

At its June 1989 session, the Executive Council approved a regular budget of SwF 87,871,700 for 1990-1991. Supplementary estimates of SwF 4,800,000 were added later in the year.

NOTE: For further details regarding WMO activities, see *World Meteorological Organization Annual Report 1989.*

HEADQUARTERS

World Meteorological Organization
41, Avenue Giuseppe-Motta
(Case postale No. 2300)
CH-1211 Geneva 2, Switzerland
Telephone: (41) (22) 730-81-11
Fax: (41) (22) 734-23-26
Cable address: METEOMONO GENEVA
Telex: 41-41 99 OMMCH
E-mail: ipa@www.wmo.ch
Homepage: http://www.wmo.ch

Chapter XIV

International Maritime Organization (IMO)

The International Maritime Organization (IMO), which began work in 1959 as the Intergovernmental Maritime Consultative Organization, continued during its thirtieth anniversary year in 1989 to focus on developing international shipping standards and treaties with the aim of improving maritime safety and preventing pollution from ships.

In April, an international conference at IMO headquarters in London adopted the International Convention on Salvage to replace the 1910 convention on the law of salvage. A set of amendments to the International Convention for the Safety of Life at Sea (SOLAS), 1974, entered into force in October 1989. During the year, the IMO Maritime Safety Committee adopted another series of amendments, which were expected to enter into force on 1 February 1992.

In September 1989, the International Maritime Prize for 1988 was awarded to Emil Jansen of Norway, who had been involved in IMO's work since 1966 and had served as Chairman of the Maritime Safety Committee until his retirement in 1988. The prize is awarded annually to the individual or organization judged to have made the most significant contribution to IMO objectives.

The theme for World Maritime Day, which was celebrated at IMO headquarters on 2 September, was "IMO—The First Thirty Years".

In October, the IMO Assembly appointed William A. O'Neil of Canada as IMO Secretary-General for a four-year term beginning on 1 January 1990.

During the year, IMO membership increased to 134, with the admission of Malawi and Monaco. The organization also had one associate member, Hong Kong.

Activities in 1989

IMO Assembly

The IMO Assembly, at its sixteenth biennial session (London, 9-19 October), approved the IMO work programme and budget for the 1990-1991 biennium and the long-term work plan up to 1996. It also elected a new 32-member IMO Council—the IMO governing body between sessions of the Assembly.

Among its major actions during the session, the Assembly adopted Guidelines for the Management of Safe Ship Operation and Pollution Prevention, designed to provide shipping companies with a framework for the proper development, implementation and assessment of safety and pollution-prevention management. The Guidelines addressed responsibilities of the management, master and crew, and stressed the importance of emergency drills.

The Assembly decided to hold in November 1990 a conference on oil pollution preparedness and response, to adopt a framework convention for international co-operation in combating major oil pollution incidents. It amended Regulation 10 of the International Regulations for Preventing Collisions at Sea, 1972, to clarify the use of inshore traffic zones in the vicinity of traffic separation schemes. It also adopted six resolutions designed to assist implementation of the Global Maritime Distress and Safety System, to be introduced during the 1990s following the adoption of amendments to SOLAS.

The Assembly adopted a new Code for the Construction and Equipment of Mobile Offshore Drilling Units, to supersede the first code adopted in 1979 and for application to units built on or after 1 May 1991. Other resolutions dealt with the observance of safety zones around offshore structures; guidelines and standards for the removal of unwanted offshore installations; stability criteria for twin-pontoon column-stabilized semi-submersible units; and criteria for a range of positive stability after damage or flooding for such units.

Prevention of pollution

The new International Convention on Salvage provided for a salvor to be rewarded not only for saving the ship and/or its cargo but also for preventing a major pollution incident. The Convention was to enter into force one year after 15 States had ratified or acceded to it.

Also in 1989, the IMO Maritime Safety Committee adopted the twenty-fifth amendment to the 1965 International Maritime Dangerous Goods Code to extend its application to marine pollutants. In October, the North Sea was designated as a "special area" where the environment was under particular threat, under a new amendment to annex V of the International Convention for the Prevention of Pollution from Ships, 1973, as modified by the Protocol of 1978 relating thereto (MARPOL 73/78). The amendment would ban, in addition to plastics, the disposal into the North Sea of dunnage and wastes which were not ground up. In addition, IMO's technical assistance programme for 1989 included a number of projects designed to combat marine pollution.

Ship security and safety at sea

The IMO Maritime Safety Committee, at its fifty-seventh session, adopted several amendments to SOLAS, 1974. The main changes concerned chapters II-1 and II-2 of the Convention, concerning, respectively, ships' construction and fire protection, detection and extinction. One of the more important amendments to chapter II-1 was designed to reduce the number and size of openings in watertight bulkheads in passenger ships and to ensure they were closed in the event of an emergency. Regulations introduced as part of amendments to chapter II-2 included improvements to fixed-gas fire-extinguishing systems, smoke detection systems, arrangements for fuel and other oils, and the location and separation of spaces.

On 22 October 1989, another series of amendments to SOLAS, designed to improve the safety of ferries, entered into force. The new regulations, added to SOLAS chapter II-1 (ships' construction, subdivision, stability, machinery and electrical installation), required, among other measures, new leakage detection systems and the installation of emergency lighting for roll-on/roll-off passenger ships.

Training facilities

Total enrolment at the World Maritime University in Malmö, Sweden, was 204 students in 1989, double the number of 1988. More than 100 countries had sent students to the University since its opening in 1983. The University was established under IMO auspices to provide two-year advanced training in maritime safety administration, the technical management of shipping companies and maritime education.

During the year, two new institutions established in 1988—the International Maritime Academy and the IMO International Maritime Law Institute—were inaugurated. Located in Trieste, Italy, the Academy received nearly 100 applications from more than 60 countries for 20 places available in its first series of short-term training courses in maritime search and rescue administration, MARPOL 73/78 port State control, and marine accident and incident investigation. The Institute, in Valletta, Malta, provided suitably qualified persons, especially from developing countries, with one-year advanced training and research in international maritime law.

Secretariat

As at 31 December 1989, there were 267 full-time staff members employed at the IMO secretariat in London. Of those, 106 were in the Professional and higher categories and 161 were in the General Service and related categories. In addition, there were 11 Professional and 14 General Service staff employed on technical assistance projects.

Budget

Due to non-payment of contributions by some member States, the IMO budget for 1989 was reduced from 11,053,100 pounds sterling to 10,564,700 pounds. As a result, IMO had to cut its 1989 meetings programme from 24.5 weeks to 12.5 weeks. Contributions from member States for 1989 totalled 10,237,100 pounds. The IMO Assembly in October requested the IMO Council to make proposals for payment of arrears by instalment and for effective application of article 56 of the IMO Convention, which would prohibit any member State in arrears for more than one year from voting in the Assembly or other IMO bodies, unless the Assembly waived the provision. Also requested was a review of the apportionment system of contributions. The Assembly approved budgetary appropriations of 25,410,600 pounds for 1990-1991 (12.1 million pounds for 1990 and 13.3 million pounds for 1991).

NOTE: For details of IMO activities in 1989, see the magazine of IMO, *IMO News*, Nos. 1-3, 1989, and No. 1, 1990.

HEADQUARTERS

International Maritime Organization
4 Albert Embankment
London SE1 7SR, United Kingdom
Cable address: INTERMAR LONDON SE1
Telephone: (44) (171) 735-7611
Fax: (44) (171) 587-3210
Telex: 23588 IMOLDN G, 296979 IMOLDN G

Chapter XV

World Intellectual Property Organization (WIPO)

In 1989, the World Intellectual Property Organization (WIPO) continued development co-operation, standardization and registration activities to promote respect for the protection and use of intellectual properties, including industrial property and copyrights. During the year, the organization's development co-operation programme further expanded, as did activities related to norm-setting in the exchange of industrial property information and the international registration of marks, patents and industrial designs. During 1989, diplomatic conferences convened by WIPO adopted two new treaties—on the International Registration of Audiovisual Works and on Intellectual Property in Respect of Integrated Circuits—and a new Protocol to the Madrid Agreement Concerning the International Registration of Marks.

The governing bodies of WIPO and the unions administered by it held their twentieth series of meetings (Geneva, 25 September–4 October), and adopted a substantial programme of work and a budget for the WIPO International Bureau for the 1990-1991 biennium. New activities to be undertaken during that period included examination or preparation of: a new protocol to the Berne Convention for the Protection of Literary and Artistic Works; a new treaty on the settlement of disputes between States in the field of intellectual property; a new treaty or revision of the Lisbon Agreement on the Protection of Appellations of Origin and Their International Registration; model laws on intellectual property protection in respect of integrated circuits, as well as on counterfeiting and piracy; and a mechanism to provide services for the resolution of disputes between private parties over intellectual property rights.

During 1989, WIPO membership increased to 126 States, with the accession of Democratic Yemen, Liberia, Madagascar, Malaysia and Thailand to the 1967 Convention establishing WIPO, amended in 1979. The number of States adhering to treaties administered by WIPO also increased: to 100 parties to the Paris Convention for the Protection of Industrial Property; 84 to the Berne Convention for the Protection of Literary and Artistic Works; 24 to the Budapest Treaty on the International Recognition of the Deposit of Microorganisms for the Purposes of Patent Procedure; 35 to the Rome Convention for the Protection of Performers, Producers of Phonograms and Broadcasting Organizations; 43 to the Geneva Conven-

tion for the Protection of Producers of Phonograms against Unauthorized Duplication of their Phonograms; 34 to the Nice Agreement Concerning the International Classification of Goods and Services for the Purposes of the Registration of Marks; and 43 to the Patent Co-operation Treaty (PCT).

Activities in 1989

Development co-operation activities

During 1989, WIPO continued to assist developing countries in preparing legislation and establishing or modernizing institutions, particularly those related to patent documentation and information services. A total of some 60 developing and industrialized countries and 23 organizations, foremost among them the United Nations Development Programme, provided support for WIPO's development co-operation programme, which benefited 117 developing countries, 17 intergovernmental organizations and one regional commission. During the year, there was a sturdy growth in activities in favour of developing countries. The number of training fellowships granted rose to 376 and over 4,000 people benefited from some 100 courses, workshops, seminars and study visits organized at the national, regional and global levels. Advice on legal matters and institution building was provided to some 80 countries, while 285 advisory missions were undertaken to some 75 developing countries.

A World-wide Symposium on the International Patent System in the Twenty-first Century, organized by WIPO and the Chinese Patent Office (Beijing, November), brought together several hundred participants from more than 50 countries to discuss future trends and developments.

Under the WIPO medal awards programme, instituted in 1979 to promote inventive and innovative activities, particularly for developing countries or to their benefit, WIPO awarded in 1989 37 medals to inventors from Algeria, Benin, Bulgaria, China, Cuba, the Democratic People's Republic of Korea, France, Iraq, Italy, Japan, Malaysia, Mali, the Niger, Nigeria, the Philippines, the Republic of Korea, the USSR, the United States, Viet Nam and Yugoslavia. From the start of the programme until 31 December 1989, a total of 199 medals had been awarded to inventors and promoters of inventive activity from 49 countries.

Setting of norms and standards

The major achievements of WIPO in 1989 towards raising the standards of protection for intellectual property rights were the adoption of two new treaties and a protocol. The Treaty on the International Registration of Audiovisual Works, adopted on 18 April, provided for the establishment, under WIPO auspices, of an international register of audiovisual works to record statements concerning who was the owner of what rights in which countries. By 31 December, the Treaty had been signed by 17 States. The Treaty on Intellectual Property in Respect of Integrated Circuits was adopted on 26 May to ensure the protection of layout designs and provide for the settlement of possible disputes between contracting parties. The Protocol Relating to the Madrid Agreement Concerning the International Registration of Marks, adopted in June, introduced changes to the Madrid system intended to remove certain impediments to its wider acceptance. By 31 December, the Protocol had been signed by 28 States.

The harmonization of patent laws advanced considerably during the year. Work on the harmonization of trademark laws began in November when a new committee of experts held its first session. Important progress was made in the committee of experts on model copyright provisions and completion of the work on the text was expected in 1990.

Registration activities

Patent Co-operation Treaty. During the year, 14,874 international patent applications were filed under PCT, a 25 per cent increase over 1988. The PCT Union Assembly decided in October to convene a working group in 1990-1991 to consider further expansion of the internationalization of the grants of patents.

Madrid Agreement. A total of 19,488 registrations and renewals were applied to the International Register of Marks in 1989, an increase of 11 per cent over 1988. In addition, there were 20,380 changes and 38,366 refusals or invalidations recorded during the year. In October, the Madrid Union Assembly approved an average 8 per cent increase in registration fees, effective as of 1 April 1990. It also approved establishment of a working group in 1990-1991 to prepare new draft regulations and other measures required by the new Protocol to the Madrid Agreement.

Hague Agreement. In 1989, there were 3,176 international industrial design deposits under the Hague Agreement, reflecting a 17.5 per cent increase over 1988. With such growth expected to continue, the Assembly of the Hague Union decided in October to begin computerizing operations during 1990-1991. The Assembly also agreed on convening a working group to consider revising the Agreement or adding a protocol to it, in order to introduce further flexibility and other measures to encourage adherence to the Agreement and to make it easier to use by applicants.

Secretariat

On 1 January 1989, WIPO employed 319 staff members. Of these, 107 were in the Professional and higher categories (drawn from 40 States) and 212 were in the General Service category. In addition, during the year, 149 experts' missions were undertaken by WIPO consultants for technical assistance projects and 222 lecturers participated in meetings sponsored by WIPO.

Budget

The principal sources of income for WIPO derived from international registration services (primarily under PCT and the Madrid Agreement) and contributions from member States. During 1988-1989, WIPO income totalled 137,415,000 Swiss francs (SwF), including SwF 45,617,000 from contributions, SwF 78,133,000 from registration services and SwF 13,665,000 from the sale of publications and other miscellaneous sources. During the same period, total expenditures amounted to SwF 108,739,000.

NOTE: For further information on WIPO, see *Governing Bodies of WIPO and the Unions Administered by WIPO: Activities in the Year 1989.*

HEADQUARTERS AND OTHER OFFICE

HEADQUARTERS
World Intellectual Property Organization
34 Chemin des Colombettes
1211 Geneva 20, Switzerland
Cable address: OMPI GENEVA
Telephone: (41) (22) 730-91-11
Fax: (41) (22) 733-54-28
Telex: 412 912 OMPI CH

WIPO OFFICE AT THE UNITED NATIONS
2 United Nations Plaza, Room 560
New York, N.Y. 10017, United States
Telephone: (1) (212) 963-6813
Fax: (1) (212) 963-4801
Telex: 420544 UNH UI

Chapter XVI

International Fund for Agricultural Development (IFAD)

In 1989, the International Fund for Agricultural Development (IFAD) continued to provide concessional financial assistance to agricultural projects in low-income, food-deficit countries to increase food output while retaining environmental sustainability and focusing on support for poor rural women. The Fund paid particular attention to sub-Saharan Africa to generate durable benefits for a large number of the poor in the most deprived areas of the continent.

The year marked several important milestones for IFAD. Negotiations on the third replenishment of the Fund's resources were successfully completed and rebuilding of the Fund's lending levels was further reinforced. A wide range of additional commitments under the Special Programme for Sub-Saharan African Countries Affected by Drought and Desertification (SPA) took place and a new generation of grants for agricultural research on environmentally sound methods of smallholder crop and animal development was introduced. Particularly important in terms of IFAD's preparedness for the coming decade were the gains made in furthering the specificity of its approach to rural poverty alleviation.

The IFAD Executive Board held three regular sessions (April, September, December) and one special session (June) during the year, approving loans for 23 projects, including 7 loans under SPA, as well as 31 technical assistance grants. The Board approved a programme of work for 1990 at 214.4 million special drawing rights (SDR) and endorsed a budget of $38.85 million, plus a contingency of $500,000. It also approved the programme of work in 1990 for SPA (SDR 43.3 million) along with administrative expenses of $3.82 million with a contingency of $150,000.

IFAD membership remained at 143 in 1989, with non-original membership pending on two States, Malaysia and Myanmar. Of the current members, 21 were in category I (developed countries), 12 in Category II (oil-exporting developing countries) and 110 in Category III (other developing countries).

Resources

Successfully completed in 1989, the third replenishment of IFAD's resources generated some $570 million, well above the $476 million pledged for the second replenishment. Member States in the first two categories provided core financing, while the amount pledged in convertible currency by the third category of members rose nearly threefold. The industrialized countries of Category I responded to that increase by matching that raise threefold in their own contributions. External cofinancing contributed $186.5 million, while IFAD itself provided $121.1 million for 14 projects.

The Executive Board expressed concern about the delay in deposits of instruments of contribution and payments against pledges to IFAD's second replenishment, bearing in mind that the Governing Council called for the completion of all payments by 31 December 1987.

In 1989, IFAD continued to enter into special funding agreements with member Governments with a view to involving them more actively in those areas of its operations that were of particular interest to them. The bulk of such supplementary funding provided to the Fund was intended to support activities in selected projects. Among the contributions received during the year were $1.5 million from Italy for a technical assistance grant, $1.2 million from Denmark, $1.1 million from the Netherlands, $0.4 million from Australia and $0.3 million from Finland.

Other supplementary funding was provided by Governments and private donors to finance studies, training and workshops on specific issues, such as women's role in development and the environment, and for promotional and educational programmes.

Activities

In 1989, IFAD provided SDR 204.1 million (approximately $259.9 million) in 25 loans and SDR 9.7 million ($12.5 million) in 31 technical assistance grants, making a total of SDR 213.8 million (approximately $272.4 million) for the year under both the Regular Programme and SPA, compared with SDR 183.6 million ($242.6 million) in 1988. Average loan size rose by 27 per cent in 1989.

Agricultural and rural development projects accounted for 27 per cent and 25.6 per cent, respectively, of the projects approved. A common theme running through all components in IFAD projects was the strengthening of women's role in development; almost every project approved in 1989 provided substantial resources to increase the farm productivity and off-farm incomes of women.

IFAD technical assistance activities continued the trend towards greater specificity. Grants for agricultural research, in particular, focused on the development of environmentally safe and sustainable technologies which stressed the needs of resource-poor farmers while protecting their natural resource base.

The number of IFAD beneficiary countries rose to 93 in 1989, with loans being extended for the first time to Angola and Gabon. The beneficiary countries were spread across the developing world, with Africa accounting for 40, Asia 16, Latin America 24 and the Near East and North Africa 13.

By the end of the year, IFAD assistance to Africa under the Regular Programme amounted to SDR 690 million ($806.8 million) in loans and grants for 89 projects in 39 countries. In addition, under SPA, the Fund provided SDR 152.4 million ($193.1 million) for 20 projects in 16 countries. IFAD's total assistance to the region amounted to SDR 842.4 million ($999.9 million), or 35.3 per cent of the total project cost of $2,828.8 million.

In 1989, under the Regular and Special Programmes combined, Africa received SDR 106.6 million in assistance for 12 projects in 11 countries.

By the end of 1989, IFAD assistance to Asia amounted to SDR 872.8 million for 71 projects in 16 countries. Of the total project cost of $4,070.9 million, the Fund contributed 25.4 per cent ($1,033.2 million). During the year, the region received SDR 48.5 million in assistance for five projects in five States. The total cost of those projects amounted to $205.7 million, of which IFAD's share was $62.3 million, or 30.3 per cent. Three were primarily credit projects with rural development components, and two were to a large extent concerned with environmental preservation and maintaining an ecological balance.

IFAD assistance to Latin America and the Caribbean amounted to SDR 326.8 million ($393.5 million) for 46 projects in 24 countries by the end of 1989; of the total project cost of $1,327.8 million, the Fund contributed $393.5 million, or 29.6 per cent. In 1989, under the Regular Programme, the region received SDR 13.5 million in assistance for two projects—involving irrigation in Haiti and rural development in Guatemala—at a total cost

of $41.1 million, of which IFAD's share was $17.3 million, or 42.1 per cent.

By the end of the year, IFAD assistance to the Near East and North Africa under the Regular Programme amounted to SDR 390.4 million ($460.8 million) for 40 projects in 13 countries; of the total project costs of $2,836.1 million, the Fund contributed $461.1 million, or 16.3 per cent. In addition, under its Special Programme, IFAD provided SDR 16.3 million ($20.5 million) for three loans and one grant in three countries. Under the Regular and Special Programmes combined, the region received in 1989 SDR 37.3 million in assistance for four projects—agricultural and rural development projects in Djibouti, Somalia and Turkey, and an agricultural credit project in Yemen—at a total cost of $114.8 million, of which IFAD funded $47.7 million, or 41.6 per cent.

Secretariat

At the end of 1989, IFAD's staff totalled 198, of whom 80 drawn from 39 member States were in the Professional category, and 118 in the General Service category.

Income and expenditure

Total revenue under the Regular Programme for 1989 was $97 million, consisting of $70.5 million in investment income, including gains on the sale of investments of $0.1 million, and $26.5 million from interest and service charges on loans. Total expenses for the year amounted to $29.5 million, compared with a budget before contingency of $35.8 million. The excess of revenue over expenses for the year was $67.5 million.

Total revenue under SPA for 1989 was $12.6 million, consisting of $12.5 million of investment income and $0.1 million from interest and service charges on loans. Expenses for the year totalled $3.1 million, compared with a budget before contingency of $4.2 million. The excess of revenue over expenses for the year was $9.5 million.

NOTE: For further details on IFAD activities in 1989, see *IFAD Annual Report 1989.*

HEADQUARTERS AND OTHER OFFICES

HEADQUARTERS
International Fund for Agricultural Development
Via del Serafico, 107
00142 Rome, Italy
  Cable address: IFAD ROME
  Telephone: (39) (6) 54591
  Fax: (39) (6) 5043463
  Telex: 620330

IFAD Liaison Office
1 United Nations Plaza, Room 1208
New York, N.Y. 10017, United States
  Telephone: (1) (212) 963-0546
  Fax: (1) (212) 963-2787

IFAD Liaison Office
1775 K Street, N.W., Suite 410
Washington, D.C. 20006, United States
  Telephone: (1) (202) 331-9099
  Fax: (1) (202) 331-9366

Chapter XVII

United Nations Industrial Development Organization (UNIDO)

In 1989, the United Nations Industrial Development Organization (UNIDO) continued its activities in the areas of industrial operations, strategies and promotion. In addition, special programmes calling for multidisciplinary or interdepartmental approaches were designed to support industrial growth and restructuring, which included the first Industrial Development Decade for Africa 1980-1990 (IDDA), assistance to the least developed countries (LDCs), industrial co-operation among developing countries, integration of women in industrial development and co-operation with industrial enterprises and non-governmental organizations (NGOs).

A streamlined vision for the industrialization of developing countries was presented at the third session of the General Conference, which took place at Vienna from 20 to 24 November. Attended by 129 countries and some 700 delegates, the Conference addressed such topics as environmental protection; regional industrial programmes for Africa, Latin America and the Caribbean, and Asia and the Pacific; industrialization of LDCs; new concepts and approaches for co-operation in industrial development; mobilization of financial resources; and the 1990-1991 programme and budget.

As of 31 December 1989, 151 States were members of UNIDO.

Industrial strategies and operations

A total of 1,896 technical assistance projects with a total value of $133.8 million were implemented by UNIDO in 1989. Africa received 36.7 percent; Asia and the Pacific received 32.6 per cent; the Arab States (including the African Arab States) received 14.4 per cent; the Americas (Latin America and the Caribbean) received 9 per cent; and Europe received 3.2 per cent. Interregional and global projects accounted for 14.3 per cent.

Major emphasis continued to be placed on the analysis and formulation of the UNIDO perspective on global industrialization, embodied in *Industry and Development: Global Report*, a publication issued to member States prior to the General Conference in November, which contains a review of the latest trends in the global industrial landscape and of the near-term prospects for industrialization in developing countries. Various policy-oriented documents were also prepared for the

Conference, including reports on external debt and industrial development, as well as on the restructuring of world industrial production and redeployment.

Implementation of industrial operations

Agro-industries. Technical co-operation expenditures for agro-industries amounted to $14.6 million, some 60.5 per cent of which was financed from resources of the United Nations Development Programme (UNDP). Of a total of 162 projects under implementation, Africa accounted for 47.1 per cent; Asia and the Pacific, 39.3 per cent; Latin America and the Caribbean, 10 per cent; the Arab States (excluding those in Africa), 9.5 per cent; Europe, 1.5 per cent; and global and interregional projects, 1.6 per cent.

Projects related to agro-industries continued to focus on the production of value-added, agro-based products. Industrial promotion focused on investment, the System of Consultations, and the development and transfer of technology. Four Consultations were convened, on the food-processing industry, the electronics industry, small- and medium-scale enterprises and the capital goods industry. Measures were taken to integrate the consultation process more effectively into other activities of UNIDO, and emphasis was also placed on follow-up activities encompassing the whole of UNIDO as well as other organizations and member States.

Chemical industries. Expenditures for technical co-operation in the chemical sector amounted to $30.2 million, with a total of 356 projects. Some 58 per cent of the total implementation was financed from UNDP resources. Of the total expenditure, Africa accounted for 40.5 per cent; Asia and the Pacific, 43.3 per cent; Latin America and the Caribbean, 6.2 per cent; the Arab States (excluding those in Africa), 25.9 per cent; Europe, 4.1 per cent; and global and interregional projects, 4.9 per cent.

The UNIDO activities in the biennium 1988-1989 reflected the adoption of a more integrated approach to the chemical industry, which aimed to create more efficient and competitive products. Increased attention was given to environmental and energy aspects of the industry, such as recycling, waste utilization and waste minimization. Projects associated with the environmental impact of energy production totalled $2 million. Initial steps were taken to strengthen all of these activities by giving special attention to some of the advances in biotechnology and new materials science, from which many of the non- and low-waste technologies are derived.

Metallurgical industries. In 1989, technical co-operation expenditures in metallurgical industries amounted to $9.1 million, with 85 per cent of the total implementation financed from UNDP resources. The number of projects totalled 130, of which Africa accounted for 23.1 per cent; Asia and the Pacific, 59.7 per cent; Latin America and the Caribbean, 6.5 per cent; the Arab States (excluding those in Africa), 9.4 per cent; Europe, 2.1 per cent; and global and interregional projects, 7.4 per cent. Special attention was given to the introduction and adoption of new technologies in technical co-operation activities to ensure rationalization of the production process, improve product quality and the management of material and energy resources and to encourage the development of solutions to pressing environmental problems through increased waste utilization. Projects aimed at technology transfer, rehabilitation, restructuring and modernization were strongly promoted, and technical co-operation activities related to the establishment of small-scale metallurgical operations were increased.

Engineering industries. Technical co-operation expenditures for engineering industries amounted to $17.2 million. About 82 per cent of the total implementation was financed from UNDP resources. Of the 210 projects, Africa accounted for 34.7 per cent; Asia and the Pacific, 42.4 per cent; Latin America and the Caribbean, 9.1 per cent; the Arab States (excluding those in Africa), 13.3 per cent; Europe, 8.5 per cent; and global and interregional projects, 1.2 per cent.

The focus of these activities remained on rural development in the metal sector, the application of electronic high technology to industry, the use of computer-aided manufacturing (CAM) techniques in the machine tools sector, spare-parts manufacture in the transport industries and equipment development in the energy sector. Activities related to materials and technology for the packaging industry were also initiated, using an integrated approach to serve the industry as a whole, particularly the agro-industrial sector. Repair and maintenance continued to represent a major component of all technical assistance in engineering industries. The servicing of agricultural tools and machinery remained one of the most acute problems facing many developing countries. Therefore, UNIDO established specific maintenance and repair centres and workshops in certain African countries to help local industries maintain production equipment through the introduction of main-

tenance schemes and local production of spare parts.

Industrial planning. This area encompassed a total of 113 technical co-operation projects, with expenditures amounting to $8.1 million, of which 83 per cent was financed from UNDP resources. Of the total expenditure, Africa accounted for 56.9 per cent; Asia and the Pacific, 15.1 per cent; Latin America and the Caribbean, 19 per cent; the Arab States (excluding those in Africa), 6.4 per cent; Europe, 0.3 per cent; and global and interregional projects, 4 per cent.

There was an increase in project approvals due to greater demand for assistance in the area of planning. The quantitative targets for the sub-programme of industrial planning were exceeded, and new approaches were adopted and activities were redirected towards strategic management, enhancement of the productive performance and decision-support systems. Emphasis was placed on efficient co-operation between the public and the private sector to help developing countries adjust to rapid structural change. The introduction of industrial automation technologies, as well as the strengthening of productive performance in the capital-goods sectors continued to underlie the industrial strategies of many developing countries.

Institutional infrastructure. Expenditures in the area of institutional infrastructure totalled $15 million in 1989, of which 81 per cent was funded from UNDP resources. A total of 208 projects were implemented or under implementation. Africa accounted for 40.6 per cent; Asia and the Pacific, 22.5 per cent; Latin America and the Caribbean, 15.9 per cent; the Arab States (excluding those in Africa), 16 per cent; Europe, 1.6 per cent; and global and interregional projects, 7.2 per cent. A comprehensive and integrated approach to technical co-operation projects was adopted and applied at various levels in order to render assistance more effective. The promotion and development of small- and medium-scale industries continued to receive high priority as a major programme element. UNIDO continued to assist a number of developing countries in setting up national chambers of commerce and industry in response to the growing demand for help in the industrialization process.

Industrial management and rehabilitation. Technical co-operation expenditures in this sector amounted to $7.5 million, with 82 per cent coming from UNDP resources. A total of 103 projects were under implementation. Of the total expenditure, Africa accounted for 33.6 per cent; Asia and the Pacific, 37.7 per cent; Latin America and the Caribbean, 19.7 per cent; the Arab States (excluding those in Africa), 13 per cent; Europe, 4.8 per cent; and global and interregional projects, 0.8 per cent.

In these programmes, emphasis was placed on improving the quality of technical co-operation.

Many large-scale projects dealt with the upgrading and modernization of production and management capability. Increased attention was given to project management in establishing new production facilities, factors in plant performance and managerial improvement such as maintenance and accounting and the modernization of plants and enterprises in general. In addition, industrial management and rehabilitation were addressed by many projects related to specific sectors.

Industrial human resource development. Expenditures for fellowships and training in all technical co-operation projects implemented by UNIDO amounted to $20.2 million. Of that total, $13.6 million was spent on fellowships and study tours and $6.6 million on group training activities and meetings. Technical co-operation expenditures for training that received substantive support from the former Industrial Training Branch (renamed the Industrial Human Resource Branch in 1989) amounted to $6.4 million. About 11 per cent of the expenditure in this area was financed from UNDP resources. A total of 179 projects were implemented. Africa accounted for 42.5 per cent; Asia and the Pacific, 3.2 per cent; Latin America and the Caribbean, 2.2 per cent; the Arab States (excluding those in Africa), 0.6 per cent; Europe, 4.6 per cent; and global and interregional projects, 47.1 per cent.

During 1989, UNIDO training programmes responded to the growing needs of the developing countries for assistance in assimilating new and advanced technology. Special attention was given to strengthening the training capacity of institutions and industry in this area through the instruction of trainers in computer-based advanced training systems and the preparation of related materials. Most of the activities were undertaken in Africa within the framework of IDDA.

Feasibility studies. A total of $7 million was spent on feasibility studies in 1989. Some 64 per cent of the total was financed from UNDP resources, and 125 projects at different stages of implementation were undertaken. Of the total expenditures, Africa accounted for 51.7 per cent; Asia and the Pacific, 19.5 per cent; Latin America and the Caribbean, 1.3 per cent; the Arab States (excluding those in Africa), 29.3 per cent; and global and interregional projects, 6.9 per cent.

An increasing number of requests for project appraisals was received from industrialized countries in 1989, which were carried out on a commercial basis against payment of a fee. Continued emphasis was given to the promotion of institution-building to improve capability at the national level for industrial feasibility studies. Thirty-five pre-investment studies were undertaken in developing countries. A quarter of pre-investment studies led to actual investment during the period. In response

to the pressing need for developing countries to upgrade the level of skills required for the preparation of pre-investment studies, 50 seminars were carried out in which 900 participants were given training.

Industrial promotion

In 1989, industrial promotion focused on reinforcing links in the areas of consultations, the development and transfer of technology and industrial investment.

System of Consultations. The UNIDO System of Consultations is a mechanism for achieving the goals set out in the Lima Declaration and Plan of Action on Industrial Development and Co-operation,[a] specifically, restructuring world industry and increasing the share of developing countries in world production. Four consultations were held during 1989: the Consultation on the Food-Processing Industry with emphasis on fruit and vegetable processing (Tbilisi, USSR, 18-22 September); the First Consultation on Small- and Medium-Scale Enterprises including Co-operatives (Bari, Italy, 9-13 October); the First Consultation on the Electronics Industry (Valletta, Malta, 6-10 November); and the Third Consultation on the Capital Goods Industry with emphasis on rural transport equipment (Vienna, 4-8 December). Measures were taken to integrate the Consultation process more effectively into other activities of the organization and to enhance mutual support between the Divisions.

Several follow-ups to earlier consultations were held in 1989: the Regional Expert Group Meeting on the Development of the Non-ferrous Metals Industry in Latin America (Cordoba, Argentina, March); the Expert Group Meeting on the Pesticides Industry (Hungary, March); and the preparation for an interregional meeting on co-operation among developing countries for the development of the pharmaceutical industry. In addition, a number of technical co-operation proposals were developed as a general follow-up to consultations.

Preparatory meetings were held for consultations in 1990 on the building materials industry, emphasizing the transfer of technology within African and Asian countries, and on the food-processing industry and the wood and wood products industry. Preparatory work and substantive documentation for the selection and finalization of issues for a regional consultation on the petrochemical industry in the Arab countries, scheduled for 1991, were also undertaken.

Development and transfer of technology. A wide variety of programmes were carried out for the development and transfer of technology in 1989. A pro-

[a]YUN 1975, p. 473.

gramme of action was developed by the Conference on National and International Co-operation for the Telecommunications Industry in Africa, held in Arusha, United Republic of Tanzania, in March. The Conference reinforced the need for UNIDO involvement and for international co-operation. Two five-year projects totalling $42 million were approved by the Preparatory Committee on the Establishment of the International Centre for Genetic Engineering and Biotechnology (IGGEB), in order to increase research work in this field.

In the area of new and renewable sources of energy, special attention was given to new developments in solar energy and proposals were evaluated with emphasis on international co-operation. The Second Meeting of the Consultative Group on Solar Energy Research recommended that assistance continue to be provided to developing countries in the formulation of viable projects and studies on market development in solar energy devices.

The activities of the networking system of the Industrial and Technological Information Bank (INTIB) were further developed to provide more efficient direct services to end-users, in particular small- and medium-scale enterprises. Participants in the network included over 70 national focal points.

Industrial investment programme. UNIDO was increasingly called upon to assist developing countries in identifying sound investment projects and finding local investors and overseas partners to implement the projects. As in earlier years, this form of industrial co-operation went beyond investment to include the areas of marketing expertise, plant and equipment, technical know-how and licences, management support and training of local staff. A steady growth in technical co-operation activities of that type reflected the search by developing countries for new sources of financing, particularly foreign direct investment.

The Industrial Investment Division was restructured in 1989 to give it a clearer regional focus, directed at promoting programmes at the sectoral and subsectoral levels.

Industrial Development Decade for Africa (1980-1990)

The mid-term evaluation of the first Industrial Development Decade for Africa (IDDA) was completed and submitted to the African Ministers of Industry at their ninth meeting (Harare, Zimbabwe, May). This report, tracing a new course of development and emphasizing the need for Africa to shift dependence from external to internal engines of growth, played a major role in determining the approach to be adopted in the second Decade covering the period 1991-2000.

Technical assistance under IDDA addressed three main areas: the establishment of pilot and demonstration plants, the accelerated development of human resources and institutional infrastructure for industrial development.

In the course of the biennium 1988-1989, 34 projects valued at $4,065,974 were initiated and implemented. Short-term advisory services were used to contribute to the integrated programming exercise begun in 1989, which was intended to identify projects for funding. Under the technical assistance component, 24 programmes were drawn up for 13 countries, with an additional 22 programmes in preparation. The programmes were related to the priority area set for the biennium, namely agro-industries and related sectors such as fertilizers, pesticides and agricultural machinery.

In addition, UNIDO initiated meetings and workshops in order to secure co-operation within the framework of IDDA and to decide on future industrial development activities. As in previous years, close co-operation was maintained between the secretariats of the Organization of African Unity (OAU), the Economic Commission for Africa (ECA) and UNIDO.

Assistance to LDCs

UNIDO participated in various preparatory meetings for the Second United Nations Conference on the Least Developed Countries, which was scheduled to take place in Paris in 1990. As its contribution to the Conference, UNIDO was updating the review of the manufacturing sector in LDCs, which was prepared in 1988. Under an initiative to increase its technical assistance to LDCs, such assistance rose by 31.1 per cent. UNIDO also organized and financed visits by officials from seven countries to its headquarters in order to understand better the perceptions of individual countries. In addition, 15 programme-review and 14 project-formulation missions were undertaken during the year. To review ongoing programmes and define priority areas for UNDP action during its fifth programming cycle, UNIDO participated in UNDP country-programme mid-term reviews.

LDCs also participated in and benefited from UNIDO activities organized at the regional and subregional levels.

Industrial co-operation among developing countries

UNIDO diversified its activities related to industrial co-operation among developing countries in 1989. Programmes for economic and technical co-operation among developing countries (ECDC/TCDC) were focused on enterprise-to-enterprise co-operation, and increased attention was given to the follow-up of preliminary ECDC/TCDC agreements. Promotional activities for co-operation among developing countries in industrial development were pursued, including the examination of some 30 projects by a Solidarity Ministerial Meeting (Conakry, Guinea, December). A number of projects were implemented that resulted from previous preliminary agreements and recommendations, such as co-operation between the Republic of Korea and Turkey on the use of high-sulphur lignite without the resultant excessive pollution.

In 1989, UNIDO continued to make efforts to increase the use of resources from developing countries by awarding contracts to their organizations and institutions and by hiring their experts. Efforts were also made to ensure that bidder lists included companies from developing countries as much as possible. In 1989, 37 per cent of contracts went to organizations and institutions in 34 developing countries.

Integration of women in industrial development

The number of technical co-operation projects specifically targeting women increased in 1989. Twenty-two projects with a total value of over $4.5 million were under implementation, and a further 21 projects with a total value of $7 million were in preparation. Strong emphasis was placed on the development of a more systematic approach to the integration of women into UNIDO activities, especially into the process of industrial development. Another area of concentration was the organization of training programmes specifically for women in fields such as management, industrial project preparation, evaluation, financing and investment promotion, as well as food-processing technology. First steps were taken towards the goal of more visibly integrating women into general projects and programmes.

Environment

In response to 1987 General Assembly resolutions[b] on the environmental perspective to the year 2000, measures were undertaken to develop a comprehensive UNIDO environment programme through which environmental aspects could be systematically integrated, as appropriate, in the activities of the organization. Co-operation with other UN organizations on environmental matters was given high priority in 1989, for example in the framework for activities developed with UNEP. In 1989, a total of 41 environment-related projects were implemented and 77 were in preparation.

Secretariat

As of 31 December 1989, there were 1,358 staff members serving at UNIDO headquarters, 442 of whom were in the Professional and higher categories, and 916 in the General Service and related categories. Six hundred and ninety-eight staff members were women; 81 were Professionals and 617 were in other grades. In 1989, a total of 2,131 appointments of project personnel were processed (an increase of 221 from 1988), and a total of 1,061 expert appointments were extended. UNIDO was represented in the field by 37 Senior Industrial Development Field Advisers (SIDFAs) in developing countries, who worked with UNDP resident coordinators. At the end of 1989, 25 UNIDO Country Directors were financed by UNDP, nine from the operational budget and three from voluntary contributions from Germany and Italy. They were assisted by 69 Junior Professional Officers (JPOs) financed by 12 member Governments: Austria, Belgium, Denmark, Finland, France, Federal Republic of Germany, Italy, Japan, Netherlands, Norway, Sweden and Switzerland.

Budget

For 1989, total expenditures were $231.5 million, comprising $133.8 million for technical co-operation programmes and $97.7 million for headquarters expenditures. Financing came from member States, either directly through their assessed contributions and their voluntary contributions to the Industrial Development Fund (IDF) and trust funds, or indirectly via voluntary programmes such as UNDP. Non-governmental organizations, including enterprises being assisted on a self-financing basis, may also contribute to IDF and trust funds.

Headquarters expenditures, for example, activities other than technical co-operation projects, were financed largely from the regular budget. In 1989, that amount ($82.1 million) was supplemented by $15.6 million derived from a 13 per cent reimbursement for overheads on technical assistance delivery. At its second session, the General Conference approved the regular budget of $154.3 million for the biennium 1988-1989.

Technical co-operation activities were largely financed by the UNDP indicative planning figure. Other sources of financing included the UNDP Special Services programme (set up to respond to specific short-term, urgent requests relating to industrial development), trust funds and self-financing arrangements, IDF and the United Nations Fund for Drug Abuse Control.

[b]YUN 1987, p. 661, GA res. 42/186, and p. 679, GA res. 42/187, 11 Dec. 1987.

HEADQUARTERS AND OTHER OFFICE

HEADQUARTERS
United Nations Industrial Development Organization
Vienna International Centre
P. O. Box 300
A-1400 Vienna, Austria
  Telephone: (43) (1) 211310
  Fax: (43) (1) 232156, 2140414
  Telex: 135612
  World Wide Web: http://www.unido.org
  E-mail: unido-pinfo@unido.org

LIAISON OFFICE
UNIDO Liaison Office
1 United Nations Plaza, Room DC1-1110
New York, N.Y. 10017, United States
  Telephone: (1) (212) 963-6882
  Fax: (1) (212) 963-7904

Chapter XVIII

Interim Commission for the International Trade Organization (ICITO) and the General Agreement on Tariffs and Trade (GATT)

The United Nations Conference on Trade and Employment (Havana, Cuba, November 1947–March 1948) drew up a charter for an International Trade Organization (ITO) and established an Interim Commission for the International Trade Organization (ICITO). The members of the Conference's Preparatory Committee also negotiated tariffs among themselves and drew up the General Agreement on Tariffs and Trade (GATT). Since the charter itself was never accepted, ITO was not established. GATT—the only multilateral treaty embodying reciprocal rights and obligations laying down agreed rules for international trade—entered into force on 1 January 1948 with 23 contracting parties; ICITO provided the GATT secretariat.

As at 31 December 1989, the number of contracting parties to GATT remained at 96. Tunisia had acceded provisionally. The contracting parties accounted for nearly 90 per cent of world trade; 28 other countries, to whose territories GATT had been applied before their independence, maintained a *de facto* application of GATT pending final decisions as to their future commercial policy.

Multilateral trade negotiations

Uruguay Round

Trade Negotiations Committee

In April 1989, the Trade Negotiations Committee, the body responsible for overseeing the Uruguay Round—GATT's eighth "round" of multilateral trade negotiations, launched in 1986[a]—met in Geneva at the senior official level to complete the mid-term review of the Round, which had started in 1988.[b] In the agricultural negotiations, the Committee approved a detailed negotiating mandate for long-term reform and a short-term freeze on government support and aid. The Committee also defined the issues to be covered by the negotiations on trade-related aspects of intellectual property rights and agreed that substantive negotiations on textiles and clothing and on safeguards should begin in earnest. Following the completion of the mid-term review, the GATT Council of Representatives adopted a new trade policy review mechanism and detailed measures

to reform the dispute settlement procedures. It agreed that the Contracting Parties would meet at the ministerial level at least once every two years.

The Surveillance Body, responsible for overseeing the implementation of commitments on standstill and roll-back contained in the 1986 Ministerial Declaration on the Uruguay Round,[c] received no notifications of alleged breaches of the standstill commitment during 1989. With regard to the roll-back commitment, 20 requests had been made since 1986, most of which were addressed to the European Community (EC), Japan and the United States, but the frequency of consultations on those requests greatly diminished in 1989. The Surveillance Body also provided a forum for early-warning discussions on 30 cases of impending or threatened trade measures.

Group of Negotiations on Goods

The Group of Negotiations on Goods oversaw the work of the 14 negotiating groups that were established in 1987 to conduct the work outlined in part I of the 1986 Ministerial Declaration. The activities of the negotiating groups, which began to reconvene following the mid-term review in April, dealt with tariffs; non-tariff measures; natural-resource-based products; textiles and clothing; agriculture; tropical products; the review of GATT articles; multinational trade negotiation agreements and arrangements; safeguards; subsidies and countervailing measures; trade-related aspects of intellectual property rights; trade-related investment measures; dispute settlement; functioning of the GATT system; and services.

Implementation of the Tokyo Round agreements

The Tokyo Round—the multilateral trade negotiations that preceded the Uruguay Round—established a number of agreements covering non-tariff measures and certain sectoral matters as well as securing major tariff cuts. Each of the agreements had an overseeing committee or council.

[a]YUN 1986, p. 1210.
[b]YUN 1988, p. 982.
[c]YUN 1986, p. 1211.

Those bodies dealt with tariffs; anti-dumping practices; subsidies and countervailing measures; government procurement; technical barriers to trade; customs valuation; import licensing; bovine meat; dairy products; and civil aircraft. Settlement of disputes became an increasingly important role for some of those committees.

Other GATT activities

Contracting Parties regular session

The Contracting Parties held their forty-fifth regular session on 4 and 5 December 1989, focusing on the Uruguay Round and the importance of its success. Involvement in GATT was seen as of particular importance for the countries of Eastern Europe, which were initiating widespread political and economic reform.

Council of Representatives

The Council of Representatives, GATT's highest body between sessions of the Contracting Parties, held a special meeting on 11 December 1989 to review major activities of GATT and developments in the trading system. The Council noted some favourable developments in 1989 to which the Uruguay Round negotiations had contributed, such as the implementation of the trade policy review mechanism, the introduction of trade liberalization reform in a number of countries and an increased interest in GATT membership.

The GATT Director-General reported that, despite the contracting parties' determination to conduct trade policies within the GATT rules and framework, there were a number of actions that had been taken outside. At the end of 1989, there were approximately 249 discriminatory export restraint–type arrangements in force involving GATT contracting parties (excluding bilateral quantitative restrictions on textiles and clothing imposed under the Multifibre Arrangement). A majority of the restraints involved food and other agricultural products, textiles and clothing, footwear and machine tools.

Under the trade policy review mechanism agreed at the April mid-term review meeting, the Council was to examine, on a regular basis, each member's trade policies and practices. In December, it conducted a comprehensive examination of the trade policies of Australia, Morocco and the United States, each based on two reports, one prepared by the country concerned and the other by the GATT secretariat.

Trade and development

In 1989, the Committee on Trade and Development continued to review, discuss and negotiate issues of trade interest to developing countries. It reviewed implementation of part IV of the

General Agreement and of the Enabling Clause, an agreement resulting from the Tokyo Round, which provided for differential and more favourable treatment of developing countries in various areas of trade policy. With regard to trade between developed and developing countries, the Committee exchanged views on interlinkages between trade, money and finance, and the scope for credit and recognition for trade liberalization measures undertaken by developing countries.

In September, the Sub-Committee on Trade of Least Developed Countries reviewed issues in the Uruguay Round of particular interest to that group of countries. The Sub-Committee's Chairman proposed that the Enabling Clause be opened up further for the least developed countries (LDCs) by exempting them from quantitative restrictions and other non-tariff measures falling outside the scope of the multilateral trade negotiations agreements.

Conciliation and settlement of disputes

In April, the Council of Representatives revised GATT's dispute-settlement mechanism, as agreed at the mid-term review meeting in 1988. A number of disputes were taken up by dispute-settlement panels: a United States complaint about Canada's import restrictions on ice cream and yoghurt; a complaint by Chile about EC import restrictions on dessert apples; a United States complaint about EC import restrictions on apples; a United States complaint about payments and subsidies paid by EC to processors and producers of oilseeds and related animal-feed proteins; an Australian complaint about United States import restrictions on sugar; an EC complaint about United States restrictions on the importation of sugar and sugar-containing products; a United States complaint against EC restraints on exports of copper scrap; a complaint by Canada about Japan's tariff on imports of spruce, pine and fir dimension lumber; three separate complaints by Australia, New Zealand and the United States against the Republic of Korea's restrictions on imports of beef; a United States complaint about Norway's import restrictions on apples and pears; a complaint by Brazil about United States import restrictions on certain Brazilian products; a complaint by Canada about United States countervailing duty on Canadian pork; and an EC complaint regarding section 337 of the United States Tariff Act of 1930.

Among other matters dealt with during the year were a streamlined mechanism for reconciling the interests of contracting parties in the event of trade-damaging acts and the establishment of a working group on the export of domestically prohibited goods and other hazardous substances.

Technical assistance

In 1989, the GATT secretariat's Technical Co-operation Division organized or participated in 18 national trade policy seminars in developing countries in Africa, Asia and Latin America. It also organized a special training course on GATT dispute-settlement procedures and practices (Geneva, November). The Statistics and Information Systems Division organized a seminar/workshop on the integrated data base (Geneva, October), which was attended by some 70 representatives from 34 countries.

Training programmes

Between 1955 and the end of 1989, a total of 1,146 officials from 114 countries and 10 regional organizations had attended GATT trade policy courses. Twenty-four fellowships were granted for each course. Two such courses, one in French and the other in English, were given in 1989.

International Trade Centre

The International Trade Centre, established by GATT in 1964 and jointly operated with the United Nations Conference on Trade and Development since 1968, continued to provide trade information and trade promotion advisory services to developing countries. The Centre's technical co-operation activities amounted to $29.6 million in 1989. Some 136 national, 54 regional and 107 interregional projects were under implementation, covering one or more of the Centre's eight programme areas: institutional infrastructure for trade promotion at the national level; specialized national trade promotion services; export market development; commodity promotion; training; import operations and techniques; trade promotion for LDCs; and activities with national chambers of commerce.

Secretariat

As at 31 December 1989, the GATT secretariat employed 376 staff members—159 in the Professional and higher categories, 213 in the General Service category and 4 ungraded staff members.

Financial arrangements

Member countries of GATT contributed to the budget in accordance with a scale assessed on the basis of each country's share in the total trade of the contracting parties and associated Governments. The budget for 1989 was 64,861,000 Swiss francs.

NOTE: For further information on GATT, see *GATT Activities 1989: An Annual Review of the Work of the GATT.*

HEADQUARTERS*

World Trade Organization/
GATT Secretariat
Centre William Rappard
154, rue de Lausanne
1211 Geneva 21, Switzerland
   Cable address: OMC/WTO, GENEVE
   Telephone: (41) (22) 739-51-11
   Fax: (41) (22) 731-42-06
   Telex: 412 324 OMC/WTO CH

*Listing as of June 1997.

Appendices

Appendix I

Roster of the United Nations

(As at 31 December 1989)

MEMBER	DATE OF ADMISSION	MEMBER	DATE OF ADMISSION	MEMBER	DATE OF ADMISSION
Afghanistan	19 Nov. 1946	Germany, Federal		Peru	31 Oct. 1945
Albania	14 Dec. 1955	Republic of	18 Sep. 1973	Philippines	24 Oct. 1945
Algeria	8 Oct. 1962	Ghana	8 Mar. 1957	Poland	24 Oct. 1945
Angola	1 Dec. 1976	Greece	25 Oct. 1945	Portugal	14 Dec. 1955
Antigua and Barbuda	11 Nov. 1981	Grenada	17 Sep. 1974	Qatar	21 Sep. 1971
Argentina	24 Oct. 1945	Guatemala	21 Nov. 1945	Romania	14 Dec. 1955
Australia	1 Nov. 1945	Guinea	12 Dec. 1958	Rwanda	18 Sep. 1962
Austria	14 Dec. 1955	Guinea-Bissau	17 Sep. 1974	Saint Kitts and Nevis	23 Sep. 1983
Bahamas	18 Sep. 1973	Guyana	20 Sep. 1966	Saint Lucia	18 Sep. 1979
Bahrain	21 Sep. 1971	Haiti	24 Oct. 1945	Saint Vincent and	
Bangladesh	17 Sep. 1974	Honduras	17 Dec. 1945	the Grenadines	16 Sep. 1980
Barbados	9 Dec. 1966	Hungary	14 Dec. 1955	Samoa	15 Dec. 1976
Belgium	27 Dec. 1945	Iceland	19 Nov. 1946	Sao Tome and	
Belize	25 Sep. 1981	India	30 Oct. 1945	Principe	16 Sep. 1975
Benin	20 Sep. 1960	Indonesia[2]	28 Sep. 1950	Saudi Arabia	24 Oct. 1945
Bhutan	21 Sep. 1971	Iran (Islamic		Senegal	28 Sep. 1960
Bolivia	14 Nov. 1945	Republic of)	24 Oct. 1945	Seychelles	21 Sep. 1976
Botswana	17 Oct. 1966	Iraq	21 Dec. 1945	Sierra Leone	27 Sep. 1961
Brazil	24 Oct. 1945	Ireland	14 Dec. 1955	Singapore[3]	21 Sep. 1965
Brunei Darussalam	21 Sep. 1984	Israel	11 May 1949	Solomon Islands	19 Sep. 1978
Bulgaria	14 Dec. 1955	Italy	14 Dec. 1955	Somalia	20 Sep. 1960
Burkina Faso	20 Sep. 1960	Jamaica	18 Sep. 1962	South Africa	7 Nov. 1945
Burundi	18 Sep. 1962	Japan	18 Dec. 1956	Spain	14 Dec. 1955
Byelorussian Soviet		Jordan	14 Dec. 1955	Sri Lanka	14 Dec. 1955
Socialist Republic	24 Oct. 1945	Kenya	16 Dec. 1963	Sudan	12 Nov. 1956
Cameroon	20 Sep. 1960	Kuwait	14 May 1963	Suriname	4 Dec. 1975
Canada	9 Nov. 1945	Lao People's		Swaziland	24 Sep. 1968
Cape Verde	16 Sep. 1975	Democratic Republic	14 Dec. 1955	Sweden	19 Nov. 1946
Central African		Lebanon	24 Oct. 1945	Syrian Arab	
Republic	20 Sep. 1960	Lesotho	17 Oct. 1966	Republic[1]	24 Oct. 1945
Chad	20 Sep. 1960	Liberia	2 Nov. 1945	Thailand	16 Dec. 1946
Chile	24 Oct. 1945	Libyan Arab		Togo	20 Sep. 1960
China	24 Oct. 1945	Jamahiriya	14 Dec. 1955	Trinidad and Tobago	18 Sep. 1962
Colombia	5 Nov. 1945	Luxembourg	24 Oct. 1945	Tunisia	12 Nov. 1956
Comoros	12 Nov. 1975	Madagascar	20 Sep. 1960	Turkey	24 Oct. 1945
Congo	20 Sep. 1960	Malawi	1 Dec. 1964	Uganda	25 Oct. 1962
Costa Rica	2 Nov. 1945	Malaysia[3]	17 Sep. 1957	Ukrainian Soviet	
Côte d'Ivoire	20 Sep. 1960	Maldives	21 Sep. 1965	Socialist Republic	24 Oct. 1945
Cuba	24 Oct. 1945	Mali	28 Sep. 1960	Union of Soviet	
Cyprus	20 Sep. 1960	Malta	1 Dec. 1964	Socialist Republics	24 Oct. 1945
Czechoslovakia	24 Oct. 1945	Mauritania	27 Oct. 1961	United Arab Emirates	9 Dec. 1971
Democratic Kampuchea	14 Dec. 1955	Mauritius	24 Apr. 1968	United Kingdom of	
Democratic Yemen	14 Dec. 1967	Mexico	7 Nov. 1945	Great Britain and	
Denmark	24 Oct. 1945	Mongolia	27 Oct. 1961	Northern Ireland	24 Oct. 1945
Djibouti	20 Sep. 1977	Morocco	12 Nov. 1956	United Republic	
Dominica	18 Dec. 1978	Mozambique	16 Sep. 1975	of Tanzania[5]	14 Dec. 1961
Dominican Republic	24 Oct. 1945	Myanmar[4]	19 Apr. 1948	United States	
Ecuador	21 Dec. 1945	Nepal	14 Dec. 1955	of America	24 Oct. 1945
Egypt[1]	24 Oct. 1945	Netherlands	10 Dec. 1945	Uruguay	18 Dec. 1945
El Salvador	24 Oct. 1945	New Zealand	24 Oct. 1945	Vanuatu	15 Sep. 1981
Equatorial Guinea	12 Nov. 1968	Nicaragua	24 Oct. 1945	Venezuela	15 Nov. 1945
Ethiopia	13 Nov. 1945	Niger	20 Sep. 1960	Viet Nam	20 Sep. 1977
Fiji	13 Oct. 1970	Nigeria	7 Oct. 1960	Yemen	30 Sep. 1947
Finland	14 Dec. 1955	Norway	27 Nov. 1945	Yugoslavia	24 Oct. 1945
France	24 Oct. 1945	Oman	7 Oct. 1971	Zaire	20 Sep. 1960
Gabon	20 Sep. 1960	Pakistan	30 Sep. 1947	Zambia	1 Dec. 1964
Gambia	21 Sep. 1965	Panama	13 Nov. 1945	Zimbabwe	25 Aug. 1980
German Democratic		Papua New Guinea	10 Oct. 1975		
Republic	18 Sep. 1973	Paraguay	24 Oct. 1945		

(footnotes on next page)

(footnotes for preceding page)

[1]Egypt and Syria, both of which became Members of the United Nations on 24 October 1945, joined together—following a plebiscite held in those countries on 21 February 1958—to form the United Arab Republic. On 13 October 1961, Syria, having resumed its status as an independent State, also resumed its separate membership in the United Nations; it changed its name to the Syrian Arab Republic on 14 September 1971. The United Arab Republic continued as a Member of the United Nations and reverted to the name of Egypt on 2 September 1971.

[2]On 20 January 1965, Indonesia informed the Secretary-General that it had decided to withdraw from the United Nations. By a telegram of 19 September 1966, it notified the Secretary-General of its decision to resume participation in the activities of the United Nations. On 28 September 1966, the General Assembly took note of that decision and the President invited the representatives of Indonesia to take their seats in the Assembly.

[3]On 16 September 1963, Sabah (North Borneo), Sarawak and Singapore joined with the Federation of Malaya (which became a United Nations Member on 17 September 1957) to form Malaysia. On 9 August 1965, Singapore became an independent State and on 21 September 1965 it became a Member of the United Nations.

[4]Formerly Burma; name changed on 18 June 1989.

[5]Tanganyika was admitted to the United Nations on 14 December 1961, and Zanzibar on 16 December 1963. Following ratification, on 26 April 1964, of the Articles of Union between Tanganyika and Zanzibar, the two States became represented as a single Member: the United Republic of Tanganyika and Zanzibar; it changed its name to the United Republic of Tanzania on 1 November 1964.

Appendix II

Charter of the United Nations and Statute of the International Court of Justice

Charter of the United Nations

NOTE: The Charter of the United Nations was signed on 26 June 1945, in San Francisco, at the conclusion of the United Nations Conference on International Organization, and came into force on 24 October 1945. The Statute of the International Court of Justice is an integral part of the Charter.

Amendments to Articles 23, 27 and 61 of the Charter were adopted by the General Assembly on 17 December 1963 and came into force on 31 August 1965. A further amendment to Article 61 was adopted by the General Assembly on 20 December 1971, and came into force on 24 September 1973. An amendment to Article 109, adopted by the General Assembly on 20 December 1965, came into force on 12 June 1968.

The amendment to Article 23 enlarges the membership of the Security Council from 11 to 15. The amended Article 27 provides that decisions of the Security Council on procedural matters shall be made by an affirmative vote of nine members (formerly seven) and on all other matters by an affirmative vote of nine members (formerly seven), including the concurring votes of the five permanent members of the Security Council.

The amendment to Article 61, which entered into force on 31 August 1965, enlarged the membership of the Economic and Social Council from 18 to 27. The subsequent amendment to that Article, which entered into force on 24 September 1973, further increased the membership of the Council from 27 to 54.

The amendment to Article 109, which relates to the first paragraph of that Article, provides that a General Conference of Member States for the purpose of reviewing the Charter may be held at a date and place to be fixed by a two-thirds vote of the members of the General Assembly and by a vote of any nine members (formerly seven) of the Security Council. Paragraph 3 of Article 109, which deals with the consideration of a possible review conference during the tenth regular session of the General Assembly, has been retained in its original form in its reference to a "vote of any seven members of the Security Council", the paragraph having been acted upon in 1955 by the General Assembly, at its tenth regular session, and by the Security Council.

WE THE PEOPLES
OF THE UNITED NATIONS
DETERMINED

to save succeeding generations from the scourge of war, which twice in our lifetime has brought untold sorrow to mankind, and

to reaffirm faith in fundamental human rights, in the dignity and worth of the human person, in the equal rights of men and women and of nations large and small, and

to establish conditions under which justice and respect for the obligations arising from treaties and other sources of international law can be maintained, and

to promote social progress and better standards of life in larger freedom,

AND FOR THESE ENDS

to practice tolerance and live together in peace with one another as good neighbors, and

to unite our strength to maintain international peace and security, and

to ensure, by the acceptance of principles and the institution of methods, that armed force shall not be used, save in the common interest, and

to employ international machinery for the promotion of the economic and social advancement of all peoples,

HAVE RESOLVED TO
COMBINE OUR EFFORTS TO
ACCOMPLISH THESE AIMS.

Accordingly, our respective Governments, through representatives assembled in the city of San Francisco, who have exhibited their full powers found to be in good and due form, have agreed to the present Charter of the United Nations and do hereby establish an international organization to be known as the United Nations.

Chapter I
PURPOSES AND PRINCIPLES

Article 1

The Purposes of the United Nations are:

1. To maintain international peace and security, and to that end: to take effective collective measures for the prevention and removal of threats to the peace, and for the suppression of acts of aggression or other breaches of the peace, and to bring about by peaceful means, and in conformity with the principles of justice and international law, adjustment or settlement of international disputes or situations which might lead to a breach of the peace;

2. To develop friendly relations among nations based on respect for the principle of equal rights and self-determination of peoples, and to take other appropriate measures to strengthen universal peace;

3. To achieve international cooperation in solving international problems of an economic, social, cultural, or humanitarian character, and in promoting and encouraging respect for human rights and for fundamental freedoms for all without distinction as to race, sex, language, or religion; and

4. To be a center for harmonizing the actions of nations in the attainment of these common ends.

Article 2

The Organization and its Members, in pursuit of the Purposes stated in Article 1, shall act in accordance with the following Principles.

1. The Organization is based on the principle of the sovereign equality of all its Members.

2. All Members, in order to ensure to all of them the rights and benefits resulting from membership, shall fulfil in good faith the obligations assumed by them in accordance with the present Charter.

3. All Members shall settle their international disputes by peaceful means in such a manner that international peace and security, and justice, are not endangered.

4. All Members shall refrain in their international relations from the threat or use of force against the territorial integrity or political independence of any state, or in any other manner inconsistent with the Purposes of the United Nations.

5. All Members shall give the United Nations every assistance in any action it takes in accordance with the present Charter, and shall refrain from giving assistance to any state against which the United Nations is taking preventive or enforcement action.

6. The Organization shall ensure that states which are not Members of the United Nations act in accordance with these Principles so far as may be necessary for the maintenance of international peace and security.

7. Nothing contained in the present Charter shall authorize the United Nations to intervene in matters which are essentially within the domestic jurisdiction of any state or shall require the Members to submit such matters to settlement under the present Charter; but this principle shall not prejudice the application of enforcement measures under Chapter VII.

Chapter II
MEMBERSHIP

Article 3

The original Members of the United Nations shall be the states which, having participated in the United Nations Conference on International Organization at San Francisco, or having previously signed the Declaration by United Nations of 1 January 1942, sign the present Charter and ratify it in accordance with Article 110.

Article 4

1. Membership in the United Nations is open to all other peace-loving states which accept the obligations contained in the present Charter and, in the judgment of the Organization, are able and willing to carry out these obligations.

2. The admission of any such state to membership in the United Nations will be effected by a decision of the General Assembly upon the recommendation of the Security Council.

Article 5

A Member of the United Nations against which preventive or enforcement action has been taken by the Security Council may be suspended from the exercise of the rights and privileges of membership by the General Assembly upon the recommendation of the Security Council. The exercise of these rights and privileges may be restored by the Security Council.

Article 6

A Member of the United Nations which has persistently violated the Principles contained in the present Charter may be expelled from the Organization by the General Assembly upon the recommendation of the Security Council.

Chapter III
ORGANS

Article 7

1. There are established as the principal organs of the United Nations: a General Assembly, a Security Council, an Economic and Social Council, a Trusteeship Council, an International Court of Justice, and a Secretariat.

2. Such subsidiary organs as may be found necessary may be established in accordance with the present Charter.

Article 8

The United Nations shall place no restrictions on the eligibility of men and women to participate in any capacity and under conditions of equality in its principal and subsidiary organs.

Chapter IV
THE GENERAL ASSEMBLY

Composition

Article 9

1. The General Assembly shall consist of all the Members of the United Nations.

2. Each Member shall have not more than five representatives in the General Assembly.

Functions and powers

Article 10

The General Assembly may discuss any questions or any matters within the scope of the present Charter or relating to the powers and functions of any organs provided for in the present Charter, and, except as provided in Article 12, may make recommendations to the Members of the United Nations or to the Security Council or to both on any such questions or matters.

Article 11

1. The General Assembly may consider the general principles of cooperation in the maintenance of international peace and security, including the principles governing disarmament and the regulation of armaments, and may make recommendations with regard to such principles to the Members or to the Security Council or to both.

2. The General Assembly may discuss any questions relating to the maintenance of international peace and security brought before it by any Member of the United Nations, or by the Security Council, or by a state which is not a Member of the United Nations in accordance with Article 35, paragraph 2, and, except as provided in Article 12, may make recommendations with regard to any such questions to the state or states concerned or to the Security Council or to both. Any such question on which action is necessary shall be referred to the Security Council by the General Assembly either before or after discussion.

3. The General Assembly may call the attention of the Security Council to situations which are likely to endanger international peace and security.

4. The powers of the General Assembly set forth in this Article shall not limit the general scope of Article 10.

Article 12

1. While the Security Council is exercising in respect of any dispute or situation the functions assigned to it in the present Charter, the General Assembly shall not make any recommendation with regard to that dispute or situation unless the Security Council so requests.

2. The Secretary-General, with the consent of the Security Council, shall notify the General Assembly at each session of any matters relative to the maintenance of international peace and security which are being dealt with by the Security Council and shall similarly notify the General Assembly, or the Members of the United Nations if the General Assembly is not in session, immediately the Security Council ceases to deal with such matters.

Article 13

1. The General Assembly shall initiate studies and make recommendations for the purpose of:

    a. promoting international cooperation in the political field and encouraging the progressive development of international law and its codification;

    b. promoting international cooperation in the economic, social, cultural, educational, and health fields, and assisting in the realization of human rights and fundamental freedoms for all without distinction as to race, sex, language, or religion.

2. The further responsibilities, functions, and powers of the General Assembly with respect to matters mentioned in paragraph 1(b) above are set forth in Chapters IX and X.

Article 14

Subject to the provisions of Article 12, the General Assembly may recommend measures for the peaceful adjustment of any situation, regardless of origin, which it deems likely to impair the general welfare or friendly relations among nations, including situations resulting from a violation of the provisions of the present Charter setting forth the Purposes and Principles of the United Nations.

Article 15

1.   The General Assembly shall receive and consider annual and special reports from the Security Council; these reports shall include an account of the measures that the Security Council has decided upon or taken to maintain international peace and security.

2.   The General Assembly shall receive and consider reports from the other organs of the United Nations.

Article 16

The General Assembly shall perform such functions with respect to the international trusteeship system as are assigned to it under Chapters XII and XIII, including the approval of the trusteeship agreements for areas not designated as strategic.

Article 17

1.   The General Assembly shall consider and approve the budget of the Organization.

2.   The expenses of the Organization shall be borne by the Members as apportioned by the General Assembly.

3.   The General Assembly shall consider and approve any financial and budgetary arrangements with specialized agencies referred to in Article 57 and shall examine the administrative budgets of such specialized agencies with a view to making recommendations to the agencies concerned.

Voting

Article 18

1.   Each member of the General Assembly shall have one vote.

2.   Decisions of the General Assembly on important questions shall be made by a two-thirds majority of the members present and voting. These questions shall include: recommendations with respect to the maintenance of international peace and security, the election of the non-permanent members of the Security Council, the election of the members of the Economic and Social Council, the election of members of the Trusteeship Council in accordance with paragraph 1(c) of Article 86, the admission of new Members to the United Nations, the suspension of the rights and privileges of membership, the expulsion of Members, questions relating to the operation of the trusteeship system, and budgetary questions.

3.   Decisions on other questions, including the determination of additional categories of questions to be decided by a two-thirds majority, shall be made by a majority of the members present and voting.

Article 19

A Member of the United Nations which is in arrears in the payment of its financial contributions to the Organization shall have no vote in the General Assembly if the amount of its arrears equals or exceeds the amount of the contributions due from it for the preceding two full years. The General Assembly may, nevertheless, permit such a Member to vote if it is satisfied that the failure to pay is due to conditions beyond the control of the Member.

Procedure

Article 20

The General Assembly shall meet in regular annual sessions and in such special sessions as occasion may require. Special sessions shall be convoked by the Secretary-General at the request of the Security Council or of a majority of the Members of the United Nations.

Article 21

The General Assembly shall adopt its own rules of procedure. It shall elect its President for each session.

Article 22

The General Assembly may establish such subsidiary organs as it deems necessary for the performance of its functions.

Chapter V
THE SECURITY COUNCIL

Composition

Article 23[1]

1.   The Security Council shall consist of fifteen Members of the United Nations. The Republic of China, France, the Union of Soviet Socialist Republics, the United Kingdom of Great Britain and Northern Ireland, and the United States of America shall be permanent members of the Security Council. The General Assembly shall elect ten other Members of the United Nations to be non-permanent members of the Security Council, due regard being specially paid, in the first instance to the contribution of Members of the United Nations to the maintenance of international peace and security and to the other purposes of the Organization, and also to equitable geographical distribution.

2.   The non-permanent members of the Security Council shall be elected for a term of two years. In the first election of the non-permanent members after the increase of the membership of the Security Council from eleven to fifteen, two of the four additional members shall be chosen for a term of one year. A retiring member shall not be eligible for immediate re-election.

3.   Each member of the Security Council shall have one representative.

Functions and powers

Article 24

1.   In order to ensure prompt and effective action by the United Nations, its Members confer on the Security Council primary responsibility for the maintenance of international peace and security, and agree that in carrying out its duties under this responsibility the Security Council acts on their behalf.

2.   In discharging these duties the Security Council shall act in accordance with the Purposes and Principles of the United Nations. The specific powers granted to the Security Council for the discharge of these duties are laid down in Chapters VI, VII, VIII, and XII.

3.   The Security Council shall submit annual and, when necessary, special reports to the General Assembly for its consideration.

Article 25

The Members of the United Nations agree to accept and carry out the decisions of the Security Council in accordance with the present Charter.

Article 26

In order to promote the establishment and maintenance of international peace and security with the least diversion for armaments of the world's human and economic resources, the Security Council shall be responsible for formulating, with the

---

[1]Amended text of Article 23, which came into force on 31 August 1965. (The text of Article 23 before it was amended read as follows:

1.   The Security Council shall consist of eleven Members of the United Nations. The Republic of China, France, the Union of Soviet Socialist Republics, the United Kingdom of Great Britain and Northern Ireland, and the United States of America shall be permanent members of the Security Council. The General Assembly shall elect six other Members of the United Nations to be non-permanent members of the Security Council, due regard being specially paid, in the first instance to the contribution of Members of the United Nations to the maintenance of international peace and security and to the other purposes of the Organization, and also to equitable geographical distribution.

2.   The non-permanent members of the Security Council shall be elected for a term of two years. In the first election of non-permanent members, however, three shall be chosen for a term of one year. A retiring member shall not be eligible for immediate re-election.

3.   Each member of the Security Council shall have one representative.)

assistance of the Military Staff Committee referred to in Article 47, plans to be submitted to the Members of the United Nations for the establishment of a system for the regulation of armaments.

Voting

Article 27[2]

1.   Each member of the Security Council shall have one vote.

2.   Decisions of the Security Council on procedural matters shall be made by an affirmative vote of nine members.

3.   Decisions of the Security Council on all other matters shall be made by an affirmative vote of nine members including the concurring votes of the permanent members; provided that, in decisions under Chapter VI, and under paragraph 3 of Article 52, a party to a dispute shall abstain from voting.

Procedure

Article 28

1.   The Security Council shall be so organized as to be able to function continuously. Each member of the Security Council shall for this purpose be represented at all times at the seat of the Organization.

2.   The Security Council shall hold periodic meetings at which each of its members may, if it so desires, be represented by a member of the government or by some other specially designated representative.

3.   The Security Council may hold meetings at such places other than the seat of the Organization as in its judgment will best facilitate its work.

Article 29

The Security Council may establish such subsidiary organs as it deems necessary for the performance of its functions.

Article 30

The Security Council shall adopt its own rules of procedure, including the method of selecting its President.

Article 31

Any Member of the United Nations which is not a member of the Security Council may participate, without vote, in the discussion of any question brought before the Security Council whenever the latter considers that the interests of that Member are specially affected.

Article 32

Any Member of the United Nations which is not a member of the Security Council or any state which is not a Member of the United Nations, if it is a party to a dispute under consideration by the Security Council, shall be invited to participate, without vote, in the discussion relating to the dispute. The Security Council shall lay down such conditions as it deems just for the participation of a state which is not a Member of the United Nations.

Chapter VI
PACIFIC SETTLEMENT OF DISPUTES

Article 33

1.   The parties to any dispute, the continuance of which is likely to endanger the maintenance of international peace and security, shall, first of all, seek a solution by negotiation, enquiry, mediation, conciliation, arbitration, judicial settlement, resort to regional agencies or arrangements, or other peaceful means of their own choice.

2.   The Security Council shall, when it deems necessary, call upon the parties to settle their dispute by such means.

Article 34

The Security Council may investigate any dispute or any situation which might lead to international friction or give rise to a dispute, in order to determine whether the continuance of the dispute or situation is likely to endanger the maintenance of international peace and security.

Article 35

1.   Any Member of the United Nations may bring any dispute, or any situation of the nature referred to in Article 34, to the attention of the Security Council or of the General Assembly.

2.   A state which is not a Member of the United Nations may bring to the attention of the Security Council or of the General Assembly any dispute to which it is a party if it accepts in advance, for the purposes of the dispute, the obligations of pacific settlement provided in the present Charter.

3.   The proceedings of the General Assembly in respect of matters brought to its attention under this Article will be subject to the provisions of Articles 11 and 12.

Article 36

1.   The Security Council may, at any stage of a dispute of the nature referred to in Article 33 or of a situation of like nature, recommend appropriate procedures or methods of adjustment.

2.   The Security Council should take into consideration any procedures for the settlement of the dispute which have already been adopted by the parties.

3.   In making recommendations under this Article the Security Council should also take into consideration that legal disputes should as a general rule be referred by the parties to the International Court of Justice in accordance with the provisions of the Statute of the Court.

Article 37

1.   Should the parties to a dispute of the nature referred to in Article 33 fail to settle it by the means indicated in that Article, they shall refer it to the Security Council.

2.   If the Security Council deems that the continuance of the dispute is in fact likely to endanger the maintenance of international peace and security, it shall decide whether to take action under Article 36 or to recommend such terms of settlement as it may consider appropriate.

Article 38

Without prejudice to the provisions of Articles 33 to 37, the Security Council may, if all the parties to any dispute so request, make recommendations to the parties with a view to a pacific settlement of the dispute.

Chapter VII
ACTION WITH RESPECT TO THREATS TO THE PEACE, BREACHES OF THE PEACE, AND ACTS OF AGGRESSION

Article 39

The Security Council shall determine the existence of any threat to the peace, breach of the peace, or act of aggression and shall make recommendations, or decide what measures shall be taken in accordance with Articles 41 and 42, to maintain or restore international peace and security.

Article 40

In order to prevent an aggravation of the situation, the Security Council may, before making the recommendations or deciding upon the measures provided for in Article 39, call upon the parties concerned to comply with such provisional measures as it deems necessary or desirable. Such provisional measures shall be without prejudice to the rights, claims, or position of the parties concerned. The Security Council shall duly take account of failure to comply with such provisional measures.

---

[2]Amended text of Article 27, which came into force on 31 August 1965. (The text of Article 27 before it was amended read as follows:

1.   Each member of the Security Council shall have one vote.

2.   Decisions of the Security Council on procedural matters shall be made by an affirmative vote of seven members.

3.   Decisions of the Security Council on all other matters shall be made by an affirmative vote of seven members including the concurring votes of the permanent members; provided that, in decisions under Chapter VI, and under paragraph 3 of Article 52, a party to a dispute shall abstain from voting.)

Article 41

The Security Council may decide what measures not involving the use of armed force are to be employed to give effect to its decisions, and it may call upon the Members of the United Nations to apply such measures. These may include complete or partial interruption of economic relations and of rail, sea, air, postal, telegraphic, radio, and other means of communication, and the severance of diplomatic relations.

Article 42

Should the Security Council consider that measures provided for in Article 41 would be inadequate or have proved to be inadequate, it may take such action by air, sea, or land forces as may be necessary to maintain or restore international peace and security. Such action may include demonstrations, blockade, and other operations by air, sea, or land forces of Members of the United Nations.

Article 43

1. All Members of the United Nations, in order to contribute to the maintenance of international peace and security, undertake to make available to the Security Council, on its call and in accordance with a special agreement or agreements, armed forces, assistance, and facilities, including rights of passage, necessary for the purpose of maintaining international peace and security.

2. Such agreement or agreements shall govern the numbers and types of forces, their degree of readiness and general location, and the nature of the facilities and assistance to be provided.

3. The agreement or agreements shall be negotiated as soon as possible on the initiative of the Security Council. They shall be concluded between the Security Council and Members or between the Security Council and groups of Members and shall be subject to ratification by the signatory states in accordance with their respective constitutional processes.

Article 44

When the Security Council has decided to use force it shall, before calling upon a Member not represented on it to provide armed forces in fulfillment of the obligations assumed under Article 43, invite that Member, if the Member so desires, to participate in the decisions of the Security Council concerning the employment of contingents of that Member's armed forces.

Article 45

In order to enable the United Nations to take urgent military measures, Members shall hold immediately available national air-force contingents for combined international enforcement action. The strength and degree of readiness of these contingents and plans for their combined action shall be determined, within the limits laid down in the special agreement or agreements referred to in Article 43, by the Security Council with the assistance of the Military Staff Committee.

Article 46

Plans for the application of armed force shall be made by the Security Council with the assistance of the Military Staff Committee.

Article 47

1. There shall be established a Military Staff Committee to advise and assist the Security Council on all questions relating to the Security Council's military requirements for the maintenance of international peace and security, the employment and command of forces placed at its disposal, the regulation of armaments, and possible disarmament.

2. The Military Staff Committee shall consist of the Chiefs of Staff of the permanent members of the Security Council or their representatives. Any Member of the United Nations not permanently represented on the Committee shall be invited by the Committee to be associated with it when the efficient discharge of the Committee's responsibilities requires the participation of that Member in its work.

3. The Military Staff Committee shall be responsible under the Security Council for the strategic direction of any armed forces placed at the disposal of the Security Council. Questions relating to the command of such forces shall be worked out subsequently.

4. The Military Staff Committee, with the authorization of the Security Council and after consultation with appropriate regional agencies, may establish regional subcommittees.

Article 48

1. The action required to carry out the decisions of the Security Council for the maintenance of international peace and security shall be taken by all the Members of the United Nations or by some of them, as the Security Council may determine.

2. Such decisions shall be carried out by the Members of the United Nations directly and through their action in the appropriate international agencies of which they are members.

Article 49

The Members of the United Nations shall join in affording mutual assistance in carrying out the measures decided upon by the Security Council.

Article 50

If preventive or enforcement measures against any state are taken by the Security Council, any other state, whether a Member of the United Nations or not, which finds itself confronted with special economic problems arising from the carrying out of those measures shall have the right to consult the Security Council with regard to a solution of those problems.

Article 51

Nothing in the present Charter shall impair the inherent right of individual or collective self-defense if an armed attack occurs against a Member of the United Nations, until the Security Council has taken measures necessary to maintain international peace and security. Measures taken by Members in the exercise of this right of self-defense shall be immediately reported to the Security Council and shall not in any way affect the authority and responsibility of the Security Council under the present Charter to take at any time such action as it deems necessary in order to maintain or restore international peace and security.

Chapter VIII
REGIONAL ARRANGEMENTS

Article 52

1. Nothing in the present Charter precludes the existence of regional arrangements or agencies for dealing with such matters relating to the maintenance of international peace and security as are appropriate for regional action, provided that such arrangements or agencies and their activities are consistent with the Purposes and Principles of the United Nations.

2. The Members of the United Nations entering into such arrangements or constituting such agencies shall make every effort to achieve pacific settlement of local disputes through such regional arrangements or by such regional agencies before referring them to the Security Council.

3. The Security Council shall encourage the development of pacific settlement of local disputes through such regional arrangements or by such regional agencies either on the initiative of the states concerned or by reference from the Security Council.

4. This Article in no way impairs the application of Articles 34 and 35.

Article 53

1. The Security Council shall, where appropriate, utilize such regional arrangements or agencies for enforcement action under its authority. But no enforcement action shall be taken under regional arrangements or by regional agencies without the authorization of the Security Council, with the exception of measures against any enemy state, as defined in paragraph 2 of this Article, provided for pursuant to Article 107 or in regional arrangements directed against renewal of aggressive policy on the part of any such state, until such time as the Organization may, on request of the Governments concerned, be charged with the responsibility for preventing further aggression by such a state.

2.   The term enemy state as used in paragraph 1 of this Article applies to any state which during the Second World War has been an enemy of any signatory of the present Charter.

Article 54

The Security Council shall at all times be kept fully informed of activities undertaken or in contemplation under regional arrangements or by regional agencies for the maintenance of international peace and security.

Chapter IX
INTERNATIONAL ECONOMIC AND SOCIAL COOPERATION

Article 55

With a view to the creation of conditions of stability and well-being which are necessary for peaceful and friendly relations among nations based on respect for the principle of equal rights and self-determination of peoples, the United Nations shall promote:

a.   higher standards of living, full employment, and conditions of economic and social progress and development;
b.   solutions of international economic, social, health, and related problems; and international cultural and educational cooperation; and
c.   universal respect for, and observance of, human rights and fundamental freedoms for all without distinction as to race, sex, language, or religion.

Article 56

All Members pledge themselves to take joint and separate action in cooperation with the Organization for the achievement of the purposes set forth in Article 55.

Article 57

1.   The various specialized agencies, established by intergovernmental agreement and having wide international responsibilities, as defined in their basic instruments, in economic, social, cultural, educational, health, and related fields, shall be brought into relationship with the United Nations in accordance with the provisions of Article 63.

2.   Such agencies thus brought into relationship with the United Nations are hereinafter referred to as specialized agencies.

Article 58

The Organization shall make recommendations for the coordination of the policies and activities of the specialized agencies.

Article 59

The Organization shall, where appropriate, initiate negotiations among the states concerned for the creation of any new specialized agencies required for the accomplishment of the purposes set forth in Article 55.

Article 60

Responsibility for the discharge of the functions of the Organization set forth in this Chapter shall be vested in the General Assembly and, under the authority of the General Assembly, in the Economic and Social Council, which shall have for this purpose the powers set forth in Chapter X.

Chapter X
THE ECONOMIC AND SOCIAL COUNCIL

Composition

Article 61[3]

1.   The Economic and Social Council shall consist of fifty-four Members of the United Nations elected by the General Assembly.

2.   Subject to the provisions of paragraph 3, eighteen members of the Economic and Social Council shall be elected each year for a term of three years. A retiring member shall be eligible for immediate re-election.

3.   At the first election after the increase in the membership of the Economic and Social Council from twenty-seven to fifty-four members, in addition to the members elected in place of the nine members whose term of office expires at the end of that year, twenty-seven additional members shall be elected. Of these twenty-seven additional members, the term of office of nine members so elected shall expire at the end of one year, and of nine other members at the end of two years, in accordance with arrangements made by the General Assembly.

4.   Each member of the Economic and Social Council shall have one representative.

Functions and powers

Article 62

1.   The Economic and Social Council may make or initiate studies and reports with respect to international economic, social, cultural, educational, health, and related matters and may make recommendations with respect to any such matters to the General Assembly, to the Members of the United Nations, and to the specialized agencies concerned.

2.   It may make recommendations for the purpose of promoting respect for, and observance of, human rights and fundamental freedoms for all.

3.   It may prepare draft conventions for submission to the General Assembly, with respect to matters falling within its competence.

4.   It may call, in accordance with the rules prescribed by the United Nations, international conferences on matters falling within its competence.

Article 63

1.   The Economic and Social Council may enter into agreements with any of the agencies referred to in Article 57, defining the terms on which the agency concerned shall be brought into relationship with the United Nations. Such agreements shall be subject to approval by the General Assembly.

2.   It may coordinate the activities of the specialized agencies through consultation with and recommendations to such agencies and through recommendations to the General Assembly and to the Members of the United Nations.

Article 64

1.   The Economic and Social Council may take appropriate steps to obtain regular reports from the specialized agencies. It may make arrangements with the Members of the United Nations and with the specialized agencies to obtain reports on the steps taken to give effect to its own recommendations and to recommendations on matters falling within its competence made by the General Assembly.

2.   It may communicate its observations on these reports to the General Assembly.

Article 65

The Economic and Social Council may furnish information to the Security Council and shall assist the Security Council upon its request.

Article 66

1.   The Economic and Social Council shall perform such functions as fall within its competence in connection with the carrying out of the recommendations of the General Assembly.

---

[3]Amended text of Article 61, which came into force on 24 September 1973. (The text of Article 61 as previously amended on 31 August 1965 read as follows:

1.   The Economic and Social Council shall consist of twenty-seven Members of the United Nations elected by the General Assembly.

2.   Subject to the provisions of paragraph 3, nine members of the Economic and Social Council shall be elected each year for a term of three years. A retiring member shall be eligible for immediate re-election.

3.   At the first election after the increase in the membership of the Economic and Social Council from eighteen to twenty-seven members, in addition to the members elected in place of the six members whose term of office expires at the end of that year, nine additional members shall be elected. Of these nine additional members, the term of office of three members so elected shall expire at the end of one year, and of three other members at the end of two years, in accordance with arrangements made by the General Assembly.

4.   Each member of the Economic and Social Council shall have one representative.)

2. It may, with the approval of the General Assembly, perform services at the request of Members of the United Nations and at the request of specialized agencies.

3. It shall perform such other functions as are specified elsewhere in the present Charter or as may be assigned to it by the General Assembly.

Voting

Article 67

1. Each member of the Economic and Social Council shall have one vote.

2. Decisions of the Economic and Social Council shall be made by a majority of the members present and voting.

Procedure

Article 68

The Economic and Social Council shall set up commissions in economic and social fields and for the promotion of human rights, and such other commissions as may be required for the performance of its functions.

Article 69

The Economic and Social Council shall invite any Member of the United Nations to participate, without vote, in its deliberations on any matter of particular concern to that Member.

Article 70

The Economic and Social Council may make arrangements for representatives of the specialized agencies to participate, without vote, in its deliberations and in those of the commissions established by it, and for its representatives to participate in the deliberations of the specialized agencies.

Article 71

The Economic and Social Council may make suitable arrangements for consultation with non-governmental organizations which are concerned with matters within its competence. Such arrangements may be made with international organizations and, where appropriate, with national organizations after consultation with the Member of the United Nations concerned.

Article 72

1. The Economic and Social Council shall adopt its own rules of procedure, including the method of selecting its President.

2. The Economic and Social Council shall meet as required in accordance with its rules, which shall include provision for the convening of meetings on the request of a majority of its members.

Chapter XI
DECLARATION REGARDING NON-SELF-GOVERNING TERRITORIES

Article 73

Members of the United Nations which have or assume responsibilities for the administration of territories whose peoples have not yet attained a full measure of self-government recognize the principle that the interests of the inhabitants of these territories are paramount, and accept as a sacred trust the obligation to promote to the utmost, within the system of international peace and security established by the present Charter, the well-being of the inhabitants of these territories, and, to this end:

a. to ensure, with due respect for the culture of the peoples concerned, their political, economic, social, and educational advancement, their just treatment, and their protection against abuses;

b. to develop self-government, to take due account of the political aspirations of the peoples, and to assist them in the progressive development of their free political institutions, according to the particular circumstances of each territory and its peoples and their varying stages of advancement;

c. to further international peace and security;

d. to promote constructive measures of development, to encourage research, and to cooperate with one another and,

when and where appropriate, with specialized international bodies with a view to the practical achievement of the social, economic, and scientific purposes set forth in this Article; and

e. to transmit regularly to the Secretary-General for information purposes, subject to such limitation as security and constitutional considerations may require, statistical and other information of a technical nature relating to economic, social, and educational conditions in the territories for which they are respectively responsible other than those territories to which Chapters XII and XIII apply.

Article 74

Members of the United Nations also agree that their policy in respect of the territories to which this Chapter applies, no less than in respect of their metropolitan areas, must be based on the general principle of good-neighborliness, due account being taken of the interests and well-being of the rest of the world, in social, economic, and commercial matters.

Chapter XII
INTERNATIONAL TRUSTEESHIP SYSTEM

Article 75

The United Nations shall establish under its authority an international trusteeship system for the administration and supervision of such territories as may be placed thereunder by subsequent individual agreements. These territories are hereinafter referred to as trust territories.

Article 76

The basic objectives of the trusteeship system, in accordance with the Purposes of the United Nations laid down in Article 1 of the present Charter, shall be:

a. to further international peace and security;

b. to promote the political, economic, social, and educational advancement of the inhabitants of the trust territories, and their progressive development towards self-government or independence as may be appropriate to the particular circumstances of each territory and its peoples and the freely expressed wishes of the peoples concerned, and as may be provided by the terms of each trusteeship agreement;

c. to encourage respect for human rights and for fundamental freedoms for all without distinction as to race, sex, language, or religion, and to encourage recognition of the interdependence of the peoples of the world; and

d. to ensure equal treatment in social, economic, and commercial matters for all Members of the United Nations and their nationals, and also equal treatment for the latter in the administration of justice, without prejudice to the attainment of the foregoing objectives and subject to the provisions of Article 80.

Article 77

1. The trusteeship system shall apply to such territories in the following categories as may be placed thereunder by means of trusteeship agreements:

a. territories now held under mandate;

b. territories which may be detached from enemy states as a result of the Second World War; and

c. territories voluntarily placed under the system by states responsible for their administration.

2. It will be a matter for subsequent agreement as to which territories in the foregoing categories will be brought under the trusteeship system and upon what terms.

Article 78

The trusteeship system shall not apply to territories which have become Members of the United Nations, relationship among which shall be based on respect for the principle of sovereign equality.

Article 79

The terms of trusteeship for each territory to be placed under the trusteeship system, including any alteration or amendment, shall be agreed upon by the states directly concerned, including the mandatory power in the case of territories held under mandate by a Member of the United Nations, and shall be approved as provided for in Articles 83 and 85.

Article 80

1. Except as may be agreed upon in individual trusteeship agreements, made under Articles 77, 79, and 81, placing each territory under the trusteeship system, and until such agreements have been concluded, nothing in this Chapter shall be construed in or of itself to alter in any manner the rights whatsoever of any states or any peoples or the terms of existing international instruments to which Members of the United Nations may respectively be parties.

2. Paragraph 1 of this Article shall not be interpreted as giving grounds for delay or postponement of the negotiation and conclusion of agreements for placing mandated and other territories under the trusteeship system as provided for in Article 77.

Article 81

The trusteeship agreement shall in each case include the terms under which the trust territory will be administered and designate the authority which will exercise the administration of the trust territory. Such authority, hereinafter called the administering authority, may be one or more states or the Organization itself.

Article 82

There may be designated, in any trusteeship agreement, a strategic area or areas which may include part or all of the trust territory to which the agreement applies, without prejudice to any special agreement or agreements made under Article 43.

Article 83

1. All functions of the United Nations relating to strategic areas, including the approval of the terms of the trusteeship agreements and of their alteration or amendment, shall be exercised by the Security Council.

2. The basic objectives set forth in Article 76 shall be applicable to the people of each strategic area.

3. The Security Council shall, subject to the provisions of the trusteeship agreements and without prejudice to security considerations, avail itself of the assistance of the Trusteeship Council to perform those functions of the United Nations under the trusteeship system relating to political, economic, social, and educational matters in the strategic areas.

Article 84

It shall be the duty of the administering authority to ensure that the trust territory shall play its part in the maintenance of international peace and security. To this end the administering authority may make use of volunteer forces, facilities, and assistance from the trust territory in carrying out the obligations towards the Security Council undertaken in this regard by the administering authority, as well as for local defense and the maintenance of law and order within the trust territory.

Article 85

1. The functions of the United Nations with regard to trusteeship agreements for all areas not designated as strategic, including the approval of the terms of the trusteeship agreements and of their alteration or amendment, shall be exercised by the General Assembly.

2. The Trusteeship Council, operating under the authority of the General Assembly, shall assist the General Assembly in carrying out these functions.

Chapter XIII
THE TRUSTEESHIP COUNCIL

Composition

Article 86

1. The Trusteeship Council shall consist of the following Members of the United Nations:

a. those Members administering trust territories;
b. such of those Members mentioned by name in Article 23 as are not administering trust territories; and
c. as many other Members elected for three-year terms by the General Assembly as may be necessary to ensure that the total number of members of the Trusteeship Council is equally divided between those Members of the United Nations which administer trust territories and those which do not.

2. Each member of the Trusteeship Council shall designate one specially qualified person to represent it therein.

Functions and powers

Article 87

The General Assembly and, under its authority, the Trusteeship Council, in carrying out their functions, may:

a. consider reports submitted by the administering authority;
b. accept petitions and examine them in consultation with the administering authority;
c. provide for periodic visits to the respective trust territories at times agreed upon with the administering authority; and
d. take these and other actions in conformity with the terms of the trusteeship agreements.

Article 88

The Trusteeship Council shall formulate a questionnaire on the political, economic, social, and educational advancement of the inhabitants of each trust territory, and the administering authority for each trust territory within the competence of the General Assembly shall make an annual report to the General Assembly upon the basis of such questionnaire.

Voting

Article 89

1. Each member of the Trusteeship Council shall have one vote.

2. Decisions of the Trusteeship Council shall be made by a majority of the members present and voting.

Procedure

Article 90

1. The Trusteeship Council shall adopt its own rules of procedure, including the method of selecting its President.

2. The Trusteeship Council shall meet as required in accordance with its rules, which shall include provision for the convening of meetings on the request of a majority of its members.

Article 91

The Trusteeship Council shall, when appropriate, avail itself of the assistance of the Economic and Social Council and of the specialized agencies in regard to matters with which they are respectively concerned.

Chapter XIV
THE INTERNATIONAL COURT OF JUSTICE

Article 92

The International Court of Justice shall be the principal judicial organ of the United Nations. It shall function in accordance with the annexed Statute, which is based upon the Statute of the Permanent Court of International Justice and forms an integral part of the present Charter.

Article 93

1. All Members of the United Nations are *ipso facto* parties to the Statute of the International Court of Justice.

2. A state which is not a Member of the United Nations may become a party to the Statute of the International Court of Justice on conditions to be determined in each case by the General Assembly upon the recommendation of the Security Council.

Article 94

1. Each Member of the United Nations undertakes to comply with the decision of the International Court of Justice in any case to which it is a party.

2. If any party to a case fails to perform the obligations incumbent upon it under a judgment rendered by the Court, the other party may have recourse to the Security Council, which may, if it deems necessary, make recommendations or decide upon measures to be taken to give effect to the judgment.

Article 95

Nothing in the present Charter shall prevent Members of the United Nations from entrusting the solution of their differences to other tribunals by virtue of agreements already in existence or which may be concluded in the future.

Article 96

1. The General Assembly or the Security Council may request the International Court of Justice to give an advisory opinion on any legal question.

2. Other organs of the United Nations and specialized agencies, which may at any time be so authorized by the General Assembly, may also request advisory opinions of the Court on legal questions arising within the scope of their activities.

Chapter XV
THE SECRETARIAT

Article 97

The Secretariat shall comprise a Secretary-General and such staff as the Organization may require. The Secretary-General shall be appointed by the General Assembly upon the recommendation of the Security Council. He shall be the chief administrative officer of the Organization.

Article 98

The Secretary-General shall act in that capacity in all meetings of the General Assembly, of the Security Council, of the Economic and Social Council, and of the Trusteeship Council, and shall perform such other functions as are entrusted to him by these organs. The Secretary-General shall make an annual report to the General Assembly on the work of the Organization.

Article 99

The Secretary-General may bring to the attention of the Security Council any matter which in his opinion may threaten the maintenance of international peace and security.

Article 100

1. In the performance of their duties the Secretary-General and the staff shall not seek or receive instructions from any government or from any other authority external to the Organization. They shall refrain from any action which might reflect on their position as international officials responsible only to the Organization.

2. Each Member of the United Nations undertakes to respect the exclusively international character of the responsibilities of the Secretary-General and the staff and not to seek to influence them in the discharge of their responsibilities.

Article 101

1. The staff shall be appointed by the Secretary-General under regulations established by the General Assembly.

2. Appropriate staffs shall be permanently assigned to the Economic and Social Council, the Trusteeship Council, and, as required, to other organs of the United Nations. These staffs shall form a part of the Secretariat.

3. The paramount consideration in the employment of the staff and in the determination of the conditions of service shall be the necessity of securing the highest standards of efficiency, competence, and integrity. Due regard shall be paid to the importance of recruiting the staff on as wide a geographical basis as possible.

Chapter XVI
MISCELLANEOUS PROVISIONS

Article 102

1. Every treaty and every international agreement entered into by any Member of the United Nations after the present Charter comes into force shall as soon as possible be registered with the Secretariat and published by it.

2. No party to any such treaty or international agreement which has not been registered in accordance with the provisions of paragraph 1 of this Article may invoke that treaty or agreement before any organ of the United Nations.

Article 103

In the event of a conflict between the obligations of the Members of the United Nations under the present Charter and their obligations under any other international agreement, their obligations under the present Charter shall prevail.

Article 104

The Organization shall enjoy in the territory of each of its Members such legal capacity as may be necessary for the exercise of its functions and the fulfillment of its purposes.

Article 105

1. The Organization shall enjoy in the territory of each of its Members such privileges and immunities as are necessary for the fulfillment of its purposes.

2. Representatives of the Members of the United Nations and officials of the Organization shall similarly enjoy such privileges and immunities as are necessary for the independent exercise of their functions in connection with the Organization.

3. The General Assembly may make recommendations with a view to determining the details of the application of paragraphs 1 and 2 of this Article or may propose conventions to the Members of the United Nations for this purpose.

Chapter XVII
TRANSITIONAL SECURITY ARRANGEMENTS

Article 106

Pending the coming into force of such special agreements referred to in Article 43 as in the opinion of the Security Council enable it to begin the exercise of its responsibilities under Article 42, the parties to the Four-Nation Declaration, signed at Moscow, October 30, 1943, and France, shall, in accordance with the provisions of paragraph 5 of that Declaration, consult with one another and as occasion requires with other Members of the United Nations with a view to such joint action on behalf of the Organization as may be necessary for the purpose of maintaining international peace and security.

Article 107

Nothing in the present Charter shall invalidate or preclude action, in relation to any state which during the Second World War has been an enemy of any signatory to the present Charter, taken or authorized as a result of that war by the Governments having responsibility for such action.

Chapter XVIII
AMENDMENTS

Article 108

Amendments to the present Charter shall come into force for all Members of the United Nations when they have been adopted by a vote of two thirds of the members of the General Assembly and ratified in accordance with their respective constitutional processes by two thirds of the Members of the United Nations, including all the permanent members of the Security Council.

Article 109[4]

1. A General Conference of the Members of the United Nations for the purpose of reviewing the present Charter may be held at a date and place to be fixed by a two-thirds vote of the members of the General Assembly and by a vote of any nine members of the Security Council. Each Member of the United Nations shall have one vote in the conference.

2. Any alteration of the present Charter recommended by a two-thirds vote of the conference shall take effect when ratified in accordance with their respective constitutional processes by two thirds of the Members of the United Nations including all the permanent members of the Security Council.

3. If such a conference has not been held before the tenth annual session of the General Assembly following the coming into force of the present Charter, the proposal to call such a conference shall be placed on the agenda of that session of the General Assembly, and the conference shall be held if so decided by a majority vote of the members of the General Assembly and by a vote of any seven members of the Security Council.

Chapter XIX
RATIFICATION AND SIGNATURE

Article 110

1. The present Charter shall be ratified by the signatory states in accordance with their respective constitutional processes.

2. The ratifications shall be deposited with the Government of the United States of America, which shall notify all the signatory states of each deposit as well as the Secretary-General of the Organization when he has been appointed.

3. The present Charter shall come into force upon the deposit of ratifications by the Republic of China, France, the Union of Soviet Socialist Republics, the United Kingdom of Great Britain and Northern Ireland, and the United States of America, and by a majority of the other signatory states. A protocol of the ratifications deposited shall thereupon be drawn up by the Government of the United States

of America which shall communicate copies thereof to all the signatory states.

4. The states signatory to the present Charter which ratify it after it has come into force will become original Members of the United Nations on the date of the deposit of their respective ratifications.

Article 111

The present Charter, of which the Chinese, French, Russian, English, and Spanish texts are equally authentic, shall remain deposited in the archives of the Government of the United States of America. Duly certified copies thereof shall be transmitted by that Government to the Governments of the other signatory states.

IN FAITH WHEREOF the representatives of the Governments of the United Nations have signed the present Charter.

DONE at the city of San Francisco the twenty-sixth day of June, one thousand nine hundred and forty-five.

---

[4]Amended text of Article 109, which came into force on 12 June 1968. (The text of Article 109 before it was amended read as follows:

1. A General Conference of the Members of the United Nations for the purpose of reviewing the present Charter may be held at a date and place to be fixed by a two-thirds vote of the members of the General Assembly and by a vote of any seven members of the Security Council. Each Member of the United Nations shall have one vote in the conference.

2. Any alteration of the present Charter recommended by a two-thirds vote of the conference shall take effect when ratified in accordance with their respective constitutional processes by two thirds of the Members of the United Nations including all the permanent members of the Security Council.

3. If such a conference has not been held before the tenth annual session of the General Assembly following the coming into force of the present Charter, the proposal to call such a conference shall be placed on the agenda of that session of the General Assembly, and the conference shall be held if so decided by a majority vote of the members of the General Assembly and by a vote of any seven members of the Security Council.)

Statute of the International Court of Justice

Article 1

THE INTERNATIONAL COURT OF JUSTICE established by the Charter of the United Nations as the principal judicial organ of the United Nations shall be constituted and shall function in accordance with the provisions of the present Statute.

Chapter I
ORGANIZATION OF THE COURT

Article 2

The Court shall be composed of a body of independent judges, elected regardless of their nationality from among persons of high moral character, who possess the qualifications required in their respective countries for appointment to the highest judicial offices, or are jurisconsults of recognized competence in international law.

Article 3

1. The Court shall consist of fifteen members, no two of whom may be nationals of the same state.

2. A person who for the purposes of membership in the Court could be regarded as a national of more than one state shall be deemed to be a national of the one in which he ordinarily exercises civil and political rights.

Article 4

1. The members of the Court shall be elected by the General Assembly and by the Security Council from a list of persons nominated by the national groups in the Permanent Court of Arbitration, in accordance with the following provisions.

2. In the case of Members of the United Nations not represented in the Permanent Court of Arbitration, candidates shall be nominated by national groups appointed for this purpose by their governments under the same conditions as those prescribed for mem-

bers of the Permanent Court of Arbitration by Article 44 of the Convention of The Hague of 1907 for the pacific settlement of international disputes.

3. The conditions under which a state which is a party to the present Statute but is not a Member of the United Nations may participate in electing the members of the Court shall, in the absence of a special agreement, be laid down by the General Assembly upon recommendation of the Security Council.

Article 5

1. At least three months before the date of the election, the Secretary-General of the United Nations shall address a written request to the members of the Permanent Court of Arbitration belonging to the states which are parties to the present Statute, and to the members of the national groups appointed under Article 4, paragraph 2, inviting them to undertake, within a given time, by national groups, the nomination of persons in a position to accept the duties of a member of the Court.

2. No group may nominate more than four persons, not more than two of whom shall be of their own nationality. In no case may the number of candidates nominated by a group be more than double the number of seats to be filled.

Article 6

Before making these nominations, each national group is recommended to consult its highest court of justice, its legal faculties and schools of law, and its national academies and national sections of international academies devoted to the study of law.

Article 7

1. The Secretary-General shall prepare a list in alphabetical order of all the persons thus nominated. Save as provided in Article 12, paragraph 2, these shall be the only persons eligible.

2. The Secretary-General shall submit this list to the General Assembly and to the Security Council.

Article 8

The General Assembly and the Security Council shall proceed independently of one another to elect the members of the Court.

Article 9

At every election, the electors shall bear in mind not only that the persons to be elected should individually possess the qualifications required, but also that in the body as a whole the representation of the main forms of civilization and of the principal legal systems of the world should be assured.

Article 10

1. Those candidates who obtain an absolute majority of votes in the General Assembly and in the Security Council shall be considered as elected.

2. Any vote of the Security Council, whether for the election of judges or for the appointment of members of the conference envisaged in Article 12, shall be taken without any distinction between permanent and non-permanent members of the Security Council.

3. In the event of more than one national of the same state obtaining an absolute majority of the votes both of the General Assembly and of the Security Council, the eldest of these only shall be considered as elected.

Article 11

If, after the first meeting held for the purpose of the election, one or more seats remain to be filled, a second and, if necessary, a third meeting shall take place.

Article 12

1. If, after the third meeting, one or more seats still remain unfilled, a joint conference consisting of six members, three appointed by the General Assembly and three by the Security Council, may be formed at any time at the request of either the General Assembly or the Security Council, for the purpose of choosing by the vote of an absolute majority one name for each seat still vacant, to submit to the General Assembly and the Security Council for their respective acceptance.

2. If the joint conference is unanimously agreed upon any person who fulfils the required conditions, he may be included in its list, even though he was not included in the list of nominations referred to in Article 7.

3. If the joint conference is satisfied that it will not be successful in procuring an election, those members of the Court who have already been elected shall, within a period to be fixed by the Security Council, proceed to fill the vacant seats by selection from among those candidates who have obtained votes either in the General Assembly or in the Security Council.

4. In the event of an equality of votes among the judges, the eldest judge shall have a casting vote.

Article 13

1. The members of the Court shall be elected for nine years and may be re-elected; provided, however, that of the judges elected at the first election, the terms of five judges shall expire at the end of three years and the terms of five more judges shall expire at the end of six years.

2. The judges whose terms are to expire at the end of the above-mentioned initial periods of three and six years shall be chosen by lot to be drawn by the Secretary-General immediately after the first election has been completed.

3. The members of the Court shall continue to discharge their duties until their places have been filled. Though replaced, they shall finish any cases which they may have begun.

4. In the case of the resignation of a member of the Court, the resignation shall be addressed to the President of the Court for transmission to the Secretary-General. This last notification makes the place vacant.

Article 14

Vacancies shall be filled by the same method as that laid down for the first election, subject to the following provision: the Secretary-General shall, within one month of the occurrence of the vacancy, proceed to issue the invitations provided for in Article 5, and the date of the election shall be fixed by the Security Council.

Article 15

A member of the Court elected to replace a member whose term of office has not expired shall hold office for the remainder of his predecessor's term.

Article 16

1. No member of the Court may exercise any political or administrative function, or engage in any other occupation of a professional nature.

2. Any doubt on this point shall be settled by the decision of the Court.

Article 17

1. No member of the Court may act as agent, counsel, or advocate in any case.

2. No member may participate in the decision of any case in which he has previously taken part as agent, counsel, or advocate for one of the parties, or as a member of a national or international court, or of a commission of enquiry, or in any other capacity.

3. Any doubt on this point shall be settled by the decision of the Court.

Article 18

1. No member of the Court can be dismissed unless, in the unanimous opinion of the other members, he has ceased to fulfil the required conditions.

2. Formal notification thereof shall be made to the Secretary-General by the Registrar.

3. This notification makes the place vacant.

Article 19

The members of the Court, when engaged on the business of the Court, shall enjoy diplomatic privileges and immunities.

Article 20

Every member of the Court shall, before taking up his duties, make a solemn declaration in open court that he will exercise his powers impartially and conscientiously.

Article 21

1. The Court shall elect its President and Vice-President for three years; they may be re-elected.

2. The Court shall appoint its Registrar and may provide for the appointment of such other officers as may be necessary.

Article 22

1. The seat of the Court shall be established at The Hague. This, however, shall not prevent the Court from sitting and exercising its functions elsewhere whenever the Court considers it desirable.

2. The President and the Registrar shall reside at the seat of the Court.

Article 23

1. The Court shall remain permanently in session, except during the judicial vacations, the dates and duration of which shall be fixed by the Court.

2. Members of the Court are entitled to periodic leave, the dates and duration of which shall be fixed by the Court, having in mind the distance between The Hague and the home of each judge.

3. Members of the Court shall be bound, unless they are on leave or prevented from attending by illness or other serious reasons duly explained to the President, to hold themselves permanently at the disposal of the Court.

Article 24

1. If, for some special reason, a member of the Court considers that he should not take part in the decision of a particular case, he shall so inform the President.

2. If the President considers that for some special reason one of the members of the Court should not sit in a particular case, he shall give him notice accordingly.

3. If in any such case the member of the Court and the President disagree, the matter shall be settled by the decision of the Court.

Article 25

1. The full Court shall sit except when it is expressly provided otherwise in the present Statute.

2. Subject to the condition that the number of judges available to constitute the Court is not thereby reduced below eleven, the Rules of the Court may provide for allowing one or more judges, according to circumstances and in rotation, to be dispensed from sitting.

3. A quorum of nine judges shall suffice to constitute the Court.

Article 26

1. The Court may from time to time form one or more chambers, composed of three or more judges as the Court may determine, for dealing with particular categories of cases; for example, labor cases and cases relating to transit and communications.

2. The Court may at any time form a chamber for dealing with a particular case. The number of judges to constitute such a chamber shall be determined by the Court with the approval of the parties.

3. Cases shall be heard and determined by the chambers provided for in this Article if the parties so request.

Article 27

A judgment given by any of the chambers provided for in Articles 26 and 29 shall be considered as rendered by the Court.

Article 28

The chambers provided for in Articles 26 and 29 may, with the consent of the parties, sit and exercise their functions elsewhere than at The Hague.

Article 29

With a view to the speedy despatch of business, the Court shall form annually a chamber composed of five judges which, at the request of the parties, may hear and determine cases by summary procedure. In addition, two judges shall be selected for the purpose of replacing judges who find it impossible to sit.

Article 30

1. The Court shall frame rules for carrying out its functions. In particular, it shall lay down rules of procedure.

2. The Rules of the Court may provide for assessors to sit with the Court or with any of its chambers, without the right to vote.

Article 31

1. Judges of the nationality of each of the parties shall retain their right to sit in the case before the Court.

2. If the Court includes upon the Bench a judge of the nationality of one of the parties, any other party may choose a person to sit as judge. Such person shall be chosen preferably from among those persons who have been nominated as candidates as provided in Articles 4 and 5.

3. If the Court includes upon the Bench no judge of the nationality of the parties, each of these parties may proceed to choose a judge as provided in paragraph 2 of this Article.

4. The provisions of this Article shall apply to the case of Articles 26 and 29. In such cases, the President shall request one or, if necessary, two of the members of the Court forming the chamber to give place to the members of the Court of the nationality of the parties concerned, and, failing such, or if they are unable to be present, to the judges specially chosen by the parties.

5. Should there be several parties in the same interest, they shall, for the purpose of the preceding provisions, be reckoned as one party only. Any doubt upon this point shall be settled by the decision of the Court.

6. Judges chosen as laid down in paragraphs 2, 3 and 4 of this Article shall fulfil the conditions required by Articles 2, 17 (paragraph 2), 20, and 24 of the present Statute. They shall take part in the decision on terms of complete equality with their colleagues.

Article 32

1. Each member of the Court shall receive an annual salary.

2. The President shall receive a special annual allowance.

3. The Vice-President shall receive a special allowance for every day on which he acts as President.

4. The judges chosen under Article 31, other than members of the Court, shall receive compensation for each day on which they exercise their functions.

5. These salaries, allowances, and compensation shall be fixed by the General Assembly. They may not be decreased during the term of office.

6. The salary of the Registrar shall be fixed by the General Assembly on the proposal of the Court.

7. Regulations made by the General Assembly shall fix the conditions under which retirement pensions may be given to members of the Court and to the Registrar, and the conditions under which members of the Court and the Registrar shall have their traveling expenses refunded.

8. The above salaries, allowances, and compensation shall be free of all taxation.

Article 33

The expenses of the Court shall be borne by the United Nations in such a manner as shall be decided by the General Assembly.

Chapter II
COMPETENCE OF THE COURT

Article 34

1. Only states may be parties in cases before the Court.

2. The Court, subject to and in conformity with its Rules, may request of public international organizations information relevant to cases before it, and shall receive such information presented by such organizations on their own initiative.

3. Whenever the construction of the constituent instrument of a public international organization or of an international convention adopted thereunder is in question in a case before the Court, the Registrar shall so notify the public international organization concerned and shall communicate to it copies of all the written proceedings.

Article 35

1. The Court shall be open to the states parties to the present Statute.

2. The conditions under which the Court shall be open to other states shall, subject to the special provisions contained in treaties in force, be laid down by the Security Council, but in no case shall such conditions place the parties in a position of inequality before the Court.

3. When a state which is not a Member of the United Nations is a party to a case, the Court shall fix the amount which that party is to contribute towards the expenses of the Court. This provision shall not apply if such state is bearing a share of the expenses of the Court.

Article 36

1. The jurisdiction of the Court comprises all cases which the parties refer to it and all matters specially provided for in the Charter of the United Nations or in treaties and conventions in force.

2. The states parties to the present Statute may at any time declare that they recognize as compulsory *ipso facto* and without special agreement, in relation to any other state accepting the same obligation, the jurisdiction of the Court in all legal disputes concerning:

a. the interpretation of a treaty;

b. any question of international law;

c. the existence of any fact which, if established, would constitute a breach of an international obligation;

d. the nature or extent of the reparation to be made for the breach of an international obligation.

3. The declarations referred to above may be made unconditionally or on condition of reciprocity on the part of several or certain states, or for a certain time.

4. Such declarations shall be deposited with the Secretary-General of the United Nations, who shall transmit copies thereof to the parties to the Statute and to the Registrar of the Court.

5. Declarations made under Article 36 of the Statute of the Permanent Court of International Justice and which are still in force shall be deemed, as between the parties to the present Statute, to be acceptances of the compulsory jurisdiction of the International Court of Justice for the period which they still have to run and in accordance with their terms.

6. In the event of a dispute as to whether the Court has jurisdiction, the matter shall be settled by the decision of the Court.

Article 37

Whenever a treaty or convention in force provides for reference of a matter to a tribunal to have been instituted by the League of Nations, or to the Permanent Court of International Justice, the matter shall, as between the parties to the present Statute, be referred to the International Court of Justice.

Article 38

1. The Court, whose function is to decide in accordance with international law such disputes as are submitted to it, shall apply:

  a. international conventions, whether general or particular, establishing rules expressly recognized by the contesting states;

  b. international custom, as evidence of a general practice accepted as law;

  c. the general principles of law recognized by civilized nations;

  d. subject to the provisions of Article 59, judicial decisions and the teachings of the most highly qualified publicists of the various nations, as subsidiary means for the determination of rules of law.

2. This provision shall not prejudice the power of the Court to decide a case *ex aequo et bono*, if the parties agree thereto.

Chapter III
PROCEDURE

Article 39

1. The official languages of the Court shall be French and English. If the parties agree that the case shall be conducted in French, the judgment shall be delivered in French. If the parties agree that the case shall be conducted in English, the judgment shall be delivered in English.

2. In the absence of an agreement as to which language shall be employed, each party may, in the pleadings, use the language which it prefers; the decision of the Court shall be given in French and English. In this case the Court shall at the same time determine which of the two texts shall be considered as authoritative.

3. The Court shall, at the request of any party, authorize a language other than French or English to be used by that party.

Article 40

1. Cases are brought before the Court, as the case may be, either by the notification of the special agreement or by a written application addressed to the Registrar. In either case the subject of the dispute and the parties shall be indicated.

2. The Registrar shall forthwith communicate the application to all concerned.

3. He shall also notify the Members of the United Nations through the Secretary-General, and also any other states entitled to appear before the Court.

Article 41

1. The Court shall have the power to indicate, if it considers that circumstances so require, any provisional measures which ought to be taken to preserve the respective rights of either party.

2. Pending the final decision, notice of the measures suggested shall forthwith be given to the parties and to the Security Council.

Article 42

1. The parties shall be represented by agents.

2. They may have the assistance of counsel or advocates before the Court.

3. The agents, counsel, and advocates of parties before the Court shall enjoy the privileges and immunities necessary to the independent exercise of their duties.

Article 43

1. The procedure shall consist of two parts: written and oral.

2. The written proceedings shall consist of the communication to the Court and to the parties of memorials, counter-memorials and, if necessary, replies; also all papers and documents in support.

3. These communications shall be made through the Registrar, in the order and within the time fixed by the Court.

4. A certified copy of every document produced by one party shall be communicated to the other party.

5. The oral proceedings shall consist of the hearing by the Court of witnesses, experts, agents, counsel, and advocates.

Article 44

1. For the service of all notices upon persons other than the agents, counsel, and advocates, the Court shall apply direct to the government of the state upon whose territory the notice has to be served.

2. The same provision shall apply whenever steps are to be taken to procure evidence on the spot.

Article 45

The hearing shall be under the control of the President or, if he is unable to preside, of the Vice-President; if neither is able to preside, the senior judge present shall preside.

Article 46

The hearing in Court shall be public, unless the Court shall decide otherwise, or unless the parties demand that the public be not admitted.

Article 47

1. Minutes shall be made at each hearing and signed by the Registrar and the President.

2. These minutes alone shall be authentic.

Article 48

The Court shall make orders for the conduct of the case, shall decide the form and time in which each party must conclude its arguments, and make all arrangements connected with the taking of evidence.

Article 49

The Court may, even before the hearing begins, call upon the agents to produce any document or to supply any explanations. Formal note shall be taken of any refusal.

Article 50

The Court may, at any time, entrust any individual, body, bureau, commission, or other organization that it may select, with the task of carrying out an enquiry or giving an expert opinion.

Article 51

During the hearing any relevant questions are to be put to the witnesses and experts under the conditions laid down by the Court in the rules of procedure referred to in Article 30.

Article 52

After the Court has received the proofs and evidence within the time specified for the purpose, it may refuse to accept any further oral or written evidence that one party may desire to present unless the other side consents.

Article 53

1. Whenever one of the parties does not appear before the Court, or fails to defend its case, the other party may call upon the Court to decide in favor of its claim.

2. The Court must, before doing so, satisfy itself, not only that it has jurisdiction in accordance with Articles 36 and 37, but also that the claim is well founded in fact and law.

Article 54

1. When, subject to the control of the Court, the agents, counsel, and advocates have completed their presentation of the case, the President shall declare the hearing closed.

2. The Court shall withdraw to consider the judgment.

3. The deliberations of the Court shall take place in private and remain secret.

Article 55

1. All questions shall be decided by a majority of the judges present.

2. In the event of an equality of votes, the President or the judge who acts in his place shall have a casting vote.

Article 56

1. The judgment shall state the reasons on which it is based.

2. It shall contain the names of the judges who have taken part in the decision.

Article 57

If the judgment does not represent in whole or in part the unanimous opinion of the judges, any judge shall be entitled to deliver a separate opinion.

Article 58

The judgment shall be signed by the President and by the Registrar. It shall be read in open court, due notice having been given to the agents.

Article 59

The decision of the Court has no binding force except between the parties and in respect of that particular case.

Article 60

The judgment is final and without appeal. In the event of dispute as to the meaning or scope of the judgment, the Court shall construe it upon the request of any party.

Article 61

1. An application for revision of a judgment may be made only when it is based upon the discovery of some fact of such a nature as to be a decisive factor, which fact was, when the judgment was given, unknown to the Court and also to the party claiming revision, always provided that such ignorance was not due to negligence.

2. The proceedings for revision shall be opened by a judgment of the Court expressly recording the existence of the new fact, recognizing that it has such a character as to lay the case open to revision, and declaring the application admissible on this ground.

3. The Court may require previous compliance with the terms of the judgment before it admits proceedings in revision.

4. The application for revision must be made at latest within six months of the discovery of the new fact.

5. No application for revision may be made after the lapse of ten years from the date of the judgment.

Article 62

1. Should a state consider that it has an interest of a legal nature which may be affected by the decision in the case, it may submit a request to the Court to be permitted to intervene.

2. It shall be for the Court to decide upon this request.

Article 63

1. Whenever the construction of a convention to which states other than those concerned in the case are parties is in question, the Registrar shall notify all such states forthwith.

2. Every state so notified has the right to intervene in the proceedings; but if it uses this right, the construction given by the judgment will be equally binding upon it.

Article 64

Unless otherwise decided by the Court, each party shall bear its own costs.

Chapter IV
ADVISORY OPINIONS

Article 65

1. The Court may give an advisory opinion on any legal question at the request of whatever body may be authorized by or in accordance with the Charter of the United Nations to make such a request.

2. Questions upon which the advisory opinion of the Court is asked shall be laid before the Court by means of a written request containing an exact statement of the question upon which an opinion is required, and accompanied by all documents likely to throw light upon the question.

Article 66

1. The Registrar shall forthwith give notice of the request for an advisory opinion to all states entitled to appear before the Court.

2. The Registrar shall also, by means of a special and direct communication, notify any state entitled to appear before the Court or international organization considered by the Court, or, should it not be sitting, by the President, as likely to be able to furnish information on the question, that the Court will be prepared to receive, within a time limit to be fixed by the President, written statements, or to hear, at a public sitting to be held for the purpose, oral statements relating to the question.

3. Should any such state entitled to appear before the Court have failed to receive the special communication referred to in paragraph 2 of this Article, such state may express a desire to submit a written statement or to be heard; and the Court will decide.

4. States and organizations having presented written or oral statements or both shall be permitted to comment on the statements made by other states or organizations in the form, to the extent, and within the time limits which the Court, or, should it not be sitting, the President, shall decide in each particular case. Accordingly, the Registrar shall in due time communicate any such written statements to states and organizations having submitted similar statements.

Article 67

The Court shall deliver its advisory opinions in open court, notice having been given to the Secretary-General and to the representatives of Members of the United Nations, of other states and of international organizations immediately concerned.

Article 68

In the exercise of its advisory functions the Court shall further be guided by the provisions of the present Statute which apply in contentious cases to the extent to which it recognizes them to be applicable.

Chapter V
AMENDMENT

Article 69

Amendments to the present Statute shall be effected by the same procedure as is provided by the Charter of the United Nations for amendments to that Charter, subject however to any provisions which the General Assembly upon recommendation of the Security Council may adopt concerning the participation of states which are parties to the present Statute but are not Members of the United Nations.

Article 70

The Court shall have power to propose such amendments to the present Statute as it may deem necessary, through written communications to the Secretary-General, for consideration in conformity with the provisions of Article 69.

Appendix III

Structure of the United Nations

General Assembly

The General Assembly is composed of all the Members of the United Nations.

SESSIONS
Resumed forty-third session: 14 February–7 March, 18-20 April, 11 July and 18 September 1989.
Forty-fourth session:[1] 19 September–29 December 1989 (suspended).
Sixteenth special session: 12-14 December 1989.

OFFICERS
Resumed forty-third session
President: Dante Caputo (Argentina).
Vice-Presidents: Bahrain, China, Côte d'Ivoire, Cyprus, Denmark, Ecuador, El Salvador, France, Guinea-Bissau, Libyan Arab Jamahiriya, Malta, Nepal, Sao Tome and Principe, Swaziland, Thailand, USSR, United Kingdom, United Republic of Tanzania, United States, Vanuatu, Yugoslavia.

Forty-fourth session and sixteenth special session
President: Joseph Nanven Garba (Nigeria).[a]
Vice-Presidents:[b] Antigua and Barbuda, Bolivia, Brunei Darussalam, China, Congo, Costa Rica, France, Gambia, Iran, Iraq, Kuwait, Luxembourg, Morocco, Norway, Papua New Guinea, Poland, Sudan, USSR, United Kingdom, United States, Zimbabwe.

[a]Elected on 19 September 1989 (decision 44/302). On 12 December (decision S-16/12), the Assembly decided that the President at the forty-fourth session would serve in the same capacity at the sixteenth special session.
[b]Elected on 19 September 1989 (decision 44/304). On 12 December (decision S-16/14), the Assembly decided that the Vice-Presidents at the forty-fourth session would serve in the same capacity at the sixteenth special session.

The Assembly has four types of committees: (1) Main Committees; (2) procedural committees; (3) standing committees; (4) subsidiary and *ad hoc* bodies. In addition, it convenes conferences to deal with specific subjects.

Main Committees
Seven Main Committees have been established as follows:

Political and Security Committee (disarmament and related international security questions) (First Committee)
Special Political Committee
Economic and Financial Committee (Second Committee)
Social, Humanitarian and Cultural Committee (Third Committee)
Trusteeship Committee (including Non-Self-Governing Territories) (Fourth Committee)
Administrative and Budgetary Committee (Fifth Committee)
Legal Committee (Sixth Committee)

The General Assembly may constitute other committees, on which all Members of the United Nations have the right to be represented.

OFFICERS OF THE MAIN COMMITTEES

Resumed forty-third session

Second Committee[a]
Chairman: Hugo Navajas-Mogro (Bolivia).
Vice-Chairmen: José Fernandez (Philippines), Eloho E. Otobo (Nigeria).
Rapporteur: Pavol Sepelak (Czechoslovakia).

Fifth Committee[a]
Chairman: Michael George Okeyo (Kenya).
Vice-Chairmen: Mojtaba Arastou (Iran), Tjaco T. van den Hout (Netherlands).
Rapporteur: Flor A. de Rodríguez (Venezuela).

[a]The only Main Committees to meet at the resumed session.

Forty-fourth session[a]

[a]Chairmen elected by the Main Committees; announced by the Assembly President on 19 September 1989 (decision 44/303).

First Committee
Chairman: Adolfo Raúl Taylhardat (Venezuela).
Vice-Chairmen: Mohamed Nabil Fahmy (Egypt), Hassaan Mashahdi-Ghahvehchi (Iran).
Rapporteur: Dimitrios Platis (Greece).

Special Political Committee
Chairman: Guennadi Iossifovich Oudovenko (Ukrainian SSR).
Vice-Chairmen: Choo Siew Kioh (Malaysia), Charles S. Flemming (Saint Lucia).
Rapporteur: Nonet M. Dapul (Philippines).

Second Committee
Chairman: Ahmed Ghezal (Tunisia).
Vice-Chairmen: Badam-Ochiryn Doljintseren (Mongolia), David Bruce Payton (New Zealand).
Rapporteur: Martha Dueñas de Whist (Ecuador).

Third Committee
Chairman: Paul Désiré Kaboré (Burkina Faso).
Vice-Chairmen: Stanislav Ogurtsov (Byelorussian SSR), A. Missouri Sherman-Peter (Bahamas).
Rapporteur: Wilfried Grolig (Federal Republic of Germany).

Fourth Committee
Chairman: Robert F. Van Lierop (Vanuatu).
Vice-Chairmen: Gordon H. Bristol (Nigeria), A. M. Antony Cave (Barbados).
Rapporteur: Mohammad Saeed Al-Kindi (United Arab Emirates).

Fifth Committee
Chairman: Ahmad Fathi Al-Masri (Syrian Arab Republic).
Vice-Chairmen: Kwaku Duah Dankwa (Ghana), Ado Vaher (Canada).
Rapporteur: Etien Ninov (Bulgaria).

Sixth Committee
Chairman: Helmut Türk (Austria).
Vice-Chairmen: Ernesto S. Martínez Gondra (Argentina), Vaclav Mikulka (Czechoslovakia).
Rapporteur: Guillaume Pambou-Tchivounda (Gabon).

---

[1]The forty-fourth session of the General Assembly resumed in 1990 on 20 February, on 12 March, from 26 to 29 March, on 2 April, 17 May, 28 June and 20 July and from 10 to 17 September.

Sixteenth special session[a]

Ad Hoc Committee of the Whole of the Sixteenth Special Session
Chairman: Ann Hercus (New Zealand).[b]
Vice-Chairmen: Moumouni Adamou Djermakoye (Niger), Ruth Nita Barrow (Barbados), Robert F. Van Lierop (Vanuatu).
Rapporteur: Gerhard Richter (German Democratic Republic).

[a]On 12 December 1989 (decision S-16/13), the Assembly decided that the Chairmen of the Main Committees at the forty-fourth session would serve in the same capacity at the sixteenth special session, on the understanding that the Chairmen of the First and Sixth Committees would be replaced by another member of the same delegation.
[b]Elected by the Assembly on 12 December 1989 (decision S-16/15); other officers elected by the *Ad Hoc* Committee.

Procedural committees

General Committee
The General Committee consists of the President of the General Assembly, as Chairman, the 21 Vice-Presidents and the Chairmen of the seven Main Committees.

Credentials Committee
The Credentials Committee consists of nine members appointed by the General Assembly on the proposal of the President.

Forty-fourth session and sixteenth special session[a]
Antigua and Barbuda, Australia, China, Colombia, Malawi, Philippines, USSR, United States, Zaire *(Chairman)*.

[a]Elected on 19 September 1989 (decision 44/301). On 12 December (decision S-16/11), the Assembly decided that the Credentials Committee for the sixteenth special session would have the same composition as at the forty-fourth session.

Standing committees
The two standing committees consist of experts appointed in their individual capacity for three-year terms.

Advisory Committee on Administrative and Budgetary Questions
Members:
To serve until 31 December 1989: Michel Brochard (France); Maria Elisa de Bittencourt Berenguer (Brazil); Tadanori Inomata (Japan); Ma Longde (China); Irmeli Mustonen (Finland); Banbit A. Roy (India).
To serve until 31 December 1990: Bagbeni Adeito Nzengeya (Zaire); Even Fontaine-Ortiz (Cuba); Richard Nygard (United States); Tjaco T. van den Hout (Netherlands); Viktor A. Vislykh (USSR).
To serve until 31 December 1991: Ahmad Fathi Al-Masri (Syrian Arab Republic); Ferguson O. Iheme (Nigeria);[b] C. S. M. Mselle, *Chairman* (United Republic of Tanzania); Jozsef Tardos (Hungary); Christopher R. Thomas (Trinidad and Tobago).

[a]Resigned in September 1989; John Fox (United States) was appointed by the General Assembly on 29 September (decision 44/305 A) to fill the resultant vacancy.
[b]Resigned in October 1989; Lawrence O. C. Agubuzu (Nigeria) was appointed by the General Assembly on 19 December (decision 44/305 B) for a term of office beginning on 1 January 1990 to fill the resultant vacancy.

On 19 December 1989 (decision 44/305 B), the General Assembly appointed the following six members for a three-year term beginning on 1 January 1990 to fill the vacancies occurring on 31 December 1989: Carlos Casap (Bolivia), Yogesh Kumar Gupta (India), Tadanori Inomata (Japan), Ulrich Kalbitzer (Federal Republic of Germany), Irmeli Mustonen (Finland), Yang Hushan (China).

Committee on Contributions
Members:
To serve until 31 December 1989: Bagbeni Adeito Nzengeya (Zaire); Carlos Antonio Bivero García (Venezuela); Peter Gregg (Australia); Atilio Norberto Molteni, *Vice-Chairman* (Argentina); Dimitri Rallis (Greece); Omar Sirry (Egypt).

To serve until 31 December 1990: Amjad Ali, *Chairman* (Pakistan); Ernesto Battisti (Italy); Alain Catta (France); Yuri Chulkov (USSR); Carlos Moreira Garcia (Brazil); Wang Liansheng (China).
To serve until 31 December 1991: Kenshiroh Akimoto (Japan); John Fox (United States); Ion Gorita (Romania); Elias M. C. Kazembe (Zambia); Vanu Gopala Menon (Singapore); Assen Iliev Zlatanov (Bulgaria).

On 19 December 1989 (decision 44/316), the General Assembly appointed the following six members for a three-year term beginning on 1 January 1990 to fill the vacancies occurring on 31 December 1989: Bagbeni Adeito Nzengeya (Zaire), Sergio Chaparro Ruiz (Chile), Peter Gregg (Australia), Atilio Norberto Molteni (Argentina), Mohamed Mahmoud Ould El Ghaouth (Mauritania), Dimitri Rallis (Greece).

Subsidiary and *ad hoc* bodies
The following subsidiary and *ad hoc* bodies were in existence or functioning in 1989, or were established during the General Assembly's forty-fourth session, held from 19 September to 29 December 1989. (For other related bodies, see p. 1012.)

Ad Hoc Committee of the General Assembly for the Announcement of Voluntary Contributions to the 1990 Programme of the United Nations High Commissioner for Refugees
As soon as practicable after the opening of each regular session of the General Assembly, an *ad hoc* committee of the whole of the Assembly meets, under the chairmanship of the President of the session, to enable Governments to announce pledges of voluntary contributions to the programme of UNHCR for the following year. Also invited to announce their pledges are States which are members of specialized agencies but not Members of the United Nations. In 1989, the *Ad Hoc* Committee met on 20 November.

Ad Hoc Committee of the General Assembly for the Announcement of Voluntary Contributions to the United Nations Relief and Works Agency for Palestine Refugees in the Near East
As soon as practicable after the opening of each regular session of the General Assembly, an *ad hoc* committee of the whole of the Assembly meets, under the chairmanship of the President of the session, to enable Governments to announce pledges of voluntary contributions to the programme of UNRWA for the following year. Also invited to announce their pledges are States which are members of specialized agencies but not Members of the United Nations. In 1989, the *Ad Hoc* Committee met on 16 November.

Ad Hoc Committee of the International Conference on Kampuchea
The *Ad Hoc* Committee of the International Conference on Kampuchea held four meetings between 8 February and 12 September 1989, at United Nations Headquarters.

Members: Belgium *(Vice-Chairman)*, Japan, Malaysia *(Rapporteur)*, Nepal, Nigeria, Peru, Senegal, Sri Lanka, Sudan, Thailand.

Chairman: Absa Claude Diallo (Senegal).

Ad Hoc Committee of the Whole for the Preparation of the International Development Strategy for the Fourth United Nations Development Decade
In 1989, the *Ad Hoc* Committee of the Whole for the Preparation of the International Development Strategy for the Fourth United Nations Development Decade held three sessions at United Nations Headquarters: an organizational session from 15 to 17 March, its first session from 5 to 9 June and its second session from 11 to 15 September.

Chairman: Gamani Corea (Sri Lanka).
Vice-Chairmen: Alvaro Gurgel de Alencar (Brazil), Ahmed Djoghlaf (Algeria), Paul Laberge (Canada), Wolfgang Sproete (German Democratic Republic).
Rapporteur: Ahmed Djoghlaf (Algeria).

Ad Hoc Committee on the Drafting of an International Convention against the Recruitment, Use, Financing and Training of Mercenaries

The 35-member *Ad Hoc* Committee on the Drafting of an International Convention against the Recruitment, Use, Financing and Training of Mercenaries held its eighth session at United Nations Headquarters from 30 January to 17 February 1989.

Members: Algeria, Angola, Bangladesh, Barbados, Benin, Bulgaria, Canada, Cuba, Democratic Yemen, Ethiopia, France, German Democratic Republic, Germany, Federal Republic of, Haiti, India, Italy, Jamaica, Japan, Mongolia, Portugal, Senegal, Seychelles, Spain, Suriname, Togo, Turkey, Ukrainian SSR, USSR, United Kingdom, United States, Uruguay, Viet Nam, Yugoslavia, Zaire, Zambia.

Chairman: Gebre-Medhin Hagoss (Ethiopia).
Vice-Chairmen: Vladimir Y. Eltchenko (Ukrainian SSR), Tullio Treves (Italy), Siegfried Werners (Suriname).
Rapporteur: Hameed Mohamed Ali (Democratic Yemen).

Ad Hoc Committee on the Indian Ocean

In 1989, the 49-member *Ad Hoc* Committee on the Indian Ocean, continuing the preparatory work for the Conference on the Indian Ocean (rescheduled for 1991 at Colombo, Sri Lanka), held two sessions, at United Nations Headquarters: from 10 to 14 April and from 5 to 19 July.

Members: Australia, Bangladesh, Bulgaria, Canada, China, Democratic Yemen, Djibouti, Egypt, Ethiopia, France, German Democratic Republic, Germany, Federal Republic of, Greece, India, Indonesia, Iran, Iraq, Italy, Japan, Kenya, Liberia, Madagascar, Malaysia, Maldives, Mauritius, Mozambique, Netherlands, Norway, Oman, Pakistan, Panama, Poland, Romania, Seychelles, Singapore, Somalia, Sri Lanka, Sudan, Thailand, Uganda, USSR, United Arab Emirates, United Kingdom, United Republic of Tanzania, United States, Yemen, Yugoslavia, Zambia, Zimbabwe.

Sweden, a major maritime user of the Indian Ocean, continued to participate in the meetings as an observer.

Chairman: Daya Perera (Sri Lanka).
Vice-Chairmen: Jill Courtney (Australia), Manuel dos Santos (Mozambique), Wilhelm Grundmann (German Democratic Republic), Isslamet Poernomo (Indonesia).
Rapporteur: Jean de Dieu Rakotozafy (Madagascar).

Ad Hoc Committee on the World Disarmament Conference

The *Ad Hoc* Committee on the World Disarmament Conference did not meet in 1989.

Members: Algeria, Argentina, Austria, Belgium, Brazil, Bulgaria, Burundi, Canada, Chile, Colombia, Czechoslovakia, Egypt, Ethiopia, Hungary, India, Indonesia, Iran, Italy, Japan, Lebanon, Liberia, Mexico, Mongolia, Morocco, Netherlands, Nigeria, Pakistan, Peru, Philippines, Poland, Romania, Spain, Sri Lanka, Sweden, Tunisia, Turkey, Venezuela, Yugoslavia, Zaire, Zambia.

The USSR participates in the work of the *Ad Hoc* Committee, while China, France, the United Kingdom and the United States maintain contact with it through its Chairman, pursuant to a 1973 General Assembly resolution.[2]

WORKING GROUP
Members: Burundi, Egypt, Hungary, India, Iran, Italy, Mexico, Peru, Poland, Spain, Sri Lanka.

Advisory Committee on the United Nations Educational and Training Programme for Southern Africa

Members: Byelorussian SSR, Canada, Denmark, India, Japan, Liberia, Nigeria, Norway, United Republic of Tanzania, United States, Venezuela, Zaire, Zambia.

Chairman: Tom Eric Vraalsen (Norway).
Vice-Chairman: Isaiah Zimba Chabala (Zambia).

Advisory Committee on the United Nations Programme of Assistance in the Teaching, Study, Dissemination and Wider Appreciation of International Law

The Advisory Committee on the United Nations Programme of Assistance in the Teaching, Study, Dissemination and Wider Appreciation of International Law held its twenty-fourth session at United Nations Headquarters on 31 October 1989.

Members (until 31 December 1991): Bangladesh, Cyprus, France, Ghana, Libyan Arab Jamahiriya, Mexico, Netherlands, Romania, Turkey, USSR, United Kingdom, Venezuela, Zaire.

Chairman: Clifford Nii Amon Kotey (Ghana).

Board of Auditors

The Board of Auditors consists of three members appointed by the General Assembly for three-year terms.

Members:
To serve until 30 June 1990: Chairman of the Commission of Audit of the Philippines.
To serve until 30 June 1991: Auditor-General of Ghana.
To serve until 30 June 1992: President of the Federal Court of Audit of the Federal Republic of Germany.

On 19 December 1989 (decision 44/317), the General Assembly appointed the Chairman of the Commission of Audit of the Philippines for a three-year term beginning on 1 July 1990.

Collective Measures Committee

Established in 1950 under the General Assembly's "Uniting for Peace" resolution,[3] the Collective Measures Committee reported three times to the Assembly. In noting the third report, to its ninth (1954) session, the Assembly directed the Committee to remain in a position to pursue such further studies as it may deem desirable to strengthen the capability of the United Nations to maintain peace and to report to the Security Council and to the Assembly as appropriate.[4]

Members: Australia, Belgium, Brazil, Canada, Egypt, France, Mexico, Myanmar (Burma), Philippines, Turkey, United Kingdom, United States, Venezuela, Yugoslavia.

Committee for the United Nations Population Award

The Committee for the United Nations Population Award is composed of: *(a)* 10 representatives of United Nations Member States elected by the Economic and Social Council for a three-year period, with due regard for equitable geographical representation and the need to include Member States that had made contributions for the Award; *(b)* the Secretary-General and the UNFPA Executive Director, to serve *ex officio;* and *(c)* five individuals eminent for their significant contributions to population-related activities, selected by the Committee, to serve as honorary members in an advisory capacity for a renewable three-year term.

In 1989, the Committee held meetings at United Nations Headquarters on 5 and 12 January and on 7 and 22 February.

Members (until 31 December 1991): Byelorussian SSR, Ecuador, India, Japan, Mauritius, Mexico, Pakistan, Rwanda, Togo, Turkey.
Ex-officio members: The Secretary-General and the UNFPA Executive Director.
Honorary members (until 31 December 1991): Takeo Fukuda, Enrique Iglesias, Bradford Morse, Olusegun Obsanjo, Jean Ripert.

Chairman: Mario Moya-Palencia (Mexico).

---

[2]YUN 1973, p. 18, GA res. 3183(XXVIII), 18 Dec. 1973.
[3]YUN 1950, p. 194, GA res. 377(V), part A, para. 11, 3 Nov. 1950.
[4]YUN 1954, p. 23, GA res. 809(IX), 4 Nov. 1954.

Committee of Trustees of the United Nations Trust Fund for South Africa

Members: Chile, Morocco, Nigeria, Pakistan, Sweden.

Chairman: Jan K. Eliasson (Sweden).
Vice-Chairman: Joseph N. Garba (Nigeria).

Committee on Applications for Review of Administrative Tribunal Judgements

In 1989, the Committee on Applications for Review of Administrative Tribunal Judgements held two sessions, at United Nations Headquarters: its thirty-second on 30 January and 3 February and its thirty-third on 6 and 8 September.

Members (until 18 September 1989) (based on the composition of the General Committee at the General Assembly's forty-third session): Argentina, Bahrain, Bolivia, Canada, China, Côte d'Ivoire, Cyprus, Denmark, Ecuador, El Salvador, France, Guinea-Bissau, Kenya, Kuwait, Libyan Arab Jamahiriya, Malta, Nepal, Poland, Saint Vincent and the Grenadines, Sao Tome and Principe, Sudan, Swaziland, Thailand, USSR, United Kingdom, United Republic of Tanzania, United States, Vanuatu, Yugoslavia.

Chairman: Achol Deng (Sudan).
Rapporteur: Anthony Aust (United Kingdom).

Members (from 19 September 1989) (based on the composition of the General Committee at the General Assembly's forty-fourth session): Antigua and Barbuda, Austria, Bolivia, Brunei Darussalam, Burkina Faso, China, Congo, Costa Rica, France, Gambia, Iran, Iraq, Kuwait, Luxembourg, Morocco, Nigeria, Norway, Papua New Guinea, Poland, Sudan, Syrian Arab Republic, Tunisia, Ukrainian SSR, USSR, United Kingdom, United States, Vanuatu, Venezuela, Zimbabwe.

Committee on Arrangements for a Conference for the Purpose of Reviewing the Charter

All Members of the United Nations are members of the Committee on Arrangements for a Conference for the Purpose of Reviewing the Charter.

The Committee, established in 1955, last met in 1967, following which the General Assembly decided to keep it in being.[5]

Committee on Conferences

The Committee on Conferences is composed of 21 Member States appointed by the President of the General Assembly according to a specific pattern of equitable geographical distribution, to serve for a three-year term.

Members:[a]
To serve until 31 December 1989: Austria, Fiji, Iran, Mexico, Senegal, Tunisia, United States.
To serve until 31 December 1990: Chile, Cyprus, Egypt, Ethiopia, France, Japan, USSR.
To serve until 31 December 1991: German Democratic Republic, Ghana, Honduras, Indonesia, Jamaica, Mozambique, United Kingdom.

[a]Appointed by the President of the forty-third session of the General Assembly, as stated in his communication of 3 January 1989 to the Secretary-General.

Chairman: Franziska Friessnigg (Austria).
Vice-Chairmen: Jaime Bazán (Chile), Shamel Elsayed Nasser (Egypt), Tadanori Inomata (Japan).
Rapporteur: Michael Klett (German Democratic Republic).

On 15 December 1989 (decision 44/314), the General Assembly took note of the appointment by its President of the following members for a three-year term beginning on 1 January 1990 to fill the vacancies occurring on 31 December 1989: Austria, Iraq, Liberia, Mexico, Pakistan, Uganda, United States.

Committee on Information

In 1989, the 73-member Committee on Information held its eleventh session at United Nations Headquarters on 6 March (organizational meeting) and from 13 to 28 April (substantive meetings).

Members: Algeria, Argentina, Bangladesh, Belgium, Benin, Brazil, Bulgaria, Burundi, Chile, China, Colombia, Congo, Costa Rica, Côte d'Ivoire, Cuba, Cyprus, Denmark, Ecuador, Egypt, El Salvador, Ethiopia, Finland, France, German Democratic Republic, Germany, Federal Republic of, Ghana, Greece, Guatemala, Guinea, Guyana, Hungary, India, Indonesia, Ireland, Italy, Japan, Jordan, Kenya, Lebanon, Malta, Mexico, Mongolia, Morocco, Netherlands, Niger, Nigeria, Pakistan, Peru, Philippines, Poland, Portugal, Romania, Singapore, Somalia, Spain, Sri Lanka, Sudan, Syrian Arab Republic, Togo, Trinidad and Tobago, Tunisia, Turkey, Ukrainian SSR, USSR, United Kingdom, United Republic of Tanzania, United States, Venezuela, Viet Nam, Yemen, Yugoslavia, Zaire, Zimbabwe.

Chairman: Orobola Fasehun (Nigeria).
Vice-Chairmen: Gerhard Haensel (German Democratic Republic), Peter Janus (Netherlands), Mansoor Suhail (Pakistan).
Rapporteur: Ricardo Lagorio (Argentina).

On 8 December 1989, the General Assembly increased the membership of the Committee from 73 to 74 (decision 44/418) and appointed Nepal as a member as from 1 January 1990 (decision 44/313).

Committee on Relations with the Host Country

Members: Bulgaria, Canada, China, Costa Rica, Côte d'Ivoire, Cyprus, France, Honduras, Iraq, Mali, Senegal, Spain, USSR, United Kingdom, United States (host country).

Chairman: Constantine Moushoutas (Cyprus).
Vice-Chairmen: Bulgaria, Canada, Côte d'Ivoire.
Rapporteur: Emilia Castro de Barish (Costa Rica).

Committee on the Development and Utilization of New and Renewable Sources of Energy

The Committee on the Development and Utilization of New and Renewable Sources of Energy, open to the participation of all States as full members, did not meet in 1989.

Committee on the Exercise of the Inalienable Rights of the Palestinian People

Members: Afghanistan, Cuba, Cyprus, German Democratic Republic, Guinea, Guyana, Hungary, India, Indonesia, Lao People's Democratic Republic, Madagascar, Malaysia, Mali, Malta, Nigeria, Pakistan, Romania, Senegal, Sierra Leone, Tunisia, Turkey, Ukrainian SSR, Yugoslavia.

Chairman: Absa Claude Diallo (Senegal).
Vice-Chairmen: Shah Mohammad Dost (Afghanistan) (until 8 November), Noor Ahmad Noor (Afghanistan) (from 8 November); Oscar Oramas-Oliva (Cuba).
Rapporteur: Alexander Borg Olivier (Malta).

WORKING GROUP
Members: Afghanistan, Cuba, German Democratic Republic, Guinea, Guyana, India *(Vice-Chairman)*, Malta *(Chairman)*, Pakistan, Senegal, Tunisia, Turkey, Ukrainian SSR; Palestine Liberation Organization.

Committee on the Peaceful Uses of Outer Space

The 53-member Committee on the Peaceful Uses of Outer Space held its thirty-second session at United Nations Headquarters from 5 to 15 June 1989.

---

[5]YUN 1967, p. 291, GA res. 2285(XXII), 5 Dec. 1967.

Members: Albania, Argentina, Australia, Austria, Belgium, Benin, Brazil, Bulgaria, Burkina Faso, Cameroon, Canada, Chad, Chile, China, Colombia, Czechoslovakia, Ecuador, Egypt, France, German Democratic Republic, Germany, Federal Republic of, Greece, Hungary, India, Indonesia, Iran, Iraq, Italy, Japan, Kenya, Lebanon, Mexico, Mongolia, Morocco, Netherlands, Niger, Nigeria, Pakistan, Philippines, Poland, Romania, Sierra Leone, Spain, Sudan, Sweden, Syrian Arab Republic, USSR, United Kingdom, United States, Uruguay, Venezuela, Viet Nam, Yugoslavia.

Chairman: Peter Jankowitsch (Austria).
Vice-Chairman: Petre Tanasie (Romania).
Rapporteur: Flavio Miragaia Perri (Brazil).

LEGAL SUB-COMMITTEE
The Legal Sub-Committee, a committee of the whole, held its twenty-eighth session at United Nations Headquarters from 20 March to 7 April 1989.

Chairman: Stanislav Suja (Czechoslovakia).

SCIENTIFIC AND TECHNICAL SUB-COMMITTEE
The Scientific and Technical Sub-Committee, a committee of the whole, held its twenty-sixth session at United Nations Headquarters from 21 February to 3 March 1989.

Chairman: John H. Carver (Australia).

Disarmament Commission
In 1989, the Disarmament Commission, composed of all the Members of the United Nations, held a series of meetings between 8 and 31 May and an organizational session on 1 and 7 December, all at United Nations Headquarters.

Chairman: Bagbeni Adeito Nzengeya (Zaire).
Vice-Chairmen: Austria, Bahrain, Costa Rica, German Democratic Republic, Haiti, Romania, Sri Lanka, Togo.
Rapporteur: André Querton (Belgium).

High-level Committee on the Review of Technical Co-operation among Developing Countries
In 1989, the High-level Committee on the Review of Technical Co-operation among Developing Countries, composed of all States participating in UNDP, held its sixth session at United Nations Headquarters from 18 to 22 and on 29 September.

President: Mohammad A. Abulhasan (Kuwait).
Vice-Presidents: Charles S. Flemming (Saint Lucia), K. O. Kumi (Ghana), Selim Yenel (Turkey).
Rapporteur: Svetlozar Panov (Bulgaria).

Intergovernmental Committee on Science and Technology for Development
The Intergovernmental Committee on Science and Technology for Development, which reports to the General Assembly through the Economic and Social Council and is open to the participation of all States as full members, held its tenth session at United Nations Headquarters from 21 August to 1 September 1989.

Chairman: Celso Lafer (Brazil).
Vice-Chairmen: Oleg N. Pashkevich (Byelorussian SSR), Torsten Westlund (Sweden), Zhu Lilan (China).
Rapporteur: James M. Mugume (Uganda).

ADVISORY COMMITTEE ON SCIENCE
AND TECHNOLOGY FOR DEVELOPMENT
The 28-member Advisory Committee on Science and Technology for Development held its ninth session at Vienna from 4 to 12 September 1989.

Members:
To serve until 31 December 1989: Carlos Rafael Abeledo, *Vice-Chairman* (Argentina); Elisabeth Birman (Hungary); Harvey Brooks, *Vice-Chairman* (United States); Essam El-Din Galal (Egypt); Karl E. Ganzhorn (Federal Republic of Germany); Yoichi Kaya (Japan);

Mumtaz Ali Kazi (Pakistan); Lydia P. Makhubu, *Vice-Chairman* (Swaziland); Lourival Carmo Monaco (Brazil); Abdulrahman Salim Msangi (United Republic of Tanzania); James Mullin, *Rapporteur* (Canada); Yash Pal, *Vice-Chairman* (India); Nana Claris Efuah Pratt (Sierra Leone); Francisco R. Sagasti, *Chairman* (Peru).
To serve until 31 December 1990: Saleh Abdulrahman Al-Athel (Saudi Arabia); Ali Boussaha (Algeria); Robert Gyabaa Jones Butler (Ghana); Hyung Sup Choi (Republic of Korea); Elisabeth Helander (Finland); David Kear (New Zealand); Stefan Kwiatkowski, *Vice-Chairman* (Poland); Henry Isaac Cloore Lowe (Jamaica); Tansia Molende Monkoy (Zaire); Charles Herbert Geoffrey Oldham (United Kingdom); Omar bin Abdul Rahman (Malaysia); Daniel Resendiz Núñez (Mexico); Alexander P. Vladislavlev (USSR); Wu Yi Kang (China).

On 25 August 1989, the Intergovernmental Committee appointed the following 14 members of the Advisory Committee for a three-year term beginning on 1 January 1990 to fill the vacancies occurring on 31 December 1989: Carlos Rafael Abeledo (Argentina), Elisabeth Birman (Hungary), Harvey Brooks (United States), Karl E. Ganzhorn (Federal Republic of Germany), Seeiso Liphuko (Botswana), Joanna Olutunmbi Maduka (Nigeria), Marcos Mares Guia (Brazil), Thomas R. Odhiambo (Kenya), Yash Pal (India), Maria de Lourdes Pintassilgo (Portugal), Yangze Sherpa (Nepal), Mikoto Usui (Japan), Dulce Arnao de Uzcátegui (Venezuela), Joséphine Guidy Wandja (Côte d'Ivoire).

Intergovernmental Group to Monitor the Supply and Shipping of Oil and Petroleum Products to South Africa
The Intergovernmental Group to Monitor the Supply and Shipping of Oil and Petroleum Products to South Africa is composed of 11 Member States appointed by the Assembly President, in consultation with the regional groups and the Chairman of the Special Committee against *Apartheid*, on the basis of equitable geographical distribution and ensuring representation of oil-exporting and -shipping States.

Members: Algeria, Cuba, German Democratic Republic, Indonesia, Kuwait, New Zealand, Nicaragua, Nigeria, Norway, Ukrainian SSR, United Republic of Tanzania.

Chairman: Tom Eric Vraalsen (Norway).
Vice-Chairman: Nabeela Al-Mulla (Kuwait).
Rapporteur: Wilbert K. Chagula (United Republic of Tanzania).

Interim Committee of the General Assembly
The Interim Committee of the General Assembly, on which each Member of the United Nations has the right to appoint one representative, was originally established by the Assembly in 1947 to function between the Assembly's regular sessions. It was re-established in 1948 for a further year and in 1949[6] for an indefinite period. The Committee has not met since 1961.[7]

International Civil Service Commission
The International Civil Service Commission consists of 15 members who serve in their personal capacity as individuals of recognized competence in public administration or related fields, particularly in personnel management. They are appointed by the General Assembly, with due regard for equitable geographical distribution, for four-year terms.

The Commission held three sessions in 1989: its second special at United Nations Headquarters from 16 to 19 January, its twenty-ninth at Vienna from 6 to 23 March, and its thirtieth at United Nations Headquarters from 31 July to 25 August.

Members:
To serve until 31 December 1989: Michel Jean Bardoux (France); Claudia Cooley (United States); Antônio Fonseca Pimentel (Brazil); Alexis Stephanou (Greece); Ku Tashiro (Japan).
To serve until 31 December 1990: Richard M. Akwei, *Chairman* (Ghana); Turkia Daddah (Mauritania); Karel Houska (Czechoslo-

---

[6]YUN 1948-49, p. 411, GA res. 295(IV), 21 Nov. 1949.
[7]YUN 1961, p. 705.

vakia);[a] André Xavier Pirson (Belgium); Carlos S. Vegega, *Vice-Chairman* (Argentina).
To serve until 31 December 1992: Amjad Ali (Pakistan); Francesca Yetunde Emanuel (Nigeria); Omar Sirry (Egypt); Vladislav Petrovich Terekhov (USSR); M. A. Vellodi (India).

[a]Resigned effective 31 December 1989; Ladislav Smid (Czechoslovakia) was appointed on 19 December (decision 44/320) to fill the resultant vacancy.

On 19 December 1989 (decision 44/320), the General Assembly appointed the following for a four-year term beginning on 1 January 1990 to fill the vacancies occurring on 31 December 1989: Michel Jean Bardoux (France), Claudia Cooley (United States), António Fonseca Pimentel (Brazil), Alexis Stephanou (Greece), Ku Tashiro (Japan).

ADVISORY COMMITTEE ON POST ADJUSTMENT QUESTIONS

The Advisory Committee on Post Adjustment Questions consists of six members, of whom five are chosen from the geographical regions of Africa, Asia, Latin America, Eastern Europe, and Western Europe and other States; and one, from ICSC, who serves *ex officio* as Chairman. Members are appointed by the ICSC Chairman to serve for four-year terms.

The Advisory Committee held its fourteenth session at United Nations Headquarters from 31 May to 6 June 1989.

Members:

To serve until 31 December 1989: Jeremiah P. Banda (Zambia).
To serve until 31 December 1990: Hugues Picard (France).
To serve until 31 December 1991: Yuri Ivanov (USSR), Isaac Kerstenetzky (Brazil).
To serve until 31 December 1992: Yuki Miura (Japan).
Ex-officio member: Carlos S. Vegega, *Chairman* (Argentina).

International Law Commission

The International Law Commission consists of 34 persons of recognized competence in international law, elected by the General Assembly to serve in their individual capacity for a five-year term. Vacancies occurring within the five-year period are filled by the Commission.

The Commission held its forty-first session at Geneva from 2 May to 21 July 1989.

Members (until 31 December 1991): Bola Adesumbo Ajibola (Nigeria); Hussain M. Al-Baharna (Bahrain); Awn S. Al-Khasawneh (Jordan); Riyadh Al-Qaysi (Iraq); Gaetano Arangio-Ruiz (Italy); Julio Barboza (Argentina); Yuri G. Barsegov (USSR); J. Alan Beesley (Canada); Mohamed Bennouna, *Rapporteur* (Morocco); Boutros Boutros-Ghali (Egypt); Carlos Calero-Rodrigues (Brazil); Leonardo Díaz-González (Venezuela); Gudmundur Eiriksson (Iceland); Laurel B. Francis (Jamaica); Bernhard Graefrath, *Chairman* (German Democratic Republic); Francis Mahon Hayes (Ireland); Jorge Enrique Illueca (Panama); Andreas J. Jacovides (Cyprus); Abdul G. Koroma (Sierra Leone); Ahmed Mahiou (Algeria); Stephen C. McCaffrey (United States); Frank X. J. C. Njenga (Kenya); Motoo Ogiso (Japan); Stanislaw M. Pawlak (Poland); Pemmaraju Sreenivasa Rao, *First Vice-Chairman* (India); Edilbert Razafindralambo (Madagascar); Paul Reuter (France); Emmanuel J. Roucounas, *Second Vice-Chairman* (Greece); César Sepúlveda Gutiérrez (Mexico); Shi Jiuyong (China); Luis Solari Tudela (Peru); Doudou Thiam (Senegal); Christian Tomuschat (Federal Republic of Germany); Alexander Yankov (Bulgaria).

Investments Committee

The Investments Committee consists of nine members appointed by the Secretary-General, after consultation with the United Nations Joint Staff Pension Board and ACABQ, subject to confirmation by the General Assembly. Members serve for three-year terms.

Members:

To serve until 31 December 1989: Yves Oltramare (Switzerland); Emmanuel Noi Omaboe (Ghana); Juergen Reimnitz (Federal Republic of Germany).

To serve until 31 December 1990: Jean Guyot, *Vice-Chairman* (France); George Johnston (United States); Michiya Matsukawa (Japan).
To serve until 31 December 1991: Aloysio de Andrade Faria (Brazil); Braj Kumar Nehru, *Chairman* (India); Stanislaw Raczkowski (Poland).

In addition, during 1989, Ahmed Abdullatif (Saudi Arabia) served in an *ad hoc* consultative capacity.

On 19 December 1989 (decision 44/318), the General Assembly confirmed the appointment by the Secretary-General of Yves Oltramare (Switzerland), Emmanuel Noi Omaboe (Ghana) and Juergen Reimnitz (Federal Republic of Germany) as members for a three-year term beginning on 1 January 1990.

Joint Advisory Group on the International Trade Centre UNCTAD/GATT

The Joint Advisory Group was established in accordance with an agreement between UNCTAD and GATT with effect from 1 January 1968, the date on which their joint sponsorship of the International Trade Centre commenced.

Participation in the Group is open to all States members of UNCTAD and to all contracting parties to GATT.

The Group held its twenty-second session at Geneva from 10 to 14 April 1989.

Chairman: William Rossier (Switzerland).
Vice-Chairmen: A. El-Gowhari (Egypt), M. Lebkowski (Poland).
Rapporteur: S. Mangoma (Zimbabwe).

Joint Inspection Unit

The Joint Inspection Unit consists of not more than 11 Inspectors appointed by the General Assembly from candidates nominated by Member States following appropriate consultations, including consultations with the President of the Economic and Social Council and with the Chairman of ACC. The Inspectors, chosen for their special experience in national or international administrative and financial matters, with due regard for equitable geographical distribution and reasonable rotation, serve in their personal capacity for five-year terms.

Members:

To serve until 31 December 1990: Enrique Ferrer Vieyra (Argentina) (until 1 April 1989); Alain Gourdon (France); Richard Vognild Hennes, *Chairman* (United States); Ivan Kojio (Yugoslavia); Kabongo Tunsala, *Vice-Chairman* (Zaire).
To serve until 31 December 1992: Adib Daoudy (Syrian Arab Republic); Mohamed Salah Eldin Ibrahim (Egypt); Boris P. Prokofiev (USSR); Siegfried Schumm (Federal Republic of Germany); Norman Williams (Panama).
To serve until 31 December 1993: Raúl Quijano (Argentina) (from 1 April 1989).
To serve until 31 December 1994: Kahono Martohadinegoro (Indonesia).[a]

[a]Reappointed in 1988 (see YUN 1988, p. 1011).

On 15 December 1989 (decision 44/315 A), the General Assembly appointed Andrzej Abraszewski (Poland) and Kabongo Tunsala (Zaire) for a five-year term beginning on 1 January 1991 to fill two of the four vacancies occurring on 31 December 1990; no further appointments were made in 1989 to fill the remaining vacancies.

Negotiating Committee on the Financial Emergency of the United Nations

Established in 1975 by the General Assembly[8] to consist of 54 Member States appointed by its President on the basis of equitable geographical balance, the Negotiating Committee on the Financial Emergency of the United Nations has a membership of 48. It has not met since 1976.[9]

[8]YUN 1975, p. 957, GA res. 3538(XXX), 17 Dec. 1975.
[9]YUN 1976, pp. 889 and 1064.

Members: Argentina, Austria, Bangladesh, Bolivia, Burkina Faso, Canada, Chad, Colombia, Cuba, Ecuador, Egypt, Finland, France, Gabon, German Democratic Republic, Germany, Federal Republic of, Ghana, Greece, Grenada, India, Indonesia, Iran, Ireland, Italy, Jamaica, Japan, Jordan, Kenya, Kuwait, Libyan Arab Jamahiriya, Malawi, Mexico, Morocco, Nigeria, Pakistan, Philippines, Poland, Spain, Sudan, Swaziland, Sweden, Trinidad and Tobago, Tunisia, Turkey, USSR, United Kingdom, United States, Venezuela.

Office of the United Nations High Commissioner for Refugees (UNHCR)

EXECUTIVE COMMITTEE OF THE HIGH COMMISSIONER'S PROGRAMME
The Executive Committee held its fortieth session at Geneva from 5 to 13 October 1989.

Members: Algeria, Argentina, Australia, Austria, Belgium, Brazil, Canada, China, Colombia, Denmark, Finland, France, Germany, Federal Republic of, Greece, Holy See, Iran, Israel, Italy, Japan, Lebanon, Lesotho, Madagascar, Morocco, Namibia (represented by the United Nations Council for Namibia), Netherlands, Nicaragua, Nigeria, Norway, Pakistan, Somalia, Sudan, Sweden, Switzerland, Thailand, Tunisia, Turkey, Uganda, United Kingdom, United Republic of Tanzania, United States, Venezuela, Yugoslavia, Zaire.

Chairman: Fredo Dannenbring (Federal Republic of Germany).
Vice-Chairman: Messaoud Ait Chaalal (Algeria).
Rapporteur: Zenji Kaminaga (Japan).

United Nations High Commissioner for Refugees: Jean-Pierre Hocké.[a]
Deputy High Commissioner: Arthur Eugene Dewey.

[a]Resigned on 1 November 1989; Thorvald Stoltenberg was elected by the General Assembly on 20 November (decision 44/312) for a four-year term beginning on 1 January 1990.

SUB-COMMITTEE OF THE WHOLE
ON INTERNATIONAL PROTECTION
The Sub-Committee of the Whole on International Protection held its fourteenth meeting at Geneva on 2 and 5 October 1989.

Chairman: A. H. Jamal (United Republic of Tanzania).

SUB-COMMITTEE ON
ADMINISTRATIVE AND FINANCIAL MATTERS
The Sub-Committee on Administrative and Financial Matters, which is composed of all members of the Executive Committee, held its ninth meeting at Geneva on 3, 4 and 9 October 1989.

Chairman: Fredo Dannenbring (Federal Republic of Germany).

Panel for Inquiry and Conciliation
The Panel for Inquiry and Conciliation was created by the General Assembly in 1949[10] to consist of qualified persons, designated by United Nations Member States, each to serve for a term of five years. Information concerning the Panel's composition had from time to time been communicated to the Assembly and the Security Council; the last consolidated list was issued by the Secretary-General in a note of 20 January 1961.

Panel of External Auditors
The Panel of External Auditors consists of the members of the United Nations Board of Auditors and the appointed external auditors of the specialized agencies and IAEA.

Panel of Military Experts
The General Assembly's "Uniting for Peace" resolution[11] called for the appointment of military experts to be available, on request, to United Nations Member States wishing to obtain technical advice on the organization, training and equipment of elements within their national armed forces which could be made available,

in accordance with national constitutional processes, for service as a unit or units of the United Nations upon the recommendation of the Security Council or the Assembly.

Preparatory Committee for the United Nations Conference on Environment and Development
On 22 December 1989 (resolution 44/228), the General Assembly established the Preparatory Committee for the United Nations Conference on Environment and Development (to be held in June 1992), open to all States Members of the United Nations or members of the specialized agencies. The Committee was to hold an organizational session in March 1990.

Preparatory Committee of the Whole for the Seventeenth Special Session of the General Assembly
On 14 November 1989 (decision 44/410), the General Assembly established a preparatory committee of the whole for the seventeenth special session (to be held in February 1990), to consider the question of international co-operation against illicit production, supply, demand, trafficking and distribution of narcotic drugs, with a view to expanding the scope and increasing the effectiveness of such co-operation.
The Preparatory Committee held its first session at United Nations Headquarters on 6 and 7 December 1989.

Chairman: Peter Hohenfellner (Austria).
Vice-Chairmen: Koffi Adjoyi (Togo), Ricardo Luna (Peru), Razali Ismail (Malaysia).
Rapporteur: Anatoli Oleinik (Ukrainian SSR).

Preparatory Committee of the Whole for the Special Session of the General Assembly Devoted to International Economic Co-operation, in particular to the Revitalization of Economic Growth and Development of the Developing Countries
On 7 March 1989 (decision 43/460), the General Assembly decided to convene in April 1990 a special session devoted to international economic co-operation, in particular to the revitalization of economic growth and development of the developing countries, and established an intergovernmental preparatory committee of the whole to make the necessary preparations.
In 1989, the Preparatory Committee held, at United Nations Headquarters, an organizational session on 13 and 16 March and its first session from 31 May to 2 June.

Chairman: Constantine Zepos (Greece).
Vice-Chairmen: Ahmed Ghezal (Tunisia), Samuel R. Insanally (Guyana), Wang Baoliu (China), Evzen Zapotocky (Czechoslovakia).

Special Committee against *Apartheid*
Members: Algeria, German Democratic Republic, Ghana, Guinea, Haiti, Hungary, India, Indonesia, Malaysia, Nepal, Nigeria, Peru, Philippines, Somalia, Sudan, Syrian Arab Republic, Trinidad and Tobago, Ukrainian SSR, Zimbabwe.

Chairman: Joseph N. Garba (Nigeria).
Vice-Chairmen: Guennadi I. Oudovenko (Ukrainian SSR), Jai Pratap Rana (Nepal), Glodys St.-Phard (Haiti).
Rapporteur: Virendra Gupta (India).

SUB-COMMITTEE ON PETITIONS AND INFORMATION
Members: Algeria *(Chairman)*, German Democratic Republic, Nepal, Somalia, Trinidad and Tobago.

SUB-COMMITTEE ON THE IMPLEMENTATION
OF UNITED NATIONS RESOLUTIONS
AND COLLABORATION WITH SOUTH AFRICA
Members: Ghana *(Chairman)*, Hungary, India, Indonesia, Peru, Sudan.

---

[10]YUN 1948-49, p. 416, GA res. 268 D (III), 28 Apr. 1949.
[11]YUN 1950, p. 194, GA res. 377(V), part A, para. 10, 3 Nov. 1950.

Special Committee on Peace-keeping Operations

In 1989, the 34-member Special Committee on Peace-keeping Operations met at United Nations Headquarters from 10 to 12 April and on 1 June.

Members: Afghanistan, Algeria, Argentina *(Vice-Chairman)*, Australia, Austria, Canada *(Vice-Chairman)*, China, Denmark, Egypt *(Rapporteur)*, El Salvador, Ethiopia, France, German Democratic Republic *(Vice-Chairman)*, Guatemala, Hungary, India, Iraq, Italy, Japan *(Vice-Chairman)*, Mauritania, Mexico, Netherlands, Nigeria *(Chairman)*, Pakistan, Poland, Romania, Sierra Leone, Spain, Thailand, USSR, United Kingdom, United States, Venezuela, Yugoslavia.

WORKING GROUP

Members: France, India, Mexico, Pakistan, USSR, United Kingdom, United States, and the officers of the Special Committee.

Special Committee on the Charter of the United Nations and on the Strengthening of the Role of the Organization

The 47-member Special Committee on the Charter of the United Nations and on the Strengthening of the Role of the Organization met at United Nations Headquarters from 27 March to 14 April 1989.

Members: Algeria, Argentina, Barbados, Belgium, Brazil, China, Colombia, Congo, Cyprus, Czechoslovakia, Ecuador, Egypt, El Salvador, Finland, France, German Democratic Republic, Germany, Federal Republic of, Ghana, Greece, Guyana, India, Indonesia, Iran, Iraq, Italy, Japan, Kenya, Liberia, Mexico, Nepal, New Zealand, Nigeria, Pakistan, Philippines, Poland, Romania, Rwanda, Sierra Leone, Spain, Tunisia, Turkey, USSR, United Kingdom, United States, Venezuela, Yugoslavia, Zambia.

Chairman: James Victor Gbeho (Ghana).
Vice-Chairmen: T. L. Gill (India), Klaus Erich Scharioth (Federal Republic of Germany), Ioan Voicu (Romania).

Special Committee on the Situation with regard to the Implementation of the Declaration on the Granting of Independence to Colonial Countries and Peoples

Members: Afghanistan, Bulgaria, Chile, China, Congo, Côte d'Ivoire, Cuba, Czechoslovakia, Ethiopia, Fiji, India, Indonesia, Iran, Iraq, Mali, Norway, Sierra Leone, Syrian Arab Republic, Trinidad and Tobago, Tunisia, USSR, United Republic of Tanzania, Venezuela, Yugoslavia.

Chairman: Tesfaye Tadesse (Ethiopia).
Vice-Chairmen: Sverre Bergh Johansen (Norway), Lubomir Dolejs (Czechoslovakia), Oscar Oramas-Oliva (Cuba).
Rapporteur: Mohammad Najdat Shaheed (Syrian Arab Republic).

SUB-COMMITTEE ON PETITIONS,
INFORMATION AND ASSISTANCE
Members: Afghanistan, Bulgaria, Congo, Cuba, Czechoslovakia *(Chairman)*, Indonesia, Iran, Iraq, Mali, Sierra Leone, Syrian Arab Republic, Tunisia, United Republic of Tanzania.

SUB-COMMITTEE ON SMALL TERRITORIES
Members: Afghanistan, Bulgaria, Chile, Côte d'Ivoire, Cuba, Czechoslovakia, Ethiopia, Fiji, India, Indonesia, Iran, Iraq, Mali, Norway *(Rapporteur)*, Trinidad and Tobago, Tunisia *(Chairman)*, United Republic of Tanzania, Venezuela, Yugoslavia.

WORKING GROUP

In 1989, the Working Group of the Special Committee, which functions as a steering committee, consisted of: Congo, Fiji, Iran; the five officers of the Special Committee; and the Chairman and the Rapporteur of the Sub-Committee on Small Territories.

Special Committee to Investigate Israeli Practices Affecting the Human Rights of the Population of the Occupied Territories

Members: Senegal, Sri Lanka *(Chairman)*, Yugoslavia.

On 8 December 1989 (resolution 44/48 A), the General Assembly renamed the Committee "Special Committee to Investigate Israeli Practices Affecting the Human Rights of the Palestinian People and Other Arabs of the Occupied Territories".

Special Committee to Select the Winners of the United Nations Human Rights Prize

The Special Committee to Select the Winners of the United Nations Human Rights Prize was established pursuant to a 1966 General Assembly resolution[12] recommending that a prize or prizes in the field of human rights be awarded not more often than at five-year intervals. Prizes were awarded for the fourth time on 10 December 1988.

Members: The President of the General Assembly, the President of the Economic and Social Council, the Chairman of the Commission on Human Rights, the Chairman of the Commission on the Status of Women and the Chairman of the Sub-Commission on Prevention of Discrimination and Protection of Minorities.

United Nations Administrative Tribunal

Members:
To serve until 31 December 1989: Jerome Ackerman, *Second Vice-President* (United States); Arnold Wilfred Geoffrey Kean, *President* (United Kingdom).
To serve until 31 December 1990: Francisco Forteza (Uruguay); Ioan Voicu (Romania).
To serve until 31 December 1991: Ahmed Osman (Egypt); Roger Pinto, *First Vice-President* (France); Samarendranath Sen (India).

On 19 December 1989 (decision 44/319), the General Assembly appointed Jerome Ackerman (United States) and Arnold Wilfred Geoffrey Kean (United Kingdom) for a three-year term beginning on 1 January 1990 to fill the vacancies occurring on 31 December 1989.

United Nations Capital Development Fund

The United Nations Capital Development Fund was set up as an organ of the General Assembly to function as an autonomous organization within the United Nations framework, with the control of its policies and operations to be exercised by a 24-member Executive Board elected by the Assembly from Members of the United Nations or members of the specialized agencies or of IAEA. The chief executive officer of the Fund, the Managing Director, exercises his functions under the general direction of the Executive Board, which reports to the Assembly through the Economic and Social Council.

EXECUTIVE BOARD

The UNDP Governing Council acts as the Executive Board of the Fund—and the UNDP Administrator as its Managing Director—in conformity with measures the General Assembly adopted provisionally in 1967[13] and reconfirmed yearly thereafter. In 1981, the Assembly decided that UNDP should continue to provide the Fund with, among other things, all headquarters administrative support services;[14] the Fund thus continued to operate under the same arrangements, which remained unchanged in 1989.

Managing Director: William H. Draper III (UNDP Administrator).

United Nations Commission on International Trade Law (UNCITRAL)

The United Nations Commission on International Trade Law consists of 36 members elected by the General Assembly, in accordance with a formula providing equitable geographical representation and adequate representation of the principal economic and legal systems of the world. Members serve for six-year terms.

---

[12]YUN 1966, p. 458, GA res. 2217 A (XXI), annex, 19 Dec. 1966.
[13]YUN 1967, p. 372, GA res. 2321(XXII), 15 Dec. 1967.
[14]YUN 1981, p. 469, GA res. 36/196, 17 Dec. 1981.

The Commission held its twenty-second session at Vienna from 16 May to 2 June 1989.

Members:

To serve until the day preceding the Commission's regular annual session in 1992: Argentina, Chile, Cuba, Cyprus, Czechoslovakia, Hungary, India, Iran, Iraq, Italy, Kenya, Lesotho, Libyan Arab Jamahiriya, Netherlands, Sierra Leone, Spain, United States, Uruguay, Yugoslavia.

To serve until the day preceding the Commission's regular annual session in 1995: Bulgaria, Cameroon, Canada, China, Costa Rica, Denmark, Egypt, France, Germany, Federal Republic of, Japan, Mexico, Morocco, Nigeria, Singapore, Togo, USSR, United Kingdom.

Chairman: Jaromir Ruzicka (Czechoslovakia).
Vice-Chairmen: José M. Abascal (Mexico), Rafael Illescas (Spain), Michel Wembou-Djiena (Cameroon).
Rapporteur: Seiichi Ochiai (Japan).

WORKING GROUP ON
INTERNATIONAL CONTRACT PRACTICES
The Working Group on International Contract Practices, composed of all States members of UNCITRAL, did not meet in 1989.

WORKING GROUP ON INTERNATIONAL PAYMENTS
In 1989, the Working Group on International Payments, composed of all States members of UNCITRAL, held two sessions: its nineteenth at United Nations Headquarters from 10 to 21 July, and its twentieth at Vienna from 27 November to 8 December.

Chairman: José María Abascal Zamora (Mexico).
Rapporteur: Bradley Crawford (Canada).

WORKING GROUP ON THE
NEW INTERNATIONAL ECONOMIC ORDER
The Working Group on the New International Economic Order, composed of all States members of UNCITRAL, did not meet in 1989.

United Nations Conciliation Commission for Palestine
Members: France, Turkey, United States.

United Nations Conference on Trade and Development (UNCTAD)
Members of UNCTAD are Members of the United Nations or members of the specialized agencies or of IAEA.

TRADE AND DEVELOPMENT BOARD
The Trade and Development Board is a permanent organ of UNCTAD. It reports to UNCTAD as well as annually to the General Assembly through the Economic and Social Council. Its membership is drawn from the following list of UNCTAD members.

Part A. Afghanistan, Algeria, Angola, Bahrain, Bangladesh, Benin, Bhutan, Botswana, Brunei Darussalam, Burkina Faso, Burundi, Cameroon, Cape Verde, Central African Republic, Chad, China, Comoros, Congo, Côte d'Ivoire, Democratic Kampuchea, Democratic People's Republic of Korea, Democratic Yemen, Djibouti, Egypt, Equatorial Guinea, Ethiopia, Fiji, Gabon, Gambia, Ghana, Guinea, Guinea-Bissau, India, Indonesia, Iran, Iraq, Israel, Jordan, Kenya, Kuwait, Lao People's Democratic Republic, Lebanon, Lesotho, Liberia, Libyan Arab Jamahiriya, Madagascar, Malawi, Malaysia, Maldives, Mali, Mauritania, Mauritius, Mongolia, Morocco, Mozambique, Myanmar (Burma), Namibia, Nepal, Niger, Nigeria, Oman, Pakistan, Papua New Guinea, Philippines, Qatar, Republic of Korea, Rwanda, Samoa, Sao Tome and Principe, Saudi Arabia, Senegal, Seychelles, Sierra Leone, Singapore, Solomon Islands, Somalia, South Africa, Sri Lanka, Sudan, Swaziland, Syrian Arab Republic, Thailand, Togo, Tonga, Tunisia, Uganda, United Arab Emirates, United Republic of Tanzania, Vanuatu, Viet Nam, Yemen, Yugoslavia, Zaire, Zambia, Zimbabwe.

Part B. Australia, Austria, Belgium, Canada, Cyprus, Denmark, Finland, France, Germany, Federal Republic of, Greece, Holy See, Iceland, Ireland, Italy, Japan, Liechtenstein, Luxembourg, Malta, Monaco, Netherlands, New Zealand, Norway, Portugal, San Marino, Spain, Sweden, Switzerland, Turkey, United Kingdom, United States.

Part C. Antigua and Barbuda, Argentina, Bahamas, Barbados, Belize, Bolivia, Brazil, Chile, Colombia, Costa Rica, Cuba, Dominica, Dominican Republic, Ecuador, El Salvador, Grenada, Guatemala, Guyana, Haiti, Honduras, Jamaica, Mexico, Nicaragua, Panama, Paraguay, Peru, Saint Kitts and Nevis, Saint Lucia, Saint Vincent and the Grenadines, Suriname, Trinidad and Tobago, Uruguay, Venezuela.

Part D. Albania, Bulgaria, Byelorussian SSR, Czechoslovakia, German Democratic Republic, Hungary, Poland, Romania, Ukrainian SSR, USSR.

BOARD MEMBERS AND SESSIONS
The membership of the Board is open to all UNCTAD members. Those wishing to become members of the Board communicate their intention to the Secretary-General of UNCTAD for transmittal to the Board President, who announces the membership on the basis of such notifications.
The Board held the following sessions in 1989, at Geneva: the second part of its thirty-fifth session from 6 to 17 and on 22 March and on 19 May, and the first part of its thirty-sixth session from 2 to 13 and on 18 October.

Members: Afghanistan, Algeria, Angola, Argentina, Australia, Austria, Bahrain, Bangladesh, Barbados, Belgium, Benin, Bhutan, Bolivia, Brazil, Bulgaria, Burkina Faso, Burma (Myanmar), Burundi, Byelorussian SSR, Cameroon, Canada, Central African Republic, Chad, Chile, China, Colombia, Congo, Costa Rica, Côte d'Ivoire, Cuba, Cyprus, Czechoslovakia, Democratic People's Republic of Korea, Democratic Yemen, Denmark, Dominican Republic, Ecuador, Egypt, El Salvador, Ethiopia, Finland, France, Gabon, German Democratic Republic, Germany, Federal Republic of, Ghana, Greece, Grenada, Guatemala, Guinea, Guyana, Haiti, Honduras, Hungary, India, Indonesia, Iran, Iraq, Ireland, Israel, Italy, Jamaica, Japan, Jordan, Kenya, Kuwait, Lebanon, Liberia, Libyan Arab Jamahiriya, Liechtenstein, Luxembourg, Madagascar, Malaysia, Mali, Malta, Mauritania, Mauritius, Mexico, Mongolia, Morocco, Namibia, Nepal, Netherlands, New Zealand, Nicaragua, Nigeria, Norway, Oman, Pakistan, Panama, Papua New Guinea, Paraguay, Peru, Philippines, Poland, Portugal, Qatar, Republic of Korea, Romania, Saudi Arabia, Senegal, Sierra Leone, Singapore, Somalia, Spain, Sri Lanka, Sudan, Suriname, Sweden, Switzerland, Syrian Arab Republic, Thailand, Togo, Trinidad and Tobago, Tunisia, Turkey, Uganda, Ukrainian SSR, USSR, United Arab Emirates, United Kingdom, United Republic of Tanzania, United States, Uruguay, Venezuela, Viet Nam, Yemen, Yugoslavia, Zaire, Zambia, Zimbabwe.

OFFICERS (BUREAU) OF THE BOARD
Thirty-fifth session
President: Tobgye S. Dorji (Bhutan).
Vice-Presidents: Emilio Artacho (Spain), Emeka Ayo Azikiwe (Nigeria), Raúl España Smith (Bolivia), Farouk Kasrawi (Jordan), de Montigny Marchand (Canada), José Enrique Mejía Uclés (Honduras), Youssef Mokaddem (Tunisia), Joseph C. Petrone (United States), Gerald Philipp (German Democratic Republic), T. V. Teodorovich (USSR).
Rapporteur: Kees Jan René Klompenhouwer (Netherlands).

Thirty-sixth session
President: Oscar R. de Rojas (Venezuela).
Vice-Presidents: Morris Abram (United States), Anna Doynova (Bulgaria), Hicham Hamdan (Lebanon), Alexander Kachanov (USSR), Jean-David Levitte (France), Michael Joseph Lillis (Ireland), Wisber Loeis (Indonesia), Olli Adolf Mennander (Finland), Thomas A. Ogada (Kenya), Gustavo Adolfo Vargas (Nicaragua).
Rapporteur: Abderrazak Azaiez (Tunisia).

SUBSIDIARY ORGANS OF THE
TRADE AND DEVELOPMENT BOARD
The main committees of the Board are open to the participation of all interested UNCTAD members, on the understanding that

those wishing to attend a particular session of one or more of the main committees communicate their intention to the Secretary-General of UNCTAD during the preceding regular session of the Board. On the basis of such notifications, the Board determines the membership of the main committees.

COMMITTEE ON COMMODITIES

The Committee on Commodities did not meet in 1989.

Members: Algeria, Argentina, Australia, Austria, Bahrain, Bangladesh, Belgium, Bolivia, Brazil, Bulgaria, Burkina Faso, Burundi, Cameroon, Canada, Central African Republic, Chad, Chile, China, Colombia, Costa Rica, Côte d'Ivoire, Cuba, Czechoslovakia, Democratic People's Republic of Korea, Democratic Yemen, Denmark, Dominican Republic, Ecuador, Egypt, El Salvador, Ethiopia, Finland, France, Gabon, German Democratic Republic, Germany, Federal Republic of, Ghana, Greece, Guatemala, Guinea, Haiti, Honduras, Hungary, India, Indonesia, Iran, Iraq, Ireland, Israel, Italy, Jamaica, Japan, Jordan, Kenya, Kuwait, Liberia, Libyan Arab Jamahiriya, Madagascar, Malaysia, Malta, Mauritius, Mexico, Morocco, Myanmar (Burma), Netherlands, New Zealand, Nicaragua, Nigeria, Norway, Pakistan, Panama, Paraguay, Peru, Philippines, Poland, Portugal, Qatar, Republic of Korea, Romania, Rwanda, Saudi Arabia, Senegal, Somalia, Spain, Sri Lanka, Sudan, Sweden, Switzerland, Syrian Arab Republic, Thailand, Togo, Trinidad and Tobago, Tunisia, Turkey, Uganda, USSR, United Arab Emirates, United Kingdom, United Republic of Tanzania, United States, Uruguay, Venezuela, Viet Nam, Yemen, Yugoslavia, Zaire, Zimbabwe.

COMMITTEE ON TUNGSTEN

The Committee on Tungsten held its twenty-first session at Geneva from 4 to 8 December 1989.

Members: Argentina, Australia, Austria, Belgium, Bolivia, Brazil, Canada, China, Cyprus, France, Gabon, Germany, Federal Republic of, Italy, Japan, Mexico, Netherlands, Peru, Poland, Portugal, Republic of Korea, Romania, Rwanda, Spain, Sweden, Thailand, Turkey, USSR, United Kingdom, United States.

Chairman: Marie-Christine Colomb d'Ecotay (France).
Vice-Chairman/Rapporteur: Dong-Seok Min (Republic of Korea).

COMMITTEE ON ECONOMIC CO-OPERATION AMONG DEVELOPING COUNTRIES

The Committee on Economic Co-operation among Developing Countries held its fifth session at Geneva from 1 to 12 June 1989.

Members: Algeria, Argentina, Australia, Austria, Bahrain, Bangladesh, Belgium, Benin, Bolivia, Brazil, Bulgaria, Burma (Myanmar), Cameroon, Canada, Central African Republic, Chile, China, Colombia, Costa Rica, Côte d'Ivoire, Cuba, Cyprus, Czechoslovakia, Democratic People's Republic of Korea, Democratic Yemen, Denmark, Dominican Republic, Ecuador, Egypt, El Salvador, Ethiopia, Finland, France, Gabon, German Democratic Republic, Germany, Federal Republic of, Ghana, Greece, Guatemala, Guyana, Haiti, Honduras, Hungary, India, Indonesia, Iran, Iraq, Ireland, Israel, Italy, Jamaica, Japan, Jordan, Kenya, Kuwait, Lebanon, Liberia, Libyan Arab Jamahiriya, Madagascar, Malaysia, Malta, Mauritius, Mexico, Morocco, Netherlands, New Zealand, Nicaragua, Nigeria, Norway, Oman, Pakistan, Panama, Paraguay, Peru, Philippines, Poland, Portugal, Qatar, Republic of Korea, Romania, Saudi Arabia, Senegal, Singapore, Somalia, Spain, Sri Lanka, Sudan, Suriname, Sweden, Switzerland, Syrian Arab Republic, Thailand, Togo, Trinidad and Tobago, Tunisia, Turkey, Uganda, USSR, United Arab Emirates, United Kingdom, United Republic of Tanzania, United States, Uruguay, Venezuela, Viet Nam, Yemen, Yugoslavia, Zaire, Zambia, Zimbabwe.

Chairman: Hani Khallaf (Egypt).
Vice-Chairmen: Victoria Bataclan (Philippines), Kunihiko Makita (Japan), Samuel Owoeye (Nigeria), Christian Tanghe (Belgium), Miguel Zalles Denegri (Bolivia).
Rapporteur: Raimund Rolfs (German Democratic Republic).

COMMITTEE ON INVISIBLES AND FINANCING RELATED TO TRADE

The Committee on Invisibles and Financing related to Trade did not meet in 1989.

Members: Algeria, Argentina, Australia, Austria, Bahrain, Bangladesh, Belgium, Bolivia, Brazil, Bulgaria, Burkina Faso, Burundi, Cameroon, Canada, Central African Republic, Chad, Chile, China, Colombia, Costa Rica, Côte d'Ivoire, Cuba, Czechoslovakia, Democratic People's Republic of Korea, Democratic Yemen, Denmark, Dominican Republic, Ecuador, Egypt, El Salvador, Ethiopia, Finland, France, German Democratic Republic, Germany, Federal Republic of, Ghana, Greece, Guatemala, Guinea, Honduras, Hungary, India, Indonesia, Iran, Iraq, Ireland, Israel, Italy, Jamaica, Japan, Jordan, Kenya, Kuwait, Lebanon, Liberia, Libyan Arab Jamahiriya, Madagascar, Malaysia, Mali, Malta, Mexico, Morocco, Netherlands, New Zealand, Nicaragua, Nigeria, Norway, Pakistan, Panama, Paraguay, Peru, Philippines, Poland, Portugal, Qatar, Republic of Korea, Romania, Saudi Arabia, Senegal, Somalia, Spain, Sri Lanka, Sudan, Sweden, Switzerland, Syrian Arab Republic, Thailand, Trinidad and Tobago, Tunisia, Turkey, Uganda, USSR, United Kingdom, United Republic of Tanzania, United States, Uruguay, Venezuela, Viet Nam, Yemen, Yugoslavia, Zaire, Zimbabwe.

COMMITTEE ON MANUFACTURES

The Committee on Manufactures held its twelfth session at Geneva from 9 to 17 November 1989.

Members: Algeria, Argentina, Australia, Austria, Bahrain, Bangladesh, Belgium, Bolivia, Brazil, Bulgaria, Burkina Faso, Cameroon, Canada, Central African Republic, Chile, China, Colombia, Costa Rica, Côte d'Ivoire, Cuba, Czechoslovakia, Democratic People's Republic of Korea, Democratic Yemen, Denmark, Dominican Republic, Ecuador, Egypt, El Salvador, Ethiopia, Finland, France, German Democratic Republic, Germany, Federal Republic of, Ghana, Greece, Guatemala, Haiti, Honduras, Hungary, India, Indonesia, Iran, Iraq, Ireland, Israel, Italy, Jamaica, Japan, Jordan, Kenya, Kuwait, Liberia, Libyan Arab Jamahiriya, Madagascar, Malaysia, Mali, Malta, Mauritius, Mexico, Morocco, Netherlands, New Zealand, Nicaragua, Nigeria, Norway, Pakistan, Panama, Paraguay, Peru, Philippines, Poland, Portugal, Qatar, Republic of Korea, Romania, Saudi Arabia, Senegal, Singapore, Somalia, Spain, Sri Lanka, Sudan, Sweden, Switzerland, Syrian Arab Republic, Thailand, Trinidad and Tobago, Tunisia, Turkey, USSR, United Kingdom, United Republic of Tanzania, United States, Uruguay, Venezuela, Viet Nam, Yemen, Yugoslavia, Zaire, Zambia, Zimbabwe.

Chairman: M. Lebkowski (Poland).
Vice-Chairmen: Victoria Bataclan (Philippines), K. Komano (Japan), E. M'lingui Keffa (Côte d'Ivoire), H. Smith (United Kingdom), J. Stiglich (Peru).
Rapporteur: S. Lebdioui (Algeria).

COMMITTEE ON SHIPPING

The Committee on Shipping did not meet in 1989.

Members: Algeria, Argentina, Australia, Bahrain, Bangladesh, Belgium, Benin, Bolivia, Brazil, Bulgaria, Burkina Faso, Cameroon, Canada, Central African Republic, Chile, China, Colombia, Congo, Costa Rica, Côte d'Ivoire, Cuba, Cyprus, Czechoslovakia, Democratic People's Republic of Korea, Democratic Yemen, Denmark, Dominican Republic, Ecuador, Egypt, El Salvador, Ethiopia, Finland, France, Gabon, German Democratic Republic, Germany, Federal Republic of, Ghana, Greece, Guatemala, Guinea, Honduras, Hungary, India, Indonesia, Iran, Iraq, Israel, Italy, Jamaica, Japan, Jordan, Kenya, Kuwait, Lebanon, Liberia, Libyan Arab Jamahiriya, Madagascar, Malaysia, Malta, Mauritius, Mexico, Morocco, Netherlands, New Zealand, Nicaragua, Nigeria, Norway, Oman, Pakistan, Panama, Paraguay, Peru, Philippines, Poland, Portugal, Qatar, Republic of Korea, Romania, Saudi Arabia, Senegal, Somalia, Spain, Sri Lanka, Sudan, Sweden, Switzerland, Syrian Arab Republic, Thailand, Trinidad and Tobago, Tunisia, Turkey, Uganda, USSR, United

Arab Emirates, United Kingdom, United Republic of Tanzania, United States, Uruguay, Venezuela, Viet Nam, Yemen, Yugoslavia, Zaire.

WORKING GROUP ON INTERNATIONAL SHIPPING LEGISLATION

The Working Group on International Shipping Legislation, whose membership is identical to that of the Committee on Shipping, did not meet in 1989.

COMMITTEE ON TRANSFER OF TECHNOLOGY

The Committee on Transfer of Technology held its seventh session at Geneva from 23 January to 2 February 1989.

Members: Algeria, Argentina, Australia, Austria, Bahrain, Bangladesh, Belgium, Bolivia, Brazil, Bulgaria, Burkina Faso, Cameroon, Canada, Chile, China, Colombia, Costa Rica, Côte d'Ivoire, Cuba, Czechoslovakia, Democratic People's Republic of Korea, Democratic Yemen, Denmark, Dominican Republic, Ecuador, Egypt, El Salvador, Ethiopia, Finland, France, German Democratic Republic, Germany, Federal Republic of, Ghana, Greece, Guatemala, Haiti, Honduras, Hungary, India, Indonesia, Iran, Iraq, Ireland, Israel, Italy, Jamaica, Japan, Jordan, Kenya, Kuwait, Liberia, Libyan Arab Jamahiriya, Madagascar, Malaysia, Malta, Mauritius, Mexico, Morocco, Netherlands, New Zealand, Nicaragua, Nigeria, Norway, Pakistan, Panama, Paraguay, Peru, Philippines, Poland, Portugal, Qatar, Republic of Korea, Romania, Saudi Arabia, Senegal, Sierra Leone, Somalia, Spain, Sri Lanka, Sudan, Sweden, Switzerland, Syrian Arab Republic, Thailand, Trinidad and Tobago, Tunisia, Turkey, USSR, United Arab Emirates, United Kingdom, United Republic of Tanzania, United States, Uruguay, Venezuela, Viet Nam, Yemen, Yugoslavia, Zaire, Zimbabwe.

Chairman: I. Jankovic (Yugoslavia).
Vice-Chairmen: R. Babul (Chile), D. Coates (United Kingdom), H. Riad (Egypt), K. Scott (United States), K. V. Swaminathan (India).
Rapporteur: K. Tiltsch (German Democratic Republic).

SPECIAL COMMITTEE ON PREFERENCES

The Special Committee on Preferences, which is open to the participation of all UNCTAD members, held its sixteenth session at Geneva from 24 April to 3 May 1989.

Chairman: E. A. Hörig (Federal Republic of Germany).
Vice-Chairmen: R. Babul (Chile), Furong Bian (China), M. Helal (Egypt), A. Ivanka (Hungary), K. Natsume (Japan).
Rapporteur: Yong Siew Min (Singapore).

United Nations Council for Namibia

Members: Algeria, Angola, Australia, Bangladesh, Belgium, Botswana, Bulgaria, Burundi, Cameroon, Chile, China, Colombia, Cyprus, Egypt, Finland, Guyana, Haiti, India, Indonesia, Liberia, Mexico, Nigeria, Pakistan, Poland, Romania, Senegal, Turkey, USSR, Venezuela, Yugoslavia, Zambia.

President: Peter D. Zuze (Zambia).
Vice-Presidents: Mustafa Aksin (Turkey), Hocine Djoudi (Algeria), Chinmaya R. Gharekhan (India), Samuel R. Insanally (Guyana), Dragoslav Pejic (Yugoslavia).

COMMITTEE ON THE UNITED NATIONS FUND FOR NAMIBIA

Members: Australia, Finland, India, Nigeria, Romania, Senegal, Turkey, Venezuela *(Vice-Chairman/Rapporteur)*, Yugoslavia, Zambia; the President of the Council *(ex-officio Chairman)*.

STANDING COMMITTEE I

Members: Algeria, Cameroon *(Chairman)*, China, Colombia, Finland, Haiti, India, Indonesia, Nigeria, Poland, Senegal, Turkey, USSR, Venezuela, Zambia.

STANDING COMMITTEE II

Members: Algeria, Angola, Australia, Bangladesh, Botswana, Bulgaria, Chile, Colombia, Cyprus, Egypt, Finland, Guyana, India, Liberia, Mexico, Nigeria, Pakistan *(Chairman)*, Romania, Zambia.

STANDING COMMITTEE III

Members: Algeria, Angola, Australia, Belgium, Bulgaria *(Chairman)*, Burundi, Colombia, Cyprus, Egypt, India, Mexico *(Vice-Chairman)*, Nigeria, Pakistan, Romania, Venezuela, Yugoslavia, Zambia.

STEERING COMMITTEE

In 1989, the Steering Committee consisted of the Council's President and five Vice-Presidents, the Chairmen of its three Standing Committees and the Vice-Chairman/Rapporteur of the Committee on the United Nations Fund for Namibia.

United Nations Development Fund for Women (UNIFEM)

The United Nations Development Fund for Women is a separate entity in autonomous association with UNDP. The Director of the Fund, appointed by the UNDP Administrator, conducts all matters related to its mandate and the Administrator is accountable for its management and operations.

CONSULTATIVE COMMITTEE

The Consultative Committee on UNIFEM to advise the UNDP Administrator on all policy matters affecting the Fund's activities is composed of five Member States designated by the General Assembly President with due regard for the financing of the Fund from voluntary contributions and to equitable geographical distribution. Each State member of the Committee serves for a three-year term and designates a person with expertise in development co-operation activities, including those benefiting women.

The Committee held two sessions in 1989, at United Nations Headquarters: its twenty-fifth from 13 to 19 April, and its twenty-sixth from 28 August to 1 September.

Members (to serve until 31 December 1991): German Democratic Republic, India, Mexico, Netherlands, Senegal.

Director of UNIFEM: Margaret Snyder (until 31 January 1989), Sharon Capeling-Alakija (from 1 February).

United Nations Environment Programme (UNEP)

GOVERNING COUNCIL

The Governing Council of UNEP consists of 58 members elected by the General Assembly for four-year terms.

Seats on the Governing Council are allocated as follows: 16 to African States, 13 to Asian States, 6 to Eastern European States, 10 to Latin American States, and 13 to Western European and other States.

The Governing Council, which reports to the Assembly through the Economic and Social Council, held its fifteenth session at Nairobi, Kenya, from 15 to 26 May 1989.

Members:
To serve until 31 December 1989: Argentina, Australia, Barbados, Brazil, Burundi, China, Dominican Republic, France, Gabon, Germany, Federal Republic of, Greece, Indonesia, Iran, Iraq, Japan, Lesotho, Mauritania, Mauritius, Republic of Korea, Senegal, Sweden, Switzerland, Ukrainian SSR, USSR, United States, Venezuela, Yugoslavia, Zaire, Zimbabwe.
To serve until 31 December 1991: Bangladesh, Botswana, Bulgaria, Canada, Chile, Colombia, Costa Rica, Côte d'Ivoire, Czechoslovakia, Finland, Guyana, India, Jordan, Kenya, Libyan Arab Jamahiriya, Malta, Mexico, Netherlands, Oman, Pakistan, Poland, Rwanda, Saudi Arabia, Sri Lanka, Sudan, Togo, Turkey, Uganda, United Kingdom.

President: I. N. Topkov (Bulgaria).
Vice-Presidents: G. García (Colombia), J. Nyagah (Kenya), E. Rajakoski (Finland).
Rapporteur: S. Tell (Jordan).

Executive Director of UNEP: Mostafa Kamal Tolba.
Deputy Executive Director: William H. Mansfield III.

On 6 November 1989 (decision 44/309), the General Assembly elected the following for a four-year term beginning on 1 January 1990 to fill the vacancies occurring on 31 December 1989: Argentina, Austria, Barbados, Brazil, Burundi, China, France, Gabon, Gambia, German Democratic Republic, Germany, Federal Republic of, Indonesia, Japan, Kuwait, Lesotho, Mauritius, New Zealand, Norway, Peru, Philippines, Spain, Thailand, Tunisia, USSR, United States, Venezuela, Yugoslavia, Zaire, Zimbabwe.

COMMITTEE OF PERMANENT REPRESENTATIVES
The open-ended Committee of Permanent Representatives consists of permanent representatives to UNEP and/or Government-designated officials, to consider administrative and budgetary and programme matters, and to review progress in implementing the programme and Council decisions. It meets with the Executive Director at least five times a year.

United Nations Institute for Disarmament Research (UNIDIR)

BOARD OF TRUSTEES
On 1 January 1989, the Secretary-General's Advisory Board on Disarmament Studies was renamed Advisory Board on Disarmament Matters. The Board, composed in 1989 of 23 eminent persons selected on the basis of their personal expertise and taking into account the principle of equitable geographical representation, functions as the Board of Trustees of UNIDIR; the Director of UNIDIR reports to the General Assembly and is an *ex-officio* member of the Advisory Board when it acts as the Board of Trustees.

Members (until 31 December 1990): Oluyemi Adeniji (Nigeria); Omran El-Shafei (Egypt); Alfonso García Robles (Mexico); Ignac Golob, *Chairman* (Yugoslavia); Ryukichi Imai (Japan); Tommy Koh Thong Bee (Singapore); Boris P. Krasulin (USSR); Bjorn Inge Kristvik (Norway); Sir Ronald Mason (United Kingdom); Manfred Müller (German Democratic Republic); Joseph S. Nye, Jr. (United States); Carlos Ortiz de Rozas (Argentina); Edgard Pisani (France); Qian Jiadong (China); Maharajakrishna Rasgotra (India); Raúl Roa Kouri (Cuba); Nihal Rodrigo (Sri Lanka); Friedrich Ruth (Federal Republic of Germany); Amada Segarra (Ecuador); Agha Shahi (Pakistan); Tadeusz Strulak (Poland); Maj Britt Theorin (Sweden); Milos Vejvoda (Czechoslovakia).

Director of UNIDIR: Jayantha Dhanapala.

United Nations Institute for Training and Research (UNITAR)
The Executive Director of UNITAR, in consultation with the Board of Trustees of the Institute, reports through the Secretary-General to the General Assembly and, as appropriate, to the Economic and Social Council and other United Nations bodies.

BOARD OF TRUSTEES
The Board of Trustees of UNITAR is composed of: *(a)* not less than 11 and not more than 30 members, which may include one or more officials of the United Nations Secretariat, appointed on a broad geographical basis by the Secretary-General, in consultation with the Presidents of the General Assembly and the Economic and Social Council; and *(b)* four *ex-officio* members.
The Board held its twenty-seventh session at United Nations Headquarters from 3 to 7 April 1989.

Members:
To serve until 31 December 1989: D. H. N. Alleyne (Trinidad and Tobago); Jaime de Piniés (Secretariat); Lucio García del Solar (Argentina); Kiyoaki Kikuchi (Japan); Franz E. Muheim (Switzerland); Ali A. Treiki (Libyan Arab Jamahiriya).
To serve until 31 December 1990: Lawrence S. Eagleburger (United States);[a] Amara Essy (Côte d'Ivoire); Keijo Korhonen (Finland); Natarajan Krishnan (India); Umberto La Rocca (Italy).
To serve until 31 December 1991: Andrés Aguilar, *Chairman* (Venezuela); Rafeeuddin Ahmed (Secretariat); J. Isawa Elaigwu (Nigeria); Jacques Leprette (France); Missoum Sbih, *Vice-Chairman* (Algeria); S. Shah Nawaz (Pakistan); Victor A. Zvezdin (USSR).
Ex-officio members: The Secretary-General, the President of the General Assembly, the President of the Economic and Social Council and the Executive Director of UNITAR.

[a]Resigned on 20 January 1989.

Executive Director of UNITAR: Michel Doo Kingué.

United Nations Joint Staff Pension Board
The United Nations Joint Staff Pension Board is composed of 33 members, as follows:

Twelve appointed by the United Nations Staff Pension Committee (four from members elected by the General Assembly, four from those appointed by the Secretary-General, four from those elected by participants);
Twenty-one appointed by staff pension committees of other member organizations of the United Nations Joint Staff Pension Fund (seven from those chosen by the bodies corresponding to the General Assembly, seven from those appointed by the chief administrative officers, seven from those chosen by participants).

The Board held its thirty-eighth session at United Nations Headquarters from 12 to 21 July 1989.

Members:
United Nations
  Representing the General Assembly: Members: Yogesh Kumar Gupta (India); Sol Kuttner (United States); Michael G. Okeyo (Kenya); Victor A. Vislykh (USSR). Alternates: Tadanori Inomata (Japan); Ulrich Kalbitzer (Federal Republic of Germany); Mohand Ladjouzi (Algeria); Teodoro Maus (Mexico).
  Representing the Secretary-General: Members: Kofi A. Annan (Ghana); J. Richard Foran (Canada); Maryan Baquerot (France); Anthony J. Miller (Australia). Alternates: Matías de la Mota (Spain); Dulcie Bull (United Kingdom).
  Representing the Participants: Members: Susanna H. Johnston, *Second Vice-Chairman* (United States); Gualtiero Fulcheri (Italy); Bruce C. Hillis (Canada); Lennox Bourne (United Kingdom). Alternates: Nancy L. Sadka (Australia); George Irving (United States).
Food and Agriculture Organization of the United Nations
  Representing the Governing Body: Member: A. Bergquist (Sweden).
  Representing the Executive Head: Member: M. Bel Hadj Amor, *First Vice-Chairman* (Tunisia).
  Representing the Participants: Member: Aurelio Marcucci (Italy). Alternate: Massimo Arrigo (Italy).
World Health Organization
  Representing the Governing Body: Member: Sir John Reid (United Kingdom).
  Representing the Executive Head: Member: Warren W. Furth (United States). Alternate: Herbert R. Crockett (Canada).
  Representing the Participants: Member: M. A. Dam (United States). Alternate: V. Pedersen (Switzerland).
International Labour Organisation
  Representing the Executive Head: Member: Antonio Busca, *Rapporteur* (Italy).
  Representing the Participants: Member: E. Ryser (Switzerland). Alternate: B. Debbas (Lebanon).
United Nations Educational, Scientific and Cultural Organization
  Representing the Governing Body: Member: Gollerkery Vishvanath Rao (India).
  Representing the Executive Head: Member: Y. Kochubey (Ukrainian SSR).
United Nations Industrial Development Organization
  Representing the Governing Body: Member: E. Zador, *Chairman* (Hungary). Alternate: M. N. Oliveros (Argentina).
  Representing the Executive Head: Member: D. Haniph (Guyana).
International Civil Aviation Organization
  Representing the Governing Body: Member: F. A. Neal (United Kingdom).
  Representing the Executive Head: Member: S. Jayasekera (Sri Lanka).
International Atomic Energy Agency
  Representing the Participants: Member: W. P. Scherzer (Austria).
International Telecommunication Union
  Representing the Executive Head: Member: J. Jipguep (Cameroon). Alternate: J.-P. Baré (France).

International Maritime Organization
  Representing the Governing Body: Member: Y. Tito (Zaire).
Interim Commission for the International Trade Organization/General Agreement on Tariffs and Trade
  Representing the Participants: Member: G. Thorn (Belgium).
World Meteorological Organization
  Representing the Participants: Member: S. Mbele-Mbong (Cameroon).
World Intellectual Property Organization
  Representing the Governing Body: Member: W. Milzow (Federal Republic of Germany.
International Fund for Agricultural Development
  Representing the Participants: Member: P. Kelly (United Kingdom).

STANDING COMMITTEE OF THE PENSION BOARD
  The Standing Committee met at United Nations Headquarters on 21 July 1989.

Members (appointed at the Board's thirty-eighth session):

United Nations (Group I)
  Representing the General Assembly: Members: Sol Kuttner, Yogesh Kumar Gupta. Alternates: Victor A. Vislykh, Mohand Ladjouzi.
  Representing the Secretary-General: Members: Kofi A. Annan, J. Richard Foran. Alternates: Maryan Baquerot, Anthony J. Miller.
  Representing the Participants: Members: Susanna H. Johnston, Bruce C. Hillis. Alternates: Gualtiero Fulcheri, George Irving.
Specialized agencies (Group II)
  Representing the Governing Body: Member: Sir John Reid (WHO).
  Representing the Executive Head: Member: M. Bel Hadj Amor (FAO).
  Representing the Participants: Member: Aurelio Marcucci (FAO). Alternate: M. A. Dam (WHO).
Specialized agencies (Group III)
  Representing the Governing Body: Member: Gollerkery Vishvanath Rao (UNESCO).
  Representing the Participants: Member: E. Ryser (ILO). Alternate: B. Debbas (ILO).
Specialized agencies (Group IV)
  Representing the Governing Body: Member: M. N. Oliveros (UNIDO). Alternate: J. Morales Pedraza (IAEA).
  Representing the Executive Head: Member: J.-P. Baré (ITU).
Specialized agencies (Group V)
  Representing the Executive Head: Member: P. Rolian (GATT). Alternate: T. Myrvang (IFAD).
  Representing the Participants: Member: D. Bertaud (IMO). Alternate: S. Mbele-Mbong (WMO).

COMMITTEE OF ACTUARIES
  The Committee of Actuaries consists of five members, each representing one of the five geographical regions of the United Nations.

Members: Ajibola O. Ogunshola (Nigeria), *Region I* (African States); Kunio Takeuchi (Japan), *Region II* (Asian States); Evgeny M. Chetyrkin (USSR), *Region III* (Eastern European States); H. Pérez Montas (Dominican Republic), *Region IV* (Latin American States); Robert J. Myers (United States), *Region V* (Western European and other States).

United Nations Population Fund (UNFPA)
  The United Nations Population Fund, a subsidiary organ of the General Assembly, plays a leading role in the United Nations system in promoting population programmes and assists developing countries at their request in dealing with their population problems. It operates under the overall policy guidance of the Economic and Social Council and under the financial and administrative policy guidance of the Governing Council of UNDP.

Executive Director of UNFPA: Dr. Nafis I. Sadik.
Deputy Executive Director: Tatsuro Kunugi.

United Nations Relief and Works Agency for Palestine Refugees in the Near East (UNRWA)

ADVISORY COMMISSION OF UNRWA
  The Advisory Commission of UNRWA met at Vienna on 31 August 1989.

Members: Belgium, Egypt, France, Japan, Jordan, Lebanon, Syrian Arab Republic, Turkey, United Kingdom, United States *(Chairman)*.

WORKING GROUP ON THE FINANCING OF UNRWA
Members: France, Ghana, Japan, Lebanon, Norway *(Rapporteur)*, Trinidad and Tobago, Turkey *(Chairman)*, United Kingdom, United States.

Commissioner-General of UNRWA: Giorgio Giacomelli.
Deputy Commissioner-General: William L. Eagleton.

United Nations Scientific Advisory Committee
  Established by the General Assembly in 1954 as a seven-member advisory committee on the International Conference on the Peaceful Uses of Atomic Energy (1955), the United Nations Scientific Advisory Committee was so renamed and its mandate revised by the Assembly in 1958,[15] retaining its original composition. The Committee has not met since 1956.[16]

Members: Brazil, Canada, France, India, USSR, United Kingdom, United States.

United Nations Scientific Committee on the Effects of Atomic Radiation
  The 21-member United Nations Scientific Committee on the Effects of Atomic Radiation held its thirty-eighth session at Vienna from 8 to 12 May 1989.

Members: Argentina, Australia, Belgium, Brazil, Canada, China, Czechoslovakia, Egypt, France, Germany, Federal Republic of, India, Indonesia, Japan, Mexico, Peru, Poland, Sudan, Sweden, USSR, United Kingdom, United States.

Chairman: K. H. Lokan (Australia).
Vice-Chairman: J. Maisin (Belgium).
Rapporteur: E. Létourneau (Canada).

United Nations Special Fund
(to provide emergency relief and development assistance)

BOARD OF GOVERNORS
  The activities of the United Nations Special Fund were suspended, *ad interim*, in 1978 by the General Assembly, which assumed the functions of the Board of Governors of the Fund. In 1981,[17] the Assembly decided to continue performing these functions, within the context of its consideration of the item on development and international economic co-operation, pending consideration of the question in 1983. However, no further action had been taken by the end of 1989.

United Nations Staff Pension Committee
  The United Nations Staff Pension Committee consists of four members and four alternates elected by the General Assembly, four members and two alternates appointed by the Secretary-General, and four members and two alternates elected by the participants in the United Nations Joint Staff Pension Fund. The term of office of the elected members is three years, or until the election of their successors.

Members:
Elected by Assembly (to serve until 31 December 1991): *Members:* Yogesh Kumar Gupta (India), Sol Kuttner (United States),

---

[15]YUN 1958, p. 31, GA res. 1344(XIII), 13 Dec. 1958.
[16]YUN 1956, p. 108.
[17]YUN 1981, p. 418, GA dec. 36/424, 4 Dec. 1981.

Michael G. Okeyo (Kenya), Victor A. Vislykh (USSR). *Alternates:* Tadanori Inomata (Japan), Ulrich Kalbitzer (Federal Republic of Germany), Mohand Ladjouzi (Algeria), Teodoro Maus (Mexico).

Appointed by Secretary-General (to serve until further notice): *Members:* Kofi Annan, J. Richard Foran, Maryan Baquerot, Anthony J. Miller. *Alternates:* Matías de la Mota, Dulcie Bull.

Elected by Participants (to serve until 31 December 1989): *Members:* Susanna H. Johnston, Gualtiero Fulcheri, Bruce C. Hillis, Lennox Bourne. *Alternates:* Nancy L. Sadka, George Irving.

In 1989, the participants elected, effective 1 January 1990 for a three-year term, as members: Bruce C. Hillis, Susanna H. Johnston, Gualtiero Fulcheri, Viviana Baeza; and as alternates: Naowalak Watanaphanich, Narinder Kakar.

United Nations University

COUNCIL OF THE UNITED NATIONS UNIVERSITY

The Council of the United Nations University, the governing board of the University, reports annually to the General Assembly, to the Economic and Social Council and to the UNESCO Executive Board through the Secretary-General and the UNESCO Director-General. It consists of: *(a)* 24 members appointed jointly by the Secretary-General and the UNESCO Director-General, in consultation with the agencies and programmes concerned including UNITAR, who serve in their personal capacity for six-year terms; *(b)* the Secretary-General, the Director-General of UNESCO and the Executive Director of UNITAR, who are *ex-officio* members; and *(c)* the Rector of the University, who is normally appointed for a five-year term.

In 1989, the Council held two sessions: its thirty-third at Budapest, Hungary, from 3 to 8 July, and its thirty-fourth in Tokyo from 4 to 8 December.

Members:

To serve until 2 May 1992: Mary F. Berry (United States); Alfonso Borrero, *Vice-Chairman* (Colombia); Umberto Colombo, *Vice-Chairman* (Italy); Kuniyoshi Date (Japan); Keith B. Griffin, *Vice-Chairman* (United Kingdom); Joseph Ki-Zerbo (Burkina Faso); Candido Mendes de Almeida (Brazil); M. G. K. Menon, *Vice-Chairman* (India); Martha V. Mvungi, *Vice-Chairman* (United Republic of Tanzania); Mihaly Simai, *Vice-Chairman* (Hungary); Rehman Sobhan (Bangladesh); Justin Thorens, *Chairman* (Switzerland).

To serve until 2 May 1995:[a] Claude Frejacques (France); Sippanondha Ketudat (Thailand); Felipe E. MacGregor (Peru); Lucille Mair (Jamaica); Abdel Salam Majali (Jordan); Lydia Makhubu (Swaziland); Vladlen A. Martynov (USSR); Fatima Mernissi (Morocco); Rafael Portaencasa (Spain); Raimo Vayrynen (Finland); Josephine Guidy-Wandja (Côte d'Ivoire); Yao Erxin (China).

Ex-officio members: The Secretary-General, the Director-General of UNESCO and the Executive Director of UNITAR.

[a]Appointed in May 1989.

Rector of the United Nations University: Heitor Gurgulino de Souza.

The Council maintained four standing committees during 1989: the Committee on Finance and Budget; the Committee on Institutional and Programmatic Development; the Committee on Statutes, Rules and Guidelines; and the Committee on the Report of the Council.

United Nations Voluntary Fund for Indigenous Populations

The United Nations Voluntary Fund for Indigenous Populations provides financial assistance to representatives of indigenous communities and organizations to enable their participation in meetings of the Working Group on Indigenous Populations, a subsidiary of the Sub-Commission on Prevention of Discrimination and Protection of Minorities.

BOARD OF TRUSTEES

The Board of Trustees to advise the Secretary-General in his administration of the Fund consists of five members with relevant experience in issues affecting indigenous populations, appointed in their personal capacity by the Secretary-General for a three-year term. At least one member is a representative of a widely recognized organization of indigenous people.

The Board held its second session at Geneva from 24 to 27 April 1989.

Members: Leif Dunfjeld (Norway); Alioune Séné (Senegal); Hiwi Tauroa (New Zealand); Danilo Türk (Yugoslavia); Augusto Willemsen-Díaz, *Chairman* (Guatemala).

United Nations Voluntary Fund for Victims of Torture

BOARD OF TRUSTEES

The Board of Trustees to advise the Secretary-General in his administration of the United Nations Voluntary Fund for Victims of Torture consists of five members with wide experience in the field of human rights, appointed in their personal capacity by the Secretary-General with due regard for equitable geographical distribution and in consultation with their Governments.

The Board held its eighth session at Geneva from 24 to 28 April 1989.

Members (to serve until 31 December 1992): Elizabeth Odio Benito (Costa Rica); Waleed M. Sadi (Jordan); Ivan Tosevski (Yugoslavia); Amos Wako (Kenya); Jaap Walkate, *Chairman* (Netherlands).

World Food Council

The World Food Council, at the ministerial or plenipotentiary level, functions as an organ of the United Nations and reports to the General Assembly through the Economic and Social Council. It consists of 36 members, nominated by the Economic and Social Council and elected by the Assembly according to the following pattern: nine members from African States, eight from Asian States, seven from Latin American States, four from socialist States of Eastern Europe and eight from Western European and other States. Members serve for three-year terms.

The Council held its fifteenth session at Cairo, Egypt, from 22 to 25 May 1989.

Members:

To serve until 31 December 1989: Argentina, Burundi, Colombia, France, Hungary, India, Italy, Japan, Pakistan, Rwanda, Sweden, Tunisia.

To serve until 31 December 1990: Bulgaria, Canada, China, Côte d'Ivoire, Indonesia, Madagascar, Mexico, Thailand, Turkey, United States, Uruguay, Zambia.

To serve until 31 December 1991: Australia, Cape Verde, Cyprus, Ecuador, German Democratic Republic, Germany, Federal Republic of, Guatemala, Niger, Paraguay, Syrian Arab Republic, USSR, Zimbabwe.

President: Eduardo Pesqueira (Mexico).

Vice-Presidents: Yovtcho Roussev (Bulgaria), Rao Sikandar Iqbal (Pakistan).

Executive Director: Gerald Ion Trant.

On 23 May 1989 (decision 1989/160), the Economic and Social Council nominated the following 12 States for election by the General Assembly for a three-year term beginning on 1 January 1990 to fill the vacancies occurring on 31 December 1989: Argentina, Burundi, Democratic Yemen, Denmark, Egypt, France, Hungary, Iran, Italy, Japan, Peru, Rwanda. The Assembly elected them on 8 November (decision 44/310).

Security Council

The Security Council consists of 15 Member States of the United Nations, in accordance with the provisions of Article 23 of the United Nations Charter as amended in 1965.

MEMBERS
Permanent members: China, France, USSR, United Kingdom, United States.
Non-permanent members: Algeria, Brazil, Canada, Colombia, Ethiopia, Finland, Malaysia, Nepal, Senegal, Yugoslavia.

On 18 October 1989 (decision 44/306), the General Assembly elected Côte d'Ivoire, Cuba, Democratic Yemen, Romania and Zaire for a two-year term beginning on 1 January 1990, to replace Algeria, Brazil, Nepal, Senegal and Yugoslavia, whose terms of office were to expire on 31 December 1989.

PRESIDENTS
The presidency of the Council rotates monthly, according to the English alphabetical listing of its member States. The following served as Presidents during 1989:

Month	Member	Representative
January	Malaysia	Razali Ismail
February	Nepal	Jai Pratap Rana
March	Senegal	Absa Claude Diallo
April	USSR	Aleksandr M. Belonogov
May	United Kingdom	Sir Crispin Tickell
June	United States	Thomas R. Pickering
July	Yugoslavia	Dragoslav Pejic
August	Algeria	Hocine Djoudi
September	Brazil	Paulo Nogueira-Batista
October	Canada	L. Yves Fortier
November	China	Li Luye
December	Colombia	Enrique Peñalosa

Military Staff Committee

The Military Staff Committee consists of the chiefs of staff of the permanent members of the Security Council or their representatives. It met fortnightly throughout 1989; the first meeting was held on 13 January and the last on 30 December.

Standing committees

Each of the three standing committees of the Security Council is composed of representatives of all Council members:

Committee of Experts (to examine the provisional rules of procedure of the Council and any other matters entrusted to it by the Council)
Committee on the Admission of New Members
Committee on Council Meetings Away from Headquarters

Ad hoc bodies

Ad Hoc Committee established under resolution 507(1982)
Members: France *(Chairman)*, Guyana,[a] Jordan,[a] Uganda.[a]

[a]Not Council members in 1989.

**Committee of Experts established by the
Security Council at its 1506th meeting**
(on the question of micro-States)
The Committee of Experts consists of all the members of the Security Council. It did not meet in 1989.

**Security Council Commission established
under resolution 446(1979)**
*(to examine the situation relating to settlements in the
Arab territories occupied since 1967, including Jerusalem)*
Members:[a] Bolivia, Portugal, Zambia.

[a]Not Council members in 1989.

**Security Council Committee established by resolution 421(1977)
concerning the question of South Africa**
The Committee consists of all the members of the Security Council.

Chairman: Jai Pratap Rana (Nepal).

PEACE-KEEPING OPERATIONS AND SPECIAL MISSIONS

United Nations Truce Supervision Organization (UNTSO)
Chief of Staff: Lieutenant-General Martin Vadset.

**United Nations Military Observer Group
in India and Pakistan (UNMOGIP)**
Chief Military Observer: Brigadier-General James Parker (until 19 May 1989), Lieutenant-Colonel Mario Fiorese (Acting, 20 May–27 June), Brigadier-General Jeremiah Enright (from 28 June).

United Nations Peace-keeping Force in Cyprus (UNFICYP)
Special Representative of the Secretary-General: Oscar Héctor Camilión.
Force Commander: Major-General Günther G. Greindl (until April 1989), Major-General Clive Milner (from April).

United Nations Disengagement Observer Force (UNDOF)
Force Commander: Major-General Adolf Radauer.

United Nations Interim Force in Lebanon (UNIFIL)
Force Commander: Lieutenant-General Lars-Eric Wahlgren.

**United Nations Good Offices Mission in
Afghanistan and Pakistan (UNGOMAP)**
Representative of the Secretary-General: Diego Cordovez.
Deputy Representative of the Secretary-General: Major-General Rauli Kalervo Helminen (until 9 May 1989), Colonel Heikki Happonen (from 19 May).

United Nations Iran-Iraq Military Observer Group (UNIIMOG)
Personal Representative of the Secretary-General: Jan K. Eliasson.
Chief Military Observer: Major-General Slavko Jovic.

United Nations Angola Verification Mission (UNAVEM)
Chief Military Observer: Brigadier-General Péricles Ferreira Gomes.

United Nations Transition Assistance Group (UNTAG)
On 16 January 1989, the Security Council decided that implementation of its resolution establishing the United Nations Transition Assistance Group in Namibia[18] would begin on 1 April 1989.

Special Representative of the Secretary-General: Martti Ahtisaari.
Force Commander: Lieutenant-General Dewan Prem Chand.

**United Nations Observer Mission for the Verification of the
Electoral Process in Nicaragua (ONUVEN)**
On 25 August 1989, ONUVEN was established.

Personal Representative of the Secretary-General: Elliott Richardson.
Chief of Mission: Iqbal Riza.
Deputy Chief: Horatio Boneo.

**United Nations Observer Group
in Central America (ONUCA)**
On 7 November 1989, the Security Council established, under its authority, a United Nations Observer Group in Central America to verify compliance by Costa Rica, El Salvador, Guatemala, Honduras and Nicaragua with the undertakings in respect of security contained in the Esquipulas II Agreement.[19]

Chief Military Observer: Major-General Agustín Quesada Gómez (from 21 November 1989).

---

[18]YUN 1978, p. 915, SC res. 435(1978), 29 Sep. 1978.
[19]YUN 1987, p. 188.

Economic and Social Council

The Economic and Social Council consists of 54 Member States of the United Nations, elected by the General Assembly, each for a three-year term, in accordance with the provisions of Article 61 of the United Nations Charter as amended in 1965 and 1973.

MEMBERS

To serve until 31 December 1989: Belize, Bolivia, Bulgaria, Canada, China, Denmark, Iran, Norway, Oman, Poland, Rwanda, Somalia, Sri Lanka, Sudan, USSR, United Kingdom, Uruguay, Zaire.
To serve until 31 December 1990: Colombia, Cuba, France, Germany, Federal Republic of, Ghana, Greece, Guinea, India, Ireland, Japan, Lesotho, Liberia, Libyan Arab Jamahiriya, Portugal, Saudi Arabia, Trinidad and Tobago, Venezuela, Yugoslavia.
To serve until 31 December 1991: Bahamas, Brazil, Cameroon, Czechoslovakia, Indonesia, Iraq, Italy, Jordan, Kenya, Netherlands, New Zealand, Nicaragua, Niger, Thailand, Tunisia, Ukrainian SSR, United States, Zambia.

On 1 November 1989 (decision 44/308), the General Assembly elected the following 18 States for a three-year term beginning on 1 January 1990 to fill the vacancies occurring on 31 December 1989: Algeria, Bahrain, Bulgaria, Burkina Faso, Canada, China, Ecuador, Finland, German Democratic Republic, Iran, Jamaica, Mexico, Pakistan, Rwanda, Sweden, USSR, United Kingdom, Zaire.

SESSIONS

Organizational session for 1989: United Nations Headquarters, 19 January and 9 and 10 February.
First regular session of 1989: United Nations Headquarters, 2-24 May.
Second regular session of 1989: Geneva, 5-28 July.

OFFICERS

President: Kjeld Wilhelm Mortensen (Denmark).
Vice-Presidents: Chandrashekhar Dasgupta (India), Hassen Elghouayel (Tunisia), Guennadi I. Oudovenko (Ukrainian SSR), Felipe Héctor Paolillo (Uruguay).

Subsidiary and other related organs

SUBSIDIARY ORGANS

In addition to three regular sessional committees, the Economic and Social Council may, at each session, set up other committees or working groups, of the whole or of limited membership, and refer to them any items on the agenda for study and report.

Other subsidiary organs reporting to the Council consist of functional commissions, regional commissions, standing committees, expert bodies and *ad hoc* bodies.

The inter-agency Administrative Committee on Co-ordination also reports to the Council.

Sessional bodies

SESSIONAL COMMITTEES

Each of the sessional committees of the Economic and Social Council consists of the 54 members of the Council.

First (Economic) Committee. Chairman: Chandrashekhar Dasgupta (India). *Vice-Chairmen:* Pavol Sepelak (Czechoslovakia) (until 4 July 1989), Vladimir Duris (Czechoslovakia) (from 5 July); Henrique Moret (Cuba).
Second (Social) Committee. Chairman: Hassen Elghouayel (Tunisia). *Vice-Chairmen:* Esther María Ashton (Bolivia), Saodah Batin Akuan Syahruddin (Indonesia).

Third (Programme and Co-ordination) Committee. Chairman: Guennadi I. Oudovenko (Ukrainian SSR). *Vice-Chairmen:* Karl Borchard (Federal Republic of Germany), Alhaj Muhammad Abdullah (Ghana).

Functional commissions

Commission for Social Development

The Commission for Social Development consists of 32 members, elected for four-year terms by the Economic and Social Council according to a specific pattern of equitable geographical distribution.

The Commission held its thirty-first session at Vienna from 13 to 22 March 1989.

Members:

To serve until 31 December 1990: Argentina, Austria, Bangladesh, Cyprus, Dominican Republic, German Democratic Republic, Ghana, Liberia, Libyan Arab Jamahiriya, Norway, Togo.
To serve until 31 December 1991: France, Germany, Federal Republic of, Guatemala, Haiti, Iraq, Pakistan, Romania, Sudan, Uganda, USSR, United States.
To serve until 31 December 1992: Burundi,[a] Cameroon, Chile, China, Ecuador, Finland, Malta, Philippines, Poland, Spain.

[a]Elected on 23 May 1989 (decision 1989/160).

Chairman: Oskar Schröder (Federal Republic of Germany).
Vice-Chairmen: Eduardo Castillo-Arriola (Guatemala), Elsie MBella NGomba (Cameroon), Mita Pardo de Tavera (Philippines).
Rapporteur: Norbert Poerschke (German Democratic Republic).

Commission on Human Rights

The Commission on Human Rights consists of 43 members, elected for three-year terms by the Economic and Social Council according to a specific pattern of equitable geographical distribution.

The Commission held its forty-fifth session at Geneva from 30 January to 10 March 1989.

Members:

To serve until 31 December 1989: Brazil, France, German Democratic Republic, Iraq, Italy, Mexico, Pakistan, Philippines, Rwanda, Senegal, Somalia, Togo, United States, Yugoslavia.
To serve until 31 December 1990: Argentina, Botswana, Bulgaria, China, Gambia, Germany, Federal Republic of, Japan, Nigeria, Peru, Portugal, Sao Tome and Principe, Spain, Sri Lanka, United Kingdom, Venezuela.
To serve until 31 December 1991: Bangladesh, Belgium, Canada, Colombia, Cuba, Cyprus, Ethiopia, India, Morocco, Panama, Swaziland, Sweden, Ukrainian SSR, USSR.

Chairman: Marc Bossuyt (Belgium).
Vice-Chairmen: Claude Heller (Mexico), Zagorka Ilic (Yugoslavia), Qian Jiadong (China).
Rapporteur: Christy Ezim Mbonu (Nigeria).

On 23 May 1989 (decision 1989/160), the Economic and Social Council elected the following 14 members for a three-year term beginning on 1 January 1990 to fill the vacancies occurring on 31 December 1989: Brazil, France, Ghana, Hungary, Iraq, Italy, Madagascar, Mexico, Pakistan, Philippines, Senegal, Somalia, United States, Yugoslavia.

AD HOC WORKING GROUP OF EXPERTS
(established by Commission on Human Rights resolution 2(XXIII) of 6 March 1967)
Members: Leliel Mikuin Balanda, *Chairman/Rapporteur* (Zaire); Humberto Díaz-Casanueva, *Vice-Chairman* (Chile); Felix Er-

macora (Austria); Branimir M. Jankovic (Yugoslavia); Elly Elikunda E. Mtango (United Republic of Tanzania); Mulka Govinda Reddy (India).

GROUP OF THREE ESTABLISHED UNDER THE
INTERNATIONAL CONVENTION ON THE SUPPRESSION
AND PUNISHMENT OF THE CRIME OF *APARTHEID*

The Group of Three held its twelfth session at Geneva from 23 to 27 January 1989.

Members: Ethiopia, German Democratic Republic, Mexico.

Chairman/Rapporteur: Vicente Montemayor Cantu (Mexico).

SUB-COMMISSION ON PREVENTION OF
DISCRIMINATION AND PROTECTION OF MINORITIES

The Sub-Commission consists of 26 members elected by the Commission on Human Rights from candidates nominated by Member States of the United Nations, in accordance with a scheme to ensure equitable geographical distribution. Members serve in their individual capacity as experts, rather than as governmental representatives, each for a four-year term.

The Sub-Commission held its forty-first session at Geneva from 7 August to 1 September 1989.

Members: Yawo Agboyibor (Togo); Miguel Alfonso Martínez, *Vice-Chairman* (Cuba); Awn Shawkat Al-Khasawneh (Jordan); Judith Sefi Attah (Nigeria); Mary Concepción Bautista (Philippines); Murlidhar Chandrakant Bhandare (India); Stanislav Valentinovich Chernichenko (USSR); Erica-Irene A. Daes (Greece); Leandro Despouy (Argentina); Ion Diaconu, *Vice-Chairman* (Romania); Asbjorn Eide (Norway); Ribot Hatano, *Rapporteur* (Japan); Aidid Abdillahi Ilkahanaf (Somalia); Louis Joinet (France); Ahmed Mohamed Khalifa (Egypt); Fatma Zohra Ksentini (Algeria); Claire Palley (United Kingdom); Rafael Rivas Posada (Colombia); Alejandro Sobarzo Loaiza (Mexico); Tian Jin (China); William W. Treat (United States); Danilo Türk (Yugoslavia); Theodoor Cornelis van Boven, *Vice-Chairman* (Netherlands); Luis Varela Quirós (Costa Rica); Hamila Embarek Warzazi (Morocco); Fisseha Yimer, *Chairman* (Ethiopia).

Working Group
(established by resolution 2(XXIV) of 16 August 1971 of the Sub-Commission on Prevention of Discrimination and Protection of Minorities pursuant to Economic and Social Council resolution 1503(XLVIII))

The Working Group on Communications concerning human rights held its seventeenth session at Geneva from 24 July to 4 August 1989.

Members: Ribot Hatano (Japan); Teimuraz O. Ramishvili (USSR); Alejandro Sobarzo Loaiza (Mexico); Theodoor Cornelis van Boven (Netherlands); Fisseha Yimer, *Chairman/Rapporteur* (Ethiopia).

Working Group
(established on 21 August 1974 by resolution 11(XXVII) of the Sub-Commission on Prevention of Discrimination and Protection of Minorities)

The Working Group on Contemporary Forms of Slavery held its fourteenth session at Geneva from 31 July to 4 August and on 25 August 1989.

Members: Mary Concepción Bautista (Philippines); Ion Diaconu (Romania); Asbjorn Eide, *Chairman/Rapporteur* (Norway); Fatma Zohra Ksentini (Algeria); Luis Varela Quirós (Costa Rica).

Working Group on Detention
The Working Group on Detention met at Geneva between 9 and 23 August 1989.

Members: Miguel Alfonso Martínez, *Chairman* (Cuba); Judith Sefi Attah (Nigeria); Mary Concepción Bautista (Philippines); Louis Joinet, *Rapporteur* (France); Danilo Türk (Yugoslavia).

Working Group on Indigenous Populations
The Working Group on Indigenous Populations held its seventh session at Geneva from 31 July to 4 August 1989.

Members: Miguel Alfonso Martínez (Cuba); Erica-Irene A. Daes, *Chairman/Rapporteur* (Greece); Christie Mbonu (Nigeria); Tian Jin (China); Danilo Türk (Yugoslavia).

WORKING GROUP OF GOVERNMENTAL
EXPERTS ON THE RIGHT TO DEVELOPMENT

The Working Group of Governmental Experts on the Right to Development held its twelfth (open-ended) session at Geneva from 23 to 27 January 1989.

Chairman: Alioune Séné (Senegal).
Vice-Chairmen: Julio Heredia-Pérez (Cuba), Danilo Türk (Yugoslavia).
Vice-Chairman/Rapporteur: Kantilal Lallubhai Dalal (India).

WORKING GROUP ON ENFORCED
OR INVOLUNTARY DISAPPEARANCES

The Working Group on Enforced or Involuntary Disappearances held three sessions in 1989: its twenty-seventh at United Nations Headquarters from 17 to 21 April, and its twenty-eighth and twenty-ninth at Geneva from 28 August to 1 September and from 6 to 15 December, respectively.

Members: Jonas Kwami Dotse Foli (Ghana); Diego García-Sayán (Peru); Agha Hilaly (Pakistan); Ivan Tosevski, *Chairman/Rapporteur* (Yugoslavia); Toine van Dongen (Netherlands).

WORKING GROUPS
(to study situations revealing a consistent pattern of gross violations of human rights)

Working Group established by Commission on Human Rights decision 1988/103 of 2 March 1988:
Members: Antônio Costa Lobo (Portugal); Todor Ditchev, *Chairman/Rapporteur* (Bulgaria); Roshdi Khaled Rashid (Iraq); Aregba Polo (Togo); Jaime Stiglich (Peru).

Working Group established by Commission on Human Rights decision 1989/109 of 7 March 1989:
Members:[a] Antônio Costa Lobo (Portugal), Todor Ditchev (Bulgaria), Gmor Abdou Secka (Gambia), Armando Villanueva del Campo (Peru).

[a]The seat allocated to a member from the Asian Group was not filled in 1989.

WORKING GROUPS (OPEN-ENDED)

Working Group established by Commission on Human Rights decision 1985/112 of 14 March 1985
(to draft a declaration on the right and responsibility of individuals, groups and organs of society to promote and protect universally recognized human rights and fundamental freedoms):
Chairman/Rapporteur: Robert H. Robertson (Australia).

Working Group established by Commission on Human Rights resolution 1985/50 of 14 March 1985
(to draft a convention on the rights of the child):
Chairman/Rapporteur: Adam Lopatka (Poland).

The Working Group completed the drafting of the convention in 1989.

Working Group established by Commission on Human Rights resolution 1985/53 of 14 March 1985
(to draft a declaration on the rights of persons belonging to national, ethnic, religious and linguistic minorities):
Chairman/Rapporteur: Zagorka Ilíc (Yugoslavia).

Commission on Narcotic Drugs
The Commission on Narcotic Drugs consists of 40 members, elected for four-year terms by the Economic and Social Council

from among the Members of the United Nations and members of the specialized agencies and the parties to the Single Convention on Narcotic Drugs, 1961, with due regard for the adequate representation of *(a)* countries which are important producers of opium or coca leaves, *(b)* countries which are important in the manufacture of narcotic drugs, and *(c)* countries in which drug addiction or the illicit traffic in narcotic drugs constitutes an important problem, as well as taking into account the principle of equitable geographical distribution.

The Commission held its thirty-third session at Vienna from 6 to 17 February 1989.

Members:

To serve until 31 December 1989: Argentina, Australia, Belgium, Bulgaria, China, Ecuador, Hungary, Indonesia, Japan, Malaysia, Mali, Mexico, Nigeria, Senegal, Spain, Turkey, USSR, United Kingdom, Venezuela, Zambia.

To serve until 31 December 1991: Bolivia, Brazil, Canada, Côte d'Ivoire, Denmark, Egypt, France, Germany, Federal Republic of, India, Italy, Lebanon, Madagascar, Netherlands, Pakistan, Peru, Poland, Switzerland, Thailand, United States, Yugoslavia.

Chairman: Dilshad Najmuddin (Pakistan).
First Vice-Chairman: E. A. Babayan (USSR).
Second Vice-Chairman: R. J. Samsom (Netherlands).
Rapporteur: F. Cuevas Cancino (Mexico).

On 23 May 1989 (decision 1989/160), the Economic and Social Council elected the following 20 members for a four-year term beginning on 1 January 1990 to fill the vacancies occurring on 31 December 1989: Australia, Bahamas, Belgium, Bulgaria, China, Colombia, Ecuador, Gambia, Ghana, Hungary, Indonesia, Japan, Libyan Arab Jamahiriya, Malaysia, Mexico, Senegal, Spain, Sweden, USSR, United Kingdom.

SUB-COMMISSION ON ILLICIT DRUG TRAFFIC AND
RELATED MATTERS IN THE NEAR AND MIDDLE EAST

In 1989, the Sub-Commission held two sessions: its twenty-fourth at Vienna on 31 January and 1 February and its twenty-fifth at Ankara, Turkey, from 2 to 6 October.

Members: Afghanistan, Egypt, India, Iran, Jordan, Kuwait,[a] Lebanon,[a] Oman,[a] Pakistan, Saudi Arabia,[a] Sweden, Turkey, United Arab Emirates,[a] Yemen.[a]

[a]Membership approved by the Economic and Social Council on 22 May 1989 (decision 1989/120).

Twenty-fourth session
Chairman: Erdem Erner (Turkey).
Vice-Chairman: Ghodratollah Assadi (Iran).

Twenty-fifth session
Chairman: Erdem Erner (Turkey).
First Vice-Chairman: M. M. Bhatnagar (India).
Second Vice-Chairman: Ahmed F. Nada (Egypt).

MEETINGS OF HEADS OF NATIONAL
DRUG LAW ENFORCEMENT AGENCIES (HONLEA)

Interregional HONLEA

Interregional HONLEA examines in depth the most important aspects of the drug trafficking problem. All Member States are encouraged to participate, and competent bodies within the United Nations system as well as the International Criminal Police Organization (Interpol) and the Customs Co-operation Council are invited to offer their technical expertise.

Interregional HONLEA held its second meeting at Vienna from 11 to 15 September 1989.

Chairman: Javier Coello Trejo (Mexico).
First Vice-Chairman: M. M. Bhatnagar (India).
Second Vice-Chairman: Andras Turos (Hungary).

Third Vice-Chairman: Kamoyo G. Mwale (Zambia).
Rapporteur: Robert F. Pietersz (Netherlands).

HONLEA, Africa

A meeting to co-ordinate regional activities against illicit drug traffic, convened annually (except when Interregional HONLEA meets), is open to any State in the region, as well as to observers from Interpol, the Customs Co-operation Council, other competent international and intergovernmental organizations, and INCB. Any interested Government which is actively involved in countering illicit drug traffic in the region may be invited by the Secretary-General to send an observer at its own expense.

HONLEA, Africa, did not meet in 1989.

HONLEA, Asia and the Pacific

A meeting to co-ordinate regional activities against illicit drug traffic, convened annually (except when Interregional HONLEA meets) in one of the region's capitals, is open to any country or territory in the region approved by the Commission, as well as to observers from the Association of South-East Asian Nations, the Colombo Plan Bureau, the Customs Co-operation Council, Interpol and INCB. Any interested Government outside the region may be invited by the Secretary-General to send an observer at its own expense.

HONLEA, Asia and the Pacific, did not meet in 1989.

HONLEA, Latin America and the Caribbean

A meeting to co-ordinate regional activities against illicit drug traffic, convened annually (except when Interregional HONLEA meets) in one of the region's capitals, is open to any country or territory in the region approved by the Commission, as well as to observers from the Customs Co-operation Council, Interpol and INCB. Any interested Government outside the region may be invited by the Secretary-General to send an observer at its own expense.

HONLEA, Latin America and the Caribbean, did not meet in 1989.

Commission on the Status of Women

The Commission on the Status of Women consists of 32 members, elected for four-year terms by the Economic and Social Council according to a specific pattern of equitable geographical distribution.

The Commission held its thirty-third session at Vienna from 29 March to 7 April 1989.

Members:

To serve until 31 December 1990: Australia, Bangladesh, Côte d'Ivoire, Czechoslovakia, Gabon, Italy, Mexico, Philippines, USSR, United States, Zaire.

To serve until 31 December 1991: Burkina Faso, China, Costa Rica, Cuba, German Democratic Republic, Guatemala, Lesotho, Pakistan, Sweden, Turkey.

To serve until 31 December 1992: Austria, Brazil, Canada, Colombia, France, Japan, Morocco, Poland, Sudan, Thailand, United Republic of Tanzania.

Chairman: Johanna Dohnal (Austria).
Vice-Chairmen: Sonia Martínez (Colombia), Dagmar Molkova (Czechoslovakia), Wang Shuxian (China).
Rapporteur: Assumani Ussu Bagbeni (Zaire).

On 24 May 1989 (resolution 1989/45), the Economic and Social Council decided that the membership of the Commission should be increased to 45 and that the seats should be allocated according to the following pattern: 13 members from African States; 11 from Asian States; 4 from Eastern European States; 9 from Latin American and Caribbean States; and 8 from Western European and other States. The additional seats were to be filled at the Council's organizational session for 1990.

Population Commission

The Population Commission consists of 27 members elected for four-year terms by the Economic and Social Council according to a specific pattern of equitable geographical distribution.

The Commission held its twenty-fifth session at United Nations Headquarters from 21 February to 2 March 1989.

Members:

To serve until 31 December 1989: Burundi, China, Cuba, Iran, Malawi, Mexico, USSR, United Kingdom, United States.
To serve until 31 December 1991: Bolivia, France, Iraq, Japan, Nigeria, Poland, Rwanda, Sweden, Togo.
To serve until 31 December 1992: Bangladesh, Belgium, Brazil, Colombia, Egypt, Germany, Federal Republic of, Turkey, Uganda,[a] Ukrainian SSR.

[a]Elected on 10 February 1989 (decision 1989/104).

Chairman: Jerzy Holzer (Poland).
Vice-Chairmen: Shigemi Kono (Japan), Jonathas Niyungeko (Burundi), Luz María Valdés (Mexico).
Rapporteur: Charlotte Hoehn (Federal Republic of Germany).

On 23 May and 27 July 1989 (decisions 1989/160 and 1989/181), the Economic and Social Council elected the following for a four-year term beginning on 1 January 1990 to fill eight of the nine vacancies occurring on 31 December 1989: Botswana, China, Iran, Mexico, Panama, USSR, United Kingdom, United States. No further election was held in 1989 to fill the remaining seat, allocated to a member from African States.

Statistical Commission

The Statistical Commission consists of 24 members elected for four-year terms by the Economic and Social Council according to a specific pattern of equitable geographical distribution.

The Commission held its twenty-fifth session at United Nations Headquarters from 6 to 15 February 1989.

Members:

To serve until 31 December 1989: Argentina, Egypt, France, Germany, Federal Republic of, Spain, Togo, USSR, Zambia.
To serve until 31 December 1991: Bulgaria, China, Czechoslovakia, Ghana, Morocco, Pakistan, Panama, United States.
To serve until 31 December 1992: Brazil, Canada, Hungary, Iran, Japan, Mexico, Norway, United Kingdom.

Chairman: Luis Alberto Beccaría (Argentina).
Vice-Chairmen: Hermann Habermann (United States), M. A. Korolev (USSR), Hiroyasu Kudo (Japan).
Rapporteur: Awad Mokhtar Hallouda (Egypt).

On 23 May 1989 (decision 1989/160), the Economic and Social Council elected the following eight members for a four-year term beginning on 1 January 1990 to fill the vacancies occurring on 31 December 1989: Argentina, France, Germany, Federal Republic of, Kenya, Netherlands, Togo, USSR, Zambia.

WORKING GROUP ON INTERNATIONAL
STATISTICAL PROGRAMMES AND CO-ORDINATION

The Working Group consists of the Bureau of the Statistical Commission; the representatives to the Commission of the two major contributors to the United Nations budget, unless they are already represented in the Bureau; and one representative to the Commission from a developing country from among members of each of the following: ECA, ECLAC, ESCAP and ESCWA, unless they are also already represented in the Bureau. Members serve two-year terms.

The Working Group held its thirteenth session at Geneva from 11 to 14 September 1989.

Chairman: Luis Alberto Beccaría (Argentina).

Regional commissions

Economic and Social Commission for
Asia and the Pacific (ESCAP)

The Economic and Social Commission for Asia and the Pacific held its forty-fifth session at Bangkok, Thailand, from 27 March to 5 April 1989.

Members: Afghanistan, Australia, Bangladesh, Bhutan, Brunei Darussalam, Burma (Myanmar), China, Democratic Kampuchea, Fiji, France, India, Indonesia, Iran, Japan, Lao People's Democratic Republic, Malaysia, Maldives, Mongolia, Nauru, Nepal, Netherlands, New Zealand, Pakistan, Papua New Guinea, Philippines, Republic of Korea, Samoa, Singapore, Solomon Islands, Sri Lanka, Thailand, Tonga, Tuvalu, USSR, United Kingdom, United States, Vanuatu, Viet Nam.
Associate members: American Samoa, Commonwealth of the Northern Mariana Islands, Cook Islands, Federated States of Micronesia, Guam, Hong Kong, Kiribati, Niue, Republic of the Marshall Islands, Republic of Palau.

Switzerland, not a Member of the United Nations, participates in a consultative capacity in the work of the Commission.

Chairman: Khumbagyn Olzvoy (Mongolia).
Vice-Chairmen: James Cecil Cocker (Tonga), Datuk Kasitah Gaddam (Malaysia), B. P. Dhital (Nepal), John Giheno (Papua New Guinea), Choi Ho-Joong (Republic of Korea), Donald Kalpokas (Vanuatu), Li Daoyu (China), Takamori Makino (Japan), Mohammad A. Munim (Bangladesh), Siddhi Savetsila (Thailand), Mohammad Mohsen Sazegara (Iran), Dinesh Singh (India), Haji Ahmad Wally Skinner (Brunei Darussalam), Peter Sung (Singapore), Tran Quang Co (Viet Nam).
Rapporteur: John Gee (Australia).

Following are the main subsidiary and related bodies of the Commission:
Advisory body: Advisory Committee of Permanent Representatives and Other Representatives Designated by Members of the Commission.
Legislative bodies: Committee on Agriculture, Rural Development and the Environment; Committee on Development Planning and Statistics; Committee on Industry, Technology and Human Settlements; Committee on Natural Resources and Energy; Committee on Population and Social Development; Committee on Shipping, Transport and Communications; Committee on Trade.
Subsidiary bodies: Governing Board, Asian and Pacific Centre for Transfer of Technology; Governing Board, Regional Co-ordination Centre for Research and Development of Coarse Grains, Pulses, Roots and Tuber Crops in the Humid Tropics of Asia and the Pacific.
Related intergovernmental bodies: Asian and Pacific Development Centre; Committee for Co-ordination of Joint Prospecting for Mineral Resources in Asian Offshore Areas; Committee for Co-ordination of Joint Prospecting for Mineral Resources in South Pacific Offshore Areas; Interim Committee for Co-ordination of Investigations of the Lower Mekong Basin; Typhoon Committee.
Regional institution: Statistical Institute for Asia and the Pacific.
Intergovernmental meeting convened by ESCAP: Special Body on Land-locked Countries.

Economic and Social Commission for Western Asia (ESCWA)

The Economic and Social Commission for Western Asia held its fifteenth session at Baghdad, Iraq, on 17 and 18 May 1989.

Members: Bahrain, Democratic Yemen, Egypt, Iraq, Jordan, Kuwait, Lebanon, Oman, Palestine, Qatar, Saudi Arabia, Syrian Arab Republic, United Arab Emirates, Yemen.

Chairman: Hikmat Omar Mukhailif al-Hadithi (Iraq).
Vice-Chairmen: Motahar Abdalla al-Saidi (Yemen), Khalifa Jassim Al Thani (Qatar).
Rapporteur: Mokhtar Hashim Osman (Egypt).

The Commission's one main subsidiary organ, the Technical Committee, composed of all ESCWA members, reviews the Commission's programme of work.

Economic Commission for Africa (ECA)

The Economic Commission for Africa meets in annual session at the ministerial level known as the Conference of Ministers.

The Commission held its twenty-fourth session (fifteenth meeting of the Conference of Ministers) at Addis Ababa, Ethiopia, from 6 to 10 April 1989.

Members: Algeria, Angola, Benin, Botswana, Burkina Faso, Burundi, Cameroon, Cape Verde, Central African Republic, Chad, Comoros, Congo, Côte d'Ivoire, Djibouti, Egypt, Equatorial Guinea, Ethiopia, Gabon, Gambia, Ghana, Guinea, Guinea-Bissau, Kenya, Lesotho, Liberia, Libyan Arab Jamahiriya, Madagascar, Malawi, Mali, Mauritania, Mauritius, Morocco, Mozambique, Niger, Nigeria, Rwanda, Sao Tome and Principe, Senegal, Seychelles, Sierra Leone, Somalia, South Africa,[a] Sudan, Swaziland, Togo, Tunisia, Uganda, United Republic of Tanzania, Zaire, Zambia, Zimbabwe.

[a]On 30 July 1963, the Economic and Social Council decided that South Africa should not take part in the work of ECA until conditions for constructive co-operation had been restored by a change in South Africa's racial policy (YUN 1963, p. 274, ESC res. 974 D IV (XXXVI)).

Switzerland, not a Member of the United Nations, participates in a consultative capacity in the work of the Commission.

Chairman: Mersie Ijigu (Ethiopia).
First Vice-Chairman: Awadh Abdulmottalub Bin Mosa (Libyan Arab Jamahiriya).
Second Vice-Chairman: Pascal Gayama (Congo).
Rapporteur: Simon Ifede Ogouma (Benin).

The Commission has established the following principal legislative organs:

Conference of Ministers; Technical Preparatory Committee of the Whole; sectoral ministerial conferences, each assisted by an appropriate committee of technical officials; Council of Ministers of each Multinational Programming and Operational Centre, assisted by its committee of officials.

The Commission has also established the following subsidiary bodies:

Joint Conference of African Planners, Statisticians and Demographers; Intergovernmental Committee of Experts for Science and Technology Development; Intergovernmental Regional Committee on Human Settlements and Environment; Africa Regional Co-ordinating Committee for the Integration of Women in Development; Technical Committee of the Pan-African Documentation and Information System.

Economic Commission for Europe (ECE)

The Economic Commission for Europe held its forty-fourth session at Geneva from 11 to 21 April 1989.

Members: Albania, Austria, Belgium, Bulgaria, Byelorussian SSR, Canada, Cyprus, Czechoslovakia, Denmark, Finland, France, German Democratic Republic, Germany, Federal Republic of, Greece, Hungary, Iceland, Ireland, Italy, Luxembourg, Malta, Netherlands, Norway, Poland, Portugal, Romania, Spain, Sweden, Switzerland, Turkey, Ukrainian SSR, USSR, United Kingdom, United States, Yugoslavia.

The Holy See, Liechtenstein and San Marino, which are not Members of the United Nations, participate in a consultative capacity in the work of the Commission.

Chairman: Ercument Yavuzalp (Turkey).
Vice-Chairman: Bogumil Sujka (Poland).
Rapporteurs: Edith Reidy (United States), Igor Tourianski (Ukrainian SSR).

Following are the principal subsidiary bodies of the Commission:

Chemical Industry Committee; Coal Committee; Committee on Agricultural Problems; Committee on Electric Power; Committee on Gas; Committee on Housing, Building and Planning; Committee on the Development of Trade; Conference of European Statisticians; Inland Transport Committee; Meeting of Government Officials Responsible for Standardization Policies; Senior Advisers to ECE Governments on Energy; Senior Advisers to ECE Governments on Environmental and Water Problems; Senior Advisers to ECE Governments on Science and Technology; Senior Economic Advisers to ECE Governments; Steel Committee; Timber Committee; Working Party on Engineering Industries and Automation.

Ad hoc meetings of experts are convened for sectors of activity not dealt with by these principal bodies.

Economic Commission for Latin America and the Caribbean (ECLAC)

The Economic Commission for Latin America and the Caribbean did not meet in 1989.

Members: Antigua and Barbuda, Argentina, Bahamas, Barbados, Belize, Bolivia, Brazil, Canada, Chile, Colombia, Costa Rica, Cuba, Dominica, Dominican Republic, Ecuador, El Salvador, France, Grenada, Guatemala, Guyana, Haiti, Honduras, Jamaica, Mexico, Netherlands, Nicaragua, Panama, Paraguay, Peru, Portugal, Saint Kitts and Nevis, Saint Lucia, Saint Vincent and the Grenadines, Spain, Suriname, Trinidad and Tobago, United Kingdom, United States, Uruguay, Venezuela.
Associate members: Aruba, British Virgin Islands, Montserrat, Netherlands Antilles, United States Virgin Islands.

Switzerland, not a Member of the United Nations, participates in a consultative capacity in the work of the Commission.

The Commission has established the following principal subsidiary bodies:

Caribbean Development and Co-operation Committee; Central American Economic Co-operation Committee and its Inter-agency Committee; Committee of High-level Government Experts; Committee of the Whole; Regional Council for Planning, Latin American and Caribbean Institute for Economic and Social Planning.

The Latin American Demographic Centre forms part of the ECLAC system as an autonomous institution.

Standing committees

Commission on Human Settlements

The Commission on Human Settlements consists of 58 members elected by the Economic and Social Council for four-year terms according to a specific pattern of equitable geographical distribution; it reports to the General Assembly through the Council.

The Commission held its twelfth session at Cartagena de Indias, Colombia, from 24 April to 3 May 1989.

Members:
To serve until 31 December 1990: Argentina, Brazil, Bulgaria, Cameroon, Colombia, Ecuador, Finland, Gabon, Iran, Japan, Madagascar, Pakistan, Philippines, Sierra Leone, Togo, Turkey, Uganda, USSR, United Kingdom, United States.
To serve until 31 December 1991: Bangladesh, Botswana, Burundi, Byelorussian SSR, Cyprus, Denmark, Egypt, German Democratic Republic, Germany, Federal Republic of, Greece, India, Jamaica, Jordan, Kenya, Mexico, Norway, Peru, Sri Lanka, United Republic of Tanzania.
To serve until 31 December 1992: Bolivia, Canada, China, France, Guatemala, Hungary, Indonesia, Iraq, Italy, Lesotho, Malawi, Netherlands, Paraguay, Somalia, Swaziland, Sweden, Syrian Arab Republic, Tunisia, Yugoslavia.

Chairman: Carlos Arturo Marulanda Ramírez (Colombia).
Vice-Chairmen: Simon Essimengane (Gabon), Daniel Figgins (United States), Istvan Geczi (Hungary).
Rapporteur: W. D. Ailapperuma (Sri Lanka).

Commission on Transnational Corporations

The Commission on Transnational Corporations consists of 48 members, elected from all States for three-year terms by the Economic and Social Council according to a specific pattern of geographical distribution.

The Commission held its fifteenth session at United Nations Headquarters from 5 to 14 April 1989.

Members:
To serve until 31 December 1989: China, Colombia, Czechoslovakia, Egypt, Fiji, France, German Democratic Republic, Germany,

Federal Republic of, Iran, Japan, Peru, Sierra Leone, Suriname, Switzerland, Tunisia, Zaire.

To serve until 31 December 1990: Burundi, Byelorussian SSR, Cameroon, Canada, Ghana, India, Iraq, Italy, Jamaica, Philippines, Poland, Republic of Korea, Trinidad and Tobago, Turkey, Uganda, Venezuela.

To serve until 31 December 1991:[a] Brazil, Costa Rica, Cuba, Cyprus, Gabon, Indonesia, Mexico, Netherlands, Norway, Swaziland, USSR, United Kingdom, United States, Zaire.[b]

Expert advisers (to serve through the sixteenth session): Mark Anderson (United States), José María Basagoiti (Mexico), Ernst-Otto Czempiel (Federal Republic of Germany), Peter Frerk (Federal Republic of Germany), Roland Guyvarc'h (France), Kamal Hossain (Bangladesh), Ali Mazrui (Kenya), Laurence McQuade (United States), William Robbins (United Kingdom), Alexis Sierralta (Venezuela), Hassan Sunmonu (Nigeria), Kari Tapiola (Finland), L. M. Thapar (India), Raúl Trajtenberg (Uruguay/Argentina), Wang Linsheng (China), Nikolai G. Zaitsev (USSR).

[a]Two seats allocated to one member from African States and one from Asian States remained unfilled in 1989.
[b]Elected on 23 May 1989 (decision 1989/160).

Chairman: A. Gautier (Netherlands).
Vice-Chairmen: Marek Kulczycki (Poland), Víctor Lichtinger (Mexico), Roger Tchibota-Souamy (Gabon).
Rapporteur: Triyono Wibowo (Indonesia).

On 23 May and 27 July 1989 (decisions 1989/160 and 1989/181), the Economic and Social Council elected the following for a three-year term beginning on 1 January 1990 to fill 14 of the 16 vacancies occurring on 31 December 1989: China, Czechoslovakia, Egypt, France, German Democratic Republic, Germany, Federal Republic of, Iran, Japan, Peru, Sierra Leone, Switzerland, Tunisia, Uruguay, Zimbabwe. No further elections were held in 1989 to fill the remaining seats, allocated to one member from Asian States and one from Latin American and Caribbean States.

Committee for Programme and Co-ordination

The Committee for Programme and Co-ordination is the main subsidiary organ of the Economic and Social Council and of the General Assembly for planning, programming and co-ordination and reports directly to both. It consists of 34 members nominated by the Council and elected by the Assembly for three-year terms according to a specific pattern of equitable geographical distribution.

During 1989, the Committee held, at United Nations Headquarters, an organizational meeting on 10 April, and its twenty-ninth session from 8 May to 5 June.

Members:
To serve until 31 December 1989: Brazil, Burkina Faso, Cameroon, China, Indonesia, Japan, Tunisia.
To serve until 31 December 1990: Austria, Bahrain, Bangladesh, Canada, Colombia, Côte d'Ivoire, Cuba, Germany, Federal Republic of, India, Kenya, Mexico, Pakistan, Poland, Romania, Rwanda, Sweden, Trinidad and Tobago, United Kingdom, Uganda, Yugoslavia.
To serve until 31 December 1991: Bahamas, Benin, France, USSR, United States, Venezuela, Zambia.

Chairman: Tommo Monthe (Cameroon).
Vice-Chairmen: Andrzej Abraszewski (Poland), Yogesh Kumar Gupta (India), Ado Vaher (Canada).
Rapporteur: Norma Goicochea Estenoz (Cuba).

On 23 May 1989 (decision 1989/160), the Economic and Social Council nominated the following seven Member States for a three-year term beginning on 1 January 1990 to fill the vacancies occurring on 31 December 1989: Algeria, Argentina, Cameroon, China, Japan, Morocco, Sri Lanka. They were elected by the Assembly on 8 November (decision 44/311).

Committee on Natural Resources

The Committee on Natural Resources consists of 54 members, elected by the Economic and Social Council for four-year terms

in accordance with the geographical distribution of seats in the Council.

The Committee held its eleventh session at United Nations Headquarters from 27 March to 5 April 1989.

Members:
To serve until 31 December 1990:[a] Bolivia, Byelorussian SSR, Côte d'Ivoire, Cuba, Finland, France, German Democratic Republic, Germany, Federal Republic of, Hungary, Iran, Nigeria, Pakistan, Philippines, Poland, Swaziland, Sweden, Thailand, Togo, Turkey, Uganda, United States, Zaire.
To serve until 31 December 1992:[b] Botswana, Chile, China, Ecuador, El Salvador, Gabon,[c] Guatemala, Guinea-Bissau, Haiti, Honduras, Japan, Paraguay, Sudan, Tunisia,[d] Ukrainian SSR, USSR, Uruguay.

[a]Five seats allocated to two members from Asian States and three from Western European and other States remained unfilled in 1989.
[b]Ten seats allocated to three members from African States, three from Asian States and four from Western European and other States remained unfilled in 1989.
[c]Elected on 10 February 1989 (decision 1989/104).
[d]Elected on 23 May 1989 (decision 1989/160).

Chairman: Jürgen Brandenburg (Federal Republic of Germany).
Vice-Chairmen: Siegfried Laechelt (German Democratic Republic), Juan Salazar Sancisi (Ecuador), Roger Tchibota-Souamy (Gabon).
Rapporteur: Ashraf Qureshi (Pakistan).

Committee on Negotiations with Intergovernmental Agencies

The Committee on Negotiations with Intergovernmental Agencies, established by the Economic and Social Council on 16 February 1946, was reconstituted by the Council on 4 February 1983 for the purpose of negotiating a relationship agreement between the United Nations and UNIDO.

The Committee adjourned *sine die* on 20 November 1985 upon completion of its report on the negotiations.

Committee on Non-Governmental Organizations

The Committee on Non-Governmental Organizations consists of 19 members elected by the Economic and Social Council for a four-year term according to a specific pattern of equitable geographical representation.

In 1989, the Committee met at United Nations Headquarters between 23 January and 3 February.

Members (until 31 December 1990): Bulgaria, Burundi, Colombia, Costa Rica, Cuba, Cyprus, France, Greece, Kenya, Malawi, Nicaragua, Oman, Pakistan, Rwanda, Sao Tome and Principe, Sri Lanka, Sweden, USSR, United States.

Chairman: Annie Marie Sundbom (Sweden).
Vice-Chairman: Emil Y. Golemanov (Bulgaria).
Rapporteur: Elias Eliades (Cyprus).

Expert bodies

Ad Hoc Group of Experts on International Co-operation in Tax Matters

The *Ad Hoc* Group of Experts on International Co-operation in Tax Matters—to consist of 25 members drawn from 15 developing and 10 developed countries, appointed by the Secretary-General to serve in their individual capacity—remained at 24 in 1989, with a member from Kenya still to be appointed.

The *Ad Hoc* Group, which meets biennially, held its fifth meeting at Geneva from 6 to 12 December 1989.

Members: Julius Olasoji Akinmola (Nigeria); Mohamed Chkounda (Morocco); Maurice Hugh Collins, *Chairman* (United Kingdom); Eivany Antonio Da Silva (Brazil); V. U. Eradi (India); Mordecai S. Feinberg (United States); José Ramón Fernández-Pérez (Spain); Antonio H. Figueroa (Argentina); Mayer Gabay (Israel); Dominique Gibrat (France); Hugo Hanisch-Ovalle (Chile); Abdel

Fatah Ismail (Egypt); Marwan Koudsi (Syrian Arab Republic); Daniel Lüthi (Switzerland); Reksoprajitno Mansury, *Vice-Chairman* (Indonesia); Thomas Menck (Federal Republic of Germany); Canute R. Miller (Jamaica); Naoki Oka (Japan); Alfred Philipp (Austria); Aaron Schwartzman (Mexico); Rainer Söderholm (Finland); Mohammed Taraq (Pakistan); André Titty (Cameroon); Koenraad Van der Heeden (Netherlands).

Committee for Development Planning
The Committee for Development Planning is composed of 24 experts representing different planning systems. They are appointed by the Economic and Social Council, on nomination by the Secretary-General, to serve in their personal capacity for a term of three years.

The Committee held its twenty-fifth session at United Nations Headquarters from 9 to 12 May 1989.

Members (until 31 December 1989): Abdlatif Y. Al-Hamad, *Chairman* (Kuwait); Nicolás Ardito-Barletta (Panama); Gerasimos D. Arsenis (Greece); Edmar Bacha (Brazil); Bernard T. G. Chidzero (Zimbabwe); Hernando de Soto (Peru); Prithvi Nath Dhar (India); Adama Diallo (Senegal); Just Faaland, *Rapporteur* (Norway); Keith Broadwell Griffin (United Kingdom); Patrick Guillaumont (France); Mahbub ul Haq (Pakistan); Gerald K. Helleiner (Canada); Helen Hughes (Australia); Shinichi Ichimura (Japan); Solita Collas Monsod (Philippines); Henry Nau (United States); G. O. Nwankwo (Nigeria); Jozef Pajestka (Poland); Pu Shan (China);[a] Mihaly Simai, *Vice-Chairman* (Hungary); Udo Ernst Simonis (Federal Republic of Germany); Igor Sysoyev (USSR); Ferdinand Van Dam (Netherlands).

[a]Replaced Huan Xiang (China), who died on 28 February 1989.

Committee of Experts on the Transport of Dangerous Goods
The Committee of Experts on the Transport of Dangerous Goods is composed of experts from countries interested in the international transport of dangerous goods. The experts are made available by their Governments at the request of the Secretary-General. The membership, to be increased to 15 in accordance with a 1975 resolution of the Economic and Social Council,[20] was 14 in 1989. The Committee did not meet in 1989.

Members: Canada, China, France, Germany, Federal Republic of, India,[a] Italy, Japan, Netherlands, Norway, Poland, Sweden, USSR, United Kingdom, United States.

[a]Membership approved by the Economic and Social Council on 27 July 1989.

On 27 July 1989, the Economic and Social Council endorsed the Committee's decision to combine its two subsidiary bodies — the Group of Rapporteurs and the Group of Experts on Explosives — into a single Sub-Committee of Experts on the Transport of Dangerous Goods.

SUB-COMMITTEE OF EXPERTS
ON THE TRANSPORT OF DANGEROUS GOODS
The Sub-Committee of Experts on the Transport of Dangerous Goods, a committee of the whole, held its first session at Geneva from 31 July to 11 August 1989.

Chairman: L. Grainger (United Kingdom).
Vice-Chairmen: M. Mariat (France), J. Monteith (Canada).

Committee on Crime Prevention and Control
The Committee on Crime Prevention and Control consists of 27 members elected for four-year terms by the Economic and Social Council, according to a specific pattern of equitable geographical representation, from among experts nominated by Member States.
The Committee did not meet in 1989.

Members:
To serve until 31 December 1990: Cheng Weiqiu (China), Roger S. Clark (New Zealand), Dusan Cotic (Yugoslavia), Hedi Fessi (Tunisia), Eugène Jules Henri Frencken (Belgium), Vasily P. Ignatov (USSR), Albert Llewelyn Olawole Metzger (Sierra Leone), Benjamín Miguel-Harb (Bolivia), Jorge Arturo Montero Castro (Costa Rica), Abdul Karim Nasution (Indonesia), Victor Ramanitra (Madagascar), Simone Andrée Rozes (France), Minoru Shikita (Japan), Adolfo Luis Tamini (Argentina).

To serve until 31 December 1992: Ramón de la Cruz Ochoa (Cuba), Trevor Percival Frank De Silva (Sri Lanka), David Faulkner (United Kingdom), Ronald L. Gainer (United States), Nour El-Deen Khair (Jordan), Jacek Kubiak (Poland), Hama Mâmoudou (Niger), Farouk A. Mourad (Saudi Arabia), Salah Nour (Algeria), Bertin Pandi (Central African Republic), Gioacchino Polimeni (Italy), Miguel A. Sánchez Méndez (Colombia), Abdel Aziz Abdalla Shiddo (Sudan).

Committee on Economic, Social and Cultural Rights
The Committee on Economic, Social and Cultural Rights consists of 18 experts serving in their personal capacity, elected by the Economic and Social Council from among persons nominated by States parties to the International Covenant on Economic, Social and Cultural Rights. The experts have recognized competence in the field of human rights, with due consideration given to equitable geographical distribution and to the representation of different forms of social and legal systems. Members serve for four-year terms.

The Committee held its third session at Geneva from 6 to 24 February 1989.

Members:
To serve until 31 December 1990: Philip Alston, *Rapporteur* (Australia); Ibrahim Ali Badawi El-Sheikh, *Chairman* (Egypt); Sami Glaiel (Syrian Arab Republic); Valeri I. Kouznetsov (USSR); Jaime Alberto Marchán Romero (Ecuador); Alexandre Muterahejuru (Rwanda); Bruno Simma (Federal Republic of Germany); Chikako Taya (Japan); Javier Wimer Zambrano (Mexico).
To serve until 31 December 1992: Juan Alvarez Vita, *Vice-Chairman* (Peru); Mohamed Lamine Fofana (Guinea); María de los Angeles Jiménez Butragueño (Spain); Samba Cor Konate (Senegal); Vassil Mratchkov (Bulgaria); Wladyslaw Neneman, *Vice-Chairman* (Poland); Kenneth Osborne Rattray (Jamaica); Mikis Demetriou Sparsis, *Vice-Chairman* (Cyprus); Philippe Texier (France).

Intergovernmental Working Group of Experts on International Standards of Accounting and Reporting
The Intergovernmental Working Group of Experts on International Standards of Accounting and Reporting, which reports to the Commission on Transnational Corporations, consists of 34 members, elected for three-year terms by the Economic and Social Council according to a specific pattern of equitable geographical distribution. Each State elected appoints an expert with appropriate experience in accounting and reporting.

The Group held its seventh session at United Nations Headquarters from 7 to 17 March 1989.

Members:
To serve until 31 December 1990:[a] Brazil, Canada, China, France, Kenya, Norway, Spain, Swaziland, Switzerland, USSR, Zaire.
To serve until 31 December 1991:[b] Argentina,[c] Chile,[c] Cyprus, Czechoslovakia, Germany, Federal Republic of, India, Italy, Japan, Jordan,[c] Malawi, Netherlands, Nigeria, Peru,[c] Uganda, United Kingdom.

[a]Six seats allocated to two members each from African, Asian and Latin American and Caribbean States remained unfilled in 1989.
[b]Two seats allocated to one member each from African and Eastern European States remained unfilled in 1989.
[c]Elected on 23 May 1989 (decision 1989/160).

Chairman: S. R. Singh (India).
Vice-Chairmen: Victor P. Bogomolov (USSR), John H. N. Kosieyo (Kenya), Eliseu Martins (Brazil).
Rapporteur: John Bagnall (Canada).

United Nations Group of Experts on Geographical Names
The United Nations Group of Experts on Geographical Names represents various geographical/linguistic divisions, of which there

[20]YUN 1975, p. 734, ESC res. 1973(LIX), 30 July 1975.

were 19 in 1989, as follows: Africa Central; Africa East; Africa West; Arabic; Asia East (other than China); Asia South-East and Pacific South-West; Asia South-West (other than Arabic); Celtic; China; Dutch- and German-speaking; East Central and South-East Europe; East Mediterranean (other than Arabic); India; Latin America; Norden; Romano-Hellenic; Union of Soviet Socialist Republics; United Kingdom; United States of America/Canada.

The Group of Experts held its fourteenth session at Geneva from 17 to 26 May 1989.

Chairman: Henri Dorion (Canada).
Vice-Chairman: Abdelhadi Tazi (Morocco).
Rapporteur: P. J. Woodman (United Kingdom).

Administrative Committee on Co-ordination

The Administrative Committee on Co-ordination held three sessions in 1989: its first regular session at Geneva from 19 to 21 April; a special session at Geneva on 5 July; and its second regular session at United Nations Headquarters on 19 and 20 October.

The membership of ACC, under the chairmanship of the Secretary-General of the United Nations, includes the executive heads of ILO, FAO, UNESCO, ICAO, WHO, the World Bank, IMF, UPU, ITU, WMO, IMO, WIPO, IFAD, UNIDO, IAEA and the secretariat of the Contracting Parties to GATT.

Also taking part in the work of ACC are the United Nations Director-General for Development and International Economic Co-operation; the Under-Secretaries-General for International Economic and Social Affairs, for Administration and Management, and for Technical Co-operation for Development; and the executive heads of UNCTAD, UNDP, UNEP, UNFPA, UNHCR, UNICEF, UNITAR, UNRWA and WFP.

ACC has established subsidiary bodies on organizational, administrative and substantive questions.

Other related bodies

International Research and Training Institute for the Advancement of Women (INSTRAW)

The International Research and Training Institute for the Advancement of Women, a body of the United Nations financed through voluntary contributions, functions under the authority of a Board of Trustees.

BOARD OF TRUSTEES

The Board of Trustees is composed of 11 members serving in their individual capacity, appointed by the Economic and Social Council on the nomination of States; and *ex-officio* members. Members serve for three-year terms, with a maximum of two terms.

The Board, which reports periodically to the Council and where appropriate to the General Assembly, held its ninth session at Santo Domingo, Dominican Republic, from 20 to 24 February 1989.

Members (until 30 June 1989):
To serve until 30 June 1989: Inés Alberdi (Spain); Siga Seye (Senegal); Berta Torrijos de Arosemena, *Vice-President* (Panama).
To serve until 30 June 1990: Daniela Colombo (Italy); Tawhida O. Hadra, *Rapporteur* (Sudan); Achie Sudiarti Luhulima (Indonesia).
To serve until 30 June 1991: Fabiola Cuvi Ortiz (Ecuador); Awa Diallo (Mali); Elena Atanassova Lagadinova (Bulgaria); Gule Afruz Mahbub (Bangladesh); Kristin Tornes, *President* (Norway).

On 23 May 1989 (decision 1989/160), the Economic and Social Council appointed the following three members for a three-year term beginning on 1 July 1989 to fill the vacancies occurring on 30 June: Virginia Olivo de Celli (Venezuela), Penelope Ruth Fenwick (New Zealand), Victoria N. Okobi (Nigeria).

Members (from 1 July 1989):
To serve until 30 June 1990: Daniela Colombo (Italy), Tawhida O. Hadra (Sudan), Achie Sudiarti Luhulima (Indonesia).

To serve until 30 June 1991: Fabiola Cuvi Ortiz (Ecuador), Awa Diallo (Mali), Elena Atanassova Lagadinova (Bulgaria), Gule Afruz Mahbub (Bangladesh), Kristin Tornes (Norway).
To serve until 30 June 1992: Virginia Olivo de Celli (Venezuela), Penelope Ruth Fenwick (New Zealand), Victoria N. Okobi (Nigeria).

Ex-officio members: The Director of the Institute, and a representative of the Secretary-General, each of the regional commissions and the Institute's host country (Dominican Republic).
Director of the Institute: Dunja Pastizzi-Ferencic.

United Nations Children's Fund (UNICEF)

EXECUTIVE BOARD

The UNICEF Executive Board, which reports to the Economic and Social Council and, as appropriate, to the General Assembly, consists of 41 members elected by the Council from Member States of the United Nations or members of the specialized agencies or of IAEA, for three-year terms.

In 1989, the Board held its regular session from 17 to 28 April and (with its composition as of 1 August) an organizational session on 12 June and 20 December and a special session from 18 to 22 December, all at United Nations Headquarters.

Members (until 31 July 1989):
To serve until 31 July 1989: Canada, China, Colombia, Germany, Federal Republic of, Guyana, Lesotho, Norway, Poland, Thailand, Turkey.
To serve until 31 July 1990: Australia, Belgium, Benin, India, Indonesia, Liberia, Philippines, Switzerland, Uruguay, Yugoslavia.
To serve until 31 July 1991: Bangladesh, Bolivia, Byelorussian SSR, Cameroon, Egypt, France, Italy, Japan, Mexico, Nicaragua, Nigeria, Oman, Pakistan, Republic of Korea, Sao Tome and Principe, Sudan, Sweden, Uganda, USSR, United Kingdom, United States.

Chairman: Torild Skard (Norway).
First Vice-Chairman: Suyono Yahya (Indonesia).
Second Vice-Chairman: Stanislaw Trepczynski (Poland).
Third Vice-Chairman: Michael O. Ononaiye (Nigeria).
Fourth Vice-Chairman: Chandrashekhar Dasgupta (India).

On 23 May 1989 (decision 1989/160), the Economic and Social Council elected the following 10 members for a three-year term beginning on 1 August 1989 to fill the vacancies occurring on 31 July: Barbados, Canada, China, Finland, Germany, Federal Republic of, Netherlands, Peru, Poland, Thailand, Zimbabwe.

Members (from 1 August 1989):
To serve until 31 July 1990: Australia, Belgium, Benin, India, Indonesia, Liberia, Philippines, Switzerland, Uruguay, Yugoslavia.
To serve until 31 July 1991: Bangladesh, Bolivia, Byelorussian SSR, Cameroon, Egypt, France, Italy, Japan, Mexico, Nicaragua, Nigeria, Oman, Pakistan, Republic of Korea, Sao Tome and Principe, Sudan, Sweden, Uganda, USSR, United Kingdom, United States.
To serve until 31 July 1992: Barbados, Canada, China, Finland, Germany, Federal Republic of, Netherlands, Peru, Poland, Thailand, Zimbabwe.

Chairman: Margarita Diéguez (Mexico).
First Vice-Chairman: Lisbet Palme (Sweden).
Second Vice-Chairman: Stanislaw Trepczynski (Poland).
Third Vice-Chairman: Suyono Yahya (Indonesia).
Fourth Vice-Chairman: Paul Bamela Engo (Cameroon).

Executive Director of UNICEF: James P. Grant.

COMMITTEE ON ADMINISTRATION AND FINANCE

The Committee on Administration and Finance is a committee of the whole of the UNICEF Executive Board.

Chairman: Nicole Senécal (Canada) (until 31 July), Hoda Badran (Egypt) (from 1 August).
Vice-Chairman: Rawle Lucas (Guyana) (until 31 July), Takeshi Kagami (Japan) (from 1 August).

PROGRAMME COMMITTEE
The Programme Committee is a committee of the whole of the UNICEF Executive Board.

Chairman: Margarita Diéguez (Mexico) (until 31 July), Frank Majoor (Netherlands) (from 1 August).
Vice-Chairman: Hoda Badran (Egypt) (until 31 July), Gabriel Vidart (Uruguay) (from 1 August).

UNESCO/UNICEF Joint Committee on Education

In April 1989, the UNICEF Executive Board approved the establishment of the UNESCO/UNICEF Joint Committee on Education. The Committee consists of: six members of the UNICEF Executive Board, among whom are the chairmen of the Executive Board and the Programme Committee who serve *ex officio;* and six members of the UNESCO Executive Board.

The Joint Committee, which was to meet biennially, did not meet in 1989.

UNICEF/WHO Joint Committee on Health Policy

The UNICEF/WHO Joint Committee on Health Policy consists of: six members of the UNICEF Executive Board, among whom are the chairmen of the Executive Board and the Programme Committee who serve *ex officio;* and six members of the WHO Executive Board.

The Joint Committee, which meets biennially, held its twenty-seventh session at Geneva from 23 to 25 January 1989.

Members:
UNICEF ex-officio members: Immita Cornaz (Switzerland);[a] Margarita Diéguez, *Chairman* (Mexico).
Elected by UNICEF: Z. R. Akplogan (Benin); I. Dogramaci (Turkey); L. Vogel, *Rapporteur* (United States); Suyono Yahya (Indonesia).
Appointed by WHO: Dr. N. Blackman (Guyana);[b] J.-F. Girard (France); Dr. H. Oweis (Jordan); R. Figueira Santos, *Rapporteur* (Brazil); Dr. O. Tall (Mali); Dr. S. Tapa (Tonga).

[a]Alternate for Torild Skard.
[b]Alternate for K. G. Rahman.

United Nations Development Programme (UNDP)

GOVERNING COUNCIL

The Governing Council of UNDP, which reports to the Economic and Social Council and through it to the General Assembly, consists of 48 members, elected by the Council from Member States of the United Nations or members of the specialized agencies or of IAEA. Twenty-seven seats are allocated to developing countries as follows: 11 to African countries, 9 to Asian countries and Yugoslavia, and 7 to Latin American countries. Twenty-one seats are allocated to economically more advanced countries as follows: 17 to Western European and other countries, and 4 to Eastern European countries. The term of office is three years, one third of the members being elected each year.

In 1989, the Governing Council held, at United Nations Headquarters, an organizational meeting on 21 and 24 February, a special session from 21 to 24 February and its thirty-sixth session from 5 to 30 June.

Members:
To serve until the day preceding the February 1990 organizational session: Argentina, Burkina Faso, Colombia, Ecuador, Fiji, Finland, German Democratic Republic, Germany, Federal Republic of, India, Liberia, Netherlands, Poland, Sudan, Switzerland, Thailand, Turkey.
To serve until the day preceding the February 1991 organizational session: Austria, China, Cuba, Ghana, Guatemala, Italy, Japan, Libyan Arab Jamahiriya, Norway, Peru, Syrian Arab Republic, USSR, United Kingdom, United States, Yugoslavia, Zimbabwe.

To serve until the day preceding the February 1992 organizational session: Australia, Belgium, Brazil, Canada, Cyprus, France, Guinea-Bissau, Kenya, Mozambique, Pakistan, Philippines, Romania, Sao Tome and Principe, Spain, Sweden, Zaire.

President: Nitya Pibulsonggram (Thailand).
Vice-Presidents: Edward Obeng Kufuor (Ghana), Dominik Langenbacher (Switzerland), Ion Popescu (Romania), Juan Salazar-Sancisi (Ecuador).

On 23 May 1989 (decision 1989/160), the Economic and Social Council elected the following 16 members for a three-year term beginning on the first day of the February 1990 organizational session to fill the vacancies occurring the preceding day: Bulgaria, Denmark, Djibouti, Germany, Federal Republic of, Guyana, India, Malaysia, Mauritania, Netherlands, Nigeria, Poland, Portugal, Sri Lanka, Switzerland, Uruguay, Venezuela.

Administrator of UNDP: William H. Draper III.[a]
Associate Administrator: G. Arthur Brown (until June 1989), Andrew Joseph (from 1 October).

[a]On 1 November 1989 (decision 44/307), the General Assembly confirmed his reappointment for a further four-year term beginning on 1 January 1990.

BUDGETARY AND FINANCE COMMITTEE
The Budgetary and Finance Committee, a committee of the whole, held a series of meetings at United Nations Headquarters between 5 and 30 June 1989.

Chairman: Dominik Langenbacher (Switzerland).
Rapporteur: Malgorzata Zachorowska (Poland).

COMMITTEE OF THE WHOLE
The Governing Council resolved itself into a Committee of the Whole and held meetings between 7 and 11 June 1989 to consider matters related to programme management. The President of the Council presided.

United Nations Research Institute for Social Development (UNRISD)

BOARD OF DIRECTORS
The Board of Directors of UNRISD reports to the Economic and Social Council through the Commission for Social Development. The Board consists of:

The Chairman, appointed by the Secretary-General: Keith Griffin (United Kingdom);
Seven members, nominated by the Commission for Social Development and confirmed by the Economic and Social Council (to serve until 30 June 1989):[a] Ismail Sabri Abdallah (Egypt), Sartaj Aziz (Pakistan), Vida Cok (Yugoslavia), Louis Emmerij (Netherlands), Ulf Hannerz (Sweden); (to serve until 30 June 1991): Lucio Kowarick (Brazil);
Seven other members, as follows: a representative of the Secretary-General, the Director of the Latin American and Caribbean Institute for Economic and Social Planning, the Director of the African Institute for Economic Development and Planning, the Executive Secretary of ESCWA, the Director of UNRISD *(ex officio)*, and the representatives of two of the following specialized agencies appointed as members and observers in annual rotation: ILO and FAO (members); UNESCO and WHO (observers).

[a]One seat was vacant.

On 23 May 1989 (decision 1989/160), the Economic and Social Council confirmed the nomination by the Commission for Social Development of the following for terms beginning on 1 July to fill the vacancies occurring on 30 June: for a four-year term, Ingrid Eide (Norway), Maureen O'Neil (Canada); for a two-year term, Ismail Sabri Abdallah (Egypt), Sartaj Aziz (Pakistan), Vida Cok (Yugoslavia), Louis Emmerij (Netherlands).

On 24 May (decision 1989/132), the Council endorsed the Commission's decision to increase the number of nominated members from 7 to 10. On 6 July (decision 1989/181), the Council confirmed the nomination of the following three members for terms beginning on 6 July and ending on 30 June 1993: Lars Anell (Sweden), Tatyana Ivanovna Koryagina (USSR), Akilagpa Sawyerr (Ghana).

Director of the Institute: Dharam Ghai.

World Food Programme

COMMITTEE ON FOOD AID POLICIES AND PROGRAMMES

The Committee on Food Aid Policies and Programmes, the governing body of WFP, reports annually to the Economic and Social Council, the FAO Council and the World Food Council. It consists of 30 members, of which 15 are elected by the Economic and Social Council and 15 by the FAO Council, from Member States of the United Nations or from members of FAO. Members serve for three-year terms.

The Committee held two sessions in 1989, at Rome, Italy: its twenty-seventh from 29 May to 3 June, and its twenty-eighth from 11 to 13 December.

Members:
To serve until 31 December 1989:
  Elected by Economic and Social Council: Hungary, India, Italy, Sweden, Tunisia.
  Elected by FAO Council: Australia, Bangladesh, Canada, Saudi Arabia, United States *(Chairman)*.
To serve until 31 December 1990:
  Elected by Economic and Social Council: Belgium, Japan, Kenya *(First Vice-Chairman)*, Norway, Pakistan.
  Elected by FAO Council: Brazil, Cameroon, China, Madagascar, Netherlands.
To serve until 31 December 1991:
  Elected by Economic and Social Council: Colombia, Cuba, Denmark *(Second Vice-Chairman)*, Niger, United Kingdom.
  Elected by FAO Council: Congo, France, Germany, Federal Republic of, Mexico, Zambia.

On 23 May 1989 (decision 1989/160), the Economic and Social Council elected Finland, Hungary, India, Italy and the Sudan,

and, on 30 November 1989, the FAO Council elected Australia, Bangladesh, Canada, Guinea and the United States, all for a three-year term beginning on 1 January 1990 to fill the vacancies occurring on 31 December 1989.

Executive Director of WFP: James Charles Ingram.
Deputy Executive Director: Salahuddin Ahmed.

Conference

Fourth United Nations Regional Cartographic Conference for the Americas

The Fourth United Nations Regional Cartographic Conference for the Americas was held at United Nations Headquarters from 23 to 27 January 1989. Participating were the following 39 States:

Algeria, Argentina, Bahamas, Barbados, Bolivia, Brazil, Canada, Chile, China, Cyprus, Ecuador, El Salvador, Finland, France, Gabon, German Democratic Republic, Germany, Federal Republic of, Guinea, Holy See (Observer), Honduras, Hungary, Iraq, Mauritius, Mexico, Morocco, Norway, Peru, Poland, Qatar, Republic of Korea (Observer), Saint Vincent and the Grenadines, Saudi Arabia, Spain, Sweden, Syrian Arab Republic, USSR, United Kingdom, United States, Venezuela.

President: Fred Campbell (Canada).
First Vice-President: C. E. R. Williams (Saint Vincent and the Grenadines).
Second Vice-President: E. E. Rutsch (Argentina).
Rapporteur: Richard D. Sanchez (United States).

Chairmen of committees:
  Committee I: Z. A. Jiwani (Canada).
  Committee II: Carlos Galindo Contreras (Mexico).
  Committee III: Paulo César Teixeira Trino (Brazil).
  Committee IV: Gottfried Konecny (Federal Republic of Germany).
  Committee V: Lowell Starr (United States).

Trusteeship Council

Article 86 of the United Nations Charter lays down that the Trusteeship Council shall consist of the following:

Members of the United Nations administering Trust Territories;
Permanent members of the Security Council which do not administer Trust Territories;
As many other members elected for a three-year term by the General Assembly as will ensure that the membership of the Council is equally divided between United Nations Members which administer Trust Territories and those which do not.[a]

[a]During 1989, only one Member of the United Nations was an administering member of the Trusteeship Council, while four permanent members of the Security Council continued as non-administering members.

MEMBERS

Member administering a Trust Territory: United States.
Non-administering members: China, France, USSR, United Kingdom.

SESSIONS

Nineteenth special session: United Nations Headquarters, 16 and 17 March 1989.
Fifty-sixth session: United Nations Headquarters, 15 May to 1 August 1989.

OFFICERS

President: Jean-Michel Gaussot (France) (19th special session), John A. Birch (United Kingdom) (56th session).
Vice-President: John A. Birch (United Kingdom) (19th special session), Jean-Michel Gaussot (France) (56th session).

United Nations Visiting Mission to Palau, Trust Territory of the Pacific Islands, 1989

Members: Jean-Michel Gaussot, *Chairman* (France); J. Stephen Smith, *Vice-Chairman* (United Kingdom).

International Court of Justice

Judges of the Court

The International Court of Justice consists of 15 Judges elected for nine-year terms by the General Assembly and the Security Council.

The following were the Judges of the Court serving in 1989, listed in the order of precedence:

Judge	Country of nationality	End of term[a]
José María Ruda, *President*	Argentina	1991
Kéba Mbaye, *Vice-President*	Senegal	1991
Manfred Lachs	Poland	1994
Taslim Olawale Elias	Nigeria	1994
Shigeru Oda	Japan	1994
Roberto Ago	Italy	1997
Stephen M. Schwebel	United States	1997
Sir Robert Y. Jennings	United Kingdom	1991
Mohammed Bedjaoui	Algeria	1997
Ni Zhengyu	China	1994
Jens Evensen	Norway	1994
Nikolai K. Tarassov	USSR	1997
Gilbert Guillaume	France	1991
Mohamed Shahabuddeen	Guyana	1997
Raghunandan Swarup Pathak[b]	India	1991

[a]Term expires on 5 February of the year indicated.
[b]Elected by the General Assembly (decision 43/327) and the Security Council on 18 April 1989 to fill a vacancy resulting from the death in 1988 of Nagendra Singh (India).

Registrar: Eduardo Valencia-Ospina.
Deputy Registrar: Bernard Noble.

Chamber formed in the case concerning
Elettronica Sicula S.p.A. (ELSI)
(United States of America v. Italy)
Members: José María Ruda *(President)*, Shigeru Oda, Roberto Ago, Stephen M. Schwebel, Sir Robert Y. Jennings.

Chamber formed in the case concerning the *Land, Island and Maritime Frontier Dispute (El Salvador/Honduras)*
Members: José Sette-Camara *(President)*, Shigeru Oda, Sir Robert Y. Jennings.
Ad hoc members: Nicolas Valticos, Michel Virally.[a]

[a]Died on 27 January 1989; replaced on 13 December by Santiago Torres Bernárdez.

Chamber of Summary Procedure
(as constituted by the Court on 10 February 1989)
Members: José María Ruda *(ex officio)*, Kéba Mbaye *(ex officio)*, Sir Robert Y. Jennings, Ni Zhengyu, Jens Evensen.
Substitute members: Gilbert Guillaume, Mohamed Shahabuddeen.

Parties to the Court's Statute

All Members of the United Nations are *ipso facto* parties to the Statute of the International Court of Justice. Also parties to it in 1989 were the following non-members: Liechtenstein, Nauru, San Marino, Switzerland.

States accepting the compulsory jurisdiction of the Court

Declarations made by the following States, a number with reservations, accepting the Court's compulsory jurisdiction (or made under the Statute of the Permanent Court of International Justice and deemed to be an acceptance of the jurisdiction of the International Court) were in force at the end of 1989:

Australia, Austria, Barbados, Belgium, Botswana, Canada, Colombia, Costa Rica, Cyprus, Democratic Kampuchea, Denmark, Dominican Republic, Egypt, El Salvador, Finland, Gambia, Guinea-Bissau,[a] Haiti, Honduras, India, Japan, Kenya, Liberia, Liechtenstein, Luxembourg, Malawi, Malta, Mauritius, Mexico, Nauru, Netherlands, New Zealand, Nicaragua, Nigeria, Norway, Pakistan, Panama, Philippines, Portugal, Senegal, Somalia, Sudan, Suriname, Swaziland, Sweden, Switzerland, Togo, Uganda, United Kingdom, Uruguay, Zaire.[a]

[a]Filed its declaration of acceptance on 7 August and 8 February 1989, respectively.

United Nations organs and specialized and related agencies authorized to request advisory opinions from the Court

Authorized by the United Nations Charter to request opinions on any legal question: General Assembly, Security Council.

Authorized by the General Assembly in accordance with the Charter to request opinions on legal questions arising within the scope of their activities: Economic and Social Council, Trusteeship Council, Interim Committee of the General Assembly, Committee on Applications for Review of Administrative Tribunal Judgements, ILO, FAO, UNESCO, ICAO, WHO, World Bank, IFC, IDA, IMF, ITU, WMO, IMO, WIPO, IFAD, UNIDO, IAEA.

Committees of the Court

BUDGETARY AND ADMINISTRATIVE COMMITTEE
Members: José María Ruda *(ex officio)*, Kéba Mbaye *(ex officio)*, Taslim Olawale Elias, Stephen M. Schwebel, Mohammed Bedjaoui, Nikolai K. Tarassov, Gilbert Guillaume.

COMMITTEE ON RELATIONS
Members: Mohammed Bedjaoui, Ni Zhengyu, Jens Evensen.

LIBRARY COMMITTEE
Members: Shigeru Oda, Sir Robert Y. Jennings, Ni Zhengyu.

RULES COMMITTEE
Members: Manfred Lachs, Kéba Mbaye, Shigeru Oda, Roberto Ago, Sir Robert Y. Jennings, Ni Zhengyu, Nikolai K. Tarassov, Mohamed Shahabuddeen.

Other United Nations−related bodies

The following bodies are not subsidiary to any principal organ of the United Nations but were established by an international treaty instrument or arrangement sponsored by the United Nations and are thus related to the Organization and its work. These bodies, often referred to as "treaty organs", are serviced by the United Nations Secretariat and may be financed in part or wholly from the Organization's regular budget, as authorized by the General Assembly, to which most of them report annually.

Commission against *Apartheid* in Sports

The Commission against *Apartheid* in Sports was established under the International Convention against *Apartheid* in Sports.[21] It consists of 15 members elected by the States parties to the Convention to serve in their individual capacity, with due regard for equitable geographical distribution and for representation of the principal legal systems, particular attention being paid to the participation of persons having experience in sports administration. Members serve four-year terms, except that after the first election on 2 March 1989 nine were chosen by lot to serve for two years.

The Commission, which reports annually to the General Assembly through the Secretary-General, held its first session at United Nations Headquarters from 18 to 20 October 1989.

[21]YUN 1985, p. 167, GA res. 40/64 G, annex, article 11, 10 Dec. 1985.

Members:
To serve until 2 March 1991: Hamad Abdelaziz Al-Kawari, *Vice-Chairman* (Qatar); Ahmad Fathi Al-Masri (Syrian Arab Republic); Hocine Djoudi (Algeria); James Victor Gbeho, *Chairman* (Ghana); Lionel Hurst (Antigua and Barbuda); Besley Maycock, *Rapporteur* (Barbados); Abraham Ordia (Nigeria); Vladimir Platonov (Ukrainian SSR); Zoumana Traoré (Burkina Faso).
To serve until 2 March 1993: Raúl González Rodríguez (Mexico);[a] Allan Rae (Jamaica); Tesfaye Shafo (Ethiopia); Claudio Teehankee (Philippines); Boris Topornin (USSR); Georg Zorowka, *Vice-Chairman* (German Democratic Republic).

[a]Replaced Fernando Alanís Camino (Mexico) who resigned in May 1989.

Committee against Torture

The Committee against Torture was established under the Convention against Torture and Other Cruel, Inhuman or Degrading Treatment or Punishment.[22] It consists of 10 experts elected for four-year terms by the States parties to the Convention to serve in their personal capacity, with due regard for equitable geographical distribution and for the usefulness of the participation of some persons having legal experience.

In 1989, the Committee, which reports annually to the General Assembly, held two sessions, at Geneva: its second from 17 to 28 April and its third from 13 to 24 November.

Members:
To serve until 31 December 1989: Alexis Dipanda Mouelle, *Vice-Chairman* (Cameroon); Yuri A. Khitrin (USSR); Dimitar Nikolov Mikhailov, *Rapporteur* (Bulgaria); Bent Sorensen (Denmark); Joseph Voyame, *Chairman* (Switzerland).
To serve until 31 December 1991: Alfredo R. A. Bengzon, *Vice-Chairman* (Philippines); Peter Thomas Burns (Canada); Christine Chanet (France); Socorro Díaz Palacios (Mexico); Ricardo Gil Lavedra, *Vice-Chairman* (Argentina).

On 28 November 1989, the States parties re-elected the following for a four-year term beginning on 1 January 1990 to fill the vacancies occurring on 31 December 1989: Alexis Dipanda Mouelle (Cameroon), Yuri A. Khitrin (USSR), Dimitar Nikolov Mikhailov (Bulgaria), Bent Sorensen (Denmark), Joseph Voyame (Switzerland).

Committee on the Elimination of Discrimination against Women

The Committee on the Elimination of Discrimination against Women was established under the Convention on the Elimination of All Forms of Discrimination against Women.[23] It consists of 23 experts elected for four-year terms by the States parties to the Convention to serve in their personal capacity, with due regard for equitable geographical distribution and for representation of the different forms of civilization and principal legal systems.

The Committee, which reports annually to the General Assembly through the Economic and Social Council, held its eighth session at Vienna from 20 February to 3 March 1989.

Members:
To serve until 15 April 1990: Ryoko Akamatsu (Japan); Ivanka Corti (Italy); Hadja Assa Diallo Soumare (Mali); Ruth Escobar (Brazil); Norma M. Forde (Barbados); Guan Minqian, *Vice-Chairman* (China); Zagorka Ilic (Yugoslavia); Elvira Novikova (USSR); Lily Pilataxi de Arenas, *Vice-Chairman* (Ecuador); Pudjiwati Sayogyo (Indonesia); Mervat Tallawy (Egypt); Rose N. Ukeje, *Rapporteur* (Nigeria).
To serve until 15 April 1992: Ana Maria Alfonsín de Fasan (Argentina); Désirée P. Bernard (Guyana); Carlota Bustelo García del Real (Spain); Elizabeth Evatt, *Chairman* (Australia); Grethe Fenger-Möller (Denmark); Aida González Martínez (Mexico); Chryssanthi Laiou-Antoniou (Greece); Edith Oeser, *Vice-Chairman* (German Democratic Republic); Hanna Beate Schöpp-Schilling (Federal Republic of Germany); Kongit Sinegiorgis (Ethiopia); Kissem Walla-Tchangai (Togo).

Committee on the Elimination of Racial Discrimination

The Committee on the Elimination of Racial Discrimination was established under the International Convention on the Elimination of All Forms of Racial Discrimination.[24] It consists of 18 experts elected for four-year terms by the States parties to the Conven-tion to serve in their personal capacity, with due regard for equitable geographical distribution and for representation of the different forms of civilization and principal legal systems.

The Committee, which reports annually to the General Assembly through the Secretary-General, held its thirty-seventh session at Geneva from 7 August to 1 September 1989.

Members:
To serve until 19 January 1990: Mahmoud Aboul-Nasr (Egypt); Hamzat Ahmadu (Nigeria); Michael Parker Banton (United Kingdom); Mohamed Omer Beshir (Sudan); André Braunschweig (France); George O. Lamptey, *Chairman* (Ghana); Karl Josef Partsch, *Vice-Chairman* (Federal Republic of Germany); Agha Shahi (Pakistan); Michael E. Sherifis (Cyprus).
To serve until 19 January 1992: Eduardo Ferrero Costa (Peru); Isi Foighel (Denmark); Ivan Garvalov, *Vice-Chairman* (Bulgaria); Yuri A. Reshetov (USSR); Jorge Rhenan Segura (Costa Rica); Shanti Sadiq Ali, *Rapporteur* (India); Song Shuhua (China); Kasimir Vidas (Yugoslavia); Mario Jorge Yutzis, *Vice-Chairman* (Argentina).

Conference on Disarmament

The Conference on Disarmament, the multilateral negotiating forum on disarmament, reports annually to the General Assembly and is serviced by the United Nations Secretariat. It was composed of 40 members in 1989.

During 1989, the Conference met at Geneva from 7 February to 27 April and from 13 June to 31 August.

Members: Algeria, Argentina, Australia, Belgium, Brazil, Bulgaria, Burma (Myanmar), Canada, China, Cuba, Czechoslovakia, Egypt, Ethiopia, France, German Democratic Republic, Germany, Federal Republic of, Hungary, India, Indonesia, Iran, Italy, Japan, Kenya, Mexico, Mongolia, Morocco, Netherlands, Nigeria, Pakistan, Peru, Poland, Romania, Sri Lanka, Sweden, USSR, United Kingdom, United States, Venezuela, Yugoslavia, Zaire.

The presidency, which rotates in English alphabetical order among the members, was held by the following in 1989: February, Italy; March, Japan; April and the recess between the first and second parts of the 1989 session, Kenya; June, Mexico; July, Mongolia; August and the recess until the 1990 session, Morocco.

Human Rights Committee

The Human Rights Committee was established under the International Covenant on Civil and Political Rights.[25] It consists of 18 experts elected by the States parties to the Covenant to serve in their personal capacity for four-year terms.

In 1989, the Committee, which reports annually to the General Assembly through the Economic and Social Council, held three sessions: its thirty-fifth at United Nations Headquarters from 20 March to 7 April, its thirty-sixth at Geneva from 10 to 28 July and its thirty-seventh at Geneva from 23 October to 10 November.

Members:
To serve until 31 December 1990: Nisuke Ando (Japan); Christine Chanet (France); Joseph A. L. Cooray, *Vice-Chairman* (Sri Lanka); Vojin Dimitrijevic, *Vice-Chairman* (Yugoslavia); Omran El-Shafei (Egypt); Joseph A. Mommersteeg (Netherlands); Birame Ndiaye (Senegal); Julio Prado Vallejo (Ecuador); Bertil Wennergren (Sweden).
To serve until 31 December 1992: Francisco José Aguilar Urbina (Costa Rica); Janos Fodor (Hungary); Rosalyn Higgins (United Kingdom); Rajsoomer Lallah, *Chairman* (Mauritius); Andreas V. Mavrommatis (Cyprus); Rein A. Myullerson (USSR); Fausto Pocar, *Rapporteur* (Italy); Alejandro Serrano Caldera, *Vice-Chairman* (Nicaragua); S. Amos Wako (Kenya).

---

[22]YUN 1984, p. 815, GA res. 39/46, annex, article 17, 10 Dec. 1984.
[23]YUN 1979, p. 898, GA res. 34/180, annex, article 17, 18 Dec. 1979.
[24]YUN 1965, p. 443, GA res. 2106 A (XX), annex, article 8, 21 Dec. 1965.
[25]YUN 1966, p. 427, GA res. 2200 A (XXI), annex, part IV, 16 Dec. 1966.

International Narcotics Control Board (INCB)

The International Narcotics Control Board, established under the Single Convention on Narcotic Drugs, 1961, as amended by the 1972 Protocol, consists of 13 members, elected by the Economic and Social Council for five-year terms, three from candidates nominated by WHO and 10 from candidates nominated by Members of the United Nations and parties to the Single Convention.

The Board held two sessions in 1989, at Vienna: its forty-fifth from 16 to 26 May, and its forty-sixth from 4 to 20 October.

Members:

To serve until 1 March 1990: Dr. Cai Zhi-ji, *Second Vice-President* (China); Dr. Diego Garcés-Giraldo (Colombia); Ben J. A. Huyghe-Braeckmans, *President* (Belgium); Mohsen Kchouk, *Rapporteur* (Tunisia); Manuel Quijano Narezo (Mexico);[a,b] Sahibzada Raoof Ali Khan (Pakistan).

To serve until 1 March 1992: Sirad Atmodjo (Indonesia);[b] Dr. Nikolai K. Barkov (USSR); Abdullahi S. Elmi, *First Vice-President* (Somalia); Betty C. Gough (United States); Dr. S. Oguz Kayaalp (Turkey);[b] Paul Reuter (France); Dr. Tulio Velásquez-Quevedo (Peru).

[a]Elected on 23 May 1989 (decision 1989/160) to fill a vacancy created by the death in April of Dr. John C. Ebie (Nigeria).
[b]Elected from candidates nominated by WHO.

On 23 May 1989 (decision 1989/160), the Economic and Social Council elected the following six members for a five-year term beginning on 2 March 1990 to fill the vacancies occurring on 1 March 1990: Dr. Cai Zhi-ji (China), Huáscar Cajías Kauffmann (Bolivia), Mohsen Kchouk (Tunisia), Mohammed Abbas Mansour (Egypt), Maruthi Vasudev Narayan Rao (India), Oskar Schröder (Federal Republic of Germany).

Preparatory Commission for the International Sea-Bed Authority and for the International Tribunal for the Law of the Sea

The Preparatory Commission for the International Sea-Bed Authority and for the International Tribunal for the Law of the Sea was established by the Third United Nations Conference on the Law of the Sea. It consists of States, Namibia (represented by the United Nations Council for Namibia), self-governing associated States, territories enjoying full internal self-government and international organizations which have signed or acceded to the United Nations Convention on the Law of the Sea. As of 31 December 1989, the Commission had 159 members.

In 1989, the Commission held its seventh session at Kingston, Jamaica, from 27 February to 23 March and meetings at United Nations Headquarters from 14 August to 1 September.

Members: Afghanistan, Algeria, Angola, Antigua and Barbuda, Argentina, Australia, Austria, Bahamas, Bahrain, Bangladesh, Barbados, Belgium, Belize, Benin, Bhutan, Bolivia, Botswana, Brazil, Brunei Darussalam, Bulgaria, Burkina Faso, Burma (Myanmar), Burundi, Byelorussian SSR, Cameroon, Canada, Cape Verde, Central African Republic, Chad, Chile, China, Colombia, Comoros, Congo, Cook Islands, Costa Rica, Côte d'Ivoire, Cuba, Cyprus, Czechoslovakia, Democratic Kampuchea, Democratic People's Republic of Korea, Democratic Yemen, Denmark, Djibouti, Dominica, Dominican Republic, Egypt, El Salvador, Equatorial Guinea, Ethiopia, European Economic Community, Fiji, Finland, France, Gabon, Gambia, German Democratic Republic, Ghana, Greece, Grenada, Guatemala, Guinea, Guinea-Bissau, Guyana, Haiti, Honduras, Hungary, Iceland, India, Indonesia, Iran, Iraq, Ireland, Italy, Jamaica, Japan, Kenya, Kuwait, Lao People's Democratic Republic, Lebanon, Lesotho, Liberia, Libyan Arab Jamahiriya, Liechtenstein, Luxembourg, Madagascar, Malawi, Malaysia, Maldives, Mali, Malta, Mauritania, Mauritius, Mexico, Monaco, Mongolia, Morocco, Mozambique, Namibia (United Nations Council for), Nauru, Nepal, Netherlands, New Zealand, Nicaragua, Niger, Nigeria, Niue, Norway, Oman, Pakistan, Panama, Papua New Guinea, Paraguay, Philippines, Poland, Portugal, Qatar, Republic of Korea, Romania, Rwanda, Saint Kitts and Nevis, Saint Lucia, Saint Vincent and the Grenadines, Samoa, Sao Tome and Principe, Saudi Arabia, Senegal, Seychelles, Sierra Leone, Singapore, Solomon Islands, Somalia, South Africa, Spain, Sri Lanka, Sudan, Suriname, Swaziland, Sweden, Switzerland, Thailand, Togo, Trinidad and Tobago, Tunisia, Tuvalu, Uganda, Ukrainian SSR, USSR, United Arab Emirates, United Republic of Tanzania, Uruguay, Vanuatu, Viet Nam, Yemen, Yugoslavia, Zaire, Zambia, Zimbabwe.

Chairman: José Luis Jesus (Cape Verde).
Vice-Chairmen: Algeria, Australia, Brazil, Cameroon, Chile, China, France, India, Iraq, Japan, Liberia, Nigeria, Sri Lanka, USSR.
Rapporteur-General: Kenneth O. Rattray (Jamaica).

CREDENTIALS COMMITTEE

Members: Austria, China, Colombia, Costa Rica, Côte d'Ivoire, Hungary, Ireland, Japan, Somalia.
Chairman: Helmut Türk (Austria).

GENERAL COMMITTEE

The General Committee consists of the Commission's Chairman, the 14 Vice-Chairmen, the Rapporteur-General and the 20 officers of the four Special Commissions.

SPECIAL COMMISSIONS

The four Special Commissions are each composed of all the members of the Commission:

Special Commission 1 (on the problem of land-based producers)
Chairman: Hasjim Djalal (Indonesia).
Vice-Chairmen: Austria, Cuba, Romania, Zambia.

Special Commission 2 (on the Enterprise)
Chairman: Lennox Ballah (Trinidad and Tobago).
Vice-Chairmen: Canada, Mongolia, Senegal, Yugoslavia.

Special Commission 3 (on the mining code)
Chairman: Jaap A. Walkate (Netherlands).
Vice-Chairmen: Gabon, Mexico, Pakistan, Poland.

Special Commission 4 (on the International Tribunal for the Law of the Sea)
Chairman: Günter Goerner (German Democratic Republic).
Vice-Chairmen: Colombia, Greece, Philippines, Sudan.

Principal members of the United Nations Secretariat

(as at 31 December 1989)

Secretariat

The Secretary-General: Javier Pérez de Cuéllar

Executive Office of the Secretary-General
Under-Secretary-General, Chef de Cabinet: Virendra Dayal
   Assistant Secretary-General, Executive Assistant to the Secretary-General: Alvaro de Soto
   Assistant Secretary-General, Chief of Protocol: Aly I. Teymour

Office of the Director-General for Development and International Economic Co-operation
Under-Secretary-General, Director-General: Antoine Blanca
   Assistant Secretary-General: Enrique ter Horst

Office of the Under-Secretary-General for Special Political Affairs
Under-Secretary-General: Marrack I. Goulding

Office of the Under-Secretary-General for Political and General Assembly Affairs and Secretariat Services
Under-Secretary-General: Ronald I. Spiers

Office for Research and the Collection of Information
Assistant Secretary-General: James O. C. Jonah

Office of Legal Affairs
Under-Secretary-General, the Legal Counsel: Carl-August Fleischhauer

Office for Ocean Affairs and the Law of the Sea
Under-Secretary-General, Special Representative of the Secretary-General: Satya N. Nandan

Department of Political and Security Council Affairs
Under-Secretary-General: Vasily S. Safronchuk
  Assistant Secretary-General, Centre against Apartheid: Sotirios Mousouris

Department for Special Political Questions, Regional Co-operation, Decolonization and Trusteeship
Under-Secretary-General, Co-ordinator, Special Economic Assistance Programmes: Abdulrahim Abby Farah

Department for Disarmament Affairs
Under-Secretary-General: Yasushi Akashi

Department of International Economic and Social Affairs
Under-Secretary-General: Rafeeuddin Ahmed
  Assistant Secretary-General for Development Research and Policy Analysis: P. Göran Ohlin

Department of Technical Co-operation for Development
Under-Secretary-General: Xie Qimei

Centre for Science and Technology for Development
Assistant Secretary-General, Executive Director: Sergio C. Trindade

United Nations Centre on Transnational Corporations
Assistant Secretary-General, Executive Director: Peter Hansen

United Nations Conference on Trade and Development
Under-Secretary-General, Secretary-General of the Conference: Kenneth K. S. Dadzie
  Assistant Secretary-General, Deputy Secretary-General of the Conference: Yves Berthelot

Office of the United Nations Disaster Relief Co-ordinator
Under-Secretary-General, Disaster Relief Co-ordinator: M'Hamed Essaafi

Office of the United Nations High Commissioner for Refugees
Under-Secretary-General, High Commissioner: vacant
  Assistant Secretary-General, Deputy High Commissioner: Arthur Eugene Dewey

United Nations Environment Programme
Under-Secretary-General, Executive Director: Mostafa Kamal Tolba
  Assistant Secretary-General, Deputy Executive Director: William H. Mansfield III
  Assistant Secretary-General, Assistant Executive Director, Office of the Environment Programme: Sveneld Evteev

United Nations Centre for Human Settlements
Under-Secretary-General, Executive Director: Arcot Ramachandran
  Assistant Secretary-General, Deputy Administrator, United Nations Habitat and Human Settlements Foundation: Sumihiro Kuyama

Economic Commission for Europe
Under-Secretary-General, Executive Secretary: Gerald Hinteregger

Economic and Social Commission for Asia and the Pacific
Under-Secretary-General, Executive Secretary: Shah A. M. S. Kibria

Economic Commission for Latin America and the Caribbean
Under-Secretary-General, Executive Secretary: Gert Rosenthal

Economic Commission for Africa
Under-Secretary-General, Executive Secretary: Adebayo Adedeji

Economic and Social Commission for Western Asia
Under-Secretary-General, Executive Secretary: Tayseer Abdel Jaber

United Nations Relief and Works Agency for Palestine Refugees in the Near East
Under-Secretary-General, Commissioner-General: Giorgio Giacomelli
  Assistant Secretary-General, Deputy Commissioner-General: William L. Eagleton

World Food Council
Assistant Secretary-General, Executive Director: Gerald Ion Trant

Department of Public Information
Under-Secretary-General: Thérèse Paquet-Sévigny

Department of Conference Services
Under-Secretary-General for Conference Services and Special Assignments: Eugeniusz Wyzner

Department of Administration and Management
Acting Under-Secretary-General: Luis María Gómez

OFFICE OF PROGRAMME PLANNING, BUDGET AND FINANCE
  Assistant Secretary-General, Controller: Luis María Gómez

OFFICE OF HUMAN RESOURCES MANAGEMENT
  Assistant Secretary-General: Kofi A. Annan

OFFICE OF GENERAL SERVICES
  Assistant Secretary-General: J. Richard Foran

United Nations Office at Geneva
Under-Secretary-General, Director-General of the United Nations Office at Geneva and head of the Centre for Human Rights: Jan Martenson
  Assistant Secretary-General, Personal Representative of the Secretary-General, Secretary-General of the Conference on Disarmament: Miljan Komatina

United Nations Office at Vienna
Under-Secretary-General, Director-General of the United Nations Office at Vienna and head of the Centre for Social Development and Humanitarian Affairs: Margaret Joan Anstee

Secretariats of subsidiary organs, special representatives and other related bodies

International Court of Justice Registry
Assistant Secretary-General, Registrar: Eduardo Valencia-Ospina

International Trade Centre UNCTAD/GATT
Assistant Secretary-General, Executive Director: Göran M. Engblom

Office of the Co-ordinator for United Nations Humanitarian and Economic Assistance Programmes relating to Afghanistan
Under-Secretary-General, Co-ordinator: Sadruddin Aga Khan

Office of the Personal Representative of the Secretary-General in Afghanistan and Pakistan
Assistant Secretary-General, Personal Representative of the Secretary-General: Benon Vahe Sevan

Office of the Special Representative of the Secretary-General for Humanitarian Affairs in South-East Asia
Under-Secretary-General, Special Representative of the Secretary-General: Rafeeuddin Ahmed

Office of the Special Representative of the Secretary-General for the Promotion of the United Nations Decade of Disabled Persons
Assistant Secretary-General, Special Representative of the Secretary-General: Hans Hoegh

Office of the Special Representative of the Secretary-General for Western Sahara
Under-Secretary-General, Special Representative of the Secretary-General: Héctor Gros Espiell

United Nations Angola Verification Mission
Chief Military Observer: Brigadier-General Péricles Ferreira Gomes

United Nations Assistance for the Reconstruction and Development of Lebanon
Special Representative for the Reconstruction and Development of Lebanon: Ragnar Gudmundsson

United Nations Children's Fund
Under-Secretary-General, Executive Director: James P. Grant
  Assistant Secretary-General, Deputy Executive Director, Operations: Karin Lokhaug
  Assistant Secretary-General, Deputy Executive Director, Programmes: Richard Jolly
  Assistant Secretary-General, Deputy Executive Director for External Relations: Marco Vianello-Chiodo

United Nations Development Programme
Administrator: William H. Draper III
  Associate Administrator: Andrew Joseph
  Deputy Assistant Administrator, Bureau for Finance and Administration, and Director, Division of Finance: M. Douglas Stafford
  Assistant Administrator and Director, Bureau for Special Activities: Aldo Ajello
  Assistant Administrator and Director, Bureau for Programme Policy and Evaluation: Ryokichi Hirono
  Assistant Administrator and Director, Office for Project Services: Bernt Bernander
  Executive Director, United Nations Population Fund: Dr. Nafis I. Sadik
  Deputy Executive Director, United Nations Population Fund: Tatsuro Kunugi
  Assistant Executive Director, United Nations Population Fund: Joseph van Arendonk
  Assistant Administrator and Regional Director, Regional Bureau for Africa: Pierre-Claver Damiba
  Assistant Administrator and Regional Director, Regional Bureau for Arab States and Europe: Mohamed Abdalla Nour
  Assistant Administrator and Regional Director, Regional Bureau for Asia and the Pacific: Krishnan Singh

  Assistant Administrator and Regional Director, Regional Bureau for Latin America and the Caribbean: Augusto Ramírez Ocampo

United Nations Disengagement Observer Force
Assistant Secretary-General, Force Commander: Major-General Adolf Radauer

United Nations Fund for Drug Abuse Control
Assistant Secretary-General, Executive Director: Giuseppe di Gennaro

United Nations Good Offices Mission in Afghanistan and Pakistan
Under-Secretary-General, Representative of the Secretary-General: Diego Cordovez
  Deputy Representative: Colonel Heikki Happonen

United Nations Institute for Training and Research
Under-Secretary-General, Executive Director: Michel Doo Kingué

United Nations Interim Force in Lebanon
Assistant Secretary-General, Force Commander: Lieutenant-General Lars-Eric Wahlgren

United Nations Iran-Iraq Military Observer Group
Personal Representative of the Secretary-General for Iran-Iraq: Jan K. Eliasson
  Assistant Secretary-General, Chief Military Observer: Major-General Slavko Jovic

United Nations Military Observer Group in India and Pakistan
Chief Military Observer: Brigadier-General Jeremiah Enright

United Nations Observer Group in Central America
Chief Military Observer: Major-General Agustín Quesada Gómez

United Nations Observer Mission to Verify the Electoral Process in Nicaragua
Under-Secretary-General, Personal Representative of the Secretary-General: Elliott Richardson
  Chief of Mission: Iqbal Riza

United Nations Peace-keeping Force in Cyprus
Under-Secretary-General, Special Representative of the Secretary-General: Oscar Héctor Camilión
  Assistant Secretary-General, Force Commander: Major-General Clive Milner

United Nations Transition Assistance Group
Under-Secretary-General, Special Representative of the Secretary-General: Martti Ahtisaari
  Assistant Secretary-General, Force Commander: Lieutenant-General Dewan Prem Chand

United Nations Truce Supervision Organization
Assistant Secretary-General, Chief of Staff: Lieutenant-General Martin Vadset

United Nations University
Under-Secretary-General, Rector: Heitor Gurgulino de Souza
  Assistant Secretary-General, Director, World Institute for Development Economics Research: Lalith R. U. Jayawardena

---

On 31 December 1989, the total number of staff of the United Nations holding permanent, probationary and fixed-term appointments with service or expected service of a year or more was 13,703. Of these, 4,814 were in the Professional and higher categories and 8,889 were in the General Service, Manual Worker and Field Service categories. Of the same total, 12,236 were regular staff serving at Headquarters or other established offices and 1,467 were assigned as project personnel to technical co-operation projects. In addition, UNRWA had some 17,752 local area staff, including temporary assistance.

Appendix IV

Agendas of United Nations principal organs in 1989

This appendix lists the items on the agendas of the General Assembly, the Security Council, the Economic and Social Council and the Trusteeship Council during 1989. For the Assembly and the Economic and Social Council, the column headed "Allocation" indicates the assignment of each item to plenary meetings or committees.

Agenda item titles have been shortened by omitting mention of reports, if any, following the subject of the item. Where the subject-matter of an item is not apparent from its title, the subject is identified in square brackets; this is not part of the title.

General Assembly

Agenda items considered at the resumed forty-third session
(14, 16 and 21 February, 1 and 7 March, 18-20 April,
11 July and 18 September 1989)

Item No.	*Title*	*Allocation*
2.	Minute of silent prayer or meditation.	Plenary
8.	Adoption of the agenda and organization of work.	Plenary
15.	Elections to fill vacancies in principal organs:	
	(c) Election of a member of the International Court of Justice.	Plenary
36.	Policies of *apartheid* of the Government of South Africa.	Plenary
37.	Question of Palestine.	Plenary
46.	Armed Israeli aggression against the Iraqi nuclear installations and its grave consequences for the established international system concerning the peaceful uses of nuclear energy, the non-proliferation of nuclear weapons and international peace and security.	Plenary
47.	Question of Cyprus.	1
48.	Consequences of the prolongation of the armed conflict between Iran and Iraq.	Plenary
82.	Development and international economic co-operation.	2nd
120.	Scale of assessments for the apportionment of the expenses of the United Nations.	2
137.	Report of the Committee on Relations with the Host Country.	3
153.	Financing of the United Nations Angola Verification Mission.[4]	5th
154.	Financing of the United Nations Transition Assistance Group.[4]	5th

Agenda of the forty-fourth session
(first part, 19 September–29 December 1989)

Item No.	*Title*	*Allocation*
1.	Opening of the session by the Chairman of the delegation of Argentina.	Plenary
2.	Minute of silent prayer or meditation.	Plenary
3.	Credentials of representatives to the forty-fourth session of the General Assembly:	
	(a) Appointment of the members of the Credentials Committee;	Plenary
	(b) Report of the Credentials Committee.	Plenary
4.	Election of the President of the General Assembly.	Plenary
5.	Election of the officers of the Main Committees.	Plenary
6.	Election of the Vice-Presidents of the General Assembly.	Plenary
7.	Notification by the Secretary-General under Article 12, paragraph 2, of the Charter of the United Nations.	Plenary
8.	Adoption of the agenda and organization of work.	Plenary
9.	General debate.	Plenary

[1]Not allocated; consideration deferred to the forty-fourth session.
[2]Allocated to the Fifth Committee at the first part of the session in 1988 but considered only in plenary meeting at the resumed session.
[3]Allocated to the Sixth Committee at the first part of the session in 1988 but considered only in plenary meeting at the resumed session.
[4]Item added at the resumed session.

Item No.	*Title*	*Allocation*
10.	Report of the Secretary-General on the work of the Organization.	Plenary
11.	Report of the Security Council.	Plenary
12.	Report of the Economic and Social Council.	Plenary, 2nd, 3rd, 4th, 5th
13.	Report of the International Court of Justice.	Plenary
14.	Report of the International Atomic Energy Agency.	Plenary
15.	Elections to fill vacancies in principal organs:	
	(a) Election of five non-permanent members of the Security Council;	Plenary
	(b) Election of eighteen members of the Economic and Social Council.	Plenary
16.	Elections to fill vacancies in subsidiary organs and other elections:	
	(a) Election of twenty-nine members of the Governing Council of the United Nations Environment Programme;	Plenary
	(b) Election of twelve members of the World Food Council;	Plenary
	(c) Election of seven members of the Committee for Programme and Co-ordination;	Plenary
	(d) Election of the United Nations High Commissioner for Refugees.	Plenary
17.	Appointments to fill vacancies in subsidiary organs and other appointments:	
	(a) Appointment of members of the Advisory Committee on Administrative and Budgetary Questions;	5th
	(b) Appointment of members of the Committee on Contributions;	5th
	(c) Appointment of a member of the Board of Auditors;	5th
	(d) Confirmation of the appointment of members of the Investments Committee;	5th
	(e) Appointment of members of the United Nations Administrative Tribunal;	5th
	(f) Appointment of members of the International Civil Service Commission;	5th
	(g) Appointment of members of the Committee on Conferences;	Plenary
	(h) Appointment of members of the Joint Inspection Unit;	Plenary
	(i) Confirmation of the appointment of the Administrator of the United Nations Development Programme;	Plenary
	(j) Appointment of the United Nations Commissioner for Namibia.	Plenary
18.	Implementation of the Declaration on the Granting of Independence to Colonial Countries and Peoples.	Plenary, 4th[5]
19.	Admission of new Members to the United Nations.	Plenary
20.	Return or restitution of cultural property to the countries of origin.	Plenary
21.	Achievements of the International Year of Peace.	Plenary
22.	Co-operation between the United Nations and the Organization of the Islamic Conference.	Plenary
23.	Co-operation between the United Nations and the League of Arab States.	Plenary
24.	Co-operation between the United Nations and the Latin American Economic System.	Plenary
25.	Short-term, medium-term and long-term solutions to the problems of natural disasters in Bangladesh.	2nd
26.	Judgment of the International Court of Justice of 27 June 1986 concerning military and paramilitary activities in and against Nicaragua: need for immediate compliance.	Plenary
27.	Co-operation between the United Nations and the Organization of African Unity.	Plenary
28.	Policies of *apartheid* of the Government of South Africa.	Plenary, SPC[6]
29.	Question of the Comorian island of Mayotte.	Plenary
30.	Law of the sea.	Plenary
31.	The situation in Kampuchea.	Plenary
32.	The situation in Afghanistan and its implications for international peace and security.	Plenary
33.	Zone of peace and co-operation of the South Atlantic.	Plenary
34.	The situation in Central America: threats to international peace and security and peace initiatives.	Plenary
35.	Question of the Falkland Islands (Malvinas).	Plenary, 4th[6]
36.	Question of Namibia.	Plenary, 4th[6]
37.	The situation in the Middle East.	Plenary
38.	Review of the efficiency of the administrative and financial functioning of the United Nations.	Plenary,[7] 5th
39.	Question of Palestine.	Plenary

[5]Chapters of the report of the Special Committee on the Situation with regard to the Implementation of the Declaration on the Granting of Independence to Colonial Countries and Peoples relating to specific Territories.

[6]Hearings of organizations and individuals having an interest in the question.

[7]Consideration of the report on the United Nations intergovernmental structure and functions in the economic and social fields.

Item No.	*Title*	*Allocation*
40.	Current financial crisis of the United Nations.	5th
41.	Question of peace, stability and co-operation in South-East Asia.	Plenary
42.	Declaration of the Assembly of Heads of State and Government of the Organization of African Unity on the aerial and naval military attack against the Socialist People's Libyan Arab Jamahiriya by the present United States Administration in April 1986.	Plenary
43.	Implementation of the resolutions of the United Nations.	Plenary
44.	Launching of global negotiations on international economic co-operation for development.	Plenary
45.	Question of equitable representation on and increase in the membership of the Security Council.	Plenary
46.	Armed Israeli aggression against the Iraqi nuclear installations and its grave consequences for the established international system concerning the peaceful uses of nuclear energy, the non-proliferation of nuclear weapons and international peace and security.	Plenary
47.	Question of Cyprus.	8
48.	Consequences of the prolongation of the armed conflict between Iran and Iraq.	Plenary
49.	Implementation of General Assembly resolution 43/62 concerning the signature and ratification of Additional Protocol I of the Treaty for the Prohibition of Nuclear Weapons in Latin America (Treaty of Tlatelolco).	1st
50.	Cessation of all nuclear-test explosions.	1st
51.	Amendment of the Treaty Banning Nuclear Weapon Tests in the Atmosphere, in Outer Space and under Water.	1st
52.	Urgent need for a comprehensive nuclear-test-ban treaty.	1st
53.	Establishment of a nuclear-weapon-free zone in the region of the Middle East.	1st
54.	Establishment of a nuclear-weapon-free zone in South Asia.	1st
55.	Convention on Prohibitions or Restrictions on the Use of Certain Conventional Weapons Which May Be Deemed to Be Excessively Injurious or to Have Indiscriminate Effects.	1st
56.	Conclusion of effective international arrangements on the strengthening of the security of non-nuclear-weapon States against the use or threat of use of nuclear weapons.	1st
57.	Conclusion of effective international arrangements to assure non-nuclear-weapon States against the use or threat of use of nuclear weapons.	1st
58.	Prevention of an arms race in outer space.	1st
59.	Implementation of the Declaration on the Denuclearization of Africa.	1st
60.	Prohibition of the development and manufacture of new types of weapons of mass destruction and new systems of such weapons.	1st
61.	Reduction of military budgets.	1st
62.	Chemical and bacteriological (biological) weapons.	1st
63.	General and complete disarmament:	
	(a) Notification of nuclear tests;	1st
	(b) Relationship between disarmament and development;	1st
	(c) Prohibition of the development, production, stockpiling and use of radiological weapons;	1st
	(d) Conventional disarmament;	1st
	(e) Nuclear disarmament;	1st
	(f) Objective information on miitary matters;	1st
	(g) Implementation of General Assembly resolutions in the field of disarmament;	1st
	(h) International arms transfers;	1st
	(i) Prohibition of the production of fissionable material for weapons purposes;	1st
	(j) Naval armaments and disarmament;	1st
	(k) Prohibition of the dumping of radioactive wastes for hostile purposes;	1st
	(l) Review of the role of the United Nations in the field of disarmament;	1st
	(m) Conventional disarmament on a regional scale;	1st
	(n) Dumping of radioactive wastes.	1st
64.	Review and implementation of the Concluding Document of the Twelfth Special Session of the General Assembly:	
	(a) Regional disarmament;	1st
	(b) Disarmament and international security;	1st
	(c) Nuclear-arms freeze;	1st
	(d) World Disarmament Campaign;	1st
	(e) United Nations Regional Centre for Peace and Disarmament in Africa;	1st
	(f) Convention on the Prohibition of the Use of Nuclear Weapons;	1st
	(g) United Nations disarmament fellowship, training and advisory services programme;	1st
	(h) United Nations Regional Centre for Peace and Disarmament in Asia;	1st
	(i) United Nations Regional Centre for Peace, Disarmament and Development in Latin America and the Caribbean.	1st
65.	Scientific and technological developments and their impact on international security.	1st

[8]On 22 September 1989, the General Assembly adopted the General Committee's recommendation that the item be allocated at an appropriate time during the session.

Item No.	Title	Allocation
66.	Review of the implementation of the recommendations and decisions adopted by the General Assembly at its tenth special session:	
	(a) Report of the Disarmament Commission;	1st
	(b) Report of the Conference on Disarmament;	1st
	(c) Status of multilateral disarmament agreements;	1st
	(d) Advisory Board on Disarmament Matters;[9]	1st
	(e) United Nations Institute for Disarmament Research;	1st
	(f) Review and appraisal of the implementation of the Declaration of the 1980s as the Second Disarmament Decade;	1st
	(g) Non-use of nuclear weapons and prevention of nuclear war;	1st
	(h) Climatic effects of nuclear war, including nuclear winter;	1st
	(i) Cessation of the nuclear-arms race and nuclear disarmament;	1st
	(j) Prevention of nuclear war;	1st
	(k) Disarmament Week;	1st
	(l) Comprehensive programme of disarmament;	1st
	(m) Declaration of the 1990s as the Third Disarmament Decade.	1st
67.	Implementation of the Declaration of the Indian Ocean as a Zone of Peace.	1st
68.	Israeli nuclear armament.	1st
69.	Compliance with arms limitation and disarmament agreements.	1st
70.	Question of Antarctica.	1st
71.	Strengthening of security and co-operation in the Mediterranean region.	1st
72.	Review of the implementation of the Declaration on the Strengthening of International Security.	1st
73.	Comprehensive approach to strengthening international peace and security in accordance with the Charter of the United Nations.	1st
74.	Effects of atomic radiation.	SPC
75.	International co-operation in the peaceful uses of outer space.	SPC
76.	United Nations Relief and Works Agency for Palestine Refugees in the Near East.	SPC
77.	Report of the Special Committee to Investigate Israeli Practices Affecting the Human Rights of the Population of the Occupied Territories.	SPC
78.	Comprehensive review of the whole question of peace-keeping operations in all their aspects.	SPC
79.	Questions relating to information.	SPC
80.	Question of the Malagasy islands of Glorieuses, Juan de Nova, Europa and Bassas da India.	SPC
81.	Question of the composition of the relevant organs of the United Nations.	SPC
82.	Development and international economic co-operation:	
	(a) Preparation of an international development strategy for the fourth United Nations development decade (1991-2000);	2nd
	(b) Trade and development;	2nd
	(c) Charter of Economic Rights and Duties of States;	2nd
	(d) Effective mobilization and integration of women in development;	2nd
	(e) Economic and technical co-operation among developing countries;	2nd
	(f) Environment;	2nd
	(g) Desertification and drought;	2nd
	(h) Human settlements;	2nd
	(i) Science and technology for development;	Plenary
	(j) Environmental protection of extraterritorial spaces for present and future generations.	2nd
83.	Preparations for the special session of the General Assembly in 1990.	2nd
84.	External debt crisis and development.	2nd
85.	Protection of global climate for present and future generations of mankind.	2nd
86.	Operational activities for development:	
	(a) Comprehensive policy review of operational activities of the United Nations system;	2nd
	(b) United Nations Development Programme;	2nd
	(c) United Nations Capital Development Fund;	2nd
	(d) United Nations technical co-operation activities;	2nd
	(e) United Nations Volunteers programme.	2nd
87.	Training and research: United Nations Institute for Training and Research.	2nd
88.	Special economic and disaster relief assistance:	
	(a) Special programmes of economic assistance;	2nd
	(b) International strategy for the fight against the locust and grasshopper infestation, particularly in Africa.	2nd
89.	Implementation of the Programme of Action for the Second Decade to Combat Racism and Racial Discrimination.	3rd

---

[9]The Advisory Board on Disarmament Studies was redesignated the Advisory Board on Disarmament Matters as from 1 January 1989.

Item No.	*Title*	*Allocation*
90.	World social situation:	
	(a) World social situation;	3rd
	(b) Popular participation in its various forms as an important factor in development and in the full realization of all human rights.	3rd
91.	Twentieth anniversary of the Declaration on Social Progress and Development.	3rd
92.	National experience in achieving far-reaching social and economic changes for the purpose of social progress.	3rd
93.	Policies and programmes involving youth.	3rd
94.	International Research and Training Institute for the Advancement of Women.	3rd
95.	Preparation and organization of International Literacy Year.	3rd
96.	Alternative approaches and ways and means within the United Nations system for improving the effective enjoyment of human rights and fundamental freedoms:	
	(a) National institutions for the protection and promotion of human rights;	3rd
	(b) Right to development;	3rd
	(c) Development of public information activities in the field of human rights.	3rd
97.	Interregional Consultation on Developmental Social Welfare Policies and Programmes.	3rd
98.	International Covenants on Human Rights.	3rd
99.	Question of aging.	3rd
100.	Elimination of all forms of racial discrimination.	3rd
101.	Implementation of the World Programme of Action concerning Disabled Persons and the United Nations Decade of Disabled Persons.	3rd
102.	Crime prevention and criminal justice.	3rd
103.	Elimination of all forms of discrimination against women.	3rd
104.	Forward-looking strategies for the advancement of women to the year 2000:	
	(a) Implementation of the Nairobi Forward-looking Strategies for the Advancement of Women;	3rd
	(b) United Nations Development Fund for Women;	3rd
	(c) Improvement of the status of women in the Secretariat;	3rd
	(d) Implementation of the Declaration on the Participation of Women in Promoting International Peace and Co-operation;	3rd
	(e) National experience relating to the improvement of the situation of women in rural areas.	3rd
105.	Importance of the universal realization of the right of peoples to self-determination and of the speedy granting of independence to colonial countries and peoples for the effective guarantee and observance of human rights.	3rd
106.	Elimination of all forms of religious intolerance.	3rd
107.	Human rights and scientific and technological developments.	3rd
108.	Adoption of a convention on the rights of the child.	3rd
109.	Effective implementation of international instruments on human rights, including reporting obligations under international instruments on human rights.	3rd
110.	Office of the United Nations High Commissioner for Refugees:	
	(a) International Conference on the Plight of Refugees, Returnees and Displaced Persons in Southern Africa;	3rd
	(b) International Conference on Central American Refugees;	3rd
	(c) International Conference on Indo-Chinese Refugees.	3rd
111.	International campaign against traffic in drugs:	
	(a) United Nations Convention against Illicit Traffic in Narcotic Drugs and Psychotropic Substances;	3rd
	(b) International campaign against drug abuse and illicit trafficking.	3rd
112.	Torture and other cruel, inhuman or degrading treatment or punishment.	3rd
113.	Families in the development process.	3rd
114.	Enhancing the effectiveness of the principle of periodic and genuine elections.	3rd
115.	Preparation of an instrument on human rights based on solidarity.	3rd
116.	Information from Non-Self-Governing Territories transmitted under Article 73 *e* of the Charter of the United Nations.	4th
117.	Activities of foreign economic and other interests which are impeding the implementation of the Declaration on the Granting of Independence to Colonial Countries and Peoples in Namibia and in all other Territories under colonial domination and efforts to eliminate colonialism, *apartheid* and racial discrimination in southern Africa.	4th
118.	Implementation of the Declaration on the Granting of Independence to Colonial Countries and Peoples by the specialized agencies and the international institutions associated with the United Nations.	4th
119.	United Nations Educational and Training Programme for Southern Africa.	4th
120.	Offers by Member States of study and training facilities for inhabitants of Non-Self-Governing Territories.	4th

Item No.	*Title*	*Allocation*
121.	Financial reports and audited financial statements, and reports of the Board of Auditors:	
	(a) United Nations Development Programme;	5th
	(b) United Nations Children's Fund;	5th
	(c) United Nations Relief and Works Agency for Palestine Refugees in the Near East;	5th
	(d) United Nations Institute for Training and Research;	5th
	(e) Voluntary funds administered by the United Nations High Commissioner for Refugees;	5th
	(f) United Nations Population Fund.	5th
122.	Programme budget for the biennium 1988-1989.	5th
123.	Proposed programme budget for the biennium 1990-1991.	5th
124.	Programme planning.	5th
125.	Financial emergency of the United Nations.	5th
126.	Administrative and budgetary co-ordination of the United Nations with the specialized agencies and the International Atomic Energy Agency:	
	(a) Report of the Advisory Committee on Administrative and Budgetary Questions;	5th
	(b) Harmonization of the statutes, rules and practices of the administrative tribunals of the International Labour Organisation and of the United Nations.	5th
127.	Joint Inspection Unit.	5th
128.	Pattern of conferences.	5th
129.	Scale of assessments for the apportionment of the expenses of the United Nations.	5th
130.	Personnel questions:	
	(a) Composition of the Secretariat;	5th
	(b) Respect for the privileges and immunities of officials of the United Nations and the specialized agencies and related organizations;	5th
	(c) Other personnel questions.	5th
131.	United Nations common system.	5th
132.	United Nations pension system.	5th
133.	Financing of the United Nations peace-keeping forces in the Middle East:	
	(a) United Nations Disengagement Observer Force;	5th
	(b) United Nations Interim Force in Lebanon;	5th
	(c) Review of the rates of reimbursement to the Governments of troop-contributing States.	5th
134.	Financing of the United Nations Iran-Iraq Military Observer Group.	5th
135.	Financing of the United Nations Angola Verification Mission.	5th
136.	Financing of the United Nations Transition Assistance Group.	5th
137.	Administrative and budgetary aspects of the financing of the United Nations peace-keeping operations.	5th
138.	United Nations Programme of Assistance in the Teaching, Study, Dissemination and Wider Appreciation of International Law.	6th
139.	Measures to prevent international terrorism which endangers or takes innocent human lives or jeopardizes fundamental freedoms and study of the underlying causes of those forms of terrorism and acts of violence which lie in misery, frustration, grievance and despair and which cause some people to sacrifice human lives, including their own, in an attempt to effect radical changes:	
	(a) Report of the Secretary-General;	6th
	(b) Convening, under the auspices of the United Nations, of an international conference to define terrorism and to differentiate it from the struggle of peoples for national liberation.	6th
140.	Progressive development of the principles and norms of international law relating to the new international economic order.	6th
141.	Peaceful settlement of disputes between States.	6th
142.	Draft Code of Crimes against the Peace and Security of Mankind.	6th
143.	Report of the United Nations Commission on International Trade Law on the work of its twenty-second session.	6th
144.	Report of the *Ad Hoc* Committee on the Drafting of an International Convention against the Recruitment, Use, Financing and Training of Mercenaries.	6th
145.	Report of the International Law Commission on the work of its forty-first session.	6th
146.	Report of the Special Committee on the Charter of the United Nations and on the Strengthening of the Role of the Organization.	6th
147.	Report of the Committee on Relations with the Host Country.	6th
148.	Observer status for the Council of Europe in the General Assembly.	Plenary
149.	United Nations Decade of International Law.	Plenary
150.	Protection and security of small States.	SPC
151.	Education and information for disarmament.	1st
152.	International criminal responsibility of individuals and entities engaged in illicit trafficking in narcotic drugs across national frontiers and other transnational criminal activities: establishment of an international criminal court with jurisdiction over such crimes.	6th
153.	Emergency assistance to the Sudan.	2nd

Item No.	*Title*	*Allocation*
154.	Operation Lifeline Sudan.	Plenary
155.	African Alternative Framework to Structural Adjustment Programmes for Socio-Economic Recovery and Transformation.	Plenary
156.	Emergency assistance to Antigua and Barbuda, the British Virgin Islands, Dominica, Montserrat and Saint Kitts and Nevis.	Plenary
157.	Special session of the General Assembly to consider the question of international co-operation against illicit production, supply, demand, trafficking and distribution of narcotic drugs, with a view to expanding the scope and increasing the effectiveness of such co-operation.	Plenary
158.	Enhancing international peace, security and international co-operation in all its aspects in accordance with the Charter of the United Nations.	Plenary
159.	Financing of the United Nations Observer Group in Central America.	5th
160.	International assistance for the economic rehabilitation of Angola.	Plenary
161.	Emergency humanitarian assistance to Romania.	Plenary

Agenda of the sixteenth special session
(12-14 December 1989)

Item No.	*Title*	*Allocation*
1.	Opening of the session by the Chairman of the delegation of Nigeria.	Plenary
2.	Minute of silent prayer or meditation.	Plenary
3.	Credentials of representatives to the sixteenth special session of the General Assembly:	
	(a) Appointment of the members of the Credentials Committee;	Plenary
	(b) Report of the Credentials Committee.	Plenary
4.	Election of the President of the General Assembly.	Plenary
5.	Organization of the session.	Plenary
6.	Adoption of the agenda.	Plenary
7.	*Apartheid* and its destructive consequences in southern Africa.	10

Security Council
Agenda items considered during 1989

Item No.[11]   *Title*

1. Letter dated 4 January 1989 from the Chargé d'affaires a.i. of the Permanent Mission of the Libyan Arab Jamahiriya to the United Nations addressed to the President of the Security Council; letter dated 4 January 1989 from the Chargé d'affaires a.i. of the Permanent Mission of Bahrain to the United Nations addressed to the President of the Security Council (Libyan Arab Jamahiriya v. United States in connection with the downing of two Libyan reconnaissance aircraft).

2. Date of an election to fill a vacancy in the International Court of Justice.

3. The situation in Namibia.

4. The situation in the Middle East.

5. The situation between Iran and Iraq.

6. The situation in the occupied Arab territories.

7. The situation relating to Afghanistan.

8. Election of a member of the International Court of Justice.

9. Letter dated 25 April 1989 from the Permanent Representative of Panama to the United Nations addressed to the President of the Security Council (Panama v. United States wherein Panama contested actions of the United States military in Panama, while the United States alleged election fraud in Panama).

10. The situation in Cyprus.

11. Marking of plastic or sheet explosives for the purposes of detection.

12. Central America: efforts towards peace.

13. The question of hostage-taking and abduction.

14. Consideration of the draft report of the Security Council to the General Assembly covering the period from 16 June 1988 to 15 June 1989.

15. Letter dated 27 November 1989 from the Permanent Representative of El Salvador to the United Nations addressed to the President of the Security Council; letter dated 28 November 1989 from the Permanent Representative of Nicaragua to the United Nations addressed to the President of the Security Council (El Salvador v. Sandinista Government of Nicaragua).

16. The situation in Panama.

---

[10]Allocated to the *Ad Hoc* Committee of the Whole of the Sixteenth Special Session.
[11]Numbers indicate the order in which items were taken up in 1989.

Economic and Social Council
Agenda of the organizational session for 1989
(⚫ January and 9 and 10 February 1989)

Item No.	Title	Allocation
1.	Election of the Bureau.	Plenary
2.	Adoption of the agenda and other organizational matters.	Plenary
3.	Basic programme of work of the Council for 1989 and 1990.	Plenary
4.	Elections to subsidiary bodies of the Council and confirmation of representatives on the functional commissions.	Plenary
5.	Provisional agenda for the first regular session of 1989 and related organizational matters.	Plenary

Agenda of the first regular session of 1989
(2-24 May 1989)

Item No.	Title	Allocation
1.	Adoption of the agenda and other organizational matters.	Plenary
2.	Implementation of the Programme of Action for the Second Decade to Combat Racism and Racial Discrimination.	Plenary
3.	Non-governmental organizations.	Plenary
4.	United Nations University.	1st
5.	Public administration and finance.	1st
6.	Statistical and cartographic questions:	
	(a) Statistics;	1st
	(b) Cartography.	1st
7.	Natural resources.	1st
8.	Transnational corporations.	1st
9.	Human rights questions:	
	(a) International Covenants on Human Rights;	2nd
	(b) Human rights.	2nd
10.	Women:	
	(a) Convention on the Elimination of All Forms of Discrimination against Women;	2nd
	(b) Advancement of women.	2nd
11.	Social development:	
	(a) World social situation;	2nd
	(b) Social policy and social development.	2nd
12.	Narcotic drugs.	2nd
13.	Elections and nominations.	Plenary
14.	Consideration of the provisional agenda for the second regular session of 1989.	Plenary

Agenda of the second regular session of 1989
(5-28 July 1989)

Item No.	Title	Allocation
1.	Adoption of the agenda and other organizational matters.	Plenary
2.	General discussion of international economic and social policy, including regional and sectoral developments.	Plenary
3.	Special session of the General Assembly devoted to international economic co-operation, in particular to the revitalization of the economic growth and development of the developing countries.	Plenary
4.	Revitalization of the Economic and Social Council.	Plenary
5.	Permanent sovereignty over national resources in the occupied Palestinian and other Arab territories.	Plenary
6.	Regional co-operation.	1st
7.	Development and international economic co-operation:	
	(a) Trade and development;	1st
	(b) Food and agriculture;	1st
	(c) Preparation of the international development strategy for the fourth United Nations development decade;	1st
	(d) Population;	1st
	(e) Human settlements;	1st
	(f) Environment;	1st

Item No.	Title	Allocation
(g) Desertification and drought;		1st
(h) Transport of dangerous goods;		1st
(i) Effective mobilization and integration of women in development.		1st
8. Operational activities for development:		
(a) Triennial comprehensive policy review of operational activities of the United Nations system;		3rd
(b) Reports of governing bodies;		3rd
(c) Human resources development and the activities of the United Nations system in that field.		3rd
9. Co-ordination questions:		
(a) Reports of the Committee for Programme and Co-ordination and the Administrative Committee on Co-ordination;		3rd
(b) World Decade for Cultural Development;		3rd
(c) Prevention and control of acquired immunodeficiency syndrome (AIDS);		3rd
(d) World Tourism Organization;		3rd
(e) Economic and technical aspects of marine affairs;		3rd
(f) Co-operation in the field of informatics.		3rd
10. Implementation of the Declaration on the Granting of Independence to Colonial Countries and Peoples by the specialized agencies and the international institutions associated with the United Nations.		3rd
11. Programme and related questions:		
(a) Proposed programme budget for the biennium 1990-1991;		3rd
(b) Calendar of conferences and meetings for 1990 and 1991.		3rd
12. Co-operation for natural disaster reduction:		
(a) International decade for natural disaster reduction;		3rd
(b) International strategy for the fight against locust and grasshopper infestation, particularly in Africa.		3rd
13. Special economic and humanitarian assistance:		
(a) Special programmes of economic assistance;		3rd
(b) Humanitarian assistance.		3rd
14. Report of the United Nations High Commissioner for Refugees.		Plenary
15. Elections and nominations.		Plenary

Trusteeship Council
Agenda of the nineteenth special session
(16 and 17 March 1989)

Item No.	Title

1. Adoption of the agenda.

2. Report of the Secretary-General on credentials.

3. Letters dated 1 and 3 March 1989, respectively, from the Acting Permanent Representative of the United States of America to the United Nations addressed to the Secretary-General inviting the Trusteeship Council at its earliest convenience to send a visiting mission to observe the current conditions in Palau, and requesting that a special session of the Council be convened at the earliest possible date to consider that invitation.

4. Examination of petitions related to item 3 of the agenda.

Agenda of the fifty-sixth session
(15-25 and 31 May, 1 June and 1 August 1989)

Item No.	Title

1. Adoption of the agenda.

2. Report of the Secretary-General on credentials.

3. Election of the President and the Vice-President.

4. Examination of the annual report of the Administering Authority for the year ended 30 September 1988: Trust Territory of the Pacific Islands.

5. Examination of petitions.

6. Report of the United Nations Visiting Mission to Palau, Trust Territory of the Pacific Islands, 1989.

7. Offers by Member States of study and training facilities for inhabitants of Trust Territories.

8. Dissemination of information on the United Nations and the International Trusteeship System in Trust Territories.

9. Co-operation with the Committee on the Elimination of Racial Discrimination.

| *Item No.* | *Title* |

10. Second Decade to Combat Racism and Racial Discrimination.

11. Attainment of self-government or independence by the Trust Territories and the situation in Trust Territories with regard to the implementation of the Declaration on the Granting of Independence to Colonial Countries and Peoples.

12. Co-operation with the Special Committee on the Situation with regard to the Implementation of the Declaration on the Granting of Independence to Colonial Countries and Peoples.

13. Adoption of the report of the Trusteeship Council to the Security Council.

Appendix V

United Nations information centres and services
(as at 15 April 1997)

ACCRA. United Nations Information Centre
Gamel Abdul Nassar/Liberia Roads
(P.O. Box 2339)
Accra, Ghana
   Serving: Ghana, Sierra Leone

ADDIS ABABA. United Nations Information
Service, Economic Commission for Africa
Africa Hall
(P.O. Box 3001)
Addis Ababa, Ethiopia
   Serving: Ethiopia

ALGIERS. United Nations Information Centre
19, Avenue Chahid El Ouali, Mustapha Sayed
(Boîte Postale 823, Alger-Gare, Algeria)
Algiers, Algeria
   Serving: Algeria

AMMAN (relocated from Baghdad). United
Nations Information Service, Economic
and Social Commission for Western Asia
28 Abdul Hameed Sharaf Street
(P.O. Box 927115)
Amman, Jordan
   Serving: Iraq, Jordan

ANKARA. United Nations Information Centre
197 Atatürk Bulvari
(P.K. 407)
Ankara, Turkey
   Serving: Turkey

ANTANANARIVO. United Nations Informa-
tion Centre
22 Rue Rainitovo, Antasahavola
(Boîte Postale 1348)
Antananarivo, Madagascar
   Serving: Madagascar

ASUNCION. United Nations Information
Centre
Estrella 345, Edificio City (3er piso)
(Casilla de Correo 1107)
Asunción, Paraguay
   Serving: Paraguay

ATHENS. United Nations Information Centre
36 Amalia Avenue
GR-10558 Athens, Greece
   Serving: Cyprus, Greece, Israel

BANGKOK. United Nations Information Serv-
ice, Economic and Social Commission for
Asia and the Pacific
United Nations Building
Rajdamnern Avenue
Bangkok 10200, Thailand
   Serving: Cambodia, Hong Kong, Lao
People's Democratic Republic, Malaysia,
Singapore, Thailand, Viet Nam

BEIRUT. United Nations Information Centre
Apt. No. 1, Fakhoury Building
Montée Bain Militaire, Ardati Street
(P.O. Box 4656)
Beirut, Lebanon
   Serving: Kuwait, Lebanon, Syrian
Arab Republic

BONN. United Nations Information Centre
Haus Carstanjen
Martin-Luther-King-Str. 8
(P.O. Box 260111, D-53153, Bonn)
D-53175, Bonn, Germany
   Serving: Germany

BRAZZAVILLE. United Nations Information
Centre
Avenue Foch, Case Ortf 15
(P.O. Box 13210 or 1018)
Brazzaville, Congo
   Serving: Congo

BRUSSELS. United Nations Information
Centre
Avenue de Broqueville 40
1200 Brussels, Belgium
   Serving: Belgium, Luxembourg,
Netherlands; liaison with EC

BUCHAREST. United Nations Information
Centre
16 Aurel Vlaicu
(P.O. Box 1-701)
Bucharest, Romania
   Serving: Romania

BUENOS AIRES. United Nations Information Centre
Junín 1940 (1er piso)
1113 Buenos Aires, Argentina
   Serving: Argentina, Uruguay

BUJUMBURA. United Nations Information
Centre
117 Avenue de la Révolution
(Boîte Postale 2160)
Bujumbura, Burundi
   Serving: Burundi

CAIRO. United Nations Information Centre
1 Osoris Street
Garden City
(Boîte Postale 262)
Cairo, Egypt
   Serving: Egypt, Saudi Arabia

COLOMBO. United Nations Information
Centre
202-204 Bauddhaloka Mawatha
(P.O. Box 1505, Colombo)
Colombo 7, Sri Lanka
   Serving: Sri Lanka

COPENHAGEN. United Nations Information
Centre
Midtermolen 3
DK-2100 Copenhagen V, Denmark
   Serving: Denmark, Finland, Iceland,
Norway, Sweden

DAKAR. United Nations Information Centre
12 Avenue Roume, Immeuble UNESCO
(Boîte Postale 154)
Dakar, Senegal
   Serving: Cape Verde, Côte d'Ivoire, Gam-
bia, Guinea, Guinea-Bissau, Mauritania,
Senegal

DAR ES SALAAM. United Nations Informa-
tion Centre
Marogoro Road/Sokoine Drive
Old Boma Building (ground floor)
(P.O. Box 9224)
Dar es Salaam, United Republic of Tanzania
   Serving: United Republic of Tanzania

DHAKA. United Nations Information Centre
House 60, Road 11A
Dhanmondi
(G.P.O. Box 3658, Dhaka 1000)
Dhaka, Bangladesh
   Serving: Bangladesh

GENEVA. United Nations Information Service,
United Nations Office at Geneva
Palais des Nations
1211 Geneva 10, Switzerland
   Serving: Bulgaria, Switzerland

HARARE. United Nations Information Centre
Zimre Centre, 3rd floor
L. Takawira Street/Union Avenue
(P.O. Box 4408)
Harare, Zimbabwe
   Serving: Zimbabwe

ISLAMABAD. United Nations Information
Centre
House No. 26
88th Street, G-6/3
(P.O. Box 1107)
Islamabad, Pakistan
   Serving: Pakistan

JAKARTA. United Nations Information Centre
Gedung Dewan Pers (5th floor)
32-34 Jalan Kebon Sirih
Jakarta, Indonesia
   Serving: Indonesia

KABUL. United Nations Information Centre
Shah Mahmoud Ghazi Watt
(P.O. Box 5)
Kabul, Afghanistan
   Serving: Afghanistan

KATHMANDU. United Nations Information
Centre
Pulchowk, Patan
(P.O. Box 107, Pulchowk)
Kathmandu, Nepal
Serving: Nepal

KHARTOUM. United Nations Information
Centre
United Nations Compound
Gamma'a Avenue
(P.O. Box 913)
Khartoum, Sudan
Serving: Somalia, Sudan

KINSHASA. United Nations Information Centre
Bâtiment Deuxième République
Boulevard du 30 Juin
(Boîte Postale 7248)
Kinshasa, Zaire
Serving: Zaire

LAGOS. United Nations Information Centre
17 Kingsway Road, Ikoyi
(P.O. Box 1068)
Lagos, Nigeria
Serving: Nigeria

LA PAZ. United Nations Information Centre
Av. Mariscal
Santa Cruz No. 1350
(Apartado Postal 9072)
La Paz, Bolivia
Serving: Bolivia

LIMA. United Nations Information Centre
Lord Cochrane 130
San Isidro (L-27)
(P.O. Box 14-0199)
Lima, Peru
Serving: Peru

LISBON. United Nations Information Centre
Rua Latino Coelho, 1
Edificio Aviz, Bloco A-1, 10°
1000 Lisbon, Portugal
Serving: Portugal

LOME. United Nations Information Centre
107 Boulevard du 13 Janvier
(Boîte Postale 911)
Lomé, Togo
Serving: Benin, Togo

LONDON. United Nations Information Centre
Millbank Tower (21st floor)
21-24 Millbank
London SW1P 4QH, England
Serving: Ireland, United Kingdom

LUSAKA. United Nations Information Centre
P.O. Box 32905
Lusaka 10101, Zambia
Serving: Botswana, Malawi, Swaziland,
Zambia

MADRID. United Nations Information Centre
Avenida General Perón, 32-1
(P.O. Box 3400, 28080 Madrid)
28020 Madrid, Spain
Serving: Spain

MANAGUA. United Nations Information
Centre
Del Portón del Hospital Militar
1 c. al lago y 1 c. abajo
(Apartado Postal 3260)
Managua, Nicaragua
Serving: Nicaragua

MANAMA. United Nations Information
Centre
Villa 131, Road 2803
Segaya
(P.O. Box 26004, Manama)
Manama 328, Bahrain
Serving: Bahrain, Qatar, United Arab
Emirates

MANILA. United Nations Information
Centre
NEDA Building
106 Amorsolo Street
Legaspi Village, Makati
(P.O. Box 7285 ADC (DAPO), Pasay City)
Metro Manila, Philippines
Serving: Papua New Guinea, Philip-
pines, Solomon Islands

MASERU. United Nations Information
Centre
Letsie Road
Food Aid Compound
Behind Hotel Victoria
(P.O. Box 301, Maseru 100)
Maseru, Lesotho
Serving: Lesotho

MEXICO CITY. United Nations Information
Centre
Presidente Masaryk 29-6° piso
11570 México, D.F., Mexico
Serving: Cuba, Dominican Republic,
Mexico

MOSCOW. United Nations Information
Centre
4/16 Ulitsa Lunacharskogo
Moscow 121002, Russian Federation
Serving: Russian Federation

NAIROBI. United Nations Information
Centre
United Nations Office
Gigiri
(P.O. Box 30552)
Nairobi, Kenya
Serving: Kenya, Seychelles, Uganda

NEW DELHI. United Nations Information
Centre
55 Lodi Estate
New Delhi 110003, India
Serving: Bhutan, India

OUAGADOUGOU. United Nations Informa-
tion Centre
Avenue Georges Konseiga
Secteur No. 4
(Boîte Postale 135)
Ouagadougou 01, Burkina Faso
Serving: Burkina Faso, Chad, Mali,
Niger

PANAMA CITY. United Nations Informa-
tion Centre
Calle Gerardo Ortega y Ave. Samuel Lewis
Banco Central Hispano Building (1st floor)
(P.O. Box 6-9083 El Dorado)
Panama City, Panama
Serving: Panama

PARIS. United Nations Information Centre
1 Rue Miollis
75732, Paris Cedex 15, France
Serving: France

PORT OF SPAIN. United Nations Informa-
tion Centre
2nd floor, Bretton Hall
16 Victoria Avenue
(P.O. Box 130)
Port of Spain, Trinidad, W.I.
Serving: Antigua and Barbuda, Ba-
hamas, Barbados, Belize, Dominica,
Grenada, Guyana, Jamaica, Netherlands
Antilles, Saint Kitts and Nevis, Saint
Lucia, Saint Vincent and the Grenadines,
Suriname, Trinidad and Tobago

PRAGUE. United Nations Information
Centre
Panska 5
11000 Prague 1, Czech Republic
Serving: Czech Republic

PRETORIA. United Nations Information
Centre
Metro Park Building
351 Schoeman Street
P.O. Box 12677
Tramshed 0126
Pretoria, South Africa
Serving: South Africa

RABAT. United Nations Information Centre
Angle Charia Ibnouzaid
Et Zankat Roundanat, No. 6
(Boîte Postale 601)
Rabat, Morocco
Serving: Morocco

RIO DE JANEIRO. United Nations Informa-
tion Centre
Palácio Itamaraty
Av. Marechal Floriano 196
20080-002 Rio de Janeiro, RJ Brazil
Serving: Brazil

ROME. United Nations Information Centre
Palazzetto Venezia
Piazza San Marco 50
00186 Rome, Italy
Serving: Holy See, Italy, Malta, San
Marino

SANA'A. United Nations Information
Centre
Handhal Street, 4
Al-Boniya Area
(P.O. Box 237)
Sana'a, Yemen
Serving: Yemen

SAN SALVADOR. United Nations Information Centre
Edificio Escalón (2º piso)
Paseo General Escalón y 87 Avenida Norte
Colonia Escalón
(Apartado Postal 2157)
San Salvador, El Salvador

> *Serving:* El Salvador

SANTA FE DE BOGOTA. United Nations Information Centre
Calle 100 No. 8A-55, Of. 815
(Apartado Aéreo 058964)
Santa Fé de Bogotá 2, Colombia

> *Serving:* Colombia, Ecuador, Venezuela

SANTIAGO. United Nations Information Service, Economic Commission for Latin America and the Caribbean
Edificio Naciones Unidas
Avenida Dag Hammarskjöld
(Avenida Dag Hammarskjöld s/n, Casilla 179-D)
Santiago, Chile

> *Serving:* Chile

SYDNEY. United Nations Information Centre
46-48 York Street, 5th floor
(G.P.O. Box 4045, Sydney, N.S.W. 2001)
Sydney, N.S.W. 2000, Australia

> *Serving:* Australia, Fiji, Kiribati, Nauru, New Zealand, Samoa, Tonga, Tuvalu, Vanuatu

TEHRAN. United Nations Information Centre
185 Ghaem Magham Farahani Avenue
(P.O. Box 15875-4557, Tehran)
Tehran, 15868 Iran

> *Serving:* Iran

TOKYO. United Nations Information Centre
UNU Building (8th floor)
53-70 Jingumae 5-chome, Shibuya-ku
Tokyo 150, Japan

> *Serving:* Japan

TRIPOLI. United Nations Information Centre
Muzzafar Al Aftas Street
Hay El-Andalous (2)
(P.O. Box 286)
Tripoli, Libyan Arab Jamahiriya

> *Serving:* Libyan Arab Jamahiriya

TUNIS. United Nations Information Centre
61 Boulevard Bab-Benat
(Boîte Postale 863)
Tunis, Tunisia

> *Serving:* Tunisia

VIENNA. United Nations Information Service, United Nations Office at Vienna
Vienna International Centre
Wagramer Strasse 5
(P.O. Box 500, A-1400 Vienna)
A-1220 Vienna, Austria

> *Serving:* Austria, Hungary, Slovakia

WARSAW. United Nations Information Centre
Al. Niepodleglosci 186
00-608 Warszawa
(UN Centre, P.O.Box 1, 02-514 Warsaw 12)
Poland

> *Serving:* Poland

WASHINGTON, D.C. United Nations Information Centre
1775 K Street, N.W., Suite 400
Washington, D.C. 20006, United States

> *Serving:* United States

WINDHOEK. United Nations Information Centre
372 Paratus Building
Independence Avenue
(Private Bag 13351)
Windhoek, Namibia

> *Serving:* Namibia

YANGON. United Nations Information Centre
6 Natmauk Road
(P.O. Box 230)
Yangon, Myanmar

> *Serving:* Myanmar

YAOUNDE. United Nations Information Centre
Immeuble Kamdem, Rue Joseph Clère
(Boîte Postale 836)
Yaoundé, Cameroon

> *Serving:* Cameroon, Central African Republic, Gabon

Indexes

USING THE SUBJECT INDEX

To assist the researcher in reading and searching the Yearbook index, three typefaces have been employed.

ALL BOLD CAPITAL LETTERS are used for major subject entries (including chapter topics) e.g., **DEVELOPMENT**, **DISARMAMENT**, as well as country names (e.g., **THAILAND**), region names (e.g., **AFRICA**), and principal UN organs (e.g., **GENERAL ASSEMBLY**).

SMALL CAPITAL LETTERS are used to highlight major sub-topics, e.g., NUCLEAR DISARMAMENT, territories (ST. HELENA), sub-regions (CARIBBEAN) and official names of specialized agencies (e.g., UNIVERSAL POSTAL UNION) and regional commissions (e.g., ECONOMIC COMMISSION FOR EUROPE).

Regular body text is used for single entries and cross-reference entries, e.g., drift-net fishing, Nelson Mandela, social welfare.

1—An asterisk (*) before an entry indicates the presence of a text (reproduced in full) of General Assembly, Security Council or Economic and Social Council resolutions and decisions.

2—Under major subject entries, alphabetical entries are preceded by listings of major UN bodies and other machinery that deal with the subject, and programmes and projects related to the subject.

3—Entries, which are heavily cross-referenced, appear under key substantive words, as well as under the first word of official titles.

4—United Nations bodies are listed under major subject entries and alphabetically by both their formal names and acronyms.

A list of major topics and major sub-topics follows.

(Index abbreviations which appear below supplement those on page xv in the list of ''Abbreviations commonly used in the Yearbook''.)

MAJOR TOPICS, COUNTRY AND REGIONAL ENTRIES
(in ALL BOLD CAPS)

Afghanistan	Development	Iraq
Africa	Disarmament	Israel
Albania	Djibouti	Italy
Algeria	Dominican Republic	Jamaica
Americas	Drug abuse/control	Japan
Angola	Economic and Social Council	Jordan
Antigua and Barbuda	Ecuador	Kampuchea
Argentina	Egypt	Labour
Asia & the Pacific	El Salvador	Latin America and Caribbean
Australia	Environment	Law of the sea
Bangladesh	Equatorial Guinea	Lebanon
Benin	Ethiopia	Lesotho
Botswana	Europe	Libyan Arab Jamahiriya
Brunei Darussalam	Food	Madagascar
Cameroon	France	Malawi
Central African Republic	General Assembly	Malaysia
Central America	Greece	Maldives
Chad	Guatemala	Mauritania
Charter of UN	Guinea-Bissau	Middle East
Children	Haiti	Morocco
Chile	Health	Mozambique
China	Honduras	Myanmar
Colombia	Human rights	Namibia
Comoros	Human settlements	Nepal
Costa Rica	India	New Zealand
Côte d'Ivoire	Indonesia	Nicaragua
Crime prevention	Industrial development	Nigeria
Cuba	Information	Norway
Cyprus	International Court of Justice	Outer space
Decolonization	International law	Pakistan
Democratic Yemen	International peace and security	
Denmark	Iran	

Panama
Paraguay
Peace-keeping
Population
Portugal
Refugees
Romania
Saint Kitts and Nevis
Secretariat, UN
Security Council

Senegal
Sierra Leone
Social development
Somalia
South Africa
Spain
Sri Lanka
Sudan
Syrian Arab Republic
Trade

Trusteeship Council
Trusteeship System, UN
Turkey
Union of Soviet Socialist Republics
United Kingdom
United Nations
United States
Vanuatu
Viet Nam
Women

MAJOR SUB-TOPICS, TERRITORIES, SUB-REGIONS, SPECIALIZED AGENCIES, REGIONAL COMMISSIONS
(*in* SMALL CAPS)

aging
agriculture
AIDS
American Samoa
Anguilla
Antarctica
apartheid
atomic energy
Bermuda
British Virgin Islands
Caribbean
Cayman Islands
chemicals
civil and political rights
civil aviation
climate change
commodities
conferences and meetings, UN
co-ordination, UN
cultural development
desertification
developing countries
Development Programme, UN
diplomatic relations
disabled
disaster relief
East Asia
East Timor
Eastern Europe
Economic Commission for Africa (ECA)
Economic Commission for Europe (ECE)
Economic Commission for Latin America and
   the Caribbean (ECLAC)
economic co-operation, international
Economic and Social Commission for Asia
   and the Pacific (ESCAP)
Economic and Social Commission for Western Asia (ESCWA)
economic, social and cultural rights
education
energy
financing and programming, UN

Food and Agricultural Organization of the
   United Nations (FAO)
General Agreement on Tariffs and Trade
   (GATT)
Gibraltar
Guam
humanitarian assistance
intellectual property
International Atomic Energy Agency (IAEA)
International Bank for Reconstruction and
   Development (IBRD/World Bank)
International Civil Aviation Organization
   (ICAO)
International Development Association (IDA)
International Finance Corporation (IFC)
International Fund for Agricultural Develop-
   ment (IFAD)
International Labour Organisation (ILO)
International Maritime Organization (IMO)
International Monetary Fund (IMF)
International Telecommunication Union (ITU)
international trade
Jerusalem
literacy
maritime issues
Marshall Islands
Mediterranean
meteorology
Montserrat
natural resources
Nauru
Near East
New Caledonia
non-governmental organizations
North Africa
North America
nuclear disarmament
nutrition
occupied territories
operational activities for development
ozone layer
Pacific
Palau

Palestine, question of
Pitcairn
postal services
reform
St. Helena
science and technology for development
Secretary-General, UN
South America
South Asia
South-East Asia
Southern Africa
Soviet Union
specialized agencies
staff, UN
statistics
technical co-operation
telecommunications
Tokelau
torture
trade, international
trade law, international
transnational corporations
transport
Turks and Caicos Islands
United Nations Educational, Scientific and
   Cultural Organization (UNESCO)
United Nations Industrial Development Or-
   ganization (UNIDO)
United States Virgin Islands
Universal Postal Union (UPU)
violations, human rights
water
weather
Western Asia
Western Europe
Western Sahara
World Bank Group
World Health Organization (WHO)
World Intellectual Property Organization
   (WIPO)
World Meteorological Organization (WMO)
youth

ABBREVIATIONS

adm.   administration/administrative
adv.   advisory
agr.   agriculture
AIDS   acquired immunodeficiency syndrome
appt.   appointment
assn.   association
asst.   assistance
Bd.   Board
budg.   budgetary

Cent. Am.   Central America(n)
Cf.   Conference
Cm.   Commission
cns.   countries
conv.   convention
corp.   corporation
co-op.   co-operation
co-ord.   co-ordination
crim.   criminal

Ct.	Committee	mtg.	meeting
Ctr.	Centre	natl.	national
cult.	cultural	org.	organization(al)
decl.	declaration	Pal.	Palestinian
dept.	department	pers.	personal
dev.	development	pop.	population
div.	division	prep.	preparation/preparatory
dvg.	developing	prog.	programme
dis.	disarmament	prop.	proposed
dr.	draft	Rapp.	Rapporteur
EC	European Community	reg.	regional
econ.	economic	Rep.	Representative
env.	environment(al)	res.	resource(s)
fin.	financial	rpt.	report
gl.	global	rts.	rights
gov.	government(al)	sess.	session
grp.	group	soc.	social
HIV	human immunodeficiency virus	sp.	special
hum.	human	sr.	senior
info.	information	stat.	statistics/statistical
Inst.	Institute	std.	standard
intergov.	intergovernmental	strat.	strategy
intl.	international	Sub-Cm.	Sub-Commission
isl.	island	Sub-Ct.	Sub-Committee
jt.	joint	symp.	symposium
mgt.	management	tech.	technical
min.	minimum	terr.	territory
Mt.	Mount	wk.	working

Subject index

A

F

G

GUATEMALA 519, 923

Guidelines of Riyadh (juvenile delinquency) 621

GUINEA-BISSAU 816-17

Gulf Co-operation Council (GCC) 273

H

Habitat, see under Human settlements
Habitat and Human Settlements Foundation, UN 470
Hague Academy of Intl. Law 851
Hague Agreement/Industrial Design (WIPO) 957
Hague Decl. on Tourism 384

HAITI 519-20, 530

Harare Decl. (OAU) 126, 127, 129
harmful chemical substances, list 433
harmful products, consolidated list of, review 432
harmonization of measurements (env.) 432
Harmonized Commodity Description and Coding System 733
hazardous wastes 573, see also Environment
transboundary movements of (Basel Conv.)
15, 417, 419, 420, 573

HEALTH 577-88, see also AIDS, disabled, Drug abuse, nutrition
Scientific Ct./Effects of Atomic Radiation
(38th sess.) 577-78
World Health Organization (WHO) 201, 577,
930-33

Bamako Initiative 672-73, 676-77
Chemical Safety, WHO/ILO/UNEP Intl. Prog.
on 577, 932
*Disabled Persons, UN Decade of 581-88
Elderly, Gl. Prog. on Health for (WHO) 932
Health for All, Gl. Strat. (1981) 930
Immunization, Expanded Prog. on (WHO)
933
World Health Day 931

accident & injury prevention, world cf. 931
diarrhoeal diseases control 676 (UNICEF),
932-33 (WHO)
child immunization 676
disease prevention/control 932-33
family planning 931
health policy, Jt. Ct. on (UNICEF/WHO) 681
hum. resources for 930
& hum. rts. 574
intl. classification of diseases 930
malaria, Expert Ct. (WHO) 933
*mental health 574, 931-32
non-smoking prog. (WHO) 931
No-Tobacco Day 931
occupational health, Ct. (ILO/WHO) 932

primary health care (UNICEF) 676, see also
Bamako Initiative
protection/promotion 931-32
public info./education 931

Health for All, Gl. Strat. (1981) 930
Helsinki Decl. (ozone layer) 419, 441
Helsinki Inst. (crime prevention) 636
Higgins, Lt. Col. William 203, 830, 896
*High Commissioner for Refugees, Office of the UN
(UNHCR) 693-97, see also Refugees
HIV/AIDS, see AIDS

HONDURAS 169-70, 171, 530, 816, 817, see also
Central America

Hopi-Navajo relocation 481
Horn of Africa, Intergov. Authority on Drought & Dev.
in 250, see also desertification, Environment
*host country relations 847-48
*Ct. on 847-48
membership 990
*hostage-taking/abduction 498, 830-31, see also
under Human rights, detention
1979 Conv. on prevention of 828
household surveys 737, see also under statistics
human dev. index 309
Human Development Report 1990 (UNDP) 308-309
human immunodeficiency virus (HIV), see AIDS
*human resources dev. 594-97

HUMAN RIGHTS 12 (SG rpt.), 472-576
Centre for Human Rights 514-15, 517
Commission on Human Rights 213, 512-14
*enlargement 513-14
membership 1002
Sub-Cm. on Prevention of Discrimination
& Protection of Minorities 514
Human Rights Ct. 485, 521
membership 1013

Hum. Rts. Day (10 Dec.) 515
*Intl. Covenants on Hum. Rts. 523-26
Civil & Political (see below)
Economic, Social & Cultural (see below)
*World Public Info. Campaign for Hum. Rts.
472, 506, 507, 515, 524

advisory services 517-21
Equatorial Guinea 518-19
Guatemala 519
Haiti 519-20
Paraguay 520-21
Voluntary Fund for 518
African Cm. on Hum. & Peoples' Rts. 517,
518
*alternative approaches to improve enjoyment
of 509-11
& fundamental freedoms 503
*interdependence of hum. rts. 505-506

M

O

P

Postal Administration, UN (UNPA) 910

POSTAL SERVICES see Universal Postal Union (UPU)

*poverty eradication in dvg. cns. 288-89, 614
Power Reactor Info. System (IAEA) 914
preferences, generalized system of (GSP), see Trade Preferences, Sp. Ct. on 997
prevention of armed conflicts 8 (SG rpt.)
Prevention of Food Losses Prog. (FAO) 923
*prevention of nuclear war 47-48
price stats. (Intl. Comparison Prog.) 732-33
primary health care (UNICEF) 676-77, see also Bamako Initiative
*Prisoners, Standard Minimum Rules for Treatment (1955) 634, see also Crime Prevention
privileges and immunities (UN), Conv. (1946) 817-18
procurement 319, see also Dev. Prog. (UNDP)
*Programme and Co-ordination, Ct. (CPC) 747-49, 878, see also co-ordination
    membership 1007
*prohibition of use of nuclear weapons (dr. Conv.) 49-50
Project Services, UN Office (financing) 321
prostitution, child 569
Protocol of Geneva (1988) (Namibia) 795
psychotropic substances, see Drug abuse
*Psychotropic Substances, Conv. (1971) 715-17
public administration 254, 294-95
    & finance, UN prog. in, 9th & 10th mtgs. of experts 294-95
    tech. co-op 295
public information, UN, see under Information
*Public Information, Department of (DPI) 102, 103-104, 106-107, see also under Information
Puerto Rico 763-64

R

racial discrimination, see under Human rights
Racial Discrimination, Intl. Conv. on (1965) 473, 476
Racial Discrimination, 2nd Decade for Action to Combat Racism and (1983-1993) (action programme) 472
radiation protection prog. 913
Radiation, UN Scientific Ct. on Effects of Atomic (UNSCEAR) 108-109
Radio Consultative Ct. 946
radioactive wastes
    *dumping (in Africa) 71-72
    management 914
        Management Adv. Ct. 914
radiological (mass destruction) weapons, see under Disarmament
Railway Co-op. Grp., Asia/Pacific 260
Railway Grp., Intergov. 260
Rarotonga, Treaty of (1985) (South Pacific) 39
Red Cross, Intl. Ct. of 214
Red Sea (pollution) 446

*REFORM (UN) 17, 747, 865-67, 891, see also under UN, financing & programming
    *Econ. & Soc. Council revitalization, restructuring 739-43, see also under regions, econ. cms.
    *financial crisis emergency 862-64
    Group of 18 741, 747, 861, 866, 867
    restructuring, effects of 891

REFUGEES 17 (SG rpt.), 693-713
    *Office of UN High Commissioner 693-97
        Commissioner, resignation and appointment 693
        Executive Ct. 693
            prog. policy 693-94

    Afghanistan 540
    African 699-707
    Asian 707
    *asst. 697-711
    Central American, Intl. Cf. on 163, 343, 709
    El Salvador 551
    fin. & adm. questions 696-97
        contributions 697
    Indo-Chinese 179
        Intl. Cf. on Indo-Chinese Refugees 707
    law (intl. instruments) 711-12
    Nansen Medal 693
    in Near East, see Middle East
    protection 711
    reg. activities 699-711
    rights of 712
    women & children 662, 712

*regional disarmament 76-77
regional econ. co-op. 243-76, see also Econ. Cm. for Africa (ECA), Econ. Cm. for Europe (ECE), Econ. Cm. for Latin America/Caribbean (ECLAC), Econ. & Social Cm. for Asia/Pacific (ESCAP), Econ. & Social Cm. for Western Asia (ESCWA) or under name of region
    Executive Secretaries mtgs. 243
    *trade facilitation 244
Regional Trade Information Network (ESCAP) 260
Register of Entertainers, Actors and Others Who Have Performed in *Apartheid* South Africa 145-46
Register of Sports Contacts with South Africa 144, 145
*religious intolerance 478
    1981 Decl. on Elimination of 477-79
remote sensing 95
renewable energy sources, new and 405
research on TNCs 395-96
Research, UN Inst. for Disarmament (UNIDIR) 90-91
*research and training (UN) 598-602
Research and Training, UN Inst. for (UNITAR) 598-601
*resources, net transfer of 375-76
*restitution (return) of cultural property 641-43
restrictive business practices 370

V

W

Index of resolutions and decisions

Numbers in italics indicate that the text is summarized rather than reprinted in full. (For dates of sessions, refer to Appendix III.)

How to obtain volumes of the *Yearbook*

The 1985 to 1989 and 1991 to 1995 volumes of the *Yearbook of the United Nations* are sold and distributed in the United States, Canada and Mexico by Kluwer Law International, 101 Philip Drive, Norwell, Massachusetts 02061; in all other countries by Kluwer Law International, P.O. Box 85889, 2508 CN The Hague, Netherlands.

Recent volumes of the *Yearbook* may also be obtained in many bookstores throughout the world and from United Nations Publications, Sales Section, Room DC2-853, United Nations, New York, N.Y. 10017, or from United Nations Publications, Palais des Nations, Office C-115, 1211 Geneva 10, Switzerland.

Older editions are available in microfiche.

Yearbook of the United Nations, 1995
Vol. 49. Sales No. E.96.I.1 $150.

Yearbook of the United Nations, 1994
Vol. 48. Sales No. E.95.I.1 $150.

Yearbook of the United Nations, 1993
Vol. 47. Sales No. E.94.I.1 $150.

Yearbook of the United Nations, 1992
Vol. 46. Sales No. E.93.I.1 $150.

Yearbook of the United Nations, 1991
Vol. 45. Sales No. E.92.I.1 $115.

Yearbook of the United Nations, 1988
Vol. 42. Sales No. E.93.I.100 $150.

Yearbook of the United Nations, 1987
Vol. 41. Sales No. E.91.I.1 $105.

Yearbook of the United Nations, 1986
Vol. 40. Sales No. E.90.I.1 $95.

Yearbook of the United Nations, 1985
Vol. 39. Sales No. E.88.I.1 $95.

Yearbook of the United Nations, 1984
Vol. 38. Sales No. E.87.I.1 $90.

Yearbook of the United Nations, 1983
Vol. 37. Sales No. E.86.I.1 $85.

Yearbook of the United Nations, 1982
Vol. 36. Sales No. E.85.I.1 $75.

Yearbook of the United Nations, 1981
Vol. 35. Sales No. E.84.I.1 $75.

Yearbook of the United Nations, 1980
Vol. 34. Sales No. E.83.I.1 $72.

Yearbook of the United Nations
Special Edition
UN Fiftieth Anniversary
1945-1995
Sales No. E.95.I.50 $95.

The Yearbook *in microfiche*

Yearbook Volumes 1-41 (1946-1987) are now available in microfiche. Individual volumes are also available, and prices can be obtained by contacting the following: United Nations Publications, Sales Section, Room DC2-853, United Nations, New York, N.Y. 10017, or United Nations Publications, Palais des Nations, Office C-115, 1211 Geneva 10, Switzerland.

NOTES

NOTES

NOTES

NOTES

NOTES

NOTES

NOTES

NOTES

NOTES

NOTES

NOTES